California
FAMILY LAWS AND RULES

Volume 1

Family Code to Probate Code

Mat#42996079

© 2023 Thomson Reuters

ISBN: 978-1-668-71816-2

This publication was created to provide you with accurate and authoritative information concerning the subject matter covered; however, this publication was not necessarily prepared by persons licensed to practice law in a particular jurisdiction. The publisher is not engaged in rendering legal or other professional advice, and this publication is not a substitute for the advice of an attorney. If you require legal or other expert advice, you should seek the services of a competent attorney or other professional.

West and West's are registered in the U.S. Patent and Trademark Office.
Thomson Reuters Westlaw is a trademark of Thomson Reuters and its affiliates.

PREFACE

California Family Laws and Rules features the complete text of the California Family Code, along with selected sections from other codes and selected state court rules, in order to provide comprehensive coverage of California family law. It also includes related federal statutes, as well as materials regarding Indian Child Custody Proceedings and interstate placement of children. In order to aid in research and analysis, cross references and research references are included for California statutes.

WHAT'S NEW

In order to accommodate the growth of this title and to enhance ease of use, it has been divided into two volumes. Includes all laws through c. 997 of the 2022 portion of the 2021-2022 Regular Session, and propositions voted on at the Nov. 8, 2022 election.

ADDITIONAL INFORMATION

All California legislative enactments in 2022 are effective January 1, 2023, unless indicated otherwise. Additions or changes in statutes affected by 2022 legislation are indicated by underlining; deletions are indicated by asterisks.

With the exception of the Family Code, repealed statutes are omitted.

Codified legislation which is subject to a governor's veto is followed by an italicized note indicating that fact. For the text of the message, please consult the Historical and Statutory Notes for the provision in *West's Annotated California Codes* or the material pertaining to the legislation affecting the provision in *West's California Legislative Service*.

For official election results, see *https://electionresults.sos.ca.gov*.

Section captions have been prepared by the publisher, unless specifically indicated otherwise.

CONTACT US

For additional information or research assistance, contact the Reference Attorneys at 1-800-REF-ATTY (1-800-733-2889) or by Live Chat: Access via Westlaw. Contact our U.S. legal editorial department directly with your questions and suggestions by e-mail at editors.us-legal@tr.com.

Thank you for subscribing to this product. Should you have any questions regarding this product, please contact Customer Service at 1-800-328-4880 or by submitting an online request through our Support center on legal.thomsonreuters.com. If you would like to inquire about related publications, or to place an order, please contact us at 1-888-728-7677 or visit us at legal.thomsonreuters.com.

THE PUBLISHER

January 2023

THOMSON REUTERS PROVIEW™

This title is one of many now available on your tablet as an eBook.

Take your research mobile. Powered by the Thomson Reuters ProView™ app, our eBooks deliver the same trusted content as your print resources, but in a compact, on-the-go format.

ProView eBooks are designed for the way you work. You can add your own notes and highlights to the text, and all of your annotations will transfer electronically to every new edition of your eBook.

You can also instantly verify primary authority with built-in links to Westlaw® and KeyCite®, so you can be confident that you're accessing the most current and accurate information.

To find out more about ProView eBooks and available discounts, call 1-800-328-9352.

TABLE OF SECTIONS AFFECTED

This table indicates sections affected by 2022 legislation

Family Code

Sec.	Effect	Chap.	Sec.
211.5	Added	385	2
1816	Amended	197	3
3011	Amended	28	45
3040	Amended	385	3
3421	Amended	810	4
3424	Amended	810	5
3427	Amended	810	6
3428	Amended	810	7
3453.5	Added	810	8
4007.5	Amended	573	2
4054	Amended	573	3
4058	Amended	573	4
4077	Added	573	5
4204	Amended	420	15
6216	Amended	76	2
6307	Repealed	420	16
	Added	420	17
6308	Amended	420	18
6344	Repealed	591	1
	Added	591	2
6345	Amended	88	1
7613	Amended	159	1
7643	Amended	420	19
7643.5	Amended	420	20
8609.5	Amended	159	2
8713	Amended	159	3
8714	Amended	159	4
8802	Amended	159	5
8803	Amended	159	6
8910	Amended	159	7
8912	Amended	159	8
9000	Amended	159	9
9100	Amended	870	1
9324	Amended	159	10
17400	Amended	215	3
17404.4	Amended	420	21
17504.1	Redes. as 17504.4 and Amended	573	6
17504.2	Added	573	7
17504.4	Redes. from 17504.1 and Amended	573	6

TABLE OF SECTIONS AFFECTED

Sec.	Effect	Chap.	Sec.
17504.6	Added	573	8
17520.5	Added	830	1
17552	Amended	755	2

TABLE OF CONTENTS

Volume 1
FAMILY CODE

Division		Page
1.	Preliminary Provisions and Definitions	1
Part		
1.	Preliminary Provisions	1
2.	Definitions	3
3.	Indian Children	7
2.	General Provisions	9
Part		
1.	Jurisdiction	9
2.	General Procedural Provisions	10
3.	Temporary Restraining Order in Summons	12
4.	Ex Parte Temporary Restraining Orders	13
5.	Attorney's Fees and Costs	15
6.	Enforcement of Judgments and Orders	16
7.	Tribal Marriages and Divorces	17
2.5	Domestic Partner Registration	17
Part		
1.	Definitions	17
2.	Registration	20
3.	Termination	22
4.	Legal Effect	24
5.	Preemption	24
3.	Marriage	24
Part		
1.	Validity of Marriage	24
2.	Marriage License	29
3.	Solemnization of Marriage	33
4.	Confidential Marriage	37
5.	Remote Marriage License Issuance and Solemnization	42
4.	Rights and Obligations During Marriage	43
Part		
1.	General Provisions	43
2.	Characterization of Marital Property	46
3.	Liability of Marital Property	54
4.	Management and Control of Marital Property	59
5.	Marital Agreements	62
5.	Conciliation Proceedings	66
Part		
1.	Family Conciliation Court Law	67
2.	Statewide Coordination of Family Mediation and Conciliation Services	73
6.	Nullity, Dissolution, and Legal Separation	74
Part		
1.	General Provisions	74

TABLE OF CONTENTS

Part		Page
2.	Judicial Determination of Void or Voidable Marriage	93
3.	Dissolution of Marriage and Legal Separation	97

Division

7. Division of Property 108
   Part
   1. Definitions 108
   2. General Provisions 108
   3. Presumption Concerning Property Held in Joint Form 110
   4. Special Rules for Division of Community Estate 111
   5. Retirement Plan Benefits 113
   6. Debts and Liabilities 114
   7. Reimbursements 116
   8. Jointly Held Separate Property 118
   9. Real Property Located in Another State 119

8. Custody of Children 119
   Part
   1. Definitions and General Provisions 120
   2. Right to Custody of Minor Child 124
   3. Uniform Child Custody Jurisdiction and Enforcement Act 165

9. Support 176
   Part
   1. Definitions and General Provisions 176
   2. Child Support 199
   3. Spousal Support 224
   4. Support of Parents 233
   5. Enforcement of Support Orders 235
   6. Uniform Interstate Family Support Act 265

10. Prevention of Domestic Violence 280
    Part
    1. Short Title and Definitions 280
    2. General Provisions 283
    3. Emergency Protective Orders 285
    4. Protective Orders and Other Domestic Violence Prevention Orders ... 289
    5. Uniform Interstate Enforcement of Domestic Violence Protection Orders Act ... 306
    6. Uniform Recognition and Enforcement of Canadian Domestic Violence Protection Orders Act ... 309

11. Minors 311
    Part
    1. Age of Majority 311
    1.5 Caregivers 312
    2. Rights and Liabilities; Civil Actions and Proceedings 314
    3. Contracts 315
    4. Medical Treatment 321
    5. Enlistment in Armed Forces 325
    6. Emancipation of Minors Law 326

12. Parent and Child Relationship 330
    Part
    1. Rights of Parents 331

VIII

TABLE OF CONTENTS

Part		Page
2.	Presumption Concerning Child of Marriage and Genetic Testing to Determine Parentage	332
3.	Uniform Parentage Act	344
4.	Freedom from Parental Custody and Control	367
5.	Interstate Compact on Placement of Children	380
6.	Foster Care Placement Considerations	387
7.	Surrogacy and Donor Facilitators, Assisted Reproduction Agreements for Gestational Carriers, and Oocyte Donations	387

Division

13.	Adoption		389
	Part		
	1.	Definitions	389
	2.	Adoption of Unmarried Minors	393
	3.	Adoption of Adults and Married Minors	448
14.	Family Law Facilitator Act		453
15.	Friend of the Court Act [Repealed]		455
16.	Family Law Information Centers [Repealed]		455
17.	Support Services		455
	Chapter		
	1.	Department of Child Support Services	456
	2.	Child Support Enforcement	466
	5.	Complaint Resolution	513
20.	Pilot Projects		514
	Part		
	1.	Family Law Pilot Projects	514
	2.	Paternity Pilot Projects [Inoperative]	520

BUSINESS AND PROFESSIONS CODE

Division

2.	Healing Arts		521
	Chapter		
	1.	General Provisions	521
	1.2	Expedited Licensure Process	521
	13.	Licensed Marriage and Family Therapists	522

CIVIL CODE

Division

1.	Persons		549
	Part		
	2.	Personal Rights	549
2.	Property		554
	Part		
	1.	Property In General	554
3.	Obligations		557
	Part		
	2.	Contracts	557
	3.	Obligations Imposed by Law	558
	4.	Obligations Arising from Particular Transactions	559

IX

TABLE OF CONTENTS

CODE OF CIVIL PROCEDURE

Part		Page
1.	Of Courts of Justice	569
	Title	
	1. Organization and Jurisdiction	569
	2. Judicial Officers	575
	3. Persons Specially Invested with Powers of a Judicial Nature	582
	5. Persons Specially Invested with Ministerial Powers Relating to Courts of Justice	583
2.	Of Civil Actions	584
	Title	
	2. Of the Time of Commencing Civil Actions	584
	3. Of the Parties to Civil Actions	609
	4. Of the Place of Trial, Reclassification, and Coordination of Civil Actions	613
	4.5 Recording Notice of Certain Actions	616
	5. Jurisdiction and Service of Process	620
	6. Of the Pleadings in Civil Actions	621
	7. Other Provisional Remedies in Civil Actions	624
	7a. Pretrial Conferences	639
	8. Of the Trial and Judgment in Civil Actions	640
	9. Enforcement of Judgments	656
	13. Appeals in Civil Actions	687
	14. Of Miscellaneous Provisions	690
3.	Of Special Proceedings of a Civil Nature	698
	Title	
	3. Of Summary Proceedings	698
	5. Of Contempts	700
	8. Change of Names	705
	11. Money Judgments of Other Jurisdictions	709
	11.7 Recovery of Preferences and Exempt Property in an Assignment for the Benefit of Creditors	714
4.	Miscellaneous Provisions	717
	Title	
	2. Of the Kinds and Degrees of Evidence	717
	3. Of the Production of Evidence	717
	4. Civil Discovery Act	724

EDUCATION CODE

Title		Page
1.	General Education Code Provisions	795
	Division	
	1. General Education Code Provisions	795
2.	Elementary and Secondary Education	801
	Division	
	4. Instruction and Services	801
3.	Postsecondary Education	808
	Division	
	7. Community Colleges	808

TABLE OF CONTENTS

Division			Page
8.	California State University		809
9.	University of California		810

EVIDENCE CODE

Division
5. Burden of Proof; Burden of Producing Evidence; Presumptions and Inferences ... 811
   Chapter
   3. Presumptions and Inferences ... 811
8. Privileges ... 811
   Chapter
   4. Particular Privileges ... 811
10. Hearsay Evidence ... 821
    Chapter
    2. Exceptions to the Hearsay Rule ... 821
11. Writings ... 824
    Chapter
    2. Secondary Evidence of Writings ... 824

GOVERNMENT CODE

Title
2. Government of the State of California ... 831
   Division
   3. Executive Department ... 831
   5. Personnel ... 834
3. Government of Counties ... 836
   Division
   2. Officers ... 836
   4. Employees ... 838
5. Local Agencies ... 839
   Division
   1. Cities and Counties ... 839
8. The Organization and Government of Courts ... 839
   Chapter
   2. The Judicial Council ... 839

HEALTH AND SAFETY CODE

Division
2. Licensing Provisions ... 841
   Chapter
   2. Health Facilities ... 841
   3. California Community Care Facilities Act ... 845
8. Cemeteries ... 846
   Part
   3. Private Cemeteries ... 846
102. Vital Records and Health Statistics ... 847
   Part
   1. Vital Records ... 847

XI

TABLE OF CONTENTS

INSURANCE CODE

Division		Page
1.	General Rules Governing Insurance	861
	Part	
	1. The Contract	861
3.	The Insurance Commissioner	861
	Chapter	
	2. Powers and Duties	861

PENAL CODE

Part		Page
1.	Of Crimes and Punishments	865
	Title	
	5. Of Crimes By and Against the Executive Power of the State	865
	7. Of Crimes Against Public Justice	865
	9. Of Crimes Against the Person Involving Sexual Assault, and Crimes Against Public Decency and Good Morals	871
	13. Of Crimes Against Property	892
	15. Miscellaneous Crimes	893
	17. Rights of Victims and Witnesses of Crime	897
2.	Of Criminal Procedure	899
	Title	
	6. Pleadings and Proceedings Before Trial	899
	12. Of Special Proceedings of a Criminal Nature	902
4.	Prevention of Crimes and Apprehension of Criminals	903
	Title	
	5. Law Enforcement Response to Domestic Violence	903
	5.3 Family Justice Centers and Multidisciplinary Teams	906
	6. California Council on Criminal Justice	910
6.	Control of Deadly Weapons	911
	Title	
	4. Firearms	911

PROBATE CODE

Division		Page
2.	General Provisions	913
	Part	
	3. Contractual Arrangements Relating to Rights at Death	913
3.	General Provisions of a Procedural Nature	915
	Part	
	3. Appeals	915
4.	Guardianship, Conservatorship, and Other Protective Proceedings	916
	Part	
	1. Definitions and General Provisions	916
	2. Guardianship	926
	3. Conservatorship	937
	4. Provisions Common to Guardianship and Conservatorship	977
	5. Public Guardian	1045

TABLE OF CONTENTS

Part		Page
6.	Management or Disposition of Community Property Where Spouse Lacks Legal Capacity	1052
7.	Capacity Determinations and Health Care Decisions for Adult Without Conservator	1064
8.	Other Protective Proceedings	1068
9.	California Uniform Transfers to Minors Act	1079

Division
6. Wills and Intestate Succession 1089

Part		
1.	Wills	1089
2.	Intestate Succession	1090
3.	Family Protection	1091

11. Construction of Wills, Trusts, and Other Instruments 1098

Part
6. Family Protection: Omitted Spouses and Children 1098

Volume 2

REVENUE AND TAXATION CODE

Division
2. Other Taxes 1

Part
10.2 Administration of Franchise and Income Tax Laws 1

VEHICLE CODE

Division
6.7 Unattended Child in Motor Vehicle Safety Act 15

Chapter
1. General Provisions 15
2. Offenses 15
3. Educational Provisions 15

9. Civil Liability 16

Chapter
2. Civil Liability of Persons Signing License Applications of Minors 16

WELFARE AND INSTITUTIONS CODE

General Provisions 19

Division
2. Children 19

Part
1. Delinquents and Wards of the Juvenile Court 19

9. Public Social Services 175

Part
2. Administration 175
3. Aid and Medical Assistance 176
4. Services for the Care of Children 325
4.4 Family Preservation Services 427
6. Miscellaneous Provisions 428

XIII

TABLE OF CONTENTS

UNITED STATES CODE

Title		Page
22.	Foreign Relations and Intercourse	439
	Chapter	
	97. International Child Abduction Remedies	439
25.	Indians	443
	Chapter	
	21. Indian Child Welfare	443
28.	Judiciary and Judicial Procedure	449
	Part	
	V. Procedure	449
34.	Crime Control and Law Enforcement	452
	Subtitle	
	IV. Criminal Records and Information	452
42.	The Public Health and Welfare	456
	Chapter	
	7. Social Security	456
	67. Child Abuse Prevention and Treatment and Adoption Reform	560

DEPARTMENT OF THE INTERIOR
BUREAU OF INDIAN AFFAIRS GUIDELINES FOR STATE COURTS AND AGENCIES IN INDIAN CHILD CUSTODY PROCEEDINGS
(Page 589)

INTERSTATE COMPACT ON THE PLACEMENT OF CHILDREN REGULATIONS
(Page 605)

RULES OF COURT

Title		Page
2.	Trial Court Rules	629
	Division	
	4. Court Records	629
5.	Family and Juvenile Rules	632
	Division	
	1. Family Rules	641
	2. Rules Applicable in Family and Juvenile Proceedings	695
7.	Probate Rules	707
	Chapter	
	7. Spousal or Domestic Partner Property Petitions	707
9.	Rules on Law Practice, Attorneys, and Judges	707
	Division	
	2. Attorney Admission and Disciplinary Proceedings and Review of State Bar Proceedings	707

STANDARDS OF JUDICIAL ADMINISTRATION

Title		Page
5.	Standards for Cases Involving Children and Families	708

TABLE OF CONTENTS

APPENDIX C TO CALIFORNIA RULES OF COURT
GUIDELINES FOR THE OPERATION OF FAMILY LAW INFORMATION CENTERS
AND FAMILY LAW FACILITATORS OFFICES
(Page 714)

RULES OF THE STATE BAR OF CALIFORNIA
THE STANDARDS FOR CERTIFICATION AND RECERTIFICATION IN FAMILY LAW
(Page 716)

TABLE OF JUDICIAL COUNCIL FORMS
(Page 719)

INDEX
(Page I–1)

FAMILY CODE

Division	Section		Division	Section
1. Preliminary Provisions and Definitions	1		9. Support	3500
2. General Provisions	200		10. Prevention of Domestic Violence	6200
2.5. Domestic Partner Registration	297		11. Minors	6500
3. Marriage	300		12. Parent and Child Relationship	7500
4. Rights and Obligations During Marriage	700		13. Adoption	8500
5. Conciliation Proceedings	1800		14. Family Law Facilitator Act	10000
6. Nullity, Dissolution, and Legal Separation	2000		15. Friend of the Court Act [Repealed]	
7. Division of Property	2500		16. Family Law Information Centers [Repealed]	
8. Custody of Children	3000		17. Support Services	17000
			20. Pilot Projects	20000

Division 1

PRELIMINARY PROVISIONS AND DEFINITIONS

Part	Section
1. Preliminary Provisions	1
2. Definitions	50
3. Indian Children	170

Part 1

PRELIMINARY PROVISIONS

Section
1. Title of code.
2. Continuation of existing statutes; construction.
3. Construction as provision of uniform act.
4. Change in code; operative date; application of new law; filings; orders; liability for action taken before operative date.
5. Construction of headings.
6. Construction of code.
7. References to statutes; application.
8. Definitions.
9. Present, past, and future tenses.
10. Numbers; singular and plural.
11. Husband, wife, spouses, and married persons.
12. Meaning of "shall" and "may".
13. Severability.

§ 1. Title of code

This code shall be known as the Family Code. *(Stats.1992, c. 162 (A.B.2650), § 10, operative Jan. 1, 1994.)*

Cross References

Construction of code, see Family Code § 6.
Construction of statutes, generally, see Government Code § 9603.
Operation of statutes and resolutions, see Government Code § 9600 et seq.
Similar provisions, see Civil Code § 21; Probate Code § 1.

§ 2. Continuation of existing statutes; construction

A provision of this code, insofar as it is substantially the same as a previously existing provision relating to the same subject matter, shall be considered as a restatement and continuation thereof and not as a new enactment, and a reference in a statute to the provision of this code shall be deemed to include a reference to the previously existing provision unless a contrary intent appears. *(Stats.1992, c. 162 (A.B.2650), § 10, operative Jan. 1, 1994. Amended by Stats.1993, c. 219 (A.B.1500), § 78.)*

Cross References

Construction of code, see Family Code § 6.
General rules for construction to be as prescribed in preliminary provisions of codes, see Government Code § 9603.
Operation of statutes, see Government Code § 9600 et seq.
Restatements and continuations of statutes, generally, see Government Code § 9604.
Similar provisions, see Corporations Code § 2; Probate Code § 2.

§ 3. Construction as provision of uniform act

A provision of this code, insofar as it is the same in substance as a provision of a uniform act, shall be construed to effectuate the general purpose to make uniform the law in those states which enact that provision. *(Stats.1992, c. 162 (A.B.2650), § 10, operative Jan. 1, 1994.)*

Cross References

General rules for construction to be as prescribed in preliminary provisions of codes, see Government Code § 9603.
Interstate Compact on Placement of Children, see Family Code § 7900 et seq.
Operation of statutes, see Government Code § 9600 et seq.
State defined for purposes of this Code, see Family Code § 145.
Uniform Act on Blood Tests to Determine Paternity, see Family Code § 7550 et seq.
Uniform Child Custody Jurisdiction and Enforcement Act, see Family Code § 3400 et seq.
Uniform Divorce Recognition Act, see Family Code § 2090 et seq.
Uniform Interstate Enforcement of Domestic Violence Protection Orders Act, see Family Code § 6400 et seq.
Uniform Interstate Family Act, see Family Code § 5700.101 et seq.
Uniform Parentage Act, see Family Code § 7600 et seq.
Uniform Premarital Agreement Act, see Family Code § 1600 et seq.

Research References

Forms

1 California Transactions Forms--Family Law § 1:71, Binding Agreement With Specific Family Code Waivers.

§ 4. Change in code; operative date; application of new law; filings; orders; liability for action taken before operative date

(a) As used in this section:

(1) "New law" means either of the following, as the case may be:

(A) The act that enacted this code:

(B) The act that makes a change in this code, whether effectuated by amendment, addition, or repeal of a provision of this code.

(2) "Old law" means the applicable law in effect before the operative date of the new law.

(3) "Operative date" means the operative date of the new law.

(b) This section governs the application of the new law except to the extent otherwise expressly provided in the new law.

(c) Subject to the limitations provided in this section, the new law applies on the operative date to all matters governed by the new law, regardless of whether an event occurred or circumstance existed before, on, or after the operative date, including, but not limited to, commencement of a proceeding, making of an order, or taking of an action.

(d) If a document or paper is filed before the operative date, the contents, execution, and notice thereof are governed by the old law and not by the new law; but subsequent proceedings taken after the operative date concerning the document or paper, including an objection or response, a hearing, an order, or other matter relating thereto is governed by the new law and not by the old law.

(e) If an order is made before the operative date, or an action on an order is taken before the operative date, the validity of the order or action is governed by the old law and not by the new law. Nothing in this subdivision precludes proceedings after the operative date to modify an order made, or alter a course of action commenced, before the operative date to the extent proceedings for modification of an order or alteration of a course of action of that type are otherwise provided in the new law.

(f) No person is liable for an action taken before the operative date that was proper at the time the action was taken, even though the action would be improper if taken on or after the operative date, and the person has no duty, as a result of the enactment of the new law, to take any step to alter the course of action or its consequences.

(g) If the new law does not apply to a matter that occurred before the operative date, the old law continues to govern the matter notwithstanding its repeal or amendment by the new law.

(h) If a party shows, and the court determines, that application of a particular provision of the new law or of the old law in the manner required by this section or by the new law would substantially interfere with the effective conduct of the proceedings or the rights of the parties or other interested persons in connection with an event that occurred or circumstance that existed before the operative date, the court may, notwithstanding this section or the new law, apply either the new law or the old law to the extent reasonably necessary to mitigate the substantial interference. *(Stats.1992, c. 162 (A.B. 2650), § 10, operative Jan. 1, 1994.)*

Cross References

General rules for construction to be as prescribed in preliminary provisions of codes, see Government Code § 9603.
Judgment and order defined for purposes of this Code, see Family Code § 100.
Operation of statutes, see Government Code § 9600 et seq.
Person defined for purposes of this Code, see Family Code § 105.
Proceeding defined for purposes of this Code, see Family Code § 110.
Similar provisions, see Probate Code § 3.

§ 5. Construction of headings

Division, part, chapter, article, and section headings do not in any manner affect the scope, meaning, or intent of this code. *(Stats.1992, c. 162 (A.B.2650), § 10, operative Jan. 1, 1994.)*

Cross References

Construction of headings, see Business and Professions Code § 9; Corporations Code § 6; Evidence Code § 5.
General rules for construction to be as prescribed in preliminary provisions of codes, see Government Code § 9603.
Operation of statutes, see Government Code § 9600 et seq.

§ 6. Construction of code

Unless the provision or context otherwise requires, the general provisions and rules of construction in this part govern the construction of this code. *(Stats.1992, c. 162 (A.B.2650), § 10, operative Jan. 1, 1994.)*

Cross References

General rules for construction to be as prescribed in preliminary provisions of codes, see Government Code § 9603.
Operation of statutes, see Government Code § 9600 et seq.
Similar provisions, see Probate Code § 6.

§ 7. References to statutes; application

Whenever a reference is made to a portion of this code or to another law, the reference applies to all amendments and additions regardless of when made. *(Stats.1992, c. 162 (A.B.2650), § 10, operative Jan. 1, 1994.)*

Cross References

General rules for construction to be as prescribed in preliminary provisions of codes, see Government Code § 9603.
Operation of statutes, see Government Code § 9600 et seq.
Similar provisions, see Probate Code § 7.

§ 8. Definitions

Unless otherwise expressly stated:

(a) "Division" means a division of this code.

(b) "Part" means a part of the division in which that term occurs.

(c) "Chapter" means a chapter of the division or part, as the case may be, in which that term occurs.

(d) "Article" means an article of the chapter in which that term occurs.

(e) "Section" means a section of this code.

(f) "Subdivision" means a subdivision of the section in which that term occurs.

(g) "Paragraph" means a paragraph of the subdivision in which that term occurs.

(h) "Subparagraph" means a subparagraph of the paragraph in which that term occurs. *(Stats.1992, c. 162 (A.B.2650), § 10, operative Jan. 1, 1994.)*

Cross References

General rules for construction to be as prescribed in preliminary provisions of codes, see Government Code § 9603.
Operation of statutes, see Government Code § 9600 et seq.
Preliminary provisions, see Civil Code § 14; Probate Code § 8.

§ 9. Present, past, and future tenses

The present tense includes the past and future tenses, and the future, the present. *(Stats.1992, c. 162 (A.B.2650), § 10, operative Jan. 1, 1994.)*

Cross References

General rules for construction to be as prescribed in preliminary provisions of codes, see Government Code § 9603.
Operation of statutes, see Government Code § 9600 et seq.
Tenses, see Civil Code § 14; Labor Code § 11.

§ 10. Numbers; singular and plural

The singular number includes the plural, and the plural, the singular. *(Stats.1992, c. 162 (A.B.2650), § 10, operative Jan. 1, 1994.)*

Cross References

General rules for construction to be as prescribed in preliminary provisions of codes, see Government Code § 9603.

Numbers, singular and plural, see Civil Code § 14; Probate Code § 10.
Operation of statutes, see Government Code § 9600 et seq.

§ 11. Husband, wife, spouses, and married persons

A reference to "husband" and "wife," "spouses," or "married persons," or a comparable term, includes persons who are lawfully married to each other and persons who were previously lawfully married to each other, as is appropriate under the circumstances of the particular case. *(Stats.1992, c. 162 (A.B.2650), § 10, operative Jan. 1, 1994.)*

Cross References

Construction of code, generally, see Family Code § 6.
General rules for construction to be as prescribed in preliminary provisions of codes, see Government Code § 9603.
Operation of statutes, see Government Code § 9600 et seq.
Person defined for purposes of this Code, see Family Code § 105.

§ 12. Meaning of "shall" and "may"

"Shall" is mandatory and "may" is permissive. "Shall not" and "may not" are prohibitory. *(Stats.1992, c. 162 (A.B.2650), § 10, operative Jan. 1, 1994.)*

Cross References

General rules for construction to be as prescribed in preliminary provisions of codes, see Government Code § 9603.
Operation of statutes, see Government Code § 9600 et seq.
Similar provisions, see Probate Code § 12.

§ 13. Severability

If a provision or clause of this code or its application to any person or circumstances is held invalid, the invalidity does not affect other provisions or applications of the code which can be given effect without the invalid provision or application, and to this end the provisions of this code are severable. *(Stats.1992, c. 162 (A.B.2650), § 10, operative Jan. 1, 1994.)*

Cross References

General rules for construction to be as prescribed in preliminary provisions of codes, see Government Code § 9603.
Operation of statutes, see Government Code § 9600 et seq.
Person defined for purposes of this Code, see Family Code § 105.
Severability, see Business and Professions Code § 24; Corporations Code § 19; Probate Code § 11.

Part 2

DEFINITIONS

Section
50. Applicability of part.
55, 57. Inoperative.
58. Child for whom support may be ordered.
60. Inoperative.
63. Community estate.
65. Community property.
67. County.
70. Date of separation.
75. Inoperative.
80. Employee benefit plan.
92. Family support.
95. Income and expense declaration.
100. Judgment; order.
105. Person.
110. Proceeding.
113. Property.
115. Property declaration.
125. Quasi-community property.
126. Petitioner.

Section
127. Respondent.
130. Separate property.
142. Spousal support.
143. Spouse.
145. State.
150. Support.
155. Support order.

§ 50. Applicability of part

Unless the provision or context otherwise requires, the definitions and rules of construction in this part govern the construction of this code. *(Stats.1992, c. 162 (A.B.2650), § 10, operative Jan. 1, 1994.)*

Cross References

General rules for construction to be as prescribed in preliminary provisions of codes, see Government Code § 9603.
Operation of statutes, see Government Code § 9600 et seq.
Similar provisions, see Family Code §§ 6, 900, 6900; Probate Code § 20.

§§ 55, 57. Inoperative

§ 58. Child for whom support may be ordered

"Child for whom support may be ordered" means a minor child and a child for whom support is authorized under Section 3587, 3901, or 3910. *(Added by Stats.1993, c. 219 (A.B.1500), § 79.)*

Cross References

Minor defined for purposes of this Code, see Family Code § 6500.
Support defined for purposes of this Code, see Family Code § 150.

§ 60. Inoperative

§ 63. Community estate

"Community estate" includes both community property and quasi-community property. *(Added by Stats.1993, c. 219 (A.B.1500), § 79.3.)*

Cross References

Community property defined elsewhere, see Civil Code § 687; Family Code § 760.
Community property defined for purposes of this Code, see Family Code § 65.
Community property subject to enforcement of money judgment, see Code of Civil Procedure § 695.020.
Homestead exemptions, see Code of Civil Procedure § 704.710 et seq.
Liability of quasi-community property, see Family Code § 912.
Partition of real and personal property, see Code of Civil Procedure § 872.010 et seq.
Property defined for purposes of this Code, see Family Code § 113.
Quasi-community property defined, see Family Code § 125.
Real property includes leasehold interests in real property, see Family Code § 700.

Research References

Forms

7PT1 Am. Jur. Pl. & Pr. Forms Community Property § 2, Statutory References.
7PT1 Am. Jur. Pl. & Pr. Forms Community Property § 39, Complaint, Petition, or Declaration—For Divorce or Other Legal Separation—Allegation of Quasi-Community Property.
Asset Protection: Legal Planning, Strategies and Forms ¶ 4.03, Community Property.
1 California Transactions Forms--Estate Planning § 1:26, Quasi-Community Property; Separate Property.
2 California Transactions Forms--Estate Planning § 10:5, Quasi-Community Property.

§ 65. Community property

"Community property" is property that is community property under Part 2 (commencing with Section 760) of Division 4. *(Stats.1992, c. 162 (A.B.2650), § 10, operative Jan. 1, 1994.)*

§ 65

Cross References

Community property, defined, characterization of marital property, see Family Code § 760 et seq.
Division of property, dissolution or legal separation proceedings, see Family Code § 2500 et seq.
Liability of marital property, see Family Code § 900 et seq.
Management and control of marital property, see Family Code § 1100 et seq.
Presumptions, nature of marital property, see Family Code §§ 802, 803.
Property defined for purposes of this Code, see Family Code § 113.
Property rights during marriage, see Family Code § 750 et seq.
Quasi-community property, defined, see Family Code § 125.
Reimbursement, community property, see Family Code § 920.
Special rules for division of community estate, see Family Code § 2600 et seq.
Transitional provisions, marital property, see Family Code §§ 930, 931.
Transmutation of community property, see Family Code § 850 et seq.

Research References

Forms

7PT1 Am. Jur. Pl. & Pr. Forms Community Property § 2, Statutory References.

§ 67. County

"County" includes city and county. *(Stats.1992, c. 162 (A.B.2650), § 10, operative Jan. 1, 1994.)*

Cross References

Similar provisions, see Civil Code § 14.

§ 70. Date of separation

(a) "Date of separation" means the date that a complete and final break in the marital relationship has occurred, as evidenced by both of the following:

(1) The spouse has expressed to the other spouse the intent to end the marriage.

(2) The conduct of the spouse is consistent with the intent to end the marriage.

(b) In determining the date of separation, the court shall take into consideration all relevant evidence.

(c) It is the intent of the Legislature in enacting this section to abrogate the decisions in In re Marriage of Davis (2015) 61 Cal.4th 846 and In re Marriage of Norviel (2002) 102 Cal.App.4th 1152. *(Added by Stats.2016, c. 114 (S.B.1255), § 1, eff. Jan. 1, 2017. Amended by Stats.2019, c. 115 (A.B.1817), § 1, eff. Jan. 1, 2020.)*

Cross References

Temporary or permanent support to abusive spouse, rebuttable presumption disfavoring award, evidence, see Family Code § 4325.
Violent sexual felony, domestic violence felony, prohibited awards, see Family Code § 4324.5.

Research References

Forms

California Practice Guide: Rutter Family Law Forms Form 1:32, Glossary of Common Family Law Terms, Phrases and Concepts (Enclosure to Form 1:31).
1 California Transactions Forms--Family Law § 2:80, Information to Ascertain Before Drafting Agreement.
1 California Transactions Forms--Family Law § 2:108.50, Statement Attached to Judgment Granting Dissolution of Marriage.

§ 75. Inoperative

§ 80. Employee benefit plan

"Employee benefit plan" includes public and private retirement, pension, annuity, savings, profit sharing, stock bonus, stock option, thrift, vacation pay, and similar plans of deferred or fringe benefit compensation, whether of the defined contribution or defined benefit type whether or not such plan is qualified under the Employee Retirement Income Security Act of 1974 (P.L. 93-406) (ERISA), as amended. The term also includes "employee benefit plan" as defined in Section 3 of ERISA (29 U.S.C.A. Sec. 1002(3)). *(Stats. 1992, c. 162 (A.B.2650), § 10, operative Jan. 1, 1994. Amended by Stats.1994, c. 1269 (A.B.2208), § 9.)*

Cross References

Division of plan benefits, see Family Code § 2610.
Joinder of parties, pension plan as party in dissolution, etc., proceedings, see Family Code § 2060 et seq.

Research References

Forms

California Practice Guide: Rutter Family Law Forms Form 1:32, Glossary of Common Family Law Terms, Phrases and Concepts (Enclosure to Form 1:31).
West's California Code Forms, Family § 2060, Comment Overview—Application and Order for Joinder.
West's California Judicial Council Forms FL-374, Notice of Appearance and Response of Employee Benefit Plan.
West's California Judicial Council Forms FL-460, Qualified Domestic Relations Order for Support (Earnings Assignment Order for Support).

§ 92. Family support

"Family support" means an agreement between the parents, or an order or judgment, that combines child support and spousal support without designating the amount to be paid for child support and the amount to be paid for spousal support. *(Stats.1992, c. 162 (A.B. 2650), § 10, operative Jan. 1, 1994.)*

Cross References

Abandoned child, duty to support parents, see Family Code § 4410 et seq.
Agreements for support, see Family Code § 3580 et seq.
County officers, payments to, see Family Code § 4200 et seq.
Court designated officers, payment of spousal support, see Family Code § 4350 et seq.
Court orders, see Family Code § 4000 et seq.
Death of supporting party, continuation of support, see Family Code § 4360.
Discovery, modification or termination proceedings, see Family Code § 3660 et seq.
Duty of parent, see Family Code § 3900 et seq.
Duty of support, spousal support, see Family Code § 4300 et seq.
Fines and penalties, delinquent payments, see Family Code § 4720 et seq.
Interstate Family Support Act,
 Generally, see Family Code § 5700.101 et seq.
 Practice and procedure rules, see Family Code § 210 et seq.
Judgment and order defined for purposes of this Code, see Family Code § 100.
Modification or termination of support, see Family Code § 3650 et seq.
Order for support, enforcement, see Family Code § 4500 et seq.
Parents, duty, see Family Code § 3900 et seq.
Reporting of delinquent payments, see Family Code §§ 4700, 4701.
Spousal support defined for purposes of this Code, see Family Code § 142.
Support defined for purposes of this Code, see Family Code § 150.
Support generally, see Family Code § 3500 et seq.
Support of spouse from separate property, see Family Code § 4301.
Termination of support, see Family Code § 3650 et seq.

Research References

Forms

California Practice Guide: Rutter Family Law Forms Form 1:32, Glossary of Common Family Law Terms, Phrases and Concepts (Enclosure to Form 1:31).
1 California Transactions Forms--Family Law § 2:66, Overview.

§ 95. Income and expense declaration

"Income and expense declaration" means the form for an income and expense declaration in family law matters adopted by the Judicial Council. *(Stats.1992, c. 162 (A.B.2650), § 10, operative Jan. 1, 1994.)*

Cross References

Practice and procedure rules, see Family Code § 210 et seq.

Property declaration defined, see Family Code § 115.

§ 100. Judgment; order

"Judgment" and "order" include a decree, as appropriate under the circumstances. *(Stats.1992, c. 162 (A.B.2650), § 10, operative Jan. 1, 1994.)*

Cross References

Decree,
    Uniform Child Custody Jurisdiction and Enforcement Act, see Family Code § 3400 et seq.
    Uniform Interstate Family Support Act, see Family Code § 5700.101 et seq.
Enforcement of judgments or orders, see Family Code §§ 290, 291.
Judgment defined, see Code of Civil Procedure § 577.
Marriage annulment, dissolution or legal separation proceedings,
    Pendency of proceedings, orders during, see Family Code § 2045.
    Summons, orders in summons, see Family Code § 2040.
Order, defined, see Code of Civil Procedure § 1003.
Orders pending proceedings, notice and hearing, see Family Code § 6340 et seq.
Protective and restraining orders, attorney's fees and costs, see Family Code § 2030 et seq.
Protective and temporary restraining orders, see Family Code § 7700 et seq.
Registration and enforcement of orders, see Family Code § 6380 et seq.

§ 105. Person

"Person" includes a natural person, firm, association, organization, partnership, business trust, corporation, limited liability company, or public entity. *(Added by Stats.1993, c. 219 (A.B.1500), § 80. Amended by Stats.1994, c. 1010 (S.B.2053), § 107.)*

§ 110. Proceeding

"Proceeding" includes an action. *(Added by Stats.1993, c. 219 (A.B.1500), § 81.)*

§ 113. Property

"Property" includes real and personal property and any interest therein. *(Added by Stats.2000, c. 808 (A.B.1358), § 21, eff. Sept. 28, 2000.)*

Cross References

Community estate defined, see Family Code § 63.
Quasi-community property defined, see Family Code § 125.

§ 115. Property declaration

"Property declaration" means the form for a property declaration in family law matters adopted by the Judicial Council. *(Stats.1992, c. 162 (A.B.2650), § 10, operative Jan. 1, 1994.)*

Cross References

Income and expense declaration, see Family Code § 95.
Property defined for purposes of this Code, see Family Code § 113.
Rules of practice and procedure, see Family Code § 210 et seq.

Research References

Forms

West's California Judicial Council Forms FL-160, Property Declaration (Also Available in Spanish).
West's California Judicial Council Forms FL-161, Continuation of Property Declaration.

§ 125. Quasi-community property

"Quasi-community property" means all real or personal property, wherever situated, acquired before or after the operative date of this code in any of the following ways:

(a) By either spouse while domiciled elsewhere which would have been community property if the spouse who acquired the property had been domiciled in this state at the time of its acquisition.

(b) In exchange for real or personal property, wherever situated, which would have been community property if the spouse who acquired the property so exchanged had been domiciled in this state at the time of its acquisition. *(Stats.1992, c. 162 (A.B.2650), § 10, operative Jan. 1, 1994.)*

Cross References

Characterization of marital property, see Family Code § 760 et seq.
Community property defined for purposes of this Code, see Family Code § 65.
Damages, satisfaction of judgment, separate property, see Family Code § 781.
Division of property, dissolution or legal separation proceedings, see Family Code § 2500 et seq.
Earnings and accumulations during period of separation, see Family Code § 771.
Earnings or accumulations after entry of judgment of legal separation, classification, see Family Code § 772.
Liability of marital property, see Family Code § 900 et seq.
Management and control of marital property, see Family Code § 1100 et seq.
Personal property defined, see Civil Code § 663.
Presumptions, nature of marital property, see Family Code §§ 802, 803.
Property defined for purposes of this Code, see Family Code § 113.
Real property defined, see Civil Code §§ 14, 658.
References to husband, wife, spouses and married persons, persons included for purposes of this Code, see Family Code § 11.
Reimbursement, community property, see Family Code § 920.
Separate property, satisfaction of judgment, see Family Code § 781.
Separate property of married persons, see Family Code § 770 et seq.
Special rules for division of community estate, see Family Code § 2600 et seq.
State defined for purposes of this Code, see Family Code § 145.
Transitional provisions, marital property, see Family Code §§ 930, 931.
Transmutation of community property, see Family Code § 850 et seq.

Research References

Forms

7PT1 Am. Jur. Pl. & Pr. Forms Community Property § 39, Complaint, Petition, or Declaration—For Divorce or Other Legal Separation—Allegation of Quasi-Community Property.
Asset Protection: Legal Planning, Strategies and Forms ¶ 4.03, Community Property.
California Practice Guide: Rutter Family Law Forms Form 1:32, Glossary of Common Family Law Terms, Phrases and Concepts (Enclosure to Form 1:31).
1 California Transactions Forms--Estate Planning § 1:26, Quasi-Community Property; Separate Property.
2 California Transactions Forms--Estate Planning § 10:5, Quasi-Community Property.
4 California Transactions Forms--Estate Planning § 19:19, Quasi-Community Property.
1 California Transactions Forms--Family Law § 1:27, Complete Agreement.
West's California Code Forms, Family § 1611 Form 1, Premarital Agreement.

§ 126. Petitioner

"Petitioner" includes plaintiff, where appropriate. *(Added by Stats.1999, c. 980 (A.B.1671), § 1.)*

§ 127. Respondent

"Respondent" includes defendant, where appropriate. *(Stats. 1992, c. 162 (A.B.2650), § 10, operative Jan. 1, 1994.)*

§ 130. Separate property

"Separate property" is property that is separate property under Part 2 (commencing with Section 760) of Division 4. *(Stats.1992, c. 162 (A.B.2650), § 10, operative Jan. 1, 1994.)*

Cross References

Division of property, see Family Code § 2500 et seq.
Earnings and accumulations during period of separation, see Family Code § 771.
Earnings or accumulations after entry of judgment of legal separation, see Family Code § 772.
Liability of marital property, see Family Code § 900 et seq.
Management and control of marital property, see Family Code § 1100 et seq.
Presumptions, nature of marital property, see Family Code §§ 802, 803.

§ 130

Property defined for purposes of this Code, see Family Code § 113.
Property rights during marriage, see Family Code § 750 et seq.
Reimbursement, community property, see Family Code § 920.
Separate property,
   Defined, see Family Code §§ 2502, 3515.
   Married persons, see Family Code § 770 et seq.
   Satisfaction of judgment for damages, see Family Code § 781.
Special rules for division of community estate, see Family Code § 2600 et seq.
Support, separate property defined, see Family Code § 3515.
Transitional provisions, marital property, see Family Code §§ 930, 931.
Transmutation of community property, see Family Code § 850 et seq.

§ 142. Spousal support

"Spousal support" means support of the spouse of the obligor. *(Stats.1992, c. 162 (A.B.2650), § 10, operative Jan. 1, 1994.)*

Cross References

Agreements for support, see Family Code § 3580 et seq.
Application of definitions, see Family Code § 50.
Assets, deposits, securing future support payments, see Family Code §§ 4303, 4320 et seq.
County officers, payments to, see Family Code § 4200 et seq.
Court designated officers, payment of support to, see Family Code § 4350 et seq.
Court orders, see Family Code § 4000 et seq.
Death of supporting party, continuation of support, see Family Code § 4360.
Discovery, modification or termination proceedings, see Family Code § 3660 et seq.
Duty of support, spousal support, see Family Code § 4300 et seq.
Interstate Family Support Act,
   Generally, see Family Code § 5700.101 et seq.
   Practice and procedure rules, see Family Code § 210 et seq.
Modification of support, see Family Code § 3650 et seq.
Order for support, enforcement, see Family Code § 4500 et seq.
Penalties, delinquent payments, see Family Code § 4722.
References to husband, wife, spouses and married persons, persons included for purposes of this Code, see Family Code § 11.
Reporting of delinquent payments, see Family Code §§ 4700, 4701.
Support defined for purposes of this Code, see Family Code § 150.
Support generally, see Family Code § 3500 et seq.
Termination of support, see Family Code § 3650 et seq.

§ 143. Spouse

"Spouse" includes "registered domestic partner," as required by Section 297.5. *(Added by Stats.2016, c. 50 (S.B.1005), § 35, eff. Jan. 1, 2017.)*

§ 145. State

"State" means a state of the United States, the District of Columbia, or a commonwealth, territory, or insular possession subject to the jurisdiction of the United States. *(Stats.1992, c. 162 (A.B.2650), § 10, operative Jan. 1, 1994. Amended by Stats.1999, c. 661 (A.B.825), § 3.)*

Cross References

Interstate Family Support Act,
   Generally, see Family Code § 5700.101 et seq.
   Practice and procedure rules, see Family Code § 210 et seq.
Uniform Child Custody Jurisdiction and Enforcement Act, definitions, see Family Code § 3402.

§ 150. Support

"Support" refers to a support obligation owing on behalf of a child, spouse, or family, or an amount owing pursuant to Section 17402. It also includes past due support or arrearage when it exists. "Support," when used with reference to a minor child or a child described in Section 3901, includes maintenance and education. *(Stats.1992, c. 162 (A.B.2650), § 10, operative Jan. 1, 1994. Amended by Stats.1993, c. 219 (A.B.1500), § 82; Stats.2000, c. 808 (A.B.1358), § 22, eff. Sept. 28, 2000.)*

Cross References

Abandoned child, duty to support parents, see Family Code § 4410 et seq.
Agreements for support, see Family Code § 3580 et seq.
County officers, payments to, see Family Code § 4200 et seq.
Court designated officers, payment of support to, see Family Code § 4350 et seq.
Court orders, see Family Code § 4000 et seq.
Death of supporting party, continuation of support, see Family Code § 4360.
Discovery, modification or termination proceedings, see Family Code § 3660 et seq.
Duty of parent, see Family Code § 3900 et seq.
Duty of support, spousal support, see Family Code § 4300 et seq.
Interstate Family Support Act,
   Generally, see Family Code § 5700.101 et seq.
   Practice and procedure rules, see Family Code § 210 et seq.
Minor defined for purposes of this Code, see Family Code § 6500.
Modification of support, see Family Code § 3650 et seq.
Order for support, enforcement, see Family Code § 4500 et seq.
Penalties, delinquent payments, see Family Code § 4722.
References to husband, wife, spouses and married persons, persons included for purposes of this Code, see Family Code § 11.
Reporting of delinquent payments, see Family Code §§ 4700, 4701.
Support generally, see Family Code § 3500 et seq.
Termination of support, see Family Code § 3650 et seq.

Research References

Forms

West's California Code Forms, Family § 3900, Comment Overview—Duty of Parent to Support Child.
West's California Judicial Council Forms FL–343, Spousal, Domestic Partner, or Family Support Order Attachment.

§ 155. Support order

"Support order" means a judgment or order of support in favor of an obligee, whether temporary or final, or subject to modification, termination, or remission, regardless of the kind of action or proceeding in which it is entered. For the purposes of Section 685.020 of the Code of Civil Procedure, only the initial support order, whether temporary or final, whether or not the order is contained in a judgment, shall be considered an installment judgment. No support order or other order or notice issued, which sets forth the amount of support owed for prior periods of time or establishes a periodic payment to liquidate the support owed for prior periods, shall be considered a money judgment for purposes of subdivision (b) of Section 685.020 of the Code of Civil Procedure. *(Stats.1992, c. 162 (A.B.2650), § 10, operative Jan. 1, 1994. Amended by Stats.2002, c. 539 (S.B.97), § 2.)*

Cross References

Agreements for support, see Family Code § 3580 et seq.
Application of definitions, see Family Code § 50.
County officers, payments to, see Family Code § 4200 et seq.
Court designated officers, payment of support to, see Family Code § 4350 et seq.
Court orders, see Family Code § 4000 et seq.
Death of supporting party, continuation of support, see Family Code § 4360.
Discovery, modification or termination proceedings, see Family Code § 3660 et seq.
Interstate Family Support Act,
   Generally, see Family Code § 5700.101 et seq.
   Practice and procedure rules, see Family Code § 210 et seq.
Judgment and order defined for purposes of this Code, see Family Code § 100.
Modification of support, see Family Code § 3650 et seq.
Order for support, enforcement, see Family Code § 4500 et seq.
Penalties, delinquent payments, see Family Code § 4722.
Proceeding defined for purposes of this Code, see Family Code § 110.
Reporting of delinquent payments, see Family Code §§ 4700, 4701.
Sister state money–judgments, definitions, "sister state judgment", see Code of Civil Procedure § 1710.10.
Support defined for purposes of this Code, see Family Code § 150.
Support generally, see Family Code § 3500 et seq.

Termination of support, see Family Code § 3650 et seq.

Part 3
INDIAN CHILDREN

Section
170. Definitions; eligible membership in more than one tribe.
175. Legislative findings and declarations.
177. Governing law in Indian child custody proceedings.
180. Notice of proceedings; parties; requirements; time to send.
185. Indian child of tribe not recognized to have tribal status under federal law; tribal participation at hearings.

§ 170. Definitions; eligible membership in more than one tribe

(a) As used in this code, unless the context otherwise requires, the terms "Indian," "Indian child," "Indian child's tribe," "Indian custodian," "Indian organization," "Indian tribe," "reservation," and "tribal court" shall be defined as provided in Section 1903 of the Indian Child Welfare Act (25 U.S.C. Sec. 1901 et seq.).

(b) When used in connection with an Indian child custody proceeding, the terms "extended family member" and "parent" shall be defined as provided in Section 1903 of the Indian Child Welfare Act.

(c) "Indian child custody proceeding" means a "child custody proceeding" within the meaning of Section 1903 of the Indian Child Welfare Act, including a voluntary or involuntary proceeding that may result in an Indian child's temporary or long-term foster care or guardianship placement if the parent or Indian custodian cannot have the child returned upon demand, termination of parental rights, or adoptive placement. An "Indian child custody proceeding" does not include a proceeding under this code commenced by the parent of an Indian child to determine the custodial rights of the child's parents, unless the proceeding involves a petition to declare an Indian child free from the custody or control of a parent or involves a grant of custody to a person or persons other than a parent, over the objection of a parent.

(d) If an Indian child is a member of more than one tribe or is eligible for membership in more than one tribe, the court shall make a determination, in writing together with the reasons for it, as to which tribe is the Indian child's tribe for purposes of the Indian child custody proceeding. The court shall make that determination as follows:

(1) If the Indian child is or becomes a member of only one tribe, that tribe shall be designated as the Indian child's tribe, even though the child is eligible for membership in another tribe.

(2) If an Indian child is or becomes a member of more than one tribe, or is not a member of any tribe but is eligible for membership in more than one tribe, the tribe with which the child has the more significant contacts shall be designated as the Indian child's tribe. In determining which tribe the child has the more significant contacts with, the court shall consider, among other things, the following factors:

(A) The length of residence on or near the reservation of each tribe and frequency of contact with each tribe.

(B) The child's participation in activities of each tribe.

(C) The child's fluency in the language of each tribe.

(D) Whether there has been a previous adjudication with respect to the child by a court of one of the tribes.

(E) Residence on or near one of the tribes' reservations by the child's parents, Indian custodian or extended family members.

(F) Tribal membership of custodial parent or Indian custodian.

(G) Interest asserted by each tribe in response to the notice specified in Section 180.

(H) The child's self identification.

(3) If an Indian child becomes a member of a tribe other than the one designated by the court as the Indian child's tribe under paragraph (2), actions taken based on the court's determination prior to the child's becoming a tribal member shall continue to be valid. *(Added by Stats.2006, c. 838 (S.B.678), § 1.)*

Research References

Forms

1 California Transactions Forms--Family Law § 3:7, Custody Issues Outside the Scope of the Family Code.
2 California Transactions Forms--Family Law § 6:143, Overview of Indian Child Welfare Act (ICWA).
2 California Transactions Forms--Family Law § 6:144, Scope and Implementation of ICWA.
2 California Transactions Forms--Family Law § 6:145, Definitions.
West's California Judicial Council Forms ADOPT-200, Adoption Request.

§ 175. Legislative findings and declarations

(a) The Legislature finds and declares the following:

(1) There is no resource that is more vital to the continued existence and integrity of recognized Indian tribes than their children, and the State of California has an interest in protecting Indian children who are members of, or are eligible for membership in, an Indian tribe. The state is committed to protecting the essential tribal relations and best interest of an Indian child by promoting practices, in accordance with the Indian Child Welfare Act (25 U.S.C. Sec. 1901 et seq.) and other applicable law, designed to prevent the child's involuntary out-of-home placement and, whenever the placement is necessary or ordered, by placing the child, whenever possible, in a placement that reflects the unique values of the child's tribal culture and is best able to assist the child in establishing, developing, and maintaining a political, cultural, and social relationship with the child's tribe and tribal community.

(2) It is in the interest of an Indian child that the child's membership in the child's Indian tribe and connection to the tribal community be encouraged and protected, regardless of any of the following:

(A) Whether the child is in the physical custody of an Indian parent or Indian custodian at the commencement of a child custody proceeding.

(B) Whether the parental rights of the child's parents have been terminated.

(C) Where the child has resided or been domiciled.

(b) In all Indian child custody proceedings the court shall consider all of the findings contained in subdivision (a), strive to promote the stability and security of Indian tribes and families, comply with the federal Indian Child Welfare Act, and seek to protect the best interest of the child. Whenever an Indian child is removed from a foster care home or institution, guardianship, or adoptive placement for the purpose of further foster care, guardianship, or adoptive placement, placement of the child shall be in accordance with the Indian Child Welfare Act.

(c) A determination by an Indian tribe that an unmarried person, who is under the age of 18 years, is either (1) a member of an Indian tribe or (2) eligible for membership in an Indian tribe and a biological child of a member of an Indian tribe shall constitute a significant political affiliation with the tribe and shall require the application of the federal Indian Child Welfare Act to the proceedings.

(d) In any case in which this code or other applicable state or federal law provides a higher standard of protection to the rights of the parent or Indian custodian of an Indian child, or the Indian

§ 175

child's tribe, than the rights provided under the Indian Child Welfare Act, the court shall apply the higher standard.

(e) Any Indian child, the Indian child's tribe, or the parent or Indian custodian from whose custody the child has been removed, may petition the court to invalidate an action in an Indian child custody proceeding for foster care, guardianship placement, or termination of parental rights if the action violated Sections 1911, 1912, and 1913 of the Indian Child Welfare Act (25 U.S.C. Sec. 1901 et seq.). Nothing in this section is intended to prohibit, restrict, or otherwise limit any rights under Section 1914 of the Indian Child Welfare Act (25 U.S.C. Sec. 1901 et seq.). *(Added by Stats.2006, c. 838 (S.B.678), § 1.)*

Cross References

Person defined for purposes of this Code, see Family Code § 105.
Proceeding defined for purposes of this Code, see Family Code § 110.
Removal of Indian child from custody of parents by state or local authority, notice to tribe, see Welfare and Institutions Code § 305.5.
State defined for purposes of this Code, see Family Code § 145.

Research References

Forms

1 California Transactions Forms--Family Law § 3:8, No Statutory Custody Preferences.
2 California Transactions Forms--Family Law § 6:143, Overview of Indian Child Welfare Act (ICWA).

§ 177. Governing law in Indian child custody proceedings

(a) In an Indian child custody proceeding, the court shall apply Sections 224.2 to 224.6, inclusive, and Sections 305.5, 361.31, and 361.7 of the Welfare and Institutions Code, and the following rules from the California Rules of Court, as they read on January 1, 2007:

(1) Paragraph (7) of subdivision (b) of Rule 5.530.

(2) Subdivision (i) of Rule 5.534.

(b) In the provisions cited in subdivision (a), references to social workers, probation officers, county welfare department, or probation department shall be construed as meaning the party seeking a foster care placement, guardianship, or adoption under this code.

(c) This section shall only apply to proceedings involving an Indian child. *(Added by Stats.2006, c. 838 (S.B.678), § 1. Amended by Stats.2007, c. 130 (A.B.299), § 85.)*

Research References

Forms

1 California Transactions Forms--Family Law § 3:4, Subject Matter Jurisdiction for Custody Determinations.
2 California Transactions Forms--Family Law § 6:143, Overview of Indian Child Welfare Act (ICWA).
2 California Transactions Forms--Family Law § 6:149, Rights of Indian Child's Tribe.
West's California Judicial Council Forms ICWA–020, Parental Notification of Indian Status (Also Available in Spanish).
West's California Judicial Council Forms ICWA–040, Notice of Designation of Tribal Representative in a Court Proceeding Involving an Indian Child.
West's California Judicial Council Forms ICWA–050, Notice of Petition and Petition to Transfer Case Involving an Indian Child to Tribal Jurisdiction.
West's California Judicial Council Forms ICWA–060, Order on Petition to Transfer Case Involving an Indian Child to Tribal Jurisdiction.

§ 180. Notice of proceedings; parties; requirements; time to send

(a) In an Indian child custody proceeding notice shall comply with subdivision (b) of this section.

(b) Any notice sent under this section shall be sent to the minor's parent or legal guardian, Indian custodian, if any, and the Indian child's tribe and shall comply with all of the following requirements:

(1) Notice shall be sent by registered or certified mail with return receipt requested. Additional notice by first-class mail is recommended, but not required.

(2) Notice to the tribe shall be to the tribal chairperson, unless the tribe has designated another agent for service.

(3) Notice shall be sent to all tribes of which the child may be a member or eligible for membership until the court makes a determination as to which tribe is the Indian child's tribe in accordance with subdivision (d) of Section 170, after which notice need only be sent to the tribe determined to be the Indian child's tribe.

(4) Notice, to the extent required by federal law, shall be sent to the Secretary of the Interior's designated agent, the Sacramento Area Director, Bureau of Indian Affairs. If the identity or location of the Indian child's tribe is known, a copy of the notice shall also be sent directly to the Secretary of the Interior unless the Secretary of the Interior has waived that notice in writing and the person responsible for giving notice under this section has filed proof of the waiver with the court.

(5) In addition to the information specified in other sections of this article, notice shall include all of the following information:

(A) The name, birthdate, and birthplace of the Indian child, if known.

(B) The name of any Indian tribe in which the child is a member or may be eligible for membership, if known.

(C) All names known of the Indian child's biological parents, grandparents, and great-grandparents, or Indian custodians, including maiden, married, and former names or aliases, as well as their current and former addresses, birthdates, places of birth and death, tribal enrollment numbers, and any other identifying information, if known.

(D) A copy of the petition by which the proceeding was initiated.

(E) A copy of the child's birth certificate, if available.

(F) The location, mailing address, and telephone number of the court and all parties notified pursuant to this section.

(G) A statement of the following:

(i) The absolute right of the child's parents, Indian custodians, and tribe to intervene in the proceeding.

(ii) The right of the child's parents, Indian custodians, and tribe to petition the court to transfer the proceeding to the tribal court of the Indian child's tribe, absent objection by either parent and subject to declination by the tribal court.

(iii) The right of the child's parents, Indian custodians, and tribe to, upon request, be granted up to an additional 20 days from the receipt of the notice to prepare for the proceeding.

(iv) The potential legal consequences of the proceedings on the future custodial rights of the child's parents or Indian custodians.

(v) That if the parents or Indian custodians are unable to afford counsel, counsel will be appointed to represent the parents or Indian custodians pursuant to Section 1912 of the Indian Child Welfare Act (25 U.S.C. Sec. 1901 et seq.).

(vi) That the information contained in the notice, petition, pleading, and other court documents is confidential, so any person or entity notified shall maintain the confidentiality of the information contained in the notice concerning the particular proceeding and not reveal it to anyone who does not need the information in order to exercise the tribe's rights under the Indian Child Welfare Act (25 U.S.C. Sec. 1901 et seq.).

(c) Notice shall be sent whenever it is known or there is reason to know that an Indian child is involved, and for every hearing thereafter, including, but not limited to, the hearing at which a final adoption order is to be granted. After a tribe acknowledges that the child is a member or eligible for membership in that tribe, or after the Indian child's tribe intervenes in a proceeding, the information set out in subparagraphs (C), (D), (E), and (G) of paragraph (5) of subdivision (b) need not be included with the notice.

(d) Proof of the notice, including copies of notices sent and all return receipts and responses received, shall be filed with the court in advance of the hearing except as permitted under subdivision (e).

(e) No proceeding shall be held until at least 10 days after receipt of notice by the parent, Indian custodian, the tribe, or the Bureau of Indian Affairs. The parent, Indian custodian, or the tribe shall, upon request, be granted up to 20 additional days to prepare for the proceeding. Nothing herein shall be construed as limiting the rights of the parent, Indian custodian, or tribe to 10 days' notice if a lengthier notice period is required under this code.

(f) With respect to giving notice to Indian tribes, a party shall be subject to court sanctions if that person knowingly and willfully falsifies or conceals a material fact concerning whether the child is an Indian child, or counsels a party to do so.

(g) The inclusion of contact information of any adult or child that would otherwise be required to be included in the notification pursuant to this section, shall not be required if that person is at risk of harm as a result of domestic violence, child abuse, sexual abuse, or stalking. *(Added by Stats.2006, c. 838 (S.B.678), § 1.)*

Research References
Forms

2 California Transactions Forms--Family Law § 6:143, Overview of Indian Child Welfare Act (ICWA).

West's California Judicial Council Forms ADOPT–200, Adoption Request.

West's California Judicial Council Forms ICWA–030(A), Attachment to Notice of Child Custody Proceeding for Indian Child (Also Available in Spanish).

§ 185. Indian child of tribe not recognized to have tribal status under federal law; tribal participation at hearings

(a) In a custody proceeding involving a child who would otherwise be an Indian child based on the definition contained in paragraph (4) of Section 1903 of the federal Indian Child Welfare Act (25 U.S.C. Sec. 1901 et seq.), but is not an Indian child based on status of the child's tribe, as defined in paragraph (8) of Section 1903 of the federal Indian Child Welfare Act (25 U.S.C. Sec. 1901 et seq.), the court may permit the tribe from which the child is descended to participate in the proceeding upon request of the tribe.

(b) If the court permits a tribe to participate in a proceeding, the tribe may do all of the following, upon consent of the court:

(1) Be present at the hearing.

(2) Address the court.

(3) Request and receive notice of hearings.

(4) Request to examine court documents relating to the proceeding.

(5) Present information to the court that is relevant to the proceeding.

(6) Submit written reports and recommendations to the court.

(7) Perform other duties and responsibilities as requested or approved by the court.

(c) If more than one tribe requests to participate in a proceeding under subdivision (a), the court may limit participation to the tribe with which the child has the most significant contacts, as determined in accordance with paragraph (2) of subdivision (d) of Section 170.

(d) This section is intended to assist the court in making decisions that are in the best interest of the child by permitting a tribe in the circumstances set out in subdivision (a) to inform the court and parties to the proceeding about placement options for the child within the child's extended family or the tribal community, services and programs available to the child and the child's parents as Indians, and other unique interests the child or the child's parents may have as Indians. This section shall not be construed to make the Indian Child Welfare Act (25 U.S.C. Sec. 1901 et seq.), or any state law implementing the Indian Child Welfare Act, applicable to the proceedings, or to limit the court's discretion to permit other interested persons to participate in these or any other proceedings.

(e) This section shall only apply to proceedings involving an Indian child. *(Added by Stats.2006, c. 838 (S.B.678), § 1.)*

Division 2

GENERAL PROVISIONS

Part	Section
1. Jurisdiction	200
2. General Procedural Provisions	210
3. Temporary Restraining Order in Summons	231
4. Ex Parte Temporary Restraining Orders	240
5. Attorney's Fees and Costs	270
6. Enforcement of Judgments and Orders	290
7. Tribal Marriages and Divorces	295

Part 1

JURISDICTION

Section
200. Jurisdiction in superior court.

§ 200. Jurisdiction in superior court

The superior court has jurisdiction in proceedings under this code. *(Stats.1992, c. 162 (A.B.2650), § 10, operative Jan. 1, 1994.)*

Cross References

Appealable judgments and orders, see Code of Civil Procedure § 904.1.
Dissolution, nullity proceedings or legal separation, scope of jurisdiction, see Family Code §§ 2010, 2011.
Expedited child support order, jurisdiction of court, see Family Code § 3623.
Family conciliation courts,
 Coextensive jurisdiction, see Family Code § 1834.
 Jurisdiction, designation of court, see Family Code § 1810.
 Petition invoking jurisdiction, see Family Code § 1831.
 Proceedings for conciliation, see Family Code § 1830 et seq.
Interstate Compact on the Placement of Children, jurisdictional provisions, see Family Code § 7901.
Proceeding defined for purposes of this Code, see Family Code § 110.
Proceedings not involving minors, see Family Code § 1842.
Uniform Child Custody Jurisdiction and Enforcement Act,
 Conduct as grounds for declining jurisdiction, see Family Code § 3428.
 Grounds, see Family Code § 3421.
 Inconvenient forum, see Family Code § 3427.
 Modification of custody decree of another state, see Family Code § 3423.
 Notice to person outside the state, submission to jurisdiction, see Family Code § 3408.
 Simultaneous proceedings in other states, effect on jurisdiction, see Family Code § 3426.
Uniform Parentage Act,
 Jurisdiction and venue, see Family Code § 7620.
 Modification of judgment or order, jurisdiction and manner, see Family Code § 7642.

Research References
Forms

1 California Transactions Forms--Family Law § 4:104, Paternity Acknowledgment.

§ 200   GENERAL PROVISIONS

West's California Code Forms, Family § 303 Form 1, Order and Notices to Minor on Request Marry or Establish Domestic Partnership.
West's California Code Forms, Family § 4303 Form 1, Complaint by Spouse to Enforce Duty of Spousal Support.
West's California Code Forms, Family § 4400, Comment Overview—Duty of Adult Children to Support Parents.

Part 2
GENERAL PROCEDURAL PROVISIONS

Section
210. Rules for practice and procedure.
211. Provision by rule for practice and procedure.
211.5. Resources for veterans; communication with Department of Veteran Affairs; development and amendment of rules and forms.
212. Verification of pleadings.
213. Responsive declaration to seek affirmative relief alternative to moving party's requested relief; proceedings.
214. Joinder of issues of fact; private trial.
215. Modification of judgment or order; service of notice.
216. Mediators or evaluators appointed by or connected to the court; limitations upon communication with said persons; exceptions.
217. Hearing on motion; live, competent testimony to be received; refusal to hear testimony for good cause with written reasons; service of witness list.
218. Postjudgment pleadings; automatic reopening of discovery.

§ 210. Rules for practice and procedure

Except to the extent that any other statute or rules adopted by the Judicial Council provide applicable rules, the rules of practice and procedure applicable to civil actions generally, including the provisions of Title 3a (commencing with Section 391) of Part 2 of the Code of Civil Procedure, apply to, and constitute the rules of practice and procedure in, proceedings under this code. (Stats.1992, c. 162 (A.B.2650), § 10, operative Jan. 1, 1994. Amended by Stats.2002, c. 1118 (A.B.1938), § 2.)

Cross References

Adoption of minors,
  Appeal from order as to father's consent, see Family Code § 7669.
  Appeal from order as to withdrawal of consent, see Family Code § 8815.
  Department or agency disapproval, appeal from, see Family Code § 8820.
  Stepparent adoption, appeal from order as to consent, see Family Code § 9005.
Appeal of bifurcated issues, see Family Code § 2025.
Disposition of property, revision on appeal, see Family Code § 2555.
Dissolution of marriage, effect of appeal from judgment, see Family Code § 2341.
Judgment nunc pro tunc, entry where no appeal taken, see Family Code § 2346.
Parental custody and control,
  Appeal from order freeing child, indigent appellant, see Family Code § 7895.
  Appeal from order or judgment freeing child, see Family Code § 7894.
  Inspection of court papers on appeal from proceedings, see Family Code § 7805.
Proceeding defined for purposes of this Code, see Family Code § 110.
Similar provisions, see Probate Code § 1000.
Special rules regarding stay on appeal, provisions relating to child custody and exclusion from family dwelling, see Code of Civil Procedure § 917.7.
Summary dissolution proceedings, appeal in, see Family Code §§ 2400, 2404.
Superior courts, appealable judgments and orders, see Code of Civil Procedure § 904.1.
Support orders or judgments, appealable as in civil actions, see Family Code § 3554.

Valuation of property by court for purposes of arbitration, appeal, see Family Code § 2554.

§ 211. Provision by rule for practice and procedure

Notwithstanding any other provision of law, the Judicial Council may provide by rule for the practice and procedure in proceedings under this code. (Stats.1992, c. 162 (A.B.2650), § 10, operative Jan. 1, 1994.)

Cross References

Child support payments, duties relating to procedure for deposit of money, see Family Code § 4552.
Judicial Council,
  Child support guidelines, study and report, see Family Code § 4067.
  Consumer price index, adjustment of dollar amounts, see Family Code § 2400.
  Determining eligibility for payment of counsel, see Family Code § 3153.
  Family mediation and conciliation services, statewide coordination, see Family Code § 1850 et seq.
  Forms, see Family Code §§ 95, 115, 2062, 2250, 2331, 2401, 2402.
  Mediation, uniform standards of practice, see Family Code § 3162.
  Summary dissolution procedure, brochure description, see Family Code § 2406.
  Training program, see Family Code § 1816.
Proceeding defined for purposes of this Code, see Family Code § 110.
Similar provisions, see Family Code §§ 2021, 2025, 2070, 2321.
Temporary restraining orders, generally, see Code of Civil Procedure § 513.010 et seq.

Research References

Forms

West's California Judicial Council Forms FL–260, Petition for Custody and Support of Minor Children (Also Available in Spanish).
West's California Judicial Council Forms FL–270, Response to Petition for Custody and Support of Minor Children (Also Available in Spanish).

§ 211.5. Resources for veterans; communication with Department of Veteran Affairs; development and amendment of rules and forms

(a)(1) Commencing January 1, 2024, in proceedings under this code, a court shall provide self-identified veterans with a list of resources for veterans, including information about how to contact the local office of the Department of Veterans Affairs.

(2) The veteran may, at their discretion, provide the information about their veteran status on the Judicial Council military service form, file the form with the court, and serve it on the other parties to the action.

(b)(1) When a person files a form identifying the person as a veteran pursuant to paragraph (2) of subdivision (a), the court shall transmit a copy of the form to the Department of Veterans Affairs.

(2) Upon receipt of a copy of the form, the Department of Veterans Affairs shall, within a reasonable time, contact the person using the information provided on the form.

(c) On or before January 1, 2024, the Judicial Council may amend or develop the rules and forms necessary to implement this section. (Added by Stats.2022, c. 385 (S.B.1182), § 2, eff. Jan. 1, 2023.)

§ 212. Verification of pleadings

A petition, response, application, opposition, or other pleading filed with the court under this code shall be verified. (Stats.1992, c. 162 (A.B.2650), § 10, operative Jan. 1, 1994.)

Cross References

Similar provisions, see Code of Civil Procedure § 446.

Research References

Forms

2 California Transactions Forms--Family Law § 6:41, Initiating the Adoption.

2 California Transactions Forms--Family Law § 6:47, Matters to Consider in Drafting Petition for Independent Adoption of Unmarried Minor.
2 California Transactions Forms--Family Law § 6:98, Form Drafting Considerations.
2 California Transactions Forms--Family Law § 6:112, Form Drafting Considerations.
2 California Transactions Forms--Family Law § 6:162, Termination of Adoption.

§ 213. Responsive declaration to seek affirmative relief alternative to moving party's requested relief; proceedings

(a) In a hearing on an order to show cause, or on a modification thereof, or in a hearing on a motion, other than for contempt, the responding party may seek affirmative relief alternative to that requested by the moving party, on the same issues raised by the moving party, by filing a responsive declaration within the time set by statute or rules of court.

(b) This section applies in any of the following proceedings:

(1) A proceeding for dissolution of marriage, for nullity of marriage, or for legal separation of the parties.

(2) A proceeding relating to a protective order described in Section 6218.

(3) Any other proceeding in which there is at issue the visitation, custody, or support of a child. *(Stats.1992, c. 162 (A.B.2650), § 10, operative Jan. 1, 1994. Amended by Stats.1993, c. 219 (A.B.1500), § 83.)*

Cross References

Abuse of child, emergency protective order, see Family Code § 6250 et seq.
Custody of minors, protective and temporary orders, see Family Code § 7700.
Dissolution of marriage and legal separation,
  Generally, see Family Code § 2300 et seq.
  General procedural provisions, see Family Code § 2330 et seq.
Domestic violence protective order,
  In general, see Family Code § 6200 et seq.
  Defined, see Family Code § 6218.
  Mutual restraining orders, conditions for issuance, see Family Code § 6305.
  Remedies in addition to other remedies, see Family Code § 6227.
Emergency protective orders, see Family Code § 6240 et seq.
Ex parte orders issuable, temporary restraining orders, see Family Code § 6320 et seq.
Judgment and order defined for purposes of this Code, see Family Code § 100.
Proceeding defined for purposes of this Code, see Family Code § 110.
Support defined for purposes of this Code, see Family Code § 150.
Support of minors, see Family Code § 3900 et seq.
Temporary restraining orders, see Family Code § 7700 et seq.
Termination of parental rights, see Family Code § 7660 et seq.
Visitation, compensation, failure to assume responsibility, interference with rights, see Family Code § 3028.

Research References

Forms

West's California Judicial Council Forms FL–685, Response to Governmental Notice of Motion or Order to Show Cause.

§ 214. Joinder of issues of fact; private trial

Except as otherwise provided in this code or by court rule, the court may, when it considers it necessary in the interests of justice and the persons involved, direct the trial of any issue of fact joined in a proceeding under this code to be private, and may exclude all persons except the officers of the court, the parties, their witnesses, and counsel. *(Stats.1992, c. 162 (A.B.2650), § 10, operative Jan. 1, 1994.)*

Cross References

Adoption, exclusion from all court proceedings, see Family Code § 8611.
Conciliation proceedings, mandatory exclusion from, see Family Code § 1818.
Courts, public proceedings required, see Code of Civil Procedure § 124.
Marriage, confidential marriages, see Family Code § 500 et seq.
Person defined for purposes of this Code, see Family Code § 105.

Proceeding defined for purposes of this Code, see Family Code § 110.
Proceedings for termination of parental custody and control, exclusion from, see Family Code § 7884.
Uniform Parentage Act, confidentiality, see Family Code § 7643.

§ 215. Modification of judgment or order; service of notice

(a) Except as provided in subdivision (b) or (c), after entry of a judgment of dissolution of marriage, nullity of marriage, legal separation of the parties, or paternity, or after a permanent order in any other proceeding in which there was at issue the visitation, custody, or support of a child, no modification of the judgment or order, and no subsequent order in the proceedings, is valid unless any prior notice otherwise required to be given to a party to the proceeding is served, in the same manner as the notice is otherwise permitted by law to be served, upon the party. For the purposes of this section, service upon the attorney of record is not sufficient.

(b) A postjudgment motion to modify a custody, visitation, or child support order may be served on the other party or parties by first-class mail or airmail, postage prepaid, to the persons to be served. For any party served by mail, the proof of service shall include an address verification.

(c) This section does not apply if the court has ordered an issue or issues bifurcated for separate trial in advance of the disposition of the entire case. In those cases, service of a motion on any outstanding matter shall be served either upon the attorney of record, if the parties are represented, or upon the parties, if unrepresented. However, if there has been no pleading filed in the action for a period of six months after the entry of the bifurcated judgment, service shall be upon both the party, at the party's last known address, and the attorney of record. *(Stats.1992, c. 162 (A.B.2650), § 10, operative Jan. 1, 1994. Amended by Stats.1993, c. 219 (A.B. 1500), § 84; Stats.1999, c. 980 (A.B.1671), § 2; Stats.2010, c. 352 (A.B.939), § 2; Stats.2016, c. 67 (A.B.1735), § 1, eff. Jan. 1, 2017.)*

Cross References

Judgment and order defined for purposes of this Code, see Family Code § 100.
Manner of service of writs, notices, and other papers, service on attorney of creditor or debtor, see Code of Civil Procedure § 684.010.
Proceeding defined for purposes of this Code, see Family Code § 110.
Support, earnings assignment orders, stay of service of process, see Family Code §§ 5260, 5261.
Support defined for purposes of this Code, see Family Code § 150.

Research References

Forms

West's California Judicial Council Forms FL–334, Declaration Regarding Address Verification—Postjudgment Request to Modify a Child Custody, Visitation, or Child Support Order.
West's California Judicial Council Forms FL–683, Order to Show Cause (Governmental).
West's California Judicial Council Forms FL–684, Request for Order and Supporting Declaration (Governmental).
West's California Judicial Council Forms FL–686, Proof of Service by Mail.

§ 216. Mediators or evaluators appointed by or connected to the court; limitations upon communication with said persons; exceptions

(a) In the absence of a stipulation by the parties to the contrary, there shall be no ex parte communication between the attorneys for any party to an action and any court-appointed or court-connected evaluator or mediator, or between a court-appointed or court-connected evaluator or mediator and the court, in any proceedings under this code, except with regard to the scheduling of appointments.

(b) There shall be no ex parte communications between counsel appointed by the court pursuant to Section 3150 and a court-appointed or court-connected evaluator or mediator, except when it is expressly authorized by the court or undertaken pursuant to paragraph (5) of subdivision (c) of Section 3151.

§ 216

(c) Subdivisions (a) and (b) shall not apply in the following situations:

(1) To allow a mediator or evaluator to address a case involving allegations of domestic violence as set forth in Sections 3113, 3181, and 3192.

(2) To allow a mediator or evaluator to address a case involving allegations of domestic violence as set forth in Rule 5.215 of the California Rules of Court.

(3) If the mediator or evaluator determines that ex parte communication is needed to inform the court of the mediator's or evaluator's belief that a restraining order is necessary to prevent an imminent risk to the physical safety of the child or the party.

(d) This section shall not be construed to limit the responsibilities a mediator or evaluator may have as a mandated reporter pursuant to Section 11165.9 of the Penal Code or the responsibilities a mediator or evaluator have to warn under Tarasoff v. Regents of the University of California (1976) 17 Cal.3d 425, Hedlund v. Superior Court (1983) 34 Cal.3d 695, and Section 43.92 of the Civil Code.

(e) The Judicial Council shall, by July 1, 2006, adopt a rule of court to implement this section. *(Added by Stats.2005, c. 489 (S.B.1088), § 1. Amended by Stats.2007, c. 130 (A.B.299), § 86; Stats.2019, c. 115 (A.B.1817), § 2, eff. Jan. 1, 2020.)*

Implementation

For implementation of this section, see its terms.

§ 217. Hearing on motion; live, competent testimony to be received; refusal to hear testimony for good cause with written reasons; service of witness list

(a) At a hearing on any order to show cause or notice of motion brought pursuant to this code, absent a stipulation of the parties or a finding of good cause pursuant to subdivision (b), the court shall receive any live, competent testimony that is relevant and within the scope of the hearing and the court may ask questions of the parties.

(b) In appropriate cases, a court may make a finding of good cause to refuse to receive live testimony and shall state its reasons for the finding on the record or in writing. The Judicial Council shall, by January 1, 2012, adopt a statewide rule of court regarding the factors a court shall consider in making a finding of good cause.

(c) A party seeking to present live testimony from witnesses other than the parties shall, prior to the hearing, file and serve a witness list with a brief description of the anticipated testimony. If the witness list is not served prior to the hearing, the court may, on request, grant a brief continuance and may make appropriate temporary orders pending the continued hearing. *(Added by Stats.2010, c. 352 (A.B.939), § 3.)*

Research References

Forms

West's California Judicial Council Forms FL-321, Witness List.

§ 218. Postjudgment pleadings; automatic reopening of discovery

With respect to the ability to conduct formal discovery in family law proceedings, when a request for order or other motion is filed and served after entry of judgment, discovery shall automatically reopen as to the issues raised in the postjudgment pleadings currently before the court. The date initially set for trial of the action specified in subdivision (a) of Section 2024.020 of the Code of Civil Procedure shall mean the date the postjudgment proceeding is set for hearing on the motion or any continuance thereof, or evidentiary trial, whichever is later. *(Added by Stats.2014, c. 169 (A.B.2586), § 1, eff. Jan. 1, 2015.)*

Part 3

TEMPORARY RESTRAINING ORDER IN SUMMONS

Section
231. Application of part.
232. Statement in summons as to enforceability of order.
233. Duration of order; enforceability; violation; punishment.
234. Ex parte orders; admissibility as evidence.
235. Modification or revocation of orders.

Cross References

Petitions or judgments for dissolution of marriage, nullity of marriage, or for legal separation of the parties, see Family Code § 2024.

§ 231. Application of part

This part applies to a temporary restraining order in a summons issued under any of the following provisions:

(a) Section 2040 (proceeding for dissolution of marriage, for nullity of marriage, or for legal separation of the parties).

(b) Section 7700 (proceeding under Uniform Parentage Act). *(Stats.1992, c. 162 (A.B.2650), § 10, operative Jan. 1, 1994. Amended by Stats.1993, c. 219 (A.B.1500), § 84.5.)*

Cross References

Judgment and order defined for purposes of this Code, see Family Code § 100.
Proceeding defined for purposes of this Code, see Family Code § 110.
Uniform Parentage Act, see Family Code § 7600 et seq.

§ 232. Statement in summons as to enforceability of order

The summons shall state on its face that the order is enforceable in any place in this state by any law enforcement agency that has received mailed notice of the order or has otherwise received a copy of the order and any officer who has been shown a copy of the order. *(Stats.1992, c. 162 (A.B.2650), § 10, operative Jan. 1, 1994.)*

Cross References

Deprivation of custody of child or right to visitation, see Penal Code § 278.5.
Intentional and knowing violation of court order to prevent harassment, disturbing the peace, or threats or acts of violence, see Penal Code § 273.6.
Judgment and order defined for purposes of this Code, see Family Code § 100.
State defined for purposes of this Code, see Family Code § 145.

Research References

Forms

West's California Judicial Council Forms FL-110, Summons (Also Available in Arabic and Chinese).
West's California Judicial Council Forms FL-210, Summons (Uniform Percentage—Petition for Custody and Support) (Incl. Spanish) (Also Available in Chinese).

§ 233. Duration of order; enforceability; violation; punishment

(a) Upon filing the petition and issuance of the summons and upon personal service of the petition and summons on the respondent or upon waiver and acceptance of service by the respondent, the temporary restraining order under this part shall be in effect against the parties until the final judgment is entered or the petition is dismissed, or until further order of the court.

(b) The temporary restraining order is enforceable in any place in this state, but is not enforceable by a law enforcement agency of a political subdivision unless that law enforcement agency has received mailed notice of the order or has otherwise received a copy of the order or the officer enforcing the order has been shown a copy of the order.

(c) A willful and knowing violation of the order included in the summons by removing a child from the state without the written consent of the other party or an order of the court is punishable as provided in Section 278.5 of the Penal Code. A willful and knowing violation of any of the other orders included in the summons is punishable as provided in Section 273.6 of the Penal Code. *(Stats. 1992, c. 162 (A.B.2650), § 10, operative Jan. 1, 1994.)*

Cross References

Deprivation of custody of child or right to visitation, see Penal Code § 278.5.
Intentional and knowing violation of court order to prevent harassment, disturbing the peace, or threats or acts of violence, see Penal Code § 273.6.
Judgment and order defined for purposes of this Code, see Family Code § 100.
Respondent defined for purposes of this Code, see Family Code § 127.
State defined for purposes of this Code, see Family Code § 145.

Research References

Forms

California Practice Guide: Rutter Family Law Forms Form 1:32, Glossary of Common Family Law Terms, Phrases and Concepts (Enclosure to Form 1:31).
West's California Judicial Council Forms FL-110, Summons (Also Available in Arabic and Chinese).
West's California Judicial Council Forms FL-210, Summons (Uniform Percentage—Petition for Custody and Support) (Incl. Spanish) (Also Available in Chinese).

§ 234. Ex parte orders; admissibility as evidence

The automatic granting of the ex parte temporary restraining order under this part is not a court determination or competent evidence in any proceeding of any prior history of the conduct so proscribed occurring between the parties. *(Stats.1992, c. 162 (A.B.2650), § 10, operative Jan. 1, 1994.)*

Cross References

Deprivation of custody of child or right to visitation, see Penal Code § 278.5.
Intentional and knowing violation of court order to prevent harassment, disturbing the peace, or threats or acts of violence, see Penal Code § 273.6.
Judgment and order defined for purposes of this Code, see Family Code § 100.
Proceeding defined for purposes of this Code, see Family Code § 110.

§ 235. Modification or revocation of orders

Nothing in this part precludes either party from applying to the court for modification or revocation of the temporary restraining order provided for in this part or for further temporary orders or an expanded temporary ex parte order. *(Stats.1992, c. 162 (A.B.2650), § 10, operative Jan. 1, 1994.)*

Cross References

Deprivation of custody of child or right to visitation, see Penal Code § 278.5.
Intentional and knowing violation of court order to prevent harassment, disturbing the peace, or threats or acts of violence, see Penal Code § 273.6.
Judgment and order defined for purposes of this Code, see Family Code § 100.

Part 4

EX PARTE TEMPORARY RESTRAINING ORDERS

Section
240. Application of part.
240.5. Repealed.
241. Notice requirement; exception.
242. Deadline for hearing on the petition.
243. Service and response.
244. Precedence of hearing and trial.
245. Continuance.
246. Grant or denial on date petition submitted.

Cross References

Electronic submission of petitions and filings, development and publication of local rules, establishment of telephone number for electronic filing inquiries, see Family Code § 6307.
Ex parte protective orders, generally, see Family Code § 2045.
Temporary restraining orders, generally, see Code of Civil Procedure § 513.010 et seq.

§ 240. Application of part

This part applies where a temporary restraining order, including a protective order as defined in Section 6218, is issued under any of the following provisions:

(a) Article 2 (commencing with Section 2045) of Chapter 4 of Part 1 of Division 6 (dissolution of marriage, nullity of marriage, or legal separation of the parties).

(b) Article 3 (commencing with Section 4620) of Chapter 3 of Part 5 of Division 9 (deposit of assets to secure future child support payments).

(c) Article 1 (commencing with Section 6320) of Chapter 2 of Part 4 of Division 10 (Domestic Violence Prevention Act), other than an order under Section 6322.5.

(d) Article 2 (commencing with Section 7710) of Chapter 6 of Part 3 of Division 12 (Uniform Parentage Act). *(Added by Stats.1993, c. 219 (A.B.1500), § 85.1. Amended by Stats.1998, c. 511 (A.B.1900), § 1.)*

Cross References

Certified copies of order under certain domestic relations laws, free copies to indigent plaintiff, see Government Code § 26833.5.
Ex parte orders, see Family Code § 7710.
Injunction, temporary restraining order, see Code of Civil Procedure § 527.
Judgment and order defined for purposes of this Code, see Family Code § 100.
Practice and procedure rules, see Family Code § 210 et seq.
Support defined for purposes of this Code, see Family Code § 150.
Temporary restraining orders, generally, see Code of Civil Procedure § 513.010 et seq.

Research References

Forms

California Practice Guide: Rutter Family Law Forms Form 1:32, Glossary of Common Family Law Terms, Phrases and Concepts (Enclosure to Form 1:31).
West's California Code Forms, Family § 2045, Comment Overview—Ex Parte Protective Orders.

§ 240.5. Repealed by Stats.2002, c. 784 (S.B.1316), § 104

§ 241. Notice requirement; exception

Except as provided in Section 6300, an order described in Section 240 may not be granted without notice to the respondent unless it appears from facts shown by the declaration in support of the petition for the order, or in the petition for the order, that great or irreparable injury would result to the petitioner before the matter can be heard on notice. *(Stats.1992, c. 162 (A.B.2650), § 10, operative Jan. 1, 1994. Amended by Stats.1993, c. 219 (A.B.1500), § 85.2; Stats.2010, c. 572 (A.B.1596), § 6, operative Jan. 1, 2012.)*

Cross References

Affidavits, generally, see Code of Civil Procedure § 2009 et seq.
Judgment and order defined for purposes of this Code, see Family Code § 100.
Respondent defined for purposes of this Code, see Family Code § 127.
Support defined for purposes of this Code, see Family Code § 150.
Temporary restraining orders, generally, see Code of Civil Procedure § 513.010 et seq.
Verification of pleadings, see Family Code § 212.

§ 242. Deadline for hearing on the petition

(a) Within 21 days, or, if good cause appears to the court, 25 days from the date that a temporary restraining order is granted or denied, a hearing shall be held on the petition. If no request for a temporary restraining order is made, the hearing shall be held within 21 days, or, if good cause appears to the court, 25 days from the date that the petition is filed.

(b) If a hearing is not held within the time provided in subdivision (a), the court may nonetheless hear the matter, but the temporary restraining order shall no longer be enforceable unless it is extended under Section 245. *(Added by Stats.1993, c. 219 (A.B.1500), § 85.4. Amended by Stats.2010, c. 572 (A.B.1596), § 7, operative Jan. 1, 2012; Stats.2015, c. 411 (A.B.1081), § 4, eff. Jan. 1, 2016.)*

Cross References

Certified copies of order under certain domestic relations laws, free copies to indigent plaintiff, see Government Code § 26833.5.
Injunctions, grants before judgment upon verified complaint or affidavits, see Code of Civil Procedure § 527.
Judgment and order defined for purposes of this Code, see Family Code § 100.
Temporary restraining orders, generally, see Code of Civil Procedure § 513.010 et seq.

Research References

Forms

West's California Judicial Council Forms DV-109, Notice of Court Hearing (Domestic Violence Prevention) (Also Available in Chinese, Korean, Spanish, and Vietnamese).

§ 243. Service and response

(a) If a petition under this part has been filed, the respondent shall be personally served with a copy of the petition, the temporary restraining order, if any, and the notice of hearing on the petition. Service shall be made at least five days before the hearing.

(b) On motion of the petitioner or on its own motion, the court may shorten the time for service on the respondent.

(c) If service on the respondent is made, the respondent may file a response that explains or denies the allegations in the petition. *(Stats.1992, c. 162 (A.B.2650), § 10, operative Jan. 1, 1994. Amended by Stats.1993, c. 219 (A.B.1500), § 85.5; Stats.1999, c. 980 (A.B.1671), § 3; Stats.2000, c. 135 (A.B.2539), § 56; Stats.2000, c. 90 (A.B.2914), § 1, eff. July 5, 2000; Stats.2010, c. 572 (A.B.1596), § 8, operative Jan. 1, 2012; Stats.2015, c. 411 (A.B.1081), § 5, eff. Jan. 1, 2016.)*

Cross References

Application for temporary restraining order, see Code of Civil Procedure § 513.010.
Certified copies of order under certain domestic relations laws, free copies to indigent plaintiff, see Government Code § 26833.5.
Injunctions, generally, see Code of Civil Procedure § 525 et seq.
Judgment and order defined for purposes of this Code, see Family Code § 100.
Respondent defined for purposes of this Code, see Family Code § 127.
Support defined for purposes of this Code, see Family Code § 150.

Research References

Forms

West's California Judicial Council Forms DV-200, Proof of Personal Service (CLETS) (Also Available in Korean, Spanish, and Vietnamese).

§ 244. Precedence of hearing and trial

(a) On the day of the hearing, the hearing on the petition shall take precedence over all other matters on the calendar that day, except older matters of the same character, and matters to which special precedence may be given by law.

(b) The hearing on the petition shall be set for trial at the earliest possible date and shall take precedence over all other matters, except older matters of the same character, and matters to which special precedence may be given by law. *(Stats.1992, c. 162 (A.B.2650), § 10, operative Jan. 1, 1994. Amended by Stats.2010, c. 572 (A.B. 1596), § 9, operative Jan. 1, 2012.)*

Cross References

Applicability of part, see Family Code § 240.
Judgment and order defined for purposes of this Code, see Family Code § 100.
Temporary restraining orders, generally, see Code of Civil Procedure § 513.010 et seq.

§ 245. Continuance

(a) The respondent shall be entitled, as a matter of course, to one continuance for a reasonable period, to respond to the petition.

(b) Either party may request a continuance of the hearing, which the court shall grant on a showing of good cause. The request may be made in writing before or at the hearing or orally at the hearing. The court may also grant a continuance on its own motion.

(c) If the court grants a continuance, any temporary restraining order that has been issued shall remain in effect until the end of the continued hearing, unless otherwise ordered by the court. In granting a continuance, the court may modify or terminate a temporary restraining order.

(d) If the court grants a continuance, the extended temporary restraining order shall state on its face the new date of expiration of the order.

(e) A fee shall not be charged for the extension of the temporary restraining order. *(Stats.1992, c. 162 (A.B.2650), § 10, operative Jan. 1, 1994. Amended by Stats.2010, c. 572 (A.B.1596), § 10, operative Jan. 1, 2012; Stats.2015, c. 411 (A.B.1081), § 6, eff. Jan. 1, 2016.)*

Cross References

Ex parte orders, survival of custody, visitation, or support order following expiration of protective order, alternative methods of service, see Family Code § 6340.
Injunctions, grants before judgment upon verified complaint or affidavits, see Code of Civil Procedure § 527.
Judgment and order defined for purposes of this Code, see Family Code § 100.
Respondent defined for purposes of this Code, see Family Code § 127.
State defined for purposes of this Code, see Family Code § 145.
Temporary restraining orders, generally, see Code of Civil Procedure § 513.010 et seq.

Research References

Forms

West's California Code Forms, Family § 6340, Comment Overview—Issuance of Orders After Notice and Hearing.
West's California Judicial Council Forms DV-115, Request to Continue Hearing (Also Available in Chinese, Korean, Spanish, and Vietnamese).
West's California Judicial Council Forms DV-115-INFO, How to Ask for a New Hearing Date (Also Available in Chinese, Korean, Spanish, and Vietnamese).
West's California Judicial Council Forms DV-116, Order on Request to Continue Court Hearing (Also Available in Korean, Spanish, and Vietnamese).
West's California Judicial Council Forms DV-200, Proof of Personal Service (CLETS) (Also Available in Korean, Spanish, and Vietnamese).
West's California Judicial Council Forms FL-309, Order on Request to Reschedule Hearing (Family Law—Governmental—Uniform Parentage—Custody and Support) (Also Available in Spanish).
West's California Judicial Council Forms FL-310, Responsive Declaration to Request to Reschedule Hearing (Family Law—Governmental—Uniform Parentage—Custody and Support).

§ 246. Grant or denial on date petition submitted

A request for a temporary restraining order described in Section 240, issued without notice, shall be granted or denied on the same day that the petition is submitted to the court, unless the petition is filed too late in the day to permit effective review, in which case the order shall be granted or denied on the next day of judicial business in sufficient time for the order to be filed that day with the clerk of the court. *(Added by Stats.1993, c. 148 (A.B.1331), § 1. Amended by Stats.2010, c. 572 (A.B.1596), § 11, operative Jan. 1, 2012.)*

§ 272

Part 5

ATTORNEY'S FEES AND COSTS

Section
270. Order for attorney's fees and costs; ability to pay.
271. Alternative basis for award; encouragement of cooperation; award as sanction; notice; property or income of sanctioned party.
272. Method of payment; enforcement of order for costs and fees.
273. Attorney's fees awarded against governmental agencies.
274. Attempted murder of a spouse; attorney's fees and costs; notice and hearing; source of funds.
275. Inoperative.

Cross References

Attorney in an action or special proceeding, ability to change before or after judgment or final determination, see Code of Civil Procedure § 284.
Attorneys, State Bar Act, see Business and Professions Code § 6000.
Attorney's fees and costs, generally, see Code of Civil Procedure § 1021.
Withdrawal of attorneys of record in domestic relations proceedings, see Code of Civil Procedure § 285.1.

§ 270. Order for attorney's fees and costs; ability to pay

If a court orders a party to pay attorney's fees or costs under this code, the court shall first determine that the party has or is reasonably likely to have the ability to pay. *(Added by Stats.1993, c. 219 (A.B.1500), § 87.)*

Cross References

Attorney's fees and costs, generally, see Code of Civil Procedure § 1021.
Judgment and order defined for purposes of this Code, see Family Code § 100.
Right to custody of minor child, failure to assume caretaker responsibility, application of this section, see Family Code § 3028.

Research References

Forms

West's California Code Forms, Family § 270, Comment Overview—Attorney's Fees.
West's California Judicial Council Forms FL–157, Spousal or Domestic Partner Support Declaration Attachment (Also Available in Spanish).
West's California Judicial Council Forms FL–158, Supporting Declaration for Attorney's Fees and Costs Attachment.
West's California Judicial Council Forms FL–319, Request for Attorney's Fees and Costs Attachment.
West's California Judicial Council Forms FL–346, Attorney's Fees and Costs Order Attachment.
West's California Judicial Council Forms FL–349, Spousal or Domestic Partner Support Factors Under Family Code Section 4320—Attachment.

§ 271. Alternative basis for award; encouragement of cooperation; award as sanction; notice; property or income of sanctioned party

(a) Notwithstanding any other provision of this code, the court may base an award of attorney's fees and costs on the extent to which the conduct of each party or attorney furthers or frustrates the policy of the law to promote settlement of litigation and, where possible, to reduce the cost of litigation by encouraging cooperation between the parties and attorneys. An award of attorney's fees and costs pursuant to this section is in the nature of a sanction. In making an award pursuant to this section, the court shall take into consideration all evidence concerning the parties' incomes, assets, and liabilities. The court shall not impose a sanction pursuant to this section that imposes an unreasonable financial burden on the party against whom the sanction is imposed. In order to obtain an award under this section, the party requesting an award of attorney's fees and costs is not required to demonstrate any financial need for the award.

(b) An award of attorney's fees and costs as a sanction pursuant to this section shall be imposed only after notice to the party against whom the sanction is proposed to be imposed and opportunity for that party to be heard.

(c) An award of attorney's fees and costs as a sanction pursuant to this section is payable only from the property or income of the party against whom the sanction is imposed, except that the award may be against the sanctioned party's share of the community property. *(Added by Stats.1993, c. 219 (A.B.1500), § 87.)*

Cross References

Attorneys, State Bar Act, see Business and Professions Code § 6000.
Attorney's fees and costs, generally, see Code of Civil Procedure § 1021.
Community property defined for purposes of this Code, see Family Code § 65.
Judgment and order defined for purposes of this Code, see Family Code § 100.
Property defined for purposes of this Code, see Family Code § 113.

Research References

Forms

California Practice Guide: Rutter Family Law Forms Form 14:4, Request for Order Re Attorney Fees and Costs as Sanctions (Family Code §271).
West's California Code Forms, Family § 270, Comment Overview—Attorney's Fees.

§ 272. Method of payment; enforcement of order for costs and fees

(a) Where the court orders one of the parties to pay attorney's fees and costs for the benefit of the other party, the fees and costs may, in the discretion of the court, be made payable in whole or in part to the attorney entitled thereto.

(b) Subject to subdivision (c), the order providing for payment of the attorney's fees and costs may be enforced directly by the attorney in the attorney's own name or by the party in whose behalf the order was made.

(c) If the attorney has ceased to be the attorney for the party in whose behalf the order was made, the attorney may enforce the order only if it appears of record that the attorney has given to the former client or successor counsel 10 days' written notice of the application for enforcement of the order. During the 10-day period, the client may file in the proceeding a motion directed to the former attorney for partial or total reallocation of fees and costs to cover the services and cost of successor counsel. On the filing of the motion, the enforcement of the order by the former attorney shall be stayed until the court has resolved the motion. *(Added by Stats.1993, c. 219 (A.B.1500), § 87.)*

Cross References

Attorney in an action or special proceeding, ability to change before or after judgment or final determination, see Code of Civil Procedure § 284.
Judgment and order defined for purposes of this Code, see Family Code § 100.
Proceeding defined for purposes of this Code, see Family Code § 110.
Withdrawal of attorneys of record in domestic relations proceedings, see Code of Civil Procedure § 285.1.

Research References

Forms

West's California Code Forms, Family § 270, Comment Overview—Attorney's Fees.
West's California Code Forms, Family § 272 Form 1, Notice of Enforcement of Attorney's Fees Award.

§ 272

West's California Code Forms, Family § 272 Form 2, Declaration in Support of Motion for Reallocation of Attorney's Fees.

§ 273. Attorney's fees awarded against governmental agencies

Notwithstanding any other provision of this code, the court shall not award attorney's fees against any governmental agency involved in a family law matter or child support proceeding except when sanctions are appropriate pursuant to Section 128.5 of the Code of Civil Procedure or Section 271 of this code. *(Added by Stats.1994, c. 1269 (A.B.2208), § 10.)*

Cross References

Attorney's fees and costs, generally, see Code of Civil Procedure § 1021.
Proceeding defined for purposes of this Code, see Family Code § 110.
Support defined for purposes of this Code, see Family Code § 150.
Withdrawal of attorneys of record in domestic relations proceedings, see Code of Civil Procedure § 285.1.

§ 274. Attempted murder of a spouse; attorney's fees and costs; notice and hearing; source of funds

(a) Notwithstanding any other provision of law, if the injured spouse is entitled to a remedy authorized pursuant to Section 4324, the injured spouse shall be entitled to an award of reasonable attorney's fees and costs as a sanction pursuant to this section.

(b) An award of attorney's fees and costs as a sanction pursuant to this section shall be imposed only after notice to the party against whom the sanction is proposed to be imposed and opportunity for that party to be heard.

(c) An award of attorney's fees and costs as a sanction pursuant to this section is payable only from the property or income of the party against whom the sanction is imposed, except that the award may be against the sanctioned party's share of the community property. In order to obtain an award under this section, the party requesting an award of attorney's fees and costs is not required to demonstrate any financial need for the award. *(Added by Stats.1995, c. 364 (A.B.16), § 1. Amended by Stats.2006, c. 538 (S.B.1852), § 156.)*

Cross References

Community property defined for purposes of this Code, see Family Code § 65.
Judgment and order defined for purposes of this Code, see Family Code § 100.
Property defined for purposes of this Code, see Family Code § 113.
References to husband, wife, spouses and married persons, persons included for purposes of this Code, see Family Code § 11.
Withdrawal of attorneys of record in domestic relations proceedings, see Code of Civil Procedure § 285.1.

§ 275. Inoperative

Part 6

ENFORCEMENT OF JUDGMENTS AND ORDERS

Section
290. Methods of enforcement.
291. Judgment for possession or sale of property; enforceability; renewal; laches; enforcement after death; self-help materials; definition.
292. Judicial Council; modification and creation of contempt forms; content.

§ 290. Methods of enforcement

A judgment or order made or entered pursuant to this code may be enforced by the court by execution, the appointment of a receiver, or contempt, or by any other order as the court in its discretion determines from time to time to be necessary. *(Stats.1992, c. 162 (A.B.2650), § 10, operative Jan. 1, 1994. Amended by Stats.2000, c. 808 (A.B.1358), § 23, eff. Sept. 28, 2000; Stats.2006, c. 86 (A.B.2126), § 2.)*

Cross References

Contempt proceedings, see Code of Civil Procedure § 1209 et seq.
Enforcement of judgments, see Code of Civil Procedure § 680.010 et seq.
Execution, enforcement by writ without prior court approval, see Family Code § 5100 et seq.
Execution of judgments, generally, see Code of Civil Procedure § 699.010 et seq.
Judgment and order defined for purposes of this Code, see Family Code § 100.
Receivers, generally, see Code of Civil Procedure § 564 et seq.
Renewal of judgment, application for, see Code of Civil Procedure § 683.130.
Support orders, enforcement, see Family Code § 4500 et seq.
Uninsured health care costs, payment procedures, judicial relief, see Family Code § 4063.

Research References

Forms
8C Am. Jur. Pl. & Pr. Forms Divorce and Separation § 375, Introductory Comments.
West's California Code Forms, Family § 270, Comment Overview—Attorney's Fees.
West's California Code Forms, Family § 290, Comment Overview—Enforcement of Judgments and Orders.

§ 291. Judgment for possession or sale of property; enforceability; renewal; laches; enforcement after death; self-help materials; definition

(a) A money judgment or judgment for possession or sale of property that is made or entered under this code, including a judgment for child, family, or spousal support, is enforceable until paid in full or otherwise satisfied.

(b) A judgment described in this section is exempt from any requirement that a judgment be renewed. Failure to renew a judgment described in this section has no effect on the enforceability of the judgment.

(c) A judgment described in this section may be renewed pursuant to Article 2 (commencing with Section 683.110) of Chapter 3 of Division 1 of Title 9 of Part 2 of the Code of Civil Procedure. An application for renewal of a judgment described in this section, whether or not payable in installments, may be filed:

(1) If the judgment has not previously been renewed as to past due amounts, at any time.

(2) If the judgment has previously been renewed, the amount of the judgment as previously renewed and any past due amount that became due and payable after the previous renewal may be renewed at any time after a period of at least five years has elapsed from the time the judgment was previously renewed.

(d) In an action to enforce a judgment for child, family, or spousal support, the defendant may raise, and the court may consider, the defense of laches only with respect to any portion of the judgment that is owed to the state.

(e) Nothing in this section supersedes the law governing enforcement of a judgment after the death of the judgment creditor or judgment debtor.

(f) On or before January 1, 2008, the Judicial Council shall develop self-help materials that include: (1) a description of the remedies available for enforcement of a judgment under this code, and (2) practical advice on how to avoid disputes relating to the enforcement of a support obligation. The self-help materials shall be made available to the public through the Judicial Council self-help Internet Web site.

(g) As used in this section, "judgment" includes an order. *(Added by Stats.2006, c. 86 (A.B.2126), § 4. Amended by Stats.2007, c. 130 (A.B.299), § 87.)*

Cross References

Contempt proceedings, see Code of Civil Procedure § 1209 et seq.

Enforcement of support orders, period for enforcement and renewal governed by these provisions, see Family Code § 4502.
Execution of judgments, generally, see Code of Civil Procedure § 699.010 et seq.
Judgment and order defined for purposes of this Code, see Family Code § 100.
Property defined for purposes of this Code, see Family Code § 113.
Renewal of judgment, application for, see Code of Civil Procedure § 683.130.
Support orders, enforcement, see Family Code § 4500 et seq.

Research References

Forms

8C Am. Jur. Pl. & Pr. Forms Divorce and Separation § 375, Introductory Comments.
West's California Code Forms, Family § 5104, Comment Overview—Enforcement by Writ of Execution.

§ 292. Judicial Council; modification and creation of contempt forms; content

(a) The Judicial Council shall modify the title of its existing form, "Order to Show Cause and Declaration for Contempt (Family Law)," to "Order to Show Cause and Affidavit for Contempt (Family Law)."

(b) The Judicial Council shall prescribe a form entitled "Affidavit of Facts Constituting Contempt" that a party seeking to enforce a judgment or order made or entered pursuant to this code by contempt may use as an attachment to the Judicial Council form entitled "Order to Show Cause and Affidavit for Contempt (Family Law)." The form shall provide in the simplest language possible:

(1) The basic information needed to sustain a cause of action for contempt, including, but not limited to, the elements of a cause of action for contempt.

(2) Instructions on how to prepare and submit the Order to Show Cause and Affidavit for Contempt (Family Law) and the Affidavit of Facts Constituting Contempt.

(3) Lines for the date and a signature made under penalty of perjury.

(c) Section 1211.5 of the Code of Civil Procedure shall apply to the Order to Show Cause and Affidavit for Contempt (Family Law) and the Affidavit of Facts Constituting Contempt. (Added by Stats.1995, c. 904 (A.B.965), § 2.)

Cross References

Contempts, generally, see Code of Civil Procedure § 1209 et seq.

Family law matters, filing of Judicial Council form entitled "Order to Show Cause and Affidavit for Contempt (Family Law)", compliance, see Code of Civil Procedure § 1211.
Judgment and order defined for purposes of this Code, see Family Code § 100.

Research References

Forms

West's California Judicial Council Forms FL–410, Order to Show Cause and Affidavit for Contempt.
West's California Judicial Council Forms FL–411, Affidavit of Facts Constituting Contempt (Financial and Injunctive Orders).
West's California Judicial Council Forms FL–412, Affidavit of Facts Constituting Contempt (Domestic Violence/Custody and Visitation).

Part 7

TRIBAL MARRIAGES AND DIVORCES

Section
295. Validity of marriages and divorces.

§ 295. Validity of marriages and divorces

(a) For the purpose of application of the laws of succession set forth in the Probate Code to a decedent, and for the purpose of determining the validity of a marriage under the laws of this state, an alliance entered into before 1958, which, by custom of the Indian tribe, band, or group of which the parties to the alliance, or either of them, are members, is commonly recognized in the tribe, band, or group as marriage, is deemed a valid marriage under the laws of this state.

(b) In the case of these marriages and for the purposes described in subdivision (a), a separation, which, by custom of the Indian tribe, band, or group of which the separating parties, or either of them, are members, is commonly recognized in the tribe, band, or group as a dissolution of marriage, is deemed a valid divorce under the laws of this state. (Stats.1992, c. 162 (A.B.2650), § 10, operative Jan. 1, 1994.)

Cross References

Adoption, children of Indian ancestry, certificate of degree of Indian blood, see Family Code § 8619.
Intestate succession, generally, see Probate Code § 6400 et seq.
State defined for purposes of this Code, see Family Code § 145.

Division 2.5

DOMESTIC PARTNER REGISTRATION

Part	Section
1. Definitions	297
2. Registration	298
3. Termination	299
4. Legal Effect	299.2
5. Preemption	299.6

Cross References

Approval of contracts, contracts for acquisition of goods or services with contractors who discriminate against employees with domestic partners, see Public Contract Code § 10295.3.
State employees' health benefits, filing of valid Declaration of Domestic Partnership form or establishing valid domestic partnership, see Government Code § 22872.

Part 1

DEFINITIONS

Section
297. Domestic partners and partnership; establishment.
297.1. Domestic partnership with underage person; court order and written consent of parents.
297.5. Rights, protections and benefits; responsibilities; obligations and duties under law; date of registration as equivalent of date of marriage.

§ 297. Domestic partners and partnership; establishment

(a) Domestic partners are two adults who have chosen to share one another's lives in an intimate and committed relationship of mutual caring.

(b) A domestic partnership shall be established in California when both persons file a Declaration of Domestic Partnership with the Secretary of State pursuant to this division, and, at the time of filing, all of the following requirements are met:

(1) Neither person is married to someone else or is a member of another domestic partnership with someone else that has not been terminated, dissolved, or adjudged a nullity.

(2) The two persons are not related by blood in a way that would prevent them from being married to each other in this state.

(3) Both persons are at least 18 years of age, except as provided in Section 297.1.

(4) Both persons are capable of consenting to the domestic partnership. *(Added by Stats.1999, c. 588 (A.B.26), § 2. Amended by Stats.2001, c. 893 (A.B.25), § 3; Stats.2003, c. 421 (A.B.205), § 3, operative Jan. 1, 2005; Stats.2011, c. 721 (S.B.651), § 1; Stats.2019, c. 135 (S.B.30), § 1, eff. Jan. 1, 2020.)*

Cross References

Adult defined for purposes of this Code, see Family Code § 6501.
Capacity of conservatee to marry or enter domestic partnership, determination, see Probate Code § 1901.
Capacity to bind or obligate conservatorship estate, rights not limited, see Probate Code § 1871.
Confidential domestic partnership, see Family Code § 298.7.
County employees retirement law, retired members, election to change or elect optional retirement allowance to provide for domestic partner, see Government Code § 31760.7.
Domestic partner and spousal eligibility for medical assistance, definitions, undue hardship from ineligibility period, see Welfare and Institutions Code § 14015.12.
Domestic partner defined for purposes of Probate Code, see Probate Code § 37.
Domestic partner desiring to adopt a child of his or her domestic partner, filing a petition in county in which the petitioner resides, see Family Code § 9000.
Domestic partners, negligent infliction of emotional distress, damages, see Civil Code § 1714.01.
Domestic partnership defined for purposes of state government personnel, see Government Code § 22869.
Domestic violence incident reports and face sheets, see Family Code § 6228.
Health care service plans, domestic partners, coverage, see Health and Safety Code § 1374.58.
Health care surrogates, domestic partner of patient, see Probate Code § 4716.
Health facilities, visitation rights of domestic partners, domestic partner's children, and domestic partner of patient's parent or child, see Health and Safety Code § 1261.
Housing, age limitations, necessity for senior citizen housing, see Civil Code § 51.3.
Human experimentation, investigators within institutions holding a federal assurance, see Health and Safety Code § 24178.
Individual access to health care coverage, open, annual, and special enrollment periods, triggering events, effective dates of coverage, limitations on eligibility rules, single risk pool considerations, see Health and Safety Code § 1399.849.
Individual access to health insurance, open, annual, and special enrollment periods, triggering events, effective dates of coverage, limitations on eligibility rules, single risk pool considerations, see Insurance Code § 10965.3.
Judges' retirement law, domestic partnership, see Government Code § 75004.5.
Judges retirement system, definitions, see Government Code § 75502.
Life and disability insurance, domestic partners, coverage, see Insurance Code § 10121.7.
Paid family leave, definitions, see Unemployment Insurance Code § 3302.
Person defined for purposes of this Code, see Family Code § 105.
Personal income tax, domestic partner of taxpayer, treatment as spouse, dependent, or member of family for purposes of tax statutes, see Revenue and Taxation Code § 17021.7.
Powers and duties of guardian or conservator of the estate, payments from principal and income, see Probate Code § 2430.
Public employees' retirement system, domestic partnership, see Government Code § 20065.5.
Retirement of legislators, domestic partnership, see Government Code § 9351.4.
Riverside County, establishment or preservation of senior housing, see Civil Code § 51.11.
San Mateo County, survivor's optional death benefits and allowances, domestic partners, see Government Code § 31780.2
State defined for purposes of this Code, see Family Code § 145.
State employees' health benefits, domestic partners, see Government Code § 22867 et seq.
State Teachers' Retirement System, election to receive actuarially modified retirement allowance payable throughout life, see Education Code § 24300.1.
State teachers' retirement system, registered domestic partner of member included as spouse, see Education Code §§ 22007.5, 22171.
State teachers' retirement system cash balance plan, registered domestic partner of member included as spouse, see Education Code §§ 26002.5, 26140.
Unemployment compensation, claimants who left employment to accompany domestic partner to location impractical to commute from,
  Disqualification from benefits, voluntary leaving employment without good cause, see Unemployment Insurance Code § 1256.
  Extended duration benefits, ruling as to cause of termination of exhaustee's employment, see Unemployment Insurance Code § 3701.
  Federal-state extended benefits, submission of facts by employer affecting eligibility, see Unemployment Insurance Code § 4701.
  Reserve accounts, employer's right to notify department of cause of claimant's leaving, see Unemployment Insurance Code §§ 1030, 1032.
Victims of crime, work absences for judicial proceedings, covered employees, see Labor Code § 230.2.
Wrongful death, persons with standing, see Code of Civil Procedure § 377.60.

Research References

Forms

California Practice Guide: Rutter Family Law Forms Form 1:32, Glossary of Common Family Law Terms, Phrases and Concepts (Enclosure to Form 1:31).
1 California Transactions Forms--Family Law § 4:4, Application of Agreements to Same Sex Couples.
West's California Code Forms, Civil Procedure § 377.60 Form 2, Parties—Complaint—Wrongful Death of Domestic Partner.
West's California Code Forms, Family § 297.5, Comment Overview—Domestic Partnerships.
West's California Code Forms, Probate § 21351 Form 1, Certificate of Independent Review.
West's California Code Forms, Revenue and Taxation § 7651 Form 1, Supplier of Motor Vehicle Fuel Tax Return (CDTFA-501-Ps).
West's California Code Forms, Revenue and Taxation § 30182 Form 1, Cigarette Distributor's Tax Return (CDTFA-501-CD).
West's California Code Forms, Revenue and Taxation § 32251 Form 1, Beer Manufacturer Tax Return (CDTFA-501-Bm).
West's California Code Forms, Revenue and Taxation § 38402 Form 2, Timber Tax Return (CDTFA-401-1pt).
West's California Code Forms, Revenue and Taxation § 40063 Form 1, Consumer's Electrical Energy Surcharge Return (CDTFA-501-Ec).
West's California Code Forms, Revenue and Taxation § 41052 Form 1, Emergency Telephone Users Surcharge Return (CDTFA-501-Te).
West's California Code Forms, Revenue and Taxation § 43152.16 Form 1, Hazardous Waste Disposal Fee Return (CDTFA-501-HD)—Annual (CDTFA-501-HF).
West's California Code Forms, Revenue and Taxation § 45051 Form 1, Integrated Waste Management Fee Return (CDTFA-501-SQ).
West's California Code Forms, Revenue and Taxation § 60115 Form 1, Interstate User Diesel Fuel Tax Return (CDTFA-501-Di).
West's California Judicial Council Forms FL–100, Petition—Marriage/Domestic Partnership (Also Available in Arabic, Chinese, and Spanish).
West's California Judicial Council Forms FL–910, Request of Minor to Marry or Establish a Domestic Partnership.
West's California Judicial Council Forms FL–912, Consent for Minor to Marry or Establish a Domestic Partnership.
West's California Judicial Council Forms FL–915, Order and Notices to Minor on Request to Marry or Establish a Domestic Partnership.

§ 297.1. Domestic partnership with underage person; court order and written consent of parents

(a) A person under 18 years of age who, together with the other proposed domestic partner, otherwise meets the requirements for a domestic partnership other than the requirement of being at least 18 years of age, may establish a domestic partnership upon obtaining a court order granting permission to the underage person or persons to establish a domestic partnership.

(b)(1) The court order and written consent of the parents of each person under 18 years of age or of one of the parents or the guardian of each person under 18 years of age, except as provided in paragraph (2), shall be filed with the clerk of the court, and a certified copy of the order shall be filed with the Secretary of State with the Declaration of Domestic Partnership.

(2) If it appears to the satisfaction of the court by application of a person under 18 years of age that the person requires a written consent to establish a domestic partnership and that the minor has no parent or guardian, or has no parent or guardian capable of consenting, the court may make an order consenting to establishing the domestic partnership. The order shall be filed with the clerk of the court and a certified copy of the order shall be filed with the Secretary of State with the Declaration of Domestic Partnership.

(3) Notwithstanding any other law, immediately after the Secretary of State creates or updates the document described in Section 298.8 using the information required for the document and that is contained in a certified copy of a court order filed with the Secretary of State with the Declaration of Domestic Partnership pursuant to this subdivision, the Secretary of State may dispose of the certified copy of the court order.

(c) In determining whether to issue a court order granting permission to establish a domestic partnership, the court shall do all of the following:

(1) Require Family Court Services to separately interview the parties intending to establish a domestic partnership and, if applicable, at least one of the parents or the guardian of each party who is a minor. If more than one parent or guardian is interviewed, the parents or guardians shall be interviewed separately.

(2) Require Family Court Services to prepare and submit to the court a written report, containing any assessment of potential force, threat, persuasion, fraud, coercion, or duress by either of the parties or their family members relating to the intended domestic partnership. The report shall also contain recommendations of Family Court Services for either granting or denying the parties permission to establish a domestic partnership. If Family Court Services knows or reasonably suspects that either party is a victim of child abuse or neglect, Family Court Services shall submit a report of the known or suspected child abuse or neglect to the county child protective services agency.

(3) After receiving the report of the assessments of Family Court Services, as described in paragraph (2), separately interview in camera each of the parties prior to making a final determination regarding the court order.

(4) Consider whether there is evidence of coercion or undue influence on the minor.

(d) If the court issues an order granting the parties permission to establish a domestic partnership, and if one or both of the parties are 17 years of age or younger, the parties shall be eligible to file a Declaration of Domestic Partnership with the Secretary of State no earlier than 30 days from the time the court order was issued.

(e) As part of the court order granting permission to establish a domestic partnership, the court shall, if it considers it necessary, require the parties to the prospective domestic partnership of a minor to participate, before the domestic partnership is established, in counseling concerning social, economic, and personal responsibilities incident to the domestic partnership. The parties shall not be required to confer with counselors provided by religious organizations of any denomination. In determining whether to order the parties to participate in the counseling, the court shall consider, among other factors, the ability of the parties to pay for the counseling. The court may impose a reasonable fee to cover the cost of counseling provided by the county or the court. The fees shall be used exclusively to cover the cost of the counseling services authorized by this section.

(f)(1) Only for purposes of completing the document described in Section 298.8, and not for purposes of making a determination regarding the court order, the gender of each party intending to establish a domestic partnership, if provided, shall be documented on the court order granting permission to establish the domestic partnership.

(2) The date of birth of each party intending to establish a domestic partnership shall also be documented on the court order granting permission to establish the domestic partnership.

(g) Upon issuance of the order granting permission to establish a domestic partnership, the minor shall be provided with the following information:

(1) The rights and responsibilities of an emancipated minor, including, but not limited to, the effects of emancipation as described in Chapter 2 (commencing with Section 7050) of Part 6 of Division 11.

(2)(A) The circumstances under which a domestic partnership may be determined by a court to be void or voidable and adjudged a nullity and the procedure for obtaining that judicial determination.

(B) The procedures for termination of a domestic partnership.

(3) Telephone numbers for the National Domestic Violence Hotline and the National Sexual Assault Hotline.

(4) The conditions under which an unemancipated minor may leave home and seek to remain in a shelter or otherwise live separately from the minor's parent or guardian, and whether the consent or acquiescence of a parent or guardian is required to remain away from the home of the parent or guardian, the rights of an unemancipated minor to apply for a protective or restraining order to prevent abuse, and the rights of a minor to enter into contracts, including contracts for legal services and mental health counseling.

(h)(1) Subdivisions (c) and (d) do not apply to a minor who is 17 years of age and who has achieved a high school diploma or a high school equivalency certificate.

(2) Subdivision (d) does not apply to a minor who is 16 or 17 years of age and who is pregnant or whose prospective domestic partner is pregnant. *(Added by Stats.2011, c. 721 (S.B.651), § 2. Amended by Stats.2018, c. 660 (S.B.273), § 1, eff. Jan. 1, 2019; Stats.2019, c. 115 (A.B.1817), § 3, eff. Jan. 1, 2020; Stats.2019, c. 135 (S.B.30), § 2, eff. Jan. 1, 2020.)*

Cross References

Domestic partnership information document, annual update, contents, personal identifying information, see Family Code § 298.8.

Research References

Forms

1 California Transactions Forms--Family Law § 4:4, Application of Agreements to Same Sex Couples.
West's California Judicial Council Forms FL-910, Request of Minor to Marry or Establish a Domestic Partnership.
West's California Judicial Council Forms FL-912, Consent for Minor to Marry or Establish a Domestic Partnership.
West's California Judicial Council Forms FL-915, Order and Notices to Minor on Request to Marry or Establish a Domestic Partnership.

§ 297.5. Rights, protections and benefits; responsibilities; obligations and duties under law; date of registration as equivalent of date of marriage

(a) Registered domestic partners shall have the same rights, protections, and benefits, and shall be subject to the same responsibilities, obligations, and duties under law, whether they derive from statutes, administrative regulations, court rules, government policies, common law, or any other provisions or sources of law, as are granted to and imposed upon spouses.

(b) Former registered domestic partners shall have the same rights, protections, and benefits, and shall be subject to the same responsibilities, obligations, and duties under law, whether they derive from statutes, administrative regulations, court rules, government policies, common law, or any other provisions or sources of law, as are granted to and imposed upon former spouses.

(c) A surviving registered domestic partner, following the death of the other partner, shall have the same rights, protections, and benefits, and shall be subject to the same responsibilities, obligations, and duties under law, whether they derive from statutes, administrative regulations, court rules, government policies, common law, or any other provisions or sources of law, as are granted to and imposed upon a widow or a widower.

(d) The rights and obligations of registered domestic partners with respect to a child of either of them shall be the same as those of spouses. The rights and obligations of former or surviving registered domestic partners with respect to a child of either of them shall be the same as those of former or surviving spouses.

(e) To the extent that provisions of California law adopt, refer to, or rely upon, provisions of federal law in a way that otherwise would cause registered domestic partners to be treated differently than spouses, registered domestic partners shall be treated by California law as if federal law recognized a domestic partnership in the same manner as California law.

(f) Registered domestic partners shall have the same rights regarding nondiscrimination as those provided to spouses.

(g) No public agency in this state may discriminate against any person or couple on the ground that the person is a registered domestic partner rather than a spouse or that the couple are registered domestic partners rather than spouses, except that nothing in this section applies to modify eligibility for long-term care plans pursuant to Chapter 15 (commencing with Section 21660) of Part 3 of Division 5 of Title 2 of the Government Code.

(h) This act does not preclude any state or local agency from exercising its regulatory authority to implement statutes providing rights to, or imposing responsibilities upon, domestic partners.

(i) This section does not amend or modify any provision of the California Constitution or any provision of any statute that was adopted by initiative.

(j) Where necessary to implement the rights of registered domestic partners under this act, gender-specific terms referring to spouses shall be construed to include domestic partners.

(k)(1) For purposes of the statutes, administrative regulations, court rules, government policies, common law, and any other provision or source of law governing the rights, protections, and benefits, and the responsibilities, obligations, and duties of registered domestic partners in this state, as effectuated by this section, with respect to community property, mutual responsibility for debts to third parties, the right in particular circumstances of either partner to seek financial support from the other following the dissolution of the partnership, and other rights and duties as between the partners concerning ownership of property, any reference to the date of a marriage shall be deemed to refer to the date of registration of a domestic partnership with the state.

(2) Notwithstanding paragraph (1), for domestic partnerships registered with the state before January 1, 2005, an agreement between the domestic partners that the partners intend to be governed by the requirements set forth in Sections 1600 to 1620, inclusive, and which complies with those sections, except for the agreement's effective date, shall be enforceable as provided by Sections 1600 to 1620, inclusive, if that agreement was fully executed and in force as of June 30, 2005. *(Added by Stats.2003, c. 421 (A.B.205), § 4, operative Jan. 1, 2005. Amended by Stats.2004, c. 947 (A.B.2580), § 2; Stats.2006, c. 802 (S.B.1827), § 2.)*

Cross References

Community property defined for purposes of this Code, see Family Code § 65.
Individuals and fiduciaries, filing status, see Revenue and Taxation Code § 18521.
Internal Revenue Code, definitions, application, see Revenue and Taxation Code § 17024.5.
Judges' retirement law, domestic partnership, see Government Code § 75004.5.
Judges retirement system, definitions, see Government Code § 75502.
Person defined for purposes of this Code, see Family Code § 105.
Property defined for purposes of this Code, see Family Code § 113.
Public employees' retirement system, domestic partnership, see Government Code § 20065.5.
References to husband, wife, spouses and married persons, persons included for purposes of this Code, see Family Code § 11.
Retirement of legislators, domestic partnership, see Government Code § 9351.4.
State defined for purposes of this Code, see Family Code § 145.
Utility shutoff protection, Military Families Financial Relief Act of 2005, see Military and Veterans Code § 827.

Research References

Forms

Asset Protection: Legal Planning, Strategies and Forms ¶ A.05, Dix A.05 California (Opt Out State).
1 California Transactions Forms--Family Law § 4:4, Application of Agreements to Same Sex Couples.
West's California Code Forms, Family § 297.5, Comment Overview—Domestic Partnerships.
West's California Judicial Council Forms DE-221, Spousal or Domestic Partner Property Petition (Probate— Decedents Estates).
West's California Judicial Council Forms DE-226, Spousal or Domestic Partner Property Order (Probate—Decedents Estates).
16 West's Legal Forms PT I Intro., Introduction.

Part 2

REGISTRATION

Section	
298.	Declaration of Domestic Partnership and Notice of Termination of Domestic Partnership forms.
298.5.	Filing of Declaration of Domestic Partnership forms; registration.
298.6.	Parties to registered domestic partnership; names; procedure for change of name.
298.7.	Confidential domestic partnership.
298.8.	Domestic partnership information document; annual update; contents; personal identifying information.

§ 298. Declaration of Domestic Partnership and Notice of Termination of Domestic Partnership forms

(a)(1) The Secretary of State shall prepare forms entitled "Declaration of Domestic Partnership" and "Notice of Termination of Domestic Partnership" to meet the requirements of this division. These forms shall require the signature and seal of an acknowledgment by a notary public to be binding and valid.

(2) The instructions on the "Declaration of Domestic Partnership" form shall include both of the following:

(A) An explanation that registered domestic partners have the same rights, protections, and benefits, and are subject to the same responsibilities, obligations, and duties under law as are granted to and imposed upon spouses.

(B) An explanation of how to terminate a registered domestic partnership.

(3) When funding allows, the Secretary of State shall include on the form notice that a lesbian, gay, bisexual, and transgender specific domestic abuse brochure is available upon request.

(b)(1) These forms shall be available to the public at the office of the Secretary of State or on the Secretary of State's internet website. The Secretary of State's internet website shall include all of the information required in paragraph (2) of subdivision (a).

(2) The Secretary of State shall, by regulation, establish fees for the actual costs of processing each of these forms and shall charge these fees to persons filing the forms.

(3) There is hereby established a fee of twenty-three dollars ($23) to be charged in addition to the existing fees established by regulation to persons filing domestic partner registrations pursuant to Section 297 for development and support of a lesbian, gay, bisexual, and transgender curriculum for training workshops on domestic violence, conducted pursuant to Section 13823.15 of the Penal Code, and for the support of a grant program to promote healthy nonviolent relationships in the lesbian, gay, bisexual, and transgender community. This paragraph does not apply to persons filing a domestic partner registration when one or both of the domestic partners are 62 years of age or older.

(4) The fee established by paragraph (3) shall be deposited in the Equality in Prevention and Services for Domestic Abuse Fund, which is hereby established. The fund shall be administered by the Office of Emergency Services, and expenditures from the fund shall be used to support the purposes of paragraph (3).

(c) The Declaration of Domestic Partnership shall require each person who wants to become a domestic partner to (1) state that the person meets the requirements of Section 297 at the time the form is signed, (2) provide a mailing address, (3) state that the person consents to the jurisdiction of the Superior Courts of California for the purpose of a proceeding to obtain a judgment of dissolution or nullity of the domestic partnership or for legal separation of partners in the domestic partnership, or for any other proceeding related to the partners' rights and obligations, even if one or both partners ceases to be a resident of, or to maintain a domicile in, this state, (4) sign the form with a declaration that representations made therein are true, correct, and contain no material omissions of fact to the best knowledge and belief of the applicant, and (5) have a notary public acknowledge the signature. Both partners' signatures shall be affixed to one Declaration of Domestic Partnership form, which shall then be transmitted to the Secretary of State according to the instructions provided on the form. Filing an intentionally and materially false Declaration of Domestic Partnership shall be punishable as a misdemeanor.

(d) The Declaration of Domestic Partnership form shall contain an optional section for either party or both parties to indicate a change in name pursuant to Section 298.6. The optional section shall require a party indicating a change in name to provide the person's date of birth. *(Added by Stats.1999, c. 588 (A.B.26), § 2. Amended by Stats.2003, c. 421 (A.B.205), § 5, operative Jan. 1, 2005; Stats.2006, c. 856 (A.B.2051), § 2; Stats.2007, c. 179 (S.B.86), § 7, eff. Aug. 24, 2007; Stats.2007, c. 567 (A.B.102), § 4; Stats.2010, c. 618 (A.B.2791), § 14; Stats.2013, c. 352 (A.B.1317), § 78, eff. Sept. 26, 2013, operative July 1, 2013; Stats.2019, c. 115 (A.B.1817), § 4, eff. Jan. 1, 2020; Stats.2019, c. 135 (S.B.30), § 3, eff. Jan. 1, 2020.)*

Cross References

County defined for purposes of this Code, see Family Code § 67.
Health care service plans, domestic partners, coverage, see Health and Safety Code § 1374.58.
Judgment and order defined for purposes of this Code, see Family Code § 100.
Life and disability insurance, domestic partners, coverage, see Insurance Code § 10121.7.
Misdemeanors, definition and penalties, see Penal Code §§ 17, 19, 19.2.
Payment of wages, victims of crime, work absences for judicial proceedings, see Labor Code § 230.2.

Person defined for purposes of this Code, see Family Code § 105.
Proceeding defined for purposes of this Code, see Family Code § 110.
State defined for purposes of this Code, see Family Code § 145.

Research References

Forms

California Practice Guide: Rutter Family Law Forms Form 1:32, Glossary of Common Family Law Terms, Phrases and Concepts (Enclosure to Form 1:31).
1 California Transactions Forms--Family Law § 4:4.50, Declaration of Domestic Partnership.
5¶ 2 Nichols Cyclopedia of Legal Forms Annotated § 100:1, Definitions and Status of Persons as Spouses or Domestic or Civil Partners, Generally.
5¶ 2 Nichols Cyclopedia of Legal Forms Annotated § 100:4, Dissolution or Termination of Marital Relationship, Generally.

§ 298.5. Filing of Declaration of Domestic Partnership forms; registration

(a) Two persons desiring to become domestic partners may complete and file a Declaration of Domestic Partnership with the Secretary of State.

(b) The Secretary of State shall register the Declaration of Domestic Partnership in a registry for those partnerships, and shall return a copy of the registered form, a Certificate of Registered Domestic Partnership, and a copy of the brochure that is made available to county clerks and the Secretary of State by the State Department of Public Health pursuant to Section 358 and distributed to individuals receiving a confidential marriage license pursuant to Section 503, to the domestic partners at the mailing address provided by the domestic partners.

(c) A person who has filed a Declaration of Domestic Partnership may not file a new Declaration of Domestic Partnership or enter a civil marriage with someone other than their registered domestic partner unless the most recent domestic partnership has been terminated or a final judgment of dissolution or nullity of the most recent domestic partnership has been entered. This prohibition does not apply if the previous domestic partnership ended because one of the partners died.

(d) When funding allows, the Secretary of State shall print and make available upon request, pursuant to Section 358, a lesbian, gay, bisexual, and transgender specific domestic abuse brochure developed by the State Department of Public Health and made available to the Secretary of State to domestic partners who qualify pursuant to Section 297.

(e) The Certificate of Registered Domestic Partnership shall include the name used by each party before registration of the domestic partnership and the new name, if any, selected by each party upon registration of the domestic partnership. *(Added by Stats.1999, c. 588 (A.B.26), § 2. Amended by Stats.2003, c. 421 (A.B.205), § 6, operative Jan. 1, 2005; Stats.2006, c. 856 (A.B.2051), § 3; Stats.2007, c. 483 (S.B.1039), § 8; Stats.2007, c. 567 (A.B.102), § 5; Stats.2019, c. 135 (S.B.30), § 4, eff. Jan. 1, 2020.)*

Cross References

Judgment and order defined for purposes of this Code, see Family Code § 100.
Person defined for purposes of this Code, see Family Code § 105.
State defined for purposes of this Code, see Family Code § 145.

Research References

Forms

California Practice Guide: Rutter Family Law Forms Form 1:32, Glossary of Common Family Law Terms, Phrases and Concepts (Enclosure to Form 1:31).
5¶ 2 Nichols Cyclopedia of Legal Forms Annotated § 100:1, Definitions and Status of Persons as Spouses or Domestic or Civil Partners, Generally.

West's California Code Forms, Family § 298, Comment Overview—Declaration of Domestic Partnership.

§ 298.6. Parties to registered domestic partnership; names; procedure for change of name

(a) Parties to a registered domestic partnership shall not be required to have the same name. Neither party shall be required to change their name. A person's name shall not change upon registration as a domestic partner unless that person elects to change their name pursuant to subdivision (b).

(b)(1) One party or both parties to a registered domestic partnership may elect to change the middle or last names by which that party wishes to be known after registration of the domestic partnership by entering the new name in the space provided on the Declaration of Domestic Partnership form without intent to defraud.

(2) A person may adopt any of the following middle or last names pursuant to paragraph (1):

(A) The current last name of the other domestic partner.

(B) The last name of either domestic partner given at birth.

(C) A name combining into a single last name all or a segment of the current last name or the last name of either domestic partner given at birth.

(D) A hyphenated combination of last names.

(3)(A) An election by a person to change the person's name pursuant to paragraph (1) shall serve as a record of the name change. A certified copy of the Declaration of Domestic Partnership containing the new name, or retaining the former name, shall constitute proof that the use of the new name or retention of the former name is lawful.

(B) A certified copy of a Declaration of Domestic Partnership shall be accepted as identification establishing a true, full name for purposes of Section 12800.7 of the Vehicle Code.

(C) This section does not prohibit the Department of Motor Vehicles from accepting as identification other documents establishing a true, full name for purposes of Section 12800.7 of the Vehicle Code. Those documents may include, without limitation, a certified copy of a document that is substantially equivalent to a Certificate of Registered Domestic Partnership that records either of the following:

(i) A legal union of two persons that was validly formed in another jurisdiction and is recognized as a valid domestic partnership in this state pursuant to Section 299.2.

(ii) A legal union of domestic partners as defined by a local jurisdiction pursuant to Section 299.6.

(D) This section shall be applied in a manner consistent with the requirements of Sections 1653.5 and 12801 of the Vehicle Code.

(4) The adoption of a new name, or the choice not to adopt a new name, by means of a Declaration of Domestic Partnership pursuant to paragraph (1) shall not abrogate the right of either party to adopt a different name through usage at a future date, or to petition the superior court for a change of name pursuant to Title 8 (commencing with Section 1275) of Part 3 of the Code of Civil Procedure.

(c) This section does not abrogate the common law right of a person to change the person's name, or the right of a person to petition the superior court for a change of name pursuant to Title 8 (commencing with Section 1275) of Part 3 of the Code of Civil Procedure. *(Added by Stats.2007, c. 567 (A.B.102), § 6. Amended by Stats.2019, c. 115 (A.B.1817), § 5, eff. Jan. 1, 2020; Stats.2019, c. 135 (S.B.30), § 5, eff. Jan. 1, 2020.)*

Cross References

Marriage or domestic partnership, informational brochure, see Family Code § 358.

Research References

Forms

1 California Transactions Forms--Family Law § 4:2, Purpose of Agreement.
1 California Transactions Forms--Family Law § 4:4, Application of Agreements to Same Sex Couples.
1 California Transactions Forms--Family Law § 4:4.50, Declaration of Domestic Partnership.

§ 298.7. Confidential domestic partnership

The Secretary of State shall establish a process by which two persons, who have been living together as domestic partners and who meet the requirements of paragraphs (1) to (4), inclusive, of subdivision (b) of Section 297, may enter into a confidential domestic partnership. This process shall do all of the following:

(a) Maintain each confidential Declaration of Domestic Partnership as a permanent record that is not open to public inspection except upon order of the court issued upon a showing of good cause.

(b) Authorize the Secretary of State to charge a reasonable fee to offset costs directly connected with maintaining confidentiality of a Declaration of Domestic Partnership. *(Added by Stats.2011, c. 721 (S.B.651), § 3. Amended by Stats.2019, c. 135 (S.B.30), § 6, eff. Jan. 1, 2020.)*

§ 298.8. Domestic partnership information document; annual update; contents; personal identifying information

(a) The Secretary of State shall create a document no later than March 1, 2020, with annual updates no later than March 1 of each year thereafter, disaggregated by county, containing only the following information concerning domestic partnerships that were registered during the preceding calendar year and in which one or both of the parties were minors at the time the domestic partnership was established:

(1) The total number of those registered domestic partnerships.

(2) Itemized for each of those registered domestic partnerships, the age of each party at the time the domestic partnership was established.

(3) Itemized for each of those registered domestic partnerships, the gender of each party as documented on the court order pursuant to Section 297.1, unless the court order does not include the gender.

(b) The document shall not contain the names, addresses, or other personal identifying information of parties to a registered domestic partnership, or any information identifying a registered domestic partnership. The document shall not contain a registered domestic partnership or a copy of the court order described in Section 297.1.

(c) The Secretary of State shall make the document available to the public upon request. *(Added by Stats.2018, c. 660 (S.B.273), § 2, eff. Jan. 1, 2019.)*

Cross References

Domestic partnership with underage person, court order and written consent of parents, see Family Code § 297.1.

Part 3

TERMINATION

Section
299. Termination of registered domestic partnership; filing of Notice of Termination of Domestic Partnership; conditions; effective date; setting aside termination; jurisdiction; dissolution of marriage.

§ 299. **Termination of registered domestic partnership; filing of Notice of Termination of Domestic Partnership; conditions; effective date; setting aside termination; jurisdiction; dissolution of marriage**

(a) A registered domestic partnership may be terminated without filing a proceeding for dissolution of domestic partnership by the filing of a Notice of Termination of Domestic Partnership with the Secretary of State pursuant to this section, provided that all of the following conditions exist at the time of the filing:

(1) The Notice of Termination of Domestic Partnership is signed by both registered domestic partners.

(2) There are no children of the relationship of the parties born before or after registration of the domestic partnership or adopted by the parties after registration of the domestic partnership, and neither of the registered domestic partners, to their knowledge, is pregnant.

(3) The registered domestic partnership is not more than five years in duration.

(4) Neither party has any interest in real property wherever situated, with the exception of the lease of a residence occupied by either party which satisfies the following requirements:

(A) The lease does not include an option to purchase.

(B) The lease terminates within one year from the date of filing of the Notice of Termination of Domestic Partnership.

(5) There are no unpaid obligations in excess of the amount described in paragraph (6) of subdivision (a) of Section 2400, as adjusted by subdivision (b) of Section 2400, incurred by either or both of the parties after registration of the domestic partnership, excluding the amount of any unpaid obligation with respect to an automobile.

(6) The total fair market value of community property assets, excluding all encumbrances and automobiles, including any deferred compensation or retirement plan, is less than the amount described in paragraph (7) of subdivision (a) of Section 2400, as adjusted by subdivision (b) of Section 2400, and neither party has separate property assets, excluding all encumbrances and automobiles, in excess of that amount.

(7) The parties have executed an agreement setting forth the division of assets and the assumption of liabilities of the community property, and have executed any documents, title certificates, bills of sale, or other evidence of transfer necessary to effectuate the agreement.

(8) The parties waive any rights to support by the other domestic partner.

(9) The parties have read and understand a brochure prepared by the Secretary of State describing the requirements, nature, and effect of terminating a domestic partnership.

(10) Both parties desire that the domestic partnership be terminated.

(b) The registered domestic partnership shall be terminated effective six months after the date of filing of the Notice of Termination of Domestic Partnership with the Secretary of State pursuant to this section, provided that neither party has, before that date, filed with the Secretary of State a notice of revocation of the termination of domestic partnership, in the form and content as shall be prescribed by the Secretary of State, and sent to the other party a copy of the notice of revocation by first-class mail, postage prepaid, at the other party's last known address. The effect of termination of a domestic partnership pursuant to this section shall be the same as, and shall be treated for all purposes as, the entry of a judgment of dissolution of a domestic partnership.

(c) The termination of a domestic partnership pursuant to subdivision (b) does not prejudice nor bar the rights of either of the parties to institute an action in the superior court to set aside the termination for fraud, duress, mistake, or any other ground recognized at law or in equity. A court may set aside the termination of domestic partnership and declare the termination of the domestic partnership null and void upon proof that the parties did not meet the requirements of subdivision (a) at the time of the filing of the Notice of Termination of Domestic Partnership with the Secretary of State.

(d) The superior courts shall have jurisdiction over all proceedings relating to the dissolution of domestic partnerships, nullity of domestic partnerships, and legal separation of partners in a domestic partnership. The dissolution of a domestic partnership, nullity of a domestic partnership, and legal separation of partners in a domestic partnership shall follow the same procedures, and the partners shall possess the same rights, protections, and benefits, and be subject to the same responsibilities, obligations, and duties, as apply to the dissolution of marriage, nullity of marriage, and legal separation of spouses in a marriage, respectively, except as provided in subdivision (a), and except that, in accordance with the consent acknowledged by domestic partners in the Declaration of Domestic Partnership form, proceedings for dissolution, nullity, or legal separation of a domestic partnership registered in this state may be filed in the superior courts of this state even if neither domestic partner is a resident of, or maintains a domicile in, the state at the time the proceedings are filed.

(e) Parties to a registered domestic partnership who are also married to one another may petition the court to dissolve both their domestic partnership and their marriage in a single proceeding, in a form that shall be prescribed by the Judicial Council. *(Added by Stats.2003, c. 421 (A.B.205), § 8, operative Jan. 1, 2005. Amended by Stats.2004, c. 947 (A.B.2580), § 3; Stats.2010, c. 397 (A.B.2700), § 1.)*

Cross References

Community property defined for purposes of this Code, see Family Code § 65.
Death terminating domestic partnership, and Notice of Termination not filed prior to death, surviving partner's rights notwithstanding this section, see Probate Code § 37.
Judgment and order defined for purposes of this Code, see Family Code § 100.
Order of preference for appointment of conservator, domestic partner of proposed conservatee, see Probate Code § 1813.1.
Petitions, existence of child support, child custody, visitation, or spousal support orders, personal conduct restraining order, or bifurcated case, dismissal for delay in prosecution prohibited, see Code of Civil Procedure § 583.161.
Proceeding defined for purposes of this Code, see Family Code § 110.
Property defined for purposes of this Code, see Family Code § 113.
References to husband, wife, spouses and married persons, persons included for purposes of this Code, see Family Code § 11.
Separate property defined for purposes of this Code, see Family Code § 130.
State defined for purposes of this Code, see Family Code § 145.
State employees' health benefits, filing of valid Declaration of Domestic Partnership form or establishing valid domestic partnership, see Government Code § 22872.
State teachers' retirement system, community property, dissolution or legal separation and rights of registered domestic partners, see Education Code § 22650.
State teachers' retirement system cash balance plan, community property, dissolution or legal separation and rights of registered domestic partners, see Education Code § 27400.
Support defined for purposes of this Code, see Family Code § 150.

Research References

Forms

1 California Transactions Forms--Family Law § 1:2, Nature and Advantages of Agreement.
1 California Transactions Forms--Family Law § 4:4.60, Termination of Registered Domestic Partnership.
West's California Code Forms, Family § 299, Comment Overview—Termination of Registered Domestic Partnership.
West's California Judicial Council Forms FL–100, Petition—Marriage/Domestic Partnership (Also Available in Arabic, Chinese, and Spanish).
West's California Judicial Council Forms FL–343, Spousal, Domestic Partner, or Family Support Order Attachment.

§ 299

West's California Judicial Council Forms FL–345, Property Order Attachment to Judgment (Also Available in Spanish).
West's California Judicial Council Forms FL–435, Earnings Assignment Order for Spousal or Partner Support.
West's California Judicial Council Forms FL–800, Joint Petition for Summary Dissolution.

Part 4

LEGAL EFFECT

Section
299.2. Recognizing legal union from another jurisdiction as a valid domestic partnership.
299.3. Repealed.
299.5. Repealed.

§ 299.2. Recognizing legal union from another jurisdiction as a valid domestic partnership

A legal union of two persons, other than a marriage, that was validly formed in another jurisdiction, and that is substantially equivalent to a domestic partnership as defined in this part, shall be recognized as a valid domestic partnership in this state regardless of whether it bears the name domestic partnership. (Added by Stats. 2003, c. 421 (A.B.205), § 9, operative Jan. 1, 2005. Amended by Stats.2019, c. 135 (S.B.30), § 7, eff. Jan. 1, 2020.)

Cross References

Person defined for purposes of this Code, see Family Code § 105.
Registered domestic partnership, change of name, see Family Code § 298.6.
State defined for purposes of this Code, see Family Code § 145.
State Teachers' Retirement System, election to receive actuarially modified retirement allowance payable throughout life, see Education Code § 24300.1.
State teachers' retirement system, registered domestic partner of member included as spouse, see Education Code §§ 22007.5, 22171.
State teachers' retirement system cash balance plan, registered domestic partner of member included as spouse, see Education Code §§ 26002.5, 26140.

Research References

Forms
5¶ 2 Nichols Cyclopedia of Legal Forms Annotated § 100:4, Dissolution or Termination of Marital Relationship, Generally.

§ 299.3. Repealed by Stats.2019, c. 135 (S.B.30), § 8, eff. Jan. 1, 2020

§ 299.5. Repealed by Stats.2003, c. 421, § 11, operative Jan. 1, 2005

Part 5

PREEMPTION

Section
299.6. Preemption of local ordinances or laws.

§ 299.6. Preemption of local ordinances or laws

(a) Any local ordinance or law that provides for the creation of a "domestic partnership" shall be preempted on and after July 1, 2000, except as provided in subdivision (c).

(b) Domestic partnerships created under any local domestic partnership ordinance or law before July 1, 2000, shall remain valid. On and after July 1, 2000, domestic partnerships previously established under a local ordinance or law shall be governed by this division and the rights and duties of the partners shall be those set out in this division, except as provided in subdivision (c), provided a Declaration of Domestic Partnership is filed by the domestic partners under Section 298.5.

(c) Any local jurisdiction may retain or adopt ordinances, policies, or laws that offer rights within that jurisdiction to domestic partners as defined by Section 297 or as more broadly defined by the local jurisdiction's ordinances, policies, or laws, or that impose duties upon third parties regarding domestic partners as defined by Section 297 or as more broadly defined by the local jurisdiction's ordinances, policies, or laws, that are in addition to the rights and duties set out in this division, and the local rights may be conditioned upon the agreement of the domestic partners to assume the additional obligations set forth in this division. (Added by Stats.1999, c. 588 (A.B.26), § 2.)

Cross References

Registered domestic partnership, change of name, see Family Code § 298.6.
Statutory will form, see Probate Code § 6240.

Research References

Forms
West's California Code Forms, Probate § 6240 Form 1, California Statutory Will.

Division 3

MARRIAGE

Part	Section
1. Validity of Marriage	300
2. Marriage License	350
3. Solemnization of Marriage	400
4. Confidential Marriage	500
5. Remote Marriage License Issuance and Solemnization	550

Part 1

VALIDITY OF MARRIAGE

Section
300. Consent; issuance of license and solemnization; marriage license and marriage certificate.
301. Adults; capability to consent to and consummate marriage.
302. Minors; issuance of marriage license; requirements; court order and parental consent; filing.
303. Consent of court to marriage of minor.
304. Interview of parties intending to marry; interview of parents; separate interviews; written report; evidence of coercion or undue influence; premarital counseling; fees; registration information; solemnization requirements.
305. Proof of consent and solemnization.
306. Procedural requirements; effect of noncompliance.
306.5. Parties to marriage; names; procedure for change of name.
307. Marriage of members of religious society or denomination; requirements.
308. Validity of foreign marriages.
308.5. Repealed.

Section
309. Action to test validity of marriage.
310. Methods of dissolution.

Cross References

Capacity of conservatee to marry, determination of capacity, see Probate Code § 1901.
Destruction of marriage records, see Health and Safety Code § 102235.
Examination of marriage certificates, see Health and Safety Code §§ 102225, 102310.
Fees and charges for certified copies of marriage and marriage dissolution records, see Health and Safety Code § 100440.
Judicial determination of void or voidable marriage, see Family Code § 2200 et seq.
Record of marriage, establishment, see Health and Safety Code § 103450 et seq.
Vital records, marriage registration, see Health and Safety Code § 102100.

§ 300. Consent; issuance of license and solemnization; marriage license and marriage certificate

(a) Marriage is a personal relation arising out of a civil contract between two persons, to which the consent of the parties capable of making that contract is necessary. Consent alone does not constitute marriage. Consent must be followed by the issuance of a license and solemnization as authorized by this division, except as provided by Section 425 and Part 4 (commencing with Section 500).

(b) For purposes of this part, the document issued by the county clerk is a marriage license until it is registered with the county recorder, at which time the license becomes a marriage certificate. *(Stats.1992, c. 162 (A.B.2650), § 10, operative Jan. 1, 1994. Amended by Stats.1993, c. 219 (A.B.1500), § 88; Stats.2006, c. 816 (A.B.1102), § 1, operative Jan. 1, 2008; Stats.2014, c. 82 (S.B.1306), § 2, eff. Jan. 1, 2015.)*

Validity

Language in a prior version of this section ("between a man and a woman") was held unconstitutional as a violation of the equal protection clause in the decision of In re Marriage Cases (2008) 76 Cal.Rptr.3d 683, 43 Cal.4th 757, 183 P.3d 384, rehearing denied, on subsequent appeal 2009 WL 2515727, unpublished. See, also, Const. Art. 1, § 7.5.

Cross References

License,
 Confidential license, see Family Code § 500 et seq.
 Endorsement and return, see Family Code § 423.
 Failure to file, misdemeanor, see Penal Code § 360.
 False return, misdemeanor, see Penal Code § 360.
 Fee, see Government Code § 26840.
 Person solemnizing must require, see Family Code § 421.
Marital agreements, see Family Code § 1500 et seq.
Marital property, characterization, see Family Code § 760 et seq.
Marriage registration,
 Certificate of registry, filing, see Family Code § 359.
 Examination of marriage certificates, see Health and Safety Code §§ 102225, 102310.
 Forms, see Health and Safety Code § 103125.
Presumption of validity of marriage, see Evidence Code §§ 605, 663.
Proof of marriage,
 Bigamy, see Penal Code § 281 et seq.
 Church certificates or records, see Evidence Code §§ 1315, 1316.
 Community reputation of date or fact of marriage, see Evidence Code § 1314.
 Entries in family records, see Evidence Code § 1312.
 Hearsay rule, exception, see Evidence Code § 1310.
Real property including leasehold interests, see Family Code § 700.
Record of marriage, establishment, see Health and Safety Code § 103450 et seq.
Relations of husband and wife, see Family Code §§ 720, 721.
Uniform Premarital Agreement Act, see Fa nily Code § 1600 et seq.

Void or voidable marriage, judicial determination, see Family Code § 2200 et seq.

Research References

Forms
California Practice Guide: Rutter Family Law Forms Form 1:32, Glossary of Common Family Law Terms, Phrases and Concepts (Enclosure to Form 1:31).
1 California Transactions Forms--Family Law § 4:4, Application of Agreements to Same Sex Couples.
West's California Code Forms, Family § 400, Comment Overview—Solemnize Marriage.

§ 301. Adults; capability to consent to and consummate marriage

Two unmarried persons 18 years of age or older, who are not otherwise disqualified, are capable of consenting to and consummating marriage. *(Stats.1992, c. 162 (A.B.2650), § 10, operative Jan. 1, 1994. Amended by Stats.2014, c. 82 (S.B.1306), § 3, eff. Jan. 1, 2015.)*

Cross References

Annulment of marriage by party under legal age of consent, see Family Code § 2210.
Consent to contract, see Civil Code § 1565 et seq.
License, necessity, see Family Code § 350.
Marital agreements, see Family Code § 1500 et seq.
Marital property, characterization, see Family Code § 760 et seq.
Presumption of validity of marriage, see Evidence Code §§ 605, 663.
Proof of marriage,
 Bigamy, see Penal Code § 281 et seq.
 Church certificates or records, see Evidence Code §§ 1315, 1316.
 Community reputation of date or fact of marriage, see Evidence Code § 1314.
 Entries in family records, see Evidence Code § 1312.
 Hearsay rule, exception, see Evidence Code § 1310.
Real property including leasehold interests, see Family Code § 700.
Relations of husband and wife, see Family Code §§ 720, 721.
Uniform Premarital Agreement Act, see Family Code § 1600 et seq.

Research References

Forms
17A Am. Jur. Pl. & Pr. Forms Marriage § 1, Introductory Comments.
17A Am. Jur. Pl. & Pr. Forms Marriage § 2, Introductory Comments.

§ 302. Minors; issuance of marriage license; requirements; court order and parental consent; filing

(a) An unmarried person under 18 years of age may be issued a marriage license upon obtaining a court order granting permission to the underage person or persons to marry, in accordance with the requirements described in Section 304.

(b) The court order and written consent of at least one of the parents or the guardian of each underage person shall be filed with the clerk of the court, and a certified copy of the order shall be presented to the county clerk at the time the marriage license is issued. *(Stats.1992, c. 162 (A.B.2650), § 10, operative Jan. 1, 1994. Amended by Stats.2006, c. 816 (A.B.1102), § 2, operative Jan. 1, 2008; Stats.2014, c. 82 (S.B.1306), § 4, eff. Jan. 1, 2015; Stats.2016, c. 474 (A.B.2882), § 1, eff. Jan. 1, 2017; Stats.2018, c. 660 (S.B.273), § 3, eff. Jan. 1, 2019.)*

Cross References

Agreements by minors, see Family Code § 1501.
Annulment of marriage by party under legal age of consent, see Family Code § 2210.
Consent of court to marriage of minor, see Family Code § 303.
Consent to contract, see Civil Code § 1565 et seq.
County defined for purposes of this Code, see Family Code § 67.
Judgment and order defined for purposes of this Code, see Family Code § 100.
Jurisdiction of superior court, see Family Code § 200.
License, necessity, see Family Code § 350.
Marital agreements, see Family Code § 1500 et seq.
Marital property, characterization, see Family Code § 760 et seq.

§ 302

Person defined for purposes of this Code, see Family Code § 105.
Premarital counseling, minors, see Family Code § 304.
Presumption of validity of marriage, see Evidence Code §§ 605, 663.
Proof of marriage,
  Bigamy, see Penal Code § 281 et seq.
  Church certificates or records, see Evidence Code §§ 1315, 1316.
  Community reputation of date or fact of marriage, see Evidence Code § 1314.
  Entries in family records, see Evidence Code § 1312.
  Hearsay rule, exception, see Evidence Code § 1310.
Real property including leasehold interests, see Family Code § 700.
Relations of husband and wife, see Family Code §§ 720, 721.
Uniform Premarital Agreement Act, see Family Code § 1600 et seq.

Research References

Forms

West's California Code Forms, Family § 302, Comment Overview—Marriage of Minor.
West's California Judicial Council Forms FL–910, Request of Minor to Marry or Establish a Domestic Partnership.
West's California Judicial Council Forms FL–912, Consent for Minor to Marry or Establish a Domestic Partnership.
West's California Judicial Council Forms FL–915, Order and Notices to Minor on Request to Marry or Establish a Domestic Partnership.

§ 303. Consent of court to marriage of minor

If it appears to the satisfaction of the court by application of a minor that the minor requires a written consent to marry and that the minor has no parent or has no parent capable of consenting, the court may make an order consenting to the issuance of a marriage license and granting permission to the minor to marry, in accordance with the requirements described in Section 304. The order shall be filed with the clerk of the court and a certified copy of the order shall be presented to the county clerk at the time the marriage license is issued. *(Stats.1992, c. 162 (A.B.2650), § 10, operative Jan. 1, 1994. Amended by Stats.2006, c. 816 (A.B.1102), § 3, operative Jan. 1, 2008; Stats.2018, c. 660 (S.B.273), § 4, eff. Jan. 1, 2019.)*

Cross References

Agreements by minors, see Family Code § 1501.
Consent to contract, see Civil Code § 1565 et seq.
County defined for purposes of this Code, see Family Code § 67.
Judgment and order defined for purposes of this Code, see Family Code § 100.
Jurisdiction of superior court, see Family Code § 200.
Marital property, characterization, see Family Code § 760 et seq.
Minor defined for purposes of this Code, see Family Code § 6500.
Premarital counseling, minors, see Family Code § 304.
Presumption of validity of marriage, see Evidence Code §§ 605, 663.
Proof of marriage,
  Bigamy, see Penal Code § 281 et seq.
  Church certificates or records, see Evidence Code §§ 1315, 1316.
  Community reputation of date or fact of marriage, see Evidence Code § 1314.
  Entries in family records, see Evidence Code § 1312.
  Hearsay rule, exception, see Evidence Code § 1310.
Real property including leasehold interests, see Family Code § 700.
Relations of husband and wife, see Family Code §§ 720, 721.

Research References

Forms

West's California Code Forms, Family § 302, Comment Overview—Marriage of Minor.
West's California Code Forms, Family § 303 Form 1, Order and Notices to Minor on Request Marry or Establish Domestic Partnership.

§ 304. Interview of parties intending to marry; interview of parents; separate interviews; written report; evidence of coercion or undue influence; premarital counseling; fees; registration information; solemnization requirements

(a) In determining whether to issue a court order granting permission to marry pursuant to Section 302 or 303, the court shall do all of the following:

(1) Require Family Court Services to separately interview the parties intending to marry and, if applicable, at least one of the parents or the guardian of each party who is a minor. If more than one parent or guardian is interviewed, the parents or guardians shall be interviewed separately.

(2) Require Family Court Services to prepare and submit to the court a written report, containing any assessment of potential force, threat, persuasion, fraud, coercion, or duress by either of the parties or their family members relating to the intended marriage. The report shall also contain recommendations of Family Court Services for either granting or denying the parties permission to marry. If Family Court Services knows or reasonably suspects that either party is a victim of child abuse or neglect, Family Court Services shall submit a report of the known or suspected child abuse or neglect to the county child protective services agency.

(3) After receiving the report of the assessments of Family Court Services, as described in paragraph (2), separately interview in camera each of the parties prior to making a final determination regarding the court order.

(4) Consider whether there is evidence of coercion or undue influence on the minor.

(b) If the court issues an order granting the parties permission to marry pursuant to Section 302 or 303, and if one or both of the parties are 17 years of age or younger, the parties shall be eligible to request a marriage license no earlier than 30 days from the time the court order was issued.

(c) As part of the court order granting permission to marry under Section 302 or 303, the court shall, if it considers it necessary, require the parties to the prospective marriage of a minor to participate in premarital counseling concerning social, economic, and personal responsibilities incident to marriage. The parties shall not be required to confer with counselors provided by religious organizations of any denomination. In determining whether to order the parties to participate in the premarital counseling, the court shall consider, among other factors, the ability of the parties to pay for the counseling. The court may impose a reasonable fee to cover the cost of premarital counseling provided by the county or the court. The fees shall be used exclusively to cover the cost of the counseling services authorized by this section.

(d)(1) Only for purposes of completing the document described in Section 102233 of the Health and Safety Code, and not for purposes of making a determination regarding the court order, the gender of each party intending to marry, if provided, shall be documented on the court order granting permission to marry.

(2) The date of birth of each party intending to marry shall also be documented on the court order granting permission to marry.

(3) For purposes of the requirements on the person solemnizing the marriage under subdivision (b) of Section 423, and the requirements on the local registrar under subdivision (a) of Section 102356 of the Health and Safety Code, the court shall provide parties who are granted permission to marry with a copy of the court order granting permission to marry.

(e) Upon issuance of the order granting permission to marry, the minor shall be provided with the following information:

(1) The rights and responsibilities of an emancipated minor, including, but not limited to, the effects of emancipation as described in Chapter 2 (commencing with Section 7050) of Part 6 of Division 11.

(2)(A) The circumstances under which a marriage may be determined by a court to be void or voidable and adjudged a nullity and the procedure for obtaining that judicial determination.

(B) The procedures for legal separation or dissolution of marriage.

(3) Telephone numbers for the National Domestic Violence Hotline and the National Sexual Assault Hotline.

(4) The conditions under which an unemancipated minor may leave home and seek to remain in a shelter or otherwise live separately from the minor's parent or guardian, and whether the consent or acquiescence of a parent or guardian is required to remain away from the home of the parent or guardian, the rights of an unemancipated minor to apply for a protective or restraining order to prevent abuse, and the rights of a minor to enter into contracts, including contracts for legal services and mental health counseling.

(f)(1) Subdivisions (a) and (b) do not apply to a minor who is 17 years of age and who has achieved a high school diploma or a high school equivalency certificate.

(2) Subdivision (b) does not apply to a minor who is 16 or 17 years of age and who is pregnant or whose prospective spouse is pregnant. (Stats.1992, c. 162 (A.B.2650), § 10, operative Jan. 1, 1994. Amended by Stats.2007, c. 738 (A.B.1248), § 12; Stats.2016, c. 474 (A.B.2882), § 2, eff. Jan. 1, 2017; Stats.2018, c. 660 (S.B.273), § 5, eff. Jan. 1, 2019; Stats.2019, c. 115 (A.B.1817), § 6, eff. Jan. 1, 2020.)

Cross References

Consent to contract, see Civil Code § 1565 et seq.
County defined for purposes of this Code, see Family Code § 67.
Courts, fees and fines collected after January 1, 2006, treatment thereof, see Government Code § 68085.1.
Document concerning information on marriage certificates, annual update, personal identifying information, see Health and Safety Code § 102233.
Judgment and order defined for purposes of this Code, see Family Code § 100.
Marital agreements, see Family Code § 1500 et seq.
Minor defined for purposes of this Code, see Family Code § 6500.
Minors, issuance of marriage license, requirements, court order and parental consent, filing, see Family Code § 302.
Real property including leasehold interests, see Family Code § 700.
Relations of husband and wife, see Family Code §§ 720, 721.
Return of license, inclusion of copy of court order granting permission to marry, see Family Code § 423.
Uniform Premarital Agreement Act, see Family Code § 1600 et seq.

Research References

Forms

West's California Code Forms, Family § 302, Comment Overview—Marriage of Minor.
West's California Code Forms, Family § 303 Form 1, Order and Notices to Minor on Request Marry or Establish Domestic Partnership.
West's California Judicial Council Forms FL–910, Request of Minor to Marry or Establish a Domestic Partnership.
West's California Judicial Council Forms FL–912, Consent for Minor to Marry or Establish a Domestic Partnership.
West's California Judicial Council Forms FL–915, Order and Notices to Minor on Request to Marry or Establish a Domestic Partnership.

§ 305. Proof of consent and solemnization

Consent to and solemnization of marriage may be proved under the same general rules of evidence as facts are proved in other cases. (Stats.1992, c. 162 (A.B.2650), § 10, operative Jan. 1, 1994.)

Cross References

License,
  Confidential license, see Family Code § 500 et seq.
  Endorsement and return, see Family Code § 423.
  Failure to file, misdemeanor, see Penal Code § 360.
  False return, misdemeanor, see Penal Code § 360.
  Fee, see Government Code § 26840.
  Person solemnizing must require, see Family Code § 421.
Marital property, characterization, see Family Code § 760 et seq.
Marriage registration,
  Certificate of registry, filing, see Family Code § 359.
  Forms, see Health and Safety Code § 103125.
Presumption of validity of marriage, see Evidence Code §§ 605, 663.
Proof, generally, see Evidence Code § 190.
Proof of marriage,
  Bigamy, see Penal Code § 281 et seq.
  Church certificates or records, see Evidence Code §§ 1315, 1316.
  Community reputation of date or fact of marriage, see Evidence Code § 1314.
  Entries in family records, see Evidence Code § 1312.
  Hearsay rule, exception, see Evidence Code § 1310.
Real property including leasehold interests, see Family Code § 700.
Record of marriage, establishment, see Health and Safety Code § 103450 et seq.
Relations of husband and wife, see Family Code §§ 720, 721.

§ 306. Procedural requirements; effect of noncompliance

Except as provided in Section 307, a marriage shall be licensed, solemnized, and authenticated, and the authenticated marriage license shall be returned to the county recorder of the county where the marriage license was issued, as provided in this part. Noncompliance with this part by a nonparty to the marriage does not invalidate the marriage. (Stats.1992, c. 162 (A.B.2650), § 10, operative Jan. 1, 1994. Amended by Stats.1993, c. 219 (A.B.1500), § 89; Stats.2006, c. 816 (A.B.1102), § 4, operative Jan. 1, 2008.)

Cross References

License,
  Confidential license, see Family Code § 500 et seq.
  Endorsement and return, see Family Code § 423.
  Failure to file, misdemeanor, see Penal Code § 360.
  False return, misdemeanor, see Penal Code § 360.
  Fee, see Government Code § 26840.
  Person solemnizing must require, see Family Code § 421.
Marital agreements, see Family Code § 1500 et seq.
Marital property, characterization, see Family Code § 760 et seq.
Marriage registration,
  Certificate of registry, filing, see Family Code § 359.
  Forms, see Health and Safety Code § 103125.
Presumption of validity of marriage, see Evidence Code §§ 605, 663.
Proof of marriage,
  Bigamy, see Penal Code § 281 et seq.
  Church certificates or records, see Evidence Code §§ 1315, 1316.
  Community reputation of date or fact of marriage, see Evidence Code § 1314.
  Entries in family records, see Evidence Code § 1312.
  Hearsay rule, exception, see Evidence Code § 1310.
Real property including leasehold interests, see Family Code § 700.
Record of marriage, establishment, see Health and Safety Code § 103450 et seq.
Relations of husband and wife, see Family Code §§ 720, 721.
Uniform Premarital Agreement Act, see Family Code § 1600 et seq.

§ 306.5. Parties to marriage; names; procedure for change of name

(a) Parties to a marriage shall not be required to have the same name. Neither party shall be required to change their name. A person's name shall not change upon marriage unless that person elects to change their name pursuant to subdivision (b).

(b)(1) One party or both parties to a marriage may elect to change the middle or last names, or both, by which that party wishes to be known after solemnization of the marriage by entering the new name in the spaces provided on the marriage license application without intent to defraud.

(2) A person may adopt any of the following last names pursuant to paragraph (1):

(A) The current last name of the other spouse.

(B) The last name of either spouse given at birth.

(C) A name combining into a single last name all or a segment of the current last name or the last name of either spouse given at birth.

(D) A combination of last names.

(3) A person may adopt any of the following middle names pursuant to paragraph (1):

(A) The current last name of either spouse.

§ 306.5

(B) The last name of either spouse given at birth.

(C) A combination of the current middle name and the current last name of the person or spouse.

(D) A combination of the current middle name and the last name given at birth of the person or spouse.

(4)(A) An election by a person to change their name pursuant to paragraph (1) shall serve as a record of the name change. A certified copy of a marriage certificate containing the new name, or retaining the former name, shall constitute proof that the use of the new name or retention of the former name is lawful.

(B) A certified copy of a marriage certificate shall be accepted as identification establishing a true, full name for purposes of Section 12800.7 of the Vehicle Code.

(C) This section does not prohibit the Department of Motor Vehicles from accepting as identification other documents establishing a true, full name for purposes of Section 12800.7 of the Vehicle Code. Those documents may include, without limitation, a certified copy of a marriage certificate recording a marriage outside of this state.

(D) This section shall be applied in a manner consistent with the requirements of Sections 1653.5 and 12801 of the Vehicle Code.

(5) The adoption of a new name, or the choice not to adopt a new name, by means of a marriage license application pursuant to paragraph (1) shall only be made at the time the marriage license is issued. After a marriage certificate is registered by the local registrar, the certificate shall not be amended to add a new name or change the name adopted pursuant to paragraph (1). An amendment may be issued to correct a clerical error in the new name fields on the marriage license. In this instance, the amendment shall be signed by one of the parties to the marriage and the county clerk or a deputy clerk, and the reason for the amendment shall be stated as correcting a clerical error. A clerical error as used in this part is an error made by the county clerk, a deputy clerk, or a notary authorized to issue confidential marriage licenses, whereby the information shown in the new name field does not match the information shown on the marriage license application. This requirement does not abrogate the right of either party to adopt a different name through usage at a future date, or to petition the superior court for a change of name pursuant to Title 8 (commencing with Section 1275) of Part 3 of the Code of Civil Procedure.

(c) This section does not abrogate the common law right of a person to change their name, or the right of a person to petition the superior court for a change of name pursuant to Title 8 (commencing with Section 1275) of Part 3 of the Code of Civil Procedure. *(Added by Stats.2007, c. 567 (A.B.102), § 7, operative Jan. 1, 2009. Amended by Stats.2009, c. 512 (A.B.1143), § 1; Stats.2016, c. 474 (A.B.2882), § 3, eff. Jan. 1, 2017; Stats.2019, c. 115 (A.B.1817), § 7, eff. Jan. 1, 2020.)*

Cross References

Marriage or domestic partnership, informational brochure, see Family Code § 358.

Research References

Forms

West's California Code Forms, Family § 350, Comment Overview—Marriage License and Certificate of Registry.

West's California Code Forms, Family § 351 Form 1, Marriage License Application.

§ 307. Marriage of members of religious society or denomination; requirements

This division, so far as it relates to the solemnizing of marriage, is not applicable to members of a particular religious society or denomination not having clergy for the purpose of solemnizing marriage or entering the marriage relation, if all of the following requirements are met:

(a) The parties to the marriage sign and endorse on the form prescribed by the State Department of Public Health, showing all of the following:

(1) The fact, time, and place of entering into the marriage.

(2) The printed names, signatures, and mailing addresses of two witnesses to the ceremony.

(3) The religious society or denomination of the parties to the marriage, and that the marriage was entered into in accordance with the rules and customs of that religious society or denomination. The statement of the parties to the marriage that the marriage was entered into in accordance with the rules and customs of the religious society or denomination is conclusively presumed to be true.

(b) The License and Certificate of Non–Clergy Marriage, endorsed pursuant to subdivision (a), is returned to the county recorder of the county in which the license was issued within 10 days after the ceremony. *(Stats.1992, c. 162 (A.B.2650), § 10, operative Jan. 1, 1994. Amended by Stats.1993, c. 219 (A.B.1500), § 90; Stats.2006, c. 816 (A.B.1102), § 5, operative Jan. 1, 2008; Stats.2007, c. 483 (S.B.1039), § 9.)*

Cross References

County defined for purposes of this Code, see Family Code § 67.
Department of Health Care Services, generally, see Health and Safety Code § 100100 et seq.
License,
    Confidential license, see Family Code § 500 et seq.
    Endorsement and return, see Family Code § 423.
    Failure to file, misdemeanor, see Penal Code § 360.
    False return, misdemeanor, see Penal Code § 360.
    Fee, see Government Code § 26840.
    Person solemnizing must require, see Family Code § 421.
Marital agreements, see Family Code § 1500 et seq.
Marital property, characterization, see Family Code § 760 et seq.
Marriage registration,
    Certificate of registry, filing, see Family Code § 359.
    Forms, see Health and Safety Code § 103125.
    Marriages not solemnized by clergy, license and certificate of declaration of marriage, see Health and Safety Code § 103180.
Presumption of validity of marriage, see Evidence Code §§ 605, 663.
Proof of marriage,
    Bigamy, see Penal Code § 281 et seq.
    Church certificates or records, see Evidence Code §§ 1315, 1316.
    Community reputation of date or fact of marriage, see Evidence Code § 1314.
    Entries in family records, see Evidence Code § 1312.
    Hearsay rule, exception, see Evidence Code § 1310.
Real property including leasehold interests, see Family Code § 700.
Record of marriage, establishment, see Health and Safety Code § 103450 et seq.
Relations of husband and wife, see Family Code §§ 720, 721.
State defined for purposes of this Code, see Family Code § 145.
Uniform Premarital Agreement Act, see Family Code § 1600 et seq.

Research References

Forms

West's California Code Forms, Family § 400, Comment Overview—Solemnize Marriage.

§ 308. Validity of foreign marriages

A marriage contracted outside this state that would be valid by laws of the jurisdiction in which the marriage was contracted is valid in California. *(Added by Stats.2014, c. 82 (S.B.1306), § 6, eff. Jan. 1, 2015. Amended by Stats.2016, c. 474 (A.B.2882), § 4, eff. Jan. 1, 2017.)*

Cross References

Death of party to marriage as reputed or believed, effect, see Family Code § 2201.

Marital agreements, see Family Code § 1500 et seq.
Marital property, characterization, see Family Code § 760 et seq.
Nullity, dissolution, and legal separation, scope of jurisdiction including marriage under this section, see Family Code § 2010.
Presumption of validity of marriage, see Evidence Code §§ 605, 663.
Proof of marriage,
   Bigamy, see Penal Code § 281 et seq.
   Church certificates or records, see Evidence Code §§ 1315, 1316.
   Community reputation of date or fact of marriage, see Evidence Code § 1314.
   Entries in family records, see Evidence Code § 1312.
   Hearsay rule, exception, see Evidence Code § 1310.
Real property including leasehold interests, see Family Code § 700.
Relations of husband and wife, see Family Code §§ 720, 721.
State defined for purposes of this Code, see Family Code § 145.
Uniform Premarital Agreement Act, see Family Code § 1600 et seq.

Research References

Forms

1 California Transactions Forms--Family Law § 4:65, Effect of Valid Marriage.

§ 308.5. Repealed by Stats.2014, c. 82, § 7, eff. Jan. 1, 2015

§ 309. Action to test validity of marriage

If either party to a marriage denies the marriage, or refuses to join in a declaration of the marriage, the other party may proceed, by action pursuant to Section 103450 of the Health and Safety Code, to have the validity of the marriage determined and declared. *(Stats. 1992, c. 162 (A.B.2650), § 10, operative Jan. 1, 1994. Amended by Stats.2006, c. 816 (A.B.1102), § 6, operative Jan. 1, 2008.)*

Cross References

Absence of party to marriage for five years, effect, see Family Code § 2201.
Action commenced with filing complaint, see Code of Civil Procedure § 350.
Action defined, see Code of Civil Procedure § 22.
Commencing civil actions, see Code of Civil Procedure § 411.10 et seq.
Judgment of nullity conclusive as to parties, effect, see Family Code § 2212.
Jurisdiction in superior court, see Family Code § 200.
Marital agreements, see Family Code § 1500 et seq.
Marital property, characterization, see Family Code § 760 et seq.
Parentage of father of issue of void, annulled or dissolved marriage, see Family Code §§ 7611, 7612.
Persons under conservatorship, determination of capacity to marry, see Probate Code § 1901.
Presumption of validity of marriage, see Evidence Code §§ 605, 663.
Proof of marriage,
   Bigamy, see Penal Code § 281 et seq.
   Church certificates or records, see Evidence Code §§ 1315, 1316.
   Community reputation of date or fact of marriage, see Evidence Code § 1314.
   Entries in family records, see Evidence Code § 1312.
   Hearsay rule, exception, see Evidence Code § 1310.
Real property including leasehold interests, see Family Code § 700.
Relations of husband and wife, see Family Code §§ 720, 721.
Separation agreements, see Family Code §§ 1620, 3580.
Uniform Divorce Recognition Act, see Family Code § 2090 et seq.
Uniform Premarital Agreement Act, see Family Code § 1600 et seq.

Research References

Forms

West's California Code Forms, Family § 309, Comment Overview—Action to Test Validity of Marriage.
West's California Code Forms, Family § 309 Form 2, Judgment Establishing Validity of Marriage.

§ 310. Methods of dissolution

Marriage is dissolved only by one of the following:

(a) The death of one of the parties.

(b) A judgment of dissolution of marriage.

(c) A judgment of nullity of marriage. *(Stats.1992, c. 162 (A.B. 2650), § 10, operative Jan. 1, 1994.)*

Cross References

Absence of party to marriage for five years, effect, see Family Code § 2201.
Death of either party following entry of judgment of dissolution, see Family Code § 2344.
Death of party to marriage as reputed or believed, effect, see Family Code § 2201.
Judgment and order defined for purposes of this Code, see Family Code § 100.
Judgment of dissolution, subsequent death of party, see Family Code § 2344.
Judgment of nullity, effect, see Family Code § 2212.
Marital agreements, see Family Code § 1500 et seq.
Marital property, characterization, see Family Code § 760 et seq.
Parentage of father of issue of void, annulled or dissolved marriage, see Family Code §§ 7611, 7612.
Presumption of death, see Evidence Code § 667; Probate Code § 12401.
Presumption of validity of marriage, see Evidence Code §§ 605, 663.
Real property including leasehold interests, see Family Code § 700.
Relations of husband and wife, see Family Code §§ 720, 721.
Separation agreements, see Family Code §§ 1620, 3580.
Uniform Divorce Recognition Act, see Family Code § 2090 et seq.
Uniform Premarital Agreement Act, see Family Code § 1600 et seq.
Void or voidable marriages, judicial determination, see Family Code § 2200 et seq.

Part 2

MARRIAGE LICENSE

Section	
350.	Necessity of license; armed forces members serving overseas in conflict or war; appearance of attorney-in-fact.
351.	Contents of license.
351.5.	Certificate of registry and marriage license; address information.
351.6.	Mailing address.
352.	Grounds for denial of license.
353.	Repealed.
354.	Identification; examination of applicants; additional documentary proof; armed forces members serving overseas in war or conflict; compliance by attorney-in-fact.
355.	Forms.
356.	Expiration of license.
357.	Numbering of licenses; transmittal of list of issued licenses; notice of expiration of license.
358.	Informational brochure; preparation and publication; contents.
359.	Marriage license; completion and return to county recorder.
359.	Marriage license; completion and return to county recorder.
360.	Duplicate marriage license; affidavit; issuance; fee; licenses lost, damaged, or destroyed before marriage ceremony.

Cross References

Confidential marriage, see Family Code § 500 et seq.
Fees for marriage licenses, see Government Code § 26840.
Local marriage registrar, see Health and Safety Code § 102285.
Marriage registration, see Health and Safety Code § 103125 et seq.
Original marriage registry certificates, transmittal to state registrar, see Health and Safety Code § 102355.
Record forms, see Health and Safety Code § 102200.
State Department of Health Care Services, generally, see Health and Safety Code § 100100 et seq.
Unrecorded marriage, license and certificate of declaration of marriage, see Family Code § 425.

§ 350. Necessity of license; armed forces members serving overseas in conflict or war; appearance of attorney-in-fact

(a) Before entering a marriage, or declaring a marriage pursuant to Section 425, the parties shall first obtain a marriage license from a county clerk.

§ 350

(b) If a marriage is to be entered into pursuant to subdivision (b) of Section 420, the attorney-in-fact shall appear before the county clerk on behalf of the party who is overseas, as prescribed in subdivision (a). *(Stats.1992, c. 162 (A.B.2650), § 10, operative Jan. 1, 1994. Amended by Stats.2004, c. 476 (S.B.7), § 1, eff. Sept. 10, 2004.)*

Cross References

Civil Rights Act, see Civil Code § 51 et seq.
County defined for purposes of this Code, see Family Code § 67.
Inalienable rights, see Cal. Const. Art. 1, § 1.
License,
    Confidential marriage, see Family Code § 500 et seq.
    Failure to file, false return or record, see Penal Code § 360.
    Fees, generally, see Government Code § 26820 et seq.
    Fees for marriage licenses, see Government Code § 26840.
    Unrecorded marriage, license and certificate of declaration of marriage, see Family Code § 425.
Local marriage registrar, see Health and Safety Code § 102285.
Marriage registration, see Health and Safety Code § 103125 et seq.
Privileges and immunities, see Cal. Const. Art. 1, § 7.

Research References

Forms

West's California Code Forms, Family § 350, Comment Overview—Marriage License and Certificate of Registry.

§ 351. Contents of license

The marriage license shall show all of the following:

(a) The identity of the parties to the marriage.

(b) The parties' full given names at birth or by court order, and mailing addresses.

(c) The parties' dates of birth. *(Stats.1992, c. 162 (A.B.2650), § 10, operative Jan. 1, 1994. Amended by Stats.2006, c. 816 (A.B.1102), § 8, operative Jan. 1, 2008.)*

Cross References

Fees for marriage licenses, see Government Code § 26840.
License, unrecorded marriage, License and Certificate of Declaration of Marriage, see Family Code § 425.
Local marriage registrar, see Health and Safety Code § 102285.
Marriage license and certificate of registry, mailing address of applicant, witness, or person solemnizing, see Family Code § 351.6.
Marriage registration, see Health and Safety Code § 103125 et seq.

Research References

Forms

West's California Code Forms, Family § 350, Comment Overview—Marriage License and Certificate of Registry.

§ 351.5. Certificate of registry and marriage license; address information

Notwithstanding subdivision (b) of Section 351 or 359 of this code, or Section 103175 of the Health and Safety Code, if either of the applicants for, or any witness to, a certificate of registry of marriage and a marriage license requests, the certificate of registry and the marriage license shall show the business address or United States Postal Service post office box for that applicant or witness instead of the residential address of that person. *(Added by Stats.2006, c. 60 (S.B.1364), § 1.)*

§ 351.6. Mailing address

Notwithstanding Section 307, 351, 351.5, 359, or 422 of this code, or Section 103175 or 103180 of the Health and Safety Code, a mailing address used by an applicant, witness, or person solemnizing or performing the marriage ceremony shall be a residential address, a business address, or a United States Postal Service post office box. *(Added by Stats.2006, c. 816 (A.B.1102), § 8.5, operative Jan. 1, 2007.)*

Operative Effect

For operative effect of Stats.2006, c. 816 (A.B.1102), see § 55 of that act.

§ 352. Grounds for denial of license

For Executive Order N–58–20 (2019 CA EO 58-20), which temporarily authorizes people to obtain marriage licenses and solemnize their marriages by videoconference, due to the COVID-19 pandemic, see Historical and Statutory Notes under Family Code § 359.

For Executive Order N–71–20 (2019 CA EO 71-20), which extends certain provisions of Executive Order N–58–20, due to the COVID-19 pandemic, see Historical and Statutory Notes under Education Code § 41422.

No marriage license shall be granted if either of the applicants lacks the capacity to enter into a valid marriage or is, at the time of making the application for the license, under the influence of an intoxicating liquor or narcotic drug. *(Stats.1992, c. 162 (A.B.2650), § 10, operative Jan. 1, 1994.)*

Cross References

Civil Rights Act, see Civil Code § 51 et seq.
Conservatees, determination of capacity to marry, see Probate Code § 1901.
Inalienable rights, see Cal. Const. Art. 1, § 1.
License,
    Confidential marriage, see Family Code § 500 et seq.
    Unrecorded marriage, License and Certificate of Declaration of Marriage, see Family Code § 425.
Marriage registration, see Health and Safety Code § 103125 et seq.
Privileges and immunities, see Cal. Const. Art. 1, § 7.

§ 353. Repealed by Stats.2006, c. 816 (A.B.1102), § 9, operative Jan. 1, 2008

§ 354. Identification; examination of applicants; additional documentary proof; armed forces members serving overseas in war or conflict; compliance by attorney-in-fact

For Executive Order N–58–20 (2019 CA EO 58-20), which temporarily authorizes people to obtain marriage licenses and solemnize their marriages by videoconference, due to the COVID-19 pandemic, see Historical and Statutory Notes under Family Code § 359.

For Executive Order N–71–20 (2019 CA EO 71-20), which extends certain provisions of Executive Order N–58–20, due to the COVID-19 pandemic, see Historical and Statutory Notes under Education Code § 41422.

(a) Each applicant for a marriage license shall be required to present authentic photo identification acceptable to the county clerk as to name and date of birth. A credible witness affidavit or affidavits may be used in lieu of authentic photo identification.

(b) For the purpose of ascertaining the facts mentioned or required in this part, if the clerk deems it necessary, the clerk may examine the applicants for a marriage license on oath at the time of the application. The clerk shall reduce the examination to writing and the applicants shall sign it.

(c) If necessary, the clerk may request additional documentary proof as to the accuracy of the facts stated.

(d) Applicants for a marriage license shall not be required to state, for any purpose, their race or color.

(e) If a marriage is to be entered into pursuant to subdivision (b) of Section 420, the attorney in fact shall comply with the requirements of this section on behalf of the applicant who is overseas, if necessary. *(Stats.1992, c. 162 (A.B.2650), § 10, operative Jan. 1, 1994. Amended by Stats.2004, c. 476 (S.B.7), § 2, eff. Sept. 10, 2004; Stats.2006, c. 816 (A.B.1102), § 10, operative Jan. 1, 2008.)*

Cross References

Authentication of writings, see Evidence Code § 1400 et seq.
Authenticity of documents, see Evidence Code § 643 et seq.
Inalienable rights, see Cal. Const. Art. 1, § 1.
License,
    Confidential marriage, see Family Code § 500 et seq.
    Fees, see Government Code § 26840 et seq.
Privileges and immunities, see Cal. Const. Art. 1, § 7.
State defined for purposes of this Code, see Family Code § 145.
Unrecorded marriage, License and Certificate of Declaration of Marriage, see Family Code § 425.

§ 355. Forms

(a) The forms for the marriage license shall be prescribed by the State Department of Public Health, and shall be adapted to set forth the facts required in this part.

(b) The marriage license shall include an affidavit, which the applicants shall sign, affirming that they have received the brochure provided for in Section 358. If the marriage is to be entered into pursuant to subdivision (b) of Section 420, the attorney in fact shall sign the affidavit on behalf of the applicant who is overseas.

(c) The forms for the marriage license shall contain spaces for either party or both parties to indicate a change in name pursuant to Section 306.5. *(Stats.1992, c. 162 (A.B.2650), § 10, operative Jan. 1, 1994. Amended by Stats.2004, c. 476 (S.B.7), § 3, eff. Sept. 10, 2004; Stats.2006, c. 816 (A.B.1102), § 11, operative Jan. 1, 2008; Stats.2007, c. 483 (S.B.1039), § 10; Stats.2007, c. 567 (A.B.102), § 8, operative Jan. 1, 2009.)*

Cross References

Department of Health Care Services, generally, see Health and Safety Code § 100100 et seq.
License, opposite sex requirement, see Family Code § 300.
Record forms, see Health and Safety Code § 102200.
State defined for purposes of this Code, see Family Code § 145.

Research References

Forms

West's California Code Forms, Family § 350, Comment Overview—Marriage License and Certificate of Registry.

§ 356. Expiration of license

A marriage license issued pursuant to this part expires 90 days after its issuance. The calendar date of expiration shall be clearly noted on the face of the license. *(Stats.1992, c. 162 (A.B.2650), § 10, operative Jan. 1, 1994.)*

Cross References

Inalienable rights, see Cal. Const. Art. 1, § 1.
License,
    Opposite sex requirement, see Family Code § 300.
Unrecorded marriage, License and Certificate of Declaration of Marriage, see Family Code § 425.

Research References

Forms

West's California Code Forms, Family § 350, Comment Overview—Marriage License and Certificate of Registry.

§ 357. Numbering of licenses; transmittal of list of issued licenses; notice of expiration of license

(a) The county clerk shall number each marriage license issued and shall transmit at periodic intervals to the county recorder a list or copies of the licenses issued.

(b) Not later than 60 days after the date of issuance, the county recorder shall notify licenseholders whose marriage license has not been returned of that fact and that the marriage license will automatically expire on the date shown on its face.

(c) The county recorder shall notify the licenseholders of the obligation of the person solemnizing their marriage to return the marriage license to the recorder's office within 10 days after the ceremony. *(Stats.1992, c. 162 (A.B.2650), § 10, operative Jan. 1, 1994. Amended by Stats.1993, c. 219 (A.B.1500), § 91; Stats.2001, c. 39 (A.B.1323), § 1; Stats.2006, c. 816 (A.B.1102), § 12, operative Jan. 1, 2008.)*

Cross References

County defined for purposes of this Code, see Family Code § 67.
Inalienable rights, see Cal. Const. Art. 1, § 1.
License,
    Failure to file, false return or record, see Penal Code § 360.
    Fees, see Government Code § 26840 et seq.
    Opposite sex requirement, see Family Code § 300.
Person defined for purposes of this Code, see Family Code § 105.
Privileges and immunities, see Cal. Const. Art. 1, § 7.
Unrecorded marriage, License and Certificate of Declaration of Marriage, see Family Code § 425.

§ 358. Informational brochure; preparation and publication; contents

(a) The State Department of Public Health shall prepare and publish a brochure that shall contain the following:

(1) Information concerning the possibilities of genetic defects and diseases and a listing of centers available for the testing and treatment of genetic defects and diseases.

(2) Information concerning acquired immunodeficiency syndrome (AIDS) and the availability of testing for antibodies to the probable causative agent of AIDS.

(3) Information concerning domestic violence, including resources available to victims and a statement that physical, emotional, psychological, and sexual abuse, and assault and battery, are against the law.

(4) Information concerning options for changing a name upon solemnization of marriage pursuant to Section 306.5, or upon registration of a domestic partnership pursuant to Section 298.6. That information shall include a notice that the recording of a change in name or the absence of a change in name on a marriage license application and certificate pursuant to Section 306.5 may not be amended once the marriage license is issued, but that options to adopt a change in name in the future through usage, common law, or petitioning the superior court are preserved, as set forth in Section 306.5.

(b) The State Department of Public Health shall make the brochures available to county clerks who shall distribute a copy of the brochure to each applicant for a marriage license, including applicants for a confidential marriage license and notaries public receiving a confidential marriage license pursuant to Section 503. The department shall also make the brochure available to the Secretary of State, who shall distribute a copy of the brochure to persons who qualify as domestic partners pursuant to Section 297 and shall make the brochure available electronically on the Internet Web site of the Secretary of State.

(c) The department shall prepare a lesbian, gay, bisexual, and transgender specific domestic abuse brochure and make the brochure available to the Secretary of State who shall print and make available the brochure, as funding allows, pursuant to Section 298.5.

(d) Each notary public issuing a confidential marriage license under Section 503 shall distribute a copy of the brochure to the applicants for a confidential marriage license.

(e) To the extent possible, the State Department of Public Health shall seek to combine in a single brochure all statutorily required information for marriage license applicants. *(Stats.1992, c. 162 (A.B.2650), § 10, operative Jan. 1, 1994. Amended by Stats.1996, c. 1075 (S.B.1444), § 8; Stats.2006, c. 816 (A.B.1102), § 13; Stats.2006,*

§ 358

c. 856 (A.B.2051), § 4.5; Stats.2007, c. 483 (S.B.1039), § 11; Stats. 2007, c. 567 (A.B.102), § 9.)

Cross References

Abuse defined for purposes of the Domestic Violence Protection Act, see Family Code § 6203.
AIDS Public Health Records Confidentiality Act, see Health and Safety Code § 121025 et seq.
AIDS training, see Business and Professions Code § 32.
Communicable disease prevention and control, Human Immunodeficiency Virus (HIV), see Health and Safety Code § 120775 et seq.
County defined for purposes of this Code, see Family Code § 67.
Department of Health Care Services, generally, see Health and Safety Code § 100100 et seq.
Disclosure of AIDS test results, see Health and Safety Code § 121015.
Domestic partners, availability of lesbian, gay, bisexual, and transgender specific domestic abuse brochure, see Family Code § 298.5.
Domestic violence defined for purposes of this Code, see Family Code § 6211.
HIV antibody tests conducted for purposes of insurance application, disclosures, see Insurance Code § 799.10.
License, opposite sex requirement, see Family Code § 300.
State defined for purposes of this Code, see Family Code § 145.

Research References

Forms

West's California Code Forms, Family § 350, Comment Overview—Marriage License and Certificate of Registry.

Repeal

For repeal of this section, see its terms.

Cross References

Civil Rights Act, see Civil Code § 51.
Contents of certificate of registry, see Health and Safety Code §§ 103175, 103180.
County defined for purposes of this Code, see Family Code § 67.
Duplicate certificate of registry, see Family Code § 360.
Duty of registering, see Health and Safety Code § 103150.
Inalienable rights, see Cal. Const. Art. 1, § 1.
License,
   Confidential marriage, see Family Code § 500 et seq.
   Failure to file, false return or record, see Penal Code § 360.
   Fees, see Government Code § 26840 et seq.
   Opposite sex requirement, see Family Code § 300.
   Unrecorded marriage, License and Certificate of Declaration of Marriage, see Family Code § 425.
Marriage registration, generally, see Health and Safety Code § 103125 et seq.
Person defined for purposes of this Code, see Family Code § 105.

Research References

Forms

West's California Code Forms, Family § 350, Comment Overview—Marriage License and Certificate of Registry.
West's California Code Forms, Family § 350 Form 1, California Marriage License, Registration and Ceremony Information.

§ 359. Marriage license; completion and return to county recorder

Section operative until Jan. 1, 2024. See, also, § 359 operative Jan. 1, 2024.

For Executive Order N–58–20 (2019 CA EO 58-20), which temporarily authorizes people to obtain marriage licenses and solemnize their marriages by videoconference, due to the COVID-19 pandemic, see Historical and Statutory Notes under this section.

For Executive Order N–71–20 (2019 CA EO 71-20), which extends certain provisions of Executive Order N–58–20, due to the COVID-19 pandemic, see Historical and Statutory Notes under Education Code § 41422.

(a) Except as provided in Sections 420 and 426, or Part 5 (commencing with Section 550), applicants to be married shall first appear together in person before the county clerk to obtain a marriage license.

(b) The contents of the marriage license are provided in Part 1 (commencing with Section 102100) of Division 102 of the Health and Safety Code.

(c) The issued marriage license shall be presented to the person solemnizing the marriage by the parties to be married.

(d) The person solemnizing the marriage shall complete the solemnization sections on the marriage license, and shall cause to be entered on the marriage license the printed name, signature, and mailing address of at least one, and no more than two, witnesses to the marriage ceremony.

(e) The marriage license shall be returned by the person solemnizing the marriage to the county recorder of the county in which the license was issued within 10 days after the ceremony.

(f) As used in this division, "returned" means presented to the appropriate person in person, or postmarked, before the expiration of the specified time period.

(g) This section shall remain in effect only until January 1, 2024, and as of that date is repealed. (Stats.1992, c. 162 (A.B.2650), § 10, operative Jan. 1, 1994. Amended by Stats.1993, c. 219 (A.B.1500), § 92; Stats.1996, c. 1023 (S.B.1497), § 44, eff. Sept. 29, 1996; Stats.2001, c. 39 (A.B.1323), § 2; Stats.2006, c. 816 (A.B.1102), § 14, operative Jan. 1, 2008; Stats.2021, c. 620 (A.B.583), § 1, eff. Oct. 7, 2021.)

§ 359. Marriage license; completion and return to county recorder

Section operative Jan. 1, 2024. See, also, § 359 operative until Jan. 1, 2024.

For Executive Order N–58–20 (2019 CA EO 58-20), which temporarily authorizes people to obtain marriage licenses and solemnize their marriages by videoconference, due to the COVID-19 pandemic, see Historical and Statutory Notes under this section.

For Executive Order N–71–20 (2019 CA EO 71-20), which extends certain provisions of Executive Order N–58–20, due to the COVID-19 pandemic, see Historical and Statutory Notes under Education Code § 41422.

(a) Except as provided in Sections 420 and 426, applicants to be married shall first appear together in person before the county clerk to obtain a marriage license.

(b) The contents of the marriage license are provided in Part 1 (commencing with Section 102100) of Division 102 of the Health and Safety Code.

(c) The issued marriage license shall be presented to the person solemnizing the marriage by the parties to be married.

(d) The person solemnizing the marriage shall complete the solemnization sections on the marriage license, and shall cause to be entered on the marriage license the printed name, signature, and mailing address of at least one, and no more than two, witnesses to the marriage ceremony.

(e) The marriage license shall be returned by the person solemnizing the marriage to the county recorder of the county in which the license was issued within 10 days after the ceremony.

(f) As used in this division, "returned" means presented to the appropriate person in person, or postmarked, before the expiration of the specified time period.

(g) This section shall become operative on January 1, 2024. (Added by Stats.2021, c. 620 (A.B.583), § 2, eff. Oct. 7, 2021, operative Jan. 1, 2024.)

Cross References

Civil Rights Act, see Civil Code § 51.
Contents of certificate of registry, see Health and Safety Code §§ 103175, 103180.

County defined for purposes of this Code, see Family Code § 67.
Duplicate certificate of registry, see Family Code § 360.
Duty of registering, see Health and Safety Code § 103150.
Inalienable rights, see Cal. Const. Art. 1, § 1.
License,
   Confidential marriage, see Family Code § 500 et seq.
   Failure to file, false return or record, see Penal Code § 360.
   Fees, see Government Code § 26840 et seq.
   Opposite sex requirement, see Family Code § 300.
   Unrecorded marriage, License and Certificate of Declaration of Marriage, see Family Code § 425.
Marriage registration, generally, see Health and Safety Code § 103125 et seq.
Person defined for purposes of this Code, see Family Code § 105.

Research References

Forms

West's California Code Forms, Family § 350, Comment Overview—Marriage License and Certificate of Registry.
West's California Code Forms, Family § 350 Form 1, California Marriage License, Registration and Ceremony Information.

§ 360. Duplicate marriage license; affidavit; issuance; fee; licenses lost, damaged, or destroyed before marriage ceremony

(a) If a marriage license is lost, damaged, or destroyed after the marriage ceremony, but before it is returned to the county recorder, or deemed unacceptable for registration by the county recorder, the person solemnizing the marriage, in order to comply with Section 359, shall obtain a duplicate marriage license by filing an affidavit setting forth the facts with the county clerk of the county in which the license was issued.

(b) The duplicate marriage license shall not be issued later than one year after the date of marriage and shall be returned by the person solemnizing the marriage to the county recorder within one year of the date of marriage.

(c) The county clerk may charge a fee to cover the actual costs of issuing a duplicate marriage license.

(d) If a marriage license is lost, damaged, or destroyed before a marriage ceremony takes place, the applicants shall purchase a new marriage license and the old license shall be voided. *(Stats.1992, c. 162 (A.B.2650), § 10, operative Jan. 1, 1994. Amended by Stats.1993, c. 219 (A.B.1500), § 93; Stats.2001, c. 39 (A.B.1323), § 3; Stats.2006, c. 816 (A.B.1102), § 15, operative Jan. 1, 2008; Stats.2016, c. 474 (A.B.2882), § 5, eff. Jan. 1, 2017.)*

Cross References

Contents of certificate of registry, see Health and Safety Code §§ 103175, 103180.
County defined for purposes of this Code, see Family Code § 67.
Duty of registering, see Health and Safety Code § 103150.
Judgment and order defined for purposes of this Code, see Family Code § 100.
License,
   Confidential marriage, see Family Code § 500 et seq.
   Opposite sex requirement, see Family Code § 300.
   Unrecorded marriage, License and Certificate of Declaration of Marriage, see Family Code § 425.
Lost or destroyed documents, generally, see Evidence Code § 1601.
Marriage registration, generally, see Health and Safety Code § 103125 et seq.
Person defined for purposes of this Code, see Family Code § 105.

Research References

Forms

West's California Code Forms, Family § 350 Form 1, California Marriage License, Registration and Ceremony Information.

Part 3

SOLEMNIZATION OF MARRIAGE

Chapter	Section
1. Persons Authorized to Solemnize Marriage	400
2. Solemnization of Marriage	420

Cross References

Fee for performance of marriage, see Government Code § 26861.
Penalty for solemnizing illegal marriages, see Penal Code § 359.

CHAPTER 1. PERSONS AUTHORIZED TO SOLEMNIZE MARRIAGE

Section	
400.	Authorized persons; refusal to solemnize marriage; tax-exempt status.
400.1.	Repealed.
401.	Commissioner of civil marriages; designation of county clerk; deputies.
402.	Officials of nonprofit religious institutions.

§ 400. Authorized persons; refusal to solemnize marriage; tax-exempt status

(a) Although marriage is a personal relation arising out of a civil, and not a religious, contract, a marriage may be solemnized by a priest, minister, rabbi, or authorized person of any religious denomination who is 18 years of age or older. A person authorized by this subdivision shall not be required to solemnize a marriage that is contrary to the tenets of the person's faith. Refusal to solemnize a marriage under this subdivision, either by an individual or by a religious denomination, shall not affect the tax-exempt status of any entity.

(b) Consistent with Section 94.5 of the Penal Code and provided that any compensation received is reasonable, including payment of actual expenses, a marriage may also be solemnized by any of the following persons:

(1) A judge or retired judge, commissioner of civil marriages or retired commissioner of civil marriages, commissioner or retired commissioner, or assistant commissioner of a court of record in this state.

(2) A judge or magistrate who has resigned from office.

(3) Any of the following judges or magistrates of the United States:

(A) A justice or retired justice of the United States Supreme Court.

(B) A judge or retired judge of a court of appeals, a district court, or a court created by an act of the United States Congress the judges of which are entitled to hold office during good behavior.

(C) A judge or retired judge of a bankruptcy court or a tax court.

(D) A United States magistrate or retired magistrate.

(c) Except as provided in subdivision (d), a marriage may also be solemnized by any of the following persons who are 18 years of age or older:

(1) A Member of the Legislature or constitutional officer of this state or a Member of Congress of the United States who represents a district within this state, or a former Member of the Legislature or constitutional officer of this state or a former Member of Congress of the United States who represented a district within this state.

(2) A person that holds or formerly held an elected office of a city, county, or city and county.

(3) A city clerk of a charter city or serving in accordance with subdivision (b) of Section 36501 of the Government Code, while that person holds office.

(d)(1) A person listed in subdivision (c) shall not accept compensation for solemnizing a marriage while holding office.

§ 400

(2) A person listed in subdivision (c) shall not solemnize a marriage pursuant to this section if they have been removed from office due to committing an offense or have been convicted of an offense that involves moral turpitude, dishonesty, or fraud. *(Stats. 1992, c. 162 (A.B.2650), § 10, operative Jan. 1, 1994. Amended by Stats.1998, c. 931 (S.B.2139), § 142, eff. Sept. 28, 1998; Stats.1998, c. 932 (A.B.1094), § 31.5, operative Jan. 1, 1999; Stats.2006, c. 816 (A.B.1102), § 16, operative Jan. 1, 2008; Stats.2012, c. 834 (S.B.1140), § 1; Stats.2016, c. 211 (S.B.875), § 1, eff. Jan. 1, 2017; Stats.2016, c. 528 (A.B.2761), § 1, eff. Jan. 1, 2017; Stats.2017, c. 42 (A.B.430), § 1, eff. July 10, 2017; Stats.2019, c. 115 (A.B.1817), § 8, eff. Jan. 1, 2020.)*

Cross References

Commissioner of civil marriages, acceptance of fees or gratuities, see Penal Code § 70.5.
Foreign marriages, validity, see Family Code § 308.
Obligors, duties of support, see Family Code § 3550.
Officials of nonprofit religious institutions, authorization to solemnize marriages, see Family Code § 402.
Penalty for solemnizing illegal marriages, see Penal Code § 359.
Person defined for purposes of this Code, see Family Code § 105.
Religious society or denomination members, requirement for marriage, see Family Code § 307.
State defined for purposes of this Code, see Family Code § 145.

Research References

Forms

West's California Code Forms, Family § 350 Form 1, California Marriage License, Registration and Ceremony Information.
West's California Code Forms, Family § 400, Comment Overview—Solemnize Marriage.

§ 400.1. Repealed by Stats.2016, c. 211 (S.B.875), § 2, eff. Jan. 1, 2017; Stats.2016, c. 528 (A.B.2761), § 2, eff. Jan. 1, 2017

§ 401. Commissioner of civil marriages; designation of county clerk; deputies

(a) For each county, the county clerk is designated as a commissioner of civil marriages.

(b) The commissioner of civil marriages may appoint deputy commissioners of civil marriages who may solemnize marriages under the direction of the commissioner of civil marriages and shall perform other duties directed by the commissioner. *(Stats.1992, c. 162 (A.B.2650), § 10, operative Jan. 1, 1994.)*

Cross References

Commissioner of civil marriages, acceptance of fees or gratuities, see Penal Code § 70.5.
County clerk, fees, performance of marriage, see Government Code § 26861.
County defined for purposes of this Code, see Family Code § 67.
Fee for performance of marriage, see Government Code § 26861.
Foreign marriages, validity, see Family Code § 308.
Religious society or denomination members, requirement for marriage, see Family Code § 307.

Research References

Forms

West's California Code Forms, Family § 350 Form 1, California Marriage License, Registration and Ceremony Information.

§ 402. Officials of nonprofit religious institutions

In addition to the persons permitted to solemnize marriages under Section 400, a county may license officials of a nonprofit religious institution, whose articles of incorporation are registered with the Secretary of State, to solemnize the marriages of persons who are affiliated with or are members of the religious institution. The licensee shall possess the degree of doctor of philosophy and must perform religious services or rites for the institution on a regular basis. The marriages shall be performed without fee to the parties. *(Stats.1992, c. 162 (A.B.2650), § 10, operative Jan. 1, 1994.)*

Cross References

County defined for purposes of this Code, see Family Code § 67.
Foreign marriages, validity, see Family Code § 308.
Nonprofit Religious Corporations, see Corporations Code § 9110 et seq.
Person defined for purposes of this Code, see Family Code § 105.
Religious society or denomination members, requirement for marriage, see Family Code § 307.
State defined for purposes of this Code, see Family Code § 145.

Research References

Forms

West's California Code Forms, Family § 350 Form 1, California Marriage License, Registration and Ceremony Information.

CHAPTER 2. SOLEMNIZATION OF MARRIAGE

Section
420. Requirements for solemnization; appearance by attorney-in-fact on behalf of armed forces member serving overseas in conflict or war.
421. Duties of persons solemnizing marriage.
422. License; statement of person solemnizing marriage.
423. Return of license; inclusion of copy of court order granting permission to marry.
424. Repealed.
425. Unrecorded marriage; license and certificate of declaration of marriage; filing.
426. Physical inability of party to appear before clerk; issuance of license; requirements.

Cross References

Marriage registration, required registration, see Health and Safety Code § 103150.
Penalty for solemnizing illegal marriages, see Penal Code § 359.

§ 420. Requirements for solemnization; appearance by attorney-in-fact on behalf of armed forces member serving overseas in conflict or war

For Executive Order N–58–20 (2019 CA EO 58-20), which temporarily authorizes people to obtain marriage licenses and solemnize their marriages by videoconference, due to the COVID-19 pandemic, see Historical and Statutory Notes under Family Code § 359.

For Executive Order N–71–20 (2019 CA EO 71-20), which extends certain provisions of Executive Order N–58–20, due to the COVID-19 pandemic, see Historical and Statutory Notes under Education Code § 41422.

(a) No particular form for the ceremony of marriage is required for solemnization of the marriage, but the parties shall declare, in the physical presence of the person solemnizing the marriage and necessary witnesses, that they take each other as spouses.

(b) Notwithstanding subdivision (a), a member of the Armed Forces of the United States who is stationed overseas and serving in a conflict or a war and is unable to appear for the licensure and solemnization of the marriage may enter into that marriage by the appearance of an attorney in fact, commissioned and empowered in writing for that purpose through a power of attorney. The attorney in fact shall personally appear at the county clerk's office with the party who is not stationed overseas and present the original power of attorney duly signed by the party stationed overseas and acknowledged before a notary or witnessed by two officers of the United States Armed Forces. Copies in any form, including by facsimile, are not acceptable. The power of attorney shall state the full given names at birth, or by court order, of the parties to be married, and that the power of attorney is solely for the purpose of authorizing the attorney in fact to obtain a marriage license on the person's behalf and participate in the solemnization of the marriage. The original power of attorney shall be a part of the marriage certificate upon registration. The completion of a power of attorney shall be the sole determinant as to whether the county clerk's office and the State Registrar will accept the power of attorney.

(c) A contract of marriage, if otherwise duly made, shall not be invalidated for want of conformity to the requirements of any religious sect. (Stats.1992, c. 162 (A.B.2650), § 10, operative Jan. 1, 1994. Amended by Stats.1993, c. 219 (A.B.1500), § 94; Stats.2004, c. 476 (S.B.7), § 4, eff. Sept. 10, 2004; Stats.2005, c. 22 (S.B.1108), § 60; Stats.2006, c. 816 (A.B.1102), § 17, operative Jan. 1, 2008; Stats.2014, c. 82 (S.B.1306), § 8, eff. Jan. 1, 2015; Stats.2016, c. 130 (A.B.2128), § 1, eff. Jan. 1, 2017.)

Cross References

Confidential marriage, see Family Code § 500 et seq.
Duty of registering, see Health and Safety Code § 103150.
Foreign marriages, validity, see Family Code § 308.
Forms for application for marriage license, affidavit, signature by attorney-in-fact on behalf of overseas military member, see Family Code § 355.
License, opposite sex requirement, see Family Code § 300.
Marriage licenses, appearance of attorney-in-fact before county clerk on behalf of military member overseas, see Family Code § 350.
Marriage licenses, identification and examination requirements, compliance by attorney-in-fact on behalf of overseas military member, see Family Code § 354.
Marriage registration, generally, see Health and Safety Code § 103125 et seq.
Person defined for purposes of this Code, see Family Code § 105.
Presumption of validity of marriage, see Evidence Code §§ 605, 663.
Proof of marriage,
  Church certificates or records, see Evidence Code §§ 1315, 1316.
  Community reputation of date or fact of marriage, see Evidence Code § 1314.
  Entries in family records, see Evidence Code § 1312.
  Hearsay rule, exception, see Evidence Code § 1310.
Record of marriage, establishment, see Health and Safety Code § 103450 et seq.
References to husband, wife, spouses and married persons, persons included for purposes of this Code, see Family Code § 11.
Religious society or denomination members, requirement for marriage, see Family Code § 307.

Research References

Forms

West's California Code Forms, Family § 350 Form 1, California Marriage License, Registration and Ceremony Information.

§ 421. Duties of persons solemnizing marriage

For Executive Order N–58–20 (2019 CA EO 58-20), which temporarily authorizes people to obtain marriage licenses and solemnize their marriages by videoconference, due to the COVID-19 pandemic, see Historical and Statutory Notes under Family Code § 359.

For Executive Order N–71–20 (2019 CA EO 71-20), which extends certain provisions of Executive Order N–58–20, due to the COVID-19 pandemic, see Historical and Statutory Notes under Education Code § 41422.

Before solemnizing a marriage, the person solemnizing the marriage shall require the presentation of the marriage license. If the person solemnizing the marriage has reason to doubt the correctness of the statement of facts in the marriage license, the person must be satisfied as to the correctness of the statement of facts before solemnizing the marriage. For this purpose, the person may administer oaths and examine the parties and witnesses in the same manner as the county clerk does before issuing the license. (Stats. 1992, c. 162 (A.B.2650), § 10, operative Jan. 1, 1994.)

Cross References

Confidential marriage, see Family Code § 500 et seq.
County defined for purposes of this Code, see Family Code § 67.
Duty of registering, see Health and Safety Code § 103150.
Foreign marriages, validity, see Family Code § 308.
License,
  Failure to file, misdemeanor, see Penal Code § 360.
  False return, misdemeanor, see Penal Code § 360.
  Necessity, see Family Code § 350.
  Opposite sex requirement, see Family Code § 300.
Marriage registration,
  Generally, see Health and Safety Code § 103125 et seq.
  Certificate of registry, filing, see Family Code § 359.
Person defined for purposes of this Code, see Family Code § 105.
Presumption of validity of marriage, see Evidence Code §§ 605, 663.
Proof of marriage,
  Church certificates or records, see Evidence Code §§ 1315, 1316.
  Community reputation of date or fact of marriage, see Evidence Code § 1314.
  Entries in family records, see Evidence Code § 1312.
  Hearsay rule, exception, see Evidence Code § 1310.
Record of marriage, establishment, see Health and Safety Code § 103450 et seq.
Religious society or denomination members, requirement for marriage, see Family Code § 307.

§ 422. License; statement of person solemnizing marriage

For Executive Order N–58–20 (2019 CA EO 58-20), which temporarily authorizes people to obtain marriage licenses and solemnize their marriages by videoconference, due to the COVID-19 pandemic, see Historical and Statutory Notes under Family Code § 359.

For Executive Order N–71–20 (2019 CA EO 71-20), which extends certain provisions of Executive Order N–58–20, due to the COVID-19 pandemic, see Historical and Statutory Notes under Education Code § 41422.

The person solemnizing a marriage shall sign and print or type upon the marriage license a statement, in the form prescribed by the State Department of Public Health, showing all of the following:

(a) The fact, date (month, day, year), and place (city and county) of solemnization.

(b) The printed names, signatures, and mailing addresses of at least one, and no more than two, witnesses to the ceremony.

(c) The official position of the person solemnizing the marriage, or of the denomination of which that person is a priest, minister, rabbi, or other authorized person of any religious denomination.

(d) The person solemnizing the marriage shall also type or print their name and mailing address. (Stats.1992, c. 162 (A.B.2650), § 10, operative Jan. 1, 1994. Amended by Stats.1993, c. 219 (A.B.1500), § 95; Stats.2006, c. 816 (A.B.1102), § 18, operative Jan. 1, 2008; Stats.2007, c. 483 (S.B.1039), § 12; Stats.2019, c. 115 (A.B.1817), § 9, eff. Jan. 1, 2020.)

Cross References

Confidential marriage, see Family Code § 500 et seq.
County defined for purposes of this Code, see Family Code § 67.
Department of Health Care Services, generally, see Health and Safety Code § 100100 et seq.
Duty of registering, see Health and Safety Code § 103150.
Foreign marriages, validity, see Family Code § 308.
License,
  Failure to file, misdemeanor, see Penal Code § 360.
  False return, misdemeanor, see Penal Code § 360.
  Necessity, see Family Code § 350.
  Opposite sex requirement, see Family Code § 300.
Marriage license and certificate of registry, mailing address of applicant, witness, or person solemnizing, see Family Code § 351.6.
Marriage registration,
  Generally, see Health and Safety Code § 103125 et seq.
  Certificate of registry, filing, see Family Code § 359.
Person defined for purposes of this Code, see Family Code § 105.
Presumption of validity of marriage, see Evidence Code §§ 605, 663.
Proof of marriage,
  Church certificates or records, see Evidence Code §§ 1315, 1316.

§ 422

Community reputation of date or fact of marriage, see Evidence Code § 1314.
Entries in family records, see Evidence Code § 1312.
Hearsay rule, exception, see Evidence Code § 1310.
Record of marriage, establishment, see Health and Safety Code § 103450 et seq.
Religious society or denomination members, requirement for marriage, see Family Code § 307.
State defined for purposes of this Code, see Family Code § 145.

Research References

Forms

West's California Code Forms, Family § 350, Comment Overview—Marriage License and Certificate of Registry.
West's California Code Forms, Family § 400, Comment Overview—Solemnize Marriage.

§ 423. Return of license; inclusion of copy of court order granting permission to marry

For Executive Order N–58–20 (2019 CA EO 58-20), which temporarily authorizes people to obtain marriage licenses and solemnize their marriages by videoconference, due to the COVID-19 pandemic, see Historical and Statutory Notes under Family Code § 359.

For Executive Order N–71–20 (2019 CA EO 71-20), which extends certain provisions of Executive Order N–58–20, due to the COVID-19 pandemic, see Historical and Statutory Notes under Education Code § 41422.

(a) The person solemnizing the marriage shall return the marriage license, endorsed as required in Section 422, to the county recorder of the county in which the license was issued within 10 days after the ceremony.

(b) For purposes of Section 102356 of the Health and Safety Code, the person solemnizing the marriage shall include with the marriage license described in subdivision (a) a copy of the court order granting permission to marry described in Section 304, if one or both of the parties to the marriage were minors at the time of solemnization of the marriage. (Stats.1992, c. 162 (A.B.2650), § 10, operative Jan. 1, 1994. Amended by Stats.1993, c. 219 (A.B.1500), § 96; Stats.2001, c. 39 (A.B.1323), § 4; Stats.2018, c. 660 (S.B.273), § 6, eff. Jan. 1, 2019.)

Cross References

Confidential marriage, see Family Code § 500 et seq.
County defined for purposes of this Code, see Family Code § 67.
Document concerning information on marriage certificates in which one or both of the parties are minors, contents, personal identifying information, see Health and Safety Code § 102356.
Duty of registering, see Health and Safety Code § 103150.
Foreign marriages, validity, see Family Code § 308.
Interview of parties intending to marry, interview of parents, separate interviews, written report, evidence of coercion or undue influence, premarital counseling, fees, registration information, solemnization requirements, see Family Code § 304.
License,
    Failure to file, misdemeanor, see Penal Code § 360.
    False return, misdemeanor, see Penal Code § 360.
    Necessity, see Family Code § 350.
    Opposite sex requirement, see Family Code § 300.
Marriage registration,
    Generally, see Health and Safety Code § 103125 et seq.
    Certificate of registry, filing, see Family Code § 359.
Person defined for purposes of this Code, see Family Code § 105.
Presumption of validity of marriage, see Evidence Code §§ 605, 663.
Proof of marriage,
    Church certificates or records, see Evidence Code §§ 1315, 1316.
    Community reputation of date or fact of marriage, see Evidence Code § 1314.
    Entries in family records, see Evidence Code § 1312.
    Hearsay rule, exception, see Evidence Code § 1310.
Record of marriage, establishment, see Health and Safety Code § 103450 et seq.
Religious society or denomination members, requirement for marriage, see Family Code § 307.

Research References

Forms

West's California Code Forms, Family § 302, Comment Overview—Marriage of Minor.

§ 424. Repealed by Stats.2006, c. 816 (A.B.1102), § 19, operative Jan. 1, 2008

§ 425. Unrecorded marriage; license and certificate of declaration of marriage; filing

If no record of the solemnization of a California marriage previously contracted under this division for that marriage is known to exist, the parties may purchase a License and Certificate of Declaration of Marriage from the county clerk in the parties' county of residence one year or more from the date of the marriage. The license and certificate shall be returned to the county recorder of the county in which the license was issued. (Stats.1992, c. 162 (A.B. 2650), § 10, operative Jan. 1, 1994. Amended by Stats.1993, c. 219 (A.B.1500), § 97; Stats.2006, c. 816 (A.B.1102), § 20, operative Jan. 1, 2008.)

Cross References

Confidential marriage, see Family Code § 500 et seq.
County defined for purposes of this Code, see Family Code § 67.
Duty of registering, see Health and Safety Code § 103150.
Foreign marriages, validity, see Family Code § 308.
License,
    Failure to file, misdemeanor, see Penal Code § 360.
    False return, misdemeanor, see Penal Code § 360.
    Necessity, see Family Code § 350.
    Opposite sex requirement, see Family Code § 300.
Marriage registration,
    Generally, see Health and Safety Code § 103125 et seq.
    Certificate of registry, filing, see Family Code § 359.
Presumption of validity of marriage, see Evidence Code §§ 605, 663.
Proof of marriage,
    Church certificates or records, see Evidence Code §§ 1315, 1316.
    Community reputation of date or fact of marriage, see Evidence Code § 1314.
    Entries in family records, see Evidence Code § 1312.
    Hearsay rule, exception, see Evidence Code § 1310.
Record of marriage, establishment, see Health and Safety Code § 103450 et seq.
Religious society or denomination members, requirement for marriage, see Family Code § 307.

Research References

Forms

West's California Code Forms, Family § 309, Comment Overview—Action to Test Validity of Marriage.
West's California Code Forms, Family § 309 Form 1, Complaint to Establish Validity of Marriage.
West's California Code Forms, Family § 350 Form 1, California Marriage License, Registration and Ceremony Information.
West's California Code Forms, Family § 400, Comment Overview—Solemnize Marriage.

§ 426. Physical inability of party to appear before clerk; issuance of license; requirements

For Executive Order N–58–20 (2019 CA EO 58-20), which temporarily authorizes people to obtain marriage licenses and solemnize their marriages by videoconference, due to the COVID-19 pandemic, see Historical and Statutory Notes under Family Code § 359.

For Executive Order N–71–20 (2019 CA EO 71-20), which extends certain provisions of Executive Order N–58–20, due to the COVID-19 pandemic, see Historical and Statutory Notes under Education Code § 41422.

If for sufficient reason, as described in subdivision (d), either or both of the parties to be married are physically unable to appear in person before the county clerk, a marriage license may be issued by the county clerk to the person solemnizing the marriage if the following requirements are met:

(a) The person solemnizing the marriage physically presents an affidavit to the county clerk explaining the reason for the inability to appear.

(b) The affidavit is signed under penalty of perjury by the person solemnizing the marriage and by both parties.

(c) The signature of any party to be married who is unable to appear in person before the county clerk is authenticated by a notary public or a court prior to the county clerk issuing the marriage license.

(d) Sufficient reason includes proof of hospitalization, incarceration, or any other reason proved to the satisfaction of the county clerk. *(Added by Stats.2006, c. 816 (A.B.1102), § 21, operative Jan. 1, 2008.)*

Part 4

CONFIDENTIAL MARRIAGE

Chapter	Section
1. General Provisions	500
2. Approval of Notaries to Authorize Confidential Marriages	530

Cross References

Alameda County Board of Supervisors, domestic violence, fee increase for marriage and confidential marriage licenses, see Government Code § 26840.10.
Contra Costa County Board of Supervisors, domestic violence, fee increase for marriage and confidential marriage licenses, see Government Code § 26840.9.
County clerk, fees,
  Marriage authorization, see Government Code § 26840.8.
  Marriage certificate, see Government Code § 26840.1.
Increase of fees for support of family conciliation court and mediation services, see Government Code § 26840.3.
Marriage registration, see Health and Safety Code § 103125 et seq.
Marriage requirements, consent followed by issuance of license and solemnization, exceptions, see Family Code § 300.
Original marriage registry certificates, transmittal to state registrar, see Health and Safety Code § 102355.
Record forms, see Health and Safety Code § 102200.
Solano County Board of Supervisors, domestic violence, fee increase for marriage and confidential marriage licenses, see Government Code § 26840.11.
Solemnizing marriages, presentment of license, authorization, see Penal Code § 360.
State Department of Health Care Services, generally, see Health and Safety Code § 100100 et seq.
State Registrar of Vital Statistics, see Health and Safety Code § 102175.
Unrecorded marriage, license and certificate of declaration of marriage, see Family Code § 425.

CHAPTER 1. GENERAL PROVISIONS

Section	
500.	Unmarried persons who have been living together as spouses.
500.5.	Marriage license and marriage certificate.
501.	Issuance of license.
501.	Issuance of license.
502.	Inability to personally appear; issuance of license.
503.	Issuance of confidential marriage license upon request of notary public; fees.
504.	Duration of license.
505.	Form of license; contents.
506.	Completion of license; filing.
507.	Repealed.
508.	Application to obtain certified copy of confidential marriage license.
509.	Application to obtain certified copy of certificate; fee.
510.	Replacement of marriage certificate; issuance of duplicate license.
511.	Maintenance of marriage certificates; inspections; preservation of record; reproductions; disclosure of information.

§ 500. Unmarried persons who have been living together as spouses

When two unmarried people, not minors, have been living together as spouses, they may be married pursuant to this chapter by a person authorized to solemnize a marriage under Chapter 1 (commencing with Section 400) of Part 3. *(Stats.1992, c. 162 (A.B.2650), § 10, operative Jan. 1, 1994. Amended by Stats.2014, c. 82 (S.B.1306), § 9, eff. Jan. 1, 2015; Stats.2016, c. 474 (A.B.2882), § 6, eff. Jan. 1, 2017.)*

Cross References

Certificate of registry, preparation and filing, see Family Code § 359.
Consent of parties, see Family Code § 300 et seq.
Increase of fees for support of family conciliation court and mediation services, conditions, see Government Code § 26840.3.
License,
  Necessity, see Family Code §§ 300, 350.
  Offense of solemnization of marriage without license or authorization, see Penal Code § 360.
  Return of license to county recorder, see Family Code § 423.
Marriage authorization, additional fee upon filing, use of fee, see Government Code § 26840.8.
Marriage certificate, fee, see Government Code § 26840.1.
Marriage registration, see Health and Safety Code § 103125 et seq.
Minor defined, see Family Code § 6500.
Penalty for solemnizing illegal marriages, see Penal Code § 359.
Person defined for purposes of this Code, see Family Code § 105.
References to husband, wife, spouses and married persons, persons included for purposes of this Code, see Family Code § 11.
Solemnization requirements, see Family Code § 420 et seq.

Research References

Forms

West's California Code Forms, Family § 350 Form 1, California Marriage License, Registration and Ceremony Information.
West's California Code Forms, Family § 500, Comment Overview—Requirements for Confidential Marriages.

§ 500.5. Marriage license and marriage certificate

For purposes of this part, the document issued by the county clerk is a marriage license until it is registered with the county clerk, at which time the license becomes a marriage certificate. *(Added by Stats.2006, c. 816 (A.B.1102), § 22, operative Jan. 1, 2008.)*

Research References

Forms

West's California Code Forms, Family § 500, Comment Overview—Requirements for Confidential Marriages.

§ 501. Issuance of license

Section operative until Jan. 1, 2024. See, also, § 501 operative Jan. 1, 2024.

For Executive Order N–58–20 (2019 CA EO 58-20), which temporarily authorizes people to obtain marriage licenses and solemnize their marriages by videoconference, due to the

COVID-19 pandemic, see Historical and Statutory Notes under Family Code § 359.

For Executive Order N-71-20 (2019 CA EO 71-20), which extends certain provisions of Executive Order N-58-20, due to the COVID-19 pandemic, see Historical and Statutory Notes under Education Code § 41422.

(a) Except as provided in Section 502 or Part 5 (commencing with Section 550), a confidential marriage license shall be issued by the county clerk upon the personal appearance together of the parties to be married and their payment of the fees required by Sections 26840.1 and 26840.8 of the Government Code and any fee imposed pursuant to the authorization of Section 26840.3 of the Government Code.

(b) This section shall remain in effect only until January 1, 2024, and as of that date is repealed. *(Stats.1992, c. 162 (A.B.2650), § 10, operative Jan. 1, 1994. Amended by Stats.2006, c. 816 (A.B.1102), § 23, operative Jan. 1, 2008; Stats.2021, c. 620 (A.B.583), § 3, eff. Oct. 7, 2021.)*

Repeal

For repeal of this section, see its terms.

Cross References

Certificate of registry, preparation and filing, see Family Code § 359.
County defined for purposes of this Code, see Family Code § 67.
License,
    Necessity, see Family Code §§ 300, 350.
    Offense of solemnization of marriage without license or authorization, see Penal Code § 360.
    Return of license to county recorder, see Family Code § 423.
Marriage registration, see Health and Safety Code § 103125 et seq.
Solemnization requirements, see Family Code § 420 et seq.

Research References

Forms

West's California Code Forms, Family § 500, Comment Overview—Requirements for Confidential Marriages.

§ 501. Issuance of license

Section operative Jan. 1, 2024. See, also, § 501 operative until Jan. 1, 2024.

For Executive Order N-58-20 (2019 CA EO 58-20), which temporarily authorizes people to obtain marriage licenses and solemnize their marriages by videoconference, due to the COVID-19 pandemic, see Historical and Statutory Notes under Family Code § 359.

For Executive Order N-71-20 (2019 CA EO 71-20), which extends certain provisions of Executive Order N-58-20, due to the COVID-19 pandemic, see Historical and Statutory Notes under Education Code § 41422.

(a) Except as provided in Section 502, a confidential marriage license shall be issued by the county clerk upon the personal appearance together of the parties to be married and their payment of the fees required by Sections 26840.1 and 26840.8 of the Government Code and any fee imposed pursuant to the authorization of Section 26840.3 of the Government Code.

(b) This section shall become operative on January 1, 2024. *(Added by Stats.2021, c. 620 (A.B.583), § 4, eff. Oct. 7, 2021, operative Jan. 1, 2024.)*

Cross References

Certificate of registry, preparation and filing, see Family Code § 359.
County defined for purposes of this Code, see Family Code § 67.
License,
    Necessity, see Family Code §§ 300, 350.
    Offense of solemnization of marriage without license or authorization, see Penal Code § 360.
    Return of license to county recorder, see Family Code § 423.
Marriage registration, see Health and Safety Code § 103125 et seq.
Solemnization requirements, see Family Code § 420 et seq.

Research References

Forms

West's California Code Forms, Family § 500, Comment Overview—Requirements for Confidential Marriages.

§ 502. Inability to personally appear; issuance of license

For Executive Order N-58-20 (2019 CA EO 58-20), which temporarily authorizes people to obtain marriage licenses and solemnize their marriages by videoconference, due to the COVID-19 pandemic, see Historical and Statutory Notes under Family Code § 359.

For Executive Order N-71-20 (2019 CA EO 71-20), which extends certain provisions of Executive Order N-58-20, due to the COVID-19 pandemic, see Historical and Statutory Notes under Education Code § 41422.

If for sufficient reason, as described in subdivision (d), either or both of the parties to be married are physically unable to appear in person before the county clerk, a confidential marriage license may be issued by the county clerk to the person solemnizing the marriage if the following requirements are met:

(a) The person solemnizing the marriage physically presents an affidavit to the county clerk explaining the reason for the inability to appear.

(b) The affidavit is signed under penalty of perjury by the person solemnizing the marriage and by both parties.

(c) The signature of any party to be married who is unable to appear in person before the county clerk is authenticated by a notary public or a court prior to the county clerk issuing the confidential marriage license.

(d) Sufficient reason includes proof of hospitalization, incarceration, or any other reason proved to the satisfaction of the county clerk. *(Stats.1992, c. 162 (A.B.2650), § 10, operative Jan. 1, 1994. Amended by Stats.2006, c. 816 (A.B.1102), § 24, operative Jan. 1, 2008.)*

Cross References

Affidavit defined, see Code of Civil Procedure § 2003.
Affidavits, generally, see Code of Civil Procedure § 2009 et seq.
Certificate of registry, preparation and filing, see Family Code § 359.
County defined for purposes of this Code, see Family Code § 67.
License,
    Necessity, see Family Code §§ 300, 350.
    Offense of solemnization of marriage without license or authorization, see Penal Code § 360.
    Return of license to county recorder, see Family Code § 423.
Person defined for purposes of this Code, see Family Code § 105.
Solemnization requirements, see Family Code § 420 et seq.

Research References

Forms

West's California Code Forms, Family § 500, Comment Overview—Requirements for Confidential Marriages.

§ 503. Issuance of confidential marriage license upon request of notary public; fees

The county clerk shall issue a confidential marriage license upon the request of a notary public approved by the county clerk to issue confidential marriage licenses pursuant to Chapter 2 (commencing with Section 530) and upon payment by the notary public of the fees specified in Sections 26840.1 and 26840.8 of the Government Code. The parties shall reimburse a notary public who issues a confidential marriage license for the amount of the fees. *(Stats.1992, c. 162*

(A.B.2650), § 10, operative Jan. 1, 1994. Amended by Stats.2006, c. 816 (A.B.1102), § 25, operative Jan. 1, 2008.)

Cross References
Certificate of registry, preparation and filing, see Family Code § 359.
County defined for purposes of this Code, see Family Code § 67.
Informational brochure, distribution requirement, see Family Code § 358.
License,
    Necessity, see Family Code §§ 300, 350.
    Offense of solemnization of marriage without license or authorization, see Penal Code § 360.
    Return of license to county recorder, see Family Code § 423.
Solemnization requirements, see Family Code § 420 et seq.

Research References
Forms

West's California Code Forms, Family § 500, Comment Overview—Requirements for Confidential Marriages.

§ 504. Duration of license

A confidential marriage license is valid only for a period of 90 days after its issuance by the county clerk. *(Stats.1992, c. 162 (A.B.2650), § 10, operative Jan. 1, 1994. Amended by Stats.2014, c. 913 (A.B. 2747), § 16, eff. Jan. 1, 2015.)*

Cross References
County defined for purposes of this Code, see Family Code § 67.
License,
    Offense of solemnization of marriage without license or authorization, see Penal Code § 360.
    Return of license to county recorder, see Family Code § 423.
Marriage registration, see Health and Safety Code § 103125 et seq.
Solemnization requirements, see Family Code § 420 et seq.

Research References
Forms

West's California Code Forms, Family § 500, Comment Overview—Requirements for Confidential Marriages.

§ 505. Form of license; contents

(a) The form of the confidential marriage license shall be prescribed by the State Registrar of Vital Statistics.

(b) The form shall be designed to require that the parties to be married declare or affirm that they meet all of the requirements of this chapter.

(c) The form shall include an affidavit, which the bride and groom shall sign, affirming that they have received the brochure provided for in Section 358. *(Stats.1992, c. 162 (A.B.2650), § 10, operative Jan. 1, 1994. Amended by Stats.2006, c. 816 (A.B.1102), § 26, operative Jan. 1, 2008.)*

Cross References
Certificate of registry, preparation and filing, see Family Code § 359.
License,
    Necessity, see Family Code §§ 300, 350.
    Offense of solemnization of marriage without license or authorization, see Penal Code § 360.
    Return of license to county recorder, see Family Code § 423.
Marriage registration, see Health and Safety Code § 103125 et seq.
Person defined for purposes of this Code, see Family Code § 105.
References to husband, wife, spouses and married persons, persons included for purposes of this Code, see Family Code § 11.
Solemnization requirements, see Family Code § 420 et seq.
State defined for purposes of this Code, see Family Code § 145.
State Registrar of Vital Statistics, see Health and Safety Code § 102175.

§ 506. Completion of license; filing

For Executive Order N–58–20 (2019 CA EO 58-20), which temporarily authorizes people to obtain marriage licenses and solemnize their marriages by videoconference, due to the COVID-19 pandemic, see Historical and Statutory Notes under Family Code § 359.

For Executive Order N–71–20 (2019 CA EO 71-20), which extends certain provisions of Executive Order N–58–20, due to the COVID-19 pandemic, see Historical and Statutory Notes under Education Code § 41422.

(a) The confidential marriage license shall be presented to the person solemnizing the marriage.

(b) Upon performance of the ceremony, the solemnization section on the confidential marriage license shall be completed by the person solemnizing the marriage.

(c) The confidential marriage license shall be returned by the person solemnizing the marriage to the office of the county clerk in the county in which the license was issued within 10 days after the ceremony. *(Stats.1992, c. 162 (A.B.2650), § 10, operative Jan. 1, 1994. Amended by Stats.1993, c. 219 (A.B.1500), § 98; Stats.2001, c. 39 (A.B.1323), § 5; Stats.2006, c. 816 (A.B.1102), § 27, operative Jan. 1, 2008.)*

Cross References
Certificate of registry, preparation and filing, see Family Code § 359.
County defined for purposes of this Code, see Family Code § 67.
License,
    Necessity, see Family Code §§ 300, 350.
    Offense of solemnization of marriage without license or authorization, see Penal Code § 360.
    Return of license to county recorder, see Family Code § 423.
Marriage registration, see Health and Safety Code § 103125 et seq.
Person defined for purposes of this Code, see Family Code § 105.
Solemnization requirements, see Family Code § 420 et seq.

Research References
Forms

West's California Code Forms, Family § 500, Comment Overview—Requirements for Confidential Marriages.

§ 507. Repealed by Stats.2001, c. 39 (A.B.1323), § 6

§ 508. Application to obtain certified copy of confidential marriage license

Upon issuance of a confidential marriage license, parties shall be provided with an application to obtain a certified copy of the confidential marriage certificate from the county clerk. *(Stats.1992, c. 162 (A.B.2650), § 10, operative Jan. 1, 1994. Amended by Stats.2001, c. 39 (A.B.1323), § 7; Stats.2006, c. 816 (A.B.1102), § 28, operative Jan. 1, 2008.)*

Cross References
Certificate of registry, preparation and filing, see Family Code § 359.
County defined for purposes of this Code, see Family Code § 67.
License,
    Necessity, see Family Code §§ 300, 350.
    Offense of solemnization of marriage without license or authorization, see Penal Code § 360.
    Return of license to county recorder, see Family Code § 423.
Solemnization requirements, see Family Code § 420 et seq.

§ 509. Application to obtain certified copy of certificate; fee

(a) A party to a confidential marriage may obtain a certified copy of the confidential marriage certificate from the county clerk of the county in which the certificate is filed by submitting an application that satisfies the requirements of Chapter 14 (commencing with Section 103525) of Part 1 of Division 102 of the Health and Safety Code.

(b) Copies of a confidential marriage certificate may be issued to the parties to the marriage upon payment of the fee equivalent to that charged for copies of a marriage certificate. *(Stats.1992, c. 162 (A.B.2650), § 10, operative Jan. 1, 1994. Amended by Stats.2001, c. 39*

§ 509

(A.B.1323), § 8; Stats.2006, c. 816 (A.B.1102), § 29, operative Jan. 1, 2008; Stats.2009, c. 412 (A.B.130), § 2.)

Cross References

Certificate of registry, preparation and filing, see Family Code § 359.
County defined for purposes of this Code, see Family Code § 67.
License,
    Necessity, see Family Code §§ 300, 350.
    Offense of solemnization of marriage without license or authorization, see Penal Code § 360.
    Return of license to county recorder, see Family Code § 423.
Solemnization requirements, see Family Code § 420 et seq.

§ 510. Replacement of marriage certificate; issuance of duplicate license

(a) If a confidential marriage license is lost, damaged, or destroyed after the performance of the marriage, but before it is returned to the county clerk, or deemed unacceptable for registration by the county clerk, the person solemnizing the marriage, in order to comply with Section 506, shall obtain a duplicate marriage license by filing an affidavit setting forth the facts with the county clerk of the county in which the license was issued.

(b) The duplicate license may not be issued later than one year after the date of the marriage and shall be returned by the person solemnizing the marriage to the county clerk within one year of the date of the marriage.

(c) The county clerk may charge a fee to cover the actual costs of issuing a duplicate marriage license.

(d) If a marriage license is lost, damaged, or destroyed before a marriage ceremony takes place, the applicants shall purchase a new marriage license and the old license shall be voided. (Stats.1992, c. 162 (A.B.2650), § 10, operative Jan. 1, 1994. Amended by Stats.1993, c. 219 (A.B.1500), § 99; Stats.2001, c. 39 (A.B.1323), § 9; Stats.2006, c. 816 (A.B.1102), § 30, operative Jan. 1, 2008; Stats.2020, c. 36 (A.B.3364), § 27, eff. Jan. 1, 2021.)

Cross References

Certificate of registry, preparation and filing, see Family Code § 359.
County defined for purposes of this Code, see Family Code § 67.
License,
    Necessity, see Family Code §§ 300, 350.
    Offense of solemnization of marriage without license or authorization, see Penal Code § 360.
    Return of license to county recorder, see Family Code § 423.
Person defined for purposes of this Code, see Family Code § 105.
Solemnization requirements, see Family Code § 420 et seq.

Research References

Forms

2 California Transactions Forms--Family Law § 6:44, Documentation and Final Hearing.
2 California Transactions Forms--Family Law § 6:112, Form Drafting Considerations.
2 California Transactions Forms--Family Law § 7:13, Background Investigation.

§ 511. Maintenance of marriage certificates; inspections; preservation of record; reproductions; disclosure of information

(a) Except as provided in subdivision (b), the county clerk shall maintain confidential marriage certificates filed pursuant to Section 506 as permanent records which shall not be open to public inspection except upon order of the court issued upon a showing of good cause. The confidential marriage license is a confidential record and not open to public inspection without an order from the court.

(b) The county clerk shall keep all original certificates of confidential marriages for one year from the date of filing. After one year, the clerk may reproduce the certificates pursuant to Section 26205 of the Government Code, and dispose of the original certificates. The county clerk shall promptly seal and store at least one original negative of each microphotographic film made in a manner and place as reasonable to ensure its preservation indefinitely against loss, theft, defacement, or destruction. The microphotograph shall be made in a manner that complies with the minimum standards or guidelines, or both, recommended by the American National Standards Institute or the Association for Information and Image Management. Every reproduction shall be deemed and considered an original. A certified copy of any reproduction shall be deemed and considered a certified copy of the original.

(c) The county clerk may conduct a search for a confidential marriage certificate for the purpose of confirming the existence of a marriage, but the date of the marriage and any other information contained in the certificate shall not be disclosed except upon order of the court.

(d) The county clerk shall, not less than quarterly, transmit copies of all original confidential marriage certificates retained, or originals of reproduced confidential marriage certificates filed after January 1, 1982, to the State Registrar of Vital Statistics. The registrar may destroy the copies so transmitted after they have been indexed. The registrar may respond to an inquiry as to the existence of a marriage performed pursuant to this chapter, but shall not disclose the date of the marriage. (Stats.1992, c. 162 (A.B.2650), § 10, operative Jan. 1, 1994. Amended by Stats.1994, c. 1269 (A.B.2208), § 11; Stats.2006, c. 816 (A.B.1102), § 31, operative Jan. 1, 2008.)

Cross References

Certificate of registry, preparation and filing, see Family Code § 359.
County defined for purposes of this Code, see Family Code § 67.
Judgment and order defined for purposes of this Code, see Family Code § 100.
License,
    Necessity, see Family Code §§ 300, 350.
    Offense of solemnization of marriage without license or authorization, see Penal Code § 360.
    Return of license to county recorder, see Family Code § 423.
Register of actions, see Government Code § 69845.
Solemnization requirements, see Family Code § 420 et seq.
State defined for purposes of this Code, see Family Code § 145.
State Registrar of Vital Statistics, see Health and Safety Code § 102175.

Research References

Forms

West's California Code Forms, Family § 350 Form 1, California Marriage License, Registration and Ceremony Information.
West's California Code Forms, Family § 500, Comment Overview—Requirements for Confidential Marriages.

CHAPTER 2. APPROVAL OF NOTARIES TO AUTHORIZE CONFIDENTIAL MARRIAGES

Section
530. Compliance with chapter; violation; penalty.
531. Application by notary for approval to authorize marriage; contents; fees.
532. Proof of completion of course of instruction.
533. Validity of approval; renewal of approval; conditions.
534. List of notaries public approved to issue confidential marriage licenses; public inspection; currentness of information.
535. Suspension or revocation of approval; hearing.
536. Application fees; renewal fees; deposit of fees.

Cross References

Marriage registration, see Health and Safety Code § 103125 et seq.

Notaries public, see Government Code § 8200 et seq.

§ 530. Compliance with chapter; violation; penalty

(a) No notary public shall issue a confidential marriage license pursuant to this part unless the notary public is approved by the county clerk to issue confidential marriage licenses pursuant to this chapter.

(b) A violation of subdivision (a) is a misdemeanor punishable by a fine not to exceed one thousand dollars ($1,000) or six months in jail. *(Stats.1992, c. 162 (A.B.2650), § 10, operative Jan. 1, 1994. Amended by Stats.2006, c. 816 (A.B.1102), § 32, operative Jan. 1, 2008.)*

Cross References

Consent of parties, see Family Code § 300 et seq.
County defined for purposes of this Code, see Family Code § 67.
Marriage registration, see Health and Safety Code § 103125 et seq.
Misdemeanors, definition and penalties, see Penal Code §§ 17, 19, 19.2.
Notaries public, see Government Code § 8200 et seq.

§ 531. Application by notary for approval to authorize marriage; contents; fees

(a) An application for approval to authorize confidential marriages pursuant to this part shall be submitted to the county clerk in the county in which the notary public who is applying for the approval resides. The county clerk shall exercise reasonable discretion as to whether to approve applications.

(b) The application shall include all of the following:

(1) The full name of the applicant.

(2) The date of birth of the applicant.

(3) The applicant's current residential address and telephone number.

(4) The address and telephone number of the place where the applicant will issue confidential marriage licenses.

(5) The full name of the applicant's employer if the applicant is employed by another person.

(6) Whether or not the applicant has engaged in any of the acts specified in Section 8214.1 of the Government Code.

(c) The application shall be accompanied by the fee provided for in Section 536. *(Stats.1992, c. 162 (A.B.2650), § 10, operative Jan. 1, 1994. Amended by Stats.2001, c. 39 (A.B.1323), § 10; Stats.2006, c. 816 (A.B.1102), § 33, operative Jan. 1, 2008.)*

Cross References

County defined for purposes of this Code, see Family Code § 67.
Notaries public, see Government Code § 8200 et seq.
Person defined for purposes of this Code, see Family Code § 105.

§ 532. Proof of completion of course of instruction

No approval, or renewal of the approval, shall be granted pursuant to this chapter unless the notary public shows evidence of successful completion of a course of instruction concerning the issuance of confidential marriage licenses that was conducted by the county clerk in the county of registration. The course of instruction shall not exceed six hours in duration. *(Stats.1992, c. 162 (A.B.2650), § 10, operative Jan. 1, 1994. Amended by Stats.2006, c. 816 (A.B.1102), § 34, operative Jan. 1, 2008.)*

Cross References

County defined for purposes of this Code, see Family Code § 67.

§ 533. Validity of approval; renewal of approval; conditions

An approval to issue confidential marriage licenses pursuant to this chapter is valid for one year. The approval may be renewed for additional one-year periods provided the following conditions are met:

(a) The applicant has not violated any of the provisions provided for in Section 531.

(b) The applicant has successfully completed the course prescribed in Section 532.

(c) The applicant has paid the renewal fee provided for in Section 536. *(Stats.1992, c. 162 (A.B.2650), § 10, operative Jan. 1, 1994. Amended by Stats.2006, c. 816 (A.B.1102), § 35, operative Jan. 1, 2008.)*

§ 534. List of notaries public approved to issue confidential marriage licenses; public inspection; currentness of information

(a) The county clerk shall maintain a list of the notaries public who are approved to issue confidential marriage licenses. The list shall be available for inspection by the public.

(b) It is the responsibility of a notary public approved to issue confidential marriage licenses pursuant to this chapter to keep current the information required in paragraphs (1), (3), (4), and (5) of subdivision (b) of Section 531. This information shall be used by the county clerk to update the list required to be maintained by this section. *(Stats.1992, c. 162 (A.B.2650), § 10, operative Jan. 1, 1994. Amended by Stats.2006, c. 816 (A.B.1102), § 36, operative Jan. 1, 2008.)*

Cross References

County defined for purposes of this Code, see Family Code § 67.

§ 535. Suspension or revocation of approval; hearing

(a) If, after an approval to issue confidential marriage licenses is granted pursuant to this chapter, it is discovered that the notary public has engaged in any of the actions specified in Section 8214.1 of the Government Code, the approval shall be revoked, and the county clerk shall notify the Secretary of State for whatever action the Secretary of State deems appropriate. Any fees paid by the notary public shall be retained by the county clerk.

(b) If a notary public who is approved to authorize confidential marriages pursuant to this division is alleged to have violated a provision of this division, the county clerk shall conduct a hearing to determine if the approval of the notary public should be suspended or revoked. The notary public may present any evidence as is necessary in the notary public's defense. If the county clerk determines that the notary public has violated a provision of this division, the county clerk may place the notary public on probation or suspend or revoke the notary public's registration, and any fees paid by the notary public shall be retained by the county clerk. The county clerk shall report the findings of the hearing to the Secretary of State for whatever action the Secretary of State deems appropriate. *(Stats.1992, c. 162 (A.B.2650), § 10, operative Jan. 1, 1994. Amended by Stats.2006, c. 816 (A.B.1102), § 37, operative Jan. 1, 2008.)*

Cross References

County defined for purposes of this Code, see Family Code § 67.
Notaries public, see Government Code § 8200 et seq.
Secretary of State, generally, see Government Code § 12152 et seq.
State defined for purposes of this Code, see Family Code § 145.

§ 536. Application fees; renewal fees; deposit of fees

(a) The fee for an application for approval to authorize confidential marriages pursuant to this chapter is three hundred dollars ($300).

(b) The fee for renewal of an approval is three hundred dollars ($300).

(c) Fees received pursuant to this chapter shall be deposited in a trust fund established by the county clerk. The money in the trust fund shall be used exclusively for the administration of the programs described in this chapter. *(Stats.1992, c. 162 (A.B.2650), § 10,*

§ 536 MARRIAGE

operative Jan. 1, 1994. Amended by Stats.2006, c. 816 (A.B.1102), § 38, operative Jan. 1, 2008.)

Cross References

County defined for purposes of this Code, see Family Code § 67.

Part 5

REMOTE MARRIAGE LICENSE ISSUANCE AND SOLEMNIZATION

Section
550. Issuance of license using remote technology; exception.
552. Verification of identity.
554. Physical location of each member of couple; affidavit.
556. Marriage license; signatures and transmittal.
558. Guidance from county clerk relating to this part.
560. "Remote technology" defined.
562. Duration of part.
580 to 594. Repealed.

Repeal

For repeal of Part 5, see Family Code § 562.

§ 550. Issuance of license using remote technology; exception

Notwithstanding any other law, including, but not limited to, Section 420, a county clerk may issue a marriage license, including a confidential marriage license, or solemnize or witness a marriage ceremony under state law using remote technology pursuant to this part, except for a marriage of a minor, as set forth in Sections 302 to 304, inclusive, or any successor provisions. *(Added by Stats.2021, c. 620 (A.B.583), § 5, eff. Oct. 7, 2021.)*

Repeal

For repeal of Part 5, see Family Code § 562.

§ 552. Verification of identity

A couple seeking a marriage license or solemnization pursuant to this part shall present, in the manner requested by the county clerk, a copy of a valid government-issued photo identification to verify their identity and any additional documentary proof requested by the county clerk. *(Added by Stats.2021, c. 620 (A.B.583), § 5, eff. Oct. 7, 2021.)*

Repeal

For repeal of Part 5, see Family Code § 562.

§ 554. Physical location of each member of couple; affidavit

(a) Each member of the couple shall be physically located in the State of California while using remote technology to obtain a marriage license pursuant to this part.

(b)(1) Each member of the couple shall be in the same physical location in the State of California while using remote technology to solemnize their marriage pursuant to this part.

(2) The person solemnizing the marriage, any necessary witnesses, and the county clerk shall all be physically located in the State of California, but may be at separate physical locations from each other and the couple solemnizing their marriage.

(c) The county clerk may require a couple to complete an affidavit, in a form provided by the county clerk, affirming that they and each individual participating in a marriage solemnization using remote technology are physically present within the State of California in compliance with this part. *(Added by Stats.2021, c. 620 (A.B.583), § 5, eff. Oct. 7, 2021.)*

Repeal

For repeal of Part 5, see Family Code § 562.

§ 556. Marriage license; signatures and transmittal

(a) At the discretion of the county clerk, a couple applying for a marriage license using remote technology may sign their marriage license electronically or by original wet signature. The couple shall transmit a signed, legible copy of their marriage license by United States mail, fax, or electronic means directly to the county clerk, in the manner required by the county clerk.

(b) At the discretion of the county clerk, a marriage license issued using the procedure described in this part may be transmitted to the applicants by United States mail, fax, or electronic means.

(c) Before the solemnization of a marriage pursuant to this part, one or both of the parties to be married shall transmit the marriage license by United States mail, fax, or electronic means to the person solemnizing the marriage and any necessary witnesses, in the manner required by the county clerk.

(d) At the discretion of the county clerk, the person solemnizing the marriage or any necessary witnesses may sign the marriage license electronically or by original wet signature and transmit the signed marriage license by United States mail, fax, or electronic means, in the manner required by the county clerk.

(e) A county clerk who witnesses a marriage solemnized by someone other than the county clerk using remote technology may apply an electronic signature to the marriage license as a witness, and transmit the signed license to the person solemnizing the marriage by United States mail, fax, or electronic means. *(Added by Stats.2021, c. 620 (A.B.583), § 5, eff. Oct. 7, 2021.)*

Repeal

For repeal of Part 5, see Family Code § 562.

§ 558. Guidance from county clerk relating to this part

A county clerk may provide guidance relating to marriage license applications, marriage license issuance, and the witnessing or solemnizing of the marriage ceremony when the guidance relates to the use of their remote technology pursuant to this part. *(Added by Stats.2021, c. 620 (A.B.583), § 5, eff. Oct. 7, 2021.)*

Repeal

For repeal of Part 5, see Family Code § 562.

§ 560. "Remote technology" defined

For purposes of this part, "remote technology" means audiovideo technology that is provided by a county clerk and allows the couple, or the couple and others participating in a marriage solemnization, as applicable, to appear together from the same physical location and directly interact with each other and the county clerk. *(Added by Stats.2021, c. 620 (A.B.583), § 5, eff. Oct. 7, 2021.)*

Repeal

For repeal of Part 5, see Family Code § 562.

§ 562. Duration of part

This part shall remain in effect only until January 1, 2024, and as of that date is repealed. *(Added by Stats.2021, c. 620 (A.B.583), § 5, eff. Oct. 7, 2021.)*

§§ 580 to 594. Repealed by Stats.1994, c. 197 (A.B.3128), § 1

Division 4

RIGHTS AND OBLIGATIONS DURING MARRIAGE

Part	Section
1. General Provisions	700
2. Characterization of Marital Property	760
3. Liability of Marital Property	900
4. Management and Control of Marital Property	1100
5. Marital Agreements	1500

Cross References

Actions, married person's right to sue without spouse being joined as party, see Code of Civil Procedure § 370.
Community property,
  Debts, liability for, see Family Code §§ 910, 911.
  Defined, see Probate Code § 28; Civil Code § 687; Family Code §§ 65, 760.
  Division of, see Family Code § 2600 et seq.
  Held in revocable trust, see Probate Code § 104.
  Interests of spouses defined, see Family Code § 751.
Contractual arrangements relating to property rights of spouses at death, see Probate Code § 140 et seq.
Decedent's property, passage of title, see Probate Code §§ 7000, 7001.
Disposition of estate without administration, passage of property to surviving spouse, see Probate Code § 13500 et seq.
Division of Property Act, dissolution of marriage, community estate including out-of-state real property, see Family Code § 2660.
Effect of death of married person on community and quasi-community property, see Probate Code § 100 et seq.
Intestate succession as to community property, see Probate Code § 6401.
Inventory of estate, community and separate property, see Probate Code § 8850.
Judgment creditors seek writ of execution to enforce a judgment made, entered, or enforceable pursuant to Family Code, see Code of Civil Procedure § 699.510.
Management or disposition of community property where spouse lacks legal capacity, see Probate Code § 3000 et seq.
Nature of property, generally, see Civil Code § 654.
Personal property defined, see Civil Code § 663.
Presumptions and limitations of actions as to property acquired by wife, see Family Code § 803.
Real property as coextensive with lands, tenements, and hereditaments, see Civil Code § 14; Code of Civil Procedure § 17; Penal Code § 7.
Real property defined, see Civil Code §§ 14, 658; Evidence Code § 205; Health and Safety Code §§ 33390, 34215; Public Resources Code § 9802; Revenue and Taxation Code § 104.
Separate property of married person, defined, see Family Code §§ 130, 770.
Setting aside homestead for the benefit of decedent's spouse or child, see Probate Code § 6520 et seq.
Simultaneous death, disposition of property, see Probate Code § 220 et seq.
Surviving spouse, defined, see Probate Code § 78.

Part 1

GENERAL PROVISIONS

Chapter	Section
1. Definitions	700
2. Relation of Spouses	720
3. Property Rights During Marriage	750

CHAPTER 1. DEFINITIONS

Section
700. Leasehold interest in real property.

§ 700. Leasehold interest in real property

For the purposes of this division, a leasehold interest in real property is real property, not personal property. (Stats.1992, c. 162 (A.B.2650), § 10, operative Jan. 1, 1994.)

Cross References

Nature of property, generally, see Civil Code § 654.
Property defined for purposes of this Code, see Family Code § 113.
Real property as coextensive with lands, tenements, and hereditaments, see Civil Code § 14; Code of Civil Procedure § 17; Penal Code § 7.
Real property defined, see Civil Code § 658; Evidence Code § 205; Health and Safety Code §§ 33390, 34215; Public Resources Code § 9802; Revenue and Taxation Code § 104.

CHAPTER 2. RELATION OF SPOUSES

Section
720. Mutual obligations.
721. Contracts with each other and third parties; fiduciary relationship.

§ 720. Mutual obligations

Spouses contract toward each other obligations of mutual respect, fidelity, and support. (Stats.1992, c. 162 (A.B.2650), § 10, operative Jan. 1, 1994. Amended by Stats.2014, c. 82 (S.B.1306), § 11, eff. Jan. 1, 2015.)

Cross References

Breach of fiduciary duty, claims and remedies, see Family Code § 1101.
Community property,
  Debts, liability for, see Family Code §§ 910, 911.
  Defined, see Probate Code § 28; Civil Code § 687; Family Code §§ 65, 760.
  Division of, see Family Code § 2600 et seq.
  Held in revocable trust, see Probate Code § 104.
  Interests of spouses defined, see Family Code § 751.
Conciliation proceedings, see Family Code § 1830 et seq.
Contracts relating to property and separation, see Family Code § 1620.
Contractual arrangements relating to property rights of spouses at death, see Probate Code § 140 et seq.
Decedent's property, passage of title, see Probate Code §§ 7000, 7001.
Disposition of estate without administration, passage of property to surviving spouse, see Probate Code § 13500 et seq.
Effect of death of married person on community and quasi-community property, see Probate Code § 100 et seq.
Effect of judicial record of foreign state, see Code of Civil Procedure § 1913.
Grounds for dissolution or separation, see Family Code § 2310 et seq.
Intestate succession as to community property, see Probate Code § 6401.
Inventory of estate, community and separate property, see Probate Code § 8850.
Judgment creditors seek writ of execution to enforce a judgment made, entered, or enforceable pursuant to Family Code, see Code of Civil Procedure § 699.510.
Liability for debts of deceased spouse, see Probate Code § 13550 et seq.
Management or disposition of community property where spouse lacks legal capacity, see Probate Code § 3000 et seq.
Premarital agreements, see Family Code § 1600 et seq.
References to husband, wife, spouses and married persons, persons included for purposes of this Code, see Family Code § 11.
Separate domicile or residence for purpose of dissolution proceedings, see Family Code § 2322.
Spousal support, defined, see Family Code § 142.
Support,
  Generally, see Family Code § 3500 et seq.
  Action to enforce spouse's right, see Family Code § 4303.
  Children, see Family Code § 3900 et seq.
  Defined for purposes of this Code, see Family Code § 150.
  Separation by agreement, see Family Code § 4302.
  Spousal support, see Family Code § 4300 et seq.
  Uniform Interstate Family Act, see Family Code § 5700.101 et seq.

§ 720

Research References

Forms

2 California Transactions Forms--Estate Planning § 11:45, Introduction.

§ 721. Contracts with each other and third parties; fiduciary relationship

(a) Subject to subdivision (b), either spouse may enter into any transaction with the other, or with any other person, respecting property, which either might if unmarried.

(b) Except as provided in Sections 143, 144, 146, 16040, 16047, and 21385 of the Probate Code, in transactions between themselves, spouses are subject to the general rules governing fiduciary relationships that control the actions of persons occupying confidential relations with each other. This confidential relationship imposes a duty of the highest good faith and fair dealing on each spouse, and neither shall take any unfair advantage of the other. This confidential relationship is a fiduciary relationship subject to the same rights and duties of nonmarital business partners, as provided in Sections 16403, 16404, and 16503 of the Corporations Code, including, but not limited to, the following:

(1) Providing each spouse access at all times to any books kept regarding a transaction for the purposes of inspection and copying.

(2) Rendering upon request, true and full information of all things affecting any transaction that concerns the community property. Nothing in this section is intended to impose a duty for either spouse to keep detailed books and records of community property transactions.

(3) Accounting to the spouse, and holding as a trustee, any benefit or profit derived from any transaction by one spouse without the consent of the other spouse that concerns the community property.
(Stats.1992, c. 162 (A.B.2650), § 10, operative Jan. 1, 1994. Amended by Stats.2002, c. 310 (S.B.1936), § 1; Stats.2014, c. 82 (S.B.1306), § 12, eff. Jan. 1, 2015; Stats.2019, c. 43 (A.B.327), § 1, eff. Jan. 1, 2020.)

Cross References

Actions, married person's right to sue without spouse being joined as party, see Code of Civil Procedure § 370.
Alteration of legal relations by contract, see Family Code § 1620.
Community personal property, management and control, restrictions on disposition, see Family Code § 1100.
Community property defined for purposes of this Code, see Family Code § 65.
Contractual arrangements relating to rights at death, surviving spouse's waiver of rights,
  Enforceability generally, see Probate Code § 143.
  Enforceability under certain circumstances, see Probate Code § 144.
  Requirements, see Probate Code § 146.
Marital dissolution, interest in the community estate, claim against spouse for breach of fiduciary duty, see Family Code § 1101.
Marital dissolution, interest in the community estate, length and scope of fiduciary relationship, see Family Code § 2102.
Person defined for purposes of this Code, see Family Code § 105.
Premarital agreements, see Family Code § 1600 et seq.
Property defined for purposes of this Code, see Family Code § 113.
Protection of rights of spouse lacking legal capacity, see Probate Code § 3057.
References to husband, wife, spouses and married persons, persons included for purposes of this Code, see Family Code § 11.
Relations of partners to each other and to partnership, see Corporations Code § 16401 et seq.
Right of married person to defend suit for spouses right, see Code of Civil Procedure § 371.
Termination of agency, see Probate Code § 2355.
Trustees, duty of loyalty, see Probate Code § 16002.

Research References

Forms

California Practice Guide: Rutter Family Law Forms Form 8:1, Request for Order Re Separate Trial Re Validity of Interspousal Deed.
California Practice Guide: Rutter Family Law Forms Form 9:2, Marital Agreement.
California Practice Guide: Rutter Family Law Forms Form 9:3, Marital Settlement Agreement.
4 California Transactions Forms--Business Entities § 19:82, Consent of Spouse.
2 California Transactions Forms--Estate Planning § 10:4, Community Property.
2 California Transactions Forms--Estate Planning § 11:34, Agreement Entered Into Before January 1, 1985.
2 California Transactions Forms--Estate Planning § 11:36, Family Code §852 Transmutations and Rules Governing Fiduciary Relationships.
2 California Transactions Forms--Estate Planning § 11:40, Premarital Agreements Entered Into Before January 1, 1986.
2 California Transactions Forms--Estate Planning § 11:45, Introduction.
2 California Transactions Forms--Estate Planning § 11:47, Formalities.
2 California Transactions Forms--Estate Planning § 11:48, Governing Contractual Provisions [CC §§1550 et seq., Fam C §721(B)].
2 California Transactions Forms--Estate Planning § 11:52, Enforceability Under Probate Code § 143.
2 California Transactions Forms--Estate Planning § 11:53, Enforceability Under Probate Code § 144.
2 California Transactions Forms--Estate Planning § 11:54, Revocation and Amendment of Waiver by Agreement.
4 California Transactions Forms--Estate Planning § 19:15, Waiver of Family Protection.
1 California Transactions Forms--Family Law § 1:18, Capacity and Consent; Undue Influence.
1 California Transactions Forms--Family Law § 1:99, Waiver of Management and Control of Property.
1 California Transactions Forms--Family Law § 2:3, Comprehensive Drafting.
1 California Transactions Forms--Family Law § 2:4, Fiduciary Duty.
West's California Code Forms, Family § 850, Comment Overview—Transmutation by Agreement or Transfer.
West's California Code Forms, Family § 1500 Form 1, Marital Agreement.
West's California Code Forms, Family § 2338 Form 9, Marital Agreement—Both Spouses Employed.
West's California Code Forms, Family § 2550 Form 3, Marital Agreement.
West's California Code Forms, Probate § 3080 Form 1, Petition for Support; for Injunctive Orders; for Determination of the Character of Property; for an Accounting; for Employment of Counsel; and for Attorney Fees and Costs.

CHAPTER 3. PROPERTY RIGHTS DURING MARRIAGE

Section
750. Methods of holding property.
751. Community property; interests of parties.
752. Separate property; interest of parties.
753. Exclusion of spouse from other's dwelling.
754. Disposition of separate property residence during pendency of proceedings.
755. Employee benefit plan; payment or refund; discharge from adverse claims; notice of claims.

Cross References

Community property,
  Debts, liability for, see Family Code §§ 910, 911.
  Defined, see Probate Code § 28; Civil Code § 687; Family Code §§ 65, 760.
  Division of, see Family Code § 2600 et seq.
  Held in revocable trust, see Probate Code § 104.
  Interests of spouses defined, see Family Code § 751.
Contractual arrangements relating to property rights of spouses at death, see Probate Code § 140 et seq.
Decedent's property, passage of title, see Probate Code §§ 7000, 7001.
Disposition of estate without administration, passage of property to surviving spouse, see Probate Code § 13500 et seq.
Division of Property Act, dissolution of marriage, community estate including out-of-state real property, see Family Code § 2660.
Effect of death of married person on community and quasi-community property, see Probate Code § 100 et seq.
Intestate succession as to community property, see Probate Code § 6401.
Inventory of estate, community and separate property, see Probate Code § 8850.

Judgment creditors seek writ of execution to enforce a judgment made, entered, or enforceable pursuant to Family Code, see Code of Civil Procedure § 699.510.
Management or disposition of community property where spouse lacks legal capacity, see Probate Code § 3000 et seq.
Nature of property, generally, see Civil Code § 654.
Personal property defined, see Civil Code § 663.
Presumptions and limitations of actions as to property acquired by wife, see Family Code § 803.
Property defined, see Civil Code § 654.
Real property as coextensive with lands, tenements, and hereditaments, see Civil Code § 14; Code of Civil Procedure § 17; Penal Code § 7.
Real property defined, see Civil Code § 658; Evidence Code § 205; Health and Safety Code §§ 33390, 34215; Public Resources Code § 9802; Revenue and Taxation Code § 104.
Separate property of married person, defined, see Family Code § 770.
Setting aside homestead for the benefit of decedent's spouse or child, see Probate Code § 6520 et seq.
Simultaneous death, disposition of property, see Probate Code § 220 et seq.
Surviving spouse, defined, see Probate Code § 78.

§ 750. Methods of holding property

Spouses may hold property as joint tenants or tenants in common, or as community property, or as community property with a right of survivorship. *(Stats.1992, c. 162 (A.B.2650), § 10, operative Jan. 1, 1994. Amended by Stats.2001, c. 754 (A.B.1697), § 2; Stats.2014, c. 82 (S.B.1306), § 13, eff. Jan. 1, 2015.)*

Cross References

Alteration of legal relations by contract, see Family Code § 1620.
Community estate, defined, see Family Code § 63.
Community property, defined, see Family Code §§ 65, 760; Civil Code § 687.
Division of community estate, see Family Code § 2600 et seq.
Interest in common, interests excluded, see Civil Code § 686.
Interest in common defined, see Civil Code § 685.
Joint tenancy, definition, method of creation, see Civil Code § 683.
Joint tenancy, safe-deposit box, see Civil Code § 683.1.
Joint tenancy, severance, right of survivorship, see Civil Code § 683.2.
Liability of marital property, see Family Code § 900 et seq.
Management and control of marital property, see Family Code § 1100 et seq.
Married parties and community property, presumption and rebuttal, change of survivorship right, beneficiary, or payee by will, see Probate Code § 5305.
Multiple party accounts, see Financial Code § 1402.
Ownership, generally, see Civil Code § 669 et seq.
Property acquired by married woman before January 1, 1975, conclusiveness of presumptions, see Family Code § 803.
Property defined for purposes of this Code, see Family Code § 113.
References to husband, wife, spouses and married persons, persons included for purposes of this Code, see Family Code § 11.
Right of married person to defend suit for spouses right, see Code of Civil Procedure § 371.
Right of married person to sue without spouse being joined as party, see Code of Civil Procedure § 370.
Simultaneous death, see Probate Code § 220 et seq.
Transferees and creditors of partner, see Corporations Code § 16501 et seq.
Transmutation of property, see Family Code § 850 et seq.

Research References

Forms

7PT1 Am. Jur. Pl. & Pr. Forms Community Property § 2, Statutory References.
14 Am. Jur. Pl. & Pr. Forms Husband and Wife § 2, Introductory Comments.
West's California Code Forms, Family § 754, Comment Overview—Property Rights During Marriage.

§ 751. Community property; interests of parties

The respective interests of each spouse in community property during continuance of the marriage relation are present, existing, and equal interests. *(Stats.1992, c. 162 (A.B.2650), § 10, operative Jan. 1, 1994. Amended by Stats.2014, c. 82 (S.B.1306), § 14, eff. Jan. 1, 2015.)*

Cross References

Alteration of legal relations by contract, see Family Code § 1620.
Community estate, defined, see Family Code § 63.
Community property, defined elsewhere, see Family Code § 760; Civil Code § 687.
Community property defined for purposes of this Code, see Family Code § 65.
Division of community estate, see Family Code § 2600 et seq.
Employee retirement, death, benefit or savings plan, payments or refunds, see Family Code § 755.
Interests in property, see Civil Code § 678 et seq.
Liability of marital property, see Family Code § 900 et seq.
Life and disability insurance, discharge of insurer by payment, see Insurance Code § 10172.
Management and control of marital property, see Family Code § 1100 et seq.
Probate Code proceedings to establish death, see Probate Code § 200 et seq.
Property defined for purposes of this Code, see Family Code § 113.
Public employees' retirement system, payment or refund by system, discharge from adverse claims, see Government Code § 21263.
References to husband, wife, spouses and married persons, persons included for purposes of this Code, see Family Code § 11.
State teachers' retirement system, discharge of system from liability for payments, see Education Code § 24613.
Transferees and creditors of partner, see Corporations Code § 16501 et seq.

Research References

Forms

1 California Transactions Forms--Estate Planning § 3:75, Community Property.
2 California Transactions Forms--Estate Planning § 10:4, Community Property.
4 California Transactions Forms--Estate Planning § 19:18, Community Property.

§ 752. Separate property; interest of parties

Except as otherwise provided by statute, neither spouse has any interest in the separate property of the other. *(Stats.1992, c. 162 (A.B.2650), § 10, operative Jan. 1, 1994. Amended by Stats.2014, c. 82 (S.B.1306), § 15, eff. Jan. 1, 2015.)*

Cross References

Alteration of legal relations by contract, see Family Code § 1620.
Appeal, stay of proceedings as to judgment or order affecting custody, see Code of Civil Procedure § 917.7.
Division of community estate, see Family Code § 2600 et seq.
Domestic violence, ex parte order excluding party from dwelling, see Family Code § 6321.
Exclusion of spouse from other's dwelling, see Family Code § 753.
Harassment, temporary restraining order and injunction, see Code of Civil Procedure § 527.6.
Injunctions, generally, see Code of Civil Procedure § 525 et seq.
Liability of marital property, see Family Code § 900 et seq.
Management and control of marital property, see Family Code § 1100 et seq.
Property defined for purposes of this Code, see Family Code § 113.
References to husband, wife, spouses and married persons, persons included for purposes of this Code, see Family Code § 11.
Right of married person to defend suit for spouse's right, see Code of Civil Procedure § 371.
Right of married person to sue without spouse being joined as party, see Code of Civil Procedure § 370.
Separate property, defined, see Family Code §§ 130, 770.

Research References

Forms

West's California Code Forms, Family § 754, Comment Overview—Property Rights During Marriage.

§ 753. Exclusion of spouse from other's dwelling

Notwithstanding Section 752 and except as provided in Article 2 (commencing with Section 2045), Article 3 (commencing with Section 2047), or Article 4 (commencing with Section 2049) of Chapter 4 of Part 1 of Division 6, neither spouse may be excluded from the other's dwelling. *(Stats.1992, c. 162 (A.B.2650), § 10, operative Jan. 1, 1994. Amended by Stats.1993, c. 219 (A.B.1500), § 99.5.)*

§ 753

MARRIAGE RIGHTS AND OBLIGATIONS

Cross References

Alteration of legal relations by contract, see Family Code § 1620.
Appeal, stay of proceedings as to judgment or order affecting custody, see Code of Civil Procedure § 917.7.
Division of community estate, see Family Code § 2600 et seq.
Dwelling defined, see Business and Professions Code § 10240.2.
Dwelling unit defined, see Civil Code § 1940.
Harassment, temporary restraining order and injunction, see Code of Civil Procedure § 527.6.
Injunctions, generally, see Code of Civil Procedure § 525 et seq.
Liability of marital property, see Family Code § 900 et seq.
Management and control of marital property, see Family Code § 1100 et seq.
References to husband, wife, spouses and married persons, persons included for purposes of this Code, see Family Code § 11.

Research References

Forms

Asset Protection: Legal Planning, Strategies and Forms ¶ 12.04, Discharge.
West's California Code Forms, Family § 754, Comment Overview—Property Rights During Marriage.

§ 754. Disposition of separate property residence during pendency of proceedings

If notice of the pendency of a proceeding for dissolution of the marriage, for nullity of the marriage, or for legal separation of the parties is recorded in any county in which either spouse resides on real property that is the separate property of the other, the real property shall not for a period of three months thereafter be transferred, encumbered, or otherwise disposed of voluntarily or involuntarily without the joinder of both spouses, unless the court otherwise orders. *(Stats.1992, c. 162 (A.B.2650), § 10, operative Jan. 1, 1994. Amended by Stats.2014, c. 82 (S.B.1306), § 16, eff. Jan. 1, 2015.)*

Cross References

Alteration of legal relations by contract, see Family Code § 1620.
Appeal, stay of proceedings as to judgment or order affecting custody, see Code of Civil Procedure § 917.7.
Compulsory joinder, see Code of Civil Procedure § 389 et seq.
County defined for purposes of this Code, see Family Code § 67.
Division of community estate, see Family Code § 2600 et seq.
Family dwelling, disposition, see Family Code § 1100.
Harassment, temporary restraining order and injunction, see Code of Civil Procedure § 527.6.
Injunctions, generally, see Code of Civil Procedure § 525 et seq.
Judgment and order defined for purposes of this Code, see Family Code § 100.
Lease, transfer or encumbrance of real property, see Family Code § 1102.
Liability of marital property, see Family Code § 900 et seq.
Management and control of marital property, see Family Code § 1100 et seq.
Permissive joinder, generally, see Code of Civil Procedure § 378 et seq.
Permissive joinder of other causes of action, see Code of Civil Procedure § 427.10 et seq.
Proceeding defined for purposes of this Code, see Family Code § 110.
Property defined for purposes of this Code, see Family Code § 113.
Real property, including leasehold interests, see Family Code § 700.
Real property as coextensive with lands, tenements, and hereditaments, see Civil Code § 14; Code of Civil Procedure § 17; Penal Code § 7.
Real property defined, see Civil Code § 658; Evidence Code § 205; Health and Safety Code §§ 33390, 34215; Public Resources Code § 9802; Revenue and Taxation Code § 104.
References to husband, wife, spouses and married persons, persons included for purposes of this Code, see Family Code § 11.
Separate property defined for purposes of this Code, see Family Code § 130.
Separate property of married person, defined, see Family Code § 770.
Setting aside homestead for the benefit of decedent's spouse or child, see Probate Code § 6520 et seq.
Temporary restraining order, see Family Code § 2040 et seq.

Research References

Forms

West's California Code Forms, Family § 754, Comment Overview—Property Rights During Marriage.

§ 755. Employee benefit plan; payment or refund; discharge from adverse claims; notice of claims

(a) The terms "participant," "beneficiary," "employer," "employee organization," "named fiduciary," "fiduciary," and "administrator," as used in subdivision (b), have the same meaning as provided in Section 3 of the Employee Retirement Income Security Act of 1974 (P.L. 93-406) (ERISA), as amended (29 U.S.C.A. Sec. 1002). The term "employee benefit plan" has the same meaning as provided in Section 80 of this code. The term "trustee" shall include a "named fiduciary" as that term is employed in ERISA. The term "plan sponsor" shall include an "employer" or "employee organization," as those terms are used in ERISA (29 U.S.C.A. Sec. 1002).

(b) Notwithstanding Sections 751 and 1100, if payment or refund is made to a participant or the participant's, employee's, or former employee's beneficiary or estate pursuant to an employee benefit plan including a plan governed by the Employee Retirement Income Security Act of 1974 (P.L. 93-406), as amended, the payment or refund fully discharges the plan sponsor and the administrator, trustee, or insurance company making the payment or refund from all adverse claims thereto unless, before the payment or refund is made, the plan sponsor or the administrator of the plan has received written notice by or on behalf of some other person that the other person claims to be entitled to the payment or refund or some part thereof. Nothing in this section affects or releases the participant from claims which may exist against the participant by a person other than the plan sponsor, trustee, administrator, or other person making the benefit payment. *(Stats.1992, c. 162 (A.B.2650), § 10, operative Jan. 1, 1994. Amended by Stats.1994, c. 1269 (A.B.2208), § 12.)*

Cross References

Division of community estate, see Family Code § 2600 et seq.
Employee benefit plan defined for purposes of this Code, see Family Code § 80.
Judges' Retirement Law,
 Benefits as community property, see Government Code § 75050 et seq.
 Retirement allowance benefit if community property benefit awarded to ex-spouse, see Government Code § 75033.6.
Person defined for purposes of this Code, see Family Code § 105.
Public employees' retirement system, see Government Code § 20000 et seq.

Research References

Forms

California Practice Guide: Rutter Family Law Forms Form 8:5, Notice of Adverse Interest in Employee Benefit Plan(S).
West's California Code Forms, Family § 754, Comment Overview—Property Rights During Marriage.
West's California Code Forms, Family § 755 Form 1, Notice of Claim to Retirement Benefits.
West's California Code Forms, Family § 2060, Comment Overview—Application and Order for Joinder.

Part 2

CHARACTERIZATION OF MARITAL PROPERTY

Chapter	Section
1. Community Property	760
2. Separate Property	770
3. Damages for Injuries to Married Person	780
4. Presumptions Concerning Nature of Property	802
5. Transmutation of Property	850

Cross References

Community property,
 Debts, liability for, see Family Code §§ 910, 911.
 Defined, see Probate Code § 28; Civil Code § 687; Family Code §§ 65, 760.
 Division of, see Family Code § 2600 et seq.
 Held in revocable trust, see Probate Code § 104.
 Interests of spouses defined, see Family Code § 751.
Consumer credit contracts, evidentiary effect of delivery of notice to contract signatory, community property, see Civil Code § 1799.98.
Contractual arrangements relating to property rights of spouses at death, see Probate Code § 140 et seq.

CHARACTERIZATION OF MARITAL PROPERTY § 761

Decedent's property, passage of title, see Probate Code §§ 7000, 7001.
Disposition of estate without administration, passage of property to surviving spouse, see Probate Code § 13500 et seq.
Division of Property Act, dissolution of marriage, community estate including out-of-state real property, see Family Code § 2660.
Effect of death of married person on community and quasi-community property, see Probate Code § 100 et seq.
Intestate succession as to community property, see Probate Code § 6401.
Inventory of estate, community and separate property, see Probate Code § 8850.
Judgment creditors seek writ of execution to enforce a judgment made, entered, or enforceable pursuant to Family Code, see Code of Civil Procedure § 699.510.
Management or disposition of community property where spouse lacks legal capacity, see Probate Code § 3000 et seq.
Modification of ownership, interests in property, community property defined, see Civil Code § 687.
Nature of property, generally, see Civil Code § 654.
Personal property defined, see Civil Code § 663.
Presumptions and limitations of actions as to property acquired by wife, see Family Code § 803.
Property defined, see Civil Code § 654.
Property which may be disposed of by will, percentage of community property belonging to testator, see Probate Code § 6101.
Real property as coextensive with lands, tenements, and hereditaments, see Civil Code § 14; Code of Civil Procedure § 17; Penal Code § 7.
Real property defined, see Civil Code § 658; Evidence Code § 205; Health and Safety Code §§ 33390, 34215; Public Resources Code § 9802; Revenue and Taxation Code § 104.
Separate property of married person, defined, see Family Code § 770.
Setting aside homestead for the benefit of decedent's spouse or child, see Probate Code § 6520 et seq.
Simultaneous death, disposition of property, see Probate Code § 220 et seq.
Surviving spouse, defined, see Probate Code § 78.

CHAPTER 1. COMMUNITY PROPERTY

Section
760. "Community property" defined.
761. Property of certain revocable trusts as community property.

Cross References

Community property, interests of spouses defined, see Family Code § 751.
Community property defined, see Probate Code § 28; Civil Code § 687; Family Code §§ 65, 760.
Community property held in revocable trust, see Probate Code § 104.
Consumer credit contracts, evidentiary effect of delivery of notice to contract signatory, community property, see Civil Code § 1799.98.
Debts from community property, liability for, see Family Code §§ 910, 911.
Division of community property, see Family Code § 2600 et seq.
Effect of death of married person on community and quasi-community property, see Probate Code § 100 et seq.
Intestate succession as to community property, see Probate Code § 6401.
Inventory of estate, community and separate property, see Probate Code § 8850.
Management or disposition of community property where spouse lacks legal capacity, see Probate Code § 3000 et seq.
Modification of ownership, interests in property, community property defined, see Civil Code § 687.
Partition of real and personal property, see Code of Civil Procedure § 872.010 et seq.
Property which may be disposed of by will, percentage of community property belonging to testator, see Probate Code § 6101.

§ 760. "Community property" defined

Except as otherwise provided by statute, all property, real or personal, wherever situated, acquired by a married person during the marriage while domiciled in this state is community property.
(Stats.1992, c. 162 (A.B.2650), § 10, operative Jan. 1, 1994.)

Cross References

Community property defined elsewhere, see Probate Code § 28; Civil Code § 687.

Community property defined for purposes of this Code, see Family Code § 65.
Community property held in revocable trust, see Probate Code § 104.
Community property, interests of spouses defined, see Family Code § 751.
Consumer credit contracts, evidentiary effect of delivery of notice to contract signatory, community property, see Civil Code § 1799.98.
Contractual arrangements relating to property rights of spouses at death, see Probate Code § 140 et seq.
Death of married person, effect on community and quasi-community property, see Probate Code § 100 et seq.
Division of community property, see Family Code § 2600 et seq.
Division of Property Act, dissolution of marriage, community estate including out-of-state real property, see Family Code § 2660.
Earnings and accumulations after judgment of legal separation, see Family Code § 772.
Earnings and accumulations during period of separation, see Family Code § 771.
Intestate succession as to community property, see Probate Code § 6401.
Inventory of estate, community and separate property, see Probate Code § 8850.
Management or disposition of community property where spouse lacks legal capacity, see Probate Code § 3000 et seq.
Marital property agreements, see Family Code § 1500 et seq.
Modification of ownership, interests in property, community property defined, see Civil Code § 687.
Person defined for purposes of this Code, see Family Code § 105.
Personal injuries,
  Damages as community property, see Family Code § 780.
  Damages as separate property, see Family Code § 781.
Presumptions, see Evidence Code § 600 et seq.
Presumptions relating to nature of property, see Family Code §§ 802, 803.
Property defined for purposes of this Code, see Family Code § 113.
Property which may be disposed of by will, percentage of community property belonging to testator, see Probate Code § 6101.
References to husband, wife, spouses and married persons, persons included for purposes of this Code, see Family Code § 11.
Reimbursements between community and separate property, division of property, see Family Code § 2640.
Separate property, defined, see Family Code § 130.
Separate property of married person, defined, see Family Code § 770.
Simultaneous death, disposition of property, see Probate Code § 220 et seq.
State defined for purposes of this Code, see Family Code § 145.
Support, property subject to, see Family Code § 4008.
Surviving spouse's right in state real property of nondomiciliary decedent, see Probate Code § 120.
Transmutation of property, see Family Code § 850 et seq.

Research References

Forms
Asset Protection: Legal Planning, Strategies and Forms ¶ 4.03, Community Property.
Asset Protection: Legal Planning, Strategies and Forms ¶ 4.07, Marital Agreements.
Asset Protection: Legal Planning, Strategies and Forms ¶ 4.12, Postnuptial Agreement.
California Practice Guide: Rutter Family Law Forms Form 1:32, Glossary of Common Family Law Terms, Phrases and Concepts (Enclosure to Form 1:31).
3 California Transactions Forms--Business Transactions § 18:14, Spouses.
1 California Transactions Forms--Estate Planning § 1:22, Community Property.
2 California Transactions Forms--Estate Planning § 10:4, Community Property.
4 California Transactions Forms--Estate Planning § 19:18, Community Property.
1 California Transactions Forms--Family Law § 1:27, Complete Agreement.
1 California Transactions Forms--Family Law § 2:34, Mixed-Character Asset Described.
West's California Code Forms, Family § 803, Comment Overview—Presumptions Concerning Nature of Property.
West's California Code Forms, Family § 1611 Form 1, Premarital Agreement.
West's California Code Forms, Family § 2550, Comment Overview—Manner of Division of Community Estate.

§ 761. Property of certain revocable trusts as community property

(a) Unless the trust instrument or the instrument of transfer expressly provides otherwise, community property that is transferred

§ 761

in trust remains community property during the marriage, regardless of the identity of the trustee, if the trust, originally or as amended before or after the transfer, provides that the trust is revocable as to that property during the marriage and the power, if any, to modify the trust as to the rights and interests in that property during the marriage may be exercised only with the joinder or consent of both spouses.

(b) Unless the trust instrument expressly provides otherwise, a power to revoke as to community property may be exercised by either spouse acting alone. Community property, including any income or appreciation, that is distributed or withdrawn from a trust by revocation, power of withdrawal, or otherwise, remains community property unless there is a valid transmutation of the property at the time of distribution or withdrawal.

(c) The trustee may convey and otherwise manage and control the trust property in accordance with the provisions of the trust without the joinder or consent of either spouse unless the trust expressly requires the joinder or consent of one or both spouses.

(d) This section applies to a transfer made before, on, or after July 1, 1987.

(e) Nothing in this section affects the community character of property that is transferred before, on, or after July 1, 1987, in any manner or to a trust other than described in this section. *(Stats.1992, c. 162 (A.B.2650), § 10, operative Jan. 1, 1994. Amended by Stats.2014, c. 82 (S.B.1306), § 17, eff. Jan. 1, 2015.)*

Cross References

Community personal property, management and control, restrictions on disposition, see Family Code § 1100.
Community property defined for purposes of this Code, see Family Code § 65.
Creditors' rights against revocable trust during lifetime of settlor, see Probate Code § 18200.
Dependent children—temporary custody and detention, presumed or alleged fathers, inquiry by court, see Welfare and Institutions Code § 316.2.
Disposition of estate without administration, community property held in revocable trust, see Probate Code § 13504.
Property defined for purposes of this Code, see Family Code § 113.
Property which may be disposed of by will, percentage of community property belonging to testator, see Probate Code § 6101.
References to husband, wife, spouses and married persons, persons included for purposes of this Code, see Family Code § 11.
Support, property subject to, see Family Code § 4008.
Trust, transfer by married persons, transmutation limitations, see Family Code § 850 et seq.
Trusts revocable by settlor, see Probate Code § 15401.
Wills, disposition of interest in community property in absence of method provided by trust instrument, see Probate Code § 104.

Research References

Forms

2 California Transactions Forms--Estate Planning § 10:4, Community Property.
3 California Transactions Forms--Estate Planning § 13:10, Revocation of Trust Created by More Than One Settlor.
3 California Transactions Forms--Estate Planning § 13:17, Joinder and Consent.
3 California Transactions Forms--Estate Planning § 13:18, Revocable Trust Property Retains Community Property Status.
3 California Transactions Forms--Estate Planning § 13:19, Legal Effect of Retention of Community Character.
3 California Transactions Forms--Estate Planning § 13:20, Tax Effect of Retention of Community Character.
3 California Transactions Forms--Estate Planning § 13:21, Transmutation.
3 California Transactions Forms--Estate Planning § 13:22, Agent May Amend or Revoke.
1 California Transactions Forms--Family Law § 2:45, Trust Terms Obsolete.
1 California Transactions Forms--Family Law § 2:46, No Transmutation.

CHAPTER 2. SEPARATE PROPERTY

Section
770. Separate property of married person.
771. Earnings and accumulations after date of separation.
772. Earnings or accumulations after entry of judgment of legal separation.

Cross References

Inventory of estate, community and separate property, see Probate Code § 8850.
Nature of property, generally, see Civil Code § 654.

§ 770. Separate property of married person

(a) Separate property of a married person includes all of the following:

(1) All property owned by the person before marriage.

(2) All property acquired by the person after marriage by gift, bequest, devise, or descent.

(3) The rents, issues, and profits of the property described in this section.

(b) A married person may, without the consent of the person's spouse, convey the person's separate property. *(Stats.1992, c. 162 (A.B.2650), § 10, operative Jan. 1, 1994.)*

Cross References

Applicable provisions, see Family Code § 231.
Community property, defined, see Probate Code § 28; Civil Code § 687; Family Code §§ 65, 760.
Death or injury, liability of married person, satisfaction from separate property, see Family Code § 1000.
Disposition of property, insufficient evidence of survivorship, see Probate Code § 220.
Husband and wife agreeing to divide community property on basis of non pro rata division of aggregate value of community property or on basis of division of each individual item or asset of community property, or partly on each basis, see Probate Code § 100.
Indebtedness incurred before or during marriage, liability of separate property, see Family Code § 913.
Making community property separate property by agreement,
   Premarital and marital agreements, see Family Code §§ 1500 et seq., 1620, 1617.
   Transmutation during marriage, see Family Code §§ 850 to 853.
Person defined for purposes of this Code, see Family Code § 105.
Property acquired by married woman, rights of, see Family Code § 803.
Property defined for purposes of this Code, see Family Code § 113.
References to husband, wife, spouses and married persons, persons included for purposes of this Code, see Family Code § 11.
Reimbursements between community and separate property, division of property, see Family Code § 2640.
Separate property, defined,
   Generally, see Family Code § 130.
   Division of property, see Family Code § 2502.
Support, see Family Code § 3515.
Survivorship, right to separate property, determination, see Probate Code § 230 et seq.
Transfers, generally, see Civil Code § 1039 et seq.

Research References

Forms

7PT1 Am. Jur. Pl. & Pr. Forms Community Property § 4, Complaint, Petition, or Declaration—By Spouse—To Determine Defendant Spouse's Adverse Claims to Community Interest in Plaintiff's Real Property Acquired After Marriage.
Asset Protection: Legal Planning, Strategies and Forms ¶ 4.03, Community Property.
California Practice Guide: Rutter Family Law Forms Form 1:32, Glossary of Common Family Law Terms, Phrases and Concepts (Enclosure to Form 1:31).

2 California Transactions Forms--Estate Planning § 10:3, Separate Property.
4 California Transactions Forms--Estate Planning § 19:17, Separate Property.
1 California Transactions Forms--Family Law § 2:28, Dividing Defined Contribution Plan.
1 California Transactions Forms--Family Law § 2:34, Mixed-Character Asset Described.
West's California Code Forms, Family § 2550, Comment Overview—Manner of Division of Community Estate.

§ 771. Earnings and accumulations after date of separation

(a) The earnings and accumulations of a spouse and the minor children living with, or in the custody of, the spouse, after the date of separation of the spouses, are the separate property of the spouse.

(b) Notwithstanding subdivision (a), the earnings and accumulations of an unemancipated minor child related to a contract of a type described in Section 6750 shall remain the sole legal property of the minor child. (Stats.1992, c. 162 (A.B.2650), § 10, operative Jan. 1, 1994. Amended by Stats.1999, c. 940 (S.B.1162), § 1; Stats.2016, c. 114 (S.B.1255), § 2, eff. Jan. 1, 2017.)

Cross References

Creditors, direct payment, see Family Code § 2023.
Earnings of minors, see Family Code § 7503.
Legal separation, generally, see Family Code § 2000 et seq.
Legal separation, characterization of liabilities, community or separate property, see Family Code § 2551.
Legal separation, division of property, see Code of Civil Procedure § 259; Family Code § 2500 et seq.
Minor defined for purposes of this Code, see Family Code § 6500.
Property defined for purposes of this Code, see Family Code § 113.
References to husband, wife, spouses and married persons, persons included for purposes of this Code, see Family Code § 11.
Separate debts, confirmation, see Family Code § 2625.
Separate property,
   Defined for purposes of this Code, see Family Code § 130.
   Earnings and accumulations, see Family Code § 772.
   Joint tenancy or tenancy in common, property division, see Family Code § 2650.
Third party rights, property transfers, see Family Code § 2041.

Research References

Forms

Asset Protection: Legal Planning, Strategies and Forms ¶ 4.03, Community Property.
2 California Transactions Forms--Estate Planning § 10:3, Separate Property.
4 California Transactions Forms--Estate Planning § 19:17, Separate Property.

§ 772. Earnings or accumulations after entry of judgment of legal separation

After entry of a judgment of legal separation of the parties, the earnings or accumulations of each party are the separate property of the party acquiring the earnings or accumulations. (Stats.1992, c. 162 (A.B.2650), § 10, operative Jan. 1, 1994.)

Cross References

Earnings of minors, see Family Code § 7503.
Joint tenancy or tenancy in common, property division, see Family Code § 2650.
Judgment, decree included in, see Family Code § 100.
Judgment and order defined for purposes of this Code, see Family Code § 100.
Legal separation, generally, see Family Code § 2000 et seq.
Legal separation, division of property, see Code of Civil Procedure § 259; Family Code § 2500 et seq.
Property defined for purposes of this Code, see Family Code § 113.
Separate property defined for purposes of this Code, see Family Code § 130.

Research References

Forms

Asset Protection: Legal Planning, Strategies and Forms ¶ 4.03, Community Property.
2 California Transactions Forms--Estate Planning § 10:3, Separate Property.
4 California Transactions Forms--Estate Planning § 19:17, Separate Property.

CHAPTER 3. DAMAGES FOR INJURIES TO MARRIED PERSON

Section
780. Community property.
781. Separate property.
782. Injuries to married person by spouse; primary resort to separate property; consent of injured spouse to use of community property; indemnity.
782.5. Attempted murder or soliciting the murder of a spouse; remedies; community property interests.
783. Injuries to married person by third party; extent concurring negligence of spouse allowable as defense.

Cross References

Community property, interests of spouses defined, see Family Code § 751.
Community property defined, see Probate Code § 28; Civil Code § 687; Family Code §§ 65, 760.
Community property held in revocable trust, see Probate Code § 104.
Community property subject to enforcement of money judgement, see Code of Civil Procedure § 695.020.
Consumer credit contracts, evidentiary effect of delivery of notice to contract signatory, community property, see Civil Code § 1799.98.
Debts from community property, liability for, see Family Code §§ 910, 911.
Division of community property, see Family Code § 2600 et seq.
Effect of death of married person on community and quasi-community property, see Probate Code § 100 et seq.
Intestate succession as to community property, see Probate Code § 6401.
Inventory of estate, community and separate property, see Probate Code § 8850.
Management or disposition of community property where spouse lacks legal capacity, see Probate Code § 3000 et seq.
Modification of ownership, interests in property, community property defined, see Civil Code § 687.
Property which may be disposed of by will, percentage of community property belonging to testator, see Probate Code § 6101.

§ 780. Community property

Except as provided in Section 781 and subject to the rules of allocation set forth in Section 2603, money and other property received or to be received by a married person in satisfaction of a judgment for damages for personal injuries, or pursuant to an agreement for the settlement or compromise of a claim for such damages, is community property if the cause of action for the damages arose during the marriage. (Stats.1992, c. 162 (A.B.2650), § 10, operative Jan. 1, 1994.)

Cross References

Abstract of judgment or decree, contents, see Code of Civil Procedure § 674.
Community estate personal injury damages, division, see Family Code § 2603.
Community property, interests of spouses defined, see Family Code § 751.
Community property defined elsewhere, see Probate Code § 28; Civil Code § 687; Family Code §§ 65, 760.
Community property defined for purposes of this Code, see Family Code § 65.
Community property held in revocable trust, see Probate Code § 104.
Community property subject to enforcement of money judgement, see Code of Civil Procedure § 695.020.
Consumer credit contracts, evidentiary effect of delivery of notice to contract signatory, community property, see Civil Code § 1799.98.
Debts from community property, liability for, see Family Code §§ 910, 911.
Division of community property, generally, see Family Code § 2600 et seq.
Effect of death of married person on community and quasi-community property, see Probate Code § 100 et seq.
Intestate succession as to community property, see Probate Code § 6401.
Inventory of estate, community and separate property, see Probate Code § 8850.
Judgment and order defined for purposes of this Code, see Family Code § 100.
Management or disposition of community property where spouse lacks legal capacity, see Probate Code § 3000 et seq.

§ 780

Modification of ownership, interests in property, community property defined, see Civil Code § 687.
Person defined for purposes of this Code, see Family Code § 105.
Property defined for purposes of this Code, see Family Code § 113.
Property which may be disposed of by will, percentage of community property belonging to testator, see Probate Code § 6101.
Receivers, generally, see Code of Civil Procedure § 564 et seq.
References to husband, wife, spouses and married persons, persons included for purposes of this Code, see Family Code § 11.

Research References

Forms

3 California Transactions Forms--Business Transactions § 18:14, Spouses.
4 California Transactions Forms--Estate Planning § 19:17, Separate Property.
4 California Transactions Forms--Estate Planning § 19:18, Community Property.

§ 781. Separate property

(a) Money or other property received or to be received by a married person in satisfaction of a judgment for damages for personal injuries, or pursuant to an agreement for the settlement or compromise of a claim for those damages, is the separate property of the injured person if the cause of action for the damages arose as follows:

(1) After the entry of a judgment of dissolution of a marriage or legal separation of the parties.

(2) While the injured spouse is living separate from the other spouse.

(b) Notwithstanding subdivision (a), if the spouse of the injured person has paid expenses by reason of the personal injuries from separate property or from the community property, the spouse is entitled to reimbursement of the separate property or the community property for those expenses from the separate property received by the injured person under subdivision (a).

(c) Notwithstanding subdivision (a), if one spouse has a cause of action against the other spouse that arose during the marriage of the parties, money or property paid or to be paid by or on behalf of a party to the party's spouse of that marriage in satisfaction of a judgment for damages for personal injuries to that spouse, or pursuant to an agreement for the settlement or compromise of a claim for the damages, is the separate property of the injured spouse. *(Stats.1992, c. 162 (A.B.2650), § 10, operative Jan. 1, 1994. Amended by Stats.2019, c. 115 (A.B.1817), § 10, eff. Jan. 1, 2020.)*

Cross References

Applicable provisions, see Family Code § 231.
Community estate personal injury damages, division, see Family Code § 2603.
Community property, defined elsewhere, see Probate Code § 28; Civil Code § 687; Family Code §§ 65, 760.
Community property defined for purposes of this Code, see Family Code § 65.
Death or injury, liability of married person, satisfaction from separate property, see Family Code § 1000.
Disposition of property, insufficient evidence of survivorship, see Probate Code § 220.
Husband and wife agreeing to divide community property on basis of non pro rata division of aggregate value of community property or on basis of division of each individual item or asset of community property, or partly on each basis, see Probate Code § 100.
Indebtedness incurred before or during marriage, liability of separate property, see Family Code § 913.
Judgment and order defined for purposes of this Code, see Family Code § 100.
Making community property separate property by agreement,
 Premarital and marital agreements, see Family Code §§ 1500 et seq., 1620, 1617.
 Transmutation during marriage, see Family Code §§ 850 to 853.
Person defined for purposes of this Code, see Family Code § 105.
Property acquired by married woman, rights of, see Family Code § 803.
Property defined for purposes of this Code, see Family Code § 113.
References to husband, wife, spouses and married persons, persons included for purposes of this Code, see Family Code § 11.

Reimbursements between community and separate property, division of property, see Family Code § 2640.
Separate property, defined,
 Generally, see Family Code § 130.
 Division of property, see Family Code § 2502.
 Support, see Family Code § 3515.
Separate property of married person, defined, see Family Code § 770.
Survivorship, right to separate property, determination, see Probate Code § 230 et seq.
Transfers, generally, see Civil Code § 1039 et seq.

Research References

Forms

Asset Protection: Legal Planning, Strategies and Forms ¶ 4.03, Community Property.
2 California Transactions Forms--Estate Planning § 10:3, Separate Property.
4 California Transactions Forms--Estate Planning § 19:17, Separate Property.
West's California Code Forms, Family § 781, Comment Overview--Damages for Injuries to Married Person.
West's California Code Forms, Family § 2550, Comment Overview--Manner of Division of Community Estate.

§ 782. Injuries to married person by spouse; primary resort to separate property; consent of injured spouse to use of community property; indemnity

(a) Where an injury to a married person is caused in whole or in part by the negligent or wrongful act or omission of the person's spouse, the community property may not be used to discharge the liability of the tortfeasor spouse to the injured spouse or the liability to make contribution to a joint tortfeasor until the separate property of the tortfeasor spouse, not exempt from enforcement of a money judgment, is exhausted.

(b) This section does not prevent the use of community property to discharge a liability referred to in subdivision (a) if the injured spouse gives written consent thereto after the occurrence of the injury.

(c) This section does not affect the right to indemnity provided by an insurance or other contract to discharge the tortfeasor spouse's liability, whether or not the consideration given for the contract consisted of community property. *(Stats.1992, c. 162 (A.B.2650), § 10, operative Jan. 1, 1994.)*

Cross References

Actions by unmarried minor children, see Code of Civil Procedure § 376.
Acts forbidden by personal relations, see Civil Code § 49.
Address confidentiality for victims of domestic violence and stalking, see Government Code § 6205 et seq.
Civil actions arising out of obligations, or injuries, see Code of Civil Procedure § 25.
Community property defined for purposes of this Code, see Family Code § 65.
Creation and enforcement of obligation by operation of law, see Civil Code § 1428.
Domestic violence, prevention, see Family Code § 6200 et seq.
Domestic violence victim-counselor privilege, see Evidence Code § 1037 et seq.
Force, right to use, see Civil Code § 50.
Injuring person or property of another, or infringing upon any of his or her rights, see Civil Code § 1708.
Injury to person defined, see Code of Civil Procedure § 29.
Injury to property defined, see Code of Civil Procedure § 28.
Judgment and order defined for purposes of this Code, see Family Code § 100.
Judgments, exemptions from enforcement, see Code of Civil Procedure § 703.010.
Kinds of injuries, see Code of Civil Procedure § 27.
Law enforcement response to domestic violence, see Penal Code § 13710 et seq.
Person defined for purposes of this Code, see Family Code § 105.
Person suffering detriment may recover damages, see Civil Code § 3281.
Personal rights, see Civil Code § 43.
Presumption against persons perpetrating domestic violence, custody of children, see Family Code § 3044.
Property defined for purposes of this Code, see Family Code § 113.

CHARACTERIZATION OF MARITAL PROPERTY

References to husband, wife, spouses and married persons, persons included for purposes of this Code, see Family Code § 11.
Releases from and contributions among joint tortfeasors, see Code of Civil Procedure § 875 et seq.
Remedy for every wrong, see Civil Code § 3523.
Responsibility for willful acts and negligence, see Civil Code § 1714.
Rights, use so as not to infringe on rights of another, see Civil Code § 3514.
Separate property defined for purposes of this Code, see Family Code § 130.
Suffering from act of another, see Civil Code § 3520.
Taking advantage of own wrong prohibited, see Civil Code § 3517.
Unlawful contracts, see Civil Code § 1667 et seq.
Wrongs not actionable, see Civil Code § 43.5.

Research References

Forms

West's California Code Forms, Family § 781, Comment Overview—Damages for Injuries to Married Person.

§ 782.5. Attempted murder or soliciting the murder of a spouse; remedies; community property interests

In addition to any other remedy authorized by law, when a spouse is convicted of attempting to murder the other spouse, as punishable pursuant to subdivision (a) of Section 664 of the Penal Code, or of soliciting the murder of the other spouse, as punishable pursuant to subdivision (b) of Section 653f of the Penal Code, the injured spouse shall be entitled to an award to the injured spouse of 100 percent of the community property interest in the retirement and pension benefits of the injured spouse.

As used in this section, "injured spouse" has the same meaning as defined in Section 4324. *(Added by Stats.1995, c. 364 (A.B.16), § 2. Amended by Stats.2010, c. 65 (A.B.2674), § 1.)*

Cross References

Actions by unmarried minor children, see Code of Civil Procedure § 376.
Acts forbidden by personal relations, see Civil Code § 49.
Address confidentiality for victims of domestic violence and stalking, see Government Code § 6205 et seq.
Civil actions arising out of obligations, or injuries, see Code of Civil Procedure § 25.
Community property defined for purposes of this Code, see Family Code § 65.
Creation and enforcement of obligation by operation of law, see Civil Code § 1428.
Domestic violence, prevention, see Family Code § 6200 et seq.
Domestic violence victim-counselor privilege, see Evidence Code § 1037 et seq.
Force, right to use, see Civil Code § 50.
Injuring person or property of another, or infringing upon any of his or her rights, see Civil Code § 1708.
Injury to person defined, see Code of Civil Procedure § 29.
Injury to property defined, see Code of Civil Procedure § 28.
Judgments, exemptions from enforcement, see Code of Civil Procedure § 703.010.
Kinds of injuries, see Code of Civil Procedure § 27.
Law enforcement response to domestic violence, see Penal Code § 13710 et seq.
Person suffering detriment may recover damages, see Civil Code § 3281.
Personal rights, see Civil Code § 43.
Presumption against persons perpetrating domestic violence, custody of children, see Family Code § 3044.
Property defined for purposes of this Code, see Family Code § 113.
References to husband, wife, spouses and married persons, persons included for purposes of this Code, see Family Code § 11.
Releases from and contributions among joint tortfeasors, see Code of Civil Procedure § 875 et seq.
Remedy for every wrong, see Civil Code § 3523.
Responsibility for willful acts and negligence, see Civil Code § 1714.
Rights, use so as not to infringe on rights of another, see Civil Code § 3514.
Suffering from act of another, see Civil Code § 3520.
Taking advantage of own wrong prohibited, see Civil Code § 3517.
Unlawful contracts, see Civil Code § 1667 et seq.
Wrongs not actionable, see Civil Code § 43.5.

§ 783. Injuries to married person by third party; extent concurring negligence of spouse allowable as defense

If a married person is injured by the negligent or wrongful act or omission of a person other than the married person's spouse, the fact that the negligent or wrongful act or omission of the spouse of the injured person was a concurring cause of the injury is not a defense in an action brought by the injured person to recover damages for the injury except in cases where the concurring negligent or wrongful act or omission would be a defense if the marriage did not exist. *(Stats.1992, c. 162 (A.B.2650), § 10, operative Jan. 1, 1994.)*

Cross References

Civil actions arising out of obligations, or injuries, see Code of Civil Procedure § 25.
Domestic violence, prevention, see Family Code § 6200 et seq.
Force, right to use, see Civil Code § 50.
Injuring person or property of another, or infringing upon any of his or her rights, see Civil Code § 1708.
Injury to person defined, see Code of Civil Procedure § 29.
Injury to property defined, see Code of Civil Procedure § 28.
Joinder of parties, right of married person to sue without joinder of spouse, see Code of Civil Procedure § 370.
Judgments, exemptions from enforcement, see Code of Civil Procedure § 703.010.
Kinds of injuries, see Code of Civil Procedure § 27.
Person defined for purposes of this Code, see Family Code § 105.
Person suffering detriment may recover damages, see Civil Code § 3281.
Personal rights, see Civil Code § 43.
References to husband, wife, spouses and married persons, persons included for purposes of this Code, see Family Code § 11.
Releases from and contributions among joint tortfeasors, see Code of Civil Procedure § 875 et seq.
Remedy for every wrong, see Civil Code § 3523.
Responsibility for willful acts and negligence, see Civil Code § 1714.
Rights, use so as not to infringe on rights of another, see Civil Code § 3514.
Suffering from act of another, see Civil Code § 3520.
Taking advantage of own wrong prohibited, see Civil Code § 3517.
Unlawful contracts, see Civil Code § 1667 et seq.
Wrongs not actionable, see Civil Code § 43.5.

CHAPTER 4. PRESUMPTIONS CONCERNING NATURE OF PROPERTY

Section
802. Property acquired during marriage terminated by dissolution more than four years prior to death.
803. Property acquired by married woman before January 1, 1975; conclusiveness of presumptions.

Cross References

Community property,
 Debts, liability for, see Family Code §§ 910, 911.
 Defined, see Probate Code § 28; Civil Code § 687; Family Code §§ 65, 760.
 Division of, see Family Code § 2600 et seq.
 Held in revocable trust, see Probate Code § 104.
 Interests of spouses defined, see Family Code § 751.
Consumer credit contracts, evidentiary effect of delivery of notice to contract signatory, community property, see Civil Code § 1799.98.
Contractual arrangements relating to property rights of spouses at death, see Probate Code § 140 et seq.
Decedent's property, passage of title, see Probate Code §§ 7000, 7001.
Disposition of estate without administration, passage of property to surviving spouse, see Probate Code § 13500 et seq.
Division of Property Act, dissolution of marriage, community estate including out-of-state real property, see Family Code § 2660.
Effect of death of married person on community and quasi-community property, see Probate Code § 100 et seq.
Intestate succession as to community property, see Probate Code § 6401.
Inventory of estate, community and separate property, see Probate Code § 8850.

MARRIAGE RIGHTS AND OBLIGATIONS

Judgment creditors seek writ of execution to enforce a judgment made, entered, or enforceable pursuant to Family Code, see Code of Civil Procedure § 699.510.
Management or disposition of community property where spouse lacks legal capacity, see Probate Code § 3000 et seq.
Modification of ownership, interests in property, community property defined, see Civil Code § 687.
Nature of property, generally, see Civil Code § 654.
Personal property defined, see Civil Code § 663.
Presumptions and limitations of actions as to property acquired by wife, see Family Code § 803.
Property defined, see Civil Code § 654.
Property which may be disposed of by will, percentage of community property belonging to testator, see Probate Code § 6101.
Real property as coextensive with lands, tenements, and hereditaments, see Civil Code § 14; Code of Civil Procedure § 17; Penal Code § 7.
Real property defined, see Civil Code § 658; Evidence Code § 205; Health and Safety Code §§ 33390, 34215; Public Resources Code § 9802; Revenue and Taxation Code § 104.
Separate property of married person, defined, see Family Code § 770.
Setting aside homestead for the benefit of decedent's spouse or child, see Probate Code § 6520 et seq.
Simultaneous death, disposition of property, see Probate Code § 220 et seq.
Surviving spouse, defined, see Probate Code § 78.

§ 802. Property acquired during marriage terminated by dissolution more than four years prior to death

The presumption that property acquired during marriage is community property does not apply to any property to which legal or equitable title is held by a person at the time of the person's death if the marriage during which the property was acquired was terminated by dissolution of marriage more than four years before the death. *(Stats.1992, c. 162 (A.B.2650), § 10, operative Jan. 1, 1994.)*

Cross References

Community property defined elsewhere, see Probate Code § 28; Civil Code § 687; Family Code § 760.
Community property defined for purposes of this Code, see Family Code § 65.
Community property, interests of spouses defined, see Family Code § 751.
Contractual arrangements relating to property rights of spouses at death, see Probate Code § 140 et seq.
Decedent's property, passage of title, see Probate Code §§ 7000, 7001.
Disposition of estate without administration, passage of property to surviving spouse, see Probate Code § 13500 et seq.
Division of Property Act, dissolution of marriage, community estate including out-of-state real property, see Family Code § 2660.
Effect of death of married person on community and quasi-community property, see Probate Code § 100 et seq.
Intestate succession as to community property, see Probate Code § 6401.
Inventory of estate, community and separate property, see Probate Code § 8850.
Judgment creditors seek writ of execution to enforce a judgment made, entered, or enforceable pursuant to Family Code, see Code of Civil Procedure § 699.510.
Management or disposition of community property where spouse lacks legal capacity, see Probate Code § 3000 et seq.
Person defined for purposes of this Code, see Family Code § 105.
Presumptions, generally, see Evidence Code § 600 et seq.
Presumptions and limitations of actions as to property acquired by wife, see Family Code § 803.
Property defined for purposes of this Code, see Family Code § 113.
Property which may be disposed of by will, percentage of community property belonging to testator, see Probate Code § 6101.
Real property as coextensive with lands, tenements, and hereditaments, see Civil Code § 14; Code of Civil Procedure § 17; Penal Code § 7.
Real property defined, see Civil Code § 658; Evidence Code § 205; Health and Safety Code §§ 33390, 34215; Public Resources Code § 9802; Revenue and Taxation Code § 104.
Separate property of married person, defined, see Family Code § 770.
Setting aside homestead for the benefit of decedent's spouse or child, see Probate Code § 6520 et seq.
Simultaneous death, disposition of property, see Probate Code § 220 et seq.
Surviving spouse, defined, see Probate Code § 78.

Research References

Forms

4 California Transactions Forms--Estate Planning § 19:18, Community Property.

§ 803. Property acquired by married woman before January 1, 1975; conclusiveness of presumptions

Notwithstanding any other provision of this part, whenever any real or personal property, or any interest therein or encumbrance thereon, was acquired before January 1, 1975, by a married woman by an instrument in writing, the following presumptions apply, and are conclusive in favor of any person dealing in good faith and for a valuable consideration with the married woman or her legal representatives or successors in interest, regardless of any change in her marital status after acquisition of the property:

(a) If acquired by the married woman, the presumption is that the property is the married woman's separate property.

(b) If acquired by the married woman and any other person, the presumption is that the married woman takes the part acquired by her as tenant in common, unless a different intention is expressed in the instrument.

(c) If acquired by husband and wife by an instrument in which they are described as husband and wife, the presumption is that the property is the community property of the husband and wife, unless a different intention is expressed in the instrument. *(Stats.1992, c. 162 (A.B.2650), § 10, operative Jan. 1, 1994.)*

Cross References

Civil liability of owners and operators of vehicles, limitation on Family Code presumptions, see Vehicle Code § 17150.5.
Community property, interests of spouses defined, see Family Code § 751.
Community property defined elsewhere, see Probate Code § 28; Civil Code § 687; Family Code § 760.
Community property defined for purposes of this Code, see Family Code § 65.
Contractual arrangements relating to property rights of spouses at death, see Probate Code § 140 et seq.
Decedent's property, passage of title, see Probate Code §§ 7000, 7001.
Disposition of estate without administration, passage of property to surviving spouse, see Probate Code § 13500 et seq.
Division of Property Act, dissolution of marriage, community estate including out-of-state real property, see Family Code § 2660.
Effect of death of married person on community and quasi-community property, see Probate Code § 100 et seq.
Intestate succession as to community property, see Probate Code § 6401.
Inventory of estate, community and separate property, see Probate Code § 8850.
Judgment creditors seek writ of execution to enforce a judgment made, entered, or enforceable pursuant to Family Code, see Code of Civil Procedure § 699.510.
Management or disposition of community property where spouse lacks legal capacity, see Probate Code § 3000 et seq.
Person defined for purposes of this Code, see Family Code § 105.
Presumptions, generally, see Evidence Code § 600 et seq.
Presumptions and limitations of actions as to property acquired by wife, see Family Code § 803.
Property defined for purposes of this Code, see Family Code § 113.
Property which may be disposed of by will, percentage of community property belonging to testator, see Probate Code § 6101.
Real property as coextensive with lands, tenements, and hereditaments, see Civil Code § 14; Code of Civil Procedure § 17; Penal Code § 7.
Real property defined, see Civil Code § 658; Evidence Code § 205; Health and Safety Code §§ 33390, 34215; Public Resources Code § 9802; Revenue and Taxation Code § 104.
References to husband, wife, spouses and married persons, persons included for purposes of this Code, see Family Code § 11.
Separate property defined for purposes of this Code, see Family Code § 130.
Separate property of married person, defined, see Family Code § 770.
Setting aside homestead for the benefit of decedent's spouse or child, see Probate Code § 6520 et seq.
Simultaneous death, disposition of property, see Probate Code § 220 et seq.

Surviving spouse, defined, see Probate Code § 78.

Research References

Forms

Asset Protection: Legal Planning, Strategies and Forms ¶ 4.03, Community Property.
Asset Protection: Legal Planning, Strategies and Forms ¶ 4.12, Postnuptial Agreement.
West's California Code Forms, Family § 803, Comment Overview—Presumptions Concerning Nature of Property.

CHAPTER 5. TRANSMUTATION OF PROPERTY

Section
850. Transmutation by agreement or transfer.
851. Transmutation subject to fraudulent transfer laws.
852. Requirements.
853. Characterization of property in will; admissibility in proceedings commenced before death of testator; waiver of right to joint and survivor annuity or survivor's benefits; written joinders or consents to nonprobate transfers of community property.

Cross References

Effect of recording, or the want thereof, see Civil Code § 1213 et seq.
Leasehold interest in real property, see Family Code § 700.
Licenses to sell firearms, violations, exceptions, see Penal Code §§ 16620, 16730, 16960, 17310, and 26500 to 26588.
Property of certain revocable trusts as community property, see Family Code § 761.
Reimbursements, contributions to the acquisition of property of the community property estate, waivers and amounts, see Family Code § 2640.
Statute of frauds, see Civil Code § 1624.
Transfer of real property, method of transfer, see Civil Code § 1091.
Uniform Fraudulent Transfer Act, see Civil Code § 3439 et seq.
Written consent not a transmutation, exception, see Probate Code § 5022.

§ 850. Transmutation by agreement or transfer

Subject to Sections 851 to 853, inclusive, married persons may by agreement or transfer, with or without consideration, do any of the following:

(a) Transmute community property to separate property of either spouse.

(b) Transmute separate property of either spouse to community property.

(c) Transmute separate property of one spouse to separate property of the other spouse. *(Stats.1992, c. 162 (A.B.2650), § 10, operative Jan. 1, 1994.)*

Cross References

Community property defined for purposes of this Code, see Family Code § 65.
Licenses to sell firearms, violations, exceptions, see Penal Code §§ 16620, 16730, 16960, 17310, and 26500 to 26588.
Person defined for purposes of this Code, see Family Code § 105.
Property defined for purposes of this Code, see Family Code § 113.
Property of certain revocable trusts as community property, see Family Code § 761.
References to husband, wife, spouses and married persons, persons included for purposes of this Code, see Family Code § 11.
Separate property defined for purposes of this Code, see Family Code § 130.
Transmutations, required formalities, see Family Code § 852.
Uniform Fraudulent Transfer Act, see Civil Code § 3439 et seq.
Written consent not a transmutation, exception, see Probate Code § 5022.

Research References

Forms

Asset Protection: Legal Planning, Strategies and Forms ¶ 4.04, Determining the Character of Property.
Asset Protection: Legal Planning, Strategies and Forms ¶ 4.07, Marital Agreements.

2 California Transactions Forms--Estate Planning § 9:77, Beneficiary Designations of Community Property Interests in Plan or IRA [Prob C §§ 5000 et seq.].
2 California Transactions Forms--Estate Planning § 10:3, Separate Property.
2 California Transactions Forms--Estate Planning § 11:29, In General.
2 California Transactions Forms--Estate Planning § 11:35, Agreement Entered Into on or After January 1, 1985.
2 California Transactions Forms--Estate Planning § 11:47, Formalities.
2 California Transactions Forms--Estate Planning § 11:48, Governing Contractual Provisions [CC §§1550 et seq., Fam C §721(B)].
2 California Transactions Forms--Estate Planning § 11:59, Matters to Include in Transmutation Agreement.
2 California Transactions Forms--Estate Planning § 11:68, General Transmutation Agreement.
3 California Transactions Forms--Estate Planning § 13:21, Transmutation.
West's California Code Forms, Family § 850, Comment Overview—Transmutation by Agreement or Transfer.
West's California Code Forms, Family § 850 Form 2, Agreement Transmuting Separate Property to Community Property.
West's California Code Forms, Family § 850 Form 3, Agreement Transmuting Separate Property of Spouse to Separate Property of Other Spouse.

§ 851. Transmutation subject to fraudulent transfer laws

A transmutation is subject to the laws governing fraudulent transfers. *(Stats.1992, c. 162 (A.B.2650), § 10, operative Jan. 1, 1994.)*

Cross References

Statute of frauds, see Civil Code § 1624.
Uniform Fraudulent Transfer Act, see Civil Code § 3439 et seq.
Written consent not a transmutation, exception, see Probate Code § 5022.

Research References

Forms

Asset Protection: Legal Planning, Strategies and Forms ¶ 4.07, Marital Agreements.
2 California Transactions Forms--Estate Planning § 11:35, Agreement Entered Into on or After January 1, 1985.
West's California Code Forms, Family § 850, Comment Overview—Transmutation by Agreement or Transfer.

§ 852. Requirements

(a) A transmutation of real or personal property is not valid unless made in writing by an express declaration that is made, joined in, consented to, or accepted by the spouse whose interest in the property is adversely affected.

(b) A transmutation of real property is not effective as to third parties without notice thereof unless recorded.

(c) This section does not apply to a gift between the spouses of clothing, wearing apparel, jewelry, or other tangible articles of a personal nature that is used solely or principally by the spouse to whom the gift is made and that is not substantial in value taking into account the circumstances of the marriage.

(d) Nothing in this section affects the law governing characterization of property in which separate property and community property are commingled or otherwise combined.

(e) This section does not apply to or affect a transmutation of property made before January 1, 1985, and the law that would otherwise be applicable to that transmutation shall continue to apply. *(Stats.1992, c. 162 (A.B.2650), § 10, operative Jan. 1, 1994.)*

Cross References

Community property defined for purposes of this Code, see Family Code § 65.
Consent to nonprobate transfer, written consent not a transmutation, exception, see Probate Code § 5022.
Effect of recording, or the want thereof, see Civil Code § 1213 et seq.
Leasehold interest in real property, see Family Code § 700.
Nature of property, generally, see Civil Code § 654.
Personal property defined, see Civil Code § 663.
Presumptions and limitations of actions as to property acquired by wife, see Family Code § 803.

§ 852

MARRIAGE RIGHTS AND OBLIGATIONS

Property defined elsewhere, see Civil Code § 654.
Property defined for purposes of this Code, see Family Code § 113.
Property which may be disposed of by will, percentage of community property belonging to testator, see Probate Code § 6101.
Real property as coextensive with lands, tenements, and hereditaments, see Civil Code § 14; Code of Civil Procedure § 17; Penal Code § 7.
Real property defined, see Civil Code § 658; Evidence Code § 205; Health and Safety Code §§ 33390, 34215; Public Resources Code § 9802; Revenue and Taxation Code § 104.
References to husband, wife, spouses and married persons, persons included for purposes of this Code, see Family Code § 11.
Separate property defined for purposes of this Code, see Family Code § 130.
Separate property of married person, defined, see Family Code § 770.
Statute of frauds, see Civil Code § 1624.
Transfer of real property, method of transfer, see Civil Code § 1091.
Uniform Fraudulent Transfer Act, see Civil Code § 3439 et seq.

Research References

Forms

Asset Protection: Legal Planning, Strategies and Forms ¶ 4.04, Determining the Character of Property.
Asset Protection: Legal Planning, Strategies and Forms ¶ 4.07, Marital Agreements.
Asset Protection: Legal Planning, Strategies and Forms ¶ 13.01A, Charitable Contributions of Ira's and Other Retirement Plans.
1 California Transactions Forms--Estate Planning § 1:21, Severing Joint Tenancies in Real Property.
1 California Transactions Forms--Estate Planning § 1:24, Community Property Versus Joint Tenancy.
1 California Transactions Forms--Estate Planning § 1:25, Joint Tenancy or Community Property Treatment of Property in Revocable Trust.
2 California Transactions Forms--Estate Planning § 10:4, Community Property.
2 California Transactions Forms--Estate Planning § 10:7, Joint Tenancy.
2 California Transactions Forms--Estate Planning § 10:14, Formalities Required.
2 California Transactions Forms--Estate Planning § 10:19, Joint Tenancy Property.
2 California Transactions Forms--Estate Planning § 11:34, Agreement Entered Into Before January 1, 1985.
2 California Transactions Forms--Estate Planning § 11:35, Agreement Entered Into on or After January 1, 1985.
2 California Transactions Forms--Estate Planning § 11:36, Family Code §852 Transmutations and Rules Governing Fiduciary Relationships.
2 California Transactions Forms--Estate Planning § 11:59, Matters to Include in Transmutation Agreement.
3 California Transactions Forms--Estate Planning § 13:21, Transmutation.
4 California Transactions Forms--Estate Planning § 19:17, Separate Property.
4 California Transactions Forms--Estate Planning § 19:70, Characterization of Property.
1 California Transactions Forms--Family Law § 2:18, Reimbursement of Separate Property Contribution [Fam. Code §2640].
1 California Transactions Forms--Family Law § 2:42, Excess Tax Payments.
West's California Code Forms, Family § 850, Comment Overview--Transmutation by Agreement or Transfer.

§ 853. Characterization of property in will; admissibility in proceedings commenced before death of testator; waiver of right to joint and survivor annuity or survivor's benefits; written joinders or consents to nonprobate transfers of community property

(a) A statement in a will of the character of property is not admissible as evidence of a transmutation of the property in a proceeding commenced before the death of the person who made the will.

(b) A waiver of a right to a joint and survivor annuity or survivor's benefits under the federal Retirement Equity Act of 1984 (Public Law 98-397)[1] is not a transmutation of the community property rights of the person executing the waiver.

(c) A written joinder or written consent to a nonprobate transfer of community property on death that satisfies Section 852 is a transmutation and is governed by the law applicable to transmutations and not by Chapter 2 (commencing with Section 5010) of Part 1 of Division 5 of the Probate Code. *(Stats.1992, c. 162 (A.B.2650), § 10, operative Jan. 1, 1994. Amended by Stats.1993, c. 219 (A.B. 1500), § 100.)*

[1] See Short Title of 1984 Amendment note under 29 U.S.C.A. § 1001 for classifications of the Act.

Cross References

Community property defined for purposes of this Code, see Family Code § 65.
Consent to nonprobate transfer, written consent not a transmutation, exception, see Probate Code § 5022.
Effect of recording, or the want thereof, see Civil Code § 1213 et seq.
Leasehold interest in real property, see Family Code § 700.
Nature of property, generally, see Civil Code § 654.
Person defined for purposes of this Code, see Family Code § 105.
Personal property defined, see Civil Code § 663.
Presumptions and limitations of actions as to property acquired by wife, see Family Code § 803.
Proceeding defined for purposes of this Code, see Family Code § 110.
Property defined elsewhere, see Civil Code § 654.
Property defined for purposes of this Code, see Family Code § 113.
Property which may be disposed of by will, percentage of community property belonging to testator, see Probate Code § 6101.
Real property as coextensive with lands, tenements, and hereditaments, see Civil Code § 14; Code of Civil Procedure § 17; Penal Code § 7.
Real property defined, see Civil Code § 658; Evidence Code § 205; Health and Safety Code §§ 33390, 34215; Public Resources Code § 9802; Revenue and Taxation Code § 104.
Separate property of married person, defined, see Family Code § 770.
Transfer of real property, method of transfer, see Civil Code § 1091.

Research References

Forms

2 California Transactions Forms--Estate Planning § 11:35, Agreement Entered Into on or After January 1, 1985.
4 California Transactions Forms--Estate Planning § 19:57, Maintaining Confidentiality.
4 California Transactions Forms--Estate Planning § 19:70, Characterization of Property.
1 California Transactions Forms--Family Law § 2:46, No Transmutation.

Part 3

LIABILITY OF MARITAL PROPERTY

Chapter	Section
1. Definitions	900
2. General Rules of Liability	910
3. Reimbursement	920
4. Transitional Provisions	930
5. Liability for Death or Injury	1000

Cross References

Community property,
 Debts, liability for, see Family Code §§ 910, 911.
 Defined, see Probate Code § 28; Civil Code § 687; Family Code §§ 65, 760.
 Division of, see Family Code § 2600 et seq.
 Held in revocable trust, see Probate Code § 104.
 Interests of spouses defined, see Family Code § 751.
Consumer credit contracts, evidentiary effect of delivery of notice to contract signatory, community property, see Civil Code § 1799.98.
Contractual arrangements relating to property rights of spouses at death, see Probate Code § 140 et seq.
Decedent's property, passage of title, see Probate Code §§ 7000, 7001.
Disposition of estate without administration, passage of property to surviving spouse, see Probate Code § 13500 et seq.
Division of Property Act, dissolution of marriage, community estate including out-of-state real property, see Family Code § 2660.
Effect of death of married person on community and quasi-community property, see Probate Code § 100 et seq.
Intestate succession as to community property, see Probate Code § 6401.
Inventory of estate, community and separate property, see Probate Code § 8850.

Judgment creditors seek writ of execution to enforce a judgment made, entered, or enforceable pursuant to Family Code, see Code of Civil Procedure § 699.510.

Management or disposition of community property where spouse lacks legal capacity, see Probate Code § 3000 et seq.

Modification of ownership, interests in property, community property defined, see Civil Code § 687.

Nature of property, generally, see Civil Code § 654.

Personal property defined, see Civil Code § 663.

Presumptions and limitations of actions as to property acquired by wife, see Family Code § 803.

Property defined, see Civil Code § 654.

Property which may be disposed of by will, percentage of community property belonging to testator, see Probate Code § 6101.

Real property as coextensive with lands, tenements, and hereditaments, see Civil Code § 14; Code of Civil Procedure § 17; Penal Code § 7.

Real property defined, see Civil Code § 658; Evidence Code § 205; Health and Safety Code §§ 33390, 34215; Public Resources Code § 9802; Revenue and Taxation Code § 104.

Separate property of married person, defined, see Family Code § 770.

Setting aside homestead for the benefit of decedent's spouse or child, see Probate Code § 6520 et seq.

Simultaneous death, disposition of property, see Probate Code § 220 et seq.

Surviving spouse, defined, see Probate Code § 78.

CHAPTER 1. DEFINITIONS

Section
900. Construction of part.
901. Inoperative.
902. Debt.
903. Time debt is incurred.

§ 900. Construction of part

Unless the provision or context otherwise requires, the definitions in this chapter govern the construction of this part. *(Stats.1992, c. 162 (A.B.2650), § 10, operative Jan. 1, 1994.)*

Cross References

Consumer credit contracts, evidentiary effect of delivery of notice to contract signatory, see Civil Code § 1799.98.

Statutory construction, determination of legislative intent, see Code of Civil Procedure § 1859.

Statutory construction, general rules for statutes, see Government Code § 9603.

Statutory construction, language of writing, interpretation according to meaning in place of execution, see Code of Civil Procedure § 1858.

Statutory construction, preference to interpretations, construction in favor of natural right, see Code of Civil Procedure § 1866.

Research References

Forms

West's California Code Forms, Family § 781, Comment Overview—Damages for Injuries to Married Person.

§ 901. Inoperative

§ 902. Debt

"Debt" means an obligation incurred by a married person before or during marriage, whether based on contract, tort, or otherwise. *(Stats.1992, c. 162 (A.B.2650), § 10, operative Jan. 1, 1994.)*

Cross References

Person defined for purposes of this Code, see Family Code § 105.

References to husband, wife, spouses and married persons, persons included for purposes of this Code, see Family Code § 11.

§ 903. Time debt is incurred

A debt is "incurred" at the following time:

(a) In the case of a contract, at the time the contract is made.

(b) In the case of a tort, at the time the tort occurs.

(c) In other cases, at the time the obligation arises. *(Stats.1992, c. 162 (A.B.2650), § 10, operative Jan. 1, 1994.)*

Research References

Forms

Asset Protection: Legal Planning, Strategies and Forms ¶ 4.03, Community Property.

CHAPTER 2. GENERAL RULES OF LIABILITY

Section
910. Community estate; liability for debts.
911. Earnings of married persons; liability for premarital debts; earnings held in deposit accounts.
912. Quasi-community property; treatment.
913. Separate property of married person; liability for debt.
914. Personal liability for debts incurred by spouse; separate property applied to satisfaction of debt; statute of limitations.
915. Child or spousal support obligation not arising out of marriage; reimbursement of community.
916. Division of property; subsequent liability; right of reimbursement, interest and attorney's fees.

Cross References

Community property, debts, liability for, see Family Code §§ 910, 911.

Consumer credit contracts, evidentiary effect of delivery of notice to contract signatory, community property, see Civil Code § 1799.98.

Contractual arrangements relating to property rights of spouses at death, see Probate Code § 140 et seq.

Effect of death of married person on community and quasi-community property, see Probate Code §§ 100 et seq.

Judgment creditors seek writ of execution to enforce a judgment made, entered, or enforceable pursuant to Family Code, see Code of Civil Procedure § 699.510.

Quasi-community property, defined see Family Code § 125.

§ 910. Community estate; liability for debts

(a) Except as otherwise expressly provided by statute, the community estate is liable for a debt incurred by either spouse before or during marriage, regardless of which spouse has the management and control of the property and regardless of whether one or both spouses are parties to the debt or to a judgment for the debt.

(b) "During marriage" for purposes of this section does not include the period after the date of separation, as defined in Section 70, and before a judgment of dissolution of marriage or legal separation of the parties. *(Stats.1992, c. 162 (A.B.2650), § 10, operative Jan. 1, 1994. Amended by Stats.2016, c. 114 (S.B.1255), § 3, eff. Jan. 1, 2017.)*

Cross References

Bank account of married person, see Financial Code § 1401.

Businesses operated or managed by spouse, liability, see Family Code § 1100.

Child or spousal support obligation not arising out of marriage, reimbursement of community, see Family Code § 915.

Collection of judgment where judgment debtor is creditor of public entity, see Code of Civil Procedure § 708.710 et seq.

Community estate, defined, see Family Code § 63.

Community property, debts, liability for, see Family Code §§ 910, 911.

Conservatorship, see Probate Code § 3051.

Consumer credit contracts, evidentiary effect of delivery of notice to contract signatory, community property, see Civil Code § 1799.98.

Contractual arrangements relating to property rights of spouses at death, see Probate Code § 140 et seq.

Debt defined for purposes of this Part, see Family Code § 902.

Division of property, subsequent liability, see Family Code § 916.

Judgment and order defined for purposes of this Code, see Family Code § 100.

Judgment for child or spousal support, see Code of Civil Procedure § 703.070.

Property defined for purposes of this Code, see Family Code § 113.

References to husband, wife, spouses and married persons, persons included for purposes of this Code, see Family Code § 11.

§ 910

Right of married person to defend suit for spouse's right, see Code of Civil Procedure § 371.
Spouse of judgment debtor, earnings withholding order against, see Code of Civil Procedure § 706.109.
Time debt is incurred, see Family Code § 903.

Research References

Forms

Asset Protection: Legal Planning, Strategies and Forms ¶ 4.03, Community Property.
2 California Transactions Forms--Estate Planning § 10:14, Formalities Required.

§ 911. Earnings of married persons; liability for premarital debts; earnings held in deposit accounts

(a) The earnings of a married person during marriage are not liable for a debt incurred by the person's spouse before marriage. After the earnings of the married person are paid, they remain not liable so long as they are held in a deposit account in which the person's spouse has no right of withdrawal and are uncommingled with other property in the community estate, except property insignificant in amount.

(b) As used in this section:

(1) "Deposit account" has the meaning prescribed in paragraph (29) of subdivision (a) of Section 9102 of the Commercial Code.

(2) "Earnings" means compensation for personal services performed, whether as an employee or otherwise. *(Stats.1992, c. 162 (A.B.2650), § 10, operative Jan. 1, 1994. Amended by Stats.1999, c. 991 (S.B.45), § 42.5, operative July 1, 2001.)*

Cross References

Community estate, defined, see Family Code § 63.
Debt defined for purposes of this Part, see Family Code § 902.
Earnings and accumulations,
 After entry of judgment of separation, see Family Code § 772.
 During period of separation, see Family Code § 771.
Person defined for purposes of this Code, see Family Code § 105.
Property defined for purposes of this Code, see Family Code § 113.
References to husband, wife, spouses and married persons, persons included for purposes of this Code, see Family Code § 11.
Time debt is incurred, see Family Code § 903.

Research References

Forms

Asset Protection: Legal Planning, Strategies and Forms ¶ 4.03, Community Property.
Asset Protection: Legal Planning, Strategies and Forms ¶ 4.07, Marital Agreements.

§ 912. Quasi-community property; treatment

For the purposes of this part, quasi-community property is liable to the same extent, and shall be treated the same in all other respects, as community property. *(Stats.1992, c. 162 (A.B.2650), § 10, operative Jan. 1, 1994.)*

Cross References

Characterization of marital property, see Family Code § 760 et seq.
Community property defined for purposes of this Code, see Family Code § 65.
Effect of death of married person on community and quasi-community property, see Probate Code § 100 et seq.
Property defined for purposes of this Code, see Family Code § 113.
Quasi-community property, defined, see Family Code § 125.

§ 913. Separate property of married person; liability for debt

(a) The separate property of a married person is liable for a debt incurred by the person before or during marriage.

(b) Except as otherwise provided by statute:

(1) The separate property of a married person is not liable for a debt incurred by the person's spouse before or during marriage.

(2) The joinder or consent of a married person to an encumbrance of community estate property to secure payment of a debt incurred by the person's spouse does not subject the person's separate property to liability for the debt unless the person also incurred the debt. *(Stats.1992, c. 162 (A.B.2650), § 10, operative Jan. 1, 1994.)*

Cross References

Community estate defined for purposes of this Code, see Family Code § 63.
Consumer credit contracts, evidentiary effect of delivery of notice to contract signatory, community property, see Civil Code § 1799.98.
Contractual arrangements relating to property rights of spouses at death, see Probate Code § 140 et seq.
Debt defined for purposes of this Part, see Family Code § 902.
Person defined for purposes of this Code, see Family Code § 105.
Property defined for purposes of this Code, see Family Code § 113.
References to husband, wife, spouses and married persons, persons included for purposes of this Code, see Family Code § 11.
Separate property defined for purposes of this Code, see Family Code § 130.
Time debt is incurred, see Family Code § 903.

Research References

Forms

Asset Protection: Legal Planning, Strategies and Forms ¶ 4.03, Community Property.

§ 914. Personal liability for debts incurred by spouse; separate property applied to satisfaction of debt; statute of limitations

(a) Notwithstanding Section 913, a married person is personally liable for the following debts incurred by the person's spouse during marriage:

(1) A debt incurred for necessaries of life of the person's spouse before the date of separation of the spouses.

(2) Except as provided in Section 4302, a debt incurred for common necessaries of life of the person's spouse after the date of separation of the spouses.

(b) The separate property of a married person may be applied to the satisfaction of a debt for which the person is personally liable pursuant to this section. If separate property is so applied at a time when nonexempt property in the community estate or separate property of the person's spouse is available but is not applied to the satisfaction of the debt, the married person is entitled to reimbursement to the extent such property was available.

(c)(1) Except as provided in paragraph (2), the statute of limitations set forth in Section 366.2 of the Code of Civil Procedure shall apply if the spouse for whom the married person is personally liable dies.

(2) If the surviving spouse had actual knowledge of the debt prior to expiration of the period set forth in Section 366.2 of the Code of Civil Procedure and the personal representative of the deceased spouse's estate failed to provide the creditor asserting the claim under this section with a timely written notice of the probate administration of the estate in the manner provided for pursuant to Section 9050 of the Probate Code, the statute of limitations set forth in Section 337 or 339 of the Code of Civil Procedure, as applicable, shall apply.

(d) For purposes of this section, "date of separation" has the same meaning as set forth in Section 70. *(Stats.1992, c. 162 (A.B.2650), § 10, operative Jan. 1, 1994. Amended by Stats.1993, c. 219 (A.B. 1500), § 100.4; Stats.2001, c. 702 (A.B.539), § 1; Stats.2014, c. 71 (S.B.1304), § 53, eff. Jan. 1, 2015; Stats.2016, c. 114 (S.B.1255), § 4, eff. Jan. 1, 2017.)*

Cross References

Community estate defined for purposes of this Code, see Family Code § 63.
Consumer credit contracts, evidentiary effect of delivery of notice to contract signatory, community property, see Civil Code § 1799.98.
Contractual arrangements relating to property rights of spouses at death, see Probate Code § 140 et seq.

Debt defined for purposes of this Part, see Family Code § 902.
Person defined for purposes of this Code, see Family Code § 105.
Property defined for purposes of this Code, see Family Code § 113.
References to husband, wife, spouses and married persons, persons included for purposes of this Code, see Family Code § 11.
Reimbursement, see Family Code § 920.
Separate property defined for purposes of this Code, see Family Code § 130.
Spouses living separate by agreement, obligation of support, see Family Code § 4302.
Support, use of separate property while living together, see Family Code § 4301.
Time debt is incurred, see Family Code § 903.

Research References

Forms

Asset Protection: Legal Planning, Strategies and Forms ¶ 4.02, Common Law.
Asset Protection: Legal Planning, Strategies and Forms ¶ 4.08, Implications of Divorce.

§ 915. Child or spousal support obligation not arising out of marriage; reimbursement of community

(a) For the purpose of this part, a child or spousal support obligation of a married person that does not arise out of the marriage shall be treated as a debt incurred before marriage, regardless of whether a court order for support is made or modified before or during marriage and regardless of whether any installment payment on the obligation accrues before or during marriage.

(b) If property in the community estate is applied to the satisfaction of a child or spousal support obligation of a married person that does not arise out of the marriage, at a time when nonexempt separate income of the person is available but is not applied to the satisfaction of the obligation, the community estate is entitled to reimbursement from the person in the amount of the separate income, not exceeding the property in the community estate so applied.

(c) Nothing in this section limits the matters a court may take into consideration in determining or modifying the amount of a support order, including, but not limited to, the earnings of the spouses of the parties. *(Stats.1992, c. 162 (A.B.2650), § 10, operative Jan. 1, 1994. Amended by Stats.1993, c. 219 (A.B.1500), § 100.5.)*

Cross References

Community estate,
  Defined, see Family Code § 63.
  Liability for debts, see Family Code § 910.
Debt defined for purposes of this Part, see Family Code § 902.
Judgment and order defined for purposes of this Code, see Family Code § 100.
Person defined for purposes of this Code, see Family Code § 105.
Property defined for purposes of this Code, see Family Code § 113.
References to husband, wife, spouses and married persons, persons included for purposes of this Code, see Family Code § 11.
Spousal support defined for purposes of this Code, see Family Code § 142.
Support defined for purposes of this Code, see Family Code § 150.
Support order defined for purposes of this Code, see Family Code § 155.
Time debt is incurred, see Family Code § 903.

§ 916. Division of property; subsequent liability; right of reimbursement, interest and attorney's fees

(a) Notwithstanding any other provision of this chapter, after division of community and quasi-community property pursuant to Division 7 (commencing with Section 2500):

(1) The separate property owned by a married person at the time of the division and the property received by the person in the division is liable for a debt incurred by the person before or during marriage and the person is personally liable for the debt, whether or not the debt was assigned for payment by the person's spouse in the division.

(2) The separate property owned by a married person at the time of the division and the property received by the person in the division is not liable for a debt incurred by the person's spouse before or during marriage, and the person is not personally liable for the debt, unless the debt was assigned for payment by the person in the division of the property. Nothing in this paragraph affects the liability of property for the satisfaction of a lien on the property.

(3) The separate property owned by a married person at the time of the division and the property received by the person in the division is liable for a debt incurred by the person's spouse before or during marriage, and the person is personally liable for the debt, if the debt was assigned for payment by the person in the division of the property. If a money judgment for the debt is entered after the division, the property is not subject to enforcement of the judgment and the judgment may not be enforced against the married person, unless the person is made a party to the judgment for the purpose of this paragraph.

(b) If property of a married person is applied to the satisfaction of a money judgment pursuant to subdivision (a) for a debt incurred by the person that is assigned for payment by the person's spouse, the person has a right of reimbursement from the person's spouse to the extent of the property applied, with interest at the legal rate, and may recover reasonable attorney's fees incurred in enforcing the right of reimbursement. *(Stats.1992, c. 162 (A.B.2650), § 10, operative Jan. 1, 1994.)*

Cross References

Community property defined for purposes of this Code, see Family Code § 65.
Debt defined for purposes of this Part, see Family Code § 902.
Division of property, debts and liabilities, see Family Code § 2620 et seq.
Judgment and order defined for purposes of this Code, see Family Code § 100.
Person defined for purposes of this Code, see Family Code § 105.
Property defined for purposes of this Code, see Family Code § 113.
Quasi-community property defined for purposes of this Code, see Family Code § 125.
References to husband, wife, spouses and married persons, persons included for purposes of this Code, see Family Code § 11.
Separate property defined for purposes of this Code, see Family Code § 130.
Time debt is incurred, see Family Code § 903.

Research References

Forms

Asset Protection: Legal Planning, Strategies and Forms ¶ 4.08, Implications of Divorce.

CHAPTER 3. REIMBURSEMENT

Section
920. Conditions governing right of reimbursement.

Cross References

Dissolution of marriage, reimbursement,
  Contributions to the acquisition of property, see Family Code § 2640.
  Education or training, community contributions, see Family Code § 2641.

§ 920. Conditions governing right of reimbursement

A right of reimbursement provided by this part is subject to the following provisions:

(a) The right arises regardless of which spouse applies the property to the satisfaction of the debt, regardless of whether the property is applied to the satisfaction of the debt voluntarily or involuntarily, and regardless of whether the debt to which the property is applied is satisfied in whole or in part. The right is subject to an express written waiver of the right by the spouse in whose favor the right arises.

(b) The measure of reimbursement is the value of the property or interest in property at the time the right arises.

(c) The right shall be exercised not later than the earlier of the following times:

(1) Within three years after the spouse in whose favor the right arises has actual knowledge of the application of the property to the satisfaction of the debt.

(2) In proceedings for division of community and quasi-community property pursuant to Division 7 (commencing with Section 2500) or in proceedings upon the death of a spouse. *(Stats.1992, c. 162 (A.B.2650), § 10, operative Jan. 1, 1994.)*

Cross References

Applicability to all debts, reimbursement, see Family Code § 931.
Community property defined for purposes of this Code, see Family Code § 65.
Debt defined for purposes of this Part, see Family Code § 902.
Dissolution of marriage, reimbursement,
 Contributions to the acquisition of property, see Family Code § 2640.
 Education or training, community contributions, see Family Code § 2641.
Limitation on exercise of reimbursement right, see Family Code § 1000.
Proceeding defined for purposes of this Code, see Family Code § 110.
Property defined for purposes of this Code, see Family Code § 113.
Quasi-community property defined for purposes of this Code, see Family Code § 125.
References to husband, wife, spouses and married persons, persons included for purposes of this Code, see Family Code § 11.

Research References

Forms

Asset Protection: Legal Planning, Strategies and Forms ¶ 4.08, Implications of Divorce.

CHAPTER 4. TRANSITIONAL PROVISIONS

Section
930. Liability for debts enforced on or after Jan. 1, 1985.
931. Application of provisions governing reimbursement.

Cross References

Community estate defined, see Family Code § 63.

§ 930. Liability for debts enforced on or after Jan. 1, 1985

Except as otherwise provided by statute, this part governs the liability of separate property and property in the community estate and the personal liability of a married person for a debt enforced on or after January 1, 1985, regardless of whether the debt was incurred before, on, or after that date. *(Stats.1992, c. 162 (A.B.2650), § 10, operative Jan. 1, 1994. Amended by Stats.1993, c. 219 (A.B.1500), § 100.6.)*

Cross References

Community estate defined, see Family Code § 63.
Debt defined for purposes of this Part, see Family Code § 902.
Person defined for purposes of this Code, see Family Code § 105.
Property defined for purposes of this Code, see Family Code § 113.
References to husband, wife, spouses and married persons, persons included for purposes of this Code, see Family Code § 11.
Separate property defined for purposes of this Code, see Family Code § 130.
Time debt is incurred, see Family Code § 903.

Research References

Forms

Asset Protection: Legal Planning, Strategies and Forms ¶ 4.08, Implications of Divorce.

§ 931. Application of provisions governing reimbursement

The provisions of this part that govern reimbursement apply to all debts, regardless of whether satisfied before, on, or after January 1, 1985. *(Stats.1992, c. 162 (A.B.2650), § 10, operative Jan. 1, 1994.)*

Cross References

Debt defined for purposes of this Part, see Family Code § 902.

CHAPTER 5. LIABILITY FOR DEATH OR INJURY

Section
1000. Liability for injury or damage caused by spouse; property subject to satisfaction of liability; satisfaction out of insurance proceeds; limitation on exercise of reimbursement right.

Cross References

Effect of death of married person on community and quasi-community property, see Probate Code § 100 et seq.
Setting aside homestead for the benefit of decedent's spouse or child, see Probate Code § 6520 et seq.
Simultaneous death, disposition of property, see Probate Code § 220 et seq.
Surviving spouse, defined, see Probate Code § 78.

§ 1000. Liability for injury or damage caused by spouse; property subject to satisfaction of liability; satisfaction out of insurance proceeds; limitation on exercise of reimbursement right

(a) A married person is not liable for any injury or damage caused by the other spouse except in cases where the married person would be liable therefor if the marriage did not exist.

(b) The liability of a married person for death or injury to person or property shall be satisfied as follows:

(1) If the liability of the married person is based upon an act or omission which occurred while the married person was performing an activity for the benefit of the community, the liability shall first be satisfied from the community estate and second from the separate property of the married person.

(2) If the liability of the married person is not based upon an act or omission which occurred while the married person was performing an activity for the benefit of the community, the liability shall first be satisfied from the separate property of the married person and second from the community estate.

(c) This section does not apply to the extent the liability is satisfied out of proceeds of insurance for the liability, whether the proceeds are from property in the community estate or from separate property. Notwithstanding Section 920, no right of reimbursement under this section shall be exercised more than seven years after the spouse in whose favor the right arises has actual knowledge of the application of the property to the satisfaction of the debt. *(Stats.1992, c. 162 (A.B.2650), § 10, operative Jan. 1, 1994. Amended by Stats.1993, c. 219 (A.B.1500), § 100.7.)*

Cross References

Abstaining from injuring person or property of another, see Civil Code § 1708.
Community estate defined for purposes of this Code, see Family Code § 63.
Damages for suffering detriment from unlawful act or omission of another, see Civil Code § 3281.
Death of married person, effect on community and quasi-community property, see Probate Code § 100 et seq.
Debt defined for purposes of this Part, see Family Code § 902.
Educational loans, liabilities for death or injuries, assignment, see Family Code § 2627.
Injuries, division of,
 Generally, see Code of Civil Procedure § 27.
 Personal injuries, see Code of Civil Procedure § 29.
 Property damage, see Code of Civil Procedure § 28.
Joint tort-feasors, contribution and subrogation, see Code of Civil Procedure § 875.
Person defined for purposes of this Code, see Family Code § 105.
Persons equally liable for injury or damage, see Civil Code § 3524.
Property defined for purposes of this Code, see Family Code § 113.
References to husband, wife, spouses and married persons, persons included for purposes of this Code, see Family Code § 11.

Responsibility for willful acts and negligence, contributory negligence, see Civil Code § 1714.
Right of married person to sue without spouse being joined as party, see Code of Civil Procedure § 370.
Separate property defined for purposes of this Code, see Family Code § 130.

Research References
Forms

Asset Protection: Legal Planning, Strategies and Forms ¶ 4.03, Community Property.
West's California Code Forms, Family § 781, Comment Overview—Damages for Injuries to Married Person.

Part 4
MANAGEMENT AND CONTROL OF MARITAL PROPERTY

Section
1100. Community personal property; management and control; restrictions on disposition.
1101. Claim for breach of fiduciary duty; court ordered accounting; addition of name of spouse to community property; limitation of action; consent of spouse not required; remedies.
1102. Community real property; spouse's joinder in conveyances; application of section; limitation of actions.
1103. Management and control of community property; one or both spouses having conservator of estate or lacking legal capacity.

Cross References
Community property,
Debts, liability for, see Family Code §§ 910, 911.
Defined, see Probate Code § 28; Civil Code § 687; Family Code §§ 65, 760.
Division of, see Family Code § 2600 et seq.
Held in revocable trust, see Probate Code § 104.
Interests of spouses defined, see Family Code § 751.
Consumer credit contracts, evidentiary effect of delivery of notice to contract signatory, community property, see Civil Code § 1799.98.
Contractual arrangements relating to property rights of spouses at death, see Probate Code § 140 et seq.
Decedent's property, passage of title, see Probate Code §§ 7000, 7001.
Disposition of estate without administration, passage of property to surviving spouse, see Probate Code § 13500 et seq.
Division of Property Act, dissolution of marriage, community estate including out-of-state real property, see Family Code § 2660.
Effect of death of married person on community and quasi-community property, see Probate Code § 100 et seq.
Intestate succession as to community property, see Probate Code § 6401.
Inventory of estate, community and separate property, see Probate Code § 8850.
Judgment creditors seek writ of execution to enforce a judgment made, entered, or enforceable pursuant to Family Code, see Code of Civil Procedure § 699.510.
Management or disposition of community property where spouse lacks legal capacity, see Probate Code § 3000 et seq.
Modification of ownership, interests in property, community property defined, see Civil Code § 687.
Nature of property, generally, see Civil Code § 654.
Personal property defined, see Civil Code § 663.
Presumptions and limitations of actions as to property acquired by wife, see Family Code § 803.
Property defined, see Civil Code § 654.
Property which may be disposed of by will, percentage of community property belonging to testator, see Probate Code § 6101.
Real property as coextensive with lands, tenements, and hereditaments, see Civil Code § 14; Code of Civil Procedure § 17; Penal Code § 7.
Real property defined, see Civil Code § 658; Evidence Code § 205; Health and Safety Code §§ 33390, 34215; Public Resources Code § 9802; Revenue and Taxation Code § 104.
Separate property of married person, defined, see Family Code § 770.
Setting aside homestead for the benefit of decedent's spouse or child, see Probate Code § 6520 et seq.
Simultaneous death, disposition of property, see Probate Code § 220 et seq.
Surviving spouse, defined, see Probate Code § 78.

§ 1100. Community personal property; management and control; restrictions on disposition

(a) Except as provided in subdivisions (b), (c), and (d) and Sections 761 and 1103, either spouse has the management and control of the community personal property, whether acquired prior to or on or after January 1, 1975, with like absolute power of disposition, other than testamentary, as the spouse has of the separate estate of the spouse.

(b) A spouse may not make a gift of community personal property, or dispose of community personal property for less than fair and reasonable value, without the written consent of the other spouse. This subdivision does not apply to gifts mutually given by both spouses to third parties and to gifts given by one spouse to the other spouse.

(c) A spouse may not sell, convey, or encumber community personal property used as the family dwelling, or the furniture, furnishings, or fittings of the home, or the clothing or wearing apparel of the other spouse or minor children which is community personal property, without the written consent of the other spouse.

(d) Except as provided in subdivisions (b) and (c), and in Section 1102, a spouse who is operating or managing a business or an interest in a business that is all or substantially all community personal property has the primary management and control of the business or interest. Primary management and control means that the managing spouse may act alone in all transactions but shall give prior written notice to the other spouse of any sale, lease, exchange, encumbrance, or other disposition of all or substantially all of the personal property used in the operation of the business (including personal property used for agricultural purposes), whether or not title to that property is held in the name of only one spouse. Written notice is not, however, required when prohibited by the law otherwise applicable to the transaction.

Remedies for the failure by a managing spouse to give prior written notice as required by this subdivision are only as specified in Section 1101. A failure to give prior written notice shall not adversely affect the validity of a transaction nor of any interest transferred.

(e) Each spouse shall act with respect to the other spouse in the management and control of the community assets and liabilities in accordance with the general rules governing fiduciary relationships which control the actions of persons having relationships of personal confidence as specified in Section 721, until such time as the assets and liabilities have been divided by the parties or by a court. This duty includes the obligation to make full disclosure to the other spouse of all material facts and information regarding the existence, characterization, and valuation of all assets in which the community has or may have an interest and debts for which the community is or may be liable, and to provide equal access to all information, records, and books that pertain to the value and character of those assets and debts, upon request. *(Stats.1992, c. 162 (A.B.2650), § 10, operative Jan. 1, 1994. Amended by Stats.1993, c. 219 (A.B.1500), § 100.8.)*

Cross References
Community property defined, see Probate Code § 28; Civil Code § 687; Family Code §§ 65, 760.
Consideration, in general, see Civil Code § 1605 et seq.
Consumer credit contracts, evidentiary effect of delivery of notice to contract signatory, see Civil Code § 1799.98.
Creation of joint tenancy in personal property, see Civil Code § 683.
Death of married person, effect on community and quasi-community property, see Probate Code § 100 et seq.

§ 1100   MARRIAGE RIGHTS AND OBLIGATIONS

Effect of premarital agreements and other marital property agreements, see Family Code § 1500.
Employee retirement, death, benefit or savings plan, payments or refunds, see Family Code § 755.
Gifts, see Civil Code § 1146 et seq.
Immunity from liability of corporation, transfer agent or registrar, specified transfers, see Corporations Code § 420.
Interests of parties in community property, see Family Code § 751.
Joinder or consent by conservator, authority, court order, see Probate Code § 3072.
Leasehold interest in real property, see Family Code § 700.
Liens for service and storage of household goods and wearing apparel, see Civil Code § 3066.
Life and disability insurance, discharge of insurer by payment, see Insurance Code § 10172.
Management, control and disposition of community property where spouse lacks legal capacity, see Probate Code § 3051.
Management or disposition of community property where spouse lacks legal capacity, manner of joinder or consent, see Probate Code § 3073.
Minor defined for purposes of this Code, see Family Code § 6500.
Person defined for purposes of this Code, see Family Code § 105.
Personal property defined, see Civil Code §§ 14, 663.
Presumptions,
  Generally, see Evidence Code § 600.
  Consideration, see Evidence Code § 622.
Property defined for purposes of this Code, see Family Code § 113.
Protection of rights of spouse lacking legal capacity, see Probate Code § 3057.
Public employees' retirement system, payment or refund by system, discharge from adverse claims, see Government Code § 21263.
References to husband, wife, spouses and married persons, persons included for purposes of this Code, see Family Code § 11.
Satisfaction of joinder or consent requirements, see Probate Code § 3071.
State teachers' retirement system, discharge of system from liability for payments, see Education Code § 24613.

Research References

Forms

7PT1 Am. Jur. Pl. & Pr. Forms Community Property § 77, Statutory References.
Asset Protection: Legal Planning, Strategies and Forms ¶ 4.07, Marital Agreements.
California Practice Guide: Rutter Family Law Forms Form 9:2, Marital Agreement.
California Practice Guide: Rutter Family Law Forms Form 9:3, Marital Settlement Agreement.
4 California Transactions Forms--Business Entities § 19:82, Consent of Spouse.
3 California Transactions Forms--Business Transactions § 18:14, Spouses.
1 California Transactions Forms--Estate Planning § 7:2, Types of Gifts.
1 California Transactions Forms--Estate Planning § 7:14, Grant Deed Making Gift of Real Property.
1 California Transactions Forms--Estate Planning § 7:20, Declaration of Gift in View of Impending Death.
1 California Transactions Forms--Estate Planning § 7:26, Consent of Spouse to Gift.
1 California Transactions Forms--Estate Planning § 7:33, Restricted Endowment to Charitable Organization.
2 California Transactions Forms--Estate Planning § 10:4, Community Property.
2 California Transactions Forms--Estate Planning § 10:21, Life Insurance Generally.
2 California Transactions Forms--Estate Planning § 11:49, Introduction and Definition [Prob C § 140].
1 California Transactions Forms--Family Law § 1:99, Waiver of Management and Control of Property.
1 California Transactions Forms--Family Law § 2:3, Comprehensive Drafting.
1 California Transactions Forms--Family Law § 2:4, Fiduciary Duty.
1 California Transactions Forms--Family Law § 2:5, Disclosure Requirements.
1 California Transactions Forms--Family Law § 2:30, Overview.
1 California Transactions Forms--Family Law § 2:88, Marital Settlement Agreement.
West's California Code Forms, Family § 781, Comment Overview—Damages for Injuries to Married Person.
West's California Code Forms, Family § 1100, Comment Overview—Community Personal Property.
West's California Code Forms, Family § 1100 Form 1, Consent of Spouse to Gift by Other Spouse of Community Personal Property.
West's California Code Forms, Family § 1500 Form 1, Marital Agreement.
West's California Code Forms, Family § 2338 Form 8, Marital Agreement.
West's California Code Forms, Family § 2338 Form 9, Marital Agreement—Both Spouses Employed.
West's California Code Forms, Family § 2550 Form 3, Marital Agreement.
West's California Code Forms, Family § 2550 Form 4, Division of Property Clauses in Dissolution Settlement Agreement.
West's California Code Forms, Probate § 3080 Form 1, Petition for Support; for Injunctive Orders; for Determination of the Character of Property; for an Accounting; for Employment of Counsel; and for Attorney Fees and Costs.

§ 1101. Claim for breach of fiduciary duty; court ordered accounting; addition of name of spouse to community property; limitation of action; consent of spouse not required; remedies

(a) A spouse has a claim against the other spouse for any breach of the fiduciary duty that results in impairment to the claimant spouse's present undivided one-half interest in the community estate, including, but not limited to, a single transaction or a pattern or series of transactions, which transaction or transactions have caused or will cause a detrimental impact to the claimant spouse's undivided one-half interest in the community estate.

(b) A court may order an accounting of the property and obligations of the parties to a marriage and may determine the rights of ownership in, the beneficial enjoyment of, or access to, community property, and the classification of all property of the parties to a marriage.

(c) A court may order that the name of a spouse shall be added to community property held in the name of the other spouse alone or that the title of community property held in some other title form shall be reformed to reflect its community character, except with respect to any of the following:

(1) A partnership interest held by the other spouse as a general partner.

(2) An interest in a professional corporation or professional association.

(3) An asset of an unincorporated business if the other spouse is the only spouse involved in operating and managing the business.

(4) Any other property, if the revision would adversely affect the rights of a third person.

(d)(1) Except as provided in paragraph (2), any action under subdivision (a) shall be commenced within three years of the date a petitioning spouse had actual knowledge that the transaction or event for which the remedy is being sought occurred.

(2) An action may be commenced under this section upon the death of a spouse or in conjunction with an action for legal separation, dissolution of marriage, or nullity without regard to the time limitations set forth in paragraph (1).

(3) The defense of laches may be raised in any action brought under this section.

(4) Except as to actions authorized by paragraph (2), remedies under subdivision (a) apply only to transactions or events occurring on or after July 1, 1987.

(e) In any transaction affecting community property in which the consent of both spouses is required, the court may, upon the motion of a spouse, dispense with the requirement of the other spouse's consent if both of the following requirements are met:

(1) The proposed transaction is in the best interest of the community.

(2) Consent has been arbitrarily refused or cannot be obtained due to the physical incapacity, mental incapacity, or prolonged absence of the nonconsenting spouse.

(f) Any action may be brought under this section without filing an action for dissolution of marriage, legal separation, or nullity, or may be brought in conjunction with the action or upon the death of a spouse.

(g) Remedies for breach of the fiduciary duty by one spouse, including those set out in Sections 721 and 1100, shall include, but not be limited to, an award to the other spouse of 50 percent, or an amount equal to 50 percent, of any asset undisclosed or transferred in breach of the fiduciary duty plus attorney's fees and court costs. The value of the asset shall be determined to be its highest value at the date of the breach of the fiduciary duty, the date of the sale or disposition of the asset, or the date of the award by the court.

(h) Remedies for the breach of the fiduciary duty by one spouse, as set forth in Sections 721 and 1100, when the breach falls within the ambit of Section 3294 of the Civil Code shall include, but not be limited to, an award to the other spouse of 100 percent, or an amount equal to 100 percent, of any asset undisclosed or transferred in breach of the fiduciary duty. *(Stats.1992, c. 162 (A.B.2650), § 10, operative Jan. 1, 1994. Amended by Stats.2001, c. 703 (A.B.583), § 1.)*

Application

For application of Stats.2001, c. 703 (A.B.583), see § 8 of that act.

Cross References

Community estate defined for purposes of this Code, see Family Code § 63.
Community property defined for purposes of this Code, see Family Code § 65.
Court order to authorize particular transactions, proceeding for, see Probate Code § 3101.
Exemplary damages, when allowable, see Civil Code § 3294.
Judgment and order defined for purposes of this Code, see Family Code § 100.
Person defined for purposes of this Code, see Family Code § 105.
Property defined for purposes of this Code, see Family Code § 113.
References to husband, wife, spouses and married persons, persons included for purposes of this Code, see Family Code § 11.
Spouse lacking legal capacity, protection of rights, see Probate Code § 3057.
State teachers' retirement system,
    Election of disability and death benefit coverage, spouse's refusal to sign election document, see Education Code § 23704.
    Spouse's refusal to sign application, right to action, see Education Code § 22454.
State teachers' retirement system cash balance plan, rights to benefits, court enforcement of spousal signature requirement, see Education Code § 26704.

Research References

Forms

Asset Protection: Legal Planning, Strategies and Forms ¶ 4.08, Implications of Divorce.
2 California Transactions Forms--Estate Planning § 10:4, Community Property.
2 California Transactions Forms--Estate Planning § 10:21, Life Insurance Generally.
1 California Transactions Forms--Family Law § 1:99, Waiver of Management and Control of Property.
1 California Transactions Forms--Family Law § 2:9, Remedies for False Disclosure.
1 California Transactions Forms--Family Law § 2:81, Potential Community Assets and Obligations.
West's California Code Forms, Family § 1100, Comment Overview--Community Personal Property.

§ 1102. Community real property; spouse's joinder in conveyances; application of section; limitation of actions

(a) Except as provided in Sections 761 and 1103, either spouse has the management and control of the community real property, whether acquired prior to, or on or after January 1, 1975, but both spouses, either personally or by a duly authorized agent, are required to join in executing an instrument by which that community real property or an interest therein is leased for a longer period than one year, or is sold, conveyed, or encumbered.

(b) This section does not apply to a lease, mortgage, conveyance, or transfer of real property, or of an interest in real property, between spouses.

(c) Notwithstanding subdivision (b), both of the following shall apply:

(1) The sole lease, contract, mortgage, or deed of the husband, holding the record title to community real property, to a lessee, purchaser, or encumbrancer, in good faith without knowledge of the marriage relation, shall be presumed to be valid if executed prior to January 1, 1975.

(2) The sole lease, contract, mortgage, or deed of either spouse, holding the record title to community real property, to a lessee, purchaser, or encumbrancer, in good faith without knowledge of the marriage relation, shall be presumed to be valid if executed on or after January 1, 1975.

(d) An action to avoid an instrument mentioned in this section, affecting any property standing of record in the name of either spouse alone, executed by the spouse alone, shall not be commenced after the expiration of one year from the filing for record of that instrument in the recorder's office in the county in which the land is situated.

(e) This section does not preclude either spouse from encumbering that spouse's interest in community real property, as provided in Section 2033, to pay reasonable attorney's fees in order to retain or maintain legal counsel in a proceeding for dissolution of marriage, for nullity of marriage, or for legal separation of the parties. *(Stats.1992, c. 162 (A.B.2650), § 10, operative Jan. 1, 1994. Amended by Stats.1993, c. 219 (A.B.1500), § 101; Stats.2014, c. 82 (S.B.1306), § 18, eff. Jan. 1, 2015; Stats.2019, c. 115 (A.B.1817), § 11, eff. Jan. 1, 2020.)*

Cross References

Combining proceedings with administration of estate, see Probate Code § 202.
Community property, defined, see Family Code § 65.
County defined for purposes of this Code, see Family Code § 67.
Division of community estate, see Family Code § 2600 et seq.
False representations, sale of real estate by married person, see Penal Code § 534.
Instruments void against purchasers, see Civil Code §§ 1227, 1228.
Interest of parties in community property, see Family Code § 751.
Judgment and order defined for purposes of this Code, see Family Code § 100.
Management or disposition of community property where spouse lacks legal capacity,
    Generally, see Probate Code § 3000 et seq.
    Manner of joinder or consent, see Probate Code § 3073.
Nature of property, generally, see Civil Code § 654.
Personal property defined, see Civil Code § 663.
Presumptions and limitations of actions as to property acquired by wife, see Family Code § 803.
Presumptions, generally, see Evidence Code § 600 et seq.
Presumptions, real property acquired by wife during marriage, see Family Code § 803.
Proceeding defined for purposes of this Code, see Family Code § 110.
Property acquired during marriage, characterization of, see Family Code § 760.
Property defined elsewhere, see Civil Code § 654.
Property defined for purposes of this Code, see Family Code § 113.
Recording, effect, see Civil Code § 1213 et seq.
Real property as coextensive with lands, tenements, and hereditaments, see Civil Code § 14; Code of Civil Procedure § 17; Penal Code § 7.
Real property defined, see Civil Code §§ 14, 658; Evidence Code § 205; Health and Safety Code §§ 33390, 34215; Public Resources Code § 9802; Revenue and Taxation Code § 104.
References to husband, wife, spouses and married persons, persons included for purposes of this Code, see Family Code § 11.
Satisfaction of joinder or consent requirements, see Probate Code § 3071.
Separate property of married person, defined, see Family Code §§ 130, 770.
Setting aside homestead for the benefit of decedent's spouse or child, see Probate Code § 6520 et seq.
Simultaneous death, disposition of property, see Probate Code § 220 et seq.
Statute of frauds, see Civil Code § 1624.

§ 1102

MARRIAGE RIGHTS AND OBLIGATIONS

Transfer of real property,
  Effect, see Civil Code § 1104 et seq.
  Mode of transfer, see Civil Code § 1091 et seq.

Research References

Forms

7PT1 Am. Jur. Pl. & Pr. Forms Community Property § 19, Statutory References.
California Practice Guide: Rutter Family Law Forms Form 1:20, Ex Parte Application and Request for Order Re Objection to Family Law Attorney's Real Property Lien and Request to Stay Recordation.
3 California Transactions Forms--Business Transactions § 18:14, Spouses.
2 California Transactions Forms--Estate Planning § 10:4, Community Property.
West's California Code Forms, Family § 1100, Comment Overview—Community Personal Property.
West's California Code Forms, Family § 2033 Form 2, Trust Deed Creating Attorney's Lien.

§ 1103. Management and control of community property; one or both spouses having conservator of estate or lacking legal capacity

(a) Where one or both of the spouses either has a conservator of the estate or lacks legal capacity to manage and control community property, the procedure for management and control (which includes disposition) of the community property is that prescribed in Part 6 (commencing with Section 3000) of Division 4 of the Probate Code.

(b) Where one or both spouses either has a conservator of the estate or lacks legal capacity to give consent to a gift of community personal property or a disposition of community personal property without a valuable consideration as required by Section 1100 or to a sale, conveyance, or encumbrance of community personal property for which a consent is required by Section 1100, the procedure for that gift, disposition, sale, conveyance, or encumbrance is that prescribed in Part 6 (commencing with Section 3000) of Division 4 of the Probate Code.

(c) Where one or both spouses either has a conservator of the estate or lacks legal capacity to join in executing a lease, sale, conveyance, or encumbrance of community real property or any interest therein as required by Section 1102, the procedure for that lease, sale, conveyance, or encumbrance is that prescribed in Part 6 (commencing with Section 3000) of Division 4 of the Probate Code. *(Stats.1992, c. 162 (A.B.2650), § 10, operative Jan. 1, 1994.)*

Cross References

Community property,
  Debts, liability for, see Family Code §§ 910, 911.
  Defined, see Probate Code § 28; Civil Code § 687; Family Code §§ 65, 760.
  Division of, see Family Code § 2600 et seq.
  Held in revocable trust, see Probate Code § 104.
  Interests of spouses defined, see Family Code § 751.
  Personal property, management and control, restrictions on disposition, see Family Code § 1100.
Community property defined for purposes of this Code, see Family Code § 65.
Conservatorship or lack of legal capacity, consent or joinder, see Probate Code § 3012.
Conservatorship or lack of legal capacity of married persons, substitute for joinder or consent, see Probate Code § 3071.
Establishment of conservatorship, see Probate Code § 1800 et seq.
Property defined for purposes of this Code, see Family Code § 113.
References to husband, wife, spouses and married persons, persons included for purposes of this Code, see Family Code § 11.

Research References

Forms

7PT1 Am. Jur. Pl. & Pr. Forms Community Property § 77, Statutory References.

West's California Code Forms, Family § 781, Comment Overview—Damages for Injuries to Married Person.

Part 5
MARITAL AGREEMENTS

Chapter	Section
1. General Provisions	1500
2. Uniform Premarital Agreement Act	1600
3. Agreements Between Spouses	1620

Cross References

County employees retirement law of 1937, optional retirement allowances, notice to spouse of member's selection of benefits or change of beneficiary, see Government Code § 31760.3.
Public employees' retirement system, notice to spouse of selection of benefits or change of beneficiary, see Government Code § 21261.
State teachers' retirement system,
  Applications for benefits, spousal signature, see Education Code § 22453.
  Election of disability and death benefit coverage, requirements, see Education Code § 23703.
State teachers' retirement system cash balance plan, rights to benefits, signature of spouse required, see Education Code § 26703.

CHAPTER 1. GENERAL PROVISIONS

Section
1500. Effect of premarital agreements and other marital property agreements.
1501. Agreements by minors.
1502. Recording of agreements.
1503. Law applicable to preexisting premarital agreements.

§ 1500. Effect of premarital agreements and other marital property agreements

The property rights of spouses prescribed by statute may be altered by a premarital agreement or other marital property agreement. *(Stats.1992, c. 162 (A.B.2650), § 10, operative Jan. 1, 1994. Amended by Stats.2014, c. 82 (S.B.1306), § 19, eff. Jan. 1, 2015.)*

Cross References

Community property, defined, see Family Code § 65.
County employees retirement law of 1937, optional retirement allowances, notice to spouse of member's selection of benefits or change of beneficiary, see Government Code § 31760.3.
Debts and liabilities, see Family Code § 2620 et seq.
Division of property, see Family Code § 2500 et seq.
Jointly held separate property, division, see Family Code § 2650.
Liability of marital property, see Family Code § 900 et seq.
Presumptions, community property in joint title, see Family Code § 2580.
Property defined for purposes of this Code, see Family Code § 113.
Real property including leasehold interests, see Family Code § 700.
Real property located in another state, see Family Code § 2660.
References to husband, wife, spouses and married persons, persons included for purposes of this Code, see Family Code § 11.
Relations of husband and wife, see Family Code §§ 720, 721.
Retirement plan benefits, division, see Family Code § 2610.
Separate property, defined, see Family Code § 130.
Special rules for division of community estate, see Family Code § 2600 et seq.
Spousal support, defined, see Family Code § 142.
State teachers' retirement system,
  Applications for benefits, spousal signature, see Education Code § 22453.
  Election of disability and death benefit coverage, requirements, see Education Code § 23703.
State teachers' retirement system cash balance plan, rights to benefits, signature of spouse required, see Education Code § 26703.

Research References

Forms

Asset Protection: Legal Planning, Strategies and Forms ¶ 4.07, Marital Agreements.

2 California Transactions Forms--Estate Planning § 11:39, General Considerations.
2 California Transactions Forms--Estate Planning § 11:45, Introduction.
1 California Transactions Forms--Family Law § 1:71, Binding Agreement With Specific Family Code Waivers.
West's California Code Forms, Family § 1500, Comment Overview—Marital Agreements and Premarital Agreements.

§ 1501. Agreements by minors

A minor may make a valid premarital agreement or other marital property agreement if the minor is emancipated, is otherwise capable of contracting marriage pursuant to Section 302 or 303, or has entered or is entering a marriage that is valid in the jurisdiction where the marriage is solemnized. *(Stats.1992, c. 162 (A.B.2650), § 10, operative Jan. 1, 1994. Amended by Stats.2018, c. 660 (S.B.273), § 7, eff. Jan. 1, 2019.)*

Cross References

Age of majority, see Family Code § 6500 et seq.
Capacity of minors, see Family Code §§ 6700, 6701.
Disaffirmance of contracts, see Family Code §§ 6710 et seq., 6751.
Minor defined for purposes of this Code, see Family Code § 6500.
Property defined for purposes of this Code, see Family Code § 113.

Research References

Forms

2 California Transactions Forms--Estate Planning § 11:39, General Considerations.
West's California Code Forms, Family § 1500, Comment Overview—Marital Agreements and Premarital Agreements.

§ 1502. Recording of agreements

(a) A premarital agreement or other marital property agreement that is executed and acknowledged or proved in the manner that a grant of real property is required to be executed and acknowledged or proved may be recorded in the office of the recorder of each county in which real property affected by the agreement is situated.

(b) Recording or nonrecording of a premarital agreement or other marital property agreement has the same effect as recording or nonrecording of a grant of real property. *(Stats.1992, c. 162 (A.B.2650), § 10, operative Jan. 1, 1994.)*

Cross References

County defined for purposes of this Code, see Family Code § 67.
Property defined for purposes of this Code, see Family Code § 113.

Research References

Forms

Asset Protection: Legal Planning, Strategies and Forms ¶ 4.07, Marital Agreements.
2 California Transactions Forms--Estate Planning § 11:39, General Considerations.
2 California Transactions Forms--Estate Planning § 11:45, Introduction.
1 California Transactions Forms--Family Law § 1:8, Acknowledgment and Recordation.
West's California Code Forms, Family § 1500, Comment Overview—Marital Agreements and Premarital Agreements.

§ 1503. Law applicable to preexisting premarital agreements

Nothing in this chapter affects the validity or effect of premarital agreements made before January 1, 1986, and the validity and effect of those agreements shall continue to be determined by the law applicable to the agreements before January 1, 1986. *(Stats.1992, c. 162 (A.B.2650), § 10, operative Jan. 1, 1994.)*

Research References

Forms

1 California Transactions Forms--Family Law § 1:5, Governing Law, Form, and Execution.

CHAPTER 2. UNIFORM PREMARITAL AGREEMENT ACT

Article	Section
1. Preliminary Provisions	1600
2. Premarital Agreements	1610

Cross References

Domestic partner registration, rights, protections and benefits, responsibilities, obligations and duties under law, date of registration as equivalent of date of marriage, see Family Code § 297.5.
Other uniform acts in the Family Code,
    Uniform Act on Blood Tests to Determine Paternity, see Family Code § 7550 et seq.
    Uniform Child Custody Jurisdiction and Enforcement Act, see Family Code § 3400 et seq.
    Uniform Divorce Recognition Act, see Family Code § 2090 et seq.
    Uniform Interstate Enforcement of Domestic Violence Protection Orders Act, see Family Code § 6400 et seq.
    Uniform Interstate Family Act, see Family Code § 5700.101 et seq.
    Uniform Parentage Act, see Family Code § 7600 et seq.
Uniform act, construction of provisions, see Family Code § 3.

ARTICLE 1. PRELIMINARY PROVISIONS

Section
1600. Short title.
1601. Effective date of chapter.

§ 1600. Short title

This chapter may be cited as the Uniform Premarital Agreement Act. *(Stats.1992, c. 162 (A.B.2650), § 10, operative Jan. 1, 1994.)*

Cross References

Uniform Act, construction of provisions, see Family Code § 3.

Research References

Forms

Asset Protection: Legal Planning, Strategies and Forms ¶ 4.07, Marital Agreements.
1 California Transactions Forms--Estate Planning § 6:28, Exceptions to Omitted Spouse Statute.
1 California Transactions Forms--Estate Planning § 6:99, Omitted Spouse Made Valid Agreement Waiving Right to Share in Decedent's Estate.
2 California Transactions Forms--Estate Planning § 11:37, Introduction.
1 California Transactions Forms--Family Law § 1:2, Nature and Advantages of Agreement.
1 California Transactions Forms--Family Law § 1:5, Governing Law, Form, and Execution.
1 California Transactions Forms--Family Law § 4:7, Effect of Subsequent Marriage Between Cohabitants.
West's California Code Forms, Family § 1500, Comment Overview—Marital Agreements and Premarital Agreements.

§ 1601. Effective date of chapter

This chapter is effective on and after January 1, 1986, and applies to any premarital agreement executed on or after that date. *(Stats.1992, c. 162 (A.B.2650), § 10, operative Jan. 1, 1994.)*

Cross References

Premarital agreement defined for purposes of this Chapter, see Family Code § 1610.

§ 1601 MARRIAGE RIGHTS AND OBLIGATIONS

Uniform Act, construction of provisions, see Family Code § 3.

Research References

Forms

2 California Transactions Forms--Estate Planning § 11:41, Formalities.
1 California Transactions Forms--Family Law § 1:5, Governing Law, Form, and Execution.

ARTICLE 2. PREMARITAL AGREEMENTS

Section
1610. Definitions.
1611. Form and execution of agreement; consideration.
1612. Subject matter of premarital agreements.
1613. Effective date of agreements.
1614. Amendment or revocation of agreements.
1615. Unenforceable agreements; unconscionability; voluntariness.
1616. Void marriage, effect on agreement.
1617. Limitation of actions; equitable defenses including laches and estoppel.

Cross References

Uniform act, construction of provisions, see Family Code § 3.

§ 1610. Definitions

As used in this chapter:

(a) "Premarital agreement" means an agreement between prospective spouses made in contemplation of marriage and to be effective upon marriage.

(b) "Property" means an interest, present or future, legal or equitable, vested or contingent, in real or personal property, including income and earnings. *(Stats.1992, c. 162 (A.B.2650), § 10, operative Jan. 1, 1994.)*

Cross References

Community property defined, see Probate Code § 28; Civil Code § 687; Family Code §§ 65, 760.
Nature of property, generally, see Civil Code § 654.
Personal property defined, see Civil Code § 663.
Property defined for purposes of this Code, see Family Code § 113.
Real property as coextensive with lands, tenements, and hereditaments, see Civil Code § 14; Code of Civil Procedure § 17; Penal Code § 7.
Real property defined, see Civil Code §§ 14, 658; Evidence Code § 205; Health and Safety Code §§ 33390, 34215; Public Resources Code § 9802; Revenue and Taxation Code § 104.
References to husband, wife, spouses and married persons, persons included for purposes of this Code, see Family Code § 11.
Separate property of married person, defined, see Family Code §§ 130, 770.
Uniform Act, construction of provisions, see Family Code § 3.

Research References

Forms

California Practice Guide: Rutter Family Law Forms Form 9:1, Premarital Agreement.
1 California Transactions Forms--Estate Planning § 6:28, Exceptions to Omitted Spouse Statute.
2 California Transactions Forms--Estate Planning § 11:37, Introduction.
2 California Transactions Forms--Estate Planning § 11:39, General Considerations.
2 California Transactions Forms--Estate Planning § 11:41, Formalities.
1 California Transactions Forms--Family Law § 1:2, Nature and Advantages of Agreement.
1 California Transactions Forms--Family Law § 1:6, Subject Matter; Altering Rights.
1 California Transactions Forms--Family Law § 1:27, Complete Agreement.
1 California Transactions Forms--Family Law § 1:37, Agreement in Contemplation and Consideration of Marriage; Complex Provision.
1 California Transactions Forms--Family Law § 4:7, Effect of Subsequent Marriage Between Cohabitants.
1 California Transactions Forms--Family Law § 4:9, Rights to Income.

West's California Code Forms, Family § 1611, Comment Overview—Premarital Agreements.
West's California Code Forms, Family § 1611 Form 1, Premarital Agreement.

§ 1611. Form and execution of agreement; consideration

A premarital agreement shall be in writing and signed by both parties. It is enforceable without consideration. *(Stats.1992, c. 162 (A.B.2650), § 10, operative Jan. 1, 1994.)*

Cross References

Premarital agreement defined for purposes of this Chapter, see Family Code § 1610.
Uniform Act, construction of provisions, see Family Code § 3.

Research References

Forms

1 California Transactions Forms--Estate Planning § 6:28, Exceptions to Omitted Spouse Statute.
2 California Transactions Forms--Estate Planning § 11:41, Formalities.
1 California Transactions Forms--Family Law § 1:5, Governing Law, Form, and Execution.
1 California Transactions Forms--Family Law § 1:8, Acknowledgment and Recordation.
1 California Transactions Forms--Family Law § 1:19, Consideration.
West's California Code Forms, Family § 1611, Comment Overview—Premarital Agreements.

§ 1612. Subject matter of premarital agreements

(a) Parties to a premarital agreement may contract with respect to all of the following:

(1) The rights and obligations of each of the parties in any of the property of either or both of them whenever and wherever acquired or located.

(2) The right to buy, sell, use, transfer, exchange, abandon, lease, consume, expend, assign, create a security interest in, mortgage, encumber, dispose of, or otherwise manage and control property.

(3) The disposition of property upon separation, marital dissolution, death, or the occurrence or nonoccurrence of any other event.

(4) The making of a will, trust, or other arrangement to carry out the provisions of the agreement.

(5) The ownership rights in and disposition of the death benefit from a life insurance policy.

(6) The choice of law governing the construction of the agreement.

(7) Any other matter, including their personal rights and obligations, not in violation of public policy or a statute imposing a criminal penalty.

(b) The right of a child to support may not be adversely affected by a premarital agreement.

(c) Any provision in a premarital agreement regarding spousal support, including, but not limited to, a waiver of it, is not enforceable if the party against whom enforcement of the spousal support provision is sought was not represented by independent counsel at the time the agreement containing the provision was signed, or if the provision regarding spousal support is unconscionable at the time of enforcement. An otherwise unenforceable provision in a premarital agreement regarding spousal support may not become enforceable solely because the party against whom enforcement is sought was represented by independent counsel. *(Stats.1992, c. 162 (A.B.2650), § 10, operative Jan. 1, 1994. Amended by Stats.2001, c. 286 (S.B.78), § 1.)*

Cross References

Contracts concerning will or succession, see Probate Code § 21700.
Premarital agreement defined for purposes of this Chapter, see Family Code § 1610.
Property defined for purposes of this Chapter, see Family Code § 1610.

Property defined for purposes of this Code, see Family Code § 113.
Spousal support defined for purposes of this Code, see Family Code § 142.
Support defined for purposes of this Code, see Family Code § 150.
Surviving spouse, waiver of rights, see Probate Code § 140 et seq.
Uniform Act, construction of provisions, see Family Code § 3.

Research References
Forms

Asset Protection: Legal Planning, Strategies and Forms ¶ 4.07, Marital Agreements.
California Practice Guide: Rutter Family Law Forms Form 9:1, Premarital Agreement.
2 California Transactions Forms--Estate Planning § 11:37, Introduction.
2 California Transactions Forms--Estate Planning § 11:42, Scope of Statutory Framework.
2 California Transactions Forms--Estate Planning § 11:48, Governing Contractual Provisions [CC §§1550 et seq., Fam C §721(B)].
2 California Transactions Forms--Estate Planning § 11:60, Matters to be Included in Premarital Agreement.
2 California Transactions Forms--Estate Planning § 11:69, Premarital Agreement.
1 California Transactions Forms--Family Law § 1:2, Nature and Advantages of Agreement.
1 California Transactions Forms--Family Law § 1:6, Subject Matter; Altering Rights.
1 California Transactions Forms--Family Law § 1:105, Spousal Support.
1 California Transactions Forms--Family Law § 4:67, Agreement Becoming Prenuptial Agreement.

§ 1613. Effective date of agreements

A premarital agreement becomes effective upon marriage. *(Stats. 1992, c. 162 (A.B.2650), § 10, operative Jan. 1, 1994.)*

Cross References

Premarital agreement defined for purposes of this Chapter, see Family Code § 1610.
Uniform Act, construction of provisions, see Family Code § 3.

Research References
Forms

1 California Transactions Forms--Family Law § 1:5, Governing Law, Form, and Execution.
West's California Code Forms, Family § 1611, Comment Overview—Premarital Agreements.

§ 1614. Amendment or revocation of agreements

After marriage, a premarital agreement may be amended or revoked only by a written agreement signed by the parties. The amended agreement or the revocation is enforceable without consideration. *(Stats.1992, c. 162 (A.B.2650), § 10, operative Jan. 1, 1994.)*

Cross References

Premarital agreement defined for purposes of this Chapter, see Family Code § 1610.
Uniform Act, construction of provisions, see Family Code § 3.

Research References
Forms

2 California Transactions Forms--Estate Planning § 11:43, Amendment or Revocation After Marriage.
2 California Transactions Forms--Estate Planning § 11:47, Formalities.
2 California Transactions Forms--Estate Planning § 11:48, Governing Contractual Provisions [CC §§1550 et seq., Fam C §721(B)].
1 California Transactions Forms--Family Law § 1:5, Governing Law, Form, and Execution.
West's California Code Forms, Family § 1611, Comment Overview—Premarital Agreements.

§ 1615. Unenforceable agreements; unconscionability; voluntariness

(a) A premarital agreement is not enforceable if the party against whom enforcement is sought proves either of the following:

(1) That party did not execute the agreement voluntarily.

(2) The agreement was unconscionable when it was executed and, before execution of the agreement, all of the following applied to that party:

(A) That party was not provided a fair, reasonable, and full disclosure of the property or financial obligations of the other party.

(B) That party did not voluntarily and expressly waive, in writing, any right to disclosure of the property or financial obligations of the other party beyond the disclosure provided.

(C) That party did not have, or reasonably could not have had, an adequate knowledge of the property or financial obligations of the other party.

(b) An issue of unconscionability of a premarital agreement shall be decided by the court as a matter of law.

(c) For the purposes of subdivision (a), it shall be deemed that a premarital agreement was not executed voluntarily unless the court finds in writing or on the record all of the following:

(1) The party against whom enforcement is sought was represented by independent legal counsel at the time of signing the agreement or, after being advised to seek independent legal counsel, expressly waived, in a separate writing, representation by independent legal counsel. The advisement to seek independent legal counsel shall be made at least seven calendar days before the final agreement is signed.

(2) One of the following:

(A) For an agreement executed between January 1, 2002, and January 1, 2020, the party against whom enforcement is sought had not less than seven calendar days between the time that party was first presented with the final agreement and advised to seek independent legal counsel and the time the agreement was signed. This requirement does not apply to nonsubstantive amendments that do not change the terms of the agreement.

(B) For an agreement executed on or after January 1, 2020, the party against whom enforcement is sought had not less than seven calendar days between the time that party was first presented with the final agreement and the time the agreement was signed, regardless of whether the party is represented by legal counsel. This requirement does not apply to nonsubstantive amendments that do not change the terms of the agreement.

(3) The party against whom enforcement is sought, if unrepresented by legal counsel, was fully informed of the terms and basic effect of the agreement as well as the rights and obligations the party was giving up by signing the agreement, and was proficient in the language in which the explanation of the party's rights was conducted and in which the agreement was written. The explanation of the rights and obligations relinquished shall be memorialized in writing and delivered to the party prior to signing the agreement. The unrepresented party shall, on or before the signing of the premarital agreement, execute a document declaring that the party received the information required by this paragraph and indicating who provided that information.

(4) The agreement and the writings executed pursuant to paragraphs (1) and (3) were not executed under duress, fraud, or undue influence, and the parties did not lack capacity to enter into the agreement.

(5) Any other factors the court deems relevant. *(Stats.1992, c. 162 (A.B.2650), § 10, operative Jan. 1, 1994. Amended by Stats.2001, c. 286 (S.B.78), § 2; Stats.2019, c. 115 (A.B.1817), § 12, eff. Jan. 1, 2020; Stats.2019, c. 193 (A.B.1380), § 1, eff. Jan. 1, 2020.)*

Cross References

Contracts concerning will or succession, see Probate Code § 21700.
Premarital agreement defined for purposes of this Chapter, see Family Code § 1610.

§ 1615 MARRIAGE RIGHTS AND OBLIGATIONS

Property defined for purposes of this Chapter, see Family Code § 1610.
Property defined for purposes of this Code, see Family Code § 113.
Surviving spouse, waiver of rights, see Probate Code § 140 et seq.
Uniform Act, construction of provisions, see Family Code § 3.

Research References

Forms

Asset Protection: Legal Planning, Strategies and Forms ¶ 4.07, Marital Agreements.
California Practice Guide: Rutter Family Law Forms Form 9:1, Premarital Agreement.
1 California Transactions Forms--Estate Planning § 6:28, Exceptions to Omitted Spouse Statute.
1 California Transactions Forms--Estate Planning § 6:99, Omitted Spouse Made Valid Agreement Waiving Right to Share in Decedent's Estate.
2 California Transactions Forms--Estate Planning § 11:44, Enforceability.
1 California Transactions Forms--Family Law § 1:7, Unenforceable Agreements; Severability.
1 California Transactions Forms--Family Law § 1:71, Binding Agreement With Specific Family Code Waivers.
West's California Code Forms, Family § 1611, Comment Overview—Premarital Agreements.

§ 1616. Void marriage, effect on agreement

If a marriage is determined to be void, an agreement that would otherwise have been a premarital agreement is enforceable only to the extent necessary to avoid an inequitable result. *(Stats.1992, c. 162 (A.B.2650), § 10, operative Jan. 1, 1994.)*

Cross References

Premarital agreement defined for purposes of this Chapter, see Family Code § 1610.
Uniform Act, construction of provisions, see Family Code § 3.
Void marriage,
 Definition, see Family Code §§ 2200, 2201.
 Procedure, see Family Code § 2250 et seq.
Voidable marriage, see Family Code § 2210 et seq.

Research References

Forms

2 California Transactions Forms--Estate Planning § 11:44, Enforceability.
1 California Transactions Forms--Family Law § 1:9, Effect of Void Marriage; Limitations of Actions and Equitable Defenses.
1 California Transactions Forms--Family Law § 1:34, Waiver of Family Code §1616 Provisions.

§ 1617. Limitation of actions; equitable defenses including laches and estoppel

Any statute of limitations applicable to an action asserting a claim for relief under a premarital agreement is tolled during the marriage of the parties to the agreement. However, equitable defenses limiting the time for enforcement, including laches and estoppel, are available to either party. *(Stats.1992, c. 162 (A.B.2650), § 10, operative Jan. 1, 1994.)*

Cross References

Community property, presumptions concerning nature, see Family Code § 803.
Premarital agreement defined for purposes of this Chapter, see Family Code § 1610.

Uniform Act, construction of provisions, see Family Code § 3.

Research References

Forms

1 California Transactions Forms--Estate Planning § 6:28, Exceptions to Omitted Spouse Statute.
1 California Transactions Forms--Estate Planning § 6:99, Omitted Spouse Made Valid Agreement Waiving Right to Share in Decedent's Estate.
2 California Transactions Forms--Estate Planning § 11:44, Enforceability.
1 California Transactions Forms--Family Law § 1:9, Effect of Void Marriage; Limitations of Actions and Equitable Defenses.
1 California Transactions Forms--Family Law § 1:71, Binding Agreement With Specific Family Code Waivers.
1 California Transactions Forms--Family Law § 4:7, Effect of Subsequent Marriage Between Cohabitants.

CHAPTER 3. AGREEMENTS BETWEEN SPOUSES

Section
1620. Contracts altering legal relations of spouses; restrictions.

Cross References

Domestic partner registration, rights, protections and benefits, responsibilities, obligations and duties under law, date of registration as equivalent of date of marriage, see Family Code § 297.5.
Formerly married person, reference to married person includes, see Family Code § 11.
Surviving spouse, waiver, agreement or property settlement affecting rights on death of other spouse, see Probate Code § 140 et seq.

§ 1620. Contracts altering legal relations of spouses; restrictions

Except as otherwise provided by law, spouses cannot, by a contract with each other, alter their legal relations, except as to property. *(Stats.1992, c. 162 (A.B.2650), § 10, operative Jan. 1, 1994. Amended by Stats.2014, c. 82 (S.B.1306), § 21, eff. Jan. 1, 2015.)*

Cross References

Breach of fiduciary duties, remedies, see Family Code § 1101.
Community contributions and loans for education or training of spouse, agreements, see Family Code § 2641.
Community estate, agreements concerning division, see Family Code § 2550.
Confidential relationship between spouses, see Family Code § 721.
Consideration, recital as conclusive presumption, see Evidence Code § 622.
Fidelity, obligations of, see Family Code § 720.
Property defined for purposes of this Code, see Family Code § 113.
References to husband, wife, spouses and married persons, persons included for purposes of this Code, see Family Code § 11.
Spouses living separate by agreement, see Family Code § 4302.
Support, generally, see Family Code § 3500 et seq.
Support agreements, see Family Code § 3580 et seq.
Support order, modification or termination, agreement between parties on support, see Family Code § 3651.
Surviving spouse, waiver, agreement or property settlement affecting rights on death of other spouse, see Probate Code § 140 et seq.
Transactions between spouses, rules governing, see Family Code § 721.

Research References

Forms

2 California Transactions Forms--Estate Planning § 11:39, General Considerations.
2 California Transactions Forms--Estate Planning § 11:45, Introduction.
2 California Transactions Forms--Estate Planning § 11:48, Governing Contractual Provisions [CC §§1550 et seq., Fam C §721(B)].

Division 5

CONCILIATION PROCEEDINGS

Part	Section
1. Family Conciliation Court Law	1800
2. Statewide Coordination of Family Mediation and Conciliation Services	1850

Cross References

Conciliation courts,
  Abbreviations, use, see Code of Civil Procedure § 186.
  Adjournment, judges absence, see Code of Civil Procedure § 139.
  Business and judicial days, see Code of Civil Procedure § 133 et seq.
  Powers and duties, see Code of Civil Procedure § 128 et seq.
  Seal, affixing to documents, see Code of Civil Procedure § 153.

Part 1

FAMILY CONCILIATION COURT LAW

Chapter	Section
1. General Provisions	1800
2. Family Conciliation Courts	1810
3. Proceedings for Conciliation	1830

Cross References

Evidence affected or excluded by extrinsic policies, mediation, application of Chapter, see Evidence Code § 1117.

CHAPTER 1. GENERAL PROVISIONS

Section
1800. Short title.
1801. Purposes of part.
1802. Application of part.

§ 1800. Short title

This part may be cited as the Family Conciliation Court Law. *(Stats.1992, c. 162 (A.B.2650), § 10, operative Jan. 1, 1994.)*

Research References

Forms
2 California Transactions Forms--Business Transactions § 14:50, Confidentiality of Mediation Process.
West's California Code Forms, Family § 1830, Comment Overview—Jurisdiction.

§ 1801. Purposes of part

The purposes of this part are to protect the rights of children and to promote the public welfare by preserving, promoting, and protecting family life and the institution of matrimony, and to provide means for the reconciliation of spouses and the amicable settlement of domestic and family controversies. *(Stats.1992, c. 162 (A.B.2650), § 10, operative Jan. 1, 1994.)*

Cross References

References to husband, wife, spouses and married persons, persons included for purposes of this Code, see Family Code § 11.

Research References

Forms
West's California Code Forms, Family § 1830, Comment Overview—Jurisdiction.

§ 1802. Application of part

(a) This part applies only in counties in which the superior court determines that the social conditions in the county and the number of domestic relations cases in the courts render the procedures provided in this part necessary to the full and proper consideration of those cases and the effectuation of the purposes of this part.

(b) The determination under subdivision (a) shall be made annually in the month of January by:

(1) The judge of the superior court in counties having only one superior court judge.

(2) A majority of the judges of the superior court in counties having more than one superior court judge. *(Stats.1992, c. 162 (A.B.2650), § 10, operative Jan. 1, 1994.)*

Cross References

County defined for purposes of this Code, see Family Code § 67.

CHAPTER 2. FAMILY CONCILIATION COURTS

Section
1810. Jurisdiction; designation of court.
1811. Assignment of judges; number of sessions.
1812. Transfer of cases; reasons; duties of transferee judge.
1813. Substitute judge; appointment; powers and authority.
1814. Supervising counselor; secretary; powers and duties; other assistants; classification; compensation.
1815. Supervising and associate counselors; qualifications.
1816. Domestic violence training for evaluators; areas of basic, advanced, and updated training; eligible providers.
1817. Probation officers; duties.
1818. Privacy of hearings; conferences; confidential nature of communications; closed files; inspection of papers.
1819. Destruction of records, papers or documents in office of counselor; exception; microfilming.
1820. Joint family conciliation court services; agreement between courts.

Cross References

Privilege for official information, see Evidence Code § 1040.

§ 1810. Jurisdiction; designation of court

Each superior court shall exercise the jurisdiction conferred by this part. While sitting in the exercise of this jurisdiction, the court shall be known and referred to as the "family conciliation court." *(Stats.1992, c. 162 (A.B.2650), § 10, operative Jan. 1, 1994.)*

Cross References

Judicial power of state, courts, see Cal. Const. Art. 6, § 1.
Jurisdiction, no children involved, see Family Code § 1842.
Superior court, original jurisdiction, see Cal. Const. Art. 6, § 10.
Superior court jurisdiction of domestic proceedings, see Family Code § 200.

§ 1811. Assignment of judges; number of sessions

The presiding judge of the superior court shall annually, in the month of January, designate at least one judge to hear all cases under this part. *(Stats.1992, c. 162 (A.B.2650), § 10, operative Jan. 1, 1994. Amended by Stats.2003, c. 149 (S.B.79), § 11.)*

Cross References

Number of judges, superior court, see Government Code § 69580 et seq.
Sessions of superior court, see Government Code § 69740 et seq.

§ 1812. Transfer of cases; reasons; duties of transferee judge

(a) The judge of the family conciliation court may transfer any case before the family conciliation court pursuant to this part to the department of the presiding judge of the superior court for assignment for trial or other proceedings by another judge of the court, whenever in the opinion of the judge of the family conciliation court the transfer is necessary to expedite the business of the family conciliation court or to ensure the prompt consideration of the case.

(b) When a case is transferred pursuant to subdivision (a), the judge to whom it is transferred shall act as the judge of the family conciliation court in the matter. *(Stats.1992, c. 162 (A.B.2650), § 10, operative Jan. 1, 1994.)*

Cross References

Proceeding defined for purposes of this Code, see Family Code § 110.

§ 1813. Substitute judge; appointment; powers and authority

(a) The presiding judge of the superior court may appoint a judge of the superior court other than the judge of the family conciliation court to act as judge of the family conciliation court during any period when the judge of the family conciliation court is on vacation, absent, or for any reason unable to perform the duties as judge of the family conciliation court.

(b) The judge appointed under subdivision (a) has all of the powers and authority of a judge of the family conciliation court in cases under this part. *(Stats.1992, c. 162 (A.B.2650), § 10, operative Jan. 1, 1994.)*

Cross References

Judicial council, see Cal. Const. Art. 6, § 6.
Presiding judge, duties, see Government Code § 69508.

§ 1814. Supervising counselor; secretary; powers and duties; other assistants; classification; compensation

(a) In each county in which a family conciliation court is established, the superior court may appoint one supervising counselor of conciliation and one secretary to assist the family conciliation court in disposing of its business and carrying out its functions. When superior courts by contract have established joint family conciliation court services, the contracting courts jointly may make the appointments under this subdivision.

(b) The supervising counselor of conciliation has the power to do all of the following:

(1) Hold conciliation conferences with parties to, and hearings in, proceedings under this part, and make recommendations concerning the proceedings to the judge of the family conciliation court.

(2) Provide supervision in connection with the exercise of the counselor's jurisdiction as the judge of the family conciliation court may direct.

(3) Cause reports to be made, statistics to be compiled, and records to be kept as the judge of the family conciliation court may direct.

(4) Hold hearings in all family conciliation court cases as may be required by the judge of the family conciliation court, and make investigations as may be required by the court to carry out the intent of this part.

(5) Make recommendations relating to marriages where one or both parties are underage.

(6) Make investigations, reports, and recommendations as provided in Section 281 of the Welfare and Institutions Code under the authority provided the probation officer in that code.

(7) Act as domestic relations cases investigator.

(8) Conduct mediation of child custody and visitation disputes.

(c) The superior court, or contracting superior courts, may also appoint associate counselors of conciliation and other office assistants as may be necessary to assist the family conciliation court in disposing of its business. The associate counselors shall carry out their duties under the supervision of the supervising counselor of conciliation and have the powers of the supervising counselor of conciliation. Office assistants shall work under the supervision and direction of the supervising counselor of conciliation.

(d) The classification and salaries of persons appointed under this section shall be determined by:

(1) The superior court of the county in which a noncontracting family conciliation court operates.

(2) The superior court of the county which by contract has the responsibility to administer funds of the joint family conciliation court service. *(Stats.1992, c. 162 (A.B.2650), § 10, operative Jan. 1, 1994. Amended by Stats.2012, c. 470 (A.B.1529), § 12.)*

Cross References

County defined for purposes of this Code, see Family Code § 67.
Person defined for purposes of this Code, see Family Code § 105.
Population of counties, see Government Code § 28020.
Proceeding defined for purposes of this Code, see Family Code § 110.
Superior court officers and employees, see Government Code § 69894.3 et seq.

§ 1815. Supervising and associate counselors; qualifications

(a) A person employed as a supervising counselor of conciliation or as an associate counselor of conciliation shall have all of the following minimum qualifications:

(1) A master's degree in psychology, social work, marriage, family and child counseling, or other behavioral science substantially related to marriage and family interpersonal relationships.

(2) At least two years of experience in counseling or psychotherapy, or both, preferably in a setting related to the areas of responsibility of the family conciliation court and with the ethnic population to be served.

(3) Knowledge of the court system of California and the procedures used in family law cases.

(4) Knowledge of other resources in the community that clients can be referred to for assistance.

(5) Knowledge of adult psychopathology and the psychology of families.

(6) Knowledge of child development, child abuse, clinical issues relating to children, the effects of divorce on children, the effects of domestic violence on children, and child custody research sufficient to enable a counselor to assess the mental health needs of children.

(7) Training in domestic violence issues as described in Section 1816.

(b) The family conciliation court may substitute additional experience for a portion of the education, or additional education for a portion of the experience, required under subdivision (a).

(c) This section does not apply to any supervising counselor of conciliation who was in office on March 27, 1980. *(Stats.1992, c. 162 (A.B.2650), § 10, operative Jan. 1, 1994. Amended by Stats.2006, c. 130 (A.B.2853), § 1.)*

Cross References

Abuse defined for purposes of the Domestic Violence Protection Act, see Family Code § 6203.
Adult defined for purposes of this Code, see Family Code § 6501.
Domestic violence defined for purposes of this Code, see Family Code § 6211.
Mediators, qualifications, see Family Code § 3164.
Person defined for purposes of this Code, see Family Code § 105.
Superior court officers and employees, see Government Code § 69894.3 et seq.

§ 1816. Domestic violence training for evaluators; areas of basic, advanced, and updated training; eligible providers

(a) For purposes of this section, the following definitions apply:

(1) "Eligible provider" means the Administrative Office of the Courts or an educational institution, professional association, professional continuing education group, a group connected to the courts, or a public or private group that has been authorized by the Administrative Office of the Courts to provide domestic violence training.

(2) "Evaluator" means a supervising or associate counselor described in Section 1815, a mediator described in Section 3164, a court-connected or private child custody evaluator described in Section 3110.5, or a court-appointed investigator or evaluator as described in Section 3110 or Section 730 of the Evidence Code.

(b) An evaluator shall participate in a program of continuing instruction in domestic violence, including child abuse, as may be arranged and provided to that evaluator. This training may utilize domestic violence training programs conducted by nonprofit community organizations with an expertise in domestic violence issues.

(c) Areas of basic instruction shall include, but are not limited to, the following:

(1) The effects of domestic violence on children.

(2) The nature and extent of domestic violence.

(3) The social and family dynamics of domestic violence.

(4) Techniques for identifying and assisting families affected by domestic violence.

(5) Interviewing, documentation of, and appropriate recommendations for, families affected by domestic violence.

(6) The legal rights of, and remedies available to, victims.

(7) Availability of community and legal domestic violence resources.

(d) An evaluator shall also complete 16 hours of advanced training within a 12-month period. Four hours of that advanced training shall include community resource networking intended to acquaint the evaluator with domestic violence resources in the geographical communities where the family being evaluated may reside. Twelve hours of instruction, as approved by the Administrative Office of the Courts, shall include all of the following:

(1) The appropriate structuring of the child custody evaluation process, including, but not limited to, all of the following:

(A) Maximizing safety for clients, evaluators, and court personnel.

(B) Maintaining objectivity.

(C) Providing and gathering balanced information from the parties and controlling for bias.

(D) Providing separate sessions at separate times as described in Section 3113.

(E) Considering the impact of the evaluation report and recommendations with particular attention to the dynamics of domestic violence.

(2) The relevant sections of local, state, and federal laws, rules, or regulations.

(3) The range, availability, and applicability of domestic violence resources available to victims, including, but not limited to, all of the following:

* * *

(A) Domestic violence shelter-based programs.

(B) Counseling, including drug and alcohol counseling.

(C) Legal assistance.

(D) Job training.

(E) Parenting classes.

(F) Resources for a victim who is an immigrant.

(4) The range, availability, and applicability of domestic violence intervention available to perpetrators, including, but not limited to, all of the following:

(A) Certified treatment programs described in subdivision (c) of Section 1203.097 of the Penal Code.

(B) Drug and alcohol counseling.

(C) Legal assistance.

(D) Job training.

(E) Parenting classes.

(5) The unique issues in a family and psychological assessment in a domestic violence case, including all of the following:

(A) The effects of exposure to domestic violence and psychological trauma on children, the relationship between child physical abuse, child sexual abuse, and domestic violence, the differential family dynamics related to parent-child attachments in families with domestic violence, intergenerational transmission of familial violence, and manifestations of post-traumatic stress disorders in children.

(B) The nature and extent of domestic violence, and the relationship of gender, class, race, culture, and sexual orientation to domestic violence.

(C) Current legal, psychosocial, public policy, and mental health research related to the dynamics of family violence, the impact of victimization, the psychology of perpetration, and the dynamics of power and control in battering relationships.

(D) The assessment of family history based on the type, severity, and frequency of violence.

(E) The impact on parenting abilities of being a victim or perpetrator of domestic violence.

(F) The uses and limitations of psychological testing and psychiatric diagnosis in assessing parenting abilities in domestic violence cases.

(G) The influence of alcohol and drug use and abuse on the incidence of domestic violence.

(H) Understanding the dynamics of high conflict relationships and relationships between an abuser and victim.

(I) The importance of, and procedures for, obtaining collateral information from a probation department, children's protective services, police incident report, a pleading regarding a restraining order, medical records, a school, and other relevant sources.

(J) Accepted methods for structuring safe and enforceable child custody and parenting plans that ensure the health, safety, welfare, and best interest of the child, and safeguards for the parties.

(K) The importance of discouraging participants in child custody matters from blaming victims of domestic violence for the violence and from minimizing allegations of domestic violence, child abuse, or abuse against a family member.

(e) After an evaluator has completed the advanced training described in subdivision (d), that evaluator shall complete four hours of updated training annually that shall include, but is not limited to, all of the following:

(1) Changes in local court practices, case law, and state and federal legislation related to domestic violence.

(2) An update of current social science research and theory, including the impact of exposure to domestic violence on children.

(f) Training described in this section shall be acquired from an eligible provider and that eligible provider shall comply with all of the following:

(1) Ensure that a training instructor or consultant delivering the education and training programs either meets the training requirements of this section or is an expert in the subject matter.

(2) Monitor and evaluate the quality of courses, curricula, training, instructors, and consultants.

(3) Emphasize the importance of focusing child custody evaluations on the health, safety, welfare, and best interest of the child.

(4) Develop a procedure to verify that an evaluator completes the education and training program.

(5) Distribute a certificate of completion to each evaluator who has completed the training. That certificate shall document the number of hours of training offered, the number of hours the evaluator completed, the dates of the training, and the name of the training provider.

§ 1816

(g)(1) If there is a local court rule regarding the procedure to notify the court that an evaluator has completed training as described in this section, the evaluator shall comply with that local court rule.

(2) Except as provided in paragraph (1), an evaluator shall attach copies of the certificates of completion of the training described in subdivision (d) and the most recent updated training described in subdivision (e).

(h) An evaluator may satisfy the requirement for 12 hours of instruction described in subdivision (d) by training from an eligible provider that was obtained on or after January 1, 1996. The advanced training of that evaluator shall not be complete until that evaluator completes the four hours of community resource networking described in subdivision (d).

(i) The Judicial Council shall develop standards for the training programs. The Judicial Council shall solicit the assistance of community organizations concerned with domestic violence and child abuse and shall seek to develop training programs that will maximize coordination between conciliation courts and local agencies concerned with domestic violence. (Stats.1992, c. 162 (A.B.2650), § 10, operative Jan. 1, 1994. Amended by Stats.1993, c. 219 (A.B.1500), § 101.5; Stats.2000, c. 926 (S.B.1716), § 1; Stats.2006, c. 130 (A.B.2853), § 2; Stats.2007, c. 130 (A.B.299), § 88; Stats.2019, c. 115 (A.B.1817), § 13, eff. Jan. 1, 2020; Stats.2022, c. 197 (S.B.1493), § 3, eff. Jan. 1, 2023.)

Cross References

Abuse defined for purposes of the Domestic Violence Protection Act, see Family Code § 6203.
Domestic violence defined for purposes of this Code, see Family Code § 6211.
Privilege for official information, see Evidence Code § 1040.

Research References

Forms
1 California Transactions Forms--Family Law § 2:70, Deciding Custody.
West's California Judicial Council Forms FL-325, Declaration of Court-Connected Child Custody Evaluator Regarding Qualifications.
West's California Judicial Council Forms FL-326, Declaration of Private Child Custody Evaluator Regarding Qualifications.

§ 1817. Probation officers; duties

The probation officer in every county shall do all of the following:

(a) Give assistance to the family conciliation court that the court may request to carry out the purposes of this part, and to that end shall, upon request, make investigations and reports as requested.

(b) In cases pursuant to this part, exercise all the powers and perform all the duties granted or imposed by the laws of this state relating to probation or to probation officers. (Stats.1992, c. 162 (A.B.2650), § 10, operative Jan. 1, 1994.)

Cross References

County defined for purposes of this Code, see Family Code § 67.
Duties of probation officers, see Penal Code § 1203 et seq.; Welfare and Institutions Code § 270 et seq.
State defined for purposes of this Code, see Family Code § 145.
Wards, temporary custody and detention, role of probation officer, see Welfare and Institutions Code § 630 et seq.

§ 1818. Privacy of hearings; conferences; confidential nature of communications; closed files; inspection of papers

(a) All superior court hearings or conferences in proceedings under this part shall be held in private and the court shall exclude all persons except the officers of the court, the parties, their counsel, and witnesses. The court shall not allow ex parte communications, except as authorized by Section 216. All communications, verbal or written, from parties to the judge, commissioner, or counselor in a proceeding under this part shall be deemed to be official information within the meaning of Section 1040 of the Evidence Code.

(b) The files of the family conciliation court shall be closed. The petition, supporting affidavit, conciliation agreement, and any court order made in the matter may be opened to inspection by a party or the party's counsel upon the written authority of the judge of the family conciliation court. (Stats.1992, c. 162 (A.B.2650), § 10, operative Jan. 1, 1994. Amended by Stats.2005, c. 489 (S.B.1088), § 2.)

Cross References

Domestic violence, interagency death review teams, reporting procedures, see Penal Code § 11163.3.
Inspection of public records, see Government Code § 6250 et seq.
Judgment and order defined for purposes of this Code, see Family Code § 100.
Person defined for purposes of this Code, see Family Code § 105.
Proceeding defined for purposes of this Code, see Family Code § 110.
Publicity of court proceedings,
  Generally, see Code of Civil Procedure § 124.
  Exception to open rule, see Family Code § 214.
Sessions of superior court, see Government Code § 69740 et seq.
Written or oral communications during mediation process, admissibility, see Evidence Code § 1119.

§ 1819. Destruction of records, papers or documents in office of counselor; exception; microfilming

(a) Except as provided in subdivision (b), upon order of the judge of the family conciliation court, the supervising counselor of conciliation may destroy any record, paper, or document filed or kept in the office of the supervising counselor of conciliation which is more than two years old.

(b) Records described in subdivision (a) of child custody or visitation mediation may be destroyed when the minor or minors involved are 18 years of age.

(c) In the judge's discretion, the judge of the family conciliation court may order the microfilming of any record, paper, or document described in subdivision (a) or (b). (Stats.1992, c. 162 (A.B.2650), § 10, operative Jan. 1, 1994.)

Cross References

Board of Supervisors, destruction of certain records, conditions, see Government Code § 26205.
Inspection of public records, see Government Code § 6250 et seq.
Judgment and order defined for purposes of this Code, see Family Code § 100.
Juvenile court, release or destruction of court record, see Welfare and Institutions Code § 826.
Minor defined for purposes of this Code, see Family Code § 6500.
Recording in separate books or rolls of film or in general series, official records, see Government Code § 27323.
Retention or return of exhibits, depositions, or administrative records, destruction or disposition, see Code of Civil Procedure § 1952.

§ 1820. Joint family conciliation court services; agreement between courts

(a) A court may contract with any other court or courts to provide joint family conciliation court services.

(b) An agreement between two or more courts for the operation of a joint family conciliation court service may provide that one participating court shall be the custodian of moneys made available for the purposes of the joint services, and that the custodian court may make payments from the moneys upon audit of the appropriate auditing officer or body of the court.

(c) An agreement between two or more courts for the operation of a joint family conciliation court service may also provide:

(1) For the joint provision or operation of services and facilities or for the provision or operation of services and facilities by one participating court under contract for the other participating courts.

(2) For appointments of members of the staff of the family conciliation court including the supervising counselor.

FAMILY CONCILIATION COURT LAW

(3) That, for specified purposes, the members of the staff of the family conciliation court including the supervising counselor, but excluding the judges of the family conciliation court, shall be considered to be employees of one participating court.

(4) For other matters that are necessary or proper to effectuate the purposes of the Family Conciliation Court Law.

(d) The provisions of this part relating to family conciliation court services provided by a single court shall be equally applicable to courts which contract, pursuant to this section, to provide joint family conciliation court services. *(Stats.1992, c. 162 (A.B.2650), § 10, operative Jan. 1, 1994. Amended by Stats.2012, c. 470 (A.B.1529), § 13.)*

Cross References

County defined for purposes of this Code, see Family Code § 67.

CHAPTER 3. PROCEEDINGS FOR CONCILIATION

Section
1830. Jurisdiction.
1831. Petition; right to file; purpose.
1832. Petition; caption.
1833. Petition; contents.
1834. Blank forms; assistance in preparing and presenting petition; references; coextensive jurisdiction.
1835. Fees.
1836. Hearing; time; place; notice; citation; witnesses.
1837. Time and place of holding court; hearings in chambers or otherwise.
1838. Informal hearings; conferences; purpose; aid of specialists or experts.
1839. Orders, duration; reconciliation agreement; temporary support.
1840. Dissolution, legal separation or judgment of nullity; stay of right to file; effect of pendency of action upon conciliation proceedings.
1841. Dissolution, legal separation or judgment of nullity; minor child involved; transfer.
1842. Dissolution, legal separation or judgment of nullity; no minor children; application for and acceptance of transfer; jurisdiction.

§ 1830. Jurisdiction

(a) When a controversy exists between spouses, or when a controversy relating to child custody or visitation exists between parents regardless of their marital status, and the controversy may, unless a reconciliation is achieved, result in dissolution of the marriage, nullity of the marriage, or legal separation of the parties, or in the disruption of the household, and there is a minor child of the spouses or parents or of either of them whose welfare might be affected thereby, the family conciliation court has jurisdiction as provided in this part over the controversy and over the parties to the controversy and over all persons having any relation to the controversy.

(b) The family conciliation court also has jurisdiction over the controversy, whether or not there is a minor child of the parties or either of them, where the controversy involves domestic violence. *(Stats.1992, c. 162 (A.B.2650), § 10, operative Jan. 1, 1994.)*

Cross References

Custody of children, see Family Code § 3000 et seq.
Domestic violence defined for purposes of this Code, see Family Code § 6211.
Domestic violence prevention, see Family Code § 6200 et seq.
Jurisdiction, acceptance in cases where no minor children involved, see Family Code § 1842.
Minor defined for purposes of this Code, see Family Code § 6500.
Nullity, dissolution, and legal separation, see Family Code § 2000 et seq.
Person defined for purposes of this Code, see Family Code § 105.

References to husband, wife, spouses and married persons, persons included for purposes of this Code, see Family Code § 11.
Similar provisions, see Family Code §§ 200, 1810.
Superior court, original jurisdiction, see Cal. Const. Art. 6, § 10.
Support, generally, see Family Code § 3500 et seq.

Research References

Forms

West's California Code Forms, Family § 1830, Comment Overview—Jurisdiction.

§ 1831. Petition; right to file; purpose

Before the filing of a proceeding for determination of custody or visitation rights, for dissolution of marriage, for nullity of a voidable marriage, or for legal separation of the parties, either spouse or parent, or both, may file in the family conciliation court a petition invoking the jurisdiction of the court for the purpose of preserving the marriage by effecting a reconciliation between the parties, or for amicable settlement of the controversy between the spouses or parents, so as to avoid further litigation over the issue involved. *(Stats.1992, c. 162 (A.B.2650), § 10, operative Jan. 1, 1994.)*

Cross References

Counseling of parents and child, see Family Code § 3190 et seq.
Mediation, custody and visitation issues, see Family Code § 3160 et seq.
Proceeding defined for purposes of this Code, see Family Code § 110.
References to husband, wife, spouses and married persons, persons included for purposes of this Code, see Family Code § 11.

Research References

Forms

West's California Code Forms, Family § 1830, Comment Overview—Jurisdiction.

§ 1832. Petition; caption

The petition shall be captioned substantially as follows:

In the Superior Court of the State of California
in and for the County of _____

Upon the petition of
_____)
        (Petitioner)) Petition for
And concerning) Conciliation
_____ and) (Under the Family
_____) Conciliation
_____) Court Law)
_____, Respondents)

To the Family Conciliation Court:

(Stats.1992, c. 162 (A.B.2650), § 10, operative Jan. 1, 1994.)

Cross References

County defined for purposes of this Code, see Family Code § 67.
Petitioner defined for purposes of this Code, see Family Code § 126.
Respondent defined for purposes of this Code, see Family Code § 127.
State defined for purposes of this Code, see Family Code § 145.

§ 1833. Petition; contents

The petition shall:

(a) Allege that a controversy exists between the spouses or parents and request the aid of the court to effect a reconciliation or an amicable settlement of the controversy.

(b) State the name and age of each minor child whose welfare may be affected by the controversy.

(c) State the name and address of the petitioner or the names and addresses of the petitioners.

§ 1833

CONCILIATION PROCEEDINGS

(d) If the petition is presented by one spouse or parent only, the name of the other spouse or parent as a respondent, and state the address of that spouse or parent.

(e) Name as a respondent any other person who has any relation to the controversy, and state the address of the person if known to the petitioner.

(f) If the petition arises out of an instance of domestic violence, so state generally and without specific allegations as to the incident.

(g) State any other information the court by rule requires. *(Stats.1992, c. 162 (A.B.2650), § 10, operative Jan. 1, 1994.)*

Cross References

Domestic violence defined for purposes of this Code, see Family Code § 6211.
Minor defined for purposes of this Code, see Family Code § 6500.
Person defined for purposes of this Code, see Family Code § 105.
Petitioner defined for purposes of this Code, see Family Code § 126.
References to husband, wife, spouses and married persons, persons included for purposes of this Code, see Family Code § 11.
Respondent defined for purposes of this Code, see Family Code § 127.
State defined for purposes of this Code, see Family Code § 145.

§ 1834. Blank forms; assistance in preparing and presenting petition; references; coextensive jurisdiction

(a) The clerk of the court shall provide, at the expense of the court, blank forms for petitions for filing pursuant to this part.

(b) The probation officers of the county and the attachés and employees of the family conciliation court shall assist a person in the preparation and presentation of a petition under this part if the person requests assistance.

(c) All public officers in each county shall refer to the family conciliation court all petitions and complaints made to them in respect to controversies within the jurisdiction of the family conciliation court.

(d) The jurisdiction of the family conciliation court in respect to controversies arising out of an instance of domestic violence is not exclusive but is coextensive with any other remedies either civil or criminal in nature that may be available. *(Stats.1992, c. 162 (A.B.2650), § 10, operative Jan. 1, 1994. Amended by Stats.2012, c. 470 (A.B.1529), § 14.)*

Cross References

County defined for purposes of this Code, see Family Code § 67.
Domestic violence defined for purposes of this Code, see Family Code § 6211.
Person defined for purposes of this Code, see Family Code § 105.
Probation officers, duties, see Penal Code § 1203 et seq.; Welfare and Institutions Code § 270 et seq.
Superior court officers and employees, see Government Code § 69894.3 et seq.

§ 1835. Fees

No fee shall be charged by any officer for filing the petition. *(Stats.1992, c. 162 (A.B.2650), § 10, operative Jan. 1, 1994.)*

§ 1836. Hearing; time; place; notice; citation; witnesses

(a) The court shall fix a reasonable time and place for hearing on the petition. The court shall cause notice to be given to the respondents of the filing of the petition and of the time and place of the hearing that the court deems necessary.

(b) The court may, when it deems it necessary, issue a citation to a respondent requiring the respondent to appear at the time and place stated in the citation. The court may require the attendance of witnesses as in other civil cases. *(Stats.1992, c. 162 (A.B.2650), § 10, operative Jan. 1, 1994.)*

Cross References

Respondent defined for purposes of this Code, see Family Code § 127.

Subpoena, requiring attendance, see Code of Civil Procedure § 1985 et seq.

§ 1837. Time and place of holding court; hearings in chambers or otherwise

(a) Except as provided in subdivision (b), for the purpose of conducting hearings pursuant to this part, the family conciliation court may be convened at any time and place within the county, and the hearing may be had in chambers or otherwise.

(b) The time and place for hearing shall not be different from the time and place provided by law for the trial of civil actions if any party, before the hearing, objects to any different time or place. *(Stats.1992, c. 162 (A.B.2650), § 10, operative Jan. 1, 1994.)*

Cross References

County defined for purposes of this Code, see Family Code § 67.
Judicial holidays, see Code of Civil Procedure § 133 et seq.
Place of trial of civil actions, see Code of Civil Procedure § 392 et seq.
Session of superior court, see Government Code § 69740 et seq.

§ 1838. Informal hearings; conferences; purpose; aid of specialists or experts

(a) The hearing shall be conducted informally as a conference or a series of conferences to effect a reconciliation of the spouses or an amicable adjustment or settlement of the issues in controversy.

(b) To facilitate and promote the purposes of this part, the court may, with the consent of both parties to the proceeding, recommend or invoke the aid of medical or other specialists or scientific experts, or of the pastor or director of any religious denomination to which the parties may belong. Aid under this subdivision shall not be at the expense of the court unless the presiding judge specifically authorizes the aid, nor at the expense of the county unless the board of supervisors of the county specifically provides and authorizes the aid. *(Stats.1992, c. 162 (A.B.2650), § 10, operative Jan. 1, 1994. Amended by Stats.2012, c. 470 (A.B.1529), § 15.)*

Cross References

County defined for purposes of this Code, see Family Code § 67.
Proceeding defined for purposes of this Code, see Family Code § 110.
References to husband, wife, spouses and married persons, persons included for purposes of this Code, see Family Code § 11.

§ 1839. Orders, duration; reconciliation agreement; temporary support

(a) At or after the hearing, the court may make orders in respect to the conduct of the spouses or parents and the subject matter of the controversy that the court deems necessary to preserve the marriage or to implement the reconciliation of the spouses. No such order shall be effective for more than 30 days from the hearing of the petition unless the parties mutually consent to a continuation of the time the order remains effective.

(b) A reconciliation agreement between the parties may be reduced to writing and, with the consent of the parties, a court order may be made requiring the parties to comply fully with the agreement.

(c) During the pendency of a proceeding under this part, the superior court may order a spouse or parent, as the case may be, to pay an amount necessary for the support and maintenance of the other spouse and for the support, maintenance, and education of the minor children, as the case may be. In determining the amount, the superior court may take into consideration the recommendations of a financial referee if one is available to the court. An order made pursuant to this subdivision shall not prejudice the rights of the parties or children with respect to any subsequent order that may be made. An order made pursuant to this subdivision may be modified or terminated at any time except as to an amount that accrued before the date of filing of the notice of motion or order to show cause to modify or terminate. *(Stats.1992, c. 162 (A.B.2650), § 10, operative*

Jan. 1, 1994. Amended by Stats.1993, c. 219 (A.B.1500), § 102; Stats.2014, c. 82 (S.B.1306), § 22, eff. Jan. 1, 2015.)

Cross References

Counseling of parents and children, see Family Code § 3190 et seq.
Custody of children, see Family Code § 3000 et seq.
Judgment and order defined for purposes of this Code, see Family Code § 100.
Mediation, custody and visitation, see Family Code § 3160 et seq.
Minor defined for purposes of this Code, see Family Code § 6500.
Proceeding defined for purposes of this Code, see Family Code § 110.
References to husband, wife, spouses and married persons, persons included for purposes of this Code, see Family Code § 11.
Support defined for purposes of this Code, see Family Code § 150.

§ 1840. Dissolution, legal separation or judgment of nullity; stay of right to file; effect of pendency of action upon conciliation proceedings

(a) During a period beginning upon the filing of the petition for conciliation and continuing until 30 days after the hearing of the petition for conciliation, neither spouse shall file a petition for dissolution of marriage, for nullity of a voidable marriage, or for legal separation of the parties.

(b) After the expiration of the period under subdivision (a), if the controversy between the spouses, or the parents, has not been terminated, either spouse may institute a proceeding for dissolution of marriage, for nullity of a voidable marriage, or for legal separation of the parties, or a proceeding to determine custody or visitation of the minor child or children.

(c) The pendency of a proceeding for dissolution of marriage, for nullity of marriage, or for legal separation of the parties, or a proceeding to determine custody or visitation of the minor child or children, does not operate as a bar to the instituting of proceedings for conciliation under this part. *(Stats.1992, c. 162 (A.B.2650), § 10, operative Jan. 1, 1994.)*

Cross References

Counseling of parents and children, see Family Code § 3190 et seq.
Jurisdiction, see Family Code § 1830.
Mediation, custody and visitation issues, see Family Code § 3160 et seq.
Minor defined for purposes of this Code, see Family Code § 6500.
Nullity, dissolution, and legal separation, see Family Code § 2000 et seq.
Proceeding defined for purposes of this Code, see Family Code § 110.
References to husband, wife, spouses and married persons, persons included for purposes of this Code, see Family Code § 11.
Superior court, original jurisdiction, see Cal. Const. Art. 6, § 10.

§ 1841. Dissolution, legal separation or judgment of nullity; minor child involved; transfer

If a petition for dissolution of marriage, for nullity of marriage, or for legal separation of the parties is filed, the case may be transferred at any time during the pendency of the proceeding to the family conciliation court for proceedings for reconciliation of the spouses or amicable settlement of issues in controversy in accordance with this part if both of the following appear to the court:

(a) There is a minor child of the spouses, or of either of them, whose welfare may be adversely affected by the dissolution of the marriage or the disruption of the household or a controversy involving child custody.

(b) There is some reasonable possibility of a reconciliation being effected. *(Stats.1992, c. 162 (A.B.2650), § 10, operative Jan. 1, 1994.)*

Cross References

Counseling of parents and children, see Family Code § 3190 et seq.
Jurisdiction, see Family Code § 1830.
Mediation, custody and visitation issues, see Family Code § 3160 et seq.
Minor defined for purposes of this Code, see Family Code § 6500.
Nullity, dissolution and legal separation, see Family Code § 2000 et seq.
Proceeding defined for purposes of this Code, see Family Code § 110.
References to husband, wife, spouses and married persons, persons included for purposes of this Code, see Family Code § 11.
Superior court, original jurisdiction, see Cal. Const. Art. 6, § 10.

Research References

Forms

West's California Code Forms, Family § 1830, Comment Overview—Jurisdiction.
West's California Code Forms, Family § 1841 Form 1, Order Transferring Action to Family Conciliation Court.

§ 1842. Dissolution, legal separation or judgment of nullity; no minor children; application for and acceptance of transfer; jurisdiction

(a) If an application is made to the family conciliation court for conciliation proceedings in respect to a controversy between spouses, or a contested proceeding for dissolution of marriage, for nullity of a voidable marriage, or for legal separation of the parties, but there is no minor child whose welfare may be affected by the results of the controversy, and it appears to the court that reconciliation of the spouses or amicable adjustment of the controversy can probably be achieved, and that the work of the court in cases involving children will not be seriously impeded by acceptance of the case, the court may accept and dispose of the case in the same manner as similar cases involving the welfare of children are disposed of.

(b) If the court accepts the case under subdivision (a), the court has the same jurisdiction over the controversy and the parties to the controversy and those having a relation to the controversy that it has under this part in similar cases involving the welfare of children. *(Stats.1992, c. 162 (A.B.2650), § 10, operative Jan. 1, 1994.)*

Cross References

Counseling of parents and children, see Family Code § 3190 et seq.
Jurisdiction, see Family Code § 1830.
Mediation, custody and visitation issues, see Family Code § 3160 et seq.
Minor defined for purposes of this Code, see Family Code § 6500.
Nullity, dissolution and legal separation, see Family Code § 2000 et seq.
Proceeding defined for purposes of this Code, see Family Code § 110.
References to husband, wife, spouses and married persons, persons included for purposes of this Code, see Family Code § 11.
Superior court, original jurisdiction, see Cal. Const. Art. 6, § 10.

Part 2

STATEWIDE COORDINATION OF FAMILY MEDIATION AND CONCILIATION SERVICES

Section
1850. Duties of Judicial Council.
1851. Advisory committee.
1852. Family Law Trust Fund; deposits; disbursements.

§ 1850. Duties of Judicial Council

The Judicial Council shall do all of the following:

(a) Assist courts in implementing mediation and conciliation proceedings under this code.

(b) Establish and implement a uniform statistical reporting system relating to proceedings brought for dissolution of marriage, for nullity of marriage, or for legal separation of the parties, including, but not limited to, a custody disposition survey.

(c) Administer a program of grants to public and private agencies submitting proposals for research, study, and demonstration projects in the area of family law, including, but not limited to, all of the following:

§ 1850 CONCILIATION PROCEEDINGS

(1) The development of conciliation and mediation and other newer dispute resolution techniques, particularly as they relate to child custody and to avoidance of litigation.

(2) The establishment of criteria to ensure that a child support order is adequate.

(3) The development of methods to ensure that a child support order is paid.

(4) The study of the feasibility and desirability of guidelines to assist judges in making custody decisions.

(d) Administer a program for the training of court personnel involved in family law proceedings, which shall be available to the court personnel and which shall be totally funded from funds specified in Section 1852. The training shall include, but not be limited to, the order of preference for custody of minor children and the meaning of the custody arrangements under Part 2 (commencing with Section 3020) of Division 8.

(e) Conduct research on the effectiveness of current family law for the purpose of shaping future public policy. *(Stats.1992, c. 162 (A.B.2650), § 10, operative Jan. 1, 1994. Amended by Stats.1993, c. 219 (A.B.1500), § 102.5; Stats.2012, c. 470 (A.B.1529), § 16.)*

Cross References

Child support standards, statewide uniform guideline, see Family Code § 4050 et seq.
Counseling of parents and children, see Family Code § 3190 et seq.
County defined for purposes of this Code, see Family Code § 67.
Judgment and order defined for purposes of this Code, see Family Code § 100.
Judicial Council, generally, see Government Code § 68500 et seq.
Mediation of visitation and custody issues, see Family Code § 3160 et seq.
Minor defined for purposes of this Code, see Family Code § 6500.
Proceeding defined for purposes of this Code, see Family Code § 110.
Rules for proceedings of Judicial Council, see Family Code § 210 et seq.
Support defined for purposes of this Code, see Family Code § 150.
Support order defined for purposes of this Code, see Family Code § 155.

§ 1851. Advisory committee

The Judicial Council shall establish an advisory committee of persons representing a broad spectrum of interest in and knowledge about family law. The committee shall recommend criteria for determining grant recipients pursuant to subdivision (c) of Section 1850, which shall include proposal evaluation guidelines and procedures for submission of the results to the Legislature, the Governor, and family law courts. In accordance with established criteria, the committee shall receive grant proposals and shall recommend the priority of submitted proposals. *(Stats.1992, c. 162 (A.B.2650), § 10, operative Jan. 1, 1994.)*

Cross References

Person defined for purposes of this Code, see Family Code § 105.
Rules for proceedings of Judicial Council, see Family Code § 210 et seq.

§ 1852. Family Law Trust Fund; deposits; disbursements

(a) There is in the State Treasury the Family Law Trust Fund.

(b) Moneys collected by the state pursuant to subdivision (c) of Section 103625 of the Health and Safety Code, Section 70674 of the Government Code, and grants, gifts, or devises made to the state from private sources to be used for the purposes of this part shall be deposited into the Family Law Trust Fund.

(c) Moneys deposited in the Family Law Trust Fund shall be placed in an interest bearing account. Any interest earned shall accrue to the fund and shall be disbursed pursuant to subdivision (d).

(d) Money deposited in the Family Law Trust Fund shall be disbursed for purposes specified in this part and for other family law related activities.

(e) Moneys deposited in the Family Law Trust Fund shall be administered by the Judicial Council. The Judicial Council may, with appropriate guidelines, delegate the administration of the fund to the Administrative Office of the Courts.

(f) Any moneys in the Family Law Trust Fund that are unencumbered at the end of the fiscal year are automatically appropriated to the Family Law Trust Fund of the following year.

(g) In order to defray the costs of collection of these funds, pursuant to this section, the local registrar, county clerk, or county recorder may retain a percentage of the funds collected, not to exceed 10 percent of the fee payable to the state pursuant to subdivision (c) of Section 103625 of the Health and Safety Code. *(Stats.1992, c. 162 (A.B.2650), § 10, operative Jan. 1, 1994. Amended by Stats.1996, c. 1023 (S.B.1497), § 45, eff. Sept. 29, 1996; Stats.1997, c. 850 (A.B.233), § 5; Stats.2005, c. 75 (A.B.145), § 45, eff. July 19, 2005, operative Jan. 1, 2006.)*

Cross References

County defined for purposes of this Code, see Family Code § 67.
Health Statistics Special Fund,
   Deposits, see Health and Safety Code § 103605.
   Expenditures, purpose, see Health and Safety Code § 102247.
Judgment and order defined for purposes of this Code, see Family Code § 100.
State defined for purposes of this Code, see Family Code § 145.

Division 6

NULLITY, DISSOLUTION, AND LEGAL SEPARATION

Part		Section
1.	General Provisions	2000
2.	Judicial Determination of Void or Voidable Marriage	2200
3.	Dissolution of Marriage and Legal Separation	2300
3.5.	Attorney's Fees and Costs	2030
4.	Protective and Restraining Orders	2040
5.	Notice to Insurance Carriers	2050
6.	Employee Pension Benefit Plan as Party	2060
7.	Restoration of Wife's Former Name	2080
8.	Uniform Divorce Recognition Act	2090
9.	Disclosure of Assets and Liabilities	2100
10.	Relief From Judgment	2120

Part 1

GENERAL PROVISIONS

Chapter		Section
1.	Application of Part	2000
2.	Jurisdiction	2010
3.	Procedural Provisions	2020

CHAPTER 1. APPLICATION OF PART

Section
2000. Application of part.

GENERAL PROVISIONS

§ 2000. Application of part

This part applies to a proceeding for dissolution of marriage, for nullity of marriage, or for legal separation of the parties. *(Stats.1992, c. 162 (A.B.2650), § 10, operative Jan. 1, 1994.)*

Cross References

Collaborative law process, see Family Code § 2013.
Proceeding defined for purposes of this Code, see Family Code § 110.

CHAPTER 2. JURISDICTION

Section
2010. Scope of jurisdiction.
2011. Service by publication; scope of jurisdiction.
2012. Pendency of motion to quash service of summons or to stay or dismiss action; appearance of respondent.
2013. Collaborative law process.

§ 2010. Scope of jurisdiction

In a proceeding for dissolution of marriage, for nullity of marriage, or for legal separation of the parties, the court has jurisdiction to inquire into and render any judgment and make orders that are appropriate concerning the following:

(a) The status of the marriage, including any marriage under subdivision (c) of Section 308.

(b) The custody of minor children of the marriage.

(c) The support of children for whom support may be ordered, including children born after the filing of the initial petition or the final decree of dissolution.

(d) The support of either party.

(e) The settlement of the property rights of the parties.

(f) The award of attorney's fees and costs. *(Stats.1992, c. 162 (A.B.2650), § 10, operative Jan. 1, 1994. Amended by Stats.1993, c. 219 (A.B.1500), § 103; Stats.1994, c. 1269 (A.B.2208), § 12.5; Stats.2010, c. 397 (A.B.2700), § 2.)*

Cross References

Child for whom support may be ordered defined for purposes of this Code, see Family Code § 58.
Continuing jurisdiction, community estate or liabilities, see Family Code § 2556.
Custody of child, matters to be considered, see Family Code § 3040 et seq.
Judgment and order defined for purposes of this Code, see Family Code § 100.
Jurisdiction, division of real and personal property, see Family Code § 2650.
Minor defined, see Family Code § 6500.
Proceeding defined for purposes of this Code, see Family Code § 110.
Property defined for purposes of this Code, see Family Code § 113.
Stepparent's visitation rights, see Family Code § 3101.
Superior court jurisdiction, see Family Code § 200.
Support defined for purposes of this Code, see Family Code § 150.
Uniform Child Custody Jurisdiction and Enforcement Act, see Family Code § 3400 et seq.
Uniform Divorce Recognition Act, see Family Code § 2090 et seq.
Uniform Parentage Act, see Family Code § 7600 et seq.

Research References

Forms

California Practice Guide: Rutter Family Law Forms Form 1:32, Glossary of Common Family Law Terms, Phrases and Concepts (Enclosure to Form 1:31).
California Practice Guide: Rutter Family Law Forms Form 4:12, Request for Order to Strike Petition.
1 California Transactions Forms--Family Law § 2:55, Continuing Jurisdiction.
1 California Transactions Forms--Family Law § 3:4, Subject Matter Jurisdiction for Custody Determinations.
West's California Judicial Council Forms FL-372, Request for Joinder of Employee Benefit Plan Order.
West's California Judicial Council Forms FL-374, Notice of Appearance and Response of Employee Benefit Plan.

§ 2011. Service by publication; scope of jurisdiction

When service of summons on a spouse is made pursuant to Section 415.50 of the Code of Civil Procedure, the court, without the aid of attachment or the appointment of a receiver, shall have and may exercise the same jurisdiction over:

(a) The community real property of the spouse so served situated in this state as it has or may exercise over the community real property of a spouse who is personally served with process within this state.

(b) The quasi-community real property of the spouse so served situated in this state as it has or may exercise over the quasi-community real property of a spouse who is personally served with process within this state. *(Stats.1992, c. 162 (A.B.2650), § 10, operative Jan. 1, 1994.)*

Cross References

Community property defined, see Family Code § 65.
Property defined for purposes of this Code, see Family Code § 113.
Quasi-community property defined, see Family Code § 125.
References to husband, wife, spouses and married persons, persons included for purposes of this Code, see Family Code § 11.
State defined for purposes of this Code, see Family Code § 145.

§ 2012. Pendency of motion to quash service of summons or to stay or dismiss action; appearance of respondent

(a) During the time a motion pursuant to Section 418.10 of the Code of Civil Procedure is pending, the respondent may appear in opposition to an order made during the pendency of the proceeding and the appearance shall not be deemed a general appearance by the respondent.

(b) As used in this section, a motion pursuant to Section 418.10 of the Code of Civil Procedure is pending from the time notice of motion is served and filed until the time within which to petition for a writ of mandate has expired or, if a petition is made, until the time final judgment in the mandate proceeding is entered. *(Stats.1992, c. 162 (A.B.2650), § 10, operative Jan. 1, 1994.)*

Cross References

Judgment and order defined for purposes of this Code, see Family Code § 100.
Mandamus, purpose of writ of mandate, courts which may issue writ and parties to whom issued, see Code of Civil Procedure § 1085.
Proceeding defined for purposes of this Code, see Family Code § 110.
Respondent defined for purposes of this Code, see Family Code § 127.

§ 2013. Collaborative law process

(a) If a written agreement is entered into by the parties, the parties may utilize a collaborative law process to resolve any matter governed by this code over which the court is granted jurisdiction pursuant to Section 2000.

(b) "Collaborative law process" means the process in which the parties and any professionals engaged by the parties to assist them agree in writing to use their best efforts and to make a good faith attempt to resolve disputes related to the family law matters as referenced in subdivision (a) on an agreed basis without resorting to adversary judicial intervention. *(Added by Stats.2006, c. 496 (A.B. 402), § 2.)*

Research References

Forms

West's California Code Forms, Family § 2013, Comment Overview—Collaborative Law.

CHAPTER 3. PROCEDURAL PROVISIONS

Section
2020. Responsive pleadings.

NULLITY, DISSOLUTION, AND LEGAL SEPARATION

Section
2021. Joinder; interested parties; employee benefit plans.
2022. Evidence collected by eavesdropping; admissibility.
2023. Payment of obligation directly to creditor.
2024. Petitions or judgments for dissolution of marriage, nullity of marriage, or for legal separation of the parties; notice.
2024.5. Redacting social security numbers from pleadings, attachments, documents or other written material filed pursuant to petitions for dissolution of marriage, nullity of marriage or legal separation; exceptions.
2024.6. Sealing of pleadings listing parties' financial assets and liabilities and their location and identifying information; forms; service of copy of pleading.
2024.7. Notice of eligibility for reduced-cost or no-cost health coverage.
2025. Appeals of bifurcated issues; certification by superior court.
2026. Reconciliation of parties; amelioration of contempt.

§ 2020. Responsive pleadings

A responsive pleading, if any, shall be filed and a copy served on the petitioner within 30 days of the date of the service on the respondent of a copy of the petition and summons. *(Stats.1992, c. 162 (A.B.2650), § 10, operative Jan. 1, 1994. Amended by Stats.1998, c. 581 (A.B.2801), § 4.)*

Cross References

Petitioner defined for purposes of this Code, see Family Code § 126.
Respondent defined for purposes of this Code, see Family Code § 127.

Research References

Forms
West's California Code Forms, Family § 2020, Comment Overview—Nullity, Dissolution, and Legal Separation.
West's California Judicial Council Forms FL-120, Response—Marriage/Domestic Partnership (Also Available in Arabic, Chinese, and Spanish).

§ 2021. Joinder; interested parties; employee benefit plans

(a) Subject to subdivision (b), the court may order that a person who claims an interest in the proceeding be joined as a party to the proceeding in accordance with rules adopted by the Judicial Council pursuant to Section 211.

(b) An employee benefit plan may be joined as a party only in accordance with Chapter 6 (commencing with Section 2060). *(Stats. 1992, c. 162 (A.B.2650), § 10, operative Jan. 1, 1994. Amended by Stats.1996, c. 1061 (S.B.1033), § 3.)*

Cross References

Adverse claims, discharge of employee benefit plan from, see Family Code § 755.
Employee benefit plan defined for purposes of this Code, see Family Code § 80.
Judgment and order defined for purposes of this Code, see Family Code § 100.
Person defined for purposes of this Code, see Family Code § 105.
Proceeding defined for purposes of this Code, see Family Code § 110.

Research References

Forms
West's California Code Forms, Family § 2020, Comment Overview—Nullity, Dissolution, and Legal Separation.
West's California Judicial Council Forms FL-371, Notice of Motion and Declaration for Joinder.
West's California Judicial Council Forms FL-372, Request for Joinder of Employee Benefit Plan Order.
West's California Judicial Council Forms FL-374, Notice of Appearance and Response of Employee Benefit Plan.

§ 2022. Evidence collected by eavesdropping; admissibility

(a) Evidence collected by eavesdropping in violation of Chapter 1.5 (commencing with Section 630) of Title 15 of Part 1 of the Penal Code is inadmissible.

(b) If it appears that a violation described in subdivision (a) exists, the court may refer the matter to the proper authority for investigation and prosecution. *(Stats.1992, c. 162 (A.B.2650), § 10, operative Jan. 1, 1994.)*

Cross References

Marital communications, privilege, see Evidence Code § 980.
Mediation proceedings, restrictions on admissibility and disclosure of specified communications, see Evidence Code §§ 1119, 1120, 1122, 1127.
Wiretapping, inadmissibility of evidence, see Penal Code § 631.

Research References

Forms
1 California Transactions Forms--Family Law § 3:16, Identifying Areas of Parental Decision Making and Participation.

§ 2023. Payment of obligation directly to creditor

(a) On a determination that payment of an obligation of a party would benefit either party or a child for whom support may be ordered, the court may order one of the parties to pay the obligation, or a portion thereof, directly to the creditor.

(b) The creditor has no right to enforce the order made under this section, nor are the creditor's rights affected by the determination made under this section. *(Stats.1992, c. 162 (A.B.2650), § 10, operative Jan. 1, 1994. Amended by Stats.1993, c. 219 (A.B.1500), § 104.)*

Cross References

Child for whom support may be ordered defined, see Family Code § 58.
Judgment and order defined for purposes of this Code, see Family Code § 100.
Support defined for purposes of this Code, see Family Code § 150.

§ 2024. Petitions or judgments for dissolution of marriage, nullity of marriage, or for legal separation of the parties; notice

(a) A petition for dissolution of marriage, nullity of marriage, or legal separation of the parties, or a joint petition for summary dissolution of marriage, shall contain the following notice:

"Dissolution or annulment of your marriage may automatically cancel your spouse's rights under your will, trust, retirement benefit plan, power of attorney, pay on death bank account, transfer on death vehicle registration, survivorship rights to any property owned in joint tenancy, and any other similar thing. It does not automatically cancel your spouse's rights as beneficiary of your life insurance policy. If these are not the results that you want, you must change your will, trust, account agreement, or other similar document to reflect your actual wishes.

Dissolution or annulment of your marriage may also automatically cancel your rights under your spouse's will, trust, retirement benefit plan, power of attorney, pay on death bank account, transfer on death vehicle registration, and survivorship rights to any property owned in joint tenancy, and any other similar thing. It does not automatically cancel your rights as beneficiary of your spouse's life insurance policy.

You should review these matters, as well as any credit cards, other credit accounts, insurance policies, retirement benefit plans, and credit reports to determine whether they should be changed or whether you should take any other actions in view of the dissolution or annulment of your marriage, or your legal separation. However, some changes may require the agreement of your spouse or a court order (see Part 3 (commencing with Section 231) of Division 2 of the Family Code)."

(b) A judgment for dissolution of marriage, for nullity of marriage, or for legal separation of the parties shall contain the following notice:

"Dissolution or annulment of your marriage may automatically cancel your spouse's rights under your will, trust, retirement benefit plan, power of attorney, pay on death bank account, transfer on death vehicle registration, survivorship rights to any property owned in joint tenancy, and any other similar thing. It does not automatically cancel your spouse's rights as beneficiary of your life insurance policy. If these are not the results that you want, you must change your will, trust, account agreement, or other similar document to reflect your actual wishes.

Dissolution or annulment of your marriage may also automatically cancel your rights under your spouse's will, trust, retirement benefit plan, power of attorney, pay on death bank account, transfer on death vehicle registration, survivorship rights to any property owned in joint tenancy, and any other similar thing. It does not automatically cancel your rights as beneficiary of your spouse's life insurance policy.

You should review these matters, as well as any credit cards, other credit accounts, insurance policies, retirement benefit plans, and credit reports to determine whether they should be changed or whether you should take any other actions in view of the dissolution or annulment of your marriage, or your legal separation." *(Stats. 1992, c. 162 (A.B.2650), § 10, operative Jan. 1, 1994. Amended by Stats.1993, c. 219 (A.B.1500), § 105; Stats.2001, c. 417 (A.B.873), § 1.)*

Cross References

Judgment and order defined for purposes of this Code, see Family Code § 100.
Property defined for purposes of this Code, see Family Code § 113.
References to husband, wife, spouses and married persons, persons included for purposes of this Code, see Family Code § 11.
Wills, provisions revoked by dissolution or annulment of marriage, see Probate Code § 6122.

Research References

Forms

West's California Code Forms, Family § 2020, Comment Overview—Nullity, Dissolution, and Legal Separation.
West's California Judicial Council Forms FL–180, Judgment (Also Available in Spanish).

§ 2024.5. Redacting social security numbers from pleadings, attachments, documents or other written material filed pursuant to petitions for dissolution of marriage, nullity of marriage or legal separation; exceptions

(a) Except as provided in subdivision (b), the petitioner or respondent may redact any social security number from any pleading, attachment, document, or other written material filed with the court pursuant to a petition for dissolution of marriage, nullity of marriage, or legal separation. The Judicial Council form used to file such a petition, or a response to such a petition, shall contain a notice that the parties may redact any social security numbers from those pleadings, attachments, documents, or other material filed with the court.

(b) An abstract of support judgment, the form required pursuant to subdivision (b) of Section 4014, or any similar form created for the purpose of collecting child or spousal support payments may not be redacted pursuant to subdivision (a). *(Added by Stats.2004, c. 45 (A.B.782), § 2, eff. June 7, 2004.)*

Cross References

Department of Child Support Services, generally, see Family Code § 17000 et seq.
Judgment and order defined for purposes of this Code, see Family Code § 100.

Minor defined for purposes of this Code, see Family Code § 6500.
Petitioner defined for purposes of this Code, see Family Code § 126.
Proceeding defined for purposes of this Code, see Family Code § 110.
Respondent defined for purposes of this Code, see Family Code § 127.
Support defined for purposes of this Code, see Family Code § 150.

§ 2024.6. Sealing of pleadings listing parties' financial assets and liabilities and their location and identifying information; forms; service of copy of pleading

(a) Upon request by a party to a petition for dissolution of marriage, nullity of marriage, or legal separation, the court shall order a pleading that lists the parties' financial assets and liabilities and provides the location or identifying information about those assets and liabilities sealed. The request may be made by ex parte application. Nothing sealed pursuant to this section may be unsealed except upon petition to the court and good cause shown.

(b) Commencing not later than July 1, 2005, the Judicial Council form used to declare assets and liabilities of the parties in a proceeding for dissolution of marriage, nullity of marriage, or legal separation of the parties shall require the party filing the form to state whether the declaration contains identifying information on the assets and liabilities listed therein. If the party making the request uses a pleading other than the Judicial Council form, the pleading shall exhibit a notice on the front page, in bold capital letters, that the pleading lists and identifies financial information and is therefore subject to this section.

(c) For purposes of this section, "pleading" means a document that sets forth or declares the parties' assets and liabilities, income and expenses, a marital settlement agreement that lists and identifies the parties' assets and liabilities, or any document filed with the court incidental to the declaration or agreement that lists and identifies financial information.

(d) The party making the request to seal a pleading pursuant to subdivision (a) shall serve a copy of the pleading on the other party to the proceeding and file a proof of service with the request to seal the pleading.

(e) Nothing in this section precludes a party to a proceeding described in this section from using any document or information contained in a sealed pleading in any manner that is not otherwise prohibited by law. *(Added by Stats.2004, c. 45 (A.B.782), § 3, eff. June 7, 2004. Amended by Stats.2005, c. 22 (S.B.1108), § 61.)*

Validity

This section was held unconstitutional on its face as an undue burden on the right of public access to court records, in the case of In re Marriage of Burkle (App. 2 Dist. 2006) 37 Cal.Rptr.3d 805, 135 Cal.App.4th 1045, as modified, review denied.

Research References

Forms

West's California Code Forms, Family § 2020, Comment Overview—Nullity, Dissolution, and Legal Separation.
West's California Code Forms, Family § 2104 Form 4, Schedule of Assets and Debts.

§ 2024.7. Notice of eligibility for reduced-cost or no-cost health coverage

On and after January 1, 2014, upon the filing of a petition for dissolution of marriage, nullity of marriage, or legal separation, the court shall provide to the petitioner and the respondent a notice informing them that they may be eligible for reduced-cost coverage through the California Health Benefit Exchange established under Title 22 (commencing with Section 100500) of the Government Code or no-cost coverage through Medi-Cal. The notice shall include information on obtaining coverage pursuant to those programs, and shall be developed by the California Health Benefit Exchange.

§ 2024.7

(Added by Stats.2012, c. 851 (A.B.792), § 1. Amended by Stats.2019, c. 115 (A.B.1817), § 14, eff. Jan. 1, 2020.)

Research References

Forms

West's California Judicial Council Forms FL–110, Summons (Also Available in Arabic and Chinese).

§ 2025. Appeals of bifurcated issues; certification by superior court

Notwithstanding any other provision of law, if the court has ordered an issue or issues bifurcated for separate trial or hearing in advance of the disposition of the entire case, a court of appeal may order an issue or issues transferred to it for hearing and decision when the court that heard the issue or issues certifies that the appeal is appropriate. Certification by the court shall be in accordance with rules promulgated by the Judicial Council. *(Stats.1992, c. 162 (A.B.2650), § 10, operative Jan. 1, 1994.)*

Cross References

Judgment and order defined for purposes of this Code, see Family Code § 100.
Judicial Council, rules of practice and procedure, see Family Code § 210 et seq.
Jurisdiction in superior court, see Family Code § 200.

§ 2026. Reconciliation of parties; amelioration of contempt

The reconciliation of the parties, whether conditional or unconditional, is an ameliorating factor to be considered by the court in considering a contempt of an existing court order. *(Stats.1992, c. 162 (A.B.2650), § 10, operative Jan. 1, 1994.)*

Cross References

Conciliation,
  Family mediation and conciliation services, see Family Code § 1850.
  Petition, see Family Code § 1831 et seq.
  Stay after hearing of conciliation petition, see Family Code § 1840.
  Transfer of actions, see Family Code § 1841.
Judgment and order defined for purposes of this Code, see Family Code § 100.
Party in contempt, enforcement in judgment or order, see Code of Civil Procedure § 1218.

CHAPTER 3.5. ATTORNEY'S FEES AND COSTS

Section
2030. Award; findings; timing; modification; limitation; statewide rule of court.
2031. Applications for temporary orders.
2032. Reasonableness of award; findings; property from which fees can be awarded; allocation of fees and costs in light of complex issues.
2033. Family law attorney's real property lien; notice; objections.
2034. Denial of lien on real property; limitation of lien amount; determination of appropriate, equitable allocation.
2035 to 2039. Inoperative.

Cross References

Attorney's fees and costs, generally, see Code of Civil Procedure § 1021.
Judicial determination of void or voidable marriages, grant of attorney's fees and costs, see Family Code § 2255.

§ 2030. Award; findings; timing; modification; limitation; statewide rule of court

(a)(1) In a proceeding for dissolution of marriage, nullity of marriage, or legal separation of the parties, and in any proceeding subsequent to entry of a related judgment, the court shall ensure that each party has access to legal representation, including access early in the proceedings, to preserve each party's rights by ordering, if necessary based on the income and needs assessments, one party, except a governmental entity, to pay to the other party, or to the other party's attorney, whatever amount is reasonably necessary for attorney's fees and for the cost of maintaining or defending the proceeding during the pendency of the proceeding.

(2) When a request for attorney's fees and costs is made, the court shall make findings on whether an award of attorney's fees and costs under this section is appropriate, whether there is a disparity in access to funds to retain counsel, and whether one party is able to pay for legal representation of both parties. If the findings demonstrate disparity in access and ability to pay, the court shall make an order awarding attorney's fees and costs. A party who lacks the financial ability to hire an attorney may request, as an in pro per litigant, that the court order the other party, if that other party has the financial ability, to pay a reasonable amount to allow the unrepresented party to retain an attorney in a timely manner before proceedings in the matter go forward.

(b) Attorney's fees and costs within this section may be awarded for legal services rendered or costs incurred before or after the commencement of the proceeding.

(c) The court shall augment or modify the original award for attorney's fees and costs as may be reasonably necessary for the prosecution or defense of the proceeding, or any proceeding related thereto, including after any appeal has been concluded.

(d) Any order requiring a party who is not the spouse of another party to the proceeding to pay attorney's fees or costs shall be limited to an amount reasonably necessary to maintain or defend the action on the issues relating to that party.

(e) The Judicial Council shall, by January 1, 2012, adopt a statewide rule of court to implement this section and develop a form for the information that shall be submitted to the court to obtain an award of attorney's fees under this section. *(Added by Stats.1993, c. 219 (A.B.1500), § 106.1. Amended by Stats.2004, c. 472 (A.B.2148), § 1; Stats.2010, c. 352 (A.B.939), § 4.)*

Cross References

Attorney's fees and costs, generally, see Code of Civil Procedure § 1021.
Custody of children, award of attorney's fees and costs, see Family Code § 3121.
Domestic violence protection, protective orders and other domestic violence prevention orders, award of attorney's fees and costs, see Family Code § 6344.
Judgment and order defined for purposes of this Code, see Family Code § 100.
Judicial determination of void or voidable marriages, grant of attorney's fees and costs, see Family Code § 2255.
Proceeding defined for purposes of this Code, see Family Code § 110.
References to husband, wife, spouses and married persons, persons included for purposes of this Code, see Family Code § 11.
Uniform Parentage Act, child custody and visitation proceedings, award of attorney's fees and costs, see Family Code § 7605.

Research References

Forms

California Practice Guide: Rutter Family Law Forms Form 5:2, Request for Order Re Child Custody, Child Support, Spousal Support, Attorney Fees, etc.
California Practice Guide: Rutter Family Law Forms Form 14:1, Request for Order Re Need-Based Attorney Fees and Costs.
California Practice Guide: Rutter Family Law Forms Form 14:2, Request for Order Re Need-Based Attorney Fees and Costs (Pro Per Litigant).
California Practice Guide: Rutter Family Law Forms Form 14:3, Request for Order Re Need-Based Attorney Fees and Costs ("Borson Motion").
1 California Transactions Forms--Family Law § 2:48, Nondischargeable Debts.
1 California Transactions Forms--Family Law § 3:2, Child Custody.
West's California Code Forms, Family § 2030, Comment Overview—Attorney's Fees.
West's California Judicial Council Forms FL–150, Income and Expense Declaration (Also Available in Spanish).
West's California Judicial Council Forms FL–157, Spousal or Domestic Partner Support Declaration Attachment (Also Available in Spanish).

West's California Judicial Council Forms FL–158, Supporting Declaration for Attorney's Fees and Costs Attachment.
West's California Judicial Council Forms FL–319, Request for Attorney's Fees and Costs Attachment.
West's California Judicial Council Forms FL–346, Attorney's Fees and Costs Order Attachment.
West's California Judicial Council Forms FL–349, Spousal or Domestic Partner Support Factors Under Family Code Section 4320—Attachment.

§ 2031. Applications for temporary orders

(a)(1) Except as provided in subdivision (b), during the pendency of a proceeding for dissolution of marriage, for nullity of marriage, for legal separation of the parties, or any proceeding subsequent to entry of a related judgment, an application for a temporary order making, augmenting, or modifying an award of attorney's fees, including a reasonable retainer to hire an attorney, or costs or both shall be made by motion on notice or by an order to show cause.

(2) The court shall rule on an application within 15 days of the hearing on the motion or order to show cause.

(b) An order described in subdivision (a) may be made without notice by an oral motion in open court at either of the following times:

(1) At the time of the hearing of the cause on the merits.

(2) At any time before entry of judgment against a party whose default has been entered pursuant to Section 585 or 586 of the Code of Civil Procedure. The court shall rule on any motion made pursuant to this subdivision within 15 days and prior to the entry of any judgment. *(Added by Stats.1993, c. 219 (A.B.1500), § 106.1. Amended by Stats.2004, c. 472 (A.B.2148), § 2.)*

Cross References

Attorney's fees and costs, generally, see Code of Civil Procedure § 1021.
Computation of time, first and last days, holidays, see Civil Code § 10; Code of Civil Procedure § 12 et seq.; Government Code § 6800 et seq.
Custody of children, application for temporary order of award for attorney's fees and costs, see Family Code § 3121.
Judgment and order defined for purposes of this Code, see Family Code § 100.
Judicial determination of void or voidable marriages, grant of attorney's fees and costs, see Family Code § 2255.
Proceeding defined for purposes of this Code, see Family Code § 110.
Uniform Parentage Act, child custody and visitation proceedings, application for temporary order for award of attorney's fees and costs, see Family Code § 7605.

Research References

Forms

West's California Code Forms, Family § 2030, Comment Overview—Attorney's Fees.

§ 2032. Reasonableness of award; findings; property from which fees can be awarded; allocation of fees and costs in light of complex issues

(a) The court may make an award of attorney's fees and costs under Section 2030 or 2031 where the making of the award, and the amount of the award, are just and reasonable under the relative circumstances of the respective parties.

(b) In determining what is just and reasonable under the relative circumstances, the court shall take into consideration the need for the award to enable each party, to the extent practical, to have sufficient financial resources to present the party's case adequately, taking into consideration, to the extent relevant, the circumstances of the respective parties described in Section 4320. The fact that the party requesting an award of attorney's fees and costs has resources from which the party could pay the party's own attorney's fees and costs is not itself a bar to an order that the other party pay part or all of the fees and costs requested. Financial resources are only one factor for the court to consider in determining how to apportion the overall cost of the litigation equitably between the parties under their relative circumstances.

(c) The court may order payment of an award of attorney's fees and costs from any type of property, whether community or separate, principal or income.

(d) Either party may, at any time before the hearing of the cause on the merits, on noticed motion, request the court to make a finding that the case involves complex or substantial issues of fact or law related to property rights, visitation, custody, or support. Upon that finding, the court may in its discretion determine the appropriate, equitable allocation of attorney's fees, court costs, expert fees, and consultant fees between the parties. The court order may provide for the allocation of separate or community assets, security against these assets, and for payments from income or anticipated income of either party for the purpose described in this subdivision and for the benefit of one or both parties. Payments shall be authorized only on agreement of the parties or, in the absence thereof, by court order. The court may order that a referee be appointed pursuant to Section 639 of the Code of Civil Procedure to oversee the allocation of fees and costs. *(Added by Stats.1993, c. 219 (A.B.1500), § 106.1. Amended by Stats.2010, c. 352 (A.B.939), § 5.)*

Cross References

Judgment and order defined for purposes of this Code, see Family Code § 100.
Property defined for purposes of this Code, see Family Code § 113.
Support defined for purposes of this Code, see Family Code § 150.

Research References

Forms

California Practice Guide: Rutter Family Law Forms Form 14:1, Request for Order Re Need-Based Attorney Fees and Costs.
California Practice Guide: Rutter Family Law Forms Form 14:2, Request for Order Re Need-Based Attorney Fees and Costs (Pro Per Litigant).
California Practice Guide: Rutter Family Law Forms Form 14:3, Request for Order Re Need-Based Attorney Fees and Costs ("Borson Motion").
1 California Transactions Forms--Family Law § 3:2, Child Custody.
1 California Transactions Forms--Family Law § 3:6, Unenforceability of Limitation of Jurisdiction.
West's California Code Forms, Family § 2030, Comment Overview—Attorney's Fees.
West's California Judicial Council Forms FL–150, Income and Expense Declaration (Also Available in Spanish).
West's California Judicial Council Forms FL–157, Spousal or Domestic Partner Support Declaration Attachment (Also Available in Spanish).
West's California Judicial Council Forms FL–158, Supporting Declaration for Attorney's Fees and Costs Attachment.
West's California Judicial Council Forms FL–319, Request for Attorney's Fees and Costs Attachment.
West's California Judicial Council Forms FL–349, Spousal or Domestic Partner Support Factors Under Family Code Section 4320—Attachment.

§ 2033. Family law attorney's real property lien; notice; objections

(a) Either party may encumber the party's interest in community real property to pay reasonable attorney's fees in order to retain or maintain legal counsel in a proceeding for dissolution of marriage, for nullity of marriage, or for legal separation of the parties. This encumbrance shall be known as a "family law attorney's real property lien" and attaches only to the encumbering party's interest in the community real property.

(b) Notice of a family law attorney's real property lien shall be served either personally or on the other party's attorney of record at least 15 days before the encumbrance is recorded. This notice shall contain a declaration signed under penalty of perjury containing all of the following:

(1) A full description of the real property.

(2) The party's belief as to the fair market value of the property and documentation supporting that belief.

(3) Encumbrances on the property as of the date of the declaration.

(4) A list of community assets and liabilities and their estimated values as of the date of the declaration.

(5) The amount of the family law attorney's real property lien.

(c) The nonencumbering party may file an ex parte objection to the family law attorney's real property lien. The objection shall include a request to stay the recordation until further notice of the court and shall contain a copy of the notice received. The objection shall also include a declaration signed under penalty of perjury as to all of the following:

(1) Specific objections to the family law attorney's real property lien and to the specific items in the notice.

(2) The objector's belief as to the appropriate items or value and documentation supporting that belief.

(3) A declaration specifically stating why recordation of the encumbrance at this time would likely result in an unequal division of property or would otherwise be unjust under the circumstances of the case.

(d) Except as otherwise provided by this section, general procedural rules regarding ex parte motions apply.

(e) An attorney for whom a family law attorney's real property lien is obtained shall comply with Rule 3–300 of the Rules of Professional Conduct of the State Bar of California. *(Added by Stats.1993, c. 219 (A.B.1500), § 106.1. Amended by Stats.2019, c. 115 (A.B.1817), § 15, eff. Jan. 1, 2020.)*

Cross References

Community real property, spouse's joinder in conveyances, application of this section, see Family Code § 1102.
Judgment and order defined for purposes of this Code, see Family Code § 100.
Proceeding defined for purposes of this Code, see Family Code § 110.
Property defined for purposes of this Code, see Family Code § 113.
State defined for purposes of this Code, see Family Code § 145.

Research References

Forms

California Practice Guide: Rutter Family Law Forms Form 1:17, Family Law Attorney's Real Property Lien.
California Practice Guide: Rutter Family Law Forms Form 1:19, Notice of Family Law Attorney's Real Property Lien.
California Practice Guide: Rutter Family Law Forms Form 1:20, Ex Parte Application and Request for Order Re Objection to Family Law Attorney's Real Property Lien and Request to Stay Recordation.
West's California Code Forms, Family § 2030, Comment Overview—Attorney's Fees.
West's California Code Forms, Family § 2033 Form 2, Trust Deed Creating Attorney's Lien.
West's California Code Forms, Family § 2033 Form 3, Notice of Attorney's Real Property Lien.

§ 2034. Denial of lien on real property; limitation of lien amount; determination of appropriate, equitable allocation

(a) On application of either party, the court may deny the family law attorney's real property lien described in Section 2033 based on a finding that the encumbrance would likely result in an unequal division of property because it would impair the encumbering party's ability to meet the party's fair share of the community obligations or would otherwise be unjust under the circumstances of the case. The court may also, for good cause, limit the amount of the family law attorney's real property lien. A limitation by the court is not to be construed as a determination of reasonable attorney's fees.

(b) On receiving an objection to the establishment of a family law attorney's real property lien, the court may, on its own motion, determine whether the case involves complex or substantial issues of fact or law related to property rights, visitation, custody, or support. If the court finds that the case involves one or more of these complex or substantial issues, the court may determine the appropriate, equitable allocation of fees and costs as provided in subdivision (d) of Section 2032.

(c) The court has jurisdiction to resolve any dispute arising from the existence of a family law attorney's real property lien. *(Added by Stats.1993, c. 219 (A.B.1500), § 106.1. Amended by Stats.2010, c. 352 (A.B.939), § 6; Stats.2019, c. 115 (A.B.1817), § 16, eff. Jan. 1, 2020.)*

Cross References

Property defined for purposes of this Code, see Family Code § 113.
Support defined for purposes of this Code, see Family Code § 150.

Research References

Forms

California Practice Guide: Rutter Family Law Forms Form 1:20, Ex Parte Application and Request for Order Re Objection to Family Law Attorney's Real Property Lien and Request to Stay Recordation.
West's California Code Forms, Family § 2030, Comment Overview—Attorney's Fees.
West's California Code Forms, Family § 2033 Form 2, Trust Deed Creating Attorney's Lien.

§§ 2035 to 2039. Inoperative

CHAPTER 4. PROTECTIVE AND RESTRAINING ORDERS

Article	Section
1. Orders in Summons	2040
2. Ex Parte Orders	2045
3. Orders After Notice and Hearing	2047
4. Orders Included in Judgment	2049

Cross References

Law enforcement response to domestic violence, written policies and standards, see Penal Code § 13701.

ARTICLE 1. ORDERS IN SUMMONS

Section
2040. Temporary restraining order; contents; notice; definitions.
2041. Application of temporary restraining order provisions to rights, title and interest of purchaser for value.
2042, 2043. Inoperative.

§ 2040. Temporary restraining order; contents; notice; definitions

(a) In addition to the contents required by Section 412.20 of the Code of Civil Procedure, the summons shall contain a temporary restraining order:

(1) Restraining both parties from removing the minor child or children of the parties, if any, from the state, or from applying for a new or replacement passport for the minor child or children, without the prior written consent of the other party or an order of the court.

(2)(A) Restraining both parties from transferring, encumbering, hypothecating, concealing, or in any way disposing of, any property, real or personal, whether community, quasi-community, or separate, without the written consent of the other party or an order of the court, except in the usual course of business or for the necessities of life, and requiring each party to notify the other party of proposed extraordinary expenditures at least five business days before incurring those expenditures and to account to the court for all extraordinary expenditures made after service of the summons on that party.

(B) Notwithstanding subparagraph (A), the restraining order shall not preclude a party from using community property, quasi-community property, or the party's own separate property to pay reasonable attorney's fees and costs in order to retain legal counsel in the proceeding. A party who uses community property or quasi-community property to pay the party's attorney's retainer for fees and costs under this provision shall account to the community for the use of the property. A party who uses other property that is subsequently determined to be the separate property of the other party to pay the party's attorney's retainer for fees and costs under this provision shall account to the other party for the use of the property.

(3) Restraining both parties from cashing, borrowing against, canceling, transferring, disposing of, or changing the beneficiaries of insurance or other coverage, including life, health, automobile, and disability, held for the benefit of the parties and their child or children for whom support may be ordered.

(4) Restraining both parties from creating a nonprobate transfer or modifying a nonprobate transfer in a manner that affects the disposition of property subject to the transfer, without the written consent of the other party or an order of the court.

(b) This section does not restrain any of the following:

(1) Creation, modification, or revocation of a will.

(2) Revocation of a nonprobate transfer, including a revocable trust, pursuant to the instrument, provided that notice of the change is filed and served on the other party before the change takes effect.

(3) Elimination of a right of survivorship to property, provided that notice of the change is filed and served on the other party before the change takes effect.

(4) Creation of an unfunded revocable or irrevocable trust.

(5) Execution and filing of a disclaimer pursuant to Part 8 (commencing with Section 260) of Division 2 of the Probate Code.

(c) In all actions filed on and after January 1, 1995, the summons shall contain the following notice:

"WARNING: California law provides that, for purposes of division of property upon dissolution of marriage or legal separation, property acquired by the parties during marriage in joint form is presumed to be community property. If either party to this action should die before the jointly held community property is divided, the language of how title is held in the deed (i.e., joint tenancy, tenants in common, or community property) will be controlling and not the community property presumption. You should consult your attorney if you want the community property presumption to be written into the recorded title to the property."

(d) For the purposes of this section:

(1) "Nonprobate transfer" means an instrument, other than a will, that makes a transfer of property on death, including a revocable trust, pay on death account in a financial institution, Totten trust, transfer on death registration of personal property, revocable transfer on death deed, or other instrument of a type described in Section 5000 of the Probate Code.

(2) "Nonprobate transfer" does not include a provision for the transfer of property on death in an insurance policy or other coverage held for the benefit of the parties and their child or children for whom support may be ordered, to the extent that the provision is subject to paragraph (3) of subdivision (a).

(e) The restraining order included in the summons shall include descriptions of the notices required by paragraphs (2) and (3) of subdivision (b). *(Added by Stats.1993, c. 219 (A.B.1500), § 106.7. Amended by Stats.1994, c. 1269 (A.B.2208), § 13; Stats.1999, c. 118 (S.B.357), § 1; Stats.2000, c. 135 (A.B.2539), § 57; Stats.2001, c. 417 (A.B.873), § 2; Stats.2012, c. 276 (S.B.1206), § 2; Stats.2015, c. 293 (A.B.139), § 2, eff. Jan. 1, 2016; Stats.2019, c. 115 (A.B.1817), § 17, eff. Jan. 1, 2020.)*

Cross References

Child for whom support may be ordered defined for purposes of this Code, see Family Code § 58.
Community property defined for purposes of this Code, see Family Code § 65.
Deprivation of custody of child or right to visitation in violation of court order, see Penal Code § 278.5.
Effect of death of married person on community and quasi-community property, see Probate Code § 100.
Ex parte order regarding community, quasi-community and separate property, see Family Code § 6325.
Injunctions, generally, see Code of Civil Procedure § 526.
Injunctions, preventive relief, see Civil Code § 3420 et seq.
Intentional and knowing violation of court order to prevent harassment, disturbing the peace, or threats or acts of violence, see Penal Code § 273.6.
Judgment and order defined for purposes of this Code, see Family Code § 100.
Minor defined for purposes of this Code, see Family Code § 6500.
Proceeding defined for purposes of this Code, see Family Code § 110.
Property defined for purposes of this Code, see Family Code § 113.
Quasi-community property defined for purposes of this Code, see Family Code § 125.
Separate property defined for purposes of this Code, see Family Code § 130.
State defined for purposes of this Code, see Family Code § 145.
Support defined for purposes of this Code, see Family Code § 150.
Temporary restraining order in summons, application of this section, see Family Code § 231.
Written instruments, compliance with requirements for execution of will, rights of creditors, see Probate Code § 5000.

Research References

Forms

Asset Protection: Legal Planning, Strategies and Forms ¶ 4.04, Determining the Character of Property.
California Practice Guide: Rutter Family Law Forms Form 1:32, Glossary of Common Family Law Terms, Phrases and Concepts (Enclosure to Form 1:31).
West's California Judicial Council Forms FL–110, Summons (Also Available in Arabic and Chinese).
West's California Judicial Council Forms FL–210, Summons (Uniform Percentage—Petition for Custody and Support) (Incl. Spanish) (Also Available in Chinese).

§ 2041. Application of temporary restraining order provisions to rights, title and interest of purchaser for value

Nothing in Section 2040 adversely affects the rights, title, and interest of a purchaser for value, encumbrancer for value, or lessee for value who is without actual knowledge of the restraining order. *(Added by Stats.1993, c. 219 (A.B.1500), § 106.7.)*

Cross References

Judgment and order defined for purposes of this Code, see Family Code § 100.

§§ 2042, 2043. Inoperative

ARTICLE 2. EX PARTE ORDERS

Section
2045. Ex parte protective orders.

Cross References

County clerk, fees, certified copies of order under certain domestic relations laws, see Government Code § 26833.5.

§ 2045. Ex parte protective orders

During the pendency of the proceeding, on application of a party in the manner provided by Part 4 (commencing with Section 240) of Division 2, the court may issue ex parte any of the following orders:

(a) An order restraining any person from transferring, encumbering, hypothecating, concealing, or in any way disposing of any property, real or personal, whether community, quasi-community, or separate, except in the usual course of business or for the necessities of life, and if the order is directed against a party, requiring that party to notify the other party of any proposed extraordinary expenditures and to account to the court for all extraordinary expenditures.

§ 2045

NULLITY, DISSOLUTION, AND LEGAL SEPARATION

(b) A protective order, as defined in Section 6218, and any other order as provided in Article 1 (commencing with Section 6320) of Chapter 2 of Part 4 of Division 10. *(Added by Stats.1993, c. 219 (A.B.1500), § 106.7.)*

Cross References

Community property,
  Debts, liability for, see Family Code §§ 910, 911.
  Defined, see Civil Code § 687; Family Code §§ 65, 760; Probate Code § 28.
  Division of, see Family Code § 2600 et seq.
  Held in revocable trust, see Probate Code § 104.
  Interests of spouses defined, see Family Code § 751.
Ex parte order regarding community, quasi-community and separate property, see Family Code § 6325.
Judgment and order defined for purposes of this Code, see Family Code § 100.
Minor defined, see Family Code § 6500.
Person defined for purposes of this Code, see Family Code § 105.
Prevention of domestic violence, forms for issuance of orders, see Family Code § 6221.
Proceeding defined for purposes of this Code, see Family Code § 110.
Property defined for purposes of this Code, see Family Code § 113.
Quasi-community property defined, see Family Code § 125.
Separate property of married person, defined, see Family Code §§ 130, 770.
Support persons for victims of domestic violence, see Family Code § 6303.

Research References

Forms
California Practice Guide: Rutter Family Law Forms Form 5:5, Ex Parte Application and Request for Order Re Child Custody, Visitation and Property Control.
West's California Code Forms, Family § 2045, Comment Overview—Ex Parte Protective Orders.
West's California Judicial Council Forms FL–300, Request for Order (Also Available in Spanish).
West's California Judicial Council Forms FL–303, Declaration Regarding Notice and Service of Request for Temporary Emergency (Ex Parte) Orders (Also Available in Spanish).
West's California Judicial Council Forms FL–305, Temporary Emergency (Ex Parte) Orders (Also Available in Spanish).
West's California Judicial Council Forms FL–344, Property Order Attachment to Findings and Order After Hearing (Also Available in Spanish).

ARTICLE 3. ORDERS AFTER NOTICE AND HEARING

Section
2047. Protective orders; restraining orders.

Cross References

County clerk, fees, certified copies of order under certain domestic relations laws, see Government Code § 26833.5.

§ 2047. Protective orders; restraining orders

(a) After notice and a hearing, the court may issue a protective order, as defined in Section 6218, and any other restraining order as provided in Article 2 (commencing with Section 6340) of Chapter 2 of Part 4 of Division 10.

(b) The court may not issue a mutual protective order pursuant to subdivision (a) unless it meets the requirements of Section 6305. *(Added by Stats.1993, c. 219 (A.B.1500), § 106.7. Amended by Stats.1995, c. 246 (S.B.591), § 1.)*

Cross References

Judgment and order defined for purposes of this Code, see Family Code § 100.

Research References

Forms
West's California Code Forms, Family § 2047, Comment Overview—Orders After Notice and Hearing.

ARTICLE 4. ORDERS INCLUDED IN JUDGMENT

Section
2049. Protective orders included in judgments; restraining orders.

Cross References

County clerk, fees, certified copies of order under certain domestic relations laws, see Government Code § 26833.5.

§ 2049. Protective orders included in judgments; restraining orders

A judgment may include a protective order, as defined in Section 6218, and any other restraining order as provided in Article 3 (commencing with Section 6360) of Chapter 2 of Part 4 of Division 10. *(Added by Stats.1993, c. 219 (A.B.1500), § 106.7.)*

Cross References

County clerk, fees, certified copies of order under certain domestic relations laws, see Government Code § 26833.5.
Exclusion of spouse from other's dwelling, see Family Code § 753.
Judgment and order defined for purposes of this Code, see Family Code § 100.

Research References

Forms
West's California Code Forms, Family § 2049, Comment Overview—Orders Included in Judgment.

CHAPTER 5. NOTICE TO INSURANCE CARRIERS

Section
2050. Notice to health, life, or disability insurance carrier; form.
2051. Transmittal of order or judgment and notice.
2052. Method of notice.
2053. Insured or policyholder to furnish information to other party.

§ 2050. Notice to health, life, or disability insurance carrier; form

Upon filing of the petition, or at any time during the proceeding, a party may transmit to, or the court may order transmittal to, a health, life, or disability insurance carrier or plan the following notice in substantially the following form:

"YOU ARE HEREBY NOTIFIED, PURSUANT TO A PENDING PROCEEDING, IN RE MARRIAGE OF _____, CASE NUMBER _____, FILED IN THE SUPERIOR COURT OF THE STATE OF CALIFORNIA, COUNTY OF _____, THAT OWNERSHIP OF, OR BENEFITS PAYABLE UNDER, A POLICY OF HEALTH, LIFE, OR DISABILITY INSURANCE WHICH YOU HAVE ISSUED TO ONE OF THE PARTIES TO THIS PROCEEDING, POLICY NO. _____, IS AT ISSUE OR MAY BE AT ISSUE IN THE PROCEEDING.

YOU ARE HEREBY INSTRUCTED TO MAINTAIN THE NAMED BENEFICIARIES OR COVERED DEPENDENTS UNDER THE POLICY, UNLESS THE TERMS OF THE POLICY OR OTHER PROVISIONS OF LAW REQUIRE OTHERWISE, OR UNTIL RECEIPT OF A COURT ORDER, JUDGMENT, OR STIPULATION BETWEEN THE PARTIES PROVIDING OTHER INSTRUCTIONS.

YOU ARE FURTHER INSTRUCTED TO SEND NOTICE TO THE NAMED BENEFICIARIES, COVERED DEPENDENTS, OR OTHER SPECIFIED PERSONS UPON CANCELLATION, LAPSE, OR CHANGE OF THE COVERAGE, OR CHANGE OF DESIGNATED BENEFICIARIES UNDER THE POLICY."
(Stats.1992, c. 162 (A.B.2650), § 10, operative Jan. 1, 1994.)

Cross References

Application of part, see Family Code § 2000.
County defined for purposes of this Code, see Family Code § 67.
Health insurance coverage assignment, see Family Code § 3760 et seq.
Judgment and order defined for purposes of this Code, see Family Code § 100.
Person defined for purposes of this Code, see Family Code § 105.
Proceeding defined for purposes of this Code, see Family Code § 110.

State defined for purposes of this Code, see Family Code § 145.

Research References

Forms

California Practice Guide: Rutter Family Law Forms Form 3:7, Notice of Pending Proceeding to Health/Life/Disability Insurance Carrier (Family Code §2050).

California Practice Guide: Rutter Family Law Forms Form 6:13, Notice to Health/Life/Disability Carrier of Order to Maintain Insurance Coverage (Family Code §2051).

West's California Code Forms, Family § 2050, Comment Overview—Notice to Insurance Carrier.

§ 2051. Transmittal of order or judgment and notice

Upon the entry of an order or judgment in the proceeding requiring a party to maintain existing health, life, or disability insurance coverage for a spouse or children or after an order or judgment in the proceeding requiring a party to purchase life or disability insurance and name the spouse or children as beneficiaries and upon receipt of the name, title, and address of the insurer, or the name of the plan's trustee, administrator, or agent for service of process, a party may transmit to, or the court may order transmittal to, the insurer or plan a copy of the order or judgment endorsed by the court, together with the following notice in substantially the following form:

"PURSUANT TO A PROCEEDING, IN RE MARRIAGE OF _____, CASE NUMBER _____, IN THE SUPERIOR COURT OF THE STATE OF CALIFORNIA, COUNTY OF _____, YOUR INSURED, _____, HAS BEEN ORDERED TO MAINTAIN THE EXISTING (HEALTH) (LIFE) (DISABILITY) INSURANCE COVERAGE, POLICY NO. _____, IN FORCE FOR THE NAMED BENEFICIARIES OR COVERED DEPENDENTS AS SPECIFIED IN THE ATTACHED ORDER OR JUDGMENT.

THE ATTACHED ORDER OR JUDGMENT REQUIRES YOU TO MAINTAIN THE NAMED BENEFICIARIES UNDER THE POLICY AS IRREVOCABLE BENEFICIARIES OR COVERED DEPENDENTS OF THE POLICY AND YOU MUST ADMINISTER THE COVERAGE ACCORDINGLY, UNTIL THE DATE SPECIFIED, IF ANY, IN THE ORDER OR JUDGMENT, OR UNTIL THE RECEIPT OF A COURT ORDER, JUDGMENT, OR STIPULATION PROVIDING OTHER INSTRUCTIONS.

YOU ARE FURTHER INSTRUCTED TO SEND NOTICE TO THE NAMED BENEFICIARIES, COVERED DEPENDENTS, OR OTHER SPECIFIED PERSONS UPON ANY CANCELLATION, LAPSE, OR CHANGE OF COVERAGE, OR CHANGE OF DESIGNATED BENEFICIARIES UNDER THIS POLICY."

(Stats.1992, c. 162 (A.B.2650), § 10, operative Jan. 1, 1994.)

Cross References

Application of part, see Family Code § 2000.
County defined for purposes of this Code, see Family Code § 67.
Health insurance coverage assignment, see Family Code § 3760 et seq.
Judgment and order defined for purposes of this Code, see Family Code § 100.
Person defined for purposes of this Code, see Family Code § 105.
Proceeding defined for purposes of this Code, see Family Code § 110.
References to husband, wife, spouses and married persons, persons included for purposes of this Code, see Family Code § 11.
State defined for purposes of this Code, see Family Code § 145.

Research References

Forms

California Practice Guide: Rutter Family Law Forms Form 6:13, Notice to Health/Life/Disability Carrier of Order to Maintain Insurance Coverage (Family Code §2051).

West's California Code Forms, Family § 2050, Comment Overview—Notice to Insurance Carrier.

§ 2052. Method of notice

Notice pursuant to this chapter may be sent by first-class mail, postage prepaid, to the last known address of the covered dependents, named beneficiaries, or other specified persons who have requested receipt of notification. (Stats.1992, c. 162 (A.B.2650), § 10, operative Jan. 1, 1994.)

Cross References

Application of part, see Family Code § 2000.
Person defined for purposes of this Code, see Family Code § 105.

Research References

Forms

West's California Code Forms, Family § 2050, Comment Overview—Notice to Insurance Carrier.

§ 2053. Insured or policyholder to furnish information to other party

The insured or policyholder who is a party to the proceeding shall furnish to the other party the name, title, and address of the insurer or the insurer's agent for service of process. (Stats.1992, c. 162 (A.B.2650), § 10, operative Jan. 1, 1994.)

Cross References

Application of part, see Family Code § 2000.
Health insurance coverage assignment, see Family Code § 3760 et seq.
Proceeding defined for purposes of this Code, see Family Code § 110.

Research References

Forms

West's California Code Forms, Family § 2050, Comment Overview—Notice to Insurance Carrier.

CHAPTER 6. EMPLOYEE PENSION BENEFIT PLAN AS PARTY

Article	Section
1. Joinder of Plan	2060
2. Proceedings After Joinder	2070

Cross References

County employees retirement law of 1937, community property, legal separation or marriage dissolution, see Government Code § 31685.

ARTICLE 1. JOINDER OF PLAN

Section
2060. Application and order for joinder.
2061. Pleading of party requesting joinder.
2062. Service of documents by party requesting joinder.
2063. Employee pension benefit plan; notice of appearance; responsive pleadings.
2064. Filing fees.
2065. Default of plan.

§ 2060. Application and order for joinder

(a) Upon written application by a party, the clerk shall enter an order joining as a party to the proceeding any employee benefit plan in which either party to the proceeding claims an interest that is or may be subject to disposition by the court.

(b) An order or judgment in the proceeding is not enforceable against an employee benefit plan unless the plan has been joined as a party to the proceeding. (Stats.1992, c. 162 (A.B.2650), § 10,

§ 2060

NULLITY, DISSOLUTION, AND LEGAL SEPARATION

operative Jan. 1, 1994. Amended by Stats.1996, c. 1061 (S.B.1033), § 4.)

Cross References

Application of part to dissolution, nullity, or legal separation proceedings, see Family Code § 2000.
Discharge of employee benefit plan from adverse claims, see Family Code § 755.
Employee benefit plan defined for purposes of this Code, see Family Code § 80.
Enforcement of support orders regardless of joinder, see Family Code § 5103.
Judgment and order defined for purposes of this Code, see Family Code § 100.
Notices, and filing and service of papers, see Code of Civil Procedure § 1010 et seq.
Pension trusts, see Government Code § 53215 et seq.
Proceeding defined for purposes of this Code, see Family Code § 110.

Research References

Forms

West's California Code Forms, Family § 2060, Comment Overview—Application and Order for Joinder.
West's California Code Forms, Family § 2061 Form 1, Pleading on Joinder.
West's California Judicial Council Forms FL–370, Pleading on Joinder—Employee Benefit Plan.
West's California Judicial Council Forms FL–372, Request for Joinder of Employee Benefit Plan Order.
West's California Judicial Council Forms FL–374, Notice of Appearance and Response of Employee Benefit Plan.

§ 2061. Pleading of party requesting joinder

Upon entry of the order under Section 2060, the party requesting joinder shall file an appropriate pleading setting forth the party's claim against the plan and the nature of the relief sought. *(Stats. 1992, c. 162 (A.B.2650), § 10, operative Jan. 1, 1994.)*

Cross References

Application of part to dissolution, nullity, or legal separation proceedings, see Family Code § 2000.
Discharge of employee benefit plan from adverse claims, see Family Code § 755.
Employee benefit plan defined, see Family Code § 80.
Judgment and order defined for purposes of this Code, see Family Code § 100.
Notices, and filing and service of papers, see Code of Civil Procedure § 1010 et seq.

Research References

Forms

West's California Code Forms, Family § 2060, Comment Overview—Application and Order for Joinder.

§ 2062. Service of documents by party requesting joinder

(a) The party requesting joinder shall serve all of the following upon the employee benefit plan:

(1) A copy of the pleading on joinder.

(2) A copy of the request for joinder and order of joinder.

(3) A copy of the summons (joinder).

(4) A blank copy of a notice of appearance in form and content approved by the Judicial Council.

(b) Service shall be made in the same manner as service of papers generally. Service of the summons upon a trustee or administrator of the plan in its capacity as trustee or administrator, or upon an agent designated by the plan for service of process in its capacity as agent, constitutes service upon the plan.

(c) To facilitate identification and service, the employee spouse shall furnish to the nonemployee spouse within 30 days after written request, as to each employee benefit plan covering the employee, the name of the plan, the name, title, address, and telephone number of the plan's trustee, administrator, or agent for service of process. If necessary, the employee shall obtain the information from the plan or plan sponsor. *(Stats.1992, c. 162 (A.B.2650), § 10, operative Jan. 1, 1994. Amended by Stats.1994, c. 1269 (A.B.2208), § 15.)*

Cross References

Application of part to dissolution, nullity, or legal separation proceedings, see Family Code § 2000.
Discharge of employee benefit plan from adverse claims, see Family Code § 755.
Employee benefit plan defined for purposes of this Code, see Family Code § 80.
Judgment and order defined for purposes of this Code, see Family Code § 100.
Notices, and filing and service of papers, see Code of Civil Procedure § 1010 et seq.
References to husband, wife, spouses and married persons, persons included for purposes of this Code, see Family Code § 11.

Research References

Forms

West's California Code Forms, Family § 2060, Comment Overview—Application and Order for Joinder.
West's California Judicial Council Forms FL–375, Summons (Joinder).

§ 2063. Employee pension benefit plan; notice of appearance; responsive pleadings

(a) The employee benefit plan shall file and serve a copy of a notice of appearance upon the party requesting joinder within 30 days of the date of the service upon the plan of a copy of the joinder request and summons.

(b) The employee benefit plan may, but need not, file an appropriate responsive pleading with its notice of appearance. If the plan does not file a responsive pleading, all statements of fact and requests for relief contained in any pleading served on the plan are deemed to be controverted by the plan's notice of appearance. *(Stats.1992, c. 162 (A.B.2650), § 10, operative Jan. 1, 1994. Amended by Stats.1994, c. 1269 (A.B.2208), § 16.)*

Cross References

Application of part to dissolution, nullity, or legal separation proceedings, see Family Code § 2000.
Discharge of employee benefit plan from adverse claims, see Family Code § 755.
Employee benefit plan defined for purposes of this Code, see Family Code § 80.
Notices, and filing and service of papers, see Code of Civil Procedure § 1010 et seq.

Research References

Forms

West's California Code Forms, Family § 2060, Comment Overview—Application and Order for Joinder.
West's California Code Forms, Family § 2063 Form 1, Notice of Appearance and Response of Employee Pension Benefit Plan.

§ 2064. Filing fees

Notwithstanding any contrary provision of law, the employee benefit plan is not required to pay any fee to the clerk of the court as a condition to filing the notice of appearance or any subsequent paper in the proceeding. *(Stats.1992, c. 162 (A.B.2650), § 10, operative Jan. 1, 1994. Amended by Stats.1994, c. 1269 (A.B.2208), § 17.)*

Cross References

Application of part to dissolution, nullity, or legal separation proceedings, see Family Code § 2000.
Discharge of employee benefit plan from adverse claims, see Family Code § 755.
Employee benefit plan defined for purposes of this Code, see Family Code § 80.
Notices, and filing and service of papers, see Code of Civil Procedure § 1010 et seq.

Proceeding defined for purposes of this Code, see Family Code § 110.

§ 2065. Default of plan

If the employee benefit plan has been served and no notice of appearance, notice of motion to quash service of summons pursuant to Section 418.10 of the Code of Civil Procedure, or notice of the filing of a petition for writ of mandate as provided in that section, has been filed with the clerk of the court within the time specified in the summons or such further time as may be allowed, the clerk, upon written application of the party requesting joinder, shall enter the default of the employee benefit plan in accordance with Chapter 2 (commencing with Section 585) of Title 8 of Part 2 of the Code of Civil Procedure. *(Stats.1992, c. 162 (A.B.2650), § 10, operative Jan. 1, 1994. Amended by Stats.1994, c. 1269 (A.B.2208), § 18.)*

Cross References

Application of part to dissolution, nullity, or legal separation proceedings, see Family Code § 2000.
Discharge of employee benefit plan from adverse claims, see Family Code § 755.
Employee benefit plan defined for purposes of this Code, see Family Code § 80.
Mandamus, purpose of writ of mandate, courts which may issue writ and parties to whom issued, see Code of Civil Procedure § 1085.
Notices, and filing and service of papers, see Code of Civil Procedure § 1010 et seq.

Research References

Forms

West's California Code Forms, Family § 2060, Comment Overview—Application and Order for Joinder.
West's California Judicial Council Forms FL-370, Pleading on Joinder—Employee Benefit Plan.
West's California Judicial Council Forms FL-372, Request for Joinder of Employee Benefit Plan Order.
West's California Judicial Council Forms FL-374, Notice of Appearance and Response of Employee Benefit Plan.

ARTICLE 2. PROCEEDINGS AFTER JOINDER

Section
2070. Application of article; application of law applicable to civil actions.
2071. Notice and reply to proposed property settlement.
2072. Hearings; appearances.
2073. Order affecting plan; stay.
2074. Motion to set aside or modify; hearing.

§ 2070. Application of article; application of law applicable to civil actions

(a) This article governs a proceeding in which an employee benefit plan has been joined as a party.

(b) To the extent not in conflict with this article and except as otherwise provided by rules adopted by the Judicial Council pursuant to Section 211, all provisions of law applicable to civil actions generally apply, regardless of nomenclature, to the portion of the proceeding as to which an employee benefit plan has been joined as a party if those provisions would otherwise apply to the proceeding without reference to this article. *(Stats.1992, c. 162 (A.B.2650), § 10, operative Jan. 1, 1994. Amended by Stats.1994, c. 1269 (A.B.2208), § 19.)*

Cross References

Application of part to dissolution, nullity, or legal separation proceedings, see Family Code § 2000.
Discharge of employee benefit plan from adverse claims, see Family Code § 755.
Employee benefit plan defined for purposes of this Code, see Family Code § 80.
Judicial Council, generally, see Government Code § 68500 et seq.

Proceeding defined for purposes of this Code, see Family Code § 110.

Research References

Forms

West's California Code Forms, Family § 2060, Comment Overview—Application and Order for Joinder.
West's California Judicial Council Forms FL-372, Request for Joinder of Employee Benefit Plan Order.
West's California Judicial Council Forms FL-374, Notice of Appearance and Response of Employee Benefit Plan.

§ 2071. Notice and reply to proposed property settlement

Either party or their representatives may notify the employee benefit plan of any proposed property settlement as it concerns the plan before any hearing at which the proposed property settlement will be a matter before the court. If so notified, the plan may stipulate to the proposed settlement or advise the representative that it will contest the proposed settlement. *(Stats.1992, c. 162 (A.B. 2650), § 10, operative Jan. 1, 1994. Amended by Stats.1994, c. 1269 (A.B.2208), § 20.)*

Cross References

Application of part to dissolution, nullity, or legal separation proceedings, see Family Code § 2000.
Discharge of employee benefit plan from adverse claims, see Family Code § 755.
Employee benefit plan defined for purposes of this Code, see Family Code § 80.
Property defined for purposes of this Code, see Family Code § 113.

§ 2072. Hearings; appearances

The employee benefit plan is not required to, but may, appear at any hearing in the proceeding. For purposes of the Code of Civil Procedure, the plan shall be considered a party appearing at the trial with respect to any hearing at which the interest of the parties in the plan is an issue before the court. *(Stats.1992, c. 162 (A.B.2650), § 10, operative Jan. 1, 1994. Amended by Stats.1994, c. 1269 (A.B.2208), § 21.)*

Cross References

Application of part to dissolution, nullity, or legal separation proceedings, see Family Code § 2000.
Discharge of employee benefit plan from adverse claims, see Family Code § 755.
Employee benefit plan defined for purposes of this Code, see Family Code § 80.
Proceeding defined for purposes of this Code, see Family Code § 110.

§ 2073. Order affecting plan; stay

(a) Subject to subdivisions (b) and (c), the provisions of an order entered by stipulation of the parties or entered at or as a result of a hearing not attended by the employee benefit plan (whether or not the plan received notice of the hearing) which affect the plan or which affect any interest either the petitioner or respondent may have or claim under the plan, shall be stayed until 30 days after the order has been served upon the plan.

(b) The plan may waive all or any portion of the 30-day period under subdivision (a).

(c) If within the 30-day period, the plan files in the proceeding a motion to set aside or modify those provisions of the order affecting it, those provisions shall be stayed until the court has resolved the motion.

(d) The duration of the stay described in subdivision (a), and the time period for filing the motion to set aside or modify provisions of the order, shall be extended to 60 days if the plan files with the court and serves on all affected parties a request for extension within the 30-day period.

(e) Either spousal party may seek an order staying any other provisions of the order and associated orders or judgments related to

§ 2073

or affected by the provisions to which the plan has objected, until the court has resolved the motion, in order to protect the right of the party to seek relief under subdivision (c) of Section 2074. *(Stats. 1992, c. 162 (A.B.2650), § 10, operative Jan. 1, 1994. Amended by Stats.1994, c. 1269 (A.B.2208), § 22.)*

Cross References

Application of part to dissolution, nullity, or legal separation proceedings, see Family Code § 2000.
Discharge of employee benefit plan from adverse claims, see Family Code § 755.
Employee benefit plan defined for purposes of this Code, see Family Code § 80.
Judgment and order defined for purposes of this Code, see Family Code § 100.
Petitioner defined for purposes of this Code, see Family Code § 126.
Proceeding defined for purposes of this Code, see Family Code § 110.
Respondent defined for purposes of this Code, see Family Code § 127.

§ 2074. Motion to set aside or modify; hearing

(a) At any hearing on a motion to set aside or modify an order pursuant to Section 2073, any party may present further evidence on any issue relating to the rights of the parties under the employee benefit plan or the extent of the parties' community or quasi-community property interest in the plan, except where the parties have agreed in writing to the contrary.

(b) Any statement of decision issued by the court with respect to the order which is the subject of the motion shall take account of the evidence referred to in subdivision (a).

(c) If the provisions of the order affecting the employee benefit plan are modified or set aside, the court, on motion by either party, may set aside or modify other provisions of the order and associated orders or judgments related to or affected by the provisions affecting the plan. *(Stats.1992, c. 162 (A.B.2650), § 10, operative Jan. 1, 1994. Amended by Stats.1994, c. 1269 (A.B.2208), § 23.)*

Cross References

Adverse claims, discharge of employee benefit plan from, see Family Code § 755.
Application of part to dissolution, nullity, or legal separation proceedings, see Family Code § 2000.
Community property defined, see Family Code §§ 65, 760.
Employee benefit plan defined for purposes of this Code, see Family Code § 80.
Judgment and order defined for purposes of this Code, see Family Code § 100.
Property defined for purposes of this Code, see Family Code § 113.
Quasi-community property defined, see Family Code § 125.

Research References

Forms

West's California Code Forms, Family § 2060, Comment Overview—Application and Order for Joinder.
West's California Judicial Council Forms FL–372, Request for Joinder of Employee Benefit Plan Order.
West's California Judicial Council Forms FL–374, Notice of Appearance and Response of Employee Benefit Plan.

CHAPTER 7. RESTORATION OF WIFE'S FORMER NAME

Section
2080. Request for restoration.
2081. Grounds for denial.
2082. Common law rights.

§ 2080. Request for restoration

In a proceeding for dissolution of marriage or for nullity of marriage, but not in a proceeding for legal separation of the parties, the court, upon the request of a party, shall restore the birth name or former name of that party, regardless of whether or not a request for restoration of the name was included in the petition. *(Stats.1992, c. 162 (A.B.2650), § 10, operative Jan. 1, 1994. Amended by Stats,1996, c. 1061 (S.B.1033), § 5.)*

Cross References

Change of names, see Code of Civil Procedure § 1275 et seq.
Proceeding defined for purposes of this Code, see Family Code § 110.
Trade or business, doing business or providing services to women, prohibition against requiring use of name indicating marital status, etc., see Code of Civil Procedure § 1279.6.

Research References

Forms

West's California Code Forms, Family § 2080, Comment Overview—Request for Restoration.
West's California Judicial Council Forms FL–395, Ex Parte Application for Restoration of Former Name After Entry of Judgment and Order.

§ 2081. Grounds for denial

The restoration of a former name or birth name requested under Section 2080 shall not be denied (a) on the basis that the party has custody of a minor child who bears a different name or (b) for any other reason other than fraud. *(Stats.1992, c. 162 (A.B.2650), § 10, operative Jan. 1, 1994. Amended by Stats.1996, c. 1061 (S.B.1033), § 6.)*

Cross References

Change of names, see Code of Civil Procedure § 1275 et seq.
Minor defined for purposes of this Code, see Family Code § 6500.

Research References

Forms

West's California Code Forms, Family § 2080, Comment Overview—Request for Restoration.

§ 2082. Common law rights

Nothing in this code shall be construed to abrogate the common law right of any person to change one's name. *(Stats.1992, c. 162 (A.B.2650), § 10, operative Jan. 1, 1994.)*

Cross References

Change of names, see Code of Civil Procedure § 1275 et seq.
Person defined for purposes of this Code, see Family Code § 105.
Trade or business, doing business or providing services to women, prohibition against requiring use of names indicating marital status, etc., see Code of Civil Procedure § 1279.6.

CHAPTER 8. UNIFORM DIVORCE RECOGNITION ACT

Section
2090. Short title.
2091. Foreign divorce of parties domiciled in state; effect.
2092. Domicile; prima facie evidence.
2093. Application of title; full faith and credit.

Cross References

Other uniform acts in the Family Code,
Uniform Child Custody Jurisdiction and Enforcement Act, see Family Code § 3400 et seq.
Uniform Interstate Enforcement of Domestic Violence Protection Orders Act, see Family Code § 6400 et seq.
Uniform Interstate Family Support Act, see Family Code § 5700.101 et seq.
Uniform Parentage Act, see Family Code § 7600 et seq.
Uniform Premarital Agreement Act, see Family Code § 1600 et seq.

§ 2090. Short title

This chapter may be cited as the Uniform Divorce Recognition Act. *(Stats.1992, c. 162 (A.B.2650), § 10, operative Jan. 1, 1994.)*

Cross References

Severability of provisions, see Family Code § 13.
Uniform act, construction of provisions, see Family Code § 3.

§ 2091. Foreign divorce of parties domiciled in state; effect

A divorce obtained in another jurisdiction shall be of no force or effect in this state if both parties to the marriage were domiciled in this state at the time the proceeding for the divorce was commenced. *(Stats.1992, c. 162 (A.B.2650), § 10, operative Jan. 1, 1994.)*

Cross References

Determination of place of residence, see Government Code § 244.
Judicial record, foreign state, see Code of Civil Procedure § 1913.
Proceeding defined for purposes of this Code, see Family Code § 110.
State defined for purposes of this Code, see Family Code § 145.
Uniform act, construction of provisions, see Family Code § 3.

§ 2092. Domicile; prima facie evidence

Proof that a person hereafter obtaining a divorce from the bonds of matrimony in another jurisdiction was (a) domiciled in this state within 12 months before the commencement of the proceeding therefor, and resumed residence in this state within 18 months after the date of the person's departure therefrom, or (b) at all times after the person's departure from this state and until the person's return maintained a place of residence within this state, shall be prima facie evidence that the person was domiciled in this state when the divorce proceeding was commenced. *(Stats.1992, c. 162 (A.B.2650), § 10, operative Jan. 1, 1994.)*

Cross References

Determination of place of residence, see Government Code § 244.
Dissolution of marriage and legal separation, residency requirements, see Family Code § 2320 et seq.
Person defined for purposes of this Code, see Family Code § 105.
Prima facie evidence, see Evidence Code § 602.
Proceeding defined for purposes of this Code, see Family Code § 110.
Residence requirement in actions for dissolution of marriage, see Family Code § 2320.
State defined for purposes of this Code, see Family Code § 145.
Uniform act, construction of provisions, see Family Code § 3.

§ 2093. Application of title; full faith and credit

The application of this chapter is limited by the requirement of the Constitution of the United States that full faith and credit shall be given in each state to the public acts, records, and judicial proceedings of every other state. *(Stats.1992, c. 162 (A.B.2650), § 10, operative Jan. 1, 1994.)*

Cross References

Judicial record, foreign state, see Code of Civil Procedure § 1913.
Proceeding defined for purposes of this Code, see Family Code § 110.
State defined for purposes of this Code, see Family Code § 145.
Uniform act, construction of provisions, see Family Code § 3.

CHAPTER 9. DISCLOSURE OF ASSETS AND LIABILITIES

Section
2100. Legislative findings and declarations; disclosure of assets and liabilities.
2101. Definitions.
2102. Fiduciary relationship; length and scope of duty; termination.
2103. Declarations of disclosure; requirements.
2104. Preliminary declaration of disclosure.
2105. Final declaration of disclosure of current income and expenses; execution and service; contents; waiver; perjury or noncompliance with chapter.
2106. Entry of judgment; requirement of execution and service of declarations; exceptions; execution and filing of declaration of execution and service or of waiver.
2107. Noncomplying declarations; requests to comply; remedies.
2108. Liquidation of community or quasi-community assets to avoid market or investment risks; authority of court.
2109. Summary dissolution of marriage; required disclosures.
2110. Default judgments; declarations of disclosure.
2111. Attorney work product privilege; protective orders.
2112. Forms.
2113. Application of chapter.

§ 2100. Legislative findings and declarations; disclosure of assets and liabilities

The Legislature finds and declares the following:

(a) It is the policy of the State of California (1) to marshal, preserve, and protect community and quasi-community assets and liabilities that exist at the date of separation so as to avoid dissipation of the community estate before distribution, (2) to ensure fair and sufficient child and spousal support awards, and (3) to achieve a division of community and quasi-community assets and liabilities on the dissolution or nullity of marriage or legal separation of the parties as provided under California law.

(b) Sound public policy further favors the reduction of the adversarial nature of marital dissolution and the attendant costs by fostering full disclosure and cooperative discovery.

(c) In order to promote this public policy, a full and accurate disclosure of all assets and liabilities in which one or both parties have or may have an interest must be made in the early stages of a proceeding for dissolution of marriage or legal separation of the parties, regardless of the characterization as community or separate, together with a disclosure of all income and expenses of the parties. Moreover, each party has a continuing duty to immediately, fully, and accurately update and augment that disclosure to the extent there have been any material changes so that at the time the parties enter into an agreement for the resolution of any of these issues, or at the time of trial on these issues, each party will have a full and complete knowledge of the relevant underlying facts. *(Added by Stats.1993, c. 219 (A.B.1500), § 107. Amended by Stats.1993, c. 1101 (A.B.1469), § 3, eff. Oct. 11, 1993, operative Jan. 1, 1994; Stats.2001, c. 703 (A.B.583), § 2.)*

Application

For application of Stats.2001, c. 703 (A.B.583), see § 8 of that act.

Cross References

Asset defined for purposes of this Chapter, see Family Code § 2101.
Community estate defined, see Family Code § 63.
Community property defined, see Civil Code § 687; Family Code §§ 65, 760; Probate Code § 28.
Expenses defined for purposes of this Chapter, see Family Code § 2101.
Judgment and order defined for purposes of this Code, see Family Code § 100.
Proceeding defined for purposes of this Code, see Family Code § 110.
Quasi-community defined, see Family Code § 125.
Spousal support defined for purposes of this Code, see Family Code § 142.
State defined for purposes of this Code, see Family Code § 145.

§ 2100

Support defined for purposes of this Code, see Family Code § 150.

Research References

Forms

California Practice Guide: Rutter Family Law Forms Form 1:6, Letter to Opposing Counsel to Exchange Information.
California Practice Guide: Rutter Family Law Forms Form 9:3, Marital Settlement Agreement.
1 California Transactions Forms--Family Law § 2:4, Fiduciary Duty.
1 California Transactions Forms--Family Law § 2:5, Disclosure Requirements.
West's California Code Forms, Family § 2104, Comment Overview—Disclosure of Assets.
West's California Judicial Council Forms FL-150, Income and Expense Declaration (Also Available in Spanish).

§ 2101. Definitions

Unless the provision or context otherwise requires, the following definitions apply to this chapter:

(a) "Asset" includes, but is not limited to, any real or personal property of any nature, whether tangible or intangible, and whether currently existing or contingent.

(b) "Default judgment" does not include a stipulated judgment or any judgment pursuant to a marital settlement agreement.

(c) "Earnings and accumulations" includes income from whatever source derived, as provided in Section 4058.

(d) "Expenses" includes, but is not limited to, all personal living expenses, but does not include business related expenses.

(e) "Income and expense declaration" includes the Income and Expense Declaration forms approved for use by the Judicial Council, and any other financial statement that is approved for use by the Judicial Council in lieu of the Income and Expense Declaration, if the financial statement form satisfies all other applicable criteria.

(f) "Liability" includes, but is not limited to, any debt or obligation, whether currently existing or contingent. *(Added by Stats. 1993, c. 219 (A.B.1500), § 107. Amended by Stats.1993, c. 1101 (A.B.1469), § 4, eff. Oct. 11, 1993, operative Jan. 1, 1994; Stats.1998, c. 581 (A.B.2801), § 5.)*

Cross References

Income and expense declaration defined for purposes of this Code, see Family Code § 95.
Judgment and order defined for purposes of this Code, see Family Code § 100.
Property defined for purposes of this Code, see Family Code § 113.

§ 2102. Fiduciary relationship; length and scope of duty; termination

(a) From the date of separation to the date of the distribution of the community or quasi-community asset or liability in question, each party is subject to the standards provided in Section 721, as to all activities that affect the assets and liabilities of the other party, including, but not limited to, the following activities:

(1) The accurate and complete disclosure of all assets and liabilities in which the party has or may have an interest or obligation and all current earnings, accumulations, and expenses, including an immediate, full, and accurate update or augmentation to the extent there have been material changes.

(2) The accurate and complete written disclosure of any investment opportunity, business opportunity, or other income-producing opportunity that presents itself after the date of separation, but that results from any investment, significant business activity outside the ordinary course of business, or other income-producing opportunity of either spouse from the date of marriage to the date of separation, inclusive. The written disclosure shall be made in sufficient time for the other spouse to make an informed decision as to whether the spouse desires to participate in the investment opportunity, business, or other potential income-producing opportunity, and for the court to resolve any dispute regarding the right of the other spouse to participate in the opportunity. In the event of nondisclosure of an investment opportunity, the division of any gain resulting from that opportunity is governed by the standard provided in Section 2556.

(3) The operation or management of a business or an interest in a business in which the community may have an interest.

(b) From the date that a valid, enforceable, and binding resolution of the disposition of the asset or liability in question is reached, until the asset or liability has actually been distributed, each party is subject to the standards provided in Section 721 as to all activities that affect the assets or liabilities of the other party. Once a particular asset or liability has been distributed, the duties and standards set forth in Section 721 shall end as to that asset or liability.

(c) From the date of separation to the date of a valid, enforceable, and binding resolution of all issues relating to child or spousal support and professional fees, each party is subject to the standards provided in Section 721 as to all issues relating to the support and fees, including immediate, full, and accurate disclosure of all material facts and information regarding the income or expenses of the party. *(Added by Stats.1993, c. 219 (A.B.1500), § 107. Amended by Stats.1993, c. 1101 (A.B.1469), § 5, eff. Oct. 11, 1993, operative Jan. 1, 1994; Stats.2001, c. 703 (A.B.583), § 3; Stats.2019, c. 115 (A.B.1817), § 18, eff. Jan. 1, 2020.)*

Cross References

Asset defined for purposes of this Chapter, see Family Code § 2101.
Earnings and accumulations defined for purposes of this Chapter, see Family Code § 2101.
Expenses defined for purposes of this Chapter, see Family Code § 2101.
References to husband, wife, spouses and married persons, persons included for purposes of this Code, see Family Code § 11.
Spousal support defined for purposes of this Code, see Family Code § 142.
Support defined for purposes of this Code, see Family Code § 150.

Research References

Forms

California Practice Guide: Rutter Family Law Forms Form 8:1, Request for Order Re Separate Trial Re Validity of Interspousal Deed.
California Practice Guide: Rutter Family Law Forms Form 9:3, Marital Settlement Agreement.
California Practice Guide: Rutter Family Law Forms Form 11:6, Final Declaration of Disclosure Separate Statement (Attorney-Drafted Sample).
West's California Code Forms, Family § 2338 Form 9, Marital Agreement—Both Spouses Employed.
West's California Judicial Council Forms FL-140, Declaration of Disclosure (Also Available in Spanish).
West's California Judicial Council Forms FL-141, Declaration Regarding Service of Declaration of Disclosure and Income and Expense Declaration.
West's California Judicial Council Forms FL-144, Stipulation and Waiver of Final Declaration of Disclosure.

§ 2103. Declarations of disclosure; requirements

In order to provide full and accurate disclosure of all assets and liabilities in which one or both parties may have an interest, each party to a proceeding for dissolution of the marriage or legal separation of the parties shall serve on the other party a preliminary declaration of disclosure under Section 2104, unless service of the preliminary declaration of disclosure is waived as provided in Section 2107 or is not required pursuant to Section 2110, and a final declaration of disclosure under Section 2105, unless service of the final declaration of disclosure is waived pursuant to Section 2105, 2107, or 2110, and shall file proof of service of each with the court. *(Added by Stats.1993, c. 219 (A.B.1500), § 107. Amended by Stats.1998, c. 581 (A.B.2801), § 6; Stats.2015, c. 46 (S.B.340), § 1, eff. Jan. 1, 2016; Stats.2016, c. 474 (A.B.2882), § 7, eff. Jan. 1, 2017.)*

Cross References

Asset defined for purposes of this Chapter, see Family Code § 2101.
Declarations of disclosure, remedies for noncompliance, see Family Code § 2107.

Judgment and order defined for purposes of this Code, see Family Code § 100.
Proceeding defined for purposes of this Code, see Family Code § 110.

§ 2104. Preliminary declaration of disclosure

(a) Except by court order for good cause, as provided in Section 2107, or when service of the preliminary declaration of disclosure is not required pursuant to Section 2110, in the time period set forth in subdivision (f), each party shall serve on the other party a preliminary declaration of disclosure, executed under penalty of perjury on a form prescribed by the Judicial Council. The commission of perjury on the preliminary declaration of disclosure may be grounds for setting aside the judgment, or any part or parts thereof, pursuant to Chapter 10 (commencing with Section 2120), in addition to any and all other remedies, civil or criminal, that otherwise are available under law for the commission of perjury. The preliminary declaration of disclosure shall include all tax returns filed by the declarant within the two years prior to the date that the party served the declaration.

(b) The preliminary declaration of disclosure shall not be filed with the court, except on court order. However, the parties shall file proof of service of the preliminary declaration of disclosure with the court.

(c) The preliminary declaration of disclosure shall set forth with sufficient particularity, that a person of reasonable and ordinary intelligence can ascertain, all of the following:

(1) The identity of all assets in which the declarant has or may have an interest and all liabilities for which the declarant is or may be liable, regardless of the characterization of the asset or liability as community, quasi-community, or separate.

(2) The declarant's percentage of ownership in each asset and percentage of obligation for each liability when property is not solely owned by one or both of the parties. The preliminary declaration may also set forth the declarant's characterization of each asset or liability.

(d) A declarant may amend the preliminary declaration of disclosure without leave of the court. Proof of service of an amendment shall be filed with the court.

(e) Along with the preliminary declaration of disclosure, each party shall provide the other party with a completed income and expense declaration unless an income and expense declaration has already been provided and is current and valid.

(f) The petitioner shall serve the other party with the preliminary declaration of disclosure either concurrently with the petition for dissolution or legal separation, or within 60 days of filing the petition. When a petitioner serves the summons and petition by publication or posting pursuant to court order and the respondent files a response prior to a default judgment being entered, the petitioner shall serve the other party with the preliminary declaration of disclosure within 30 days of the response being filed. The respondent shall serve the other party with the preliminary declaration of disclosure either concurrently with the response to the petition, or within 60 days of filing the response. The time periods specified in this subdivision may be extended by written agreement of the parties or by court order. (Added by Stats.1993, c. 219 (A.B.1500), § 107. Amended by Stats.1993, c. 1101 (A.B.1469), § 6, eff. Oct. 11, 1993, operative Jan. 1, 1994; Stats.1998, c. 581 (A.B.2801), § 7; Stats.2009, c. 110 (A.B.459), § 1; Stats.2012, c. 107 (A.B.1406), § 1; Stats.2015, c. 46 (S.B.340), § 2, eff. Jan. 1, 2016; Stats.2015, c. 416 (A.B.1519), § 1.5, eff. Jan. 1, 2016; Stats.2019, c. 115 (A.B.1817), § 19, eff. Jan. 1, 2020.)

Cross References

Asset defined for purposes of this Chapter, see Family Code § 2101.
Declarations of disclosure, remedies for noncompliance, see Family Code § 2107.
Income and expense declaration defined for purposes of this Chapter, see Family Code § 2101.
Income and expense declaration defined for purposes of this Code, see Family Code § 95.
Judgment and order defined for purposes of this Code, see Family Code § 100.
Mediation, evidence otherwise admissible, see Evidence Code § 1120.
Perjury defined, see Penal Code § 118.
Person defined for purposes of this Code, see Family Code § 105.
Property defined for purposes of this Code, see Family Code § 113.
Summary dissolution, declaration requirements, see Family Code § 2109.

Research References

Forms

California Practice Guide: Rutter Family Law Forms Form 1:32, Glossary of Common Family Law Terms, Phrases and Concepts (Enclosure to Form 1:31).
1 California Transactions Forms--Family Law § 2:6, Preliminary Declaration of Disclosure.
1 California Transactions Forms--Family Law § 2:7, Final Declaration of Disclosure.
1 California Transactions Forms--Family Law § 2:8, Waiver of Final Declaration of Disclosure.
1 California Transactions Forms--Family Law § 2:9, Remedies for False Disclosure.
1 California Transactions Forms--Family Law § 2:88, Marital Settlement Agreement.
West's California Code Forms, Family § 2104, Comment Overview--Disclosure of Assets.
West's California Code Forms, Family § 2338 Form 8, Marital Agreement.
West's California Code Forms, Family § 2550 Form 4, Division of Property Clauses in Dissolution Settlement Agreement.
West's California Judicial Council Forms FL–140, Declaration of Disclosure (Also Available in Spanish).
West's California Judicial Council Forms FL–141, Declaration Regarding Service of Declaration of Disclosure and Income and Expense Declaration.
West's California Judicial Council Forms FL–144, Stipulation and Waiver of Final Declaration of Disclosure.
West's California Judicial Council Forms FL–160, Property Declaration (Also Available in Spanish).
West's California Judicial Council Forms FL–161, Continuation of Property Declaration.

§ 2105. Final declaration of disclosure of current income and expenses; execution and service; contents; waiver; perjury or noncompliance with chapter

(a) Except by court order for good cause, before or at the time the parties enter into an agreement for the resolution of property or support issues other than pendente lite support, or, if the case goes to trial, no later than 45 days before the first assigned trial date, each party, or the attorney for the party in this matter, shall serve on the other party a final declaration of disclosure and a current income and expense declaration, executed under penalty of perjury on a form prescribed by the Judicial Council, unless the parties mutually waive the final declaration of disclosure. The commission of perjury on the final declaration of disclosure by a party may be grounds for setting aside the judgment, or any part or parts thereof, pursuant to Chapter 10 (commencing with Section 2120), in addition to any and all other remedies, civil or criminal, that otherwise are available under law for the commission of perjury.

(b) The final declaration of disclosure shall include all of the following information:

(1) All material facts and information regarding the characterization of all assets and liabilities.

(2) All material facts and information regarding the valuation of all assets that are contended to be community property or in which it is contended the community has an interest.

(3) All material facts and information regarding the amounts of all obligations that are contended to be community obligations or for which it is contended the community has liability.

(4) All material facts and information regarding the earnings, accumulations, and expenses of each party that have been set forth in the income and expense declaration.

§ 2105

(c) In making an order setting aside a judgment for failure to comply with this section, the court may limit the set aside to those portions of the judgment materially affected by the nondisclosure.

(d) The parties may stipulate to a mutual waiver of the requirements of subdivision (a) concerning the final declaration of disclosure, by execution of a waiver under penalty of perjury entered into in open court or by separate stipulation. The waiver shall include all of the following representations:

(1) Both parties have complied with Section 2104 and the preliminary declarations of disclosure have been completed and exchanged.

(2) Both parties have completed and exchanged a current income and expense declaration, that includes all material facts and information regarding that party's earnings, accumulations, and expenses.

(3) Both parties have fully complied with Section 2102 and have fully augmented the preliminary declarations of disclosure, including disclosure of all material facts and information regarding the characterization of all assets and liabilities, the valuation of all assets that are contended to be community property or in which it is contended the community has an interest, and the amounts of all obligations that are contended to be community obligations or for which it is contended the community has liability.

(4) The waiver is knowingly, intelligently, and voluntarily entered into by each of the parties.

(5) Each party understands that this waiver does not limit the legal disclosure obligations of the parties, but rather is a statement under penalty of perjury that those obligations have been fulfilled. Each party further understands that noncompliance with those obligations will result in the court setting aside the judgment. (Added by Stats.1993, c. 219 (A.B.1500), § 107. Amended by Stats.1993, c. 1101 (A.B.1469), § 7, eff. Oct. 11, 1993, operative Jan. 1, 1994; Stats.1995, c. 233 (A.B.806), § 1; Stats.1996, c. 1061 (S.B.1033), § 7; Stats.1998, c. 581 (A.B.2801), § 8; Stats.2001, c. 703 (A.B.583), § 4.)

Application

For application of Stats.2001, c. 703 (A.B.583), see § 8 of that act.

Cross References

Asset defined for purposes of this Chapter, see Family Code § 2101.
Community property defined for purposes of this Code, see Family Code § 65.
Declarations of disclosure, remedies for noncompliance, see Family Code § 2107.
Earnings and accumulations defined for purposes of this Chapter, see Family Code § 2101.
Expenses defined for purposes of this Chapter, see Family Code § 2101.
Income and expense declaration defined for purposes of this Chapter, see Family Code § 2101.
Income and expense declaration defined for purposes of this Code, see Family Code § 95.
Judgment and order defined for purposes of this Code, see Family Code § 100.
Mediation, evidence otherwise admissible, see Evidence Code § 1120.
Perjury defined, see Penal Code § 118.
Property defined for purposes of this Code, see Family Code § 113.
Summary dissolution, declaration requirements, see Family Code § 2109.
Support defined for purposes of this Code, see Family Code § 150.

Research References

Forms

California Practice Guide: Rutter Family Law Forms Form 1:32, Glossary of Common Family Law Terms, Phrases and Concepts (Enclosure to Form 1:31).
California Practice Guide: Rutter Family Law Forms Form 11:6, Final Declaration of Disclosure Separate Statement (Attorney-Drafted Sample).
1 California Transactions Forms--Family Law § 2:6, Preliminary Declaration of Disclosure.
1 California Transactions Forms--Family Law § 2:7, Final Declaration of Disclosure.
1 California Transactions Forms--Family Law § 2:8, Waiver of Final Declaration of Disclosure.
1 California Transactions Forms--Family Law § 2:9, Remedies for False Disclosure.
1 California Transactions Forms--Family Law § 2:88, Marital Settlement Agreement.
West's California Code Forms, Family § 2104, Comment Overview—Disclosure of Assets.
West's California Code Forms, Family § 2338 Form 8, Marital Agreement.
West's California Code Forms, Family § 2550 Form 4, Division of Property Clauses in Dissolution Settlement Agreement.
West's California Judicial Council Forms FL-140, Declaration of Disclosure (Also Available in Spanish).
West's California Judicial Council Forms FL-141, Declaration Regarding Service of Declaration of Disclosure and Income and Expense Declaration.
West's California Judicial Council Forms FL-144, Stipulation and Waiver of Final Declaration of Disclosure.

§ 2106. Entry of judgment; requirement of execution and service of declarations; exceptions; execution and filing of declaration of execution and service or of waiver

Except as provided in subdivision (d) of Section 2105, Section 2110, or absent good cause as provided in Section 2107, judgment shall not be entered with respect to the parties' property rights without each party, or the attorney for that party in this matter, having executed and served a copy of the final declaration of disclosure and current income and expense declaration. Each party, or the party's attorney, shall execute and file with the court a declaration signed under penalty of perjury stating that service of the final declaration of disclosure and current income and expense declaration was made on the other party or that service of the final declaration of disclosure has been waived pursuant to subdivision (d) of Section 2105 or in Section 2110. (Added by Stats.1993, c. 219 (A.B.1500), § 107. Amended by Stats.1993, c. 1101 (A.B.1469), § 8, eff. Oct. 11, 1993, operative Jan. 1, 1994; Stats.1995, c. 233 (A.B.806), § 2; Stats.1996, c. 1061 (S.B.1033), § 8; Stats.1998, c. 581 (A.B.2801), § 9; Stats.2001, c. 703 (A.B.583), § 5; Stats.2002, c. 1008 (A.B.3028), § 15; Stats.2009, c. 110 (A.B.459), § 2; Stats.2019, c. 115 (A.B.1817), § 20, eff. Jan. 1, 2020.)

Cross References

Income and expense declaration defined for purposes of this Chapter, see Family Code § 2101.
Income and expense declaration defined for purposes of this Code, see Family Code § 95.
Judgment and order defined for purposes of this Code, see Family Code § 100.
Property defined for purposes of this Code, see Family Code § 113.

Research References

Forms

1 California Transactions Forms--Family Law § 2:7, Final Declaration of Disclosure.
1 California Transactions Forms--Family Law § 2:8, Waiver of Final Declaration of Disclosure.
West's California Code Forms, Family § 2104, Comment Overview—Disclosure of Assets.
West's California Judicial Council Forms FL-140, Declaration of Disclosure (Also Available in Spanish).
West's California Judicial Council Forms FL-141, Declaration Regarding Service of Declaration of Disclosure and Income and Expense Declaration.

§ 2107. Noncomplying declarations; requests to comply; remedies

(a) If one party fails to serve on the other party a preliminary declaration of disclosure under Section 2104, unless that party is not required to serve a preliminary declaration of disclosure pursuant to Section 2110, or a final declaration of disclosure under Section 2105, or fails to provide the information required in the respective declarations with sufficient particularity, and if the other party has served the respective declaration of disclosure on the noncomplying party, the complying party may, within a reasonable time, request preparation of the appropriate declaration of disclosure or further particularity.

(b) If the noncomplying party fails to comply with a request under subdivision (a), the complying party may do one or more of the following:

(1) File a motion to compel a further response.

(2) File a motion for an order preventing the noncomplying party from presenting evidence on issues that should have been covered in the declaration of disclosure.

(3) File a motion showing good cause for the court to grant the complying party's voluntary waiver of receipt of the noncomplying party's preliminary declaration of disclosure pursuant to Section 2104 or final declaration of disclosure pursuant to Section 2105. The voluntary waiver does not affect the rights enumerated in subdivision (d).

(c) If a party fails to comply with any provision of this chapter, the court shall, in addition to any other remedy provided by law, impose money sanctions against the noncomplying party. Sanctions shall be in an amount sufficient to deter repetition of the conduct or comparable conduct, and shall include reasonable attorney's fees, costs incurred, or both, unless the court finds that the noncomplying party acted with substantial justification or that other circumstances make the imposition of the sanction unjust.

(d) Except as otherwise provided in this subdivision, if a court enters a judgment when the parties have failed to comply with all disclosure requirements of this chapter, the court shall set aside the judgment. The failure to comply with the disclosure requirements does not constitute harmless error. If the court granted the complying party's voluntary waiver of receipt of the noncomplying party's preliminary declaration of disclosure pursuant to paragraph (3) of subdivision (b), the court shall set aside the judgment only at the request of the complying party, unless the motion to set aside the judgment is based on one of the following:

(1) Actual fraud if the defrauded party was kept in ignorance or in some other manner was fraudulently prevented from fully participating in the proceeding.

(2) Perjury, as defined in Section 118 of the Penal Code, in the preliminary or final declaration of disclosure, in the waiver of the final declaration of disclosure, or in the current income and expense statement.

(e) Upon the motion to set aside judgment, the court may order the parties to provide the preliminary and final declarations of disclosure that were exchanged between them. Absent a court order to the contrary, the disclosure declarations shall not be filed with the court and shall be returned to the parties. *(Added by Stats.1993, c. 219 (A.B.1500), § 107. Amended by Stats.1993, c. 1101 (A.B.1469), § 9, eff. Oct. 11, 1993, operative Jan. 1, 1994; Stats.2001, c. 703 (A.B.583), § 6; Stats.2009, c. 110 (A.B.459), § 3; Stats.2015, c. 46 (S.B.340), § 3, eff. Jan. 1, 2016.)*

Cross References

Judgment and order defined for purposes of this Code, see Family Code § 100.

Research References

Forms

California Practice Guide: Rutter Family Law Forms Form 11:3, Request for Preliminary Declaration of Disclosure.

California Practice Guide: Rutter Family Law Forms Form 11:4, Request for Order Re Service of Declaration of Disclosure.

West's California Judicial Council Forms FL–300, Request for Order (Also Available in Spanish).

West's California Judicial Council Forms FL–316, Request for Orders Regarding Noncompliance With Disclosure Requirements.

§ 2108. Liquidation of community or quasi-community assets to avoid market or investment risks; authority of court

At any time during the proceeding, the court has the authority, on application of a party and for good cause, to order the liquidation of community or quasi-community assets so as to avoid unreasonable market or investment risks, given the relative nature, scope, and extent of the community estate. However, in no event shall the court grant the application unless, as provided in this chapter, the appropriate declaration of disclosure has been served by the moving party. *(Added by Stats.1993, c. 219 (A.B.1500), § 107.)*

Cross References

Asset defined for purposes of this Chapter, see Family Code § 2101.
Community estate defined for purposes of this Code, see Family Code § 63.
Judgment and order defined for purposes of this Code, see Family Code § 100.
Proceeding defined for purposes of this Code, see Family Code § 110.

Research References

Forms

California Practice Guide: Rutter Family Law Forms Form 5:9, Request for Order to Liquidate Family Residence (Family Code §2108).

California Practice Guide: Rutter Family Law Forms Form 5:10, Responsive Declaration to Request for Order to Liquidate Family Residence (Family Code §2108).

§ 2109. Summary dissolution of marriage; required disclosures

The provisions of this chapter requiring a final declaration of disclosure do not apply to a summary dissolution of marriage, but a preliminary declaration of disclosure is required. *(Added by Stats. 1993, c. 1101 (A.B.1469), § 11, eff. Oct. 11, 1993, operative Jan. 1, 1994.)*

Cross References

Summary dissolution of marriage, see Family Code § 2400 et seq.

Research References

Forms

West's California Judicial Council Forms FL–800, Joint Petition for Summary Dissolution.

§ 2110. Default judgments; declarations of disclosure

In the case of a default judgment, the petitioner may waive the final declaration of disclosure requirements provided in this chapter, and shall not be required to serve a final declaration of disclosure on the respondent nor receive a final declaration of disclosure from the respondent. However, a preliminary declaration of disclosure by the petitioner is required unless the petitioner served the summons and petition by publication or posting pursuant to court order and the respondent has defaulted. *(Added by Stats.1993, c. 1101 (A.B.1469), § 12, eff. Oct. 11, 1993, operative Jan. 1, 1994. Amended by Stats.1994, c. 146 (A.B.3601), § 41; Stats.1998, c. 581 (A.B.2801), § 10; Stats.2015, c. 46 (S.B.340), § 4, eff. Jan. 1, 2016.)*

Cross References

Default judgment defined for purposes of this Chapter, see Family Code § 2101.
Judgment and order defined for purposes of this Code, see Family Code § 100.
Petitioner defined for purposes of this Code, see Family Code § 126.
Respondent defined for purposes of this Code, see Family Code § 127.

§ 2111. Attorney work product privilege; protective orders

A disclosure required by this chapter does not abrogate the attorney work product privilege or impede the power of the court to issue protective orders. *(Added by Stats.1993, c. 1101 (A.B.1469), § 13, eff. Oct. 11, 1993, operative Jan. 1, 1994.)*

Cross References

Judgment and order defined for purposes of this Code, see Family Code § 100.

§ 2111   NULLITY, DISSOLUTION, AND LEGAL SEPARATION

Protective order defined for purposes of this Code, see Family Code § 6218.

Research References

Forms

West's California Code Forms, Family § 2104, Comment Overview—Disclosure of Assets.

§ 2112. Forms

The Judicial Council shall adopt appropriate forms and modify existing forms to effectuate the purposes of this chapter. *(Added by Stats.1993, c. 1101 (A.B.1469), § 14, eff. Oct. 11, 1993, operative Jan. 1, 1994.)*

Research References

Forms

West's California Code Forms, Family § 2112 Form 1, Form Interrogatories.
West's California Judicial Council Forms FL–140,   Declaration of Disclosure (Also Available in Spanish).
West's California Judicial Council Forms FL–141,   Declaration Regarding Service of Declaration of Disclosure and Income and Expense Declaration.

§ 2113. Application of chapter

This chapter applies to any proceeding commenced on or after January 1, 1993. *(Formerly § 2109, added by Stats.1993, c. 219, (A.B.1500), § 107. Renumbered § 2113 and amended by Stats.1993, c. 1101 (A.B.1469), § 10, eff. Oct. 11, 1993, operative Jan. 1, 1994.)*

Cross References

Proceeding defined for purposes of this Code, see Family Code § 110.

Research References

Forms

West's California Code Forms, Family § 2104, Comment Overview—Disclosure of Assets.
West's California Judicial Council Forms FL–150,   Income and Expense Declaration (Also Available in Spanish).

CHAPTER 10.   RELIEF FROM JUDGMENT

Section
2120.   Legislative findings and declarations; public policy.
2121.   Authority of court to provide relief.
2122.   Grounds for relief; limitation of actions.
2123.   Restrictions on grounds for relief; inequitable judgments.
2124.   Attorney negligence.
2125.   Actions or motions to set aside judgment.
2126.   Valuation date of assets or liabilities for which judgment was set aside; equal division.
2127.   Actions or motions; statement of decision.
2128.   Construction of chapter with other provisions.
2129.   Application of chapter.

Cross References

Perjury committed on preliminary or final declaration of disclosure, grounds for setting aside judgment, see Family Code §§ 2104, 2105.

§ 2120. Legislative findings and declarations; public policy

The Legislature finds and declares the following:

(a) The State of California has a strong policy of ensuring the division of community and quasi-community property in the dissolution of a marriage as set forth in Division 7 (commencing with Section 2500), and of providing for fair and sufficient child and spousal support awards. These policy goals can only be implemented with full disclosure of community, quasi-community, and separate assets, liabilities, income, and expenses, as provided in Chapter 9 (commencing with Section 2100), and decisions freely and knowingly made.

(b) It occasionally happens that the division of property or the award of support, whether made as a result of agreement or trial, is inequitable when made due to the nondisclosure or other misconduct of one of the parties.

(c) The public policy of assuring finality of judgments must be balanced against the public interest in ensuring proper division of marital property, in ensuring sufficient support awards, and in deterring misconduct.

(d) The law governing the circumstances under which a judgment can be set aside, after the time for relief under Section 473 of the Code of Civil Procedure has passed, has been the subject of considerable confusion which has led to increased litigation and unpredictable and inconsistent decisions at the trial and appellate levels. *(Added by Stats.1993, c. 219 (A.B.1500), § 108.)*

Cross References

Community property defined for purposes of this Code, see Family Code § 65.
Judgment and order defined for purposes of this Code, see Family Code § 100.
Property defined for purposes of this Code, see Family Code § 113.
Quasi-community property defined for purposes of this Code, see Family Code § 125.
Spousal support defined for purposes of this Code, see Family Code § 142.
State defined for purposes of this Code, see Family Code § 145.
Support defined for purposes of this Code, see Family Code § 150.

Research References

Forms

California Practice Guide: Rutter Family Law Forms Form 16:1, Request for Order to Set Aside Judgment (Family Code §2120 et seq.).
West's California Code Forms, Family § 2104, Comment Overview—Disclosure of Assets.

§ 2121. Authority of court to provide relief

(a) In proceedings for dissolution of marriage, for nullity of marriage, or for legal separation of the parties, the court may, on any terms that may be just, relieve a spouse from a judgment, or any part or parts thereof, adjudicating support or division of property, after the six-month time limit of Section 473 of the Code of Civil Procedure has run, based on the grounds, and within the time limits, provided in this chapter.

(b) In all proceedings under this chapter, before granting relief, the court shall find that the facts alleged as the grounds for relief materially affected the original outcome and that the moving party would materially benefit from the granting of the relief. *(Added by Stats.1993, c. 219 (A.B.1500), § 108.)*

Cross References

Dissolution or legal separation, see Family Code § 2300 et seq.
Judgment and order defined for purposes of this Code, see Family Code § 100.
Nullity of marriage, proceeding, see Family Code § 2200 et seq.
Proceeding defined for purposes of this Code, see Family Code § 110.
Property defined for purposes of this Code, see Family Code § 113.
References to husband, wife, spouses and married persons, persons included for purposes of this Code, see Family Code § 11.
Support defined for purposes of this Code, see Family Code § 150.

Research References

Forms

California Practice Guide: Rutter Family Law Forms Form 16:1, Request for Order to Set Aside Judgment (Family Code §2120 et seq.).

§ 2122. Grounds for relief; limitation of actions

The grounds and time limits for a motion to set aside a judgment, or any part or parts thereof, are governed by this section and shall be one of the following:

(a) Actual fraud where the defrauded party was kept in ignorance or in some other manner was fraudulently prevented from fully participating in the proceeding. An action or motion based on fraud shall be brought within one year after the date on which the complaining party either did discover, or should have discovered, the fraud.

(b) Perjury. An action or motion based on perjury in the preliminary or final declaration of disclosure, the waiver of the final declaration of disclosure, or in the current income and expense statement shall be brought within one year after the date on which the complaining party either did discover, or should have discovered, the perjury.

(c) Duress. An action or motion based upon duress shall be brought within two years after the date of entry of judgment.

(d) Mental incapacity. An action or motion based on mental incapacity shall be brought within two years after the date of entry of judgment.

(e) As to stipulated or uncontested judgments or that part of a judgment stipulated to by the parties, mistake, either mutual or unilateral, whether mistake of law or mistake of fact. An action or motion based on mistake shall be brought within one year after the date of entry of judgment.

(f) Failure to comply with the disclosure requirements of Chapter 9 (commencing with Section 2100). An action or motion based on failure to comply with the disclosure requirements shall be brought within one year after the date on which the complaining party either discovered, or should have discovered, the failure to comply. *(Added by Stats.1993, c. 219 (A.B.1500), § 108. Amended by Stats.1993, c. 1101 (A.B.1469), § 15, eff. Oct. 11, 1993, operative Jan. 1, 1994; Stats.2001, c. 703 (A.B.583), § 7.)*

Application

For application of Stats.2001, c. 703 (A.B.583), see § 8 of that act.

Cross References

Judgment and order defined for purposes of this Code, see Family Code § 100.
Proceeding defined for purposes of this Code, see Family Code § 110.

Research References

Forms

California Practice Guide: Rutter Family Law Forms Form 16:1, Request for Order to Set Aside Judgment (Family Code §2120 et seq.).

§ 2123. Restrictions on grounds for relief; inequitable judgments

Notwithstanding any other provision of this chapter, or any other law, a judgment may not be set aside simply because the court finds that it was inequitable when made, nor simply because subsequent circumstances caused the division of assets or liabilities to become inequitable, or the support to become inadequate. *(Added by Stats.1993, c. 219 (A.B.1500), § 108.)*

Cross References

Judgment and order defined for purposes of this Code, see Family Code § 100.
Support defined for purposes of this Code, see Family Code § 150.

§ 2124. Attorney negligence

The negligence of an attorney shall not be imputed to a client to bar an order setting aside a judgment, unless the court finds that the client knew, or should have known, of the attorney's negligence and unreasonably failed to self-protect. *(Added by Stats.1993, c. 219 (A.B.1500), § 108. Amended by Stats.2019, c. 115 (A.B.1817), § 21, eff. Jan. 1, 2020.)*

Cross References

Judgment and order defined for purposes of this Code, see Family Code § 100.

§ 2125. Actions or motions to set aside judgment

When ruling on an action or motion to set aside a judgment, the court shall set aside only those provisions materially affected by the circumstances leading to the court's decision to grant relief. However, the court has discretion to set aside the entire judgment, if necessary, for equitable considerations. *(Added by Stats.1993, c. 219 (A.B.1500), § 108. Amended by Stats.1993, c. 1101 (A.B.1469), § 16, eff. Oct. 11, 1993, operative Jan. 1, 1994.)*

Cross References

Judgment and order defined for purposes of this Code, see Family Code § 100.

§ 2126. Valuation date of assets or liabilities for which judgment was set aside; equal division

As to assets or liabilities for which a judgment or part of a judgment is set aside, the date of valuation shall be subject to equitable considerations. The court shall equally divide the asset or liability, unless the court finds upon good cause shown that the interests of justice require an unequal division. *(Added by Stats.1993, c. 219 (A.B.1500), § 108.)*

Cross References

Judgment and order defined for purposes of this Code, see Family Code § 100.

§ 2127. Actions or motions; statement of decision

As to actions or motions filed under this chapter, if a timely request is made, the court shall render a statement of decision where the court has resolved controverted factual evidence. *(Added by Stats.1993, c. 219 (A.B.1500), § 108. Amended by Stats.1993, c. 1101 (A.B.1469), § 17, eff. Oct. 11, 1993, operative Jan. 1, 1994.)*

§ 2128. Construction of chapter with other provisions

(a) Nothing in this chapter prohibits a party from seeking relief under Section 2556.

(b) Nothing in this chapter changes existing law with respect to contract remedies where the contract has not been merged or incorporated into a judgment.

(c) Nothing in this chapter is intended to restrict a family law court from acting as a court of equity.

(d) Nothing in this chapter is intended to limit existing law with respect to the modification or enforcement of support orders.

(e) Nothing in this chapter affects the rights of a bona fide lessee, purchaser, or encumbrancer for value of real property. *(Added by Stats.1993, c. 219 (A.B.1500), § 108.)*

Cross References

Judgment and order defined for purposes of this Code, see Family Code § 100.
Property defined for purposes of this Code, see Family Code § 113.
Support defined for purposes of this Code, see Family Code § 150.
Support order defined for purposes of this Code, see Family Code § 155.

§ 2129. Application of chapter

This chapter applies to judgments entered on or after January 1, 1993. *(Added by Stats.1993, c. 219 (A.B.1500), § 108.)*

Cross References

Judgment and order defined for purposes of this Code, see Family Code § 100.

Part 2

JUDICIAL DETERMINATION OF VOID OR VOIDABLE MARRIAGE

Chapter	Section
1. Void Marriage	2200

NULLITY, DISSOLUTION, AND LEGAL SEPARATION

Chapter	Section
2. Voidable Marriage	2210
3. Procedural Provisions	2250

Cross References
Preliminary declaration of disclosure, service, see Family Code § 2104.
Relief from judgment adjudicating support or division of property, see Family Code § 2121.

CHAPTER 1. VOID MARRIAGE

Section
2200. Incestuous marriages.
2201. Bigamous and polygamous marriages; exceptions; absentees.

Cross References
Validity of marriage, see Family Code § 300 et seq.

§ 2200. Incestuous marriages

Marriages between parents and children, ancestors and descendants of every degree, and between siblings of the half as well as the whole blood, and between uncles or aunts and nieces or nephews, are incestuous, and void from the beginning, whether the relationship is legitimate or illegitimate. *(Stats.1992, c. 162 (A.B.2650), § 10, operative Jan. 1, 1994. Amended by Stats.2014, c. 82 (S.B.1306), § 23, eff. Jan. 1, 2015.)*

Cross References
Ex parte protective orders, see Family Code § 2045.
Persons solemnizing marriages, duties, see Family Code § 421.
Punishment for crime of incest, see Penal Code § 285.
Punishment for solemnizing incestuous or forbidden marriages, see Penal Code § 359.
Validity of marriage, see Family Code § 300 et seq.

Research References
Forms
California Practice Guide: Rutter Family Law Forms Form 1:32, Glossary of Common Family Law Terms, Phrases and Concepts (Enclosure to Form 1:31).
West's California Code Forms, Family § 2250, Comment Overview—Judgment of Nullity.

§ 2201. Bigamous and polygamous marriages; exceptions; absentees

(a) A subsequent marriage contracted by a person during the life of his or her former spouse, with a person other than the former spouse, is illegal and void, unless:

(1) The former marriage has been dissolved or adjudged a nullity before the date of the subsequent marriage.

(2) The former spouse (A) is absent, and not known to the person to be living for the period of five successive years immediately preceding the subsequent marriage, or (B) is generally reputed or believed by the person to be dead at the time the subsequent marriage was contracted.

(b) In either of the cases described in paragraph (2) of subdivision (a), the subsequent marriage is valid until its nullity is adjudged pursuant to subdivision (b) of Section 2210. *(Stats.1992, c. 162 (A.B.2650), § 10, operative Jan. 1, 1994. Amended by Stats.2014, c. 82 (S.B.1306), § 24, eff. Jan. 1, 2015.)*

Cross References
Bigamy, generally, see Penal Code § 281 et seq.
Bigamy, punishment, see Penal Code §§ 283, 284.
Person defined for purposes of this Code, see Family Code § 105.
References to husband, wife, spouses and married persons, persons included for purposes of this Code, see Family Code § 11.

Validity of marriage, see Family Code § 300 et seq.

Research References
Forms
California Practice Guide: Rutter Family Law Forms Form 1:32, Glossary of Common Family Law Terms, Phrases and Concepts (Enclosure to Form 1:31).
West's California Code Forms, Family § 2250, Comment Overview—Judgment of Nullity.

CHAPTER 2. VOIDABLE MARRIAGE

Section
2210. Judgment of nullity; causes.
2211. Limitation of actions.
2212. Effect of judgment of nullity; conclusiveness.

Cross References
Uniform Divorce Recognition Act, see Family Code § 2090 et seq.
Validity of marriage, see Family Code § 300 et seq.

§ 2210. Judgment of nullity; causes

A marriage is voidable and may be adjudged a nullity if any of the following conditions existed at the time of the marriage:

(a) The party who commences the proceeding or on whose behalf the proceeding is commenced was under 18 years of age, unless the party entered into the marriage pursuant to Section 302 or 303.

(b) The spouse of either party was living and the marriage with that spouse was then in force and that spouse (1) was absent and not known to the party commencing the proceeding to be living for a period of five successive years immediately preceding the subsequent marriage for which the judgment of nullity is sought or (2) was generally reputed or believed by the party commencing the proceeding to be dead at the time the subsequent marriage was contracted.

(c) Either party was of unsound mind, unless the party of unsound mind, after coming to reason, freely cohabited with the other as his or her spouse.

(d) The consent of either party was obtained by fraud, unless the party whose consent was obtained by fraud afterwards, with full knowledge of the facts constituting the fraud, freely cohabited with the other as his or her spouse.

(e) The consent of either party was obtained by force, unless the party whose consent was obtained by force afterwards freely cohabited with the other as his or her spouse.

(f) Either party was, at the time of marriage, physically incapable of entering into the marriage state, and that incapacity continues, and appears to be incurable. *(Stats.1992, c. 162 (A.B.2650), § 10, operative Jan. 1, 1994. Amended by Stats.2014, c. 82 (S.B.1306), § 25, eff. Jan. 1, 2015; Stats.2018, c. 660 (S.B.273), § 8, eff. Jan. 1, 2019.)*

Cross References
Actions for annulment,
  Generally, see Family Code § 2250.
  Attorney fees and costs, see Family Code § 270 et seq.
  Employee pension benefit plans, joinder, see Family Code § 2060 et seq.
  Jurisdiction, see Family Code § 2010 et seq.
  Procedure, see Family Code § 2020 et seq.
  Reconciliation proceedings, pendency of nullity proceedings, see Family Code § 1840.
Bigamous and polygamous marriages, see Family Code § 2201.
Disposition of separate property residence during pendency of proceedings, see Family Code § 754.
Enforcement of money judgments, see Family Code § 291.
Ex parte temporary restraining orders, see Family Code § 240 et seq.
Incestuous marriages, see Family Code § 2200.
Judgment and order defined for purposes of this Code, see Family Code § 100.
Practice and procedure rules, see Family Code § 210 et seq.
Proceeding defined for purposes of this Code, see Family Code § 110.

VOID OR VOIDABLE MARRIAGE § 2250

Proceedings for conciliation, see Family Code § 1830 et seq.
Protective and restraining orders, see Family Code § 2040 et seq.
Protective orders,
  Defined, see Family Code § 6218.
  Pending proceedings, notice and hearing, see Family Code § 6340 et seq.
References to husband, wife, spouses and married persons, persons included for purposes of this Code, see Family Code § 11.
Restoration of former name, see Family Code § 2080 et seq.
State defined for purposes of this Code, see Family Code § 145.
Temporary restraining order in summons, see Family Code § 231 et seq.
Validity of marriage, see Family Code § 300 et seq.

Research References

Forms

California Practice Guide: Rutter Family Law Forms Form 1:32, Glossary of Common Family Law Terms, Phrases and Concepts (Enclosure to Form 1:31).
West's California Code Forms, Family § 2250, Comment Overview—Judgment of Nullity.

§ 2211. Limitation of actions

A proceeding to obtain a judgment of nullity of marriage, for causes set forth in Section 2210, must be commenced within the periods and by the parties, as follows:

(a) For causes mentioned in subdivision (a) of Section 2210, by any of the following:

(1) The party to the marriage who was married under the age of legal consent, within four years after arriving at the age of consent.

(2) A parent, guardian, conservator, or other person having charge of the minor, at any time before the married minor has arrived at the age of legal consent.

(b) For causes mentioned in subdivision (b) of Section 2210, by either of the following:

(1) Either party during the life of the other.

(2) The former spouse.

(c) For causes mentioned in subdivision (c) of Section 2210, by the party injured, or by a relative or conservator of the party of unsound mind, at any time before the death of either party.

(d) For causes mentioned in subdivision (d) of Section 2210, by the party whose consent was obtained by fraud, within four years after the discovery of the facts constituting the fraud.

(e) For causes mentioned in subdivision (e) of Section 2210, by the party whose consent was obtained by force, within four years after the marriage.

(f) For causes mentioned in subdivision (f) of Section 2210, by the injured party, within four years after the marriage. *(Stats.1992, c. 162 (A.B.2650), § 10, operative Jan. 1, 1994. Amended by Stats.2014, c. 82 (S.B.1306), § 26, eff. Jan. 1, 2015.)*

Cross References

Actions for annulment, generally, see Family Code § 2250.
General provisions as to time of commencing actions, see Code of Civil Procedure § 350 et seq.
Judgment and order defined for purposes of this Code, see Family Code § 100.
Minors,
  Conciliation counselor recommendations on marriage, see Family Code § 1814.
  Defined for purposes of this Code, see Family Code § 6500.
  Marriage license applicants, see Family Code § 302.
Parties to civil actions in general, see Code of Civil Procedure § 367 et seq.
Person defined for purposes of this Code, see Family Code § 105.
Proceeding defined for purposes of this Code, see Family Code § 110.
References to husband, wife, spouses and married persons, persons included for purposes of this Code, see Family Code § 11.

Time of commencing actions, generally, see Code of Civil Procedure § 312 et seq.

§ 2212. Effect of judgment of nullity; conclusiveness

(a) The effect of a judgment of nullity of marriage is to restore the parties to the status of unmarried persons.

(b) A judgment of nullity of marriage is conclusive only as to the parties to the proceeding and those claiming under them. *(Stats. 1992, c. 162 (A.B.2650), § 10, operative Jan. 1, 1994.)*

Cross References

Effect of dissolution, see Family Code § 2300.
Employee pension benefit plan as party, joinder, see Family Code § 2060 et seq.
Enforcement of judgments and orders, see Family Code §§ 290, 291.
Joinder, interested parties, see Family Code § 2021.
Judgment and order defined for purposes of this Code, see Family Code § 100.
Person defined for purposes of this Code, see Family Code § 105.
Proceeding defined for purposes of this Code, see Family Code § 110.
Uniform Divorce Recognition Act, see Family Code § 2090 et seq.

Research References

Forms

West's California Code Forms, Family § 2250, Comment Overview—Judgment of Nullity.

CHAPTER 3. PROCEDURAL PROVISIONS

Section
2250. Petition for judgment of nullity; filing; service.
2251. Status of putative spouse; division of community or quasi-community property.
2252. Liability of quasi-marital property for debts of parties.
2253. Children of annulled marriage; determination of custody.
2254. Order for support; putative spouse.
2255. Grant of attorney's fees and costs.

§ 2250. Petition for judgment of nullity; filing; service

(a) A proceeding based on void or voidable marriage is commenced by filing a petition entitled "In re the marriage of _____ and _____" which shall state that it is a petition for a judgment of nullity of the marriage.

(b) A copy of the petition together with a copy of a summons in form and content approved by the Judicial Council shall be served upon the other party to the marriage in the same manner as service of papers in civil actions generally. *(Stats.1992, c. 162 (A.B.2650), § 10, operative Jan. 1, 1994.)*

Cross References

Annulment, causes for, see Family Code § 2210.
Employee pension benefit plan, notice of appearance, responsive pleadings, see Family Code § 2063.
Incestuous marriages, see Family Code § 2200.
Judgment and order defined for purposes of this Code, see Family Code § 100.
Jurisdiction in superior court, see Family Code § 200.
Jurisdiction over real property in dissolution, nullity, or separation, see Family Code § 2011.
Limitation of actions, see Family Code § 2211.
Petitions, existence of child support, child custody, visitation, or spousal support orders, personal conduct restraining order, or bifurcated case, dismissal for delay in prosecution prohibited, see Code of Civil Procedure § 583.161.
Proceeding defined for purposes of this Code, see Family Code § 110.
Responsive pleadings, see Family Code § 2020.
Restoration of former name, see Family Code § 2080 et seq.

§ 2250

State defined for purposes of this Code, see Family Code § 145.

Research References

Forms

California Practice Guide: Rutter Family Law Forms Form 1:32, Glossary of Common Family Law Terms, Phrases and Concepts (Enclosure to Form 1:31).

West's California Code Forms, Family § 2250, Comment Overview—Judgment of Nullity.

§ 2251. Status of putative spouse; division of community or quasi-community property

(a) If a determination is made that a marriage is void or voidable and the court finds that either party or both parties believed in good faith that the marriage was valid, the court shall:

(1) Declare the party or parties, who believed in good faith that the marriage was valid, to have the status of a putative spouse.

(2) If the division of property is in issue, divide, in accordance with Division 7 (commencing with Section 2500), that property acquired during the union that would have been community property or quasi-community property if the union had not been void or voidable, only upon request of a party who is declared a putative spouse under paragraph (1). This property is known as "quasi-marital property."

(b) If the court expressly reserves jurisdiction, it may make the property division at a time after the judgment. *(Stats.1992, c. 162 (A.B.2650), § 10, operative Jan. 1, 1994. Amended by Stats.2015, c. 196 (A.B.380), § 1, eff. Jan. 1, 2016.)*

Cross References

Agreements between husband and wife, see Family Code § 1620.
Characterization of marital property, see Family Code § 760 et seq.
Community property defined, see Civil Code § 687; Family Code §§ 65, 760; Probate Code § 28.
Effect of judgment of nullity, conclusiveness, see Family Code § 2211.
Judgment and order defined for purposes of this Code, see Family Code § 100.
Jurisdiction over real property in dissolution, nullity, or separation, see Family Code § 2011.
Liability of marital property, see Family Code § 900 et seq.
Presumptions concerning nature of property, see Family Code §§ 802, 803.
Property defined for purposes of this Code, see Family Code § 113.
Quasi-community property defined, see Family Code § 125.
References to husband, wife, spouses and married persons, persons included for purposes of this Code, see Family Code § 11.
Separate property of married person, see Family Code § 770 et seq.
Transmutation of property, see Family Code § 850 et seq.

Research References

Forms

West's California Code Forms, Family § 2250, Comment Overview—Judgment of Nullity.

§ 2252. Liability of quasi-marital property for debts of parties

The property divided pursuant to Section 2251 is liable for debts of the parties to the same extent as if the property had been community property or quasi-community property. *(Stats.1992, c. 162 (A.B. 2650), § 10, operative Jan. 1, 1994.)*

Cross References

Community property defined, see Civil Code § 687; Family Code §§ 65, 760; Probate Code § 28.
Effect of judgment of nullity, conclusiveness, see Family Code § 2211.
Jurisdiction over real property in dissolution, nullity, or separation, see Family Code § 2011.
Liability of property after division, see Family Code § 916.
Property defined for purposes of this Code, see Family Code § 113.
Quasi-community property, jurisdiction, see Family Code § 2011.
Quasi-community property defined, see Family Code § 125.

§ 2253. Children of annulled marriage; determination of custody

In a proceeding under this part, custody of the children shall be determined according to Division 8 (commencing with Section 3000). *(Stats.1992, c. 162 (A.B.2650), § 10, operative Jan. 1, 1994.)*

Cross References

Action for exclusive custody of children, see Family Code § 3120.
Custody investigation and report, see Family Code § 3110 et seq.
Custody of children, see Family Code § 3000 et seq.
Proceeding defined for purposes of this Code, see Family Code § 110.
Quasi-community property, support, property subject to, see Family Code § 4008.
Support, generally, see Family Code § 3500 et seq.
Uniform Parentage Act, see Family Code § 7600 et seq.
Visitation rights, see Family Code § 3100 et seq.

Research References

Forms

1 California Transactions Forms--Family Law § 3:4, Subject Matter Jurisdiction for Custody Determinations.

§ 2254. Order for support; putative spouse

The court may, during the pendency of a proceeding for nullity of marriage or upon judgment of nullity of marriage, order a party to pay for the support of the other party in the same manner as if the marriage had not been void or voidable if the party for whose benefit the order is made is found to be a putative spouse. *(Stats.1992, c. 162 (A.B.2650), § 10, operative Jan. 1, 1994.)*

Cross References

Ex parte protective orders, see Family Code § 2045.
Judgment and order defined for purposes of this Code, see Family Code § 100.
Orders during pendency of proceedings, see Family Code § 2045.
Orders for support, dissolution or separation, see Family Code § 4330.
Payment of obligation directly to creditor, see Family Code § 2023.
Proceeding defined for purposes of this Code, see Family Code § 110.
References to husband, wife, spouses and married persons, persons included for purposes of this Code, see Family Code § 11.
Spousal and child support during pendency of proceeding, see Family Code § 3600 et seq.
Support defined for purposes of this Code, see Family Code § 150.

§ 2255. Grant of attorney's fees and costs

The court may grant attorney's fees and costs in accordance with Chapter 3.5 (commencing with Section 2030) of Part 1 in proceedings to have the marriage adjudged void and in those proceedings based upon voidable marriage in which the party applying for attorney's fees and costs is found to be innocent of fraud or wrongdoing in inducing or entering into the marriage, and free from knowledge of the then existence of any prior marriage or other impediment to the contracting of the marriage for which a judgment of nullity is sought. *(Stats.1992, c. 162 (A.B.2650), § 10, operative Jan. 1, 1994. Amended by Stats.1993, c. 219 (A.B.1500), § 108.5.)*

Cross References

Approval of contract for attorney's fees for minor, see Family Code § 6602.
Attorney fees,
   Generally, see Code of Civil Procedure § 1021.
   Contract for by minor, see Family Code § 6602.
   Jurisdiction over, see Family Code § 2010.
   Modification of support, see Family Code § 3652.
Judgment and order defined for purposes of this Code, see Family Code § 100.
Payment of obligation directly to creditor, see Family Code § 2023.

Part 3

DISSOLUTION OF MARRIAGE AND LEGAL SEPARATION

Chapter	Section
1. Effect of Dissolution	2300
2. Grounds for Dissolution or Legal Separation	2310
3. Residence Requirements	2320
4. General Procedural Provisions	2330
5. Summary Dissolution	2400
6. Case Management	2450

Cross References

Declarations of disclosure, requirements, see Family Code § 2103 et seq.
Relief from judgment adjudicating support or division of property, see Family Code § 2121.

CHAPTER 1. EFFECT OF DISSOLUTION

Section
2300. Effect of dissolution.

§ 2300. Effect of dissolution

The effect of a judgment of dissolution of marriage when it becomes final is to restore the parties to the state of unmarried persons. *(Stats.1992, c. 162 (A.B.2650), § 10, operative Jan. 1, 1994.)*

Cross References

Finality of judgment,
 Effective date, see Family Code § 2340 et seq.
 Waiting period, see Family Code § 2339.
Former name, restoration of, see Family Code § 2080 et seq.
Judgment and order defined for purposes of this Code, see Family Code § 100.
Judgment of nullity, effect, conclusiveness, see Family Code § 2212.
Manner of division of community estate, see Family Code § 2550.
Person defined for purposes of this Code, see Family Code § 105.
Special rules for division of community estate, see Family Code § 2600 et seq.
State defined for purposes of this Code, see Family Code § 145.

Research References

Forms

California Practice Guide: Rutter Family Law Forms Form 1:32, Glossary of Common Family Law Terms, Phrases and Concepts (Enclosure to Form 1:31).
1 California Transactions Forms--Family Law § 2:51, Preparation of Future Returns.

CHAPTER 2. GROUNDS FOR DISSOLUTION OR LEGAL SEPARATION

Section
2310. Grounds for dissolution or legal separation.
2311. "Irreconcilable differences" defined.
2312. Permanent legal incapacity to make decisions.
2313. Support of spouse lacking legal capacity to make decisions.

Proceeding defined for purposes of this Code, see Family Code § 110.

Research References

Forms

West's California Code Forms, Family § 2250, Comment Overview—Judgment of Nullity.

§ 2310. Grounds for dissolution or legal separation

Dissolution of the marriage or legal separation of the parties may be based on either of the following grounds, which shall be pleaded generally:

(a) Irreconcilable differences, which have caused the irremediable breakdown of the marriage.

(b) Permanent legal incapacity to make decisions. *(Stats.1992, c. 162 (A.B.2650), § 10, operative Jan. 1, 1994. Amended by Stats.2014, c. 144 (A.B.1847), § 9, eff. Jan. 1, 2015.)*

Cross References

Evidence of specific acts of misconduct, admissibility, see Family Code § 2335.
Family Conciliation Court Law, see Family Code § 1830 et seq.
Irreconcilable differences defined, see Family Code § 2311.
Jurisdiction, status of marriage, see Family Code § 2010.
Jurisdiction of superior court, see Cal. Const. Art. 6, §§ 10, 11.
Petition for dissolution of marriage and legal separation, see Family Code § 2330 et seq.

Research References

Forms

California Practice Guide: Rutter Family Law Forms Form 1:32, Glossary of Common Family Law Terms, Phrases and Concepts (Enclosure to Form 1:31).

§ 2311. "Irreconcilable differences" defined

Irreconcilable differences are those grounds which are determined by the court to be substantial reasons for not continuing the marriage and which make it appear that the marriage should be dissolved. *(Stats.1992, c. 162 (A.B.2650), § 10, operative Jan. 1, 1994.)*

§ 2312. Permanent legal incapacity to make decisions

A marriage may be dissolved on the grounds of permanent legal incapacity to make decisions only upon proof, including competent medical or psychiatric testimony, that the spouse was at the time the petition was filed, and remains, permanently lacking the legal capacity to make decisions. *(Stats.1992, c. 162 (A.B.2650), § 10, operative Jan. 1, 1994. Amended by Stats.2014, c. 144 (A.B.1847), § 10, eff. Jan. 1, 2015.)*

Cross References

Commitment of defendant to state hospital, see Penal Code § 1026.
Commitment of mentally disordered persons, see Welfare and Institutions Code § 7200 et seq.
Conservatorship, see Probate Code § 1800 et seq.
Guardianship, see Probate Code § 1500.
Guardianship ad litem, see Code of Civil Procedure §§ 373, 373.5.
Legal capacity of conservatee, generally, see Probate Code § 1870 et seq.
Opinion of witness as to sanity, see Evidence Code § 870.
References to husband, wife, spouses and married persons, persons included for purposes of this Code, see Family Code § 11.

Research References

Forms

West's California Code Forms, Family § 2330, Comment Overview—Procedures.

§ 2313. Support of spouse lacking legal capacity to make decisions

No dissolution of marriage granted on the ground of permanent legal incapacity to make decisions relieves a spouse from any obligation imposed by law as a result of the marriage for the support of the spouse who lacks legal capacity to make decisions, and the court may make an order for support, or require a bond therefor, as the circumstances require. *(Stats.1992, c. 162 (A.B.2650), § 10, operative Jan. 1, 1994. Amended by Stats.2014, c. 144 (A.B.1847), § 11, eff. Jan. 1, 2015.)*

Cross References

Commitment of defendant to state hospital, see Penal Code § 1026.

§ 2313 NULLITY, DISSOLUTION, AND LEGAL SEPARATION

Commitment of mentally disordered persons, see Welfare and Institutions Code § 7200 et seq.
Conservatorship, see Probate Code § 1800 et seq.
Enforcement of right of support, see Family Code § 4303.
Guardianship, see Probate Code § 1500.
Guardianship ad litem, see Code of Civil Procedure §§ 373, 373.5.
Judgment and order defined for purposes of this Code, see Family Code § 100.
Legal capacity of conservatee, generally, see Probate Code § 1870 et seq.
Mutual duty to support, see Family Code § 720.
References to husband, wife, spouses and married persons, persons included for purposes of this Code, see Family Code § 11.
Support defined for purposes of this Code, see Family Code § 150.
Support of spouse from separate property, see Family Code § 4301.

Research References

Forms

West's California Code Forms, Family § 2330, Comment Overview—Procedures.

CHAPTER 3. RESIDENCE REQUIREMENTS

Section
2320. Entry of judgment of dissolution; entry of judgment for dissolution, nullity, or legal separation of marriage between persons of the same sex.
2321. Conversion of separation proceeding to dissolution proceeding; notice.
2322. Separate domicile or residence.

§ 2320. Entry of judgment of dissolution; entry of judgment for dissolution, nullity, or legal separation of marriage between persons of the same sex

(a) Except as provided in subdivision (b), a judgment of dissolution of marriage may not be entered unless one of the parties to the marriage has been a resident of this state for six months and of the county in which the proceeding is filed for three months next preceding the filing of the petition.

(b)(1) A judgment for dissolution, nullity, or legal separation of a marriage between persons of the same sex may be entered, even if neither spouse is a resident of, or maintains a domicile in, this state at the time the proceedings are filed, if the following apply:

(A) The marriage was entered in California.

(B) Neither party to the marriage resides in a jurisdiction that will dissolve the marriage. If the jurisdiction does not recognize the marriage, there shall be a rebuttable presumption that the jurisdiction will not dissolve the marriage.

(2) For the purposes of this subdivision, the superior court in the county where the marriage was entered shall be the proper court for the proceeding. The dissolution, nullity, or legal separation shall be adjudicated in accordance with California law. *(Stats.1992, c. 162 (A.B.2650), § 10, operative Jan. 1, 1994. Amended by Stats.2011, c. 721 (S.B.651), § 4.)*

Cross References

County defined for purposes of this Code, see Family Code § 67.
Determination of place of residence, see Government Code § 244.
Dissolution of marriage and legal separation, summary dissolution, conditions necessary at commencement of proceedings, see Family Code § 2400.
Domicile, prima facie evidence under Uniform Divorce Recognition Act, see Family Code § 2092.
Grounds for dissolution or legal separation, see Family Code § 2310 et seq.
Judgment and order defined for purposes of this Code, see Family Code § 100.
Prima facie evidence of domicile, see Family Code § 2092.
Proceeding defined for purposes of this Code, see Family Code § 110.
State defined for purposes of this Code, see Family Code § 145.

Uniform Divorce Recognition Act, see Family Code § 2090 et seq.

Research References

Forms

California Practice Guide: Rutter Family Law Forms Form 4:19, Request for Order to Quash Proceeding.
West's California Code Forms, Family § 2330, Comment Overview—Procedures.
West's California Judicial Council Forms FL–100, Petition—Marriage/Domestic Partnership (Also Available in Arabic, Chinese, and Spanish).
West's California Judicial Council Forms FL–800, Joint Petition for Summary Dissolution.

§ 2321. Conversion of separation proceeding to dissolution proceeding; notice

(a) In a proceeding for legal separation of the parties in which neither party, at the time the proceeding was commenced, has complied with the residence requirements of Section 2320, either party may, upon complying with the residence requirements, amend the party's petition or responsive pleading in the proceeding to request that a judgment of dissolution of the marriage be entered. The date of the filing of the amended petition or pleading shall be deemed to be the date of commencement of the proceeding for the dissolution of the marriage for the purposes only of the residence requirements of Section 2320.

(b) If the other party has appeared in the proceeding, notice of the amendment shall be given to the other party in the manner provided by rules adopted by the Judicial Council. If no appearance has been made by the other party in the proceeding, notice of the amendment may be given to the other party by mail to the last known address of the other party, or by personal service, if the intent of the party to so amend upon satisfaction of the residence requirements of Section 2320 is set forth in the initial petition or pleading in the manner provided by rules adopted by the Judicial Council. *(Stats.1992, c. 162 (A.B.2650), § 10, operative Jan. 1, 1994.)*

Cross References

Determination of place of residence, see Government Code § 244.
Domicile, prima facie evidence under Uniform Divorce Recognition Act, see Family Code § 2092.
Judgment and order defined for purposes of this Code, see Family Code § 100.
Proceeding defined for purposes of this Code, see Family Code § 110.

§ 2322. Separate domicile or residence

For the purpose of a proceeding for dissolution of marriage, each spouse may have a separate domicile or residence depending upon proof of the fact and not upon legal presumptions. *(Stats.1992, c. 162 (A.B.2650), § 10, operative Jan. 1, 1994. Amended by Stats.2014, c. 82 (S.B.1306), § 27, eff. Jan. 1, 2015.)*

Cross References

Determination of place of residence, see Government Code § 244.
Domicile, prima facie evidence under Uniform Divorce Recognition Act, see Family Code § 2092.
Proceeding defined for purposes of this Code, see Family Code § 110.
References to husband, wife, spouses and married persons, persons included for purposes of this Code, see Family Code § 11.

CHAPTER 4. GENERAL PROCEDURAL PROVISIONS

Section
2330. Petition.
2330.1. Supplemental complaint; paternity or child support.
2330.3. Assignment to same court and judicial officer; minimum length of judicial officer assignment.
2330.5. Financial declarations; filing; exception.
2331. Service of petitions and summons.

DISSOLUTION OF MARRIAGE AND LEGAL SEPARATION § 2330.3

Section	
2332.	Service of petition for dissolution on grounds of permanent legal incapacity to make decisions; appointment of guardian ad litem.
2333.	Irreconcilable differences; order for dissolution.
2334.	Grounds for continuance; authority of court.
2335.	Misconduct; admissibility of specific acts of misconduct.
2335.5.	Requests to enter default judgment; dissolution or legal separation; notice to defaulting spouse.
2336.	Default; proof required.
2337.	Early and separate trial on dissolution; preliminary declaration; conditions; effect on retirement plan; service on plan administrator; reservation of jurisdiction; effect of party's death.
2338.	Decisions; judgments.
2338.5.	Default judgments; dissolution or nullity of marriage, or legal separation.
2339.	Finality of judgment; waiting period.
2340.	Statement of effective date of judgment.
2341.	Appeal or motion for new trial; finality of judgment.
2342.	Joint petitions for summary dissolutions; revocation; final judgment.
2343.	Retention of jurisdiction; purposes; effect of date of termination of marital status.
2344.	Death of party after entry of judgment.
2345.	Consent to legal separation.
2346.	Judgments; nunc pro tunc entry; rights to judgment.
2347.	Judgment of legal separation; effect on subsequent judgment of dissolution.
2348.	Annual report to Judicial Council; superior court clerks.

§ 2330. Petition

(a) A proceeding for dissolution of marriage or for legal separation of the parties is commenced by filing a petition entitled "In re the marriage of _____ and _____" which shall state whether it is a petition for dissolution of the marriage or for legal separation of the parties.

(b) In a proceeding for dissolution of marriage or for legal separation of the parties, the petition shall set forth among other matters, as nearly as can be ascertained, the following facts:

(1) The date of marriage.

(2) The date of separation.

(3) The number of years from marriage to separation.

(4) The number of children of the marriage, if any, and if none a statement of that fact.

(5) The age and birth date of each minor child of the marriage. (Stats.1992, c. 162 (A.B.2650), § 10, operative Jan. 1, 1994. Amended by Stats.1998, c. 581 (A.B.2801), § 11.)

Cross References

Child or spousal support order in effect, dismissal of petition filed pursuant to this section, see Code of Civil Procedure § 583.161.
General procedural provisions, see Family Code § 210 et seq.
Joint petition for summary dissolution, revocation, date of final judgment, see Family Code § 2342.
Jurisdiction in superior court, see Family Code § 200.
Jurisdiction of conciliation court, see Family Code § 1830.
Jurisdiction of superior courts, see Cal. Const. Art. 6, §§ 10, 11.
Minor defined for purposes of this Code, see Family Code § 6500.
Petition for separation or dissolution of marriage, pending child or spousal support order, see Code of Civil Procedure § 583.161.
Proceeding defined for purposes of this Code, see Family Code § 110.
State defined for purposes of this Code, see Family Code § 145.

Verification of pleadings, see Family Code § 212.

Research References

Forms

West's California Code Forms, Family § 2330, Comment Overview—Procedures.
West's California Judicial Council Forms FL–100, Petition—Marriage/Domestic Partnership (Also Available in Arabic, Chinese, and Spanish).

§ 2330.1. Supplemental complaint; paternity or child support

In any proceeding for dissolution of marriage, for legal separation of the parties, or for the support of children, the petition or complaint may list children born before the marriage to the same parties and, pursuant to the terms of the Uniform Parentage Act, a determination of paternity may be made in the action. In addition, a supplemental complaint may be filed, in any of those proceedings, pursuant to Section 464 of the Code of Civil Procedure, seeking a judgment or order of paternity or support for a child of the mother and father of the child whose paternity and support are already in issue before the court. A supplemental complaint for paternity or support of children may be filed without leave of court either before or after final judgment in the underlying action. Service of the supplemental summons and complaint shall be made in the manner provided for the initial service of a summons by this code. (Added by Stats.1994, c. 1269 (A.B.2208), § 23.5. Amended by Stats.1998, c. 581 (A.B.2801), § 12.)

Cross References

Judgment and order defined for purposes of this Code, see Family Code § 100.
Proceeding defined for purposes of this Code, see Family Code § 110.
Support defined for purposes of this Code, see Family Code § 150.

Research References

Forms

West's California Code Forms, Family § 2330, Comment Overview—Procedures.
West's California Code Forms, Family § 3650, Comment Overview—Modification, Termination, or Set Aside of Support Orders.
West's California Judicial Council Forms FL–600, Summons and Complaint or Supplemental Complaint Regarding Parental Obligations (Governmental).
West's California Judicial Council Forms FL–610, Answer to Complaint or Supplemental Complaint Regarding Parental Obligations (Governmental).
West's California Judicial Council Forms FL–640, Notice and Motion to Cancel (Set Aside) Support Order Based on Presumed Income (Also Available in Spanish).
West's California Judicial Council Forms FL–640–INFO, Information Sheet for Notice and Motion to Cancel (Set Aside) Support Order Based on Presumed Income (Also Available in Spanish).
West's California Judicial Council Forms FL–643, Declaration of Obligor's Income During Judgment Period—Presumed Income Set Aside.

§ 2330.3. Assignment to same court and judicial officer; minimum length of judicial officer assignment

(a) All dissolution actions, to the greatest extent possible, shall be assigned to the same superior court department for all purposes, in order that all decisions in a case through final judgment shall be made by the same judicial officer. However, if the assignment will result in a significant delay of any family law matter, the dissolution action need not be assigned to the same superior court department for all purposes, unless the parties stipulate otherwise.

(b) The Judicial Council shall adopt a standard of judicial administration prescribing a minimum length of assignment of a judicial officer to a family law assignment.

(c) This section shall be operative on July 1, 1997. (Added by Stats.1996, c. 56 (S.B.389), § 2, operative July 1, 1997. Amended by Stats.2010, c. 352 (A.B.939), § 7.)

§ 2330.3

Cross References

Judgment and order defined for purposes of this Code, see Family Code § 100.

§ 2330.5. Financial declarations; filing; exception

Notwithstanding any other provision of law, if no demand for money, property, costs, or attorney's fees is contained in the petition and the judgment of dissolution of marriage is entered by default, the filing of income and expense declarations and property declarations in connection therewith shall not be required. *(Stats.1992, c. 162 (A.B.2650), § 10, operative Jan. 1, 1994.)*

Cross References

Income and expense declaration defined see Family Code § 95.
Judgment and order defined for purposes of this Code, see Family Code § 100.
Property declaration defined for purposes of this Code, see Family Code § 115.
Property defined for purposes of this Code, see Family Code § 113.

Research References

Forms
West's California Judicial Council Forms FL-165, Request to Enter Default (Uniform Parentage).

§ 2331. Service of petitions and summons

A copy of the petition, together with a copy of a summons, in form and content approved by the Judicial Council shall be served upon the other party to the marriage in the same manner as service of papers in civil actions generally. *(Stats.1992, c. 162 (A.B.2650), § 10, operative Jan. 1, 1994.)*

Cross References

Service of summons, see Code of Civil Procedure § 413.10 et seq.

§ 2332. Service of petition for dissolution on grounds of permanent legal incapacity to make decisions; appointment of guardian ad litem

(a) If the petition for dissolution of the marriage is based on the ground of permanent legal incapacity to make decisions and the spouse who lacks legal capacity to make decisions has a guardian or conservator, other than the spouse filing the petition, the petition and summons shall be served upon the spouse and the guardian or conservator. The guardian or conservator shall defend and protect the interests of the spouse who lacks legal capacity to make decisions.

(b) If the spouse who lacks legal capacity to make decisions has no guardian or conservator, or if the spouse filing the petition is the guardian or conservator, the court shall appoint a guardian ad litem, who may be the district attorney or the county counsel, if any, to defend and protect the interests of the spouse who lacks legal capacity to make decisions. If a district attorney or county counsel is appointed guardian ad litem pursuant to this subdivision, the successor in the office of district attorney or county counsel, as the case may be, succeeds as guardian ad litem, without further action by the court or parties.

(c) "Guardian or conservator" as used in this section means:

(1) With respect to the issue of the dissolution of the marriage relationship, the guardian or conservator of the person.

(2) With respect to support and property division issues, the guardian or conservator of the estate. *(Stats.1992, c. 162 (A.B.2650), § 10, operative Jan. 1, 1994. Amended by Stats.2014, c. 144 (A.B.1847), § 12, eff. Jan. 1, 2015.)*

Cross References

County defined for purposes of this Code, see Family Code § 67.
Incurable insanity, proof, see Family Code § 2312.
Person defined for purposes of this Code, see Family Code § 105.
Property defined for purposes of this Code, see Family Code § 113.
References to husband, wife, spouses and married persons, persons included for purposes of this Code, see Family Code § 11.
Service of summons, see Code of Civil Procedure § 413.10 et seq.

Support defined for purposes of this Code, see Family Code § 150.

Research References

Forms
West's California Code Forms, Family § 2330, Comment Overview—Procedures.

§ 2333. Irreconcilable differences; order for dissolution

Subject to Section 2334, if from the evidence at the hearing the court finds that there are irreconcilable differences which have caused the irremediable breakdown of the marriage, the court shall order the dissolution of the marriage or a legal separation of the parties. *(Stats.1992, c. 162 (A.B.2650), § 10, operative Jan. 1, 1994.)*

Cross References

Irreconcilable differences, defined, see Family Code § 2311.
Judgment and order defined for purposes of this Code, see Family Code § 100.

§ 2334. Grounds for continuance; authority of court

(a) If it appears that there is a reasonable possibility of reconciliation, the court shall continue the proceeding for the dissolution of the marriage or for a legal separation of the parties for a period not to exceed 30 days.

(b) During the period of the continuance, the court may make orders for the support and maintenance of the parties, the custody of the minor children of the marriage, the support of children for whom support may be ordered, attorney's fees, and for the preservation of the property of the parties.

(c) At any time after the termination of the period of the continuance, either party may move for the dissolution of the marriage or a legal separation of the parties, and the court may enter a judgment of dissolution of the marriage or legal separation of the parties. *(Stats.1992, c. 162 (A.B.2650), § 10, operative Jan. 1, 1994. Amended by Stats.1993, c. 219 (A.B.1500), § 109.)*

Cross References

Child for whom support may be ordered defined for purposes of this Code, see Family Code § 58.
Judgment and order defined for purposes of this Code, see Family Code § 100.
Minor defined for purposes of this Code, see Family Code § 6500.
Proceeding defined for purposes of this Code, see Family Code § 110.
Property defined for purposes of this Code, see Family Code § 113.
Support defined for purposes of this Code, see Family Code § 150.

§ 2335. Misconduct; admissibility of specific acts of misconduct

Except as otherwise provided by statute, in a pleading or proceeding for dissolution of marriage or legal separation of the parties, including depositions and discovery proceedings, evidence of specific acts of misconduct is improper and inadmissible. *(Stats.1992, c. 162 (A.B.2650), § 10, operative Jan. 1, 1994. Amended by Stats.1993, c. 219 (A.B.1500), § 110.)*

Cross References

Best interest of child, considerations, see Family Code § 3011.
Depositions and discovery, see Code of Civil Procedure § 2016.010 et seq.
Privilege, confidential marital communications, see Evidence Code § 980.
Proceeding defined for purposes of this Code, see Family Code § 110.
Protective order, see Family Code § 6218.

§ 2335.5. Requests to enter default judgment; dissolution or legal separation; notice to defaulting spouse

In a proceeding for dissolution of marriage or legal separation of the parties, where the judgment is to be entered by default, the petitioner shall provide the court clerk with a stamped envelope bearing sufficient postage addressed to the spouse who has defaulted, with the address of the court clerk as the return address, and the court clerk shall mail a copy of the request to enter default to that spouse in the envelope provided. A judgment of dissolution or legal separation, including relief requested in the petition, shall not be denied solely on the basis that the request to enter default was returned unopened to the court. The court clerk shall maintain any such document returned by the post office as part of the court file in the case. *(Added by Stats.1996, c. 810 (A.B.2149), § 1.)*

Cross References

Judgment and order defined for purposes of this Code, see Family Code § 100.
Petitioner defined for purposes of this Code, see Family Code § 126.
Proceeding defined for purposes of this Code, see Family Code § 110.
References to husband, wife, spouses and married persons, persons included for purposes of this Code, see Family Code § 11.

Research References

Forms

West's California Code Forms, Family § 2330, Comment Overview—Procedures.
West's California Judicial Council Forms FL–165, Request to Enter Default (Uniform Parentage).

§ 2336. Default; proof required

(a) No judgment of dissolution or of legal separation of the parties may be granted upon the default of one of the parties or upon a statement or finding of fact made by a referee; but the court shall, in addition to the statement or finding of the referee, require proof of the grounds alleged, and the proof, if not taken before the court, shall be by affidavit. In all cases where there are minor children of the parties, each affidavit or offer of proof shall include an estimate by the declarant or affiant of the monthly gross income of each party. If the declarant or affiant has no knowledge of the estimated monthly income of a party, the declarant or affiant shall state why he or she has no knowledge. In all cases where there is a community estate, each affidavit or offer of proof shall include an estimate of the value of the assets and the debts the declarant or affiant proposes to be distributed to each party, unless the declarant or affiant has filed, or concurrently files, a complete and accurate property declaration with the court.

(b) If the proof is by affidavit, the personal appearance of the affiant is required only when it appears to the court that any of the following circumstances exist:

(1) Reconciliation of the parties is reasonably possible.

(2) A proposed child custody order is not in the best interest of the child.

(3) A proposed child support order is less than a noncustodial parent is capable of paying.

(4) A personal appearance of a party or interested person would be in the best interests of justice.

(c) An affidavit submitted pursuant to this section shall contain a stipulation by the affiant that the affiant understands that proof will be by affidavit and that the affiant will not appear before the court unless so ordered by the court. *(Stats.1992, c. 162 (A.B.2650), § 10, operative Jan. 1, 1994. Amended by Stats.1996, c. 810 (A.B.2149), § 2; Stats.1998, c. 581 (A.B.2801), § 13.)*

Cross References

Community estate defined for purposes of this Code, see Family Code § 63.
Debt defined elsewhere in this Code, see Family Code § 902.
Depositions and discovery, see Code of Civil Procedure § 2016.010 et seq.
Judgment and order defined for purposes of this Code, see Family Code § 100.
Judgment on default, see Code of Civil Procedure § 585.
Minor defined for purposes of this Code, see Family Code § 6500.
Person defined for purposes of this Code, see Family Code § 105.
Property declaration defined for purposes of this Code, see Family Code § 115.
Property defined for purposes of this Code, see Family Code § 113.
State defined for purposes of this Code, see Family Code § 145.
Support defined for purposes of this Code, see Family Code § 150.
Support order defined for purposes of this Code, see Family Code § 155.

Research References

Forms

West's California Code Forms, Family § 2330, Comment Overview—Procedures.
West's California Judicial Council Forms FL–170, Declaration for Default or Uncontested Dissolution or Legal Separation (Also Available in Spanish).

§ 2337. Early and separate trial on dissolution; preliminary declaration; conditions; effect on retirement plan; service on plan administrator; reservation of jurisdiction; effect of party's death

(a) In a proceeding for dissolution of marriage, the court, upon noticed motion, may sever and grant an early and separate trial on the issue of the dissolution of the status of the marriage apart from other issues.

(b) A preliminary declaration of disclosure with a completed schedule of assets and debts shall be served on the nonmoving party with the noticed motion unless it has been served previously, or unless the parties stipulate in writing to defer service of the preliminary declaration of disclosure until a later time.

(c) The court may impose upon a party any of the following conditions on granting a severance of the issue of the dissolution of the status of the marriage, and in case of that party's death, an order of any of the following conditions continues to be binding upon that party's estate:

(1) The party shall indemnify and hold the other party harmless from any taxes, reassessments, interest, and penalties payable by the other party in connection with the division of the community estate that would not have been payable if the parties were still married at the time the division was made.

(2) Until judgment has been entered on all remaining issues and has become final, the party shall maintain all existing health and medical insurance coverage for the other party and any minor children as named dependents, so long as the party is eligible to do so. If at any time during this period the party is not eligible to maintain that coverage, the party shall, at the party's sole expense, provide and maintain health and medical insurance coverage that is comparable to the existing health and medical insurance coverage to the extent it is available. To the extent that coverage is not available, the party shall be responsible to pay, and shall demonstrate to the court's satisfaction the ability to pay, for the health and medical care for the other party and the minor children, to the extent that care would have been covered by the existing insurance coverage but for the dissolution of marital status, and shall otherwise indemnify and hold the other party harmless from any adverse consequences resulting from the loss or reduction of the existing coverage. For purposes of this subdivision, "health and medical insurance coverage" includes any coverage for which the parties are eligible under any group or individual health or other medical plan, fund, policy, or program.

(3) Until judgment has been entered on all remaining issues and has become final, the party shall indemnify and hold the other party harmless from any adverse consequences to the other party if the bifurcation results in a termination of the other party's right to a probate homestead in the residence in which the other party resides at the time the severance is granted.

(4) Until judgment has been entered on all remaining issues and has become final, the party shall indemnify and hold the other party harmless from any adverse consequences to the other party if the bifurcation results in the loss of the rights of the other party to a probate family allowance as the surviving spouse of the party.

(5) Until judgment has been entered on all remaining issues and has become final, the party shall indemnify and hold the other party harmless from any adverse consequences to the other party if the

bifurcation results in the loss of the other party's rights with respect to any retirement, survivor, or deferred compensation benefits under any plan, fund, or arrangement, or to any elections or options associated therewith, to the extent that the other party would have been entitled to those benefits or elections as the spouse or surviving spouse of the party.

(6) The party shall indemnify and hold the other party harmless from any adverse consequences if the bifurcation results in the loss of rights to social security benefits or elections to the extent the other party would have been entitled to those benefits or elections as the surviving spouse of the party.

(7)(A) The court may make an order pursuant to paragraph (3) of subdivision (b) of Section 5040 of the Probate Code, if appropriate, that a party maintain a beneficiary designation for a nonprobate transfer, as described in Section 5000 of the Probate Code, for a spouse or domestic partner for up to one-half of or, upon a showing of good cause, for all of a nonprobate transfer asset until judgment has been entered with respect to the community ownership of that asset, and until the other party's interest therein has been distributed to him or her.

(B) Except upon a showing of good cause, this paragraph does not apply to any of the following:

(i) A nonprobate transfer described in Section 5000 of the Probate Code that was not created by either party or that was acquired by either party by gift, descent, or devise.

(ii) An irrevocable trust.

(iii) A trust of which neither party is the grantor.

(iv) Powers of appointment under a trust instrument that was not created by either party or of which neither party is a grantor.

(v) The execution and filing of a disclaimer pursuant to Part 8 (commencing with Section 260) of Division 2 of the Probate Code.

(vi) The appointment of a party as a trustee.

(8) In order to preserve the ability of the party to defer the distribution of the Individual Retirement Account or annuity (IRA) established under Section 408 or 408A of the Internal Revenue Code [1] of 1986, as amended, (IRC) upon the death of the other party, the court may require that one-half, or all upon a showing of good cause, of the community interest in any IRA, by or for the benefit of the party, be assigned and transferred to the other party pursuant to Section 408(d)(6) of the Internal Revenue Code. This paragraph does not limit the power granted pursuant to subdivision (g).

(9) Upon a showing that circumstances exist that would place a substantial burden of enforcement upon either party's community property rights or would eliminate the ability of the surviving party to enforce his or her community property rights if the other party died before the division and distribution or compliance with any court-ordered payment of any community property interest therein, including, but not limited to, a situation in which preemption under federal law applies to an asset of a party, or purchase by a bona fide purchaser has occurred, the court may order a specific security interest designed to reduce or eliminate the likelihood that a postmortem enforcement proceeding would be ineffective or unduly burdensome to the surviving party. For this purpose, those orders may include, but are not limited to, any of the following:

(A) An order that the party provide an undertaking.

(B) An order to provide a security interest by Qualified Domestic Relations Order from that party's share of a retirement plan or plans.

(C) An order for the creation of a trust as defined in paragraph (2) of subdivision (a) of Section 82 of the Probate Code.

(D) An order for other arrangements as may be reasonably necessary and feasible to provide appropriate security in the event of the party's death before judgment has been entered with respect to the community ownership of that asset, and until the other party's interest therein has been distributed to him or her.

(E) If a retirement plan is not subject to an enforceable court order for the payment of spousal survivor benefits to the other party, an interim order requiring the party to pay or cause to be paid, and to post adequate security for the payment of, any survivor benefit that would have been payable to the other party on the death of the party but for the judgment granting a dissolution of the status of the marriage, pending entry of judgment on all remaining issues.

(10) Any other condition the court determines is just and equitable.

(d) Prior to, or simultaneously with, entry of judgment granting dissolution of the status of the marriage, all of the following shall occur:

(1) The party's retirement or pension plan shall be joined as a party to the proceeding for dissolution, unless joinder is precluded or made unnecessary by Title 1 of the federal Employee Retirement Income Security Act of 1974 (29 U.S.C. Sec. 1001 et seq.), as amended (ERISA), or any other applicable law.

(2) To preserve the claims of each spouse in all retirement plan benefits upon entry of judgment granting a dissolution of the status of the marriage, the court shall enter one of the following in connection with the judgment for each retirement plan in which either party is a participant:

(A) An order pursuant to Section 2610 disposing of each party's interest in retirement plan benefits, including survivor and death benefits.

(B) An interim order preserving the nonemployee party's right to retirement plan benefits, including survivor and death benefits, pending entry of judgment on all remaining issues.

(C) An attachment to the judgment granting a dissolution of the status of the marriage, as follows:

EACH PARTY (insert names and addresses) IS PROVISIONALLY AWARDED WITHOUT PREJUDICE AND SUBJECT TO ADJUSTMENT BY A SUBSEQUENT DOMESTIC RELATIONS ORDER, A SEPARATE INTEREST EQUAL TO ONE-HALF OF ALL BENEFITS ACCRUED OR TO BE ACCRUED UNDER THE PLAN (name each plan individually) AS A RESULT OF EMPLOYMENT OF THE OTHER PARTY DURING THE MARRIAGE OR DOMESTIC PARTNERSHIP AND PRIOR TO THE DATE OF SEPARATION. IN ADDITION, PENDING FURTHER NOTICE, THE PLAN SHALL, AS ALLOWED BY LAW, OR IN THE CASE OF A GOVERNMENTAL PLAN, AS ALLOWED BY THE TERMS OF THE PLAN, CONTINUE TO TREAT THE PARTIES AS MARRIED OR DOMESTIC PARTNERS FOR PURPOSES OF ANY SURVIVOR RIGHTS OR BENEFITS AVAILABLE UNDER THE PLAN TO THE EXTENT NECESSARY TO PROVIDE FOR PAYMENT OF AN AMOUNT EQUAL TO THAT SEPARATE INTEREST OR FOR ALL OF THE SURVIVOR BENEFIT IF AT THE TIME OF THE DEATH OF THE PARTICIPANT, THERE IS NO OTHER ELIGIBLE RECIPIENT OF THE SURVIVOR BENEFIT.

(e) The moving party shall promptly serve a copy of any order, interim order, or attachment entered pursuant to paragraph (2) of subdivision (d), and a copy of the judgment granting a dissolution of the status of the marriage, on the retirement or pension plan administrator.

(f) A judgment granting a dissolution of the status of the marriage shall expressly reserve jurisdiction for later determination of all other pending issues.

(g) If the party dies after the entry of judgment granting a dissolution of marriage, any obligation imposed by this section shall be enforceable against any asset, including the proceeds thereof, against which these obligations would have been enforceable prior to the person's death. *(Stats.1992, c. 162 (A.B.2650), § 10, operative*

Jan. 1, 1994. Amended by Stats.1994, c. 1269 (A.B.2208), § 24; Stats.1997, c. 56 (A.B.1098), § 1; Stats.1998, c. 581 (A.B.2801), § 14; Stats.2007, c. 141 (A.B.861), § 1; Stats.2015, c. 293 (A.B.139), § 1, eff. Jan. 1, 2016.)

[1] Internal Revenue Code sections are in Title 26 of the U.S.C.A.

Cross References

Community estate, equal division, see Family Code § 2550.
Community estate defined, see Family Code § 63.
Debt defined elsewhere in this Code, see Family Code § 902.
Employee benefit plan defined for purposes of this Code, see Family Code § 80.
Judgment and order defined for purposes of this Code, see Family Code § 100.
Minor defined for purposes of this Code, see Family Code § 6500.
Person defined for purposes of this Code, see Family Code § 105.
Petition for separation or dissolution of marriage, pending child or spousal support order, see Code of Civil Procedure § 583.161.
Proceeding defined for purposes of this Code, see Family Code § 110.
References to husband, wife, spouses and married persons, persons included for purposes of this Code, see Family Code § 11.

Research References

Forms

California Practice Guide: Rutter Family Law Forms Form 1:32, Glossary of Common Family Law Terms, Phrases and Concepts (Enclosure to Form 1:31).
California Practice Guide: Rutter Family Law Forms Form 11:13, Request for Order to Sever (Bifurcate) and Grant an Early and Separate Trial on the Issue of Dissolution of Marital Status.
1 California Transactions Forms--Family Law § 2:27, Joinder of Pension Plan.
1 California Transactions Forms--Family Law § 2:108.50, Statement Attached to Judgment Granting Dissolution of Marriage.
West's California Code Forms, Family § 2330, Comment Overview—Procedures.
West's California Judicial Council Forms FL–315, Request or Response to Request for Separate Trial.
West's California Judicial Council Forms FL–318–INFO, Retirement Plan Joinder—Information Sheet.
West's California Judicial Council Forms FL–347, Bifurcation of Status of Marriage or Domestic Partnership—Attachment.
West's California Judicial Council Forms FL–348, Pension Benefits—Attachment to Judgment (Attach to Form FL–180) (Also Available in Spanish).

§ 2338. Decisions; judgments

(a) In a proceeding for dissolution of the marriage or legal separation of the parties, the court shall file its decision and any statement of decision as in other cases.

(b) If the court determines that no dissolution should be granted, a judgment to that effect only shall be entered.

(c) If the court determines that a dissolution should be granted, a judgment of dissolution of marriage shall be entered. After the entry of the judgment and before it becomes final, neither party has the right to dismiss the proceeding without the consent of the other. *(Stats.1992, c. 162 (A.B.2650), § 10, operative Jan. 1, 1994.)*

Cross References

Decision, findings of fact and conclusions of law, see Code of Civil Procedure § 632.
Dismissal or setting aside void judgment on motion, see Code of Civil Procedure § 473.
Enforcement of judgments and orders, see Family Code §§ 290, 291.
General rules of practice and procedure, see Family Code § 210 et seq.
Impeachment of judicial record, see Code of Civil Procedure § 1916.
Judgment and order defined for purposes of this Code, see Family Code § 100.
Modification of judgment or order, see Family Code § 215.
Proceeding defined for purposes of this Code, see Family Code § 110.
Setting aside void judgment on motion, see Code of Civil Procedure § 473.

Statement of decision, necessity in absence of request, see Code of Civil Procedure § 632.

Research References

Forms

8C Am. Jur. Pl. & Pr. Forms Divorce and Separation § 282, Introductory Comments.
West's California Judicial Council Forms FL–190, Notice of Entry of Judgment (Uniform Parentage—Custody and Support).

§ 2338.5. Default judgments; dissolution or nullity of marriage, or legal separation

Where a judgment of dissolution or nullity of marriage or legal separation of the parties is to be granted upon the default of one of the parties:

(a) The signature of the spouse who has defaulted on any marital settlement agreement or on any stipulated judgment shall be notarized.

(b) The court clerk shall give notice of entry of judgment of dissolution of marriage, nullity of marriage, or legal separation to the attorney for each party or to the party, if unrepresented.

(c) For the purpose of mailing the notice of entry of judgment, the party submitting the judgment shall provide the court clerk with a stamped envelope bearing sufficient postage addressed to the attorney for the other party or to the party, if unrepresented, with the address of the court clerk as the return address. The court clerk shall maintain any such document returned by the post office as part of the court file in the case. *(Added by Stats.1996, c. 810 (A.B.2149), § 3.)*

Cross References

Judgment and order defined for purposes of this Code, see Family Code § 100.
References to husband, wife, spouses and married persons, persons included for purposes of this Code, see Family Code § 11.

§ 2339. Finality of judgment; waiting period

(a) Subject to subdivision (b) and to Sections 2340 to 2344, inclusive, no judgment of dissolution is final for the purpose of terminating the marriage relationship of the parties until six months have expired from the date of service of a copy of summons and petition or the date of appearance of the respondent, whichever occurs first.

(b) The court may extend the six-month period described in subdivision (a) for good cause shown. *(Stats.1992, c. 162 (A.B.2650), § 10, operative Jan. 1, 1994.)*

Cross References

Effect of dissolution judgment when it becomes final, see Family Code § 2300.
Impeachment of judicial record, see Code of Civil Procedure § 1916.
Joint petition for summary dissolution, revocation, see Family Code § 2342.
Judgment and order defined for purposes of this Code, see Family Code § 100.
Modification of judgment or order, see Family Code § 215.
Respondent defined for purposes of this Code, see Family Code § 127.
Uniform Divorce Recognition Act, see Family Code § 2090 et seq.

Research References

Forms

West's California Judicial Council Forms FL–970, Request and Declaration for Final Judgment of Dissolution of Marriage.

§ 2340. Statement of effective date of judgment

A judgment of dissolution of marriage shall specify the date on which the judgment becomes finally effective for the purpose of terminating the marriage relationship of the parties. *(Stats.1992, c. 162 (A.B.2650), § 10, operative Jan. 1, 1994.)*

§ 2340

Cross References

Judgment and order defined for purposes of this Code, see Family Code § 100.

Research References

Forms

West's California Judicial Council Forms FL–180, Judgment (Also Available in Spanish).

§ 2341. Appeal or motion for new trial; finality of judgment

(a) Notwithstanding Section 2340, if an appeal is taken from the judgment or a motion for a new trial is made, the dissolution of marriage does not become final until the motion or appeal has been finally disposed of, nor then, if the motion has been granted or judgment reversed.

(b) Notwithstanding any other provision of law, the filing of an appeal or of a motion for a new trial does not stay the effect of a judgment insofar as it relates to the dissolution of the marriage status and restoring the parties to the status of unmarried persons, unless the appealing or moving party specifies in the notice of appeal or motion for new trial an objection to the termination of the marriage status. No party may make such an objection to the termination of the marriage status unless such an objection was also made at the time of trial. *(Stats.1992, c. 162 (A.B.2650), § 10, operative Jan. 1, 1994.)*

Cross References

Appeal from interlocutory judgment, see Code of Civil Procedure § 904.1.
Community estate, disposition, revision on appeal, see Family Code § 2555.
Impeachment of judicial record, see Code of Civil Procedure § 1916.
Judgment and order defined for purposes of this Code, see Family Code § 100.
Modification of judgment or order, see Family Code § 215.
New trials, see Code of Civil Procedure § 656 et seq.
Person defined for purposes of this Code, see Family Code § 105.

§ 2342. Joint petitions for summary dissolutions; revocation; final judgment

Where a joint petition under Chapter 5 (commencing with Section 2400) is thereafter revoked and either party commences a proceeding pursuant to Section 2330 within 90 days from the date of the filing of the revocation, the date the judgment becomes a final judgment under Section 2339 shall be calculated by deducting the period of time which has elapsed from the date of filing the joint petition to the date of filing the revocation. *(Stats.1992, c. 162 (A.B.2650), § 10, operative Jan. 1, 1994.)*

Cross References

Judgment and order defined for purposes of this Code, see Family Code § 100.
Modification of judgment or order, see Family Code § 215.
Proceeding defined for purposes of this Code, see Family Code § 110.

§ 2343. Retention of jurisdiction; purposes; effect of date of termination of marital status

The court may, upon notice and for good cause shown, or on stipulation of the parties, retain jurisdiction over the date of termination of the marital status, or may order that the marital status be terminated at a future specified date. On the date of termination of the marital status, the parties are restored to the status of unmarried persons. *(Stats.1992, c. 162 (A.B.2650), § 10, operative Jan. 1, 1994.)*

Cross References

Judgment and order defined for purposes of this Code, see Family Code § 100.
Person defined for purposes of this Code, see Family Code § 105.

Research References

Forms

West's California Judicial Council Forms FL–180, Judgment (Also Available in Spanish).

§ 2344. Death of party after entry of judgment

(a) The death of either party after entry of the judgment does not prevent the judgment from becoming a final judgment under Sections 2339 to 2343, inclusive.

(b) Subdivision (a) does not validate a marriage by either party before the judgment becomes final, nor does it constitute a defense in a criminal prosecution against either party. *(Stats.1992, c. 162 (A.B.2650), § 10, operative Jan. 1, 1994.)*

Cross References

Judgment and order defined for purposes of this Code, see Family Code § 100.

Research References

Forms

West's California Judicial Council Forms FL–970, Request and Declaration for Final Judgment of Dissolution of Marriage.

§ 2345. Consent to legal separation

The court may not render a judgment of the legal separation of the parties without the consent of both parties unless one party has not made a general appearance and the petition is one for legal separation. *(Stats.1992, c. 162 (A.B.2650), § 10, operative Jan. 1, 1994.)*

Cross References

Judgment and order defined for purposes of this Code, see Family Code § 100.

§ 2346. Judgments; nunc pro tunc entry; rights to judgment

(a) If the court determines that a judgment of dissolution of the marriage should be granted, but by mistake, negligence, or inadvertence, the judgment has not been signed, filed, and entered, the court may cause the judgment to be signed, dated, filed, and entered in the proceeding as of the date when the judgment could have been signed, dated, filed, and entered originally, if it appears to the satisfaction of the court that no appeal is to be taken in the proceeding or motion made for a new trial, to annul or set aside the judgment, or for relief under Chapter 8 (commencing with Section 469) of Title 6 of Part 2 of the Code of Civil Procedure.

(b) The court may act under subdivision (a) on its own motion or upon the motion of either party to the proceeding. In contested cases, the motion of a party shall be with notice to the other party.

(c) The court may cause the judgment to be entered nunc pro tunc as provided in this section, even though the judgment may have been previously entered, where through mistake, negligence, or inadvertence the judgment was not entered as soon as it could have been entered under the law if applied for.

(d) The court shall not cause a judgment to be entered nunc pro tunc as provided in this section as of a date before trial in the matter, before the date of an uncontested judgment hearing in the matter, or before the date of submission to the court of an application for judgment on affidavit pursuant to Section 2336. Upon the entry of the judgment, the parties have the same rights with regard to the dissolution of marriage becoming final on the date that it would have become final had the judgment been entered upon the date when it could have been originally entered. *(Stats.1992, c. 162 (A.B.2650), § 10, operative Jan. 1, 1994.)*

Cross References

Enforcement of judgments and orders, see Family Code §§ 290, 291.
Judgment and order defined for purposes of this Code, see Family Code § 100.

Proceeding defined for purposes of this Code, see Family Code § 110.
Relief from judgment or order taken by mistake, inadvertence, surprise or neglect, see Code of Civil Procedure § 473.

Research References

Forms

California Practice Guide: Rutter Family Law Forms Form 15:8, Request for Order Re Entry of Judgment of Dissolution Nunc Pro Tunc.

West's California Code Forms, Family § 2330, Comment Overview—Procedures.

West's California Judicial Council Forms FL–180, Judgment (Also Available in Spanish).

§ 2347. Judgment of legal separation; effect on subsequent judgment of dissolution

A judgment of legal separation of the parties does not bar a subsequent judgment of dissolution of the marriage granted pursuant to a petition for dissolution filed by either party. *(Stats.1992, c. 162 (A.B.2650), § 10, operative Jan. 1, 1994.)*

Cross References

Judgment and order defined for purposes of this Code, see Family Code § 100.

§ 2348. Annual report to Judicial Council; superior court clerks

(a) In addition to the requirements of Section 103200 of the Health and Safety Code, the clerk of the superior court of each county shall report annually to the Judicial Council the number of judgments entered in the county during the preceding calendar year or other 12–month period as required by the Judicial Council for each of the following:

(1) Dissolution of marriage.

(2) Legal separation of the parties.

(3) Nullity of marriage.

(b) After the Judicial Branch Statistical Information System (JBSIS) is operational statewide, the clerk of the superior court of each county shall also report annually to the Judicial Council the number of each of those judgments specified in paragraphs (1), (2), and (3) of subdivision (a), entered in the county during the preceding calendar year or other 12–month period as required by the Judicial Council, that include orders relating to child custody, visitation, or support.

(c) The Judicial Council shall include in its annual report to the Legislature on court statistics the number of each of the types of judgments entered in the state reported pursuant to subdivisions (a) and (b).

(d) The Judicial Council shall establish the applicable 12–month reporting period, the due date, and forms to be used, for submission of data pursuant to subdivisions (a) and (b). Until the Judicial Branch Statistical Information System (JBSIS) is operational statewide, the clerk of the superior court may report the data described in subdivision (a) using existing data collection systems, according to current Judicial Council statistical reporting regulations. *(Added by Stats.1998, c. 225 (A.B.913), § 1.)*

Cross References

County defined for purposes of this Code, see Family Code § 67.
Judgment and order defined for purposes of this Code, see Family Code § 100.
State defined for purposes of this Code, see Family Code § 145.
Support defined for purposes of this Code, see Family Code § 150.

CHAPTER 5. SUMMARY DISSOLUTION

Section

2400. Conditions necessary at commencement of proceedings.

2401. Joint petition; filing; form; contents.

Section

2402. Revocation of joint petition; termination of proceedings; notice; filing; copy to other party.

2403. Entry of judgment of dissolution; notice.

2404. Final judgment as final adjudication of rights and obligations.

2405. Actions to set aside final judgment.

2406. Brochure to describe proceedings; availability; distribution; contents and form.

§ 2400. Conditions necessary at commencement of proceedings

(a) A marriage may be dissolved by the summary dissolution procedure provided in this chapter if all of the following conditions exist at the time the proceeding is commenced:

(1) Either party has met the jurisdictional requirements of Chapter 3 (commencing with Section 2320) with regard to dissolution of marriage.

(2) Irreconcilable differences have caused the irremediable breakdown of the marriage and the marriage should be dissolved.

(3) There are no children of the relationship of the parties born before or during the marriage or adopted by the parties during the marriage, and neither party, to that party's knowledge, is pregnant.

(4) The marriage is not more than five years in duration as of the date of separation of the parties.

(5) Neither party has any interest in real property wherever situated, with the exception of the lease of a residence occupied by either party which satisfies the following requirements:

(A) The lease does not include an option to purchase.

(B) The lease terminates within one year from the date of the filing of the petition.

(6) There are no unpaid obligations in excess of four thousand dollars ($4,000) incurred by either or both of the parties after the date of their marriage, excluding the amount of any unpaid obligation with respect to an automobile.

(7) The total fair market value of community property assets, excluding all encumbrances and automobiles, including any deferred compensation or retirement plan, is less than twenty-five thousand dollars ($25,000), and neither party has separate property assets, excluding all encumbrances and automobiles, in excess of twenty-five thousand dollars ($25,000).

(8) The parties have executed an agreement setting forth the division of assets and the assumption of liabilities of the community, and have executed any documents, title certificates, bills of sale, or other evidence of transfer necessary to effectuate the agreement.

(9) The parties waive any rights to spousal support.

(10) The parties, upon entry of the judgment of dissolution of marriage pursuant to Section 2403, irrevocably waive their respective rights to appeal and their rights to move for a new trial.

(11) The parties have read and understand the summary dissolution brochure provided for in Section 2406.

(12) The parties desire that the court dissolve the marriage.

(b) On January 1, 1985, and on January 1 of each odd-numbered year thereafter, the amounts in paragraph (6) of subdivision (a) shall be adjusted to reflect any change in the value of the dollar. On January 1, 1993, and on January 1 of each odd-numbered year thereafter, the amounts in paragraph (7) of subdivision (a) shall be adjusted to reflect any change in the value of the dollar. The adjustments shall be made by multiplying the base amounts by the percentage change in the California Consumer Price Index as compiled by the Department of Industrial Relations, with the result rounded to the nearest thousand dollars. The Judicial Council shall compute and publish the amounts. *(Stats.1992, c. 162 (A.B.2650), § 10, operative Jan. 1, 1994. Amended by Stats.1993, c. 219 (A.B.*

§ 2400

1500), § 110.2; Stats.2010, c. 352 (A.B.939), § 8; Stats.2014, c. 82 (S.B.1306), § 28, eff. Jan. 1, 2015.)

Cross References

Actions to set aside judgments, see Family Code § 2405.
Community property defined for purposes of this Code, see Family Code § 65.
Irreconcilable differences defined, see Family Code § 2311.
Judgment and order defined for purposes of this Code, see Family Code § 100.
Proceeding defined for purposes of this Code, see Family Code § 110.
Property defined for purposes of this Code, see Family Code § 113.
References to husband, wife, spouses and married persons, persons included for purposes of this Code, see Family Code § 11.
Separate property defined for purposes of this Code, see Family Code § 130.
Spousal support defined for purposes of this Code, see Family Code § 142.
Support defined for purposes of this Code, see Family Code § 150.

Research References

Forms

1 California Transactions Forms--Family Law § 4:4.60, Termination of Registered Domestic Partnership.
West's California Code Forms, Family § 2401, Comment Overview—Summary Dissolution.
West's California Judicial Council Forms FL–800, Joint Petition for Summary Dissolution.
West's California Judicial Council Forms FL–810, Summary Dissolution Information (Also Available in Spanish).

§ 2401. Joint petition; filing; form; contents

(a) A proceeding for summary dissolution of the marriage shall be commenced by filing a joint petition in the form prescribed by the Judicial Council.

(b) The petition shall be signed under oath by both spouses, and shall include all of the following:

(1) A statement that as of the date of the filing of the joint petition all of the conditions set forth in Section 2400 have been met.

(2) The mailing address of each spouse.

(3) A statement whether a spouse elects to have his or her former name restored, and, if so, the name to be restored. *(Stats.1992, c. 162 (A.B.2650), § 10, operative Jan. 1, 1994. Amended by Stats.2014, c. 82 (S.B.1306), § 29, eff. Jan. 1, 2015.)*

Cross References

Jurisdiction in superior court, see Family Code § 200.
Proceeding defined for purposes of this Code, see Family Code § 110.
References to husband, wife, spouses and married persons, persons included for purposes of this Code, see Family Code § 11.

Research References

Forms

West's California Code Forms, Family § 2401, Comment Overview—Summary Dissolution.

§ 2402. Revocation of joint petition; termination of proceedings; notice; filing; copy to other party

(a) At any time before the filing of application for judgment pursuant to Section 2403, either party to the marriage may revoke the joint petition and thereby terminate the summary dissolution proceeding filed pursuant to this chapter.

(b) The revocation shall be effected by filing with the clerk of the court where the proceeding was commenced a notice of revocation in such form and content as shall be prescribed by the Judicial Council.

(c) The revoking party shall send a copy of the notice of revocation to the other party by first-class mail, postage prepaid, at the other party's last known address. *(Stats.1992, c. 162 (A.B.2650), § 10, operative Jan. 1, 1994.)*

Cross References

Judgment and order defined for purposes of this Code, see Family Code § 100.

Proceeding defined for purposes of this Code, see Family Code § 110.

Research References

Forms

California Practice Guide: Rutter Family Law Forms Form 2:5, Notice of Revocation of Joint Petition for Summary Dissolution.
West's California Code Forms, Family § 2401, Comment Overview—Summary Dissolution.
West's California Judicial Council Forms FL–830, Notice of Revocation of Joint Petition for Summary Dissolution.

§ 2403. Entry of judgment of dissolution; notice

When six months have expired from the date of the filing of the joint petition for summary dissolution, the court shall, unless a revocation has been filed pursuant to Section 2402, enter the judgment dissolving the marriage. The judgment restores to the parties the status of single persons, and either party may marry after the entry of the judgment. The clerk shall send a notice of entry of judgment to each of the parties at the party's last known address. *(Stats.1992, c. 162 (A.B.2650), § 10, operative Jan. 1, 1994. Amended by Stats.2010, c. 352 (A.B.939), § 9.)*

Cross References

Actions to set aside judgments, see Family Code § 2405.
Judgment and order defined for purposes of this Code, see Family Code § 100.
Person defined for purposes of this Code, see Family Code § 105.

Research References

Forms

West's California Code Forms, Family § 2401, Comment Overview—Summary Dissolution.
West's California Judicial Council Forms FL–820, Request for Judgment, Judgment of Dissolution of Marriage, and Notice of Entry of Judgment.
West's California Judicial Council Forms FL–825, Judgment of Dissolution and Notice of Entry of Judgment.

§ 2404. Final judgment as final adjudication of rights and obligations

Entry of the judgment pursuant to Section 2403 constitutes:

(a) A final adjudication of the rights and obligations of the parties with respect to the status of the marriage and property rights.

(b) A waiver of their respective rights to spousal support, rights to appeal, and rights to move for a new trial. *(Stats.1992, c. 162 (A.B.2650), § 10, operative Jan. 1, 1994.)*

Cross References

Judgment and order defined for purposes of this Code, see Family Code § 100.
Property defined for purposes of this Code, see Family Code § 113.
Spousal support defined for purposes of this Code, see Family Code § 142.
Support defined for purposes of this Code, see Family Code § 150.

Research References

Forms

West's California Code Forms, Family § 2401, Comment Overview—Summary Dissolution.

§ 2405. Actions to set aside final judgment

(a) Entry of the judgment pursuant to Section 2403 does not prejudice nor bar the rights of either of the parties to institute an action to set aside the judgment for fraud, duress, accident, mistake, or other grounds recognized at law or in equity or to make a motion pursuant to Section 473 of the Code of Civil Procedure.

(b) The court shall set aside a judgment entered pursuant to Section 2403 regarding all matters except the status of the marriage, upon proof that the parties did not meet the requirements of Section 2400 at the time the petition was filed. *(Stats.1992, c. 162 (A.B. 2650), § 10, operative Jan. 1, 1994.)*

Cross References

Judgment and order defined for purposes of this Code, see Family Code § 100.

Research References

Forms

West's California Code Forms, Family § 2401, Comment Overview—Summary Dissolution.

§ 2406. Brochure to describe proceedings; availability; distribution; contents and form

(a) Each superior court shall make available a brochure, the contents and form of which shall be prescribed by the Judicial Council, describing the requirements, nature, and effect of proceedings under this chapter. The brochure shall be printed and distributed by the Judicial Council in both English and Spanish.

(b) The brochure shall state, in nontechnical language, all the following:

(1) It is in the best interests of the parties to consult an attorney regarding the dissolution of their marriage. The services of an attorney may be obtained through lawyer referral services, group or prepaid legal services, or legal aid organizations.

(2) The parties should not rely exclusively on this brochure which is not intended as a guide for self-representation in proceedings under this chapter.

(3) A concise summary of the provisions and procedures of this chapter and Sections 2320 and 2322 and Sections 2339 to 2344, inclusive.

(4) The nature of services of the conciliation court, where available.

(5) Neither party to the marriage can in the future obtain spousal support from the other.

(6) A statement in boldface type to the effect that upon entry of the judgment, the rights and obligations of the parties to the marriage with respect to the marriage, including property and spousal support rights, will be permanently adjudicated without right of appeal, except that neither party will be barred from instituting an action to set aside the judgment for fraud, duress, accident, mistake, or other grounds at law or in equity, or to make a motion pursuant to Section 473 of the Code of Civil Procedure.

(7) The parties to the marriage retain the status of married persons and cannot remarry until the judgment dissolving the marriage is entered.

(8) Other matters as the Judicial Council considers appropriate. (Stats.1992, c. 162 (A.B.2650), § 10, operative Jan. 1, 1994.)

Cross References

Judgment and order defined for purposes of this Code, see Family Code § 100.
Person defined for purposes of this Code, see Family Code § 105.
Proceeding defined for purposes of this Code, see Family Code § 110.
Property defined for purposes of this Code, see Family Code § 113.
References to husband, wife, spouses and married persons, persons included for purposes of this Code, see Family Code § 11.
Spousal support defined for purposes of this Code, see Family Code § 142.
State defined for purposes of this Code, see Family Code § 145.
Support defined for purposes of this Code, see Family Code § 150.

Research References

Forms

West's California Code Forms, Family § 2406 Form 1, Summary Dissolution Information.
West's California Judicial Council Forms FL–800, Joint Petition for Summary Dissolution.

West's California Judicial Council Forms FL–810, Summary Dissolution Information (Also Available in Spanish).

CHAPTER 6. CASE MANAGEMENT

Section
2450. Family centered case resolution; purpose; order.
2451. Family centered case resolution plan; contents; appointment of experts; statewide rule of court.
2452. Increase of procedures.

§ 2450. Family centered case resolution; purpose; order

(a) The purpose of family centered case resolution is to benefit the parties by providing judicial assistance and management to the parties in actions for dissolution of marriage for the purpose of expediting the processing of the case, reducing the expense of litigation, and focusing on early resolution by settlement. Family centered case resolution is a tool to allow the courts to better assist families. It does not increase the authority of the court to appoint any third parties to the case.

(b) The court may order a family centered case resolution plan as provided in Section 2451. If the court orders family centered case resolution, it shall state the family centered case resolution plan in writing or on the record. (Added by Stats.1996, c. 56 (S.B.389), § 3. Amended by Stats.2010, c. 352 (A.B.939), § 10.)

Cross References

Judgment and order defined for purposes of this Code, see Family Code § 100.

Research References

Forms

California Practice Guide: Rutter Family Law Forms Form 1:32, Glossary of Common Family Law Terms, Phrases and Concepts (Enclosure to Form 1:31).
West's California Judicial Council Forms FL–174, Family Centered Case Resolution Order.

§ 2451. Family centered case resolution plan; contents; appointment of experts; statewide rule of court

(a) A court-ordered family centered case resolution plan must be in conformance with due process requirements and may include, but is not limited to, all of the following:

(1) Early neutral case evaluation.

(2) Alternative dispute resolution consistent with the requirements of subdivision (a) of Section 3181.

(3) Limitations on discovery, including temporary suspension pending exploration of settlement. There is a rebuttable presumption that an attorney who carries out discovery as provided in a family centered case resolution plan has fulfilled his or her duty of care to the client as to the existence of community property.

(4) Use of telephone conference calls to ascertain the status of the case, encourage cooperation, and assist counsel in reaching agreement. However, if the court is required to issue an order other than by stipulation, a hearing shall be held.

(5) If stipulated by the parties, modification or waiver of the requirements of procedural statutes.

(6) A requirement that any expert witness be selected by the parties jointly or be appointed by the court. However, if at any time the court determines that the issues for which experts are required cannot be settled under these conditions, the court shall permit each party to employ his or her own expert.

(7) Bifurcation of issues for trial.

(b) This section does not provide any additional authority to the court to appoint experts beyond that permitted under other provisions of law.

§ 2451

(c) The Judicial Council shall, by January 1, 2012, adopt a statewide rule of court to implement this section.

(d) The changes made to this section by the act adding this subdivision [1] shall become operative on January 1, 2012. *(Added by Stats.1996, c. 56 (S.B.389), § 3. Amended by Stats.2010, c. 352 (A.B.939), § 11, operative Jan. 1, 2012.)*

[1] Stats.2010, c. 352 (A.B.939).

Cross References

Community property defined for purposes of this Code, see Family Code § 65.
Judgment and order defined for purposes of this Code, see Family Code § 100.
Property defined for purposes of this Code, see Family Code § 113.

Research References

Forms
California Practice Guide: Rutter Family Law Forms Form 1:32, Glossary of Common Family Law Terms, Phrases and Concepts (Enclosure to Form 1:31).
West's California Judicial Council Forms FL-174, Family Centered Case Resolution Order.

§ 2452. Increase of procedures

The Judicial Council may, by rule, increase the procedures set forth in this chapter. *(Added by Stats.1996, c. 56 (S.B.389), § 3. Amended by Stats.2014, c. 311 (A.B.2745), § 1, eff. Jan. 1, 2015.)*

Division 7

DIVISION OF PROPERTY

Part	Section
1. Definitions	2500
2. General Provisions	2550
3. Presumption Concerning Property Held in Joint Form	2580
4. Special Rules for Division of Community Estate	2600
5. Retirement Plan Benefits	2610
6. Debts and Liabilities	2620
7. Reimbursements	2640
8. Jointly Held Separate Property	2650
9. Real Property Located in Another State	2660

Cross References

Dissolution actions, division of property, public policy, see Family Code § 2120.
Nonprobate transfers of community property, revocability of written consent, see Probate Code § 5030.
Public policy regarding division of community and quasi-community property, see Family Code § 2120.
Void or voidable marriages, division of property pursuant to this division, see Family Code § 2251.

Part 1

DEFINITIONS

Section
2500. Construction of division.
2501. Inoperative.
2502. Separate property.

§ 2500. Construction of division

Unless the provision or context otherwise requires, the definitions in this part govern the construction of this division. *(Stats.1992, c. 162 (A.B.2650), § 10, operative Jan. 1, 1994.)*

Cross References

Nonprobate transfers of community property, revocability of written consent, see Probate Code § 5030.
Public policy regarding division of community and quasi-community property, see Family Code § 2120.

Research References

Forms
West's California Code Forms, Family § 2550, Comment Overview—Manner of Division of Community Estate.
West's California Judicial Council Forms FL-160, Property Declaration (Also Available in Spanish).
West's California Judicial Council Forms FL-161, Continuation of Property Declaration.
West's California Judicial Council Forms FL-345, Property Order Attachment to Judgment (Also Available in Spanish).

§ 2501. Inoperative

§ 2502. Separate property

"Separate property" does not include quasi-community property. *(Stats.1992, c. 162 (A.B.2650), § 10, operative Jan. 1, 1994.)*

Cross References

Community property defined for purposes of this Code, see Family Code § 65.
Property defined for purposes of this Code, see Family Code § 113.
Quasi-community property defined, see Family Code § 125.
Separate property defined, see Family Code §§ 130, 770.
Similar provisions, see Family Code § 3515.

Research References

Forms
1 California Transactions Forms--Estate Planning § 1:26, Quasi-Community Property; Separate Property.

Part 2

GENERAL PROVISIONS

Section
2550. Manner of division of community estate.
2551. Characterization of liabilities; confirmation or assignment.
2552. Valuation of assets and liabilities.
2553. Powers of court.
2554. Failure to agree to voluntary division of property; submission to arbitration.
2555. Disposition of community estate; revision on appeal.
2556. Community property or debts; continuing jurisdiction.

§ 2550. Manner of division of community estate

Except upon the written agreement of the parties, or on oral stipulation of the parties in open court, or as otherwise provided in this division, in a proceeding for dissolution of marriage or for legal separation of the parties, the court shall, either in its judgment of dissolution of the marriage, in its judgment of legal separation of the parties, or at a later time if it expressly reserves jurisdiction to make such a property division, divide the community estate of the parties equally. *(Stats.1992, c. 162 (A.B.2650), § 10, operative Jan. 1, 1994.)*

GENERAL PROVISIONS § 2553

Cross References

Agreements between parties concerning their property, see Family Code § 1620.
Bankruptcy, obligations of property settlement discharged, see Family Code § 3592.
Care and ownership of pet animal, see Family Code § 2605.
Characterization of marital property, see Family Code § 760 et seq.
Community estate defined for purposes of this Code, see Family Code § 63.
Death of married person, effect on community and quasi-community property, see Probate Code § 100 et seq.
Educational loans, assignment, see Family Code § 2627.
Homestead property,
  General provisions, see Code of Civil Procedure §§ 704.710 et seq., 704.910 et seq.
  Administration of estates, see Probate Code § 6520 et seq.
Jointly held property, presumptions, see Family Code § 2581.
Jointly held separate property, division, see Family Code § 2650.
Judgment and order defined for purposes of this Code, see Family Code § 100.
Marital debt incurred prior to separation date, division, see Family Code § 2622.
Marriage dissolution proceedings, joint California income tax liabilities, revision by court, see Family Code § 2628.
Partition of real and personal property, see Code of Civil Procedure § 872.010 et seq.
Presumptions, nature of marital property, see Family Code §§ 802, 803.
Proceeding defined for purposes of this Code, see Family Code § 110.
Property defined for purposes of this Code, see Family Code § 113.
Property rights during marriage, see Family Code § 750 et seq.
Real property located in another state, see Family Code § 2660.
Rules for division of community estate, see Family Code § 2600 et seq.
Subsequent liability, division of community estate, see Family Code § 916.

Research References

Forms

7PT1 Am. Jur. Pl. & Pr. Forms Community Property § 39, Complaint, Petition, or Declaration—For Divorce or Other Legal Separation—Allegation of Quasi-Community Property.
Asset Protection: Legal Planning, Strategies and Forms ¶ 4.08, Implications of Divorce.
California Practice Guide: Rutter Family Law Forms Form 1:32, Glossary of Common Family Law Terms, Phrases and Concepts (Enclosure to Form 1:31).
1 California Transactions Forms--Estate Planning § 1:23, Aggregate or Asset-By-Asset Division of Community Property.
1 California Transactions Forms--Estate Planning § 1:26, Quasi-Community Property; Separate Property.
1 California Transactions Forms--Estate Planning § 1:36, Conflicts Between Clients.
2 California Transactions Forms--Estate Planning § 10:4, Community Property.
2 California Transactions Forms--Estate Planning § 10:5, Quasi-Community Property.
1 California Transactions Forms--Family Law § 2:12, Overview.
1 California Transactions Forms--Family Law § 2:13, Equalizing Payments.
West's California Code Forms, Family § 2338 Form 6, Provision in Judgment—Awarding Community Estate.
West's California Code Forms, Family § 2550, Comment Overview—Manner of Division of Community Estate.

§ 2551. Characterization of liabilities; confirmation or assignment

For the purposes of division and in confirming or assigning the liabilities of the parties for which the community estate is liable, the court shall characterize liabilities as separate or community and confirm or assign them to the parties in accordance with Part 6 (commencing with Section 2620). *(Stats.1992, c. 162 (A.B.2650), § 10, operative Jan. 1, 1994.)*

Cross References

Characterization of marital property, see Family Code § 760 et seq.
Community estate debts, confirmation or division, see Family Code § 2620.
Community estate defined for purposes of this Code, see Family Code § 63.
Death of married person, effect on community and quasi-community property, see Probate Code § 100 et seq.
Educational loans, assignment, see Family Code § 2627.
Homestead property,
  General provisions, see Code of Civil Procedure §§ 704.710 et seq., 704.910 et seq.
  Administration of estates, see Probate Code § 6520 et seq.
Marital debt incurred prior to separation date, division, see Family Code § 2622.
Marriage dissolution proceedings, joint California income tax liabilities, revision by court, see Family Code § 2628.
Partition of real and personal property, see Code of Civil Procedure § 872.010 et seq.
Presumptions, nature of marital property, see Family Code §§ 802, 803.
Property rights during marriage, see Family Code § 750 et seq.

§ 2552. Valuation of assets and liabilities

(a) For the purpose of division of the community estate upon dissolution of marriage or legal separation of the parties, except as provided in subdivision (b), the court shall value the assets and liabilities as near as practicable to the time of trial.

(b) Upon 30 days' notice by the moving party to the other party, the court for good cause shown may value all or any portion of the assets and liabilities at a date after separation and before trial to accomplish an equal division of the community estate of the parties in an equitable manner. *(Stats.1992, c. 162 (A.B.2650), § 10, operative Jan. 1, 1994.)*

Cross References

Characterization of marital property, see Family Code § 760 et seq.
Community estate debts, confirmation or division, see Family Code § 2620.
Community estate defined, see Family Code § 63.
Computation of time, see Code of Civil Procedure §§ 12, 12a; Government Code § 6800 et seq.
Death of married person, effect on community and quasi-community property, see Probate Code § 100 et seq.
Educational loans, assignment, see Family Code § 2627.
Homestead property,
  General provisions, see Code of Civil Procedure §§ 704.710 et seq., 704.910 et seq.
  Administration of estates, see Probate Code § 6520 et seq.
Marital debt incurred prior to separation date, division, see Family Code § 2622.
Marriage dissolution proceedings, joint California income tax liabilities, revision by court, see Family Code § 2628.
Notice, actual and constructive, defined, see Civil Code § 18.
Partition of real and personal property, see Code of Civil Procedure § 872.010 et seq.
Presumptions, nature of marital property, see Family Code §§ 802, 803.
Property rights during marriage, see Family Code § 750 et seq.

Research References

Forms

California Practice Guide: Rutter Family Law Forms Form 8:8, Request for Order Re Separate Trial Re Alternate Valuation Date (Community Bank Accounts).
1 California Transactions Forms--Family Law § 2:32, Date of Valuation.
West's California Code Forms, Family § 2550, Comment Overview—Manner of Division of Community Estate.

§ 2553. Powers of court

The court may make any orders the court considers necessary to carry out the purposes of this division. *(Stats.1992, c. 162 (A.B. 2650), § 10, operative Jan. 1, 1994.)*

Cross References

Characterization of marital property, see Family Code § 760 et seq.
Death of married person, effect on community and quasi-community property, see Probate Code § 100 et seq.
Homestead property,
  General provisions, see Code of Civil Procedure §§ 704.710 et seq., 704.910 et seq.
  Administration of estates, see Probate Code § 6520 et seq.
Judgment and order defined for purposes of this Code, see Family Code § 100.
Partition of real and personal property, see Code of Civil Procedure § 872.010 et seq.

§ 2553 DIVISION OF PROPERTY

Presumptions, nature of marital property, see Family Code §§ 802, 803.
Property rights during marriage, see Family Code § 750 et seq.

Research References

Forms

7PT1 Am. Jur. Pl. & Pr. Forms Community Property § 35, Statutory References.

§ 2554. Failure to agree to voluntary division of property; submission to arbitration

(a) Notwithstanding any other provision of this division, in any case in which the parties do not agree in writing to a voluntary division of the community estate of the parties, the issue of the character, the value, and the division of the community estate may be submitted by the court to arbitration for resolution pursuant to Chapter 2.5 (commencing with Section 1141.10) of Title 3 of Part 3 of the Code of Civil Procedure, if the total value of the community and quasi-community property in controversy in the opinion of the court does not exceed fifty thousand dollars ($50,000). The decision of the court regarding the value of the community and quasi-community property for purposes of this section is not appealable.

(b) The court may submit the matter to arbitration at any time it believes the parties are unable to agree upon a division of the property. *(Stats.1992, c. 162 (A.B.2650), § 10, operative Jan. 1, 1994.)*

Cross References

Appeals from order in arbitration, see Code of Civil Procedure §§ 1294, 1294.2.
Appeals in civil actions, generally, see Code of Civil Procedure § 901 et seq.
Appeals in criminal cases,
　Appeals from Superior Courts, see Penal Code § 1235 et seq.
　Appeals to Superior Courts, see Penal Code § 1466 et seq.
Arbitration, generally, see Code of Civil Procedure § 1281 et seq.
Characterization of marital property, see Family Code § 760 et seq.
Community estate defined, see Family Code § 63.
Community property defined for purposes of this Code, see Family Code § 65.
Death of married person, effect on community and quasi-community property, see Probate Code § 100 et seq.
Division of community estate, special rules, see Family Code § 2600 et seq.
Division of quasi-marital property, see Family Code §§ 2251, 2252.
Homestead property,
　General provisions, see Code of Civil Procedure §§ 704.710 et seq., 704.910 et seq.
　Administration of estates, see Probate Code § 6520 et seq.
Partition of real and personal property, see Code of Civil Procedure § 872.010 et seq.
Presumptions, nature of marital property, see Family Code §§ 802, 803.
Property defined for purposes of this Code, see Family Code § 113.
Property rights during marriage, see Family Code § 750 et seq.
Quasi-community property defined for purposes of this Code, see Family Code § 125.
Writings, authentication and proof of, see Evidence Code § 1400 et seq.

Research References

Forms

26 West's Legal Forms § 1:3, Statutes Mandating or Encouraging Alternative Dispute Resolution.

§ 2555. Disposition of community estate; revision on appeal

The disposition of the community estate, as provided in this division, is subject to revision on appeal in all particulars, including those which are stated to be in the discretion of the court. *(Stats.1992, c. 162 (A.B.2650), § 10, operative Jan. 1, 1994.)*

Cross References

Appealable judgments and orders, see Code of Civil Procedure § 904.1.
Appeals from order in arbitration, see Code of Civil Procedure §§ 1294, 1294.2.
Appeals in civil actions, generally, see Code of Civil Procedure § 901 et seq.
Appeals in criminal cases,
　Appeals from Superior Courts, see Penal Code § 1235 et seq.
　Appeals to Superior Courts, see Penal Code § 1466 et seq.
Characterization of marital property, see Family Code § 760 et seq.
Community estate, defined, see Family Code § 63.
Death of married person, effect on community and quasi-community property, see Probate Code § 100 et seq.
Division of quasi-marital property, see Family Code §§ 2251, 2252.
Homestead property,
　General provisions, see Code of Civil Procedure §§ 704.710 et seq., 704.910 et seq.
　Administration of estates, see Probate Code § 6520 et seq.
Interlocutory judgments, appeals permitted, including character of property, see Code of Civil Procedure § 904.1.
Partition of real and personal property, see Code of Civil Procedure § 872.010 et seq.
Presumptions, nature of marital property, see Family Code §§ 802, 803.
Property rights during marriage, see Family Code § 750 et seq.
Superior courts, appealable judgments and orders, see Code of Civil Procedure § 904.1.

§ 2556. Community property or debts; continuing jurisdiction

In a proceeding for dissolution of marriage, for nullity of marriage, or for legal separation of the parties, the court has continuing jurisdiction to award community estate assets or community estate liabilities to the parties that have not been previously adjudicated by a judgment in the proceeding. A party may file a postjudgment motion or order to show cause in the proceeding in order to obtain adjudication of any community estate asset or liability omitted or not adjudicated by the judgment. In these cases, the court shall equally divide the omitted or unadjudicated community estate asset or liability, unless the court finds upon good cause shown that the interests of justice require an unequal division of the asset or liability. *(Stats.1992, c. 162 (A.B.2650), § 10, operative Jan. 1, 1994. Amended by Stats.1993, c. 219 (A.B.1500), § 111.)*

Cross References

Characterization of marital property, see Family Code § 760 et seq.
Community estate defined for purposes of this Code, see Family Code § 63.
Death of married person, effect on community and quasi-community property, see Probate Code § 100 et seq.
Division of quasi-marital property, see Family Code §§ 2251, 2252.
Homestead property,
　General provisions, see Code of Civil Procedure §§ 704.710 et seq., 704.910 et seq.
　Administration of estates, see Probate Code § 6520 et seq.
Judgment and order defined for purposes of this Code, see Family Code § 100.
Jurisdiction in superior court, see Family Code § 200.
Partition of real and personal property, see Code of Civil Procedure § 872.010 et seq.
Presumptions, nature of marital property, see Family Code §§ 802, 803.
Proceeding defined for purposes of this Code, see Family Code § 110.
Property rights during marriage, see Family Code § 750 et seq.

Research References

Forms

Asset Protection: Legal Planning, Strategies and Forms ¶ 4.08, Implications of Divorce.

Part 3

PRESUMPTION CONCERNING PROPERTY HELD IN JOINT FORM

Section
2580.　Legislative findings and declarations; public policy.
2581.　Division of property; presumptions.

§ 2580. Legislative findings and declarations; public policy

The Legislature hereby finds and declares as follows:

(a) It is the public policy of this state to provide uniformly and consistently for the standard of proof in establishing the character of property acquired by spouses during marriage in joint title form, and for the allocation of community and separate interests in that property between the spouses.

(b) The methods provided by case and statutory law have not resulted in consistency in the treatment of spouses' interests in property they hold in joint title, but rather, have created confusion as to which law applies to property at a particular point in time, depending on the form of title, and, as a result, spouses cannot have reliable expectations as to the characterization of their property and the allocation of the interests therein, and attorneys cannot reliably advise their clients regarding applicable law.

(c) Therefore, a compelling state interest exists to provide for uniform treatment of property. Thus, former Sections 4800.1 and 4800.2 of the Civil Code, as operative on January 1, 1987, and as continued in Sections 2581 and 2640 of this code, apply to all property held in joint title regardless of the date of acquisition of the property or the date of any agreement affecting the character of the property, and those sections apply in all proceedings commenced on or after January 1, 1984. However, those sections do not apply to property settlement agreements executed before January 1, 1987, or proceedings in which judgments were rendered before January 1, 1987, regardless of whether those judgments have become final. *(Added by Stats.1993, c. 219 (A.B.1500), § 111.6. Amended by Stats.1993, c. 876 (S.B.1068), § 15.2, eff. Oct. 6, 1993, operative Jan. 1, 1994.)*

Cross References

Attorneys, State Bar Act, see Business and Professions Code § 6000.
Judgment and order defined for purposes of this Code, see Family Code § 100.
Proceeding defined for purposes of this Code, see Family Code § 110.
Property defined for purposes of this Code, see Family Code § 113.
References to husband, wife, spouses and married persons, persons included for purposes of this Code, see Family Code § 11.
State defined for purposes of this Code, see Family Code § 145.

Research References

Forms

Asset Protection: Legal Planning, Strategies and Forms ¶ 4.03, Community Property.
1 California Transactions Forms--Family Law § 1:90, Real and Personal Property.

§ 2581. Division of property; presumptions

For the purpose of division of property on dissolution of marriage or legal separation of the parties, property acquired by the parties during marriage in joint form, including property held in tenancy in common, joint tenancy, or tenancy by the entirety, or as community property, is presumed to be community property. This presumption is a presumption affecting the burden of proof and may be rebutted by either of the following:

(a) A clear statement in the deed or other documentary evidence of title by which the property is acquired that the property is separate property and not community property.

(b) Proof that the parties have made a written agreement that the property is separate property. *(Added by Stats.1993, c. 219 (A.B. 1500), § 111.7.)*

Cross References

Burden of proof, generally, see Evidence Code § 500 et seq.
Community property defined for purposes of this Code, see Family Code § 65.
Nonprobate transfers, ownership between parties and their creditors and successors, married parties, see Probate Code § 5305.
Presumptions,
    Generally, see Evidence Code § 600 et seq.
    Relating to community property, see Family Code § 760.
    Relating to leasehold interests, see Family Code § 700.
    Relating to the nature of property, see Family Code § 803 et seq.

Property defined for purposes of this Code, see Family Code § 113.
Reimbursement for separate property contributions to acquisition of community property, see Family Code § 2640.
Separate property,
    Defined, see Family Code §§ 130, 770.
    Earnings and accumulations after entry of judgment of legal separation, see Family Code § 772.
    Earnings and accumulations during separation period, see Family Code § 771.

Research References

Forms

Asset Protection: Legal Planning, Strategies and Forms ¶ 4.01, Introduction.
Asset Protection: Legal Planning, Strategies and Forms ¶ 4.03, Community Property.
2 California Transactions Forms--Estate Planning § 10:6, Tenancy in Common.
2 California Transactions Forms--Estate Planning § 10:7, Joint Tenancy.
2 California Transactions Forms--Estate Planning § 10:19, Joint Tenancy Property.
1 California Transactions Forms--Family Law § 1:90, Real and Personal Property.

Part 4

SPECIAL RULES FOR DIVISION OF COMMUNITY ESTATE

Section
2600. Powers of court.
2601. Conditional award of an asset of the community estate to one party.
2602. Additional award or offset against existing property; award of amount determined to have been misappropriated.
2603. Community estate personal injury damages; assignment.
2603.5. Civil damages in a domestic violence action; enforcement of judgment.
2604. Community estates of less than $5,000; award of entire estate.
2605. Care and ownership of pet animal.

§ 2600. Powers of court

Notwithstanding Sections 2550 to 2552, inclusive, the court may divide the community estate as provided in this part. *(Stats.1992, c. 162 (A.B.2650), § 10, operative Jan. 1, 1994.)*

Cross References

Characterization of marital property, see Family Code § 760 et seq.
Community estate defined, see Family Code § 63.
Community property, see Family Code § 760.
Death of married person, effect on community and quasi-community property, see Probate Code § 100 et seq.
Division of quasi-marital property, see Family Code §§ 2251, 2252.
Homestead property,
    General provisions, see Code of Civil Procedure §§ 704.710 et seq., 704.910 et seq.
    Administration of estates, see Probate Code § 6520 et seq.
Partition of real and personal property, see Code of Civil Procedure § 872.010 et seq.
Presumptions, nature of marital property, see Family Code §§ 802, 803.
Property rights during marriage, see Family Code § 750 et seq.

Research References

Forms

7PT1 Am. Jur. Pl. & Pr. Forms Community Property § 2, Statutory References.

§ 2600

West's California Code Forms, Family § 2338 Form 6, Provision in Judgment—Awarding Community Estate.

§ 2601. Conditional award of an asset of the community estate to one party

Where economic circumstances warrant, the court may award an asset of the community estate to one party on such conditions as the court deems proper to effect a substantially equal division of the community estate. *(Stats.1992, c. 162 (A.B.2650), § 10, operative Jan. 1, 1994.)*

Cross References

Characterization of marital property, see Family Code § 760 et seq.
Community estate defined, see Family Code § 63.
Community property, see Family Code § 760.
Death of married person, effect on community and quasi-community property, see Probate Code § 100 et seq.
Division of quasi-marital property, see Family Code §§ 2251, 2252.
Homestead property,
 General provisions, see Code of Civil Procedure §§ 704.710 et seq., 704.910 et seq.
 Administration of estates, see Probate Code § 6520 et seq.
Marital debt incurred prior to separation date, division, see Family Code § 2622.
Partition of real and personal property, see Code of Civil Procedure § 872.010 et seq.
Presumptions, nature of marital property, see Family Code §§ 802, 803.
Property rights during marriage, see Family Code § 750 et seq.

Research References

Forms

1 California Transactions Forms--Estate Planning § 1:23, Aggregate or Asset-By-Asset Division of Community Property.
1 California Transactions Forms--Family Law § 2:13, Equalizing Payments.

§ 2602. Additional award or offset against existing property; award of amount determined to have been misappropriated

As an additional award or offset against existing property, the court may award, from a party's share, the amount the court determines to have been deliberately misappropriated by the party to the exclusion of the interest of the other party in the community estate. *(Stats.1992, c. 162 (A.B.2650), § 10, operative Jan. 1, 1994.)*

Cross References

Characterization of marital property, see Family Code § 760 et seq.
Community estate defined, see Family Code § 63.
Community property, see Family Code § 760.
Death of married person, effect on community and quasi-community property, see Probate Code § 100 et seq.
Division of quasi-marital property, see Family Code §§ 2251, 2252.
Marital debt incurred prior to separation date, division, see Family Code § 2622.
Partition of real and personal property, see Code of Civil Procedure § 872.010 et seq.
Presumptions, nature of marital property, see Family Code §§ 802, 803.
Property defined for purposes of this Code, see Family Code § 113.
Property rights during marriage, see Family Code § 750 et seq.

§ 2603. Community estate personal injury damages; assignment

(a) "Community estate personal injury damages" as used in this section means all money or other property received or to be received by a person in satisfaction of a judgment for damages for the person's personal injuries or pursuant to an agreement for the settlement or compromise of a claim for the damages, if the cause of action for the damages arose during the marriage but is not separate property as described in Section 781, unless the money or other property has been commingled with other assets of the community estate.

(b) Community estate personal injury damages shall be assigned to the party who suffered the injuries unless the court, after taking into account the economic condition and needs of each party, the time that has elapsed since the recovery of the damages or the accrual of the cause of action, and all other facts of the case, determines that the interests of justice require another disposition. In such a case, the community estate personal injury damages shall be assigned to the respective parties in such proportions as the court determines to be just, except that at least one-half of the damages shall be assigned to the party who suffered the injuries. *(Stats.1992, c. 162 (A.B.2650), § 10, operative Jan. 1, 1994.)*

Cross References

Characterization of marital property, see Family Code § 760 et seq.
Community estate defined, see Family Code § 63.
Community property,
 Generally, see Family Code § 760.
 Damages as community property, see Family Code § 780.
Death of married person, effect on community and quasi-community property, see Probate Code § 100 et seq.
Division of quasi-marital property, see Family Code §§ 2251, 2252.
Judgment and order defined for purposes of this Code, see Family Code § 100.
Marital debt incurred prior to separation date, division, see Family Code § 2622.
Partition of real and personal property, see Code of Civil Procedure § 872.010 et seq.
Person defined for purposes of this Code, see Family Code § 105.
Presumptions, nature of marital property, see Family Code §§ 802, 803.
Property defined for purposes of this Code, see Family Code § 113.
Property rights during marriage, see Family Code § 750 et seq.
Separate property defined for purposes of this Code, see Family Code § 130.

Research References

Forms

West's California Code Forms, Family § 2338 Form 7, Provision in Judgment—Awarding Community Estate Personal Injury Damages.
West's California Code Forms, Family § 2550, Comment Overview—Manner of Division of Community Estate.

§ 2603.5. Civil damages in a domestic violence action; enforcement of judgment

The court may, if there is a judgment for civil damages for an act of domestic violence perpetrated by one spouse against the other spouse, enforce that judgment against the abusive spouse's share of community property, if a proceeding for dissolution of marriage or legal separation of the parties is pending prior to the entry of final judgment. *(Added by Stats.2004, c. 299 (A.B.2018), § 1.)*

§ 2604. Community estates of less than $5,000; award of entire estate

If the net value of the community estate is less than five thousand dollars ($5,000) and one party cannot be located through the exercise of reasonable diligence, the court may award all the community estate to the other party on conditions the court deems proper in its judgment of dissolution of marriage or legal separation of the parties. *(Stats.1992, c. 162 (A.B.2650), § 10, operative Jan. 1, 1994.)*

Cross References

Characterization of marital property, see Family Code § 760 et seq.
Community estate defined, see Family Code § 63.
Community property, see Family Code § 760.
Death of married person, effect on community and quasi-community property, see Probate Code § 100 et seq.
Division of quasi-marital property, see Family Code §§ 2251, 2252.
Homestead property,
 General provisions, see Code of Civil Procedure §§ 704.710 et seq., 704.910 et seq.
 Administration of estates, see Probate Code § 6520 et seq.
Judgment and order defined for purposes of this Code, see Family Code § 100.
Marital debt incurred prior to separation date, division, see Family Code § 2622.
Partition of real and personal property, see Code of Civil Procedure § 872.010 et seq.
Presumptions, nature of marital property, see Family Code §§ 802, 803.

Property rights during marriage, see Family Code § 750 et seq.

Research References

Forms

West's California Code Forms, Family § 2338 Form 6, Provision in Judgment—Awarding Community Estate.

§ 2605. Care and ownership of pet animal

(a) The court, at the request of a party to proceedings for dissolution of marriage or for legal separation of the parties, may enter an order, prior to the final determination of ownership of a pet animal, to require a party to care for the pet animal. The existence of an order providing for the care of a pet animal during the course of proceedings for dissolution of marriage or for legal separation of the parties shall not have any impact on the court's final determination of ownership of the pet animal.

(b) Notwithstanding any other law, including, but not limited to, Section 2550, the court, at the request of a party to proceedings for dissolution of marriage or for legal separation of the parties, may assign sole or joint ownership of a pet animal taking into consideration the care of the pet animal.

(c) For purposes of this section, the following definitions shall apply:

(1) "Care" includes, but is not limited to, the prevention of acts of harm or cruelty, as described in Section 597 of the Penal Code, and the provision of food, water, veterinary care, and safe and protected shelter.

(2) "Pet animal" means any animal that is community property and kept as a household pet. *(Added by Stats.2018, c. 820 (A.B. 2274), § 1, eff. Jan. 1, 2019.)*

Part 5

RETIREMENT PLAN BENEFITS

Section
2610. Retirement plans; orders to ensure benefits.
2611. Final tribal court order; recognition of retirement and deferred compensation plans; jurisdiction to modify.

Cross References

Characterization of marital property, see Family Code § 760 et seq.
Community property, legal separation or dissolution of marriage, division of account into two separate accounts, see Government Code § 22970.70.
County employees retirement law of 1937, community property, legal separation or marriage dissolution, see Government Code § 31685.
Death of married person, effect on community and quasi-community property, see Probate Code § 100 et seq.
Discharge of payment or refund from adverse claims, notice of claim, see Family Code § 755.
Division of community property interests in judge's retirement system, see Government Code § 75050.
Division of quasi-marital property, see Family Code §§ 2251, 2252.
Employee benefit plan defined, see Family Code § 80.
Judges' retirement law,
  Community property, former spouses of judges, see Government Code § 75059.1.
  Community property, legal separation or dissolution of marriage of member, see Government Code § 75050.
  Community property, legal separation or dissolution of marriage of retired member, see Government Code § 75059.
  Extended service incentive program, beneficiaries, see Government Code § 75088.4.
  Payment of benefits, beneficiary designation, see Government Code § 75074.
Judges' retirement system II, community property, legal separation or dissolution of marriage of member, see Government Code § 75551.
Notice of claim, payment or refund of benefits, see Family Code § 755.
Partition of real and personal property, see Code of Civil Procedure § 872.010 et seq.
Presumptions, nature of marital property, see Family Code §§ 802, 803.
Property rights during marriage, see Family Code § 750 et seq.
Public employees' retirement system,
  Generally, see Government Code § 20000 et seq.
  Community property, marriage dissolutions or legal separations, see Government Code § 21290.
  Death benefits, designation of beneficiary, see Government Code § 21490.
State peace officers' and firefighters' defined contribution plan, community property, earnings attributable to periods of service during marriage, see Government Code § 22960.75.
State teachers' retirement system,
  Cash balance plan, determination of community property rights, payment to spouse, see Education Code § 27405.
  Designation of beneficiary, revocation, see Education Code § 23300.
  Retirement allowance or retirement annuity, community property rights of nonmember spouse, see Education Code § 22655.

§ 2610. Retirement plans; orders to ensure benefits

(a) Except as provided in subdivision (b), the court shall make whatever orders are necessary or appropriate to ensure that each party receives the party's full community property share in any retirement plan, whether public or private, including all survivor and death benefits, including, but not limited to, any of the following:

(1) Order the disposition of retirement benefits payable upon or after the death of either party in a manner consistent with Section 2550.

(2) Order a party to elect a survivor benefit annuity or other similar election for the benefit of the other party, as specified by the court, when a retirement plan provides for that election, provided that no court shall order a retirement plan to provide increased benefits determined on the basis of actuarial value.

(3) Upon the agreement of the nonemployee spouse, order the division of accumulated community property contributions and service credit as provided in the following or similar enactments:

(A) Article 2 (commencing with Section 21290) of Chapter 9 of Part 3 of Division 5 of Title 2 of the Government Code.

(B) Chapter 12 (commencing with Section 22650) of Part 13 of Division 1 of Title 1 of the Education Code.

(C) Article 8.4 (commencing with Section 31685) of Chapter 3 of Part 3 of Division 4 of Title 3 of the Government Code.

(D) Article 2.5 (commencing with Section 75050) of Chapter 11 of Title 8 of the Government Code.

(E) Chapter 15 (commencing with Section 27400) of Part 14 of Division 1 of Title 1 of the Education Code.

(4) Order a retirement plan to make payments directly to a nonmember party of the nonmember party's community property interest in retirement benefits.

(b) A court shall not make an order that requires a retirement plan to do either of the following:

(1) Make payments in a manner that will result in an increase in the amount of benefits provided by the plan.

(2) Make the payment of benefits to a party at any time before the member retires, except as provided in paragraph (3) of subdivision (a), unless the plan so provides.

(c) This section shall not be applied retroactively to payments made by a retirement plan to a person who retired or died prior to January 1, 1987, or to payments made to a person who retired or died prior to June 1, 1988, for plans subject to paragraph (3) of subdivision (a). *(Stats.1992, c. 162 (A.B.2650), § 10, operative Jan. 1, 1994. Amended by Stats.1993, c. 219 (A.B.1500), § 112; Stats.1994, c. 670 (S.B.1500), § 1; Stats.1994, c. 1269 (A.B.2208), § 25.5; Stats. 1998, c. 965 (A.B.2765), § 322; Stats.2009, c. 130 (A.B.966), § 1; Stats.2019, c. 115 (A.B.1817), § 22, eff. Jan. 1, 2020.)*

§ 2610

Validity

This section was held preempted by ERISA in the decision of Branco v. UFCW-Northern California Employers Joint Pension Plan, C.A.9 (Cal.)2002, 279 F.3d 1154.

Cross References

Characterization of marital property, see Family Code § 760 et seq.
Community property, legal separation or dissolution of marriage, division of account into two separate accounts, see Government Code § 22970.70.
Community property defined for purposes of this Code, see Family Code § 65.
County employees retirement law of 1937, community property, legal separation or marriage dissolution, see Government Code § 31685.
Death of married person, effect on community and quasi-community property, see Probate Code § 100 et seq.
Discharge of payment or refund from adverse claims, notice of claim, see Family Code § 755.
Division of quasi-marital property, see Family Code §§ 2251, 2252.
Employee benefit plan, defined, see Family Code § 80.
Judges' retirement law, community property,
    Former spouses of judges, see Government Code § 75059.1.
    Legal separation or dissolution of marriage of member, see Government Code § 75050.
    Legal separation or dissolution of marriage of retired member, see Government Code § 75059.
Judges' retirement law, payment of benefits, beneficiary designation, see Government Code § 75074.
Judges' retirement system II, community property, legal separation or dissolution of marriage of member, see Government Code § 75551.
Judgment and order defined for purposes of this Code, see Family Code § 100.
Notice of claim, payment or refund of benefits, see Family Code § 755.
Partition of real and personal property, see Code of Civil Procedure § 872.010 et seq.
Person defined for purposes of this Code, see Family Code § 105.
Presumptions, nature of marital property, see Family Code §§ 802, 803.
Property defined for purposes of this Code, see Family Code § 113.
Property rights during marriage, see Family Code § 750 et seq.
Public employees' retirement system,
    Generally, see Government Code § 20000 et seq.
    Community property, marriage dissolutions or legal separations, see Government Code § 21290.
        Death benefits, designation of beneficiary, see Government Code § 21490.
        Flexible Beneficiary Option 4, see Government Code § 21477.
References to husband, wife, spouses and married persons, persons included for purposes of this Code, see Family Code § 11.
State peace officers' and firefighters' defined contribution plan, community property, earnings attributable to periods of service during marriage, see Government Code § 22960.75.
State teachers' retirement system,
    Cash balance plan, determination of community property rights, payment to spouse, see Education Code § 27405.
    Designation of beneficiary, revocation, see Education Code § 23300.
    Retirement allowance or retirement annuity, community property rights of nonmember spouse, see Education Code § 22655.

Research References

Forms

California Practice Guide: Rutter Family Law Forms Form 8:6, Qualified Domestic Relations Order (QDRO).
2 California Transactions Forms--Estate Planning § 9:76, Community Property Interest in Retirement Benefits.
2 California Transactions Forms--Estate Planning § 10:4, Community Property.
4 California Transactions Forms--Estate Planning § 19:16, Overview.
1 California Transactions Forms--Family Law § 2:23, Overview.
West's California Code Forms, Family § 2060, Comment Overview—Application and Order for Joinder.
West's California Code Forms, Family § 2550, Comment Overview—Manner of Division of Community Estate.
West's California Judicial Council Forms FL–347, Bifurcation of Status of Marriage or Domestic Partnership—Attachment.
West's California Judicial Council Forms FL–348, Pension Benefits—Attachment to Judgment (Attach to Form FL-180) (Also Available in Spanish).

§ 2611. Final tribal court order; recognition of retirement and deferred compensation plans; jurisdiction to modify

(a) A final order of a tribal court that creates or recognizes the existence of the right of a spouse, former spouse, child, or other dependent of a participant in a retirement plan or other plan of deferred compensation to receive all or a portion of the benefits payable with respect to such plan participant, and that relates to the provision of child support, spousal support payments, or marital property rights to such spouse, former spouse, child, or other dependent, that is filed in accordance with Section 1733.1 of the Code of Civil Procedure shall be recognized as an order made pursuant to the domestic relations laws of this state.

(b) The filing of the tribal court order does not confer any jurisdiction on a court of this state to modify or enforce the tribal court order. *(Added by Stats.2021, c. 58 (A.B.627), § 7, eff. Jan. 1, 2022.)*

Part 6

DEBTS AND LIABILITIES

Section
2620. Community estate debts; confirmation or division.
2621. Premarital debts; confirmation.
2622. Marital debts incurred before the date of separation; division.
2623. Marital debts incurred after the date of separation; confirmation.
2624. Marital debts incurred after entry of judgment of dissolution or after entry of judgment of legal separation; confirmation.
2625. Separate debts incurred before date of separation; confirmation.
2626. Reimbursements.
2627. Educational loans; liabilities for death or injuries; assignment.
2628. Joint California income tax liabilities; revision by court in marriage dissolution proceeding.

Cross References

Characterization of marital property, see Family Code § 760 et seq.
Community estate defined, see Family Code § 63.
Community property, see Family Code § 760.
Court characterization, liabilities as separate or community, distribution to parties, see Family Code § 2551.
Death of married person, effect on community and quasi-community property, see Probate Code § 100 et seq.
Division of quasi-marital property, see Family Code §§ 2251, 2252.
General rules regarding liability of marital property, see Family Code § 910 et seq.
Homestead property,
    General provisions, see Code of Civil Procedure §§ 704.710 et seq., 704.910 et seq.
    Administration of estates, see Probate Code § 6520 et seq.
Liability of marital property, see Family Code § 900 et seq.
Marriage dissolution proceedings, joint California income tax liabilities, revision by court, see Family Code § 2628.
Partition of real and personal property, see Code of Civil Procedure § 872.010 et seq.
Presumptions, nature of marital property, see Family Code §§ 802, 803.
Property rights during marriage, see Family Code § 750 et seq.
References to husband, wife, spouses and married persons, persons included for purposes of this Code, see Family Code § 11.
Time, valuation date for liabilities, see Family Code § 2552.

§ 2620. Community estate debts; confirmation or division

The debts for which the community estate is liable which are unpaid at the time of trial, or for which the community estate becomes liable after trial, shall be confirmed or divided as provided in this part. *(Stats.1992, c. 162 (A.B.2650), § 10, operative Jan. 1, 1994.)*

Cross References

Characterization of marital property, see Family Code § 760 et seq.
Community estate defined, see Family Code § 63.
Community property, see Family Code § 760.
Court characterization, liabilities as separate or community, distribution to parties, see Family Code § 2551.
Death of married person, effect on community and quasi-community property, see Probate Code § 100 et seq.
Division of quasi-marital property, see Family Code §§ 2251, 2252.
Educational loans, assignment, see Family Code § 2627.
General rules regarding liability of marital property, see Family Code § 910 et seq.
Homestead property,
  General provisions, see Code of Civil Procedure §§ 704.710 et seq., 704.910 et seq.
  Administration of estates, see Probate Code § 6520 et seq.
Liability of marital property, see Family Code § 900 et seq.
Marriage dissolution proceedings, joint California income tax liabilities, revision by court, see Family Code § 2628.
Partition of real and personal property, see Code of Civil Procedure § 872.010 et seq.
Presumptions, nature of marital property, see Family Code §§ 802, 803.
Property rights during marriage, see Family Code § 750 et seq.
Time, valuation date for liabilities, see Family Code § 2552.

Research References

Forms

West's California Code Forms, Family § 2550, Comment Overview—Manner of Division of Community Estate.

§ 2621. Premarital debts; confirmation

Debts incurred by either spouse before the date of marriage shall be confirmed without offset to the spouse who incurred the debt. *(Stats.1992, c. 162 (A.B.2650), § 10, operative Jan. 1, 1994.)*

Cross References

Characterization of marital property, see Family Code § 760 et seq.
Death of married person, effect on community and quasi-community property, see Probate Code § 100 et seq.
Division of quasi-marital property, see Family Code §§ 2251, 2252.
Educational loans, assignment, see Family Code § 2627.
General rules regarding liability of marital property, see Family Code § 910 et seq.
Homestead property,
  General provisions, see Code of Civil Procedure §§ 704.710 et seq., 704.910 et seq.
  Administration of estates, see Probate Code § 6520 et seq.
Liability of marital property, see Family Code § 900 et seq.
Marriage dissolution proceedings, joint California income tax liabilities, revision by court, see Family Code § 2628.
Partition of real and personal property, see Code of Civil Procedure § 872.010 et seq.
Presumptions, nature of marital property, see Family Code §§ 802, 803.
Property rights during marriage, see Family Code § 750 et seq.
References to husband, wife, spouses and married persons, persons included for purposes of this Code, see Family Code § 11.

§ 2622. Marital debts incurred before the date of separation; division

(a) Except as provided in subdivision (b), debts incurred by either spouse after the date of marriage but before the date of separation shall be divided as set forth in Sections 2550 to 2552, inclusive, and Sections 2601 to 2604, inclusive.

(b) To the extent that community debts exceed total community and quasi-community assets, the excess of debt shall be assigned as the court deems just and equitable, taking into account factors such as the parties' relative ability to pay. *(Stats.1992, c. 162 (A.B.2650), § 10, operative Jan. 1, 1994.)*

Cross References

Characterization of marital property, see Family Code § 760 et seq.
Death of married person, effect on community and quasi-community property, see Probate Code § 100 et seq.
Division of quasi-marital property, see Family Code §§ 2251, 2252.
Educational loans, assignment, see Family Code § 2627.
General rules regarding liability of marital property, see Family Code § 910 et seq.
Homestead property,
  General provisions, see Code of Civil Procedure §§ 704.710 et seq., 704.910 et seq.
  Administration of estates, see Probate Code § 6520 et seq.
Liability of marital property, see Family Code § 900 et seq.
Marriage dissolution proceedings, joint California income tax liabilities, revision by court, see Family Code § 2628.
Partition of real and personal property, see Code of Civil Procedure § 872.010 et seq.
Presumptions, nature of marital property, see Family Code §§ 802, 803.
Property rights during marriage, see Family Code § 750 et seq.
References to husband, wife, spouses and married persons, persons included for purposes of this Code, see Family Code § 11.

§ 2623. Marital debts incurred after the date of separation; confirmation

Debts incurred by either spouse after the date of separation but before entry of a judgment of dissolution of marriage or legal separation of the parties shall be confirmed as follows:

(a) Debts incurred by either spouse for the common necessaries of life of either spouse or the necessaries of life of the children of the marriage for whom support may be ordered, in the absence of a court order or written agreement for support or for the payment of these debts, shall be confirmed to either spouse according to the parties' respective needs and abilities to pay at the time the debt was incurred.

(b) Debts incurred by either spouse for nonnecessaries of that spouse or children of the marriage for whom support may be ordered shall be confirmed without offset to the spouse who incurred the debt. *(Stats.1992, c. 162 (A.B.2650), § 10, operative Jan. 1, 1994. Amended by Stats.1993, c. 219 (A.B.1500), § 113.)*

Cross References

Agreements for support of adult children, see Family Code § 3587.
Characterization of marital property, see Family Code § 760 et seq.
Death of married person, effect on community and quasi-community property, see Probate Code § 100 et seq.
Division of quasi-marital property, see Family Code §§ 2251, 2252.
Educational loans, assignment, see Family Code § 2627.
General rules regarding liability of marital property, see Family Code § 910 et seq.
Homestead property,
  General provisions, see Code of Civil Procedure §§ 704.710 et seq., 704.910 et seq.
  Administration of estates, see Probate Code § 6520 et seq.
Judgment and order defined for purposes of this Code, see Family Code § 100.
Liability of marital property, see Family Code § 900 et seq.
Marriage dissolution proceedings, joint California income tax liabilities, revision by court, see Family Code § 2628.
Partition of real and personal property, see Code of Civil Procedure § 872.010 et seq.
Presumptions, nature of marital property, see Family Code §§ 802, 803.
Property rights during marriage, see Family Code § 750 et seq.
References to husband, wife, spouses and married persons, persons included for purposes of this Code, see Family Code § 11.
Support, generally, see Family Code § 3500 et seq.
Support agreements,
  Generally, see Family Code § 3580 et seq.
  Child support agreements, see Family Code § 3585 et seq.
  Spousal support agreements, see Family Code § 3590 et seq.

§ 2623

Support defined for purposes of this Code, see Family Code § 150.

§ 2624. Marital debts incurred after entry of judgment of dissolution or after entry of judgment of legal separation; confirmation

Debts incurred by either spouse after entry of a judgment of dissolution of marriage but before termination of the parties' marital status or after entry of a judgment of legal separation of the parties shall be confirmed without offset to the spouse who incurred the debt. *(Stats.1992, c. 162 (A.B.2650), § 10, operative Jan. 1, 1994.)*

Cross References

Characterization of marital property, see Family Code § 760 et seq.
Death of married person, effect on community and quasi-community property, see Probate Code § 100 et seq.
Division of quasi-marital property, see Family Code §§ 2251, 2252.
Educational loans, assignment, see Family Code § 2627.
General rules regarding liability of marital property, see Family Code § 910 et seq.
Homestead property,
  General provisions, see Code of Civil Procedure §§ 704.710 et seq., 704.910 et seq.
  Administration of estates, see Probate Code § 6520 et seq.
Judgment and order defined for purposes of this Code, see Family Code § 100.
Liability of marital property, see Family Code § 900 et seq.
Marriage dissolution proceedings, joint California income tax liabilities, revision by court, see Family Code § 2628.
Partition of real and personal property, see Code of Civil Procedure § 872.010 et seq.
Presumptions, nature of marital property, see Family Code §§ 802, 803.
Property rights during marriage, see Family Code § 750 et seq.
References to husband, wife, spouses and married persons, persons included for purposes of this Code, see Family Code § 11.

§ 2625. Separate debts incurred before date of separation; confirmation

Notwithstanding Sections 2620 to 2624, inclusive, all separate debts, including those debts incurred by a spouse during marriage and before the date of separation that were not incurred for the benefit of the community, shall be confirmed without offset to the spouse who incurred the debt. *(Stats.1992, c. 162 (A.B.2650), § 10, operative Jan. 1, 1994.)*

Cross References

Characterization of marital property, see Family Code § 760 et seq.
Death of married person, effect on community and quasi-community property, see Probate Code § 100 et seq.
Division of quasi-marital property, see Family Code §§ 2251, 2252.
General rules regarding liability of marital property, see Family Code § 910 et seq.
Homestead property,
  General provisions, see Code of Civil Procedure §§ 704.710 et seq., 704.910 et seq.
  Administration of estates, see Probate Code § 6520 et seq.
Liability of marital property, see Family Code § 900 et seq.
Partition of real and personal property, see Code of Civil Procedure § 872.010 et seq.
Presumptions, nature of marital property, see Family Code §§ 802, 803.
Property rights during marriage, see Family Code § 750 et seq.
References to husband, wife, spouses and married persons, persons included for purposes of this Code, see Family Code § 11.

§ 2626. Reimbursements

The court has jurisdiction to order reimbursement in cases it deems appropriate for debts paid after separation but before trial. *(Stats.1992, c. 162 (A.B.2650), § 10, operative Jan. 1, 1994.)*

Cross References

Characterization of marital property, see Family Code § 760 et seq.
Death of married person, effect on community and quasi-community property, see Probate Code § 100 et seq.
Division of quasi-marital property, see Family Code §§ 2251, 2252.
General rules regarding liability of marital property, see Family Code § 910 et seq.

Homestead property,
  General provisions, see Code of Civil Procedure §§ 704.710 et seq., 704.910 et seq.
  Administration of estates, see Probate Code § 6520 et seq.
Judgment and order defined for purposes of this Code, see Family Code § 100.
Liability of marital property, see Family Code § 900 et seq.
Partition of real and personal property, see Code of Civil Procedure § 872.010 et seq.
Presumptions, nature of marital property, see Family Code §§ 802, 803.
Property rights during marriage, see Family Code § 750 et seq.

Research References

Forms

California Practice Guide: Rutter Family Law Forms Form 1:32, Glossary of Common Family Law Terms, Phrases and Concepts (Enclosure to Form 1:31).

§ 2627. Educational loans; liabilities for death or injuries; assignment

Notwithstanding Sections 2550 to 2552, inclusive, and Sections 2620 to 2624, inclusive, educational loans shall be assigned pursuant to Section 2641 and liabilities subject to paragraph (2) of subdivision (b) of Section 1000 shall be assigned to the spouse whose act or omission provided the basis for the liability, without offset. *(Stats. 1992, c. 162 (A.B.2650), § 10, operative Jan. 1, 1994.)*

Cross References

Characterization of marital property, see Family Code § 760 et seq.
Death of married person, effect on community and quasi-community property, see Probate Code § 100 et seq.
Division of quasi-marital property, see Family Code §§ 2251, 2252.
General rules regarding liability of marital property, see Family Code § 910 et seq.
Homestead property,
  General provisions, see Code of Civil Procedure §§ 704.710 et seq., 704.910 et seq.
  Administration of estates, see Probate Code § 6520 et seq.
Liability of marital property, see Family Code § 900 et seq.
Partition of real and personal property, see Code of Civil Procedure § 872.010 et seq.
Presumptions, nature of marital property, see Family Code §§ 802, 803.
Property rights during marriage, see Family Code § 750 et seq.
References to husband, wife, spouses and married persons, persons included for purposes of this Code, see Family Code § 11.

§ 2628. Joint California income tax liabilities; revision by court in marriage dissolution proceeding

Notwithstanding Sections 2550 to 2552, inclusive, and Sections 2620 to 2624, inclusive, joint California income tax liabilities may be revised by a court in a proceeding for dissolution of marriage, provided the requirements of Section 19006 of the Revenue and Taxation Code are satisfied. *(Added by Stats.2002, c. 374 (A.B.2979), § 1.)*

Cross References

Proceeding defined for purposes of this Code, see Family Code § 110.
Tax levies, see Government Code § 29100 et seq.; Revenue and Taxation Code § 2151 et seq.

Part 7

REIMBURSEMENTS

Section
2640. Contribution to the acquisition of property of the community property estate; waivers; amount of reimbursement.
2641. Community contributions to education or training.

Cross References

Burden of proof, generally, see Evidence Code § 500 et seq.

Characterization of marital property, see Family Code § 760 et seq.
Community estate defined, see Family Code § 63.
Community property,
  Generally, see Family Code § 760.
  Multiple-party accounts of married persons, presumption notwithstanding this section, see Probate Code § 5305.
Death of married person, effect on community and quasi-community property, see Probate Code § 100 et seq.
Division of quasi-marital property, see Family Code §§ 2251, 2252.
General rules regarding liability of marital property, see Family Code § 910 et seq.
Homestead property,
  General provisions, see Code of Civil Procedure §§ 704.710 et seq., 704.910 et seq.
  Administration of estates, see Probate Code § 6520 et seq.
Liability of marital property, see Family Code § 900 et seq.
Multiple-party accounts of married persons, presumption of community property notwithstanding this section, see Probate Code § 5305.
Partition of real and personal property, see Code of Civil Procedure § 872.010 et seq.
Presumptions, nature of marital property, see Family Code §§ 802, 803.
Property held in joint title, application of section, see Family Code § 2580.
Property rights during marriage, see Family Code § 750 et seq.
Reimbursement,
  General provisions, see Family Code § 920.
  Transitional provisions, see Family Code § 931.
Separate property,
  Defined, see Family Code § 770.
  In relation to quasi-community property, see Family Code § 2502.

§ 2640. Contribution to the acquisition of property of the community property estate; waivers; amount of reimbursement

(a) "Contributions to the acquisition of property," as used in this section, include downpayments, payments for improvements, and payments that reduce the principal of a loan used to finance the purchase or improvement of the property but do not include payments of interest on the loan or payments made for maintenance, insurance, or taxation of the property.

(b) In the division of the community estate under this division, unless a party has made a written waiver of the right to reimbursement or has signed a writing that has the effect of a waiver, the party shall be reimbursed for the party's contributions to the acquisition of property of the community property estate to the extent the party traces the contributions to a separate property source. The amount reimbursed shall be without interest or adjustment for change in monetary values and may not exceed the net value of the property at the time of the division.

(c) A party shall be reimbursed for the party's separate property contributions to the acquisition of property of the other spouse's separate property estate during the marriage, unless there has been a transmutation in writing pursuant to Chapter 5 (commencing with Section 850) of Part 2 of Division 4, or a written waiver of the right to reimbursement. The amount reimbursed shall be without interest or adjustment for change in monetary values and may not exceed the net value of the property at the time of the division. *(Stats.1992, c. 162 (A.B.2650), § 10, operative Jan. 1, 1994. Amended by Stats.1993, c. 219 (A.B.1500), § 114.5; Stats.2004, c. 119 (S.B.1407), § 1.)*

Cross References

Characterization of marital property, see Family Code § 760 et seq.
Community estate defined, see Family Code § 63.
Community property,
  Generally, see Family Code § 760.
  Multiple-party accounts of married persons, presumption notwithstanding this section, see Probate Code § 5305.
Death of married person, effect on community and quasi-community property, see Probate Code § 100 et seq.
Division of quasi-marital property, see Family Code §§ 2251, 2252.
General rules regarding liability of marital property, see Family Code § 910 et seq.
Homestead property,
  General provisions, see Code of Civil Procedure §§ 704.710 et seq., 704.910 et seq.
  Administration of estates, see Probate Code § 6520 et seq.
Liability of marital property, see Family Code § 900 et seq.
Multiple-party accounts of married persons, presumption of community property notwithstanding this section, see Probate Code § 5305.
Partition of real and personal property, see Code of Civil Procedure § 872.010 et seq.
Presumptions, nature of marital property, see Family Code §§ 802, 803.
Property defined for purposes of this Code, see Family Code § 113.
Property held in joint title, application of section, see Family Code § 2580.
Property rights during marriage, see Family Code § 750 et seq.
Reimbursement,
  General provisions, see Family Code § 920.
  Transitional provisions, see Family Code § 931.
Separate property,
  Generally, see Family Code § 770.
  In relation to quasi-community property, see Family Code § 2502.
Separate property defined for purposes of this Code, see Family Code § 130.
Writings, authentication and proof of, see Evidence Code § 1400 et seq.

Research References

Forms

Asset Protection: Legal Planning, Strategies and Forms ¶ 4.08, Implications of Divorce.
1 California Transactions Forms--Estate Planning § 1:25, Joint Tenancy or Community Property Treatment of Property in Revocable Trust.
1 California Transactions Forms--Estate Planning § 2:13, Separate Versus Community Property Issues.
2 California Transactions Forms--Estate Planning § 10:45, Property Characterization Agreement.
2 California Transactions Forms--Estate Planning § 11:49, Introduction and Definition [Prob C § 140].
1 California Transactions Forms--Family Law § 1:90, Real and Personal Property.
1 California Transactions Forms--Family Law § 2:17, Drafting Principles Regarding Disposition of Residence.
1 California Transactions Forms--Family Law § 2:18, Reimbursement of Separate Property Contribution [Fam. Code §2640].
1 California Transactions Forms--Family Law § 2:81, Potential Community Assets and Obligations.
1 California Transactions Forms--Family Law § 2:88, Marital Settlement Agreement.
1 California Transactions Forms--Family Law § 2:97, Confirmation of Capital Gains Tax and Division of Proceeds After Separate Property Reimbursement [Fam C § 2640].
West's California Code Forms, Family § 2338 Form 8, Marital Agreement.

§ 2641. Community contributions to education or training

(a) "Community contributions to education or training" as used in this section means payments made with community or quasi-community property for education or training or for the repayment of a loan incurred for education or training, whether the payments were made while the parties were resident in this state or resident outside this state.

(b) Subject to the limitations provided in this section, upon dissolution of marriage or legal separation of the parties:

(1) The community shall be reimbursed for community contributions to education or training of a party that substantially enhances the earning capacity of the party. The amount reimbursed shall be with interest at the legal rate, accruing from the end of the calendar year in which the contributions were made.

(2) A loan incurred during marriage for the education or training of a party shall not be included among the liabilities of the community for the purpose of division pursuant to this division but shall be assigned for payment by the party.

(c) The reimbursement and assignment required by this section shall be reduced or modified to the extent circumstances render such a disposition unjust, including, but not limited to, any of the following:

§ 2641
DIVISION OF PROPERTY

(1) The community has substantially benefited from the education, training, or loan incurred for the education or training of the party. There is a rebuttable presumption, affecting the burden of proof, that the community has not substantially benefited from community contributions to the education or training made less than 10 years before the commencement of the proceeding, and that the community has substantially benefited from community contributions to the education or training made more than 10 years before the commencement of the proceeding.

(2) The education or training received by the party is offset by the education or training received by the other party for which community contributions have been made.

(3) The education or training enables the party receiving the education or training to engage in gainful employment that substantially reduces the need of the party for support that would otherwise be required.

(d) Reimbursement for community contributions and assignment of loans pursuant to this section is the exclusive remedy of the community or a party for the education or training and any resulting enhancement of the earning capacity of a party. However, nothing in this subdivision limits consideration of the effect of the education, training, or enhancement, or the amount reimbursed pursuant to this section, on the circumstances of the parties for the purpose of an order for support pursuant to Section 4320.

(e) This section is subject to an express written agreement of the parties to the contrary. *(Stats.1992, c. 162 (A.B.2650), § 10, operative Jan. 1, 1994.)*

Cross References

Burden of proof, generally, see Evidence Code § 500 et seq.
Community estate defined, see Family Code § 63.
Community property, see Family Code § 760.
Community property defined for purposes of this Code, see Family Code § 65.
Death of married person, effect on community and quasi-community property, see Probate Code § 100 et seq.
Judgment and order defined for purposes of this Code, see Family Code § 100.
Partition of real and personal property, see Code of Civil Procedure § 872.010 et seq.
Presumptions, see Evidence Code § 600 et seq.
Proceeding defined for purposes of this Code, see Family Code § 110.
Property defined for purposes of this Code, see Family Code § 113.
Quasi-community property defined for purposes of this Code, see Family Code § 125.
Reimbursement,
   General provisions, see Family Code § 920.
   Transitional provisions, see Family Code § 931.
State defined for purposes of this Code, see Family Code § 145.
Support, generally, see Family Code § 3500 et seq.
Support defined for purposes of this Code, see Family Code § 150.

Research References

Forms

Asset Protection: Legal Planning, Strategies and Forms ¶ 4.07, Marital Agreements.
2 California Transactions Forms--Estate Planning § 11:49, Introduction and Definition [Prob C § 140].
1 California Transactions Forms--Family Law § 2:88, Marital Settlement Agreement.
West's California Code Forms, Family § 2338 Form 8, Marital Agreement.
West's California Code Forms, Family § 2550, Comment Overview—Manner of Division of Community Estate.

Part 8

JOINTLY HELD SEPARATE PROPERTY

Section
2650. Jurisdiction; division of real and personal property.

Cross References

Actions for partition, see Code of Civil Procedure § 872.010 et seq.
Agreement of parties, equal division of community estate in absence of, see Family Code § 2550.
Characterization of marital property, see Family Code § 760 et seq.
Community estate defined, see Family Code § 63.
Community property,
   Generally, see Family Code § 760.
   Interests of spouses, see Family Code § 751.
Death of married person, effect on community and quasi-community property, see Probate Code § 100 et seq.
Division of quasi-marital property, see Family Code §§ 2251, 2252.
Dwelling, excluding spouse from, see Family Code § 753.
Equal division, community estate, see Family Code § 2550.
General rules regarding liability of marital property, see Family Code § 910 et seq.
Homestead property,
   General provisions, see Code of Civil Procedure §§ 704.710 et seq., 704.910 et seq.
   Administration of estates, see Probate Code § 6520 et seq.
Jurisdiction over property of spouse, service by publication, see Family Code § 2011.
Jurisdictional scope, see Family Code § 2010 et seq.
Liability of marital property, see Family Code § 900 et seq.
Methods of holding property, see Family Code § 750.
Partition of real and personal property, see Code of Civil Procedure § 872.010 et seq.
Pendency of proceedings, limitation on disposition of separate property residence, see Family Code § 754.
Presumptions, nature of marital property, see Family Code §§ 802, 803.
Property rights during marriage, see Family Code § 750 et seq.
Real property situated in another state, see Family Code § 2660.
Scope of jurisdiction, see Family Code § 2010.
Separate property,
   Generally, see Family Code § 770.
   Defined, see Family Code § 130.
   Interests of spouses, see Family Code § 752.
Service of process, jurisdiction over property of spouse served by publication, see Family Code § 2011.

§ 2650. Jurisdiction; division of real and personal property

In a proceeding for division of the community estate, the court has jurisdiction, at the request of either party, to divide the separate property interests of the parties in real and personal property, wherever situated and whenever acquired, held by the parties as joint tenants or tenants in common. The property shall be divided together with, and in accordance with the same procedure for and limitations on, division of community estate. *(Stats.1992, c. 162 (A.B.2650), § 10, operative Jan. 1, 1994.)*

Cross References

Actions for partition, see Code of Civil Procedure § 872.010 et seq.
Agreement of parties, equal division of community estate in absence of, see Family Code § 2550.
Characterization of marital property, see Family Code § 760 et seq.
Community estate defined, see Family Code § 63.
Community property,
   Generally, see Family Code § 760.
   Interests of spouses, see Family Code § 751.
Death of married person, effect on community and quasi-community property, see Probate Code § 100 et seq.
Division of quasi-marital property, see Family Code §§ 2251, 2252.
Dwelling, excluding spouse from, see Family Code § 753.
Equal division, community estate, see Family Code § 2550.
General rules regarding liability of marital property, see Family Code § 910 et seq.
Homestead property,
   General provisions, see Code of Civil Procedure §§ 704.710 et seq., 704.910 et seq.
   Administration of estates, see Probate Code § 6520 et seq.
Jurisdiction over property of spouse, service by publication, see Family Code § 2011.
Jurisdictional scope, see Family Code § 2010 et seq.
Liability of marital property, see Family Code § 900 et seq.
Methods of holding property, see Family Code § 750.

DEFINITIONS AND GENERAL PROVISIONS

Partition of real and personal property, see Code of Civil Procedure § 872.010 et seq.
Pendency of proceedings, limitation on disposition of separate property residence, see Family Code § 754.
Presumptions, nature of marital property, see Family Code §§ 802, 803.
Proceeding defined for purposes of this Code, see Family Code § 110.
Property defined for purposes of this Code, see Family Code § 113.
Property rights during marriage, see Family Code § 750 et seq.
Real property situated in another state, see Family Code § 2660.
Scope of jurisdiction, see Family Code § 2010.
Separate property,
   Generally, see Family Code § 770.
   Defined for purposes of this Code, see Family Code § 130.
   Interests of spouses, see Family Code § 752.
Service of process, jurisdiction over property of spouse served by publication, see Family Code § 2011.

Research References

Forms

West's California Code Forms, Family § 2550, Comment Overview—Manner of Division of Community Estate.

Part 9

REAL PROPERTY LOCATED IN ANOTHER STATE

Section
2660. Division of real property situated in another state.

Cross References

Characterization of marital property, see Family Code § 760 et seq.
Death of married person, effect on community and quasi-community property, see Probate Code § 100 et seq.
Division of quasi-marital property, see Family Code §§ 2251, 2252.
General rules regarding liability of marital property, see Family Code § 910 et seq.
Homestead property,
   General provisions, see Code of Civil Procedure §§ 704.710 et seq., 704.910 et seq.
   Administration of estates, see Probate Code § 6520 et seq.
Jurisdiction,
   Community property, see Family Code § 2011.
   Superior court, see Cal. Const. Art. 6, §§ 10, 11; Family Code § 200.
Liability of marital property, see Family Code § 900 et seq.
Partition of real and personal property, see Code of Civil Procedure § 872.010 et seq.
Presumptions, nature of marital property, see Family Code §§ 802, 803.
Property rights during marriage, see Family Code § 750 et seq.

§ 2660. Division of real property situated in another state

(a) Except as provided in subdivision (b), if the property subject to division includes real property situated in another state, the court shall, if possible, divide the community property and quasi-community property as provided for in this division in such a manner that it is not necessary to change the nature of the interests held in the real property situated in the other state.

(b) If it is not possible to divide the property in the manner provided for in subdivision (a), the court may do any of the following in order to effect a division of the property as provided for in this division:

(1) Require the parties to execute conveyances or take other actions with respect to the real property situated in the other state as are necessary.

(2) Award to the party who would have been benefited by the conveyances or other actions the money value of the interest in the property that the party would have received if the conveyances had been executed or other actions taken. *(Stats.1992, c. 162 (A.B.2650), § 10, operative Jan. 1, 1994.)*

Cross References

Characterization of marital property, see Family Code § 760 et seq.
Community property defined for purposes of this Code, see Family Code § 65.
Death of married person, effect on community and quasi-community property, see Probate Code § 100 et seq.
Division of quasi-marital property, see Family Code §§ 2251, 2252.
General rules regarding liability of marital property, see Family Code § 910 et seq.
Homestead property,
   General provisions, see Code of Civil Procedure §§ 704.710 et seq., 704.910 et seq.
   Administration of estates, see Probate Code § 6520 et seq.
Judgment and order defined for purposes of this Code, see Family Code § 100.
Jurisdiction,
   Community property, see Family Code § 2011.
   Superior court, see Cal. Const. Art. 6, §§ 10, 11; Family Code § 200.
Liability of marital property, see Family Code § 900 et seq.
Partition of real and personal property, see Code of Civil Procedure § 872.010 et seq.
Presumptions, nature of marital property, see Family Code §§ 802, 803.
Property defined for purposes of this Code, see Family Code § 113.
Property rights during marriage, see Family Code § 750 et seq.
Quasi-community property defined for purposes of this Code, see Family Code § 125.
State defined for purposes of this Code, see Family Code § 145.

Research References

Forms

4 California Transactions Forms--Estate Planning § 19:19, Quasi-Community Property.
West's California Code Forms, Family § 2550, Comment Overview—Manner of Division of Community Estate.
West's California Judicial Council Forms FL–160, Property Declaration (Also Available in Spanish).
West's California Judicial Council Forms FL–161, Continuation of Property Declaration.
West's California Judicial Council Forms FL–345, Property Order Attachment to Judgment (Also Available in Spanish).

Division 8

CUSTODY OF CHILDREN

Part	Section
1. Definitions and General Provisions	3000
2. Right to Custody of Minor Child	3020
3. Uniform Child Custody Jurisdiction and Enforcement Act	3400

Cross References

California Work Opportunity and Responsibility to Kids Act, see Welfare and Institutions Code § 11200 et seq.
Child support, generally, see Family Code § 3900 et seq.
Child welfare services, see Welfare and Institutions Code § 16500 et seq.
Custody agreements, modification, see Family Code § 3179.
Custody and visitation proceedings, controlled substances or alcohol abuse testing of parent, see Family Code § 3041.5.
Dependent children, custody over, juvenile court's jurisdiction, see Welfare and Institutions Code § 304.
Dependent children, supervision program, see Welfare and Institutions Code § 301.
Dependent children, temporary custody and detention, see Welfare and Institutions Code § 305.

CUSTODY OF CHILDREN

Dependent children of the juvenile court, hearing to terminate parental rights or establish guardianship, see Welfare and Institutions Code § 366.26.
District attorney, action where child taken or detained in violation of custody order, see Family Code § 3131.
Domestic violence,
  Prevention, generally, see Family Code § 6200 et seq.
  Support person for victims, see Family Code § 6303.
Family Conciliation Court Law, see Family Code § 1800 et seq.
Family mediation and conciliation services, statewide coordination, see Family Code § 1850 et seq.
Freedom from parental custody and control, stay of proceedings and effect upon jurisdiction under these provisions, see Family Code § 7807.
Guardian, appointment of, see Family Code § 7893.
Investigation and report involving custody, status, and welfare of minor, see Welfare and Institutions Code § 281.
Minor defined, see Family Code § 6500.
Order of preference for custody, best interest of child as factor to be considered, see Family Code § 3040.
Pendente lite relief of custody or visitation order on finding of parent-child relationship, see Family Code § 7604.
Presumption of joint custody, see Family Code § 3080.
Removal from custody and placement in foster home or institution, order for, see Welfare and Institutions Code § 387.
Removal of child from parental custody, preferential consideration of relative's request for placement of child with relative, see Welfare and Institutions Code § 361.3.
Spousal and child support during pendency of proceedings, see Family Code § 3600 et seq.
Support duty, actions to enforce, see Family Code § 4000.
Termination of parental rights of father, filing of petition, stay of proceedings affecting a child under these provisions pending final determination of parental rights of the father, see Family Code § 7662.
Uniform Child Custody Jurisdiction and Enforcement Act, see Family Code § 3400 et seq.
Uniform Divorce Recognition Act, see Family Code § 2090 et seq.
Uniform Interstate Enforcement of Domestic Violence Protection Orders Act, see Family Code § 6400 et seq.
Uniform Interstate Family Support Act, see Family Code § 5700.101 et seq.
Uniform Parentage Act, see Family Code § 7600 et seq.
Uniform Premarital Agreement Act, see Family Code § 1600 et seq.
Visitation rights,
  Generally, see Family Code § 3100 et seq.
  Close relatives where parent is deceased, see Family Code § 3102.
  Grandparents, see Family Code §§ 3103, 3104.
  Mediation of stepparent or grandparent visitation issues, see Family Code §§ 3171, 3178, 3185.
  Stepparents, see Family Code § 3101.

Part 1

DEFINITIONS AND GENERAL PROVISIONS

Chapter	Section
1. Definitions	3000
2. General Provisions	3010

Cross References

California Work Opportunity and Responsibility to Kids Act, see Welfare and Institutions Code § 11200 et seq.
Child support, generally, see Family Code § 3900 et seq.
Child welfare services, see Welfare and Institutions Code § 16500 et seq.
Minor defined, see Family Code § 6500.
Uniform Child Custody Jurisdiction and Enforcement Act, see Family Code § 3400 et seq.
Uniform Divorce Recognition Act, see Family Code § 2090 et seq.
Uniform Interstate Family Support Act, see Family Code § 5700.101 et seq.
Uniform Parentage Act, see Family Code § 7600 et seq.
Uniform Premarital Agreement Act, see Family Code § 1600 et seq.

CHAPTER 1. DEFINITIONS

Section
3000. Construction of division.
3002. Joint custody.
3003. Joint legal custody.
3004. Joint physical custody.
3006. Sole legal custody.
3007. Sole physical custody.

§ 3000. Construction of division

Unless the provision or context otherwise requires, the definitions in this chapter govern the construction of this division. *(Stats.1992, c. 162 (A.B.2650), § 10, operative Jan. 1, 1994.)*

Cross References

Freedom from parental custody and control, stay of proceedings and effect upon jurisdiction under these provisions, see Family Code § 7807.
Similar provisions, see Family Code § 50.

Research References

Forms

1 California Transactions Forms--Family Law § 2:70, Deciding Custody.
1 California Transactions Forms--Family Law § 3:2, Child Custody.
1 California Transactions Forms--Family Law § 3:4, Subject Matter Jurisdiction for Custody Determinations.

§ 3002. Joint custody

"Joint custody" means joint physical custody and joint legal custody. *(Stats.1992, c. 162 (A.B.2650), § 10, operative Jan. 1, 1994.)*

Cross References

California Work Opportunity and Responsibility to Kids Act, see Welfare and Institutions Code § 11200 et seq.
Child support, generally, see Family Code § 3900 et seq.
Child welfare services, see Welfare and Institutions Code § 16500 et seq.
Custody agreements, modification, see Family Code § 3179.
Custody and visitation proceedings, controlled substances or alcohol abuse testing of parent, see Family Code § 3041.5.
Dependent children, custody over, juvenile court's jurisdiction, see Welfare and Institutions Code § 304.
Dependent children, supervision program, see Welfare and Institutions Code § 301.
Dependent children, temporary custody and detention, see Welfare and Institutions Code § 305.
Dependent children of the juvenile court, hearing to terminate parental rights or establish guardianship, see Welfare and Institutions Code § 366.26.
Domestic violence,
  Prevention, generally, see Family Code § 6200 et seq.
  Support person for victims, see Family Code § 6303.
Family Conciliation Court Law, see Family Code § 1800 et seq.
Freedom from parental custody and control, see Family Code § 7800 et seq.
Guardian, appointment of, see Family Code § 7893.
Minor defined, see Family Code § 6500.
Order of preference for custody, best interest of child as factor to be considered, see Family Code § 3040.
Pendente lite relief of custody or visitation order on finding of parent-child relationship, see Family Code § 7604.
Presumption of joint custody, see Family Code § 3080.
Removal from custody and placement in foster home or institution, order for, see Welfare and Institutions Code § 387.
Removal of child from parental custody, preferential consideration of relative's request for placement of child with relative, see Welfare and Institutions Code § 361.3.
Termination of parental rights of father, see Family Code § 7662.
Uniform Child Custody Jurisdiction and Enforcement Act, see Family Code § 3400 et seq.
Visitation rights,
  Generally, see Family Code § 3100 et seq.
  Close relatives where parent is deceased, see Family Code § 3102.
  Grandparents, see Family Code §§ 3103, 3104.
  Mediation of stepparent or grandparent visitation issues, see Family Code §§ 3171, 3178, 3185.
  Stepparents, see Family Code § 3101.

DEFINITIONS AND GENERAL PROVISIONS § 3006

Research References

Forms

1 California Transactions Forms--Family Law § 2:69, Terminology of Custody.
2 California Transactions Forms--Family Law § 5:2, Overview.

§ 3003. Joint legal custody

"Joint legal custody" means that both parents shall share the right and the responsibility to make the decisions relating to the health, education, and welfare of a child. *(Stats.1992, c. 162 (A.B.2650), § 10, operative Jan. 1, 1994.)*

Cross References

California Work Opportunity and Responsibility to Kids Act, see Welfare and Institutions Code § 11200 et seq.
Child support, generally, see Family Code § 3900 et seq.
Child welfare services, see Welfare and Institutions Code § 16500 et seq.
Custody agreements, modification, see Family Code § 3179.
Custody and visitation proceedings, controlled substances or alcohol abuse testing of parent, see Family Code § 3041.5.
Dependent children, custody over, juvenile court's jurisdiction, see Welfare and Institutions Code § 304.
Dependent children, supervision program, see Welfare and Institutions Code § 301.
Dependent children, temporary custody and detention, see Welfare and Institutions Code § 305.
Dependent children of the juvenile court, hearing to terminate parental rights or establish guardianship, see Welfare and Institutions Code § 366.26.
Domestic violence,
  Prevention, generally, see Family Code § 6200 et seq.
  Support person for victims, see Family Code § 6303.
Family Conciliation Court Law, see Family Code § 1800 et seq.
Freedom from parental custody and control, see Family Code § 7800 et seq.
Guardian, appointment of, see Family Code § 7893.
Minor defined, see Family Code § 6500.
Order of preference for custody, best interest of child as factor to be considered, see Family Code § 3040.
Pendente lite relief of custody or visitation order on finding of parent-child relationship, see Family Code § 7604.
Presumption of joint custody, see Family Code § 3080.
Removal from custody and placement in foster home or institution, order for, see Welfare and Institutions Code § 387.
Removal of child from parental custody, preferential consideration of relative's request for placement of child with relative, see Welfare and Institutions Code § 361.3.
Termination of parental rights of father, see Family Code § 7662.
Uniform Child Custody Jurisdiction and Enforcement Act, see Family Code § 3400 et seq.
Visitation rights,
  Generally, see Family Code § 3100 et seq.
  Close relatives where parent is deceased, see Family Code § 3102.
  Grandparents, see Family Code §§ 3103, 3104.
  Mediation of stepparent or grandparent visitation issues, see Family Code §§ 3171, 3178, 3185.
  Stepparents, see Family Code § 3101.

Research References

Forms

1 California Transactions Forms--Family Law § 2:69, Terminology of Custody.
1 California Transactions Forms--Family Law § 3:9, Statutory Custody Definitions.
1 California Transactions Forms--Family Law § 3:15, Overview; Scope of Agreement.
1 California Transactions Forms--Family Law § 3:53, Sample Basic Custody Provisions.
2 California Transactions Forms--Family Law § 5:16, School and Extracurricular Activities; Religious Upbringing; Medical Care.
West's California Judicial Council Forms FL–341(C), Children's Holiday Schedule Attachment (Also Available in Spanish).
West's California Judicial Council Forms FL–341(D), Additional Provisions—Physical Custody Attachment (Also Available in Spanish).
West's California Judicial Council Forms FL–341(E), Joint Legal Custody Attachment (Also Available in Spanish).

§ 3004. Joint physical custody

"Joint physical custody" means that each of the parents shall have significant periods of physical custody. Joint physical custody shall be shared by the parents in such a way so as to assure a child of frequent and continuing contact with both parents, subject to Sections 3011 and 3020. *(Stats.1992, c. 162 (A.B.2650), § 10, operative Jan. 1, 1994. Amended by Stats.1997, c. 849 (A.B.200), § 1.)*

Cross References

California Work Opportunity and Responsibility to Kids Act, see Welfare and Institutions Code § 11200 et seq.
Child support, generally, see Family Code § 3900 et seq.
Child welfare services, see Welfare and Institutions Code § 16500 et seq.
Custody agreements, modification, see Family Code § 3179.
Custody and visitation proceedings, controlled substances or alcohol abuse testing of parent, see Family Code § 3041.5.
Dependent children, custody over, juvenile court's jurisdiction, see Welfare and Institutions Code § 304.
Dependent children, supervision program, see Welfare and Institutions Code § 301.
Dependent children, temporary custody and detention, see Welfare and Institutions Code § 305.
Dependent children of the juvenile court, hearing to terminate parental rights or establish guardianship, see Welfare and Institutions Code § 366.26.
Domestic violence,
  Prevention, generally, see Family Code § 6200 et seq.
  Support person for victims, see Family Code § 6303.
Family Conciliation Court Law, see Family Code § 1800 et seq.
Freedom from parental custody and control, see Family Code § 7800 et seq.
Guardian, appointment of, see Family Code § 7893.
Minor defined, see Family Code § 6500.
Order of preference for custody, best interest of child as factor to be considered, see Family Code § 3040.
Pendente lite relief of custody or visitation order on finding of parent-child relationship, see Family Code § 7604.
Presumption of joint custody, see Family Code § 3080.
Removal from custody and placement in foster home or institution, order for, see Welfare and Institutions Code § 387.
Removal of child from parental custody, preferential consideration of relative's request for placement of child with relative, see Welfare and Institutions Code § 361.3.
Termination of parental rights of father, see Family Code § 7662.
Uniform Child Custody Jurisdiction and Enforcement Act, see Family Code § 3400 et seq.
Visitation rights,
  Generally, see Family Code § 3100 et seq.
  Close relatives where parent is deceased, see Family Code § 3102.
  Grandparents, see Family Code §§ 3103, 3104.
  Mediation of stepparent or grandparent visitation issues, see Family Code §§ 3171, 3178, 3185.
  Stepparents, see Family Code § 3101.

Research References

Forms

1 California Transactions Forms--Family Law § 2:69, Terminology of Custody.
1 California Transactions Forms--Family Law § 3:18, Overview.
1 California Transactions Forms--Family Law § 3:53, Sample Basic Custody Provisions.

§ 3006. Sole legal custody

"Sole legal custody" means that one parent shall have the right and the responsibility to make the decisions relating to the health, education, and welfare of a child. *(Stats.1992, c. 162 (A.B.2650), § 10, operative Jan. 1, 1994.)*

Cross References

California Work Opportunity and Responsibility to Kids Act, see Welfare and Institutions Code § 11200 et seq.
Child support, generally, see Family Code § 3900 et seq.
Child welfare services, see Welfare and Institutions Code § 16500 et seq.
Custody agreements, modification, see Family Code § 3179.

§ 3006

Custody and visitation proceedings, controlled substances or alcohol abuse testing of parent, see Family Code § 3041.5.
Dependent children, custody over, juvenile court's jurisdiction, see Welfare and Institutions Code § 304.
Dependent children, supervision program, see Welfare and Institutions Code § 301.
Dependent children, temporary custody and detention, see Welfare and Institutions Code § 305.
Dependent children of the juvenile court, hearing to terminate parental rights or establish guardianship, see Welfare and Institutions Code § 366.26.
Domestic violence,
  Prevention, generally, see Family Code § 6200 et seq.
  Support person for victims, see Family Code § 6303.
Family Conciliation Court Law, see Family Code § 1800 et seq.
Freedom from parental custody and control, see Family Code § 7800 et seq.
Guardian, appointment of, see Family Code § 7893.
Minor defined, see Family Code § 6500.
Order of preference for custody, best interest of child as factor to be considered, see Family Code § 3040.
Pendente lite relief of custody or visitation order on finding of parent-child relationship, see Family Code § 7604.
Presumption of joint custody, see Family Code § 3080.
Removal from custody and placement in foster home or institution, order for, see Welfare and Institutions Code § 387.
Removal of child from parental custody, preferential consideration of relative's request for placement of child with relative, see Welfare and Institutions Code § 361.3.
Termination of parental rights of father, see Family Code § 7662.
Uniform Child Custody Jurisdiction and Enforcement Act, see Family Code § 3400 et seq.
Visitation rights,
  Generally, see Family Code § 3100 et seq.
  Close relatives where parent is deceased, see Family Code § 3102.
  Grandparents, see Family Code §§ 3103, 3104.
  Mediation of stepparent or grandparent visitation issues, see Family Code §§ 3171, 3178, 3185.
  Stepparents, see Family Code § 3101.

Research References

Forms

1 California Transactions Forms--Family Law § 2:69, Terminology of Custody.

§ 3007. Sole physical custody

"Sole physical custody" means that a child shall reside with and be under the supervision of one parent, subject to the power of the court to order visitation. *(Stats.1992, c. 162 (A.B.2650), § 10, operative Jan. 1, 1994.)*

Cross References

California Work Opportunity and Responsibility to Kids Act, see Welfare and Institutions Code § 11200 et seq.
Child support, generally, see Family Code § 3900 et seq.
Child welfare services, see Welfare and Institutions Code § 16500 et seq.
Custody agreements, modification, see Family Code § 3179.
Custody and visitation proceedings, controlled substances or alcohol abuse testing of parent, see Family Code § 3041.5.
Dependent children, custody over, juvenile court's jurisdiction, see Welfare and Institutions Code § 304.
Dependent children, supervision program, see Welfare and Institutions Code § 301.
Dependent children, temporary custody and detention, see Welfare and Institutions Code § 305.
Dependent children of the juvenile court, hearing to terminate parental rights or establish guardianship, see Welfare and Institutions Code § 366.26.
Domestic violence,
  Prevention, generally, see Family Code § 6200 et seq.
  Support person for victims, see Family Code § 6303.
Family Conciliation Court Law, see Family Code § 1800 et seq.
Freedom from parental custody and control, see Family Code § 7800 et seq.
Guardian, appointment of, see Family Code § 7893.
Judgment and order defined for purposes of this Code, see Family Code § 100.
Minor defined, see Family Code § 6500.
Order of preference for custody, best interest of child as factor to be considered, see Family Code § 3040.

Pendente lite relief of custody or visitation order on finding of parent-child relationship, see Family Code § 7604.
Presumption of joint custody, see Family Code § 3080.
Removal from custody and placement in foster home or institution, order for, see Welfare and Institutions Code § 387.
Removal of child from parental custody, preferential consideration of relative's request for placement of child with relative, see Welfare and Institutions Code § 361.3.
Termination of parental rights of father, see Family Code § 7662.
Uniform Child Custody Jurisdiction and Enforcement Act, see Family Code § 3400 et seq.
Visitation rights,
  Generally, see Family Code § 3100 et seq.
  Close relatives where parent is deceased, see Family Code § 3102.
  Grandparents, see Family Code §§ 3103, 3104.
  Mediation of stepparent or grandparent visitation issues, see Family Code §§ 3171, 3178, 3185.
  Stepparents, see Family Code § 3101.

Research References

Forms

1 California Transactions Forms--Family Law § 2:69, Terminology of Custody.
1 California Transactions Forms--Family Law § 3:9, Statutory Custody Definitions.
2 California Transactions Forms--Family Law § 5:2, Overview.

CHAPTER 2. GENERAL PROVISIONS

Section
3010. Custody of unemancipated minor children.
3011. Best interests of child; considerations.
3012. Use of telepresence in child custody proceedings.
3013 to 3018. Inoperative.

§ 3010. Custody of unemancipated minor children

(a) The mother of an unemancipated minor child and the father, if presumed to be the father under Section 7611, are equally entitled to the custody of the child.

(b) If one parent is dead, is unable or refuses to take custody, or has abandoned the child, the other parent is entitled to custody of the child. *(Added by Stats.1993, c. 219 (A.B.1500), § 115.5.)*

Cross References

California Work Opportunity and Responsibility to Kids Act, see Welfare and Institutions Code § 11200 et seq.
Child support, generally, see Family Code § 3900 et seq.
Child welfare services, see Welfare and Institutions Code § 16500 et seq.
Custody agreements, modification, see Family Code § 3179.
Custody and visitation proceedings, controlled substances or alcohol abuse testing of parent, see Family Code § 3041.5.
Dependent children, custody over, juvenile court's jurisdiction, see Welfare and Institutions Code § 304.
Dependent children, supervision program, see Welfare and Institutions Code § 301.
Dependent children, temporary custody and detention, see Welfare and Institutions Code § 305.
Dependent children of the juvenile court, hearing to terminate parental rights or establish guardianship, see Welfare and Institutions Code § 366.26.
Domestic violence,
  Prevention, generally, see Family Code § 6200 et seq.
  Support person for victims, see Family Code § 6303.
Earnings, payment to minor, see Family Code § 7503.
Emancipation of child, conditions, see Family Code § 7002.
Family Conciliation Court Law, see Family Code § 1800 et seq.
Freedom from parental custody and control, see Family Code § 7800 et seq.
Guardian, appointment of, see Family Code § 7893.
Juvenile court, jurisdiction over children's care and custody, see Welfare and Institutions Code § 300.
Minor defined for purposes of this Code, see Family Code § 6500.
Order of preference for custody, best interest of child as factor to be considered, see Family Code § 3040.
Pendente lite relief of custody or visitation order on finding of parent-child relationship, see Family Code § 7604.

Presumption of joint custody, see Family Code § 3080.
Relinquishment of parental right of controlling child and receiving earnings, see Family Code § 7504.
Removal from custody and placement in foster home or institution, order for, see Welfare and Institutions Code § 387.
Removal of child from parental custody, preferential consideration of relative's request for placement of child with relative, see Welfare and Institutions Code § 361.3.
Termination of parental rights of father, see Family Code § 7662.
Uniform Child Custody Jurisdiction and Enforcement Act, see Family Code § 3400 et seq.
Uniform Parentage Act, see Family Code § 7600 et seq.
Visitation rights,
  Generally, see Family Code § 3100 et seq.
  Close relatives where parent is deceased, see Family Code § 3102.
  Grandparents, see Family Code §§ 3103, 3104.
  Mediation of stepparent or grandparent visitation issues, see Family Code §§ 3171, 3178, 3185.
  Stepparents, see Family Code § 3101.

Research References

Forms

2 California Transactions Forms--Family Law § 5:2, Overview.

§ 3011. Best interests of child; considerations

(a) In making a determination of the best interests of the child in a proceeding described in Section 3021, the court shall, among any other factors it finds relevant and consistent with Section 3020, consider all of the following:

(1) The health, safety, and welfare of the child.

(2)(A) A history of abuse by one parent or any other person seeking custody against any of the following:

(i) A child to whom the parent or person seeking custody is related by blood or affinity or with whom the parent or person seeking custody has had a caretaking relationship, no matter how temporary.

(ii) The other parent.

(iii) A parent, current spouse, or cohabitant, of the parent or person seeking custody, or a person with whom the parent or person seeking custody has a dating or engagement relationship.

(B) As a prerequisite to considering allegations of abuse, the court may require independent corroboration, including, but not limited to, written reports by law enforcement agencies, child protective services or other social welfare agencies, courts, medical facilities, or other public agencies or private nonprofit organizations providing services to victims of sexual assault or domestic violence. As used in this paragraph, "abuse against a child" means "child abuse and neglect" as defined in Section 11165.6 of the Penal Code and abuse against any other person described in clause (ii) or (iii) of subparagraph (A) means "abuse" as defined in Section 6203.

(3) The nature and amount of contact with both parents, except as provided in Section 3046.

(4) The habitual or continual illegal use of controlled substances, the habitual or continual abuse of alcohol, or the habitual or continual abuse of prescribed controlled substances by either parent. Before considering these allegations, the court may first require independent corroboration, including, but not limited to, written reports from law enforcement agencies, courts, probation departments, social welfare agencies, medical facilities, rehabilitation facilities, or other public agencies or nonprofit organizations providing drug and alcohol abuse services. As used in this paragraph, "controlled substances" has the same meaning as defined in the California Uniform Controlled Substances Act (Division 10 (commencing with Section 11000) of the Health and Safety Code).

(5)(A) When allegations about a parent pursuant to paragraph (2) or (4) have been brought to the attention of the court in the current proceeding, and the court makes an order for sole or joint custody or unsupervised visitation to that parent, the court shall state its reasons in writing or on the record. In these circumstances, the court shall ensure that any order regarding custody or visitation is specific as to time, day, place, and manner of transfer of the child as set forth in subdivision (c) of Section 6323.

(B) This paragraph does not apply if the parties stipulate in writing or on the record regarding custody or visitation.

(b) Notwithstanding subdivision (a), the court shall not consider the sex, gender identity, gender expression, or sexual orientation of a parent, legal guardian, or relative in determining the best interests of the child. (Added by Stats.1993, c. 219 (A.B.1500), § 115.5. Amended by Stats.1996, c. 835 (A.B.2474), § 1; Stats.1996, c. 836 (S.B.384), § 1.5; Stats.1997, c. 849 (A.B.200), § 2; Stats.1999, c. 980 (A.B. 1671), § 4; Stats.2012, c. 258 (A.B.2365), § 1; Stats.2018, c. 941 (A.B.2044), § 1, eff. Jan. 1, 2019; Stats.2019, c. 115 (A.B.1817), § 23, eff. Jan. 1, 2020; Stats.2019, c. 551 (S.B.495), § 1, eff. Jan. 1, 2020; Stats.2020, c. 370 (S.B.1371), § 115, eff. Jan. 1, 2021; Stats.2021, c. 768 (S.B.654), § 1, eff. Jan. 1, 2022; Stats.2022, c. 28 (S.B.1380), § 45, eff. Jan. 1, 2023.)

Cross References

Abuse defined for purposes of the Domestic Violence Prevention Act, see Family Code § 6203.
Affinity defined for purposes of this Code, see Family Code § 6205.
Child welfare services, see Welfare and Institutions Code § 16500 et seq.
Custody and visitation proceedings, controlled substances or alcohol abuse testing of parent, see Family Code § 3041.5.
Custody of children, presumption against person perpetrating domestic violence, see Family Code § 3044.
Dependent children, custody over, juvenile court's jurisdiction, see Welfare and Institutions Code § 304.
Dependent children, supervision program, see Welfare and Institutions Code § 301.
Dependent children, temporary custody and detention, see Welfare and Institutions Code § 305.
Dependent children of the juvenile court, hearing to terminate parental rights or establish guardianship, see Welfare and Institutions Code § 366.26.
Determination of child's residence for purpose of public assistance, see Welfare and Institutions Code § 11102.
Domestic violence,
  Defined for purposes of this Code, see Family Code § 6211.
  Prevention, generally, see Family Code § 6200 et seq.
  Support person for victims, see Family Code § 6303.
Guardian, fixing residence of ward, see Probate Code § 2352.
Information available for juvenile court proceedings regarding best interest of child, see Welfare and Institutions Code § 204.
Information available for probate guardianship proceeding and guardianship investigator regarding best interest of child, confidentiality, see Probate Code § 1514.5.
Joint custody orders, visitation rights, and domestic and violence prevention orders, see Family Code § 3044.
Judgment and order defined for purposes of this Code, see Family Code § 100.
Order of preference for custody, best interest of child as factor, see Family Code § 3040.
Orders, restraining removal of child from state, see Family Code § 3063.
Pendente lite relief of custody or visitation order on finding of parent-child relationship, see Family Code § 7604.
Person defined for purposes of this Code, see Family Code § 105.
Presumption of joint custody, see Family Code § 3080.
Proceeding defined for purposes of this Code, see Family Code § 110.
References to husband, wife, spouses and married persons, persons included for purposes of this Code, see Family Code § 11.
Removal from custody and placement in foster home or institution, order for, see Welfare and Institutions Code § 387.
Removal of child from parental custody, preferential consideration of relative's request for placement of child with relative, see Welfare and Institutions Code § 361.3.
Rules determining residence of minors, see Government Code § 244; Welfare and Institutions Code § 17.1.
State defined for purposes of this Code, see Family Code § 145.
Termination of parental rights of father, see Family Code § 7662.
Uniform Child Custody Jurisdiction and Enforcement Act, see Family Code § 3400 et seq.
Visitation rights,
  Generally, see Family Code § 3100 et seq.

§ 3011

Close relatives where parent is deceased, see Family Code § 3102.
Grandparents, see Family Code §§ 3103, 3104.
Mediation of stepparent or grandparent visitation issues, see Family Code §§ 3171, 3178, 3185.
Stepparents, see Family Code § 3101.
Writings, authentication and proof of, see Evidence Code § 1400 et seq.

Research References

Forms

California Practice Guide: Rutter Family Law Forms Form 1:32, Glossary of Common Family Law Terms, Phrases and Concepts (Enclosure to Form 1:31).
California Practice Guide: Rutter Family Law Forms Form 5:5, Ex Parte Application and Request for Order Re Child Custody, Visitation and Property Control.
California Practice Guide: Rutter Family Law Forms Form 7:19.2, Request for Order Re Move-Away Request.
1 California Transactions Forms--Family Law § 2:70, Deciding Custody.
1 California Transactions Forms--Family Law § 2:76, Drug and Alcohol Use.
1 California Transactions Forms--Family Law § 3:2, Child Custody.
1 California Transactions Forms--Family Law § 3:8, No Statutory Custody Preferences.
1 California Transactions Forms--Family Law § 3:11, Permanent Custody.
1 California Transactions Forms--Family Law § 3:16, Identifying Areas of Parental Decision Making and Participation.
2 California Transactions Forms--Family Law § 5:2, Overview.
West's California Code Forms, Family § 3120, Comment Overview—Action for Exclusive Custody.
West's California Judicial Council Forms GC-212, Confidential Guardian Screening Form.

§ 3012. Use of telepresence in child custody proceedings

(a) If a party's deportation or detention by the United States Immigration and Customs Enforcement of the Department of Homeland Security will have a material effect on the person's ability, or anticipated ability, to appear in person at a child custody proceeding, the court shall, upon motion of the party, allow the party to present testimony and evidence and participate in mandatory child custody mediation by electronic means, including, but not limited to, telephone, video teleconferencing, or other electronic means that provide remote access to the hearing, to the extent that this technology is reasonably available to the court and protects the due process rights of all parties.

(b) This section does not authorize the use of electronic recording for the purpose of taking the official record of these proceedings.
(Added by Stats.2015, c. 69 (A.B.365), § 1, eff. Jan. 1, 2016. Amended by Stats.2019, c. 115 (A.B.1817), § 24, eff. Jan. 1, 2020.)

§§ 3013 to 3018. Inoperative

Part 2

RIGHT TO CUSTODY OF MINOR CHILD

Chapter	Section
1. General Provisions	3020
2. Matters to be Considered in Granting Custody	3040
3. Temporary Custody Order During Pendency of Proceeding	3060
4. Joint Custody	3080
5. Visitation Rights	3100
6. Custody Investigation and Report	3110
7. Action for Exclusive Custody	3120
8. Location of Missing Party or Child	3130
9. Check to Determine Whether Child is Missing Person	3140
10. Appointment of Counsel to Represent Child	3150
11. Mediation of Custody and Visitation Issues	3160
12. Counseling of Parents and Child	3190
13. Supervised Visitation and Exchange Services, Education, and Counseling	3200

Cross References

Adoption, generally, see Family Code § 8500 et seq.
Adoption proceedings, termination of parental rights, see Family Code § 7664 et seq.
Best interests of child, considerations, see Family Code § 3011.
California Work Opportunity and Responsibility to Kids Act, see Welfare and Institutions Code § 11200 et seq.
Child support, generally, see Family Code § 3900 et seq.
Child welfare services, see Welfare and Institutions Code § 16500 et seq.
Custody and visitation proceedings, controlled substances or alcohol abuse testing of parent, see Family Code § 3041.5.
Dependent children, custody over, juvenile court's jurisdiction, see Welfare and Institutions Code § 304.
Dependent children, judgments and orders, determinations prior to order for removal, see Welfare and Institutions Code § 361.2.
Domestic violence,
 Defined for purposes of this Code, see Family Code § 6211.
 Prevention, generally, see Family Code § 6200 et seq.
 Support person for victims, see Family Code § 6303.
Guardian, appointment of, see Family Code § 7893.
Marital dissolution and separation, generally, see Family Code § 2300 et seq.
Mediation of custody and visitation issues, modification of agreements, see Family Code § 3179.
Minor defined, see Family Code § 6500.
Order of preference for custody, best interest of child as factor to be considered, see Family Code § 3040.
Parental Kidnapping Prevention Act, see Family Code § 3134.5.
Parental rights to services and earnings of child, see Family Code § 7500.
Pendente lite relief of custody or visitation order on finding of parent-child relationship, see Family Code § 7604.
Presumption of joint custody, see Family Code § 3080.
Removal from custody and placement in foster home or institution, order for, see Welfare and Institutions Code § 387.
Removal of child from custody of parents, preferential consideration of relative's request for placement of child with relative, see Welfare and Institutions Code § 361.3.
Termination of parental rights of father, see Family Code § 7662.
Uniform Child Custody Jurisdiction and Enforcement Act, see Family Code § 3400 et seq.
Visitation rights,
 Generally, see Family Code § 3100 et seq.
 Close relatives where parent is deceased, see Family Code § 3102.
 Grandparents, see Family Code §§ 3103, 3104.
 Mediation of stepparent or grandparent visitation issues, see Family Code §§ 3171, 3178, 3185.
 Stepparents, see Family Code § 3101.

CHAPTER 1. GENERAL PROVISIONS

Section	
3020.	Legislative findings and declarations; public policy.
3021.	Application of part.
3022.	Order for custody.
3022.3.	Statement of decision.
3022.5.	Motion by parent for reconsideration of child custody order after conviction of spouse for false accusation of child abuse against parent.
3023.	Sole contested issue or order for separate trial on issue; preference for trial date.
3024.	Notice to other parent of change of residence of child.
3025.	Parental access to records.
3025.5.	Psychological evaluations of children; confidentiality; exceptions; confidential information contained in child custody evaluation reports.
3026.	Family reunification services.
3027.	Allegations of child abuse or child sexual abuse.
3027.1.	False accusations of child abuse or neglect during child custody proceedings; knowledge; penalties.

RIGHT TO CUSTODY OF MINOR CHILD § 3020

Section
- 3027.5. Sexual abuse of child; report or treatment; limitations on custody or visitation.
- 3028. Compensation; failure to assume caretaker responsibility; thwarting of other parent's visitation or custody rights; attorney's fees.
- 3029. Noncustodial parent's liability for support if custodial parent is receiving AFDC assistance; order.
- 3030. Sex offenders; murderers; custody and visitation; child support; disclosure of information relating to custodial parent.
- 3030.5. Modification or termination of order for physical or legal custody or unsupervised visitation order; sex offenders required to be registered.
- 3031. Protective or restraining orders; findings; transfer of children; detail specific custody or visitation orders; required presence of third party.
- 3032. Pilot program to provide interpreter in child custody or protective order cases; lack of English proficiency and financial ability of party; report to Legislature.

Cross References
Appointment of guardian, see Probate Code § 1514.

§ 3020. Legislative findings and declarations; public policy

(a) The Legislature finds and declares that it is the public policy of this state to ensure that the health, safety, and welfare of children shall be the court's primary concern in determining the best interests of children when making any orders regarding the physical or legal custody or visitation of children. The Legislature further finds and declares that children have the right to be safe and free from abuse, and that the perpetration of child abuse or domestic violence in a household where a child resides is detrimental to the health, safety, and welfare of the child.

(b) The Legislature finds and declares that it is the public policy of this state to ensure that children have frequent and continuing contact with both parents after the parents have separated or dissolved their marriage, or ended their relationship, and to encourage parents to share the rights and responsibilities of child rearing in order to effect this policy, except when the contact would not be in the best interests of the child, as provided in subdivisions (a) and (c) of this section and Section 3011.

(c) When the policies set forth in subdivisions (a) and (b) of this section are in conflict, a court's order regarding physical or legal custody or visitation shall be made in a manner that ensures the health, safety, and welfare of the child and the safety of all family members.

(d) The Legislature finds and declares that it is the public policy of this state to ensure that the sex, gender identity, gender expression, or sexual orientation of a parent, legal guardian, or relative is not considered in determining the best interests of the child. (Stats.1992, c. 162 (A.B.2650), § 10, operative Jan. 1, 1994. Amended by Stats.1993, c. 219 (A.B.1500), § 116; Stats.1997, c. 849 (A.B.200), § 3; Stats.1999, c. 980 (A.B.1671), § 5; Stats.2018, c. 941 (A.B.2044), § 2, eff. Jan. 1, 2019; Stats.2019, c. 551 (S.B.495), § 2, eff. Jan. 1, 2020.)

Cross References
Abuse defined for purposes of the Domestic Violence Prevention Act, see Family Code § 6203.
Adoption, generally, see Family Code § 8500 et seq.
Adoption proceedings, termination of parental rights, see Family Code § 7664 et seq.
Best interests of child, considerations, see Family Code § 3011.
California Work Opportunity and Responsibility to Kids Act, see Welfare and Institutions Code § 11200 et seq.
Child support, generally, see Family Code § 3900 et seq.
Child welfare services, see Welfare and Institutions Code § 16500 et seq.
Custody and visitation proceedings, controlled substances or alcohol abuse testing of parent, see Family Code § 3041.5.
Custody of children, presumption against person perpetrating domestic violence, see Family Code § 3044.
Custody of unemancipated minor children, generally, see Family Code § 3010.
Dependent children, custody over, juvenile court's jurisdiction, see Welfare and Institutions Code § 304.
Dependent children, supervision program, see Welfare and Institutions Code § 301.
Dependent children, temporary custody and detention, see Welfare and Institutions Code § 305.
Dependent children of the juvenile court, hearing to terminate parental rights or establish guardianship, see Welfare and Institutions Code § 366.26.
Domestic violence,
  Defined for purposes of this Code, see Family Code § 6211.
  Prevention, generally, see Family Code § 6200 et seq.
  Support person for victims, see Family Code § 6303.
Family Conciliation Court Law, see Family Code § 1800 et seq.
Family mediation and conciliation services, statewide coordination, see Family Code § 1850 et seq.
Freedom from parental custody and control, see Family Code § 7800 et seq.
Guardian, appointment of, see Family Code § 7893.
Guardianship proceedings, exclusive jurisdiction, consolidation with visitation and custody cases, see Probate Code § 2204.
Inapplicability of law, proceedings for declaration of freedom from parental custody and control, see Family Code § 7807.
Joint custody orders, visitation rights, and domestic and violence prevention orders, see Family Code § 3044.
Judgment and order defined for purposes of this Code, see Family Code § 100.
Marital dissolution and separation, generally, see Family Code § 2300 et seq.
Mediation of custody and visitation issues, modification of agreements, see Family Code § 3179.
Minor defined, see Family Code § 6500.
Order of preference for custody, best interest of child as factor to be considered, see Family Code § 3040.
Parental rights to services and earnings of child, see Family Code § 7500.
Pendente lite relief of custody or visitation order on finding of parent-child relationship, see Family Code § 7604.
Presumption of joint custody, see Family Code § 3080.
Removal from custody and placement in foster home or institution, order for, see Welfare and Institutions Code § 387.
State defined for purposes of this Code, see Family Code § 145.
Termination of parental rights of father, see Family Code § 7662.
Uniform Child Custody Jurisdiction and Enforcement Act, see Family Code § 3400 et seq.
Visitation rights,
  Generally, see Family Code § 3100 et seq.
  Close relatives where parent is deceased, see Family Code § 3102.
  Grandparents, see Family Code §§ 3103, 3104.
Mediation of stepparent or grandparent visitation issues, see Family Code §§ 3171, 3178, 3185.
Stepparents, see Family Code § 3101.

Research References
Forms
California Practice Guide: Rutter Family Law Forms Form 1:32, Glossary of Common Family Law Terms, Phrases and Concepts (Enclosure to Form 1:31).
California Practice Guide: Rutter Family Law Forms Form 5:2, Request for Order Re Child Custody, Child Support, Spousal Support, Attorney Fees, etc.
California Practice Guide: Rutter Family Law Forms Form 5:5, Ex Parte Application and Request for Order Re Child Custody, Visitation and Property Control.
1 California Transactions Forms--Family Law § 2:70, Deciding Custody.
1 California Transactions Forms--Family Law § 3:2, Child Custody.
1 California Transactions Forms--Family Law § 3:4, Subject Matter Jurisdiction for Custody Determinations.
1 California Transactions Forms--Family Law § 3:8, No Statutory Custody Preferences.
1 California Transactions Forms--Family Law § 3:11, Permanent Custody.
1 California Transactions Forms--Family Law § 4:104, Paternity Acknowledgment.
2 California Transactions Forms--Family Law § 5:2, Overview.
2 California Transactions Forms--Family Law § 5:3, Rights of Nonparents Generally.

§ 3020

2 California Transactions Forms--Family Law § 5:9, Use of Parenting Agreement to Define Rights and Responsibilities Relating to Child on Termination of Partners' Relationship Where Both Partners Are Biological Parents.

West's California Code Forms, Family § 3022, Comment Overview—Order for Custody.

West's California Code Forms, Family § 7841 Form 1, Petition for Freedom from Parental Control—Abandonment.

West's California Code Forms, Probate § 1514 Form 1, Order Appointing Guardian of Minor—Judicial Council Form GC-240.

West's California Judicial Council Forms DV-140, Child Custody and Visitation Order (Also Available in Chinese, Korean, Spanish, and Vietnamese).

West's California Judicial Council Forms FL-341, Child Custody and Visitation (Parenting Time) Order Attachment (Also Available in Spanish).

West's California Judicial Council Forms FL-356, Confidential Request for Special Immigrant Juvenile Findings—Family Law (Also Available in Spanish).

West's California Judicial Council Forms JV-200, Custody Order—Juvenile—Final Judgment (Also Available in Spanish).

West's California Judicial Council Forms JV-205, Visitation Order—Juvenile (Also Available in Spanish).

§ 3021. Application of part

This part applies in any of the following:

(a) A proceeding for dissolution of marriage.

(b) A proceeding for nullity of marriage.

(c) A proceeding for legal separation of the parties.

(d) An action for exclusive custody pursuant to Section 3120.

(e) A proceeding to determine physical or legal custody or for visitation in a proceeding pursuant to the Domestic Violence Prevention Act (Division 10 (commencing with Section 6200)).

In an action under Section 6323, nothing in this subdivision shall be construed to authorize physical or legal custody, or visitation rights, to be granted to any party to a Domestic Violence Prevention Act proceeding who has not established a parent and child relationship pursuant to paragraph (2) of subdivision (a) of Section 6323.

(f) A proceeding to determine physical or legal custody or visitation in an action pursuant to the Uniform Parentage Act (Part 3 (commencing with Section 7600) of Division 12).

(g) A proceeding to determine physical or legal custody or visitation in an action brought by the district attorney pursuant to Section 17404. *(Added by Stats.1993, c. 219 (A.B.1500), § 116.11. Amended by Stats.1996, c. 1075 (S.B.1444), § 9; Stats.1997, c. 396 (S.B.564), § 1; Stats.1999, c. 980 (A.B.1671), § 6; Stats.2000, c. 135 (A.B.2539), § 58.)*

Cross References

Best interests of child, considerations, see Family Code § 3011.
Custody and visitation proceedings, controlled substances or alcohol abuse testing of parent, see Family Code § 3041.5.
District attorney, powers and duties, see Government Code § 26500 et seq.
Domestic violence,
  Defined for purposes of this Code, see Family Code § 6211.
  Prevention, generally, see Family Code § 6200 et seq.
  Support person for victims, see Family Code § 6303.
Guardianship proceedings, custody or visitation proceedings pending in more than one court, determination of venue, see Probate Code § 2204.
Juvenile court law, assumption of jurisdiction regardless of custody by one or both parents, see Welfare and Institutions Code § 302.
Marital dissolution and separation, generally, see Family Code § 2300 et seq.
Order of preference for custody, best interest of child as factor to be considered, see Family Code § 3040.
Proceeding defined for purposes of this Code, see Family Code § 110.
Uniform Child Custody Jurisdiction and Enforcement Act, see Family Code § 3400 et seq.
Visitation rights,
  Generally, see Family Code § 3100 et seq.
  Close relatives where parent is deceased, see Family Code § 3102.
  Grandparents, see Family Code §§ 3103, 3104.

Mediation of stepparent or grandparent visitation issues, see Family Code §§ 3171, 3178, 3185.
Stepparents, see Family Code § 3101.

Research References

Forms

California Practice Guide: Rutter Family Law Forms Form 5:5, Ex Parte Application and Request for Order Re Child Custody, Visitation and Property Control.

California Practice Guide: Rutter Family Law Forms Form 7:17, Notice of Motion and Declaration for Joinder (Grandparent Visitation Claim).

California Practice Guide: Rutter Family Law Forms Form 7:18, Complaint for Joinder (Grandparent Visitation Claim).

California Practice Guide: Rutter Family Law Forms Form 7:19, Memorandum in Support of Motion and Declaration for Joinder (Grandparent Visitation Claim).

1 California Transactions Forms--Family Law § 3:4, Subject Matter Jurisdiction for Custody Determinations.

2 California Transactions Forms--Family Law § 5:2, Overview.

§ 3022. Order for custody

The court may, during the pendency of a proceeding or at any time thereafter, make an order for the custody of a child during minority that seems necessary or proper. *(Formerly § 3021, enacted by Stats.1992, c. 162 (A.B.2650), § 10, operative Jan. 1, 1994. Renumbered § 3022 and amended by Stats.1993, c. 219 (A.B.1500), § 116.12.)*

Cross References

Appeals, court orders not automatically stayed by, see Code of Civil Procedure § 917.7.
Best interests of child, considerations, see Family Code § 3011.
Child welfare services, see Welfare and Institutions Code § 16500 et seq.
Custody agreements, modification, see Family Code § 3179.
Custody and visitation proceedings, controlled substances or alcohol abuse testing of parent, see Family Code § 3041.5.
Custody of unemancipated minor children, generally, see Family Code § 3010.
Dependent children, custody over, juvenile court's jurisdiction, see Welfare and Institutions Code § 304.
Dependent children, supervision program, see Welfare and Institutions Code § 301.
Dependent children, temporary custody and detention, see Welfare and Institutions Code § 305.
Dependent children of the juvenile court, hearing to terminate parental rights or establish guardianship, see Welfare and Institutions Code § 366.26.
Domestic violence,
  Defined for purposes of this Code, see Family Code § 6211.
  Prevention, generally, see Family Code § 6200 et seq.
  Support person for victims, see Family Code § 6303.
Freedom from parental custody and control, see Family Code § 7800 et seq.
Guardian, appointment of, see Family Code § 7893.
Inapplicability of law, proceedings for declaration of freedom from parental custody and control, see Family Code § 7807.
Judgment and order defined for purposes of this Code, see Family Code § 100.
Marital dissolution and separation, generally, see Family Code § 2300 et seq.
Mediation of custody and visitation issues, modification of agreements, see Family Code § 3179.
Minor defined, see Family Code § 6500.
Order of preference for custody, best interest of child as factor to be considered, see Family Code § 3040.
Parental rights to services and earnings of child, see Family Code § 7500.
Pendente lite relief of custody or visitation order on finding of parent-child relationship, see Family Code § 7604.
Petitions, existence of child support, child custody, visitation, or spousal support orders, personal conduct restraining order, or bifurcated case, dismissal for delay in prosecution prohibited, see Code of Civil Procedure § 583.161.
Presumption of joint custody, see Family Code § 3080.
Proceeding defined for purposes of this Code, see Family Code § 110.
Removal from custody and placement in foster home or institution, order for, see Welfare and Institutions Code § 387.
Spousal and child support during pendency of proceeding, see Family Code § 3600 et seq.
Termination of parental rights of father, see Family Code § 7662.
Uniform Child Custody Jurisdiction and Enforcement Act, see Family Code § 3400 et seq.

Uniform Parentage Act, see Family Code § 7600 et seq.
Uniform Premarital Agreement Act, see Family Code § 1600 et seq.
Visitation rights,
  Generally, see Family Code § 3100 et seq.
  Close relatives where parent is deceased, see Family Code § 3102.
  Grandparents, see Family Code §§ 3103, 3104.
  Mediation of stepparent or grandparent visitation issues, see Family Code §§ 3171, 3178, 3185.
  Stepparents, see Family Code § 3101.

Research References
Forms

California Practice Guide: Rutter Family Law Forms Form 5:2, Request for Order Re Child Custody, Child Support, Spousal Support, Attorney Fees, etc.
California Practice Guide: Rutter Family Law Forms Form 5:5, Ex Parte Application and Request for Order Re Child Custody, Visitation and Property Control.
California Practice Guide: Rutter Family Law Forms Form 17:5, Request for Order Re Modification of Child Custody, Visitation and Child Support.
1 California Transactions Forms--Family Law § 2:70, Deciding Custody.
1 California Transactions Forms--Family Law § 3:2, Child Custody.
1 California Transactions Forms--Family Law § 3:11, Permanent Custody.
West's California Code Forms, Family § 3022, Comment Overview—Order for Custody.
West's California Code Forms, Family § 7841 Form 1, Petition for Freedom from Parental Control—Abandonment.
West's California Judicial Council Forms DV-140, Child Custody and Visitation Order (Also Available in Chinese, Korean, Spanish, and Vietnamese).
West's California Judicial Council Forms FL-341, Child Custody and Visitation (Parenting Time) Order Attachment (Also Available in Spanish).

§ 3022.3. Statement of decision

Upon the trial of the question of fact in a proceeding to determine the custody of a minor child, the court shall, upon the request of either party, issue a statement of the decision explaining the factual and legal basis for its decision pursuant to Section 632 of the Code of Civil Procedure. *(Added by Stats.2006, c. 496 (A.B.402), § 3.)*

§ 3022.5. Motion by parent for reconsideration of child custody order after conviction of spouse for false accusation of child abuse against parent

A motion by a parent for reconsideration of an existing child custody order shall be granted if the motion is based on the fact that the other parent was convicted of a crime in connection with falsely accusing the moving parent of child abuse. *(Added by Stats.1995, c. 406 (S.B.558), § 1.)*

Cross References

Best interests of child, considerations, see Family Code § 3011.
Domestic violence,
  Abuse defined for purposes of the Domestic Violence Prevention Act, see Family Code § 6203.
  Defined for purposes of this Code, see Family Code § 6211.
  Prevention, generally, see Family Code § 6200 et seq.
  Support person for victims, see Family Code § 6303.
Judgment and order defined for purposes of this Code, see Family Code § 100.
Marital dissolution and separation, generally, see Family Code § 2300 et seq.
Parent convicted under certain Penal Code provisions, see Family Code § 3030.
Perjury and subornation of perjury, see Penal Code § 118 et seq.
Sending minors to immoral places, see Penal Code § 273f.
Society for prevention of cruelty to children, prosecutions by, see Penal Code § 273c.
Uniform Interstate Enforcement of Domestic Violence Protection Orders Act, see Family Code § 6400 et seq.
Willful cruelty or unjustifiable punishment of child, see Penal Code § 273a.

Research References
Forms

West's California Code Forms, Family § 3022, Comment Overview—Order for Custody.

§ 3023. Sole contested issue or order for separate trial on issue; preference for trial date

(a) If custody of a minor child is the sole contested issue, the case shall be given preference over other civil cases, except matters to which special precedence may be given by law, for assigning a trial date and shall be given an early hearing.

(b) If there is more than one contested issue and one of the issues is the custody of a minor child, the court, as to the issue of custody, shall order a separate trial. The separate trial shall be given preference over other civil cases, except matters to which special precedence may be given by law, for assigning a trial date. *(Stats. 1992, c. 162 (A.B.2650), § 10, operative Jan. 1, 1994. Amended by Stats.1993, c. 219 (A.B.1500), § 116.14.)*

Cross References

Best interests of child, considerations, see Family Code § 3011.
Child support, separate trial on issue, see Family Code § 4003.
Custody agreements, modification, see Family Code § 3179.
Custody and visitation proceedings, controlled substances or alcohol abuse testing of parent, see Family Code § 3041.5.
Custody of unemancipated minor children, generally, see Family Code § 3010.
Dependent children, custody over, juvenile court's jurisdiction, see Welfare and Institutions Code § 304.
Dependent children, supervision program, see Welfare and Institutions Code § 301.
Dependent children, temporary custody and detention, see Welfare and Institutions Code § 305.
Domestic violence, support person for victims, see Family Code § 6303.
Hearing on award of custody to nonparent, excluding public, see Family Code § 3041.
Judgment and order defined for purposes of this Code, see Family Code § 100.
Marital dissolution and separation, generally, see Family Code § 2300 et seq.
Mediation of custody and visitation issues, modification of agreements, see Family Code § 3179.
Minor defined, see Family Code § 6500.
Order of preference for custody, best interest of child as factor to be considered, see Family Code § 3040.
Spousal and child support during pendency of proceeding, see Family Code § 3600 et seq.
Termination of parental rights of father, see Family Code § 7662.

§ 3024. Notice to other parent of change of residence of child

In making an order for custody, if the court does not consider it inappropriate, the court may specify that a parent shall notify the other parent if the parent plans to change the residence of the child for more than 30 days, unless there is prior written agreement to the removal. The notice shall be given before the contemplated move, by mail, return receipt requested, postage prepaid, to the last known address of the parent to be notified. A copy of the notice shall also be sent to that parent's counsel of record. To the extent feasible, the notice shall be provided within a minimum of 45 days before the proposed change of residence so as to allow time for mediation of a new agreement concerning custody. This section does not affect orders made before January 1, 1989. *(Stats.1992, c. 162 (A.B.2650), § 10, operative Jan. 1, 1994.)*

Cross References

Arbitration, generally, see Code of Civil Procedure § 1281 et seq.
California Work Opportunity and Responsibility to Kids Act, see Welfare and Institutions Code § 11200 et seq.
Child welfare services, see Welfare and Institutions Code § 16500 et seq.
Computation of time, see Code of Civil Procedure §§ 12, 12a; Government Code § 6800 et seq.
Conciliation proceedings, generally, see Family Code § 1800 et seq.

§ 3024

Counsel, right to, see Cal. Const. Art. 1, § 15, cl. 3.
Custody of unemancipated minor children, generally, see Family Code § 3010.
Dependent children, custody over, juvenile court's jurisdiction, see Welfare and Institutions Code § 304.
District attorney, action where child taken or detained in violation of custody order, see Family Code § 3131.
Family mediation and conciliation services, statewide coordination, see Family Code § 1850 et seq.
Judgment and order defined for purposes of this Code, see Family Code § 100.
Mediation of custody and visitation issues, generally, see Family Code § 3160 et seq.
Notice, actual and constructive, defined, see Civil Code § 18.
Uniform Child Custody Jurisdiction and Enforcement Act, see Family Code § 3400 et seq.
Uniform Interstate Enforcement of Domestic Violence Protection Orders Act, see Family Code § 6400 et seq.
Uniform Interstate Family Support Act, see Family Code § 5700.101 et seq.

Research References
Forms

1 California Transactions Forms--Family Law § 2:74, Move-Away Cases.
1 California Transactions Forms--Family Law § 2:88, Marital Settlement Agreement.
1 California Transactions Forms--Family Law § 3:16, Identifying Areas of Parental Decision Making and Participation.
West's California Judicial Council Forms FL–341(D), Additional Provisions—Physical Custody Attachment (Also Available in Spanish).

§ 3025. Parental access to records

Notwithstanding any other provision of law, access to records and information pertaining to a minor child, including, but not limited to, medical, dental, and school records, shall not be denied to a parent because that parent is not the child's custodial parent. *(Stats.1992, c. 162 (A.B.2650), § 10, operative Jan. 1, 1994.)*

Cross References

California Work Opportunity and Responsibility to Kids Act, see Welfare and Institutions Code § 11200 et seq.
Confidential information and records, disclosure to parent or guardian, minor removed from physical custody of parent or guardian, see Welfare and Institutions Code § 5328.03.
Disclosure of minor's mental health records, minor removed from custody of parent or guardian, see Civil Code § 56.106.
Minor defined, see Family Code § 6500.
Minor removed from physical custody of parent or guardian, mental health records, psychotherapist duty not to permit inspection or obtaining of copies, see Health and Safety Code § 123116.
Uniform Child Custody Jurisdiction and Enforcement Act, see Family Code § 3400 et seq.

Research References
Forms

1 California Transactions Forms--Family Law § 2:75, Access to Records.
1 California Transactions Forms--Family Law § 2:88, Marital Settlement Agreement.
1 California Transactions Forms--Family Law § 3:16, Identifying Areas of Parental Decision Making and Participation.
2 California Transactions Forms--Family Law § 5:21, Access to Information.
2 California Transactions Forms--Family Law § 5:31, Parenting Agreement Providing for Joint Legal and Sole Physical Custody Where Both Partners Are Biological Parents of Child.
2 California Transactions Forms--Family Law § 5:33, Parenting Agreement Providing for Joint Legal and Sole Physical Custody Where Neither or Only One Partner is Biological Parent of Child.
West's California Code Forms, Family § 2338 Form 8, Marital Agreement.
West's California Code Forms, Family § 3081 Form 2, Clauses Regarding Custody and Visitation.
West's California Judicial Council Forms FL–341, Child Custody and Visitation (Parenting Time) Order Attachment (Also Available in Spanish).

CUSTODY OF CHILDREN

West's California Judicial Council Forms FL–341(E), Joint Legal Custody Attachment (Also Available in Spanish).

§ 3025.5. Psychological evaluations of children; confidentiality; exceptions; confidential information contained in child custody evaluation reports

(a) In a proceeding involving child custody or visitation rights, if a report containing psychological evaluations of a child or recommendations regarding custody of, or visitation with, a child is submitted to the court, including, but not limited to, a report created pursuant to Chapter 6 (commencing with Section 3110) of this part and a recommendation made to the court pursuant to Section 3183, that information shall be contained in a document that shall be placed in the confidential portion of the court file of the proceeding, and may not be disclosed, except to the following persons:

(1) A party to the proceeding and the party's attorney.

(2) A federal or state law enforcement officer, the licensing entity of a child custody evaluator, a judicial officer, court employee, or family court facilitator of the superior court of the county in which the action was filed, or an employee or agent of that facilitator, acting within the scope of the facilitator's duties.

(3) Counsel appointed for the child pursuant to Section 3150.

(4) Any other person upon order of the court for good cause.

(b) Confidential information contained in a report prepared pursuant to Section 3111 that is disclosed to the licensing entity of a child custody evaluator pursuant to subdivision (a) shall remain confidential and shall only be used for purposes of investigating allegations of unprofessional conduct by the child custody evaluator, or in a criminal, civil, or administrative proceeding involving the child custody evaluator. All confidential information, including, but not limited to, the identity of any minors, shall retain their confidential nature in a criminal, civil, or administrative proceeding resulting from the investigation of unprofessional conduct and shall be sealed at the conclusion of the proceeding and shall not subsequently be released. Names that are confidential shall be listed in attachments separate from the general pleadings. If the confidential information does not result in a criminal, civil, or administrative proceeding, it shall be sealed after the licensing entity decides that no further action will be taken in the matter of suspected licensing violations. *(Added by Stats.2004, c. 102 (S.B.1284), § 1. Amended by Stats.2012, c. 470 (A.B.1529), § 17; Stats.2014, c. 283 (A.B.1843), § 2, eff. Jan. 1, 2015; Stats.2019, c. 115 (A.B.1817), § 25, eff. Jan. 1, 2020.)*

Research References
Forms

West's California Judicial Council Forms FL–329, Confidential Child Custody Evaluation Report.
West's California Judicial Council Forms FL–329–INFO, Child Custody Evaluation Information Sheet (Also Available in Spanish).

§ 3026. Family reunification services

Family reunification services shall not be ordered as a part of a child custody or visitation rights proceeding. Nothing in this section affects the applicability of Section 16507 of the Welfare and Institutions Code. *(Stats.1992, c. 162 (A.B.2650), § 10, operative Jan. 1, 1994. Amended by Stats.1993, c. 219 (A.B.1500), § 116.16.)*

Cross References

Best interests of child, considerations, see Family Code § 3011.
Custody of unemancipated minor children, generally, see Family Code § 3010.
Dependent children, custody over, juvenile court's jurisdiction, see Welfare and Institutions Code § 304.
Domestic violence,
  Defined for purposes of this Code, see Family Code § 6211.
  Prevention, generally, see Family Code § 6200 et seq.
  Support person for victims, see Family Code § 6303.
Family Conciliation Court Law, see Family Code § 1800 et seq.

Family mediation and conciliation services, statewide coordination, see Family Code § 1850 et seq.
Marital dissolution and separation, generally, see Family Code § 2300 et seq.
Proceeding defined for purposes of this Code, see Family Code § 110.

§ 3027. Allegations of child abuse or child sexual abuse

(a) If allegations of child abuse, including child sexual abuse, are made during a child custody proceeding and the court has concerns regarding the child's safety, the court may take any reasonable, temporary steps as the court, in its discretion, deems appropriate under the circumstances to protect the child's safety until an investigation can be completed. Nothing in this section shall affect the applicability of Section 16504 or 16506 of the Welfare and Institutions Code.

(b) If allegations of child abuse, including child sexual abuse, are made during a child custody proceeding, the court may request that the local child welfare services agency conduct an investigation of the allegations pursuant to Section 328 of the Welfare and Institutions Code. Upon completion of the investigation, the agency shall report its findings to the court. *(Added by Stats.2000, c. 926 (S.B.1716), § 3. Amended by Stats.2010, c. 352 (A.B.939), § 12.)*

Cross References

Abuse defined for purposes of the Domestic Violence Prevention Act, see Family Code § 6203.
Corporal punishment or injury of child, felony, see Penal Code § 273d.
Degrading, immoral, or vicious practices, or habitual drunkenness, in presence of children, see Penal Code § 273g.
Domestic violence,
  Defined for purposes of this Code, see Family Code § 6211.
  Prevention, generally, see Family Code § 6200 et seq.
  Support person for victims, see Family Code § 6303.
Marital dissolution and separation, generally, see Family Code § 2300 et seq.
Parent convicted under certain Penal Code provisions, see Family Code § 3030.
Perjury and subornation of perjury, see Penal Code § 118 et seq.
Proceeding defined for purposes of this Code, see Family Code § 110.
Sending minors to immoral places, see Penal Code § 273f.
Society for prevention of cruelty to children, prosecutions by, see Penal Code § 273c.
Willful cruelty or unjustifiable punishment of child, see Penal Code § 273a.

§ 3027.1. False accusations of child abuse or neglect during child custody proceedings; knowledge; penalties

(a) If a court determines, based on the investigation described in Section 3027 or other evidence presented to it, that an accusation of child abuse or neglect made during a child custody proceeding is false and the person making the accusation knew it to be false at the time the accusation was made, the court may impose reasonable money sanctions, not to exceed all costs incurred by the party accused as a direct result of defending the accusation, and reasonable attorney's fees incurred in recovering the sanctions, against the person making the accusation. For the purposes of this section, "person" includes a witness, a party, or a party's attorney.

(b) On motion by any person requesting sanctions under this section, the court shall issue its order to show cause why the requested sanctions should not be imposed. The order to show cause shall be served on the person against whom the sanctions are sought and a hearing thereon shall be scheduled by the court to be conducted at least 15 days after the order is served.

(c) The remedy provided by this section is in addition to any other remedy provided by law. *(Formerly § 3027, enacted by Stats.1992, c. 162 (A.B.2650), § 10, operative Jan. 1, 1994. Amended by Stats.1993, c. 219 (A.B.1500), § 116.17; Stats.1994, c. 688 (A.B.2845), § 1. Renumbered § 3027.1 and amended by Stats.2000, c. 926 (S.B.1716), § 2.)*

Cross References

Abuse defined for purposes of the Domestic Violence Prevention Act, see Family Code § 6203.
Attorney's fees and costs, generally, see Code of Civil Procedure § 1021.
Best interests of child, considerations, see Family Code § 3011.
Computation of time, see Code of Civil Procedure §§ 12, 12a; Government Code § 6800 et seq.
Corporal punishment or injury of child, felony, see Penal Code § 273d.
Degrading, immoral, or vicious practices, or habitual drunkenness, in presence of children, see Penal Code § 273g.
Domestic violence,
  Defined for purposes of this Code, see Family Code § 6211.
  Prevention, generally, see Family Code § 6200 et seq.
  Support person for victims, see Family Code § 6303.
Judgment and order defined for purposes of this Code, see Family Code § 100.
Marital dissolution and separation, generally, see Family Code § 2300 et seq.
Parent convicted under certain Penal Code provisions, see Family Code § 3030.
Perjury and subornation of perjury, see Penal Code § 118 et seq.
Person defined for purposes of this Code, see Family Code § 105.
Proceeding defined for purposes of this Code, see Family Code § 110.
Sending minors to immoral places, see Penal Code § 273f.
Society for prevention of cruelty to children, prosecutions by, see Penal Code § 273c.
Uniform Interstate Enforcement of Domestic Violence Protection Orders Act, see Family Code § 6400 et seq.
Willful cruelty or unjustifiable punishment of child, see Penal Code § 273a.

Research References

Forms

California Practice Guide: Rutter Family Law Forms Form 7:10, Request for Order Re Sanctions for False Child Abuse Allegations.
West's California Code Forms, Civil § 47 Form 2, Affirmative Defense—Defamation—Official Proceeding Privilege.

§ 3027.5. Sexual abuse of child; report or treatment; limitations on custody or visitation

(a) A parent shall not be placed on supervised visitation, or be denied custody of or visitation with the parent's child, and custody or visitation rights shall not be limited, solely because the parent did any of the following:

(1) Lawfully reported suspected sexual abuse of the child.

(2) Otherwise acted lawfully, based on a reasonable belief, to determine if the child was the victim of sexual abuse.

(3) Sought treatment for the child from a licensed mental health professional for suspected sexual abuse.

(b) The court may order supervised visitation or limit a parent's custody or visitation if the court finds substantial evidence that the parent, with the intent to interfere with the other parent's lawful contact with the child, made a report of child sexual abuse, during a child custody proceeding or at any other time, that the reporting parent knew was false at the time it was made. A limitation of custody or visitation, including an order for supervised visitation, pursuant to this subdivision, or a statute regarding the making of a false child abuse report, shall be imposed only after the court has determined that the limitation is necessary to protect the health, safety, and welfare of the child, and the court has considered the state's policy of ensuring that children have frequent and continuing contact with both parents as declared in subdivision (b) of Section 3020. *(Added by Stats.1999, c. 985 (S.B.792), § 1. Amended by Stats.2019, c. 115 (A.B.1817), § 26, eff. Jan. 1, 2020.)*

Cross References

Abuse defined for purposes of the Domestic Violence Prevention Act, see Family Code § 6203.
Best interests of child, considerations, see Family Code § 3011.
Corporal punishment or injury of child, felony, see Penal Code § 273d.
Degrading, immoral, or vicious practices, or habitual drunkenness, in presence of children, see Penal Code § 273g.
Domestic violence,
  Defined for purposes of this Code, see Family Code § 6211.
  Prevention, generally, see Family Code § 6200 et seq.
  Support person for victims, see Family Code § 6303.
Judgment and order defined for purposes of this Code, see Family Code § 100.

§ 3027.5

Marital dissolution and separation, generally, see Family Code § 2300 et seq.
Parent convicted under certain Penal Code provisions, see Family Code § 3030.
Perjury and subornation of perjury, see Penal Code § 118 et seq.
Proceeding defined for purposes of this Code, see Family Code § 110.
Sending minors to immoral places, see Penal Code § 273f.
Society for prevention of cruelty to children, prosecutions by, see Penal Code § 273c.
State defined for purposes of this Code, see Family Code § 145.
Uniform Interstate Enforcement of Domestic Violence Protection Orders Act, see Family Code § 6400 et seq.
Willful cruelty or unjustifiable punishment of child, see Penal Code § 273a.

§ 3028. Compensation; failure to assume caretaker responsibility; thwarting of other parent's visitation or custody rights; attorney's fees

(a) The court may order financial compensation for periods when a parent fails to assume the caretaker responsibility or when a parent has been thwarted by the other parent when attempting to exercise custody or visitation rights contemplated by a custody or visitation order, including, but not limited to, an order for joint physical custody, or by a written or oral agreement between the parents.

(b) The compensation shall be limited to (1) the reasonable expenses incurred for or on behalf of a child, resulting from the other parent's failure to assume caretaker responsibility or (2) the reasonable expenses incurred by a parent for or on behalf of a child, resulting from the other parent's thwarting of the parent's efforts to exercise custody or visitation rights. The expenses may include the value of caretaker services but are not limited to the cost of services provided by a third party during the relevant period.

(c) The compensation may be requested by noticed motion or an order to show cause, which shall allege, under penalty of perjury, (1) a minimum of one hundred dollars ($100) of expenses incurred or (2) at least three occurrences of failure to exercise custody or visitation rights or (3) at least three occurrences of the thwarting of efforts to exercise custody or visitation rights within the six months before filing of the motion or order.

(d) Attorney's fees shall be awarded to the prevailing party upon a showing of the nonprevailing party's ability to pay as required by Section 270. *(Stats.1992, c. 162 (A.B.2650), § 10, operative Jan. 1, 1994. Amended by Stats.1993, c. 219 (A.B.1500), § 116.18.)*

Cross References

Attorney's fees and costs, payment to attorney, see Family Code § 272.
California Work Opportunity and Responsibility to Kids Act, see Welfare and Institutions Code § 11200 et seq.
Custody agreements, modification, see Family Code § 3179.
Custody of unemancipated minor children, generally, see Family Code § 3010.
Freedom from parental custody and control, see Family Code § 7800 et seq.
Joint legal custody defined, see Family Code § 3003.
Joint physical custody defined, see Family Code § 3004.
Judgment and order defined for purposes of this Code, see Family Code § 100.
Noncustodial parent's duty of support, failure of custodial parent to implement other parent's custody or visitation rights, see Family Code § 3556.
Support, generally, see Family Code § 3500 et seq.
Support duty, actions to enforce, see Family Code § 4000.
Uniform Child Custody Jurisdiction and Enforcement Act, see Family Code § 3400 et seq.
Uniform Interstate Family Support Act, see Family Code § 5700.101 et seq.
Uniform Parentage Act, custody and support, see Family Code § 7600 et seq.
Visitation rights,
   Generally, see Family Code § 3100 et seq.
   Close relatives where parent is deceased, see Family Code § 3102.
   Grandparents, see Family Code §§ 3103, 3104.
   Mediation of stepparent or grandparent visitation issues, see Family Code §§ 3171, 3178, 3185.
   Stepparents, see Family Code § 3101.

§ 3029. Noncustodial parent's liability for support if custodial parent is receiving AFDC assistance; order

An order granting custody to a parent who is receiving, or in the opinion of the court is likely to receive, assistance pursuant to the Family Economic Security Act of 1982 (Chapter 2 (commencing with Section 11200) of Part 3 of Division 9 of the Welfare and Institutions Code) for the maintenance of the child shall include an order pursuant to Chapter 2 (commencing with Section 4000) of Part 2 of Division 9 of this code, directing the noncustodial parent to pay any amount necessary for the support of the child, to the extent of the noncustodial parent's ability to pay. *(Added by Stats.1993, c. 219 (A.B.1500), § 116.19.)*

Cross References

California Work Opportunity and Responsibility to Kids Act, see Welfare and Institutions Code § 11200 et seq.
Child support, generally, see Family Code § 3900 et seq.
Child support agreements, generally, see Family Code § 3585 et seq.
Child support orders pending proceeding, see Family Code § 3600 et seq.
Judgment and order defined for purposes of this Code, see Family Code § 100.
Support defined for purposes of this Code, see Family Code § 150.
Support duty, actions to enforce, see Family Code § 4000.
Uniform Child Custody Jurisdiction and Enforcement Act, see Family Code § 3400 et seq.
Uniform Interstate Family Support Act, see Family Code § 5700.101 et seq.

§ 3030. Sex offenders; murderers; custody and visitation; child support; disclosure of information relating to custodial parent

(a)(1) No person shall be granted physical or legal custody of, or unsupervised visitation with, a child if the person is required to be registered as a sex offender under Section 290 of the Penal Code where the victim was a minor, or if the person has been convicted under Section 273a, 273d, or 647.6 of the Penal Code, unless the court finds that there is no significant risk to the child and states its reasons in writing or on the record. The child may not be placed in a home in which that person resides, nor permitted to have unsupervised visitation with that person, unless the court states the reasons for its findings in writing or on the record.

(2) No person shall be granted physical or legal custody of, or unsupervised visitation with, a child if anyone residing in the person's household is required, as a result of a felony conviction in which the victim was a minor, to register as a sex offender under Section 290 of the Penal Code, unless the court finds there is no significant risk to the child and states its reasons in writing or on the record. The child may not be placed in a home in which that person resides, nor permitted to have unsupervised visitation with that person, unless the court states the reasons for its findings in writing or on the record.

(3) The fact that a child is permitted unsupervised contact with a person who is required, as a result of a felony conviction in which the victim was a minor, to be registered as a sex offender under Section 290 of the Penal Code, shall be prima facie evidence that the child is at significant risk. When making a determination regarding significant risk to the child, the prima facie evidence shall constitute a presumption affecting the burden of producing evidence. However, this presumption shall not apply if there are factors mitigating against its application, including whether the party seeking custody or visitation is also required, as the result of a felony conviction in which the victim was a minor, to register as a sex offender under Section 290 of the Penal Code.

(b) No person shall be granted custody of, or visitation with, a child if the person has been convicted under Section 261 of the Penal Code and the child was conceived as a result of that violation.

(c) No person shall be granted custody of, or unsupervised visitation with, a child if the person has been convicted of murder in the first degree, as defined in Section 189 of the Penal Code, and the victim of the murder was the other parent of the child who is the subject of the order, unless the court finds that there is no risk to the child's health, safety, and welfare, and states the reasons for its finding in writing or on the record. In making its finding, the court may consider, among other things, the following:

(1) The wishes of the child, if the child is of sufficient age and capacity to reason so as to form an intelligent preference.

(2) Credible evidence that the convicted parent was a victim of abuse, as defined in Section 6203, committed by the deceased parent. That evidence may include, but is not limited to, written reports by law enforcement agencies, child protective services or other social welfare agencies, courts, medical facilities, or other public agencies or private nonprofit organizations providing services to victims of domestic abuse.

(3) Testimony of an expert witness, qualified under Section 1107 of the Evidence Code, that the convicted parent experiences intimate partner battering.

Unless and until a custody or visitation order is issued pursuant to this subdivision, no person shall permit or cause the child to visit or remain in the custody of the convicted parent without the consent of the child's custodian or legal guardian.

(d) The court may order child support that is to be paid by a person subject to subdivision (a), (b), or (c) to be paid through the local child support agency, as authorized by Section 4573 of the Family Code and Division 17 (commencing with Section 17000) of this code.

(e) The court shall not disclose, or cause to be disclosed, the custodial parent's place of residence, place of employment, or the child's school, unless the court finds that the disclosure would be in the best interest of the child. *(Added by Stats.1993, c. 219 (A.B. 1500), § 116.20. Amended by Stats.1993–94, 1st Ex.Sess., c. 5 (S.B.25), § 1, eff. Nov. 30, 1994; Stats.1997, c. 594 (A.B.1222), § 1; Stats.1998, c. 131 (A.B.1645), § 1; Stats.1998, c. 485 (A.B.2803), § 64; Stats.1998, c. 704 (A.B.2745), § 1.5; Stats.1998, c. 705 (A.B. 2386), § 1.5; Stats.2000, c. 808 (A.B.1358), § 26, eff. Sept. 28, 2000; Stats.2005, c. 215 (A.B.220), § 2; Stats.2005, c. 483 (S.B.594), § 2.5; Stats.2006, c. 207 (A.B.2893), § 1.)*

Cross References

Abuse defined for purposes of the Domestic Violence Prevention Act, see Family Code § 6203.
Best interests of child, considerations, see Family Code § 3011.
Child support, generally, see Family Code § 3900 et seq.
Child welfare services, see Welfare and Institutions Code § 16500 et seq.
Custody and visitation proceedings, controlled substances or alcohol abuse testing of parent, see Family Code § 3041.5.
Dependent children, custody over, juvenile court's jurisdiction, see Welfare and Institutions Code § 304.
Dependent children, supervision program, see Welfare and Institutions Code § 301.
Dependent children, temporary custody and detention, see Welfare and Institutions Code § 305.
Dependent children of the juvenile court, hearing to terminate parental rights or establish guardianship, see Welfare and Institutions Code § 366.26.
District attorney, action where child taken or detained in violation of custody order, see Family Code § 3131.
Domestic violence,
  Defined for purposes of this Code, see Family Code § 6211.
  Prevention, generally, see Family Code § 6200 et seq.
  Support person for victims, see Family Code § 6303.
Expedited child support orders, see Family Code § 3620 et seq.
Foster care, visitation, see Welfare and Institutions Code § 362.1.
Health insurance coverage for supported children, see Family Code § 3750 et seq.
Judgment and order defined for purposes of this Code, see Family Code § 100.
Minor defined for purposes of this Code, see Family Code § 6500.
Modification, termination, or setting aside of support order, see Family Code § 3650 et seq.
Person defined for purposes of this Code, see Family Code § 105.
Removal from custody and placement in foster home or institution, order for, see Welfare and Institutions Code § 387.
State defined for purposes of this Code, see Family Code § 145.
Support, generally, see Family Code § 3500 et seq.
Support defined for purposes of this Code, see Family Code § 150.
Uniform Child Custody Jurisdiction and Enforcement Act, see Family Code § 3400 et seq.
Writings, authentication and proof of, see Evidence Code § 1400 et seq.

Research References

Forms

West's California Code Forms, Family § 3022, Comment Overview—Order for Custody.

§ 3030.5. Modification or termination of order for physical or legal custody or unsupervised visitation order; sex offenders required to be registered

(a) Upon the motion of one or both parents, or the legal guardian or custodian, or upon the court's own motion, an order granting physical or legal custody of, or unsupervised visitation with, a child may be modified or terminated if either of the following circumstances has occurred since the order was entered, unless the court finds that there is no significant risk to the child and states its reasons in writing or on the record:

(1) The person who has been granted physical or legal custody of, or unsupervised visitation with the child is required, as a result of a felony conviction in which the victim was a minor, to be registered as a sex offender under Section 290 of the Penal Code.

(2) The person who has been granted physical or legal custody of, or unsupervised visitation with, the child resides with another person who is required, as a result of a felony conviction in which the victim was a minor, to be registered as a sex offender under Section 290 of the Penal Code.

(b) The fact that a child is permitted unsupervised contact with a person who is required, as a result of a felony conviction in which the victim was a minor, to be registered as a sex offender under Section 290 of the Penal Code, shall be prima facie evidence that the child is at significant risk. When making a determination regarding significant risk to the child, the prima facie evidence shall constitute a presumption affecting the burden of producing evidence. However, this presumption shall not apply if there are factors mitigating against its application, including whether the party seeking custody or visitation is also required, as the result of a felony conviction in which the victim was a minor, to register as a sex offender under Section 290 of the Penal Code.

(c) The court shall not modify an existing custody or visitation order upon the ex parte petition of one party pursuant to this section without providing notice to the other party and an opportunity to be heard. This notice provision applies only when the motion for custody or visitation change is based solely on the fact that the child is allowed unsupervised contact with a person required, as a result of a felony conviction in which the victim was a minor, to register as a sex offender under Section 290 of the Penal Code and does not affect the court's ability to remove a child upon an ex parte motion when there is a showing of immediate harm to the child. *(Added by Stats.2005, c. 483 (S.B.594), § 3.)*

Cross References

Judgment and order defined for purposes of this Code, see Family Code § 100.
Person defined for purposes of this Code, see Family Code § 105.
Uniform Child Custody Jurisdiction and Enforcement Act, see Family Code § 3400 et seq.

§ 3031. Protective or restraining orders; findings; transfer of children; detail specific custody or visitation orders; required presence of third party

(a) Where the court considers the issue of custody or visitation the court is encouraged to make a reasonable effort to ascertain whether or not any emergency protective order, protective order, or other restraining order is in effect that concerns the parties or the minor. The court is encouraged not to make a custody or visitation order that is inconsistent with the emergency protective order, protective

§ 3031

order, or other restraining order, unless the court makes both of the following findings:

(1) The custody or visitation order cannot be made consistent with the emergency protective order, protective order, or other restraining order.

(2) The custody or visitation order is in the best interest of the minor.

(b) Whenever custody or visitation is granted to a parent in a case in which domestic violence is alleged and an emergency protective order, protective order, or other restraining order has been issued, the custody or visitation order shall specify the time, day, place, and manner of transfer of the child for custody or visitation to limit the child's exposure to potential domestic conflict or violence and to ensure the safety of all family members. Where the court finds a party is staying in a place designated as a shelter for victims of domestic violence or other confidential location, the court's order for time, day, place, and manner of transfer of the child for custody or visitation shall be designed to prevent disclosure of the location of the shelter or other confidential location.

(c) When making an order for custody or visitation in a case in which domestic violence is alleged and an emergency protective order, protective order, or other restraining order has been issued, the court shall consider whether the best interest of the child, based upon the circumstances of the case, requires that any custody or visitation arrangement shall be limited to situations in which a third person, specified by the court, is present, or whether custody or visitation shall be suspended or denied. *(Added by Stats.1993, c. 219 (A.B.1500), § 116.30. Amended by Stats.1994, c. 320 (A.B.356), § 1.)*

Cross References

Best interest of child, see Family Code § 3011.
Domestic violence,
  Defined for purposes of this Code, see Family Code § 6211.
  Prevention, generally, see Family Code § 6200 et seq.
  Support person for victims, see Family Code § 6303.
Emergency protective order defined for purposes of this Code, see Family Code § 6215.
Judgment and order defined for purposes of this Code, see Family Code § 100.
Minor defined, see Family Code § 6500.
Person defined for purposes of this Code, see Family Code § 105.
Removal from custody and placement in foster home or institution, order for, see Welfare and Institutions Code § 387.
Uniform Child Custody Jurisdiction and Enforcement Act, see Family Code § 3400 et seq.
Uniform Interstate Enforcement of Domestic Violence Protection Orders Act, see Family Code § 6400 et seq.

Research References

Forms

1 California Transactions Forms--Family Law § 3:2, Child Custody.
West's California Judicial Council Forms DV–150, Supervised Visitation and Exchange Order.
West's California Judicial Council Forms FL–341(A), Supervised Visitation Order (Also Available in Spanish).
West's California Judicial Council Forms FL–356, Confidential Request for Special Immigrant Juvenile Findings—Family Law (Also Available in Spanish).

§ 3032. Pilot program to provide interpreter in child custody or protective order cases; lack of English proficiency and financial ability of party; report to Legislature

(a) The Judicial Council shall establish a state-funded one-year pilot project beginning July 1, 1999, in at least two counties, including Los Angeles County, pursuant to which, in any child custody proceeding, including mediation proceedings pursuant to Section 3170, any action or proceeding under Division 10 (commencing with Section 6200), any action or proceeding under the Uniform Parentage Act (Part 3 commencing with Section 7600) of Division 12, and any proceeding for dissolution or nullity of marriage or legal

CUSTODY OF CHILDREN

separation of the parties in which a protective order as been granted or is being sought pursuant to Section 6221, the court shall, notwithstanding Section 68092 of the Government Code, appoint an interpreter to interpret the proceedings at court expense, if both of the following conditions are met:

(1) One or both of the parties is unable to participate fully in the proceeding due to a lack of proficiency in the English language.

(2) The party who needs an interpreter appears in forma pauperis, pursuant to Section 68511.3 of the Government Code, or the court otherwise determines that the parties are financially unable to pay the cost of an interpreter. In all other cases where an interpreter is required pursuant to this section, interpreter fees shall be paid as provided in Section 68092 of the Government Code.

(3) This section shall not prohibit the court doing any of the following when an interpreter is not present:

(A) Issuing an order when the necessity for the order outweighs the necessity for an interpreter.

(B) Extending the duration of a previously issued temporary order if an interpreter is not readily available.

(C) Issuing a permanent order where a party who requires an interpreter fails to make appropriate arrangements for an interpreter after receiving proper notice of the hearing, including notice of the requirement to have an interpreter present, along with information about obtaining an interpreter.

(b) The Judicial Council shall submit its findings and recommendations with respect to the pilot project to the Legislature by January 31, 2001. Measurable objectives of the program may include increased utilization of the court by parties not fluent in English, increased efficiency in proceedings, increased compliance with orders, enhanced coordination between courts and culturally relevant services in the community, increased client satisfaction, and increased public satisfaction. *(Added by Stats.1998, c. 981 (A.B.1884), § 2.)*

Cross References

Arbitration, generally, see Code of Civil Procedure § 1281 et seq.
Conciliation proceedings, generally, see Family Code § 1800 et seq.
County defined for purposes of this Code, see Family Code § 67.
Family mediation and conciliation services, statewide coordination, see Family Code § 1850 et seq.
Judgment and order defined for purposes of this Code, see Family Code § 100.
Mediation of custody and visitation issues, generally, see Family Code § 3160 et seq.
Notice, actual and constructive, defined, see Civil Code § 18.
Proceeding defined for purposes of this Code, see Family Code § 110.
Protective order defined for purposes of this Code, see Family Code § 6218.
State defined for purposes of this Code, see Family Code § 145.

CHAPTER 2. MATTERS TO BE CONSIDERED IN GRANTING CUSTODY

Section
3040. Order of preference; child with more than two parents.
3041. Custody award to nonparent; findings of court; hearing.
3041.5. Controlled substances or alcohol abuse testing of persons seeking custody or visitation; grounds for testing; confidentiality of results; penalties for unauthorized disclosure.
3042. Preference of child; custody or visitation; examination of child witnesses; addressing the court; means other than direct testimony; determination of wish to express preference; rule of court.
3043. Nomination of guardian by parent.
3044. Presumption against persons perpetrating domestic violence.

RIGHT TO CUSTODY OF MINOR CHILD § 3040

Section	
3046.	Party absence or relocation from residence; consideration; interference with contact; application.
3047.	Military duty, temporary duty, mobilization, or deployment as justification; modification of custody or visitation orders; ability to appear at hearing; relocation of nondeploying parent; deployment as basis for inconvenience; legislative intent.
3048.	Required contents for custody or visitation orders; risk of child abduction; risk factors and preventative measures; notation of preventative conditions on minute order of court proceedings; Child Abduction Unit; child custody order forms.
3049.	Disabled parents; legislative intent.

Cross References

Action for exclusive custody, see Family Code § 3120.
Best interest of child, see Family Code § 3011.
Child custody,
  Generally, see Family Code § 3020 et seq.
  Joint custody, see Family Code §§ 3002, 3080 et seq.
  Joint legal custody, see Family Code § 3003.
  Joint physical custody, see Family Code § 3004.
  Sole legal custody, see Family Code § 3006.
  Sole physical custody, see Family Code § 3007.
Child support, generally, see Family Code § 3900 et seq.
Child welfare services, see Welfare and Institutions Code § 16500 et seq.
Custody agreements, modification, see Family Code § 3179.
Dependent children, custody over, juvenile court's jurisdiction, see Welfare and Institutions Code § 304.
Guardian, appointment of, see Family Code § 7893.
Joint custody, presumption, see Family Code § 3080.
Marital dissolution and separation, generally, see Family Code § 2300 et seq.
Parent convicted under certain Penal Code provisions, see Family Code § 3030.
Pendente lite relief of custody or visitation order on finding of parent-child relationship, see Family Code § 7604.
Uniform Child Custody Jurisdiction and Enforcement Act, see Family Code § 3400 et seq.

§ 3040. Order of preference; child with more than two parents

(a) Custody should be granted in the following order of preference according to the best interest of the child as provided in Sections 3011 and 3020:

(1) To both parents jointly pursuant to Chapter 4 (commencing with Section 3080) or to either parent. In making an order granting custody to either parent, the court shall consider, among other factors, which parent is more likely to allow the child frequent and continuing contact with the noncustodial parent, consistent with Sections 3011 and 3020. The court, in its discretion, may require the parents to submit to the court a plan for the implementation of the custody order.

(2) If to neither parent, to the person or persons in whose home the child has been living in a wholesome and stable environment.

(3) To any other person or persons deemed by the court to be suitable and able to provide adequate and proper care and guidance for the child.

(b) The immigration status of a parent, legal guardian, or relative shall not disqualify the parent, legal guardian, or relative from receiving custody under subdivision (a).

(c) The court shall not consider the sex, gender identity, gender expression, or sexual orientation of a parent, legal guardian, or relative in determining the best interest of the child under subdivision (a).

(d)(1) Commencing January 1, 2024, if a court finds that the effects of a parent's, legal guardian's, or relative's history of or current mental illness are a factor in determining the best interest of the child under subdivision (a), the court shall do both of the following:

(A) Provide the parent, legal guardian, or relative with a list of local resources for mental health treatment.

(B) State its reasons for the finding in writing or on the record.

(2) This subdivision does not relieve a court from ensuring that the health, safety, and welfare of the child is the court's primary concern in determining the best interests of children when making any order regarding the physical or legal custody, or visitation, of the child.

(e) This section establishes neither a preference nor a presumption for or against joint legal custody, joint physical custody, or sole custody, but allows the court and the family the widest discretion to choose a parenting plan that is in the best interest of the child, consistent with this section.

(f) In cases where a child has more than two parents, the court shall allocate custody and visitation among the parents based on the best interest of the child, including, but not limited to, addressing the child's need for continuity and stability by preserving established patterns of care and emotional bonds. The court may order that not all parents share legal or physical custody of the child if the court finds that it would not be in the best interest of the child as provided in Sections 3011 and 3020. (Added by Stats.1993, c. 219 (A.B.1500), § 116.50. Amended by Stats.1997, c. 849 (A.B.200), § 4; Stats.2012, c. 845 (S.B.1064), § 1; Stats.2013, c. 564 (S.B.274), § 2; Stats.2019, c. 551 (S.B.495), § 3, eff. Jan. 1, 2020; Stats.2022, c. 385 (S.B.1182), § 3, eff. Jan. 1, 2023.)

Cross References

Action for exclusive custody, see Family Code § 3120.
Best interest of child, see Family Code § 3011.
Child custody,
  Generally, see Family Code § 3020 et seq.
  Joint custody, see Family Code §§ 3002, 3080 et seq.
  Joint legal custody, see Family Code § 3003.
  Joint physical custody, see Family Code § 3004.
  Sole legal custody, see Family Code § 3006.
  Sole physical custody, see Family Code § 3007.
Child support, generally, see Family Code § 3900 et seq.
Child welfare services, see Welfare and Institutions Code § 16500 et seq.
Custody agreements, modification, see Family Code § 3179.
Dependent children, custody over, juvenile court's jurisdiction, see Welfare and Institutions Code § 304.
Guardian, appointment of, see Family Code § 7893.
Joint custody, presumption, see Family Code § 3080.
Judgment and order defined for purposes of this Code, see Family Code § 100.
Marital dissolution and separation, generally, see Family Code § 2300 et seq.
Parent convicted under certain Penal Code provisions, see Family Code § 3030.
Pendente lite relief of custody or visitation order on finding of parent-child relationship, see Family Code § 7604.
Person defined for purposes of this Code, see Family Code § 105.
Presumptions, see Evidence Code § 600 et seq.
Uniform Child Custody Jurisdiction and Enforcement Act, see Family Code § 3400 et seq.

Research References

Forms

4 California Transactions Forms--Estate Planning § 19:94, Appointment of Guardian of Person.
1 California Transactions Forms--Family Law § 2:70, Deciding Custody.
1 California Transactions Forms--Family Law § 3:7, Custody Issues Outside the Scope of the Family Code.
1 California Transactions Forms--Family Law § 3:8, No Statutory Custody Preferences.
1 California Transactions Forms--Family Law § 3:11, Permanent Custody.
2 California Transactions Forms--Family Law § 5:2, Overview.
West's California Code Forms, Family § 3022, Comment Overview--Order for Custody.
West's California Code Forms, Family § 3040, Comment Overview--Matters to be Considered in Granting Custody.
West's California Code Forms, Family § 7841 Form 1, Petition for Freedom from Parental Control--Abandonment.

§ 3040

CUSTODY OF CHILDREN

West's California Code Forms, Probate § 1514 Form 1, Order Appointing Guardian of Minor—Judicial Council Form GC-240.

West's California Judicial Council Forms DV-140, Child Custody and Visitation Order (Also Available in Chinese, Korean, Spanish, and Vietnamese).

West's California Judicial Council Forms FL-341, Child Custody and Visitation (Parenting Time) Order Attachment (Also Available in Spanish).

§ 3041. Custody award to nonparent; findings of court; hearing

(a) Before making an order granting custody to a person other than a parent, over the objection of a parent, the court shall make a finding that granting custody to a parent would be detrimental to the child and that granting custody to the nonparent is required to serve the best interest of the child. Allegations that parental custody would be detrimental to the child, other than a statement of that ultimate fact, shall not appear in the pleadings. The court may, in its discretion, exclude the public from the hearing on this issue.

(b) Subject to subdivision (d), a finding that parental custody would be detrimental to the child shall be supported by clear and convincing evidence.

(c) As used in this section, "detriment to the child" includes the harm of removal from a stable placement of a child with a person who has assumed, on a day-to-day basis, the role of the child's parent, fulfilling both the child's physical needs and the child's psychological needs for care and affection, and who has assumed that role for a substantial period of time. A finding of detriment does not require a finding of unfitness of the parents.

(d) Notwithstanding subdivision (b), if the court finds by a preponderance of the evidence that the person to whom custody may be given is a person described in subdivision (c), this finding shall constitute a finding that the custody is in the best interest of the child and that parental custody would be detrimental to the child absent a showing by a preponderance of the evidence to the contrary.

(e) Notwithstanding subdivisions (a) to (d), inclusive, if the child is an Indian child, when an allegation is made that parental custody would be detrimental to the child, before making an order granting custody to a person other than a parent, over the objection of a parent, the court shall apply the evidentiary standards described in subdivisions (d), (e), and (f) of Section 1912 of the Indian Child Welfare Act (25 U.S.C. Sec. 1901 et seq.) and Sections 224.6 and 361.7 of the Welfare and Institutions Code and the placement preferences and standards set out in Section 361.31 of the Welfare and Institutions Code and Section 1922 of the Indian Child Welfare Act (25 U.S.C. Sec. 1901 et seq.). *(Added by Stats.1993, c. 219 (A.B.1500), § 116.50. Amended by Stats.2002, c. 1118 (A.B.1938), § 3; Stats.2006, c. 838 (S.B.678), § 2; Stats.2019, c. 115 (A.B.1817), § 27, eff. Jan. 1, 2020.)*

Cross References

Adoption, generally, see Family Code § 8500 et seq.
Adoption proceedings, termination of parental rights, see Family Code § 7664 et seq.
Best interest of child, see Family Code § 3011.
Custody agreements, modification, see Family Code § 3179.
Dependent children of the juvenile court, hearing to terminate parental rights or establish guardianship, see Welfare and Institutions Code § 366.26.
Guardian, appointment of, see Family Code § 7893.
Joint guardians or conservators, appointment, see Probate Code § 2105.
Judgment and order defined for purposes of this Code, see Family Code § 100.
Marital dissolution and separation, generally, see Family Code § 2300 et seq.
Person defined for purposes of this Code, see Family Code § 105.
Removal from custody and placement in foster home or institution, order for, see Welfare and Institutions Code § 387.
Termination of parental rights of father, see Family Code § 7662.
Uniform Child Custody Jurisdiction and Enforcement Act, see Family Code § 3400 et seq.
Uniform Interstate Enforcement of Domestic Violence Protection Orders Act, see Family Code § 6400 et seq.
Uniform Parentage Act, see Family Code § 7600 et seq.

Withdrawal of petition for adoption, see Family Code § 8804.

Research References

Forms

California Practice Guide: Rutter Family Law Forms Form 7:16, Memorandum in Support of Motion and Declaration for Joinder (Nonparent Custody Claim).
2 California Transactions Forms--Family Law § 5:3, Rights of Nonparents Generally.
2 California Transactions Forms--Family Law § 5:4, Rights of De Facto Parents.
2 California Transactions Forms--Family Law § 5:26, Inheritance and Custody on Death.
2 California Transactions Forms--Family Law § 6:11, Initiating Proceeding Under Uniform Parentage Act [Fam. Code, §§7600 to 7730].
West's California Code Forms, Family § 3022, Comment Overview—Order for Custody.
West's California Code Forms, Probate § 1510 Form 1, Petition for Appointment of Guardian of Estate of Minor—Judicial Council Form GC-210.
West's California Code Forms, Probate § 1514 Form 1, Order Appointing Guardian of Minor—Judicial Council Form GC-240.

§ 3041.5. Controlled substances or alcohol abuse testing of persons seeking custody or visitation; grounds for testing; confidentiality of results; penalties for unauthorized disclosure

In any custody or visitation proceeding brought under this part, as described in Section 3021, or any guardianship proceeding brought under the Probate Code, the court may order any person who is seeking custody of, or visitation with, a child who is the subject of the proceeding to undergo testing for the illegal use of controlled substances and the use of alcohol if there is a judicial determination based upon a preponderance of evidence that there is the habitual, frequent, or continual illegal use of controlled substances or the habitual or continual abuse of alcohol by the parent, legal custodian, person seeking guardianship, or person seeking visitation in a guardianship. This evidence may include, but may not be limited to, a conviction within the last five years for the illegal use or possession of a controlled substance. The court shall order the least intrusive method of testing for the illegal use of controlled substances or the habitual or continual abuse of alcohol by either or both parents, the legal custodian, person seeking guardianship, or person seeking visitation in a guardianship. If substance abuse testing is ordered by the court, the testing shall be performed in conformance with procedures and standards established by the United States Department of Health and Human Services for drug testing of federal employees. The parent, legal custodian, person seeking guardianship, or person seeking visitation in a guardianship who has undergone drug testing shall have the right to a hearing, if requested, to challenge a positive test result. A positive test result, even if challenged and upheld, shall not, by itself, constitute grounds for an adverse custody or guardianship decision. Determining the best interests of the child requires weighing all relevant factors. The court shall also consider any reports provided to the court pursuant to the Probate Code. The results of this testing shall be confidential, shall be maintained as a sealed record in the court file, and may not be released to any person except the court, the parties, their attorneys, the Judicial Council, until completion of its authorized study of the testing process, and any person to whom the court expressly grants access by written order made with prior notice to all parties. Any person who has access to the test results may not disseminate copies or disclose information about the test results to any person other than a person who is authorized to receive the test results pursuant to this section. Any breach of the confidentiality of the test results shall be punishable by civil sanctions not to exceed two thousand five hundred dollars ($2,500). The results of the testing may not be used for any purpose, including any criminal, civil, or administrative proceeding, except to assist the court in determining, for purposes of the proceeding, the best interest of the child pursuant to Section 3011 and the content of the order or judgment determining custody or visitation. The court may order either party, or both parties, to pay the costs of the drug or alcohol testing ordered pursuant to this section. As used in this section, "controlled substances" has the same meaning as defined in the California Uniform Controlled Substances Act (Division 10 (commencing with Section 11000) of the Health and Safety Code). *(Added by Stats.2004, c. 19 (A.B.1108), § 1, eff. Feb. 23, 2004. Amended by Stats.2005, c. 302 (A.B.541), § 1; Stats.2007, c. 152 (S.B.403), § 1; Stats.2008, c. 57 (S.B.1255), § 1; Stats.2009, c. 140 (A.B.1164), § 66; Stats.2012, c. 258 (A.B.2365), § 2.)*

Cross References

Abuse defined for purposes of the Domestic Violence Prevention Act, see Family Code § 6203.
Administrative Procedure Act, see Government Code §§ 11340 et seq., 11370 et seq., 11400 et seq., 11500 et seq.
Administrative proceedings, judicial review, see Government Code § 11523.
Best interests of child, considerations, see Family Code § 3011.
Department of Health Care Services, generally, see Health and Safety Code § 100100 et seq.
Domestic violence,
   Defined for purposes of this Code, see Family Code § 6211.
   Prevention, generally, see Family Code § 6200 et seq.
   Support person for victims, see Family Code § 6303.
Judgment and order defined for purposes of this Code, see Family Code § 100.
Notice, actual and constructive, defined, see Civil Code § 18.
Person defined for purposes of this Code, see Family Code § 105.
Proceeding defined for purposes of this Code, see Family Code § 110.
Removal from custody and placement in foster home or institution, order for, see Welfare and Institutions Code § 387.
State defined for purposes of this Code, see Family Code § 145.
Uniform Child Custody Jurisdiction and Enforcement Act, see Family Code § 3400 et seq.
Uniform Interstate Enforcement of Domestic Violence Protection Orders Act, see Family Code § 6400 et seq.

§ 3042. Preference of child; custody or visitation; examination of child witnesses; addressing the court; means other than direct testimony; determination of wish to express preference; rule of court

(a) If a child is of sufficient age and capacity to reason so as to form an intelligent preference as to custody or visitation, the court shall consider, and give due weight to, the wishes of the child in making an order granting or modifying custody or visitation.

(b) In addition to the requirements of subdivision (b) of Section 765 of the Evidence Code, the court shall control the examination of a child witness so as to protect the best interest of the child.

(c) If the child is 14 years of age or older and wishes to address the court regarding custody or visitation, the child shall be permitted to do so, unless the court determines that doing so is not in the child's best interest, in which case, the court shall state its reasons for that finding on the record.

(d) This section does not prevent a child who is less than 14 years of age from addressing the court regarding custody or visitation, if the court determines that is appropriate pursuant to the child's best interest.

(e) If the court precludes the calling of a child as a witness, the court shall provide alternative means of obtaining input from the child and other information regarding the child's preferences.

(f)(1) Except as provided in paragraph (2), the court shall not permit a child addressing the court regarding custody or visitation to do so in the presence of the parties. The court shall provide an alternative to having the child address the court in the presence of the parties in order to obtain input directly from the child.

(2) Notwithstanding paragraph (1), the court may permit the child addressing the court regarding custody or visitation to do so in the presence of the parties if the court determines that doing so is in the child's best interest and states its reasons for that finding on the record. In determining the child's best interest under this paragraph, the court shall consider whether addressing the court regarding custody or visitation in the presence of the parties is likely to be detrimental to the child.

(g) To assist the court in determining whether the child wishes to express a preference or to provide other input regarding custody or visitation to the court, a minor's counsel, an evaluator, an investigator, or a child custody recommending counselor shall indicate to the judge that the child wishes to address the court, or the judge may make that inquiry in the absence of that request. A party or a party's attorney may also indicate to the judge that the child wishes to address the court or judge.

(h) If a child informs the minor's counsel, an evaluator, an investigator, or a child custody recommending counselor at any point that the child has changed their choice with respect to addressing the court, the minor's counsel, evaluator, investigator, or child custody recommending counselor shall, as soon as feasible, indicate to the judge, the parties or their attorneys, and other professionals serving on the case that the child has changed their preference.

(i) This section does not require the child to express to the court a preference or to provide other input regarding custody or visitation.

(j) The Judicial Council shall, no later than January 1, 2023, develop or amend rules as necessary to implement this section. *(Added by Stats.1993, c. 219 (A.B.1500), § 116.50. Amended by Stats.1994, c. 596 (S.B.1700), § 1; Stats.1995, c. 91 (S.B.975), § 38; Stats.2010, c. 187 (A.B.1050), § 1; Stats.2019, c. 115 (A.B.1817), § 28, eff. Jan. 1, 2020; Stats.2021, c. 768 (S.B.654), § 2, eff. Jan. 1, 2022.)*

Cross References

Action for exclusive custody, see Family Code § 3120.
Best interests of child, considerations, see Family Code § 3011.
Child custody,
   Generally, see Family Code § 3020 et seq.
   Joint custody, see Family Code §§ 3002, 3080 et seq.
   Joint legal custody, see Family Code § 3003.
   Joint physical custody, see Family Code § 3004.
   Sole legal custody, see Family Code § 3006.
   Sole physical custody, see Family Code § 3007.
Child welfare services, see Welfare and Institutions Code § 16500 et seq.
Custody agreements, modification, see Family Code § 3179.
Dependent children, custody over, juvenile court's jurisdiction, see Welfare and Institutions Code § 304.
Freedom from parental custody and control, see Family Code § 7800 et seq.
Guardian, appointment of, see Family Code § 7893.
Hearing in chambers to determine child's wishes regarding custody, see Family Code § 7891.
Judgment and order defined for purposes of this Code, see Family Code § 100.
Marital dissolution and separation, generally, see Family Code § 2300 et seq.
Pendente lite relief of custody or visitation order on finding of parent-child relationship, see Family Code § 7604.
Uniform Child Custody Jurisdiction and Enforcement Act, see Family Code § 3400 et seq.
Uniform Parentage Act, see Family Code § 7600 et seq.

Research References

Forms

4 California Transactions Forms--Estate Planning § 19:94, Appointment of Guardian of Person.
1 California Transactions Forms--Family Law § 3:12, Preferences of the Child.

§ 3043. Nomination of guardian by parent

In determining the person or persons to whom custody should be granted under paragraph (2) or (3) of subdivision (a) of Section 3040, the court shall consider and give due weight to the nomination of a guardian of the person of the child by a parent under Article 1 (commencing with Section 1500) of Chapter 1 of Part 2 of Division 4 of the Probate Code. *(Added by Stats.1993, c. 219 (A.B.1500), § 116.50.)*

Cross References

Best interests of child, considerations, see Family Code § 3011.
Child custody, generally, see Family Code § 3020 et seq.

§ 3043

Child welfare services, see Welfare and Institutions Code § 16500 et seq.
Custody agreements, modification, see Family Code § 3179.
Dependent children, custody over, juvenile court's jurisdiction, see Welfare and Institutions Code § 304.
Freedom from parental custody and control, see Family Code § 7800 et seq.
Guardian, appointment of, see Family Code § 7893.
Marital dissolution and separation, generally, see Family Code § 2300 et seq.
Person defined for purposes of this Code, see Family Code § 105.
Uniform Child Custody Jurisdiction and Enforcement Act, see Family Code § 3400 et seq.

Research References

Forms

4 California Transactions Forms--Estate Planning § 19:94, Appointment of Guardian of Person.
West's California Code Forms, Family § 7841 Form 1, Petition for Freedom from Parental Control—Abandonment.
West's California Judicial Council Forms DV–140, Child Custody and Visitation Order (Also Available in Chinese, Korean, Spanish, and Vietnamese).
West's California Judicial Council Forms FL–341, Child Custody and Visitation (Parenting Time) Order Attachment (Also Available in Spanish).

§ 3044. Presumption against persons perpetrating domestic violence

(a) Upon a finding by the court that a party seeking custody of a child has perpetrated domestic violence within the previous five years against the other party seeking custody of the child, or against the child or the child's siblings, or against a person in subparagraph (A) of paragraph (2) of subdivision (a) of Section 3011 with whom the party has a relationship, there is a rebuttable presumption that an award of sole or joint physical or legal custody of a child to a person who has perpetrated domestic violence is detrimental to the best interest of the child, pursuant to Sections 3011 and 3020. This presumption may only be rebutted by a preponderance of the evidence.

(b) To overcome the presumption set forth in subdivision (a), the court shall find that paragraph (1) is satisfied and shall find that the factors in paragraph (2), on balance, support the legislative findings in Section 3020.

(1) The perpetrator of domestic violence has demonstrated that giving sole or joint physical or legal custody of a child to the perpetrator is in the best interest of the child pursuant to Sections 3011 and 3020. In determining the best interest of the child, the preference for frequent and continuing contact with both parents, as set forth in subdivision (b) of Section 3020, or with the noncustodial parent, as set forth in paragraph (1) of subdivision (a) of Section 3040, may not be used to rebut the presumption, in whole or in part.

(2) Additional factors:

(A) The perpetrator has successfully completed a batterer's treatment program that meets the criteria outlined in subdivision (c) of Section 1203.097 of the Penal Code.

(B) The perpetrator has successfully completed a program of alcohol or drug abuse counseling, if the court determines that counseling is appropriate.

(C) The perpetrator has successfully completed a parenting class, if the court determines the class to be appropriate.

(D) The perpetrator is on probation or parole, and has or has not complied with the terms and conditions of probation or parole.

(E) The perpetrator is restrained by a protective order or restraining order, and has or has not complied with its terms and conditions.

(F) The perpetrator of domestic violence has committed further acts of domestic violence.

(G) The court has determined, pursuant to Section 6322.5, that the perpetrator is a restrained person in possession or control of a firearm or ammunition in violation of Section 6389.

(c) For purposes of this section, a person has "perpetrated domestic violence" when the person is found by the court to have intentionally or recklessly caused or attempted to cause bodily injury, or sexual assault, or to have placed a person in reasonable apprehension of imminent serious bodily injury to that person or to another, or to have engaged in behavior involving, but not limited to, threatening, striking, harassing, destroying personal property, or disturbing the peace of another, for which a court may issue an ex parte order pursuant to Section 6320 to protect the other party seeking custody of the child or to protect the child and the child's siblings.

(d)(1) For purposes of this section, the requirement of a finding by the court shall be satisfied by, among other things, and not limited to, evidence that a party seeking custody has been convicted within the previous five years, after a trial or a plea of guilty or no contest, of a crime against the other party that comes within the definition of domestic violence contained in Section 6211 and of abuse contained in Section 6203, including, but not limited to, a crime described in subdivision (e) of Section 243 of, or Section 261, 273.5, 422, or 646.9 of, or former Section 262 of, the Penal Code.

(2) The requirement of a finding by the court shall also be satisfied if a court, whether that court hears or has heard the child custody proceedings or not, has made a finding pursuant to subdivision (a) based on conduct occurring within the previous five years.

(e) When a court makes a finding that a party has perpetrated domestic violence, the court may not base its findings solely on conclusions reached by a child custody evaluator or on the recommendation of the Family Court Services staff, but shall consider any relevant, admissible evidence submitted by the parties.

(f)(1) It is the intent of the Legislature that this subdivision be interpreted consistently with the decision in Jaime G. v. H.L. (2018) 25 Cal.App.5th 794, which requires that the court, in determining that the presumption in subdivision (a) has been overcome, make specific findings on each of the factors in subdivision (b).

(2) If the court determines that the presumption in subdivision (a) has been overcome, the court shall state its reasons in writing or on the record as to why paragraph (1) of subdivision (b) is satisfied and why the factors in paragraph (2) of subdivision (b), on balance, support the legislative findings in Section 3020.

(g) In an evidentiary hearing or trial in which custody orders are sought and where there has been an allegation of domestic violence, the court shall make a determination as to whether this section applies prior to issuing a custody order, unless the court finds that a continuance is necessary to determine whether this section applies, in which case the court may issue a temporary custody order for a reasonable period of time, provided the order complies with Sections 3011 and 3020.

(h) In a custody or restraining order proceeding in which a party has alleged that the other party has perpetrated domestic violence in accordance with the terms of this section, the court shall inform the parties of the existence of this section and shall give them a copy of this section prior to custody mediation in the case. (Added by Stats.1999, c. 445 (A.B.840), § 1. Amended by Stats.2003, c. 243 (S.B.265), § 1; Stats.2018, c. 941 (A.B.2044), § 3, eff. Jan. 1, 2019; Stats.2019, c. 115 (A.B.1817), § 29, eff. Jan. 1, 2020; Stats.2021, c. 124 (A.B.938), § 26, eff. Jan. 1, 2022; Stats.2021, c. 213 (A.B.1579), § 1, eff. Jan. 1, 2022; Stats.2021, c. 626 (A.B.1171), § 10, eff. Jan. 1, 2022; Stats.2021, c. 685 (S.B.320), § 2.7, eff. Jan. 1, 2022.)

Cross References

Abuse defined for purposes of the Domestic Violence Prevention Act, see Family Code § 6203.
Arbitration, generally, see Code of Civil Procedure § 1281 et seq.
Best interests of child, considerations, see Family Code § 3011.
Conciliation proceedings, generally, see Family Code § 1800 et seq.
Domestic violence,
    Defined for purposes of this Code, see Family Code § 6211.

Prevention, generally, see Family Code § 6200 et seq.
Support person for victims, see Family Code § 6303.
Family mediation and conciliation services, statewide coordination, see Family Code § 1850 et seq.
Judgment and order defined for purposes of this Code, see Family Code § 100.
Mediation of custody and visitation issues, generally, see Family Code § 3160 et seq.
Person defined for purposes of this Code, see Family Code § 105.
Presumptions, see Evidence Code § 600 et seq.
Proceeding defined for purposes of this Code, see Family Code § 110.
Property defined for purposes of this Code, see Family Code § 113.
Protective order defined for purposes of this Code, see Family Code § 6218.
Removal from custody and placement in foster home or institution, order for, see Welfare and Institutions Code § 387.
Uniform Child Custody Jurisdiction and Enforcement Act, see Family Code § 3400 et seq.
Uniform Interstate Enforcement of Domestic Violence Protection Orders Act, see Family Code § 6400 et seq.

§ 3046. Party absence or relocation from residence; consideration; interference with contact; application

(a) If a party is absent or relocates from the family residence, the court shall not consider the absence or relocation as a factor in determining custody or visitation in either of the following circumstances:

(1) The absence or relocation is of short duration and the court finds that, during the period of absence or relocation, the party has demonstrated an interest in maintaining custody or visitation, the party maintains, or makes reasonable efforts to maintain, regular contact with the child, and the party's behavior demonstrates no intent to abandon the child.

(2) The party is absent or relocates because of an act or acts of actual or threatened domestic or family violence by the other party.

(b) The court may consider attempts by one party to interfere with the other party's regular contact with the child in determining if the party has satisfied the requirements of subdivision (a).

(c) This section does not apply to either of the following:

(1) A party against whom a protective or restraining order has been issued excluding the party from the dwelling of the other party or the child, or otherwise enjoining the party from assault or harassment against the other party or the child, including, but not limited to, orders issued under Part 4 (commencing with Section 6300) of Division 10, orders preventing civil harassment or workplace violence issued pursuant to Section 527.6 or 527.8 of the Code of Civil Procedure, and criminal protective orders issued pursuant to Section 136.2 of the Penal Code.

(2) A party who abandons a child as provided in Section 7822. *(Added by Stats.1999, c. 980 (A.B.1671), § 7. Amended by Stats.2006, c. 538 (S.B.1852), § 157.)*

Cross References

Best interests of child, considerations, see Family Code § 3011.
Child welfare services, see Welfare and Institutions Code § 16500 et seq.
Custody agreements, modification, see Family Code § 3179.
Dependent children, custody over, juvenile court's jurisdiction, see Welfare and Institutions Code § 304.
Freedom from parental custody and control, see Family Code § 7800 et seq.
Judgment and order defined for purposes of this Code, see Family Code § 100.
Marital dissolution and separation, generally, see Family Code § 2300 et seq.
Protective order defined for purposes of this Code, see Family Code § 6218.
Uniform Child Custody Jurisdiction and Enforcement Act, see Family Code § 3400 et seq.
Visitation rights,
  Generally, see Family Code § 3100 et seq.
  Close relatives where parent is deceased, see Family Code § 3102.
  Grandparents, see Family Code §§ 3103, 3104.
  Mediation of stepparent or grandparent visitation issues, see Family Code §§ 3171, 3178, 3185.
  Stepparents, see Family Code § 3101.

Research References
Forms
1 California Transactions Forms--Family Law § 2:70, Deciding Custody.
1 California Transactions Forms--Family Law § 3:16, Identifying Areas of Parental Decision Making and Participation.

§ 3047. Military duty, temporary duty, mobilization, or deployment as justification; modification of custody or visitation orders; ability to appear at hearing; relocation of nondeploying parent; deployment as basis for inconvenience; legislative intent

(a) A party's absence, relocation, or failure to comply with custody and visitation orders shall not, by itself, be sufficient to justify a modification of a custody or visitation order if the reason for the absence, relocation, or failure to comply is the party's activation to military duty or temporary duty, mobilization in support of combat or other military operation, or military deployment out of state.

(b)(1) If a party with sole or joint physical custody or visitation receives temporary duty, deployment, or mobilization orders from the military that require the party to move a substantial distance from the party's residence or otherwise has a material effect on the ability of the party to exercise custody or visitation rights, any necessary modification of the existing custody order shall be deemed a temporary custody order made without prejudice, which shall be subject to review and reconsideration upon the return of the party from military deployment, mobilization, or temporary duty.

(2) If the temporary order is reviewed upon return of the party from military deployment, mobilization, or temporary duty, there shall be a presumption that the custody order shall revert to the order that was in place before the modification, unless the court determines that it is not in the best interest of the child. The court shall not, as part of its review of the temporary order upon the return of the deploying party, order a child custody evaluation under Section 3111 of this code or Section 730 of the Evidence Code, unless the party opposing reversion of the order makes a prima facie showing that reversion is not in the best interest of the child.

(3)(A) If the court makes a temporary custody order, it shall consider any appropriate orders to ensure that the relocating party can maintain frequent and continuing contact with the child by means that are reasonably available.

(B) Upon a motion by the relocating party, the court may grant reasonable visitation rights to a stepparent, grandparent, or other family member if the court does all of the following:

(i) Finds that there is a preexisting relationship between the family member and the child that has engendered a bond such that visitation is in the best interest of the child.

(ii) Finds that the visitation will facilitate the child's contact with the relocating party.

(iii) Balances the interest of the child in having visitation with the family member against the right of the parents to exercise parental authority.

(C) This paragraph does not increase the authority of the persons described in subparagraph (B) to seek visitation orders independently.

(D) The granting of visitation rights to a nonparent pursuant to subparagraph (B) shall not impact the calculation of child support.

(c) If a party's deployment, mobilization, or temporary duty will have a material effect on the party's ability, or anticipated ability, to appear in person at a regularly scheduled hearing, the court shall do either of the following:

(1) Upon motion of the party, hold an expedited hearing to determine custody and visitation issues prior to the departure of the party.

(2) Upon motion of the party, allow the party to present testimony and evidence and participate in court-ordered child custody media-

§ 3047

tion by electronic means, including, but not limited to, telephone, video teleconferencing, or the internet, to the extent that this technology is reasonably available to the court and protects the due process rights of all parties.

(d) A relocation by a nondeploying parent during a period of a deployed parent's absence while a temporary modification order for a parenting plan is in effect shall not, by itself, terminate the exclusive and continuing jurisdiction of the court for purposes of later determining custody or parenting time under this chapter.

(e) When a court of this state has issued a custody or visitation order, the absence of a child from this state during the deployment of a parent shall be considered a "temporary absence" for purposes of the Uniform Child Custody Jurisdiction and Enforcement Act (Part 3 (commencing with Section 3400)), and the court shall retain exclusive continuing jurisdiction under Section 3422.

(f) The deployment of a parent shall not be used as a basis to assert inconvenience of the forum under Section 3427.

(g) For purposes of this section, the following terms have the following meanings:

(1) "Deployment" means the temporary transfer of a member of the Armed Forces in active-duty status in support of combat or some other military operation.

(2) "Mobilization" means the transfer of a member of the National Guard or Military Reserve to extended active-duty status, but does not include National Guard or Military Reserve annual training.

(3) "Temporary duty" means the transfer of a servicemember from one military base to a different location, usually another base, for a limited period of time to accomplish training or to assist in the performance of a noncombat mission.

(h) It is the intent of the Legislature that this section provide a fair, efficient, and expeditious process to resolve child custody and visitation issues when a party receives temporary duty, deployment, or mobilization orders from the military, as well as at the time that the party returns from service and files a motion to revert back to the custody order in place before the deployment. The Legislature intends that family courts shall, to the extent feasible within existing resources and court practices, prioritize the calendaring of these cases, avoid unnecessary delay or continuances, and ensure that parties who serve in the military are not penalized for their service by a delay in appropriate access to their children. (Added by Stats.2005, c. 154 (S.B.1082), § 1, eff. Aug. 30, 2005. Amended by Stats.2010, c. 466 (A.B.2416), § 1; Stats.2012, c. 116 (A.B.1807), § 1; Stats.2013, c. 76 (A.B.383), § 59; Stats.2019, c. 115 (A.B.1817), § 30, eff. Jan. 1, 2020.)

Cross References

Arrears collection enhancement process, see Family Code § 17560.
Modification, termination, or set-aside of support orders, power of court, see Family Code § 3651.
Modification, termination, or set-aside of support orders, retroactive application, see Family Code § 3653.
United States military and National Guard service members, modification of child support, form, motion by local child support agency, see Family Code § 17440.

§ 3048. Required contents for custody or visitation orders; risk of child abduction; risk factors and preventative measures; notation of preventative conditions on minute order of court proceedings; Child Abduction Unit; child custody order forms

(a) Notwithstanding any other law, in a proceeding to determine child custody or visitation with a child, every custody or visitation order shall contain all of the following:

(1) The basis for the court's exercise of jurisdiction.

(2) The manner in which notice and opportunity to be heard were given.

(3) A clear description of the custody and visitation rights of each party.

(4) A provision stating that a violation of the order may subject the party in violation to civil or criminal penalties, or both.

(5) Identification of the country of habitual residence of the child or children.

(b)(1) In cases in which the court becomes aware of facts that may indicate that there is a risk of abduction of a child, the court shall, either on its own motion or at the request of a party, determine whether measures are needed to prevent the abduction of the child by one parent. To make that determination, the court shall consider the risk of abduction of the child, obstacles to location, recovery, and return if the child is abducted, and potential harm to the child if the child is abducted. To determine whether there is a risk of abduction, the court shall consider the following factors:

(A) Whether a party has previously taken, enticed away, kept, withheld, or concealed a child in violation of the right of custody or of visitation of a person.

(B) Whether a party has previously threatened to take, entice away, keep, withhold, or conceal a child in violation of the right of custody or of visitation of a person.

(C) Whether a party lacks strong ties to this state.

(D) Whether a party has strong familial, emotional, or cultural ties to another state or country, including foreign citizenship. This factor shall be considered only if evidence exists in support of another factor specified in this section.

(E) Whether a party has no financial reason to stay in this state, including whether the party is unemployed, is able to work anywhere, or is financially independent.

(F) Whether a party has engaged in planning activities that would facilitate the removal of a child from the state, including quitting a job, selling the primary residence, terminating a lease, closing a bank account, liquidating other assets, hiding or destroying documents, applying for a passport, applying to obtain a birth certificate or school or medical records, or purchasing airplane or other travel tickets, with consideration given to whether a party is carrying out a safety plan to flee from domestic violence.

(G) Whether a party has a history of a lack of parental cooperation or child abuse, or there is substantiated evidence that a party has perpetrated domestic violence.

(H) Whether a party has a criminal record.

(2) If the court makes a finding that there is a need for preventative measures after considering the factors listed in paragraph (1), the court shall consider taking one or more of the following measures to prevent the abduction of the child:

(A) Ordering supervised visitation.

(B) Requiring a parent to post a bond in an amount sufficient to serve as a financial deterrent to abduction, the proceeds of which may be used to offset the cost of recovery of the child in the event there is an abduction.

(C) Restricting the right of the custodial or noncustodial parent to remove the child from the county, the state, or the country.

(D) Restricting the right of the custodial parent to relocate with the child, unless the custodial parent provides advance notice to, and obtains the written agreement of, the noncustodial parent, or obtains the approval of the court, before relocating with the child.

(E) Requiring the surrender of passports and other travel documents.

(F) Prohibiting a parent from applying for a new or replacement passport for the child.

(G) Requiring a parent to notify a relevant foreign consulate or embassy of passport restrictions and to provide the court with proof of that notification.

(H) Requiring a party to register a California order in another state as a prerequisite to allowing a child to travel to that state for visits, or to obtain an order from another country containing terms identical to the custody and visitation order issued in the United States (recognizing that these orders may be modified or enforced pursuant to the laws of the other country), as a prerequisite to allowing a child to travel to that country for visits.

(I) Obtaining assurances that a party will return from foreign visits by requiring the traveling parent to provide the court or the other parent or guardian with any of the following:

(i) The travel itinerary of the child.

(ii) Copies of round trip airline tickets.

(iii) A list of addresses and telephone numbers where the child can be reached at all times.

(iv) An open airline ticket for the left-behind parent in case the child is not returned.

(J) Including provisions in the custody order to facilitate use of the Uniform Child Custody Jurisdiction and Enforcement Act (Part 3 (commencing with Section 3400)) and the Hague Convention on the Civil Aspects of International Child Abduction (implemented pursuant to 42 U.S.C. Sec. 11601 et seq.), such as identifying California as the home state of the child or otherwise defining the basis for the California court's exercise of jurisdiction under Part 3 (commencing with Section 3400), identifying the United States as the country of habitual residence of the child pursuant to the Hague Convention, defining custody rights pursuant to the Hague Convention, obtaining the express agreement of the parents that the United States is the country of habitual residence of the child, or that California or the United States is the most appropriate forum for addressing custody and visitation orders.

(K) Authorizing the assistance of law enforcement.

(3) If the court imposes any or all of the conditions listed in paragraph (2), those conditions shall be specifically noted on the minute order of the court proceedings.

(4) If the court determines there is a risk of abduction that is sufficient to warrant the application of one or more of the prevention measures authorized by this section, the court shall inform the parties of the telephone number and address of the Child Abduction Unit in the office of the district attorney in the county where the custody or visitation order is being entered.

(c) The Judicial Council shall make the changes to its child custody order forms that are necessary for the implementation of subdivision (b).

(d) This section does not affect the applicability of Section 278.7 of the Penal Code. *(Added by Stats.2002, c. 856 (A.B.2441), § 2. Amended by Stats.2003, c. 62 (S.B.600), § 86; Stats.2003, c. 52 (A.B.1516) § 1, eff. July 14, 2003; Stats.2019, c. 115 (A.B.1817), § 31, eff. Jan. 1, 2020.)*

Cross References

Abuse defined for purposes of the Domestic Violence Prevention Act, see Family Code § 6203.
Best interests of child, considerations, see Family Code § 3011.
Child welfare services, see Welfare and Institutions Code § 16500 et seq.
County defined for purposes of this Code, see Family Code § 67.
Dependent children, custody over, juvenile court's jurisdiction, see Welfare and Institutions Code § 304.
District attorney, powers and duties, see Government Code § 26500 et seq.
Domestic violence,
  Defined for purposes of this Code, see Family Code § 6211.
  Prevention, generally, see Family Code § 6200 et seq.
  Support person for victims, see Family Code § 6303.
Judgment and order defined for purposes of this Code, see Family Code § 100.
Notice, actual and constructive, defined, see Civil Code § 18.
Person defined for purposes of this Code, see Family Code § 105.
Proceeding defined for purposes of this Code, see Family Code § 110.
Protective order defined for purposes of this Code, see Family Code § 6218.
State defined for purposes of this Code, see Family Code § 145.
Uniform Child Custody Jurisdiction and Enforcement Act, see Family Code § 3400 et seq.
Uniform Interstate Enforcement of Domestic Violence Protection Orders Act, see Family Code § 6400 et seq.
Visitation rights,
  Generally, see Family Code § 3100 et seq.
  Close relatives where parent is deceased, see Family Code § 3102.
  Grandparents, see Family Code §§ 3103, 3104.
  Mediation of stepparent or grandparent visitation issues, see Family Code §§ 3171, 3178, 3185.
  Stepparents, see Family Code § 3101.

Research References

Forms

California Practice Guide: Rutter Family Law Forms Form 9:3, Marital Settlement Agreement.
West's California Code Forms, Family § 2338 Form 9, Marital Agreement—Both Spouses Employed.
West's California Code Forms, Family § 3081 Form 3, Clauses Regarding Custody and Visitation—Additional Clauses.
West's California Judicial Council Forms DV–108, Request for Order: No Travel With Children (Also Available in Chinese, Korean, Spanish, and Vietnamese).
West's California Judicial Council Forms DV–145, Order: No Travel With Children (Also Available in Chinese, Korean, Spanish, and Vietnamese).
West's California Judicial Council Forms FL–312, Request for Child Abduction Prevention Orders (Also Available in Spanish).
West's California Judicial Council Forms FL–341, Child Custody and Visitation (Parenting Time) Order Attachment (Also Available in Spanish).
West's California Judicial Council Forms FL–341(B), Child Abduction Prevention Order Attachment (Also Available in Spanish).

§ 3049. Disabled parents; legislative intent

It is the intent of the Legislature in enacting this section to codify the decision of the California Supreme Court in In re Marriage of Carney (1979) 24 Cal.3d 725, with respect to custody and visitation determinations by the court involving a disabled parent. *(Added by Stats.2010, c. 179 (S.B.1188), § 1.)*

Research References

Forms

1 California Transactions Forms--Family Law § 3:11, Permanent Custody.

CHAPTER 3. TEMPORARY CUSTODY ORDER DURING PENDENCY OF PROCEEDING

Section
3060. Petition for temporary custody order.
3061. Agreement or understanding on custody; temporary custody order.
3062. Ex parte temporary custody orders; hearing; extension of order if responding party avoiding jurisdiction.
3063. Order restraining removal of child from state.
3064. Restrictions on ex parte orders granting or modifying custody order.

Cross References

Child custody, generally, see Family Code § 3020 et seq.
Child welfare services, see Welfare and Institutions Code § 16500 et seq.
Dependent children, custody over, juvenile court's jurisdiction, see Welfare and Institutions Code § 304.
District attorney, action for taking or detaining child in violation of custody order, see Family Code § 3131.
District attorney, temporary custody order at request of, see Family Code § 3133.

CUSTODY OF CHILDREN

Ex parte temporary restraining orders issued without notice, see Family Code § 242.
Uniform Child Custody Jurisdiction and Enforcement Act, see Family Code § 3400 et seq.

§ 3060. Petition for temporary custody order

A petition for a temporary custody order, containing the statement required by Section 3429, may be included with the initial filing of the petition or action or may be filed at any time after the initial filing. *(Stats.1992, c. 162 (A.B.2650), § 10, operative Jan. 1, 1994. Amended by Stats.1993, c. 219 (A.B.1500), § 116.60; Stats.2019, c. 497 (A.B. 991), § 110, eff. Jan. 1, 2020.)*

Cross References

Child custody, generally, see Family Code § 3020 et seq.
Child welfare services, see Welfare and Institutions Code § 16500 et seq.
Custody agreements, modification, see Family Code § 3179.
Dependent children, custody over, juvenile court's jurisdiction, see Welfare and Institutions Code § 304.
District attorney, action for taking or detaining child in violation of custody order, see Family Code § 3131.
District attorney, temporary custody order at request of, see Family Code § 3133.
Ex parte temporary restraining orders issued without notice, see Family Code § 242.
Judgment and order defined for purposes of this Code, see Family Code § 100.
Jurisdiction of court, see Family Code § 3400 et seq.
Uniform Child Custody Jurisdiction and Enforcement Act, see Family Code § 3400 et seq.

Research References

Forms

1 California Transactions Forms--Family Law § 3:10, Temporary Custody.

§ 3061. Agreement or understanding on custody; temporary custody order

If the parties have agreed to or reached an understanding on the custody or temporary custody of their children, a copy of the agreement or an affidavit as to their understanding shall be attached to the petition or action. As promptly as possible after this filing, the court shall, except in exceptional circumstances, enter an order granting temporary custody in accordance with the agreement or understanding or in accordance with any stipulation of the parties. *(Stats.1992, c. 162 (A.B.2650), § 10, operative Jan. 1, 1994. Amended by Stats.1993, c. 219 (A.B.1500), § 116.61.)*

Cross References

Ex parte temporary restraining orders issued without notice, see Family Code § 242.
Judgment and order defined for purposes of this Code, see Family Code § 100.
Uniform Child Custody Jurisdiction and Enforcement Act, see Family Code § 3400 et seq.
Uniform Parentage Act, see Family Code § 7600 et seq.

Research References

Forms

1 California Transactions Forms--Family Law § 2:70, Deciding Custody.
1 California Transactions Forms--Family Law § 3:10, Temporary Custody.

§ 3062. Ex parte temporary custody orders; hearing; extension of order if responding party avoiding jurisdiction

(a) In the absence of an agreement, understanding, or stipulation, the court may, if jurisdiction is appropriate, enter an ex parte temporary custody order, set a hearing date within 20 days, and issue an order to show cause on the responding party. If the responding party does not appear or respond within the time set, the temporary custody order may be extended as necessary, pending the termination of the proceedings.

(b) If, despite good faith efforts, service of the ex parte order and order to show cause has not been effected in a timely fashion and there is reason to believe, based on an affidavit, or other manner of proof made under penalty of perjury, by the petitioner, that the responding party has possession of the minor child and seeks to avoid the jurisdiction of the court or is concealing the whereabouts of the child, then the hearing date may be reset and the ex parte order extended up to an additional 90 days. After service has been effected, either party may request ex parte that the hearing date be advanced or the ex parte order be dissolved or modified. *(Stats.1992, c. 162 (A.B.2650), § 10, operative Jan. 1, 1994.)*

Cross References

Computation of time, see Code of Civil Procedure §§ 12, 12a; Government Code § 6800 et seq.
District attorney, action to locate missing party and child, securing compliance with order to appear, see Family Code § 3130.
Ex parte temporary restraining orders issued without notice, see Family Code § 242.
Judgment and order defined for purposes of this Code, see Family Code § 100.
Minor defined, see Family Code § 6500.
Petitioner defined for purposes of this Code, see Family Code § 126.
Proceeding defined for purposes of this Code, see Family Code § 110.
Uniform Child Custody Jurisdiction and Enforcement Act, see Family Code § 3400 et seq.
Uniform Parentage Act, see Family Code § 7600 et seq.

Research References

Forms

California Practice Guide: Rutter Family Law Forms Form 5:5, Ex Parte Application and Request for Order Re Child Custody, Visitation and Property Control.
West's California Judicial Council Forms FL–303, Declaration Regarding Notice and Service of Request for Temporary Emergency (Ex Parte) Orders (Also Available in Spanish).
West's California Judicial Council Forms FL–305, Temporary Emergency (Ex Parte) Orders (Also Available in Spanish).

§ 3063. Order restraining removal of child from state

In conjunction with any ex parte order seeking or modifying an order of custody, the court shall enter an order restraining the person receiving custody from removing the child from the state pending notice and a hearing on the order seeking or modifying custody. *(Stats.1992, c. 162 (A.B.2650), § 10, operative Jan. 1, 1994.)*

Cross References

District attorney,
  Action to locate missing party and child, securing compliance with order to appear, see Family Code § 3130.
  Violation of custody order, action for child taken or detained, see Family Code § 3131.
Ex parte temporary restraining orders issued without notice, see Family Code § 242.
Judgment and order defined for purposes of this Code, see Family Code § 100.
Minor defined, see Family Code § 6500.
Notice, actual and constructive, defined, see Civil Code § 18.
Person defined for purposes of this Code, see Family Code § 105.
State defined for purposes of this Code, see Family Code § 145.
Uniform Child Custody Jurisdiction and Enforcement Act, see Family Code § 3400 et seq.
Uniform Parentage Act, see Family Code § 7600 et seq.

Research References

Forms

West's California Judicial Council Forms DV–105, Request for Child Custody and Visitation Orders (Also Available in Chinese, Korean, Spanish, and Vietnamese).

§ 3064. Restrictions on ex parte orders granting or modifying custody order

(a) The court shall refrain from making an order granting or modifying a custody order on an ex parte basis unless there has been a showing of immediate harm to the child or immediate risk that the child will be removed from the State of California.

(b) "Immediate harm to the child" includes, but is not limited to, the following:

(1) Having a parent who has committed acts of domestic violence, where the court determines that the acts of domestic violence are of recent origin or are a part of a demonstrated and continuing pattern of acts of domestic violence.

(2) Sexual abuse of the child, where the court determines that the acts of sexual abuse are of recent origin or are a part of a demonstrated and continuing pattern of acts of sexual abuse. *(Stats.1992, c. 162 (A.B.2650), § 10, operative Jan. 1, 1994. Amended by Stats.2008, c. 54 (A.B.2960), § 1.)*

Cross References

Domestic violence,
   Defined for purposes of this Code, see Family Code § 6211.
   Prevention, generally, see Family Code § 6200 et seq.
   Support person for victims, see Family Code § 6303.
Ex parte temporary restraining orders issued without notice, see Family Code § 242.
Judgment and order defined for purposes of this Code, see Family Code § 100.
State defined for purposes of this Code, see Family Code § 145.
Uniform Child Custody Jurisdiction and Enforcement Act, see Family Code § 3400 et seq.
Uniform Parentage Act, see Family Code § 7600 et seq.

Research References

Forms

1 California Transactions Forms--Family Law § 3:10, Temporary Custody.
West's California Judicial Council Forms FL-303, Declaration Regarding Notice and Service of Request for Temporary Emergency (Ex Parte) Orders (Also Available in Spanish).
West's California Judicial Council Forms FL-305, Temporary Emergency (Ex Parte) Orders (Also Available in Spanish).

CHAPTER 4. JOINT CUSTODY

Section
3080. Presumption of joint custody.
3081. Application by parents; custody investigation.
3082. Statement of reasons for grant or denial.
3083. Contents and construction of joint legal custody order.
3084. Rights of parents to physical control of child.
3085. Grant of joint legal custody without joint physical custody.
3086. Orders of joint physical custody or joint legal custody; designation of primary caretaker and primary home of child.
3087. Modification or termination of joint custody order; statement of reasons.
3088. Modification of custody order to joint custody order.
3089. Conciliation court; consultation by court or parties.

Cross References

Best interest of child,
   Considerations, see Family Code § 3011.
   Order of preference for custody, best interest of child as factor, see Family Code § 3040.
Burden of proof, generally, see Evidence Code § 500 et seq.
Custody agreements, modification, see Family Code § 3179.
District attorney, actions, child taken or detained in violation of custody order, see Family Code § 3131.
Joint custody defined, see Family Code § 3002.
Joint physical custody defined, see Family Code § 3004.
Uniform Child Custody Jurisdiction and Enforcement Act, see Family Code § 3400 et seq.
Uniform Parentage Act, see Family Code § 7600 et seq.
Visitation rights, generally, see Family Code § 3100 et seq.

§ 3080. Presumption of joint custody

There is a presumption, affecting the burden of proof, that joint custody is in the best interest of a minor child, subject to Section 3011, where the parents have agreed to joint custody or so agree in open court at a hearing for the purpose of determining the custody of the minor child. *(Stats.1992, c. 162 (A.B.2650), § 10, operative Jan. 1, 1994. Amended by Stats.1993, c. 219 (A.B.1500), § 116.70.)*

Cross References

Best interest of child,
   Considerations, see Family Code § 3011.
   Order of preference for custody, best interest of child as factor, see Family Code § 3040.
Burden of proof, generally, see Evidence Code § 500 et seq.
Custody agreements, modification, see Family Code § 3179.
District attorney, actions, child taken or detained in violation of custody order, see Family Code § 3131.
Joint custody defined, see Family Code § 3002.
Joint physical custody defined, see Family Code § 3004.
Minor defined, see Family Code § 6500.
Presumptions, see Evidence Code § 600 et seq.
Uniform Child Custody Jurisdiction and Enforcement Act, see Family Code § 3400 et seq.
Uniform Parentage Act, see Family Code § 7600 et seq.
Visitation rights, generally, see Family Code § 3100 et seq.

Research References

Forms

1 California Transactions Forms--Family Law § 3:8, No Statutory Custody Preferences.
West's California Code Forms, Family § 3080, Comment Overview—Joint Custody.

§ 3081. Application by parents; custody investigation

On application of either parent, joint custody may be ordered in the discretion of the court in cases other than those described in Section 3080, subject to Section 3011. For the purpose of assisting the court in making a determination whether joint custody is appropriate under this section, the court may direct that an investigation be conducted pursuant to Chapter 6 (commencing with Section 3110). *(Stats.1992, c. 162 (A.B.2650), § 10, operative Jan. 1, 1994. Amended by Stats.1993, c. 219 (A.B.1500), § 116.71.)*

Cross References

Appeal, order not automatically stayed by, see Code of Civil Procedure § 917.7.
Best interest of child,
   Considerations, see Family Code § 3011.
   Order of preference for custody, best interest of child as factor, see Family Code § 3040.
California Work Opportunity and Responsibility to Kids Act, see Welfare and Institutions Code § 11200 et seq.
District attorney, actions, child taken or detained in violation of custody order, see Family Code § 3131.
Joint custody defined, see Family Code § 3002.
Joint physical custody defined, see Family Code § 3004.
Uniform Child Custody Jurisdiction and Enforcement Act, see Family Code § 3400 et seq.
Visitation rights, generally, see Family Code § 3100 et seq.

Research References

Forms

West's California Code Forms, Family § 3080, Comment Overview—Joint Custody.

§ 3082. Statement of reasons for grant or denial

When a request for joint custody is granted or denied, the court, upon the request of any party, shall state in its decision the reasons for granting or denying the request. A statement that joint physical custody is, or is not, in the best interest of the child is not sufficient to

§ 3082

satisfy the requirements of this section. *(Stats.1992, c. 162 (A.B. 2650), § 10, operative Jan. 1, 1994.)*

Cross References

Best interest of child,
    Considerations, see Family Code § 3011.
    Order of preference for custody, best interest of child as factor, see Family Code § 3040.
California Work Opportunity and Responsibility to Kids Act, see Welfare and Institutions Code § 11200 et seq.
District attorney, actions, child taken or detained in violation of custody order, see Family Code § 3131.
Joint custody defined, see Family Code § 3002.
Joint physical custody defined, see Family Code § 3004.
State defined for purposes of this Code, see Family Code § 145.
Uniform Child Custody Jurisdiction and Enforcement Act, see Family Code § 3400 et seq.
Visitation rights, generally, see Family Code § 3100 et seq.

Research References

Forms

West's California Code Forms, Family § 3080, Comment Overview—Joint Custody.

§ 3083. Contents and construction of joint legal custody order

In making an order of joint legal custody, the court shall specify the circumstances under which the consent of both parents is required to be obtained in order to exercise legal control of the child and the consequences of the failure to obtain mutual consent. In all other circumstances, either parent acting alone may exercise legal control of the child. An order of joint legal custody shall not be construed to permit an action that is inconsistent with the physical custody order unless the action is expressly authorized by the court. *(Stats.1992, c. 162 (A.B.2650), § 10, operative Jan. 1, 1994.)*

Cross References

Best interest of child,
    Considerations, see Family Code § 3011.
    Order of preference for custody, best interest of child as factor, see Family Code § 3040.
California Work Opportunity and Responsibility to Kids Act, see Welfare and Institutions Code § 11200 et seq.
District attorney, actions, child taken or detained in violation of custody order, see Family Code § 3131.
Joint custody defined, see Family Code § 3002.
Joint physical custody defined, see Family Code § 3004.
Judgment and order defined for purposes of this Code, see Family Code § 100.
Visitation rights, generally, see Family Code § 3100 et seq.

Research References

Forms

1 California Transactions Forms--Family Law § 3:9, Statutory Custody Definitions.
1 California Transactions Forms--Family Law § 3:15, Overview; Scope of Agreement.
1 California Transactions Forms--Family Law § 3:17, Deciding How to Implement and Enforce the Agreement.
2 California Transactions Forms--Family Law § 5:16, School and Extracurricular Activities; Religious Upbringing; Medical Care.
2 California Transactions Forms--Family Law § 5:26, Inheritance and Custody on Death.
West's California Code Forms, Family § 3080, Comment Overview—Joint Custody.
West's California Judicial Council Forms FL–341(C), Children's Holiday Schedule Attachment (Also Available in Spanish).
West's California Judicial Council Forms FL–341(D), Additional Provisions—Physical Custody Attachment (Also Available in Spanish).
West's California Judicial Council Forms FL–341(E), Joint Legal Custody Attachment (Also Available in Spanish).

§ 3084. Rights of parents to physical control of child

In making an order of joint physical custody, the court shall specify the rights of each parent to physical control of the child in sufficient detail to enable a parent deprived of that control to implement laws for relief of child snatching and kidnapping. *(Stats.1992, c. 162 (A.B.2650), § 10, operative Jan. 1, 1994.)*

Cross References

Best interest of child,
    Considerations, see Family Code § 3011.
    Order of preference for custody, best interest of child as factor, see Family Code § 3040.
California Work Opportunity and Responsibility to Kids Act, see Welfare and Institutions Code § 11200 et seq.
Joint custody defined, see Family Code § 3002.
Joint physical custody defined, see Family Code § 3004.
Judgment and order defined for purposes of this Code, see Family Code § 100.
Uniform Child Custody Jurisdiction and Enforcement Act, see Family Code § 3400 et seq.
Visitation rights, generally, see Family Code § 3100 et seq.

Research References

Forms

1 California Transactions Forms--Family Law § 3:9, Statutory Custody Definitions.
1 California Transactions Forms--Family Law § 3:18, Overview.

§ 3085. Grant of joint legal custody without joint physical custody

In making an order for custody with respect to both parents, the court may grant joint legal custody without granting joint physical custody. *(Stats.1992, c. 162 (A.B.2650), § 10, operative Jan. 1, 1994. Amended by Stats.1993, c. 219 (A.B.1500), § 116.72.)*

Cross References

Best interest of child,
    Considerations, see Family Code § 3011.
    Order of preference for custody, best interest of child as factor, see Family Code § 3040.
California Work Opportunity and Responsibility to Kids Act, see Welfare and Institutions Code § 11200 et seq.
Joint custody defined, see Family Code § 3002.
Joint physical custody defined, see Family Code § 3004.
Judgment and order defined for purposes of this Code, see Family Code § 100.
Uniform Child Custody Jurisdiction and Enforcement Act, see Family Code § 3400 et seq.
Visitation rights, generally, see Family Code § 3100 et seq.

Research References

Forms

1 California Transactions Forms--Family Law § 3:9, Statutory Custody Definitions.

§ 3086. Orders of joint physical custody or joint legal custody; designation of primary caretaker and primary home of child

In making an order of joint physical custody or joint legal custody, the court may specify one parent as the primary caretaker of the child and one home as the primary home of the child, for the purposes of determining eligibility for public assistance. *(Stats.1992, c. 162 (A.B.2650), § 10, operative Jan. 1, 1994.)*

Cross References

Best interest of child,
    Considerations, see Family Code § 3011.
    Order of preference for custody, best interest of child as factor, see Family Code § 3040.
California Work Opportunity and Responsibility to Kids Act, see Welfare and Institutions Code § 11200 et seq.
Compensation, failure to assume caretaker responsibility, see Family Code § 3028.
Joint custody defined, see Family Code § 3002.
Joint physical custody defined, see Family Code § 3004.
Judgment and order defined for purposes of this Code, see Family Code § 100.
Uniform Child Custody Jurisdiction and Enforcement Act, see Family Code § 3400 et seq.

Visitation rights, generally, see Family Code § 3100 et seq.

Research References

Forms

1 California Transactions Forms--Family Law § 3:9, Statutory Custody Definitions.
1 California Transactions Forms--Family Law § 3:18, Overview.

§ 3087. Modification or termination of joint custody order; statement of reasons

An order for joint custody may be modified or terminated upon the petition of one or both parents or on the court's own motion if it is shown that the best interest of the child requires modification or termination of the order. If either parent opposes the modification or termination order, the court shall state in its decision the reasons for modification or termination of the joint custody order. *(Stats. 1992, c. 162 (A.B.2650), § 10, operative Jan. 1, 1994.)*

Cross References

Appeals, orders not automatically stayed, see Code of Civil Procedure § 917.7.
Best interest of child,
  Considerations, see Family Code § 3011.
  Order of preference for custody, best interest of child as factor, see Family Code § 3040.
California Work Opportunity and Responsibility to Kids Act, see Welfare and Institutions Code § 11200 et seq.
Joint custody defined, see Family Code § 3002.
Joint physical custody defined, see Family Code § 3004.
Judgment and order defined for purposes of this Code, see Family Code § 100.
State defined for purposes of this Code, see Family Code § 145.
Uniform Child Custody Jurisdiction and Enforcement Act, see Family Code § 3400 et seq.
Visitation rights, generally, see Family Code § 3100 et seq.

Research References

Forms

1 California Transactions Forms--Family Law § 3:18, Overview.

§ 3088. Modification of custody order to joint custody order

An order for the custody of a minor child entered by a court in this state or any other state may, subject to the jurisdictional requirements in Sections 3403 and 3414, be modified at any time to an order for joint custody in accordance with this chapter. *(Stats.1992, c. 162 (A.B.2650), § 10, operative Jan. 1, 1994. Amended by Stats.1993, c. 219 (A.B.1500), § 116.73.)*

Cross References

Best interest of child,
  Considerations, see Family Code § 3011.
  Order of preference for custody, best interest of child as factor, see Family Code § 3040.
California Work Opportunity and Responsibility to Kids Act, see Welfare and Institutions Code § 11200 et seq.
Joint custody defined, see Family Code § 3002.
Joint physical custody defined, see Family Code § 3004.
Judgment and order defined for purposes of this Code, see Family Code § 100.
Minor defined, see Family Code § 6500.
State defined for purposes of this Code, see Family Code § 145.
Uniform Child Custody Jurisdiction and Enforcement Act, see Family Code § 3400 et seq.
Visitation rights, generally, see Family Code § 3100 et seq.

§ 3089. Conciliation court; consultation by court or parties

In counties having a conciliation court, the court or the parties may, at any time, pursuant to local rules of court, consult with the conciliation court for the purpose of assisting the parties to formulate a plan for implementation of the custody order or to resolve a controversy which has arisen in the implementation of a plan for custody. *(Stats.1992, c. 162 (A.B.2650), § 10, operative Jan. 1, 1994.)*

Cross References

Best interest of child,
  Considerations, see Family Code § 3011.
  Order of preference for custody, best interest of child as factor, see Family Code § 3040.
California Work Opportunity and Responsibility to Kids Act, see Welfare and Institutions Code § 11200 et seq.
Conciliation proceedings, generally, see Family Code § 1800 et seq.
County defined for purposes of this Code, see Family Code § 67.
Family mediation and conciliation services, statewide coordination, see Family Code § 1850 et seq.
Joint custody defined, see Family Code § 3002.
Joint physical custody defined, see Family Code § 3004.
Judgment and order defined for purposes of this Code, see Family Code § 100.
Minor defined, see Family Code § 6500.
Uniform Child Custody Jurisdiction and Enforcement Act, see Family Code § 3400 et seq.
Visitation rights, generally, see Family Code § 3100 et seq.

Research References

Forms

1 California Transactions Forms--Family Law § 3:17, Deciding How to Implement and Enforce the Agreement.

CHAPTER 5. VISITATION RIGHTS

Section

3100. Joint custody orders; visitation rights; domestic violence prevention orders; transfer of children; detail specific orders; confidentiality of shelter locations.
3101. Stepparent's visitation rights.
3102. Deceased parent; visitation rights of close relatives; adoption of child.
3103. Grandparent's rights; custody proceeding.
3104. Grandparent's rights; petition by grandparent; notice; protective order directed to grandparent; rebuttable presumptions; conflict with rights of non-party birth parent; change of residence of child; discretion of court.
3105. Former legal guardians; visitation rights.

Cross References

Best interest of child,
  Considerations, see Family Code § 3011.
  Order of preference for custody, best interest of child as factor, see Family Code § 3040.
Jurisdiction in superior court, see Family Code § 200.
Mediation of stepparent or grandparent visitation issues, see Family Code §§ 3171, 3178, 3185.
Modification of custody agreements reached through mediation, see Family Code § 3179.
Uniform Child Custody Jurisdiction and Enforcement Act, see Family Code § 3400 et seq.

§ 3100. Joint custody orders; visitation rights; domestic violence prevention orders; transfer of children; detail specific orders; confidentiality of shelter locations

(a) In making an order pursuant to Chapter 4 (commencing with Section 3080), the court shall grant reasonable visitation rights to a parent when it is shown that the visitation would be in the best interest of the child, as defined in Section 3011, and consistent with Section 3020. In the discretion of the court, reasonable visitation rights may be granted to any other person having an interest in the welfare of the child.

(b) If a protective order, as defined in Section 6218, has been directed to a parent, the court shall consider whether the best interest of the child requires that any visitation by that parent be limited to situations in which a third person, specified by the court, is present, or whether visitation shall be suspended, limited, or denied. The court shall include in its deliberations a consideration of the nature of

§ 3100

the acts from which the parent was enjoined and the period of time that has elapsed since that order. A parent may submit to the court the name of a person that the parent deems suitable to be present during visitation.

(c) If visitation is ordered in a case in which domestic violence is alleged and an emergency protective order, protective order, or other restraining order has been issued, the visitation order shall specify the time, day, place, and manner of transfer of the child, so as to limit the child's exposure to potential domestic conflict or violence and to ensure the safety of all family members. If a criminal protective order has been issued pursuant to Section 136.2 of the Penal Code, the visitation order shall make reference to, and, unless there is an emergency protective order that has precedence in enforcement pursuant to paragraph (1) of subdivision (c) of Section 136.2 of the Penal Code or a no-contact order, as described in Section 6320, acknowledge the precedence of enforcement of, an appropriate criminal protective order.

(d) If the court finds a party is staying in a place designated as a shelter for victims of domestic violence or other confidential location, the court's order for time, day, place, and manner of transfer of the child for visitation shall be designed to prevent disclosure of the location of the shelter or other confidential location. *(Stats.1992, c. 162 (A.B.2650), § 10, operative Jan. 1, 1994. Amended by Stats.1993, c. 219 (A.B.1500), § 116.74; Stats.1994, c. 320 (A.B.356), § 2; Stats.2005, c. 465 (A.B.118), § 1; Stats.2013, c. 263 (A.B.176), § 1, operative July 1, 2014; Stats.2018, c. 941 (A.B.2044), § 4, eff. Jan. 1, 2019.)*

Cross References

Appeals, orders not automatically stayed, see Code of Civil Procedure § 917.7.
Best interest of child,
  Considerations, see Family Code § 3011.
  Order of preference for custody, best interest of child as factor, see Family Code § 3040.
Court orders available in response to good cause belief of harm to, intimidation of, or dissuasion of victim or witness, see Penal Code § 136.2.
Custody or visitation, parent convicted under Penal Code provisions, see Family Code § 3030.
District attorney, actions, taking or detaining child in violation of visitation order, see Family Code § 3131.
Domestic violence defined for purposes of this Code, see Family Code § 6211.
Domestic violence prevention, generally, see Family Code § 6200 et seq.
Emergency protective order defined for purposes of this Code, see Family Code § 6215.
Judgment and order defined for purposes of this Code, see Family Code § 100.
Jurisdiction in superior court, see Family Code § 200.
Mediation of stepparent or grandparent visitation issues, see Family Code §§ 3171, 3178, 3185.
Modification of custody agreements reached through mediation, see Family Code § 3179.
Parent convicted under certain penal provisions, unsupervised visitation with child, see Family Code § 3030.
Person defined for purposes of this Code, see Family Code § 105.
Protective order defined, see Family Code § 6218.
Uniform Child Custody Jurisdiction and Enforcement Act, see Family Code § 3400 et seq.

Research References

Forms

California Practice Guide: Rutter Family Law Forms Form 5:5, Ex Parte Application and Request for Order Re Child Custody, Visitation and Property Control.
California Practice Guide: Rutter Family Law Forms Form 7:19, Memorandum in Support of Motion and Declaration for Joinder (Grandparent Visitation Claim).
1 California Transactions Forms--Family Law § 3:13, Rights of Third Parties.
1 California Transactions Forms--Family Law § 4:104, Paternity Acknowledgment.
2 California Transactions Forms--Family Law § 5:2, Overview.
West's California Code Forms, Family § 3103, Comment Overview—Visitation Rights.
West's California Judicial Council Forms DV–140, Child Custody and Visitation Order (Also Available in Chinese, Korean, Spanish, and Vietnamese).
West's California Judicial Council Forms DV–150, Supervised Visitation and Exchange Order.
West's California Judicial Council Forms FL–341, Child Custody and Visitation (Parenting Time) Order Attachment (Also Available in Spanish).
West's California Judicial Council Forms FL–341(A), Supervised Visitation Order (Also Available in Spanish).

§ 3101. Stepparent's visitation rights

(a) Notwithstanding any other provision of law, the court may grant reasonable visitation to a stepparent, if visitation by the stepparent is determined to be in the best interest of the minor child.

(b) If a protective order, as defined in Section 6218, has been directed to a stepparent to whom visitation may be granted pursuant to this section, the court shall consider whether the best interest of the child requires that any visitation by the stepparent be denied.

(c) Visitation rights may not be ordered under this section that would conflict with a right of custody or visitation of a birth parent who is not a party to the proceeding.

(d) As used in this section:

(1) "Birth parent" means "birth parent" as defined in Section 8512.

(2) "Stepparent" means a person who is a party to the marriage that is the subject of the proceeding, with respect to a minor child of the other party to the marriage. *(Added by Stats.1993, c. 219 (A.B.1500), § 116.76.)*

Cross References

Appeals, orders not automatically stayed, see Code of Civil Procedure § 917.7.
Best interests of child,
  Considerations, see Family Code § 3011.
  Order of preference for custody, best interest of child as factor, see Family Code § 3040.
Custody or visitation, parent convicted under Penal Code provisions, see Family Code § 3030.
District attorney, actions, taking or detaining child in violation of visitation order, see Family Code § 3131.
Judgment and order defined for purposes of this Code, see Family Code § 100.
Mediation of stepparent or grandparent visitation issues, see Family Code §§ 3171, 3178, 3185.
Minor defined for purposes of this Code, see Family Code § 6500.
Modification of custody agreements reached through mediation, see Family Code § 3179.
Person defined for purposes of this Code, see Family Code § 105.
Proceeding defined for purposes of this Code, see Family Code § 110.
Temporary custody order, district attorney order, see Family Code § 3133.
Uniform Child Custody Jurisdiction and Enforcement Act, see Family Code § 3400 et seq.

Research References

Forms

1 California Transactions Forms--Family Law § 3:7, Custody Issues Outside the Scope of the Family Code.
1 California Transactions Forms--Family Law § 3:13, Rights of Third Parties.
2 California Transactions Forms--Family Law § 5:3, Rights of Nonparents Generally.
2 California Transactions Forms--Family Law § 5:10, Use of Parenting Agreement to Define Rights and Responsibilities Relating to Child on Termination of Partners' Relationship Where Neither or Only One Partner is Biological Parent.

§ 3102. Deceased parent; visitation rights of close relatives; adoption of child

(a) If either parent of an unemancipated minor child is deceased, the children, siblings, parents, and grandparents of the deceased parent may be granted reasonable visitation with the child during the child's minority upon a finding that the visitation would be in the best interest of the minor child.

(b) In granting visitation pursuant to this section to a person other than a grandparent of the child, the court shall consider the amount of personal contact between the person and the child before the application for the visitation order.

(c) This section does not apply if the child has been adopted by a person other than a stepparent or grandparent of the child. Any visitation rights granted pursuant to this section before the adoption of the child automatically terminate if the child is adopted by a person other than a stepparent or grandparent of the child. *(Stats.1992, c. 162 (A.B.2650), § 10, operative Jan. 1, 1994. Amended by Stats.1993, c. 219 (A.B.1500), § 116.77; Stats.1994, c. 164 (A.B. 3042), § 1.)*

Cross References

Appeals, orders not automatically stayed, see Code of Civil Procedure § 917.7.
Best interest of child,
   Considerations, see Family Code § 3011.
   Order of preference for custody, best interest of child as factor, see Family Code § 3040.
Emancipation of minors, conditions, see Family Code § 7002.
Judgment and order defined for purposes of this Code, see Family Code § 100.
Jurisdiction in superior court, see Family Code § 200.
Mediation of custody and visitation issues, see Family Code § 3160 et seq.
Mediation of stepparent or grandparent visitation, see Family Code §§ 3171, 3178, 3185.
Minor defined for purposes of this Code, see Family Code § 6500.
Modification of custody agreements reached through mediation, see Family Code § 3179.
Person defined for purposes of this Code, see Family Code § 105.
Removal of child from parental custody, preferential consideration of relative's request for placement of child with relative, see Welfare and Institutions Code § 361.3.
Uniform Child Custody Jurisdiction and Enforcement Act, see Family Code § 3400 et seq.

Research References

Forms

2 California Transactions Forms--Family Law § 5:3, Rights of Nonparents Generally.
2 California Transactions Forms--Family Law § 5:10, Use of Parenting Agreement to Define Rights and Responsibilities Relating to Child on Termination of Partners' Relationship Where Neither or Only One Partner is Biological Parent.
West's California Code Forms, Family § 3103, Comment Overview—Visitation Rights.

§ 3103. Grandparent's rights; custody proceeding

(a) Notwithstanding any other provision of law, in a proceeding described in Section 3021, the court may grant reasonable visitation to a grandparent of a minor child of a party to the proceeding if the court determines that visitation by the grandparent is in the best interest of the child.

(b) If a protective order as defined in Section 6218 has been directed to the grandparent during the pendency of the proceeding, the court shall consider whether the best interest of the child requires that visitation by the grandparent be denied.

(c) The petitioner shall give notice of the petition to each of the parents of the child, any stepparent, and any person who has physical custody of the child, by certified mail, return receipt requested, postage prepaid, to the person's last known address, or to the attorneys of record of the parties to the proceeding.

(d) There is a rebuttable presumption affecting the burden of proof that the visitation of a grandparent is not in the best interest of a minor child if the child's parents agree that the grandparent should not be granted visitation rights.

(e) Visitation rights may not be ordered under this section if that would conflict with a right of custody or visitation of a birth parent who is not a party to the proceeding.

(f) Visitation ordered pursuant to this section shall not create a basis for or against a change of residence of the child, but shall be one of the factors for the court to consider in ordering a change of residence.

(g) When a court orders grandparental visitation pursuant to this section, the court in its discretion may, based upon the relevant circumstances of the case:

(1) Allocate the percentage of grandparental visitation between the parents for purposes of the calculation of child support pursuant to the statewide uniform guideline (Article 2 (commencing with Section 4050) of Chapter 2 of Part 2 of Division 9).

(2) Notwithstanding Sections 3930 and 3951, order a parent or grandparent to pay to the other, an amount for the support of the child or grandchild. For purposes of this paragraph, "support" means costs related to visitation such as any of the following:

(A) Transportation.

(B) Provision of basic expenses for the child or grandchild, such as medical expenses, day care costs, and other necessities.

(h) As used in this section, "birth parent" means "birth parent" as defined in Section 8512. *(Added by Stats.1993, c. 219 (A.B.1500), § 116.78. Amended by Stats.1993, c. 832 (S.B.306), § 1.)*

Cross References

Appeals, orders not automatically stayed, see Code of Civil Procedure § 917.7.
Best interests of child,
   Considerations, see Family Code § 3011.
   Order of preference for custody, best interest of child as factor, see Family Code § 3040.
Burden of proof, generally, see Evidence Code § 500 et seq.
Child support, generally, see Family Code § 3900 et seq.
Custody or visitation, parent convicted under Penal Code provisions, see Family Code § 3030.
District attorney, actions, taking or detaining child in violation of visitation order, see Family Code § 3131.
Fees for mediation services, see Government Code § 26840.3.
Judgment and order defined for purposes of this Code, see Family Code § 100.
Mediation of stepparent or grandparent visitation issues, see Family Code §§ 3171, 3178, 3185.
Minor defined for purposes of this Code, see Family Code § 6500.
Notice, actual and constructive, defined, see Civil Code § 18.
Person defined for purposes of this Code, see Family Code § 105.
Petitioner defined for purposes of this Code, see Family Code § 126.
Presumptions, see Evidence Code § 600 et seq.
Proceeding defined for purposes of this Code, see Family Code § 110.
Support, generally, see Family Code § 3500 et seq.
Support defined for purposes of this Code, see Family Code § 150.
Temporary custody order, district attorney order, see Family Code § 3133.
Uniform Child Custody Jurisdiction and Enforcement Act, see Family Code § 3400 et seq.

Research References

Forms

California Practice Guide: Rutter Family Law Forms Form 7:17, Notice of Motion and Declaration for Joinder (Grandparent Visitation Claim).
California Practice Guide: Rutter Family Law Forms Form 7:18, Complaint for Joinder (Grandparent Visitation Claim).
California Practice Guide: Rutter Family Law Forms Form 7:19, Memorandum in Support of Motion and Declaration for Joinder (Grandparent Visitation Claim).
1 California Transactions Forms--Family Law § 3:7, Custody Issues Outside the Scope of the Family Code.
2 California Transactions Forms--Family Law § 5:3, Rights of Nonparents Generally.
2 California Transactions Forms--Family Law § 5:5, Rights of Grandparents and Close Relatives.
2 California Transactions Forms--Family Law § 5:10, Use of Parenting Agreement to Define Rights and Responsibilities Relating to Child on Termination of Partners' Relationship Where Neither or Only One Partner is Biological Parent.

§ 3103

West's California Code Forms, Family § 3103, Comment Overview—Visitation Rights.

§ 3104. Grandparent's rights; petition by grandparent; notice; protective order directed to grandparent; rebuttable presumptions; conflict with rights of non-party birth parent; change of residence of child; discretion of court

(a) On petition to the court by a grandparent of a minor child, the court may grant reasonable visitation rights to the grandparent if the court does both of the following:

(1) Finds that there is a preexisting relationship between the grandparent and the grandchild that has engendered a bond such that visitation is in the best interest of the child.

(2) Balances the interest of the child in having visitation with the grandparent against the right of the parents to exercise their parental authority.

(b) A petition for visitation under this section shall not be filed while the natural or adoptive parents are married, unless one or more of the following circumstances exist:

(1) The parents are currently living separately and apart on a permanent or indefinite basis.

(2) One of the parents has been absent for more than one month without the other spouse knowing the whereabouts of the absent spouse.

(3) One of the parents joins in the petition with the grandparents.

(4) The child is not residing with either parent.

(5) The child has been adopted by a stepparent.

(6) One of the parents is incarcerated or involuntarily institutionalized.

At any time that a change of circumstances occurs such that none of these circumstances exist, the parent or parents may move the court to terminate grandparental visitation and the court shall grant the termination.

(c) The petitioner shall give notice of the petition to each of the parents of the child, any stepparent, and any person who has physical custody of the child, by personal service pursuant to Section 415.10 of the Code of Civil Procedure.

(d) If a protective order as defined in Section 6218 has been directed to the grandparent during the pendency of the proceeding, the court shall consider whether the best interest of the child requires that any visitation by that grandparent should be denied.

(e) There is a rebuttable presumption that the visitation of a grandparent is not in the best interest of a minor child if the natural or adoptive parents agree that the grandparent should not be granted visitation rights.

(f) There is a rebuttable presumption affecting the burden of proof that the visitation of a grandparent is not in the best interest of a minor child if the parent who has been awarded sole legal and physical custody of the child in another proceeding, or the parent with whom the child resides if there is currently no operative custody order objects to visitation by the grandparent.

(g) Visitation rights may not be ordered under this section if that would conflict with a right of custody or visitation of a birth parent who is not a party to the proceeding.

(h) Visitation ordered pursuant to this section shall not create a basis for or against a change of residence of the child, but shall be one of the factors for the court to consider in ordering a change of residence.

(i) When a court orders grandparental visitation pursuant to this section, the court in its discretion may, based upon the relevant circumstances of the case:

(1) Allocate the percentage of grandparental visitation between the parents for purposes of the calculation of child support pursuant to the statewide uniform guideline (Article 2 (commencing with Section 4050) of Chapter 2 of Part 2 of Division 9).

(2) Notwithstanding Sections 3930 and 3951, order a parent or grandparent to pay to the other, an amount for the support of the child or grandchild. For purposes of this paragraph, "support" means costs related to visitation such as any of the following:

(A) Transportation.

(B) Provision of basic expenses for the child or grandchild, such as medical expenses, day care costs, and other necessities.

(j) As used in this section, "birth parent" means "birth parent" as defined in Section 8512. *(Added by Stats.1993, c. 832 (S.B.306), § 2. Amended by Stats.2006, c. 138 (A.B.2517), § 1; Stats.2014, c. 328 (A.B.1628), § 1, eff. Jan. 1, 2015.)*

Cross References

Best interest of child,
   Considerations, see Family Code § 3011.
   Order of preference for custody, best interest of child as factor, see Family Code § 3040.
Burden of proof, generally, see Evidence Code § 500 et seq.
Child support, generally, see Family Code § 3900 et seq.
Judgment and order defined for purposes of this Code, see Family Code § 100.
Minor defined for purposes of this Code, see Family Code § 6500.
Modification of custody agreements reached through mediation, see Family Code § 3179.
Notice, actual and constructive, defined, see Civil Code § 18.
Person defined for purposes of this Code, see Family Code § 105.
Petitioner defined for purposes of this Code, see Family Code § 126.
Presumptions, see Evidence Code § 600 et seq.
Proceeding defined for purposes of this Code, see Family Code § 110.
References to husband, wife, spouses and married persons, persons included for purposes of this Code, see Family Code § 11.
Support, generally, see Family Code § 3500 et seq.
Support defined for purposes of this Code, see Family Code § 150.
Uniform Child Custody Jurisdiction and Enforcement Act, see Family Code § 3400 et seq.

Research References

Forms

California Practice Guide: Rutter Family Law Forms Form 7:17, Notice of Motion and Declaration for Joinder (Grandparent Visitation Claim).
California Practice Guide: Rutter Family Law Forms Form 7:18, Complaint for Joinder (Grandparent Visitation Claim).
California Practice Guide: Rutter Family Law Forms Form 7:19, Memorandum in Support of Motion and Declaration for Joinder (Grandparent Visitation Claim).
1 California Transactions Forms--Family Law § 3:7, Custody Issues Outside the Scope of the Family Code.
2 California Transactions Forms--Family Law § 5:3, Rights of Nonparents Generally.
2 California Transactions Forms--Family Law § 5:5, Rights of Grandparents and Close Relatives.
2 California Transactions Forms--Family Law § 5:10, Use of Parenting Agreement to Define Rights and Responsibilities Relating to Child on Termination of Partners' Relationship Where Neither or Only One Partner is Biological Parent.
West's California Code Forms, Family § 3103, Comment Overview—Visitation Rights.

§ 3105. Former legal guardians; visitation rights

(a) The Legislature finds and declares that a parent's fundamental right to provide for the care, custody, companionship, and management of the parent's children, while compelling, is not absolute. Children have a fundamental right to maintain healthy, stable relationships with a person who has served in a significant, judicially approved parental role.

(b) The court may grant reasonable visitation rights to a person who previously served as the legal guardian of a child, if visitation is determined to be in the best interest of the minor child.

(c) In the absence of a court order granting or denying visitation between a former legal guardian and a former minor ward, and if a dependency proceeding is not pending, a former legal guardian may maintain an independent action for visitation with the former minor ward. If the child does not have at least one living parent, visitation shall not be determined in a proceeding under the Family Code, but shall instead be determined in a guardianship proceeding that may be initiated for that purpose. *(Added by Stats.2004, c. 301 (A.B.2292), § 1. Amended by Stats.2019, c. 115 (A.B.1817), § 32, eff. Jan. 1, 2020.)*

CHAPTER 6. CUSTODY INVESTIGATION AND REPORT

Section
3110. Court-appointed investigator.
3110.5. Child custody evaluator.
3111. Child custody evaluations; confidentiality and use of report; monetary sanction for unwarranted disclosure; adoption of form regarding confidentiality.
3112. Repayment of expenses.
3113. Domestic violence history between parties; custody investigation procedures.
3114. Appointment of counsel for minor children; recommendations.
3115. Cross–examination of court–appointed investigator; waiver of right.
3116. Investigator's duty to assist court; scope of duty.
3117. Standards for court–connected child custody actions; guidelines for cross–examination of court–appointed investigators; deadline.
3118. Child sex abuse allegations; child custody evaluation, investigation or assessment.

Cross References

Child custody, confidential psychological evaluations and recommendations, exceptions, see Family Code § 3025.5.
Department of Consumer Affairs, complaints about licensees, notification upon receipt of child custody evaluation report, see Business and Professions Code § 129.
Investigation and report involving custody, status, and welfare of minor, see Welfare and Institutions Code § 281.
Mediation proceedings, recommendation of investigation prior to hearing, see Family Code § 3183.

§ 3110. Court-appointed investigator

As used in this chapter, "court-appointed investigator" means a probation officer, domestic relations investigator, or court-appointed evaluator directed by the court to conduct an investigation pursuant to this chapter. *(Added by Stats.1993, c. 219 (A.B.1500), § 116.81.)*

Cross References

Mediation proceedings, recommendation of investigation prior to hearing, see Family Code § 3183.

Research References

Forms

California Practice Guide: Rutter Family Law Forms Form 1:32, Glossary of Common Family Law Terms, Phrases and Concepts (Enclosure to Form 1:31).
1 California Transactions Forms--Family Law § 2:70, Deciding Custody.

§ 3110.5. Child custody evaluator

(a) A person may be a court-connected or private child custody evaluator under this chapter only if the person has completed the domestic violence and child abuse training program described in Section 1816 and has complied with Rules 5.220 and 5.230 of the California Rules of Court.

(b)(1) On or before January 1, 2002, the Judicial Council shall formulate a statewide rule of court that establishes education, experience, and training requirements for all child custody evaluators appointed pursuant to this chapter, Section 730 of the Evidence Code, or Chapter 15 (commencing with Section 2032.010) of Title 4 of Part 4 of the Code of Civil Procedure.

(A) The rule shall require a child custody evaluator to declare under penalty of perjury that the evaluator meets all of the education, experience, and training requirements specified in the rule and, if applicable, possesses a license in good standing. The Judicial Council shall establish forms to implement this section. The rule shall permit court-connected evaluators to conduct evaluations if they meet all of the qualifications established by the Judicial Council. The education, experience, and training requirements to be specified for court-connected evaluators shall include, but not be limited to, knowledge of the psychological and developmental needs of children and parent and child relationships.

(B) The rule shall require all evaluators to utilize comparable interview, assessment, and testing procedures for all parties that are consistent with generally accepted clinical, forensic, scientific, diagnostic, or medical standards. The rule shall also require evaluators to inform each adult party of the purpose, nature, and method of the evaluation.

(C) The rule may allow courts to permit the parties to stipulate to an evaluator of their choosing with the approval of the court under the circumstances set forth in subdivision (d). The rule may require courts to provide general information about how parties can contact qualified child custody evaluators in their county.

(2) On or before January 1, 2004, the Judicial Council shall include in the statewide rule of court created pursuant to this section a requirement that all court-connected and private child custody evaluators receive training in the nature of child sexual abuse. The Judicial Council shall develop standards for this training that shall include, but not be limited to, the following:

(A) Children's patterns of hiding and disclosing sexual abuse occurring in a family setting.

(B) The effects of sexual abuse on children.

(C) The nature and extent of child sexual abuse.

(D) The social and family dynamics of child sexual abuse.

(E) Techniques for identifying and assisting families affected by child sexual abuse.

(F) Legal rights, protections, and remedies available to victims of child sexual abuse.

(c) In addition to the education, experience, and training requirements established by the Judicial Council pursuant to subdivision (b), on or after January 1, 2005, a person may be a child custody evaluator under this chapter, Section 730 of the Evidence Code, or Chapter 15 (commencing with Section 2032.010) of Title 4 of Part 4 of the Code of Civil Procedure only if the person meets one of the following criteria:

(1) The person is licensed as a physician under Chapter 5 (commencing with Section 2000) of Division 2 of the Business and Professions Code and either is a board certified psychiatrist or has completed a residency in psychiatry.

(2) The person is licensed as a psychologist under Chapter 6.6 (commencing with Section 2900) of Division 2 of the Business and Professions Code.

(3) The person is licensed as a marriage and family therapist under Chapter 13 (commencing with Section 4980) of Division 2 of the Business and Professions Code.

(4) The person is licensed as a clinical social worker under Article 4 (commencing with Section 4996) of Chapter 14 of Division 2 of the Business and Professions Code.

§ 3110.5

(5) The person is licensed as a professional clinical counselor under Chapter 16 (commencing with Section 4999.10) of Division 2 of the Business and Professions Code.

(6) The person is a court-connected evaluator who has been certified by the court as meeting all of the qualifications for court-connected evaluators as specified by the Judicial Council pursuant to subdivision (b).

(d) Subdivision (c) does not apply in a case in which the court determines that there are no evaluators who meet the criteria of subdivision (c) who are willing and available, within a reasonable period of time, to perform child custody evaluations. In those cases, the parties may stipulate to an individual who does not meet the criteria of subdivision (c), subject to approval by the court.

(e) A child custody evaluator who is licensed by the Medical Board of California, the Board of Psychology, or the Board of Behavioral Sciences shall be subject to disciplinary action by that board for unprofessional conduct, as defined in the licensing law applicable to that licensee.

(f) On or after January 1, 2005, a court-connected or private child custody evaluator may not evaluate, investigate, or mediate an issue of child custody in a proceeding pursuant to this division unless that person has completed child sexual abuse training as required by this section. *(Added by Stats.1999, c. 932 (S.B.433), § 1. Amended by Stats.2000, c. 926 (S.B.1716), § 4; Stats.2004, c. 182 (A.B.3081), § 33, operative July 1, 2005; Stats.2004, c. 811 (A.B.3079), § 1; Stats.2004, c. 811 (A.B.3079), § 1.5, operative July 1, 2005; Stats.2018, c. 389 (A.B.2296), § 11, eff. Jan. 1, 2019; Stats.2019, c. 115 (A.B.1817), § 33, eff. Jan. 1, 2020; Stats.2021, c. 440 (A.B.462), § 6, eff. Jan. 1, 2022.)*

Cross References

Abuse defined for purposes of the Domestic Violence Prevention Act, see Family Code § 6203.
Adult defined for purposes of this Code, see Family Code § 6501.
Conciliation proceedings, generally, see Family Code § 1800 et seq.
County defined for purposes of this Code, see Family Code § 67.
Domestic violence defined for purposes of this Code, see Family Code § 6211.
Family mediation and conciliation services, statewide coordination, see Family Code § 1850 et seq.
Mediation of custody and visitation issues, generally, see Family Code § 3160 et seq.
Person defined for purposes of this Code, see Family Code § 105.
Proceeding defined for purposes of this Code, see Family Code § 110.

Research References

Forms
1 California Transactions Forms--Family Law § 2:70, Deciding Custody.
West's California Code Forms, Family § 3110, Comment Overview—Custody Investigation and Report.
West's California Judicial Council Forms FL-325, Declaration of Court-Connected Child Custody Evaluator Regarding Qualifications.
West's California Judicial Council Forms FL-326, Declaration of Private Child Custody Evaluator Regarding Qualifications.
West's California Judicial Council Forms FL-327, Order Appointing Child Custody Evaluator.

§ 3111. Child custody evaluations; confidentiality and use of report; monetary sanction for unwarranted disclosure; adoption of form regarding confidentiality

(a) In a contested proceeding involving child custody or visitation rights, the court may appoint a child custody evaluator to conduct a child custody evaluation in cases where the court determines it is in the best interest of the child. The child custody evaluation shall be conducted in accordance with the standards adopted by the Judicial Council pursuant to Section 3117, and all other standards adopted by the Judicial Council regarding child custody evaluations. If directed by the court, the court-appointed child custody evaluator shall file a written confidential report on the evaluation. At least 10 days before a hearing regarding custody of the child, the report shall be filed with the clerk of the court in which the custody hearing will be conducted and served on the parties or their attorneys, and any other counsel appointed for the child pursuant to Section 3150. A child custody evaluation, investigation, or assessment, and a resulting report, may be considered by the court only if it is conducted in accordance with the requirements set forth in the standards adopted by the Judicial Council pursuant to Section 3117; however, this does not preclude the consideration of a child custody evaluation report that contains nonsubstantive or inconsequential errors or both.

(b) The report shall not be made available other than as provided in subdivision (a) or Section 3025.5, or as described in Section 204 of the Welfare and Institutions Code or Section 1514.5 of the Probate Code. Any information obtained from access to a juvenile court case file, as defined in subdivision (e) of Section 827 of the Welfare and Institutions Code, is confidential and shall only be disseminated as provided by paragraph (4) of subdivision (a) of Section 827 of the Welfare and Institutions Code.

(c) The report may be received in evidence on stipulation of all interested parties and is competent evidence as to all matters contained in the report.

(d) If the court determines that an unwarranted disclosure of a written confidential report has been made, the court may impose a monetary sanction against the disclosing party. The sanction shall be in an amount sufficient to deter repetition of the conduct, and may include reasonable attorney's fees, costs incurred, or both, unless the court finds that the disclosing party acted with substantial justification or that other circumstances make the imposition of the sanction unjust. The court shall not impose a sanction pursuant to this subdivision that imposes an unreasonable financial burden on the party against whom the sanction is imposed.

(e) The Judicial Council shall, by January 1, 2010, do the following:

(1) Adopt a form to be served with every child custody evaluation report that informs the report recipient of the confidentiality of the report and the potential consequences for the unwarranted disclosure of the report.

(2) Adopt a rule of court to require that, when a court-ordered child custody evaluation report is served on the parties, the form specified in paragraph (1) shall be included with the report.

(f) For purposes of this section, a disclosure is unwarranted if it is done either recklessly or maliciously, and is not in the best interest of the child. *(Added by Stats.1993, c. 219 (A.B.1500), § 116.81. Amended by Stats.1996, c. 761 (S.B.1995), § 1; Stats.1999, c. 932 (S.B.433), § 2; Stats.2002, c. 1008 (A.B.3028), § 16; Stats.2004, c. 574 (A.B.2228), § 1; Stats.2005, c. 22 (S.B.1108), § 62; Stats.2008, c. 215 (A.B.1877), § 1; Stats.2014, c. 283 (A.B.1843), § 3, eff. Jan. 1, 2015; Stats.2015, c. 130 (S.B.594), § 1, eff. Jan. 1, 2016; Stats.2019, c. 115 (A.B.1817), § 34, eff. Jan. 1, 2020.)*

Cross References

Attorneys, State Bar Act, see Business and Professions Code § 6000.
Computation of time, see Code of Civil Procedure §§ 12, 12a; Government Code § 6800 et seq.
Counsel, right to, see Cal. Const. Art. 1, § 15, cl. 3.
Investigation and report involving custody, status, and welfare of minor, see Welfare and Institutions Code § 281.
Joint custody, investigation, see Family Code § 3081.
Juvenile case file inspection, confidentiality, release, probation reports, destruction of records, and liability, see Welfare and Institutions Code § 827.
Mediation proceedings, recommendation of investigation prior to hearing, see Family Code § 3183.
Modification of custody or visitation orders, justifications, military duty, see Family Code § 3047.
Proceeding defined for purposes of this Code, see Family Code § 110.

Protective orders and other domestic violence prevention orders, criminal history search, prior restraining orders, see Family Code § 6306.

Research References

Forms

California Practice Guide: Rutter Family Law Forms Form 1:32, Glossary of Common Family Law Terms, Phrases and Concepts (Enclosure to Form 1:31).

California Practice Guide: Rutter Family Law Forms Form 7:5, Stipulation Appointing Child Custody Evaluator (Attorney-Drafted).

1 California Transactions Forms--Family Law § 2:70, Deciding Custody.

West's California Code Forms, Family § 3110, Comment Overview—Custody Investigation and Report.

West's California Judicial Council Forms FL-327, Order Appointing Child Custody Evaluator.

West's California Judicial Council Forms FL-328, Notice Regarding Confidentiality of Child Custody Evaluation Report.

West's California Judicial Council Forms FL-329-INFO, Child Custody Evaluation Information Sheet (Also Available in Spanish).

§ 3112. Repayment of expenses

(a) Where a court-appointed investigator is directed by the court to conduct a custody investigation or evaluation pursuant to this chapter or to undertake visitation work, including necessary evaluation, supervision, and reporting, the court shall inquire into the financial condition of the parent, guardian, or other person charged with the support of the minor. If the court finds the parent, guardian, or other person able to pay all or part of the expense of the investigation, report, and recommendation, the court may make an order requiring the parent, guardian, or other person to repay the court the amount the court determines proper.

(b) The repayment shall be made to the court. The court shall keep suitable accounts of the expenses and repayments and shall deposit the collections as directed by the Judicial Council. *(Added by Stats.1993, c. 219 (A.B.1500), § 116.81. Amended by Stats.2000, c. 926 (S.B.1716), § 5.)*

Cross References

County financial evaluation officer, financial evaluations and collections, see Government Code § 27752.

Courts, fees and fines collected after January 1, 2006, treatment thereof, see Government Code § 68085.1.

Investigation and report involving custody, status, and welfare of minor, see Welfare and Institutions Code § 281.

Judgment and order defined for purposes of this Code, see Family Code § 100.

Mediation proceedings, recommendation of investigation prior to hearing, see Family Code § 3183.

Minor defined for purposes of this Code, see Family Code § 6500.

Person defined for purposes of this Code, see Family Code § 105.

Support, generally, see Family Code § 3500 et seq.

Support defined for purposes of this Code, see Family Code § 150.

§ 3113. Domestic violence history between parties; custody investigation procedures

Where there has been a history of domestic violence between the parties, or where a protective order as defined in Section 6218 is in effect, at the request of the party alleging domestic violence in a written declaration under penalty of perjury or at the request of a party who is protected by the order, the parties shall meet with the court-appointed investigator separately and at separate times. *(Added by Stats.1993, c. 219 (A.B.1500), § 116.81.)*

Cross References

Domestic violence defined for purposes of this Code, see Family Code § 6211.
Judgment and order defined for purposes of this Code, see Family Code § 100.

§ 3114. Appointment of counsel for minor children; recommendations

Nothing in this chapter prohibits a court-appointed investigator from recommending to the court that counsel be appointed pursuant to Chapter 10 (commencing with Section 3150) to represent the minor child. In making that recommendation, the court-appointed investigator shall inform the court of the reasons why it would be in the best interest of the child to have counsel appointed. *(Added by Stats.1993, c. 219 (A.B.1500), § 116.81.)*

Cross References

Best interest of child,
  Considerations, see Family Code § 3011.
  Order of preference for custody, best interest of child as factor, see Family Code § 3040.
Counsel, right to, see Cal. Const. Art. 1, § 15, cl. 3.
Minor defined for purposes of this Code, see Family Code § 6500.

§ 3115. Cross-examination of court-appointed investigator; waiver of right

A statement, whether written or oral, or conduct shall not be held to constitute a waiver by a party of the right to cross-examine the court-appointed investigator, unless the statement is made, or the conduct occurs, after the report has been received by a party or the party's attorney. *(Added by Stats.1993, c. 219 (A.B.1500), § 116.81. Amended by Stats.1996, c. 761 (S.B.1995), § 2; Stats.2019, c. 115 (A.B.1817), § 35, eff. Jan. 1, 2020.)*

Cross References

Application of part, see Family Code § 3021.
Investigation and report involving custody, status, and welfare of minor, see Welfare and Institutions Code § 281.

§ 3116. Investigator's duty to assist court; scope of duty

Nothing in this chapter limits the duty of a court-appointed investigator to assist the appointing court in the transaction of the business of the court. *(Added by Stats.1993, c. 219 (A.B.1500), § 116.81.)*

Cross References

Application of part, see Family Code § 3021.
Mediation proceedings, recommendation of investigation prior to hearing, see Family Code § 3183.
Superior court, jurisdiction, see Family Code § 200.

§ 3117. Standards for court-connected child custody actions; guidelines for cross-examination of court-appointed investigators; deadline

The Judicial Council shall, by January 1, 1999, do both of the following:

(a) Adopt standards for full and partial court-connected evaluations, investigations, and assessments related to child custody.

(b) Adopt procedural guidelines for the expeditious and cost-effective cross-examination of court-appointed investigators, including, but not limited to, the use of electronic technology whereby the court-appointed investigator may not need to be present in the courtroom. These guidelines shall in no way limit the requirement that the court-appointed investigator be available for the purposes of cross-examination. These guidelines shall also provide for written notification to the parties of the right to cross-examine these investigators after the parties have had a reasonable time to review the investigator's report. *(Added by Stats.1996, c. 761 (S.B.1995), § 3.)*

Cross References

Mediation proceedings, recommendation of investigation prior to hearing, see Family Code § 3183.

§ 3118. Child sex abuse allegations; child custody evaluation, investigation or assessment

(a) In any contested proceeding involving child custody or visitation rights, where the court has appointed a child custody evaluator or has referred a case for a full or partial court-connected evaluation, investigation, or assessment, and the court determines that there is a

§ 3118

serious allegation of child sexual abuse, the court shall require an evaluation, investigation, or assessment pursuant to this section. When the court has determined that there is a serious allegation of child sexual abuse, any child custody evaluation, investigation, or assessment conducted subsequent to that determination shall be considered by the court only if the evaluation, investigation, or assessment is conducted in accordance with the minimum requirements set forth in this section in determining custody or visitation rights, except as specified in paragraph (1). For purposes of this section, a serious allegation of child sexual abuse means an allegation of child sexual abuse, as defined in Section 11165.1 of the Penal Code, that is based in whole or in part on statements made by the child to law enforcement, a child welfare services agency investigator, any person required by statute to report suspected child abuse, or any other court-appointed personnel, or that is supported by substantial independent corroboration as provided for in subparagraph (B) of paragraph (2) of subdivision (a) of Section 3011. When an allegation of child abuse arises in any other circumstances in any proceeding involving child custody or visitation rights, the court may require an evaluator or investigator to conduct an evaluation, investigation, or assessment pursuant to this section. The order appointing a child custody evaluator or investigator pursuant to this section shall provide that the evaluator or investigator have access to all juvenile court records pertaining to the child who is the subject of the evaluation, investigation, or assessment. The order shall also provide that any juvenile court records or information gained from those records remain confidential and shall only be released as specified in Section 3111.

(1) This section does not apply to any emergency court-ordered partial investigation that is conducted for the purpose of assisting the court in determining what immediate temporary orders may be necessary to protect and meet the immediate needs of a child. This section does apply when the emergency is resolved and the court is considering permanent child custody or visitation orders.

(2) This section does not prohibit a court from considering evidence relevant to determining the safety and protection needs of the child.

(3) Any evaluation, investigation, or assessment conducted pursuant to this section shall be conducted by an evaluator or investigator who meets the qualifications set forth in Section 3110.5.

(b) The evaluator or investigator shall, at a minimum, do all of the following:

(1) Consult with the agency providing child welfare services and law enforcement regarding the allegations of child sexual abuse, and obtain recommendations from these professionals regarding the child's safety and the child's need for protection.

(2) Review and summarize the child welfare services agency file. No document contained in the child welfare services agency file may be photocopied, but a summary of the information in the file, including statements made by the children and the parents, and the recommendations made or anticipated to be made by the child welfare services agency to the juvenile court, may be recorded by the evaluator or investigator, except for the identity of the reporting party. The evaluator's or investigator's notes summarizing the child welfare services agency information shall be stored in a file separate from the evaluator's or investigator's file and may only be released to either party under order of the court.

(3) Obtain from a law enforcement investigator all available information obtained from criminal background checks of the parents and any suspected perpetrator that is not a parent, including information regarding child abuse, domestic violence, or substance abuse.

(4) Review the results of a multidisciplinary child interview team (hereafter MDIT) interview if available, or if not, or if the evaluator or investigator believes the MDIT interview is inadequate for purposes of the evaluation, investigation, or assessment, interview the child or request an MDIT interview, and shall wherever possible avoid repeated interviews of the child.

(5) Request a forensic medical examination of the child from the appropriate agency, or include in the report required by paragraph (6) a written statement explaining why the examination is not needed.

(6) File a confidential written report with the clerk of the court in which the custody hearing will be conducted and which shall be served on the parties or their attorneys at least 10 days prior to the hearing. On and after January 1, 2021, this report shall be made on the form adopted pursuant to subdivision (i). This report may not be made available other than as provided in this subdivision. This report shall address the safety of the child and shall include, but not be limited to, the following:

(A) Documentation of material interviews, including any MDIT interview of the child or the evaluator or investigator, written documentation of interviews with both parents by the evaluator or investigator, and interviews with other witnesses who provided relevant information.

(B) A summary of any law enforcement investigator's investigation, including information obtained from the criminal background check of the parents and any suspected perpetrator that is not a parent, including information regarding child abuse, domestic violence, or substance abuse.

(C) Relevant background material, including, but not limited to, a summary of a written report from any therapist treating the child for suspected child sexual abuse, excluding any communication subject to Section 1014 of the Evidence Code, reports from other professionals, and the results of any forensic medical examination and any other medical examination or treatment that could help establish or disprove whether the child has been the victim of sexual abuse.

(D) The written recommendations of the evaluator or investigator regarding the therapeutic needs of the child and how to ensure the safety of the child.

(E) A summary of the following information: whether the child and the child's parents are or have been the subject of a child abuse investigation and the disposition of that investigation; the name, location, and telephone number of the children's services worker; the status of the investigation and the recommendations made or anticipated to be made regarding the child's safety; and any dependency court orders or findings that might have a bearing on the custody dispute.

(F) Any information regarding the presence of domestic violence or substance abuse in the family that has been obtained from a child protective agency in accordance with paragraphs (1) and (2), a law enforcement agency, medical personnel or records, prior or currently treating therapists, excluding any communication subject to Section 1014 of the Evidence Code, or from interviews conducted or reviewed for this evaluation, investigation, or assessment.

(G) Which, if any, family members are known to have been deemed eligible for assistance from the Victims of Crime Program due to child abuse or domestic violence.

(H) Any other information the evaluator or investigator believes would be helpful to the court in determining what is in the best interests of the child.

(c) If the evaluator or investigator obtains information as part of a family court mediation, that information shall be maintained in the family court file, which is not subject to subpoena by either party. If, however, the members of the family are the subject of an ongoing child welfare services investigation, or the evaluator or investigator has made a child welfare services referral, the evaluator or investigator shall so inform the family law judicial officer in writing and this information shall become part of the family law file. This subdivision may not be construed to authorize or require a mediator to disclose any information not otherwise authorized or required by law to be disclosed.

(d) In accordance with subdivision (d) of Section 11167 of the Penal Code, the evaluator or investigator may not disclose any information regarding the identity of any person making a report of suspected child abuse. This section is not intended to limit any disclosure of information by any agency that is otherwise required by law or court order.

(e) The evaluation, investigation, or assessment standards set forth in this section represent minimum requirements of evaluation and the court shall order further evaluation beyond these minimum requirements when necessary to determine the safety needs of the child.

(f) If the court orders an evaluation, investigation, or assessment pursuant to this section, the court shall consider whether the best interests of the child require that a temporary order be issued that limits visitation with the parent against whom the allegations have been made to situations in which a third person specified by the court is present or whether visitation will be suspended or denied in accordance with Section 3011.

(g) An evaluation, investigation, or assessment pursuant to this section shall be suspended if a petition is filed to declare the child a dependent child of the juvenile court pursuant to Section 300 of the Welfare and Institutions Code, and all information gathered by the evaluator or investigator shall be made available to the juvenile court.

(h) This section shall not be construed to authorize a court to issue any orders in a proceeding pursuant to this division regarding custody or visitation with respect to a minor child who is the subject of a dependency hearing in juvenile court or to otherwise supersede Section 302 of the Welfare and Institutions Code.

(i) On or before January 1, 2021, the Judicial Council shall adopt a mandatory form that shall be used for all evaluations, investigations, or assessments conducted pursuant to this section. The form shall provide a standardized template for all information necessary to provide a full and complete analysis of the allegations raised in the proceeding. *(Added by Stats.2000, c. 926 (S.B.1716), § 6. Amended by Stats.2002, c. 305 (S.B.1704), § 1; Stats.2003, c. 62 (S.B.600), § 87; Stats.2019, c. 115 (A.B.1817), § 36, eff. Jan. 1, 2020; Stats.2019, c. 127 (A.B.1179), § 1, eff. Jan. 1, 2020; Stats.2021, c. 124 (A.B.938), § 27, eff. Jan. 1, 2022.)*

Cross References

Abuse defined for purposes of the Domestic Violence Prevention Act, see Family Code § 6203.
Arbitration, generally, see Code of Civil Procedure § 1281 et seq.
Attorneys, State Bar Act, see Business and Professions Code § 6000.
Computation of time, see Code of Civil Procedure §§ 12, 12a; Government Code § 6800 et seq.
Conciliation proceedings, generally, see Family Code § 1800 et seq.
Domestic violence defined for purposes of this Code, see Family Code § 6211.
Family mediation and conciliation services, statewide coordination, see Family Code § 1850 et seq.
Inspection of public records, exemptions from disclosure, child sexual abuse reports, reports filed in contested child custody or visitation proceeding, see Government Code § 6276.10.
Judgment and order defined for purposes of this Code, see Family Code § 100.
Juvenile case file inspection, confidentiality, release, see Welfare and Institutions Code § 827.
Mediation of custody and visitation issues, generally, see Family Code § 3160 et seq.
Minor defined for purposes of this Code, see Family Code § 6500.
Person defined for purposes of this Code, see Family Code § 105.
Proceeding defined for purposes of this Code, see Family Code § 110.
Writings, authentication and proof of, see Evidence Code § 1400 et seq.

Research References

Forms

California Practice Guide: Rutter Family Law Forms Form 1:32, Glossary of Common Family Law Terms, Phrases and Concepts (Enclosure to Form 1:31).
California Practice Guide: Rutter Family Law Forms Form 7:5, Stipulation Appointing Child Custody Evaluator (Attorney-Drafted).
West's California Judicial Council Forms FL-327, Order Appointing Child Custody Evaluator.
West's California Judicial Council Forms FL-327(A), Additional Orders Regarding Child Custody Evaluations Under Family Code Section 3118.
West's California Judicial Council Forms FL-329, Confidential Child Custody Evaluation Report.
West's California Judicial Council Forms FL-329-INFO, Child Custody Evaluation Information Sheet (Also Available in Spanish).

CHAPTER 7. ACTION FOR EXCLUSIVE CUSTODY

Section
3120. Action for exclusive custody; order.
3121. Attorney's fees and costs; findings; temporary order; default; statewide rule of court.

Cross References

Applicable law, see Family Code § 3021.
Best interest of child,
   Considerations, see Family Code § 3011.
   Order of preference for custody, best interest of child as factor, see Family Code § 3040.
Parental Kidnapping Prevention Act, see Family Code § 3134.5.
Sole legal custody, see Family Code § 3006.
Sole physical custody, see Family Code § 3007.
Uniform Child Custody Jurisdiction and Enforcement Act, see Family Code § 3400 et seq.

§ 3120. Action for exclusive custody; order

Without filing a petition for dissolution of marriage or legal separation of the parties, a spouse may bring an action for the exclusive custody of the children of the marriage. The court may, during the pendency of the action, or at the final hearing thereof, or afterwards, make such order regarding the support, care, custody, education, and control of the children of the marriage as may be just and in accordance with the natural rights of the parents and the best interest of the children. The order may be modified or terminated at any time thereafter as the natural rights of the parties and the best interest of the children may require. *(Stats.1992, c. 162 (A.B.2650), § 10, operative Jan. 1, 1994. Amended by Stats.2014, c. 82 (S.B.1306), § 30, eff. Jan. 1, 2015.)*

Cross References

Applicable law, see Family Code § 3021.
Best interest of child,
   Considerations, see Family Code § 3011.
   Order of preference for custody, best interest of child as factor, see Family Code § 3040.
Judgment and order defined for purposes of this Code, see Family Code § 100.
Order, including decree, see Family Code § 100.
References to husband, wife, spouses and married persons, persons included for purposes of this Code, see Family Code § 11.
Sole legal custody, see Family Code § 3006.
Sole physical custody, see Family Code § 3007.
Support, generally, see Family Code § 3500 et seq.
Support defined for purposes of this Code, see Family Code § 150.
Uniform Child Custody Jurisdiction and Enforcement Act, see Family Code § 3400 et seq.

Research References

Forms

1 California Transactions Forms--Family Law § 3:4, Subject Matter Jurisdiction for Custody Determinations.
West's California Code Forms, Family § 3120, Comment Overview—Action for Exclusive Custody.
West's California Judicial Council Forms FL-230, Declaration for Default or Uncontested Judgment (Uniform Parentage, Custody and Support) (Also Available in Spanish).
West's California Judicial Council Forms FL-250, Judgment (Uniform Parentage—Custody and Support) (Also Available in Spanish).

§ 3120 CUSTODY OF CHILDREN

West's California Judicial Council Forms FL–260, Petition for Custody and Support of Minor Children (Also Available in Spanish).

West's California Judicial Council Forms FL–270, Response to Petition for Custody and Support of Minor Children (Also Available in Spanish).

§ 3121. Attorney's fees and costs; findings; temporary order; default; statewide rule of court

(a) In any proceeding pursuant to Section 3120, and in any proceeding subsequent to entry of a related judgment, the court shall ensure that each party has access to legal representation, including access early in the proceedings, to preserve each party's rights by ordering, if necessary based on the income and needs assessments, one party, except a government entity, to pay to the other party, or to the other party's attorney, whatever amount is reasonably necessary for attorney's fees and for the cost of maintaining or defending the proceeding during the pendency of the proceeding.

(b) When a request for attorney's fees and costs is made, the court shall make findings on whether an award of attorney's fees and costs under this section is appropriate, whether there is a disparity in access to funds to retain counsel, and whether one party is able to pay for legal representation of both parties. If the findings demonstrate disparity in access and ability to pay, the court shall make an order awarding attorney's fees and costs. A party who lacks the financial ability to hire an attorney may request, as an in pro per litigant, that the court order the other party, if that other party has the financial ability, to pay a reasonable amount to allow the unrepresented party to retain an attorney in a timely manner before proceedings in the matter go forward.

(c) Attorney's fees and costs within this section may be awarded for legal services rendered or costs incurred before or after the commencement of the proceeding.

(d) The court shall augment or modify the original award for attorney's fees and costs as may be reasonably necessary for the prosecution or defense of a proceeding described in Section 3120, or any proceeding related thereto, including after any appeal has been concluded.

(e) Except as provided in subdivision (f), an application for a temporary order making, augmenting, or modifying an award of attorney's fees, including a reasonable retainer to hire an attorney, or costs, or both, shall be made by motion on notice or by an order to show cause during the pendency of any proceeding described in Section 3120.

(f) The court shall rule on an application for fees under this section within 15 days of the hearing on the motion or order to show cause. An order described in subdivision (a) may be made without notice by an oral motion in open court at either of the following times:

(1) At the time of the hearing of the cause on the merits.

(2) At any time before entry of judgment against a party whose default has been entered pursuant to Section 585 or 586 of the Code of Civil Procedure. The court shall rule on any motion made pursuant to this subdivision within 15 days and prior to the entry of any judgment.

(g) The Judicial Council shall, by January 1, 2012, adopt a statewide rule of court to implement this section and develop a form for the information that shall be submitted to the court to obtain an award of attorney's fees under this section. (Added by Stats.2004, c. 472 (A.B.2148), § 3. Amended by Stats.2006, c. 538 (S.B.1852), § 158; Stats.2010, c. 352 (A.B.939), § 13.)

Cross References

Attorney's fees and costs, generally, see Code of Civil Procedure § 1021.
Computation of time, first and last days, holidays, see Civil Code § 10; Code of Civil Procedure § 12 et seq.; Government Code § 6800 et seq.
Dissolution and legal separation, award of attorney's fees and costs, see Family Code § 2030.
Judgment and order defined for purposes of this Code, see Family Code § 100.
Proceeding defined for purposes of this Code, see Family Code § 110.

Research References

Forms

West's California Code Forms, Family § 3120, Comment Overview—Action for Exclusive Custody.

West's California Judicial Council Forms FL–158, Supporting Declaration for Attorney's Fees and Costs Attachment.

West's California Judicial Council Forms FL–319, Request for Attorney's Fees and Costs Attachment.

West's California Judicial Council Forms FL–346, Attorney's Fees and Costs Order Attachment.

CHAPTER 8. LOCATION OF MISSING PARTY OR CHILD

Section
3130. Custody petitions or temporary custody orders; duties of district attorney.
3131. Custody or visitation orders; duties of district attorney.
3132. District attorney to act on behalf of court.
3133. Temporary custody orders; temporary sole physical custody.
3134. Payment of district attorney's expenses.
3134.5. Protective custody warrant; order to freeze assets; service; dismissal of warrant; order terminated, modified, or vacated; service of notice of dismissal.
3135. Effect of Part 3 on authority of district attorney or arresting agency.

Cross References

California Work Opportunity and Responsibility to Kids Act, see Welfare and Institutions Code § 11200 et seq.
Child abduction, sentencing, relevant factors and circumstances, see Penal Code § 278.6.
Expenses for return of child detained or concealed from lawful custodian, see Penal Code § 279.
Parental Kidnapping Prevention Act, see Family Code § 3134.5.
Uniform Child Custody Jurisdiction and Enforcement Act, see Family Code § 3400 et seq.
Utility customer information, access during child abduction or concealment investigations, see Public Utilities Code § 588.

§ 3130. Custody petitions or temporary custody orders; duties of district attorney

If a petition to determine custody of a child has been filed in a court of competent jurisdiction, or if a temporary order pending determination of custody has been entered in accordance with Chapter 3 (commencing with Section 3060), and the whereabouts of a party in possession of the child are not known, or there is reason to believe that the party may not appear in the proceedings although ordered to appear personally with the child pursuant to Section 3430, the district attorney shall take all actions necessary to locate the party and the child and to procure compliance with the order to appear with the child for purposes of adjudication of custody. The petition to determine custody may be filed by the district attorney. (Stats. 1992, c. 162 (A.B.2650), § 10, operative Jan. 1, 1994. Amended by Stats.2008, c. 699 (S.B.1241), § 2.)

Cross References

California Work Opportunity and Responsibility to Kids Act, see Welfare and Institutions Code § 11200 et seq.
District attorney, powers and duties, see Government Code § 26500 et seq.
Judgment and order defined for purposes of this Code, see Family Code § 100.
Proceeding defined for purposes of this Code, see Family Code § 110.
Uniform Child Custody Jurisdiction and Enforcement Act, see Family Code § 3400 et seq.

§ 3131. Custody or visitation orders; duties of district attorney

If a custody or visitation order has been entered by a court of competent jurisdiction and the child is taken or detained by another person in violation of the order, the district attorney shall take all actions necessary to locate and return the child and the person who violated the order and to assist in the enforcement of the custody or visitation order or other order of the court by use of an appropriate civil or criminal proceeding. *(Stats.1992, c. 162 (A.B.2650), § 10, operative Jan. 1, 1994.)*

Cross References

California Work Opportunity and Responsibility to Kids Act, see Welfare and Institutions Code § 11200 et seq.
District attorney, powers and duties, see Government Code § 26500 et seq.
Judgment and order defined for purposes of this Code, see Family Code § 100.
Order, including decree, see Family Code § 100.
Person defined for purposes of this Code, see Family Code § 105.
Proceeding defined for purposes of this Code, see Family Code § 110.
Uniform Child Custody Jurisdiction and Enforcement Act, see Family Code § 3400 et seq.
Utility customer information, access during child abduction or concealment investigations, see Public Utilities Code § 588.

§ 3132. District attorney to act on behalf of court

In performing the functions described in Sections 3130 and 3131, the district attorney shall act on behalf of the court and shall not represent any party to the custody proceedings. *(Stats.1992, c. 162 (A.B.2650), § 10, operative Jan. 1, 1994.)*

Cross References

Attorneys, State Bar Act, see Business and Professions Code § 6000.
California Work Opportunity and Responsibility to Kids Act, see Welfare and Institutions Code § 11200 et seq.
District attorney, powers and duties, see Government Code § 26500 et seq.
Proceeding defined for purposes of this Code, see Family Code § 110.
Uniform Child Custody Jurisdiction and Enforcement Act, see Family Code § 3400 et seq.
Utility customer information, access during child abduction or concealment investigations, see Public Utilities Code § 588.

§ 3133. Temporary custody orders; temporary sole physical custody

If the district attorney represents to the court, by a written declaration under penalty of perjury, that a temporary custody order is needed to recover a child who is being detained or concealed in violation of a court order or a parent's right to custody, the court may issue an order, placing temporary sole physical custody in the parent or person recommended by the district attorney to facilitate the return of the child to the jurisdiction of the court, pending further hearings. If the court determines that it is not in the best interest of the child to place temporary sole physical custody in the parent or person recommended by the district attorney, the court shall appoint a person to take charge of the child and return the child to the jurisdiction of the court. *(Stats.1992, c. 162 (A.B.2650), § 10, operative Jan. 1, 1994.)*

Cross References

Best interests of child,
  Considerations, see Family Code § 3011.
  Order of preference for custody, best interest of child as factor, see Family Code § 3040.
California Work Opportunity and Responsibility to Kids Act, see Welfare and Institutions Code § 11200 et seq.
District attorney, powers and duties, see Government Code § 26500 et seq.
Judgment and order defined for purposes of this Code, see Family Code § 100.
Person defined for purposes of this Code, see Family Code § 105.
Sole physical custody defined, see Family Code § 3007.
Uniform Child Custody Jurisdiction and Enforcement Act, see Family Code § 3400 et seq.
Utility customer information, access during child abduction or concealment investigations, see Public Utilities Code § 588.

§ 3134. Payment of district attorney's expenses

(a) When the district attorney incurs expenses pursuant to this chapter, including expenses incurred in a sister state, payment of the expenses may be advanced by the county subject to reimbursement by the state, and shall be audited by the Controller and paid by the State Treasury according to law.

(b) The court in which the custody proceeding is pending or which has continuing jurisdiction shall, if appropriate, allocate liability for the reimbursement of actual expenses incurred by the district attorney to either or both parties to the proceedings, and that allocation shall constitute a judgment for the state for the funds advanced pursuant to this section. The county shall take reasonable action to enforce that liability and shall transmit all recovered funds to the state. *(Stats.1992, c. 162 (A.B.2650), § 10, operative Jan. 1, 1994.)*

Cross References

Child abduction, sentencing, relevant factors and circumstances, see Penal Code § 278.6.
County defined for purposes of this Code, see Family Code § 67.
District attorney, powers and duties, see Government Code § 26500 et seq.
Expenses for return of child detained or concealed from lawful custodian, see Penal Code § 279.
Judgment and order defined for purposes of this Code, see Family Code § 100.
Proceeding defined for purposes of this Code, see Family Code § 110.
State Controller, generally, see Government Code § 12402 et seq.
State defined for purposes of this Code, see Family Code § 145.
Utility customer information, access during child abduction or concealment investigations, see Public Utilities Code § 588.

§ 3134.5. Protective custody warrant; order to freeze assets; service; dismissal of warrant; order terminated, modified, or vacated; service of notice of dismissal

(a) Upon request of the district attorney, the court may issue a protective custody warrant to secure the recovery of an unlawfully detained or concealed child. The request by the district attorney shall include a written declaration under penalty of perjury that a warrant for the child is necessary in order for the district attorney to perform the duties described in Sections 3130 and 3131. The protective custody warrant for the child shall contain an order that the arresting agency shall place the child in protective custody, or return the child as directed by the court. The protective custody warrant for the child may also contain an order to freeze the California assets of the party alleged to be in possession of the child. The protective custody warrant may be served in any county in the same manner as a warrant of arrest and may be served at any time of the day or night. For purposes of this subdivision, "assets" means funds held in a depository institution, as defined in subdivision (a) of Section 1420 of the Financial Code, in California.

(b) Upon a declaration of the district attorney that the child has been recovered or that the warrant is otherwise no longer required, the court may dismiss the warrant without further court proceedings.

(c) Upon noticed motion, any order to freeze assets pursuant to subdivision (a) may be terminated, modified, or vacated by the court upon a finding that the release of the assets will not jeopardize the safety or best interest of the child.

(d) If an asset freeze order is entered pursuant to subdivision (a), and the court subsequently dismisses the warrant pursuant to subdivision (b), notice of the dismissal shall be immediately served on the depository institutions holding any assets pursuant to the freeze order. *(Added by Stats.1996, c. 988 (A.B.2936), § 1.5. Amended by Stats.2012, c. 276 (S.B.1206), § 3.)*

§ 3134.5

Cross References

Child abduction, sentencing, relevant factors and circumstances, see Penal Code § 278.6.
County defined for purposes of this Code, see Family Code § 67.
District attorney, powers and duties, see Government Code § 26500 et seq.
Expenses for return of child detained or concealed from lawful custodian, see Penal Code § 279.
Judgment and order defined for purposes of this Code, see Family Code § 100.
Proceeding defined for purposes of this Code, see Family Code § 110.
Uniform Child Custody Jurisdiction and Enforcement Act, see Family Code § 3400 et seq.
Utility customer information, access during child abduction or concealment investigations, see Public Utilities Code § 588.

§ 3135. Effect of Part 3 on authority of district attorney or arresting agency

Part 3 (commencing with Section 3400) does not limit the authority of a district attorney or arresting agency to act pursuant to this chapter, Section 279.6 of the Penal Code, or any other applicable law. *(Added by Stats.1999, c. 867 (S.B.668), § 1.)*

Cross References

District attorney, powers and duties, see Government Code § 26500 et seq.

CHAPTER 9. CHECK TO DETERMINE WHETHER CHILD IS MISSING PERSON

Section
3140. Parent not appearing in court or by counsel; submission of child's birth certificate; missing children.

§ 3140. Parent not appearing in court or by counsel; submission of child's birth certificate; missing children

(a) Subject to subdivisions (b) and (c), before granting or modifying a custody order in a case in which one or both parents of the child have not appeared either personally or by counsel, the court shall require the parent, petitioner, or other party appearing in the case to submit a certified copy of the child's birth certificate to the court. The court or its designee shall forward the certified copy of the birth certificate to the local police or sheriff's department which shall check with the National Crime Information Center Missing Person System to ascertain whether the child has been reported missing or is the victim of an abduction and shall report the results of the check to the court.

(b) If the custody matter before the court also involves a petition for the dissolution of marriage or the adjudication of paternity rights or duties, this section applies only to a case in which there is no proof of personal service of the petition on the absent parent.

(c) For good cause shown, the court may waive the requirements of this section. *(Stats.1992, c. 162 (A.B.2650), § 10, operative Jan. 1, 1994.)*

Cross References

California Parent Locator Service and Central Registry, see Family Code § 17506.
Certified copy and verification of records, see Health and Safety Code § 103526.
Counsel, right to, see Cal. Const. Art. 1, § 15, cl. 3.
Judgment and order defined for purposes of this Code, see Family Code § 100.
Person defined for purposes of this Code, see Family Code § 105.
Petitioner defined for purposes of this Code, see Family Code § 126.
Proof of service, see Code of Civil Procedure § 417.10 et seq.
Uniform Child Custody Jurisdiction and Enforcement Act, see Family Code § 3400 et seq.

Uniform Parentage Act, see Family Code § 7600 et seq.

CHAPTER 10. APPOINTMENT OF COUNSEL TO REPRESENT CHILD

Section
3150. Appointment of private counsel.
3151. Duties and rights of private counsel.
3151.5. Repealed.
3152. Reports or files of local child protective services agencies; release; review.
3153. Compensation and expenses of private counsel.
3155 to 3159. Inoperative.

Cross References

Attorney fees, generally, see Family Code § 270 et seq.
Best interests of child,
    Considerations, see Family Code § 3011.
    Order of preference for custody, best interest of child as factor, see Family Code § 3040.
Cost of counsel appointed to represent minor as court operation for funding purposes, see Government Code § 77003.
Custody investigation and report, recommendation for appointment of counsel, see Family Code § 3114.
Mediation proceedings, recommendation that counsel be appointed to represent minor child, see Family Code § 3184.
State funding of trial courts, court operations defined, see Government Code § 77003.

§ 3150. Appointment of private counsel

(a) If the court determines that it would be in the best interest of the minor child, the court may appoint private counsel to represent the interests of the child in a custody or visitation proceeding, provided that the court and counsel comply with the requirements set forth in Rules 5.240, 5.241, and 5.242 of the California Rules of Court.

(b) Upon entering an appearance on behalf of a child pursuant to this chapter, counsel shall continue to represent that child unless relieved by the court upon the substitution of other counsel by the court or for cause. *(Stats.1992, c. 162 (A.B.2650), § 10, operative Jan. 1, 1994. Amended by Stats.1993, c. 219 (A.B.1500), § 116.85; Stats.2010, c. 352 (A.B.939), § 14.)*

Cross References

Attorney fees, generally, see Family Code § 270 et seq.
Best interests of child,
    Considerations, see Family Code § 3011.
    Order of preference for custody, best interest of child as factor, see Family Code § 3040.
Child custody, confidential psychological evaluations and recommendations, exceptions, see Family Code § 3025.5.
Cost of counsel appointed to represent minor as court operation for funding purposes, see Government Code § 77003.
Counsel, right to, see Cal. Const. Art. 1, § 15, cl. 3.
Custody investigation and report, recommendation for appointment of counsel, see Family Code § 3114.
Disclosure of juvenile case file and records when child is subject of family law or probate guardianship case, persons who may inspect or receive copies of records, see Welfare and Institutions Code § 827.10.
Juvenile court law, records, inspection of juvenile court documents, see Welfare and Institutions Code § 827.
Mediation proceedings, recommendation that counsel be appointed to represent minor child, see Family Code § 3184.
Minor defined, see Family Code § 6500.
Proceeding defined for purposes of this Code, see Family Code § 110.
Uniform Child Custody Jurisdiction and Enforcement Act, see Family Code § 3400 et seq.

Research References

Forms
1 California Transactions Forms--Family Law § 2:72, Counsel for the Children.

West's California Judicial Council Forms FL–322, Declaration of Counsel for a Child Regarding Qualifications (Also Available in Spanish).

West's California Judicial Council Forms FL–323, Order Appointing Counsel for a Child (Also Available in Chinese, Korean, Spanish, and Vietnamese).

West's California Judicial Council Forms FL–323–INFO, Attorney for Child in a Family Law Case—Information Sheet (Also Available in Chinese, Korean, Spanish, and Vietnamese).

§ 3151. Duties and rights of private counsel

(a) The child's counsel appointed under this chapter is charged with the representation of the child's best interests. The role of the child's counsel is to gather evidence that bears on the best interests of the child, and present that admissible evidence to the court in any manner appropriate for the counsel of a party. If the child so desires, the child's counsel shall present the child's wishes to the court. The counsel's duties, unless under the circumstances it is inappropriate to exercise the duty, include interviewing the child, reviewing the court files and all accessible relevant records available to both parties, and making any further investigations as the counsel considers necessary to ascertain evidence relevant to the custody or visitation hearings.

(b) Counsel shall serve notices and pleadings on all parties, consistent with requirements for parties. Counsel shall not be called as a witness in the proceeding. Counsel may introduce and examine counsel's own witnesses, present arguments to the court concerning the child's welfare, and participate further in the proceeding to the degree necessary to represent the child adequately.

(c) The child's counsel shall have the following rights:

(1) Reasonable access to the child.

(2) Standing to seek affirmative relief on behalf of the child.

(3) Notice of any proceeding, and all phases of that proceeding, including a request for examination affecting the child.

(4) The right to take any action that is available to a party to the proceeding, including, but not limited to, the following: filing pleadings, making evidentiary objections, and presenting evidence and being heard in the proceeding, which may include, but shall not be limited to, presenting motions and orders to show cause, and participating in settlement conferences, trials, seeking writs, appeals, and arbitrations.

(5) Access to the child's medical, dental, mental health, and other health care records, school and educational records, and the right to interview school personnel, caretakers, health care providers, mental health professionals, and others who have assessed the child or provided care to the child. The release of this information to counsel shall not constitute a waiver of the confidentiality of the reports, files, and any disclosed communications. Counsel may interview mediators; however, the provisions of Sections 3177 and 3182 shall apply.

(6) The right to reasonable advance notice of and the right to refuse any physical or psychological examination or evaluation, for purposes of the proceeding, which has not been ordered by the court.

(7) The right to assert or waive any privilege on behalf of the child.

(8) The right to seek independent psychological or physical examination or evaluation of the child for purposes of the pending proceeding, upon approval by the court. (Stats.1992, c. 162 (A.B. 2650), § 10, operative Jan. 1, 1994. Amended by Stats.1997, c. 449 (A.B.1526), § 1; Stats.2010, c. 352 (A.B.939), § 15.)

Cross References

Appeals from order in arbitration, see Code of Civil Procedure §§ 1294, 1294.2.
Appeals in civil actions, generally, see Code of Civil Procedure § 901 et seq.
Appeals in criminal cases,
　Appeals from Superior Courts, see Penal Code § 1235 et seq.
　Appeals to Superior Courts, see Penal Code § 1466 et seq.
Arbitration, generally, see Code of Civil Procedure § 1281 et seq.
Attorney fees, generally, see Family Code § 270 et seq.
Attorneys, State Bar Act, see Business and Professions Code § 6000.
Child custody, confidential psychological evaluations and recommendations, exceptions, see Family Code § 3025.5.
Computation of time, see Code of Civil Procedure §§ 12, 12a; Government Code § 6800 et seq.
Conciliation proceedings, generally, see Family Code § 1800 et seq.
Cost of counsel appointed to represent minor as court operation for funding purposes, see Government Code § 77003.
Counsel, right to, see Cal. Const. Art. 1, § 15, cl. 3.
Family mediation and conciliation services, statewide coordination, see Family Code § 1850 et seq.
Judgment and order defined for purposes of this Code, see Family Code § 100.
Notice, actual and constructive, defined, see Civil Code § 18.
Proceeding defined for purposes of this Code, see Family Code § 110.
State defined for purposes of this Code, see Family Code § 145.
Uniform Child Custody Jurisdiction and Enforcement Act, see Family Code § 3400 et seq.

Research References

Forms

1 California Transactions Forms--Family Law § 2:72, Counsel for the Children.
West's California Judicial Council Forms FL–323, Order Appointing Counsel for a Child (Also Available in Chinese, Korean, Spanish, and Vietnamese).

§ 3151.5. Repealed by Stats.2012, c. 107 (A.B.1406), § 2

§ 3152. Reports or files of local child protective services agencies; release; review

(a) The child's counsel may, upon noticed motion to all parties and the local child protective services agency, request the court to authorize release of relevant reports or files, concerning the child represented by the counsel, of the relevant local child protective services agency.

(b) The court shall review the reports or files in camera in order to determine whether they are relevant to the pending action and whether and to what extent they should be released to the child's counsel.

(c) Neither the review by the court nor the release to counsel shall constitute a waiver of the confidentiality of the reports and files. Counsel shall not disclose the contents or existence of the reports or files to anyone unless otherwise permitted by law. (Stats.1992, c. 162 (A.B.2650), § 10, operative Jan. 1, 1994.)

Cross References

Attorney fees, generally, see Family Code § 270 et seq.
Best interests of child,
　Considerations, see Family Code § 3011.
　Order of preference for custody, best interest of child as factor, see Family Code § 3040.
Cost of counsel appointed to represent minor as court operation for funding purposes, see Government Code § 77003.
Counsel, right to, see Cal. Const. Art. 1, § 15, cl. 3.
Custody investigation and report, recommendation for appointment of counsel, see Family Code § 3114.
Judgment and order defined for purposes of this Code, see Family Code § 100.
Juvenile court law, records, inspection of juvenile court documents, see Welfare and Institutions Code § 827.
Mediation proceedings, recommendation that counsel be appointed to represent minor child, see Family Code § 3184.
State funding of trial courts, court operations defined, see Government Code § 77003.
Uniform Child Custody Jurisdiction and Enforcement Act, see Family Code § 3400 et seq.

Research References

Forms

West's California Judicial Council Forms FL–323, Order Appointing Counsel for a Child (Also Available in Chinese, Korean, Spanish, and Vietnamese).

§ 3152

West's California Judicial Council Forms FL-323-INFO, Attorney for Child in a Family Law Case—Information Sheet (Also Available in Chinese, Korean, Spanish, and Vietnamese).

§ 3153. Compensation and expenses of private counsel

(a) If the court appoints counsel under this chapter to represent the child, counsel shall receive a reasonable sum for compensation and expenses, the amount of which shall be determined by the court. Except as provided in subdivision (b), this amount shall be paid by the parties in the proportions the court deems just.

(b) Upon its own motion or that of a party, the court shall determine whether both parties together are financially unable to pay all or a portion of the cost of counsel appointed pursuant to this chapter, and the portion of the cost of that counsel which the court finds the parties are unable to pay shall be paid by the county. The Judicial Council shall adopt guidelines to assist in determining financial eligibility for county payment of counsel appointed by the court pursuant to this chapter. *(Stats.1992, c. 162 (A.B.2650), § 10, operative Jan. 1, 1994.)*

Cross References

Attorney fees, generally, see Family Code § 270 et seq.
Cost of counsel appointed to represent minor as court operation for funding purposes, see Government Code § 77003.
Counsel, right to, see Cal. Const. Art. 1, § 15, cl. 3.
County defined for purposes of this Code, see Family Code § 67.
Courts, fees and fines collected after January 1, 2006, treatment thereof, see Government Code § 68085.1.
Judicial Council, practice and procedure rules, see Family Code § 210 et seq.

Research References

Forms

1 California Transactions Forms--Family Law § 2:72, Counsel for the Children.

§§ 3155 to 3159. Inoperative

CHAPTER 11. MEDIATION OF CUSTODY AND VISITATION ISSUES

Article	Section
1. General Provisions	3160
2. Availability of Mediation	3170
3. Mediation Proceedings	3175

Cross References

County clerk, increase of fees for support of family conciliation court and mediation services, conditions, see Government Code § 26840.3.
Evidence affected or excluded by extrinsic policies, mediation, application of Chapter, see Evidence Code § 1117.
Fees for conciliation court and mediation services, see Government Code § 26840.3.
Increase of fees for support of family conciliation court and mediation services, see Government Code § 26840.3.
Witnesses, competency, judges, arbitrators or mediators as witnesses, see Evidence Code § 703.5.

ARTICLE 1. GENERAL PROVISIONS

Section
3160. Mediators; availability; duties of court.
3161. Purpose of mediation proceedings.
3162. Uniform standards of practice; contents; adoption by Judicial Council.
3163. Local rules; development.
3164. Qualifications of mediators.
3165. Continuing education; clinical supervisors of evaluators, investigators, and mediators.

Cross References

Juvenile case file inspection, confidentiality, release, see Welfare and Institutions Code § 827.

§ 3160. Mediators; availability; duties of court

Each superior court shall make a mediator available. The court is not required to institute a family conciliation court in order to provide mediation services. *(Added by Stats.1993, c. 219 (A.B.1500), § 116.87.)*

Cross References

Arbitration, generally, see Code of Civil Procedure § 1281 et seq.
Conciliation proceedings, generally, see Family Code § 1800 et seq.
Family mediation and conciliation services, statewide coordination, see Family Code § 1850 et seq.
Fees for conciliation court and mediation services, see Government Code § 26840.3.
Judgment and order defined for purposes of this Code, see Family Code § 100.

Research References

Forms

1 Alternative Dispute Resolution § 1:9 (4th ed.), Statutes Mandating or Encouraging Alternative Dispute Resolution.
California Practice Guide: Rutter Family Law Forms Form 1:32, Glossary of Common Family Law Terms, Phrases and Concepts (Enclosure to Form 1:31).
2 California Transactions Forms--Business Transactions § 14:50, Confidentiality of Mediation Process.
1 California Transactions Forms--Family Law § 2:70, Deciding Custody.
1 California Transactions Forms--Family Law § 3:16, Identifying Areas of Parental Decision Making and Participation.
1 California Transactions Forms--Family Law § 3:59, Basis for Modification of Physical Custody.
1 California Transactions Forms--Family Law § 3:87, Appointment of a Special Master.
West's California Code Forms, Family § 3160, Comment Overview—Mediation of Custody and Visitation Issues.
26 West's Legal Forms § 1:3, Statutes Mandating or Encouraging Alternative Dispute Resolution.

§ 3161. Purpose of mediation proceedings

The purposes of a mediation proceeding are as follows:

(a) To reduce acrimony that may exist between the parties.

(b) To develop an agreement assuring the child close and continuing contact with both parents that is in the best interest of the child, consistent with Sections 3011 and 3020.

(c) To effect a settlement of the issue of visitation rights of all parties that is in the best interest of the child. *(Added by Stats.1993, c. 219 (A.B.1500), § 116.87. Amended by Stats.1997, c. 849 (A.B. 200), § 5.)*

Cross References

Arbitration, generally, see Code of Civil Procedure § 1281 et seq.
Best interest of child,
  Considerations, see Family Code § 3011.
  Order of preference for custody, best interest of child as factor, see Family Code § 3040.
Conciliation proceedings, generally, see Family Code § 1800 et seq.
Family mediation and conciliation services, statewide coordination, see Family Code § 1850 et seq.
Fees for conciliation court and mediation services, see Government Code § 26840.3.
Proceeding defined for purposes of this Code, see Family Code § 110.
Visitation rights,
  Generally, see Family Code § 3100 et seq.
  Close relatives where parent is deceased, see Family Code § 3102.
  Grandparents, see Family Code §§ 3103, 3104.
  Mediation of stepparent or grandparent visitation issues, see Family Code §§ 3171, 3178, 3185.
  Stepparents, see Family Code § 3101.

Research References

Forms

1 Alternative Dispute Resolution § 23:7 (4th ed.), Child Custody Disputes. West's California Code Forms, Family § 3160, Comment Overview—Mediation of Custody and Visitation Issues.

§ 3162. Uniform standards of practice; contents; adoption by Judicial Council

(a) Mediation of cases involving custody and visitation concerning children shall be governed by uniform standards of practice adopted by the Judicial Council.

(b) The standards of practice shall include, but not be limited to, all of the following:

(1) Provision for the best interest of the child and the safeguarding of the rights of the child to frequent and continuing contact with both parents, consistent with Sections 3011 and 3020.

(2) Facilitation of the transition of the family by detailing factors to be considered in decisions concerning the child's future.

(3) The conducting of negotiations in such a way as to equalize power relationships between the parties.

(c) In adopting the standards of practice, the Judicial Council shall consider standards developed by recognized associations of mediators and attorneys and other relevant standards governing mediation of proceedings for the dissolution of marriage.

(d) The Judicial Council shall offer training with respect to the standards to mediators. *(Added by Stats.1993, c. 219 (A.B.1500), § 116.87. Amended by Stats.1997, c. 849 (A.B.200), § 6.)*

Cross References

Arbitration, generally, see Code of Civil Procedure § 1281 et seq.
Best interest of child,
    Considerations, see Family Code § 3011.
    Order of preference for custody, best interest of child as factor, see Family Code § 3040.
Child custody or visitation mediation, record destruction, see Family Code § 1819.
Family mediation and conciliation services, statewide coordination, see Family Code § 1850.
Proceeding defined for purposes of this Code, see Family Code § 110.

§ 3163. Local rules; development

Courts shall develop local rules to respond to requests for a change of mediators or to general problems relating to mediation. *(Added by Stats.1993, c. 219 (A.B.1500), § 116.87.)*

Cross References

Arbitration, generally, see Code of Civil Procedure § 1281 et seq.
Conciliation proceedings, generally, see Family Code § 1800 et seq.
Family mediation and conciliation services, statewide coordination, see Family Code § 1850 et seq.

§ 3164. Qualifications of mediators

(a) The mediator may be a member of the professional staff of a family conciliation court, probation department, or mental health services agency, or may be any other person or agency designated by the court.

(b) The mediator shall meet the minimum qualifications required of a counselor of conciliation as provided in Section 1815. *(Added by Stats.1993, c. 219 (A.B.1500), § 116.87.)*

Cross References

Conciliation proceedings, generally, see Family Code § 1800 et seq.
Domestic violence training for counselors and mediators, see Family Code § 1816.
Family mediation and conciliation services, statewide coordination, see Family Code § 1850 et seq.
Person defined for purposes of this Code, see Family Code § 105.

§ 3165. Continuing education; clinical supervisors of evaluators, investigators, and mediators

Any person, regardless of administrative title, hired on or after January 1, 1998, who is responsible for clinical supervision of evaluators, investigators, or mediators or who directly supervises or administers the Family Court Services evaluation or mediation programs shall meet the same continuing education requirements specified in Section 1816 for supervising and associate counselors of conciliation. *(Added by Stats.1996, c. 761 (S.B.1995), § 4.)*

Cross References

Arbitration, generally, see Code of Civil Procedure § 1281 et seq.
Conciliation proceedings, generally, see Family Code § 1800 et seq.
Domestic violence training for counselors and mediators, see Family Code § 1816.
Family mediation and conciliation services, statewide coordination, see Family Code § 1850 et seq.
Person defined for purposes of this Code, see Family Code § 105.

ARTICLE 2. AVAILABILITY OF MEDIATION

Section
3170. Setting matters for mediation; guidelines for handling domestic violence cases.
3171. Stepparent or grandparent visitation; setting matter for mediation; waiver of parental right to object or require a hearing.
3172. Paternity disputes; availability of mediation proceedings.
3173. Mediation of disputes relating to existing custody or visitation orders; filing of petition.
3174. Inoperative.

Cross References

Best interest of the child,
    Considerations, see Family Code § 3011.
    Order of preference for custody, best interest of child as factor, see Family Code § 3040.
Fees for conciliation court and mediation services, see Government Code § 26840.3.
Mediation of stepparent or grandparent visitation issues, see Family Code §§ 3178, 3185.

§ 3170. Setting matters for mediation; guidelines for handling domestic violence cases

(a) If it appears on the face of a petition, application, or other pleading to obtain or modify a temporary or permanent custody or visitation order that custody, visitation, or both are contested, the court shall set the contested issues for mediation.

(b) Domestic violence cases shall be handled by Family Court Services in accordance with a separate written protocol approved by the Judicial Council. The Judicial Council shall adopt guidelines for services, other than services provided under this chapter, that courts or counties may offer to parents who have been unable to resolve their disputes. These services may include, but are not limited to, parent education programs, booklets, video recordings, or referrals to additional community resources.

(c) This section shall become operative on January 1, 2020. *(Added by Stats.2017, c. 330 (A.B.1692), § 2, eff. Jan. 1, 2018, operative Jan. 1, 2020.)*

Cross References

Arbitration, generally, see Code of Civil Procedure § 1281 et seq.
Child support commissioners, referral of actions or proceedings, see Family Code § 4251.
Conciliation proceedings, generally, see Family Code § 1800 et seq.

§ 3170

Contested issues of child custody and visitation set out for mediation, see Family Code § 20019.
County defined for purposes of this Code, see Family Code § 67.
Domestic violence,
  Defined for purposes of this Code, see Family Code § 6211.
  Prevention, generally, see Family Code § 6200 et seq.
  Support person for victims, see Family Code § 6303.
Family mediation and conciliation services, statewide coordination, see Family Code § 1850 et seq.
Judgment and order defined for purposes of this Code, see Family Code § 100.
Mediation, before or concurrent with hearing, see Family Code § 3175.

Research References

Forms

1 Alternative Dispute Resolution § 1:9 (4th ed.), Statutes Mandating or Encouraging Alternative Dispute Resolution.
1 Alternative Dispute Resolution § 4:4 (4th ed.), Mandated Mediation.
1 Alternative Dispute Resolution § 23:7 (4th ed.), Child Custody Disputes.
1 Alternative Dispute Resolution § 24:1 (4th ed.), Generally.
1 California Transactions Forms--Family Law § 2:70, Deciding Custody.

§ 3171. Stepparent or grandparent visitation; setting matter for mediation; waiver of parental right to object or require a hearing

(a) If a stepparent or grandparent has petitioned, or otherwise applied, for a visitation order pursuant to Chapter 5 (commencing with Section 3100), the court shall set the matter for mediation.

(b) A natural or adoptive parent who is not a party to the proceeding is not required to participate in the mediation proceeding, but failure to participate is a waiver of that parent's right to object to a settlement reached by the other parties during mediation or to require a hearing on the matter. *(Added by Stats.1993, c. 219 (A.B.1500), § 116.87.)*

Cross References

Arbitration, generally, see Code of Civil Procedure § 1281 et seq.
Best interest of the child,
  Considerations, see Family Code § 3011.
  Order of preference for custody, best interest of child as factor, see Family Code § 3040.
Conciliation proceedings, generally, see Family Code § 1800 et seq.
Family mediation and conciliation services, statewide coordination, see Family Code § 1850 et seq.
Fees for conciliation court and mediation services, see Government Code § 26840.3.
Judgment and order defined for purposes of this Code, see Family Code § 100.
Mediation of stepparent or grandparent visitation issues, see Family Code §§ 3178, 3185.
Proceeding defined for purposes of this Code, see Family Code § 110.
Visitation rights of grandparents, see Family Code §§ 3103, 3104.
Visitation rights of stepparents, see Family Code § 3101 et seq.

§ 3172. Paternity disputes; availability of mediation proceedings

Mediation shall not be denied to the parties on the basis that paternity is at issue in a proceeding before the court. *(Added by Stats.1993, c. 219 (A.B.1500), § 116.87.)*

Cross References

Arbitration, generally, see Code of Civil Procedure § 1281 et seq.
Conciliation proceedings, generally, see Family Code § 1800 et seq.
Family mediation and conciliation services, statewide coordination, see Family Code § 1850 et seq.
Fees for mediation services, see Government Code § 26840.3.
Proceeding defined for purposes of this Code, see Family Code § 110.
Uniform Parentage Act, see Family Code § 7600 et seq.

§ 3173. Mediation of disputes relating to existing custody or visitation orders; filing of petition

(a) Upon an order of the presiding judge of a superior court authorizing the procedure in that court, a petition may be filed pursuant to this chapter for mediation of a dispute relating to an existing order for custody, visitation, or both.

(b) The mediation of a dispute concerning an existing order shall be set not later than 60 days after the filing of the petition. *(Added by Stats.1993, c. 219 (A.B.1500), § 116.87. Amended by Stats.2012, c. 470 (A.B.1529), § 19.)*

Cross References

Arbitration, generally, see Code of Civil Procedure § 1281 et seq.
Computation of time, see Code of Civil Procedure §§ 12, 12a; Government Code § 6800 et seq.
Conciliation proceedings, generally, see Family Code § 1800 et seq.
Family mediation and conciliation services, statewide coordination, see Family Code § 1850 et seq.
Fees for mediation services, see Government Code § 26840.3.
Judgment and order defined for purposes of this Code, see Family Code § 100.

§ 3174. Inoperative

ARTICLE 3. MEDIATION PROCEEDINGS

Section
3175. Setting matter before or concurrent with hearing.
3176. Notice of mediation and hearing.
3177. Confidentiality of proceedings.
3178. Restrictions on mediation agreements.
3179. Modification of agreements.
3180. Duties of mediators.
3181. Domestic violence history between the parties; separate meetings; intake forms.
3182. Authority of mediators; exclusion of counsel; exclusion of domestic violence support person.
3183. Child custody recommending counseling; written report provided to parties and counsel; investigation when agreement not reached; restraining order to protect child well-being.
3184. Appointment of counsel to represent minor child; recommendations.
3185. Failure to reach mediation agreement; visitation rights hearing.
3186. Report of agreement; confirmation or incorporation of agreement in order.
3188. Confidential mediation program.

Cross References

Fees for conciliation court and mediation services, see Government Code § 26840.3.
Mediation of stepparent or grandparent visitation issues, see Family Code §§ 3171, 3178, 3185.

§ 3175. Setting matter before or concurrent with hearing

If a matter is set for mediation pursuant to this chapter, the mediation shall be set before or concurrent with the setting of the matter for hearing. *(Added by Stats.1993, c. 219 (A.B.1500), § 116.87.)*

Cross References

Arbitration, generally, see Code of Civil Procedure § 1281 et seq.
Conciliation proceedings, generally, see Family Code § 1800 et seq.
Family mediation and conciliation services, statewide coordination, see Family Code § 1850 et seq.
Fees for mediation services, see Government Code § 26840.3.

Research References

Forms

1 Alternative Dispute Resolution § 23:7 (4th ed.), Child Custody Disputes.

§ 3176. Notice of mediation and hearing

(a) Notice of mediation and of any hearing to be held pursuant to this chapter shall be given to the following persons:

(1) Where mediation is required to settle a contested issue of custody or visitation, to each party and to each party's counsel of record.

(2) Where a stepparent or grandparent seeks visitation rights, to the stepparent or grandparent seeking visitation rights, to each parent of the child, and to each parent's counsel of record.

(b) Notice shall be given by certified mail, return receipt requested, postage prepaid, to the last known address.

(c) Notice of mediation pursuant to Section 3188 shall state that all communications involving the mediator shall be kept confidential between the mediator and the disputing parties. *(Added by Stats. 1993, c. 219 (A.B.1500), § 116.87. Amended by Stats.2002, c. 1077 (S.B.174), § 1.)*

Cross References

Arbitration, generally, see Code of Civil Procedure § 1281 et seq.
Conciliation proceedings, generally, see Family Code § 1800 et seq.
Counsel, right to, see Cal. Const. Art. 1, § 15, cl. 3.
Family mediation and conciliation services, statewide coordination, see Family Code § 1850 et seq.
Fees for conciliation court and mediation services, see Government Code § 26840.3.
Mediation of stepparent or grandparent visitation issues, see Family Code §§ 3171, 3178, 3185.
Notice, actual and constructive, defined, see Civil Code § 18.
Person defined for purposes of this Code, see Family Code § 105.
State defined for purposes of this Code, see Family Code § 145.
Visitation rights of grandparents, see Family Code §§ 3103, 3104.
Visitation rights of stepparents, see Family Code § 3101 et seq.

§ 3177. Confidentiality of proceedings

Mediation proceedings pursuant to this chapter shall be held in private and shall be confidential. All communications, verbal or written, from the parties to the mediator made in the proceeding are official information within the meaning of Section 1040 of the Evidence Code. *(Added by Stats.1993, c. 219 (A.B.1500), § 116.87.)*

Cross References

Arbitration, generally, see Code of Civil Procedure § 1281 et seq.
Conciliation proceedings, generally, see Family Code § 1800 et seq.
Domestic violence, interagency death review teams, reporting procedures, see Penal Code § 11163.3.
Family mediation and conciliation services, statewide coordination, see Family Code § 1850 et seq.
Fees for conciliation court and mediation services, see Government Code § 26840.3.
Mediation of stepparent or grandparent visitation issues, see Family Code §§ 3171, 3178, 3185.
Proceeding defined for purposes of this Code, see Family Code § 110.
Visitation rights of grandparents, see Family Code §§ 3103, 3104.
Visitation rights of stepparents, see Family Code § 3101 et seq.

§ 3178. Restrictions on mediation agreements

An agreement reached by the parties as a result of mediation shall be limited as follows:

(a) Where mediation is required to settle a contested issue of custody or visitation, the agreement shall be limited to the resolution of issues relating to parenting plans, custody, visitation, or a combination of these issues.

(b) Where a stepparent or grandparent seeks visitation rights, the agreement shall be limited to the resolution of issues relating to visitation. *(Added by Stats.1993, c. 219 (A.B.1500), § 116.87.)*

Cross References

Arbitration, generally, see Code of Civil Procedure § 1281 et seq.
Conciliation proceedings, generally, see Family Code § 1800 et seq.
Family mediation and conciliation services, statewide coordination, see Family Code § 1850 et seq.
Fees for conciliation court and mediation services, see Government Code § 26840.3.
Mediation of stepparent or grandparent visitation issues, see Family Code §§ 3171, 3178, 3185.
Visitation rights of grandparents, see Family Code §§ 3103, 3104.
Visitation rights of stepparents, see Family Code § 3101 et seq.

§ 3179. Modification of agreements

A custody or visitation agreement reached as a result of mediation may be modified at any time at the discretion of the court, subject to Chapter 1 (commencing with Section 3020), Chapter 2 (commencing with Section 3040), Chapter 4 (commencing with Section 3080), and Chapter 5 (commencing with Section 3100). *(Added by Stats.1993, c. 219 (A.B.1500), § 116.87.)*

Cross References

Arbitration, generally, see Code of Civil Procedure § 1281 et seq.
Conciliation proceedings, generally, see Family Code § 1800 et seq.
Family mediation and conciliation services, statewide coordination, see Family Code § 1850 et seq.
Fees for conciliation court and mediation services, see Government Code § 26840.3.
Mediation of stepparent or grandparent visitation issues, see Family Code §§ 3171, 3178, 3185.
Visitation rights of grandparents, see Family Code §§ 3103, 3104.
Visitation rights of stepparents, see Family Code § 3101 et seq.

§ 3180. Duties of mediators

(a) In mediation proceedings pursuant to this chapter, the mediator has the duty to assess the needs and interests of the child involved in the controversy, and is entitled to interview the child when the mediator considers the interview appropriate or necessary.

(b) The mediator shall use their best efforts to effect a settlement of the custody or visitation dispute that is in the best interest of the child, as provided in Section 3011. *(Added by Stats.1993, c. 219 (A.B.1500), § 116.87. Amended by Stats.2019, c. 115 (A.B.1817), § 37, eff. Jan. 1, 2020.)*

Cross References

Arbitration, generally, see Code of Civil Procedure § 1281 et seq.
Best interest of child,
 Considerations, see Family Code § 3011.
 Order of preference for custody, best interest of child as factor, see Family Code § 3040.
Conciliation proceedings, generally, see Family Code § 1800 et seq.
Family mediation and conciliation services, statewide coordination, see Family Code § 1850 et seq.
Fees for conciliation court and mediation services, see Government Code § 26840.3.
Mediation of stepparent or grandparent visitation issues, see Family Code §§ 3171, 3178, 3185.
Proceeding defined for purposes of this Code, see Family Code § 110.
Visitation rights of grandparents, see Family Code §§ 3103, 3104.
Visitation rights of stepparents, see Family Code § 3101 et seq.

§ 3181. Domestic violence history between the parties; separate meetings; intake forms

(a) In a proceeding in which mediation is required pursuant to this chapter, where there has been a history of domestic violence between the parties or where a protective order as defined in Section 6218 is in effect, at the request of the party alleging domestic violence in a written declaration under penalty of perjury or protected by the order, the mediator appointed pursuant to this chapter shall meet with the parties separately and at separate times.

(b) Any intake form that an agency charged with providing family court services requires the parties to complete before the commencement of mediation shall state that, if a party alleging domestic violence in a written declaration under penalty of perjury or a party protected by a protective order so requests, the mediator will meet with the parties separately and at separate times. *(Added by Stats.1993, c. 219 (A.B.1500), § 116.87.)*

Cross References

Arbitration, generally, see Code of Civil Procedure § 1281 et seq.
Conciliation proceedings, generally, see Family Code § 1800 et seq.
Domestic violence,
   Defined for purposes of this Code, see Family Code § 6211.
   Prevention, generally, see Family Code § 6200 et seq.
   Support person for victims, see Family Code § 6303.
Family mediation and conciliation services, statewide coordination, see Family Code § 1850 et seq.
Judgment and order defined for purposes of this Code, see Family Code § 100.
Perjury and subornation of perjury, see Penal Code § 118 et seq.
Proceeding defined for purposes of this Code, see Family Code § 110.
State defined for purposes of this Code, see Family Code § 145.

§ 3182. Authority of mediators; exclusion of counsel; exclusion of domestic violence support person

(a) The mediator has authority to exclude counsel from participation in the mediation proceedings pursuant to this chapter if, in the mediator's discretion, exclusion of counsel is appropriate or necessary.

(b) The mediator has authority to exclude a domestic violence support person from a mediation proceeding as provided in Section 6303. *(Added by Stats.1993, c. 219 (A.B.1500), § 116.87.)*

Cross References

Arbitration, generally, see Code of Civil Procedure § 1281 et seq.
Conciliation proceedings, generally, see Family Code § 1800 et seq.
Counsel, right to, see Cal. Const. Art. 1, § 15, cl. 3.
Domestic violence, support person for victims, see Family Code § 6303.
Domestic violence defined for purposes of this Code, see Family Code § 6211.
Family mediation and conciliation services, statewide coordination, see Family Code § 1850 et seq.
Fees for conciliation court and mediation services, see Government Code § 26840.3.
Person defined for purposes of this Code, see Family Code § 105.
Proceeding defined for purposes of this Code, see Family Code § 110.
Support defined for purposes of this Code, see Family Code § 150.

Research References

Forms
26 West's Legal Forms App 2B, Uniform Mediation Act.

§ 3183. Child custody recommending counseling; written report provided to parties and counsel; investigation when agreement not reached; restraining order to protect child well-being

(a) Except as provided in Section 3188, the mediator may, consistent with local court rules, submit a recommendation to the court as to the custody of or visitation with the child, if the mediator has first provided the parties and their attorneys, including counsel for any minor children, with the recommendations in writing in advance of the hearing. The court shall make an inquiry at the hearing as to whether the parties and their attorneys have received the recommendations in writing. If the mediator is authorized to submit a recommendation to the court pursuant to this subdivision, the mediation and recommendation process shall be referred to as "child custody recommending counseling" and the mediator shall be referred to as a "child custody recommending counselor." Mediators who make those recommendations are considered mediators for purposes of Chapter 11 (commencing with Section 3160), and shall be subject to all requirements for mediators for all purposes under this code and the California Rules of Court. On and after January 1, 2012, all court communications and information regarding the child custody recommending counseling process shall reflect the change in the name of the process and the name of the providers.

(b) If the parties have not reached agreement as a result of the mediation proceedings, the mediator may recommend to the court that an investigation be conducted pursuant to Chapter 6 (commencing with Section 3110) or that other services be offered to assist the parties to effect a resolution of the controversy before a hearing on the issues.

(c) In appropriate cases, the mediator may recommend that restraining orders be issued, pending determination of the controversy, to protect the well-being of the child involved in the controversy. *(Added by Stats.1993, c. 219 (A.B.1500), § 116.87. Amended by Stats.1996, c. 761 (S.B.1995), § 6; Stats.2002, c. 1077 (S.B.174), § 2; Stats.2010, c. 352 (A.B.939), § 16.)*

Cross References

Arbitration, generally, see Code of Civil Procedure § 1281 et seq.
Best interest of child,
   Considerations, see Family Code § 3011.
   Order of preference for custody, best interest of child as factor, see Family Code § 3040.
Child custody, confidential psychological evaluations and recommendations, exceptions, see Family Code § 3025.5.
Conciliation proceedings, generally, see Family Code § 1800 et seq.
Custody or visitation, preference of child, determination of wish to express preference, see Family Code § 3042.
Family mediation and conciliation services, statewide coordination, see Family Code § 1850 et seq.
Fees for conciliation court and mediation services, see Government Code § 26840.3.
Judgment and order defined for purposes of this Code, see Family Code § 100.
Proceeding defined for purposes of this Code, see Family Code § 110.

§ 3184. Appointment of counsel to represent minor child; recommendations

Except as provided in Section 3188, nothing in this chapter prohibits the mediator from recommending to the court that counsel be appointed, pursuant to Chapter 10 (commencing with Section 3150), to represent the minor child. In making this recommendation, the mediator shall inform the court of the reasons why it would be in the best interest of the minor child to have counsel appointed. *(Added by Stats.1993, c. 219 (A.B.1500), § 116.87. Amended by Stats.2002, c. 1077 (S.B.174), § 3.)*

Cross References

Best interest of child,
   Considerations, see Family Code § 3011.
   Order of preference for custody, best interest of child as factor, see Family Code § 3040.
Conciliation proceedings, generally, see Family Code § 1800 et seq.
Counsel, right to, see Cal. Const. Art. 1, § 15, cl. 3.
Family mediation and conciliation services, statewide coordination, see Family Code § 1850 et seq.
Minor defined for purposes of this Code, see Family Code § 6500.

§ 3185. Failure to reach mediation agreement; visitation rights hearing

(a) If issues that may be resolved by agreement pursuant to Section 3178 are not resolved by an agreement of all the parties who participate in mediation, the mediator shall inform the court in writing and the court shall set the matter for hearing on the unresolved issues.

(b) Where a stepparent or grandparent requests visitation, each natural or adoptive parent and the stepparent or grandparent shall be given an opportunity to appear and be heard on the issue of visitation. *(Added by Stats.1993, c. 219 (A.B.1500), § 116.87.)*

Cross References

Arbitration, generally, see Code of Civil Procedure § 1281 et seq.
Conciliation proceedings, generally, see Family Code § 1800 et seq.
Family mediation and conciliation services, statewide coordination, see Family Code § 1850 et seq.
Mediation of stepparent or grandparent visitation issues, see Family Code §§ 3171, 3178.
Visitation rights of grandparents, see Family Code §§ 3103, 3104.
Visitation rights of stepparents, see Family Code § 3101 et seq.

Writings, authentication and proof of, see Evidence Code § 1400 et seq.

§ 3186. Report of agreement; confirmation or incorporation of agreement in order

(a) An agreement reached by the parties as a result of mediation shall be reported to counsel for the parties by the mediator on the day set for mediation or as soon thereafter as practical, but before the agreement is reported to the court.

(b) An agreement may not be confirmed or otherwise incorporated in an order unless each party, in person or by counsel of record, has affirmed and assented to the agreement in open court or by written stipulation.

(c) An agreement may be confirmed or otherwise incorporated in an order if a party fails to appear at a noticed hearing on the issue involved in the agreement. *(Added by Stats.1993, c. 219 (A.B.1500), § 116.87.)*

Cross References

Arbitration, generally, see Code of Civil Procedure § 1281 et seq.
Conciliation proceedings, generally, see Family Code § 1800 et seq.
Counsel, right to, see Cal. Const. Art. 1, § 15, cl. 3.
Family mediation and conciliation services, statewide coordination, see Family Code § 1850 et seq.
Fees for conciliation court and mediation services, see Government Code § 26840.3.
Judgment and order defined for purposes of this Code, see Family Code § 100.
Person defined for purposes of this Code, see Family Code § 105.

§ 3188. Confidential mediation program

(a) Any court selected by the Judicial Council under subdivision (c) may voluntarily adopt a confidential mediation program that provides for all of the following:

(1) The mediator may not make a recommendation as to custody or visitation to anyone other than the disputing parties, except as otherwise provided in this section.

(2) If total or partial agreement is reached in mediation, the mediator may report this fact to the court. If both parties consent in writing, where there is a partial agreement, the mediator may report to the court a description of the issues still in dispute, without specific reference to either party.

(3) In making the recommendation described in Section 3184, the mediator may not inform the court of the reasons why it would be in the best interest of the minor child to have counsel appointed.

(4) If the parties have not reached agreement as a result of the initial mediation, this section does not prohibit the court from requiring subsequent mediation that may result in a recommendation as to custody or visitation with the child if the subsequent mediation is conducted by a different mediator with no prior involvement with the case or knowledge of any communications, as defined in Section 1040 of the Evidence Code, with respect to the initial mediation. The court, however, shall inform the parties that the mediator will make a recommendation to the court regarding custody or visitation in the event that the parties cannot reach agreement on these issues.

(5) If an initial screening or intake process indicates that the case involves serious safety risks to the child, such as domestic violence, sexual abuse, or serious substance abuse, the mediator may provide an initial emergency assessment service that includes a recommendation to the court concerning temporary custody or visitation orders in order to expeditiously address those safety issues.

(b) This section shall become operative upon the appropriation of funds in the annual Budget Act sufficient to implement this section.

(c) This section shall apply only in four or more superior courts selected by the Judicial Council that currently allow a mediator to make custody recommendations to the court and have more than 1,000 family law case filings per year. The Judicial Council may also make this section applicable to additional superior courts that have fewer than 1,000 family law case filings per year. *(Added by Stats.2002, c. 1077 (S.B.174), § 4. Amended by Stats.2012, c. 470 (A.B.1529), § 20.)*

Cross References

Abuse defined for purposes of the Domestic Violence Prevention Act, see Family Code § 6203.
Arbitration, generally, see Code of Civil Procedure § 1281 et seq.
Conciliation proceedings, generally, see Family Code § 1800 et seq.
Counsel, right to, see Cal. Const. Art. 1, § 15, cl. 3.
County defined for purposes of this Code, see Family Code § 67.
Domestic violence defined for purposes of this Code, see Family Code § 6211.
Family mediation and conciliation services, statewide coordination, see Family Code § 1850 et seq.
Fees for conciliation court and mediation services, see Government Code § 26840.3.
Judgment and order defined for purposes of this Code, see Family Code § 100.
Mediation of stepparent or grandparent visitation issues, see Family Code §§ 3171, 3178.
Minor defined for purposes of this Code, see Family Code § 6500.
Writings, authentication and proof of, see Evidence Code § 1400 et seq.

CHAPTER 12. COUNSELING OF PARENTS AND CHILD

Section
3190. Court order to participate in counseling; costs.
3191. Goals of outpatient counseling.
3192. Separate counseling sessions; history of abuse in family relationship.

§ 3190. Court order to participate in counseling; costs

(a) The court may require parents or any other party involved in a custody or visitation dispute, and the minor child, to participate in outpatient counseling with a licensed mental health professional, or through other community programs and services that provide appropriate counseling, including, but not limited to, mental health or substance abuse services, for not more than one year, provided that the program selected has counseling available for the designated period of time, if the court finds both of the following:

(1) The dispute between the parents, between the parent or parents and the child, between the parent or parents and another party seeking custody or visitation rights with the child, or between a party seeking custody or visitation rights and the child, poses a substantial danger to the best interest of the child.

(2) The counseling is in the best interest of the child.

(b) In determining whether a dispute, as described in paragraph (1) of subdivision (a), poses a substantial danger to the best interest of the child, the court shall consider, in addition to any other factors the court determines relevant, any history of domestic violence, as defined in Section 6211, within the past five years between the parents, between the parent or parents and the child, between the parent or parents and another party seeking custody or visitation rights with the child, or between a party seeking custody or visitation rights and the child.

(c) Subject to Section 3192, if the court finds that the financial burden created by the order for counseling does not otherwise jeopardize a party's other financial obligations, the court shall fix the cost and shall order the entire cost of the services to be borne by the parties in the proportions the court deems reasonable.

(d) The court, in its finding, shall set forth reasons why it has found both of the following:

(1) The dispute poses a substantial danger to the best interest of the child and the counseling is in the best interest of the child.

(2) The financial burden created by the court order for counseling does not otherwise jeopardize a party's other financial obligations.

§ 3190

(e) The court shall not order the parties to return to court upon the completion of counseling. Any party may file a new order to show cause or motion after counseling has been completed, and the court may again order counseling consistent with this chapter. *(Stats.1992, c. 162 (A.B.2650), § 10, operative Jan. 1, 1994. Amended by Stats.1993, c. 219 (A.B.1500), § 116.90; Stats.1993, c. 301, (A.B.197), § 1; Stats.1993, c. 876 (S.B.1068), § 15.4, eff. Oct. 6, 1993, operative Jan. 1, 1994; Stats.1994, c. 1269 (A.B.2208), § 30; Stats. 1998, c. 229 (A.B.1837), § 1.)*

Cross References

Abuse defined for purposes of the Domestic Violence Prevention Act, see Family Code § 6203.
Best interests of child,
   Considerations, see Family Code § 3011.
   Order of preference for custody, best interest of child, see Family Code § 3040.
Judgment and order defined for purposes of this Code, see Family Code § 100.
Minor defined for purposes of this Code, see Family Code § 6500.

Research References

Forms

1 California Transactions Forms--Family Law § 2:76, Drug and Alcohol Use.

§ 3191. Goals of outpatient counseling

The counseling pursuant to this chapter shall be specifically designed to facilitate communication between the parties regarding their minor child's best interest, to reduce conflict regarding custody or visitation, and to improve the quality of parenting skills of each parent. *(Stats.1992, c. 162 (A.B.2650), § 10, operative Jan. 1, 1994. Amended by Stats.1993, c. 219 (A.B.1500), § 116.91.)*

Cross References

Best interest of child,
   Considerations, see Family Code § 3011.
   Order of preference for custody, best interest of child as factor, see Family Code § 3040.
Minor defined for purposes of this Code, see Family Code § 6500.

§ 3192. Separate counseling sessions; history of abuse in family relationship

In a proceeding in which counseling is ordered pursuant to this chapter, where there has been a history of abuse by either parent against the child or by one parent against the other parent and a protective order, as defined in Section 6218, is in effect, the court may order the parties to participate in counseling separately and at separate times. Each party shall bear the cost of the party's own counseling separately, unless good cause is shown for a different apportionment. The costs associated with a minor child participating in counseling shall be apportioned in accordance with Section 4062. *(Stats.1992, c. 162 (A.B.2650), § 10, operative Jan. 1, 1994. Amended by Stats.1993, c. 219 (A.B.1500), § 116.92; Stats.1994, c. 1269 (A.B.2208), § 31; Stats.2019, c. 115 (A.B.1817), § 38, eff. Jan. 1, 2020.)*

Cross References

Abuse defined for purposes of the Domestic Violence Prevention Act, see Family Code § 6203.
Domestic violence defined, see Family Code § 6211.
Domestic violence prevention, see Family Code § 6200 et seq.
Emergency protective orders, generally, see Family Code § 6240 et seq.
Judgment and order defined for purposes of this Code, see Family Code § 100.
Minor defined for purposes of this Code, see Family Code § 6500.
Perjury and subornation of perjury, see Penal Code § 118 et seq.
Proceeding defined for purposes of this Code, see Family Code § 110.

Protective order defined, see Family Code § 6218.

CHAPTER 13. SUPERVISED VISITATION AND EXCHANGE SERVICES, EDUCATION, AND COUNSELING

Section
3200. Supervised visitation provider standards; guidelines.
3200.5. Standards for professional or nonprofessional supervised visitation providers; cases of domestic violence or child abuse or neglect; court to determine provider based on best interest of child; definitions; training; child to provider ratio; duties of professional providers.
3201. Administration of supervised visitation.
3201.5. Administration of programs; education about protecting children during family disruption.
3202. Uniform Standards of Practice for Providers of Supervised Visitation; eligible providers.
3203. Establishment and administration of programs by family law division of county superior courts.
3204. Judicial Council; application for grants from the federal Administration for Children and Families; legislative intent; reports.

§ 3200. Supervised visitation provider standards; guidelines

The Judicial Council shall develop standards for supervised visitation providers in accordance with the guidelines set forth in this section. For the purposes of the development of these standards, the term "provider" shall include any individual who functions as a visitation monitor, as well as supervised visitation centers. Provisions shall be made within the standards to allow for the diversity of supervised visitation providers.

(a) When developing standards, the Judicial Council shall consider all of the following issues:

(1) The provider's qualifications, experience, and education.

(2) Safety and security procedures, including ratios of children per supervisor.

(3) Any conflict of interest.

(4) Maintenance and disclosure of records, including confidentiality policies.

(5) Procedures for screening, delineation of terms and conditions, and termination of supervised visitation services.

(6) Procedures for emergency or extenuating situations.

(7) Orientation to and guidelines for cases in which there are allegations of domestic violence, child abuse, substance abuse, or special circumstances.

(8) The legal obligations and responsibilities of supervisors.

(b) The Judicial Council shall consult with visitation centers, mothers' groups, fathers' groups, judges, the State Bar of California, children's advocacy groups, domestic violence prevention groups, Family Court Services, and other groups it regards as necessary in connection with these standards.

(c) It is the intent of the Legislature that the safety of children, adults, and visitation supervisors be a precondition to providing visitation services. Once safety is assured, the best interest of the child is the paramount consideration at all stages and particularly in deciding the manner in which supervision is provided. *(Added by Stats.1996, c. 387 (S.B.1643), § 1. Amended by Stats.2004, c. 193 (S.B.111), § 17.)*

Cross References

Abuse defined for purposes of the Domestic Violence Prevention Act, see Family Code § 6203.

Adult defined for purposes of this Code, see Family Code § 6501.
Domestic violence defined for purposes of this Code, see Family Code § 6211.
Legislative intent, construction of statutes, see Code of Civil Procedure § 1859.
State defined for purposes of this Code, see Family Code § 145.

Research References

Forms

2 California Transactions Forms--Family Law § 5:2, Overview.

2 California Transactions Forms--Family Law § 5:9, Use of Parenting Agreement to Define Rights and Responsibilities Relating to Child on Termination of Partners' Relationship Where Both Partners Are Biological Parents.

West's California Code Forms, Family § 3022, Comment Overview—Order for Custody.

§ 3200.5. Standards for professional or nonprofessional supervised visitation providers; cases of domestic violence or child abuse or neglect; court to determine provider based on best interest of child; definitions; training; child to provider ratio; duties of professional providers

(a) Any standards for supervised visitation providers adopted by the Judicial Council pursuant to Section 3200 shall conform to this section. A provider, as described in Section 3200, shall be a professional provider or nonprofessional provider.

(b) In any case in which the court has determined that there is domestic violence or child abuse or neglect, as defined in Section 11165.6 of the Penal Code, and the court determines supervision is necessary, the court shall consider whether to use a professional or nonprofessional provider based upon the child's best interest.

(c) For the purposes of this section, the following definitions apply:

(1) "Nonprofessional provider" means any person who is not paid for providing supervised visitation services.

(2) "Professional provider" means any person paid for providing supervised visitation services, or an independent contractor, employee, intern, or volunteer operating independently or through a supervised visitation center or agency.

(d) Unless otherwise ordered by the court or stipulated by the parties, a nonprofessional provider shall:

(1) Have no record of a conviction for child molestation, child abuse, or other crimes against a person.

(2) Have proof of automobile insurance if transporting the child.

(3) Have no current or past court order in which the provider is the person being supervised.

(4) Agree to adhere to and enforce the court order regarding supervised visitation.

(e) A professional provider shall:

(1) Be at least 21 years of age.

(2) Have no record of a conviction for driving under the influence (DUI) within the last five years.

(3) Not have been on probation or parole for the last 10 years.

(4) Have no record of a conviction for child molestation, child abuse, or other crimes against a person.

(5) Have proof of automobile insurance if transporting the child.

(6) Have no civil, criminal, or juvenile restraining orders within the last 10 years.

(7) Have no current or past court order in which the provider is the person being supervised.

(8) Be able to speak the language of the party being supervised and of the child, or the provider must provide a neutral interpreter over 18 years of age who is able to do so.

(9) Agree to adhere to and enforce the court order regarding supervised visitation.

(10)(A) Complete 24 hours of training prior to providing visitation services, including at least 12 hours of classroom instruction in the following subjects:

(i) The role of a professional provider.

(ii) Child abuse reporting laws.

(iii) Recordkeeping procedures.

(iv) Screening, monitoring, and termination of visitation.

(v) Developmental needs of children.

(vi) Legal responsibilities and obligations of a provider.

(vii) Cultural sensitivity.

(viii) Conflicts of interest, including the acceptance of gifts.

(ix) Confidentiality.

(x) Issues relating to substance abuse, child abuse, sexual abuse, and domestic violence.

(xi) Basic knowledge of family and juvenile law.

(B) Of the 24 hours of training required pursuant to subparagraph (A), at a minimum, three hours shall be on the screening, monitoring, and termination of visitation, three hours shall be on the developmental needs of children, three hours shall be on issues relating to substance abuse, child abuse, sexual abuse, and domestic violence, and one hour shall be on basic knowledge of family law.

(C) Notwithstanding the requirement for classroom instruction in subparagraph (A), on and after January 1, 2021, a professional provider shall complete the training required pursuant to clause (ii) of subparagraph (A), relating to child abuse reporting laws, by completing an online training course required for mandated reporters that is provided by the State Department of Social Services. This online training requirement is not intended to increase the total number of training hours required by this paragraph.

(11) Complete a Live Scan criminal background check, at the expense of the provider or the supervised visitation center or agency, prior to providing visitation services.

(12) Sign the Judicial Council Declaration of Supervised Visitation Provider form that the person meets the training and qualifications of a provider. A professional provider shall sign a separate, updated form each time the professional provider submits a report to the court.

(13)(A) Beginning January 1, 2021, be registered as a trustline provider pursuant to Chapter 3.35 (commencing with Section 1596.60) of Division 2 of the Health and Safety Code.

(B) Notwithstanding any other law, if a person is denied trustline registration by the State Department of Social Services pursuant to Section 1596.605 or 1596.607 of the Health and Safety Code, or if the State Department of Social Services revokes a person's trustline registration pursuant to Section 1596.608 of the Health and Safety Code, that person shall be ineligible to be a professional provider.

(f) The ratio of children to a professional provider shall be contingent on:

(1) The degree of risk factors present in each case.

(2) The nature of supervision required in each case.

(3) The number and ages of the children to be supervised during a visit.

(4) The number of people visiting the child during the visit.

(5) The duration and location of the visit.

(6) The experience of the provider.

(g) Professional providers of supervised visitation shall:

(1) Advise the parties before commencement of supervised visitation that no confidential privilege exists.

§ 3200.5

(2) Report suspected child abuse to the appropriate agency, as provided by law, and inform the parties of the provider's obligation to make those reports.

(3) Suspend or terminate visitation under subdivision (h).

(h) Professional providers shall:

(1) Prepare a written contract to be signed by the parties before commencement of the supervised visitation. The contract should inform each party of the terms and conditions of supervised visitation.

(2) Review custody and visitation orders relevant to the supervised visitation.

(3) Keep a record for each case, including, at least, all of the following:

(A) A written record of each contact and visit.

(B) Who attended the visit.

(C) Any failure to comply with the terms and conditions of the visitation.

(D) Any incidence of abuse, as required by law.

(i)(1) Each provider shall make every reasonable effort to provide a safe visit for the child and the noncustodial party.

(2) If a provider determines that the rules of the visit have been violated, the child has become acutely distressed, or the safety of the child or the provider is at risk, the visit may be temporarily interrupted, rescheduled at a later date, or terminated.

(3) All interruptions or terminations of visits shall be recorded in the case file.

(4) All providers shall advise both parties of the reasons for the interruption or termination of a visit.

(j) A professional provider shall state the reasons for temporary suspension or termination of supervised visitation in writing and shall provide the written statement to both parties, their attorneys, the attorney for the child, and the court. (Added by Stats.2012, c. 692 (A.B.1674), § 1. Amended by Stats.2013, c. 76 (A.B.383), § 60; Stats.2019, c. 823 (A.B.1165), § 1, eff. Jan. 1, 2020.)

Cross References

Child Care Provider Registration, definitions, see Health and Safety Code § 1596.60.

Professional supervised visitation provider, required registration, see Health and Safety Code § 1596.657.

Research References

Forms

West's California Judicial Council Forms FL–324(NP), Declaration of Supervised Visitation Provider (Nonprofessional).

West's California Judicial Council Forms FL–324(P), Declaration of Supervised Visitation Provider (Professional).

§ 3201. Administration of supervised visitation

Any supervised visitation maintained or imposed by the court shall be administered in accordance with Standard 5.20 of the California Standards of Judicial Administration recommended by the Judicial Council. (Added by Stats.1999, c. 985 (S.B.792), § 2. Amended by Stats.2021, c. 213 (A.B.1579), § 2, eff. Jan. 1, 2022.)

§ 3201.5. Administration of programs; education about protecting children during family disruption

(a) The programs described in this chapter shall be administered by the family law division of the superior court in the county.

(b) For purposes of this chapter, "education about protecting children during family disruption" includes education on parenting skills and the impact of parental conflict on children, how to put a parenting agreement into effect, and the responsibility of both parents to comply with custody and visitation orders. (Formerly § 3201, added by Stats.1999, c. 1004 (A.B.673), § 2. Renumbered § 3201.5 and amended by Stats.2015, c. 303 (A.B.731), § 145, eff. Jan. 1, 2016.)

Cross References

County defined for purposes of this Code, see Family Code § 67.
Judgment and order defined for purposes of this Code, see Family Code § 100.

§ 3202. Uniform Standards of Practice for Providers of Supervised Visitation; eligible providers

(a) All supervised visitation and exchange programs funded pursuant to this chapter shall comply with all requirements of the Uniform Standards of Practice for Providers of Supervised Visitation set forth in Standard 5.20 of the Standards of Judicial Administration as amended. The family law division of the superior court may contract with eligible providers of supervised visitation and exchange services, education, and group counseling to provide services under this chapter.

(b) As used in this section, "eligible provider" means:

(1) For providers of supervised visitation and exchange services, a local public agency or nonprofit entity that satisfies the Uniform Standards of Practice for Providers of Supervised Visitation.

(2) For providers of group counseling, a professional licensed to practice psychotherapy in this state, including, but not limited to, a licensed psychiatrist, licensed psychologist, licensed clinical social worker, licensed marriage and family therapist, or licensed professional clinical counselor; or a mental health intern working under the direct supervision of a professional licensed to practice psychotherapy.

(3) For providers of education, a professional with a bachelor's or master's degree in human behavior, child development, psychology, counseling, family-life education, or a related field, having specific training in issues relating to child and family development, substance abuse, child abuse, domestic violence, effective parenting, and the impact of divorce and interparental conflict on children; or an intern working under the supervision of that professional. (Added by Stats.1999, c. 1004 (A.B.673), § 3. Amended by Stats.2011, c. 381 (S.B.146), § 24; Stats.2013, c. 61 (S.B.826), § 1.)

Cross References

Abuse defined for purposes of the Domestic Violence Prevention Act, see Family Code § 6203.
Domestic violence defined for purposes of this Code, see Family Code § 6211.
State defined for purposes of this Code, see Family Code § 145.

§ 3203. Establishment and administration of programs by family law division of county superior courts

Subject to the availability of federal funding for the purposes of this chapter, the family law division of the superior court in each county may establish and administer a supervised visitation and exchange program, programs for education about protecting children during family disruption, and group counseling programs for parents and children under this chapter. The programs shall allow parties and children to participate in supervised visitation between a custodial party and a noncustodial party or joint custodians, and to participate in the education and group counseling programs, irrespective of whether the parties are or are not married to each other or are currently living separately and apart on a permanent or temporary basis. (Added by Stats.1999, c. 1004 (A.B.673), § 4.)

Cross References

County defined for purposes of this Code, see Family Code § 67.

§ 3204. Judicial Council; application for grants from the federal Administration for Children and Families; legislative intent; reports

(a) The Judicial Council shall annually submit an application to the federal Administration for Children and Families, pursuant to

Section 669B of the "1996 Federal Personal Responsibility and Work Opportunity Recovery Act" (PRWORA), for a grant to fund child custody and visitation programs pursuant to this chapter.

The Judicial Council shall be charged with the administration of the grant funds.

(b)(1) It is the intention of the Legislature that, effective October 1, 2000, the grant funds described in subdivision (a) shall be used to fund the following three types of programs: supervised visitation and exchange services, education about protecting children during family disruption, and group counseling for parents and children, as set forth in this chapter. Contracts shall follow a standard request for proposal procedure, that may include multiple year funding. Requests for proposals shall meet all state and federal requirements for receiving access and visitation grant funds.

(2) The grant funds shall be awarded with the intent of approving as many requests for proposals as possible while assuring that each approved proposal would provide beneficial services and satisfy the overall goals of the program under this chapter. The Judicial Council shall determine the final number and amount of grants. Requests for proposals shall be evaluated based on the following criteria:

(A) Availability of services to a broad population of parties.

(B) The ability to expand existing services.

(C) Coordination with other community services.

(D) The hours of service delivery.

(E) The number of counties or regions participating.

(F) Overall cost-effectiveness.

(G) The purpose of the program to promote and encourage healthy parent and child relationships between noncustodial parents and their children, while ensuring the health, safety, and welfare of the children.

(3) Special consideration for grant funds shall be given to proposals that coordinate supervised visitation and exchange services, education, and group counseling with existing court-based programs and services.

(c) The family law division of the superior court in each county shall approve sliding scale fees that are based on the ability to pay for all parties, including low-income families, participating in a supervised visitation and exchange, education, and group counseling programs under this chapter.

(d) The Judicial Council shall, on March 1, 2002, and on the first day of March of each subsequent even-numbered year, report to the Legislature on the programs funded pursuant to this chapter and whether and to what extent those programs are achieving the goal of promoting and encouraging healthy parent and child relationships between noncustodial or joint custodial parents and their children while ensuring the health, safety, and welfare of children, and the other goals described in this chapter. *(Added by Stats.1999, c. 1004 (A.B.673), § 5. Amended by Stats.2007, c. 738 (A.B.1248), § 13.)*

Cross References

County defined for purposes of this Code, see Family Code § 67.
Legislative intent, construction of statutes, see Code of Civil Procedure § 1859.
State defined for purposes of this Code, see Family Code § 145.

Part 3

UNIFORM CHILD CUSTODY JURISDICTION AND ENFORCEMENT ACT

Chapter	Section
1. General Provisions	3400
2. Jurisdiction	3421
3. Enforcement	3441
4. Miscellaneous Provisions	3461

Cross References

Child abduction,
  Exception, belief of bodily injury or emotional harm, see Penal Code § 278.7.
  Protective custody, circumstances, see Penal Code § 279.6.
Child custody provisions, appeals, automatic stay provisions, see Code of Civil Procedure § 917.7.
Modification of custody or visitation orders, justifications, military duty, see Family Code § 3047.
Other uniform acts in the Family Code,
  Uniform Divorce Recognition Act, see Family Code § 2090 et seq.
  Uniform Interstate Enforcement of Domestic Violence Protection Orders Act, see Family Code § 6400 et seq.
  Uniform Interstate Family Support Act, see Family Code § 5700.101 et seq.
  Uniform Parentage Act, see Family Code § 7600 et seq.
  Uniform Premarital Agreement Act, see Family Code § 1600 et seq.
Uniform act, construction of provisions, see Family Code § 3.

CHAPTER 1. GENERAL PROVISIONS

Section
3400. Short title.
3401. Repealed.
3402. Definitions.
3403. Adoption proceedings; emergency medical care.
3404. Native American children.
3405. Foreign countries; application of this Part; recognition of foreign custody determinations; exception.
3406. Binding effect of custody determinations.
3407. Questions regarding jurisdiction; priority handling.
3408. Notice to persons outside California.
3409. Child custody proceedings; parties; immunity from personal jurisdiction in other proceedings.
3410. Communication between courts.
3411. Witnesses in another state; testimony by deposition; documentary evidence transmitted by technological means.
3412. Request of another court to hold hearing or enter an order; preservation of pleadings and records.
3413 to 3420. Repealed.

§ 3400. Short title

This part may be cited as the Uniform Child Custody Jurisdiction and Enforcement Act. *(Added by Stats.1999, c. 867 (S.B.668), § 3.)*

Cross References

Uniform act, construction of provisions, see Family Code § 3.

Research References

Forms

1 California Transactions Forms--Family Law § 3:4, Subject Matter Jurisdiction for Custody Determinations.
2 California Transactions Forms--Family Law § 6:119, Continuing Jurisdiction.
2 California Transactions Forms--Family Law § 7:33, Parentage Testing.
West's California Code Forms, Family § 3400, Comment Overview—Uniform Child Custody Jurisdiction and Enforcement Act.
West's California Judicial Council Forms FL–105, Declaration Under Uniform Child Custody Jurisdiction and Enforcement Act (UCCJEA) (Also Available in Spanish).
West's California Judicial Council Forms FL–105(A), Attachment to Declaration Under Uniform Child Custody Jurisdiction and Enforcement Act (UCCJEA).
West's California Judicial Council Forms FL–260, Petition for Custody and Support of Minor Children (Also Available in Spanish).
West's California Judicial Council Forms FL–270, Response to Petition for Custody and Support of Minor Children (Also Available in Spanish).

§ 3400

West's California Judicial Council Forms GC–120, Declaration Under Uniform Child Custody Jurisdiction and Enforcement Act (UCCJEA) (Also Available in Spanish).

West's California Judicial Council Forms GC–120(A), Attachment to Declaration Under Uniform Child Custody Jurisdiction and Enforcement Act (UCCJEA).

§ 3401. Repealed by Stats.1999, c. 867 (S.B.668), § 2

§ 3402. Definitions

As used in this part:

(a) "Abandoned" means left without provision for reasonable and necessary care or supervision.

(b) "Child" means an individual who has not attained 18 years of age.

(c) "Child custody determination" means a judgment, decree, or other order of a court providing for the legal custody, physical custody, or visitation with respect to a child. The term includes a permanent, temporary, initial, and modification order. The term does not include an order relating to child support or other monetary obligation of an individual.

(d) "Child custody proceeding" means a proceeding in which legal custody, physical custody, or visitation with respect to a child is an issue. The term includes a proceeding for dissolution of marriage, legal separation of the parties, neglect, abuse, dependency, guardianship, paternity, termination of parental rights, and protection from domestic violence, in which the issue may appear. The term does not include a proceeding involving juvenile delinquency, contractual emancipation, or enforcement under Chapter 3 (commencing with Section 3441).

(e) "Commencement" means the filing of the first pleading in a proceeding.

(f) "Court" means an entity authorized under the law of a state to establish, enforce, or modify a child custody determination.

(g) "Home state" means the state in which a child lived with a parent or a person acting as a parent for at least six consecutive months immediately before the commencement of a child custody proceeding. In the case of a child less than six months of age, the term means the state in which the child lived from birth with any of the persons mentioned. A period of temporary absence of any of the mentioned persons is part of the period.

(h) "Initial determination" means the first child custody determination concerning a particular child.

(i) "Issuing court" means the court that makes a child custody determination for which enforcement is sought under this part.

(j) "Issuing state" means the state in which a child custody determination is made.

(k) "Modification" means a child custody determination that changes, replaces, supersedes, or is otherwise made after a previous determination concerning the same child, whether or not it is made by the court that made the previous determination.

(*l*) "Person" means an individual, corporation, business trust, estate, trust, partnership, limited liability company, association, joint venture, or government; governmental subdivision, agency, or instrumentality; public corporation; or any other legal or commercial entity.

(m) "Person acting as a parent" means a person, other than a parent, who: (1) has physical custody of the child or has had physical custody for a period of six consecutive months, including any temporary absence, within one year immediately before the commencement of a child custody proceeding; and (2) has been awarded legal custody by a court or claims a right to legal custody under the law of this state.

(n) "Physical custody" means the physical care and supervision of a child.

(o) "State" means a state of the United States, the District of Columbia, Puerto Rico, the United States Virgin Islands, or any territory or insular possession subject to the jurisdiction of the United States.

(p) "Tribe" means an Indian tribe or band, or Alaskan Native village, that is recognized by federal law or formally acknowledged by a state.

(q) "Warrant" means an order issued by a court authorizing law enforcement officers to take physical custody of a child. *(Added by Stats.1999, c. 867 (S.B.668), § 3.)*

Cross References

Abuse defined for purposes of the Domestic Violence Prevention Act, see Family Code § 6203.
Child support, generally, see Family Code § 3900 et seq.
Domestic violence defined for purposes of this Code, see Family Code § 6211.
Expedited child support orders, see Family Code § 3620 et seq.
Health insurance coverage for supported children, see Family Code § 3750 et seq.
Judgment and order defined for purposes of this Code, see Family Code § 100.
Modification, termination, or setting aside of support order, see Family Code § 3650 et seq.
Person defined for purposes of this Code, see Family Code § 105.
Proceeding defined for purposes of this Code, see Family Code § 110.
State defined for purposes of this Code, see Family Code § 145.
Support, generally, see Family Code § 3500 et seq.
Support defined for purposes of this Code, see Family Code § 150.
Uniform act, construction of provisions, see Family Code § 3.

Research References

Forms

West's California Code Forms, Probate § 1510 Form 3, Declaration Under Uniform Child Custody Jurisdiction and Enforcement Act (UCCJEA)-Judicial Council Form FL-105/GC-120.

§ 3403. Adoption proceedings; emergency medical care

This part does not govern an adoption proceeding or a proceeding pertaining to the authorization of emergency medical care for a child. *(Added by Stats.1999, c. 867 (S.B.668), § 3.)*

Cross References

Proceeding defined for purposes of this Code, see Family Code § 110.
Temporary emergency jurisdiction, see Family Code § 3424.
Uniform act, construction of provisions, see Family Code § 3.

Research References

Forms

2 California Transactions Forms--Family Law § 6:119, Continuing Jurisdiction.
2 California Transactions Forms--Family Law § 7:39, Adoption and Termination of Parental Rights.

§ 3404. Native American children

(a) A child custody proceeding that pertains to an Indian child as defined in the Indian Child Welfare Act (25 U.S.C. Sec. 1901 et seq.) is not subject to this part to the extent that it is governed by the Indian Child Welfare Act.

(b) A court of this state shall treat a tribe as if it were a state of the United States for the purpose of applying this chapter and Chapter 2 (commencing with Section 3421).

(c) A child custody determination made by a tribe under factual circumstances in substantial conformity with the jurisdictional standards of this part must be recognized and enforced under Chapter 3 (commencing with Section 3441). *(Added by Stats.1999, c. 867 (S.B.668), § 3.)*

Cross References

Proceeding defined for purposes of this Code, see Family Code § 110.
State defined for purposes of this Code, see Family Code § 145.

Uniform act, construction of provisions, see Family Code § 3.

Research References

Forms

1 California Transactions Forms--Family Law § 3:4, Subject Matter Jurisdiction for Custody Determinations.

§ 3405. Foreign countries; application of this Part; recognition of foreign custody determinations; exception

(a) A court of this state shall treat a foreign country as if it were a state of the United States for the purpose of applying this chapter and Chapter 2 (commencing with Section 3421).

(b) Except as otherwise provided in subdivision (c), a child custody determination made in a foreign country under factual circumstances in substantial conformity with the jurisdictional standards of this part must be recognized and enforced under Chapter 3 (commencing with Section 3441).

(c) A court of this state need not apply this part if the child custody law of a foreign country violates fundamental principles of human rights. *(Added by Stats.1999, c. 867 (S.B.668), § 3.)*

Cross References

State defined for purposes of this Code, see Family Code § 145.
Uniform act, construction of provisions, see Family Code § 3.

§ 3406. Binding effect of custody determinations

A child custody determination made by a court of this state that had jurisdiction under this part binds all persons who have been served in accordance with the laws of this state or notified in accordance with Section 3408 or who have submitted to the jurisdiction of the court, and who have been given an opportunity to be heard. As to those persons, the determination is conclusive as to all decided issues of law and fact except to the extent the determination is modified. *(Added by Stats.1999, c. 867 (S.B.668), § 3.)*

Cross References

Person defined for purposes of this Code, see Family Code § 105.
State defined for purposes of this Code, see Family Code § 145.
Uniform act, construction of provisions, see Family Code § 3.

§ 3407. Questions regarding jurisdiction; priority handling

If a question of existence or exercise of jurisdiction under this part is raised in a child custody proceeding, the question, upon request of a party, must be given priority on the calendar and handled expeditiously. *(Added by Stats.1999, c. 867 (S.B.668), § 3.)*

Cross References

Proceeding defined for purposes of this Code, see Family Code § 110.
Uniform act, construction of provisions, see Family Code § 3.

§ 3408. Notice to persons outside California

(a) Notice required for the exercise of jurisdiction when a person is outside this state may be given in a manner prescribed by the law of this state for service of process or by the law of the state in which the service is made. Notice must be given in a manner reasonably calculated to give actual notice but may be by publication if other means are not effective.

(b) Proof of service may be made in the manner prescribed by the law of this state or by the law of the state in which the service is made.

(c) Notice is not required for the exercise of jurisdiction with respect to a person who submits to the jurisdiction of the court. *(Added by Stats.1999, c. 867 (S.B.668), § 3.)*

Cross References

Notice, actual and constructive, defined, see Civil Code § 18.
Person defined for purposes of this Code, see Family Code § 105.
Proof of service, see Code of Civil Procedure § 417.10 et seq.
Service of process, generally, see Code of Civil Procedure § 410.10 et seq.
State defined for purposes of this Code, see Family Code § 145.
Uniform act, construction of provisions, see Family Code § 3.

§ 3409. Child custody proceedings; parties; immunity from personal jurisdiction in other proceedings

(a) A party to a child custody proceeding, including a modification proceeding, or a petitioner or respondent in a proceeding to enforce or register a child custody determination, is not subject to personal jurisdiction in this state for another proceeding or purpose solely by reason of having participated, or of having been physically present for the purpose of participating, in the proceeding.

(b) A person who is subject to personal jurisdiction in this state on a basis other than physical presence is not immune from service of process in this state. A party present in this state who is subject to the jurisdiction of another state is not immune from service of process allowable under the laws of that state.

(c) The immunity granted by subdivision (a) does not extend to civil litigation based on acts unrelated to the participation in a proceeding under this part committed by an individual while present in this state. *(Added by Stats.1999, c. 867 (S.B.668), § 3.)*

Cross References

Person defined for purposes of this Code, see Family Code § 105.
Petitioner defined for purposes of this Code, see Family Code § 126.
Proceeding defined for purposes of this Code, see Family Code § 110.
Respondent defined for purposes of this Code, see Family Code § 127.
Service of process, generally, see Code of Civil Procedure § 410.10 et seq.
State defined for purposes of this Code, see Family Code § 145.
Uniform act, construction of provisions, see Family Code § 3.

Research References

Forms

West's California Code Forms, Family § 3400, Comment Overview—Uniform Child Custody Jurisdiction and Enforcement Act.
West's California Code Forms, Family § 7841 Form 1, Petition for Freedom from Parental Control—Abandonment.
West's California Judicial Council Forms FL-100, Petition—Marriage/Domestic Partnership (Also Available in Arabic, Chinese, and Spanish).

§ 3410. Communication between courts

(a) A court of this state may communicate with a court in another state concerning a proceeding arising under this part.

(b) The court may allow the parties to participate in the communication. If the parties are not able to participate in the communication, they must be given the opportunity to present facts and legal arguments before a decision on jurisdiction is made.

(c) Communication between courts on schedules, calendars, court records, and similar matters may occur without informing the parties. A record need not be made of the communication.

(d) Except as otherwise provided in subdivision (c), a record must be made of a communication under this section. The parties must be informed promptly of the communication and granted access to the record.

(e) For the purposes of this section, "record" means information that is inscribed on a tangible medium or that is stored in an electronic or other medium and is retrievable in perceivable form. *(Added by Stats.1999, c. 867 (S.B.668), § 3.)*

Cross References

Proceeding defined for purposes of this Code, see Family Code § 110.
State defined for purposes of this Code, see Family Code § 145.

§ 3410   CUSTODY OF CHILDREN

Uniform act, construction of provisions, see Family Code § 3.

§ 3411. Witnesses in another state; testimony by deposition; documentary evidence transmitted by technological means

(a) In addition to other procedures available to a party, a party to a child custody proceeding may offer testimony of witnesses who are located in another state, including testimony of the parties and the child, by deposition or other means allowable in this state for testimony taken in another state. The court, on its own motion, may order that the testimony of a person be taken in another state and may prescribe the manner in which and the terms upon which the testimony is taken.

(b) A court of this state may permit an individual residing in another state to be deposed or to testify by telephone, audiovisual means, or other electronic means before a designated court or at another location in that state. A court of this state shall cooperate with courts of other states in designating an appropriate location for the deposition or testimony.

(c) Documentary evidence transmitted from another state to a court of this state by technological means that do not produce an original writing may not be excluded from evidence on an objection based on the means of transmission. *(Added by Stats.1999, c. 867 (S.B.668), § 3.)*

Cross References

Judgment and order defined for purposes of this Code, see Family Code § 100.
Person defined for purposes of this Code, see Family Code § 105.
Proceeding defined for purposes of this Code, see Family Code § 110.
State defined for purposes of this Code, see Family Code § 145.
Uniform act, construction of provisions, see Family Code § 3.
Writings, authentication and proof of, see Evidence Code § 1400 et seq.

§ 3412. Request of another court to hold hearing or enter an order; preservation of pleadings and records

(a) A court of this state may request the appropriate court of another state to do all of the following:

(1) Hold an evidentiary hearing.

(2) Order a person to produce or give evidence pursuant to procedures of that state.

(3) Order that an evaluation be made with respect to the custody of a child involved in a pending proceeding.

(4) Forward to the court of this state a certified copy of the transcript of the record of the hearing, the evidence otherwise presented, and any evaluation prepared in compliance with the request.

(5) Order a party to a child custody proceeding or any person having physical custody of the child to appear in the proceeding with or without the child.

(b) Upon request of a court of another state, a court of this state may hold a hearing or enter an order described in subdivision (a).

(c) Travel and other necessary and reasonable expenses incurred under subdivisions (a) and (b) may be assessed against the parties according to the law of this state.

(d) A court of this state shall preserve the pleadings, orders, decrees, records of hearings, evaluations, and other pertinent records with respect to a child custody proceeding until the child attains 18 years of age. Upon appropriate request by a court or law enforcement official of another state, the court shall forward a certified copy of those records. *(Added by Stats.1999, c. 867 (S.B.668), § 3.)*

Cross References

Judgment and order defined for purposes of this Code, see Family Code § 100.
Person defined for purposes of this Code, see Family Code § 105.
Proceeding defined for purposes of this Code, see Family Code § 110.
State defined for purposes of this Code, see Family Code § 145.

Uniform act, construction of provisions, see Family Code § 3.

§§ 3413 to 3420. Repealed by Stats.1999, c. 867 (S.B.668), § 2

CHAPTER 2. JURISDICTION

Section
3421. Jurisdiction to make initial child custody determination.
3422. Continuing jurisdiction.
3423. Modification of custody determination made by court of another state.
3424. Temporary emergency jurisdiction.
3425. Notice and opportunity to be heard.
3426. Simultaneous proceedings in another state.
3427. Inconvenient forum; declining to exercise jurisdiction.
3428. Declining to exercise jurisdiction due to unjustifiable conduct of person.
3429. Required information in first pleading.
3430. Appearance by party and child.

§ 3421. Jurisdiction to make initial child custody determination

(a) Except as otherwise provided in Section 3424, a court of this state has jurisdiction to make an initial child custody determination only if any of the following are true:

(1) This state is the home state of the child on the date of the commencement of the proceeding, or was the home state of the child within six months before the commencement of the proceeding and the child is absent from this state but a parent or person acting as a parent continues to live in this state.

(2) A court of another state does not have jurisdiction under paragraph (1), or a court of the home state of the child has declined to exercise jurisdiction on the grounds that this state is the more appropriate forum under Section 3427 or 3428, and both of the following are true:

(A) The child and the child's parents, or the child and at least one parent or a person acting as a parent, have a significant connection with this state other than mere physical presence.

(B) Substantial evidence is available in this state concerning the child's care, protection, training, and personal relationships.

(3) All courts having jurisdiction under paragraph (1) or (2) have declined to exercise jurisdiction on the ground that a court of this state is the more appropriate forum to determine the custody of the child under Section 3427 or 3428.

(4) No court of any other state would have jurisdiction under the criteria specified in paragraph (1), (2), or (3).

(b) Subdivision (a) is the exclusive jurisdictional basis for making a child custody determination by a court of this state.

(c) Physical presence of, or personal jurisdiction over, a party or a child is not necessary or sufficient to make a child custody determination.

(d) <u>The presence of a child in this state for the purpose of obtaining gender-affirming health care or gender-affirming mental health care, as defined by Section 16010.2 of the Welfare and Institutions Code, is sufficient to meet the requirements of paragraph (2) of subdivision (a).</u> *(Added by Stats.1999, c. 867 (S.B.668), § 3. Amended by Stats.2022, c. 810 (S.B.107), § 4, eff. Jan. 1, 2023.)*

Cross References

Person defined for purposes of this Code, see Family Code § 105.
Proceeding defined for purposes of this Code, see Family Code § 110.
State defined for purposes of this Code, see Family Code § 145.

Uniform act, construction of provisions, see Family Code § 3.

Research References

Forms

19 Am. Jur. Pl. & Pr. Forms Parent and Child § 6, Introductory Comments.
1 California Transactions Forms--Family Law § 3:4, Subject Matter Jurisdiction for Custody Determinations.
West's California Code Forms, Probate § 1510 Form 3, Declaration Under Uniform Child Custody Jurisdiction and Enforcement Act (UCCJEA)- Judicial Council Form FL-105/GC-120.

§ 3422. Continuing jurisdiction

(a) Except as otherwise provided in Section 3424, a court of this state that has made a child custody determination consistent with Section 3421 or 3423 has exclusive, continuing jurisdiction over the determination until either of the following occurs:

(1) A court of this state determines that neither the child, nor the child and one parent, nor the child and a person acting as a parent have a significant connection with this state and that substantial evidence is no longer available in this state concerning the child's care, protection, training, and personal relationships.

(2) A court of this state or a court of another state determines that the child, the child's parents, and any person acting as a parent do not presently reside in this state.

(b) A court of this state that has made a child custody determination and does not have exclusive, continuing jurisdiction under this section may modify that determination only if it has jurisdiction to make an initial determination under Section 3421. *(Added by Stats.1999, c. 867 (S.B.668), § 3.)*

Cross References

Modification of custody or visitation orders, justifications, military duty, see Family Code § 3047.
Order for parties outside the state to appear with or without the child, see Family Code § 3430.
Person defined for purposes of this Code, see Family Code § 105.
Simultaneous proceedings in another state, permissible state court actions, see Family Code § 3426.
State defined for purposes of this Code, see Family Code § 145.
Uniform act, construction of provisions, see Family Code § 3.

Research References

Forms

1 California Transactions Forms--Family Law § 3:4, Subject Matter Jurisdiction for Custody Determinations.
1 California Transactions Forms--Family Law § 3:16, Identifying Areas of Parental Decision Making and Participation.

§ 3423. Modification of custody determination made by court of another state

Except as otherwise provided in Section 3424, a court of this state may not modify a child custody determination made by a court of another state unless a court of this state has jurisdiction to make an initial determination under paragraph (1) or (2) of subdivision (a) of Section 3421 and either of the following determinations is made:

(a) The court of the other state determines it no longer has exclusive, continuing jurisdiction under Section 3422 or that a court of this state would be a more convenient forum under Section 3427.

(b) A court of this state or a court of the other state determines that the child, the child's parents, and any person acting as a parent do not presently reside in the other state. *(Added by Stats.1999, c. 867 (S.B.668), § 3.)*

Cross References

Order for parties outside the state to appear with or without the child, see Family Code § 3430.
Person defined for purposes of this Code, see Family Code § 105.
Simultaneous proceedings in another state, permissible state court actions, see Family Code § 3426.
State defined for purposes of this Code, see Family Code § 145.
Uniform act, construction of provisions, see Family Code § 3.

Research References

Forms

1 California Transactions Forms--Family Law § 3:16, Identifying Areas of Parental Decision Making and Participation.

§ 3424. Temporary emergency jurisdiction

(a) A court of this state has temporary emergency jurisdiction if the child is present in this state and the child has been abandoned or it is necessary in an emergency to protect the child because the child, or a sibling or parent of the child, is subjected to, or threatened with, mistreatment or abuse, or because the child has been unable to obtain gender-affirming health care or gender-affirming mental health care, as defined by Section 16010.2 of the Welfare and Institutions Code.

(b) If there is no previous child custody determination that is entitled to be enforced under this part and a child custody proceeding has not been commenced in a court of a state having jurisdiction under Sections 3421 to 3423, inclusive, a child custody determination made under this section remains in effect until an order is obtained from a court of a state having jurisdiction under Sections 3421 to 3423, inclusive. If a child custody proceeding has not been or is not commenced in a court of a state having jurisdiction under Sections 3421 to 3423, inclusive, a child custody determination made under this section becomes a final determination, if it so provides and this state becomes the home state of the child.

(c) If there is a previous child custody determination that is entitled to be enforced under this part, or a child custody proceeding has been commenced in a court of a state having jurisdiction under Sections 3421 to 3423, inclusive, any order issued by a court of this state under this section must specify in the order a period that the court considers adequate to allow the person seeking an order to obtain an order from the state having jurisdiction under Sections 3421 to 3423, inclusive. The order issued in this state remains in effect until an order is obtained from the other state within the period specified or the period expires.

(d) A court of this state that has been asked to make a child custody determination under this section, upon being informed that a child custody proceeding has been commenced in, or a child custody determination has been made by, a court of a state having jurisdiction under Sections 3421 to 3423, inclusive, shall immediately communicate with the other court. A court of this state which is exercising jurisdiction pursuant to Sections 3421 to 3423, inclusive, upon being informed that a child custody proceeding has been commenced in, or a child custody determination has been made by, a court of another state under a statute similar to this section shall immediately communicate with the court of that state to resolve the emergency, protect the safety of the parties and the child, and determine a period for the duration of the temporary order.

(e) It is the intent of the Legislature in enacting subdivision (a) that the grounds on which a court may exercise temporary emergency jurisdiction be expanded. It is further the intent of the Legislature that these grounds include those that existed under Section 3403 of the Family Code as that section read on December 31, 1999, particularly including cases involving domestic violence. *(Added by Stats.1999, c. 867 (S.B.668), § 3. Amended by Stats.2022, c. 810 (S.B.107), § 5, eff. Jan. 1, 2023.)*

Cross References

Abuse defined for purposes of the Domestic Violence Prevention Act, see Family Code § 6203.
Domestic violence defined for purposes of this Code, see Family Code § 6211.
Judgment and order defined for purposes of this Code, see Family Code § 100.
Legislative intent, construction of statutes, see Code of Civil Procedure § 1859.

§ 3424

Person defined for purposes of this Code, see Family Code § 105.
Proceeding defined for purposes of this Code, see Family Code § 110.
State defined for purposes of this Code, see Family Code § 145.
Uniform act, construction of provisions, see Family Code § 3.

§ 3425. Notice and opportunity to be heard

(a) Before a child custody determination is made under this part, notice and an opportunity to be heard in accordance with the standards of Section 3408 must be given to all persons entitled to notice under the law of this state as in child custody proceedings between residents of this state, any parent whose parental rights have not been previously terminated, and any person having physical custody of the child.

(b) This part does not govern the enforceability of a child custody determination made without notice or an opportunity to be heard.

(c) The obligation to join a party and the right to intervene as a party in a child custody proceeding under this part are governed by the law of this state as in child custody proceedings between residents of this state. *(Added by Stats.1999, c. 867 (S.B.668), § 3. Amended by Stats.2008, c. 699 (S.B.1241), § 3.)*

Cross References

Notice, actual and constructive, defined, see Civil Code § 18.
Person defined for purposes of this Code, see Family Code § 105.
Proceeding defined for purposes of this Code, see Family Code § 110.
State defined for purposes of this Code, see Family Code § 145.
Uniform act, construction of provisions, see Family Code § 3.

§ 3426. Simultaneous proceedings in another state

(a) Except as otherwise provided in Section 3424, a court of this state may not exercise its jurisdiction under this chapter if, at the time of the commencement of the proceeding, a proceeding concerning the custody of the child has been commenced in a court of another state having jurisdiction substantially in conformity with this part, unless the proceeding has been terminated or is stayed by the court of the other state because a court of this state is a more convenient forum under Section 3427.

(b) Except as otherwise provided in Section 3424, a court of this state, before hearing a child custody proceeding, shall examine the court documents and other information supplied by the parties pursuant to Section 3429. If the court determines that a child custody proceeding has been commenced in a court in another state having jurisdiction substantially in accordance with this part, the court of this state shall stay its proceeding and communicate with the court of the other state. If the court of the state having jurisdiction substantially in accordance with this part does not determine that the court of this state is a more appropriate forum, the court of this state shall dismiss the proceeding.

(c) In a proceeding to modify a child custody determination, a court of this state shall determine whether a proceeding to enforce the determination has been commenced in another state. If a proceeding to enforce a child custody determination has been commenced in another state, the court may do any of the following:

(1) Stay the proceeding for modification pending the entry of an order of a court of the other state enforcing, staying, denying, or dismissing the proceeding for enforcement.

(2) Enjoin the parties from continuing with the proceeding for enforcement.

(3) Proceed with the modification under conditions it considers appropriate. *(Added by Stats.1999, c. 867 (S.B.668), § 3.)*

Cross References

Judgment and order defined for purposes of this Code, see Family Code § 100.
Proceeding defined for purposes of this Code, see Family Code § 110.
State defined for purposes of this Code, see Family Code § 145.

Uniform act, construction of provisions, see Family Code § 3.

§ 3427. Inconvenient forum; declining to exercise jurisdiction

(a) A court of this state that has jurisdiction under this part to make a child custody determination may decline to exercise its jurisdiction at any time if it determines that it is an inconvenient forum under the circumstances and that a court of another state is a more appropriate forum. The issue of inconvenient forum may be raised upon motion of a party, the court's own motion, or request of another court.

(b) Before determining whether it is an inconvenient forum, a court of this state shall consider whether it is appropriate for a court of another state to exercise jurisdiction. For this purpose, the court shall allow the parties to submit information and shall consider all relevant factors, including:

(1) Whether domestic violence has occurred and is likely to continue in the future and which state could best protect the parties and the child.

(2) The length of time the child has resided outside this state.

(3) The distance between the court in this state and the court in the state that would assume jurisdiction.

(4) The degree of financial hardship to the parties in litigating in one forum over the other.

(5) Any agreement of the parties as to which state should assume jurisdiction.

(6) The nature and location of the evidence required to resolve the pending litigation, including testimony of the child.

(7) The ability of the court of each state to decide the issue expeditiously and the procedures necessary to present the evidence.

(8) The familiarity of the court of each state with the facts and issues in the pending litigation.

(c) If a court of this state determines that it is an inconvenient forum and that a court of another state is a more appropriate forum, it shall stay the proceedings upon condition that a child custody proceeding be promptly commenced in another designated state and may impose any other condition the court considers just and proper.

(d) A court of this state may decline to exercise its jurisdiction under this part if a child custody determination is incidental to an action for dissolution of marriage or another proceeding while still retaining jurisdiction over the dissolution of marriage or other proceeding.

(e) If it appears to the court that it is clearly an inappropriate forum, the court may require the party who commenced the proceeding to pay, in addition to the costs of the proceeding in this state, necessary travel and other expenses, including attorney's fees, incurred by the other parties or their witnesses. Payment is to be made to the clerk of the court for remittance to the proper party.

<u>(f)(1) In a case where the provision of gender-affirming health care or gender-affirming mental health care to the child is at issue, a court of this state shall not determine that it is an inconvenient forum where the law or policy of the other state that may take jurisdiction limits the ability of a parent to obtain gender-affirming health care or gender-affirming mental health care for their child.</u>

<u>(2) For the purposes of this section, "gender-affirming health care" and "gender-affirming mental health care" have the same meaning as defined by Section 16010.2 of the Welfare and Institutions Code.</u> *(Added by Stats.1999, c. 867 (S.B.668), § 3. Amended by Stats.2022, c. 810 (S.B.107), § 6, eff. Jan. 1, 2023.)*

Cross References

Attorney's fees and costs, generally, see Code of Civil Procedure § 1021.
Domestic violence defined for purposes of this Code, see Family Code § 6211.
Proceeding defined for purposes of this Code, see Family Code § 110.
State defined for purposes of this Code, see Family Code § 145.

Uniform act, construction of provisions, see Family Code § 3.

Research References

Forms

1 California Transactions Forms--Family Law § 3:4, Subject Matter Jurisdiction for Custody Determinations.

§ 3428. Declining to exercise jurisdiction due to unjustifiable conduct of person

(a) Except as otherwise provided in Section 3424 or by any other law of this state, if a court of this state has jurisdiction under this part because a person seeking to invoke its jurisdiction has engaged in unjustifiable conduct, the court shall decline to exercise its jurisdiction unless one of the following are true:

(1) The parents and all persons acting as parents have acquiesced in the exercise of jurisdiction.

(2) A court of the state otherwise having jurisdiction under Sections 3421 to 3423, inclusive, determines that this state is a more appropriate forum under Section 3427.

(3) No court of any other state would have jurisdiction under the criteria specified in Sections 3421 to 3423, inclusive.

(b) If a court of this state declines to exercise its jurisdiction pursuant to subdivision (a), it may fashion an appropriate remedy to ensure the safety of the child and prevent a repetition of the unjustifiable conduct, including staying the proceeding until a child custody proceeding is commenced in a court having jurisdiction under Sections 3421 to 3423, inclusive.

(c) If a court dismisses a petition or stays a proceeding because it declines to exercise its jurisdiction pursuant to subdivision (a), it shall assess against the party seeking to invoke its jurisdiction necessary and reasonable expenses including costs, communication expenses, attorney's fees, investigative fees, expenses for witnesses, travel expenses, and child care during the course of the proceedings, unless the party from whom fees are sought establishes that the assessment would be clearly inappropriate. The court may not assess fees, costs, or expenses against this state unless authorized by law other than this part.

(d) In making a determination under this section, a court shall not consider as a factor weighing against the petitioner any taking of the child, or retention of the child after a visit or other temporary relinquishment of physical custody, from the person who has legal custody, if there is evidence that the taking or retention of the child was a result of domestic violence against the petitioner, as defined in Section 6211, or for the purposes of obtaining gender-affirming health care or gender-affirming mental health care, as defined by Section 16010.2 of the Welfare and Institutions Code, for the child and the law or policy of the other state limits the ability of a parent to obtain gender-affirming health care or gender-affirming mental health care for their child. *(Added by Stats.1999, c. 867 (S.B.668), § 3. Amended by Stats.2022, c. 810 (S.B.107), § 7, eff. Jan. 1, 2023.)*

Cross References

Attorney's fees and costs, generally, see Code of Civil Procedure § 1021.
Person defined for purposes of this Code, see Family Code § 105.
Petitioner defined for purposes of this Code, see Family Code § 126.
Proceeding defined for purposes of this Code, see Family Code § 110.
State defined for purposes of this Code, see Family Code § 145.
Uniform act, construction of provisions, see Family Code § 3.

§ 3429. Required information in first pleading

(a) In a child custody proceeding, each party, in its first pleading or in an attached affidavit, shall give information, if reasonably ascertainable, under oath as to the child's present address or whereabouts, the places where the child has lived during the last five years, and the names and present addresses of the persons with whom the child has lived during that period. However, where there are allegations of domestic violence or child abuse, any addresses of the party alleging violence or abuse and of the child which are unknown to the other party are confidential and may not be disclosed in the pleading or affidavit. The pleading or affidavit must state whether the party:

(1) Has participated, as a party or witness or in any other capacity, in any other proceeding concerning the custody of, or visitation with, the child and, if so, identify the court, the case number, and the date of the child custody determination, if any.

(2) Knows of any proceeding that could affect the current proceeding, including proceedings for enforcement and proceedings relating to domestic violence, protective orders, termination of parental rights, and adoptions and, if so, identify the court, the case number, and the nature of the proceeding.

(3) Knows the names and addresses of any person not a party to the proceeding who has physical custody of the child or claims rights of legal custody or physical custody of, or visitation with, the child and, if so, the names and addresses of those persons.

(b) If the information required by subdivision (a) is not furnished, the court, upon motion of a party or its own motion, may stay the proceeding until the information is furnished.

(c) If the declaration as to any of the items described in paragraphs (1) to (3), inclusive, of subdivision (a) is in the affirmative, the declarant shall give additional information under oath as required by the court. The court may examine the parties under oath as to details of the information furnished and other matters pertinent to the court's jurisdiction and the disposition of the case.

(d) Each party has a continuing duty to inform the court of any proceeding in this or any other state that could affect the current proceeding. *(Added by Stats.1999, c. 867 (S.B.668), § 3.)*

Cross References

Abuse defined for purposes of the Domestic Violence Prevention Act, see Family Code § 6203.
Domestic violence defined for purposes of this Code, see Family Code § 6211.
Judgment and order defined for purposes of this Code, see Family Code § 100.
Person defined for purposes of this Code, see Family Code § 105.
Petition for temporary custody order, see Family Code § 3060.
Proceeding defined for purposes of this Code, see Family Code § 110.
Protective order defined for purposes of this Code, see Family Code § 6218.
State defined for purposes of this Code, see Family Code § 145.
Uniform act, construction of provisions, see Family Code § 3.

Research References

Forms

West's California Judicial Council Forms FL-580, Registration of Out-Of-State Custody Decree.

§ 3430. Appearance by party and child

(a) In a child custody proceeding in this state, the court may order a party to the proceeding who is in this state to appear before the court in person with or without the child. The court may order any person who is in this state and who has physical custody or control of the child to appear in person with the child.

(b) If a party to a child custody proceeding whose presence is desired by the court is outside this state, the court may order that a notice given pursuant to Section 3408 include a statement directing the party to appear in person with or without the child and informing the party that failure to appear may result in a decision adverse to the party.

(c) The court may enter any orders necessary to ensure the safety of the child and of any person ordered to appear under this section.

(d) If a party to a child custody proceeding who is outside this state is directed to appear under subdivision (b) or desires to appear personally before the court with or without the child, the court may require another party to pay reasonable and necessary travel and other expenses of the party so appearing and of the child. *(Added by Stats.1999, c. 867 (S.B.668), § 3.)*

Cross References

Judgment and order defined for purposes of this Code, see Family Code § 100.
Notice, actual and constructive, defined, see Civil Code § 18.
Person defined for purposes of this Code, see Family Code § 105.
Proceeding defined for purposes of this Code, see Family Code § 110.
State defined for purposes of this Code, see Family Code § 145.
Uniform act, construction of provisions, see Family Code § 3.

CHAPTER 3. ENFORCEMENT

Section
3441. "Petitioner" and "respondent" defined.
3442. Orders made under the Hague Convention on the Civil Aspects of International Child Abduction.
3443. Recognition and enforcement of out-of-state custody decrees.
3444. Temporary order enforcing out-of-state visitation order.
3445. Registration of out-of-state custody determination; method; duties of court; notice; contesting validity of registration; confirmation of registered order.
3446. Enforcement of registered child custody determination.
3447. Pending proceeding in another state to modify order.
3448. Petition; verification; contents; order directing respondent to appear.
3449. Service of petition and order.
3450. Order for immediate physical custody; fees and costs; inferences; spousal privilege.
3451. Warrant to take physical custody.
3452. Prevailing party; award of necessary and reasonable expenses.
3453. Full faith and credit to order issued by another state.
3453.5. Law of another state allowing removal of child based on parent or child allowing child to receive gender-affirming health care or gender-affirming mental health care; not enforceable or applicable in this state.
3454. Appeals.
3455. Locating missing child or party; district attorney authorized to proceed pursuant to § 3130 et seq.
3456. Law enforcement officers; locating child or party.
3457. Expenses incurred under § 3455 or 3456.

§ 3441. "Petitioner" and "respondent" defined

In this chapter:

(a) "Petitioner" means a person who seeks enforcement of an order for return of a child under the Hague Convention on the Civil Aspects of International Child Abduction or enforcement of a child custody determination.

(b) "Respondent" means a person against whom a proceeding has been commenced for enforcement of an order for return of a child under the Hague Convention on the Civil Aspects of International Child Abduction or enforcement of a child custody determination. *(Added by Stats.1999, c. 867 (S.B.668), § 3.)*

Cross References

Judgment and order defined for purposes of this Code, see Family Code § 100.
Person defined for purposes of this Code, see Family Code § 105.
Petitioner defined for purposes of this Code, see Family Code § 126.
Proceeding defined for purposes of this Code, see Family Code § 110.
Respondent defined for purposes of this Code, see Family Code § 127.

Uniform act, construction of provisions, see Family Code § 3.

§ 3442. Orders made under the Hague Convention on the Civil Aspects of International Child Abduction

Under this chapter, a court of this state may enforce an order for the return of a child made under the Hague Convention on the Civil Aspects of International Child Abduction as if it were a child custody determination. *(Added by Stats.1999, c. 867 (S.B.668), § 3.)*

Cross References

Judgment and order defined for purposes of this Code, see Family Code § 100.
State defined for purposes of this Code, see Family Code § 145.
Uniform act, construction of provisions, see Family Code § 3.

§ 3443. Recognition and enforcement of out-of-state custody decrees

(a) A court of this state shall recognize and enforce a child custody determination of a court of another state if the latter court exercised jurisdiction in substantial conformity with this part or the determination was made under factual circumstances meeting the jurisdictional standards of this part and the determination has not been modified in accordance with this part.

(b) A court of this state may utilize any remedy available under other laws of this state to enforce a child custody determination made by a court of another state. The remedies provided in this chapter are cumulative and do not affect the availability of other remedies to enforce a child custody determination. *(Added by Stats.1999, c. 867 (S.B.668), § 3.)*

Cross References

State defined for purposes of this Code, see Family Code § 145.
Uniform act, construction of provisions, see Family Code § 3.

§ 3444. Temporary order enforcing out-of-state visitation order

(a) A court of this state which does not have jurisdiction to modify a child custody determination may issue a temporary order enforcing either:

(1) A visitation schedule made by a court of another state.

(2) The visitation provisions of a child custody determination of another state that does not provide for a specific visitation schedule.

(b) If a court of this state makes an order under paragraph (2) of subdivision (a), it shall specify in the order a period that it considers adequate to allow the petitioner to obtain an order from a court having jurisdiction under the criteria specified in Chapter 2 (commencing with Section 3421). The order remains in effect until an order is obtained from the other court or the period expires. *(Added by Stats.1999, c. 867 (S.B.668), § 3.)*

Cross References

Judgment and order defined for purposes of this Code, see Family Code § 100.
Petitioner defined for purposes of this Code, see Family Code § 126.
State defined for purposes of this Code, see Family Code § 145.
Uniform act, construction of provisions, see Family Code § 3.

§ 3445. Registration of out-of-state custody determination; method; duties of court; notice; contesting validity of registration; confirmation of registered order

(a) A child custody determination issued by a court of another state may be registered in this state, with or without a simultaneous request for enforcement, by sending all of the following to the appropriate court in this state:

(1) A letter or other document requesting registration.

(2) Two copies, including one certified copy, of the determination sought to be registered, and a statement under penalty of perjury that to the best of the knowledge and belief of the person seeking registration the order has not been modified.

(3) Except as otherwise provided in Section 3429, the name and address of the person seeking registration and any parent or person acting as a parent who has been awarded custody or visitation in the child custody determination sought to be registered.

(b) On receipt of the documents required by subdivision (a), the registering court shall do both of the following:

(1) Cause the determination to be filed as a foreign judgment, together with one copy of any accompanying documents and information, regardless of their form.

(2) Serve notice upon the persons named pursuant to paragraph (3) of subdivision (a) and provide them with an opportunity to contest the registration in accordance with this section.

(c) The notice required by paragraph (2) of subdivision (b) shall state all of the following:

(1) That a registered determination is enforceable as of the date of the registration in the same manner as a determination issued by a court of this state.

(2) That a hearing to contest the validity of the registered determination must be requested within 20 days after service of the notice.

(3) That failure to contest the registration will result in confirmation of the child custody determination and preclude further contest of that determination with respect to any matter that could have been asserted.

(d) A person seeking to contest the validity of a registered order must request a hearing within 20 days after service of the notice. At that hearing, the court shall confirm the registered order unless the person contesting registration establishes any of the following:

(1) That the issuing court did not have jurisdiction under Chapter 2 (commencing with Section 3421).

(2) That the child custody determination sought to be registered has been vacated, stayed, or modified by a court having jurisdiction to do so under Chapter 2 (commencing with Section 3421).

(3) That the person contesting registration was entitled to notice, but notice was not given in accordance with the standards of Section 3408, in the proceedings before the court that issued the order for which registration is sought.

(e) If a timely request for a hearing to contest the validity of the registration is not made, the registration is confirmed as a matter of law and the person requesting registration and all persons served shall be notified of the confirmation.

(f) Confirmation of a registered order, whether by operation of law or after notice and hearing, precludes further contest of the order with respect to any matter that could have been asserted at the time of registration. *(Added by Stats.1999, c. 867 (S.B.668), § 3.)*

Cross References

Computation of time, see Code of Civil Procedure §§ 12, 12a; Government Code § 6800 et seq.
Judgment and order defined for purposes of this Code, see Family Code § 100.
Notice, actual and constructive, defined, see Civil Code § 18.
Person defined for purposes of this Code, see Family Code § 105.
Proceeding defined for purposes of this Code, see Family Code § 110.
State defined for purposes of this Code, see Family Code § 145.
Uniform act, construction of provisions, see Family Code § 3.

Research References

Forms

West's California Judicial Council Forms FL–580, Registration of Out-Of-State Custody Decree.

West's California Judicial Council Forms FL–585, Request for Hearing Regarding Registration of Out-Of-State Custody Decree.

§ 3446. Enforcement of registered child custody determination

(a) A court of this state may grant any relief normally available under the law of this state to enforce a registered child custody determination made by a court of another state.

(b) A court of this state shall recognize and enforce, but may not modify, except in accordance with Chapter 2 (commencing with Section 3421), a registered child custody determination of a court of another state. *(Added by Stats.1999, c. 867 (S.B.668), § 3.)*

Cross References

State defined for purposes of this Code, see Family Code § 145.
Uniform act, construction of provisions, see Family Code § 3.

§ 3447. Pending proceeding in another state to modify order

If a proceeding for enforcement under this chapter is commenced in a court of this state and the court determines that a proceeding to modify the determination is pending in a court of another state having jurisdiction to modify the determination under Chapter 2 (commencing with Section 3421), the enforcing court shall immediately communicate with the modifying court. The proceeding for enforcement continues unless the enforcing court, after consultation with the modifying court, stays or dismisses the proceeding. *(Added by Stats.1999, c. 867 (S.B.668), § 3.)*

Cross References

Proceeding defined for purposes of this Code, see Family Code § 110.
State defined for purposes of this Code, see Family Code § 145.
Uniform act, construction of provisions, see Family Code § 3.

§ 3448. Petition; verification; contents; order directing respondent to appear

(a) A petition under this chapter must be verified. Certified copies of all orders sought to be enforced and of any order confirming registration must be attached to the petition. A copy of a certified copy of an order may be attached instead of the original.

(b) A petition for enforcement of a child custody determination must state all of the following:

(1) Whether the court that issued the determination identified the jurisdictional basis it relied upon in exercising jurisdiction and, if so, what the basis was.

(2) Whether the determination for which enforcement is sought has been vacated, stayed, or modified by a court whose decision must be enforced under this part and, if so, identify the court, the case number, and the nature of the proceeding.

(3) Whether any proceeding has been commenced that could affect the current proceeding, including proceedings relating to domestic violence, protective orders, termination of parental rights, and adoptions and, if so, identify the court, the case number, and the nature of the proceeding.

(4) The present physical address of the child and the respondent, if known.

(5) Whether relief in addition to the immediate physical custody of the child and attorney's fees is sought, including a request for assistance from law enforcement officials and, if so, the relief sought.

(6) If the child custody determination has been registered and confirmed under Section 3445, the date and place of registration.

(c) Upon the filing of a petition, the court shall issue an order directing the respondent to appear in person with or without the child at a hearing and may enter any order necessary to ensure the safety of the parties and the child. The hearing must be held on the next judicial day after service of the order unless that date is impossible. In that event, the court shall hold the hearing on the

§ 3448 CUSTODY OF CHILDREN

first judicial day possible. The court may extend the date of hearing at the request of the petitioner.

(d) An order issued under subdivision (c) must state the time and place of the hearing and advise the respondent that, at the hearing, the court will order that the petitioner may take immediate physical custody of the child and the payment of fees, costs, and expenses under Section 3452, and may schedule a hearing to determine whether further relief is appropriate, unless the respondent appears and establishes either of the following:

(1) That the child custody determination has not been registered and confirmed under Section 3445 and all of the following are true:

(A) The issuing court did not have jurisdiction under Chapter 2 (commencing with Section 3421).

(B) The child custody determination for which enforcement is sought has been vacated, stayed, or modified by a court having jurisdiction to do so under Chapter 2 (commencing with Section 3421).

(C) The respondent was entitled to notice, but notice was not given in accordance with the standards of Section 3408, in the proceedings before the court that issued the order for which enforcement is sought.

(2) That the child custody determination for which enforcement is sought was registered and confirmed under Section 3445, but has been vacated, stayed, or modified by a court of a state having jurisdiction to do so under Chapter 2 (commencing with Section 3421). *(Added by Stats.1999, c. 867 (S.B.668), § 3. Amended by Stats.2008, c. 699 (S.B.1241), § 4.)*

Cross References

Domestic violence defined for purposes of this Code, see Family Code § 6211.
Judgment and order defined for purposes of this Code, see Family Code § 100.
Notice, actual and constructive, defined, see Civil Code § 18.
Person defined for purposes of this Code, see Family Code § 105.
Petitioner defined for purposes of this Code, see Family Code § 126.
Proceeding defined for purposes of this Code, see Family Code § 110.
Protective order defined for purposes of this Code, see Family Code § 6218.
Respondent defined for purposes of this Code, see Family Code § 127.
State defined for purposes of this Code, see Family Code § 145.
Uniform act, construction of provisions, see Family Code § 3.

§ 3449. Service of petition and order

Except as otherwise provided in Section 3451, the petition and order shall be served, by any method authorized by the law of this state, upon the respondent and any person who has physical custody of the child. *(Added by Stats.1999, c. 867 (S.B.668), § 3.)*

Cross References

Judgment and order defined for purposes of this Code, see Family Code § 100.
Person defined for purposes of this Code, see Family Code § 105.
Respondent defined for purposes of this Code, see Family Code § 127.
State defined for purposes of this Code, see Family Code § 145.
Uniform act, construction of provisions, see Family Code § 3.

§ 3450. Order for immediate physical custody; fees and costs; inferences; spousal privilege

(a) Unless the court issues a temporary emergency order pursuant to Section 3424, upon a finding that a petitioner is entitled to immediate physical custody of the child, the court shall order that the petitioner may take immediate physical custody of the child unless the respondent establishes either of the following:

(1) That the child custody determination has not been registered and confirmed under Section 3445 and one of the following is true:

(A) The issuing court did not have jurisdiction under Chapter 2 (commencing with Section 3421).

(B) The child custody determination for which enforcement is sought has been vacated, stayed, or modified by a court of a state having jurisdiction to do so under Chapter 2 (commencing with Section 3421).

(C) The respondent was entitled to notice, but notice was not given in accordance with the standards of Section 3408, in the proceedings before the court that issued the order for which enforcement is sought.

(2) That the child custody determination for which enforcement is sought was registered and confirmed under Section 3445 but has been vacated, stayed, or modified by a court of a state having jurisdiction to do so under Chapter 2 (commencing with Section 3421).

(b) The court shall award the fees, costs, and expenses authorized under Section 3452 and may grant additional relief, including a request for the assistance of law enforcement officials, and set a further hearing to determine whether additional relief is appropriate.

(c) If a party called to testify refuses to answer on the ground that the testimony may be self-incriminating, the court may draw an adverse inference from the refusal.

(d) A privilege against disclosure of communications between spouses and a defense of immunity based on the relationship of spouses or parent and child may not be invoked in a proceeding under this chapter. *(Added by Stats.1999, c. 867 (S.B.668), § 3. Amended by Stats.2014, c. 82 (S.B.1306), § 31, eff. Jan. 1, 2015.)*

Cross References

Judgment and order defined for purposes of this Code, see Family Code § 100.
Notice, actual and constructive, defined, see Civil Code § 18.
Petitioner defined for purposes of this Code, see Family Code § 126.
Proceeding defined for purposes of this Code, see Family Code § 110.
References to husband, wife, spouses and married persons, persons included for purposes of this Code, see Family Code § 11.
Respondent defined for purposes of this Code, see Family Code § 127.
State defined for purposes of this Code, see Family Code § 145.
Uniform act, construction of provisions, see Family Code § 3.

§ 3451. Warrant to take physical custody

(a) Upon the filing of a petition seeking enforcement of a child custody determination, the petitioner may file a verified application for the issuance of a warrant to take physical custody of the child if the child is imminently likely to suffer serious physical harm or be removed from this state.

(b) If the court, upon the testimony of the petitioner or other witness, finds that the child is imminently likely to suffer serious physical harm or be removed from this state, it may issue a warrant to take physical custody of the child. The petition must be heard on the next judicial day after the warrant is executed unless that date is impossible. In that event, the court shall hold the hearing on the first judicial day possible. The application for the warrant must include the statements required by subdivision (b) of Section 3448.

(c) A warrant to take physical custody of a child must do all of the following:

(1) Recite the facts upon which a conclusion of imminent serious physical harm or removal from the jurisdiction is based.

(2) Direct law enforcement officers to take physical custody of the child immediately.

(3) Provide for the placement of the child pending final relief.

(d) The respondent must be served with the petition, warrant, and order immediately after the child is taken into physical custody.

(e) A warrant to take physical custody of a child is enforceable throughout this state. If the court finds on the basis of the testimony of the petitioner or other witness that a less intrusive remedy is not effective, it may authorize law enforcement officers to enter private property to take physical custody of the child. If required by exigent circumstances of the case, the court may authorize law enforcement officers to make a forcible entry at any hour.

(f) The court may impose conditions upon placement of a child to ensure the appearance of the child and the child's custodian. *(Added by Stats.1999, c. 867 (S.B.668), § 3.)*

Cross References

Judgment and order defined for purposes of this Code, see Family Code § 100.
Petitioner defined for purposes of this Code, see Family Code § 126.
Property defined for purposes of this Code, see Family Code § 113.
Respondent defined for purposes of this Code, see Family Code § 127.
State defined for purposes of this Code, see Family Code § 145.
Uniform act, construction of provisions, see Family Code § 3.

§ 3452. Prevailing party; award of necessary and reasonable expenses

(a) The court shall award the prevailing party, including a state, necessary and reasonable expenses incurred by or on behalf of the party, including costs, communication expenses, attorney's fees, investigative fees, expenses for witnesses, travel expenses, and child care during the course of the proceedings, unless the party from whom fees or expenses are sought establishes that the award would be clearly inappropriate.

(b) The court may not assess fees, costs, or expenses against a state unless authorized by law other than this part. *(Added by Stats.1999, c. 867 (S.B.668), § 3.)*

Cross References

Attorney's fees and costs, generally, see Code of Civil Procedure § 1021.
Proceeding defined for purposes of this Code, see Family Code § 110.
State defined for purposes of this Code, see Family Code § 145.
Uniform act, construction of provisions, see Family Code § 3.

§ 3453. Full faith and credit to order issued by another state

A court of this state shall accord full faith and credit to an order issued by another state, and consistent with this part, enforce a child custody determination by a court of another state unless the order has been vacated, stayed, or modified by a court having jurisdiction to do so under Chapter 2 (commencing with Section 3421). *(Added by Stats.1999, c. 867 (S.B.668), § 3.)*

Cross References

Judgment and order defined for purposes of this Code, see Family Code § 100.
State defined for purposes of this Code, see Family Code § 145.
Uniform act, construction of provisions, see Family Code § 3.

§ 3453.5. Law of another state allowing removal of child based on parent or child allowing child to receive gender-affirming health care or gender-affirming mental health care; not enforceable or applicable in this state

(a) A law of another state that authorizes a state agency to remove a child from their parent or guardian based on the parent or guardian allowing their child to receive gender-affirming health care or gender-affirming mental health care is against the public policy of this state and shall not be enforced or applied in a case pending in a court in this state.

(b) For the purpose of this subdivision, "gender-affirming health care" and "gender-affirming mental health care" shall have the same meaning as provided in Section 16010.2 of the Welfare and Institutions Code. *(Added by Stats.2022, c. 810 (S.B.107), § 8, eff. Jan. 1, 2023.)*

§ 3454. Appeals

An appeal may be taken from a final order in a proceeding under this chapter in accordance with expedited appellate procedures in other civil cases. Unless the court enters a temporary emergency order under Section 3424, the enforcing court may not stay an order enforcing a child custody determination pending appeal. *(Added by Stats.1999, c. 867 (S.B.668), § 3.)*

Cross References

Appeals from order in arbitration, see Code of Civil Procedure §§ 1294, 1294.2.
Appeals in civil actions, generally, see Code of Civil Procedure § 901 et seq.
Appeals in criminal cases,
  Appeals from Superior Courts, see Penal Code § 1235 et seq.
  Appeals to Superior Courts, see Penal Code § 1466 et seq.
Child custody provisions, appeals, automatic stay provisions, see Code of Civil Procedure § 917.7.
Judgment and order defined for purposes of this Code, see Family Code § 100.
Proceeding defined for purposes of this Code, see Family Code § 110.
Uniform act, construction of provisions, see Family Code § 3.

§ 3455. Locating missing child or party; district attorney authorized to proceed pursuant to § 3130 et seq.

(a) In a case arising under this part or involving the Hague Convention on the Civil Aspects of International Child Abduction, a district attorney is authorized to proceed pursuant to Chapter 8 (commencing with Section 3130) of Part 2.

(b) A district attorney acting under this section acts on behalf of the court and may not represent any party. *(Added by Stats.1999, c. 867 (S.B.668), § 3.)*

Cross References

Attorneys, State Bar Act, see Business and Professions Code § 6000.
District attorney, powers and duties, see Government Code § 26500 et seq.
Uniform act, construction of provisions, see Family Code § 3.

§ 3456. Law enforcement officers; locating child or party

At the request of a district attorney acting under Section 3455, a law enforcement officer may take any lawful action reasonably necessary to locate a child or a party and assist the district attorney with responsibilities under Section 3455. *(Added by Stats.1999, c. 867 (S.B.668), § 3.)*

Cross References

Attorneys, State Bar Act, see Business and Professions Code § 6000.
District attorney, powers and duties, see Government Code § 26500 et seq.
Uniform Act, construction of provisions, see Family Code § 3.

§ 3457. Expenses incurred under § 3455 or 3456

The court may assess all direct expenses and costs incurred by a district attorney under Section 3455 or 3456 pursuant to the provisions of Section 3134. *(Added by Stats.1999, c. 867 (S.B.668), § 3.)*

Cross References

District attorney, powers and duties, see Government Code § 26500 et seq.
Uniform act, construction of provisions, see Family Code § 3.

CHAPTER 4. MISCELLANEOUS PROVISIONS

Section
3461. Construction of act; promoting uniformity.
3462. Severability.
3465. Proceedings begun before effective date of this act.

§ 3461. Construction of act; promoting uniformity

In applying and construing this Uniform Child Custody Jurisdiction and Enforcement Act, consideration shall be given to the need to promote uniformity of the law with respect to its subject matter among states that enact it. *(Added by Stats.1999, c. 867 (S.B.668), § 3.)*

Cross References

State defined for purposes of this Code, see Family Code § 145.

§ 3461

Uniform act, construction of provisions, see Family Code § 3.

§ 3462. Severability

If any provision of this part or its application to any person or circumstance is held invalid, the invalidity does not affect other provisions or applications of this part that can be given effect without the invalid provision or application, and to this end the provisions of this part are severable. *(Added by Stats.1999, c. 867 (S.B.668), § 3.)*

Cross References

Person defined for purposes of this Code, see Family Code § 105.
Uniform act, construction of provisions, see Family Code § 3.

§ 3465. Proceedings begun before effective date of this act

A motion or other request for relief made in a child custody proceeding or to enforce a child custody determination that was commenced before the effective date of this part is governed by the law in effect at the time the motion or other request was made. *(Added by Stats.1999, c. 867 (S.B.668), § 3.)*

Cross References

Proceeding defined for purposes of this Code, see Family Code § 110.
Uniform act, construction of provisions, see Family Code § 3.

Research References

Forms

1 California Transactions Forms--Family Law § 2:70, Deciding Custody.
1 California Transactions Forms--Family Law § 3:2, Child Custody.
2 California Transactions Forms--Family Law § 6:119, Continuing Jurisdiction.

Division 9

SUPPORT

Part	Section
1. Definitions and General Provisions	3500
2. Child Support	3900
3. Spousal Support	4300
4. Support of Parents	4400
5. Enforcement of Support Orders	4500
6. Uniform Interstate Family Support Act	5700.101

Cross References

Amount of child support, conditions determining, see Family Code § 4005.
Bankruptcy, effect on child support, see Family Code § 4013.
Bond for support, see Penal Code § 270b.
California Work Opportunity and Responsibility to Kids Act, see Welfare and Institutions Code § 11200 et seq.
Child for whom support may be ordered, defined, see Family Code § 58.
Child support, generally, see Family Code § 3900 et seq.
Child Support Delinquency Reporting Law, see Family Code §§ 4700, 4701.
Child support duty, actions to enforce, see Family Code § 4000.
Child welfare services, see Welfare and Institutions Code § 16500 et seq.
Community property, subject to child support, see Family Code § 4008.
Compensation, failure to assume caretaker responsibility or thwarting other parent with regard to custody or visitation rights, see Family Code § 3028.
Compensation to relatives and strangers, see Family Code § 3951.
Contempt of court, order for child, spousal, or family support, suspension of proceedings, see Penal Code § 166.5.
Contingencies terminating child support, see Family Code § 4007.
Counties, right to proceed on behalf of child, see Family Code § 4002.
Desertion of child, see Penal Code § 271.
Estate of parent, source of support, see Family Code § 3952.
Failure to support spouse or children, see Penal Code § 270 et seq.
Freedom from parental custody and control, stay of proceedings and effect upon jurisdiction under these provisions, see Family Code § 7807.
Nonminor dependents, opening of separate court file, access to file, see Welfare and Institutions Code § 362.5.
Order for child support, retroactive application, see Family Code § 4009.
Parent and child relationship, see Probate Code § 6450.
Payment of reasonable value of necessaries to others who support child, see Family Code § 3950.
Presumption of child support amount established by formula, see Family Code § 4057.
Priority of child support payments, see Family Code § 4011.
Public assistance, use or intended use to support child, see Family Code § 4004.
Quasi-community property, property subject to child support, see Family Code § 4008.
Security for payment of child support, see Family Code § 4012.
Separate trial, child support proceedings, see Family Code § 4003.
Spousal and child support during pendency of proceedings, see Family Code § 3600 et seq.
Statewide uniform child support guidelines, see Family Code § 4050 et seq.
Support order, modification or termination,
   Authority of court, see Family Code § 3651.
   Discovery, see Family Code § 3660 et seq.
   Retroactive application of modification, see Family Code § 3653.
Termination of child support, effect of contingencies, see Family Code § 4007.
Termination of parental rights of father, filing of petition, stay of proceedings affecting a child under these provisions pending final determination of parental rights of the father, see Family Code § 7662.
Uniform Child Custody Jurisdiction and Enforcement Act, see Family Code § 3400 et seq.
Uniform Divorce Recognition Act, see Family Code § 2090 et seq.
Uniform Interstate Family Support Act, see Family Code § 5700.101 et seq.
Uniform Parentage Act, see Family Code § 7600 et seq.
Uniform Premarital Agreement Act, see Family Code § 1600 et seq.

Part 1

DEFINITIONS AND GENERAL PROVISIONS

Chapter	Section
1. Definitions	3500
2. General Provisions	3550
3. Support Agreements	3580
4. Spousal and Child Support During Pendency of Proceeding	3600
5. Expedited Child Support Order	3620
6. Modification, Termination, or Set Aside of Support Orders	3650
7. Health Insurance	3750
8. Deferred Sale of Home Order	3800
9. Software Used to Determine Support	3830

Cross References

California Work Opportunity and Responsibility to Kids Act, see Welfare and Institutions Code § 11200 et seq.
Child for whom support may be ordered, defined, see Family Code § 58.
Child support, generally, see Family Code § 3900 et seq.
Child Support Delinquency Reporting Law, see Family Code §§ 4700, 4701.
Child welfare services, see Welfare and Institutions Code § 16500 et seq.
Domestic violence prevention orders, authorization to issue orders for spousal support that would otherwise be authorized under these provisions, see Family Code § 6341.
Spousal and child support during pendency of proceedings, see Family Code § 3600 et seq.
Statewide uniform child support guidelines, see Family Code § 4050 et seq.
Uniform Child Custody Jurisdiction and Enforcement Act, see Family Code § 3400 et seq.
Uniform Divorce Recognition Act, see Family Code § 2090 et seq.
Uniform Interstate Family Support Act, see Family Code § 5700.101 et seq.

Uniform Parentage Act, see Family Code § 7600 et seq.
Uniform Premarital Agreement Act, see Family Code § 1600 et seq.

CHAPTER 1. DEFINITIONS

Section
3500. Construction of division.
3515. Separate property; quasi-community property.

Cross References

Community property defined for purposes of this Code, see Family Code § 65.
Definitions,
    Family support, see Family Code § 92.
    Married person, see Family Code § 11.
    Spousal support, see Family Code § 142.
    Support, see Family Code § 150.
    Support order, see Family Code § 155.
Quasi-community property defined, see Family Code § 125.
Separate property defined in section 760 et seq., see Family Code § 130.

§ 3500. Construction of division

Unless the provision or context otherwise requires, the definitions in this chapter govern the construction of this division. *(Stats.1992, c. 162 (A.B.2650), § 10, operative Jan. 1, 1994.)*

Cross References

Definitions,
    Family support, see Family Code § 92.
    Married person, see Family Code § 11.
    Spousal support, see Family Code § 142.
    Support, see Family Code § 150.
    Support order, see Family Code § 155.

Research References

Forms
West's California Code Forms, Family § 4300, Comment Overview—Duty to Support Spouse.
West's California Code Forms, Family § 6340, Comment Overview—Issuance of Orders After Notice and Hearing.

§ 3515. Separate property; quasi-community property

"Separate property" does not include quasi-community property. *(Stats.1992, c. 162 (A.B.2650), § 10, operative Jan. 1, 1994.)*

Cross References

Community property defined for purposes of this Code, see Family Code § 65.
Property defined for purposes of this Code, see Family Code § 113.
Quasi-community property defined, see Family Code § 125.
Separate property defined in section 760 et seq., see Family Code § 130.
Similar provision, see Family Code § 2502.

CHAPTER 2. GENERAL PROVISIONS

Section
3550. Obligee; obligor; duties of support of obligors.
3551. Inapplicability of privilege; competency of husband and wife to testify.
3552. State and federal income tax returns; submission to court; examination and discovery.
3554. Appeals.
3555. Support paid through county officer; forwarding of payments.
3556. Child support; failure or refusal to implement custody or visitation rights.
3557. Award of attorney's fees.
3558. Child or family support proceedings; court-ordered job training, placement, or vocation rehabilitation; documentation.

Cross References

Appeals from superior court judgment or order, see Code of Civil Procedure § 904.1.
References to husband, wife, spouses and married persons, persons included for purposes of this Code, see Family Code § 11.
Rules of practice and procedure, see Family Code § 210.
Spousal support defined for purposes of this Code, see Family Code § 142.
State defined for purposes of this Code, see Family Code § 145.
Support defined for purposes of this Code, see Family Code § 150.

§ 3550. Obligee; obligor; duties of support of obligors

(a) As used in this section:

(1) "Obligee" means a person to whom a duty of support is owed.

(2) "Obligor" means a person who owes a duty of support.

(b) An obligor present or resident in this state has the duty of support as defined in Sections 3900, 3901, 3910, 4300, and 4400, regardless of the presence or residence of the obligee. *(Stats.1992, c. 162 (A.B.2650), § 10, operative Jan. 1, 1994.)*

Cross References

Person defined for purposes of this Code, see Family Code § 105.
State defined for purposes of this Code, see Family Code § 145.
Support defined for purposes of this Code, see Family Code § 150.

Research References

Forms
West's California Code Forms, Family § 4300, Comment Overview—Duty to Support Spouse.

§ 3551. Inapplicability of privilege; competency of husband and wife to testify

Laws attaching a privilege against the disclosure of communications between spouses are inapplicable under this division. Spouses are competent witnesses to testify to any relevant matter, including marriage and parentage. *(Stats.1992, c. 162 (A.B.2650), § 10, operative Jan. 1, 1994. Amended by Stats.2014, c. 82 (S.B.1306), § 32, eff. Jan. 1, 2015.)*

Cross References

Privileged marital communications, see Evidence Code § 980 et seq.
References to husband, wife, spouses and married persons, persons included for purposes of this Code, see Family Code § 11.

§ 3552. State and federal income tax returns; submission to court; examination and discovery

(a) In a proceeding involving child, family, or spousal support, no party to the proceeding may refuse to submit copies of the party's state and federal income tax returns to the court, whether individual or joint.

(b) The tax returns may be examined by the other party and are discoverable by the other party. A party also may be examined by the other party as to the contents of a tax return submitted pursuant to this section.

(c) If the court finds that it is relevant to the case to retain the tax return, the tax return shall be sealed and maintained as a confidential record of the court. If the court finds that the tax return is not relevant to disposition of the case, all copies of the tax return shall be returned to the party who submitted it. *(Stats.1992, c. 162 (A.B. 2650), § 10, operative Jan. 1, 1994.)*

Cross References

Child support, generally, see Family Code § 3900 et seq.
Proceeding defined for purposes of this Code, see Family Code § 110.
Spousal support defined for purposes of this Code, see Family Code § 142.
State defined for purposes of this Code, see Family Code § 145.
Support defined for purposes of this Code, see Family Code § 150.
Tax levies, see Government Code § 29100 et seq.; Revenue and Taxation Code § 2151 et seq.

§ 3552

Tax returns,
  Discovery, proceedings for modification or termination of support order, see Family Code § 3665.
  Expedited support order proceedings, see Family Code § 3629.

Research References

Forms

West's California Judicial Council Forms FL–150, Income and Expense Declaration (Also Available in Spanish).

§ 3554. Appeals

An appeal may be taken from an order or judgment under this division as in other civil actions. *(Stats.1992, c. 162 (A.B.2650), § 10, operative Jan. 1, 1994.)*

Cross References

Appeals from order in arbitration, see Code of Civil Procedure §§ 1294, 1294.2.
Appeals from superior court judgment or order, see Code of Civil Procedure § 904.1.
Appeals in civil actions, generally, see Code of Civil Procedure § 901 et seq.
Appeals in criminal cases,
  Appeals from Superior Courts, see Penal Code § 1235 et seq.
  Appeals to Superior Courts, see Penal Code § 1466 et seq.
Judgment and order defined for purposes of this Code, see Family Code § 100.
Rules of practice and procedure, see Family Code § 210.

§ 3555. Support paid through county officer; forwarding of payments

Where support is ordered to be paid through the county officer designated by the court on behalf of a child or other party not receiving public assistance pursuant to the Family Economic Security Act of 1982 (Chapter 2 (commencing with Section 11200) of Part 3 of Division 9 of the Welfare and Institutions Code), the designated county officer shall forward the support received to the designated payee within the time standards prescribed by federal law and the Department of Child Support Services. *(Stats.1992, c. 162 (A.B. 2650), § 10, operative Jan. 1, 1994. Amended by Stats.1993, c. 219 (A.B.1500), § 120; Stats.2000, c. 808 (A.B.1358), § 27, eff. Sept. 28, 2000.)*

Cross References

Agreements discharged in bankruptcy, see Family Code § 3592.
Bankruptcy, discharge of child support obligation, see Family Code § 4013.
Cohabitation with person of opposite sex, termination of support, presumption in absence of agreement, see Family Code § 4323.
Consideration,
  Generally, see Civil Code § 1605 et seq.
  Recital as conclusive presumption, see Evidence Code § 622.
Contracts altering spouses' legal relations, see Family Code § 1620.
County defined for purposes of this Code, see Family Code § 67.
County officers,
  Designation for payment of child support, see Family Code § 4200 et seq.
  Designation for payment of spousal support payments, see Family Code § 4350 et seq.
  Notice of change of address under earnings assignment order for support, see Family Code § 5237.
Department of Child Support Services, generally, see Family Code § 17000 et seq.
District attorney,
  Health insurance coverage for child, providing information, see Family Code § 3752.
  Support paid through district attorney for child not receiving public assistance, see Family Code § 4573.
Modification or termination, support order based on agreement, see Family Code § 3651.
Mutual obligation of support, see Family Code § 720.
Spouse living separate by agreement, no support unless stipulated, see Family Code § 4302.
Support defined for purposes of this Code, see Family Code § 150.
Support of children, see Family Code § 3900 et seq.
Transactions with each other and third parties, fiduciary relationship of spouses, see Family Code § 721.

Uniform Interstate Family Support Act, see Family Code § 5700.101 et seq.

§ 3556. Child support; failure or refusal to implement custody or visitation rights

The existence or enforcement of a duty of support owed by a noncustodial parent for the support of a minor child is not affected by a failure or refusal by the custodial parent to implement any rights as to custody or visitation granted by a court to the noncustodial parent. *(Stats.1992, c. 162 (A.B.2650), § 10, operative Jan. 1, 1994.)*

Cross References

Child custody, see Family Code § 3020 et seq.
Child support, generally, see Family Code § 3900 et seq.
Custody or visitation rights, parental interference, compensation, see Family Code § 3028.
Minor defined for purposes of this Code, see Family Code § 6500.
Support defined for purposes of this Code, see Family Code § 150.

§ 3557. Award of attorney's fees

(a) Notwithstanding any other provision of law, absent good cause to the contrary, the court, in order to ensure that each party has access to legal representation to preserve each party's rights, upon determining (1) an award of attorney's fees and cost under this section is appropriate, (2) there is a disparity in access to funds to retain counsel, and (3) one party is able to pay for legal representation for both parties, shall award reasonable attorney's fees to any of the following persons:

(1) A custodial parent or other person to whom payments should be made in any action to enforce any of the following:

(A) An existing order for child support.

(B) A penalty incurred pursuant to Chapter 5 (commencing with Section 4720) of Part 5 of Division 9.

(2) A supported spouse in an action to enforce an existing order for spousal support.

(b) This section shall not be construed to allow an award of attorney's fees to or against a governmental entity. *(Added by Stats.1993, c. 219 (A.B.1500), § 120.3. Amended by Stats.1994, c. 1269 (A.B.2208), § 31.2; Stats.2010, c. 352 (A.B.939), § 17.)*

Cross References

Child support, generally, see Family Code § 3900 et seq.
Child support, modification or termination of order, attorney fees and court costs, see Family Code § 3652.
Child support agreements, generally, see Family Code § 3585 et seq.
Child support orders pending proceeding, see Family Code § 3600 et seq.
Expedited child support orders, see Family Code § 3620 et seq.
Health insurance coverage for supported children, see Family Code § 3750 et seq.
Judgment and order defined for purposes of this Code, see Family Code § 100.
Marital dissolution or legal separation proceedings, consideration of motions for temporary spousal support, child support, and counsel fees and costs prior to determining motion to transfer, see Code of Civil Procedure § 396b.
Modification, termination, or setting aside of support order, see Family Code § 3650 et seq.
Orders for support, dissolution or separation, see Family Code § 4330.
Person defined for purposes of this Code, see Family Code § 105.
References to husband, wife, spouses and married persons, persons included for purposes of this Code, see Family Code § 11.
Spousal support defined for purposes of this Code, see Family Code § 142.
Support agreement, adult child, court approval, see Family Code § 3587.
Support defined for purposes of this Code, see Family Code § 150.

Research References

Forms

West's California Judicial Council Forms FL–158, Supporting Declaration for Attorney's Fees and Costs Attachment.
West's California Judicial Council Forms FL–319, Request for Attorney's Fees and Costs Attachment.

West's California Judicial Council Forms FL–346, Attorney's Fees and Costs Order Attachment.

§ 3558. Child or family support proceedings; court-ordered job training, placement, or vocation rehabilitation; documentation

In a proceeding involving child or family support, a court may require either parent to attend job training, job placement and vocational rehabilitation, and work programs, as designated by the court, at regular intervals and times and for durations specified by the court, and provide documentation of participation in the programs, in a format that is acceptable to the court, in order to enable the court to make a finding that good faith attempts at job training and placement have been undertaken by the parent. *(Added by Stats. 1996, c. 490 (A.B.932), § 1.)*

Cross References

Child support, generally, see Family Code § 3900 et seq.
Family support defined for purposes of this Code, see Family Code § 92.
Health insurance coverage for supported children, see Family Code § 3750 et seq.
Judgment and order defined for purposes of this Code, see Family Code § 100.
Proceeding defined for purposes of this Code, see Family Code § 110.
Support defined for purposes of this Code, see Family Code § 150.

CHAPTER 3. SUPPORT AGREEMENTS

Article	Section
1. General Provisions	3580
2. Child Support	3585
3. Spousal Support	3590

Cross References

California Work Opportunity and Responsibility to Kids Act, see Welfare and Institutions Code § 11200 et seq.
Child support, generally, see Family Code § 3900 et seq.

ARTICLE 1. GENERAL PROVISIONS

Section
3580. Immediate separation agreements; consent to support agreements.

Cross References

California Work Opportunity and Responsibility to Kids Act, see Welfare and Institutions Code § 11200 et seq.
Child support, generally, see Family Code § 3900 et seq.
Support order, modification or termination,
  Authority of court, see Family Code § 3651.
  Discovery, see Family Code § 3660 et seq.
  Retroactive application, see Family Code § 3653.

§ 3580. Immediate separation agreements; consent to support agreements

Subject to this chapter and to Section 3651, spouses may agree, in writing, to an immediate separation, and may provide in the agreement for the support of either of them and of their children during the separation or upon the dissolution of their marriage. The mutual consent of the parties is sufficient consideration for the agreement. *(Stats.1992, c. 162 (A.B.2650), § 10, operative Jan. 1, 1994. Amended by Stats.2014, c. 82 (S.B.1306), § 33, eff. Jan. 1, 2015.)*

Cross References

Child support, generally, see Family Code § 3900 et seq.
References to husband, wife, spouses and married persons, persons included for purposes of this Code, see Family Code § 11.
Spousal support, liability, spouse living separate by agreement, see Family Code § 4302.
Support defined for purposes of this Code, see Family Code § 150.

Writings, authentication and proof of, see Evidence Code § 1400 et seq.

Research References

Forms
2 California Transactions Forms--Estate Planning § 11:48, Governing Contractual Provisions [CC §§1550 et seq., Fam C §721(B)].
1 California Transactions Forms--Family Law § 2:52, Overview.
1 California Transactions Forms--Family Law § 2:53, Temporary Support.
1 California Transactions Forms--Family Law § 2:63, Authority for Child Support.
West's California Code Forms, Family § 3580, Comment Overview—Support Agreements.

ARTICLE 2. CHILD SUPPORT

Section
3585. Severability of child support provisions; orders based on agreements.
3586. Child support and spousal support agreements; failure to designate amount of payments.
3587. Approval of stipulated agreements to pay support for adult children.

Cross References

Failure to support child, see Penal Code § 270 et seq.
Support order, modification or termination,
  Authority of court, see Family Code § 3651.
  Discovery, see Family Code § 3660 et seq.
  Retroactive application, see Family Code § 3653.

§ 3585. Severability of child support provisions; orders based on agreements

The provisions of an agreement between the parents for child support shall be deemed to be separate and severable from all other provisions of the agreement relating to property and support of either spouse. An order for child support based on the agreement shall be imposed by law and shall be made under the power of the court to order child support. *(Stats.1992, c. 162 (A.B.2650), § 10, operative Jan. 1, 1994. Amended by Stats.2014, c. 82 (S.B.1306), § 34, eff. Jan. 1, 2015.)*

Cross References

Child support, generally, see Family Code § 3900 et seq.
Expedited child support orders, see Family Code § 3620 et seq.
Health insurance coverage for supported children, see Family Code § 3750 et seq.
Judgment and order defined for purposes of this Code, see Family Code § 100.
Modification, termination, or setting aside of support order, see Family Code § 3650 et seq.
Property defined for purposes of this Code, see Family Code § 113.
References to husband, wife, spouses and married persons, persons included for purposes of this Code, see Family Code § 11.
Support defined for purposes of this Code, see Family Code § 150.
Support order, modification or termination,
  Authority of court, see Family Code § 3651.
  Discovery, see Family Code § 3660 et seq.
  Retroactive application of modification, see Family Code § 3653.

Research References

Forms
1 California Transactions Forms--Family Law § 2:63, Authority for Child Support.
West's California Code Forms, Family § 3580, Comment Overview—Support Agreements.
West's California Code Forms, Family § 3585, Comment Overview—Child Support.

§ 3586. Child support and spousal support agreements; failure to designate amount of payments

If an agreement between the parents combines child support and spousal support without designating the amount to be paid for child

§ 3586

support and the amount to be paid for spousal support, the court is not required to make a separate order for child support. *(Stats.1992, c. 162 (A.B.2650), § 10, operative Jan. 1, 1994.)*

Cross References

Child support, generally, see Family Code § 3900 et seq.
Enforcement of support order, see Family Code § 4500 et seq.
Expedited child support orders, see Family Code § 3620 et seq.
Family support defined, see Family Code § 92.
Health insurance coverage for supported children, see Family Code § 3750 et seq.
Judgment and order defined for purposes of this Code, see Family Code § 100.
Modification, termination, or setting aside of support order, see Family Code § 3650 et seq.
Mutual obligation of support, see Family Code § 720.
Spousal support defined for purposes of this Code, see Family Code § 142.
Support defined for purposes of this Code, see Family Code § 150.
Transactions with each other and third parties, fiduciary relationship of spouses, see Family Code § 721.
Uniform Interstate Family Support Act, see Family Code § 5700.101 et seq.

Research References

Forms

West's California Code Forms, Family § 3585, Comment Overview—Child Support.

§ 3587. Approval of stipulated agreements to pay support for adult children

Notwithstanding any other provision of law, the court has the authority to approve a stipulated agreement by the parents to pay for the support of an adult child or for the continuation of child support after a child attains the age of 18 years and to make a support order to effectuate the agreement. *(Stats.1992, c. 162 (A.B.2650), § 10, operative Jan. 1, 1994.)*

Cross References

Adult defined for purposes of this Code, see Family Code § 6501.
Child for whom support may be ordered defined, see Family Code § 58.
Child support, generally, see Family Code § 3900 et seq.
Failure to support child, see Penal Code § 270 et seq.
Health insurance coverage for supported children, see Family Code § 3750 et seq.
Judgment and order defined for purposes of this Code, see Family Code § 100.
Mutual obligation of support, see Family Code § 720.
Support defined for purposes of this Code, see Family Code § 150.
Support order defined for purposes of this Code, see Family Code § 155.
Transactions with each other and third parties, fiduciary relationship of spouses, see Family Code § 721.
Uniform Interstate Family Support Act, see Family Code § 5700.101 et seq.

Research References

Forms

1 California Transactions Forms--Family Law § 3:26, Voluntary Support After Age of Majority.
West's California Code Forms, Family § 3585, Comment Overview—Child Support.

ARTICLE 3. SPOUSAL SUPPORT

Section
3590. Severability of support provisions; orders based on agreements.
3591. Modification or termination of agreements.
3592. Discharge in bankruptcy; power of court to make new orders.
3593. Application of §§ 3590 and 3591.

Cross References

Failure to support spouse, see Penal Code § 270a.
Support order, modification or termination,
 Authority of court, see Family Code § 3651.

Discovery, see Family Code § 3660 et seq.
Retroactive application, see Family Code § 3653.

§ 3590. Severability of support provisions; orders based on agreements

The provisions of an agreement for support of either party shall be deemed to be separate and severable from the provisions of the agreement relating to property. An order for support of either party based on the agreement shall be law-imposed and shall be made under the power of the court to order spousal support. *(Stats.1992, c. 162 (A.B.2650), § 10, operative Jan. 1, 1994.)*

Cross References

Agreements for child support, see Family Code § 3585 et seq.
Failure to support spouse, see Penal Code § 270a.
Judgment and order defined for purposes of this Code, see Family Code § 100.
Property defined for purposes of this Code, see Family Code § 113.
Spousal support defined for purposes of this Code, see Family Code § 142.
Support defined for purposes of this Code, see Family Code § 150.

Research References

Forms

West's California Code Forms, Family § 3590, Comment Overview—Spousal Support.

§ 3591. Modification or termination of agreements

(a) Except as provided in subdivisions (b) and (c), the provisions of an agreement for the support of either party are subject to subsequent modification or termination by court order.

(b) An agreement may not be modified or terminated as to an amount that accrued before the date of the filing of the notice of motion or order to show cause to modify or terminate.

(c) An agreement for spousal support may not be modified or revoked to the extent that a written agreement, or, if there is no written agreement, an oral agreement entered into in open court between the parties, specifically provides that the spousal support is not subject to modification or termination. *(Stats.1992, c. 162 (A.B.2650), § 10, operative Jan. 1, 1994.)*

Cross References

Judgment and order defined for purposes of this Code, see Family Code § 100.
Notice, actual and constructive, defined, see Civil Code § 18.
Spousal support defined for purposes of this Code, see Family Code § 142.
Support defined for purposes of this Code, see Family Code § 150.

Research References

Forms

1 California Transactions Forms--Family Law § 2:61, Modifiability.

§ 3592. Discharge in bankruptcy; power of court to make new orders

If an obligation under an agreement for settlement of property to a spouse or for support of a spouse is discharged in bankruptcy, the court may make all proper orders for the support of the spouse, as the court determines are just, having regard for the circumstances of the parties and the amount of the obligations under the agreement that are discharged. *(Stats.1992, c. 162 (A.B.2650), § 10, operative Jan. 1, 1994.)*

Cross References

Judgment and order defined for purposes of this Code, see Family Code § 100.
Property defined for purposes of this Code, see Family Code § 113.
References to husband, wife, spouses and married persons, persons included for purposes of this Code, see Family Code § 11.
Support defined for purposes of this Code, see Family Code § 150.

§ 3593. Application of §§ 3590 and 3591

Sections 3590 and 3591 are effective only with respect to a property settlement agreement entered into on or after January 1, 1970, and do not affect an agreement entered into before January 1, 1970, as to which Chapter 1308 of the Statutes of 1967 shall apply. *(Stats.1992, c. 162 (A.B.2650), § 10, operative Jan. 1, 1994.)*

Cross References

Property defined for purposes of this Code, see Family Code § 113.

CHAPTER 4. SPOUSAL AND CHILD SUPPORT DURING PENDENCY OF PROCEEDING

Section
3600. Support orders.
3601. Duration of child support orders.
3602. Reconciliation.
3603. Time for modification or termination of orders; exceptions.
3604. Rights of the parties or children with respect to subsequent orders.

Cross References

Child support, generally, see Family Code § 3900 et seq.
Failure to support spouse or children, see Penal Code § 270 et seq.
Marital dissolution or legal separation proceedings, consideration of motions for temporary spousal support, child support, and counsel fees and costs prior to determining motion to transfer, see Code of Civil Procedure § 396b.
References to husband, wife, spouses and married persons, persons included for purposes of this Code, see Family Code § 11.
Support defined for purposes of this Code, see Family Code § 150.
Uniform Interstate Family Support Act, see Family Code § 5700.101 et seq.

§ 3600. Support orders

During the pendency of any proceeding for dissolution of marriage or for legal separation of the parties or under Division 8 (commencing with Section 3000) (custody of children) or in any proceeding where there is at issue the support of a minor child or a child for whom support is authorized under Section 3901 or 3910, the court may order (a) either spouse to pay any amount that is necessary for the support of the other spouse, consistent with the requirements of subdivisions (i) and (m) of Section 4320 and Section 4325, or (b) either or both parents to pay any amount necessary for the support of the child, as the case may be. *(Stats.1992, c. 162 (A.B.2650), § 10, operative Jan. 1, 1994. Amended by Stats.2001, c. 293 (S.B.1221), § 1; Stats.2002, c. 759 (A.B.3033), § 1; Stats.2014, c. 82 (S.B.1306), § 35, eff. Jan. 1, 2015.)*

Cross References

Child custody, see Family Code § 3020 et seq.
Child support, generally, see Family Code § 3900 et seq.
Failure to support spouse or children, see Penal Code § 270 et seq.
Judgment and order defined for purposes of this Code, see Family Code § 100.
Marital dissolution or legal separation proceedings, consideration of motions for temporary spousal support, child support, and counsel fees and costs prior to determining motion to transfer, see Code of Civil Procedure § 396b.
Minor defined for purposes of this Code, see Family Code § 6500.
Proceeding defined for purposes of this Code, see Family Code § 110.
References to husband, wife, spouses and married persons, persons included for purposes of this Code, see Family Code § 11.
Support defined for purposes of this Code, see Family Code § 150.
Uniform Interstate Family Support Act, see Family Code § 5700.101 et seq.

Research References

Forms

California Practice Guide: Rutter Family Law Forms Form 1:32, Glossary of Common Family Law Terms, Phrases and Concepts (Enclosure to Form 1:31).
California Practice Guide: Rutter Family Law Forms Form 5:2, Request for Order Re Child Custody, Child Support, Spousal Support, Attorney Fees, etc.
California Practice Guide: Rutter Family Law Forms Form 6:11, Request for Order Re Guideline Child Support, Temporary "Guideline" Spousal Support and Family Code §4062 "Add-On" Child Support.
California Practice Guide: Rutter Family Law Forms Form 6:23, Request for Order Re Temporary "Guideline" Spousal Support and Family Code §4360 Provision for Support After Death of Supporting Party.
1 California Transactions Forms--Family Law § 2:52, Overview.
1 California Transactions Forms--Family Law § 2:53, Temporary Support.
1 California Transactions Forms--Family Law § 2:63, Authority for Child Support.
1 California Transactions Forms--Family Law § 3:21, Jurisdiction for Orders to Pay Child Support.
West's California Code Forms, Family § 3600, Comment Overview—Spousal and Child Support During Pendency of Proceeding.

§ 3601. Duration of child support orders

(a) An order for child support entered pursuant to this chapter continues in effect until the order (1) is terminated by the court or (2) terminates by operation of law pursuant to Sections 3900, 3901, 4007, and 4013.

(b) Subject to Section 3602, subdivision (a) applies notwithstanding any other provision of law and notwithstanding that the proceeding has not been brought to trial within the time limits specified in Chapter 1.5 (commencing with Section 583.110) of Title 8 of Part 2 of the Code of Civil Procedure. *(Stats.1992, c. 162 (A.B.2650), § 10, operative Jan. 1, 1994. Amended by Stats.1993, c. 219 (A.B.1500), § 121.)*

Cross References

Child support, generally, see Family Code § 3900 et seq.
Expedited child support orders, see Family Code § 3620 et seq.
Health insurance coverage for supported children, see Family Code § 3750 et seq.
Judgment and order defined for purposes of this Code, see Family Code § 100.
Marital dissolution or legal separation proceedings, consideration of motions for temporary spousal support, child support, and counsel fees and costs prior to determining motion to transfer, see Code of Civil Procedure § 396b.
Modification, termination, or setting aside of support order, see Family Code § 3650 et seq.
Proceeding defined for purposes of this Code, see Family Code § 110.
Support defined for purposes of this Code, see Family Code § 150.
Uniform Interstate Family Support Act, see Family Code § 5700.101 et seq.

§ 3602. Reconciliation

Unless the order specifies otherwise, an order made pursuant to this chapter is not enforceable during any period in which the parties have reconciled and are living together. *(Stats.1992, c. 162 (A.B. 2650), § 10, operative Jan. 1, 1994.)*

Cross References

Child support, generally, see Family Code § 3900 et seq.
Judgment and order defined for purposes of this Code, see Family Code § 100.
Marital dissolution or legal separation proceedings, consideration of motions for temporary spousal support, child support, and counsel fees and costs prior to determining motion to transfer, see Code of Civil Procedure § 396b.
Uniform Interstate Family Support Act, see Family Code § 5700.101 et seq.

§ 3603. Time for modification or termination of orders; exceptions

An order made pursuant to this chapter may be modified or terminated at any time except as to an amount that accrued before the date of the filing of the notice of motion or order to show cause to modify or terminate. *(Stats.1992, c. 162 (A.B.2650), § 10, operative Jan. 1, 1994.)*

Cross References

Child support, generally, see Family Code § 3900 et seq.
Judgment and order defined for purposes of this Code, see Family Code § 100.

§ 3603

Marital dissolution or legal separation proceedings, consideration of motions for temporary spousal support, child support, and counsel fees and costs prior to determining motion to transfer, see Code of Civil Procedure § 396b.
Notice, actual and constructive, defined, see Civil Code § 18.
Support order, modification or termination,
    Authority of court, see Family Code § 3651.
    Discovery, see Family Code § 3660 et seq.
    Retroactive application, see Family Code § 3653.
Uniform Interstate Family Support Act, see Family Code § 5700.101 et seq.

§ 3604. Rights of the parties or children with respect to subsequent orders

An order made pursuant to this chapter does not prejudice the rights of the parties or the child with respect to any subsequent order which may be made. *(Stats.1992, c. 162 (A.B.2650), § 10, operative Jan. 1, 1994.)*

Cross References

Child support, generally, see Family Code § 3900 et seq.
Judgment and order defined for purposes of this Code, see Family Code § 100.
Marital dissolution or legal separation proceedings, consideration of motions for temporary spousal support, child support, and counsel fees and costs prior to determining motion to transfer, see Code of Civil Procedure § 396b.
Uniform Interstate Family Support Act, see Family Code § 5700.101 et seq.

Research References

Forms

West's California Code Forms, Family § 3600, Comment Overview—Spousal and Child Support During Pendency of Proceeding.

CHAPTER 5. EXPEDITED CHILD SUPPORT ORDER

Section
3620. Expedited support order.
3621. Amount of support orders.
3622. Application for order; forms and required information.
3623. Jurisdiction of court.
3624. Effective date of expedited support order; service of application; effect of failure to respond.
3625. Response to application; service; effect of filing.
3626. Time set for hearing.
3627. Notice of hearing.
3628. Failure to give notice of hearing.
3629. Submission of state and federal income tax returns; review and examination; enforcement.
3630. Amount of expedited support order.
3631. Order after hearing.
3632. Effective date of order after hearing; retroactive effect.
3633. Time for modification or termination of order.
3634. Forms; preparation by Judicial Council.

Cross References

Child support, generally, see Family Code § 3900 et seq.
Support defined for purposes of this Code, see Family Code § 150.
Support order, modification or termination,
    Authority of court, see Family Code § 3651.
    Discovery, see Family Code § 3660 et seq.
    Retroactive application of modification, see Family Code § 3653.
Support order defined for purposes of this Code, see Family Code § 155.
Uniform Interstate Family Support Act, see Family Code § 5700.101 et seq.

§ 3620. Expedited support order

An order under this chapter shall be known as an expedited support order. *(Stats.1992, c. 162 (A.B.2650), § 10, operative Jan. 1, 1994.)*

Cross References

Child support, generally, see Family Code § 3900 et seq.
Judgment and order defined for purposes of this Code, see Family Code § 100.
Support defined for purposes of this Code, see Family Code § 150.
Support order, modification or termination,
    Authority of court, see Family Code § 3651.
    Discovery, see Family Code § 3660 et seq.
    Retroactive application of modification, see Family Code § 3653.
Support order defined for purposes of this Code, see Family Code § 155.
Uniform Interstate Family Support Act, see Family Code § 5700.101 et seq.

Research References

Forms

West's California Judicial Council Forms FL-150, Income and Expense Declaration (Also Available in Spanish).
West's California Judicial Council Forms FL-380, Application for Expedited Child Support Order.
West's California Judicial Council Forms FL-381, Response to Application for Expedited Child Support Order and Notice of Hearing.
West's California Judicial Council Forms FL-382, Expedited Child Support Order.

§ 3621. Amount of support orders

In an action for child support that has been filed and served, the court may, without a hearing, make an order requiring a parent or parents to pay for the support of their minor child or children during the pendency of that action, pursuant to this chapter, the amount required by Section 4055 or, if the income of the obligated parent or parents is unknown to the applicant, then the minimum amount of support as provided in Section 11452 of the Welfare and Institutions Code. *(Stats.1992, c. 162 (A.B.2650), § 10, operative Jan. 1, 1994. Amended by Stats.1993, c. 219 (A.B.1500), § 122.)*

Cross References

Child support, generally, see Family Code § 3900 et seq.
Health insurance coverage for supported children, see Family Code § 3750 et seq.
Judgment and order defined for purposes of this Code, see Family Code § 100.
Minor defined for purposes of this Code, see Family Code § 6500.
Modification, termination, or setting aside of support order, see Family Code § 3650 et seq.
Support defined for purposes of this Code, see Family Code § 150.
Support order, modification or termination,
    Authority of court, see Family Code § 3651.
    Discovery, see Family Code § 3660 et seq.
    Retroactive application of modification, see Family Code § 3653.
Uniform Interstate Family Support Act, see Family Code § 5700.101 et seq.

Research References

Forms

West's California Code Forms, Family § 3620, Comment Overview—Expedited Child Support Order.

§ 3622. Application for order; forms and required information

The court shall make an expedited support order upon the filing of all of the following:

(a) An application for an expedited child support order, setting forth the minimum amount the obligated parent or parents are required to pay pursuant to Section 4055 of this code or the minimum basic standards of adequate care for Region 1 as specified in Sections 11452 and 11452.018 of the Welfare and Institutions Code.

(b) An income and expense declaration for both parents, completed by the applicant.

(c) A worksheet setting forth the basis of the amount of support requested.

(d) A proposed expedited child support order. *(Stats.1992, c. 162 (A.B.2650), § 10, operative Jan. 1, 1994. Amended by Stats.1993, c. 219 (A.B.1500), § 123; Stats.1997, c. 14 (A.B.239), § 2, eff. May 30, 1997.)*

Cross References

Child support, generally, see Family Code § 3900 et seq.
Health insurance coverage for supported children, see Family Code § 3750 et seq.
Income and expense declaration defined, see Family Code § 95.
Judgment and order defined for purposes of this Code, see Family Code § 100.
Jurisdiction in superior court, see Family Code § 200.
Modification, termination, or setting aside of support order, see Family Code § 3650 et seq.
Support defined for purposes of this Code, see Family Code § 150.
Support order, modification or termination,
   Authority of court, see Family Code § 3651.
   Discovery, see Family Code § 3660 et seq.
   Retroactive application of modification, see Family Code § 3653.
Support order defined for purposes of this Code, see Family Code § 155.
Uniform Interstate Family Support Act, see Family Code § 5700.101 et seq.

Research References

Forms

West's California Code Forms, Family § 3620, Comment Overview—Expedited Child Support Order.

§ 3623. Jurisdiction of court

(a) An application for the expedited support order confers jurisdiction on the court to hear only the issue of support of the child or children for whom support may be ordered.

(b) Nothing in this chapter prevents either party from bringing before the court at the hearing other separately noticed issues otherwise relevant and proper to the action in which the application for the expedited support order has been filed. *(Stats.1992, c. 162 (A.B.2650), § 10, operative Jan. 1, 1994. Amended by Stats.1993, c. 219 (A.B.1500), § 124.)*

Cross References

Child for whom support may be ordered defined for purposes of this Code, see Family Code § 58.
Child support, generally, see Family Code § 3900 et seq.
Health insurance coverage for supported children, see Family Code § 3750 et seq.
Judgment and order defined for purposes of this Code, see Family Code § 100.
Jurisdiction in superior court, see Family Code § 200.
Modification, termination, or setting aside of support order, see Family Code § 3650 et seq.
Support defined for purposes of this Code, see Family Code § 150.
Support order, modification or termination,
   Authority of court, see Family Code § 3651.
   Discovery, see Family Code § 3660 et seq.
   Retroactive application of modification, see Family Code § 3653.
Support order defined for purposes of this Code, see Family Code § 155.
Uniform Interstate Family Support Act, see Family Code § 5700.101 et seq.

§ 3624. Effective date of expedited support order; service of application; effect of failure to respond

(a) Subject to Section 3625, an expedited support order becomes effective 30 days after service on the obligated parent of all of the following:

(1) The application for an expedited child support order.

(2) The proposed expedited child support order, which shall include a notice of consequences of failure to file a response.

(3) The completed income and expense declaration for both parents.

(4) A worksheet setting forth the basis of the amount of support requested.

(5) Three blank copies of the income and expense declaration form.

(6) Three blank copies of the response to an application for expedited child support order and notice of hearing form.

(b) Service on the obligated parent of the application and other required documents as set forth in subdivision (a) shall be by personal service or by any method available under Sections 415.10 to 415.40, inclusive, of the Code of Civil Procedure.

(c) Unless there is a response to the application for an expedited support order as provided in Section 3625, the expedited support order shall be effective on the obligated parent without further action by the court. *(Stats.1992, c. 162 (A.B.2650), § 10, operative Jan. 1, 1994.)*

Cross References

Child support, generally, see Family Code § 3900 et seq.
Computation of time, see Code of Civil Procedure §§ 12, 12a; Government Code § 6800 et seq.
Health insurance coverage for supported children, see Family Code § 3750 et seq.
Income and expense declaration defined, see Family Code § 95.
Judgment and order defined for purposes of this Code, see Family Code § 100.
Modification, termination, or setting aside of support order, see Family Code § 3650 et seq.
Notice, actual and constructive, defined, see Civil Code § 18.
Support defined for purposes of this Code, see Family Code § 150.
Support order, modification or termination,
   Authority of court, see Family Code § 3651.
   Discovery, see Family Code § 3660 et seq.
   Retroactive application of modification, see Family Code § 3653.
Support order defined for purposes of this Code, see Family Code § 155.
Uniform Interstate Family Support Act, see Family Code § 5700.101 et seq.

Research References

Forms

West's California Code Forms, Family § 3620, Comment Overview—Expedited Child Support Order.

§ 3625. Response to application; service; effect of filing

(a) A response to the application for the proposed expedited support order and the obligated parent's income and expense declaration may be filed with the court at any time before the effective date of the expedited support order and, on filing, shall be served upon the applicant by any method by which a response to a notice of motion may be served.

(b) The response to the application for an expedited support order shall state the objections of the obligated parent to the proposed expedited support order.

(c) The simultaneous filing of the response to the application for an expedited support order and the obligated parent's income and expense declaration shall stay the effective date of the expedited support order.

(d) No fee shall be charged for, or in connection with, the filing of the response. *(Stats.1992, c. 162 (A.B.2650), § 10, operative Jan. 1, 1994.)*

Cross References

Child support, generally, see Family Code § 3900 et seq.
Income and expense declaration defined, see Family Code § 95.
Judgment and order defined for purposes of this Code, see Family Code § 100.
Notice, actual and constructive, defined, see Civil Code § 18.
State defined for purposes of this Code, see Family Code § 145.
Support defined for purposes of this Code, see Family Code § 150.
Support order defined for purposes of this Code, see Family Code § 155.
Uniform Interstate Family Support Act, see Family Code § 5700.101 et seq.

Research References

Forms

West's California Code Forms, Family § 3620, Comment Overview—Expedited Child Support Order.

§ 3626. Time set for hearing

The obligated parent shall cause the court clerk to, and the court clerk shall, set a hearing on the application for the expedited support order not less than 20 nor more than 30 days after the filing of the

§ 3626

response to the application for the expedited support order and income and expense declaration. *(Stats.1992, c. 162 (A.B.2650), § 10, operative Jan. 1, 1994.)*

Cross References

Child support, generally, see Family Code § 3900 et seq.
Computation of time, see Code of Civil Procedure §§ 12, 12a; Government Code § 6800 et seq.
Income and expense declaration defined for purposes of this Code, see Family Code § 95.
Judgment and order defined for purposes of this Code, see Family Code § 100.
Support defined for purposes of this Code, see Family Code § 150.
Support order defined for purposes of this Code, see Family Code § 155.
Uniform Interstate Family Support Act, see Family Code § 5700.101 et seq.

Research References

Forms

West's California Code Forms, Family § 3620, Comment Overview—Expedited Child Support Order.

§ 3627. Notice of hearing

The obligated parent shall give notice of the hearing to the other parties or their counsel by first-class mail not less than 15 days before the hearing. *(Stats.1992, c. 162 (A.B.2650), § 10, operative Jan. 1, 1994.)*

Cross References

Child support, generally, see Family Code § 3900 et seq.
Computation of time, see Code of Civil Procedure §§ 12, 12a; Government Code § 6800 et seq.
Counsel, right to, see Cal. Const. Art. 1, § 15, cl. 3.
Notice, actual and constructive, defined, see Civil Code § 18.
Uniform Interstate Family Support Act, see Family Code § 5700.101 et seq.

§ 3628. Failure to give notice of hearing

If notice of the hearing is not given as provided in Section 3627, the expedited support order becomes effective as provided in Section 3624, subject to the relief available to the responding party as provided by Section 473 of the Code of Civil Procedure or any other available relief whether in law or in equity. *(Stats.1992, c. 162 (A.B.2650), § 10, operative Jan. 1, 1994.)*

Cross References

Child support, generally, see Family Code § 3900 et seq.
Judgment and order defined for purposes of this Code, see Family Code § 100.
Notice, actual and constructive, defined, see Civil Code § 18.
Support defined for purposes of this Code, see Family Code § 150.
Support order defined for purposes of this Code, see Family Code § 155.
Uniform Interstate Family Support Act, see Family Code § 5700.101 et seq.

§ 3629. Submission of state and federal income tax returns; review and examination; enforcement

(a) At the hearing on the application for the expedited support order, all parties who are parents of the child or children who are the subject of the action shall produce copies of their most recently filed federal and state income tax returns.

(b) A tax return so submitted may be reviewed by the other parties, and a party also may be examined by the other parties as to the contents of the return.

(c) Except as provided in subdivision (d), a party who fails to submit documents to the court as required by this chapter shall not be granted the relief that the party has requested.

(d) The court may grant the requested relief if the party submits a declaration under penalty of perjury that (1) no such document exists, or (2) in the case of a tax return, it cannot be produced, but a copy has been requested from the Internal Revenue Service or Franchise Tax Board. *(Stats.1992, c. 162 (A.B.2650), § 10, operative Jan. 1, 1994.)*

Cross References

Child support, generally, see Family Code § 3900 et seq.
Judgment and order defined for purposes of this Code, see Family Code § 100.
State defined for purposes of this Code, see Family Code § 145.
Support defined for purposes of this Code, see Family Code § 150.
Support order defined for purposes of this Code, see Family Code § 155.
Tax levies, see Government Code § 29100 et seq.; Revenue and Taxation Code § 2151 et seq.
Tax returns, support proceedings, see Family Code § 3552.
Uniform Interstate Family Support Act, see Family Code § 5700.101 et seq.

§ 3630. Amount of expedited support order

(a) Except as provided in subdivision (b), the amount of the expedited support order shall be the minimum amount the obligated parent is required to pay as set forth in the application.

(b) If a hearing is held on the application, the court shall order an amount of support in accordance with Article 2 (commencing with Section 4050) of Chapter 2 of Part 2. *(Stats.1992, c. 162 (A.B.2650), § 10, operative Jan. 1, 1994.)*

Cross References

Child support, generally, see Family Code § 3900 et seq.
Judgment and order defined for purposes of this Code, see Family Code § 100.
Support defined for purposes of this Code, see Family Code § 150.
Support order defined for purposes of this Code, see Family Code § 155.
Uniform Interstate Family Support Act, see Family Code § 5700.101 et seq.

§ 3631. Order after hearing

When there is a hearing, the resulting order shall be called an order after hearing. *(Stats.1992, c. 162 (A.B.2650), § 10, operative Jan. 1, 1994.)*

Cross References

Child support, generally, see Family Code § 3900 et seq.
Judgment and order defined for purposes of this Code, see Family Code § 100.
Uniform Interstate Family Support Act, see Family Code § 5700.101 et seq.

§ 3632. Effective date of order after hearing; retroactive effect

An order after hearing shall become effective not more than 30 days after the filing of the response to the application for the expedited support order and may be given retroactive effect to the date of the filing of the application. *(Stats.1992, c. 162 (A.B.2650), § 10, operative Jan. 1, 1994.)*

Cross References

Child support, generally, see Family Code § 3900 et seq.
Computation of time, see Code of Civil Procedure §§ 12, 12a; Government Code § 6800 et seq.
Judgment and order defined for purposes of this Code, see Family Code § 100.
Support defined for purposes of this Code, see Family Code § 150.
Support order defined for purposes of this Code, see Family Code § 155.
Uniform Interstate Family Support Act, see Family Code § 5700.101 et seq.

§ 3633. Time for modification or termination of order

An order entered under this chapter may be modified or terminated at any time on the same basis as any other order for child support. *(Stats.1992, c. 162 (A.B.2650), § 10, operative Jan. 1, 1994.)*

Cross References

Child support, generally, see Family Code § 3900 et seq.
Health insurance coverage for supported children, see Family Code § 3750 et seq.
Judgment and order defined for purposes of this Code, see Family Code § 100.
Modification or termination of support order, see Family Code § 3650 et seq.
Support defined for purposes of this Code, see Family Code § 150.

Uniform Interstate Family Support Act, see Family Code § 5700.101 et seq.

§ 3634. Forms; preparation by Judicial Council

The Judicial Council shall prepare all forms necessary to give effect to this chapter. (Stats.1992, c. 162 (A.B.2650), § 10, operative Jan. 1, 1994.)

Cross References

Child support, generally, see Family Code § 3900 et seq.
Income and expense declaration defined, see Family Code § 95.
Judicial Council, rules of practice and procedure, see Family Code § 210 et seq.
Property declaration defined, see Family Code § 115.
Uniform Interstate Family Support Act, see Family Code § 5700.101 et seq.

Research References

Forms

West's California Judicial Council Forms FL–150, Income and Expense Declaration (Also Available in Spanish).
West's California Judicial Council Forms FL–380, Application for Expedited Child Support Order.
West's California Judicial Council Forms FL–381, Response to Application for Expedited Child Support Order and Notice of Hearing.
West's California Judicial Council Forms FL–382, Expedited Child Support Order.

CHAPTER 6. MODIFICATION, TERMINATION, OR SET ASIDE OF SUPPORT ORDERS

Article	Section
1. General Provisions	3650
2. Discovery Before Commencing Modification or Termination Proceeding	3660
3. Simplified Procedure for Modification of Support Order	3680
4. Relief From Orders	3690

Cross References

Child support, generally, see Family Code § 3900 et seq.
Support order pending proceeding, modification or termination, see Family Code § 3603.

ARTICLE 1. GENERAL PROVISIONS

Section	
3650.	Support order.
3651.	Powers of court; application of section.
3652.	Attorney's fees and court costs.
3653.	Retroactive application of modification or termination of support orders.
3654.	Statement of decision.

§ 3650. Support order

Unless the provision or context otherwise requires, as used in this chapter, "support order" means a child, family, or spousal support order. (Stats.1992, c. 162 (A.B.2650), § 10, operative Jan. 1, 1994. Amended by Stats.1993, c. 219 (A.B.1500), § 124.5.)

Cross References

Child support, generally, see Family Code § 3900 et seq.
Expedited child support orders, see Family Code § 3620 et seq.
Health insurance coverage for supported children, see Family Code § 3750 et seq.
Judgment and order defined for purposes of this Code, see Family Code § 100.
Spousal support defined for purposes of this Code, see Family Code § 142.
Support defined for purposes of this Code, see Family Code § 150.
Support order defined, see Family Code § 155.

Uniform Interstate Family Support Act, see Family Code § 5700.101 et seq.

Research References

Forms

West's California Code Forms, Family § 4405 Form 1, Notice of Motion and Motion to Modify Order for Support.

§ 3651. Powers of court; application of section

(a) Except as provided in subdivisions (c) and (d) and subject to Article 3 (commencing with Section 3680) and Sections 3552, 3587, and 4004, a support order may be modified or terminated at any time as the court determines to be necessary.

(b) Upon the filing of a supplemental complaint pursuant to Section 2330.1, a child support order in the original proceeding may be modified in conformity with the statewide uniform guideline for child support to provide for the support of all of the children of the same parents who were named in the initial and supplemental pleadings, to consolidate arrearages and wage assignments for children of the parties, and to consolidate orders for support.

(c)(1) Except as provided in paragraph (2) and subdivision (b), a support order may not be modified or terminated as to an amount that accrued before the date of the filing of the notice of motion or order to show cause to modify or terminate.

(2) If a party to a support order is activated to United States military duty or National Guard service and deployed out of state, the servicemember may file and serve a notice of activation of military service and request to modify a support order, in lieu of a notice of motion or order to show cause, by informing the court and the other party of the request to modify the support order based on the change in circumstance. The servicemember shall indicate the date of deployment and, if possible, the court shall schedule the hearing prior to that date. If the court cannot hear the matter prior to the date of deployment out of state, and the servicemember complies with the conditions set forth in the Servicemembers Civil Relief Act, Section 522 of the Appendix of Title 50 of the United States Code, the court shall grant a stay of proceedings consistent with the timelines for stays set forth in that section. If, after granting the mandatory stay required by Section 522 of the Appendix of Title 50 of the United States Code, the court fails to grant the discretionary stay described under the law, it shall comply with the federal mandate to appoint counsel to represent the interests of the deployed servicemember. The court may not proceed with the matter if it does not appoint counsel, unless the servicemember is represented by other counsel. If the court stays the proceeding until after the return of the service member, the servicemember shall request the court to set the matter for hearing within 90 days of return from deployment or the matter shall be taken off calendar and the existing order may not be made retroactive pursuant to subdivision (c) of Section 3653.

(3) A servicemember who does not file a notice of activation of military service and request to modify a support order or order to show cause or notice of motion prior to deployment out of state nonetheless shall not be subject to penalties otherwise authorized by Chapter 5 (commencing with Section 4720) of Part 5 on the amount of child support that would not have accrued if the order had been modified pursuant to paragraph (2), absent a finding by the court of good cause. Any such finding shall be stated on the record.

(4) Notwithstanding any other law, interest shall not accrue on that amount of a child support obligation that would not have become due and owing if the activated servicemember modified the support order upon activation to reflect the change in income due to the activation. Upon a finding by the court that good cause did not exist for the servicemember's failure to seek, or delay in seeking, the modification, interest shall accrue as otherwise allowed by law.

(d) An order for spousal support may not be modified or terminated to the extent that a written agreement or, if there is no written agreement, an oral agreement entered into in open court

§ 3651

between the parties, specifically provides that the spousal support is not subject to modification or termination.

(e) This section applies whether or not the support order is based upon an agreement between the parties.

(f) This section is effective only with respect to a property settlement agreement entered into on or after January 1, 1970, and does not affect an agreement entered into before January 1, 1970, as to which Chapter 1308 of the Statutes of 1967 shall apply.

(g)(1) The Judicial Council, no later than 90 days after the effective date of the act adding this section, shall develop forms and procedures necessary to implement paragraph (2) of subdivision (c). The Judicial Council shall ensure that all forms adopted pursuant to this section are in plain language.

(2) The form developed by the Judicial Council, in addition to other items the Judicial Council determines to be necessary or appropriate, shall include the following:

(A) The date of deployment and all information relevant to the determination of the amount of child support, including whether the servicemember's employer will supplement the servicemember's income during the deployment.

(B) A notice informing the opposing party that, absent a finding of good cause, the order will be made retroactive to the date of service of the form or the date of deployment, whichever is later.

(C) Notice that the requesting party must notify the court and the other party upon return from military duty and seek to bring any unresolved request for modification to hearing within 90 days of return, or else lose the right to modify the order pursuant to this section. *(Stats.1992, c. 162 (A.B.2650), § 10, operative Jan. 1, 1994. Amended by Stats.1994, c. 1269 (A.B.2208), § 31.4; Stats.1997, c. 599 (A.B.573), § 6; Stats.2005, c. 154 (S.B.1082), § 2, eff. Aug. 30, 2005; Stats.2019, c. 115 (A.B.1817), § 39, eff. Jan. 1, 2020.)*

Cross References

Arrears collection enhancement process, see Family Code § 17560.
Child support, generally, see Family Code § 3900 et seq.
Child support guidelines, modification of orders, see Family Code § 4076.
Discovery proceeding, modification or termination, see Family Code § 3660 et seq.
Expedited child support orders, see Family Code § 3620 et seq.
Health insurance coverage for supported children, see Family Code § 3750 et seq.
Judgment and order defined for purposes of this Code, see Family Code § 100.
Modification of custody or visitation order, military service as justification, see Family Code § 3047.
Modification or termination of child or spousal support order, pendency of proceedings, see Family Code § 3603.
Modification or termination of spousal support agreement, see Family Code § 3591.
Notice, actual and constructive, defined, see Civil Code § 18.
Proceeding defined for purposes of this Code, see Family Code § 110.
Property defined for purposes of this Code, see Family Code § 113.
Retroactivity, modification or termination, see Family Code § 3653.
Service of notice, validity of modification of judgment or order, see Family Code § 215.
Spousal support defined for purposes of this Code, see Family Code § 142.
Support agreements, generally, see Family Code § 3580 et seq.
Support defined for purposes of this Code, see Family Code § 150.
Support order defined for purposes of this Code, see Family Code § 155.
Suspension of money judgment or order for support of a child, exceptions, resumption of obligation, administrative adjustment, evaluation, see Family Code § 4007.5.
Uniform Interstate Family Support Act, see Family Code § 5700.101 et seq.
United States military and National Guard service members, modification of child support, form, motion by local child support agency, see Family Code § 17440.

Research References

Forms

1 California Transactions Forms--Family Law § 2:61, Modifiability.

West's California Code Forms, Family § 3585, Comment Overview—Child Support.
West's California Code Forms, Family § 3650, Comment Overview—Modification, Termination, or Set Aside of Support Orders.
West's California Code Forms, Family § 4405 Form 1, Notice of Motion and Motion to Modify Order for Support.
West's California Judicial Council Forms FL-343, Spousal, Domestic Partner, or Family Support Order Attachment.

§ 3652. Attorney's fees and court costs

Except as against a governmental agency, an order modifying, terminating, or setting aside a support order may include an award of attorney's fees and court costs to the prevailing party. *(Stats.1992, c. 162 (A.B.2650), § 10, operative Jan. 1, 1994. Amended by Stats.1994, c. 1269 (A.B.2208), § 31.6; Stats.1999, c. 653 (A.B.380), § 3.)*

Cross References

Attorney fees, generally, see Family Code § 3557.
Attorney's fees and costs, generally, see Code of Civil Procedure § 1021.
Child support, generally, see Family Code § 3900 et seq.
Judgment and order defined for purposes of this Code, see Family Code § 100.
Support defined for purposes of this Code, see Family Code § 150.
Support order, modification or termination,
 Authority of court, see Family Code § 3651.
 Discovery, see Family Code § 3660 et seq.
 Retroactive application of modification, see Family Code § 3653.
Support order defined for purposes of this Code, see Family Code § 155.
Uniform Interstate Family Support Act, see Family Code § 5700.101 et seq.

Research References

Forms

West's California Code Forms, Family § 3650, Comment Overview—Modification, Termination, or Set Aside of Support Orders.

§ 3653. Retroactive application of modification or termination of support orders

(a) An order modifying or terminating a support order may be made retroactive to the date of the filing of the notice of motion or order to show cause to modify or terminate, or to any subsequent date, except as provided in subdivision (b) or by federal law (42 U.S.C. Sec. 666(a)(9)).

(b) If an order modifying or terminating a support order is entered due to the unemployment of either the support obligor or the support obligee, the order shall be made retroactive to the later of the date of the service on the opposing party of the notice of motion or order to show cause to modify or terminate or the date of unemployment, subject to the notice requirements of federal law (42 U.S.C. Sec. 666(a)(9)), unless the court finds good cause not to make the order retroactive and states its reasons on the record.

(c) If an order modifying or terminating a support order is entered due to a change in income resulting from the activation to United States military service or National Guard duty and deployment out of state for either the support obligor or the support obligee, the order shall be made retroactive to the later of the date of the service on the opposing party of the notice of activation, notice of motion, order to show cause to modify or terminate, or the date of activation, subject to the notice requirements of federal law (42 U.S.C. Sec. 666(a)(9)), unless the court finds good cause not to make the order retroactive and states its reasons on the record. Good cause shall include, but not be limited to, a finding by the court that the delay in seeking the modification was not reasonable under the circumstances faced by the service member.

(d) If an order decreasing or terminating a support order is entered retroactively pursuant to this section, the support obligor may be entitled to, and the support obligee may be ordered to repay, according to the terms specified in the order, any amounts previously paid by the support obligor pursuant to the prior order that are in excess of the amounts due pursuant to the retroactive order. The court may order that the repayment by the support obligee shall be made over any period of time and in any manner, including, but not limited to, by an offset against future support payments or wage assignment, as the court deems just and reasonable. In determining whether to order a repayment, and in establishing the terms of repayment, the court shall consider all of the following factors:

(1) The amount to be repaid.

(2) The duration of the support order prior to modification or termination.

(3) The financial impact on the support obligee of any particular method of repayment such as an offset against future support payments or wage assignment.

(4) Any other facts or circumstances that the court deems relevant. *(Stats.1992, c. 162 (A.B.2650), § 10, operative Jan. 1, 1994. Amended by Stats.1998, c. 854 (A.B.960), § 1; Stats.1999, c. 653 (A.B.380), § 4; Stats.2005, c. 154 (S.B.1082), § 3, eff. Aug. 30, 2005.)*

Cross References

Arrears collection enhancement process, see Family Code § 17560.
Child support, generally, see Family Code § 3900 et seq.
Child support enforcement, support obligations, disabled obligors receiving SSI/SSP or social security disability insurance benefits, see Family Code § 17400.5.
Judgment and order defined for purposes of this Code, see Family Code § 100.
Modification of custody or visitation order, military service as justification, see Family Code § 3047.
Notice, actual and constructive, defined, see Civil Code § 18.
Retroactivity of,
 Child support order, see Family Code § 4009.
 Spousal support order, see Family Code § 4333.
State defined for purposes of this Code, see Family Code § 145.
Support defined for purposes of this Code, see Family Code § 150.
Support order, modification or termination,
 Authority of court, see Family Code § 3651.
 Discovery, see Family Code § 3660 et seq.
Support order defined for purposes of this Code, see Family Code § 155.
Uniform Interstate Family Support Act, see Family Code § 5700.101 et seq.
United States military and National Guard service members, modification of child support, form, motion by local child support agency, see Family Code § 17440.

Research References

Forms

West's California Code Forms, Family § 3650, Comment Overview—Modification, Termination, or Set Aside of Support Orders.
West's California Judicial Council Forms FL–343, Spousal, Domestic Partner, or Family Support Order Attachment.

§ 3654. Statement of decision

At the request of either party, an order modifying, terminating, or setting aside a support order shall include a statement of decision. *(Stats.1992, c. 162 (A.B.2650), § 10, operative Jan. 1, 1994. Amended by Stats.1999, c. 653 (A.B.380), § 5.)*

Cross References

Child support, generally, see Family Code § 3900 et seq.
Judgment and order defined for purposes of this Code, see Family Code § 100.
Support defined for purposes of this Code, see Family Code § 150.
Support order defined for purposes of this Code, see Family Code § 155.
Uniform Interstate Family Support Act, see Family Code § 5700.101 et seq.

Research References

Forms

West's California Judicial Council Forms FL–343, Spousal, Domestic Partner, or Family Support Order Attachment.

ARTICLE 2. DISCOVERY BEFORE COMMENCING MODIFICATION OR TERMINATION PROCEEDING

Section
3660. Purpose of article.

Section
3662. Methods of discovery; restrictions.
3663. Discovery requests; restrictions.
3664. Requests for current income and expense declaration; authorized forms; requests to employer for income and benefit information; service.
3665. Attachments to income and expense declaration; tax returns; disclosure.
3666. Enforcement of article.
3667. Incomplete or inaccurate income and expense declaration; penalties.
3668. Forms; adoption by Judicial Council.

Cross References

Support order, modification or termination,
 Authority of court, see Family Code § 3651.
 Retroactive application, see Family Code § 3653.

§ 3660. Purpose of article

The purpose of this article is to permit inexpensive discovery of facts before the commencement of a proceeding for modification or termination of an order for child, family, or spousal support. *(Stats.1992, c. 162 (A.B.2650), § 10, operative Jan. 1, 1994.)*

Cross References

Affidavits, see Code of Civil Procedure § 2009 et seq.
Child support, generally, see Family Code § 3900 et seq.
Discovery, generally, see Code of Civil Procedure § 2016.010 et seq.
Expedited child support orders, see Family Code § 3620 et seq.
Health insurance coverage for supported children, see Family Code § 3750 et seq.
Judgment and order defined for purposes of this Code, see Family Code § 100.
Notaries public, duty to take depositions, see Government Code § 8205.
Proceeding defined for purposes of this Code, see Family Code § 110.
Spousal support defined for purposes of this Code, see Family Code § 142.
Support defined for purposes of this Code, see Family Code § 150.

Research References

Forms

1 California Transactions Forms--Family Law § 3:52, Simplified Method of Discovery for Purposes of Modification of Child Support or Family Support.
West's California Code Forms, Family § 3660, Comment Overview—Discovery Before Commencing Modification or Termination Proceeding.

§ 3662. Methods of discovery; restrictions

Methods of discovery other than that described in this article may only be used if a motion for modification or termination of the support order is pending. *(Stats.1992, c. 162 (A.B.2650), § 10, operative Jan. 1, 1994.)*

Cross References

Affidavits, see Code of Civil Procedure § 2009 et seq.
Discovery, generally, see Code of Civil Procedure § 2016.010 et seq.
Judgment and order defined for purposes of this Code, see Family Code § 100.
Notaries public, duty to take depositions, see Government Code § 8205.
Support defined for purposes of this Code, see Family Code § 150.
Support order defined for purposes of this Code, see Family Code § 155.

Research References

Forms

West's California Code Forms, Family § 3620, Comment Overview—Expedited Child Support Order.
West's California Code Forms, Family § 3660, Comment Overview—Discovery Before Commencing Modification or Termination Proceeding.

§ 3663. Discovery requests; restrictions

In the absence of a pending motion for modification or termination of a support order, a request for discovery pursuant to this

§ 3663

article may be undertaken not more frequently than once every 12 months. *(Stats.1992, c. 162 (A.B.2650), § 10, operative Jan. 1, 1994.)*

Cross References

Affidavits, see Code of Civil Procedure § 2009 et seq.
Discovery, generally, see Code of Civil Procedure § 2016.010 et seq.
Judgment and order defined for purposes of this Code, see Family Code § 100.
Support defined for purposes of this Code, see Family Code § 150.
Support order defined for purposes of this Code, see Family Code § 155.

Research References

Forms

West's California Code Forms, Family § 3620, Comment Overview—Expedited Child Support Order.
West's California Code Forms, Family § 3660, Comment Overview—Discovery Before Commencing Modification or Termination Proceeding.

§ 3664. Requests for current income and expense declaration; authorized forms; requests to employer for income and benefit information; service

(a) At any time following a judgment of dissolution of marriage or legal separation of the parties, or a determination of parentage, that provides for payment of support, either the party ordered to pay support or the party to whom support was ordered to be paid or that party's assignee, without leave of court, may serve a request on the other party for the production of a completed current income and expense declaration in the form adopted by the Judicial Council.

(b) If there is no response within 35 days of service of the request or if the responsive income and expense declaration is incomplete as to any wage information, including the attachment of pay stubs and income tax returns, the requesting party may serve a request on the employer of the other party for information limited to the income and benefits provided to the party in the form adopted by the Judicial Council. The employer may require the requesting party to pay the reasonable costs of copying this information for the requesting party. The date specified in the request served on the employer for the production of income and benefit information shall not be less than 15 days from the date this request is issued.

(c) The requesting party shall serve or cause to be served on the employee described in this section, or on the employee's attorney, a copy of the request served on the employer prior to the date specified in the request served on the employer for the production of income and benefit information. This copy shall be accompanied by a notice, in a typeface that is intended to call attention to its terms, that indicates all of the following:

(1) That information limited to the income and benefits provided to the employee by the employer is being sought from the employer named in the request for production.

(2) That the information may be protected by right of privacy.

(3) That, if the employee objects to the production of this information by the employer to the requesting party, the employee shall notify the court, in writing, of this objection prior to the date specified in the request served on the employer for the production of income and benefit information.

(4) That, if the requesting party does not agree, in writing, to cancel or narrow the scope of the request for the production of this information by the employer, the employee should consult an attorney regarding the employee's right to privacy and how to protect this right.

(d) The employee described in this section may, prior to the date specified in the request served on the employer for the production of income and benefit information, bring a motion pursuant to Section 1987.1 of the Code of Civil Procedure to quash or modify this request in the same manner as a subpoena duces tecum. Notice of this motion shall be given to the employer prior to the date specified in the request served on the employer for the production of income and benefit information. An employer is not required to produce information limited to the income and benefits of the employee, except upon order of the court or upon agreement of the parties, employers, and employee affected.

(e) Service of a request for production of an income and expense declaration or for income and benefit information pursuant to this section or a copy thereof shall be by certified mail, postage prepaid, return receipt requested, to the last known address of the party to be served, or by personal service.

(f) The form adopted by the Judicial Council for purposes of the request on an employer described in subdivision (b) shall state that compliance with the request is voluntary, except upon order of the court or upon agreement of the parties, employers, and employee affected. *(Stats.1992, c. 162 (A.B.2650), § 10, operative Jan. 1, 1994. Amended by Stats.1995, c. 506 (A.B.413), § 2; Stats.2019, c. 115 (A.B.1817), § 40, eff. Jan. 1, 2020.)*

Cross References

Admissibility of income and benefit information forms, see Evidence Code § 1567.
Affidavits, see Code of Civil Procedure § 2009 et seq.
Computation of time, see Code of Civil Procedure §§ 12, 12a; Government Code § 6800 et seq.
Income and expense declaration defined, see Family Code § 95.
Judgment and order defined for purposes of this Code, see Family Code § 100.
Notaries public, duty to take depositions, see Government Code § 8205.
Notice, actual and constructive, defined, see Civil Code § 18.
State defined for purposes of this Code, see Family Code § 145.
Support defined for purposes of this Code, see Family Code § 150.
Tax levies, see Government Code § 29100 et seq.; Revenue and Taxation Code § 2151 et seq.
Writings, authentication and proof of, see Evidence Code § 1400 et seq.

Research References

Forms

1 California Transactions Forms--Family Law § 3:52, Simplified Method of Discovery for Purposes of Modification of Child Support or Family Support.
West's California Code Forms, Family § 3620, Comment Overview—Expedited Child Support Order.
West's California Code Forms, Family § 3660, Comment Overview—Discovery Before Commencing Modification or Termination Proceeding.
West's California Judicial Council Forms FL–396, Request for Production of an Income and Expense Declaration After Judgment.
West's California Judicial Council Forms FL–397, Request for Income and Benefit Information from Employer.

§ 3665. Attachments to income and expense declaration; tax returns; disclosure

(a) A copy of the prior year's federal and state personal income tax returns shall be attached to the income and expense declaration of each party.

(b) A party shall not disclose the contents or provide copies of the other party's tax returns to anyone except the court, the party's attorney, the party's accountant, or other financial consultant assisting with matters relating to the proceeding, or any other person permitted by the court.

(c) The tax returns shall be controlled by the court as provided in Section 3552. *(Stats.1992, c. 162 (A.B.2650), § 10, operative Jan. 1, 1994.)*

Cross References

Affidavits, see Code of Civil Procedure § 2009 et seq.
Income and expense declaration defined, see Family Code § 95.
Notaries public, duty to take depositions, see Government Code § 8205.
Person defined for purposes of this Code, see Family Code § 105.
Proceeding defined for purposes of this Code, see Family Code § 110.
State defined for purposes of this Code, see Family Code § 145.
Tax levies, see Government Code § 29100 et seq.; Revenue and Taxation Code § 2151 et seq.

DEFINITIONS AND GENERAL PROVISIONS

Tax returns, support proceedings, see Family Code § 3552.

Research References

Forms

1 California Transactions Forms--Family Law § 3:52, Simplified Method of Discovery for Purposes of Modification of Child Support or Family Support.

West's California Code Forms, Family § 3660, Comment Overview—Discovery Before Commencing Modification or Termination Proceeding.

West's California Judicial Council Forms FL-396, Request for Production of an Income and Expense Declaration After Judgment.

§ 3666. Enforcement of article

This article may be enforced in the manner specified in Sections 1991, 1991.1, 1991.2, 1992, and 1993 of the Code of Civil Procedure and in the Civil Discovery Act (Title 4 (commencing with Section 2016.010) of Part 4 of the Code of Civil Procedure), and any other statutes applicable to the enforcement of procedures for discovery. (Stats.1992, c. 162 (A.B.2650), § 10, operative Jan. 1, 1994. Amended by Stats.2004, c. 182 (A.B.3081), § 34, operative July 1, 2005.)

Cross References

Affidavits, see Code of Civil Procedure § 2009 et seq.
Discovery, generally, see Code of Civil Procedure § 2016.010 et seq.
Notaries public, duty to take depositions, see Government Code § 8205.

§ 3667. Incomplete or inaccurate income and expense declaration; penalties

Upon the subsequent filing of a motion for modification or termination of the support order by the requesting party, if the court finds that the income and expense declaration submitted by the responding party pursuant to this article was incomplete, inaccurate, or missing the prior year's federal and state personal income tax returns, or that the declaration was not submitted in good faith, the court may order sanctions against the responding party in the form of payment of all costs of the motion, including the filing fee and the costs of the depositions and subpoenas necessary to be utilized in order to obtain complete and accurate information. This section is applicable regardless of whether a party has utilized subdivision (b) of Section 3664. (Stats.1992, c. 162 (A.B.2650), § 10, operative Jan. 1, 1994. Amended by Stats.1995, c. 506 (A.B.413), § 3.)

Cross References

Affidavits, see Code of Civil Procedure § 2009 et seq.
Income and expense declaration defined, see Family Code § 95.
Judgment and order defined for purposes of this Code, see Family Code § 100.
Notaries public, duty to take depositions, see Government Code § 8205.
State defined for purposes of this Code, see Family Code § 145.
Support defined for purposes of this Code, see Family Code § 150.
Support order defined for purposes of this Code, see Family Code § 155.
Tax levies, see Government Code § 29100 et seq.; Revenue and Taxation Code § 2151 et seq.

§ 3668. Forms; adoption by Judicial Council

The Judicial Council shall adopt forms which shall be used in the procedure provided by this article. (Stats.1992, c. 162 (A.B.2650), § 10, operative Jan. 1, 1994.)

Cross References

Affidavits, see Code of Civil Procedure § 2009 et seq.
Judicial Council, rules of practice and procedure, see Family Code § 210 et seq.

Research References

Forms

West's California Judicial Council Forms FL-396, Request for Production of an Income and Expense Declaration After Judgment.

ARTICLE 3. SIMPLIFIED PROCEDURE FOR MODIFICATION OF SUPPORT ORDER

Section
3680. Legislative findings and declaration.

§§ 3681 to 3685
Repealed

Section
3680.5. Local child support agency; monitoring; modifications.
3681 to 3685. Repealed.
3686. Repealed.
3687 to 3689. Repealed.

§ 3680. Legislative findings and declaration

(a) The Legislature finds and declares the following:

(1) There is currently no simple method available to parents to quickly modify their support orders when circumstances warrant a change in the amount of support.

(2) The lack of a simple method for parents to use to modify support orders has led to orders in which the amount of support ordered is inappropriate based on the parents' financial circumstances.

(3) Parents should not have to incur significant costs or experience significant delays in obtaining an appropriate support order.

(b) Therefore, it is the intent of the Legislature that the Judicial Council adopt rules of court and forms for a simplified method to modify support orders. This simplified method should be designed to be used by parents who are not represented by counsel. (Added by Stats.1996, c. 957 (A.B.1058), § 5.)

Cross References

Counsel, right to, see Cal. Const. Art. 1, § 15, cl. 3.
Judgment and order defined for purposes of this Code, see Family Code § 100.
Legislative intent, construction of statutes, see Code of Civil Procedure § 1859.
Support defined for purposes of this Code, see Family Code § 150.
Support order defined for purposes of this Code, see Family Code § 155.

Research References

Forms

West's California Code Forms, Family § 3680, Comment Overview—Simplified Procedure for Modification of Support Order.

West's California Code Forms, Family § 3680 Form 1, Notice of Motion and Motion for Simplified Modification of Order for Child, Spousal, or Family Support.

West's California Code Forms, Family § 3680 Form 6, Responsive Declaration to Motion for Simplified Modification of Order for Child, Spousal, or Family Support.

West's California Judicial Council Forms FL-390, Notice of Motion and Motion for Simplified Modification of Order for Child, Spousal, or Family Support.

West's California Judicial Council Forms FL-391, Information Sheet—Simplified Way to Change Child, Spousal, or Family Support.

West's California Judicial Council Forms FL-392, Responsive Declaration to Motion for Simplified Modification of Order for Child, Spousal, or Family Support.

West's California Judicial Council Forms FL-393, Information Sheet—How to Oppose a Request to Change Child, Spousal, or Family Support.

§ 3680.5. Local child support agency; monitoring; modifications

(a) The local child support agency shall monitor child support cases and seek modifications, when needed.

(b) At least once every three years, the local child support agency shall review, and, if appropriate, seek modification of, each child support case for which assistance is being provided under the CalWORKs program, pursuant to Chapter 2 (commencing with Section 11200) of Part 3 of Division 9 of the Welfare and Institutions Code. (Added by Stats.1999, c. 652 (S.B.240), § 3. Amended by Stats.2007, c. 488 (A.B.176), § 1.)

Cross References

Child support, generally, see Family Code § 3900 et seq.
Support defined for purposes of this Code, see Family Code § 150.

§§ 3681 to 3685. Repealed by Stats.1994, c. 415 (S.B.1715), § 1

§ 3686 Repealed

§ 3686. Repealed by Stats.1994, c. 415 (S.B.1715), § 1; Stats.1994, c. 1269 (A.B.2208), § 32

§§ 3687 to 3689. Repealed by Stats.1994, c. 415 (S.B.1715), § 1

ARTICLE 4. RELIEF FROM ORDERS

Section
3690. Authority to grant relief; findings; limitations operation.
3691. Grounds and time limits.
3692. Limits on set aside; inequity or changed circumstances.
3693. Set aside of materially affected provisions.
3694. Repealed.

§ 3690. Authority to grant relief; findings; limitations operation

(a) The court may, on any terms that may be just, relieve a party from a support order, or any part or parts thereof, after the six-month time limit of Section 473 of the Code of Civil Procedure has run, based on the grounds, and within the time limits, provided in this article.

(b) In all proceedings under this division, before granting relief, the court shall find that the facts alleged as the grounds for relief materially affected the original order and that the moving party would materially benefit from the granting of the relief.

(c) Nothing in this article shall limit or modify the provisions of Section 17432 or 17433.

(d) This section shall only be operative if Assembly Bill 196,[1] of the 1999–2000 Regular Session, is enacted and becomes operative. *(Added by Stats.1999, c. 653 (A.B.380), § 6.)*

[1] Stats.1999, c. 478 (A.B.196).

Cross References

Judgment and order defined for purposes of this Code, see Family Code § 100.
Proceeding defined for purposes of this Code, see Family Code § 110.
Support defined for purposes of this Code, see Family Code § 150.
Support order defined for purposes of this Code, see Family Code § 155.

Research References

Forms
California Practice Guide: Rutter Family Law Forms Form 16:2, Request for Hearing and Application to Set Aside Support Order Under Family Code Section 3691.
California Practice Guide: Rutter Family Law Forms Form 16:3, Responsive Declaration to Application to Set Aside Support Order.
California Practice Guide: Rutter Family Law Forms Form 16:4, Order After Hearing on Motion to Set Aside Support Order.
West's California Code Forms, Family § 3690, Comment Overview—Relief from Order.
West's California Judicial Council Forms FL–360, Request for Hearing and Application to Set Aside Support Order Under Family Code Section 3691.
West's California Judicial Council Forms FL–365, Responsive Declaration to Application to Set Aside Support Order.
West's California Judicial Council Forms FL–367, Order After Hearing on Motion to Set Aside Support Order.

§ 3691. Grounds and time limits

The grounds and time limits for an action or motion to set aside a support order, or part thereof, are governed by this section and shall be one of the following:

(a) Actual fraud. Where the defrauded party was kept in ignorance or in some other manner, other than through the party's own lack of care or attention, was fraudulently prevented from fully participating in the proceeding. An action or motion based on fraud shall be brought within six months after the date on which the complaining party discovered or reasonably should have discovered the fraud.

(b) Perjury. An action or motion based on perjury shall be brought within six months after the date on which the complaining party discovered or reasonably should have discovered the perjury.

(c) Lack of Notice.

(1) When service of a summons has not resulted in notice to a party in time to defend the action for support and a default or default judgment has been entered against the party in the action, the party may serve and file a notice of motion to set aside the default and for leave to defend the action. The notice of motion shall be served and filed within a reasonable time, but in no event later than six months after the party obtains or reasonably should have obtained notice (A) of the support order, or (B) that the party's income and assets are subject to attachment pursuant to the order.

(2) A notice of motion to set aside a support order pursuant to this subdivision shall be accompanied by an affidavit showing, under oath, that the party's lack of notice in time to defend the action was not caused by avoidance of service or inexcusable neglect. The party shall serve and file with the notice a copy of the answer, motion, or other pleading proposed to be filed in the action.

(3) The court may not set aside or otherwise relieve a party from a support order pursuant to this subdivision if service of the summons was accomplished in accordance with existing requirements of law regarding service of process. *(Added by Stats.1999, c. 653 (A.B.380), § 6. Amended by Stats.2019, c. 115 (A.B.1817), § 41, eff. Jan. 1, 2020.)*

Cross References

Judgment and order defined for purposes of this Code, see Family Code § 100.
Notice, actual and constructive, defined, see Civil Code § 18.
Persons upon whom summons may be served, see Code of Civil Procedure § 416.10 et seq.
Proceeding defined for purposes of this Code, see Family Code § 110.
Proof of service, see Code of Civil Procedure § 417.10 et seq.
Service of process, generally, see Code of Civil Procedure § 410.10 et seq.
Support defined for purposes of this Code, see Family Code § 150.
Support order defined for purposes of this Code, see Family Code § 155.

Research References

Forms
California Practice Guide: Rutter Family Law Forms Form 16:2, Request for Hearing and Application to Set Aside Support Order Under Family Code Section 3691.
West's California Code Forms, Family § 3690, Comment Overview—Relief from Order.

§ 3692. Limits on set aside; inequity or changed circumstances

Notwithstanding any other provision of this article, or any other law, a support order may not be set aside simply because the court finds that it was inequitable when made, nor simply because subsequent circumstances caused the support ordered to become excessive or inadequate. *(Added by Stats.1999, c. 653 (A.B.380), § 6.)*

Cross References

Judgment and order defined for purposes of this Code, see Family Code § 100.
Support defined for purposes of this Code, see Family Code § 150.
Support order defined for purposes of this Code, see Family Code § 155.

§ 3693. Set aside of materially affected provisions

When ruling on an action or motion to set aside a support order, the court shall set aside only those provisions materially affected by the circumstances leading to the court's decision to grant relief. However, the court has discretion to set aside the entire order, if necessary, for equitable considerations. *(Added by Stats.1999, c. 653 (A.B.380), § 6.)*

Cross References

Judgment and order defined for purposes of this Code, see Family Code § 100.

Support defined for purposes of this Code, see Family Code § 150.
Support order defined for purposes of this Code, see Family Code § 155.

Research References

Forms

West's California Judicial Council Forms FL–360, Request for Hearing and Application to Set Aside Support Order Under Family Code Section 3691.

West's California Judicial Council Forms FL–365, Responsive Declaration to Application to Set Aside Support Order.

West's California Judicial Council Forms FL–367, Order After Hearing on Motion to Set Aside Support Order.

§ 3694. Repealed by Stats.1994, c. 415 (S.B.1715), § 1

CHAPTER 7. HEALTH INSURANCE

Article	Section
1. Health Insurance Coverage for Supported Child	3750
2. Health Insurance Coverage Assignment	3760
3. Assignment of Reimbursement Rights Under Health Plan [Repealed]	

Cross References

Classes of insurance, life and disability insurance, small employer health insurance, purchasing pool for small employers, persons or entities subject to chapter, compliance with specified standards, see Insurance Code § 10731.2.

Grandfathered small employer carrier requirements, life and disability insurance, compliance with standards in this Chapter, see Insurance Code § 10755.02.1.

Grandfathered small employer healthcare service plans, requirements for offering coverage to eligible employees or dependents not working or residing in approved service area, see Health and Safety Code § 1357.610.

Health care benefits, coverage of children, see Labor Code § 2803.5.

Health care service plans, standards, compliance with specified requirements, see Health and Safety Code § 1374.3.

Nongrandfathered small employer carrier requirements, life and disability insurance, compliance with standards in this Chapter, see Insurance Code § 10753.02.1.

Small employer health insurance,
Persons or entities subject to chapter, see Insurance Code § 10702.1.
Purchasing pool for small employers, compliance with specified standards, see Insurance Code § 10731.2.
Voluntary reinsurance mechanism, compliance with specified standards, see Insurance Code § 10719.1.

Specified plans and policies, coverage of newborn infants or adopted minors, see Insurance Code § 10119.

ARTICLE 1. HEALTH INSURANCE COVERAGE FOR SUPPORTED CHILD

Section
3750. Health insurance coverage.
3751. Maintenance of health insurance coverage; cost of insurance; application by parents for coverage; continuation of coverage for supported child upon attainment of limiting age for dependent child.
3751.5. Denial of enrollment; prohibited grounds; court or administrative order requiring parent to provide coverage; duties of employers or insurers.
3752. Notice to the local child support agency designated as assigned payee for child support; policy information to be provided to custodial parent.
3752.5. Notice of availability of coverage; continuation of health insurance coverage upon child or adult attaining limiting age; modification of form of order by Judicial Council.
3753. Health insurance cost; separation from child support.

§ 3750. Health insurance coverage

"Health insurance coverage" as used in this article includes all of the following:

(a) Vision care and dental care coverage whether the vision care or dental care coverage is part of existing health insurance coverage or is issued as a separate policy or plan.

(b) Provision for the delivery of health care services by a fee for service, health maintenance organization, preferred provider organization, or any other type of health care delivery system under which medical services could be provided to a dependent child of an absent parent. (Stats.1992, c. 162 (A.B.2650), § 10, operative Jan. 1, 1994. Amended by Stats.1994, c. 147 (A.B.2377), § 1, eff. July 11, 1994; Stats.1996, c. 1062 (A.B.1832), § 1.)

Cross References

Dissolution, nullity, or legal separation proceedings, notice to insurance carriers, see Family Code § 2050 et seq.

Health insurance coverage, consideration in determining child support, see Family Code § 4006.

Health insurance coverage, enrollment of supported child in plan available to obligor through employer, see Family Code § 3761.

§ 3751. Maintenance of health insurance coverage; cost of insurance; application by parents for coverage; continuation of coverage for supported child upon attainment of limiting age for dependent child

(a)(1) Support orders issued or modified pursuant to this chapter shall include a provision requiring the child support obligor to keep the agency designated under Title IV–D of the Social Security Act (42 U.S.C. Sec. 651 et seq.) informed of whether the obligor has health insurance coverage at a reasonable cost and, if so, the health insurance policy information.

(2) When an amount is set for current support, the court shall require that health insurance coverage for a supported child shall be maintained by either or both parents if that insurance is available at no cost or at a reasonable cost to the parent. Health insurance coverage shall be rebuttably presumed to be reasonable in cost if the cost to the responsible parent providing medical support does not exceed 5 percent of the parent's gross income. In applying the 5 percent for the cost of health insurance, the cost is the difference between self-only and family coverage. If the obligor is entitled to a low-income adjustment as provided in paragraph (7) of subdivision (b) of Section 4055, medical support shall be deemed not reasonable, unless the court determines that not requiring medical support would be unjust and inappropriate in the particular case. If the court determines that the cost of health insurance coverage is not reasonable, the court shall state its reasons on the record. If the court determines that, although the obligor is entitled to a low-income adjustment, not requiring medical support would be unjust and inappropriate, the court shall state its reasons on the record.

(b) If the court determines that health insurance coverage is not available at no cost or at a reasonable cost, the court's order for support shall contain a provision that specifies that health insurance coverage shall be obtained if it becomes available at no cost or at a reasonable cost. Upon health insurance coverage at no cost or at a reasonable cost becoming available to a parent, the parent shall apply for that coverage.

(c) The court's order for support shall require the parent who, at the time of the order or subsequently, provides health insurance coverage for a supported child to seek continuation of coverage for the child upon attainment of the limiting age for a dependent child under the health insurance coverage if the child meets the criteria specified under Section 1373 of the Health and Safety Code or Section 10277 or 10278 of the Insurance Code and that health insurance coverage is available at no cost or at a reasonable cost to the parent or parents, as applicable. (Stats.1992, c. 162 (A.B.2650), § 10, operative Jan. 1, 1994. Amended by Stats.1993, c. 876 (S.B.

§ 3751

1068), § 16, eff. Oct. 6, 1993, operative Jan. 1, 1994; Stats.1994, c. 1269 (A.B.2208), § 33; Stats.2007, c. 617 (A.B.910), § 1; Stats.2010, c. 103 (S.B.580), § 1; Stats.2019, c. 115 (A.B.1817), § 42, eff. Jan. 1, 2020.)

Cross References

Child support, generally, see Family Code § 3900 et seq.
Dissolution, nullity, or legal separation proceedings, notice to insurance carriers, see Family Code § 2050 et seq.
Health insurance coverage, consideration in determining child support, see Family Code § 4006.
Judgment and order defined for purposes of this Code, see Family Code § 100.
State defined for purposes of this Code, see Family Code § 145.
Support defined for purposes of this Code, see Family Code § 150.
Support order defined for purposes of this Code, see Family Code § 155.

Research References

Forms

California Practice Guide: Rutter Family Law Forms Form 5:1, Stipulation to Orders Pending Trial (Attorney-Drafted).
California Practice Guide: Rutter Family Law Forms Form 5:2, Request for Order Re Child Custody, Child Support, Spousal Support, Attorney Fees, etc.
California Practice Guide: Rutter Family Law Forms Form 6:2, Stipulation Re Child Support and Order Thereon (Attorney-Drafted).
California Practice Guide: Rutter Family Law Forms Form 11:20, Sample Trial Brief.
West's California Judicial Council Forms FL–684, Request for Order and Supporting Declaration (Governmental).

§ 3751.5. Denial of enrollment; prohibited grounds; court or administrative order requiring parent to provide coverage; duties of employers or insurers

(a) Notwithstanding any other provision of law, an employer or insurer shall not deny enrollment of a child under the health insurance coverage of a child's parent on any of the following grounds:

(1) The child was born out of wedlock.

(2) The child is not claimed as a dependent on the parent's federal income tax return.

(3) The child does not reside with the parent or within the insurer's service area.

(b) Notwithstanding any other provision of law, in any case in which a parent is required by a court or administrative order to provide health insurance coverage for a child and the parent is eligible for family health coverage through an employer or an insurer, the employer or insurer shall do all of the following, as applicable:

(1) Permit the parent to enroll under health insurance coverage any child who is otherwise eligible to enroll for that coverage, without regard to any enrollment period restrictions.

(2) If the parent is enrolled in health insurance coverage but fails to apply to obtain coverage of the child, enroll that child under the health coverage upon presentation of the court order or request by the local child support agency, the other parent or person having custody of the child, or the Medi–Cal program.

(3) The employer or insurer shall not disenroll or eliminate coverage of a child unless either of the following applies:

(A) The employer has eliminated family health insurance coverage for all of the employer's employees.

(B) The employer or insurer is provided with satisfactory written evidence that either of the following apply:

(i) The court order or administrative order is no longer in effect or is terminated pursuant to Section 3770.

(ii) The child is or will be enrolled in comparable health insurance coverage through another insurer that will take effect not later than the effective date of the child's disenrollment.

(c) In any case in which health insurance coverage is provided for a child pursuant to a court or administrative order, the insurer shall do all of the following:

(1) Provide any information, including, but not limited to, the health insurance membership or identification card regarding the child, the evidence of coverage and disclosure form, and any other information provided to the covered parent about the child's health care coverage to the noncovered parent having custody of the child or any other person having custody of the child and to the local child support agency when requested by the local child support agency.

(2) Permit the noncovered parent or person having custody of the child, or a provider with the approval of the noncovered parent or person having custody, to submit claims for covered services without the approval of the covered parent.

(3) Make payment on claims submitted in accordance with subparagraph (2) directly to the noncovered parent or person having custody, the provider, or to the Medi–Cal program. Payment on claims for services provided to the child shall be made to the covered parent for claims submitted or paid by the covered parent.

(d) For purposes of this section, "insurer" includes every health care service plan, self-insured welfare benefit plan, including those regulated pursuant to the Employee Retirement Income Security Act of 1974 (29 U.S.C. Sec. 1001, et seq.), self-funded employer plan, disability insurer, nonprofit hospital service plan, labor union trust fund, employer, and any other similar plan, insurer, or entity offering a health coverage plan.

(e) For purposes of this section, "person having custody of the child" is defined as a legal guardian, a caregiver who is authorized to enroll the child in school or to authorize medical care for the child pursuant to Section 6550, or a person with whom the child resides.

(f) For purposes of this section, "employer" has the meaning provided in Section 5210.

(g) For purposes of this section, the insurer shall notify the covered parent and noncovered parent having custody of the child or any other person having custody of the child in writing at any time that health insurance for the child is terminated.

(h) The requirements of subdivision (g) shall not apply unless the court, employer, or person having custody of the child provides the insurer with one of the following:

(1) A qualified medical child support order that meets the requirements of subdivision (a) of Section 1169 of Title 29 of the United States Code.

(2) A health insurance coverage assignment or assignment order made pursuant to Section 3761.

(3) A national medical support notice made pursuant to Section 3773.

(i) The noncovered parent or person having custody of the child may contact the insurer, by telephone or in writing, and request information about the health insurance coverage for the child. Upon request of the noncovered parent or person having custody of the child, the insurer shall provide the requested information that is specific to the health insurance coverage for the child. (Added by Stats.1996, c. 1062 (A.B.1832), § 2. Amended by Stats.1997, c. 599 (A.B.573), § 7; Stats.2000, c. 808 (A.B.1358), § 28, eff. Sept. 28, 2000; Stats.2000, c. 809 (A.B.2130), § 1; Stats.2001, c. 755 (S.B.943), § 2, eff. Oct. 12, 2001.)

Cross References

Administrative Procedure Act, see Government Code §§ 11340 et seq., 11370 et seq., 11400 et seq., 11500 et seq.
Administrative proceedings, judicial review, see Government Code § 11523.
Child custody, see Family Code § 3020 et seq.
Child support, generally, see Family Code § 3900 et seq.
Disability insurance, dependent child coverage, children not residing with employee, insured or policyholder, see Insurance Code § 10121.6.

DEFINITIONS AND GENERAL PROVISIONS

Expedited child support orders, see Family Code § 3620 et seq.
Health care service plans, preexisting condition provisions and late enrollees, see Health and Safety Code § 1357.50.
Judgment and order defined for purposes of this Code, see Family Code § 100.
Modification, termination, or setting aside of support order, see Family Code § 3650 et seq.
Notice, actual and constructive, defined, see Civil Code § 18.
Person defined for purposes of this Code, see Family Code § 105.
State defined for purposes of this Code, see Family Code § 145.
Support defined for purposes of this Code, see Family Code § 150.
Support order defined for purposes of this Code, see Family Code § 155.
Tax levies, see Government Code § 29100 et seq.; Revenue and Taxation Code § 2151 et seq.
Writings, authentication and proof of, see Evidence Code § 1400 et seq.

§ 3752. Notice to the local child support agency designated as assigned payee for child support; policy information to be provided to custodial parent

(a) If the local child support agency has been designated as the assigned payee for child support, the court shall order the parent to notify the local child support agency upon applying for and obtaining health insurance coverage for the child within a reasonable period of time.

(b) The local child support agency shall obtain a completed medical form from the parent in accordance with Section 17422 and shall forward the completed form to the State Department of Health Services.

(c) In those cases where the local child support agency is providing medical support enforcement services, the local child support agency shall provide the parent or person having custody of the child with information pertaining to the health insurance policy that has been secured for the child. *(Stats.1992, c. 162 (A.B.2650), § 10, operative Jan. 1, 1994. Amended by Stats.2000, c. 808 (A.B.1358), § 30, eff. Sept. 28, 2000.)*

Cross References

Child custody, see Family Code § 3020 et seq.
Child support, generally, see Family Code § 3900 et seq.
Department of Health Care Services, generally, see Health and Safety Code § 100100 et seq.
Dissolution, nullity, or legal separation proceedings, notice to insurance carriers, see Family Code § 2050 et seq.
Expedited child support orders, see Family Code § 3620 et seq.
Health insurance coverage, consideration in determining child support, see Family Code § 4006.
Judgment and order defined for purposes of this Code, see Family Code § 100.
Modification, termination, or setting aside of support order, see Family Code § 3650 et seq.
Person defined for purposes of this Code, see Family Code § 105.
State defined for purposes of this Code, see Family Code § 145.
Support defined for purposes of this Code, see Family Code § 150.

§ 3752.5. Notice of availability of coverage; continuation of health insurance coverage upon child or adult attaining limiting age; modification of form of order by Judicial Council

(a) A child support order issued or modified pursuant to this division shall include a provision requiring the child support obligor to keep the obligee informed of whether the obligor has health insurance made available through the obligor's employer or has other group health insurance and, if so, the health insurance policy information. The support obligee under a child support order shall inform the support obligor of whether the obligee has health insurance made available through the employer or other group health insurance and, if so, the health insurance policy information.

(b) A child support order issued or modified pursuant to this division shall include a provision requiring the child support obligor and obligee to provide the information described in subdivision (a) for a child or an adult who meets the criteria for continuation of health insurance coverage upon attaining the limiting age pursuant to Section 1373 of the Health and Safety Code or Section 10277 or 10278 of the Insurance Code.

(c) The Judicial Council shall modify the form of the order for health insurance coverage (family law) to notify child support obligors of the requirements of this section and of Section 3752. Notwithstanding any other provision of law, the Judicial Council shall not be required to modify the form of the order for health insurance coverage (family law) to include the provisions described in subdivision (b) until January 1, 2010. *(Added by Stats.1993, c. 876 (S.B.1068), § 17, eff. Oct. 6, 1993, operative Jan. 1, 1994. Amended by Stats.2007, c. 617 (A.B.910), § 2.)*

Cross References

Child support, generally, see Family Code § 3900 et seq.
Expedited child support orders, see Family Code § 3620 et seq.
Judgment and order defined for purposes of this Code, see Family Code § 100.
Modification, termination, or setting aside of support order, see Family Code § 3650 et seq.
Support defined for purposes of this Code, see Family Code § 150.
Support order defined for purposes of this Code, see Family Code § 155.

Research References

Forms

California Practice Guide: Rutter Family Law Forms Form 5:1, Stipulation to Orders Pending Trial (Attorney-Drafted).
California Practice Guide: Rutter Family Law Forms Form 6:2, Stipulation Re Child Support and Order Thereon (Attorney-Drafted).
California Practice Guide: Rutter Family Law Forms Form 11:20, Sample Trial Brief.

§ 3753. Health insurance cost; separation from child support

The cost of the health insurance shall be in addition to the child support amount ordered under Article 2 (commencing with Section 4050), with allowance for the costs of health insurance actually obtained given due consideration under subdivision (d) of Section 4059. *(Added by Stats.1994, c. 1269 (A.B.2208), § 36.)*

Cross References

Child support, generally, see Family Code § 3900 et seq.
Expedited child support orders, see Family Code § 3620 et seq.
Modification, termination, or setting aside of support order, see Family Code § 3650 et seq.
Support defined for purposes of this Code, see Family Code § 150.

ARTICLE 2. HEALTH INSURANCE COVERAGE ASSIGNMENT

Section
3760. Definitions.
3761. Application for health insurance coverage assignment; assignment order.
3762. Denial of health insurance coverage assignment order; findings of court.
3763. Time for order of health insurance coverage assignment order; modification.
3764. Effective date of assignment; copy of order and information to obligor; service of assignment order.
3765. Motion to quash assignment; grounds.
3766. Commencement of coverage; selection of plan.
3767. Duties of employer or health insurance provider.
3768. Failure to comply with a valid assignment order; liability.
3769. Discrimination prohibited; violation; penalty.
3770. Termination of assignment order; grounds.
3771. Information provided to the local child support agency.
3772. Forms; adoption by Judicial Council.
3773. Title IV–D cases where support enforcement services are provided by local child support agency.

SUPPORT

Cross References

Child support enforcement, generally, see Family Code § 17400 et seq.
Health insurance coverage, medical insurance form, see Family Code § 17422.
Medical insurance form, submission to local child support agency, see Family Code § 17424.

§ 3760. Definitions

As used in this article, unless the provision or context otherwise requires:

(a) "Employer" includes the United States government and any public entity as defined in Section 811.2 of the Government Code.

(b) "Health insurance," "health insurance plan," "health insurance coverage," "health care services," or "health insurance coverage assignment" includes vision care and dental care coverage whether the vision care or dental care coverage is part of existing health insurance coverage or is issued as a separate policy or plan.

(c) "Health insurance coverage assignment" or "assignment order" means an order made under Section 3761.

(d) "National medical support notice" means the notice required by Section 666(a)(19) of Title 42 of the United States Code with respect to an order made pursuant to Section 3773. *(Stats.1992, c. 162 (A.B.2650), § 10, operative Jan. 1, 1994. Amended by Stats.2000, c. 119 (S.B.2045), § 1.)*

Cross References

Judgment and order defined for purposes of this Code, see Family Code § 100.
Notice, actual and constructive, defined, see Civil Code § 18.
State defined for purposes of this Code, see Family Code § 145.
Support defined for purposes of this Code, see Family Code § 150.

Research References

Forms

14B Am. Jur. Pl. & Pr. Forms Insurance § 180, Statutory References.
West's California Judicial Council Forms FL–470, Application and Order for Health Insurance Coverage.

§ 3761. Application for health insurance coverage assignment; assignment order

(a) Upon application by a party or local child support agency in any proceeding where the court has ordered either or both parents to maintain health insurance coverage under Article 1 (commencing with Section 3750), the court shall order the employer of the obligor parent or other person providing health insurance to the obligor to enroll the supported child in the health insurance plan available to the obligor through the employer or other person and to deduct the appropriate premium or costs, if any, from the earnings of the obligor unless the court makes a finding of good cause for not making the order.

(b)(1) The application shall state that the party or local child support agency seeking the assignment order has given the obligor a written notice of the intent to seek a health insurance coverage assignment order in the event of a default in instituting coverage required by court order on behalf of the parties' child and that the notice was transmitted by first-class mail, postage prepaid, or personally served at least 15 days before the date of the filing of the application for the order. The written notice of the intent to seek an assignment order required by this subdivision may be given at the time of filing a petition or complaint for support or at any later time, but shall be given at least 15 days before the date of filing the application under this section. The obligor may at any time waive the written notice required by this subdivision.

(2) The party or local child support agency seeking the assignment order shall file a certificate of service showing the method and date of service of the order and the statements required under Section 3772 upon the employer or provider of health insurance.

(c) The total amount that may be withheld from earnings for all obligations, including health insurance assignments, is limited by subdivision (a) of Section 706.052 of the Code of Civil Procedure or Section 1673 of Title 15 of the United States Code, whichever is less. *(Stats.1992, c. 162 (A.B.2650), § 10, operative Jan. 1, 1994. Amended by Stats.1993, c. 219 (A.B.1500), § 127; Stats.1994, c. 1269 (A.B. 2208), § 37; Stats.2000, c. 808 (A.B.1358), § 31, eff. Sept. 28, 2000.)*

Cross References

Child support, generally, see Family Code § 3900 et seq.
Child support enforcement, generally, see Family Code § 17400 et seq.
Computation of time, see Code of Civil Procedure §§ 12, 12a; Government Code § 6800 et seq.
Dissolution, nullity, or legal separation proceedings, notice to insurance carriers, see Family Code § 2050 et seq.
Earnings defined, see Family Code § 5206.
Expedited child support orders, see Family Code § 3620 et seq.
Health insurance coverage, medical insurance form, see Family Code § 17422.
Judgment and order defined for purposes of this Code, see Family Code § 100.
Medical insurance form, submission to local child support agency, see Family Code § 17424.
Modification, termination, or setting aside of support order, see Family Code § 3650 et seq.
Notice, actual and constructive, defined, see Civil Code § 18.
Person defined for purposes of this Code, see Family Code § 105.
Proceeding defined for purposes of this Code, see Family Code § 110.
State defined for purposes of this Code, see Family Code § 145.
Support defined for purposes of this Code, see Family Code § 150.

Research References

Forms

West's California Code Forms, Family § 3760, Comment Overview—Health Insurance Coverage Assignment.
West's California Judicial Council Forms FL–478, Request and Notice of Hearing Regarding Health Insurance Assignment.
West's California Judicial Council Forms FL–478–INFO, Information Sheet and Instructions for Request and Notice of Hearing Regarding Health Insurance Assignment.
West's California Judicial Council Forms FL–650, Statement for Registration of California Support Order (Governmental).
West's California Judicial Council Forms FL–684, Request for Order and Supporting Declaration (Governmental).

§ 3762. Denial of health insurance coverage assignment order; findings of court

Good cause for not making a health insurance coverage assignment order shall be limited to either of the following:

(a) The court finds that one of the conditions listed in subdivision (a) of Section 3765 or in Section 3770 exists.

(b) The court finds that the health insurance coverage assignment order would cause extraordinary hardship to the obligor. The court shall specify the nature of the extraordinary hardship and, whenever possible, a date by which the obligor shall obtain health insurance coverage or be subject to a health insurance coverage assignment. *(Stats.1992, c. 162 (A.B.2650), § 10, operative Jan. 1, 1994. Amended by Stats.1994, c. 1269 (A.B.2208), § 38.)*

Cross References

Child support enforcement, generally, see Family Code § 17400 et seq.
Health insurance coverage, medical insurance form, see Family Code § 17422.
Judgment and order defined for purposes of this Code, see Family Code § 100.
Medical insurance form, submission to local child support agency, see Family Code § 17424.

Research References

Forms

West's California Code Forms, Family § 3760, Comment Overview—Health Insurance Coverage Assignment.

§ 3763. Time for order of health insurance coverage assignment order; modification

(a) The health insurance coverage assignment order may be ordered at the time of trial or entry of a judgment ordering health insurance coverage. The order operates as an assignment and is binding on any existing or future employer of the obligor parent, or other person providing health insurance to the obligor, upon whom a copy of the order has been served.

(b) The order of assignment may be modified at any time by the court. *(Stats.1992, c. 162 (A.B.2650), § 10, operative Jan. 1, 1994. Amended by Stats.1994, c. 1269 (A.B.2208), § 39.)*

Cross References

Child support enforcement, generally, see Family Code § 17400 et seq.
Dissolution, nullity, or legal separation proceedings, notice to insurance carriers, see Family Code § 2050 et seq.
Health insurance coverage, medical insurance form, see Family Code § 17422.
Judgment and order defined for purposes of this Code, see Family Code § 100.
Medical insurance form, submission to local child support agency, see Family Code § 17424.
Person defined for purposes of this Code, see Family Code § 105.

§ 3764. Effective date of assignment; copy of order and information to obligor; service of assignment order

(a) A health insurance coverage assignment order does not become effective until 20 days after service by the applicant of the assignment order on the employer.

(b) Within 10 days after service of the order, the employer or other person providing health insurance to the obligor shall deliver a copy of the order to the obligor, together with a written statement of the obligor's rights and the relevant procedures under the law to move to quash the order.

(c) Service of a health insurance coverage assignment order on any employer or other person providing health insurance may be made by first class mail in the manner prescribed in Section 1013 of the Code of Civil Procedure. *(Stats.1992, c. 162 (A.B.2650), § 10, operative Jan. 1, 1994. Amended by Stats.1994, c. 1269 (A.B.2208), § 40.)*

Cross References

Child support enforcement, generally, see Family Code § 17400 et seq.
Computation of time, see Code of Civil Procedure §§ 12, 12a; Government Code § 6800 et seq.
Dissolution, nullity, or legal separation proceedings, notice to insurance carriers, see Family Code § 2050 et seq.
Health insurance coverage, medical insurance form, see Family Code § 17422.
Judgment and order defined for purposes of this Code, see Family Code § 100.
Medical insurance form, submission to local child support agency, see Family Code § 17424.
Person defined for purposes of this Code, see Family Code § 105.

§ 3765. Motion to quash assignment; grounds

(a) The obligor may move to quash a health insurance coverage assignment order as provided in this section if the obligor declares under penalty of perjury that there is error on any of the following grounds:

(1) No order to maintain health insurance has been issued under Article 1 (commencing with Section 3750).

(2) The amount to be withheld for premiums is greater than that permissible under Article 1 (commencing with Section 3750) or greater than the amount otherwise ordered by the court.

(3) The amount of the increased premium is unreasonable.

(4) The alleged obligor is not the obligor from whom health insurance coverage is due.

(5) The child is or will be otherwise provided health care coverage.

(6) The employer's choice of coverage is inappropriate.

(b) The motion and notice of motion to quash the assignment order, including the declaration required by subdivision (a), shall be filed with the court issuing the assignment order within 15 days after delivery of a copy of the order to the obligor pursuant to subdivision (b) of Section 3764. The court clerk shall set the motion for hearing not less than 15 days, nor more than 30 days, after receipt of the notice of motion. The clerk shall, within five days after receipt of the notice of motion, deliver a copy of the notice of motion to (1) the district attorney personally or by first-class mail, and (2) the applicant and the employer or other person providing health insurance, at the appropriate addresses contained in the application, by first-class mail.

(c) Upon a finding of error described in subdivision (a), the court shall quash the assignment. *(Stats.1992, c. 162 (A.B.2650), § 10, operative Jan. 1, 1994. Amended by Stats.1994, c. 1269 (A.B.2208), § 41.)*

Cross References

Child support enforcement, generally, see Family Code § 17400 et seq.
Computation of time, see Code of Civil Procedure §§ 12, 12a; Government Code § 6800 et seq.
District attorney, powers and duties, see Government Code § 26500 et seq.
Health insurance coverage, medical insurance form, see Family Code § 17422.
Judgment and order defined for purposes of this Code, see Family Code § 100.
Medical insurance form, submission to local child support agency, see Family Code § 17424.
Notice, actual and constructive, defined, see Civil Code § 18.
Person defined for purposes of this Code, see Family Code § 105.

Research References

Forms

West's California Judicial Council Forms FL–478, Request and Notice of Hearing Regarding Health Insurance Assignment.
West's California Judicial Council Forms FL–478–INFO, Information Sheet and Instructions for Request and Notice of Hearing Regarding Health Insurance Assignment.

§ 3766. Commencement of coverage; selection of plan

(a) The employer, or other person providing health insurance, shall take steps to commence coverage, consistent with the order for the health insurance coverage assignment, within 30 days after service of the assignment order upon the obligor under Section 3764 unless the employer or other person providing health insurance coverage receives an order issued pursuant to Section 3765 to quash the health insurance coverage assignment. The employer, or the person providing health insurance, shall commence coverage at the earliest possible time and, if applicable, consistent with the group plan enrollment rules.

(b) If the obligor has made a selection of health coverage prior to the issuance of the court order, the selection shall not be superseded unless the child to be enrolled in the plan will not be provided benefits or coverage where the child resides or the court order specifically directs other health coverage.

(c) If the obligor has not enrolled in an available health plan, there is a choice of coverage, and the court has not ordered coverage by a specific plan, the employer or other person providing health insurance shall enroll the child in the plan that will provide reasonable benefits or coverage where the child resides. If that coverage is not available, the employer or other person providing health insurance shall, within 20 days, return the assignment order to the attorney or person initiating the assignment.

(d) If an assignment order is served on an employer or other person providing health insurance and no coverage is available for the supported child, the employer or other person shall, within 20 days, return the assignment to the attorney or person initiating the assignment. *(Stats.1992, c. 162 (A.B.2650), § 10, operative Jan. 1, 1994. Amended by Stats.1994, c. 1269 (A.B.2208), § 42; Stats.2002, c. 927 (A.B.3032), § 2.)*

Cross References

Child support enforcement, generally, see Family Code § 17400 et seq.
Computation of time, see Code of Civil Procedure §§ 12, 12a; Government Code § 6800 et seq.
Dissolution, nullity, or legal separation proceedings, notice to insurance carriers, see Family Code § 2050 et seq.

§ 3766

Health insurance coverage, medical insurance form, see Family Code § 17422.
Judgment and order defined for purposes of this Code, see Family Code § 100.
Medical insurance form, submission to local child support agency, see Family Code § 17424.
Person defined for purposes of this Code, see Family Code § 105.

§ 3767. Duties of employer or health insurance provider

The employer or other person providing health insurance shall do all of the following:

(a) Notify the applicant for the assignment order or notice of assignment of the commencement date of the coverage of the child.

(b) Provide evidence of coverage and any information necessary for the child to obtain benefits through the coverage to both parents or the person having custody of the child and to the local child support agency when requested by the local child support agency.

(c) Upon request by the parents or person having custody of the child, provide all forms and other documentation necessary for the purpose of submitting claims to the insurance carrier which the employer or other person providing health insurance usually provides to insureds. *(Stats.1992, c. 162 (A.B.2650), § 10, operative Jan. 1, 1994. Amended by Stats.1996, c. 1062 (A.B.1832), § 3; Stats.1997, c. 599 (A.B.573), § 8; Stats.2001, c. 755 (S.B.943), § 3, eff. Oct. 12, 2001.)*

Cross References

Child custody, see Family Code § 3020 et seq.
Child support, generally, see Family Code § 3900 et seq.
Child support enforcement, generally, see Family Code § 17400 et seq.
Health insurance coverage, medical insurance form, see Family Code § 17422.
Judgment and order defined for purposes of this Code, see Family Code § 100.
Medical insurance form, submission to local child support agency, see Family Code § 17424.
Notice, actual and constructive, defined, see Civil Code § 18.
Person defined for purposes of this Code, see Family Code § 105.
Support defined for purposes of this Code, see Family Code § 150.

§ 3768. Failure to comply with a valid assignment order; liability

(a) An employer or other person providing health insurance who willfully fails to comply with a valid health insurance coverage assignment order entered and served on the employer or other person pursuant to this article is liable to the applicant for the amount incurred in health care services that would otherwise have been covered under the insurance policy but for the conduct of the employer or other person that was contrary to the assignment order.

(b) Willful failure of an employer or other person providing health insurance to comply with a health insurance coverage assignment order is punishable as contempt of court under Section 1218 of the Code of Civil Procedure. *(Stats.1992, c. 162 (A.B.2650), § 10, operative Jan. 1, 1994. Amended by Stats.1994, c. 1269 (A.B.2208), § 43.)*

Cross References

Child support enforcement, generally, see Family Code § 17400 et seq.
Dissolution, nullity, or legal separation proceedings, notice to insurance carriers, see Family Code § 2050 et seq.
Health insurance coverage, medical insurance form, see Family Code § 17422.
Judgment and order defined for purposes of this Code, see Family Code § 100.
Medical insurance form, submission to local child support agency, see Family Code § 17424.
Person defined for purposes of this Code, see Family Code § 105.

§ 3769. Discrimination prohibited; violation; penalty

No employer shall use a health insurance coverage assignment order as grounds for refusing to hire a person or for discharging or taking disciplinary action against an employee. An employer who violates this section may be assessed a civil penalty of a maximum of five hundred dollars ($500). *(Stats.1992, c. 162 (A.B.2650), § 10, operative Jan. 1, 1994. Amended by Stats.1994, c. 1269 (A.B.2208), § 44.)*

Cross References

Child support enforcement, generally, see Family Code § 17400 et seq.
Health insurance coverage, medical insurance form, see Family Code § 17422.
Judgment and order defined for purposes of this Code, see Family Code § 100.
Medical insurance form, submission to local child support agency, see Family Code § 17424.
Person defined for purposes of this Code, see Family Code § 105.

§ 3770. Termination of assignment order; grounds

Upon notice of motion by the obligor, the court shall terminate a health insurance coverage assignment order if any of the following conditions exist:

(a) A new order has been issued under Article 1 (commencing with Section 3750) that is inconsistent with the existing assignment.

(b) The employer or other person providing health insurance has discontinued that coverage to the obligor.

(c) The court determines that there is good cause, consistent with Section 3762, to terminate the assignment.

(d) The death or emancipation of the child for whom the health insurance has been obtained. *(Stats.1992, c. 162 (A.B.2650), § 10, operative Jan. 1, 1994. Amended by Stats.1994, c. 1269 (A.B.2208), § 45.)*

Cross References

Child support enforcement, generally, see Family Code § 17400 et seq.
Health insurance coverage, medical insurance form, see Family Code § 17422.
Judgment and order defined for purposes of this Code, see Family Code § 100.
Medical insurance form, submission to local child support agency, see Family Code § 17424.
Notice, actual and constructive, defined, see Civil Code § 18.
Person defined for purposes of this Code, see Family Code § 105.

§ 3771. Information provided to the local child support agency

Upon request of the local child support agency the employer shall provide the following information to the local child support agency within 30 days:

(a) The social security number of the absent parent.

(b) The home address of the absent parent.

(c) Whether the absent parent has a health insurance policy and, if so, the policy names and numbers, and the names of the persons covered.

(d) Whether the health insurance policy provides coverage for dependent children of the absent parent who do not reside in the absent parent's home.

(e) If there is a subsequent lapse in health insurance coverage, the employer shall notify the local child support agency, giving the date the coverage ended, the reason for the lapse in coverage and, if the lapse is temporary, the date upon which coverage is expected to resume. *(Stats.1992, c. 162 (A.B.2650), § 10, operative Jan. 1, 1994. Amended by Stats.2000, c. 808 (A.B.1358), § 32, eff. Sept. 28, 2000.)*

Cross References

Child support, generally, see Family Code § 3900 et seq.
Child support enforcement, generally, see Family Code § 17400 et seq.
Computation of time, see Code of Civil Procedure §§ 12, 12a; Government Code § 6800 et seq.
Health insurance coverage, medical insurance form, see Family Code § 17422.
Medical insurance form, submission to local child support agency, see Family Code § 17424.
Person defined for purposes of this Code, see Family Code § 105.
Support defined for purposes of this Code, see Family Code § 150.

Research References

Forms

West's California Code Forms, Family § 3760, Comment Overview—Health Insurance Coverage Assignment.

West's California Judicial Council Forms FL-475, Employer's Health Insurance Return.

§ 3772. Forms; adoption by Judicial Council

The Judicial Council shall adopt forms for the health insurance coverage assignment required or authorized by this article, including, but not limited to, the application, the order, the statement of the obligor's rights, and an employer's return form which shall include information on the limitations on the total amount that may be withheld from earnings for obligations, including health insurance assignments, under subdivision (a) of Section 706.052 of the Code of Civil Procedure and Section 1673 of Title 15 of the United States Code, and the information required by Section 3771. The parties and child shall be sufficiently identified on the forms by the inclusion of birth dates, social security numbers, and any other information the Judicial Council determines is necessary. *(Stats.1992, c. 162 (A.B. 2650), § 10, operative Jan. 1, 1994. Amended by Stats.1994, c. 1269 (A.B.2208), § 46.)*

Cross References

Child support enforcement, generally, see Family Code § 17400 et seq.
Health insurance coverage, medical insurance form, see Family Code § 17422.
Judgment and order defined for purposes of this Code, see Family Code § 100.
Judicial Council, rules of practice and procedure, see Family Code § 210 et seq.
Medical insurance form, submission to local child support agency, see Family Code § 17424.
State defined for purposes of this Code, see Family Code § 145.

Research References

Forms

West's California Judicial Council Forms FL-470, Application and Order for Health Insurance Coverage.
West's California Judicial Council Forms FL-475, Employer's Health Insurance Return.

§ 3773. Title IV-D cases where support enforcement services are provided by local child support agency

(a) This section applies only to Title IV-D cases where support enforcement services are being provided by the local child support agency pursuant to Section 17400.

(b) After the court has ordered that a parent provide health insurance coverage, the local child support agency shall serve on the employer a national medical support notice in lieu of the health insurance coverage assignment order. The national medical support notice may be combined with the order/notice to withhold income for child support that is authorized by Section 5246.

(c) A national medical support notice shall have the same force and effect as a health insurance coverage assignment order.

(d) The obligor shall have the same right to move to quash or terminate a national medical support notice as provided in this article for a health insurance coverage assignment order. *(Added by Stats.1997, c. 599 (A.B.573), § 9. Amended by Stats.1998, c. 858 (A.B.2169), § 1; Stats.2000, c. 119 (S.B.2045), § 2.)*

Cross References

Child support, generally, see Family Code § 3900 et seq.
Child support enforcement, generally, see Family Code § 17400 et seq.
Expedited child support orders, see Family Code § 3620 et seq.
Health insurance coverage, medical insurance form, see Family Code § 17422.
Judgment and order defined for purposes of this Code, see Family Code § 100.
Medical insurance form, submission to local child support agency, see Family Code § 17424.
Modification, termination, or setting aside of support order, see Family Code § 3650 et seq.
Notice, actual and constructive, defined, see Civil Code § 18.

Support defined for purposes of this Code, see Family Code § 150.

Research References

Forms

West's California Judicial Council Forms FL-478, Request and Notice of Hearing Regarding Health Insurance Assignment.
West's California Judicial Council Forms FL-478-INFO, Information Sheet and Instructions for Request and Notice of Hearing Regarding Health Insurance Assignment.

ARTICLE 3. ASSIGNMENT OF REIMBURSEMENT RIGHTS UNDER HEALTH PLAN [REPEALED]

§§ 3780 to 3782. Repealed by Stats.1997, c. 599 (A.B.573), §§ 10 to 12

CHAPTER 8. DEFERRED SALE OF HOME ORDER

Section
3800. Definitions.
3801. Determination of economic feasibility of deferred sale.
3802. Grant or denial of order; discretion of court.
3803. Contents of order.
3804. Recordation of order.
3805. Inoperative.
3806. Payment of maintenance and capital improvement costs; order.
3807. Time for modification or termination of orders; exceptions.
3808. Remarriage or other change in circumstances; rebuttable presumption.
3809. Reservation of jurisdiction.
3810. Application of chapter.

Cross References

Burden of proof, generally, see Evidence Code § 500 et seq.
Presumption of child support amount established by formula, see Family Code § 4057.
Spousal support defined for purposes of this Code, see Family Code § 142.
Support defined for purposes of this Code, see Family Code § 150.

§ 3800. Definitions

As used in this chapter:

(a) "Custodial parent" means a party awarded physical custody of a child.

(b) "Deferred sale of home order" means an order that temporarily delays the sale and awards the temporary exclusive use and possession of the family home to a custodial parent of a minor child or child for whom support is authorized under Sections 3900 and 3901 or under Section 3910, whether or not the custodial parent has sole or joint custody, in order to minimize the adverse impact of dissolution of marriage or legal separation of the parties on the welfare of the child.

(c) "Resident parent" means a party who has requested or who has already been awarded a deferred sale of home order. *(Stats. 1992, c. 162 (A.B.2650), § 10, operative Jan. 1, 1994.)*

Cross References

Child custody, see Family Code § 3020 et seq.
Child support, generally, see Family Code § 3900 et seq.
Judgment and order defined for purposes of this Code, see Family Code § 100.
Minor defined for purposes of this Code, see Family Code § 6500.

§ 3800

Support defined for purposes of this Code, see Family Code § 150.

Research References

Forms

1 California Transactions Forms--Family Law § 3:38, Deferred Sale of Residence.

§ 3801. Determination of economic feasibility of deferred sale

(a) If one of the parties has requested a deferred sale of home order pursuant to this chapter, the court shall first determine whether it is economically feasible to maintain the payments of any note secured by a deed of trust, property taxes, insurance for the home during the period the sale of the home is deferred, and the condition of the home comparable to that at the time of trial.

(b) In making this determination, the court shall consider all of the following:

(1) The resident parent's income.

(2) The availability of spousal support, child support, or both spousal and child support.

(3) Any other sources of funds available to make those payments.

(c) It is the intent of the Legislature, by requiring the determination under this section, to do all of the following:

(1) Avoid the likelihood of possible defaults on the payments of notes and resulting foreclosures.

(2) Avoid inadequate insurance coverage.

(3) Prevent deterioration of the condition of the family home.

(4) Prevent any other circumstance which would jeopardize both parents' equity in the home. *(Stats.1992, c. 162 (A.B.2650), § 10, operative Jan. 1, 1994.)*

Cross References

Child support, generally, see Family Code § 3900 et seq.
Judgment and order defined for purposes of this Code, see Family Code § 100.
Legislative intent, construction of statutes, see Code of Civil Procedure § 1859.
Property defined for purposes of this Code, see Family Code § 113.
Spousal support defined for purposes of this Code, see Family Code § 142.
Support defined for purposes of this Code, see Family Code § 150.
Tax levies, see Government Code § 29100 et seq.; Revenue and Taxation Code § 2151 et seq.

Research References

Forms

1 California Transactions Forms--Family Law § 3:38, Deferred Sale of Residence.

§ 3802. Grant or denial of order; discretion of court

(a) If the court determines pursuant to Section 3801 that it is economically feasible to consider ordering a deferred sale of the family home, the court may grant a deferred sale of home order to a custodial parent if the court determines that the order is necessary in order to minimize the adverse impact of dissolution of marriage or legal separation of the parties on the child.

(b) In exercising its discretion to grant or deny a deferred sale of home order, the court shall consider all of the following:

(1) The length of time the child has resided in the home.

(2) The child's placement or grade in school.

(3) The accessibility and convenience of the home to the child's school and other services or facilities used by and available to the child, including child care.

(4) Whether the home has been adapted or modified to accommodate any physical disabilities of a child or a resident parent in a manner that a change in residence may adversely affect the ability of the resident parent to meet the needs of the child.

(5) The emotional detriment to the child associated with a change in residence.

(6) The extent to which the location of the home permits the resident parent to continue employment.

(7) The financial ability of each parent to obtain suitable housing.

(8) The tax consequences to the parents.

(9) The economic detriment to the nonresident parent in the event of a deferred sale of home order.

(10) Any other factors the court deems just and equitable. *(Stats.1992, c. 162 (A.B.2650), § 10, operative Jan. 1, 1994.)*

Cross References

Child custody, see Family Code § 3020 et seq.
Judgment and order defined for purposes of this Code, see Family Code § 100.
Tax levies, see Government Code § 29100 et seq.; Revenue and Taxation Code § 2151 et seq.

Research References

Forms

1 California Transactions Forms--Family Law § 3:38, Deferred Sale of Residence.

§ 3803. Contents of order

A deferred sale of home order shall state the duration of the order and may include the legal description and assessor's parcel number of the real property which is subject to the order. *(Stats.1992, c. 162 (A.B.2650), § 10, operative Jan. 1, 1994.)*

Cross References

Judgment and order defined for purposes of this Code, see Family Code § 100.
Property defined for purposes of this Code, see Family Code § 113.
State defined for purposes of this Code, see Family Code § 145.

§ 3804. Recordation of order

A deferred sale of home order may be recorded in the office of the county recorder of the county in which the real property is located. *(Stats.1992, c. 162 (A.B.2650), § 10, operative Jan. 1, 1994.)*

Cross References

County defined for purposes of this Code, see Family Code § 67.
Judgment and order defined for purposes of this Code, see Family Code § 100.
Property defined for purposes of this Code, see Family Code § 113.

§ 3805. Inoperative

§ 3806. Payment of maintenance and capital improvement costs; order

The court may make an order specifying the parties' respective responsibilities for the payment of the costs of routine maintenance and capital improvements. *(Stats.1992, c. 162 (A.B.2650), § 10, operative Jan. 1, 1994.)*

Cross References

Judgment and order defined for purposes of this Code, see Family Code § 100.

§ 3807. Time for modification or termination of orders; exceptions

Except as otherwise agreed to by the parties in writing, a deferred sale of home order may be modified or terminated at any time at the discretion of the court. *(Stats.1992, c. 162 (A.B.2650), § 10, operative Jan. 1, 1994.)*

Cross References

Judgment and order defined for purposes of this Code, see Family Code § 100.

CHILD SUPPORT

Writings, authentication and proof of, see Evidence Code § 1400 et seq.

§ 3808. Remarriage or other change in circumstances; rebuttable presumption

Except as otherwise agreed to by the parties in writing, if the party awarded the deferred sale of home order remarries, or if there is otherwise a change in circumstances affecting the determinations made pursuant to Section 3801 or 3802 or affecting the economic status of the parties or the children on which the award is based, a rebuttable presumption, affecting the burden of proof, is created that further deferral of the sale is no longer an equitable method of minimizing the adverse impact of the dissolution of marriage or legal separation of the parties on the children. (Stats.1992, c. 162 (A.B.2650), § 10, operative Jan. 1, 1994.)

Cross References

Burden of proof, generally, see Evidence Code § 500 et seq.
Judgment and order defined for purposes of this Code, see Family Code § 100.
Presumptions, see Evidence Code § 600 et seq.
Writings, authentication and proof of, see Evidence Code § 1400 et seq.

Research References

Forms

1 California Transactions Forms--Family Law § 3:38, Deferred Sale of Residence.

§ 3809. Reservation of jurisdiction

In making an order pursuant to this chapter, the court shall reserve jurisdiction to determine any issues that arise with respect to the deferred sale of home order including, but not limited to, the maintenance of the home and the tax consequences to each party. (Stats.1992, c. 162 (A.B.2650), § 10, operative Jan. 1, 1994.)

Cross References

Judgment and order defined for purposes of this Code, see Family Code § 100.
Tax levies, see Government Code § 29100 et seq.; Revenue and Taxation Code § 2151 et seq.

§ 3810. Application of chapter

This chapter is applicable regardless of whether the deferred sale of home order is made before or after January 1, 1989. (Stats.1992, c. 162 (A.B.2650), § 10, operative Jan. 1, 1994.)

Cross References

Judgment and order defined for purposes of this Code, see Family Code § 100.

Research References

Forms

1 California Transactions Forms--Family Law § 3:38, Deferred Sale of Residence.

CHAPTER 9. SOFTWARE USED TO DETERMINE SUPPORT

Section
3830. Conformation of software to rules of court; analysis; costs.

§ 3830. Conformation of software to rules of court; analysis; costs

(a) On and after January 1, 1994, no court shall use any computer software to assist in determining the appropriate amount of child support or spousal support obligations, unless the software conforms to rules of court adopted by the Judicial Council prescribing standards for the software, which shall ensure that it performs in a manner consistent with the applicable statutes and rules of court for determination of child support or spousal support.

(b) The Judicial Council may contract with an outside agency or organization to analyze software to ensure that it conforms to the standards established by the Judicial Council. The cost of this analysis shall be paid by the applicant software producers and fees therefor shall be established by the Judicial Council in an amount that in the aggregate will defray its costs of administering this section. (Added by Stats.1993, c. 219 (A.B.1500), § 129.)

Cross References

Child support, generally, see Family Code § 3900 et seq.
Civil actions, computer assistance, pro per court documents, see Code of Civil Procedure § 1062.20.
Spousal support defined for purposes of this Code, see Family Code § 142.
Support defined for purposes of this Code, see Family Code § 150.

Research References

Forms

California Practice Guide: Rutter Family Law Forms Form 5:2, Request for Order Re Child Custody, Child Support, Spousal Support, Attorney Fees, etc.
California Practice Guide: Rutter Family Law Forms Form 6:11, Request for Order Re Guideline Child Support, Temporary "Guideline" Spousal Support and Family Code §4062 "Add-On" Child Support.
1 California Transactions Forms--Family Law § 2:64, Amount of Support.
1 California Transactions Forms--Family Law § 3:22, Mandatory Compliance With Statewide Guidelines.
1 California Transactions Forms--Family Law § 3:112, Alternating the Dependency Exemption.

Part 2

CHILD SUPPORT

Chapter	Section
1. Duty of Parent to Support Child	3900
2. Court-Ordered Child Support	4000

Cross References

Action for injury to child, see Code of Civil Procedure § 376.
Amount of support, conditions determining, see Family Code § 4005.
Bankruptcy, effect, see Family Code § 4013.
Bond for support, see Penal Code § 270b.
California Work Opportunity and Responsibility to Kids Act, see Welfare and Institutions Code § 11200 et seq.
Child Support Delinquency Reporting Law, see Family Code §§ 4700, 4701.
Child welfare services, see Welfare and Institutions Code § 16500 et seq.
Compensation, failure to assume caretaker responsibility or thwarting other parent with regard to custody or visitation rights, see Family Code § 3028.
Compensation to relatives and strangers, see Family Code § 3951.
Counties, right to proceed on behalf of child, see Family Code § 4002.
Desertion of child, see Penal Code § 271.
Duration of order for child support during pendency of proceedings, see Family Code § 3601.
Estate of parent, source of support, see Family Code § 3952.
Failure to support child, see Penal Code § 270 et seq.
Guardian ad litem, appointment of, see Code of Civil Procedure §§ 372, 373, 373.5.
Minor, defined, see Family Code § 6500.
Order for support, retroactive application, see Family Code § 4009.
Parent and child relationship, see Probate Code § 6450.
Payment of reasonable value of necessaries to others who support child, see Family Code § 3950.
Petition for separation or dissolution of marriage, dismissal prohibited where child support order has not been terminated, see Code of Civil Procedure § 583.161.
Presumption of child support amount established by formula, see Family Code § 4057.
Priority of support payments, see Family Code § 4011.
Public assistance, use or intended use to support child, see Family Code § 4004.
Quasi-community property, property subject to support, see Family Code § 4008.
Security for payment of support, see Family Code § 4012.

SUPPORT

Separate trial, support proceedings, see Family Code § 4003.
Spousal and child support during pendency of proceedings, see Family Code § 3600 et seq.
Statewide uniform child support guidelines, see Family Code § 4050 et seq.
Support duty, actions to enforce, see Family Code § 4000.
Support order, modification or termination,
   Authority of court, see Family Code § 3651.
   Discovery, see Family Code § 3660 et seq.
   Retroactive application of modification, see Family Code § 3653.
Termination of support, effect of contingencies, see Family Code § 4007.
Uniform Interstate Family Support Act, see Family Code § 5700.101 et seq.
Venue of actions, see Code of Civil Procedure § 395.

CHAPTER 1. DUTY OF PARENT TO SUPPORT CHILD

Article	Section
1. Support of Minor Child	3900
2. Support of Adult Child	3910
3. Support of Grandchild	3930
4. Liability to Others Who Provide Support for Child	3950

Cross References

Amount of support, conditions determining, see Family Code § 4005.
Bankruptcy, effect, see Family Code § 4013.
Bond for support, see Penal Code § 270b.
California Work Opportunity and Responsibility to Kids Act, see Welfare and Institutions Code § 11200 et seq.
Child Support Delinquency Reporting Law, see Family Code §§ 4700, 4701.
Child welfare services, see Welfare and Institutions Code § 16500 et seq.
Compensation, failure to assume caretaker responsibility or thwarting other parent with regard to custody or visitation rights, see Family Code § 3028.
Compensation to relatives and strangers, see Family Code § 3951.
Counties, right to proceed on behalf of child, see Family Code § 4002.
Desertion of child, see Penal Code § 271.
Duration of order for child support during pendency of proceedings, see Family Code § 3601.
Estate of parent, source of support, see Family Code § 3952.
Failure to support child, see Penal Code § 270 et seq.
Guardian ad litem, appointment of, see Code of Civil Procedure §§ 372, 373, 373.5.
Order for support, retroactive application, see Family Code § 4009.
Parent and child relationship, see Probate Code § 6450.
Payment of reasonable value of necessaries to others who support child, see Family Code § 3950.
Petition for separation or dissolution of marriage, dismissal prohibited where child support order has not been terminated, see Code of Civil Procedure § 583.161.
Presumption of child support amount established by formula, see Family Code § 4057.
Priority of support payments, see Family Code § 4011.
Public assistance, use or intended use to support child, see Family Code § 4004.
Quasi-community property, property subject to support, see Family Code § 4008.
Security for payment of support, see Family Code § 4012.
Separate trial, support proceedings, see Family Code § 4003.
Spousal and child support during pendency of proceedings, see Family Code § 3600 et seq.
Statewide uniform child support guidelines, see Family Code § 4050 et seq.
Support duty, actions to enforce, see Family Code § 4000.
Support order, modification or termination,
   Authority of court, see Family Code § 3651.
   Discovery, see Family Code § 3660 et seq.
   Retroactive application of modification, see Family Code § 3653.
Termination of support, effect of contingencies, see Family Code § 4007.
Uniform Interstate Family Support Act, see Family Code § 5700.101 et seq.
Venue of actions, see Code of Civil Procedure § 395.

ARTICLE 1. SUPPORT OF MINOR CHILD

Section
3900. Equal duty of parents to support child.
3901. Duration of duty of support.
3902. Property of child; allowance to parent.

Cross References

Abandonment and desertion situations, bond for support, see Penal Code § 270b.
Amount of support, conditions determining, see Family Code § 4005.
Bankruptcy, effect, see Family Code § 4013.
California Work Opportunity and Responsibility to Kids Act, see Welfare and Institutions Code § 11200 et seq.
Child for whom support may be ordered, defined, see Family Code § 58.
Child Support Delinquency Reporting Law, see Family Code §§ 4700, 4701.
Child welfare services, see Welfare and Institutions Code § 16500 et seq.
Community property, subject to support, see Family Code § 4008.
Compensation, failure to assume caretaker responsibility or thwarting other parent with regard to custody or visitation rights, see Family Code § 3028.
Compensation to relatives and strangers, see Family Code § 3951.
Counties, right to proceed on behalf of child, see Family Code § 4002.
Duration of order for child support during pendency of proceedings, see Family Code § 3601.
Expedited child support orders, see Family Code § 3620 et seq.
Failure to support child, see Penal Code § 270 et seq.
Guardian ad litem, appointment of, see Code of Civil Procedure §§ 372, 373, 373.5.
Health insurance, see Family Code § 3750 et seq.
Order for support, retroactive application, see Family Code § 4009.
Petition for separation or dissolution of marriage, dismissal prohibited where child support order has not been terminated, see Code of Civil Procedure § 583.161.
Priority of support payments, see Family Code § 4011.
Public assistance, use or intended use to support child, see Family Code § 4004.
Security for payment of support, see Family Code § 4012.
Separate trial, support proceedings, see Family Code § 4003.
Statewide uniform child support guidelines, see Family Code § 4050 et seq.
Support agreements, see Family Code § 3580 et seq.
Support duty, actions to enforce, see Family Code § 4000.
Support orders, modification or termination, see Family Code § 3650 et seq.
Support pending proceeding, see Family Code § 3600 et seq.
Termination of support, effect of contingencies, see Family Code § 4007.

§ 3900. Equal duty of parents to support child

Subject to this division, the father and mother of a minor child have an equal responsibility to support their child in the manner suitable to the child's circumstances. *(Stats.1992, c. 162 (A.B.2650), § 10, operative Jan. 1, 1994.)*

Cross References

Action for support, see Family Code § 4000.
Agreements for child support, see Family Code § 3585 et seq.
Amount of support, conditions determining, see Family Code § 4005.
Bankruptcy, effect, see Family Code § 4013.
Child Support Delinquency Reporting Law, see Family Code §§ 4700, 4701.
Compensation, failure to assume caretaker responsibility or thwarting other parent with regard to custody or visitation rights, see Family Code § 3028.
Compensation to relatives and strangers, see Family Code § 3951.
Counties, right to proceed on behalf of child, see Family Code § 4002.
Desertion of child, see Penal Code § 271.
Duration of order for child support during pendency of proceedings, see Family Code § 3601.
Duty of parent, see Family Code §§ 3910, 3930.
Estate of parent, source of support, see Family Code § 3952.
Failure to implement custody or visitation rights, see Family Code § 3556.
Failure to support child, see Penal Code § 270 et seq.
Liability for support to applicant for aid, see Welfare And Institutions Code § 12350.
Minor defined for purposes of this Code, see Family Code § 6500.
Order for support, effective date, see Family Code § 4009.
Parent and child relationship, see Probate Code § 6450.
Payment of reasonable value of necessaries to others who support child, see Family Code § 3950.
Petition for separation or dissolution of marriage, pending child or spousal support order, see Code of Civil Procedure § 583.161.
Presence or residence of person owing support in state, see Family Code § 3550.

Presumption of child support amount established by formula, see Family Code § 4057.
Priority of payment, see Family Code § 4011.
Public assistance, use to support child, see Family Code § 4004.
Quasi-community property, property subject to support, see Family Code § 4008.
Security for payment of support, see Family Code § 4012.
Separate trial, support proceedings, see Family Code § 4003.
Spousal and child support during pendency of proceedings, see Family Code § 3600 et seq.
Statewide uniform child support guidelines, see Family Code § 4050 et seq.
Support defined for purposes of this Code, see Family Code § 150.
Support order, modification or termination,
   Authority of court, see Family Code § 3651.
   Discovery, see Family Code § 3660 et seq.
   Retroactive application of modification, see Family Code § 3653.
Termination of support, effect of contingencies, see Family Code § 4007.
Uniform Interstate Family Support Act, see Family Code § 5700.101 et seq.
Venue of actions, see Code of Civil Procedure § 395.

Research References

Forms

California Practice Guide: Rutter Family Law Forms Form 1:32, Glossary of Common Family Law Terms, Phrases and Concepts (Enclosure to Form 1:31).
1 California Transactions Forms--Family Law § 3:3, Child Support.
1 California Transactions Forms--Family Law § 4:104, Paternity Acknowledgment.
2 California Transactions Forms--Family Law § 7:43, Characterization of Payments as Child Support.
West's California Code Forms, Family § 3900, Comment Overview—Duty of Parent to Support Child.
West's California Judicial Council Forms FL–230, Declaration for Default or Uncontested Judgment (Uniform Parentage, Custody and Support) (Also Available in Spanish).
West's California Judicial Council Forms FL–250, Judgment (Uniform Parentage—Custody and Support) (Also Available in Spanish).
West's California Judicial Council Forms FL–260, Petition for Custody and Support of Minor Children (Also Available in Spanish).
West's California Judicial Council Forms FL–270, Response to Petition for Custody and Support of Minor Children (Also Available in Spanish).
West's California Judicial Council Forms FL–684, Request for Order and Supporting Declaration (Governmental).

§ 3901. Duration of duty of support

(a)(1) The duty of support imposed by Section 3900 continues as to an unmarried child who has attained 18 years of age, is a full-time high school student, unless excused pursuant to paragraph (2), and who is not self-supporting, until the time the child completes the 12th grade or attains 19 years of age, whichever occurs first.

(2) A child is excused from the requirement to be a full-time high school student for purposes of paragraph (1) if the child has a medical condition documented by a physician that prevents full-time school attendance.

(b) This section does not limit a parent's ability to agree to provide additional support or the court's power to inquire whether an agreement to provide additional support has been made. *(Stats. 1992, c. 162 (A.B.2650), § 10, operative Jan. 1, 1994. Amended by Stats.1993, c. 219 (A.B.1500), § 130; Stats.2018, c. 504 (A.B.3248), § 2, eff. Jan. 1, 2019.)*

Cross References

Action for support, see Family Code § 4000.
Amount of support, conditions determining, see Family Code § 4053.
Bankruptcy, effect, see Family Code § 4013.
Child for whom support may be ordered, defined, see Family Code § 58.
Child support agreements, see Family Code § 3580 et seq.
Child Support Delinquency Reporting Law, see Family Code §§ 4700, 4701.
Civil action against parent, enforcement of duty of support, see Family Code § 4000.
Compensation to relatives and strangers, see Family Code § 3951.
Counties, right to proceed on behalf of child, see Family Code § 4002.

Duration of order for child support during pendency of proceedings, see Family Code § 3601.
Duty of parent, see Family Code §§ 3910, 3930.
Enforcement of support orders, see Family Code § 4500 et seq.
Estate of parent, source of support, see Family Code § 3952.
Expedited child support order, see Family Code § 3620 et seq.
Failure to implement custody or visitation rights, see Family Code § 3556.
Order for support, effective date, see Family Code § 4009.
Payment of reasonable value of necessaries to others who support child, see Family Code § 3950.
Pendency of proceeding, child support during, see Family Code § 3600 et seq.
Petition for separation or dissolution of marriage, pending child or spousal support order, see Code of Civil Procedure § 583.161.
Place of trial, action to enforce support, see Code of Civil Procedure § 395.
Presence or residence of person owing support in state, see Family Code § 3550.
Public assistance, use to support child, see Family Code § 4004.
Quasi-community property, property subject to support, see Family Code § 4008.
Security for payment of support, see Family Code § 4012.
Separate trial, support proceedings, see Family Code § 4003.
Spousal and child support during pendency of proceedings, see Family Code § 3600 et seq.
Spousal support, termination of child support as change of circumstances, see Family Code § 4326.
Support defined for purposes of this Code, see Family Code § 150.
Termination of support, effect of contingencies, see Family Code § 4007.
Uniform Interstate Family Support Act, see Family Code § 5700.101 et seq.

Research References

Forms

California Practice Guide: Rutter Family Law Forms Form 1:32, Glossary of Common Family Law Terms, Phrases and Concepts (Enclosure to Form 1:31).
1 California Transactions Forms--Family Law § 3:25, Duration of Child Support Obligation.
1 California Transactions Forms--Family Law § 3:26, Voluntary Support After Age of Majority.
West's California Code Forms, Family § 3900, Comment Overview—Duty of Parent to Support Child.
West's California Code Forms, Family § 4000, Comment Overview—Court-Ordered Child Support.
West's California Judicial Council Forms FL–430, Ex Parte Application to Issue, Modify, or Terminate an Earnings Assignment Order.
West's California Judicial Council Forms FL–684, Request for Order and Supporting Declaration (Governmental).

§ 3902. Property of child; allowance to parent

The court may direct that an allowance be made to the parent of a child for whom support may be ordered out of the child's property for the child's past or future support, on conditions that are proper, if the direction is for the child's benefit. *(Stats.1992, c. 162 (A.B.2650), § 10, operative Jan. 1, 1994. Amended by Stats.1993, c. 219 (A.B. 1500), § 131.)*

Cross References

Action for support, see Family Code § 4000.
Agreements for child support, see Family Code § 3585 et seq.
Amount of support, conditions determining, see Family Code § 4005.
Bankruptcy, effect, see Family Code § 4013.
Child for whom support may be ordered defined for purposes of this Code, see Family Code § 58.
Child Support Delinquency Reporting Law, see Family Code §§ 4700, 4701.
Compensation to relatives and strangers, see Family Code § 3951.
Counties, right to proceed on behalf of child, see Family Code § 4002.
Duty of parent, see Family Code §§ 3900, 3910, 3930.
Education and maintenance of minor children, included in support, see Family Code § 150.
Estate of parent, source of support, see Family Code § 3952.
Expedited child support orders, see Family Code § 3620 et seq.
Failure to implement custody or visitation rights, see Family Code § 3556.
Health insurance coverage for supported children, see Family Code § 3750 et seq.
Maintenance and education of minor children, inclusion in support, see Family Code § 150.

§ 3902

Modification, termination, or setting aside of support order, see Family Code § 3650 et seq.
Order for support, effective date, see Family Code § 4009.
Payment of reasonable value of necessaries to others who support child, see Family Code § 3950.
Place of trial, action to enforce support, see Code of Civil Procedure § 395.
Priority of payment, see Family Code § 4011.
Property defined for purposes of this Code, see Family Code § 113.
Public assistance, use to support child, see Family Code § 4004.
Quasi-community property, property subject to support, see Family Code § 4008.
Security for payment of support, see Family Code § 4012.
Separate trial, support proceedings, see Family Code § 4003.
Support defined for purposes of this Code, see Family Code § 150.
Termination of support, effect of contingencies, see Family Code § 4007.
Uniform Interstate Family Support Act, see Family Code § 5700.101 et seq.

Research References

Forms

1 California Transactions Forms--Family Law § 3:43, Use of Child's Property or Income.
West's California Code Forms, Family § 3900, Comment Overview—Duty of Parent to Support Child.

ARTICLE 2. SUPPORT OF ADULT CHILD

Section
3910. Duty to support incapacitated adult child.

§ 3910. Duty to support incapacitated adult child

(a) The father and mother have an equal responsibility to maintain, to the extent of their ability, a child of whatever age who is incapacitated from earning a living and without sufficient means.

(b) Nothing in this section limits the duty of support under Sections 3900 and 3901. *(Stats.1992, c. 162 (A.B.2650), § 10, operative Jan. 1, 1994.)*

Cross References

Action for support, see Family Code § 4000.
Agreement for support of adult child, court order to effectuate, see Family Code § 3587.
Agreements for child support, see Family Code § 3585 et seq.
Amount of support, conditions determining, see Family Code § 4005.
Bankruptcy, effect, see Family Code § 4013.
Bond for support, see Penal Code § 270b.
Child for whom support may be ordered, defined, see Family Code § 58.
Child Support Delinquency Reporting Law, see Family Code §§ 4700, 4701.
Compensation to relatives and strangers, see Family Code § 3951.
Counties, right to proceed on behalf of child, see Family Code § 4002.
Estate of parent, source of support, see Family Code § 3952.
Failure of parent to provide for minor children, see Penal Code § 270.
Failure to implement custody or visitation rights, see Family Code § 3556.
Obligors, duties of support, see Family Code § 3550.
Order for support,
  Generally, see Family Code § 4001.
  Effective date, see Family Code § 4009.
Effectuation of agreement for support of adult child, see Family Code § 3587.
Payment of reasonable value of necessaries to others who support child, see Family Code § 3950.
Place of trial, action to enforce support, see Code of Civil Procedure § 395.
Presence or residence of person owing support in state, see Family Code § 3550.
Priority of payment, see Family Code § 4011.
Public assistance, use to support child, see Family Code § 4004.
Quasi-community property, property subject to support, see Family Code § 4008.
Relative's liability for support or aid, see Welfare and Institutions Code §§ 12350, 17200.
Security for payment of support, see Family Code § 4012.
Separate trial, support proceedings, see Family Code § 4003.
State Supplementary Program for Aged, Blind and Disabled relative's liability for recipient's support, see Welfare and Institutions Code § 12350.

Support defined for purposes of this Code, see Family Code § 150.
Termination of support, effect of contingencies, see Family Code § 4007.
Uniform Interstate Family Support Act, see Family Code § 5700.101 et seq.

Research References

Forms

California Practice Guide: Rutter Family Law Forms Form 6:7, Request for Order Re Child Support (Needy, Incapacitated Adult Child).
1 California Transactions Forms--Family Law § 3:27, Support for Incapacitated Adult Child.
West's California Code Forms, Family § 3900, Comment Overview—Duty of Parent to Support Child.
West's California Code Forms, Family § 3910, Comment Overview—Support of Adult Child.
West's California Code Forms, Family § 4000, Comment Overview—Court-Ordered Child Support.
West's California Code Forms, Family § 4400, Comment Overview—Duty of Adult Children to Support Parents.

ARTICLE 3. SUPPORT OF GRANDCHILD

Section
3930. Duty to support grandchild.

§ 3930. Duty to support grandchild

A parent does not have the duty to support a child of the parent's child. *(Stats.1992, c. 162 (A.B.2650), § 10, operative Jan. 1, 1994. Amended by Stats.1993, c. 219 (A.B.1500), § 132.)*

Cross References

Agreements for child support, see Family Code § 3585 et seq.
Authority of court to order support payments by grandparents, see Family Code § 3103.
Grandparent's rights, see Family Code § 3104.
Support defined for purposes of this Code, see Family Code § 150.

Research References

Forms

2 California Transactions Forms--Family Law § 5:5, Rights of Grandparents and Close Relatives.
West's California Code Forms, Family § 3930, Comment Overview—Support of Grandchild.
West's California Code Forms, Family § 3950, Comment Overview—Liability to Others Who Provide Support for Child.

ARTICLE 4. LIABILITY TO OTHERS WHO PROVIDE SUPPORT FOR CHILD

Section
3950. Necessaries furnished to child.
3951. Circumstances where liability is not incurred.
3952. Estate of deceased parent; action for support of child.

§ 3950. Necessaries furnished to child

If a parent neglects to provide articles necessary for the parent's child who is under the charge of the parent, according to the circumstances of the parent, a third person may in good faith supply the necessaries and recover their reasonable value from the parent. *(Stats.1992, c. 162 (A.B.2650), § 10, operative Jan. 1, 1994.)*

Cross References

Action for support, see Family Code § 4000.
Agreements for child support, see Family Code § 3585 et seq.
Amount of support, conditions determining, see Family Code § 4005.
Bankruptcy, effect, see Family Code § 4013.
Child Support Delinquency Reporting Law, see Family Code §§ 4700, 4701.
Compensation to relatives and strangers, see Family Code § 3951.
Counties, right to proceed on behalf of child, see Family Code § 4002.
Criminal penalties, failure to provide necessaries for child, see Penal Code § 270.

CHILD SUPPORT

Duty of parent, see Family Code §§ 3900, 3910, 3930.
Estate of parent, source of support, see Family Code § 3952.
Failure to implement custody or visitation rights, see Family Code § 3556.
Failure to provide necessaries for child, criminal penalties, see Penal Code § 270.
Minor's contract for necessaries not disaffirmable, see Family Code §§ 6712, 6751.
Order for support, effective date, see Family Code § 4009.
Person defined for purposes of this Code, see Family Code § 105.
Place of trial, action to enforce support, see Code of Civil Procedure § 395.
Priority of payment, see Family Code § 4011.
Public assistance, use to support child, see Family Code § 4004.
Quasi-community property, property subject to support, see Family Code § 4008.
Security for payment of support, see Family Code § 4012.
Separate trial, support proceedings, see Family Code § 4003.
Support, defined, see Family Code § 150.
Termination of support, effect of contingencies, see Family Code § 4007.
Uniform Interstate Family Support Act, see Family Code § 5700.101 et seq.

Research References

Forms

West's California Code Forms, Family § 3950, Comment Overview—Liability to Others Who Provide Support for Child.
West's California Code Forms, Family § 4400, Comment Overview—Duty of Adult Children to Support Parents.

§ 3951. Circumstances where liability is not incurred

(a) A parent is not bound to compensate the other parent, or a relative, for the voluntary support of the parent's child, without an agreement for compensation.

(b) A parent is not bound to compensate a stranger for the support of a child who has abandoned the parent without just cause.

(c) Nothing in this section relieves a parent of the obligation to support a child during any period in which the state, county, or other governmental entity provides support for the child. (Stats.1992, c. 162 (A.B.2650), § 10, operative Jan. 1, 1994.)

Cross References

Action for support, see Family Code § 4000.
Agreements for child support, see Family Code § 3585 et seq.
Agreements for support of adult children, see Family Code § 3587.
Amount of support, conditions determining, see Family Code § 4005.
Authority of court to order support payments by grandparents, see Family Code § 3103.
Bankruptcy, effect, see Family Code § 4013.
Child Support Delinquency Reporting Law, see Family Code §§ 4700, 4701.
Counties, right to proceed on behalf of child, see Family Code § 4002.
County defined for purposes of this Code, see Family Code § 67.
Duty of parent, see Family Code §§ 3900, 3910, 3930.
Failure to implement custody or visitation rights, see Family Code § 3556.
Health insurance coverage for supported children, see Family Code § 3750 et seq.
Minor's contract for necessaries not disaffirmable, see Family Code §§ 6712, 6751.
Order for support, effective date, see Family Code § 4009.
Place of trial, action to enforce support, see Code of Civil Procedure § 395.
Priority of payment, see Family Code § 4011.
Public assistance, use to support child, see Family Code § 4004.
Quasi-community property, property subject to support, see Family Code § 4008.
Security for payment of support, see Family Code § 4012.
Separate trial, support proceedings, see Family Code § 4003.
State defined for purposes of this Code, see Family Code § 145.
Support defined for purposes of this Code, see Family Code § 150.
Termination of support, effect of contingencies, see Family Code § 4007.
Uniform Interstate Family Support Act, see Family Code § 5700.101 et seq.

Research References

Forms

2 California Transactions Forms—Family Law § 5:5, Rights of Grandparents and Close Relatives.

West's California Code Forms, Family § 3950, Comment Overview—Liability to Others Who Provide Support for Child.

§ 3952. Estate of deceased parent; action for support of child

If a parent chargeable with the support of a child dies leaving the child chargeable to the county or leaving the child confined in a state institution to be cared for in whole or in part at the expense of the state, and the parent leaves an estate sufficient for the child's support, the supervisors of the county or the director of the state department having jurisdiction over the institution may claim provision for the child's support from the parent's estate, and for this purpose has the same remedies as a creditor against the estate of the parent and may obtain reimbursement from the successor of the deceased parent to the extent provided in Division 8 (commencing with Section 13000) of the Probate Code. (Stats.1992, c. 162 (A.B.2650), § 10, operative Jan. 1, 1994.)

Cross References

Action for support, see Family Code § 4000.
Action to enforce support obligation, place of trial, see Code of Civil Procedure § 395.
Administration of estate, claims submitted to personal representative, see Probate Code § 9000 et seq.
Agreements for child support, see Family Code § 3585 et seq.
Amount of support, conditions determining, see Family Code § 4005.
Bankruptcy, effect, see Family Code § 4013.
Child Support Delinquency Reporting Law, see Family Code §§ 4700, 4701.
Counties, right to proceed on behalf of child, see Family Code § 4002.
County defined for purposes of this Code, see Family Code § 67.
Duty of parent, see Family Code §§ 3900, 3910, 3930.
Failure to implement custody or visitation rights, see Family Code § 3556.
Limitation on liability of successor, see Probate Code § 13112.
Minor's contract for necessaries not disaffirmable, see Family Code §§ 6712, 6751.
Order for support, effective date, see Family Code § 4009.
Payment of reasonable value of necessaries to others who support child, see Family Code § 3950.
Priority of payment, see Family Code § 4011.
Public assistance, use to support child, see Family Code § 4004.
Quasi-community property, property subject to support, see Family Code § 4008.
Security for payment of support, see Family Code § 4012.
Separate trial, support proceedings, see Family Code § 4003.
State defined for purposes of this Code, see Family Code § 145.
Support defined for purposes of this Code, see Family Code § 150.
Termination of support, effect of contingencies, see Family Code § 4007.
Uniform Interstate Family Support Act, see Family Code § 5700.101 et seq.

Research References

Forms

4 California Transactions Forms--Estate Planning § 19:11, Child Support.
West's California Code Forms, Family § 3950, Comment Overview—Liability to Others Who Provide Support for Child.

CHAPTER 2. COURT–ORDERED CHILD SUPPORT

Article	Section
1. General Provisions	4000
2. Statewide Uniform Guideline	4050
3. Payment to Court Designated County Officer; Enforcement by District Attorney	4200
4. Child Support Commissioners	4250

Cross References

Abandonment and desertion situations, bond for support, see Penal Code § 270b.
California Work Opportunity and Responsibility to Kids Act, see Welfare and Institutions Code § 11200 et seq.
Child for whom support may be ordered, defined, see Family Code § 58.
Child welfare services, see Welfare and Institutions Code § 16500 et seq.
Desertion of child, see Penal Code § 271.

SUPPORT

Duration of order for child support during pendency of proceedings, see Family Code § 3601.
Emancipation of minors, warning that court may void or rescind declaration and parents may become liable for support and medical insurance coverage pursuant to this chapter, see Family Code § 7121.
Estate of parent, source of support, see Family Code § 3952.
Failure to support child, see Penal Code § 270 et seq.
Guardian, appointment of, see Family Code § 7893.
Guardian ad litem, appointment of, see Code of Civil Procedure §§ 372, 373, 373.5.
Minor, defined, see Family Code § 6500.
Parent and child relationship, see Probate Code § 6450.
Petition for separation or dissolution of marriage, dismissal prohibited where child support order has not been terminated, see Code of Civil Procedure § 583.161.
Presumption of child support amount established by formula, see Family Code § 4057.
Spousal and child support during pendency of proceedings, see Family Code § 3600 et seq.
Statewide uniform child support guidelines, see Family Code § 4050 et seq.
Support order, modification or termination,
  Authority of court, see Family Code § 3651.
  Discovery, see Family Code § 3660 et seq.
  Retroactive application of modification, see Family Code § 3653.
Uniform Interstate Family Support Act, see Family Code § 5700.101 et seq.
Venue of action for support, see Code of Civil Procedure § 395.

ARTICLE 1. GENERAL PROVISIONS

Section
4000. Actions to enforce parent's duty to support.
4001. Order for support.
4002. Enforcement of right of support; reimbursement of county.
4003. Separate trial; calendar preference; joinder with custody.
4004. Disclosure of party receiving or intending to receive public assistance for maintenance of child.
4005. Circumstances forming basis for child support order; findings.
4006. Health insurance coverage; consideration by court.
4007. Termination of duty to pay support on happening of contingency; notice of contingency.
4007.5. Suspension of money judgment or order for support of a child; exceptions; resumption of obligation; administrative adjustment; evaluation.
4008. Property which may be subjected to support of children.
4009. Retroactive application of order for support.
4010. Information on procedures to modify support order.
4011. Priority of payments; creditors.
4012. Security for payment of child support.
4013. Duty for child support discharged in bankruptcy; order for child support.
4014. Notice of obligation to provide name and address of employer; notice of information to be filed with the court.

Cross References

Emancipation of minors, warning that court may void or rescind declaration and parents may become liable for support and medical insurance coverage pursuant to this chapter, see Family Code § 7121.
Statewide uniform child support guidelines, see Family Code § 4050 et seq.

§ 4000. Actions to enforce parent's duty to support

If a parent has the duty to provide for the support of the parent's child and willfully fails to so provide, the other parent, or the child by a guardian ad litem, may bring an action against the parent to enforce the duty. (Stats.1992, c. 162 (A.B.2650), § 10, operative Jan. 1, 1994.)

Cross References

Abandonment and desertion situations, bond for support, see Penal Code § 270b.
Child for whom support may be ordered, defined, see Family Code § 58.
Conciliation Court Law, see Family Code § 1800 et seq.
Emancipation of minors, notice of declaration proceedings, warning that court may void or rescind declaration and parents may become liable for support and medical insurance coverage pursuant to this chapter, see Family Code § 7121.
Enforcement of support orders, generally, see Family Code § 4500 et seq.
Estate of parent, source of support, see Family Code § 3952.
Failure to implement custody or visitation rights, effect, see Family Code § 3556.
Failure to support child, see Penal Code § 270 et seq.
Guardian, appointment of, see Family Code § 7893.
Guardian ad litem, appointment of, see Code of Civil Procedure §§ 372, 373, 373.5.
Incapacitated child of any age, duty to support, see Family Code § 3910.
Jurisdiction of superior court, see Family Code § 200; Cal. Const. Art. 6, §§ 10, 11.
Parent and child relationship, see Family Code § 7500 et seq.
Presumption of child support amount established by formula, see Family Code § 4057.
Public assistance, support order required where parent is recipient, see Family Code § 4004.
Statewide uniform child support guidelines, see Family Code § 4050 et seq.
Support,
  Generally, see Family Code § 3500 et seq.
  Defined, see Family Code § 150.
  Parental duty to provide, see Family Code § 3900 et seq.
Support agreement, adult child, court approval, see Family Code § 3587.
Uniform Interstate Family Support Act, see Family Code § 5700.101 et seq.

Research References

Forms
1 California Transactions Forms--Family Law § 2:88, Marital Settlement Agreement.
1 California Transactions Forms--Family Law § 2:91, Add-On Expenses in Conjunction With Family Support.
West's California Code Forms, Family § 2338 Form 8, Marital Agreement.
West's California Code Forms, Family § 3585 Form 2, Child Support Provisions.
West's California Code Forms, Family § 3900, Comment Overview—Duty of Parent to Support Child.
West's California Code Forms, Family § 4000, Comment Overview—Court-Ordered Child Support.
West's California Code Forms, Family § 4001 Form 1, Order for Support of Child.

§ 4001. Order for support

In any proceeding where there is at issue the support of a minor child or a child for whom support is authorized under Section 3901 or 3910, the court may order either or both parents to pay an amount necessary for the support of the child. (Stats.1992, c. 162 (A.B.2650), § 10, operative Jan. 1, 1994.)

Cross References

Abandonment and desertion situations, bond for support, see Penal Code § 270b.
Amount of support, conditions determining, see Family Code § 4005.
Bankruptcy, effect, see Family Code § 4013.
California Work Opportunity and Responsibility to Kids Act, see Welfare and Institutions Code § 11200 et seq.
Child for whom support may be ordered, defined, see Family Code § 58.
Child welfare services, see Welfare and Institutions Code § 16500 et seq.
Duration of order for child support during pendency of proceedings, see Family Code § 3601.
Emancipation of minors, warning that court may void or rescind declaration and parents may become liable for support and medical insurance coverage pursuant to this chapter, see Family Code § 7121.
Enforcement of support orders, generally, see Family Code § 4500 et seq.
Estate of parent, source of support, see Family Code § 3952.
Failure to assume caretaker responsibility or thwarting other parent attempting to exercise custody or visitation rights, compensation, see Family Code § 3028.

CHILD SUPPORT § 4006

Failure to implement custody or visitation rights, effect, see Family Code § 3556.
Future child support payments,
  Deposit of assets to secure, see Family Code § 4600 et seq.
  Deposits to secure, see Family Code § 4550 et seq.
Judgment and order defined for purposes of this Code, see Family Code § 100.
Minor defined for purposes of this Code, see Family Code § 6500.
Order for support, retroactive application, see Family Code § 4009.
Proceeding defined for purposes of this Code, see Family Code § 110.
Public assistance, support order required where parent is receiving, see Family Code § 4004.
Quasi-community property, property subject to support, see Family Code § 4008.
Statewide uniform child support guidelines, see Family Code § 4050 et seq.
Support,
  Generally, see Family Code § 3500 et seq.
  Defined, see Family Code § 150.
Support order, modification or termination,
  Authority of court, see Family Code § 3651.
  Discovery, see Family Code § 3660 et seq.
  Retroactive application of modification, see Family Code § 3653.
Uniform Interstate Family Support Act, see Family Code § 5700.101 et seq.
Venue of action for support, see Code of Civil Procedure § 395.

Research References

Forms

1 California Transactions Forms--Family Law § 2:63, Authority for Child Support.
1 California Transactions Forms--Family Law § 3:21, Jurisdiction for Orders to Pay Child Support.
West's California Code Forms, Family § 4000, Comment Overview—Court-Ordered Child Support.
West's California Judicial Council Forms FL–683, Order to Show Cause (Governmental).
West's California Judicial Council Forms FL–684, Request for Order and Supporting Declaration (Governmental).

§ 4002. Enforcement of right of support; reimbursement of county

(a) The county may proceed on behalf of a child to enforce the child's right of support against a parent.

(b) If the county furnishes support to a child, the county has the same right as the child to secure reimbursement and obtain continuing support. The right of the county to reimbursement is subject to any limitation otherwise imposed by the law of this state.

(c) The court may order the parent to pay the county reasonable attorney's fees and court costs in a proceeding brought by the county pursuant to this section. *(Stats.1992, c. 162 (A.B.2650), § 10, operative Jan. 1, 1994.)*

Cross References

Attorney's fees and costs, generally, see Code of Civil Procedure § 1021.
Counties,
  Enforcement of duty to provide spousal support, see Family Code § 4303.
  Enforcement of duty to support parent, see Family Code § 4403.
County defined for purposes of this Code, see Family Code § 67.
Emancipation of minors, notice of declaration proceedings, warning that court may void or rescind declaration and parents may become liable for support and medical insurance coverage pursuant to this chapter, see Family Code § 7121.
Enforcement of support orders, generally, see Family Code § 4500 et seq.
Judgment and order defined for purposes of this Code, see Family Code § 100.
Proceeding defined for purposes of this Code, see Family Code § 110.
State defined for purposes of this Code, see Family Code § 145.
Support, generally, see Family Code § 3500 et seq.
Support defined for purposes of this Code, see Family Code § 150.

Research References

Forms

West's California Code Forms, Family § 3900, Comment Overview—Duty of Parent to Support Child.
West's California Code Forms, Family § 4000, Comment Overview—Court-Ordered Child Support.
West's California Judicial Council Forms FL–683, Order to Show Cause (Governmental).
West's California Judicial Council Forms FL–684, Request for Order and Supporting Declaration (Governmental).

§ 4003. Separate trial; calendar preference; joinder with custody

In any case in which the support of a child is at issue, the court may, upon a showing of good cause, order a separate trial on that issue. The separate trial shall be given preference over other civil cases, except matters to which special precedence may be given by law, for assigning a trial date. If the court has also ordered a separate trial on the issue of custody pursuant to Section 3023, the two issues shall be tried together. *(Stats.1992, c. 162 (A.B.2650), § 10, operative Jan. 1, 1994. Amended by Stats.1993, c. 219 (A.B. 1500), § 133.)*

Cross References

Emancipation of minors, warning that court may void or rescind declaration and parents may become liable for support and medical insurance coverage pursuant to this chapter, see Family Code § 7121.
Enforcement of support orders, generally, see Family Code § 4500 et seq.
Judgment and order defined for purposes of this Code, see Family Code § 100.
Support, generally, see Family Code § 3500 et seq.
Support defined for purposes of this Code, see Family Code § 150.
Venue of action for support, see Code of Civil Procedure § 395.

§ 4004. Disclosure of party receiving or intending to receive public assistance for maintenance of child

In a proceeding where there is at issue the support of a child, the court shall require the parties to reveal whether a party is currently receiving, or intends to apply for, public assistance under the Family Economic Security Act of 1982 (Chapter 2 (commencing with Section 11200) of Part 3 of Division 9 of the Welfare and Institutions Code) for the maintenance of the child. *(Stats.1992, c. 162 (A.B.2650), § 10, operative Jan. 1, 1994. Amended by Stats.1993, c. 219 (A.B. 1500), § 134.)*

Cross References

Health insurance coverage for supported children, see Family Code § 3750 et seq.
Proceeding defined for purposes of this Code, see Family Code § 110.
Support defined for purposes of this Code, see Family Code § 150.

§ 4005. Circumstances forming basis for child support order; findings

At the request of either party, the court shall make appropriate findings with respect to the circumstances on which the order for support of a child is based. *(Added by Stats.1994, c. 1269 (A.B.2208), § 47.)*

Cross References

Expedited child support orders, see Family Code § 3620 et seq.
Health insurance coverage for supported children, see Family Code § 3750 et seq.
Judgment and order defined for purposes of this Code, see Family Code § 100.
Modification, termination, or setting aside of support order, see Family Code § 3650 et seq.
Support defined for purposes of this Code, see Family Code § 150.

§ 4006. Health insurance coverage; consideration by court

In a proceeding for child support under this code, including, but not limited to, Division 17 (commencing with Section 17000), the court shall consider the health insurance coverage, if any, of the parties to the proceeding. *(Stats.1992, c. 162 (A.B.2650), § 10, operative Jan. 1, 1994. Amended by Stats.2000, c. 808 (A.B.1358), § 33, eff. Sept. 28, 2000.)*

§ 4006

Cross References

Emancipation of minors, warning that court may void or rescind declaration and parents may become liable for support and medical insurance coverage pursuant to this chapter, see Family Code § 7121.
Health insurance coverage, see Family Code § 3750 et seq.
Proceeding defined for purposes of this Code, see Family Code § 110.
Support defined for purposes of this Code, see Family Code § 150.

§ 4007. Termination of duty to pay support on happening of contingency; notice of contingency

(a) If a court orders a person to make specified payments for support of a child during the child's minority, or until the child is married or otherwise emancipated, or until the death of, or the occurrence of a specified event as to, a child for whom support is authorized under Section 3901 or 3910, the obligation of the person ordered to pay support terminates on the happening of the contingency. The court may, in the original order for support, order the custodial parent or other person to whom payments are to be made to notify the person ordered to make the payments, or the person's attorney of record, of the happening of the contingency.

(b) If the custodial parent or other person having physical custody of the child, to whom payments are to be made, fails to notify the person ordered to make the payments, or the attorney of record of the person ordered to make the payments, of the happening of the contingency and continues to accept support payments, the person shall refund all moneys received that accrued after the happening of the contingency, except that the overpayments shall first be applied to any support payments that are then in default. *(Stats.1992, c. 162 (A.B.2650), § 10, operative Jan. 1, 1994.)*

Cross References

Child custody, see Family Code § 3020 et seq.
Duration of order for child support during pendency of proceedings, see Family Code § 3601.
Enforcement of support orders, generally, see Family Code § 4500 et seq.
Expedited child support orders, see Family Code § 3620 et seq.
Health insurance coverage for supported children, see Family Code § 3750 et seq.
Judgment and order defined for purposes of this Code, see Family Code § 100.
Modification, termination, or setting aside of support order, see Family Code § 3650 et seq.
Person defined for purposes of this Code, see Family Code § 105.
Petition for separation or dissolution of marriage, pending child or spousal support order, see Code of Civil Procedure § 583.161.
Similar provisions, see Family Code § 4334.
Support, generally, see Family Code § 3500 et seq.
Support defined for purposes of this Code, see Family Code § 150.
Support order, modification or termination,
 Authority of court, see Family Code § 3651.
 Discovery, see Family Code § 3660 et seq.
 Retroactive application of modification, see Family Code § 3653.
Support order defined for purposes of this Code, see Family Code § 155.
Uniform Interstate Family Support Act, see Family Code § 5700.101 et seq.

Research References

Forms

West's California Judicial Council Forms FL-684, Request for Order and Supporting Declaration (Governmental).

§ 4007.5. Suspension of money judgment or order for support of a child; exceptions; resumption of obligation; administrative adjustment; evaluation

(a) Every money judgment or order for support of a child shall be suspended, by operation of law, for any period exceeding 90 consecutive days in which the person ordered to pay support is incarcerated or involuntarily institutionalized, unless * * * the person owing support has the means to pay support while incarcerated or involuntarily institutionalized.

* * *

(b) The child support obligation shall <u>be suspended effective on the first day of the first full month of incarceration or involuntary institutionalization and shall</u> resume on the first day of the first full month after the release of the person owing support in the amount previously ordered, and that amount is presumed to be appropriate under federal and state law. This section does not preclude a person owing support from seeking a modification of the child support order pursuant to Section 3651, based on a change in circumstances or any other appropriate reason.

(c)(1) A local child support agency enforcing a child support order under Title IV–D of the Social Security Act (42 U.S.C. Sec. 651 et seq.) may, upon written notice of the proposed adjustment to the support obligor and obligee along with a blank form provided for the support obligor or obligee to object to the administrative adjustment to the local child support agency, administratively adjust account balances for a money judgment or order for support of a child suspended pursuant to subdivision (a) if all of the following occurs:

(A) The agency verifies that arrears and interest were accrued in violation of this section.

(B) The agency verifies that * * *<u>, to the extent known to the agency, the person owing support does not have the means to pay support while incarcerated or involuntarily institutionalized</u>.

(C) Neither the support obligor nor obligee objects, within 30 days of receipt of the notice of proposed adjustment, whether in writing or by telephone, to the administrative adjustment by the local child support agency.

(2) If either the support obligor or obligee objects to the administrative adjustment set forth in this subdivision, the agency shall not adjust the order, but shall file a motion with the court to seek to adjust the arrears and shall serve copies of the motion on the parties, who may file an objection to the agency's motion with the court. The obligor's arrears shall not be adjusted unless the court approves the adjustment.

(3) The agency may perform this adjustment without regard to whether it was enforcing the child support order at the time the parent owing support qualified for relief under this section.

(d) This section does not prohibit the local child support agency or a party from petitioning a court for a determination of child support or arrears amounts.

(e) For purposes of this section, the following definitions shall apply:

(1) "Incarcerated or involuntarily institutionalized" includes, but is not limited to, involuntary confinement to * * * <u>a federal or</u> state prison, a county jail, a juvenile facility operated by the Division of Juvenile Facilities in the Department of Corrections and Rehabilitation, or a mental health facility.

(2) "Suspend" means that the payment due on the current child support order, an arrears payment on a preexisting arrears balance, or interest on arrears created during a qualifying period of incarceration pursuant to this section is, by operation of law, set to zero dollars ($0) for the period in which the person owing support is incarcerated or involuntarily institutionalized.

(f) This section applies to * * * any child support * * * <u>obligation that accrues</u> on or after the enactment of this section regardless of when the child support order was established.

(g) The Department of Child Support Services shall, by <u>July 1, * * * 2023</u> and in consultation with the Judicial Council, develop forms to implement this section.

(h) On or before January 1, <u>2026</u>, the Department of Child Support Services * * *<u>, in consultation with the Judicial Council,</u> shall conduct an evaluation of the effectiveness of the administrative adjustment process authorized by this section and shall report the results of the review, as well as any recommended changes, to the Assembly Judiciary Committee and the Senate Judiciary Committee.

The evaluation shall include a review of the ease of the process to both the obligor and obligee, as well as an analysis of the number of cases administratively adjusted, the number of cases adjusted in court, and the number of cases not adjusted.

(i) It is the intent of the Legislature to ensure qualified persons are provided the support suspension by operation of law for qualified periods of incarceration or involuntary institutionalization that existed during the operative terms of the earlier versions of this statute regardless of whether the judicial or administrative determination of arrears is made before or after the repeal of the statute, if the earlier version of the statute provided for the money judgment or order for support to be suspended by operation of law. This subdivision is declarative of existing law. *(Added by Stats.2020, c. 217 (A.B.2325), § 2, eff. Jan. 1, 2021. Amended by Stats.2022, c. 573 (A.B.207), § 2, eff. Sept. 27, 2022.)*

Research References

Forms

West's California Judicial Council Forms FL–192, Notice of Rights and Responsibilities Health-Care Costs and Reimbursement Procedures (Translations Also Available).

West's California Judicial Council Forms FL–490, Application to Determine Arrears (Also Available in Spanish).

West's California Judicial Council Forms FL–676, Request for Determination of Support Arrears (Also Available in Spanish).

West's California Judicial Council Forms FL–676–INFO, Information Sheet Request for Determination of Support Arrears.

§ 4008. Property which may be subjected to support of children

The community property, the quasi-community property, and the separate property may be subjected to the support of the children in the proportions the court determines are just. *(Stats.1992, c. 162 (A.B.2650), § 10, operative Jan. 1, 1994.)*

Cross References

Community property defined for purposes of this Code, see Family Code § 65.
Property defined for purposes of this Code, see Family Code § 113.
Quasi-community property, defined, see Family Code § 125.
Separate property, defined, see Family Code §§ 130, 3515.
Spousal support, order of resort to property for payment, see Family Code § 4338.
Support defined for purposes of this Code, see Family Code § 150.

§ 4009. Retroactive application of order for support

An original order for child support may be made retroactive to the date of filing the petition, complaint, or other initial pleading. If the parent ordered to pay support was not served with the petition, complaint, or other initial pleading within 90 days after filing and the court finds that the parent was not intentionally evading service, the child support order shall be effective no earlier than the date of service. *(Stats.1992, c. 162 (A.B.2650), § 10, operative Jan. 1, 1994. Amended by Stats.1999, c. 653 (A.B.380), § 8; Stats.2000, c. 808 (A.B.1358), § 34, eff. Sept. 28, 2000; Stats.2004, c. 305 (A.B.2669), § 3.)*

Cross References

Computation of time, see Code of Civil Procedure §§ 12, 12a; Government Code § 6800 et seq.
Emancipation of minors, warning that court may void or rescind declaration and parents may become liable for support and medical insurance coverage pursuant to this chapter, see Family Code § 7121.
Enforcement of support orders, generally, see Family Code § 4500 et seq.
Expedited child support orders, see Family Code § 3620 et seq.
Health insurance coverage for supported children, see Family Code § 3750 et seq.
Judgment and order defined for purposes of this Code, see Family Code § 100.
Modification, termination, or setting aside of support order, see Family Code § 3650 et seq.
Retroactivity,
   Order modifying or terminating child support order, see Family Code § 3653.
   Spousal support order, see Family Code § 4333.
Support, generally, see Family Code § 3500 et seq.
Support defined for purposes of this Code, see Family Code § 150.
Support order, modification or termination,
   Authority of court, see Family Code § 3651.
   Discovery, see Family Code § 3660 et seq.
Support order defined for purposes of this Code, see Family Code § 155.

Research References

Forms

1 California Transactions Forms--Family Law § 1:104, Children and Obligations from Former Marriage.

1 California Transactions Forms--Family Law § 3:104, Basic Child Support Agreement.

1 California Transactions Forms--Family Law § 3:109, Extracurricular Activities.

West's California Judicial Council Forms FL–684, Request for Order and Supporting Declaration (Governmental).

§ 4010. Information on procedures to modify support order

In a proceeding in which the court orders a payment for the support of a child, the court shall, at the time of providing written notice of the order, provide the parties with a document describing the procedures by which the order may be modified. *(Stats.1992, c. 162 (A.B.2650), § 10, operative Jan. 1, 1994. Amended by Stats.1993, c. 219 (A.B.1500), § 136.)*

Cross References

Emancipation of minors, warning that court may void or rescind declaration and parents may become liable for support and medical insurance coverage pursuant to this chapter, see Family Code § 7121.
Expedited child support orders, see Family Code § 3620 et seq.
Health insurance coverage for supported children, see Family Code § 3750 et seq.
Judgment and order defined for purposes of this Code, see Family Code § 100.
Modification or termination of support orders, see Family Code § 3650 et seq.
Notice, actual and constructive, defined, see Civil Code § 18.
Proceeding defined for purposes of this Code, see Family Code § 110.
Statewide uniform child support guidelines, see Family Code § 4050 et seq.
Support defined for purposes of this Code, see Family Code § 150.

Research References

Forms

West's California Judicial Council Forms FL–192, Notice of Rights and Responsibilities Health-Care Costs and Reimbursement Procedures (Translations Also Available).

§ 4011. Priority of payments; creditors

Payment of child support ordered by the court shall be made by the person owing the support payment before payment of any debts owed to creditors. *(Stats.1992, c. 162 (A.B.2650), § 10, operative Jan. 1, 1994.)*

Cross References

Creditor defined, see Civil Code § 3430.
Expedited child support orders, see Family Code § 3620 et seq.
Health insurance coverage for supported children, see Family Code § 3750 et seq.
Modification, termination, or setting aside of support order, see Family Code § 3650 et seq.
Person defined for purposes of this Code, see Family Code § 105.
Support defined for purposes of this Code, see Family Code § 150.

Research References

Forms

1 California Transactions Forms--Family Law § 3:3, Child Support.

§ 4012. Security for payment of child support

Upon a showing of good cause, the court may order a parent required to make a payment of child support to give reasonable

§ 4012

security for the payment. *(Stats.1992, c. 162 (A.B.2650), § 10, operative Jan. 1, 1994.)*

Cross References

Bond for support, see Penal Code § 270b.
Expedited child support orders, see Family Code § 3620 et seq.
Failure to support child, see Penal Code § 270 et seq.
Health insurance coverage for supported children, see Family Code § 3750 et seq.
Judgment and order defined for purposes of this Code, see Family Code § 100.
Modification, termination, or setting aside of support order, see Family Code § 3650 et seq.
Payment of spousal support, security for, see Family Code § 4339.
Securing future child support payments,
 Deposit of assets, see Family Code § 4600 et seq.
 Deposit of money, see Family Code § 4550 et seq.
Security for payment of spousal support, see Family Code § 4339.
Support defined for purposes of this Code, see Family Code § 150.

Research References

Forms
1 California Transactions Forms--Family Law § 2:43, Life Insurance.

§ 4013. Duty for child support discharged in bankruptcy; order for child support

If obligations for support of a child are discharged in bankruptcy, the court may make all proper orders for the support of the child that the court determines are just. *(Stats.1992, c. 162 (A.B.2650), § 10, operative Jan. 1, 1994.)*

Cross References

Agreement for property settlement or support of spouse discharged in bankruptcy, see Family Code § 3592.
California Work Opportunity and Responsibility to Kids Act, see Welfare and Institutions Code § 11200 et seq.
Child for whom support may be ordered, defined, see Family Code § 58.
Child support agreements, generally, see Family Code § 3585 et seq.
Child welfare services, see Welfare and Institutions Code § 16500 et seq.
Expedited child support orders, see Family Code § 3620 et seq.
Failure to support child, see Penal Code § 270 et seq.
Health insurance coverage for supported children, see Family Code § 3750 et seq.
Judgment and order defined for purposes of this Code, see Family Code § 100.
Modification, termination, or setting aside of support order, see Family Code § 3650 et seq.
Petition for separation or dissolution of marriage, pending child or spousal support order, see Code of Civil Procedure § 583.161.
Spousal and child support during pendency of proceedings, see Family Code § 3600 et seq.
Support, defined, see Family Code § 150.
Support order, modification or termination,
 Authority of court, see Family Code § 3651.
 Discovery, see Family Code § 3660 et seq.
 Retroactive application of modification, see Family Code § 3653.
Termination of support, effect of contingencies, see Family Code § 4007.
Uniform Interstate Family Support Act, see Family Code § 5700.101 et seq.

§ 4014. Notice of obligation to provide name and address of employer; notice of information to be filed with the court

(a) An order for child support issued or modified pursuant to this chapter shall include a provision requiring the obligor and child support obligee to notify the other parent or, if the order requires payment through an agency designated under Title IV-D of the Social Security Act (42 U.S.C. Sec. 651 et seq.), the agency named in the order, of the name and address of the person's current employer.

(b) The requirements set forth in this subdivision apply only in cases when the local child support agency is not providing child support services pursuant to Section 17400. To the extent required by federal law, and subject to applicable confidentiality provisions of state or federal law, a judgment for paternity and an order for child support entered or modified pursuant to any law shall include a provision requiring the child support obligor and obligee to file with the court all of the following information:

(1) Residential and mailing address.

(2) Social security number, individual taxpayer identification number, or other uniform identification number.

(3) Telephone number.

(4) Driver's license number or identification card number issued by the Department of Motor Vehicles.

(5) Name, address, and telephone number of the employer.

(6) Any other information prescribed by the Judicial Council.

The judgment or order shall specify that each parent is responsible for providing the parent's own information, that the information must be filed with the court within 10 days of the court order, and that new or different information must be filed with the court within 10 days after any event causing a change in the previously provided information.

(c) The requirements set forth in this subdivision shall only apply in cases in which the local child support agency is not providing child support services pursuant to Section 17400. Once the child support registry, as described in Section 17391 is operational, a judgment for parentage and an order for child support entered or modified pursuant to any law shall include a provision requiring the child support obligor and obligee to file and keep updated the information specified in subdivision (b) with the child support registry.

(d) The Judicial Council shall develop forms to implement this section. The forms shall be developed so as not to delay the implementation of the Statewide Child Support Registry described in Section 17391 and shall be available no later than 30 days prior to the implementation of the Statewide Child Support Registry. *(Added by Stats.1993, c. 876 (S.B.1068), § 18, eff. Oct. 6, 1993, operative Jan. 1, 1994. Amended by Stats.1997, c. 599 (A.B.573), § 13; Stats.1998, c. 858 (A.B.2169), § 2; Stats.2004, c. 339 (A.B.1704), § 2; Stats.2016, c. 474 (A.B.2882), § 8, eff. Jan. 1, 2017; Stats.2018, c. 838 (S.B.695), § 5, eff. Jan. 1, 2019; Stats.2019, c. 115 (A.B.1817), § 43, eff. Jan. 1, 2020.)*

Cross References

Computation of time, see Code of Civil Procedure §§ 12, 12a; Government Code § 6800 et seq.
Expedited child support orders, see Family Code § 3620 et seq.
Health insurance coverage for supported children, see Family Code § 3750 et seq.
Judgment and order defined for purposes of this Code, see Family Code § 100.
Modification, termination, or setting aside of support order, see Family Code § 3650 et seq.
Redacting social security numbers from material filed pursuant to petitions for dissolution of marriage, nullity of marriage or legal separation, exception set out for this section, see Family Code § 2024.5.
State defined for purposes of this Code, see Family Code § 145.
Support defined for purposes of this Code, see Family Code § 150.

Research References

Forms
West's California Code Forms, Family § 4000, Comment Overview—Court-Ordered Child Support.
West's California Judicial Council Forms FL-191, Child Support Case Registry Form (Also Available in Spanish).
West's California Judicial Council Forms FL-684, Request for Order and Supporting Declaration (Governmental).

ARTICLE 2. STATEWIDE UNIFORM GUIDELINE

Section
4050. Legislative intent; compliance with federal law.
4051. Repealed.
4052. Adherence of courts to uniform guidelines.

Section

4052.5. Child with more than two parents; application of uniform guideline; amount of support adjusted if presumption rebutted; effect on existing guidelines, regulations, etc.
4053. Implementation of statewide uniform guideline; principles to be followed by court.
4054. Review of statewide uniform guideline by Judicial Council; recommendations to Legislature.
4055. Statewide uniform guideline for determining child support.
4056. Amount differing from guideline formula; information used in determining statewide uniform guideline amount.
4057. Amount of child support established by formula; rebuttable presumption.
4057.5. Income of obligor parent's subsequent spouse or nonmarital partner; consideration.
4058. Annual gross income of parents.
4059. Annual net disposable income of parents.
4060. Computation of monthly net disposable income.
4061. Additional support for children; computation.
4062. Additional child support.
4063. Uninsured health care costs; payment procedures.
4064. Adjustment of award to accommodate parent's seasonal or fluctuating income.
4065. Stipulated agreements for child support awards; conditions; modification.
4066. "Family support" designation; maximization of tax benefits.
4067. Legislative review of statewide uniform guideline.
4068. Model worksheets for determination of amount of support due; form to assist courts in making findings and orders; development of simplified income and expense form.
4069. Establishment of statewide uniform guideline as change of circumstances.
4070. Financial hardship; income deductions.
4071. Financial hardship; evidence.
4071.5. Repealed.
4072. Deduction for hardship expenses; statement by court of reasons for supporting deductions; statement of amount and underlying facts; duration.
4073. Considerations of court in deciding whether or not to allow hardship deduction.
4074. Application of article to all awards for support of children.
4075. Tax treatment of spousal support and separate maintenance; application of article.
4076. Modification of child support orders; two-step phase-in of formula amount of support; conditions.
4077. Identification of additional legislative changes required to comply with federal child support regulations.
4100 to 4105. Inoperative.

Cross References

Construction of code, continuation of existing statutes, see Family Code § 2.
Emancipation of minors, notice of declaration proceedings, warning that court may void or rescind declaration and parents may become liable for support and medical insurance coverage pursuant to this chapter, see Family Code § 7121.
Support of wards and dependent children, liability for costs of support, see Welfare and Institutions Code § 903.
Temporary child support orders issued pursuant to San Mateo County Pilot Project, compliance with uniform guidelines, see Family Code § 20018.

Uniform Interstate Family Support Act, see Family Code § 5700.101 et seq.

§ 4050. Legislative intent; compliance with federal law

In adopting the statewide uniform guideline provided in this article, it is the intention of the Legislature to ensure that this state remains in compliance with federal regulations for child support guidelines. *(Added by Stats.1993, c. 219 (A.B.1500), § 138.)*

Cross References

Construction of code, continuation of existing statutes, see Family Code § 2.
Legislative intent, construction of statutes, see Code of Civil Procedure § 1859.
State defined for purposes of this Code, see Family Code § 145.
Support defined for purposes of this Code, see Family Code § 150.
Uniform Interstate Family Support Act, see Family Code § 5700.101 et seq.

Research References

Forms

California Practice Guide: Rutter Family Law Forms Form 1:32, Glossary of Common Family Law Terms, Phrases and Concepts (Enclosure to Form 1:31).
California Practice Guide: Rutter Family Law Forms Form 5:1, Stipulation to Orders Pending Trial (Attorney-Drafted).
California Practice Guide: Rutter Family Law Forms Form 6:2, Stipulation Re Child Support and Order Thereon (Attorney-Drafted).
California Practice Guide: Rutter Family Law Forms Form 11:20, Sample Trial Brief.
California Practice Guide: Rutter Family Law Forms Form 17:1, Stipulation and Order for Modification of Spousal Support, Child Support, Custody and Visitation.
1 California Transactions Forms--Family Law § 3:3, Child Support.
1 California Transactions Forms--Family Law § 3:22, Mandatory Compliance With Statewide Guidelines.
West's California Code Forms, Family § 3900, Comment Overview—Duty of Parent to Support Child.
West's California Code Forms, Family § 4050, Comment Overview—Statewide Uniform Guideline.
West's California Code Forms, Family § 4068 Form 2, Financial Statement—Simplified.
West's California Judicial Council Forms FL-150, Income and Expense Declaration (Also Available in Spanish).
West's California Judicial Council Forms FL-684, Request for Order and Supporting Declaration (Governmental).

§ 4051. Repealed by Stats.2015, c. 303 (A.B.731), § 148, eff. Jan. 1, 2016

§ 4052. Adherence of courts to uniform guidelines

The court shall adhere to the statewide uniform guideline and may depart from the guideline only in the special circumstances set forth in this article. *(Added by Stats.1993, c. 219 (A.B.1500), § 138.)*

Research References

Forms

California Practice Guide: Rutter Family Law Forms Form 5:2, Request for Order Re Child Custody, Child Support, Spousal Support, Attorney Fees, etc.
California Practice Guide: Rutter Family Law Forms Form 6:11, Request for Order Re Guideline Child Support, Temporary "Guideline" Spousal Support and Family Code §4062 "Add-On" Child Support.
West's California Code Forms, Family § 4050, Comment Overview—Statewide Uniform Guideline.

§ 4052.5. Child with more than two parents; application of uniform guideline; amount of support adjusted if presumption rebutted; effect on existing guidelines, regulations, etc.

(a) The statewide uniform guideline, as required by federal regulations, shall apply in any case in which a child has more than two parents. The court shall apply the guideline by dividing child support obligations among the parents based on income and amount of time spent with the child by each parent, pursuant to Section 4053.

(b) Consistent with federal regulations, after calculating the amount of support owed by each parent under the guideline, the

§ 4052.5

presumption that the guideline amount of support is correct may be rebutted if the court finds that the application of the guideline in that case would be unjust or inappropriate due to special circumstances, pursuant to Section 4057. If the court makes that finding, the court shall divide child support obligations among the parents in a manner that is just and appropriate based on income and amount of time spent with the child by each parent, applying the principles set forth in Section 4053 and this article.

(c) Nothing in this section shall be construed to require reprogramming of the California Child Support Enforcement System, a change to the statewide uniform guideline for determining child support set forth in Section 4055, or a revision by the Department of Child Support Services of its regulations, policies, procedures, forms, or training materials. *(Added by Stats.2013, c. 564 (S.B.274), § 3. Amended by Stats.2016, c. 474 (A.B.2882), § 9, eff. Jan. 1, 2017.)*

§ 4053. Implementation of statewide uniform guideline; principles to be followed by court

In implementing the statewide uniform guideline, the courts shall adhere to the following principles:

(a) A parent's first and principal obligation is to support the parent's minor children according to the parent's circumstances and station in life.

(b) Both parents are mutually responsible for the support of their children.

(c) The guideline takes into account each parent's actual income and level of responsibility for the children.

(d) Each parent should pay for the support of the children according to the parent's ability.

(e) The guideline seeks to place the interests of children as the state's top priority.

(f) Children should share in the standard of living of both parents. Child support may therefore appropriately improve the standard of living of the custodial household to improve the lives of the children.

(g) Child support orders in cases in which both parents have high levels of responsibility for the children should reflect the increased costs of raising the children in two homes and should minimize significant disparities in the children's living standards in the two homes.

(h) The financial needs of the children should be met through private financial resources as much as possible.

(i) It is presumed that a parent having primary physical responsibility for the children contributes a significant portion of available resources for the support of the children.

(j) The guideline seeks to encourage fair and efficient settlements of conflicts between parents and seeks to minimize the need for litigation.

(k) The guideline is intended to be presumptively correct in all cases, and only under special circumstances should child support orders fall below the child support mandated by the guideline formula.

(*l*) Child support orders shall ensure that children actually receive fair, timely, and sufficient support reflecting the state's high standard of living and high costs of raising children compared to other states. *(Added by Stats.1993, c. 219 (A.B.1500), § 138. Amended by Stats.2019, c. 115 (A.B.1817), § 44, eff. Jan. 1, 2020.)*

Cross References

Child custody, see Family Code § 3020 et seq.
Emancipation of minors, warning that court may void or rescind declaration and parents may become liable for support and medical insurance coverage pursuant to this chapter, see Family Code § 7121.
Expedited child support orders, see Family Code § 3620 et seq.
Health insurance coverage for supported children, see Family Code § 3750 et seq.

Judgment and order defined for purposes of this Code, see Family Code § 100.
Minor defined for purposes of this Code, see Family Code § 6500.
Modification, termination, or setting aside of support order, see Family Code § 3650 et seq.
Presumption of child support amount established by formula, see Family Code § 4057.
State defined for purposes of this Code, see Family Code § 145.
Support defined for purposes of this Code, see Family Code § 150.
Support order defined for purposes of this Code, see Family Code § 155.
Uniform Interstate Family Support Act, see Family Code § 5700.101 et seq.

Research References

Forms

California Practice Guide: Rutter Family Law Forms Form 6:8, Request for Order Re Child Support (Guideline Based on Earning Capacity in Lieu of Actual Income).
1 California Transactions Forms--Family Law § 2:64, Amount of Support.
1 California Transactions Forms--Family Law § 2:65, Add-Ons.
1 California Transactions Forms--Family Law § 3:23, Legislative Principles.
1 California Transactions Forms--Family Law § 3:36, Permitted Adjustments.
1 California Transactions Forms--Family Law § 3:39, Extraordinarily High Income.
West's California Code Forms, Family § 4000, Comment Overview—Court-Ordered Child Support.
West's California Code Forms, Family § 4050, Comment Overview—Statewide Uniform Guideline.

§ 4054. Review of statewide uniform guideline by Judicial Council; recommendations to Legislature

(a) The Judicial Council shall periodically review the statewide uniform guideline to recommend to the Legislature appropriate revisions.

(b) The review shall include * * * <u>all of the following:</u>

<u>(1) Economic data on the cost of raising children * * *:</u>

<u>(2) Labor market data, such as unemployment rates, employment rates, hours worked, and earnings, by occupation and skill level for the state and local job markets.</u>

<u>(3) The impact of guideline policies and amounts on custodial and noncustodial parents who have family incomes below 200 percent of the federal poverty level.</u>

<u>(4) Factors that influence employment rates among custodial and noncustodial parents and compliance with child support orders.</u>

<u>(5) An</u> analysis of case data, gathered through sampling or other methods, on the actual application of<u>, and deviations from,</u> the guideline after the guideline's operative date * * *<u>, as well as the rates of orders entered by default, orders entered based on presumed income and earning capacity, and orders determined using the low-income adjustment.</u>

<u>(6) An</u> analysis of guidelines and studies from other states, and other research and studies available to or undertaken by the Judicial Council.

<u>(7) A comparison of payments on child support orders by case characteristics, including whether the order was entered by default, based on earning capacity or presumed income, or determined using the low-income adjustment.</u>

<u>(8) Any additional factors required by federal regulations.</u>

(c) Any recommendations for revisions to the guideline shall be made to ensure that the guideline results in appropriate child support orders, to limit deviations from the guideline, or otherwise to help ensure that the guideline is in compliance with federal law.

(d) The Judicial Council may also review and report on other matters, including, but not limited to, the following:

(1) The treatment of the income of a subsequent spouse or nonmarital partner.

(2) The treatment of children from prior or subsequent relationships.

(3) The application of the guideline in a case where a payer parent has extraordinarily low or extraordinarily high income, or where each parent has primary physical custody of one or more of the children of the marriage.

(4) The benefits and limitations of a uniform statewide spousal support guideline and the interrelationship of that guideline with the state child support guideline.

(5) Whether the use of gross or net income in the guideline is preferable.

(6) Whether the guideline affects child custody litigation or the efficiency of the judicial process.

(7) Whether the various assumptions used in computer software used by some courts to calculate child support comport with state law and should be made available to parties and counsel.

(e) The initial review by the Judicial Council shall be submitted to the Legislature and to the Department of Child Support Services on or before December 31, 1993, and subsequent reviews shall occur at least every four years thereafter unless federal law requires a different interval.

(f) In developing its recommendations, the Judicial Council shall consult with a broad cross-section of groups involved in child support issues, including, but not limited to, the following:

(1) Custodial and noncustodial parents.

(2) Representatives of established women's rights and fathers' rights groups.

(3) Representatives of established organizations that advocate for the economic well-being of children.

(4) Members of the judiciary, district attorney's offices, the Attorney General's office, and the Department of Child Support Services.

(5) Certified family law specialists.

(6) Academicians specializing in family law.

(7) Persons representing low-income parents.

(8) Persons representing recipients of assistance under the Cal-WORKs program seeking child support services.

(9) Persons representing currently or formerly incarcerated parents.

(g) In developing its recommendations, the Judicial Council shall seek public comment and shall be guided by the legislative intent that children share in the standard of living of both of their parents. *(Added by Stats.1993, c. 219 (A.B.1500), § 138. Amended by Stats.2002, c. 927 (A.B.3032), § 2.5; Stats.2022, c. 573 (A.B.207), § 3, eff. Sept. 27, 2022.)*

Cross References

Attorney General, generally, see Government Code § 12500 et seq.
Child custody, see Family Code § 3020 et seq.
Counsel, right to, see Cal. Const. Art. 1, § 15, cl. 3.
Department of Child Support Services, generally, see Family Code § 17000 et seq.
District attorney, powers and duties, see Government Code § 26500 et seq.
Expedited child support orders, see Family Code § 3620 et seq.
Health insurance coverage for supported children, see Family Code § 3750 et seq.
Judgment and order defined for purposes of this Code, see Family Code § 100.
Legislative intent, construction of statutes, see Code of Civil Procedure § 1859.
Legislative review of state uniform support guideline, consideration of Judicial Council's recommendations, see Family Code § 4067.
Modification, termination, or setting aside of support order, see Family Code § 3650 et seq.
Person defined for purposes of this Code, see Family Code § 105.
References to husband, wife, spouses and married persons, persons included for purposes of this Code, see Family Code § 11.
Spousal support defined for purposes of this Code, see Family Code § 142.
State defined for purposes of this Code, see Family Code § 145.
Support defined for purposes of this Code, see Family Code § 150.
Support order defined for purposes of this Code, see Family Code § 155.

§ 4055. Statewide uniform guideline for determining child support

(a) The statewide uniform guideline for determining child support orders is as follows: $CS = K[HN - (H\%)(TN)]$.

(b)(1) The components of the formula are as follows:

(A) CS = child support amount.

(B) K = amount of both parents' income to be allocated for child support as set forth in paragraph (3).

(C) HN = high earner's net monthly disposable income.

(D) $H\%$ = approximate percentage of time that the high earner has or will have primary physical responsibility for the children compared to the other parent. In cases in which parents have different time-sharing arrangements for different children, $H\%$ equals the average of the approximate percentages of time the high earner parent spends with each child.

(E) TN = total net monthly disposable income of both parties.

(2) To compute net disposable income, see Section 4059.

(3) K (amount of both parents' income allocated for child support) equals one plus $H\%$ (if $H\%$ is less than or equal to 50 percent) or two minus $H\%$ (if $H\%$ is greater than 50 percent) times the following fraction:

Total Net Disposable Income Per Month	K
$0–800	0.20 + TN/16,000
$801–6,666	0.25
$6,667–10,000	0.10 + 1,000/TN
Over $10,000	0.12 + 800/TN

For example, if $H\%$ equals 20 percent and the total monthly net disposable income of the parents is $1,000, $K = (1 + 0.20) \times 0.25$, or 0.30. If $H\%$ equals 80 percent and the total monthly net disposable income of the parents is $1,000, $K = (2 - 0.80) \times 0.25$, or 0.30.

(4) For more than one child, multiply CS by:

2 children	1.6
3 children	2
4 children	2.3
5 children	2.5
6 children	2.625
7 children	2.75
8 children	2.813
9 children	2.844
10 children	2.86

(5) If the amount calculated under the formula results in a positive number, the higher earner shall pay that amount to the lower earner. If the amount calculated under the formula results in a negative number, the lower earner shall pay the absolute value of that amount to the higher earner.

(6) In any default proceeding where proof is by affidavit pursuant to Section 2336, or in any proceeding for child support in which a party fails to appear after being duly noticed, $H\%$ shall be set at zero in the formula if the noncustodial parent is the higher earner or at 100 if the custodial parent is the higher earner, where there is no evidence presented demonstrating the percentage of time that the noncustodial parent has primary physical responsibility for the children. $H\%$ shall not be set as described in paragraph (3) if the moving party in a default proceeding is the noncustodial parent or if the party who fails to appear after being duly noticed is the custodial parent. A statement by the party who is not in default as to the percentage of time that the noncustodial parent has primary physical responsibility for the children shall be deemed sufficient evidence.

(7) In all cases in which the net disposable income per month of the obligor is less than one thousand five hundred dollars ($1,500),

§ 4055

adjusted annually for cost-of-living increases, there is a rebuttable presumption that the obligor is entitled to a low-income adjustment. The Judicial Council shall annually determine the amount of the net disposable income adjustment based on the change in the annual California Consumer Price Index for All Urban Consumers, published by the California Department of Industrial Relations, Division of Labor Statistics and Research. The presumption may be rebutted by evidence showing that the application of the low-income adjustment would be unjust and inappropriate in the particular case. In determining whether the presumption is rebutted, the court shall consider the principles provided in Section 4053, and the impact of the contemplated adjustment on the respective net incomes of the obligor and the obligee. The low-income adjustment shall reduce the child support amount otherwise determined under this section by an amount that is no greater than the amount calculated by multiplying the child support amount otherwise determined under this section by a fraction, the numerator of which is 1,500, adjusted annually for cost-of-living increases, minus the obligor's net disposable income per month, and the denominator of which is 1,500, adjusted annually for cost-of-living increases.

(8) Unless the court orders otherwise, the order for child support shall allocate the support amount so that the amount of support for the youngest child is the amount of support for one child, and the amount for the next youngest child is the difference between that amount and the amount for two children, with similar allocations for additional children. However, this paragraph does not apply to cases in which there are different time-sharing arrangements for different children or where the court determines that the allocation would be inappropriate in the particular case.

(c) If a court uses a computer to calculate the child support order, the computer program shall not automatically default affirmatively or negatively on whether a low-income adjustment is to be applied. If the low-income adjustment is applied, the computer program shall not provide the amount of the low-income adjustment. Instead, the computer program shall ask the user whether or not to apply the low-income adjustment, and if answered affirmatively, the computer program shall provide the range of the adjustment permitted by paragraph (7) of subdivision (b). *(Added by Stats.1993, c. 219 (A.B.1500), § 138. Amended by Stats.1993, c. 1156 (S.B.541), § 1; Stats.1994, c. 906 (A.B.923), § 1.5; Stats.1998, c. 581 (A.B.2801), § 15; Stats.2003, c. 225 (A.B.1752), § 1, eff. Aug. 11, 2003; Stats. 2012, c. 646 (A.B.2393), § 1; Stats.2013, c. 76 (A.B.383), § 61; Stats.2017, c. 730 (S.B.469), § 1, eff. Jan. 1, 2018; Stats.2020, c. 36 (A.B.3364), § 28, eff. Jan. 1, 2021.)*

Cross References

Affidavits, see Code of Civil Procedure § 2009 et seq.
Child custody, see Family Code § 3020 et seq.
Expedited child support orders, see Family Code § 3620 et seq.
Financial hardship, see Family Code § 4071.
Health insurance coverage for supported children, see Family Code § 3750 et seq.
Judgment and order defined for purposes of this Code, see Family Code § 100.
Modification, termination, or setting aside of support order, see Family Code § 3650 et seq.
Presumption of child support amount established by formula, see Family Code § 4057.
Presumptions, see Evidence Code § 600 et seq.
Proceeding defined for purposes of this Code, see Family Code § 110.
Support defined for purposes of this Code, see Family Code § 150.
Support order defined for purposes of this Code, see Family Code § 155.
Uniform Interstate Family Support Act, see Family Code § 5700.101 et seq.

Research References

Forms

California Practice Guide: Rutter Family Law Forms Form 5:19, Non-Guideline Child Support Findings Attachment.
1 California Transactions Forms--Family Law § 2:64, Amount of Support.
1 California Transactions Forms--Family Law § 3:22, Mandatory Compliance With Statewide Guidelines.
1 California Transactions Forms--Family Law § 3:36, Permitted Adjustments.
1 California Transactions Forms--Family Law § 3:112, Alternating the Dependency Exemption.
West's California Code Forms, Family § 4050, Comment Overview—Statewide Uniform Guideline.
West's California Code Forms, Family § 4068 Form 2, Financial Statement—Simplified.
West's California Judicial Council Forms FL–342, Child Support Information and Order Attachment (Also Available in Spanish).

§ 4056. Amount differing from guideline formula; information used in determining statewide uniform guideline amount

(a) To comply with federal law, the court shall state, in writing or on the record, the following information whenever the court is ordering an amount for support that differs from the statewide uniform guideline formula amount under this article:

(1) The amount of support that would have been ordered under the guideline formula.

(2) The reasons the amount of support ordered differs from the guideline formula amount.

(3) The reasons the amount of support ordered is consistent with the best interests of the children.

(b) At the request of any party, the court shall state in writing or on the record the following information used in determining the guideline amount under this article:

(1) The net monthly disposable income of each parent.

(2) The actual federal income tax filing status of each parent (for example, single, married, married filing separately, or head of household and number of exemptions).

(3) Deductions from gross income for each parent.

(4) The approximate percentage of time pursuant to paragraph (1) of subdivision (b) of Section 4055 that each parent has primary physical responsibility for the children compared to the other parent. *(Added by Stats.1993, c. 219 (A.B.1500), § 138. Amended by Stats.1993, c. 1156 (S.B.541), § 2.)*

Cross References

Best interest of child,
   Considerations, see Family Code § 3011.
   Order of preference for custody, best interest of child as factor, see Family Code § 3040.
State defined for purposes of this Code, see Family Code § 145.
Support defined for purposes of this Code, see Family Code § 150.
Tax levies, see Government Code § 29100 et seq.; Revenue and Taxation Code § 2151 et seq.
Writings, authentication and proof of, see Evidence Code § 1400 et seq.

Research References

Forms

California Practice Guide: Rutter Family Law Forms Form 1:32, Glossary of Common Family Law Terms, Phrases and Concepts (Enclosure to Form 1:31).
1 California Transactions Forms--Family Law § 2:64, Amount of Support.
1 California Transactions Forms--Family Law § 2:65, Add-Ons.
1 California Transactions Forms--Family Law § 2:88, Marital Settlement Agreement.
1 California Transactions Forms--Family Law § 3:28, Statutory Findings as Basis for Support.
1 California Transactions Forms--Family Law § 3:32, Determination of Net Monthly Disposable Income.
West's California Code Forms, Family § 2338 Form 8, Marital Agreement.
West's California Code Forms, Family § 3585 Form 2, Child Support Provisions.
West's California Code Forms, Family § 4050, Comment Overview—Statewide Uniform Guideline.
West's California Judicial Council Forms FL–342(A), Non-Guideline Support Findings Attachment.

§ 4057. Amount of child support established by formula; rebuttable presumption

(a) The amount of child support established by the formula provided in subdivision (a) of Section 4055 is presumed to be the correct amount of child support to be ordered.

(b) The presumption of subdivision (a) is a rebuttable presumption affecting the burden of proof and may be rebutted by admissible evidence showing that application of the formula would be unjust or inappropriate in the particular case, consistent with the principles set forth in Section 4053, because one or more of the following factors is found to be applicable by a preponderance of the evidence, and the court states in writing or on the record the information required in subdivision (a) of Section 4056:

(1) The parties have stipulated to a different amount of child support under subdivision (a) of Section 4065.

(2) The sale of the family residence is deferred pursuant to Chapter 8 (commencing with Section 3800) of Part 1 and the rental value of the family residence where the children reside exceeds the mortgage payments, homeowner's insurance, and property taxes. The amount of any adjustment pursuant to this paragraph shall not be greater than the excess amount.

(3) The parent being ordered to pay child support has an extraordinarily high income and the amount determined under the formula would exceed the needs of the children.

(4) A party is not contributing to the needs of the children at a level commensurate with that party's custodial time.

(5) Application of the formula would be unjust or inappropriate due to special circumstances in the particular case. These special circumstances include, but are not limited to, the following:

(A) Cases in which the parents have different time-sharing arrangements for different children.

(B) Cases in which both parents have substantially equal time-sharing of the children and one parent has a much lower or higher percentage of income used for housing than the other parent.

(C) Cases in which the children have special medical or other needs that could require child support that would be greater than the formula amount.

(D) Cases in which a child is found to have more than two parents. (Added by Stats.1993, c. 219 (A.B.1500), § 138. Amended by Stats.1993, c. 935 (S.B.145), § 1; Stats.1993, c. 1156 (S.B.541), § 3.5; Stats.2013, c. 564 (S.B.274), § 4.)

Cross References

Agreements for support of adult children, see Family Code § 3587.
Burden of proof, generally, see Evidence Code § 500 et seq.
Child custody, see Family Code § 3020 et seq.
Expedited child support orders, see Family Code § 3620 et seq.
Health insurance coverage for supported children, see Family Code § 3750 et seq.
Modification, termination, or setting aside of support order, see Family Code § 3650 et seq.
Presumptions, see Evidence Code § 600 et seq.
Property defined for purposes of this Code, see Family Code § 113.
State defined for purposes of this Code, see Family Code § 145.
Support agreements,
　Generally, see Family Code § 3580 et seq.
　Child support agreements, see Family Code § 3585 et seq.
　Spousal support agreements, see Family Code § 3590 et seq.
Support defined for purposes of this Code, see Family Code § 150.
Support of wards and dependent children, liability for costs of support, see Welfare and Institutions Code § 903.
Tax levies, see Government Code § 29100 et seq.; Revenue and Taxation Code § 2151 et seq.
West's California Judicial Council Forms FL-693, Guideline Findings Attachment (Governmental).
Writings, authentication and proof of, see Evidence Code § 1400 et seq.

Research References

Forms

California Practice Guide: Rutter Family Law Forms Form 6:10, Responsive Declaration to Request for Order Re Child Support Based on Guideline Formula (Extraordinarily High Income Earner Rebuttal).
1 California Transactions Forms--Family Law § 2:64, Amount of Support.
1 California Transactions Forms--Family Law § 2:88, Marital Settlement Agreement.
1 California Transactions Forms--Family Law § 3:36, Permitted Adjustments.
1 California Transactions Forms--Family Law § 3:39, Extraordinarily High Income.
West's California Code Forms, Family § 2338 Form 8, Marital Agreement.
West's California Code Forms, Family § 3585 Form 2, Child Support Provisions.
West's California Code Forms, Family § 4050, Comment Overview--Statewide Uniform Guideline.
West's California Judicial Council Forms FL-693, Guideline Findings Attachment (Governmental).

§ 4057.5. Income of obligor parent's subsequent spouse or nonmarital partner; consideration

(a)(1) The income of the obligor parent's subsequent spouse or nonmarital partner shall not be considered when determining or modifying child support, except in an extraordinary case where excluding that income would lead to extreme and severe hardship to any child subject to the child support award, in which case the court shall also consider whether including that income would lead to extreme and severe hardship to any child supported by the obligor or by the obligor's subsequent spouse or nonmarital partner.

(2) The income of the obligee parent's subsequent spouse or nonmarital partner shall not be considered when determining or modifying child support, except in an extraordinary case where excluding that income would lead to extreme and severe hardship to any child subject to the child support award, in which case the court shall also consider whether including that income would lead to extreme and severe hardship to any child supported by the obligee or by the obligee's subsequent spouse or nonmarital partner.

(b) For purposes of this section, an extraordinary case may include a parent who voluntarily or intentionally quits work or reduces income, or who intentionally remains unemployed or underemployed and relies on a subsequent spouse's income.

(c) If any portion of the income of either parent's subsequent spouse or nonmarital partner is allowed to be considered pursuant to this section, discovery for the purposes of determining income shall be based on W2 and 1099 income tax forms, except where the court determines that application would be unjust or inappropriate.

(d) If any portion of the income of either parent's subsequent spouse or nonmarital partner is allowed to be considered pursuant to this section, the court shall allow a hardship deduction based on the minimum living expenses for one or more stepchildren of the party subject to the order.

(e) The enactment of this section constitutes cause to bring an action for modification of a child support order entered prior to the operative date of this section. (Added by Stats.1993, c. 935 (S.B.145), § 2. Amended by Stats.1994, c. 1140 (S.B.279), § 1; Stats.1994, c. 1269 (A.B.2208), § 47.5.)

Cross References

Discovery, generally, see Code of Civil Procedure § 2016.010 et seq.
Expedited child support orders, see Family Code § 3620 et seq.
Health insurance coverage for supported children, see Family Code § 3750 et seq.
Judgment and order defined for purposes of this Code, see Family Code § 100.
Modification, termination, or setting aside of support order, see Family Code § 3650 et seq.
References to husband, wife, spouses and married persons, persons included for purposes of this Code, see Family Code § 11.

§ 4057.5

Support defined for purposes of this Code, see Family Code § 150.
Support order defined for purposes of this Code, see Family Code § 155.
Tax levies, see Government Code § 29100 et seq.; Revenue and Taxation Code § 2151 et seq.

Research References
Forms
1 California Transactions Forms--Family Law § 3:35, Consideration of New Spouse's Income for Tax Purposes.

§ 4058. Annual gross income of parents

(a) The annual gross income of each parent means income from whatever source derived, except as specified in subdivision (c) and includes, but is not limited to, the following:

(1) Income such as commissions, salaries, royalties, wages, bonuses, rents, dividends, pensions, interest, trust income, annuities, workers' compensation benefits, unemployment insurance benefits, disability insurance benefits, social security benefits, and spousal support actually received from a person not a party to the proceeding to establish a child support order under this article.

(2) Income from the proprietorship of a business, such as gross receipts from the business reduced by expenditures required for the operation of the business.

(3) In the discretion of the court, employee benefits or self-employment benefits, taking into consideration the benefit to the employee, any corresponding reduction in living expenses, and other relevant facts.

(b)(1) The court may, in its discretion, consider the earning capacity of a parent in lieu of the parent's income, consistent with the best interests of the children, taking into consideration the overall welfare and developmental needs of the children, and the time that parent spends with the children.

(2) When determining the earning capacity of the parent pursuant to this subdivision, the court shall consider the specific circumstances of the parent, to the extent known. Those circumstances include, but are not limited to, the parent's assets, residence, employment and earnings history, job skills, educational attainment, literacy, age, health, criminal record and other employment barriers, and record of seeking work, as well as the local job market, the availability of employers willing to hire the parent, prevailing earnings levels in the local community, and other relevant background factors affecting the parent's ability to earn.

(3) Notwithstanding any other law, the incarceration or involuntary institutionalization of a parent shall not be treated as voluntary unemployment in establishing or modifying support orders regardless of the nature of the offense. "Incarcerated or involuntarily institutionalized" has the same meaning as subdivision (e) of Section 4007.5.

(c) Annual gross income does not include any income derived from child support payments actually received, and income derived from any public assistance program, eligibility for which is based on a determination of need. Child support received by a party for children from another relationship shall not be included as part of that party's gross or net income. (Added by Stats.1993, c. 219 (A.B.1500), § 138. Amended by Stats.2018, c. 178 (A.B.2780), § 1, eff. Jan. 1, 2019; Stats.2022, c. 573 (A.B.207), § 4, eff. Sept. 27, 2022.)

Cross References

Best interest of the child,
 Considerations, see Family Code § 3011.
 Order of preference for custody, best interest of child as factor, see Family Code § 3040.
Expedited child support orders, see Family Code § 3620 et seq.
Health insurance coverage for supported children, see Family Code § 3750 et seq.
Judgment and order defined for purposes of this Code, see Family Code § 100.
Modification, termination, or setting aside of support order, see Family Code § 3650 et seq.
Person defined for purposes of this Code, see Family Code § 105.
Proceeding defined for purposes of this Code, see Family Code § 110.
Spousal support defined for purposes of this Code, see Family Code § 142.
Support defined for purposes of this Code, see Family Code § 150.
Support order defined for purposes of this Code, see Family Code § 155.
Workers' compensation, see Labor Code § 3200 et seq.

Research References
Forms
California Practice Guide: Rutter Family Law Forms Form 6:8, Request for Order Re Child Support (Guideline Based on Earning Capacity in Lieu of Actual Income).
1 California Transactions Forms--Family Law § 3:29, Determination of Gross Income.
West's California Code Forms, Family § 4050, Comment Overview—Statewide Uniform Guideline.

§ 4059. Annual net disposable income of parents

The annual net disposable income of each parent shall be computed by deducting from the parent's annual gross income the actual amounts attributable to the following items or other items permitted under this article:

(a) The state and federal income tax liability resulting from the parties' taxable income. Federal and state income tax deductions shall bear an accurate relationship to the tax status of the parties (that is, single, married, married filing separately, or head of household) and number of dependents. State and federal income taxes shall be those actually payable (not necessarily current withholding) after considering appropriate filing status, all available exclusions, deductions, and credits. Unless the parties stipulate otherwise, the tax effects of spousal support shall not be considered in determining the net disposable income of the parties for determining child support, but shall be considered in determining spousal support consistent with Chapter 3 (commencing with Section 4330) of Part 3.

(b) Deductions attributed to the employee's contribution or the self-employed worker's contribution pursuant to the Federal Insurance Contributions Act (FICA), or an amount not to exceed that allowed under FICA for persons not subject to FICA, provided that the deducted amount is used to secure retirement or disability benefits for the parent.

(c) Deductions for mandatory union dues and retirement benefits, provided that they are required as a condition of employment.

(d) Deductions for health insurance or health plan premiums for the parent and for any children the parent has an obligation to support and deductions for state disability insurance premiums.

(e) Any child or spousal support actually being paid by the parent pursuant to a court order, to or for the benefit of a person who is not a subject of the order to be established by the court. In the absence of a court order, child support actually being paid, not to exceed the amount established by the guideline, for natural or adopted children of the parent not residing in that parent's home, who are not the subject of the order to be established by the court, and of whom the parent has a duty of support. Unless the parent proves payment of the support, a deduction shall not be allowed under this subdivision.

(f) Job–related expenses, if allowed by the court after consideration of whether the expenses are necessary, the benefit to the employee, and any other relevant facts.

(g) A deduction for hardship, as defined by Sections 4070 to 4073, inclusive, and applicable published appellate court decisions. The amount of the hardship shall not be deducted from the amount of child support, but shall be deducted from the income of the party to whom it applies. In applying any hardship under paragraph (2) of subdivision (a) of Section 4071, the court shall seek to provide equity between competing child support orders. The Judicial Council shall develop a formula for calculating the maximum hardship deduction and shall submit it to the Legislature for its consideration on or before July 1, 1995. *(Added by Stats.1993, c. 219 (A.B.1500), § 138. Amended by Stats.1994, c. 1056 (A.B.3258), § 1; Stats.2019, c. 115 (A.B.1817), § 45, eff. Jan. 1, 2020.)*

Cross References

Agreements for support of adult children, see Family Code § 3587.
Expedited child support orders, see Family Code § 3620 et seq.
Health insurance coverage for supported children, see Family Code § 3750 et seq.
Judgment and order defined for purposes of this Code, see Family Code § 100.
Modification, termination, or setting aside of support order, see Family Code § 3650 et seq.
Person defined for purposes of this Code, see Family Code § 105.
Spousal support defined for purposes of this Code, see Family Code § 142.
State defined for purposes of this Code, see Family Code § 145.
Support agreements,
   Generally, see Family Code § 3580 et seq.
   Child support agreements, see Family Code § 3585 et seq.
   Spousal support agreements, see Family Code § 3590 et seq.
Support defined for purposes of this Code, see Family Code § 150.
Support order defined for purposes of this Code, see Family Code § 155.
Tax levies, see Government Code § 29100 et seq.; Revenue and Taxation Code § 2151 et seq.

Research References

Forms

1 California Transactions Forms--Family Law § 3:29, Determination of Gross Income.
1 California Transactions Forms--Family Law § 3:32, Determination of Net Monthly Disposable Income.
1 California Transactions Forms--Family Law § 3:33, Adjustments for Tax Filing Status, Itemized Deductions, and Credits.

§ 4060. Computation of monthly net disposable income

The monthly net disposable income shall be computed by dividing the annual net disposable income by 12. If the monthly net disposable income figure does not accurately reflect the actual or prospective earnings of the parties at the time the determination of support is made, the court may adjust the amount appropriately. *(Added by Stats.1993, c. 219 (A.B.1500), § 138.)*

Cross References

Support defined for purposes of this Code, see Family Code § 150.

Research References

Forms

1 California Transactions Forms--Family Law § 3:32, Determination of Net Monthly Disposable Income.
1 California Transactions Forms--Family Law § 3:40, Bonuses and Other Nonrecurring Income.

§ 4061. Additional support for children; computation

The amounts in Section 4062 shall be considered additional support for the children and shall be computed in accordance with the following:

(a) If there needs to be an apportionment of expenses pursuant to Section 4062, the expenses shall be divided one-half to each parent, unless either parent requests a different apportionment pursuant to subdivision (b) and presents documentation which demonstrates that a different apportionment would be more appropriate.

(b) If requested by either parent, and the court determines it is appropriate to apportion expenses under Section 4062 other than one-half to each parent, the apportionment shall be as follows:

(1) The basic child support obligation shall first be computed using the formula set forth in subdivision (a) of Section 4055, as adjusted for any appropriate rebuttal factors in subdivision (b) of Section 4057.

(2) Any additional child support required for expenses pursuant to Section 4062 shall thereafter be ordered to be paid by the parents in proportion to their net disposable incomes as adjusted pursuant to subdivisions (c) and (d).

(c) In cases where spousal support is or has been ordered to be paid by one parent to the other, for purposes of allocating additional expenses pursuant to Section 4062, the gross income of the parent paying spousal support shall be decreased by the amount of the spousal support paid and the gross income of the parent receiving the spousal support shall be increased by the amount of the spousal support received for as long as the spousal support order is in effect and is paid.

(d) For purposes of computing the adjusted net disposable income of the parent paying child support for allocating any additional expenses pursuant to Section 4062, the net disposable income of the parent paying child support shall be reduced by the amount of any basic child support ordered to be paid under subdivision (a) of Section 4055. However, the net disposable income of the parent receiving child support shall not be increased by any amount of child support received. *(Added by Stats.1993, c. 219 (A.B.1500), § 138. Amended by Stats.2010, c. 103 (S.B.580), § 2.)*

Cross References

Expedited child support orders, see Family Code § 3620 et seq.
Health insurance coverage for supported children, see Family Code § 3750 et seq.
Judgment and order defined for purposes of this Code, see Family Code § 100.
Modification, termination, or setting aside of support order, see Family Code § 3650 et seq.
Spousal support defined for purposes of this Code, see Family Code § 142.
Support defined for purposes of this Code, see Family Code § 150.
Support order defined for purposes of this Code, see Family Code § 155.

Research References

Forms

California Practice Guide: Rutter Family Law Forms Form 5:2, Request for Order Re Child Custody, Child Support, Spousal Support, Attorney Fees, etc.
1 California Transactions Forms--Family Law § 2:65, Add-Ons.
1 California Transactions Forms--Family Law § 3:44, Mandatory Additional Child Support.

§ 4062. Additional child support

(a) The court shall order the following as additional child support:

(1) Child care costs related to employment or to reasonably necessary education or training for employment skills.

(2) The reasonable uninsured health care costs for the children as provided in Section 4063.

(b) The court may order the following as additional child support:

(1) Costs related to the educational or other special needs of the children.

(2) Travel expenses for visitation. *(Added by Stats.1993, c. 219 (A.B.1500), § 138. Amended by Stats.1994, c. 466 (S.B.1807), § 1.)*

Cross References

Court order to participate in counseling, apportionment of costs, see Family Code § 3190.
Expedited child support orders, see Family Code § 3620 et seq.
Health insurance coverage for supported children, see Family Code § 3750 et seq.
Judgment and order defined for purposes of this Code, see Family Code § 100.
Modification, termination, or setting aside of support order, see Family Code § 3650 et seq.

§ 4062

Support defined for purposes of this Code, see Family Code § 150.

Research References

Forms

California Practice Guide: Rutter Family Law Forms Form 5:2, Request for Order Re Child Custody, Child Support, Spousal Support, Attorney Fees, etc.

California Practice Guide: Rutter Family Law Forms Form 6:11, Request for Order Re Guideline Child Support, Temporary "Guideline" Spousal Support and Family Code §4062 "Add-On" Child Support.

1 California Transactions Forms--Family Law § 2:65, Add-Ons.

1 California Transactions Forms--Family Law § 3:44, Mandatory Additional Child Support.

1 California Transactions Forms--Family Law § 3:45, Discretionary Additional Child Support.

West's California Code Forms, Family § 4050, Comment Overview—Statewide Uniform Guideline.

West's California Judicial Council Forms FL–192, Notice of Rights and Responsibilities Health-Care Costs and Reimbursement Procedures (Translations Also Available).

§ 4063. Uninsured health care costs; payment procedures

(a) When making an order pursuant to paragraph (2) of subdivision (a) of Section 4062, the court shall:

(1) Advise each parent, in writing or on the record, of the parent's rights and liabilities, including financial responsibilities.

(2) Include in its order the time period for a parent to reimburse the other parent for the reimbursing parent's share of the reasonable additional child support costs subject to the requirements of this section.

(b) Unless there has been an assignment of rights pursuant to Section 11477 of the Welfare and Institutions Code, when either parent accrues or pays costs pursuant to an order under this section, that parent shall provide the other parent with an itemized statement of the costs within a reasonable time, but not more than 30 days after accruing the costs. These costs shall then be paid as follows:

(1) If a parent has already paid all of these costs, that parent shall provide proof of payment and a request for reimbursement of that parent's court-ordered share to the other parent.

(2) If a parent has paid the parent's court-ordered share of the costs only, that parent shall provide proof of payment to the other parent, request the other parent to pay the remainder of the costs directly to the provider, and provide the reimbursing parent with any necessary information about how to make the payment to the provider.

(3) The other parent shall make the reimbursement or pay the remaining costs within the time period specified by the court, or, if no period is specified, within a reasonable time not to exceed 30 days from notification of the amount due, or according to any payment schedule set by the health care provider for either parent unless the parties agree in writing to another payment schedule or the court finds good cause for setting another payment schedule.

(4) If the reimbursing parent disputes a request for payment, that parent shall pay the requested amount and thereafter may seek judicial relief under this section and Section 290. If the reimbursing parent fails to pay the other parent as required by this subdivision, the other parent may seek judicial relief under this section and Section 290.

(c) Either parent may file a noticed motion to enforce an order issued pursuant to this section. In addition to the court's powers under Section 290, the court may award filing costs and reasonable attorney's fees if it finds that either party acted without reasonable cause regarding the party's obligations pursuant to this section.

(d) There is a rebuttable presumption that the costs actually paid for the uninsured health care needs of the children are reasonable, except as provided in subdivision (e).

(e) Except as provided in subdivision (g):

(1) The health care insurance coverage, including, but not limited to, coverage for emergency treatment, provided by a parent pursuant to a court order, shall be the coverage to be utilized at all times, consistent with the requirements of that coverage, unless the other parent can show that the health care insurance coverage is inadequate to meet the child's needs.

(2) If either parent obtains health care insurance coverage in addition to that provided pursuant to the court order, that parent shall bear sole financial responsibility for the costs of that additional coverage and the costs of any care or treatment obtained pursuant thereto in excess of the costs that would have been incurred under the health care insurance coverage provided for in the court order.

(f) Except as provided in subdivision (g):

(1) If the health care insurance coverage provided by a parent pursuant to a court order designates a preferred health care provider, that preferred provider shall be used at all times, consistent with the terms and requirements of that coverage.

(2) If either parent uses a health care provider other than the preferred provider inconsistent with the terms and requirements of the court-ordered health care insurance coverage, the parent obtaining that care shall bear the sole responsibility for any nonreimbursable health care costs in excess of the costs that would have been incurred under the court-ordered health care insurance coverage had the preferred provider been used.

(g) When ruling on a motion made pursuant to this section, in order to ensure that the health care needs of the child under this section are met, the court shall consider all relevant facts, including, but not limited to, the following:

(1) The geographic access and reasonable availability of necessary health care for the child that complies with the terms of the health care insurance coverage paid for by either parent pursuant to a court order. Health insurance shall be rebuttably presumed to be accessible if services to be provided are within 50 miles of the residence of the child subject to the support order. If the court determines that health insurance is not accessible, the court shall state the reason on the record.

(2) The necessity of emergency medical treatment that may have precluded the use of the health care insurance, or the preferred health care provider required under the insurance, provided by either parent pursuant to a court order.

(3) The special medical needs of the child.

(4) The reasonable inability of a parent to pay the full amount of reimbursement within a 30–day period and the resulting necessity for a court-ordered payment schedule. *(Added by Stats.1994, c. 466 (S.B.1807), § 3. Amended by Stats.2010, c. 103 (S.B.580), § 3; Stats.2019, c. 115 (A.B.1817), § 46, eff. Jan. 1, 2020.)*

Cross References

Attorney's fees and costs, generally, see Code of Civil Procedure § 1021.

Computation of time, see Code of Civil Procedure §§ 12, 12a; Government Code § 6800 et seq.

Health insurance coverage for supported children, see Family Code § 3750 et seq.

Judgment and order defined for purposes of this Code, see Family Code § 100.

Presumptions, see Evidence Code § 600 et seq.

Support defined for purposes of this Code, see Family Code § 150.

Writings, authentication and proof of, see Evidence Code § 1400 et seq.

Research References

Forms

California Practice Guide: Rutter Family Law Forms Form 5:2, Request for Order Re Child Custody, Child Support, Spousal Support, Attorney Fees, etc.

California Practice Guide: Rutter Family Law Forms Form 11:20, Sample Trial Brief.

1 California Transactions Forms--Family Law § 3:44, Mandatory Additional Child Support.

West's California Code Forms, Family § 4050, Comment Overview—Statewide Uniform Guideline.
West's California Judicial Council Forms FL-192, Notice of Rights and Responsibilities Health-Care Costs and Reimbursement Procedures (Translations Also Available).

§ 4064. Adjustment of award to accommodate parent's seasonal or fluctuating income

The court may adjust the child support order as appropriate to accommodate seasonal or fluctuating income of either parent. *(Added by Stats.1993, c. 219 (A.B.1500), § 138.)*

Cross References

Expedited child support orders, see Family Code § 3620 et seq.
Health insurance coverage for supported children, see Family Code § 3750 et seq.
Judgment and order defined for purposes of this Code, see Family Code § 100.
Modification, termination, or setting aside of support order, see Family Code § 3650 et seq.
Support defined for purposes of this Code, see Family Code § 150.
Support order defined for purposes of this Code, see Family Code § 155.

Research References

Forms

1 California Transactions Forms--Family Law § 3:41, Seasonal or Fluctuating Income.

§ 4065. Stipulated agreements for child support awards; conditions; modification

(a) Unless prohibited by applicable federal law, the parties may stipulate to a child support amount subject to approval of the court. However, the court shall not approve a stipulated agreement for child support below the guideline formula amount unless the parties declare all of the following:

(1) They are fully informed of their rights concerning child support.

(2) The order is being agreed to without coercion or duress.

(3) The agreement is in the best interests of the children involved.

(4) The needs of the children will be adequately met by the stipulated amount.

(5) The right to support has not been assigned to the county pursuant to Section 11477 of the Welfare and Institutions Code and no public assistance application is pending.

(b) The parties may, by stipulation, require the child support obligor to designate an account for the purpose of paying the child support obligation by electronic funds transfer pursuant to Section 4508.

(c) A stipulated agreement of child support is not valid unless the local child support agency has joined in the stipulation by signing it in any case in which the local child support agency is providing services pursuant to Section 17400. The local child support agency shall not stipulate to a child support order below the guideline amount if the children are receiving assistance under the CalWORKs program, if an application for public assistance is pending, or if the parent receiving support has not consented to the order.

(d) If the parties to a stipulated agreement stipulate to a child support order below the amount established by the statewide uniform guideline, no change of circumstances need be demonstrated to obtain a modification of the child support order to the applicable guideline level or above. *(Added by Stats.1993, c. 219 (A.B.1500), § 138. Amended by Stats.1993, c. 1156 (S.B.541), § 4; Stats.1999, c. 980 (A.B.1671), § 8; Stats.2000, c. 135 (A.B.2539), § 59; Stats.2000, c. 808 (A.B.1358), § 35, eff. Sept. 28, 2000.)*

Cross References

Agreements for support of adult children, see Family Code § 3587.
County defined for purposes of this Code, see Family Code § 67.
Expedited child support orders, see Family Code § 3620 et seq.
Health insurance coverage for supported children, see Family Code § 3750 et seq.
Judgment and order defined for purposes of this Code, see Family Code § 100.
Modification, termination, or setting aside of support order, see Family Code § 3650 et seq.
Presumption of child support amount established by formula, see Family Code § 4057.
Support agreements,
    Generally, see Family Code § 3580 et seq.
    Child support agreements, see Family Code § 3585 et seq.
    Spousal support agreements, see Family Code § 3590 et seq.
Support defined for purposes of this Code, see Family Code § 150.
Support order defined for purposes of this Code, see Family Code § 155.

Research References

Forms

California Practice Guide: Rutter Family Law Forms Form 5:1, Stipulation to Orders Pending Trial (Attorney-Drafted).
California Practice Guide: Rutter Family Law Forms Form 17:1, Stipulation and Order for Modification of Spousal Support, Child Support, Custody and Visitation.
1 California Transactions Forms--Family Law § 2:63, Authority for Child Support.
1 California Transactions Forms--Family Law § 2:64, Amount of Support.
1 California Transactions Forms--Family Law § 2:65, Add-Ons.
1 California Transactions Forms--Family Law § 2:88, Marital Settlement Agreement.
1 California Transactions Forms--Family Law § 2:91, Add-On Expenses in Conjunction With Family Support.
1 California Transactions Forms--Family Law § 2:93.50, Child Support Provision Regarding Electronic Transfer of Funds.
1 California Transactions Forms--Family Law § 3:37, Stipulation of the Parties.
1 California Transactions Forms--Family Law § 3:112, Alternating the Dependency Exemption.
1 California Transactions Forms--Family Law § 3:112.50, Designation of Electronic Fund Transfer Account Number.
West's California Code Forms, Family § 2338 Form 8, Marital Agreement.
West's California Code Forms, Family § 3585 Form 2, Child Support Provisions.
West's California Code Forms, Family § 4050, Comment Overview—Statewide Uniform Guideline.
West's California Judicial Council Forms FL-350, Stipulation to Establish or Modify Child Support and Order (Also Available in Spanish).
West's California Judicial Council Forms FL-693, Guideline Findings Attachment (Governmental).

§ 4066. "Family support" designation; maximization of tax benefits

Orders and stipulations otherwise in compliance with the statewide uniform guideline may designate as "family support" an unallocated total sum for support of the spouse and any children without specifically labeling all or any portion as "child support" as long as the amount is adjusted to reflect the effect of additional deductibility. The amount of the order shall be adjusted to maximize the tax benefits for both parents. *(Added by Stats.1993, c. 219 (A.B.1500), § 138.)*

Cross References

Agreements for support of adult children, see Family Code § 3587.
Family support defined for purposes of this Code, see Family Code § 92.
Judgment and order defined for purposes of this Code, see Family Code § 100.
References to husband, wife, spouses and married persons, persons included for purposes of this Code, see Family Code § 11.
Support agreements,
    Generally, see Family Code § 3580 et seq.
    Child support agreements, see Family Code § 3585 et seq.
    Spousal support agreements, see Family Code § 3590 et seq.
Support defined for purposes of this Code, see Family Code § 150.

§ 4066

Tax levies, see Government Code § 29100 et seq.; Revenue and Taxation Code § 2151 et seq.

Research References

Forms

California Practice Guide: Rutter Family Law Forms Form 1:32, Glossary of Common Family Law Terms, Phrases and Concepts (Enclosure to Form 1:31).
1 California Transactions Forms--Family Law § 3:24, Family Support.
1 California Transactions Forms--Family Law § 3:25, Duration of Child Support Obligation.

§ 4067. Legislative review of statewide uniform guideline

It is the intent of the Legislature that the statewide uniform guideline shall be reviewed by the Legislature at least every four years and shall be revised by the Legislature as appropriate to ensure that its application results in the determination of appropriate child support amounts. The review shall include consideration of changes required by applicable federal laws and regulations or recommended from time to time by the Judicial Council pursuant to Section 4054. *(Added by Stats.1993, c. 219 (A.B.1500), § 138.)*

Cross References

Health insurance coverage for supported children, see Family Code § 3750 et seq.
Legislative intent, construction of statutes, see Code of Civil Procedure § 1859.
Support defined for purposes of this Code, see Family Code § 150.

§ 4068. Model worksheets for determination of amount of support due; form to assist courts in making findings and orders; development of simplified income and expense form

(a) The Judicial Council may develop the following:

(1) Model worksheets to assist parties in determining the approximate amount of child support due under the formula provided in subdivision (a) of Section 4055 and the approximate percentage of time each parent has primary physical responsibility for the children.

(2) A form to assist the courts in making the findings and orders required by this article.

(b) The Judicial Council, in consultation with representatives of the State Department of Social Services, the California Family Support Council, the Senate Judiciary Committee, the Assembly Judiciary Committee, the Family Law Section of the State Bar of California, a legal services organization providing representation on child support matters, a custodial parent group, and a noncustodial parent group, shall develop a simplified income and expense form for determining child support under the formula provided in subdivision (a) of Section 4055, by June 1, 1995. The Judicial Council, also in consultation with these groups, shall develop factors to use to determine when the simplified income and expense form may be used and when the standard income and expense form must be used. *(Added by Stats.1993, c. 219 (A.B.1500), § 138. Amended by Stats.1994, c. 415 (S.B.1715), § 2; Stats.1994, c. 953 (A.B.2142), § 1.)*

Cross References

Child custody, see Family Code § 3020 et seq.
Family support defined for purposes of this Code, see Family Code § 92.
Judgment and order defined for purposes of this Code, see Family Code § 100.
State defined for purposes of this Code, see Family Code § 145.
Support defined for purposes of this Code, see Family Code § 150.

Research References

Forms

West's California Code Forms, Family § 4050, Comment Overview—Statewide Uniform Guideline.
West's California Code Forms, Family § 4068 Form 2, Financial Statement—Simplified.

West's California Judicial Council Forms FL-155, Financial Statement (Simplified) (Also Available in Spanish).

§ 4069. Establishment of statewide uniform guideline as change of circumstances

The establishment of the statewide uniform guideline constitutes a change of circumstances. *(Added by Stats.1993, c. 219 (A.B.1500), § 138. Amended by Stats.1993, c. 1156 (S.B.541), § 5.)*

Research References

Forms

West's California Judicial Council Forms FL-342, Child Support Information and Order Attachment (Also Available in Spanish).

§ 4070. Financial hardship; income deductions

If a parent is experiencing extreme financial hardship due to justifiable expenses resulting from the circumstances enumerated in Section 4071, on the request of a party, the court may allow the income deductions under Section 4059 that may be necessary to accommodate those circumstances. *(Added by Stats.1993, c. 219 (A.B.1500), § 138.)*

Research References

Forms

1 California Transactions Forms--Family Law § 2:65, Add-Ons.
1 California Transactions Forms--Family Law § 3:32, Determination of Net Monthly Disposable Income.
1 California Transactions Forms--Family Law § 3:34, Hardship Deductions.

§ 4071. Financial hardship; evidence

(a) Circumstances evidencing hardship include the following:

(1) Extraordinary health expenses for which the parent is financially responsible, and uninsured catastrophic losses.

(2) The minimum basic living expenses of either parent's natural or adopted children for whom the parent has the obligation to support from other marriages or relationships who reside with the parent. The court, on its own motion or on the request of a party, may allow these income deductions as necessary to accommodate these expenses after making the deductions allowable under paragraph (1).

(b) The maximum hardship deduction under paragraph (2) of subdivision (a) for each child who resides with the parent may be equal to, but shall not exceed, the support allocated each child subject to the order. For purposes of calculating this deduction, the amount of support per child established by the statewide uniform guideline shall be the total amount ordered divided by the number of children and not the amount established under paragraph (8) of subdivision (b) of Section 4055.

(c) The Judicial Council may develop tables in accordance with this section to reflect the maximum hardship deduction, taking into consideration the parent's net disposable income before the hardship deduction, the number of children for whom the deduction is being given, and the number of children for whom the support award is being made. *(Added by Stats.1993, c. 219 (A.B.1500), § 138. Amended by Stats.1993, c. 1156 (S.B.541), § 6.)*

Cross References

Computation of annual net disposable income of parents, see Family Code § 4059.
Computation of monthly net disposable income of parents, see Family Code § 4060.
Expedited child support orders, see Family Code § 3620 et seq.
Health insurance coverage for supported children, see Family Code § 3750 et seq.
Judgment and order defined for purposes of this Code, see Family Code § 100.
Modification, termination, or setting aside of support order, see Family Code § 3650 et seq.

Support defined for purposes of this Code, see Family Code § 150.

Research References

Forms

1 California Transactions Forms--Family Law § 2:88, Marital Settlement Agreement.
1 California Transactions Forms--Family Law § 3:34, Hardship Deductions.
West's California Code Forms, Family § 2338 Form 8, Marital Agreement.
West's California Code Forms, Family § 3585 Form 2, Child Support Provisions.

§ 4071.5. Repealed by Stats.1999, c. 653 (A.B.380), § 9

§ 4072. Deduction for hardship expenses; statement by court of reasons for supporting deductions; statement of amount and underlying facts; duration

(a) If a deduction for hardship expenses is allowed, the court shall do both of the following:

(1) State the reasons supporting the deduction in writing or on the record.

(2) Document the amount of the deduction and the underlying facts and circumstances.

(b) Whenever possible, the court shall specify the duration of the deduction. *(Added by Stats.1993, c. 219 (A.B.1500), § 138.)*

Cross References

Computation of annual net disposable income of parents, see Family Code § 4059.
Computation of monthly net disposable income of parents, see Family Code § 4060.
State defined for purposes of this Code, see Family Code § 145.
Writings, authentication and proof of, see Evidence Code § 1400 et seq.

§ 4073. Considerations of court in deciding whether or not to allow hardship deduction

The court shall be guided by the goals set forth in this article when considering whether or not to allow a financial hardship deduction, and, if allowed, when determining the amount of the deduction. *(Added by Stats.1993, c. 219 (A.B.1500), § 138.)*

Cross References

Computation of annual net disposable income of parents, see Family Code § 4059.
Computation of monthly net disposable income of parents, see Family Code § 4060.

Research References

Forms

1 California Transactions Forms--Family Law § 3:32, Determination of Net Monthly Disposable Income.

§ 4074. Application of article to all awards for support of children

This article applies to an award for the support of children, including those awards designated as "family support," that contain provisions for the support of children as well as for the support of the spouse. *(Added by Stats.1993, c. 219 (A.B.1500), § 138.)*

Cross References

Family support defined for purposes of this Code, see Family Code § 92.
References to husband, wife, spouses and married persons, persons included for purposes of this Code, see Family Code § 11.
Support defined for purposes of this Code, see Family Code § 150.

§ 4075. Tax treatment of spousal support and separate maintenance; application of article

This article shall not be construed to affect the treatment of spousal support and separate maintenance payments pursuant to Section 71 of the Internal Revenue Code of 1954 (26 U.S.C. Sec. 71). *(Added by Stats.1993, c. 219 (A.B.1500), § 138.)*

Cross References

Spousal support defined for purposes of this Code, see Family Code § 142.
Support defined for purposes of this Code, see Family Code § 150.

§ 4076. Modification of child support orders; two-step phase-in of formula amount of support; conditions

(a) When the court is requested to modify a child support order issued prior to July 1, 1992, for the purpose of conforming to the statewide child support guideline, and it is not using its discretionary authority to depart from the guideline pursuant to paragraph (3), (4), or (5) of subdivision (b) of Section 4057, and the amount of child support to be ordered is the amount provided under the guideline formula in subdivision (a) of Section 4055, the court may, in its discretion, order a two-step phase-in of the formula amount of support to provide the obligor with time for transition to the full formula amount if all of the following are true:

(1) The period of the phase-in is carefully limited to the time necessary for the obligor to rearrange the obligor's financial obligations in order to meet the full formula amount of support.

(2) The obligor is immediately being ordered to pay not less than 30 percent of the amount of the child support increase, in addition to the amount of child support required under the prior order.

(3) The obligor has not unreasonably increased their financial obligations following notice of the motion for modification of support, has no arrearages owing, and has a history of good faith compliance with prior support orders.

(b) When the court grants a request for a phase-in pursuant to this section, the court shall state the following in writing:

(1) The specific reasons why (A) the immediate imposition of the full formula amount of support would place an extraordinary hardship on the obligor, and (B) this extraordinary hardship on the obligor would outweigh the hardship caused the supported children by the temporary phase-in of the full formula amount of support.

(2) The full guideline amount of support, the date and amount of each phase-in, and the date that the obligor must commence paying the full formula amount of support, which shall not be later than one year after the filing of the motion for modification of support.

(c) When the court orders a phase-in pursuant to this section, and the court thereafter determines that the obligor has violated the phase-in schedule or has intentionally lowered the income available for the payment of child support during the phase-in period, the court may order the immediate payment of the full formula amount of child support and the difference in the amount of support that would have been due without the phase-in and the amount of support due with the phase-in, in addition to any other penalties provided for by law. *(Added by Stats.1993, c. 1156 (S.B.541), § 7.5. Amended by Stats.2019, c. 115 (A.B.1817), § 47, eff. Jan. 1, 2020.)*

Cross References

Expedited child support orders, see Family Code § 3620 et seq.
Health insurance coverage for supported children, see Family Code § 3750 et seq.
Judgment and order defined for purposes of this Code, see Family Code § 100.
Modification, termination, or setting aside of support order, see Family Code § 3650 et seq.
Notice, actual and constructive, defined, see Civil Code § 18.
State defined for purposes of this Code, see Family Code § 145.
Support defined for purposes of this Code, see Family Code § 150.
Support order defined for purposes of this Code, see Family Code § 155.
Writings, authentication and proof of, see Evidence Code § 1400 et seq.

Research References

Forms

1 California Transactions Forms--Family Law § 3:21, Jurisdiction for Orders to Pay Child Support.
West's California Code Forms, Family § 4068 Form 2, Financial Statement—Simplified.

§ 4076

West's California Judicial Council Forms FL–150, Income and Expense Declaration (Also Available in Spanish).

West's California Judicial Council Forms FL–684, Request for Order and Supporting Declaration (Governmental).

§ 4077. Identification of additional legislative changes required to comply with federal child support regulations

The Department of Child Support Services and the Judicial Council shall meet and confer, no later than November 21, 2022, and each entity shall submit its own report to the Assembly Committee on Budget and the Senate Committee on Budget and Fiscal Review and the Assembly and Senate Committees on Judiciary on what additional legislative changes are required to comply with the federal child support regulations revised in 81 Federal Register 93492 (Sec. 20, 2016), if any, which shall consider the most recent review of the statewide child support guideline completed pursuant to Section 4054, and identify any points of agreement and any difference of interpretation, perspective, or opinion between the entities regarding the legislative changes required. (Added by Stats.2022, c. 573 (A.B.207), § 5, eff. Sept. 27, 2022.)

§§ 4100 to 4105. Inoperative

ARTICLE 3. PAYMENT TO COURT DESIGNATED COUNTY OFFICER; ENFORCEMENT BY DISTRICT ATTORNEY

Section
4200. Child support orders to parents receiving welfare; duties of court.
4201. Child support orders; payment to county officer; appearance by local child support agency in enforcement proceeding.
4202. Parents residing in different counties.
4203. Charges and expenses.
4204. Child support assigned to county; local child support agency providing child support enforcement services; notice regarding where payments should be directed.
4205. Notice requesting meeting with support obligor; contents.

Cross References

Emancipation of minors, warning that court may void or rescind declaration and parents may become liable for support and medical insurance coverage pursuant to this chapter, see Family Code § 7121.

§ 4200. Child support orders to parents receiving welfare; duties of court

In any proceeding where a court makes or has made an order requiring the payment of child support to a parent receiving welfare moneys for the maintenance of children for whom support may be ordered, the court shall do both of the following:

(a) Direct that the payments of support shall be made to the county officer designated by the court for that purpose. Once the State Disbursement Unit is implemented pursuant to Section 17309, all payments shall be directed to the State Disbursement Unit instead of the county officer designated by the court.

(b) Direct the local child support agency to appear on behalf of the welfare recipient in any proceeding to enforce the order. (Stats.1992, c. 162 (A.B.2650), § 10, operative Jan. 1, 1994. Amended by Stats.1993, c. 219 (A.B.1500), § 140; Stats.1997, c. 599 (A.B.573), § 14; Stats.2000, c. 808 (A.B.1358) § 36, eff. Sept. 28, 2000; Stats.2003, c. 387 (A.B.739), § 2.)

Cross References

Attorney fees, generally, see Family Code § 270 et seq.
Child for whom support may be ordered defined for purposes of this Code, see Family Code § 58.

Child support services, role of state department, see Family Code § 4701.
County defined for purposes of this Code, see Family Code § 67.
County officers,
  Designation for payment of spousal support payments, see Family Code § 4350 et seq.
  Financial evaluation officers, see Government Code § 27750 et seq.
  Notice of change of address, earnings assignment order for support, see Family Code § 5237.
Deposit of assets to secure future child support payments, see Family Code § 4600 et seq.
Deposit of money to secure future child support payments, see Family Code § 4550 et seq.
Domestic relations investigators, duties, see Family Code § 3110.
Expedited child support orders, see Family Code § 3620 et seq.
Forwarding support payments paid through county officers, see Family Code § 3555.
Health insurance coverage for supported children, see Family Code § 3750 et seq.
Judgment and order defined for purposes of this Code, see Family Code § 100.
Jurisdiction of superior court, generally, see Cal. Const. Art. 6, §§ 10, 11.
Jurisdiction of superior court, proceedings under this code, see Family Code § 200.
Local child support agency,
  Health insurance coverage for child, providing information, see Family Code § 3752.
  Support paid through local child support agency for child not receiving public assistance, see Family Code § 4573.
Modification, termination, or setting aside of support order, see Family Code § 3650 et seq.
Order for support, custodial parent receiving AFDC assistance, see Family Code § 3029.
Probation officers, duties, see Penal Code § 1203.10; Welfare and Institutions Code § 281.
Proceeding defined for purposes of this Code, see Family Code § 110.
Similar procedures, spousal support payments, see Family Code § 4350 et seq.
State defined for purposes of this Code, see Family Code § 145.
Support defined for purposes of this Code, see Family Code § 150.

Research References

Forms

West's California Code Forms, Family § 4200, Comment Overview—Child Support Orders to Parents.
West's California Judicial Council Forms FL–632, Notice Regarding Payment of Support (Governmental).
West's California Judicial Council Forms FL–684, Request for Order and Supporting Declaration (Governmental).

§ 4201. Child support orders; payment to county officer; appearance by local child support agency in enforcement proceeding

In any proceeding where a court makes or has made an order requiring the payment of child support to the person having custody of a child for whom support may be ordered, the court may do either or both of the following:

(a) Direct that the payments shall be made to the county officer designated by the court for that purpose. Once the State Disbursement Unit is implemented pursuant to Section 17309, all payments shall be directed to the State Disbursement Unit instead of the county officer designated by the court.

(b) Direct the local child support agency to appear on behalf of the minor children in any proceeding to enforce the order. (Stats.1992, c. 162 (A.B.2650), § 10, operative Jan. 1, 1994. Amended by Stats.1993, c. 219 (A.B.1500), § 141; Stats.1997, c. 599 (A.B.573), § 15; Stats.2000, c. 808 (A.B.1358), § 37, eff. Sept. 28, 2000; Stats.2003, c. 387 (A.B.739), § 3.)

Cross References

Attorney fees, generally, see Family Code § 270 et seq.
Child custody, see Family Code § 3020 et seq.
Child for whom support may be ordered defined for purposes of this Code, see Family Code § 58.
Child support services, role of state department, see Family Code § 4701.
County defined for purposes of this Code, see Family Code § 67.

County officers,
   Designation for payment of spousal support payments, see Family Code § 4350 et seq.
   Financial evaluation officers, see Government Code § 27750 et seq.
   Notice of change of address, earnings assignment order for support, see Family Code § 5237.
Deposit of assets to secure future child support payments, see Family Code § 4600 et seq.
Deposit of money to secure future child support payments, see Family Code § 4550 et seq.
Domestic relations investigators, duties, see Family Code § 3110.
Expedited child support orders, see Family Code § 3620 et seq.
Forwarding support payments paid through county officers, see Family Code § 3555.
Health insurance coverage for supported children, see Family Code § 3750 et seq.
Judgment and order defined for purposes of this Code, see Family Code § 100.
Jurisdiction of superior court, proceedings under code, see Family Code § 200.
Local child support agency,
   Health insurance coverage for child, providing information, see Family Code § 3752.
   Support paid through local child support agency for child not receiving public assistance, see Family Code § 4573.
Minor defined for purposes of this Code, see Family Code § 6500.
Modification, termination, or setting aside of support order, see Family Code § 3650 et seq.
Officer designated to act as trustee, service charge for cost, see Welfare and Institutions Code § 279.
Person defined for purposes of this Code, see Family Code § 105.
Probation officers, duties, see Penal Code § 1203.10; Welfare and Institutions Code § 281.
Proceeding defined for purposes of this Code, see Family Code § 110.
State defined for purposes of this Code, see Family Code § 145.
Support defined for purposes of this Code, see Family Code § 150.

Research References

Forms

West's California Code Forms, Family § 4200, Comment Overview—Child Support Orders to Parents.
West's California Judicial Council Forms FL–632, Notice Regarding Payment of Support (Governmental).

§ 4202. Parents residing in different counties

(a) Notwithstanding any other provision of law, in a proceeding where the custodial parent resides in one county and the parent ordered to pay support resides in another county, the court may direct payment to be made to the county officer designated by the court for those purposes in the county of residence of the custodial parent, and may direct the local child support agency of either county to enforce the order.

(b) If the court directs the local child support agency of the county of residence of the noncustodial parent to enforce the order, the expenses of the local child support agency with respect to the enforcement is a charge upon the county of residence of the noncustodial parent. *(Stats.1992, c. 162 (A.B.2650), § 10, operative Jan. 1, 1994. Amended by Stats.2000, c. 808 (A.B.1358), § 38, eff. Sept. 28, 2000; Stats.2004, c. 339 (A.B.1704), § 3.)*

Cross References

Attorney fees, generally, see Family Code § 270 et seq.
Child custody, see Family Code § 3020 et seq.
Child support services, role of state department, see Family Code § 4701.
County defined for purposes of this Code, see Family Code § 67.
County officers,
   Designation for payment of spousal support payments, see Family Code § 4350 et seq.
   Financial evaluation officers, see Government Code § 27750 et seq.
   Notice of change of address, earnings assignment order for support, see Family Code § 5237.
Deposit of assets to secure future child support payments, see Family Code § 4600 et seq.
Deposit of money to secure future child support payments, see Family Code § 4550 et seq.
Domestic relations investigators, duties, see Family Code § 3110.
Expedited child support orders, see Family Code § 3620 et seq.
Forwarding support payments paid through county officers, see Family Code § 3555.
Health insurance coverage for supported children, see Family Code § 3750 et seq.
Judgment and order defined for purposes of this Code, see Family Code § 100.
Local child support agency,
   Health insurance coverage for child, providing information, see Family Code § 3752.
   Support paid through local child support agency for child not receiving public assistance, see Family Code § 4573.
Modification, termination, or setting aside of support order, see Family Code § 3650 et seq.
Probation officers, duties, see Penal Code § 1203.10; Welfare and Institutions Code § 281.
Proceeding defined for purposes of this Code, see Family Code § 110.
Support defined for purposes of this Code, see Family Code § 150.

§ 4203. Charges and expenses

(a) Except as provided in Section 4202, expenses of the county officer designated by the court, and expenses of the local child support agency incurred in the enforcement of an order of the type described in Section 4200 or 4201, are a charge upon the county where the proceedings are pending.

(b) Fees for service of process in the enforcement of an order of the type described in Section 4200 or 4201 are a charge upon the county where the process is served. *(Stats.1992, c. 162 (A.B.2650), § 10, operative Jan. 1, 1994. Amended by Stats.2000, c. 808 (A.B.1358), § 39, eff. Sept. 28, 2000.)*

Cross References

Attorney fees, generally, see Family Code § 270 et seq.
Child support services, role of state department, see Family Code § 4701.
County defined for purposes of this Code, see Family Code § 67.
County officers,
   Designation for payment of spousal support payments, see Family Code § 4350 et seq.
   Financial evaluation officers, see Government Code § 27750 et seq.
   Notice of change of address, earnings assignment order for support, see Family Code § 5237.
Deposit of assets to secure future child support payments, see Family Code § 4600 et seq.
Deposit of money to secure future child support payments, see Family Code § 4550 et seq.
Domestic relations investigators, duties, see Family Code § 3110.
Expedited child support orders, see Family Code § 3620 et seq.
Forwarding support payments paid through county officers, see Family Code § 3555.
Health insurance coverage for supported children, see Family Code § 3750 et seq.
Judgment and order defined for purposes of this Code, see Family Code § 100.
Local child support agency, health insurance coverage for child, providing information, see Family Code § 3752.
Modification, termination, or setting aside of support order, see Family Code § 3650 et seq.
Probation officers, duties, see Penal Code § 1203.10; Welfare and Institutions Code § 281.
Proceeding defined for purposes of this Code, see Family Code § 110.
Service of process, generally, see Code of Civil Procedure § 410.10 et seq.
Support defined for purposes of this Code, see Family Code § 150.

§ 4204. Child support assigned to county; local child support agency providing child support enforcement services; notice regarding where payments should be directed

Notwithstanding any other * * * law, in any proceeding where the court has made an order requiring the payment of child support * * * and the child support is subsequently assigned to the county pursuant to Section 11477 of the Welfare and Institutions Code or the * * * <u>support obligor or obligee</u> has requested <u>a</u> local child support agency to provide child support enforcement services pursuant to Section 17400, the local child support agency <u>shall</u> issue a notice directing that the payments shall be made to the local child

§ 4204

support agency, another county office, or the State Disbursement Unit pursuant to Section 17309. Additionally, the local child support agency shall provide notice when it is no longer providing services under Part D of Title IV of the federal Social Security Act (42 U.S.C. Sec. 651 et seq.). The * * * local child support agency shall * * * serve the notice on both the support obligor and obligee in compliance with Section 1013 of the Code of Civil Procedure * * * and file the notice with the * * * court. *(Added by Stats.1997, c. 599 (A.B.573), § 16. Amended by Stats.2000, c. 808 (A.B.1358), § 40, eff. Sept. 28, 2000; Stats.2003, c. 387 (A.B.739), § 4; Stats.2022, c. 420 (A.B.2960), § 15, eff. Jan. 1, 2023.)*

Cross References

Child custody, see Family Code § 3020 et seq.
County defined for purposes of this Code, see Family Code § 67.
Expedited child support orders, see Family Code § 3620 et seq.
Health insurance coverage for supported children, see Family Code § 3750 et seq.
Judgment and order defined for purposes of this Code, see Family Code § 100.
Modification, termination, or setting aside of support order, see Family Code § 3650 et seq.
Notice, actual and constructive, defined, see Civil Code § 18.
Person defined for purposes of this Code, see Family Code § 105.
Proceeding defined for purposes of this Code, see Family Code § 110.
State defined for purposes of this Code, see Family Code § 145.
Support defined for purposes of this Code, see Family Code § 150.
Support order defined for purposes of this Code, see Family Code § 155.

Research References

Forms

West's California Judicial Council Forms FL-632, Notice Regarding Payment of Support (Governmental).
West's California Judicial Council Forms FL-684, Request for Order and Supporting Declaration (Governmental).

§ 4205. Notice requesting meeting with support obligor; contents

Any notice from the local child support agency requesting a meeting with the support obligor for any purpose authorized under this part shall contain a statement advising the support obligor of the obligor's right to have an attorney present at the meeting. *(Added by Stats.1998, c. 854 (A.B.960), § 2. Amended by Stats.2000, c. 808 (A.B.1358), § 41, eff. Sept. 28, 2000; Stats.2019, c. 115 (A.B.1817), § 48, eff. Jan. 1, 2020.)*

Cross References

Notice, actual and constructive, defined, see Civil Code § 18.
Support defined for purposes of this Code, see Family Code § 150.

Research References

Forms

West's California Code Forms, Family § 4200, Comment Overview—Child Support Orders to Parents.

ARTICLE 4. CHILD SUPPORT COMMISSIONERS

Section
4250. Legislative findings and declarations.
4251. Provision of commissioners; referral of actions or proceedings; authority of commissioners.
4252. Appointment of subordinate judicial officers as child support commissioners; priority of cases; number of commissioner positions allotted to each court; responsibility of Judicial Council.
4253. Default orders.

Cross References

Acknowledgment of satisfaction of matured installments under installment judgment, child or spousal support orders, see Code of Civil Procedure § 724.250.

Emancipation of minors, warning that court may void or rescind declaration and parents may become liable for support and medical insurance coverage pursuant to this chapter, see Family Code § 7121.
Trial Court Operations Fund, establishment by board of supervisors, deposits, see Government Code § 77009.

§ 4250. Legislative findings and declarations

(a) The Legislature finds and declares the following:

(1) Child and spousal support are serious legal obligations.

(2) The current system for obtaining, modifying, and enforcing child and spousal support orders is inadequate to meet the future needs of California's children due to burgeoning caseloads within local child support agencies and the growing number of parents who are representing themselves in family law actions.

(3) The success of California's child support enforcement program depends upon its ability to establish and enforce child support orders quickly and efficiently.

(4) There is a compelling state interest in creating an expedited process in the courts that is cost-effective and accessible to families, for establishing and enforcing child support orders in cases being enforced by the local child support agency.

(5) There is a compelling state interest in having a simple, speedy, conflict-reducing system, that is both cost-effective and accessible to families, for resolving all issues concerning children, including support, health insurance, custody, and visitation in family law cases that do not involve enforcement by the local child support agency.

(b) Therefore, it is the intent of the Legislature to: (1) provide for commissioners to hear child support cases being enforced by the local child support agency; (2) adopt uniform and simplified procedures for all child support cases; and (3) create an Office of the Family Law Facilitator in the courts to provide education, information, and assistance to parents with child support issues. *(Added by Stats.1996, c. 957 (A.B.1058), § 6. Amended by Stats.2000, c. 808 (A.B.1358), § 42, eff. Sept. 28, 2000.)*

Cross References

Child custody, see Family Code § 3020 et seq.
Expedited child support orders, see Family Code § 3620 et seq.
Health insurance coverage for supported children, see Family Code § 3750 et seq.
Judgment and order defined for purposes of this Code, see Family Code § 100.
Legislative intent, construction of statutes, see Code of Civil Procedure § 1859.
Modification, termination, or setting aside of support order, see Family Code § 3650 et seq.
Spousal support defined for purposes of this Code, see Family Code § 142.
State defined for purposes of this Code, see Family Code § 145.
Support defined for purposes of this Code, see Family Code § 150.
Support order defined for purposes of this Code, see Family Code § 155.

Research References

Forms

West's California Code Forms, Family § 4250, Comment Overview—Child Support Commissioners.

§ 4251. Provision of commissioners; referral of actions or proceedings; authority of commissioners

(a) Commencing July 1, 1997, each superior court shall provide sufficient commissioners to hear Title IV-D child support cases filed by the local child support agency. The number of child support commissioners required in each county shall be determined by the Judicial Council as prescribed by paragraph (3) of subdivision (b) of Section 4252. All actions or proceedings filed by the local child support agency in a support action or proceeding in which enforcement services are being provided pursuant to Section 17400, for an order to establish, modify, or enforce child or spousal support, including actions to establish parentage, shall be referred for hearing to a child support commissioner unless a child support commissioner is not available due to exceptional circumstances, as prescribed by the

Judicial Council pursuant to paragraph (7) of subdivision (b) of Section 4252. All actions or proceedings filed by a party other than the local child support agency to modify or enforce a support order established by the local child support agency or for which enforcement services are being provided pursuant to Section 17400 shall be referred for hearing to a child support commissioner unless a child support commissioner is not available due to exceptional circumstances, as prescribed by the Judicial Council pursuant to paragraph (7) of subdivision (b) of Section 4252.

(b) The commissioner shall act as a temporary judge unless an objection is made by the local child support agency or any other party. The Judicial Council shall develop a notice that shall be included on all forms and pleadings used to initiate a child support action or proceeding that advises the parties of their right to review by a superior court judge and how to exercise that right. The parties shall also be advised by the court prior to the commencement of the hearing that the matter is being heard by a commissioner who shall act as a temporary judge unless any party objects to the commissioner acting as a temporary judge. While acting as a temporary judge, the commissioner shall receive no compensation other than compensation as a commissioner.

(c) If a party objects to the commissioner acting as a temporary judge, the commissioner may hear the matter and make findings of fact and a recommended order. Within 10 court days, a judge shall ratify the recommended order unless either party objects to the recommended order, or where a recommended order is in error. In both cases, the judge shall issue a temporary order and schedule a hearing de novo within 10 court days. A party may waive the right to the review hearing at any time.

(d) The commissioner, where appropriate, shall do any of the following:

(1) Review and determine ex parte applications for orders and writs.

(2) Take testimony.

(3) Establish a record, evaluate evidence, and make recommendations or decisions.

(4) Enter judgments or orders based upon voluntary acknowledgments of support liability and parentage and stipulated agreements respecting the amount of child support to be paid.

(5) Enter default orders and judgments pursuant to Section 4253.

(6) In actions in which parentage is at issue, order the mother, child, and alleged father to submit to genetic tests.

(e) The commissioner shall, upon application of a party, join issues concerning custody, visitation, and protective orders in the action filed by the local child support agency, subject to Section 17404. After joinder, the commissioner shall:

(1) Refer the parents for mediation of disputed custody or visitation issues pursuant to Section 3170.

(2) Accept stipulated agreements concerning custody, visitation, and protective orders and enter orders pursuant to the agreements.

(3) Refer contested issues of custody, visitation, and protective orders to a judge or to another commissioner for hearing. A child support commissioner may hear contested custody, visitation, and restraining order issues only if the court has adopted procedures to segregate the costs of hearing Title IV-D child support issues from the costs of hearing other issues pursuant to applicable federal requirements.

(f) The local child support agency shall be served notice by the moving party of any proceeding under this section in which support is at issue. An order for support that is entered without the local child support agency having received proper notice shall be voidable upon the motion of the local child support agency. *(Added by Stats.1996, c. 957 (A.B.1058), § 6. Amended by Stats.1998, c. 932 (A.B.1094), § 32;*

Stats.2000, c. 808 (A.B.1358), § 43, eff. Sept. 28, 2000; Stats.2019, c. 115 (A.B.1817), § 49, eff. Jan. 1, 2020.)

Cross References

Agreements for support of adult children, see Family Code § 3587.
Arbitration, generally, see Code of Civil Procedure § 1281 et seq.
Child custody, see Family Code § 3020 et seq.
Computation of time, see Code of Civil Procedure §§ 12, 12a; Government Code § 6800 et seq.
Conciliation proceedings, generally, see Family Code § 1800 et seq.
County defined for purposes of this Code, see Family Code § 67.
Court commissioners, powers and duties with respect to this section, see Code of Civil Procedure § 259.
Emancipation of minors, warning that court may void or rescind declaration and parents may become liable for support and medical insurance coverage pursuant to this chapter, see Family Code § 7121.
Expedited child support orders, see Family Code § 3620 et seq.
Family mediation and conciliation services, statewide coordination, see Family Code § 1850 et seq.
Health insurance coverage for supported children, see Family Code § 3750 et seq.
Judgment and order defined for purposes of this Code, see Family Code § 100.
Mediation of custody and visitation issues, generally, see Family Code § 3160 et seq.
Modification, termination, or setting aside of support order, see Family Code § 3650 et seq.
Notice, actual and constructive, defined, see Civil Code § 18.
Proceeding defined for purposes of this Code, see Family Code § 110.
Protective order defined for purposes of this Code, see Family Code § 6218.
Spousal support defined for purposes of this Code, see Family Code § 142.
Superior court judges, conversion of subordinate judicial officers to temporary judgeships, exemption for positions established by this section, see Government Code § 69615.
Support agreements,
  Generally, see Family Code § 3580 et seq.
  Child support agreements, see Family Code § 3585 et seq.
  Spousal support agreements, see Family Code § 3590 et seq.
Support defined for purposes of this Code, see Family Code § 150.
Support order defined for purposes of this Code, see Family Code § 155.

Research References

Forms

West's California Judicial Council Forms FL-665, Findings and Recommendation of Commissioner (Also Available in Spanish).
West's California Judicial Council Forms FL-666, Notice of Objection (Governmental).
West's California Judicial Council Forms FL-667, Review of Commissioner's Findings of Fact and Recommendation (Governmental).
West's California Judicial Council Forms FL-683, Order to Show Cause (Governmental).

§ 4252. Appointment of subordinate judicial officers as child support commissioners; priority of cases; number of commissioner positions allotted to each court; responsibility of Judicial Council

(a) The superior court shall appoint one or more subordinate judicial officers as child support commissioners to perform the duties specified in Section 4251. The child support commissioners' first priority always shall be to hear Title IV-D child support cases. The child support commissioners shall specialize in hearing child support cases, and their primary responsibility shall be to hear Title IV-D child support cases. Notwithstanding Section 71622 of the Government Code, the number of child support commissioner positions allotted to each court shall be determined by the Judicial Council in accordance with caseload standards developed pursuant to paragraph (3) of subdivision (b), subject to appropriations in the annual Budget Act.

(b) The Judicial Council shall do all of the following:

(1) Establish minimum qualifications for child support commissioners.

(2) Establish minimum educational and training requirements for child support commissioners and other court personnel that are

§ 4252

assigned to Title IV–D child support cases. Training programs shall include both federal and state laws concerning child support and related issues.

(3) Establish caseload, case processing, and staffing standards for child support commissioners on or before April 1, 1997, which shall set forth the maximum number of cases that each child support commissioner can process. These standards shall be reviewed and, if appropriate, revised by the Judicial Council every two years.

(4) Adopt uniform rules of court and forms for use in Title IV–D child support cases.

(5) Offer technical assistance to courts regarding issues relating to implementation and operation of the child support commissioner system, including assistance related to funding, staffing, and the sharing of resources between courts.

(6) Establish procedures for the distribution of funding to the courts for child support commissioners, family law facilitators pursuant to Division 14 (commencing with Section 10000), and related allowable costs.

(7) Adopt rules that define the exceptional circumstances in which judges may hear Title IV–D child support matters as provided in subdivision (a) of Section 4251.

(8) Undertake other actions as appropriate to ensure the successful implementation and operation of child support commissioners in the counties.

(c) As used in this article, "Title IV–D" means Title IV–D of the federal Social Security Act (42 U.S.C. Sec. 651 et seq.). *(Added by Stats.1996, c. 957 (A.B.1058), § 6. Amended by Stats.1998, c. 249 (A.B.2498), § 1; Stats.1999, c. 83 (S.B.966), § 49; Stats.2002, c. 784 (S.B.1316), § 105.)*

Cross References

County defined for purposes of this Code, see Family Code § 67.
Health insurance coverage for supported children, see Family Code § 3750 et seq.
State defined for purposes of this Code, see Family Code § 145.
Support defined for purposes of this Code, see Family Code § 150.

§ 4253. Default orders

Notwithstanding any other provision of law, when hearing child support matters, a commissioner or referee may enter default orders if the defendant does not respond to notice or other process within the time prescribed to respond to that notice. *(Added by Stats.1996, c. 957 (A.B.1058), § 6.)*

Cross References

Expedited child support orders, see Family Code § 3620 et seq.
Health insurance coverage for supported children, see Family Code § 3750 et seq.
Judgment and order defined for purposes of this Code, see Family Code § 100.
Modification, termination, or setting aside of support order, see Family Code § 3650 et seq.
Notice, actual and constructive, defined, see Civil Code § 18.
Support defined for purposes of this Code, see Family Code § 150.

Part 3

SPOUSAL SUPPORT

Chapter	Section
1. Duty to Support Spouse	4300
2. Factors to be Considered in Ordering Support	4320
3. Spousal Support Upon Dissolution or Legal Separation	4330
4. Payment to Court–Designated Officer; Enforcement by District Attorney	4350
5. Provision for Support After Death of Supporting Party	4360

Cross References

Actions for support, see Family Code § 17404.
Attorney's fees and costs, generally, see Family Code § 270 et seq.
Cohabitation with person of opposite sex, presumption of decreased need for support, see Family Code § 4323.
Contract of spouses for mutual respect, fidelity, and support, see Family Code § 720.
Domestic violence prevention orders, authorization to issue orders for spousal support that would otherwise be authorized under these provisions, see Family Code § 6341.
Enforcement of support orders, see Family Code § 4500 et seq.
Factors to be considered in ordering support, see Family Code § 4320 et seq.
Immediate separation agreements, spousal support provisions, see Family Code § 3580.
Order for spousal support, see Family Code § 4330.
Presence or residence of person owing support in state, see Family Code § 3550.
Punishment for failure to provide support for spouse, see Penal Code § 270a.
Putative spouse, order for support, see Family Code § 2254.
References to husband, wife, spouses and married persons, persons included for purposes of this Code, see Family Code § 11.
Spousal support, willful violation of order to pay, punishment, see Penal Code § 270.6.
State Supplementary Program for Aged, Blind and Disabled relative's liability for support to applicant for aid, see Welfare and Institutions Code § 12350.
Support, generally, see Family Code § 3500 et seq.
Support defined for purposes of this Code, see Family Code § 150.
Uniform Interstate Family Support Act, see Family Code § 5700.101 et seq.

CHAPTER 1. DUTY TO SUPPORT SPOUSE

Section
4300. Individual's duty of support.
4301. Support of spouse from separate property.
4302. Support of spouse living separate by agreement.
4303. Enforcement of duty of support; reimbursement of county.

Cross References

Actions for support, see Family Code § 17404.
Cohabitation with person of opposite sex, presumption of decreased need for support, see Family Code § 4323.
Contract of spouses for mutual respect, fidelity, and support, see Family Code § 720.
Enforcement of support orders, see Family Code § 4500 et seq.
Factors to be considered in ordering support, see Family Code § 4320 et seq.
Immediate separation agreements, spousal support provisions, see Family Code § 3580.
Order for spousal support, see Family Code § 4330.
Presence or residence of person owing support in state, see Family Code § 3550.
Punishment for failure to provide support for spouse, see Penal Code § 270a.
Putative spouse, order for support, see Family Code § 2254.
Support, generally, see Family Code § 3500 et seq.
Support defined for purposes of this Code, see Family Code § 150.
Uniform Interstate Family Support Act, see Family Code § 5700.101 et seq.

§ 4300. Individual's duty of support

Subject to this division, a person shall support the person's spouse. *(Stats.1992, c. 162 (A.B.2650), § 10, operative Jan. 1, 1994.)*

Cross References

Actions for support, see Family Code § 17404.
Attorney's fees and costs, generally, see Family Code § 270 et seq.
Cohabitation with person of opposite sex, presumption of decreased need for support, see Family Code § 4323.
Contract of spouses for mutual respect, fidelity, and support, see Family Code § 720.
Enforcement of support orders, see Family Code § 4500 et seq.
Factors to be considered in ordering support, see Family Code § 4320 et seq.
Immediate separation agreements, spousal support provisions, see Family Code § 3580.
Order for spousal support, see Family Code § 4330.

Person defined for purposes of this Code, see Family Code § 105.
Presence or residence of person owing support in state, see Family Code § 3550.
Punishment for failure to provide support for spouse, see Penal Code § 270a.
Putative spouse, order for support, see Family Code § 2254.
References to husband, wife, spouses and married persons, persons included for purposes of this Code, see Family Code § 11.
State Supplementary Program for Aged, Blind and Disabled relative's liability for support to applicant for aid, see Welfare and Institutions Code § 12350.
Support, generally, see Family Code § 3500 et seq.
Support defined for purposes of this Code, see Family Code § 150.
Uniform Interstate Family Support Act, see Family Code § 5700.101 et seq.

Research References
Forms

1 Alternative Dispute Resolution § 22:5 (4th ed.), Parties.
14 Am. Jur. Pl. & Pr. Forms Husband and Wife § 64, Introductory Comments.
1 California Transactions Forms--Family Law § 2:52, Overview.
West's California Code Forms, Family § 4300, Comment Overview—Duty to Support Spouse.
West's California Code Forms, Probate § 3080 Form 1, Petition for Support; for Injunctive Orders; for Determination of the Character of Property; for an Accounting; for Employment of Counsel; and for Attorney Fees and Costs.
West's California Judicial Council Forms FL–150, Income and Expense Declaration (Also Available in Spanish).

§ 4301. Support of spouse from separate property

Subject to Section 914, a person shall support the person's spouse while they are living together out of the separate property of the person when there is no community property or quasi-community property. *(Stats.1992, c. 162 (A.B.2650), § 10, operative Jan. 1, 1994.)*

Cross References

Actions for support, see Family Code § 17404.
Attorney's fees and costs, generally, see Family Code § 270 et seq.
Community property, defined in § 760 et seq., see Family Code § 65.
Consumer credit contracts, evidentiary effect of delivery of notice to contract signatory, see Civil Code § 1799.98.
Enforcement of support orders, see Family Code § 4500 et seq.
Mutual obligations of husband and wife, contract for respect, fidelity and support, see Family Code § 720.
Order for spousal support, see Family Code § 4330.
Person defined for purposes of this Code, see Family Code § 105.
Personal liability for debts incurred by spouse, separate property, see Family Code §§ 913, 914.
Property defined for purposes of this Code, see Family Code § 113.
Punishment for failure to provide support for spouse, see Penal Code § 270a.
Quasi-community property, defined, see Family Code § 125.
References to husband, wife, spouses and married persons, persons included for purposes of this Code, see Family Code § 11.
Separate property,
  Defined, see Family Code § 3515.
  Defined in § 760 et seq., see Family Code § 130.
  Personal liability for debts incurred by spouse, see Family Code § 914.
State Supplementary Program for Aged, Blind and Disabled relative's liability for support to applicant for aid, see Welfare and Institutions Code § 12350.
Support, generally, see Family Code § 3500 et seq.
Support defined for purposes of this Code, see Family Code § 150.
Uniform Interstate Family Support Act, see Family Code § 5700.101 et seq.

§ 4302. Support of spouse living separate by agreement

A person is not liable for support of the person's spouse when the person is living separate from the spouse by agreement unless support is stipulated in the agreement. *(Stats.1992, c. 162 (A.B. 2650), § 10, operative Jan. 1, 1994.)*

Cross References

Actions for support, see Family Code § 17404.
Attorney's fees and costs, generally, see Family Code § 270 et seq.
Consumer credit contracts, evidentiary effect of delivery of notice to contract signatory, see Civil Code § 1799.98.
Enforcement of support orders, see Family Code § 4500 et seq.
Mutual obligations of husband and wife, contract for respect, fidelity and support, see Family Code § 720.
Order for spousal support, see Family Code § 4330.
Person defined for purposes of this Code, see Family Code § 105.
Personal liability for debts incurred by spouse, see Family Code § 914.
Punishment for failure to provide support for spouse, see Penal Code § 270a.
References to husband, wife, spouses and married persons, persons included for purposes of this Code, see Family Code § 11.
Separation agreement, spousal support in, see Family Code § 3580.
Spousal support agreements, generally, see Family Code § 3590 et seq.
State Supplementary Program for Aged, Blind and Disabled relative's liability for support to applicant for aid, see Welfare and Institutions Code § 12350.
Support, generally, see Family Code § 3500 et seq.
Support defined for purposes of this Code, see Family Code § 150.
Uniform Interstate Family Support Act, see Family Code § 5700.101 et seq.

Research References
Forms

Asset Protection: Legal Planning, Strategies and Forms ¶ 4.02, Common Law.

§ 4303. Enforcement of duty of support; reimbursement of county

(a) The obligee spouse, or the county on behalf of the obligee spouse, may bring an action against the obligor spouse to enforce the duty of support.

(b) If the county furnishes support to a spouse, the county has the same right as the spouse to whom the support was furnished to secure reimbursement and obtain continuing support. The right of the county to reimbursement is subject to any limitation otherwise imposed by the law of this state.

(c) The court may order the obligor to pay the county reasonable attorney's fees and court costs in a proceeding brought by the county under this section. *(Stats.1992, c. 162 (A.B.2650), § 10, operative Jan. 1, 1994.)*

Cross References

Actions for support, see Family Code § 17404.
Attorney's fees and costs, generally, see Code of Civil Procedure § 1021; Family Code § 270 et seq.
County defined for purposes of this Code, see Family Code § 67.
Enforcement of support orders, see Family Code § 4500 et seq.
Judgment and order defined for purposes of this Code, see Family Code § 100.
Jurisdiction of superior court, see Cal. Const. Art. 6, §§ 10, 11.
Jurisdiction of superior court, proceedings under code, see Family Code § 200.
Mutual obligations of husband and wife, contract for respect, fidelity and support, see Family Code § 720.
Order for spousal support, see Family Code § 4330.
Proceeding defined for purposes of this Code, see Family Code § 110.
Punishment for failure to provide support for spouse, see Penal Code § 270a.
References to husband, wife, spouses and married persons, persons included for purposes of this Code, see Family Code § 11.
Similar provisions, see Family Code §§ 4002, 4403.
State defined for purposes of this Code, see Family Code § 145.
State Supplementary Program for Aged, Blind and Disabled relative's liability for support to applicant for aid, see Welfare and Institutions Code § 12350.
Support, generally, see Family Code § 3500 et seq.
Support defined for purposes of this Code, see Family Code § 150.
Support order, defined, see Family Code § 155.
Uniform Interstate Family Support Act, see Family Code § 5700.101 et seq.

Research References
Forms

1 California Transactions Forms--Family Law § 2:52, Overview.
West's California Code Forms, Family § 4300, Comment Overview—Duty to Support Spouse.

CHAPTER 2. FACTORS TO BE CONSIDERED IN ORDERING SUPPORT

Section
4320. Determination of amount due for support; considerations.

Section	
4321.	Denial of support from separate property of other party; grounds.
4322.	Childless party has or acquires a separate estate sufficient for support; prohibition on order or continuation of support.
4323.	Cohabitation with nonmarital partner; rebuttable presumption of decreased need for support; modification or termination of support.
4324.	Attempted murder or soliciting the murder of spouse; prohibited awards.
4324.5.	Violent sexual felony; domestic violence felony; prohibited awards.
4325.	Temporary or permanent support to abusive spouse; rebuttable presumption disfavoring award; evidence.
4326.	Termination of child support as change of circumstances; time for filing motion to modify spousal support; appointment of vocational training counselor; exceptions.

§ 4320. Determination of amount due for support; considerations

In ordering spousal support under this part, the court shall consider all of the following circumstances:

(a) The extent to which the earning capacity of each party is sufficient to maintain the standard of living established during the marriage, taking into account all of the following:

(1) The marketable skills of the supported party; the job market for those skills; the time and expenses required for the supported party to acquire the appropriate education or training to develop those skills; and the possible need for retraining or education to acquire other, more marketable skills or employment.

(2) The extent to which the supported party's present or future earning capacity is impaired by periods of unemployment that were incurred during the marriage to permit the supported party to devote time to domestic duties.

(b) The extent to which the supported party contributed to the attainment of an education, training, a career position, or a license by the supporting party.

(c) The ability of the supporting party to pay spousal support, taking into account the supporting party's earning capacity, earned and unearned income, assets, and standard of living.

(d) The needs of each party based on the standard of living established during the marriage.

(e) The obligations and assets, including the separate property, of each party.

(f) The duration of the marriage.

(g) The ability of the supported party to engage in gainful employment without unduly interfering with the interests of dependent children in the custody of the party.

(h) The age and health of the parties.

(i) All documented evidence of any history of domestic violence, as defined in Section 6211, between the parties or perpetrated by either party against either party's child, including, but not limited to, consideration of:

(1) A plea of nolo contendere.

(2) Emotional distress resulting from domestic violence perpetrated against the supported party by the supporting party.

(3) Any history of violence against the supporting party by the supported party.

(4) Issuance of a protective order after a hearing pursuant to Section 6340.

(5) A finding by a court during the pendency of a divorce, separation, or child custody proceeding, or other proceeding under Division 10 (commencing with Section 6200), that the spouse has committed domestic violence.

(j) The immediate and specific tax consequences to each party.

(k) The balance of the hardships to each party.

(*l*) The goal that the supported party shall be self-supporting within a reasonable period of time. Except in the case of a marriage of long duration as described in Section 4336, a "reasonable period of time" for purposes of this section generally shall be one-half the length of the marriage. However, nothing in this section is intended to limit the court's discretion to order support for a greater or lesser length of time, based on any of the other factors listed in this section, Section 4336, and the circumstances of the parties.

(m) The criminal conviction of an abusive spouse shall be considered in making a reduction or elimination of a spousal support award in accordance with Section 4324.5 or 4325.

(n) Any other factors the court determines are just and equitable.
(Stats.1992, c. 162 (A.B.2650), § 10, operative Jan. 1, 1994. Amended by Stats.1996, c. 1163 (S.B.509), § 1; Stats.1999, c. 284 (A.B.808), § 1; Stats.1999, c. 846 (A.B.391), § 1.5; Stats.2001, c. 293 (S.B.1221), § 2; Stats.2012, c. 718 (A.B.1522), § 1; Stats.2013, c. 455 (A.B.681), § 1; Stats.2015, c. 137 (S.B.28), § 1, eff. Jan. 1, 2016; Stats.2018, c. 938 (A.B.929), § 1, eff. Jan. 1, 2019.)

Cross References

Agreements for spousal support, see Family Code § 3580 et seq.
Annuity, insurance, or trust to provide support in event of death of supporting spouse, see Family Code § 4360.
Attorney's fees and costs, applications for temporary orders, see Family Code § 2031.
Child custody, see Family Code § 3020 et seq.
Community contributions to education or training, reimbursement, see Family Code § 2641.
Enforcement of support orders, see Family Code § 4500 et seq.
Judgment and order defined for purposes of this Code, see Family Code § 100.
Modification or termination of support order, see Family Code § 3650 et seq.
Property defined for purposes of this Code, see Family Code § 113.
References to husband, wife, spouses and married persons, persons included for purposes of this Code, see Family Code § 11.
Retirement plans, division, see Family Code § 2610.
Separate property defined for purposes of this Code, see Family Code § 130.
Similar provisions, see Family Code § 4404.
Spousal support defined for purposes of this Code, see Family Code § 142.
Support, generally, see Family Code § 3500 et seq.
Support defined for purposes of this Code, see Family Code § 150.
Support of spouse discharged in bankruptcy, agreement for support, order, see Family Code § 3592.
Tax levies, see Government Code § 29100 et seq.; Revenue and Taxation Code § 2151 et seq.

Research References

Forms
California Practice Guide: Rutter Family Law Forms Form 9:3, Marital Settlement Agreement.
California Practice Guide: Rutter Family Law Forms Form 11:20, Sample Trial Brief.
California Practice Guide: Rutter Family Law Forms HIGHLIGHTS, 2021 Update.
1 California Transactions Forms--Family Law § 2:54, Permanent Support.
1 California Transactions Forms--Family Law § 2:62, Grounds for Modification Post-Judgment.
1 California Transactions Forms--Family Law § 2:88, Marital Settlement Agreement.
1 California Transactions Forms--Family Law § 2:92, Family Support.
West's California Code Forms, Family § 2338 Form 8, Marital Agreement.
West's California Code Forms, Family § 2338 Form 9, Marital Agreement--Both Spouses Employed.
West's California Code Forms, Family § 3590 Form 3, Spousal Support Provisions.

West's California Code Forms, Family § 3590 Form 4, Spousal Support Provisions—Good Faith Efforts.
West's California Code Forms, Family § 3600, Comment Overview—Spousal and Child Support During Pendency of Proceeding.
West's California Code Forms, Family § 4300, Comment Overview—Duty to Support Spouse.
West's California Code Forms, Family § 4303 Form 1, Complaint by Spouse to Enforce Duty of Spousal Support.
West's California Code Forms, Family § 4330, Comment Overview—Spousal Support Upon Dissolution or Legal Separation.
West's California Judicial Council Forms FL–157, Spousal or Domestic Partner Support Declaration Attachment (Also Available in Spanish).
West's California Judicial Council Forms FL–158, Supporting Declaration for Attorney's Fees and Costs Attachment.
West's California Judicial Council Forms FL–343, Spousal, Domestic Partner, or Family Support Order Attachment.
West's California Judicial Council Forms FL–349, Spousal or Domestic Partner Support Factors Under Family Code Section 4320—Attachment.

§ 4321. Denial of support from separate property of other party; grounds

In a judgment of dissolution of marriage or legal separation of the parties, the court may deny support to a party out of the separate property of the other party in any of the following circumstances:

(a) The party has separate property, or is earning the party's own livelihood, or there is community property or quasi-community property sufficient to give the party proper support.

(b) The custody of the children has been awarded to the other party, who is supporting them. *(Stats.1992, c. 162 (A.B.2650), § 10, operative Jan. 1, 1994. Amended by Stats.1993, c. 219 (A.B.1500), § 141.5.)*

Cross References

Child custody, see Family Code § 3020 et seq.
Community property defined for purposes of this Code, see Family Code § 65.
Judgment and order defined for purposes of this Code, see Family Code § 100.
Property defined for purposes of this Code, see Family Code § 113.
Putative spouse, support of, see Family Code § 2254.
Quasi-community property defined, see Family Code § 125.
Separate property defined, see Family Code §§ 130, 3515.
State Supplementary Program for Aged, Blind and Disabled relative's liability for support to applicant for aid, see Welfare and Institutions Code § 12350.
Support, generally, see Family Code § 3500 et seq.
Support defined for purposes of this Code, see Family Code § 150.

§ 4322. Childless party has or acquires a separate estate sufficient for support; prohibition on order or continuation of support

In an original or modification proceeding, where there are no children, and a party has or acquires a separate estate, including income from employment, sufficient for the party's proper support, no support shall be ordered or continued against the other party. *(Stats.1992, c. 162 (A.B.2650), § 10, operative Jan. 1, 1994.)*

Cross References

Proceeding defined for purposes of this Code, see Family Code § 110.
Support, generally, see Family Code § 3500 et seq.
Support defined for purposes of this Code, see Family Code § 150.

§ 4323. Cohabitation with nonmarital partner; rebuttable presumption of decreased need for support; modification or termination of support

(a)(1) Except as otherwise agreed to by the parties in writing, there is a rebuttable presumption, affecting the burden of proof, of decreased need for spousal support if the supported party is cohabiting with a nonmarital partner. Upon a determination that circumstances have changed, the court may modify or terminate the spousal support as provided for in Chapter 6 (commencing with Section 3650) of Part 1.

(2) Holding oneself out to be the spouse of the person with whom one is cohabiting is not necessary to constitute cohabitation as the term is used in this subdivision.

(b) The income of a supporting spouse's subsequent spouse or nonmarital partner shall not be considered when determining or modifying spousal support.

(c) Nothing in this section precludes later modification or termination of spousal support on proof of change of circumstances. *(Stats.1992, c. 162 (A.B.2650), § 10, operative Jan. 1, 1994. Amended by Stats.1993, c. 935 (S.B.145), § 3; Stats.2014, c. 82 (S.B.1306), § 36, eff. Jan. 1, 2015.)*

Cross References

Burden of proof, generally, see Evidence Code §§ 500 et seq., 660 et seq.
Person defined for purposes of this Code, see Family Code § 105.
Presumptions, generally, see Evidence Code § 600 et seq.
References to husband, wife, spouses and married persons, persons included for purposes of this Code, see Family Code § 11.
Spousal support agreements, generally, see Family Code § 3590 et seq.
Spousal support defined for purposes of this Code, see Family Code § 142.
Support, generally, see Family Code § 3500 et seq.
Support defined for purposes of this Code, see Family Code § 150.
Writings, authentication and proof of, see Evidence Code § 1400 et seq.

Research References

Forms

1 California Transactions Forms--Family Law § 2:56, Effect of Death, Remarriage, or Cohabitation.

§ 4324. Attempted murder or soliciting the murder of spouse; prohibited awards

In addition to any other remedy authorized by law, when a spouse is convicted of attempting to murder the other spouse, as punishable pursuant to subdivision (a) of Section 664 of the Penal Code, or of soliciting the murder of the other spouse, as punishable pursuant to subdivision (b) of Section 653f of the Penal Code, the injured spouse shall be entitled to a prohibition of any temporary or permanent award for spousal support or medical, life, or other insurance benefits or payments from the injured spouse to the other spouse.

As used in this section, "injured spouse" means the spouse who has been the subject of the attempted murder or the solicitation of murder for which the other spouse was convicted, whether or not actual physical injury occurred. *(Added by Stats.1995, c. 364 (A.B.16), § 3. Amended by Stats.2010, c. 65 (A.B.2674), § 2.)*

Cross References

Attempted murder or soliciting the murder of a spouse, remedies, community property interests, see Family Code § 782.5.
References to husband, wife, spouses and married persons, persons included for purposes of this Code, see Family Code § 11.
Spousal support defined for purposes of this Code, see Family Code § 142.
Support defined for purposes of this Code, see Family Code § 150.

Research References

Forms

West's California Code Forms, Family § 4330, Comment Overview—Spousal Support Upon Dissolution or Legal Separation.

§ 4324.5. Violent sexual felony; domestic violence felony; prohibited awards

(a) In any proceeding for dissolution of marriage where there is a criminal conviction for a violent sexual felony or a domestic violence felony perpetrated by one spouse against the other spouse and the petition for dissolution is filed before five years following the conviction and any time served in custody, on probation, or on parole, the following shall apply:

(1) An award of spousal support to the convicted spouse from the injured spouse is prohibited.

§ 4324.5

(2) If economic circumstances warrant, the court shall order the attorney's fees and costs incurred by the parties to be paid from the community assets. The injured spouse shall not be required to pay any attorney's fees of the convicted spouse out of the injured spouse's separate property.

(3) At the request of the injured spouse, the date of separation, as defined in Section 70, shall be the date of the incident giving rise to the conviction, or earlier, if the court finds circumstances that justify an earlier date.

(4) The injured spouse shall be entitled to 100 percent of the community property interest in the retirement and pension benefits of the injured spouse.

(b) As used in this section, the following definitions apply:

(1) "Domestic violence felony" means a felony offense for an act of abuse, as described in Section 6203, perpetrated by one spouse against the other spouse.

(2) "Injured spouse" means the spouse who has been the subject of the violent sexual felony or domestic violence felony for which the other spouse was convicted.

(3) "Violent sexual felony" means those offenses described in paragraphs (3), (4), (5), (11), and (18) of subdivision (c) of Section 667.5 of the Penal Code.

(c) If a convicted spouse presents documented evidence of the convicted spouse's history as a victim of a violent sexual offense, as described in paragraphs (3), (4), (5), (11), and (18) of subdivision (c) of Section 667.5 of the Penal Code, or domestic violence, as defined in Section 6211, perpetrated by the other spouse, the court may determine, based on the facts of the particular case, that one or more of paragraphs (1) to (4), inclusive, of subdivision (a) do not apply.

(d) The changes made to this section by the bill that added this subdivision shall only apply to convictions that occur on or after January 1, 2019. *(Added by Stats.2012, c. 718 (A.B.1522), § 2. Amended by Stats.2018, c. 850 (S.B.1129), § 1, eff. Jan. 1, 2019.)*

§ 4325. Temporary or permanent support to abusive spouse; rebuttable presumption disfavoring award; evidence

(a) In a proceeding for dissolution of marriage where there is a criminal conviction for a domestic violence misdemeanor or a criminal conviction for a misdemeanor that results in a term of probation pursuant to Section 1203.097 of the Penal Code perpetrated by one spouse against the other spouse entered by the court within five years prior to the filing of the dissolution proceeding or during the course of the dissolution proceeding, there shall be a rebuttable presumption that the following shall apply:

(1) An award of spousal support to the convicted spouse from the injured spouse is prohibited.

(2) If economic circumstances warrant, the court shall order the attorney's fees and costs incurred by the parties to be paid from the community assets. The injured spouse shall not be required to pay any attorney's fees of the convicted spouse out of the injured spouse's separate property.

(3) At the request of the injured spouse, the date of separation, as defined in Section 70, shall be the date of the incident giving rise to the conviction, or earlier, if the court finds circumstances that justify an earlier date.

(b) The court may consider documented evidence of a convicted spouse's history as a victim of domestic violence, as defined in Section 6211, perpetrated by the other spouse, or any other factors the court deems just and equitable, as conditions for rebutting this presumption.

(c) The rebuttable presumption created in this section may be rebutted by a preponderance of the evidence.

(d) The court may determine, based on the facts of a particular case, that the injured spouse is entitled to up to 100 percent of the community property interest in the injured spouse's retirement and pension benefits. In determining whether and how to apportion the community property interest in the retirement and pension benefits of the injured spouse, the court shall consider all of the following factors:

(1) The misdemeanor domestic violence conviction, as well as documented evidence of other instances of domestic violence, as defined in Section 6211, between the parties or perpetrated by either party against either party's child, including, but not limited to, consideration of emotional distress resulting from domestic violence. The court shall also consider documented evidence of a convicted spouse's history as a victim of domestic violence, as defined in Section 6211, perpetrated by the other spouse.

(2) The duration of the marriage and when, based on documented evidence, incidents of domestic violence, as defined in Section 6211, occurred.

(3) The extent to which the convicted spouse's present or future earning capacity is impaired by periods of unemployment that were incurred during the marriage to permit the convicted spouse to devote time to domestic duties.

(4) The extent to which the convicted spouse contributed to the attainment of an education, training, a career position, or a license by the injured spouse.

(5) The balance of the hardships to each party.

(6) Any other factors the court determines are just and equitable.

(e) As used in this section, the following definitions apply:

(1) "Domestic violence misdemeanor" means a misdemeanor offense for an act of abuse, as described in paragraphs (1) to (3), inclusive, of subdivision (a) of Section 6203, perpetrated by one spouse against the other spouse.

(2) "Injured spouse" means the spouse who has been the subject of the domestic violence misdemeanor for which the other spouse was convicted.

(f) The changes made to this section by the bill that added this subdivision shall only apply to convictions that occur on or after January 1, 2019. *(Added by Stats.2001, c. 293 (S.B.1221), § 3. Amended by Stats.2018, c. 850 (S.B.1129), § 2, eff. Jan. 1, 2019; Stats.2019, c. 115 (A.B.1817), § 50, eff. Jan. 1, 2020.)*

Cross References

Burden of proof, generally, see Evidence Code § 500 et seq.
Domestic violence defined for purposes of this Code, see Family Code § 6211.
Presumptions, see Evidence Code § 600 et seq.
Proceeding defined for purposes of this Code, see Family Code § 110.
References to husband, wife, spouses and married persons, persons included for purposes of this Code, see Family Code § 11.
Spousal support defined for purposes of this Code, see Family Code § 142.
Support defined for purposes of this Code, see Family Code § 150.

Research References

Forms

1 California Transactions Forms--Family Law § 2:54, Permanent Support.
West's California Code Forms, Family § 3600, Comment Overview—Spousal and Child Support During Pendency of Proceeding.

§ 4326. Termination of child support as change of circumstances; time for filing motion to modify spousal support; appointment of vocational training counselor; exceptions

(a) Except as provided in subdivision (d), in a proceeding in which a spousal support order exists or in which the court has retained jurisdiction over a spousal support order, if a companion child support order is in effect, the termination of child support pursuant to subdivision (a) of Section 3901 constitutes a change of circumstances that may be the basis for a request by either party for modification of spousal support.

(b) A motion to modify spousal support based on the change of circumstances described in subdivision (a) shall be filed by either party no later than six months from the date the child support order terminates.

(c) If a motion to modify a spousal support order pursuant to subdivision (a) is filed, either party may request the appointment of a vocational training counselor pursuant to Section 4331.

(d) Notwithstanding subdivision (a), termination of the child support order does not constitute a change of circumstances under subdivision (a) in any of the following circumstances:

(1) The child and spousal support orders are the result of a marital settlement agreement or judgment and the marital settlement agreement or judgment contains a provision regarding what is to occur when the child support order terminates.

(2) The child and spousal support orders are the result of a marital settlement agreement or judgment, which provides that the spousal support order is nonmodifiable or that spousal support is waived and the court's jurisdiction over spousal support has been terminated.

(3) The court's jurisdiction over spousal support was previously terminated.

(e) Notwithstanding subdivision (b), a party whose six-month deadline to file expired between January 1, 2014, and September 30, 2014, may file a motion pursuant to this section until December 31, 2014. *(Added by Stats.2014, c. 202 (A.B.414), § 1, eff. Aug. 15, 2014.)*

CHAPTER 3. SPOUSAL SUPPORT UPON DISSOLUTION OR LEGAL SEPARATION

Section
4330. Order of support; advice to support recipient.
4331. Examination by vocational training counselor; order; payment of expenses and costs.
4332. Findings of court; standard of living during marriage; other circumstances.
4333. Retroactive application of order.
4334. Orders for contingent periods of time; termination; notification.
4335. Termination of spousal support order; extension of order.
4336. Retention of jurisdiction; application of section.
4337. Termination of support order; death; remarriage.
4338. Enforcement of order for support; property to be utilized by court.
4339. Security for payment.

Cross References

Spousal and child support during pendency of proceedings, see Family Code § 3600 et seq.
Spousal support, willful violation of order to pay, punishment, see Penal Code § 270.6.
Statewide uniform child support guidelines, see Family Code § 4050 et seq.
Support order, modification or termination,
  Authority of court, see Family Code § 3651.
  Discovery, see Family Code § 3660 et seq.
  Retroactive application of modification, see Family Code § 3653.

§ 4330. Order of support; advice to support recipient

(a) In a judgment of dissolution of marriage or legal separation of the parties, the court may order a party to pay for the support of the other party an amount, for a period of time, that the court determines is just and reasonable, based on the standard of living established during the marriage, taking into consideration the circumstances as provided in Chapter 2 (commencing with Section 4320).

(b) When making an order for spousal support, the court may advise the recipient of support that the recipient should make reasonable efforts to assist in providing for their support needs, taking into account the particular circumstances considered by the court pursuant to Section 4320, unless, in the case of a marriage of long duration as provided for in Section 4336, the court decides this warning is inadvisable. *(Stats.1992, c. 162 (A.B.2650), § 10, operative Jan. 1, 1994. Amended by Stats.1996, c. 1163 (S.B.509), § 2; Stats.1999, c. 846 (A.B.391), § 2; Stats.2019, c. 115 (A.B.1817), § 51, eff. Jan. 1, 2020.)*

Cross References

Duty to support spouse, see Family Code § 4300 et seq.
Enforcement of spousal support, see Family Code §§ 4303, 4351, 5100.
Factors considered in ordering support, see Family Code § 4320 et seq.
Judgment and order defined for purposes of this Code, see Family Code § 100.
Modification or termination of support order, see Family Code § 3650 et seq.
Spousal and child support during pendency of proceedings, see Family Code § 3600 et seq.
Spousal support defined for purposes of this Code, see Family Code § 142.
State Supplementary Program for Aged, Blind and Disabled relative's liability for support to applicant for aid, see Welfare and Institutions Code § 12350.
Statewide uniform child support guidelines, see Family Code § 4050 et seq.
Support, generally, see Family Code § 3500 et seq.
Support defined for purposes of this Code, see Family Code § 150.

Research References

Forms

California Practice Guide: Rutter Family Law Forms Form 1:32, Glossary of Common Family Law Terms, Phrases and Concepts (Enclosure to Form 1:31).
California Practice Guide: Rutter Family Law Forms Form 9:3, Marital Settlement Agreement.
1 California Transactions Forms--Family Law § 2:52, Overview.
1 California Transactions Forms--Family Law § 2:54, Permanent Support.
1 California Transactions Forms--Family Law § 2:62, Grounds for Modification Post-Judgment.
1 California Transactions Forms--Family Law § 2:88, Marital Settlement Agreement.
1 California Transactions Forms--Family Law § 2:92, Family Support.
West's California Code Forms, Family § 2338 Form 8, Marital Agreement.
West's California Code Forms, Family § 2338 Form 9, Marital Agreement—Both Spouses Employed.
West's California Code Forms, Family § 3590 Form 3, Spousal Support Provisions.
West's California Code Forms, Family § 3590 Form 4, Spousal Support Provisions—Good Faith Efforts.
West's California Code Forms, Family § 4330, Comment Overview—Spousal Support Upon Dissolution or Legal Separation.
West's California Judicial Council Forms FL-343, Spousal, Domestic Partner, or Family Support Order Attachment.

§ 4331. Examination by vocational training counselor; order; payment of expenses and costs

(a) In a proceeding for dissolution of marriage or for legal separation of the parties, the court may order a party to submit to an examination by a vocational training counselor. The examination shall include an assessment of the party's ability to obtain employment based upon the party's age, health, education, marketable skills, employment history, and the current availability of employment opportunities. The focus of the examination shall be on an assessment of the party's ability to obtain employment that would allow the party to maintain their marital standard of living.

(b) The order may be made only on motion, for good cause, and on notice to the party to be examined and to all parties. The order shall specify the time, place, manner, conditions, scope of the examination, and the person or persons by whom it is to be made.

(c) A party who does not comply with an order under this section is subject to the same consequences provided for failure to comply with an examination ordered pursuant to Chapter 15 (commencing

§ 4331

with Section 2032.010) of Title 4 of Part 4 of the Code of Civil Procedure.

(d) "Vocational training counselor" for the purpose of this section means an individual with sufficient knowledge, skill, experience, training, or education in interviewing, administering, and interpreting tests for analysis of marketable skills, formulating career goals, planning courses of training and study, and assessing the job market, to qualify as an expert in vocational training under Section 720 of the Evidence Code.

(e) A vocational training counselor shall have at least the following qualifications:

(1) A master's degree in the behavioral sciences, or other postgraduate degree that the court finds provides sufficient training to perform a vocational evaluation.

(2) Qualification to administer and interpret inventories for assessing career potential.

(3) Demonstrated ability in interviewing clients and assessing marketable skills with an understanding of age constraints, physical and mental health, previous education and experience, and time and geographic mobility constraints.

(4) Knowledge of current employment conditions, job market, and wages in the indicated geographic area.

(5) Knowledge of education and training programs in the area with costs and time plans for these programs.

(f) The court may order the supporting spouse to pay, in addition to spousal support, the necessary expenses and costs of the counseling, retraining, or education. *(Stats.1992, c. 162 (A.B.2650), § 10, operative Jan. 1, 1994. Amended by Stats.2004, c. 182 (A.B.3081), § 35, operative July 1, 2005; Stats.2018, c. 178 (A.B.2780), § 2, eff. Jan. 1, 2019; Stats.2019, c. 115 (A.B.1817), § 52, eff. Jan. 1, 2020.)*

Cross References

Judgment and order defined for purposes of this Code, see Family Code § 100.
Mental and physical examinations, see Code of Civil Procedure § 2032.010 et seq.
Notice, actual and constructive, defined, see Civil Code § 18.
Officer designated to act as trustee, service charge to defray cost, see Welfare and Institutions Code § 279.
Person defined for purposes of this Code, see Family Code § 105.
Proceeding defined for purposes of this Code, see Family Code § 110.
References to husband, wife, spouses and married persons, persons included for purposes of this Code, see Family Code § 11.
Spousal support defined for purposes of this Code, see Family Code § 142.
Support, generally, see Family Code § 3500 et seq.
Support defined for purposes of this Code, see Family Code § 150.

Research References

Forms

California Practice Guide: Rutter Family Law Forms Form 6:14, Request for Order Re Vocational Examination.

§ 4332. Findings of court; standard of living during marriage; other circumstances

In a proceeding for dissolution of marriage or for legal separation of the parties, the court shall make specific factual findings with respect to the standard of living during the marriage, and, at the request of either party, the court shall make appropriate factual determinations with respect to other circumstances. *(Stats.1992, c. 162 (A.B.2650), § 10, operative Jan. 1, 1994.)*

Cross References

Factors to be considered in ordering spousal support, see Family Code § 4320 et seq.
Proceeding defined for purposes of this Code, see Family Code § 110.

Support, generally, see Family Code § 3500 et seq.

Research References

Forms

1 California Transactions Forms--Family Law § 2:54, Permanent Support.

§ 4333. Retroactive application of order

An order for spousal support in a proceeding for dissolution of marriage or for legal separation of the parties may be made retroactive to the date of filing the notice of motion or order to show cause, or to any subsequent date. *(Stats.1992, c. 162 (A.B.2650), § 10, operative Jan. 1, 1994.)*

Cross References

Judgment and order defined for purposes of this Code, see Family Code § 100.
Notice, actual and constructive, defined, see Civil Code § 18.
Proceeding defined for purposes of this Code, see Family Code § 110.
Spousal support defined for purposes of this Code, see Family Code § 142.
Support, generally, see Family Code § 3500 et seq.
Support defined for purposes of this Code, see Family Code § 150.
Support order, modification or termination, retroactive application, see Family Code § 3653.

Research References

Forms

1 California Transactions Forms--Family Law § 2:53, Temporary Support.

§ 4334. Orders for contingent periods of time; termination; notification

(a) If a court orders spousal support for a contingent period of time, the obligation of the supporting party terminates on the happening of the contingency. The court may, in the order, order the supported party to notify the supporting party, or the supporting party's attorney of record, of the happening of the contingency.

(b) If the supported party fails to notify the supporting party, or the attorney of record of the supporting party, of the happening of the contingency and continues to accept spousal support payments, the supported party shall refund payments received that accrued after the happening of the contingency, except that the overpayments shall first be applied to spousal support payments that are then in default. *(Stats.1992, c. 162 (A.B.2650), § 10, operative Jan. 1, 1994.)*

Cross References

Attorney's fees and costs, generally, see Family Code § 270 et seq.
Child support for contingent period of time, see Family Code § 4007.
Judgment and order defined for purposes of this Code, see Family Code § 100.
Spousal support defined for purposes of this Code, see Family Code § 142.
Support, generally, see Family Code § 3500 et seq.
Support defined for purposes of this Code, see Family Code § 150.

§ 4335. Termination of spousal support order; extension of order

An order for spousal support terminates at the end of the period provided in the order and shall not be extended unless the court retains jurisdiction in the order or under Section 4336. *(Stats.1992, c. 162 (A.B.2650), § 10, operative Jan. 1, 1994.)*

Cross References

Attorney's fees and costs, generally, see Family Code § 270 et seq.
Judgment and order defined for purposes of this Code, see Family Code § 100.
Spousal support defined for purposes of this Code, see Family Code § 142.
Support, generally, see Family Code § 3500 et seq.
Support defined for purposes of this Code, see Family Code § 150.

§ 4336. Retention of jurisdiction; application of section

(a) Except on written agreement of the parties to the contrary or a court order terminating spousal support, the court retains jurisdiction indefinitely in a proceeding for dissolution of marriage or for legal separation of the parties where the marriage is of long duration.

(b) For the purpose of retaining jurisdiction, there is a presumption affecting the burden of producing evidence that a marriage of 10 years or more, from the date of marriage to the date of separation, is a marriage of long duration. However, the court may consider periods of separation during the marriage in determining whether the marriage is in fact of long duration. Nothing in this subdivision precludes a court from determining that a marriage of less than 10 years is a marriage of long duration.

(c) Nothing in this section limits the court's discretion to terminate spousal support in later proceedings on a showing of changed circumstances.

(d) This section applies to the following:

(1) A proceeding filed on or after January 1, 1988.

(2) A proceeding pending on January 1, 1988, in which the court has not entered a permanent spousal support order or in which the court order is subject to modification. *(Stats.1992, c. 162 (A.B.2650), § 10, operative Jan. 1, 1994.)*

Cross References

Judgment and order defined for purposes of this Code, see Family Code § 100.
Jurisdiction of superior court,
  Generally, see Cal. Const. Art. 6, §§ 10, 11.
  Proceedings under code, see Family Code § 200.
Presumptions, see Evidence Code § 600 et seq.
Proceeding defined for purposes of this Code, see Family Code § 110.
Spousal support agreements, generally, see Family Code § 3590 et seq.
Spousal support defined for purposes of this Code, see Family Code § 142.
Support, generally, see Family Code § 3500 et seq.
Support defined for purposes of this Code, see Family Code § 150.
Support order defined for purposes of this Code, see Family Code § 155.

Research References

Forms

California Practice Guide: Rutter Family Law Forms Form 6:24, Request for Order Re Modification Contingent Termination of Spousal Support Jurisdiction ("Richmond Order").
1 California Transactions Forms--Family Law § 2:55, Continuing Jurisdiction.

§ 4337. Termination of support order; death; remarriage

Except as otherwise agreed by the parties in writing, the obligation of a party under an order for the support of the other party terminates upon the death of either party or the remarriage of the other party. *(Stats.1992, c. 162 (A.B.2650), § 10, operative Jan. 1, 1994.)*

Cross References

Death of supporting party, provision for support, see Family Code § 4360.
Judgment and order defined for purposes of this Code, see Family Code § 100.
Spousal support agreements, generally, see Family Code § 3590 et seq.
Support, generally, see Family Code § 3500 et seq.
Support defined for purposes of this Code, see Family Code § 150.
Writings, authentication and proof of, see Evidence Code § 1400 et seq.

Research References

Forms

4 California Transactions Forms--Estate Planning § 19:11, Child Support.
1 California Transactions Forms--Family Law § 2:56, Effect of Death, Remarriage, or Cohabitation.
West's California Judicial Council Forms FL-343, Spousal, Domestic Partner, or Family Support Order Attachment.

§ 4338. Enforcement of order for support; property to be utilized by court

In the enforcement of an order for spousal support, the court shall resort to the property described below in the order indicated:

(a) The earnings, income, or accumulations of either spouse after the date of separation, as defined in Section 70, which would have been community property if the spouse had not been separated from the other spouse.

(b) The community property.

(c) The quasi-community property.

(d) The other separate property of the party required to make the support payments. *(Stats.1992, c. 162 (A.B.2650), § 10, operative Jan. 1, 1994. Amended by Stats.2016, c. 114 (S.B.1255), § 5, eff. Jan. 1, 2017.)*

Cross References

Community property,
  Defined, see Family Code § 65.
  Division on dissolution or legal separation, see Family Code § 2550 et seq.
Judgment and order defined for purposes of this Code, see Family Code § 100.
Jurisdiction of superior court,
  Generally, see Cal. Const. Art. 6, §§ 10, 11.
  Proceedings under code, see Family Code § 200.
Jurisdiction over community property, see Family Code § 2011.
Property defined for purposes of this Code, see Family Code § 113.
Quasi-community property, defined, see Family Code § 125.
References to husband, wife, spouses and married persons, persons included for purposes of this Code, see Family Code § 11.
Separate property, defined, see Family Code §§ 130, 3515.
Spousal support defined for purposes of this Code, see Family Code § 142.
Support, generally, see Family Code § 3500 et seq.
Support defined for purposes of this Code, see Family Code § 150.
Support order, judgment or order of support, see Family Code § 155.

§ 4339. Security for payment

The court may order the supporting party to give reasonable security for payment of spousal support. *(Stats.1992, c. 162 (A.B. 2650), § 10, operative Jan. 1, 1994.)*

Cross References

Child support provisions,
  Deposit of assets, see Family Code § 4600 et seq.
  Deposit of money, see Family Code § 4550 et seq.
  Security for payment, see Family Code § 4012.
Judgment and order defined for purposes of this Code, see Family Code § 100.
Spousal support defined for purposes of this Code, see Family Code § 142.
Support, generally, see Family Code § 3500 et seq.
Support defined for purposes of this Code, see Family Code § 150.

Research References

Forms

1 California Transactions Forms--Family Law § 2:43, Life Insurance.
West's California Judicial Council Forms FL-150, Income and Expense Declaration (Also Available in Spanish).

CHAPTER 4. PAYMENT TO COURT–DESIGNATED OFFICER; ENFORCEMENT BY DISTRICT ATTORNEY

Section
4350. Payments to county officer.
4351. Referral of enforcement to local child support agency; enforcement proceedings; notice requesting meeting with support obligor; contents.
4352. Expenses and charges.

Cross References

Acknowledgment of satisfaction of matured installments under installment judgment, child or spousal support orders, see Code of Civil Procedure § 724.250.
Spousal support, willful violation of order to pay, punishment, see Penal Code § 270.6.

§ 4350. Payments to county officer

In any proceeding where a court makes or has made an order requiring the payment of spousal support, the court may direct that payment shall be made to the county officer designated by the court for that purpose. The court may include in its order made pursuant

§ 4350

to this section any service charge imposed under the authority of Section 279 of the Welfare and Institutions Code. *(Stats.1992, c. 162 (A.B.2650), § 10, operative Jan. 1, 1994.)*

Cross References

County defined for purposes of this Code, see Family Code § 67.
Judgment and order defined for purposes of this Code, see Family Code § 100.
Proceeding defined for purposes of this Code, see Family Code § 110.
Similar provisions, see Family Code § 4200 et seq.
Spousal support defined for purposes of this Code, see Family Code § 142.
Support defined for purposes of this Code, see Family Code § 150.
Support payments, forwarding payments made through county officers, see Family Code § 3555.

Research References

Forms

West's California Code Forms, Family § 4350, Comment Overview—Payment to Court-Designated Officer.
West's California Judicial Council Forms FL–632, Notice Regarding Payment of Support (Governmental).

§ 4351. Referral of enforcement to local child support agency; enforcement proceedings; notice requesting meeting with support obligor; contents

(a) In a proceeding where the court has entered an order pursuant to Section 4350, the court may also refer the matter of enforcement of the spousal support order to the local child support agency. The local child support agency may bring those enforcement proceedings it determines to be appropriate.

(b) Notwithstanding subdivision (a), when the local child support agency is required to appear on behalf of a welfare recipient in a proceeding to enforce an order requiring payment of child support, the local child support agency shall also enforce any order requiring payment to the welfare recipient of spousal support that is in arrears.

(c) This section does not prohibit the district attorney or the local child support agency from bringing an action or initiating process to enforce or punish the failure to obey an order for spousal support under any law that empowers the district attorney or the local child support agency to bring an action or initiate a process, whether or not there has been a referral by the court pursuant to this chapter.

(d) Any notice from the district attorney or the local child support agency requesting a meeting with the support obligor for any purpose authorized under this part shall contain a statement advising the support obligor of the obligor's right to have an attorney present at the meeting. *(Stats.1992, c. 162 (A.B.2650), § 10, operative Jan. 1, 1994. Amended by Stats.1998, c. 854 (A.B.960), § 3; Stats.1999, c. 83 (S.B.966), § 50; Stats.2000, c. 808 (A.B.1358), § 44, eff. Sept. 28, 2000; Stats.2019, c. 115 (A.B.1817), § 53, eff. Jan. 1, 2020.)*

Cross References

Child support, generally, see Family Code § 3900 et seq.
District attorney, powers and duties, see Government Code § 26500 et seq.
Expedited child support orders, see Family Code § 3620 et seq.
Health insurance coverage for supported children, see Family Code § 3750 et seq.
Judgment and order defined for purposes of this Code, see Family Code § 100.
Modification, termination, or setting aside of support order, see Family Code § 3650 et seq.
Notice, actual and constructive, defined, see Civil Code § 18.
Proceeding defined for purposes of this Code, see Family Code § 110.
Similar provisions, see Family Code § 4200 et seq.
Spousal support, willful violation of order to pay, punishment, see Penal Code § 270.6.
Spousal support defined for purposes of this Code, see Family Code § 142.
Support defined for purposes of this Code, see Family Code § 150.

Support order defined for purposes of this Code, see Family Code § 155.

Research References

Forms

West's California Code Forms, Family § 4350, Comment Overview—Payment to Court-Designated Officer.
West's California Judicial Council Forms FL–632, Notice Regarding Payment of Support (Governmental).

§ 4352. Expenses and charges

(a) Insofar as expenses of the county officer designated by the court and expenses of the local child support agency incurred in the enforcement of an order referred by the court under this chapter exceed any service charge imposed under Section 279 of the Welfare and Institutions Code, the expenses are a charge upon the county where the proceedings are pending.

(b) Fees for service of process in the enforcement of an order referred by the court under this chapter are a charge upon the county where the process is served. *(Stats.1992, c. 162 (A.B.2650), § 10, operative Jan. 1, 1994. Amended by Stats.2000, c. 808 (A.B.1358), § 45, eff. Sept. 28, 2000.)*

Cross References

Charges and expenses, see Family Code § 4203.
Child support, generally, see Family Code § 3900 et seq.
County defined for purposes of this Code, see Family Code § 67.
Expedited child support orders, see Family Code § 3620 et seq.
Health insurance coverage for supported children, see Family Code § 3750 et seq.
Judgment and order defined for purposes of this Code, see Family Code § 100.
Modification, termination, or setting aside of support order, see Family Code § 3650 et seq.
Officer designated to act as trustee, service charge to defray cost, see Welfare and Institutions Code § 279.
Proceeding defined for purposes of this Code, see Family Code § 110.
Service of process, generally, see Code of Civil Procedure § 410.10 et seq.
Support defined for purposes of this Code, see Family Code § 150.

CHAPTER 5. PROVISION FOR SUPPORT AFTER DEATH OF SUPPORTING PARTY

Section
4360. Needs of supported spouse; annuity, life insurance, or trust; modification or termination of order.

§ 4360. Needs of supported spouse; annuity, life insurance, or trust; modification or termination of order

(a) For the purpose of Section 4320, where it is just and reasonable in view of the circumstances of the parties, the court, in determining the needs of a supported spouse, may include an amount sufficient to purchase an annuity for the supported spouse or to maintain insurance for the benefit of the supported spouse on the life of the spouse required to make the payment of support, or may require the spouse required to make the payment of support to establish a trust to provide for the support of the supported spouse, so that the supported spouse will not be left without means of support in the event that the spousal support is terminated by the death of the party required to make the payment of support.

(b) Except as otherwise agreed to by the parties in writing, an order made under this section may be modified or terminated at the discretion of the court at any time before the death of the party required to make the payment of support. *(Stats.1992, c. 162 (A.B.2650), § 10, operative Jan. 1, 1994.)*

Cross References

Death or remarriage, effect on spousal support, see Family Code § 4337.
Judgment and order defined for purposes of this Code, see Family Code § 100.
References to husband, wife, spouses and married persons, persons included for purposes of this Code, see Family Code § 11.

Spousal support agreements, generally, see Family Code § 3590 et seq.
Spousal support defined for purposes of this Code, see Family Code § 142.
Support defined for purposes of this Code, see Family Code § 150.
Writings, authentication and proof of, see Evidence Code § 1400 et seq.

Research References

Forms

California Practice Guide: Rutter Family Law Forms Form 6:23, Request for Order Re Temporary "Guideline" Spousal Support and Family Code §4360 Provision for Support After Death of Supporting Party.
1 California Transactions Forms--Family Law § 2:43, Life Insurance.

Part 4

SUPPORT OF PARENTS

Chapter Section
1. General Provisions 4400
2. Relief from Duty to Support Parent Who Abandoned Child 4410

CHAPTER 1. GENERAL PROVISIONS

Section
4400. Duty of adult children to support parents.
4401. Promise of adult child to pay for necessaries.
4402. Cumulative nature of duties.
4403. Enforcement of right of support; reimbursement of county.
4404. Determination of amount due for support; circumstances.
4405. Jurisdiction to modify or terminate order of support.

§ 4400. Duty of adult children to support parents

Except as otherwise provided by law, an adult child shall, to the extent of the adult child's ability, support a parent who is in need and unable to self-maintain by work. *(Stats.1992, c. 162 (A.B.2650), § 10, operative Jan. 1, 1994. Amended by Stats.2019, c. 115 (A.B.1817), § 54, eff. Jan. 1, 2020.)*

Cross References

Abandonment of children, relief from duty to support parent, see Family Code § 4410 et seq.
Adoption of adults and married minors, legal relationship of parent and child, see Family Code § 9305.
Adult child, failure to provide for indigent parent, see Penal Code § 270c.
Adult defined for purposes of this Code, see Family Code § 6501.
Bond for support, see Penal Code § 270b.
Charge against responsible relatives for county aid provided an indigent, see Welfare and Institutions Code § 17300.
Freedom from parental custody and control, see Family Code § 7800 et seq.
Presence or residence of person owing support in state, see Family Code § 3550.
State Supplementary Program for Aged, Blind and Disabled relative's liability for support, see Welfare and Institutions Code § 12350.
Support defined for purposes of this Code, see Family Code § 150.

Research References

Forms

West's California Code Forms, Family § 4400, Comment Overview—Duty of Adult Children to Support Parents.
West's California Code Forms, Family § 4405 Form 2, Order Modifying Order for Support.

§ 4401. Promise of adult child to pay for necessaries

The promise of an adult child to pay for necessaries previously furnished to a parent described in Section 4400 is binding. *(Stats. 1992, c. 162 (A.B.2650), § 10, operative Jan. 1, 1994.)*

Cross References

Adult defined for purposes of this Code, see Family Code § 6501.
Bond for support, see Penal Code § 270b.
Charge against responsible relatives for county aid provided an indigent, see Welfare and Institutions Code § 17300.
Failure of adult child to provide for indigent parent, see Penal Code § 270c.
State Supplementary Program for Aged, Blind and Disabled relative's liability for recipient's support, see Welfare and Institutions Code § 12350.

Research References

Forms

West's California Code Forms, Family § 4400, Comment Overview—Duty of Adult Children to Support Parents.

§ 4402. Cumulative nature of duties

The duty of support under this part is cumulative and not in substitution for any other duty. *(Stats.1992, c. 162 (A.B.2650), § 10, operative Jan. 1, 1994.)*

Cross References

Failure of adult child to provide for indigent parent, see Penal Code § 270c.
Freedom from parental custody and control, see Family Code § 7800 et seq.
Support defined for purposes of this Code, see Family Code § 150.

Research References

Forms

West's California Code Forms, Family § 4400, Comment Overview—Duty of Adult Children to Support Parents.

§ 4403. Enforcement of right of support; reimbursement of county

(a) Subject to subdivision (b):

(1) A parent, or the county on behalf of the parent, may bring an action against the child to enforce the duty of support under this part.

(2) If the county furnishes support to a parent, the county has the same right as the parent to whom the support was furnished to secure reimbursement and obtain continuing support.

(b) The right of the county to proceed on behalf of the parent or to obtain reimbursement is subject to any limitation otherwise imposed by the law of this state.

(c) The court may order the child to pay the county reasonable attorney's fees and court costs in a proceeding by the county under this section. *(Stats.1992, c. 162 (A.B.2650), § 10, operative Jan. 1, 1994.)*

Cross References

Adoption of adults and married minors, legal relationship of parent and child, see Family Code § 9305.
Attorney's fees and costs, generally, see Code of Civil Procedure § 1021.
County defined for purposes of this Code, see Family Code § 67.
Failure of adult child to provide for indigent parent, see Penal Code § 270c.
Freedom from parental custody and control, see Family Code § 7800 et seq.
Judgment and order defined for purposes of this Code, see Family Code § 100.
Proceeding defined for purposes of this Code, see Family Code § 110.
Similar provisions, see Family Code §§ 4002, 4303.
State defined for purposes of this Code, see Family Code § 145.
Support defined for purposes of this Code, see Family Code § 150.
Uniform Interstate Family Support Act, see Family Code § 5700.101 et seq.

Research References

Forms

West's California Code Forms, Family § 4400, Comment Overview—Duty of Adult Children to Support Parents.

§ 4404. Determination of amount due for support; circumstances

In determining the amount to be ordered for support, the court shall consider the following circumstances of each party:

(a) Earning capacity and needs.

(b) Obligations and assets.

§ 4404

(c) Age and health.

(d) Standard of living.

(e) Other factors the court deems just and equitable. *(Stats.1992, c. 162 (A.B.2650), § 10, operative Jan. 1, 1994.)*

Cross References

Adoption of adults and married minors, legal relationship of parent and child, see Family Code § 9305.
Failure of adult child to provide for indigent parent, see Penal Code § 270c.
Freedom from parental custody and control, see Family Code § 7800 et seq.
Similar provisions, see Family Code § 4320.
Support defined for purposes of this Code, see Family Code § 150.

Research References

Forms

West's California Code Forms, Family § 4400, Comment Overview—Duty of Adult Children to Support Parents.
West's California Code Forms, Family § 4400 Form 1, Complaint to Enforce Reciprocal Duty of Support of Needy Parent.
West's California Code Forms, Family § 4405 Form 1, Notice of Motion and Motion to Modify Order for Support.

§ 4405. Jurisdiction to modify or terminate order of support

The court retains jurisdiction to modify or terminate an order for support where justice requires. *(Stats.1992, c. 162 (A.B.2650), § 10, operative Jan. 1, 1994.)*

Cross References

Adoption of adults and married minors, legal relationship of parent and child, see Family Code § 9305.
Failure of adult child to provide for indigent parent, see Penal Code § 270c.
Freedom from parental custody and control, see Family Code § 7800 et seq.
Judgment and order defined for purposes of this Code, see Family Code § 100.
Jurisdiction of superior court,
  Generally, see Cal. Const. Art. 6, §§ 10, 11.
  Proceedings under code, see Family Code § 200.
Modification or termination of support, see Family Code § 3650 et seq.
Support defined for purposes of this Code, see Family Code § 150.

Research References

Forms

West's California Code Forms, Family § 4405 Form 1, Notice of Motion and Motion to Modify Order for Support.

CHAPTER 2. RELIEF FROM DUTY TO SUPPORT PARENT WHO ABANDONED CHILD

Section
4410. Petition for relief from duty; filing.
4411. Grounds for order.
4412. Time for hearing; service of citation and petition.
4413. Jurisdiction; notice to district attorney or county counsel.
4414. Order for relief; effect of order.

Cross References

Abandonment and neglect of children, see Penal Code § 270 et seq.
Adoption of adults and married minors, legal relationship of parent and child, see Family Code § 9305.
Adoptive parents, legal relationship to children, see Family Code § 8616.
Adult defined for purposes of this Code, see Family Code § 6501.
Birth parents, responsibility toward adopted children, see Family Code § 8617.
County defined for purposes of this Code, see Family Code § 67.
Failure of adult child to provide for indigent parent, see Penal Code § 270c.
Judgment and order defined for purposes of this Code, see Family Code § 100.
Jurisdiction, superior court, see Family Code § 200.
Petitioner defined for purposes of this Code, see Family Code § 126.
Pleadings, verification, see Family Code § 212.
Relinquishment of child to department or licensed adoption agency, termination of parental rights, see Family Code § 8700.
State defined for purposes of this Code, see Family Code § 145.
Support defined for purposes of this Code, see Family Code § 150.

§ 4410. Petition for relief from duty; filing

An adult child may file a petition in the county where a parent of the child resides requesting that the court make an order freeing the petitioner from the obligation otherwise imposed by law to support the parent. If the parent does not reside in this state, the petition shall be filed in the county where the adult child resides. *(Stats.1992, c. 162 (A.B.2650), § 10, operative Jan. 1, 1994.)*

Cross References

Abandonment and neglect of children, see Penal Code § 270 et seq.
Adoption of adults and married minors, legal relationship of parent and child, see Family Code § 9305.
Adoptive parents, legal relationship to children, see Family Code § 8616.
Adult defined for purposes of this Code, see Family Code § 6501.
Birth parents, responsibility toward adopted children, see Family Code § 8617.
County defined for purposes of this Code, see Family Code § 67.
Judgment and order defined for purposes of this Code, see Family Code § 100.
Jurisdiction, superior court, see Family Code § 200.
Petitioner defined for purposes of this Code, see Family Code § 126.
Pleadings, verification, see Family Code § 212.
Relinquishment of child to department or licensed adoption agency, termination of parental rights, see Family Code § 8700.
State defined for purposes of this Code, see Family Code § 145.
Support defined for purposes of this Code, see Family Code § 150.

Research References

Forms

West's California Code Forms, Family § 4410, Comment Overview—Petition for Relief from Duty to Support Parent Who Abandoned Child.
West's California Code Forms, Family § 4410 Form 3, Notice of Pendency of Proceedings to Obtain Relief from Obligation to Support Parent Who Abandoned Child.

§ 4411. Grounds for order

The court shall make the order requested pursuant to Section 4410 only if the petition alleges and the court finds all of the following:

(a) The child was abandoned by the parent when the child was a minor.

(b) The abandonment continued for a period of two or more years before the time the child attained the age of 18 years.

(c) During the period of abandonment the parent was physically and mentally able to provide support for the child. *(Stats.1992, c. 162 (A.B.2650), § 10, operative Jan. 1, 1994.)*

Cross References

Abandonment and neglect of children, see Penal Code § 270 et seq.
Adoption of adults and married minors, legal relationship of parent and child, see Family Code § 9305.
Adoptive parents, legal relationship to children, see Family Code § 8616.
Birth parents, responsibility toward adopted children, see Family Code § 8617.
Child support, generally, see Family Code § 3900 et seq.
Judgment and order defined for purposes of this Code, see Family Code § 100.
Minor defined for purposes of this Code, see Family Code § 6500.
Relinquishment of child to department or licensed adoption agency, termination of parental rights, see Family Code § 8700.
Support defined for purposes of this Code, see Family Code § 150.

Research References

Forms

West's California Code Forms, Family § 4410, Comment Overview—Petition for Relief from Duty to Support Parent Who Abandoned Child.

§ 4412. Time for hearing; service of citation and petition

On the filing of a petition under this chapter, the clerk shall set the matter for hearing by the court and shall issue a citation, stating the time and place of the hearing, directed to the parent and to the parent's conservator, if any, or, if the parent is deceased, the personal representative of the parent's estate. At least five days before the date of the hearing, the citation and a copy of the petition shall be personally served on each person to whom it is directed, in the same manner as provided by law for the service of summons. *(Stats.1992, c. 162 (A.B.2650), § 10, operative Jan. 1, 1994.)*

Cross References

Computation of time, see Code of Civil Procedure §§ 12, 12a; Government Code § 6800 et seq.
Person defined for purposes of this Code, see Family Code § 105.
Persons upon whom summons may be served, see Code of Civil Procedure § 416.10 et seq.
Proof of service, see Code of Civil Procedure § 417.10 et seq.

Research References

Forms

West's California Code Forms, Family § 4410, Comment Overview—Petition for Relief from Duty to Support Parent Who Abandoned Child.
West's California Code Forms, Family § 4410 Form 2, Citation—Petition to Obtain Relief from Obligation to Support Parent.
West's California Code Forms, Family § 4410 Form 4, Order Granting Relief from Obligation to Support Parent.

§ 4413. Jurisdiction; notice to district attorney or county counsel

If the parent is a resident of this state, the court does not have jurisdiction to make an order under this chapter until 30 days after the county counsel, or the district attorney in a county not having a county counsel, of the county in which the parent resides has been served with notice of the pendency of the proceeding. *(Stats.1992, c. 162 (A.B.2650), § 10, operative Jan. 1, 1994.)*

Cross References

Abandonment and neglect of children, see Penal Code § 270 et seq.
Adoption of adults and married minors, legal relationship of parent and child, see Family Code § 9305.
Adoptive parents, legal relationship to children, see Family Code § 8616.
Birth parents, responsibility toward adopted children, see Family Code § 8617.
Computation of time, see Code of Civil Procedure §§ 12, 12a; Government Code § 6800 et seq.
Counsel, right to, see Cal. Const. Art. 1, § 15, cl. 3.
County defined for purposes of this Code, see Family Code § 67.
District attorney, powers and duties, see Government Code § 26500 et seq.
Judgment and order defined for purposes of this Code, see Family Code § 100.
Notice, actual and constructive, defined, see Civil Code § 18.
Proceeding defined for purposes of this Code, see Family Code § 110.
Relinquishment of child to department or licensed adoption agency, termination of parental rights, see Family Code § 8700.
State defined for purposes of this Code, see Family Code § 145.

Research References

Forms

West's California Code Forms, Family § 4410, Comment Overview—Petition for Relief from Duty to Support Parent Who Abandoned Child.
West's California Code Forms, Family § 4410 Form 3, Notice of Pendency of Proceedings to Obtain Relief from Obligation to Support Parent Who Abandoned Child.
West's California Code Forms, Family § 4410 Form 4, Order Granting Relief from Obligation to Support Parent.

§ 4414. Order for relief; effect of order

(a) If, upon hearing, the court determines that the requirements of Section 4411 are satisfied, the court shall make an order that the petitioner is relieved from the obligation otherwise imposed by law to support the parent.

(b) An order under this section also releases the petitioner with respect to any state law under which a child is required to do any of the following:

(1) Pay for the support, care, maintenance, and the like of a parent.

(2) Reimburse the state or a local public agency for furnishing the support, care, maintenance, or the like of a parent. *(Stats.1992, c. 162 (A.B.2650), § 10, operative Jan. 1, 1994.)*

Cross References

Abandonment and neglect of children, see Penal Code § 270 et seq.
Adoption of adults and married minors, legal relationship of parent and child, see Family Code § 9305.
Adoptive parents, legal relationship to children, see Family Code § 8616.
Birth parents, responsibility toward adopted children, see Family Code § 8617.
Judgment and order defined for purposes of this Code, see Family Code § 100.
Orders, term including decree as appropriate, see Family Code § 100.
Petitioner defined for purposes of this Code, see Family Code § 126.
Relinquishment of child to department or licensed adoption agency, termination of parental rights, see Family Code § 8700.
State defined for purposes of this Code, see Family Code § 145.
Support defined for purposes of this Code, see Family Code § 150.

Research References

Forms

West's California Code Forms, Family § 4410, Comment Overview—Petition for Relief from Duty to Support Parent Who Abandoned Child.

Part 5

ENFORCEMENT OF SUPPORT ORDERS

Chapter	Section
1. General Provisions	4500
2. Deposit of Money to Secure Future Child Support Payments	4550
3. Deposit of Assets to Secure Future Child Support Payments	4600
4. Child Support Delinquency Reporting	4700
5. Civil Penalty for Child Support Delinquency	4720
6. Uniform Interstate Family Support Act [Repealed]	
7. Enforcement by Writ of Execution	5100
8. Earnings Assignment Order	5200
9. Private Child Support Collectors	5610

CHAPTER 1. GENERAL PROVISIONS

Section
4500. Orders enforceable under this code.
4501. Family support orders.
4502. Judgments or orders for support; enforcement and renewal; governing provisions.
4503. Actions to recover arrearages; limitation of actions.
4504. Payments received from the federal government under specified federal acts or from specified agencies due to retirement or disability of noncustodial parent; application for benefits on behalf of each eligible child; cooperation requirements; credit toward amount ordered to be paid by court.
4505. Default due to unemployment; allegation by parent; list of places applied for employment.
4506. Certification of abstract of judgment; contents; form; notice of support judgment.
4506.1. Obligations enforced pursuant to Title IV–D of the Social Security Act; filing and recording abstract of support judgment.
4506.2. Enforcement of obligation pursuant to Title IV–D of the Social Security Act; filing and recording record of substitution of payee.
4506.3. Notice directing payment of support to local child support agency and notice that support has been assigned; single form.

SUPPORT

Section
4507. Payment of court order for support in accordance with Government Code § 1151.5.
4508. Electronic funds transfer; designation of account; application of section.

§ 4500. Orders enforceable under this code

An order for child, family, or spousal support that is made, entered, or enforceable in this state is enforceable under this code, whether or not the order was made or entered pursuant to this code. *(Stats.1992, c. 162 (A.B.2650), § 10, operative Jan. 1, 1994.)*

Cross References

Child support, generally, see Family Code § 3900 et seq.
Duty to provide for spouse, enforcement of, see Family Code § 4303.
Employee benefit plan, enforcement against, see Family Code § 5103.
Enforcement of judgments and orders, see Family Code §§ 290, 291.
Entry of judgment, see Code of Civil Procedure § 664 et seq.
Expedited child support orders, see Family Code § 3620 et seq.
Health insurance coverage for supported children, see Family Code § 3750 et seq.
Judgment and order defined for purposes of this Code, see Family Code § 100.
Modification, termination, or setting aside of support order, see Family Code § 3650 et seq.
Order, term including decree as appropriate, see Family Code § 100.
Spousal support defined for purposes of this Code, see Family Code § 142.
Spousal support order, enforcement by district attorney, see Family Code § 4351.
State defined for purposes of this Code, see Family Code § 145.
State Supplementary Program for Aged, Blind and Disabled relative's liability for support to applicant for aid, see Welfare and Institutions Code § 12350.
Support agreement, adult child, court approval, see Family Code § 3587.
Support defined for purposes of this Code, see Family Code § 150.
Support order, defined, see Family Code § 155.
Writ of execution, enforcement by, see Family Code § 5100 et seq.

Research References

Forms

West's California Code Forms, Family § 4500, Comment Overview—Enforcement of Support Orders.

§ 4501. Family support orders

A family support order is enforceable in the same manner and to the same extent as a child support order. *(Stats.1992, c. 162 (A.B.2650), § 10, operative Jan. 1, 1994.)*

Cross References

Child support, generally, see Family Code § 3900 et seq.
Duty to provide for spouse, enforcement of, see Family Code § 4303.
Employee benefit plan, enforcement against, see Family Code § 5103.
Enforcement of judgments and orders, see Family Code §§ 290, 291.
Expedited child support orders, see Family Code § 3620 et seq.
Family support, defined, see Family Code § 92.
Health insurance coverage for supported children, see Family Code § 3750 et seq.
Judgment and order defined for purposes of this Code, see Family Code § 100.
Modification, termination, or setting aside of support order, see Family Code § 3650 et seq.
Order, term including decree where appropriate, see Family Code § 100.
Spousal support order, enforcement by district attorney, see Family Code § 4351.
Support defined for purposes of this Code, see Family Code § 150.
Support order defined for purposes of this Code, see Family Code § 155.
Writ of execution, enforcement by, see Family Code § 5100 et seq.

Research References

Forms

West's California Code Forms, Family § 4500, Comment Overview—Enforcement of Support Orders.

§ 4502. Judgments or orders for support; enforcement and renewal; governing provisions

The period for enforcement and procedure for renewal of a judgment or order for child, family, or spousal support is governed by Section 291. *(Added by Stats.2006, c. 86 (A.B.2126), § 6.)*

Cross References

Application for renewal of judgment, filing time, see Code of Civil Procedure § 683.130.
Child support, generally, see Family Code § 3900 et seq.
Duty to provide for spouse, enforcement of, see Family Code § 4303.
Employee benefit plan, enforcement against, see Family Code § 5103.
Enforcement and renewal of judgments, application, see Code of Civil Procedure § 683.110.
Enforcement of judgments and orders, see Family Code §§ 290, 291.
Judgment and order defined for purposes of this Code, see Family Code § 100.
Judgment or order for possession or sale of property, period of enforceability, see Family Code § 291.
Laches and enforcement of premarital agreements, see Family Code § 1617.
Spousal support defined for purposes of this Code, see Family Code § 142.
Spousal support order, enforcement by district attorney, see Family Code § 4351.
State defined for purposes of this Code, see Family Code § 145.
Support defined for purposes of this Code, see Family Code § 150.
Writ of execution, enforcement by, see Family Code § 5100 et seq.

Research References

Forms

West's California Code Forms, Family § 4500, Comment Overview—Enforcement of Support Orders.

§ 4503. Actions to recover arrearages; limitation of actions

If a parent has been ordered to make payments for the support of a minor child, an action to recover an arrearage in those payments may be maintained at any time within the period otherwise specified for the enforcement of such a judgment, notwithstanding the fact that the child has attained the age of 18 years. *(Stats.1992, c. 162 (A.B.2650), § 10, operative Jan. 1, 1994.)*

Cross References

Child support, generally, see Family Code § 3900 et seq.
Child support payments, priority, see Family Code § 4011.
Duty to provide for spouse, enforcement of, see Family Code § 4303.
Enforcement of judgments, generally, see Code of Civil Procedure § 680.010.
Enforcement of judgments and orders, see Family Code §§ 290, 291.
Expedited child support orders, see Family Code § 3620 et seq.
Health insurance coverage for supported children, see Family Code § 3750 et seq.
Judgment and order defined for purposes of this Code, see Family Code § 100.
Minor defined for purposes of this Code, see Family Code § 6500.
Modification, termination, or setting aside of support order, see Family Code § 3650 et seq.
Spousal support order, enforcement by district attorney, see Family Code § 4351.
Support, payment of education and maintenance expenses of minor children, see Family Code § 150.
Support defined for purposes of this Code, see Family Code § 150.
Writ of execution, enforcement by, see Family Code § 5100 et seq.

Research References

Forms

West's California Code Forms, Family § 4500, Comment Overview—Enforcement of Support Orders.
West's California Judicial Council Forms FL–626, Stipulation and Order Waiving Unassigned Arrears (Governmental) (Also Available in Chinese, Korean, Spanish, Tagalog, and Vietnamese).

§ 4504. Payments received from the federal government under specified federal acts or from specified agencies due to retirement or disability of noncustodial parent; application for benefits on behalf of each eligible child; cooperation requirements; credit toward amount ordered to be paid by court

(a) If the noncustodial parent is receiving payments from the federal government pursuant to the Social Security Act or Railroad Retirement Act, or from the Department of Veterans Affairs because of the retirement or disability of the noncustodial parent and the noncustodial parent notifies the custodial person, or notifies the local child support agency in a case being enforced by the local child support agency pursuant to Title IV–D of the Social Security Act, then the custodial parent or other child support obligee shall contact the appropriate federal agency within 30 days of receiving notification that the noncustodial parent is receiving those payments to verify eligibility for each child to receive payments from the federal government because of the disability of the noncustodial parent. If the child is potentially eligible for those payments, the custodial parent or other child support obligee shall apply for and cooperate with the appropriate federal agency for the receipt of those benefits on behalf of each child. The noncustodial parent shall cooperate with the custodial parent or other child support obligee in making that application and shall provide any information necessary to complete the application.

(b) If the court has ordered a noncustodial parent to pay for the support of a child, payments for the support of the child made by the federal government pursuant to the Social Security Act or Railroad Retirement Act, or by the Department of Veterans Affairs because of the retirement or disability of the noncustodial parent and received by the custodial parent or other child support obligee shall be credited toward the amount ordered by the court to be paid by the noncustodial parent for support of the child unless the payments made by the federal government were taken into consideration by the court in determining the amount of support to be paid. Any payments shall be credited in the order set forth in Section 695.221 of the Code of Civil Procedure.

(c) If the custodial parent or other child support obligee refuses to apply for those benefits or fails to cooperate with the appropriate federal agency in completing the application but the child or children otherwise are eligible to receive those benefits, the noncustodial parent shall be credited toward the amount ordered by the court to be paid for that month by the noncustodial parent for support of the child or children in the amount of payment that the child or children would have received that month had the custodial parent or other child support obligee completed an application for the benefits if the noncustodial parent provides evidence to the local child support agency indicating the amount the child or children would have received. The credit for those payments shall continue until the child or children would no longer be eligible for those benefits or the order for child support for the child or children is no longer in effect, whichever occurs first. *(Stats.1992, c. 162 (A.B.2650), § 10, operative Jan. 1, 1994. Amended by Stats.1996, c. 912 (A.B.1751), § 2; Stats.2001, c. 651 (A.B.891), § 1; Stats.2004, c. 305 (A.B.2669), § 4.)*

Cross References

Child custody, see Family Code § 3020 et seq.
Child support, generally, see Family Code § 3900 et seq.
Computation of time, see Code of Civil Procedure §§ 12, 12a; Government Code § 6800 et seq.
Employee benefit plan, enforcement against, see Family Code § 5103.
Enforcement of judgments and orders, see Family Code §§ 290, 291.
Expedited child support orders, see Family Code § 3620 et seq.
Health insurance coverage for supported children, see Family Code § 3750 et seq.
Judgment and order defined for purposes of this Code, see Family Code § 100.
Modification, termination, or setting aside of support order, see Family Code § 3650 et seq.
Person defined for purposes of this Code, see Family Code § 105.
Spousal support order, enforcement by district attorney, see Family Code § 4351.
Support defined for purposes of this Code, see Family Code § 150.
Writ of execution, enforcement by, see Family Code § 5100 et seq.

Research References

Forms

California Practice Guide: Rutter Family Law Forms Form 6:9, Responsive Declaration to Request for Order Re Child Support Based on Earning Capacity.

§ 4505. Default due to unemployment; allegation by parent; list of places applied for employment

(a) A court may require a parent who alleges that the parent's default in a child or family support order is due to the parent's unemployment to submit to the appropriate child support enforcement agency or any other entity designated by the court, including, but not limited to, the court itself, each two weeks, or at a frequency deemed appropriate by the court, a list of at least five different places the parent has applied for employment.

(b) This section shall become operative on January 1, 2011. *(Added by Stats.2007, c. 249 (S.B.523), § 2, operative Jan. 1, 2011.)*

Cross References

Child support, generally, see Family Code § 3900 et seq.
Enforcement of judgments and orders, see Family Code §§ 290, 291.
Expedited child support orders, see Family Code § 3620 et seq.
Family support defined for purposes of this Code, see Family Code § 92.
Health insurance coverage for supported children, see Family Code § 3750 et seq.
Judgment and order defined for purposes of this Code, see Family Code § 100.
Modification, termination, or setting aside of support order, see Family Code § 3650 et seq.
Spousal support order, enforcement by district attorney, see Family Code § 4351.
Support defined for purposes of this Code, see Family Code § 150.
Support order defined for purposes of this Code, see Family Code § 155.
Writ of execution, enforcement by, see Family Code § 5100 et seq.

§ 4506. Certification of abstract of judgment; contents; form; notice of support judgment

(a) An abstract of a judgment ordering a party to pay spousal, child, or family support to the other party shall be certified by the clerk of the court where the judgment was entered and shall contain all of the following:

(1) The title of the court where the judgment is entered and the cause and number of the proceeding.

(2) The date of entry of the judgment and of any renewal of the judgment.

(3) Where the judgment and any renewals are entered in the records of the court.

(4) The name and last known address of the party ordered to pay support.

(5) The name and address of the party to whom support payments are ordered to be paid.

(6) Only the last four digits of the social security number, birth date, and driver's license number of the party who is ordered to pay support. If any of those numbers are not known to the party to whom support payments are to be paid, that fact shall be indicated on the abstract of the court judgment. This paragraph shall not apply to documents created prior to January 1, 2010.

(7) Whether a stay of enforcement has been ordered by the court and, if so, the date the stay ends.

(8) The date of issuance of the abstract.

(9) Any other information deemed reasonable and appropriate by the Judicial Council.

(b) The Judicial Council may develop a form for an abstract of a judgment ordering a party to pay child, family, or spousal support to another party which contains the information required by subdivision (a).

(c) Notwithstanding any other provision of law, when a support obligation is being enforced pursuant to Title IV–D of the Social Security Act, the agency enforcing the obligation may record a notice of support judgment. The notice of support judgment shall contain the same information as the form adopted by the Judicial Council pursuant to subdivision (b) and Section 4506.1. The notice of support judgment shall have the same force and effect as an abstract

§ 4506

of judgment certified by the clerk of the court where the judgment was entered. The local child support agency or other Title IV-D agency shall not be subject to any civil liability as a consequence of causing a notice of support judgment to be recorded.

(d) As used in this section, "judgment" includes an order for child, family, or spousal support. *(Stats.1992, c. 162 (A.B.2650), § 10, operative Jan. 1, 1994. Amended by Stats.2002, c. 927 (A.B.3032), § 3; Stats.2009, c. 552 (S.B.40), § 3.)*

Cross References

Abstract of judgment, amendment, see Code of Civil Procedure § 674.
Child support, generally, see Family Code § 3900 et seq.
Enforcement of judgments and orders, see Family Code §§ 290, 291.
Expedited child support orders, see Family Code § 3620 et seq.
Family support defined for purposes of this Code, see Family Code § 92.
Health insurance coverage for supported children, see Family Code § 3750 et seq.
Judgment and order defined for purposes of this Code, see Family Code § 100.
Lien for child support against real property, digitized or digital electronic record, see Family Code § 17523.5.
Modification, termination, or setting aside of support order, see Family Code § 3650 et seq.
Notice, actual and constructive, defined, see Civil Code § 18.
Proceeding defined for purposes of this Code, see Family Code § 110.
Spousal support defined for purposes of this Code, see Family Code § 142.
Spousal support order, enforcement by district attorney, see Family Code § 4351.
Support defined for purposes of this Code, see Family Code § 150.
Writ of execution, enforcement by, see Family Code § 5100 et seq.

Research References

Forms

West's California Code Forms, Family § 4500, Comment Overview—Enforcement of Support Orders.

§ 4506.1. Obligations enforced pursuant to Title IV-D of the Social Security Act; filing and recording abstract of support judgment

Notwithstanding any other provision of law, when a support obligation is being enforced pursuant to Title IV-D of the Social Security Act, the agency enforcing the obligation may file and record an abstract of support judgment as authorized by Section 4506 and substitute the office address of the agency designated to receive support payments for the address of the party to whom support was ordered to be paid. *(Added by Stats.1994, c. 1269 (A.B.2208), § 48.)*

Cross References

Judgment and order defined for purposes of this Code, see Family Code § 100.
Support defined for purposes of this Code, see Family Code § 150.

§ 4506.2. Enforcement of obligation pursuant to Title IV-D of the Social Security Act; filing and recording record of substitution of payee

(a) Notwithstanding any other provision of law, when a support obligation is being enforced pursuant to Title IV-D of the Social Security Act, the agency enforcing the obligation may file and record a substitution of payee, if a judgment or abstract of judgment has previously been recorded pursuant to Section 697.320 of the Code of Civil Procedure by the support obligee or by a different governmental agency.

(b) Notwithstanding any other provision of law, when the Title IV-D agency ceases enforcement of a support obligation at the request of the support obligee, the agency may file and record a substitution of payee, if a judgment or abstract of judgment has been previously recorded pursuant to Section 697.320 of the Code of Civil Procedure.

(c) The substitution of payee shall contain all of the following:

(1) The name and address of the governmental agency or substituted payee filing the substitution and a notice that the substituted payee is to be contacted when notice to a lienholder may or must be given.

(2) The title of the court, the cause, and number of the proceeding where the substituted payee has registered the judgment.

(3) The name and last known address of the party ordered to pay support.

(4) The recorder identification number or book and page of the recorded document to which the substitution of payee applies.

(5) Any other information deemed reasonable and appropriate by the Judicial Council.

(d) The recorded substitution of payee shall not affect the priorities created by earlier recordations of support judgments or abstracts of support judgments.

(e) An agency enforcing the support obligation pursuant to Title IV-D of the Social Security Act is not required to obtain prior court approval or a clerk's certification when filing and recording a substitution of payee under this section. *(Added by Stats.1994, c. 1269 (A.B.2208), § 48.2. Amended by Stats.1997, c. 599 (A.B.573), § 17.)*

Cross References

Judgment and order defined for purposes of this Code, see Family Code § 100.
Notice, actual and constructive, defined, see Civil Code § 18.
Proceeding defined for purposes of this Code, see Family Code § 110.
Support defined for purposes of this Code, see Family Code § 150.

§ 4506.3. Notice directing payment of support to local child support agency and notice that support has been assigned; single form

The Judicial Council, in consultation with the California Family Support Council, the Department of Child Support Services, and title insurance industry representatives, shall develop a single form, which conforms with the requirements of Section 27361.6 of the Government Code, for the substitution of payee, for notice directing payment of support to the local child support agency pursuant to Section 4204, and for notice that support has been assigned pursuant to Section 11477 of the Welfare and Institutions Code. The form shall be available no later than July 1, 1998. *(Added by Stats.1994, c. 1269 (A.B.2208), § 48.4. Amended by Stats.1996, c. 957 (A.B.1058), § 7; Stats.1997, c. 599 (A.B.573), § 18; Stats.2000, c. 808 (A.B.1358), § 46, eff. Sept. 28, 2000.)*

Cross References

Child support, generally, see Family Code § 3900 et seq.
Department of Child Support Services, generally, see Family Code § 17000 et seq.
Family support defined for purposes of this Code, see Family Code § 92.
Notice, actual and constructive, defined, see Civil Code § 18.
Support defined for purposes of this Code, see Family Code § 150.

Research References

Forms

West's California Judicial Council Forms FL-632, Notice Regarding Payment of Support (Governmental).

§ 4507. Payment of court order for support in accordance with Government Code § 1151.5

When a court orders a person to make payment for child support or family support, the court may order that individual to make that payment as provided in Section 1151.5 of the Government Code. *(Added by Stats.1993, c. 176 (A.B.877), § 1.)*

Cross References

Child support, generally, see Family Code § 3900 et seq.
Expedited child support orders, see Family Code § 3620 et seq.
Family support defined for purposes of this Code, see Family Code § 92.

Health insurance coverage for supported children, see Family Code § 3750 et seq.
Judgment and order defined for purposes of this Code, see Family Code § 100.
Modification, termination, or setting aside of support order, see Family Code § 3650 et seq.
Person defined for purposes of this Code, see Family Code § 105.
Support defined for purposes of this Code, see Family Code § 150.

§ 4508. Electronic funds transfer; designation of account; application of section

(a) This section does not apply to any child support obligor who is subject to an earnings assignment order pursuant to Chapter 8 (commencing with Section 5200).

(b) Except as provided in subdivision (a), every order or judgment to pay child support may require a child support obligor to designate an account for the purpose of paying the child support obligation by electronic funds transfer, as defined in subdivision (a) of Section 6479.5 of the Revenue and Taxation Code. The order or judgment may require the obligor to deposit funds in an interest-bearing account with a state or federally chartered commercial bank, a savings and loan association, or in shares of a federally insured credit union doing business in this state, and shall require the obligor to maintain funds in the account sufficient to pay the monthly child support obligation. The court may order that each payment be electronically transferred to either the obligee's account or the local child support agency account. The obligor shall be required to notify the obligee if the depository institution or the account number is changed. No interest shall accrue on any amount subject to electronic funds transfer as long as funds are maintained in the account that are sufficient to pay the monthly child support obligation. *(Added by Stats.1994, c. 906 (A.B.923), § 2. Amended by Stats.1999, c. 980 (A.B.1671), § 9; Stats.2001, c. 755 (S.B.943), § 4, eff. Oct. 12, 2001.)*

Cross References

Child support, generally, see Family Code § 3900 et seq.
Expedited child support orders, see Family Code § 3620 et seq.
Health insurance coverage for supported children, see Family Code § 3750 et seq.
Judgment and order defined for purposes of this Code, see Family Code § 100.
Modification, termination, or setting aside of support order, see Family Code § 3650 et seq.
State defined for purposes of this Code, see Family Code § 145.
Support defined for purposes of this Code, see Family Code § 150.

Research References

Forms
1 California Transactions Forms--Family Law § 2:63, Authority for Child Support.
1 California Transactions Forms--Family Law § 2:93.50, Child Support Provision Regarding Electronic Transfer of Funds.
1 California Transactions Forms--Family Law § 3:37, Stipulation of the Parties.
1 California Transactions Forms--Family Law § 3:112.50, Designation of Electronic Fund Transfer Account Number.

CHAPTER 2. DEPOSIT OF MONEY TO SECURE FUTURE CHILD SUPPORT PAYMENTS

Article	Section
1. General Provisions	4550
2. Order for Deposit of Money	4560
3. Application to Reduce or Eliminate Deposit	4565
4. Use of Deposit to Make Delinquent Support Payment	4570

ARTICLE 1. GENERAL PROVISIONS

Section
4550. "Child support obligee" defined.
4551. Application of chapter.
4552. Rules of court; promulgation and publication of forms by Judicial Council.
4553. Construction of chapter; compliance with federal law.
4554. Application of chapter.

Cross References

Assets, deposit to secure future child support payments, see Family Code § 4600 et seq.

§ 4550. "Child support obligee" defined

"Child support obligee" as used in this chapter means either the parent, guardian, or other person to whom child support has been ordered to be paid or the local child support agency designated by the court to receive the payment. The local child support agency is the "child support obligee" for the purposes of this chapter for all cases in which an application for services has been filed under Part D of Title IV of the Social Security Act (42 U.S.C. Sec. 651 et seq.). *(Stats.1992, c. 162 (A.B.2650), § 10, operative Jan. 1, 1994; Stats.2001, c. 755 (S.B.943), § 5, eff. Oct. 12, 2001.)*

Cross References

Child support, generally, see Family Code § 3900 et seq.
Delinquent payments, use of security deposit to cover, see Family Code § 4570 et seq.
Expedited child support orders, see Family Code § 3620 et seq.
Health insurance coverage for supported children, see Family Code § 3750 et seq.
Hearing, reduction or elimination of security deposit, see Family Code § 4567.
Modification, termination, or setting aside of support order, see Family Code § 3650 et seq.
Order for security deposit, see Family Code § 4560 et seq.
Person defined for purposes of this Code, see Family Code § 105.
Reduction or elimination of security deposit, see Family Code § 4565 et seq.
Support defined for purposes of this Code, see Family Code § 150.

§ 4551. Application of chapter

Except as provided in this section, this chapter:

(a) Does not apply to a temporary child support order.

(b) Applies to an application for modification of child support filed on or after January 1, 1992, but this chapter does not constitute the basis for the modification.

(c) Applies to an application for modification of child support in a case where the child support obligee has previously waived the establishment of a child support trust account pursuant to subdivision (b) of Section 4560 and now seeks the establishment of the child support trust account.

(d) Applies to an order or judgment entered by the court on or after January 1, 1993, ordering a child support obligor to pay a then existing child support arrearage that the child support obligor has unlawfully failed to pay as of the date of that order or judgment, including the arrearages which were incurred before January 1, 1992. *(Stats.1992, c. 162 (A.B.2650), § 10, operative Jan. 1, 1994.)*

Cross References

Child support, generally, see Family Code § 3900 et seq.
Expedited child support orders, see Family Code § 3620 et seq.
Health insurance coverage for supported children, see Family Code § 3750 et seq.
Judgment and order defined for purposes of this Code, see Family Code § 100.
Modification, termination, or setting aside of support order, see Family Code § 3650 et seq.
Support defined for purposes of this Code, see Family Code § 150.

§ 4551

Support order defined for purposes of this Code, see Family Code § 155.

§ 4552. Rules of court; promulgation and publication of forms by Judicial Council

The Judicial Council shall promulgate such rules of court and publish such related judicial forms as the Judicial Council determines are necessary and appropriate to implement this chapter. In taking these steps, the Judicial Council shall ensure the uniform statewide application of this chapter and compliance with Part D of Title IV of the Social Security Act (42 U.S.C. Sec. 651 et seq.) and any regulations promulgated thereunder. *(Stats.1992, c. 162 (A.B.2650), § 10, operative Jan. 1, 1994.)*

Cross References

Judicial Council, rules for proceedings, see Family Code § 210 et seq.

§ 4553. Construction of chapter; compliance with federal law

Nothing in this chapter shall be construed to permit any action or omission by the state or any of its political subdivisions that would place the state in noncompliance with any requirement of federal law, including, but not limited to, the state reimbursement requirements of Part D of Title IV of the Social Security Act (42 U.S.C. Sec. 651 et seq.) and any regulations promulgated thereunder. *(Stats. 1992, c. 162 (A.B.2650), § 10, operative Jan. 1, 1994.)*

Cross References

State defined for purposes of this Code, see Family Code § 145.

§ 4554. Application of chapter

This chapter applies notwithstanding any other law. *(Stats.1992, c. 162 (A.B.2650), § 10, operative Jan. 1, 1994.)*

ARTICLE 2. ORDER FOR DEPOSIT OF MONEY

Section
4560. Child support security deposit; trust account.
4561. Deposit of funds.
4562. Evidence of deposit.
4563. Dissolution of account; return of funds.

Cross References

Assets, deposit to secure future child support payments, see Family Code § 4600 et seq.

§ 4560. Child support security deposit; trust account

(a) Except as provided in subdivision (b) or in Article 3 (commencing with Section 4565), every order or judgment to pay child support may also require the payment by the child support obligor of up to one year's child support or such lesser amount as is equal to the child support amount due to be paid by the child support obligor between the time of the date of the order and the date when the support obligation will be terminated by operation of law. This amount shall be known as the "child support security deposit."

(b) Unless expressly waived by the child support obligee, the court may order the establishment of a child support trust account pursuant to this chapter in every proceeding in which a child support obligation is imposed by order of the court. Among other reasons, the court may decline to establish a child support trust account upon its finding that an adequately funded child support trust account already exists pursuant to this chapter for the benefit of the child or children involved in the proceeding or that the child support obligor has provided adequate alternative security which is equivalent to the child support security deposit otherwise required by this chapter. *(Stats.1992, c. 162 (A.B.2650), § 10, operative Jan. 1, 1994.)*

Cross References

Application of chapter, see Family Code § 4551.
Child support, generally, see Family Code § 3900 et seq.
Expedited child support orders, see Family Code § 3620 et seq.
Grounds for application to reduce or eliminate deposit, see Family Code § 4565.
Health insurance coverage for supported children, see Family Code § 3750 et seq.
Judgment and order defined for purposes of this Code, see Family Code § 100.
Modification, termination, or setting aside of support order, see Family Code § 3650 et seq.
Proceeding defined for purposes of this Code, see Family Code § 110.
Security deposit of assets to secure future payments, see Family Code § 4600 et seq.
Support defined for purposes of this Code, see Family Code § 150.

Research References

Forms

1 California Transactions Forms--Family Law § 3:48, Deposit Into Trust Account.
West's California Code Forms, Family § 4560, Comment Overview—Deposit of Money to Secure Future Child Support Payments.
West's California Judicial Council Forms FL–400, Order for Child Support Security Deposit and Evidence of Deposit.

§ 4561. Deposit of funds

If a child support security deposit is ordered, the court shall order that the moneys be deposited by the child support obligor in an interest-bearing account with a state or federally chartered commercial bank, a trust company authorized to transact trust business in this state, or a savings and loan association, or in shares of a federally insured credit union doing business in this state and having a trust department, subject to withdrawal only upon authorization of the court. The moneys so deposited shall be used exclusively to guarantee the monthly payment of child support. *(Stats.1992, c. 162 (A.B.2650), § 10, operative Jan. 1, 1994.)*

Cross References

Child support, generally, see Family Code § 3900 et seq.
Expedited child support orders, see Family Code § 3620 et seq.
Health insurance coverage for supported children, see Family Code § 3750 et seq.
Judgment and order defined for purposes of this Code, see Family Code § 100.
Modification, termination, or setting aside of support order, see Family Code § 3650 et seq.
State defined for purposes of this Code, see Family Code § 145.
Support defined for purposes of this Code, see Family Code § 150.

§ 4562. Evidence of deposit

The court shall also order that evidence of the deposit shall be provided by the child support obligor in the form specified by the court, which shall be served upon the child support obligee and filed with the court within a reasonable time specified by the court, not to exceed 30 days. *(Stats.1992, c. 162 (A.B.2650), § 10, operative Jan. 1, 1994.)*

Cross References

Child support, generally, see Family Code § 3900 et seq.
Computation of time, see Code of Civil Procedure §§ 12, 12a; Government Code § 6800 et seq.
Judgment and order defined for purposes of this Code, see Family Code § 100.
Support defined for purposes of this Code, see Family Code § 150.

Research References

Forms

West's California Judicial Council Forms FL–400, Order for Child Support Security Deposit and Evidence of Deposit.

§ 4563. Dissolution of account; return of funds

An account established pursuant to this chapter shall be dissolved and any remaining funds in the account shall be returned to the support obligor, with any interest earned thereon, upon the full payment and cessation of the child support obligation as provided by court order or operation of law. *(Stats.1992, c. 162 (A.B.2650), § 10, operative Jan. 1, 1994.)*

Cross References

Child support, generally, see Family Code § 3900 et seq.
Expedited child support orders, see Family Code § 3620 et seq.
Health insurance coverage for supported children, see Family Code § 3750 et seq.
Judgment and order defined for purposes of this Code, see Family Code § 100.
Modification, termination, or setting aside of support order, see Family Code § 3650 et seq.
Support defined for purposes of this Code, see Family Code § 150.

Research References

Forms

1 California Transactions Forms--Family Law § 3:48, Deposit Into Trust Account.

ARTICLE 3. APPLICATION TO REDUCE OR ELIMINATE DEPOSIT

Section
4565. Filing of application; grounds for relief.
4566. Notice of application; response.
4567. Hearing; entry of orders; reduction of amount of deposit.

Cross References

Assets, deposit to secure future child support payments, see Family Code § 4600 et seq.

§ 4565. Filing of application; grounds for relief

(a) Before entry of a child support order pursuant to Section 4560, the court shall give the child support obligor reasonable notice and opportunity to file an application to reduce or eliminate the child support security deposit on either of the following grounds:

(1) The obligor has provided adequate alternative equivalent security to assure timely payment of the amount required by Section 4560.

(2) The obligor is unable, without undue financial hardship, to pay the support deposit required by Section 4560.

(b) The application shall be supported by all reasonable and necessary financial and other information required by the court to establish the existence of either ground for relief.

(c) After the filing of an application, the child support obligor shall also serve the application and supporting financial and other information submitted pursuant to subdivision (b) upon the child support obligee and any other party to the proceeding. *(Stats.1992, c. 162 (A.B.2650), § 10, operative Jan. 1, 1994. Amended by Stats.2007, c. 441 (S.B.892), § 1.)*

Cross References

Assets, deposit for security of future payments, see Family Code § 4600 et seq.
Child support, generally, see Family Code § 3900 et seq.
Expedited child support orders, see Family Code § 3620 et seq.
Health insurance coverage for supported children, see Family Code § 3750 et seq.
Judgment and order defined for purposes of this Code, see Family Code § 100.
Modification, termination, or setting aside of support order, see Family Code § 3650 et seq.
Notice, actual and constructive, defined, see Civil Code § 18.
Support defined for purposes of this Code, see Family Code § 150.
Support order defined for purposes of this Code, see Family Code § 155.

Research References

Forms

West's California Code Forms, Family § 4560, Comment Overview—Deposit of Money to Secure Future Child Support Payments.

§ 4566. Notice of application; response

Upon the filing of an application under Section 4565 with the court and the service of the application upon the child support obligee and any other party to the proceedings, the court shall provide notice and opportunity for any party opposing the application to file responsive financial and other information setting forth the factual and legal bases for the party's opposition. *(Stats.1992, c. 162 (A.B.2650), § 10, operative Jan. 1, 1994.)*

Cross References

Child support, generally, see Family Code § 3900 et seq.
Notice, actual and constructive, defined, see Civil Code § 18.
Proceeding defined for purposes of this Code, see Family Code § 110.
Support defined for purposes of this Code, see Family Code § 150.
Support order, defined, see Family Code § 155.

§ 4567. Hearing; entry of orders; reduction of amount of deposit

The court shall then provide an opportunity for hearing, and shall thereafter enter its order exercising its discretion under all the facts and circumstances as disclosed in the admissible evidence before it so as to maximize the payment and deposit of the amount required by Section 4560, or an equivalent adequate security for the payment thereof, without imposition of undue financial hardship on the support obligor. If the court finds that the deposit of the amount required by Section 4560 would impose an undue financial hardship upon the child support obligor, the court shall reduce this amount to an amount that the child support obligor can pay as the child support security deposit without undue financial hardship. *(Stats.1992, c. 162 (A.B.2650), § 10, operative Jan. 1, 1994.)*

Cross References

Assets, deposit for security of future payments, see Family Code § 4600 et seq.
Child support, generally, see Family Code § 3900 et seq.
Judgment and order defined for purposes of this Code, see Family Code § 100.
Support defined for purposes of this Code, see Family Code § 150.
Support order, defined, see Family Code § 155.

ARTICLE 4. USE OF DEPOSIT TO MAKE DELINQUENT SUPPORT PAYMENT

Section
4570. Disbursement of funds; use of funds; replenishment of account.
4571. Service upon support obligor.
4572. Service upon depository institution and local child support agency.
4573. Support payments ordered paid through local child support agency; duties.

Cross References

Assets, deposit to secure future child support payments, see Family Code § 4600 et seq.

§ 4570. Disbursement of funds; use of funds; replenishment of account

(a) Upon the application of the child support obligee stating that the support payment is 10 or more days late, the court shall immediately order disbursement of funds from the account established pursuant to this chapter solely for the purpose of providing the amount of child support then in arrears.

§ 4570

(b) Funds so disbursed shall be used exclusively for the support, maintenance, and education of the child or children subject to the child support order.

(c) The court shall also order the account to be replenished by the child support obligor in the same amounts as are expended from the account to pay the amount of child support which the child support obligor has failed to pay the child support obligee in a timely manner. *(Stats.1992, c. 162 (A.B.2650), § 10, operative Jan. 1, 1994.)*

Cross References

Child support, generally, see Family Code § 3900 et seq.
Computation of time, see Code of Civil Procedure §§ 12, 12a; Government Code § 6800 et seq.
Expedited child support orders, see Family Code § 3620 et seq.
Health insurance coverage for supported children, see Family Code § 3750 et seq.
Judgment and order defined for purposes of this Code, see Family Code § 100.
Modification, termination, or setting aside of support order, see Family Code § 3650 et seq.
Pleadings, verification, see Family Code § 212.
Support defined for purposes of this Code, see Family Code § 150.
Support order defined for purposes of this Code, see Family Code § 155.

Research References

Forms

1 California Transactions Forms--Family Law § 3:48, Deposit Into Trust Account.
West's California Code Forms, Family § 4570, Comment Overview—Use of Deposit to Make Delinquent Support Payment.

§ 4571. Service upon support obligor

The court shall cause a copy of the application, as well as its order to disburse and replenish funds, to be served upon the child support obligor, who shall be subject to contempt of court for failure to comply with the order. *(Stats.1992, c. 162 (A.B.2650), § 10, operative Jan. 1, 1994.)*

Cross References

Child support, generally, see Family Code § 3900 et seq.
Judgment and order defined for purposes of this Code, see Family Code § 100.
Pleadings, verification, see Family Code § 212.
Service of notice, validity of modification of judgment or order, see Family Code § 215.
Support defined for purposes of this Code, see Family Code § 150.
Support order, defined, see Family Code § 155.

Research References

Forms

West's California Code Forms, Family § 4570, Comment Overview—Use of Deposit to Make Delinquent Support Payment.

§ 4572. Service upon depository institution and local child support agency

The court shall cause a copy of its order to disburse and replenish funds to be served upon the depository institution where the child support security deposit is maintained, and upon the child support agency with jurisdiction over the case. *(Stats.1992, c. 162 (A.B.2650), § 10, operative Jan. 1, 1994. Amended by Stats.2001, c. 755 (S.B.943), § 6, eff. Oct. 12, 2001.)*

Cross References

Child support, generally, see Family Code § 3900 et seq.
Judgment and order defined for purposes of this Code, see Family Code § 100.
Service of notice, validity of modification of judgment or order, see Family Code § 215.
Support defined for purposes of this Code, see Family Code § 150.

Support order, defined, see Family Code § 155.

§ 4573. Support payments ordered paid through local child support agency; duties

If support is ordered to be paid through the local child support agency on behalf of a child not receiving public assistance pursuant to the Family Economic Security Act of 1982 (Chapter 2 (commencing with Section 11200) of Part 3 of Division 9 of the Welfare and Institutions Code), the local child support agency shall forward the support received pursuant to this chapter to the custodial parent or other person having care or control of the child or children involved. *(Stats.1992, c. 162 (A.B.2650), § 10, operative Jan. 1, 1994. Amended by Stats.1993, c. 219 (A.B.1500), § 144; Stats.2000, c. 808 (A.B.1358), § 47, eff. Sept. 28, 2000.)*

Cross References

Child custody, see Family Code § 3020 et seq.
Child support, generally, see Family Code § 3900 et seq.
District attorneys,
 Spousal support, see Family Code § 4350 et seq.
 Support enforcement, see Family Code § 4200 et seq.
Expedited child support orders, see Family Code § 3620 et seq.
Forwarding support payments, county officers, see Family Code § 3555.
Health insurance coverage for supported children, see Family Code § 3750 et seq.
Modification, termination, or setting aside of support order, see Family Code § 3650 et seq.
Person defined for purposes of this Code, see Family Code § 105.
Right to custody of minor child, sex offenders, murderers, see Family Code § 3030.
Support defined for purposes of this Code, see Family Code § 150.
Support order defined, see Family Code § 155.

Research References

Forms

1 California Transactions Forms--Family Law § 3:48, Deposit Into Trust Account.

CHAPTER 3. DEPOSIT OF ASSETS TO SECURE FUTURE CHILD SUPPORT PAYMENTS

Article	Section
1. General Provisions	4600
2. Order for Deposit of Assets	4610
3. Ex Parte Restraining Orders	4620
4. Use or Sale of Assets to Make Support Payments	4630
5. Return of Assets of Obligor	4640

ARTICLE 1. GENERAL PROVISIONS

Section
4600. Purpose of chapter.
4601. "Deposit holder" defined.
4602. Statement of disbursements and receipts by deposit holder.
4603. Liability of deposit holder.
4604. Payment of fees and costs of deposit holders; hearing.

Cross References

Money, deposit to secure future child support payments, see Family Code § 4550 et seq.

§ 4600. Purpose of chapter

The purpose of this chapter is to provide an extraordinary remedy for cases of bad faith failure to pay child support obligations. *(Stats.1992, c. 162 (A.B.2650), § 10, operative Jan. 1, 1994.)*

Cross References

Child support, generally, see Family Code § 3900 et seq.
Support defined for purposes of this Code, see Family Code § 150.

Research References

Forms

1 California Transactions Forms--Family Law § 3:49, Deposit of Assets.

§ 4601. "Deposit holder" defined

"Deposit holder" as used in this chapter means the district attorney, county officer, or trustee designated by the court to receive assets deposited pursuant to this chapter to secure future support payments. *(Stats.1992, c. 162 (A.B.2650), § 10, operative Jan. 1, 1994.)*

Cross References

County defined for purposes of this Code, see Family Code § 67.
District attorney, powers and duties, see Government Code § 26500 et seq.
Support defined for purposes of this Code, see Family Code § 150.

§ 4602. Statement of disbursements and receipts by deposit holder

If requested by an obligor-parent, the deposit holder shall prepare a statement setting forth disbursements and receipts made under this chapter. *(Stats.1992, c. 162 (A.B.2650), § 10, operative Jan. 1, 1994.)*

§ 4603. Liability of deposit holder

The deposit holder who is responsible for any money or property and for any disbursements under this chapter is not liable for any action undertaken in good faith and in conformance with this chapter. *(Stats.1992, c. 162 (A.B.2650), § 10, operative Jan. 1, 1994.)*

Cross References

Property defined for purposes of this Code, see Family Code § 113.

§ 4604. Payment of fees and costs of deposit holders; hearing

(a) If the deposit holder incurs fees or costs under this chapter which are not compensated by the deduction under subdivision (c) of Section 4630 (including, but not limited to, fees or costs incurred in a sale of assets pursuant to this chapter and in the preparation of a statement pursuant to Section 4602), the court shall, after a hearing, order the obligor-parent to pay the reasonable fees and costs incurred by the deposit holder. The hearing shall be held not less than 20 days after the deposit holder serves notice of motion or order to show cause upon the obligor-parent.

(b) Fees and costs ordered to be paid under this section shall be in addition to any deposit made under this chapter but shall not exceed whichever of the following is less:

(1) Five percent of one year's child support obligation.

(2) The total amount ordered deposited under Section 4614. *(Stats.1992, c. 162 (A.B.2650), § 10, operative Jan. 1, 1994.)*

Cross References

Attorney's fees and costs, generally, see Family Code § 270 et seq.
Child support, generally, see Family Code § 3900 et seq.
Computation of time, see Code of Civil Procedure §§ 12, 12a; Government Code § 6800 et seq.
Judgment and order defined for purposes of this Code, see Family Code § 100.
Notice, actual and constructive, defined, see Civil Code § 18.
Support defined for purposes of this Code, see Family Code § 150.

ARTICLE 2. ORDER FOR DEPOSIT OF ASSETS

Section
4610. Notice and hearing; order to deposit assets.
4611. Presumptions; rebuttal.
4612. Grounds for defense of obligor-parent alleged to be in arrears.

Section
4613. Issuance of orders; conditions.
4614. Designation of assets subject to order.
4615. Performance bonds.
4616. Sale of assets; hearing; notice.
4617. Deposit of real property; certification of order as abstract of judgment; recordation.

Cross References

Money, deposit to secure future child support payments, see Family Code § 4550 et seq.

§ 4610. Notice and hearing; order to deposit assets

(a) Subject to Sections 4613, 4614, and 4615, in any proceeding where the court has ordered either or both parents to pay any amount for the support of a child for whom support may be ordered, upon an order to show cause or notice of motion, application, and declaration signed under penalty of perjury by the person or county officer to whom support has been ordered to have been paid stating that the parent or parents so ordered is in arrears in payment in a sum equal to the amount of 60 days of payments, the court shall issue to the parent or parents ordered to pay support, following notice and opportunity for a hearing, an order requiring that the parent or parents deposit assets to secure future support payments with the deposit holder designated by the court.

(b) In a proceeding under this article, upon request of any party, the court may also issue an ex parte restraining order as specified in Section 4620. *(Stats.1992, c. 162 (A.B.2650), § 10, operative Jan. 1, 1994. Amended by Stats.1993, c. 219 (A.B.1500), § 145.)*

Cross References

Authority to use or sell assets, see Family Code § 4630.
Child for whom support may be ordered defined for purposes of this Code, see Family Code § 58.
Child support, generally, see Family Code § 3900 et seq.
Computation of time, see Code of Civil Procedure §§ 12, 12a; Government Code § 6800 et seq.
County defined for purposes of this Code, see Family Code § 67.
Expedited child support orders, see Family Code § 3620 et seq.
Health insurance coverage for supported children, see Family Code § 3750 et seq.
Judgment and order defined for purposes of this Code, see Family Code § 100.
Modification, termination, or setting aside of support order, see Family Code § 3650 et seq.
Motion to stop use or sale of assets, see Family Code § 4631.
Notice, actual and constructive, defined, see Civil Code § 18.
Person defined for purposes of this Code, see Family Code § 105.
Proceeding defined for purposes of this Code, see Family Code § 110.
Return of assets and release of real property, see Family Code §§ 4640, 4641.
Support defined for purposes of this Code, see Family Code § 150.

Research References

Forms

1 California Transactions Forms--Family Law § 3:49, Deposit of Assets.

§ 4611. Presumptions; rebuttal

In a proceeding under this chapter, an obligor-parent shall rebut both of the following presumptions:

(a) The nonpayment of child support was willful, without good faith.

(b) The obligor had the ability to pay the support. *(Stats.1992, c. 162 (A.B.2650), § 10, operative Jan. 1, 1994.)*

Cross References

Burden of proof, see Evidence Code § 660 et seq.
Child support, generally, see Family Code § 3900 et seq.
Presumptions, see Evidence Code § 600 et seq.
Proceeding defined for purposes of this Code, see Family Code § 110.

§ 4611

Support defined for purposes of this Code, see Family Code § 150.

Research References

Forms

1 California Transactions Forms--Family Law § 3:49, Deposit of Assets.

§ 4612. Grounds for defense of obligor-parent alleged to be in arrears

An obligor-parent alleged to be in arrears may use any of the following grounds as a defense to the motion filed pursuant to this article or as a basis for filing a motion to stop a sale or use of assets under Section 4631:

(a) Child support payments are not in arrears.

(b) Laches.

(c) There has been a change in the custody of the children.

(d) There is a pending motion for reduction in support due to a reduction in income.

(e) Illness or disability.

(f) Unemployment.

(g) Serious adverse impact on the immediate family of the obligor-parent residing with the obligor-parent that outweighs the impact of denial of the motion or stopping the sale on obligee.

(h) Serious impairment of the ability of the obligor-parent to generate income.

(i) Other emergency conditions. *(Stats.1992, c. 162 (A.B.2650), § 10, operative Jan. 1, 1994.)*

Cross References

Child custody, see Family Code § 3020 et seq.
Child support, generally, see Family Code § 3900 et seq.
List of places applied for employment, submittal, see Family Code § 4505.
Motion to stop sale or use of assets, grounds, see Family Code § 4632.
Priority, child support payments, see Family Code § 4011.
Support defined for purposes of this Code, see Family Code § 150.

Research References

Forms

1 California Transactions Forms--Family Law § 3:49, Deposit of Assets.

§ 4613. Issuance of orders; conditions

The court shall not issue an order pursuant to this article unless the court determines that one or more of the following conditions exist:

(a) The obligor-parent is not receiving salary or wages subject to an assignment pursuant to Chapter 8 (commencing with Section 5200) and there is reason to believe that the obligor-parent has earned income from some source of employment.

(b) An assignment of a portion of salary or wages pursuant to Chapter 8 (commencing with Section 5200) would not be sufficient to meet the amount of the support obligation, for reasons other than a change of circumstances which would qualify for a reduction in the amount of child support ordered.

(c) The job history of the obligor-parent shows that an assignment of a portion of salary or wages pursuant to Chapter 8 (commencing with Section 5200), would be difficult to enforce or would not be a practical means for securing the payment of the support obligation, due to circumstances including, but not limited to, multiple concurrent or consecutive employers. *(Stats.1992, c. 162 (A.B.2650), § 10, operative Jan. 1, 1994.)*

Cross References

Child support, generally, see Family Code § 3900 et seq.
Expedited child support orders, see Family Code § 3620 et seq.
Health insurance coverage for supported children, see Family Code § 3750 et seq.

Judgment and order defined for purposes of this Code, see Family Code § 100.
Modification, termination, or setting aside of support order, see Family Code § 3650 et seq.
Support defined for purposes of this Code, see Family Code § 150.
Support order, defined, see Family Code § 155.

§ 4614. Designation of assets subject to order

The designation of assets subject to an order pursuant to this article shall be based upon concern for maximizing the liquidity and ready conversion into cash of the deposited asset. In all instances, the assets shall include a sum of money up to or equal in value to one year of support payments or six thousand dollars ($6,000) whichever is less, or any other assets, personal or real, designated by the court which equal in value up to one year of payments for support of the child, or six thousand dollars ($6,000), whichever is less, subject to Section 703.070 of the Code of Civil Procedure. *(Stats.1992, c. 162 (A.B.2650), § 10, operative Jan. 1, 1994. Amended by Stats.1993, c. 219 (A.B.1500), § 146.)*

Cross References

Child support, generally, see Family Code § 3900 et seq.
Judgment and order defined for purposes of this Code, see Family Code § 100.
Support defined for purposes of this Code, see Family Code § 150.

§ 4615. Performance bonds

In lieu of depositing cash or other assets as provided in Section 4614, the obligor-parent may, if approved by the court, provide a performance bond secured by real property or other assets of the obligor-parent and equal in value to one year of payments. *(Stats. 1992, c. 162 (A.B.2650), § 10, operative Jan. 1, 1994.)*

Cross References

Property defined for purposes of this Code, see Family Code § 113.

Research References

Forms

1 California Transactions Forms--Family Law § 3:49, Deposit of Assets.

§ 4616. Sale of assets; hearing; notice

Upon deposit of an asset which is not readily convertible into money, the court may, after a hearing, order the sale of that asset and the deposit of the proceeds with the deposit holder. Not less than 20 days written notice of the hearing shall be served on the obligor-parent. *(Stats.1992, c. 162 (A.B.2650), § 10, operative Jan. 1, 1994.)*

Cross References

Computation of time, see Code of Civil Procedure §§ 12, 12a; Government Code § 6800 et seq.
Judgment and order defined for purposes of this Code, see Family Code § 100.
Notice, actual and constructive, defined, see Civil Code § 18.
Sale of property levied upon, see Code of Civil Procedure § 701.510 et seq.

Research References

Forms

1 California Transactions Forms--Family Law § 3:49, Deposit of Assets.

§ 4617. Deposit of real property; certification of order as abstract of judgment; recordation

(a) If the asset ordered to be deposited is real property, the order shall be certified as an abstract of judgment in accordance with Section 674 of the Code of Civil Procedure.

(b) A deposit of real property is made effective by recordation of the certified abstract with the county recorder.

(c) The deposited real property and the rights, benefits, and liabilities attached to that property shall continue in the possession of the legal owner.

(d) For purposes of Section 701.545 of the Code of Civil Procedure, the date of the issuance of the order to deposit assets shall be

ENFORCEMENT OF SUPPORT ORDERS § 4631

construed as the date notice of levy on an interest in real property was served on the judgment debtor. *(Stats.1992, c. 162 (A.B.2650), § 10, operative Jan. 1, 1994.)*

Cross References

County defined for purposes of this Code, see Family Code § 67.
Judgment and order defined for purposes of this Code, see Family Code § 100.
Notice, actual and constructive, defined, see Civil Code § 18.
Property defined for purposes of this Code, see Family Code § 113.

Research References

Forms

1 California Transactions Forms--Family Law § 3:49, Deposit of Assets.

ARTICLE 3. EX PARTE RESTRAINING ORDERS

Section
4620. Issuance of orders; notification and account of extraordinary expenditures; expiration of order.

Cross References

Money, deposit to secure future child support payments, see Family Code § 4550 et seq.

§ 4620. Issuance of orders; notification and account of extraordinary expenditures; expiration of order

(a) During the pendency of a proceeding under this chapter, upon the application of either party in the manner provided by Part 4 (commencing with Section 240) of Division 2, the court may, without a hearing, issue ex parte orders restraining any person from transferring, encumbering, hypothecating, concealing, or in any way disposing of any property, real or personal, whether community, quasi-community, or separate, except in the usual course of business or for the necessities of life, and if the order is directed against a party, requiring the party to notify the other party of any proposed extraordinary expenditures and to account to the court for all such extraordinary expenditures.

(b) The matter shall be made returnable not later than 20 days, or if good cause appears to the court, 25 days from the date of the order at which time the ex parte order shall expire.

(c) The court, at the hearing, shall determine for which property the obligor-parent shall be required to report extraordinary expenditures and shall specify what is deemed an extraordinary expenditure for purposes of this subdivision.

(d) An order issued pursuant to this section after the hearing shall state on its face the date of expiration of the order, which shall expire in one year or upon deposit of assets or money pursuant to Article 2 (commencing with Section 4610), whichever first occurs. *(Stats.1992, c. 162 (A.B.2650), § 10, operative Jan. 1, 1994.)*

Cross References

Computation of time, see Code of Civil Procedure §§ 12, 12a; Government Code § 6800 et seq.
Judgment and order defined for purposes of this Code, see Family Code § 100.
Notice requirements ex parte temporary restraining orders, see Family Code § 241.
Person defined for purposes of this Code, see Family Code § 105.
Proceeding defined for purposes of this Code, see Family Code § 110.
Proceeding on notice and hearing, ex parte restraining order, see Family Code § 4610.
Property defined for purposes of this Code, see Family Code § 113.
State defined for purposes of this Code, see Family Code § 145.

Research References

Forms

West's California Judicial Council Forms FL-303, Declaration Regarding Notice and Service of Request for Temporary Emergency (Ex Parte) Orders (Also Available in Spanish).

ARTICLE 4. USE OR SALE OF ASSETS TO MAKE SUPPORT PAYMENTS

Section
4630. Authority to use or sell assets; conduct of sale.
4631. Motion to stop use or sale of assets; time of hearing.
4632. Grounds for filing motion to stop sale or use of assets.

Cross References

Money, deposit to secure future child support payments, see Family Code § 4550 et seq.

§ 4630. Authority to use or sell assets; conduct of sale

(a) Upon an obligor-parent's failure, within the time specified by the court, to make reasonable efforts to cure the default in child support payments or to comply with a court-approved payment plan, if payments continue in arrears, the deposit holder shall, not less than 25 days after providing the obligor-parent or parents with a written notice served personally or with return receipt requested, unless a motion or order to show cause has been filed to stop the use or sale, use the money or sell or otherwise process the deposited assets for an amount sufficient to pay the arrearage and the amount ordered by the court for the support currently due for the child for whom support may be ordered.

(b) Assets deposited pursuant to an order issued under Article 2 (commencing with Section 4610) shall be construed as being assets subject to levy pursuant to Article 6 (commencing with Section 701.510) of Chapter 3 of Division 2 of Title 9 of Part 2 of the Code of Civil Procedure. The sale of assets shall be conducted in accordance with Article 6 (commencing with Section 701.510) and Article 7 (commencing with Section 701.810) of Chapter 3 of Division 2 of Title 9 of Part 2 of the Code of Civil Procedure.

(c) The deposit holder may deduct from the deposited money the sum of one dollar ($1) for each payment made pursuant to this section. *(Stats.1992, c. 162 (A.B.2650), § 10, operative Jan. 1, 1994. Amended by Stats.1993, c. 219 (A.B.1500), § 147.)*

Cross References

Child for whom support may be ordered defined for purposes of this Code, see Family Code § 58.
Child support, generally, see Family Code § 3900 et seq.
Computation of time, see Code of Civil Procedure §§ 12, 12a; Government Code § 6800 et seq.
Expedited child support orders, see Family Code § 3620 et seq.
Health insurance coverage for supported children, see Family Code § 3750 et seq.
Judgment and order defined for purposes of this Code, see Family Code § 100.
Modification, termination, or setting aside of support order, see Family Code § 3650 et seq.
Notice, actual and constructive, defined, see Civil Code § 18.
Priority, child support payments, see Family Code § 4011.
Support defined for purposes of this Code, see Family Code § 150.

§ 4631. Motion to stop use or sale of assets; time of hearing

(a) An obligor-parent may file a motion to stop the use of the money or the sale of the asset under this article within 15 days after service of notice on the obligor-parent pursuant to Section 4630.

(b) The clerk of the court shall set the motion for hearing not less than 20 days after service of the notice of motion and the motion on the person or county officer to whom support has been ordered to have been paid. *(Stats.1992, c. 162 (A.B.2650), § 10, operative Jan. 1, 1994.)*

Cross References

Computation of time, see Code of Civil Procedure §§ 12, 12a; Government Code § 6800 et seq.
County defined for purposes of this Code, see Family Code § 67.
Notice, actual and constructive, defined, see Civil Code § 18.
Person defined for purposes of this Code, see Family Code § 105.

§ 4631

Support defined for purposes of this Code, see Family Code § 150.

§ 4632. Grounds for filing motion to stop sale or use of assets

An obligor-parent alleged to be in arrears under this article may use any ground set forth in Section 4612 as a basis for filing a motion under Section 4631 to stop a sale or use of assets under this article. *(Stats.1992, c. 162 (A.B.2650), § 10, operative Jan. 1, 1994.)*

ARTICLE 5. RETURN OF ASSETS OF OBLIGOR

Section
4640. Conditions for return of assets.
4641. Release of real property; duties of deposit holder.

Cross References

Money, deposit to secure future child support payments, see Family Code § 4550 et seq.

§ 4640. Conditions for return of assets

The deposit holder shall return all assets subject to court order under Article 2 (commencing with Section 4610) to the obligor-parent when both of the following occur:

(a) One year has elapsed since the court issued the order described under Article 2 (commencing with Section 4610).

(b) The obligor-parent has made all support payments on time during that one-year period. *(Stats.1992, c. 162 (A.B.2650), § 10, operative Jan. 1, 1994.)*

Cross References

Judgment and order defined for purposes of this Code, see Family Code § 100.
Support defined for purposes of this Code, see Family Code § 150.

§ 4641. Release of real property; duties of deposit holder

If the deposited asset is real property and the requirements of Section 4640 have been satisfied, the deposit holder shall do all of the following:

(a) Prepare a release in accordance with Section 697.370 of the Code of Civil Procedure.

(b) Request the clerk of the court where the order to deposit assets was made to certify the release.

(c) Record the certified release in the office of the county recorder where the certified abstract was recorded under Section 4617. *(Stats.1992, c. 162 (A.B.2650), § 10, operative Jan. 1, 1994.)*

Cross References

County defined for purposes of this Code, see Family Code § 67.
Judgment and order defined for purposes of this Code, see Family Code § 100.
Property defined for purposes of this Code, see Family Code § 113.

Research References

Forms
1 California Transactions Forms--Family Law § 3:49, Deposit of Assets.

CHAPTER 4. CHILD SUPPORT DELINQUENCY REPORTING

Section
4700. Short title.
4701. Statewide automated system for reporting.

§ 4700. Short title

This chapter may be cited as the Child Support Delinquency Reporting Law. *(Stats.1992, c. 162 (A.B.2650), § 10, operative Jan. 1, 1994.)*

Cross References

Child support, generally, see Family Code § 3900 et seq.
Support defined for purposes of this Code, see Family Code § 150.

§ 4701. Statewide automated system for reporting

(a) The Department of Child Support Services shall administer a statewide automated system for the reporting of court-ordered child support obligations to credit reporting agencies.

(b) The department shall design and develop standards for the system in conjunction with representatives of the California Family Support Council and the credit reporting industry.

(c) The standards for the system shall be consistent with credit reporting industry standards and reporting format and with the department's statewide central automated system for support enforcement.

(d) The standards shall include, but not be limited to, all of the following:

(1) Court-ordered child support obligations and delinquent payments, including amounts owed and by whom. The California local child support agencies, on a monthly basis, shall update this information, and then submit it to the department which, in turn, shall consolidate and transmit it to the credit reporting agencies.

(2) Before the initial reporting of a court-ordered child support obligation or a delinquent payment, the local child support agency shall attempt to notify the obligor parent of the proposed action and give 30 days to contest in writing the accuracy of the information, or to pay the arrearage, if any, in compliance with the due process requirements of the laws of this state.

(e) The department and the local child support agencies are responsible for the accuracy of information provided pursuant to this section, and the information shall be based upon the data available at the time the information is provided. Each of these organizations and the credit reporting agencies shall follow reasonable procedures to ensure maximum possible accuracy of the information provided. Neither the department, nor the local child support agencies are liable for any consequences of the failure of a parent to contest the accuracy of the information within the time allowed under paragraph (2) of subdivision (d). *(Stats.1992, c. 162 (A.B.2650), § 10, operative Jan. 1, 1994. Amended by Stats.2000, c. 808 (A.B.1358), § 48, eff. Sept. 28, 2000.)*

Cross References

Child support, generally, see Family Code § 3900 et seq.
Computation of time, see Code of Civil Procedure §§ 12, 12a; Government Code § 6800 et seq.
Department of Child Support Services, generally, see Family Code § 17000 et seq.
Expedited child support orders, see Family Code § 3620 et seq.
Family support defined for purposes of this Code, see Family Code § 92.
Health insurance coverage for supported children, see Family Code § 3750 et seq.
Modification, termination, or setting aside of support order, see Family Code § 3650 et seq.
State defined for purposes of this Code, see Family Code § 145.
Support defined for purposes of this Code, see Family Code § 150.
Writings, authentication and proof of, see Evidence Code § 1400 et seq.

CHAPTER 5. CIVIL PENALTY FOR CHILD SUPPORT DELINQUENCY

Section
4720. "Support" defined.
4721. Application of chapter; legislative intent; timely payments.
4722. Notice of delinquency; penalties.
4723. Execution and contents of notice.
4724. Service of notice.

ENFORCEMENT OF SUPPORT ORDERS § 4724

Section
4725. Motion for judgment; enforcement.
4726. Penalties; exceptions.
4727. Amount of penalties.
4728. Enforcement of penalties; priorities.
4729. Enforcement of child support obligations by local child support agency or other agency.
4730. Hearings to set or modify amount of child support; consideration of penalties.
4731. Subsequent notices of delinquency.
4732. Adoption of forms or notices by Judicial Counsel.
4733. Penalties; payment to custodian of child.
4800 to 4854. Repealed.

Cross References

Modification, termination or set aside of support orders, powers of court, see Family Code § 3651.
United States military and National Guard service members, modification of child support, form, motion by local child support agency, see Family Code § 17440.

§ 4720. "Support" defined

"Support" for the purposes of this chapter means support as defined in Section 150. *(Stats.1992, c. 162 (A.B.2650), § 10, operative Jan. 1, 1994.)*

Cross References

Attorney fees and costs, generally, see Family Code § 270 et seq.
Support defined for purposes of this Code, see Family Code § 150.

Research References

Forms
California Practice Guide: Rutter Family Law Forms Form 6:19, Request for Order to Determine Arrearages and to Show Cause Why Family Code §4720 et seq. Penalties Should Not Be Imposed.
West's California Judicial Council Forms FL–485, Notice of Delinquency.
West's California Judicial Council Forms FL–490, Application to Determine Arrears (Also Available in Spanish).

§ 4721. Application of chapter; legislative intent; timely payments

(a) This chapter applies only to installments of child support that are due on or after January 1, 1992.

(b) It is the intent of the Legislature that the penalties provided under this chapter shall be applied in egregious instances of noncompliance with child support orders.

(c) It is the intent of the Legislature that for the purposes of this chapter, payments made through wage assignments are considered timely regardless of the date of receipt by the local child support agency or obligee. *(Stats.1992, c. 162 (A.B.2650), § 10, operative Jan. 1, 1994. Amended by Stats.1994, c. 959 (A.B.3072), § 2, eff. Sept. 28, 1994; Stats.2000, c. 808 (A.B.1358), § 49, eff. Sept. 28, 2000.)*

Cross References

Child support, generally, see Family Code § 3900 et seq.
Expedited child support orders, see Family Code § 3620 et seq.
Health insurance coverage for supported children, see Family Code § 3750 et seq.
Judgment and order defined for purposes of this Code, see Family Code § 100.
Legislative intent, construction of statutes, see Code of Civil Procedure § 1859.
Modification, termination, or setting aside of support order, see Family Code § 3650 et seq.
Support defined for purposes of this Code, see Family Code § 150.
Support order defined for purposes of this Code, see Family Code § 155.

§ 4722. Notice of delinquency; penalties

(a) Any person with a court order for child support, the payments on which are more than 30 days in arrears, may file and then serve a notice of delinquency, as described in this chapter.

(b) Except as provided in Section 4726, and subject to Section 4727, any amount of child support specified in a notice of delinquency that remains unpaid for more than 30 days after the notice of delinquency has been filed and served shall incur a penalty of 6 percent of the delinquent payment for each month that it remains unpaid, up to a maximum of 72 percent of the unpaid balance due. *(Stats.1992, c. 162 (A.B.2650), § 10, operative Jan. 1, 1994.)*

Cross References

Child support, generally, see Family Code § 3900 et seq.
Computation of time, see Code of Civil Procedure §§ 12, 12a; Government Code § 6800 et seq.
Expedited child support orders, see Family Code § 3620 et seq.
Health insurance coverage for supported children, see Family Code § 3750 et seq.
Judgment and order defined for purposes of this Code, see Family Code § 100.
Modification, termination, or setting aside of support order, see Family Code § 3650 et seq.
Notice, actual and constructive, defined, see Civil Code § 18.
Person defined for purposes of this Code, see Family Code § 105.
Support defined for purposes of this Code, see Family Code § 150.

Research References

Forms
West's California Code Forms, Family § 4720, Comment Overview—Civil Penalty for Child Support Delinquency.

§ 4723. Execution and contents of notice

(a) The notice of delinquency shall be signed under penalty of perjury by the support obligee.

(b) The notice of delinquency shall state all of the following:

(1) The amount that the child support obligor is in arrears.

(2) The installments of support due, the amounts, if any, that have been paid, and the balance due.

(3) That any unpaid installment of child support will incur a penalty of 6 percent of the unpaid support per month until paid, to a maximum of 72 percent of the original amount of the unpaid support, unless the support arrearage is paid within 30 days of the date of service of the notice of delinquency.

(c) In the absence of a protective order prohibiting the support obligor from knowing the whereabouts of the child or children for whom support is payable, or otherwise excusing the requirements of this subdivision, the notice of delinquency shall also include a current address and telephone number of all of the children for whom support is due and, if different from that of the support obligee, the address at which court papers may be served upon the support obligee. *(Stats.1992, c. 162 (A.B.2650), § 10, operative Jan. 1, 1994.)*

Cross References

Child support, generally, see Family Code § 3900 et seq.
Computation of time, see Code of Civil Procedure §§ 12, 12a; Government Code § 6800 et seq.
Health insurance coverage for supported children, see Family Code § 3750 et seq.
Judgment and order defined for purposes of this Code, see Family Code § 100.
Notice, actual and constructive, defined, see Civil Code § 18.
Protective order defined for purposes of this Code, see Family Code § 6218.
State defined for purposes of this Code, see Family Code § 145.
Support defined for purposes of this Code, see Family Code § 150.

§ 4724. Service of notice

The notice of delinquency may be served personally or by certified mail or in any manner provided for service of summons. *(Stats.1992, c. 162 (A.B.2650), § 10, operative Jan. 1, 1994.)*

Cross References

Notice, actual and constructive, defined, see Civil Code § 18.
Persons upon whom summons may be served, see Code of Civil Procedure § 416.10 et seq.

§ 4725. Motion for judgment; enforcement

If the child support owed, or any arrearages, interest, or penalty, remains unpaid more than 30 days after serving the notice of delinquency, the support obligee may file a motion to obtain a judgment for the amount owed, which shall be enforceable in any manner provided by law for the enforcement of judgments. *(Stats. 1992, c. 162 (A.B.2650), § 10, operative Jan. 1, 1994.)*

Cross References

Child support, generally, see Family Code § 3900 et seq.
Computation of time, see Code of Civil Procedure §§ 12, 12a; Government Code § 6800 et seq.
Judgment and order defined for purposes of this Code, see Family Code § 100.
Notice, actual and constructive, defined, see Civil Code § 18.
Support defined for purposes of this Code, see Family Code § 150.

§ 4726. Penalties; exceptions

No penalties may be imposed pursuant to this chapter if, in the discretion of the court, all of the following conditions are met:

(a) Within a timely fashion after service of the notice of delinquency, the support obligor files and serves a motion to determine arrearages and to show cause why the penalties provided in this chapter should not be imposed.

(b) At the hearing on the motion filed by the support obligor, the court finds that the support obligor has proved any of the following:

(1) The child support payments were not 30 days in arrears as of the date of service of the notice of delinquency and are not in arrears as of the date of the hearing.

(2) The support obligor suffered serious illness, disability, or unemployment which substantially impaired the ability of the support obligor to comply fully with the support order and the support obligor has made every possible effort to comply with the support order.

(3) The support obligor is a public employee and for reasons relating to fiscal difficulties of the employing entity the obligor has not received a paycheck for 30 or more days.

(4) It would not be in the interests of justice to impose a penalty. *(Stats.1992, c. 162 (A.B.2650), § 10, operative Jan. 1, 1994.)*

Cross References

Child support, generally, see Family Code § 3900 et seq.
Computation of time, see Code of Civil Procedure §§ 12, 12a; Government Code § 6800 et seq.
Judgment and order defined for purposes of this Code, see Family Code § 100.
Notice, actual and constructive, defined, see Civil Code § 18.
Penalties, delinquent child support, see Family Code § 4722.
Support defined for purposes of this Code, see Family Code § 150.
Support order defined for purposes of this Code, see Family Code § 155.

Research References

Forms

California Practice Guide: Rutter Family Law Forms Form 6:19, Request for Order to Determine Arrearages and to Show Cause Why Family Code §4720 et seq. Penalties Should Not be Imposed.
West's California Code Forms, Family § 4720, Comment Overview—Civil Penalty for Child Support Delinquency.

§ 4727. Amount of penalties

Any penalty due under this chapter shall not be greater than 6 percent per month of the original amount of support arrearages or support installment, nor may the penalties on any arrearage amount or support installment exceed 72 percent of the original amount due, regardless of whether or not the installments have been listed on more than one notice of delinquency. *(Stats.1992, c. 162 (A.B.2650), § 10, operative Jan. 1, 1994.)*

Cross References

Notice, actual and constructive, defined, see Civil Code § 18.
Penalties, delinquent child support, see Family Code § 4722.
Support defined for purposes of this Code, see Family Code § 150.

Research References

Forms

West's California Code Forms, Family § 4720, Comment Overview—Civil Penalty for Child Support Delinquency.

§ 4728. Enforcement of penalties; priorities

Penalties due pursuant to this chapter may be enforced by the issuance of a writ of execution in the same manner as a writ of execution may be issued for unpaid installments of child support, as described in Chapter 7 (commencing with Section 5100), except that payment of penalties under this chapter may not take priority over payment of arrearages or current support. *(Stats.1992, c. 162 (A.B.2650), § 10, operative Jan. 1, 1994.)*

Cross References

Child support, generally, see Family Code § 3900 et seq.
Support defined for purposes of this Code, see Family Code § 150.

§ 4729. Enforcement of child support obligations by local child support agency or other agency

The local child support agency or any other agency providing support enforcement services pursuant to Title IV–D of the federal Social Security Act may not enforce child support obligations utilizing the penalties provided for by this chapter. *(Stats.1992, c. 162 (A.B.2650), § 10, operative Jan. 1, 1994. Amended by Stats.1993, c. 219 (A.B.1500), § 148; Stats.1994, c. 959 (A.B.3072), § 3, eff. Sept. 28, 1994; Stats.2000, c. 808 (A.B.1358), § 50, eff. Sept. 28, 2000.)*

Cross References

Child support, generally, see Family Code § 3900 et seq.
Support defined for purposes of this Code, see Family Code § 150.

§ 4730. Hearings to set or modify amount of child support; consideration of penalties

At any hearing to set or modify the amount payable for the support of a child, the court shall not consider any penalties imposed under this chapter in determining the amount of current support to be paid. *(Stats.1992, c. 162 (A.B.2650), § 10, operative Jan. 1, 1994. Amended by Stats.1993, c. 219 (A.B.1500), § 149.)*

Cross References

Child support, generally, see Family Code § 3900 et seq.
Support defined for purposes of this Code, see Family Code § 150.

§ 4731. Subsequent notices of delinquency

A subsequent notice of delinquency may be served and filed at any time. The subsequent notice shall indicate those child support arrearages and ongoing installments that have been listed on a previous notice. *(Stats.1992, c. 162 (A.B.2650), § 10, operative Jan. 1, 1994.)*

Cross References

Child support, generally, see Family Code § 3900 et seq.
Notice, actual and constructive, defined, see Civil Code § 18.
Support defined for purposes of this Code, see Family Code § 150.

§ 4732. Adoption of forms or notices by Judicial Counsel

The Judicial Council shall adopt forms or notices for the use of the procedures provided by this chapter. *(Stats.1992, c. 162 (A.B.2650), § 10, operative Jan. 1, 1994.)*

Cross References

Notice, actual and constructive, defined, see Civil Code § 18.

Research References

Forms

West's California Judicial Council Forms FL–490, Application to Determine Arrears (Also Available in Spanish).

§ 4733. Penalties; payment to custodian of child

Penalties collected pursuant to this chapter shall be paid to the custodian of the child who is the subject of the child support judgment or order, whether or not the child is a recipient of public assistance. *(Added by Stats.1993, c. 219 (A.B.1500), § 150.)*

Cross References

Child custody, see Family Code § 3020 et seq.
Child support, generally, see Family Code § 3900 et seq.
Expedited child support orders, see Family Code § 3620 et seq.
Health insurance coverage for supported children, see Family Code § 3750 et seq.
Judgment and order defined for purposes of this Code, see Family Code § 100.
Modification, termination, or setting aside of support order, see Family Code § 3650 et seq.
Support defined for purposes of this Code, see Family Code § 150.

Research References

Forms

West's California Judicial Council Forms FL–485, Notice of Delinquency.

§§ 4800 to 4854. Repealed by Stats.1997, c. 194 (S.B.568), § 1

CHAPTER 6. UNIFORM INTERSTATE FAMILY SUPPORT ACT [REPEALED]

§§ 4900 to 4903. Repealed by Stats.2015, c. 493 (S.B.646), § 2, eff. Jan. 1, 2016

§§ 4905 to 4914. Repealed by Stats.2015, c. 493 (S.B.646), § 2, eff. Jan. 1, 2016

§§ 4915 to 4933. Repealed by Stats.2015, c. 493 (S.B.646), § 2, eff. Jan. 1, 2016

§ 4935. Repealed by Stats.2015, c. 493 (S.B.646), § 2, eff. Jan. 1, 2016

§§ 4940 to 4946. Repealed by Stats.2015, c. 493 (S.B.646), § 2, eff. Jan. 1, 2016

§§ 4950 to 4964. Repealed by Stats.2015, c. 493 (S.B.646), § 2, eff. Jan. 1, 2016

§ 4965. Repealed by Stats.2015, c. 493 (S.B.646), § 2, eff. Jan. 1, 2016

§§ 4970, 4971. Repealed by Stats.2015, c. 493 (S.B.646), § 2, eff. Jan. 1, 2016

§§ 4975 to 5005. Repealed by Stats.2015, c. 493 (S.B.646), § 2, eff. Jan. 1, 2016

CHAPTER 7. ENFORCEMENT BY WRIT OF EXECUTION

Section
5100. Enforcement of support orders without prior court approval.
5101, 5102. Repealed.
5103. Enforcement of support against employee pension benefit plan.
5104. Application for writ.

Cross References

Enforcement of judgments and orders, generally, see Family Code §§ 290, 291.
Enforcement of money judgments by writ of execution, see Code of Civil Procedure § 699.010 et seq.

§ 5100. Enforcement of support orders without prior court approval

Notwithstanding Section 290, a child, family, or spousal support order may be enforced by a writ of execution or a notice of levy pursuant to Section 706.030 of the Code of Civil Procedure or Section 17522 of this code without prior court approval. *(Stats.1992, c. 162 (A.B.2650), § 10, operative Jan. 1, 1994. Amended by Stats.1993, c. 876 (S.B.1068), § 21, eff. Oct. 6, 1993, operative Jan. 1, 1994; Stats.1994, c. 1269 (A.B.2208), § 49.2; Stats.1997, c. 599 (A.B.573), § 19; Stats.2000, c. 808 (A.B.1358), § 54, eff. Sept. 28, 2000.)*

Cross References

Attorney's fees and costs, generally, see Family Code § 270 et seq.
Child support, generally, see Family Code § 3900 et seq.
Child support payments, priority, see Family Code § 4011.
Enforcement of judgments and orders, generally, see Family Code §§ 290, 291.
Expedited child support orders, see Family Code § 3620 et seq.
Health insurance coverage for supported children, see Family Code § 3750 et seq.
Judgment and order defined for purposes of this Code, see Family Code § 100.
Modification, termination, or setting aside of support order, see Family Code § 3650 et seq.
Notice, actual and constructive, defined, see Civil Code § 18.
Spousal support defined for purposes of this Code, see Family Code § 142.
Support defined for purposes of this Code, see Family Code § 150.
Support judgment, renewal, see Family Code § 4502.
Support order defined for purposes of this Code, see Family Code § 155.
Support orders enforceable under this code, see Family Code § 4500.

Research References

Forms

California Practice Guide: Rutter Family Law Forms Form 18:7, Application for Issuance of Writ of Execution (Family Code §5100 et seq.).
West's California Code Forms, Family § 5104, Comment Overview—Enforcement by Writ of Execution.

§§ 5101, 5102. Repealed by Stats.2000, c. 808 (A.B.1358), §§ 55, 56, eff. Sept. 28, 2000

§ 5103. Enforcement of support against employee pension benefit plan

(a) Notwithstanding Section 2060, an order for the payment of child, family, or spousal support may be enforced against an employee benefit plan regardless of whether the plan has been joined as a party to the proceeding in which the support order was obtained.

(b) Notwithstanding Section 697.710 of the Code of Civil Procedure, an execution lien created by a levy on the judgment debtor's right to payment of benefits from an employee benefit plan to enforce an order for the payment of child, family, or spousal support continues until the date the plan has withheld and paid over to the levying officer, as provided in Section 701.010 of the Code of Civil Procedure, the full amount specified in the notice of levy, unless the plan is directed to stop withholding and paying over before that time by court order or by the levying officer.

(c) A writ of execution pursuant to which a levy is made on the judgment debtor's right to payment of benefits from an employee benefit plan under an order for the payment of child, family, or spousal support shall be returned not later than one year after the date the execution lien expires under subdivision (b). *(Stats.1992, c.*

§ 5103

162 (A.B.2650), § 10, operative Jan. 1, 1994. Amended by Stats.1994, c. 1269 (A.B.2208), § 50.)

Cross References

Attorney's fees and costs, generally, see Family Code § 270 et seq.
Child support, generally, see Family Code § 3900 et seq.
Child support payments, priority, see Family Code § 4011.
Employee benefit plan defined for purposes of this Code, see Family Code § 80.
Enforcement of money judgments by writ of execution, see Code of Civil Procedure § 699.010 et seq.
Execution liens, creation and duration, see Code of Civil Procedure § 697.710.
Expedited child support orders, see Family Code § 3620 et seq.
Family support order, enforceable in same manner as child support, see Family Code § 4501.
Health insurance coverage for supported children, see Family Code § 3750 et seq.
Judgment and order defined for purposes of this Code, see Family Code § 100.
Modification, termination, or setting aside of support order, see Family Code § 3650 et seq.
Notice, actual and constructive, defined, see Civil Code § 18.
Proceeding defined for purposes of this Code, see Family Code § 110.
Spousal support defined for purposes of this Code, see Family Code § 142.
Support defined for purposes of this Code, see Family Code § 150.
Support order defined for purposes of this Code, see Family Code § 155.
Writ of execution and notice of levy, time for return, report and accounting, see Code of Civil Procedure § 699.560.

Research References

Forms

West's California Code Forms, Family § 2060, Comment Overview—Application and Order for Joinder.

§ 5104. Application for writ

(a) The application for a writ of execution shall be accompanied by an affidavit stating the total amount due and unpaid that is authorized to be enforced pursuant to Sections 5100 to 5103, inclusive, on the date of the application.

(b) If interest on the overdue installments is sought, the affidavit shall state the total amount of the interest and the amount of each due and unpaid installment and the date it became due.

(c) The affidavit shall be filed in the action and a copy shall be attached to the writ of execution delivered to the levying officer. The levying officer shall serve the copy of the affidavit on the judgment debtor when the writ of execution is first served on the judgment debtor pursuant to a levy under the writ. *(Stats.1992, c. 162 (A.B.2650), § 10, operative Jan. 1, 1994.)*

Cross References

Attorney's fees and costs, generally, see Family Code § 270 et seq.
Enforcement of money judgments by writ of execution, see Code of Civil Procedure § 699.010 et seq.
Execution liens, creation and duration, see Code of Civil Procedure § 697.710.
Judgment and order defined for purposes of this Code, see Family Code § 100.
Judgment for support, see Family Code § 4502.
Renewal, application for, see Code of Civil Procedure § 683.130.
State defined for purposes of this Code, see Family Code § 145.

Research References

Forms

California Practice Guide: Rutter Family Law Forms Form 18:7, Application for Issuance of Writ of Execution (Family Code §5100 et seq.).
West's California Code Forms, Family § 5104, Comment Overview—Enforcement by Writ of Execution.

CHAPTER 8. EARNINGS ASSIGNMENT ORDER

Article	Section
1. Definitions	5200
2. General Provisions	5230
3. Support Orders Issued or Modified Before July 1, 1990	5250
4. Stay of Service of Assignment Order	5260
5. Motion to Quash Assignment Order	5270
6. Information Concerning Address and Employment of Obligor	5280
7. Prohibited Practices	5290
8. Judicial Council Forms	5295
9. Intercounty Support Obligations	5600

Cross References

Abandonment and neglect of children, support order included in order granting probation, see Penal Code § 270h.
Wage garnishment, definitions, see Code of Civil Procedure § 706.011.

ARTICLE 1. DEFINITIONS

Section
5200. Construction of chapter.
5201. "Arrearage" or "arrearages" defined.
5202. Assignment order; earnings assignment order for support.
5204. "Due date of support payments" defined.
5206. "Earnings" defined.
5208. "Earnings assignment order for support" defined.
5210. "Employer" defined.
5212. "IV-D Case" defined.
5214. "Obligee" or "assigned obligee" defined.
5216. "Obligor" defined.
5220. "Timely payment" defined.

§ 5200. Construction of chapter

Unless the provision or context otherwise requires, the definitions in this article govern the construction of this chapter. *(Stats.1992, c. 162 (A.B.2650), § 10, operative Jan. 1, 1994.)*

Cross References

Assignment of wages, validity and exceptions, see Labor Code § 300.
Contracts with state agencies, child and family support obligations, see Public Contract Code § 7110.
Enforcement of support of spouse who has conservator, application of income and principal for support and maintenance, see Probate Code § 3088.
Support, defined, see Family Code § 150.

Research References

Forms

3 California Transactions Forms--Business Transactions § 16:83, Exclusions.

§ 5201. "Arrearage" or "arrearages" defined

"Arrearage" or "arrearages" is the amount necessary to satisfy a support judgment or order pursuant to Section 695.210 of the Code of Civil Procedure. *(Added by Stats.1997, c. 599 (A.B.573), § 21.)*

Cross References

Judgment and order defined for purposes of this Code, see Family Code § 100.
Support defined for purposes of this Code, see Family Code § 150.

§ 5202. Assignment order; earnings assignment order for support

"Assignment order" has the same meaning as "earnings assignment order for support." *(Stats.1992, c. 162 (A.B.2650), § 10, operative Jan. 1, 1994.)*

Cross References

Judgment and order defined for purposes of this Code, see Family Code § 100.

Support defined for purposes of this Code, see Family Code § 150.

§ 5204. "Due date of support payments" defined

"Due date of support payments" is the date specifically stated in the order of support or, if no date is stated in the support order, the last day of the month in which the support payment is to be paid. *(Stats.1992, c. 162 (A.B.2650), § 10, operative Jan. 1, 1994.)*

Cross References

Judgment and order defined for purposes of this Code, see Family Code § 100.
Support defined for purposes of this Code, see Family Code § 150.
Support order defined for purposes of this Code, see Family Code § 155.

§ 5206. "Earnings" defined

"Earnings," to the extent that they are subject to an earnings assignment order for support under Chapter 4 (commencing with Section 703.010) of Division 2 of Title 9 of Part 2 of the Code of Civil Procedure, include:

(a) Wages, salary, bonus, money, and benefits described in Sections 704.110, 704.113, and 704.115 of the Code of Civil Procedure.

(b) Payments due for services of independent contractors, interest, dividends, rents, royalties, residuals, patent rights, or mineral or other natural resource rights.

(c) Payments or credits due or becoming due as a result of written or oral contracts for services or sales whether denominated as wages, salary, commission, bonus, or otherwise.

(d) Payments due for workers' compensation temporary disability benefits.

(e) Payments due as a result of disability from benefits described in Section 704.130 of the Code of Civil Procedure.

(f) Any other payments or credits due or becoming due, regardless of source. *(Stats.1992, c. 162 (A.B.2650), § 10, operative Jan. 1, 1994. Amended by Stats.1993, c. 219 (A.B.1500), § 152.5; Stats.1997, c. 599 (A.B.573), § 22.)*

Cross References

Judgment and order defined for purposes of this Code, see Family Code § 100.
Support defined for purposes of this Code, see Family Code § 150.
Workers' compensation, see Labor Code § 3200 et seq.

§ 5208. "Earnings assignment order for support" defined

(a) "Earnings assignment order for support" means an order that assigns to an obligee a portion of the earnings of a support obligor due or to become due in the future.

(b) Commencing January 1, 2000, all earnings assignment orders for support in any action in which child support or family support is ordered shall be issued on an "order/notice to withhold income for child support" mandated by Section 666 of Title 42 of the United States Code. *(Stats.1992, c. 162 (A.B.2650), § 10, operative Jan. 1, 1994. Amended by Stats.1999, c. 480 (S.B.542), § 1.)*

Cross References

Child support, generally, see Family Code § 3900 et seq.
Collection of tax, referral of child support delinquencies, see Revenue and Taxation Code § 19271.
Enforcement of money judgments, workers' compensation claim or award, temporary benefits, see Code of Civil Procedure § 704.160.
Expedited child support orders, see Family Code § 3620 et seq.
Family support defined for purposes of this Code, see Family Code § 92.
Health insurance coverage for supported children, see Family Code § 3750 et seq.
Judgment and order defined for purposes of this Code, see Family Code § 100.
Modification, termination, or setting aside of support order, see Family Code § 3650 et seq.
Notice, actual and constructive, defined, see Civil Code § 18.
State defined for purposes of this Code, see Family Code § 145.

Support defined for purposes of this Code, see Family Code § 150.

Research References

Forms

California Practice Guide: Rutter Family Law Forms Form 1:32, Glossary of Common Family Law Terms, Phrases and Concepts (Enclosure to Form 1:31).
West's California Judicial Council Forms FL–435, Earnings Assignment Order for Spousal or Partner Support.
West's California Judicial Council Forms FL–460, Qualified Domestic Relations Order for Support (Earnings Assignment Order for Support).
West's California Judicial Council Forms FL–461, Attachment to Qualified Domestic Relations Order for Support (Earnings Assignment Order for Support).

§ 5210. "Employer" defined

"Employer" includes all of the following:

(a) A person for whom an individual performs services as an employee, as defined in Section 706.011 of the Code of Civil Procedure.

(b) The United States government and any public entity as defined in Section 811.2 of the Government Code.

(c) Any person or entity paying earnings as defined under Section 5206. *(Stats.1992, c. 162 (A.B.2650), § 10, operative Jan. 1, 1994.)*

Cross References

Person defined for purposes of this Code, see Family Code § 105.
State defined for purposes of this Code, see Family Code § 145.

§ 5212. "IV–D Case" defined

"IV–D Case" means any case being established, modified, or enforced by the local child support agency pursuant to Section 654 of Title 42 of the United States Code (Section 454 of the Social Security Act). *(Stats.1992, c. 162 (A.B.2650), § 10, operative Jan. 1, 1994. Amended by Stats.1999, c. 480 (S.B.542), § 2.)*

Cross References

Child support, generally, see Family Code § 3900 et seq.
State defined for purposes of this Code, see Family Code § 145.
Support defined for purposes of this Code, see Family Code § 150.

§ 5214. "Obligee" or "assigned obligee" defined

"Obligee" or "assigned obligee" means either the person to whom support has been ordered to be paid, the local child support agency, or other person designated by the court to receive the payment. The local child support agency is the obligee for all Title IV–D cases as defined under Section 5212 or in which an application for services has been filed under Part D (commencing with Section 651) and Part E (commencing with Section 670) of Subchapter IV of Chapter 7 of Title 42 of the United States Code (Title IV–D or IV–E of the Social Security Act). *(Stats.1992, c. 162 (A.B.2650), § 10, operative Jan. 1, 1994. Amended by Stats.2000, c. 808 (A.B.1358), § 57, eff. Sept. 28, 2000; Stats.2001, c. 755 (S.B.943), § 7, eff. Oct. 12, 2001.)*

Cross References

Child support, generally, see Family Code § 3900 et seq.
Expedited child support orders, see Family Code § 3620 et seq.
Health insurance coverage for supported children, see Family Code § 3750 et seq.
Modification, termination, or setting aside of support order, see Family Code § 3650 et seq.
Person defined for purposes of this Code, see Family Code § 105.
State defined for purposes of this Code, see Family Code § 145.
Support defined for purposes of this Code, see Family Code § 150.

§ 5214

Wage garnishment, withholding order for support, see Code of Civil Procedure § 706.030.

§ 5216. "Obligor" defined

"Obligor" means a person owing a duty of support. *(Stats.1992, c. 162 (A.B.2650), § 10, operative Jan. 1, 1994.)*

Cross References

Person defined for purposes of this Code, see Family Code § 105.
Support defined for purposes of this Code, see Family Code § 150.

§ 5220. "Timely payment" defined

"Timely payment" means receipt of support payments by the obligee or assigned obligee within five days of the due date. *(Stats.1992, c. 162 (A.B.2650), § 10, operative Jan. 1, 1994.)*

Cross References

Computation of time, see Code of Civil Procedure §§ 12, 12a; Government Code § 6800 et seq.
Support defined for purposes of this Code, see Family Code § 150.

ARTICLE 2. GENERAL PROVISIONS

Section
5230. Support orders; inclusion of earnings assignment order.
5230.1. Earning assignment or income withholding order of another state; enforceability; applicable law.
5230.5. Allegation of child support arrearage amount; perjury.
5231. Binding effect of assignment order upon employers.
5232. Service of order on employer.
5233. Commencement of withholding.
5234. Delivery to obligor by employer; copy of order; statement of rights.
5235. Duties of employer; withholding and forwarding of support; liability.
5236. Simplification of wage withholding.
5237. Notice of obligee of change of address; effect of failure to notify.
5238. Assignments including both current support and arrearages; priority; multiple assignment orders for the same employee; proration of withheld payments.
5239. Arrearages of support payments; computation.
5240. Payment of past due support; termination of service of order of assignment; grounds; ex parte relief.
5241. Wilful failure to withhold or forward support; penalties; actions to collect withheld sums not forwarded; electronic transfer and employer awareness.
5242. Lien on earnings; service of order.
5243. Priority of order.
5244. Local child support agency; enforcement or collection duties.
5245. Enforcement of support obligations; authority of local child support agency to use civil and criminal remedies.
5246. Assignment of earnings; notice to employer; employer's duties; application of section.
5247. Civil liability of local child support agency or employer.

§ 5230. Support orders; inclusion of earnings assignment order

(a) When the court orders a party to pay an amount for support or orders a modification of the amount of support to be paid, the court shall include in its order an earnings assignment order for support that orders the employer of the obligor to pay to the obligee that portion of the obligor's earnings due or to become due in the future as will be sufficient to pay an amount to cover both of the following:

(1) The amount ordered by the court for support.

(2) An amount which shall be ordered by the court to be paid toward the liquidation of any arrearage.

(b) An earnings assignment order for support shall be issued, and shall be effective and enforceable pursuant to Section 5231, notwithstanding the absence of the name, address, or other identifying information regarding the obligor's employer. *(Stats.1992, c. 162 (A.B.2650), § 10, operative Jan. 1, 1994. Amended by Stats.1993, c. 876 (S.B.1068), § 22.5, eff. Oct. 6, 1993, operative Jan. 1, 1994; Stats.1997, c. 599 (A.B.573), § 23; Stats.2000, c. 808 (A.B.1358), § 57.3, eff. Sept. 28, 2000.)*

Cross References

Arrearages, computation, see Family Code § 5239.
Delinquent payments of support, use of security deposit, see Family Code § 4570 et seq.
Enforcement of support orders, see Family Code § 4500 et seq.
Forms, Judicial Council, see Family Code § 5295.
Judgment and order defined for purposes of this Code, see Family Code § 100.
Practices prohibited, see Family Code § 5290.
Priority of support obligations, see Family Code § 5238.
Priority over other assignments, see Family Code § 5243.
Provisions of earnings assignment orders when not included with support order, see Family Code § 5250 et seq.
Security deposit, delinquent payments, see Family Code § 4570 et seq.
Stay of assignment orders, see Family Code §§ 5260, 5261.
Support defined for purposes of this Code, see Family Code § 150.
Support order, defined, see Family Code § 155.
Support order issued or modified before July 1, 1990, procedure for obtaining assignment order, see Family Code § 5251 et seq.
Withholding, commencement of, see Family Code § 5233.

Research References

Forms

California Practice Guide: Rutter Family Law Forms Form 1:32, Glossary of Common Family Law Terms, Phrases and Concepts (Enclosure to Form 1:31).
California Practice Guide: Rutter Family Law Forms Form 9:3, Marital Settlement Agreement.
3 California Transactions Forms--Business Transactions § 16:83, Exclusions.
1 California Transactions Forms--Family Law § 3:46, Earnings Assignment.
West's California Code Forms, Family § 2338 Form 9, Marital Agreement—Both Spouses Employed.
West's California Code Forms, Family § 5230, Comment Overview—Earnings Assignment Order.
West's California Code Forms, Government § 37103 Form 5, Standard Provisions for City Personal Services Contracts.
West's California Judicial Council Forms FL–430, Ex Parte Application to Issue, Modify, or Terminate an Earnings Assignment Order.

§ 5230.1. Earning assignment or income withholding order of another state; enforceability; applicable law

(a) An earnings assignment or income withholding order for support issued by a court or administrative agency of another state is binding upon an employer of the obligor to the same extent as an earnings assignment order made by a court of this state.

(b) When an employer receives an earnings assignment order or an income withholding order for support from a court or administrative agency in another state, all of the provisions of this chapter shall apply. *(Added by Stats.1997, c. 599 (A.B.573), § 24.)*

Cross References

Administrative Procedure Act, see Government Code §§ 11340 et seq., 11370 et seq., 11400 et seq., 11500 et seq.
Administrative proceedings, judicial review, see Government Code § 11523.
Judgment and order defined for purposes of this Code, see Family Code § 100.
State defined for purposes of this Code, see Family Code § 145.

Support defined for purposes of this Code, see Family Code § 150.

Research References

Forms

West's California Code Forms, Family § 5230, Comment Overview—Earnings Assignment Order.

§ 5230.5. Allegation of child support arrearage amount; perjury

Any obligee alleging arrearages in child support shall specify the amount thereof under penalty of perjury. *(Added by Stats.1994, c. 1140 (S.B.279), § 2.)*

Cross References

Child support, generally, see Family Code § 3900 et seq.
Support defined for purposes of this Code, see Family Code § 150.

Research References

Forms

West's California Judicial Council Forms FL–420, Declaration of Payment History (Governmental—Uniform Parentage Act).
West's California Judicial Council Forms FL–421, Payment History Attachment (Governmental—Uniform Parentage Act).

§ 5231. Binding effect of assignment order upon employers

Unless stayed pursuant to Article 4 (commencing with Section 5260), an assignment order is effective and binding upon any existing or future employer of the obligor upon whom a copy of the order is served in compliance with Sections 5232 and 5233, notwithstanding the absence of the name, address, or other identifying information regarding the obligor's employer, or the inclusion of incorrect information regarding the support obligor's employer. *(Stats.1992, c. 162 (A.B.2650), § 10, operative Jan. 1, 1994. Amended by Stats.2000, c. 808 (A.B.1358), § 57.5, eff. Sept. 28, 2000.)*

Cross References

Enforcement of support orders, see Family Code § 4500 et seq.
Judgment and order defined for purposes of this Code, see Family Code § 100.
Support defined for purposes of this Code, see Family Code § 150.

Research References

Forms

West's California Code Forms, Family § 5230, Comment Overview—Earnings Assignment Order.

§ 5232. Service of order on employer

Service on an employer of an assignment order may be made by first-class mail in the manner prescribed in Section 1013 of the Code of Civil Procedure. The obligee shall serve the documents specified in Section 5234. *(Stats.1992, c. 162 (A.B.2650), § 10, operative Jan. 1, 1994. Amended by Stats.1997, c. 599 (A.B.573), § 25.)*

Cross References

Enforcement of support orders, see Family Code § 4500 et seq.
Judgment and order defined for purposes of this Code, see Family Code § 100.

Research References

Forms

1 California Transactions Forms--Family Law § 3:46, Earnings Assignment.

§ 5233. Commencement of withholding

Unless the order states a later date, beginning as soon as possible after service of the order on the employer but not later than 10 days after service of the order on the employer, the employer shall commence withholding pursuant to the assignment order from all earnings payable to the employee. *(Stats.1992, c. 162 (A.B.2650), § 10, operative Jan. 1, 1994.)*

Cross References

Computation of time, see Code of Civil Procedure §§ 12, 12a; Government Code § 6800 et seq.
Enforcement of support orders, see Family Code § 4500 et seq.
Judgment and order defined for purposes of this Code, see Family Code § 100.
State defined for purposes of this Code, see Family Code § 145.

Research References

Forms

1 California Transactions Forms--Family Law § 3:46, Earnings Assignment.

§ 5234. Delivery to obligor by employer; copy of order; statement of rights

Within 10 days of service of an assignment order or an order/notice to withhold income for child support on an employer, the employer shall deliver both of the following to the obligor:

(a) A copy of the assignment order or the order/notice to withhold income for child support.

(b) A written statement of the obligor's rights under the law to seek to quash, modify, or stay service of the earnings assignment order, together with a blank form that the obligor can file with the court to request a hearing to quash, modify, or stay service of the earnings assignment order with instructions on how to file the form and obtain a hearing date. *(Stats.1992, c. 162 (A.B.2650), § 10, operative Jan. 1, 1994. Amended by Stats.1997, c. 599 (A.B.573), § 26; Stats.1999, c. 480 (S.B.542), § 3.)*

Cross References

Child support, generally, see Family Code § 3900 et seq.
Computation of time, see Code of Civil Procedure §§ 12, 12a; Government Code § 6800 et seq.
Enforcement of support orders, see Family Code § 4500 et seq.
Expedited child support orders, see Family Code § 3620 et seq.
Health insurance coverage for supported children, see Family Code § 3750 et seq.
Judgment and order defined for purposes of this Code, see Family Code § 100.
Modification, termination, or setting aside of support order, see Family Code § 3650 et seq.
Notice, actual and constructive, defined, see Civil Code § 18.
Support defined for purposes of this Code, see Family Code § 150.

§ 5235. Duties of employer; withholding and forwarding of support; liability

(a) The employer shall continue to withhold and forward support as required by the assignment order until served with notice terminating the assignment order. If an employer withholds support as required by the assignment order, the obligor shall not be held in contempt or subject to criminal prosecution for nonpayment of the support that was withheld by the employer but not received by the obligee. If the employer withheld the support but failed to forward the payments to the obligee, the employer shall be liable for the payments, including interest, as provided in Section 5241.

(b) Within 10 days of service of a substitution of payee on the employer, the employer shall forward all subsequent support to the governmental entity or other payee that sent the substitution.

(c) The employer shall send the amounts withheld to the obligee within the timeframe specified in federal law and shall report to the obligee the date on which the amount was withheld from the obligor's wages.

(d) The employer may deduct from the earnings of the employee the sum of one dollar and fifty cents ($1.50) for each payment made pursuant to the order.

(e) Once the State Disbursement Unit as required by Section 17309 is operational, the employer shall send all earnings withheld pursuant to this chapter to the State Disbursement Unit instead of the obligee. *(Stats.1992, c. 162 (A.B.2650), § 10, operative Jan. 1, 1994. Amended by Stats.1993, c. 876 (S.B.1068), § 23, eff. Oct. 6, 1993, operative Jan. 1, 1994; Stats.1994, c. 1269 (A.B.2208), § 50.2;*

§ 5235

Stats.1997, c. 599 (A.B.573), § 27; Stats.1998, c. 854 (A.B.960), § 4; Stats.2000, c. 808 (A.B.1358), § 58, eff. Sept. 28, 2000; Stats.2003, c. 387 (A.B.739), § 5; Stats.2004, c. 520 (A.B.2530), § 3.)

Cross References

Computation of time, see Code of Civil Procedure §§ 12, 12a; Government Code § 6800 et seq.
Enforcement of support orders, see Family Code § 4500 et seq.
Judgment and order defined for purposes of this Code, see Family Code § 100.
Notice, actual and constructive, defined, see Civil Code § 18.
State defined for purposes of this Code, see Family Code § 145.
Support defined for purposes of this Code, see Family Code § 150.

Research References

Forms

1 California Transactions Forms--Family Law § 3:46, Earnings Assignment.

§ 5236. Simplification of wage withholding

The state agency or the local agency, designated to enforce support obligations as required by federal law, shall allow employers to simplify the process of assignment order withholding by forwarding, as ordered by the court, the amounts of support withheld under more than one order in a consolidated check, accompanied by an itemized accounting providing names, social security number or other identifying number, and the amount attributable to each obligor. (Stats. 1992, c. 162 (A.B.2650), § 10, operative Jan. 1, 1994.)

Cross References

Enforcement of support orders, see Family Code § 4500 et seq.
Judgment and order defined for purposes of this Code, see Family Code § 100.
State defined for purposes of this Code, see Family Code § 145.
Support defined for purposes of this Code, see Family Code § 150.

§ 5237. Notice of obligee of change of address; effect of failure to notify

(a) Except as provided in subdivisions (b) and (c), the obligee shall notify the employer of the obligor, by first-class mail, postage prepaid, of any change of address within a reasonable period of time after the change.

(b) Where payments have been ordered to be made to a county officer designated by the court, the obligee who is the parent, guardian, or other person entitled to receive payment through the designated county officer shall notify the designated county officer by first-class mail, postage prepaid, of any address change within a reasonable period of time after the change.

(c) If the obligee is receiving support payments from the State Disbursement Unit as required by Section 17309, the obligee shall notify the State Disbursement Unit instead of the employer of the obligor as provided in subdivision (a).

(d)(1) Except as set forth in paragraph (2), if the employer, designated county officer, or the State Disbursement Unit is unable to deliver payments under the assignment order for a period of six months due to the failure of the obligee to notify the employer, designated county officer, or State Disbursement Unit, of a change of address, the employer, designated county officer, or State Disbursement Unit shall not make any further payments under the assignment order and shall return all undeliverable payments to the obligor.

(2) If payments are being directed to the State Disbursement Unit pursuant to subdivision (e) of Section 5235, but the case is not otherwise receiving services from the Title IV–D agency, and the State Disbursement Unit is unable to deliver payments under the assignment order for a period of 45 days due to the failure of the obligee to notify the employer, designated county officer, or State Disbursement Unit of a change of address, the Title IV–D agency shall take the following actions:

(A) Immediately return the undeliverable payments to the obligor if the obligee cannot be located.

(B) Notify the employer to suspend withholding pursuant to the wage assignment until the employer or Title IV-D agency is notified of the obligee's whereabouts. (Stats.1992, c. 162 (A.B.2650), § 10, operative Jan. 1, 1994. Amended by Stats.1997, c. 599 (A.B.573), § 28; Stats.2000, c. 808 (A.B.1358), § 59, eff. Sept. 28, 2000; Stats.2003, c. 387 (A.B.739), § 6; Stats.2004, c. 806 (A.B.2358), § 1.)

Cross References

County defined for purposes of this Code, see Family Code § 67.
Enforcement of support orders, see Family Code § 4500 et seq.
Judgment and order defined for purposes of this Code, see Family Code § 100.
Person defined for purposes of this Code, see Family Code § 105.
State defined for purposes of this Code, see Family Code § 145.
Support defined for purposes of this Code, see Family Code § 150.

§ 5238. Assignments including both current support and arrearages; priority; multiple assignment orders for the same employee; proration of withheld payments

(a) Where an assignment order or assignment orders include both current support and payments towards the liquidation of arrearages, priority shall be given first to the current child support obligation, then the current spousal support obligation, and thereafter to the liquidation of child and then spousal support arrearages.

(b) Where there are multiple assignment orders for the same employee, the employer shall prorate the withheld payments as follows:

(1) If the obligor has more than one assignment for support, the employer shall add together the amount of support due for each assignment.

(2) If 50 percent of the obligor's net disposable earnings will not pay in full all of the assignments for support, the employer shall prorate it first among all of the current support assignments in the same proportion that each assignment bears to the total current support owed.

(3) The employer shall apply any remainder to the assignments for arrearage support in the same proportion that each assignment bears to the total arrearage owed. (Stats.1992, c. 162 (A.B.2650), § 10, operative Jan. 1, 1994. Amended by Stats.1997, c. 599 (A.B.573), § 29.)

Cross References

Child support, generally, see Family Code § 3900 et seq.
Enforcement of support orders, see Family Code § 4500 et seq.
Judgment and order defined for purposes of this Code, see Family Code § 100.
Priority over other assignments, see Family Code § 5243.
Spousal support defined for purposes of this Code, see Family Code § 142.
Support defined for purposes of this Code, see Family Code § 150.

§ 5239. Arrearages of support payments; computation

Arrearages of support payments shall be computed on the basis of the payments owed and unpaid on the date that the obligor has been given notice of the assignment order as required by Section 5234. (Stats.1992, c. 162 (A.B.2650), § 10, operative Jan. 1, 1994.)

Cross References

Enforcement of support orders, see Family Code § 4500 et seq.
Judgment and order defined for purposes of this Code, see Family Code § 100.
Notice, actual and constructive, defined, see Civil Code § 18.
Support defined for purposes of this Code, see Family Code § 150.

§ 5240. Payment of past due support; termination of service of order of assignment; grounds; ex parte relief

(a) Upon the filing and service of a motion and a notice of motion by the obligor, the court shall terminate the service of an assignment order if past due support has been paid in full, including any interest due, and if any of the following conditions exist:

(1) With regard to orders for spousal support, the death or remarriage of the spouse to whom support is owed.

(2) With regard to orders for child support, the death or emancipation of the child for whom support is owed.

(3) The court determines that there is good cause, as defined in Section 5260, to terminate the assignment order. This subdivision does not apply if there has been more than one application for an assignment order.

(4) The obligor meets the conditions of an alternative arrangement specified in paragraph (2) of subdivision (b) of Section 5260, and a wage assignment has not been previously terminated and subsequently initiated.

(5) There is no longer a current order for support.

(6) The termination of the stay of an assignment order under Section 5261 was improper, but only if that termination was based upon the obligor's failure to make timely support payments as described in subdivision (b) of Section 5261.

(7) The employer or agency designated to provide services under Title IV–D of the Social Security Act or the State Disbursement Unit is unable to deliver payment for a period of six months due to the failure of the obligee to notify that employer or agency or the State Disbursement Unit of a change in the obligee's address.

(b) In lieu of filing and serving a motion and a notice of motion pursuant to subdivision (a), an obligor may request ex parte relief, except ex parte relief shall not be available in the circumstances described in paragraphs (3) and (4) of subdivision (a). *(Stats.1992, c. 162 (A.B.2650), § 10, operative Jan. 1, 1994. Amended by Stats.1993, c. 876 (S.B.1068), § 24, eff. Oct. 6, 1993, operative Jan. 1, 1994; Stats.1997, c. 599 (A.B.573), § 30; Stats.2003, c. 387 (A.B.739), § 7; Stats.2012, c. 77 (A.B.1727), § 1.)*

Cross References

Child support, generally, see Family Code § 3900 et seq.
Enforcement of support orders, see Family Code § 4500 et seq.
Expedited child support orders, see Family Code § 3620 et seq.
Health insurance coverage for supported children, see Family Code § 3750 et seq.
Judgment and order defined for purposes of this Code, see Family Code § 100.
Modification, termination, or setting aside of support order, see Family Code § 3650 et seq.
Notice, actual and constructive, defined, see Civil Code § 18.
References to husband, wife, spouses and married persons, persons included for purposes of this Code, see Family Code § 11.
Spousal support defined for purposes of this Code, see Family Code § 142.
State defined for purposes of this Code, see Family Code § 145.
Support defined for purposes of this Code, see Family Code § 150.
Termination, stay of assignment order, see Family Code § 5261.

Research References

Forms

West's California Judicial Council Forms FL–430, Ex Parte Application to Issue, Modify, or Terminate an Earnings Assignment Order.

§ 5241. Wilful failure to withhold or forward support; penalties; actions to collect withheld sums not forwarded; electronic transfer and employer awareness

(a) An employer who willfully fails to withhold and forward support pursuant to a currently valid assignment order entered and served upon the employer pursuant to this chapter is liable to the obligee for the amount of support not withheld, forwarded, or otherwise paid to the obligee, including any interest thereon.

(b) If an employer withholds support as required by the assignment order, the obligor shall not be held in contempt or subject to criminal prosecution for nonpayment of the support that was withheld by the employer but not received by the obligee. In addition, the employer is liable to the obligee for any interest incurred as a result of the employer's failure to timely forward the withheld support pursuant to an assignment earnings order.

(c) In addition to any other penalty or liability provided by law, willful failure by an employer to comply with an assignment order is punishable as a contempt pursuant to Section 1218 of the Code of Civil Procedure.

(d) If an employer withholds support, as required by the assignment order, but fails to forward the support to the obligee, the local child support agency shall take appropriate action to collect the withheld sums from the employer. The child support obligee or the local child support agency upon application may obtain an order requiring payment of support by electronic transfer from the employer's bank account if the employer has willfully failed to comply with the assignment order or if the employer has failed to comply with the assignment order on three separate occasions within a 12-month period. Where a court finds that an employer has willfully failed to comply with the assignment order or has otherwise failed to comply with the assignment order on three separate occasions within a 12-month period, the court may impose a civil penalty, in addition to any other penalty required by law, of up to 50 percent of the support amount that has not been received by the obligee.

(e) To facilitate employer awareness, the local child support agency shall make reasonable efforts to notify any employer subject to an assignment order pursuant to this chapter of the electronic fund transfer provision and enhanced penalties provided by this act.

(f) Notwithstanding any other provision of law, any penalty payable pursuant to this subdivision shall be payable directly to the obligee. The local child support agency shall not be required to establish or collect this penalty on behalf of the obligee. The penalty shall not be included when determining the income of the obligee for the purpose of determining the eligibility of the obligee for benefits payable pursuant to state supplemental income programs. A court may issue the order requiring payment of support by electronic transfer from the employer's bank account and impose the penalty described in this subdivision, after notice and hearing. This provision shall not be construed to expand or limit the duties and obligations of the Labor Commissioner, as set forth in Section 200 and following of the Labor Code. *(Stats.1992, c. 162 (A.B.2650), § 10, operative Jan. 1, 1994. Amended by Stats.1993, c. 745 (S.B.788), § 2; Stats.1993, c. 876 (S.B.1068), § 25, eff. Oct. 6, 1993, operative Jan. 1, 1994; Stats.1998, c. 854 (A.B.960), § 5; Stats.2000, c. 808 (A.B.1358), § 60, eff. Sept. 28, 2000; Stats.2001, c. 371 (A.B.1426), § 1; Stats.2003, c. 308 (A.B.738), § 2.)*

Cross References

Attorney's fees and costs, generally, see Family Code § 270 et seq.
Child support, generally, see Family Code § 3900 et seq.
Civil penalty, using assignment order as grounds for refusing to hire or for discharging or taking disciplinary action, see Family Code § 5290.
Enforcement of support orders, see Family Code § 4500 et seq.
Expedited child support orders, see Family Code § 3620 et seq.
Health insurance coverage for supported children, see Family Code § 3750 et seq.
Judgment and order defined for purposes of this Code, see Family Code § 100.
Modification, termination, or setting aside of support order, see Family Code § 3650 et seq.
Notice, actual and constructive, defined, see Civil Code § 18.
State defined for purposes of this Code, see Family Code § 145.
Support defined for purposes of this Code, see Family Code § 150.

§ 5242. Lien on earnings; service of order

Service of the assignment order creates a lien on the earnings of the employee and the property of the employer to the same extent as the service of an earnings withholding order as provided in Section 706.029 of the Code of Civil Procedure. *(Stats.1992, c. 162 (A.B.2650), § 10, operative Jan. 1, 1994.)*

Cross References

Enforcement of support orders, see Family Code § 4500 et seq.
Judgment and order defined for purposes of this Code, see Family Code § 100.

Property defined for purposes of this Code, see Family Code § 113.

§ 5243. Priority of order

An assignment order for support has priority as against any attachment, execution, or other assignment as specified in Section 706.031 of the Code of Civil Procedure. *(Stats.1992, c. 162 (A.B.2650), § 10, operative Jan. 1, 1994. Amended by Stats.1993, c. 876 (S.B.1068), § 26, eff. Oct. 6, 1993, operative Jan. 1, 1994.)*

Cross References

Enforcement of support orders, see Family Code § 4500 et seq.
Judgment and order defined for purposes of this Code, see Family Code § 100.
Priority of support obligations, see Family Code § 5238.
Support defined for purposes of this Code, see Family Code § 150.

§ 5244. Local child support agency; enforcement or collection duties

A reference to the local child support agency in this chapter applies only when the local child support agency is otherwise ordered or required to act pursuant to law. Nothing in this chapter shall be deemed to mandate additional enforcement or collection duties upon the local child support agency beyond those otherwise imposed by law. *(Stats.1992, c. 162 (A.B.2650), § 10, operative Jan. 1, 1994. Amended by Stats.2000, c. 808 (A.B.1358), § 61, eff. Sept. 28, 2000.)*

Cross References

Child support, generally, see Family Code § 3900 et seq.
Enforcement of support orders, see Family Code § 4500 et seq.
Expedited child support orders, see Family Code § 3620 et seq.
Health insurance coverage for supported children, see Family Code § 3750 et seq.
Modification, termination, or setting aside of support order, see Family Code § 3650 et seq.
Support defined for purposes of this Code, see Family Code § 150.

§ 5245. Enforcement of support obligations; authority of local child support agency to use civil and criminal remedies

Nothing in this chapter limits the authority of the local child support agency to use any other civil and criminal remedies to enforce support obligations, regardless of whether or not the child or the obligee who is the parent, guardian, or other person entitled to receive payment is the recipient of welfare moneys. *(Stats.1992, c. 162 (A.B.2650), § 10, operative Jan. 1, 1994. Amended by Stats.1993, c. 219 (A.B.1500), § 153; Stats.2000, c. 808 (A.B.1358), § 62, eff. Sept. 28, 2000.)*

Cross References

Child support, generally, see Family Code § 3900 et seq.
Enforcement of support orders, see Family Code § 4500 et seq.
Person defined for purposes of this Code, see Family Code § 105.
Support defined for purposes of this Code, see Family Code § 150.

§ 5246. Assignment of earnings; notice to employer; employer's duties; application of section

(a) This section applies only to Title IV–D cases where support enforcement services are being provided by the local child support agency pursuant to Section 17400.

(b) In lieu of an earnings assignment order signed by a judicial officer, the local child support agency may serve on the employer a notice of assignment in the manner specified in Section 5232. An order/notice to withhold income for child support shall have the same force and effect as an earnings assignment order signed by a judicial officer. An order/notice to withhold income for child support, when used under this section, shall be considered a notice and shall not require the signature of a judicial officer.

(c) Pursuant to Section 666 of Title 42 of the United States Code, the federally mandated order/notice to withhold income for child support shall be used for the purposes described in this section.

(d)(1) An order/notice to withhold income may not reduce the current amount withheld for court-ordered child support.

(2) If the underlying court order for support does not provide for an arrearage payment, or if an additional arrearage accrues after the date of the court order for support, the local child support agency may send an order/notice to withhold income for child support that shall be used for the purposes described in this section directly to the employer that specifies the updated arrearage amount and directs the employer to withhold an additional amount to be applied towards liquidation of the arrearages not to exceed the maximum amount permitted by Section 1673(b) of Title 15 of the United States Code.

(3) Notwithstanding paragraph (2), if an obligor is disabled, meets the SSI resource test, and is receiving Supplemental Security Income/State Supplementary Payments (SSI/SSP) or, but for excess income as described in Section 416.1100 et seq. of Part 416 of Title 20 of the Code of Federal Regulations, would be eligible to receive SSI/SSP, pursuant to Section 12200 of the Welfare and Institutions Code, and the obligor has supplied the local child support agency with proof of eligibility for and, if applicable, receipt of, SSI/SSP or Social Security Disability Insurance benefits, then the order/notice to withhold income issued by the local child support agency for the liquidation of the arrearage shall not exceed 5 percent of the obligor's total monthly Social Security Disability payments under Title II of the Social Security Act.

(e) If the obligor requests a hearing, a hearing date shall be scheduled within 20 days of the filing of the request with the court. The clerk of the court shall provide notice of the hearing to the local child support agency and the obligor no later than 10 days prior to the hearing.

(1) If, at the hearing, the obligor establishes that they are not the obligor or good cause or an alternative arrangement as provided in Section 5260, the court may order that service of the order/notice to withhold income for child support be quashed. If the court quashes service of the order/notice to withhold income for child support, the local child support agency shall notify the employer within 10 days.

(2) If the obligor contends at the hearing that the payment of arrearages at the rate specified in the order/notice to withhold income for child support is excessive or that the total arrearages owing is incorrect, and if it is determined that payment of the arrearages at the rate specified in this section creates an undue hardship upon the obligor or that the withholding would exceed the maximum amount permitted by Section 1673(b) of Title 15 of the United States Code Annotated, the rate at which the arrearages must be paid shall be reduced to a rate that is fair and reasonable considering the circumstances of the parties and the best interest of the child. If it is determined at a hearing that the total amount of arrearages calculated is erroneous, the court shall modify the amount calculated to the correct amount. If the court modifies the total amount of arrearages owed or reduces the monthly payment due on the arrearages, the local child support agency shall serve the employer with an amended order/notice to withhold income for child support within 10 days.

(f) If an obligor's current support obligation has terminated by operation of law, the local child support agency may serve an order/notice to withhold income for child support on the employer that directs the employer to continue withholding from the obligor's earnings an amount to be applied towards liquidation of the arrearages, not to exceed the maximum amount permitted by Section 1673(b) of Title 15 of the United States Code, until the employer is notified by the local child support agency that the arrearages have been paid in full. The employer shall provide the obligor with a copy of the order/notice to withhold income for child support and a blank form that the obligor may file with the court to request a hearing to modify or quash the assignment with instructions on how to file the form and obtain a hearing date. The obligor shall be entitled to the same rights to a hearing as specified in subdivision (e).

(g) The local child support agency shall retain a copy of the order/notice to withhold income for child support and shall file a copy with the court whenever a hearing concerning the order/notice to withhold income for child support is requested.

(h) The local child support agency may transmit an order/notice to withhold income for child support and other forms required by this section to the employer through electronic means. *(Added by Stats.1996, c. 957 (A.B.1058), § 8. Amended by Stats.1997, c. 599 (A.B.573), § 31; Stats.1999, c. 480 (S.B.542), § 4; Stats.2000, c. 808 (A.B.1358), § 62.3, eff. Sept. 28, 2000; Stats.2001, c. 111 (A.B.429), § 1, eff. July 30, 2001; Stats.2001, c. 651 (A.B.891), § 2; Stats.2019, c. 115 (A.B.1817), § 55, eff. Jan. 1, 2020.)*

Cross References

Child support, generally, see Family Code § 3900 et seq.
Collection of tax, referral of child support delinquencies, see Revenue and Taxation Code § 19271.
Computation of time, see Code of Civil Procedure §§ 12, 12a; Government Code § 6800 et seq.
Expedited child support orders, see Family Code § 3620 et seq.
Health insurance coverage for supported children, see Family Code § 3750 et seq.
Judgment and order defined for purposes of this Code, see Family Code § 100.
Modification, termination, or setting aside of support order, see Family Code § 3650 et seq.
Notice, actual and constructive, defined, see Civil Code § 18.
State defined for purposes of this Code, see Family Code § 145.
Support defined for purposes of this Code, see Family Code § 150.

Research References

Forms

West's California Code Forms, Family § 5246 Form 1, Request for Hearing Regarding Wage and Earnings Assignment.
West's California Judicial Council Forms FL-450, Request for Hearing Regarding Earnings Assignment (Governmental—UIFSA).

§ 5247. Civil liability of local child support agency or employer

Neither the local child support agency nor an employer shall be subject to any civil liability for any amount withheld and paid to the obligee, the local child support agency, or the State Disbursement Unit pursuant to an earnings assignment order or notice of assignment. *(Added by Stats.1997, c. 599 (A.B.573), § 32. Amended by Stats.2000, c. 808 (A.B.1358), § 63, eff. Sept. 28, 2000; Stats.2003, c. 387 (A.B.739), § 8.)*

Cross References

Child support, generally, see Family Code § 3900 et seq.
Judgment and order defined for purposes of this Code, see Family Code § 100.
Notice, actual and constructive, defined, see Civil Code § 18.
State defined for purposes of this Code, see Family Code § 145.
Support defined for purposes of this Code, see Family Code § 150.

ARTICLE 3. SUPPORT ORDERS ISSUED OR MODIFIED BEFORE JULY 1, 1990

Section
5250. Application of article.
5251. Procedure for obtaining assignment.
5252. Application for assignment order; false declarations or notices; punishment.
5253. Issuance of assignment order.

§ 5250. Application of article

For a support order first issued or modified before July 1, 1990, this article provides a procedure for obtaining an earnings assignment order for support when the court in ordering support or modification of support did not issue an assignment order. *(Stats.1992, c. 162 (A.B.2650), § 10, operative Jan. 1, 1994.)*

Cross References

Judgment and order defined for purposes of this Code, see Family Code § 100.
Support defined for purposes of this Code, see Family Code § 150.
Support order defined for purposes of this Code, see Family Code § 155.

§ 5251. Procedure for obtaining assignment

The obligee seeking issuance of an assignment order to enforce a support order described in Section 5250 may use the procedure set forth in this article by filing an application under Section 5252, or by notice of motion or order to show cause, or pursuant to subdivision (b) of Section 5230. *(Stats.1992, c. 162 (A.B.2650), § 10, operative Jan. 1, 1994.)*

Cross References

Judgment and order defined for purposes of this Code, see Family Code § 100.
Notice, actual and constructive, defined, see Civil Code § 18.
Support defined for purposes of this Code, see Family Code § 150.
Support order defined for purposes of this Code, see Family Code § 155.

§ 5252. Application for assignment order; false declarations or notices; punishment

(a) An assignment order under this article may be issued only upon an application signed under penalty of perjury by the obligee that the obligor is in default in support payments in a sum equal to the amount of support payable for one month, for any other occurrence specified by the court in the support order, or earlier by court order if requested by the local child support agency or the obligor.

(b) If the order for support does not contain a provision for an earnings assignment order for support, the application shall state that the obligee has given the obligor a written notice of the obligee's intent to seek an assignment order if there is a default in support payments and that the notice was transmitted by first-class mail, postage prepaid, or personally served at least 15 days before the date of the filing of the application. The written notice of the intent to seek an assignment order may be given at any time, including at the time of filing a petition or complaint in which support is requested or at any time subsequent thereto. The obligor may at any time waive the written notice required by this subdivision.

(c) In addition to any other penalty provided by law, the filing of the application with knowledge of the falsity of the declaration or notice is punishable as a contempt pursuant to Section 1209 of the Code of Civil Procedure. *(Stats.1992, c. 162 (A.B.2650), § 10, operative Jan. 1, 1994. Amended by Stats.2000, c. 808 (A.B.1358), § 64, eff. Sept. 28, 2000.)*

Cross References

Child support, generally, see Family Code § 3900 et seq.
Computation of time, see Code of Civil Procedure §§ 12, 12a; Government Code § 6800 et seq.
Expedited child support orders, see Family Code § 3620 et seq.
Health insurance coverage for supported children, see Family Code § 3750 et seq.
Judgment and order defined for purposes of this Code, see Family Code § 100.
Modification, termination, or setting aside of support order, see Family Code § 3650 et seq.
Notice, actual and constructive, defined, see Civil Code § 18.
State defined for purposes of this Code, see Family Code § 145.
Support defined for purposes of this Code, see Family Code § 150.
Support order defined for purposes of this Code, see Family Code § 155.

Research References

Forms

West's California Judicial Council Forms FL-430, Ex Parte Application to Issue, Modify, or Terminate an Earnings Assignment Order.

§ 5253. Issuance of assignment order

Upon receipt of the application, the court shall issue, without notice to the obligor, an assignment order requiring the employer of

§ 5253

the obligor to pay to the obligee or the State Disbursement Unit that portion of the earnings of the obligor due or to become due in the future as will be sufficient to pay an amount to cover both of the following:

(a) The amount ordered by the court for support.

(b) An amount which shall be ordered by the court to be paid toward the liquidation of any arrearage or past due support amount. *(Stats.1992, c. 162 (A.B.2650), § 10, operative Jan. 1, 1994. Amended by Stats.1997, c. 599 (A.B.573), § 33; Stats.2003, c. 387 (A.B.739), § 9.)*

Cross References

Earnings assignment order for support, defined, see Family Code § 5208.
Forms, Judicial Council, see Family Code § 5295.
Judgment and order defined for purposes of this Code, see Family Code § 100.
Notice, actual and constructive, defined, see Civil Code § 18.
State defined for purposes of this Code, see Family Code § 145.
Support defined for purposes of this Code, see Family Code § 150.

ARTICLE 4. STAY OF SERVICE OF ASSIGNMENT ORDER

Section
5260. Finding of good cause necessary to stay order; restrictions.
5261. Termination of stay; declaration; falsification of declaration; penalty.

§ 5260. Finding of good cause necessary to stay order; restrictions

(a) The court may order that service of the assignment order be stayed only if the court makes a finding of good cause or if an alternative arrangement exists for payment in accordance with paragraph (2) of subdivision (b). Notwithstanding any other provision of law, service of wage assignments issued for foreign orders for support, and service of foreign orders for the assignment of wages registered pursuant to Chapter 6 (commencing with Section 5700.601) of Part 6 shall not be stayed pursuant to this subdivision.

(b) For purposes of this section, good cause or an alternative arrangement for staying an assignment order is as follows:

(1) Good cause for staying a wage assignment exists only when all of the following conditions exist:

(A) The court provides a written explanation of why the stay of the wage assignment would be in the best interests of the child.

(B) The obligor has a history of uninterrupted, full, and timely payment, other than through a wage assignment or other mandatory process of previously ordered support, during the previous 12 months.

(C) The obligor does not owe an arrearage for prior support.

(D) The obligor proves, and the court finds, by clear and convincing evidence that service of the wage assignment would cause extraordinary hardship upon the obligor. Whenever possible, the court shall specify a date that any stay ordered under this section will automatically terminate.

(2) An alternative arrangement for staying a wage assignment order shall require a written agreement between the parties that provides for payment of the support obligation as ordered other than through the immediate service of a wage assignment. Any agreement between the parties which includes the staying of a service of a wage assignment shall include the concurrence of the local child support agency in any case in which support is ordered to be paid through a county officer designated for that purpose. The execution of an agreement pursuant to this paragraph shall not preclude a party from thereafter seeking a wage assignment in accordance with the procedures specified in Section 5261 upon violation of the agreement. *(Stats.1992, c. 162 (A.B.2650), § 10, operative Jan. 1, 1994. Amended by Stats.1993, c. 219 (A.B.1500), § 153.2; Stats.1993, c. 876 (S.B.1068), § 27, eff. Oct. 6, 1993, operative Jan. 1, 1994; Stats.1994, c.*

1269 (A.B.2208), § 50.4; Stats.2000, c. 808 (A.B.1358), § 65, eff. Sept. 28, 2000; Stats.2001, c. 755 (S.B.943), § 8, eff. Oct. 12, 2001; Stats.2015, c. 493 (S.B.646), § 3, eff. Jan. 1, 2016.)

Cross References

Agreements for support of adult children, see Family Code § 3587.
Binding affect of assignment order, see Family Code § 5231.
Child support, generally, see Family Code § 3900 et seq.
County defined for purposes of this Code, see Family Code § 67.
Expedited child support orders, see Family Code § 3620 et seq.
Grounds for motion to quash assignment order, see Family Code § 5270.
Health insurance coverage for supported children, see Family Code § 3750 et seq.
Judgment and order defined for purposes of this Code, see Family Code § 100.
Modification, termination, or setting aside of support order, see Family Code § 3650 et seq.
Service of assignment order on employer, see Family Code § 5232.
Support agreements,
  Generally, see Family Code § 3580 et seq.
  Child support agreements, see Family Code § 3585 et seq.
  Spousal support agreements, see Family Code § 3590 et seq.
Support defined for purposes of this Code, see Family Code § 150.
Support order included with earnings assignment order, see Family Code § 5230.
Termination of service of earnings assignment order, see Family Code § 5240.

Research References

Forms

1 California Transactions Forms--Family Law § 3:46, Earnings Assignment.
1 California Transactions Forms--Family Law § 3:104, Basic Child Support Agreement.
West's California Code Forms, Family § 5260, Comment Overview—Stay of Service of Assignment Order.
West's California Judicial Council Forms FL–455, Stay of Service of Earnings Assignment Order and Order.

§ 5261. Termination of stay; declaration; falsification of declaration; penalty

(a) If service of the assignment order has been ordered stayed, the stay shall terminate pursuant to subdivision (b) upon the obligor's failure to make timely support payments or earlier by court order if requested by the local child support agency or by the obligor. The stay shall terminate earlier by court order if requested by any other obligee who can establish that good cause, as defined in Section 5260, no longer exists.

(b) To terminate a stay of the service of the assignment order, the obligee shall file a declaration signed under penalty of perjury by the obligee that the obligor is in arrears in payment of any portion of the support. At the time of filing the declaration, the stay shall terminate by operation of law without notice to the obligor.

(c) In addition to any other penalty provided by law, the filing of a declaration under subdivision (b) with knowledge of the falsity of its contents is punishable as a contempt pursuant to Section 1209 of the Code of Civil Procedure. *(Stats.1992, c. 162 (A.B.2650), § 10, operative Jan. 1, 1994. Amended by Stats.2000, c. 808 (A.B.1358), § 66, eff. Sept. 28, 2000.)*

Cross References

Child support, generally, see Family Code § 3900 et seq.
Expedited child support orders, see Family Code § 3620 et seq.
Forms, Judicial Council, see Family Code § 5295.
Health insurance coverage for supported children, see Family Code § 3750 et seq.
Judgment and order defined for purposes of this Code, see Family Code § 100.
Modification, termination, or setting aside of support order, see Family Code § 3650 et seq.
Notice, actual and constructive, defined, see Civil Code § 18.
Service of assignment order on employer, see Family Code § 5232.
Support defined for purposes of this Code, see Family Code § 150.
Support order included with earnings assignment order, see Family Code § 5230.

Termination of service of order of assignment, see Family Code § 5240.

Research References

Forms

1 California Transactions Forms--Family Law § 3:46, Earnings Assignment.
West's California Code Forms, Family § 5260, Comment Overview—Stay of Service of Assignment Order.
West's California Judicial Council Forms FL–455, Stay of Service of Earnings Assignment Order and Order.

ARTICLE 5. MOTION TO QUASH ASSIGNMENT ORDER

Section
5270. Grounds for motion.
5271. Motion and notice of motion to quash; filing; hearing; service on obligee.
5272. Error or excess in amount of current support or arrearage; modification of order.

§ 5270. Grounds for motion

(a) An obligor may move to quash an assignment order on any of the following grounds:

(1) The assignment order does not correctly state the amount of current or overdue support ordered by the courts.

(2) The alleged obligor is not the obligor from whom support is due.

(3) The amount to be withheld exceeds that allowable under federal law in subsection (b) of Section 1673 of Title 15 of the United States Code.

(b) If an assignment order is sought under Article 3 (commencing with Section 5250), the party ordered to pay support may also move to quash the service of the order based upon Section 5260.

(c) The obligor shall state under oath the ground on which the motion to quash is made.

(d) If an assignment order which has been issued and served on a prior employer is served on the obligor's new employer, the obligor does not have the right to move to quash the assignment order on any grounds which the obligor previously raised when the assignment order was served on the prior employer or on any grounds which the obligor could have raised when the assignment order was served on the prior employer but failed to raise. *(Stats.1992, c. 162 (A.B.2650), § 10, operative Jan. 1, 1994.)*

Cross References

Judgment and order defined for purposes of this Code, see Family Code § 100.
State defined for purposes of this Code, see Family Code § 145.
Support defined for purposes of this Code, see Family Code § 150.

§ 5271. Motion and notice of motion to quash; filing; hearing; service on obligee

(a) The motion and notice of motion to quash the assignment order shall be filed with the court issuing the order within 10 days after delivery of the copy of the assignment order to the obligor by the employer.

(b) The clerk of the court shall set the motion to quash for hearing within not less than 15 days, nor more than 20 days, after receipt of the notice of motion.

(c) The obligor shall serve personally or by first-class mail, postage prepaid, a copy of the motion and notice of motion on the obligee named in the assignment order no less than 10 days before the date of the hearing. *(Stats.1992, c. 162 (A.B.2650), § 10, operative Jan. 1, 1994.)*

Cross References

Computation of time, see Code of Civil Procedure §§ 12, 12a; Government Code § 6800 et seq.

Judgment and order defined for purposes of this Code, see Family Code § 100.
Notice, actual and constructive, defined, see Civil Code § 18.

§ 5272. Error or excess in amount of current support or arrearage; modification of order

A finding of error in the amount of the current support or arrearage or that the amount exceeds federal or state limits is not grounds to vacate the assignment order. The court shall modify the order to reflect the correct or allowable amount of support or arrearages. The fact that the obligor may have subsequently paid the arrearages does not relieve the court of its duty to enter the assignment order. *(Stats.1992, c. 162 (A.B.2650), § 10, operative Jan. 1, 1994.)*

Cross References

Arrearages, computation of, see Family Code § 5239.
Judgment and order defined for purposes of this Code, see Family Code § 100.
State defined for purposes of this Code, see Family Code § 145.
Support defined for purposes of this Code, see Family Code § 150.

ARTICLE 6. INFORMATION CONCERNING ADDRESS AND EMPLOYMENT OF OBLIGOR

Section
5280. Obligor's whereabouts or identity of employer unknown; duties of local child support agency.
5281. Duty of obligor to inform obligee of change of employment.
5282. Duty of employer to inform obligee of obligor's change of employment.
5283. Repealed.

§ 5280. Obligor's whereabouts or identity of employer unknown; duties of local child support agency

If the obligee making the application under this chapter also states that the whereabouts of the obligor or the identity of the obligor's employer is unknown to the party to whom support has been ordered to be paid, the local child support agency shall do both of the following:

(a) Contact the California parent locator service maintained by the Department of Justice in the manner prescribed in Section 17506.

(b) Upon receiving the requested information, notify the court of the last known address of the obligor and the name and address of the obligor's last known employer. *(Stats.1992, c. 162 (A.B.2650), § 10, operative Jan. 1, 1994. Amended by Stats.2000, c. 808 (A.B. 1358), § 67, eff. Sept. 28, 2000.)*

Cross References

Change of address of obligee, notice to employer, see Family Code § 5237.
Child support, generally, see Family Code § 3900 et seq.
Employer, duties of, see Family Code §§ 5233 et seq., 5241.
Expedited child support orders, see Family Code § 3620 et seq.
Health insurance coverage for supported children, see Family Code § 3750 et seq.
Modification, termination, or setting aside of support order, see Family Code § 3650 et seq.
Obligor, defined, see Family Code § 5216.
Service on employer, see Family Code § 5232.
State defined for purposes of this Code, see Family Code § 145.
Support defined for purposes of this Code, see Family Code § 150.

§ 5281. Duty of obligor to inform obligee of change of employment

An assignment order required or authorized by this chapter shall include a requirement that the obligor notify the obligee of any change of employment and of the name and address of the obligor's new employer within 10 days of obtaining new employment. *(Stats. 1992, c. 162 (A.B.2650), § 10, operative Jan. 1, 1994.)*

§ 5281

Cross References

Change of address of obligee, notice to employer, see Family Code § 5237.
Computation of time, see Code of Civil Procedure §§ 12, 12a; Government Code § 6800 et seq.
Judgment and order defined for purposes of this Code, see Family Code § 100.
Obligor, defined, see Family Code § 5216.
Service on employer, see Family Code § 5232.

§ 5282. Duty of employer to inform obligee of obligor's change of employment

After the obligor has left employment with the employer, the employer, at the time the next payment is due on the assignment order, shall notify the obligee designated in the assignment order by first-class mail, postage prepaid, to the last known address of the obligee that the obligor has left employment. *(Stats.1992, c. 162 (A.B.2650), § 10, operative Jan. 1, 1994.)*

Cross References

Judgment and order defined for purposes of this Code, see Family Code § 100.
Obligee, defined, see Family Code § 5214.
Obligor, defined, see Family Code § 5216.
Service on employer, see Family Code § 5232.

§ 5283. Repealed by Stats.1997, c. 599 (A.B.573), § 34

ARTICLE 7. PROHIBITED PRACTICES

Section
5290. Use of assignment order under chapter as basis of adverse employment action; violations; civil penalty.

§ 5290. Use of assignment order under chapter as basis of adverse employment action; violations; civil penalty

No employer shall use an assignment order authorized by this chapter as grounds for refusing to hire a person, or for discharging, taking disciplinary action against, denying a promotion to, or for taking any other action adversely affecting the terms and conditions of employment of, an employee. An employer who engages in the conduct prohibited by this section may be assessed a civil penalty of a maximum of five hundred dollars ($500). *(Stats.1992, c. 162 (A.B.2650), § 10, operative Jan. 1, 1994. Amended by Stats.2004, c. 369 (A.B.1706), § 1.)*

Cross References

Judgment and order defined for purposes of this Code, see Family Code § 100.
Person defined for purposes of this Code, see Family Code § 105.

ARTICLE 8. JUDICIAL COUNCIL FORMS

Section
5295. Forms.
5500 to 5552. Repealed.

§ 5295. Forms

The Judicial Council shall prescribe forms necessary to carry out the requirements of this chapter, including the following:

(a) The written statement of the obligor's rights.

(b) The earnings assignment order for support.

(c) The instruction guide for obligees and obligors.

(d) The application forms required under Sections 5230, 5252, and 5261.

(e) The notice form required under Section 5252.

(f) Revised judgment and assignment order forms as necessary. *(Stats.1992, c. 162 (A.B.2650), § 10, operative Jan. 1, 1994.)*

Cross References

Judgment and order defined for purposes of this Code, see Family Code § 100.
Notice, actual and constructive, defined, see Civil Code § 18.
Support defined for purposes of this Code, see Family Code § 150.

Research References

Forms

3 California Transactions Forms--Business Transactions § 16:83, Exclusions.
3 California Transactions Forms--Business Transactions § 16:84, Form Drafting Principles.
3 California Transactions Forms--Business Transactions § 16:88, Assignment of Wages or Salary (General).

§§ 5500 to 5552. Repealed by Stats.1993, c. 219 (A.B.1500), § 153.5

ARTICLE 9. INTERCOUNTY SUPPORT OBLIGATIONS

Section
5600. Registration of order for support or earnings withholding obtained in another county.
5601. Registration by local child support agency of support order made in another county; procedures; motion to vacate; notice of registration.
5602. Registration of order by obligee; procedure; notice.
5603. Motion to vacate registration; procedure; hearing.
5604. Effect of previous determination of paternity made by another state.
5605, 5606. Repealed.

§ 5600. Registration of order for support or earnings withholding obtained in another county

(a) A local child support agency or obligee may register an order for support or earnings withholding, or both, obtained in another county of the state.

(b) An obligee may register a support order in the court of another county of this state in the manner, with the effect, and for the purposes provided in this part. The orders may be registered in any county in which the obligor, the obligee, or the child who is the subject of the order resides, or in any county in which the obligor has income, assets, or any other property. *(Added by Stats.1997, c. 599 (A.B.573), § 35. Amended by Stats.2000, c. 808 (A.B.1358), § 68, eff. Sept. 28, 2000.)*

Cross References

Child support, generally, see Family Code § 3900 et seq.
County defined for purposes of this Code, see Family Code § 67.
Expedited child support orders, see Family Code § 3620 et seq.
Health insurance coverage for supported children, see Family Code § 3750 et seq.
Judgment and order defined for purposes of this Code, see Family Code § 100.
Modification, termination, or setting aside of support order, see Family Code § 3650 et seq.
Property defined for purposes of this Code, see Family Code § 113.
State defined for purposes of this Code, see Family Code § 145.
Support defined for purposes of this Code, see Family Code § 150.
Support order defined for purposes of this Code, see Family Code § 155.

Research References

Forms

West's California Code Forms, Family § 5600, Comment Overview—Intercounty Support Obligations.

§ 5601. Registration by local child support agency of support order made in another county; procedures; motion to vacate; notice of registration

(a) When the local child support agency is responsible for the enforcement of a support order pursuant to Section 17400, the local child support agency may register a support order made in another county by utilizing the procedures set forth in Section 5602 or by filing all of the following in the superior court of the agency's county:

(1) An endorsed file copy of the most recent support order or a copy thereof.

(2) A statement of arrearages, including an accounting of amounts ordered and paid each month, together with any added costs, fees, and interest.

(3) A statement prepared by the local child support agency showing the post office address of the local child support agency, the last known place of residence or post office address of the obligor; the most recent address of the obligor set forth in the licensing records of the Department of Motor Vehicles, if known; and a list of other states and counties in California that are known to the local child support agency in which the original order of support and any modifications are registered.

(b) The filing of the documents described in subdivision (a) constitutes registration under this chapter.

(c) Promptly upon registration, the local child support agency, in compliance with the requirements of Section 1013 of the Code of Civil Procedure, or in any other manner as provided by law, shall serve the obligor with copies of the documents described in subdivision (a).

(d) If a motion to vacate registration is filed under Section 5603, a party may introduce into evidence copies of pleadings, documents, or orders that have been filed in the original court or other courts where the support order has been registered or modified. Certified copies of the documents shall not be required unless a party objects to the authenticity or accuracy of the document, in which case it shall be the responsibility of the party who is asserting the authenticity of the document to obtain a certified copy of the questioned document.

(e) Upon registration, the clerk of the court shall forward a notice of registration to the courts in other counties and states in which the original order for support and any modifications were issued or registered. Further proceedings regarding the obligor's support obligations shall not be filed in other counties.

(f) The procedure prescribed by this section may also be used to register support or wage and earnings assignment orders of other California jurisdictions that previously have been registered for purposes of enforcement only pursuant to the Uniform Interstate Family Support Act (Part 6 (commencing with Section 5700.101)) in another California county. The local child support agency may register such an order by filing an endorsed file copy of the registered California order plus any subsequent orders, including procedural amendments.

(g) The Judicial Council shall develop the forms necessary to effectuate this section. These forms shall be available no later than July 1, 1998. *(Added by Stats.1997, c. 599 (A.B.573), § 35. Amended by Stats.2000, c. 808 (A.B.1358), § 69, eff. Sept. 28, 2000; Stats.2015, c. 493 (S.B.646), § 4, eff. Jan. 1, 2016; Stats.2019, c. 115 (A.B.1817), § 56, eff. Jan. 1, 2020.)*

Cross References

Child support, generally, see Family Code § 3900 et seq.
County defined for purposes of this Code, see Family Code § 67.
Expedited child support orders, see Family Code § 3620 et seq.
Family support defined for purposes of this Code, see Family Code § 92.
Health insurance coverage for supported children, see Family Code § 3750 et seq.
Judgment and order defined for purposes of this Code, see Family Code § 100.
Modification, termination, or setting aside of support order, see Family Code § 3650 et seq.
Notice, actual and constructive, defined, see Civil Code § 18.
Proceeding defined for purposes of this Code, see Family Code § 110.
State defined for purposes of this Code, see Family Code § 145.
Support defined for purposes of this Code, see Family Code § 150.
Support order defined for purposes of this Code, see Family Code § 155.

Research References

Forms

West's California Code Forms, Family § 5230, Comment Overview—Earnings Assignment Order.
West's California Code Forms, Family § 5600, Comment Overview—Intercounty Support Obligations.
West's California Judicial Council Forms FL-650, Statement for Registration of California Support Order (Governmental).
West's California Judicial Council Forms FL-651, Notice of Registration of California Support Order (Governmental).

§ 5602. Registration of order by obligee; procedure; notice

(a) An obligee other than the local child support agency may register an order issued in this state using the same procedures specified in subdivision (a) of Section 5601, except that the obligee shall prepare and file the statement of registration. The statement shall be verified and signed by the obligee showing the mailing address of the obligee, the last known place of residence or mailing address of the obligor, and a list of other states and counties in California in which, to the obligee's knowledge, the original order of support and any modifications are registered.

(b) Upon receipt of the documents described in subdivision (a) of Section 5601, the clerk of the court shall file them without payment of a filing fee or other cost to the obligee. The filing constitutes registration under this chapter.

(c) Promptly upon registration, the clerk of the court shall send, by any form of mail requiring a return receipt from the addressee only, to the obligor at the address given a notice of the registration with a copy of the registered support order and the post office address of the obligee. Proof shall be made to the satisfaction of the court that the obligor personally received the notice of registration by mail or other method of service. A return receipt signed by the obligor shall be satisfactory evidence of personal receipt. *(Added by Stats.1997, c. 599 (A.B.573), § 35. Amended by Stats.2000, c. 808 (A.B.1358), § 70, eff. Sept. 28, 2000.)*

Cross References

Child support, generally, see Family Code § 3900 et seq.
County defined for purposes of this Code, see Family Code § 67.
Expedited child support orders, see Family Code § 3620 et seq.
Health insurance coverage for supported children, see Family Code § 3750 et seq.
Judgment and order defined for purposes of this Code, see Family Code § 100.
Modification, termination, or setting aside of support order, see Family Code § 3650 et seq.
Notice, actual and constructive, defined, see Civil Code § 18.
State defined for purposes of this Code, see Family Code § 145.
Support defined for purposes of this Code, see Family Code § 150.
Support order defined for purposes of this Code, see Family Code § 155.

Research References

Forms

West's California Code Forms, Family § 5230, Comment Overview—Earnings Assignment Order.
West's California Code Forms, Family § 5600, Comment Overview—Intercounty Support Obligations.
West's California Judicial Council Forms FL-440, Statement for Registration of California Support Order.

§ 5603. Motion to vacate registration; procedure; hearing

(a) An obligor shall have 20 days after the service of notice of the registration of a California order of support in which to file a noticed motion requesting the court to vacate the registration or for other relief. In an action under this section, there shall be no joinder of actions, coordination of actions, or cross-complaints, and the claims or defenses shall be limited strictly to the identity of the obligor, the validity of the underlying California support order, or the accuracy of the obligee's statement of the amount of support remaining unpaid

§ 5603

unless the amount has been previously established by a judgment or order. The obligor shall serve a copy of the motion, personally or by first-class mail, on the local child support agency, private attorney representing the obligee, or obligee who is self-representing who filed the request for registration of the order, not less than 15 days prior to the date on which the motion is to be heard. If service is by mail, Section 1013 of the Code of Civil Procedure applies. If the obligor does not file the motion within 20 days, the registered California support order and all other documents filed pursuant to subdivision (a) of Section 5601 or Section 5602 are confirmed.

(b) At the hearing on the motion to vacate the registration of the order, the obligor may present only matters that would be available to the obligor as defenses in an action to enforce a support judgment. If the obligor shows, and the court finds, that an appeal from the order is pending or that a stay of execution has been granted, the court shall stay enforcement of the order until the appeal is concluded, the time for appeal has expired, or the order is vacated, upon satisfactory proof that the obligor has furnished security for payment of the support ordered. If the obligor shows, and the court finds, any ground upon which enforcement of a California support order may be stayed, the court shall stay enforcement of the order for an appropriate period if the obligor furnishes security for payment of support. *(Added by Stats.1997, c. 599 (A.B.573), § 35. Amended by Stats.2000, c. 808 (A.B.1358), § 71, eff. Sept. 28, 2000; Stats.2019, c. 115 (A.B.1817), § 57, eff. Jan. 1, 2020.)*

Cross References

Appeals from order in arbitration, see Code of Civil Procedure §§ 1294, 1294.2.
Appeals in civil actions, generally, see Code of Civil Procedure § 901 et seq.
Appeals in criminal cases,
 Appeals from Superior Courts, see Penal Code § 1235 et seq.
 Appeals to Superior Courts, see Penal Code § 1466 et seq.
Attorneys, State Bar Act, see Business and Professions Code § 6000.
Child support, generally, see Family Code § 3900 et seq.
Computation of time, see Code of Civil Procedure §§ 12, 12a; Government Code § 6800 et seq.
Judgment and order defined for purposes of this Code, see Family Code § 100.
Notice, actual and constructive, defined, see Civil Code § 18.
Support defined for purposes of this Code, see Family Code § 150.
Support order defined for purposes of this Code, see Family Code § 155.

Research References

Forms

West's California Code Forms, Family § 5230, Comment Overview—Earnings Assignment Order.
West's California Judicial Council Forms FL–440, Statement for Registration of California Support Order.
West's California Judicial Council Forms FL–445, Request for Hearing Regarding Registration of California Support Order (Family Law–Governmental).
West's California Judicial Council Forms FL–650, Statement for Registration of California Support Order (Governmental).

§ 5604. Effect of previous determination of paternity made by another state

A previous determination of paternity made by another state, whether established through voluntary acknowledgment procedures in effect in that state or through an administrative or judicial process shall be given full faith and credit by the courts in this state, and shall have the same effect as a paternity determination made in this state and may be enforced and satisfied in a like manner. *(Added by Stats.1997, c. 599 (A.B.573), § 35.)*

Cross References

Administrative Procedure Act, see Government Code §§ 11340 et seq., 11370 et seq., 11400 et seq., 11500 et seq.
Administrative proceedings, judicial review, see Government Code § 11523.
State defined for purposes of this Code, see Family Code § 145.

§§ 5605, 5606. Repealed by Stats.1993, c. 219 (A.B.1500), § 153.5

CHAPTER 9. PRIVATE CHILD SUPPORT COLLECTORS

Section
5610. "Private child support collector" defined.
5611. Contract for child support collection between private child support collector and obligee; contents; notice of cancellation.
5612. Advertising disclosures.
5613. Cancellation or termination of contract with private child support collector.
5614. Duties of private child support collector; prohibited acts.
5615. Remedies for violations of chapter; attorney acting as private child support collector subject to statutes, rules, and cases governing attorney conduct.
5616. Court orders for child support and child support agreements; inclusion of provision for separate money judgment to pay fee of private child support collector; enforcement; assignment.
5650 to 5700. Repealed.

§ 5610. "Private child support collector" defined

For the purposes of this chapter, "private child support collector" means any individual, corporation, attorney, nonprofit organization, or other nongovernmental entity who is engaged by an obligee to collect child support ordered by a court or other tribunal for a fee or other consideration. The term does not include any attorney who addresses issues of ongoing child support or child support arrearages in the course of an action to establish parentage or a child support obligation, a proceeding under Division 10 (commencing with Section 6200), a proceeding for dissolution of marriage, legal separation, or nullity of marriage, or in postjudgment or modification proceedings related to any of those actions. A "private child support collector" includes any private, nongovernmental attorney whose business is substantially comprised of the collection or enforcement of child support. As used in this section, substantially means that at least 50 percent of the attorney's business, either in terms of remuneration or time spent, is comprised of the activity of seeking to collect or enforce child support obligations for other individuals. *(Added by Stats.2006, c. 797 (A.B.2781), § 1.)*

§ 5611. Contract for child support collection between private child support collector and obligee; contents; notice of cancellation

(a) A contract for the collection of child support between a private child support collector and an obligee shall be in writing and written in simple language, in at least 10–point type, signed by the private child support collector and the obligee. The contract shall be delivered to the obligee in a paper form that the obligee may retain for their records. The contract shall include all of the following:

(1) An explanation of the fees imposed by contract and otherwise permitted by law and an example of how they are calculated and deducted.

(2) A statement that the amount of fees to be charged is set by the agency and is not set by state law.

(3) A statement that the private child support collector cannot charge fees on current support if the obligee received any current child support during the 6 months preceding execution of the contract with the private collector.

(4) An explanation of the nature of the services to be provided.

(5) The expected duration of the contract, stated as a length of time or as an amount to be collected by the collection agency.

(6) An explanation of the opportunities available to the obligee or private child support collector to cancel the contract or other conditions under which the contract terminates.

(7) The mailing address, street address, telephone numbers, facsimile numbers, and internet address or location of the private child support collector.

(8) A statement that the private child support collector is not a governmental entity and that governmental entities in California provide child support collection and enforcement services free of charge.

(9) A statement that the private child support collector collects only money owed to the obligee and not support assigned to the state or county due to the receipt of CalWORKs or Temporary Assistance to Needy Families.

(10) A statement that the private child support collector will not retain fees from collections that are primarily attributable to the actions of a governmental entity or any other person or entity and is required by law to refund any fees improperly retained.

(11) A statement that the obligee may continue to receive, or may pursue, services through a governmental entity to collect support, and the private child support collection agency will not require or request that the obligee cease or refrain from engaging those services.

(12) A notice that the private child support collector is required to keep and maintain case records for a period of four years and four months, after the expiration of the contract and may thereafter destroy or otherwise dispose of the records. The obligee may, prior to destruction or disposal, retrieve those portions of the records that are not confidential.

(13) A "Notice of Cancellation," which shall be included with the contract and which shall contain, in the same size font as the contract, the following statement, written in the same language as the contract:

"Notice of Cancellation
You may cancel this contract, without any penalty or obligation, within 15 business days from the date the contract is signed or you receive this notice, whichever is later, or at any time if the private child support collector commits a material breach of any provision of the contract or a material violation of any provision of this chapter with respect to the obligee or the obligor, or _____ (all other reasons for cancellation permitted).
To cancel this contract, mail or deliver a signed copy of this cancellation notice or any other written notice to _____(name of private child support collector) at _____ (address for mail or delivery) no later than midnight on _____(date).
I am canceling this contract._____(date) _____(signature)"

(14) The following statement by the obligee on the first page of the contract:

"I understand that this contract calls for (name of private child support collector) to collect money owed to me, and not money owed to the state or county. If child support is owed to the state or county because I am receiving or have received program benefits from CalWORKs or Temporary Assistance to Needy Families, then (name of private child support collector) cannot collect that money for me. If I start to receive program benefits from CalWORKs or Temporary Assistance to Needy Families during this contract, I must notify (name of private child support collector) in writing."

"I declare by my signature below that the child support to be collected for me pursuant to this contract is not assigned to the state or county as of the time I sign this contract. I agree that I will give written notice to the private child support collector if I apply for program benefits under CalWORKs or Temporary Assistance to Needy Families during the term of this contract."

(15)(A) The following statement by the obligee immediately above the signature line of the contract:

"I understand that (name of private child support collector) will charge a fee for all the current child support and arrears it collects for me until the entire contract amount is collected or the contract terminates for another reason. I also understand that depending on the frequency and size of payments, it could take years for the amount specified in my contract to be collected. This means that if (name of private child support collector) is collecting my current support by wage withholding or other means, I will not receive the full amount of my periodic court-ordered current support until the contract terminates since (name of private child support collector) will be deducting its fee from the periodic court-ordered current support it collects for me."

(B) The statement required by subparagraph (A) shall:

(i) Be in a type size that is at least equal to one-quarter of the largest type size used in the contract. In no event shall the disclosure be printed in less than 8–point type.

(ii) Be in a contrasting style, and contrasting color or bold type, that is equally or more visible than the type used in the contract.

(b) The disclosures required by paragraph (1) of subdivision (a) of Section 5612 shall be printed in the contract, as follows:

(1) In a type size that is at least equal to one-quarter of the largest type size used in the contract. In no event shall the disclosure be printed in less than 8–point type.

(2) In a contrasting style, and contrasting color or bold type that is equally or more visible than the type used in the contract.

(3) Immediately above, below, or beside the stated fee without any intervening words, pictures, marks, or symbols.

(4) In the same language as the contract. *(Added by Stats.2006, c. 797 (A.B.2781), § 1. Amended by Stats.2019, c. 115 (A.B.1817), § 58, eff. Jan. 1, 2020.)*

§ 5612. Advertising disclosures

(a) Each private child support collector:

(1) That charges any initial fee, processing fee, application fee, filing fee, or other fee or assessment that must be paid by an obligee regardless of whether any child support collection is made on behalf of the obligee shall make the following disclosure in every radio, television, or print advertisement intended for a target audience consisting primarily of California residents:

"(Name of private child support collector) is not a governmental entity and charges an upfront fee for its services even if it does not collect anything."

(2) That does not charge any fee or assessment specified in paragraph (1) shall make the following disclosure in every radio, television, or print advertisement aired for a target audience consisting primarily of California residents:

"(Name of private child support collector) is not a governmental entity and charges a fee for its services."

(b) The disclosures required in subdivision (a) shall also be stated during the first 30 seconds of any initial telephone conversation with an obligee and in the private child support collector's contract. *(Added by Stats.2006, c. 797 (A.B.2781), § 1.)*

§ 5613. Cancellation or termination of contract with private child support collector

(a) An obligee shall have the right to cancel a contract with a private support collector under either of the following circumstances:

(1) Within 15 business days of the later of signing the contract, or receiving a blank notice of cancellation form, or at any time if the

§ 5613

private child support collector commits a material breach of any provision of the contract or a material violation of any provision of this chapter with respect to the obligee or the obligor.

(2) At the end of any 12-month period in which the total amount collected by the private child support collector is less than 50 percent of the amount scheduled to be paid under a payment plan.

(b) A contract shall automatically terminate when the contract term has expired or the contract amount has been collected, whichever occurs first. *(Added by Stats.2006, c. 797 (A.B.2781), § 1.)*

§ 5614. Duties of private child support collector; prohibited acts

(a) A private child support collector shall do all of the following:

(1)(A) Provide to an obligee all of the following information:

(i) The name of, and any other identifying information relating to, an obligor who made child support payments collected by the private child support collector.

(ii) The amount of support collected by the private child support collector.

(iii) The date on which each amount was received by the private child support collector.

(iv) The date on which each amount received by the private child support collector was sent to the obligee.

(v) The amount of the payment sent to the obligee.

(vi) The source of payment of support collected and the actions affirmatively taken by the private child support collector that resulted in the payment.

(vii) The amount and percentage of each payment kept by the private child support collector as its fee.

(B) The information required by subparagraph (A) shall be made available, at the option of the obligee, by mail, telephone, or via secure Internet access. If provided by mail, the notice shall be sent at least quarterly and, if provided by any other method, the information shall be updated and made available at least monthly. Information accessed by telephone and the Internet shall be up to date.

(2) Maintain records of all child support collections made on behalf of a client who is an obligee. The records required under this section shall be maintained by the private child support collector for the duration of the contract plus a period of four years and four months from the date of the last child support payment collected by the private child support collector on behalf of an obligee. In addition to information required by paragraph (1), the private child support collector shall maintain the following:

(A) A copy of the order establishing the child support obligation under which a collection was made by the private child support collector.

(B) Records of all correspondence between the private child support collector and the obligee or obligor in a case.

(C) Any other pertinent information relating to the child support obligation, including any case, cause, or docket number of the court having jurisdiction over the matter and official government payment records obtained by the private child support collector on behalf of, and at the request of, the obligee.

(3) Safeguard case records in a manner reasonably expected to prevent intentional or accidental disclosure of confidential information pertaining to the obligee or obligor, including providing necessary protections for records maintained in an automated system.

(4) Ensure that every person who contracts with a private child support collector has the right to review all files and documents, both paper and electronic, in the possession of the private child support collector for the information specified in this paragraph regarding that obligee's case that are not required by law to be kept confidential. The obligee, during regular business hours, shall be provided reasonable access to and copies of the files and records of the private child support collector regarding all moneys received, collection attempts made, fees retained or paid to the private child support collector, and moneys disbursed to the obligee. The private child support collector may not charge a fee for access to the files and records, but may require the obligee to pay up to three cents ($0.03) per page for the copies prior to their release.

(5) Provide, prior to commencing collection activities, written notice of a contract with an obligee to the local child support agency that is enforcing the obligee's support order, if known, or the local child support agency for the county in which the obligee resides as of the time the contract is signed by the obligee. The notice shall identify the obligee, the obligor, and the amount of the arrearage claimed by the obligee.

(b) A private child support collector shall not do any of the following:

(1) Charge fees on current support if the obligee received any current child support during the six months preceding execution of the contract with the private child support collector. A private child support collector shall inquire of the obligee and record the month and year of the last current support payment and may rely on information provided by the obligee in determining whether a fee may be charged on current support.

(2) Improperly retain fees from collections that are primarily attributable to the actions of a governmental entity. The private child support collector shall refund all of those fees to the obligee immediately upon discovery or notice of the improper retention of fees.

(3) Collect or attempt to collect child support by means of conduct that is prohibited of a debt collector collecting a consumer debt under Sections 1788.10 to 1788.16, inclusive, of the Civil Code. This chapter does not modify, alter, or amend the definition of a debt or a debt collector under the Rosenthal Fair Debt Collection Practices Act (Title 1.6C (commencing with Section 1788) of Part 4 of Division 3 of the Civil Code).

(4) Misstate the amount of the fee that may be lawfully paid to the private child support collector for the performance of the contract or the identity of the person who is obligated to pay that fee.

(5) Make a false representation of the amount of child support to be collected. A private child support collector is not in violation of this paragraph if it reasonably relied on sufficient documentation provided by the government entity collecting child support, a court with jurisdiction over the support obligation, or from the obligee, or upon sufficient documentation provided by the obligor.

(6) Ask a party other than the obligor to pay the child support obligation, unless that party is legally responsible for the obligation or is the legal representative of the obligor.

(7) On or after January 1, 2007, require, as a condition of providing services to the obligee, that the obligee waive any right or procedure provided for in state law regarding the right to file and pursue a civil action, or that the obligee agree to resolve disputes in a jurisdiction outside of California or to the application of laws other than those of California, as provided by law. Any waiver by the obligee of the right to file and pursue a civil action, the right to file and pursue a civil action in California, or the right to rely upon California law as provided by law must be knowing, voluntary, and not made a condition of doing business with the private child support collector. Any waiver, including, but not limited to, an agreement to arbitrate or regarding choice of forum or choice of law, that is required as a condition of doing business with the private child support collector, shall be presumed involuntary, unconscionable, against public policy, and unenforceable. The private child support collector has the burden of proving that any waiver of rights, including an agreement to arbitrate a claim or regarding choice of forum or choice of law, was knowing, voluntary, and not made a condition of the contract with the obligee. *(Added by Stats.2006, c.*

797 (A.B.2781), § 1. Amended by Stats.2007, c. 130 (A.B.299), § 89; Stats.2018, c. 504 (A.B.3248), § 3, eff. Jan. 1, 2019.)

§ 5615. Remedies for violations of chapter; attorney acting as private child support collector subject to statutes, rules, and cases governing attorney conduct

(a)(1) A person may bring an action for actual damages incurred as a result of a violation of this chapter.

(2) In addition to actual damages, a private child support collector who willfully and knowingly violates the provisions of this chapter shall be liable for a civil penalty in an amount determined by the court, which may not be less than one hundred dollars ($100) nor more than one thousand dollars ($1,000).

(3)(A) The prevailing party in any action pursuant to this chapter shall be entitled to recover the costs of the action. Reasonable attorney's fees, which shall be based on the time necessarily expended to enforce the liability, shall be awarded to a prevailing party, other than the private child support collector, asserting rights under this chapter. Reasonable attorney's fees may be awarded to a prevailing private child support collector if the court finds that the party bringing the action did not prosecute the action in good faith.

(B) In an action by an obligor under this chapter, the private child support collector shall have no civil liability under this chapter to the obligor under any circumstance in which a debt collector would not have civil liability under Section 1788.30 of the Civil Code.

(4) A private child support collector is not in violation of this chapter if the private child support collector shows, by a preponderance of the evidence, that the action complained of was not intentional and resulted from a bona fide error that occurred notwithstanding the use of reasonable procedures to avoid the error.

(5) The remedies provided in this section are cumulative and are in addition to any other procedures, rights, or remedies available under any other law.

(b) Any waiver of the rights, requirements, and remedies provided by this chapter violates public policy and is void.

(c) Notwithstanding any other provision of this chapter, including provisions establishing a right of cancellation and requiring notice thereof, any contract for the collection of child support between an attorney who is a "private child support collector" pursuant to Section 5610 shall conform to the statutes, rules, and case law governing attorney conduct, including the provisions of law providing that a contract with an attorney is cancelable by the attorney's client at any time. Upon cancellation of that contract, the attorney may seek compensation as provided by law, including, if applicable, a claim for the reasonable value of any services rendered to the attorney's client pursuant to the doctrine of quantum meruit, provided those services lead to the collection of support and the compensation is limited to what would have been collected had the contract been in effect. To the extent that the provisions of this chapter are in conflict with the provisions of state law governing the conduct of attorneys, this chapter shall control. If there is no conflict, an attorney who is a "private child support collector" pursuant to Section 5610 shall conform to the provisions of this chapter. *(Added by Stats.2006, c. 797 (A.B.2781), § 1.)*

§ 5616. Court orders for child support and child support agreements; inclusion of provision for separate money judgment to pay fee of private child support collector; enforcement; assignment

(a) Every court order for child support issued on or after January 1, 2010, and every child support agreement providing for the payment of child support approved by a court on or after January 1, 2010, shall include a separate money judgment owed by the child support obligor to pay a fee not to exceed 33 and ⅓ percent of the total amount in arrears, and not to exceed 50 percent of the fee as charged by a private child support collector pursuant to a contract complying with this chapter and any other child support collections costs expressly permitted by the child support order for the collection efforts undertaken by the private child support collector. The money judgment shall be in favor of the private child support collector and the child support obligee, jointly, but shall not constitute a private child support collector lien on real property unless an abstract of judgment is recorded pursuant to subdivision (d). Except as provided in subdivision (c), the money judgment may be enforced by the private child support collector by any means available to the obligee for the enforcement of the child support order without any additional action or order by the court. Nothing in this chapter shall be construed to grant the private child support collector any enforcement remedies beyond those authorized by federal or state law. Any fee collected from the obligor pursuant to a contract complying with this chapter, shall not constitute child support.

(b) If the child support order makes the obligor responsible for payment of collection fees and costs, fees that are deducted by a private child support collector may not be credited against child support arrearages or interest owing on arrearages or any other money owed by the obligor to the obligee.

(c) If the order for child support requires payment of collection fees and costs by the obligor, then not later than five days after the date that the private child support collector makes its first collection, written notice shall be provided to the obligor of (1) the amount of arrearages subject to collection, (2) the amount of the collection that shall be applied to the arrearage, and (3) the amount of the collection that shall be applied to the fees and costs of collection. The notice shall provide that, in addition to any other procedures available, the obligor has 30 days to file a motion to contest the amount of collection fees and costs assessed against the obligor.

(d) Any fees or monetary obligations resulting from the contract between an obligee parent and a private child support collector, or moneys owed to a private child support collector by the obligor parent or obligee parent as a result of the private child support collector's efforts, does not create a lien on real property, unless an abstract of judgment is obtained from the court and recorded by the private child support collector against the real property in the county in which it is located, nor shall that amount be added to any existing lien created by a recorded abstract of support or be added to an obligation on any abstract of judgment. A private child support collector lien shall have the force, effect, and priority of a judgment lien.

(e) An assignment to a private child support collector is a voluntary assignment for the purpose of collecting the domestic support obligation as defined in Section 101 of Title 11 of the United States Bankruptcy Code (11 U.S.C. Sec. 101 (14 A)). *(Added by Stats.2006, c. 797 (A.B.2781), § 1. Amended by Stats.2011, c. 296 (A.B.1023), § 92.)*

Research References

Forms

California Practice Guide: Rutter Family Law Forms Form 5:1, Stipulation to Orders Pending Trial (Attorney-Drafted).

California Practice Guide: Rutter Family Law Forms Form 6:2, Stipulation Re Child Support and Order Thereon (Attorney-Drafted).

California Practice Guide: Rutter Family Law Forms Form 11:20, Sample Trial Brief.

California Practice Guide: Rutter Family Law Forms Form 17:1, Stipulation and Order for Modification of Spousal Support, Child Support, Custody and Visitation.

§§ 5650 to 5700. Repealed by Stats.1993, c. 219 (A.B.1500), § 153.5

Part 6
UNIFORM INTERSTATE FAMILY SUPPORT ACT

Chapter	Section
1. General Provisions	5700.101

SUPPORT

Chapter	Section
2. Jurisdiction	5700.201
3. Civil Provisions of General Application	5700.301
4. Establishment of Support Order or Determination of Parentage	5700.401
5. Enforcement of Support Order Without Registration	5700.501
6. Registration, Enforcement, and Modification of Support Order	5700.601
7. Support Proceeding Under Convention	5700.701
8. Interstate Rendition	5700.801
9. Miscellaneous Provisions	5700.901

CHAPTER 1. GENERAL PROVISIONS

Section
5700.101. Short title; federal mandate.
5700.102. Definitions.
5700.103. State tribunal and state enforcement agency.
5700.104. Cumulative remedies.
5700.105. Application of part to resident of foreign country and foreign support proceeding.

§ 5700.101. Short title; federal mandate

(a) This part may be cited as the Uniform Interstate Family Support Act.

(b) There is a federal mandate set forth in Section 666(f) of Title 42 of the United States Code requiring California to adopt and have in effect the Uniform Interstate Family Support Act, including any amendments officially adopted by the National Council of Commissioners on Uniform State Laws as of September 30, 2008. *(Added by Stats.2015, c. 493 (S.B.646), § 5, eff. Jan. 1, 2016.)*

Research References

Forms
19 Am. Jur. Pl. & Pr. Forms Parent and Child § 56, Introductory Comments.

§ 5700.102. Definitions

In this part:

(1) "Child" means an individual, whether over or under the age of majority, who is or is alleged to be owed a duty of support by the individual's parent or who is or is alleged to be the beneficiary of a support order directed to the parent.

(2) "Child–support order" means a support order for a child, including a child who has attained the age of majority under the law of the issuing state or foreign country.

(3) "Convention" means the Convention on the International Recovery of Child Support and Other Forms of Family Maintenance, concluded at The Hague on November 23, 2007.

(4) "Duty of support" means an obligation imposed or imposable by law to provide support for a child, spouse, or former spouse, including an unsatisfied obligation to provide support.

(5) "Foreign country" means a country, including a political subdivision thereof, other than the United States, that authorizes the issuance of support orders and:

(A) Which has been declared under the law of the United States to be a foreign reciprocating country;

(B) Which has established a reciprocal arrangement for child support with this state as provided in Section 5700.308;

(C) Which has enacted a law or established procedures for the issuance and enforcement of support orders which are substantially similar to the procedures under this part; or

(D) In which the Convention is in force with respect to the United States.

(6) "Foreign support order" means a support order of a foreign tribunal.

(7) "Foreign tribunal" means a court, administrative agency, or quasi-judicial entity of a foreign country which is authorized to establish, enforce, or modify support orders or to determine parentage of a child. The term includes a competent authority under the Convention.

(8) "Home state" means the state or foreign country in which a child lived with a parent or a person acting as parent for at least six consecutive months immediately preceding the time of filing of a petition or comparable pleading for support and, if a child is less than six months old, the state or foreign country in which the child lived from birth with any of them. A period of temporary absence of any of them is counted as part of the six-month or other period.

(9) "Income" includes earnings or other periodic entitlements to money from any source and any other property subject to withholding for support under the law of this state.

(10) "Income–withholding order" means an order or other legal process directed to an obligor's employer, or other debtor, as defined by Section 5208, to withhold support from the income of the obligor.

(11) "Initiating tribunal" means the tribunal of a state or foreign country from which a petition or comparable pleading is forwarded or in which a petition or comparable pleading is filed for forwarding to another state or foreign country.

(12) "Issuing foreign country" means the foreign country in which a tribunal issues a support order or a judgment determining parentage of a child.

(13) "Issuing state" means the state in which a tribunal issues a support order or a judgment determining parentage of a child.

(14) "Issuing tribunal" means the tribunal of a state or foreign country that issues a support order or a judgment determining parentage of a child.

(15) "Law" includes decisional and statutory law and rules and regulations having the force of law.

(16) "Obligee" means:

(A) an individual to whom a duty of support is or is alleged to be owed or in whose favor a support order or a judgment determining parentage of a child has been issued;

(B) a foreign country, state, or political subdivision of a state to which the rights under a duty of support or support order have been assigned or which has independent claims based on financial assistance provided to an individual obligee in place of child support;

(C) an individual seeking a judgment determining parentage of the individual's child; or

(D) a person that is a creditor in a proceeding under Chapter 7.

(17) "Obligor" means an individual, or the estate of a decedent that:

(A) owes or is alleged to owe a duty of support;

(B) is alleged but has not been adjudicated to be a parent of a child;

(C) is liable under a support order; or

(D) is a debtor in a proceeding under Chapter 7.

(18) "Outside this state" means a location in another state or a country other than the United States, whether or not the country is a foreign country.

(19) "Person" means an individual, corporation, business trust, estate, trust, partnership, limited liability company, association, joint venture, public corporation, government or governmental subdivision, agency, or instrumentality, or any other legal or commercial entity.

(20) "Record" means information that is inscribed on a tangible medium or that is stored in an electronic or other medium and is retrievable in perceivable form.

(21) "Register" means to file in a tribunal of this state a support order or judgment determining parentage of a child issued in another state or a foreign country.

(22) "Registering tribunal" means a tribunal in which a support order or judgment determining parentage of a child is registered.

(23) "Responding state" means a state in which a petition or comparable pleading for support or to determine parentage of a child is filed or to which a petition or comparable pleading is forwarded for filing from another state or a foreign country.

(24) "Responding tribunal" means the authorized tribunal in a responding state or foreign country.

(25) "Spousal–support order" means a support order for a spouse or former spouse of the obligor.

(26) "State" means a state of the United States, the District of Columbia, Puerto Rico, the United States Virgin Islands, or any territory or insular possession under the jurisdiction of the United States. The term includes an Indian nation or tribe.

(27) "Support enforcement agency" means a public official, governmental entity, or private agency authorized to:

(A) seek enforcement of support orders or laws relating to the duty of support;

(B) seek establishment or modification of child support;

(C) request determination of parentage of a child;

(D) attempt to locate obligors or their assets; or

(E) request determination of the controlling child-support order.

(28) "Support order" means a judgment, decree, order, decision, or directive, whether temporary, final, or subject to modification, issued in a state or foreign country for the benefit of a child, a spouse, or a former spouse, which provides for monetary support, health care, arrearages, retroactive support, or reimbursement for financial assistance provided to an individual obligee in place of child support. The term may include related costs and fees, interest, income withholding, automatic adjustment, reasonable attorney's fees, and other relief.

(29) "Tribunal" means a court, administrative agency, or quasi-judicial entity authorized to establish, enforce, or modify support orders or to determine parentage of a child. *(Added by Stats.2015, c. 493 (S.B.646), § 5, eff. Jan. 1, 2016.)*

Research References

Forms

West's California Judicial Council Forms FL–590A, UIFSA Child Support Order Jurisdictional Attachment.

§ 5700.103. State tribunal and state enforcement agency

(a) The superior court is the tribunal of this state.

(b) The Department of Child Support Services is the support enforcement agency of this state. *(Added by Stats.2015, c. 493 (S.B.646), § 5, eff. Jan. 1, 2016.)*

§ 5700.104. Cumulative remedies

(a) Remedies provided by this part are cumulative and do not affect the availability of remedies under other law or the recognition of a foreign support order on the basis of comity.

(b) This part does not:

(1) provide the exclusive method of establishing or enforcing a support order under the law of this state; or

(2) grant a tribunal of this state jurisdiction to render judgment or issue an order relating to child custody or visitation in a proceeding under this part. *(Added by Stats.2015, c. 493 (S.B.646), § 5, eff. Jan. 1, 2016.)*

§ 5700.105. Application of part to resident of foreign country and foreign support proceeding

(a) A tribunal of this state shall apply Chapters 1 through 6 and, as applicable, Chapter 7, to a support proceeding involving:

(1) a foreign support order;

(2) a foreign tribunal; or

(3) an obligee, obligor, or child residing in a foreign country.

(b) A tribunal of this state that is requested to recognize and enforce a support order on the basis of comity may apply the procedural and substantive provisions of Chapters 1 through 6.

(c) Chapter 7 applies only to a support proceeding under the Convention. In such a proceeding, if a provision of Chapter 7 is inconsistent with Chapters 1 through 6, Chapter 7 controls. *(Added by Stats.2015, c. 493 (S.B.646), § 5, eff. Jan. 1, 2016.)*

CHAPTER 2. JURISDICTION

Section
5700.201. Bases for jurisdiction over nonresident.
5700.202. Duration of personal jurisdiction.
5700.203. Initiating and responding tribunal of state.
5700.204. Simultaneous proceedings.
5700.205. Continuing, exclusive jurisdiction to modify child-support order.
5700.206. Initiating tribunal to request tribunal of another state to enforce; continuing jurisdiction to enforce child-support order.
5700.207. Determination of controlling child-support order.
5700.208. Child-support order for two or more obligees.
5700.209. Credit for payments.
5700.210. Application of part to nonresident subject to personal jurisdiction.
5700.211. Continuing, exclusive jurisdiction to modify spousal-support order.

§ 5700.201. Bases for jurisdiction over nonresident

(a) In a proceeding to establish or enforce a support order or to determine parentage of a child, a tribunal of this state may exercise personal jurisdiction over a nonresident individual or the individual's guardian or conservator if:

(1) the individual is personally served with notice within this state;

(2) the individual submits to the jurisdiction of this state by consent in a record, by entering a general appearance, or by filing a responsive document having the effect of waiving any contest to personal jurisdiction;

(3) the individual resided with the child in this state;

(4) the individual resided in this state and provided prenatal expenses or support for the child;

(5) the child resides in this state as a result of the acts or directives of the individual;

(6) the individual engaged in sexual intercourse in this state and the child may have been conceived by that act of intercourse;

(7) the individual has filed a declaration of paternity pursuant to Chapter 3 (commencing with Section 7570) of Part 2 of Division 12, maintained in this state by the Department of Child Support Services; or

(8) there is any other basis consistent with the constitutions of this state and the United States for the exercise of personal jurisdiction.

(b) The bases of personal jurisdiction set forth in subsection (a) or in any other law of this state may not be used to acquire personal

§ 5700.201

jurisdiction for a tribunal of this state to modify a child-support order of another state unless the requirements of Section 5700.611 are met, or, in the case of a foreign support order, unless the requirements of Section 5700.615 are met. *(Added by Stats.2015, c. 493 (S.B.646), § 5, eff. Jan. 1, 2016.)*

§ 5700.202. Duration of personal jurisdiction

Personal jurisdiction acquired by a tribunal of this state in a proceeding under this part or other law of this state relating to a support order continues as long as a tribunal of this state has continuing, exclusive jurisdiction to modify its order or continuing jurisdiction to enforce its order as provided by Sections 5700.205, 5700.206, and 5700.211. *(Added by Stats.2015, c. 493 (S.B.646), § 5, eff. Jan. 1, 2016.)*

§ 5700.203. Initiating and responding tribunal of state

Under this part, a tribunal of this state may serve as an initiating tribunal to forward proceedings to a tribunal of another state, and as a responding tribunal for proceedings initiated in another state or a foreign country. *(Added by Stats.2015, c. 493 (S.B.646), § 5, eff. Jan. 1, 2016.)*

§ 5700.204. Simultaneous proceedings

(a) A tribunal of this state may exercise jurisdiction to establish a support order if the petition or comparable pleading is filed after a pleading is filed in another state or a foreign country only if:

(1) the petition or comparable pleading in this state is filed before the expiration of the time allowed in the other state or the foreign country for filing a responsive pleading challenging the exercise of jurisdiction by the other state or the foreign country;

(2) the contesting party timely challenges the exercise of jurisdiction in the other state or the foreign country; and

(3) if relevant, this state is the home state of the child.

(b) A tribunal of this state may not exercise jurisdiction to establish a support order if the petition or comparable pleading is filed before a petition or comparable pleading is filed in another state or a foreign country if:

(1) the petition or comparable pleading in the other state or foreign country is filed before the expiration of the time allowed in this state for filing a responsive pleading challenging the exercise of jurisdiction by this state;

(2) the contesting party timely challenges the exercise of jurisdiction in this state; and

(3) if relevant, the other state or foreign country is the home state of the child. *(Added by Stats.2015, c. 493 (S.B.646), § 5, eff. Jan. 1, 2016.)*

§ 5700.205. Continuing, exclusive jurisdiction to modify child-support order

(a) A tribunal of this state that has issued a child-support order consistent with the law of this state has and shall exercise continuing, exclusive jurisdiction to modify its child-support order if the order is the controlling order and:

(1) at the time of the filing of a request for modification this state is the residence of the obligor, the individual obligee, or the child for whose benefit the support order is issued; or

(2) even if this state is not the residence of the obligor, the individual obligee, or the child for whose benefit the support order is issued, the parties consent in a record or in open court that the tribunal of this state may continue to exercise jurisdiction to modify its order.

(b) A tribunal of this state that has issued a child-support order consistent with the law of this state may not exercise continuing, exclusive jurisdiction to modify the order if:

(1) all of the parties who are individuals file consent in a record with the tribunal of this state that a tribunal of another state that has jurisdiction over at least one of the parties who is an individual or that is located in the state of residence of the child may modify the order and assume continuing, exclusive jurisdiction; or

(2) its order is not the controlling order.

(c) If a tribunal of another state has issued a child-support order pursuant to the Uniform Interstate Family Support Act or a law substantially similar to that Act which modifies a child-support order of a tribunal of this state, tribunals of this state shall recognize the continuing, exclusive jurisdiction of the tribunal of the other state.

(d) A tribunal of this state that lacks continuing, exclusive jurisdiction to modify a child-support order may serve as an initiating tribunal to request a tribunal of another state to modify a support order issued in that state.

(e) A temporary support order issued ex parte or pending resolution of a jurisdictional conflict does not create continuing, exclusive jurisdiction in the issuing tribunal. *(Added by Stats.2015, c. 493 (S.B.646), § 5, eff. Jan. 1, 2016.)*

Research References

Forms

West's California Judicial Council Forms FL–590A, UIFSA Child Support Order Jurisdictional Attachment.

§ 5700.206. Initiating tribunal to request tribunal of another state to enforce; continuing jurisdiction to enforce child-support order

(a) A tribunal of this state that has issued a child-support order consistent with the law of this state may serve as an initiating tribunal to request a tribunal of another state to enforce:

(1) the order if the order is the controlling order and has not been modified by a tribunal of another state that assumed jurisdiction pursuant to the Uniform Interstate Family Support Act; or

(2) a money judgment for arrears of support and interest on the order accrued before a determination that an order of a tribunal of another state is the controlling order.

(b) A tribunal of this state having continuing jurisdiction over a support order may act as a responding tribunal to enforce the order. *(Added by Stats.2015, c. 493 (S.B.646), § 5, eff. Jan. 1, 2016.)*

§ 5700.207. Determination of controlling child-support order

(a) If a proceeding is brought under this part and only one tribunal has issued a child-support order, the order of that tribunal controls and must be recognized.

(b) If a proceeding is brought under this part, and two or more child-support orders have been issued by tribunals of this state, another state, or a foreign country with regard to the same obligor and same child, a tribunal of this state having personal jurisdiction over both the obligor and individual obligee shall apply the following rules and by order shall determine which order controls and must be recognized:

(1) If only one of the tribunals would have continuing, exclusive jurisdiction under this part, the order of that tribunal controls.

(2) If more than one of the tribunals would have continuing, exclusive jurisdiction under this part:

(A) an order issued by a tribunal in the current home state of the child controls; or

(B) if an order has not been issued in the current home state of the child, the order most recently issued controls.

(3) If none of the tribunals would have continuing, exclusive jurisdiction under this part, the tribunal of this state shall issue a child-support order, which controls.

(c) If two or more child-support orders have been issued for the same obligor and same child, upon request of a party who is an individual or that is a support enforcement agency, a tribunal of this state having personal jurisdiction over both the obligor and the obligee who is an individual shall determine which order controls under subsection (b). The request may be filed with a registration for enforcement or registration for modification pursuant to Chapter 6, or may be filed as a separate proceeding.

(d) A request to determine which is the controlling order must be accompanied by a copy of every child-support order in effect and the applicable record of payments. The requesting party shall give notice of the request to each party whose rights may be affected by the determination.

(e) The tribunal that issued the controlling order under subsection (a), (b), or (c) has continuing jurisdiction to the extent provided in Section 5700.205 or 5700.206.

(f) A tribunal of this state that determines by order which is the controlling order under subsection (b)(1) or (2) or (c), or that issues a new controlling order under subsection(b)(3), shall state in that order:

(1) the basis upon which the tribunal made its determination;

(2) the amount of prospective support, if any; and

(3) the total amount of consolidated arrears and accrued interest, if any, under all of the orders after all payments made are credited as provided by Section 5700.209.

(g) Within 30 days after issuance of an order determining which is the controlling order, the party obtaining the order shall file a certified copy of it in each tribunal that issued or registered an earlier order of child support. A party or support enforcement agency obtaining the order that fails to file a certified copy is subject to appropriate sanctions by a tribunal in which the issue of failure to file arises. The failure to file does not affect the validity or enforceability of the controlling order.

(h) An order that has been determined to be the controlling order, or a judgment for consolidated arrears of support and interest, if any, made pursuant to this section must be recognized in proceedings under this part. *(Added by Stats.2015, c. 493 (S.B.646), § 5, eff. Jan. 1, 2016.)*

§ 5700.208. Child-support order for two or more obligees

In responding to registrations or petitions for enforcement of two or more child-support orders in effect at the same time with regard to the same obligor and different individual obligees, at least one of which was issued by a tribunal of another state or a foreign country, a tribunal of this state shall enforce those orders in the same manner as if the orders had been issued by a tribunal of this state. *(Added by Stats.2015, c. 493 (S.B.646), § 5, eff. Jan. 1, 2016.)*

§ 5700.209. Credit for payments

A tribunal of this state shall credit amounts collected for a particular period pursuant to any child-support order against the amounts owed for the same period under any other child-support order for support of the same child issued by a tribunal of this state, another state, or a foreign country. *(Added by Stats.2015, c. 493 (S.B.646), § 5, eff. Jan. 1, 2016.)*

§ 5700.210. Application of part to nonresident subject to personal jurisdiction

A tribunal of this state exercising personal jurisdiction over a nonresident in a proceeding under this part, under other law of this state relating to a support order, or recognizing a foreign support order may receive evidence from outside this state pursuant to Section 5700.316, communicate with a tribunal outside this state pursuant to Section 5700.317, and obtain discovery through a tribunal outside this state pursuant to Section 5700.318. In all other respects, Chapters 3 through 6 do not apply, and the tribunal shall apply the procedural and substantive law of this state. *(Added by Stats.2015, c. 493 (S.B.646), § 5, eff. Jan. 1, 2016.)*

§ 5700.211. Continuing, exclusive jurisdiction to modify spousal-support order

(a) A tribunal of this state issuing a spousal-support order consistent with the law of this state has continuing, exclusive jurisdiction to modify the spousal-support order throughout the existence of the support obligation.

(b) A tribunal of this state may not modify a spousal-support order issued by a tribunal of another state or a foreign country having continuing, exclusive jurisdiction over that order under the law of that state or foreign country.

(c) A tribunal of this state that has continuing, exclusive jurisdiction over a spousal-support order may serve as:

(1) an initiating tribunal to request a tribunal of another state to enforce the spousal-support order issued in this state; or

(2) a responding tribunal to enforce or modify its own spousal-support order. *(Added by Stats.2015, c. 493 (S.B.646), § 5, eff. Jan. 1, 2016.)*

CHAPTER 3. CIVIL PROVISIONS OF GENERAL APPLICATION

Section
5700.301. Proceedings under part.
5700.302. Proceeding by minor parent.
5700.303. Application of law of state.
5700.304. Duties of initiating tribunal.
5700.305. Duties and powers of responding tribunal.
5700.306. Inappropriate tribunal.
5700.307. Duties of support enforcement agency.
5700.308. Duty of Attorney General or Department of Child Support Services.
5700.309. Private counsel.
5700.310. Duties of state information agency.
5700.311. Pleadings and accompanying documents.
5700.312. Nondisclosure of information in exceptional circumstances.
5700.313. Costs and fees.
5700.314. Limited immunity of petitioner.
5700.315. Nonparentage as defense.
5700.316. Special rules of evidence and procedure.
5700.317. Communications between tribunals.
5700.318. Assistance with discovery.
5700.319. Receipt and disbursement of payments.

§ 5700.301. Proceedings under part

(a) Except as otherwise provided in this part, this chapter applies to all proceedings under this part.

(b) An individual petitioner or a support enforcement agency may initiate a proceeding authorized under this part by filing a petition in an initiating tribunal for forwarding to a responding tribunal or by filing a petition or a comparable pleading directly in a tribunal of another state or a foreign country which has or can obtain personal jurisdiction over the respondent. *(Added by Stats.2015, c. 493 (S.B.646), § 5, eff. Jan. 1, 2016.)*

§ 5700.302. Proceeding by minor parent

A minor parent, or a guardian or other legal representative of a minor parent, may maintain a proceeding on behalf of or for the benefit of the minor's child. *(Added by Stats.2015, c. 493 (S.B.646), § 5, eff. Jan. 1, 2016.)*

§ 5700.303

§ 5700.303. Application of law of state

Except as otherwise provided in this part, a responding tribunal of this state shall:

(1) apply the procedural and substantive law generally applicable to similar proceedings originating in this state and may exercise all powers and provide all remedies available in those proceedings; and

(2) determine the duty of support and the amount payable in accordance with the law and support guidelines of this state. *(Added by Stats.2015, c. 493 (S.B.646), § 5, eff. Jan. 1, 2016.)*

§ 5700.304. Duties of initiating tribunal

(a) Upon the filing of a petition authorized by this part, an initiating tribunal of this state shall forward the petition and its accompanying documents:

(1) to the responding tribunal or appropriate support enforcement agency in the responding state; or

(2) if the identity of the responding tribunal is unknown, to the state information agency of the responding state with a request that they be forwarded to the appropriate tribunal and that receipt be acknowledged.

(b) If requested by the responding tribunal, a tribunal of this state shall issue a certificate or other document and make findings required by the law of the responding state. If the responding tribunal is in a foreign country, upon request the tribunal of this state shall specify the amount of support sought, convert that amount into the equivalent amount in the foreign currency under applicable official or market exchange rate as publicly reported, and provide any other documents necessary to satisfy the requirements of the responding foreign tribunal. *(Added by Stats.2015, c. 493 (S.B.646), § 5, eff. Jan. 1, 2016.)*

§ 5700.305. Duties and powers of responding tribunal

(a) When a responding tribunal of this state receives a petition or comparable pleading from an initiating tribunal or directly pursuant to Section 5700.301(b), it shall cause the petition or pleading to be filed and notify the petitioner where and when it was filed.

(b) A responding tribunal of this state, to the extent not prohibited by other law, may do one or more of the following:

(1) establish or enforce a support order, modify a child-support order, determine the controlling child-support order, or determine parentage of a child;

(2) order an obligor to comply with a support order, specifying the amount and the manner of compliance;

(3) order income withholding;

(4) determine the amount of any arrearages, and specify a method of payment;

(5) enforce orders by civil or criminal contempt, or both;

(6) set aside property for satisfaction of the support order;

(7) place liens and order execution on the obligor's property;

(8) order an obligor to keep the tribunal informed of the obligor's current residential address, electronic-mail address, telephone number, employer, address of employment, and telephone number at the place of employment;

(9) issue a bench warrant for an obligor who has failed after proper notice to appear at a hearing ordered by the tribunal and enter the bench warrant in any local and state computer systems for criminal warrants;

(10) order the obligor to seek appropriate employment by specified methods;

(11) award reasonable attorney's fees and other fees and costs; and

(12) grant any other available remedy.

(c) A responding tribunal of this state shall include in a support order issued under this part, or in the documents accompanying the order, the calculations on which the support order is based.

(d) A responding tribunal of this state may not condition the payment of a support order issued under this part upon compliance by a party with provisions for visitation.

(e) If a responding tribunal of this state issues an order under this part, the tribunal shall send a copy of the order to the petitioner and the respondent and to the initiating tribunal, if any.

(f) If requested to enforce a support order, arrears, or judgment or modify a support order stated in a foreign currency, a responding tribunal of this state shall convert the amount stated in the foreign currency to the equivalent amount in dollars under the applicable official or market exchange rate as publicly reported. *(Added by Stats.2015, c. 493 (S.B.646), § 5, eff. Jan. 1, 2016.)*

§ 5700.306. Inappropriate tribunal

If a petition or comparable pleading is received by an inappropriate tribunal of this state, the tribunal shall forward the pleading and accompanying documents to an appropriate tribunal of this state or another state and notify the petitioner where and when the pleading was sent. *(Added by Stats.2015, c. 493 (S.B.646), § 5, eff. Jan. 1, 2016.)*

§ 5700.307. Duties of support enforcement agency

(a) A support enforcement agency of this state, upon request, shall provide services to a petitioner in a proceeding under this part.

(b) A support enforcement agency of this state that is providing services to the petitioner shall:

(1) take all steps necessary to enable an appropriate tribunal of this state, another state, or a foreign country to obtain jurisdiction over the respondent;

(2) request an appropriate tribunal to set a date, time, and place for a hearing;

(3) make a reasonable effort to obtain all relevant information, including information as to income and property of the parties;

(4) within 14 days, exclusive of Saturdays, Sundays, and legal holidays, after receipt of notice in a record from an initiating, responding, or registering tribunal, send a copy of the notice to the petitioner;

(5) within 14 days, exclusive of Saturdays, Sundays, and legal holidays, after receipt of communication in a record from the respondent or the respondent's attorney, send a copy of the communication to the petitioner; and

(6) notify the petitioner if jurisdiction over the respondent cannot be obtained.

(c) A support enforcement agency of this state that requests registration of a child-support order in this state for enforcement or for modification shall make reasonable efforts:

(1) to ensure that the order to be registered is the controlling order; or

(2) if two or more child-support orders exist and the identity of the controlling order has not been determined, to ensure that a request for such a determination is made in a tribunal having jurisdiction to do so.

(d) A support enforcement agency of this state that requests registration and enforcement of a support order, arrears, or judgment stated in a foreign currency shall convert the amounts stated in the foreign currency into the equivalent amounts in dollars under the applicable official or market exchange rate as publicly reported.

(e) A support enforcement agency of this state shall issue or request a tribunal of this state to issue a child-support order and an income-withholding order that redirect payment of current support, arrears, and interest if requested to do so by a support enforcement agency of another state pursuant to Section 5700.319.

(f) This part does not create or negate a relationship of attorney and client or other fiduciary relationship between a support enforcement agency or the attorney for the agency and the individual being assisted by the agency. *(Added by Stats.2015, c. 493 (S.B.646), § 5, eff. Jan. 1, 2016.)*

Research References

Forms

West's California Judicial Council Forms FL–530, Judgment Regarding Parental Obligations (UIFSA) (Also Available in Spanish).

§ 5700.308. Duty of Attorney General or Department of Child Support Services

(a) If the Attorney General or the Department of Child Support Services determines that the support enforcement agency is neglecting or refusing to provide services to an individual, the Attorney General or the department may order the agency to perform its duties under this part or may provide those services directly to the individual.

(b) The Department of Child Support Services, in consultation with the Attorney General, may determine that a foreign country has established a reciprocal arrangement for child support with this state and take appropriate action for notification of the determination. *(Added by Stats.2015, c. 493 (S.B.646), § 5, eff. Jan. 1, 2016.)*

§ 5700.309. Private counsel

An individual may employ private counsel to represent the individual in proceedings authorized by this part. *(Added by Stats.2015, c. 493 (S.B.646), § 5, eff. Jan. 1, 2016.)*

§ 5700.310. Duties of state information agency

(a) The Department of Child Support Services is the state information agency under this part.

(b) The state information agency shall:

(1) compile and maintain a current list, including addresses, of the tribunals in this state which have jurisdiction under this part and any support enforcement agencies in this state and transmit a copy to the state information agency of every other state;

(2) maintain a register of names and addresses of tribunals and support enforcement agencies received from other states;

(3) forward to the appropriate tribunal in the county in this state in which the obligee who is an individual or the obligor resides, or in which the obligor's property is believed to be located, all documents concerning a proceeding under this part received from another state or a foreign country; and

(4) obtain information concerning the location of the obligor and the obligor's property within this state not exempt from execution, by such means as postal verification and federal or state locator services, examination of telephone directories, requests for the obligor's address from employers, and examination of governmental records, including, to the extent not prohibited by other law, those relating to real property, vital statistics, law enforcement, taxation, motor vehicles, driver's licenses, and social security. *(Added by Stats.2015, c. 493 (S.B.646), § 5, eff. Jan. 1, 2016.)*

§ 5700.311. Pleadings and accompanying documents

(a) In a proceeding under this part, a petitioner seeking to establish a support order, to determine parentage of a child, or to register and modify a support order of a tribunal of another state or a foreign country must file a petition. Unless otherwise ordered under Section 5700.312, the petition or accompanying documents must provide, so far as known, the name, residential address, and social security numbers of the obligor and the obligee or the parent and alleged parent, and the name, sex, residential address, social security number, and date of birth of each child for whose benefit support is sought or whose parentage is to be determined. Unless filed at the time of registration, the petition must be accompanied by a copy of any support order known to have been issued by another tribunal. The petition may include any other information that may assist in locating or identifying the respondent.

(b) The petition must specify the relief sought. The petition and accompanying documents must conform substantially with the requirements imposed by the forms mandated by federal law for use in cases filed by a support enforcement agency. *(Added by Stats.2015, c. 493 (S.B.646), § 5, eff. Jan. 1, 2016.)*

Research References

Forms

West's California Judicial Council Forms FL–510, Summons (UIFSA).

West's California Judicial Council Forms FL–520, Response to Uniform Support Petition (UIFSA).

§ 5700.312. Nondisclosure of information in exceptional circumstances

If a party alleges in an affidavit or a pleading under oath that the health, safety, or liberty of a party or child would be jeopardized by disclosure of specific identifying information, that information must be sealed and may not be disclosed to the other party or the public. After a hearing in which a tribunal takes into consideration the health, safety, or liberty of the party or child, the tribunal may order disclosure of information that the tribunal determines to be in the interest of justice. *(Added by Stats.2015, c. 493 (S.B.646), § 5, eff. Jan. 1, 2016.)*

§ 5700.313. Costs and fees

(a) The petitioner may not be required to pay a filing fee or other costs.

(b) If an obligee prevails, a responding tribunal of this state may assess against an obligor filing fees, reasonable attorney's fees, other costs, and necessary travel and other reasonable expenses incurred by the obligee and the obligee's witnesses. The tribunal may not assess fees, costs, or expenses against the obligee or the support enforcement agency of either the initiating or responding state or foreign country, except as provided by other law. Attorney's fees may be taxed as costs, and may be ordered paid directly to the attorney, who may enforce the order in the attorney's own name. Payment of support owed to the obligee has priority over fees, costs, and expenses.

(c) The tribunal shall order the payment of costs and reasonable attorney's fees if it determines that a hearing was requested primarily for delay. In a proceeding under Chapter 6, a hearing is presumed to have been requested primarily for delay if a registered support order is confirmed or enforced without change. *(Added by Stats. 2015, c. 493 (S.B.646), § 5, eff. Jan. 1, 2016.)*

§ 5700.314. Limited immunity of petitioner

(a) Participation by a petitioner in a proceeding under this part before a responding tribunal, whether in person, by private attorney, or through services provided by the support enforcement agency, does not confer personal jurisdiction over the petitioner in another proceeding.

(b) A petitioner is not amenable to service of civil process while physically present in this state to participate in a proceeding under this part.

(c) The immunity granted by this section does not extend to civil litigation based on acts unrelated to a proceeding under this part committed by a party while physically present in this state to participate in the proceeding. *(Added by Stats.2015, c. 493 (S.B.646), § 5, eff. Jan. 1, 2016.)*

§ 5700.315. Nonparentage as defense

A party whose parentage of a child has been previously determined by or pursuant to law may not plead nonparentage as a defense to a proceeding under this part. *(Added by Stats.2015, c. 493 (S.B.646), § 5, eff. Jan. 1, 2016.)*

§ 5700.316. Special rules of evidence and procedure

(a) The physical presence of a nonresident party who is an individual in a tribunal of this state is not required for the establishment, enforcement, or modification of a support order or the rendition of a judgment determining parentage of a child.

(b) An affidavit, a document substantially complying with federally mandated forms, or a document incorporated by reference in any of them, which would not be excluded under the hearsay rule if given in person, is admissible in evidence if given under penalty of perjury by a party or witness residing outside this state.

(c) A copy of the record of child-support payments certified as a true copy of the original by the custodian of the record may be forwarded to a responding tribunal. The copy is evidence of facts asserted in it, and is admissible to show whether payments were made.

(d) Copies of bills for testing for parentage of a child, and for prenatal and postnatal health care of the mother and child, furnished to the adverse party at least 10 days before trial, are admissible in evidence to prove the amount of the charges billed and that the charges were reasonable, necessary, and customary.

(e) Documentary evidence transmitted from outside this state to a tribunal of this state by telephone, telecopier, or other electronic means that do not provide an original record may not be excluded from evidence on an objection based on the means of transmission.

(f) In a proceeding under this part, a tribunal of this state shall permit a party or witness residing outside this state to be deposed or to testify under penalty of perjury by telephone, audiovisual means, or other electronic means at a designated tribunal or other location. A tribunal of this state shall cooperate with other tribunals in designating an appropriate location for the deposition or testimony.

(g) If a party called to testify at a civil hearing refuses to answer on the ground that the testimony may be self-incriminating, the trier of fact may draw an adverse inference from the refusal.

(h) A privilege against disclosure of communications between spouses does not apply in a proceeding under this part.

(i) The defense of immunity based on the relationship of husband and wife or parent and child does not apply in a proceeding under this part.

(j) A voluntary acknowledgment of paternity, certified as a true copy, is admissible to establish parentage of the child. *(Added by Stats.2015, c. 493 (S.B.646), § 5, eff. Jan. 1, 2016.)*

§ 5700.317. Communications between tribunals

A tribunal of this state may communicate with a tribunal outside this state in a record or by telephone, electronic mail, or other means, to obtain information concerning the laws, the legal effect of a judgment, decree, or order of that tribunal, and the status of a proceeding. A tribunal of this state may furnish similar information by similar means to a tribunal outside this state. *(Added by Stats.2015, c. 493 (S.B.646), § 5, eff. Jan. 1, 2016.)*

§ 5700.318. Assistance with discovery

A tribunal of this state may:

(1) request a tribunal outside this state to assist in obtaining discovery; and

(2) upon request, compel a person over which it has jurisdiction to respond to a discovery order issued by a tribunal outside this state. *(Added by Stats.2015, c. 493 (S.B.646), § 5, eff. Jan. 1, 2016.)*

§ 5700.319. Receipt and disbursement of payments

(a) A support enforcement agency or tribunal of this state shall disburse promptly any amounts received pursuant to a support order, as directed by the order. The agency or tribunal shall furnish to a requesting party or tribunal of another state or a foreign country a certified statement by the custodian of the record of the amounts and dates of all payments received.

(b) If neither the obligor, nor the obligee who is an individual, nor the child resides in this state, upon request from the support enforcement agency of this state or another state, the Department of Child Support Services or a tribunal of this state shall:

(1) direct that the support payment be made to the support enforcement agency in the state in which the obligee is receiving services; and

(2) issue and send to the obligor's employer a conforming income-withholding order or an administrative notice of change of payee, reflecting the redirected payments.

(c) The support enforcement agency of this state receiving redirected payments from another state pursuant to a law similar to subsection (b) shall furnish to a requesting party or tribunal of the other state a certified statement by the custodian of the record of the amount and dates of all payments received. *(Added by Stats.2015, c. 493 (S.B.646), § 5, eff. Jan. 1, 2016.)*

CHAPTER 4. ESTABLISHMENT OF SUPPORT ORDER OR DETERMINATION OF PARENTAGE

Section
5700.401. Issuance of support orders; temporary child-support orders.
5700.402. Proceeding to determine parentage.

§ 5700.401. Issuance of support orders; temporary child-support orders

(a) If a support order entitled to recognition under this part has not been issued, a responding tribunal of this state with personal jurisdiction over the parties may issue a support order if:

(1) the individual seeking the order resides outside this state; or

(2) the support enforcement agency seeking the order is located outside this state.

(b) The tribunal may issue a temporary child-support order if the tribunal determines that such an order is appropriate and the individual ordered to pay is:

(1) a presumed father of the child;

(2) petitioning to have his paternity adjudicated;

(3) identified as the father of the child through genetic testing;

(4) an alleged father who has declined to submit to genetic testing;

(5) shown by clear and convincing evidence to be the father of the child;

(6) an acknowledged father as provided by applicable state law;

(7) the mother of the child; or

(8) an individual who has been ordered to pay child support in a previous proceeding and the order has not been reversed or vacated.

(c) Upon finding, after notice and opportunity to be heard, that an obligor owes a duty of support, the tribunal shall issue a support order directed to the obligor and may issue other orders pursuant to Section 5700.305. *(Added by Stats.2015, c. 493 (S.B.646), § 5, eff. Jan. 1, 2016.)*

§ 5700.402. Proceeding to determine parentage

A tribunal of this state authorized to determine parentage of a child may serve as a responding tribunal in a proceeding to determine parentage of a child brought under this part or a law or procedure substantially similar to this part. (Added by Stats.2015, c. 493 (S.B.646), § 5, eff. Jan. 1, 2016.)

CHAPTER 5. ENFORCEMENT OF SUPPORT ORDER WITHOUT REGISTRATION

Section
5700.501. Employer's receipt of income-withholding order of another state.
5700.502. Employer's compliance with income-withholding order of another state.
5700.503. Employer's compliance with two or more income-withholding orders.
5700.504. Immunity from civil liability.
5700.505. Penalties for noncompliance.
5700.506. Contest by obligor.
5700.507. Administrative enforcement of orders.

§ 5700.501. Employer's receipt of income-withholding order of another state

An income-withholding order issued in another state may be sent by or on behalf of the obligee, or by the support enforcement agency, to the person defined as the obligor's employer under Section 5210 without first filing a petition or comparable pleading or registering the order with a tribunal of this state. (Added by Stats.2015, c. 493 (S.B.646), § 5, eff. Jan. 1, 2016.)

§ 5700.502. Employer's compliance with income-withholding order of another state

(a) Upon receipt of an income-withholding order, the obligor's employer shall immediately provide a copy of the order to the obligor.

(b) The employer shall treat an income-withholding order issued in another state which appears regular on its face as if it had been issued by a tribunal of this state.

(c) Except as otherwise provided in subsection (d) and Section 5700.503, the employer shall withhold and distribute the funds as directed in the withholding order by complying with terms of the order which specify:

(1) the duration and amount of periodic payments of current child support, stated as a sum certain;

(2) the person designated to receive payments and the address to which the payments are to be forwarded;

(3) medical support, whether in the form of periodic cash payment, stated as a sum certain, or ordering the obligor to provide health insurance coverage for the child under a policy available through the obligor's employment;

(4) the amount of periodic payments of fees and costs for a support enforcement agency, the issuing tribunal, and the obligee's attorney, stated as sums certain; and

(5) the amount of periodic payments of arrearages and interest on arrearages, stated as sums certain.

(d) An employer shall comply with the law of the state of the obligor's principal place of employment for withholding from income with respect to:

(1) the employer's fee for processing an income-withholding order;

(2) the maximum amount permitted to be withheld from the obligor's income; and

(3) the times within which the employer must implement the withholding order and forward the child-support payment. (Added by Stats.2015, c. 493 (S.B.646), § 5, eff. Jan. 1, 2016.)

§ 5700.503. Employer's compliance with two or more income-withholding orders

If an obligor's employer receives two or more income-withholding orders with respect to the earnings of the same obligor, the employer satisfies the terms of the orders if the employer complies with the law of the state of the obligor's principal place of employment to establish the priorities for withholding and allocating income withheld for two or more child-support obligees. (Added by Stats.2015, c. 493 (S.B.646), § 5, eff. Jan. 1, 2016.)

§ 5700.504. Immunity from civil liability

An employer that complies with an income-withholding order issued in another state in accordance with this chapter is not subject to civil liability to an individual or agency with regard to the employer's withholding of child support from the obligor's income. (Added by Stats.2015, c. 493 (S.B.646), § 5, eff. Jan. 1, 2016.)

§ 5700.505. Penalties for noncompliance

An employer that willfully fails to comply with an income-withholding order issued in another state and received for enforcement is subject to the same penalties that may be imposed for noncompliance with an order issued by a tribunal of this state. (Added by Stats.2015, c. 493 (S.B.646), § 5, eff. Jan. 1, 2016.)

§ 5700.506. Contest by obligor

(a) An obligor may contest the validity or enforcement of an income-withholding order issued in another state and received directly by an employer in this state by registering the order in a tribunal of this state and filing a contest to that order as provided in Chapter 6, or otherwise contesting the order in the same manner as if the order had been issued by a tribunal of this state.

(b) The obligor shall give notice of the contest to:

(1) a support enforcement agency providing services to the obligee;

(2) each employer that has directly received an income-withholding order relating to the obligor; and

(3) the person designated to receive payments in the income-withholding order or, if no person is designated, to the obligee. (Added by Stats.2015, c. 493 (S.B.646), § 5, eff. Jan. 1, 2016.)

§ 5700.507. Administrative enforcement of orders

(a) A party or support enforcement agency seeking to enforce a support order or an income-withholding order, or both, issued in another state or a foreign support order may send the documents required for registering the order to a support enforcement agency of this state.

(b) Upon receipt of the documents, the support enforcement agency, without initially seeking to register the order, shall consider and, if appropriate, use any administrative procedure authorized by the law of this state to enforce a support order or an income-withholding order, or both. If the obligor does not contest administrative enforcement, the order need not be registered. If the obligor contests the validity or administrative enforcement of the order, the support enforcement agency shall register the order pursuant to this part. (Added by Stats.2015, c. 493 (S.B.646), § 5, eff. Jan. 1, 2016.)

CHAPTER 6. REGISTRATION, ENFORCEMENT, AND MODIFICATION OF SUPPORT ORDER

Article	Section
1. Registration for Enforcement of Support Order	5700.601
2. Contest of Validity or Enforcement	5700.605
3. Registration and Modification of Child-Support Order of Another State	5700.609

SUPPORT

Article	Section
4. Registration and Modification of Foreign Child-Support Order	5700.615

ARTICLE 1. REGISTRATION FOR ENFORCEMENT OF SUPPORT ORDER

Section
5700.601. Registration of order for enforcement.
5700.602. Procedure to register order for enforcement.
5700.603. Effect of registration for enforcement.
5700.604. Choice of law.

§ 5700.601. Registration of order for enforcement

A support order or income-withholding order issued in another state or a foreign support order may be registered in this state for enforcement. *(Added by Stats.2015, c. 493 (S.B.646), § 5, eff. Jan. 1, 2016.)*

§ 5700.602. Procedure to register order for enforcement

(a) Except as otherwise provided in Section 5700.706, a support order or income-withholding order of another state or a foreign support order may be registered in this state by sending the following records to the appropriate tribunal in this state:

(1) a letter of transmittal to the tribunal requesting registration and enforcement;

(2) two copies, including one certified copy, of the order to be registered, including any modification of the order;

(3) a sworn statement by the person requesting registration or a certified statement by the custodian of the records showing the amount of any arrearage;

(4) the name of the obligor and, if known:

(A) the obligor's address and social security number;

(B) the name and address of the obligor's employer and any other source of income of the obligor; and

(C) a description and the location of property of the obligor in this state not exempt from execution; and

(5) except as otherwise provided in Section 5700.312, the name and address of the obligee and, if applicable, the person to whom support payments are to be remitted.

(b) On receipt of a request for registration, the registering tribunal shall cause the order to be filed as an order of a tribunal of another state or a foreign support order, together with one copy of the documents and information, regardless of their form.

(c) A petition or comparable pleading seeking a remedy that must be affirmatively sought under other law of this state may be filed at the same time as the request for registration or later. The pleading must specify the grounds for the remedy sought.

(d) If two or more orders are in effect, the person requesting registration shall:

(1) furnish to the tribunal a copy of every support order asserted to be in effect in addition to the documents specified in this section;

(2) specify the order alleged to be the controlling order, if any; and

(3) specify the amount of consolidated arrears, if any.

(e) A request for a determination of which is the controlling order may be filed separately or with a request for registration and enforcement or for registration and modification. The person requesting registration shall give notice of the request to each party whose rights may be affected by the determination. *(Added by Stats.2015, c. 493 (S.B.646), § 5, eff. Jan. 1, 2016.)*

§ 5700.603. Effect of registration for enforcement

(a) A support order or income-withholding order issued in another state or a foreign support order is registered when the order is filed in the registering tribunal of this state.

(b) A registered support order issued in another state or a foreign country is enforceable in the same manner and is subject to the same procedures as an order issued by a tribunal of this state.

(c) Except as otherwise provided in this part, a tribunal of this state shall recognize and enforce, but may not modify, a registered support order if the issuing tribunal had jurisdiction. *(Added by Stats.2015, c. 493 (S.B.646), § 5, eff. Jan. 1, 2016.)*

Research References

Forms

West's California Judicial Council Forms FL–570, Notice of Registration of Out-Of-State Support Order.

§ 5700.604. Choice of law

(a) Except as otherwise provided in subsection (d), the law of the issuing state or foreign country governs:

(1) the nature, extent, amount, and duration of current payments under a registered support order;

(2) the computation and payment of arrearages and accrual of interest on the arrearages under the support order; and

(3) the existence and satisfaction of other obligations under the support order.

(b) In a proceeding for arrears under a registered support order, the statute of limitation of this state, or of the issuing state or foreign country, whichever is longer, applies.

(c) A responding tribunal of this state shall apply the procedures and remedies of this state to enforce current support and collect arrears and interest due on a support order of another state or a foreign country registered in this state.

(d) After a tribunal of this state or another state determines which is the controlling order and issues an order consolidating arrears, if any, a tribunal of this state shall prospectively apply the law of the state or foreign country issuing the controlling order, including its law on interest on arrears, on current and future support, and on consolidated arrears. *(Added by Stats.2015, c. 493 (S.B.646), § 5, eff. Jan. 1, 2016.)*

ARTICLE 2. CONTEST OF VALIDITY OR ENFORCEMENT

Section
5700.605. Notice of registration of order.
5700.606. Procedure to contest validity or enforcement of registered support order.
5700.607. Contest of registration or enforcement.
5700.608. Confirmed order.

§ 5700.605. Notice of registration of order

(a) When a support order or income-withholding order issued in another state or a foreign support order is registered, the registering tribunal of this state shall notify the nonregistering party. The notice must be accompanied by a copy of the registered order and the documents and relevant information accompanying the order.

(b) A notice must inform the nonregistering party:

(1) that a registered support order is enforceable as of the date of registration in the same manner as an order issued by a tribunal of this state;

(2) that a hearing to contest the validity or enforcement of the registered order must be requested within 20 days after notice unless the registered order is under Section 5700.707;

(3) that failure to contest the validity or enforcement of the registered order in a timely manner will result in confirmation of the order and enforcement of the order and the alleged arrearages; and

(4) of the amount of any alleged arrearages.

(c) If the registering party asserts that two or more orders are in effect, a notice must also:

(1) identify the two or more orders and the order alleged by the registering party to be the controlling order and the consolidated arrears, if any;

(2) notify the nonregistering party of the right to a determination of which is the controlling order;

(3) state that the procedures provided in subsection (b) apply to the determination of which is the controlling order; and

(4) state that failure to contest the validity or enforcement of the order alleged to be the controlling order in a timely manner may result in confirmation that the order is the controlling order.

(d) Upon registration of an income-withholding order for enforcement, the support enforcement agency or the registering tribunal shall notify the obligor's employer pursuant to Chapter 8 (commencing with Section 5200) of Part 5. *(Added by Stats.2015, c. 493 (S.B.646), § 5, eff. Jan. 1, 2016.)*

Research References

Forms

West's California Judicial Council Forms FL–570, Notice of Registration of Out-Of-State Support Order.

§ 5700.606. Procedure to contest validity or enforcement of registered support order

(a) A nonregistering party seeking to contest the validity or enforcement of a registered support order in this state shall request a hearing within the time required by Section 5700.605. The nonregistering party may seek to vacate the registration, to assert any defense to an allegation of noncompliance with the registered order, or to contest the remedies being sought or the amount of any alleged arrearages pursuant to Section 5700.607.

(b) If the nonregistering party fails to contest the validity or enforcement of the registered support order in a timely manner, the order is confirmed by operation of law.

(c) If a nonregistering party requests a hearing to contest the validity or enforcement of the registered support order, the registering tribunal shall schedule the matter for hearing and give notice to the parties of the date, time, and place of the hearing. *(Added by Stats.2015, c. 493 (S.B.646), § 5, eff. Jan. 1, 2016.)*

Research References

Forms

West's California Judicial Council Forms FL–575, Request for Hearing Regarding Registration of Out-Of-State Support Order.

§ 5700.607. Contest of registration or enforcement

(a) A party contesting the validity or enforcement of a registered support order or seeking to vacate the registration has the burden of proving one or more of the following defenses:

(1) the issuing tribunal lacked personal jurisdiction over the contesting party;

(2) the order was obtained by fraud;

(3) the order has been vacated, suspended, or modified by a later order;

(4) the issuing tribunal has stayed the order pending appeal;

(5) there is a defense under the law of this state to the remedy sought;

(6) full or partial payment has been made;

(7) the statute of limitation under Section 5700.604 precludes enforcement of some or all of the alleged arrearages; or

(8) the alleged controlling order is not the controlling order.

(b) If a party presents evidence establishing a full or partial defense under subsection (a), a tribunal may stay enforcement of a registered support order, continue the proceeding to permit production of additional relevant evidence, and issue other appropriate orders. An uncontested portion of the registered support order may be enforced by all remedies available under the law of this state.

(c) If the contesting party does not establish a defense under subsection (a) to the validity or enforcement of a registered support order, the registering tribunal shall issue an order confirming the order. *(Added by Stats.2015, c. 493 (S.B.646), § 5, eff. Jan. 1, 2016.)*

Research References

Forms

West's California Judicial Council Forms FL–575, Request for Hearing Regarding Registration of Out-Of-State Support Order.

§ 5700.608. Confirmed order

Confirmation of a registered support order, whether by operation of law or after notice and hearing, precludes further contest of the order with respect to any matter that could have been asserted at the time of registration. *(Added by Stats.2015, c. 493 (S.B.646), § 5, eff. Jan. 1, 2016.)*

ARTICLE 3. REGISTRATION AND MODIFICATION OF CHILD–SUPPORT ORDER OF ANOTHER STATE

Section
5700.609. Procedure to register child-support order of another state for modification.
5700.610. Effect of registration for modification.
5700.611. Modification of child-support order of another state.
5700.612. Recognition of order modified in another state.
5700.613. Jurisdiction to modify child-support order of another state when individual parties reside in this state.
5700.614. Notice to issuing tribunal of modification.

§ 5700.609. Procedure to register child-support order of another state for modification

A party or support enforcement agency seeking to modify, or to modify and enforce, a child-support order issued in another state shall register that order in this state in the same manner provided in Sections 5700.601 through 5700.608 if the order has not been registered. A petition for modification may be filed at the same time as a request for registration, or later. The pleading must specify the grounds for modification. *(Added by Stats.2015, c. 493 (S.B.646), § 5, eff. Jan. 1, 2016.)*

§ 5700.610. Effect of registration for modification

A tribunal of this state may enforce a child-support order of another state registered for purposes of modification, in the same manner as if the order had been issued by a tribunal of this state, but the registered support order may be modified only if the requirements of Section 5700.611 or 5700.613 have been met. *(Added by Stats.2015, c. 493 (S.B.646), § 5, eff. Jan. 1, 2016.)*

§ 5700.611. Modification of child-support order of another state

(a) If Section 5700.613 does not apply, upon petition a tribunal of this state may modify a child-support order issued in another state which is registered in this state if, after notice and hearing, the tribunal finds that:

(1) the following requirements are met:

§ 5700.611

(A) neither the child, nor the obligee who is an individual, nor the obligor resides in the issuing state;

(B) a petitioner who is a nonresident of this state seeks modification; and

(C) the respondent is subject to the personal jurisdiction of the tribunal of this state; or

(2) this state is the residence of the child, or a party who is an individual is subject to the personal jurisdiction of the tribunal of this state, and all of the parties who are individuals have filed consents in a record in the issuing tribunal for a tribunal of this state to modify the support order and assume continuing, exclusive jurisdiction.

(b) Modification of a registered child-support order is subject to the same requirements, procedures, and defenses that apply to the modification of an order issued by a tribunal of this state and the order may be enforced and satisfied in the same manner.

(c) A tribunal of this state may not modify any aspect of a child-support order that may not be modified under the law of the issuing state, including the duration of the obligation of support. If two or more tribunals have issued child-support orders for the same obligor and same child, the order that controls and must be so recognized under Section 5700.207 establishes the aspects of the support order which are nonmodifiable.

(d) In a proceeding to modify a child-support order, the law of the state that is determined to have issued the initial controlling order governs the duration of the obligation of support. The obligor's fulfillment of the duty of support established by that order precludes imposition of a further obligation of support by a tribunal of this state.

(e) On the issuance of an order by a tribunal of this state modifying a child-support order issued in another state, the tribunal of this state becomes the tribunal having continuing, exclusive jurisdiction.

(f) Notwithstanding subsections (a) through (e) and Section 5700.201(b), a tribunal of this state retains jurisdiction to modify an order issued by a tribunal of this state if:

(1) one party resides in another state; and

(2) the other party resides outside the United States. *(Added by Stats.2015, c. 493 (S.B.646), § 5, eff. Jan. 1, 2016.)*

Research References

Forms

West's California Judicial Council Forms FL–590A, UIFSA Child Support Order Jurisdictional Attachment.

§ 5700.612. Recognition of order modified in another state

If a child-support order issued by a tribunal of this state is modified by a tribunal of another state which assumed jurisdiction pursuant to the Uniform Interstate Family Support Act, a tribunal of this state:

(1) may enforce its order that was modified only as to arrears and interest accruing before the modification;

(2) may provide appropriate relief for violations of its order which occurred before the effective date of the modification; and

(3) shall recognize the modifying order of the other state, upon registration, for the purpose of enforcement. *(Added by Stats.2015, c. 493 (S.B.646), § 5, eff. Jan. 1, 2016.)*

§ 5700.613. Jurisdiction to modify child-support order of another state when individual parties reside in this state

(a) If all of the parties who are individuals reside in this state and the child does not reside in the issuing state, a tribunal of this state has jurisdiction to enforce and to modify the issuing state's child-support order in a proceeding to register that order.

(b) A tribunal of this state exercising jurisdiction under this section shall apply the provisions of Chapters 1 and 2, and this chapter, and the procedural and substantive law of this state to the proceeding for enforcement or modification. Chapters 3, 4, 5, 7, and 8 do not apply. *(Added by Stats.2015, c. 493 (S.B.646), § 5, eff. Jan. 1, 2016.)*

Research References

Forms

West's California Judicial Council Forms FL–590A, UIFSA Child Support Order Jurisdictional Attachment.

§ 5700.614. Notice to issuing tribunal of modification

Within 30 days after issuance of a modified child-support order, the party obtaining the modification shall file a certified copy of the order with the issuing tribunal that had continuing, exclusive jurisdiction over the earlier order, and in each tribunal in which the party knows the earlier order has been registered. A party who obtains the order and fails to file a certified copy is subject to appropriate sanctions by a tribunal in which the issue of failure to file arises. The failure to file does not affect the validity or enforceability of the modified order of the new tribunal having continuing, exclusive jurisdiction. *(Added by Stats.2015, c. 493 (S.B.646), § 5, eff. Jan. 1, 2016.)*

ARTICLE 4. REGISTRATION AND MODIFICATION OF FOREIGN CHILD–SUPPORT ORDER

Section

5700.615. Jurisdiction to modify child-support order of foreign country.

5700.616. Procedure to register child-support order of foreign country for modification.

§ 5700.615. Jurisdiction to modify child-support order of foreign country

(a) Except as otherwise provided in Section 5700.711, if a foreign country lacks or refuses to exercise jurisdiction to modify its child-support order pursuant to its laws, a tribunal of this state may assume jurisdiction to modify the child-support order and bind all individuals subject to the personal jurisdiction of the tribunal whether the consent to modification of a child-support order otherwise required of the individual pursuant to Section 5700.611 has been given or whether the individual seeking modification is a resident of this state or of the foreign country.

(b) An order issued by a tribunal of this state modifying a foreign child-support order pursuant to this section is the controlling order. *(Added by Stats.2015, c. 493 (S.B.646), § 5, eff. Jan. 1, 2016.)*

Research References

Forms

West's California Judicial Council Forms FL–590A, UIFSA Child Support Order Jurisdictional Attachment.

§ 5700.616. Procedure to register child-support order of foreign country for modification

A party or support enforcement agency seeking to modify, or to modify and enforce, a foreign child-support order not under the Convention may register that order in this state under Sections 5700.601 through 5700.608 if the order has not been registered. A petition for modification may be filed at the same time as a request for registration, or at another time. The petition must specify the grounds for modification. *(Added by Stats.2015, c. 493 (S.B.646), § 5, eff. Jan. 1, 2016.)*

CHAPTER 7. SUPPORT PROCEEDING UNDER CONVENTION

Section
5700.701. Definitions.
5700.702. Applicability.
5700.703. Relationship of Department of Child Support Services to United States central authority.
5700.704. Initiation by Department of Child Support Services of support proceeding under Convention.
5700.705. Direct request.
5700.706. Registration of Convention support order.
5700.707. Contest of registered Convention support order.
5700.708. Recognition and enforcement of registered Convention support order.
5700.709. Partial enforcement.
5700.710. Foreign support agreement.
5700.711. Modification of Convention child-support order.
5700.712. Personal information; limit on use.
5700.713. Record in original language; English translation.

§ 5700.701. Definitions

In this chapter:

(1) "Application" means a request under the Convention by an obligee or obligor, or on behalf of a child, made through a central authority for assistance from another central authority.

(2) "Central authority" means the entity designated by the United States or a foreign country described in Section 5700.102(5)(D) to perform the functions specified in the Convention.

(3) "Convention support order" means a support order of a tribunal of a foreign country described in Section 5700.102(5)(D).

(4) "Direct request" means a petition filed by an individual in a tribunal of this state in a proceeding involving an obligee, obligor, or child residing outside the United States.

(5) "Foreign central authority" means the entity designated by a foreign country described in Section 5700.102(5)(D) to perform the functions specified in the Convention.

(6) "Foreign support agreement":

(A) means an agreement for support in a record that:

(i) is enforceable as a support order in the country of origin;

(ii) has been:

(I) formally drawn up or registered as an authentic instrument by a foreign tribunal; or

(II) authenticated by, or concluded, registered, or filed with a foreign tribunal; and

(iii) may be reviewed and modified by a foreign tribunal; and

(B) includes a maintenance arrangement or authentic instrument under the Convention.

(7) "United States central authority" means the Secretary of the United States Department of Health and Human Services. *(Added by Stats.2015, c. 493 (S.B.646), § 5, eff. Jan. 1, 2016.)*

§ 5700.702. Applicability

This chapter applies only to a support proceeding under the Convention. In such a proceeding, if a provision of this chapter is inconsistent with Chapters 1 through 6, this chapter controls. *(Added by Stats.2015, c. 493 (S.B.646), § 5, eff. Jan. 1, 2016.)*

§ 5700.703. Relationship of Department of Child Support Services to United States central authority

The Department of Child Support Services is recognized as the agency designated by the United States central authority to perform specific functions under the Convention. *(Added by Stats.2015, c. 493 (S.B.646), § 5, eff. Jan. 1, 2016.)*

§ 5700.704. Initiation by Department of Child Support Services of support proceeding under Convention

(a) In a support proceeding under this chapter, the Department of Child Support Services shall:

(1) transmit and receive applications; and

(2) initiate or facilitate the institution of a proceeding regarding an application in a tribunal of this state.

(b) The following support proceedings are available to an obligee under the Convention:

(1) recognition or recognition and enforcement of a foreign support order;

(2) enforcement of a support order issued or recognized in this state;

(3) establishment of a support order if there is no existing order, including, if necessary, determination of parentage of a child;

(4) establishment of a support order if recognition of a foreign support order is refused under Section 5700.708(b)(2), (4), or (9);

(5) modification of a support order of a tribunal of this state; and

(6) modification of a support order of a tribunal of another state or a foreign country.

(c) The following support proceedings are available under the Convention to an obligor against which there is an existing support order:

(1) recognition of an order suspending or limiting enforcement of an existing support order of a tribunal of this state;

(2) modification of a support order of a tribunal of this state; and

(3) modification of a support order of a tribunal of another state or a foreign country.

(d) A tribunal of this state may not require security, bond, or deposit, however described, to guarantee the payment of costs and expenses in proceedings under the Convention. *(Added by Stats. 2015, c. 493 (S.B.646), § 5, eff. Jan. 1, 2016.)*

§ 5700.705. Direct request

(a) A petitioner may file a direct request seeking establishment or modification of a support order or determination of parentage of a child. In the proceeding, the law of this state applies.

(b) A petitioner may file a direct request seeking recognition and enforcement of a support order or support agreement. In the proceeding, Sections 5700.706 through 5700.713 apply.

(c) In a direct request for recognition and enforcement of a Convention support order or foreign support agreement:

(1) a security, bond, or deposit is not required to guarantee the payment of costs and expenses; and

(2) an obligee or obligor that in the issuing country has benefited from free legal assistance is entitled to benefit, at least to the same extent, from any free legal assistance provided for by the law of this state under the same circumstances.

(d) A petitioner filing a direct request is not entitled to assistance from the Department of Child Support Services.

(e) This chapter does not prevent the application of laws of this state that provide simplified, more expeditious rules regarding a direct request for recognition and enforcement of a foreign support order or foreign support agreement. *(Added by Stats.2015, c. 493 (S.B.646), § 5, eff. Jan. 1, 2016.)*

§ 5700.706. Registration of Convention support order

(a) Except as otherwise provided in this chapter, a party who is an individual or a support enforcement agency seeking recognition of a

§ 5700.706

Convention support order shall register the order in this state as provided in Chapter 6.

(b) Notwithstanding Sections 5700.311 and 5700.602(a), a request for registration of a Convention support order must be accompanied by:

(1) a complete text of the support order or an abstract or extract of the support order drawn up by the issuing foreign tribunal, which may be in the form recommended by the Hague Conference on Private International Law;

(2) a record stating that the support order is enforceable in the issuing country;

(3) if the respondent did not appear and was not represented in the proceedings in the issuing country, a record attesting, as appropriate, either that the respondent had proper notice of the proceedings and an opportunity to be heard or that the respondent had proper notice of the support order and an opportunity to be heard in a challenge or appeal on fact or law before a tribunal;

(4) a record showing the amount of arrears, if any, and the date the amount was calculated;

(5) a record showing a requirement for automatic adjustment of the amount of support, if any, and the information necessary to make the appropriate calculations; and

(6) if necessary, a record showing the extent to which the applicant received free legal assistance in the issuing country.

(c) A request for registration of a Convention support order may seek recognition and partial enforcement of the order.

(d) A tribunal of this state may vacate the registration of a Convention support order without the filing of a contest under Section 5700.707 only if, acting on its own motion, the tribunal finds that recognition and enforcement of the order would be manifestly incompatible with public policy.

(e) The tribunal shall promptly notify the parties of the registration or the order vacating the registration of a Convention support order. *(Added by Stats.2015, c. 493 (S.B.646), § 5, eff. Jan. 1, 2016.)*

Research References

Forms

West's California Judicial Council Forms FL–592, Notice of Registration of an International Hague Convention Support Order.

§ 5700.707. Contest of registered Convention support order

(a) Except as otherwise provided in this chapter, Sections 5700.605 through 5700.608 apply to a contest of a registered Convention support order.

(b) A party contesting a registered Convention support order shall file a contest not later than 30 days after notice of the registration, but if the contesting party does not reside in the United States, the contest must be filed not later than 60 days after notice of the registration.

(c) If the nonregistering party fails to contest the registered Convention support order by the time specified in subsection (b), the order is enforceable.

(d) A contest of a registered Convention support order may be based only on grounds set forth in Section 5700.708. The contesting party bears the burden of proof.

(e) In a contest of a registered Convention support order, a tribunal of this state:

(1) is bound by the findings of fact on which the foreign tribunal based its jurisdiction; and

(2) may not review the merits of the order.

(f) A tribunal of this state deciding a contest of a registered Convention support order shall promptly notify the parties of its decision.

(g) A challenge or appeal, if any, does not stay the enforcement of a Convention support order unless there are exceptional circumstances. *(Added by Stats.2015, c. 493 (S.B.646), § 5, eff. Jan. 1, 2016.)*

Research References

Forms

West's California Judicial Council Forms FL–592, Notice of Registration of an International Hague Convention Support Order.

§ 5700.708. Recognition and enforcement of registered Convention support order

(a) Except as otherwise provided in subsection (b), a tribunal of this state shall recognize and enforce a registered Convention support order.

(b) The following grounds are the only grounds on which a tribunal of this state may refuse recognition and enforcement of a registered Convention support order:

(1) recognition and enforcement of the order is manifestly incompatible with public policy, including the failure of the issuing tribunal to observe minimum standards of due process, which include notice and an opportunity to be heard;

(2) the issuing tribunal lacked personal jurisdiction consistent with Section 5700.201;

(3) the order is not enforceable in the issuing country;

(4) the order was obtained by fraud in connection with a matter of procedure;

(5) a record transmitted in accordance with Section 5700.706 lacks authenticity or integrity;

(6) a proceeding between the same parties and having the same purpose is pending before a tribunal of this state and that proceeding was the first to be filed;

(7) the order is incompatible with a more recent support order involving the same parties and having the same purpose if the more recent support order is entitled to recognition and enforcement under this part in this state;

(8) payment, to the extent alleged arrears have been paid in whole or in part;

(9) in a case in which the respondent neither appeared nor was represented in the proceeding in the issuing foreign country:

(A) if the law of that country provides for prior notice of proceedings, the respondent did not have proper notice of the proceedings and an opportunity to be heard; or

(B) if the law of that country does not provide for prior notice of the proceedings, the respondent did not have proper notice of the order and an opportunity to be heard in a challenge or appeal on fact or law before a tribunal; or

(10) the order was made in violation of Section 5700.711.

(c) If a tribunal of this state does not recognize a Convention support order under subsection (b)(2), (4), or (9):

(1) the tribunal may not dismiss the proceeding without allowing a reasonable time for a party to request the establishment of a new Convention support order; and

(2) the Department of Child Support Services shall take all appropriate measures to request a child-support order for the obligee if the application for recognition and enforcement was received under Section 5700.704. *(Added by Stats.2015, c. 493 (S.B.646), § 5, eff. Jan. 1, 2016.)*

§ 5700.709. Partial enforcement

If a tribunal of this state does not recognize and enforce a Convention support order in its entirety, it shall enforce any severable part of the order. An application or direct request may seek recognition and partial enforcement of a Convention support order. *(Added by Stats.2015, c. 493 (S.B.646), § 5, eff. Jan. 1, 2016.)*

§ 5700.710. Foreign support agreement

(a) Except as otherwise provided in subsections (c) and (d), a tribunal of this state shall recognize and enforce a foreign support agreement registered in this state.

(b) An application or direct request for recognition and enforcement of a foreign support agreement must be accompanied by:

(1) a complete text of the foreign support agreement; and

(2) a record stating that the foreign support agreement is enforceable as an order of support in the issuing country.

(c) A tribunal of this state may vacate the registration of a foreign support agreement only if, acting on its own motion, the tribunal finds that recognition and enforcement would be manifestly incompatible with public policy.

(d) In a contest of a foreign support agreement, a tribunal of this state may refuse recognition and enforcement of the agreement if it finds:

(1) recognition and enforcement of the agreement is manifestly incompatible with public policy;

(2) the agreement was obtained by fraud or falsification;

(3) the agreement is incompatible with a support order involving the same parties and having the same purpose in this state, another state, or a foreign country if the support order is entitled to recognition and enforcement under this act in this state; or

(4) the record submitted under subsection (b) lacks authenticity or integrity.

(e) A proceeding for recognition and enforcement of a foreign support agreement must be suspended during the pendency of a challenge to or appeal of the agreement before a tribunal of another state or a foreign country. *(Added by Stats.2015, c. 493 (S.B.646), § 5, eff. Jan. 1, 2016.)*

§ 5700.711. Modification of Convention child-support order

(a) A tribunal of this state may not modify a Convention child-support order if the obligee remains a resident of the foreign country where the support order was issued unless:

(1) the obligee submits to the jurisdiction of a tribunal of this state, either expressly or by defending on the merits of the case without objecting to the jurisdiction at the first available opportunity; or

(2) the foreign tribunal lacks or refuses to exercise jurisdiction to modify its support order or issue a new support order.

(b) If a tribunal of this state does not modify a Convention child-support order because the order is not recognized in this state, Section 5700.708(c) applies. *(Added by Stats.2015, c. 493 (S.B.646), § 5, eff. Jan. 1, 2016.)*

§ 5700.712. Personal information; limit on use

Personal information gathered or transmitted under this chapter may be used only for the purposes for which it was gathered or transmitted. *(Added by Stats.2015, c. 493 (S.B.646), § 5, eff. Jan. 1, 2016.)*

§ 5700.713. Record in original language; English translation

A record filed with a tribunal of this state under this chapter must be in the original language and, if not in English, must be accompanied by an English translation. *(Added by Stats.2015, c. 493 (S.B.646), § 5, eff. Jan. 1, 2016.)*

CHAPTER 8. INTERSTATE RENDITION

Section
5700.801. Grounds for rendition.
5700.802. Conditions of rendition.

§ 5700.801. Grounds for rendition

(a) For purposes of this chapter, "governor" includes an individual performing the functions of governor or the executive authority of a state covered by this part.

(b) The Governor may:

(1) demand that the governor of another state surrender an individual found in the other state who is charged criminally in this state with having failed to provide for the support of an obligee; or

(2) on the demand of the governor of another state, surrender an individual found in this state who is charged criminally in the other state with having failed to provide for the support of an obligee.

(c) A provision for extradition of individuals not inconsistent with this act applies to the demand even if the individual whose surrender is demanded was not in the demanding state when the crime was allegedly committed and has not fled therefrom. *(Added by Stats. 2015, c. 493 (S.B.646), § 5, eff. Jan. 1, 2016.)*

§ 5700.802. Conditions of rendition

(a) Before making a demand that the governor of another state surrender an individual charged criminally in this state with having failed to provide for the support of an obligee, the Governor may require a prosecutor of this state to demonstrate that at least 60 days previously the obligee had initiated proceedings for support pursuant to this act or that the proceeding would be of no avail.

(b) If, under this act or a law substantially similar to this act, the Governor of another state makes a demand that the Governor of this state surrender an individual charged criminally in that state with having failed to provide for the support of a child or other individual to whom a duty of support is owed, the Governor may require a prosecutor to investigate the demand and report whether a proceeding for support has been initiated or would be effective. If it appears that a proceeding would be effective but has not been initiated, the Governor may delay honoring the demand for a reasonable time to permit the initiation of a proceeding.

(c) If a proceeding for support has been initiated and the individual whose rendition is demanded prevails, the Governor may decline to honor the demand. If the petitioner prevails and the individual whose rendition is demanded is subject to a support order, the Governor may decline to honor the demand if the individual is complying with the support order. *(Added by Stats.2015, c. 493 (S.B.646), § 5, eff. Jan. 1, 2016.)*

CHAPTER 9. MISCELLANEOUS PROVISIONS

Section
5700.901. Uniformity of application and construction.
5700.902. Transitional provision.
5700.903. Severability.
5700.905. Emergency regulations.
5701 to 5807. Repealed.

§ 5700.901. Uniformity of application and construction

In applying and construing this uniform act, consideration must be given to the need to promote uniformity of the law with respect to its subject matter among states that enact it. *(Added by Stats.2015, c. 493 (S.B.646), § 5, eff. Jan. 1, 2016.)*

§ 5700.902. Transitional provision

This part applies to proceedings begun on or after January 1, 2016, to establish a support order or determine parentage of a child or to

§ 5700.902

register, recognize, enforce, or modify a prior support order, determination, or agreement, whenever issued or entered. *(Added by Stats.2015, c. 493 (S.B.646), § 5, eff. Jan. 1, 2016.)*

§ 5700.903. Severability

If any provision of this part or its application to any person or circumstance is held invalid, the invalidity does not affect other provisions or applications of this part which can be given effect without the invalid provision or application, and to this end the provisions of this part are severable. *(Added by Stats.2015, c. 493 (S.B.646), § 5, eff. Jan. 1, 2016.)*

§ 5700.905. Emergency regulations

The Department of Child Support Services may adopt emergency regulations as appropriate to implement this part. *(Added by Stats.2015, c. 493 (S.B.646), § 5, eff. Jan. 1, 2016.)*

§§ 5701 to 5807. Repealed by Stats.1993, c. 219 (A.B.1500), § 153.5

Division 10

PREVENTION OF DOMESTIC VIOLENCE

Part	Section
1. Short Title and Definitions	6200
2. General Provisions	6220
3. Emergency Protective Orders	6240
4. Protective Orders and Other Domestic Violence Prevention Orders	6300
5. Uniform Interstate Enforcement of Domestic Violence Protection Orders Act	6400
6. Uniform Recognition and Enforcement of Canadian Domestic Violence Protection Orders Act	6450

Cross References

Acceptance of Judicial Council form, summons, order, or other notices by email, fax, or in-person delivery, fee, court fee waiver or exemption, see Government Code § 26666.5.

Applicable law, see Family Code § 3021.

Arrest with and without warrant, citizen's arrest by domestic victim, protective or restraining order, see Penal Code § 836.

Carrying loaded firearms, punishment, exceptions, see Penal Code §§ 25850 to 26100.

Certified copies of orders issued pursuant to this Division, no fees charged to indigent plaintiffs, see Government Code § 7076.

Civil actions for abuse of elderly or dependent adults, protective orders, see Welfare and Institutions Code § 15657.03.

County clerk, fees, certified copies of order under certain domestic relations laws, see Government Code § 7076.

Court interpreter services provided in civil actions, reimbursement by Judicial Council, prioritization where funding is insufficient, see Evidence Code § 756.

Dependent children, jurisdiction, custody of child, restraining order, see Welfare and Institutions Code § 304.

Determination of amount due for spousal support, considerations, see Family Code § 4320.

Dissolution of injunction, exceptions, see Code of Civil Procedure § 529.

Domestic violence prevention order, contempt for failure to comply, see Code of Civil Procedure § 1218.

Elder abuse and dependent adult civil protection, see Welfare and Institutions Code § 15600 et seq.

Freedom from parental custody and control, stay of proceedings and effect upon jurisdiction under these provisions, see Family Code § 7807.

Gun-Free School Zone Act, see Penal Code § 626.9.

Law enforcement response to domestic violence, written policies and standards, see Penal Code § 13701.

License plates, application for new and different plates by domestic violence victims, conditions for issuance, see Vehicle Code § 4467.

Minors, incompetent persons or persons for whom conservator appointed, see Code of Civil Procedure § 372.

Orders or injunctions, sheriff or marshal providing service of process, payment of fee prohibited, see Government Code § 6103.3.

Parties to civil actions, minor under age 12, appearance conditions, see Code of Civil Procedure § 374.

Petitions, existence of child support, child custody, visitation, or spousal support orders, personal conduct restraining order, or bifurcated case, dismissal for delay in prosecution prohibited, see Code of Civil Procedure § 583.161.

Temporary restraining order and injunction, domestic violence, see Code of Civil Procedure § 527.6.

Termination of parental rights of father, filing of petition, stay of proceedings affecting a child under these provisions pending final determination of parental rights of the father, see Family Code § 7662.

Unlawful carrying and possession of weapons, justifiable violation of Penal Code § 25400, see Penal Code § 25600.

Witnesses, interpreters and translators, hearings or proceedings related to domestic violence, see Evidence Code § 756.

Part 1

SHORT TITLE AND DEFINITIONS

Section
6200. Short title.
6201. Construction of code; application of definitions.
6203. "Abuse" defined.
6205. "Affinity" defined.
6209. "Cohabitant" defined.
6210. "Dating relationship" defined.
6211. "Domestic violence" defined.
6215. "Emergency protective order" defined.
6216. "Firearm" and "firearm precursor part" defined.
6218. "Protective order" defined.
6219. Demonstration project to identify best practices in domestic violence court cases; participation in project; findings and recommendations.

Cross References

Proceedings in English, translations of court orders and court order forms, see Code of Civil Procedure § 185.

§ 6200. Short title

This division may be cited as the Domestic Violence Prevention Act. *(Added by Stats.1993, c. 219 (A.B.1500), § 154.)*

Cross References

Unemployment compensation benefits, eligibility, leaving work for good cause due to domestic violence, see Unemployment Insurance Code § 1256.

Research References

Forms

1 California Transactions Forms--Family Law § 3:4, Subject Matter Jurisdiction for Custody Determinations.

1 California Transactions Forms--Family Law § 4:14, Domestic Violence and Restraining Orders.

West's California Code Forms, Civil Procedure § 372 Form 8, Parties—Notice of Motion for Order Appointing Guardian Ad Litem for Minor 12 Years or Older to Assist Minor in Obtaining Protective Order.

West's California Code Forms, Civil Procedure § 372 Form 9, Parties—Order Appointing Guardian Ad Litem for Minor 12 Years or Older to Assist Minor in Obtaining Protective Order.

West's California Code Forms, Family § 2045, Comment Overview—Ex Parte Protective Orders.
West's California Code Forms, Family § 6200, Comment Overview—Prevention of Domestic Violence.
West's California Judicial Council Forms DV-100, Request for Domestic Violence Restraining Order (Also Available in Chinese, Korean, Spanish, and Vietnamese).
West's California Judicial Council Forms DV-101, Description of Abuse (Also Available in Chinese, Korean, Spanish, and Vietnamese).
West's California Judicial Council Forms DV-110, Temporary Restraining Order (Clets—Tro) (Also Available in Chinese, Korean, Spanish, and Vietnamese).
West's California Judicial Council Forms DV-120, Response to Request for Domestic Violence Restraining Order (Also Available in Korean, Spanish, and Vietnamese).
West's California Judicial Council Forms DV-130, Restraining Order After Hearing (Clets—Oah) (Order of Protection) (Also Available in Korean, Spanish, and Vietnamese).
West's California Judicial Council Forms FL-311, Child Custody and Visitation (Parenting Time) Application Attachment (Also Available in Spanish).

§ 6201. Construction of code; application of definitions

Unless the provision or context otherwise requires, the definitions in this part govern the construction of this code. *(Added by Stats.1993, c. 219 (A.B.1500), § 154.)*

§ 6203. "Abuse" defined

(a) For purposes of this act, "abuse" means any of the following:

(1) To intentionally or recklessly cause or attempt to cause bodily injury.

(2) Sexual assault.

(3) To place a person in reasonable apprehension of imminent serious bodily injury to that person or to another.

(4) To engage in any behavior that has been or could be enjoined pursuant to Section 6320.

(b) Abuse is not limited to the actual infliction of physical injury or assault. *(Added by Stats.1993, c. 219 (A.B.1500), § 154. Amended by Stats.1998, c. 581 (A.B.2801), § 16; Stats.2014, c. 635 (A.B.2089), § 2, eff. Jan. 1, 2015; Stats.2015, c. 303 (A.B.731), § 149, eff. Jan. 1, 2016.)*

Cross References

Abandonment and neglect of children, criminal history search, prior restraining orders, see Penal Code § 273.75.
Child abuse and neglect reporting, child abuse or neglect defined, see Penal Code § 11165.6.
Criminal history, use when setting bond or considering plea agreement, see Penal Code § 273.75.
Domestic violence, interagency death review teams, reporting procedures, see Penal Code § 11163.3.
Emergency protective orders, grounds for issuance, persons in danger of domestic violence or abuse, see Family Code § 6250.
Evidence of character, habit, or custom, battered women's syndrome, abuse and domestic violence, see Evidence Code § 1107.
Person defined for purposes of this Code, see Family Code § 105.
Presumption against persons perpetrating domestic violence, custody of children, see Family Code § 3044.
Protective orders to prevent domestic violence, issuance of order upon affidavit, see Family Code § 6300.
Protective orders to prevent domestic violence, persons who may be granted order, see Family Code § 6301.
Rights of victims and witnesses, domestic violence or abuse counselors, presence at law enforcement interviews, see Penal Code § 679.05.

Research References

Forms
West's California Code Forms, Family § 6200, Comment Overview—Prevention of Domestic Violence.

§ 6205. "Affinity" defined

"Affinity," when applied to the marriage relation, signifies the connection existing in consequence of marriage between each of the married persons and the blood relatives of the other. *(Added by Stats.1993, c. 219 (A.B.1500), § 154.)*

Cross References

Person defined for purposes of this Code, see Family Code § 105.
References to husband, wife, spouses and married persons, persons included for purposes of this Code, see Family Code § 11.

§ 6209. "Cohabitant" defined

"Cohabitant" means a person who regularly resides in the household. "Former cohabitant" means a person who formerly regularly resided in the household. *(Added by Stats.1993, c. 219 (A.B.1500), § 154.)*

Cross References

Arrest with and without warrant, citizen's arrest by domestic victim, protective or restraining order, see Penal Code § 836.
Domestic violence incidents, temporary custody of firearms by officers, subsequent procedures, see Penal Code § 18250.
Person defined for purposes of this Code, see Family Code § 105.

Research References

Forms
1 California Transactions Forms--Family Law § 4:3, Validity and Scope of Agreement.
1 California Transactions Forms--Family Law § 4:14, Domestic Violence and Restraining Orders.

§ 6210. "Dating relationship" defined

"Dating relationship" means frequent, intimate associations primarily characterized by the expectation of affection or sexual involvement independent of financial considerations. *(Added by Stats.2001, c. 110 (A.B.362), § 1.)*

Cross References

Battery committed against former spouse, fiancee, or victim who has or had dating relationship with defendant, see Penal Code § 243.

§ 6211. "Domestic violence" defined

"Domestic violence" is abuse perpetrated against any of the following persons:

(a) A spouse or former spouse.

(b) A cohabitant or former cohabitant, as defined in Section 6209.

(c) A person with whom the respondent is having or has had a dating or engagement relationship.

(d) A person with whom the respondent has had a child, where the presumption applies that the male parent is the father of the child of the female parent under the Uniform Parentage Act (Part 3 (commencing with Section 7600) of Division 12).

(e) A child of a party or a child who is the subject of an action under the Uniform Parentage Act, where the presumption applies that the male parent is the father of the child to be protected.

(f) Any other person related by consanguinity or affinity within the second degree. *(Added by Stats.1993, c. 219 (A.B.1500), § 154.)*

Cross References

Action for damages suffered as result of domestic violence, see Code of Civil Procedure § 340.15.
Address confidentiality for victims of domestic violence and stalking, definitions, see Government Code § 6205.5.
Arraignment of the defendant, presence of defendant, domestic violence, see Penal Code § 977.
Authority to compromise misdemeanors for which victim has civil action, see Penal Code § 1377.
Cancellation and failure to renew certain property insurance, victims of domestic violence, see Insurance Code § 676.9.
Change of names, orders to show cause, publication or posting, see Code of Civil Procedure § 1277.

§ 6211

PREVENTION OF DOMESTIC VIOLENCE

Child abuse and neglect reporting, child abuse or neglect defined, see Penal Code § 11165.6.

Community conflict resolution programs, referral of cases by district attorney, considerations, see Penal Code § 14152.

Conditions preventing deferral of sentencing from being offered, see Penal Code § 1001.98.

Criminal history, use when setting bond or considering plea agreement, see Penal Code § 273.75.

Domestic violence, admissibility of other acts evidence, see Evidence Code § 1109.

Domestic violence, interagency death review teams, reporting procedures, see Penal Code § 11163.3.

Domestic violence incidents, temporary custody of firearms, domestic violence defined, see Penal Code §§ 16490, 18250.

Domestic violence offenses, community conflict resolution program referrals prohibited, see Penal Code § 14152.

Domestic violence offenses, compromise prohibited, see Penal Code § 1377.

Domestic violence victim–Counselor privilege, see Evidence Code § 1037.7.

Emergency protective orders, grounds for issuance, persons in danger of domestic violence or abuse, see Family Code § 6250.

Evidence of character, habit, or custom, battered women's syndrome, abuse and domestic violence, see Evidence Code § 1107.

Imprisonment to compel performance of acts, exemption of sexual assault and domestic violence victims who refuse to testify, see Code of Civil Procedure § 1219.

Lease not to be terminated based on domestic or sexual assault against tenant, landlord's liability for compliance, form for affirmative defense to unlawful detainer action, see Code of Civil Procedure § 1161.3.

Legal actions by domestic violence and sexual assault victims, see Labor Code § 230.

Life and disability insurance,
  Discriminatory practices, victims of domestic violence, see Insurance Code § 10144.3.
  Victims of domestic violence, health care service plans, see Insurance Code § 10144.2.

Notification to victim or witness of release of person convicted of stalking or domestic violence, see Penal Code § 646.92.

Offer of diversion to misdemeanor defendant, charged offenses not eligible for diversion, see Penal Code § 1001.95.

Payment of wages, employers with twenty-five or more employees, domestic violence and sexual assault victims, see Labor Code § 230.1.

Person defined for purposes of this Code, see Family Code § 105.

Point-of-service health care service plan contracts, victims of domestic violence, see Health and Safety Code § 1374.75.

Powers and duties of housing authorities, annual report of activities to department, see Health and Safety Code § 34328.1.

Powers of courts, contempt orders, execution of sentence and stay pending appeal, see Code of Civil Procedure § 128.

Presumption against persons perpetrating domestic violence, custody of children, see Family Code § 3044.

Probation revocation or modification, discharge, conditions, see Penal Code § 1203.3.

Protective orders to prevent domestic violence, issuance of order upon affidavit, see Family Code § 6300.

Protective orders to prevent domestic violence, persons who may be granted order, see Family Code § 6301.

References to husband, wife, spouses and married persons, persons included for purposes of this Code, see Family Code § 11.

Respondent defined for purposes of this Code, see Family Code § 127.

Rights of victims and witnesses, domestic violence or abuse counselors, presence at law enforcement interviews, see Penal Code § 679.05.

Summoning law enforcement assistance or emergency assistance by victim of abuse, victim of crime, or individual in emergency, local agency ordinance, etc. limiting right prohibited, see Government Code § 53165.

Summoning law enforcement assistance or emergency assistance, lease or rental agreement provisions prohibiting or limiting right void, see Civil Code § 1946.8.

Suspension of money judgment or order for support of a child, exceptions, resumption of obligation, administrative adjustment, evaluation, see Family Code § 4007.5.

Temporary or permanent support, spouse convicted of domestic violence, presumption disfavoring award, see Family Code § 4325.

Terms of probation for crime of domestic violence, see Penal Code § 1203.097.

Unlawful detainer, commission of nuisance upon premises, see Code of Civil Procedure § 1161.

Victims of domestic violence, notice and conditions of perpetrator's parole, see Penal Code § 3053.2.

Victims of domestic violence, sexual assault, or stalking, written notice to terminate tenancy, requirements, see Civil Code § 1946.7.

Violent sexual felony, domestic violence felony, prohibited awards, see Family Code § 4324.5.

Research References

Forms

California Practice Guide: Rutter Family Law Forms Form 1:32, Glossary of Common Family Law Terms, Phrases and Concepts (Enclosure to Form 1:31).

1 California Transactions Forms--Family Law § 2:54, Permanent Support.

1 California Transactions Forms--Family Law § 4:14, Domestic Violence and Restraining Orders.

West's California Code Forms, Family § 6300, Comment Overview—Protective Orders.

§ 6215. "Emergency protective order" defined

"Emergency protective order" means an order issued under Part 3 (commencing with Section 6240). *(Added by Stats.1993, c. 219 (A.B.1500), § 154.)*

Cross References

Judgment and order defined for purposes of this Code, see Family Code § 100.

§ 6216. "Firearm" and "firearm precursor part" defined

* * * For the purposes of this division, "firearm" includes the frame or receiver of the weapon * * *, including a completed frame or receiver or a firearm precursor part. "Firearm precursor part" has the same meaning as in subdivision (a) of Section 16531 of the Penal Code.

* * * *(Added by Stats.2021, c. 682 (A.B.1057), § 1, eff. Jan. 1, 2022, operative July 1, 2022. Amended by Stats.2022, c. 76 (A.B.1621), § 2, eff. June 30, 2022.)*

§ 6218. "Protective order" defined

"Protective order" means an order that includes any of the following restraining orders, whether issued ex parte, after notice and hearing, or in a judgment:

(a) An order described in Section 6320 enjoining specific acts of abuse.

(b) An order described in Section 6321 excluding a person from a dwelling.

(c) An order described in Section 6322 enjoining other specified behavior. *(Added by Stats.1993, c. 219 (A.B.1500), § 154.)*

Cross References

Abandonment and neglect of children, intentional and knowing violation of court order to prevent harassment, disturbing the peace, or threats or acts of violence, see Penal Code § 273.6.

Community conflict resolution programs, referral of cases by district attorney, considerations, see Penal Code § 14152.

Contempt of court, conduct constituting, see Penal Code § 166.

Criminal identification and statistics, public housing authorities, access to information, see Penal Code § 11105.03.

Dependent children, jurisdiction, custody of child, restraining order, see Welfare and Institutions Code § 304.

Judgment and order defined for purposes of this Code, see Family Code § 100.

Juvenile court law, protective order, parentage, custody, or visitation order, see Welfare and Institutions Code § 726.5.

License plates, application for new and different plates by domestic violence victims, conditions for issuance, see Vehicle Code § 4467.

Person defined for purposes of this Code, see Family Code § 105.

Relinquishment of firearms, persons subject to restraining orders, see Code of Civil Procedure § 527.9.

Search warrants, grounds for issuance, firearm owned by, in possession of, or in custody and control of person against whom protective order has been issued under this section, see Penal Code § 1524.

Termination of juvenile court jurisdiction, pending proceedings relating to parental marriage or custody order, see Welfare and Institutions Code § 362.4.

Unlawful carrying and possession of firearms, specified convictions, see Penal Code §§ 29800 to 29875.

Research References

Forms

West's California Code Forms, Family § 6200, Comment Overview—Prevention of Domestic Violence.

West's California Code Forms, Family § 6250, Comment Overview—Issuance and Effect of Emergency Protective Order.

West's California Judicial Council Forms JV-245, Request for Restraining Order—Juvenile (Also Available in Chinese, Korean, Spanish, and Vietnamese).

West's California Judicial Council Forms JV-250, Notice of Hearing and Temporary Restraining Order—Juvenile (Also Available in Chinese, Korean, Spanish, and Vietnamese).

West's California Judicial Council Forms JV-255, Restraining Order—Juvenile (Clets–Juv) (Also Available in Chinese, Korean, Spanish, and Vietnamese).

§ 6219. Demonstration project to identify best practices in domestic violence court cases; participation in project; findings and recommendations

Subject to adequate, discretionary funding from a city or a county, the superior courts in San Diego County and in Santa Clara County may develop a demonstration project to identify the best practices in civil, juvenile, and criminal court cases involving domestic violence. The superior courts in any other county that is able and willing may also participate in the demonstration project. The superior courts participating in this demonstration project shall report their findings and recommendations to the Judicial Council and the Legislature on or before May 1, 2004. The Judicial Council may make those recommendations available to any court or county. *(Added by Stats.2002, c. 192 (A.B.1909), § 1.)*

Cross References

County defined for purposes of this Code, see Family Code § 67.

Part 2

GENERAL PROVISIONS

Section
6220. Purpose.
6221. Application of division; forms for issuance of orders.
6222. Application, responsive pleading, or show cause order seeking to acquire, modify, or enforce a protective order; subpoena filed in connection; fees.
6223. Custody or visitation order; application of Part 2 of Division 8.
6224. Statement on face of order; expiration date and notice.
6225. Explicit statement of address not required.
6226. Forms and instructions; promulgation by Judicial Council.
6226.5. Confidentiality program provision in "Can a Domestic Violence Restraining Order Help Me?" form.
6227. Remedies in this chapter additional to other remedies.
6228. Access to Domestic Violence Reports Act of 1999.
6229. Minor under 12 years of age appearing without counsel.

§ 6220. Purpose

The purpose of this division is to prevent acts of domestic violence, abuse, and sexual abuse and to provide for a separation of the persons involved in the domestic violence for a period sufficient to enable these persons to seek a resolution of the causes of the violence. *(Added by Stats.1993, c. 219 (A.B.1500), § 154. Amended by Stats.2014, c. 635 (A.B.2089), § 3, eff. Jan. 1, 2015.)*

Cross References

Domestic violence defined for purposes of this Code, see Family Code § 6211.
Person defined for purposes of this Code, see Family Code § 105.
Prevention of domestic violence, issuance of order upon affidavit or testimony, see Family Code § 6300.
Protective orders and other domestic violence protection orders, confidentiality of information relating to minors, see Family Code § 6301.5.

§ 6221. Application of division; forms for issuance of orders

(a) Unless the provision or context otherwise requires, this division applies to any order described in this division, whether the order is issued in a proceeding brought pursuant to this division, in an action brought pursuant to the Uniform Parentage Act (Part 3 (commencing with Section 7600) of Division 12), or in a proceeding for dissolution of marriage, for nullity of marriage, or for legal separation of the parties.

(b) Nothing in this division affects the jurisdiction of the juvenile court.

(c) Any order issued by a court to which this division applies shall be issued on forms adopted by the Judicial Council of California and that have been approved by the Department of Justice pursuant to subdivision (i) of Section 6380. However, the fact that an order issued by a court pursuant to this section was not issued on forms adopted by the Judicial Council and approved by the Department of Justice shall not, in and of itself, make the order unenforceable. *(Added by Stats.1993, c. 219 (A.B.1500), § 154. Amended by Stats.1999, c. 661 (A.B.825), § 4.)*

Cross References

Court interpreter services provided in civil actions, reimbursement by Judicial Council, prioritization where funding is insufficient, see Evidence Code § 756.
Electronic transmission of data filed with the court with respect to protective orders, see Family Code § 6380.
Judgment and order defined for purposes of this Code, see Family Code § 100.
Proceeding defined for purposes of this Code, see Family Code § 110.
Witnesses, interpreters and translators, hearings or proceedings related to domestic violence, see Evidence Code § 756.

Research References

Forms

West's California Code Forms, Family § 6200, Comment Overview—Prevention of Domestic Violence.
West's California Code Forms, Family § 6220, Comment Overview—General Provisions.
West's California Code Forms, Family § 6380, Comment Overview—Registration and Enforcement of Orders.

§ 6222. Application, responsive pleading, or show cause order seeking to acquire, modify, or enforce a protective order; subpoena filed in connection; fees

There is no filing fee for an application, a responsive pleading, or an order to show cause that seeks to obtain, modify, or enforce a protective order or other order authorized by this division when the request for the other order is necessary to obtain or give effect to a protective order. There is no fee for a subpoena filed in connection with that application, responsive pleading, or order to show cause. There is no fee for any filings related to a petition filed pursuant to Part 4 (commencing with 6300) of this division. *(Added by Stats. 2002, c. 1009 (A.B.2030), § 4, operative Jan. 1, 2007. Amended by Stats.2006, c. 476 (A.B.2695), § 3; Stats.2021, c. 686 (S.B.538), § 1, eff. Jan. 1, 2022.)*

Cross References

Harassment, temporary restraining order or injunction, fee waiver, see Code of Civil Procedure § 527.6.
Judgment and order defined for purposes of this Code, see Family Code § 100.
Petitioner defined for purposes of this Code, see Family Code § 126.
Proceeding defined for purposes of this Code, see Family Code § 110.

Protective order defined for purposes of this Code, see Family Code § 6218.

Research References

Forms

West's California Code Forms, Family § 6220, Comment Overview—General Provisions.

§ 6223. Custody or visitation order; application of Part 2 of Division 8

A custody or visitation order issued in a proceeding brought pursuant to this division is subject to Part 2 (commencing with Section 3020) of Division 8 (custody of children). *(Added by Stats.1993, c. 219 (A.B.1500), § 154.)*

Cross References

Judgment and order defined for purposes of this Code, see Family Code § 100.
Proceeding defined for purposes of this Code, see Family Code § 110.

Research References

Forms

1 California Transactions Forms--Family Law § 3:4, Subject Matter Jurisdiction for Custody Determinations.

§ 6224. Statement on face of order; expiration date and notice

An order described in this division shall state on its face the date of expiration of the order and the following statements in substantially the following form:

"This order is effective when made. The law enforcement agency shall enforce it immediately on receipt. It is enforceable anywhere in California by any law enforcement agency that has received the order or is shown a copy of the order. If proof of service on the restrained person has not been received, the law enforcement agency shall advise the restrained person of the terms of the order and then shall enforce it." *(Added by Stats.1993, c. 219 (A.B.1500), § 154.)*

Cross References

Intentional and knowing violations of court orders to prevent harassment or domestic violence, see Penal Code § 273.6.
Judgment and order defined for purposes of this Code, see Family Code § 100.
Person defined for purposes of this Code, see Family Code § 105.
State defined for purposes of this Code, see Family Code § 145.
Temporary restraining orders or injunctions, victims of domestic violence, see Code of Civil Procedure § 527.6.

Research References

Forms

West's California Judicial Council Forms FL–300, Request for Order (Also Available in Spanish).

§ 6225. Explicit statement of address not required

A petition for an order described in this division is valid and the order is enforceable without explicitly stating the address of the petitioner or the petitioner's place of residence, school, employment, the place where the petitioner's child is provided child care services, or the child's school. *(Added by Stats.1993, c. 219 (A.B.1500), § 154.)*

Cross References

Judgment and order defined for purposes of this Code, see Family Code § 100.
Petitioner defined for purposes of this Code, see Family Code § 126.

§ 6226. Forms and instructions; promulgation by Judicial Council

The Judicial Council shall prescribe the form of the orders and any other documents required by this division and shall promulgate forms and instructions for applying for orders described in this division. *(Added by Stats.1993, c. 219 (A.B.1500), § 154.)*

Cross References

Judgment and order defined for purposes of this Code, see Family Code § 100.

Research References

Forms

West's California Judicial Council Forms FL–300, Request for Order (Also Available in Spanish).

§ 6226.5. Confidentiality program provision in "Can a Domestic Violence Restraining Order Help Me?" form

(a) On or before January 1, 2023, the Judicial Council shall amend the Judicial Council form entitled "Can a Domestic Violence Restraining Order Help Me?" to include a brief description of the address confidentiality program established under Chapter 3.1 (commencing with Section 6205) of Division 7 of Title 1 of the Government Code, the benefits of enrollment in the program for victims of domestic violence, and the internet address for the Secretary of State's internet web page that contains more detailed information about the program.

(b) On or before January 1, 2023, the Judicial Council shall make the Judicial Council form available in English and in at least the other languages described in Section 1632 of the Civil Code. The Judicial Council may make the form available in additional languages. *(Added by Stats.2021, c. 457 (A.B.277), § 1, eff. Jan. 1, 2022.)*

§ 6227. Remedies in this chapter additional to other remedies

The remedies provided in this division are in addition to any other civil or criminal remedies that may be available to the petitioner. *(Added by Stats.1993, c. 219 (A.B.1500), § 154.)*

Cross References

Petitioner defined for purposes of this Code, see Family Code § 126.

§ 6228. Access to Domestic Violence Reports Act of 1999

(a) State and local law enforcement agencies shall provide, upon request and without charging a fee, one copy of all incident report face sheets, one copy of all incident reports, or both, to a victim, or the victim's representative as defined in subdivision (g), of a crime that constitutes an act of any of the following:

(1) Domestic violence, as defined in Section 6211.

(2) Sexual assault, as defined in Sections 261, 261.5, 262, 265, 266, 266a, 266b, 266c, 266g, 266j, 267, 269, 273.4, 285, 286, 287, 288, 288.5, 289, or 311.4 of, or former Section 288a of, the Penal Code.

(3) Stalking, as defined in Section 1708.7 of the Civil Code or Section 646.9 of the Penal Code.

(4) Human trafficking, as defined in Section 236.1 of the Penal Code.

(5) Abuse of an elder or a dependent adult, as defined in Section 15610.07 of the Welfare and Institutions Code.

(b)(1) A copy of an incident report face sheet shall be made available during regular business hours to a victim or the victim's representative no later than 48 hours after being requested, unless the state or local law enforcement agency informs the victim or the victim's representative of the reasons why, for good cause, the incident report face sheet is not available, in which case the incident report face sheet shall be made available no later than five working days after the request is made.

(2) A copy of the incident report shall be made available during regular business hours to a victim or the victim's representative no later than five working days after being requested, unless the state or local law enforcement agency informs the victim or the victim's representative of the reasons why, for good cause, the incident report is not available, in which case the incident report shall be made available no later than 10 working days after the request is made.

(c) A person requesting copies under this section shall present state or local law enforcement with the person's identification, including a current, valid driver's license, a state-issued identification card, or a passport. If the person is a representative of the victim and the victim is deceased, the representative shall also present a certified copy of the death certificate or other satisfactory evidence of the death of the victim at the time a request is made. If the person is a representative of the victim and the victim is alive and not the subject of a conservatorship, the representative shall also present a written authorization, signed by the victim, making the person the victim's personal representative.

(d)(1) This section shall apply to requests for domestic violence face sheets or incident reports made within five years from the date of completion of the incident report.

(2) This section shall apply to requests for sexual assault, stalking, human trafficking, or abuse of an elder or a dependent adult face sheets or incident reports made within two years from the date of completion of the incident report.

(e) This section shall be known and may be cited as the Access to Domestic Violence Reports Act of 1999.

(f) For purposes of this section, "victim" includes a minor who is 12 years of age or older.

(g)(1) For purposes of this section, if the victim is deceased, a "representative of the victim" means any of the following:

(A) The surviving spouse.

(B) A surviving child of the decedent who has attained 18 years of age.

(C) A domestic partner, as defined in subdivision (a) of Section 297.

(D) A surviving parent of the decedent.

(E) A surviving adult relative.

(F) The personal representative of the victim, as defined in Section 58 of the Probate Code, if one is appointed.

(G) The public administrator if one has been appointed.

(2) For purposes of this section, if the victim is not deceased, a "representative of the victim" means any of the following:

(A) A parent, guardian, or adult child of the victim, or an adult sibling of a victim 12 years of age or older, who shall present to law enforcement identification pursuant to subdivision (c). A guardian shall also present to law enforcement a copy of the letters of guardianship demonstrating that the person is the appointed guardian of the victim.

(B) An attorney for the victim, who shall present to law enforcement identification pursuant to subdivision (c) and written proof that the person is the attorney for the victim.

(C) A conservator of the victim who shall present to law enforcement identification pursuant to subdivision (c) and a copy of the letters of conservatorship demonstrating that the person is the appointed conservator of the victim.

(3) A representative of the victim does not include any person who has been convicted of murder in the first degree, as defined in Section 189 of the Penal Code, of the victim, or any person identified in the incident report face sheet as a suspect. (Added by Stats.1999, c. 1022 (A.B.403), § 1. Amended by Stats.2002, c. 377 (S.B.1265), § 1; Stats.2010, c. 363 (A.B.1738), § 1; Stats.2011, c. 296 (A.B.1023), § 93; Stats.2016, c. 875 (A.B.1678), § 1, eff. Jan. 1, 2017; Stats.2018, c. 423 (S.B.1494), § 24, eff. Jan. 1, 2019; Stats.2019, c. 115 (A.B. 1817), § 59, eff. Jan. 1, 2020.)

Cross References

Adult defined for purposes of this Code, see Family Code § 6501.
Person defined for purposes of this Code, see Family Code § 105.
References to husband, wife, spouses and married persons, persons included for purposes of this Code, see Family Code § 11.
State defined for purposes of this Code, see Family Code § 145.

§ 6229. Minor under 12 years of age appearing without counsel

A minor, under 12 years of age, accompanied by a duly appointed and acting guardian ad litem, shall be permitted to appear in court without counsel for the limited purpose of requesting or opposing a request for a temporary restraining order or injunction, or both, under this division as provided in Section 374 of the Code of Civil Procedure. (Added by Stats.2010, c. 572 (A.B.1596), § 12, operative Jan. 1, 2012.)

Part 3

EMERGENCY PROTECTIVE ORDERS

Chapter	Section
1. General Provisions	6240
2. Issuance and Effect of Emergency Protective Order	6250
3. Duties of Law Enforcement Officer	6270

Cross References

Child abduction,
  Definitions, custody, proceeding, see Penal Code § 277.
  Protective custody, circumstances, see Penal Code § 279.6.
Freedom from parental custody and control, application of proceedings to domestic violence orders, see Family Code § 7807.
Termination of parental rights of father, application of provisions relating to filing of petition to terminate upon jurisdiction of court pursuant to this Part with respect to domestic violence orders, see Family Code § 7662.
Victims of domestic violence, sexual assault, or stalking, written notice to terminate tenancy, requirements, see Civil Code § 1946.7.

CHAPTER 1. GENERAL PROVISIONS

Section
6240. Definitions.
6241. Designation of judge, commissioner, or referee to orally issue emergency protective orders.

Cross References

Lease not to be terminated based on domestic or sexual assault against tenant, landlord's liability for compliance, form for affirmative defense to unlawful detainer action, see Code of Civil Procedure § 1161.3.
Tenant protected by restraining order against another tenant, change of locks on dwelling unit, definitions, see Civil Code § 1941.6.
Tenant protected by restraining order against non-tenant, change of locks on dwelling unit, definitions, see Civil Code § 1941.5.

§ 6240. Definitions

As used in this part:

(a) "Judicial officer" means a judge, commissioner, or referee designated under Section 6241.

(b) "Law enforcement officer" means one of the following officers who requests or enforces an emergency protective order under this part:

(1) A police officer.

(2) A sheriff's officer.

(3) A peace officer of the Department of the California Highway Patrol.

(4) A peace officer of the University of California Police Department.

(5) A peace officer of the California State University and College Police Departments.

§ 6240

(6) A peace officer of the Department of Parks and Recreation, as defined in subdivision (f) of Section 830.2 of the Penal Code.

(7) A peace officer of the Department of General Services of the City of Los Angeles, as defined in subdivision (c) of Section 830.31 of the Penal Code.

(8) A housing authority patrol officer, as defined in subdivision (d) of Section 830.31 of the Penal Code.

(9) A peace officer for a district attorney, as defined in Section 830.1 or 830.35 of the Penal Code.

(10) A parole officer, probation officer, or deputy probation officer, as defined in Section 830.5 of the Penal Code.

(11) A peace officer of a California Community College police department, as defined in subdivision (a) of Section 830.32.

(12) A peace officer employed by a police department of a school district, as defined in subdivision (b) of Section 830.32.

(c) "Abduct" means take, entice away, keep, withhold, or conceal. *(Added by Stats.1993, c. 219 (A.B.1500), § 154. Amended by Stats.1993, c. 1229 (A.B.224), § 1; Gov.Reorg.Plan No. 1 of 1995, § 4, eff. July 12, 1995; Stats.1996, c. 305 (A.B.3103), § 5; Stats.1996, c. 988 (A.B.2936), § 3; Stats.1999, c. 659 (S.B.355), § 1; Stats.2004, c. 250 (S.B.1391), § 1.)*

Cross References

Emergency protective order defined for purposes of this Code, see Family Code § 6215.
Freedom from parental custody and control, stay of proceedings and effect upon jurisdiction under these provisions, see Family Code § 7807.
Judgment and order defined for purposes of this Code, see Family Code § 100.
State defined for purposes of this Code, see Family Code § 145.

Research References

Forms

West's California Judicial Council Forms EPO–001, Emergency Protective Order (CLETS-EPO) (Also Available in Chinese, Korean, Spanish, and Vietnamese).

§ 6241. Designation of judge, commissioner, or referee to orally issue emergency protective orders

The presiding judge of the superior court in each county shall designate at least one judge, commissioner, or referee to be reasonably available to issue orally, by telephone or otherwise, emergency protective orders at all times whether or not the court is in session. *(Added by Stats.1993, c. 219 (A.B.1500), § 154.)*

Cross References

County defined for purposes of this Code, see Family Code § 67.
Emergency protective order defined for purposes of this Code, see Family Code § 6215.
Judgment and order defined for purposes of this Code, see Family Code § 100.

Research References

Forms

West's California Code Forms, Family § 6240, Comment Overview—Emergency Protective Orders.

CHAPTER 2. ISSUANCE AND EFFECT OF EMERGENCY PROTECTIVE ORDER

Section
6250. Grounds for issuance.
6250.3. Valid orders.
6250.5. Issuance of ex parte emergency protective orders to peace officers.
6251. Findings of court.
6252. Inclusion of other orders.

Section
6252.5. Addresses or locations of persons protected under court order; prohibition upon certain enjoined parties from acting to obtain such information.
6253. Contents of orders.
6254. Availability of orders; effect of vacation of household.
6255. Issuance of orders without prejudice.
6256. Expiration of orders.
6257. Application for restraining orders under Welfare and Institutions Code § 213.5.

Cross References

Domestic violence prevention, emergency protective orders, precedence over other restraining or protective orders for enforcement purposes, see Penal Code § 136.2.

§ 6250. Grounds for issuance

A judicial officer may issue an ex parte emergency protective order where a law enforcement officer asserts reasonable grounds to believe any of the following:

(a) That a person is in immediate and present danger of domestic violence, based on the person's allegation of a recent incident of abuse or threat of abuse by the person against whom the order is sought.

(b) That a child is in immediate and present danger of abuse by a family or household member, based on an allegation of a recent incident of abuse or threat of abuse by the family or household member.

(c) That a child is in immediate and present danger of being abducted by a parent or relative, based on a reasonable belief that a person has an intent to abduct the child or flee with the child from the jurisdiction or based on an allegation of a recent threat to abduct the child or flee with the child from the jurisdiction.

(d) That an elder or dependent adult is in immediate and present danger of abuse as defined in Section 15610.07 of the Welfare and Institutions Code, based on an allegation of a recent incident of abuse or threat of abuse by the person against whom the order is sought, except that no emergency protective order shall be issued based solely on an allegation of financial abuse. *(Added by Stats.1993, c. 219 (A.B.1500), § 154. Amended by Stats.1996, c. 988 (A.B.2936), § 4; Stats.1999, c. 561 (A.B.59), § 1; Stats.2003, c. 468 (S.B.851), § 3.)*

Cross References

Adult defined for purposes of this Code, see Family Code § 6501.
Domestic violence defined for purposes of this Code, see Family Code § 6211.
Emergency protective order defined for purposes of this Code, see Family Code § 6215.
Judgment and order defined for purposes of this Code, see Family Code § 100.
Officer to inform that order may be sought, request for person in immediate and present danger, see Family Code § 6275.
Person defined for purposes of this Code, see Family Code § 105.

Research References

Forms

California Practice Guide: Rutter Family Law Forms Form 1:32, Glossary of Common Family Law Terms, Phrases and Concepts (Enclosure to Form 1:31).
West's California Code Forms, Family § 6250, Comment Overview—Issuance and Effect of Emergency Protective Order.

§ 6250.3. Valid orders

An emergency protective order is valid only if it is issued by a judicial officer after making the findings required by Section 6251 and pursuant to a specific request by a law enforcement officer. *(Added by Stats.2006, c. 82 (A.B.1787), § 1.)*

§ 6250.5. Issuance of ex parte emergency protective orders to peace officers

A judicial officer may issue an ex parte emergency protective order to a peace officer defined in subdivisions (a) and (b) of Section 830.32 if the issuance of that order is consistent with an existing memorandum of understanding between the college or school police department where the peace officer is employed and the sheriff or police chief of the city in whose jurisdiction the peace officer's college or school is located and the peace officer asserts reasonable grounds to believe that there is a demonstrated threat to campus safety. *(Added by Stats.1999, c. 659 (S.B.355), § 1.5.)*

Cross References

Emergency protective order defined for purposes of this Code, see Family Code § 6215.
Judgment and order defined for purposes of this Code, see Family Code § 100.

Research References

Forms

West's California Code Forms, Family § 6250, Comment Overview—Issuance and Effect of Emergency Protective Order.

§ 6251. Findings of court

An emergency protective order may be issued only if the judicial officer finds both of the following:

(a) That reasonable grounds have been asserted to believe that an immediate and present danger of domestic violence exists, that a child is in immediate and present danger of abuse or abduction, or that an elder or dependent adult is in immediate and present danger of abuse as defined in Section 15610.07 of the Welfare and Institutions Code.

(b) That an emergency protective order is necessary to prevent the occurrence or recurrence of domestic violence, child abuse, child abduction, or abuse of an elder or dependent adult. *(Added by Stats.1993, c. 219 (A.B.1500), § 154. Amended by Stats.1996, c. 988 (A.B.2936), § 5; Stats.1999, c. 561 (A.B.59), § 2.)*

Cross References

Abuse defined for purposes of the Domestic Violence Protection Act, see Family Code § 6203.
Adult defined for purposes of this Code, see Family Code § 6501.
Domestic violence defined for purposes of this Code, see Family Code § 6211.
Emergency protective order defined for purposes of this Code, see Family Code § 6215.
Judgment and order defined for purposes of this Code, see Family Code § 100.

Research References

Forms

West's California Code Forms, Family § 6250, Comment Overview—Issuance and Effect of Emergency Protective Order.

§ 6252. Inclusion of other orders

An emergency protective order may include any of the following specific orders, as appropriate:

(a) A protective order, as defined in Section 6218.

(b) An order determining the temporary care and control of any minor child of the endangered person and the person against whom the order is sought.

(c) An order authorized in Section 213.5 of the Welfare and Institutions Code, including provisions placing the temporary care and control of the endangered child and any other minor children in the family or household with the parent or guardian of the endangered child who is not a restrained party.

(d) An order determining the temporary care and control of any minor child who is in danger of being abducted.

(e) An order authorized by Section 15657.03 of the Welfare and Institutions Code. *(Added by Stats.1993, c. 219 (A.B.1500), § 154. Amended by Stats.1996, c. 988 (A.B.2936), § 6; Stats.1999, c. 561 (A.B.59), § 3.)*

Cross References

Emergency protective order defined for purposes of this Code, see Family Code § 6215.
Guardian, defined, see Probate Code §§ 2350, 2400.
Judgment and order defined for purposes of this Code, see Family Code § 100.
Minor defined for purposes of this Code, see Family Code § 6500.
Parent or guardian, defined, see Family Code § 6903.
Person defined for purposes of this Code, see Family Code § 105.

Research References

Forms

West's California Code Forms, Family § 6250, Comment Overview—Issuance and Effect of Emergency Protective Order.

§ 6252.5. Addresses or locations of persons protected under court order; prohibition upon certain enjoined parties from acting to obtain such information

(a) The court shall order that any party enjoined pursuant to an order issued under this part be prohibited from taking any action to obtain the address or location of a protected party or a protected party's family members, caretakers, or guardian, unless there is good cause not to make that order.

(b) The Judicial Council shall promulgate forms necessary to effectuate this section. *(Added by Stats.2005, c. 472 (A.B.978), § 2.)*

Research References

Forms

West's California Code Forms, Family § 6250, Comment Overview—Issuance and Effect of Emergency Protective Order.

§ 6253. Contents of orders

An emergency protective order shall include all of the following:

(a) A statement of the grounds asserted for the order.

(b) The date and time the order expires.

(c) The address of the superior court for the district or county in which the endangered person or child in danger of being abducted resides.

(d) The following statements, which shall be printed in English and Spanish:

(1) "To the Protected Person: This order will last only until the date and time noted above. If you wish to seek continuing protection, you will have to apply for an order from the court, at the address noted above. You may seek the advice of an attorney as to any matter connected with your application for any future court orders. The attorney should be consulted promptly so that the attorney may assist you in making your application."

(2) "To the Restrained Person: This order will last until the date and time noted above. The protected party may, however, obtain a more permanent restraining order from the court. You may seek the advice of an attorney as to any matter connected with the application. The attorney should be consulted promptly so that the attorney may assist you in responding to the application."

(e) In the case of an endangered child, the following statement, which shall be printed in English and Spanish: "This order will last only until the date and time noted above. You may apply for a more permanent restraining order under Section 213.5 of the Welfare and Institutions Code from the court at the address noted above. You may seek the advice of an attorney in connection with the application for a more permanent restraining order."

(f) In the case of a child in danger of being abducted, the following statement, which shall be printed in English and Spanish: "This

§ 6253

order will last only until the date and time noted above. You may apply for a child custody order from the court, at the address noted above. You may seek the advice of an attorney as to any matter connected with the application. The attorney should be consulted promptly so that the attorney may assist you in responding to the application." *(Added by Stats.1993, c. 219 (A.B.1500), § 154. Amended by Stats.1996, c. 988 (A.B.2936), § 7.)*

Cross References

County defined for purposes of this Code, see Family Code § 67.
Emergency protective order defined for purposes of this Code, see Family Code § 6215.
Judgment and order defined for purposes of this Code, see Family Code § 100.
Person defined for purposes of this Code, see Family Code § 105.

Research References

Forms

West's California Code Forms, Family § 6250, Comment Overview—Issuance and Effect of Emergency Protective Order.

§ 6254. Availability of orders; effect of vacation of household

The fact that the endangered person has left the household to avoid abuse does not affect the availability of an emergency protective order. *(Added by Stats.1993, c. 219 (A.B.1500), § 154.)*

Cross References

Abuse defined for purposes of the Domestic Violence Protection Act, see Family Code § 6203.
Emergency protective order defined for purposes of this Code, see Family Code § 6215.
Judgment and order defined for purposes of this Code, see Family Code § 100.
Person defined for purposes of this Code, see Family Code § 105.

Research References

Forms

West's California Code Forms, Family § 6250, Comment Overview—Issuance and Effect of Emergency Protective Order.

§ 6255. Issuance of orders without prejudice

An emergency protective order shall be issued without prejudice to any person. *(Added by Stats.1993, c. 219 (A.B.1500), § 154.)*

Cross References

Emergency protective order defined for purposes of this Code, see Family Code § 6215.
Judgment and order defined for purposes of this Code, see Family Code § 100.
Person defined for purposes of this Code, see Family Code § 105.

§ 6256. Expiration of orders

An emergency protective order expires at the earlier of the following times:

(a) The close of judicial business on the fifth court day following the day of its issuance.

(b) The seventh calendar day following the day of its issuance. *(Added by Stats.1993, c. 219 (A.B.1500), § 154. Amended by Stats.1993, c. 1229 (A.B.224), § 2.)*

Cross References

Emergency protective order defined for purposes of this Code, see Family Code § 6215.
Judgment and order defined for purposes of this Code, see Family Code § 100.

Research References

Forms

West's California Code Forms, Family § 6250, Comment Overview—Issuance and Effect of Emergency Protective Order.

§ 6257. Application for restraining orders under Welfare and Institutions Code § 213.5

If an emergency protective order concerns an endangered child, the child's parent or guardian who is not a restrained person, or a person having temporary custody of the endangered child, may apply to the court for a restraining order under Section 213.5 of the Welfare and Institutions Code. *(Added by Stats.1993, c. 219 (A.B. 1500), § 154.)*

Cross References

Emergency protective order defined for purposes of this Code, see Family Code § 6215.
Guardian, defined, see Probate Code §§ 2350, 2400.
Judgment and order defined for purposes of this Code, see Family Code § 100.
Parent or guardian, defined, see Family Code § 6903.
Person defined for purposes of this Code, see Family Code § 105.

Research References

Forms

West's California Code Forms, Family § 6250, Comment Overview—Issuance and Effect of Emergency Protective Order.

CHAPTER 3. DUTIES OF LAW ENFORCEMENT OFFICER

Section
6270. Reduction of orders to writing.
6271. Duties of officer who requested order.
6272. Enforcement of orders; liability of officers enforcing orders.
6273. Repealed.
6274. Stalking; emergency protective order.
6275. Conditions under which an officer is to inform a person for whom emergency protective order may be sought.

§ 6270. Reduction of orders to writing

A law enforcement officer who requests an emergency protective order shall reduce the order to writing and sign it. *(Added by Stats.1993, c. 219 (A.B.1500), § 154.)*

Cross References

Emergency protective order defined for purposes of this Code, see Family Code § 6215.
Judgment and order defined for purposes of this Code, see Family Code § 100.

§ 6271. Duties of officer who requested order

A law enforcement officer who requests an emergency protective order shall do all of the following:

(a) Serve the order on the restrained person, if the restrained person can reasonably be located.

(b) Give a copy of the order to the protected person or, if the protected person is a minor child, to a parent or guardian of the endangered child who is not a restrained person, if the parent or guardian can reasonably be located, or to a person having temporary custody of the endangered child.

(c) File a copy of the order with the court as soon as practicable after issuance.

(d) Have the order entered into the computer database system for protective and restraining orders maintained by the Department of Justice. *(Added by Stats.1993, c. 219 (A.B.1500), § 154. Amended by Stats.2013, c. 145 (A.B.238), § 1.)*

Cross References

Emergency protective order defined for purposes of this Code, see Family Code § 6215.
Guardian, defined, see Probate Code §§ 2350, 2400.
Judgment and order defined for purposes of this Code, see Family Code § 100.
Minor defined for purposes of this Code, see Family Code § 6500.
Parent or guardian, defined, see Family Code § 6903.

Person defined for purposes of this Code, see Family Code § 105.

§ 6272. Enforcement of orders; liability of officers enforcing orders

(a) A law enforcement officer shall use every reasonable means to enforce an emergency protective order.

(b) A law enforcement officer who acts in good faith to enforce an emergency protective order is not civilly or criminally liable. *(Added by Stats.1993, c. 219 (A.B.1500), § 154.)*

Cross References

Emergency protective order defined for purposes of this Code, see Family Code § 6215.

Judgment and order defined for purposes of this Code, see Family Code § 100.

§ 6273. Repealed by Stats.2013, c. 145 (A.B.238), § 2

§ 6274. Stalking; emergency protective order

A peace officer, as defined in Section 830.1 or 830.2 of the Penal Code, may seek an emergency protective order relating to stalking under Section 646.91 of the Penal Code if the requirements of that section are complied with. *(Added by Stats.1997, c. 169 (A.B.350), § 1.)*

Cross References

Emergency protective order defined for purposes of this Code, see Family Code § 6215.

Judgment and order defined for purposes of this Code, see Family Code § 100.

Research References

Forms

West's California Code Forms, Family § 6274, Comment Overview—Stalking.

§ 6275. Conditions under which an officer is to inform a person for whom emergency protective order may be sought

(a) A law enforcement officer who responds to a situation in which the officer believes that there may be grounds for the issuance of an emergency protective order pursuant to Section 6250 of this code or Section 646.91 of the Penal Code, shall inform the person for whom an emergency protective order may be sought, or, if that person is a minor, the minor's parent or guardian, provided that the parent or guardian is not the person against whom the emergency protective order may be obtained, that the person may request the officer to request an emergency protective order pursuant to this part.

(b) Notwithstanding Section 6250, and pursuant to this part, an officer shall request an emergency protective order if the officer believes that the person requesting an emergency protective order is in immediate and present danger. *(Added by Stats.2006, c. 479 (A.B.2139), § 1. Amended by Stats.2019, c. 115 (A.B.1817), § 60, eff. Jan. 1, 2020.)*

Research References

Forms

West's California Code Forms, Family § 6250, Comment Overview—Issuance and Effect of Emergency Protective Order.
West's California Code Forms, Family § 6274, Comment Overview—Stalking.
West's California Judicial Council Forms EPO–001, Emergency Protective Order (CLETS-EPO) (Also Available in Chinese, Korean, Spanish, and Vietnamese).

Part 4

PROTECTIVE ORDERS AND OTHER DOMESTIC VIOLENCE PREVENTION ORDERS

Chapter	Section
1. General Provisions	6300
2. Issuance of Orders	6320
3. Registration and Enforcement of Orders	6380

Cross References

Application, responsive pleading, or show cause order seeking to acquire, modify, or enforce a protective order, subpoena filed in connection, fees, see Family Code § 6222.

Domestic violence incidents, temporary custody of firearms by officers, subsequent procedures, see Penal Code §§ 18250 to 18275.

Freedom from parental custody and control, stay of proceedings and effect upon jurisdiction under these provisions, see Family Code § 7807.

License plates, application for new and different plates by domestic violence victims, conditions for issuance, see Vehicle Code § 4467.

Termination of parental rights of father, application of provisions relating to filing of petition to terminate upon jurisdiction of court pursuant to this Part with respect to domestic violence orders, see Family Code § 7662.

Victims of domestic violence, sexual assault, or stalking, written notice to terminate tenancy, requirements, see Civil Code § 1946.7.

CHAPTER 1. GENERAL PROVISIONS

Section	
6300.	Issuance of order upon affidavit or testimony.
6301.	Persons who may be granted order.
6301.5.	Confidentiality of information relating to minors.
6302.	Notice of hearing.
6303.	Support persons for victims of domestic violence; powers and duties; discretion of court.
6304.	Protective orders; court to inform parties of terms of orders.
6305.	Mutual orders; personal appearance of parties; application for relief.
6306.	Criminal history search; prior restraining orders.
6306.5.	Electronically submitted petitions seeking domestic violence restraining orders.
6306.6.	Domestic violence restraining orders visible on superior court's internet website.
6307.	Repealed.
6307.	Electronic submission of petitions and filings; availability of electronic filing and self-help center information on homepage; adoption of rules and forms for implementation.
6308.	Remote appearance of party, support person, and witness; development and publication of local rules.

Cross References

Lease not to be terminated based on domestic or sexual assault against tenant, landlord's liability for compliance, form for affirmative defense to unlawful detainer action, see Code of Civil Procedure § 1161.3.

Tenant protected by restraining order against another tenant, change of locks on dwelling unit, definitions, see Civil Code § 1941.6.

Tenant protected by restraining order against non-tenant, change of locks on dwelling unit, definitions, see Civil Code § 1941.5.

§ 6300. Issuance of order upon affidavit or testimony

(a) An order may be issued under this part to restrain any person for the purpose specified in Section 6220, if an affidavit or testimony and any additional information provided to the court pursuant to Section 6306, shows, to the satisfaction of the court, reasonable proof of a past act or acts of abuse. The court may issue an order under this part based solely on the affidavit or testimony of the person requesting the restraining order.

(b) An ex parte restraining order issued pursuant to Article 1 (commencing with Section 6320) shall not be denied solely because the other party was not provided with notice. *(Added by Stats.1993, c. 219 (A.B.1500), § 154. Amended by Stats.2001, c. 572 (S.B.66), § 2; Stats.2014, c. 635 (A.B.2089), § 4, eff. Jan. 1, 2015; Stats.2018, c. 219 (A.B.2694), § 1, eff. Jan. 1, 2019.)*

§ 6300   PREVENTION OF DOMESTIC VIOLENCE

Implementation

Implementation of Stats.2001, c. 572 (S.B.66), see § 7 of that act.

Cross References

Abuse defined for purposes of the Domestic Violence Protection Act, see Family Code § 6203.
Domestic violence defined for purposes of this Code, see Family Code § 6211.
Judgment and order defined for purposes of this Code, see Family Code § 100.
Person defined for purposes of this Code, see Family Code § 105.

Research References

Forms

West's California Code Forms, Family § 6200, Comment Overview—Prevention of Domestic Violence.
West's California Code Forms, Family § 6300, Comment Overview—Protective Orders.

§ 6301. Persons who may be granted order

(a) An order under this part may be granted to any person described in Section 6211, including a minor pursuant to subdivision (b) of Section 372 of the Code of Civil Procedure.

(b) The right to petition for relief shall not be denied because the petitioner has vacated the household to avoid abuse, and in the case of a marital relationship, notwithstanding that a petition for dissolution of marriage, for nullity of marriage, or for legal separation of the parties has not been filed.

(c) The length of time since the most recent act of abuse is not, by itself, determinative. The court shall consider the totality of the circumstances in determining whether to grant or deny a petition for relief. *(Added by Stats.1993, c. 219 (A.B.1500), § 154. Amended by Stats.1996, c. 727 (A.B.2155), § 3; Stats.2014, c. 635 (A.B.2089), § 5, eff. Jan. 1, 2015; Stats.2015, c. 303 (A.B.731), § 150, eff. Jan. 1, 2016.)*

Cross References

Abuse defined for purposes of the Domestic Violence Protection Act, see Family Code § 6203.
Judgment and order defined for purposes of this Code, see Family Code § 100.
Minor defined for purposes of this Code, see Family Code § 6500.
Person defined for purposes of this Code, see Family Code § 105.
Petitioner defined for purposes of this Code, see Family Code § 126.

Research References

Forms

West's California Code Forms, Family § 6300, Comment Overview—Protective Orders.

§ 6301.5. Confidentiality of information relating to minors

(a) A minor or the minor's legal guardian may petition the court to have information regarding a minor that was obtained in connection with a request for a protective order pursuant to this division, including, but not limited to, the minor's name, address, and the circumstances surrounding the request for a protective order with respect to that minor, be kept confidential, except as provided in subdivision (d).

(b) The court may order the information specified in subdivision (a) be kept confidential if the court expressly finds all of the following:

(1) The minor's right to privacy overcomes the right of public access to the information.

(2) There is a substantial probability that the minor's interest will be prejudiced if the information is not kept confidential.

(3) The order to keep the information confidential is narrowly tailored.

(4) No less restrictive means exist to protect the minor's privacy.

(c)(1) If the request is granted, except as provided in subdivision (d), information regarding the minor shall be maintained in a confidential case file and shall not become part of the public file in the proceeding, any other proceeding initiated under the Family Code, or any other civil proceeding between the parties. Except as provided in paragraph (2), if the court determines that disclosure of confidential information has been made without a court order, the court may impose a sanction of up to one thousand dollars ($1,000). The minor who has alleged abuse as defined under this division shall not be sanctioned for disclosure of the confidential information. If the court imposes a sanction, the court shall first determine whether the person has, or is reasonably likely to have, the ability to pay.

(2) Confidential information may be disclosed without a court order pursuant to subdivision (d) only in the following circumstances:

(A) By the minor's legal guardian who petitioned to keep the information confidential pursuant to this section or the protected party in an order pursuant to this division, provided that the disclosure effectuates the purpose of this division specified in Section 6220 or is in the minor's best interest. A legal guardian or a protected party who makes a disclosure under this subparagraph is subject to the sanction in paragraph (1) only if the disclosure was malicious.

(B) By a person to whom confidential information is disclosed, provided that the disclosure effectuates the purpose of this division specified in Section 6220 or is in the best interest of the minor, no more information than necessary is disclosed, and a delay would be caused by first obtaining a court order to authorize the disclosure of the information. A person who makes a disclosure pursuant to this subparagraph is subject to the sanction in paragraph (1) if the person discloses the information in a manner that recklessly or maliciously disregards these requirements.

(d)(1) Confidential information shall be made available to both of the following:

(A) Law enforcement pursuant to Section 6380, to the extent necessary and only for the purpose of enforcing the protective order.

(B) The respondent to allow the respondent to comply with the order for confidentiality and to allow the respondent to comply with and respond to the protective order. A notice shall be provided to the respondent that identifies the specific information that has been made confidential and shall include a statement that disclosure is punishable by a monetary fine.

(2) At any time, the court on its own may authorize a disclosure of any portion of the confidential information to certain individuals or entities as necessary to effectuate the purpose of this division specified in Section 6220, including implementation of the protective order, or if it is in the best interest of the minor, including, but not limited to, disclosure to educational institutions, childcare providers, medical or mental health providers, professional or nonprofessional supervisors for visitation, the Department of Child Support Services, attorneys for the parties or the minor, judicial officers, court employees, child custody evaluators, family court mediators, and court reporters.

(3) The court may authorize a disclosure of any portion of the confidential information to any person that files a petition if the court determines disclosure would effectuate the purpose of this division specified in Section 6220 or if the court determines that disclosure is in the best interest of the minor. The party who petitioned the court to keep the information confidential pursuant to this section shall be served personally or by first-class mail with a copy of the petition and afforded an opportunity to object to the disclosure. *(Added by Stats.2017, c. 384 (A.B.953), § 2, eff. Jan. 1, 2018. Amended by Stats.2019, c. 294 (A.B.925), § 2, eff. Jan. 1, 2020.)*

Research References

Forms

West's California Judicial Council Forms DV–160, Request to Keep Minor's Information Confidential (Domestic Violence Prevention) (Also Available in Chinese, Korean, Spanish, and Vietnamese).

West's California Judicial Council Forms DV–160–INFO, Privacy Protection for a Minor (Person Under 18 Years Old) (Domestic Violence Prevention).
West's California Judicial Council Forms DV–165, Order on Request to Keep Minor's Information Confidential (Also Available in Chinese, Korean, Spanish, and Vietnamese).
West's California Judicial Council Forms DV–170, Notice of Order Protecting Information of Minor (Domestic Violence Prevention) (Also Available in Chinese, Korean, Spanish, and Vietnamese).
West's California Judicial Council Forms DV–175, Cover Sheet for Confidential Information (Domestic Violence Prevention) (Also Available in Chinese, Korean, Spanish, and Vietnamese).
West's California Judicial Council Forms DV–176, Request for Release of Minor's Confidential Information.
West's California Judicial Council Forms DV–177, Notice of Request for Release of Minor's Confidential Information.
West's California Judicial Council Forms DV–178, Response to Request for Release of Minor's Confidential Information.
West's California Judicial Council Forms DV–179, Order on Request for Release of Minor's Confidential Information.

§ 6302. Notice of hearing

A notice of hearing under this part shall notify the respondent that, if the respondent does not attend the hearing, the court may make orders against the respondent that could last up to five years. *(Added by Stats.2010, c. 572 (A.B.1596), § 14, operative Jan. 1, 2012. Amended by Stats.2019, c. 115 (A.B.1817), § 61, eff. Jan. 1, 2020.)*

§ 6303. Support persons for victims of domestic violence; powers and duties; discretion of court

(a) It is the function of a support person to provide moral and emotional support for a person who alleges to be a victim of domestic violence. The person who alleges to be a victim of domestic violence may select any individual to act as a support person. No certification, training, or other special qualification is required for an individual to act as a support person. The support person shall assist the person in feeling more confident that the person will not be injured or threatened by the other party during the proceedings where the person and the other party must be present in close proximity. The support person is not present as a legal adviser and shall not give legal advice.

(b) A support person shall be permitted to accompany either party to any proceeding to obtain a protective order, as defined in Section 6218. Where the party is not represented by an attorney, the support person may sit with the party at the table that is generally reserved for the party and the party's attorney.

(c) Notwithstanding any other law to the contrary, if a court has issued a protective order, a support person shall be permitted to accompany a party protected by the order during any mediation orientation or mediation session, including separate mediation sessions, held pursuant to a proceeding described in Section 3021. Family Court Services, and any agency charged with providing family court services, shall advise the party protected by the order of the right to have a support person during mediation. A mediator may exclude a support person from a mediation session if the support person participates in the mediation session, or acts as an advocate, or the presence of a particular support person is disruptive or disrupts the process of mediation. The presence of the support person does not waive the confidentiality of the mediation, and the support person is bound by the confidentiality of the mediation.

(d) In a proceeding subject to this section, a support person shall be permitted to accompany a party in court where there are allegations or threats of domestic violence and, where the party is not represented by an attorney, may sit with the party at the table that is generally reserved for the party and the party's attorney.

(e) This section does not preclude a court from exercising its discretion to remove a person from the courtroom when it would be in the interest of justice to do so, or when the court believes the person is prompting, swaying, or influencing the party protected by the order. *(Added by Stats.1993, c. 219 (A.B.1500), § 154. Amended by Stats.1996, c. 761 (S.B.1995), § 7; Stats.2012, c. 470 (A.B.1529), § 21; Stats.2019, c. 115 (A.B.1817), § 62, eff. Jan. 1, 2020.)*

Cross References

Domestic violence defined for purposes of this Code, see Family Code § 6211.
Judgment and order defined for purposes of this Code, see Family Code § 100.
Person defined for purposes of this Code, see Family Code § 105.
Proceeding defined for purposes of this Code, see Family Code § 110.
Support defined for purposes of this Code, see Family Code § 150.

§ 6304. Protective orders; court to inform parties of terms of orders

When making a protective order, as defined in Section 6218, where both parties are present in court, the court shall inform both the petitioner and the respondent of the terms of the order, including notice that the respondent is prohibited from owning, possessing, purchasing, or receiving or attempting to own, possess, purchase, or receive a firearm or ammunition, and including notice of the penalty for violation. Information provided shall include how any firearms or ammunition still in the restrained party's possession are to be relinquished, according to local procedures, and the process for submitting a receipt to the court showing proof of relinquishment. *(Added by Stats.1993, c. 219 (A.B.1500), § 154. Amended by Stats.1999, c. 662 (S.B.218), § 2; Stats.2010, c. 572 (A.B.1596), § 15, operative Jan. 1, 2012; Stats.2021, c. 685 (S.B.320), § 3, eff. Jan. 1, 2022.)*

Cross References

Intentional and knowing violation of court order to prevent harassment or domestic violence, penalties, see Penal Code § 273.6.
Judgment and order defined for purposes of this Code, see Family Code § 100.
Petitioner defined for purposes of this Code, see Family Code § 126.
Respondent defined for purposes of this Code, see Family Code § 127.
Unlawful ownership or possession of firearms in violation of protective order, penalties, see Penal Code §§ 29800 to 29875.

§ 6305. Mutual orders; personal appearance of parties; application for relief

(a) The court shall not issue a mutual order enjoining the parties from specific acts of abuse described in Section 6320 unless both of the following apply:

(1) Both parties personally appear and each party presents written evidence of abuse or domestic violence in an application for relief using a mandatory Judicial Council restraining order application form. For purposes of this paragraph, written evidence of abuse or domestic violence in a responsive pleading does not satisfy the party's obligation to present written evidence of abuse or domestic violence. By July 1, 2016, the Judicial Council shall modify forms as necessary to provide notice of this information.

(2) The court makes detailed findings of fact indicating that both parties acted as a primary aggressor and that neither party acted primarily in self-defense.

(b) For purposes of subdivision (a), in determining if both parties acted primarily as aggressors, the court shall consider the provisions concerning dominant aggressors set forth in paragraph (3) of subdivision (c) of Section 836 of the Penal Code. *(Added by Stats.1993, c. 219 (A.B.1500), § 154. Amended by Stats.1995, c. 246 (S.B.591), § 2; Stats.2014, c. 635 (A.B.2089), § 6, eff. Jan. 1, 2015; Stats.2015, c. 73 (A.B.536), § 1, eff. Jan. 1, 2016.)*

Cross References

Abuse defined for purposes of the Domestic Violence Protection Act, see Family Code § 6203.
Domestic violence defined for purposes of this Code, see Family Code § 6211.
Intentional and knowing violation of court order to prevent harassment or domestic violence, penalties, see Penal Code § 273.6.

Judgment and order defined for purposes of this Code, see Family Code § 100.

Research References

Forms

West's California Code Forms, Family § 2047, Comment Overview—Orders After Notice and Hearing.

§ 6306. Criminal history search; prior restraining orders

(a) Prior to a hearing on the issuance or denial of an order under this part, the court shall ensure that a search is or has been conducted to determine if the subject of the proposed order has a prior criminal conviction for a violent felony specified in Section 667.5 of the Penal Code or a serious felony specified in Section 1192.7 of the Penal Code; has a misdemeanor conviction involving domestic violence, weapons, or other violence; has an outstanding warrant; is currently on parole or probation; has a registered firearm; or has a prior restraining order or a violation of a prior restraining order. The search shall be conducted of all records and databases readily available and reasonably accessible to the court, including, but not limited to, the following:

(1) The California Sex and Arson Registry (CSAR).

(2) The Supervised Release File.

(3) State summary criminal history information maintained by the Department of Justice pursuant to Section 11105 of the Penal Code.

(4) The Federal Bureau of Investigation's nationwide database.

(5) Locally maintained criminal history records or databases.

However, a record or database need not be searched if the information available in that record or database can be obtained as a result of a search conducted in another record or database.

(b)(1) Prior to deciding whether to issue an order under this part or when determining appropriate temporary custody and visitation orders, the court shall consider the following information obtained pursuant to a search conducted under subdivision (a): a conviction for a violent felony specified in Section 667.5 of the Penal Code or a serious felony specified in Section 1192.7 of the Penal Code; a misdemeanor conviction involving domestic violence, weapons, or other violence; an outstanding warrant; parole or probation status; a prior restraining order; and a violation of a prior restraining order.

(2) Information obtained as a result of the search that does not involve a conviction described in this subdivision shall not be considered by the court in making a determination regarding the issuance of an order pursuant to this part. That information shall be destroyed and shall not become part of the public file in this or any other civil proceeding.

(c)(1) After issuing its ruling, the court shall advise the parties that they may request the information described in subdivision (b) upon which the court relied. The court shall admonish the party seeking the proposed order that it is unlawful, pursuant to Sections 11142 and 13303 of the Penal Code, to willfully release the information, except as authorized by law.

(2) Upon the request of either party to obtain the information described in subdivision (b) upon which the court relied, the court shall release the information to the parties or, upon either party's request, to the party's attorney in that proceeding.

(3) The party seeking the proposed order may release the information to the party's counsel, court personnel, and court-appointed mediators for the purpose of seeking judicial review of the court's order or for purposes of court proceedings under Section 213.5 of the Welfare and Institutions Code.

(d) Information obtained as a result of the search conducted pursuant to subdivision (a) and relied upon by the court shall be maintained in a confidential case file and shall not become part of the public file in the proceeding or any other civil proceeding. However, the contents of the confidential case file shall be disclosed to the court-appointed mediator assigned to the case or to a child custody evaluator appointed by the court pursuant to Section 3111 of this code or Section 730 of the Evidence Code. All court-appointed mediators and child custody evaluators appointed or contracted by the court pursuant to Section 3111 of this code or Section 730 of the Evidence Code who receive information from the search conducted pursuant to subdivision (a) shall be subject to, and shall comply with, the California Law Enforcement Telecommunications System policies, practices, and procedures adopted pursuant to Section 15160 of the Government Code.

(e) If the results of the search conducted pursuant to subdivision (a) indicate that an outstanding warrant exists against the subject of the order, the court shall order the clerk of the court to immediately notify, by the most effective means available, appropriate law enforcement officials of the issuance and contents of a protective order and of any other information obtained through the search that the court determines is appropriate. The law enforcement officials so notified shall take all actions necessary to execute any outstanding warrants or any other actions, with respect to the restrained person, as appropriate and as soon as practicable.

(f) If the results of the search conducted pursuant to subdivision (a) indicate that the subject of the order owns a registered firearm or if the court receives evidence of the subject's possession of a firearm or ammunition, the court shall make a written record as to whether the subject has relinquished the firearm or ammunition and provided proof of the required storage, sale, or relinquishment of the firearm or ammunition. If evidence of compliance with firearms prohibitions is not provided pursuant to subdivision (c) of Section 6389, the court shall order the clerk of the court to immediately notify, by the most effective means available, appropriate law enforcement officials of the issuance and contents of a protective order, information about the firearm or ammunition, and of any other information obtained through the search that the court determines is appropriate. The law enforcement officials so notified shall take all actions necessary to obtain those and any other firearms or ammunition owned, possessed, or controlled by the restrained person and to address any violation of the order with respect to firearms or ammunition as appropriate and as soon as practicable.

(g) If the results of the search conducted pursuant to subdivision (a) indicate that the subject of the order is currently on parole or probation, the court shall order the clerk of the court to immediately notify, by the most effective means available, the appropriate parole or probation officer of the issuance and contents of a protective order issued by the court and of any other information obtained through the search that the court determines is appropriate. That officer shall take all actions necessary to revoke parole or probation, or any other actions, with respect to the restrained person, as appropriate and as soon as practicable.

(h) This section shall not delay the granting of an application for an order that may otherwise be granted without the information resulting from the database search. If the court finds that a protective order under this part should be granted on the basis of the affidavit presented with the petition, the court shall issue the protective order and shall then ensure that a search is conducted pursuant to subdivision (a) prior to the hearing. (Added by Stats.2001, c. 572 (S.B.66), § 3. Amended by Stats.2012, c. 765 (S.B.1433), § 1; Stats.2014, c. 54 (S.B.1461), § 2, eff. Jan. 1, 2015; Stats.2019, c. 115 (A.B.1817), § 63, eff. Jan. 1, 2020; Stats.2021, c. 685 (S.B.320), § 4, eff. Jan. 1, 2022.)

Cross References

Domestic violence defined for purposes of this Code, see Family Code § 6211.
Felonies, definition and penalties, see Penal Code §§ 17, 18.
Judgment and order defined for purposes of this Code, see Family Code § 100.
Juvenile court law, proceedings to declare a minor child a dependent child, see Welfare and Institutions Code § 213.5.
Misdemeanors, definition and penalties, see Penal Code §§ 17, 19, 19.2.
Person defined for purposes of this Code, see Family Code § 105.

PROTECTIVE AND PREVENTION ORDERS

Procedure prior to hearing on issuance, renewal, or termination of order, see Penal Code § 18110.
Proceeding defined for purposes of this Code, see Family Code § 110.
Protective order defined for purposes of this Code, see Family Code § 6218.
State defined for purposes of this Code, see Family Code § 145.

§ 6306.5. Electronically submitted petitions seeking domestic violence restraining orders

(a)(1) Petitions seeking domestic violence restraining orders under Chapter 2 (commencing with Section 6320) and domestic violence temporary restraining orders under Part 4 (commencing with Section 240) of Division 2 may be submitted electronically in every trial court. Courts shall accept these filings consistent with the timeframe in Section 246.

(2) The notice of court date, copies of the request to mail on respondent, and the temporary restraining order, if granted, shall be remitted to the petitioner electronically.

(3) Notwithstanding paragraph (2), the petitioner may elect to receive documents by regular mail or to retrieve documents from the court.

(b) The Judicial Council shall develop or amend rules and forms as necessary to implement this section.

(c) There shall be no fee for any filings related to a petition submitted electronically in accordance with this section.

(d) This section shall become operative only upon an appropriation of funds for this purpose in the annual Budget Act or other statute. *(Added by Stats.2021, c. 681 (A.B.887), § 1, eff. Jan. 1, 2022.)*

Contingent Operation

Operation of this section is contingent upon availability of funding in the annual Budget Act, by its own terms.

§ 6306.6. Domestic violence restraining orders visible on superior court's internet website

(a) Information about access to self-help services regarding domestic violence restraining orders shall be prominently visible on the superior court's internet website.

(b) The Judicial Council shall develop or amend rules as necessary to implement this section. *(Added by Stats.2021, c. 681 (A.B.887), § 2, eff. Jan. 1, 2022.)*

§ 6307. Repealed by Stats.2022, c. 420 (A.B.2960), § 16, eff. Jan. 1, 2023

§ 6307. Electronic submission of petitions and filings; availability of electronic filing and self-help center information on homepage; adoption of rules and forms for implementation

Section operative July 1, 2023.

(a)(1) A court or court facility that receives petitions for domestic violence restraining orders under this part or domestic violence temporary restraining orders under Part 4 (commencing with Section 240) of Division 2 shall permit those petitions and any filings related to those petitions to be submitted electronically. The court or court facility shall, based on the time of receipt, act on these filings consistent with Section 246.

(2) The request, notice of the court date, copies of the request to serve on the respondent, and the temporary restraining order, if granted, shall be provided to the petitioner electronically, unless the petitioner notes, at the time of electronic filing, that these documents will be picked up from the court or court facility.

(b)(1) Information regarding electronic filing and access to the court's self-help center shall be prominently displayed on each court's homepage.

(2) Each self-help center shall maintain and make available information related to domestic violence restraining orders pursuant to this section.

(c) The Judicial Council may adopt or amend rules and forms to implement this section.

(d) This section shall become operative on July 1, 2023. *(Added by Stats.2022, c. 420 (A.B.2960), § 17, eff. Jan. 1, 2023, operative July 1, 2023.)*

§ 6308. Remote appearance of party, support person, and witness; development and publication of local rules

* * * A party, support person as defined in Section 6303, or witness may appear remotely at the hearing on a petition for a domestic violence restraining order. The superior court of each county shall develop local rules and instructions for remote appearances permitted under this section, which shall be posted on its internet website.

* * * *(Added by Stats.2021, c. 686 (S.B.538), § 3, eff. Jan. 1, 2022. Amended by Stats.2022, c. 420 (A.B.2960), § 18, eff. Jan. 1, 2023.)*

CHAPTER 2. ISSUANCE OF ORDERS

Article	Section
1. Ex Parte Orders	6320
2. Orders Issuable After Notice and Hearing	6340
3. Orders Included in Judgment	6360

ARTICLE 1. EX PARTE ORDERS

Section	
6320.	Ex parte order enjoining contact, credibly or falsely impersonating, or destroying personal property; protection for companion animals.
6320.5.	Order denying petition for ex parte order; reasons; right to noticed hearing; right to waive hearing.
6321.	Ex parte order excluding party from dwelling.
6322.	Ex parte order enjoining specified behavior.
6322.5.	Restrained person having firearm or ammunition; determination of violation of Section 6389.
6322.7.	Addresses or locations of persons protected under court order; prohibition upon certain enjoined parties from acting to obtain such information.
6323.	Ex parte orders regarding temporary custody and visitation of minor children; stipulation of parentage; considerations.
6323.5.	Ex parte provision restraining a party from accessing records and information pertaining to the health care, education, daycare, recreational activities, or employment of a minor child of the parties; protocols relating to the provider's compliance; release of information or records.
6324.	Ex parte order regarding real or personal property.
6325.	Ex parte order regarding community, quasi-community and separate property.
6325.5.	Ex parte order regarding insurance coverage.
6326.	Issuance or denial on date application submitted.
6327.	Ex parte orders; application of Part 4 of Division 2.

Cross References

Ex parte temporary restraining orders, generally, see Family Code § 240 et seq.
Nullity, dissolution, and legal separation, ex parte protective orders, generally, see Family Code § 2045.
Uniform Parentage Act, issuance of ex parte orders, see Family Code § 7710.

Witnesses, interpreters and translators, hearings or proceedings related to domestic violence, see Evidence Code § 756.

§ 6320. Ex parte order enjoining contact, credibly or falsely impersonating, or destroying personal property; protection for companion animals

(a) The court may issue an ex parte order enjoining a party from molesting, attacking, striking, stalking, threatening, sexually assaulting, battering, credibly impersonating as described in Section 528.5 of the Penal Code, falsely personating as described in Section 529 of the Penal Code, harassing, telephoning, including, but not limited to, making annoying telephone calls as described in Section 653m of the Penal Code, destroying personal property, contacting, either directly or indirectly, by mail or otherwise, coming within a specified distance of, or disturbing the peace of the other party, and, in the discretion of the court, on a showing of good cause, of other named family or household members.

(b) On a showing of good cause, the court may include in a protective order a grant to the petitioner of the exclusive care, possession, or control of any animal owned, possessed, leased, kept, or held by either the petitioner or the respondent or a minor child residing in the residence or household of either the petitioner or the respondent. The court may order the respondent to stay away from the animal and forbid the respondent from taking, transferring, encumbering, concealing, molesting, attacking, striking, threatening, harming, or otherwise disposing of the animal.

(c) As used in this subdivision (a), "disturbing the peace of the other party" refers to conduct that, based on the totality of the circumstances, destroys the mental or emotional calm of the other party. This conduct may be committed directly or indirectly, including through the use of a third party, and by any method or through any means including, but not limited to, telephone, online accounts, text messages, internet-connected devices, or other electronic technologies. This conduct includes, but is not limited to, coercive control, which is a pattern of behavior that in purpose or effect unreasonably interferes with a person's free will and personal liberty. Examples of coercive control include, but are not limited to, unreasonably engaging in any of the following:

(1) Isolating the other party from friends, relatives, or other sources of support.

(2) Depriving the other party of basic necessities.

(3) Controlling, regulating, or monitoring the other party's movements, communications, daily behavior, finances, economic resources, or access to services.

(4) Compelling the other party by force, threat of force, or intimidation, including threats based on actual or suspected immigration status, to engage in conduct from which the other party has a right to abstain or to abstain from conduct in which the other party has a right to engage.

(5) Engaging in reproductive coercion, which consists of control over the reproductive autonomy of another through force, threat of force, or intimidation, and may include, but is not limited to, unreasonably pressuring the other party to become pregnant, deliberately interfering with contraception use or access to reproductive health information, or using coercive tactics to control, or attempt to control, pregnancy outcomes.

(d) This section does not limit any remedies available under this act or any other provision of law. (Added by Stats.2013, c. 260 (A.B.157), § 2, operative July 1, 2014. Amended by Stats.2020, c. 248 (S.B.1141), § 2, eff. Jan. 1, 2021; Stats.2021, c. 135 (S.B.374), § 1, eff. Jan. 1, 2022.)

Cross References

Abandonment and neglect of children, intentional and knowing violation of court order to prevent harassment, disturbing the peace, or threats or acts of violence, see Penal Code § 273.6.

Contempt of court, conduct constituting, see Penal Code § 166.
Court orders available in response to good cause belief of harm to, intimidation of, or dissuasion of victim or witness, see Penal Code § 136.2.
Interstate enforcement of domestic violence protection orders, more than one order issued, enforcement of no-contact order, see Family Code § 6405.
Judgment and order defined for purposes of this Code, see Family Code § 100.
More than one order issued, enforcement of no-contact order, see Family Code § 6383.
Property defined for purposes of this Code, see Family Code § 113.
Suspension of money judgment or order for support of a child, exceptions, resumption of obligation, administrative adjustment, evaluation, see Family Code § 4007.5.
Uniform Recognition and Enforcement of Canadian Domestic Violence Protection Orders Act, multiple protective orders, priority of enforcement, see Family Code § 6457.

Research References

Forms

California Practice Guide: Rutter Family Law Forms Form 1:32, Glossary of Common Family Law Terms, Phrases and Concepts (Enclosure to Form 1:31).
West's California Code Forms, Family § 6320, Comment Overview—Ex Parte Orders.
West's California Code Forms, Family § 6340, Comment Overview—Issuance of Orders After Notice and Hearing.
West's California Judicial Council Forms FL–300, Request for Order (Also Available in Spanish).
West's California Judicial Council Forms JV–245, Request for Restraining Order—Juvenile (Also Available in Chinese, Korean, Spanish, and Vietnamese).

§ 6320.5. Order denying petition for ex parte order; reasons; right to noticed hearing; right to waive hearing

(a) An order denying a petition for an ex parte order pursuant to Section 6320 shall include the reasons for denying the petition.

(b) An order denying a jurisdictionally adequate petition for an ex parte order, pursuant to Section 6320, shall provide the petitioner the right to a noticed hearing on the earliest date that the business of the court will permit, but not later than 21 days or, if good cause appears to the court, 25 days from the date of the order. The petitioner shall serve on the respondent, at least five days before the hearing, copies of all supporting papers filed with the court, including the application and affidavits.

(c) Notwithstanding subdivision (b), upon the denial of the ex parte order pursuant to Section 6320, the petitioner shall have the option of waiving the right to a noticed hearing. However, this section does not preclude a petitioner who waives the right to a noticed hearing from refiling a new petition, without prejudice, at a later time. (Added by Stats.2008, c. 263 (A.B.2553), § 1. Amended by Stats.2010, c. 572 (A.B.1596), § 17, operative Jan. 1, 2012; Stats.2019, c. 115 (A.B.1817), § 64, eff. Jan. 1, 2020.)

Research References

Forms

West's California Judicial Council Forms DV–112, Waiver of Hearing on Denied Request for Temporary Restraining Order (Also Available in Chinese, Korean, Spanish, and Vietnamese).

§ 6321. Ex parte order excluding party from dwelling

(a) The court may issue an ex parte order excluding a party from the family dwelling, the dwelling of the other party, the common dwelling of both parties, or the dwelling of the person who has care, custody, and control of a child to be protected from domestic violence for the period of time and on the conditions the court determines, regardless of which party holds legal or equitable title or is the lessee of the dwelling.

(b) The court may issue an order under subdivision (a) only on a showing of all of the following:

(1) Facts sufficient for the court to ascertain that the party who will stay in the dwelling has a right under color of law to possession of the premises.

(2) That the party to be excluded has assaulted or threatens to assault the other party or any other person under the care, custody, and control of the other party, or any minor child of the parties or of the other party.

(3) That physical or emotional harm would otherwise result to the other party, to any person under the care, custody, and control of the other party, or to any minor child of the parties or of the other party. *(Added by Stats.1993, c. 219 (A.B.1500), § 154.)*

Cross References

Domestic violence defined for purposes of this Code, see Family Code § 6211.
Ex parte temporary restraining orders, generally, see Family Code § 240 et seq.
Exclusion of spouse from other's dwelling, see Family Code § 753.
Judgment and order defined for purposes of this Code, see Family Code § 100.
Minor defined for purposes of this Code, see Family Code § 6500.
Nullity, dissolution, and legal separation, ex parte protective orders, generally, see Family Code § 2045.
Person defined for purposes of this Code, see Family Code § 105.
Uniform Parentage Act, issuance of ex parte orders, see Family Code § 7710.

Research References

Forms

California Practice Guide: Rutter Family Law Forms Form 1:32, Glossary of Common Family Law Terms, Phrases and Concepts (Enclosure to Form 1:31).
West's California Code Forms, Family § 6320, Comment Overview—Ex Parte Orders.
West's California Code Forms, Family § 6340, Comment Overview—Issuance of Orders After Notice and Hearing.
West's California Judicial Council Forms JV-245, Request for Restraining Order—Juvenile (Also Available in Chinese, Korean, Spanish, and Vietnamese).

§ 6322. Ex parte order enjoining specified behavior

The court may issue an ex parte order enjoining a party from specified behavior that the court determines is necessary to effectuate orders under Section 6320 or 6321. *(Added by Stats.1993, c. 219 (A.B.1500), § 154.)*

Cross References

Ex parte temporary restraining orders, generally, see Family Code § 240 et seq.
Judgment and order defined for purposes of this Code, see Family Code § 100.
Nullity, dissolution, and legal separation, ex parte protective orders, generally, see Family Code § 2045.
Uniform Parentage Act, issuance of ex parte orders, see Family Code § 7710.

Research References

Forms

California Practice Guide: Rutter Family Law Forms Form 1:32, Glossary of Common Family Law Terms, Phrases and Concepts (Enclosure to Form 1:31).
West's California Judicial Council Forms JV-245, Request for Restraining Order—Juvenile (Also Available in Chinese, Korean, Spanish, and Vietnamese).

§ 6322.5. Restrained person having firearm or ammunition; determination of violation of Section 6389

(a) When relevant information is presented to the court at a noticed hearing that a restrained person has a firearm or ammunition, the court shall consider that information and determine, by a preponderance of the evidence, whether the person subject to a protective order has a firearm or ammunition in, or subject to, their immediate possession or control in violation of Section 6389.

(b)(1) In making the determination required pursuant to subdivision (a), the court may consider whether the restrained person filed a firearm relinquishment, storage, or sales receipt or if an exemption from the firearm prohibition was granted pursuant to subdivision (h) of Section 6389.

(2) The court may make the determination at a noticed hearing when a domestic violence protective order is issued, at a subsequent review hearing, or at any subsequent family or juvenile law hearing while the order remains in effect.

(3) If the court makes a determination that the restrained person has a firearm or ammunition in violation of Section 6389, the court shall make a written record of the determination and provide a copy to any party who is present at the hearing and, upon request, to any party not present at the hearing.

(c)(1) When presented with information pursuant to subdivision (a), the court may set a review hearing to determine whether there has been a violation of Section 6389.

(2) The review hearing shall be held within 10 court days after the noticed hearing at which the information was presented. If the restrained person is not present when the court sets the review hearing, the protected person shall provide notice of the review hearing to the restrained person at least two court days before the review hearing, in accordance with Section 414.10 of the Code of Civil Procedure, by personal service or by mail to the restrained person's last known address.

(3) The court may, for good cause, extend the date of the review hearing for a reasonable period or remove it from the calendar.

(4) The court shall order the restrained person to appear at the hearing.

(5) The court may conduct the review hearing in the absence of the protected person.

(6) This section does not prohibit the court from permitting a party or witness to appear through technology that enables remote appearances, as determined by the court.

(d) The determination made pursuant to this section may be considered by the court in issuing an order to show cause for contempt pursuant to paragraph (5) of subdivision (a) of Section 1209 of the Code of Civil Procedure or an order for monetary sanctions pursuant to Section 177.5 of the Code of Civil Procedure. *(Added by Stats.2021, c. 685 (S.B.320), § 5, eff. Jan. 1, 2022.)*

Cross References

Custody of children, presumption against person perpetrating domestic violence, see Family Code § 3044.
Proceedings to declare a minor child a dependent child, ex parte orders, see Welfare and Institutions Code § 213.5.

§ 6322.7. Addresses or locations of persons protected under court order; prohibition upon certain enjoined parties from acting to obtain such information

(a) The court shall order that any party enjoined pursuant to an order issued under this part be prohibited from taking any action to obtain the address or location of any protected person, unless there is good cause not to make that order.

(b) The Judicial Council shall develop forms necessary to effectuate this section. *(Added by Stats.2005, c. 472 (A.B.978), § 3. Amended by Stats.2010, c. 572 (A.B.1596), § 18, operative Jan. 1, 2012.)*

Research References

Forms

West's California Code Forms, Family § 6320, Comment Overview—Ex Parte Orders.

§ 6323. Ex parte orders regarding temporary custody and visitation of minor children; stipulation of parentage; considerations

(a) Subject to Section 3064:

§ 6323

(1) The court may issue an ex parte order determining the temporary custody and visitation of a minor child, on the conditions the court determines, to a party who has established a parent and child relationship pursuant to paragraph (2). The parties shall inform the court if a custody or visitation order has already been issued in any other proceeding.

(2)(A) In making a determination of the best interest of the child, in order to limit the child's exposure to potential domestic violence, and to ensure the safety of all family members, if the party who has obtained the restraining order has established a parent and child relationship and the other party has not established that relationship, the court may award temporary sole legal and physical custody to the party to whom the restraining order was issued and may make an order of no visitation to the other party pending the establishment of a parent and child relationship between the child and the other party.

(B) A party may establish a parent and child relationship for purposes of subparagraph (A) only by offering proof of any of the following:

(i) The party gave birth to the child.

(ii) The child is conclusively presumed to be a child of the marriage between the parties, pursuant to Section 7540, or the party has been determined by a court to be a parent of the child, pursuant to Section 7541.

(iii) Legal adoption or pending legal adoption of the child by the party.

(iv) The party has signed a valid voluntary declaration of paternity, which has been in effect more than 60 days prior to the issuance of the restraining order, and that declaration has not been rescinded or set aside.

(v) A determination made by the juvenile court that there is a parent and child relationship between the party offering the proof and the child.

(vi) A determination of parentage made in a proceeding to determine custody or visitation in a case brought by the local child support agency pursuant to Chapter 2 (commencing with Section 17400) of Division 17.

(vii) The party has been determined to be the parent of the child through a proceeding under the Uniform Parentage Act (Part 3 (commencing with Section 7600) of Division 12).

(viii) Both parties stipulate, in writing or on the record, for purposes of this proceeding, that they are the parents of the child.

(b)(1) Except as provided in paragraph (2), the court shall not make a finding of paternity in this proceeding, and an order issued pursuant to this section shall be without prejudice in any other action brought to establish a parent and child relationship.

(2) The court may accept a stipulation of paternity by the parties and, if paternity is uncontested, enter a judgment establishing paternity, subject to the set-aside provisions in Section 7646.

(c) When making an order for custody or visitation pursuant to this section, the court's order shall specify the time, day, place, and manner of transfer of the child for custody or visitation to limit the child's exposure to potential domestic conflict or violence and to ensure the safety of all family members. If the court finds a party is staying in a place designated as a shelter for victims of domestic violence or other confidential location, the court's order for time, day, place, and manner of transfer of the child for custody or visitation shall be designed to prevent disclosure of the location of the shelter or other confidential location.

(d) When making an order for custody or visitation pursuant to this section, the court shall consider whether the best interest of the child, based upon the circumstances of the case, requires that a visitation or custody arrangement shall be limited to situations in which a third person, specified by the court, is present, or whether visitation or custody shall be suspended or denied.

(e) When determining whether visitation should be suspended, denied, or limited to situations in which a third person is present pursuant to subdivision (d), the court shall consider a determination made pursuant to Section 6322.5 that the party is a restrained person in possession or control of a firearm or ammunition in violation of Section 6389. *(Added by Stats.1993, c. 219 (A.B.1500), § 154. Amended by Stats.1994, c. 320 (A.B.356), § 3; Stats.1997, c. 396 (S.B.564), § 2; Stats.2010, c. 352 (A.B.939), § 18; Stats.2019, c. 497 (A.B.991), § 111, eff. Jan. 1, 2020; Stats.2019, c. 115 (A.B.1817), § 65, eff. Jan. 1, 2020; Stats.2021, c. 685 (S.B.320), § 6, eff. Jan. 1, 2022.)*

Cross References

Custody or visitation orders, proceedings to declare a minor child a dependent child of the court, required procedures, see Welfare and Institutions Code § 213.5.
Destruction of court records, notice, retention periods, see Government Code § 68152.
Domestic violence defined for purposes of this Code, see Family Code § 6211.
Ex parte temporary restraining orders, generally, see Family Code § 240 et seq.
Judgment and order defined for purposes of this Code, see Family Code § 100.
Minor defined for purposes of this Code, see Family Code § 6500.
Nullity, dissolution, and legal separation, ex parte protective orders, generally, see Family Code § 2045.
Person defined for purposes of this Code, see Family Code § 105.
Proceeding defined for purposes of this Code, see Family Code § 110.
Uniform Parentage Act, issuance of ex parte orders, see Family Code § 7710.

Research References

Forms

1 California Transactions Forms--Family Law § 3:4, Subject Matter Jurisdiction for Custody Determinations.
West's California Judicial Council Forms DV-180, Agreement and Judgment of Parentage (Also Available in Chinese, Korean, Spanish, and Vietnamese).

§ 6323.5. Ex parte provision restraining a party from accessing records and information pertaining to the health care, education, daycare, recreational activities, or employment of a minor child of the parties; protocols relating to the provider's compliance; release of information or records

(a) For purposes of this section, the following definitions apply:

(1) "Discretionary services organization" includes any organization that provides nonessential services to children, such as recreational activities, entertainment, and summer camps. "Discretionary services organization" also includes a place of employment of a minor described in subdivision (b).

(2) "Essential care provider" includes a public or private school, health care facility, daycare facility, dental facility, or other similar organization that frequently provides essential social, health, or care services to children.

(b)(1) Notwithstanding Section 3025, and in accordance with Section 6322, a court may include in an ex parte order a provision restraining a party from accessing records and information pertaining to the health care, education, daycare, recreational activities, or employment of a minor child of the parties.

(2) A parent or guardian may provide a copy of an order with a provision specified in paragraph (1) to an essential care provider or a discretionary services organization, or both.

(c)(1)(A) An essential care provider shall, on or before February 1, 2023, develop protocols relating to the provider's compliance with the order described in subdivision (b), including, at a minimum, designating the appropriate personnel responsible for receiving the protective order, establishing a means of ensuring that the restrained party is not able to access the records or information, and implementing a procedure for submission of a copy of an order and for providing the party that submits the copy of the order with documentation indicating when, and to whom, the copy of the order was submitted.

(B) A discretionary services organization that is provided an order described in subdivision (b), shall develop the protocols specified in paragraph (1) within 30 days of receipt of the first order.

(2) If an essential care provider or discretionary services organization is provided with a copy of an order described in subdivision (b), the essential care provider or discretionary services organization shall not release information or records pertaining to the child to the restrained party. This requirement applies regardless of whether the essential care provider or discretionary services organization has finalized the protocols described in paragraph (1).

(d) The Judicial Council shall develop or update any forms or rules of court that are necessary to implement this section.

(e) This section shall become operative on January 1, 2023. *(Added by Stats.2021, c. 129 (S.B.24), § 2, eff. Jan. 1, 2022, operative Jan. 1, 2023.)*

§ 6324. Ex parte order regarding real or personal property

The court may issue an ex parte order determining the temporary use, possession, and control of real or personal property of the parties and the payment of any liens or encumbrances coming due during the period the order is in effect. *(Added by Stats.1993, c. 219 (A.B.1500), § 154.)*

Cross References

Ex parte temporary restraining orders, generally, see Family Code § 240 et seq.
Judgment and order defined for purposes of this Code, see Family Code § 100.
Nullity, dissolution, and legal separation, ex parte protective orders, generally, see Family Code § 2045.
Property defined for purposes of this Code, see Family Code § 113.
Uniform Parentage Act, issuance of ex parte orders, see Family Code § 7710.

Research References

Forms

California Practice Guide: Rutter Family Law Forms Form 1:32, Glossary of Common Family Law Terms, Phrases and Concepts (Enclosure to Form 1:31).
California Practice Guide: Rutter Family Law Forms Form 5:5, Ex Parte Application and Request for Order Re Child Custody, Visitation and Property Control.
West's California Judicial Council Forms DV-250, Proof of Service by Mail (CLETS) (Domestic Violence Prevention) (Also Available in Chinese, Korean, Spanish, and Vietnamese).
West's California Judicial Council Forms FL-344, Property Order Attachment to Findings and Order After Hearing (Also Available in Spanish).

§ 6325. Ex parte order regarding community, quasi-community and separate property

The court may issue an ex parte order restraining a married person from specified acts in relation to community, quasi-community, and separate property as provided in Section 2045. *(Added by Stats.1993, c. 219 (A.B.1500), § 154.)*

Cross References

Ex parte temporary restraining orders, generally, see Family Code § 240 et seq.
Judgment and order defined for purposes of this Code, see Family Code § 100.
Nullity, dissolution, and legal separation, ex parte protective orders, generally, see Family Code § 2045.
Person defined for purposes of this Code, see Family Code § 105.
Property defined for purposes of this Code, see Family Code § 113.
References to husband, wife, spouses and married persons, persons included for purposes of this Code, see Family Code § 11.
Separate property defined for purposes of this Code, see Family Code § 130.

Uniform Parentage Act, issuance of ex parte orders, see Family Code § 7710.

Research References

Forms

California Practice Guide: Rutter Family Law Forms Form 1:32, Glossary of Common Family Law Terms, Phrases and Concepts (Enclosure to Form 1:31).
West's California Code Forms, Family § 6320, Comment Overview—Ex Parte Orders.

§ 6325.5. Ex parte order regarding insurance coverage

(a) The court may issue an ex parte order restraining any party from cashing, borrowing against, canceling, transferring, disposing of, or changing the beneficiaries of any insurance or other coverage held for the benefit of the parties, or their child or children, if any, for whom support may be ordered, or both.

(b) This section shall become operative on July 1, 2014. *(Added by Stats.2013, c. 261 (A.B.161), § 1, operative July 1, 2014.)*

§ 6326. Issuance or denial on date application submitted

An ex parte order under this article shall be issued or denied on the same day that the application is submitted to the court, unless the application is filed too late in the day to permit effective review, in which case the order shall be issued or denied on the next day of judicial business in sufficient time for the order to be filed that day with the clerk of the court. A petition for an ex parte order pursuant to this article shall not be denied solely because the other party was not provided with notice. *(Added by Stats.1993, c. 148 (A.B.1331), § 2. Amended by Stats.2018, c. 219 (A.B.2694), § 2, eff. Jan. 1, 2019.)*

Cross References

Ex parte temporary restraining orders, generally, see Family Code § 240 et seq.
Judgment and order defined for purposes of this Code, see Family Code § 100.
Nullity, dissolution, and legal separation, ex parte protective orders, generally, see Family Code § 2045.
Uniform Parentage Act, issuance of ex parte orders, see Family Code § 7710.

Research References

Forms

West's California Judicial Council Forms FL-300, Request for Order (Also Available in Spanish).

§ 6327. Ex parte orders; application of Part 4 of Division 2

Part 4 (commencing with Section 240) of Division 2 applies to the issuance of any ex parte order under this article, other than an order under Section 6322.5. *(Formerly § 6326, added by Stats.1993, c. 219 (A.B.1500), § 154. Renumbered § 6327 and amended by Stats.1993, c. 876 (S.B.1068), § 27.2, eff. Oct. 6, 1993, operative Jan. 1, 1994. Amended by Stats.1998, c. 511 (A.B.1900), § 6.)*

Cross References

Judgment and order defined for purposes of this Code, see Family Code § 100.

ARTICLE 2. ORDERS ISSUABLE AFTER NOTICE AND HEARING

Section
6340. Ex parte orders; survival of custody, visitation, or support order following expiration of protective order; alternative methods of service; court statement upon denial.
6341. Married parties with no other child support order; presumptive father; considerations; order to pay child support; order to pay spousal support; considerations; effect of order in proceedings for dissolution, nullity of marriage or legal separation.
6342. Orders for restitution.

PREVENTION OF DOMESTIC VIOLENCE

Section
6342.5. Order determining use, possession, and control of real or personal property; debts incurred as result of domestic violence.
6343. Batterer's program; order to participate; enrollment; resource list.
6344. Order for payment of attorney's fees and costs; grounds for determination.
6345. Duration of orders.
6346. Custody and visitation orders; notice and hearing.
6347. Order directing wireless telephone service provider to transfer billing responsibility and rights to requesting party.

Cross References

Establishing parent and child relationship, restraining orders issued after notice and hearing, see Family Code § 7720.

Nullity, dissolution, and legal separation, protective orders, issuance after notice and hearing, see Family Code § 2047.

§ 6340. Ex parte orders; survival of custody, visitation, or support order following expiration of protective order; alternative methods of service; court statement upon denial

(a)(1) The court may issue any of the orders described in Article 1 (commencing with Section 6320) after notice and a hearing. When determining whether to make any orders under this subdivision, the court shall consider whether failure to make any of these orders may jeopardize the safety of the petitioner and the children for whom the custody or visitation orders are sought. If the court makes any order for custody, visitation, or support, that order shall survive the termination of any protective order. The Judicial Council shall provide notice of this provision on any Judicial Council forms related to this subdivision.

(2)(A) If at the time of a hearing with respect to an order issued pursuant to this part based on an ex parte temporary restraining order, the court determines that, after diligent effort, the petitioner has been unable to accomplish personal service, and that there is reason to believe that the restrained party is evading service, the court may permit an alternative method of service designed to give reasonable notice of the action to the respondent. Alternative methods of service include, but are not limited to, the following:

(i) Service by publication pursuant to the standards set forth in Section 415.50 of the Code of Civil Procedure.

(ii) Service by first-class mail sent to the respondent at the most current address for the respondent that is available to the court or delivering a copy of the pleadings and orders at the respondent's home or place of employment, pursuant to the standards set forth in Sections 415.20 to 415.40, inclusive, of the Code of Civil Procedure.

(B) If the court permits an alternative method of service under this paragraph, the court shall grant a continuance to allow for the alternative service pursuant to Section 245.

(b) The court shall, upon denying a petition under this part, provide a brief statement of the reasons for the decision in writing or on the record. A decision stating "denied" is insufficient.

(c) The court may issue an order described in Section 6321 excluding a person from a dwelling if the court finds that physical or emotional harm would otherwise result to the other party, to a person under the care, custody, and control of the other party, or to a minor child of the parties or of the other party. *(Added by Stats.1993, c. 219 (A.B.1500), § 154. Amended by Stats.2004, c. 472 (A.B.2148), § 4; Stats.2010, c. 352 (A.B.939), § 19; Stats.2014, c. 635 (A.B.2089), § 7, eff. Jan. 1, 2015; Stats.2018, c. 219 (A.B.2694), § 3, eff. Jan. 1, 2019.)*

Cross References

Determination of amount due for spousal support, considerations, see Family Code § 4320.

Ex parte temporary restraining orders, generally, see Family Code § 240 et seq.

Intentional and knowing violations of court orders to prevent harassment or domestic violence, penalties, see Penal Code § 273.6.

Judgment and order defined for purposes of this Code, see Family Code § 100.

Minor defined for purposes of this Code, see Family Code § 6500.

Nullity, dissolution, and legal separation, ex parte protective orders, generally, see Family Code § 2045.

Person defined for purposes of this Code, see Family Code § 105.

Uniform Parentage Act, issuance of ex parte orders, see Family Code § 7710.

Research References

Forms

West's California Code Forms, Family § 6340, Comment Overview—Issuance of Orders After Notice and Hearing.

West's California Judicial Council Forms DV–117, Order Granting Alternative Service.

West's California Judicial Council Forms DV–140, Child Custody and Visitation Order (Also Available in Chinese, Korean, Spanish, and Vietnamese).

West's California Judicial Council Forms DV–205–INFO, What If the Person I Want Protection from is Avoiding (Evading) Service?

West's California Judicial Council Forms DV–210, Summons (Domestic Violence Prevention).

West's California Judicial Council Forms DV–250, Proof of Service by Mail (CLETS) (Domestic Violence Prevention) (Also Available in Chinese, Korean, Spanish, and Vietnamese).

West's California Judicial Council Forms FL–341, Child Custody and Visitation (Parenting Time) Order Attachment (Also Available in Spanish).

§ 6341. Married parties with no other child support order; presumptive father; considerations; order to pay child support; order to pay spousal support; considerations; effect of order in proceedings for dissolution, nullity of marriage or legal separation

(a) If the parties are married to each other and no other child support order exists or if there is a presumption under Section 7611 that the respondent is the natural father of a minor child and the child is in the custody of the petitioner, after notice and a hearing, the court may, if requested by the petitioner, order a party to pay an amount necessary for the support and maintenance of the child if the order would otherwise be authorized in an action brought pursuant to Division 9 (commencing with Section 3500) or the Uniform Parentage Act (Part 3 (commencing with Section 7600) of Division 12). When determining whether to make any orders under this subdivision, the court shall consider whether failure to make any of these orders may jeopardize the safety of the petitioner and the children for whom child support is requested, including safety concerns related to the financial needs of the petitioner and the children. The Judicial Council shall provide notice of this provision on any Judicial Council forms related to this subdivision.

(b) An order issued pursuant to subdivision (a) of this section shall be without prejudice in an action brought pursuant to the Uniform Parentage Act (Part 3 (commencing with Section 7600) of Division 12).

(c) If the parties are married to each other and no spousal support order exists, after notice and a hearing, the court may order the respondent to pay spousal support in an amount, if any, that would otherwise be authorized in an action pursuant to Part 1 (commencing with Section 3500) or Part 3 (commencing with Section 4300) of Division 9. When determining whether to make any orders under this subdivision, the court shall consider whether failure to make any of these orders may jeopardize the safety of the petitioner, including safety concerns related to the financial needs of the petitioner. The Judicial Council shall provide notice of this provision on any Judicial Council forms related to this subdivision.

(d) An order issued pursuant to subdivision (c) shall be without prejudice in a proceeding for dissolution of marriage, nullity of marriage, or legal separation of the parties. *(Added by Stats.1993, c. 219 (A.B.1500), § 154. Amended by Stats.1999, c. 980 (A.B.1671),*

§ 13; Stats.2004, c. 472 (A.B.2148), § 5; Stats.2005, c. 22 (S.B.1108), § 63.)

Cross References

Judgment and order defined for purposes of this Code, see Family Code § 100.
Minor defined for purposes of this Code, see Family Code § 6500.
Petitioner defined for purposes of this Code, see Family Code § 126.
Respondent defined for purposes of this Code, see Family Code § 127.
Support defined for purposes of this Code, see Family Code § 150.
Support order defined for purposes of this Code, see Family Code § 155.

Research References

Forms

West's California Code Forms, Family § 6340, Comment Overview—Issuance of Orders After Notice and Hearing.

§ 6342. Orders for restitution

(a) After notice and a hearing, the court may issue any of the following orders:

(1) An order that restitution be paid to the petitioner for loss of earnings and out-of-pocket expenses, including, but not limited to, expenses for medical care and temporary housing, incurred as a direct result of the abuse inflicted by the respondent or any actual physical injuries sustained from the abuse.

(2) An order that restitution be paid by the petitioner for out-of-pocket expenses incurred by a party as a result of an ex parte order that is found by the court to have been issued on facts shown at a noticed hearing to be insufficient to support the order.

(3) An order that restitution be paid by the respondent to any public or private agency for the reasonable cost of providing services to the petitioner required as a direct result of the abuse inflicted by the respondent or any actual injuries sustained therefrom.

(b) An order for restitution under this section shall not include damages for pain and suffering. *(Added by Stats.1993, c. 219 (A.B.1500), § 154.)*

Cross References

Abuse defined for purposes of the Domestic Violence Protection Act, see Family Code § 6203.
Judgment and order defined for purposes of this Code, see Family Code § 100.
Petitioner defined for purposes of this Code, see Family Code § 126.
Respondent defined for purposes of this Code, see Family Code § 127.
Support defined for purposes of this Code, see Family Code § 150.

Research References

Forms

West's California Code Forms, Family § 6340, Comment Overview—Issuance of Orders After Notice and Hearing.

§ 6342.5. Order determining use, possession, and control of real or personal property; debts incurred as result of domestic violence

(a) After notice and a hearing, the court may issue an order determining the use, possession, and control of real or personal property of the parties during the period the order is in effect and the payment of any liens or encumbrances coming due during that period.

(b) The order described in subdivision (a) may include a finding that specific debts were incurred as the result of domestic violence and without the consent of a party. For purposes of this subdivision, the acts that may support this finding include, but are not limited to, the crimes proscribed by Section 530.5 of the Penal Code. This finding does not affect the priority of any lien or other security interest.

(c) The Judicial Council shall adopt appropriate forms and modify existing forms, as necessary, to effectuate this section.

(d) This section shall be operative on January 1, 2022. *(Added by Stats.2020, c. 245 (A.B.2517), § 1, eff. Jan. 1, 2021, operative Jan. 1, 2022.)*

§ 6343. Batterer's program; order to participate; enrollment; resource list

(a) After notice and a hearing, the court may issue an order requiring the restrained party to participate in a batterer's program approved by the probation department as provided in Section 1203.097 of the Penal Code.

(b)(1) Commencing July 1, 2016, if the court orders a restrained party to participate in a batterer's program pursuant to subdivision (a), the restrained party shall do all of the following:

(A) Register for the program by the deadline ordered by the court. If no deadline is ordered by the court, the restrained party shall register no later than 30 days from the date the order was issued.

(B) At the time of enrollment, sign all necessary program consent forms for the program to release proof of enrollment, attendance records, and completion or termination reports to the court and the protected party, or the protected party's attorney. The court and the protected party may provide to the program a fax number or mailing address for purposes of receiving proof of enrollment, attendance records, and completion or termination reports.

(C) Provide the court and the protected party with the name, address, and telephone number of the program.

(2) By July 1, 2016, the Judicial Council shall revise or promulgate forms as necessary to effectuate this subdivision.

(c) The courts shall, in consultation with local domestic violence shelters and programs, develop a resource list of referrals to appropriate community domestic violence programs and services to be provided to each applicant for an order under this section. *(Added by Stats.1993, c. 219 (A.B.1500), § 154. Amended by Stats.1993, c. 876 (S.B.1068), § 27.3, eff. Oct. 6, 1993, operative Jan. 1, 1994; Stats.1999, c. 662 (S.B.218), § 3; Stats.2015, c. 72 (A.B.439), § 1, eff. Jan. 1, 2016; Stats.2019, c. 115 (A.B.1817), § 66, eff. Jan. 1, 2020.)*

Cross References

Domestic violence defined for purposes of this Code, see Family Code § 6211.
Judgment and order defined for purposes of this Code, see Family Code § 100.

Research References

Forms

West's California Code Forms, Family § 6340, Comment Overview—Issuance of Orders After Notice and Hearing.
West's California Judicial Council Forms DV–805, Proof of Enrollment for Batterer Intervention Program (Also Available in Chinese, Korean, Spanish, and Vietnamese).
West's California Judicial Council Forms DV–815, Batterer Intervention Program Progress Report (Also Available in Chinese, Korean, Spanish, and Vietnamese).

§ 6344. Order for payment of attorney's fees and costs; grounds for determination

(a) After notice and a hearing, a court, upon request, shall issue an order for the payment of attorney's fees and costs for a prevailing petitioner.

(b) After notice and a hearing, the court, upon request, may issue an order for the payment of attorney's fees and costs for a prevailing respondent only if the respondent establishes by a preponderance of the evidence that the petition or request is frivolous or solely intended to abuse, intimidate, or cause unnecessary delay.

(c) Before a court awards attorney's fees and costs pursuant to this section, the court shall first determine pursuant to Section 270 that the party ordered to pay has, or is reasonably likely to have, the ability to pay. *(Added by Stats.2022, c. 591 (A.B.2369), § 2, eff. Jan. 1, 2023.)*

Cross References

Custody of children, award of attorney's fees and costs, see Family Code § 3121.
Dissolution and separation, award of attorney's fees and costs, see Family Code §§ 2030, 2031.
Judgment and order defined for purposes of this Code, see Family Code § 100.
Payment of appointed counsel's fees and costs, enforcement of protective order, see Family Code § 6386.
Uniform Parentage Act, child custody and visitation proceedings, award of attorney's fees and costs, see Family Code § 7605.

§ 6345. Duration of orders

(a) In the discretion of the court, the personal conduct, stay-away, and residence exclusion orders contained in a court order issued after notice and a hearing under this article may have a duration of not more than five years, subject to termination or modification by further order of the court either on written stipulation filed with the court or on the motion of a party. These orders may be renewed, upon the request of a party, either for five or more years, or permanently, at the discretion of the court, without a showing of further abuse since the issuance of the original order * * *. Renewals and subsequent renewals shall be subject to termination * * *, modification, or subsequent renewal by further order of the court either on written stipulation filed with the court or on the motion of a party. The request for renewal may be brought at any time within the three months before the expiration of the orders.

(b) Notwithstanding subdivision (a), the duration of any orders, other than the protective orders described in subdivision (a), that are also contained in a court order issued after notice and a hearing under this article, including, but not limited to, orders for custody, visitation, support, and disposition of property, shall be governed by the law relating to those specific subjects.

(c) The failure to state the expiration date on the face of the form creates an order with a duration of three years from the date of issuance.

(d) If an action is filed for the purpose of terminating or modifying a protective order prior to the expiration date specified in the order by a party other than the protected party, the party who is protected by the order shall be given notice, pursuant to subdivision (b) of Section 1005 of the Code of Civil Procedure, of the proceeding by personal service or, if the protected party has satisfied the requirements of Chapter 3.1 (commencing with Section 6205) of Division 7 of Title 1 of the Government Code, by service on the Secretary of State. If the party who is protected by the order cannot be notified prior to the hearing for modification or termination of the protective order, the court shall deny the motion to modify or terminate the order without prejudice or continue the hearing until the party who is protected can be properly noticed and may, upon a showing of good cause, specify another method for service of process that is reasonably designed to afford actual notice to the protected party. The protected party may waive the right to notice if the protected party is physically present in court and does not challenge the sufficiency of the notice. *(Added by Stats.1993, c. 219 (A.B.1500), § 154. Amended by Stats.1995, c. 907 (A.B.935), § 2; Stats.2005, c. 125 (A.B.99), § 1; Stats.2010, c. 572 (A.B.1596), § 19, operative Jan. 1, 2012; Stats.2011, c. 101 (A.B.454), § 4; Stats.2019, c. 115 (A.B.1817), § 67, eff. Jan. 1, 2020; Stats.2022, c. 88 (S.B.935), § 1, eff. Jan. 1, 2023.)*

Cross References

Abuse defined for purposes of the Domestic Violence Protection Act, see Family Code § 6203.
Judgment and order defined for purposes of this Code, see Family Code § 100.
Property defined for purposes of this Code, see Family Code § 113.
Protective order defined for purposes of this Code, see Family Code § 6218.
State defined for purposes of this Code, see Family Code § 145.
Support defined for purposes of this Code, see Family Code § 150.

Research References

Forms

West's California Code Forms, Family § 6340, Comment Overview—Issuance of Orders After Notice and Hearing.
West's California Judicial Council Forms DV–200, Proof of Personal Service (CLETS) (Also Available in Korean, Spanish, and Vietnamese).
West's California Judicial Council Forms DV–400, Findings and Order to Terminate Restraining Order After Hearing (Clets—Cancel) (Also Available in Spanish).
West's California Judicial Council Forms DV–700, Request to Renew Restraining Order (Also Available in Chinese, Korean, Spanish, and Vietnamese).
West's California Judicial Council Forms DV–710, Notice of Hearing to Renew Restraining Order (Also Available in Chinese, Korean, Spanish, and Vietnamese).
West's California Judicial Council Forms DV–720, Response to Request to Renew Restraining Order (Also Available in Chinese, Korean, Spanish, and Vietnamese).
West's California Judicial Council Forms DV–730, Order to Renew Domestic Violence Restraining Order (Also Available in Chinese, Korean, Spanish, and Vietnamese).

§ 6346. Custody and visitation orders; notice and hearing

The court may make appropriate custody and visitation orders pursuant to the Uniform Parentage Act (Part 3 (commencing with Section 7600) of Division 12) after notice and a hearing under this section when the party who has requested custody or visitation has not established a parent and child relationship under subparagraph (B) of paragraph (2) of subdivision (a) of Section 6323, but has taken steps to establish that relationship by filing an action under the Uniform Parentage Act. *(Added by Stats.1997, c. 396 (S.B.564), § 3.)*

Cross References

Judgment and order defined for purposes of this Code, see Family Code § 100.

§ 6347. Order directing wireless telephone service provider to transfer billing responsibility and rights to requesting party

(a) Commencing July 1, 2016, in order to ensure that the requesting party can maintain an existing wireless telephone number, and the wireless numbers of any minor children in the care of the requesting party, the court may issue an order, after notice and a hearing, directing a wireless telephone service provider to transfer the billing responsibility for and rights to the wireless telephone number or numbers to the requesting party, if the requesting party is not the accountholder.

(b)(1) The order transferring billing responsibility for and rights to the wireless telephone number or numbers to a requesting party shall be a separate order that is directed to the wireless telephone service provider. The order shall list the name and billing telephone number of the accountholder, the name and contact information of the person to whom the telephone number or numbers will be transferred, and each telephone number to be transferred to that person. The court shall ensure that the contact information of the requesting party is not provided to the accountholder in proceedings held pursuant to Division 10 (commencing with Section 6200).

(2) The order shall be served on the wireless service provider's agent for service of process listed with the Secretary of State.

(3) Where the wireless service provider cannot operationally or technically effectuate the order due to certain circumstances, including, but not limited to, any of the following, the wireless service provider shall notify the requesting party within 72 hours of receipt of the order:

(A) When the accountholder has already terminated the account.

(B) When differences in network technology prevent the functionality of a device on the network.

(C) When there are geographic or other limitations on network or service availability.

(c)(1) Upon transfer of billing responsibility for and rights to a wireless telephone number or numbers to a requesting party pursuant to subdivision (b) by a wireless telephone service provider, the requesting party shall assume all financial responsibility for the transferred wireless telephone number or numbers, monthly service costs, and costs for any mobile device associated with the wireless telephone number or numbers.

(2) This section shall not preclude a wireless service provider from applying any routine and customary requirements for account establishment to the requesting party as part of this transfer of billing responsibility for a wireless telephone number or numbers and any devices attached to that number or numbers, including, but not limited to, identification, financial information, and customer preferences.

(d) This section shall not affect the ability of the court to apportion the assets and debts of the parties as provided for in law, or the ability to determine the temporary use, possession, and control of personal property pursuant to Sections 6324 and 6340.

(e) No cause of action shall lie against any wireless telephone service provider, its officers, employees, or agents, for actions taken in accordance with the terms of a court order issued pursuant to this section.

(f) The Judicial Council shall, on or before July 1, 2016, develop any forms or rules necessary to effectuate this section. *(Added by Stats.2015, c. 415 (A.B.1407), § 2, eff. Jan. 1, 2016.)*

Research References

Forms

West's California Judicial Council Forms DV–900, Order Transferring Wireless Phone Account (Also Available in Chinese, Korean, Spanish, and Vietnamese).

West's California Judicial Council Forms DV–901, Attachment to Order Transferring Wireless Phone Account (Also Available in Chinese, Korean, Spanish, and Vietnamese).

ARTICLE 3. ORDERS INCLUDED IN JUDGMENT

Section
6360. Judgments which may include protective orders.
6361. Statements on face of order included in judgment.

Cross References

Establishing parent and child relationship, restraining orders included in judgment, see Family Code § 7730.
Protective and restraining orders included in judgments, see Family Code § 2049.

§ 6360. Judgments which may include protective orders

A judgment entered in a proceeding for dissolution of marriage, for nullity of marriage, for legal separation of the parties, in a proceeding brought pursuant to this division, or in an action brought pursuant to the Uniform Parentage Act (Part 3 (commencing with Section 7600) of Division 12) may include a protective order as defined in Section 6218. *(Added by Stats.1993, c. 219 (A.B.1500), § 154.)*

Cross References

Judgment and order defined for purposes of this Code, see Family Code § 100.
Proceeding defined for purposes of this Code, see Family Code § 110.

§ 6361. Statements on face of order included in judgment

If an order is included in a judgment pursuant to this article, the judgment shall state on its face both of the following:

(a) Which provisions of the judgment are the orders.

(b) The date of expiration of the orders, which shall be not more than five years from the date the judgment is issued, unless extended by the court after notice and a hearing. *(Added by Stats.1993, c. 219 (A.B.1500), § 154. Amended by Stats.2005, c. 125 (A.B.99), § 2.)*

Cross References

Judgment and order defined for purposes of this Code, see Family Code § 100.
State defined for purposes of this Code, see Family Code § 145.

CHAPTER 3. REGISTRATION AND ENFORCEMENT OF ORDERS

Section
6380. California Law Enforcement Telecommunications System; information transmitted to Department of Justice; California Restraining and Protective Order System.
6380.5. Repealed.
6381. Enforceability of orders; receipt of copy by law enforcement agency; California Restraining and Protective Order System.
6382. Availability of information concerning orders; law enforcement officers.
6383. Service of order; verification; verbal notice; report; civil liability.
6384. Personal service of order not required; forms for orders.
6385. Proof of service of protective orders; personal descriptive information; purchase or receipt of firearm.
6386. Appointment of counsel; payment of attorney fees and costs.
6387. Copies of order to be provided to petitioner.
6388. Willful and knowing violation of order; penalty.
6389. Firearm or ammunition ownership, possession, purchase, or receipt; relinquishment order; use immunity; storage fee; order content; exemption; sale; penalty.
6390. Repealed.

§ 6380. California Law Enforcement Telecommunications System; information transmitted to Department of Justice; California Restraining and Protective Order System

(a) Each county, with the approval of the Department of Justice, shall, by July 1, 1996, develop a procedure, using existing systems, for the electronic transmission of data, as described in subdivision (b), to the Department of Justice. The data shall be electronically transmitted through the California Law Enforcement Telecommunications System (CLETS) of the Department of Justice by law enforcement personnel, or with the approval of the Department of Justice, court personnel, or another appropriate agency capable of maintaining and preserving the integrity of both the CLETS and the California Restraining and Protective Order System, as described in subdivision (e). Data entry is required to be entered only once under the requirements of this section, unless the order is served at a later time. A portion of all fees payable to the Department of Justice under subdivision (a) of Section 1203.097 of the Penal Code for the entry of the information required under this section, based upon the proportion of the costs incurred by the local agency and those incurred by the Department of Justice, shall be transferred to the local agency actually providing the data. All data with respect to criminal court protective orders issued, modified, extended, or terminated under Section 136.2 of the Penal Code, and all data filed with the court on the required Judicial Council forms with respect to protective orders, including their issuance, modification, extension, or termination, to which this division applies pursuant to Section 6221, shall be transmitted by the court or its designee within one business day to law enforcement personnel by either one of the following methods:

(1) Transmitting a physical copy of the order to a local law enforcement agency authorized by the Department of Justice to enter orders into CLETS.

(2) With the approval of the Department of Justice, entering the order into CLETS directly.

(b) Upon the issuance of a protective order to which this division applies pursuant to Section 6221, or the issuance of a temporary restraining order or injunction relating to harassment, unlawful violence, or the threat of violence pursuant to Section 527.6, 527.8, or 527.85 of the Code of Civil Procedure, or the issuance of a criminal court protective order under Section 136.2 of the Penal Code, or the issuance of a juvenile court restraining order related to domestic violence pursuant to Section 213.5, 304, or 362.4 of the Welfare and Institutions Code, or the issuance of a protective order pursuant to Section 15657.03 of the Welfare and Institutions Code, or upon registration with the court clerk of a domestic violence protective or restraining order issued by the tribunal of another state, as defined in Section 6401, and including any of the foregoing orders issued in connection with an order for modification of a custody or visitation order issued pursuant to a dissolution, legal separation, nullity, or paternity proceeding the Department of Justice shall be immediately notified of the contents of the order and the following information:

(1) The name, race, date of birth, and other personal descriptive information of the respondent as required by a form prescribed by the Department of Justice.

(2) The names of the protected persons.

(3) The date of issuance of the order.

(4) The duration or expiration date of the order.

(5) The terms and conditions of the protective order, including stay-away, no-contact, residency exclusion, custody, and visitation provisions of the order.

(6) The department or division number and the address of the court.

(7) Whether or not the order was served upon the respondent.

(8) The terms and conditions of any restrictions on the ownership or possession of firearms.

All available information shall be included; however, the inability to provide all categories of information shall not delay the entry of the information available.

(c) The information conveyed to the Department of Justice shall also indicate whether the respondent was present in court to be informed of the contents of the court order. The respondent's presence in court shall provide proof of service of notice of the terms of the protective order. The respondent's failure to appear shall also be included in the information provided to the Department of Justice.

(d)(1) Within one business day of service, a law enforcement officer who served a protective order shall submit the proof of service directly into the Department of Justice California Restraining and Protective Order System, including the officer's name and law enforcement agency, and shall transmit the original proof of service form to the issuing court.

(2) Within one business day of receipt of proof of service by a person other than a law enforcement officer, the clerk of the court shall submit the proof of service of a protective order directly into the Department of Justice California Restraining and Protective Order System, including the name of the person who served the order. If the court is unable to provide this notification to the Department of Justice by electronic transmission, the court shall, within one business day of receipt, transmit a copy of the proof of service to a local law enforcement agency. The local law enforcement agency shall submit the proof of service directly into the Department of Justice California Restraining and Protective Order System within one business day of receipt from the court.

(e) The Department of Justice shall maintain a California Restraining and Protective Order System and shall make available to court clerks and law enforcement personnel, through computer access, all information regarding the protective and restraining orders and injunctions described in subdivision (b), whether or not served upon the respondent.

(f) If a court issues a modification, extension, or termination of a protective order, it shall be on forms adopted by the Judicial Council of California and that have been approved by the Department of Justice, and the transmitting agency for the county shall immediately notify the Department of Justice, by electronic transmission, of the terms of the modification, extension, or termination.

(g) The Judicial Council shall assist local courts charged with the responsibility for issuing protective orders by developing informational packets describing the general procedures for obtaining a domestic violence restraining order and indicating the appropriate Judicial Council forms. The informational packets shall include a design, that local courts shall complete, that describes local court procedures and maps to enable applicants to locate filing windows and appropriate courts, and shall also include information on how to return proofs of service, including mailing addresses and fax numbers. The court clerk shall provide a fee waiver form to all applicants for domestic violence protective orders. The court clerk shall provide all Judicial Council forms required by this chapter to applicants free of charge. The informational packet shall also contain a statement that the protective order is enforceable in any state, as defined in Section 6401, and general information about agencies in other jurisdictions that may be contacted regarding enforcement of an order issued by a court of this state.

(h) For the purposes of this part, "electronic transmission" shall include computer access through the California Law Enforcement Telecommunications System (CLETS).

(i) Only protective and restraining orders issued on forms adopted by the Judicial Council of California and that have been approved by the Department of Justice shall be transmitted to the Department of Justice. However, this provision does not apply to a valid protective or restraining order related to domestic or family violence issued by a tribunal of another state, as defined in Section 6401. Those orders shall, upon request, be registered pursuant to Section 6404.

(j)(1) All protective orders subject to transmittal to CLETS pursuant to this section are required to be so transmitted.

(2) This subdivision does not constitute a change in, but is declaratory of, existing law. (Added by Stats.1994, c. 872 (A.B.3034), § 2. Amended by Stats.1995, c. 731 (A.B.233), § 1; Stats.1996, c. 1139 (A.B.2647), § 1; Stats.1996, c. 1140 (A.B.2231), § 1.5; Stats. 1998, c. 187 (A.B.1531), § 1; Stats.1998, c. 581 (A.B.2801), § 17; Stats.1998, c. 702 (A.B.2177), § 1; Stats.1998, c. 707 (S.B.1682), § 2.7; Stats.1999, c. 83 (S.B.966), § 52; Stats.1999, c. 561 (A.B.59), § 4; Stats.1999, c. 661 (A.B.825), § 5.5; Stats.2001, c. 698 (A.B.160), § 2; Stats.2001, c. 816 (A.B.731), § 1.5; Stats.2002, c. 265 (S.B.1627), § 1; Stats.2005, c. 631 (S.B.720), § 2; Stats.2010, c. 572 (A.B.1596), § 20, operative Jan. 1, 2012; Stats.2018, c. 89 (S.B.1089), § 2, eff. Jan. 1, 2019; Stats.2019, c. 497 (A.B.991), § 112, eff. Jan. 1, 2020; Stats.2019, c. 115 (A.B.1817), § 68, eff. Jan. 1, 2020.)

Cross References

Arrest with and without warrant, citizen's arrest by domestic victim, protective or restraining order, see Penal Code § 836.
County defined for purposes of this Code, see Family Code § 67.
Court orders available in response to good cause belief of harm to, intimidation of, or dissuasion of victim or witness, see Penal Code § 136.2.
Criminal procedure, judgment and execution, domestic violence victims, see Penal Code § 1203.097.
Domestic violence defined for purposes of this Code, see Family Code § 6211.
Domestic violence prevention order, contempt for failure to comply, see Code of Civil Procedure § 1218.

Employees subject to unlawful violence or threat of violence at the workplace, temporary restraining order, injunction, see Code of Civil Procedure § 527.8.

Judgment and order defined for purposes of this Code, see Family Code § 100.

Juvenile court law, proceedings to declare a minor child a dependent child, see Welfare and Institutions Code § 213.5.

Officers authorized to maintain order on school campus or facility, threat of violence made off school campus, temporary restraining order and injunction, violation of restraining order, see Code of Civil Procedure § 527.85.

Person defined for purposes of this Code, see Family Code § 105.

Proceeding defined for purposes of this Code, see Family Code § 110.

Protective order defined for purposes of this Code, see Family Code § 6218.

Registration of Canadian domestic violence protection order, see Family Code § 6454.

Respondent defined for purposes of this Code, see Family Code § 127.

State defined for purposes of this Code, see Family Code § 145.

Temporary restraining order and injunction, domestic violence, see Code of Civil Procedure § 527.6.

Research References

Forms

West's California Code Forms, Family § 6300, Comment Overview—Protective Orders.

West's California Code Forms, Family § 6380, Comment Overview—Registration and Enforcement of Orders.

West's California Code Forms, Family § 6400, Comment Overview—Uniform Interstate Enforcement of Violence Protection Orders Act.

West's California Judicial Council Forms JV–250, Notice of Hearing and Temporary Restraining Order—Juvenile (Also Available in Chinese, Korean, Spanish, and Vietnamese).

West's California Judicial Council Forms JV–255, Restraining Order—Juvenile (Clets—Juv) (Also Available in Chinese, Korean, Spanish, and Vietnamese).

§ 6380.5. Repealed by Stats.2001, c. 816 (A.B.731), § 2

§ 6381. Enforceability of orders; receipt of copy by law enforcement agency; California Restraining and Protective Order System

(a) Notwithstanding Section 6380 and subject to subdivision (b), an order issued under this part is enforceable in any place in this state.

(b) An order issued under this part is not enforceable by a law enforcement agency of a political subdivision unless that law enforcement agency has received a copy of the order, or the officer enforcing the order has been shown a copy of the order or has obtained information, through the California Restraining and Protective Order System maintained by the Department of Justice, of the contents of the order, as described in subdivision (b).

(c) The data contained in the California Restraining and Protective Order System shall be deemed to be original, self-authenticating, documentary evidence of the court orders. Oral notification of the terms of the orders shall be sufficient notice for enforcement under subdivision (g) of Section 136.2 and Section 273.6 of the Penal Code. *(Added by Stats.1993, c. 219 (A.B.1500), § 154. Amended by Stats.1994, c. 872 (A.B.3034), § 3; Stats.1999, c. 661 (A.B.825), § 7; Stats.2019, c. 115 (A.B.1817), § 69, eff. Jan. 1, 2020.)*

Cross References

Domestic violence defined for purposes of this Code, see Family Code § 6211.

Judgment and order defined for purposes of this Code, see Family Code § 100.

State defined for purposes of this Code, see Family Code § 145.

Research References

Forms

West's California Code Forms, Family § 6380, Comment Overview—Registration and Enforcement of Orders.

§ 6382. Availability of information concerning orders; law enforcement officers

Each appropriate law enforcement agency shall make available to any law enforcement officer responding to the scene of reported domestic violence, through an existing system for verification, information as to the existence, terms, and current status of an order issued under this part. *(Added by Stats.1993, c. 219 (A.B.1500), § 154.)*

Cross References

Domestic violence defined for purposes of this Code, see Family Code § 6211.

Judgment and order defined for purposes of this Code, see Family Code § 100.

Research References

Forms

West's California Code Forms, Family § 6380, Comment Overview—Registration and Enforcement of Orders.

§ 6383. Service of order; verification; verbal notice; report; civil liability

(a) A temporary restraining order or emergency protective order issued under this part shall, on request of the petitioner, be served on the respondent, whether or not the respondent has been taken into custody, by a law enforcement officer who is present at the scene of reported domestic violence involving the parties to the proceeding.

(b) The petitioner shall provide the officer with an endorsed copy of the order and a proof of service that the officer shall complete and transmit to the issuing court.

(c) It is a rebuttable presumption that the proof of service was signed on the date of service.

(d) Upon receiving information at the scene of a domestic violence incident that a protective order has been issued under this part, or that a person who has been taken into custody is the respondent to that order, if the protected person cannot produce an endorsed copy of the order, a law enforcement officer shall immediately inquire of the California Restraining and Protective Order System to verify the existence of the order.

(e) If the law enforcement officer determines that a protective order has been issued, but not served, the officer shall immediately notify the respondent of the terms of the order and where a written copy of the order can be obtained, and the officer shall, at that time, also enforce the order. The law enforcement officer's verbal notice of the terms of the order shall constitute service of the order and is sufficient notice for the purposes of this section and for the purposes of Sections 273.6 and 29825 of the Penal Code.

(f) If a report is required under Section 13730 of the Penal Code, or if no report is required, then in the daily incident log, the officer shall provide the name and assignment of the officer notifying the respondent pursuant to subdivision (e) and the case number of the order.

(g) Upon service of the order outside of the court, a law enforcement officer shall advise the respondent to go to the local court to obtain a copy of the order containing the full terms and conditions of the order.

(h)(1) There shall be no civil liability on the part of, and no cause of action for false arrest or false imprisonment against, a peace officer who makes an arrest pursuant to a protective or restraining order that is regular upon its face, if the peace officer, in making the arrest, acts in good faith and has reasonable cause to believe that the person against whom the order is issued has notice of the order and has committed an act in violation of the order.

(2) If there is more than one order issued and one of the orders is an emergency protective order that has precedence in enforcement pursuant to paragraph (1) of subdivision (c) of Section 136.2 of the Penal Code, the peace officer shall enforce the emergency protective order. If there is more than one order issued, none of the orders issued is an emergency protective order that has precedence in enforcement, and one of the orders issued is a no-contact order, as described in Section 6320, the peace officer shall enforce the no-contact order. If there is more than one civil order regarding the

§ 6383 PREVENTION OF DOMESTIC VIOLENCE

same parties and neither an emergency protective order that has precedence in enforcement nor a no-contact order has been issued, the peace officer shall enforce the order that was issued last. If there are both civil and criminal orders regarding the same parties and neither an emergency protective order that has precedence in enforcement nor a no-contact order has been issued, the peace officer shall enforce the criminal order issued last, subject to the provisions of subdivisions (h) and (i) of Section 136.2 of the Penal Code. This section does not exonerate a peace officer from liability for the unreasonable use of force in the enforcement of the order. The immunities afforded by this section shall not affect the availability of any other immunity that may apply, including, but not limited to, Sections 820.2 and 820.4 of the Government Code. *(Added by Stats.1993, c. 219 (A.B.1500), § 154. Amended by Stats.1994, c. 872 (A.B.3034), § 4; Stats.1997, c. 347 (A.B.356), § 1; Stats.1999, c. 661 (A.B.825), § 8; Stats.2001, c. 698 (A.B.160), § 3; Stats.2005, c. 467 (A.B.429), § 2; Stats.2010, c. 178 (S.B.1115), § 24, operative Jan. 1, 2012; Stats.2013, c. 263 (A.B.176), § 2, operative July 1, 2014; Stats.2014, c. 71 (S.B.1304), § 54, eff. Jan. 1, 2015; Stats.2019, c. 115 (A.B.1817), § 70, eff. Jan. 1, 2020.)*

Cross References

Domestic violence defined for purposes of this Code, see Family Code § 6211.
Emergency protective order defined for purposes of this Code, see Family Code § 6215.
Judgment and order defined for purposes of this Code, see Family Code § 100.
Person defined for purposes of this Code, see Family Code § 105.
Petitioner defined for purposes of this Code, see Family Code § 126.
Proceeding defined for purposes of this Code, see Family Code § 110.
Respondent defined for purposes of this Code, see Family Code § 127.

Research References

Forms

West's California Code Forms, Family § 6380, Comment Overview—Registration and Enforcement of Orders.

§ 6384. Personal service of order not required; forms for orders

(a) If a respondent named in an order issued under this part after a hearing has not been served personally with the order but has received actual notice of the existence and substance of the order through personal appearance in court to hear the terms of the order from the court, no additional proof of service is required for enforcement of the order.

If a respondent named in a temporary restraining order or emergency protective order is personally served with the order and notice of hearing with respect to a restraining order or protective order based on the temporary restraining order or emergency protective order, but the respondent does not appear at the hearing either in person or by counsel, and the terms and conditions of the restraining order or protective order issued at the hearing are identical to the temporary restraining or emergency protective order, except for the duration of the order, the restraining order or protective order issued at the hearing may be served on the respondent by first-class mail sent to the respondent at the most current address for the respondent that is available to the court.

(b) The Judicial Council forms for orders issued under this part shall contain a statement in substantially the following form:

"If you have been personally served with a temporary restraining order and notice of hearing, but you do not appear at the hearing either in person or by a lawyer, and a restraining order that is the same as this temporary restraining order except for the expiration date is issued at the hearing, a copy of the order will be served on you by mail at the following address: _____.

If that address is not correct or you wish to verify that the temporary restraining order was converted to a restraining order at the hearing without substantive change and to find out the duration of that order, contact the clerk of the court." *(Added by Stats.1993,*

c. 219 (A.B.1500), § 154. Amended by Stats.1997, c. 347 (A.B.356), § 2; Stats.2010, c. 572 (A.B.1596), § 21, operative Jan. 1, 2012.)

Cross References

Emergency protective order defined for purposes of this Code, see Family Code § 6215.
Judgment and order defined for purposes of this Code, see Family Code § 100.
Person defined for purposes of this Code, see Family Code § 105.

§ 6385. Proof of service of protective orders; personal descriptive information; purchase or receipt of firearm

(a) Proof of service of the protective order is not required for the purposes of Section 6380 if the order indicates on its face that both parties were personally present at the hearing at which the order was issued and that, for the purpose of Section 6384, no proof of service is required, or if the order was served by a law enforcement officer pursuant to Section 6383.

(b) The failure of the petitioner to provide the Department of Justice with the personal descriptive information regarding the person restrained does not invalidate the protective order.

(c) There is no civil liability on the part of, and no cause of action arises against, an employee of a local law enforcement agency, a court, or the Department of Justice, acting within the scope of employment, if a person described in Section 29825 of the Penal Code unlawfully purchases or receives or attempts to purchase or receive a firearm and a person is injured by that firearm or a person who is otherwise entitled to receive a firearm is denied a firearm and either wrongful action is due to a failure of a court to provide the notification provided for in this chapter. *(Added by Stats.1993, c. 219 (A.B.1500), § 154. Amended by Stats.1994, c. 872 (A.B.3034), § 5; Stats.1995, c. 731 (A.B.233), § 2; Stats.2002, c. 265 (S.B.1627), § 2; Stats.2010, c. 178 (S.B.1115), § 25, operative Jan. 1, 2012.)*

Cross References

Judgment and order defined for purposes of this Code, see Family Code § 100.
Person defined for purposes of this Code, see Family Code § 105.
Petitioner defined for purposes of this Code, see Family Code § 126.
Protective order defined for purposes of this Code, see Family Code § 6218.
Transmission of firearm purchaser information, procedures, see Penal Code §§ 28200 to 28250.

Research References

Forms

West's California Code Forms, Family § 6380, Comment Overview—Registration and Enforcement of Orders.

§ 6386. Appointment of counsel; payment of attorney fees and costs

(a) The court may, in its discretion, appoint counsel to represent the petitioner in a proceeding to enforce the terms of a protective order, as defined in Section 6218.

(b) In a proceeding in which private counsel was appointed by the court pursuant to subdivision (a), the court may order the respondent to pay reasonable attorney's fees and costs incurred by the petitioner. *(Added by Stats.1993, c. 219 (A.B.1500), § 154.)*

Cross References

Judgment and order defined for purposes of this Code, see Family Code § 100.
Petitioner defined for purposes of this Code, see Family Code § 126.
Proceeding defined for purposes of this Code, see Family Code § 110.
Respondent defined for purposes of this Code, see Family Code § 127.

§ 6387. Copies of order to be provided to petitioner

The court shall order the clerk of the court to provide to a petitioner, without cost, up to three certified, stamped, and endorsed copies of any order issued under this part, and of an extension, modification, or termination of the order. *(Added by Stats.1993, c.*

219 (A.B.1500), § 154. Amended by Stats.2001, c. 176 (S.B.210), § 5; Stats.2010, c. 572 (A.B.1596), § 22, operative Jan. 1, 2012.)

Cross References

Judgment and order defined for purposes of this Code, see Family Code § 100.
Petitioner defined for purposes of this Code, see Family Code § 126.

§ 6388. Willful and knowing violation of order; penalty

A willful and knowing violation of a protective order, as defined in Section 6218, is a crime punishable as provided by Section 273.6 of the Penal Code. *(Added by Stats.1993, c. 219 (A.B.1500), § 154.)*

Cross References

Judgment and order defined for purposes of this Code, see Family Code § 100.

§ 6389. Firearm or ammunition ownership, possession, purchase, or receipt; relinquishment order; use immunity; storage fee; order content; exemption; sale; penalty

(a) A person subject to a protective order, as defined in Section 6218, shall not own, possess, purchase, or receive a firearm or ammunition while that protective order is in effect. A person who owns, possesses, purchases, or receives, or attempts to purchase or receive a firearm or ammunition while the protective order is in effect is punishable pursuant to Section 29825 of the Penal Code.

(b) On all forms providing notice that a protective order has been requested or granted, the Judicial Council shall include a notice that, upon service of the order, the respondent shall be ordered to relinquish possession or control of any firearms or ammunition and not to purchase or receive or attempt to purchase or receive any firearms or ammunition for a period not to exceed the duration of the restraining order.

(c)(1) Upon issuance of a protective order, as defined in Section 6218, the court shall order the respondent to relinquish any firearm or ammunition in the respondent's immediate possession or control or subject to the respondent's immediate possession or control.

(2) The relinquishment ordered pursuant to paragraph (1) shall occur by immediately surrendering the firearm or ammunition in a safe manner, upon request of a law enforcement officer, to the control of the officer, after being served with the protective order. A law enforcement officer serving a protective order that indicates that the respondent possesses weapons or ammunition shall request that the firearm or ammunition be immediately surrendered. Alternatively, if a request is not made by a law enforcement officer, the relinquishment shall occur within 24 hours of being served with the order, by either surrendering the firearm or ammunition in a safe manner to the control of local law enforcement officials, or by selling, transferring, or relinquishing for storage pursuant to Section 29830 of the Penal Code, the firearm or ammunition to a licensed gun dealer, as specified in Article 1 (commencing with Section 26700) and Article 2 (commencing with Section 26800) of Chapter 2 of Division 6 of Title 4 of Part 6 of the Penal Code. The law enforcement officer or licensed gun dealer taking possession of the firearm or ammunition pursuant to this subdivision shall issue a receipt to the person relinquishing the firearm or ammunition at the time of relinquishment. A person ordered to relinquish a firearm or ammunition pursuant to this subdivision shall, within 48 hours after being served with the order, do both of the following:

(A) File, with the court that issued the protective order, the receipt showing the firearm or ammunition was surrendered to a local law enforcement agency or sold to a licensed gun dealer. Failure to timely file a receipt shall constitute a violation of the protective order.

(B) File a copy of the receipt described in subparagraph (A) with the law enforcement agency that served the protective order. Failure to timely file a copy of the receipt shall constitute a violation of the protective order.

(3) The forms for protective orders adopted by the Judicial Council and approved by the Department of Justice shall require the petitioner to describe the number, types, and locations of any firearms or ammunition presently known by the petitioner to be possessed or controlled by the respondent.

(4) A court holding a hearing on this matter shall review the file to determine whether the receipt has been filed and inquire of the respondent whether they have complied with the requirement. Violations of the firearms prohibition of any restraining order under this section shall be reported to the prosecuting attorney in the jurisdiction where the order has been issued within two business days of the court hearing unless the restrained party provides a receipt showing compliance at a subsequent hearing or by direct filing with the clerk of the court.

(5) Every law enforcement agency in the state shall develop, adopt, and implement written policies and standards for law enforcement officers who request immediate relinquishment of firearms or ammunition.

(d) If the respondent declines to relinquish possession of a firearm or ammunition based on the assertion of the right against self-incrimination, as provided by the Fifth Amendment to the United States Constitution and Section 15 of Article I of the California Constitution, the court may grant use immunity for the act of relinquishing the firearm or ammunition required under this section.

(e) A local law enforcement agency may charge the respondent a fee for the storage of a firearm or ammunition pursuant to this section. This fee shall not exceed the actual cost incurred by the local law enforcement agency for the storage of the firearm or ammunition. For purposes of this subdivision, "actual cost" means expenses directly related to taking possession of a firearm or ammunition, storing the firearm or ammunition, and surrendering possession of the firearm or ammunition to a licensed dealer as defined in Section 26700 of the Penal Code or to the respondent.

(f) The restraining order requiring a person to relinquish a firearm or ammunition pursuant to subdivision (c) shall state on its face that the respondent is prohibited from owning, possessing, purchasing, or receiving a firearm or ammunition while the protective order is in effect and that the firearm or ammunition shall be relinquished to the local law enforcement agency for that jurisdiction or sold to a licensed gun dealer, and that proof of surrender or sale shall be filed with the court within a specified period of receipt of the order. The order shall also state on its face the expiration date for relinquishment. This section does not limit a respondent's right under existing law to petition the court at a later date for modification of the order.

(g) The restraining order requiring a person to relinquish a firearm or ammunition pursuant to subdivision (c) shall prohibit the person from possessing or controlling a firearm or ammunition for the duration of the order. At the expiration of the order, the local law enforcement agency shall return possession of the surrendered firearm or ammunition to the respondent, within five days after the expiration of the relinquishment order, unless the local law enforcement agency determines that (1) the firearm or ammunition has been stolen, (2) the respondent is prohibited from possessing a firearm or ammunition because the respondent is in a prohibited class for the possession of firearms or ammunition, as defined in Chapter 2 (commencing with Section 29800) and Chapter 3 (commencing with Section 29900) of Division 9 of Title 4 of Part 6 of the Penal Code, Section 30305 of the Penal Code, and Sections 8100 and 8103 of the Welfare and Institutions Code, or (3) another successive restraining order is issued against the respondent under this section. If the local law enforcement agency determines that the respondent is the legal owner of a firearm or ammunition deposited with the local law enforcement agency and is prohibited from possessing a firearm or ammunition, the respondent shall be entitled to sell or transfer the firearm or ammunition to a licensed dealer as defined in Section 26700 of the Penal Code. If the firearm or ammunition has been stolen, the firearm or ammunition shall be restored to the lawful owner upon the owner identifying the firearm and ammunition and providing proof of ownership.

(h) The court may, as part of the relinquishment order, grant an exemption from the relinquishment requirements of this section for a particular firearm or ammunition if the respondent can show that a particular firearm or ammunition is necessary as a condition of continued employment and that the current employer is unable to reassign the respondent to another position where a firearm or ammunition is unnecessary. If an exemption is granted pursuant to this subdivision, the order shall provide that the firearm or ammunition shall be in the physical possession of the respondent only during scheduled work hours and during travel to and from the place of employment. When a peace officer is required, as a condition of employment, to carry a firearm or ammunition and whose personal safety depends on the ability to carry a firearm or ammunition a court may allow the peace officer to continue to carry a firearm or ammunition, either on duty or off duty, if the court finds by a preponderance of the evidence that the officer does not pose a threat of harm. Prior to making this finding, the court shall require a mandatory psychological evaluation of the peace officer and may require the peace officer to enter into counseling or other remedial treatment program to deal with any propensity for domestic violence.

(i) During the period of the relinquishment order, a respondent is entitled to make one sale of all firearms or ammunition that are in the possession of a local law enforcement agency pursuant to this section. A licensed gun dealer, who presents a local law enforcement agency with a bill of sale indicating that all firearms or ammunition owned by the respondent that are in the possession of the local law enforcement agency have been sold by the respondent to the licensed gun dealer, shall be given possession of those firearms or ammunition, at the location where a respondent's firearms or ammunition are stored, within five days of presenting the local law enforcement agency with a bill of sale.

(j) The disposition of any unclaimed property under this section shall be made pursuant to Section 1413 of the Penal Code.

(k) The relinquishment of a firearm to a law enforcement agency pursuant to subdivision (g) or the return of a firearm to a person pursuant to subdivision (g) shall not be subject to the requirements of Section 27545 of the Penal Code.

(*l*) If the respondent notifies the court that the respondent owns a firearm or ammunition that is not in their immediate possession, the court may limit the order to exclude that firearm or ammunition if the judge is satisfied the respondent is unable to gain access to that firearm or ammunition while the protective order is in effect.

(m) A respondent to a protective order who violates an order issued pursuant to this section shall be punished under the provisions of Section 29825 of the Penal Code. *(Added by Stats.1994, c. 871 (S.B.1278), § 2. Amended by Stats.1999, c. 662 (S.B.218), § 5; Stats.2003, c. 498 (S.B.226), § 5; Stats.2004, c. 250 (S.B.1391), § 2; Stats.2006, c. 467 (S.B.585), § 1; Stats.2010, c. 178 (S.B.1115), § 26, operative Jan. 1, 2012; Stats.2010, c. 572 (A.B.1596), § 23, operative Jan. 1, 2012; Stats.2011, c. 285 (A.B.1402), § 6; Stats.2012, c. 765 (S.B.1433), § 2; Stats.2019, c. 115 (A.B.1817), § 71, eff. Jan. 1, 2020; Stats.2021, c. 685 (S.B.320), § 7, eff. Jan. 1, 2022.)*

Cross References

Abandonment and neglect of children, intentional and knowing violation of court order to prevent harassment, disturbing the peace, or threats or acts of violence, see Penal Code § 273.6.
Carrying an unloaded firearm that is not a handgun in an incorporated city or city and county, exemption for complying with this section, see Penal Code § 26405.
Certain sales, deliveries, transfers, or returns of firearms, application of Penal Code § 26500, see Penal Code § 26540.
Contempt of court, conduct constituting, see Penal Code § 166.
Criminal history search, prior restraining orders, see Family Code § 6306.
Custody of children, presumption against person perpetrating domestic violence, see Family Code § 3044.
Domestic violence defined for purposes of this Code, see Family Code § 6211.
Ex parte orders, restrained person having firearm or ammunition, determination of violation of this section, see Family Code § 6322.5.
Ex parte orders regarding temporary custody and visitation of minor children, stipulation of parentage, considerations, see Family Code § 6323.
Firearms reported stolen, lost, found, recovered, held for safekeeping, surrendered, relinquished, or under observation, entry into Department of Justice Automated Firearms System, see Penal Code § 11108.2.
Judgment and order defined for purposes of this Code, see Family Code § 100.
Open carrying of unloaded handgun, exemption pursuant to this section, see Penal Code § 26379.
Person defined for purposes of this Code, see Family Code § 105.
Persons or business enterprises selling more than 500 rounds of ammunition in 30-day period, vendor license requirement, exemption for compliance with this section, see Penal Code § 30342.
Proceedings to declare a minor child a dependent child, ex parte orders, see Welfare and Institutions Code § 213.5.
Property defined for purposes of this Code, see Family Code § 113.
Respondent defined for purposes of this Code, see Family Code § 127.
Search warrants, grounds for issuance, firearm owned by, in possession of, or in custody and control of person subject to firearms prohibition under this section, see Penal Code § 1524.
State defined for purposes of this Code, see Family Code § 145.
Transportation of firearm in order to comply with specified provisions, see Penal Code § 25555.

Research References

Forms

California Practice Guide: Rutter Family Law Forms Form 1:32, Glossary of Common Family Law Terms, Phrases and Concepts (Enclosure to Form 1:31).
West's California Judicial Council Forms DV–800, Proof of Firearms Turned In, Sold, or Stored.
West's California Judicial Council Forms JV–250, Notice of Hearing and Temporary Restraining Order—Juvenile (Also Available in Chinese, Korean, Spanish, and Vietnamese).
West's California Judicial Council Forms JV–255, Restraining Order—Juvenile (Clets—Juv) (Also Available in Chinese, Korean, Spanish, and Vietnamese).

§ 6390. Repealed by Stats.2002, c. 784 (S.B.1316), § 106.

Part 5

UNIFORM INTERSTATE ENFORCEMENT OF DOMESTIC VIOLENCE PROTECTION ORDERS ACT

Section
6400. Short title.
6401. Definitions.
6402. Judicial enforcement of order.
6403. Nonjudicial enforcement of order.
6404. Registration of order.
6405. Immunity from civil liability; multiple orders; precedence in enforcement; unreasonable use of force.
6406. Other remedies.
6407. Uniformity of application and construction.
6408. Severability clause.
6409. Application of Part.

Cross References

Abandonment and neglect of children, intentional and knowing violation of court order to prevent harassment, disturbing the peace, or threats or acts of violence, see Penal Code § 273.6.
Lease not to be terminated based on domestic or sexual assault against tenant, landlord's liability for compliance, form for affirmative defense to unlawful detainer action, see Code of Civil Procedure § 1161.3.
Other uniform acts in the Family Code,
    Uniform Act on Blood Tests to Determine Paternity, see Family Code § 7550 et seq.

Uniform Child Custody Jurisdiction and Enforcement Act, see Family Code § 3400 et seq.
Uniform Divorce Recognition Act, see Family Code § 2090 et seq.
Uniform Interstate Family Act, see Family Code § 5700.101 et seq.
Uniform Parentage Act, see Family Code § 7600 et seq.
Uniform Premarital Agreement Act, see Family Code § 1600 et seq.
Tenant protected by restraining order against another tenant, change of locks on dwelling unit, definitions, see Civil Code § 1941.6.
Tenant protected by restraining order against non-tenant, change of locks on dwelling unit, definitions, see Civil Code § 1941.5.
Uniform act, construction of provisions, see Family Code § 3.

§ 6400. Short title

This part may be cited as the Uniform Interstate Enforcement of Domestic Violence Protection Orders Act. *(Added by Stats.2001, c. 816 (A.B.731), § 3.)*

Cross References

Freedom from parental custody and control, stay of proceedings and effect upon jurisdiction under these provisions, see Family Code § 7807.
Judgment and order defined for purposes of this Code, see Family Code § 100.
Uniform act, construction of provisions, see Family Code § 3.

§ 6401. Definitions

In this part:

(1) "Foreign protection order" means a protection order issued by a tribunal of another state.

(2) "Issuing state" means the state whose tribunal issues a protection order.

(3) "Mutual foreign protection order" means a foreign protection order that includes provisions in favor of both the protected individual seeking enforcement of the order and the respondent.

(4) "Protected individual" means an individual protected by a protection order.

(5) "Protection order" means an injunction or other order, issued by a tribunal under the domestic violence, family violence, or antistalking laws of the issuing state, to prevent an individual from engaging in violent or threatening acts against, harassment of, contact or communication with, or physical proximity to, another individual.

(6) "Respondent" means the individual against whom enforcement of a protection order is sought.

(7) "State" means a state of the United States, the District of Columbia, Puerto Rico, the United States Virgin Islands, or any territory or insular possession subject to the jurisdiction of the United States. The term includes an Indian tribe or band, or any branch of the United States military, that has jurisdiction to issue protection orders.

(8) "Tribunal" means a court, agency, or other entity authorized by law to issue or modify a protection order. *(Added by Stats.2001, c. 816 (A.B.731), § 3. Amended by Stats.2003, c. 134 (S.B.399), § 1.)*

Cross References

Domestic violence defined for purposes of this Code, see Family Code § 6211.
Judgment and order defined for purposes of this Code, see Family Code § 100.
Respondent defined for purposes of this Code, see Family Code § 127.
State defined for purposes of this Code, see Family Code § 145.
Uniform act, construction of provisions, see Family Code § 3.

§ 6402. Judicial enforcement of order

(a) A person authorized by the law of this state to seek enforcement of a protection order may seek enforcement of a valid foreign protection order in a tribunal of this state. The tribunal shall enforce the terms of the order, including terms that provide relief that a tribunal of this state would lack power to provide but for this section. The tribunal shall enforce the order, whether the order was obtained by independent action or in another proceeding, if it is an order issued in response to a complaint, petition, or motion filed by or on behalf of an individual seeking protection. In a proceeding to enforce a foreign protection order, the tribunal shall follow the procedures of this state for the enforcement of protection orders.

(b) A tribunal of this state may not enforce a foreign protection order issued by a tribunal of a state that does not recognize the standing of a protected individual to seek enforcement of the order.

(c) A tribunal of this state shall enforce the provisions of a valid foreign protection order which govern custody and visitation, if the order was issued in accordance with the jurisdictional requirements governing the issuance of custody and visitation orders in the issuing state.

(d) A foreign protection order is valid if it meets all of the following criteria:

(1) Identifies the protected individual and the respondent.

(2) Is currently in effect.

(3) Was issued by a tribunal that had jurisdiction over the parties and subject matter under the law of the issuing state.

(4) Was issued after the respondent was given reasonable notice and had an opportunity to be heard before the tribunal issued the order or, in the case of an order ex parte, the respondent was given notice and has had or will have an opportunity to be heard within a reasonable time after the order was issued, in a manner consistent with the rights of the respondent to due process.

(e) A foreign protection order valid on its face is prima facie evidence of its validity.

(f) Absence of any of the criteria for validity of a foreign protection order is an affirmative defense in an action seeking enforcement of the order.

(g) A tribunal of this state may enforce provisions of a mutual foreign protection order which favor a respondent only if both of the following are true:

(1) The respondent filed a written pleading seeking a protection order from the tribunal of the issuing state.

(2) The tribunal of the issuing state made specific findings in favor of the respondent. *(Added by Stats.2001, c. 816 (A.B.731), § 3. Amended by Stats.2003, c. 134 (S.B.399), § 2.)*

Cross References

Judgment and order defined for purposes of this Code, see Family Code § 100.
Person defined for purposes of this Code, see Family Code § 105.
Prima facie evidence, see Evidence Code § 602.
Proceeding defined for purposes of this Code, see Family Code § 110.
Respondent defined for purposes of this Code, see Family Code § 127.
State defined for purposes of this Code, see Family Code § 145.
Uniform act, construction of provisions, see Family Code § 3.

Research References

Forms

West's California Code Forms, Family § 6400, Comment Overview—Uniform Interstate Enforcement of Violence Protection Orders Act.

§ 6403. Nonjudicial enforcement of order

(a) A law enforcement officer of this state, upon determining that there is probable cause to believe that a valid foreign protection order exists and that the order has been violated, shall enforce the order as if it were the order of a tribunal of this state. Presentation of a protection order that identifies both the protected individual and the respondent and, on its face, is currently in effect constitutes, in and of itself, probable cause to believe that a valid foreign protection order exists. For the purposes of this section, the protection order may be inscribed on a tangible medium or may have been stored in an electronic or other medium if it is retrievable in perceivable form. Presentation of a certified copy of a protection order is not required for enforcement.

(b) If a foreign protection order is not presented, a law enforcement officer of this state may consider other information in determining whether there is probable cause to believe that a valid foreign protection order exists.

(c) If a law enforcement officer of this state determines that an otherwise valid foreign protection order cannot be enforced because the respondent has not been notified or served with the order, the officer shall inform the respondent of the order, make a reasonable effort to serve the order upon the respondent, and allow the respondent a reasonable opportunity to comply with the order before enforcing the order. Verbal notice of the terms of the order is sufficient notice for the purposes of this section.

(d) Registration or filing of an order in this state is not required for the enforcement of a valid foreign protection order pursuant to this part. *(Added by Stats.2001, c. 816 (A.B.731), § 3.)*

Cross References

Judgment and order defined for purposes of this Code, see Family Code § 100.
Respondent defined for purposes of this Code, see Family Code § 127.
State defined for purposes of this Code, see Family Code § 145.
Uniform act, construction of provisions, see Family Code § 3.

Research References

Forms

West's California Code Forms, Family § 6400, Comment Overview—Uniform Interstate Enforcement of Violence Protection Orders Act.

§ 6404. Registration of order

(a) A foreign protection order shall, upon request of the person in possession of the order, be registered with a court of this state in order to be entered in the California Restraining and Protective Order System established under Section 6380. The Judicial Council shall adopt rules of court to do the following:

(1) Set forth the process whereby a person in possession of a foreign protection order may voluntarily register the order with a court of this state for entry into the California Restraining and Protective Order System.

(2) Require the sealing of foreign protection orders and provide access only to law enforcement, the person who registered the order upon written request with proof of identification, the defense after arraignment on criminal charges involving an alleged violation of the order, or upon further order of the court.

(b) A fee shall not be charged for the registration of a foreign protection order. The court clerk shall provide all Judicial Council forms required by this part to a person in possession of a foreign protection order free of charge. *(Added by Stats.2001, c. 816 (A.B.731), § 3. Amended by Stats.2019, c. 115 (A.B.1817), § 72, eff. Jan. 1, 2020.)*

Cross References

Domestic violence defined for purposes of this Code, see Family Code § 6211.
Judgment and order defined for purposes of this Code, see Family Code § 100.
Person defined for purposes of this Code, see Family Code § 105.
Registration of Canadian domestic violence protection order, see Family Code § 6454.
State defined for purposes of this Code, see Family Code § 145.
Uniform act, construction of provisions, see Family Code § 3.

Research References

Forms

West's California Code Forms, Family § 6400, Comment Overview—Uniform Interstate Enforcement of Violence Protection Orders Act.
West's California Judicial Council Forms DV–600, Order to Register Out-Of-State or Tribal Court Protective/Restraining Order (Also Available in Chinese, Korean, Spanish, and Vietnamese).

§ 6405. Immunity from civil liability; multiple orders; precedence in enforcement; unreasonable use of force

(a) There shall be no civil liability on the part of, and no cause of action for false arrest or false imprisonment against, a peace officer who makes an arrest pursuant to a foreign protection order that is regular upon its face, if the peace officer, in making the arrest, acts in good faith and has reasonable cause to believe that the person against whom the order is issued has notice of the order and has committed an act in violation of the order.

(b) If there is more than one order issued and one of the orders is an emergency protective order that has precedence in enforcement pursuant to paragraph (1) of subdivision (c) of Section 136.2 of the Penal Code, the peace officer shall enforce the emergency protective order. If there is more than one order issued, none of the orders issued is an emergency protective order that has precedence in enforcement, and one of the orders issued is a no-contact order, as described in Section 6320, the peace officer shall enforce the no-contact order. If there is more than one civil order regarding the same parties and neither an emergency protective order that has precedence in enforcement nor a no-contact order has been issued, the peace officer shall enforce the order that was issued last. If there are both civil and criminal orders regarding the same parties and neither an emergency protective order that has precedence in enforcement nor a no-contact order has been issued, the peace officer shall enforce the criminal order issued last.

(c) Nothing in this section shall be deemed to exonerate a peace officer from liability for the unreasonable use of force in the enforcement of the order. The immunities afforded by this section shall not affect the availability of any other immunity that may apply, including, but not limited to, Sections 820.2 and 820.4 of the Government Code. *(Added by Stats.2001, c. 816 (A.B.731), § 3. Amended by Stats.2013, c. 263 (A.B.176), § 3, operative July 1, 2014.)*

Cross References

Judgment and order defined for purposes of this Code, see Family Code § 100.
Person defined for purposes of this Code, see Family Code § 105.
Uniform act, construction of provisions, see Family Code § 3.

§ 6406. Other remedies

A protected individual who pursues remedies under this part is not precluded from pursuing other legal or equitable remedies against the respondent. *(Added by Stats.2001, c. 816 (A.B.731), § 3.)*

Cross References

Respondent defined for purposes of this Code, see Family Code § 127.
Uniform act, construction of provisions, see Family Code § 3.

§ 6407. Uniformity of application and construction

In applying and construing this part, consideration shall be given to the need to promote uniformity of the law with respect to its subject matter among states that also have adopted the act cited in Section 6400. *(Added by Stats.2001, c. 816 (A.B.731), § 3.)*

Cross References

State defined for purposes of this Code, see Family Code § 145.
Uniform act, construction of provisions, see Family Code § 3.

§ 6408. Severability clause

If any provision of this part or its application to any person or circumstance is held invalid, the invalidity does not affect other provisions or applications of this part which can be given effect without the invalid provision or application, and to this end the provisions of this part are severable. *(Added by Stats.2001, c. 816 (A.B.731), § 3.)*

Cross References

Person defined for purposes of this Code, see Family Code § 105.

Uniform act, construction of provisions, see Family Code § 3.

§ 6409. Application of Part

This part applies to protection orders issued before January 1, 2002, and to continuing actions for enforcement of foreign protection orders commenced before January 1, 2002. A request for enforcement of a foreign protection order made on or after January 1, 2002, for violations of a foreign protection order occurring before January 1, 2002, is governed by this part. *(Added by Stats.2001, c. 816 (A.B.731), § 3.)*

Cross References

Judgment and order defined for purposes of this Code, see Family Code § 100.
Uniform act, construction of provisions, see Family Code § 3.

Part 6

UNIFORM RECOGNITION AND ENFORCEMENT OF CANADIAN DOMESTIC VIOLENCE PROTECTION ORDERS ACT

Section
6450. Short title.
6451. Definitions.
6452. Enforcement of Canadian domestic violence protection order by law enforcement officer.
6453. Enforcement of Canadian domestic violence protection order by tribunal.
6454. Registration of Canadian domestic violence protection order.
6455. Immunity.
6456. Other remedies.
6457. Multiple protective orders; priority of enforcement.
6458. Relation to Electronic Signatures in Global and National Commerce Act.
6459. Transition.
6460. Severability.

§ 6450. Short title

This part may be cited as the Uniform Recognition and Enforcement of Canadian Domestic Violence Protection Orders Act. *(Added by Stats.2017, c. 98 (S.B.204), § 1, eff. Jan. 1, 2018.)*

§ 6451. Definitions

In this part:

(a) "Canadian domestic violence protection order" means a judgment or part of a judgment or order issued in English in a civil proceeding by a court of Canada under law of the issuing jurisdiction that relates to domestic violence and prohibits a respondent from doing any of the following:

(1) Being in physical proximity to a protected individual or following a protected individual.

(2) Directly or indirectly contacting or communicating with a protected individual or other individual described in the order.

(3) Being within a certain distance of a specified place or location associated with a protected individual.

(4) Molesting, annoying, harassing, or engaging in threatening conduct directed at a protected individual.

(b) "Domestic protection order" means an injunction or other order issued by a tribunal that relates to domestic or family violence laws to prevent an individual from engaging in violent or threatening acts against, harassment of, direct or indirect contact or communication with, or being in physical proximity to, another individual.

(c) "Issuing court" means the court that issues a Canadian domestic violence protection order.

(d) "Law enforcement officer" means an individual authorized by law of this state to enforce a domestic protection order.

(e) "Person" means an individual, estate, business or nonprofit entity, public corporation, government or governmental subdivision, agency, or instrumentality, or other legal entity.

(f) "Protected individual" means an individual protected by a Canadian domestic violence protection order.

(g) "Record" means information that is inscribed on a tangible medium or that is stored in an electronic or other medium and is retrievable in perceivable form.

(h) "Respondent" means an individual against whom a Canadian domestic violence protection order is issued.

(i) "State" means a state of the United States, the District of Columbia, Puerto Rico, the United States Virgin Islands, or any territory or insular possession subject to the jurisdiction of the United States. The term includes a federally recognized Indian tribe.

(j) "Tribunal" means a court, agency, or other entity authorized by law to establish, enforce, or modify a domestic protection order. *(Added by Stats.2017, c. 98 (S.B.204), § 1, eff. Jan. 1, 2018.)*

§ 6452. Enforcement of Canadian domestic violence protection order by law enforcement officer

(a) If a law enforcement officer determines under subdivision (b) or (c) that there is probable cause to believe a valid Canadian domestic violence protection order exists and the order has been violated, the officer shall enforce the terms of the Canadian domestic violence protection order as if the terms were in an order of a tribunal of this state. Presentation to a law enforcement officer of a certified copy of a Canadian domestic violence protection order is not required for enforcement.

(b) Presentation to a law enforcement officer of a record of a Canadian domestic violence protection order that identifies both a protected individual and a respondent and on its face is in effect constitutes probable cause to believe that a valid order exists.

(c) If a record of a Canadian domestic violence protection order is not presented as provided in subdivision (b), a law enforcement officer may consider other information in determining whether there is probable cause to believe that a valid Canadian domestic violence protection order exists.

(d) If a law enforcement officer determines that an otherwise valid Canadian domestic violence protection order cannot be enforced because the respondent has not been notified of or served with the order, the officer shall notify the protected individual that the officer will make reasonable efforts to contact the respondent, consistent with the safety of the protected individual. After notice to the protected individual and consistent with the safety of the individual, the officer shall make a reasonable effort to inform the respondent of the order, notify the respondent of the terms of the order, provide a record of the order, if available, to the respondent, and allow the respondent a reasonable opportunity to comply with the order before the officer enforces the order. Verbal notice of the terms of the order is sufficient for purposes of this subdivision.

(e) If a law enforcement officer determines that an individual is a protected individual, the officer shall inform the individual of available local victim services. *(Added by Stats.2017, c. 98 (S.B.204), § 1, eff. Jan. 1, 2018.)*

§ 6453. Enforcement of Canadian domestic violence protection order by tribunal

(a) A tribunal of this state may issue an order enforcing or refusing to enforce a Canadian domestic violence protection order on application of any of the following:

(1) A protected party or other person authorized by law of this state other than this part to seek enforcement of a domestic protection order.

(2) A respondent.

(b) In a proceeding under subdivision (a), the tribunal of this state shall follow the procedures of this state for enforcement of a domestic protection order. An order entered under this section is limited to the enforcement of the terms of the Canadian domestic violence protection order as described in subdivision (a) of Section 6451.

(c) A Canadian domestic violence protection order is enforceable under this section if all of the following apply:

(1) The order identifies a protected individual and a respondent.

(2) The order is valid and in effect.

(3) The issuing court had jurisdiction over the parties and the subject matter under law applicable in the issuing court.

(4) The order was issued after either of the following:

(A) The respondent was given reasonable notice and had an opportunity to be heard before the court issued the order.

(B) In the case of an ex parte order, the respondent was given reasonable notice and had or will have an opportunity to be heard within a reasonable time after the order was issued, in a manner consistent with the right of the respondent to due process.

(d) A Canadian domestic violence protection order valid on its face is prima facie evidence of its enforceability under this section.

(e) A claim that a Canadian domestic violence protection order does not comply with subdivision (c) is an affirmative defense in a proceeding seeking enforcement of the order. If the tribunal of this state determines that the order is not enforceable, the tribunal of this state shall issue an order that the Canadian domestic violence protection order is not enforceable under this section and Section 6452 and may not be registered under Section 6454.

(f) This section applies to enforcement of a provision of a Canadian domestic violence protection order against a party to the order in which each party is a protected individual and respondent only if both of the following apply:

(1) The party seeking enforcement of the order filed a pleading requesting the order from the issuing court.

(2) The court made detailed findings of fact indicating that both parties acted as a primary aggressor and that neither party acted primarily in self-defense. *(Added by Stats.2017, c. 98 (S.B.204), § 1, eff. Jan. 1, 2018.)*

§ 6454. Registration of Canadian domestic violence protection order

(a) An individual may register a Canadian domestic violence protection order in this state. To register the order, the individual must present a certified copy of the order to a court of this state to be entered into the California Restraining and Protective Order System established under Section 6380, pursuant to procedures set forth in Section 6404.

(b) A fee shall not be charged for the registration of a Canadian domestic violence protection order under this section.

(c) Registration in this state or filing under law of this state other than this part of a Canadian domestic violence protection order is not required for its enforcement under this part. *(Added by Stats.2017, c. 98 (S.B.204), § 1, eff. Jan. 1, 2018. Amended by Stats.2019, c. 115 (A.B.1817), § 73, eff. Jan. 1, 2020.)*

Research References

Forms

West's California Judicial Council Forms DV–630, Order to Register Canadian Domestic Violence Protective/Restraining Order (Also Available in Chinese, Korean, Spanish, and Vietnamese).

§ 6455. Immunity

(a) There shall be no civil liability on the part of, and no cause of action for false arrest or false imprisonment against, a law enforcement officer who makes an arrest pursuant to a Canadian domestic violence protection order that is regular upon its face, if the law enforcement officer, in making the arrest, acts in good faith and has reasonable cause to believe that the person against whom the order is issued has notice of the order and has committed an act in violation of the order.

(b) Nothing in this section shall be deemed to exonerate a law enforcement officer from liability for the unreasonable use of force in the enforcement of the order. The immunities afforded by this section shall not affect the availability of any other immunity that may apply, including, but not limited to, Sections 820.2 and 820.4 of the Government Code. *(Added by Stats.2017, c. 98 (S.B.204), § 1, eff. Jan. 1, 2018.)*

§ 6456. Other remedies

An individual who seeks a remedy under this part may seek other legal or equitable remedies. *(Added by Stats.2017, c. 98 (S.B.204), § 1, eff. Jan. 1, 2018.)*

§ 6457. Multiple protective orders; priority of enforcement

If there is more than one order issued and one of the orders is an emergency protective order that has precedence in enforcement pursuant to paragraph (1) of subdivision (c) of Section 136.2 of the Penal Code, the law enforcement officer shall enforce the emergency protective order. If there is more than one order issued, none of the orders issued is an emergency protective order that has precedence in enforcement, and one of the orders issued is a no-contact order, as described in Section 6320, the law enforcement officer shall enforce the no-contact order. If there is more than one civil order regarding the same parties and neither an emergency protective order that has precedence in enforcement nor a no-contact order has been issued, the law enforcement officer shall enforce the order that was issued last. If there are both civil and criminal orders regarding the same parties and neither an emergency protective order that has precedence in enforcement nor a no-contact order has been issued, the law enforcement officer shall enforce the criminal order issued last. *(Added by Stats.2017, c. 98 (S.B.204), § 1, eff. Jan. 1, 2018.)*

§ 6458. Relation to Electronic Signatures in Global and National Commerce Act

This part modifies, limits, or supersedes the federal Electronic Signatures in Global and National Commerce Act (15 U.S.C. Sec. 7001 et seq.), but does not modify, limit, or supersede Section 101(c) of that act (15 U.S.C. Sec. 7001(c)), or authorize electronic delivery of any of the notices described in Section 103(b) of that act (15 U.S.C. Sec. 7003(b)). *(Added by Stats.2017, c. 98 (S.B.204), § 1, eff. Jan. 1, 2018.)*

§ 6459. Transition

This part applies to a Canadian domestic violence protection order issued before, on, or after January 1, 2018, and to a continuing action for enforcement of a Canadian domestic violence protection order commenced before, on, or after January 1, 2018. A request for enforcement of a Canadian domestic violence protection order made on or after January 1, 2018, for a violation of the order occurring before, on, or after January 1, 2018, is governed by this part. *(Added by Stats.2017, c. 98 (S.B.204), § 1, eff. Jan. 1, 2018.)*

§ 6460. Severability

If any provision of this part or its application to any person or circumstance is held invalid, the invalidity does not affect other provisions or applications of this part that can be given effect without the invalid provision or application, and to this end the provisions of this part are severable. (Added by Stats.2017, c. 98 (S.B.204), § 1, eff. Jan. 1, 2018.)

Division 11

MINORS

Part		Section
1.	Age of Majority	6500
1.5.	Caregivers	6550
2.	Rights and Liabilities; Civil Actions and Proceedings	6600
3.	Contracts	6700
4.	Medical Treatment	6900
5.	Enlistment in Armed Forces	6950
6.	Emancipation of Minors Law	7000

Cross References

Contracts, capacity of minors and persons of unsound mind, see Civil Code § 1557.

Freedom from parental custody and control, stay of proceedings and effect upon jurisdiction under these provisions, see Family Code § 7807.

Minor defined for purposes of the California Uniform Transfers to Minors Act, see Probate Code § 3901.

Termination of parental rights of father, filing of petition, stay of proceedings affecting a child pending final determination of parental rights, see Family Code § 7662.

Part 1

AGE OF MAJORITY

Section
6500. "Minor" defined.
6501. "Adult" defined.
6502. Transitional provisions.

Cross References

Abandonment and neglect of children, see Penal Code § 270 et seq.
Academic achievement, release of individual records, see Education Code § 60607.
Actions for injuries to children, see Code of Civil Procedure § 376.
Adoption, children of Indian ancestry, certification of degree of Indian blood available to adopted child upon age of majority, see Family Code § 8619.
Annulment of marriage, see Family Code § 2210.
Armed forces enlistment, consent, see Family Code § 6950.
Capability of minors to consent to and consummate marriage, see Family Code § 302.
Child defined for purposes of the Uniform Interstate Family Support Act, see Family Code § 5700.102.
Child support,
  Duration of duty to support, see Family Code § 3901.
  Enforcement, local child support agencies, jurisdiction, see Family Code § 17400.
  Support of adult child, compensation, see Family Code § 7506.
Conditions for emancipation, see Family Code § 7002.
Consent of court to marriage of minor, see Family Code § 303.
Contracts, generally, see Family Code § 6700 et seq.
Contracts, capacity of minors to form, see Civil Code § 1556.
Disabilities of minority, effect on limitations period, see Code of Civil Procedure §§ 328, 352.
Emancipation of minors, see Family Code § 7000 et seq.
Freedom from parental custody and control, stay of proceedings and effect upon jurisdiction under these provisions, see Family Code § 7807.
Guardianship, termination upon majority, see Probate Code § 1600.
Medical treatment, see Family Code § 6900 et seq.
Minor considered an adult, emancipation, see Family Code § 7050.
Minor defined for purposes of the California Uniform Transfers to Minors Act, see Probate Code § 3901.
Parental authority, termination upon guardianship, marriage, or age of majority, see Family Code § 7505.
Premarital counseling, minors, see Family Code § 304.
Rights and liabilities of minors, generally, see Family Code § 6600 et seq.
Special education beyond age of majority, responsible local educational agencies, see Education Code § 56041.
State Teachers' Retirement System, minors entitled to benefits, payments to persons entitled to custody, see Education Code § 24612.
Student residency requirements, student who remains in state after parent moves elsewhere, see Education Code § 68070.

§ 6500. "Minor" defined

A minor is an individual who is under 18 years of age. The period of minority is calculated from the first minute of the day on which the individual is born to the same minute of the corresponding day completing the period of minority. (Stats.1992, c. 162 (A.B.2650), § 10, operative Jan. 1, 1994.)

Cross References

Abandonment and neglect of children, see Penal Code § 270 et seq.
Academic achievement, release of individual records, see Education Code § 60607.
Actions for injuries to children, see Code of Civil Procedure § 376.
Adoption, children of Indian ancestry, certification of degree of Indian blood available to adopted child upon age of majority, see Family Code § 8619.
Annulment of marriage, see Family Code § 2210.
Armed forces enlistment, consent, see Family Code § 6950.
Capability of minors to consent to and consummate marriage, see Family Code § 302.
Child defined for purposes of the Uniform Interstate Family Support Act, see Family Code § 5700.102.
Child support,
  Duration of duty to support, see Family Code § 3901.
  Enforcement, local child support agencies, jurisdiction, see Family Code § 17400.
  Support of adult child, compensation, see Family Code § 7506.
Conditions for emancipation, see Family Code § 7002.
Consent of court to marriage of minor, see Family Code § 303.
Contracts, generally, see Family Code § 6700 et seq.
Contracts, capacity of minors to form, see Civil Code § 1556.
Disabilities of minority, effect on limitations period, see Code of Civil Procedure §§ 328, 352.
Emancipation of minors, see Family Code § 7000 et seq.
Freedom from parental custody and control, stay of proceedings and effect upon jurisdiction under these provisions, see Family Code § 7807.
Guardianship, termination upon majority, see Probate Code § 1600.
Medical treatment, see Family Code § 6900 et seq.
Minor considered an adult, emancipation, see Family Code § 7050.
Minor defined for purposes of the California Uniform Transfers to Minors Act, see Probate Code § 3901.
Parental authority, termination upon guardianship, marriage, or age of majority, see Family Code § 7505.
Premarital counseling, minors, see Family Code § 304.
Public Employees' Retirement System, death benefits, surviving spouse, see Government Code § 21548.
Rights and liabilities of minors, generally, see Family Code § 6600 et seq.
School finance, state financial management and control, adults and minors, see Education Code § 41053.
Special education beyond age of majority, responsible local educational agencies, see Education Code § 56041.
State Teachers' Retirement System, minors entitled to benefits, payments to persons entitled to custody, see Education Code § 24612.

§ 6500   MINORS

Student residency requirements, student who remains in state after parent moves elsewhere, see Education Code § 68070.

Research References

Forms

14A Am. Jur. Pl. & Pr. Forms Infants § 1, Introductory Comments.
California Practice Guide: Rutter Family Law Forms Form 1:32, Glossary of Common Family Law Terms, Phrases and Concepts (Enclosure to Form 1:31).
1 California Transactions Forms--Business Entities § 5:103, Voting Rights-- Administrator, Executor, Guardian, or Conservator.
1 California Transactions Forms--Business Transactions § 6:9, Parties Who May Contract.
1 California Transactions Forms--Business Transactions § 6:10, Minors.
2 California Transactions Forms--Business Transactions § 8:53, Model Release for Images Included in Website.
3 California Transactions Forms--Business Transactions § 17:25, Minors.
1 California Transactions Forms--Estate Planning § 1:29, Options Involving Gifts to Minors.
1 California Transactions Forms--Estate Planning § 2:5, Necessity of Privity Between Estate Planner and Ultimate Beneficiary.
1 California Transactions Forms--Estate Planning § 6:15, Minors' Capacity to Take Devised Property.
1 California Transactions Forms--Estate Planning § 6:53, Matters to Consider in Drafting Gifts to Minors.
2 California Transactions Forms--Estate Planning § 11:39, General Considerations.
2 California Transactions Forms--Estate Planning § 11:48, Governing Contractual Provisions [CC §§1550 et seq., Fam C §721(B)].
3 California Transactions Forms--Estate Planning § 18:53, Irrevocable Asset Protection Discretionary Trust for Children With Spendthrift Provisions.
1 California Transactions Forms--Family Law § 1:2, Nature and Advantages of Agreement.
1 California Transactions Forms--Family Law § 2:63, Authority for Child Support.
1 California Transactions Forms--Family Law § 3:53, Sample Basic Custody Provisions.

§ 6501. "Adult" defined

An adult is an individual who is 18 years of age or older. *(Stats.1992, c. 162 (A.B.2650), § 10, operative Jan. 1, 1994.)*

Cross References

Adult defined for purposes of the California Uniform Transfers to Minors Act, see Probate Code § 3901.
Adult status, emancipated minors, see Family Code § 7050.
Conditions for emancipation, see Family Code § 7002.
Emancipation of minors, see Family Code § 7000 et seq.
Unruh Civil Rights Act, see Civil Code § 51 et seq.

Research References

Forms

1 California Transactions Forms--Business Transactions § 6:10, Minors.
1 California Transactions Forms--Estate Planning § 6:17, Guardian of Estate or of Property.

§ 6502. Transitional provisions

(a) The use of or reference to the words "age of majority," "age of minority," "adult," "minor," or words of similar intent in any instrument, order, transfer, or governmental communication made in this state:

(1) Before March 4, 1972, makes reference to individuals 21 years of age and older, or younger than 21 years of age.

(2) On or after March 4, 1972, makes reference to individuals 18 years of age and older, or younger than 18 years of age.

(b) Nothing in subdivision (a) or in Chapter 1748 of the Statutes of 1971 prevents amendment of any court order, will, trust, contract, transfer, or instrument to refer to the 18-year-old age of majority if the court order, will, trust, contract, transfer, or instrument satisfies all of the following conditions:

(1) It was in existence on March 4, 1972.

(2) It is subject to amendment by law, and amendment is allowable or not prohibited by its terms.

(3) It is otherwise subject to the laws of this state. *(Stats.1992, c. 162 (A.B.2650), § 10, operative Jan. 1, 1994.)*

Cross References

Adult and minor defined for purposes of the California Uniform Transfers to Minors Act, see Probate Code § 3901.
Judgment and order defined for purposes of this Code, see Family Code § 100.
Minor defined for purposes of this Code, see Family Code § 6500.
State defined for purposes of this Code, see Family Code § 145.

Research References

Forms

1 California Transactions Forms--Business Entities § 5:103, Voting Rights-- Administrator, Executor, Guardian, or Conservator.
1 California Transactions Forms--Business Transactions § 6:10, Minors.

Part 1.5

CAREGIVERS

Section
6550. Authorization affidavits; scope of authority; reliance on affidavit.
6552. Form of authorization affidavit.

Cross References

Minors, caregivers, form of authorization affidavit, see Family Code § 6552.

§ 6550. Authorization affidavits; scope of authority; reliance on affidavit

(a) A caregiver's authorization affidavit that meets the requirements of this part authorizes a caregiver 18 years of age or older who completes items 1 to 4, inclusive, of the affidavit provided in Section 6552 and signs the affidavit to enroll a minor in school and consent to school-related medical care on behalf of the minor. A caregiver who is a relative and who completes items 1 to 8, inclusive, of the affidavit provided in Section 6552 and signs the affidavit shall have the same rights to authorize medical care and dental care for the minor that are given to guardians under Section 2353 of the Probate Code. The medical care authorized by this caregiver who is a relative may include mental health treatment subject to the limitations of Section 2356 of the Probate Code.

(b) The decision of a caregiver to consent to or to refuse medical or dental care for a minor shall be superseded by any contravening decision of the parent or other person having legal custody of the minor, provided the decision of the parent or other person having legal custody of the minor does not jeopardize the life, health, or safety of the minor.

(c) A person who acts in good faith reliance on a caregiver's authorization affidavit to provide medical or dental care, without actual knowledge of facts contrary to those stated on the affidavit, is not subject to criminal liability or to civil liability to any person, and is not subject to professional disciplinary action, for that reliance if the applicable portions of the affidavit are completed. This subdivision applies even if medical or dental care is provided to a minor in contravention of the wishes of the parent or other person having legal custody of the minor as long as the person providing the medical or dental care has no actual knowledge of the wishes of the parent or other person having legal custody of the minor.

(d) A person who relies on the affidavit has no obligation to make any further inquiry or investigation.

(e) Nothing in this section relieves any individual from liability for violations of other provisions of law.

(f) If the minor stops living with the caregiver, the caregiver shall notify any school, health care provider, or health care service plan that has been given the affidavit. The affidavit is invalid after the school, health care provider, or health care service plan receives notice that the minor is no longer living with the caregiver.

(g) A caregiver's authorization affidavit shall be invalid, unless it substantially contains, in not less than 10–point boldface type or a reasonable equivalent thereof, the warning statement beginning with the word "warning" specified in Section 6552. The warning statement shall be enclosed in a box with 3–point rule lines.

(h) For purposes of this part, the following terms have the following meanings:

(1) "Person" includes an individual, corporation, partnership, association, the state, or any city, county, city and county, or other public entity or governmental subdivision or agency, or any other legal entity.

(2) "Relative" means a spouse, parent, stepparent, brother, sister, stepbrother, stepsister, half brother, half sister, uncle, aunt, niece, nephew, first cousin, or any person denoted by the prefix "grand" or "great," or the spouse of any of the persons specified in this definition, even after the marriage has been terminated by death or dissolution.

(3) "School-related medical care" means medical care that is required by state or local governmental authority as a condition for school enrollment, including immunizations, physical examinations, and medical examinations conducted in schools for pupils. *(Added by Stats.1994, c. 98 (S.B.592), § 4 eff. June 6, 1994. Amended by Stats.1996, c. 563 (S.B.392), § 1.5; Stats.2004, c. 895 (A.B.2855), § 12.)*

Cross References

California Victim Compensation and Government Claims Board, applications for compensation, filing, see Government Code § 13952.
Compulsory education law, residency requirements for school attendance, see Education Code § 48204.
County defined for purposes of this Code, see Family Code § 67.
General instructional programs, apportionments for independent study by pupils, policy requirements, see Education Code § 51747.
Health facilities, regulations, surrender of custody of minor, see Health and Safety Code § 1283.
Minor defined for purposes of this Code, see Family Code § 6500.
Person defined for purposes of this Code, see Family Code § 105.
References to husband, wife, spouses and married persons, persons included for purposes of this Code, see Family Code § 11.
State defined for purposes of this Code, see Family Code § 145.

Research References

Forms
West's California Code Forms, Education § 48980 Form 1, Notice to Parents and Guardians Regarding Statutory Rights.
West's California Code Forms, Family § 6550, Comment Overview—Authorization Affidavits.
West's California Code Forms, Family § 6552 Form 1, Caregiver's Authorization Affidavit.
West's California Code Forms, Family § 6900, Comment Overview—Consent by Person Having Care of Minor.
West's California Judicial Council Forms GC–205, Guardianship Pamphlet (Also Available in Chinese, Korean, Spanish, and Vietnamese).

§ 6552. Form of authorization affidavit

The caregiver's authorization affidavit shall be in substantially the following form:

Caregiver's Authorization Affidavit

Use of this affidavit is authorized by Part 1.5 (commencing with Section 6550) of Division 11 of the California Family Code.

Instructions: Completion of items 1–4 and the signing of the affidavit is sufficient to authorize enrollment of a minor in school and authorize school-related medical care. Completion of items 5–8 is additionally required to authorize any other medical care. Print clearly.

The minor named below lives in my home and I am 18 years of age or older.

1. Name of minor: _____
2. Minor's birth date: _____
3. My name (adult giving authorization): _____
4. My home address: _____
  _____
5. ☐ I am a grandparent, aunt, uncle, or other qualified relative of the minor (see back of this form for a definition of "qualified relative").
6. Check one or both (for example, if one parent was advised and the other cannot be located):
  ☐ I have advised the parent(s) or other person(s) having legal custody of the minor of my intent to authorize medical care, and have received no objection.
  ☐ I am unable to contact the parent(s) or other person(s) having legal custody of the minor at this time, to notify them of my intended authorization.
7. My date of birth: _____
8. My California driver's license or identification card number: _____

Warning: Do not sign this form if any of the statements above are incorrect, or you will be committing a crime punishable by a fine, imprisonment, or both.

I declare under penalty of perjury under the laws of the State of California that the foregoing is true and correct.
Dated: _____ Signed: _____

Notices:

1. This declaration does not affect the rights of the minor's parents or legal guardian regarding the care, custody, and control of the minor, and does not mean that the caregiver has legal custody of the minor.

2. A person who relies on this affidavit has no obligation to make any further inquiry or investigation.

Additional Information:

TO CAREGIVERS:

1. "Qualified relative," for purposes of item 5, means a spouse, parent, stepparent, brother, sister, stepbrother, stepsister, half brother, half sister, uncle, aunt, niece, nephew, first cousin, or any person denoted by the prefix "grand" or "great," or the spouse of any of the persons specified in this definition, even after the marriage has been terminated by death or dissolution.

2. The law may require you, if you are not a relative or a currently licensed, certified, or approved foster parent, to obtain resource family approval pursuant to Section 1517 of the Health and Safety Code or Section 16519.5 of the Welfare and Institutions Code in order to care for a minor. If you have any questions, please contact your local department of social services.

3. If the minor stops living with you, you are required to notify any school, health care provider, or health care service plan to which you have given this affidavit. The affidavit is invalid after the school, health care provider, or health care service plan receives notice that the minor no longer lives with you.

4. If you do not have the information requested in item 8 (California driver's license or I.D.), provide another form of identification such as your social security number or Medi–Cal number.

TO SCHOOL OFFICIALS:

1. Section 48204 of the Education Code provides that this affidavit constitutes a sufficient basis for a determination of residency of the minor, without the requirement of a guardianship or other custody order, unless the school district determines from actual facts that the minor is not living with the caregiver.

2. The school district may require additional reasonable evidence that the caregiver lives at the address provided in item 4.

TO HEALTH CARE PROVIDERS AND HEALTH CARE SERVICE PLANS:

1. A person who acts in good faith reliance upon a caregiver's authorization affidavit to provide medical or dental care, without actual knowledge of facts contrary to those stated on the affidavit, is not subject to criminal liability or to civil liability to any person, and is not subject to professional disciplinary action, for that reliance if the applicable portions of the form are completed.

2. This affidavit does not confer dependency for health care coverage purposes. *(Added by Stats.1994, c. 98 (S.B.592), § 4, eff. June 6, 1994. Amended by Stats.1994, c. 1269 (A.B.2208), § 50.6; Stats.2004, c. 895 (A.B.2855), § 13; Stats.2016, c. 612 (A.B.1997), § 6, eff. Jan. 1, 2017.)*

Cross References

Adult defined for purposes of this Code, see Family Code § 6501.
Judgment and order defined for purposes of this Code, see Family Code § 100.
Minor defined for purposes of this Code, see Family Code § 6500.
Person defined for purposes of this Code, see Family Code § 105.
References to husband, wife, spouses and married persons, persons included for purposes of this Code, see Family Code § 11.
State defined for purposes of this Code, see Family Code § 145.

Research References

Forms

West's California Code Forms, Family § 6550, Comment Overview—Authorization Affidavits.
West's California Code Forms, Family § 6552 Form 1, Caregiver's Authorization Affidavit.

West's California Code Forms, Family § 6910 Form 2, Authorization by Parent to Allow Another Person to Consent to Minor's Medical Care.

Part 2

RIGHTS AND LIABILITIES; CIVIL ACTIONS AND PROCEEDINGS

Section
6600. Minors; civil liability.
6601. Enforcement of minor's rights.
6602. Approval of contract for attorney's fees for minor; fees in absence of contract.

Cross References

Computer data access and fraud, offense of minor imputed to parent or guardian, see Penal Code § 502.
Criminal liability, capacity of minors, see Penal Code § 26.
Firearms, storage in places accessible to children, liability, see Penal Code §§ 25100 to 25130.
Liability of parent or guardian,
　Willful misconduct of minors, see Civil Code § 1714.1.
　Willful pupil misconduct, see Education Code § 48904.
Petty theft, retail merchandise, see Penal Code § 490.5.

§ 6600. Minors; civil liability

A minor is civilly liable for a wrong done by the minor, but is not liable in exemplary damages unless at the time of the act the minor was capable of knowing that the act was wrongful. *(Stats.1992, c. 162 (A.B.2650), § 10, operative Jan. 1, 1994.)*

Cross References

Computer data access and fraud, offense of minor imputed to parent or guardian, see Penal Code § 502.
Criminal liability, capacity of minors, see Penal Code § 26.
Firearms, storage in places accessible to children, liability, see Penal Code §§ 25100 to 25130.
Liability of parent or guardian,
　Willful misconduct of minors, see Civil Code § 1714.1.
　Willful pupil misconduct, see Education Code § 48904.
Minor defined for purposes of this Code, see Family Code § 6500.
Petty theft, retail merchandise, see Penal Code § 490.5.

Research References

Forms

1 California Transactions Forms--Estate Planning § 1:29, Options Involving Gifts to Minors.

§ 6601. Enforcement of minor's rights

A minor may enforce the minor's rights by civil action or other legal proceedings in the same manner as an adult, except that a guardian must conduct the action or proceedings. *(Stats.1992, c. 162 (A.B.2650), § 10, operative Jan. 1, 1994.)*

Cross References

Actions and proceedings, representation by guardian of estate, see Probate Code § 2462.
Appearances, minor required to appear either by guardian of estate or guardian ad litem, see Code of Civil Procedure § 372.
Appointment of guardians, generally, see Probate Code § 1510 et seq.
Compromise and settlement,
　Actions and proceedings by guardian, see Probate Code § 2500 et seq.
　Minor's disputed claim, see Probate Code § 3600 et seq.
Emancipation of minors,
　Compromise of claim by minor, minor suing in own name, see Family Code § 7050.
　Conditions, see Family Code § 7002.
Guardians ad litem, appointment, generally, see Code of Civil Procedure § 373.
Guardians ad litem, appointment in probate proceedings, see Probate Code § 1003.

Minor defined for purposes of this Code, see Family Code § 6500.
Proceeding defined for purposes of this Code, see Family Code § 110.
Workers' compensation proceedings, appointment of trustee or guardian ad litem, see Labor Code §§ 5307.5, 5408.

Research References

Forms

West's California Code Forms, Family § 7500, Comment Overview—Rights of Parents.

§ 6602. Approval of contract for attorney's fees for minor; fees in absence of contract

A contract for attorney's fees for services in litigation, made by or on behalf of a minor, is void unless the contract is approved, on petition by an interested person, by the court in which the litigation is pending or by the court having jurisdiction of the guardianship estate of the minor. If the contract is not approved and a judgment is recovered by or on behalf of the minor, the attorney's fees chargeable against the minor shall be fixed by the court rendering the judgment. *(Stats.1992, c. 162 (A.B.2650), § 10, operative Jan. 1, 1994.)*

Cross References

Attorney's fees and costs, generally, see Family Code § 270 et seq.
Emancipation of minors, see Family Code §§ 7002, 7050.
Guardianship or protective proceedings, interested person defined, see Probate Code § 1424.
Guardianship or protective proceedings, judgment for minor, order directing payment of attorney's fees, see Probate Code § 3601.
Judgment and order defined for purposes of this Code, see Family Code § 100.
Minor defined for purposes of this Code, see Family Code § 6500.
Person defined for purposes of this Code, see Family Code § 105.

Part 3

CONTRACTS

Chapter	Section
1. Capacity to Contract	6700
2. Disaffirmance of Contracts	6710
3. Contracts in Art, Entertainment, and Professional Sports	6750

Cross References

Contracts, capacity of minors governed by this Division, see Civil Code § 1557.
Contracts, incapacity of minors to form, see Civil Code § 1556.
Contracts for attorney's fees for litigation services provided to minors, approval by court, see Family Code § 6602.

CHAPTER 1. CAPACITY TO CONTRACT

Section
6700. Authority to contract.
6701. Restrictions on authority to contract.

Cross References

Contracts, capacity of minors governed by this Division, see Civil Code § 1557.
Contracts, incapacity of minors to form, see Civil Code § 1556.
Contracts for attorney's fees for litigation services provided to minors, approval by court, see Family Code § 6602.

§ 6700. Authority to contract

Except as provided in Section 6701, a minor may make a contract in the same manner as an adult, subject to the power of disaffirmance under Chapter 2 (commencing with Section 6710), and subject to Part 1 (commencing with Section 300) of Division 3 (validity of marriage). *(Stats.1992, c. 162 (A.B.2650), § 10, operative Jan. 1, 1994.)*

Cross References

Age of majority, see Family Code § 6500 et seq.
Contracts, capacity of minors governed by this Division, see Civil Code § 1557.
Contracts, defined, see Civil Code § 1549.
Contracts, incapacity of minors to form, see Civil Code § 1556.
Contracts for attorney's fees for litigation services provided to minors, approval by court, see Family Code § 6602.
Drug or alcohol treatment, consent, see Family Code § 6929.
Emancipation of minors, see Family Code §§ 7002, 7050.
Medical treatment, consent to, see Family Code §§ 6922, 6924.
Minor defined for purposes of this Code, see Family Code § 6500.

Research References

Forms

1 California Transactions Forms--Business Transactions § 6:10, Minors.
3 California Transactions Forms--Business Transactions § 17:25, Minors.

§ 6701. Restrictions on authority to contract

A minor cannot do any of the following:

(a) Give a delegation of power.

(b) Make a contract relating to real property or any interest therein.

(c) Make a contract relating to any personal property not in the immediate possession or control of the minor. *(Stats.1992, c. 162 (A.B.2650), § 10, operative Jan. 1, 1994.)*

Cross References

Contract, defined, see Civil Code § 1549.
Contracts, capacity of minors governed by this Division, see Civil Code § 1557.
Contracts, incapacity of minors to form, see Civil Code § 1556.
Contracts for attorney's fees for litigation services provided to minors, approval by court, see Family Code § 6602.
Emancipation of minors, see Family Code §§ 7002, 7050.
Minor defined for purposes of this Code, see Family Code § 6500.
Property defined for purposes of this Code, see Family Code § 113.

Research References

Forms

1 California Transactions Forms--Business Transactions § 6:10, Minors.
1 California Transactions Forms--Business Transactions § 6:11, Void Contracts of Minors.
1 California Transactions Forms--Business Transactions § 6:12, Voidable Contracts of Minors.
2 California Transactions Forms--Business Transactions § 15:5, Qualifications.
3 California Transactions Forms--Business Transactions § 17:25, Minors.

CHAPTER 2. DISAFFIRMANCE OF CONTRACTS

Section
6710. Right of disaffirmance.
6711. Obligations entered into under express statutory authority.
6712. Contracts minors cannot disaffirm; conditions.
6713. Recovery from good faith purchaser.

Cross References

Contracts, capacity of minors governed by this Division, see Civil Code § 1557.
Contracts, incapacity of minors to form, see Civil Code § 1556.
Contracts for attorney's fees for litigation services provided to minors, approval by court, see Family Code § 6602.

§ 6710. Right of disaffirmance

Except as otherwise provided by statute, a contract of a minor may be disaffirmed by the minor before majority or within a reasonable time afterwards or, in case of the minor's death within that period, by the minor's heirs or personal representative. *(Stats.1992, c. 162 (A.B.2650), § 10, operative Jan. 1, 1994.)*

§ 6710

Cross References

Approval of court, contracts in arts, entertainment, or professional sports, see Family Code § 6751.
Contract, defined, see Civil Code § 1549.
Contracts, capacity of minors governed by this Division, see Civil Code § 1557.
Contracts, incapacity of minors to form, see Civil Code § 1556.
Contracts for attorney's fees for litigation services provided to minors, approval by court, see Family Code § 6602.
Emancipation of minors, see Family Code §§ 7002, 7050.
Good faith purchasers, protection, see Family Code § 6713.
Minor defined for purposes of this Code, see Family Code § 6500.
Obligations of minors not disaffirmable, see Family Code §§ 6751, 6921.

Research References

Forms

1 California Transactions Forms--Business Transactions § 6:10, Minors.
1 California Transactions Forms--Business Transactions § 6:12, Voidable Contracts of Minors.
3 California Transactions Forms--Business Transactions § 17:25, Minors.
West's California Code Forms, Family § 6710, Comment Overview—Right of Disaffirmance.
West's California Code Forms, Family § 6710 Form 1, Notice of Disaffirmance of Contract Made by Minor.
West's California Code Forms, Family § 6710 Form 2, Complaint by Minor to Recover Consideration Paid Under Contract Subsequently Disaffirmed.

§ 6711. Obligations entered into under express statutory authority

A minor cannot disaffirm an obligation, otherwise valid, entered into by the minor under the express authority or direction of a statute. *(Stats.1992, c. 162 (A.B.2650), § 10, operative Jan. 1, 1994.)*

Cross References

Contract, defined, see Civil Code § 1549.
Contracts, capacity of minors governed by this Division, see Civil Code § 1557.
Contracts, incapacity of minors to form, see Civil Code § 1556.
Contracts for attorney's fees for litigation services provided to minors, approval by court, see Family Code § 6602.
Minor defined for purposes of this Code, see Family Code § 6500.

Research References

Forms

1 California Transactions Forms--Business Transactions § 6:10, Minors.
1 California Transactions Forms--Business Transactions § 6:13, Contracts Enforceable Against Minors.
West's California Code Forms, Family § 6710, Comment Overview—Right of Disaffirmance.

§ 6712. Contracts minors cannot disaffirm; conditions

A contract, otherwise valid, entered into during minority, may not be disaffirmed on that ground either during the actual minority of the person entering into the contract, or at any time thereafter, if all of the following requirements are satisfied:

(a) The contract is to pay the reasonable value of things necessary for the support of the minor or the minor's family.

(b) These things have been actually furnished to the minor or to the minor's family.

(c) The contract is entered into by the minor when not under the care of a parent or guardian able to provide for the minor or the minor's family. *(Stats.1992, c. 162 (A.B.2650), § 10, operative Jan. 1, 1994.)*

Cross References

Contract, defined, see Civil Code § 1549.
Contracts, capacity of minors governed by this Division, see Civil Code § 1557.
Contracts, incapacity of minors to form, see Civil Code § 1556.
Contracts for attorney's fees for litigation services provided to minors, approval by court, see Family Code § 6602.
Emancipation of minors, see Family Code §§ 7002, 7050.
Minor defined for purposes of this Code, see Family Code § 6500.
Person defined for purposes of this Code, see Family Code § 105.

Support defined for purposes of this Code, see Family Code § 150.

Research References

Forms

1 California Transactions Forms--Business Transactions § 6:13, Contracts Enforceable Against Minors.
1 California Transactions Forms--Estate Planning § 1:29, Options Involving Gifts to Minors.
West's California Code Forms, Family § 6710, Comment Overview—Right of Disaffirmance.

§ 6713. Recovery from good faith purchaser

If, before the contract of a minor is disaffirmed, goods the minor has sold are transferred to another purchaser who bought them in good faith for value and without notice of the transferor's defect of title, the minor cannot recover the goods from an innocent purchaser. *(Stats.1992, c. 162 (A.B.2650), § 10, operative Jan. 1, 1994.)*

Cross References

Contract, defined, see Civil Code § 1549.
Contracts, capacity of minors governed by this Division, see Civil Code § 1557.
Contracts, incapacity of minors to form, see Civil Code § 1556.
Contracts for attorney's fees for litigation services provided to minors, approval by court, see Family Code § 6602.
Emancipation of minors, see Family Code §§ 7002, 7050.
Minor defined for purposes of this Code, see Family Code § 6500.

Research References

Forms

1 California Transactions Forms--Business Transactions § 6:10, Minors.
1 California Transactions Forms--Business Transactions § 6:13, Contracts Enforceable Against Minors.
2 California Transactions Forms--Family Law § 7:72, Parentage.
West's California Code Forms, Family § 6710, Comment Overview—Right of Disaffirmance.
West's California Code Forms, Family § 6713 Form 1, Affirmative Defense—Goods Not Recoverable from Innocent Purchaser.

CHAPTER 3. CONTRACTS IN ART, ENTERTAINMENT, AND PROFESSIONAL SPORTS

Section
6750. Application of chapter.
6751. Disaffirmance of contracts approved by court.
6752. Providing copy of minor's birth certificate to other party; percentage of minor's gross earnings set aside in trust for minor's benefit; exceptions; trustee of funds; deposits or disbursements; The Actors' Fund of America as trustee of unclaimed set-aside funds; entitlement of beneficiary of such fund to imputed interest; forwarding of unclaimed funds to The Actors' Fund of America; application of Unclaimed Property Law.
6753. Establishment of Coogan Trust Account; consent of court required for withdrawals; written statement; handling of funds.

Cross References

Contracts,
  Capacity of minors governed by this Division, see Civil Code § 1557.
  Incapacity of minors to form, see Civil Code § 1556.
Contracts for attorney's fees for litigation services provided to minors, approval by court, see Family Code § 6602.
Labor Commissioner's written consent for employment of minor, effect of failure to timely establish Coogan Trust Account, see Labor Code § 1308.9.

Minors, occupations requiring consent of commissioner, misdemeanors, see Labor Code § 1308.5.

§ 6750. Application of chapter

(a) This chapter applies to the following contracts entered into between an unemancipated minor and a third party on or after January 1, 2000:

(1) A contract pursuant to which a minor is employed or agrees to render artistic or creative services, either directly or through a third party, including, but not limited to, a personal services corporation (loan–out company), or through a casting agency. "Artistic or creative services" includes, but is not limited to, services as an actor, actress, dancer, musician, comedian, singer, stuntperson, voice-over artist, or other performer or entertainer, or as a songwriter, musical producer or arranger, writer, director, producer, production executive, choreographer, composer, conductor, or designer.

(2) A contract pursuant to which a minor agrees to purchase, or otherwise secure, sell, lease, license, or otherwise dispose of literary, musical, or dramatic properties, or use of a person's likeness, voice recording, performance, or story of or incidents in the person's life, either tangible or intangible, or any rights therein for use in motion pictures, television, the production of sound recordings in any format now known or hereafter devised, the legitimate or living stage, or otherwise in the entertainment field.

(3) A contract pursuant to which a minor is employed or agrees to render services as a participant or player in a sport.

(b)(1) If a minor is employed or agrees to render services directly for a person or entity, that person or entity shall be considered the minor's employer for purposes of this chapter.

(2) If a minor's services are being rendered through a third-party individual or personal services corporation (loan–out company), the person to whom or entity to which that third party is providing the minor's services shall be considered the minor's employer for purposes of this chapter.

(3) If a minor renders services as an extra, background performer, or in a similar capacity through an agency or service that provides one or more of those performers for a fee (casting agency), the agency or service shall be considered the minor's employer for the purposes of this chapter.

(c)(1) For purposes of this chapter, the minor's "gross earnings" means the total compensation payable to the minor under the contract or, if the minor's services are being rendered through a third-party individual or personal services corporation (loan–out company), the total compensation payable to that third party for the services of the minor.

(2) Notwithstanding paragraph (1), with respect to contracts pursuant to which a minor is employed or agrees to render services as a musician, singer, songwriter, musical producer, or arranger only, for purposes of this chapter, the minor's "gross earnings" means the total amount paid to the minor pursuant to the contract, including the payment of any advances to the minor pursuant to the contract, but excluding deductions to offset those advances or other expenses incurred by the employer pursuant to the contract, or, if the minor's services are being rendered through a third-party individual or personal services corporation (loan–out company), the total amount payable to that third party for the services of the minor. *(Stats.1992, c. 162 (A.B.2650), § 10, operative Jan. 1, 1994. Amended by Stats.1999, c. 940 (S.B.1162), § 2; Stats.2003, c. 667 (S.B.210), § 1; Stats.2019, c. 115 (A.B.1817), § 74, eff. Jan. 1, 2020.)*

Cross References

Contract, defined, see Civil Code § 1549.
Contracts, capacity of minors governed by this Division, see Civil Code § 1557.
Contracts, incapacity of minors to form, see Civil Code § 1556.
Contracts for attorney's fees for litigation services provided to minors, approval by court, see Family Code § 6602.

Emancipated minor, description, see Family Code § 7002.
Labor Commissioner's written consent for employment of minor, effect of failure to timely establish Coogan Trust Account, see Labor Code § 1308.9.
Licensed talent agencies, minor's right to disaffirm contract, see Labor Code § 1700.37.
Minor defined for purposes of this Code, see Family Code § 6500.
Person defined for purposes of this Code, see Family Code § 105.
Property defined for purposes of this Code, see Family Code § 113.

Research References

Forms

2 California Transactions Forms--Business Transactions § 8:53, Model Release for Images Included in Website.
2 California Transactions Forms--Business Transactions § 10:8, Employment of Minors.
West's California Code Forms, Family § 6710, Comment Overview—Right of Disaffirmance.
West's California Code Forms, Family § 6751, Comment Overview—Minor's Employment Contract.

§ 6751. Disaffirmance of contracts approved by court

(a) A contract, otherwise valid, of a type described in Section 6750, entered into during minority, cannot be disaffirmed on that ground either during the minority of the person entering into the contract, or at any time thereafter, if the contract has been approved by the superior court in any county in which the minor resides or is employed or in which any party to the contract has its principal office in this state for the transaction of business.

(b) Approval of the court may be given on petition of any party to the contract, after such reasonable notice to all other parties to the contract as is fixed by the court, with opportunity to such other parties to appear and be heard.

(c) Approval of the court given under this section extends to the whole of the contract and all of its terms and provisions, including, but not limited to, any optional or conditional provisions contained in the contract for extension, prolongation, or termination of the term of the contract.

(d) For the purposes of any proceeding under this chapter, a parent or legal guardian, as the case may be, entitled to the physical custody, care, and control of the minor at the time of the proceeding shall be considered the minor's guardian ad litem for the proceeding, unless the court shall determine that appointment of a different individual as guardian ad litem is required in the best interests of the minor. *(Stats.1992, c. 162 (A.B.2650), § 10, operative Jan. 1, 1994. Amended by Stats.1999, c. 940 (S.B.1162), § 3.)*

Cross References

Contract, defined, see Civil Code § 1549.
Contracts, capacity of minors governed by this Division, see Civil Code § 1557.
Contracts, incapacity of minors to form, see Civil Code § 1556.
Contracts for attorney's fees for litigation services provided to minors, approval by court, see Family Code § 6602.
County defined for purposes of this Code, see Family Code § 67.
Emancipation of minors, see Family Code §§ 7002, 7050.
Minor defined for purposes of this Code, see Family Code § 6500.
Person defined for purposes of this Code, see Family Code § 105.
Proceeding defined for purposes of this Code, see Family Code § 110.
State defined for purposes of this Code, see Family Code § 145.
Talent agencies, limitation on minor's right to disaffirm, see Labor Code § 1700.37.

Research References

Forms

1 California Transactions Forms--Business Transactions § 6:10, Minors.
1 California Transactions Forms--Business Transactions § 6:13, Contracts Enforceable Against Minors.
2 California Transactions Forms--Business Transactions § 10:8, Employment of Minors.
West's California Code Forms, Family § 6710, Comment Overview—Right of Disaffirmance.

§ 6751

West's California Code Forms, Family § 6751, Comment Overview—Minor's Employment Contract.

West's California Code Forms, Family § 6751 Form 1, Petition by Employer for Approval of Minor's Employment Contract.

§ 6752. Providing copy of minor's birth certificate to other party; percentage of minor's gross earnings set aside in trust for minor's benefit; exceptions; trustee of funds; deposits or disbursements; The Actors' Fund of America as trustee of unclaimed set-aside funds; entitlement of beneficiary of such fund to imputed interest; forwarding of unclaimed funds to The Actors' Fund of America; application of Unclaimed Property Law

(a) A parent or guardian entitled to the physical custody, care, and control of a minor who enters into a contract of a type described in Section 6750 shall provide a certified copy of the minor's birth certificate indicating the minor's minority to the other party or parties to the contract and in addition, in the case of a guardian, a certified copy of the court document appointing the person as the minor's legal guardian.

(b)(1) Notwithstanding any other statute, in an order approving a minor's contract of a type described in Section 6750, the court shall require that 15 percent of the minor's gross earnings pursuant to the contract be set aside by the minor's employer, except an employer of a minor for services as an extra, background performer, or in a similar capacity, as described in paragraph (3) of subdivision (b) of Section 6750. These amounts shall be held in trust, in an account or other savings plan, and preserved for the benefit of the minor in accordance with Section 6753.

(2) The court shall require that at least one parent or legal guardian, as the case may be, entitled to the physical custody, care, and control of the minor at the time the order is issued be appointed as trustee of the funds ordered to be set aside in trust for the benefit of the minor, unless the court shall determine that appointment of a different individual, individuals, entity, or entities as trustee or trustees is required in the best interest of the minor.

(3) Within 10 business days after commencement of employment, the trustee or trustees of the funds ordered to be set aside in trust shall provide the minor's employer with a true and accurate photocopy of the trustee's statement pursuant to Section 6753. Upon presentation of the trustee's statement offered pursuant to this subdivision, the employer shall provide the parent or guardian with a written acknowledgment of receipt of the statement.

(4) The minor's employer shall deposit or disburse the 15 percent of the minor's gross earnings pursuant to the contract within 15 business days after receiving a true and accurate copy of the trustee's statement pursuant to subdivision (c) of Section 6753, a certified copy of the minor's birth certificate, and, in the case of a guardian, a certified copy of the court document appointing the person as the minor's guardian. Notwithstanding any other law, pending receipt of these documents, the minor's employer shall hold, for the benefit of the minor, the 15 percent of the minor's gross earnings pursuant to the contract. This paragraph does not apply to an employer of a minor for services as an extra, background performer, or in a similar capacity, as described in paragraph (3) of subdivision (b) of Section 6750.

(5) When making the initial deposit of funds, the minor's employer shall provide written notification to the financial institution or company that the funds are subject to Section 6753. Upon receipt of the court order, the minor's employer shall provide the financial institution with a copy of the order.

(6) Once the minor's employer deposits the set-aside funds pursuant to Section 6753, in trust, in an account or other savings plan, the minor's employer shall have no further obligation or duty to monitor or account for the funds. The trustee or trustees of the trust shall be the only individual, individuals, entity, or entities with the obligation or duty to monitor and account for those funds once they have been deposited by the minor's employer. The trustee or trustees shall do an annual accounting of the funds held in trust, in an account or other savings plan, in accordance with Sections 16062 and 16063 of the Probate Code.

(7) The court shall have continuing jurisdiction over the trust established pursuant to the order and may at any time, upon petition of the parent or legal guardian, the minor, through the minor's guardian ad litem, or the trustee or trustees, on good cause shown, order that the trust be amended or terminated, notwithstanding the provisions of the declaration of trust. An order amending or terminating a trust may be made only after reasonable notice to the beneficiary and, if the beneficiary is then a minor, to the parent or guardian, if any, and to the trustee or trustees of the funds with opportunity for all parties to appear and be heard.

(8) A parent or guardian entitled to the physical custody, care, and control of the minor shall promptly notify the minor's employer, in writing, of any change in facts that affect the employer's obligation or ability to set aside the funds in accordance with the order, including, but not limited to, a change of financial institution or account number, or the existence of a new or amended order issued pursuant to paragraph (7) amending or terminating the employer's obligations under this section. The written notification shall be accompanied by a true and accurate photocopy of the trustee's statement pursuant to Section 6753 and, if applicable, a true and accurate photocopy of the new or amended order.

(9)(A) If a parent, guardian, or trustee fails to provide the minor's employer with a true and accurate photocopy of the trustee's statement pursuant to Section 6753 within 180 days after the commencement of employment, the employer shall forward to The Actors' Fund of America 15 percent of the minor's gross earnings pursuant to the contract, together with the minor's name and, if known, the minor's social security number, birth date, last known address, telephone number, email address, dates of employment, and title of the project on which the minor was employed, and shall notify the parent, guardian, or trustee of that transfer by certified mail to the last known address. Upon receipt of those forwarded funds, The Actors' Fund of America shall become the trustee of those funds and the minor's employer shall have no further obligation or duty to monitor or account for the funds.

(B) The Actors' Fund of America shall make its best efforts to notify the parent, guardian, or trustee of their responsibilities to provide a true and accurate photocopy of the trustee's statement pursuant to Section 6753, and in the case of a guardian, a certified copy of the court document appointing the person as the minor's legal guardian. Within 15 business days after receiving those documents, The Actors' Fund of America shall deposit or disburse the funds as directed by the trustee's statement. When making that deposit or disbursal of the funds, The Actors' Fund of America shall provide to the financial institution notice that the funds are subject to Section 6753 and a copy of each applicable order, and shall thereafter have no further obligation or duty to monitor or account for the funds.

(C) The Actors' Fund of America shall notify each beneficiary of their entitlement to the funds that it holds for the beneficiary within 60 days after the date on which its records indicated that the beneficiary has attained 18 years of age or the date on which it received notice that the minor has been emancipated, by sending that notice to the last known address for the beneficiary or, if it has no specific separate address for the beneficiary, to the beneficiary's parent or guardian.

(c)(1) Notwithstanding any other statute, for any minor's contract of a type described in Section 6750 that is not being submitted for approval by the court pursuant to Section 6751, or for which the court has issued a final order denying approval, 15 percent of the minor's gross earnings pursuant to the contract shall be set aside by the minor's employer, except an employer of a minor for services as an extra, background performer, or in a similar capacity, as described in paragraph (3) of subdivision (b) of Section 6750. These amounts shall be held in trust, in an account or other savings plan, and preserved for the benefit of the minor in accordance with Section 6753. At least one parent or legal guardian, as the case may be, entitled to the physical custody, care, and control of the minor, shall be the trustee of the funds set aside for the benefit of the minor, unless the court, upon petition by the parent or legal guardian, the minor, through the minor's guardian ad litem, or the trustee or trustees of the trust, shall determine that appointment of a different individual, individuals, entity, or entities as trustee or trustees is required in the best interest of the minor.

(2) Within 10 business days of commencement after employment, a parent or guardian, as the case may be, entitled to the physical custody, care, and control of the minor shall provide the minor's employer with a true and accurate photocopy of the trustee's statement pursuant to Section 6753 and in addition, in the case of a guardian, a certified copy of the court document appointing the person as the minor's legal guardian. Upon presentation of the trustee's statement offered pursuant to this subdivision, the employer shall provide the parent or guardian with a written acknowledgment of receipt of the statement.

(3) The minor's employer shall deposit 15 percent of the minor's gross earnings pursuant to the contract within 15 business days of receiving the trustee's statement pursuant to Section 6753, or if the court denies approval of the contract, within 15 business days of receiving a final order denying approval of the contract. Notwithstanding any other statute, pending receipt of the trustee's statement or the final court order, the minor's employer shall hold for the benefit of the minor the 15 percent of the minor's gross earnings pursuant to the contract. When making the initial deposit of funds, the minor's employer shall provide written notification to the financial institution or company that the funds are subject to Section 6753. This paragraph does not apply to an employer of a minor for services as an extra, background performer, or in a similar capacity, as described in paragraph (3) of subdivision (b) of Section 6750.

(4) Once the minor's employer deposits the set-aside funds in trust, in an account or other savings plan pursuant to Section 6753, the minor's employer shall have no further obligation or duty to monitor or account for the funds. The trustee or trustees of the trust shall be the only individual, individuals, entity, or entities with the obligation or duty to monitor and account for those funds once they have been deposited by the minor's employer. The trustee or trustees shall do an annual accounting of the funds held in trust, in an account or other savings plan, in accordance with Sections 16062 and 16063 of the Probate Code.

(5) Upon petition of the parent or legal guardian, the minor, through the minor's guardian ad litem, or the trustee or trustees of the trust, to the superior court in a county in which the minor resides or in which the trust is established, the court may at any time, on good cause shown, order that the trust be amended or terminated, notwithstanding the provisions of the declaration of trust. An order amending or terminating a trust may be made only after reasonable notice to the beneficiary and, if the beneficiary is then a minor, to the parent or guardian, if any, and to the trustee or trustees of the funds with opportunity for all parties to appear and be heard.

(6) A parent or guardian entitled to the physical custody, care, and control of the minor shall promptly notify the minor's employer in writing of any change in facts that affect the employer's obligation or ability to set aside funds for the benefit of the minor in accordance with this section, including, but not limited to, a change of financial institution or account number, or the existence of a new or amended order issued pursuant to paragraph (5) amending or terminating the employer's obligations under this section. The written notification shall be accompanied by a true and accurate photocopy of the trustee's statement and attachments pursuant to Section 6753 and, if applicable, a true and accurate photocopy of the new or amended order.

(7)(A) If a parent, guardian, or trustee fails to provide the minor's employer with a true and accurate photocopy of the trustee's statement pursuant to Section 6753, within 180 days after commencement of employment, the employer shall forward to The Actors' Fund of America the 15 percent of the minor's gross earnings pursuant to the contract, together with the minor's name and, if known, the minor's social security number, birth date, last known address, telephone number, email address, dates of employment, and the title of the project on which the minor was employed, and shall notify the parent, guardian, or trustee of that transfer by certified mail to the last known address. Upon receipt of those forwarded funds, The Actors' Fund of America shall become the trustee of those funds and the minor's employer shall have no further obligation or duty to monitor or account for the funds.

(B) The Actors' Fund of America shall make best efforts to notify the parent, guardian, or trustee of their responsibilities to provide a true and accurate photocopy of the trustee's statement pursuant to Section 6753 and in the case of a guardian, a certified copy of the court document appointing the person as the minor's legal guardian. After receiving those documents, The Actors' Fund of America shall deposit or disburse the funds as directed by the trustee's statement, and in accordance with Section 6753, within 15 business days. When making that deposit or disbursal of the funds, The Actors' Fund of America shall provide notice to the financial institution that the funds are subject to Section 6753, and shall thereafter have no further obligation or duty to monitor or account for the funds.

(C) The Actors' Fund of America shall notify each beneficiary of their entitlement to the funds that it holds for the beneficiary, within 60 days after the date on which its records indicate that the beneficiary has attained 18 years of age or on the date on which it received notice that the minor has been emancipated, by sending that notice to the last known address that it has for the beneficiary, or to the beneficiary's parent or guardian, where it has no specific separate address for the beneficiary.

(d) Where a parent or guardian is entitled to the physical custody, care, and control of a minor who enters into a contract of a type described in Section 6750, the relationship between the parent or guardian and the minor is a fiduciary relationship that is governed by the law of trusts, whether or not a court has issued a formal order to that effect. The parent or guardian acting in a fiduciary relationship, shall, with the earnings and accumulations of the minor under the contract, pay all liabilities incurred by the minor under the contract, including, but not limited to, payments for taxes on all earnings, including taxes on the amounts set aside under subdivisions (b) and (c) of this section, and payments for personal or professional services rendered to the minor or the business related to the contract. This subdivision does not alter any other existing responsibilities of a parent or legal guardian to provide for the support of a minor child.

(e)(1) Except as otherwise provided in this subdivision, The Actors' Fund of America, as trustee of unclaimed set-aside funds, shall manage and administer those funds in the same manner as a trustee under the Probate Code. Notwithstanding the foregoing, The Actors' Fund of America is not required to open separate, segregated individual trust accounts for each beneficiary but may hold the set-aside funds in a single, segregated master account for all beneficiaries, provided it maintains accounting records for each beneficiary's interest in the master account.

(2) The Actors' Fund of America shall have the right to transfer funds from the master account, or from a beneficiary's segregated account to its general account in an amount equal to the beneficiary's balance. The Actors' Fund of America shall have the right to use those funds transferred to its general account to provide programs and services for young performers. This use of the funds does not limit or alter The Actors' Fund of America's obligation to disburse the set-aside funds to the beneficiary, or the beneficiary's parent, guardian, trustee, or estate pursuant to this chapter.

§ 6752

(3)(A) Upon receiving a certified copy of the beneficiary's birth certificate, or United States passport, and a true and accurate photocopy of the trustee's statement pursuant to Section 6753, The Actors' Fund of America shall transfer the beneficiary's balance to the trust account established for the beneficiary.

(B) The Actors' Fund of America shall disburse the set-aside funds to a beneficiary who has attained 18 years of age, after receiving proof of the beneficiary's identity and a certified copy of the beneficiary's birth certificate or United States passport, or to a beneficiary who has been emancipated, after receiving proof of the beneficiary's identity and appropriate documentation evidencing the beneficiary's emancipation.

(C) The Actors' Fund of America shall disburse the set-aside funds to the estate of a deceased beneficiary after receiving appropriate documentation evidencing the death of the beneficiary and the claimant's authority to collect those funds on behalf of the beneficiary.

(f)(1) The beneficiary of an account held by The Actors' Fund of America pursuant to this section shall be entitled to receive imputed interest on the balance in the account for the entire period during which the account is held at a rate equal to the lesser of the federal reserve rate in effect on the last business day of the prior calendar quarter or the national average money market rate as published in the New York Times on the last Sunday of the prior calendar quarter, adjusted quarterly.

(2) The Actors' Fund of America may assess and deduct from the balance in the beneficiary's account reasonable management, administrative, and investment expenses, including beneficiary-specific fees for initial setup, account notifications and account disbursements, and a reasonably allocable share of management, administrative, and investment expenses of the master account. Fees may not be charged to a beneficiary's account during the first year that the account is held by The Actors' Fund of America.

(3) Notwithstanding paragraph (2), the amount paid on any claim made by a beneficiary or the beneficiary's parent or guardian after The Actors' Fund of America receives and holds funds pursuant to this section may not be less than the amount of the funds received plus the imputed interest.

(g) Notwithstanding any provision of this chapter to the contrary, a minor's employer holding set-aside funds under this chapter, which funds remain unclaimed 180 days after the effective date hereof, shall forward those unclaimed funds to The Actors' Fund of America, along with the minor's name and, if known, the minor's social security number, birth date, last known address, telephone number, email address, dates of employment, and the title of the project on which the minor was employed, and shall notify the parent, guardian, or trustee of that transfer by certified mail to the last known address. Upon receipt of those forwarded funds by The Actors' Fund of America, the minor's employer shall have no further obligation or duty to monitor or account for the funds.

(h) All funds received by The Actors' Fund of America pursuant to this section shall be exempt from the application of the Unclaimed Property Law (Title 10 (commencing with Section 1300) of Part 3 of the Code of Civil Procedure), including, but not limited to, Section 1510 of the Code of Civil Procedure. *(Added by Stats.1999, c. 940 (S.B.1162), § 5. Amended by Stats.2003, c. 667 (S.B.210), § 2; Stats.2013, c. 102 (A.B.533), § 1; Stats.2019, c. 115 (A.B.1817), § 75, eff. Jan. 1, 2020.)*

Cross References

Contract, defined, see Civil Code § 1549.
Contracts, capacity of minors governed by this Division, see Civil Code § 1557.
Contracts, incapacity of minors to form, see Civil Code § 1556.
Contracts for attorney's fees for litigation services provided to minors, approval by court, see Family Code § 6602.
County defined for purposes of this Code, see Family Code § 67.
Guardian defined, see Probate Code §§ 2350, 2400.
Judgment and order defined for purposes of this Code, see Family Code § 100.
Jurisdiction of superior court, see Family Code § 200.
Minor defined for purposes of this Code, see Family Code § 6500.
Parent or guardian defined, see Family Code § 6903.
Person defined for purposes of this Code, see Family Code § 105.
Property defined for purposes of this Code, see Family Code § 113.
State defined for purposes of this Code, see Family Code § 145.
Support defined for purposes of this Code, see Family Code § 150.

Research References

Forms

2 California Transactions Forms--Business Transactions § 10:8, Employment of Minors.
West's California Code Forms, Family § 6751, Comment Overview--Minor's Employment Contract.
West's California Code Forms, Family § 6751 Form 2, Order Approving Minor's Employment Contract.
West's California Code Forms, Family § 6752 Form 1, Parental Consent to Court Order With Savings Provision.
West's California Code Forms, Family § 6753 Form 1, Petition to Terminate Trust or Savings Plan Established by Court Order.
West's California Code Forms, Family § 6753 Form 2, Order Terminating Trust or Savings Plan Established by Court Order.

§ 6753. Establishment of Coogan Trust Account; consent of court required for withdrawals; written statement; handling of funds

(a) The trustee or trustees shall establish a trust account, that shall be known as a Coogan Trust Account, pursuant to this section at a bank, savings and loan institution, credit union, brokerage firm, or company registered under the Investment Company Act of 1940, that is located in the State of California, unless a similar trust has been previously established, for the purpose of preserving for the benefit of the minor the portion of the minor's gross earnings pursuant to paragraph (1) of subdivision (b) of Section 6752 or pursuant to paragraph (1) of subdivision (c) of Section 6752. The trustee or trustees shall establish the trust pursuant to this section within seven business days after the minor's contract is signed by the minor, the third-party individual or personal services corporation (loan-out company), and the employer.

(b) Except as otherwise provided in this section, prior to the date on which the beneficiary of the trust attains the age of 18 years or the issuance of a declaration of emancipation of the minor under Section 7122, no withdrawal by the beneficiary or any other individual, individuals, entity, or entities may be made of funds on deposit in trust without written order of the superior court pursuant to paragraph (7) of subdivision (b) or paragraph (5) of subdivision (c) of Section 6752. Upon reaching the age of 18 years, the beneficiary may withdraw the funds on deposit in trust only after providing a certified copy of the beneficiary's birth certificate to the financial institution where the trust is located.

(c) The trustee or trustees shall, within 10 business days after the minor's contract is signed by the minor, the third-party individual or personal services corporation (loan-out company), and the employer, prepare a written statement under penalty of perjury that shall include the name, address, and telephone number of the financial institution, the name of the account, the number of the account, the name of the minor beneficiary, the name of the trustee or trustees of the account, and any additional information needed by the minor's employer to deposit into the account the portion of the minor's gross earnings prescribed by paragraph (1) of subdivision (b) or paragraph (1) of subdivision (c) of Section 6752. The trustee or trustees shall attach to the written statement a true and accurate photocopy of any information received from the financial institution confirming the creation of the account, such as an account agreement, account terms, passbook, or other similar writings.

(d) The trust shall be established in California either with a financial institution that is and remains insured at all times by the Federal Deposit Insurance Corporation (FDIC), the Securities Investor Protection Corporation (SIPC), or the National Credit

Union Share Insurance Fund (NCUSIF) or their respective successors, or with a company that is and remains registered under the Investment Company Act of 1940. The trustee or trustees of the trust shall be the only individual, individuals, entity, or entities with the obligation or duty to ensure that the funds remain in trust, in an account or other savings plan insured in accordance with this section, or with a company that is and remains registered under the Investment Company Act of 1940 as authorized by this section.

(e) Upon application by the trustee or trustees to the financial institution or company in which the trust is held, the trust funds shall be handled by the financial institution or company in one or more of the following methods:

(1) The financial institution or company may transfer funds to another account or other savings plan at the same financial institution or company, provided that the funds transferred shall continue to be held in trust, and subject to this chapter.

(2) The financial institution or company may transfer funds to another financial institution or company, provided that the funds transferred shall continue to be held in trust, and subject to this chapter and that the transferring financial institution or company has provided written notification to the financial institution or company to which the funds will be transferred that the funds are subject to this section and written notice of the requirements of this chapter.

(3) The financial institution or company may use all or a part of the funds to purchase, in the name of and for the benefit of the minor, (A) investment funds offered by a company registered under the Investment Company Act of 1940, provided that if the underlying investments are equity securities, the investment fund is a broad-based index fund or invests broadly across the domestic or a foreign regional economy, is not a sector fund, and has assets under management of at least two hundred fifty million dollars ($250,000,-000); or (B) government securities and bonds, certificates of deposit, money market instruments, money market accounts, or mutual funds investing solely in those government securities and bonds, certificates, instruments, and accounts, that are available at the financial institution where the trust fund or other savings plan is held, provided that the funds shall continue to be held in trust and subject to this chapter, those purchases shall have a maturity date on or before the date upon which the minor will attain the age of 18 years, and any proceeds accruing from those purchases shall be redeposited into that account or accounts or used to further purchase any of those or similar securities, bonds, certificates, instruments, funds, or accounts. *(Added by Stats.1999, c. 940 (S.B.1162), § 7. Amended by Stats.2003, c. 667 (S.B.210), § 3.)*

Cross References

Contracts, capacity of minors governed by this Division, see Civil Code § 1557.
Contracts, incapacity of minors to form, see Civil Code § 1556.
Contracts for attorney's fees for litigation services provided to minors, approval by court, see Family Code § 6602.
Judgment and order defined for purposes of this Code, see Family Code § 100.
Minor defined for purposes of this Code, see Family Code § 6500.
State defined for purposes of this Code, see Family Code § 145.

Research References

Forms

2 California Transactions Forms--Business Transactions § 8:53, Model Release for Images Included in Website.
2 California Transactions Forms--Business Transactions § 10:8, Employment of Minors.
West's California Code Forms, Family § 6751 Form 2, Order Approving Minor's Employment Contract.
West's California Code Forms, Family § 6753 Form 1, Petition to Terminate Trust or Savings Plan Established by Court Order.

West's California Code Forms, Family § 6753 Form 2, Order Terminating Trust or Savings Plan Established by Court Order.

Part 4

MEDICAL TREATMENT

Chapter	Section
1. Definitions	6900
2. Consent by Person Having Care of Minor or by Court	6910
3. Consent by Minor	6920

CHAPTER 1. DEFINITIONS

Section
6900. Construction of part.
6901. "Dental care" defined.
6902. "Medical care" defined.
6903. "Parent or guardian" defined.

§ 6900. Construction of part

Unless the provision or context otherwise requires, the definitions in this chapter govern the construction of this part. *(Stats.1992, c. 162 (A.B.2650), § 10, operative Jan. 1, 1994.)*

§ 6901. "Dental care" defined

"Dental care" means X-ray examination, anesthetic, dental or surgical diagnosis or treatment, and hospital care by a dentist licensed under the Dental Practice Act.[1] *(Stats.1992, c. 162 (A.B.2650), § 10, operative Jan. 1, 1994.)*

[1] See Business and Professions Code § 1600 et seq.

Research References

Forms

2 California Transactions Forms--Family Law § 6:65, Medical Authorization.

§ 6902. "Medical care" defined

"Medical care" means X-ray examination, anesthetic, medical or surgical diagnosis or treatment, and hospital care under the general or special supervision and upon the advice of or to be rendered by a physician and surgeon licensed under the Medical Practice Act.[1] *(Stats.1992, c. 162 (A.B.2650), § 10, operative Jan. 1, 1994.)*

[1] See Business and Professions Code § 2000 et seq.

Research References

Forms

2 California Transactions Forms--Family Law § 6:65, Medical Authorization.

§ 6903. "Parent or guardian" defined

"Parent or guardian" means either parent if both parents have legal custody, or the parent or person having legal custody, or the guardian, of a minor. *(Stats.1992, c. 162 (A.B.2650), § 10, operative Jan. 1, 1994.)*

Cross References

Guardian defined, see Probate Code §§ 2350, 2400.
Minor defined for purposes of this Code, see Family Code § 6500.
Person defined for purposes of this Code, see Family Code § 105.

Research References

Forms

2 California Transactions Forms--Family Law § 6:65, Medical Authorization.

CHAPTER 2. CONSENT BY PERSON HAVING CARE OF MINOR OR BY COURT

Section
6910. Medical treatment of minor; adult entrusted with consensual power.

MINORS

Section
6911. Consent by court; conditions.

§ 6910. Medical treatment of minor; adult entrusted with consensual power

The parent, guardian, or caregiver of a minor who is a relative of the minor and who may authorize medical care and dental care under Section 6550, may authorize in writing an adult into whose care a minor has been entrusted to consent to medical care or dental care, or both, for the minor. *(Stats.1992, c. 162 (A.B.2650), § 10, operative Jan. 1, 1994. Amended by Stats.1996, c. 563 (S.B.392), § 2.)*

Cross References

Dental care defined, see Family Code § 6901.
Emancipation of minors, see Family Code §§ 7002, 7050.
Foster care licensees, consent to medical and dental care, see Health and Safety Code § 1530.6.
Guardian's rights to consent to medical treatment, see Probate Code § 2353.
Medical care defined, see Family Code § 6902.
Minor defined for purposes of this Code, see Family Code § 6500.
Parent or guardian defined, see Family Code § 6903.

Research References

Forms
2 California Transactions Forms--Family Law § 6:65, Medical Authorization.
West's California Code Forms, Family § 6900, Comment Overview—Consent by Person Having Care of Minor.
West's California Code Forms, Family § 6910 Form 1, Authorization by Parent to Allow Adopting Parents to Consent to Minor's Medical Care.

§ 6911. Consent by court; conditions

(a) Upon application by a minor, the court may summarily grant consent for medical care or dental care or both for the minor if the court determines all of the following:

(1) The minor is 16 years of age or older and resides in this state.

(2) The consent of a parent or guardian is necessary to permit the medical care or dental care or both, and the minor has no parent or guardian available to give the consent.

(b) No fee may be charged for proceedings under this section. *(Stats.1992, c. 162 (A.B.2650), § 10, operative Jan. 1, 1994.)*

Cross References

Dental care defined, see Family Code § 6901.
Guardian defined, see Probate Code §§ 2350, 2400.
Medical care defined, see Family Code § 6902.
Minor defined for purposes of this Code, see Family Code § 6500.
Parent or guardian defined, see Family Code § 6903.
Proceeding defined for purposes of this Code, see Family Code § 110.
State defined for purposes of this Code, see Family Code § 145.

Research References

Forms
West's California Code Forms, Family § 6900, Comment Overview—Consent by Person Having Care of Minor.

CHAPTER 3. CONSENT BY MINOR

Section
6920. Capacity of minor to consent.
6921. Effect of minority upon consent.
6922. Conditions for consent of minor; liability of parents or guardians; notification of minor's parents or guardians.
6924. Mental health treatment or counseling services; involvement of parents or guardians; liability of parents or guardians.
6925. Prevention or treatment of pregnancy.

Section
6926. Diagnosis or treatment of infectious, contagious, or communicable diseases; consent by minor to certain medical care; liability of parents or guardians.
6927. Diagnosis or treatment for rape.
6928. Diagnosis or treatment for sexual assault.
6929. Diagnosis or treatment of drug and alcohol abuse; liability for cost of services; disclosure of medical information.
6930. Diagnosis and treatment for intimate partner violence; minors; applicability of section; report by health practitioner.

Cross References

California Council on Criminal Justice, minimum standards for examination and treatment of victims of sexual assault or attempted sexual assault, see Penal Code § 13823.11.
Medical, surgical or dental care, recommendation of physician and surgeon, court order, release of information, construction of section, see Welfare and Institutions Code § 369.

§ 6920. Capacity of minor to consent

Subject to the limitations provided in this chapter, notwithstanding any other provision of law, a minor may consent to the matters provided in this chapter, and the consent of the minor's parent or guardian is not necessary. *(Stats.1992, c. 162 (A.B.2650), § 10, operative Jan. 1, 1994.)*

Cross References

Blood donations, minor's right to consent, see Health and Safety Code § 1607.5.
Emancipation of minors, see Family Code §§ 7002, 7050.
Guardian defined, see Probate Code §§ 2350, 2400.
Minor defined for purposes of this Code, see Family Code § 6500.
Parent or guardian defined, see Family Code § 6903.
Statutory authority, obligations entered under, disaffirmance not allowed, see Family Code § 6711.

§ 6921. Effect of minority upon consent

A consent given by a minor under this chapter is not subject to disaffirmance because of minority. *(Stats.1992, c. 162 (A.B.2650), § 10, operative Jan. 1, 1994.)*

Cross References

Minor defined for purposes of this Code, see Family Code § 6500.

Research References

Forms
West's California Code Forms, Family § 6920, Comment Overview—Consent by Minor.

§ 6922. Conditions for consent of minor; liability of parents or guardians; notification of minor's parents or guardians

(a) A minor may consent to the minor's medical care or dental care if all of the following conditions are satisfied:

(1) The minor is 15 years of age or older.

(2) The minor is living separate and apart from the minor's parents or guardian, whether with or without the consent of a parent or guardian and regardless of the duration of the separate residence.

(3) The minor is managing the minor's own financial affairs, regardless of the source of the minor's income.

(b) The parents or guardian are not liable for medical care or dental care provided pursuant to this section.

(c) A physician and surgeon or dentist may, with or without the consent of the minor patient, advise the minor's parent or guardian of the treatment given or needed if the physician and surgeon or dentist has reason to know, on the basis of the information given by the minor, the whereabouts of the parent or guardian. *(Stats.1992, c. 162 (A.B.2650), § 10, operative Jan. 1, 1994.)*

Cross References

Dental care defined, see Family Code § 6901.
Emancipation of minors, see Family Code §§ 7002, 7050.
Guardian defined, see Probate Code §§ 2350, 2400.
Medical care defined, see Family Code § 6902.
Minor defined for purposes of this Code, see Family Code § 6500.
Parent or guardian defined, see Family Code § 6903.
Uniform Controlled Substances Act, medical marijuana program, see Health and Safety Code § 11362.7.

Research References

Forms

West's California Code Forms, Family § 6920, Comment Overview—Consent by Minor.
West's California Code Forms, Family § 6922 Form 1, Consent by Minor Living Apart from Parents to Medical Care.

§ 6924. Mental health treatment or counseling services; involvement of parents or guardians; liability of parents or guardians

(a) As used in this section:

(1) "Mental health treatment or counseling services" means the provision of mental health treatment or counseling on an outpatient basis by any of the following:

(A) A governmental agency.

(B) A person or agency having a contract with a governmental agency to provide the services.

(C) An agency that receives funding from community united funds.

(D) A runaway house or crisis resolution center.

(E) A professional person, as defined in paragraph (2).

(2) "Professional person" means any of the following:

(A) A person designated as a mental health professional in Sections 622 to 626, inclusive, of Article 8 of Subchapter 3 of Chapter 1 of Title 9 of the California Code of Regulations.

(B) A marriage and family therapist as defined in Chapter 13 (commencing with Section 4980) of Division 2 of the Business and Professions Code.

(C) A licensed educational psychologist as defined in Article 5 (commencing with Section 4986) of Chapter 13 of Division 2 of the Business and Professions Code.

(D) A credentialed school psychologist as described in Section 49424 of the Education Code.

(E) A clinical psychologist as defined in Section 1316.5 of the Health and Safety Code.

(F) The chief administrator of an agency referred to in paragraph (1) or (3).

(G) A person registered as an associate marriage and family therapist, as defined in Chapter 13 (commencing with Section 4980) of Division 2 of the Business and Professions Code, while working under the supervision of a licensed professional specified in subdivision (g) of Section 4980.03 of the Business and Professions Code.

(H) A licensed professional clinical counselor, as defined in Chapter 16 (commencing with Section 4999.10) of Division 2 of the Business and Professions Code.

(I) A person registered as an associate professional clinical counselor, as defined in Chapter 16 (commencing with Section 4999.10) of Division 2 of the Business and Professions Code, while working under the supervision of a licensed professional specified in subdivision (h) of Section 4999.12 of the Business and Professions Code.

(3) "Residential shelter services" means any of the following:

(A) The provision of residential and other support services to minors on a temporary or emergency basis in a facility that services only minors by a governmental agency, a person or agency having a contract with a governmental agency to provide these services, an agency that receives funding from community funds, or a licensed community care facility or crisis resolution center.

(B) The provision of other support services on a temporary or emergency basis by any professional person as defined in paragraph (2).

(b) A minor who is 12 years of age or older may consent to mental health treatment or counseling on an outpatient basis, or to residential shelter services, if both of the following requirements are satisfied:

(1) The minor, in the opinion of the attending professional person, is mature enough to participate intelligently in the outpatient services or residential shelter services.

(2) The minor (A) would present a danger of serious physical or mental harm to self or to others without the mental health treatment or counseling or residential shelter services, or (B) is the alleged victim of incest or child abuse.

(c) A professional person offering residential shelter services, whether as an individual or as a representative of an entity specified in paragraph (3) of subdivision (a), shall make their best efforts to notify the parent or guardian of the provision of services.

(d) The mental health treatment or counseling of a minor authorized by this section shall include involvement of the minor's parent or guardian unless, in the opinion of the professional person who is treating or counseling the minor, the involvement would be inappropriate. The professional person who is treating or counseling the minor shall state in the client record whether and when the person attempted to contact the minor's parent or guardian, and whether the attempt to contact was successful or unsuccessful, or the reason why, in the professional person's opinion, it would be inappropriate to contact the minor's parent or guardian.

(e) The minor's parents or guardian are not liable for payment for mental health treatment or counseling services provided pursuant to this section unless the parent or guardian participates in the mental health treatment or counseling, and then only for services rendered with the participation of the parent or guardian. The minor's parents or guardian are not liable for payment for any residential shelter services provided pursuant to this section unless the parent or guardian consented to the provision of those services.

(f) This section does not authorize a minor to receive convulsive therapy or psychosurgery as defined in subdivisions (f) and (g) of Section 5325 of the Welfare and Institutions Code, or psychotropic drugs without the consent of the minor's parent or guardian. *(Stats.1992, c. 162 (A.B.2650), § 10, operative Jan. 1, 1994. Amended by Stats.1993, c. 219 (A.B.1500), § 155; Stats.2000, c. 519 (A.B.2161), § 1; Stats.2009, c. 26 (S.B.33), § 22; Stats.2011, c. 381 (S.B.146), § 25; Stats.2018, c. 703 (S.B.1491), § 46, eff. Jan. 1, 2019; Stats.2019, c. 497 (A.B.991), § 113, eff. Jan. 1, 2020; Stats.2019, c. 115 (A.B.1817), § 76, eff. Jan. 1, 2020.)*

Cross References

Abuse defined for purposes of the Domestic Violence Protection Act, see Family Code § 6203.
Basic health care, financial responsibility of parents for person under twenty-one years, see Welfare and Institutions Code § 14010.
Consent by parent or guardian not necessary, see Family Code § 6920.
Consent not subject to disaffirmance, see Family Code § 6921.
Emancipation of minors, see Family Code §§ 7002, 7050.
Guardian defined, see Probate Code § 2350.
Minor defined for purposes of this Code, see Family Code § 6500.
Person defined for purposes of this Code, see Family Code § 105.
Psychotherapist-patient privilege, see Evidence Code § 1010.
State defined for purposes of this Code, see Family Code § 145.

§ 6924

Support defined for purposes of this Code, see Family Code § 150.

Research References

Forms

West's California Code Forms, Family § 6920, Comment Overview—Consent by Minor.

§ 6925. Prevention or treatment of pregnancy

(a) A minor may consent to medical care related to the prevention or treatment of pregnancy.

(b) This section does not authorize a minor:

(1) To be sterilized without the consent of the minor's parent or guardian.

(2) To receive an abortion without the consent of a parent or guardian other than as provided in Section 123450 of the Health and Safety Code. *(Stats.1992, c. 162 (A.B.2650), § 10, operative Jan. 1, 1994. Amended by Stats.1996, c. 1023 (S.B.1497), § 46, eff. Sept. 29, 1996.)*

Cross References

Basic health care, financial responsibility of parents for person under twenty-one years, see Welfare and Institutions Code § 14010.
Consent by parent or guardian unnecessary, see Family Code § 6920.
Consent not subject to disaffirmance, see Family Code § 6921.
Emancipation of minors, see Family Code §§ 7002, 7050.
Guardian defined, see Probate Code §§ 2350, 2400.
Medical care defined, see Family Code § 6902.
Minor defined for purposes of this Code, see Family Code § 6500.
Parent or guardian defined, see Family Code § 6903.

Research References

Forms

West's California Code Forms, Family § 6920, Comment Overview—Consent by Minor.

§ 6926. Diagnosis or treatment of infectious, contagious, or communicable diseases; consent by minor to certain medical care; liability of parents or guardians

(a) A minor who is 12 years of age or older and who may have come into contact with an infectious, contagious, or communicable disease may consent to medical care related to the diagnosis or treatment of the disease, if the disease or condition is one that is required by law or regulation adopted pursuant to law to be reported to the local health officer, or is a related sexually transmitted disease, as may be determined by the State Public Health Officer.

(b) A minor who is 12 years of age or older may consent to medical care related to the prevention of a sexually transmitted disease.

(c) The minor's parents or guardian are not liable for payment for medical care provided pursuant to this section. *(Stats.1992, c. 162 (A.B.2650), § 10, operative Jan. 1, 1994. Amended by Stats.2011, c. 652 (A.B.499), § 1.)*

Cross References

Basic health care, financial responsibility of parents for person under twenty-one years, see Welfare and Institutions Code § 14010.
Consent by parent or guardian unnecessary, see Family Code § 6920.
Consent not subject to disaffirmance, see Family Code § 6921.
Emancipation of minors, see Family Code §§ 7002, 7050.
Establishment and administration of program to subsidize costs of medications for prevention of HIV infection and related medical expenses, recipient requirements, funding, confidentiality of information, see Health and Safety Code § 120972.
Guardian defined, see Probate Code §§ 2350, 2400.
Minor defined for purposes of this Code, see Family Code § 6500.
Parent or guardian defined, see Family Code § 6903.
Primary care clinic to offer HIV test consistent with federal recommendation and guidelines, testing of minors 12 years of age or older, communication of results, see Health and Safety Code § 120991.

State defined for purposes of this Code, see Family Code § 145.

Research References

Forms

West's California Code Forms, Family § 6920, Comment Overview—Consent by Minor.

§ 6927. Diagnosis or treatment for rape

A minor who is 12 years of age or older and who is alleged to have been raped may consent to medical care related to the diagnosis or treatment of the condition and the collection of medical evidence with regard to the alleged rape. *(Stats.1992, c. 162 (A.B.2650), § 10, operative Jan. 1, 1994.)*

Cross References

Basic health care, financial responsibility of parents for person under twenty-one years, see Welfare and Institutions Code § 14010.
Consent by parent or guardian unnecessary, see Family Code § 6920.
Consent not subject to disaffirmance, see Family Code § 6921.
Emancipation of minors, see Family Code §§ 7002, 7050.
Medical care defined, see Family Code § 6902.
Minor defined for purposes of this Code, see Family Code § 6500.
Sexual assault victims, examination and treatment, consent by minors without parental consent, see Penal Code § 13823.11.

Research References

Forms

West's California Code Forms, Family § 6920, Comment Overview—Consent by Minor.

§ 6928. Diagnosis or treatment for sexual assault

(a) "Sexually assaulted" as used in this section includes, but is not limited to, conduct coming within Section 261, 286, or 287 of the Penal Code.

(b) A minor who is alleged to have been sexually assaulted may consent to medical care related to the diagnosis and treatment of the condition, and the collection of medical evidence with regard to the alleged sexual assault.

(c) The professional person providing medical treatment shall attempt to contact the minor's parent or guardian and shall note in the minor's treatment record the date and time the professional person attempted to contact the parent or guardian and whether the attempt was successful or unsuccessful. This subdivision does not apply if the professional person reasonably believes that the minor's parent or guardian committed the sexual assault on the minor. *(Stats.1992, c. 162 (A.B.2650), § 10, operative Jan. 1, 1994. Amended by Stats.2018, c. 423 (S.B.1494), § 25, eff. Jan. 1, 2019.)*

Cross References

Basic health care, financial responsibility of parents for person under twenty-one years, see Welfare and Institutions Code § 14010.
Consent by parent or guardian unnecessary, see Family Code § 6920.
Consent not subject to disaffirmance, see Family Code § 6921.
Emancipation of minors, see Family Code §§ 7002, 7050.
Guardian defined, see Probate Code §§ 2350, 2400.
Medical care defined, see Family Code § 6902.
Minor defined for purposes of this Code, see Family Code § 6500.
Parent or guardian defined, see Family Code § 6903.
Person defined for purposes of this Code, see Family Code § 105.
Sexual assault victims, examination and treatment, consent by minors without parental consent, see Penal Code § 13823.11.

Research References

Forms

West's California Code Forms, Family § 6920, Comment Overview—Consent by Minor.

§ 6929. Diagnosis or treatment of drug and alcohol abuse; liability for cost of services; disclosure of medical information

(a) As used in this section:

(1) "Counseling" means the provision of counseling services by a provider under a contract with the state or a county to provide alcohol or drug abuse counseling services pursuant to Part 2 (commencing with Section 5600) of Division 5 of the Welfare and Institutions Code or pursuant to Division 10.5 (commencing with Section 11750) of the Health and Safety Code.

(2) "Drug or alcohol" includes, but is not limited to, any substance listed in any of the following:

(A) Section 380 or 381 of the Penal Code.

(B) Division 10 (commencing with Section 11000) of the Health and Safety Code.

(C) Subdivision (f) of Section 647 of the Penal Code.

(3) "LAAM" means levoalphacetylmethadol as specified in paragraph (10) of subdivision (c) of Section 11055 of the Health and Safety Code.

(4) "Professional person" means a physician and surgeon, registered nurse, psychologist, clinical social worker, professional clinical counselor, marriage and family therapist, registered marriage and family therapist intern when appropriately employed and supervised pursuant to Section 4980.43 of the Business and Professions Code, psychological assistant when appropriately employed and supervised pursuant to Section 2913 of the Business and Professions Code, associate clinical social worker when appropriately employed and supervised pursuant to Section 4996.18 of the Business and Professions Code, or registered clinical counselor intern when appropriately employed and supervised pursuant to Section 4999.42 of the Business and Professions Code.

(b) A minor who is 12 years of age or older may consent to medical care and counseling relating to the diagnosis and treatment of a drug- or alcohol-related problem.

(c) The treatment plan of a minor authorized by this section shall include the involvement of the minor's parent or guardian, if appropriate, as determined by the professional person or treatment facility treating the minor. The professional person providing medical care or counseling to a minor shall state in the minor's treatment record whether and when the professional person attempted to contact the minor's parent or guardian, and whether the attempt to contact the parent or guardian was successful or unsuccessful, or the reason why, in the opinion of the professional person, it would not be appropriate to contact the minor's parent or guardian.

(d) The minor's parent or guardian is not liable for payment for care provided to a minor pursuant to this section, except that if the minor's parent or guardian participates in a counseling program pursuant to this section, the parent or guardian is liable for the cost of the services provided to the minor and the parent or guardian.

(e) This section does not authorize a minor to receive replacement narcotic abuse treatment, in a program licensed pursuant to Article 3 (commencing with Section 11875) of Chapter 1 of Part 3 of Division 10.5 of the Health and Safety Code, without the consent of the minor's parent or guardian.

(f) It is the intent of the Legislature that the state shall respect the right of a parent or legal guardian to seek medical care and counseling for a drug- or alcohol-related problem of a minor child when the child does not consent to the medical care and counseling, and nothing in this section shall be construed to restrict or eliminate this right.

(g) Notwithstanding any other law, when a parent or legal guardian has sought the medical care and counseling for a drug- or alcohol-related problem of a minor child, the physician and surgeon shall disclose medical information concerning the care to the minor's parent or legal guardian upon the parent's or guardian's request, even if the minor child does not consent to disclosure, without liability for the disclosure. *(Stats.1992, c. 162 (A.B.2650), § 10, operative Jan. 1, 1994. Amended by Stats.1995, c. 455 (A.B.1113), § 1,* eff. Sept. 5, 1995; Stats.1996, c. 656 (A.B.2883), § 1; Stats.2002, c. 1013 (S.B.2026), § 79; Stats.2004, c. 59 (A.B.2182), § 1; Stats.2009, c. 26 (S.B.33), § 23; Stats.2011, c. 381 (S.B.146), § 26; Stats.2019, c. 115 (A.B.1817), § 77, eff. Jan. 1, 2020.)

Cross References

Abuse defined for purposes of the Domestic Violence Protection Act, see Family Code § 6203.
Basic health care, financial responsibility of parents for person under twenty-one years, see Welfare and Institutions Code § 14010.
Consent by parent or guardian unnecessary, see Family Code § 6920.
Consent not subject to disaffirmance, see Family Code § 6921.
County defined for purposes of this Code, see Family Code § 67.
Emancipation of minors, see Family Code §§ 7002, 7050.
Guardian defined, see Probate Code §§ 2350, 2400.
Medical care defined, see Family Code § 6902.
Minor defined for purposes of this Code, see Family Code § 6500.
Parent or guardian defined, see Family Code § 6903.
Person defined for purposes of this Code, see Family Code § 105.
State defined for purposes of this Code, see Family Code § 145.

Research References

Forms

West's California Code Forms, Family § 6920, Comment Overview—Consent by Minor.

§ 6930. Diagnosis and treatment for intimate partner violence; minors; applicability of section; report by health practitioner

(a) A minor who is 12 years of age or older and who states that the minor is injured as a result of intimate partner violence may consent to medical care related to the diagnosis or treatment of the injury and the collection of medical evidence with regard to the alleged intimate partner violence.

(b)(1) For purposes of this section, "intimate partner violence" means an intentional or reckless infliction of bodily harm that is perpetrated by a person with whom the minor has or has had a sexual, dating, or spousal relationship.

(2) This section does not apply when a minor is an alleged victim of rape, as defined in Section 261 of the Penal Code, in which case Section 6927 shall apply, and does not apply when a minor is alleged to have been sexually assaulted, as described in Section 6928, in which case that section shall apply.

(c) If the health practitioner providing treatment believes that the injuries described in subdivision (a) require a report pursuant to Section 11160 of the Penal Code, the health practitioner shall do both of the following:

(1) Inform the minor that the report will be made.

(2) Attempt to contact the minor's parent or guardian and inform them of the report. The health practitioner shall note in the minor's treatment record the date and time of the attempt to contact the parent or guardian and whether the attempt was successful or unsuccessful. This paragraph does not apply if the health practitioner reasonably believes that the minor's parent or guardian committed the intimate partner violence on the minor. *(Added by Stats.2018, c. 1003 (A.B.3189), § 1, eff. Jan. 1, 2019. Amended by Stats.2019, c. 115 (A.B.1817), § 78, eff. Jan. 1, 2020; Stats.2021, c. 626 (A.B.1171), § 11, eff. Jan. 1, 2022.)*

Part 5

ENLISTMENT IN ARMED FORCES

Section
6950. Consent of court; conditions.

§ 6950. Consent of court; conditions

(a) Upon application by a minor, the court may summarily grant consent for enlistment by the minor in the armed forces of the United States if the court determines all of the following:

(1) The minor is 16 years of age or older and resides in this state.

(2) The consent of a parent or guardian is necessary to permit the enlistment, and the minor has no parent or guardian available to give the consent.

(b) No fee may be charged for proceedings under this section. *(Stats.1992, c. 162 (A.B.2650), § 10, operative Jan. 1, 1994.)*

Cross References

Armed forces defined, see Government Code § 18540.
Emancipation of minors, see Family Code § 7002.
Guardian defined, see Probate Code §§ 2350, 2400.
Minor defined for purposes of this Code, see Family Code § 6500.
Parent or guardian defined, see Family Code § 6903.
Proceeding defined for purposes of this Code, see Family Code § 110.
State defined for purposes of this Code, see Family Code § 145.

Part 6

EMANCIPATION OF MINORS LAW

Chapter	Section
1. General Provisions	7000
2. Effect of Emancipation	7050
3. Court Declaration of Emancipation	7110

Cross References

California Work Opportunity and Responsibility to Kids Act, support enforcement and child abduction records, authorized disclosure of information, see Welfare and Institutions Code § 11478.1.
Employment of minors, permits to work full time, see Education Code § 49130.
Minors in foster care adjudged wards of court, placement goals, see Welfare and Institutions Code § 727.3.
Provision of housing for homeless youth, age discrimination, see Government Code § 12957.
Termination or modification of guardianship under Probate Code, see Welfare and Institutions Code § 728.

CHAPTER 1. GENERAL PROVISIONS

Section
7000. Short title.
7001. Purpose of part.
7002. Emancipated minor; description.

Cross References

Executive department, agencies, facilitating and supporting development and operation of housing for homeless youth, see Government Code § 11139.3.

§ 7000. Short title

This part may be cited as the Emancipation of Minors Law. *(Stats.1992, c. 162 (A.B.2650), § 10, operative Jan. 1, 1994.)*

Cross References

Employment of minors, permits to work full time, conditions, see Education Code § 49130.
Minor defined for purposes of this Code, see Family Code § 6500.
State agencies, discrimination, development and operation of housing for homeless youth, see Government Code § 11139.3.

Research References

Forms
1 California Transactions Forms--Family Law § 1:2, Nature and Advantages of Agreement.
West's California Code Forms, Family § 7110, Comment Overview—Emancipation of Minor.
West's California Judicial Council Forms EM–100, Petition for Declaration of Emancipation of Minor, Order Prescribing Notice, Declaration of Emancipation, and Order Denying Petition.
West's California Judicial Council Forms EM–109, Notice of Hearing—Emancipation of Minor.
West's California Judicial Council Forms EM–115, Emancipation of Minor Income and Expense Declaration.
West's California Judicial Council Forms EM–130, Declaration of Emancipation of Minor After Hearing.
West's California Judicial Council Forms EM–140, Emancipated Minor's Application to California Department of Motor Vehicles.

§ 7001. Purpose of part

It is the purpose of this part to provide a clear statement defining emancipation and its consequences and to permit an emancipated minor to obtain a court declaration of the minor's status. This part is not intended to affect the status of minors who may become emancipated under the decisional case law that was in effect before the enactment of Chapter 1059 of the Statutes of 1978. *(Stats.1992, c. 162 (A.B.2650), § 10, operative Jan. 1, 1994.)*

Cross References

Minor defined for purposes of this Code, see Family Code § 6500.

§ 7002. Emancipated minor; description

A person under the age of 18 years is an emancipated minor if any of the following conditions is satisfied:

(a) The person has entered into a valid marriage, or has established a valid domestic partnership, regardless of whether the marriage or the domestic partnership has been dissolved.

(b) The person is on active duty with the Armed Forces of the United States.

(c) The person has received a declaration of emancipation pursuant to Section 7122. *(Stats.1992, c. 162 (A.B.2650), § 10, operative Jan. 1, 1994. Amended by Stats.2018, c. 660 (S.B.273), § 9, eff. Jan. 1, 2019.)*

Cross References

Armed forces, defined, see Government Code § 18540.
Armed forces enlistment, see Family Code § 6950.
Dissolution of marriage, see Family Code § 310.
Employment of minors, permits to work full time, see Education Code § 49130.
Guardianship, majority, death, adoption, or emancipation of ward, see Probate Code § 1600.
Minor defined for purposes of this Code, see Family Code § 6500.
Minors in foster care adjudged wards of court, placement goals, see Welfare and Institutions Code § 727.3.
Person defined for purposes of this Code, see Family Code § 105.
State defined for purposes of this Code, see Family Code § 145.
State government's role to alleviate problems related to the inappropriate use of alcoholic beverages, see Health and Safety Code § 11834.02.
Termination or modification of guardianship under Probate Code, see Welfare and Institutions Code § 728.
Uniform Controlled Substances Act, medical marijuana program, see Health and Safety Code § 11362.7.

Research References

Forms
California Practice Guide: Rutter Family Law Forms Form 9:3, Marital Settlement Agreement.

1 California Transactions Forms—Business Transactions § 6:11, Void Contracts of Minors.
1 California Transactions Forms—Estate Planning § 6:16, Guardian of Person.
West's California Code Forms, Family § 2338 Form 9, Marital Agreement—Both Spouses Employed.
West's California Code Forms, Family § 7002, Comment Overview—Emancipated Minors.
West's California Code Forms, Probate § 1601 Form 1, Petition for Termination of Guardianship—Judicial Council Form GC-255.

CHAPTER 2. EFFECT OF EMANCIPATION

Section
7050. Purposes for which emancipated minors are considered an adult.
7051. Insurance contracts.
7052. Powers of emancipated minor with respect to shares of stock and similar property.

Cross References
Domestic partnership with underage person, court order and written consent of parents, see Family Code § 297.1.

§ 7050. Purposes for which emancipated minors are considered an adult

An emancipated minor shall be considered as being an adult for the following purposes:

(a) The minor's right to support by the minor's parents.

(b) The right of the minor's parents to the minor's earnings and to control the minor.

(c) The application of Sections 300 and 601 of the Welfare and Institutions Code.

(d) Ending all vicarious or imputed liability of the minor's parents or guardian for the minor's torts. Nothing in this section affects any liability of a parent, guardian, spouse, or employer imposed by the Vehicle Code, or any vicarious liability that arises from an agency relationship.

(e) The minor's capacity to do any of the following:

(1) Consent to medical, dental, or psychiatric care, without parental consent, knowledge, or liability.

(2) Enter into a binding contract or give a delegation of power.

(3) Buy, sell, lease, encumber, exchange, or transfer an interest in real or personal property, including, but not limited to, shares of stock in a domestic or foreign corporation or a membership in a nonprofit corporation.

(4) Sue or be sued in the minor's own name.

(5) Compromise, settle, arbitrate, or otherwise adjust a claim, action, or proceeding by or against the minor.

(6) Make or revoke a will.

(7) Make a gift, outright or in trust.

(8) Convey or release contingent or expectant interests in property, including marital property rights and any right of survivorship incident to joint tenancy, and consent to a transfer, encumbrance, or gift of marital property.

(9) Exercise or release the minor's powers as donee of a power of appointment unless the creating instrument otherwise provides.

(10) Create for the minor's own benefit or for the benefit of others a revocable or irrevocable trust.

(11) Revoke a revocable trust.

(12) Elect to take under or against a will.

(13) Renounce or disclaim any interest acquired by testate or intestate succession or by inter vivos transfer, including exercise of the right to surrender the right to revoke a revocable trust.

(14) Make an election referred to in Section 13502 of, or an election and agreement referred to in Section 13503 of, the Probate Code.

(15) Establish the minor's own residence.

(16) Apply for a work permit pursuant to Section 49110 of the Education Code without the request of the minor's parents.

(17) Enroll in a school or college. (Stats.1992, c. 162 (A.B.2650), § 10, operative Jan. 1, 1994.)

Cross References
Adult defined, see Family Code § 6501.
Basic health care, financial responsibility of parents for person under twenty-one years, see Welfare and Institutions Code § 14010.
Contracts,
 Capacity of minors governed by this Division, see Civil Code § 1557.
 Incapacity of minors to form, see Civil Code § 1556.
 Restrictions on authority of minors, see Family Code § 6701.
 Right of disaffirmance, see Family Code § 6710.
Criminal liability, capacity of minors, see Penal Code § 26.
Liability of parents and guardians for willful misconduct of minors, see Civil Code § 1714.1.
Medical treatment, consent by minor, generally, see Family Code § 6900 et seq.
Minor defined for purposes of this Code, see Family Code § 6500.
Proceeding defined for purposes of this Code, see Family Code § 110.
Property defined for purposes of this Code, see Family Code § 113.
References to husband, wife, spouses and married persons, persons included for purposes of this Code, see Family Code § 11.
Support defined for purposes of this Code, see Family Code § 150.
Uniform Controlled Substances Act, medical marijuana program, see Health and Safety Code § 11362.7.

Research References
Forms
1 California Transactions Forms—Business Transactions § 6:11, Void Contracts of Minors.
4 California Transactions Forms—Estate Planning § 19:32, Persons Who May Make Will.
4 California Transactions Forms—Estate Planning § 19:43, Who May Execute.
1 California Transactions Forms—Family Law § 1:2, Nature and Advantages of Agreement.
West's California Code Forms, Family § 302, Comment Overview—Marriage of Minor.
West's California Code Forms, Family § 7002, Comment Overview—Emancipated Minors.
West's California Code Forms, Family § 7002 Form 2, Consent by Married Minor to Medical Care.
West's California Code Forms, Family § 7002 Form 3, Consent by Minor in Military to Medical Care.

§ 7051. Insurance contracts

An insurance contract entered into by an emancipated minor has the same effect as if it were entered into by an adult and, with respect to that contract, the minor has the same rights, duties, and liabilities as an adult. (Stats.1992, c. 162 (A.B.2650), § 10, operative Jan. 1, 1994.)

Cross References
Adult defined for purposes of this Code, see Family Code § 6501.
Contracts, restrictions on authority of minors, see Family Code § 6701.
Contracts, right of disaffirmance by minors, see Family Code § 6710.
Life and disability insurance, insurance of minors, see Insurance Code § 10112.
Minor defined for purposes of this Code, see Family Code § 6500.

§ 7052. Powers of emancipated minor with respect to shares of stock and similar property

With respect to shares of stock in a domestic or foreign corporation held by an emancipated minor, a membership in a nonprofit corporation held by an emancipated minor, or other property held by an emancipated minor, the minor may do all of the following:

§ 7052

(a) Vote in person, and give proxies to exercise any voting rights, with respect to the shares, membership, or property.

(b) Waive notice of any meeting or give consent to the holding of any meeting.

(c) Authorize, ratify, approve, or confirm any action that could be taken by shareholders, members, or property owners. *(Stats.1992, c. 162 (A.B.2650), § 10, operative Jan. 1, 1994.)*

Cross References

Contracts, restrictions on authority of minors, see Family Code § 6701.
Contracts, right of disaffirmance by minors, see Family Code § 6710.
Corporations, immunity from liability for transfer of shares by or to minors, see Corporations Code § 420.
Minor defined for purposes of this Code, see Family Code § 6500.
Person defined for purposes of this Code, see Family Code § 105.
Property defined for purposes of this Code, see Family Code § 113.

CHAPTER 3. COURT DECLARATION OF EMANCIPATION

Article	Section
1. General Provisions	7110
2. Procedure for Declaration	7120
3. Voiding or Rescinding Declaration	7130
4. Identification Cards and Information	7140

ARTICLE 1. GENERAL PROVISIONS

Section
7110. Legislative intent; minimum expense; forms.
7111. Issuance of declaration of emancipation; effect on public social service benefits.

§ 7110. Legislative intent; minimum expense; forms

It is the intent of the Legislature that proceedings under this part be as simple and inexpensive as possible. To that end, the Judicial Council is requested to prepare and distribute to the clerks of the superior courts appropriate forms for the proceedings that are suitable for use by minors acting as their own counsel. *(Stats.1992, c. 162 (A.B.2650), § 10, operative Jan. 1, 1994.)*

Cross References

Minor defined for purposes of this Code, see Family Code § 6500.
Proceeding defined for purposes of this Code, see Family Code § 110.

Research References

Forms

West's California Code Forms, Family § 7110 Form 1, Petition for Declaration of Emancipation of Minor.

§ 7111. Issuance of declaration of emancipation; effect on public social service benefits

The issuance of a declaration of emancipation does not entitle the minor to any benefits under Division 9 (commencing with Section 10000) of the Welfare and Institutions Code which would not otherwise accrue to an emancipated minor. *(Stats.1992, c. 162 (A.B.2650), § 10, operative Jan. 1, 1994.)*

Cross References

Minor defined for purposes of this Code, see Family Code § 6500.

ARTICLE 2. PROCEDURE FOR DECLARATION

Section
7120. Petitions for declaration of emancipation; contents.
7121. Notice of declaration proceedings.

Section
7122. Findings of court; issuance of declaration of emancipation.
7123. Grant or denial of petition; filing of petition for writ of mandate.

§ 7120. Petitions for declaration of emancipation; contents

(a) A minor may petition the superior court of the county in which the minor resides or is temporarily domiciled for a declaration of emancipation.

(b) The petition shall set forth with specificity all of the following facts:

(1) The minor is at least 14 years of age.

(2) The minor willingly lives separate and apart from the minor's parents or guardian with the consent or acquiescence of the minor's parents or guardian.

(3) The minor is managing their own financial affairs. As evidence of this, the minor shall complete and attach a declaration of income and expenses as provided in Judicial Council form FL–150.

(4) The source of the minor's income is not derived from any activity declared to be a crime by the laws of this state or the laws of the United States. *(Stats.1992, c. 162 (A.B.2650), § 10, operative Jan. 1, 1994. Amended by Stats.1993, c. 219 (A.B.1500), § 156; Stats. 2004, c. 811 (A.B.3079), § 3; Stats.2019, c. 115 (A.B.1817), § 79, eff. Jan. 1, 2020.)*

Cross References

County defined for purposes of this Code, see Family Code § 67.
Guardian defined, see Probate Code §§ 2350, 2400.
Minor defined for purposes of this Code, see Family Code § 6500.
Parent or guardian defined, see Family Code § 6903.
State defined for purposes of this Code, see Family Code § 145.
Uniform Controlled Substances Act, medical marijuana program, see Health and Safety Code § 11362.7.

Research References

Forms

West's California Code Forms, Family § 7110, Comment Overview—Emancipation of Minor.

§ 7121. Notice of declaration proceedings

(a) Before the petition for a declaration of emancipation is heard, notice the court determines is reasonable shall be given to the minor's parents, guardian, or other person entitled to the custody of the minor, or proof shall be made to the court that their addresses are unknown or that for other reasons the notice cannot be given.

(b) The clerk of the court shall also notify the local child support agency of the county in which the matter is to be heard of the proceeding. If the minor is a ward of the court, notice shall be given to the probation department. If the child is a dependent child of the court, notice shall be given to the county welfare department.

(c) The notice shall include a form whereby the minor's parents, guardian, or other person entitled to the custody of the minor may give their written consent to the petitioner's emancipation. The notice shall include a warning that a court may void or rescind the declaration of emancipation and the parents may become liable for support and medical insurance coverage pursuant to Chapter 2 (commencing with Section 4000) of Part 2 of Division 9 and Sections 17400, 17402, 17404, and 17422. *(Stats.1992, c. 162 (A.B.2650), § 10, operative Jan. 1, 1994. Amended by Stats.1993, c. 219 (A.B.1500), § 157; Stats.2003, c. 365 (A.B.1710), § 1.)*

Cross References

County defined for purposes of this Code, see Family Code § 67.
Minor defined for purposes of this Code, see Family Code § 6500.
Person defined for purposes of this Code, see Family Code § 105.
Petitioner defined for purposes of this Code, see Family Code § 126.

Proceeding defined for purposes of this Code, see Family Code § 110.
Support defined for purposes of this Code, see Family Code § 150.

Research References

Forms

West's California Code Forms, Family § 7110, Comment Overview—Emancipation of Minor.

§ 7122. Findings of court; issuance of declaration of emancipation

(a) The court shall sustain the petition if it finds that the minor is a person described by Section 7120 and that emancipation would not be contrary to the minor's best interest.

(b) If the petition is sustained, the court shall forthwith issue a declaration of emancipation, which shall be filed by the clerk of the court.

(c) A declaration is conclusive evidence that the minor is emancipated. (Stats.1992, c. 162 (A.B.2650), § 10, operative Jan. 1, 1994. Amended by Stats.2002, c. 784 (S.B.1316), § 107.)

Cross References

Jurisdiction, superior court, see Family Code § 200.
Minor defined for purposes of this Code, see Family Code § 6500.
Person defined for purposes of this Code, see Family Code § 105.

Research References

Forms

1 California Transactions Forms--Estate Planning § 6:16, Guardian of Person.
West's California Code Forms, Family § 7110, Comment Overview—Emancipation of Minor.

§ 7123. Grant or denial of petition; filing of petition for writ of mandate

(a) If the petition is denied, the minor has a right to file a petition for a writ of mandate.

(b) If the petition is sustained, the parents or guardian have a right to file a petition for a writ of mandate if they have appeared in the proceeding and opposed the granting of the petition. (Stats.1992, c. 162 (A.B.2650), § 10, operative Jan. 1, 1994.)

Cross References

Guardian defined, see Probate Code §§ 2350, 2400.
Mandamus, purpose of writ of mandate, courts which may issue writ and parties to whom issued, see Code of Civil Procedure § 1085.
Minor defined for purposes of this Code, see Family Code § 6500.
Parent or guardian defined, see Family Code § 6903.
Proceeding defined for purposes of this Code, see Family Code § 110.

Research References

Forms

West's California Code Forms, Family § 7110, Comment Overview—Emancipation of Minor.

ARTICLE 3. VOIDING OR RESCINDING DECLARATION

Section
7130. Grounds for voiding or rescinding declaration.
7131. Filing of petitions to void declarations.
7132. Filing of petitions to rescind declarations.
7133. Notice of petition to void or rescind declaration.
7134. Issuance of order.
7135. Effect upon contractual and property obligations.

§ 7130. Grounds for voiding or rescinding declaration

(a) A declaration of emancipation obtained by fraud or by the withholding of material information is voidable.

(b) A declaration of emancipation of a minor who is indigent and has no means of support is subject to rescission. (Stats.1992, c. 162 (A.B.2650), § 10, operative Jan. 1, 1994.)

Cross References

Minor defined for purposes of this Code, see Family Code § 6500.
Support defined for purposes of this Code, see Family Code § 150.

§ 7131. Filing of petitions to void declarations

A petition to void a declaration of emancipation on the ground that the declaration was obtained by fraud or by the withholding of material information may be filed by any person or by any public or private agency. The petition shall be filed in the court that made the declaration. (Stats.1992, c. 162 (A.B.2650), § 10, operative Jan. 1, 1994.)

Cross References

Person defined for purposes of this Code, see Family Code § 105.

§ 7132. Filing of petitions to rescind declarations

(a) A petition to rescind a declaration of emancipation on the ground that the minor is indigent and has no means of support may be filed by the minor declared emancipated, by the minor's conservator, or by the district attorney of the county in which the minor resides. The petition shall be filed in the county in which the minor or the conservator resides.

(b) The minor may be considered indigent if the minor's only source of income is from public assistance benefits. The court shall consider the impact of the rescission of the declaration of emancipation on the minor and shall find the rescission of the declaration of emancipation will not be contrary to the best interest of the minor before granting the order to rescind. (Stats.1992, c. 162 (A.B.2650), § 10, operative Jan. 1, 1994. Amended by Stats.1993, c. 219 (A.B. 1500), § 158.)

Cross References

County defined for purposes of this Code, see Family Code § 67.
Judgment and order defined for purposes of this Code, see Family Code § 100.
Jurisdiction, superior court, see Family Code § 200.
Minor defined for purposes of this Code, see Family Code § 6500.
Support defined for purposes of this Code, see Family Code § 150.

§ 7133. Notice of petition to void or rescind declaration

(a) Before a petition under this article is heard, notice the court determines is reasonable shall be given to the minor's parents or guardian, or proof shall be made to the court that their addresses are unknown or that for other reasons the notice cannot be given.

(b) The notice to parents shall state that if the declaration of emancipation is voided or rescinded, the parents may be liable to provide support and medical insurance coverage for the child pursuant to Chapter 2 (commencing with Section 4000) of Part 2 of Division 9 of this code and Sections 11350, 11350.1, 11475.1, and 11490 of the Welfare and Institutions Code.

(c) No liability accrues to a parent or guardian not given actual notice, as a result of voiding or rescinding the declaration of emancipation, until that parent or guardian is given actual notice. (Stats.1992, c. 162 (A.B.2650), § 10, operative Jan. 1, 1994. Amended by Stats.1993, c. 219 (A.B.1500), § 159.)

Cross References

Guardian defined, see Probate Code §§ 2350, 2400.
Minor defined for purposes of this Code, see Family Code § 6500.
Parent or guardian defined, see Family Code § 6903.
State defined for purposes of this Code, see Family Code § 145.

§ 7133

Support defined for purposes of this Code, see Family Code § 150.

§ 7134. Issuance of order

If the petition is sustained, the court shall forthwith issue an order voiding or rescinding the declaration of emancipation, which shall be filed by the clerk of the court. *(Stats.1992, c. 162 (A.B.2650), § 10, operative Jan. 1, 1994. Amended by Stats.2002, c. 784 (S.B.1316), § 108.)*

Cross References

Judgment and order defined for purposes of this Code, see Family Code § 100.

§ 7135. Effect upon contractual and property obligations

Voiding or rescission of the declaration of emancipation does not alter any contractual obligation or right or any property right or interest that arose during the period that the declaration was in effect. *(Stats.1992, c. 162 (A.B.2650), § 10, operative Jan. 1, 1994.)*

Cross References

Property defined for purposes of this Code, see Family Code § 113.

ARTICLE 4. IDENTIFICATION CARDS AND INFORMATION

Section
7140. Entry of identifying information into department of motor vehicles records systems; statement of emancipation upon identification card.
7141. Reliance on representation of emancipation; effect.
7142. Liability of public entities or employees.
7143. Notification to Department of Motor Vehicles upon voiding or rescission of declaration of emancipation; invalidation of identification cards.

§ 7140. Entry of identifying information into department of motor vehicles records systems; statement of emancipation upon identification card

On application of a minor declared emancipated under this chapter, the Department of Motor Vehicles shall enter identifying information in its law enforcement computer network, and the fact of emancipation shall be stated on the department's identification card issued to the emancipated minor. *(Stats.1992, c. 162 (A.B.2650), § 10, operative Jan. 1, 1994.)*

Cross References

Minor defined for purposes of this Code, see Family Code § 6500.

Research References

Forms

West's California Code Forms, Family § 7110, Comment Overview—Emancipation of Minor.

§ 7141. Reliance on representation of emancipation; effect

A person who, in good faith, has examined a minor's identification card and relies on a minor's representation that the minor is emancipated, has the same rights and obligations as if the minor were in fact emancipated at the time of the representation. *(Stats.1992, c. 162 (A.B.2650), § 10, operative Jan. 1, 1994.)*

Cross References

Minor defined for purposes of this Code, see Family Code § 6500.
Person defined for purposes of this Code, see Family Code § 105.

§ 7142. Liability of public entities or employees

No public entity or employee is liable for any loss or injury resulting directly or indirectly from false or inaccurate information contained in the Department of Motor Vehicles records system or identification cards as provided in this part. *(Stats.1992, c. 162 (A.B.2650), § 10, operative Jan. 1, 1994.)*

§ 7143. Notification to Department of Motor Vehicles upon voiding or rescission of declaration of emancipation; invalidation of identification cards

If a declaration of emancipation is voided or rescinded, notice shall be sent immediately to the Department of Motor Vehicles which shall remove the information relating to emancipation in its law enforcement computer network. Any identification card issued stating emancipation shall be invalidated. *(Stats.1992, c. 162 (A.B. 2650), § 10, operative Jan. 1, 1994.)*

Division 12

PARENT AND CHILD RELATIONSHIP

Part	Section
1. Rights of Parents	7500
2. Presumption Concerning Child of Marriage and Genetic Testing to Determine Parentage	7540
3. Uniform Parentage Act	7600
4. Freedom from Parental Custody and Control	7800
5. Interstate Compact on Placement of Children	7900
6. Foster Care Placement Considerations	7950
7. Surrogacy and Donor Facilitators, Assisted Reproduction Agreements for Gestational Carriers, and Oocyte Donations	7960

Cross References

Adjudication of parentage, establishment of new birth certificate, see Health and Safety Code § 102725.
Adoption,
  Adoptive parent defined, see Family Code § 8503.
  Cessation of birth parents' responsibilities toward child, see Family Code § 8617.
  Legal relationship of adoptive parents and adults or married minors, see Family Code § 9305.
  Legal relationship of adoptive parents and unmarried minor child, see Family Code § 8616.
Birth parent defined, see Family Code § 8512.
Child defined for purposes of the Probate Code, see Probate Code § 26.
Child defined for purposes of the Uniform Interstate Family Support Act, see Family Code § 5700.102.
Child support, equal duty of parents to support child, see Family Code § 3900.
Child support enforcement, California Parent Locator Service and Central Registry, see Family Code § 17506.
Disclosure of records establishing parent and child relationship,
  Child abduction records, see Family Code § 17514.
  Support services, see Family Code § 17212.
Hearsay exceptions, statements concerning family history, see Evidence Code § 1310 et seq.
Intestate succession, parent and child relationship,
  Natural parents, see Probate Code § 6453.
  Out-of-wedlock births, conditions for inheritance based on relationship, see Probate Code § 6452.
  Relationship severed by adoption, see Probate Code § 6451.
Parent defined for purposes of the Probate Code, see Probate Code § 54.
Parent or guardian defined, see Family Code § 6903.
Presumption affecting the burden of proof defined, see Evidence Code § 605.

Void marriages, incest, see Family Code § 2200.

Part 1
RIGHTS OF PARENTS

Section
7500. Services and earnings of child.
7501. Residence of children; determination by parents; restrictions; public policy.
7502. Property of child; control.
7503. Payment of earnings to minor.
7504. Relinquishment of parental rights; abandonment.
7505. Parental authority; termination.
7506. Support of adult child; compensation.
7507. Abuse of parental authority; remedy.

Cross References

Freedom from parental custody and control, stay of proceedings and effect upon jurisdiction under these provisions, see Family Code § 7807.
Termination of parental rights of father, filing of petition, stay of proceedings affecting a child pending final determination of parental rights, see Family Code § 7662.

§ 7500. Services and earnings of child

(a) The mother of an unemancipated minor child, and the father, if presumed to be the father under Section 7611, are equally entitled to the services and earnings of the child.

(b) If one parent is dead, is unable or refuses to take custody, or has abandoned the child, the other parent is entitled to the services and earnings of the child.

(c) This section shall not apply to any services or earnings of an unemancipated minor child related to a contract of a type described in Section 6750. *(Added by Stats.1993, c. 219 (A.B.1500), § 162. Amended by Stats.1999, c. 940 (S.B.1162), § 8.)*

Cross References

Emancipated minor, description, see Family Code § 7002.
Freedom from parental custody and control, stay of proceedings and effect upon jurisdiction under these provisions, see Family Code § 7807.
Minor defined for purposes of this Code, see Family Code § 6500.

§ 7501. Residence of children; determination by parents; restrictions; public policy

(a) A parent entitled to the custody of a child has a right to change the residence of the child, subject to the power of the court to restrain a removal that would prejudice the rights or welfare of the child.

(b) It is the intent of the Legislature to affirm the decision in In re Marriage of Burgess (1996) 13 Cal.4th 25, and to declare that ruling to be the public policy and law of this state. *(Added by Stats.1993, c. 219 (A.B.1500), § 164. Amended by Stats.2003, c. 674 (S.B.156), § 1.)*

Cross References

State defined for purposes of this Code, see Family Code § 145.

Research References

Forms
1 California Transactions Forms--Family Law § 2:74, Move-Away Cases.
1 California Transactions Forms--Family Law § 3:16, Identifying Areas of Parental Decision Making and Participation.
1 California Transactions Forms--Family Law § 3:18, Overview.
1 California Transactions Forms--Family Law § 3:76, Procedure in Event of Moveaway.
West's California Code Forms, Family § 7500, Comment Overview—Rights of Parents.

West's California Code Forms, Family § 7501 Form 1, Notice of Motion and Supporting Declaration for Order Restraining Change of Residence of Child.
West's California Code Forms, Family § 7501 Form 2, Order Restraining Change of Residence of Child.

§ 7502. Property of child; control

The parent, as such, has no control over the property of the child. *(Added by Stats.1993, c. 219 (A.B.1500), § 165.)*

Cross References

Property defined for purposes of this Code, see Family Code § 113.

§ 7503. Payment of earnings to minor

The employer of a minor shall pay the earnings of the minor to the minor until the parent or guardian entitled to the earnings gives the employer notice that the parent or guardian claims the earnings. *(Added by Stats.1993, c. 219 (A.B.1500), § 166.)*

Cross References

Guardian defined, see Probate Code §§ 2350, 2400.
Minor defined for purposes of this Code, see Family Code § 6500.
Parent or guardian defined, see Family Code § 6903.

Research References

Forms
West's California Code Forms, Family § 7503 Form 1, Notice by Parent or Guardian Claiming Wages of Child.

§ 7504. Relinquishment of parental rights; abandonment

The parent, whether solvent or insolvent, may relinquish to the child the right of controlling the child and receiving the child's earnings. Abandonment by the parent is presumptive evidence of that relinquishment. *(Added by Stats.1993, c. 219 (A.B.1500), § 167.)*

Research References

Forms
West's California Code Forms, Family § 7500, Comment Overview—Rights of Parents.

§ 7505. Parental authority; termination

The authority of a parent ceases on any of the following:

(a) The appointment, by a court, of a guardian of the person of the child.

(b) The marriage of the child.

(c) The child attaining the age of majority. *(Added by Stats.1993, c. 219 (A.B.1500), § 168.)*

Cross References

Age of majority, see Family Code § 6500 et seq.
Person defined for purposes of this Code, see Family Code § 105.

Research References

Forms
West's California Code Forms, Family § 7500, Comment Overview—Rights of Parents.

§ 7506. Support of adult child; compensation

Where a child, after attaining the age of majority, continues to serve and to be supported by the parent, neither party is entitled to compensation, in the absence of an agreement for the compensation. *(Added by Stats.1993, c. 219 (A.B.1500), § 169.)*

§ 7506 PARENT AND CHILD RELATIONSHIP

Cross References

Age of majority, see Family Code § 6500 et seq.

Research References

Forms

West's California Code Forms, Family § 7506, Comment Overview—Support of Adult Child.

§ 7507. Abuse of parental authority; remedy

The abuse of parental authority is the subject of judicial cognizance in a civil action brought by the child, or by the child's relative within the third degree, or by the supervisors of the county where the child resides; and when the abuse is established, the child may be freed from the dominion of the parent, and the duty of support and education enforced. *(Added by Stats.1993, c. 219 (A.B.1500), § 170.)*

Cross References

Abuse defined for purposes of the Domestic Violence Protection Act, see Family Code § 6203.
County defined for purposes of this Code, see Family Code § 67.
Support defined for purposes of this Code, see Family Code § 150.

Research References

Forms

West's California Code Forms, Family § 7500, Comment Overview—Rights of Parents.

Part 2

PRESUMPTION CONCERNING CHILD OF MARRIAGE AND GENETIC TESTING TO DETERMINE PARENTAGE

Chapter	Section
1. Child of Wife Cohabiting With Husband	7540
2. Genetic Testing to Determine Parentage	7550
3. Establishment of Parentage by Voluntary Declaration	7570

Cross References

Assisted reproduction agreements for gestational carriers, rebuttal of presumptions, see Family Code § 7962.
Freedom from parental custody and control, stay of proceedings and effect upon jurisdiction under these provisions, see Family Code § 7807.
Termination of parental rights of father, filing of petition, stay of proceedings affecting a child under these provisions pending final determination of parental rights of the father, see Family Code § 7662.

CHAPTER 1. CHILD OF WIFE COHABITING WITH HUSBAND

Section
7540. Conclusive presumption as child of marriage; exceptions.
7541. Resolution of question of parentage upon finding of court based upon genetic testing that spouse who is presumed parent is not genetic parent of child; action to challenge parentage.

Cross References

Action to determine existence or nonexistence of father and child relationship, exception for cases under this Chapter, see Family Code § 7630.
Consent required for adoption, presumed fathers, see Family Code § 8604.

§ 7540. Conclusive presumption as child of marriage; exceptions

(a) Except as provided in Section 7541, the child of spouses who cohabited at the time of conception and birth is conclusively presumed to be a child of the marriage.

(b) The conclusive marital presumption in subdivision (a) does not apply if the court determines that the husband of the woman who gave birth was impotent or sterile at the time of conception and that the child was not conceived through assisted reproduction. *(Added by Stats.2018, c. 876 (A.B.2684), § 5, eff. Jan. 1, 2019.)*

Cross References

Hearsay exceptions, statements concerning family history, see Evidence Code § 1310 et seq.
Presumption affecting burden of proof, establishment of parent and child relationship, see Evidence Code § 605.
Presumptions,
  Rebuttable presumption, natural father, see Family Code § 7612.
  Status as natural father, see Family Code § 7611.
References to husband, wife, spouses and married persons, persons included for purposes of this Code, see Family Code § 11.
Uniform Parentage Act, setting aside or vacating judgment of paternity, see Family Code § 7646.
Void voluntary declaration of parentage, conditions, notice, see Family Code § 7573.5.

Research References

Forms

California Practice Guide: Rutter Family Law Forms Form 6:4, Request for Order Re Genetic Testing.
1 California Transactions Forms--Family Law § 3:126, Request for Hearing and Application to Set Aside Voluntary Declaration of Paternity [Form FL-280].
1 California Transactions Forms--Family Law § 3:126.50, Information Sheet for Completing Request for Hearing and Application to Set Aside Voluntary Declaration of Paternity [Form FL-281].
1 California Transactions Forms--Family Law § 3:127, Responsive Declaration to Application to Set Aside Voluntary Declaration of Paternity [Form FL-285].
1 California Transactions Forms--Family Law § 3:128, Order After Hearing on Motion to Set Aside Voluntary Declaration of Paternity [Form FL-290].
1 California Transactions Forms--Family Law § 4:105, Declaration of Paternity.
2 California Transactions Forms--Family Law § 5:4, Rights of De Facto Parents.
2 California Transactions Forms--Family Law § 5:9, Use of Parenting Agreement to Define Rights and Responsibilities Relating to Child on Termination of Partners' Relationship Where Both Partners Are Biological Parents.
2 California Transactions Forms--Family Law § 5:9.50, Voiding of a Voluntary Declaration of Parentage.
2 California Transactions Forms--Family Law § 6:3, Definitions.
2 California Transactions Forms--Family Law § 6:8, Consent for Adoption of Unmarried Minor.
2 California Transactions Forms--Family Law § 6:11, Initiating Proceeding Under Uniform Parentage Act [Fam. Code, §§7600 to 7730].
2 California Transactions Forms--Family Law § 6:40, Structuring the Adoption.
2 California Transactions Forms--Family Law § 6:47, Matters to Consider in Drafting Petition for Independent Adoption of Unmarried Minor.
2 California Transactions Forms--Family Law § 6:72, Petition to Terminate Parental Rights of Alleged Father.
2 California Transactions Forms--Family Law § 6:74, Petition to Terminate Parental Rights of Alleged Father Served With Notice of Alleged Paternity Without Timely Response.
2 California Transactions Forms--Family Law § 6:75, Order Terminating Parental Rights of Alleged Father Served With Notice of Alleged Paternity Without Timely Response.
2 California Transactions Forms--Family Law § 6:76, Ex Parte Application for Order to Terminate Parental Rights of Alleged Father Who Waived Notice or Denied Paternity.
2 California Transactions Forms--Family Law § 7:8, Traditional Surrogacy Agreements.

2 California Transactions Forms--Family Law § 7:45, Artificial Insemination Surrogacy Agreement Between Intended Father and Surrogate Couple.
2 California Transactions Forms--Family Law § 7:46, In Vitro Surrogacy Agreement Between Intended Parents and Surrogate Couple; Intended Parents Are Genetic Parents.
2 California Transactions Forms--Family Law § 7:47, In Vitro Fertilization Surrogacy Agreement Between Intended Mother and Surrogate Using Donated Genetic Material.
2 California Transactions Forms--Family Law § 7:60, Overview; Paternity of Child [Fam C § 7613].
West's California Code Forms, Family § 7540, Comment Overview—Conclusive Presumption as Child of Marriage.
West's California Code Forms, Family § 7610, Comment Overview—Establishing Parent and Child Relationship.
West's California Code Forms, Family § 7645, Comment Overview—Setting Aside or Vacating Judgment of Paternity.
West's California Judicial Council Forms JV–505, Statement Regarding Parentage (Juvenile) (Also Available in Spanish).

§ 7541. Resolution of question of parentage upon finding of court based upon genetic testing that spouse who is presumed parent is not genetic parent of child; action to challenge parentage

(a) If the court finds that the spouse who is a presumed parent under Section 7540 is not a genetic parent of the child pursuant to Chapter 2 (commencing with Section 7550), the question of parentage shall be resolved in accordance with all other applicable provisions of this division, including, but not limited to, Section 7612.

(b) An action to challenge the parentage of the spouse who is a presumed parent under Section 7540 shall be filed and served not later than two years from the child's date of birth and may only be filed by any of the following:

(1) By either spouse.

(2) By a person who is a presumed parent under Section 7611 or by the child, through or by the child's guardian ad litem, to establish the parentage of the person who is a presumed parent under Section 7611.

(c) The petition or motion to challenge a presumption under Section 7540 pursuant to this section shall be supported by a declaration under oath submitted by the moving party stating the factual basis for placing the issue of parentage before the court.

(d) Genetic testing may not be used to challenge parentage, in either of the following cases:

(1) A case that reached final judgment of parentage on or before September 30, 1980.

(2) A case challenging the parentage of a spouse who is a parent pursuant to Section 7962 or subdivision (a) of Section 7613, except to resolve a dispute regarding whether the child was conceived through assisted reproduction. *(Formerly § 7501, enacted by Stats.1992, c. 162 (A.B.2650), § 10, operative Jan. 1, 1994. Renumbered § 7541 and amended by Stats.1993, c. 219 (A.B.1500), § 163. Amended by Stats.1998, c. 581 (A.B.2801), § 18; Stats.2018, c. 876 (A.B.2684), § 6, eff. Jan. 1, 2019; Stats.2019, c. 115 (A.B.1817), § 80, eff. Jan. 1, 2020.)*

Cross References

Hearsay exceptions, statements concerning family history, see Evidence Code § 1310 et seq.
Judgment and order defined for purposes of this Code, see Family Code § 100.
Presumption affecting the burden of proof defined, see Evidence Code § 605.
References to husband, wife, spouses and married persons, persons included for purposes of this Code, see Family Code § 11.

Research References

Forms

California Practice Guide: Rutter Family Law Forms Form 6:4, Request for Order Re Genetic Testing.
2 California Transactions Forms--Family Law § 6:3, Definitions.
2 California Transactions Forms--Family Law § 6:11, Initiating Proceeding Under Uniform Parentage Act [Fam. Code, §§7600 to 7730].

2 California Transactions Forms--Family Law § 7:45, Artificial Insemination Surrogacy Agreement Between Intended Father and Surrogate Couple.
2 California Transactions Forms--Family Law § 7:46, In Vitro Surrogacy Agreement Between Intended Parents and Surrogate Couple; Intended Parents Are Genetic Parents.
2 California Transactions Forms--Family Law § 7:47, In Vitro Fertilization Surrogacy Agreement Between Intended Mother and Surrogate Using Donated Genetic Material.
2 California Transactions Forms--Family Law § 7:60, Overview; Paternity of Child [Fam C § 7613].
2 California Transactions Forms--Family Law § 7:64, Exception to Application of Fam C § 7613 in Certain Surrogacy Cases.
2 California Transactions Forms--Family Law § 7:72, Parentage.
West's California Code Forms, Family § 7540, Comment Overview—Conclusive Presumption as Child of Marriage.
West's California Judicial Council Forms JV–505, Statement Regarding Parentage (Juvenile) (Also Available in Spanish).

CHAPTER 2. GENETIC TESTING TO DETERMINE PARENTAGE

Section
7550.   Application of chapter.
7550.5. Definitions.
7551.   Order for genetic tests in civil actions involving parentage; exceptions; applications.
7551.5. Genetic test facilitation for enforcement purposes.
7552.   Type of genetic testing; qualifications of experts performing tests; specimen used in testing; selection of frequencies for use in calculating relationship index; additional testing.
7552.5. Genetic test results; copy to parties; declaration; admittance into evidence without foundation; written objections; expert witnesses.
7553.   Compensation of experts.
7554.   Determination of parentage.
7555.   Person identified as genetic parent; challenge to genetic testing results; more than one person, other than mother, identified as genetic parent.
7556.   Application of part to criminal actions.
7557.   Right of parties to produce other expert evidence; payment of fees.
7558.   Administrative order for genetic testing.
7559.   Payment of cost of initial genetic testing.
7560.   Additional genetic testing upon request of person who contests results of initial testing.
7562.   Genetic testing of deceased person.

Cross References

Parent and child relationship, setting aside or vacating judgment of paternity, established father not biological father, see Family Code § 7648.
Uniform act, construction of provisions, see Family Code § 3.
Uniform Parentage Act, see Family Code § 7600 et seq.

§ 7550. Application of chapter

This chapter shall govern both of the following:

(a) The genetic testing of a person who either voluntarily submits to genetic testing or is ordered to submit to genetic testing pursuant to an order of a court or local child support agency.

(b) The use of genetic testing in a proceeding to determine parentage. *(Added by Stats.2018, c. 876 (A.B.2684), § 9, eff. Jan. 1, 2019.)*

Research References

Forms

2 California Transactions Forms--Family Law § 6:2, Governing Law.

2 California Transactions Forms--Family Law § 6:11, Initiating Proceeding Under Uniform Parentage Act [Fam. Code, §§7600 to 7730].

§ 7550.5. Definitions

The following definitions shall apply to this chapter:

(a) "Combined relationship index" means the product of all tested relationship indices.

(b) "Ethnic or racial group" means, for the purpose of genetic testing, a recognized group that a person identifies as the person's ancestry, or part of the ancestry, or that is identified by other information.

(c) "Genetic testing" means any genetic testing that complies with Section 7552.

(d) "Hypothesized genetic relationship" means an asserted genetic relationship between a person and a child.

(e) "Probability of parentage" means, for the ethnic or racial group to which a person alleged to be a parent belongs, the probability that a hypothesized genetic relationship is supported, compared to the probability that a genetic relationship is supported between the child and a random person of the ethnic or racial group used in the hypothesized genetic relationship, expressed as a percentage incorporating the combined relationship index and a prior probability.

(f) "Relationship index" means a likelihood ratio that compares the probability of a genetic marker given a hypothesized genetic relationship and the probability of the genetic marker given a genetic relationship between the child and a random person of the ethnic or racial group used in the hypothesized genetic relationship. *(Added by Stats.2018, c. 876 (A.B.2684), § 10, eff. Jan. 1, 2019.)*

§ 7551. Order for genetic tests in civil actions involving parentage; exceptions; applications

(a) Except as provided in subdivisions (b) and (c), in a civil action or proceeding in which parentage is a relevant fact, the court may, upon its own initiative or upon suggestion made by or on behalf of any person who is involved, and shall upon motion of any party to the action or proceeding made at a time so as not to delay the proceedings unduly, order the woman who gave birth, the child, and the alleged genetic parent to submit to genetic testing.

(b)(1) Genetic testing shall not be used for any of the following purposes:

(A) To challenge the parentage of a person who is a parent pursuant to subdivision (a) of Section 7613, except to resolve a dispute whether the child was conceived through assisted reproduction.

(B) To challenge the parentage of a person who is a parent pursuant to Section 7962, except to resolve a dispute whether the gestational carrier surrogate is a genetic parent.

(C) To establish the parentage of a person who is a donor pursuant to subdivision (b) or (c) of Section 7613, except to resolve a dispute whether the child was conceived through assisted reproduction.

(2) If the child has a presumed parent pursuant to Section 7540, a motion for genetic testing is governed by Section 7541.

(3) If the child has a parent whose parentage has been previously established in a judgment, a request for genetic testing shall be governed by Section 7647.7.

(4) A court shall not order genetic testing if the genetic testing would be used to establish the parentage of a person who is prohibited under this division from establishing parentage based on evidence of genetic testing.

(c) A court shall not order in utero genetic testing.

(d) In any case under this division in which genetic testing is ordered, the following shall apply:

(1) If a party refuses to submit to genetic testing, the court may resolve the question of parentage against that party or enforce its order if the rights of others and the interests of justice so require.

(2) The refusal of a party to submit to genetic testing is admissible in evidence in any proceeding to determine parentage.

(3) If two or more persons are subject to court-ordered genetic testing, the court may order that the testing be completed concurrently or sequentially.

(4) Genetic testing of a woman who gave birth to a child is not a condition precedent to the testing of the child and a person whose genetic parentage of the child is being determined. If the woman is unavailable for genetic testing, the court may order genetic testing of the child and each person whose genetic parentage of the child is at issue.

(5) An order under this division for genetic testing is enforceable by contempt. *(Added by Stats.2018, c. 876 (A.B.2684), § 12, eff. Jan. 1, 2019.)*

Cross References

Aid and medical assistance, eligibility, submission to genetic testing to determine paternity, see Welfare and Institutions Code § 11477.
Child support commissioners, paternity, power to order genetic tests, see Family Code § 4251.
Child support enforcement proceedings, continuance allowed for genetic testing, see Family Code § 17404.
Civil action, definition includes civil proceeding, see Evidence Code § 120.
Evidence, discretion of court to exclude, see Evidence Code § 352.
Evidence, only relevant evidence admissible, see Evidence Code § 350.
Judgment and order defined for purposes of this Code, see Family Code § 100.
Person defined for purposes of this Code, see Family Code § 105.
Presumption as natural father, evidence rebutting presumption, see Family Code § 7612.
Presumption as natural father, status, see Family Code § 7611.
Proceeding defined for purposes of this Code, see Family Code § 110.
State defined for purposes of this Code, see Family Code § 145.
Support orders, issuance, paternity established through genetic testing, see Family Code § 5700.401.
Uniform act, construction of provisions, see Family Code § 3.

Research References

Forms

California Practice Guide: Rutter Family Law Forms Form 6:4, Request for Order Re Genetic Testing.
West's California Code Forms, Family § 7550, Comment Overview—Blood Tests to Determine Parentage.
West's California Judicial Council Forms FL–627, Order for Genetic (Parentage) Testing.
West's California Judicial Council Forms FL–684, Request for Order and Supporting Declaration (Governmental).

§ 7551.5. Genetic test facilitation for enforcement purposes

All hospitals, local child support agencies, welfare offices, and family courts shall facilitate genetic tests for purposes of enforcement of this chapter. This may include having a health care professional available for purposes of extracting samples to be used for genetic testing. *(Added by Stats.1999, c. 652 (S.B.240), § 6.)*

Cross References

Support defined for purposes of this Code, see Family Code § 150.
Uniform act, construction of provisions, see Family Code § 3.

§ 7552. Type of genetic testing; qualifications of experts performing tests; specimen used in testing; selection of frequencies for use in calculating relationship index; additional testing

(a) Genetic testing shall be of a type reasonably relied on by experts in the field of genetic testing and performed in a testing laboratory accredited by either of the following:

(1) The AABB, formerly known as the American Association of Blood Banks, or a successor organization.

(2) An accrediting body designated by the Secretary of the United States Department of Health and Human Services.

(b) A specimen used in genetic testing may consist of a sample or a combination of samples of blood, buccal cells, bone, hair, or other body tissue or fluid. The specimen used in the testing need not be of the same kind for each person undergoing genetic testing.

(c) Based on the ethnic or racial group of a person undergoing genetic testing, a testing laboratory shall determine the databases from which to select frequencies for use in calculating a relationship index. If a person or a local child support agency objects to the laboratory's choice, the following rules shall apply:

(1) Not later than 30 days after receipt of the report of the test, the objecting person or local child support agency may request the court to require the laboratory to recalculate the relationship index using an ethnic or racial group different from that used by the laboratory.

(2) The person or local child support agency objecting to the choice of laboratories under this subdivision shall do either of the following:

(A) If the requested frequencies are not available to the laboratory for the ethnic or racial group requested, provide the requested frequencies compiled in a manner recognized by accrediting bodies.

(B) Engage another laboratory to perform the calculations.

(3) The laboratory may use its own statistical estimate if there is a question of which ethnic or racial group is appropriate. The laboratory shall calculate the frequencies using statistics, if available, for any other ethnic or racial group requested.

(d) If, after recalculation of the relationship index pursuant to subdivision (c) using a different ethnic or racial group, genetic testing does not identify a person as a genetic parent of the child, the court may require a person who has been tested to submit to additional genetic testing to identify a genetic parent. *(Added by Stats.2018, c. 876 (A.B.2684), § 14, eff. Jan. 1, 2019.)*

Cross References

Appointment of expert witnesses, generally, see Evidence Code § 730 et seq.
Civil action, defined to include civil proceeding, see Evidence Code § 120.
Evidence, discretion of court to exclude, see Evidence Code § 352.
Evidence, only relevant evidence admissible, see Evidence Code § 350.
Examination of expert witnesses, see Evidence Code §§ 721, 722, 801 et seq.
Examination of witnesses, generally, see Evidence Code § 760 et seq.
Judgment and order defined for purposes of this Code, see Family Code § 100.
Person defined for purposes of this Code, see Family Code § 105.
State defined for purposes of this Code, see Family Code § 145.
Uniform act, construction of provisions, see Family Code § 3.

Research References

Forms

California Practice Guide: Rutter Family Law Forms Form 6:4, Request for Order Re Genetic Testing.

§ 7552.5. Genetic test results; copy to parties; declaration; admittance into evidence without foundation; written objections; expert witnesses

(a) A copy of the results of all genetic testing performed under Section 7551 or 7558 shall be served upon all parties, by any method of service authorized under Chapter 5 (commencing with Section 1010) of Title 14 of Part 2 of the Code of Civil Procedure except personal service, no later than 20 days prior to a hearing in which the genetic test results may be admitted into evidence. The genetic test results shall be accompanied by a declaration under penalty of perjury of the custodian of records or other qualified employee of the laboratory that conducted the genetic tests, stating in substance each of the following:

(1) The declarant is the duly authorized custodian of the records or other qualified employee of the laboratory, and has authority to certify the records.

(2) A statement that establishes in detail the chain of custody of all genetic samples collected, including the date on which the genetic sample was collected, the identity of each person from whom a genetic sample was collected, the identity of the person who performed or witnessed the collecting of the genetic samples and packaged them for transmission to the laboratory, the date on which the genetic samples were received by the laboratory, the identity of the person who unpacked the samples and forwarded them to the person who performed the laboratory analysis of the genetic sample, and the identification and qualifications of all persons who performed the laboratory analysis and published the results.

(3) A statement that establishes that the procedures used by the laboratory to conduct the tests for which the test results are attached are used in the laboratory's ordinary course of business to ensure accuracy and proper identification of genetic samples.

(4) The genetic test results were prepared at or near the time of completion of the genetic tests by personnel of the business qualified to perform genetic tests in the ordinary course of business.

(b) The genetic test results shall be admitted into evidence at the hearing or trial to establish parentage, without the need for foundation testimony of authenticity and accuracy, unless a written objection to the genetic test results is filed with the court and served on all other parties, by a party no later than five days prior to the hearing or trial in which parentage is at issue.

(c) If a written objection is filed with the court and served on all parties within the time specified in subdivision (b), experts appointed by the court shall be called by the court as witnesses to testify to their findings and are subject to cross-examination by the parties. *(Added by Stats.1994, c. 1266 (A.B.3804), § 3.7. Amended by Stats.1997, c. 599 (A.B.573), § 38; Stats.1999, c. 652 (S.B.240), § 7; Stats.2018, c. 876 (A.B.2684), § 15, eff. Jan. 1, 2019.)*

Cross References

Evidence, discretion of court to exclude, see Evidence Code § 352.
Evidence, only relevant evidence admissible, see Evidence Code § 350.
Person defined for purposes of this Code, see Family Code § 105.
Uniform act, construction of provisions, see Family Code § 3.

Research References

Forms

California Practice Guide: Rutter Family Law Forms Form 6:4, Request for Order Re Genetic Testing.
West's California Judicial Council Forms FL–627, Order for Genetic (Parentage) Testing.

§ 7553. Compensation of experts

(a) The compensation of each expert witness appointed by the court shall be fixed at a reasonable amount. It shall be paid as the court shall order. Except as provided in subdivision (b), the court may order that it be paid by the parties in the proportions and at the times the court prescribes, or that the proportion of any party be paid by the county, and that, after payment by the parties or the county or both, all or part or none of it be taxed as costs in the action or proceeding.

(b) If the expert witness is appointed for the court's needs, the compensation shall be paid by the court. *(Stats.1992, c. 162 (A.B.2650), § 10, operative Jan. 1, 1994. Amended by Stats.2012, c. 470 (A.B.1529), § 22.)*

Cross References

Appointment of expert witnesses, generally, see Evidence Code § 730 et seq.
Attorney's fees and costs, generally, see Family Code § 270 et seq.
Civil action defined to include civil proceeding, see Evidence Code § 120.
Compensation of witnesses, see Government Code § 68092.5.

§ 7553

County defined for purposes of this Code, see Family Code § 67.
Judgment and order defined for purposes of this Code, see Family Code § 100.
Proceeding defined for purposes of this Code, see Family Code § 110.
Uniform act, construction of provisions, see Family Code § 3.

§ 7554. Determination of parentage

(a) If the woman who gave birth to the child is the only other person who is a parent or has a claim to parentage of the child under this division, the court shall find the person who is the alleged father or genetic parent who is not a donor under Section 7613 to be a parent of the child if the person meets any of the following:

(1) Is identified pursuant to Section 7555 as a genetic parent of the child and the identification is not successfully challenged.

(2) Admits parentage in a pleading, when making an appearance, or during a hearing, the court accepts the admission, and the court determines that the person is a genetic parent of the child.

(3) Declines to submit to genetic testing ordered by the court or a local child support agency, in which case, the court may find that the person is a parent of the child even if the person denies a genetic relationship with the child.

(4) Is in default after service of process and the court determines the person to be a genetic parent of the child.

(5) Is neither identified nor excluded as a genetic parent by genetic testing and, based on other evidence, the court determines the person to be a genetic parent of the child.

(b) If more than one person other than the woman who gave birth asserts a claim under this division to be the child's parent, parentage shall be determined under provisions of this division. *(Added by Stats.2018, c. 876 (A.B.2684), § 17, eff. Jan. 1, 2019. Amended by Stats.2019, c. 115 (A.B.1817), § 81, eff. Jan. 1, 2020.)*

Cross References

Aid and medical assistance, eligibility, submission to genetic testing to determine paternity, see Welfare and Institutions Code § 11477.
Child support commissioners, paternity, power to order genetic tests, see Family Code § 4251.
Child support enforcement proceedings, continuance allowed for genetic testing, see Family Code § 17404.
Civil action, definition includes civil proceeding, see Evidence Code § 120.
Evidence, discretion of court to exclude, see Evidence Code § 352.
Evidence, only relevant evidence admissible, see Evidence Code § 350.
Hearsay exceptions, statements concerning family history, see Evidence Code § 1310 et seq.
Intestate succession, parent and child relationship,
 Natural parents, see Probate Code § 6453.
 Out-of-wedlock births, conditions for inheritance based on relationship, see Probate Code § 6452.
 Relationship severed by adoption, see Probate Code § 6451.
Presumed father and child relationship, written promise to furnish support, enforceability, see Family Code § 7614.
Presumption affecting the burden of proof defined, see Evidence Code § 605.
Presumption as natural father, evidence rebutting presumption, see Family Code § 7612.
Presumption as natural father, status, see Family Code § 7611.
Support orders, issuance, paternity established through genetic testing, see Family Code § 5700.401.
Uniform act, construction of provisions, see Family Code § 3.

§ 7555. Person identified as genetic parent; challenge to genetic testing results; more than one person, other than mother, identified as genetic parent

(a) Subject to a challenge under subdivision (b), a person is identified under this part as a genetic parent of a child if genetic testing complies with this part and the results of the testing disclose both of the following:

(1) The person has at least a 99 percent probability of parentage, using a prior probability of 0.50, as calculated by using the combined relationship index obtained in the testing.

(2) A combined relationship index of at least 100 to 1.

(b) A person identified pursuant to subdivision (a) as a genetic parent of the child may challenge the genetic testing results only by other genetic testing satisfying the requirements of this chapter that either excludes the person as a genetic parent of the child or identifies another person as a possible genetic parent of the child other than the woman who gave birth to the child or the person challenging parentage.

(c) If more than one person, other than the woman who gave birth to the child, is identified by genetic testing as a possible genetic parent of the child, the court shall order each person to submit to further genetic testing to identify a genetic parent. *(Added by Stats.2018, c. 876 (A.B.2684), § 19, eff. Jan. 1, 2019.)*

Cross References

Burden of proof, generally, see Evidence Code § 500 et seq.
Hearsay exceptions, statements concerning family history, see Evidence Code § 1310 et seq.
Presumed father and child relationship, written promise to furnish support, enforceability, see Family Code § 7614.
Presumption affecting the burden of proof, defined, see Evidence Code § 605.
Presumption as natural father, evidence rebutting presumption, see Family Code § 7612.
Presumption as natural father, status, see Family Code § 7611.
Uniform act, construction of provisions, see Family Code § 3.

§ 7556. Application of part to criminal actions

This part applies to criminal actions subject to the following limitations and provisions:

(a) An order for genetic testing shall be made only upon application of a party or on the court's initiative.

(b) The compensation of the experts, other than an expert witness appointed by the court for the court's needs, shall be paid by the county under order of court. The compensation of an expert witness appointed for the court's needs shall be paid by the court.

(c) The court may direct a verdict of acquittal if the person is found not to be a genetic parent pursuant to Section 7555, otherwise the case shall be submitted for determination upon all the evidence. *(Stats.1992, c. 162 (A.B.2650), § 10, operative Jan. 1, 1994. Amended by Stats.2012, c. 470 (A.B.1529), § 23; Stats.2018, c. 876 (A.B.2684), § 20, eff. Jan. 1, 2019.)*

Cross References

County defined for purposes of this Code, see Family Code § 67.
Definitions,
 Criminal action, see Evidence Code § 130.
 Evidence, see Evidence Code § 140.
Expert testimony, instruction on effect of, see Penal Code § 1127b.
Judgment and order defined for purposes of this Code, see Family Code § 100.
Uniform act, construction of provisions, see Family Code § 3.
Voluntary declaration of paternity by minor parents, inadmissible in certain criminal prosecutions, see Family Code § 7577.

§ 7557. Right of parties to produce other expert evidence; payment of fees

Nothing in this part prevents a party to an action or proceeding from producing other expert evidence on the matter covered by this part; but, where other expert witnesses are called by a party to the action or proceeding, their fees shall be paid by the party calling them and only ordinary witness fees shall be taxed as costs in the action or proceeding. *(Stats.1992, c. 162 (A.B.2650), § 10, operative Jan. 1, 1994.)*

Cross References

Civil action, defined to include civil proceeding, see Evidence Code § 120.
Number of expert witnesses, limitation by court, see Evidence Code § 723.
Proceeding defined for purposes of this Code, see Family Code § 110.
Similar provisions, see Evidence Code § 733.

DETERMINATION OF PARENTAGE

Uniform act, construction of provisions, see Family Code § 3.

Research References

Forms

2 California Transactions Forms--Family Law § 6:2, Governing Law.
2 California Transactions Forms--Family Law § 6:11, Initiating Proceeding Under Uniform Parentage Act [Fam. Code, §§7600 to 7730].

§ 7558. Administrative order for genetic testing

(a) This section applies only to cases where support enforcement services are being provided by the local child support agency pursuant to Section 17400.

(b) In any civil action or proceeding in which parentage is a relevant fact, and in which the issue of parentage is contested, the local child support agency may issue an administrative order requiring the mother, child, and the alleged father to submit to genetic testing if any of the following conditions exist:

(1) The person alleging parentage has signed a statement under penalty of perjury that sets forth facts that establish a reasonable possibility that the person is the child's genetic parent.

(2) The person denying parentage has signed a statement under penalty of perjury that sets forth facts that establish a reasonable possibility that the person is not a genetic parent of the child.

(3) The alleged father has filed an answer in the action or proceeding in which parentage is a relevant fact and has requested that genetic tests be performed.

(4) The woman who gave birth to the child and the alleged father agree in writing to submit to genetic tests.

(c) Notwithstanding subdivision (b), the local child support agency may not order a person to submit to genetic tests in any of the following instances:

(1) The person has been found to have good cause for failure to cooperate in the determination of parentage pursuant to Section 11477 of the Welfare and Institutions Code.

(2) A case in which more than one person other than the woman who gave birth asserts a claim under this division to be the child's parent.

(3) A case involving a child conceived through assisted reproduction.

(d) The local child support agency shall pay the costs of any genetic tests that are ordered under subdivision (b), subject to the county obtaining a court order for reimbursement from the alleged father if parentage is established pursuant to Section 7553.

(e) This section does not prohibit a person who has been ordered by the local child support agency to submit to genetic tests pursuant to this section from filing a notice of motion with the court in the action or proceeding in which parentage is a relevant fact seeking relief from the local child support agency's order to submit to genetic tests. In that event, the court shall resolve the issue of whether genetic tests should be ordered as provided in Section 7551. When a person refuses to submit to the tests after receipt of the administrative order pursuant to this section and fails to seek relief from the court from the administrative order either prior to the scheduled tests or within 10 days after the tests are scheduled, the court may resolve the question of parentage against that person or enforce the administrative order if the rights of others or the interest of justice so require. Except as provided in subdivision (c), a person's refusal to submit to tests ordered by the local child support agency is admissible in evidence in any proceeding to determine parentage if a notice of motion is not filed within the timeframes specified in this subdivision.

(f) If the original test result is contested, the local child support agency shall order an additional test only upon request and advance payment of the contestant.

(g) The local child support agency shall not order in utero genetic testing.

(h) The local child support agency shall administer this section consistent with federal law. *(Added by Stats.1997, c. 599 (A.B.573), § 40. Amended by Stats.2000, c. 808 (A.B.1358), § 72, eff. Sept. 28, 2000; Stats.2018, c. 876 (A.B.2684), § 21, eff. Jan. 1, 2019.)*

Cross References

Child support enforcement proceedings, continuance allowed for genetic testing, see Family Code § 17404.
County defined for purposes of this Code, see Family Code § 67.
Judgment and order defined for purposes of this Code, see Family Code § 100.
Person defined for purposes of this Code, see Family Code § 105.
Proceeding defined for purposes of this Code, see Family Code § 110.
Support defined for purposes of this Code, see Family Code § 150.
Uniform act, construction of provisions, see Family Code § 3.

§ 7559. Payment of cost of initial genetic testing

Payment of the cost of initial genetic testing shall be made in advance when agreed to by the parties or ordered by the court pursuant to Section 7640. *(Added by Stats.2018, c. 876 (A.B.2684), § 22, eff. Jan. 1, 2019.)*

§ 7560. Additional genetic testing upon request of person who contests results of initial testing

The court or local child support agency shall order additional genetic testing upon the request of a person who contests the results of the initial testing under Section 7555. *(Added by Stats.2018, c. 876 (A.B.2684), § 23, eff. Jan. 1, 2019.)*

§ 7562. Genetic testing of deceased person

If a person seeking genetic testing demonstrates good cause, the court may order genetic testing of a deceased person. *(Added by Stats.2018, c. 876 (A.B.2684), § 24, eff. Jan. 1, 2019.)*

CHAPTER 3. ESTABLISHMENT OF PARENTAGE BY VOLUNTARY DECLARATION

Section

7570. Legislative findings and declarations.
7571. Voluntary declaration of parentage; liability of health care provider; payment.
7572. Written informational materials; contents; regulations.
7573. Voluntary declaration of parentage; signed record; force and effect.
7573.5. Void voluntary declaration of parentage; conditions; notice.
7574. Voluntary declaration of parentage; form.
7575. Rescission of voluntary declaration of parentage; form; limitations.
7576. Challenging voluntary declaration of parentage; limitations.
7577. Rules applying to challenge of valid voluntary declaration of parentage brought by person not signatory to declaration.
7578. Parties to proceeding to challenge declaration; nonsuspension of legal responsibilities during the pendency of proceeding; new birth certificate.
7580. Voluntary declaration of parentage; minor parents; validity; rescission; presumption; admissibility.
7581. Voluntary declaration of paternity; presumption; admissibility of evidence; rebuttal; construction with other presumptions of paternity.

Cross References

Child support enforcement, opportunity to sign voluntary declaration of paternity, see Family Code § 17410.

Consent required for adoption, presumed fathers, see Family Code § 8604.

§ 7570. Legislative findings and declarations

(a) The Legislature hereby finds and declares as follows:

(1) There is a compelling state interest in establishing parentage for all children. Establishing parentage is the first step toward a child support award, which, in turn, provides children with equal rights and access to benefits, including, but not limited to, social security, health insurance, survivors' benefits, military benefits, and inheritance rights.

(2) A simple administrative system allowing for establishment of voluntary parentage will result in a significant increase in the ease of establishing parentage, a significant increase in parentage establishment, an increase in the number of children who have greater access to child support and other benefits, and a significant decrease in the time and money required to establish parentage due to the removal of the need for a lengthy and expensive court process to determine and establish parentage and is in the public interest.

(b) This section shall become operative on January 1, 2020. *(Added by Stats.2018, c. 876 (A.B.2684), § 27, eff. Jan. 1, 2019, operative Jan. 1, 2020.)*

Cross References

State defined for purposes of this Code, see Family Code § 145.
Support defined for purposes of this Code, see Family Code § 150.

Research References

Forms

5 Am. Jur. Pl. & Pr. Forms Bastards § 1, Introductory Comments.
2 California Transactions Forms--Family Law § 5:8, Effect of Birth Certificate Paternity Designation; Declaration of Paternity.
2 California Transactions Forms--Family Law § 5:9, Use of Parenting Agreement to Define Rights and Responsibilities Relating to Child on Termination of Partners' Relationship Where Both Partners Are Biological Parents.
2 California Transactions Forms--Family Law § 7:38, Parentage and Birth Certificate.
2 California Transactions Forms--Family Law § 7:86, Overview.
West's California Code Forms, Family § 7610, Comment Overview—Establishing Parent and Child Relationship.

§ 7571. Voluntary declaration of parentage; liability of health care provider; payment

(a) On and after January 1, 1995, upon the event of a live birth, prior to an unmarried mother or a mother who gave birth to a child conceived through assisted reproduction leaving a hospital, the person responsible for registering live births under Section 102405 of the Health and Safety Code shall provide to the woman giving birth and shall attempt to provide, at the place of birth, to the person identified by the woman giving birth as either the only possible genetic parent other than the woman who gave birth or the intended parent of a child conceived through assisted reproduction, a voluntary declaration of parentage together with the written materials described in Section 7572. Staff in the hospital shall witness the signatures of parents signing a voluntary declaration of parentage and shall forward the signed declaration to the Department of Child Support Services within 20 days of the date the declaration was signed. A copy of the declaration shall be made available to each of the attesting parents.

(b) A health care provider shall not be subject to civil, criminal, or administrative liability for a negligent act or omission relative to the accuracy of the information provided, or for filing the declaration with the appropriate state or local agencies.

(c) The local child support agency shall pay the sum of ten dollars ($10) to birthing hospitals and other entities that provide prenatal services for each completed declaration of parentage that is filed with the Department of Child Support Services, provided that the local child support agency and the hospital or other entity providing prenatal services has entered into a written agreement that specifies the terms and conditions for the payment as required by federal law.

(d) If the declaration is not registered by the person responsible for registering live births at the hospital, it may be completed by the attesting parents, notarized, and mailed to the Department of Child Support Services at any time after the child's birth.

(e) Prenatal clinics shall offer prospective parents the opportunity to sign a voluntary declaration of parentage. In order to be paid for their services as provided in subdivision (c), prenatal clinics must ensure that the form is witnessed and forwarded to the Department of Child Support Services within 20 days of the date the declaration was signed.

(f) Declarations shall be made available without charge at all local child support agency offices, offices of local registrars of births and deaths, courts, and county welfare departments within this state. Staff in these offices shall witness the signatures of parents wishing to sign a voluntary declaration of parentage and shall be responsible for forwarding the signed declaration to the Department of Child Support Services within 20 days of the date the declaration was signed.

(g) The Department of Child Support Services, at its option, may pay the sum of ten dollars ($10) to local registrars of births and deaths, county welfare departments, or courts for each completed declaration of parentage that is witnessed by staff in these offices and filed with the Department of Child Support Services. In order to receive payment, the Department of Child Support Services and the entity shall enter into a written agreement that specifies the terms and conditions for payment as required by federal law. The Department of Child Support Services shall study the effect of the ten dollar ($10) payment on obtaining completed voluntary declaration of parentage forms.

(h) The Department of Child Support Services and local child support agencies shall publicize the availability of the declarations. The local child support agency shall make the declaration, together with the written materials described in subdivision (a) of Section 7572, available upon request to any parent and any agency or organization that is required to offer parents the opportunity to sign a voluntary declaration of parentage. The local child support agency shall also provide qualified staff to answer parents' questions regarding the declaration and the process of establishing parentage.

(i) Copies of the declaration and any rescissions filed with the Department of Child Support Services shall be made available only to the parents, the child, the local child support agency, the county welfare department, the county counsel, the State Department of Public Health, and the courts.

(j) Publicly funded or licensed health clinics, pediatric offices, Head Start programs, child care centers, social services providers, prisons, and schools may offer parents the opportunity to sign a voluntary declaration of parentage. In order to be paid for their services as provided in subdivision (c), publicly funded or licensed health clinics, pediatric offices, Head Start programs, child care centers, social services providers, prisons, and schools shall ensure that the form is witnessed and forwarded to the Department of Child Support Services.

(k) An agency or organization required to offer parents the opportunity to sign a voluntary declaration of parentage shall also identify parents who are willing to sign, but were unavailable when the child was born. The organization shall then contact these parents within 10 days and again offer the parent the opportunity to sign a voluntary declaration of parentage.

(*l*) This section shall become operative on January 1, 2020. *(Added by Stats.2018, c. 876 (A.B.2684), § 29, eff. Jan. 1, 2019, operative Jan. 1, 2020.)*

DETERMINATION OF PARENTAGE § 7573

Cross References

Certificates of birth following adoption, legitimation, court determination of paternity, and acknowledgment, availability of records, see Health and Safety Code § 102768.
County defined for purposes of this Code, see Family Code § 67.
Department of Child Support Services, generally, see Family Code § 17000 et seq.
Department of Health Care Services, generally, see Health and Safety Code § 100100 et seq.
Judgment and order defined for purposes of this Code, see Family Code § 100.
Person defined for purposes of this Code, see Family Code § 105.
Records, certificates of birth following adoption, legitimation, court determination of paternity, and acknowledgment, addition of father's name to birth certificate, see Health and Safety Code § 102766.
State defined for purposes of this Code, see Family Code § 145.
Support defined for purposes of this Code, see Family Code § 150.

Research References

Forms

2 California Transactions Forms--Family Law § 5:9, Use of Parenting Agreement to Define Rights and Responsibilities Relating to Child on Termination of Partners' Relationship Where Both Partners Are Biological Parents.
West's California Code Forms, Family § 7570, Comment Overview—Establishment of Parentage by Voluntary Declaration.
West's California Code Forms, Family § 7574 Form 1, Voluntary Declaration of Parentage.
West's California Code Forms, Family § 7644 Form 1, Voluntary Declaration of Paternity.

§ 7572. Written informational materials; contents; regulations

(a) The Department of Child Support Services, in consultation with the State Department of Health Care Services, the California Association of Hospitals and Health Systems, and other affected health provider organizations, shall work cooperatively to develop written materials to assist providers and parents in complying with this chapter. This written material shall be updated periodically by the Department of Child Support Services to reflect changes in law, procedures, or public need.

(b) The written materials for unmarried parents or parents of a child conceived through assisted reproduction that shall be attached to the form specified in Section 7574 and shall contain the following information:

(1) A signed voluntary declaration of parentage that is filed with the Department of Child Support Services legally establishes parentage.

(2) The legal rights and obligations of both parents and the child that result from the establishment of parentage.

(3) An alleged father's constitutional rights to have the issue of parentage decided by a court; to notice of any hearing on the issue of parentage; to have an opportunity to present the alleged father's case to the court, including the right to present and cross-examine witnesses; to be represented by an attorney; and to have an attorney appointed if the alleged father cannot afford one in a parentage action filed by a local child support agency.

(4) That by signing the voluntary declaration of parentage, the father is voluntarily waiving the father's constitutional rights.

(c) Parents shall also be given oral notice of the rights and responsibilities specified in subdivision (b). Oral notice may be accomplished through the use of audio or video recorded programs developed by the Department of Child Support Services to the extent permitted by federal law.

(d) The Department of Child Support Services shall, free of charge, make available to hospitals, clinics, and other places of birth any and all informational and training materials for the program under this chapter, as well as the declaration of parentage form. The Department of Child Support Services shall make training available to every participating hospital, clinic, local registrar of births and deaths, and other place of birth no later than June 30, 1999.

(e) The Department of Child Support Services may adopt regulations, including emergency regulations, necessary to implement this chapter. *(Added by Stats.2018, c. 876 (A.B.2684), § 31, eff. Jan. 1, 2019, operative Jan. 1, 2020. Amended by Stats.2019, c. 115 (A.B. 1817), § 82, eff. Jan. 1, 2020.)*

Cross References

Department of Child Support Services, generally, see Family Code § 17000 et seq.
Department of Health Care Services, generally, see Health and Safety Code § 100100 et seq.
State defined for purposes of this Code, see Family Code § 145.
Support defined for purposes of this Code, see Family Code § 150.

Research References

Forms

1 California Transactions Forms--Family Law § 4:105, Declaration of Paternity.

§ 7573. Voluntary declaration of parentage; signed record; force and effect

(a) The following persons may sign a voluntary declaration of parentage to establish the parentage of the child:

(1) An unmarried woman who gave birth to the child and another person who is a genetic parent.

(2) A married or unmarried woman who gave birth to the child and another person who is a parent under Section 7613 of a child conceived through assisted reproduction.

(b) A voluntary declaration of parentage shall be in a record signed by the woman who gave birth to the child and by either the only possible genetic parent other than the woman who gave birth or the intended parent of a child conceived through assisted reproduction, and the signatures shall be attested by a notary or witnessed.

(c) Except as provided by Section 7580, a voluntary declaration of parentage takes effect on the filing of the document with the Department of Child Support Services.

(d) Except as provided in Sections 7573.5, 7575, 7576, 7577, and 7580, a completed voluntary declaration of parentage that complies with this chapter and that has been filed with the Department of Child Support Services is equivalent to a judgment of parentage of the child and confers on the declarant all rights and duties of a parent.

(e) The court shall give full faith and credit to a voluntary declaration of parentage effective in another state if the declaration was in a signed record and otherwise complies with the law of the other state.

(f) This section shall become operative on January 1, 2020. *(Added by Stats.2018, c. 876 (A.B.2684), § 33, eff. Jan. 1, 2019, operative Jan. 1, 2020.)*

Cross References

Department of Child Support Services, generally, see Family Code § 17000 et seq.
Judgment and order defined for purposes of this Code, see Family Code § 100.
Support defined for purposes of this Code, see Family Code § 150.

Research References

Forms

2 California Transactions Forms--Family Law § 5:9, Use of Parenting Agreement to Define Rights and Responsibilities Relating to Child on Termination of Partners' Relationship Where Both Partners Are Biological Parents.
2 California Transactions Forms--Family Law § 6:3, Definitions.

§ 7573 PARENT AND CHILD RELATIONSHIP

West's California Judicial Council Forms JV–500, Paternity Inquiry (Also Available in Spanish).

§ 7573.5. Void voluntary declaration of parentage; conditions; notice

(a) A voluntary declaration of parentage is void if, at the time of signing, any of the following are true:

(1) A person other than the woman who gave birth to the child or a person seeking to establish parentage through a voluntary declaration of parentage is a presumed parent under Section 7540 or subdivision (a), (b), or (c) of Section 7611.

(2) A court has entered a judgment of parentage of the child.

(3) Another person has signed a valid voluntary declaration of parentage.

(4) The child has a parent under Section 7613 or 7962 other than the signatories.

(5) The person seeking to establish parentage is a sperm or ova donor under subdivision (b) or (c) of Section 7613.

(6) The person seeking to establish parentage asserts that the person is a parent under Section 7613 and the child was not conceived through assisted reproduction.

(b) In an action in which a party is seeking a determination that a voluntary declaration of parentage is void under this section, notice shall be provided pursuant to Section 7635. *(Added by Stats.2018, c. 876 (A.B.2684), § 34, eff. Jan. 1, 2019, operative Jan. 1, 2020. Amended by Stats.2019, c. 115 (A.B.1817), § 83, eff. Jan. 1, 2020.)*

Research References

Forms

2 California Transactions Forms--Family Law § 5:9.50, Voiding of a Voluntary Declaration of Parentage.

West's California Judicial Council Forms FL–280, Request for Hearing and Application to Cancel (Set Aside) Voluntary Declaration of Parentage or Paternity (Also Available in Spanish).

West's California Judicial Council Forms FL–281, Information Sheet for Completing Request for Hearing and Application to Cancel (Set Aside) Voluntary Declaration of Parentage or Paternity (Also Available in Spanish).

West's California Judicial Council Forms FL–285, Responsive Declaration to Application to Cancel (Set Aside) Voluntary Declaration of Parentage or Paternity (Also Available in Spanish).

§ 7574. Voluntary declaration of parentage; form

(a) The voluntary declaration of parentage shall be executed on a form developed by the Department of Child Support Services in consultation with the State Department of Public Health and groups addressing child support, child custody, assisted reproduction issues, and lesbian, gay, bisexual, and transgender rights.

(b) The form described in subdivision (a) shall contain, at a minimum, all of the following:

(1) The name and the signature of the woman who gave birth to the child.

(2) The name and the signature of the person seeking to establish parentage.

(3) The name of the child.

(4) The date of birth of the child.

(5) For a voluntary declaration of parentage signed pursuant to paragraph (1) of subdivision (a) of Section 7573, all of the following:

(A) A statement by the woman who gave birth that the woman is unmarried and understands the written materials described in Section 7572, that the person who is signing the voluntary declaration of parentage is the only possible genetic parent other than the woman who gave birth, that the woman who gave birth consents to the establishment of parentage by the genetic parent signing the voluntary declaration of parentage, and that the woman who gave birth understands that a challenge by a signatory to a valid declaration of parentage is permitted only under limited circumstances and is barred two years after the effective date of the declaration.

(B) A statement by the person signing the voluntary declaration of parentage that the person has read and understands the written materials described in Section 7572, understands that by signing the voluntary declaration of parentage the person is waiving rights as described in the written materials, that the person is the genetic parent of the child, that the person consents to the establishment of parentage by signing the voluntary declaration of parentage, that the person is assuming all the rights and responsibilities of a parent and wishes to be named on the child's birth certificate, and that the person understands that a challenge by a signatory to a valid declaration of parentage is permitted only under limited circumstances and is barred two years after the effective date of the declaration.

(6) For a voluntary declaration of parentage signed pursuant to paragraph (2) of subdivision (a) of Section 7573, all of the following:

(A) A statement by the woman who gave birth that the woman has read and understands the written materials described in Section 7572, that the person who is signing the voluntary declaration of parentage is the intended parent of a child conceived through assisted reproduction, that the woman who gave birth consents to the establishment of parentage by the other person signing the voluntary declaration of parentage, and that the woman who gave birth understands that a challenge by a signatory to a valid declaration of parentage is permitted only under limited circumstances and is barred two years after the effective date of the declaration.

(B) A statement that the person seeking to establish parentage has read and understands the written materials described in Section 7572, understands that by signing the voluntary declaration of parentage the person is waiving rights as described in the written materials, that the person is the intended parent of the child conceived through assisted reproduction, that the person consents to the establishment of parentage by signing the voluntary declaration of parentage, that the person is assuming all the rights and responsibilities of a parent and wishes to be named on the child's birth certificate, and that the person understands that a challenge by a signatory to a valid declaration of parentage is permitted only under limited circumstances and is barred two years after the effective date of the declaration.

(7) The name and the signature of the person who witnesses the signing of the declaration. *(Added by Stats.2018, c. 876 (A.B.2684), § 36, eff. Jan. 1, 2019, operative Jan. 1, 2020. Amended by Stats.2019, c. 115 (A.B.1817), § 84, eff. Jan. 1, 2020.)*

Cross References

Department of Child Support Services, generally, see Family Code § 17000 et seq.
Department of Health Care Services, generally, see Health and Safety Code § 100100 et seq.
Family support defined for purposes of this Code, see Family Code § 92.
Hearsay exceptions, statements concerning family history, see Evidence Code § 1310 et seq.
Intestate succession, parent and child relationship,
  Natural parents, see Probate Code § 6453.
  Out-of-wedlock births, conditions for inheritance based on relationship, see Probate Code § 6452.
  Relationship severed by adoption, see Probate Code § 6451.
Person defined for purposes of this Code, see Family Code § 105.
Presumption affecting the burden of proof defined, see Evidence Code § 605.
State defined for purposes of this Code, see Family Code § 145.
Support defined for purposes of this Code, see Family Code § 150.

Research References

Forms

1 California Transactions Forms--Family Law § 4:105, Declaration of Paternity.

2 California Transactions Forms--Family Law § 5:9, Use of Parenting Agreement to Define Rights and Responsibilities Relating to Child on Termination of Partners' Relationship Where Both Partners Are Biological Parents.

West's California Code Forms, Family § 7570, Comment Overview—Establishment of Parentage by Voluntary Declaration.

§ 7575. Rescission of voluntary declaration of parentage; form; limitations

(a) Either parent may rescind the voluntary declaration of parentage by filing a rescission form with the Department of Child Support Services within 60 days of the date of execution of the declaration by the attesting parents, whichever signature is later, unless a court order for custody, visitation, or child support has been entered in an action in which the signatory seeking to rescind was a party. The Department of Child Support Services shall develop a form to be used by parents to rescind the declaration of parentage and instructions on how to complete and file the rescission with the Department of Child Support Services. The form shall include a declaration under penalty of perjury completed by the person filing the rescission form that certifies that a copy of the rescission form was sent by any form of mail requiring a return receipt to the other person who signed the voluntary declaration of parentage. A copy of the return receipt shall be attached to the rescission form when filed with the Department of Child Support Services. The form and instructions shall be written in simple, easy to understand language and shall be made available at the local family support office and the office of local registrar of births and deaths. The department shall, upon written request, provide to a court or commissioner a copy of any rescission form filed with the department that is relevant to proceedings before the court or commissioner.

(b) This section shall become operative on January 1, 2020. *(Added by Stats.2018, c. 876 (A.B.2684), § 38, eff. Jan. 1, 2019, operative Jan. 1, 2020.)*

Cross References

Burden of proof, generally, see Evidence Code § 500 et seq.

Certificates of birth following adoption, legitimation, court determination of paternity, and acknowledgment, removal of father's name from birth certificate following rescission, see Health and Safety Code § 102767.

Department of Child Support Services, generally, see Family Code § 17000 et seq.

Determination of father and child relationship, voluntary declaration of paternity, child custody and support actions, see Family Code § 7644.

Family support defined for purposes of this Code, see Family Code § 92.

Hearsay exceptions, statements concerning family history, see Evidence Code § 1310 et seq.

Intestate succession, parent and child relationship,
  Natural parents, see Probate Code § 6453.
  Out-of-wedlock births, conditions for inheritance based on relationship, see Probate Code § 6452.
  Relationship severed by adoption, see Probate Code § 6451.

Judgment and order defined for purposes of this Code, see Family Code § 100.

Person defined for purposes of this Code, see Family Code § 105.

Presumption affecting the burden of proof defined, see Evidence Code § 605.

Proceeding defined for purposes of this Code, see Family Code § 110.

Ruling to set aside voluntary declaration of paternity, factors considered by court, see Family Code § 7630.

Support defined for purposes of this Code, see Family Code § 150.

Uniform Parentage Act, setting aside or vacating judgment of paternity, see Family Code § 7646.

Research References

Forms

1 California Transactions Forms--Family Law § 3:126, Request for Hearing and Application to Set Aside Voluntary Declaration of Paternity [Form FL-280].

1 California Transactions Forms--Family Law § 3:126.50, Information Sheet for Completing Request for Hearing and Application to Set Aside Voluntary Declaration of Paternity [Form FL-281].

1 California Transactions Forms--Family Law § 3:127, Responsive Declaration to Application to Set Aside Voluntary Declaration of Paternity [Form FL-285].

1 California Transactions Forms--Family Law § 3:128, Order After Hearing on Motion to Set Aside Voluntary Declaration of Paternity [Form FL-290].

1 California Transactions Forms--Family Law § 4:105, Declaration of Paternity.

2 California Transactions Forms--Family Law § 5:4, Rights of De Facto Parents.

2 California Transactions Forms--Family Law § 5:9, Use of Parenting Agreement to Define Rights and Responsibilities Relating to Child on Termination of Partners' Relationship Where Both Partners Are Biological Parents.

2 California Transactions Forms--Family Law § 6:3, Definitions.

2 California Transactions Forms--Family Law § 6:8, Consent for Adoption of Unmarried Minor.

2 California Transactions Forms--Family Law § 6:11, Initiating Proceeding Under Uniform Parentage Act [Fam. Code, §§7600 to 7730].

2 California Transactions Forms--Family Law § 6:40, Structuring the Adoption.

2 California Transactions Forms--Family Law § 6:47, Matters to Consider in Drafting Petition for Independent Adoption of Unmarried Minor.

2 California Transactions Forms--Family Law § 6:72, Petition to Terminate Parental Rights of Alleged Father.

2 California Transactions Forms--Family Law § 6:74, Petition to Terminate Parental Rights of Alleged Father Served With Notice of Alleged Paternity Without Timely Response.

2 California Transactions Forms--Family Law § 6:75, Order Terminating Parental Rights of Alleged Father Served With Notice of Alleged Paternity Without Timely Response.

2 California Transactions Forms--Family Law § 6:76, Ex Parte Application for Order to Terminate Parental Rights of Alleged Father Who Waived Notice or Denied Paternity.

2 California Transactions Forms--Family Law § 7:38, Parentage and Birth Certificate.

2 California Transactions Forms--Family Law § 7:86, Overview.

West's California Code Forms, Family § 7570, Comment Overview—Establishment of Parentage by Voluntary Declaration.

West's California Code Forms, Family § 7575 Form 2, Request for Hearing and Application to Set Aside Voluntary Declaration of Parentage or Paternity.

West's California Code Forms, Family § 7575 Form 3, Responsive Declaration to Application to Set Aside Voluntary Declaration of Parentage or Paternity.

West's California Judicial Council Forms FL-272, Notice of Motion to Cancel (Set Aside) Judgment of Parentage (Also Available in Spanish).

§ 7576. Challenging voluntary declaration of parentage; limitations

(a) After the period for rescission provided in Section 7575 expires, but not later than two years after the effective date provided in subdivision (c) of Section 7573 of a voluntary declaration of parentage, a signatory of the voluntary declaration of parentage may commence a proceeding to challenge the declaration on the basis of fraud, duress, or material mistake of fact.

(b) The limitations period provided in subdivision (a) shall not apply if the voluntary declaration of parentage is void under Section 7573.5.

(c) This section shall become operative on January 1, 2020. *(Added by Stats.2018, c. 876 (A.B.2684), § 40, eff. Jan. 1, 2019, operative Jan. 1, 2020.)*

Research References

Forms

West's California Judicial Council Forms FL-273, Declaration in Support of Motion to Cancel (Set Aside) Judgment of Parentage (Also Available in Spanish).

West's California Judicial Council Forms FL-274, Information Sheet for Completing Notice of Motion to Cancel (Set Aside) Judgment of Parentage (Also Available in Spanish).

West's California Judicial Council Forms FL-276, Response to Notice of Motion to Cancel (Set Aside) Judgment of Parentage (Also Available in Spanish).

§ 7576

West's California Judicial Council Forms FL–278, Order After Hearing on Motion to Cancel (Set Aside) Judgment of Parentage (Also Available in Spanish).

West's California Judicial Council Forms FL–280, Request for Hearing and Application to Cancel (Set Aside) Voluntary Declaration of Parentage or Paternity (Also Available in Spanish).

West's California Judicial Council Forms FL–281, Information Sheet for Completing Request for Hearing and Application to Cancel (Set Aside) Voluntary Declaration of Parentage or Paternity (Also Available in Spanish).

West's California Judicial Council Forms FL–285, Responsive Declaration to Application to Cancel (Set Aside) Voluntary Declaration of Parentage or Paternity (Also Available in Spanish).

West's California Judicial Council Forms FL–290, Order After Hearing on Motion to Cancel (Set Aside) Voluntary Declaration of Parentage or Paternity (Also Available in Spanish).

§ 7577. Rules applying to challenge of valid voluntary declaration of parentage brought by person not signatory to declaration

The following rules apply in an action to challenge a valid voluntary declaration of parentage brought by a person who is not a signatory to the declaration. This section does not apply to a voluntary declaration of parentage that is void under Section 7573.5.

(a) A person has standing under this section if the person is an alleged genetic parent who is not a donor under Section 7613, is a presumed parent under Section 7611, or any person who has standing under Section 7630.

(b) The petition challenging a voluntary declaration of parentage pursuant to this section shall be supported by a declaration under oath alleging specific facts to support standing under this section.

(c) If the court holds a hearing to determine standing, the hearing shall be held on an expedited basis. If the person challenging the voluntary declaration of parentage is an alleged genetic parent, genetic testing shall be ordered on an expedited basis.

(d) The action shall be filed not later than two years after the effective date of the declaration. This limitations period does not apply if the voluntary declaration of parentage is void under Section 7573.5.

(e) Notice shall be provided to the signatories of the declaration and to any person entitled to notice under Section 7635. A person who asserts a claim to parentage under this division shall be joined in the action.

(f) With respect to whether the voluntary declaration of parentage should be set aside, the person petitioning to set aside the voluntary declaration of parentage shall have the burden of proof by a preponderance of the evidence.

(g) The court may grant the petition to set aside the voluntary declaration of parentage only if the court finds that setting aside the voluntary declaration of parentage is in the best interest of the child, based on consideration of all of the following factors:

(1) The age of the child.

(2) The length of time since the effective date of the voluntary declaration of parentage.

(3) The nature, duration, and quality of any relationship between the person who signed the voluntary declaration of parentage and the child, including the duration and frequency of any time periods during which the child and the person resided in the same household or enjoyed a parent and child relationship.

(4) The request of the person who signed the voluntary declaration of parentage that the parent and child relationship continue.

(5) If the person challenges a voluntary declaration of parentage signed pursuant to paragraph (1) of subdivision (a) of Section 7573, the court shall additionally consider all of the following:

(A) Notice by the genetic parent of the child that the genetic parent does not oppose preservation of the relationship between the person who signed the declaration of parentage and the child.

(B) Whether any conduct of the person who signed the voluntary declaration has impaired the ability to ascertain the identity of, or obtain support from, the genetic parent.

(6) Additional factors deemed by the court to be relevant to its determination of the best interest of the child.

(h) If the voluntary declaration of parentage is challenged by a person who is presumed to be a parent under subdivision (d) of Section 7611, the court's ruling on the petition to set aside the voluntary declaration of parentage shall, in addition to the factors under subdivision (g), also take into account the nature, duration, and quality of the relationship between the petitioning party and the child and the benefit or detriment to the child of continuing that relationship.

(i) If the court denies the petition to set aside the voluntary declaration of parentage, the court shall state on the record the basis for the denial of the action and any supporting facts.

(j)(1) If the court grants the petition to set aside the voluntary declaration of parentage, the court shall adjudicate parentage pursuant to Section 7612.

(2) An order for custody, visitation, or child support shall remain in effect until the court determines that the voluntary declaration of parentage should be set aside, subject to the court's power to modify the orders as otherwise provided by law.

(k) This section does not prejudice or bar the rights of a person who is not a signatory and has standing under subdivision (a) to file an action or motion to set aside the voluntary declaration of parentage on any of the grounds described in, and within the time limits specified in, Section 473 of the Code of Civil Procedure. If the action or motion to set aside a judgment is required to be filed within a specified time period under Section 473 of the Code of Civil Procedure, the period within which the action or motion to set aside the voluntary declaration of parentage must be filed shall commence on the date that the court makes an initial order for custody, visitation, or child support based upon a voluntary declaration of parentage.

(*l*) This section does not restrict a court from acting as a court of equity.

(m) The Judicial Council shall develop the forms and procedures necessary to effectuate this section. *(Added by Stats.2018, c. 876 (A.B.2684), § 42, eff. Jan. 1, 2019, operative Jan. 1, 2020. Amended by Stats.2019, c. 115 (A.B.1817), § 85, eff. Jan. 1, 2020.)*

Research References

Forms

1 California Transactions Forms--Family Law § 4:105, Declaration of Paternity.

West's California Judicial Council Forms FL–272, Notice of Motion to Cancel (Set Aside) Judgment of Parentage (Also Available in Spanish).

West's California Judicial Council Forms FL–273, Declaration in Support of Motion to Cancel (Set Aside) Judgment of Parentage (Also Available in Spanish).

West's California Judicial Council Forms FL–274, Information Sheet for Completing Notice of Motion to Cancel (Set Aside) Judgment of Parentage (Also Available in Spanish).

West's California Judicial Council Forms FL–276, Response to Notice of Motion to Cancel (Set Aside) Judgment of Parentage (Also Available in Spanish).

West's California Judicial Council Forms FL–278, Order After Hearing on Motion to Cancel (Set Aside) Judgment of Parentage (Also Available in Spanish).

West's California Judicial Council Forms FL–280, Request for Hearing and Application to Cancel (Set Aside) Voluntary Declaration of Parentage or Paternity (Also Available in Spanish).

West's California Judicial Council Forms FL–281, Information Sheet for Completing Request for Hearing and Application to Cancel (Set Aside) Voluntary Declaration of Parentage or Paternity (Also Available in Spanish).

§ 7578. Parties to proceeding to challenge declaration; nonsuspension of legal responsibilities during the pendency of proceeding; new birth certificate

(a) Every signatory to a voluntary declaration of parentage shall be made a party to a proceeding to challenge the declaration.

(b) By signing a voluntary declaration, a signatory submits to personal jurisdiction in this state in a proceeding to challenge the declaration, effective on the filing of the declaration with the Department of Child Support Services.

(c) The court shall not suspend the legal responsibilities arising from a voluntary declaration of parentage, including the duty to pay child support, during the pendency of a proceeding to challenge the voluntary declaration of parentage, unless the party challenging the declaration shows good cause.

(d) A party challenging a voluntary declaration of parentage has the burden of proof by a preponderance of the evidence.

(e) If the judgment or order of the court is at variance with the child's birth certificate, the court shall order that a new birth certificate be issued as prescribed in Article 2 (commencing with Section 102725) of Chapter 5 of Part 1 of Division 102 of the Health and Safety Code.

(f) This section shall become operative on January 1, 2020. *(Added by Stats.2018, c. 876 (A.B.2684), § 43, eff. Jan. 1, 2019, operative Jan. 1, 2020.)*

§ 7580. Voluntary declaration of parentage; minor parents; validity; rescission; presumption; admissibility

(a) Notwithstanding subdivision (c) of Section 7573, a voluntary declaration of parentage that is signed by a minor parent does not establish parentage until 60 days after both signatories have reached 18 years of age or are emancipated, whichever first occurs.

(b) A person who signs a voluntary declaration of parentage as a minor may rescind the voluntary declaration of parentage at any time up to 60 days after the signatory reaches 18 years of age or becomes emancipated, whichever first occurs.

(c) A voluntary declaration of parentage signed by a minor creates a rebuttable presumption for or against parentage until the date that it establishes parentage as specified in subdivision (a).

(d) A voluntary declaration of parentage signed by a minor shall be admissible as evidence in a civil action to establish parentage of the minor named in the voluntary declaration.

(e) A voluntary declaration of parentage that is signed by a minor shall not be admissible as evidence in a criminal prosecution for violation of Section 261.5 of the Penal Code. *(Added by Stats.2018, c. 876 (A.B.2684), § 44, eff. Jan. 1, 2019, operative Jan. 1, 2020. Amended by Stats.2019, c. 115 (A.B.1817), § 86, eff. Jan. 1, 2020.)*

Cross References

Minor defined for purposes of this Code, see Family Code § 6500.

Research References

Forms

1 California Transactions Forms--Family Law § 3:126, Request for Hearing and Application to Set Aside Voluntary Declaration of Paternity [Form FL-280].

1 California Transactions Forms--Family Law § 3:126.50, Information Sheet for Completing Request for Hearing and Application to Set Aside Voluntary Declaration of Paternity [Form FL-281].

1 California Transactions Forms--Family Law § 3:127, Responsive Declaration to Application to Set Aside Voluntary Declaration of Paternity [Form FL-285].

1 California Transactions Forms--Family Law § 3:128, Order After Hearing on Motion to Set Aside Voluntary Declaration of Paternity [Form FL-290].

1 California Transactions Forms--Family Law § 4:105, Declaration of Paternity.

2 California Transactions Forms--Family Law § 5:4, Rights of De Facto Parents.

2 California Transactions Forms--Family Law § 5:9, Use of Parenting Agreement to Define Rights and Responsibilities Relating to Child on Termination of Partners' Relationship Where Both Partners Are Biological Parents.

2 California Transactions Forms--Family Law § 6:8, Consent for Adoption of Unmarried Minor.

2 California Transactions Forms--Family Law § 6:11, Initiating Proceeding Under Uniform Parentage Act [Fam. Code, §§7600 to 7730].

2 California Transactions Forms--Family Law § 6:40, Structuring the Adoption.

2 California Transactions Forms--Family Law § 6:72, Petition to Terminate Parental Rights of Alleged Father.

2 California Transactions Forms--Family Law § 6:74, Petition to Terminate Parental Rights of Alleged Father Served With Notice of Alleged Paternity Without Timely Response.

2 California Transactions Forms--Family Law § 6:75, Order Terminating Parental Rights of Alleged Father Served With Notice of Alleged Paternity Without Timely Response.

2 California Transactions Forms--Family Law § 6:76, Ex Parte Application for Order to Terminate Parental Rights of Alleged Father Who Waived Notice or Denied Paternity.

2 California Transactions Forms--Family Law § 7:38, Parentage and Birth Certificate.

2 California Transactions Forms--Family Law § 7:86, Overview.

§ 7581. Voluntary declaration of paternity; presumption; admissibility of evidence; rebuttal; construction with other presumptions of paternity

The following provisions shall apply for voluntary declarations signed on or before December 31, 1996.

(a) Except as provided in subdivision (d), the child of a woman and a man executing a declaration of paternity under this chapter is conclusively presumed to be the man's child. The presumption under this section has the same force and effect as the presumption under Section 7540.

(b) A voluntary declaration of paternity shall be recognized as the basis for the establishment of an order for child custody or support.

(c) In an action to rebut the presumption created by this section, a voluntary declaration of paternity shall be admissible as evidence to determine paternity of the child named in the voluntary declaration of paternity.

(d) The presumption established by this section may be rebutted by any person by requesting genetic testing pursuant to Chapter 2 (commencing with Section 7550). The notice of motion for genetic testing pursuant to this section shall be supported by a declaration under oath submitted by the moving party stating the factual basis for placing the issue of paternity before the court. The notice of motion for genetic testing shall be made within three years from the date of execution of the declaration by the attesting father, or by the attesting mother, whichever signature is later. The two-year statute of limitations specified in subdivision (b) of Section 7541 is inapplicable for purposes of this section.

(e) A presumption under this section shall override all statutory presumptions of paternity, except a presumption arising under Section 7540, a claim made pursuant to Section 7555, or as provided in Section 7612.

(f) This section shall become operative on January 1, 2020. *(Added by Stats.2018, c. 876 (A.B.2684), § 45, eff. Jan. 1, 2019, operative Jan. 1, 2020.)*

§ 7581   PARENT AND CHILD RELATIONSHIP

Cross References

Determination of father and child relationship, voluntary declaration of paternity, child custody and support actions, see Family Code § 7644.
Judgment and order defined for purposes of this Code, see Family Code § 100.
Person defined for purposes of this Code, see Family Code § 105.
Presumed father and child relationship, written promise to furnish support, enforceability, see Family Code § 7614.
Support defined for purposes of this Code, see Family Code § 150.

Termination of juvenile court jurisdiction, pending proceedings relating to parental marriage or custody order, see Welfare and Institutions Code § 362.4.
Termination of parental rights of father, filing of petition, stay of proceedings affecting a child pending final determination of parental rights, see Family Code § 7662.
Uniform act, construction of provisions, see Family Code § 3.
Witnesses, interpreters and translators, hearings or proceedings related to domestic violence, see Evidence Code § 756.

Part 3

UNIFORM PARENTAGE ACT

Chapter	Section
1. General Provisions	7600
2. Establishing Parent and Child Relationship	7610
3. Jurisdiction and Venue	7620
4. Determination of Parent and Child Relationship	7630
5. Termination of Parental Rights in Adoption Proceedings	7660
6. Protective and Restraining Orders	7700

Cross References

Adoption, termination of parental rights of father, stay of proceedings under these provisions, see Family Code § 7662.
Applicable law, see Family Code § 3021.
Arrest with and without warrant, citizen's arrest by domestic victim, protective or restraining order, see Penal Code § 836.
Change of names,
   Orders to show cause, publication or posting, see Code of Civil Procedure § 1277.
   Orders without hearings, see Code of Civil Procedure § 1278.
Court interpreter services provided in civil actions, reimbursement by Judicial Council, prioritization where funding is insufficient, see Evidence Code § 756.
Dissolution of marriage and legal separation, supplemental complaint, determination of paternity pursuant to these provisions, see Family Code § 2330.1.
Domestic violence defined, see Family Code § 6211.
Domestic violence incidents, temporary custody of firearms by officers, subsequent procedures, see Penal Code §§ 18250 to 18500.
Family Law Facilitator Act, application of division to these provisions, see Family Code § 10003.
Family law pilot projects, Santa Clara County, application to proceedings pursuant to these provisions, see Family Code § 20031.
Freedom from parental custody and control, stay of proceedings and effect upon jurisdiction under these provisions, see Family Code § 7807.
Intestate succession, natural parents, see Probate Code § 6453.
Judgments which may include protective orders, see Family Code § 6360.
Juvenile court law, protective order, parentage, custody, or visitation order, see Welfare and Institutions Code § 726.5.
Orders included in judgments, required statements, see Family Code § 6361.
Other uniform acts in the Family Code,
   Uniform Act on Blood Tests to Determine Paternity, see Family Code § 7550 et seq.
   Uniform Child Custody Jurisdiction and Enforcement Act, see Family Code § 3400 et seq.
   Uniform Divorce Recognition Act, see Family Code § 2090 et seq.
   Uniform Interstate Enforcement of Domestic Violence Protection Orders Act, see Family Code § 6400 et seq.
   Uniform Interstate Family Act, see Family Code § 5700.101 et seq.
   Uniform Premarital Agreement Act, see Family Code § 1600 et seq.
Place of trial, court having jurisdiction of subject matter but not proper court, see Code of Civil Procedure § 396b.
Prevention of domestic violence, application of division to these provisions, forms, see Family Code § 6221.
Right to custody defined, see Penal Code § 277.
Right to custody of minor child, application to physical or legal custody or visitation proceedings pursuant to these provision, see Family Code § 3021.
Santa Clara County Pilot Project, hearings subject to project, see Family Code § 20031.

CHAPTER 1. GENERAL PROVISIONS

Section	
7600.	Short title.
7601.	"Natural parent" defined; "parent and child relationship" defined; finding of parent and child relationship with more than two parents; interpretation of reference to two parents.
7602.	Application regardless of marital status of parents.
7603.	Application of § 3140.
7604.	Pendente lite relief of custody or visitation order on finding of parent-child relationship.
7604.5.	Pregnancy, childbirth and genetic testing bills as evidence.
7605.	Attorney's fees and costs; court findings; standard for awarding fees and costs; augmentation or modification; temporary orders; time for determination of application.
7606.	"Assisted reproduction" and "assisted reproduction agreement" defined.

Cross References

Stepparent adoption, procedures, see Family Code § 9000.5.
Uniform act, construction of provisions, see Family Code § 3.

§ 7600. Short title

This part may be cited as the Uniform Parentage Act. *(Stats.1992, c. 162 (A.B.2650), § 10, operative Jan. 1, 1994.)*

Cross References

Freedom from parental custody and control, stay of proceedings and effect upon jurisdiction under these provisions, see Family Code § 7807.
Petitions, existence of child support, child custody, visitation, or spousal support orders, personal conduct restraining order, or bifurcated case, dismissal for delay in prosecution prohibited, see Code of Civil Procedure § 583.161.
Severability of provisions, see Family Code § 13.
Uniform acts, construction of provisions from, see Family Code § 3.
Uniform Interstate Family Support Act, proceedings to determine parentage, see Family Code § 5700.402.

Research References

Forms

1 California Transactions Forms--Estate Planning § 6:11, Existence of Relationship.
1 California Transactions Forms--Estate Planning § 6:52, Matters to Consider in Drafting Class Gifts.
1 California Transactions Forms--Family Law § 3:4, Subject Matter Jurisdiction for Custody Determinations.
2 California Transactions Forms--Family Law § 5:1, Nature and Purpose of Parenting Agreement.
2 California Transactions Forms--Family Law § 5:9, Use of Parenting Agreement to Define Rights and Responsibilities Relating to Child on Termination of Partners' Relationship Where Both Partners Are Biological Parents.
2 California Transactions Forms--Family Law § 5:30, Parenting Agreement Providing for Joint Legal and Joint Physical Custody Where Both Partners Are Biological Parents of Child.
2 California Transactions Forms--Family Law § 5:31, Parenting Agreement Providing for Joint Legal and Sole Physical Custody Where Both Partners Are Biological Parents of Child.
2 California Transactions Forms--Family Law § 6:2, Governing Law.

2 California Transactions Forms--Family Law § 6:3, Definitions.
2 California Transactions Forms--Family Law § 6:10, Initiating Proceeding Under Fam. Code, §§7800 et seq.
2 California Transactions Forms--Family Law § 7:6, Overview; Gestational Surrogacy Agreements.
2 California Transactions Forms--Family Law § 7:7, Gestational Surrogacy Agreements Using Donated Egg and Sperm.
2 California Transactions Forms--Family Law § 7:28, Overview.
2 California Transactions Forms--Family Law § 7:45, Artificial Insemination Surrogacy Agreement Between Intended Father and Surrogate Couple.
2 California Transactions Forms--Family Law § 7:46, In Vitro Surrogacy Agreement Between Intended Parents and Surrogate Couple; Intended Parents Are Genetic Parents.
2 California Transactions Forms--Family Law § 7:47, In Vitro Fertilization Surrogacy Agreement Between Intended Mother and Surrogate Using Donated Genetic Material.
West's California Code Forms, Family § 6200, Comment Overview—Prevention of Domestic Violence.
West's California Code Forms, Family § 6340, Comment Overview—Issuance of Orders After Notice and Hearing.
West's California Judicial Council Forms DV–180, Agreement and Judgment of Parentage (Also Available in Chinese, Korean, Spanish, and Vietnamese).
West's California Judicial Council Forms FL–230, Declaration for Default or Uncontested Judgment (Uniform Parentage, Custody and Support) (Also Available in Spanish).
West's California Judicial Council Forms FL–235, Advisement and Waiver of Rights Re: Establishment of Parental Relationship (Also Available in Spanish).
West's California Judicial Council Forms FL–240, Stipulation for Entry of Judgment Re: Establishment of Parental Relationship (Also Available in Spanish).
West's California Judicial Council Forms FL–250, Judgment (Uniform Parentage—Custody and Support) (Also Available in Spanish).
West's California Judicial Council Forms FL–260, Petition for Custody and Support of Minor Children (Also Available in Spanish).
West's California Judicial Council Forms FL–270, Response to Petition for Custody and Support of Minor Children (Also Available in Spanish).

§ 7601. "Natural parent" defined; "parent and child relationship" defined; finding of parent and child relationship with more than two parents; interpretation of reference to two parents

(a) "Natural parent" as used in this code means a nonadoptive parent established under this part, whether biologically related to the child or not.

(b) "Parent and child relationship" as used in this part means the legal relationship existing between a child and the child's natural or adoptive parents incident to which the law confers or imposes rights, privileges, duties, and obligations. The term includes the mother and child relationship and the father and child relationship.

(c) This part does not preclude a finding that a child has a parent and child relationship with more than two parents.

(d) For purposes of state law, administrative regulations, court rules, government policies, common law, and any other provision or source of law governing the rights, protections, benefits, responsibilities, obligations, and duties of parents, any reference to two parents shall be interpreted to apply to every parent of a child where that child has been found to have more than two parents under this part. *(Stats.1992, c. 162 (A.B.2650), § 10, operative Jan. 1, 1994. Amended by Stats.2013, c. 510 (A.B.1403), § 1; Stats.2013, c. 564 (S.B.274), § 5.5.)*

Cross References

Adoption, legal relationship of adoptive parents and child, see Family Code § 8616.
Adoptive parent defined, see Family Code § 8503.
Birth parent defined, see Family Code § 8512.
Domestic violence defined, see Family Code § 6211.
Domestic violence, ex parte orders regarding temporary custody and visitation of minor children, see Family Code § 6323.
Effect of judgment or order determining parent and child relationship, see Family Code § 7636.
Hearsay exceptions, statements concerning family history, see Evidence Code § 1310 et seq.
Intestate succession, parent and child relationship, natural parents, see Probate Code § 6453.
Presumption affecting the burden of proof, defined, see Evidence Code § 605.
Uniform act, construction of provisions, see Family Code § 3.

Research References
Forms

1 California Transactions Forms--Family Law § 3:4, Subject Matter Jurisdiction for Custody Determinations.
2 California Transactions Forms--Family Law § 5:9, Use of Parenting Agreement to Define Rights and Responsibilities Relating to Child on Termination of Partners' Relationship Where Both Partners Are Biological Parents.

§ 7602. Application regardless of marital status of parents

The parent and child relationship extends equally to every child and to every parent, regardless of the marital status of the parents. *(Stats.1992, c. 162 (A.B.2650), § 10, operative Jan. 1, 1994.)*

Cross References

Adoption, legal relationship of adoptive parents and child, see Family Code § 8616.
Adoptive parent defined, see Family Code § 8503.
Birth parent defined, see Family Code § 8512.
Domestic violence, ex parte orders regarding temporary custody and visitation of minor children, see Family Code § 6323.
Intestate succession, parent and child relationship, natural parents, see Probate Code § 6453.
Uniform act, construction of provisions, see Family Code § 3.

§ 7603. Application of § 3140

Section 3140 is applicable to proceedings pursuant to this part. *(Stats.1992, c. 162 (A.B.2650), § 10, operative Jan. 1, 1994.)*

Cross References

Certified copy and verification of records, see Health and Safety Code § 103526.
Proceeding defined for purposes of this Code, see Family Code § 110.
Uniform act, construction of provisions, see Family Code § 3.

§ 7604. Pendente lite relief of custody or visitation order on finding of parent-child relationship

A court may order pendente lite relief consisting of a custody or visitation order pursuant to Part 2 (commencing with Section 3020) of Division 8, if the court finds both of the following:

(a) A parent and child relationship exists pursuant to Section 7540 or 7541.

(b) The custody or visitation order would be in the best interest of the child. *(Stats.1992, c. 162 (A.B.2650), § 10, operative Jan. 1, 1994. Amended by Stats.1993, c. 219 (A.B.1500), § 175.5; Stats.2018, c. 876 (A.B.2684), § 46, eff. Jan. 1, 2019.)*

Cross References

Domestic violence, protective order, defined, see Family Code §§ 6211, 6218.
Judgment and order defined for purposes of this Code, see Family Code § 100.
Uniform act, construction of provisions, see Family Code § 3.

Research References
Forms

1 California Transactions Forms--Family Law § 3:4, Subject Matter Jurisdiction for Custody Determinations.
2 California Transactions Forms--Family Law § 5:9, Use of Parenting Agreement to Define Rights and Responsibilities Relating to Child on Termination of Partners' Relationship Where Both Partners Are Biological Parents.
West's California Judicial Council Forms DV–140, Child Custody and Visitation Order (Also Available in Chinese, Korean, Spanish, and Vietnamese).

§ 7604.5. Pregnancy, childbirth and genetic testing bills as evidence

Notwithstanding any other provision of law, bills for pregnancy, childbirth, and genetic testing shall be admissible as evidence without third-party foundation testimony and shall constitute prima facie evidence of costs incurred for those services. *(Added by Stats.1997, c. 599 (A.B.573), § 44.)*

Cross References

Prima facie evidence, see Evidence Code § 602.
Uniform act, construction of provisions, see Family Code § 3.

§ 7605. Attorney's fees and costs; court findings; standard for awarding fees and costs; augmentation or modification; temporary orders; time for determination of application

(a) In any proceeding to establish physical or legal custody of a child or a visitation order under this part, and in any proceeding subsequent to entry of a related judgment, the court shall ensure that each party has access to legal representation to preserve each party's rights by ordering, if necessary based on the income and needs assessments, one party, except a government entity, to pay to the other party, or to the other party's attorney, whatever amount is reasonably necessary for attorney's fees and for the cost of maintaining or defending the proceeding during the pendency of the proceeding.

(b) When a request for attorney's fees and costs is made under this section, the court shall make findings on whether an award of attorney's fees and costs is appropriate, whether there is a disparity in access to funds to retain counsel, and whether one party is able to pay for legal representation of both parties. If the findings demonstrate disparity in access and ability to pay, the court shall make an order awarding attorney's fees and costs. A party who lacks the financial ability to hire an attorney may request, as an in pro per litigant, that the court order the other party, if that other party has the financial ability, to pay a reasonable amount to allow the unrepresented party to retain an attorney in a timely manner before proceedings in the matter go forward.

(c) Attorney's fees and costs within this section may be awarded for legal services rendered or costs incurred before or after the commencement of the proceeding.

(d) The court shall augment or modify the original award for attorney's fees and costs as may be reasonably necessary for the prosecution or defense of a proceeding described in subdivision (a), or any proceeding related thereto, including after any appeal has been concluded.

(e) Except as provided in subdivision (f), an application for a temporary order making, augmenting, or modifying an award of attorney's fees, including a reasonable retainer to hire an attorney, or costs, or both, shall be made by motion on notice or by an order to show cause during the pendency of any proceeding described in subdivision (a).

(f) The court shall rule on an application for fees under this section within 15 days of the hearing on the motion or order to show cause. An order described in subdivision (a) may be made without notice by an oral motion in open court at either of the following times:

(1) At the time of the hearing of the cause on the merits.

(2) At any time before entry of judgment against a party whose default has been entered pursuant to Section 585 or 586 of the Code of Civil Procedure. The court shall rule on any motion made pursuant to this subdivision within 15 days and prior to the entry of any judgment. *(Added by Stats.2004, c. 472 (A.B.2148), § 7.*

Amended by Stats.2006, c. 538 (S.B.1852), § 160; Stats.2012, c. 107 (A.B.1406), § 3.)

Cross References

Attorney's fees and costs, generally, see Code of Civil Procedure § 1021.
Computation of time, first and last days, holidays, see Civil Code § 10; Code of Civil Procedure § 12 et seq.; Government Code § 6800 et seq.
Custody of children, award of attorney's fees and costs, see Family Code § 3121.
Dissolution and separation, award of attorney's fees and costs, see Family Code §§ 2030, 2031.
Domestic violence protection, protective orders and other domestic violence prevention orders, award of attorney's fees and costs, see Family Code § 6344.
Judgment and order defined for purposes of this Code, see Family Code § 100.
Proceeding defined for purposes of this Code, see Family Code § 110.

Research References

Forms

West's California Judicial Council Forms FL–158, Supporting Declaration for Attorney's Fees and Costs Attachment.
West's California Judicial Council Forms FL–319, Request for Attorney's Fees and Costs Attachment.
West's California Judicial Council Forms FL–346, Attorney's Fees and Costs Order Attachment.

§ 7606. "Assisted reproduction" and "assisted reproduction agreement" defined

As used in this part, the following definitions shall apply:

(a) "Assisted reproduction" means conception by any means other than sexual intercourse.

(b) "Assisted reproduction agreement" means a written contract that includes a person who intends to be the legal parent of a child or children born through assisted reproduction and that defines the terms of the relationship between the parties to the contract. *(Added by Stats.2006, c. 806 (S.B.1325), § 1.)*

Research References

Forms

2 California Transactions Forms--Family Law § 7:8.50, Surrogacy Facilitator.

CHAPTER 2. ESTABLISHING PARENT AND CHILD RELATIONSHIP

Section
7610. Method of establishment.
7611. Status as natural parent; presumption; conditions.
7611.5. Presumption against natural father status; Section 7611 inapplicable.
7612. Presumption as natural parent; rebuttable presumption; conflicting presumptions; more than two persons with claim to parentage; person's offer or refusal to sign voluntary declaration of parentage.
7613. Conception through assisted reproduction with semen or ova donated by donor other than spouse; consent of another intended parent; treatment as natural parent; treatment of semen or ova donors.
7613.5. Intended parent; use of forms.
7614. Written promise to furnish support; enforcement; confidentiality.

Cross References

Hearsay exceptions, statements concerning family history, see Evidence Code § 1310 et seq.
Intestate succession, parent and child relationship,
 Natural parents, see Probate Code § 6453.
 Out-of-wedlock births, conditions for inheritance based on relationship, see Probate Code § 6452.
 Relationship severed by adoption, see Probate Code § 6451.

Presumption affecting the burden of proof defined, see Evidence Code § 605.
Uniform act, construction of provisions, see Family Code § 3.

§ 7610. Method of establishment

The parent and child relationship may be established as follows:

(a) Between a child and the natural parent, it may be established by proof of having given birth to the child, or under this part.

(b) Between a child and an adoptive parent, it may be established by proof of adoption. *(Stats.1992, c. 162 (A.B.2650), § 10, operative Jan. 1, 1994. Amended by Stats.2013, c. 510 (A.B.1403), § 2.)*

Cross References

Adoptive parent defined, see Family Code § 8503.
Assisted reproduction agreements for gestational carriers, requirements, rebuttal of presumptions, see Family Code § 7962.
Birth parent defined, see Family Code § 8512.
Domestic violence, ex parte orders regarding temporary custody and visitation of minor children, see Family Code § 6323.
Hearsay exceptions, statements concerning family history, see Evidence Code § 1310 et seq.
Intestate succession, parent and child relationship,
  Natural parents, see Probate Code § 6453.
  Out-of-wedlock births, conditions for inheritance based on relationship, see Probate Code § 6452.
  Relationship severed by adoption, see Probate Code § 6451.
Presumption affecting the burden of proof defined, see Evidence Code § 605.

Research References

Forms

2 California Transactions Forms--Family Law § 7:63, Application of Fam C § 7613 to Egg Donors.
West's California Code Forms, Family § 7610, Comment Overview—Establishing Parent and Child Relationship.

§ 7611. Status as natural parent; presumption; conditions

A person is presumed to be the natural parent of a child if the person meets the conditions provided in Chapter 1 (commencing with Section 7540) or Chapter 3 (commencing with Section 7570) of Part 2 or in any of the following subdivisions:

(a) The presumed parent and the child's natural mother are, or have been, married to each other and the child is born during the marriage, or within 300 days after the marriage is terminated by death, annulment, declaration of invalidity, or divorce, or after a judgment of separation is entered by a court.

(b) Before the child's birth, the presumed parent and the child's natural mother have attempted to marry each other by a marriage solemnized in apparent compliance with law, although the attempted marriage is or could be declared invalid, and either of the following is true:

(1) If the attempted marriage could be declared invalid only by a court, the child is born during the attempted marriage, or within 300 days after its termination by death, annulment, declaration of invalidity, or divorce.

(2) If the attempted marriage is invalid without a court order, the child is born within 300 days after the termination of cohabitation.

(c) After the child's birth, the presumed parent and the child's natural mother have married, or attempted to marry, each other by a marriage solemnized in apparent compliance with law, although the attempted marriage is or could be declared invalid, and either of the following is true:

(1) With the presumed parent's consent, the presumed parent is named as the child's parent on the child's birth certificate.

(2) The presumed parent is obligated to support the child under a written voluntary promise or by court order.

(d) The presumed parent receives the child into their home and openly holds out the child as their natural child.

(e) The child is in utero after the death of the decedent and the conditions set forth in Section 249.5 of the Probate Code are satisfied. *(Stats.1992, c. 162 (A.B.2650), § 10, operative Jan. 1, 1994. Amended by Stats.1993, c. 219 (A.B.1500), § 176; Stats.1994, c. 1269 (A.B.2208), § 53; Stats.2004, c. 775 (A.B.1910), § 1; Stats.2013, c. 510 (A.B.1403), § 3; Stats.2019, c. 115 (A.B.1817), § 87, eff. Jan. 1, 2020.)*

Validity

This section was held unconstitutional in the case of In re Jerry P. (App. 2 Dist. 2002) 116 Cal.Rptr.2d 123, 95 Cal.App.4th 793, modified on denial of rehearing, review granted and opinion superseded 119 Cal.Rptr.2d 856, 46 P.3d 331, publication ordered 121 Cal.Rptr.2d 106, 47 P.3d 988, review dismissed, cause remanded 124 Cal.Rptr.2d 718, 53 P.3d 133.

Cross References

Abandonment and neglect of children, willful infliction of corporal injury, see Penal Code § 273.5.
Action for determination of father and child relationship, see Family Code § 7630.
Adoption, child of presumed father, relinquishment or consent by mother, see Family Code § 7660.
Assisted reproduction agreements for gestational carriers, requirements, rebuttal of presumptions, see Family Code § 7962.
Consent required for adoption, presumed fathers, see Family Code § 8604.
Domestic violence, ex parte orders regarding temporary custody and visitation of minor children, see Family Code § 6323.
Domestic violence incidents, temporary custody of firearms, domestic violence defined, see Penal Code §§ 18250 to 18500.
Filing petition to terminate parental rights of father, conditions, see Family Code § 7662.
Hearsay exceptions, statements concerning family history, see Evidence Code § 1310 et seq.
Intestate succession, parent and child relationship,
  Natural parents, see Probate Code § 6453.
  Out-of-wedlock births, conditions for inheritance based on relationship, see Probate Code § 6452.
  Relationship severed by adoption, see Probate Code § 6451.
Judgment and order defined for purposes of this Code, see Family Code § 100.
Presumption affecting the burden of proof defined, see Evidence Code § 605.
Punishment for kidnapping, victim under 14 years of age, see Penal Code § 208.
State defined for purposes of this Code, see Family Code § 145.
Support defined for purposes of this Code, see Family Code § 150.
Void voluntary declaration of parentage, conditions, notice, see Family Code § 7573.5.

Research References

Forms

1 California Transactions Forms--Family Law § 3:126, Request for Hearing and Application to Set Aside Voluntary Declaration of Paternity [Form FL-280].
1 California Transactions Forms--Family Law § 3:126.50, Information Sheet for Completing Request for Hearing and Application to Set Aside Voluntary Declaration of Paternity [Form FL-281].
1 California Transactions Forms--Family Law § 3:127, Responsive Declaration to Application to Set Aside Voluntary Declaration of Paternity [Form FL-285].
1 California Transactions Forms--Family Law § 3:128, Order After Hearing on Motion to Set Aside Voluntary Declaration of Paternity [Form FL-290].
1 California Transactions Forms--Family Law § 4:105, Declaration of Paternity.
2 California Transactions Forms--Family Law § 5:4, Rights of De Facto Parents.
2 California Transactions Forms--Family Law § 5:9, Use of Parenting Agreement to Define Rights and Responsibilities Relating to Child on Termination of Partners' Relationship Where Both Partners Are Biological Parents.
2 California Transactions Forms--Family Law § 5:9.50, Voiding of a Voluntary Declaration of Parentage.
2 California Transactions Forms--Family Law § 6:3, Definitions.

§ 7611

2 California Transactions Forms--Family Law § 6:8, Consent for Adoption of Unmarried Minor.
2 California Transactions Forms--Family Law § 6:11, Initiating Proceeding Under Uniform Parentage Act [Fam. Code, §§ 7600 to 7730].
2 California Transactions Forms--Family Law § 6:40, Structuring the Adoption.
2 California Transactions Forms--Family Law § 6:47, Matters to Consider in Drafting Petition for Independent Adoption of Unmarried Minor.
2 California Transactions Forms--Family Law § 6:72, Petition to Terminate Parental Rights of Alleged Father.
2 California Transactions Forms--Family Law § 6:74, Petition to Terminate Parental Rights of Alleged Father Served With Notice of Alleged Paternity Without Timely Response.
2 California Transactions Forms--Family Law § 6:75, Order Terminating Parental Rights of Alleged Father Served With Notice of Alleged Paternity Without Timely Response.
2 California Transactions Forms--Family Law § 6:76, Ex Parte Application for Order to Terminate Parental Rights of Alleged Father Who Waived Notice or Denied Paternity.
2 California Transactions Forms--Family Law § 6:77, Order Terminating Parental Rights of Alleged Father Who Waived Notice.
2 California Transactions Forms--Family Law § 7:38, Parentage and Birth Certificate.
2 California Transactions Forms--Family Law § 7:86, Overview.
2 California Transactions Forms--Family Law § 7:96, California Statutory Form for Assisted Reproduction—Intent to be Parents—Married Spouses or Registered Domestic Partners Using Assisted Reproduction to Conceive a Child (Form 1).
2 California Transactions Forms--Family Law § 7:97, California Statutory Form for Assisted Reproduction—Intent to be Parents—Unmarried, Intended Parents Using Intended Parent's Sperm to Conceive a Child (Form 2).
2 California Transactions Forms--Family Law § 7:98, California Statutory Form for Assisted Reproduction—Intent to be Parents—Intended Parents Conceiving a Child Using Eggs from One Parent and the Other Parent Will Give Birth (Form 3).
2 California Transactions Forms--Family Law § 7:98.50, California Statutory Form for Assisted Reproduction—Intent to be Parents—Intended Parents Using Known Sperm, Egg Donor to Conceive Child (Form 4).
West's California Code Forms, Family § 6340, Comment Overview—Issuance of Orders After Notice and Hearing.
West's California Code Forms, Family § 7540, Comment Overview—Conclusive Presumption as Child of Marriage.
West's California Code Forms, Family § 7610, Comment Overview—Establishing Parent and Child Relationship.
West's California Code Forms, Family § 7613 Form 1, Consent by Husband to Artificial Insemination of Wife.
West's California Code Forms, Family § 7630, Comment Overview—Determining Parent and Child Relationship.
West's California Code Forms, Family § 7630 Form 2, Complaint to Establish Nonexistence of Parental Relationship.
West's California Code Forms, Family § 7660, Comment Overview—Termination of Parental Rights in Adoption Proceedings.
West's California Code Forms, Family § 8600, Comment Overview—Adoption of Unmarried Minors.
West's California Judicial Council Forms JV–505, Statement Regarding Parentage (Juvenile) (Also Available in Spanish).

§ 7611.5. Presumption against natural father status; Section 7611 inapplicable

Where Section 7611 does not apply, a man shall not be presumed to be the natural father of a child if either of the following is true:

(a) The child was conceived as a result of an act in violation of Section 261 of the Penal Code and the father was convicted of that violation.

(b) The child was conceived as a result of an act in violation of Section 261.5 of the Penal Code, the father was convicted of that violation, and the mother was under the age of 15 years and the father was 21 years of age or older at the time of conception. *(Added by Stats.1993, c. 219 (A.B.1500), § 177.)*

Cross References

Freedom from parental custody and control, parent convicted of felony, right of action, see Family Code § 7825.

Hearsay exceptions, statements concerning family history, see Evidence Code § 1310 et seq.
Intestate succession, parent and child relationship,
Natural parents, see Probate Code § 6453.
Out-of-wedlock births, conditions for inheritance based on relationship, see Probate Code § 6452.
Relationship severed by adoption, see Probate Code § 6451.
Presumption affecting the burden of proof defined, see Evidence Code § 605.

Research References

Forms
West's California Judicial Council Forms JV–505, Statement Regarding Parentage (Juvenile) (Also Available in Spanish).

§ 7612. Presumption as natural parent; rebuttable presumption; conflicting presumptions; more than two persons with claim to parentage; person's offer or refusal to sign voluntary declaration of parentage

(a) Except as provided in Chapter 1 (commencing with Section 7540) and Chapter 3 (commencing with Section 7570) of Part 2, a presumption under Section 7611 is a rebuttable presumption affecting the burden of proof and may be rebutted in an appropriate action only by clear and convincing evidence.

(b) If two or more presumptions arise under Section 7611 that conflict with each other, or if one or more presumptions under Section 7611 conflict with a claim by a person identified as a genetic parent pursuant to Section 7555, the presumption that on the facts is founded on the weightier considerations of policy and logic controls. If one of the presumed parents is also a presumed parent under Section 7540, the presumption arising under Section 7540 may only be rebutted pursuant to Section 7541.

(c) In an appropriate action, a court may find that more than two persons with a claim to parentage under this division are parents if the court finds that recognizing only two parents would be detrimental to the child. In determining detriment to the child, the court shall consider all relevant factors, including, but not limited to, the harm of removing the child from a stable placement with a parent who has fulfilled the child's physical needs and the child's psychological needs for care and affection, and who has assumed that role for a substantial period of time. A finding of detriment to the child does not require a finding of unfitness of any of the parents or persons with a claim to parentage.

(d) Unless a court orders otherwise after making the determination specified in subdivision (c), a presumption under Section 7611 is rebutted by a judgment establishing parentage of the child by another person.

(e) A person's offer or refusal to sign a voluntary declaration of parentage may be considered as a factor, but shall not be determinative, as to the issue of legal parentage in a proceeding regarding the establishment or termination of parental rights.

(f) This section shall become operative on January 1, 2020. *(Added by Stats.2018, c. 876 (A.B.2684), § 48, eff. Jan. 1, 2019, operative Jan. 1, 2020.)*

Cross References

Abandonment and neglect of children, willful infliction of corporal injury, see Penal Code § 273.5.
Burden of proof, generally, see Evidence Code § 500 et seq.
Domestic violence, ex parte orders regarding temporary custody and visitation of minor children, see Family Code § 6323.
Domestic violence incidents, temporary custody of firearms, domestic violence defined, see Penal Code §§ 18250 to 18500.
Hearsay exceptions, statements concerning family history, see Evidence Code § 1310 et seq.
Intestate succession, parent and child relationship,
Natural parents, see Probate Code § 6453.
Out-of-wedlock births, conditions for inheritance based on relationship, see Probate Code § 6452.
Relationship severed by adoption, see Probate Code § 6451.

Judgment and order defined for purposes of this Code, see Family Code § 100.
Presumption affecting the burden of proof defined, see Evidence Code § 605.

Research References

Forms

1 California Transactions Forms--Family Law § 3:126, Request for Hearing and Application to Set Aside Voluntary Declaration of Paternity [Form FL-280].
1 California Transactions Forms--Family Law § 3:126.50, Information Sheet for Completing Request for Hearing and Application to Set Aside Voluntary Declaration of Paternity [Form FL-281].
1 California Transactions Forms--Family Law § 3:127, Responsive Declaration to Application to Set Aside Voluntary Declaration of Paternity [Form FL-285].
1 California Transactions Forms--Family Law § 3:128, Order After Hearing on Motion to Set Aside Voluntary Declaration of Paternity [Form FL-290].
1 California Transactions Forms--Family Law § 4:105, Declaration of Paternity.
2 California Transactions Forms--Family Law § 5:4, Rights of De Facto Parents.
2 California Transactions Forms--Family Law § 5:9, Use of Parenting Agreement to Define Rights and Responsibilities Relating to Child on Termination of Partners' Relationship Where Both Partners Are Biological Parents.
2 California Transactions Forms--Family Law § 6:3, Definitions.
2 California Transactions Forms--Family Law § 6:8, Consent for Adoption of Unmarried Minor.
2 California Transactions Forms--Family Law § 6:11, Initiating Proceeding Under Uniform Parentage Act [Fam. Code, §§ 7600 to 7730].
2 California Transactions Forms--Family Law § 6:40, Structuring the Adoption.
2 California Transactions Forms--Family Law § 6:47, Matters to Consider in Drafting Petition for Independent Adoption of Unmarried Minor.
2 California Transactions Forms--Family Law § 6:72, Petition to Terminate Parental Rights of Alleged Father.
2 California Transactions Forms--Family Law § 6:74, Petition to Terminate Parental Rights of Alleged Father Served With Notice of Alleged Paternity Without Timely Response.
2 California Transactions Forms--Family Law § 6:75, Order Terminating Parental Rights of Alleged Father Served With Notice of Alleged Paternity Without Timely Response.
2 California Transactions Forms--Family Law § 6:76, Ex Parte Application for Order to Terminate Parental Rights of Alleged Father Who Waived Notice or Denied Paternity.
2 California Transactions Forms--Family Law § 7:38, Parentage and Birth Certificate.
2 California Transactions Forms--Family Law § 7:86, Overview.
West's California Judicial Council Forms JV-505, Statement Regarding Parentage (Juvenile) (Also Available in Spanish).

§ 7613. Conception through assisted reproduction with semen or ova donated by donor other than spouse; consent of another intended parent; treatment as natural parent; treatment of semen or ova donors

(a)(1) If a woman conceives through assisted reproduction with semen or ova or both donated by a donor who is not the woman's spouse, with the consent of another intended parent, that intended parent is treated in law as if that intended parent is the natural parent of a child thereby conceived. The other intended parent's consent shall be in writing and signed by the other intended parent and the woman conceiving through assisted reproduction.

(2) Failure to consent in writing, as required by paragraph (1), does not preclude the court from finding that the intended parent consented if the court finds by clear and convincing evidence that, prior to the conception of the child, the woman and the intended parent had an oral agreement that the woman and the intended parent would both be parents of the child.

(b)(1) The donor of semen provided to a licensed physician and surgeon or to a licensed sperm bank for use in assisted reproduction by a woman other than the donor's spouse is treated in law as if the donor is not the natural parent of a child thereby conceived, unless otherwise agreed to in a writing signed by the donor and the woman prior to the conception of the child.

(2) If the semen is not provided to a licensed physician and surgeon or a licensed sperm bank as specified in paragraph (1), the donor of semen for use in assisted reproduction by a woman other than the donor's spouse is treated in law as if the donor is not the natural parent of a child thereby conceived if either of the following are met:

(A) The donor and the woman agreed in a writing signed prior to conception that the donor would not be a parent.

(B) A court finds by clear and convincing evidence that the child was conceived through assisted reproduction and that, prior to the conception of the child, the woman and the donor had an oral agreement that the donor would not be a parent.

(3) Paragraphs (1) and (2) do not apply to a man who provided semen for use in assisted reproduction by a woman other than the man's spouse pursuant to a written agreement signed by the man and the woman prior to conception of the child stating that they intended for the man to be a parent.

(c) * * * A person providing ova for use in assisted reproduction by a person other than the provider's spouse or nonmarital partner is treated in law as if the provider is not the natural parent of a child thereby conceived unless the court finds satisfactory evidence that the * * * provider of the ova, and * * * each recipient, intended for * * * that provider to have parental rights.

(d)(1) A provider of an embryo for use in assisted reproduction to an intended parent who is not the provider's spouse or nonmarital partner is treated in law as if the provider is not the natural parent of a child thereby conceived unless the court finds satisfactory evidence that the provider and the intended parent intended for the provider to be a parent.

(2) If the provider of ova, semen, or embryos is not the original source of the ova or sperm, each original provider's written consent to the donation is required unless that person has executed a writing to consent, waive, or relinquish their right to the genetic material, or as otherwise ordered by a court of law. (Stats.1992, c. 162 (A.B.2650), § 10, operative Jan. 1, 1994. Amended by Stats.2008, c. 534 (S.B.1726), § 2; Stats.2011, c. 185 (A.B.1349), § 4; Stats.2013, c. 510 (A.B.1403), § 5; Stats.2015, c. 566 (A.B.960), § 1, eff. Jan. 1, 2016; Stats.2016, c. 385 (A.B.2349), § 2, eff. Jan. 1, 2017; Stats.2018, c. 876 (A.B.2684), § 49, eff. Jan. 1, 2019; Stats.2019, c. 115 (A.B.1817), § 88, eff. Jan. 1, 2020; Stats.2022, c. 159 (A.B.2495), § 1, eff. Jan. 1, 2023.)

Cross References

Adoption, cessation of birth parents' responsibilities toward child, see Family Code § 8617.
Assisted reproduction agreements for gestational carriers, requirements, rebuttal of presumptions, see Family Code § 7962.
Birth parent defined, see Family Code § 8512.
Child support, equal duty of parents to support child, see Family Code § 3900.
Conception by surgical procedure, blood tests not allowed to challenge paternity, see Family Code § 7541.
Custody of children, generally, see Family Code § 3000 et seq.
Domestic violence, ex parte orders regarding temporary custody and visitation of minor children, see Family Code § 6323.
Domestic violence incidents, temporary custody of firearms, domestic violence defined, see Penal Code §§ 18250 to 18500.
Duty of parent to support child, see Family Code § 3900 et seq.
Enforcement of contract by third party beneficiary, see Civil Code § 1559.
Father and child relationship, action to determine existence or nonexistence, see Family Code § 7630.
Filing petition to terminate parental rights of father, conditions, see Family Code § 7662.
Hearsay exceptions, statements concerning family history, see Evidence Code § 1310 et seq.
Independent adoptions, consent of birth parents, see Family Code § 8814.
Intestate succession, parent and child relationship,
    Natural parents, see Probate Code § 6453.

§ 7613

Out-of-wedlock births, conditions for inheritance based on relationship, see Probate Code § 6452.

Relationship severed by adoption, see Probate Code § 6451.

Judgment and order defined for purposes of this Code, see Family Code § 100.

Mother and child relationship, action to determine existence or nonexistence, see Family Code § 7650.

Parent and child relationship, setting aside or vacating paternity judgments, artificial insemination and surrogacy agreements, see Family Code § 7648.9.

Presumption affecting the burden of proof defined, see Evidence Code § 605.

Production of evidence, burden of proof, see Evidence Code §§ 500, 550.

References to husband, wife, spouses and married persons, persons included for purposes of this Code, see Family Code § 11.

Void voluntary declaration of parentage, conditions, notice, see Family Code § 7573.5.

Written instrument, presumption of consideration, see Civil Code § 1614.

Research References

Forms

1 California Transactions Forms--Family Law § 3:126, Request for Hearing and Application to Set Aside Voluntary Declaration of Paternity [Form FL-280].

1 California Transactions Forms--Family Law § 3:126.50, Information Sheet for Completing Request for Hearing and Application to Set Aside Voluntary Declaration of Paternity [Form FL-281].

1 California Transactions Forms--Family Law § 3:127, Responsive Declaration to Application to Set Aside Voluntary Declaration of Paternity [Form FL-285].

1 California Transactions Forms--Family Law § 3:128, Order After Hearing on Motion to Set Aside Voluntary Declaration of Paternity [Form FL-290].

1 California Transactions Forms--Family Law § 4:105, Declaration of Paternity.

2 California Transactions Forms--Family Law § 5:4, Rights of De Facto Parents.

2 California Transactions Forms--Family Law § 5:9, Use of Parenting Agreement to Define Rights and Responsibilities Relating to Child on Termination of Partners' Relationship Where Both Partners Are Biological Parents.

2 California Transactions Forms--Family Law § 5:9.50, Voiding of a Voluntary Declaration of Parentage.

2 California Transactions Forms--Family Law § 5:11, Use of Parenting Agreement to Define Rights and Responsibilities Relating to Child During Relationship Between Same-Sex Partners.

2 California Transactions Forms--Family Law § 5:34, Parenting Agreement Between Lesbian Partners Where One Partner is Egg Mother and One Partner is Gestational Mother.

2 California Transactions Forms--Family Law § 5:35, Parenting Agreement Between Lesbian Partners Where One Partner is Both Gestational and Egg Mother.

2 California Transactions Forms--Family Law § 6:3, Definitions.

2 California Transactions Forms--Family Law § 6:8, Consent for Adoption of Unmarried Minor.

2 California Transactions Forms--Family Law § 6:11, Initiating Proceeding Under Uniform Parentage Act [Fam. Code, §§7600 to 7730].

2 California Transactions Forms--Family Law § 6:40, Structuring the Adoption.

2 California Transactions Forms--Family Law § 6:47, Matters to Consider in Drafting Petition for Independent Adoption of Unmarried Minor.

2 California Transactions Forms--Family Law § 6:72, Petition to Terminate Parental Rights of Alleged Father.

2 California Transactions Forms--Family Law § 6:74, Petition to Terminate Parental Rights of Alleged Father Served With Notice of Alleged Paternity Without Timely Response.

2 California Transactions Forms--Family Law § 6:75, Order Terminating Parental Rights of Alleged Father Served With Notice of Alleged Paternity Without Timely Response.

2 California Transactions Forms--Family Law § 6:76, Ex Parte Application for Order to Terminate Parental Rights of Alleged Father Who Waived Notice or Denied Paternity.

2 California Transactions Forms--Family Law § 7:7, Gestational Surrogacy Agreements Using Donated Egg and Sperm.

2 California Transactions Forms--Family Law § 7:8, Traditional Surrogacy Agreements.

2 California Transactions Forms--Family Law § 7:33, Parentage Testing.

2 California Transactions Forms--Family Law § 7:45, Artificial Insemination Surrogacy Agreement Between Intended Father and Surrogate Couple.

2 California Transactions Forms--Family Law § 7:46, In Vitro Surrogacy Agreement Between Intended Parents and Surrogate Couple; Intended Parents Are Genetic Parents.

2 California Transactions Forms--Family Law § 7:47, In Vitro Fertilization Surrogacy Agreement Between Intended Mother and Surrogate Using Donated Genetic Material.

2 California Transactions Forms--Family Law § 7:49, Nonconsent of Surrogate's Husband [Fam C § 7613].

2 California Transactions Forms--Family Law § 7:54, Introduction.

2 California Transactions Forms--Family Law § 7:60, Overview; Paternity of Child [Fam C § 7613].

2 California Transactions Forms--Family Law § 7:61, Requirement of Physician Involvement.

2 California Transactions Forms--Family Law § 7:62, Effect of Failure to Certify Consent.

2 California Transactions Forms--Family Law § 7:63, Application of Fam C § 7613 to Egg Donors.

2 California Transactions Forms--Family Law § 7:64, Exception to Application of Fam C § 7613 in Certain Surrogacy Cases.

2 California Transactions Forms--Family Law § 7:67, Selecting Physician.

2 California Transactions Forms--Family Law § 7:68, Overview.

2 California Transactions Forms--Family Law § 7:79, Waiver of Parental Rights by Donor, Acceptance of Parental Rights by Recipient.

2 California Transactions Forms--Family Law § 7:90, Artificial Insemination Agreement Between Husband, Wife, and Licensed Physician.

2 California Transactions Forms--Family Law § 7:91, Implantation Agreement Between Husband, Wife, and Licensed Physician.

2 California Transactions Forms--Family Law § 7:92, Sperm Donation Agreement Between Sperm Donor and Agency.

2 California Transactions Forms--Family Law § 7:93, Sperm Donation Agreement Between Sperm Donor and Recipients for Insemination of Recipients' Surrogate.

2 California Transactions Forms--Family Law § 7:94, Egg Donation Agreement Between Egg Donor and Agency.

2 California Transactions Forms--Family Law § 7:95, Agreement Between Agency and Recipients to Utilize Eggs from Anonymous Donor.

2 California Transactions Forms--Family Law § 7:96, California Statutory Form for Assisted Reproduction—Intent to be Parents—Married Spouses or Registered Domestic Partners Using Assisted Reproduction to Conceive a Child (Form 1).

2 California Transactions Forms--Family Law § 7:97, California Statutory Form for Assisted Reproduction—Intent to be Parents—Unmarried, Intended Parents Using Intended Parent's Sperm to Conceive a Child (Form 2).

2 California Transactions Forms--Family Law § 7:98, California Statutory Form for Assisted Reproduction—Intent to be Parents—Intended Parents Conceiving a Child Using Eggs from One Parent and the Other Parent Will Give Birth (Form 3).

2 California Transactions Forms--Family Law § 7:98.50, California Statutory Form for Assisted Reproduction—Intent to be Parents—Intended Parents Using Known Sperm, Egg Donor to Conceive Child (Form 4).

West's California Code Forms, Family § 7610, Comment Overview—Establishing Parent and Child Relationship.

West's California Code Forms, Family § 7613 Form 1, Consent by Husband to Artificial Insemination of Wife.

§ 7613.5. Intended parent; use of forms

(a) An intended parent may, but is not required to, use the forms set forth in this section to demonstrate the intent to be a legal parent of a child conceived through assisted reproduction. These forms shall satisfy the writing requirement specified in Section 7613, and are designed to provide clarity regarding the intentions, at the time of conception, of intended parents using assisted reproduction. These forms do not affect any presumptions of parentage based on Section 7611, and do not preclude a court from considering any other claims to parentage under California statute or case law.

(b) These forms apply only in very limited circumstances. Please read the forms carefully to see if you qualify for use of the forms.

(c) These forms do not apply to assisted reproduction agreements for gestational carriers or surrogacy agreements.

(d) This section does not require the use of one of these forms to satisfy the writing requirement of Section 7613.

UNIFORM PARENTAGE ACT § 7613.5

(e) The following are the optional California Statutory Forms for Assisted Reproduction:

California Statutory Forms for Assisted Reproduction, Form 1:

<u>Two Married or Unmarried People Using Assisted Reproduction to Conceive a Child</u>
Use this form if: You and another intended parent, who may be your spouse or registered domestic partner, are conceiving a child through assisted reproduction using sperm and/or egg donation; and one of you will be giving birth.

WARNING: Signing this form does not terminate the parentage claim of a sperm donor. A sperm donor's claim to parentage is terminated if the sperm is provided to a licensed physician and surgeon or to a licensed sperm bank prior to insemination, or if you conceive without having sexual intercourse and you have a written agreement signed by you and the donor that you will conceive using assisted reproduction and do not intend for the donor to be a parent, as required by Section 7613(b) of the Family Code.

The laws about parentage of a child are complicated. **You are strongly encouraged to consult with an attorney about your rights.** Even if you do not fill out this form, a spouse or domestic partner of the parent giving birth is presumed to be a legal parent of any child born during the marriage or domestic partnership.

_____

This form demonstrates your intent to be parents of the child you plan to conceive through assisted reproduction using sperm and/or egg donation.

I, _____ (print name of person not giving birth), intend to be a parent of a child that _____ (print name of person giving birth) will or has conceived through assisted reproduction using sperm and/or egg donation. I consent to the use of assisted reproduction by the person who will give birth. <u>I INTEND to be a parent of the child conceived.</u>

SIGNATURES

Intended parent who will give birth: _____
(print name)
_____ (signature)
_____(date)

Intended parent who will not give birth: _____
(print name)
_____ (signature)
_____(date)

_____

NOTARY ACKNOWLEDGMENT

State of California
County of _____)

On _____ before me, _____
(insert name and title of the officer)
personally appeared _____,

who proved to me on the basis of satisfactory evidence to be the person(s) whose name(s) is/are subscribed to the within instrument and acknowledged to me that he/she/they executed the same in his/her/their authorized capacity, and that by his/her/their signature(s) on the instrument the person(s), or the entity upon behalf of which the person(s) acted, executed the instrument.

I certify under PENALTY OF PERJURY under the laws of the State of California that the foregoing paragraph is true and correct.

WITNESS my hand and official seal.

Signature_____ (Seal)

California Statutory Forms for Assisted Reproduction, Form 2:

<u>Unmarried, Intended Parents Using Intended Parent's Sperm to Conceive a Child</u>
Use this form if: (1) Neither you or the other person are married or in a registered domestic partnership (including a registered domestic partnership or civil union from another state); (2) one of you will give birth to a child conceived through assisted reproduction using the intended parent's sperm; and (3) you both intend to be parents of that child.

Do <u>not</u> use this form if you are conceiving using a surrogate.

WARNING: If you do not sign this form, or a similar agreement, you may be treated as a sperm donor if you conceive without having sexual intercourse according to Section 7613(b) of the Family Code.

The laws about parentage of a child are complicated. **You are strongly encouraged to consult with an attorney about your rights.**

_____

This form demonstrates your intent to be parents of the child you plan to conceive through assisted reproduction using sperm donation.

I, _____ (print name of parent giving birth), plan to use assisted reproduction with another intended parent who is providing sperm to conceive the child. I am not married and am not in a registered domestic partnership (including a registered domestic partnership or civil union from another jurisdiction), and <u>I INTEND for the person providing sperm to be a parent of the child to be conceived.</u>

I, _____ (print name of parent providing sperm), plan to use assisted reproduction to conceive a child using my sperm with the parent giving birth. I am not married and am not in a registered domestic partnership (including a registered domestic partnership or civil union from another jurisdiction), and <u>I INTEND to be a parent of the child to be conceived.</u>

SIGNATURES

Intended parent giving birth: _____ (print name)

§ 7613.5 PARENT AND CHILD RELATIONSHIP

_____ (signature)
_____ (date)

Intended parent providing sperm: _____ (print name)
_____ (signature)
_____ (date)

NOTARY ACKNOWLEDGMENT

State of California
County of _____)

On _____ before me, _____ (insert name and title of the officer) personally appeared _____, who proved to me on the basis of satisfactory evidence to be the person(s) whose name(s) is/are subscribed to the within instrument and acknowledged to me that he/she/they executed the same in his/her/their authorized capacity, and that by his/her/their signature(s) on the instrument the person(s), or the entity upon behalf of which the person(s) acted, executed the instrument.

I certify under PENALTY OF PERJURY under the laws of the State of California that the foregoing paragraph is true and correct.

WITNESS my hand and official seal.

Signature_____ (Seal)

_____

California Statutory Forms for Assisted Reproduction, Form 3:

<u>Intended Parents Conceiving a Child Using Eggs from One Parent and the Other Parent Will Give Birth</u>
Use this form if: You are conceiving a child using the eggs from one of you and the other person will give birth to the child; (2) and you both intend to be parents to that child.

Do <u>not</u> use this form if you are conceiving using a surrogate.

WARNING: Signing this form does not terminate the parentage claim of a sperm donor. A sperm donor's claim to parentage is terminated if the sperm is provided to a licensed physician and surgeon or to a licensed sperm bank prior to insemination, or if you conceive without having sexual intercourse and you have a written agreement signed by you and the donor that you will conceive using assisted reproduction and do not intend for the donor to be a parent, as required by Section 7613(b) of the Family Code.

The laws about parentage of a child are complicated. **You are strongly encouraged to consult with an attorney about your rights.**

_____

This form demonstrates your intent to be parents of the child you plan to conceive through assisted reproduction using eggs from one parent and the other parent will give birth to the child.

I, _____ (print name of parent giving birth), plan to use assisted reproduction to conceive and give birth to a child with another person who will provide eggs to conceive the child. <u>I INTEND for the person providing eggs to be a parent of the child to be conceived.</u>

I, _____ (print name of parent providing eggs), plan to use assisted reproduction to conceive a child with another person who will give birth to the child conceived using my eggs. <u>I INTEND to be a parent of the child to be conceived.</u>

SIGNATURES

Intended parent giving birth: _____ (print name)
_____ (signature)
_____ (date)

Intended parent providing eggs: _____ (print name)
_____ (signature)
_____ (date)

NOTARY ACKNOWLEDGMENT

State of California
County of _____)

On _____ before me, _____ (insert name and title of the officer) personally appeared _____, who proved to me on the basis of satisfactory evidence to be the person(s) whose name(s) is/are subscribed to the within instrument and acknowledged to me that he/she/they executed the same in his/her/their authorized capacity, and that by his/her/their signature(s) on the instrument the person(s), or the entity upon behalf of which the person(s) acted, executed the instrument.

I certify under PENALTY OF PERJURY under the laws of the State of California that the foregoing paragraph is true and correct.

WITNESS my hand and official seal.

Signature_____ (Seal)

_____

California Statutory Forms for Assisted Reproduction, Form 4:

<u>Intended Parent(s) Using a Known Sperm and/or Egg Donor(s) to Conceive a Child</u>
Use this form if: You are using a known sperm and/or egg donor(s), or embryo donation, to conceive a child and you do not intend for the donor(s) to be a parent.

Do <u>not</u> use this form if you are conceiving using a surrogate.

If you do not sign this form or a similar agreement, your sperm donor may be treated as a parent unless the sperm is provided to a licensed physician and surgeon or to a licensed sperm bank prior to insemination, or a court finds by clear and convincing evidence that you planned to conceive through assisted reproduction and did not intend for the donor to be a parent, as required by Section 7613(b) of the Family Code. If you do not sign this form or a similar agreement, your egg donor may be treated as a parent unless a court finds that there is satisfactory evidence that you planned to conceive through assisted reproduction and did not intend for the donor to be a parent, as required by Section 7613(c) of the Family Code.

The laws about parentage of a child are complicated. **You are strongly encouraged to consult with an attorney about your rights.**

_____

This form demonstrates your intent that your sperm and/or egg or embryo donor(s) will not be a parent or parents of the child you plan to conceive through assisted reproduction.

I, _____ (print name of parent giving birth), plan to use assisted reproduction to conceive using a sperm and/or egg donor(s) or embryo donation, and I DO NOT INTEND for the sperm and/or egg or embryo donor(s) to be a parent of the child to be conceived.

(If applicable) I, _____ (print name of sperm donor), plan to donate my sperm to _____ (print name of parent giving birth and second parent if applicable). I am not married to and am not in a registered domestic partnership (including a registered domestic partnership or a civil union from another jurisdiction) with _____ (print name of parent giving birth), and I DO NOT INTEND to be a parent of the child to be conceived.

(If applicable) I, _____ (print name of egg donor), plan to donate my ova to _____ (print name of parent giving birth and second parent if applicable). I am not married to and am not in a registered domestic partnership (including a registered domestic partnership or a civil union from another jurisdiction) with _____ (print name of parent giving birth), or any intimate and nonmarital relationship with _____ (print name of parent giving birth) and I DO NOT INTEND to be a parent of the child to be conceived.

(If applicable) I, _____ (print name of intended parent not giving birth), INTEND to be a parent of the child that _____ (print name of parent giving birth) will conceive through assisted reproduction using sperm and/or egg donation and I DO NOT INTEND for the sperm and/or egg or embryo donor(s) to be a parent. I consent to the use of assisted reproduction by the person who will give birth.

SIGNATURES

Intended parent giving birth: _____ (print name)
_____ (signature)
_____ (date)

(If applicable) Sperm Donor: _____ (print name)
_____ (signature)
_____ (date)

(If applicable) Egg Donor: _____ (print name)
_____ (signature)
_____ (date)

(If applicable) Intended parent not giving birth: _____ (print name)
_____ (signature)
_____ (date)

NOTARY ACKNOWLEDGMENT

State of California
County of _____)

On _____ before me, _____ (insert name and title of the officer) personally appeared _____ who proved to me on the basis of satisfactory evidence to be the person(s) whose name(s) is/are subscribed to the within instrument and acknowledged to me that he/she/they executed the same in his/her/their authorized capacity, and that by his/her/their signature(s) on the instrument the person(s), or the entity upon behalf of which the person(s) acted, executed the instrument.

I certify under PENALTY OF PERJURY under the laws of the State of California that the foregoing paragraph is true and correct.

WITNESS my hand and official seal.

Signature _____ (Seal)

(Added by Stats.2014, c. 636 (A.B.2344), § 1, eff. Jan. 1, 2015. Amended by Stats.2015, c. 566 (A.B.960), § 2, eff. Jan. 1, 2016; Stats.2016, c. 86 (S.B.1171), § 130, eff. Jan. 1, 2017; Stats.2019, c. 115 (A.B.1817), § 89, eff. Jan. 1, 2020.)

Research References

Forms

2 California Transactions Forms--Family Law § 7:96, California Statutory Form for Assisted Reproduction—Intent to be Parents—Married Spouses or Registered Domestic Partners Using Assisted Reproduction to Conceive a Child (Form 1).

2 California Transactions Forms--Family Law § 7:97, California Statutory Form for Assisted Reproduction—Intent to be Parents—Unmarried, Intended Parents Using Intended Parent's Sperm to Conceive a Child (Form 2).

2 California Transactions Forms--Family Law § 7:98, California Statutory Form for Assisted Reproduction—Intent to be Parents—Intended Parents Conceiving a Child Using Eggs from One Parent and the Other Parent Will Give Birth (Form 3).

2 California Transactions Forms--Family Law § 7:98.50, California Statutory Form for Assisted Reproduction—Intent to be Parents—Intended Parents Using Known Sperm, Egg Donor to Conceive Child (Form 4).

§ 7614. Written promise to furnish support; enforcement; confidentiality

(a) A promise in writing to furnish support for a child, growing out of a presumed parent or alleged father and child relationship, does not require consideration and, subject to Section 7632, is enforceable according to its terms.

(b) In the best interest of the child or the other parent, the court may, and upon the promisor's request shall, order the promise to be kept in confidence and designate a person or agency to receive and disburse on behalf of the child all amounts paid in performance of the promise. (Stats.1992, c. 162 (A.B.2650), § 10, operative Jan. 1, 1994. Amended by Stats.2013, c. 510 (A.B.1403), § 6.)

Cross References

Best interest of child, considerations, see Family Code § 3011.
Child support, equal duty of parents to support child, see Family Code § 3900.
Judgment and order defined for purposes of this Code, see Family Code § 100.
Paternity, rebuttable presumption, see Family Code § 7555.
Person defined for purposes of this Code, see Family Code § 105.
Support defined for purposes of this Code, see Family Code § 150.

CHAPTER 3. JURISDICTION AND VENUE

Section
7620. Intent to become legal parent by assisted reproduction in state; consent to jurisdiction; jurisdiction to determine parentage; venue.

Cross References

Uniform act, construction of provisions, see Family Code § 3.

§ 7620. Intent to become legal parent by assisted reproduction in state; consent to jurisdiction; jurisdiction to determine parentage; venue

(a) A person who has sexual intercourse or causes conception with the intent to become a legal parent by assisted reproduction in this state, or who enters into an assisted reproduction agreement for gestational carriers in this state, thereby submits to the jurisdiction of the courts of this state as to an action brought under this part with respect to a child who may have been conceived by that act of intercourse or assisted reproduction, or who may have been conceived as a result of that assisted reproduction agreement.

(b) If a child is conceived pursuant to an assisted reproduction agreement for gestational carriers, as defined in Section 7960 and as described in Section 7962, the courts of this state shall have jurisdiction over a proceeding to determine parentage of the child if any of the following conditions is satisfied:

(1) One or more of the parties to the assisted reproduction agreement for gestational carriers resides in this state, or resided in this state at the time the assisted reproduction agreement for gestational carriers was executed.

(2) The medical procedures leading to conception, including in vitro fertilization or embryo transfer, or both, were carried out in this state.

(3) The child is born in this state.

(c) An action under this part shall be brought in one of the following:

(1) The county in which the child resides or is found.

(2) If the child is the subject of a pending or proposed adoption, any county in which a licensed California adoption agency to which the child has been relinquished or is proposed to be relinquished maintains an office.

(3) If the child is the subject of a pending or proposed adoption, the county in which an office of the department or a public adoption agency investigating the petition is located.

(4) If the parent is deceased, the county in which proceedings for probate of the estate of the parent of the child have been or could be commenced.

(5) If the child was conceived pursuant to an assisted reproduction agreement for gestational carriers, any county described in subdivision (e) of Section 7962. (Stats.1992, c. 162 (A.B.2650), § 10, operative Jan. 1, 1994. Amended by Stats.2003, c. 251 (S.B.182), § 1; Stats.2005, c. 627 (S.B.302), § 1; Stats.2006, c. 806 (S.B.1325), § 2; Stats.2009, c. 492 (A.B.941), § 1; Stats.2013, c. 510 (A.B.1403), § 7; Stats.2016, c. 385 (A.B.2349), § 3, eff. Jan. 1, 2017.)

Cross References

County defined for purposes of this Code, see Family Code § 67.
Jurisdiction of superior court,
 Generally, see Cal. Const. Art. 6, §§ 10, 11.
 Proceedings under this code, see Family Code § 200.
Person defined for purposes of this Code, see Family Code § 105.
Proceeding defined for purposes of this Code, see Family Code § 110.
State defined for purposes of this Code, see Family Code § 145.
Uniform Interstate Family Support Act, bases for jurisdiction over nonresident, see Family Code § 5700.201.

Research References

Forms
2 California Transactions Forms--Family Law § 6:11, Initiating Proceeding Under Uniform Parentage Act [Fam. Code, §§ 7600 to 7730].
2 California Transactions Forms--Family Law § 6:72, Petition to Terminate Parental Rights of Alleged Father.

CHAPTER 4. DETERMINATION OF PARENT AND CHILD RELATIONSHIP

Article	Section
1. Determination of Parent and Child Relationship	7630
1.5. Setting Aside or Vacating Judgment of Parentage	7645
2. Determination of Mother and Child Relationship	7650

Cross References

California Work Opportunity and Responsibility to Kids Act, paternity not established, adoption being considered, see Welfare and Institutions Code § 11479.
Uniform act, construction of provisions, see Family Code § 3.

ARTICLE 1. DETERMINATION OF PARENT AND CHILD RELATIONSHIP

Section
7630. Action to determine existence or nonexistence of parent and child relationship; consolidated actions; notice of proceedings.
7631. Repealed.
7632. Agreement among parties does not bar action.
7633. Time for action, order or judgment.
7634. Action brought by local child support agency; review of current practices.
7635. Parties to action; representation of child by guardian ad litem or private counsel; notice; alignment.
7635.5. Right of alleged father to have genetic testing to determine parentage; right to make motion to set aside or vacate judgment.
7636. Effect of judgment or order; exceptions.
7637. Contents of judgment or order.
7638. Procedures to change name of child.
7639. Order for issuance of new birth certificate.
7640. Fees and costs.
7641. Obligation of parent; enforcement; parties; persons payable; willful failure to obey; civil contempt.
7642. Modification or set aside of judgment or order; jurisdiction; manner.

UNIFORM PARENTAGE ACT § 7630

Section	
7643.	Hearing or trial in closed court; papers and records; inspection and copying.
7643.5.	Hearing or trial in closed court for actions on or after January 1, 2023; papers and records; inspection and copying; designation of action or proceeding.
7644.	Voluntary declaration of parentage; child custody and support actions; force and effect.

Cross References

Uniform act, construction of provisions, see Family Code § 3.

§ 7630. Action to determine existence or nonexistence of parent and child relationship; consolidated actions; notice of proceedings

(a) A child, the child's natural mother, a person presumed to be the child's parent under subdivision (a), (b), or (c) of Section 7611, a person seeking to be adjudicated as a parent or donor under Section 7613, an adoption agency to whom the child has been relinquished, or a prospective adoptive parent of the child may bring an action as follows:

(1) At any time for the purpose of declaring the existence of the parent and child relationship presumed under subdivision (a), (b), or (c) of Section 7611, or established pursuant to Section 7613.

(2) For the purpose of declaring the nonexistence of the parent and child relationship presumed under subdivision (a), (b), or (c) of Section 7611 only if the action is brought within a reasonable time after obtaining knowledge of relevant facts. After the presumption has been rebutted, parentage of the child by another person may be determined in the same action, if that person has been made a party.

(3) At any time for the purpose of declaring the nonexistence of the parent and child relationship of a donor under Section 7613.

(b) Any interested party may bring an action at any time for the purpose of determining the existence or nonexistence of the parent and child relationship presumed under subdivision (d) or (e) of Section 7611.

(c) Except as to cases coming within Chapter 1 (commencing with Section 7540) of Part 2 or when paragraph (2) of subdivision (a) applies, an action to determine parentage may be brought by the child, a personal representative of the child, the Department of Child Support Services, a presumed parent or the personal representative or a parent of that presumed parent if that parent has died or is a minor, or, when the natural mother is the only presumed parent or an action under Section 300 of the Welfare and Institutions Code or adoption is pending, a man alleged or claiming to be the father or the personal representative or a parent of the alleged father if the alleged father has died or is a minor.

(d)(1) If a proceeding has been filed under Chapter 2 (commencing with Section 7820) of Part 4, an action under subdivision (a) or (b) shall be consolidated with that proceeding. The parental rights of the presumed parent shall be determined as set forth in Sections 7820 to 7829, inclusive.

(2) If a proceeding pursuant to Section 7662 has been filed under Chapter 5 (commencing with Section 7660), an action under subdivision (c) shall be consolidated with that proceeding. The parental rights of the alleged father shall be determined as set forth in Section 7664.

(3) The consolidated action under paragraph (1) or (2) shall be heard in the court in which the proceeding under Section 7662 or Chapter 2 (commencing with Section 7820) of Part 4 is filed, unless the court finds, by clear and convincing evidence, that transferring the action to the other court poses a substantial hardship to the petitioner. Mere inconvenience does not constitute a sufficient basis for a finding of substantial hardship. If the court determines there is a substantial hardship, the consolidated action shall be heard in the court in which the parentage action is filed.

(e)(1) If a prospective adoptive parent who has physical custody of the child, a licensed California adoption agency that has legal custody of the child or to which the mother proposes to relinquish the child for adoption, or a person whom the mother has designated as the prospective adoptive parent in a written statement executed before a hospital social worker, an adoption service provider, an adoption agency representative, or a notary public, has not been joined as a party to an action to determine the existence of a parent and child relationship under subdivision (a), (b), or (c), or an action for custody by a person claiming to be a parent under this division, the court shall join the prospective adoptive parent or licensed California adoption agency as a party upon application or on its own motion, without the necessity of a motion for joinder. A joined party shall not be required to pay a fee in connection with this action.

(2) If a person brings an action to determine parentage and custody of a child who the person has reason to believe is in the physical or legal custody of an adoption agency, or of one or more persons other than the child's parent who are prospective adoptive parents, the person shall serve the entire pleading on, and give notice of all proceedings to, the adoption agency or the prospective adoptive parents, or both.

(f) A party to an assisted reproduction agreement may bring an action at any time to establish a parent and child relationship consistent with the intent expressed in that assisted reproduction agreement.

(g)(1) In an action to determine the existence of the parent and child relationship brought pursuant to subdivision (b), if the child's other parent has died and there are no existing court orders or pending court actions involving custody or guardianship of the child, then the persons having physical custody of the child shall be served with notice of the proceeding at least 15 days prior to the hearing, either by mail or in a manner authorized by the court. If a person identified as having physical custody of the child cannot be located, the court shall prescribe the manner of giving notice.

(2) If known to the person bringing the parentage action, relatives within the second degree of the child shall be given notice of the proceeding at least 15 days prior to the hearing, either by mail or in a manner authorized by the court. If a person identified as a relative of the second degree of the child cannot be located, or the relative's whereabouts are unknown or cannot be ascertained, the court shall prescribe the manner of giving notice, or shall dispense with giving notice to that person.

(3) Proof of notice pursuant to this subdivision shall be filed with the court before the proceeding to determine the existence of the parent and child relationship is heard. *(Stats.1992, c. 162 (A.B.2650), § 10, operative Jan. 1, 1994. Amended by Stats.2000, c. 808 (A.B. 1358), § 76, eff. Sept. 28, 2000; Stats.2001, c. 353 (A.B.538), § 1; Stats.2003, c. 251 (S.B.182), § 2; Stats.2004, c. 775 (A.B.1910), § 2; Stats.2005, c. 627 (S.B.302), § 2; Stats.2006, c. 806 (S.B.1325), § 3; Stats.2007, c. 47 (S.B.313), § 1; Stats.2008, c. 534 (S.B.1726), § 3; Stats.2010, c. 588 (A.B.2020), § 1; Stats.2012, c. 155 (A.B.1337), § 1; Stats.2013, c. 510 (A.B.1403), § 8; Stats.2014, c. 763 (A.B.1701), § 1, eff. Jan. 1, 2015; Stats.2018, c. 876 (A.B.2684), § 51, eff. Jan. 1, 2019; Stats.2019, c. 115 (A.B.1817), § 90, eff. Jan. 1, 2020; Stats.2021, c. 124 (A.B.938), § 28, eff. Jan. 1, 2022.)*

Cross References

Action to determine mother and child relationship, see Family Code § 7650.
Action to enforce parent's duty to support, see Family Code § 4000.
Aid to dependent children, action to establish parental liability for support, see Welfare and Institutions Code § 11479.
Artificial insemination, see Family Code § 7613.
Assisted reproduction agreements for gestational carriers, requirements, actions to establish parent-child relationship, judgment or order, see Family Code § 7962.
Blood tests to determine paternity, see Family Code § 7550 et seq.
Department of Child Support Services, generally, see Family Code § 17000 et seq.

§ 7630

Ex parte orders terminating parental rights, see Family Code § 7667.
Fees and costs, see Family Code § 7640.
Intestate succession, natural parents, see Probate Code § 6453.
Jurisdiction, actions filed under this section, see Welfare and Institutions Code § 316.2.
Juvenile court law, disposition hearing, parentage inquiries, see Welfare and Institutions Code § 726.4.
Juvenile court law, protective order, parentage, custody, or visitation order, see Welfare and Institutions Code § 726.5.
Minor defined for purposes of this Code, see Family Code § 6500.
Petitioner defined for purposes of this Code, see Family Code § 126.
Presumed parent, filing of petition to set aside voluntary declaration of paternity pursuant to this section, see Family Code § 7612.
Proceeding defined for purposes of this Code, see Family Code § 110.
Promise to furnish support, effect of, see Family Code § 7614.
Representation of child, see Family Code § 7635.
Required paternity determination by court, actions filed under this section, see Welfare and Institutions Code § 316.2.
Support defined for purposes of this Code, see Family Code § 150.
Termination of juvenile court jurisdiction, pending proceedings relating to parental marriage or custody order, see Welfare and Institutions Code § 362.4.
Termination of parental rights in adoption proceedings, failure of alleged father to bring action for determination of father and child relationship, see Family Code § 7666.

Research References

Forms

1 California Transactions Forms--Estate Planning § 6:11, Existence of Relationship.
1 California Transactions Forms--Estate Planning § 6:52, Matters to Consider in Drafting Class Gifts.
1 California Transactions Forms--Family Law § 3:126, Request for Hearing and Application to Set Aside Voluntary Declaration of Paternity [Form FL-280].
1 California Transactions Forms--Family Law § 3:126.50, Information Sheet for Completing Request for Hearing and Application to Set Aside Voluntary Declaration of Paternity [Form FL-281].
1 California Transactions Forms--Family Law § 3:127, Responsive Declaration to Application to Set Aside Voluntary Declaration of Paternity [Form FL-285].
1 California Transactions Forms--Family Law § 3:128, Order After Hearing on Motion to Set Aside Voluntary Declaration of Paternity [Form FL-290].
1 California Transactions Forms--Family Law § 4:105, Declaration of Paternity.
2 California Transactions Forms--Family Law § 5:9, Use of Parenting Agreement to Define Rights and Responsibilities Relating to Child on Termination of Partners' Relationship Where Both Partners Are Biological Parents.
2 California Transactions Forms--Family Law § 6:8, Consent for Adoption of Unmarried Minor.
2 California Transactions Forms--Family Law § 6:11, Initiating Proceeding Under Uniform Parentage Act [Fam. Code, §§ 7600 to 7730].
2 California Transactions Forms--Family Law § 6:40, Structuring the Adoption.
2 California Transactions Forms--Family Law § 6:42, Rights of Birth Father.
2 California Transactions Forms--Family Law § 6:71, Notice of Alleged Paternity.
2 California Transactions Forms--Family Law § 6:72, Petition to Terminate Parental Rights of Alleged Father.
2 California Transactions Forms--Family Law § 6:75, Order Terminating Parental Rights of Alleged Father Served With Notice of Alleged Paternity Without Timely Response.
2 California Transactions Forms--Family Law § 6:78, Petition to Terminate Parental Rights of Alleged Father Who Cannot be Located.
2 California Transactions Forms--Family Law § 7:28, Overview.
2 California Transactions Forms--Family Law § 7:30, Parties to Proceeding.
2 California Transactions Forms--Family Law § 7:38, Parentage and Birth Certificate.
2 California Transactions Forms--Family Law § 7:86, Overview.
West's California Code Forms, Family § 7630, Comment Overview--Determining Parent and Child Relationship.
West's California Judicial Council Forms FL-200, Petition to Determine Parental Relationship (Uniform Parentage) (Uniform Parentage) (Also Available in Spanish).
West's California Judicial Council Forms FL-220, Response to Petition to Determine Parental Relationship (Uniform Parentage) (Also Available in Spanish).

§ 7631. Repealed by Stats.2010, c. 588 (A.B.2020), § 2

§ 7632. Agreement among parties does not bar action

Regardless of its terms, an agreement between an alleged father or a presumed parent and the other parent or child does not bar an action under this chapter. *(Stats.1992, c. 162 (A.B.2650), § 10, operative Jan. 1, 1994. Amended by Stats.2013, c. 510 (A.B.1403), § 9.)*

Cross References

Juvenile court law, protective order, parentage, custody, or visitation order, see Welfare and Institutions Code § 726.5.
Presumed father and child relationship, written promise to furnish support, enforceability, see Family Code § 7614.
Termination of juvenile court jurisdiction, pending proceedings relating to parental marriage or custody order, see Welfare and Institutions Code § 362.4.

§ 7633. Time for action, order or judgment

An action under this chapter may be brought, an order or judgment may be entered before the birth of the child, and enforcement of that order or judgment shall be stayed until the birth of the child. *(Stats.1992, c. 162 (A.B.2650), § 10, operative Jan. 1, 1994. Amended by Stats.2006, c. 806 (S.B.1325), § 4.)*

Cross References

Assisted reproduction agreements for gestational carriers, requirements, actions to establish parent-child relationship, judgment or order, see Family Code § 7962.
Juvenile court law, protective order, parentage, custody, or visitation order, see Welfare and Institutions Code § 726.5.
Termination of juvenile court jurisdiction, pending proceedings relating to parental marriage or custody order, see Welfare and Institutions Code § 362.4.

Research References

Forms

2 California Transactions Forms--Family Law § 7:28, Overview.

§ 7634. Action brought by local child support agency; review of current practices

(a) The local child support agency may, in the local child support agency's discretion, bring an action under this chapter in any case in which the local child support agency believes it to be appropriate.

(b) The Department of Child Support Services may review the current practices of service of process used by the local child support agencies pursuant to subdivision (a), and may develop methods to increase the number of persons served using personal delivery. *(Stats.1992, c. 162 (A.B.2650), § 10, operative Jan. 1, 1994. Amended by Stats.2000, c. 808 (A.B.1358), § 77, eff. Sept. 28, 2000; Stats.2004, c. 849 (A.B.252), § 2.)*

Cross References

Department of Child Support Services, local child support agencies established, see Family Code § 17304.
Juvenile court law, protective order, parentage, custody, or visitation order, see Welfare and Institutions Code § 726.5.
Support defined for purposes of this Code, see Family Code § 150.
Support enforcement, district attorneys, see Family Code § 4200 et seq.
Support obligations, local child support agencies, authorized actions, see Family Code § 17400.
Termination of juvenile court jurisdiction, pending proceedings relating to parental marriage or custody order, see Welfare and Institutions Code § 362.4.

§ 7635. Parties to action; representation of child by guardian ad litem or private counsel; notice; alignment

(a) The child may, if under the age of 12 years, and shall, if 12 years of age or older, be made a party to the action. If the child is a minor and a party to the action, the child shall be represented by a guardian ad litem appointed by the court. The guardian ad litem need not be represented by counsel if the guardian ad litem is a relative of the child.

(b) A natural parent, each person presumed to be a parent under Section 7611 or 7540, each person who is a parent of the child under Section 7613 or 7962, and each person alleged to be the genetic parent unless precluded under this division from establishing parentage based on genetic testing, shall be given notice of the action in the manner prescribed in Section 7666 and an opportunity to be heard, and shall be made a party if they request to be joined. Appointment of a guardian ad litem shall not be required for a minor who is a parent of the child who is the subject of the petition to establish parental relationship, unless the minor parent is unable to understand the nature of the proceedings or to assist counsel in preparing the case.

(c) The court may align the parties.

(d) In any initial or subsequent proceeding under this chapter where custody of, or visitation with, a minor child is in issue, the court may, if it determines it would be in the best interest of the minor child, appoint private counsel to represent the interests of the minor child pursuant to Chapter 10 (commencing with Section 3150) of Part 2 of Division 8. *(Stats.1992, c. 162 (A.B.2650), § 10, operative Jan. 1, 1994. Amended by Stats.1994, c. 1269 (A.B.2208), § 55; Stats.2008, c. 181 (S.B.1612), § 2; Stats.2013, c. 510 (A.B.1403), § 10; Stats.2018, c. 876 (A.B.2684), § 52, eff. Jan. 1, 2019.)*

Cross References
Fees and costs, see Family Code § 7640.
Guardians, generally, see Code of Civil Procedure §§ 373, 373.5; Probate Code § 1500 et seq.
Minor defined for purposes of this Code, see Family Code § 6500.
Proceeding defined for purposes of this Code, see Family Code § 110.
Void voluntary declaration of parentage, conditions, notice, see Family Code § 7573.5.

Research References
Forms
2 California Transactions Forms--Family Law § 5:9.50, Voiding of a Voluntary Declaration of Parentage.
West's California Judicial Council Forms FL–935, Application and Order for and Appointment of Guardian Ad Litem of Minor—Family Law.

§ 7635.5. Right of alleged father to have genetic testing to determine parentage; right to make motion to set aside or vacate judgment

In any action brought pursuant to this article, if the alleged father is present in court for the action, the court shall inform the alleged father of the alleged father's right to have genetic testing performed to determine the biological parentage of the child. The court shall further inform the alleged father of the alleged father's right to move to set aside or vacate a judgment of parentage pursuant to Section 7646 within two years of the date notice of the action to establish parentage is received, and that after that time has expired the alleged father may not move to set aside or vacate the judgment of parentage, regardless of whether genetic testing shows the alleged father not to be the biological father of the child. *(Added by Stats.2004, c. 849 (A.B.252), § 3. Amended by Stats.2019, c. 115 (A.B.1817), § 91, eff. Jan. 1, 2020.)*

§ 7636. Effect of judgment or order; exceptions

The judgment or order of the court determining the existence or nonexistence of the parent and child relationship is determinative for all purposes except for actions brought pursuant to Section 270 of the Penal Code. *(Stats.1992, c. 162 (A.B.2650), § 10, operative Jan. 1, 1994.)*

Cross References
Judgment and order defined for purposes of this Code, see Family Code § 100.
Jurisdiction of superior court, see Family Code § 200.

Research References
Forms
West's California Code Forms, Family § 7630, Comment Overview—Determining Parent and Child Relationship.
West's California Judicial Council Forms FL–190, Notice of Entry of Judgment (Uniform Parentage—Custody and Support).

§ 7637. Contents of judgment or order

The judgment or order may contain any other provision directed against the appropriate party to the proceeding, concerning the duty of support, the custody and guardianship of the child, visitation privileges with the child, the furnishing of bond or other security for the payment of the judgment, or any other matter in the best interest of the child. The judgment or order may direct the parent to pay the reasonable expenses of the mother's pregnancy and confinement. *(Stats.1992, c. 162 (A.B.2650), § 10, operative Jan. 1, 1994. Amended by Stats.1993, c. 219 (A.B.1500), § 179; Stats.2013, c. 510 (A.B.1403), § 11.)*

Cross References
Determination of father and child relationship, voluntary declaration of paternity, child custody and support actions, see Family Code § 7644.
Judgment and order defined for purposes of this Code, see Family Code § 100.
Proceeding defined for purposes of this Code, see Family Code § 110.
Support defined for purposes of this Code, see Family Code § 150.

Research References
Forms
1 California Transactions Forms--Family Law § 3:4, Subject Matter Jurisdiction for Custody Determinations.
2 California Transactions Forms--Family Law § 5:9, Use of Parenting Agreement to Define Rights and Responsibilities Relating to Child on Termination of Partners' Relationship Where Both Partners Are Biological Parents.
2 California Transactions Forms--Family Law § 7:28, Overview.
West's California Code Forms, Family § 7630, Comment Overview—Determining Parent and Child Relationship.
West's California Judicial Council Forms FL–190, Notice of Entry of Judgment (Uniform Parentage—Custody and Support).

§ 7638. Procedures to change name of child

The procedure in an action under this part to change the name of a minor or adult child for whom a parent and child relationship is established pursuant to Section 7636, upon application in accordance with Title 8 (commencing with Section 1275) of Part 3 of the Code of Civil Procedure shall conform to those provisions, except that the application for the change of name may be included with the petition filed under this part and except as provided in Sections 1277 and 1278 of the Code of Civil Procedure. *(Stats.1992, c. 162 (A.B.2650), § 10, operative Jan. 1, 1994.)*

Cross References
Adjudication of parentage, establishment of new birth certificate, see Health and Safety Code § 102725.
Change of name, hearings, see Code of Civil Procedure § 1278.
Change of names, application or petition, see Code of Civil Procedure § 1276.
Jurisdiction of superior court, see Family Code § 200.
Minor defined for purposes of this Code, see Family Code § 6500.

§ 7639. Order for issuance of new birth certificate

If the judgment or order of the court is at variance with the child's birth certificate, the court shall order that a new birth certificate be issued as prescribed in Article 2 (commencing with Section 102725)

§ 7639

of Chapter 5 of Part 1 of Division 102 of the Health and Safety Code. *(Stats.1992, c. 162 (A.B.2650), § 10, operative Jan. 1, 1994. Amended by Stats.1996, c. 1023 (S.B.1497), § 48, eff. Sept. 29, 1996.)*

Cross References

Judgment and order defined for purposes of this Code, see Family Code § 100.

Research References

Forms

2 California Transactions Forms--Family Law § 5:8, Effect of Birth Certificate Paternity Designation; Declaration of Paternity.

§ 7640. Fees and costs

The court may order reasonable fees of counsel, experts, and the child's guardian ad litem, and other costs of the action and pretrial proceedings, including genetic testing, to be paid by the parties, excluding any governmental entity, in proportions and at times determined by the court. The court may apply the standards set forth in Sections 2032 and 7605 in making this determination. *(Stats.1992, c. 162 (A.B.2650), § 10, operative Jan. 1, 1994. Amended by Stats.1994, c. 1269 (A.B.2208), § 55.2; Stats.2018, c. 876 (A.B.2684), § 53, eff. Jan. 1, 2019.)*

Cross References

Attorney's fees and costs, generally, see Family Code § 270 et seq.
Judgment and order defined for purposes of this Code, see Family Code § 100.
Proceeding defined for purposes of this Code, see Family Code § 110.

Research References

Forms

West's California Code Forms, Family § 7630, Comment Overview—Determining Parent and Child Relationship.
West's California Judicial Council Forms FL–157, Spousal or Domestic Partner Support Declaration Attachment (Also Available in Spanish).
West's California Judicial Council Forms FL–349, Spousal or Domestic Partner Support Factors Under Family Code Section 4320—Attachment.

§ 7641. Obligation of parent; enforcement; parties; persons payable; willful failure to obey; civil contempt

(a) If there is a voluntary declaration of paternity in place, or parentage or a duty of support has been acknowledged or adjudicated under this part or under prior law, the obligation of the parent may be enforced in the same or other proceedings by any of the following:

(1) The other parent.

(2) The child.

(3) The public authority that has furnished or may furnish the reasonable expenses of pregnancy, confinement, education, support, or funeral.

(4) Any other person, including a private agency, to the extent the person has furnished or is furnishing these expenses.

(b) The court may order support payments to be made to any of the following:

(1) The other parent.

(2) The clerk of the court.

(3) A person, corporation, or agency designated to administer the payments for the benefit of the child under the supervision of the court.

(c) Willful failure to obey the judgment or order of the court is a civil contempt of the court. All remedies for the enforcement of judgments, including imprisonment for contempt, apply. *(Stats.1992, c. 162 (A.B.2650), § 10, operative Jan. 1, 1994. Amended by Stats.2013, c. 510 (A.B.1403), § 12.)*

Cross References

Enforcement of judgments and orders, see Family Code §§ 290, 291.

Judgment and order defined for purposes of this Code, see Family Code § 100.
Person defined for purposes of this Code, see Family Code § 105.
Proceeding defined for purposes of this Code, see Family Code § 110.
Support defined for purposes of this Code, see Family Code § 150.

Research References

Forms

2 California Transactions Forms--Family Law § 7:60, Overview; Paternity of Child [Fam C § 7613].
West's California Code Forms, Family § 7630, Comment Overview—Determining Parent and Child Relationship.

§ 7642. Modification or set aside of judgment or order; jurisdiction; manner

The court has continuing jurisdiction to modify or set aside a judgment or order made under this part. A judgment or order relating to an adoption may only be modified or set aside in the same manner and under the same conditions as an order of adoption may be modified or set aside under Section 9100 or 9102. *(Stats.1992, c. 162 (A.B.2650), § 10, operative Jan. 1, 1994. Amended by Stats.1999, c. 653 (A.B.380), § 11.)*

Cross References

Enforcement of judgments and orders, see Family Code §§ 290, 291.
Judgment and order defined for purposes of this Code, see Family Code § 100.

Research References

Forms

2 California Transactions Forms--Family Law § 5:9, Use of Parenting Agreement to Define Rights and Responsibilities Relating to Child on Termination of Partners' Relationship Where Both Partners Are Biological Parents.
2 California Transactions Forms--Family Law § 6:58, Independent Adoption Placement Agreement—Indian Child [Dss Form Ad 925].
2 California Transactions Forms--Family Law § 6:148, Rights of Indian Parents of Indian Children.
2 California Transactions Forms--Family Law § 6:154.30, Indian Child Inquiry Attachment [ICWA-010(A)].
2 California Transactions Forms--Family Law § 6:154.50, Information Sheet on Indian Child Inquiry Attachment and Notice of Child Custody Proceeding for Indian Child [ICWA-005-Info].
2 California Transactions Forms--Family Law § 6:154.60, Notice of Child Custody Proceeding for Indian Child [ICWA-030].
2 California Transactions Forms--Family Law § 6:154.65, Attachment to Notice of Child Custody Proceeding for Indian Child [ICWA-030(A)].
2 California Transactions Forms--Family Law § 6:154.70, Parental Notification of Indian Status [ICWA-020].
2 California Transactions Forms--Family Law § 6:154.80, Notice of Designation of Tribal Representative and Notice of Intervention in a Court Proceeding Involving an Indian Child [ICWA-040].
2 California Transactions Forms--Family Law § 6:155, Attachment to Petition for Adoption of Indian Child [Judicial Council Form Adopt-220].
2 California Transactions Forms--Family Law § 6:155.30, Notice of Petition and Petition to Transfer Case Involving an Indian Child to Tribal Jurisdiction [ICWA-050].
2 California Transactions Forms--Family Law § 6:155.50, Order on Petition to Transfer Case Involving an Indian Child to Tribal Jurisdiction [ICWA-060].
2 California Transactions Forms--Family Law § 6:156, Consent to Termination of Parental Rights and Certification—Adoption of an Indian Child [Form Adopt-225].
2 California Transactions Forms--Family Law § 6:156.50, Consent to Adoption by Parents of Indian Child [Dss Form Ad 859].
2 California Transactions Forms--Family Law § 6:156.55, Independent Adoption Placement Agreement (Indian Child) [Form Ad 925].
West's California Code Forms, Family § 7630, Comment Overview—Determining Parent and Child Relationship.

§ 7643. Hearing or trial in closed court; papers and records; inspection and copying

(a) Notwithstanding any other law concerning public hearings and records, a hearing or trial held under this part may be held in closed court without admittance of any person other than those necessary to the action or proceeding. Except as provided in subdivision (b), all papers and records, other than the final judgment, pertaining to the action or proceeding, whether part of the permanent record of the court or of a file in a public agency or elsewhere, are subject to inspection and copying only in exceptional cases upon an order of the court for good cause shown.

(b)(1) Papers and records pertaining to the action or proceeding that are part of the permanent record of the court are subject to inspection and copying by the parties to the action, their attorneys, and by agents acting pursuant to written authorization from the parties to the action or their attorneys. An attorney shall obtain the consent of the party to the action * * * before authorizing an agent to inspect and copy the permanent record. An attorney shall also state on the written authorization that the attorney has obtained the consent of the party to authorize an agent to inspect and copy the permanent record.

(2) For purposes of establishing parentage and establishing and enforcing child support orders, papers and records pertaining to the action or proceeding that are part of the permanent record of the court are subject to inspection and copying by any local child support agency, as defined in subdivision (h) of Section 17000.

(c) This section applies only to actions filed * * * before January 1, 2023. *(Stats.1992, c. 162 (A.B.2650), § 10, operative Jan. 1, 1994. Amended by Stats.2008, c. 50 (A.B.1679), § 1; Stats.2010, c. 212 (A.B.2767), § 5; Stats.2018, c. 504 (A.B.3248), § 4, eff. Jan. 1, 2019; Stats.2019, c. 115 (A.B.1817), § 92, eff. Jan. 1, 2020; Stats.2021, c. 52 (A.B.429), § 1, eff. Jan. 1, 2022; Stats.2022, c. 420 (A.B.2960), § 19, eff. Jan. 1, 2023.)*

Cross References

Judgment and order defined for purposes of this Code, see Family Code § 100.
Person defined for purposes of this Code, see Family Code § 105.
Proceeding defined for purposes of this Code, see Family Code § 110.

Research References

Forms

2 California Transactions Forms--Family Law § 5:9, Use of Parenting Agreement to Define Rights and Responsibilities Relating to Child on Termination of Partners' Relationship Where Both Partners Are Biological Parents.
West's California Code Forms, Family § 7630, Comment Overview—Determining Parent and Child Relationship.

§ 7643.5. Hearing or trial in closed court for actions on or after January 1, 2023; papers and records; inspection and copying; designation of action or proceeding

(a) Notwithstanding any other law concerning public hearings and records, a hearing or trial held under this part for an action filed on or after January 1, 2023, under Section 7613, subdivision (f) of Section 7630, or Part 7 (commencing with Section 7960), may be held in closed court without admittance of any person other than those necessary to the action or proceeding. Except as provided in subdivision (b), all papers and records, other than the final judgment, pertaining to the action or proceeding, whether part of the permanent record of the court or of a file in a public agency or elsewhere, are subject to inspection and copying only in exceptional cases upon an order of the court for good cause shown.

(b)(1) Papers and records pertaining to the action or proceeding that are part of the permanent record of the court are subject to inspection and copying by the parties to the action, their attorneys, and by agents acting pursuant to written authorization from the parties to the action or their attorneys. An attorney shall obtain the consent of the party to the action * * * before authorizing an agent to inspect and copy the permanent record. An attorney shall also state on the written authorization that the attorney has obtained the consent of the party to authorize an agent to inspect and copy the permanent record.

(2) For purposes of establishing parentage and establishing and enforcing child support orders, papers and records pertaining to the action or proceeding that are part of the permanent record of the court are subject to inspection and copying by any local child support agency, as defined in subdivision (h) of Section 17000.

(c) On or before January 1, 2023, the Judicial Council shall create a new form or modify an existing form, as it deems appropriate, that requires a party initiating an action or proceeding filed under Section 7613, subdivision (f) of Section 7630, or Part 7 (commencing with Section 7960) to designate the action or proceeding as filed under the identified statutory provision.

(d) Notwithstanding Section 4, * * * this section shall apply to all actions filed * * * before January 1, 2023. *(Added by Stats.2021, c. 52 (A.B.429), § 2, eff. Jan. 1, 2022. Amended by Stats.2022, c. 420 (A.B.2960), § 20, eff. Jan. 1, 2023.)*

§ 7644. Voluntary declaration of parentage; child custody and support actions; force and effect

(a) Notwithstanding any other law, an action for child custody and support and for other relief as provided in Section 7637 may be filed based upon a voluntary declaration of parentage as provided in Chapter 3 (commencing with Section 7570) of Part 2.

(b) Except as provided in Section 7581, the voluntary declaration of parentage shall be given the same force and effect as a judgment of parentage entered by a court of competent jurisdiction. The court shall make appropriate orders as specified in Section 7637 based upon the voluntary declaration of parentage unless evidence is presented that the voluntary declaration of parentage has been rescinded by the parties, set aside as provided in Section 7575, 7576, or 7577, or is void under Section 7573.5.

(c) The Judicial Council shall develop the forms and procedures necessary to implement this section.

(d) This section shall become operative on January 1, 2020. *(Added by Stats.2018, c. 876 (A.B.2684), § 55, eff. Jan. 1, 2019, operative Jan. 1, 2020.)*

Cross References

Judgment and order defined for purposes of this Code, see Family Code § 100.
Support defined for purposes of this Code, see Family Code § 150.

ARTICLE 1.5. SETTING ASIDE OR VACATING JUDGMENT OF PARENTAGE

Section	
7645.	Definitions.
7646.	Setting aside or vacating judgments establishing parentage; time periods for bringing motion; application; reconsideration of motion.
7647.	Requirements for granting motion to set aside or vacate parentage judgment; proof of service.
7647.5.	Appointment of guardian ad litem.
7647.7.	Genetic testing.
7648.	Denial of motion to set aside or vacate judgment establishing parentage; factors.
7648.1.	Statement of basis for denial of motion.
7648.2.	Support enforcement services; administrative orders; payment of costs of genetic testing.
7648.3.	Prohibition against setting aside or vacating paternity judgment; circumstances.
7648.4.	Orders for child support and arrearages based on previous judgment of paternity; reimbursement.
7648.8.	Termination of adoption; effect on obligations.
7648.9.	Assisted reproduction and surrogacy agreements.
7649.	Rights and remedies available under other provisions of law.

PARENT AND CHILD RELATIONSHIP

Section

7649.5. Distribution from estate of decedent made in good faith reliance on judgement establishing paternity; finality; appeal; liability of estate, trust, personal representative or trustee.

§ 7645. Definitions

For purposes of this article, the following definitions shall apply:

(a) "Child" means the child of a previously established father or mother, as determined by the superior court in a judgment that is the subject of a motion brought pursuant to this article, or as a matter of law.

(b) "Judgment" means a judgment, order, or decree entered in a court of this state that establishes parentage, including a determination of parentage made pursuant to a petition filed under Section 300, 601, or 602 of the Welfare and Institutions Code. For purposes of this article, "judgment" does not include a judgment in any action for marital dissolution, legal separation, or nullity.

(c) "Previously established father" means a person identified as the father of a child in a judgment that is the subject of a motion brought pursuant to this article.

(d) "Previously established mother" means a person identified as the mother of a child in a judgment that is the subject of a motion brought pursuant to this article. *(Added by Stats.2004, c. 849 (A.B.252), § 4. Amended by Stats.2018, c. 876 (A.B.2684), § 57, eff. Jan. 1, 2019.)*

§ 7646. Setting aside or vacating judgments establishing parentage; time periods for bringing motion; application; reconsideration of motion

(a) Notwithstanding any other law, a judgment establishing parentage may be set aside or vacated upon a motion by a previously established parent, the child, or the legal representative of any of these persons if genetic testing indicates that the previously established father of a child is not the genetic father of the child. The motion shall be brought within one of the following time periods:

(1) Within a two-year period commencing with the date on which the previously established father knew or should have known of a judgment that established the father's parentage of the child or commencing with the date the previously established father knew or should have known of the existence of an action to adjudicate the issue of parentage, whichever is first, except as provided in paragraph (2).

(2) In the case of a previously established father who is the legal father as a result of a default judgment as of the effective date of this section, within a two-year period from January 1, 2005, to December 31, 2006, inclusive.

(b) Subdivision (a) does not apply if the child is presumed to be a child of a marriage pursuant to Section 7540, the previously established parent is a parent under Section 7613 or 7962, or the action is barred by paragraph (2) of subdivision (a) of Section 7630.

(c) Reconsideration of a motion brought under paragraph (3)[1] of subdivision (a) may be requested and granted if the following requirements are met:

(1) The motion was filed with the court between September 24, 2006, and December 31, 2006, inclusive.

(2) The motion was denied solely on the basis that it was untimely.

(3) The request for reconsideration of the motion is filed on or before December 31, 2009. *(Added by Stats.2004, c. 849 (A.B.252), § 4. Amended by Stats.2008, c. 58 (S.B.1333), § 1; Stats.2018, c. 876 (A.B.2684), § 58, eff. Jan. 1, 2019; Stats.2019, c. 115 (A.B.1817), § 93, eff. Jan. 1, 2020.)*

[1] So in enrolled bill.

Cross References

Ex parte orders regarding temporary custody and visitation of minor children, stipulation of paternity, see Family Code § 6323.
Uniform Parentage Act, right to genetic testing, see Family Code § 7635.5.

Research References

Forms

West's California Code Forms, Family § 7645, Comment Overview—Setting Aside or Vacating Judgment of Paternity.
West's California Judicial Council Forms FL–272, Notice of Motion to Cancel (Set Aside) Judgment of Parentage (Also Available in Spanish).
West's California Judicial Council Forms FL–273, Declaration in Support of Motion to Cancel (Set Aside) Judgment of Parentage (Also Available in Spanish).
West's California Judicial Council Forms FL–274, Information Sheet for Completing Notice of Motion to Cancel (Set Aside) Judgment of Parentage (Also Available in Spanish).
West's California Judicial Council Forms FL–276, Response to Notice of Motion to Cancel (Set Aside) Judgment of Parentage (Also Available in Spanish).
West's California Judicial Council Forms FL–278, Order After Hearing on Motion to Cancel (Set Aside) Judgment of Parentage (Also Available in Spanish).

§ 7647. Requirements for granting motion to set aside or vacate parentage judgment; proof of service

(a) A court may grant a motion to set aside or vacate a judgment establishing parentage only if all of the following conditions are met:

(1) The motion is filed in a court of proper venue.

(2) The motion contains, at a minimum, all of the following information, if known:

(A) The legal name, age, county of residence, and residence address of the child.

(B) The names, mailing addresses, and counties of residence, or, if deceased, the date and place of death, of the following persons:

(i) The previously established parents and the alleged father of the child.

(ii) The guardian of the child, if any.

(iii) Any person who has physical custody of the child.

(iv) The guardian ad litem of the child, if any, as appointed pursuant to Section 7647.5.

(C) A declaration that the person filing the motion believes that the previously established father is not the genetic father of the child, the specific reasons for this belief, and a declaration that the person desires that the motion be granted. The moving party is not required to present evidence of genetic testing indicating that the previously established father is not the genetic father of the child in order to bring this motion pursuant to Section 7646.

(D) A declaration that the marital presumption set forth in Section 7540 does not apply and that an action is not barred under paragraph (2) of subdivision (a) of Section 7630.

(3) The court finds that the previously established father is not a genetic parent pursuant to Section 7555.

(b) The motion shall include a proof of service upon the following persons, excluding the person bringing the motion:

(1) The parties to the action resulting in the judgment of parentage.

(2) The local child support agency, if services are being provided to the child pursuant to Title IV–D or IV–E of the Social Security Act (42 U.S.C. Sec. 651 et seq. and 42 U.S.C. Sec. 670 et seq.).

(3) The child's guardian ad litem, if any. *(Added by Stats.2004, c. 849 (A.B.252), § 4. Amended by Stats.2018, c. 876 (A.B.2684), § 59, eff. Jan. 1, 2019.)*

Research References

Forms

West's California Code Forms, Family § 7645, Comment Overview—Setting Aside or Vacating Judgment of Paternity.

§ 7647.5. Appointment of guardian ad litem

A guardian ad litem may be appointed for the child to represent the best interests of the child in an action brought pursuant to this article. *(Added by Stats.2004, c. 849 (A.B.252), § 4.)*

§ 7647.7. Genetic testing

Any genetic testing used to support the motion to set aside or vacate shall be conducted in accordance with Section 7552. The court shall, at the request of any person authorized to make a motion pursuant to this article, or may upon its own motion, order genetic testing to assist the court in making a determination whether the previously established father is the genetic father of the child. *(Added by Stats.2004, c. 849 (A.B.252), § 4. Amended by Stats.2018, c. 876 (A.B.2684), § 60, eff. Jan. 1, 2019.)*

§ 7648. Denial of motion to set aside or vacate judgment establishing parentage; factors

The court may deny the motion to set aside or vacate a judgment establishing parentage if it determines that denial of the motion is in the best interest of the child, after consideration of the following factors:

(a) The age of the child.

(b) The length of time since the entry of the judgment establishing parentage.

(c) The nature, duration, and quality of any relationship between the previously established father and the child, including the duration and frequency of any time periods during which the child and the previously established father resided in the same household or enjoyed a parent and child relationship.

(d) The request of the previously established father that the parent and child relationship continue.

(e) Notice by the biological father of the child that the biological father does not oppose preservation of the relationship between the previously established father and the child.

(f) The benefit or detriment to the child in establishing the genetic father as the parent of the child.

(g) Whether the conduct of the previously established father has impaired the ability to ascertain the identity of, or get support from, the biological father.

(h) Additional factors deemed by the court to be relevant to its determination of the best interest of the child. *(Added by Stats.2004, c. 849 (A.B.252), § 4. Amended by Stats.2018, c. 876 (A.B.2684), § 61, eff. Jan. 1, 2019; Stats.2019, c. 115 (A.B.1817), § 94, eff. Jan. 1, 2020.)*

§ 7648.1. Statement of basis for denial of motion

If the court denies a motion pursuant to Section 7648, the court shall state on the record the basis for the denial of that motion and any supporting facts. *(Added by Stats.2004, c. 849 (A.B.252), § 4.)*

§ 7648.2. Support enforcement services; administrative orders; payment of costs of genetic testing

(a) This section applies only to cases where support enforcement services are being provided by a local child support agency pursuant to Section 17400.

(b) Upon receipt of any motion brought pursuant to Section 7646, the local child support agency may issue an administrative order requiring the mother, child, and the previously established father to submit to genetic testing if all of the conditions of paragraphs (1) and (2) of subdivision (a) of Section 7647 are satisfied.

(c) The local child support agency shall pay the costs of any genetic tests that are ordered under subdivision (b) or are ordered by a court for cases in which the local child support agency is providing services under Title IV–D of the Social Security Act (42 U.S.C. Sec. 651 et seq.).

(d) Nothing in this section prohibits any person who has been ordered by a local child support agency to submit to genetic tests pursuant to this section from filing a notice of motion with the court seeking relief from the local child support agency's order to submit to genetic tests. In that event, the court shall resolve the issue of whether genetic tests should be ordered as provided in Section 7647.7. If any person refuses to submit to the tests after receipt of the administrative order pursuant to this section and fails to seek relief from the court from the administrative order either prior to the scheduled tests or within 10 days after the tests are scheduled, the court may resolve the question of paternity against that person or enforce the administrative order if the rights of others or the interest of justice so require. *(Added by Stats.2004, c. 849 (A.B.252), § 4.)*

§ 7648.3. Prohibition against setting aside or vacating paternity judgment; circumstances

A court may not issue an order setting aside or vacating a judgment establishing paternity pursuant to this article under any of the following circumstances:

(a) The judgment was made or entered by a tribunal of another state, even if the enforcement of that judgment is sought in this state.

(b) The judgment was made or entered in this state and genetic tests were conducted prior to the entry of the judgment which did not exclude the previously established father as the biological father of the child. *(Added by Stats.2004, c. 849 (A.B.252), § 4.)*

§ 7648.4. Orders for child support and arrearages based on previous judgment of paternity; reimbursement

Notwithstanding any other provision of law, if the court grants a motion to set aside or vacate a paternity judgment pursuant to this article, the court shall vacate any order for child support and arrearages issued on the basis of that previous judgment of paternity. The previously established father has no right of reimbursement for any amount of support paid prior to the granting of the motion. *(Added by Stats.2004, c. 849 (A.B.252), § 4.)*

§ 7648.8. Termination of adoption; effect on obligations

This article does not establish a basis for termination of any adoption, and does not affect any obligation of an adoptive parent to an adoptive child. *(Added by Stats.2004, c. 849 (A.B.252), § 4.)*

§ 7648.9. Assisted reproduction and surrogacy agreements

This article does not establish a basis for setting aside or vacating a judgment establishing paternity with regard to a child conceived by assisted reproduction pursuant to Section 7613 or a child conceived pursuant to a surrogacy agreement. *(Added by Stats.2004, c. 849 (A.B.252), § 4. Amended by Stats.2013, c. 510 (A.B.1403), § 14.)*

§ 7649. Rights and remedies available under other provisions of law

This article does not limit the rights and remedies available under any other law with regard to setting aside or vacating a judgment of parentage. *(Added by Stats.2004, c. 849 (A.B.252), § 4. Amended by Stats.2018, c. 876 (A.B.2684), § 62, eff. Jan. 1, 2019.)*

§ 7649.5. Distribution from estate of decedent made in good faith reliance on judgement establishing paternity; finality; appeal; liability of estate, trust, personal representative or trustee

Notwithstanding any other provision of this article, a distribution from the estate of a decedent or payment made by a trustee, insurance company, pension fund, or any other person or entity that was made in good faith reliance on a judgment establishing paternity

§ 7649.5

that is final for purposes of direct appeal, may not be set aside or subject to direct or collateral attack because of the entry of an order setting aside or vacating a judgment under this article. An estate, trust, personal representative, trustee, or any other person or entity that made that distribution or payment may not incur any liability to any person because of the distribution or payment or because of the entry of an order under this article. (Added by Stats.2004, c. 849 (A.B.252), § 4.)

ARTICLE 2. DETERMINATION OF MOTHER AND CHILD RELATIONSHIP

Section
7650. Action to determine existence or nonexistence of mother and child relationship; parties; law governing.

Cross References

Uniform act, construction of provisions, see Family Code § 3.

§ 7650. Action to determine existence or nonexistence of mother and child relationship; parties; law governing

(a) Any interested person may bring an action to determine the existence or nonexistence of a mother and child relationship. Insofar as practicable, the provisions of this division applicable to the father and child relationship apply.

(b) A woman is presumed to be the natural mother of a child if the child is in utero after the death of the decedent and the conditions set forth in Section 249.5 of the Probate Code are satisfied. (Stats.1992, c. 162 (A.B.2650), § 10, operative Jan. 1, 1994. Amended by Stats.2004, c. 775 (A.B.1910), § 2.3; Stats.2018, c. 876 (A.B.2684), § 63, eff. Jan. 1, 2019.)

Cross References

Action to determine father and child relationship, see Family Code § 7630.
Paternity, orders for genetic tests, see Family Code § 7551 et seq.
Person defined for purposes of this Code, see Family Code § 105.

CHAPTER 5. TERMINATION OF PARENTAL RIGHTS IN ADOPTION PROCEEDINGS

Section
7660. Relinquishment or consent by mother; notice to and rights of presumed parent.
7660.5. Waiver of right to notice by presumed father; adoption proceedings under Indian Child Welfare Act.
7661. Relinquishment or consent by other parent; notice to and rights of mother.
7662. Filing of petition to terminate parental rights of alleged father; conditions.
7663. Inquiry to identify all alleged fathers and presumed parents; report.
7664. Identification of biological father or possible fathers; notice of proceedings; default; claim of parental rights; determination and order concerning parental rights.
7665. Termination of unknown biological father's parental rights; entry of order.
7666. Notice of proceedings.
7667. Time of hearing; ex parte orders terminating parental rights.
7668. Continuance of proceedings; purpose.
7669. Order requiring or dispensing with alleged father's consent for adoption; appeal from order and judgment.
7670. Filing fee.

Section
7671. Multiple fathers or multiple children; single petition to terminate parental rights.

Cross References

Action to determine existence or nonexistence of father and child relationship, consolidated actions and jurisdiction, see Family Code § 7630.
Adoption, consent of birth parents not required in certain cases, see Family Code § 8606.
Agency adoptions,
  Notice to birth parent on termination of parental rights, disclosure of name and address, see Family Code § 8703.
  Relinquishment of child to department or licensed adoption agency, termination of parental rights, see Family Code § 8700.
Dependents of juvenile court, exclusive means for terminating parental rights, see Family Code § 7808.
Hearings terminating parental rights or establishing guardianship of children adjudged dependent children of court, see Welfare and Institutions Code § 366.26.
Uniform act, construction of provisions, see Family Code § 3.

§ 7660. Relinquishment or consent by mother; notice to and rights of presumed parent

If a mother relinquishes for or consents to, or proposes to relinquish for or consent to, the adoption of a child who has a presumed parent under Section 7611, the presumed parent shall be given notice of the adoption proceeding and have the rights provided under Part 2 (commencing with Section 8600) of Division 13, unless that parent's relationship to the child has been previously terminated or determined by a court not to exist or the presumed parent has voluntarily relinquished for or consented to the adoption of the child. (Stats.1992, c. 162 (A.B.2650), § 10, operative Jan. 1, 1994. Amended by Stats.2000, c. 937 (A.B.2433), § 1; Stats.2013, c. 510 (A.B.1403), § 15.)

Cross References

Action for determination of father and child relationship, see Family Code § 7630.
Adoption, consent of birth parents required, see Family Code § 8604.
Proceeding defined for purposes of this Code, see Family Code § 110.

Research References

Forms
2 California Transactions Forms--Family Law § 6:71, Notice of Alleged Paternity.
West's California Code Forms, Family § 7660, Comment Overview—Termination of Parental Rights in Adoption Proceedings.
West's California Judicial Council Forms ADOPT–200, Adoption Request.

§ 7660.5. Waiver of right to notice by presumed father; adoption proceedings under Indian Child Welfare Act

Notwithstanding any other provision of law, a presumed father may waive the right to notice of any adoption proceeding by executing a form developed by the department before an authorized representative of the department, an authorized representative of a licensed public or private adoption agency, or a notary public or other person authorized to perform notarial acts. The waiver of notice form may be validly executed before or after the birth of the child, and once signed no notice, relinquishment for, or consent to adoption of the child shall be required from the father for the adoption to proceed. This shall be a voluntary and informed waiver without undue influence. If the child is an Indian child as defined under the Indian Child Welfare Act (ICWA), [1] any waiver of consent by an Indian presumed father shall be executed in accordance with the requirements for voluntary adoptions set forth in Section 1913 of Title 25 of the United States Code. The waiver shall not affect the rights of any known federally recognized Indian tribe or tribes from which the child or the presumed father may be descended to notification of, or participation in, adoption proceedings as provided by the ICWA. Notice that the waiver has been executed shall be given to any known federally recognized Indian tribe or tribes from which the child or the presumed father may be descended, as required by the ICWA. *(Added by Stats.2004, c. 858 (S.B.1357), § 1. Amended by Stats.2008, c. 534 (S.B.1726), § 4.)*

¹ See 25 U.S.C.A. § 1901 et seq.

Cross References

Adoption, consent of birth parents required, see Family Code § 8604.

§ 7661. Relinquishment or consent by other parent; notice to and rights of mother

If the other parent relinquishes for or consents to, or proposes to relinquish for or consent to, the adoption of a child, the mother shall be given notice of the adoption proceeding and have the rights provided under Part 2 (commencing with Section 8600) of Division 13, unless the mother's relationship to the child has been previously terminated by a court or the mother has voluntarily relinquished for or consented to the adoption of the child. *(Stats.1992, c. 162 (A.B.2650), § 10, operative Jan. 1, 1994. Amended by Stats.2013, c. 510 (A.B.1403), § 16.)*

Cross References

Adoption, consent of birth parents required, see Family Code § 8604.
Persons to whom notice to be given, see Family Code § 7666.
Proceeding defined for purposes of this Code, see Family Code § 110.

Research References

Forms

West's California Code Forms, Family § 7660, Comment Overview—Termination of Parental Rights in Adoption Proceedings.
West's California Judicial Council Forms ADOPT-200, Adoption Request.

§ 7662. Filing of petition to terminate parental rights of alleged father; conditions

(a) If a mother relinquishes for or consents to, or proposes to relinquish for or consent to, the adoption of a child, or if a child otherwise becomes the subject of an adoption proceeding, the agency or person to whom the child has been or is to be relinquished, or the mother or the person having physical or legal custody of the child, or the prospective adoptive parent, shall file a petition to terminate the parental rights of the alleged father, unless one of the following occurs:

(1) The alleged father's relationship to the child has been previously terminated or determined not to exist by a court.

(2) The alleged father has been served as prescribed in Section 7666 with a written notice alleging that the alleged father is or could be the biological father of the child to be adopted or placed for adoption and has failed to bring an action for the purpose of declaring the existence of the father and child relationship pursuant to subdivision (c) of Section 7630 within 30 days of service of the notice or the birth of the child, whichever is later.

(3) The alleged father has executed a written form developed by the department to waive notice, to deny parentage, relinquish the child for adoption, or consent to the adoption of the child.

(b) The alleged father may validly execute a waiver or denial of parentage before or after the birth of the child, and, once signed, no notice of, relinquishment for, or consent to adoption of the child shall be required from the alleged father for the adoption to proceed.

(c) Except as provided in this subdivision and subdivision (d), all proceedings affecting a child, including proceedings under Divisions 8 (commencing with Section 3000) to 11 (commencing with Section 6500), inclusive, Part 1 (commencing with Section 7500) to Part 3 (commencing with Section 7600), inclusive, of this division, and Part 1 (commencing with Section 1400), Part 2 (commencing with Section 1500), and Part 4 (commencing with Section 2100) of Division 4 of the Probate Code, and any motion or petition for custody or visitation filed in a proceeding under this part, shall be stayed. The petition to terminate parental rights under this section is the only matter that may be heard during the stay until the court issues a final ruling on the petition.

(d) This section does not limit the jurisdiction of the court pursuant to Part 3 (commencing with Section 6240) and Part 4 (commencing with Section 6300) of Division 10 with respect to domestic violence orders, or pursuant to Article 6 (commencing with Section 300) of Chapter 2 of Part 1 of Division 2 of the Welfare and Institutions Code with respect to dependency proceedings. *(Stats. 1992, c. 162 (A.B.2650), § 10, operative Jan. 1, 1994. Amended by Stats.2000, c. 937 (A.B.2433), § 2; Stats.2003, c. 251 (S.B.182), § 3; Stats.2008, c. 534 (S.B.1726), § 5; Stats.2010, c. 588 (A.B.2020), § 3; Stats.2013, c. 510 (A.B.1403), § 17; Stats.2014, c. 763 (A.B.1701), § 2, eff. Jan. 1, 2015; Stats.2019, c. 115 (A.B.1817), § 95, eff. Jan. 1, 2020.)*

Cross References

Action to determine existence or nonexistence of father and child relationship, consolidated actions and jurisdiction, see Family Code § 7630.
Adoption of unmarried minors, consent of birth parents required, see Family Code § 8604.
Domestic violence defined for purposes of this Code, see Family Code § 6211.
Filing fee charged for petition, see Family Code § 7670.
Judgment and order defined for purposes of this Code, see Family Code § 100.
Person defined for purposes of this Code, see Family Code § 105.
Proceeding defined for purposes of this Code, see Family Code § 110.
Prospective adoptive parent, defined, see Family Code § 8542.

Research References

Forms

2 California Transactions Forms--Family Law § 6:8, Consent for Adoption of Unmarried Minor.
2 California Transactions Forms--Family Law § 6:11, Initiating Proceeding Under Uniform Parentage Act [Fam. Code, §§7600 to 7730].
2 California Transactions Forms--Family Law § 6:40, Structuring the Adoption.
2 California Transactions Forms--Family Law § 6:69, Transmittal Letter to Department of Social Services.
2 California Transactions Forms--Family Law § 6:70, Appearance, Waiver of Notice, and Statement Regarding Paternity.
2 California Transactions Forms--Family Law § 6:71, Notice of Alleged Paternity.
2 California Transactions Forms--Family Law § 6:72, Petition to Terminate Parental Rights of Alleged Father.
2 California Transactions Forms--Family Law § 6:74, Petition to Terminate Parental Rights of Alleged Father Served With Notice of Alleged Paternity Without Timely Response.
2 California Transactions Forms--Family Law § 6:75, Order Terminating Parental Rights of Alleged Father Served With Notice of Alleged Paternity Without Timely Response.
2 California Transactions Forms--Family Law § 6:76, Ex Parte Application for Order to Terminate Parental Rights of Alleged Father Who Waived Notice or Denied Paternity.
2 California Transactions Forms--Family Law § 6:77, Order Terminating Parental Rights of Alleged Father Who Waived Notice.
West's California Code Forms, Family § 7660, Comment Overview—Termination of Parental Rights in Adoption Proceedings.

§ 7663. Inquiry to identify all alleged fathers and presumed parents; report

(a) In an effort to identify all alleged fathers and presumed parents, the court shall cause inquiry to be made of the mother and any other appropriate person by one of the following:

(1) The State Department of Social Services.

(2) A licensed county adoption agency.

(3) The licensed adoption agency to which the child is to be relinquished.

(4) In the case of a stepparent adoption, the licensed clinical social worker, licensed marriage and family therapist, or licensed professional clinical counselor who is performing the investigation pursuant to Section 9001, if applicable. In the case of a stepparent adoption

§ 7663 PARENT AND CHILD RELATIONSHIP

in which a licensed clinical social worker, licensed marriage and family therapist, or licensed professional clinical counselor is not performing the investigation pursuant to Section 9001, the board of supervisors may assign those inquiries to a licensed county adoption agency, the county department designated by the board of supervisors to administer the public social services program, or the county probation department.

(b) The inquiry shall include all of the following:

(1) Whether the mother was married at the time of conception of the child or at any time thereafter.

(2) Whether the mother was cohabiting with a man at the time of conception or birth of the child.

(3) Whether the mother has received support payments or promises of support with respect to the child or in connection with the pregnancy.

(4) Whether any person has formally or informally acknowledged or declared possible parentage of the child.

(5) The names and whereabouts, if known, of every person presumed or alleged to be the parent of the child, and the efforts made to give notice of the proposed adoption to each person identified.

(c) The agency that completes the inquiry shall file a written report of the findings with the court. *(Stats.1992, c. 162 (A.B.2650), § 10, operative Jan. 1, 1994. Amended by Stats.2011, c. 462 (A.B.687), § 1; Stats.2012, c. 638 (A.B.1757), § 1; Stats.2013, c. 510 (A.B.1403), § 18; Stats.2018, c. 389 (A.B.2296), § 12, eff. Jan. 1, 2019; Stats.2019, c. 115 (A.B.1817), § 96, eff. Jan. 1, 2020.)*

Cross References

Adoption, consent of birth parents required, see Family Code § 8604.
County defined for purposes of this Code, see Family Code § 67.
Juvenile court, wards and dependent children, inspection of case file, see Welfare and Institutions Code § 827.
Licensed adoption agency defined, see Family Code § 8530.
Paternity, conclusive presumption as child of marriage, see Family Code § 7540.
Paternity, voluntary declaration, see Family Code § 7573 et seq.
Person defined for purposes of this Code, see Family Code § 105.
State defined for purposes of this Code, see Family Code § 145.
Support defined for purposes of this Code, see Family Code § 150.

Research References

Forms

2 California Transactions Forms--Family Law § 6:78, Petition to Terminate Parental Rights of Alleged Father Who Cannot be Located.

§ 7664. Identification of biological father or possible fathers; notice of proceedings; default; claim of parental rights; determination and order concerning parental rights

(a) If, after the inquiry, the biological father is identified to the satisfaction of the court, or if more than one man is identified as a possible biological father, notice of the proceeding shall be given in accordance with Section 7666. If an alleged biological father fails to appear or, if appearing, fails to claim parental rights, those parental rights with reference to the child shall be terminated.

(b) If the biological father or a man claiming to be the biological father claims parental rights, the court shall determine biological parentage. The court shall then determine if it is in the best interest of the child that the biological father retain parental rights, or that an adoption of the child be allowed to proceed. The court, in making that determination, may consider all relevant evidence, including the efforts made by the biological father to obtain custody, the age and prior placement of the child, and the effects of a change of placement on the child.

(c) If the court finds that it is in the best interest of the child that the biological father should be allowed to retain parental rights, the court shall order that the biological father's consent is necessary for an adoption. If the court finds that the man claiming parental rights is not the biological father, or that if the man is the biological father it is in the child's best interest that an adoption be allowed to proceed, the court shall order that the consent of that man is not required for an adoption. This finding terminates all parental rights and responsibilities with respect to the child. *(Stats.1992, c. 162 (A.B.2650), § 10, operative Jan. 1, 1994. Amended by Stats.2011, c. 462 (A.B.687), § 2; Stats.2013, c. 510 (A.B.1403), § 19; Stats.2019, c. 115 (A.B.1817), § 97, eff. Jan. 1, 2020.)*

Cross References

Action to determine existence or nonexistence of father and child relationship, consolidated actions and jurisdiction, see Family Code § 7630.
Adoption, consent of birth parents required, see Family Code § 8604.
Best interest of child, considerations, see Family Code § 3011.
Judgment and order defined for purposes of this Code, see Family Code § 100.
Person defined for purposes of this Code, see Family Code § 105.
Proceeding defined for purposes of this Code, see Family Code § 110.

Research References

Forms

2 California Transactions Forms--Family Law § 6:3, Definitions.
2 California Transactions Forms--Family Law § 6:8, Consent for Adoption of Unmarried Minor.
2 California Transactions Forms--Family Law § 6:11, Initiating Proceeding Under Uniform Parentage Act [Fam. Code, §§7600 to 7730].
2 California Transactions Forms--Family Law § 6:40, Structuring the Adoption.
2 California Transactions Forms--Family Law § 6:72, Petition to Terminate Parental Rights of Alleged Father.
2 California Transactions Forms--Family Law § 6:74, Petition to Terminate Parental Rights of Alleged Father Served With Notice of Alleged Paternity Without Timely Response.
2 California Transactions Forms--Family Law § 6:76, Ex Parte Application for Order to Terminate Parental Rights of Alleged Father Who Waived Notice or Denied Paternity.
2 California Transactions Forms--Family Law § 6:77, Order Terminating Parental Rights of Alleged Father Who Waived Notice.

§ 7665. Termination of unknown biological father's parental rights; entry of order

If, after the inquiry, the court is unable to identify the biological father or any possible biological father and no person has appeared claiming to be the biological father and claiming custodial rights, the court shall enter an order terminating the unknown biological father's parental rights with reference to the child. *(Stats.1992, c. 162 (A.B.2650), § 10, operative Jan. 1, 1994. Amended by Stats.2013, c. 510 (A.B.1403), § 20.)*

Cross References

Adoption, consent of both parents not required in certain cases, see Family Code § 8606.
Judgment and order defined for purposes of this Code, see Family Code § 100.
Person defined for purposes of this Code, see Family Code § 105.
Protective and temporary custody orders, see Family Code § 7700 et seq.
Selection and implementation hearings, see Welfare and Institutions Code § 294.

Research References

Forms

2 California Transactions Forms--Family Law § 6:78, Petition to Terminate Parental Rights of Alleged Father Who Cannot be Located.
West's California Code Forms, Family § 7660, Comment Overview--Termination of Parental Rights in Adoption Proceedings.

§ 7666. Notice of proceedings

(a) Except as provided in subdivision (b), notice of the proceeding shall be given to every person identified as the biological father or a possible biological father in accordance with the Code of Civil Procedure for the service of process in a civil action in this state at least 10 days before the date of the proceeding, except that publication or posting of the notice of the proceeding is not required, and service on the parent or guardian of a biological father or possible biological father who is a minor is not required unless the minor has previously provided written authorization to serve the minor's parent or guardian. Proof of giving the notice shall be filed with the court before the petition is heard.

(b) Notice to a man identified as or alleged to be the biological father is not required, and the court shall issue an order dispensing with that notice under any of the following circumstances:

(1) The relationship to the child has been previously terminated or determined not to exist by a court.

(2) The alleged father has executed a written form to waive notice, deny parentage, relinquish the child for adoption, or consent to the adoption of the child.

(3) The whereabouts or identity of the alleged father are unknown or cannot be ascertained.

(4) The alleged father has been served with written notice of alleged parentage and the proposed adoption, and has failed to bring an action pursuant to subdivision (c) of Section 7630 within 30 days of service of the notice or the birth of the child, whichever is later. *(Stats.1992, c. 162 (A.B.2650), § 10, operative Jan. 1, 1994. Amended by Stats.2002, c. 260 (S.B.1512), § 1; Stats.2011, c. 462 (A.B.687), § 3; Stats.2013, c. 510 (A.B.1403), § 21; Stats.2014, c. 763 (A.B. 1701), § 3, eff. Jan. 1, 2015; Stats.2019, c. 115 (A.B.1817), § 98, eff. Jan. 1, 2020.)*

Cross References

Judgment and order defined for purposes of this Code, see Family Code § 100.
Person defined for purposes of this Code, see Family Code § 105.
Proceeding defined for purposes of this Code, see Family Code § 110.
Selection and implementation hearings, see Welfare and Institutions Code § 294.
Service of process, generally, see Code of Civil Procedure § 410.10 et seq.
State defined for purposes of this Code, see Family Code § 145.

Research References

Forms

2 California Transactions Forms--Family Law § 6:8, Consent for Adoption of Unmarried Minor.
2 California Transactions Forms--Family Law § 6:40, Structuring the Adoption.
2 California Transactions Forms--Family Law § 6:42, Rights of Birth Father.
2 California Transactions Forms--Family Law § 6:78, Petition to Terminate Parental Rights of Alleged Father Who Cannot be Located.
2 California Transactions Forms--Family Law § 6:79, Order Terminating Parental Rights of Alleged Father Who Cannot be Located.
West's California Code Forms, Family § 7630, Comment Overview—Determining Parent and Child Relationship.
West's California Code Forms, Family § 7660, Comment Overview—Termination of Parental Rights in Adoption Proceedings.

§ 7667. Time of hearing; ex parte orders terminating parental rights

(a) Notwithstanding any other law, an action to terminate the parental rights of an alleged father of a child as specified in this part shall be set for hearing not more than 45 days after filing of the petition, except as provided in subdivision (c).

(b) The matter so set shall have precedence over all other civil matters on the date set for trial, except an action to terminate parental rights pursuant to Part 4 (commencing with Section 7800).

(c) The court may dispense with a hearing and issue an ex parte order terminating parental rights if any of the following applies:

(1) The identity or whereabouts of the alleged father are unknown.

(2) The alleged father has validly executed a waiver of the right to notice or a denial of parentage.

(3) The alleged father has been served with written notice of alleged parentage and the proposed adoption, and has failed to bring an action pursuant to subdivision (c) of Section 7630 within 30 days of service of the notice or the birth of the child, whichever is later. *(Stats.1992, c. 162 (A.B.2650), § 10, operative Jan. 1, 1994. Amended by Stats.2010, c. 588 (A.B.2020), § 4; Stats.2011, c. 462 (A.B.687), § 4; Stats.2013, c. 510 (A.B.1403), § 22; Stats.2019, c. 115 (A.B. 1817), § 99, eff. Jan. 1, 2020.)*

Cross References

Judgment and order defined for purposes of this Code, see Family Code § 100.
Proceeding defined for purposes of this Code, see Family Code § 110.
State defined for purposes of this Code, see Family Code § 145.

Research References

Forms

2 California Transactions Forms--Family Law § 6:11, Initiating Proceeding Under Uniform Parentage Act [Fam. Code, §§7600 to 7730].
2 California Transactions Forms--Family Law § 6:72, Petition to Terminate Parental Rights of Alleged Father.

§ 7668. Continuance of proceedings; purpose

(a) The court may continue the proceedings for not more than 30 days as necessary to appoint counsel and to enable counsel to prepare for the case adequately or for other good cause.

(b) In order to obtain an order for a continuance of the hearing, written notice shall be filed within two court days of the date set for the hearing, together with affidavits or declarations detailing specific facts showing that a continuance is necessary, unless the court for good cause entertains an oral motion for continuance.

(c) Continuances shall be granted only upon a showing of good cause. Neither a stipulation between counsel nor the convenience of the parties is in and of itself a good cause.

(d) A continuance shall be granted only for that period of time shown to be necessary by the evidence considered at the hearing on the motion. If a continuance is granted, the facts proven which require the continuance shall be entered upon the minutes of the court. *(Stats.1992, c. 162 (A.B.2650), § 10, operative Jan. 1, 1994.)*

Cross References

Judgment and order defined for purposes of this Code, see Family Code § 100.
Proceeding defined for purposes of this Code, see Family Code § 110.

§ 7669. Order requiring or dispensing with alleged father's consent for adoption; appeal from order and judgment

(a) An order requiring or dispensing with an alleged father's consent for the adoption of a child may be appealed from in the same manner as an order of the juvenile court declaring a person to be a ward of the juvenile court and is conclusive and binding upon the alleged father.

(b) After making the order, the court has no power to set aside, change, or modify that order.

(c) Nothing in this section limits the right to appeal from the order and judgment. *(Stats.1992, c. 162 (A.B.2650), § 10, operative Jan. 1, 1994. Amended by Stats.2002, c. 260 (S.B.1512), § 2; Stats.2003, c. 251 (S.B.182), § 4; Stats.2013, c. 510 (A.B.1403), § 23.)*

Cross References

Adoption, consent of birth parents required, see Family Code § 8604.
Judgment and order defined for purposes of this Code, see Family Code § 100.
Person defined for purposes of this Code, see Family Code § 105.

Research References

Forms

West's California Code Forms, Family § 7660, Comment Overview—Termination of Parental Rights in Adoption Proceedings.

§ 7670. Filing fee

There shall be no filing fee charged for a petition filed pursuant to Section 7662. *(Stats.1992, c. 162 (A.B.2650), § 10, operative Jan. 1, 1994.)*

§ 7670

Research References

Forms

2 California Transactions Forms--Family Law § 6:11, Initiating Proceeding Under Uniform Parentage Act [Fam. Code, §§7600 to 7730].
2 California Transactions Forms--Family Law § 6:71, Notice of Alleged Paternity.
2 California Transactions Forms--Family Law § 6:72, Petition to Terminate Parental Rights of Alleged Father.

§ 7671. Multiple fathers or multiple children; single petition to terminate parental rights

A single petition may be filed pursuant to Section 7662 to terminate the parental rights of the alleged father or fathers of two or more biological siblings or to terminate the parental rights of two or more alleged fathers of the same child. A petition filed in accordance with this section may be granted in whole or in part in accordance with the procedures set forth in this chapter. The court shall retain discretion to bifurcate any case in which the petition was filed in accordance with this section, and shall do so whenever it is necessary to protect the interests of a party or a child who is the subject of the proceeding. *(Added by Stats.2014, c. 763 (A.B.1701), § 4, eff. Jan. 1, 2015.)*

Research References

Forms

2 California Transactions Forms--Family Law § 6:8, Consent for Adoption of Unmarried Minor.
2 California Transactions Forms--Family Law § 6:11, Initiating Proceeding Under Uniform Parentage Act [Fam. Code, §§7600 to 7730].
2 California Transactions Forms--Family Law § 6:40, Structuring the Adoption.
2 California Transactions Forms--Family Law § 6:72, Petition to Terminate Parental Rights of Alleged Father.

CHAPTER 6. PROTECTIVE AND RESTRAINING ORDERS

Article	Section
1. Orders in Summons	7700
2. Ex Parte Orders	7710
3. Orders After Notice and Hearing	7720
4. Orders Included in Judgment	7730

Cross References

Law enforcement response to domestic violence, written policies and standards, see Penal Code § 13701.
Uniform act, construction of provisions, see Family Code § 3.

ARTICLE 1. ORDERS IN SUMMONS

Section
7700. Temporary restraining orders contained in summons.

Cross References

Uniform act, construction of provisions, see Family Code § 3.

§ 7700. Temporary restraining orders contained in summons

In addition to the contents required by Section 412.20 of the Code of Civil Procedure, in a proceeding under this part the summons shall contain a temporary restraining order restraining all parties, without the prior written consent of the other party or an order of the court, from removing from the state any minor child for whom the proceeding seeks to establish a parent and child relationship. *(Added by Stats.1993, c. 219 (A.B.1500), § 179.6.)*

Cross References

Abuse of children, see Penal Code §§ 273a, 273d.
Applicable provisions, see Family Code § 231.
Application of part, see Family Code § 240.
Duration and enforceability of order, see Family Code §§ 232, 233.
Ex parte orders, admissibility, see Family Code § 234.
Judgment and order defined for purposes of this Code, see Family Code § 100.
Minor defined for purposes of this Code, see Family Code § 6500.
Modification or revocation of orders, see Family Code § 235.
Proceeding defined for purposes of this Code, see Family Code § 110.
Spousal abusers, see Penal Code § 273.8 et seq.
State defined for purposes of this Code, see Family Code § 145.
Temporary restraining order in summons, generally, see Family Code § 231 et seq.

Research References

Forms

West's California Judicial Council Forms FL-110, Summons (Also Available in Arabic and Chinese).
West's California Judicial Council Forms FL-210, Summons (Uniform Percentage—Petition for Custody and Support) (Incl. Spanish) (Also Available in Chinese).

ARTICLE 2. EX PARTE ORDERS

Section
7710. Issuance of orders.
7711, 7712. Inoperative.

Cross References

Certified copies of orders issued pursuant to this Article, no fees charged to indigent plaintiffs, see Government Code § 70676.
Ex parte temporary restraining orders, generally, see Family Code § 240 et seq.
Nullity, dissolution, and legal separation, ex parte protective orders, generally, see Family Code § 2045.
Uniform act, construction of provisions, see Family Code § 3.
Uniform Parentage Act, issuance of ex parte orders, see Family Code § 7710.

§ 7710. Issuance of orders

During the pendency of a proceeding under this part, on application of a party in the manner provided by Part 4 (commencing with Section 240) of Division 2, the court may issue ex parte a protective order as defined in Section 6218 and any other order as provided in Article 1 (commencing with Section 6320) of Chapter 2 of Part 4 of Division 10. *(Added by Stats.1993, c. 219 (A.B.1500), § 179.6.)*

Cross References

Abuse of children, see Penal Code §§ 273a, 273d.
Admissibility of evidence, ex parte orders, see Family Code § 234.
Applicable provisions, order to show cause, see Family Code § 242.
Certified copies of orders for indigent plaintiffs, exemption from fees, see Government Code § 70676.
Domestic Violence Prevention Act, see Family Code § 6200 et seq.
Dwelling, order excluding party following notice and hearing, see Family Code § 6340.
Judgment and order defined for purposes of this Code, see Family Code § 100.
Jurisdiction, superior court, see Family Code § 200.
Minors, incompetent persons or persons for whom conservator appointed, see Code of Civil Procedure § 372.
Parties to civil actions, minor under age 12, appearance conditions, see Code of Civil Procedure § 374.
Proceeding defined for purposes of this Code, see Family Code § 110.
Protective order, defined, see Family Code § 6218.
Return of orders, see Family Code § 242.
Similar provisions, see Family Code §§ 2045, 6250, 6320.
Spousal abusers, see Penal Code § 273.8 et seq.
Witnesses, interpreters and translators, hearings or proceedings related to domestic violence, see Evidence Code § 756.

Research References

Forms

West's California Judicial Council Forms FL-303, Declaration Regarding Notice and Service of Request for Temporary Emergency (Ex Parte) Orders (Also Available in Spanish).

§§ 7711, 7712. Inoperative

FREEDOM FROM CUSTODY AND CONTROL

ARTICLE 3. ORDERS AFTER NOTICE AND HEARING

Section
7720. Protective and restraining orders; issuance after notice and hearing.
7721, 7722. Inoperative.

Cross References

Certified copies of orders issued pursuant to this Article, no fees charged to indigent plaintiffs, see Government Code § 70676.
Uniform act, construction of provisions, see Family Code § 3.

§ 7720. Protective and restraining orders; issuance after notice and hearing

(a) After notice and a hearing, the court may issue a protective order as defined in Section 6218 and any other restraining order as provided in Article 2 (commencing with Section 6340) of Chapter 2 of Part 4 of Division 10.

(b) The court may not issue a mutual protective order pursuant to subdivision (a) unless it meets the requirements of Section 6305. *(Added by Stats.1993, c. 219 (A.B.1500), § 179.6. Amended by Stats.1995, c. 246 (S.B.591), § 3.)*

Cross References

Judgment and order defined for purposes of this Code, see Family Code § 100.
Minors, incompetent persons or persons for whom conservator appointed, see Code of Civil Procedure § 372.
Parties to civil actions, minor under age twelve, appearance conditions, see Code of Civil Procedure § 374.

§§ 7721, 7722. Inoperative

ARTICLE 4. ORDERS INCLUDED IN JUDGMENT

Section
7730. Protective and restraining orders; inclusion in judgment.
7731 to 7750. Inoperative.

Cross References

Certified copies of orders issued pursuant to this Article, no fees charged to indigent plaintiffs, see Government Code § 70676.
Uniform act, construction of provisions, see Family Code § 3.

§ 7730. Protective and restraining orders; inclusion in judgment

A judgment entered in a proceeding under this part may include a protective order as defined in Section 6218 and any other restraining order as provided in Article 3 (commencing with Section 6360) of Chapter 2 of Part 4 of Division 10. *(Added by Stats.1993, c. 219 (A.B.1500), § 179.6.)*

Cross References

Judgment and order defined for purposes of this Code, see Family Code § 100.
Proceeding defined for purposes of this Code, see Family Code § 110.

Research References

Forms
2 California Transactions Forms--Family Law § 6:2, Governing Law.
2 California Transactions Forms--Family Law § 6:3, Definitions.
2 California Transactions Forms--Family Law § 6:10, Initiating Proceeding Under Fam. Code, §§ 7800 et seq.

§§ 7731 to 7750. Inoperative

Part 4

FREEDOM FROM PARENTAL CUSTODY AND CONTROL

Chapter	Section
1. General Provisions	7800
2. Circumstances Where Proceeding May Be Brought	7820
3. Procedure	7840

Cross References

Abandonment and neglect of children, see Penal Code § 270 et seq.
Abuse of parental authority, remedy, see Family Code § 7507.
Actions affecting prisoner's parental or marital rights, see Penal Code § 2625.
Adoption, generally, see Family Code § 8500 et seq.
Agency adoptions, notice to birth parent on termination of parental rights, disclosure of name and address, see Family Code § 8703.
Child abuse and confidentiality of identity of persons reporting, see Penal Code § 11167.
Child support, generally, see Family Code § 3900 et seq.
Child support, enforcement of orders, see Family Code § 4500 et seq.
Child welfare, foster care for specified time period, termination of parental rights, see Welfare and Institutions Code § 16508.1.
Custody of children, see Family Code §§ 3000 et seq., 3020 et seq.
Custody proceedings,
 Defined for purposes of child abduction offenses, see Penal Code § 277.
 Defined for purposes of the Uniform Child Custody Jurisdiction and Enforcement Act, see Family Code § 3402.
Dependent children, judgments and orders, see Welfare and Institutions Code § 360 et seq.
Dependent children, temporary custody and detention, presumed or alleged fathers, inquiry by court, see Welfare and Institutions Code § 316.2.
Domestic violence, prevention, see Family Code § 6200 et seq.
Enforcement of judgments and orders, see Family Code §§ 290, 291.
Hearings, termination of parental rights, guardianship of dependent children, see Welfare and Institutions Code § 366.26 et seq.
Judgment and orders, dependency proceedings, see Welfare and Institutions Code § 360 et seq.
Jurisdiction, superior court, see Family Code § 200.
Juvenile court, detention of dependent children, see Welfare and Institutions Code § 367.
Limitations on parental control, see Welfare and Institutions Code § 361.
Minors,
 Age of majority, see Family Code § 6500 et seq.
 Civil actions, see Family Code § 6600 et seq.
 Contracts, see Family Code § 6700 et seq.
 Emancipation, see Family Code § 7000 et seq.
 Rights and liabilities, see Family Code § 6600 et seq.
Notice that parental rights may be terminated, see Welfare and Institutions Code § 294.
Parental custody, generally, see Family Code §§ 3000 et seq., 3020 et seq.
Parental relationship, determination, see Family Code § 7600 et seq.
Protective and temporary custody orders, see Family Code § 7700 et seq.
Temporary orders, custody and protection of children, see Family Code § 7700 et seq.
Wards, termination of parental rights, minors in foster care, see Welfare and Institutions Code §§ 706.6, 725 et seq.

CHAPTER 1. GENERAL PROVISIONS

Section
7800. Purpose of part.
7801. Liberal construction.
7802. Proceeding for declaration of freedom from parental custody and control.
7803. Effect of declaration of freedom.
7804. Appointment of party to act in minor's behalf.
7805. Inspection of petitions, reports, and court records and briefs.
7806. Filing fees.
7807. Applicability of proceedings; stay of proceedings under specified statutory provisions.

PARENT AND CHILD RELATIONSHIP

Section
7808. Application of part.
7810. Repealed.

§ 7800. Purpose of part

The purpose of this part is to serve the welfare and best interest of a child by providing the stability and security of an adoptive home when those conditions are otherwise missing from the child's life. *(Stats.1992, c. 162 (A.B.2650), § 10, operative Jan. 1, 1994.)*

Research References

Forms

2 California Transactions Forms--Family Law § 6:10, Initiating Proceeding Under Fam. Code, §§ 7800 et seq.

2 California Transactions Forms--Family Law § 7:39, Adoption and Termination of Parental Rights.

West's California Code Forms, Probate § 1510 Form 1, Petition for Appointment of Guardian of Estate of Minor—Judicial Council Form GC-210.

§ 7801. Liberal construction

This part shall be liberally construed to serve and protect the interests and welfare of the child. *(Stats.1992, c. 162 (A.B.2650), § 10, operative Jan. 1, 1994.)*

§ 7802. Proceeding for declaration of freedom from parental custody and control

A proceeding may be brought under this part for the purpose of having a minor child declared free from the custody and control of either or both parents. *(Stats.1992, c. 162 (A.B.2650), § 10, operative Jan. 1, 1994.)*

Cross References

Abuse of parental authority, see Family Code § 7507.
Adoption proceedings, hearings to terminate parental rights of father, application to proceedings pursuant to these provisions, see Family Code § 7667.
Age of majority, see Family Code § 6500 et seq.
Dependency proceedings, judgments and orders, see Welfare and Institutions Code § 360 et seq.
Emancipation of minors, see Family Code § 7000 et seq.
Enforcement of judgments and orders,
  Generally, see Family Code §§ 290, 291.
  Effect of order, see Family Code § 7894.
Hearings, termination of parental rights, guardianship of dependent children, see Welfare and Institutions Code § 366.26 et seq.
Jurisdiction of superior court, see Family Code § 200.
Juvenile courts, detention of dependent children, see Welfare and Institutions Code § 367.
Limitations on parental control, see Welfare and Institutions Code § 361.
Minor defined for purposes of this Code, see Family Code § 6500.
Minors, age of majority, see Family Code § 6500 et seq.
Notice that parental rights may be terminated, see Welfare and Institutions Code § 294.
Parent and child relationship, determination, see Family Code § 7600 et seq.
Parental custody, generally, see Family Code §§ 3000 et seq., 3020 et seq.
Proceeding defined for purposes of this Code, see Family Code § 110.
Proceeding to declare minor free from parental custody and control, see Family Code § 7820 et seq.
Removal of children from parental custody, see Welfare and Institutions Code § 360 et seq.

§ 7803. Effect of declaration of freedom

A declaration of freedom from parental custody and control pursuant to this part terminates all parental rights and responsibilities with regard to the child. *(Stats.1992, c. 162 (A.B.2650), § 10, operative Jan. 1, 1994.)*

Cross References

Abandonment and neglect of children, see Penal Code § 270 et seq.
Abuse of parental authority, remedy, see Family Code § 7507.
Adoption, generally, see Family Code § 8500 et seq.
Child support,
  Generally, see Family Code § 3900 et seq.
  Enforcement of orders, see Family Code § 4500 et seq.
Dependent children, judgments and orders, see Welfare and Institutions Code § 360 et seq.
Domestic violence, prevention, see Family Code § 6200 et seq.
Enforcement of judgments and orders, see Family Code §§ 290, 291.
Hearings, termination of parental rights, guardianship of dependent children, see Welfare and Institutions Code § 366.26 et seq.
Jurisdiction, superior court, see Family Code § 200.
Juvenile court, detention of dependent children, see Welfare and Institutions Code § 367.
Limitations on parental control, see Welfare and Institutions Code § 361.
Minors,
  Contracts, see Family Code § 6700 et seq.
  Emancipation, see Family Code § 7000 et seq.
  Rights and liabilities, civil actions and proceedings, see Family Code § 6600 et seq.
Notice that parental rights may be terminated, see Welfare and Institutions Code § 294.
Parental custody, generally, see Family Code §§ 3000 et seq., 3020 et seq.
Parental relationship, determination, see Family Code § 7600 et seq.
Protective and temporary custody orders, see Family Code § 7700 et seq.

Research References

Forms

West's California Code Forms, Family § 7890, Comment Overview—Hearing and Subsequent Proceedings.

§ 7804. Appointment of party to act in minor's behalf

In a proceeding under this part, the court may appoint a suitable party to act in behalf of the child and may order such further notice of the proceedings to be given as the court deems proper. *(Stats. 1992, c. 162 (A.B.2650), § 10, operative Jan. 1, 1994.)*

Cross References

Appointment of counsel, proceedings under this Part, see Family Code § 7860 et seq.
Appointment of counsel for dependent children and parents or guardians, see Welfare and Institutions Code § 317.
Appointment of legal counsel, see Probate Code § 1470 et seq.
Guardianship, conservatorship and other protective proceedings, see Probate Code § 1400 et seq.
Judgment and order defined for purposes of this Code, see Family Code § 100.
Proceeding defined for purposes of this Code, see Family Code § 110.

§ 7805. Inspection of petitions, reports, and court records and briefs

(a) A petition filed in a proceeding under this part, or a report of the probation officer or county department designated by the board of supervisors to administer the public social services program filed in a proceeding under this part, may be inspected only by the following persons:

(1) Court personnel.

(2) The child who is the subject of the proceeding.

(3) The parents or guardian of the child.

(4) The attorneys for the parties.

(5) Any other person designated by the judge.

(b) In a proceeding before the court of appeal or Supreme Court to review a judgment or order entered in a proceeding under this part, the court record and briefs filed by the parties may be inspected only by the following persons:

(1) Court personnel.

(2) A party to the proceeding.

(3) The attorneys for the parties.

(4) Any other person designated by the presiding judge of the court before which the matter is pending.

(c) Notwithstanding any other provision of law, if it is believed that the welfare of the child will be promoted thereby, the court and the probation officer may furnish information, pertaining to a petition under this part, to any of the following:

(1) The State Department of Social Services.

(2) A county welfare department.

(3) A public welfare agency.

(4) A private welfare agency licensed by the State Department of Social Services. *(Stats.1992, c. 162 (A.B.2650), § 10, operative Jan. 1, 1994.)*

Cross References

County defined for purposes of this Code, see Family Code § 67.
Family conciliation court proceedings, inspection of papers, see Family Code § 1818.
Judgment and order defined for purposes of this Code, see Family Code § 100.
Jurisdiction of superior court, see Family Code § 200.
Person defined for purposes of this Code, see Family Code § 105.
Proceeding defined for purposes of this Code, see Family Code § 110.
State defined for purposes of this Code, see Family Code § 145.

§ 7806. Filing fees

There shall be no filing fee charged for a proceeding brought under this part. *(Stats.1992, c. 162 (A.B.2650), § 10, operative Jan. 1, 1994.)*

Cross References

Attorney's fees and costs, generally, see Family Code § 270 et seq.
Proceeding defined for purposes of this Code, see Family Code § 110.

Research References

Forms

West's California Code Forms, Family § 7840, Comment Overview—Freedom from Parental Control.

§ 7807. Applicability of proceedings; stay of proceedings under specified statutory provisions

(a) Sections 3020, 3022, 3040 to 3043, inclusive, and 3409 do not apply in a proceeding under this part.

(b) Except as provided in this subdivision and subdivision (c), all proceedings affecting a child, including proceedings under Divisions 8 (commencing with Section 3000) to 11 (commencing with Section 6500), inclusive, Part 1 (commencing with Section 7500) to Part 3 (commencing with Section 7600), inclusive, of this division, and Part 1 (commencing with Section 1400), Part 2 (commencing with Section 1500), and Part 4 (commencing with Section 2100) of Division 4 of the Probate Code, and any motion or petition for custody or visitation filed in a proceeding under this part, shall be stayed. The petition to free the minor from parental custody and control under this section is the only matter that may be heard during the stay until the court issues a final ruling on the petition.

(c) This section does not limit the jurisdiction of the court pursuant to Part 3 (commencing with Section 6240) and Part 4 (commencing with Section 6300) of Division 10 with respect to domestic violence orders, or pursuant to Article 6 (commencing with Section 300) of Chapter 2 of Part 1 of Division 2 of the Welfare and Institutions Code with respect to dependency proceedings. *(Stats. 1992, c. 162 (A.B.2650), § 10, operative Jan. 1, 1994. Amended by Stats.1993, c. 219 (A.B.1500), § 179.9; Stats.2002, c. 260 (S.B.1512), § 3; Stats.2014, c. 763 (A.B.1701), § 5, eff. Jan. 1, 2015.)*

Cross References

Domestic violence defined for purposes of this Code, see Family Code § 6211.
Judgment and order defined for purposes of this Code, see Family Code § 100.
Proceeding defined for purposes of this Code, see Family Code § 110.

Research References

Forms

West's California Code Forms, Family § 7841 Form 1, Petition for Freedom from Parental Control—Abandonment.

§ 7808. Application of part

This part does not apply to a minor adjudged a dependent child of the juvenile court pursuant to subdivision (c) of Section 360 of the Welfare and Institutions Code on and after January 1, 1989, during the period in which the minor is a dependent child of the court. For those minors, the exclusive means for the termination of parental rights are provided in the following statutes:

(a) Section 366.26 of the Welfare and Institutions Code.

(b) Sections 8604 to 8606, inclusive, and 8700 of this code.

(c) Chapter 5 (commencing with Section 7660) of Part 3 of this division of this code. *(Stats.1992, c. 162 (A.B.2650), § 10, operative Jan. 1, 1994. Amended by Stats.1994, c. 1269 (A.B.2208), § 55.4.)*

Cross References

Minor defined for purposes of this Code, see Family Code § 6500.

§ 7810. Repealed by Stats.2006, c. 838 (S.B.678), § 3

CHAPTER 2. CIRCUMSTANCES WHERE PROCEEDING MAY BE BROUGHT

Section
7820. Application of chapter.
7821. Findings; sufficiency of evidence.
7822. Abandoned children; right to action; declaration of abandonment; Indian children.
7823. Neglected or cruelly treated children; right to action.
7824. Parents suffering from disability due to alcohol, or controlled substances, or moral depravity; right of action.
7825. Parent convicted of felony; consideration of criminal record prior to felony conviction; right of action.
7826. Parent declared developmentally disabled or mentally ill; right to action.
7827. Mentally disabled parent; right to action.
7828, 7829. Repealed.

Cross References

Abandonment and neglect of children, see Penal Code § 270 et seq.
Abuse of parental authority, remedy, see Family Code § 7507.
Action to determine existence or nonexistence of father and child relationship, consolidated actions and jurisdiction, see Family Code § 7630.
Adoption, generally, see Family Code § 8500 et seq.
Child support,
  Generally, see Family Code § 3900 et seq.
  Enforcement of orders, see Family Code § 4500 et seq.
Child welfare, foster care for specified time period, termination of parental rights, see Welfare and Institutions Code § 16508.1.
Child welfare services, reunification of family, see Welfare and Institutions Code § 361.5.
Custody of children, see Family Code §§ 3000 et seq., 3020 et seq.
Custody proceedings,
  Defined for purposes of child abduction offenses, see Penal Code § 277.
  Defined for purposes of the Uniform Child Custody Jurisdiction and Enforcement Act, see Family Code § 3402.
Dependent children, judgments and orders, see Welfare and Institutions Code § 360 et seq.
Domestic violence, prevention, see Family Code § 6200 et seq.
Enforcement of judgments and orders, see Family Code §§ 290, 291.
Hearings, termination of parental rights, guardianship of dependent children, see Welfare and Institutions Code § 366.26 et seq.
Jurisdiction, juvenile court, cases of abuse, neglect or cruelty, and children of incarcerated parents, see Welfare and Institutions Code § 300.

PARENT AND CHILD RELATIONSHIP

Jurisdiction, superior court, see Family Code § 200.
Juvenile court, detention of dependent children, see Welfare and Institutions Code § 367.
Limitations on parental control, see Welfare and Institutions Code § 361.
Minors,
  Age of majority, see Family Code § 6500 et seq.
  Contracts, see Family Code § 6700 et seq.
  Emancipation, see Family Code § 7000 et seq.
  Rights and liabilities, civil actions and proceedings, see Family Code § 6600 et seq.
Notice that parental rights may be terminated, see Welfare and Institutions Code § 294.
Parental custody, generally, see Family Code §§ 3000 et seq., 3020 et seq.
Parental relationship, determination, see Family Code § 7600 et seq.
Proceeding to have child declared free from custody and control of one or both parents, generally, see Probate Code § 1516.5.
Protective and temporary custody orders, see Family Code § 7700 et seq.
Wards, termination of parental rights, minors in foster care, see Welfare and Institutions Code §§ 706.6, 725 et seq.

§ 7820. Application of chapter

A proceeding may be brought under this part for the purpose of having a child under the age of 18 years declared free from the custody and control of either or both parents if the child comes within any of the descriptions set out in this chapter. *(Stats.1992, c. 162 (A.B.2650), § 10, operative Jan. 1, 1994.)*

Cross References

Action to determine existence or nonexistence of father and child relationship, consolidated actions and jurisdiction, see Family Code § 7630.
Child abuse and confidentiality of identity of persons reporting, see Penal Code § 11167.
Child support,
  Generally, see Family Code § 3900 et seq.
  Enforcement of orders, see Family Code § 4500 et seq.
Child welfare, foster care for specified time period, termination of parental rights, see Welfare and Institutions Code § 16508.1.
Custody of children, see Family Code §§ 3000 et seq., 3020 et seq.
Custody proceedings,
  Defined for purposes of child abduction offenses, see Penal Code § 277.
  Defined for purposes of the Uniform Child Custody Jurisdiction and Enforcement Act, see Family Code § 3402.
Dependent children, judgments and orders, see Welfare and Institutions Code § 360 et seq.
Dependent children, temporary custody and detention, presumed or alleged fathers, inquiry by court, see Welfare and Institutions Code § 316.2.
Domestic violence, prevention, see Family Code § 6200 et seq.
Enforcement of judgments and orders, see Family Code §§ 290, 291.
Hearings, termination of parental rights, guardianship of dependent children, see Welfare and Institutions Code § 366.26 et seq.
Jurisdiction, superior court, see Family Code § 200.
Juvenile court, detention of dependent children, see Welfare and Institutions Code § 367.
Limitations on parental control, see Welfare and Institutions Code § 361.
Minors,
  Age of majority, see Family Code § 6500 et seq.
  Contracts, see Family Code § 6700 et seq.
  Emancipation, see Family Code § 7000 et seq.
  Rights and liabilities, civil actions and proceedings, see Family Code § 6600 et seq.
Notice that parental rights may be terminated, see Welfare and Institutions Code § 366.23.
Parental custody, generally, see Family Code §§ 3000 et seq., 3020 et seq.
Parental relationship, determination, see Family Code § 7600 et seq.
Proceeding defined for purposes of this Code, see Family Code § 110.
Proceeding to have child declared free from custody and control of one or both parents, see Probate Code § 1516.5.
Protective and temporary custody orders, see Family Code § 7700 et seq.
Wards, termination of parental rights, minors in foster care, see Welfare and Institutions Code §§ 706.6, 725 et seq.

§ 7821. Findings; sufficiency of evidence

A finding pursuant to this chapter shall be supported by clear and convincing evidence, except as otherwise provided. *(Stats.1992, c. 162 (A.B.2650), § 10, operative Jan. 1, 1994. Amended by Stats.2006, c. 838 (S.B.678), § 4.)*

Cross References

Action to determine existence or nonexistence of father and child relationship, consolidated actions and jurisdiction, see Family Code § 7630.
Burden of proof, defined, see Evidence Code § 115.

§ 7822. Abandoned children; right to action; declaration of abandonment; Indian children

(a) A proceeding under this part may be brought if any of the following occur:

(1) The child has been left without provision for the child's identification by the child's parent or parents.

(2) The child has been left by both parents or the sole parent in the care and custody of another person for a period of six months without any provision for the child's support, or without communication from the parent or parents, with the intent on the part of the parent or parents to abandon the child.

(3) One parent has left the child in the care and custody of the other parent for a period of one year without any provision for the child's support, or without communication from the parent, with the intent on the part of the parent to abandon the child.

(b) The failure to provide identification, failure to provide support, or failure to communicate is presumptive evidence of the intent to abandon. If the parent or parents have made only token efforts to support or communicate with the child, the court may declare the child abandoned by the parent or parents. In the event that a guardian has been appointed for the child, the court may still declare the child abandoned if the parent or parents have failed to communicate with or support the child within the meaning of this section.

(c) If the child has been left without provision for the child's identification and the whereabouts of the parents are unknown, a petition may be filed after the 120th day following the discovery of the child and citation by publication may be commenced. The petition may not be heard until after the 180th day following the discovery of the child.

(d) If the parent has agreed for the child to be in the physical custody of another person or persons for adoption and has not signed an adoption placement agreement pursuant to Section 8801.3, a consent to adoption pursuant to Section 8814, or a relinquishment to a licensed adoption agency pursuant to Section 8700, evidence of the adoptive placement shall not in itself preclude the court from finding an intent on the part of that parent to abandon the child. If the parent has placed the child for adoption pursuant to Section 8801.3, consented to adoption pursuant to Section 8814, or relinquished the child to a licensed adoption agency pursuant to Section 8700, and has then either revoked the consent or rescinded the relinquishment, but has not taken reasonable action to obtain custody of the child, evidence of the adoptive placement shall not in itself preclude the court from finding an intent on the part of that parent to abandon the child.

(e) Notwithstanding subdivisions (a), (b), (c), and (d), if the parent of an Indian child has transferred physical care, custody, and control of the child to an Indian custodian, that action shall not be deemed to constitute an abandonment of the child, unless the parent manifests the intent to abandon the child by either of the following:

(1) Failing to resume physical care, custody, and control of the child upon the request of the Indian custodian provided that, if the Indian custodian is unable to make a request because the parent has failed to keep the Indian custodian apprised of the parent's whereabouts and the Indian custodian has made reasonable efforts to determine the whereabouts of the parent without success, there may be evidence of intent to abandon.

(2) Failing to substantially comply with any obligations assumed by the parent in the agreement with the Indian custodian despite the Indian custodian's objection to the noncompliance. *(Stats.1992, c. 162 (A.B.2650), § 10, operative Jan. 1, 1994. Amended by Stats.2006, c. 838 (S.B.678), § 5; Stats.2007, c. 47 (S.B.313), § 2; Stats.2019, c. 115 (A.B.1817), § 100, eff. Jan. 1, 2020.)*

Cross References

Abandonment and neglect of children, see Penal Code § 270 et seq.
Abuse of parental authority, remedy, see Family Code § 7507.
Action to determine existence or nonexistence of father and child relationship, consolidated actions and jurisdiction, see Family Code § 7630.
Adoption of unmarried minors, authority of court to declare child abandoned, see Family Code § 8607.
Age of majority, see Family Code § 6500 et seq.
Child abduction, loss of right to custody due to abandonment, see Penal Code § 277.
Child Abuse and Neglect Reporting Act, see Penal Code § 11164 et seq.
Child support,
  Generally, see Family Code § 3900 et seq.
  Enforcement of orders, see Family Code § 4500 et seq.
Custody of unemancipated minor children, see Family Code § 3010.
Dependent children, judgments and orders, see Welfare and Institutions Code § 360 et seq.
Enforcement of judgments and orders, see Family Code §§ 290, 291.
Hearings, termination of parental rights, guardianship of dependent children, see Welfare and Institutions Code § 366.26 et seq.
Jurisdiction, juvenile court, cases of abuse, neglect or cruelty, see Welfare and Institutions Code § 300.
Jurisdiction of superior court, see Family Code § 200.
Juvenile court, detention of dependent children, see Welfare and Institutions Code § 367.
Limitations on parental control, see Welfare and Institutions Code § 361.
Notice that parental rights may be terminated, see Welfare and Institutions Code § 294.
Parental custody, generally, see Family Code §§ 3000 et seq., 3020 et seq.
Petition for adoption, abandoned child, see Family Code § 8802.
Proceeding defined for purposes of this Code, see Family Code § 110.
Protective and temporary custody orders, see Family Code § 7700 et seq.
Support, relief from duty to support parent who abandoned child, see Family Code § 4411.
Support defined for purposes of this Code, see Family Code § 150.
Temporary emergency jurisdiction over abandoned children, see Family Code § 3424.

Research References

Forms

2 California Transactions Forms--Family Law § 6:10, Initiating Proceeding Under Fam. Code, §§7800 et seq.
2 California Transactions Forms--Family Law § 6:107, Adoption Without Consent of Noncustodial Parent.
2 California Transactions Forms--Family Law § 7:39, Adoption and Termination of Parental Rights.
West's California Code Forms, Family § 7840, Comment Overview—Freedom from Parental Control.
West's California Judicial Council Forms ADOPT–200, Adoption Request.

§ 7823. Neglected or cruelly treated children; right to action

(a) A proceeding under this part may be brought if all of the following requirements are satisfied:

(1) The child has been neglected or cruelly treated by either or both parents. A finding that a parent committed severe sexual abuse, as described in paragraph (6) of subdivision (b) of Section 361.5 of the Welfare and Institutions Code, against the child shall be prima facie evidence that the parent has neglected or cruelly treated the child within the meaning of this subdivision.

(2) The child has been a dependent child of the juvenile court under any subdivision of Section 300 of the Welfare and Institutions Code and the parent or parents have been deprived of the child's custody for one year before the filing of a petition pursuant to this part.

(b) Physical custody by the parent or parents for insubstantial periods of time does not interrupt the running of the one-year period. *(Stats.1992, c. 162 (A.B.2650), § 10, operative Jan. 1, 1994. Amended by Stats.2018, c. 83 (A.B.2792), § 1, eff. Jan. 1, 2019.)*

Cross References

Abandonment and neglect of children, see Penal Code § 270 et seq.
Abuse of children,
  Generally, see Penal Code §§ 273a, 273d.
  Sexual abuse, see Penal Code § 1000.12.
Abuse of parental authority, see Family Code § 7507.
Action to determine existence or nonexistence of father and child relationship, consolidated actions and jurisdiction, see Family Code § 7630.
Child Abuse and Neglect Reporting Act, see Penal Code § 11164 et seq.
Dependent children, judgments and orders, see Welfare and Institutions Code § 360 et seq.
Domestic violence prevention, see Family Code § 6200 et seq.
Hearings, termination of parental rights, guardianship of dependent children, see Welfare and Institutions Code § 366.26 et seq.
Juvenile court, detention of dependent children, see Welfare and Institutions Code § 367.
Juvenile court, jurisdiction, cases of abuse, neglect or cruelty, see Welfare and Institutions Code § 300.
Limitations on parental control, see Welfare and Institutions Code § 361.
Notice that parental rights may be terminated, see Welfare and Institutions Code § 294.
Parental custody, generally, see Family Code §§ 3000 et seq., 3020 et seq.
Proceeding defined for purposes of this Code, see Family Code § 110.
Protective and temporary custody orders, see Family Code § 7700 et seq.
Removal of children from parental custody, see Welfare and Institutions Code § 360 et seq.

Research References

Forms

West's California Code Forms, Family § 7840, Comment Overview—Freedom from Parental Control.

§ 7824. Parents suffering from disability due to alcohol, or controlled substances, or moral depravity; right of action

(a) "Disability" as used in this section means any physical or mental incapacity which renders the parent or parents unable to care for and control the child adequately.

(b) A proceeding under this part may be brought where all of the following requirements are satisfied:

(1) The child is one whose parent or parents (A) suffer a disability because of the habitual use of alcohol, or any of the controlled substances specified in Schedules I to V, inclusive, of Division 10 (commencing with Section 11000) of the Health and Safety Code, except when these controlled substances are used as part of a medically prescribed plan, or (B) are morally depraved.

(2) The child has been a dependent child of the juvenile court, and the parent or parents have been deprived of the child's custody continuously for one year immediately before the filing of a petition pursuant to this part.

(c) Physical custody by the parent or parents for insubstantial periods of time does not interrupt the running of the one-year period. *(Stats.1992, c. 162 (A.B.2650), § 10, operative Jan. 1, 1994.)*

Cross References

Abandonment and neglect of children, see Penal Code § 270 et seq.
Abuse of children,
  Generally, see Penal Code §§ 273a, 273d.
  Sexual abuse, see Penal Code § 1000.12.
Abuse of parental authority, see Family Code § 7507.
Action to determine existence or nonexistence of father and child relationship, consolidated actions and jurisdiction, see Family Code § 7630.
Dependent children, judgments and orders, see Welfare and Institutions Code § 360 et seq.
Domestic violence prevention, see Family Code § 6200 et seq.
Juvenile court, detention of dependent children, see Welfare and Institutions Code § 367.

§ 7824

Limitations on parental control, see Welfare and Institutions Code § 361.
Notice that parental rights may be terminated, see Welfare and Institutions Code § 294.
Proceeding defined for purposes of this Code, see Family Code § 110.
Removal of children from parental custody, see Welfare and Institutions Code § 360 et seq.

Research References

Forms

West's California Code Forms, Family § 7840, Comment Overview—Freedom from Parental Control.

§ 7825. Parent convicted of felony; consideration of criminal record prior to felony conviction; right of action

(a) A proceeding under this part may be brought where both of the following requirements are satisfied:

(1) The child is one whose parent or parents are convicted of a felony.

(2) The facts of the crime of which the parent or parents were convicted are of such a nature so as to prove the unfitness of the parent or parents to have the future custody and control of the child. In making a determination pursuant to this section, the court may consider the parent's criminal record prior to the felony conviction to the extent that the criminal record demonstrates a pattern of behavior substantially related to the welfare of the child or the parent's ability to exercise custody and control regarding the child.

(b) The mother of a child may bring a proceeding under this part against the father of the child, where the child was conceived as a result of an act in violation of Section 261 of the Penal Code, and where the father was convicted of that violation. For purposes of this subdivision, there is a conclusive presumption that the father is unfit to have custody or control of the child. (Stats.1992, c. 162 (A.B.2650), § 10, operative Jan. 1, 1994. Amended by Stats.1997, c. 594 (A.B.1222), § 2; Stats.2006, c. 806 (S.B.1325), § 5; Stats.2019, c. 115 (A.B.1817), § 101, eff. Jan. 1, 2020.)

Cross References

Abandonment and neglect of children, see Penal Code § 270 et seq.
Abuse of children,
   Generally, see Penal Code §§ 273a, 273d.
   Sexual abuse, see Penal Code § 1000.12.
Abuse of parental authority, see Family Code § 7507.
Action to determine existence or nonexistence of father and child relationship, consolidated actions and jurisdiction, see Family Code § 7630.
Dependent children, judgments and orders, see Welfare and Institutions Code § 360 et seq.
Domestic violence prevention, see Family Code § 6200 et seq.
Felonies, definition and penalties, see Penal Code §§ 17, 18.
Juvenile court, detention of dependent children, see Welfare and Institutions Code § 367.
Juvenile court, jurisdiction over children of incarcerated parents, see Welfare and Institutions Code § 300.
Limitations on parental control, see Welfare and Institutions Code § 361.
Notice that parental rights may be terminated, see Welfare and Institutions Code § 294.
Presumption against natural father status, acts in violation of Penal Code §§ 261, 261.5, see Family Code § 7611.5.
Prisoners, service and notice in dependency proceedings, see Penal Code § 2625.
Proceeding defined for purposes of this Code, see Family Code § 110.

Research References

Forms

2 California Transactions Forms--Family Law § 6:10, Initiating Proceeding Under Fam. Code, §§7800 et seq.

West's California Code Forms, Family § 7840, Comment Overview—Freedom from Parental Control.

§ 7826. Parent declared developmentally disabled or mentally ill; right to action

A proceeding under this part may be brought where both of the following requirements are satisfied:

(a) The child is one whose parent or parents have been declared by a court of competent jurisdiction, wherever situated, to be developmentally disabled or mentally ill.

(b) In the state or country in which the parent or parents reside or are hospitalized, the Director of State Hospitals or the Director of Developmental Services, or their equivalent, if any, and the executive director of the hospital, if any, of which the parent or parents are inmates or patients, certify that the parent or parents so declared to be developmentally disabled or mentally ill will not be capable of supporting or controlling the child in a proper manner. (Stats.1992, c. 162 (A.B.2650), § 10, operative Jan. 1, 1994. Amended by Stats.2012, c. 440 (A.B.1488), § 6, eff. Sept. 22, 2012.)

Cross References

Abandonment and neglect of children, see Penal Code § 270 et seq.
Abuse of children,
   Generally, see Penal Code §§ 273a, 273d.
   Sexual abuse, see Penal Code § 1000.12.
Abuse of parental authority, see Family Code § 7507.
Action to determine existence or nonexistence of father and child relationship, consolidated actions and jurisdiction, see Family Code § 7630.
Dependent children, judgments and orders, see Welfare and Institutions Code § 360 et seq.
Domestic violence prevention, see Family Code § 6200 et seq.
Juvenile court, detention of dependent children, see Welfare and Institutions Code § 367.
Limitations on parental control, see Welfare and Institutions Code § 361.
Notice that parental rights may be terminated, see Welfare and Institutions Code § 294.
Proceeding defined for purposes of this Code, see Family Code § 110.
State defined for purposes of this Code, see Family Code § 145.

Research References

Forms

West's California Code Forms, Family § 7840, Comment Overview—Freedom from Parental Control.

§ 7827. Mentally disabled parent; right to action

(a) "Mentally disabled" as used in this section means that a parent or parents suffer a mental incapacity or disorder that renders the parent or parents unable to care for and control the child adequately.

(b) A proceeding under this part may be brought if the child is one whose parent or parents are mentally disabled and are likely to remain so in the foreseeable future.

(c) Except as provided in subdivision (d), the evidence of any two experts, each of whom shall be a physician and surgeon, certified either by the American Board of Psychiatry and Neurology or under Section 6750 of the Welfare and Institutions Code, a licensed psychologist who has a doctoral degree in psychology and at least five years of postgraduate experience in the diagnosis and treatment of emotional and mental disorders, is required to support a finding under this section. In addition to this requirement, the court shall have the discretion to call a licensed marriage and family therapist, a licensed professional clinical counselor, or a licensed clinical social worker, either of whom shall have at least five years of relevant postlicensure experience, in circumstances in which the court determines that this testimony is in the best interest of the child and is warranted by the circumstances of the particular family or parenting issues involved. However, the court may not call a licensed marriage and family therapist, licensed professional clinical counselor, or licensed clinical social worker pursuant to this section who is the adoption service provider, as defined in Section 8502, of the child who is the subject of the petition to terminate parental rights.

(d) If the parent or parents reside in another state or in a foreign country, the evidence required by this section may be supplied by the affidavits of two experts, each of whom shall be either of the following:

(1) A physician and surgeon who is a resident of that state or foreign country, and who has been certified by a medical organization or society of that state or foreign country to practice psychiatric or neurological medicine.

(2) A licensed psychologist who has a doctoral degree in psychology and at least five years of postgraduate experience in the diagnosis and treatment of emotional and mental disorders and who is licensed in that state or authorized to practice in that country.

(e) If the rights of a parent are sought to be terminated pursuant to this section, and the parent does not have an attorney, the court shall appoint an attorney for the parent pursuant to Article 4 (commencing with Section 7860) of Chapter 3, whether or not a request for the appointment is made by the parent. *(Stats.1992, c. 162 (A.B.2650), § 10, operative Jan. 1, 1994. Amended by Stats.1996, c. 288 (S.B.2027), § 1; Stats.2002, c. 1013 (S.B.2026), § 80; Stats. 2018, c. 389 (A.B.2296), § 13, eff. Jan. 1, 2019.)*

Cross References

Abandonment and neglect of children, see Penal Code § 270 et seq.
Abuse of children,
    Generally, see Penal Code §§ 273a, 273d.
    Sexual abuse, see Penal Code § 1000.12.
Abuse of parental authority, see Family Code § 7507.
Action to determine existence or nonexistence of father and child relationship, consolidated actions and jurisdiction, see Family Code § 7630.
Dependent children, judgments and orders, see Welfare and Institutions Code § 360 et seq.
Domestic violence prevention, see Family Code § 6200 et seq.
Juvenile court, detention of dependent children, see Welfare and Institutions Code § 367.
Limitations on parental control, see Welfare and Institutions Code § 361.
Notice that parental rights may be terminated, see Welfare and Institutions Code § 294.
Proceeding defined for purposes of this Code, see Family Code § 110.
State defined for purposes of this Code, see Family Code § 145.
Support defined for purposes of this Code, see Family Code § 150.

Research References

Forms
2 California Transactions Forms--Family Law § 6:10, Initiating Proceeding Under Fam. Code, §§7800 et seq.
West's California Code Forms, Family § 7840, Comment Overview—Freedom from Parental Control.

§§ 7828, 7829. Repealed by Stats.2012, c. 638 (A.B.1757), §§ 2, 3

CHAPTER 3. PROCEDURE

Article	Section
1. Authorized Petitioners	7840
2. Venue	7845
3. Investigation and Report	7850
4. Appointment of Counsel	7860
5. Time for Hearing; Continuance	7870
6. Notice of Proceeding and Attendance at Hearing	7880
7. Hearing and Subsequent Proceedings	7890

Cross References

Abandonment and neglect of children, see Penal Code § 270 et seq.
Abuse of parental authority, remedy, see Family Code § 7507.
Adoption, generally, see Family Code § 8500 et seq.
Adoption of unmarried minors, generally, see Family Code § 8600 et seq.
Agency adoption, see Family Code §§ 8506, 8621, 8622.
California Community Care Facilities Act, see Health and Safety Code § 1500 et seq.
Child Abuse and Neglect Reporting Act, see Penal Code § 11164 et seq.
Child support, generally, see Family Code § 3900 et seq.
Child support, enforcement of orders, see Family Code § 4500 et seq.
Dependent children, judgments and orders, see Welfare and Institutions Code § 360 et seq.
Domestic violence, prevention, see Family Code § 6200 et seq.
Enforcement of judgments and orders, see Family Code §§ 290, 291.
Hearings, termination of parental rights, guardianship of dependent children, see Welfare and Institutions Code § 366.26 et seq.
Jurisdiction of superior court, see Family Code § 200.
Juvenile court, detention of dependent children, see Welfare and Institutions Code § 367.
Limitations on parental control, see Welfare and Institutions Code § 361.
Minors,
    Age of majority, see Family Code § 6500 et seq.
    Contracts, see Family Code § 6700 et seq.
    Emancipation, see Family Code § 7000 et seq.
    Rights and liabilities, civil actions and proceedings, see Family Code § 6600 et seq.
Notice of proceedings and attendance at hearing, see Family Code § 7880 et seq.
Notice that parental rights may be terminated, see Welfare and Institutions Code § 294.
Parental custody, generally, see Family Code §§ 3000 et seq., 3020 et seq.
Parental relationship, determination, see Family Code § 7600 et seq.
Pleadings, verification requirements, see Family Code § 212.
Protective and temporary custody orders, see Family Code § 7700 et seq.
Termination of parental rights, guardianship of dependent children, see Welfare and Institutions Code § 366.26 et seq.
Venue, see Family Code § 7845.
Verification of pleadings, see Family Code § 212.

ARTICLE 1. AUTHORIZED PETITIONERS

Section
7840. Right of specified entities to file petition.
7841. Right of interested persons to file petition.
7842. Single petition to free child from custody and control of both parents.

§ 7840. Right of specified entities to file petition

(a) A petition may be filed under this part for an order or judgment declaring a child free from the custody and control of either or both parents by any of the following:

(1) The State Department of Social Services, a county welfare department, a licensed private or public adoption agency, a county adoption department, or a county probation department which is planning adoptive placement of the child with a licensed adoption agency.

(2) The State Department of Social Services acting as an adoption agency in counties which are not served by a county adoption agency.

(b) The fact that a child is in a foster care home subject to the requirements of Chapter 3 (commencing with Section 1500) of Division 2 of the Health and Safety Code does not prevent the filing of a petition under subdivision (a).

(c) The county counsel or, if there is no county counsel, the district attorney of the county specified in Section 7845 shall, in a proper case, institute the proceeding upon the request of any of the state or county agencies mentioned in subdivision (a). The proceeding shall be instituted pursuant to this part within 30 days of the request.

(d) If, at the time of the filing of a petition by a department or agency specified in subdivision (a), the child is in the custody of the petitioner, the petitioner may continue to have custody of the child pending the hearing on the petition unless the court, in its discretion, makes such other order regarding custody pending the hearing as it

§ 7840

finds will best serve and protect the interest and welfare of the child. *(Stats.1992, c. 162 (A.B.2650), § 10, operative Jan. 1, 1994.)*

Cross References

Adoption agencies, see Family Code § 8500 et seq.
County defined for purposes of this Code, see Family Code § 67.
Hearings, termination of parental rights, guardianship of dependent children, see Welfare and Institutions Code § 366.25 et seq.
Judgment and order defined for purposes of this Code, see Family Code § 100.
Petitioner defined for purposes of this Code, see Family Code § 126.
Proceeding defined for purposes of this Code, see Family Code § 110.
State defined for purposes of this Code, see Family Code § 145.

Research References

Forms

West's California Code Forms, Family § 7840, Comment Overview—Freedom from Parental Control.

§ 7841. Right of interested persons to file petition

(a) An interested person may file a petition under this part for an order or judgment declaring a child free from the custody and control of either or both parents.

(b) For purposes of this section, an "interested person" is one who has a direct interest in the action, and includes, but is not limited to, a person who has filed, or who intends to file within a period of 6 months, an adoption petition under Section 8714, 8802, or 9000, or a licensed adoption agency to whom the child has been relinquished by the other parent. *(Stats.1992, c. 162 (A.B.2650), § 10, operative Jan. 1, 1994. Amended by Stats.2007, c. 47 (S.B.313), § 3.)*

Cross References

County clerk, enumeration of instances not subject to fees, see Government Code § 26857.
Fees for adoption proceedings, proceedings to declare a minor free from parental custody or control, criminal actions, and service to public entities, see Government Code § 70633.
Judgment and order defined for purposes of this Code, see Family Code § 100.
Notice of proceedings and attendance at hearing, see Family Code § 7880 et seq.
Notification to investigate, see Family Code § 7850.
Person defined for purposes of this Code, see Family Code § 105.
Superior court jurisdiction, see Family Code § 200.
Venue, see Family Code § 7845.

Research References

Forms

West's California Code Forms, Family § 7840, Comment Overview—Freedom from Parental Control.
West's California Code Forms, Family § 7894 Form 1, Judgment Declaring Minor Free from Parental Control.

§ 7842. Single petition to free child from custody and control of both parents

A single petition may be filed under this part to free a child, or more than one child if the children are biological siblings, from the custody and control of both parents. A petition filed in accordance with this section may be granted in whole or in part in accordance with the procedures set forth in this chapter. The court shall retain discretion to bifurcate any case in which the petition was filed in accordance with this section, and shall do so whenever it is necessary to protect the interests of a party or a child who is the subject of the proceeding. *(Added by Stats.2014, c. 763 (A.B.1701), § 6, eff. Jan. 1, 2015.)*

ARTICLE 2. VENUE

Section
7845. Filing of petition.

§ 7845. Filing of petition

The petition shall be filed in any of the following:

(a) The county in which a minor described in Chapter 2 (commencing with Section 7820) resides or is found.

(b) The county in which any of the acts which are set forth in Chapter 2 (commencing with Section 7820) are alleged to have occurred.

(c) The county in which a petition for the adoption of the child has been filed or the adoption agency to which the child has been relinquished or proposed to be relinquished has an office. *(Stats. 1992, c. 162 (A.B.2650), § 10, operative Jan. 1, 1994. Amended by Stats.2009, c. 492 (A.B.941), § 2.)*

Cross References

County defined for purposes of this Code, see Family Code § 67.
Jurisdiction of superior court, see Family Code § 200.
Minor defined for purposes of this Code, see Family Code § 6500.

Research References

Forms

West's California Code Forms, Family § 7840, Comment Overview—Freedom from Parental Control.

ARTICLE 3. INVESTIGATION AND REPORT

Section
7850. Notification to investigate; scope of investigation.
7851. Recommendations to court; contents of report.
7851.5. Costs in connection with termination of parental rights; liability of petitioner; investigation cost; monetary limit.
7852. "Qualified court investigator" defined.

§ 7850. Notification to investigate; scope of investigation

Upon the filing of a petition under Section 7841, the clerk of the court shall, in accordance with the direction of the court, immediately notify the juvenile probation officer, qualified court investigator, licensed clinical social worker, licensed marriage and family therapist, licensed professional clinical counselor, or the county department designated by the board of supervisors to administer the public social services program, who shall immediately investigate the circumstances of the child and the circumstances which are alleged to bring the child within any provision of Chapter 2 (commencing with Section 7820). *(Stats.1992, c. 162 (A.B.2650), § 10, operative Jan. 1, 1994. Amended by Stats.1993, c. 219 (A.B.1500), § 180; Stats.2002, c. 260 (S.B.1512), § 4; Stats.2018, c. 389 (A.B.2296), § 14, eff. Jan. 1, 2019.)*

Cross References

County defined for purposes of this Code, see Family Code § 67.
Petition, right of specified entities to file, see Family Code § 7840.

§ 7851. Recommendations to court; contents of report

(a) The juvenile probation officer, qualified court investigator, licensed clinical social worker, licensed marriage and family therapist, licensed professional clinical counselor, or the county department shall render to the court a written report of the investigation with a recommendation of the proper disposition to be made in the proceeding in the best interest of the child.

(b) The report shall include all of the following:

(1) A statement that the person making the report explained to the child the nature of the proceeding to end parental custody and control.

(2) A statement of the child's feelings and thoughts concerning the pending proceeding.

(3) A statement of the child's attitude towards the child's parent or parents and particularly whether or not the child would prefer living with the parent or parents.

(4) A statement that the child was informed of the child's right to attend the hearing on the petition and the child's feelings concerning attending the hearing.

(c) If the age, or the physical, emotional, or other condition of the child precludes the child's meaningful response to the explanations, inquiries, and information required by subdivision (b), a description of the condition shall satisfy the requirement of that subdivision.

(d) The court shall receive the report in evidence and shall read and consider its contents in rendering the court's judgment. *(Stats. 1992, c. 162 (A.B.2650), § 10, operative Jan. 1, 1994. Amended by Stats.1993, c. 219 (A.B.1500), § 181; Stats.2002, c. 260 (S.B.1512), § 5; Stats.2018, c. 389 (A.B.2296), § 15, eff. Jan. 1, 2019; Stats.2019, c. 115 (A.B.1817), § 102, eff. Jan. 1, 2020.)*

Cross References

County defined for purposes of this Code, see Family Code § 67.
Judgment and order defined for purposes of this Code, see Family Code § 100.
Juvenile court, wards and dependent children, inspection of case file, see Welfare and Institutions Code § 827.
Person defined for purposes of this Code, see Family Code § 105.
Proceeding defined for purposes of this Code, see Family Code § 110.
Proceeding to have child declared free from custody and control of one or both parents, see Probate Code § 1516.5.

§ 7851.5. Costs in connection with termination of parental rights; liability of petitioner; investigation cost; monetary limit

The petitioner shall be liable for all reasonable costs incurred in connection with the termination of parental rights, including, but not limited to, costs incurred for the investigation required by this article. However, public agencies and nonprofit organizations are exempt from payment of the costs of the investigation. The liability of a petitioner for costs under this section shall not exceed nine hundred dollars ($900). The court may defer, waive, or reduce the costs when the payment would cause an economic hardship which would be detrimental to the welfare of the child. *(Added by Stats.1994, c. 1286 (A.B.2902), § 1.)*

Cross References

Courts, fees and fines collected after January 1, 2006, treatment thereof, see Government Code § 68085.1.
Petitioner defined for purposes of this Code, see Family Code § 126.

§ 7852. "Qualified court investigator" defined

"Qualified court investigator," as used in this article, has the meaning provided by Section 8543. *(Added by Stats.1993, c. 219 (A.B.1500), § 182.)*

ARTICLE 4. APPOINTMENT OF COUNSEL

Section
7860. Procedures for appointment.
7861. Appointment of counsel for child; consideration of interests of child.
7862. Appointment of counsel for parent.
7863. Compensation and expenses.
7864. Continuance of proceedings; purpose.

Cross References

Appointment of counsel, generally, see Welfare and Institutions Code §§ 317, 366.26.
Appointment of counsel on appeal, indigent appellants, see Family Code § 7895.
Appointment of legal counsel, see Probate Code § 1470 et seq.
Attorney's fees and costs, generally, see Family Code § 270 et seq.
Custody proceedings, representation of children, see Family Code § 3150 et seq.
Dependency proceedings, review hearings, right to counsel, see Welfare and Institutions Code § 292.
Duties and rights of private counsel, custody proceedings, see Family Code § 3151.
Mentally disabled parents, mandatory appointment of counsel, see Family Code § 7827.
Public defender's office, see Government Code § 27700.
Right to counsel, generally, see Cal. Const. Art. 1, § 15, cl. 3; Penal Code § 686.
Temporary custody and detention, appointment of counsel, see Welfare and Institutions Code § 634.

§ 7860. Procedures for appointment

At the beginning of the proceeding on a petition filed pursuant to this part, counsel shall be appointed as provided in this article. The public defender or private counsel may be appointed as counsel pursuant to this article. The same counsel shall not be appointed to represent both the child and the child's parent. *(Stats.1992, c. 162 (A.B.2650), § 10, operative Jan. 1, 1994.)*

Cross References

Appointment of counsel, generally, see Welfare and Institutions Code §§ 317, 366.26.
Appointment of counsel on appeal, indigent appellants, see Family Code § 7895.
Appointment of legal counsel, see Probate Code § 1470 et seq.
Attorney's fees and costs, generally, see Family Code § 270 et seq.
Custody proceedings, representation of children, see Family Code § 3150 et seq.
Dependency proceedings, review hearings, right to counsel, see Welfare and Institutions Code § 292.
Duties and rights of private counsel, custody proceedings, see Family Code § 3151.
Mentally disabled parents, mandatory appointment of counsel, see Family Code § 7827.
Proceeding defined for purposes of this Code, see Family Code § 110.
Public defender's office, see Government Code § 27700.
Right to counsel, generally, see Penal Code § 686.
Temporary custody and detention, appointment of counsel, see Welfare and Institutions Code § 634.

Research References

Forms

West's California Code Forms, Family § 7880, Comment Overview—Notice of Proceeding and Attendance at Hearing.
West's California Judicial Council Forms ADOPT-200, Adoption Request.

§ 7861. Appointment of counsel for child; consideration of interests of child

The court shall consider whether the interests of the child require the appointment of counsel. If the court finds that the interests of the child require representation by counsel, the court shall appoint counsel to represent the child, whether or not the child is able to afford counsel. The child shall not be present in court unless the child so requests or the court so orders. *(Stats.1992, c. 162 (A.B.2650), § 10, operative Jan. 1, 1994.)*

Cross References

Appointment of counsel, generally, see Welfare and Institutions Code §§ 317, 366.26.
Appointment of counsel on appeal, see Family Code § 7895.
Appointment of legal counsel, see Probate Code § 1470 et seq.
Attorney's fees and costs, generally, see Family Code § 270 et seq.
Custody proceedings, representation of children, see Family Code § 3150 et seq.
Dependency proceedings, review hearings, right to counsel, see Welfare and Institutions Code § 292.
Judgment and order defined for purposes of this Code, see Family Code § 100.
Public defender's office, see Government Code § 27700.
Right to counsel, see Penal Code § 686.

§ 7861

Temporary custody and detention, appointment of counsel, see Welfare and Institutions Code § 634.

§ 7862. Appointment of counsel for parent

If a parent appears without counsel and is unable to afford counsel, the court shall appoint counsel for the parent, unless that representation is knowingly and intelligently waived. *(Stats.1992, c. 162 (A.B.2650), § 10, operative Jan. 1, 1994.)*

Cross References

Appointment of counsel, generally, see Welfare and Institutions Code §§ 317, 366.26.
Appointment of counsel on appeal, indigent appellants, see Family Code § 7895.
Appointment of legal counsel, see Probate Code § 1470 et seq.
Attorney's fees and costs, generally, see Family Code § 270 et seq.
Custody proceedings, representation of children, see Family Code § 3150 et seq.
Dependency proceedings, review hearings, right to counsel, see Welfare and Institutions Code § 292.
Duties and rights of private counsel, custody proceedings, see Family Code § 3151.
Mentally disabled parents, mandatory appointment of counsel, see Family Code § 7827.
Public defender's office, see Government Code § 27700.
Right to counsel, generally, see Cal. Const. Art. 1, § 15, cl. 3; Penal Code § 686.
Temporary custody and detention, appointment of counsel, see Welfare and Institutions Code § 634.

Research References

Forms

West's California Code Forms, Family § 7881 Form 1, Citation to Parent.

§ 7863. Compensation and expenses

Private counsel appointed under this article shall receive a reasonable sum for compensation and expenses, the amount of which shall be determined by the court. The amount so determined shall be paid by the real parties in interest, other than the child, in proportions the court deems just. However, if the court finds that any of the real parties in interest are unable to afford counsel, the amount shall be paid out of the general fund of the county. *(Stats.1992, c. 162 (A.B.2650), § 10, operative Jan. 1, 1994.)*

Cross References

Appointment of counsel, see Welfare and Institutions Code §§ 317, 366.26.
Attorney's fees and costs, generally, see Family Code § 270 et seq.
County defined for purposes of this Code, see Family Code § 67.
Right to counsel on appeal, see Family Code § 7895.
Support of minors, representation of children, see Family Code § 3150 et seq.

§ 7864. Continuance of proceedings; purpose

The court may continue the proceeding for not to exceed 30 days as necessary to appoint counsel and to enable counsel to become acquainted with the case. *(Stats.1992, c. 162 (A.B.2650), § 10, operative Jan. 1, 1994.)*

Cross References

Appointment of counsel, see Welfare and Institutions Code §§ 317, 366.26.
Attorney's fees and costs, generally, see Family Code § 270 et seq.
Proceeding defined for purposes of this Code, see Family Code § 110.
Right to counsel on appeal, see Family Code § 7895.
Support of minors, representation of children, see Family Code § 3150 et seq.

Research References

Forms

West's California Code Forms, Family § 7880, Comment Overview—Notice of Proceeding and Attendance at Hearing.

ARTICLE 5. TIME FOR HEARING; CONTINUANCE

Section
7870. Setting for trial; precedence over other civil matters; continuances.

Section
7871. Grounds for continuance.

§ 7870. Setting for trial; precedence over other civil matters; continuances

(a) It is the public policy of this state that judicial proceedings to declare a child free from parental custody and control shall be fully determined as expeditiously as possible.

(b) Notwithstanding any other provision of law, a proceeding to declare a child free from parental custody and control pursuant to this part shall be set for hearing not more than 45 days after the filing of the petition. If, at the time set for hearing, or at any continuance thereof, service has been completed and no interested person appears to contest, the court may issue an order based on the verified pleadings and any other evidence as may be submitted. If any interested person appears to contest the matter, the court shall set the matter for trial. The matter so set has precedence over all other civil matters on the date set for trial.

(c) The court may continue the proceeding as provided in Section 7864 or Section 7871. *(Stats.1992, c. 162 (A.B.2650), § 10, operative Jan. 1, 1994. Amended by Stats.2012, c. 638 (A.B.1757), § 4.)*

Cross References

Proceeding defined for purposes of this Code, see Family Code § 110.
State defined for purposes of this Code, see Family Code § 145.

Research References

Forms

West's California Code Forms, Family § 7840, Comment Overview—Freedom from Parental Control.

§ 7871. Grounds for continuance

(a) A continuance may be granted only upon a showing of good cause. Neither a stipulation between counsel nor the convenience of the parties is in and of itself a good cause.

(b) Unless the court for good cause entertains an oral motion for continuance, written notice of a motion for a continuance of the hearing shall be filed within two court days of the date set for the hearing, together with affidavits or declarations detailing specific facts showing that a continuance is necessary.

(c) A continuance shall be granted only for that period of time shown to be necessary by the evidence considered at the hearing on the motion. Whenever a continuance is granted, the facts proven which require the continuance shall be entered upon the minutes of the court. *(Stats.1992, c. 162 (A.B.2650), § 10, operative Jan. 1, 1994.)*

Cross References

Continuance, appointment of counsel and enabling counsel to become familiar with case, see Family Code § 7864.

Research References

Forms

West's California Code Forms, Family § 7840, Comment Overview—Freedom from Parental Control.

ARTICLE 6. NOTICE OF PROCEEDING AND ATTENDANCE AT HEARING

Section
7880. Citation requiring appearance of person having custody or control of child and child at hearing.
7881. Notice of proceeding by service of citation on parents or relatives; contents.
7882. Filing of affidavit as to parent who cannot be served or whose residence is unknown; publication of citation.

Section
7883. Failure to appear; contempt.
7884. Admission to proceedings.

Cross References

Dependent children, selection and implementation hearings, notice, see Welfare and Institutions Code § 294.
Dependent children, status review hearings, notice, see Welfare and Institutions Code § 366.21.
Hearings terminating parental rights or establishing guardianship, see Welfare and Institutions Code § 366.26.
Petition, right of interested persons to file, see Family Code § 7841.
Service of process, generally, see Code of Civil Procedure § 410.10 et seq.

§ 7880. Citation requiring appearance of person having custody or control of child and child at hearing

(a) Upon the filing of the petition, a citation shall issue requiring any person having the custody or control of the child, or the person with whom the child is, to appear at a time and place stated in the citation.

(b) The citation shall also require the person to appear with the child except that, if the child is under the age of 10 years, appearance with the child is required only upon order of the court after necessity has been shown.

(c) Service of the citation shall be made in the manner prescribed by law for service of civil process at least 10 days before the time stated in the citation for the appearance. The party or attorney responsible for serving the citation shall do so in a timely manner in order to maximize the response time available to the party being served. (Stats.1992, c. 162 (A.B.2650), § 10, operative Jan. 1, 1994. Amended by Stats.2012, c. 638 (A.B.1757), § 5.)

Cross References

Contempt, failure to appear, see Family Code § 7883.
Dependent children, selection and implementation hearings, notice, see Welfare and Institutions Code § 294.
Dependent children, status review hearings, notice, see Welfare and Institutions Code § 366.21.
Hearings, see Welfare and Institutions Code § 366.26.
Judgment and order defined for purposes of this Code, see Family Code § 100.
Person defined for purposes of this Code, see Family Code § 105.
Petition, right of interested persons to file, see Family Code § 7841.
Service of process, generally, see Code of Civil Procedure § 410.10 et seq.

Research References

Forms

West's California Code Forms, Family § 7840, Comment Overview—Freedom from Parental Control.
West's California Code Forms, Family § 7880, Comment Overview—Notice of Proceeding and Attendance at Hearing.

§ 7881. Notice of proceeding by service of citation on parents or relatives; contents

(a) Notice of the proceeding shall be given by service of a citation on the father or mother of the child, if the place of residence of the father or mother is known to the petitioner. If the place of residence of the father or mother is not known to the petitioner, then the citation shall be served on the grandparents and adult brothers, sisters, uncles, aunts, and first cousins of the child, if there are any and if their residences and relationships to the child are known to the petitioner.

(b) The citation shall advise the person or persons that they may appear at the time and place stated in the citation. The citation shall also advise the person or persons of the rights and procedures set forth in Article 4 (commencing with Section 7860). If the petition is filed for the purpose of freeing the child for placement for adoption, the citation shall so state.

(c) The citation shall be served in the manner provided by law for the service of a summons in a civil action, other than by publication.

If one parent has relinquished the child for the purpose of adoption, or has signed a consent for adoption as provided in Sections 8700, 8814, or 9003, notice as provided in this section need not be given to the parent who has signed the relinquishment or consent.

(d) Service of the citations required by this section shall be made at least 10 days before the time stated in the citation for the appearance. (Stats.1992, c. 162 (A.B.2650), § 10, operative Jan. 1, 1994.)

Cross References

Actions affecting prisoner's parental or marital rights, see Penal Code § 2625.
Dependent children, selection and implementation hearings, notice, see Welfare and Institutions Code § 294.
Dependent children, status review hearings, notice, see Welfare and Institutions Code § 366.21.
Hearings, see Welfare and Institutions Code § 366.26.
Person defined for purposes of this Code, see Family Code § 105.
Petitioner defined for purposes of this Code, see Family Code § 126.
Proceeding defined for purposes of this Code, see Family Code § 110.
Service of process, generally, see Code of Civil Procedure § 410.10 et seq.
State defined for purposes of this Code, see Family Code § 145.

Research References

Forms

West's California Code Forms, Family § 7840, Comment Overview—Freedom from Parental Control.
West's California Code Forms, Family § 7880, Comment Overview—Notice of Proceeding and Attendance at Hearing.

§ 7882. Filing of affidavit as to parent who cannot be served or whose residence is unknown; publication of citation

(a) If the parent of the child or a person alleged to be or claiming to be the parent cannot, with reasonable diligence, be served as provided for in Section 7881, or if the parent's place of residence is not known to the petitioner, the petitioner or the petitioner's agent or attorney shall make and file an affidavit stating the name of the parent or alleged parent and their place of residence, if known to the petitioner, and the name of the parent or alleged parent whose place of residence is unknown to the petitioner.

(b) Upon the filing of the affidavit, the court shall make an order that (1) the service shall be made by the publication of a citation requiring the parent or alleged parent to appear at the time and place stated in the citation and (2) the citation shall be published pursuant to Section 6064 of the Government Code in a newspaper to be named and designated in the order as most likely to give notice to the parent or alleged parent to be served.

(c) In case of publication where the residence of a parent or alleged parent is known, the court shall also direct a copy of the citation to be forthwith served upon that parent or alleged parent by mail by deposit in the post office properly addressed and with the postage thereon fully prepaid, directed to that parent or alleged parent at the place of residence. When publication is ordered, service of a copy of the citation in the manner provided for in Section 7881 is equivalent to publication and deposit in the post office.

(d) If one or both of the parents of the child are unknown or if the names of one or both of the child's parents are uncertain, that fact shall be set forth in the affidavit and the court shall order the citation to be directed to either or both of the child's parents, naming and otherwise describing the child, and to all persons claiming to be a parent of the child.

(e) Service is complete at the expiration of the time prescribed by the order for publication or when service is made as provided for in Section 7881, whichever event first occurs. (Stats.1992, c. 162 (A.B.2650), § 10, operative Jan. 1, 1994. Amended by Stats.2019, c. 115 (A.B.1817), § 103, eff. Jan. 1, 2020.)

Cross References

Actions affecting prisoner's parental or marital rights, see Penal Code § 2625.

§ 7882

Dependent children, selection and implementation hearings, notice, see Welfare and Institutions Code § 294.
Dependent children, status review hearings, notice, see Welfare and Institutions Code § 366.21.
Hearings, see Welfare and Institutions Code § 366.26.
Judgment and order defined for purposes of this Code, see Family Code § 100.
Person defined for purposes of this Code, see Family Code § 105.
Petitioner defined for purposes of this Code, see Family Code § 126.
Service of process, generally, see Code of Civil Procedure § 410.10 et seq.
State defined for purposes of this Code, see Family Code § 145.

Research References

Forms

West's California Code Forms, Family § 7880, Comment Overview—Notice of Proceeding and Attendance at Hearing.

§ 7883. Failure to appear; contempt

If a person personally served with a citation within this state as provided in Section 7880 fails without reasonable cause to appear and abide by the order of the court, or to bring the child before the court if so required in the citation, the failure constitutes a contempt of court. (Stats.1992, c. 162 (A.B.2650), § 10, operative Jan. 1, 1994.)

Cross References

Judgment and order defined for purposes of this Code, see Family Code § 100.
Person defined for purposes of this Code, see Family Code § 105.
State defined for purposes of this Code, see Family Code § 145.

Research References

Forms

West's California Code Forms, Family § 7880 Form 1, Citation to Person Having Custody.
West's California Code Forms, Family § 7881 Form 1, Citation to Parent.

§ 7884. Admission to proceedings

(a) Unless requested by the child concerning whom the petition has been filed and any parent or guardian present, the public shall not be admitted to a proceeding under this part.

(b) Notwithstanding subdivision (a), the judge may admit those persons the judge determines have a direct and legitimate interest in the particular case or in the work of the court. (Stats.1992, c. 162 (A.B.2650), § 10, operative Jan. 1, 1994.)

Cross References

Guardian defined, see Probate Code §§ 2350, 2400.
Hearing to terminate parental rights, dependent children, see Welfare and Institutions Code § 366.26.
Parent or guardian defined, see Family Code § 6903.
Person defined for purposes of this Code, see Family Code § 105.
Proceeding defined for purposes of this Code, see Family Code § 110.

ARTICLE 7. HEARING AND SUBSEQUENT PROCEEDINGS

Section
7890. Consideration of wishes of child.
7891. In chambers hearing; notice of right to attend; waiver.
7892. Testimony of child in chambers and outside presence of child's parents; conditions.
7892.5. Declaration that Indian child is free from custody or control of parent.
7893. Guardianship or referral to adoption agency.
7894. Effect of order.
7895. Appointment of counsel for appellant; indigent appellant; free copy of transcripts.

Cross References

Abandonment and neglect of children, see Penal Code § 270 et seq.
Abuse of parental authority, remedy, see Family Code § 7507.
Adoption, generally, see Family Code § 8500 et seq.
Child custody, best interest of child, considerations, see Family Code § 3011.
Child support, generally, see Family Code § 3900 et seq.
Child support, enforcement of orders, see Family Code § 4500 et seq.
Dependent children, judgments and orders, see Welfare and Institutions Code § 360 et seq.
Domestic violence, prevention, see Family Code § 6200 et seq.
Enforcement of judgments and orders, see Family Code §§ 290, 291.
Hearings, termination of parental rights, guardianship of dependent children, see Welfare and Institutions Code § 366.26 et seq.
Jurisdiction, superior court, see Family Code § 200.
Juvenile court, detention of dependent children, see Welfare and Institutions Code § 367.
Limitations on parental control, see Welfare and Institutions Code § 361.
Minors,
  Age of majority, see Family Code § 6500 et seq.
  Contracts, see Family Code § 6700 et seq.
  Emancipation, see Family Code § 7000 et seq.
  Rights and liabilities, civil actions and proceedings, see Family Code § 6600 et seq.
Notice that parental rights may be terminated, see Welfare and Institutions Code § 366.23.
Parental custody, generally, see Family Code §§ 3000 et seq., 3020 et seq.
Parental relationship, determination, see Family Code § 7600 et seq.
Protective and temporary custody orders, see Family Code § 7700 et seq.

§ 7890. Consideration of wishes of child

In a proceeding under this part, the court shall consider the wishes of the child, bearing in mind the age of the child, and shall act in the best interest of the child. (Stats.1992, c. 162 (A.B.2650), § 10, operative Jan. 1, 1994.)

Cross References

Abandonment and neglect of children, see Penal Code § 270 et seq.
Abuse of parental authority, remedy, see Family Code § 7507.
Adoption, generally, see Family Code § 8500 et seq.
Child custody, best interest of child, considerations, see Family Code § 3011.
Child support,
  Generally, see Family Code § 3900 et seq.
  Enforcement of orders, see Family Code § 4500 et seq.
Dependent children, judgments and orders, see Welfare and Institutions Code § 360 et seq.
Domestic violence, prevention, see Family Code § 6200 et seq.
Enforcement of judgments and orders, see Family Code §§ 290, 291.
Hearings, termination of parental rights, guardianship of dependent children, see Welfare and Institutions Code § 366.26 et seq.
Jurisdiction, superior court, see Family Code § 200.
Juvenile court, detention of dependent children, see Welfare and Institutions Code § 367.
Limitations on parental control, see Welfare and Institutions Code § 361.
Minors,
  Age of majority, see Family Code § 6500 et seq.
  Contracts, see Family Code § 6700 et seq.
  Emancipation, see Family Code § 7000 et seq.
  Rights and liabilities, civil actions and proceedings, see Family Code § 6600 et seq.
Notice that parental rights may be terminated, see Welfare and Institutions Code § 294.
Parental custody, generally, see Family Code §§ 3000 et seq., 3020 et seq.
Parental relationship, determination, see Family Code § 7600 et seq.
Proceeding defined for purposes of this Code, see Family Code § 110.
Protective and temporary custody orders, see Family Code § 7700 et seq.

Research References

Forms

West's California Code Forms, Family § 7840, Comment Overview—Freedom from Parental Control.
West's California Code Forms, Family § 7890, Comment Overview—Hearing and Subsequent Proceedings.

§ 7891. In chambers hearing; notice of right to attend; waiver

(a) Except as otherwise provided in this section, if the child who is the subject of the petition is 10 years of age or older, the child shall be heard by the court in chambers on at least the following matters:

(1) The feelings and thoughts of the child concerning the custody proceeding about to take place.

(2) The feelings and thoughts of the child about the child's parent or parents.

(3) The child's preference as to custody, according to Section 3042.

(b) The court shall inform the child of the child's right to attend the hearing. However, counsel for the child may waive the hearing in chambers by the court.

(c) This section does not apply if the child is confined because of illness or other incapacity to an institution or residence and is therefore unable to attend. *(Stats.1992, c. 162 (A.B.2650), § 10, operative Jan. 1, 1994. Amended by Stats.1993, c. 219 (A.B.1500), § 182.5.)*

Cross References

Hearings terminating parental rights or establishing guardianship, see Welfare and Institutions Code § 366.26.
Proceeding defined for purposes of this Code, see Family Code § 110.

Research References

Forms

1 California Transactions Forms--Family Law § 3:12, Preferences of the Child.
West's California Code Forms, Family § 7840, Comment Overview—Freedom from Parental Control.

§ 7892. Testimony of child in chambers and outside presence of child's parents; conditions

(a) The testimony of the child may be taken in chambers and outside the presence of the child's parent or parents if the child's parent or parents are represented by counsel, the counsel is present, and any of the following circumstances exist:

(1) The court determines that testimony in chambers is necessary to ensure truthful testimony.

(2) The child is likely to be intimidated by a formal courtroom setting.

(3) The child is afraid to testify in front of the child's parent or parents.

(b) The testimony of a child also may be taken in chambers and outside the presence of the guardian or guardians of a child under the circumstances specified in subdivision (a).

(c) A finding pursuant to this section shall be supported by clear and convincing evidence.

(d) After testimony in chambers, the parent or parents of the child may elect to have the court reporter read back the testimony or have the testimony summarized by counsel for the parent or parents. *(Stats.1992, c. 162 (A.B.2650), § 10, operative Jan. 1, 1994.)*

Cross References

Hearings terminating parental rights or establishing guardianship, see Welfare and Institutions Code § 366.26.

Research References

Forms

West's California Code Forms, Family § 7840, Comment Overview—Freedom from Parental Control.

§ 7892.5. Declaration that Indian child is free from custody or control of parent

The court shall not declare an Indian child free from the custody or control of a parent, unless both of the following apply:

(a) The court finds, supported by clear and convincing evidence, that active efforts were made in accordance with Section 361.7 of the Welfare and Institutions Code.

(b) The court finds, supported by evidence beyond a reasonable doubt, including testimony of one or more "qualified expert witnesses" as described in Section 224.5 of the Welfare and Institutions Code, that the continued custody of the child by the parent is likely to result in serious emotional or physical damage to the child.

(c) This section shall only apply to proceedings involving an Indian child. *(Added by Stats.2006, c. 838 (S.B.678), § 6.)*

Research References

Forms

West's California Judicial Council Forms ADOPT-200, Adoption Request.

§ 7893. Guardianship or referral to adoption agency

(a) If the court, by order or judgment, declares a child free from the custody and control of both parents under this part, or one parent if the other no longer has custody and control, the court shall at the same time take one of the following actions:

(1) Appoint a guardian for the child.

(2) At the request of the State Department of Social Services or a licensed adoption agency, or where the court finds it is in the child's best interest, refer the child to a licensed adoption agency for adoptive placement by the agency.

(b) When the court refers the child to a licensed adoption agency for adoptive placement by the agency:

(1) The agency is responsible for the care of the child and is entitled to the exclusive custody and control of the child at all times until a petition for adoption has been granted.

(2) After the referral, no petition for guardianship may be filed without the consent of the agency.

(3) No petition for adoption may be heard until the appellate rights of the natural parents have been exhausted. *(Stats.1992, c. 162 (A.B.2650), § 10, operative Jan. 1, 1994.)*

Cross References

Abandonment and neglect of children, see Penal Code § 270 et seq.
Adoption, generally, see Family Code § 8500 et seq.
Adoption of unmarried minors, consent of birth parents not required in certain cases, see Family Code § 8606.
Dependent children, juvenile court proceedings for appointment of guardian, etc., see Welfare and Institutions Code § 366.26.
Judgment and order defined for purposes of this Code, see Family Code § 100.
Parent and child, generally, see Family Code § 7500 et seq.
Relations of husband and wife, generally, see Family Code §§ 720, 721.
State defined for purposes of this Code, see Family Code § 145.
Uniform Interstate Family Support Act, see Family Code § 5700.101 et seq.

Research References

Forms

West's California Code Forms, Family § 7890, Comment Overview—Hearing and Subsequent Proceedings.

§ 7894. Effect of order

(a) An order and judgment of the court declaring a child free from the custody and control of a parent or parents under this part is conclusive and binding upon the child, upon the parent or parents, and upon all other persons who have been served with citations by publication or otherwise as provided in this part.

(b) After making the order and judgment, the court has no power to set aside, change, or modify it.

(c) Nothing in this section limits the right to appeal from the order and judgment. *(Stats.1992, c. 162 (A.B.2650), § 10, operative Jan. 1, 1994.)*

Cross References

Adoption of unmarried minors, consent of birth parents not required in certain cases, see Family Code § 8606.

§ 7894

Appeal from judgment freeing dependent children from parental custody and control, see Code of Civil Procedure § 45.
Conclusiveness of judgment and order, see Welfare and Institutions Code § 366.26.
Judgment and order defined for purposes of this Code, see Family Code § 100.
Person defined for purposes of this Code, see Family Code § 105.

Research References

Forms

West's California Code Forms, Family § 7890, Comment Overview—Hearing and Subsequent Proceedings.

§ 7895. Appointment of counsel for appellant; indigent appellant; free copy of transcripts

(a) Upon appeal from a judgment freeing a child who is a dependent child of the juvenile court from parental custody and control, the appellate court shall appoint counsel for the appellant as provided by this section.

(b) Upon motion by the appellant and a finding that the appellant is unable to afford counsel, the appellate court shall appoint counsel for the indigent appellant, and appellant's counsel shall be provided a free copy of the reporter's and clerk's transcript. All of those costs are a charge against the court.

(c) The reporter's and clerk's transcripts shall be prepared and transmitted immediately after filing of the notice of appeal, at court expense and without advance payment of fees. If the appellant is able to afford counsel, the court may seek reimbursement from the appellant for the cost of the transcripts under subdivision (c) of Section 68511.3 of the Government Code as though the appellant had been granted permission to proceed in forma pauperis. *(Stats. 1992, c. 162 (A.B.2650), § 10, operative Jan. 1, 1994. Amended by Stats.2000, c. 447 (S.B.1533), § 4; Stats.2001, c. 754 (A.B.1697), § 3.)*

Cross References

Appeal from judgment freeing dependent child from parental custody and control, see Code of Civil Procedure § 45.
Appointment of counsel, generally, see Family Code § 7860 et seq.
Attorney's fees and costs, generally, see Family Code § 270 et seq.
Judgment and order defined for purposes of this Code, see Family Code § 100.

Part 5

INTERSTATE COMPACT ON PLACEMENT OF CHILDREN

Section	
7900.	Adoption.
7901.	Provisions.
7901.1.	Request outside state; home study to assess safety and suitability of child placement; requirements.
7902.	Financial responsibility for child placed pursuant to compact.
7903.	"Appropriate public authorities" defined.
7904.	"Appropriate authority in receiving state" defined.
7905.	Agreements with party states; approval of financial obligations.
7906.	Requirements for visitation, inspection or supervision in another state.
7906.5.	Request inside state; home study to assess safety and suitability of child placement; requirements.
7907.	Application of laws restricting out-of-state placements.
7907.3.	Bringing or sending of Indian child into another state.
7907.5.	Placement for adoption with state resident or nonresident; application of Interstate Compact on Placement of Children.
7908.	Jurisdiction of courts to place children adjudged wards of the court in out-of-state facilities.

Section	
7908.5.	"Jurisdiction" defined; legislative intent.
7909.	"Executive head" defined; appointment of compact administrator.
7910.	Refusal to grant approval of placement in violation of state law; requirements for placement in out-of-state residential facility.
7911.	Authority of State Department of Social Services; out-of-state placements.
7911.1.	Out-of-state placements; investigation authority; certification standards; denial or discontinuance of certification.
7912.	Out-of-state placements; rights of child; reports.
7913.	Placement determinations by licensed private adoption agency; authority; limitations.

Cross References

Adoption of unmarried minors, requirements for placement of child for adoption, see Family Code § 8801.3.
Juvenile case file inspection, confidentiality, release, see Welfare and Institutions Code § 827.
Nonminor dependents, opening of separate court file, access to file, see Welfare and Institutions Code § 362.5.

§ 7900. Adoption

The Interstate Compact on Placement of Children as set forth in Section 7901 is hereby adopted and entered into with all other jurisdictions joining therein. *(Stats.1992, c. 162 (A.B.2650), § 10, operative Jan. 1, 1994.)*

Cross References

Adoption of unmarried minors, requirements for placement of child for adoption, see Family Code § 8801.3.

Research References

Forms

2 California Transactions Forms--Family Law § 6:2, Governing Law.
2 California Transactions Forms--Family Law § 6:116, Purpose and Background of Interstate Compact.
West's California Code Forms, Family § 7900, Comment Overview—Interstate Compact on Placement of Children.
West's California Judicial Council Forms JV-565, Request for Assistance With Expedited Placement Under the Interstate Compact on the Placement of Children.
West's California Judicial Council Forms JV-567, Expedited Placement Under the Interstate Compact on the Placement of Children: Findings and Orders.

§ 7901. Provisions

The provisions of the interstate compact referred to in Section 7900 are as follows:

INTERSTATE COMPACT ON THE PLACEMENT OF CHILDREN

Article 1. Purpose and Policy

It is the purpose and policy of the party states to cooperate with each other in the interstate placement of children to the end that:

(a) Each child requiring placement shall receive the maximum opportunity to be placed in a suitable environment and with persons or institutions having appropriate qualifications and facilities to provide a necessary and desirable degree and type of care.

(b) The appropriate authorities in a state where a child is to be placed may have full opportunity to ascertain the circumstances of the proposed placement, thereby promoting full compliance with applicable requirements for the protection of the child.

(c) The proper authorities of the state from which the placement is made may obtain the most complete information on the basis on which to evaluate a projected placement before it is made.

(d) Appropriate jurisdictional arrangements for the care of children will be promoted.

Article 2. Definitions

As used in this compact:

(a) "Child" means a person who, by reason of minority, is legally subject to parental, guardianship, or similar control.

(b) "Sending agency" means a party state, or officer or employee thereof; subdivision of a party state, or officer or employee thereof; a court of a party state; a person, corporation, association, charitable agency, or other entity that sends, brings, or causes to be sent or brought any child to another party state.

(c) "Receiving state" means the state to which a child is sent, brought, or caused to be sent or brought, whether by public authorities or private persons or agencies, and whether for placement with state or local public authorities or for placement with private agencies or persons.

(d) "Placement" means the arrangement for the care of a child in a family free or boarding home or in a child-caring agency or institution, but does not include any institution caring for persons with developmental disabilities or mental health disorders or any institution primarily educational in character, and any hospital or other medical facility.

Article 3. Conditions for Placement

(a) A sending agency shall not send, bring, or cause to be sent or brought into any other party state any child for placement in foster care or as a preliminary to a possible adoption unless the sending agency complies with each and every requirement set forth in this article and with the applicable laws of the receiving state governing the placement of children therein.

(b) Before sending, bringing, or causing any child to be sent or brought into a receiving state for placement in foster care or as a preliminary to a possible adoption, the sending agency shall furnish the appropriate public authorities in the receiving state written notice of the intention to send, bring, or place the child in the receiving state. The notice shall contain:

(1) The name, date, and place of birth of the child.

(2) The identity and address or addresses of the parents or legal guardian.

(3) The name and address of the person, agency, or institution to or with which the sending agency proposes to send, bring, or place the child.

(4) A full statement of the reasons for the proposed action and evidence of the authority pursuant to which the placement is proposed to be made.

(c) Any public officer or agency in a receiving state that receives notice pursuant to paragraph (b) of this article may request of the sending agency, or any other appropriate officer or agency of or in the sending agency's state, and shall be entitled to receive therefrom, supporting or additional information it deems necessary under the circumstances to carry out the purpose and policy of this compact.

(d) The child shall not be sent, brought, or caused to be sent or brought into the receiving state until the appropriate public authorities in the receiving state notify the sending agency, in writing, to the effect that the proposed placement does not appear to be contrary to the interest of the child.

Article 4. Penalty for Illegal Placement

The sending, bringing, or causing to be sent or brought into any receiving state of a child in violation of the terms of this compact shall constitute a violation of the laws respecting the placement of children of both the state in which the sending agency is located or from which it sends or brings the child and of the receiving state. A violation may be punished or subjected to penalty in either jurisdiction in accordance with its laws. In addition to liability for any punishment or penalty, any violation shall constitute full and sufficient grounds for the suspension or revocation of any license, permit, or other legal authorization held by the sending agency that empowers or allows it to place or care for children.

Article 5. Continuing Jurisdiction

(a) The sending agency shall retain jurisdiction over the child sufficient to determine all matters in relation to the custody, supervision, care, treatment, and disposition of the child that it would have had if the child had remained in the sending agency's state, until the child is adopted, reaches majority, becomes self-supporting, or is discharged with the concurrence of the appropriate authority in the receiving state. That jurisdiction shall also include the power to effect or cause the return of the child or the child's transfer to another location and custody pursuant to law. The sending agency shall continue to have financial responsibility for support and maintenance of the child during the period of the placement. Nothing contained herein shall defeat a claim of jurisdiction by a receiving state sufficient to deal with an act of delinquency or crime committed therein.

(b) When the sending agency is a public agency, it may enter into an agreement with an authorized public or private agency in the receiving state providing for the performance of one or more services in respect of that case by the latter as agent for the sending agency.

(c) This compact shall not be construed to prevent a private charitable agency authorized to place children in the receiving state from performing services or acting as agent in that state for a private charitable agency of the sending state or to prevent the agency in the receiving state from discharging financial responsibility for the support and maintenance of a child who has been placed on behalf of the sending agency without relieving the responsibility set forth in paragraph (a) of this article.

Article 6. Institutional Care of Delinquent Children

A child adjudicated delinquent may be placed in an institution in another party jurisdiction pursuant to this compact but that placement shall not be made unless the child is given a court hearing on notice to the parent or guardian with opportunity to be heard, before being sent to the other party jurisdiction for institutional care and the court finds that both of the following exist:

(a) Equivalent facilities for the child are not available in the sending agency's jurisdiction.

(b) Institutional care in the other jurisdiction is in the best interest of the child and will not produce undue hardship.

Article 7. Compact Administrator

The executive head of each jurisdiction party to this compact shall designate an officer who shall be general coordinator of activities under this compact in that jurisdiction and who, acting jointly with like officers of other party jurisdictions, shall have power to promulgate rules and regulations to carry out more effectively the terms and provisions of this compact.

Article 8. Limitations

This compact shall not apply to:

(a) The sending or bringing of a child into a receiving state by the child's parent, stepparent, grandparent, adult brother or sister, adult uncle or aunt, or the child's guardian and leaving the child with any such relative or nonagency guardian in the receiving state.

(b) Any placement, sending, or bringing of a child into a receiving state pursuant to any other interstate compact to which both the state from which the child is sent or brought and the receiving state are party, or to any other agreement between those states that has the force of law.

Article 9. Enactment and Withdrawal

This compact shall be open to joinder by any state, territory, or possession of the United States, the District of Columbia, the Commonwealth of Puerto Rico, and, with the consent of Congress, the government of Canada or any province thereof. It shall become effective with respect to any of these jurisdictions when that jurisdiction has enacted the same into law. Withdrawal from this compact shall be by the enactment of a statute repealing the same, but shall not take effect until two years after the effective date of the statute and until written notice of the withdrawal has been given by the withdrawing state to the Governor of each other party jurisdiction. Withdrawal of a party state shall not affect the rights, duties, and obligations under this compact of any sending agency therein with respect to a placement made before the effective date of withdrawal.

Article 10. Construction and Severability

The provisions of this compact shall be liberally construed to effectuate the purposes thereof. The provisions of this compact shall be severable and if any phrase, clause, sentence, or provision of this compact is declared to be contrary to the constitution of any party state or of the United States or the applicability thereof to any government, agency, person, or circumstance is held invalid, the validity of the remainder of this compact and the applicability thereof to any government, agency, person, or circumstance shall not be affected thereby. If this compact shall be held contrary to the constitution of any state party thereto, the compact shall remain in full force and effect as to the remaining states and in full force and effect as to the state affected as to all severable matters. *(Stats.1992, c. 162 (A.B.2650), § 10, operative Jan. 1, 1994. Amended by Stats.2002, c. 260 (S.B.1512), § 6; Stats.2014, c. 144 (A.B.1847), § 13, eff. Jan. 1, 2015; Stats.2019, c. 115 (A.B.1817), § 104, eff. Jan. 1, 2020.)*

Cross References

Adoption of unmarried minors, requirements for placement of child for adoption, see Family Code § 8801.3.
Delinquent children, jurisdiction of courts to place, see Family Code § 7908.
Person defined for purposes of this Code, see Family Code § 105.
State defined for purposes of this Code, see Family Code § 145.
Support defined for purposes of this Code, see Family Code § 150.

Research References

Forms

2 California Transactions Forms--Family Law § 6:116, Purpose and Background of Interstate Compact.
2 California Transactions Forms--Family Law § 6:117, Exclusions from Interstate Compact.
2 California Transactions Forms--Family Law § 6:118, Penalties for Noncompliance With ICPC.
2 California Transactions Forms--Family Law § 6:119, Continuing Jurisdiction.
2 California Transactions Forms--Family Law § 6:120, Compliance With Law of Sending State.
2 California Transactions Forms--Family Law § 6:125, Interstate Travel by Birth Mother Prior to Child's Birth.
2 California Transactions Forms--Family Law § 6:137.50, Notice to Recipient State.
West's California Code Forms, Family § 7900, Comment Overview—Interstate Compact on Placement of Children.

§ 7901.1. Request outside state; home study to assess safety and suitability of child placement; requirements

(a) Within 60 days of receipt of a request from another state to conduct a study of a home environment for purposes of assessing the safety and suitability of placing a child in the home, a county child welfare agency shall, directly or by contract, do both of the following:

(1) Conduct and complete the study.

(2) Return a report to the requesting state on the results of the study. The report shall address the extent to which placement in the home would meet the needs of the child.

(b) Except as provided in subdivision (c), in the case of a home study commenced on or before September 30, 2008, if the agency fails to comply with subdivision (a) within the 60–day period as a result of circumstances beyond the control of the agency, the agency shall have 75 days to comply with subdivision (a). The agency shall document the circumstances involved and certify that completing the home study is in the best interests of the child. For purposes of this subdivision, "circumstances beyond the control of the agency" include, but are not limited to, the failure of a federal agency to provide the results of a background check or the failure of any entity to provide completed medical forms, if the background check or records were requested by the agency at least 45 days before the end of the 60–day period.

(c) Subdivision (b) shall not be construed to require the agency to have completed, within the applicable period, the parts of the home study involving the education and training of the prospective foster or adoptive parents.

(d) The agency shall treat any report described in subdivision (a) that is received from another state, an Indian tribe, or a private agency under contract with another state, as meeting any requirements imposed by the state for the completion of a home study before placing a child in the home, unless, within 14 days after receipt of the report, the agency determines, based on grounds that are specific to the content of the report, that making a decision in reliance on the report would be contrary to the welfare of the child.

(e) A county is not restricted from contracting with a private agency for the conduct of a home study described in subdivision (a).

(f) The department shall work with counties to identify barriers to meeting the timeframes specified in this section and to develop recommendations to reduce or eliminate those barriers. *(Added by Stats.2007, c. 583 (S.B.703), § 1.)*

§ 7902. Financial responsibility for child placed pursuant to compact

Financial responsibility for a child placed pursuant to the Interstate Compact on the Placement of Children shall be determined in accordance with Article 5 of the compact in the first instance. However, in the event of partial or complete default of performance thereunder, the provisions of other state laws also may be invoked. *(Stats.1992, c. 162 (A.B.2650), § 10, operative Jan. 1, 1994.)*

Cross References

State defined for purposes of this Code, see Family Code § 145.

§ 7903. "Appropriate public authorities" defined

The phrase "appropriate public authorities" as used in Article 3 of the Interstate Compact on the Placement of Children means, with reference to this state, the State Department of Social Services, and that department shall receive and act with reference to notices required by Article 3 of the compact. *(Stats.1992, c. 162 (A.B.2650), § 10, operative Jan. 1, 1994.)*

Cross References

State defined for purposes of this Code, see Family Code § 145.

Research References

Forms

West's California Code Forms, Family § 7900, Comment Overview—Interstate Compact on Placement of Children.

§ 7904. "Appropriate authority in receiving state" defined

The phrase "appropriate authority in receiving state" as used in paragraph (a) of Article 5 of the Interstate Compact on the

Placement of Children, with reference to this state, means the State Department of Social Services. *(Stats.1992, c. 162 (A.B.2650), § 10, operative Jan. 1, 1994.)*

Cross References

State defined for purposes of this Code, see Family Code § 145.

Research References

Forms

West's California Code Forms, Family § 7900, Comment Overview—Interstate Compact on Placement of Children.

§ 7905. Agreements with party states; approval of financial obligations

The officers and agencies of this state and its subdivisions having authority to place children are hereby empowered to enter into agreements with appropriate officers or agencies of or in other party states pursuant to paragraph (b) of Article 5 of the Interstate Compact on the Placement of Children. Any such agreement which contains a financial commitment or imposes a financial obligation on this state or subdivision or agency thereof is not binding unless it has the approval in writing of the Controller in the case of the state and of the chief local fiscal officer in the case of a subdivision of the state. *(Stats.1992, c. 162 (A.B.2650), § 10, operative Jan. 1, 1994.)*

Cross References

State Controller, generally, see Government Code § 12402 et seq.
State defined for purposes of this Code, see Family Code § 145.

§ 7906. Requirements for visitation, inspection or supervision in another state

Any requirements for visitation, inspection, or supervision of children, homes, institutions, or other agencies in another party state which may apply under the law of this state shall be deemed to be met if performed pursuant to an agreement entered into by appropriate officers or agencies of this state or a subdivision thereof as contemplated by paragraph (b) of Article 5 of the Interstate Compact on the Placement of Children. *(Stats.1992, c. 162 (A.B. 2650), § 10, operative Jan. 1, 1994.)*

Cross References

State defined for purposes of this Code, see Family Code § 145.

§ 7906.5. Request inside state; home study to assess safety and suitability of child placement; requirements

(a) Within 60 days after an officer or agency of this state, or its political subdivision, receives a request from another state to conduct a study of a home environment for purposes of assessing the safety and suitability of placing a child, who is in the custody of the requesting state, in the home, the county child welfare agency shall, directly or indirectly, do both of the following:

(1) Conduct and complete the home study.

(2) Return to the requesting state a report on the results of the home study, which shall address the extent to which placement in the home would meet the needs of the child.

(b) A licensed private adoption agency may agree to provide the services listed in subdivision (a), and upon that agreement, shall comply with the requirements of paragraphs (1) and (2) of subdivision (a).

(c) Notwithstanding subdivision (a), in the case of a home study commenced on or before September 30, 2008, if the county fails to comply with subdivision (a) within the 60–day period as a result of circumstances beyond the control of the state, including, but not limited to, failure by a federal agency to provide the results of a background check or failure of any entity to provide completed medical forms requested by the state at least 45 days before the end of the 60–day period, the county shall have 75 days to comply with subdivision (a) if the county documents the circumstances involved and certifies that completing the home study is in the best interest of the child.

(d) Nothing in this section shall be construed to require the county to have completed, within the applicable period, those portions of the home study concerning the education and training of the prospective foster parent or adoptive parent.

(e) The county shall treat any report described in subdivision (a) that is received from another state, an Indian tribe, or a private agency under contract with another state, as meeting any requirements imposed by the state for the completion of a home study before placing a child in the home, unless, within 14 days after receipt of the report, the county determines, based on grounds that are specific to the content of the report, that making a decision in reliance on the report would be contrary to the welfare of the child.

(f) A county is not restricted from contracting with a private agency for the conduct of a home study described in subdivision (a). *(Added by Stats.2007, c. 583 (S.B.703), § 2.)*

§ 7907. Application of laws restricting out-of-state placements

No provision of law restricting out-of-state placement of children for adoption shall apply to placements made pursuant to the Interstate Compact on the Placement of Children. *(Stats.1992, c. 162 (A.B.2650), § 10, operative Jan. 1, 1994.)*

Cross References

State defined for purposes of this Code, see Family Code § 145.

§ 7907.3. Bringing or sending of Indian child into another state

The Interstate Compact on the Placement of Children shall not apply to any placement, sending, or bringing of an Indian child into another state pursuant to a transfer of jurisdiction to a tribal court under Section 1911 of the Indian Child Welfare Act (25 U.S.C. Sec. 1901 et seq.). *(Added by Stats.2006, c. 838 (S.B.678), § 7.)*

§ 7907.5. Placement for adoption with state resident or nonresident; application of Interstate Compact on Placement of Children

(a) A child who is born in this state and placed for adoption in this state with a resident of this state is not subject to the provisions of the Interstate Compact on the Placement of Children.

(b) A child who is born in this state and placed for adoption with a person who is not a resident of this state is subject to the provisions of the Interstate Compact on the Placement of Children, regardless of whether the adoption petition is filed in this state. In interstate placements, this state shall be deemed the sending state for any child born in the state. *(Added by Stats.2004, c. 858 (S.B.1357), § 2.)*

Cross References

State defined for purposes of this Code, see Family Code § 145.

§ 7908. Jurisdiction of courts to place children adjudged wards of the court in out-of-state facilities

A court having jurisdiction to place children adjudged wards of the court may place a ward in an out-of-state facility, as defined in subdivision (b) of Section 7910, pursuant to Section 727.1 of the Welfare and Institutions Code and Article 6 of the Interstate Compact on the Placement of Children and shall retain jurisdiction as provided in Article 5 of the compact. *(Stats.1992, c. 162 (A.B.2650), § 10, operative Jan. 1, 1994. Amended by Stats.2021, c. 86 (A.B.153), § 3, eff. July 16, 2021.)*

Cross References

Juvenile courts, delinquency proceedings, see Welfare and Institutions Code § 602 et seq.

§ 7908

State defined for purposes of this Code, see Family Code § 145.

§ 7908.5. "Jurisdiction" defined; legislative intent

For the purposes of an interstate adoption placement, the term "jurisdiction" as used in Article 5 of the Interstate Compact on the Placement of Children means "jurisdiction over or legal responsibility for the child." It is the intent of the Legislature that this section make a technical clarification to the Interstate Compact on the Placement of Children and not a substantive change. *(Added by Stats.2002, c. 260 (S.B.1512), § 7.)*

§ 7909. "Executive head" defined; appointment of compact administrator

"Executive head" as used in Article 7 of the Interstate Compact on the Placement of Children means the Governor. The Governor shall appoint a compact administrator in accordance with the terms of Article 7 of the compact. *(Stats.1992, c. 162 (A.B.2650), § 10, operative Jan. 1, 1994.)*

Cross References

Governor, see Government Code § 12001 et seq.

§ 7910. Refusal to grant approval of placement in violation of state law; requirements for placement in out-of-state residential facility

(a) Approval of an interstate placement of a child for adoption shall not be granted by the Compact Administrator if the placement is in violation of either Section 8801 of this code or Section 273 of the Penal Code.

(b)(1) The Compact Administrator shall not submit to a receiving state a request to place a dependent or ward for whom a county child welfare agency or county probation department has placement and care responsibility in an out-of-state residential facility, unless the requirements of Section 7911.1 of this code and Section 361.21 of, or subdivision (b) of Section 727.1 of, the Welfare and Institutions Code are met.

(2) For the purpose of this section, an "out-of-state residential facility" is a facility that is located in a state outside of California, is licensed or otherwise approved by the applicable state or tribal authority, and provides an integrated program of specialized and intensive care and supervision, services and supports, treatment, and short-term, 24–hour, trauma-informed care and supervision to children. An out-of-state residential facility may be called another name, including a group home, a residential treatment facility, or a residential care treatment facility. *(Stats.1992, c. 162 (A.B.2650), § 10, operative Jan. 1, 1994. Amended by Stats.2021, c. 86 (A.B.153), § 4, eff. July 16, 2021.)*

§ 7911. Authority of State Department of Social Services; out-of-state placements

(a) The Legislature finds and declares all of the following:

(1) The health and safety of California children placed by a county child welfare agency or probation department out of state pursuant to the provisions of the Interstate Compact on the Placement of Children are a matter of statewide concern.

(2) The State Department of Social Services has full authority to require any placement of a child in an out-of-state residential facility by a county child welfare agency or county probation department be approved on a child-specific basis after the county has exhausted in-state placement and services options that meet the needs of the child and participated in the department's technical assistance program. Before the juvenile court approves the placement pursuant to Section 361.21 of, or subdivision (b) of Section 727.1 of, the Welfare and Institutions Code, the State Department of Social Services shall certify the out-of-state residential facility pursuant to Section 7911.1. Before processing an application for out-of-state placement in a residential facility pursuant to the Interstate Compact on the Placement of Children, the Compact Administrator shall verify that the placement was approved by the juvenile court and that it has been certified by the department.

(3) The Legislature further finds and declares that certification of facilities licensed under a separate state's licensing standards has not been sufficient to ensure that the stringent California short-term residential therapeutic programs requirements are maintained to safeguard the health, safety, and well-being of California's foster children and youth. Further research demonstrates that dependents and wards in foster care placements are generally better served when they are able to maintain and develop local community supports closer to their families and communities.

(b)(1) On and after July 1, 2021, foster care placements by county child welfare agencies or probation departments into out-of-state residential facilities shall not be made, except in the limited circumstances authorized by Section 361.21 of, or subdivision (b) of Section 727.1 of, the Welfare and Institutions Code, as applicable. Unless placement of a child in an out-of-state residential facility does not require certification pursuant to subdivision (h) of Section 7911.1, the Compact Administrator shall not seek approval of placement in an out-of-state residential facility from the receiving state unless all of the following criteria are met:

(A) The Compact Administrator has received from the county placing agency documentation that it has complied with the requirements of Section 16010.9 of the Welfare and Institutions Code.

(B) The Compact Administrator has received documentation that the out-of-state residential facility has been certified by the State Department of Social Services, including documentation that the director of the State Department of Social Services has approved the certification.

(C) The Compact Administrator has received a copy of the juvenile court order authorizing placement of the child in the out-of-state residential facility pursuant to Section 361.21 or 727.1 of the Welfare and Institutions Code.

(2) On and after July 1, 2022, county child welfare agencies or probation departments shall not make new placements in out-of-state residential facilities, except for placements described in subdivision (h) of Section 7911.1.

(c) Notwithstanding any other law, on and after July 1, 2022, the State Department of Social Services shall not certify any new out-of-state residential facilities for placement by county child welfare agencies or probation departments. On and after July 1, 2022, the Compact Administrator shall not seek approval of any new placements by county child welfare agencies or probation departments in out-of-state residential facilities.

(d) The state shall decertify all out-of-state residential facilities for placement by county child welfare agencies or probation departments on January 1, 2023, and ensure that all children and youth placed in out of state residential facilities have been returned to California by that date.

(e) This section is declaratory of existing law with respect to the Governor's designation of the State Department of Social Services to act as the Compact Administrator and of that department to act as the single state agency charged with supervision of public social services under Section 10600 of the Welfare and Institutions Code. *(Added by Stats.2021, c. 86 (A.B.153), § 6, eff. July 16, 2021.)*

Cross References

Abuse defined for purposes of the Domestic Violence Protection Act, see Family Code § 6203.
County defined for purposes of this Code, see Family Code § 67.
Minor defined for purposes of this Code, see Family Code § 6500.

State defined for purposes of this Code, see Family Code § 145.

§ 7911.1. Out-of-state placements; investigation authority; certification standards; denial or discontinuance of certification

(a) Notwithstanding any other law, the State Department of Social Services or its designee shall investigate any threat to the health and safety of children placed by a California county child welfare agency or probation department in an out-of-state residential facility, as defined in subdivision (b) of Section 7910, pursuant to the provisions of the Interstate Compact on the Placement of Children. This authority shall include the authority to interview children or staff in private or review their file at the out-of-state residential facility or wherever the child or files may be at the time of the investigation. Notwithstanding any other law, the State Department of Social Services or its designee shall require certified out-of-state residential facilities to comply with the reporting requirements applicable to short-term residential therapeutic programs licensed in California for each child in care, regardless of whether or not the child is a California placement, by submitting a copy of the required reports to the Compact Administrator within regulatory timeframes. The Compact Administrator, within one business day of receiving a serious incident report from a certified out-of-state residential facility, shall verbally notify any county child welfare agency or probation department with a child placed at the certified out-of-state residential facility of the serious incident report. The Compact Administrator, within five business days of receiving a written serious incident report from a certified out-of-state residential facility, shall forward a copy of the written serious incident report to any county child welfare agency or probation department with a child placed at the certified out-of-state residential facility.

(b) Any contract, memorandum of understanding, or agreement entered into pursuant to paragraph (b) of Article 5 of the Interstate Compact on the Placement of Children regarding the placement of a child out of state by a California county social services agency or probation department shall include the language set forth in subdivision (a).

(c) Upon receipt of a request from a county child welfare agency or probation department for a child-specific certification of a placement in an out-of-state residential facility, the State Department of Social Services or its designee shall expedite the review of the request in order to determine any additional information needed, shall communicate with the requesting county agency regarding its review including regular status updates, and shall, in a timely manner, determine whether it will issue a child-specific certification to the out-of-state residential facility pursuant to this section.

(1) The licensing standards applicable to an out-of-state residential facility certified by the department shall be those required of short-term residential therapeutic programs operated in this state.

(2) Before issuing a child-specific certification to the out-of-state residential facility, the department shall do all of the following:

(A) Review documentation provided by the county placing agency pursuant to subdivision (e) of Section 16010.9 of the Welfare and Institutions Code.

(B) Perform an on-site inspection of the out-of-state residential facility's physical site.

(C) At a minimum, review all of the following sections of the out-of-state residential facility's program statement:

(i) Core Services and Supports.

(ii) Trauma Informed Interventions and Treatment Practices.

(iii) Personal Rights.

(iv) House Rules.

(v) Discipline Policies and Procedures.

(vi) Emergency Intervention Plan (Including Runaway Plan).

(D) Review the out-of-state residential facility's serious incident reports.

(E) Review the out-of-state residential facility's current license. In order for the out-of-state residential facility to receive a certification, the out-of-state residential facility shall have a current license, or an equivalent approval, in good standing issued by the appropriate authority or authorities of the state in which it is operating.

(F) Review the out-of-state residential facility's licensing history, including any substantiated complaints.

(G) Review the documentation provided by the State Department of Health Care Services pursuant to subdivision (d).

(H) Obtain approval from the director of the department of the child-specific certification for the out-of-state residential facility. Director approval may be given after all of the requirements of subparagraphs (A) to (G), inclusive, have been satisfied.

(3) The department shall not issue a child-specific certification to the out-of-state residential facility if the out-of-state residential facility fails to cooperate during the certification process, including failing to provide any of the documentation listed in paragraph (2).

(4) If all the requirements of paragraph (2) have been satisfied, the department shall certify the out-of-state residential facility pursuant to this section. The department shall provide written documentation of this certification to the county placing agency.

(5) The child-specific certification is discontinued, effective immediately, upon the child transitioning out of the out-of-state residential facility's program.

(d) The licensing standards applicable to out-of-state residential facilities certified by the department, as described in subdivision (c), shall include the licensing standards for mental health program approval described in Section 1562.01 of the Health and Safety Code. These standards shall be satisfied if the State Department of Health Care Services determines that the out-of-state residential facility has an equivalent mental health program approval in the state in which it is operating. Upon receipt of a request for the State Department of Health Care Services to determine whether an out-of-state residential facility has an equivalent mental health program approval in the state in which it is operation, the State Department of Health Care Services shall expedite the review of the request in order to determine any additional information needed, shall communicate with the requesting county agency regarding its review including regular status updates, and shall, in a timely manner, make its determination. If an out-of-state residential facility cannot satisfy the licensing standards for an equivalent mental health program approval, the department shall not certify the facility.

(e) Failure by an out-of-state residential facility to make children or staff available as required by subdivision (a) for a private interview or make files available for review shall be grounds to deny or discontinue the certification.

(f) Certifications made pursuant to this section shall be reviewed as often as necessary to ensure the health and safety of children in care. At a minimum, certifications made pursuant to this section shall be reviewed semiannually. The department shall complete a full review of the facility's program statement semiannually.

(g)(1) The department may deny or discontinue the certification of the out-of-state residential facility if the department makes a finding that the out-of-state residential facility is not operating in compliance with the requirements of this section. The department shall engage with counties that have one or more youth at a facility proposed for decertification to allow for a transition to occur, to the extent possible while ensuring the youths' safety and well-being.

(2) If the out-of-state residential facility disagrees with any decision by the department to deny or discontinue the certification, the out-of-state residential facility may appeal the decision immediately upon receipt of the notice of decertification. If the out-of-state residential facility decides to appeal the decision, the appeal shall be

submitted to the department not later than 30 calendar days after the out-of-state residential facility receives the decision. The out-of-state residential facility's appeal shall be in writing and include all information, including supporting documents, that forms the basis of the appeal. The department shall issue a final determination not later than 30 calendar days after receipt of the appeal. If the out-of-state residential facility disagrees with the department's determination, the out-of-state residential facility may file a writ pursuant to paragraph (3). If the out-of-state residential facility decides to file a writ, the writ shall be filed not later than 30 calendar days after the out-of-state residential facility receives the final determination.

(3) Any judicial proceeding to contest the department's determination as to the status of the out-of-state residential facility's certificate shall be held in California pursuant to Section 1085 of the Code of Civil Procedure.

(h) The certification requirements of this section shall not impact any of the following:

(1) Placement of emotionally disturbed children made pursuant to an individualized education program developed pursuant to the federal Individuals with Disabilities Education Act (20 U.S.C. Sec. 1400 et seq.) if the placement is not funded with federal or state foster care funds.

(2) Placement of Indian children, as defined by the Indian Child Welfare Act of 1978 (25 U.S.C. Sec. 1901 et.[1] seq.) and Section 224.1 of the Welfare and Institutions Code.

(i) Failure by an out-of-state residential facility to obtain or maintain its certification, as required by this section, shall preclude the use of any public funds, whether county, state, or federal, in the payment for the placement of any child in that out-of-state residential facility pursuant to the Interstate Compact on the Placement of Children.

(j) Notwithstanding the rulemaking provisions of the Administrative Procedure Act (Chapter 3.5 (commencing with Section 11340) of Part 1 of Division 3 of Title 2 of the Government Code), the State Department of Social Services and the State Department of Health Care Services may implement, interpret, or make specific this section by means of all-county letters, written directives, interim licensing standards, or similar written instructions from the department until regulations are adopted. These all-county letters, written directives, interim licensing standards, or similar written instructions shall have the same force and effect as regulations until the adoption of regulations. *(Added by Stats.2021, c. 86 (A.B.153), § 8, eff. July 16, 2021.)*

[1] So in enrolled bill.

Cross References

Abuse defined for purposes of the Domestic Violence Protection Act, see Family Code § 6203.
Aid to Families with Dependent Children—Foster Care, placement requirements for eligibility, see Welfare and Institutions Code § 11402.
County defined for purposes of this Code, see Family Code § 67.
Dependent children, judgments and orders, periodic status review, see Welfare and Institutions Code § 366.
Dependent children, placement in out-of-state group home, see Welfare and Institutions Code § 361.21.
Judgment and order defined for purposes of this Code, see Family Code § 100.
Juvenile court law, information required in case plan where foster care is being considered, see Welfare and Institutions Code § 706.6.
Minor adjudged a ward of the court, choice of placement, conditions upon out-of-state placement at certain facilities, see Welfare and Institutions Code § 727.1.
Proceeding defined for purposes of this Code, see Family Code § 110.
State child welfare services, case plans, see Welfare and Institutions Code § 16501.1.

State defined for purposes of this Code, see Family Code § 145.

Research References

Forms

West's California Code Forms, Family § 7900, Comment Overview—Interstate Compact on Placement of Children.

§ 7912. Out-of-state placements; rights of child; reports

(a) The Legislature finds and declares that the health and safety of children placed in out-of-state residential facilities pursuant to the Interstate Compact on the Placement of Children is a matter of statewide concern. The Legislature therefore affirms its intention that children placed by a county child welfare agency or probation department in out-of-state residential facilities be accorded the same personal rights and safeguards of a child placed in a California licensed short-term residential therapeutic program. This section is in clarification of existing law.

(b)(1) On or before September 1, 2021, and each month thereafter, the department shall report to the relevant policy and fiscal committees of the Legislature the number of children placed by a county child welfare agency or probation department in out-of-state residential facilities pursuant to the Interstate Compact on the Placement of Children.

(2) On or before January 1, 2022, and every six months thereafter until facilities are decertified and all children returned to California on or before January 1, 2023, the department, in consultation with the counties, shall report to the relevant policy and fiscal committees of the Legislature on the capacity for serving all child welfare and probation-supervised foster children within California or in home-based settings outside of the state. The report shall also include all of the following data, as applicable:

(A) The number of children served by out-of-state residential facilities, disaggregated by child welfare services agency and probation department supervision.

(B) Data measures related to ongoing transition planning efforts, including child and family team meetings, child-specific recruitment and family finding activities, and multiagency care coordination efforts that occurred for each child before and during placement in the out-of-state residential facility.

(C) The lengths of stay of each child placed in an out-of-state residential facility by a California child welfare agency or probation department.

(D) The total number of all serious incident reports received regarding out-of-state residential facilities, and descriptions of the types of incidents reported.

(E) The total number of serious incident reports received regarding California children placed in out-of-state residential facilities, and descriptions of the types of incidents reported.

(3) Reports made pursuant to this subdivision shall not include any demographic data that would permit identification of any child or nonminor dependent. *(Added by Stats.1998, c. 311 (S.B.933), § 11, eff. Aug. 19, 1998. Amended by Stats.2015, c. 773 (A.B.403), § 4, eff. Jan. 1, 2016; Stats.2016, c. 612 (A.B.1997), § 9, eff. Jan. 1, 2017; Stats.2021, c. 86 (A.B.153), § 9, eff. July 16, 2021.)*

Cross References

County defined for purposes of this Code, see Family Code § 67.
State defined for purposes of this Code, see Family Code § 145.

Research References

Forms

2 California Transactions Forms--Family Law § 6:2, Governing Law.

§ 7913. Placement determinations by licensed private adoption agency; authority; limitations

(a) When a full service licensed private adoption agency has provided adoption-related services to a birth parent or prospective adoptive parent, that agency is delegated the authority to determine whether the placement shall or shall not be made pursuant to the Interstate Compact on the Placement of Children, and to sign the compact forms documenting that determination and date of placement.

(b) For children entering California in independent adoptions, prior to making a determination regarding placement and as soon as feasible, the private adoption agency shall notify the appropriate district office or delegated county adoption agency of the matter and verify that the preplacement interview of the prospective adoptive parent or parents has been completed.

(c) This section shall not apply to a child who is a dependent of the court or a child subject to a petition filed under Section 300 of the Welfare and Institutions Code. *(Added by Stats.2011, c. 462 (A.B. 687), § 5.)*

Part 6

FOSTER CARE PLACEMENT CONSIDERATIONS

Section
7950. Relatives; race, color or national origin.
7951. Placement of less than 30 days.
7952. Statement to court by minor.
7953, 7954. Repealed.

§ 7950. Relatives; race, color or national origin

(a) With full consideration for the proximity of the natural parents to the placement so as to facilitate visitation and family reunification, when a placement in foster care is being made, the following considerations shall be used:

(1) Placement shall, if possible, be made in the home of a relative, unless the placement would not be in the best interest of the child. Diligent efforts shall be made by an agency or entity to which this subdivision applies, to locate an appropriate relative, as defined in paragraph (2) of subdivision (f) of Section 319 of the Welfare and Institutions Code. At any permanency hearing in which the court terminates reunification services, or at any postpermanency hearing for a child not placed for adoption, the court shall find that the agency or entity to which this subdivision applies has made diligent efforts to locate an appropriate relative and that each relative whose name has been submitted to the agency or entity as a possible caretaker, either by the relative or by other persons, has been evaluated as an appropriate placement resource.

(2) An agency or entity that receives any state assistance and is involved in foster care placements shall not do either of the following:

(A) Deny to any person the opportunity to become a foster parent on the basis of the race, color, or national origin of the person or the child involved.

(B) Delay or deny the placement of a child into foster care on the basis of the race, color, or national origin of the foster parent or the child involved.

(b) Subdivision (a) does not affect the application of the Indian Child Welfare Act of 1978 (25 U.S.C. Sec. 1901 et seq.).

(c) This section does not preclude a search for an appropriate relative being conducted simultaneously with a search for a foster family. *(Added by Stats.1995, c. 884 (S.B.1743), § 2. Amended by Stats.2003, c. 323 (S.B.984), § 1; Stats.2003, c. 469 (S.B.947), § 3; Stats.2015, c. 425 (S.B.794), § 1, eff. Jan. 1, 2016; Stats.2019, c. 115 (A.B.1817), § 106, eff. Jan. 1, 2020.)*

Cross References

Dependents, removal of child from custody of parents, preferential consideration of relative's request for placement of child, see Welfare and Institutions Code § 361.3.
Foster care placement,
  Legislative intent, see Welfare and Institutions Code § 16000.
  Relative caregiver or nonrelative extended family member caregiver, see Welfare and Institutions Code § 16003.
Hearings, terminating parental rights or establishing guardianship of minors adjudged dependent children, see Welfare and Institutions Code § 366.26.
Minor under supervision of a probation officer, choice of placement for foster care, priority list, see Welfare and Institutions Code § 727.1.
Person defined for purposes of this Code, see Family Code § 105.
State child welfare services, case plans, see Welfare and Institutions Code § 16501.1.
State defined for purposes of this Code, see Family Code § 145.

§ 7951. Placement of less than 30 days

This part does not apply in determining the foster care setting in which the child may be placed for a period not intended to exceed 30 days. *(Added by Stats.1995, c. 884 (A.B.1743), § 2.)*

§ 7952. Statement to court by minor

A minor 10 years of age or older being considered for placement in a foster home has the right to make a brief statement to the court making a decision on placement. The court may disregard any preferences expressed by the minor. The minor's right to make a statement is not limited to the initial placement, but continues for any proceedings concerning continued placement or a decision to return to parental custody. *(Added by Stats.1995, c. 884 (A.B.1743), § 2.)*

Cross References

Freedom from parental custody and control, in chambers hearing, statement of child, see Family Code § 7891.
Minor defined for purposes of this Code, see Family Code § 6500.
Proceeding defined for purposes of this Code, see Family Code § 110.

§§ 7953, 7954. Repealed by Stats.1995, c. 884 (A.B.1743), § 1

Part 7

SURROGACY AND DONOR FACILITATORS, ASSISTED REPRODUCTION AGREEMENTS FOR GESTATIONAL CARRIERS, AND OOCYTE DONATIONS

Section
7960. Definitions.
7961. Nonattorney surrogacy or donor facilitators; directing clients to deposit funds; financial interest or agency prohibited; disbursement; applicability.
7962. Assisted reproduction agreements for gestational carriers; requirements; actions to establish parent and child relationship; rebuttal of presumptions; judgment or order; confidentiality; presumption of validity.

§ 7960. Definitions

For purposes of this part, the following terms have the following meanings:

(a) "Assisted reproduction agreement" has the same meaning as defined in subdivision (b) of Section 7606.

(b) "Fund management agreement" means the agreement between the intended parents and the surrogacy or donor facilitator relating to the fee or other valuable consideration for services rendered or that will be rendered by the surrogacy or donor facilitator.

(c) "Intended parent" means an individual, married or unmarried, who manifests the intent to be legally bound as the parent of a child resulting from assisted reproduction.

(d) "Nonattorney surrogacy or donor facilitator" means a surrogacy or donor practitioner who is not an attorney in good standing licensed to practice law in this state.

(e) "Surrogacy or donor facilitator" means a person or organization that engages in either of the following activities:

(1) Advertising for the purpose of soliciting parties to an assisted reproduction agreement or for the donation of oocytes for use by a person other than the provider of the oocytes, or acting as an intermediary between the parties to an assisted reproduction agreement or oocyte donation.

(2) Charging a fee or other valuable consideration for services rendered relating to an assisted reproduction agreement or oocyte donation.

(f) "Surrogate" means a woman who bears and carries a child for another through medically assisted reproduction and pursuant to a written agreement, as set forth in Sections 7606 and 7962. Within the definition of surrogate are two different and distinct types:

(1) "Traditional surrogate" means a woman who agrees to gestate an embryo, in which the woman is the gamete donor and the embryo was created using the sperm of the intended father or a donor arranged by the intended parent or parents.

(2) "Gestational carrier" means a woman who is not an intended parent and who agrees to gestate a genetically unrelated embryo pursuant to an assisted reproduction agreement.

(g) "Donor" means a woman who provides oocytes for use by another for the purpose of assisting the recipient of the oocytes in having a child or children. *(Added by Stats.2010, c. 138 (A.B.2426), § 1. Amended by Stats.2012, c. 466 (A.B.1217), § 2; Stats.2015, c. 91 (A.B.1049), § 3, eff. Jan. 1, 2016; Stats.2019, c. 115 (A.B.1817), § 107, eff. Jan. 1, 2020.)*

Research References

Forms
2 California Transactions Forms--Family Law § 7:8.50, Surrogacy Facilitator.

§ 7961. Nonattorney surrogacy or donor facilitators; directing clients to deposit funds; financial interest or agency prohibited; disbursement; applicability

(a) A nonattorney surrogacy or donor facilitator shall direct the client to deposit all client funds into either of the following:

(1) An independent, bonded escrow depository maintained by a licensed, independent, bonded escrow company.

(2) A trust account maintained by an attorney.

(b) For purposes of this section, a nonattorney surrogacy or donor facilitator may not have a financial interest in any escrow company holding client funds. A nonattorney surrogacy or donor facilitator and any of its directors or employees shall not be an agent of any escrow company holding client funds.

(c) Client funds may only be disbursed by the attorney or escrow agent as set forth in the assisted reproduction agreement and fund management agreement.

(d) This section shall not apply to funds that are both of the following:

(1) Not provided for in the fund management agreement.

(2) Paid directly to a medical doctor for medical services or a psychologist for psychological services. *(Added by Stats.2010, c. 138 (A.B.2426), § 1. Amended by Stats.2015, c. 91 (A.B.1049), § 4, eff. Jan. 1, 2016.)*

Research References

Forms
2 California Transactions Forms--Family Law § 7:8.50, Surrogacy Facilitator.

§ 7962. Assisted reproduction agreements for gestational carriers; requirements; actions to establish parent and child relationship; rebuttal of presumptions; judgment or order; confidentiality; presumption of validity

(a) An assisted reproduction agreement for gestational carriers shall contain, but shall not be limited to, all of the following information:

(1) The date on which the assisted reproduction agreement for gestational carriers was executed.

(2) The persons from which the gametes originated, unless donated gametes were used, in which case the assisted reproduction agreement does not need to specify the name of the donor but shall specify whether the donated gamete or gametes were eggs, sperm, or embryos, or all.

(3) The identity of the intended parent or parents.

(4) Disclosure of how the intended parents will cover the medical expenses of the gestational carrier and of the newborn or newborns. If health care coverage is used to cover those medical expenses, the disclosure shall include a review of the health care policy provisions related to coverage for surrogate pregnancy, including any possible liability of the gestational carrier, third-party liability liens or other insurance coverage, and any notice requirements that could affect coverage or liability of the gestational carrier. The review and disclosure do not constitute legal advice. If coverage of liability is uncertain, a statement of that fact shall be sufficient to meet the requirements of this section.

(b) Prior to executing the written assisted reproduction agreement for gestational carriers, a surrogate and the intended parent or intended parents shall be represented by separate independent licensed attorneys of their choosing.

(c) The assisted reproduction agreement for gestational carriers shall be executed by the parties and the signatures on the assisted reproduction agreement for gestational carriers shall be notarized or witnessed by an equivalent method of affirmation as required in the jurisdiction where the assisted reproduction agreement for gestational carriers is executed.

(d) The parties to an assisted reproduction agreement for gestational carriers shall not undergo an embryo transfer procedure, or commence injectable medication in preparation for an embryo transfer for assisted reproduction purposes, until the assisted reproduction agreement for gestational carriers has been fully executed as required by subdivisions (b) and (c) of this section.

(e) An action to establish the parent and child relationship between the intended parent or parents and the child as to a child conceived pursuant to an assisted reproduction agreement for gestational carriers may be filed before the child's birth and may be filed in the county where the child is anticipated to be born, the county where the intended parent or intended parents reside, the county where the surrogate resides, the county where the assisted reproduction agreement for gestational carriers is executed, or the county where medical procedures pursuant to the agreement are to be performed. A copy of the assisted reproduction agreement for gestational carriers shall be lodged in the court action filed for the purpose of establishing the parent and child relationship. The parties to the assisted reproduction agreement for gestational carriers shall attest, under penalty of perjury, and to the best of their knowledge and belief, as to the parties' compliance with this section in entering into the assisted reproduction agreement for gestational carriers. Submitting those declarations shall not constitute a waiver, under Section 912 of the Evidence Code, of the lawyer-client privilege described in Article 3 (commencing with Section 950) of Chapter 4 of Division 8 of the Evidence Code.

(f)(1) A notarized assisted reproduction agreement for gestational carriers signed by all the parties, with the attached declarations of independent attorneys, and lodged with the superior court in accordance with this section, shall rebut any presumptions contained within Part 2 (commencing with Section 7540), subdivision (a) of Section 7610, and Sections 7611 and 7613, as to the gestational carrier surrogate, or the gestational carrier surrogate's spouse or partner, being a parent of the child or children.

(2) Upon petition of any party to a properly executed assisted reproduction agreement for gestational carriers, the court shall issue a judgment or order establishing a parent and child relationship, whether pursuant to Section 7630 or otherwise. The judgment or order may be issued before or after the child's or children's birth subject to the limitations of Section 7633. Subject to proof of compliance with this section, the judgment or order shall establish the parent and child relationship of the intended parent or intended parents identified in the surrogacy agreement and shall establish that the surrogate, and the surrogate's spouse or partner, is not a parent of, and has no parental rights or duties with respect to, the child or children. The judgment or order shall be issued forthwith and without further hearing or evidence, unless the court or a party to the assisted reproduction agreement for gestational carriers has a good faith, reasonable belief that the assisted reproduction agreement for gestational carriers or attorney declarations were not executed in accordance with this section. Upon motion by a party to the assisted reproduction agreement for gestational carriers, the matter shall be scheduled for hearing before a judgment or order is issued. This section * * * does not prevent a court from finding and declaring that the intended parent is, or intended parents are, the parent or parents of the child where compliance with this section has not been met; however, the court shall require sufficient proof entitling the parties to the relief sought.

(g) The petition, relinquishment or consent, agreement, order, report to the court from any investigating agency, and any power of attorney and deposition filed in the office of the clerk of the court pursuant to this part shall not be open to inspection by any person other than the parties to the proceeding and their attorneys and the State Department of Social Services, except upon the written authority of a judge of the superior court. A judge of the superior court shall not authorize anyone to inspect the petition, relinquishment or consent, agreement, order, report to the court from any investigating agency, or power of attorney or deposition, or any portion of those documents, except in exceptional circumstances and where necessary. The petitioner may be required to pay the expense of preparing the copies of the documents to be inspected.

(h) Upon the written request of any party to the proceeding and the order of any judge of the superior court, the clerk of the court shall not provide any documents referred to in subdivision (g) for inspection or copying to any other person, unless the name of the gestational carrier or any information tending to identify the gestational carrier is deleted from the documents or copies thereof.

(i) An assisted reproduction agreement for gestational carriers executed in accordance with this section is presumptively valid and shall not be rescinded or revoked without a court order. For purposes of this part, any failure to comply with the requirements of this section shall rebut the presumption of the validity of the assisted reproduction agreement for gestational carriers. *(Added by Stats. 2012, c. 466 (A.B.1217), § 3. Amended by Stats.2014, c. 636 (A.B.2344), § 2, eff. Jan. 1, 2015; Stats.2016, c. 385 (A.B.2349), § 4, eff. Jan. 1, 2017; Stats.2017, c. 326 (A.B.1396), § 1, eff. Jan. 1, 2018; Stats.2019, c. 115 (A.B.1817), § 108, eff. Jan. 1, 2020.)*

Cross References

Intent to become legal parent by assisted reproduction, consent to jurisdiction, jurisdiction to determine parentage, venue, see Family Code § 7620.
Void voluntary declaration of parentage, conditions, notice, see Family Code § 7573.5.

Research References

Forms
2 California Transactions Forms--Family Law § 5:9.50, Voiding of a Voluntary Declaration of Parentage.
2 California Transactions Forms--Family Law § 7:8.50, Surrogacy Facilitator.

Division 13
ADOPTION

Part	Section
1. Definitions	8500
2. Adoption of Unmarried Minors	8600
3. Adoption of Adults and Married Minors	9300

Cross References

Abandonment and neglect of children, criminal penalties for failure to provide care for minor child, see Penal Code § 270 et seq.
Adoption of alcohol or drug-exposed and HIV positive children, see Welfare and Institutions Code § 16135 et seq.
Aid for adoption of children, see Welfare and Institutions Code § 16115 et seq.
California Community Care Facilities act, private adoption agency, executive director or supervisor qualifications, see Health and Safety Code § 1502.6.
Child defined for purposes of the Probate Code, see Probate Code § 26.
Child support, enforcement of support, Uniform Interstate Family Support Act, see Family Code § 5700.101 et seq.
Child support, parental duty of support, generally, see Family Code § 3900 et seq.
Construction of wills, trusts, and other instruments, rules for interpretation applied to adoptees, see Probate Code § 21115.
County adoption agencies, license, see Welfare and Institutions Code § 16100.
Freedom from parental custody and control, generally, see Family Code § 7800 et seq.
Interstate adoption assistance agreements, see Welfare and Institutions Code § 16170 et seq.
Intestate succession, parent and child relationship, effect of adoption, see Probate Code § 6451.
Liability of parent or guardian for willful misconduct of minors, see Civil Code § 1714.1.
Parent and child relationship,
  Generally, see Family Code § 7500 et seq.
  Defined for purposes of Uniform Parentage Act, see Family Code § 7601.
  Establishing relationship, see Family Code § 7610 et seq.
Parent defined for purposes of the Probate Code, see Probate Code § 54.
Parent or guardian defined, see Family Code § 6903.
Parental authority, termination upon guardianship, marriage, or age of majority, see Family Code § 7505.
Parental rights, termination in adoption proceedings, see Family Code § 7660 et seq.
Post-adoptive sibling contact, jurisdiction over post-adoption agreements, see Welfare and Institutions Code § 366.29.

Part 1
DEFINITIONS

Section
8500. Construction of division.

ADOPTION

Section
8502. "Adoption service provider" defined.
8503. "Adoptive parent" defined.
8506. "Agency adoption" defined.
8509. "Applicant" defined.
8512. "Birth parent" defined.
8513. "County adoption agency" defined.
8514. "Days" defined.
8515. "Delegated county adoption agency" defined.
8518. "Department" defined.
8521. "Full-service adoption agency" defined.
8524. "Independent adoption" defined.
8527. "Intercountry adoption" defined.
8530. "Licensed adoption agency" defined.
8533. "Noncustodial adoption agency" defined.
8539. "Place for adoption" defined.
8542. "Prospective adoptive parent" defined.
8543. "Qualified court investigator" defined.
8545. "Special needs child" defined.
8548. "Stepparent adoption" defined.

§ 8500. Construction of division

Unless the provision or context otherwise requires, the definitions in this part govern the construction of this division. *(Stats.1992, c. 162 (A.B.2650), § 10, operative Jan. 1, 1994.)*

Cross References
Age of majority, see Family Code § 6500 et seq.

Research References
Forms
1B Am. Jur. Pl. & Pr. Forms Adoption § 3, Statutory References.
2 California Transactions Forms--Family Law § 6:2, Governing Law.
2 California Transactions Forms--Family Law § 6:83, Nature of Agency Adoption—Governing Law.

§ 8502. "Adoption service provider" defined

(a) "Adoption service provider" means any of the following:

(1) A licensed private adoption agency.

(2) An individual who has presented satisfactory evidence to the department that the individual is a licensed clinical social worker who also has a minimum of five years of experience providing professional social work services while employed by a licensed California adoption agency or the department.

(3) In a state other than California, or a country other than the United States, an adoption agency licensed or otherwise approved under the laws of that state or country, or an individual who is licensed or otherwise certified as a clinical social worker under the laws of that state or country.

(4) An individual who has presented satisfactory evidence to the department that the individual is a licensed marriage and family therapist who has a minimum of five years of experience providing professional adoption casework services while employed by a licensed California adoption agency or the department. The department shall review the qualifications of each individual to determine if the individual has performed professional adoption casework services for five years as required by this section while employed by a licensed California adoption agency or the department.

(5) An individual who has presented satisfactory evidence to the department that the individual is a licensed professional clinical counselor who has a minimum of five years' experience providing professional adoption casework services while employed by a licensed California adoption agency or the department. The department shall review the credentials of each individual to determine if the individual has performed professional adoption casework services as required by this paragraph.

(b) If, in the case of a birth parent located in California, at least three adoption service providers are not reasonably available, or, in the case of a birth parent located outside of California or outside of the United States who has contacted at least three potential adoption service providers and been unsuccessful in obtaining the services of an adoption service provider who is reasonably available and willing to provide services, independent legal counsel for the birth parent may serve as an adoption service provider pursuant to subdivision (e) of Section 8801.5. "Reasonably available" means that an adoption service provider is all of the following:

(1) Available within five days for an advisement of rights pursuant to Section 8801.5, or within 24 hours for the signing of the placement agreement pursuant to paragraph (3) of subdivision (b) of Section 8801.3.

(2) Within 100 miles of the birth mother.

(3) Available for a cost not exceeding five hundred dollars ($500) to make an advisement of rights and to witness the signing of the placement agreement.

(c) If an attorney acts as an adoption service provider, the fee to make an advisement of rights and to witness the signing of the placement agreement shall not exceed five hundred dollars ($500). *(Added by Stats.1993, c. 758 (S.B.792), § 3, operative Jan. 1, 1995. Amended by Stats.1994, c. 585 (A.B.3336), § 1; Stats.1997, c. 559 (S.B.1121), § 1; Stats.2002, c. 1013 (S.B.2026), § 81; Stats.2004, c. 858 (S.B.1357), § 3; Stats.2018, c. 389 (A.B.2296), § 16, eff. Jan. 1, 2019; Stats.2019, c. 115 (A.B.1817), § 109, eff. Jan. 1, 2020.)*

Cross References
Independent adoptions of unmarried minors, duties of adoption service providers, see Family Code § 8801.7.
Paying or receiving money or thing of value to parent for placement for, or consent to, adoption of child, see Penal Code § 273.
State defined for purposes of this Code, see Family Code § 145.
Unprofessional conduct, effect on licensee or registrant, see Business and Professions Code § 4992.3.

Research References
Forms
2 California Transactions Forms--Family Law § 6:34, Role of Adoption Service Provider.
2 California Transactions Forms--Family Law § 6:40, Structuring the Adoption.

§ 8503. "Adoptive parent" defined

"Adoptive parent" means a person who has obtained an order of adoption of a minor child or, in the case of an adult adoption, an adult. *(Stats.1992, c. 162 (A.B.2650), § 10, operative Jan. 1, 1994.)*

Cross References
Access to records, confidentiality of information compiled to determine status as adoptive parents, see Civil Code § 1798.38.
Adult defined for purposes of this Code, see Family Code § 6501.
Age of majority, see Family Code § 6500 et seq.
Agency adoptions, denial prohibited on basis of race, color or national origin of person or child, see Family Code § 8708.
Disclosure of information, see Family Code § 9200 et seq.
Judgment and order defined for purposes of this Code, see Family Code § 100.
Minor defined for purposes of this Code, see Family Code § 6500.
Parent and child relationship defined for purposes of the Uniform Parentage Act, see Family Code § 7601.
Parent defined for purposes of the Probate Code, see Probate Code § 54.
Person defined for purposes of this Code, see Family Code § 105.

Research References
Forms
2 California Transactions Forms--Family Law § 6:3, Definitions.

§ 8506. "Agency adoption" defined

"Agency adoption" means the adoption of a minor, other than an intercountry adoption, in which the department, county adoption agency, or licensed adoption agency is a party to, or joins in, the adoption petition. *(Stats.1992, c. 162 (A.B.2650), § 10, operative Jan. 1, 1994. Amended by Stats.2012, c. 35 (S.B.1013), § 2, eff. June 27, 2012.)*

Cross References

Adoption Assistance Program, conditions for payment of benefits, see Welfare and Institutions Code § 16120.
Agency adoptions, see Family Code § 8700 et seq.
Department defined, see Family Code § 8518.
Intercountry adoption defined, see Family Code § 8527.
Licensed adoption agency defined, see Family Code § 8530.
Minor defined for purposes of this Code, see Family Code § 6500.

Research References

Forms
2 California Transactions Forms--Family Law § 6:4, Types of Adoptions.
2 California Transactions Forms--Family Law § 6:83, Nature of Agency Adoption—Governing Law.

§ 8509. "Applicant" defined

"Applicant" means a person who has submitted a written application to adopt a child from the department, county adoption agency, or licensed adoption agency and who is being considered by the adoption agency for the adoptive placement of a child. *(Stats.1992, c. 162 (A.B.2650), § 10, operative Jan. 1, 1994. Amended by Stats.2012, c. 35 (S.B.1013), § 3, eff. June 27, 2012.)*

Cross References

Age of majority, see Family Code § 6500 et seq.
Department defined, see Family Code § 8518.
Disclosure of information, see Family Code § 9200 et seq.
Licensed adoption agency defined, see Family Code § 8530.
Person defined for purposes of this Code, see Family Code § 105.

§ 8512. "Birth parent" defined

"Birth parent" means the biological parent or, in the case of a person previously adopted, the adoptive parent. *(Stats.1992, c. 162 (A.B.2650), § 10, operative Jan. 1, 1994.)*

Cross References

Adoptive parent defined, see Family Code § 8503.
Adult adoptions, see Family Code § 9300 et seq.
Advisement of rights, role of counselors, see Family Code § 8801.5.
Disclosure of information, see Family Code § 9200 et seq.
Parent and child relationship defined for purposes of the Uniform Parentage Act, see Family Code § 7601.
Parent defined for purposes of the Probate Code, see Probate Code § 54.
Person defined for purposes of this Code, see Family Code § 105.

Research References

Forms
2 California Transactions Forms--Family Law § 6:3, Definitions.

§ 8513. "County adoption agency" defined

"County adoption agency" means an adoption agency operated by a county or consortium of counties. *(Added by Stats.2012, c. 35 (S.B.1013), § 4, eff. June 27, 2012.)*

Cross References

Resource family approval program, confidentiality of written report, see Welfare and Institutions Code § 16519.555.

§ 8514. "Days" defined

"Days" means calendar days, unless otherwise specified. *(Added by Stats.1994, c. 585 (A.B.3336), § 2.)*

§ 8515. "Delegated county adoption agency" defined

"Delegated county adoption agency" means a county adoption agency that has agreed to provide the services described in Chapter 3 (commencing with Section 8800) of Part 2. *(Stats.1992, c. 162 (A.B.2650), § 10, operative Jan. 1, 1994. Amended by Stats.2012, c. 35 (S.B.1013), § 5, eff. June 27, 2012.)*

Cross References

County defined for purposes of this Code, see Family Code § 67.
Licensed adoption agency defined, see Family Code § 8530.

§ 8518. "Department" defined

"Department" means the State Department of Social Services. *(Stats.1992, c. 162 (A.B.2650), § 10, operative Jan. 1, 1994.)*

Cross References

State defined for purposes of this Code, see Family Code § 145.

§ 8521. "Full-service adoption agency" defined

(a) "Full-service adoption agency" means a licensed or authorized entity engaged in the business of providing adoption services, that does all of the following:

(1) Assumes care, custody, and control of a child through relinquishment of the child to the agency or involuntary termination of parental rights to the child.

(2) Assesses the birth parents, prospective adoptive parents, or child.

(3) Places children for adoption.

(4) Supervises adoptive placements.

(b) Private full-service adoption agencies shall be organized and operated on a nonprofit basis. As a condition of licensure to provide intercountry adoption services, a private full-service adoption agency shall be accredited by the Council on Accreditation, or supervised by an accredited primary provider, or acting as an exempted provider, in compliance with Subpart F (commencing with Section 96.29) of Part 96 of Title 22 of the Code of Federal Regulations. *(Stats.1992, c. 162 (A.B.2650), § 10, operative Jan. 1, 1994. Amended by Stats.2007, c. 583 (S.B.703), § 3; Stats.2012, c. 35 (S.B.1013), § 6, eff. June 27, 2012.)*

Cross References

Birth parent, defined, see Family Code § 8512.
Prospective adoptive parent, defined, see Family Code § 8542.

§ 8524. "Independent adoption" defined

"Independent adoption" means the adoption of a child in which neither the department, county adoption agency, nor agency licensed by the department is a party to, or joins in, the adoption petition. *(Stats.1992, c. 162 (A.B.2650), § 10, operative Jan. 1, 1994. Amended by Stats.2012, c. 35 (S.B.1013), § 7, eff. June 27, 2012.)*

Cross References

Adoption Assistance Program, conditions for payment of benefits, see Welfare and Institutions Code § 16120.
Department defined, see Family Code § 8518.
Independent adoptions, see Family Code § 8800 et seq.
Licensed adoption agency defined, see Family Code § 8530.
Temporary custody of minor in hospital care by peace officer where release of minor to prospective adoptive parent poses an immediate danger, conditions requiring a warrant, see Welfare and Institutions Code § 305.6.

Research References

Forms
2 California Transactions Forms--Family Law § 6:4, Types of Adoptions.

§ 8527. "Intercountry adoption" defined

"Intercountry adoption" means the adoption of a foreign-born child for whom federal law makes a special immigration visa available. Intercountry adoption includes completion of the adop-

§ 8527

tion in the child's native country or completion of the adoption in this state. *(Stats.1992, c. 162 (A.B.2650), § 10, operative Jan. 1, 1994.)*

Cross References

Intercountry adoptions, generally, see Family Code § 8900 et seq.
State defined for purposes of this Code, see Family Code § 145.

Research References

Forms

2 California Transactions Forms--Family Law § 6:139, Overview of Intercountry Adoption.

§ 8530. "Licensed adoption agency" defined

"Licensed adoption agency" means an agency licensed by the department to provide adoption services. *(Stats.1992, c. 162 (A.B. 2650), § 10, operative Jan. 1, 1994. Amended by Stats.2012, c. 35 (S.B.1013), § 8, eff. June 27, 2012.)*

Cross References

Child Abuse and Neglect Reporting Act, adoption agencies, information from child abuse index, see Penal Code § 11170.5.
County defined for purposes of this Code, see Family Code § 67.
Department defined, see Family Code § 8518.
Resource family approval program, confidentiality of written report, see Welfare and Institutions Code § 16519.555.

§ 8533. "Noncustodial adoption agency" defined

(a) "Noncustodial adoption agency" means any licensed entity engaged in the business of providing adoption services, which does all of the following:

(1) Assesses the prospective adoptive parents.

(2) Cooperatively matches children freed for adoption, who are under the care, custody, and control of a licensed adoption agency, for adoption, with assessed and approved prospective adoptive parents.

(3) Cooperatively supervises adoptive placements with a full-service adoption agency, but does not disrupt a placement or remove a child from a placement.

(b) Private noncustodial adoption agencies shall be organized and operated on a nonprofit basis. As a condition of licensure to provide intercountry adoption services, a noncustodial adoption agency shall be accredited by the Council on Accreditation, or supervised by an accredited primary provider, or acting as an exempted provider, in compliance with Subpart F (commencing with Section 96.29) of Part 96 of Title 22 of the Code of Federal Regulations. *(Stats.1992, c. 162 (A.B.2650), § 10, operative Jan. 1, 1994. Amended by Stats.2007, c. 583 (S.B.703), § 4.)*

Cross References

Birth parent defined, see Family Code § 8512.
Full-service adoption agency defined, see Family Code § 8521.
Licensed adoption agency defined, see Family Code § 8530.
Prospective adoptive parent defined, see Family Code § 8542.

§ 8539. "Place for adoption" defined

"Place for adoption" means, in the case of an independent adoption, the selection of a prospective adoptive parent or parents for a child by the birth parent or parents and the completion of an adoptive placement agreement on a form prescribed by the department by the birth parent or parents placing the child with prospective adoptive parents.

This section shall become operative on January 1, 1995. *(Added by Stats.1993, c. 758 (S.B.792), § 4, operative Jan. 1, 1995.)*

Research References

Forms

2 California Transactions Forms--Family Law § 6:3, Definitions.

§ 8542. "Prospective adoptive parent" defined

"Prospective adoptive parent" means a person who has filed or intends to file a petition under Part 2 (commencing with Section 8600) to adopt a child who has been or who is to be placed in the person's physical care or a petition under Part 3 (commencing with Section 9300) to adopt an adult. *(Stats.1992, c. 162 (A.B.2650), § 10, operative Jan. 1, 1994.)*

Cross References

Adoption facilitators, information provided by birth parents reported to prospective adoptive parent, see Family Code § 8628.
Adult defined for purposes of this Code, see Family Code § 6501.
Age of majority, see Family Code § 6500 et seq.
Appearance before court,
    Adult adoptions, see Family Code § 9324.
    Independent adoptions, see Family Code § 8823.
    Intercountry adoptions, see Family Code § 8913.
    Stepparent adoptions, see Family Code § 9007.
Consideration of criminal record, fingerprinting,
    Independent adoptions, see Family Code § 8811.
    Intercountry adoptions, see Family Code § 8908.
Dependency proceedings, eligibility assessment of prospective adoptive parent, see Welfare and Institutions Code §§ 361.5 et seq., 727.31.
Disclosure of information, see Family Code § 9200 et seq.
Independent adoptions,
    Attorney's fees, medical fees and expenses, counseling fees or living expenses of birth mother, request for payment, see Family Code § 8812.
    Preplacement evaluations, see Family Code § 8811.5.
    Selection of prospective adoptive parent, see Family Code § 8801.
Person defined for purposes of this Code, see Family Code § 105.

§ 8543. "Qualified court investigator" defined

"Qualified court investigator" means a superior court investigator with the same minimum qualifications as a probation officer or county welfare worker designated to conduct stepparent adoption investigations in stepparent adoption proceedings and proceedings to declare a minor free from parental custody and control. *(Added by Stats.1993, c. 219 (A.B.1500), § 185.)*

Cross References

County defined for purposes of this Code, see Family Code § 67.
Minor defined for purposes of this Code, see Family Code § 6500.
Proceeding defined for purposes of this Code, see Family Code § 110.

§ 8545. "Special needs child" defined

"Special needs child" means a child for whom all of the following are true:

(a) It has been determined that the child cannot or should not be returned to the parent's home, as evidenced by a petition for termination of parental rights, a court order terminating parental rights, or a signed relinquishment.

(b) The child has at least one of the following characteristics that is a barrier to adoption:

(1) Adoptive placement without financial assistance is unlikely because of membership in a sibling group that should remain intact, or by virtue of race, ethnicity, color, language, age of three years or older, or parental background of a medical or behavioral nature that can be determined to adversely affect the development of the child.

(2) Adoptive placement without financial assistance is unlikely because the child has a mental, physical, emotional, or medical disability that has been certified by a licensed professional competent to make an assessment and operating within the scope of that person's profession. This paragraph shall also apply to children with a developmental disability as defined in subdivision (a) of Section 4512 of the Welfare and Institutions Code, including those deter-

mined to require out-of-home nonmedical care as described in Section 11464 of the Welfare and Institutions Code.

(c) The need for adoption subsidy is evidenced by an unsuccessful search for an adoptive home to take the child without financial assistance, as documented in the case file of the prospective adoptive child. The requirement for this search shall be waived when it would be against the best interest of the child because of the existence of significant emotional ties with prospective adoptive parents while in the care of these persons as a foster child. *(Stats.1992, c. 162 (A.B.2650), § 10, operative Jan. 1, 1994. Amended by Stats.2009, c. 339 (S.B.597), § 1; Stats.2019, c. 115 (A.B.1817), § 110, eff. Jan. 1, 2020.)*

Cross References

Adoption of alcohol or drug-exposed and HIV positive children, see Welfare and Institutions Code § 16135 et seq.
Age of majority, see Family Code § 6500 et seq.
Aid for adoption of children, see Welfare and Institutions Code § 16115 et seq.
Foster care placement, sibling groups, preference for placement together and visitation, see Welfare and Institutions Code § 16002.
Interstate adoption assistance agreements, see Welfare and Institutions Code § 16170 et seq.
Out-of-home placement, case plan provisions for sibling visitation and relationship development, see Welfare and Institutions Code § 16501.1.
Report of special needs of child to be adopted provided to adoptive parents, see Family Code § 8733.

Research References

Forms

1 California Transactions Forms—Family Law § 3:45, Discretionary Additional Child Support.
2 California Transactions Forms—Family Law § 6:23, Adoption Tax Credit and Exclusion.

§ 8548. "Stepparent adoption" defined

"Stepparent adoption" means an adoption of a child by a stepparent where one birth parent retains custody and control of the child. *(Stats.1992, c. 162 (A.B.2650), § 10, operative Jan. 1, 1994.)*

Cross References

Age of majority, see Family Code § 6500 et seq.
Birth parent defined, see Family Code § 8512.
Disclosure of information, see Family Code § 9200 et seq.
Stepparent adoptions, generally, see Family Code § 9000 et seq.

Research References

Forms

2 California Transactions Forms—Family Law § 6:2, Governing Law.
2 California Transactions Forms—Family Law § 6:4, Types of Adoptions.
2 California Transactions Forms—Family Law § 6:104, Nature and Purpose of Stepparent Adoption.

Part 2

ADOPTION OF UNMARRIED MINORS

Chapter	Section
1. General Provisions	8600
1.5. Adoption Facilitators	8623
2. Agency Adoptions	8700
2.5. Adoptions by Relative Caregivers or Foster Parents	8730
3. Independent Adoptions	8800
4. Intercountry Adoptions	8900
5. Stepparent Adoptions	9000
6. Vacation of Adoption	9100
7. Disclosure of Information	9200
8. Adoption Proceedings: Conflict of Laws	9210

Cross References

Relinquishment or consent to adoption by father, notice and rights of mother under these provisions, see Family Code § 7661.
Relinquishment or consent to adoption by mother, notice and rights of presumed father under these provisions, see Family Code § 7660.

CHAPTER 1. GENERAL PROVISIONS

Section	
8600.	Children eligible for adoption.
8600.5.	Tribal customary adoption not applicable to this part.
8601.	Adoptive parent; age requirements; exception.
8601.5.	Nunc pro tunc entry of orders of adoption.
8602.	Consent of child.
8603.	Married adoptive parent; consent of spouse.
8604.	Birth parents; presumed fathers; consent; temporary custody orders.
8605.	Children without presumed father; consent of mother required.
8606.	Consent of birth parents not required in specified cases.
8606.5.	Consent to adoption of Indian children.
8607.	Forms; contents.
8608.	Form and content of medical reports on child and biological parents; adoption of regulations.
8609.	Advertisement of placement or other adoptive services; unlicensed persons or organizations; misdemeanor.
8609.5.	Location of filing an adoption request for a nondependent minor.
8610.	Accounting report; filing by petitioners; contents; application.
8611.	Hearings.
8612.	Examination by court; agreement; execution; order of adoption.
8613.	Prospective adoptive parent in military, or in service for governmental entity, red cross, or charitable or religious organization; appearance by counsel; execution of agreement; deposition; adoption order.
8613.5.	Waiver of personal appearance of prospective adoptive parent.
8613.7.	Notice of eligibility for reduced-cost or no-cost health coverage.
8614.	Certificate of adoption.
8615.	New birth certificate.
8616.	Legal relationship of parent and child.
8616.5.	Postadoption contact agreements.
8617.	Existing parents' responsibilities toward child; cessation; waiver prior to finalization of adoption; application of section.
8618.	Adopted child may take adoptive parent's family name.
8619.	Children of Indian ancestry; information; certificate of degree of Indian blood.
8619.5.	Children of Indian ancestry; vacated or set aside final decrees or voluntary return by adoptive parents; return of custody.
8620.	Determination of identity as Indian child for purposes of relinquishment or adoption placement; procedures; civil penalty for violations.
8621.	Regulations.
8622.	Service limitations; notice.

§ 8600. Children eligible for adoption

An unmarried minor may be adopted by an adult as provided in this part. *(Stats.1992, c. 162 (A.B.2650), § 10, operative Jan. 1, 1994.)*

§ 8600

Cross References

Adoptive parents, criminal record, see Penal Code § 11105.3.
Age of majority, see Family Code § 6500 et seq.
Birth parents, money or benefits for consent or placement of children, see Penal Code § 273.
Disclosure of information, see Family Code § 9200 et seq.
Foster homes, alternative methods, see Welfare and Institutions Code § 396 et seq.
Juvenile delinquents and dependents,
   Jurisdiction, see Welfare and Institutions Code § 366.3.
   Priorities and preferences, foster parents and relatives, see Welfare and Institutions Code §§ 361.2 et seq., 366.26.
Minor defined for purposes of this Code, see Family Code § 6500.
Priorities and preferences, adoptive parents, see Welfare and Institutions Code §§ 361.2 et seq., 366.26.

Research References

Forms

2 California Transactions Forms--Family Law § 5:6, Obtaining Rights Through Adoption.
2 California Transactions Forms--Family Law § 6:2, Governing Law.
2 California Transactions Forms--Family Law § 6:6, Who May Adopt.
2 California Transactions Forms--Family Law § 6:47, Matters to Consider in Drafting Petition for Independent Adoption of Unmarried Minor.
2 California Transactions Forms--Family Law § 6:112, Form Drafting Considerations.
West's California Code Forms, Family § 7660, Comment Overview—Termination of Parental Rights in Adoption Proceedings.
West's California Code Forms, Family § 8600, Comment Overview—Adoption of Unmarried Minors.
West's California Code Forms, Family § 9100, Comment Overview—Vacation of Adoption.

§ 8600.5. Tribal customary adoption not applicable to this part

Tribal customary adoption as defined in Section 366.24 of the Welfare and Institutions Code and as applied to Indian Children who are dependents of the court, does not apply to this part. *(Added by Stats.2009, c. 287 (A.B.1325), § 1, operative July 1, 2010. Amended by Stats.2012, c. 35 (S.B.1013), § 9, eff. June 27, 2012.)*

Research References

Forms

2 California Transactions Forms--Family Law § 6:143, Overview of Indian Child Welfare Act (ICWA).

§ 8601. Adoptive parent; age requirements; exception

(a) Except as otherwise provided in subdivision (b), a prospective adoptive parent or parents shall be at least 10 years older than the child.

(b) If the court is satisfied that the adoption of a child by a stepparent, or by a sister, brother, aunt, uncle, or first cousin and, if that person is married, by that person and that person's spouse, is in the best interest of the parties and is in the public interest, it may approve the adoption without regard to the ages of the child and the prospective adoptive parent or parents. *(Stats.1992, c. 162 (A.B. 2650), § 10, operative Jan. 1, 1994.)*

Cross References

Adoptive parents, criminal record, see Penal Code § 11105.3.
Age of majority, see Family Code § 6500 et seq.
Birth parents, money or benefits for consent or placement of children, see Penal Code § 273.
Foster homes, alternative methods, see Welfare and Institutions Code § 396 et seq.
Juvenile delinquents and dependents,
   Jurisdiction, see Welfare and Institutions Code § 366.3.
   Priorities and preferences, foster parents and relatives, see Welfare and Institutions Code §§ 361.2 et seq., 366.26.
Person defined for purposes of this Code, see Family Code § 105.
Priorities and preferences, adoptive parents, see Welfare and Institutions Code §§ 361.2 et seq., 366.26.
Prospective adoptive parent, defined, see Family Code § 8542.

References to husband, wife, spouses and married persons, persons included for purposes of this Code, see Family Code § 11.
Siblings, release of information on, see Family Code § 9205.
Stepparent adoptions,
   Consent of birth parents, see Family Code § 9003.
   Investigations, see Family Code § 9001.
   Petition, requisites, see Family Code § 9000.
   Withdrawal of consent by birth parents, see Family Code § 9005.

Research References

Forms

2 California Transactions Forms--Family Law § 5:6, Obtaining Rights Through Adoption.
2 California Transactions Forms--Family Law § 6:6, Who May Adopt.
2 California Transactions Forms--Family Law § 6:7, Who May be Adopted.
2 California Transactions Forms--Family Law § 6:47, Matters to Consider in Drafting Petition for Independent Adoption of Unmarried Minor.
1¶ 1 Nichols Cyclopedia of Legal Forms Annotated § 7:4, Statutory Provisions—Who May be Adopted.
West's California Code Forms, Family § 8600, Comment Overview—Adoption of Unmarried Minors.

§ 8601.5. Nunc pro tunc entry of orders of adoption

(a) A court may issue an order of adoption and declare that it shall be entered nunc pro tunc when it will serve public policy and the best interests of the child, such as cases where adoption finalization has been delayed beyond the child's 18th birthday due to factors beyond the control of the prospective adoptive family and the proposed adoptee.

(b) The request for nunc pro tunc entry of the order shall be stated in the adoption request or an amendment thereto, and shall set forth specific facts in support thereof.

(c) To the extent that a child's eligibility for any publicly funded benefit program is or could be altered by the entry of an order of adoption, the change in eligibility shall not be determined as of the nunc pro tunc date, but shall be determined as of the date of the adoption finalization hearing.

(d) The nunc pro tunc date shall not precede the date upon which the parental rights of the birth parent or parents were initially terminated, whether voluntarily or involuntarily. *(Added by Stats. 2011, c. 462 (A.B.687), § 6.)*

Research References

Forms

West's California Judicial Council Forms ADOPT-200, Adoption Request.
West's California Judicial Council Forms ADOPT-215, Adoption Order (Also Available in Spanish).

§ 8602. Consent of child

The consent of a child, if over the age of 12 years, is necessary to the child's adoption. *(Stats.1992, c. 162 (A.B.2650), § 10, operative Jan. 1, 1994.)*

Cross References

Age of majority, see Family Code § 6500 et seq.
Birth parents, money or benefits for consent or placement of children, see Penal Code § 273.

Research References

Forms

1B Am. Jur. Pl. & Pr. Forms Adoption § 94, Person Other Than Natural Parent—Child.
1B Am. Jur. Pl. & Pr. Forms Adoption § 126, Statutory References.
2 California Transactions Forms--Family Law § 6:7, Who May be Adopted.
2 California Transactions Forms--Family Law § 6:8, Consent for Adoption of Unmarried Minor.
2 California Transactions Forms--Family Law § 6:47, Matters to Consider in Drafting Petition for Independent Adoption of Unmarried Minor.
West's California Code Forms, Family § 8600, Comment Overview—Adoption of Unmarried Minors.

West's California Code Forms, Family § 8612 Form 2, Adoption Agreement.
West's California Judicial Council Forms ADOPT-210, Adoption Agreement (Also Available in Spanish).

§ 8603. Married adoptive parent; consent of spouse

(a) A married person, not lawfully separated from the person's spouse, shall not adopt a child without the consent of the spouse, provided that the spouse is capable of giving that consent.

(b) The consent of the spouse shall not establish any parental rights or responsibilities on the part of the consenting spouse unless that person has consented to adopt the child in a writing filed with the court and is named in the final decree as an adoptive parent. The court shall not name the consenting spouse as an adoptive parent in the final decree unless the consenting spouse has filed a written consent to adopt the child with the court and has an approved adoption home study.

(c) The court may dispense with the consent of a spouse who cannot be located after diligent search, or a spouse determined by the court to lack the capacity to consent. A spouse for whom consent was dispensed shall not be named as an adoptive parent in the final decree. (Stats.1992, c. 162 (A.B.2650), § 10, operative Jan. 1, 1994. Amended by Stats.2014, c. 763 (A.B.1701), § 7, eff. Jan. 1, 2015; Stats.2019, c. 115 (A.B.1817), § 111, eff. Jan. 1, 2020.)

Cross References

Adoptive parents, criminal record, see Penal Code § 11105.3.
Age of majority, see Family Code § 6500 et seq.
Birth parents, money or benefits for consent or placement of children, see Penal Code § 273.
Foster homes, alternative methods, see Welfare and Institutions Code § 396 et seq.
Juvenile delinquents and dependents, jurisdiction, see Welfare and Institutions Code § 366.3.
Juvenile delinquents and dependents, priorities and preferences, foster parents and relatives, see Welfare and Institutions Code §§ 361.2 et seq., 366.26.
Marriage, generally, see Family Code § 300 et seq.
Person defined for purposes of this Code, see Family Code § 105.
Priorities and preferences, adoptive parents, see Welfare and Institutions Code §§ 361.2 et seq., 366.26.
References to husband, wife, spouses and married persons, persons included for purposes of this Code, see Family Code § 11.

Research References

Forms

2 California Transactions Forms--Family Law § 6:6, Who May Adopt.
2 California Transactions Forms--Family Law § 6:8, Consent for Adoption of Unmarried Minor.
2 California Transactions Forms--Family Law § 6:105, Consent of Custodial Parent.
2 California Transactions Forms--Family Law § 6:115, Consent to Stepparent Adoption by Custodial Parent.
1¶ 1 Nichols Cyclopedia of Legal Forms Annotated § 7:4, Statutory Provisions—Who May be Adopted.
West's California Code Forms, Family § 8600, Comment Overview—Adoption of Unmarried Minors.

§ 8604. Birth parents; presumed fathers; consent; temporary custody orders

(a) Except as provided in subdivision (b), a child having a presumed father under Section 7611 shall not be adopted without the consent of the child's birth parents, if living. The consent of a presumed father is not required for the child's adoption unless the person became a presumed father as described in Chapter 1 (commencing with Section 7540) or Chapter 3 (commencing with Section 7570) of Part 2 of Division 12, or subdivision (a), (b), or (c) of Section 7611 before the mother's relinquishment or consent becomes irrevocable or before the mother's parental rights have been terminated.

(b) If one birth parent has been awarded custody by judicial order, or has custody by agreement of both parents, and the other birth parent for a period of one year willfully fails to communicate with, and to pay for, the care, support, and education of the child when able to do so, then the birth parent having sole custody may consent to the adoption, but only after the birth parent not having custody has been served with a copy of a citation in the manner provided by law for the service of a summons in a civil action that requires the birth parent not having custody to appear at the time and place set for the appearance in court under Section 8718, 8823, 8913, or 9007.

(c) Failure of a birth parent to pay for the care, support, and education of the child for the period of one year or failure of a birth parent to communicate with the child for the period of one year is prima facie evidence that the failure was willful and without lawful excuse. If the birth parent or parents have made only token efforts to support or communicate with the child, the court may disregard those token efforts.

(d)(1) If the birth mother of a child for whom there is not a presumed father leaves the child in the physical care of a licensed private adoption agency, in the physical care of a prospective adoptive parent who has an approved preplacement evaluation or private agency adoption home study, or in the hospital after designating a licensed private adoption agency or an approved prospective adoptive parent in a signed document, completed with a hospital social worker, adoption service provider, licensed private adoption agency worker, notary, or attorney, but fails to sign a placement agreement, consent, or relinquishment for adoption, the approved prospective adoptive parent or the licensed private adoption agency may apply for, and the court may issue, a temporary custody order placing the child in the care and custody of the applicant.

(2) A temporary custody order issued pursuant to this subdivision shall include all of the following:

(A) A requirement that the applicant keep the court informed of the child's residence at all times.

(B) A requirement that the child shall not be removed from the state or concealed within the state.

(C) The expiration date of the order, which shall not be more than six months after the order is issued.

(3) A temporary custody order issued pursuant to this subdivision may be voided upon the birth mother's request to have the child returned to the birth mother's care and custody. (Stats.1992, c. 162 (A.B.2650), § 10, operative Jan. 1, 1994. Amended by Stats.2005, c. 627 (S.B.302), § 3; Stats.2007, c. 47 (S.B.313), § 4; Stats.2014, c. 763 (A.B.1701), § 8, eff. Jan. 1, 2015; Stats.2019, c. 115 (A.B.1817), § 112, eff. Jan. 1, 2020.)

Cross References

Adoptive parents, criminal record, see Penal Code § 11105.3.
Age of majority, see Family Code § 6500 et seq.
Appeal from order requiring or dispensing with father's consent to adoption, see Family Code § 7669.
Birth parent defined, see Family Code § 8512.
Birth parents, money or benefits for consent or placement of children, see Penal Code § 273.
Child support, generally, see Family Code § 3585 et seq.
Custody of children, generally, see Family Code § 3000 et seq.
Duty of parent to support child, see Family Code § 3900 et seq.
Foster homes, alternative methods, see Welfare and Institutions Code § 396 et seq.
Judgment and order defined for purposes of this Code, see Family Code § 100.
Juvenile delinquents and dependents,
  Jurisdiction, see Welfare and Institutions Code § 366.3.
  Priorities and preferences, foster parents and relatives, see Welfare and Institutions Code §§ 361.2 et seq., 366.26.
Order, term including decree, see Family Code § 100.
Parent and child relationship, generally, see Family Code § 7500 et seq.
Prima facie evidence, see Evidence Code § 602.
Priorities and preferences, adoptive parents, see Welfare and Institutions Code §§ 361.2 et seq., 366.26.

§ 8604

Proceedings relating to freedom from parental custody and control, application of part, see Family Code § 7808.
Relinquishment or consent to adoption by father or mother, notice and rights, see Family Code § 7660.
Right to custody of minor child, see Family Code § 3020 et seq.
Support defined for purposes of this Code, see Family Code § 150.

Research References

Forms

2 California Transactions Forms--Family Law § 6:3, Definitions.
2 California Transactions Forms--Family Law § 6:8, Consent for Adoption of Unmarried Minor.
2 California Transactions Forms--Family Law § 6:47, Matters to Consider in Drafting Petition for Independent Adoption of Unmarried Minor.
2 California Transactions Forms--Family Law § 6:72, Petition to Terminate Parental Rights of Alleged Father.
2 California Transactions Forms--Family Law § 6:107, Adoption Without Consent of Noncustodial Parent.
West's California Code Forms, Family § 8600, Comment Overview—Adoption of Unmarried Minors.
West's California Judicial Council Forms ADOPT–200, Adoption Request.

§ 8605. Children without presumed father; consent of mother required

A child not having a presumed father under Section 7611 may not be adopted without the consent of the child's mother, if living. *(Stats.1992, c. 162 (A.B.2650), § 10, operative Jan. 1, 1994.)*

Cross References

Adoptive parents, criminal record, see Penal Code § 11105.3.
Age of majority, see Family Code § 6500 et seq.
Birth parents, money or benefits for consent or placement of children, see Penal Code § 273.
Blood tests to determine paternity, see Family Code § 7550 et seq.
Child of wife cohabiting with her husband, presumptions, see Family Code §§ 7500, 7501.
Determination of parent and child relationship, see Family Code § 7630 et seq.
Foster homes, alternative methods, see Welfare and Institutions Code § 396 et seq.
Juvenile delinquents and dependents, jurisdiction, see Welfare and Institutions Code § 366.3.
Parent and child relationship, generally, see Family Code § 7500 et seq.
Priorities and preferences, adoptive or foster parents and relatives, see Welfare and Institutions Code §§ 361.2 et seq., 366.26.
Proceedings relating to freedom from parental custody and control, application of part, see Family Code § 7808.
Right to custody of minor child, see Family Code § 3020 et seq.
Uniform Parentage Act, see Family Code § 7600 et seq.

Research References

Forms

2 California Transactions Forms--Family Law § 6:3, Definitions.
2 California Transactions Forms--Family Law § 6:8, Consent for Adoption of Unmarried Minor.
2 California Transactions Forms--Family Law § 6:40, Structuring the Adoption.
2 California Transactions Forms--Family Law § 6:47, Matters to Consider in Drafting Petition for Independent Adoption of Unmarried Minor.
2 California Transactions Forms--Family Law § 6:72, Petition to Terminate Parental Rights of Alleged Father.
1¶ 1 Nichols Cyclopedia of Legal Forms Annotated § 7:5, Statutory Provisions—Consent to Adoption.

§ 8606. Consent of birth parents not required in specified cases

Notwithstanding Sections 8604 and 8605, the consent of a birth parent is not necessary in the following cases:

(a) Where the birth parent has been judicially deprived of the custody and control of the child (1) by a court order declaring the child to be free from the custody and control of either or both birth parents pursuant to Part 4 (commencing with Section 7800) of Division 12 of this code, or Section 366.25 or 366.26 of the Welfare and Institutions Code, or (2) by a similar order of a court of another jurisdiction, pursuant to a law of that jurisdiction authorizing the order.

(b) Where the birth parent has, in a judicial proceeding in another jurisdiction, voluntarily surrendered the right to the custody and control of the child pursuant to a law of that jurisdiction providing for the surrender.

(c) Where the birth parent has deserted the child without provision for identification of the child.

(d) Where the birth parent has relinquished the child for adoption as provided in Section 8700.

(e) Where the birth parent has relinquished the child for adoption to a licensed or authorized child-placing agency in another jurisdiction pursuant to the law of that jurisdiction. *(Stats.1992, c. 162 (A.B.2650), § 10, operative Jan. 1, 1994.)*

Cross References

Abandoned children, proceedings for freedom from parental custody and control, see Family Code § 7822.
Abandonment and neglect of children, see Penal Code § 270 et seq.
Adoptive parents, criminal record, see Penal Code § 11105.3.
Age of majority, see Family Code § 6500 et seq.
Birth parent, defined, see Family Code § 8512.
Birth parents, money or benefits for consent or placement of children, see Penal Code § 273.
Child support, generally, see Family Code § 3900 et seq.
Court-ordered child support, see Family Code § 4000 et seq.
Custody of children, generally, see Family Code § 3000 et seq.
Emancipation of minors, see Family Code § 7000 et seq.
Foster homes, alternative methods, see Welfare and Institutions Code § 396 et seq.
Freedom from parental custody and control, see Family Code § 7800 et seq.
Judgment and order defined for purposes of this Code, see Family Code § 100.
Juvenile delinquents and dependents,
  Jurisdiction, see Welfare and Institutions Code § 366.3.
  Priorities and preferences, foster parents and relatives, see Welfare and Institutions Code §§ 361.2 et seq., 366.26.
Licensed adoption agency defined, see Family Code § 8530.
Parent and child relationship, generally, see Family Code § 7500 et seq.
Priorities and preferences, adoptive parents, see Welfare and Institutions Code §§ 361.2 et seq., 366.26.
Proceeding defined for purposes of this Code, see Family Code § 110.
Proceedings relating to freedom from parental custody and control, application of part, see Family Code § 7808.
Prospective adoptive parent, defined, see Family Code § 8542.
Support of minor children, see Family Code § 3900 et seq.

Research References

Forms

2 California Transactions Forms--Family Law § 6:8, Consent for Adoption of Unmarried Minor.
West's California Judicial Council Forms ADOPT–200, Adoption Request.
West's California Judicial Council Forms ADOPT–210, Adoption Agreement (Also Available in Spanish).

§ 8606.5. Consent to adoption of Indian children

(a) Notwithstanding any other section in this part, and in accordance with Section 1913 of the Indian Child Welfare Act (25 U.S.C. Sec. 1901 et seq.), consent to adoption given by an Indian child's parent is not valid unless both of the following occur:

(1) The consent is executed in writing at least 10 days after the child's birth and recorded before a judge.

(2) The judge certifies that the terms and consequences of the consent were fully explained in detail in English and were fully understood by the parent or that they were interpreted into a language that the parent understood.

(b) The parent of an Indian child may withdraw consent to adoption for any reason at any time prior to the entry of a final decree of adoption and the child shall be returned to the parent.

(c) After the entry of a final decree of adoption of an Indian child, the Indian child's parent may withdraw consent to the adoption upon the grounds that consent was obtained through fraud or duress and may petition the court to vacate the decree. Upon a finding that consent was obtained through fraud or duress, the court shall vacate the decree and return the child to the parent, provided that no adoption that has been effective for at least two years may be invalidated unless otherwise permitted under state law. *(Added by Stats.2006, c. 838 (S.B.678), § 8. Amended by Stats.2019, c. 115 (A.B.1817), § 113, eff. Jan. 1, 2020.)*

Research References

Forms

2 California Transactions Forms--Family Law § 6:143, Overview of Indian Child Welfare Act (ICWA).
2 California Transactions Forms--Family Law § 6:148, Rights of Indian Parents of Indian Children.
2 California Transactions Forms--Family Law § 6:156, Consent to Termination of Parental Rights and Certification—Adoption of an Indian Child [Form Adopt-225].

§ 8607. Forms; contents

All forms adopted by the department authorizing the release of an infant from a health facility to the custody of persons other than the person entitled to custody of the child pursuant to Section 3010 and authorizing these other persons to obtain medical care for the infant shall contain a statement in boldface type delineating the various types of adoptions available, the birth parents' rights with regard thereto, including, but not limited to, rights with regard to revocation of consent to adoption, and a statement regarding the authority of the court under Part 4 (commencing with Section 7800) of Division 12 to declare the child abandoned by the birth parent or parents. *(Stats.1992, c. 162 (A.B.2650), § 10, operative Jan. 1, 1994.)*

Cross References

Abandoned children, authority of court to declare child placed for adoption without required consent abandoned, see Family Code § 7822.
Abandonment and neglect of children, see Penal Code § 270 et seq.
Agency adoptions, rescission of relinquishment for adoption by birth parent, see Family Code § 8700.
Birth parent defined, see Family Code § 8512.
Department defined, see Family Code § 8518.
Independent adoptions, revocation of consent by birth parents, see Family Code § 8814.5.
Person defined for purposes of this Code, see Family Code § 105.

§ 8608. Form and content of medical reports on child and biological parents; adoption of regulations

(a) The department shall adopt regulations specifying the form and content of the reports required by Sections 8706, 8817, and 8909. In addition to any other material that may be required by the department, the form shall include inquiries designed to elicit information on any illness, disease, or defect of a genetic or hereditary nature.

(b) All county adoption agencies and licensed adoption agencies shall cooperate with and assist the department in devising a plan that will effectuate the effective and discreet transmission to adoptees or prospective adoptive parents of pertinent medical information reported to the department, county adoption agency, or licensed adoption agency, upon the request of the person reporting the medical information. *(Stats.1992, c. 162 (A.B.2650), § 10, operative Jan. 1, 1994. Amended by Stats.2012, c. 35 (S.B.1013), § 10, eff. June 27, 2012.)*

Cross References

Confidentiality of medical information, exemptions from limitations, see Civil Code § 56.30.
Department defined, see Family Code § 8518.
Disclosure of information, see Family Code § 9200 et seq.
Licensed adoption agency defined, see Family Code § 8530.
Person defined for purposes of this Code, see Family Code § 105.
Prospective adoptive parent, defined, see Family Code § 8542.
Similar provisions, see Family Code § 9202.

§ 8609. Advertisement of placement or other adoptive services; unlicensed persons or organizations; misdemeanor

(a) Any person or organization that, without holding a valid and unrevoked license to place children for adoption issued by the department, advertises in any periodical or newspaper, by radio, or other public medium, that he, she, or it will place children for adoption, or accept, supply, provide, or obtain children for adoption, or that causes any advertisement to be published in or by any public medium soliciting, requesting, or asking for any child or children for adoption is guilty of a misdemeanor.

(b) Any person, other than a birth parent, or any organization, association, or corporation that, without holding a valid and unrevoked license to place children for adoption issued by the department, places any child for adoption is guilty of a misdemeanor. *(Stats.1992, c. 162 (A.B.2650), § 10, operative Jan. 1, 1994.)*

Cross References

Birth parent, defined, see Family Code § 8512.
Department defined, see Family Code § 8518.
Issuance of license to county adoption agency, see Welfare and Institutions Code § 16100.
Misdemeanor, see Penal Code §§ 17, 19, 19.2.
Person defined for purposes of this Code, see Family Code § 105.
Reimbursement to county for cost of child care prior to adoption, see Welfare and Institutions Code § 16105.

Research References

Forms

2 California Transactions Forms--Family Law § 6:2, Governing Law.

§ 8609.5. Location of filing an adoption request for a nondependent minor

An adoption request for the adoption or readoption of a nondependent minor may be filed with the court in the county in which one of the following applies:

(a) The petitioner resides.

(b) The child was born or resides at the time of filing.

(c) An office of the agency that placed the child or is filing the petition for adoption is located.

(d) An office of the department or a public adoption agency that is investigating the petition is located.

(e) The county in which a placing birth parent or parents resided when the adoptive placement agreement, consent, or relinquishment was signed.

(f) The county in which a placing birth parent or parents resided when the petition was filed.

(g) The county in which the child was freed for adoption. *(Added by Stats.2012, c. 638 (A.B.1757), § 6. Amended by Stats.2022, c. 159 (A.B.2495), § 2, eff. Jan. 1, 2023.)*

Cross References

Intercounty adoptions, petition for adoption, notification of department, contents, guardianship petitions, order of adoption, see Family Code § 8912.
Petition for adoption, content, guardianship petition, and order of adoption, see Family Code § 8714.
Petition for adoption, contents and order of adoption, see Family Code § 8802.

§ 8610. Accounting report; filing by petitioners; contents; application

(a) The petitioners in a proceeding for adoption of a child shall file with the court a full accounting report of all disbursements of anything of value made or agreed to be made by them or on their

§ 8610

behalf in connection with the birth of the child, the placement of the child with the petitioners, any medical or hospital care received by the child's birth mother or by the child in connection with the child's birth, any other expenses of either birth parent, or the adoption. The accounting report shall be made under penalty of perjury and shall be submitted to the court on or before the date set for the hearing on the adoption petition, unless the court grants an extension of time.

(b) The accounting report shall be itemized in detail and shall show the services relating to the adoption or to the placement of the child for adoption that were received by the petitioners, by either birth parent, by the child, or by any other person for whom payment was made by or on behalf of the petitioners. The report shall also include the dates of each payment, the names and addresses of each attorney, physician and surgeon, hospital, licensed adoption agency, or other person or organization who received any funds of the petitioners in connection with the adoption or the placement of the child with them, or participated in any way in the handling of those funds, either directly or indirectly.

(c) This section does not apply to an adoption by a stepparent where one birth parent or adoptive parent retains custody and control of the child. *(Stats.1992, c. 162 (A.B.2650), § 10, operative Jan. 1, 1994.)*

Cross References

Adoptive parent, defined, see Family Code § 8503.
Adoptive parents, criminal record, see Family Code §§ 8712, 8811; Penal Code § 11105.3.
Attorney's fees, medical fees and expenses, counseling fees or living expenses of birth mother, request for payment, see Family Code § 8812.
Birth parent, defined, see Family Code § 8512.
Disclosure of information, see Family Code § 9200 et seq.
Licensed adoption agency defined, see Family Code § 8530.
Person defined for purposes of this Code, see Family Code § 105.
Petitioner defined for purposes of this Code, see Family Code § 126.
Proceeding defined for purposes of this Code, see Family Code § 110.

Research References

Forms

2 California Transactions Forms--Family Law § 6:14, Accounting Report.
2 California Transactions Forms--Family Law § 6:25, Matters to Consider in Preparing Accounting Report [Fam. Code, §8610].
2 California Transactions Forms--Family Law § 6:44, Documentation and Final Hearing.
2 California Transactions Forms--Family Law § 6:54, Request by Birth Parent for Financial Assistance.
2 California Transactions Forms--Family Law § 6:83, Nature of Agency Adoption—Governing Law.
2 California Transactions Forms--Family Law § 6:90, Adoptive Placement Agreement.
2 California Transactions Forms--Family Law § 6:112, Form Drafting Considerations.
West's California Code Forms, Family § 8600, Comment Overview—Adoption of Unmarried Minors.
West's California Judicial Council Forms ADOPT–230, Adoption Expenses.

§ 8611. Hearings

All court hearings in an adoption proceeding shall be held in private, and the court shall exclude all persons except the officers of the court, the parties, their witnesses, counsel, and representatives of the agencies present to perform their official duties under the law governing adoptions. *(Stats.1992, c. 162 (A.B.2650), § 10, operative Jan. 1, 1994.)*

Cross References

Disclosure of information, see Family Code § 9200 et seq.
Person defined for purposes of this Code, see Family Code § 105.
Private trial, see Family Code § 214.
Proceeding defined for purposes of this Code, see Family Code § 110.
Public sittings of courts of justice, see Code of Civil Procedure § 124.
Superior court, jurisdiction, see Family Code § 200.

Withdrawal of consent, birth parents, hearing, see Family Code §§ 8815, 9005.
Withdrawal or denial of petition, hearing, see Family Code §§ 8720, 8805, 8822, 8917, 8918.

Research References

Forms

2 California Transactions Forms--Family Law § 6:12, Conduct of Hearing.
2 California Transactions Forms--Family Law § 6:111, Hearing on Stepparent Adoption Petition.

§ 8612. Examination by court; agreement; execution; order of adoption

(a) The court shall examine all persons appearing before it pursuant to this part. The examination of each person shall be conducted separately but within the physical presence of every other person unless the court, in its discretion, orders otherwise.

(b) The prospective adoptive parent or parents shall execute and acknowledge an agreement in writing that the child will be treated in all respects as their lawful child.

(c) If satisfied that the interest of the child will be promoted by the adoption, the court may make and enter an order of adoption of the child by the prospective adoptive parent or parents. *(Stats.1992, c. 162 (A.B.2650), § 10, operative Jan. 1, 1994.)*

Cross References

Adoptive parent defined, see Family Code § 8503.
Best interests of child, presumption of agency decisions, see Family Code § 8704.
Judgment and order defined for purposes of this Code, see Family Code § 100.
Person defined for purposes of this Code, see Family Code § 105.
Personal income tax, adoption costs, qualifying adoptions, see Revenue and Taxation Code § 17052.25.
Private trial, see Family Code § 214.
Prospective adoptive parent defined, see Family Code § 8542.

Research References

Forms

2 California Transactions Forms--Family Law § 6:111, Hearing on Stepparent Adoption Petition.
West's California Code Forms, Family § 8612 Form 2, Adoption Agreement.
West's California Judicial Council Forms ADOPT–210, Adoption Agreement (Also Available in Spanish).
West's California Judicial Council Forms ADOPT–215, Adoption Order (Also Available in Spanish).
West's California Judicial Council Forms JV–505, Statement Regarding Parentage (Juvenile) (Also Available in Spanish).

§ 8613. Prospective adoptive parent in military, or in service for governmental entity, red cross, or charitable or religious organization; appearance by counsel; execution of agreement; deposition; adoption order

(a) If the prospective adoptive parent is commissioned or enlisted in the military service, or auxiliary thereof, of the United States, or of any of its allies, or is engaged in service on behalf of any governmental entity of the United States, or in the American Red Cross, or in any other recognized charitable or religious organization, so that it is impossible or impracticable, because of the prospective adoptive parent's absence from this state, or otherwise, to make an appearance in person, and the circumstances are established by satisfactory evidence, the appearance may be made for the prospective adoptive parent by counsel, commissioned and empowered in writing for that purpose. The power of attorney may be incorporated in the adoption petition.

(b) Where the prospective adoptive parent is permitted to appear by counsel, the agreement may be executed and acknowledged by the counsel, or may be executed by the absent party before a notary public, or any other person authorized to take acknowledgments including the persons authorized by Sections 1183 and 1183.5 of the Civil Code.

(c) Where the prospective adoptive parent is permitted to appear by counsel, or otherwise, the court may, in its discretion, cause an examination of the prospective adoptive parent, other interested person, or witness to be made upon deposition, as it deems necessary. The deposition shall be taken upon commission, as prescribed by the Code of Civil Procedure, and the expense thereof shall be borne by the petitioner.

(d) The petition, relinquishment or consent, agreement, order, report to the court from any investigating agency, and any power of attorney and deposition shall be filed in the office of the clerk of the court.

(e) The provisions of this section permitting an appearance through counsel are equally applicable to the spouse of a prospective adoptive parent who resides with the prospective adoptive parent outside this state.

(f) Where, pursuant to this section, neither prospective adoptive parent need appear before the court, the child proposed to be adopted need not appear. If the law otherwise requires that the child execute any document during the course of the hearing, the child may do so through counsel.

(g) Where none of the parties appears, the court may not make an order of adoption until after a report has been filed with the court pursuant to Section 8715, 8807, 8914, or 9001. *(Stats.1992, c. 162 (A.B.2650), § 10, operative Jan. 1, 1994. Amended by Stats.1993, c. 1158 (S.B.1152), § 1; Stats.2002, c. 784 (S.B.1316), § 109.)*

Cross References

Adoptive parent defined, see Family Code § 8503.
Adoptive parents, criminal record, see Penal Code § 11105.3.
Appearance before court, adoptive parents, see Family Code § 8718.
Birth parents, money or benefits for consent or placement of children, see Penal Code § 273.
Foster homes, alternative methods, see Welfare and Institutions Code § 396 et seq.
Judgment and order defined for purposes of this Code, see Family Code § 100.
Juvenile delinquents and dependents, jurisdiction, see Welfare and Institutions Code § 366.3.
Person defined for purposes of this Code, see Family Code § 105.
Petitioner defined for purposes of this Code, see Family Code § 126.
Priorities and preferences, adoptive or foster parents and relatives, see Welfare and Institutions Code §§ 361.2 et seq., 366.26.
Prospective adoptive parents defined, see Family Code § 8542.
References to husband, wife, spouses and married persons, persons included for purposes of this Code, see Family Code § 11.
State defined for purposes of this Code, see Family Code § 145.

Research References

Forms

2 California Transactions Forms--Family Law § 6:13, Appearance in Person or by Counsel.
2 California Transactions Forms--Family Law § 6:28, Power of Attorney for Counsel to Appear at Final Hearing on Behalf of Petitioners Who Are Absent from California.
2 California Transactions Forms--Family Law § 6:44, Documentation and Final Hearing.
2 California Transactions Forms--Family Law § 6:111, Hearing on Stepparent Adoption Petition.
West's California Code Forms, Family § 8600, Comment Overview—Adoption of Unmarried Minors.

§ 8613.5. Waiver of personal appearance of prospective adoptive parent

(a)(1) If it is impossible or impracticable for either prospective adoptive parent to make an appearance in person, and the circumstances are established by clear and convincing documentary evidence, the court may, in its discretion, do either of the following:

(A) Waive the personal appearance of the prospective adoptive parent. The appearance may be made for the prospective adoptive parent by counsel, commissioned and empowered in writing for that purpose. The power of attorney may be incorporated in the adoption petition.

(B) Authorize the prospective adoptive parent to appear by telephone, videoconference, or other remote electronic means that the court deems reasonable, prudent, and reliable.

(2) For purposes of this section, if the circumstances that make an appearance in person by a prospective adoptive parent impossible or impracticable are temporary in nature or of a short duration, the court shall not waive the personal appearance of that prospective adoptive parent.

(b) If the prospective adoptive parent is permitted to appear by counsel, the agreement may be executed and acknowledged by the counsel, or may be executed by the absent party before a notary public, or any other person authorized to take acknowledgments including the persons authorized by Sections 1183 and 1183.5 of the Civil Code.

(c) If the prospective adoptive parent is permitted to appear by counsel, or otherwise, the court may, in its discretion, cause an examination of the prospective adoptive parent, other interested person, or witness to be made upon deposition, as it deems necessary. The deposition shall be taken upon commission, as prescribed by the Code of Civil Procedure, and the expense thereof shall be borne by the petitioner.

(d) The petition, relinquishment or consent, agreement, order, report to the court from any investigating agency, and any power of attorney and deposition shall be filed in the office of the clerk of the court.

(e) The provisions of this section permitting an appearance by counsel or electronically pursuant to subparagraph (B) of paragraph (1) of subdivision (a) are equally applicable to the spouse of a prospective adoptive parent who resides with the prospective adoptive parent outside this state.

(f) If, pursuant to this section, neither prospective adoptive parent need appear before the court, the child proposed to be adopted need not appear. If the law otherwise requires that the child execute any document during the course of the hearing, the child may do so through counsel.

(g) If none of the parties appear, the court may not make an order of adoption until after a report has been filed with the court pursuant to Section 8715, 8807, 8914, or 9001. *(Added by Stats.2006, c. 806 (S.B.1325), § 6. Amended by Stats.2014, c. 763 (A.B.1701), § 9, eff. Jan. 1, 2015.)*

Research References

Forms

West's California Code Forms, Family § 8600, Comment Overview—Adoption of Unmarried Minors.

§ 8613.7. Notice of eligibility for reduced-cost or no-cost health coverage

On and after January 1, 2014, the court shall provide to any petitioner for adoption pursuant to this part a notice informing the petitioner that they may be eligible for reduced-cost coverage through the California Health Benefit Exchange established under Title 22 (commencing with Section 100500) of the Government Code or no-cost coverage through Medi-Cal. The notice shall include information on obtaining coverage pursuant to those programs, and shall be developed by the California Health Benefit Exchange. *(Added by Stats.2012, c. 851 (A.B.792), § 2. Amended by Stats.2019, c. 115 (A.B.1817), § 114, eff. Jan. 1, 2020.)*

§ 8614. Certificate of adoption

Upon the request of the adoptive parents or the adopted child, a clerk of the superior court may issue a certificate of adoption that states the date and place of adoption, the birthday of the child, the names of the adoptive parents, and the name the child has taken.

§ 8614

Unless the child has been adopted by a stepparent or by a relative, as defined in subdivision (c) of Section 8616.5, the certificate shall not state the name of the birth parents of the child. *(Stats.1992, c. 162 (A.B.2650), § 10, operative Jan. 1, 1994. Amended by Stats.1997, c. 793 (A.B.1544), § 2; Stats.2002, c. 784 (S.B.1316), § 110; Stats.2003, c. 251 (S.B.182), § 5.)*

Cross References

Adoptive parent defined, see Family Code § 8503.
Birth parent defined, see Family Code § 8512.
Disclosure of information, see Family Code § 9200 et seq.
State defined for purposes of this Code, see Family Code § 145.

Research References

Forms

2 California Transactions Forms--Family Law § 6:15, Certificate of Adoption--Birth Certificate.
West's California Code Forms, Family § 8600, Comment Overview--Adoption of Unmarried Minors.
West's California Code Forms, Family § 8614 Form 1, Certificate of Adoption.

§ 8615. New birth certificate

(a) Notwithstanding any other law, an action may be brought in the county in which the petitioner resides for the purpose of obtaining for a child adopted by the petitioner a new birth certificate specifying that a deceased spouse of the petitioner who was in the home at the time of the initial placement of the child is a parent of the child.

(b) In an adoption proceeding, the petitioner may request that the new birth certificate specify that a deceased spouse of the petitioner who was in the home at the time of the initial placement of the child is a parent of the child.

(c) The inclusion of the name of a deceased person in a birth certificate issued pursuant to a court order under this section does not affect any matter of testate or intestate succession, and is not competent evidence on the issue of the relationship between the adopted child and the deceased person in any action or proceeding. *(Stats.1992, c. 162 (A.B.2650), § 10, operative Jan. 1, 1994.)*

Cross References

Age of majority, see Family Code § 6500 et seq.
Certificates of birth following adoption, legitimation, court determination of paternity, and acknowledgment,
  Inclusion of name of deceased adopting parent, see Health and Safety Code § 102660.
  Preparation of additional amended record, see Health and Safety Code § 102670.
Certificates of birth following adoption, see Health and Safety Code § 102625 et seq.
County defined for purposes of this Code, see Family Code § 67.
Disclosure of birth parent information to child, see Family Code §§ 8702, 8818, 9203.
Disclosure of information, see Family Code § 9200 et seq.
Indian blood, certificate of degree of, see Family Code § 8619.
Judgment and order defined for purposes of this Code, see Family Code § 100.
Person defined for purposes of this Code, see Family Code § 105.
Petitioner defined for purposes of this Code, see Family Code § 126.
Proceeding defined for purposes of this Code, see Family Code § 110.
References to husband, wife, spouses and married persons, persons included for purposes of this Code, see Family Code § 11.

Research References

Forms

2 California Transactions Forms--Family Law § 6:15, Certificate of Adoption--Birth Certificate.
West's California Code Forms, Family § 8600, Comment Overview--Adoption of Unmarried Minors.

West's California Code Forms, Family § 8615 Form 2, Order Requiring New Birth Certificate--Deceased Spouse as Parent.

§ 8616. Legal relationship of parent and child

After adoption, the adopted child and the adoptive parents shall sustain towards each other the legal relationship of parent and child and have all the rights and are subject to all the duties of that relationship. *(Stats.1992, c. 162 (A.B.2650), § 10, operative Jan. 1, 1994.)*

Cross References

Adoption of adults and married minors, legal relationship of parent and child, see Family Code § 9305.
Adoptive parent defined, see Family Code § 8503.
Age of majority, see Family Code § 6500 et seq.
Child defined for purposes of the Probate Code, see Probate Code § 26.
Child support, generally, see Family Code § 3900 et seq.
Criminal record, adoptive parents, see Family Code §§ 8712, 8811; Penal Code § 11105.3.
Custody of children, generally, see Family Code § 3000 et seq.
Custody of minor children, see Family Code § 3020 et seq.
Disclosure of information, see Family Code § 9200 et seq.
Intestate succession, parent and child relationship,
  Foster parents or stepparents, see Probate Code § 6454.
  Natural parents, see Probate Code § 6453.
  Out-of-wedlock births, conditions for inheritance based on relationship, see Probate Code § 6452.
Relationship severed by adoption, see Probate Code § 6451.
Parent and child relationship, generally, see Family Code § 7500 et seq.
Parent defined for purposes of the Probate Code, see Probate Code § 54.

Research References

Forms

2 California Transactions Forms--Family Law § 6:16, Legal Relationship Following Adoption of Unmarried Minor.
2 California Transactions Forms--Family Law § 6:18, Intestate Succession Rights.

§ 8616.5. Postadoption contact agreements

(a) The Legislature finds and declares that some adoptive children may benefit from either direct or indirect contact with birth relatives, including the birth parent or parents or any siblings, or an Indian tribe, after being adopted. Postadoption contact agreements are intended to ensure children of an achievable level of continuing contact when contact is beneficial to the children and the agreements are voluntarily executed by birth relatives, including the birth parent or parents or any siblings, or an Indian tribe, and adoptive parents. Nothing in this section requires all of the listed parties to participate in the development of a postadoption contact agreement in order for the agreement to be executed.

(b)(1) Nothing in the adoption laws of this state shall be construed to prevent the adopting parent or parents, the birth relatives, including the birth parent or parents or any siblings, or an Indian tribe, and the child from voluntarily executing a written agreement to permit continuing contact between the birth relatives, including the birth parent or parents or any siblings, or an Indian tribe, and the child if the agreement is found by the court to have been executed voluntarily and to be in the best interests of the child at the time the adoption petition is granted.

(2) The terms of any postadoption contact agreement executed under this section shall be limited to, but need not include, all of the following:

(A) Provisions for visitation between the child and a birth parent or parents and other birth relatives, including siblings, and the child's Indian tribe if the case is governed by the Indian Child Welfare Act (25 U.S.C. Sec. 1901 et seq,).

(B) Provisions for future contact between a birth parent or parents or other birth relatives, including siblings, or both, and the child or an adoptive parent, or both, and in cases governed by the Indian Child Welfare Act, the child's Indian tribe.

(C) Provisions for the sharing of information about the child in the future.

(3) The terms of any postadoption contact agreement with birth relatives, including siblings, other than the child's birth parent or parents shall be limited to the sharing of information about the child, unless the child has a preexisting relationship with the birth relative.

(c) At the time an adoption decree is entered pursuant to a petition filed pursuant to Section 8714, 8714.5, 8802, 8912, or 9000, the court entering the decree may grant postadoption privileges if an agreement for those privileges has been executed, including agreements executed pursuant to subdivision (f) of Section 8620. The hearing to grant the adoption petition and issue an order of adoption may be continued as necessary to permit parties who are in the process of negotiating a postadoption agreement to reach a final agreement.

(d) The child who is the subject of the adoption petition shall be considered a party to the postadoption contact agreement. The written consent to the terms and conditions of the postadoption contact agreement and any subsequent modifications of the agreement by a child who is 12 years of age or older is a necessary condition to the granting of privileges regarding visitation, contact, or sharing of information about the child, unless the court finds by a preponderance of the evidence that the agreement, as written, is in the best interests of the child. Any child who has been found to come within Section 300 of the Welfare and Institutions Code or who is the subject of a petition for jurisdiction of the juvenile court under Section 300 of the Welfare and Institutions Code shall be represented by an attorney for purposes of consent to the postadoption contact agreement.

(e) A postadoption contact agreement shall contain the following warnings in bold type:

(1) After the adoption petition has been granted by the court, the adoption cannot be set aside due to the failure of an adopting parent, a birth parent, a birth relative, including a sibling, an Indian tribe, or the child to follow the terms of this agreement or a later change to this agreement.

(2) A disagreement between the parties or litigation brought to enforce or modify the agreement shall not affect the validity of the adoption and shall not serve as a basis for orders affecting the custody of the child.

(3) A court will not act on a petition to change or enforce this agreement unless the petitioner has participated, or attempted to participate, in good faith in mediation or other appropriate dispute resolution proceedings to resolve the dispute.

(f) Upon the granting of the adoption petition and the issuing of the order of adoption of a child who is a dependent of the juvenile court, juvenile court dependency jurisdiction shall be terminated. Enforcement of the postadoption contact agreement shall be under the continuing jurisdiction of the court granting the petition of adoption. The court may not order compliance with the agreement absent a finding that the party seeking the enforcement participated, or attempted to participate, in good faith in mediation or other appropriate dispute resolution proceedings regarding the conflict, prior to the filing of the enforcement action, and that the enforcement is in the best interests of the child. Documentary evidence or offers of proof may serve as the basis for the court's decision regarding enforcement. No testimony or evidentiary hearing shall be required. The court shall not order further investigation or evaluation by any public or private agency or individual absent a finding by clear and convincing evidence that the best interests of the child may be protected or advanced only by that inquiry and that the inquiry will not disturb the stability of the child's home to the detriment of the child.

(g) The court may not award monetary damages as a result of the filing of the civil action pursuant to subdivision (e).

(h) A postadoption contact agreement may be modified or terminated only if either of the following occurs:

(1) All parties, including the child if the child is 12 years of age or older at the time of the requested termination or modification, have signed a modified postadoption contact agreement and the agreement is filed with the court that granted the petition of adoption.

(2) The court finds all of the following:

(A) The termination or modification is necessary to serve the best interests of the child.

(B) There has been a substantial change of circumstances since the original agreement was executed and approved by the court.

(C) The party seeking the termination or modification has participated, or attempted to participate, in good faith in mediation or other appropriate dispute resolution proceedings prior to seeking court approval of the proposed termination or modification.

Documentary evidence or offers of proof may serve as the basis for the court's decision. No testimony or evidentiary hearing shall be required. The court shall not order further investigation or evaluation by any public or private agency or individual absent a finding by clear and convincing evidence that the best interests of the child may be protected or advanced only by that inquiry and that the inquiry will not disturb the stability of the child's home to the detriment of the child.

(i) All costs and fees of mediation or other appropriate dispute resolution proceedings shall be borne by each party, excluding the child. All costs and fees of litigation shall be borne by the party filing the action to modify or enforce the agreement when no party has been found by the court as failing to comply with an existing postadoption contact agreement. Otherwise, a party, other than the child, found by the court as failing to comply without good cause with an existing agreement shall bear all the costs and fees of litigation.

(j) The Judicial Council shall adopt rules of court and forms for motions to enforce, terminate, or modify postadoption contact agreements.

(k) The court shall not set aside a decree of adoption, rescind a relinquishment, or modify an order to terminate parental rights or any other prior court order because of the failure of a birth parent, adoptive parent, birth relative, including a sibling, an Indian tribe, or the child to comply with any or all of the original terms of, or subsequent modifications to, the postadoption contact agreement, except as follows:

(1) Prior to issuing the order of adoption, in an adoption involving an Indian child, the court may, upon a petition of the birth parent, birth relative, including a sibling, or an Indian tribe, order the parties to engage in family mediation services for the purpose of reaching a postadoption contact agreement if the prospective adoptive parent fails to negotiate in good faith to execute a postadoption contact agreement, after having agreed to enter into negotiations, provided that the failure of the parties to reach an agreement is not in and of itself proof of bad faith.

(2) Prior to issuing the order of adoption, if the parties fail to negotiate in good faith to execute a postadoption contact agreement during the negotiations entered into pursuant to, and in accordance with, paragraph (1), the court may modify prior orders or issue new orders as necessary to ensure the best interest of the Indian child is met, including, but not limited to, requiring parties to engage in further family mediation services for the purpose of reaching a postadoption contact agreement, initiating guardianship proceeding in lieu of adoption, or authorizing a change of adoptive placement for the child.

(*l*) As used in this section, "sibling" means a person related to the identified child by blood, adoption, or affinity through a common

§ 8616.5

legal or biological parent. *(Formerly § 8714.7, added by Stats.1997, c. 793 (A.B.1544), § 5. Amended by Stats.2000, c. 910 (A.B.2921), § 4; Stats.2000, c. 930 (S.B.2157), § 3. Renumbered § 8616.5 and amended by Stats.2003, c. 251 (S.B.182), § 8. Amended by Stats.2004, c. 858 (S.B.1357), § 4; Stats.2006, c. 838 (S.B.678), § 9; Stats.2009, c. 492 (A.B.941), § 3; Stats.2016, c. 719 (S.B.1060), § 1, eff. Jan. 1, 2017.)*

Cross References

Adoptive parent defined, see Family Code § 8503.
Birth parent defined, see Family Code § 8512.
Certificate of adoption, restrictions on statement of names of the birth parents of the child, see Family Code § 8614.
Dependent children, hearings, see Welfare and Institutions Code § 358.1.
Filing requirements for postadoption contact agreements, see Family Code § 8714.
Foster care placement, sibling interaction, meeting regarding postadoption sibling contact agreement, see Welfare and Institutions Code § 16002.
Hearings terminating parental rights or establishing guardianship of children adjudged dependent children of court, see Welfare and Institutions Code § 366.26.
Independent adoptions, postadoption contact agreement to be filed with petition for adoption, see Family Code § 8802.
Intercountry adoptions, postadoption contact agreement to be filed with petition for adoption, see Family Code § 8912.
Judgment and order defined for purposes of this Code, see Family Code § 100.
Out-of-home placement, case plan provisions for sibling visitation and relationship development, see Welfare and Institutions Code § 16501.1.
Petitioner defined for purposes of this Code, see Family Code § 126.
Proceeding defined for purposes of this Code, see Family Code § 110.
State defined for purposes of this Code, see Family Code § 145.
Stepparent adoptions, postadoption contact agreement to be filed with petition for adoption, see Family Code § 9000.

Research References

Forms

2 California Transactions Forms--Family Law § 6:15, Certificate of Adoption---Birth Certificate.
2 California Transactions Forms--Family Law § 6:55, Agreement for Continuing Contact.
2 California Transactions Forms--Family Law § 6:97, Kinship Adoption.
2 California Transactions Forms--Family Law § 6:100, Postadoption Contact Agreement [Form Adopt-310].
West's California Code Forms, Family § 8700, Comment Overview—Relinquishment of Child to Department of Social Services or a Licensed Adoption Agency.
West's California Code Forms, Family § 8714.5 Form 1, Contact After Adoption Agreement.
West's California Code Forms, Family § 8714.5 Form 2, Request to Enforce, Change, End Contact After Adoption Agreement.
West's California Code Forms, Family § 8714.5 Form 3, Answer to Request to Enforce, Change, End Contact After Adoption Agreement.
West's California Code Forms, Family § 8714.5 Form 4, Order to Enforce, Change, End Contact After Adoption Agreement.
West's California Judicial Council Forms ADOPT–310, Contact After Adoption Agreement.
West's California Judicial Council Forms ADOPT–315, Request To: Enforce, Change, End Contact After Adoption Agreement.
West's California Judicial Council Forms ADOPT–320, Answer to Request To: Enforce, Change, End Contact After Adoption Agreement.
West's California Judicial Council Forms ADOPT–325, Judge's Order To: Enforce, Change, End Contact After Adoption Agreement.

§ 8617. Existing parents' responsibilities toward child; cessation; waiver prior to finalization of adoption; application of section

(a) Except as provided in subdivision (b), the existing parent or parents of an adopted child are, from the time of the adoption, relieved of all parental duties towards, and all responsibility for, the adopted child, and have no right over the child.

(b) The termination of the parental duties and responsibilities of the existing parent or parents under subdivision (a) may be waived if both the existing parent or parents and the prospective adoptive parent or parents sign a waiver at any time prior to the finalization of the adoption. The waiver shall be filed with the court.

(c) This section applies to all adoptions except intercountry adoptions governed by Chapter 4 (commencing with Section 8900). *(Stats.1992, c. 162 (A.B.2650), § 10, operative Jan. 1, 1994. Amended by Stats.2013, c. 564 (S.B.274), § 7; Stats.2019, c. 192 (A.B.1373), § 1, eff. Jan. 1, 2020.)*

Cross References

Age of majority, see Family Code § 6500 et seq.
Birth parent,
   Defined, see Family Code § 8512.
   Money or benefits for consent or placement of children, see Penal Code § 273.
Duty of parent to support child, see Family Code § 3900 et seq.
Intercountry adoptions of unmarried minors, guardianship to prospective adoptive parents, see Family Code § 8903.
Parent and child relationship, generally, see Family Code § 7500 et seq.
Priorities and preferences, foster parents and relatives, see Welfare and Institutions Code §§ 361.2 et seq., 366.26.
Similar provisions, see Family Code § 9306.

Research References

Forms

2 California Transactions Forms--Family Law § 6:16, Legal Relationship Following Adoption of Unmarried Minor.
2 California Transactions Forms--Family Law § 6:18, Intestate Succession Rights.
2 California Transactions Forms--Family Law § 6:106, Consent of Noncustodial Parent.
2 California Transactions Forms--Family Law § 6:134, Financial Responsibility Agreement.

§ 8618. Adopted child may take adoptive parent's family name

A child adopted pursuant to this part may take the family name of the adoptive parent. *(Stats.1992, c. 162 (A.B.2650), § 10, operative Jan. 1, 1994.)*

Cross References

Adoptive parent defined, see Family Code § 8503.
Age of majority, see Family Code § 6500 et seq.
Disclosure of information, see Family Code § 9200 et seq.
Similar provisions, see Family Code § 9304.

§ 8619. Children of Indian ancestry; information; certificate of degree of Indian blood

The department shall adopt rules and regulations it determines are reasonably necessary to ensure that the birth parent or parents of Indian ancestry, seeking to relinquish a child for adoption, provide sufficient information to the department, county adoption agency, or licensed adoption agency so that a certificate of degree of Indian blood can be obtained from the Bureau of Indian Affairs. The department shall immediately request a certificate of degree of Indian blood from the Bureau of Indian Affairs upon obtaining the information. A copy of all documents pertaining to the degree of Indian blood and tribal enrollment, including a copy of the certificate of degree of Indian blood, shall become a permanent record in the adoption files and shall be housed in a central location and made available to authorized personnel from the Bureau of Indian Affairs when required to determine the adopted person's eligibility to receive services or benefits because of the adopted person's status as an Indian. This information shall be made available to the adopted person upon reaching the age of majority. *(Stats.1992, c. 162 (A.B.2650), § 10, operative Jan. 1, 1994. Amended by Stats.2012, c. 35 (S.B.1013), § 11, eff. June 27, 2012.)*

Cross References

Age of majority, see Family Code § 6500 et seq.
Birth parent defined, see Family Code § 8512.
Certificates of birth following adoption, see Health and Safety Code § 102625 et seq.
Department defined, see Family Code § 8518.
Licensed adoption agency defined, see Family Code § 8530.

Person defined for purposes of this Code, see Family Code § 105.
Tribal marriages and divorces, validity, see Family Code § 295.

Research References

Forms

2 California Transactions Forms--Family Law § 6:143, Overview of Indian Child Welfare Act (ICWA).

West's California Code Forms, Family § 8600, Comment Overview—Adoption of Unmarried Minors.

§ 8619.5. Children of Indian ancestry; vacated or set aside final decrees or voluntary return by adoptive parents; return of custody

Whenever a final decree of adoption of an Indian child has been vacated or set aside or the adoptive parent voluntary consents to termination of parental rights to the child, a biological parent or prior Indian custodian may petition for return of custody and the court shall grant that petition unless there is a showing, in a proceeding subject to the provisions of Section 1912 of the Indian Child Welfare Act (25 U.S.C. Sec. 1901 et seq.), that the return of custody is not in the best interest of the child. *(Added by Stats.2006, c. 838 (S.B.678), § 10. Amended by Stats.2019, c. 115 (A.B.1817), § 115, eff. Jan. 1, 2020.)*

Research References

Forms

2 California Transactions Forms--Family Law § 6:143, Overview of Indian Child Welfare Act (ICWA).

§ 8620. Determination of identity as Indian child for purposes of relinquishment or adoption placement; procedures; civil penalty for violations

(a)(1) If a parent is seeking to relinquish a child pursuant to Section 8700 or execute an adoption placement agreement pursuant to Section 8801.3, the department, county adoption agency, licensed adoption agency, or adoption service provider, as applicable, shall ask the child and the child's parent or custodian whether the child is, or may be, a member of, or eligible for membership in an Indian tribe or whether the child has been identified as a member of an Indian organization. The department, county adoption agency, licensed adoption agency, or adoption service provider, as applicable, shall complete the forms provided for this purpose by the department and shall make this completed form a part of the file.

(2) If there is any oral or written information that indicates that the child is, or may be, an Indian child, the department, county adoption agency, licensed adoption agency, or adoption service provider, as applicable, shall obtain the following information:

(A) The name of the child involved, and the actual date and place of birth of the child.

(B) The name, address, date of birth, and tribal affiliation of the birth parents, maternal and paternal grandparents, and maternal and paternal great-grandparents of the child.

(C) The name and address of extended family members of the child who have a tribal affiliation.

(D) The name and address of the Indian tribes or Indian organizations of which the child is, or may be, a member.

(E) A statement of the reasons why the child is, or may be, an Indian.

(3)(A) The department, county adoption agency, licensed adoption agency, attorney for the prospective adoptive parents, or adoption service provider shall send a notice, which shall include information obtained pursuant to paragraph (2) and a request for confirmation of the child's Indian status, to any parent and any custodian of the child, and to any Indian tribe of which the child is, or may be, a member or eligible for membership. If any of the information required under paragraph (2) cannot be obtained, the notice shall indicate that fact.

(B) The notice sent pursuant to subparagraph (A) shall describe the nature of the proceeding and advise the recipient of the Indian tribe's right to intervene in the proceeding on its own behalf or on behalf of a tribal member relative of the child.

(b) The department shall adopt regulations to ensure that if a child who is being voluntarily relinquished for adoption, pursuant to Section 8700, is an Indian child, the parent of the child shall be advised of the right to withdraw consent and thereby rescind the relinquishment of an Indian child for any reason at any time prior to entry of a final decree of termination of parental rights or adoption, pursuant to Section 1913 of Title 25 of the United States Code.

(c) If a child who is the subject of an adoption proceeding after being relinquished for adoption pursuant to Section 8700, is an Indian child, the child's Indian tribe may intervene in that proceeding on behalf of a tribal member relative of the child.

(d) Any notice sent under this section shall comply with Section 180.

(e) If all prior notices required by this section have been provided to an Indian tribe, the Indian tribe receiving those prior notices is encouraged to provide notice to the department and to the licensed adoption agency, county adoption agency, or adoption service provider, not later than five calendar days prior to the date of the hearing to determine whether or not the final adoption order is to be granted, indicating whether or not it intends to intervene in the proceeding required by this section, either on its own behalf or on behalf of a tribal member who is a relative of the child.

(f) The Legislature finds and declares that some adoptive children may benefit from either direct or indirect contact with an Indian tribe. The adoption laws of this state shall not be construed to prevent the adopting parent or parents, the birth relatives, including the birth parent or parents, an Indian tribe, and the child, from voluntarily entering into a written agreement to permit continuing contact between the Indian tribe and the child, if the agreement is found by the court to have been entered into voluntarily and to be in the best interest of the child at the time the adoption petition is granted.

(g) With respect to giving notice to Indian tribes in the case of voluntary placements of Indian children pursuant to this section, a person, other than a birth parent of the child, shall be subject to a civil penalty if that person knowingly and willfully:

(1) Falsifies, conceals, or covers up by trick, scheme, or device, a material fact concerning whether the child is an Indian child or the parent is an Indian.

(2) Makes a false, fictitious, or fraudulent statement, omission, or representation.

(3) Falsifies a written document knowing that the document contains a false, fictitious, or fraudulent statement or entry relating to a material fact.

(4) Assists a person in physically removing a child from the State of California in order to obstruct the application of notification.

(h) Civil penalties for a violation of subdivision (g) by a person other than a birth parent of the child are as follows:

(1) For the initial violation, a person shall be fined not more than ten thousand dollars ($10,000).

(2) For any subsequent violation, a person shall be fined not more than twenty thousand dollars ($20,000). *(Added by Stats.2003, c. 469 (S.B.947), § 4. Amended by Stats.2006, c. 838 (S.B.678), § 11; Stats.2010, c. 588 (A.B.2020), § 5; Stats.2012, c. 35 (S.B.1013), § 12, eff. June 27, 2012; Stats.2019, c. 115 (A.B.1817), § 116, eff. Jan. 1, 2020.)*

§ 8620   ADOPTION

Cross References

Adoption service provider defined, see Family Code § 8502.
Disciplinary actions against attorneys, notification of State Bar, see Business and Professions Code § 6086.7.
Judgment and order defined for purposes of this Code, see Family Code § 100.
Person defined for purposes of this Code, see Family Code § 105.
Proceeding defined for purposes of this Code, see Family Code § 110.
State defined for purposes of this Code, see Family Code § 145.

Research References

Forms
2 California Transactions Forms--Family Law § 6:83, Nature of Agency Adoption—Governing Law.
2 California Transactions Forms--Family Law § 6:143, Overview of Indian Child Welfare Act (ICWA).
West's California Code Forms, Family § 8600, Comment Overview—Adoption of Unmarried Minors.

§ 8621. Regulations

The department shall adopt regulations regarding the provision of adoption services by the department, county adoption agencies, licensed adoption agencies, and other adoption service providers, and shall monitor the provision of those services by county adoption agencies, licensed adoption agencies, and other adoption providers. The department shall report violations of regulations to the appropriate licensing authority.

This section shall become operative on January 1, 1995. *(Added by Stats.1993, c. 758 (S.B.792), § 6, operative Jan. 1, 1995. Amended by Stats.2012, c. 35 (S.B.1013), § 13, eff. June 27, 2012.)*

Cross References

Adoption service provider defined, see Family Code § 8502.
Department defined, see Family Code § 8518.
Licensed adoption agency defined, see Family Code § 8530.

§ 8622. Service limitations; notice

A licensed private adoption agency whose services are limited to a particular target population shall inform all birth parents and prospective adoptive parents of its service limitations before commencing any services, signing any documents or agreements, or accepting any fees.

This section shall become operative on January 1, 1995. *(Added by Stats.1993, c. 758 (S.B.792), § 6.2, operative Jan. 1, 1995.)*

Cross References

Birth parent defined, see Family Code § 8512.
Licensed adoption agency defined, see Family Code § 8530.
Prospective adoptive parent defined, see Family Code § 8542.

Research References

Forms
2 California Transactions Forms--Family Law § 6:83, Nature of Agency Adoption—Governing Law.

CHAPTER 1.5. ADOPTION FACILITATORS

Section
8623. Description.
8624. Advertising.
8625. Prohibitions; misrepresentation; photolisting or advertising specific information about particular minor children.
8626. Description of services; disclosure of status.
8627. Representation of multiple parties; written agreements.
8628. Information provided by birthparents; report to prospective adoptive parents.
8629. Contracts; revocation without penalty.

Section
8630. Fees and expenses; adoption accounting report.
8631. Contracts; requirements.
8632. Contracts; verbal explanation of terms.
8632.5. Statewide registration and enforcement process for adoption facilitators.
8633. Civil penalty.
8634. Construction of contract; remedies.
8635. Repealed.
8636. Licensure requirement; surety bond.
8637. Attorneys; facilitating adoptions; application of law.
8638. Remedies.
8639. Civil penalty for failure to be in the registry; appeal; regulations.

§ 8623. Description

A person or organization is an adoption facilitator if the person or organization is not licensed as an adoption agency by the State of California and engages in either of the following activities:

(a) Advertises for the purpose of soliciting parties to an adoption or locating children for an adoption or acting as an intermediary between the parties to an adoption.

(b) Charges a fee or other valuable consideration for services rendered relating to an adoption. *(Added by Stats.1996, c. 1135 (S.B.2035), § 1. Amended by Stats.2007, c. 130 (A.B.299), § 90.)*

Cross References

Person defined for purposes of this Code, see Family Code § 105.
State defined for purposes of this Code, see Family Code § 145.

Research References

Forms
2 California Transactions Forms--Family Law § 6:3, Definitions.

§ 8624. Advertising

Any advertising by an adoption facilitator shall:

(a) Identify the name of the party placing the advertisement and shall state that the party is an adoption facilitator.

(b) Be subject to Section 17500 of the Business and Professions Code.

(c) Provide, in any written advertisement, the disclosure required by subdivision (a) in print that is the same size and typeface as the name required pursuant to subdivision (a) or any telephone number specified in the advertisement, whichever is the larger print size.

(d) Provide the disclosure required by subdivision (a) in the same color as the most prominent print in the advertisement where the advertisement contains more than one color.

(e) Present the disclosure required by subdivision (a) in a readily understandable manner and at the same speed and volume, if applicable, as the rest of the advertisement if the advertisement is a television advertisement. *(Added by Stats.1996, c. 1135 (S.B.2035), § 1.)*

Cross References

State defined for purposes of this Code, see Family Code § 145.

§ 8625. Prohibitions; misrepresentation; photolisting or advertising specific information about particular minor children

An adoption facilitator shall not:

(a) Mislead a person into believing, or imply by any document, including any form of advertising or by oral communications, that the adoption facilitator is a licensed adoption agency.

(b) Represent to any person that the adoption facilitator is able to provide services for which the adoption facilitator is not properly licensed.

(c) Make use of photolisting to advertise minor children for placement in adoption.

(d) Post in any advertising specific information about particular minor children who are available for adoption placement. *(Added by Stats.1996, c. 1135 (S.B.2035), § 1. Amended by Stats.2006, c. 754 (S.B.1758), § 2; Stats.2019, c. 115 (A.B.1817), § 117, eff. Jan. 1, 2020.)*

Cross References

Person defined for purposes of this Code, see Family Code § 105.

§ 8626. Description of services; disclosure of status

An adoption facilitator shall disclose in the first oral communication in which there is a description of services, that the facilitator is not a licensed adoption agency. *(Added by Stats.1996, c. 1135 (S.B.2035), § 1.)*

§ 8627. Representation of multiple parties; written agreements

If the facilitator is acting on behalf of more than one party, all of the parties on whose behalf the facilitator is acting shall have signed a written agreement authorizing the facilitator to act on behalf of all of the parties. *(Added by Stats.1996, c. 1135 (S.B.2035), § 1.)*

§ 8628. Information provided by birthparents; report to prospective adoptive parents

An adoption facilitator shall report in writing to the prospective adoptive parents all information that is provided to the facilitator by the birthparents concerning a particular child. *(Added by Stats.1996, c. 1135 (S.B.2035), § 1.)*

Cross References

Birth parent defined, see Family Code § 8512.
Prospective adoptive parent defined, see Family Code § 8542.

§ 8629. Contracts; revocation without penalty

For a period of 72 hours after signing a contract or after the payment of any fee, the birthparents or the prospective adoptive parents may revoke the contract and request the return of any fees paid, without penalty, except for any reasonable fees actually earned by the facilitator and which are supported by written records or documentation. *(Added by Stats.1996, c. 1135 (S.B.2035), § 1.)*

Cross References

Birth parent defined, see Family Code § 8512.
Prospective adoptive parent defined, see Family Code § 8542.

§ 8630. Fees and expenses; adoption accounting report

The amount of fees paid to an adoption facilitator and any fees or expenses an adoption facilitator pays to a third party shall be reported to the court in the adoption accounting report as an adoption-related expense. *(Added by Stats.1996, c. 1135 (S.B.2035), § 1.)*

§ 8631. Contracts; requirements

All contracts entered into by an adoption facilitator shall be in writing and, at a minimum, shall include the following:

(a) A statement that the adoption facilitator is not licensed by the State of California as an adoption agency.

(b) A statement disclosing on whose behalf the facilitator is acting.

(c) A statement that the information provided by any party is not confidential but that this waiver of confidentiality shall only apply to the parties to the facilitation contract and any disclosures required by Chapter 7 (commencing with Section 9200) of Part 2 of Division 13.

(d) A statement that the adoption facilitator cannot provide any services for which the facilitator is not properly licensed, such as legal or therapeutic counseling.

(e) A list of all the services that the adoption facilitator is required to provide under the contract.

(f) Notice that for a period of 72 hours after signing the contract any party may revoke the contract, and if a fee has been paid by the prospective adoptive parents, they may, within that 72-hour period, request the return of the fees paid, except for any reasonable fee actually earned by the facilitator that is supported by written record or documentation. *(Added by Stats.1996, c. 1135 (S.B.2035), § 1.)*

Cross References

Prospective adoptive parent defined, see Family Code § 8542.
State defined for purposes of this Code, see Family Code § 145.

Research References

Forms

2 California Transactions Forms--Family Law § 6:3, Definitions.

§ 8632. Contracts; verbal explanation of terms

The adoption facilitator shall also explain the terms of the written contract verbally to the prospective adoptive parents and the birthparents. *(Added by Stats.1996, c. 1135 (S.B.2035), § 1.)*

Cross References

Birth parent defined, see Family Code § 8512.
Prospective adoptive parent defined, see Family Code § 8542.

§ 8632.5. Statewide registration and enforcement process for adoption facilitators

(a) The department shall establish and adopt regulations for a statewide registration and enforcement process for adoption facilitators. The department shall also establish and adopt regulations to require adoption facilitators to post a bond as required by this section.

(b) The department may adapt the process it uses to register adoption service providers in order to provide a similar registration process for adoption facilitators. The process used by the department shall include a procedure for determining the status of bond compliance by adoption facilitators, a means for accepting or denying organizations seeking inclusion in the adoption facilitator registry, a means for removing adoption facilitators from the adoption facilitator registry, and an appeals process for those entities denied inclusion in or removed from the adoption facilitator registry. The department may deny or revoke inclusion in the registry for adoption facilitators to an applicant who does not possess a criminal record clearance or exemption issued by the department pursuant to Section 1522 of the Health and Safety Code and the criminal record clearance regulations applicable to personnel of private adoption agencies. Criminal record clearances and exemptions granted to adoption facilitators are not transferable.

(c) Upon the establishment by the department of a registration process, all adoption facilitators that operate independently from a licensed public or private adoption agency or an adoption attorney in this state shall be required to register with the department.

(d) An adoption facilitator, when posting a bond, shall also file with the department a disclosure form containing the adoption facilitator's name, date of birth, residence address, business address, residence telephone number, business telephone number, and the number of adoptions facilitated for the previous year. Along with the disclosure form, the adoption facilitator shall provide all of the following information to the department:

(1) Proof that the facilitator and any member of the staff who provides direct adoption services has completed two years of college courses, with at least half of the units and hours focusing on social work or a related field.

(2) Proof that the facilitator and any member of the staff who provides direct adoption services has a minimum of three years of

experience employed by a public or private adoption agency licensed by the department, a registered adoption facilitator, or an adoption attorney who assists in bringing adopting persons and placing parents together for the purpose of adoption placement.

(A) An adoption facilitator and any member of the staff subject to this paragraph may waive the educational and experience requirements by satisfying all of the following requirements:

(i) Over five years of work experience providing direct adoption services for a licensed adoption agency.

(ii) Have not been found liable of malfeasance in connection with providing adoption services.

(iii) Provide three separate letters of support attesting to the adoption facilitator's or member's ethics and work providing direct adoption services from any of the following:

(I) A licensed public or private adoption agency.

(II) A member of the Academy of California Adoption Lawyers.

(III) The State Department of Social Services.

(B) An adoption facilitator who is registered with the department may also register staff members under the designation of "trainee." A trainee may provide direct adoption services without meeting the requirements of this paragraph. Any trainee registered with the department shall be directly supervised by an individual who meets all registration requirements.

(3) A valid business license.

(4) A valid, current, government-issued identification to determine the adoption facilitator's identity, such as a California driver's license, identification card, passport, or other form of identification that is acceptable to the department.

(5) Fingerprint images for a background check to be used by the department for the purposes described in this section.

(e) The State Department of Social Services may submit fingerprint images of adoption facilitators to the Department of Justice for the purpose of obtaining criminal offender record information regarding state- and federal-level convictions and arrests, including arrests for which the Department of Justice establishes that the person is free on bail or on the person's own recognizance pending trial or appeal.

(1) The Department of Justice shall forward to the Federal Bureau of Investigation requests for federal summary criminal history information received pursuant to this section. The Department of Justice shall review the information returned from the Federal Bureau of Investigation and compile and disseminate a response to the department.

(2) The Department of Justice shall provide a response to the department pursuant to subdivision (m) of Section 11105 of the Penal Code.

(3) The department shall request from the Department of Justice subsequent arrest notification service, as provided pursuant to Section 11105.2 of the Penal Code.

(4) The Department of Justice shall charge a fee sufficient to cover the cost of processing the request described in this section.

(5) The department may only release an applicant's criminal record information search response as provided in subparagraph (G) of paragraph (3) of subdivision (a) of Section 1522 of the Health and Safety Code.

(f) The department may impose a fee upon applicants for each set of classifiable fingerprint cards that it processes pursuant to paragraph (5) of subdivision (d).

(g) The department shall post on its internet website the registration and bond requirements required by this chapter and a list of adoption facilitators in compliance with the registration and bond requirements of this chapter. The department shall ensure that the information is current and shall update the information at least once every 30 days.

(h) The department shall develop the disclosure form required pursuant to subdivision (d) and shall make it available to any adoption facilitator posting a bond.

(i) The department may charge adoption facilitators an annual filing fee to recover all costs associated with the requirements of this section and that fee shall be set by regulation.

(j) The department may create an Adoption Facilitator Account for deposit of fees received from registrants.

(k) On or before January 1, 2008, the department shall make recommendations for the registry program to the Legislature, including a recommendation on how to implement a department program to accept and compile complaints against registered adoption facilitators and to provide public access to those complaints, by specific facilitator, through the department's internet website.

(*l*) The adoption facilitator registry established pursuant to this section shall become operative on the first day of the first month following an appropriation from the Adoption Facilitator Account to the State Department of Social Services for the startup costs and the costs of administration of the adoption facilitator registry. *(Added by Stats.2006, c. 754 (S.B.1758), § 3. Amended by Stats.2007, c. 130 (A.B.299), § 91; Stats.2008, c. 534 (S.B.1726), § 6; Stats.2019, c. 115 (A.B.1817), § 118, eff. Jan. 1, 2020; Stats.2019, c. 27 (S.B.80), § 3, eff. June 27, 2019.)*

§ 8633. Civil penalty

Any person or entity that violates this chapter is subject to a civil penalty of one thousand dollars ($1,000) or the amount of the contract fees, whichever is greater. *(Added by Stats.1996, c. 1135 (S.B.2035), § 1.)*

Cross References

Person defined for purposes of this Code, see Family Code § 105.

§ 8634. Construction of contract; remedies

Any contract entered into pursuant to this chapter is subject to the rules and remedies relating to contracts generally. *(Added by Stats.1996, c. 1135 (S.B.2035), § 1.)*

Cross References

Contracts, generally, see Civil Code § 1549 et seq.

§ 8635. Repealed by Stats.2006, c. 754 (S.B.1758), § 4

§ 8636. Licensure requirement; surety bond

(a) Prior to engaging in the business of, or acting in the capacity of, an adoption facilitator, any person shall (1) obtain a business license in the appropriate jurisdiction, and (2) post a bond in the amount of twenty-five thousand dollars ($25,000), executed by a corporate surety admitted to do business in this state, with the department in accordance with Section 8632.5.

(b) The surety bond required by subdivision (a) shall be in favor of, and payable to, the people of the State of California and shall be for the benefit of any person damaged by fraud, misstatement, misrepresentation, unlawful act or omission, or failure to provide the services of the adoption facilitator, or the agents, representatives, or employees of the adoption facilitator, while acting within the scope of that employment or agency.

(c) Whenever there is a recovery from a bond required by subdivision (a), the person shall replenish the bond or file a new bond if the former bond cannot be replenished in accordance with subdivision (a) before that person may conduct further business as an adoption facilitator.

(d) An adoption facilitator shall notify the department in writing within 30 days when a surety bond required by this section is renewed, and of any change of name, address, telephone number, or agent for service of process. *(Added by Stats.1996, c. 1135 (S.B. 2035), § 1. Amended by Stats.2006, c. 754 (S.B.1758), § 5.)*

Cross References

Person defined for purposes of this Code, see Family Code § 105.

Research References

Forms

2 California Transactions Forms--Family Law § 6:3, Definitions.

§ 8637. Attorneys; facilitating adoptions; application of law

Notwithstanding the provisions of this chapter, an attorney who provides services specified in Section 8623 related to facilitating an adoption shall be subject only to those provisions of law regulating the practice of law. *(Added by Stats.1996, c. 1135 (S.B.2035), § 1.)*

Research References

Forms

2 California Transactions Forms--Family Law § 6:3, Definitions.

§ 8638. Remedies

(a) Any person aggrieved by any violation of this chapter may bring a civil action for damages, rescission, injunctive relief, or any other civil or equitable remedy.

(b) If the court finds that a person has violated this chapter, it shall award actual damages, plus an amount equal to treble the amount of the actual damages or one thousand dollars ($1,000) per violation, whichever is greater.

(c) In any civil action under this chapter, a prevailing party may recover reasonable attorney's fees and costs.

(d) The Attorney General, a district attorney, or a city attorney may bring a civil action for injunctive relief, restitution, or other equitable relief against the adoption facilitator in the name of the people of the State of California.

(e) Any other person who, based upon information or belief, claims a violation of this chapter has been committed may bring a civil action for injunctive relief on behalf of the general public. *(Added by Stats.1996, c. 1135 (S.B.2035), § 1. Amended by Stats. 2006, c. 754 (S.B.1758), § 6.)*

Cross References

Contracts, damages and interest, see Civil Code §§ 3300, 3287 and 3291.
Person defined for purposes of this Code, see Family Code § 105.

§ 8639. Civil penalty for failure to be in the registry; appeal; regulations

(a) Notwithstanding any other provision of this chapter, any adoption facilitator who operates without having met the requirements established in Section 8632.5 for inclusion into the adoption facilitator registry may be assessed by the department an immediate civil penalty in the amount of one hundred dollars ($100) per day of the violation.

(b) The civil penalty authorized in subdivision (a) shall be imposed if an adoption facilitator is involved in the facilitation of adoptions and the adoption facilitator refuses to seek inclusion in the adoption facilitator registry or if the adoption facilitator's application for inclusion into the adoption facilitator registry is denied and the adoption facilitator continues to facilitate adoptions, unless other available remedies, including criminal prosecution, are deemed more effective by the department.

(c) An adoption facilitator may appeal the assessment to the director.

(d) The department shall adopt regulations implementing this section, including the appeal process authorized in subdivision (c). *(Added by Stats.2008, c. 534 (S.B.1726), § 7.)*

CHAPTER 2. AGENCY ADOPTIONS

Section
8700. Relinquishment of child to department, county adoption agency, or licensed adoption agency; minor parents; rescission; termination of parental rights.
8700.5. Waiver of the right to revoke relinquishment; interview and witness; relinquishment final and irrevocable; conditions rendering waiver void.
8701. Right of birth parents to request information on status of adoption.
8702. Statement presented to birth parents at time of relinquishment; content; form.
8703. Written notice to birth parent upon termination of parental rights; contents.
8704. Responsibilities of department, county adoption agency, or licensed adoption agency; termination of placement; adoption petition; removal of child; consent to adoption.
8704.5. Foster care license or certification or resource family approval not required for placement of child by licensed private adoption agency; supervisory visits.
8705. Consent to adoption of child; deceased persons; court order granting agency custody; guardian appointed.
8706. Medical report; background of child and biological parents; contents; blood sample.
8707. Photo-listing service.
8707.1. Recruitment of potential adoptive parents; ethnic, racial, and cultural diversity.
8708. Race, color, or national origin of adoptive parent or child; nonresident status of adoptive parent.
8709. Consideration of religious background; best interest of child.
8710. Adoptive placement with relatives; placement criteria.
8710.1. Exchange system; child without adoptive placement plan within department or agency jurisdiction.
8710.2. Exchange system; establishment.
8710.3. Exchange system; registration of families.
8710.4. Exchange system; information access.
8711. Application of §§ 8708 to 8710.4.
8711.5. Regulations.
8712. Applicants; information required to be provided; fingerprints; criminal records; prohibited placements; fees.
8713. Removal of child from county in which placed; permission; proceedings; concealment of child; violation.
8714. Petition for adoption; content; guardianship petition; order of adoption.
8714.5. Legislative findings and declarations; adoptions by relatives; adoption petition; order of adoption; contents.
8714.7. Renumbered.
8715. Report of department or agency; submission to court.
8716. Fee paid by adoptive parents; exception.
8717. Report or findings submitted to court; copy to attorney for petitioner.
8718. Appearance before court; adoptive parents and child.
8719. Withdrawal of petition; dismissal of proceedings; notification of department.
8720. Denial or withdrawal of petition; referral to superior court for review; hearing; notice.

Cross References

Agency adoptions defined, see Family Code § 8506.

ADOPTION

Termination of parental rights in adoption proceedings, see Family Code § 7660 et seq.

§ 8700. Relinquishment of child to department, county adoption agency, or licensed adoption agency; minor parents; rescission; termination of parental rights

(a) Either birth parent may relinquish a child to the department, county adoption agency, or licensed adoption agency for adoption by a written statement signed before two subscribing witnesses and acknowledged before an authorized official of the department, county adoption agency, or licensed adoption agency. The relinquishment, when reciting that the person making it is entitled to the sole custody of the child and acknowledged before the officer, is prima facie evidence of the right of the person making it to the sole custody of the child and the person's sole right to relinquish.

(b) A relinquishing parent who is a minor has the right to relinquish a child for adoption to the department, county adoption agency, or licensed adoption agency, and the relinquishment is not subject to revocation by the relinquishing parent by reason of the minority, or because the parent or guardian of the relinquishing minor parent was not served with notice that the relinquishing minor parent relinquished the child for adoption, unless the relinquishing minor parent has previously provided written authorization to serve the relinquishing minor's parent or guardian with that notice.

(c) If a parent resides outside this state and the other parent has relinquished the child for adoption pursuant to subdivision (a) or (d), the parent residing out of state may relinquish the child by a written statement signed before a notary on a form prescribed by the department, and previously signed by an authorized official of the department, county adoption agency, or licensed adoption agency that signifies the willingness of the department, county adoption agency, or licensed adoption agency to accept the relinquishment.

(d) If a parent and child reside outside this state and the other parent has not relinquished the child for adoption to the department, county adoption agency, or licensed adoption agency, the parent residing out of state may relinquish the child to the department, county adoption agency, or licensed adoption agency by a written statement signed by the relinquishing parent, after the following requirements have been satisfied:

(1) Prior to signing the relinquishment, the relinquishing parent shall have received, from a representative of an agency licensed or otherwise approved to provide adoption services under the laws of the relinquishing parent's state of residence, the same counseling and advisement services as if the relinquishing parent resided in this state.

(2) The relinquishment shall be signed before a representative of an agency licensed or otherwise approved to provide adoption services under the laws of the relinquishing parent's state of residence whenever possible or before a licensed social worker on a form prescribed by the department, and previously signed by an authorized official of the department, county adoption agency, or licensed adoption agency, that signifies the willingness of the department, county adoption agency, or licensed adoption agency to accept the relinquishment.

(e)(1) The relinquishment authorized by this section has no effect until a certified copy is sent to, and filed with, the department. The county adoption agency or licensed adoption agency shall send that copy by certified mail, return receipt requested, or by overnight courier or messenger, with proof of delivery, to the department no earlier than the end of the business day following the signing thereof. The agency shall inform the birth parent that during this time period the birth parent may request that the relinquishment be withdrawn and that, if the birth parent makes the request, the relinquishment shall be withdrawn. The relinquishment shall be final 10 business days after receipt of the filing by the department, unless any of the following applies:

(A) The department sends written acknowledgment of receipt of the relinquishment prior to the expiration of that 10–day period, at which time the relinquishment shall be final.

(B) A longer period of time is necessary due to a pending court action or some other cause beyond control of the department.

(C) The birth parent signs a waiver of right to revoke relinquishment pursuant to Section 8700.5, in which case the relinquishment shall become final as provided in that section.

(2) After the relinquishment is final, it may be rescinded only by the mutual consent of the department, county adoption agency, or licensed adoption agency to which the child was relinquished and the birth parent or parents relinquishing the child.

(f) The relinquishing parent may name in the relinquishment the person or persons with whom the relinquishing parent intends that placement of the child for adoption be made by the department, county adoption agency, or licensed adoption agency.

(g) Notwithstanding subdivision (e), if the relinquishment names the person or persons with whom placement by the department, county adoption agency, or licensed adoption agency is intended and the child is not placed in the home of the named person or persons or the child is removed from the home prior to the granting of the adoption, the department, county adoption agency, or licensed adoption agency shall mail a notice by certified mail, return receipt requested, to the birth parent signing the relinquishment within 72 hours of the decision not to place the child for adoption or the decision to remove the child from the home.

(h) The relinquishing parent has 30 days from the date on which the notice described in subdivision (g) was mailed to rescind the relinquishment.

(1) If the relinquishing parent requests rescission during the 30–day period, the department, county adoption agency, or licensed adoption agency shall rescind the relinquishment.

(2) If the relinquishing parent does not request rescission during the 30–day period, the department, county adoption agency, or licensed adoption agency shall select adoptive parents for the child.

(3) If the relinquishing parent and the department, county adoption agency, or licensed adoption agency wish to identify a different person or persons during the 30–day period with whom the child is intended to be placed, the initial relinquishment shall be rescinded and a new relinquishment identifying the person or persons completed.

(i) Subject to the requirements of subdivision (b) of Section 361 of the Welfare and Institutions Code, a parent may sign a relinquishment of a child described in paragraph (1) of subdivision (b) of Section 361 of the Welfare and Institutions Code. If the relinquishment is to a licensed private adoption agency, the parent shall be advised, in writing, that the relinquishment shall have no effect and will be not be filed with, or acknowledged by, the department, unless the court approves the relinquishment pursuant to paragraph (3) of subdivision (b) of Section 361 of the Welfare and Institutions Code. If the court issues an order approving the relinquishment, the licensed private adoption agency shall file the relinquishment and the order with the department. If the court denies the relinquishment, the licensed private adoption agency shall void the relinquishment and inform the parent of that fact.

(j) The filing of the relinquishment with the department terminates all parental rights and responsibilities with regard to the child, except as provided in subdivisions (g) and (h).

(k) The department shall adopt regulations to administer the provisions of this section. *(Stats.1992, c. 162 (A.B.2650), § 10, operative Jan. 1, 1994. Amended by Stats.1993, c. 219 (A.B.1500), § 189; Stats.1994, c. 1269 (A.B.2208), § 56; Stats.1997, c. 793 (A.B.1544), § 3; Stats.1998, c. 1056 (A.B.2773), § 1; Stats.2004, c. 306 (A.B.2674), § 1; Stats.2006, c. 806 (S.B.1325), § 7; Stats.2008, c. 534 (S.B.1726), § 8; Stats.2012, c. 35 (S.B.1013), § 14, eff. June 27,*

2012; Stats.2012, c. 638 (A.B.1757), § 7; Stats.2014, c. 763 (A.B. 1701), § 10, eff. Jan. 1, 2015; Stats.2019, c. 115 (A.B.1817), § 119, eff. Jan. 1, 2020.)

Cross References

Abandoned children, declaration of abandonment, see Family Code § 7822.
Adoptive parents, criminal record, see Penal Code § 11105.3.
Birth parent,
 Defined, see Family Code § 8512.
 Money or benefits for consent or placement of children, see Penal Code § 273.
Department defined, see Family Code § 8518.
Foster homes, alternative methods, see Welfare and Institutions Code § 396 et seq.
Independent adoption, consent, see Family Code § 8814.
Juvenile delinquents and dependents, jurisdiction, see Welfare and Institutions Code § 366.3.
Juvenile delinquents and dependents, priorities and preferences, foster parents and relatives, see Welfare and Institutions Code §§ 361.2 et seq., 366.26.
Licensed adoption agency defined, see Family Code § 8530.
Minor defined for purposes of this Code, see Family Code § 6500.
Notices in dependent child proceedings, selection and implementation hearings, see Welfare and Institutions Code § 294.
Person defined for purposes of this Code, see Family Code § 105.
Prima facie evidence, see Evidence Code § 602.
Proceedings relating to freedom from parental custody and control, application of part, see Family Code § 7808.
Relinquishment of child or execution of adoption placement agreement, determination of child's identity as member of Indian tribe or organization, see Family Code § 8620.
Removal of child from parental custody, search for relative and furnishing identifying information, see Welfare and Institutions Code § 361.3.
Similar provisions, see Family Code § 8814.
State child welfare services, voluntary out-of-home placement, see Welfare and Institutions Code § 16507.6.
State defined for purposes of this Code, see Family Code § 145.
Stepparent adoption, consent, see Family Code § 9003.
Temporary custody of minor in hospital without warrant, conditions requiring a warrant, see Welfare and Institutions Code § 305.6.
Termination of parental rights in adoption proceedings, see Family Code § 7660 et seq.

Research References

Forms

2 California Transactions Forms--Family Law § 6:3, Definitions.
2 California Transactions Forms--Family Law § 6:5, Issues Common to All Types of Adoptions.
2 California Transactions Forms--Family Law § 6:32, Nature of Independent Adoption—Relinquishment Versus Consent.
2 California Transactions Forms--Family Law § 6:83, Nature of Agency Adoption—Governing Law.
2 California Transactions Forms--Family Law § 6:84, Relinquishment as Distinguished from Consent.
2 California Transactions Forms--Family Law § 6:85, Identified or Designated Adoption.
2 California Transactions Forms--Family Law § 6:87, Required Formalities of Relinquishment.
2 California Transactions Forms--Family Law § 6:88, Revocation of Relinquishment Prior to Filing.
2 California Transactions Forms--Family Law § 6:148, Rights of Indian Parents of Indian Children.
2 California Transactions Forms--Family Law § 7:39, Adoption and Termination of Parental Rights.
1¶ 1 Nichols Cyclopedia of Legal Forms Annotated § 7:6, Statutory Provisions—Relinquishment of Child to Another to Obtain Adoption.
West's California Code Forms, Family § 8600, Comment Overview—Adoption of Unmarried Minors.
West's California Code Forms, Family § 8700, Comment Overview—Relinquishment of Child to Department of Social Services or a Licensed Adoption Agency.
West's California Code Forms, Family § 8700 Form 1, Relinquishment by Parent Residing in California.
West's California Code Forms, Family § 9102 Form 1, Petition to Vacate Adoption—Procedural Defect.

West's California Judicial Council Forms ADOPT–200, Adoption Request.

§ 8700.5. Waiver of the right to revoke relinquishment; interview and witness; relinquishment final and irrevocable; conditions rendering waiver void

(a) A relinquishing birth parent may elect to sign a waiver of the right to revoke relinquishment in the presence of any of the following:

(1) A representative of the department or the delegated county adoption agency, or any public adoption agency of another state.

(2) A judicial officer of a court of record, within or outside of California, if the birth parent is represented by independent legal counsel.

(3) An authorized representative of a licensed private adoption agency within or outside of California, including a representative of the adoption agency that witnessed or accepted the relinquishment, if the birth parent is represented by independent legal counsel.

(b) The waiver of the right to revoke relinquishment may not be signed until the department, delegated county adoption agency, or public adoption agency of another state has completed an interview, unless the waiver is signed in the presence of a judicial officer of a court of record of any state or an authorized representative of a private adoption agency licensed within or outside of California. If the waiver is signed in the presence of a judicial officer, the interview and witnessing of the signing of the waiver shall be conducted by the judicial officer. If the waiver is signed in the presence of an authorized representative of a licensed adoption agency, the interview shall be conducted by the independent legal counsel for the birth parent or parents, who shall:

(1) Review the waiver with the birth parent or parents.

(2) Counsel the birth parent or parents about the nature of the intended waiver.

(3) Sign and deliver to the birth parent or parents and the licensed adoption agency a certificate in substantially the following form:

"I, (name of attorney), have counseled my client, (name of client), about the nature and legal effect of the waiver of the right to revoke the relinquishment for adoption. I am so disassociated from the interest of the prospective adoptive parent(s) and the licensed adoption agency as to be in a position to advise my client impartially and confidentially as to the consequences of the waiver. My client is aware that California law provides an indeterminate period, usually 2 to 10 business days, during which a birth parent may revoke a relinquishment for adoption. On the basis of this counsel, I conclude that it is the intent of my client to waive the right to revoke, and to make a permanent and irrevocable relinquishment for adoption. My client understands that upon signing this waiver, my client will not be able to regain custody of the child unless the prospective adoptive parent or parents agree to withdraw the petition for adoption or the court denies the adoption petition."

(c) If the placing birth parent signs the waiver in front of a judicial officer or the department, the relinquishment shall become final and irrevocable at the time the waiver is signed. If the waiver is signed in the presence of an authorized representative of a private licensed adoption agency, the relinquishment shall become final and irrevocable at the close of the next business day after the relinquishment was signed, or at the close of the next business day after expiration of any holding period specified in writing, whichever is later.

(d) The licensed adoption agency shall submit the waiver and certificate to the department with the relinquishment, unless the relinquishment was submitted to the department before the waiver was signed, in which case the waiver and certificate shall be submitted to the department no later than two business days after signing.

§ 8700.5

(e) A waiver executed pursuant to this section shall be void if any of the following occur:

(1) The relinquishment is determined to be invalid.

(2) The relinquishment is revoked during any holding period specified in writing.

(3) The relinquishment is rescinded pursuant to Section 8700.

(f) This section does not limit the birth parent's right to rescind the relinquishment pursuant to Section 8700. *(Added by Stats.2012, c. 638 (A.B.1757), § 8. Amended by Stats.2013, c. 743 (A.B.848), § 1; Stats.2019, c. 115 (A.B.1817), § 120, eff. Jan. 1, 2020.)*

§ 8701. Right of birth parents to request information on status of adoption

At or before the time a relinquishment is signed, the department, county adoption agency, or licensed adoption agency shall advise the birth parent signing the relinquishment, verbally and in writing, that the birth parent may, at any time in the future, request from the department, county adoption agency, or licensed adoption agency all known information about the status of the child's adoption, except for personal, identifying information about the adoptive family. The birth parent shall be advised that this information includes, but is not limited to, all of the following:

(a) Whether the child has been placed for adoption.

(b) The approximate date that an adoption was completed.

(c) If the adoption was not completed or was vacated, for any reason, whether adoptive placement of the child is again being considered. *(Stats.1992, c. 162 (A.B.2650), § 10, operative Jan. 1, 1994. Amended by Stats.2012, c. 35 (S.B.1013), § 15, eff. June 27, 2012.)*

Cross References

Birth parent defined, see Family Code § 8512.
Birth parents, money or benefits for consent, see Penal Code § 273.
Criminal record, adoptive parents, see Family Code §§ 8712, 8811; Penal Code § 11105.3.
Department defined, see Family Code § 8518.
Disclosure of information, see Family Code § 9200 et seq.
Independent adoptions, request for information by birth parents about the status of child's adoption, see Family Code § 8813.
Licensed adoption agency defined, see Family Code § 8530.

§ 8702. Statement presented to birth parents at time of relinquishment; content; form

For Executive Order N–75–20 (2019 CA EO 75-20), concerning a number of different COVID-19-related provisions, including pharmacy testing, remote adoption paperwork, and community development grants, see Historical and Statutory Notes under Government Code § 12730.

(a) The department shall adopt a statement to be presented to the birth parents at the time a relinquishment is signed and to prospective adoptive parents at the time of the home study. The statement shall, in a clear and concise manner and in words calculated to ensure the confidence of the birth parents in the integrity of the adoption process, communicate to the birth parents of a child who is the subject of an adoption petition all of the following facts:

(1) It is in the child's best interest that the birth parent keep the department, county adoption agency, or licensed adoption agency to whom the child was relinquished for adoption informed of any health problems that the parent develops that could affect the child.

(2) It is extremely important that the birth parent keep an address current with the department, county adoption agency, or licensed adoption agency to whom the child was relinquished for adoption in order to permit a response to inquiries concerning medical or social history.

(3) Section 9203 of the Family Code authorizes a person who has been adopted and who attains the age of 21 years to request the department, county adoption agency, or the licensed adoption agency to disclose the name and address of the adoptee's birth parents. Consequently, it is of the utmost importance that the birth parent indicate whether to allow this disclosure by checking the appropriate box provided on the form.

(4) The birth parent may change the decision whether to permit disclosure of the birth parent's name and address, at any time, by sending a notarized letter to that effect, by certified mail, return receipt requested, to the department, county adoption agency, or to the licensed adoption agency that joined in the adoption petition.

(5) The relinquishment will be filed in the office of the clerk of the court in which the adoption takes place. The file is not open to inspection by any persons other than the parties to the adoption proceeding, their attorneys, and the department, except upon order of a judge of the superior court.

(b) The department shall adopt a form to be signed by the birth parents at the time the relinquishment is signed, which shall provide as follows:

"Section 9203 of the Family Code authorizes a person who has been adopted and who attains the age of 21 years to make a request to the State Department of Social Services, county adoption agency, or licensed adoption agency that joined in the adoption petition, for the name and address of the adoptee's birth parents. Indicate by checking one of the boxes below whether or not you wish your name and address to be disclosed:

☐ YES

☐ NO

☐ UNCERTAIN AT THIS TIME; WILL NOTIFY AGENCY AT LATER DATE." *(Stats.1992, c. 162 (A.B.2650), § 10, operative Jan. 1, 1994. Amended by Stats.2002, c. 784 (S.B.1316), § 111; Stats.2012, c. 35 (S.B.1013), § 16, eff. June 27, 2012.)*

Cross References

Birth parent defined, see Family Code § 8512.
Department defined, see Family Code § 8518.
Independent adoption, statement to birth parents, see Family Code § 8818.
Judgment and order defined for purposes of this Code, see Family Code § 100.
Licensed adoption agency defined, see Family Code § 8530.
Person defined for purposes of this Code, see Family Code § 105.
Proceeding defined for purposes of this Code, see Family Code § 110.
Prospective adoptive parent defined, see Family Code § 8542.
State defined for purposes of this Code, see Family Code § 145.

Research References

Forms

West's California Code Forms, Family § 8700, Comment Overview—Relinquishment of Child to Department of Social Services or a Licensed Adoption Agency.

§ 8703. Written notice to birth parent upon termination of parental rights; contents

When the parental rights of a birth parent are terminated pursuant to Chapter 5 (commencing with Section 7660) of Part 3 of Division 12 or Part 4 (commencing with Section 7800) of Division 12, or pursuant to Section 366.25 or 366.26 of the Welfare and Institutions Code, the department, county adoption agency, or licensed adoption agency responsible for the adoptive placement of the child shall send a written notice to the birth parent, if the birth parent's address is known, that contains the following statement:

(a) "You are encouraged to keep the department or this agency informed of your current address in order to permit a response to any inquiry concerning medical or social history made by or on behalf of the child who was the subject of the court action terminating parental rights.

(b) Section 9203 of the Family Code authorizes a person who has been adopted and who attains the age of 21 years to make a request to the State Department of Social Services, county adoption agency, or licensed adoption agency, that joined in the adoption petition, for the name and address of the adoptee's birth parents. Indicate by checking one of the boxes below whether or not you wish your name and address to be disclosed:

( ) YES

( ) NO

( ) UNCERTAIN AT THIS TIME; WILL NOTIFY AGENCY AT LATER DATE" *(Stats.1992, c. 162 (A.B.2650), § 10, operative Jan. 1, 1994. Amended by Stats.2000, c. 910 (A.B.2921), § 1; Stats.2012, c. 35 (S.B.1013), § 17, eff. June 27, 2012.)*

Cross References

Birth parent defined, see Family Code § 8512.
Department defined, see Family Code § 8518.
Independent adoption, termination of parental rights, notice, see Family Code § 8819.
Judgment and order defined for purposes of this Code, see Family Code § 100.
Licensed adoption agency defined, see Family Code § 8530.
Person defined for purposes of this Code, see Family Code § 105.
State defined for purposes of this Code, see Family Code § 145.

Research References

Forms

West's California Code Forms, Family § 7840, Comment Overview—Freedom from Parental Control.

§ 8704. Responsibilities of department, county adoption agency, or licensed adoption agency; termination of placement; adoption petition; removal of child; consent to adoption

(a) The department, county adoption agency, or licensed adoption agency to which a child has been freed for adoption by either relinquishment or termination of parental rights is responsible for the care of the child, and is entitled to the exclusive custody and control of the child until an order of adoption is granted. Any placement for temporary care, or for adoption, made by the department, county adoption agency, or licensed adoption agency may be terminated in its discretion at any time before the granting of an order of adoption. In the event of termination of any placement for temporary care or for adoption, the child shall be returned promptly to the physical custody of the department, county adoption agency, or licensed adoption agency.

(b) No petition may be filed to adopt a child relinquished to the department, county adoption agency, or licensed adoption agency or a child declared free from the custody and control of either or both birth parents and referred to the department, county adoption agency, or licensed adoption agency for adoptive placement, except by the prospective adoptive parents with whom the child has been placed for adoption by the department, county adoption agency, or licensed adoption agency. After the adoption petition has been filed, the department, county adoption agency, or licensed adoption agency may remove the child from the prospective adoptive parents only with the approval of the court, upon motion by the department, county adoption agency, or licensed adoption agency after notice to the prospective adoptive parents, supported by an affidavit or affidavits stating the grounds on which removal is sought. If the department, county adoption agency, or licensed adoption agency refuses to consent to the adoption of a child by the person or persons with whom the department, county adoption agency, or licensed adoption agency placed the child for adoption, the court may nevertheless order the adoption if it finds that the refusal to consent is not in the child's best interest. *(Stats.1992, c. 162 (A.B.2650), § 10, operative Jan. 1, 1994. Amended by Stats.1995, c. 884 (A.B.1743), § 3; Stats.2012, c. 35 (S.B.1013), § 18, eff. June 27, 2012.)*

Cross References

Adoptive parents, criminal record, see Penal Code § 11105.3.
Birth parent defined, see Family Code § 8512.
Birth parents, money or benefits for consent or placement of children, see Penal Code § 273.
Department defined, see Family Code § 8518.
Disclosure of information, see Family Code § 9200 et seq.
Foster homes, alternative methods, see Welfare and Institutions Code § 396 et seq.
Freedom from parental custody and control, proceedings, see Family Code § 7820 et seq.
Judgment and order defined for purposes of this Code, see Family Code § 100.
Jurisdiction of superior court, see Family Code § 200.
Juvenile court, removal of child from parental control, see Welfare and Institutions Code § 726.
Juvenile delinquents and dependents,
  Jurisdiction, see Welfare and Institutions Code § 366.3.
  Priorities and preferences, foster parents and relatives, see Welfare and Institutions Code §§ 361.2 et seq., 366.26.
Licensed adoption agency defined, see Family Code § 8530.
Person defined for purposes of this Code, see Family Code § 105.
Priorities and preferences, adoptive parents, see Welfare and Institutions Code §§ 361.2 et seq., 366.26.
Prospective adoptive parent defined, see Family Code § 8542.

Research References

Forms

2 California Transactions Forms--Family Law § 6:86, Role of Agency.
2 California Transactions Forms--Family Law § 6:99, Agency Consent.
West's California Code Forms, Family § 8704 Form 1, Notice of Motion and Motion for Order Removing Child from Prospective Adoptive Parents.

§ 8704.5. Foster care license or certification or resource family approval not required for placement of child by licensed private adoption agency; supervisory visits

(a) A foster care license or certification or resource family approval shall not be required for placement of a nondependent child who is relinquished for adoption to a licensed private adoption agency, if the child is placed in the care of prospective adoptive parents who have an approved adoption home study that meets the criteria established by the department for home studies conducted within the state.

(b) During a preadoptive placement made pursuant to subdivision (a), the licensed private adoption agency shall conduct in-home supervisory visits no less than once every 30 days, until the child has been legally freed and formally placed for adoption. *(Added by Stats.2011, c. 462 (A.B.687), § 7. Amended by Stats.2017, c. 732 (A.B.404), § 2, eff. Jan. 1, 2018.)*

Cross References

California Community Care Facilities Act, exempt facilities and care or living arrangements, see Health and Safety Code § 1505.

Research References

Forms

2 California Transactions Forms--Family Law § 6:86, Role of Agency.
2 California Transactions Forms--Family Law § 6:99, Agency Consent.

§ 8705. Consent to adoption of child; deceased persons; court order granting agency custody; guardian appointed

(a) Where a child is in the custody of a public agency or licensed adoption agency, if it is established that the persons whose consent to the adoption is required by law are deceased, an action may be brought by the department, county adoption agency, or licensed adoption agency requesting the court to make an order establishing that the requesting agency has the right to custody and control of the child and the authority to place the child for adoption. The department, county adoption agency, or licensed adoption agency bringing the action shall give notice in the form prescribed by the

§ 8705

court to all known relatives of the child up to and including the third degree of lineal or collateral consanguinity.

(b) This section does not apply where a guardian of the person of the child has been appointed pursuant to nomination by a will. *(Stats.1992, c. 162 (A.B.2650), § 10, operative Jan. 1, 1994. Amended by Stats.2012, c. 35 (S.B.1013), § 19, eff. June 27, 2012.)*

Cross References

Adoptive parents, criminal record, see Penal Code § 11105.3.
Birth parents, money or benefits for consent or placement of children, see Penal Code § 273.
Department defined, see Family Code § 8518.
Foster homes, alternative methods, see Welfare and Institutions Code § 396 et seq.
Judgment and order defined for purposes of this Code, see Family Code § 100.
Juvenile delinquents and dependents,
    Jurisdiction, see Welfare and Institutions Code § 366.3.
    Priorities and preferences, foster parents and relatives, see Welfare and Institutions Code §§ 361.2 et seq., 366.26.
Licensed adoption agency defined, see Family Code § 8530.
Person defined for purposes of this Code, see Family Code § 105.

§ 8706. Medical report; background of child and biological parents; contents; blood sample

(a) An agency may not place a child for adoption unless a written report on the child's medical background and, if available, the medical background of the child's biological parents so far as ascertainable, has been submitted to the prospective adoptive parents and they have acknowledged in writing the receipt of the report.

(b) The report on the child's background shall contain all known diagnostic information, including current medical reports on the child, psychological evaluations, and scholastic information, as well as all known information regarding the child's developmental history and family life.

(c)(1) The biological parents may provide a blood sample at a clinic or hospital approved by the State Department of Health Services. The biological parents' failure to provide a blood sample shall not affect the adoption of the child.

(2) The blood sample shall be stored at a laboratory under contract with the State Department of Health Services for a period of 30 years following the adoption of the child.

(3) The purpose of the stored sample of blood is to provide a blood sample from which DNA testing can be done at a later date after entry of the order of adoption at the request of the adoptive parents or the adopted child. The cost of drawing and storing the blood samples shall be paid for by a separate fee in addition to the fee required under Section 8716. The amount of this additional fee shall be based on the cost of drawing and storing the blood samples but at no time shall the additional fee be more than one hundred dollars ($100).

(d)(1) The blood sample shall be stored and released in such a manner as to not identify any party to the adoption.

(2) Any results of the DNA testing shall be stored and released in such a manner as to not identify any party to the adoption. *(Stats.1992, c. 162 (A.B.2650), § 10, operative Jan. 1, 1994. Amended by Stats.1996, c. 1053 (A.B.3241), § 1.)*

Cross References

Department defined, see Family Code § 8518.
Department of Health Care Services, generally, see Health and Safety Code § 100100 et seq.
Disclosure of information, see Family Code § 9200 et seq.
Independent adoption, medical report, see Family Code § 8817.
Intercountry adoptions, medical report on child and biological parents, form and contents, see Family Code § 8909.
Judgment and order defined for purposes of this Code, see Family Code § 100.
Medical report form and contents, regulations, see Family Code § 8608.

Placement history or underlying source documents, disclosure of records to prospective caretakers, see Welfare and Institutions Code § 16010.
Prospective adoptive parent defined, see Family Code § 8542.
State defined for purposes of this Code, see Family Code § 145.

§ 8707. Photo-listing service

(a) The department shall establish a statewide photo-listing service to serve all county adoption agencies and licensed adoption agencies in the state as a means of recruiting adoptive families. The department shall adopt regulations governing the operations of the photo-listing service and shall establish procedures for monitoring compliance with this section.

(b) The photo-listing service shall maintain child specific information that, except as provided in this section, contains a photograph and description of each child who has been legally freed for adoption and whose case plan goal is adoption. Registration of children with the photo-listing service and notification by the licensed adoption agency of changes in a child's photo-listing status shall be reflected in the photo-listing service within 30 working days of receipt of the registration or notification.

(c) The photo-listing service shall be provided to all county adoption agencies, licensed adoption agencies, adoption support groups, and state, regional, and national photo-listings and exchanges requesting copies of the photo-listing service.

(d) All children legally freed for adoption whose case plan goal is adoption shall be photo-listed, unless deferred as provided in subdivision (e) or (f). Adoption agencies shall send a recent photograph and description of each legally freed child to the photo-listing service within 15 working days of the time a child is legally freed for adoption. When adoption has become the case plan goal for a particular child, the adoption agency may photo-list that child before the child becomes legally freed for adoption.

(e) A child shall be deferred from the photo-listing service when the child's foster parents or other identified individuals who have applied to adopt the child are meeting the county adoption agency's or licensed adoption agency's requests for required documentation and are cooperating in the completion of a home study being conducted by the agency.

(f) A child who is 12 years old or older may be deferred from the photo-listing service if the child does not consent to being adopted.

(g) Within 15 working days following a one-year period in which a child is listed in the photo-listing service, the county adoption agency or licensed adoption agency shall submit a revised description and photograph of the child.

(h) County adoption agencies and licensed adoption agencies shall notify the photo-listing service, by telephone, of any adoptive placements or of significant changes in a child's photo-listing status within two working days of the change.

(i) The department shall establish procedures for semiannual review of the photo-listing status of all legally freed children whose case plan goal is adoption, including those who are registered with the photo-listing service and those whose registration has been deferred. *(Stats.1992, c. 162 (A.B.2650), § 10, operative Jan. 1, 1994. Amended by Stats.1998, c. 1056 (A.B.2773), § 2; Stats.2012, c. 35 (S.B.1013), § 20, eff. June 27, 2012.)*

Cross References

Department defined, see Family Code § 8518.
Disclosure of information, see Family Code § 9200 et seq.
Licensed adoption agency defined, see Family Code § 8530.
State defined for purposes of this Code, see Family Code § 145.
Support defined for purposes of this Code, see Family Code § 150.

§ 8707.1. Recruitment of potential adoptive parents; ethnic, racial, and cultural diversity

(a) The agency responsible for recruitment of potential adoptive parents shall make diligent efforts to recruit individuals who reflect the ethnic, racial, and cultural diversity of children for whom adoptive homes are needed.

(b) This section shall not be construed to affect the application of the federal Indian Child Welfare Act. *(Added by Stats.2014, c. 772 (S.B.1460), § 1, eff. Jan. 1, 2015.)*

§ 8708. Race, color, or national origin of adoptive parent or child; nonresident status of adoptive parent

(a) The adoption agency to which a child has been freed for adoption by either relinquishment or termination of parental rights shall not do any of the following:

(1) Deny to any person the opportunity to become an adoptive parent on the basis of the race, color, or national origin of the person or the child involved.

(2) Delay or deny the placement of a child for adoption on the basis of the race, color, or national origin of the adoptive parent or the child involved.

(3) Delay or deny the placement of a child for adoption solely because the prospective, approved adoptive family resides outside the jurisdiction of the department, county adoption agency, or licensed adoption agency. For purposes of this paragraph, an approved adoptive family means a family approved pursuant to the California adoptive applicant assessment standards or approved as a resource family pursuant to Section 1517 of the Health and Safety Code or Section 16519.5 of the Welfare and Institutions Code. If the adoptive applicant assessment was conducted in another state according to that state's standards, the California placing agency shall determine whether the standards of the other state substantially meet the standards and criteria established in California adoption regulations.

(b) This section shall not be construed to affect the application of the federal Indian Child Welfare Act (25 U.S.C. Sec. 1901 and following). *(Added by Stats.1995, c. 884 (A.B.1743), § 4. Amended by Stats.1998, c. 1056 (A.B.2773), § 3; Stats.2003, c. 323 (S.B.984), § 2; Stats.2012, c. 35 (S.B.1013), § 21, eff. June 27, 2012; Stats.2017, c. 732 (A.B.404), § 3, eff. Jan. 1, 2018.)*

Cross References

Adoptive parent defined, see Family Code § 8503.
Department defined, see Family Code § 8518.
Freedom from parental custody and control, proceedings, see Family Code § 7820 et seq.
Hearings terminating parental rights or establishing guardianship of children adjudged dependent children of court, see Welfare and Institutions Code § 366.26.
Licensed adoption agency defined, see Family Code § 8530.
Person defined for purposes of this Code, see Family Code § 105.
Public social services, opportunity for hearing, recipient defined, see Welfare and Institutions Code § 10950.
State defined for purposes of this Code, see Family Code § 145.

Research References

Forms

2 California Transactions Forms--Family Law § 6:94, Consideration of Race, Color, National Origin, or Religion as Factor in Placement.
2 California Transactions Forms--Family Law § 6:95, Nonresident Status of Adoptive Family.

§ 8709. Consideration of religious background; best interest of child

(a) The department, county adoption agency, or licensed adoption agency to which a child has been freed for adoption by either relinquishment or termination of parental rights may consider the child's religious background in determining an appropriate placement.

(b) This section shall not be construed to affect the application of the federal Indian Child Welfare Act (25 U.S.C. Sec. 1901 and following). *(Added by Stats.1995, c. 884 (A.B.1743), § 6. Amended by Stats.2003, c. 323 (S.B.984), § 3; Stats.2012, c. 35 (S.B.1013), § 22, eff. June 27, 2012.)*

Cross References

Freedom from parental custody and control, proceedings, see Family Code § 7820 et seq.
Hearings terminating parental rights or establishing guardianship of children adjudged dependent children of court, see Welfare and Institutions Code § 366.26.

Research References

Forms

2 California Transactions Forms--Family Law § 6:94, Consideration of Race, Color, National Origin, or Religion as Factor in Placement.

§ 8710. Adoptive placement with relatives; placement criteria

(a) If a child is being considered for adoption, the department, county adoption agency, or licensed adoption agency shall first consider adoptive placement in the home of a relative or, in the case of an Indian child, according to the placement preferences and standards set out in subdivisions (c), (d), (e), (f), (g), (h), and (i) of Section 361.31 of the Welfare and Institutions Code. However, if the birth parent refuses to consider a relative or sibling placement, if a relative is not available, if placement with an available relative is not in the child's best interest, or if placement would permanently separate the child from other siblings who are being considered for adoption or who are in foster care and an alternative placement would not require the permanent separation, the foster parent or parents of the child shall be considered with respect to the child along with all other prospective adoptive parents where all of the following conditions are present:

(1) The child has been in foster care with the foster parent or parents for a period of more than four months.

(2) The child has substantial emotional ties to the foster parent or parents.

(3) The child's removal from the foster home would be seriously detrimental to the child's well-being.

(4) The foster parent or parents have made a written request to be considered to adopt the child.

(b) In the case of an Indian child whose foster parent or parents or other prospective adoptive parents do not fall within the placement preferences established in subdivision (c) or (d) of Section 361.31 of the Welfare and Institutions Code, the foster parent or parents or other prospective adoptive parents shall only be considered if the court finds, supported by clear and convincing evidence, that good cause exists to deviate from these placement preferences.

(c) This section does not apply to a child who has been adjudged a dependent of the juvenile court pursuant to Section 300 of the Welfare and Institutions Code.

(d) Upon a request to move a child from a prospective adoptive home for the purpose of placement with siblings or other relatives, the court shall consider the best interests of the child. *(Added by Stats.1995, c. 884 (A.B.1743), § 8. Amended by Stats.2006, c. 838 (S.B.678), § 12; Stats.2010, c. 588 (A.B.2020), § 6; Stats.2012, c. 35 (S.B.1013), § 23, eff. June 27, 2012.)*

Cross References

Hearings terminating parental rights or establishing guardianship, adoptive placement, preference for foster parents, see Welfare and Institutions Code § 366.26.
Licensed adoption agency defined, see Family Code § 8530.
Out-of-home placement, case plan provisions for sibling visitation and relationship development, see Welfare and Institutions Code § 16501.1.

§ 8710

Prospective adoptive parent defined, see Family Code § 8542.

Research References

Forms

2 California Transactions Forms--Family Law § 6:96, Placement Preference for Foster Parents and Extended Family.

§ 8710.1. Exchange system; child without adoptive placement plan within department or agency jurisdiction

If there is not an adoptive placement plan for a child with an approved adoptive family, as defined in subdivision (c) of Section 8708, within the department's, county adoption agency's, or licensed adoption agency's jurisdiction, then the department, county adoption agency, or licensed adoption agency shall register the child with the exchange system described in Section 8710.2. *(Added by Stats.1998, c. 1056 (A.B.2773), § 4. Amended by Stats.2012, c. 35 (S.B.1013), § 24, eff. June 27, 2012.)*

Cross References

Department defined, see Family Code § 8518.
Licensed adoption agency defined, see Family Code § 8530.

§ 8710.2. Exchange system; establishment

In order to preclude the delays or denials described in paragraph (3) of subdivision (a) of Section 8708, the department shall establish a statewide exchange system that interjurisdictionally matches waiting children and approved adoptive families. The department may create a new statewide exchange system, modify an existing statewide exchange system, such as the photo-listing service described in Section 8707, or designate an existing exchange system, such as the Adoption Exchange Enhancement Program, as the statewide exchange system for purposes of this section. *(Added by Stats.1998, c. 1056 (A.B.2773), § 5. Amended by Stats.2019, c. 497 (A.B.991), § 114, eff. Jan. 1, 2020.)*

Cross References

Department defined, see Family Code § 8518.
Judgment and order defined for purposes of this Code, see Family Code § 100.

Research References

Forms

2 California Transactions Forms--Family Law § 6:95, Nonresident Status of Adoptive Family.

§ 8710.3. Exchange system; registration of families

If the department, county adoption agency, or licensed adoption agency has approved a family for adoption pursuant to subdivision (c) of Section 8708 and that family may be appropriate for placement of a child who has been adjudged a dependent child of the juvenile court, the department, county adoption agency, or licensed adoption agency shall register the family with the statewide exchange system established pursuant to Section 8710.2, except in either of the following circumstances:

(a) The family refuses to consent to the registration.

(b) A specific child or children have already been identified for adoptive placement with the family. *(Added by Stats.1998, c. 1056 (A.B.2773), § 6. Amended by Stats.2012, c. 35 (S.B.1013), § 25, eff. June 27, 2012.)*

Cross References

Department defined, see Family Code § 8518.
Licensed adoption agency defined, see Family Code § 8530.

§ 8710.4. Exchange system; information access

(a) The department shall ensure that information regarding families and children registered with the statewide exchange system described in Section 8710.2 is accessible by licensed adoption agency personnel throughout the state. Provision shall be made for secure Internet, telephone, and facsimile access by authorized licensed adoption agency personnel.

(b) Information regarding children maintained by the statewide exchange system described in Section 8710.2 shall be confidential and shall not be disclosed to any parties other than authorized adoption agency personnel, except when consent to disclosure has been received in writing from the birth parents or the court that has jurisdiction. *(Added by Stats.1998, c, 1056 (A.B.2773), § 7.)*

Cross References

Department defined, see Family Code § 8518.
Disclosure of information, see Family Code § 9200 et seq.
Licensed adoption agency defined, see Family Code § 8530.
State defined for purposes of this Code, see Family Code § 145.

§ 8711. Application of §§ 8708 to 8710.4

Sections 8708 to 8710.4, inclusive, apply only in determining the placement of a child who has been relinquished for adoption or has been declared free from the custody and control of the birth parents. *(Stats.1992, c. 162 (A.B.2650), § 10, operative Jan. 1, 1994. Amended by Stats.1998, c. 1056 (A.B.2773), § 8.)*

Cross References

Birth parent defined, see Family Code § 8512.
Freedom from parental custody and control, proceedings, see Family Code § 7820 et seq.

§ 8711.5. Regulations

The department shall adopt regulations to administer the provisions of Sections 8708 to 8711, inclusive. *(Added by Stats.1995, c. 884 (A.B.1743), § 9.)*

Cross References

Department defined, see Family Code § 8518.

§ 8712. Applicants; information required to be provided; fingerprints; criminal records; prohibited placements; fees

(a)(1) The department, county adoption agency, or licensed adoption agency shall require each person who files an application for adoption to be fingerprinted and shall secure from an appropriate law enforcement agency any criminal record of that person to determine whether the person has ever been convicted of a crime other than a minor traffic violation. The department, county adoption agency, or licensed adoption agency may also secure the person's full criminal record, if any, with the exception of any convictions for which relief has been granted pursuant to Section 1203.49 of the Penal Code. A federal-level criminal offender record request to the Department of Justice shall be submitted with fingerprint images and related information required by the Department of Justice for the purposes of obtaining information as to the existence and content of a record of an out-of-state or federal conviction or arrest of a person or information regarding any out-of-state or federal crimes or arrests for which the Department of Justice establishes that the person is free on bail, or on their own recognizance pending trial or appeal. The Department of Justice shall forward to the Federal Bureau of Investigation any requests for federal summary criminal history information received pursuant to this section. The Department of Justice shall review the information returned from the Federal Bureau of Investigation and shall compile and disseminate a response to the department, county adoption agency, or licensed adoption agency.

(2) The department, county adoption agency, or licensed adoption agency may obtain arrest or conviction records or reports from any law enforcement agency as necessary to the performance of its duties, as provided in this section.

(b) Notwithstanding subdivision (c), the criminal record, if any, shall be taken into consideration when evaluating the prospective adoptive parent, and an assessment of the effects of any criminal history on the ability of the prospective adoptive parent to provide adequate and proper care and guidance to the child shall be included in the report to the court.

(c) The department, county adoption agency, or licensed adoption agency shall not give final approval for an adoptive placement in any home in which the prospective adoptive parent or any adult living in the prospective adoptive home has been convicted of an offense for which an exemption cannot be granted pursuant to subparagraph (A) of paragraph (2) of subdivision (g) of Section 1522 of the Health and Safety Code.

(d) Any fee charged by a law enforcement agency for fingerprinting or for checking or obtaining the criminal record of the applicant shall be paid by the applicant. The department, county adoption agency, or licensed adoption agency may defer, waive, or reduce the fee when its payment would cause economic hardship to prospective adoptive parents detrimental to the welfare of the adopted child, when the child has been in the foster care of the prospective adoptive parents for at least one year, or if necessary for the placement of a special-needs child. *(Stats.1992, c. 162 (A.B.2650), § 10, operative Jan. 1, 1994. Amended by Stats.2007, c. 464 (A.B.340), § 1; Stats.2008, c. 701 (A.B.2651), § 1, eff. Sept. 30, 2008; Stats.2012, c. 35 (S.B.1013), § 26, eff. June 27, 2012; Stats.2014, c. 708 (A.B.1585), § 1, eff. Jan. 1, 2015; Stats.2015, c. 303 (A.B.731), § 151, eff. Jan. 1, 2016; Stats.2016, c. 612 (A.B.1997), § 10, eff. Jan. 1, 2017; Stats.2017, c. 733 (S.B.213), § 1, eff. Jan. 1, 2018; Stats.2019, c. 115 (A.B.1817), § 121, eff. Jan. 1, 2020.)*

Cross References

Applicant defined, see Family Code § 8509.
California Community Care Facilities Act, fingerprints and criminal records, see Health and Safety Code § 1522.
Criminal records access, state child welfare agency, see Welfare and Institutions Code § 16504.5.
Criminal records, adoptive parents, see Penal Code § 11105.3.
Department defined, see Family Code § 8518.
Disclosure of information, see Family Code § 9200 et seq.
Federally recognized tribe, license or approval of a home for the purpose of foster or adoptive placement of an Indian child, authorization and procedure, see Welfare and Institutions Code § 10553.12.
Foster care pilot program to establish a family approval process, see Welfare and Institutions Code § 16519.5.
Implementation of unified, family friendly, and child-centered resource family approval process, continuation of licensure and oversight processes for foster family homes licensed prior to January 1, 2017, see Health and Safety Code § 1517.1.
Implementation of unified, family friendly, and child-centered resource family approval process, duties of foster family agencies and Department of Social Services, see Health and Safety Code § 1517.
Independent adoptions, fingerprinting and investigation of criminal record, see Family Code § 8811.
Intercountry adoptions, fingerprinting and investigation of criminal record, see Family Code § 8908.
Licensed adoption agency defined, see Family Code § 8530.
Minor defined for purposes of this Code, see Family Code § 6500.
Person defined for purposes of this Code, see Family Code § 105.
Prospective adoptive parent defined, see Family Code § 8542.
Resource families currently approved by foster family agency or county, approval by subsequent foster family agency, requirements, forfeiture of approval, see Health and Safety Code § 1517.5.
Special-needs child defined, see Family Code § 8545.
Stepparent adoptions, investigation, see Family Code § 9001.
Tribe or tribal organization, placement of child into foster or adoptive care, request for criminal history information, see Penal Code § 11105.08.

§ 8713. Removal of child from county in which placed; permission; proceedings; concealment of child; violation

(a) In no event may a child who has been freed for adoption be removed from the county in which the child was placed, by any person who has not petitioned to adopt the child, without first obtaining the written consent of the department, county adoption agency, or licensed adoption agency responsible for the child.

(b) During the pendency of an adoption proceeding:

(1) The child proposed to be adopted shall not be concealed from the * * * agency that is investigating the adoption or from the court with jurisdiction over the adoption proceeding * * *.

(2) The child shall not be removed from the county * * * of the * * * petitioner's residence at the time of placement, unless the petitioners or other interested persons first obtain permission for the removal from the court, after giving advance written notice of intent to obtain the court's permission to the department, county adoption agency, or licensed adoption agency responsible for the child. Upon proof of giving notice, permission may be granted by the court if, within a period of 15 days after the date of giving notice, no objections are filed with the court by the department, county adoption agency, or licensed adoption agency responsible for the child. If the department, county adoption agency, or licensed adoption agency files objections within the 15-day period, upon the request of the petitioners the court shall immediately set the matter for hearing and give to the objector, the petitioners, and the party or parties requesting permission for the removal reasonable notice of the hearing by certified mail, return receipt requested, to the address of each as shown in the records of the adoption proceeding. Upon a finding that the objections are without good cause, the court may grant the requested permission for removal of the child, subject to any limitations that appear to be in the child's best interest.

(c) This section does not apply in any of the following situations:

(1) When the child is absent for a period of not more than 30 days from the county * * * of the * * * petitioner's residence at the time of placement, unless a notice of recommendation of denial of petition has been personally served on the petitioners or the court has issued an order prohibiting the child's removal from the county of the petitioner's residence at the time of placement, pending consideration of any of the following:

(A) The suitability of the petitioners.

(B) The care provided the child.

(C) The availability of the legally required agency consents to the adoption.

(2) Where the child has been returned to and remains in the custody and control of the child's birth parent or parents.

(3) Where written consent for the removal of the child is obtained from the department, county adoption agency, or licensed adoption agency responsible for the child.

(d) A violation of this section is a violation of Section 280 of the Penal Code.

(e) Neither this section nor Section 280 of the Penal Code may be construed to render lawful any act that is unlawful under any other applicable law. *(Stats.1992, c. 162 (A.B.2650), § 10, operative Jan. 1, 1994. Amended by Stats.2012, c. 35 (S.B.1013), § 27, eff. June 27, 2012; Stats.2022, c. 159 (A.B.2495), § 3, eff. Jan. 1, 2023.)*

Cross References

Adoptive parents, criminal record, see Penal Code § 11105.3.
Birth parent, money or benefits for consent or placement of children, see Penal Code § 273.
Birth parent defined, see Family Code § 8512.
Child abduction, violations of specified adoption proceedings, punishment, see Penal Code § 280.
County defined for purposes of this Code, see Family Code § 67.
Department defined, see Family Code § 8518.
Foster homes, alternative methods, see Welfare and Institutions Code § 396 et seq.
Independent adoption, removal and concealment of child, see Family Code § 8803.
Intercountry adoption, removal and concealment, see Family Code § 8910.
Judgment and order defined for purposes of this Code, see Family Code § 100.
Juvenile delinquents and dependents,
Jurisdiction, see Welfare and Institutions Code § 366.3.

§ 8713

Priorities and preferences, foster parents and relatives, see Welfare and Institutions Code §§ 361.2 et seq., 366.26.
Licensed adoption agency defined, see Family Code § 8530.
Person defined for purposes of this Code, see Family Code § 105.
Petitioner defined for purposes of this Code, see Family Code § 126.
Priorities and preferences, adoptive parents, see Welfare and Institutions Code §§ 361.2 et seq., 366.26.
Proceeding defined for purposes of this Code, see Family Code § 110.
Similar provisions, see Family Code §§ 8803, 8910.

Research References

Forms

2 California Transactions Forms--Family Law § 6:2, Governing Law.
2 California Transactions Forms--Family Law § 6:90, Adoptive Placement Agreement.

§ 8714. Petition for adoption; content; guardianship petition; order of adoption

(a) A person desiring to adopt a nondependent child may for that purpose file an adoption request in a county authorized by Section 8609.5. A person desiring to adopt a child who has been adjudged to be a dependent of the juvenile court pursuant to Section 300 of the Welfare and Institutions Code, freed for adoption by the juvenile court, and placed for adoption with the petitioner, may file the adoption request either in the county where the petitioner resides or in the county where the child was freed for adoption.

(b) The court clerk shall immediately notify the department at Sacramento in writing of the pendency of the proceeding and of any subsequent action taken.

(c) If the petitioner has entered into a postadoption contact agreement * * * as set forth in Section 8616.5, the agreement, signed by the participating parties, shall be * * * filed with the * * * court in accordance with Section 8616.5.

(d) The caption of the adoption petition shall contain the names of the petitioners, but not the child's name. The petition shall state the child's sex and date of birth. The name the child had before adoption shall appear in the joinder signed by the licensed adoption agency.

(e) If the child is the subject of a guardianship petition, the adoption petition shall so state and shall include the caption and docket number or have attached a copy of the letters of the guardianship or temporary guardianship. The petitioners shall notify the court of any petition for guardianship or temporary guardianship filed after the adoption petition. The guardianship proceeding shall be consolidated with the adoption proceeding.

(f) The order of adoption shall contain the child's adopted name * * * and the name the child had before adoption. (Stats.1992, c. 162 (A.B.2650), § 10, operative Jan. 1, 1994. Amended by Stats.1993, c. 219 (A.B.1500), § 190; Stats.2000, c. 910 (A.B.2921), § 2; Stats. 2000, c. 930 (S.B.2157), § 1; Stats.2002, c. 1112 (A.B.746), § 1; Stats.2003, c. 251 (S.B.182), § 6; Stats.2012, c. 638 (A.B.1757), § 9; Stats.2016, c. 474 (A.B.2882), § 10, eff. Jan. 1, 2017; Stats.2022, c. 159 (A.B.2495), § 4, eff. Jan. 1, 2023.)

Cross References

Adoptive parents, criminal record, see Penal Code § 11105.3.
Birth parents, money or benefits for consent or placement of children, see Penal Code § 273.
Child Abuse and Neglect Reporting Act, notice to child protection agencies or district attorneys, availability of information, see Penal Code § 11170.
County defined for purposes of this Code, see Family Code § 67.
Disclosure of information, see Family Code § 9200 et seq.
Foster homes, alternative methods, see Welfare and Institutions Code § 396 et seq.
Guardianship proceedings, exclusive jurisdiction, consolidation of guardianship and adoption proceedings, see Probate Code § 2205.
Independent adoption, petition, see Family Code § 8802.
Intercountry adoption, petition, see Family Code § 8912.
Judgment and order defined for purposes of this Code, see Family Code § 100.
Jurisdiction of superior court, see Family Code § 200.
Juvenile delinquents and dependents, jurisdiction, see Welfare and Institutions Code § 366.3.
Person defined for purposes of this Code, see Family Code § 105.
Petitioner defined for purposes of this Code, see Family Code § 126.
Priorities and preferences, adoptive or foster parents and relatives, see Welfare and Institutions Code §§ 361.2 et seq., 366.26.
Proceeding defined for purposes of this Code, see Family Code § 110.
Similar provisions, see Family Code §§ 8802, 8912, 9000.
State defined for purposes of this Code, see Family Code § 145.
Stepparent adoption, petition, see Family Code § 9000.

Research References

Forms

2 California Transactions Forms--Family Law § 6:13, Appearance in Person or by Counsel.
2 California Transactions Forms--Family Law § 6:98, Form Drafting Considerations.
West's California Judicial Council Forms ADOPT-200, Adoption Request.
West's California Judicial Council Forms ADOPT-215, Adoption Order (Also Available in Spanish).
West's California Judicial Council Forms JV-505, Statement Regarding Parentage (Juvenile) (Also Available in Spanish).

§ 8714.5. Legislative findings and declarations; adoptions by relatives; adoption petition; order of adoption; contents

(a) The Legislature finds and declares the following:

(1) It is the intent of the Legislature to expedite legal permanency for children who cannot return to their parents and to remove barriers to adoption by relatives of children who are already in the dependency system or who are at risk of entering the dependency system.

(2) This goal will be achieved by empowering families, including extended families, to care for their own children safely and permanently whenever possible, by preserving existing family relationships, thereby causing the least amount of disruption to the child and the family, and by recognizing the importance of sibling and half-sibling relationships.

(b) A relative desiring to adopt a child may for that purpose file a petition in the county in which the petitioner resides. Where a child has been adjudged to be a dependent of the juvenile court pursuant to Section 300 of the Welfare and Institutions Code, and thereafter has been freed for adoption by the juvenile court, the petition may be filed either in the county where the petitioner resides or in the county where the child was freed for adoption.

(c) Upon the filing of a petition for adoption by a relative, the clerk of the court shall immediately notify the State Department of Social Services in Sacramento in writing of the pendency of the proceeding and of any subsequent action taken.

(d) If the adopting relative has entered into a postadoption contact agreement with the birth parent as set forth in Section 8616.5 the agreement, signed by the participating parties, shall be attached to and filed with the petition for adoption under subdivision (b).

(e) The caption of the adoption petition shall contain the name of the relative petitioner. The petition shall state the child's name, sex, and date of birth.

(f) If the child is the subject of a guardianship petition, the adoption petition shall so state and shall include the caption and docket number or have attached a copy of the letters of the guardianship or temporary guardianship. The petitioner shall notify the court of any petition for adoption. The guardianship proceeding shall be consolidated with the adoption proceeding, and the consolidated case shall be heard and decided in the court in which the adoption is pending.

(g) The order of adoption shall contain the child's adopted name and, if requested by the adopting relative, or if requested by the child who is 12 years of age or older, the name the child had before adoption.

(h) For purposes of this section, "relative" means an adult who is related to the child or the child's half-sibling by blood or affinity, including all relatives whose status is preceded by the words "step," "great," "great-great," or "grand," or the spouse of any of these persons, even if the marriage was terminated by death or dissolution. *(Added by Stats.1997, c. 793 (A.B.1544), § 4. Amended by Stats.2000, c. 910 (A.B.2921), § 3; Stats.2000, c. 930 (S.B.2157), § 2; Stats.2002, c. 784 (S.B.1316), § 112; Stats.2003, c. 251 (S.B.182), § 7; Stats.2008, c. 534 (S.B.1726), § 9.)*

Cross References

Adult defined for purposes of this Code, see Family Code § 6501.
Affinity defined for purposes of this Code, see Family Code § 6205.
County defined for purposes of this Code, see Family Code § 67.
Guardianship proceedings, exclusive jurisdiction, consolidation of guardianship and adoption proceedings, see Probate Code § 2205.
Judgment and order defined for purposes of this Code, see Family Code § 100.
Person defined for purposes of this Code, see Family Code § 105.
Petitioner defined for purposes of this Code, see Family Code § 126.
Post-adoptive sibling contact, jurisdiction over post-adoption agreements, see Welfare and Institutions Code § 366.29.
Proceeding defined for purposes of this Code, see Family Code § 110.
References to husband, wife, spouses and married persons, persons included for purposes of this Code, see Family Code § 11.
State defined for purposes of this Code, see Family Code § 145.

Research References

Forms

2 California Transactions Forms--Family Law § 6:55, Agreement for Continuing Contact.
2 California Transactions Forms--Family Law § 6:97, Kinship Adoption.
2 California Transactions Forms--Family Law § 6:100, Postadoption Contact Agreement [Form Adopt-310].
West's California Code Forms, Family § 8700, Comment Overview—Relinquishment of Child to Department of Social Services or a Licensed Adoption Agency.
West's California Judicial Council Forms ADOPT-200, Adoption Request.
West's California Judicial Council Forms ADOPT-215, Adoption Order (Also Available in Spanish).
West's California Judicial Council Forms ADOPT-310, Contact After Adoption Agreement.
West's California Judicial Council Forms ADOPT-315, Request To: Enforce, Change, End Contact After Adoption Agreement.
West's California Judicial Council Forms ADOPT-320, Answer to Request To: Enforce, Change, End Contact After Adoption Agreement.
West's California Judicial Council Forms ADOPT-325, Judge's Order To: Enforce, Change, End Contact After Adoption Agreement.
West's California Judicial Council Forms JV-505, Statement Regarding Parentage (Juvenile) (Also Available in Spanish).

§ 8714.7. Renumbered § 8616.5 and amended by Stats.2003, c. 251 (S.B.182), § 8

§ 8715. Report of department or agency; submission to court

(a) The department, county adoption agency, or licensed adoption agency, whichever is a party to, or joins in, the petition, shall submit a full report of the facts of the case to the court.

(b) If the child has been adjudged to be a dependent of the juvenile court pursuant to Section 300 of the Welfare and Institutions Code, and has thereafter been freed for adoption by the juvenile court, the report required by this section shall describe whether the requirements of subdivision (e) of Section 16002 of the Welfare and Institutions Code have been completed and what, if any, plan exists for facilitation of postadoptive contact between the child who is the subject of the adoption petition and the child's siblings and half siblings.

(c) If a petition for adoption has been filed with a postadoption contact agreement pursuant to Section 8616.5, the report shall address whether the postadoption contact agreement has been entered into voluntarily, and whether it is in the best interest of the child who is the subject of the petition.

(d) The department may also submit a report in those cases in which a county adoption agency, or licensed adoption agency is a party or joins in the adoption petition.

(e) If a petitioner is a resident of a state other than California, an updated and current home study report, conducted and approved by a licensed adoption agency or other authorized resource in the state in which the petitioner resides, shall be reviewed and endorsed by the department, county adoption agency, or licensed adoption agency, if the standards and criteria established for a home study report in the other state are substantially commensurate with the home study standards and criteria established in California adoption regulations. *(Stats.1992, c. 162 (A.B.2650), § 10, operative Jan. 1, 1994. Amended by Stats.1997, c. 793 (A.B.1544), § 6; Stats.1998, c. 1072 (A.B.2196), § 1; Stats.2000, c. 910 (A.B.2921), § 4.5; Stats.2000, c. 930 (S.B. 2157), § 4; Stats.2002, c. 1112 (A.B.746), § 2; Stats.2003, c. 251 (S.B.182), § 9; Stats.2012, c. 35 (S.B.1013), § 28, eff. June 27, 2012; Stats.2019, c. 115 (A.B.1817), § 122, eff. Jan. 1, 2020.)*

Cross References

Department defined, see Family Code § 8518.
Hearings terminating parental rights or establishing guardianship of children adjudged dependent children of court, see Welfare and Institutions Code § 366.26.
Independent adoption, report, see Family Code § 8807.
Intercountry adoption, report, see Family Code § 8914.
Licensed adoption agency defined, see Family Code § 8530.
Mandatory nature of requirements, see Family Code § 12.
Out-of-home placement, case plan provisions for sibling visitation and relationship development, see Welfare and Institutions Code § 16501.1.
Petitioner defined for purposes of this Code, see Family Code § 126.
State defined for purposes of this Code, see Family Code § 145.
Stepparent adoption, report, see Family Code § 9001.
Waiver of personal appearance of prospective adoptive parent, see Family Code § 8613.5.

Research References

Forms

2 California Transactions Forms--Family Law § 6:13, Appearance in Person or by Counsel.

§ 8716. Fee paid by adoptive parents; exception

Where a petition is filed for the adoption of a child who has been placed for adoption by a county adoption agency, licensed county adoption agency, or the department, the county adoption agency, licensed adoption agency, or department may, at the time of filing a favorable report with the court, require the petitioners to pay to the agency, as agent of the state, or to the department, a fee of five hundred dollars ($500). The county adoption agency, licensed adoption agency, or department may defer, waive, or reduce the fee if its payment would cause economic hardship to the prospective adoptive parents detrimental to the welfare of the adopted child, if the child has been in the foster care of the prospective adoptive parents for at least one year, or if necessary for the placement of a special-needs child. *(Stats.1992, c. 162 (A.B.2650), § 10, operative Jan. 1, 1994. Amended by Stats.2012, c. 35 (S.B.1013), § 29, eff. June 27, 2012.)*

Cross References

Adoptive parent defined, see Family Code § 8503.
County adoption agencies, cost of administration, see Welfare and Institutions Code § 16101.
County defined for purposes of this Code, see Family Code § 67.
Department defined, see Family Code § 8518.
Independent adoption, report fee, see Family Code § 8810.
Jurisdiction, superior court, see Family Code § 200.
Petitioner defined for purposes of this Code, see Family Code § 126.
Prospective adoptive parent defined, see Family Code § 8542.
Special-needs child defined, see Family Code § 8545.
State defined for purposes of this Code, see Family Code § 145.

§ 8716

Stepparent adoption, report fee, see Family Code § 9002.

Research References

Forms

2 California Transactions Forms--Family Law § 6:93, Agency Fees.

§ 8717. Report or findings submitted to court; copy to attorney for petitioner

When any report or findings are submitted to the court by the department, county adoption agency, or licensed adoption agency, a copy of the report or findings, whether favorable or unfavorable, shall be given to the petitioner's attorney in the proceeding, if the petitioner has an attorney of record, or to the petitioner. *(Stats.1992, c. 162 (A.B.2650), § 10, operative Jan. 1, 1994. Amended by Stats.2012, c. 35 (S.B.1013), § 30, eff. June 27, 2012.)*

Cross References

Department defined, see Family Code § 8518.
Disclosure of information, see Family Code § 9200 et seq.
Independent adoption, copy of report, see Family Code § 8821.
Intercountry adoption, copy of report, see Family Code § 8915.
Licensed adoption agency defined, see Family Code § 8530.
Petitioner defined for purposes of this Code, see Family Code § 126.
Proceeding defined for purposes of this Code, see Family Code § 110.

§ 8718. Appearance before court; adoptive parents and child

The prospective adoptive parents and the child proposed to be adopted shall appear before the court pursuant to Sections 8612 and 8613. *(Stats.1992, c. 162 (A.B.2650), § 10, operative Jan. 1, 1994.)*

Cross References

Independent adoption, appearance, see Family Code § 8823.
Intercountry adoption, appearance before court, see Family Code § 8913.
Jurisdiction of superior court, see Family Code § 200.
Prospective adoptive parent defined, see Family Code § 8542.
Stepparent adoption, appearance, see Family Code § 9007.

§ 8719. Withdrawal of petition; dismissal of proceedings; notification of department

If the petitioners move to withdraw the adoption petition or to dismiss the proceeding, the court clerk shall immediately notify the department at Sacramento of the action. *(Stats.1992, c. 162 (A.B. 2650), § 10, operative Jan. 1, 1994.)*

Cross References

Independent adoption, notice of withdrawal or dismissal, see Family Code § 8804.
Intercountry adoption, notice of withdrawal or dismissal, see Family Code § 8916.
Jurisdiction of superior court, see Family Code § 200.
Petitioner defined for purposes of this Code, see Family Code § 126.
Proceeding defined for purposes of this Code, see Family Code § 110.
Stepparent adoption, notice of withdrawal or dismissal, see Family Code § 9006.

§ 8720. Denial or withdrawal of petition; referral to superior court for review; hearing; notice

(a) If the department, county adoption agency, or licensed adoption agency finds that the home of the petitioners is not suitable for the child or that the required agency consents are not available and the department, county adoption agency, or licensed adoption agency recommends that the petition be denied, or if the petitioners desire to withdraw the petition and the department, county adoption agency, or licensed adoption agency recommends that the petition be denied, the clerk upon receipt of the report of the department, county adoption agency, or licensed adoption agency shall immediately refer it to the court for review.

(b) Upon receipt of the report, the court shall set a date for a hearing of the petition and shall give reasonable notice of the hearing to the department, county adoption agency, or licensed adoption agency, the petitioners, and, if necessary, the birth parents, by certified mail, return receipt requested, to the address of each as shown in the proceeding.

(c) The department, county adoption agency, or licensed adoption agency shall appear to represent the child. *(Stats.1992, c. 162 (A.B.2650), § 10, operative Jan. 1, 1994. Amended by Stats.2012, c. 35 (S.B.1013), § 31, eff. June 27, 2012.)*

Cross References

Birth parent defined, see Family Code § 8512.
Department defined, see Family Code § 8518.
Independent adoption, unfavorable recommendation, see Family Code § 8822.
Intercountry adoption, unfavorable recommendation, see Family Code § 8917.
Jurisdiction of superior court, see Family Code § 200.
Licensed adoption agency defined, see Family Code § 8530.
Petitioner defined for purposes of this Code, see Family Code § 126.
Proceeding defined for purposes of this Code, see Family Code § 110.

Research References

Forms

2 California Transactions Forms--Family Law § 6:83, Nature of Agency Adoption—Governing Law.

CHAPTER 2.5. ADOPTIONS BY RELATIVE CAREGIVERS OR FOSTER PARENTS

Section

8730. Abbreviated home study assessments; requirements.
8731. Adoption sought by foster parent; time for initiation; assessment or home study.
8732. Adoption sought by foster parent of six months or relative caregiver; medical examination and report.
8733. Report of special needs of child to be adopted; supply to adopting parents.
8734. Adoption training programs.
8735. Information to department when foster parent or relative caregiver denied right to adopt.
8736. Chapter provisions as grounds for removal of child from placement.

Cross References

Hearings terminating parental rights or establishing guardianship, adoptive placement, preferences, see Welfare and Institutions Code § 366.26.
Placement of child in home of relative or prospective guardian, prior background check, see Welfare and Institutions Code § 361.4.

§ 8730. Abbreviated home study assessments; requirements

(a) Subject to the requirements of subdivision (b), the department, county adoption agency, or licensed adoption agency may provide an abbreviated home study assessment for any of the following:

(1) A licensed or certified foster parent with whom the child has lived for a minimum of six months.

(2) An approved relative caregiver or nonrelated extended family member with whom the child has had an ongoing and significant relationship.

(3) A court-appointed relative guardian of the child who has been investigated and approved pursuant to the guardianship investigation process and has had physical custody of the child for at least one year.

(4) A prospective adoptive parent who has completed an agency-supervised adoption within the last two years.

(b) Unless otherwise ordered by a court with jurisdiction over the child, home study assessments completed pursuant to subdivision (a) shall include, at minimum, all of the following:

(1) A criminal records check, as required by all applicable state and federal statutes and regulations.

(2) A determination that the applicant has sufficient financial stability to support the child and ensure that an adoption assistance program payment or other government assistance to which the child is entitled is used exclusively to meet the child's needs. In making this determination, the experience of the applicant only while the child was in the applicant's care shall be considered. For purposes of this section, the applicant shall be required to provide verification of employment records or income or both.

(3) A determination that the applicant has not abused or neglected the child while the child has been in the applicant's care and has fostered the healthy growth and development of the child. This determination shall include a review of the disciplinary practices of the applicant to ensure that the practices are age appropriate and do not physically or emotionally endanger the child.

(4) A determination that the applicant is not likely to abuse or neglect the child in the future and that the applicant can protect the child, ensure necessary care and supervision, and foster the child's healthy growth and development.

(5) A determination that the applicant can address issues that may affect the child's well-being, including, but not limited to, the child's physical health, mental health, and educational needs.

(6) An interview with the applicant, an interview with each individual residing in the home, and an interview with the child to be adopted.

(7) A review by the department, county adoption agency, or licensed adoption agency of all previous guardianship investigation reports, home study assessments, and preplacement evaluations of each applicant. Notwithstanding any other law regarding the confidential nature of these reports, upon the written request of the department, county adoption agency, or licensed adoption agency that is accompanied by a signed release from the applicant, the department, county adoption agency, or licensed adoption agency may receive a copy of any of these reports from a court, investigating agency, or other person or entity in possession of the report. The department, county adoption agency, or licensed adoption agency shall document attempts to obtain the report and, if applicable, the reason the report is unavailable.

(c) The department may promulgate regulations as necessary or appropriate to implement this section.

(d) This section does not apply to independent adoptions filed pursuant to Chapter 3 (commencing with Section 8800). *(Added by Stats.1998, c. 983 (A.B.2286), § 3. Amended by Stats.2012, c. 35 (S.B.1013), § 32, eff. June 27, 2012; Stats.2013, c. 743 (A.B.848), § 2; Stats.2014, c. 71 (S.B.1304), § 55, eff. Jan. 1, 2015; Stats.2019, c. 115 (A.B.1817), § 123, eff. Jan. 1, 2020.)*

Cross References

Abuse defined for purposes of the Domestic Violence Protection Act, see Family Code § 6203.
Adoptive placement with relatives or foster parents, criteria, see Family Code § 8710.
Department defined, see Family Code § 8518.
Hearings terminating parental rights or establishing guardianship, adoptive placement, preferences, see Welfare and Institutions Code § 366.26.
Judgment and order defined for purposes of this Code, see Family Code § 100.
Licensed adoption agency defined, see Family Code § 8530.
Placement of child in home of relative or prospective guardian, prior background check, see Welfare and Institutions Code § 361.4.
Prospective adoptive parent defined, see Family Code § 8542.
Support defined for purposes of this Code, see Family Code § 150.

§ 8731. Adoption sought by foster parent; time for initiation; assessment or home study

If the prospective adoptive parent of a child is a foster parent, the assessment or home study described in Section 8730 shall not be initiated until the child to be adopted has resided in the home of the foster parent for at least six months. *(Added by Stats.1998, c. 983 (A.B.2286), § 3.)*

Cross References

Prospective adoptive parent defined, see Family Code § 8542.

§ 8732. Adoption sought by foster parent of six months or relative caregiver; medical examination and report

A report of a medical examination of the foster parent with whom the child has lived for a minimum of six months or the relative caregiver who has had an ongoing and significant relationship with the child shall be included in the assessment of each applicant unless the department, county adoption agency, or licensed adoption agency determines that, based on other available information, this report is unnecessary. *(Added by Stats.1998, c. 983 (A.B.2286), § 3. Amended by Stats.2012, c. 35 (S.B.1013), § 33, eff. June 27, 2012; Stats.2020, c. 104 (A.B.2944), § 2, eff. Sept. 18, 2020.)*

Cross References

Adult defined for purposes of this Code, see Family Code § 6501.
Applicant defined, see Family Code § 8509.

§ 8733. Report of special needs of child to be adopted; supply to adopting parents

The department, county adoption agency, or licensed adoption agency shall require the adoptive parent to be provided with information related to the specific needs of the child to be adopted, that, as determined by the licensed adoption agency, may include information regarding the following: issues surrounding birth parents, the effects of abuse and neglect on children, cultural and racial issues, sexuality, contingency planning for children in the event of the parents' death or disability, financial assistance for adopted children, common childhood disabilities, including, but not limited to, emotional disturbances, attention deficit disorder, learning disabilities, speech and hearing impairment, and dyslexia, the importance of sibling and half-sibling relationships, and other issues related to adoption and child development and the availability of counseling to deal with these issues. *(Added by Stats.1998, c. 983 (A.B.2286), § 3. Amended by Stats.2012, c. 35 (S.B.1013), § 34, eff. June 27, 2012.)*

Cross References

Abuse defined for purposes of the Domestic Violence Protection Act, see Family Code § 6203.
Adoption of alcohol or drug-exposed and HIV positive children, see Welfare and Institutions Code § 16135 et seq.
Adoptive parent defined, see Family Code § 8503.
Aid for adoption of children, see Welfare and Institutions Code § 16115 et seq.
Birth parent defined, see Family Code § 8512.
Department defined, see Family Code § 8518.
Foster care placement, preference for sibling groups, visitation, see Welfare and Institutions Code § 16002.
Licensed adoption agency defined, see Family Code § 8530.
Special-needs child defined, see Family Code § 8545.

§ 8734. Adoption training programs

The department shall encourage adoption agencies to make adoption training programs available to prospective adoptive families. *(Added by Stats.1998, c. 983 (A.B.2286), § 3.)*

Cross References

Department defined, see Family Code § 8518.
Prospective adoptive parent defined, see Family Code § 8542.

§ 8735. Information to department when foster parent or relative caregiver denied right to adopt

The department shall adopt regulations requiring county adoption agencies and licensed adoption agencies to inform the agency responsible for the foster care placement when a relative caregiver or foster parent has been denied approval to adopt based on an inability of the relative caregiver or foster parent to provide for the mental

§ 8735

and emotional health, safety, and security of the child and to recommend either that the relative caregiver or foster parent be provided with additional support and supervision or that the child be removed from the home of the relative caregiver or foster parent. *(Added by Stats.1998, c. 983 (A.B.2286), § 3. Amended by Stats.2012, c. 35 (S.B.1013), § 35, eff. June 27, 2012.)*

Cross References

Department defined, see Family Code § 8518.
Support defined for purposes of this Code, see Family Code § 150.

§ 8736. Chapter provisions as grounds for removal of child from placement

The requirements of this chapter shall not be used as basis for removing a child who has been placed with a relative caregiver or foster parent prior to January 1, 1999, unless the noncompliance with the standards described therein present a danger to the health, safety, or emotional well-being of the child. *(Added by Stats.1998, c. 983 (A.B.2286), § 3.)*

CHAPTER 3. INDEPENDENT ADOPTIONS

Section
8800. Attorney-client relationship; professional conduct; conflict of interest; birth parents right to revoke consent; dual representation.
8801. Selection of prospective adoptive parents.
8801.3. Placement of child for adoption; requirements.
8801.5. Birth parents; advice of rights; role of counselor.
8801.7. Duties of adoption service provider; duty of care.
8802. Petition for adoption; contents; order of adoption.
8803. Concealment of child; removal of child from county; permission for removal; objections; hearing; application of section; violations.
8804. Withdrawal of petition.
8805. Removal of child from home of petitioners; transfer of care of child to department or agency.
8806. Acceptance of consent of birth parent; ascertainment of whether child is proper subject for adoption; determination of suitability of home.
8807. Investigation of proposed independent adoption; report; filing with court.
8808. Interview of petitioners and persons from whom consent is required; filing of petition.
8809. Repealed.
8810. Petition fees; use of revenues; reduction of fee.
8811. Adoptive parents; fingerprints; criminal record; prohibited placements; fee; waiver.
8811.5. Preplacement evaluations.
8812. Attorney's fees, medical fees and expenses, counseling fees, or living expenses of birth mother; request for payment by adoptive parents.
8813. Request for information about the status of the child's adoption; notification of birth parents of rights.
8814. Consent of birth parent or parents; out-of-state birth parent; minor birth parent.
8814.5. Revocation of consent; actions taken within 30 days of signing consent.
8815. Withdrawal of consent.
8816. Consent of agency or department when consent of birth parent not required; prerequisites.
8817. Report on medical background of child and biological parents; contents; blood sample.
8818. Statement to birth parents; contents; disclosure form; birth parent information.
8819. Termination of parental rights of birth parent; notification.

Section
8820. Failure of department or agency to accept consent of birth parent or give consent where appropriate; appeal; proceedings.
8821. Report or findings of department or agency; submission of copy to attorney for petitioner.
8822. Denial or withdrawal of petition; referral to superior court for review; hearing; notice.
8823. Prospective adoptive parents; appearance before court.

Cross References

Independent adoptions, defined, see Family Code § 8524.

§ 8800. Attorney-client relationship; professional conduct; conflict of interest; birth parents right to revoke consent; dual representation

(a) The Legislature finds and declares that an attorney's ability to effectively represent a client may be seriously impaired when conflict of interest deprives the client of the attorney's undivided loyalty and effort. The Legislature further finds and declares that the relation between attorney and client is a fiduciary relation of the very highest character, and binds the attorney to the most conscientious fidelity.

(b) The Legislature finds that Rule 2–111(A)(2) of the State Bar Rules of Professional Conduct provides that an attorney shall not withdraw from employment until the attorney has taken reasonable steps to avoid foreseeable prejudice to the rights of the client, including giving due notice to the client, allowing time for employment of other counsel, delivering to the client all papers and property to which the client is entitled, and complying with applicable laws and rules.

(c) The Legislature declares that in an independent adoption proceeding, whether or not written consent is obtained, multiple representation by an attorney should be avoided whenever a birth parent displays the slightest reason for the attorney to believe any controversy might arise. The Legislature finds and declares that it is the duty of the attorney, when a conflict of interest occurs, to withdraw promptly from any case, advise the parties to retain independent counsel, refrain from taking positions in opposition to any of these former clients, and thereafter maintain an impartial, fair, and open attitude toward the new attorneys.

(d) Notwithstanding any other law, it is unethical for an attorney to undertake the representation of both the prospective adoptive parents and the birth parents of a child in any negotiations or proceedings in connection with an adoption unless a written consent is obtained from both parties. The written consent shall include all of the following:

(1) A notice to the birth parents, in the form specified in this section, of their right to have an independent attorney advise and represent them in the adoption proceeding and that the prospective adoptive parents may be required to pay the reasonable attorney's fees up to a maximum of five hundred dollars ($500) for that representation, unless a higher fee is agreed to by the parties.

(2) A notice to the birth parents that they may waive their right to an independent attorney and may be represented by the attorney representing the prospective adoptive parents.

(3) A waiver by the birth parents of representation by an independent attorney.

(4) An agreement that the attorney representing the prospective adoptive parents shall represent the birth parents.

(e) Upon the petition or motion of any party, or upon motion of the court, the court may appoint an attorney to represent a child's birth parent or parents in negotiations or proceedings in connection with the child's adoption.

(f) The birth parent or parents may have an attorney, other than the attorney representing the interests of the prospective adoptive parents, to advise them fully of the adoption procedures and of their legal rights. The birth parent or parents also may retain an attorney to represent them in negotiations or proceedings in connection with the child's adoption. The court may award attorney's fees and costs for just cause and based upon the ability of the parties to pay those fees and costs.

(g) In the initial communication between the attorney retained by or representing the prospective adoptive parents and the birth parents, or as soon thereafter as reasonable, but before any written consent for dual representation, the attorney shall advise the birth parents of their rights regarding an independent attorney and that it is possible to waive the independent attorney.

(h) The attorney retained by or representing the prospective adoptive parents shall inform the prospective adoptive parents in writing that the birth parent or parents can revoke consent to the adoption pursuant to Section 8814.5 and that any moneys expended in negotiations or proceedings in connection with the child's adoption are not reimbursable. The prospective adoptive parents shall sign a statement to indicate their understanding of this information.

(i) Written consent to dual representation shall be filed with the court before the filing of the birth parent's consent to adoption. *(Stats.1992, c. 162 (A.B.2650), § 10, operative Jan. 1, 1994. Amended by Stats.1993, c. 450 (S.B.255), § 1; Stats.1993, c. 450 (S.B.255), § 2, operative Jan. 1, 1995; Stats.2019, c. 115 (A.B.1817), § 124, eff. Jan. 1, 2020.)*

Cross References

Birth parent, defined, see Family Code § 8512.
Proceeding defined for purposes of this Code, see Family Code § 110.
Property defined for purposes of this Code, see Family Code § 113.
Prospective adoptive parent, defined, see Family Code § 8542.
State defined for purposes of this Code, see Family Code § 145.

Research References

Forms

2 California Transactions Forms--Family Law § 6:21, Ethical Considerations.
2 California Transactions Forms--Family Law § 6:40, Structuring the Adoption.
2 California Transactions Forms--Family Law § 6:48, Consent to Representation of Multiple Parties by Counsel.
2 California Transactions Forms--Family Law § 6:49, Statement of Representation.
2 California Transactions Forms--Family Law § 6:50, Independent Adoption Retainer Agreement.
2 California Transactions Forms--Family Law § 6:52, Birth Mother Representation Agreement.
2 California Transactions Forms--Family Law § 6:54, Request by Birth Parent for Financial Assistance.
2 California Transactions Forms--Family Law § 6:84, Relinquishment as Distinguished from Consent.
2 California Transactions Forms--Family Law § 7:39, Adoption and Termination of Parental Rights.
West's California Code Forms, Family § 8800, Comment Overview—Independent Adoptions.
West's California Code Forms, Family § 8800 Form 1, Consent to Representation of Multiple Parties.

§ 8801. Selection of prospective adoptive parents

(a) The selection of a prospective adoptive parent or parents shall be personally made by the child's birth parent or parents and may not be delegated to an agent. The act of selection by the birth parent or parents shall be based upon personal knowledge of the prospective adoptive parent or parents.

(b) "Personal knowledge" as used in this section includes, but is not limited to, substantially correct knowledge of all of the following regarding the prospective adoptive parents: their full legal names, ages, religion, race or ethnicity, length of current marriage and number of previous marriages, employment, whether other children or adults reside in their home, whether there are other children who do not reside in their home and the child support obligation for these children and any failure to meet these obligations, any health conditions curtailing their normal daily activities or reducing their normal life expectancies, any convictions for crimes other than minor traffic violations, any removals of children from their care due to child abuse or neglect, and their general area of residence or, upon request, their address. *(Added by Stats.1993, c. 758 (S.B.792), § 6.4, operative Jan. 1, 1995. Amended by Stats.2019, c. 115 (A.B.1817), § 125, eff. Jan. 1, 2020.)*

Cross References

Abuse defined for purposes of the Domestic Violence Protection Act, see Family Code § 6203.
Adoptive parents, criminal record, see Penal Code § 11105.3.
Adult defined for purposes of this Code, see Family Code § 6501.
Birth parent,
 Defined, see Family Code § 8512.
 Money or benefits for consent or placement of children, see Penal Code § 273.
Disclosure of information, see Family Code § 9200 et seq.
Foster homes, alternative methods, see Welfare and Institutions Code § 396 et seq.
Juvenile delinquents and dependents,
 Jurisdiction, see Welfare and Institutions Code § 366.3.
 Priorities and preferences, adoptive parents, see Welfare and Institutions Code §§ 361.2 et seq., 366.26.
 Priorities and preferences, foster parents and relatives, see Welfare and Institutions Code §§ 361.2 et seq., 366.26.
Minor defined for purposes of this Code, see Family Code § 6500.
Prospective adoptive parent, defined, see Family Code § 8542.
Support defined for purposes of this Code, see Family Code § 150.

Research References

Forms

2 California Transactions Forms--Family Law § 6:3, Definitions.
2 California Transactions Forms--Family Law § 6:34, Role of Adoption Service Provider.
2 California Transactions Forms--Family Law § 6:36, Independent Adoption Placement Agreement.
2 California Transactions Forms--Family Law § 6:39, Advising Prospective Adoptive Parents.
2 California Transactions Forms--Family Law § 6:40, Structuring the Adoption.
2 California Transactions Forms--Family Law § 6:45, Matters to Consider in Initial Interview and Representation of Adoptive Parents.
2 California Transactions Forms--Family Law § 6:46, Matters to Consider in Structuring the Adoption.
2 California Transactions Forms--Family Law § 6:133, Statement of Intent to Adopt and Statement of Personal Knowledge.

§ 8801.3. Placement of child for adoption; requirements

A child shall not be considered to have been placed for adoption unless each of the following is true:

(a) Each birth parent placing the child for adoption has been advised of their rights, and if desired, has been counseled pursuant to Section 8801.5.

(b) The adoption service provider, each prospective adoptive parent, and each birth parent placing the child have signed an adoption placement agreement on a form prescribed by the department. The signing of the agreement shall satisfy all of the following requirements:

(1) Each birth parent shall have been advised of their rights pursuant to Section 8801.5 at least 10 days before signing the agreement, unless the adoption service provider finds exigent circumstances that shall be set forth in the adoption placement agreement.

(2) The agreement may not be signed by either the birth parents or the prospective adoptive parents until the time of discharge of the birth mother from the hospital. However, if the birth mother remains hospitalized for a period longer than the hospitalization of the child, the agreement may be signed by all parties at the time of or

§ 8801.3

after the child's discharge from the hospital but prior to the birth mother's discharge from the hospital if the birth mother's competency to sign is verified by the attending physician and surgeon before signing the agreement.

(3) The birth parents and prospective adoptive parents shall sign the agreement in the presence of an adoption service provider.

(4) The adoption service provider who witnesses the signatures shall keep the original of the adoption placement agreement and immediately forward it and supporting documentation as required by the department to the department or delegated county adoption agency.

(5) The child is not deemed to be placed for adoption with the prospective adoptive parents until the adoption placement agreement has been signed and witnessed.

(6) If the birth parent is not located in this state or country, the adoption placement agreement shall be signed before an adoption service provider or, for purposes of identification of the birth parent only, before a notary or other person authorized to perform notarial acts in the state or country in which the birth parent is located. This paragraph is not applicable to intercountry adoptions, as defined in Section 8527, which shall be governed by Chapter 4 (commencing with Section 8900).

(c) The adoption placement agreement form shall include all of the following:

(1) A statement that the birth parent received the advisement of rights and the date upon which it was received.

(2) A statement that the birth parent understands that the placement is for the purpose of adoption and that if the birth parent takes no further action, on the 31st day after signing the adoption placement agreement, the agreement shall become a permanent and irrevocable consent to the adoption.

(3) A statement that the birth parent signs the agreement having personal knowledge of certain facts regarding the prospective adoptive parents as provided in Section 8801.

(4) A statement that the adoptive parents have been informed of the basic health and social history of the birth parents.

(5) A consent to the adoption that may be revoked as provided by Section 8814.5.

(d) The adoption placement agreement shall also meet the requirements of the Interstate Compact on the Placement of Children in Section 7901. *(Added by Stats.1993, c. 758 (S.B.792), § 7, operative Jan. 1, 1995. Amended by Stats.1994, c. 585 (A.B.3336), § 3; Stats.2000, c. 937 (A.B.2433), § 3; Stats.2001, c. 688 (S.B.104), § 1; Stats.2019, c. 115 (A.B.1817), § 126, eff. Jan. 1, 2020.)*

Cross References

Abandoned children, declaration of abandonment, see Family Code § 7822.
Adoption service provider, defined, see Family Code § 8502.
Birth parent, defined, see Family Code § 8512.
County defined for purposes of this Code, see Family Code § 67.
Department defined, see Family Code § 8518.
Person defined for purposes of this Code, see Family Code § 105.
Prospective adoptive parent, defined, see Family Code § 8542.
Relinquishment of child or execution of adoption placement agreement, determination of child's identity as member of Indian tribe or organization, see Family Code § 8620.
State defined for purposes of this Code, see Family Code § 145.

Research References

Forms

2 California Transactions Forms--Family Law § 6:3, Definitions.
2 California Transactions Forms--Family Law § 6:32, Nature of Independent Adoption—Relinquishment Versus Consent.
2 California Transactions Forms--Family Law § 6:34, Role of Adoption Service Provider.
2 California Transactions Forms--Family Law § 6:36, Independent Adoption Placement Agreement.
2 California Transactions Forms--Family Law § 6:40, Structuring the Adoption.
2 California Transactions Forms--Family Law § 6:123, Applicability of ICPC.
2 California Transactions Forms--Family Law § 7:8, Traditional Surrogacy Agreements.

§ 8801.5. Birth parents; advice of rights; role of counselor

(a) Each birth parent placing a child for adoption shall be advised of their rights by an adoption service provider.

(b) The birth parent shall be advised of their rights in a face-to-face meeting in which the birth parent may ask questions and have questions answered, as provided by Section 8801.3.

(c) The department shall prescribe the format and process for advising birth parents of their rights, the content of which shall include, but not be limited to, the following:

(1) The alternatives to adoption.

(2) The alternative types of adoption, including a description of the full procedures and timeframes involved in each type.

(3) The full rights and responsibilities of the birth parent with respect to adoption, including the need to keep the department informed of the birth parent's current address in case of a medical emergency requiring contact and of providing a full health history.

(4) The right to separate legal counsel paid for by the prospective adoptive parents upon the request of the birth parent, as provided for by Section 8800.

(5) The right to a minimum of three separate counseling sessions, each to be held on different days, to be paid for by the prospective adoptive parents upon the request of the birth parents, as provided for by subdivision (d).

(d) Each person advised pursuant to this section shall be offered at least three separate counseling sessions, to be held on different days. Each counseling session shall be not less than 50 minutes in duration. The counseling may be provided by the adoption service provider who informs the birth parent of their rights, or by another adoption service provider, or by a licensed psychotherapist, as defined by Section 1010 of the Evidence Code, as elected by the person, and after having been informed of these choices.

(e) The counselor owes a duty of care to the birth parent being counseled, similar to the duty of care established by a psychotherapist-patient relationship, regardless of who pays the fees of the counselor. A counselor shall not have a contractual relationship with the adoptive parents, an attorney for the adoptive parents, or any other individual or an organization performing any type of services for the adoptive parents and for which the adoptive parents are paying a fee, except as relates to payment of the birth parents' fee.

(f) The advisement and counseling fees shall be paid by the prospective adoptive parents at the request of the birth parent.

(g) Failure to fulfill the duties specified in this section shall not be construed as a basis for setting aside the consent or the adoption, but may give rise to a cause of action for malpractice or negligence against those professionals or agencies serving as adoption service providers that are responsible for fulfilling the duties. *(Added by Stats.1993, c. 758 (S.B.792), § 8, operative Jan. 1, 1995. Amended by Stats.1994, c. 585 (A.B.3336), § 4; Stats.1997, c. 559 (S.B.1121), § 2; Stats.2019, c. 115 (A.B.1817), § 127, eff. Jan. 1, 2020.)*

Cross References

Adoption service provider, defined, see Family Code § 8502.
Birth parent, defined, see Family Code § 8512.
Department defined, see Family Code § 8518.
Person defined for purposes of this Code, see Family Code § 105.
Prospective adoptive parent, defined, see Family Code § 8542.

Statement presented to birth parents at time of relinquishment, content, see Family Code § 8702.

Research References

Forms

2 California Transactions Forms--Family Law § 6:3, Definitions.
2 California Transactions Forms--Family Law § 6:34, Role of Adoption Service Provider.
2 California Transactions Forms--Family Law § 6:39, Advising Prospective Adoptive Parents.
2 California Transactions Forms--Family Law § 6:40, Structuring the Adoption.
2 California Transactions Forms--Family Law § 6:46, Matters to Consider in Structuring the Adoption.

§ 8801.7. Duties of adoption service provider; duty of care

(a) An adoption service provider shall also witness the signature of the adoption placement agreement and offer to interview the birth parent after the placement of the child with prospective adoptive parents. The interview shall occur within 10 working days after the placement of the child for adoption and shall include a consideration of any concerns or problems the birth parent has with the placement, a readvisement of the rights of the birth parent, and the taking of the health and social history of the birth parent, if not taken previously.

(b) The adoption service provider shall immediately notify the department or delegated county adoption agency if the birth parent is not interviewed as provided in subdivision (a) or if there are any concerns regarding the placement. If the birth parent wishes to revoke the consent, the adoption service provider shall assist the birth parent in obtaining the return of the child.

(c) The adoption service provider owes a very high duty of care to the birth parent being advised, regardless of who pays the provider's fees. The duty of care specifically does not include a duty to investigate information provided by the birth parents, prospective adoptive parents, or their attorneys or agents. No adoption service provider shall have a contractual relationship with prospective adoptive parents, an attorney or representative for prospective adoptive parents, or any individual or organization providing services of any type to prospective adoptive parents for which the adoptive parents are paying a fee, except as relates to the payment of the fees for the advising and counseling of the birth parents.

(d) This section shall become operative on January 1, 1995. *(Added by Stats.1993, c. 758 (S.B.792), § 9, operative Jan. 1, 1995.)*

Cross References

Adoption service provider, defined, see Family Code § 8502.
Birth parent, defined, see Family Code § 8512.
County defined for purposes of this Code, see Family Code § 67.
Delegated county adoption agency, see Family Code § 8515.
Department defined, see Family Code § 8518.
Medical reports on child and biological parents, form and contents, see Family Code § 8608.
Prospective adoptive parent, defined, see Family Code § 8542.

Research References

Forms

2 California Transactions Forms--Family Law § 6:34, Role of Adoption Service Provider.
2 California Transactions Forms--Family Law § 6:40, Structuring the Adoption.
2 California Transactions Forms--Family Law § 6:148, Rights of Indian Parents of Indian Children.

§ 8802. Petition for adoption; contents; order of adoption

(a) * * * Any of the following <u>adult</u> persons who desire to adopt a child may, for that purpose, file an adoption request in a county authorized by Section 8609.5:

* * * <u>(1) A person</u> who is related to the child or the child's half sibling by blood or affinity, including all relatives whose status is preceded by the words "step," "great," "great-great," or "grand," or the spouse of any of these persons, even if the marriage was terminated by death or dissolution.

<u>(2) A person named in the will of a deceased parent as an intended adoptive parent where the child has no other parent.</u>

<u>(3) A person with whom a child has been placed for adoption, in which case a copy of the independent adoption placement agreement shall be attached to the petition.</u>

* * * <u>(4) A person</u> who has been the child's legal guardian for more than one year. * * * However, if the * * * <u>guardian was nominated</u> * * * <u>by a parent</u> for a purpose other than adoption <u>and for a specified time period, or if the guardianship was established pursuant to Section 360 of the Welfare and Institutions Code, the</u> guardianship shall have been in existence for * * * <u>at least three years, unless parental rights have already been terminated.</u>

<u>(5)</u> If the child is alleged to have been abandoned pursuant to Section 7822, a * * * <u>person who has been the child's legal guardian for more than six months. The legal guardian may file a petition pursuant to Section 7822 in the same court and concurrently with</u> * * * <u>the adoption request.</u>

<u>(6) A person named in a court order terminating parental rights as the child's legal guardian or prospective adoptive parent.</u>

* * * (b) The court clerk shall immediately notify the department <u>in</u> Sacramento in writing of the pendency of the proceeding and of any subsequent action taken.

* * *

* * * (c) The adoption request shall contain an allegation that the petitioners will file promptly with the department or delegated county adoption agency information required by the department in the investigation of the proposed adoption. The omission of the allegation from * * * <u>the adoption request</u> does not affect the jurisdiction of the court to proceed or the validity of an adoption order or other order based on the * * * <u>adoption request</u>.

<u>(d)</u> The caption of the adoption <u>request</u> shall contain the names of the petitioners, but not the child's name. The * * * <u>body of the adoption request</u> shall state the child's sex and date of birth and the name the child had before adoption.

<u>(e)</u> If the child is the subject of a guardianship petition, the adoption <u>request</u> shall so state and shall include the caption and docket number or have attached a copy of the letters of the guardianship or temporary guardianship. The petitioners shall notify the court of any petition for guardianship or temporary guardianship filed after the adoption <u>request</u>. The guardianship proceeding shall be consolidated with the adoption proceeding, and the consolidated case shall be heard and decided in the court in which the adoption is pending.

<u>(f)</u> The order of adoption shall contain the child's adopted name * * * <u>and</u> the name the child had before adoption. *(Added by Stats.1993, c. 758 (S.B.792), § 9.2, operative Jan. 1, 1995. Amended by Stats.1996, c. 510 (A.B.2165), § 1; Stats.2000, c. 937 (A.B.2433), § 4; Stats.2002, c. 1112 (A.B.746), § 3; Stats.2003, c. 62 (S.B.600), § 88; Stats.2003, c. 81 (A.B.416), § 1; Stats.2004, c. 858 (S.B.1357), § 5; Stats.2007, c. 47 (S.B.313), § 5; Stats.2008, c. 534 (S.B.1726), § 10; Stats.2012, c. 638 (A.B.1757), § 10; Stats.2022, c. 159 (A.B.2495), § 5, eff. Jan. 1, 2023.)*

Cross References

Adoptive parent, defined, see Family Code § 8503.
Adoptive parents, criminal record, see Penal Code § 11105.3.
Adult defined for purposes of this Code, see Family Code § 6501.
Affinity defined for purposes of this Code, see Family Code § 6205.
Agency adoption, petition, see Family Code § 8714.
Birth parents, money or benefits for consent or placement of children, see Penal Code § 273.
Child abuse and neglect reporting act, notice to child protection agencies or district attorneys, availability of information, see Penal Code § 11170.

§ 8802

County defined for purposes of this Code, see Family Code § 67.
Department defined, see Family Code § 8518.
Disclosure of information, see Family Code § 9200 et seq.
Foster homes, alternative methods, see Welfare and Institutions Code § 396 et seq.
Guardianship proceedings, exclusive jurisdiction, consolidation of guardianship and adoption proceedings, see Probate Code § 2205.
Intercountry adoption, petition, see Family Code § 8912.
Judgment and order defined for purposes of this Code, see Family Code § 100.
Jurisdiction of superior court, see Family Code § 200.
Juvenile delinquents and dependents,
   Jurisdiction, see Welfare and Institutions Code § 366.3.
  Priorities and preferences, adoptive parents, see Welfare and Institutions Code §§ 361.2 et seq., 366.26.
  Priorities and preferences, foster parents and relatives, see Welfare and Institutions Code §§ 361.2 et seq., 366.26.
Person defined for purposes of this Code, see Family Code § 105.
Petitioner defined for purposes of this Code, see Family Code § 126.
Proceeding defined for purposes of this Code, see Family Code § 110.
References to husband, wife, spouses and married persons, persons included for purposes of this Code, see Family Code § 11.
State defined for purposes of this Code, see Family Code § 145.
Stepparent adoption petition, see Family Code § 9000.

Research References

Forms

2 California Transactions Forms--Family Law § 6:40, Structuring the Adoption.
2 California Transactions Forms--Family Law § 6:41, Initiating the Adoption.
2 California Transactions Forms--Family Law § 6:46, Matters to Consider in Structuring the Adoption.
2 California Transactions Forms--Family Law § 6:47, Matters to Consider in Drafting Petition for Independent Adoption of Unmarried Minor.
West's California Judicial Council Forms ADOPT-200, Adoption Request.

§ 8803. Concealment of child; removal of child from county; permission for removal; objections; hearing; application of section; violations

(a) During the pendency of an adoption proceeding:

(1) The child proposed to be adopted shall not be concealed from the * * * agency that is investigating the adoption, or from the court with jurisdiction over the adoption proceeding * * *.

(2) The child shall not be removed from the county * * * of the * * * petitioner's residence at the time of placement, unless the petitioners or other interested persons first obtain permission for the removal from the court, after giving advance written notice of intent to obtain the court's permission to the department or delegated county adoption agency responsible for the investigation of the proposed adoption. Upon proof of giving notice, permission may be granted by the court if, within a period of 15 days after the date of giving notice, no objections are filed with the court by the department or delegated county adoption agency. If the department or delegated county adoption agency files objections within the 15–day period, upon the request of the petitioners the court shall immediately set the matter for hearing and give to the objector, the petitioners, and the party or parties requesting permission for the removal reasonable notice of the hearing by certified mail, return receipt requested, to the address of each as shown in the records of the adoption proceeding. Upon a finding that the objections are without good cause, the court may grant the requested permission for removal of the child, subject to any limitations that appear to be in the child's best interest.

(b) This section does not apply in any of the following situations:

(1) When the child is absent for a period of not more than 30 days from the county * * * of the * * * petitioner's residence at the time of placement, unless a notice of recommendation of denial of petition has been personally served on the petitioners or the court has issued an order prohibiting the child's removal from the county of the petitioner's residence at the time of placement, pending consideration of any of the following:

(A) The suitability of the petitioners.

(B) The care provided the child.

(C) The availability of the legally required consents to the adoption.

(2) Where the child has been returned to and remains in the custody and control of the child's birth parent or parents.

(c) A violation of this section is a violation of Section 280 of the Penal Code.

(d) Neither this section nor Section 280 of the Penal Code may be construed to render lawful any act that is unlawful under any other applicable law. *(Stats.1992, c. 162 (A.B.2650), § 10, operative Jan. 1, 1994. Amended by Stats.2022, c. 159 (A.B.2495), § 6, eff. Jan. 1, 2023.)*

Cross References

Agency adoption, removal and concealment, see Family Code § 8713.
Birth parent, defined, see Family Code § 8512.
County defined for purposes of this Code, see Family Code § 67.
Delegated county adoption agency defined, see Family Code § 8515.
Department defined, see Family Code § 8518.
Intercountry adoption, removal and concealment, see Family Code § 8910.
Judgment and order defined for purposes of this Code, see Family Code § 100.
Person defined for purposes of this Code, see Family Code § 105.
Petitioner defined for purposes of this Code, see Family Code § 126.
Proceeding defined for purposes of this Code, see Family Code § 110.
Removal or concealment of child pending adoption proceedings, see Penal Code § 280.

Research References

Forms

2 California Transactions Forms--Family Law § 6:2, Governing Law.

§ 8804. Withdrawal of petition

(a) Whenever the petitioners move to withdraw the petition for the adoption or to dismiss the proceeding, the clerk of the court in which the proceeding is pending shall immediately notify the department at Sacramento of the action. The department or the delegated county adoption agency shall file a full report with the court recommending a suitable plan for the child in every case where the petitioners move to withdraw the petition for the adoption or where the department or delegated county adoption agency recommends that the petition for adoption be denied and shall appear before the court for the purpose of representing the child.

(b) Notwithstanding the withdrawal or dismissal of the petition, the court may retain jurisdiction over the child for the purposes of making any order for the child's custody that the court deems to be in the child's best interest.

(c) If a birth parent who did not place a child for adoption as specified in Section 8801.3 has refused to give the required consent, or a birth parent revokes consent as specified in Section 8814.5, the child shall be restored to the care and custody of the birth parent or parents, unless the court orders otherwise, subject to Section 3041. *(Added by Stats.1993, c. 758 (S.B.792), § 10, operative Jan. 1, 1995. Amended by Stats.2002, c. 1118 (A.B.1938), § 4; Stats.2014, c. 763 (A.B.1701), § 11, eff. Jan. 1, 2015.)*

Cross References

Agency adoption, notice of withdrawal or dismissal, see Family Code § 8719.
Birth parent, defined, see Family Code § 8512.
County defined for purposes of this Code, see Family Code § 67.
Delegated county adoption agency defined, see Family Code § 8515.
Department defined, see Family Code § 8518.
Disclosure of information, see Family Code § 9200 et seq.
Intercountry adoption, notice of withdrawal or dismissal, see Family Code § 8916.
Judgment and order defined for purposes of this Code, see Family Code § 100.
Petitioner defined for purposes of this Code, see Family Code § 126.
Proceeding defined for purposes of this Code, see Family Code § 110.

Stepparent adoption, notice of withdrawal or dismissal, see Family Code § 9006.

§ 8805. Removal of child from home of petitioners; transfer of care of child to department or agency

At the hearing, if the court sustains the recommendation of the department or delegated county adoption agency that the child be removed from the home of the petitioners because the department or agency recommends denial or if the petitioners move to withdraw the petition or if the court dismisses the petition and does not return the child to the birth parents, the court shall commit the child to the care of the department or delegated county adoption agency, whichever made the recommendation, for the department or agency to arrange adoptive placement or to make a suitable plan. In those counties not served by a delegated county adoption agency, the county welfare department shall act as the agent of the department and shall provide care for the child in accordance with rules and regulations established by the department. *(Stats.1992, c. 162 (A.B.2650), § 10, operative Jan. 1, 1994.)*

Cross References

Aid for adoption of children, benefits payment, conditions, see Welfare and Institutions Code § 16120.
County adoption agencies, adjustments, see Welfare and Institutions Code § 16106.
County defined for purposes of this Code, see Family Code § 67.
Delegated county adoption agency defined, see Family Code § 8515.
Department defined, see Family Code § 8518.
Petitioner defined for purposes of this Code, see Family Code § 126.

§ 8806. Acceptance of consent of birth parent; ascertainment of whether child is proper subject for adoption; determination of suitability of home

The department or delegated county adoption agency shall accept the consent of the birth parents to the adoption of the child by the petitioners and, before filing its report with the court, shall ascertain whether the child is a proper subject for adoption and whether the proposed home is suitable for the child. *(Stats.1992, c. 162 (A.B.2650), § 10, operative Jan. 1, 1994.)*

Cross References

Birth parent,
  Consent required, see Family Code § 8604.
  Defined, see Family Code § 8512.
Money or benefits for consent or placement of children, see Penal Code § 273.
County defined for purposes of this Code, see Family Code § 67.
Delegated county adoption agency defined, see Family Code § 8515.
Department defined, see Family Code § 8518.
Petitioner defined for purposes of this Code, see Family Code § 126.

§ 8807. Investigation of proposed independent adoption; report; filing with court

(a) Except as provided in subdivisions (b) and (c), within 180 days after receiving 50 percent of the fee, the department or delegated county adoption agency shall investigate the proposed independent adoption and, after the remaining balance of the fee is paid, submit to the court a full report of the facts disclosed by its inquiry with a recommendation regarding the granting of the petition. If the petitioners have a valid preplacement evaluation or a valid private agency adoption home study, as described in paragraph (2) of subdivision (a) of Section 8810, and no new information has been discovered and no new event has occurred subsequent to the approval of the evaluation or home study that creates a reasonable belief that further investigation is necessary, the department or delegated county adoption agency may elect not to reinvestigate any matters covered in the evaluation or home study, except that the department shall complete all background clearances required by law.

(b) If the investigation establishes that there is a serious question concerning the suitability of the petitioners, the care provided to the child, or the availability of the consent to adoption, the report shall be filed immediately.

(c) In its discretion, the court may allow additional time for the filing of the report, after at least five days' notice to the petitioner or petitioners and an opportunity for the petitioner or petitioners to be heard with respect to the request for additional time.

(d) If a petitioner is a resident of a state other than California, an updated and current home study report, conducted and approved by a licensed adoption agency or other authorized resource in the state in which the petitioner resides, shall be reviewed and endorsed by the department or delegated county adoption agency, if the standards and criteria established for a home study report in the other state are substantially commensurate with the home study standards and criteria established in California adoption regulations. *(Added by Stats.2008, c. 759 (A.B.1279), § 8, eff. Sept. 30, 2008, operative Oct. 1, 2008. Amended by Stats.2014, c. 763 (A.B.1701), § 12, eff. Jan. 1, 2015.)*

Cross References

Agency adoption, report of department, see Family Code § 8715.
County defined for purposes of this Code, see Family Code § 67.
Delegated county adoption agency defined, see Family Code § 8515.
Department defined, see Family Code § 8518.
Disclosure of information, see Family Code § 9200 et seq.
Independent adoptions, defined, see Family Code § 8524.
Intercountry adoptions, report of department or agency, see Family Code § 8914.
Petitioner defined for purposes of this Code, see Family Code § 126.
State defined for purposes of this Code, see Family Code § 145.
Stepparent adoptions, report of county welfare department or probation officer, see Family Code § 9001.
Waiver of personal appearance of prospective adoptive parent, see Family Code § 8613.5.

Research References

Forms
2 California Transactions Forms--Family Law § 6:13, Appearance in Person or by Counsel.
2 California Transactions Forms--Family Law § 6:35, Home Study Preplacement Certification Versus Postplacement Study.

§ 8808. Interview of petitioners and persons from whom consent is required; filing of petition

(a) The department or delegated county adoption agency shall interview the petitioners within 45 working days, excluding legal holidays, after the department or delegated county adoption agency receives 50 percent of the investigation fee together with a stamped file copy of the adoption petition.

(b) The department or delegated county adoption agency shall interview all persons from whom consent is required and whose addresses are known. The interview with the placing parent or parents shall include, but not be limited to, discussion of any concerns or problems that the parent has with the placement and, if the placing parent was not interviewed as provided in Section 8801.7, the content required in that interview. At the interview, the agency shall give the parent an opportunity to sign either a statement revoking the consent, or a waiver of the right to revoke consent, as provided in Section 8814.5, unless the parent has already signed a waiver or the time period allowed to revoke consent has expired.

(c) In order to facilitate the interview described in this section, within five business days of filing the petition, the petitioners shall provide the department or delegated county adoption agency a stamped file copy of the petition together with 50 percent of the fee, a copy of any valid preplacement evaluation or any valid private agency adoption home study, as described in paragraph (2) of subdivision (a) of Section 8810, and the names, addresses, and telephone numbers of all parties to be interviewed, if known.

§ 8808

(Added by Stats.2008, c. 759 (A.B.1279), § 10, eff. Sept. 30, 2008, operative Oct. 1, 2008. Amended by Stats.2014, c. 763 (A.B.1701), § 13, eff. Jan. 1, 2015.)

Cross References

Birth parents, money or benefits for consent or placement of children, see Penal Code § 273.
Delegated county adoption agency defined, see Family Code § 8515.
Department defined, see Family Code § 8518.
Person defined for purposes of this Code, see Family Code § 105.
Petitioner defined for purposes of this Code, see Family Code § 126.

Research References

Forms

2 California Transactions Forms--Family Law § 6:3, Definitions.
West's California Code Forms, Family § 8800, Comment Overview—Independent Adoptions.

§ 8809. Repealed by Stats.1992, c. 162 (A.B.2650), § 10, operative Jan. 1, 1993

§ 8810. Petition fees; use of revenues; reduction of fee

(a) Except as otherwise provided in this section, whenever a petition is filed under this chapter for the adoption of a child, the petitioner shall pay a nonrefundable fee to the department or to the delegated county adoption agency for the cost of investigating the adoption petition. Fifty percent of the payment shall be made to the department or delegated county adoption agency at the time the adoption petition is filed, and the remaining balance shall be paid no later than the date determined by the department or the delegated county adoption agency in an amount as follows:

(1) For petitions filed on and after October 1, 2008, four thousand five hundred dollars ($4,500).

(2) For petitioners who have a valid preplacement evaluation less than one year old pursuant to Section 8811.5, or a valid private agency adoption home study less than two years old at the time of filing a petition, one thousand five hundred fifty dollars ($1,550) for a postplacement evaluation pursuant to Sections 8806 and 8807.

(b) Revenues produced by fees collected by the department pursuant to subdivision (a) shall be used, when appropriated by the Legislature, to fund only the direct costs associated with the state program for independent adoptions. Revenues produced by fees collected by the delegated county adoption agency pursuant to subdivision (a) shall be used by the county to fund the county program for independent adoptions.

(c) The department or delegated county adoption agency may reduce the fee to no less than five hundred dollars ($500) when the prospective adoptive parents are lower income, according to the income limits published by the Department of Housing and Community Development, and when making the required payment would be detrimental to the welfare of an adopted child. The department shall develop additional guidelines regarding income and assets to determine the financial criteria for reduction of the fee under this subdivision. *(Added by Stats.2008, c. 759 (A.B.1279), § 12, eff. Sept. 30, 2008, operative Oct. 1, 2008. Amended by Stats.2012, c. 638 (A.B.1757), § 11; Stats.2013, c. 743 (A.B.848), § 3.)*

Cross References

Agency adoption, fee for report, see Family Code § 8716.
Delegated county adoption agency defined, see Family Code § 8515.
Department defined, see Family Code § 8518.
Independent adoption, defined, see Family Code § 8524.
Petitioner defined for purposes of this Code, see Family Code § 126.
Prospective adoptive parent, defined, see Family Code § 8542.
State defined for purposes of this Code, see Family Code § 145.

Stepparent adoption, fee for report, see Family Code § 9002.

Research References

Forms

2 California Transactions Forms--Family Law § 6:31, Accounting Report—Adoptions [Judicial Council Form Adopt-230].
2 California Transactions Forms--Family Law § 6:35, Home Study Preplacement Certification Versus Postplacement Study.
2 California Transactions Forms--Family Law § 6:69, Transmittal Letter to Department of Social Services.

§ 8811. Adoptive parents; fingerprints; criminal record; prohibited placements; fee; waiver

(a) The department or delegated county adoption agency shall require each person who files an adoption petition to be fingerprinted and shall secure from an appropriate law enforcement agency any criminal record of that person to determine if the person has ever been convicted of a crime other than a minor traffic violation. The department or delegated county adoption agency may also secure the person's full criminal record, if any, with the exception of any convictions for which relief has been granted pursuant to Section 1203.49 of the Penal Code. Any federal-level criminal offender record requests to the Department of Justice shall be submitted with fingerprint images and related information required by the Department of Justice for the purposes of obtaining information as to the existence and content of a record of an out-of-state or federal conviction or arrest of a person or information regarding any out-of-state or federal crimes or arrests for which the Department of Justice establishes that the person is free on bail, or on their own recognizance pending trial or appeal. The Department of Justice shall forward to the Federal Bureau of Investigation any requests for federal summary criminal history information received pursuant to this section. The Department of Justice shall review the information returned from the Federal Bureau of Investigation and shall compile and disseminate a response to the department or delegated county adoption agency.

(b) Notwithstanding subdivision (c), the criminal record, if any, shall be taken into consideration when evaluating the prospective adoptive parent, and an assessment of the effects of any criminal history on the ability of the prospective adoptive parent to provide adequate and proper care and guidance to the child shall be included in the report to the court.

(c)(1) The department or a delegated county adoption agency shall not give final approval for an adoptive placement in any home in which the prospective adoptive parent or any adult living in the prospective adoptive home has either of the following:

(A) A felony conviction for child abuse or neglect, spousal abuse, crimes against a child, including child pornography, or for a crime involving violence, including rape, sexual assault, or homicide, but not including other physical assault and battery. For purposes of this subdivision, crimes involving violence means those violent crimes contained in clause (i) of subparagraph (A), and subparagraph (B), of paragraph (1) of subdivision (g) of Section 1522 of the Health and Safety Code.

(B) A felony conviction that occurred within the last five years for physical assault, battery, or a drug- or alcohol-related offense.

(2) This subdivision shall become operative on October 1, 2008, and shall remain operative only to the extent that compliance with its provisions is required by federal law as a condition of receiving funding under Title IV–E of the federal Social Security Act (42 U.S.C. Sec. 670 et seq.).

(d) A fee charged by a law enforcement agency for fingerprinting or for checking or obtaining the criminal record of the petitioner shall be paid by the petitioner. The department or delegated county adoption agency may defer, waive, or reduce the fee if its payment would cause economic hardship to the prospective adoptive parents detrimental to the welfare of the adopted child, if the child has been in the foster care of the prospective adoptive parents for at least one year, or if necessary for the placement of a special-needs child. *(Stats.1992, c. 162 (A.B.2650), § 10, operative Jan. 1, 1994. Amended by Stats.2008, c. 701 (A.B.2651), § 2, eff. Sept. 30, 2008; Stats.2014, c. 708 (A.B.1585), § 2, eff. Jan. 1, 2015; Stats.2015, c. 303 (A.B.731), § 152, eff. Jan. 1, 2016; Stats.2016, c. 86 (S.B.1171), § 131, eff. Jan. 1, 2017; Stats.2019, c. 115 (A.B.1817), § 128, eff. Jan. 1, 2020.)*

Cross References

Agency adoption investigations, see Family Code § 8712.
County defined for purposes of this Code, see Family Code § 67.
Criminal record, application to adopt a child, see Penal Code § 11105.3.
Delegated county adoption agency defined, see Family Code § 8515.
Department defined, see Family Code § 8518.
Disclosure of information, see Family Code § 9200 et seq.
Intercountry adoptions, investigations, see Family Code § 8908.
Minor defined for purposes of this Code, see Family Code § 6500.
Person defined for purposes of this Code, see Family Code § 105.
Petitioner defined for purposes of this Code, see Family Code § 126.
Prospective adoptive parent, defined, see Family Code § 8542.
Special-needs child, defined, see Family Code § 8545.
Stepparent adoptions, fingerprinting and investigation of criminal record, see Family Code § 9001.

§ 8811.5. Preplacement evaluations

(a) A licensed private or public adoption agency of the state of the petitioners' residency may certify prospective adoptive parents by a preplacement evaluation that contains a finding that an individual is suited to be an adoptive parent.

(b) The preplacement evaluation shall include an investigation pursuant to standards included in the regulations governing independent adoption investigations established by the department. Fees for the investigation shall be commensurate with those fees charged for a comparable investigation conducted by the department or by a delegated licensed county adoption agency.

(c) The preplacement evaluation, whether it is conducted for the purpose of initially certifying prospective adoptive parents or for renewing that certification, shall be completed no more than one year prior to the signing of an adoption placement agreement. The cost for renewal of that certification shall be in proportion to the extent of the work required to prepare the renewal that is attributable to changes in family circumstances. *(Added by Stats.1996, c. 510 (A.B.2165), § 3. Amended by Stats.2004, c. 128 (A.B.2492), § 1.)*

Cross References

Adoptive parent, defined, see Family Code § 8503.
County defined for purposes of this Code, see Family Code § 67.
Delegated county adoption agency defined, see Family Code § 8515.
Department defined, see Family Code § 8518.
Licensed adoption agency defined, see Family Code § 8530.
Prospective adoptive parent, defined, see Family Code § 8542.

Research References

Forms
2 California Transactions Forms--Family Law § 6:35, Home Study Preplacement Certification Versus Postplacement Study.
2 California Transactions Forms--Family Law § 6:69, Transmittal Letter to Department of Social Services.

§ 8812. Attorney's fees, medical fees and expenses, counseling fees, or living expenses of birth mother; request for payment by adoptive parents

Any request by a birth parent or birth parents for payment by the prospective adoptive parents of attorney's fees, medical fees and expenses, counseling fees, or living expenses of the birth mother shall be in writing. The birth parent or parents shall, by first-class mail or other agreed upon means to ensure receipt, provide the prospective adoptive parents written receipts for any money provided to the birth parent or birth parents. The prospective adoptive parents shall provide the receipts to the court when the accounting report required pursuant to Section 8610 is filed. *(Added by Stats.1993, c. 450 (S.B.255), § 3.)*

Cross References

Birth parent, defined, see Family Code § 8512.
Prospective adoptive parent, defined, see Family Code § 8542.

Research References

Forms
2 California Transactions Forms--Family Law § 6:40, Structuring the Adoption.
2 California Transactions Forms--Family Law § 6:46, Matters to Consider in Structuring the Adoption.
2 California Transactions Forms--Family Law § 6:54, Request by Birth Parent for Financial Assistance.

§ 8813. Request for information about the status of the child's adoption; notification of birth parents of rights

At or before the time a consent to adoption is signed, the department or delegated county adoption agency shall advise the birth parent signing the consent, verbally and in writing, that the birth parent may, at any time in the future, request from the department or agency, all known information about the status of the child's adoption, except for personal, identifying information about the adoptive family. The birth parent shall be advised that this information includes, but is not limited to, all of the following:

(a) Whether the child has been placed for adoption.

(b) The approximate date that an adoption was completed.

(c) If the adoption was not completed or was vacated, for any reason, whether adoptive placement of the child is again being considered. *(Stats.1992, c. 162 (A.B.2650), § 10, operative Jan. 1, 1994.)*

Cross References

County defined for purposes of this Code, see Family Code § 67.

§ 8814. Consent of birth parent or parents; out-of-state birth parent; minor birth parent

For Executive Order N–75–20 (2019 CA EO 75-20), concerning a number of different COVID-19-related provisions, including pharmacy testing, remote adoption paperwork, and community development grants, see Historical and Statutory Notes under Government Code § 12730.

(a) Except as provided in Section 7662, the consent of the birth parent or parents who did not place the child for adoption, as described in Section 8801.3, to the adoption shall be signed in the presence of an agent of the department or of a delegated county adoption agency on a form prescribed by the department. The consent shall be filed with the clerk of the appropriate superior court.

(b) The consent described in subdivision (a), when reciting that the person giving it is entitled to the sole custody of the child and when acknowledged before that agent, is prima facie evidence of the right of the person making it to the sole custody of the child and that person's sole right to consent.

(c) If the birth parent described in subdivision (a) is located outside this state for an extended period of time unrelated to the adoption at the time of signing the consent, the consent may be signed before a notary or other person authorized to perform notarial acts, and in that case the consent of the department or of the delegated county adoption agency is also necessary.

(d) A birth parent who is a minor has the right to sign a consent for the adoption of the birth parent's child and the consent is not subject to revocation by the birth parent by reason of minority, or because the parent or guardian of the consenting minor parent was not served with notice that the minor parent consented to the adoption, unless the minor parent has previously provided written

§ 8814

authorization to serve the minor parent's parent or guardian with that notice. *(Added by Stats.1993, c. 758 (S.B.792), § 12, operative Jan. 1, 1995. Amended by Stats.1994, c. 585 (A.B.3336), § 5, operative Jan. 1, 1995; Stats.1996, c. 510 (A.B.2165), § 4; Stats.2014, c. 763 (A.B.1701), § 14, eff. Jan. 1, 2015; Stats.2019, c. 115 (A.B.1817), § 129, eff. Jan. 1, 2020.)*

Cross References

Abandoned children, declaration of abandonment, see Family Code § 7822.
Agency adoption consent, see Family Code § 8700.
Birth parent,
   Defined, see Family Code § 8512.
   Money or benefits for consent or placement of children, see Penal Code § 273.
County defined for purposes of this Code, see Family Code § 67.
Delegated county adoption agency defined, see Family Code § 8515.
Department defined, see Family Code § 8518.
Minor defined for purposes of this Code, see Family Code § 6500.
Person defined for purposes of this Code, see Family Code § 105.
Prima facie evidence, see Evidence Code § 602.
State defined for purposes of this Code, see Family Code § 145.
Stepparent adoption consent, see Family Code § 9003.

Research References

Forms

2 California Transactions Forms--Family Law § 6:5, Issues Common to All Types of Adoptions.

§ 8814.5. Revocation of consent; actions taken within 30 days of signing consent

(a) After a consent to the adoption is signed by the birth parent or parents pursuant to Section 8801.3 or 8814, the birth parent or parents signing the consent shall have 30 days to take one of the following actions:

(1) Sign and deliver to the department or delegated county adoption agency a written statement revoking the consent and requesting the child to be returned to the birth parent or parents. After revoking consent, in cases where the birth parent or parents have not regained custody, or the birth parent or parents have failed to make efforts to exercise their rights under subdivision (b) of Section 8815, a written notarized statement reinstating the original consent may be signed and delivered to the department or delegated county adoption agency, in which case the revocation of consent shall be void and the remainder of the original 30–day period shall commence. After revoking consent, in cases in which the birth parent or parents have regained custody or made efforts to exercise their rights under subdivision (b) of Section 8815 by requesting the return of the child, upon the delivery of a written notarized statement reinstating the original consent to the department or delegated county adoption agency, the revocation of consent shall be void and a new 30–day period shall commence. The birth mother shall be informed of the operational timelines associated with this section at the time of signing of the statement reinstating the original consent.

(2)(A) Sign a waiver of the right to revoke consent on a form prescribed by the department in the presence of any of the following:

(i) A representative of the department or delegated county adoption agency.

(ii) A judicial officer of a court of record if the birth parent is represented by independent legal counsel.

(iii) An adoption service provider, including, but not limited to, the adoption service provider who advised the birth mother and witnessed the signing of the consent, if the birth parent or parents are represented by independent legal counsel. The adoption service provider shall ensure that the waiver is delivered to the department, the petitioners, or their counsel no earlier than the end of the business day following the signing of the waiver. The adoption service provider shall inform the birth parent that during this time period the birth parent may request that the waiver be withdrawn and that, if that request is made, the waiver shall be withdrawn.

(B) An adoption service provider may assist the birth parent or parents in any activity where the primary purpose of that activity is to facilitate the signing of the waiver with the department, a delegated county agency, or a judicial officer. The adoption service provider or another person designated by the birth parent or parents may also be present at any interview conducted pursuant to this section to provide support to the birth parent or parents, except when the interview is conducted by independent legal counsel for the birth parent or parents.

(C) The waiver of the right to revoke consent may not be signed until an interview has been completed by the department or delegated county adoption agency unless the waiver of the right to revoke consent is signed in the presence of a judicial officer of a court of record or an adoption service provider as specified in this section. If the waiver is signed in the presence of a judicial officer, the interview and the witnessing of the signing of the waiver shall be conducted by the judicial officer. If the waiver is signed in the presence of an adoption service provider, the interview shall be conducted by the independent legal counsel for the birth parent or parents. If the waiver is to be signed in the presence of an adoption service provider, prior to the waiver being signed the waiver shall be reviewed by the independent legal counsel who (i) counsels the birth parent or parents about the nature of the intended waiver and (ii) signs and delivers to the birth parent or parents and the department a certificate in substantially the following form:

I, (name of attorney), have counseled my client, (name of client), on the nature and legal effect of the waiver of right to revoke consent to adoption. I am so disassociated from the interest of the petitioner(s)/prospective adoptive parent(s) as to be in a position to advise my client impartially and confidentially as to the consequences of the waiver. (Name of client) is aware that California law provides for a 30–day period during which a birth parent may revoke consent to adoption. On the basis of this counsel, I conclude that it is the intent of (name of client) to waive the right to revoke, and make a permanent and irrevocable consent to adoption. (Name of client) understands that they will not be able to regain custody of the child unless the petitioner(s)/prospective adoptive parent(s) agree(s) to withdraw their petition for adoption or the court denies the adoption petition.

(D) Within 10 working days of a request made after the department or the delegated county adoption agency has received a copy of the petition for the adoption and the names and addresses of the persons to be interviewed, the department or the delegated county adoption agency shall interview, at the department or agency office, any birth parent requesting to be interviewed.

(E) Notwithstanding subparagraphs (A) and (C), the interview, and the witnessing of the signing of a waiver of the right to revoke consent of a birth parent residing outside of California or located outside of California for an extended period of time unrelated to the adoption may be conducted in the state where the birth parent is located, by any of the following:

(i) A representative of a public adoption agency in that state.

(ii) A judicial officer in that state where the birth parent is represented by independent legal counsel.

(iii) An adoption service provider.

(3) Allow the consent to become a permanent consent on the 31st day after signing.

(b) The consent may not be revoked after a waiver of the right to revoke consent has been signed or after 30 days, beginning on the date the consent was signed or as provided in paragraph (1) of subdivision (a), whichever occurs first. *(Added by Stats.1993, c. 758*

(S.B.792), § 13, operative Jan. 1, 1995. Amended by Stats.1994, c. 585 (A.B.3336), § 6, operative Jan. 1, 1995; Stats.1996, c. 510 (A.B.2165), § 5; Stats.2000, c. 937 (A.B.2433), § 5; Stats.2001, c. 688 (S.B.104), § 2; Stats.2002, c. 664 (A.B.3034), § 79; Stats.2003, c. 251 (S.B.182), § 10; Stats.2008, c. 534 (S.B.1726), § 11; Stats.2009, c. 492 (A.B. 941), § 4; Stats.2010, c. 588 (A.B.2020), § 7; Stats.2019, c. 115 (A.B.1817), § 130, eff. Jan. 1, 2020.)

Cross References

Adoption service provider, defined, see Family Code § 8502.
Agency adoptions, rescission of relinquishment for adoption by birth parent, see Family Code § 8700.
Birth parent, defined, see Family Code § 8512.
County defined for purposes of this Code, see Family Code § 67.
Delegated county adoption agency defined, see Family Code § 8515.
Department defined, see Family Code § 8518.
Person defined for purposes of this Code, see Family Code § 105.
Prospective adoptive parent, defined, see Family Code § 8542.
State defined for purposes of this Code, see Family Code § 145.
Stepparent adoptions, withdrawal of consent, see Family Code § 9005.
Support defined for purposes of this Code, see Family Code § 150.
Temporary custody of minor in hospital without warrant, conditions requiring a warrant, see Welfare and Institutions Code § 305.6.

Research References

Forms

2 California Transactions Forms--Family Law § 6:3, Definitions.
2 California Transactions Forms--Family Law § 6:32, Nature of Independent Adoption—Relinquishment Versus Consent.
2 California Transactions Forms--Family Law § 6:33, Reasons for Independent Adoption.
2 California Transactions Forms--Family Law § 6:37, Placing Parent's Right to Revoke Consent to Adoption.
2 California Transactions Forms--Family Law § 6:38, Waiver of Placing Parent's Right to Revoke Consent to Adoption.
2 California Transactions Forms--Family Law § 6:50, Independent Adoption Retainer Agreement.
2 California Transactions Forms--Family Law § 6:60, Waiver of Right to Revoke Consent to Adoption: Independent Adoption Program [Department of Social Services Form Ad 929].
2 California Transactions Forms--Family Law § 6:68, Receipt for Child.
2 California Transactions Forms--Family Law § 6:84, Relinquishment as Distinguished from Consent.
2 California Transactions Forms--Family Law § 6:148, Rights of Indian Parents of Indian Children.

§ 8815. Withdrawal of consent

(a) Once the revocable consent to adoption has become permanent as provided in Section 8814.5, the consent to the adoption by the prospective adoptive parents may not be withdrawn.

(b) Before the time when the revocable consent becomes permanent as provided in Section 8814.5, the birth parent or parents may request return of the child. In that case the child shall immediately be returned to the requesting birth parent or parents, unless a court orders otherwise.

(c) If the person or persons with whom the child has been placed have concerns that the birth parent or parents requesting return of the child are unfit or present a danger of harm to the child, that person or those persons may report their concerns to the appropriate child welfare agency. These concerns shall not be a basis for failure to immediately return the child, unless a court orders otherwise. *(Added by Stats.1993, c. 758 (S.B.792), § 16, operative Jan. 1, 1995. Amended by Stats.2014, c. 763 (A.B.1701), § 15, eff. Jan. 1, 2015.)*

Cross References

Agency adoptions, rescission of relinquishment for adoption by birth parent, see Family Code § 8700.
Birth parent, defined, see Family Code § 8512.
Independent adoptions, revocation of consent by birth parents, see Family Code § 8814.5.
Person defined for purposes of this Code, see Family Code § 105.
Prospective adoptive parent, defined, see Family Code § 8542.

Stepparent adoptions, withdrawal of consent, see Family Code § 9005.
Temporary custody of minor in hospital without warrant, conditions requiring a warrant, see Welfare and Institutions Code § 305.6.

Research References

Forms

2 California Transactions Forms--Family Law § 6:37, Placing Parent's Right to Revoke Consent to Adoption.
2 California Transactions Forms--Family Law § 6:38, Waiver of Placing Parent's Right to Revoke Consent to Adoption.
2 California Transactions Forms--Family Law § 6:60, Waiver of Right to Revoke Consent to Adoption: Independent Adoption Program [Department of Social Services Form Ad 929].

§ 8816. Consent of agency or department when consent of birth parent not required; prerequisites

In an independent adoption where the consent of the birth parent or parents is not necessary, the department or delegated county adoption agency shall, before the hearing of the petition, file its consent to the adoption with the clerk of the court in which the petition is filed. The consent may not be given unless the child's welfare will be promoted by the adoption. *(Stats.1992, c. 162 (A.B.2650), § 10, operative Jan. 1, 1994.)*

Cross References

Birth parent,
    Defined, see Family Code § 8512.
    Money or benefits for consent or placement of children, see Penal Code § 273.
County defined for purposes of this Code, see Family Code § 67.
Delegated county adoption agency defined, see Family Code § 8515.
Department defined, see Family Code § 8518.
Independent adoption, defined, see Family Code § 8524.
Jurisdiction of superior court, see Family Code § 200.

§ 8817. Report on medical background of child and biological parents; contents; blood sample

(a) A written report on the child's medical background, and if available, the medical background of the child's biological parents so far as ascertainable, shall be made by the department or delegated county adoption agency as part of the study required by Section 8806.

(b) The report on the child's background shall contain all known diagnostic information, including current medical reports on the child, psychological evaluations, and scholastic information, as well as all known information regarding the child's developmental history and family life.

(c) The report shall be submitted to the prospective adoptive parents who shall acknowledge its receipt in writing.

(d)(1) The biological parents may provide a blood sample at a clinic or hospital approved by the State Department of Health Services. The biological parents' failure to provide a blood sample shall not affect the adoption of the child.

(2) The blood sample shall be stored at a laboratory under contract with the State Department of Health Services for a period of 30 years following the adoption of the child.

(3) The purpose of the stored sample of blood is to provide a blood sample from which DNA testing can be done at a later date after entry of the order of adoption at the request of the adoptive parents or the adopted child. The cost of drawing and storing the blood samples shall be paid for by a separate fee in addition to the fee required under Section 8810. The amount of this additional fee shall be based on the cost of drawing and storing the blood samples but at no time shall the additional fee be more than one hundred dollars ($100).

(e)(1) The blood sample shall be stored and released in such a manner as to not identify any party to the adoption.

(2) Any results of the DNA testing shall be stored and released in such a manner as to not identify any party to the adoption.

§ 8817

(Stats.1992, c. 162 (A.B.2650), § 10, operative Jan. 1, 1994. Amended by Stats.1996, c. 1053 (A.B.3241), § 2.)

Cross References

Agency adoption medical report, see Family Code § 8706.
Confidentiality of medical information, exemptions from limitations, see Civil Code § 56.30.
County defined for purposes of this Code, see Family Code § 67.
Delegated county adoption agency defined, see Family Code § 8515.
Department defined, see Family Code § 8518.
Department of Health Care Services, generally, see Health and Safety Code § 100100 et seq.
Disclosure of information, see Family Code § 9200 et seq.
Intercountry adoption medical report, see Family Code § 8909.
Judgment and order defined for purposes of this Code, see Family Code § 100.
Prospective adoptive parent, defined, see Family Code § 8542.
Rules and regulations,
 Availability of medical reports, see Family Code § 9202.
 Medical reports, form and content, see Family Code § 8608.
State defined for purposes of this Code, see Family Code § 145.

§ 8818. Statement to birth parents; contents; disclosure form; birth parent information

For Executive Order N–75–20 (2019 CA EO 75-20), concerning a number of different COVID-19-related provisions, including pharmacy testing, remote adoption paperwork, and community development grants, see Historical and Statutory Notes under Government Code § 12730.

(a) The department shall adopt a statement to be presented to the birth parents at the time the consent to adoption is signed and to prospective adoptive parents at the time of the home study. The statement shall, in a clear and concise manner and in words calculated to ensure the confidence of the birth parents in the integrity of the adoption process, communicate to the birth parent of a child who is the subject of an adoption petition all of the following facts:

(1) It is in the child's best interest that the birth parents keep the department informed of any health problems that the parent develops that could affect the child.

(2) It is extremely important that the birth parent keep an address current with the department in order to permit a response to inquiries concerning medical or social history.

(3) Section 9203 of the Family Code authorizes a person who has been adopted and who attains the age of 21 years to request the department to disclose the name and address of the adoptee's birth parents. Consequently, it is of the utmost importance that the birth parent indicate whether to allow this disclosure by checking the appropriate box provided on the form.

(4) The birth parent may change the decision whether to permit disclosure of the birth parent's name and address, at any time, by sending a notarized letter to that effect, by certified mail, return receipt requested, to the department.

(5) The consent will be filed in the office of the clerk of the court in which the adoption takes place. The file is not open to inspection by any persons other than the parties to the adoption proceeding, their attorneys, and the department, except upon order of a judge of the superior court.

(b) The department shall adopt a form to be signed by the birth parents at the time the consent to adoption is signed, which shall provide as follows:

"Section 9203 of the Family Code authorizes a person who has been adopted and who attains the age of 21 years to make a request to the State Department of Social Services, or the licensed adoption agency that joined in the adoption petition, for the name and address of the adoptee's birth parents. Indicate by checking one of the boxes below whether or not you wish your name and address to be disclosed:

☐ YES
☐ NO
☐ UNCERTAIN AT THIS TIME; WILL NOTIFY AGENCY AT LATER DATE."

(Stats.1992, c. 162 (A.B.2650), § 10, operative Jan. 1, 1994. Amended by Stats.2002, c. 784 (S.B.1316), § 113.)

Cross References

Agency adoption, statement to birth parents, see Family Code § 8702.
Birth parent, defined, see Family Code § 8512.
Department defined, see Family Code § 8518.
Disclosure of information, see Family Code § 9200 et seq.
Judgment and order defined for purposes of this Code, see Family Code § 100.
Person defined for purposes of this Code, see Family Code § 105.
Proceeding defined for purposes of this Code, see Family Code § 110.
Prospective adoptive parent, defined, see Family Code § 8542.
State defined for purposes of this Code, see Family Code § 145.

§ 8819. Termination of parental rights of birth parent; notification

When the parental rights of a birth parent are terminated pursuant to Chapter 5 (commencing with Section 7660) of Part 3 of Division 12 or Part 4 (commencing with Section 7800) of Division 12, the department or delegated county adoption agency shall send a written notice to the birth parent, if the birth parent's address is known, that contains the following statement:

"You are encouraged to keep the department or this agency informed of your current address in order to permit a response to any inquiry concerning medical or social history made by or on behalf of the child who was the subject of the court action terminating parental rights." (Stats.1992, c. 162 (A.B.2650), § 10, operative Jan. 1, 1994.)

Cross References

Adoptive parents, criminal record, see Penal Code § 11105.3.
Agency adoption, notice of termination of parental rights, see Family Code § 8703.
Birth parent,
 Defined, see Family Code § 8512.
 Money or benefits for consent or placement of children, see Penal Code § 273.
County defined for purposes of this Code, see Family Code § 67.
Delegated county adoption agency defined, see Family Code § 8515.
Department defined, see Family Code § 8518.
Foster care of children, see Welfare and Institutions Code § 396 et seq.
Judgment and order defined for purposes of this Code, see Family Code § 100.
Juvenile delinquents and dependents,
 Jurisdiction, see Welfare and Institutions Code § 366.3.
 Priorities and preferences, foster parents and relatives, see Welfare and Institutions Code §§ 361.2 et seq., 366.26.

§ 8820. Failure of department or agency to accept consent of birth parent or give consent where appropriate; appeal; proceedings

(a) The birth parent or parents or the petitioner may appeal in either of the following cases:

(1) If for a period of 180 days from the date of paying 50 percent of the fee, or upon the expiration of any extension of the period granted by the court, the department or delegated county adoption agency fails or refuses to accept the consent of the birth parent or parents to the adoption.

(2) In a case where the consent of the department or delegated county adoption agency is required by this chapter, if the department or agency fails or refuses to file or give its consent to the adoption after full payment has been received.

(b) The appeal shall be filed in the court in which the adoption petition is filed. The court clerk shall immediately notify the department or delegated county adoption agency of the appeal and the department or agency shall, within 10 days, file a report of its findings and the reasons for its failure or refusal to consent to the adoption or to accept the consent of the birth parent or parents.

(c) After the filing of the report by the department or delegated county adoption agency, the court may, if it deems that the welfare of the child will be promoted by that adoption, allow the signing of the consent by the birth parent or parents in open court or, if the appeal is from the refusal of the department or delegated county adoption agency to consent thereto, grant the petition without the consent.

(d) This section shall become operative on October 1, 2008. *(Added by Stats.2008, c. 759 (A.B.1279), § 14, eff. Sept. 30, 2008, operative Oct. 1, 2008.)*

Cross References

Birth parent, defined, see Family Code § 8512.
Birth parents, money or benefits for consent or placement of children, see Penal Code § 273.
Delegated county adoption agency defined, see Family Code § 8515.
Department defined, see Family Code § 8518.
Petitioner defined for purposes of this Code, see Family Code § 126.

Research References

Forms

2 California Transactions Forms--Family Law § 6:5, Issues Common to All Types of Adoptions.
West's California Code Forms, Family § 8800, Comment Overview—Independent Adoptions.

§ 8821. Report or findings of department or agency; submission of copy to attorney for petitioner

When any report or findings are submitted to the court by the department or a delegated county adoption agency, a copy of the report or findings, whether favorable or unfavorable, shall be given to the petitioner's attorney in the proceeding, if the petitioner has an attorney of record, or to the petitioner. *(Stats.1992, c. 162 (A.B. 2650), § 10, operative Jan. 1, 1994.)*

Cross References

Agency adoptions, copy of report, see Family Code § 8717.
County defined for purposes of this Code, see Family Code § 67.
Delegated county adoption agency defined, see Family Code § 8515.
Department defined, see Family Code § 8518.
Disclosure of information, see Family Code § 9200 et seq.
Intercountry adoption, copy of report, see Family Code § 8915.
Petitioner defined for purposes of this Code, see Family Code § 126.
Proceeding defined for purposes of this Code, see Family Code § 110.

§ 8822. Denial or withdrawal of petition; referral to superior court for review; hearing; notice

(a) If the findings of the department or delegated county adoption agency are that the home of the petitioners is not suitable for the child or that the required consents are not available and the department or agency recommends that the petition be denied, or if the petitioners desire to withdraw the petition and the department or agency recommends that the petition be denied, the clerk upon receipt of the report of the department or agency shall immediately refer it to the court for review.

(b) Upon receipt of the report, the court shall set a date for a hearing of the petition and shall give reasonable notice of the hearing to the department or delegated county adoption agency, the petitioners, and the birth parents by certified mail, return receipt requested, to the address of each as shown in the proceeding.

(c) The department or delegated county adoption agency shall appear to represent the child. *(Stats.1992, c. 162 (A.B.2650), § 10, operative Jan. 1, 1994.)*

Cross References

Agency adoption, unfavorable recommendations, see Family Code § 8720.
Birth parent, defined, see Family Code § 8512.
County defined for purposes of this Code, see Family Code § 67.
Delegated county adoption agency defined, see Family Code § 8515.
Department defined, see Family Code § 8518.

Intercountry adoption, unfavorable recommendations, see Family Code § 8917.
Jurisdiction of superior court, see Family Code § 200.
Petitioner defined for purposes of this Code, see Family Code § 126.
Proceeding defined for purposes of this Code, see Family Code § 110.

Research References

Forms

2 California Transactions Forms--Family Law § 6:5, Issues Common to All Types of Adoptions.

§ 8823. Prospective adoptive parents; appearance before court

The prospective adoptive parents and the child proposed to be adopted shall appear before the court pursuant to Sections 8612 and 8613. *(Stats.1992, c. 162 (A.B.2650), § 10, operative Jan. 1, 1994.)*

Cross References

Adult adoptions, appearance, see Family Code § 9324.
Agency adoption, appearance, see Family Code § 8718.
Intercountry adoptions, appearance, see Family Code § 8913.
Prospective adoptive parent, defined, see Family Code § 8542.
Stepparent adoptions, appearance, see Family Code § 9007.

CHAPTER 4. INTERCOUNTRY ADOPTIONS

Section
8900. Service providers; licensure conditions; primary provider; written agreement.
8900.5. Definitions.
8901. Administration of program.
8902. Agency services.
8903. Intercountry adoptions finalized in state; care, custody and control of child; Medi–Cal eligibility.
8904. Intercountry adoptions finalized in foreign country; agency services.
8905. Domestic and foreign adoption agencies; work with state agencies; written agreement required.
8906. Financial responsibility for child; transfer or sharing between agency and prospective adoptive parents.
8907. Fees; program funding.
8908. Applicants; fingerprints; criminal record; prohibited placement; fee; waiver.
8909. Medical report on child and biological parents; contents; blood sample.
8910. Removal of child from county; concealment of child; permission for removal; objections; hearing; notice; application of section.
8911. Conditions of placement; filing of petition.
8912. Petition for adoption; notification of department; contents; guardianship petitions; order of adoption.
8913. Adoptive parent and child; appearance before court.
8914. Agency as party to petition; report of facts; submission to court.
8915. Report or findings of agency; copy to attorney or petitioner.
8916. Withdrawal of petition; dismissal of proceedings; notification of department; agency report; recommendations; jurisdiction.
8917. Denial or withdrawal of petition; referral to court for review.
8918. Hearing; recommendation of removal of child sustained; transfer of child to care of agency.
8919. Adoptions finalized in foreign country; petition for readoption; penalty for failure to file; human trafficking prevention; birth certificate.
8919.5. Adoptions finalized in foreign country; reporting arrival of adoptee in state.

ADOPTION

Section	
8920.	Separation from sibling group through readoption; agreements for visitation; enforcement; best interest of child.
8921.	Services of adoption facilitator.
8923.	Complaint procedures.
8924.	Emigration of child to convention country.
8925.	Hague adoption certificate or custody declaration.

Cross References

Intercountry adoptions, defined, see Family Code § 8527.

§ 8900. Service providers; licensure conditions; primary provider; written agreement

(a) Intercountry adoption services described in this chapter shall be exclusively provided by private adoption agencies licensed by the department specifically to provide these services. As a condition of licensure to provide intercountry adoption services, any private full-service adoption agency and any noncustodial adoption agency shall be accredited by the Council on Accreditation, or supervised by an accredited primary provider, or acting as an exempted provider, in compliance with Subpart F (commencing with Section 96.29) of Part 96 of Title 22 of the Code of Federal Regulations.

(b) A private full-service adoption agency or a noncustodial adoption agency, when acting as the primary provider and using a supervised provider, shall ensure that each supervised provider operates under a written agreement with the primary provider pursuant to subdivision (b) of Section 96.45 of Title 22 of the Code of Federal Regulations.

(c) The primary provider shall provide to the department a copy of the written agreement with each supervised provider containing all provisions required pursuant to subdivision (b) of Section 96.45 of Title 22 of the Code of Federal Regulations. *(Stats.1992, c. 162 (A.B.2650), § 10, operative Jan. 1, 1994. Amended by Stats.2007, c. 583 (S.B.703), § 5.)*

Cross References

Department defined, see Family Code § 8518.
Intercountry adoption, defined, see Family Code § 8527.

Research References

Forms

2 California Transactions Forms--Family Law § 6:138, Prohibition of Intercountry Independent Adoption.
2 California Transactions Forms--Family Law § 6:139, Overview of Intercountry Adoption.
West's California Code Forms, Family § 8900, Comment Overview—Intercountry Adoptions.
West's California Judicial Council Forms ADOPT-200, Adoption Request.
West's California Judicial Council Forms ADOPT-215, Adoption Order (Also Available in Spanish).
West's California Judicial Council Forms ADOPT-216, Verification of Compliance With Hague Adoption Convention Attachment (Also Available in Spanish).

§ 8900.5. Definitions

As used in this chapter:

(a) "Accredited agency" means an agency that has been accredited by an accrediting entity, in accordance with the standards in Subpart F (commencing with Section 96.29) of Part 96 of Title 22 of the Code of Federal Regulations, to provide adoption services in the United States in cases subject to the convention. Accredited agency does not include a temporarily accredited agency.

(b) "Adoption service" means any of the following services:

(1) Identifying a child for adoption and arranging an adoption.

(2) Securing the necessary consent to termination of parental rights and to adoption.

(3) Performing a background study on a child or a home study on any prospective adoptive parent, and reporting on the study.

(4) Making nonjudicial determinations of the best interests of a child and the appropriateness of an adoptive placement for the child.

(5) Monitoring a case after a child has been placed with any prospective adoptive parent until final adoption.

(6) If necessary because of a disruption before final adoption, assuming custody and providing or facilitating child care or any other social service pending an alternative placement.

(c) "Central authority" means the entity designated under paragraph (1) of Article 6 of the convention by a convention country. The United States Department of State is designated as the United States Central Authority pursuant to the federal Intercountry Adoption Act of 2000 (42 U.S.C. Sec. 14911).

(d) "Convention" means the Hague Convention on Protection of Children and Co-operation in Respect of Intercountry Adoption, May 29, 1993.

(e) "Convention adoption" means the adoption of a child resident in a convention country by a United States citizen, or an adoption of a child resident in the United States by an individual or individuals residing in a convention country, if, in connection with the adoption, the child has moved or will move between the United States and the convention country.

(f) "Convention country" means a country that is party to the convention and with which the convention is in force for the United States.

(g) "Exempted provider" means a social work professional or organization that performs a home study on any prospective adoptive parent, or a child background study, or both, in the United States in connection with a convention adoption, and who is not currently providing and has not previously provided any other adoption service in the case.

(h) "Hague adoption certificate" means a certificate issued by the secretary in an outgoing case (where the child is emigrating from the United States to another convention country) certifying that a child has been adopted in the United States in accordance with the convention and, except as provided in subdivision (b) of Section 97.4 of Title 22 of the Code of Federal Regulations, the Intercountry Adoption Act of 2000 (42 U.S.C. Sec. 14901 et seq.; the IAA).

(i) "Hague custody declaration" means a declaration issued by the secretary in an outgoing case (where the child is emigrating from the United States to another convention country) declaring that custody of a child for purposes of adoption has been granted in the United States in accordance with the convention and, except as provided in subdivision (b) of Section 97.4 of Title 22 of the Code of Federal Regulations, the IAA.

(j) "Legal service" means any service, other than those defined in this section as an adoption service, that relates to the provision of legal advice and information or to the drafting of legal instruments. Legal service includes, but is not limited to, any of the following services:

(1) Drafting contracts, powers of attorney, and other legal instruments.

(2) Providing advice and counsel to an adoptive parent on completing forms for the State Department of Health Care Services or the United States Department of State.

(3) Providing advice and counsel to accredited agencies, temporarily accredited agencies, approved persons, or prospective adoptive parents on how to comply with the convention, the IAA, and any regulations implementing the IAA.

(k) "Primary provider" means the accredited agency that is identified pursuant to Section 96.14 of Title 22 of the Code of Federal Regulations as responsible for ensuring that all adoption services are provided and responsible for supervising any supervised providers when used.

(*l*) "Public domestic authority" means an authority operated by a state, local, or tribal government.

(m) "Secretary" means the United States Secretary of State, and includes any official of the United States Department of State exercising the authority of the Secretary of State under the convention, the IAA, or any regulations implementing the IAA, pursuant to a delegation of authority.

(n) "Supervised provider" means any agency, person, or other nongovernmental entity that is providing any adoption service in a convention adoption under the supervision and responsibility of an accredited agency that is acting as the primary provider in the case. *(Added by Stats.2007, c. 583 (S.B.703), § 6.)*

Research References

Forms

West's California Judicial Council Forms ADOPT–215, Adoption Order (Also Available in Spanish).

West's California Judicial Council Forms ADOPT–216, Verification of Compliance With Hague Adoption Convention Attachment (Also Available in Spanish).

§ 8901. Administration of program

The department shall adopt regulations to administer the intercountry adoption program. *(Stats.1992, c. 162 (A.B.2650), § 10, operative Jan. 1, 1994.)*

Cross References

Department defined, see Family Code § 8518.

Research References

Forms

West's California Code Forms, Family § 8900, Comment Overview—Intercountry Adoptions.

West's California Judicial Council Forms ADOPT–216, Verification of Compliance With Hague Adoption Convention Attachment (Also Available in Spanish).

§ 8902. Agency services

For intercountry adoptions that will be finalized in this state, the licensed adoption agency shall provide all of the following services:

(a) Assessment of the suitability of the applicant's home.

(b) Placement of the foreign-born child in an approved home.

(c) Postplacement supervision.

(d) Submission to the court of a report on the intercountry adoptive placement with a recommendation regarding the granting of the petition.

(e) Services to applicants seeking to adopt related children living in foreign countries. The Legislature recognizes that these children have an impelling need for adoptive placement with their relatives. *(Stats.1992, c. 162 (A.B.2650), § 10, operative Jan. 1, 1994.)*

Cross References

Agency adoption, petition, see Family Code § 8714.
Applicant, defined, see Family Code § 8509.
Intercountry adoption, defined, see Family Code § 8527.
Licensed adoption agency defined, see Family Code § 8530.
State defined for purposes of this Code, see Family Code § 145.

Research References

Forms

2 California Transactions Forms--Family Law § 6:139, Overview of Intercountry Adoption.

West's California Judicial Council Forms ADOPT–215, Adoption Order (Also Available in Spanish).

West's California Judicial Council Forms ADOPT–216, Verification of Compliance With Hague Adoption Convention Attachment (Also Available in Spanish).

West's California Judicial Council Forms JV–505, Statement Regarding Parentage (Juvenile) (Also Available in Spanish).

§ 8903. Intercountry adoptions finalized in state; care, custody and control of child; Medi–Cal eligibility

(a) For each intercountry adoption finalized in this state, the licensed adoption agency shall assume all responsibilities for the child including care, custody, and control as if the child had been relinquished for adoption in this state from the time the child left the child's native country.

(b) Notwithstanding subdivision (a), if the child's native country requires and has given full guardianship to the prospective adoptive parents, the prospective adoptive parents shall assume all responsibilities for the child including care, custody, control, and financial support.

(c) If the licensed adoption agency or prospective adoptive parents fail to meet the responsibilities under subdivision (a) or (b) and the child becomes a dependent of the court pursuant to Section 300 of the Welfare and Institutions Code, the state shall assume responsibility for the cost of care for the child. When the child becomes a dependent of the court and if, for any reason, is ineligible for AFDC under Section 14005.1 of the Welfare and Institutions Code and loses Medi–Cal eligibility, the child shall be deemed eligible for Medi–Cal under Section 14005.4 of the Welfare and Institutions Code and the State Director of Health Services has authority to provide payment for the medical services to the child that are necessary to meet the child's needs. *(Stats.1992, c. 162 (A.B.2650), § 10, operative Jan. 1, 1994.)*

Cross References

Adoptive parents, criminal record, see Penal Code § 11105.3.
Birth parents, money or benefits for consent or placement of children, see Penal Code § 273.
Foster care of children, see Welfare and Institutions Code § 396 et seq.
Intercountry adoption, defined, see Family Code § 8527.
Juvenile delinquents and dependents,
  Jurisdiction, see Welfare and Institutions Code § 366.3.
  Priorities and preferences, foster parents and relatives, see Welfare and Institutions Code §§ 361.2 et seq., 366.26.
Licensed adoption agency defined, see Family Code § 8530.
Prospective adoptive parent, defined, see Family Code § 8542.
State defined for purposes of this Code, see Family Code § 145.
Support defined for purposes of this Code, see Family Code § 150.

Research References

Forms

2 California Transactions Forms--Family Law § 6:139, Overview of Intercountry Adoption.

West's California Judicial Council Forms ADOPT–216, Verification of Compliance With Hague Adoption Convention Attachment (Also Available in Spanish).

§ 8904. Intercountry adoptions finalized in foreign country; agency services

For an intercountry adoption that will be finalized in a foreign country, the licensed adoption agency shall provide all of the following services:

(a) Assessment of the suitability of the applicant's home.

(b) Certification to the United States Citizenship and Immigration Services that this state's intercountry adoption requirements have been met.

(c) Readoption services as required by the United States Citizenship and Immigration Services.

(d) Postadoption services pursuant to any written agreement between the licensed adoption agency and any other person or entity

§ 8904

for which the postadoption services have been paid. *(Stats.1992, c. 162 (A.B.2650), § 10, operative Jan. 1, 1994. Amended by Stats.1993, c. 219 (A.B.1500), § 202; Stats.2019, c. 805 (A.B.677), § 1, eff. Jan. 1, 2020.)*

Cross References

Intercountry adoption, defined, see Family Code § 8527.
Licensed adoption agency defined, see Family Code § 8530.
State defined for purposes of this Code, see Family Code § 145.

Research References

Forms

2 California Transactions Forms--Family Law § 6:139, Overview of Intercountry Adoption.
West's California Judicial Council Forms ADOPT–216, Verification of Compliance With Hague Adoption Convention Attachment (Also Available in Spanish).

§ 8905. Domestic and foreign adoption agencies; work with state agencies; written agreement required

Licensed adoption agencies may work only with domestic and foreign adoption agencies with whom they have written agreements that specify the responsibilities of each. The agreements may not violate any statute or regulation of the United States or of this state. *(Stats.1992, c. 162 (A.B.2650), § 10, operative Jan. 1, 1994.)*

Cross References

Licensed adoption agency defined, see Family Code § 8530.
State defined for purposes of this Code, see Family Code § 145.

Research References

Forms

2 California Transactions Forms--Family Law § 6:140, Specifying Nation of Origin of Child.
West's California Judicial Council Forms ADOPT–200, Adoption Request.
West's California Judicial Council Forms ADOPT–216, Verification of Compliance With Hague Adoption Convention Attachment (Also Available in Spanish).

§ 8906. Financial responsibility for child; transfer or sharing between agency and prospective adoptive parents

Nothing in this chapter may be construed to prohibit the licensed adoption agency from entering into an agreement with the prospective adoptive parents to share or transfer financial responsibility for the child. *(Stats.1992, c. 162 (A.B.2650), § 10, operative Jan. 1, 1994.)*

Cross References

Licensed adoption agency defined, see Family Code § 8530.
Prospective adoptive parent, defined, see Family Code § 8542.

§ 8907. Fees; program funding

The costs incurred by a licensed adoption agency pursuant to programs established by this chapter shall be funded by fees charged by the agency for services required by this chapter. The agency's fee schedule is required to be approved by the department initially and whenever it is altered. *(Stats.1992, c. 162 (A.B.2650), § 10, operative Jan. 1, 1994.)*

Cross References

Department defined, see Family Code § 8518.
Licensed adoption agency defined, see Family Code § 8530.
Stepparent adoptions, report of county welfare department or probation officer, see Family Code § 9001.

§ 8908. Applicants; fingerprints; criminal record; prohibited placement; fee; waiver

(a) A licensed adoption agency shall require each person filing an application for adoption to be fingerprinted and shall secure from an appropriate law enforcement agency any criminal record of that person to determine if the person has ever been convicted of a crime other than a minor traffic violation. The licensed adoption agency may also secure the person's full criminal record, if any, with the exception of any convictions for which relief has been granted pursuant to Section 1203.49 of the Penal Code. Any federal-level criminal offender record requests to the Department of Justice shall be submitted with fingerprint images and related information required by the Department of Justice for the purposes of obtaining information as to the existence and content of a record of an out-of-state or federal conviction or arrest of a person or information regarding any out-of-state or federal crimes or arrests for which the Department of Justice establishes that the person is free on bail, or on their own recognizance pending trial or appeal. The Department of Justice shall forward to the Federal Bureau of Investigation any requests for federal summary criminal history information received pursuant to this section. The Department of Justice shall review the information returned from the Federal Bureau of Investigation and shall compile and disseminate a fitness determination to the licensed adoption agency.

(b) Notwithstanding subdivision (c), the criminal record, if any, shall be taken into consideration when evaluating the prospective adoptive parent, and an assessment of the effects of any criminal history on the ability of the prospective adoptive parent to provide adequate and proper care and guidance to the child shall be included in the report to the court.

(c)(1) A licensed adoption agency shall not give final approval for an adoptive placement in any home in which the prospective adoptive parent, or any adult living in the prospective adoptive home, has a felony conviction for either of the following:

(A) A felony conviction for child abuse or neglect, spousal abuse, crimes against a child, including child pornography, or for a crime involving violence, including rape, sexual assault, or homicide, but not including other physical assault and battery. For purposes of this subdivision, crimes involving violence means those violent crimes contained in clause (i) of subparagraph (A), and subparagraph (B), of paragraph (1) of subdivision (g) of Section 1522 of the Health and Safety Code.

(B) A felony conviction that occurred within the last five years for physical assault, battery, or a drug- or alcohol-related offense.

(2) This subdivision shall become operative on October 1, 2008, and shall remain operative only to the extent that compliance with its provisions is required by federal law as a condition of receiving funding under Title IV–E of the federal Social Security Act (42 U.S.C. Sec. 670 et seq.).

(d) Any fee charged by a law enforcement agency for fingerprinting or for checking or obtaining the criminal record of the applicant shall be paid by the applicant. The licensed adoption agency may defer, waive, or reduce the fee if its payment would cause economic hardship to the prospective adoptive parents detrimental to the welfare of the adopted child. *(Stats.1992, c. 162 (A.B.2650), § 10, operative Jan. 1, 1994. Amended by Stats.2008, c. 701 (A.B.2651), § 3, eff. Sept. 30, 2008; Stats.2014, c. 708 (A.B.1585), § 3, eff. Jan. 1, 2015; Stats.2015, c. 303 (A.B.731), § 153, eff. Jan. 1, 2016; Stats.2016, c. 86 (S.B.1171), § 132, eff. Jan. 1, 2017; Stats.2019, c. 115 (A.B.1817), § 131, eff. Jan. 1, 2020.)*

Cross References

Criminal record, adoptive parents, see Penal Code § 11105.3.
Disclosure of information, see Family Code § 9200 et seq.
Investigations,
  Agency adoption, see Family Code § 8712.
  Independent adoption, see Family Code § 8811.
  Stepparent adoption, see Family Code § 9001.
Licensed adoption agency defined, see Family Code § 8530.
Minor defined for purposes of this Code, see Family Code § 6500.
Person defined for purposes of this Code, see Family Code § 105.

Prospective adoptive parent, defined, see Family Code § 8542.

Research References

Forms

West's California Judicial Council Forms ADOPT–200, Adoption Request.
West's California Judicial Council Forms ADOPT–216, Verification of Compliance With Hague Adoption Convention Attachment (Also Available in Spanish).

§ 8909. Medical report on child and biological parents; contents; blood sample

(a) An agency may not place a child for adoption unless a written report on the child's medical background and, if available, the medical background of the child's biological parents so far as ascertainable, has been submitted to the prospective adoptive parents and they have acknowledged in writing the receipt of the report.

(b) The report on the child's background shall contain all known diagnostic information, including current medical reports on the child, psychological evaluations, and scholastic information, as well as all known information regarding the child's developmental history and family life.

(c)(1) The biological parents may provide a blood sample at a clinic or hospital approved by the State Department of Health Services. The biological parents' failure to provide a blood sample shall not affect the adoption of the child.

(2) The blood sample shall be stored at a laboratory under contract with the State Department of Health Services for a period of 30 years following the adoption of the child.

(3) The purpose of the stored sample of blood is to provide a blood sample from which DNA testing can be done at a later date after entry of the order of adoption at the request of the adoptive parents or the adopted child. The cost of drawing and storing the blood samples shall be paid for by a separate fee in addition to any fee required under Section 8907. The amount of this additional fee shall be based on the cost of drawing and storing the blood samples but at no time shall the additional fee be more than one hundred dollars ($100).

(d)(1) The blood sample shall be stored and released in such a manner as to not identify any party to the adoption.

(2) Any results of the DNA testing shall be stored and released in such a manner as to not identify any party to the adoption.
(Stats.1992, c. 162 (A.B.2650), § 10, operative Jan. 1, 1994. Amended by Stats.1996, c. 1053 (A.B.3241), § 3.)

Cross References

Agency adoption, medical report, see Family Code § 8706.
Confidentiality of medical information, exemptions from limitations, see Civil Code § 56.30.
Department of Health Care Services, generally, see Health and Safety Code § 100100 et seq.
Disclosure of information, see Family Code § 9200 et seq.
Independent adoption medical report, see Family Code § 8817.
Judgment and order defined for purposes of this Code, see Family Code § 100.
Prospective adoptive parent, defined, see Family Code § 8542.
Rules and regulations,
   Medical reports, availability, see Family Code § 9202.
   Medical reports, form and content, see Family Code § 8608.
State defined for purposes of this Code, see Family Code § 145.

Research References

Forms

2 California Transactions Forms--Family Law § 6:141, Required Medical Report on Child and Birth Parents.

§ 8910. Removal of child from county; concealment of child; permission for removal; objections; hearing; notice; application of section

(a) In no event may a child who has been placed for adoption be removed from the county in which the child was placed, by any person who has not petitioned to adopt the child, without first obtaining the written consent of the licensed adoption agency responsible for the child.

(b) During the pendency of an adoption proceeding:

(1) The child proposed to be adopted shall not be concealed from the * * * agency that is investigating the adoption or from the court with jurisdiction over the adoption proceeding * * *.

(2) The child shall not be removed from the county * * * of the * * * petitioner's residence at the time of placement, unless the petitioners or other interested persons first obtain permission for the removal from the court, after giving advance written notice of intent to obtain the court's permission to the licensed adoption agency responsible for the child. Upon proof of giving notice, permission may be granted by the court if, within a period of 15 days after the date of giving notice, no objections are filed with the court by the licensed adoption agency responsible for the child. If the licensed adoption agency files objections within the 15-day period, upon the request of the petitioners the court shall immediately set the matter for hearing and give to the objector, the petitioners, and the party or parties requesting permission for the removal reasonable notice of the hearing by certified mail, return receipt requested, to the address of each as shown in the records of the adoption proceeding. Upon a finding that the objections are without good cause, the court may grant the requested permission for removal of the child, subject to any limitations that appear to be in the child's best interest.

(c) This section does not apply in any of the following situations:

(1) When the child is absent for a period of not more than 30 days from the county * * * of the * * * petitioner's residence at the time of placement, unless a notice of recommendation of denial of petition has been personally served on the petitioners or the court has issued an order prohibiting the removal of the child from the county of the petitioner's residence at the time of placement, pending consideration of any of the following:

(A) The suitability of the petitioners.

(B) The care provided the child.

(C) The availability of the legally required agency consents to the adoption.

(2) Where the child has been returned to and remains in the custody and control of the child's birth parent or parents.

(3) Where written consent for the removal of the child is obtained from the licensed adoption agency responsible for the child.

(d) A violation of this section is a violation of Section 280 of the Penal Code.

(e) Neither this section nor Section 280 of the Penal Code may be construed to render lawful any act that is unlawful under any other applicable law. *(Stats.1992, c. 162 (A.B.2650), § 10, operative Jan. 1, 1994. Amended by Stats.2022, c. 159 (A.B.2495), § 7, eff. Jan. 1, 2023.)*

Cross References

Agency adoption, removal and concealment, see Family Code § 8713.
Birth parent, defined, see Family Code § 8512.
Child abduction, violations of specified adoption proceedings, punishment, see Penal Code § 280.
County defined for purposes of this Code, see Family Code § 67.
Independent adoptions, removal and concealment, see Family Code § 8803.
Judgment and order defined for purposes of this Code, see Family Code § 100.
Licensed adoption agency defined, see Family Code § 8530.
Person defined for purposes of this Code, see Family Code § 105.
Petitioner defined for purposes of this Code, see Family Code § 126.
Proceeding defined for purposes of this Code, see Family Code § 110.

Research References

Forms

2 California Transactions Forms--Family Law § 6:2, Governing Law.

§ 8910

West's California Code Forms, Family § 8900, Comment Overview—Intercountry Adoptions.
West's California Code Forms, Family § 8910 Form 2, Notice of Filing Petition for Permission to Remove Child from County.
West's California Judicial Council Forms ADOPT-216, Verification of Compliance With Hague Adoption Convention Attachment (Also Available in Spanish).

§ 8911. Conditions of placement; filing of petition

As a condition of placement, the prospective adoptive parents shall file a petition to adopt the child under Section 8912 within 30 days of placement. *(Stats.1992, c. 162 (A.B.2650), § 10, operative Jan. 1, 1994.)*

Cross References

Prospective adoptive parent, defined, see Family Code § 8542.
Stepparent adoption investigations, see Family Code § 9001.

Research References

Forms

West's California Judicial Council Forms ADOPT-216, Verification of Compliance With Hague Adoption Convention Attachment (Also Available in Spanish).

§ 8912. Petition for adoption; notification of department; contents; guardianship petitions; order of adoption

(a) An international adoption or readoption request may be filed by a resident of this state in a county authorized by Section 8609.5. The court clerk shall immediately notify the department at Sacramento in writing of the pendency of the proceeding and of any subsequent action taken.

(b) The caption of the adoption <u>request</u> shall contain the names of the petitioners, but not the child's name. The <u>request</u> shall state the child's sex * * *, date of birth * * *, <u>and the name the child had before adoption</u> * * *.

(c) If the child is the subject of a guardianship petition, the adoption <u>request</u> shall so state and shall include the caption and docket number or have attached a copy of the letters of the guardianship or temporary guardianship. The petitioners shall notify the court of any petition for guardianship or temporary guardianship filed after the adoption petition. The guardianship proceeding shall be consolidated with the adoption proceeding.

(d) The order of adoption shall contain the child's adopted name * * * <u>and the name the child had before adoption</u>.

(e) If the petitioner has entered into a postadoption contact agreement * * * as set forth in Section 8616.5, the agreement, signed by the participating parties, shall be * * * filed with the * * * <u>court in accordance with that section</u>. *(Stats.1992, c. 162 (A.B.2650), § 10, operative Jan. 1, 1994. Amended by Stats.2004, c. 858 (S.B.1357), § 6; Stats.2012, c. 638 (A.B.1757), § 12; Stats.2022, c. 159 (A.B.2495), § 8, eff. Jan. 1, 2023.)*

Cross References

Agency adoption petition, see Family Code § 8714.
Child abuse and neglect reporting act, notice to child protection agencies or district attorneys, availability of information, see Penal Code § 11170.
County defined for purposes of this Code, see Family Code § 67.
Department defined, see Family Code § 8518.
Independent adoption petition, see Family Code § 8802.
Judgment and order defined for purposes of this Code, see Family Code § 100.
Person defined for purposes of this Code, see Family Code § 105.
Petitioner defined for purposes of this Code, see Family Code § 126.
Proceeding defined for purposes of this Code, see Family Code § 110.
State defined for purposes of this Code, see Family Code § 145.

Stepparent adoption petition, see Family Code § 9000.

Research References

Forms

2 California Transactions Forms--Family Law § 6:139, Overview of Intercountry Adoption.
West's California Judicial Council Forms ADOPT-200, Adoption Request.
West's California Judicial Council Forms ADOPT-215, Adoption Order (Also Available in Spanish).
West's California Judicial Council Forms ADOPT-216, Verification of Compliance With Hague Adoption Convention Attachment (Also Available in Spanish).
West's California Judicial Council Forms JV-505, Statement Regarding Parentage (Juvenile) (Also Available in Spanish).

§ 8913. Adoptive parent and child; appearance before court

The prospective adoptive parents and the child proposed to be adopted shall appear before the court pursuant to Sections 8612 and 8613. *(Stats.1992, c. 162 (A.B.2650), § 10, operative Jan. 1, 1994.)*

Cross References

Adult adoptions, appearance before court, see Family Code § 9324.
Agency adoption appearances, see Family Code § 8718.
Independent adoption appearances, see Family Code § 8823.
Prospective adoptive parent, defined, see Family Code § 8542.
Stepparent adoption appearances, see Family Code § 9007.

Research References

Forms

2 California Transactions Forms--Family Law § 6:139, Overview of Intercountry Adoption.

§ 8914. Agency as party to petition; report of facts; submission to court

If the licensed adoption agency is a party to or joins in the adoption petition, it shall submit a full report of the facts of the case to the court. The department may also submit a report. *(Stats.1992, c. 162 (A.B.2650), § 10, operative Jan. 1, 1994.)*

Cross References

Agency adoption, report of department or agency, see Family Code § 8715.
Department defined, see Family Code § 8518.
Independent adoption, report of department or agency, see Family Code § 8807.
Licensed adoption agency defined, see Family Code § 8530.
Stepparent adoption, report of county welfare department or probation officer, see Family Code § 9001.
Waiver of personal appearance of prospective adoptive parent, see Family Code § 8613.5.

Research References

Forms

2 California Transactions Forms--Family Law § 6:13, Appearance in Person or by Counsel.

§ 8915. Report or findings of agency; copy to attorney or petitioner

When any report or findings are submitted to the court by a licensed adoption agency, a copy of the report or findings, whether favorable or unfavorable, shall be given to the petitioner's attorney in the proceeding, if the petitioner has an attorney of record, or to the petitioner. *(Stats.1992, c. 162 (A.B.2650), § 10, operative Jan. 1, 1994.)*

Cross References

Agency adoption, copy of report, see Family Code § 8717.
Disclosure of information, see Family Code § 9200 et seq.
Independent adoption, copy of report, see Family Code § 8821.
Licensed adoption agency defined, see Family Code § 8530.
Petitioner defined for purposes of this Code, see Family Code § 126.

Proceeding defined for purposes of this Code, see Family Code § 110.

§ 8916. Withdrawal of petition; dismissal of proceedings; notification of department; agency report; recommendations; jurisdiction

(a) If the petitioners move to withdraw the adoption petition or to dismiss the proceeding, the court clerk shall immediately notify the department at Sacramento of the action. The licensed adoption agency shall file a full report with the court recommending a suitable plan for the child in every case where the petitioners desire to withdraw the adoption petition or where the licensed adoption agency recommends that the adoption petition be denied and shall appear before the court for the purpose of representing the child.

(b) Notwithstanding the petitioners' withdrawal or dismissal, the court may retain jurisdiction over the child for the purpose of making any order for the child's custody that the court deems to be in the child's best interest. *(Stats.1992, c. 162 (A.B.2650), § 10, operative Jan. 1, 1994.)*

Cross References

Agency adoption, notice of withdrawal or dismissal, see Family Code § 8719.
Department defined, see Family Code § 8518.
Independent adoption, notice of withdrawal or dismissal, see Family Code § 8804.
Judgment and order defined for purposes of this Code, see Family Code § 100.
Licensed adoption agency defined, see Family Code § 8530.
Petitioner defined for purposes of this Code, see Family Code § 126.
Proceeding defined for purposes of this Code, see Family Code § 110.
Stepparent adoption, notice of withdrawal or dismissal, see Family Code § 9006.

§ 8917. Denial or withdrawal of petition; referral to court for review

(a) If the licensed adoption agency finds that the home of the petitioners is not suitable for the child or that the required agency consents are not available and the agency recommends that the petition be denied, or if the petitioners desire to withdraw the petition and the agency recommends that the petition be denied, the clerk upon receipt of the report of the licensed adoption agency shall immediately refer it to the court for review.

(b) Upon receipt of the report, the court shall set a date for a hearing of the petition and shall give reasonable notice of the hearing to the licensed adoption agency and the petitioners by certified mail, return receipt requested, to the address of each as shown in the proceeding.

(c) The licensed adoption agency shall appear to represent the child. *(Stats.1992, c. 162 (A.B.2650), § 10, operative Jan. 1, 1994.)*

Cross References

Agency adoption, unfavorable recommendation, see Family Code § 8720.
Independent adoption, unfavorable recommendation, see Family Code § 8822.
Jurisdiction of superior court, see Family Code § 200.
Licensed adoption agency defined, see Family Code § 8530.
Petitioner defined for purposes of this Code, see Family Code § 126.
Proceeding defined for purposes of this Code, see Family Code § 110.

§ 8918. Hearing; recommendation of removal of child sustained; transfer of child to care of agency

At the hearing, if the court sustains the recommendation that the child be removed from the home of the petitioners because the licensed adoption agency has recommended denial or the petitioners desire to withdraw the petition or the court dismisses the petition and does not return the child to the child's parents, the court shall commit the child to the care of the licensed adoption agency for the agency to arrange adoptive placement or to make a suitable plan. *(Stats.1992, c. 162 (A.B.2650), § 10, operative Jan. 1, 1994.)*

Cross References

Aid for adoption of children, benefits payment, conditions, see Welfare and Institutions Code § 16120.
County adoption agencies, adjustments, see Welfare and Institutions Code § 16106.
Licensed adoption agency defined, see Family Code § 8530.
Petitioner defined for purposes of this Code, see Family Code § 126.

§ 8919. Adoptions finalized in foreign country; petition for readoption; penalty for failure to file; human trafficking prevention; birth certificate

(a) In order to establish a record by which an adoptee can prove the facts of the foreign adoption, a state resident who has finalized an intercountry adoption in a foreign country shall file the petition to readopt within the earlier of 60 days of the adoptee's entry into the United States or the adoptee's 16th birthday. The petition shall include all of the following:

(1) A certified or otherwise official copy of the foreign decree, order, or certification of adoption that reflects finalization of the adoption in the foreign country.

(2) A certified or otherwise official copy of the child's foreign birth certificate.

(3) A certified translation of all documents described in this subdivision that are not written in English. The court shall accept the certified translation, if any, that was completed abroad for purposes of obtaining the child's visa or passport.

(4) Proof that the child was granted lawful entry into the United States as an immediate relative of the adoptive parent or parents.

(5) A report from at least one postplacement home visit by an intercountry adoption agency or a contractor of that agency licensed to provide intercountry adoption services in the State of California.

(6) A copy of the home study report previously completed for the international finalized adoption by an adoption agency authorized to provide intercountry adoption services pursuant to Section 8900.

(b) A readoption order shall not be granted unless the court receives a copy of the reports listed in paragraphs (5) and (6) of subdivision (a). The court shall consider the postplacement visit or visits and the previously completed home study when deciding whether to grant or deny the petition for readoption.

(c) If an adoptive parent who has adopted a child through an intercountry adoption that is finalized in a foreign country fails to file a petition pursuant to this section by the earlier of 60 days of the child's entry into the United States or the child's 16th birthday or fails to provide a copy of the petition to each adoption agency that provided the adoption services to the adoptive parent, then the adoption agency that facilitated the adoption shall file a petition within 90 days of the child's entry into the United States, and shall provide a file-marked copy of the petition to the adoptive parent and to any other adoption agency that provided services to the adoptive parent within five business days of filing. An adoptive parent shall be liable to the adoption agency for all costs and fees incurred as a result of good faith actions taken by the adoption agency to fulfill its requirement pursuant to this subdivision. If the adoption agency fails to file a petition as required by this subdivision, the department may take appropriate disciplinary action against the adoption agency if it is licensed in the State of California and the department has actual or constructive knowledge that the petition was not filed.

(d) If the court finds that the child may be the subject of human trafficking or may be a child who is described in Section 300 of the Welfare and Institutions Code, the court shall, in accordance with existing law, notify all appropriate authorities.

(e) Within 10 business days, the clerk of the court shall submit to the State Registrar the order granting the petition to readopt. Upon receipt, the State Registrar shall issue a delayed registration of birth in accordance with Section 102695 of the Health and Safety Code that lists the adoptive parent or parents as the child's legal parent or parents.

(f) A state resident who has adopted a child through an intercountry adoption that is finalized in a foreign country may obtain a birth certificate for that child pursuant to Section 102635 or 103450 of the Health and Safety Code. *(Added by Stats.2019, c. 805 (A.B.677), § 3, eff. Jan. 1, 2020.)*

Cross References

Judgment and order defined for purposes of this Code, see Family Code § 100.
State defined for purposes of this Code, see Family Code § 145.

Research References

Forms
2 California Transactions Forms--Family Law § 6:139, Overview of Intercountry Adoption.
2 California Transactions Forms--Family Law § 6:142, Readoption of Child Adopted in Foreign Country.
West's California Code Forms, Family § 7840, Comment Overview—Freedom from Parental Control.
West's California Judicial Council Forms ADOPT–200, Adoption Request.
West's California Judicial Council Forms ADOPT–210, Adoption Agreement (Also Available in Spanish).
West's California Judicial Council Forms ADOPT–216, Verification of Compliance With Hague Adoption Convention Attachment (Also Available in Spanish).

§ 8919.5. Adoptions finalized in foreign country; reporting arrival of adoptee in state

(a) An intercountry adoption agency shall report the arrival of an adoptee whose adoption was finalized in a foreign country to the department within 14 calendar days of the adoptee's arrival in California.

(b) If the adoption agency fails to report to the department pursuant to subdivision (a), the department may take appropriate disciplinary action against the adoption agency if it is licensed in the State of California. *(Added by Stats.2019, c. 805 (A.B.677), § 4, eff. Jan. 1, 2020.)*

Research References

Forms
West's California Judicial Council Forms ADOPT–200, Adoption Request.
West's California Judicial Council Forms ADOPT–210, Adoption Agreement (Also Available in Spanish).

§ 8920. Separation from sibling group through readoption; agreements for visitation; enforcement; best interest of child

(a) A child who was adopted as part of a sibling group and who has been separated from the child's sibling or siblings through readoption by a resident of this state may petition the court to enforce any agreement for visitation to which the separate adoptive families of the siblings subscribed prior to the child's readoption or to order visitation if such agreement does not exist. The court may order that the agreement be enforced or grant visitation rights upon a finding that visitation is in the best interest of the child.

(b) In making a finding that enforcement of an existing agreement or the granting of visitation rights is in the best interest of the child under subdivision (a), the court shall take into consideration the nature and extent of the child's sibling relationship, including, but not limited to, whether the child was raised with a sibling in the same home, whether the child shares significant common experiences or has close and strong bonds with a sibling, and whether ongoing contact with a sibling is in the child's best interest, including the child's long-term interest.

(c) As used in this section, "sibling" means full-siblings or half-siblings.

(d) As used in this section, "readoption" means the process by which a child who belongs to a foreign-born sibling group that was adopted together through an intercountry adoption is subsequently adopted by a different set of adoptive parents who are residents of the state. *(Added by Stats.2003, c. 19 (S.B.169), § 1. Amended by Stats.2019, c. 115 (A.B.1817), § 132, eff. Jan. 1, 2020.)*

Cross References

Adoptive parent, defined, see Family Code § 8503.
Judgment and order defined for purposes of this Code, see Family Code § 100.
Out-of-home placement, case plan provisions for sibling visitation and relationship development, see Welfare and Institutions Code § 16501.1.
Post-adoptive sibling contact, jurisdiction over post-adoption agreements, see Welfare and Institutions Code § 366.29.
State defined for purposes of this Code, see Family Code § 145.

§ 8921. Services of adoption facilitator

An adoption facilitator shall not offer, provide, or facilitate any adoption service, as described in this chapter, in connection with a convention adoption unless it is registered and posts a bond pursuant to Section 8632.5, and is approved by the accrediting entity pursuant to Subpart F (commencing with Section 96.29) of Part 96 of Title 22 of the Code of Federal Regulations. *(Added by Stats.2007, c. 583 (S.B.703), § 7.)*

§ 8923. Complaint procedures

(a) A complaint against an accredited agency or approved person in connection with a convention adoption shall be filed according to the procedures set forth in Subpart J (commencing with Section 96.68) of Part 96 of Title 22 of the Code of Federal Regulations.

(b) Each private full-service adoption agency and noncustodial adoption agency licensed by the department under this chapter shall notify the department of any complaint filed against it pursuant to Subpart J (commencing with Section 96.68) of Part 96 of Title 22 of the Code of Federal Regulations.

(c) The department may revoke the license of any agency that fails to comply with the provisions of this chapter and Part 96 of Title 22 of the Code of Federal Regulations. *(Added by Stats.2007, c. 583 (S.B.703), § 8.)*

§ 8924. Emigration of child to convention country

(a) For cases in which a child is emigrating from California to a convention country, an accredited agency or approved person providing any adoption service described in this chapter, shall perform all of the following:

(1) A background study on the child prepared in accordance with all requirements set forth in subdivisions (a) and (b) of Section 96.53 of Title 22 of the Code of Federal Regulations, Section 8706, and applicable state law.

(2) Consents are obtained in accordance with subdivision (c) of Section 96.53 of Title 22 of the Code of Federal Regulations and applicable state law.

(3) If the child is 12 years of age or older, the agency or person has given due consideration to the child's wishes or opinions before determining that an intercountry adoption is in the child's best interests and in accordance with applicable state law.

(4) Transmission to the United States Department of State or other competent authority, or accredited bodies of the convention country, of the child background study, proof that the necessary consents have been obtained, and the reasons for the determination that the placement is in the child's best interests.

(b) The accredited agency shall comply with all placement standards set forth in Section 96.54 of Title 22 of the Code of Federal Regulations for children emigrating from California to a convention country.

(c) The accredited agency shall keep the central authority of the convention country and the Secretary informed as necessary about the adoption process and the measures taken to complete it for children emigrating from California to a convention country, in accordance with all communication and coordination functions set forth in Section 96.55 of Title 22 of the Code of Federal Regulations.

(d) For all convention and nonconvention adoption cases involving children emigrating from California to a convention country, the agency, person, or public domestic authority providing adoption services shall report information to the Secretary in accordance with Part 99 of Title 22 of the Code of Federal Regulations. *(Added by Stats.2007, c. 583 (S.B.703), § 9.)*

Research References

Forms

West's California Judicial Council Forms ADOPT–200, Adoption Request.
West's California Judicial Council Forms ADOPT–216, Verification of Compliance With Hague Adoption Convention Attachment (Also Available in Spanish).

§ 8925. Hague adoption certificate or custody declaration

A Hague adoption certificate or, in outgoing cases, a Hague custody declaration, obtained pursuant to Part 97 of Title 22 of the Code of Federal Regulations shall be recognized as a final valid adoption for purposes of all state and local laws. *(Added by Stats.2007, c. 583 (S.B.703), § 10.)*

Research References

Forms

West's California Judicial Council Forms ADOPT–200, Adoption Request.
West's California Judicial Council Forms ADOPT–216, Verification of Compliance With Hague Adoption Convention Attachment (Also Available in Spanish).

CHAPTER 5. STEPPARENT ADOPTIONS

Section
9000. Petition for adoption; caption; contents; guardianship petition; order of adoption.
9000.5. Procedures.
9001. Review of investigation and written report.
9002. Costs.
9003. Consent of birth parents to adoption; execution; filing; out-of-state procedure; prima facie evidence of custody; minor birth parents.
9004. Consent form; notice; contents.
9005. Withdrawal of consent; court approval; motion or petition; form; hearing; notice; probation officer, court investigator or welfare department report; court order; appeal.
9006. Withdrawal of petition or dismissal by petitioner; notification of probation officer, court investigator or welfare department; consent refused by birth parent.
9007. Prospective adoptive parents; appearance before court.

Cross References

Domestic partner, defined, see Family Code § 297.
Stepparent adoptions, defined, see Family Code § 8548.

§ 9000. Petition for adoption; caption; contents; guardianship petition; order of adoption

(a) A stepparent desiring to adopt a child of the stepparent's spouse may for that purpose file a petition in <u>any</u> county * * * <u>authorized by Section 8609.5</u>.

(b) A domestic partner, as defined in Section 297, desiring to adopt a child of the other domestic partner may, for that purpose, file a petition in <u>any</u> county * * * <u>authorized pursuant to Section 8609.5</u>.

(c) The caption of the adoption petition shall contain the names of the petitioners, but not the child's name. The petition shall state the child's sex and date of birth and the name the child had before adoption.

(d) If the child is the subject of a guardianship petition, the adoption petition shall so state and shall include the caption and docket number or have attached a copy of the letters of the guardianship or temporary guardianship. The petitioners shall notify the court of any petition for guardianship or temporary guardianship filed after the adoption petition. The guardianship proceeding shall be consolidated with the adoption proceeding.

(e) The order of adoption shall contain the child's adopted name * * * <u>and the name the child had before adoption</u>.

(f) If the petitioner has entered into a postadoption contact agreement * * * <u>pursuant to Section 8616.5</u>, the agreement * * * shall be * * * filed with the * * * <u>court in accordance with that section</u>.

(g) For the purposes of this chapter, stepparent adoption includes adoption by a domestic partner, as defined in Section 297. *(Stats. 1992, c. 162 (A.B.2650), § 10, operative Jan. 1, 1994. Amended by Stats.2001, c. 893 (A.B.25), § 5; Stats.2004, c. 858 (S.B.1357), § 7; Stats.2019, c. 115 (A.B.1817), § 133, eff. Jan. 1, 2020; Stats.2022, c. 159 (A.B.2495), § 9, eff. Jan. 1, 2023.)*

Cross References

Adoptive parents, criminal record, see Penal Code § 11105.3.
Agency adoption petition, see Family Code § 8714.
Birth parents, money or benefits for consent or placement of children, see Penal Code § 273.
Child abuse and neglect reporting act, notice to child protection agencies or district attorneys, availability of information, see Penal Code § 11170.
County defined for purposes of this Code, see Family Code § 67.
Foster care of children, see Welfare and Institutions Code § 396 et seq.
Independent adoption petition, see Family Code § 8802.
Intercountry adoption petition, see Family Code § 8912.
Judgment and order defined for purposes of this Code, see Family Code § 100.
Jurisdiction of superior court, see Family Code § 200.
Juvenile delinquents and dependents,
  Jurisdiction, see Welfare and Institutions Code § 366.3.
  Priorities and preferences, foster parents and relatives, see Welfare and Institutions Code §§ 361.2 et seq., 366.26.
Petitioner defined for purposes of this Code, see Family Code § 126.
Proceeding defined for purposes of this Code, see Family Code § 110.
References to husband, wife, spouses and married persons, persons included for purposes of this Code, see Family Code § 11.
State defined for purposes of this Code, see Family Code § 145.

Research References

Forms

2 California Transactions Forms--Family Law § 6:108, Petition for Stepparent Adoption.
2 California Transactions Forms--Family Law § 6:112, Form Drafting Considerations.
West's California Code Forms, Family § 9000, Comment Overview—Stepparent Adoptions.
West's California Judicial Council Forms ADOPT–200, Adoption Request.
West's California Judicial Council Forms ADOPT–215, Adoption Order (Also Available in Spanish).
West's California Judicial Council Forms JV–505, Statement Regarding Parentage (Juvenile) (Also Available in Spanish).

§ 9000.5. Procedures

(a) The procedures provided in this section apply to a stepparent adoption where the child was born during the marriage or domestic partnership, including a registered domestic partnership or civil union from another jurisdiction, and either of the following circumstances applies:

(1) One of the spouses or partners gave birth to the child.

(2) The child was born through a gestational surrogacy process brought about by one or both of the spouses or partners, and the

§ 9000.5

parentage of only one spouse or partner was established pursuant to the Uniform Parentage Act (Part 3 (commencing with Section 7600) of Division 12) or another parentage proceeding related to the surrogacy.

(b)(1) The following are not required in stepparent adoptions under this section unless otherwise ordered by the court for good cause:

(A) A home investigation pursuant to Section 9001 or a home study.

(B) Costs incurred pursuant to Section 9002.

(C) A hearing pursuant to Section 9007.

(2) In stepparent adoptions under this section, the parties shall not be required to have been married or in a domestic partnership, including a registered domestic partnership or civil union from another jurisdiction, for a minimum period of time prior to the adoption being granted or to provide verification of their income or education.

(c) For stepparent adoptions filed under this section, the following shall be filed with the petition for adoption:

(1) A copy of the parties' marriage certificate, registered domestic partner certificate, or civil union from another jurisdiction.

(2) A copy of the child's birth certificate.

(3) Declarations by the parent who gave birth, or who caused the birth through gestational surrogacy, and the spouse or partner who is adopting explaining the circumstances of the child's conception in detail sufficient to identify whether there may be other persons with a claim to parentage of the child who are required to be provided notice of, or who must consent to, the adoption.

(d) The court may order a hearing to ascertain whether there are additional persons who must be provided notice of, or who must consent to, the adoption if it appears from the face of the pleadings and the evidence that proper notice or consent have not been provided.

(e) The court shall grant the stepparent adoption under this section upon finding both of the following:

(1) That the parent who gave birth, or who caused the birth through gestational surrogacy, and the spouse or partner who is adopting were married or in a domestic partnership, including a registered domestic partnership or civil union from another jurisdiction, at the time of the child's birth.

(2) Any other person with a claim to parentage of the child who is required to be provided notice of, or who must consent to, the adoption has been noticed or provided consent to the adoption. *(Added by Stats.2014, c. 636 (A.B.2344), § 3, eff. Jan. 1, 2015. Amended by Stats.2019, c. 192 (A.B.1373), § 2, eff. Jan. 1, 2020; Stats.2021, c. 199 (A.B.746), § 1, eff. Jan. 1, 2022.)*

Research References

Forms

West's California Judicial Council Forms ADOPT–200, Adoption Request.
West's California Judicial Council Forms ADOPT–205, Declaration Confirming Parentage in Stepparent Adoption.
West's California Judicial Council Forms ADOPT–206, Declaration Confirming Parentage in Stepparent Adoption: Gestational Surrogacy.
West's California Judicial Council Forms ADOPT–210, Adoption Agreement (Also Available in Spanish).
West's California Judicial Council Forms ADOPT–215, Adoption Order (Also Available in Spanish).

§ 9001. Review of investigation and written report

(a) Except as provided in Section 9000.5, before granting or denying a stepparent adoption request, the court shall review and consider a written investigative report. The report in a stepparent adoption case shall not require a home study unless so ordered by the court upon request of an investigator or interested person, or on the court's own motion. "Home study" as used in this section means a physical investigation of the premises where the child is residing.

(b) At the time of filing the adoption request, the petitioner shall inform the court in writing if the petitioner is electing to have the investigation and written report completed by a licensed clinical social worker, a licensed marriage and family therapist, a licensed professional clinical counselor, or a private licensed adoption agency, in which cases the petitioner shall not be required to pay an investigation fee pursuant to Section 9002 at the time of filing, but shall pay these fees directly to the investigator. Absent that notification, the court may, at the time of filing, collect an investigation fee pursuant to Section 9002, and may assign one of the following to complete the investigation: a probation officer, a qualified court investigator, or the county welfare department, if so authorized by the board of supervisors of the county where the action is pending.

(c) If a private licensed adoption agency conducts the investigation, it shall assign the investigation to a licensed clinical social worker, licensed professional clinical counselor, or licensed marriage and family therapist associated with the agency. A grievance regarding the investigation shall be directed to the licensing authority of the clinical social worker, licensed professional clinical counselor, or marriage and family therapist, as applicable.

(d) This section does not require the State Department of Social Services to issue regulations for stepparent adoptions. *(Stats.1992, c. 162 (A.B.2650), § 10, operative Jan. 1, 1994. Amended by Stats.1993, c. 219 (A.B.1500), § 204; Stats.2001, c. 353 (A.B.538), § 3; Stats.2010, c. 588 (A.B.2020), § 8; Stats.2014, c. 636 (A.B.2344), § 4, eff. Jan. 1, 2015; Stats.2016, c. 702 (A.B.2872), § 1, eff. Jan. 1, 2017; Stats.2018, c. 389 (A.B.2296), § 17, eff. Jan. 1, 2019.)*

Cross References

County defined for purposes of this Code, see Family Code § 67.
Disclosure of information, see Family Code § 9200 et seq.
Investigations,
    Agency adoption, see Family Code § 8712.
    Independent adoption, see Family Code § 8811.
    Intercountry adoption, see Family Code § 8908.
Judgment and order defined for purposes of this Code, see Family Code § 100.
Juvenile court, wards and dependent children, inspection of case file, see Welfare and Institutions Code § 827.
Person defined for purposes of this Code, see Family Code § 105.
Petitioner defined for purposes of this Code, see Family Code § 126.
Proceeding defined for purposes of this Code, see Family Code § 110.
Report, department or agency,
    Agency adoption, see Family Code § 8715.
    Independent adoption, see Family Code § 8807.
    Intercountry adoption, see Family Code § 8914.
Stepparent adoption, defined, see Family Code § 8548.
Termination of parental rights in adoption proceedings, inquiry to identify natural father and report, see Family Code § 7663.
Waiver of personal appearance of prospective adoptive parent, see Family Code § 8613.5.

Research References

Forms

2 California Transactions Forms--Family Law § 6:13, Appearance in Person or by Counsel.
2 California Transactions Forms--Family Law § 6:104, Nature and Purpose of Stepparent Adoption.
2 California Transactions Forms--Family Law § 6:109, Investigation of Stepparent Adoption.
West's California Code Forms, Family § 9000, Comment Overview—Stepparent Adoptions.
West's California Judicial Council Forms ADOPT–200, Adoption Request.

§ 9002. Costs

Except as provided in Section 9000.5, in a stepparent adoption, the prospective adoptive parent is liable for all reasonable costs incurred in connection with the stepparent adoption, including, but not limited to, costs incurred for the investigation required by Section 9001, up to a maximum of seven hundred dollars ($700). The court, probation officer, qualified court investigator, or county welfare department may defer, waive, or reduce the fee if its payment would cause economic hardship to the prospective adoptive parent detrimental to the welfare of the adopted child. *(Stats.1992, c. 162 (A.B.2650), § 10, operative Jan. 1, 1994. Amended by Stats.1993, c. 219 (A.B.1500), § 205; Stats.1993, c. 494 (A.B.1430), § 1; Stats.2001, c. 893 (A.B.25), § 6; Stats.2014, c. 636 (A.B.2344), § 5, eff. Jan. 1, 2015.)*

Cross References

Agency adoption report fee, see Family Code § 8716.
County defined for purposes of this Code, see Family Code § 67.
Courts, fees and fines collected after January 1, 2006, treatment thereof, see Government Code § 68085.1.
Independent adoption report fee, see Family Code § 8810.
Prospective adoptive parent, defined, see Family Code § 8542.
Qualified court investigator, defined, see Family Code § 8543.
Stepparent adoption, defined, see Family Code § 8548.

Research References

Forms

2 California Transactions Forms--Family Law § 6:109, Investigation of Stepparent Adoption.
West's California Judicial Council Forms ADOPT–200, Adoption Request.

§ 9003. Consent of birth parents to adoption; execution; filing; out-of-state procedure; prima facie evidence of custody; minor birth parents

(a) In a stepparent adoption, the consent of either or both birth parents shall be signed in the presence of a notary public, court clerk, probation officer, qualified court investigator, authorized representative of a licensed adoption agency, or county welfare department staff member of any county of this state. The petitioner, petitioner's counsel, or person before whom the consent is signed shall immediately file the consent with the clerk of the court where the adoption request is filed. If the request has not been filed at the time the consent has been signed, the consent shall be filed simultaneously with the adoption request. Upon filing of the adoption request, the clerk shall immediately notify the probation officer or, at the option of the board of supervisors, the county welfare department of that county.

(b) If the birth parent of a child to be adopted is outside this state at the time of signing the consent, the consent may be signed before an authorized representative of an adoption agency licensed in the state or country where the consent is being signed, a notary, or other person authorized to perform notarial acts.

(c) The consent, when reciting that the person giving it is entitled to sole custody of the child and when acknowledged before any authorized witness specified in subdivision (a), is prima facie evidence of the right of the person signing the consent to the sole custody of the child and that person's sole right to consent.

(d) A birth parent who is a minor has the right to sign a consent for the adoption of the birth parent's child and the consent is not subject to revocation by reason of the minority. *(Stats.1992, c. 162 (A.B.2650), § 10, operative Jan. 1, 1994. Amended by Stats.1993, c. 219 (A.B.1500), § 206; Stats.2005, c. 627 (S.B.302), § 4; Stats.2011, c. 462 (A.B.687), § 8.)*

Cross References

Agency adoption consents, see Family Code § 8700.
Birth parent,
  Defined, see Family Code § 8512.
  Money or benefits for consent or placement of children, see Penal Code § 273.
County defined for purposes of this Code, see Family Code § 67.
Independent adoption consents, see Family Code § 8814.
Jurisdiction of superior court, see Family Code § 200.
Juvenile delinquents and dependents,
  Jurisdiction, see Welfare and Institutions Code § 366.3.
  Priorities and preferences, foster parents and relatives, see Welfare and Institutions Code §§ 361.2 et seq., 366.26.
Minor defined for purposes of this Code, see Family Code § 6500.
Person defined for purposes of this Code, see Family Code § 105.
Prima facie evidence, see Evidence Code § 602.
Qualified court investigator, defined, see Family Code § 8543.
State defined for purposes of this Code, see Family Code § 145.
Stepparent adoption, defined, see Family Code § 8548.

Research References

Forms

2 California Transactions Forms--Family Law § 6:105, Consent of Custodial Parent.
2 California Transactions Forms--Family Law § 6:106, Consent of Noncustodial Parent.
2 California Transactions Forms--Family Law § 6:115, Consent to Stepparent Adoption by Custodial Parent.
2 California Transactions Forms--Family Law § 7:39, Adoption and Termination of Parental Rights.
1¶ 1 Nichols Cyclopedia of Legal Forms Annotated § 7:5, Statutory Provisions—Consent to Adoption.
West's California Judicial Council Forms ADOPT–210, Adoption Agreement (Also Available in Spanish).

§ 9004. Consent form; notice; contents

In a stepparent adoption, the form prescribed by the department for the consent of the birth parent shall contain substantially the following notice:

"Notice to the parent who gives the child for adoption: If you and your child lived together at any time as parent and child, the adoption of your child through a stepparent adoption does not affect the child's right to inherit your property or the property of other blood relatives." *(Stats.1992, c. 162 (A.B.2650), § 10, operative Jan. 1, 1994. Amended by Stats.2001, c. 893 (A.B.25), § 7.)*

Cross References

Birth parent, defined, see Family Code § 8512.
Department defined, see Family Code § 8518.
Intestate succession, parent and child relationship, effect of adoption, see Probate Code § 6451.
Property defined for purposes of this Code, see Family Code § 113.
Stepparent adoption, defined, see Family Code § 8548.

Research References

Forms

2 California Transactions Forms--Family Law § 6:114, Consent of Noncustodial Parent.

§ 9005. Withdrawal of consent; court approval; motion or petition; form; hearing; notice; probation officer, court investigator or welfare department report; court order; appeal

(a) Consent of the birth parent to the adoption of the child through a stepparent adoption may not be withdrawn except with court approval. Request for that approval may be made by motion, or a birth parent seeking to withdraw consent may file with the clerk of the court where the adoption petition is pending, a petition for approval of withdrawal of consent, without the necessity of paying a fee for filing the petition. The petition or motion shall be in writing, and shall set forth the reasons for withdrawal of consent, but otherwise may be in any form.

(b) The court clerk shall set the matter for hearing and shall give notice thereof to the probation officer, qualified court investigator, or county welfare department, to the prospective adoptive parent, and to the birth parent or parents by certified mail, return receipt requested, to the address of each as shown in the proceeding, at least 10 days before the time set for hearing.

(c) The probation officer, qualified court investigator, or county welfare department shall, before the hearing of the motion or petition for withdrawal, file a full report with the court and shall appear at the hearing to represent the interests of the child.

(d) At the hearing, the parties may appear in person or with counsel. The hearing shall be held in chambers, but the court reporter shall report the proceedings and, on court order, the fee therefor shall be paid from the county treasury. If the court finds that withdrawal of the consent to adoption is reasonable in view of all the circumstances and that withdrawal of the consent is in the child's best interest, the court shall approve the withdrawal of the consent. Otherwise the court shall withhold its approval. Consideration of the child's best interest shall include, but is not limited to, an assessment of the child's age, the extent of bonding with the prospective adoptive parent, the extent of bonding or the potential to bond with the birth parent, and the ability of the birth parent to provide adequate and proper care and guidance to the child. If the court approves the withdrawal of consent, the adoption proceeding shall be dismissed.

(e) A court order granting or withholding approval of a withdrawal of consent to an adoption may be appealed in the same manner as an order of the juvenile court declaring a person to be a ward of the juvenile court. *(Stats.1992, c. 162 (A.B.2650), § 10, operative Jan. 1, 1994. Amended by Stats.1993, c. 219 (A.B.1500), § 207; Stats.2001, c. 893 (A.B.25), § 8.)*

Cross References

Abuse of parental authority, see Family Code § 7507.
Birth parent, defined, see Family Code § 8512.
County defined for purposes of this Code, see Family Code § 67.
Criminal record, adoptive parents, see Penal Code § 11105.3.
Custody of children, generally, see Family Code §§ 3000 et seq., 3020 et seq.
Dependent children, judgments and orders, see Welfare and Institutions Code § 360 et seq.
Disclosure of information, see Family Code § 9200 et seq.
Enforcement of judgments and orders, see Family Code §§ 290, 291.
Independent adoption, motion or petition to withdraw consent, see Family Code § 8815.
Judgment and order defined for purposes of this Code, see Family Code § 100.
Jurisdiction of superior court, see Family Code § 200.
Juvenile court, detention of children, see Welfare and Institutions Code § 367.
Juvenile delinquents and dependents, jurisdiction, see Welfare and Institutions Code § 366.3.
Limitations on parental control, see Welfare and Institutions Code § 361.
Notice that parental rights may be terminated, see Welfare and Institutions Code § 294.
Parent and child relationship, determination, see Family Code § 7600 et seq.
Person defined for purposes of this Code, see Family Code § 105.
Proceeding defined for purposes of this Code, see Family Code § 110.
Prospective adoptive parent, defined, see Family Code § 8542.
Protective and restraining orders, see Family Code § 7700 et seq.
Qualified court investigator, defined, see Family Code § 8543.
Removal of children from parental custody, see Welfare and Institutions Code § 360 et seq.
Termination of parental rights, guardianship of dependent children, see Welfare and Institutions Code § 366.26 et seq.

Research References

Forms

2 California Transactions Forms--Family Law § 6:110, Withdrawal of Consent Once Given—Withdrawal or Dismissal of Adoption Petition.
2 California Transactions Forms--Family Law § 7:39, Adoption and Termination of Parental Rights.

§ 9006. Withdrawal of petition or dismissal by petitioner; notification of probation officer, court investigator or welfare department; consent refused by birth parent

(a) If the petitioner moves to withdraw the adoption petition or to dismiss the proceeding, the court clerk shall immediately notify the probation officer, qualified court investigator, or county welfare department of the action, unless a home investigation was not required pursuant to Section 9000.5.

(b) If a birth parent has refused to give the required consent, the adoption petition shall be dismissed. *(Stats.1992, c. 162 (A.B.2650), § 10, operative Jan. 1, 1994. Amended by Stats.1993, c. 219 (A.B.1500), § 208; Stats.2014, c. 636 (A.B.2344), § 6, eff. Jan. 1, 2015.)*

Cross References

Agency adoption, notice of withdrawal or dismissal, see Family Code § 8719.
Birth parent, defined, see Family Code § 8512.
County defined for purposes of this Code, see Family Code § 67.
Independent adoption, notice of withdrawal or dismissal, see Family Code § 8804.
Petitioner defined for purposes of this Code, see Family Code § 126.
Proceeding defined for purposes of this Code, see Family Code § 110.
Qualified court investigator, defined, see Family Code § 8543.

Research References

Forms

2 California Transactions Forms--Family Law § 6:107, Adoption Without Consent of Noncustodial Parent.
2 California Transactions Forms--Family Law § 6:110, Withdrawal of Consent Once Given—Withdrawal or Dismissal of Adoption Petition.

§ 9007. Prospective adoptive parents; appearance before court

Except as provided in Section 9000.5, the prospective adoptive parent and the child proposed to be adopted shall appear before the court pursuant to Sections 8612, 8613, and 8613.5. *(Stats.1992, c. 162 (A.B.2650), § 10, operative Jan. 1, 1994. Amended by Stats.2009, c. 492 (A.B.941), § 5; Stats.2014, c. 636 (A.B.2344), § 7, eff. Jan. 1, 2015.)*

Cross References

Adult adoptions, see Family Code § 9324.
Appearance,
  Agency adoption, see Family Code § 8718.
  Independent adoption, see Family Code § 8823.
  Intercountry adoption, see Family Code § 8913.
Prospective adoptive parent, defined, see Family Code § 8542.

Research References

Forms

2 California Transactions Forms--Family Law § 6:111, Hearing on Stepparent Adoption Petition.
West's California Code Forms, Family § 9000, Comment Overview—Stepparent Adoptions.

CHAPTER 6. VACATION OF ADOPTION

Section
9100. Developmental disability or mental illness prior to adoption; setting aside order of adoption; petition; limitation of action; notification of department.
9101. Decree or order of adoption set aside; proceedings; care and custody of child.
9102. Limitation of actions; findings of fact; duty of department.

§ 9100. Developmental disability or mental illness prior to adoption; setting aside order of adoption; petition; limitation of action; notification of department

(a) If a child adopted pursuant to the law of this state shows evidence of a developmental disability or mental illness as a result of conditions existing before the adoption to an extent that the child cannot be relinquished to an adoption agency on the grounds that * * * a plan of adoption is not currently suitable, and of which conditions the adoptive parents or parent had no knowledge or notice before the entry of the order of adoption, a petition setting forth those facts may be filed by the adoptive parents or parent with the court that granted the adoption petition. If these facts are proved to the satisfaction of the court, it may make an order setting aside the order of adoption.

(b) The petition shall be filed within five years after the entry of the order of adoption.

(c)(1) The court clerk shall immediately notify the department at Sacramento of the petition. Within 60 days after the notice, the department shall file a full report with the court and shall appear before the court for the purpose of representing the adopted child.

(2) Notwithstanding any other law, an adoption case file, including a juvenile case file, as defined in subdivision (e) of Section 827 of the Welfare and Institutions Code, may be inspected and copied by the department for the purpose of completing the duties pursuant to this subdivision. *(Stats.1992, c. 162 (A.B.2650), § 10, operative Jan. 1, 1994. Amended by Stats.2022, c. 870 (A.B.2711), § 1, eff. Jan. 1, 2023.)*

Cross References

Action to determine parent and child relationship, modification of order of adoption, application of this section, see Family Code § 7642.
Adoptive parent, defined, see Family Code § 8503.
Department defined, see Family Code § 8518.
Judgment and order defined for purposes of this Code, see Family Code § 100.
Juvenile case file inspection, confidentiality, release, probation reports, destruction of records, liability, see Welfare and Institutions Code § 827.
Removal of child from parental custody, search for relative and furnishing identifying information, see Welfare and Institutions Code § 361.3.
State defined for purposes of this Code, see Family Code § 145.

Research References

Forms

West's California Code Forms, Family § 7630, Comment Overview—Determining Parent and Child Relationship.
West's California Code Forms, Family § 9100, Comment Overview—Vacation of Adoption.

§ 9101. Decree or order of adoption set aside; proceedings; care and custody of child

(a) If an order of adoption is set aside as provided in Section 9100, the court making the order shall direct the district attorney, the county counsel, or the county welfare department to take appropriate action under the Welfare and Institutions Code. The court may also make any order relative to the care, custody, or confinement of the child pending the proceeding the court sees fit.

(b) The county in which the proceeding for adoption was had is liable for the child's support until the child is able to be self-supporting. *(Stats.1992, c. 162 (A.B.2650), § 10, operative Jan. 1, 1994. Amended by Stats.2019, c. 115 (A.B.1817), § 134, eff. Jan. 1, 2020.)*

Cross References

County defined for purposes of this Code, see Family Code § 67.
Judgment and order defined for purposes of this Code, see Family Code § 100.
Order, including decree as appropriate, see Family Code § 100.
Proceeding defined for purposes of this Code, see Family Code § 110.
Support defined for purposes of this Code, see Family Code § 150.

Research References

Forms

West's California Code Forms, Family § 9100, Comment Overview—Vacation of Adoption.

§ 9102. Limitation of actions; findings of fact; duty of department

(a) Except as provided in Section 9100, an action or proceeding of any kind to vacate, set aside, or otherwise nullify an order of adoption on any ground, except fraud, shall be commenced within one year after entry of the order.

(b) Except as provided in Section 9100, an action or proceeding of any kind to vacate, set aside, or nullify an order of adoption, based on fraud, shall be commenced within three years after entry of the order, or within 90 days of discovery of the fraud, whichever is earlier.

(c) In any action to set aside an order of adoption pursuant to this section or Section 9100, the court shall first determine whether the facts presented are legally sufficient to set aside the order of adoption. If the facts are not legally sufficient, the petition shall be denied. If the facts are legally sufficient, the court's final ruling on the matter shall take into consideration the best interests of the child, in conjunction with all other factors required by law.

(d) The department shall not be required under any circumstances to investigate a petition filed pursuant to this section or to represent a child who is the subject of a proceeding under this section. *(Stats.1992, c. 162 (A.B.2650), § 10, operative Jan. 1, 1994. Amended by Stats.1995, c. 567 (A.B.898), § 1; Stats.2000, c. 937 (A.B.2433), § 6; Stats.2011, c. 462 (A.B.687), § 9.)*

Cross References

Action to determine parent and child relationship, modification of order of adoption, application of this section, see Family Code § 7642.
Judgment and order defined for purposes of this Code, see Family Code § 100.
Proceeding defined for purposes of this Code, see Family Code § 110.
Removal of child from parental custody, search for relative and furnishing identifying information, see Welfare and Institutions Code § 361.3.

Research References

Forms

2 California Transactions Forms--Family Law § 6:89, Revocation of Relinquishment After Filing Due to Fraud or Procedural Irregularity.
West's California Code Forms, Family § 7630, Comment Overview—Determining Parent and Child Relationship.
West's California Code Forms, Family § 9100, Comment Overview—Vacation of Adoption.

CHAPTER 7. DISCLOSURE OF INFORMATION

Section
9200. Inspection of documents; authorization; fee; deletion of identification of birth parents; certificate of adoption.
9201. Adoption services; identification; adoption petitions; research.
9202. Medical report; request of adopted person or adoptive parents; access.
9202.5. Blood sample; access.
9203. Disclosure of identity of birth parents; application of section.
9203.1. Disclosure of adoption homestudy; form; time for response; fees.
9204. Consent between adult adoptee and birth parents to arrange for contact between the parties.
9205. Contact with sibling; request; form.
9206. Release of letters, photographs, or other items of personal property; requests; release form; fees.
9208. Children of Indian ancestry; notice to United States Secretary of the Interior.
9209. Children of Indian ancestry; adoptees who have reached age eighteen; access to information.

§ 9200. Inspection of documents; authorization; fee; deletion of identification of birth parents; certificate of adoption

(a) The petition, relinquishment or consent, agreement, order, report to the court from any investigating agency, and any power of attorney and deposition filed in the office of the clerk of the court pursuant to this part is not open to inspection by any person other than the parties to the proceeding and their attorneys and the department, except upon the written authority of the judge of the superior court. A judge of the superior court may not authorize anyone to inspect the petition, relinquishment or consent, agreement,

§ 9200

order, report to the court from any investigating agency, or power of attorney or deposition or any portion of any of these documents, except in exceptional circumstances and for good cause approaching the necessitous. The petitioner may be required to pay the expenses for preparing the copies of the documents to be inspected.

(b) Upon written request of any party to the proceeding and upon the order of any judge of the superior court, the clerk of the court shall not provide any documents referred to in this section for inspection or copying to any other person, unless the name of the child's birth parents or any information tending to identify the child's birth parents is deleted from the documents or copies thereof.

(c) Upon the request of the adoptive parents or the child, a clerk of the court may issue a certificate of adoption that states the date and place of adoption, the child's birth date, the names of the adoptive parents, and the name the child has taken. Unless the child has been adopted by a stepparent, the certificate shall not state the name of the child's birth parents. *(Stats.1992, c. 162 (A.B.2650), § 10, operative Jan. 1, 1994. Amended by Stats.2002, c. 784 (S.B. 1316), § 114.)*

Cross References

Adoptive parent, defined, see Family Code § 8503.
Birth parent, defined, see Family Code § 8512.
Certificate of live birth, confidentiality of second section, access, see Health and Safety Code § 102430.
Judgment and order defined for purposes of this Code, see Family Code § 100.
Person defined for purposes of this Code, see Family Code § 105.
Petitioner defined for purposes of this Code, see Family Code § 126.
Proceeding defined for purposes of this Code, see Family Code § 110.
State defined for purposes of this Code, see Family Code § 145.
Stepparent adoption, defined, see Family Code § 8548.

§ 9201. Adoption services; identification; adoption petitions; research

(a) Except as otherwise permitted or required by statute, neither the department nor a licensed adoption agency shall release information that would identify persons who receive, or have received, adoption services.

(b) Employees of the department and licensed adoption agencies shall release to the department at Sacramento any requested information, including identifying information, for the purposes of recordkeeping and monitoring, evaluation, and regulation of the provision of adoption services.

(c) Prior to the placement of a child for adoption, the department or licensed adoption agency may, upon the written request of both a birth and a prospective adoptive parent, arrange for contact between these birth and prospective adoptive parents that may include the sharing of identifying information regarding these parents.

(d) The department and any licensed adoption agency may, upon written authorization for the release of specified information by the subject of that information, share information regarding a prospective adoptive parent or birth parent with other social service agencies, including the department, other licensed adoption agencies, counties or licensed foster family agencies for purposes of approving a resource family pursuant to subparagraph (A) of paragraph (4) of subdivision (p) of Section 16519.5 of the Welfare and Institutions Code, or providers of health care as defined in Section 56.05 of the Civil Code.

(e) Notwithstanding any other law, the department and any licensed adoption agency may furnish information relating to an adoption petition or to a child in the custody of the department or any licensed adoption agency to the juvenile court, county welfare department, public welfare agency, private welfare agency licensed by the department, provider of foster care services, potential adoptive parent, or provider of health care as defined in Section 56.05 of the Civil Code, if it is believed the child's welfare will be promoted thereby.

(f) The department and any licensed adoption agency may make adoption case records, including identifying information, available for research purposes, provided that the research will not result in the disclosure of the identity of the child or the parties to the adoption to anyone other than the entity conducting the research. *(Stats.1992, c. 162 (A.B.2650), § 10, operative Jan. 1, 1994. Amended by Stats.2000, c. 910 (A.B.2921), § 5; Stats.2006, c. 538 (S.B.1852), § 161; Stats.2016, c. 612 (A.B.1997), § 11, eff. Jan. 1, 2017.)*

Cross References

County defined for purposes of this Code, see Family Code § 67.
Department defined, see Family Code § 8518.
Licensed adoption agency defined, see Family Code § 8530.
Person defined for purposes of this Code, see Family Code § 105.
Prospective adoptive parent, defined, see Family Code § 8542.

§ 9202. Medical report; request of adopted person or adoptive parents; access

(a) Notwithstanding any other law, the department or licensed adoption agency that made a medical report required by Section 8706, 8817, or 8909 shall provide a copy of the medical report, in the manner the department prescribes by regulation, to any of the following persons upon the person's request:

(1) A person who has been adopted pursuant to this part and who has attained the age of 18 years or who presents a certified copy of the person's marriage certificate.

(2) The adoptive parent of a person under the age of 18 years who has been adopted pursuant to this part.

(b) A person who is denied access to a medical report pursuant to regulations adopted pursuant to this section may petition the court for review of the reasonableness of the department's or licensed adoption agency's decision.

(c) The names and addresses of any persons contained in the report shall be removed unless the person requesting the report has previously received the information. *(Stats.1992, c. 162 (A.B.2650), § 10, operative Jan. 1, 1994. Amended by Stats.2000, c. 910 (A.B. 2921), § 6.)*

Cross References

Adoptive parent, defined, see Family Code § 8503.
Department defined, see Family Code § 8518.
Jurisdiction of superior court, see Family Code § 200.
Licensed adoption agency defined, see Family Code § 8530.
Medical reports, rules and regulations, see Family Code § 8608.
Person defined for purposes of this Code, see Family Code § 105.

§ 9202.5. Blood sample; access

(a) Notwithstanding any other law, the laboratory that is storing a blood sample pursuant to Section 8706, 8817, or 8909 shall provide access to the blood sample to only the following persons upon the person's request:

(1) A person who has been adopted pursuant to this part.

(2) The adoptive parent of a person under the age of 18 years who has been adopted pursuant to this part. The adoptive parent may receive access to the blood sample only after entry of the order of adoption.

(b) The birth parent or parents shall be given access to any DNA test results related to the blood sample on request.

(c) Except as provided in subdivision (b), no person other than the adoptive parent and the adopted child shall have access to the blood sample or any DNA test results related to the blood sample, unless the adoptive parent or the child authorizes another person or entity to have that access. *(Added by Stats.1996, c. 1053 (A.B.3241), § 4.)*

Cross References

Adoptive parent, defined, see Family Code § 8503.
Birth parent, defined, see Family Code § 8512.

Judgment and order defined for purposes of this Code, see Family Code § 100.
Person defined for purposes of this Code, see Family Code § 105.

§ 9203. Disclosure of identity of birth parents; application of section

For Executive Order N–75–20 (2019 CA EO 75-20), concerning a number of different COVID-19-related provisions, including pharmacy testing, remote adoption paperwork, and community development grants, see Historical and Statutory Notes under Government Code § 12730.

(a) The department or a licensed adoption agency shall do the following:

(1) Upon the request of a person who has been adopted pursuant to this part and who has attained 21 years of age, disclose the identity of the person's birth parent or parents and their most current address shown in the records of the department or licensed adoption agency, if the birth parent or parents have indicated consent to the disclosure in writing.

(2) Upon the request of the birth parent of a person who has been adopted pursuant to this part and who has attained 21 years of age, disclose the adopted name of the adoptee and the adoptee's most current address shown in the records of the department or licensed adoption agency, if the adult adoptee has indicated in writing, pursuant to the registration program developed by the department, that the adult adoptee wishes the adult adoptee's name and address to be disclosed.

(3) Upon the request of the adoptive parent of a person under 21 years of age who has been adopted pursuant to this part, disclose the identity of a birth parent and the birth parent's most current address shown in the records of the department or licensed adoption agency if the department or licensed adoption agency finds that a medical necessity or other extraordinary circumstances justify the disclosure.

(b) The department shall prescribe the form of the request required by this section. The form shall provide for an affidavit to be executed by the requester that to the best of the requester's knowledge the requester is an adoptee, the adoptee's birth parent, or the adoptee's adoptive parent. The department may adopt regulations requiring any additional means of identification from a requester that it deems necessary. The request shall advise an adoptee that if the adoptee consents, the adoptee's adoptive parents will be notified of the filing of the request before the release of the name and address of the adoptee's birth parent.

(c) Subdivision (a) is not applicable if a birth parent or an adoptee has indicated a desire that the name or address of the birth parent or adoptee not be disclosed.

(d) Within 20 working days of receipt of a request for information pursuant to this section, the department shall either respond to the request or forward the request to a licensed adoption agency that was a party to the adoption.

(e) Notwithstanding any other law, the department shall announce the availability of the present method of arranging contact among an adult adoptee, the adult adoptee's birth parents, and adoptive parents authorized by Section 9204 utilizing a means of communication appropriate to inform the public effectively.

(f) The department or licensed adoption agency may charge a reasonable fee in an amount the department establishes by regulation to cover the costs of processing requests for information made pursuant to subdivision (a). The department or licensed adoption agency shall waive fees authorized by this section for a person who is receiving public assistance pursuant to Part 3 (commencing with Section 11000) of Division 9 of the Welfare and Institutions Code. The revenue resulting from the fees so charged shall be utilized by the department or licensed adoption agency to increase existing staff as needed to process these requests. Fees received by the department shall be deposited in the Adoption Information Fund. This revenue shall be in addition to any other funds appropriated in support of the state adoption program.

(g) This section applies only to adoptions in which the relinquishment for or consent to adoption was signed or the birth parent's rights were involuntarily terminated by court action on or after January 1, 1984. *(Stats.1992, c. 162 (A.B.2650), § 10, operative Jan. 1, 1994. Amended by Stats.2000, c. 910 (A.B.2921), § 7; Stats.2019, c. 115 (A.B.1817), § 135, eff. Jan. 1, 2020.)*

Cross References

Adoptive parent, defined, see Family Code § 8503.
Adult defined for purposes of this Code, see Family Code § 6501.
Agency adoptions, statement presented to birth parents at time of relinquishment, see Family Code § 8702.
Birth parent, defined, see Family Code § 8512.
Certificate of live birth, confidentiality of second section, access, see Health and Safety Code § 102430.
Department defined, see Family Code § 8518.
Independent adoptions, statement to birth parents, contents, see Family Code § 8818.
Licensed adoption agency defined, see Family Code § 8530.
Person defined for purposes of this Code, see Family Code § 105.
State defined for purposes of this Code, see Family Code § 145.
Support defined for purposes of this Code, see Family Code § 150.

Research References

Forms

1¶ 1 Nichols Cyclopedia of Legal Forms Annotated § 7:15, Voluntary Adoption Registries.

§ 9203.1. Disclosure of adoption homestudy; form; time for response; fees

For Executive Order N–75–20 (2019 CA EO 75-20), concerning a number of different COVID-19-related provisions, including pharmacy testing, remote adoption paperwork, and community development grants, see Historical and Statutory Notes under Government Code § 12730.

(a) The department or a licensed adoption agency shall, upon the request of a prospective adoptive parent, disclose an adoption homestudy and any updates to an adoption homestudy to a county or licensed foster family agency for the purpose of approving the prospective adoptive parent as a resource family pursuant to subparagraph (A) of paragraph (4) of subdivision (p) of Section 16519.5 of the Welfare and Institutions Code.

(b) The department shall prescribe the form of the request described in subdivision (a).

(c) The department or a licensed adoption agency shall respond to a request made pursuant to subdivision (a) within 20 working days of receiving it.

(d) The department or a licensed adoption agency may charge a fee to cover the reasonable costs of processing requests made pursuant to subdivision (a). The department or a licensed adoption agency shall waive fees authorized by this subdivision for any person who is receiving public assistance pursuant to Part 3 (commencing with Section 11000) of Division 9 of the Welfare and Institutions Code. *(Added by Stats.2016, c. 612 (A.B.1997), § 12, eff. Jan. 1, 2017.)*

§ 9204. Consent between adult adoptee and birth parents to arrange for contact between the parties

For Executive Order N–75–20 (2019 CA EO 75-20), concerning a number of different COVID-19-related provisions, including pharmacy testing, remote adoption paperwork, and community development grants, see Historical and Statutory Notes under Government Code § 12730.

(a) Notwithstanding any other law, if an adult adoptee and the adult adoptee's birth parents have each filed a written consent with

§ 9204

the department or licensed adoption agency, the department or licensed adoption agency may arrange for contact between those persons. Neither the department nor a licensed adoption agency may solicit, directly or indirectly, the execution of a written consent.

(b) The written consent authorized by this section shall be in a form prescribed by the department. *(Stats.1992, c. 162 (A.B.2650), § 10, operative Jan. 1, 1994.)*

Cross References

Adoptive parent, defined, see Family Code § 8503.
Adult defined for purposes of this Code, see Family Code § 6501.
Birth parent, defined, see Family Code § 8512.
Department defined, see Family Code § 8518.
Licensed adoption agency defined, see Family Code § 8530.
Person defined for purposes of this Code, see Family Code § 105.

§ 9205. Contact with sibling; request; form

For Executive Order N–75–20 (2019 CA EO 75-20), concerning a number of different COVID-19-related provisions, including pharmacy testing, remote adoption paperwork, and community development grants, see Historical and Statutory Notes under Government Code § 12730.

(a) Notwithstanding any other law, the department, county adoption agency, or licensed adoption agency that joined in the adoption petition shall release the names and addresses of siblings to one another if both of the siblings have attained 18 years of age and have filed the following with the department or agency:

(1) A current address.

(2) A written request for contact with any sibling whose existence is known to the person making the request.

(3) A written waiver of the person's rights with respect to the disclosure of the person's name and address to the sibling, if the person is an adoptee.

(b) Upon inquiry and proof that a person is the sibling of an adoptee who has filed a waiver pursuant to this section, the department, county adoption agency, or licensed adoption agency may advise the sibling that a waiver has been filed by the adoptee. The department, county adoption agency, or licensed adoption agency may charge a reasonable fee, not to exceed fifty dollars ($50), for providing the service required by this section.

(c) An adoptee may revoke a waiver filed pursuant to this section by giving written notice of revocation to the department or agency.

(d) The department shall adopt a form for the request authorized by this section. The form shall provide for an affidavit to be executed by a person seeking to employ the procedure provided by this section that, to the best of the person's knowledge, the person is an adoptee or sibling of an adoptee. The form also shall contain a notice of an adoptee's rights pursuant to subdivision (c) and a statement that information will be disclosed only if there is a currently valid waiver on file with the department or agency. The department may adopt regulations requiring any additional means of identification from a person making a request pursuant to this section as it deems necessary.

(e) The department, county adoption agency, or licensed adoption agency may not solicit the execution of a waiver authorized by this section. However, the department shall announce the availability of the procedure authorized by this section, utilizing a means of communication appropriate to inform the public effectively.

(f) Notwithstanding the age requirement described in subdivision (a), an adoptee or sibling who is under 18 years of age may file a written waiver of confidentiality for the release of the person's name, address, and telephone number pursuant to this section provided that, if an adoptee, the adoptive parent consents, and, if a sibling, the sibling's legal parent or guardian consents. If the sibling is under the jurisdiction of the dependency court and has no legal parent or guardian able or available to provide consent, the dependency court may provide that consent.

(g) Notwithstanding subdivisions (a) and (e), an adoptee or sibling who seeks contact with the other for whom no waiver is on file may petition the court to appoint a confidential intermediary. If the sibling being sought is the adoptee, the intermediary shall be the department, county adoption agency, or licensed adoption agency that provided adoption services as described in Section 8521 or 8533. If the sibling being sought was formerly under the jurisdiction of the juvenile court, but is not an adoptee, the intermediary shall be the department, the county child welfare agency that provided services to the dependent child, or the licensed adoption agency that provided adoption services to the sibling seeking contact, as appropriate. If the court finds that the agency that conducted the adoptee's adoption is unable, due to economic hardship, to serve as the intermediary, then the agency shall provide all records related to the adoptee or the sibling to the court and the court shall appoint an alternate confidential intermediary. The court shall grant the petition unless it finds that it would be detrimental to the adoptee or sibling with whom contact is sought. The intermediary shall have access to all records of the adoptee or the sibling and shall make all reasonable efforts to locate and attempt to obtain the consent of the adoptee, sibling, or adoptive or birth parent, as required to make the disclosure authorized by this section. The confidential intermediary shall notify any located adoptee, sibling, or adoptive or birth parent that consent is optional, not required by law, and does not affect the status of the adoption. If that individual denies the request for consent, the confidential intermediary shall not make any further attempts to obtain consent. The confidential intermediary shall use information found in the records of the adoptee or the sibling for authorized purposes only, and may not disclose that information without authorization. If contact is sought with an adoptee or sibling who is under 18 years of age, the confidential intermediary shall contact and obtain the consent of that child's legal parent before contacting the child. If the sibling is under 18 years of age, under the jurisdiction of the dependency court, and has no legal parent or guardian able or available to provide consent, the intermediary shall obtain that consent from the dependency court. If the adoptee is seeking information regarding a sibling who is known to be a dependent child of the juvenile court, the procedures set forth in subdivision (b) of Section 388 of the Welfare and Institutions Code shall be utilized. If the adoptee is foreign born and was the subject of an intercountry adoption as defined in Section 8527, the adoption agency may fulfill the reasonable efforts requirement by utilizing all information in the agency's case file, and any information received upon request from the foreign adoption agency that conducted the adoption, if any, to locate and attempt to obtain the consent of the adoptee, sibling, or adoptive or birth parent. If that information is neither in the agency's case file, nor received from the foreign adoption agency, or if the attempts to locate are unsuccessful, then the agency shall be relieved of any further obligation to search for the adoptee or the sibling.

(h) For purposes of this section, "sibling" means a biological sibling, half-sibling, or step-sibling of the adoptee.

(i) It is the intent of the Legislature that implementation of some or all of the changes made to this section by Chapter 386 of the Statutes of 2006 shall continue, to the extent possible.

(j) Beginning in the 2011–12 fiscal year, and each fiscal year thereafter, funding and expenditures for programs and activities under this section shall be in accordance with the requirements provided in Sections 30025 and 30026.5 of the Government Code. *(Stats.1992, c. 162 (A.B.2650), § 10, operative Jan. 1, 1994. Amended by Stats.2006, c. 386 (A.B.2488), § 1; Stats.2007, c. 130 (A.B.299), § 93; Stats.2008, c. 759 (A.B.1279), § 15, eff. Sept. 30, 2008; Stats.2010, c. 725 (A.B.1612), § 2, eff. Oct. 19, 2010; Stats.2011, c. 8 (S.B.72), § 1, eff. March 24, 2011; Stats.2012, c. 35 (S.B.1013), § 36,* eff. June 27, 2012; Stats.2019, c. 115 (A.B.1817), § 136, eff. Jan. 1, 2020.)

Cross References

Adoptive parent, defined, see Family Code § 8503.
Birth parent, defined, see Family Code § 8512.
Department defined, see Family Code § 8518.
Judgment and order defined for purposes of this Code, see Family Code § 100.
Out-of-home placement, case plan provisions for sibling visitation and relationship development, see Welfare and Institutions Code § 16501.1.
Person defined for purposes of this Code, see Family Code § 105.
Post-adoptive sibling contact, jurisdiction over post-adoption agreements, see Welfare and Institutions Code § 366.29.

Research References

Forms

West's California Judicial Council Forms ADOPT–330, Request for Appointment of Confidential Intermediary.
West's California Judicial Council Forms ADOPT–331, Order for Appointment of Confidential Intermediary.

§ 9206. Release of letters, photographs, or other items of personal property; requests; release form; fees

(a) Notwithstanding any other law, the department or licensed adoption agency shall release any letters, photographs, or other items of personal property in its possession to an adoptee, birth parent, or adoptive parent, upon written request. The material may be requested by any of the following persons:

(1) The adoptee, if the adoptee has attained the age of 18 years.

(2) The adoptive parent or parents, on behalf of an adoptee under the age of 18 years, as long as instructions to the contrary have not been made by the depositor.

(3) The birth parent or parents.

(b) Notwithstanding any other law, all identifying names and addresses shall be deleted from the letters, photographs, or items of personal property before delivery to the requester.

(c) Letters, photographs, and other items of personal property deposited on or after January 1, 1985, shall be accompanied by a release form or similar document signed by the person depositing the material, specifying to whom the material may be released. At its discretion, the department or licensed adoption agency may refuse for deposit items of personal property that, because of value or bulk, would pose storage problems.

(d) Notwithstanding subdivisions (a) and (b), only the following photographs deposited before January 1, 1985, shall be released:

(1) Photographs of the adoptee that have been requested by the adoptee.

(2) Photographs that have been deposited by the adoptee, the adoptive parent or parents, or the birth parent or parents, and for which there is a letter or other document on file indicating that person's consent to the release of the photographs.

(e) The department and licensed adoption agencies may charge a fee to cover the actual costs of any services required by this section in excess of normal postadoptive services provided by the department or agency. The department shall develop a fee schedule that shall be implemented by the department and licensed adoption agencies in assessing charges to the person who deposits the material or the person to whom the material is released. The fee may be waived by the department or licensed adoption agencies in cases in which it is established that a financial hardship exists.

(f) "Photograph" as used in this section means a photograph of the person depositing the photograph or the person making the request for the release. (Stats.1992, c. 162 (A.B.2650), § 10, operative Jan. 1, 1994.)

Cross References

Adoptive parent, defined, see Family Code § 8503.
Birth parent, defined, see Family Code § 8512.
Department defined, see Family Code § 8518.
Licensed adoption agency defined, see Family Code § 8530.
Person defined for purposes of this Code, see Family Code § 105.
Property defined for purposes of this Code, see Family Code § 113.

Research References

Forms

2 California Transactions Forms--Family Law § 6:2, Governing Law.

§ 9208. Children of Indian ancestry; notice to United States Secretary of the Interior

(a) The clerk of the superior court entering a final order of adoption concerning an Indian child shall provide the United States Secretary of the Interior or a designee with a copy of the order within 30 days of the date of the order, together with any information necessary to show the following:

(1) The name and tribal affiliation of the child.

(2) The names and addresses of the biological parents.

(3) The names and addresses of the adoptive parents.

(4) The identity of any agency having files or information relating to that adoptive placement.

(b) If the court records contain an affidavit of the biological parent or parents that their identity remain confidential, the court shall include that affidavit with the other information. (Added by Stats.2006, c. 838 (S.B.678), § 13. Amended by Stats.2019, c. 115 (A.B.1817), § 137, eff. Jan. 1, 2020.)

Research References

Forms

2 California Transactions Forms--Family Law § 6:143, Overview of Indian Child Welfare Act (ICWA).
West's California Judicial Council Forms ADOPT–200, Adoption Request.

§ 9209. Children of Indian ancestry; adoptees who have reached age eighteen; access to information

(a) Upon application by an Indian individual who has reached the age of 18 years and who was the subject of an adoptive placement, the court which entered the final decree of adoption shall inform that individual of the tribal affiliation, if any, of the individual's biological parents and provide any other information as may be necessary to protect any rights flowing from the individual's tribal relationship, including, but not limited to, tribal membership rights or eligibility for federal or tribal programs or services available to Indians.

(b) If the court records contain an affidavit of the biological parent or parents that their identity remain confidential, the court shall inform the individual that the Secretary of the Interior may, upon request, certify to the individual's tribe that the individual's parentage and other circumstances of birth entitle the individual to membership under the criteria established by the tribe. (Added by Stats.2006, c. 838 (S.B.678), § 14.)

CHAPTER 8. ADOPTION PROCEEDINGS: CONFLICT OF LAWS

Section
9210. Actions commenced under this part; conditions required for California court jurisdiction; exceptions.
9211. Repealed.
9212. Prospective adoptive parents residing outside of the state; applicability of §§ 9210 and 9211.
9213. Renumbered.

§ 9210. Actions commenced under this part; conditions required for California court jurisdiction; exceptions

(a) Except as otherwise provided in subdivisions (b) and (c), a court of this state has jurisdiction over a proceeding for the adoption of a minor commenced under this part if any of the following applies:

(1) Immediately before commencement of the proceeding, the minor lived in this state with a parent, a guardian, a prospective adoptive parent, or another person acting as parent, for at least six consecutive months, excluding periods of temporary absence, or, in the case of a minor under six months of age, lived in this state with any of those individuals from soon after birth and there is available in this state substantial evidence concerning the minor's present or future care.

(2) Immediately before commencement of the proceeding, the prospective adoptive parent lived in this state for at least six consecutive months, excluding periods of temporary absence, and there is available in this state substantial evidence concerning the minor's present or future care.

(3) The agency that placed the minor for adoption is located in this state and both of the following apply:

(A) The minor and the minor's parents, or the minor and the prospective adoptive parent, have a significant connection with this state.

(B) There is available in this state substantial evidence concerning the minor's present or future care.

(4) The minor and the prospective adoptive parent are physically present in this state and the minor has been abandoned or it is necessary in an emergency to protect the minor because the minor has been subjected to or threatened with mistreatment or abuse or is otherwise neglected.

(5) It appears that no other state would have jurisdiction under requirements substantially in accordance with paragraphs (1) to (4), inclusive, or another state has declined to exercise jurisdiction on the ground that this state is the more appropriate forum to hear a petition for adoption of the minor, and there is available in this state substantial evidence concerning the minor's present or future care.

(b) A court of this state may not exercise jurisdiction over a proceeding for adoption of a minor if at the time the petition for adoption is filed a proceeding concerning the custody or adoption of the minor is pending in a court of another state exercising jurisdiction substantially in conformity with this part, unless the proceeding is stayed by the court of the other state because this state is a more appropriate forum or for another reason.

(c) If a court of another state has issued a decree or order concerning the custody of a minor who may be the subject of a proceeding for adoption in this state, a court of this state may not exercise jurisdiction over a proceeding for adoption of the minor, unless both of the following apply:

(1) The requirements for modifying an order of a court of another state under this part are met, the court of another state does not have jurisdiction over a proceeding for adoption substantially in conformity with paragraphs (1) to (4), inclusive, of subdivision (a), or the court of another state has declined to assume jurisdiction over a proceeding for adoption.

(2) The court of this state has jurisdiction under this section over the proceeding for adoption.

(d) For purposes of subdivisions (b) and (c), "a court of another state" includes, in the case of an Indian child, a tribal court having and exercising jurisdiction over a custody proceeding involving the Indian child. *(Added by Stats.2002, c. 260 (S.B.1512), § 8. Amended by Stats.2003, c. 62 (S.B.600), § 89; Stats.2006, c. 838 (S.B.678), § 15.)*

Cross References

Abuse defined for purposes of the Domestic Violence Protection Act, see Family Code § 6203.
Guardian, defined, see Probate Code §§ 2350, 2400.
Judgment and order defined for purposes of this Code, see Family Code § 100.
Minor defined for purposes of this Code, see Family Code § 6500.
Parent or guardian, defined, see Family Code § 6903.
Person defined for purposes of this Code, see Family Code § 105.
Proceeding defined for purposes of this Code, see Family Code § 110.
Prospective adoptive parent, defined, see Family Code § 8542.
State defined for purposes of this Code, see Family Code § 145.

§ 9211. Repealed by Stats.2012, c. 638 (A.B.1757), § 13

§ 9212. Prospective adoptive parents residing outside of the state; applicability of §§ 9210 and 9211

(a) Sections 9210 and 9211 apply to interstate adoptions if the prospective adoptive parents reside outside of the state.

(b) This section shall become operative only if Assembly Bill 746 of the 2001–02 Regular Session is enacted.[1] If Assembly Bill 746 is not enacted, the application of Sections 9210 and 9211 is not intended to expand jurisdiction to apply to interstate adoptions if the prospective adoptive parents reside outside of the state. *(Added by Stats.2002, c. 260 (S.B.1512), § 8. Amended by Stats.2003, c. 62 (S.B.600), § 90.)*

[1] Assembly Bill 746 was enacted as Stats.2002, c. 1112 (A.B.746).

Cross References

Guardian, defined, see Probate Code §§ 2350, 2400.
Parent or guardian, defined, see Family Code § 6903.
Prospective adoptive parent, defined, see Family Code § 8542.
State defined for purposes of this Code, see Family Code § 145.

§ 9213. Renumbered § 9321.5 and amended by Stats.2012, c. 162 (S.B.1171), § 48

Part 3

ADOPTION OF ADULTS AND MARRIED MINORS

Chapter	Section
1. General Provisions	9300
2. Procedure for Adult Adoption	9320
3. Procedure for Terminating Adult Adoption	9340

CHAPTER 1. GENERAL PROVISIONS

Section
9300. Adoption of adults or married minors; authority.
9301. Consent of spouse of adoptive parent.
9302. Consent of spouse of proposed adoptee; consent of others not required.
9303. Restrictions on adoption of more than one unrelated adult.
9304. Adoptee may take adoptive parent's family name.
9305. Legal relationship of parent and child.
9306. Birth parents; relief of parental duties; exceptions; waiver.
9307. Open and public hearing.

§ 9300. Adoption of adults or married minors; authority

(a) An adult may be adopted by another adult, including a stepparent, as provided in this part.

(b) A married minor may be adopted in the same manner as an adult under this part. *(Stats.1992, c. 162 (A.B.2650), § 10, operative Jan. 1, 1994. Amended by Stats.1993, c. 266 (S.B.970), § 1.)*

Cross References

Adult defined for purposes of this Code, see Family Code § 6501.
Age of majority, see Family Code § 6500 et seq.
Consent of court to marriage of minor, see Family Code § 303.
Dependent children, hearing to consider permanent plan of adoption for nonminor dependent, nonminor dependent not prevented from filing adoption petition pursuant to this section, see Welfare and Institutions Code § 366.31.
Emancipation of Minors Law, see Family Code § 7000 et seq.
Minor defined for purposes of this Code, see Family Code § 6500.
Minors, capability to consent to and consummate marriage, see Family Code § 302.
Stepparent adoptions, generally, see Family Code § 9000 et seq.

Research References

Forms

1B Am. Jur. Pl. & Pr. Forms Adoption § 240, Statutory References.
2 California Transactions Forms--Family Law § 6:2, Governing Law.
2 California Transactions Forms--Family Law § 6:4, Types of Adoptions.
2 California Transactions Forms--Family Law § 6:7, Who May be Adopted.
2 California Transactions Forms--Family Law § 6:158, Governing Law—Venue and Procedure.
2 California Transactions Forms--Family Law § 6:164, Agreement of Adult Adoption.
West's California Code Forms, Family § 9302 Form 2, Consent of Spouse of Adopted Adult.

§ 9301. Consent of spouse of adoptive parent

A married person who is not lawfully separated from the person's spouse may not adopt an adult without the consent of the spouse, provided that the spouse is capable of giving that consent. *(Stats. 1992, c. 162 (A.B.2650), § 10, operative Jan. 1, 1994.)*

Cross References

Adult defined for purposes of this Code, see Family Code § 6501.
Legal separation, generally, see Family Code § 2300 et seq.
Person defined for purposes of this Code, see Family Code § 105.
References to husband, wife, spouses and married persons, persons included for purposes of this Code, see Family Code § 11.
Validity of marriage, see Family Code § 300 et seq.

Research References

Forms

2 California Transactions Forms--Family Law § 6:9, Consent for Adoption of Married Minor or Adult.
2 California Transactions Forms--Family Law § 6:163, Matters to Consider in Adoption of Adult or Married Minor.
West's California Code Forms, Family § 9301, Comment Overview—Adoption of Adults and Married Minors.

§ 9302. Consent of spouse of proposed adoptee; consent of others not required

(a) A married person who is not lawfully separated from the person's spouse may not be adopted without the consent of the spouse, provided that the spouse is capable of giving that consent.

(b) The consent of the parents of the proposed adoptee, of the department, or of any other person is not required. *(Stats.1992, c. 162 (A.B.2650), § 10, operative Jan. 1, 1994.)*

Cross References

Birth parent, defined, see Family Code § 8512.
Department defined, see Family Code § 8518.
Legal separation, generally, see Family Code § 2300 et seq.
Person defined for purposes of this Code, see Family Code § 105.
References to husband, wife, spouses and married persons, persons included for purposes of this Code, see Family Code § 11.
Validity of marriage, see Family Code § 300 et seq.

Research References

Forms

2 California Transactions Forms--Family Law § 6:9, Consent for Adoption of Married Minor or Adult.
2 California Transactions Forms--Family Law § 6:163, Matters to Consider in Adoption of Adult or Married Minor.
West's California Code Forms, Family § 9301, Comment Overview—Adoption of Adults and Married Minors.

§ 9303. Restrictions on adoption of more than one unrelated adult

(a) A person may not adopt more than one unrelated adult under this part within one year of the person's adoption of an unrelated adult, unless the proposed adoptee is the biological sibling of a person previously adopted pursuant to this part or unless the proposed adoptee is disabled or physically handicapped.

(b) A person may not adopt an unrelated adult under this part within one year of an adoption of another person under this part by the prospective adoptive parent's spouse, unless the proposed adoptee is a biological sibling of a person previously adopted pursuant to this part. *(Stats.1992, c. 162 (A.B.2650), § 10, operative Jan. 1, 1994.)*

Cross References

Adult defined for purposes of this Code, see Family Code § 6501.
Foster care placement, sibling groups, see Welfare and Institutions Code § 16002.
Person defined for purposes of this Code, see Family Code § 105.
Post-adoptive sibling contact, jurisdiction over post-adoption agreements, see Welfare and Institutions Code § 366.29.
Prospective adoptive parent, defined, see Family Code § 8542.
References to husband, wife, spouses and married persons, persons included for purposes of this Code, see Family Code § 11.

Research References

Forms

2 California Transactions Forms--Family Law § 6:6, Who May Adopt.
2 California Transactions Forms--Family Law § 6:159, Limitations on Adult Adoption.

§ 9304. Adoptee may take adoptive parent's family name

A person adopted pursuant to this part may take the family name of the adoptive parent. *(Stats.1992, c. 162 (A.B.2650), § 10, operative Jan. 1, 1994.)*

Cross References

Adoption of unmarried minors, ability of adopted child to take adoptive parent's family name, see Family Code § 8618.
Adoptive parent, defined, see Family Code § 8503.
Person defined for purposes of this Code, see Family Code § 105.

§ 9305. Legal relationship of parent and child

After adoption, the adoptee and the adoptive parent or parents shall sustain towards each other the legal relationship of parent and child and have all the rights and are subject to all the duties of that relationship. *(Stats.1992, c. 162 (A.B.2650), § 10, operative Jan. 1, 1994.)*

Cross References

Abandonment and neglect of children, criminal penalties for failure to provide care for minor child, see Penal Code § 270 et seq.
Adoption of unmarried minors, legal relationship of parent and child, see Family Code § 8616.
Adoptive parent, defined, see Family Code § 8503.
Birth parent, defined, see Family Code § 8512.
Child, defined for purposes of the Probate Code, see Probate Code § 26.
Construction of wills, trusts, and other instruments, rules for interpretation applied to adoptees, see Probate Code § 21115.
Enforcement of support, Uniform Interstate Family Support Act, see Family Code § 5700.101 et seq.

§ 9305

Intestate succession, parent and child relationship,
   Adoption, effect of, see Probate Code § 6451.
   Foster parents or stepparents, see Probate Code § 6454.
   Natural parents, see Probate Code § 6453.
   Out-of-wedlock births, conditions for inheritance based on relationship, see Probate Code § 6452.
Liability of parent or guardian for willful misconduct of minors, see Civil Code § 1714.1.
Parent, defined for purposes of the Probate Code, see Probate Code § 54.
Parent and child relationship,
   Generally, see Family Code § 7500 et seq.
   Defined for purposes of Uniform Parentage Act, see Family Code § 7601.
   Establishing, see Family Code § 7610 et seq.
Parent or guardian, defined, see Family Code § 6903.
Parental authority, termination upon guardianship, marriage, or age of majority, see Family Code § 7505.
Support of adult child, duty to support incapacitated adult child, see Family Code § 3910.
Support of minor child, duration of duty to support, see Family Code § 3900.

Research References

Forms

2 California Transactions Forms--Family Law § 6:17, Legal Relationship Following Adoption of Married Minor or Adult.
2 California Transactions Forms--Family Law § 6:18, Intestate Succession Rights.
2 California Transactions Forms--Family Law § 6:161, Estate Planning Considerations.

§ 9306. Birth parents; relief of parental duties; exceptions; waiver

(a) Except as provided in subdivisions (b) and (c), the birth parents of a person adopted pursuant to this part are, from the time of the adoption, relieved of all parental duties towards, and all responsibility for, the adopted person, and have no right over the adopted person.

(b) If an adult is adopted by the spouse of a birth parent, the parental rights and responsibilities of that birth parent are not affected by the adoption.

(c) An adult being adopted pursuant to this part may waive the termination of the parental duties and responsibilities of an existing parent or parents under subdivision (a) by signing a waiver at any time prior to the finalization of the adoption. The waiver may be included in the adoption agreement or in a separate writing filed with the court. *(Stats.1992, c. 162 (A.B.2650), § 10, operative Jan. 1, 1994. Amended by Stats.1993, c. 266 (S.B.970), § 2; Stats.2019, c. 192 (A.B.1373), § 3, eff. Jan. 1, 2020.)*

Cross References

Abandonment and neglect of children, criminal penalties for failure to provide care for minor child, see Penal Code § 270 et seq.
Adoption of unmarried minors, birth parents, cessation of legal responsibilities toward child, see Family Code § 8617.
Adoptive parent, defined, see Family Code § 8503.
Adult defined for purposes of this Code, see Family Code § 6501.
Birth parent, defined, see Family Code § 8512.
Child, defined for purposes of the Probate Code, see Probate Code § 26.
Construction of wills, trusts, and other instruments, rules for interpretation applied to adoptees, see Probate Code § 21115.
Enforcement of support, Uniform Interstate Family Support Act, see Family Code § 5700.101 et seq.
Freedom from parental custody and control, generally, see Family Code § 7800 et seq.
Intestate succession, parent and child relationship,
   Adoption, effect of, see Probate Code § 6451.
   Foster parents or stepparents, see Probate Code § 6454.
   Natural parents, see Probate Code § 6453.
   Out-of-wedlock births, conditions for inheritance based on relationship, see Probate Code § 6452.
Liability of parent or guardian for willful misconduct of minors, see Civil Code § 1714.1.
Parent, defined for purposes of the Probate Code, see Probate Code § 54.
Parent and child relationship,
   Generally, see Family Code § 7500 et seq.
   Defined for purposes of Uniform Parentage Act, see Family Code § 7601.
   Establishing, see Family Code § 7610 et seq.
Parent or guardian, defined, see Family Code § 6903.
Parental authority, termination upon guardianship, marriage, or age of majority, see Family Code § 7505.
Parental rights, termination in adoption proceedings, see Family Code § 7660 et seq.
Person defined for purposes of this Code, see Family Code § 105.
References to husband, wife, spouses and married persons, persons included for purposes of this Code, see Family Code § 11.
Support of adult child, duty to support incapacitated adult child, see Family Code § 3910.
Support of minor child, duration of duty to support, see Family Code § 3900.

Research References

Forms

2 California Transactions Forms--Family Law § 6:17, Legal Relationship Following Adoption of Married Minor or Adult.
2 California Transactions Forms--Family Law § 6:161, Estate Planning Considerations.

§ 9307. Open and public hearing

A hearing with regard to adoption under Chapter 2 (commencing with Section 9320) or termination of a parent and child relationship under Chapter 3 (commencing with Section 9340) may, in the discretion of the court, be open and public. *(Stats.1992, c. 162 (A.B.2650), § 10, operative Jan. 1, 1994.)*

Research References

Forms

2 California Transactions Forms--Family Law § 6:12, Conduct of Hearing.

CHAPTER 2. PROCEDURE FOR ADULT ADOPTION

Section
9320.   Adoption agreement; execution; content.
9321.   Petition for approval of adoption agreement; filing; contents of petition.
9321.5. Petitions for adult adoption; filing; residents; nonresidents; venue.
9322.   Setting matter for hearing.
9323.   Notice of hearing; appearances and objections of interested persons.
9324.   Mandatory appearances by prospective adoptive parent and proposed adoptee; exceptions.
9325.   Investigation and report.
9326.   Notice of hearing of proposed adoption of developmentally disabled adult.
9327.   Report on proposed adoption of developmentally disabled adult.
9328.   Hearing; order of adoption or denial of petitions.

§ 9320. Adoption agreement; execution; content

(a) An adult may adopt another adult who is younger, except the spouse of the prospective adoptive parent, by an adoption agreement approved by the court, as provided in this chapter.

(b) The adoption agreement shall be in writing, executed by the prospective adoptive parent and the proposed adoptee, and shall state that the parties agree to assume toward each other the legal relationship of parent and child and to have all of the rights and be subject to all of the duties and responsibilities of that relationship. *(Stats.1992, c. 162 (A.B.2650), § 10, operative Jan. 1, 1994.)*

Cross References

Adult defined for purposes of this Code, see Family Code § 6501.
Prospective adoptive parent, defined, see Family Code § 8542.

References to husband, wife, spouses and married persons, persons included for purposes of this Code, see Family Code § 11.
State defined for purposes of this Code, see Family Code § 145.

Research References

Forms

2 California Transactions Forms--Family Law § 6:6, Who May Adopt.
2 California Transactions Forms--Family Law § 6:7, Who May be Adopted.
2 California Transactions Forms--Family Law § 6:9, Consent for Adoption of Married Minor or Adult.
2 California Transactions Forms--Family Law § 6:159, Limitations on Adult Adoption.
2 California Transactions Forms--Family Law § 6:160, Adoption Agreement—Petition for Approval of Adoption Agreement.
2 California Transactions Forms--Family Law § 6:163, Matters to Consider in Adoption of Adult or Married Minor.
2 California Transactions Forms--Family Law § 6:164, Agreement of Adult Adoption.
2 California Transactions Forms--Family Law § 6:165, Petition for Adoption (Adult).
West's California Code Forms, Family § 9320, Comment Overview—Procedure for Adult Adoption.

§ 9321. Petition for approval of adoption agreement; filing; contents of petition

(a) The prospective adoptive parent and the proposed adoptee may file in the county in which either person resides a petition for approval of the adoption agreement.

(b) The petition for approval of the adoption agreement shall state all of the following:

(1) The length and nature of the relationship between the prospective adoptive parent and the proposed adoptee.

(2) The degree of kinship, if any.

(3) The reason the adoption is sought.

(4) A statement as to why the adoption would be in the best interest of the prospective adoptive parent, the proposed adoptee, and the public.

(5) The names and addresses of any living birth parents or adult children of the proposed adoptee.

(6) Whether the prospective adoptive parent or the prospective adoptive parent's spouse has previously adopted any other adult and, if so, the name of the adult, together with the date and place of the adoption. *(Stats.1992, c. 162 (A.B.2650), § 10, operative Jan. 1, 1994.)*

Cross References

Adoptive parent, defined, see Family Code § 8503.
Adult defined for purposes of this Code, see Family Code § 6501.
Birth parent, defined, see Family Code § 8512.
County defined for purposes of this Code, see Family Code § 67.
Jurisdiction of superior court, see Family Code § 200.
Person defined for purposes of this Code, see Family Code § 105.
Prospective adoptive parent, defined, see Family Code § 8542.
References to husband, wife, spouses and married persons, persons included for purposes of this Code, see Family Code § 11.
State defined for purposes of this Code, see Family Code § 145.
Verification of pleadings, see Family Code § 212.

Research References

Forms

2 California Transactions Forms--Family Law § 6:9, Consent for Adoption of Married Minor or Adult.
2 California Transactions Forms--Family Law § 6:158, Governing Law—Venue and Procedure.
2 California Transactions Forms--Family Law § 6:160, Adoption Agreement—Petition for Approval of Adoption Agreement.
2 California Transactions Forms--Family Law § 6:163, Matters to Consider in Adoption of Adult or Married Minor.
2 California Transactions Forms--Family Law § 6:165, Petition for Adoption (Adult).
West's California Code Forms, Family § 9320, Comment Overview—Procedure for Adult Adoption.

§ 9321.5. Petitions for adult adoption; filing; residents; nonresidents; venue

(a) Notwithstanding Section 9321, a person who is a resident of this state may file a petition for adult adoption with the court in any of the following:

(1) The county in which the prospective adoptive parent resides.

(2) The county in which the proposed adoptee was born or resides at the time the petition was filed.

(3) The county in which an office of the public or private agency that placed the proposed adoptee for foster care or adoption as a minor or dependent child is located.

(b) A petitioner who is not a resident of this state may file a petition for adult adoption with the court in a county specified in paragraph (3) of subdivision (a). *(Formerly § 9213, added by Stats.2011, c. 462 (A.B.687), § 10. Renumbered § 9321.5 and amended by Stats.2012, c. 162 (S.B.1171), § 48.)*

Research References

Forms

2 California Transactions Forms--Family Law § 6:158, Governing Law—Venue and Procedure.
2 California Transactions Forms--Family Law § 6:165, Petition for Adoption (Adult).
2 California Transactions Forms--Family Law § 6:168, Decree of Adoption of Adult or Married Minor.

§ 9322. Setting matter for hearing

When the petition for approval of the adoption agreement is filed, the court clerk shall set the matter for hearing. *(Stats.1992, c. 162 (A.B.2650), § 10, operative Jan. 1, 1994.)*

Research References

Forms

West's California Code Forms, Family § 9320, Comment Overview—Procedure for Adult Adoption.

§ 9323. Notice of hearing; appearances and objections of interested persons

The court may require notice of the time and place of the hearing to be served on any other interested person and any interested person may appear and object to the proposed adoption. *(Stats. 1992, c. 162 (A.B.2650), § 10, operative Jan. 1, 1994.)*

Cross References

Person defined for purposes of this Code, see Family Code § 105.
Prospective adoptive parent, defined, see Family Code § 8542.

Research References

Forms

West's California Code Forms, Family § 9320, Comment Overview—Procedure for Adult Adoption.

§ 9324. Mandatory appearances by prospective adoptive parent and proposed adoptee; exceptions

Both the prospective adoptive parent and the proposed adoptee shall appear at the hearing in person, unless * * * <u>the court allows otherwise pursuant to Section 8613.5</u>. *(Stats.1992, c. 162 (A.B.2650), § 10, operative Jan. 1, 1994. Amended by Stats.2022, c. 159 (A.B. 2495), § 10, eff. Jan. 1, 2023.)*

Cross References

Person defined for purposes of this Code, see Family Code § 105.

§ 9324

Prospective adoptive parent, defined, see Family Code § 8542.

Research References

Forms

2 California Transactions Forms--Family Law § 6:167, Power of Attorney for Counsel to Appear on Behalf of Party to Adoption of Adult or Married Minor.

§ 9325. Investigation and report

No investigation or report to the court by any public officer or agency is required, but the court may require the county probation officer or the department to investigate the circumstances of the proposed adoption and report thereon, with recommendations, to the court before the hearing. *(Stats.1992, c. 162 (A.B.2650), § 10, operative Jan. 1, 1994.)*

Cross References

County defined for purposes of this Code, see Family Code § 67.
Department defined, see Family Code § 8518.

Research References

Forms

2 California Transactions Forms--Family Law § 6:158, Governing Law—Venue and Procedure.
West's California Code Forms, Family § 9320, Comment Overview—Procedure for Adult Adoption.

§ 9326. Notice of hearing of proposed adoption of developmentally disabled adult

The prospective adoptive parent shall mail or personally serve notice of the hearing and a copy of the petition to the director of the regional center for the developmentally disabled, established pursuant to Chapter 5 (commencing with Section 4620) of Division 4.5 of the Welfare and Institutions Code, and to any living birth parents or adult children of the proposed adoptee, at least 30 days before the day of the hearing on an adoption petition in any case in which both of the following conditions exist:

(a) The proposed adoptee is an adult with developmental disabilities.

(b) The prospective adoptive parent is a provider of board and care, treatment, habilitation, or other services to persons with developmental disabilities or is a spouse or employee of a provider. *(Stats.1992, c. 162 (A.B.2650), § 10, operative Jan. 1, 1994.)*

Cross References

Adult defined for purposes of this Code, see Family Code § 6501.
Birth parent, defined, see Family Code § 8512.
Person defined for purposes of this Code, see Family Code § 105.
Prospective adoptive parent, defined, see Family Code § 8542.
References to husband, wife, spouses and married persons, persons included for purposes of this Code, see Family Code § 11.

Research References

Forms

2 California Transactions Forms--Family Law § 6:158, Governing Law—Venue and Procedure.

§ 9327. Report on proposed adoption of developmentally disabled adult

If the prospective adoptive parent is a provider of board and care, treatment, habilitation, or other services to persons with developmental disabilities, or is a spouse or employee of a provider, and seeks to adopt an unrelated adult with developmental disabilities, the regional center for the developmentally disabled notified pursuant to Section 9326 shall file a written report with the court regarding the suitability of the proposed adoption in meeting the needs of the proposed adoptee and regarding any known previous adoption by the prospective adoptive parent. *(Stats.1992, c. 162 (A.B.2650), § 10, operative Jan. 1, 1994.)*

Cross References

Adult defined for purposes of this Code, see Family Code § 6501.
Person defined for purposes of this Code, see Family Code § 105.
Prospective adoptive parent, defined, see Family Code § 8542.
References to husband, wife, spouses and married persons, persons included for purposes of this Code, see Family Code § 11.

Research References

Forms

2 California Transactions Forms--Family Law § 6:158, Governing Law—Venue and Procedure.
West's California Code Forms, Family § 9320, Comment Overview—Procedure for Adult Adoption.

§ 9328. Hearing; order of adoption or denial of petitions

(a) At the hearing the court shall examine the parties, or the counsel of any party not present in person.

(b) If the court is satisfied that the adoption will be in the best interests of the persons seeking the adoption and in the public interest and that there is no reason why the petition should not be granted, the court shall approve the adoption agreement and make an order of adoption declaring that the person adopted is the child of the adoptive parent. Otherwise, the court shall withhold approval of the agreement and deny the petition.

(c) In determining whether or not the adoption of any person pursuant to this part is in the best interests of the persons seeking the adoption or the public interest, the court may consider evidence, oral or written, whether or not it is in conformity with the Evidence Code. *(Stats.1992, c. 162 (A.B.2650), § 10, operative Jan. 1, 1994.)*

Cross References

Adoptive parent, defined, see Family Code § 8503.
Judgment and order defined for purposes of this Code, see Family Code § 100.
Person defined for purposes of this Code, see Family Code § 105.
Prospective adoptive parent, defined, see Family Code § 8542.

Research References

Forms

2 California Transactions Forms--Family Law § 6:5, Issues Common to All Types of Adoptions.
2 California Transactions Forms--Family Law § 6:164, Agreement of Adult Adoption.
West's California Code Forms, Family § 9320, Comment Overview—Procedure for Adult Adoption.

CHAPTER 3. PROCEDURE FOR TERMINATING ADULT ADOPTION

Section
9340. Filing of petition; contents of petition; consent to termination; order.

§ 9340. Filing of petition; contents of petition; consent to termination; order

(a) Any person who has been adopted under this part may, upon written notice to the adoptive parent, file a petition to terminate the relationship of parent and child. The petition shall state the name and address of the petitioner, the name and address of the adoptive parent, the date and place of the adoption, and the circumstances upon which the petition is based.

(b) If the adoptive parent consents in writing to the termination, an order terminating the relationship of parent and child may be issued by the court without further notice.

(c) If the adoptive parent does not consent in writing to the termination, a written response shall be filed within 30 days of the date of mailing of the notice, and the matter shall be set for hearing. The court may require an investigation by the county probation officer or the department. *(Stats.1992, c. 162 (A.B.2650), § 10, operative Jan. 1, 1994.)*

Cross References

Adoptive parent, defined, see Family Code § 8503.
County defined for purposes of this Code, see Family Code § 67.
Department defined, see Family Code § 8518.
Judgment and order defined for purposes of this Code, see Family Code § 100.

Person defined for purposes of this Code, see Family Code § 105.
Petitioner defined for purposes of this Code, see Family Code § 126.
State defined for purposes of this Code, see Family Code § 145.
Verification of pleadings, see Family Code § 212.

Research References

Forms

2 California Transactions Forms--Family Law § 6:2, Governing Law.
2 California Transactions Forms--Family Law § 6:158, Governing Law-- Venue and Procedure.
2 California Transactions Forms--Family Law § 6:162, Termination of Adoption.

Division 14

FAMILY LAW FACILITATOR ACT

Section
10000. Short title.
10001. Legislative findings and declarations.
10002. Family law facilitator office; appointment of facilitator.
10003. Application of division.
10004. Facilitator services.
10005. Additional facilitator duties.
10006. Access to court hearing; protocol.
10007. Cost to parties.
10008. Child support obligations; services provided; services of facilitator.
10010. Standards for office.
10011. Title IV-D funding; federal approval.
10012. Domestic violence history; separate meetings with parties.
10013. Facilitator; attorney-client relationship; notice.
10014. Person employed or supervised by facilitator; public comments; ethical requirements.
10015. Forms.

Cross References

Child support commissioners and family law facilitators, program funding provided to Judicial Council, see Family Code § 17712.
Title IV-D state plan administration, see Family Code § 17202.
Trial Court Operations Fund, establishment by board of supervisors, deposits, see Government Code § 77009.

§ 10000. Short title

This division shall be known and may be cited as the Family Law Facilitator Act. *(Added by Stats.1996, c. 957 (A.B.1058), § 9.)*

Research References

Forms

California Practice Guide: Rutter Family Law Forms Form 1:32, Glossary of Common Family Law Terms, Phrases and Concepts (Enclosure to Form 1:31).

§ 10001. Legislative findings and declarations

(a) The Legislature finds and declares the following:

(1) Child and spousal support are serious legal obligations. The entry of a child support order is frequently delayed while parents engage in protracted litigation concerning custody and visitation. The current system for obtaining child and spousal support orders is suffering because the family courts are unduly burdened with heavy case loads and do not have sufficient personnel to meet increased demands on the courts.

(2) Reports to the Legislature regarding the family law pilot projects in the Superior Courts of the Counties of Santa Clara and San Mateo indicate that the pilot projects have provided a cost-effective and efficient method for the courts to process family law cases that involve unrepresented litigants with issues concerning child support, spousal support, and health insurance.

(3) The reports to the Legislature further indicate that the pilot projects in both counties have been successful in making the process of obtaining court orders concerning child support, spousal support, and health insurance more accessible to unrepresented parties. Surveys conducted by both counties indicate a high degree of satisfaction with the services provided by the pilot projects.

(4) There is a compelling state interest in having a speedy, conflict-reducing system for resolving issues of child support, spousal support, and health insurance that is cost-effective and accessible to families that cannot afford legal representation.

(b) Therefore, it is the intent of the Legislature to make the services provided in the family law pilot projects in the Counties of Santa Clara and San Mateo available to unrepresented parties in the superior courts of all California counties. *(Added by Stats.1996, c. 957 (A.B.1058), § 9.)*

Cross References

County defined for purposes of this Code, see Family Code § 67.
Judgment and order defined for purposes of this Code, see Family Code § 100.
Spousal support defined for purposes of this Code, see Family Code § 142.
State defined for purposes of this Code, see Family Code § 145.
Support defined for purposes of this Code, see Family Code § 150.
Support order defined for purposes of this Code, see Family Code § 155.

§ 10002. Family law facilitator office; appointment of facilitator

Each superior court shall maintain an office of the family law facilitator. The office of the family law facilitator shall be staffed by an attorney licensed to practice law in this state who has mediation or litigation experience, or both, in the field of family law. The family law facilitator shall be appointed by the superior court. *(Added by Stats.1996, c. 957 (A.B.1058), § 9.)*

Cross References

State defined for purposes of this Code, see Family Code § 145.

§ 10003. Application of division

This division shall apply to all actions or proceedings for temporary or permanent child support, spousal support, health insurance, child custody, or visitation in a proceeding for dissolution of marriage, nullity of marriage, legal separation, or exclusive child custody, or pursuant to the Uniform Parentage Act (Part 3 (commencing with Section 7600) of Division 12) or the Domestic Violence Prevention Act (Division 10 (commencing with Section 6200)). *(Added by Stats.1996, c. 957 (A.B.1058), § 9. Amended by Stats.1999, c. 652 (S.B.240), § 12.)*

§ 10003 FAMILY LAW FACILITATOR ACT

Cross References

Proceeding defined for purposes of this Code, see Family Code § 110.
Spousal support defined for purposes of this Code, see Family Code § 142.
Support defined for purposes of this Code, see Family Code § 150.

§ 10004. Facilitator services

Services provided by the family law facilitator shall include, but are not limited to, the following: providing educational materials to parents concerning the process of establishing parentage and establishing, modifying, and enforcing child support and spousal support in the courts; distributing necessary court forms and voluntary declarations of paternity; providing assistance in completing forms; preparing support schedules based upon statutory guidelines; and providing referrals to the local child support agency, family court services, and other community agencies and resources that provide services for parents and children. In counties where a family law information center exists, the family law facilitator shall provide assistance on child support issues. *(Added by Stats.1996, c. 957 (A.B.1058), § 9. Amended by Stats.1999, c. 652 (S.B.240), § 13.)*

Cross References

County defined for purposes of this Code, see Family Code § 67.
Spousal support defined for purposes of this Code, see Family Code § 142.
Support defined for purposes of this Code, see Family Code § 150.

§ 10005. Additional facilitator duties

(a) By local rule, the superior court may designate additional duties of the family law facilitator, which may include, but are not limited to, the following:

(1) Meeting with litigants to mediate issues of child support, spousal support, and maintenance of health insurance, subject to Section 10012. Actions in which one or both of the parties are unrepresented by counsel shall have priority.

(2) Drafting stipulations to include all issues agreed to by the parties, which may include issues other than those specified in Section 10003.

(3) If the parties are unable to resolve issues with the assistance of the family law facilitator, prior to or at the hearing, and at the request of the court, the family law facilitator shall review the paperwork, examine documents, prepare support schedules, and advise the judge whether or not the matter is ready to proceed.

(4) Assisting the clerk in maintaining records.

(5) Preparing formal orders consistent with the court's announced order in cases where both parties are unrepresented.

(6) Serving as a special master in proceedings and making findings to the court unless the family law facilitator has served as a mediator in that case.

(7) Providing the services specified in Section 10004 concerning the issues of child custody and visitation as they relate to calculating child support, if funding is provided for that purpose.

(b) If staff and other resources are available and the duties listed in subdivision (a) have been accomplished, the duties of the family law facilitator may also include the following:

(1) Assisting the court with research and any other responsibilities that will enable the court to be responsive to the litigants' needs.

(2) Developing programs for bar and community outreach through day and evening programs, video recordings, and other innovative means that will assist unrepresented and financially disadvantaged litigants in gaining meaningful access to family court. These programs shall specifically include information concerning underutilized legislation, such as expedited child support orders (Chapter 5 (commencing with Section 3620) of Part 1 of Division 9), and preexisting, court-sponsored programs, such as supervised visitation and appointment of attorneys for children. *(Added by Stats. 1996, c. 957 (A.B.1058), § 9. Amended by Stats.1997, c. 599 (A.B.573), § 45; Stats.1999, c. 652 (S.B.240), § 13.5; Stats.2009, c. 88 (A.B.176), § 39; Stats.2019, c. 115 (A.B.1817), § 138, eff. Jan. 1, 2020.)*

Cross References

Judgment and order defined for purposes of this Code, see Family Code § 100.
Proceeding defined for purposes of this Code, see Family Code § 110.
Spousal support defined for purposes of this Code, see Family Code § 142.
State defined for purposes of this Code, see Family Code § 145.
Support defined for purposes of this Code, see Family Code § 150.
Support order defined for purposes of this Code, see Family Code § 155.

§ 10006. Access to court hearing; protocol

The court shall adopt a protocol wherein all litigants, both unrepresented by counsel and represented by counsel, have ultimate access to a hearing before the court. *(Added by Stats.1996, c. 957 (A.B.1058), § 9.)*

§ 10007. Cost to parties

The court shall provide the family law facilitator at no cost to the parties. *(Added by Stats.1996, c. 957 (A.B.1058), § 9.)*

§ 10008. Child support obligations; services provided; services of facilitator

(a) Except as provided in subdivision (b), nothing in this chapter shall be construed to apply to a child for whom services are provided or required to be provided by a local child support agency pursuant to Section 17400.

(b) In cases in which the services of the local child support agency are provided pursuant to Section 17400, either parent may utilize the services of the family law facilitator that are specified in Section 10004. In order for a custodial parent who is receiving the services of the local child support agency pursuant to Section 17400 to utilize the services specified in Section 10005 relating to support, the custodial parent must obtain written authorization from the local child support agency. It is not the intent of the Legislature in enacting this section to limit the duties of local child support agencies with respect to seeking child support payments or to in any way limit or supersede other provisions of this code respecting temporary child support. *(Added by Stats.1996, c. 957 (A.B.1058), § 9. Amended by Stats.2000, c. 808 (A.B.1358), § 78, eff. Sept. 28, 2000.)*

Cross References

Judgment and order defined for purposes of this Code, see Family Code § 100.
Support defined for purposes of this Code, see Family Code § 150.

§ 10010. Standards for office

The Judicial Council shall adopt minimum standards for the office of the family law facilitator and any forms or rules of court that are necessary to implement this division. *(Added by Stats.1996, c. 957 (A.B.1058), § 9.)*

§ 10011. Title IV–D funding; federal approval

The Director of the State Department of Social Services shall seek approval from the United States Department of Health and Human Services, Office of Child Support Enforcement, to utilize funding under Title IV–D of the Social Security Act [1] for the services provided pursuant to this division. *(Added by Stats.1996, c. 957 (A.B.1058), § 9.)*

[1] See 42 U.S.C.A. § 651 et seq.

Cross References

Department of Health Care Services, generally, see Health and Safety Code § 100100 et seq.
State defined for purposes of this Code, see Family Code § 145.
Support defined for purposes of this Code, see Family Code § 150.

DEPARTMENT OF CHILD SUPPORT SERVICES

Title IV-D state plan administration, see Family Code § 17202.

§ 10012. Domestic violence history; separate meetings with parties

(a) In a proceeding in which mediation is required pursuant to paragraph (1) of subdivision (a) of Section 10005, where there has been a history of domestic violence between the parties or where a protective order as defined in Section 6218 is in effect, at the request of the party alleging domestic violence in a written declaration under penalty of perjury or protected by the order, the family law facilitator shall meet with the parties separately and at separate times.

(b) Any intake form that the office of the family law facilitator requires the parties to complete before the commencement of mediation shall state that, if a party alleging domestic violence in a written declaration under penalty of perjury or a party protected by a protective order so requests, the mediator will meet with the parties separately and at separate times. *(Added by Stats.1996, c. 957 (A.B.1058), § 9.)*

Cross References

Domestic violence defined for purposes of this Code, see Family Code § 6211.
Judgment and order defined for purposes of this Code, see Family Code § 100.
Proceeding defined for purposes of this Code, see Family Code § 110.
State defined for purposes of this Code, see Family Code § 145.

§ 10013. Facilitator; attorney-client relationship; notice

The family law facilitator shall not represent any party. No attorney-client relationship is created between a party and the family law facilitator as a result of any information or services provided to the party by the family law facilitator. The family law facilitator shall give conspicuous notice that no attorney-client relationship exists between the facilitator, its staff, and the family law litigant. The notice shall include the advice that the absence of an attorney-client relationship means that communications between the party and the family law facilitator are not privileged and that the family law facilitator may provide services to the other party. *(Added by Stats.1999, c. 652 (S.B.240), § 14.)*

§ 10014. Person employed or supervised by facilitator; public comments; ethical requirements

A person employed by, or directly supervised by, the family law facilitator shall not make any public comment about a pending or impending proceeding in the court as provided by paragraph (9) of subdivision (B) of Canon 3 of the Code of Judicial Ethics. All persons employed by or directly supervised by the family law facilitator shall be provided a copy of paragraph (9) of subdivision (B) of Canon 3 of the Code of Judicial Ethics, and shall be required to sign an acknowledgment that the person is aware of its provisions. *(Added by Stats.1999, c. 652 (S.B.240), § 15. Amended by Stats.2019, c. 115 (A.B.1817), § 139, eff. Jan. 1, 2020.)*

Cross References

Person defined for purposes of this Code, see Family Code § 105.
Proceeding defined for purposes of this Code, see Family Code § 110.

§ 10015. Forms

The Judicial Council shall create any necessary forms to advise the parties of the types of services provided, that there is no attorney-client relationship, that the family law facilitator is not responsible for the outcome of any case, that the family law facilitator does not represent any party and will not appear in court on the party's behalf, and that the other party may also be receiving information and services from the family law facilitator. *(Added by Stats.1999, c. 652 (S.B.240), § 15.5.)*

Research References

Forms

West's California Judicial Council Forms FL-940, Office of the Family Law Facilitator Disclosure (Also Available in Chinese, Korean, Spanish, and Vietnamese).

Division 15

FRIEND OF THE COURT ACT [REPEALED]

§§ 10100 to 10102. Repealed by Stats.1999, c. 1004 (A.B.673), § 6

Division 16

FAMILY LAW INFORMATION CENTERS [REPEALED]

§§ 15000 to 15012. Repealed by Stats.1999, c. 886 (S.B.874), § 2, operative Jan. 1, 2004

Division 17

SUPPORT SERVICES

Chapter	Section
1. Department of Child Support Services	17000
2. Child Support Enforcement	17400
5. Complaint Resolution	17800

Cross References

Consumer credit reporting agencies act, definitions involving this division, see Civil Code § 1785.3.
Definitions governing this division, see Family Code § 3500 et seq.
Enforcement of support judgments, authority of local child support agencies, delivery of writ of execution, see Code of Civil Procedure § 689.040.

SUPPORT SERVICES

Right to custody of minor child, sex offenders, murderers, see Family Code § 3030.

CHAPTER 1. DEPARTMENT OF CHILD SUPPORT SERVICES

Article	Section
1. General	17000
2. Organization	17200
3. Director of Child Support Services	17300
4. Statewide Registry for Child Support	17390

Cross References

Child support delinquency, statewide automated system for reporting administered by the department, see Family Code § 4701.

Review of statewide uniform guidelines for child support by Judicial Council, recommendations submitted to the Legislature and department, see Family Code § 4054.

Uniform Interstate Family Support Act,
  Duties of state information agency, see Family Code § 5700.310.
  Reciprocal arrangements for child support established by foreign countries, determination by the department, see Family Code § 5700.308.

ARTICLE 1. GENERAL

Section
17000. Definitions.

§ 17000. Definitions

The definitions contained in this section, and definitions applicable to Division 9 (commencing with Section 3500), shall govern the construction of this division, unless the context requires otherwise.

(a) "Child support debt" means the amount of money owed as child support pursuant to a court order.

(b) "Child support order" means a court order for the payment of a set or determinable amount of support by a parent or a court order requiring a parent to provide for health insurance coverage. "Child support order" includes any court order for spousal support or for medical support to the extent these obligations are to be enforced by a single state agency for child support under Title IV–D.

(c) "Court" means any superior court of this state and any court or tribunal of another state that has jurisdiction to determine the liability of persons for the support of another person.

(d) "Court order" means a judgment, decree, or order of any court of this state that orders the payment of a set or determinable amount of support by a parent. It does not include any order or decree of any proceeding in which a court did not order support.

(e) "Department" means the Department of Child Support Services.

(f) "Dependent child" means any of the following:

(1) Any person under 18 years of age who is not emancipated, self-supporting, married, or a member of the Armed Forces of the United States.

(2) Any unmarried person who is at least 18 years of age but who has not reached 19 years of age, is not emancipated, and is a student regularly attending high school or a program of vocational or technical training designed to train that person for gainful employment.

(g) "Director" means the Director of Child Support Services or an authorized representative.

(h) "Local child support agency" means the county department of child support services created pursuant to this chapter and with which the department has entered into a cooperative agreement, to secure child and spousal support, medical support, and determine paternity. Local child support agency includes county programs in multiple counties that have been consolidated into a single agency pursuant to subdivision (a) of Section 17304.

(i) "Parent" means the natural or adoptive father or mother of a dependent child, and includes any person who has an enforceable obligation to support a dependent child.

(j) "Public assistance" means any amount paid under the California Work Opportunity and Responsibility to Kids Act (Chapter 2 (commencing with Section 11200) of Part 3 of Division 9 of the Welfare and Institutions Code), or any Medi–Cal benefit, for the benefit of any dependent child or the caretaker of a child.

(k) "Public assistance debt" means any amount paid under the California Work Opportunity and Responsibility to Kids Act, contained in Chapter 2 (commencing with Section 11200) of Part 3 of Division 9 of the Welfare and Institutions Code, for the benefit of a dependent child or the caretaker of a child for whom the department is authorized to seek recoupment under this division, subject to applicable federal law.

(*l*) "Title IV-D" or "IV-D" means Part D of Title IV of the federal Social Security Act (42 U.S.C. Sec. 651 et seq.). *(Added by Stats.1999, c. 478 (A.B.196), § 1. Amended by Stats.1999, c. 480 (S.B.542), § 5; Stats.2000, c. 808 (A.B.1358), § 78.3, eff. Sept. 28, 2000; Stats.2003, c. 308 (A.B.738), § 3; Stats.2019, c. 115 (A.B.1817), § 140, eff. Jan. 1, 2020.)*

Cross References

Collection of tax, changes and transition of authority and responsibilities from county or district attorneys to local child support agency, see Revenue and Taxation Code § 19275.
County defined for purposes of this Code, see Family Code § 67.
County employees retirement law of 1937, local prosecutor, local public defender, local public defender investigator defined, see Government Code § 31469.2.
Judgment and order defined for purposes of this Code, see Family Code § 100.
Person defined for purposes of this Code, see Family Code § 105.
Proceeding defined for purposes of this Code, see Family Code § 110.
Public employees' retirement system, safety member classification–contracting agencies and schools, see Government Code § 20423.6.
Spousal support defined for purposes of this Code, see Family Code § 142.
State defined for purposes of this Code, see Family Code § 145.
Support defined for purposes of this Code, see Family Code § 150.
Support order defined for purposes of this Code, see Family Code § 155.

Research References

Forms

California Practice Guide: Rutter Family Law Forms Form 1:32, Glossary of Common Family Law Terms, Phrases and Concepts (Enclosure to Form 1:31).
West's California Code Forms, Family § 4200, Comment Overview—Child Support Orders to Parents.
West's California Code Forms, Family § 4500, Comment Overview—Enforcement of Support Orders.
West's California Code Forms, Family § 5230, Comment Overview—Earnings Assignment Order.

ARTICLE 2. ORGANIZATION

Section
17200. Creation and duties.
17202. Title IV–D state plan administration; state plan functions.
17204. Director and administrative units.
17206. Structure and staff.
17208. Cost reduction; speed and efficiency; enforcement through local agencies; federal funds; administrative service fee.
17210. Local agency accessibility.
17211. Child Support Assurance Demonstration Project; county demonstration projects to provide employ-

Section
ment and training services to nonsupporting noncustodial parents.
17212. Privacy rights; confidentiality of records.

Cross References

Definitions governing this Division, see Family Code §§ 3500 et seq., 17000.

§ 17200. Creation and duties

The Department of Child Support Services is hereby created within the California Health and Human Services Agency. The department shall administer all services and perform all functions necessary to establish, collect, and distribute child support. *(Added by Stats.1999, c. 478 (A.B.196), § 1.)*

Cross References

Child support delinquency, statewide automated system for reporting administered by the department, see Family Code § 4701.
Review of statewide uniform guidelines for child support by Judicial Council, recommendations submitted to the Legislature and department, see Family Code § 4054.
Support defined for purposes of this Code, see Family Code § 150.
Uniform Interstate Family Support Act,
  Duties of state information agency, see Family Code § 5700.310.
  Reciprocal arrangements for child support established by foreign countries, determination by the department, see Family Code § 5700.308.

Research References

Forms
1 California Transactions Forms--Family Law § 3:3, Child Support.
1 California Transactions Forms--Family Law § 3:21, Jurisdiction for Orders to Pay Child Support.

§ 17202. Title IV–D state plan administration; state plan functions

(a) The department is hereby designated the single organizational unit whose duty it shall be to administer the Title IV–D state plan for securing child and spousal support, medical support, and determining paternity. State plan functions shall be performed by other agencies as required by law, by delegation of the department, or by cooperative agreements.

(b) The department shall appoint the local child support agency, as defined in Section 17304, or any other entity receiving federal tax information in performance of its child support duties as its designee for purposes of paragraph (26) of subdivision (b) of Section 11105 of the Penal Code.

(c) For purposes of this section, "federal tax information" is as defined in Section 1044 of the Government Code. *(Added by Stats.1999, c. 478 (A.B.196), § 1. Amended by Stats.2017, c. 19 (A.B.111), § 7, eff. June 27, 2017.)*

Cross References

Spousal support defined for purposes of this Code, see Family Code § 142.
State defined for purposes of this Code, see Family Code § 145.
Support defined for purposes of this Code, see Family Code § 150.
Title IV–D funding, federal approval, see Family Code § 10011.

§ 17204. Director and administrative units

The department consists of the director and such division or other administrative units as the director may find necessary. *(Added by Stats.1999, c. 478 (A.B.196), § 1.)*

§ 17206. Structure and staff

The department shall ensure that there is an adequate organizational structure and sufficient staff to perform functions delegated to any governmental unit relating to Part D (commencing with Section 651) of Subchapter 4 of Chapter 7 of Title 42 of the United States Code, including a sufficient number of attorneys to ensure that all requirements of due process are satisfied in the establishment and enforcement of child support orders. *(Added by Stats.1999, c. 478 (A.B.196), § 1.)*

Cross References

Judgment and order defined for purposes of this Code, see Family Code § 100.
State defined for purposes of this Code, see Family Code § 145.
Support defined for purposes of this Code, see Family Code § 150.
Support order defined for purposes of this Code, see Family Code § 155.

§ 17208. Cost reduction; speed and efficiency; enforcement through local agencies; federal funds; administrative service fee

(a) The department shall reduce the cost of, and increase the speed and efficiency of, child support enforcement operations. It is the intent of the Legislature to operate the child support enforcement program through local child support agencies without a net increase in state General Fund or county general fund costs, considering all increases to the General Fund as a result of increased collections and welfare recoupment.

(b) The department shall maximize the use of federal funds available for the costs of administering a child support services department, and to the maximum extent feasible, obtain funds from federal financial incentives for the efficient collection of child support, to defray the remaining costs of administration of the department consistent with effective and efficient support enforcement.

(c) Effective October 1, 2019, the Department of Child Support Services shall impose an administrative service fee in the amount of thirty-five dollars ($35) on a never-assisted custodial party receiving services from the California child support program for order establishment, enforcement, and collection services provided. The annual amount of child support payments collected on behalf of the custodial party must be five hundred fifty dollars ($550) or more before an administrative service fee is imposed pursuant to this subdivision. The fee shall be deducted from the custodial party's collection payment at the time the collection payments for that year have reached levels specified by the department. *(Added by Stats. 1999, c. 478 (A.B.196), § 1. Amended by Stats.2009–2010, 4th Ex.Sess., c. 4 (A.B.4), § 1, eff. July 28, 2009; Stats.2019, c. 27 (S.B.80), § 4, eff. June 27, 2019.)*

Cross References

County defined for purposes of this Code, see Family Code § 67.
State defined for purposes of this Code, see Family Code § 145.
Support defined for purposes of this Code, see Family Code § 150.
Title IV–D funding, federal approval, see Family Code § 10011.

§ 17210. Local agency accessibility

The department shall ensure that the local child support agency offices and services are reasonably accessible throughout the counties, and shall establish systems for informing the public, including custodial and noncustodial parents of dependent children, of its services and operations. *(Added by Stats.1999, c. 478 (A.B.196), § 1.)*

Cross References

County defined for purposes of this Code, see Family Code § 67.
Support defined for purposes of this Code, see Family Code § 150.

§ 17211. Child Support Assurance Demonstration Project; county demonstration projects to provide employment and training services to nonsupporting noncustodial parents

The department shall administer the Child Support Assurance Demonstration Project established by Article 5 (commencing with Section 18241) of Chapter 3.3 of Part 6 of the Welfare and Institutions Code, and the county demonstration projects to provide employment and training services to nonsupporting noncustodial parents authorized by Section 18205.5 of the Welfare and Institutions Code. However, the department may contract with the State

Department of Social Services to continue development and implementation of these demonstration projects until they have been fully implemented. After the demonstration projects have been fully implemented, the department shall consult with the State Department of Social Services on the administration of the projects. The contracts for evaluation of the demonstration projects shall continue to be maintained by the State Department of Social Services. The department shall be responsible for the final evaluation of the projects. *(Added by Stats.1999, c. 478 (A.B.196), § 1. Amended by Stats.1999, c. 480 (S.B.542), § 6.)*

Cross References

County defined for purposes of this Code, see Family Code § 67.
State defined for purposes of this Code, see Family Code § 145.
Support defined for purposes of this Code, see Family Code § 150.

§ 17212. Privacy rights; confidentiality of records

(a) It is the intent of the Legislature to protect individual rights of privacy, and to facilitate and enhance the effectiveness of the child and spousal support enforcement program, by ensuring the confidentiality of support enforcement and child abduction records, and to thereby encourage the full and frank disclosure of information relevant to all of the following:

(1) The establishment or maintenance of parent and child relationships and support obligations.

(2) The enforcement of the child support liability of absent parents.

(3) The enforcement of spousal support liability of the spouse or former spouse to the extent required by the state plan under Section 17604 and Part 6 (commencing with Section 5700.101) of Division 9.

(4) The location of absent parents.

(5) The location of parents and children abducted, concealed, or detained by them.

(b)(1)(A) Except as provided in subdivision (c), all files, applications, papers, documents, and records established or maintained by a public entity pursuant to the administration and implementation of the child and spousal support enforcement program established pursuant to Part D (commencing with Section 651) of Subchapter IV of Chapter 7 of Title 42 of the United States Code and this division, shall be confidential, and shall not be open to examination or released for disclosure for any purpose not directly connected with the administration of the child and spousal support enforcement program. A public entity shall not disclose any file, application, paper, document, or record, or the information contained therein, except as expressly authorized by this section.

(B) For purposes of this section, "public entity" does not include the court. This subparagraph is declaratory of existing law.

(2) Information shall not be released or the whereabouts of one party or the child disclosed to another party, or to the attorney of any other party, if a protective order has been issued by a court or administrative agency with respect to the party, a good cause claim under Section 11477.04 of the Welfare and Institutions Code has been approved or is pending, or the public agency responsible for establishing paternity or enforcing support has reason to believe that the release of the information may result in physical or emotional harm to the party or the child. When a local child support agency is prohibited from releasing information pursuant to this subdivision, the information shall be omitted from any pleading or document to be submitted to the court and this subdivision shall be cited in the pleading or other document as the authority for the omission. The information shall be released only upon an order of the court pursuant to paragraph (6) of subdivision (c).

(3) Notwithstanding any other law, a proof of service filed by the local child support agency shall not disclose the address where service of process was accomplished. Instead, the local child support agency shall keep the address in its own records. The proof of service shall specify that the address is on record at the local child support agency and that the address may be released only upon an order from the court pursuant to paragraph (6) of subdivision (c). The local child support agency shall, upon request by a party served, release to that person the address where service was effected.

(c) Disclosure of the information described in subdivision (b) is authorized as follows:

(1) All files, applications, papers, documents, and records as described in subdivision (b) shall be available and may be used by a public entity for all administrative, civil, or criminal investigations, actions, proceedings, or prosecutions conducted in connection with the administration of the child and spousal support enforcement program approved under Part D (commencing with Section 651) of Subchapter IV of Chapter 7 of Title 42 of the United States Code and to the county welfare department responsible for administering a program operated under a state plan pursuant to Part A, Subpart 1 or 2 of Part B, or Part E of Subchapter IV of Chapter 7 of Title 42 of the United States Code.

(2) A document requested by a person who wrote, prepared, or furnished the document may be examined by or disclosed to that person or a designee.

(3) The payment history of an obligor pursuant to a support order may be examined by or released to the court, the obligor, or the person on whose behalf enforcement actions are being taken or that person's designee.

(4) An income and expense declaration of either parent may be released to the other parent for the purpose of establishing or modifying a support order.

(5) Public records subject to disclosure under the California Public Records Act (Division 10 (commencing with Section 7920.000) of Title 1 of the Government Code) may be released.

(6) After a noticed motion and a finding by the court, in a case in which establishment or enforcement actions are being taken, that release or disclosure to the obligor or obligee is required by due process of law, the court may order a public entity that possesses an application, paper, document, or record as described in subdivision (b) to make that item available to the obligor or obligee for examination or copying, or to disclose to the obligor or obligee the contents of that item. Article 9 (commencing with Section 1040) of Chapter 4 of Division 8 of the Evidence Code shall not be applicable to proceedings under this part. At any hearing of a motion filed pursuant to this section, the court shall inquire of the local child support agency and the parties appearing at the hearing if there is reason to believe that release of the requested information may result in physical or emotional harm to a party. If the court determines that harm may occur, the court shall issue any protective orders or injunctive orders restricting the use and disclosure of the information as are necessary to protect the individuals.

(7) To the extent not prohibited by federal law or regulation, information indicating the existence or imminent threat of a crime against a child, or location of a concealed, detained, or abducted child, or the location of the concealing, detaining, or abducting person, may be disclosed to a district attorney, an appropriate law enforcement agency, or to a state or county child protective agency, or may be used in any judicial proceedings to prosecute that crime or to protect the child.

(8) The social security number, most recent address, and the place of employment of the absent parent may be released to an authorized person as defined in Section 653(c) of Title 42 of the United States Code, only if the authorized person has filed a request for the information, and only if the information has been provided to the California Parent Locator Service by the federal Parent Locator Service pursuant to Section 653 of Title 42 of the United States Code.

(9) A parent's or relative's name, social security number, most recent address, telephone number, place of employment, or other contact information may be released to a county child welfare agency or county probation department pursuant to subdivision (c) of Section 17506.

(d)(1) "Administration and implementation of the child and spousal support enforcement program," as used in this division, means the carrying out of the state and local plans for establishing, modifying, and enforcing child support obligations, enforcing spousal support orders, and determining paternity pursuant to Part D (commencing with Section 651) of Subchapter IV of Chapter 7 of Title 42 of the United States Code and this article.

(2) For purposes of this division, "obligor" means a person owing a duty of support.

(3) As used in this division, "putative parent" shall refer to any person reasonably believed to be the parent of a child for whom the local child support agency is attempting to establish paternity or establish, modify, or enforce support pursuant to Section 17400.

(e) A person who willfully, knowingly, and intentionally violates this section is guilty of a misdemeanor.

(f) This section does not compel the disclosure of information relating to a deserting parent who is a recipient of aid under a public assistance program for which federal aid is paid to this state, if that information is required to be kept confidential by the federal law or regulations relating to the program. *(Added by Stats.1999, c. 478 (A.B.196), § 1. Amended by Stats.1999, c. 653 (A.B.380), § 12; Stats.2000, c. 808 (A.B.1358), § 79, eff. Sept. 28, 2000; Stats.2001, c. 755 (S.B.943), § 10, eff. Oct. 12, 2001; Stats.2012, c. 637 (A.B.1751), § 2; Stats.2014, c. 772 (S.B.1460), § 2, eff. Jan. 1, 2015; Stats.2015, c. 493 (S.B.646), § 7, eff. Jan. 1, 2016; Stats.2016, c. 474 (A.B.2882), § 11, eff. Jan. 1, 2017; Stats.2019, c. 115 (A.B.1817), § 141, eff. Jan. 1, 2020; Stats.2020, c. 36 (A.B.3364), § 30, eff. Jan. 1, 2021; Stats.2021, c. 615 (A.B.474), § 106, eff. Jan. 1, 2022, operative Jan. 1, 2023.)*

Cross References

County defined for purposes of this Code, see Family Code § 67.
Financial Institution Data Match System, violation of these provisions for misuse of information for other than enforcement and collection of child support delinquency, see Family Code § 17453.
Judgment and order defined for purposes of this Code, see Family Code § 100.
Misdemeanors, definition and penalties, see Penal Code §§ 17, 19 and 19.2.
Person defined for purposes of this Code, see Family Code § 105.
Proceeding defined for purposes of this Code, see Family Code § 110.
Protective order defined for purposes of this Code, see Family Code § 6218.
References to husband, wife, spouses and married persons, persons included for purposes of this Code, see Family Code § 11.
Similar provisions, see Welfare and Institutions Code § 11478.1.
Social security numbers, confidentiality in forms used in collection of child support payments, see Family Code § 2024.5.
Spousal support defined for purposes of this Code, see Family Code § 142.
State defined for purposes of this Code, see Family Code § 145.
Support defined for purposes of this Code, see Family Code § 150.
Support order defined for purposes of this Code, see Family Code § 155.

ARTICLE 3. DIRECTOR OF CHILD SUPPORT SERVICES

Section
17300. Appointment; salary; deputies.
17302. Duties.
17303. Legislative findings and declarations.
17304. County departments of child support services; duties; criminal enforcement; state plan for local agency functions; cooperative agreements; consolidation; oversight responsibility; district attorney responsibility, assets, and staff; administrators.
17305. Transition from district attorney to local agency.

Section
17306. Uniform forms, policies, and procedures for local agencies; duties of department.
17306.1. Implementation of revised local child support agency funding methodology; working sessions; written update describing recommended changes.
17307. Legislative findings and declarations with respect to authority and discretion of Department of Child Support Services to prevent, correct, or remedy effects of changes in timing of receipt of child support payments resulting solely from initial implementation of federally required State Disbursement Unit.
17308. Automated child support system.
17309. State Disbursement Unit.
17309.5. Employers required to make child support payments by electronic fund transfer; election to make payments; definitions.
17310. Regulations and general policies.
17311. Establishment and operation of Child Support Payment Trust Fund; legislative intent; General Fund loan.
17311.5. Trust agreement to receive or disburse child support collections; provisions of agreement; approved investment securities.
17311.7. Child support payment made to family through State Disbursement Unit; "alternate caregiver" defined.
17312. Regulations, orders, or standards.
17314. Staff; regional state administrators.
17316. Involvement with agency supervised by department.
17318. Application of Government Code § 11000 et seq.
17320. Temporary Assistance to Needy Families grant; federal penalties.
17325. Direct deposit of child support payments; qualifying account; requirements; definitions.

Cross References

Definitions governing this Division, see Family Code §§ 3500 et seq., 17000.

§ 17300. Appointment; salary; deputies

(a) With the consent of the Senate, the Governor shall appoint, to serve at the Governor's pleasure, an executive officer who shall be director of the department. In making the appointment the Governor shall consider training, demonstrated ability, experience, and leadership in organized child support enforcement administration. The director shall receive the salary provided for by Chapter 6 (commencing with Section 11550) of Part 1 of Division 3 of Title 2 of the Government Code.

(b) The Governor also may appoint, to serve at the Governor's pleasure, not to exceed two chief deputy directors of the department, and one deputy director of the department. The salaries of the chief deputy directors and the deputy director shall be fixed in accordance with law. *(Added by Stats.1999, c. 478 (A.B.196), § 1. Amended by Stats.1999, c. 480 (S.B.542), § 6.5; Stats.2019, c. 115 (A.B.1817), § 142, eff. Jan. 1, 2020.)*

Cross References

Support defined for purposes of this Code, see Family Code § 150.

§ 17302. Duties

The director shall do all of the following:

(a) Be responsible for the management of the department.

(b) Administer all federal and state laws and regulations pertaining to the administration of child support enforcement obligations.

(c) Perform all duties as may be prescribed by law, and any other administrative and executive duties imposed by law.

§ 17302

(d) Observe, and report to the Governor, the Legislature, and the public on, the conditions of child support enforcement activities throughout the state pursuant to subdivision (e) of Section 17602. (Added by Stats.1999, c. 478 (A.B.196), § 1. Amended by Stats.1999, c. 480 (S.B.542), § 7.)

Cross References

State defined for purposes of this Code, see Family Code § 145.
Support defined for purposes of this Code, see Family Code § 150.

§ 17303. Legislative findings and declarations

The Legislature finds and declares all of the following:

(a) Title IV–D of the federal Social Security Act, contained in Part D (commencing with Section 651) of Subchapter 4 of Chapter 7 of Title 42 of the United States Code, requires that there be a single state agency for child support enforcement. California's child support enforcement system is extremely complex, involving numerous state and local agencies. The state's system was divided between the State Department of Social Services, the Attorney General's office, the Franchise Tax Board, the Employment Development Department, the Department of Motor Vehicles, and the 58 county district attorneys' offices.

(b) The lack of coordination and integration between state and local child support agencies has been a major impediment to getting support to the children of this state. An effective child support enforcement program must have strong leadership and effective state oversight and management to best serve the needs of the children of the state.

(c) The state would benefit by centralizing its obligation to hold counties responsible for collecting support. Oversight would be best accomplished by direct management by the state.

(d) A single state agency for child support enforcement with strong leadership and direct accountability for local child support agencies will benefit the taxpayers of the state by reducing the inefficiencies introduced by involving multiple layers of government in child support enforcement operations. (Added by Stats.1999, c. 478 (A.B.196), § 1.)

Cross References

Attorney General, generally, see Government Code § 12500 et seq.
County defined for purposes of this Code, see Family Code § 67.
State defined for purposes of this Code, see Family Code § 145.
Support defined for purposes of this Code, see Family Code § 150.

§ 17304. County departments of child support services; duties; criminal enforcement; state plan for local agency functions; cooperative agreements; consolidation; oversight responsibility; district attorney responsibility, assets, and staff; administrators

To address the concerns stated by the Legislature in Section 17303, each county shall establish a new county department of child support services. Each department is also referred to in this division as the local child support agency. The local child support agency shall be separate and independent from any other county department and shall be responsible for promptly and effectively establishing, modifying, and enforcing child support obligations, including medical support, enforcing spousal support orders established by a court of competent jurisdiction, and determining paternity in the case of a child born out of wedlock. The local child support agency shall refer all cases requiring criminal enforcement services to the district attorney and the district attorney shall prosecute those cases, as appropriate. If a district attorney fails to comply with this section, the director shall notify the Attorney General and the Attorney General shall take appropriate action to secure compliance. The director shall be responsible for implementing and administering all aspects of the state plan that direct the functions to be performed by the local child support agencies relating to their Title IV–D operations. In developing the new system, all of the following shall apply:

(a) The director shall negotiate and enter into cooperative agreements with county and state agencies to carry out the requirements of the state plan and provide services relating to the establishment of paternity or the establishment, modification, or enforcement of child support obligations as required pursuant to Section 654 of Title 42 of the United States Code. The cooperative agreements shall require that the local child support agencies are reasonably accessible to the citizens of each county and are visible and accountable to the public for their activities. The director, in consultation with the impacted counties, may consolidate the local child support agencies, or any function of the agencies, in more than one county into a single local child support agency, if the director determines that the consolidation will increase the efficiency of the state Title IV–D program and each county has at least one local child support office accessible to the public.

(b) The director shall have direct oversight and supervision of the Title IV–D operations of the local child support agency, and no other local or state agency shall have any authority over the local child support agency as to any function relating to its Title IV–D operations. The local child support agency shall be responsible for the performance of child support enforcement activities required by law and regulation in a manner prescribed by the department. The administrator of the local child support agency shall be responsible for reporting to and responding to the director on all aspects of the child support program.

(c) Nothing in this section prohibits the local child support agency, with the prior approval of the director, from entering into cooperative arrangements with other county departments, as necessary to carry out the responsibilities imposed by this section pursuant to plans of cooperation submitted to the department and approved by the director. The local child support agency may not enter into a cooperative agreement or contract with any county department or independently elected official, including the office of the district attorney, to run, supervise, manage, or oversee the Title IV–D functions of the local child support agency. Until September 1, 2004, the local child support agency may enter into a cooperative agreement or contract of restricted scope and duration with a district attorney to utilize individual attorneys as necessary to carry out limited attorney services. Any cooperative agreement or contract for the attorney services shall be subject to approval by the department and contingent upon a written finding by the department that either the relatively small size of the local child support agency program, or other serious programmatic needs, arising as a result of the transition make it most efficient and cost-effective to contract for limited attorney services. The department shall ensure that any cooperative agreement or contract for attorney services provides that all attorneys be supervised by, and report directly to, the local child support agency, and comply with all state and federal child support laws and regulations. The office of the Legislative Analyst shall review and assess the efficiency and effectiveness of that cooperative agreement or contract, and shall report its findings to the Legislature by January 1, 2004. Within 60 days of receipt of a plan of cooperation or contract from the local child support agency, the department shall either approve the plan of cooperation or contract or notify the agency that the plan is denied. If an agency is notified that the plan is denied, the agency shall have the opportunity to resubmit a revised plan of cooperation or contract. If the director fails to respond in writing within 60 days of receipt, the plan shall otherwise be deemed approved. Nothing in this section shall be deemed an approval of program costs relative to the cooperative arrangements entered into by the counties with other county departments.

(d) In order to minimize the disruption of services provided and to capitalize on the expertise of employees, the director shall create a program that builds on existing staff and facilities to the fullest extent possible. All assets of the family support division in the district attorney's office shall become assets of the local child support agency.

(e)(1)(A) Except as provided in subparagraph (B), all employees and other personnel who serve the office of the district attorney and perform child support collection and enforcement activities shall become the employees and other personnel of the county child support agency at their existing or equivalent classifications, and at their existing salaries and benefits that include, but are not limited to, accrued and unused vacation, sick leave, personal leave, and health and pension plans.

(B) The Title IV–D director is entitled to become an employee of the local child support agency or may be selected as the administrator pursuant to the provisions of subdivision (f).

(2) Permanent employees of the office of the district attorney on the effective date of this chapter shall be deemed qualified, and no other qualifications shall be required for employment or retention in the county child support agency. Probationary employees on the effective date of this chapter shall retain their probationary status and rights, and shall not be deemed to have transferred, so as to require serving a new probationary period.

(3) Employment seniority of an employee of the office of the district attorney on the effective date of this chapter shall be counted toward seniority in the county child support agency and all time spent in the same, equivalent, or higher classification shall be counted toward classification seniority.

(4) An employee organization that has been recognized as the representative or exclusive representative of an established appropriate bargaining unit of employees who perform child support collection and enforcement activities shall continue to be recognized as the representative or exclusive representative of the same employees of the county.

(5) An existing memorandum of understanding or agreement between the county or the office of the district attorney and the employee organization shall remain in effect and be fully binding on the parties involved for the term of the agreement.

(6) Nothing in this section shall be construed to limit the rights of employees or employee organizations to bargain in good faith on matters of wages, hours, or other terms and conditions of employment, including the negotiation of workplace standards within the scope of bargaining as authorized by state and federal law.

(7)(A) Except as provided in subparagraph (B), a public agency shall, in implementing programs affected by the act of addition or amendment of this chapter to this code, perform program functions exclusively through the use of merit civil service employees of the public agency.

(B) Prior to transition from the district attorney to the local child support agency under Section 17305, the district attorney may continue existing contracts and their renewals, as appropriate. After the transition under Section 17305, any contracting out of program functions shall be approved by the director consistent with Section 31000 and following of the Government Code, except as otherwise provided in subdivision (c) with regard to attorney services. The director shall approve or disapprove a proposal to contract out within 60 days. Failure of the director to respond to a request to contract out within 60 days after receipt of the request shall be deemed approval, unless the director submits an extension to respond, which in no event shall be longer than 30 days.

(f) The administrator of the local child support agency shall be an employee of the county selected by the board of supervisors, or in the case of a city and county, selected by the mayor, pursuant to the qualifications established by the department. The administrator may hire staff, including attorneys, to fulfill the functions required by the agency and in conformity with any staffing requirements adopted by the department, including all those set forth in Section 17306. All staff shall be employees of the county and shall comply with all local, state, and federal child support laws, regulations, and directives.
(Added by Stats.1999, c. 478 (A.B.196), § 1. Amended by Stats.1999, c. 480 (S.B.542), § 8; Stats.2000, c. 808 (A.B.1358), § 80, eff. Sept. 28, 2000; Stats.2001, c. 755 (S.B.943), § 11, eff. Oct. 12, 2001.)

Cross References

Annual automation cooperation agreement, see Welfare and Institutions Code § 10081.
Attorney General, generally, see Government Code § 12500 et seq.
County defined for purposes of this Code, see Family Code § 67.
County employees retirement law of 1937, local prosecutor, local public defender, local public defender investigator defined, see Government Code § 31469.2.
Family support defined for purposes of this Code, see Family Code § 92.
Judgment and order defined for purposes of this Code, see Family Code § 100.
Local summary criminal history information, furnishing to authorized persons, see Penal Code § 13300.
Public employees' retirement system, safety member classification–contracting agencies and schools, see Government Code § 20423.6.
Spousal support defined for purposes of this Code, see Family Code § 142.
State defined for purposes of this Code, see Family Code § 145.
State summary criminal history information, see Penal Code § 11105.
Support defined for purposes of this Code, see Family Code § 150.
Support order defined for purposes of this Code, see Family Code § 155.
Support paid through county officers and forwarded to payee, see Family Code § 3555.

Research References

Forms

1 California Transactions Forms--Family Law § 3:3, Child Support.
1 California Transactions Forms--Family Law § 3:21, Jurisdiction for Orders to Pay Child Support.
West's California Judicial Council Forms FL–684, Request for Order and Supporting Declaration (Governmental).

§ 17305. Transition from district attorney to local agency

(a) In order to achieve an orderly and timely transition to the new system with minimal disruption of services, the director shall begin the transition from the office of the district attorney to the local child support agencies pursuant to Section 17304, commencing January 1, 2001. The director shall transfer the appropriate number of counties, equaling at least 50 percent of the statewide caseload into the new system by January 1, 2002. The transition shall be completed by January 1, 2003. A county that has appointed an administrator for the local child support agency and has complied with the requirements of subdivision (b) may transition prior to January 1, 2001, subject to the approval of the director. In determining the order in which counties will be transferred from the office of the district attorney to the local child support agencies, the director shall do all of the following:

(1) Consider the performance of the counties in establishing and collecting child support.

(2) Minimize the disruption of the services provided by the counties.

(3) Optimize the chances of a successful transition.

(b) In order to achieve an orderly transition with minimal disruption of services, a county shall submit a plan of transition which shall be approved by the department prior to transition.

(c) The director shall consult with the district attorney to achieve an orderly transition and to minimize the disruption of services. Each district attorney shall cooperate in the transition as requested by the director.

(d) To minimize any disruption of services provided under the child support enforcement program during the transition, each district attorney shall:

(1) Continue to be designated the single organizational unit whose duty it shall be to administer the Title IV–D state plan for securing child and spousal support, medical support, and determining paterni-

ty for that county until such time as the county is notified by the director that the county has been transferred pursuant to subdivision (a) or sooner under Section 17602.

(2) At a minimum, maintain all levels of funding, staffing, and services as of January 1, 1999, to administer the Title IV–D state plan for securing child and spousal support, medical support, and determining paternity. If the director determines that a district attorney has lowered the funding, staffing, or services of the child support enforcement program, the director may withhold part or all state and federal funds, including incentive funds, from the district attorney. Before the director withholds part of or all state and federal funds, including incentive funds, the district attorney shall have the opportunity to demonstrate good cause for any reductions in funding, staffing, or services. Good cause exceptions for reductions shall include, but not be limited to, natural staff attrition and caseload changes. *(Added by Stats.1999, c. 478 (A.B.196), § 1. Amended by Stats.1999, c. 480 (S.B.542), § 9.)*

Cross References

County defined for purposes of this Code, see Family Code § 67.
Judgment and order defined for purposes of this Code, see Family Code § 100.
Spousal support defined for purposes of this Code, see Family Code § 142.
State defined for purposes of this Code, see Family Code § 145.
Support defined for purposes of this Code, see Family Code § 150.

§ 17306. Uniform forms, policies, and procedures for local agencies; duties of department

(a) The Department of Child Support Services shall develop uniform forms, policies, and procedures to be employed statewide by all local child support agencies. Pursuant to this subdivision, the department shall:

(1) Adopt uniform procedures and forms.

(2) Establish standard caseload-to-staffing ratios, adjusted as appropriate to meet the varying needs of local programs.

(3) Institute a consistent statewide policy on the appropriateness of closing cases to ensure that, without relying solely on federal minimum requirements, all cases are fully and pragmatically pursued for collections prior to closing.

(4) Evaluate the best practices for the establishment, enforcement, and collection of child support, for the purpose of determining which practices should be implemented statewide in an effort to improve performance by local child support agencies. In evaluating the best practices, the director shall review existing practices in better performing counties within California, as well as practices implemented by other state Title IV–D programs nationwide.

(5) Evaluate the best practices for the management of effective child support enforcement operations for the purpose of determining what management structure should be implemented statewide in an effort to improve the establishment, enforcement, and collection of child support by local child support agencies, including an examination of the need for attorneys in management level positions. In evaluating the best practices, the director shall review existing practices in better performing counties within California, as well as practices implemented by other state Title IV–D programs nationwide.

(6) Set priorities for the use of specific enforcement mechanisms for use by local child support agencies. As part of establishing these priorities, the director shall set forth caseload processing priorities to target enforcement efforts and services in a way that will maximize collections.

(7) Develop uniform training protocols, require periodic training of all child support staff, and conduct training sessions as appropriate.

(8) Review and approve annual budgets submitted by the local child support agencies to ensure each local child support agency operates an effective and efficient program that complies with all federal and state laws, regulations, and directives, including the directive to hire sufficient staff.

(b) The director shall submit any forms intended for use in court proceedings to the Judicial Council for approval at least six months prior to the implementation of the use of the forms.

(c) In adopting the forms, policies, and procedures, the director shall consult with appropriate organizations representing stakeholders in California, such as the California State Association of Counties, the Child Support Directors Association of California, labor organizations, parent advocates, child support commissioners, family law facilitators, and the appropriate committees of the Legislature. *(Added by Stats.1999, c. 478 (A.B.196), § 1. Amended by Stats.1999, c. 480 (S.B.542), § 10; Stats.2001, c. 111 (A.B.429), § 2, eff. July 30, 2001; Stats.2002, c. 927 (A.B.3032), § 3.5; Stats. 2004, c. 806 (A.B.2358), § 2; Stats.2016, c. 474 (A.B.2882), § 12, eff. Jan. 1, 2017; Stats.2019, c. 27 (S.B.80), § 5, eff. June 27, 2019.)*

Cross References

Collection of child support, referral of child support delinquencies, see Revenue and Taxation Code § 19271.
County defined for purposes of this Code, see Family Code § 67.
Family support defined for purposes of this Code, see Family Code § 92.
Proceeding defined for purposes of this Code, see Family Code § 110.
State defined for purposes of this Code, see Family Code § 145.
State subventions, see Government Code § 7903.
Support defined for purposes of this Code, see Family Code § 150.

§ 17306.1. Implementation of revised local child support agency funding methodology; working sessions; written update describing recommended changes

(a) Commencing with the 2019–20 fiscal year, the department shall implement a revised local child support agency funding methodology that was developed in consultation with the California Child Support Directors Association. The methodology shall consist of both of the following components in the 2019–20 fiscal year:

(1) Casework operations, which consists of a statewide standard case-to-staff ratio, the respective labor costs for each local child support agency, and an operating expense and equipment complement based on a percentage of staffing costs. The department shall propose a specific ratio informed by the working sessions described in subdivision (c) and as part of the required update to the Legislature required by subdivision (d).

(2) Call center operations, which consists of a standard statewide ratio of calls to call center agents, the respective labor costs for each local child support agency, and an operating expense and equipment complement based on a percentage of staffing costs.

(b) Any increased state costs that result, either directly or indirectly, from implementation of the funding methodology described in subdivision (a) shall be implemented to the extent of an appropriation of funds in the annual Budget Act.

(c)(1) The Department of Child Support Services shall convene a series of stakeholder working sessions to develop the ongoing methodology, which shall take effect in the 2020–21 fiscal year. There shall be at least three working sessions during the summer and fall of 2019, beginning as early as possible after July 1, 2019.

(2) The working sessions shall include, but not be limited to, representatives from the Child Support Directors Association, the Legislative Analyst's Office, the Department of Finance, consultants from the Assembly and Senate Health and Human Services budget subcommittees, any other interested Legislative consultants, antipoverty advocates, advocacy organizations representing custodial and noncustodial parents, including fathers' rights advocates, impacted families, and any other interested advocates or stakeholders for the child support program.

(3) The working sessions shall do all of the following:

(A) Further refine or change the local child support agency funding methodology defined in subdivision (a), including accounting for performance incentives to be provided in future years.

(B) Discuss additional strategies that might improve the customer service, pragmatic collectability, and cost efficiency of the child support program and assess fiscal impact to operations and collections.

(C) Consider any policy changes that may affect the workload and associated funding needs of the local child support agencies and assess fiscal impact to operations and collections.

(D) Consider the ways that child support collection improves outcomes for children, impacts the well-being of children in relationship to their parents who are ordered to pay support, particularly their fathers, and impacts the racial wealth gap and further analyze the impact that child support has on parents ordered to pay support who do not have the capacity to pay.

(d) The department shall provide a written update describing recommended changes to the funding methodology described in subdivision (a) to the relevant policy committees and budget subcommittee of the Legislature on February 1, 2020. The written update shall include, but not be limited to, a description of the programmatic and policy changes discussed in the working sessions, the feasibility of implementing the discussed programmatic and policy changes, the impact that the discussed programmatic and policy changes would have on operations, collections, and families served, and additional required statutory changes. *(Added by Stats.2019, c. 27 (S.B.80), § 6, eff. June 27, 2019. Amended by Stats.2020, c. 370 (S.B.1371), § 116, eff. Jan. 1, 2021.)*

§ 17307. Legislative findings and declarations with respect to authority and discretion of Department of Child Support Services to prevent, correct, or remedy effects of changes in timing of receipt of child support payments resulting solely from initial implementation of federally required State Disbursement Unit

(a) The Legislature hereby finds and declares that the Department of Child Support Services has the authority and discretion to prevent, correct, or remedy the effects of changes in the timing of the receipt of child support payments resulting solely from the initial implementation of the federally required State Disbursement Unit. This authority shall not be construed to supplant existing statutory appropriation and technology project approval processes, limits, and requirements.

(b) The Legislature hereby finds and declares that this section is declaratory of existing law. *(Added by Stats.2006, c. 75 (A.B.1808), § 6, eff. July 12, 2006.)*

§ 17308. Automated child support system

The director shall assume responsibility for implementing and managing all aspects of a single statewide automated child support system that will comply with state and federal requirements. The director may delegate responsibility to, or enter into an agreement with, any agency or entity that it deems necessary to satisfy this requirement. *(Added by Stats.1999, c. 478 (A.B.196), § 1.)*

Cross References

State defined for purposes of this Code, see Family Code § 145.
Support defined for purposes of this Code, see Family Code § 150.

§ 17309. State Disbursement Unit

Effective October 1, 1998, the state shall operate a State Disbursement Unit as required by federal law (42 U.S.C. Secs. 654 (27), 654a(g), and 654b). *(Added by Stats.1999, c. 478 (A.B.196), § 1. Amended by Stats.2003, c. 387 (A.B.739), § 10.)*

Cross References

Deposit of child support payments upon implementation of State Disbursement Unit, see Government Code § 24351.5.
State defined for purposes of this Code, see Family Code § 145.
Wage garnishment, withholding order for support, see Code of Civil Procedure § 706.030.

§ 17309.5. Employers required to make child support payments by electronic fund transfer; election to make payments; definitions

(a) An employer who is required to withhold and, by electronic fund transfer, pay tax pursuant to Section 19011 of the Revenue and Taxation Code or Section 13021 of the Unemployment Insurance Code, shall make child support payments to the State Disbursement Unit by electronic fund transfer. All child support payments required to be made to the State Disbursement Unit shall be remitted to the State Disbursement Unit by electronic fund transfer pursuant to Division 11 (commencing with Section 11101) of the Commercial Code.

(b) An employer not required to make payment to the State Disbursement Unit pursuant to paragraph (a), may elect to make payment by electronic fund transfer under the following conditions:

(1) The election shall be made in a form, and shall contain information, as prescribed by the Director of the Department of Child Support Services, and shall be subject to approval of the department.

(2) The election may be terminated upon written request to the Department of Child Support Services.

(c) For the purposes of this section:

(1) "Electronic fund transfer" means any transfer of funds, other than a transaction originated by check, draft, or similar paper instrument, that is initiated through an electronic terminal, telephonic instrument, or computer or magnetic tape, so as to order, instruct, or authorize a financial institution to debit or credit an account. Electronic fund transfers shall be accomplished by an automated clearinghouse debit, an automated clearinghouse credit, or by Federal Reserve Wire Transfer (Fedwire).

(2) "Automated clearinghouse" means any federal reserve bank, or an organization established in agreement with the National Automated Clearinghouse Association, that operates as a clearinghouse for transmitting or receiving entries between banks or bank accounts and that authorizes an electronic transfer of funds between these banks or bank accounts.

(3) "Automated clearinghouse debit" means a transaction in which the state, through its designated depository bank, originates an automated clearinghouse transaction debiting the person's bank account and crediting the state's bank account for the amount of tax. Banking costs incurred for the automated clearinghouse debit transaction shall be paid by the state.

(4) "Automated clearinghouse credit" means an automated clearinghouse transaction in which the person, through their own bank, originates an entry crediting the state's bank account and debiting the person's own bank account. Banking costs incurred for the automated clearinghouse credit transaction charged to the state shall be paid by the person originating the credit.

(5) "Fedwire transfer" means a transaction originated by a person and utilizing the national electronic payment system to transfer funds through the federal reserve banks, when that person debits their own bank account and credits the state's bank account. Electronic fund transfers pursuant to this section may be made by Fedwire only if payment cannot, for good cause, be made according to subdivision (a), and the use of Fedwire is preapproved by the department. Banking costs incurred for the Fedwire transaction charged to the person and to the state shall be paid by the person originating the transaction. *(Added by Stats.2004, c. 806 (A.B.2358), § 3. Amended by Stats.2019, c. 115 (A.B.1817), § 143, eff. Jan. 1, 2020.)*

§ 17310. Regulations and general policies

(a) The director shall formulate, adopt, amend, or repeal regulations and general policies affecting the purposes, responsibilities, and jurisdiction of the department that are consistent with law and necessary for the administration of the state plan for securing child support and enforcing spousal support orders and determining paternity.

(b) Notwithstanding any other provision of law, all regulations, including, but not limited to, regulations of the State Department of Social Services and the State Department of Health Services, relating to child support enforcement shall remain in effect and shall be fully enforceable by the department. The department may readopt, amend, or repeal the regulations in accordance with Section 17312 as necessary and appropriate. *(Added by Stats.1999, c. 478 (A.B.196), § 1. Amended by Stats.1999, c. 480 (S.B.542), § 11.)*

Cross References

Department of Health Care Services, generally, see Health and Safety Code § 100100 et seq.
Judgment and order defined for purposes of this Code, see Family Code § 100.
Spousal support defined for purposes of this Code, see Family Code § 142.
State defined for purposes of this Code, see Family Code § 145.
Support defined for purposes of this Code, see Family Code § 150.
Support order defined for purposes of this Code, see Family Code § 155.

§ 17311. Establishment and operation of Child Support Payment Trust Fund; legislative intent; General Fund loan

(a) The Child Support Payment Trust Fund is hereby created in the State Treasury. The department shall administer the fund.

(b)(1) The state may deposit child support payments received by the State Disbursement Unit, including those amounts that result in overpayment of child support, into the Child Support Payment Trust Fund, for the purpose of processing and providing child support payments. Notwithstanding Section 13340 of the Government Code, the fund is continuously appropriated for the purposes of disbursing child support payments from the State Disbursement Unit.

(2) The state share of the interest and other earnings that accrue on the fund shall be available to the department and used to offset the following General Fund costs in this order:

(A) Any transfers made to the Child Support Payment Trust Fund from the General Fund.

(B) The cost of administering the State Disbursement Unit, subject to appropriation by the Legislature.

(C) Other child support program activities, subject to appropriation by the Legislature.

(c) The department may establish and administer a revolving account in the Child Support Payment Trust Fund in an amount not to exceed six hundred million dollars ($600,000,000) to ensure the timely disbursement of child support. This amount may be adjusted by the Director of Finance upon notification of the Legislature as required, to meet payment timeframes required under federal law.

(d) It is the intent of the Legislature to provide transfers from the General Fund to provide startup funds for the Child Support Payment Trust Fund so that, together with the balances transferred pursuant to Section 17311.7, the Child Support Payment Trust Fund will have sufficient cash on hand to make all child support payments within the required timeframes.

(e) Notwithstanding any other law, an ongoing loan shall be made available from the General Fund, from funds not otherwise appropriated, to the Child Support Payment Trust Fund, not to exceed one hundred fifty million dollars ($150,000,000) to ensure the timely disbursement of child support payments when funds have not been recorded to the Child Support Payment Trust Fund or due to other fund liabilities, including, but not limited to, Internal Revenue Service negative adjustments to tax intercept payments. Whenever an adjustment of this amount is required to meet payment timeframes under federal law, the amount shall be adjusted after approval of the Director of Finance. In conjunction with the Department of Finance and the Controller's office, the department shall establish repayment procedures to ensure the outstanding loan balance does not exceed the average daily cash needs. The ongoing evaluation of the fund as detailed in these procedures shall occur no less frequently than monthly.

(f) Notwithstanding any other law, the Controller may use the moneys in the Child Support Payment Trust Fund for loans to the General Fund as provided in Sections 16310 and 16381 of the Government Code. However, interest shall be paid on all moneys loaned to the General Fund from the Child Support Payment Trust Fund. Interest payable shall be computed at a rate determined by the Pooled Money Investment Board to be the current earning rate of the fund from which loaned. This subdivision does not authorize any transfer that will interfere with the carrying out of the object for which the Child Support Payment Trust Fund was created. *(Added by Stats.2003, c. 387 (A.B.739), § 11. Amended by Stats.2005, c. 78 (S.B.68), § 6, eff. July 19, 2005; Stats.2009–2010, 3rd Ex.Sess., c. 9 (A.B.13), § 4, eff. Feb. 20, 2009.)*

Cross References

Judgment and order defined for purposes of this Code, see Family Code § 100.
State defined for purposes of this Code, see Family Code § 145.
Support defined for purposes of this Code, see Family Code § 150.

§ 17311.5. Trust agreement to receive or disburse child support collections; provisions of agreement; approved investment securities

(a) The department may enter into a trust agreement with a trustee or fiscal intermediary to receive or disburse child support collections. The trust agreement may contain provisions the department deems reasonable and proper for the security of the child support payments. Any trust accounts created by the trust agreements may be held outside the State Treasury.

(b) For the 2012–13 fiscal year only, trust account moneys may be invested in any of the types of securities listed in Section 16430 of the Government Code or alternatives offering comparable security, including, but not limited to, mutual funds and money market funds. This subdivision does not authorize investments or transfers that would interfere with carrying out the objective for which the Child Support Payment Trust Fund was created. *(Added by Stats.2003, c. 387 (A.B.739), § 12. Amended by Stats.2012, c. 47 (S.B.1041), § 1, eff. June 27, 2012.)*

Cross References

State defined for purposes of this Code, see Family Code § 145.
Support defined for purposes of this Code, see Family Code § 150.

§ 17311.7. Child support payment made to family through State Disbursement Unit; "alternate caregiver" defined

(a) Any payment required to be made to a family through the State Disbursement Unit shall be made directly to the obligee parent in the child support order requiring the payment, the conservator or guardian of the obligee parent, a special needs trust for the benefit of the obligee parent, the guardian of the person and the estate of the child subject to the order, any caregiver relative having custody or responsibility for the child, pursuant to a written record, or an alternate caregiver to whom the obligee under the child support order directs, in a written record, that payments be made.

(b) For purposes of this section, "alternate caregiver" means a nonrelative caregiver who is designated in writing by the obligee parent to take care of the child for a limited time. *(Added by Stats.2018, c. 504 (A.B.3248), § 6, eff. Jan. 1, 2019.)*

§ 17312. Regulations, orders, or standards

(a) The department shall adopt regulations, orders, or standards of general application to implement, interpret, or make specific the law enforced by the department. Regulations, orders, and standards shall be adopted, amended, or repealed by the director only in accordance with Chapter 3.5 (commencing with Section 11340) of Part 1 of Division 3 of Title 2 of the Government Code.

(b) In adopting regulations, the department shall strive for clarity of language that may be readily understood by those administering public social services or subject to those regulations.

(c) The rules of the department need not specify or include the detail of forms, reports, or records, but shall include the essential authority by which any person, agency, organization, association, or institution subject to the supervision or investigation of the department is required to use, submit, or maintain the forms, reports, or records.

(d) The department's regulations and other materials shall be made available pursuant to the California Code of Regulations and in the same manner as are materials of the State Department of Social Services under the provisions of Section 205.70 of Title 45 of the Code of Federal Regulations. *(Added by Stats.1999, c. 478 (A.B.196), § 1. Amended by Stats.1999, c. 480 (S.B.542), § 12.)*

Cross References

Judgment and order defined for purposes of this Code, see Family Code § 100.
Person defined for purposes of this Code, see Family Code § 105.
State defined for purposes of this Code, see Family Code § 145.

§ 17314. Staff; regional state administrators

(a) Subject to the State Civil Service Act (Part 2 (commencing with Section 18500) of Division 5 of Title 2 of the Government Code), the director shall appoint any assistants and other employees that are necessary for the administration of the affairs of the department and shall prescribe their duties and, subject to the approval of the Department of Finance, fix their salaries.

(b) As the director adopts a plan for a local child support agency to assume responsibility for child support enforcement activities in any county served by a district attorney pursuant to Section 17304, the director shall hire a sufficient number of regional state administrators to oversee the local child support agencies to ensure compliance with all state and federal laws and regulations. The regions shall be divided based on the total caseload of each local child support agency. The responsibilities of the regional state administrators shall include all of the following:

(1) Conducting regular and comprehensive site visits to the local child support agencies assigned to their region and preparing quarterly reports to be submitted to the department. The local child support agencies shall fully cooperate with all reasonable requests made by the regional state administrators, including providing all requested data on the local child support agency's program.

(2) Notifying a local child support agency of any potential or actual noncompliance with any state or federal law or regulation by the agency and working with the local child support agency to develop an immediate plan to ensure compliance.

(3) Participating in program monitoring teams as set forth in subdivision (c) of Section 17602.

(4) Participating in meetings with all regional state administrators and the director on at least a monthly basis to promote statewide uniformity as to the functions and structure of the local child support agencies. The regional state administrators may recommend proposals for approval and adoption by the director to achieve this goal.

(5) Responding to requests for management or technical assistance regarding program operations by local child support agencies. *(Added by Stats.1999, c. 478 (A.B.196), § 1.)*

Cross References

County defined for purposes of this Code, see Family Code § 67.
Department of Finance, generally, see Government Code § 13000 et seq.

Public officers and employees, incompatible activities, see Government Code § 1125 et seq.
State defined for purposes of this Code, see Family Code § 145.
Support defined for purposes of this Code, see Family Code § 150.

§ 17316. Involvement with agency supervised by department

No person, while holding the office of director, shall be a trustee, manager, director, or other officer or employee of any agency performing any function supervised by the department or any institution that is subject to examination, inspection, or supervision by the department. *(Added by Stats.1999, c. 478 (A.B.196), § 1.)*

Cross References

Person defined for purposes of this Code, see Family Code § 105.
Public officers and employees, incompatible activities, see Government Code § 1125 et seq.

§ 17318. Application of Government Code § 11000 et seq.

Except as otherwise expressly provided, Part 1 (commencing with Section 11000) of Division 3 of Title 2 of the Government Code, as it may be added to or amended from time to time, shall apply to the conduct of the department. *(Added by Stats.1999, c. 478 (A.B.196), § 1.)*

§ 17320. Temporary Assistance to Needy Families grant; federal penalties

The department shall coordinate with the State Department of Social Services to avoid the imposition of any federal penalties that cause a reduction in the state's Temporary Assistance to Needy Families grant, payable pursuant to Section 603(a)(1) of Title 42 of the United States Code. *(Added by Stats.1999, c. 478 (A.B.196), § 1.)*

Cross References

State defined for purposes of this Code, see Family Code § 145.

§ 17325. Direct deposit of child support payments; qualifying account; requirements; definitions

(a)(1) Notwithstanding any other law, if child support payments are directly deposited to an account of the recipient's choice, as authorized under the federal Electronic Fund Transfer Act (EFTA) (15 U.S.C. Sec. 1693 et seq.), the payments may only be deposited to an account that meets the requirements of a qualifying account, as defined in paragraph (2), for deposit of child support payments.

(2) For purposes of this section, a "qualifying account" is one of the following:

(A) A demand deposit or savings account at an insured depository financial institution that is offered directly by the insured depository financial institution on its internet website or through its branches and that is in the name of the person entitled to the receipt of child support payments.

(B) A prepaid account, or a demand deposit or savings account offered by, or through, an entity other than an insured depository financial institution, that meets all of the following:

(i) The account is held at an insured depository financial institution.

(ii) The account is set up to meet the requirements for direct or passthrough deposit or share insurance payable to the person entitled to the receipt of child support payments by the Federal Deposit Insurance Corporation in accordance with Part 330 of Title 12 of the Code of Federal Regulations, or the National Credit Union Share Insurance Fund in accordance with Part 745 of Title 12 of the Code of Federal Regulations.

(iii) The account is not attached to a credit or overdraft feature that is automatically repaid from the account unless the credit or overdraft feature has no fee, charge, or cost, whether direct, required, voluntary, or involuntary, or the credit or overdraft feature

§ 17325

complies with the requirements for credit offered in connection with a prepaid account under the federal Truth in Lending Act (15 U.S.C. Sec. 1601 et seq.) and its implementing regulations.

(iv) The account complies with all of the requirements, and provides the holder of the account with all of the consumer protections, that apply to an account under the rules implementing the EFTA.

(3) A person or entity that is not an insured depository financial institution that offers, maintains, or manages an account that does not comply with paragraph (2) shall not solicit, accept, or facilitate the direct deposit of child support payments to the account.

(b) For purposes of this section, the department shall not be held liable for authorizing a direct deposit of child support payments into an account designated by the recipient that does not comply with paragraph (2) of subdivision (a). The department has no obligation to determine whether an account at the insured depository financial institution of the recipient's choice is a qualifying account as described in subdivision (a).

(c) For the purposes of this section, the following definitions shall apply:

(1) "Insured depository financial institution" means a state or national bank, a state or federal savings and loan association, a mutual savings bank, or a state or federal credit union that holds deposits insured by the Federal Deposit Insurance Corporation or the National Credit Union Administration.

(2) "Prepaid account" has the same meaning as that term is defined in regulations under the EFTA. *(Added by Stats.2014, c. 180 (A.B.2252), § 1, eff. Jan. 1, 2015. Amended by Stats.2014, c. 720 (A.B.1614), § 1, eff. Jan. 1, 2015; Stats.2015, c. 416 (A.B.1519), § 2, eff. Jan. 1, 2016; Stats.2021, c. 546 (S.B.497), § 1, eff. Jan. 1, 2022.)*

ARTICLE 4. STATEWIDE REGISTRY FOR CHILD SUPPORT

Section
17390. Legislative findings and declarations; utilization of California Child Support Enforcement System or its replacement.
17391. Development of implementation plan for Statewide Child Support Registry; duties of clerks of court and department.
17392. Development of forms necessary for implementation of Statewide Child Support Registry; information to be transmitted.
17393. Development of forms necessary for implementation or article.

§ 17390. Legislative findings and declarations; utilization of California Child Support Enforcement System or its replacement

(a) The Legislature finds and declares that there is no single statewide database containing statistical data regarding child support orders.

(b) The California Child Support Enforcement System or its replacement may be utilized to provide a single statewide registry of all child support orders in California, including orders for cases under Title IV–D of the Social Security Act [1] and all cases with child support orders. *(Added by Stats.2016, c. 474 (A.B.2882), § 13, eff. Jan. 1, 2017.)*

[1] See 42 U.S.C.A. § 651 et seq.

§ 17391. Development of implementation plan for Statewide Child Support Registry; duties of clerks of court and department

(a) The department shall develop an implementation plan for the Statewide Child Support Registry. The Statewide Child Support Registry shall be operated by the agency responsible for operation of the California Child Support Enforcement System or its replacement. The Statewide Child Support Registry shall include storage and data retrieval of the data elements specified in Section 17392 for all California child support orders. The Statewide Child Support Registry will operate to ensure that all data in the Statewide Child Support Registry can be accessed and integrated for statistical analysis and reporting purposes with all child support order data contained in the California Child Support Enforcement System.

(b) Each clerk of the court shall provide the information specified in Section 17392 within 20 days to the department or the Statewide Child Support Registry from each new or modified child support order, including child support arrearage orders.

(c) The department shall maintain a system for compiling the child support data received from the clerks of the court, ensure that all child support data received from the clerks of the court are entered into the Statewide Child Support Registry within five business days of receipt in the Statewide Child Support Registry, and ensure that the Statewide Child Support Registry is fully implemented statewide.

(d) The department shall provide aggregate data on a periodic basis on the data maintained by the Statewide Child Support Registry to the Judicial Council, the appropriate agencies of the executive branch, and the Legislature for statistical analysis and review. The data shall not include individual identifying information for specific cases.

(e) Any information maintained by the Statewide Child Support Registry received from clerks of the court shall be provided to local child support agencies, the courts, and others as provided by law. *(Added by Stats.2016, c. 474 (A.B.2882), § 13, eff. Jan. 1, 2017.)*

§ 17392. Development of forms necessary for implementation of Statewide Child Support Registry; information to be transmitted

(a) The Judicial Council shall develop any forms that may be necessary to implement the Statewide Child Support Registry. The forms may be in electronic form or in hardcopy, as appropriate. The forms shall be developed so as not to delay implementation, and shall be available no later than 30 days prior to the implementation, of the Statewide Child Support Registry.

(b) The information transmitted from the clerks of the court to the Statewide Child Support Registry shall include all of the following:

(1) Any information required under federal law.

(2) Any other information the department and the Judicial Council find appropriate. *(Added by Stats.2016, c. 474 (A.B.2882), § 13, eff. Jan. 1, 2017.)*

§ 17393. Development of forms necessary for implementation or article

The Judicial Council shall develop the forms necessary to implement this article. *(Added by Stats.2016, c. 474 (A.B.2882), § 13, eff. Jan. 1, 2017.)*

CHAPTER 2. CHILD SUPPORT ENFORCEMENT

Article	Section
1. Support Obligations	17400
1.5. Delinquent Child Support Obligations and Financial Institution Data Match	17450
2. Collections and Enforcement	17500
3. Program Compliance	17600
4. Program Costs	17700

Cross References

Definitions governing this Division, see Family Code §§ 3500 et seq., 17000.

Security freeze on credit report, see Civil Code § 1785.11.2.

ARTICLE 1. SUPPORT OBLIGATIONS

Section
17400. Local child support agencies; responsibilities; authorized actions; forms; venue
17400.5. Disabled obligors receiving SSI/SSP or social security disability insurance benefits; duty of local child support agency under certain circumstances to move to modify child support obligations.
17401. Residence or work address information; establishment or enforcement action by agency.
17401.5. Child support service hearings; notice and information.
17402. CalWORKs aid due to separation from or desertion of child; noncustodial parent obligation to county.
17402.1. Remittance to the department of federal and state public assistance child support payments; promulgation of regulations.
17404. Procedure in actions, including parties, joinder, issues, parentage, pleading, notice, modification of order, forms, etc.
17404.1. Pleading pursuant to Uniform Interstate Family Support Act; summons or order to show cause; proposed judgment; service; set aside of portion of judgment.
17404.2. Pleading pursuant to Uniform Interstate Family Support Act; jurisdiction; transfer to appropriate court or state.
17404.3. Hearings by telephone, audiovisual means or other electronic means; adoption of rules.
17404.4. Issuance of notice to change payee on support order; filing of notice.
17405. Local child support agency; interview of custodial parent.
17406. Attorney-client relationship between Attorney General or local agency and any person; stipulated order resolving complaint for paternity or support; notice; civil action against noncustodial parent.
17407. Support order or support-related order; appeal taken or opposed by Attorney General; expenses.
17407.5. State reciprocity; declaration; full force and effect unless specified condition is met.
17408. Consolidation of multiple court files; consolidation of orders.
17410. Voluntary declaration of paternity.
17412. Voluntary declaration of parentage; child support action.
17414. Parentage stipulation.
17415. Public assistance application where parent absent or parentage not established; welfare department referral to local child support agency.
17416. Agency agreement with noncustodial parent.
17418. Number of children; computation of support.
17420. Earnings assignment order for support.
17422. Medical insurance form; health insurance coverage.
17424. Medical insurance form; submission.
17428. Supplemental complaint and judgment.
17430. Default judgment; amendment.
17432. Setting aside part of judgment or order concerning amount of child support to be paid.
17433. Relief from default judgment; mistaken identity; remedies.
17433.5. Interest accruing on obligation for current child, spousal, family, or medical support due in a given month.

Section
17434. Booklet about support; toll-free information hotline.
17440. United States military and National Guard service members; modification of child support; form; motion by local child support agency.
17441. Repealed.

§ 17400. Local child support agencies; responsibilities; authorized actions; forms; venue

(a)(1) Each county shall maintain a local child support agency, as specified in Section 17304, that shall have the responsibility for promptly and effectively establishing, modifying, and enforcing child support obligations, including medical support, enforcing spousal support orders established by a court of competent jurisdiction, and determining paternity in the case of a child born out of wedlock. The local child support agency shall take appropriate action, including criminal action in cooperation with the district attorneys, to establish, modify, and enforce child support and, if appropriate, enforce spousal support orders if the child is receiving public assistance, including Medi-Cal, and, if requested, shall take the same actions on behalf of a child who is not receiving public assistance, including Medi-Cal.

(2)(A) Provided that no reduction in aid or payment to a custodial parent would result, the local child support agency shall cease enforcement of child support arrearages assigned to the state and other fees and costs owed to the state that the department or the local child support agency has determined to be uncollectible. If enforcement is ceased pursuant to this paragraph, cases shall be closed to the maximum extent permitted under Section 303.11 of Title 45 of the Code of Federal Regulations, as adopted under Section 118203 of Title 22 of the California Code of Regulations.

(B) In determining the meaning of uncollectible for purposes of arrearages assigned to the state and other fees and costs owed to the state, the department and the local child support agency shall consider, but not be limited to, the following factors:

(i) Income and assets available to pay the arrearage or other fees and costs.

(ii) Source of income.

(iii) Age of the arrearage or other fees and costs.

(iv) The number of support orders.

(v) Employment history.

(vi) Payment history.

(vii) Incarceration history.

(viii) Whether the order was based on imputed income.

(ix) Other readily ascertainable debts.

(C) Notwithstanding subparagraph (B), the department and a local child support agency shall deem an arrearage assigned to the state or fees and costs owed to the state as uncollectible if the noncustodial parent's sole income is from any of the following:

(i) Supplemental Security Income/State Supplementary Program for the Aged, Blind, and Disabled (SSI/SSP) benefits.

(ii) A combination of SSI/SSP benefits and Social Security Disability Insurance (SSDI) benefits.

(iii) Cash Assistance Program for Aged, Blind, and Disabled Legal Immigrants (CAPI) benefits.

(iv) Veterans Administration Disability Compensation Benefits in an amount equal to or less than the amount the noncustodial parent would receive in SSI/SSP benefits.

(D) Notwithstanding the Administrative Procedure Act (Chapter 3.5 (commencing with Section 11340) of Part 1 of Division 3 of Title 2 of the Government Code), the department may implement and administer this subdivision through a child support services letter or

§ 17400

similar instruction until regulations are adopted. Thereafter, the department shall adopt regulations to implement this subdivision by July 1, 2024.

(b)(1) Notwithstanding Sections 25203 and 26529 of the Government Code, attorneys employed within the local child support agency may direct, control, and prosecute civil actions and proceedings in the name of the county in support of child support activities of the Department of Child Support Services and the local child support agency.

(2) Notwithstanding any other law, and except for pleadings or documents required to be signed under penalty of perjury, a local child support agency may substitute original signatures of the agent of the local child support agency with any form of electronic signatures, including, but not limited to, typed, digital, or facsimile images of signatures, digital signatures, or other computer-generated signatures, on pleadings filed for the purpose of establishing, modifying, or enforcing paternity, child support, or medical support. A substituted signature used by a local child support agency shall have the same effect as an original signature, including, but not limited to, the requirements of Section 128.7 of the Code of Civil Procedure.

(3) Notwithstanding any other law, effective July 1, 2016, a local child support agency may electronically file pleadings signed by an agent of the local child support agency under penalty of perjury. An original signed pleading shall be executed prior to, or on the same day as, the day of electronic filing. Original signed pleadings shall be maintained by the local child support agency for the period of time prescribed by subdivision (a) of Section 68152 of the Government Code. A local child support agency may maintain the original signed pleading by way of an electronic copy in the Statewide Automated Child Support System. The Judicial Council, by July 1, 2016, shall develop rules to implement this subdivision.

(4)(A) Notwithstanding any other law, a local child support agency may substitute any original signatures, including, but not limited to, signatures of agents of the local child support agencies, support obligors, support obligees, other parents, witnesses, and the attorneys for the parties to the action, with a printed copy or electronic image of an electronic signature obtained in compliance with the rules of court adopted pursuant to paragraph (2) of subdivision (e) of Section 1010.6 of the Code of Civil Procedure, on pleadings or documents filed for the purpose of establishing, modifying, or enforcing paternity, child support, or medical support. If the pleading or document is signed under the penalty of perjury or the signature does not belong to an agent of the local child support agency, the local child support agency represents, by the act of filing, that the declarant electronically signed the pleading or document before, or on the same day as, the date of filing.

(B) The local child support agency shall maintain the electronic form of the pleading or document bearing the original electronic signature for the period of time prescribed by subdivision (a) of Section 68152 of the Government Code, and shall make it available for review upon the request of the court or any party to the action or proceeding in which it is filed. Printed copies or electronic images of electronic signatures used by a local child support agency in this manner shall have the same effect as an original signature, including, but not limited to, the requirements of Section 128.7 of the Code of Civil Procedure.

(c) Actions brought by the local child support agency to establish paternity or child support or to enforce child support obligations shall be completed within the time limits set forth by federal law. The local child support agency's responsibility applies to spousal support only if the spousal support obligation has been reduced to an order of a court of competent jurisdiction. In any action brought for modification or revocation of an order that is being enforced under Title IV-D of the Social Security Act (42 U.S.C. Sec. 651 et seq.), the effective date of the modification or revocation shall be as prescribed by federal law (42 U.S.C. Sec. 666(a)(9)), or any subsequent date.

(d)(1) The Judicial Council, in consultation with the department, the Senate Committee on Judiciary, the Assembly Committee on Judiciary, and a legal services organization providing representation on child support matters, shall develop simplified summons, complaint, and answer forms for any action for support brought pursuant to this section or Section 17404. The Judicial Council may combine the summons and complaint in a single form.

(2) The simplified complaint form shall provide notice of the amount of child support that is sought pursuant to the guidelines set forth in Article 2 (commencing with Section 4050) of Chapter 2 of Part 2 of Division 9 based upon the income or income history of the support obligor as known to the local child support agency. If the support obligor's income or income history is unknown to the local child support agency, the complaint shall inform the support obligor that income shall be presumed to be the amount of the minimum wage, at 40 hours per week, established by the Industrial Welfare Commission pursuant to Section 1182.11 of the Labor Code unless information concerning the support obligor's income is provided to the court. The complaint form shall be accompanied by a proposed judgment. The complaint form shall include a notice to the support obligor that the proposed judgment will become effective if the obligor fails to file an answer with the court within 30 days of service. Except as provided in paragraph (2) of subdivision (a) of Section 17402, if the proposed judgment is entered by the court, the support order in the proposed judgment shall be effective as of the first day of the month following the filing of the complaint.

(3)(A) The simplified answer form shall be written in simple English and shall permit a defendant to answer and raise defenses by checking applicable boxes. The answer form shall include instructions for completion of the form and instructions for proper filing of the answer.

(B) The answer form shall be accompanied by a blank income and expense declaration or simplified financial statement and instructions on how to complete the financial forms. The answer form shall direct the defendant to file the completed income and expense declaration or simplified financial statement with the answer, but shall state that the answer will be accepted by a court without the income and expense declaration or simplified financial statement.

(C) The clerk of the court shall accept and file answers, income and expense declarations, and simplified financial statements that are completed by hand provided they are legible.

(4)(A) The simplified complaint form prepared pursuant to this subdivision shall be used by the local child support agency or the Attorney General in all cases brought under this section or Section 17404.

(B) The simplified answer form prepared pursuant to this subdivision shall be served on all defendants with the simplified complaint. Failure to serve the simplified answer form on all defendants shall not invalidate any judgment obtained. However, failure to serve the answer form may be used as evidence in any proceeding under Section 17432 of this code or Section 473 of the Code of Civil Procedure.

(C) The Judicial Council shall add language to the governmental summons, for use by the local child support agency with the governmental complaint to establish parental relationship and child support, informing defendants that a blank answer form should have been received with the summons and additional copies may be obtained from either the local child support agency or the superior court clerk.

(e) In any action brought or enforcement proceedings instituted by the local child support agency pursuant to this section for payment of child or spousal support, an action to recover an arrearage in support payments may be maintained by the local child support agency at any time within the period otherwise specified for the enforcement of a support judgment, notwithstanding the fact that the child has attained the age of majority.

(f) The county shall undertake an outreach program to inform the public that the services described in subdivisions (a) to (c), inclusive, are available to persons not receiving public assistance. There shall be prominently displayed in every public area of every office of the agencies established by this section a notice, in clear and simple language prescribed by the Director of Child Support Services, that the services provided in subdivisions (a) to (c), inclusive, are provided to all individuals, whether or not they are recipients of public assistance.

(g)(1) In any action to establish a child support order brought by the local child support agency in the performance of duties under this section, the local child support agency may make a motion for an order effective during the pendency of that action, for the support, maintenance, and education of the child or children that are the subject of the action. This order shall be referred to as an order for temporary support. This order has the same force and effect as a like or similar order under this code.

(2) The local child support agency shall file a motion for an order for temporary support within the following time limits:

(A) If the defendant is the mother, a presumed father under Section 7611, or any father if the child is at least six months old when the defendant files the answer, the time limit is 90 days after the defendant files an answer.

(B) In any other case in which the defendant has filed an answer prior to the birth of the child or not more than six months after the birth of the child, then the time limit is nine months after the birth of the child.

(3) If more than one child is the subject of the action, the limitation on reimbursement shall apply only as to those children whose parental relationship and age would bar recovery were a separate action brought for support of that child or those children.

(4) If the local child support agency fails to file a motion for an order for temporary support within the time limits specified in this section, the local child support agency shall be barred from obtaining a judgment of reimbursement for any support provided for that child during the period between the date the time limit expired and the date the motion was filed, or, if no motion is filed, when a final judgment is entered.

(5) Except as provided in Section 17304, this section does not prohibit the local child support agency from entering into cooperative arrangements with other county departments as necessary to carry out the responsibilities imposed by this section pursuant to plans of cooperation with the departments approved by the Department of Child Support Services.

(6) This section does not otherwise limit the ability of the local child support agency from securing and enforcing orders for support of a spouse or former spouse as authorized under any other law.

(h) As used in this article, "enforcing obligations" includes, but is not limited to, all of the following:

(1) The use of all interception and notification systems operated by the department for the purpose of aiding in the enforcement of support obligations.

(2) The obtaining by the local child support agency of an initial order for child support that may include medical support or that is for medical support only, by civil or criminal process.

(3) The initiation of a motion or order to show cause to increase an existing child support order, and the response to a motion or order to show cause brought by an obligor parent to decrease an existing child support order, or the initiation of a motion or order to show cause to obtain an order for medical support, and the response to a motion or order to show cause brought by an obligor parent to decrease or terminate an existing medical support order, without regard to whether the child is receiving public assistance.

(4) The response to a notice of motion or order to show cause brought by an obligor parent to decrease an existing spousal support order if the child or children are residing with the obligee parent and the local child support agency is also enforcing a related child support obligation owed to the obligee parent by the same obligor.

(5) The referral of child support delinquencies to the department under subdivision (c) of Section 17500 in support of the local child support agency.

(i) As used in this section, "out of wedlock" means that the biological parents of the child were not married to each other at the time of the child's conception.

(j)(1) The local child support agency is the public agency responsible for administering wage withholding for current support for the purposes of Title IV–D of the Social Security Act (42 U.S.C. Sec. 651 et seq.).

(2) This section does not limit the authority of the local child support agency granted by other sections of this code or otherwise granted by law.

(k) In the exercise of the authority granted under this article, the local child support agency may intervene, pursuant to subdivision (b) of Section 387 of the Code of Civil Procedure, by ex parte application, in any action under this code, or other proceeding in which child support is an issue or a reduction in spousal support is sought. By notice of motion, order to show cause, or responsive pleading served upon all parties to the action, the local child support agency may request any relief that is appropriate that the local child support agency is authorized to seek.

(*l*) The local child support agency shall comply with all regulations and directives established by the department that set time standards for responding to requests for assistance in locating noncustodial parents, establishing paternity, establishing child support awards, and collecting child support payments.

(m) As used in this article, medical support activities that the local child support agency is authorized to perform are limited to the following:

(1) The obtaining and enforcing of court orders for health insurance coverage.

(2) Any other medical support activity mandated by federal law or regulation.

(n)(1) Notwithstanding any other law, venue for an action or proceeding under this division shall be determined as follows:

(A) Venue shall be in the superior court in the county that is currently expending public assistance.

(B) If public assistance is not currently being expended, venue shall be in the superior court in the county where the child who is entitled to current support resides or is domiciled.

(C) If current support is no longer payable through, or enforceable by, the local child support agency, venue shall be in the superior court in the county that last provided public assistance for actions to enforce arrearages assigned pursuant to Section 11477 of the Welfare and Institutions Code.

(D) If subparagraphs (A), (B), and (C) do not apply, venue shall be in the superior court in the county of residence of the support obligee.

(E) If the support obligee does not reside in California, and subparagraphs (A), (B), (C), and (D) do not apply, venue shall be in the superior court of the county of residence of the obligor.

(2) Notwithstanding paragraph (1), if the child becomes a resident of another county after an action under this part has been filed, venue may remain in the county where the action was filed until the action is completed.

§ 17400

(*o*) The local child support agency of one county may appear on behalf of the local child support agency of any other county in an action or proceeding under this part.

(p) This section shall become operative January 1, 2023. *(Added by Stats.2021, c. 85 (A.B.135), § 4, eff. July 16, 2021, operative Jan. 1, 2023. Amended by Stats.2021, c. 696 (A.B.172), § 3, eff. Oct. 8, 2021, operative Jan. 1, 2023; Stats.2022, c. 215 (A.B.2961), § 3, eff. Jan. 1, 2023.)*

Cross References

Aid and medical assistance, conditions of eligibility for medical services, see Welfare and Institutions Code § 14008.6.

Attorney General, generally, see Government Code § 12500 et seq.

Child support pilot project for Counties of Alameda, Fresno, Orange, San Mateo and Santa Clara, expedited modification orders, see Family Code § 17441.

Collection of child support,
  Referral of child support delinquencies, see Revenue and Taxation Code § 19271.
  Statewide automated system for reporting delinquency administered by the department, see Family Code § 4701.

Collection of judgment where judgment debtor is creditor of public entity, judgment for support, see Code of Civil Procedure § 708.730.

Contempt of court, order for child, spousal, or family support, suspension of proceedings, see Penal Code § 166.5.

County defined for purposes of this Code, see Family Code § 67.

Default in support order due to unemployment, proof that obligor is actively seeking employment, see Family Code § 4505.

Emancipation of minors, notice of declaration proceedings, warning that court may void or rescind declaration and parents may become liable for support and medical insurance coverage pursuant to this section, see Family Code § 7121.

Enforcement of money judgments, service of earnings assignment orders for support on public entity, see Code of Civil Procedure § 704,114.

Family support defined for purposes of this Code, see Family Code § 92.

Filing fees for issues relating to cases involving child support agency services, see Government Code § 70672.

Filing of abstract or copy of money judgment and affidavit where money owed by state agency, judgment for support, see Code of Civil Procedure § 708.740.

Franchise Tax Board,
  Generally, see Government Code § 15700 et seq.
  Powers and duties, see Revenue and Taxation Code § 19501 et seq.

Good cause for noncooperation with child support enforcement, see Welfare and Institutions Code § 11477.02.

Governmental access to financial records, exceptions, authorized acts, see Government Code § 7480.

Income and expense declaration defined for purposes of this Code, see Family Code § 95.

Judgment and order defined for purposes of this Code, see Family Code § 100.

Juvenile court law, liability for costs of support, see Welfare and Institutions Code § 903.

Minors, age of majority, see Family Code § 6500 et seq.

Notice of obligation to provide name and address of employer, filing information with court, see Family Code § 4014.

Obligor, defined for purposes of this Division, see Family Code § 17212.

Parent and child relationship, setting aside or vacating judgment of paternity, support enforcement services, see Family Code § 7648.2.

Person defined for purposes of this Code, see Family Code § 105.

Proceeding defined for purposes of this Code, see Family Code § 110.

Recovery of moneys or incurred costs for support of juveniles, order to show cause, see Welfare and Institutions Code § 903.4.

References to husband, wife, spouses and married persons, persons included for purposes of this Code, see Family Code § 11.

Spousal support defined for purposes of this Code, see Family Code § 142.

State defined for purposes of this Code, see Family Code § 145.

Support defined for purposes of this Code, see Family Code § 150.

Support order defined for purposes of this Code, see Family Code § 155.

Unemployment compensation, service-recipients, contracts with service-providers, see Unemployment Insurance Code § 1088.8.

Venue, actions by or against a city, county, city and county, or local agency, see Code of Civil Procedure § 394.

Research References

Forms

California Practice Guide: Rutter Family Law Forms Form 1:32, Glossary of Common Family Law Terms, Phrases and Concepts (Enclosure to Form 1:31).

West's California Code Forms, Family § 4250, Comment Overview—Child Support Commissioners.

West's California Judicial Council Forms FL–415, Findings and Order Regarding Contempt (Domestic Violence Prevention—Uniform Parentage—Governmental).

West's California Judicial Council Forms FL–600, Summons and Complaint or Supplemental Complaint Regarding Parental Obligations (Governmental).

West's California Judicial Council Forms FL–605, Notice and Acknowledgment of Receipt.

West's California Judicial Council Forms FL–610, Answer to Complaint or Supplemental Complaint Regarding Parental Obligations (Governmental).

West's California Judicial Council Forms FL–615, Stipulation for Judgment or Supplemental Judgment Regarding Parental Obligations and Judgment (Also Available in Spanish).

West's California Judicial Council Forms FL–616, Declaration for Amended Proposed Judgment (Governmental).

West's California Judicial Council Forms FL–620, Request to Enter Default Judgment (Governmental).

West's California Judicial Council Forms FL–625, Stipulation and Order (Also Available in Spanish).

West's California Judicial Council Forms FL–627, Order for Genetic (Parentage) Testing.

West's California Judicial Council Forms FL–630, Judgment Regarding Parental Obligations (Also Available in Spanish).

West's California Judicial Council Forms FL–632, Notice Regarding Payment of Support (Governmental).

West's California Judicial Council Forms FL–634, Notice of Change of Responsibility for Managing Child Support Case (Governmental) (Also Available in Spanish).

West's California Judicial Council Forms FL–635, Notice of Entry of Judgment and Proof of Service by Mail (Governmental).

West's California Judicial Council Forms FL–640, Notice and Motion to Cancel (Set Aside) Support Order Based on Presumed Income (Also Available in Spanish).

West's California Judicial Council Forms FL–640–INFO, Information Sheet for Notice and Motion to Cancel (Set Aside) Support Order Based on Presumed Income (Also Available in Spanish).

West's California Judicial Council Forms FL–643, Declaration of Obligor's Income During Judgment Period—Presumed Income Set Aside.

West's California Judicial Council Forms FL–646, Response of Local Child Support Agency to Notice of Intent to Take Independent Action to Enforce Support Order (Governmental).

West's California Judicial Council Forms FL–650, Statement for Registration of California Support Order (Governmental).

West's California Judicial Council Forms FL–660, Ex Parte Motion by Local Child Support Agency and Declaration for Joinder of Other Parent (Governmental).

West's California Judicial Council Forms FL–670, Notice of Motion for Judicial Review of License Denial (Governmental).

West's California Judicial Council Forms FL–675, Order After Judicial Review of License Denial (Governmental).

West's California Judicial Council Forms FL–678, Order Determining Claim of Exemption or Third-Party Claim (Governmental).

West's California Judicial Council Forms FL–683, Order to Show Cause (Governmental).

West's California Judicial Council Forms FL–684, Request for Order and Supporting Declaration (Governmental).

West's California Judicial Council Forms FL–687, Order After Hearing (Also Available in Spanish).

West's California Judicial Council Forms FL–688, Short Form Order After Hearing (Also Available in Spanish).

West's California Judicial Council Forms FL–692, Minutes and Order or Judgment (Also Available in Spanish).

§ 17400.5. Disabled obligors receiving SSI/SSP or social security disability insurance benefits; duty of local child support agency under certain circumstances to move to modify child support obligations

If an obligor has an ongoing child support order being enforced by a local child support agency pursuant to Title IV–D of the Social Security Act and the obligor is disabled, meets the SSI resource test, and is receiving Supplemental Security Income/State Supplemental Payments (SSI/SSP) or, but for excess income as described in Section 416.1100 et seq. of Part 416 of Title 20 of the Code of Federal Regulations, would be eligible to receive as SSI/SSP, pursuant to Section 12200 of the Welfare and Institutions Code, and the obligor has supplied the local child support agency with proof of eligibility for, and, if applicable, receipt of, SSI/SSP or Social Security Disability Insurance benefits, then the local child support agency shall prepare and file a motion to modify the support obligation within 30 days of receipt of verification from the noncustodial parent or any other source of the receipt of SSI/SSP or Social Security Disability Insurance benefits. The local child support agency shall serve the motion on both the noncustodial parent and custodial person and any modification of the support order entered pursuant to the motion shall be effective as provided in Section 3653 of the Family Code. *(Added by Stats.2001, c. 651 (A.B.891), § 3. Amended by Stats.2002, c. 787 (S.B.1798), § 1; Stats.2019, c. 115 (A.B.1817), § 145, eff. Jan. 1, 2020.)*

Cross References

Judgment and order defined for purposes of this Code, see Family Code § 100.
Person defined for purposes of this Code, see Family Code § 105.
State defined for purposes of this Code, see Family Code § 145.
Support defined for purposes of this Code, see Family Code § 150.
Support order defined for purposes of this Code, see Family Code § 155.

§ 17401. Residence or work address information; establishment or enforcement action by agency

If the parent who is receiving support enforcement services provides to the local child support agency substantial, credible, information regarding the residence or work address of the support obligor, the agency shall initiate an establishment or enforcement action and serve the defendant, if service is required, within 60 days and inform the parent in writing when those actions have been taken. If the address or any other information provided by the support obligee is determined by the local child support agency to be inaccurate and if, after reasonable diligence, the agency is unable to locate and serve the support obligor within that 60–day period, the local child support agency shall inform the support obligee in writing of those facts. The requirements of this section shall be in addition to the time standards established by the Department of Child Support Services pursuant to subdivision (*l*) of Section 17400. *(Added by Stats.1999, c. 653 (A.B.380), § 14. Amended by Stats.2000, c. 808 (A.B.1358), § 83, eff. Sept. 28, 2000; Stats.2001, c. 755 (S.B.943), § 12, eff. Oct. 12, 2001.)*

Cross References

Support defined for purposes of this Code, see Family Code § 150.

§ 17401.5. Child support service hearings; notice and information

(a) All of the following shall include notice of, and information about, the child support service hearings available pursuant to Section 17801, provided that there is federal financial participation available as set forth in subdivision (j) of Section 17801:

(1) The booklet required by subdivision (a) of Section 17434.

(2) Any notice required by subdivision (c) or (h) of Section 17406.

(b) To the extent not otherwise required by law, the local child support agency shall provide notice of, and information about, the child support services hearings available pursuant to Section 17801 in any regularly issued notices to custodial and noncustodial parents subject to Section 17400, provided that there is federal financial participation available as set forth in subdivision (e) of Section 17801.

Notice of and information about the child support service hearings and the child support complaint resolution process required under Section 17800 shall be easily accessible and shall be provided in a single section of the booklet. *(Formerly § 17401, added by Stats. 1999, c. 803 (A.B.472), § 1. Renumbered § 17401.5 and amended by Stats.2000, c. 808 (A.B.1358), § 84, eff. Sept. 28, 2000.)*

Cross References

Support defined for purposes of this Code, see Family Code § 150.

§ 17402. CalWORKs aid due to separation from or desertion of child; noncustodial parent obligation to county

(a) In any case of separation or desertion of a parent or parents from a child or children that results in aid under Chapter 2 (commencing with Section 11200) of Part 3 of Division 9 of the Welfare and Institutions Code being granted to that family, the noncustodial parent or parents shall be obligated to the county for an amount equal to the amount specified in an order for the support and maintenance of the family issued by a court of competent jurisdiction.

(b) The local child support agency shall take appropriate action pursuant to this section as provided in subdivision (*l*) of Section 17400. The local child support agency may establish liability for child support as provided in subdivision (a) when public assistance was provided by another county or by other counties.

(c) The amount of the obligation established for each parent with a liability under subdivision (a) shall be determined by using the appropriate child support guideline currently in effect and shall be computed as follows:

(1) If one parent remains as a custodial parent, the support shall be computed according to the guideline.

(2) If the parents reside together and neither father nor mother remains as a custodial parent, the guideline support shall be computed by combining the noncustodial parents' incomes. The combined incomes shall be used as the high earner's net monthly disposable income in the guideline formula. Income shall not be attributed to the caretaker or governmental agency. The amount of guideline support resulting shall be proportionately shared between the noncustodial parents based upon their net monthly disposable incomes.

(3) If the parents reside apart and neither father nor mother remains as a custodial parent, the guideline support shall be computed separately for each parent by treating each parent as a noncustodial parent. Income shall not be attributed to the caretaker or government agency.

(d) A parent shall pay the amount of support specified in the support order to the local child support agency. *(Added by Stats.1999, c. 478 (A.B.196), § 1. Amended by Stats.1999, c. 653 (A.B.380), § 15; Stats.2000, c. 808 (A.B.1358), § 84.3, eff. Sept. 28, 2000; Stats.2004, c. 305 (A.B.2669), § 5.)*

Cross References

Child support pilot project for Counties of Alameda, Fresno, Orange, San Mateo and Santa Clara, expedited modification orders, see Family Code § 17441.
County defined for purposes of this Code, see Family Code § 67.
Emancipation of minors, notice of declaration proceedings, warning that court may void or rescind declaration and parents may become liable for support and medical insurance coverage pursuant to this section, see Family Code § 7121.
Enforcement of money judgments, workers' compensation claim or award, temporary benefits, see Code of Civil Procedure § 704.160.
Judgment and order defined for purposes of this Code, see Family Code § 100.

§ 17402

Parentage determinations, family law and juvenile departments, exchange of documents, see Welfare and Institutions Code § 903.41.

Support defined for purposes of this Code, see Family Code § 150.

Support order defined for purposes of this Code, see Family Code § 155.

Venue, actions by or against a city, county, city and county, or local agency, see Code of Civil Procedure § 394.

Research References

Forms

- West's California Code Forms, Family § 4500, Comment Overview—Enforcement of Support Orders.
- West's California Judicial Council Forms FL–415, Findings and Order Regarding Contempt (Domestic Violence Prevention—Uniform Parentage—Governmental).
- West's California Judicial Council Forms FL–600, Summons and Complaint or Supplemental Complaint Regarding Parental Obligations (Governmental).
- West's California Judicial Council Forms FL–615, Stipulation for Judgment or Supplemental Judgment Regarding Parental Obligations and Judgment (Also Available in Spanish).
- West's California Judicial Council Forms FL–620, Request to Enter Default Judgment (Governmental).
- West's California Judicial Council Forms FL–625, Stipulation and Order (Also Available in Spanish).
- West's California Judicial Council Forms FL–630, Judgment Regarding Parental Obligations (Also Available in Spanish).
- West's California Judicial Council Forms FL–684, Request for Order and Supporting Declaration (Governmental).
- West's California Judicial Council Forms FL–687, Order After Hearing (Also Available in Spanish).
- West's California Judicial Council Forms FL–688, Short Form Order After Hearing (Also Available in Spanish).

§ 17402.1. Remittance to the department of federal and state public assistance child support payments; promulgation of regulations

(a) Each local child support agency shall, on a monthly basis, remit to the department both the federal and state public assistance child support payments received pursuant to Section 17402.

(b) The department shall promulgate regulations to implement this section. (Added by Stats.2001, c. 111 (A.B.429), § 4, eff. July 30, 2001.)

Cross References

State defined for purposes of this Code, see Family Code § 145.
Support defined for purposes of this Code, see Family Code § 150.

§ 17404. Procedure in actions, including parties, joinder, issues, parentage, pleading, notice, modification of order, forms, etc.

(a) Notwithstanding any other statute, in any action brought by the local child support agency for the support of a minor child or children, the action may be prosecuted in the name of the county on behalf of the child, children, or a parent of the child or children. The parent who has requested or is receiving support enforcement services of the local child support agency shall not be a necessary party to the action but may be subpoenaed as a witness. Except as provided in subdivision (e), in an action under this section there shall be no joinder of actions, or coordination of actions, or cross-complaints, and the issues shall be limited strictly to the question of parentage, if applicable, and child support, including an order for medical support. A final determination of parentage may be made in any action under this section as an incident to obtaining an order for support. An action for support or parentage pursuant to this section shall not be delayed or stayed because of the pendency of any other action between the parties.

(b)(1) Judgment in an action brought pursuant to this section, and in an action brought pursuant to Section 17402, if at issue, may be rendered pursuant to a noticed motion, that shall inform the defendant that in order to exercise the right to trial, the defendant shall appear at the hearing on the motion.

(2) If the defendant appears at the hearing on the motion, the court shall inquire of the defendant if the defendant desires to subpoena evidence and witnesses, if parentage is at issue and genetic tests have not already been conducted whether the defendant desires genetic tests, and if the defendant desires a trial. If the defendant's answer is in the affirmative, a continuance shall be granted to allow the defendant to exercise those rights. A continuance shall not postpone the hearing to more than 90 days from the date of service of the motion. If a continuance is granted, the court may make an order for temporary support without prejudice to the right of the court to make an order for temporary support as otherwise allowed by law.

(c) In any action to enforce a spousal support order the action may be pled in the name of the county in the same manner as an action to establish a child support obligation. The same restrictions on joinder of actions, coordination of actions, cross-complaints, and delay because of the pendency of any other action as relates to actions to establish a child support obligation shall also apply to actions to enforce a spousal support order.

(d) This section does not prevent the parties from bringing an independent action under other provisions of this code and litigating the issues of support, custody, visitation, or protective orders. In that event, any support, custody, visitation, or protective order issued by the court in an action pursuant to this section shall be filed in the action commenced under the other provisions of this code and shall continue in effect until modified by a subsequent order of the court. To the extent that the orders conflict, the court order last issued shall supersede all other orders and be binding upon all parties in that action.

(e)(1) After a support order, including a temporary support order and an order for medical support only, has been entered in an action brought pursuant to this section, the parent who has requested or is receiving support enforcement services of the local child support agency shall become a party to the action brought pursuant to this section, only in the manner and to the extent provided by this section, and only for the purposes allowed by this section.

(2) Notice of the parent's status as a party shall be given to the parent by the local child support agency in conjunction with the notice required by subdivision (e) of Section 17406. The complaint shall contain this notice. Service of the complaint on the parent in compliance with Section 1013 of the Code of Civil Procedure, or as otherwise provided by law, shall constitute compliance with this section. In all actions commenced under the procedures and forms in effect on or before December 31, 1996, the parent who has requested or is receiving support enforcement services of the local child support agency shall not become a party to the action until joined as a party pursuant to an ex parte application or noticed motion for joinder filed by the local child support agency or a noticed motion filed by either parent. The local child support agency shall serve a copy of any order for joinder of a parent obtained by the local child support agency's application on both parents in compliance with Section 1013 of the Code of Civil Procedure.

(3) Once both parents are parties to an action brought pursuant to this section in cases where Title IV–D services are currently being provided, the local child support agency shall be required, within five days of receipt, to mail the nonmoving party in the action all pleadings relating solely to the support issue in the action that have been served on the local child support agency by the moving party in the action, as provided in subdivision (f) of Section 17406. There shall be a rebuttable presumption that service on the local child support agency consistent with the provisions of this paragraph constitutes valid service on the nonmoving party. Where this procedure is used to effectuate service on the nonmoving party, the pleadings shall be served on the local child support agency not less than 30 days prior to the hearing.

(4) The parent who has requested or is receiving support enforcement services of the local child support agency is a party to an action

brought under this section for issues relating to the support, custody, and visitation of a child, and for restraining orders, and for no other purpose. The local child support agency shall not be required to serve or receive service of papers, pleadings, or documents, or participate in, or attend any hearing or proceeding relating to issues of custody or visitation, except as otherwise required by law. Orders concerning custody and visitation may be made in an action pursuant to this subdivision only if orders concerning custody and visitation have not been previously made by a court of competent jurisdiction in this state or another state and the court has jurisdiction and is the proper venue for custody and visitation determinations. All issues regarding custody and visitation shall be heard and resolved in the manner provided by this code. Except as otherwise provided by law, the local child support agency shall control support and parentage litigation brought pursuant to this section, and the manner, method, and procedures used in establishing parentage and in establishing and enforcing support obligations unless and until the parent who requested or is receiving support enforcement services has requested in writing that the local child support agency close the case and the case has been closed in accordance with state and federal regulation or policy.

(f)(1) A parent who has requested or is receiving support enforcement services of the local child support agency may take independent action to modify a support order made pursuant to this section while support enforcement services are being provided by the local child support agency. The parent shall serve the local child support agency with notice of any action filed to modify the support order and provide the local child support agency with a copy of the modified order within 15 calendar days after the date the order is issued.

(2) A parent who has requested or is receiving support enforcement services of the local child support agency may take independent action to enforce a support order made pursuant to this section while support enforcement services are being provided by the local child support agency with the written consent of the local child support agency. At least 30 days prior to filing an independent enforcement action, the parent shall provide the local child support agency with written notice of the parent's intent to file an enforcement action that includes a description of the type of enforcement action the parent intends to file. Within 30 days of receiving the notice, the local child support agency shall either provide written consent for the parent to proceed with the independent enforcement action or notify the parent that the local child support agency objects to the parent filing the proposed independent enforcement action. The local child support agency may object only if the local child support agency is currently using an administrative or judicial method to enforce the support obligation or if the proposed independent enforcement action would interfere with an investigation being conducted by the local child support agency. If the local child support agency does not respond to the parent's written notice within 30 days, the local child support agency shall be deemed to have given consent.

(3) The court shall order that all payments of support shall be made to the local child support agency in any action filed under this section by the parent who has requested, or is receiving, support enforcement services of the local child support agency unless support enforcement services have been terminated by the local child support agency by case closure as provided by state and federal law. Any order obtained by a parent prior to support enforcement services being terminated in which the local child support agency did not receive proper notice pursuant to this section shall be voidable upon the motion of the local child support agency.

(g) Any notice from the local child support agency requesting a meeting with the support obligor for any purpose authorized under this section shall contain a statement advising the support obligor of the right to have an attorney present at the meeting.

(h) For the purpose of this section, "a parent who is receiving support enforcement services" includes a parent who has assigned their rights to support pursuant to Section 11477 of the Welfare and Institutions Code.

(i) The Judicial Council shall develop forms to implement this section. *(Added by Stats.1999, c. 478 (A.B.196), § 1. Amended by Stats.1999, c. 480 (S.B.542), § 14; Stats.2000, c. 808 (A.B.1358), § 84.5, eff. Sept. 28, 2000; Stats.2001, c. 755 (S.B.943), § 13, eff. Oct. 12, 2001; Stats.2019, c. 115 (A.B.1817), § 146, eff. Jan. 1, 2020.)*

Cross References

Blood tests to determine paternity, see Family Code § 7550 et seq.
Child support commissioners, power to order genetic tests to determine paternity, see Family Code § 4251.
Child support pilot project for Counties of Alameda, Fresno, Orange, San Mateo and Santa Clara, expedited modification orders, see Family Code § 17441.
County defined for purposes of this Code, see Family Code § 67.
Emancipation of minors, notice of declaration proceedings, warning that court may void or rescind declaration and parents may become liable for support and medical insurance coverage pursuant to this section, see Family Code § 7121.
Enforcement of money judgments, workers' compensation claim or award, temporary benefits, see Code of Civil Procedure § 704.160.
Good cause for noncooperation with child support enforcement, see Welfare and Institutions Code § 11477.02.
Issuance of support orders, paternity established through genetic testing, see Family Code § 5700.401.
Judgment and order defined for purposes of this Code, see Family Code § 100.
Minor defined for purposes of this Code, see Family Code § 6500.
Notice directing payment of support to local child support agencies, see Family Code § 4506.3.
Proceeding defined for purposes of this Code, see Family Code § 110.
Protective order defined for purposes of this Code, see Family Code § 6218.
Spousal support defined for purposes of this Code, see Family Code § 142.
State defined for purposes of this Code, see Family Code § 145.
Support defined for purposes of this Code, see Family Code § 150.
Support order defined for purposes of this Code, see Family Code § 155.
Uniform Parentage Act, see Family Code § 7600 et seq.
Venue, actions by or against a city, county, city and county, or local agency, see Code of Civil Procedure § 394.

Research References

Forms

1 California Transactions Forms--Family Law § 3:2, Child Custody.
West's California Judicial Council Forms FL–334, Declaration Regarding Address Verification—Postjudgment Request to Modify a Child Custody, Visitation, or Child Support Order.
West's California Judicial Council Forms FL–415, Findings and Order Regarding Contempt (Domestic Violence Prevention—Uniform Parentage—Governmental).
West's California Judicial Council Forms FL–600, Summons and Complaint or Supplemental Complaint Regarding Parental Obligations (Governmental).
West's California Judicial Council Forms FL–610, Answer to Complaint or Supplemental Complaint Regarding Parental Obligations (Governmental).
West's California Judicial Council Forms FL–620, Request to Enter Default Judgment (Governmental).
West's California Judicial Council Forms FL–625, Stipulation and Order (Also Available in Spanish).
West's California Judicial Council Forms FL–630, Judgment Regarding Parental Obligations (Also Available in Spanish).
West's California Judicial Council Forms FL–645, Notice to Local Child Support Agency of Intent to Take Independent Action to Enforce Support Order (Governmental).
West's California Judicial Council Forms FL–646, Response of Local Child Support Agency to Notice of Intent to Take Independent Action to Enforce Support Order (Governmental).
West's California Judicial Council Forms FL–660, Ex Parte Motion by Local Child Support Agency and Declaration for Joinder of Other Parent (Governmental).
West's California Judicial Council Forms FL–661, Notice of Motion and Declaration for Joinder of Other Parent in Governmental Action.
West's California Judicial Council Forms FL–661–INFO, Information Sheet for Notice of Motion and Declaration for Joinder of Other Parent in Governmental Action.

§ 17404

West's California Judicial Council Forms FL–662, Responsive Declaration to Motion for Joinder of Other Parent—Consent Order of Joinder.

West's California Judicial Council Forms FL–662–INFO, Information Sheet for Responsive Declaration to Motion for Joinder of Other Parent—Consent Order of Joinder.

West's California Judicial Council Forms FL–663, Stipulation and Order for Joinder of Other Parent (Governmental) (Also Available in Chinese, Korean, Spanish, Tagalog, and Vietnamese).

West's California Judicial Council Forms FL–684, Request for Order and Supporting Declaration (Governmental).

West's California Judicial Council Forms FL–687, Order After Hearing (Also Available in Spanish).

West's California Judicial Council Forms FL–688, Short Form Order After Hearing (Also Available in Spanish).

§ 17404.1. Pleading pursuant to Uniform Interstate Family Support Act; summons or order to show cause; proposed judgment; service; set aside of portion of judgment

(a) Upon receipt of a petition or comparable pleading pursuant to Part 6 (commencing with Section 5700.101) of Division 9, the local child support agency or petitioner may either (1) request the issuance of a summons or (2) request the court to issue an order requiring the respondent to appear personally at a specified time and place to show cause why an order should not be issued as prayed in the petition or comparable pleading on file.

(b) The respondent may also be served with a proposed judgment consistent with the relief sought in the petition or other comparable pleading. If the respondent's income or income history is unknown to the local child support agency, the local child support agency may serve a form of proposed judgment with the petition and other documents on the respondent that shall inform the respondent that income shall be presumed to be the amount of the state minimum wage, at 40 hours per week, unless information concerning the respondent's income is provided to the court. The respondent shall also receive notice that the proposed judgment will become effective if the respondent fails to file a response with the court within 30 days after service.

(c) If a summons is issued for a petition or comparable pleading pursuant to Part 6 (commencing with Section 5700.101) of Division 9, the local child support agency or petitioner shall cause a copy of the summons, petition, and other documents to be served upon the respondent according to law.

(d) If an order to show cause is issued on a petition or comparable pleading pursuant to Part 6 (commencing with Section 5700.101) of Division 9 requiring the respondent to appear at a specified time and place to respond to the petition, a copy of the order to show cause, the petition, and other documents shall be served upon the respondent at least 15 days prior to the hearing.

(e) A petition or comparable pleading served upon a respondent in accordance with this section shall be accompanied by a blank responsive form that shall permit the respondent to answer the petition and raise any defenses by checking applicable boxes and by a blank income and expense declaration or simplified financial statement together with instructions for completion of the forms.

(f) In any action pursuant to Part 6 (commencing with Section 5700.101) of Division 9 in which the judgment was obtained pursuant to presumed income, as set forth in this section, the court may set aside that part of the judgment or order concerning the amount of child support to be paid on the grounds specified and in the manner set forth in Section 17432. *(Added by Stats.2015, c. 493 (S.B.646), § 8, eff. Jan. 1, 2016. Amended by Stats.2019, c. 115 (A.B.1817), § 147, eff. Jan. 1, 2020.)*

Research References

Forms

West's California Judicial Council Forms FL–530, Judgment Regarding Parental Obligations (UIFSA) (Also Available in Spanish).

§ 17404.2. Pleading pursuant to Uniform Interstate Family Support Act; jurisdiction; transfer to appropriate court or state

(a) If, prior to filing, a petition or comparable pleading pursuant to Part 6 (commencing with Section 5700.101) of Division 9 is received by the local child support agency or the superior court and the county in which the pleadings are received is not the appropriate jurisdiction for trial of the action, the court or the local child support agency shall forward the pleadings and any accompanying documents to the appropriate court of this state or to the jurisdiction of another state without filing the pleadings or order of the court, and shall notify the petitioner, the California Central Registry, and the local child support agency of the receiving county where and when the pleading was sent.

(b) If, after a petition or comparable pleading has been filed with the superior court of a county pursuant to Part 6 (commencing with Section 5700.101) of Division 9, it appears that the respondent is not or is no longer a resident of the county in which the action has been filed, upon ex parte application by the local child support agency or petitioner, the court shall transfer the action to the appropriate court of this state or to the appropriate jurisdiction of another state and shall notify the petitioner, the respondent, the California Central Registry, and the local child support agency of the receiving county where and when the pleading was sent.

(c) If, after entry of an order by a court of this state or an order of another state registered in a court of this state for enforcement or modification pursuant to Part 6 (commencing with Section 5700.101) of Division 9, it appears that the respondent is not or is no longer a resident of the county in which the foreign order has been registered, upon ex parte application by the local child support agency of the transferring or receiving county or the petitioner, the court shall transfer the registered order and all documents subsequently filed in that action to the appropriate court of this state and shall notify the petitioner, the respondent, the California Central Registry, and the local child support agency of the transferring and receiving county where and when the registered order and all other appropriate documents were sent. Transfer of certified copies of documents shall meet the requirements of this section.

(d) If, in an action initiated in a court of this state pursuant to Part 6 (commencing with Section 5700.101) of Division 9 or a predecessor law for interstate enforcement of support, the petitioner is no longer a resident of the county in which the action has been filed, upon ex parte application by the petitioner or the local child support agency, the court shall transfer the action to the appropriate court of this state and shall notify the responding jurisdiction where and when the action was transferred.

(e) Notwithstanding subdivisions (b) and (c), if the respondent becomes a resident of another county or jurisdiction after an action or registered order has been filed pursuant to Part 6 (commencing with Section 5700.101) of Division 9, the action may remain in the county where the action was filed until the action is completed. *(Added by Stats.2015, c. 493 (S.B.646), § 9, eff. Jan. 1, 2016.)*

Research References

Forms

West's California Judicial Council Forms FL–560, Ex Parte Application for Transfer and Order (UIFSA).

§ 17404.3. Hearings by telephone, audiovisual means or other electronic means; adoption of rules

Hearings by telephone, audiovisual means, or other electronic means shall be permitted in child support cases in which the local child support agency is providing child support services. The Judicial Council shall adopt court rules implementing this provision and subdivision (f) of Section 5700.316 on or before July 1, 2016. *(Added by Stats.2015, c. 493 (S.B.646), § 10, eff. Jan. 1, 2016.)*

§ 17404.4. Issuance of notice to change payee on support order; filing of notice

In exercising the jurisdiction under Section 5700.319, either the department or the local child support agency shall issue a notice to change payee on a support order issued in this state, upon request from the support enforcement agency of another state where a custodial party has either assigned the right to receive support or has requested support enforcement services. Notice of the administrative change of payee shall be filed with the court in which the order was issued or last registered. *(Added by Stats.2015, c. 493 (S.B.646), § 11, eff. Jan. 1, 2016. Amended by Stats.2022, c. 420 (A.B.2960), § 21, eff. Jan. 1, 2023.)*

§ 17405. **Local child support agency; interview of custodial parent**

In carrying out duties under this article, the local child support agency shall interview the custodial parent within 10 business days of opening a child support case. This interview shall solicit financial and all other information about the noncustodial parent. This information shall be acted upon immediately. The local child support agency shall reinterview the custodial parent as needed. *(Added by Stats.1999, c. 652 (S.B.240), § 16.)*

Cross References

Support defined for purposes of this Code, see Family Code § 150.

§ 17406. **Attorney-client relationship between Attorney General or local agency and any person; stipulated order resolving complaint for paternity or support; notice; civil action against noncustodial parent**

(a) In all actions involving paternity or support, including, but not limited to, other proceedings under this code, and under Division 9 (commencing with Section 10000) of the Welfare and Institutions Code, the local child support agency and the Attorney General represent the public interest in establishing, modifying, and enforcing support obligations. No attorney-client relationship shall be deemed to have been created between the local child support agency or Attorney General and any person by virtue of the action of the local child support agency or the Attorney General in carrying out these statutory duties.

(b) Subdivision (a) is declaratory of existing law.

(c) In all requests for services of the local child support agency or Attorney General pursuant to Section 17400 relating to actions involving paternity or support, not later than the same day an individual makes a request for these services in person, and not later than five working days after either (1) a case is referred for services from the county welfare department, (2) receipt of a request by mail for an application for services, or (3) an individual makes a request for services by telephone, the local child support agency or Attorney General shall give notice to the individual requesting services or on whose behalf services have been requested that the local child support agency or Attorney General does not represent the individual or the children who are the subject of the case, that no attorney-client relationship exists between the local child support agency or Attorney General and those persons, and that no such representation or relationship shall arise if the local child support agency or Attorney General provides the services requested. Notice shall be in bold print and in plain English and shall be translated into the language understandable by the recipient when reasonable. The notice shall include the advice that the absence of an attorney-client relationship means that communications from the recipient are not privileged and that the local child support agency or Attorney General may provide support enforcement services to the other parent in the future.

(d) The local child support agency or Attorney General shall give the notice required pursuant to subdivision (c) to all recipients of services under Section 17400 who have not otherwise been provided that notice, not later than the date of the next annual notice required under Section 11476.2 of the Welfare and Institutions Code. This notice shall include notification to the recipient of services under Section 17400 that the recipient may inspect the clerk's file at the office of the clerk of the court, and that, upon request, the local child support agency, or, if appropriate, the Attorney General, will furnish a copy of the most recent order entered in the case.

(e) The local child support agency or, if appropriate, the Attorney General shall serve a copy of the complaint for paternity or support, or both, on recipients of support services under Section 17400, as specified in paragraph (2) of subdivision (e) of Section 17404. A notice shall accompany the complaint that informs the recipient that the local child support agency or Attorney General may enter into a stipulated order resolving the complaint, and that the recipient shall assist the prosecuting attorney, by sending all information on the noncustodial parent's earnings and assets to the prosecuting attorney.

(f)(1)(A) The local child support agency or Attorney General shall provide written notice to recipients of services under Section 17400 of the initial date and time, and purpose of every hearing in a civil action for paternity or support.

(B) Once the parent who has requested or is receiving support enforcement services becomes a party to the action pursuant to subdivision (e) of Section 17404, in lieu of the above, the local child support agency or Attorney General shall serve on a parent all pleadings relating to paternity or support that have been served on the local child support agency by the other parent. The pleading shall be accompanied by a notice.

(C) The notice provided subject to subparagraphs (A) and (B) shall include the following language:

IMPORTANT NOTICE

It may be important that you attend the hearing. The local child support agency does not represent you or your children. You may have information about the other parent, such as information about that parent's income or assets that will not be presented to the court unless you attend the hearing. You have the right to attend the hearing and to be heard in court and tell the court what you think the court should do with the child support order. This hearing could change your rights or your children's rights to support.

(2) The notice shall state the purpose of the hearing or be attached to the motion or other pleading which caused the hearing to be scheduled.

(3) The notice shall be provided separate from all other material and shall be in at least 14–point type. The failure of the local child support agency or Attorney General to provide the notice required pursuant to subparagraph (A) of paragraph (1) does not affect the validity of any order.

(4)(A) The notice required pursuant to subparagraph (A) of paragraph (1) shall be provided not later than seven calendar days prior to the hearing, or, if the local child support agency or Attorney General receives notice of the hearing less than seven days prior to the hearing, within two days of the receipt by the local child support agency or Attorney General of the notice of the hearing.

(B) Service of the notice and the pleadings required pursuant to subparagraph (B) of paragraph (1) shall be completed not later than five days after receipt of the pleadings served on the local child support agency by the parent.

(5) The local child support agency or Attorney General shall, in order to implement this subdivision, make reasonable efforts to ensure that the local child support agency or Attorney General has current addresses for all parties to the child support action.

(g) The local child support agency or Attorney General shall give notice to recipients of services under Section 17400 of every order obtained by the local child support agency or Attorney General that establishes or modifies the support obligation for the recipient or the children who are the subject of the order, by sending a copy of the order to the recipient. The notice shall be made within the time specified by federal law after the order has been filed. The local

§ 17406

child support agency or Attorney General shall also give notice to these recipients of every order obtained in any other jurisdiction that establishes or modifies the support obligation for the recipient or the children who are the subject of the order, and which is received by the local child support agency or Attorney General, by sending a copy of the order to the recipient within the timeframe specified by federal law after the local child support agency or Attorney General has received a copy of the order. In any action enforced under Part 6 (commencing with Section 5700.101) of Division 9, the notice shall be made in compliance with the requirements of that chapter. The failure of the local child support agency or Attorney General to comply with this subdivision does not affect the validity of any order.

(h) The local child support agency or Attorney General shall give notice to the noncustodial parent against whom a civil action is filed that the local child support agency or Attorney General is not the attorney representing any individual, including, but not limited to, the custodial parent, the child, or the noncustodial parent.

(i) This section does not preclude a person who is receiving services under Section 17400 from filing and prosecuting an independent action to establish, modify, and enforce an order for current support on behalf of that person or a child if that person is not receiving public assistance.

(j) A person who is receiving services under Section 17400 but who is not currently receiving public assistance on their own behalf or on behalf of a child shall be asked to execute, or consent to, any stipulation establishing or modifying a support order in any action in which that person is named as a party, before the stipulation is filed. The local child support agency or Attorney General may not submit to the court for approval a stipulation to establish or modify a support order in the action without first obtaining the signatures of all parties to the action, their attorneys of record, or persons authorized to act on their behalf. Any stipulation approved by the court in violation of this subdivision shall be void.

(k) The local child support agency or Attorney General may not enter into a stipulation that reduces the amount of past due support, including interest and penalties accrued pursuant to an order of current support, on behalf of a person who is receiving support enforcement services under Section 17400 and who is owed support arrearages that exceed unreimbursed public assistance paid to the recipient of the support enforcement services, without first obtaining the consent of the person who is receiving services under Section 17400 on their own behalf or on behalf of the child.

(*l*) The notices required in this section shall be provided in the following manner:

(1) In all cases in which the person receiving services under Section 17400 resides in California, notice shall be provided by mailing the item by first-class mail to the last known address of, or personally delivering the item to, that person.

(2) In all actions enforced under Part 6 (commencing with Section 5700.101) of Division 9, unless otherwise specified, notice shall be provided by mailing the item by first-class mail to the initiating court.

(m) Notwithstanding any other provision of this section, the notices provided for pursuant to subdivisions (c) to (g), inclusive, are not required in foster care cases. *(Added by Stats.1999, c. 478 (A.B.196), § 1. Amended by Stats.1999, c. 480 (S.B.542), § 15; Stats.2000, c. 808 (A.B.1358), § 84.7, eff. Sept. 28, 2000; Stats.2001, c. 176 (S.B.210), § 6; Stats.2004, c. 339 (A.B.1704), § 7; Stats.2015, c. 493 (S.B.646), § 12, eff. Jan. 1, 2016; Stats.2019, c. 115 (A.B.1817), § 148, eff. Jan. 1, 2020.)*

Cross References

Arrears collection enhancement process, development of program, requirements regarding acceptance of offers in compromise, see Family Code § 17560.
Attorney General, generally, see Government Code § 12500 et seq.
County defined for purposes of this Code, see Family Code § 67.

SUPPORT SERVICES

Judgment and order defined for purposes of this Code, see Family Code § 100.
Person defined for purposes of this Code, see Family Code § 105.
Proceeding defined for purposes of this Code, see Family Code § 110.
State defined for purposes of this Code, see Family Code § 145.
Support defined for purposes of this Code, see Family Code § 150.
Support order defined for purposes of this Code, see Family Code § 155.

Research References

Forms

West's California Judicial Council Forms FL–334, Declaration Regarding Address Verification—Postjudgment Request to Modify a Child Custody, Visitation, or Child Support Order.
West's California Judicial Council Forms FL–560, Ex Parte Application for Transfer and Order (UIFSA).
West's California Judicial Council Forms FL–605, Notice and Acknowledgment of Receipt.
West's California Judicial Council Forms FL–615, Stipulation for Judgment or Supplemental Judgment Regarding Parental Obligations and Judgment (Also Available in Spanish).
West's California Judicial Council Forms FL–616, Declaration for Amended Proposed Judgment (Governmental).
West's California Judicial Council Forms FL–627, Order for Genetic (Parentage) Testing.
West's California Judicial Council Forms FL–635, Notice of Entry of Judgment and Proof of Service by Mail (Governmental).
West's California Judicial Council Forms FL–646, Response of Local Child Support Agency to Notice of Intent to Take Independent Action to Enforce Support Order (Governmental).
West's California Judicial Council Forms FL–650, Statement for Registration of California Support Order (Governmental).
West's California Judicial Council Forms FL–660, Ex Parte Motion by Local Child Support Agency and Declaration for Joinder of Other Parent (Governmental).
West's California Judicial Council Forms FL–670, Notice of Motion for Judicial Review of License Denial (Governmental).
West's California Judicial Council Forms FL–675, Order After Judicial Review of License Denial (Governmental).
West's California Judicial Council Forms FL–678, Order Determining Claim of Exemption or Third-Party Claim (Governmental).
West's California Judicial Council Forms FL–683, Order to Show Cause (Governmental).
West's California Judicial Council Forms FL–684, Request for Order and Supporting Declaration (Governmental).
West's California Judicial Council Forms FL–688, Short Form Order After Hearing (Also Available in Spanish).
West's California Judicial Council Forms FL–692, Minutes and Order or Judgment (Also Available in Spanish).
West's California Judicial Council Forms FL–697, Declaration for Default or Uncontested Judgment (Governmental).

§ 17407. Support order or support-related order; appeal taken or opposed by Attorney General; expenses

(a) If the Attorney General is of the opinion that a support order or support-related order is erroneous and presents a question of law warranting an appeal, or that an order is sound and should be defended on appeal, in the public interest the Attorney General may:

(1) Perfect or oppose an appeal to the proper appellate court if the order was issued by a court of this state.

(2) If the order was issued in another state, cause an appeal to be taken or opposed in the other state.

(b) In either case, expenses of the appeal may be paid on order of the Attorney General from funds appropriated for the Office of the Attorney General. *(Added by Stats.1999, c. 652 (S.B.240), § 17.)*

Cross References

Attorney General, generally, see Government Code § 12500 et seq.
Judgment and order defined for purposes of this Code, see Family Code § 100.
State defined for purposes of this Code, see Family Code § 145.
Support defined for purposes of this Code, see Family Code § 150.

Support order defined for purposes of this Code, see Family Code § 155.

§ 17407.5. State reciprocity; declaration; full force and effect unless specified condition is met

A declaration of state reciprocity issued by the Attorney General on or before December 31, 2015, and a declaration issued pursuant to subdivision (b) of Section 5700.308, shall remain in full force and effect unless one of the following occurs:

(a) The declaration is revoked or declared invalid by the Attorney General, in consultation with the department, or by the other party to the reciprocity agreement.

(b) The declaration is superseded by a subsequent federal bilateral agreement with the other party.

(c) The declaration is superseded by the other party's ratification of or accession to the Hague Convention on the International Recovery of Child Support and Other Forms of Family Maintenance. *(Added by Stats.2015, c. 493 (S.B.646), § 13, eff. Jan. 1, 2016.)*

§ 17408. Consolidation of multiple court files; consolidation of orders

(a) Notwithstanding Section 17404, upon noticed motion of the local child support agency, the superior court may consolidate or combine support or reimbursement arrearages owed by one obligor to one obligee in two or more court files into a single court file, or combine or consolidate two or more orders for current child support into a single court file. A motion to consolidate may be made by a local child support agency only if it is seeking to enforce the orders being consolidated. The motion shall be filed only in the court file the local child support agency is seeking to have designated as the primary file.

(b) Orders may be consolidated regardless of the nature of the underlying action, whether initiated under the Welfare and Institutions Code, this code, or another law. Orders for support shall not be consolidated unless the children involved have the same mother and father and venue is proper pursuant to Section 17400.

(c) Upon consolidation of orders, the court shall designate which court file the support orders are being consolidated into the primary file, and which court files are subordinate. Upon consolidation, the court shall order the local child support agency to file a notice in the subordinate court actions indicating the support orders in those actions were consolidated into the primary file. The notice shall state the date of the consolidation, the name of the court, and the primary file number.

(d) Upon consolidation of orders, the superior court shall not issue further orders pertaining to support in a subordinate court file; and all enforcement and modification of support orders shall occur in the primary court action.

(e) After consolidation of court orders, a single wage assignment for current support and arrearages may be issued when possible. *(Added by Stats.1999, c. 478 (A.B.196), § 1.)*

Cross References

Judgment and order defined for purposes of this Code, see Family Code § 100.
State defined for purposes of this Code, see Family Code § 145.
Support defined for purposes of this Code, see Family Code § 150.
Support order defined for purposes of this Code, see Family Code § 155.

Research References

Forms

West's California Judicial Council Forms FL–920, Notice of Consolidation.

§ 17410. Voluntary declaration of paternity

In any action filed by the local child support agency pursuant to Section 17402 or 17404, the local child support agency shall provide the mother and the alleged father the opportunity to voluntarily acknowledge paternity by signing a paternity declaration as described in Section 7574 prior to a hearing or trial where the paternity of a minor child is at issue. The opportunity to voluntarily acknowledge paternity may be provided either before or after an action pursuant to Section 17402 or 17404 is filed and served upon the alleged father. For the purpose of meeting the requirements of this section, the local child support agency may afford the defendant an opportunity to enter into a stipulation for judgment of paternity after an action for paternity has been filed in lieu of the voluntary declaration of paternity. *(Added by Stats.1999, c. 478 (A.B.196), § 1.)*

Cross References

Judgment and order defined for purposes of this Code, see Family Code § 100.
Minor defined for purposes of this Code, see Family Code § 6500.
Support defined for purposes of this Code, see Family Code § 150.

§ 17412. Voluntary declaration of parentage; child support action

(a) Notwithstanding any other law, an action for child support may be brought by the local child support agency on behalf of a minor child or caretaker parent based upon a voluntary declaration of parentage as provided in Chapter 3 (commencing with Section 7570) of Part 2 of Division 12.

(b) Except as provided in Sections 7580 and 7581, the voluntary declaration of parentage shall be given the same force and effect as a judgment for parentage entered by a court of competent jurisdiction. The court shall make appropriate orders for support of the minor child based upon the voluntary declaration of parentage unless evidence is presented that the voluntary declaration of parentage has been rescinded by the parties or set aside by a court as provided in Section 7575, 7576, or 7577.

(c) The Judicial Council shall develop the forms and procedures necessary to implement this section.

(d) This section shall become operative on January 1, 2020. *(Added by Stats.2018, c. 876 (A.B.2684), § 65, eff. Jan. 1, 2019, operative Jan. 1, 2020.)*

Cross References

Judgment and order defined for purposes of this Code, see Family Code § 100.
Minor defined for purposes of this Code, see Family Code § 6500.
Support defined for purposes of this Code, see Family Code § 150.

§ 17414. Parentage stipulation

In any action or proceeding brought by the local child support agency to establish parentage pursuant to Section 17400, the court shall enter a judgment establishing parentage upon the filing of a written stipulation between the parties provided that the stipulation is accompanied by a written advisement and waiver of rights which is signed by the defendant. The written advisement and waiver of rights shall be developed by the Judicial Council. *(Added by Stats.1999, c. 478 (A.B.196), § 1.)*

Cross References

Judgment and order defined for purposes of this Code, see Family Code § 100.
Proceeding defined for purposes of this Code, see Family Code § 110.
Support defined for purposes of this Code, see Family Code § 150.

§ 17415. Public assistance application where parent absent or parentage not established; welfare department referral to local child support agency

(a) It shall be the duty of the county welfare department to refer all cases in which a parent is absent from the home, or in which the parents are unmarried and parentage has not been established by the completion and filing of a voluntary declaration of paternity pursuant to Section 7573 or a court of competent jurisdiction, to the local child support agency immediately at the time the application for public assistance, including Medi–Cal benefits, or certificate of eligibility, is signed by the applicant or recipient, except as provided in Section 17552 and Sections 11477 and 11477.04 of the Welfare and Institutions Code. If an applicant is found to be ineligible, the applicant

§ 17415

shall be notified in writing that the referral of the case to the local child support agency may be terminated at the applicant's request. The county welfare department shall cooperate with the local child support agency and shall make available all pertinent information pursuant to Section 17505.

(b) Upon referral from the county welfare department, the local child support agency shall investigate the question of nonsupport or paternity and shall take all steps necessary to obtain child support for the needy child, enforce spousal support as part of the state plan under Section 17604, and determine paternity in the case of a child born out of wedlock. Upon the advice of the county welfare department that a child is being considered for adoption, the local child support agency shall delay the investigation and other actions with respect to the case until advised that the adoption is no longer under consideration. The granting of public assistance or Medi–Cal benefits to an applicant shall not be delayed or contingent upon investigation by the local child support agency.

(c) In cases where Medi–Cal benefits are the only assistance provided, the local child support agency shall provide child and spousal support services unless the recipient of the services notifies the local child support agency that only services related to securing health insurance benefits are requested.

(d) Whenever a court order has been obtained, any contractual agreement for support between the local child support agency or the county welfare department and the noncustodial parent shall be deemed null and void to the extent that it is not consistent with the court order.

(e) Whenever a family that has been receiving public assistance, including Medi–Cal, ceases to receive assistance, including Medi–Cal, the local child support agency shall, to the extent required by federal regulations, continue to enforce support payments from the noncustodial parent until the individual on whose behalf the enforcement efforts are made sends written notice to the local child support agency requesting that enforcement services be discontinued.

(f) The local child support agency shall, when appropriate, utilize reciprocal arrangements adopted with other states in securing support from an absent parent. In individual cases where utilization of reciprocal arrangements has proven ineffective, the local child support agency may forward to the Attorney General a request to utilize federal courts in order to obtain or enforce orders for child or spousal support. If reasonable efforts to collect amounts assigned pursuant to Section 11477 of the Welfare and Institutions Code have failed, the local child support agency may request that the case be forwarded to the United States Treasury Department for collection in accordance with federal regulations. The Attorney General, when appropriate, shall forward these requests to the Secretary of Health and Human Services, or a designated representative. *(Added by Stats.1999, c. 478 (A.B.196), § 1. Amended by Stats.1999, c. 480 (S.B.542), § 16; Stats.2001, c. 463 (A.B.1449), § 1; Stats.2014, c. 29 (S.B.855), § 1, eff. June 20, 2014.)*

Implementation

For implementation relating to Stats.2001, c. 463 (A.B.1449), see § 6 of that Act.

Cross References

Attorney General, generally, see Government Code § 12500 et seq.
County defined for purposes of this Code, see Family Code § 67.
Establishment of Approved Relative Caregiver Funding Option Program, payment rate, conditions of participation, funds to be used, children under the jurisdiction of juvenile court, see Welfare and Institutions Code § 11461.3.
Judgment and order defined for purposes of this Code, see Family Code § 100.
Juvenile court law, liability for costs of support, see Welfare and Institutions Code § 903.
Spousal support defined for purposes of this Code, see Family Code § 142.
State defined for purposes of this Code, see Family Code § 145.

Support defined for purposes of this Code, see Family Code § 150.

§ 17416. Agency agreement with noncustodial parent

(a) When the local child support agency has undertaken enforcement of support, the local child support agency may enter into an agreement with the noncustodial parent, on behalf of a minor child or children, a spouse, or former spouse for the entry of a judgment without action determining paternity, if applicable, and for periodic child and spousal support payments based on the noncustodial parent's reasonable ability to pay or, if for spousal support, an amount previously ordered by a court of competent jurisdiction. An agreement for entry of a judgment under this section may be executed prior to the birth of the child and may include a provision that the judgment is not to be entered until after the birth of the child.

(b) A judgment based on the agreement shall be entered only if one of the following requirements is satisfied:

(1) The noncustodial parent is represented by legal counsel and the attorney signs a certificate stating: "I have examined the proposed judgment and have advised my client concerning their rights in connection with this matter and the consequences of signing or not signing the agreement for the entry of the judgment and my client, after being so advised, has agreed to the entry of the judgment."

(2) A judge of the court in which the judgment is to be entered, after advising the noncustodial parent concerning their rights in connection with the matter and the consequences of agreeing or not agreeing to the entry of the judgment, makes a finding that the noncustodial parent has appeared before the judge and the judge has determined that under the circumstances of the particular case the noncustodial parent has willingly, knowingly, and intelligently waived due process rights in agreeing to the entry of the judgment.

(c) The clerk shall file the agreement, together with any certificate of the attorney or finding of the court, without the payment of any fees or charges. If the requirements of this section are satisfied, the court shall enter judgment thereon without action. The provisions of Article 4 (commencing with Section 4200) of Chapter 2 of Part 2 of Division 9 or Chapter 4 (commencing with Section 4350) of Part 3 of Division 9 shall apply to the judgment. A judgment for support so entered may be enforced by any means by which any other judgment for support may be enforced.

(d) Upon request of the local child support agency in any case under this section, the clerk shall set the matter for hearing by the court. The hearing shall be held within 10 days after the clerk receives the request. The local child support agency may require the person who signed the agreement for the entry of judgment to attend the hearing by process of subpoena in the same manner as the attendance of a witness in a civil action may be required. The presence of the person who signed the agreement for entry of judgment at the hearing shall constitute the presence of the person in court at the time the order is pronounced for the purposes of Section 1209.5 of the Code of Civil Procedure if the court makes the findings required by paragraph (2) of subdivision (b).

(e) The local child support agency shall cause the following to be served, in the manner specified in Section 415.10, 415.20, 415.30, or 415.40 of the Code of Civil Procedure, upon the person who signed the agreement for entry of the judgment and shall file proof of service thereof with the court:

(1) A copy of the judgment as entered.

(2) If the judgment includes an order for child or spousal support payments, a notice stating the substance of the following: "The court has continuing authority to make an order increasing or decreasing the amount of the child or spousal support payments. You have the right to request that the court order the child and spousal support payments be decreased or eliminated entirely."

(f) An order for child and spousal support included in a judgment entered under this section may be modified or revoked as provided in Article 1 (commencing with Section 3650) of Chapter 6 of Part 1 of Division 9 and in (1) Article 1 (commencing with Section 4000) of Chapter 2 of Part 2 of Division 9 or (2) Chapter 2 (commencing with Section 4320) and Chapter 3 (commencing with Section 4330) of Part 3 of Division 9. The court may modify the order to make the support payments payable to a different person.

(g) For the purposes of this section, in making a determination of the noncustodial parent's reasonable ability to pay, any relevant circumstances set out in Section 4005 shall be considered.

(h) After arrest and before plea or trial, or after conviction or plea of guilty, under Section 270 of the Penal Code, if the defendant appears before the court in which the criminal action is pending and the requirements of paragraph (1) or (2) of subdivision (b) have been satisfied, the court may suspend proceedings or sentence in the criminal action, but this does not limit the later institution of a civil or criminal action or limit the use of any other procedures available to enforce the judgment entered pursuant to this section.

(i) Nothing in this section applies to a case where a civil action has been commenced. *(Added by Stats.1999, c. 478 (A.B.196), § 1. Amended by Stats.2019, c. 115 (A.B.1817), § 149, eff. Jan. 1, 2020.)*

Cross References

Judgment and order defined for purposes of this Code, see Family Code § 100.
Minor defined for purposes of this Code, see Family Code § 6500.
Person defined for purposes of this Code, see Family Code § 105.
Proceeding defined for purposes of this Code, see Family Code § 110.
References to husband, wife, spouses and married persons, persons included for purposes of this Code, see Family Code § 11.
Spousal support defined for purposes of this Code, see Family Code § 142.
Support defined for purposes of this Code, see Family Code § 150.
Venue, actions by or against a city, county, city and county, or local agency, see Code of Civil Procedure § 394.

§ 17418. Number of children; computation of support

In enforcing the provisions of this division, the local child support agency shall inquire of both the custodial and noncustodial parent as to the number of minor children each is legally obligated to support. The local child support agency shall consider the needs of all of these children in computing the level of support requested to be ordered by the court. *(Added by Stats.1999, c. 478 (A.B.196), § 1.)*

Cross References

Minor defined for purposes of this Code, see Family Code § 6500.
Support defined for purposes of this Code, see Family Code § 150.

§ 17420. Earnings assignment order for support

After judgment in any court action brought to enforce the support obligation of a noncustodial parent pursuant to the provisions of this division, the court shall issue an earnings assignment order for support pursuant to Chapter 8 (commencing with Section 5200) of Part 5 of Division 9. *(Added by Stats.1999, c. 478 (A.B.196), § 1.)*

Cross References

Judgment and order defined for purposes of this Code, see Family Code § 100.
Support defined for purposes of this Code, see Family Code § 150.

§ 17422. Medical insurance form; health insurance coverage

(a) The state medical insurance form required in Article 1 (commencing with Section 3750) of Chapter 7 of Part 1 of Division 9 shall include, but shall not be limited to, all of the following:

(1) The parent or parents' names, addresses, and social security numbers.

(2) The name and address of each parent's place of employment.

(3) The name or names, addresses, policy number or numbers, and coverage type of the medical insurance policy or policies of the parents, if any.

(4) The name, CalWORKs case number, social security number, and Title IV–E foster care case number or Medi–Cal case numbers of the parents and children covered by the medical insurance policy or policies.

(b)(1) In an action brought or enforcement proceeding instituted by the local child support agency under this division for payment of child or spousal support, a completed state medical insurance form shall be obtained and sent by the local child support agency to the State Department of Health Care Services in the manner prescribed by the State Department of Health Care Services.

(2) Where it has been determined under Section 3751 that health insurance coverage is not available at no or reasonable cost, the local child support agency shall seek a provision in the support order that provides for health insurance coverage should it become available at no or reasonable cost.

(3) Health insurance coverage shall be considered reasonable in cost if the cost to the responsible parent providing medical support does not exceed 5 percent of the parent's gross income. In applying the 5 percent for the cost of health insurance, the cost is the difference between self-only and family coverage. If the obligor is entitled to a low-income adjustment as provided in paragraph (7) of subdivision (b) of Section 4055, health insurance shall not be enforced, unless the court determines that not requiring medical support would be unjust and inappropriate in the particular case. As used in this section, "health insurance coverage" also includes providing for the delivery of health care services by a fee for service, health maintenance organization, preferred provider organization, or any other type of health care delivery system under which medical services could be provided to the dependent child or children of an absent parent.

(c)(1) The local child support agency shall request employers and other groups offering health insurance coverage that is being enforced under this division to notify the local child support agency if there has been a lapse in insurance coverage. The local child support agency shall be responsible for forwarding information pertaining to the health insurance policy secured for the dependent children for whom the local child support agency is enforcing the court-ordered medical support to the custodial parent.

(2) The local child support agency shall periodically communicate with the State Department of Health Care Services to determine if there have been lapses in health insurance coverage for public assistance applicants and recipients. The State Department of Health Care Services shall notify the local child support agency when there has been a lapse in court-ordered insurance coverage.

(3) The local child support agency shall take appropriate action, civil or criminal, to enforce the obligation to obtain health insurance when there has been a lapse in insurance coverage or failure by the responsible parent to obtain insurance as ordered by the court.

(4) The local child support agency shall inform all individuals upon their application for child support enforcement services that medical support enforcement services are available. *(Added by Stats.1999, c. 478 (A.B.196), § 1. Amended by Stats.2000, c. 119 (S.B.2045), § 3; Stats.2002, c. 927 (A.B.3032), § 4; Stats.2010, c. 103 (S.B.580), § 4; Stats.2019, c. 115 (A.B.1817), § 150, eff. Jan. 1, 2020.)*

Cross References

Department of Health Care Services, generally, see Health and Safety Code § 100100 et seq.
Emancipation of minors, notice of declaration proceedings, warning that court may void or rescind declaration and parents may become liable for support and medical insurance coverage pursuant to this section, see Family Code § 7121.
Judgment and order defined for purposes of this Code, see Family Code § 100.
Proceeding defined for purposes of this Code, see Family Code § 110.

§ 17422

Spousal support defined for purposes of this Code, see Family Code § 142.
State defined for purposes of this Code, see Family Code § 145.
Support defined for purposes of this Code, see Family Code § 150.
Support order defined for purposes of this Code, see Family Code § 155.

Research References

Forms

West's California Judicial Council Forms FL–684, Request for Order and Supporting Declaration (Governmental).

§ 17424. Medical insurance form; submission

(a) A parent who has been served with a medical insurance form shall complete and return the form to the local child support agency's office within 20 calendar days of the date the form was served.

(b) The local child support agency shall send the completed medical insurance form to the department in the manner prescribed by the department. *(Added by Stats.1999, c. 478 (A.B.196), § 1.)*

Cross References

Support defined for purposes of this Code, see Family Code § 150.

§ 17428. Supplemental complaint and judgment

In any action or judgment brought or obtained pursuant to Section 17400, 17402, 17404, or 17416, a supplemental complaint may be filed, pursuant to Section 464 of the Code of Civil Procedure and Section 2330.1, either before or after a final judgment, seeking a judgment or order of paternity or support for a child of the mother and father of the child whose paternity and support are already in issue before the court. A supplemental judgment entered in the proceedings shall include, when appropriate and requested in the supplemental complaint, an order establishing or modifying support for all children named in the original or supplemental actions in conformity with the statewide uniform guideline for child support. A supplemental complaint for paternity or support of children may be filed without leave of court either before or after final judgment in the underlying action. Service of the supplemental summons and complaint shall be made in the manner provided for the initial service of a summons by the Code of Civil Procedure. *(Added by Stats.1999, c. 478 (A.B.196), § 1.)*

Cross References

Judgment and order defined for purposes of this Code, see Family Code § 100.
Proceeding defined for purposes of this Code, see Family Code § 110.
Support defined for purposes of this Code, see Family Code § 150.

Research References

Forms

West's California Judicial Council Forms FL–600, Summons and Complaint or Supplemental Complaint Regarding Parental Obligations (Governmental).

West's California Judicial Council Forms FL–640, Notice and Motion to Cancel (Set Aside) Support Order Based on Presumed Income (Also Available in Spanish).

West's California Judicial Council Forms FL–640–INFO, Information Sheet for Notice and Motion to Cancel (Set Aside) Support Order Based on Presumed Income (Also Available in Spanish).

West's California Judicial Council Forms FL–643, Declaration of Obligor's Income During Judgment Period—Presumed Income Set Aside.

§ 17430. Default judgment; amendment

(a) Notwithstanding any other law, in an action filed by the local child support agency pursuant to Section 17400, 17402, or 17404, a judgment shall be entered without hearing, without the presentation of any other evidence or further notice to the defendant, upon the filing of proof of service by the local child support agency evidencing that more than 30 days have passed since the simplified summons and complaint, proposed judgment, blank answer, blank income and expense declaration, and all notices required by this division were served on the defendant.

(b) If the defendant fails to file an answer with the court within 30 days of having been served as specified in subdivision (d) of Section 17400, or at any time before the default judgment is entered, the proposed judgment filed with the original summons and complaint shall be conformed by the court as the final judgment and a copy provided to the local child support agency, unless the local child support agency has filed a declaration and amended proposed judgment pursuant to subdivision (c).

(c) If the local child support agency receives additional financial information within 30 days of service of the complaint and proposed judgment on the defendant and the additional information would result in a support order that is different from the amount in the proposed judgment, the local child support agency shall file a declaration setting forth the additional information and an amended proposed judgment. The declaration and amended proposed judgment shall be served on the defendant in compliance with Section 1013 of the Code of Civil Procedure or otherwise as provided by law. The defendant's time to answer or otherwise appear shall be extended to 30 days from the date of service of the declaration and amended proposed judgment.

(d) Upon entry of the judgment, the clerk of the court shall provide a conformed copy of the judgment to the local child support agency. The local child support agency shall mail by first-class mail, postage prepaid, a notice of entry of judgment by default and a copy of the judgment to the defendant to the address where the summons and complaint were served and last known address if different from that address. *(Added by Stats.1999, c. 478 (A.B.196), § 1. Amended by Stats.1999, c. 480 (S.B.542), § 17; Stats.1999, c. 652 (S.B.240), § 17.5; Stats.2000, c. 808 (A.B.1358), § 85, eff. Sept. 28, 2000; Stats.2002, c. 927 (A.B.3032), § 5; Stats.2019, c. 115 (A.B.1817), § 151, eff. Jan. 1, 2020.)*

Cross References

Income and expense declaration defined for purposes of this Code, see Family Code § 95.
Judgment and order defined for purposes of this Code, see Family Code § 100.
Support defined for purposes of this Code, see Family Code § 150.
Support order defined for purposes of this Code, see Family Code § 155.

Research References

Forms

West's California Judicial Council Forms FL–600, Summons and Complaint or Supplemental Complaint Regarding Parental Obligations (Governmental).

West's California Judicial Council Forms FL–620, Request to Enter Default Judgment (Governmental).

West's California Judicial Council Forms FL–625, Stipulation and Order (Also Available in Spanish).

West's California Judicial Council Forms FL–630, Judgment Regarding Parental Obligations (Also Available in Spanish).

West's California Judicial Council Forms FL–635, Notice of Entry of Judgment and Proof of Service by Mail (Governmental).

West's California Judicial Council Forms FL–640, Notice and Motion to Cancel (Set Aside) Support Order Based on Presumed Income (Also Available in Spanish).

West's California Judicial Council Forms FL–640–INFO, Information Sheet for Notice and Motion to Cancel (Set Aside) Support Order Based on Presumed Income (Also Available in Spanish).

West's California Judicial Council Forms FL–643, Declaration of Obligor's Income During Judgment Period—Presumed Income Set Aside.

§ 17432. Setting aside part of judgment or order concerning amount of child support to be paid

(a) In any action filed by the local child support agency pursuant to Section 17400, 17402, or 17404, the court may, on any terms that may be just, set aside that part of the judgment or order concerning the amount of child support to be paid. This relief may be granted after the six- month time limit of Section 473 of the Code of Civil Procedure has elapsed, based on the grounds, and within the time limits, specified in this section.

(b) This section shall apply only to judgments or orders for support that were based upon presumed income as specified in subdivision (d) of Section 17400 and that were entered after the entry of the default of the defendant under Section 17430. This section shall apply only to the amount of support ordered and not that portion of the judgment or order concerning the determination of parentage.

(c) The court may set aside the child support order contained in a judgment described in subdivision (b) if the defendant's income was substantially different for the period of time during which judgment was effective compared with the income the defendant was presumed to have. A "substantial difference" means that amount of income that would result in an order for support that deviates from the order entered by default by 10 percent or more.

(d) Application for relief under this section shall be filed together with an income and expense declaration or simplified financial statement or other information concerning income for any relevant years. The Judicial Council may combine the application for relief under this section and the proposed answer into a single form.

(e) The burden of proving that the actual income of the defendant deviated substantially from the presumed income shall be on the party seeking to set aside the order.

(f) A motion for relief under this section shall be filed within one year of the first collection of money by the local child support agency or the obligee. The one-year time period shall run from the date that the local child support agency receives the first collection.

(g) Within three months from the date the local child support agency receives the first collection for any order established using presumed income, the local child support agency shall check all appropriate sources for income information, and if income information exists, the local child support agency shall make a determination whether the order qualifies for set aside under this section. If the order qualifies for set aside, the local child support agency shall bring a motion for relief under this section.

(h) In all proceedings under this section, before granting relief, the court shall consider the amount of time that has passed since the entry of the order, the circumstances surrounding the defendant's default, the relative hardship on the child or children to whom the duty of support is owed, the caretaker parent, and the defendant, and other equitable factors that the court deems appropriate.

(i) If the court grants the relief requested, the court shall issue a new child support order using the appropriate child support guidelines currently in effect. The new order shall have the same commencement date as the order set aside.

(j) The Judicial Council shall review and modify any relevant forms for purposes of this section. Any modifications to the forms shall be effective July 1, 2005. Prior to the implementation of any modified Judicial Council forms, the local child support agency or custodial parent may file any request to set aside a default judgment under this section using Judicial Council Form FL–680 entitled "Notice of Motion (Governmental)" and form FL–684 entitled "Request for Order and Supporting Declaration (Governmental)." (Added by Stats.1999, c. 478 (A.B.196), § 1. Amended by Stats.2002, c. 927 (A.B.3032), § 6; Stats.2003, c. 225 (A.B.1752), § 4, eff. Aug. 11, 2003; Stats.2004, c. 339 (A.B.1704), § 8.)

Cross References

Income and expense declaration defined for purposes of this Code, see Family Code § 95.
Judgment and order defined for purposes of this Code, see Family Code § 100.
Proceeding defined for purposes of this Code, see Family Code § 110.
Support defined for purposes of this Code, see Family Code § 150.

Support order defined for purposes of this Code, see Family Code § 155.

Research References

Forms

California Practice Guide: Rutter Family Law Forms Form 16:5, Notice and Motion to Cancel (Set Aside) Support Order Based on Presumed Income.
West's California Judicial Council Forms FL–640, Notice and Motion to Cancel (Set Aside) Support Order Based on Presumed Income (Also Available in Spanish).
West's California Judicial Council Forms FL–640–INFO, Information Sheet for Notice and Motion to Cancel (Set Aside) Support Order Based on Presumed Income (Also Available in Spanish).
West's California Judicial Council Forms FL–643, Declaration of Obligor's Income During Judgment Period—Presumed Income Set Aside.

§ 17433. Relief from default judgment; mistaken identity; remedies

In an action in which a judgment or order for support was entered after the entry of the default of the defendant under Section 17430, the court shall relieve the defendant from that judgment or order if the defendant establishes that the defendant was mistakenly identified in the order or in any subsequent documents or proceedings as the person having an obligation to provide support. The defendant shall also be entitled to the remedies specified in subdivisions (d) and (e) of Section 17530 with respect to any actions taken to enforce that judgment or order. This section is only intended to apply where an order has been entered against a person who is not the support obligor named in the judgment or order. (Added by Stats.1999, c. 653 (A.B.380), § 16. Amended by Stats.2000, c. 808 (A.B.1358), § 85.3, eff. Sept. 28, 2000; Stats.2019, c. 115 (A.B.1817), § 152, eff. Jan. 1, 2020.)

Cross References

Judgment and order defined for purposes of this Code, see Family Code § 100.
Person defined for purposes of this Code, see Family Code § 105.
Proceeding defined for purposes of this Code, see Family Code § 110.
Support defined for purposes of this Code, see Family Code § 150.

§ 17433.5. Interest accruing on obligation for current child, spousal, family, or medical support due in a given month

In any action enforced pursuant to this article, no interest shall accrue on an obligation for current child, spousal, family, or medical support due in a given month until the first day of the following month. (Added by Stats.2006, c. 75 (A.B.1808), § 7, eff. July 12, 2006.)

§ 17434. Booklet about support; toll-free information hotline

(a) The department shall publish a booklet describing the proper procedures and processes for the collection and payment of child and spousal support. The booklet shall be written in language understandable to the lay person and shall direct the reader to obtain the assistance of the local child support agency, the family law facilitator, or legal counsel where appropriate. The department may contract on a competitive basis with an organization or individual to write the booklet.

(b) The department shall have primary responsibility for the design and development of the contents of the booklet. The department shall solicit comment regarding the content of the booklet from the Director of the Administrative Office of the Courts. The department shall verify the appropriateness and accuracy of the contents of the booklet with at least one representative of each of the following organizations:

(1) A local child support agency.

(2) The State Attorney General's office.

(3) A community organization that advocates for the rights of custodial parents.

(4) A community organization that advocates for the rights of supporting parents.

§ 17434

(c) Upon receipt of booklets on support collection, each county welfare department shall provide a copy to each head of household whose application for public assistance under Division 9 (commencing with Section 10000) of the Welfare and Institutions Code has been approved and for whom support rights have been assigned pursuant to Section 11477 of the Welfare and Institutions Code. The department shall provide copies of the booklet to local child support agencies for distribution, and to any person upon request. The department shall also distribute the booklets to all superior courts. Upon receipt of those booklets, each clerk of the court shall provide two copies of the booklet to the petitioner or plaintiff in any action involving the support of a minor child. The moving party shall serve a copy of the booklet on the responding party.

(d) The department shall expand the information provided under its toll-free information hotline in response to inquiries regarding the process and procedures for collection and payment of child and spousal support. This toll-free number shall be advertised as providing information on child and spousal support. The hotline personnel shall not provide legal consultation or advice, but shall provide only referral services.

(e) The department shall maintain a file of referral sources to provide callers to the telephone hotline with the following information specific to the county in which the caller resides:

(1) The location and telephone number of the local child support agency, the county welfare office, the family law facilitator, and any other government agency that handles child and spousal support matters.

(2) The telephone number of the local bar association for referral to attorneys in family law practice.

(3) The name and telephone number of at least one organization that advocates the payment of child and spousal support or the name and telephone number of at least one organization that advocates the rights of supporting parents, if these organizations exist in the county. *(Added by Stats.1999, c. 478 (A.B.196), § 1. Amended by Stats.2000, c. 808 (A.B.1358), § 86, eff. Sept. 28, 2000; Stats.2016, c. 474 (A.B.2882), § 15, eff. Jan. 1, 2017.)*

Cross References

Attorney General, generally, see Government Code § 12500 et seq.
County defined for purposes of this Code, see Family Code § 67.
Family support defined for purposes of this Code, see Family Code § 92.
Minor defined for purposes of this Code, see Family Code § 6500.
Person defined for purposes of this Code, see Family Code § 105.
Petitioner defined for purposes of this Code, see Family Code § 126.
Spousal support defined for purposes of this Code, see Family Code § 142.
State defined for purposes of this Code, see Family Code § 145.
Support defined for purposes of this Code, see Family Code § 150.

§ 17440. United States military and National Guard service members; modification of child support; form; motion by local child support agency

(a) The Department of Child Support Services shall work with all branches of the United States military and the National Guard to ensure that information is made available regarding the rights and abilities of activated service members to have their support orders modified based on a change in income resulting from their activation, or other change of circumstance affecting the child support calculation, or to have a portion of their child support arrearages compromised pursuant to Section 17560.

(b) No later than 90 days after the effective date of this section, the department shall develop a form for completion by the service member that will allow the local child support agency to proceed with a motion for modification without the service member being required to appear. The form shall contain only the information necessary for the local child support agency to proceed with the motion.

(c) Within five business days of receipt of a properly completed form, the local child support agency shall bring a motion to modify the support order. The local child support agency shall bring the motion if the change in circumstances would result in any change in the dollar amount of the support order.

(d) The department shall work with the United States military to have this form and the form developed pursuant to Section 3651 distributed at all mobilization stations or other appropriate locations to ensure timely notification to all activated personnel of their rights and responsibilities. *(Added by Stats.2005, c. 154 (S.B.1082), § 4, eff. Aug. 30, 2005.)*

Cross References

Arrears collection enhancement process, see Family Code § 17560.
Modification of custody or visitation order, military service as justification, see Family Code § 3047.
Modification, termination, or set-aside of support orders, power of court, see Family Code § 3651.
Modification, termination, or set-aside of support orders, retroactive application, see Family Code § 3653.

§ 17441. Repealed by Stats.2006, c. 876 (S.B.1483), § 1, operative Jan. 1, 2010

ARTICLE 1.5. DELINQUENT CHILD SUPPORT OBLIGATIONS AND FINANCIAL INSTITUTION DATA MATCH

Section
17450. Definitions; manner of collecting child support delinquencies; return or retention; delegation of functions to Franchise Tax Board; letter of agreement and interagency agreement between department and Franchise Tax Board.
17452. Tax return information available to department; no obligation or liability incurred; privacy and confidentiality.
17453. Financial Institution Data Match System; guidelines; governmental access and misuse of information; compilation of records; identifying information; no obligation or liability incurred; notification of certain circumstances of obligors of past-due support; cost reimbursement.
17454. Request for depository institution to provide designated address for receiving notices to withhold; liability for failure to withhold; withholding delinquency and interest by depository institution from credits or things of value.
17456. Compliance without legal or equitable action; deposit accounts or accounts to be withheld; notice to each person named on account; contents and service charge.
17458. Repealed.
17460. Reciprocal agreements with other states; exchange of information with Internal Revenue Service; interagency agreements; cost reimbursement and funding.

Cross References

Collection of child support, provisions in effect until Director of Department of Child Support Services revokes delegation of authority to executive officer of Franchise Tax Board, see Revenue and Taxation Code § 19276.

§ 17450. Definitions; manner of collecting child support delinquencies; return or retention; delegation of functions to Franchise Tax Board; letter of agreement and interagency agreement between department and Franchise Tax Board

(a) For purposes of this article:

(1) "Child support delinquency" means a delinquency defined in subdivision (c) of Section 17500.

(2) "Earnings" shall include the items described in Section 5206.

(b)(1) When a delinquency is submitted to the department pursuant to subdivision (c) of Section 17500, the amount of the child support delinquency shall be collected by the department in any manner authorized under state or federal law.

(2) Any compensation, fee, commission, expense, or other fee for service incurred by the department in the collection of a child support delinquency authorized under this article shall not be an obligation of, or collected from, the obligated parent.

(c)(1) The department may return or allow a local child support agency to retain a child support delinquency for a specified purpose for collection where the department determines that the return or retention of the delinquency for the purpose so specified will enhance the collectibility of the delinquency. The department shall establish a process whereby a local child support agency may request and shall be allowed to withdraw, rescind, or otherwise recall the submittal of an account that has been submitted.

(2) If an obligor is disabled, meets the federal Supplemental Security Income resource test, and is receiving Supplemental Security Income/State Supplementary Payments (SSI/SSP), or, but for excess income as described in Section 416.1100 and following of Part 416 of Title 20 of the Code of Federal Regulations, would be eligible to receive as SSI/SSP, pursuant to Section 12200 of the Welfare and Institutions Code, and the obligor has supplied the local child support agency with proof of eligibility for, and, if applicable, receipt of, SSI/SSP or Social Security Disability Insurance benefits, then the child support delinquency shall not be referred to the department for collection, and, if referred, shall be withdrawn, rescinded, or otherwise recalled from the department by the local child support agency. The department shall not take any collection action, or if the local child support agency has already taken collection action, shall cease collection actions in the case of a disabled obligor when the delinquency is withdrawn, rescinded, or otherwise recalled by the local child support agency in accordance with the process established as described in paragraph (1).

(d) It is the intent of the Legislature that when the California Child Support Enforcement System (CSE) is fully operational, any statutes that should be modified based upon the status of the system shall be revised. During the development and implementation of CSE, the department, as the Title IV–D agency, may, through appropriate interagency agreement, delegate any and all of the functions or procedures specified in this article to the Franchise Tax Board. The Franchise Tax Board shall perform those functions or procedures as specified in Sections 19271 to 19275, inclusive, of the Revenue and Taxation Code until the director, by letter to the executive officer of the Franchise Tax Board, revokes the delegation of Title IV–D functions. Sections 19271 to 19275, inclusive, of the Revenue and Taxation Code shall be effective for these purposes until the revocation of delegation to the Franchise Tax Board.

(e) Consistent with the development and implementation of the California Child Support Enforcement System, the Franchise Tax Board and the department shall enter into a letter of agreement and an interagency agreement whereby the department shall assume responsibility for collection of child support delinquencies and the Financial Institution Data Match System as set forth in this article. The letter of agreement and interagency agreement shall, at a minimum, set forth all of the following:

(1) Contingent upon the enactment of the Budget Act, and staffing authorization from the Department of Finance and the Department of Human Resources, the department shall assume responsibility for leadership and staffing of the collection of child support delinquencies and the Financial Institution Data Match System.

(2) All employees and other personnel who staff or provide support for the collection of child support delinquencies and the Financial Institution Data Match System at the Franchise Tax Board shall become the employees of the department at their existing or equivalent classification, salaries, and benefits.

(3) Any other provisions necessary to ensure continuity of function and meet or exceed existing levels of service, including, but not limited to, agreements for continued use of automated systems used by the Franchise Tax Board to locate child support obligors and their assets. *(Added by Stats.2004, c. 806 (A.B.2358), § 6. Amended by Gov.Reorg.Plan No. 1 of 2011, § 31, eff. Sept. 9, 2011, operative July 1, 2012; Stats.2012, c. 665 (S.B.1308), § 13; Stats.2016, c. 474 (A.B. 2882), § 16, eff. Jan. 1, 2017; Stats.2019, c. 115 (A.B.1817), § 153, eff. Jan. 1, 2020.)*

§ 17452. Tax return information available to department; no obligation or liability incurred; privacy and confidentiality

(a) Subject to state and federal privacy and information security laws, the Franchise Tax Board shall make tax return information available to the department, upon request, for the purpose of collecting child support delinquencies referred to the department.

(b) For purposes of this article, the Franchise Tax Board shall incur no obligation or liability to any person arising from any of the following:

(1) Furnishing information to the department as required by this section.

(2) Failing to disclose to a taxpayer or accountholder that the name, address, social security number, or other taxpayer identification number or other identifying information of that person was included in the data exchange with the department required by this section.

(3) Any other action taken in good faith to comply with the requirements of this section.

(c) It is the intent of the Legislature that any provision of income tax return information by the Franchise Tax Board to the department pursuant to this article shall be done in accordance with the privacy and confidential information laws of this state and of the United States, and to the satisfaction of the Franchise Tax Board. *(Added by Stats.2004, c. 806 (A.B.2358), § 6.)*

§ 17453. Financial Institution Data Match System; guidelines; governmental access and misuse of information; compilation of records; identifying information; no obligation or liability incurred; notification of certain circumstances of obligors of past-due support; cost reimbursement

(a) The department, in coordination with financial institutions doing business in this state, shall operate a Financial Institution Data Match System utilizing automated data exchanges to the maximum extent feasible. The Financial Institution Data Match System shall be implemented and maintained pursuant to guidelines prescribed by the department. These guidelines shall include a structure by which financial institutions, or their designated data-processing agents, shall receive from the department the file or files of past-due support obligors compiled in accordance with subdivision (c), so that the institution shall match with its own list of accountholders to identify past-due support obligor accountholders at the institution. To the extent allowed by the federal Personal Responsibility and Work Opportunity Reconciliation Act of 1996 (P.L. 104–193),[1] the guidelines shall include an option by which financial institutions without the technical ability to process the data exchange, or without the ability to employ a third-party data processor to process the data exchange, may forward to the department a list of all accountholders and their social security numbers, so that the department shall match that list with the file or files of past-due support obligors compiled in accordance with subdivision (c).

(b) The Financial Institution Data Match System shall not be subject to any limitation set forth in Chapter 20 (commencing with Section 7460) of Division 7 of Title 1 of the Government Code. However, any use of the information provided pursuant to this

§ 17453

section for any purpose other than the enforcement and collection of a child support delinquency, as set forth in Section 17450, shall be a violation of Section 17212.

(c)(1) Until implementation of the California Child Support Automation System, each county shall compile a file of support obligors with judgments and orders that are being enforced by local child support agencies pursuant to Section 17400, and who are past due in the payment of their support obligations. The file shall be compiled, updated, and forwarded to the department, in accordance with the guidelines prescribed by the department.

(2) The department shall compile a file of obligors with support arrearages from requests made by other states for administrative enforcement in interstate cases, in accordance with federal requirements pursuant to paragraph 14 of subsection (a) of Section 666 of Title 42 of the United States Code. The file shall include, to the extent possible, the obligor's address.

(d) To effectuate the Financial Institution Data Match System, financial institutions subject to this section shall do all of the following:

(1) Provide to the department on a quarterly basis, the name, record address and other addresses, social security number or other taxpayer identification number, and other identifying information for each noncustodial parent who maintains an account at the institution and who owes past-due support, as identified by the department by name and social security number or other taxpayer identification number.

(2) Except as provided in subdivision (j), in response to a notice or order to withhold issued by the department, withhold from any accounts of the obligor the amount of any past-due support stated on the notice or order and transmit the amount to the department in accordance with Section 17454.

(e) Unless otherwise required by applicable law, a financial institution furnishing a report or providing information to the department pursuant to this section shall not disclose to a depositor, accountholder, codepositor, or coaccountholder, that the name, address, social security number, or other taxpayer identification number or other identifying information of that person has been received from, or furnished to, the department.

(f) A financial institution shall incur no obligation or liability to any person arising from any of the following:

(1) Furnishing information to the department as required by this section.

(2) Failing to disclose to a depositor, accountholder, codepositor, or coaccountholder, that the name, address, social security number, or other taxpayer identification number or other identifying information of that person was included in the data exchange with the department required by this section.

(3) Withholding or transmitting any assets in response to a notice or order to withhold issued by the department as a result of the data exchange. This paragraph shall not preclude any liability that may result if the financial institution does not comply with subdivision (b) of Section 17456.

(4) Any other action taken in good faith to comply with the requirements of this section.

(g)(1) With respect to files compiled under paragraph (1) of subdivision (c), the department shall forward to the counties, in accordance with guidelines prescribed by the department, information obtained from the financial institutions pursuant to this section. No county shall use this information for directly levying on any account. Each county shall keep the information confidential as provided by Section 17212.

(2) With respect to files compiled under paragraph (2) of subdivision (c), the amount collected by the department shall be deposited and distributed to the referring state in accordance with Section 17458.

(h) For those noncustodial parents owing past-due support for which there is a match under paragraph (1) of subdivision (d), the amount past due as indicated on the file or files compiled pursuant to subdivision (c) at the time of the match shall be a delinquency under this article for the purposes of the department taking any collection action pursuant to Section 17454.

(i) A child support delinquency need not be referred to the department for collection if a jurisdiction outside this state is enforcing the support order.

(j)(1) Each county shall notify the department upon the occurrence of the circumstances described in the following subparagraphs with respect to an obligor of past-due support:

(A) A court has ordered an obligor to make scheduled payments on a child support arrearages obligation and the obligor is in compliance with that order.

(B) An earnings assignment order or an order/notice to withhold income that includes an amount for past-due support has been served on the obligated parent's employer and earnings are being withheld pursuant to the earnings assignment order or an order/notice to withhold income.

(C) At least 50 percent of the obligated parent's earnings are being withheld for support.

(2) Notwithstanding Section 704.070 of the Code of Civil Procedure, if any of the conditions set forth in paragraph (1) exist, the assets of an obligor held by a financial institution are subject to levy as provided by paragraph (2) of subdivision (d). However, the first three thousand five hundred dollars ($3,500) of an obligor's assets are exempt from collection under this subdivision without the obligor having to file a claim of exemption.

(3) If any of the conditions set forth in paragraph (1) exist, an obligor may apply for a claim of exemption pursuant to Article 2 (commencing with Section 703.510) of Chapter 4 of Division 2 of Title 9 of Part 2 of the Code of Civil Procedure for an amount that is less than or equal to the total amount levied. The sole basis for a claim of exemption under this subdivision shall be the financial hardship for the obligor and the obligor's dependents.

(4) For the purposes of a claim of exemption made pursuant to paragraph (3), Section 688.030 of the Code of Civil Procedure shall not apply.

(5) For claims of exemption made pursuant to paragraph (3), the local child support agency responsible for enforcement of the obligor's child support order shall be the levying officer for the purpose of compliance with the provisions set forth in Article 2 (commencing with Section 703.510) of Chapter 4 of Division 2 of Title 9 of Part 2 of the Code of Civil Procedure except for the release of property required by subdivision (e) of Section 703.580 of the Code of Civil Procedure.

(6) The local child support agency shall notify the department within two business days of the receipt of a claim of exemption from an obligor. The department shall direct the financial institution subject to the order to withhold to hold any funds subject to the order pending notification by the department to remit or release the amounts held.

(7) The superior court in the county in which the local child support agency enforcing the support obligation is located shall have jurisdiction to determine the amount of exemption to be allowed. The court shall consider the needs of the obligor, the obligee, and all persons the obligor is required to support, and all other relevant circumstances in determining whether to allow any exemption pursuant to this subdivision. The court shall give effect to its determination by an order specifying the extent to which the amount levied is exempt.

(8) Within two business days of receipt of an endorsed copy of a court order issued pursuant to subdivision (e) of Section 703.580 of the Code of Civil Procedure, the local child support agency shall provide the department with a copy of the order. The department shall instruct the financial institution to remit or release the obligor's funds in accordance with the court's order.

(k) Out of any money received from the federal government for the purpose of reimbursing financial institutions for their actual and reasonable costs incurred in complying with this section, the state shall reimburse those institutions. To the extent that money is not provided by the federal government for that purpose, the state shall not reimburse financial institutions for their costs in complying with this section.

(*l*) For purposes of this section:

(1) "Account" means any demand deposit account, share or share draft account, checking or negotiable withdrawal order account, savings account, time deposit account, or a money market mutual fund account, whether or not the account bears interest.

(2) "Financial institution" has the same meaning as defined in paragraph (1) of subsection (d) of Section 669A of Title 42 of the United States Code. *(Added by Stats.2004, c. 806 (A.B.2358), § 6.)*

¹ See 42 U.S.C.A. § 601 et seq.

§ 17454. Request for depository institution to provide designated address for receiving notices to withhold; liability for failure to withhold; withholding delinquency and interest by depository institution from credits or things of value

(a) At least 45 days before sending a notice to withhold, the department shall request that a depository institution provide the department with a designated address for receiving notices to withhold.

(b) Once the depository institution has specified a designated address pursuant to subdivision (a), the department shall send all notices to that address unless the depository institution provides notification of another address. The department shall send all notices to withhold to a new designated address 30 days after notification.

(c) If a notice to withhold is mailed to the branch where the account is located or principal banking office, the depository institution shall be liable for a failure to withhold only to the extent that the accounts can be identified in information normally maintained at that location in the ordinary course of business.

(d) The department may by notice, served by magnetic media, electronic transmission, or other electronic technology, require any depository institution, as defined in the Federal Reserve Act (12 U.S.C.A. Sec. 461 (b)(1)(A)), that the department, in its sole discretion, has reason to believe may have in its possession, or under its control, any credits or other personal property or other things of value, belonging to a child support obligor, to withhold, from the credits or other personal property or other things of value, the amount of any child support delinquency, and interest, due from an obligor and transmit that amount withheld to the department at the times that it may designate, but not less than 10 business days from receipt of the notice. The notice shall state the amount due from the obligor and shall be delivered or transmitted to the branch or office reported pursuant to subdivision (a), or other address designated by that depository institution for purposes of the department serving notice by magnetic media, electronic transmission, or other electronic technology.

(e) For purposes of this section, the term "address" shall include telephone or modem number, facsimile number, or any other number designated by the depository institution to receive data by electronic means. *(Added by Stats.2004, c. 806 (A.B.2358), § 6.)*

§ 17456. Compliance without legal or equitable action; deposit accounts or accounts to be withheld; notice to each person named on account; contents and service charge

(a) Any person required to withhold and transmit any amount pursuant to this article shall comply with the requirement without resort to any legal or equitable action in a court of law or equity. Any person paying to the department any amount required by it to be withheld is not liable therefore to the person from whom withheld unless the amount withheld is refunded to the withholding agent. However, if a depository institution, as defined in the Federal Reserve Act (12 U.S.C.A. Sec. 461(b)(1)(A)) withholds and pays to the department pursuant to this article any moneys held in a deposit account in which the delinquent obligor and another person or persons have an interest, or in an account held in the name of a third party or parties in which the delinquent obligor is ultimately determined to have no interest, the depository institution paying those moneys to the department is not liable therefore to any of the persons who have an interest in the account, unless the amount withheld is refunded to the withholding agent.

(b) In the case of a deposit account or accounts for which this notice to withhold applies, the depository institution shall send a notice by first-class mail to each person named on the account or accounts included in the notice from the department, provided that a current address for each person is available to the institution. This notice shall inform each person as to the reason for the hold placed on the account or accounts, the amount subject to being withheld, and the date by which this amount is to be remitted to the department. An institution may assess the account or accounts of each person receiving this notice a reasonable service charge not to exceed three dollars ($3). *(Added by Stats.2004, c. 806 (A.B.2358), § 6.)*

§ 17458. Repealed by Stats.2016, c. 474 (A.B.2882), § 17, eff. Jan. 1, 2017

§ 17460. Reciprocal agreements with other states; exchange of information with Internal Revenue Service; interagency agreements; cost reimbursement and funding

(a) As necessary, the department shall seek reciprocal agreements with other states to improve its ability to collect child support payments from out-of-state obligated parents on behalf of custodial parents residing in California. The department may pursue agreements with the Internal Revenue Service, as permitted by federal law, to improve collections of child support delinquencies from out-of-state obligated parents through cooperative agreements with the service.

(b) The California Child Support Enforcement System shall, for purposes of this article, include the capacity to interface and exchange information, if feasible, with the Internal Revenue Service, to enable the immediate reporting and tracking of obligated parent information.

(c) The department shall enter into any interagency agreements that are necessary for the implementation of this article. State departments and boards shall cooperate with the department to the extent necessary for the implementation of this article. Out of any money received from the federal government for the purpose of reimbursing state departments and boards for their actual and reasonable costs incurred in complying with this section, the department shall reimburse those departments and boards. To the extent that money is not provided by the federal government for that purpose, and subject to the annual Budget Act, the state shall fund departments and boards for their costs in complying with this section. *(Added by Stats.2004, c. 806 (A.B.2358), § 6. Amended by Stats.2016, c. 474 (A.B.2882), § 18, eff. Jan. 1, 2017.)*

ARTICLE 2. COLLECTIONS AND ENFORCEMENT

Section	
17500.	Responsibility of department and local child support agency for collection and enforcement; administering wage withholding; submission of delinquencies; delinquency existing at time case is opened.
17501.	Repealed.
17502.	Inability to deliver child support payments due to inability to locate obligee.
17504.	First fifty dollars collected in month; payment to aid recipients; facilitation of automation changes.
17504.	Monthly child support collections; payment to aid recipients; methods of implementation until regulations are adopted.
17504.1.	Renumbered.
17504.2.	Collections in payment of assigned support obligations; passthrough to former recipients of aid; payments that cannot be delivered.
17504.4.	CalWORKs recipients or former recipients; notice of amount of assigned support payments made on behalf of recipient, former recipient, or family member.
17504.6.	Report on impact of passthrough payments on eligibility determinations for other need-based assistance programs.
17505.	State and local agencies, cooperation with local child support agencies in enforcement of support obligations; information on location of children, location and property of parents.
17506.	California Parent Locator Service and Central Registry; California Child Support Enforcement System.
17508.	Employment Development Department; access to information.
17509.	Information compare; obligor employment and earning withholding order.
17510.	Workers' compensation notification project.
17512.	Employment and income information from employer or labor organization.
17514.	Child abduction records.
17516.	Social service benefits use for support obligation.
17518.	Unemployment compensation benefits.
17520.	License applicants; compliance with support orders; license issuance, renewal, and suspension; review.
17520.5.	Denying, withholding, or suspending driver's license; support obligor at or below 70 percent median income.
17521.	Order to show cause or notice of motion for judicial review of district attorney's decision; appropriate court.
17522.	Delinquent support obligors; collection or lien enforcement by levy.
17522.5.	Issuance of levy or notice to withhold; liquidation of asset by person, financial institution, or securities intermediary in possession or control of financial asset; manner of liquidation and transfer of proceeds; value of financial assets exceeding total amount of support due; instructions for liquidation by obligor.
17523.	Lien for child support against personal property; perfection; priority; enforcement.
17523.5.	Lien for child support against real property; digitized or digital electronic record.
17524.	Statement of arrearages.
17525.	Notice of support delinquency; contents.
17526.	Statement of arrearages; review.

Section	
17528.	Public Employees' Retirement System; withholding overdue support obligations.
17530.	Support enforcement action; allegation of error due to mistaken identity; administrative and judicial remedies; penalty.
17531.	Closure of a child support case; summary criminal history information in case; deletion or purging of file.
17540.	Payment of county claims for federal and state reimbursement; waiver of time limitation.
17550.	Establishment of regulations by which the local child support agency may compromise parents' liability for public assistance debt in cases of separation or desertion of parent from child; conditions.
17552.	Regulations concerning determinations whether or not best interests of child or nonminor require case to be referred to local child support agency for child support services in situations resulting in foster care assistance, CalWORKS or Kin-GAP payments, or other specified aid; determination factors; review; nonminor dependents.
17555.	Appropriations in annual Budget Act for purpose of augmenting funding for collection responsibilities; requirements; legislative intent.
17556.	Annual report.
17560.	Arrears collection enhancement process; development of program; acceptance of offers in compromise.
17561.	Annual report on implementation of California Child Support Automation System; joint production by Office of the Chief Information Officer and Department of Child Support Services; contents.

§ 17500. Responsibility of department and local child support agency for collection and enforcement; administering wage withholding; submission of delinquencies; delinquency existing at time case is opened

(a) In carrying out its obligations under Title IV-D of the Social Security Act (42 U.S.C. Sec. 651 et seq.), the department and the local child support agency shall have the responsibility for promptly and effectively collecting and enforcing child support obligations.

(b) The department and the local child support agency are the public agencies responsible for administering wage withholding for the purposes of Title IV-D of the Social Security Act (42 U.S.C. Sec. 651 et seq.).

(c) Except as provided in Section 17450, the local child support agency shall submit child support delinquencies to the department for purposes of supplementing the collection efforts of the local child support agencies. Submissions shall be in the form and manner and at the time prescribed by the department. Collection shall be made by the department in accordance with Section 17450. For purposes of this subdivision, "child support delinquency" means an arrearage or otherwise past due amount that accrues when an obligor fails to make any court-ordered support payment when due, which is more than 60 days past due, and the aggregate amount of which exceeds one hundred dollars ($100).

(d) If a child support delinquency exists at the time a case is opened by the local child support agency, the responsibility for the collection of the child support delinquency shall be submitted to the department no later than 30 days after receipt of the case by the local child support agency. *(Added by Stats.1999, c. 478 (A.B.196), § 1. Amended by Stats.1999, c. 480 (S.B.542), § 18; Stats.2001, c. 111 (A.B.429), § 5, eff. July 30, 2001; Stats.2001, c. 651 (A.B.891), § 4; Stats.2004, c. 339 (A.B.1704), § 9; Stats.2004, c. 806 (A.B.2358), § 4.)*

Cross References

Child support delinquency, statewide automated system for reporting administered by the department, see Family Code § 4701.

Collection of tax, referral of child support delinquencies, see Revenue and Taxation Code § 19271.

Default in support order due to unemployment, proof that obligor is actively seeking employment, see Family Code § 4505.

Delinquent child support obligations and financial institutions data match, manner of collecting child support delinquencies submitted to department, see Family Code § 17450.

Franchise Tax Board,
  Generally, see Government Code § 15700 et seq.
  Powers and duties, see Revenue and Taxation Code § 19501 et seq.

Support defined for purposes of this Code, see Family Code § 150.

§ 17501. Repealed by Stats.2001, c. 111 (A.B.429), § 6, eff. July 30, 2001

§ 17502. Inability to deliver child support payments due to inability to locate obligee

A local child support agency that is collecting child support payments on behalf of a child and who is unable to deliver the payments to the obligee because the local child support agency is unable to locate the obligee shall make all reasonable efforts to locate the obligee for a period of six months. If the local child support agency is unable to locate the obligee within the six-month period, it shall return the undeliverable payments to the obligor, with written notice advising the obligor that (a) the return of the funds does not relieve the obligor of the support order, and (b) the obligor should consider placing the funds aside for purposes of child support in case the obligee appears and seeks collection of the undistributed amounts. No interest shall accrue on any past-due child support amount for which the obligor made payment to the local child support agency for six consecutive months, or on any amounts due thereafter until the obligee is located, provided that the local child support agency returned the funds to the obligor because the local child support agency was unable to locate the obligee and, when the obligee was located, the obligor made full payment for all past-due child support amounts. *(Added by Stats.1999, c. 478 (A.B.196), § 1. Amended by Stats.2004, c. 806 (A.B.2358), § 5.)*

Cross References

Judgment and order defined for purposes of this Code, see Family Code § 100.
Support defined for purposes of this Code, see Family Code § 150.
Support order defined for purposes of this Code, see Family Code § 155.

§ 17504. First fifty dollars collected in month; payment to aid recipients; facilitation of automation changes

Section operative until Jan. 1, 2022, or when the specified departments provide notice that the Statewide Automated Welfare System and the Child Support Enforcement System can perform necessary automation, whichever is later. See, also, § 17504 operative Jan. 1, 2022, or when the specified departments provide notice that the Statewide Automated Welfare System and the Child Support Enforcement System can perform necessary automation, whichever is later.

(a) The first fifty dollars ($50) of any amount of child support collected in a month in payment of the required support obligation for that month shall be paid to a recipient of aid under Article 2 (commencing with Section 11250) of Chapter 2 of Part 3 of Division 9 of the Welfare and Institutions Code, except recipients of foster care payments under Article 5 (commencing with Section 11400) of Chapter 2 of Part 3 of Division 9 of the Welfare and Institutions Code shall not be considered income or resources of the recipient family, and shall not be deducted from the amount of aid to which the family would otherwise be eligible. The local child support agency in each county shall ensure that payments are made to recipients as required by this section.

(b) This section shall become inoperative on January 1, 2022, or when the State Department of Social Services and the Department of Child Support Services notify the Legislature that the Statewide Automated Welfare System and the Child Support Enforcement System can perform the necessary automation to implement this section, as amended by the act that added this subdivision, whichever date is later, and as of that date, or, if this section becomes inoperative on a date other than January 1, 2022, on January 1 of the following year, is repealed.

(c) The State Department of Social Services shall issue an all-county letter or similar instruction no later than September 1, 2020, to facilitate automation changes necessary to implement this section and Section 17504, as added by Section 2 of the act that added this subdivision.[1] *(Added by Stats.1999, c. 478 (A.B.196), § 1. Amended by Stats.2000, c. 808 (A.B.1358), § 86.3, eff. Sept. 28, 2000; Stats.2001, c. 159 (S.B.662), § 90; Stats.2020, c. 11 (A.B.79), § 1, eff. June 29, 2020.)*

[1] Stats.2020, c. 11 (A.B.79).

Inoperative Date and Repeal

For inoperative date and repeal of this section, see its terms.

Cross References

California Work Opportunity and Responsibility to Kids Act, conditions of aid eligibility, see Welfare and Institutions Code § 11477.
County defined for purposes of this Code, see Family Code § 67.
Similar provisions, see Welfare and Institutions Code § 11475.3.
Support defined for purposes of this Code, see Family Code § 150.

§ 17504. Monthly child support collections; payment to aid recipients; methods of implementation until regulations are adopted

Section operative Jan. 1, 2022, or when the specified departments provide notice that the Statewide Automated Welfare System and the Child Support Enforcement System can perform necessary automation, whichever is later. See, also, § 17504 operative until Jan. 1, 2022, or when the specified departments provide notice that the Statewide Automated Welfare System and the Child Support Enforcement System can perform necessary automation, whichever is later.

(a) The first one hundred dollars ($100) of any amount of child support collected in a month for a family with one child, or the first two hundred dollars ($200) for a family with two or more children, in payment of the required support obligation for that month shall be paid to a recipient of aid under Article 2 (commencing with Section 11250) of Chapter 2 of Part 3 of Division 9 of the Welfare and Institutions Code, except recipients of foster care payments under Article 5 (commencing with Section 11400) of Chapter 2 of Part 3 of Division 9 of the Welfare and Institutions Code, and shall not be considered income or resources of the recipient family, and shall not be deducted from the amount of aid to which the family would otherwise be eligible. The local child support agency in each county shall ensure that payments are made to recipients as required by this section.

(b) Notwithstanding the rulemaking provisions of the Administrative Procedure Act (Chapter 3.5 (commencing with Section 11340) of Part 1 of Division 3 of Title 2 of the Government Code), the State Department of Social Services and the Department of Child Support Services may implement, interpret, or make specific this section by means of all-county letters or similar instructions from the department until regulations are adopted. These all-county letters or similar written instructions shall have the same force and effect as regulations until the adoption of regulations.

(c) This section shall become operative on January 1, 2022, or when the State Department of Social Services and the Department of Child Support Services notify the Legislature that the Statewide Automated Welfare System and Child Support Enforcement System can perform the necessary automation to implement this section,

§ 17504

whichever date is later. *(Added by Stats.2020, c. 11 (A.B.79), § 2, eff. June 29, 2020, operative contingent.)*

Cross References

California Work Opportunity and Responsibility to Kids Act, conditions of aid eligibility, see Welfare and Institutions Code § 11477.

County defined for purposes of this Code, see Family Code § 67.

Similar provisions, see Welfare and Institutions Code § 11475.3.

Support defined for purposes of this Code, see Family Code § 150.

§ 17504.1. Renumbered § 17504.4 and amended by Stats.2022, c. 573 (A.B.207), § 6, eff. Sept. 27, 2022

§ 17504.2. Collections in payment of assigned support obligations; passthrough to former recipients of aid; payments that cannot be delivered

Section operative July 1, 2023, or when the specified departments provide notice that the Statewide Automated Welfare System and the Child Support Enforcement System can perform necessary automation, whichever is later.

(a)(1) Any amount of support collected in a month in payment of an assigned support obligation shall be passed through to a former recipient of aid under Article 2 (commencing with Section 11250) of Chapter 2 of Part 3 of Division 9 of the Welfare and Institutions Code, except recipients of foster care payments under Article 5 (commencing with Section 11400) of Chapter 2 of Part 3 of Division 9 of the Welfare and Institutions Code.

(2) The local child support agency in each county shall ensure that payments are made to former recipients of aid when required by this section.

(3) The Department of Child Support Services and the local child support agencies shall provide written or electronic informational materials, which shall be developed by the Department of Child Support Services in collaboration with the Department of Social Services, to child support case participants, who are former recipients of aid, to notify them of the potential impacts of passthrough collections pursuant to this section on eligibility for public benefit programs.

(b) Notwithstanding Section 17502 of the Family Code, any passthrough payments under this section that cannot be delivered to a former recipient of aid pursuant to paragraph (2) of subdivision (a) for a period of six months shall not be returned to the obligor and shall be sent to recoup aid paid on behalf of the recipient pursuant to Section 11477 of the Welfare and Institutions Code. If the former recipient of aid makes a claim for the passthrough payment within 12 months of the payment being sent to recoupment, the payment shall be removed from recoupment and sent to the former recipient of aid. The Department of Child Support Services shall monitor the number of claims made after payments are sent for recoupment. The department shall provide that information to the Legislature no later than April 1, 2025, or two years and three months after the operative date of this section as established by subdivision (e), whichever date is later.

(c) Nothing in this section shall be construed to discontinue assignments under Section 11477 of the Welfare and Institutions Code.

(d) Notwithstanding the rulemaking provisions of the Administrative Procedure Act (Chapter 3.5 (commencing with Section 11340) of Part 1 of Division 3 of Title 2 of the Government Code), the State Department of Social Services and the Department of Child Support Services may implement, interpret, or make specific this section by means of all-county letters or similar instructions from the department until regulations are adopted. These all-county letters or similar written instructions shall have the same force and effect as regulations until the adoption of regulations.

(e) This section shall become operative on July 1, 2023, or on the date the department notifies the Legislature that the Child Support Enforcement System can perform the necessary automation to implement this section, and the Department of Child Support Services has developed and provided the written materials pursuant to subdivision (a), whichever date is later. *(Added by Stats.2022, c. 573 (A.B.207), § 7, eff. Sept. 27, 2022, operative contingent.)*

§ 17504.4. CalWORKs recipients or former recipients; notice of amount of assigned support payments made on behalf of recipient, former recipient, or family member

On a monthly basis, the local child support agency shall provide to any CalWORKs recipient or former recipient for whom an assignment pursuant to subdivision (a) of Section 11477 of the Welfare and Institutions Code is currently effective, a notice of the amount of assigned support payments made on behalf of the recipient or former recipient or any other family member for whom public assistance is received. *(Formerly § 17504.1, added by Stats.2016, c. 474 (A.B. 2882), § 19, eff. Jan. 1, 2017. Renumbered § 17504.4 and amended by Stats.2022, c. 573 (A.B.207), § 6, eff. Sept. 27, 2022.)*

§ 17504.6. Report on impact of passthrough payments on eligibility determinations for other need-based assistance programs

(a) No later than May 1, 2023, the Department of Social Services, in collaboration with the Department of Child Support Services, shall submit a report to the human services and judicial policy and fiscal committees of each house of the Legislature providing an evaluation of the impact of Section 17504.2 on an individual or family's eligibility determination for other need-based assistance programs. The report shall evaluate, but is not limited to, the following:

(1) Potential unintended impacts, both negative and positive, of this subdivision.

(2) Potential solutions to address any identified unintended impacts, including whether an opt out is necessary in order to avoid negative impact to families.

(b) This section shall remain in effect only until January 1, 2025, and as of that date is repealed. *(Added by Stats.2022, c. 573 (A.B.207), § 8, eff. Sept. 27, 2022.)*

Repeal

For repeal of this section, see its terms.

§ 17505. State and local agencies, cooperation with local child support agencies in enforcement of support obligations; information on location of children, location and property of parents

(a) All state, county, and local agencies shall cooperate with the local child support agency (1) in the enforcement of any child support obligation or to the extent required under the state plan under Part 6 (commencing with Section 5700.101) of Division 9, Section 270 of the Penal Code, and Section 17604, and (2) the enforcement of spousal support orders and in the location of parents or putative parents. The local child support agency may enter into an agreement with and shall secure from a municipal, county, or state law enforcement agency, pursuant to that agreement, state summary criminal record information through the California Law Enforcement Telecommunications System. This subdivision applies irrespective of whether the children are or are not receiving aid to families with dependent children. All state, county, and local agencies shall cooperate with the district attorney in implementing Chapter 8 (commencing with Section 3130) of Part 2 of Division 8 concerning the location, seizure, and recovery of abducted, concealed, or detained minor children.

(b) On request, all state, county, and local agencies shall supply the local child support agency of any county in this state or the California Parent Locator Service with all information on hand relative to the location, income, or property of any parents, putative parents, spouses, or former spouses, notwithstanding any other provision of law making the information confidential, and with all information on hand relative to the location and prosecution of any person who has, by means of false statement or representation or by impersonation or other fraudulent device, obtained aid for a child under this chapter.

(c) The California Child Support Automation System, or its replacement, shall be entitled to the same cooperation and information provided to the California Parent Locator Service, to the extent allowed by law. The California Child Support Automation System, or its replacement, shall be allowed access to criminal offender record information only to the extent that access is allowed by law.

(d) Information exchanged between the California Parent Locator Service or the California Child Support Automation System, or its replacement, and state, county, or local agencies as specified in Sections 653(c)(4) and 666(c)(1)(D) of Title 42 of the United State Code shall be through automated processes to the maximum extent feasible. *(Added by Stats.1999, c. 478 (A.B.196), § 1. Amended by Stats.2000, c. 808 (A.B.1358), § 87, eff. Sept. 28, 2000; Stats.2012, c. 637 (A.B.1751), § 3; Stats.2015, c. 493 (S.B.646), § 14, eff. Jan. 1, 2016.)*

Cross References

Administration of tax, disclosure of information to California Parent Locator Service, see Revenue and Taxation Code § 19548.
Collection of child support, referral of child support delinquencies, see Revenue and Taxation Code § 19271.
County defined for purposes of this Code, see Family Code § 67.
Inspection of public records, see Government Code § 6250 et seq.
Judgment and order defined for purposes of this Code, see Family Code § 100.
Minor defined for purposes of this Code, see Family Code § 6500.
Person defined for purposes of this Code, see Family Code § 105.
Property defined for purposes of this Code, see Family Code § 113.
Putative parent, defined for purposes of this Division, see Family Code § 17212.
References to husband, wife, spouses and married persons, persons included for purposes of this Code, see Family Code § 11.
Spousal support defined for purposes of this Code, see Family Code § 142.
State defined for purposes of this Code, see Family Code § 145.
Support defined for purposes of this Code, see Family Code § 150.
Support order defined for purposes of this Code, see Family Code § 155.

§ 17506. California Parent Locator Service and Central Registry; California Child Support Enforcement System

(a) There is in the department a California Parent Locator Service and Central Registry that shall collect and disseminate all of the following, with respect to any parent, putative parent, spouse, or former spouse:

(1) The full and true name of the parent together with any known aliases.

(2) Date and place of birth.

(3) Physical description.

(4) Social security number, individual taxpayer identification number, or other uniform identification number.

(5) Employment history and earnings.

(6) Military status and Veterans Administration or military service serial number.

(7) Last known address, telephone number, and date thereof.

(8) Driver's license number or identification card number issued by the Department of Motor Vehicles, driving record, and vehicle registration information.

(9) Criminal, licensing, and applicant records and information.

(10)(A) Any additional location, asset, and income information, including income tax return information obtained pursuant to Section 19548 of the Revenue and Taxation Code, and to the extent permitted by federal law, the address, telephone number, and social security number obtained from a public utility, cable television corporation, a provider of electronic digital pager communication, or a provider of mobile telephony services that may be of assistance in locating the parent, putative parent, abducting, concealing, or detaining parent, spouse, or former spouse, in establishing a parent and child relationship, in enforcing the child support liability of the absent parent, or enforcing the spousal support liability of the spouse or former spouse to the extent required by the state plan pursuant to Section 17604.

(B) For purposes of this subdivision, "income tax return information" means all of the following regarding the taxpayer:

(i) Assets.

(ii) Credits.

(iii) Deductions.

(iv) Exemptions.

(v) Identity.

(vi) Liabilities.

(vii) Nature, source, and amount of income.

(viii) Net worth.

(ix) Payments.

(x) Receipts.

(xi) Address.

(xii) Social security number, individual taxpayer identification number, or other uniform identification number.

(b) Pursuant to a letter of agreement entered into between the Department of Child Support Services and the Department of Justice, the Department of Child Support Services shall assume responsibility for the California Parent Locator Service and Central Registry. The letter of agreement shall, at a minimum, set forth all of the following:

(1) Contingent upon funding in the Budget Act, the Department of Child Support Services shall assume responsibility for leadership and staff of the California Parent Locator Service and Central Registry commencing July 1, 2003.

(2) All employees and other personnel who staff or provide support for the California Parent Locator Service and Central Registry shall, at the time of the transition, at their option, become the employees of the Department of Child Support Services at their existing or equivalent classification, salaries, and benefits.

(3) Until the department's automation system for the California Parent Locator Service and Central Registry functions is fully operational, the department shall use the automation system operated by the Department of Justice.

(4) Any other provisions necessary to ensure continuity of function and meet or exceed existing levels of service.

(c) To effectuate the purposes of this section, the California Child Support Enforcement System and the California Parent Locator Service and Central Registry shall utilize the federal Parent Locator Service to the extent necessary, and may request and shall receive from all departments, boards, bureaus, or other agencies of the state, or any of its political subdivisions, and those entities shall provide, that assistance and data that will enable the Department of Child Support Services and other public agencies to carry out their powers and duties to locate parents, spouses, and former spouses, and to identify their assets, to establish parent-child relationships, and to enforce liability for child or spousal support, and for any other obligations incurred on behalf of children, and shall also provide that information to any local child support agency in fulfilling the duties prescribed in Section 270 of the Penal Code, and in Chapter 8 (commencing with Section 3130) of Part 2 of Division 8 of this code, relating to abducted, concealed, or detained children and to any county child welfare agency or county probation department in fulfilling the duties prescribed in Article 5.5 (commencing with Section 290.1) of Chapter 2 of Part 1 of Division 2 of the Welfare and Institutions Code, and prescribed in Article 6 (commencing with

Section 300) of Chapter 2 of Part 1 of Division 2 of the Welfare and Institutions Code to identify, locate, and notify parents or relatives of children who are the subject of juvenile court proceedings, to establish parent and child relationships pursuant to Section 316.2 of the Welfare and Institutions Code, and to assess the appropriateness of placement of a child with a noncustodial parent pursuant to Section 361.2 of the Welfare and Institutions Code. Consistent with paragraph (1) of subdivision (e) of Section 309 of, and paragraph (2) of subdivision (d) of Section 628 of, the Welfare and Institutions Code, in order for county child welfare and probation departments to carry out their duties to identify and locate all grandparents, adult siblings, and other adult relatives of the child as defined in paragraph (2) of subdivision (f) of Section 319 of the Welfare and Institutions Code, including any other adult relatives suggested by the parents, county personnel are permitted to request and receive information from the California Parent Locator Service and Federal Parent Locator Service. County child welfare agencies and probation departments shall be entitled to the information described in this subdivision regardless of whether an all-county letter or similar instruction is issued pursuant to subparagraph (C) of paragraph (8) of subdivision (c) of Section 11478.1 of the Welfare and Institutions Code. The California Child Support Enforcement System shall be entitled to the same cooperation and information as the California Parent Locator Service and Central Registry to the extent allowed by law. The California Child Support Enforcement System shall be allowed access to criminal record information only to the extent that access is allowed by state and federal law.

(d)(1) To effectuate the purposes of this section, and notwithstanding any other law, regulation, or tariff, and to the extent permitted by federal law, the California Parent Locator Service and Central Registry and the California Child Support Enforcement System may request and shall receive from public utilities, as defined in Section 216 of the Public Utilities Code, customer service information, including the full name, address, telephone number, date of birth, employer name and address, and social security number of customers of the public utility, to the extent that this information is stored within the computer database of the public utility.

(2) To effectuate the purposes of this section, and notwithstanding any other law, regulation, or tariff, and to the extent permitted by federal law, the California Parent Locator Service and Central Registry and the California Child Support Enforcement System may request and shall receive from cable television corporations, as defined in Section 216.4 of the Public Utilities Code, the providers of electronic digital pager communication, as defined in Section 629.51 of the Penal Code, and the providers of mobile telephony services, as defined in Section 224.4 of the Public Utilities Code, customer service information, including the full name, address, telephone number, date of birth, employer name and address, and social security number of customers of the cable television corporation, customers of the providers of electronic digital pager communication, and customers of the providers of mobile telephony services.

(3) In order to protect the privacy of utility, cable television, electronic digital pager communication, and mobile telephony service customers, a request to a public utility, cable television corporation, provider of electronic digital pager communication, or provider of mobile telephony services for customer service information pursuant to this section shall meet the following requirements:

(A) Be submitted to the public utility, cable television corporation, provider of electronic digital pager communication, or provider of mobile telephony services in writing, on a transmittal document prepared by the California Parent Locator Service and Central Registry or the California Child Support Enforcement System and approved by all of the public utilities, cable television corporations, providers of electronic digital pager communication, and providers of mobile telephony services. The transmittal shall be deemed to be an administrative subpoena for customer service information.

(B) Have the signature of a representative authorized by the California Parent Locator Service and Central Registry or the California Child Support Enforcement System.

(C) Contain at least three of the following data elements regarding the person sought:

(i) First and last name, and middle initial, if known.

(ii) Social security number.

(iii) Driver's license number or identification card number issued by the Department of Motor Vehicles.

(iv) Birth date.

(v) Last known address.

(vi) Spouse's name.

(D) The California Parent Locator Service and Central Registry and the California Child Support Enforcement System shall ensure that each public utility, cable television corporation, provider of electronic digital pager communication services, and provider of mobile telephony services has at all times a current list of the names of persons authorized to request customer service information.

(E) The California Child Support Enforcement System and the California Parent Locator Service and Central Registry shall ensure that customer service information supplied by a public utility, cable television corporation, provider of electronic digital pager communication, or provider of mobile telephony services is applicable to the person who is being sought before releasing the information pursuant to subdivision (d).

(4) During the development of the California Child Support Enforcement System, the department shall determine the necessity of additional locate sources, including those specified in this section, based upon the cost-effectiveness of those sources.

(5) The public utility, cable television corporation, electronic digital pager communication provider, or mobile telephony service provider may charge a fee to the California Parent Locator Service and Central Registry or the California Child Support Enforcement System for each search performed pursuant to this subdivision to cover the actual costs to the public utility, cable television corporation, electronic digital pager communication provider, or mobile telephony service provider for providing this information.

(6) No public utility, cable television corporation, electronic digital pager communication provider, or mobile telephony service provider or official or employee thereof, shall be subject to criminal or civil liability for the release of customer service information as authorized by this subdivision.

(e) Notwithstanding Section 14203 of the Penal Code, any records established pursuant to this section shall be disseminated only to the Department of Child Support Services, the California Child Support Enforcement System, the California Parent Locator Service and Central Registry, the parent locator services and central registries of other states as defined by federal statutes and regulations, a local child support agency of any county in this state, and the federal Parent Locator Service. The California Child Support Enforcement System shall be allowed access to criminal offender record information only to the extent that access is allowed by law.

(f)(1) At no time shall any information received by the California Parent Locator Service and Central Registry or by the California Child Support Enforcement System be disclosed to any person, agency, or other entity, other than those persons, agencies, and entities specified pursuant to Section 17505, this section, or any other provision.

(2) This subdivision shall not otherwise affect discovery between parties in any action to establish, modify, or enforce child, family, or spousal support, that relates to custody or visitation.

(g)(1) The Department of Justice, in consultation with the Department of Child Support Services, shall promulgate rules and regulations to facilitate maximum and efficient use of the California Parent Locator Service and Central Registry. Upon implementation of the California Child Support Enforcement System, the Department of Child Support Services shall assume all responsibility for promulgating rules and regulations for use of the California Parent Locator Service and Central Registry.

(2) The Department of Child Support Services, the Public Utilities Commission, the cable television corporations, providers of electronic digital pager communication, and the providers of mobile telephony services shall develop procedures for obtaining the information described in subdivision (c) from public utilities, cable television corporations, providers of electronic digital pager communication, and providers of mobile telephony services and for compensating the public utilities, cable television corporations, providers of electronic digital pager communication, and providers of mobile telephony services for providing that information.

(h) The California Parent Locator Service and Central Registry may charge a fee not to exceed eighteen dollars ($18) for any service it provides pursuant to this section that is not performed or funded pursuant to Section 651 and following of Title 42 of the United States Code.

(i) This section shall be construed in a manner consistent with the other provisions of this article. *(Added by Stats.1999, c. 478 (A.B.196), § 1. Amended by Stats.1999, c. 652 (S.B.240), § 18; Stats.2002, c. 759 (A.B.3033), § 2; Stats.2003, c. 62 (S.B.600), § 91; Stats.2004, c. 806 (A.B.2358), § 7; Stats.2006, c. 198 (A.B.3073), § 1; Stats.2012, c. 637 (A.B.1751), § 4; Stats.2014, c. 437 (S.B.1066), § 3, eff. Jan. 1, 2015; Stats.2014, c. 772 (S.B.1460), § 3.5, eff. Jan. 1, 2015; Stats.2016, c. 474 (A.B.2882), § 20, eff. Jan. 1, 2017; Stats.2018, c. 838 (S.B.695), § 6, eff. Jan. 1, 2019.)*

Cross References

Administration of tax, disclosure of information to California Parent Locator Service, see Revenue and Taxation Code § 19548.
Child support delinquency, statewide automated system for reporting administered by the department, see Family Code § 4701.
Collection of child support, referral of child support delinquencies, see Revenue and Taxation Code § 19271.
County defined for purposes of this Code, see Family Code § 67.
Default in support order due to unemployment, proof that obligor is actively seeking employment, see Family Code § 4505.
Judgment and order defined for purposes of this Code, see Family Code § 100.
Person defined for purposes of this Code, see Family Code § 105.
Putative parent, defined for purposes of this Division, see Family Code § 17212.
References to husband, wife, spouses and married persons, persons included for purposes of this Code, see Family Code § 11.
Spousal support defined for purposes of this Code, see Family Code § 142.
State defined for purposes of this Code, see Family Code § 145.
Support defined for purposes of this Code, see Family Code § 150.

§ 17508. Employment Development Department; access to information

(a) The Employment Development Department shall, when requested by the Department of Child Support Services local child support agency, the federal Parent Locator Service, or the California Parent Locator Service, provide access to information collected pursuant to Division 1 (commencing with Section 100) of the Unemployment Insurance Code to the requesting department or agency for purposes of administering the child support enforcement program, and for purposes of verifying employment of applicants and recipients of aid under this chapter or CalFresh under Chapter 10 (commencing with Section 18900) of Part 6 of Division 9 of the Welfare and Institutions Code.

(b)(1) To the extent possible, the Employment Development Department shall share information collected under Sections 1088.5 and 1088.8 of the Unemployment Insurance Code immediately upon receipt. This sharing of information may include electronic means.

(2) This subdivision shall not authorize the Employment Development Department to share confidential information with any individuals not otherwise permitted by law to receive the information or preclude batch runs or comparisons of data. *(Added by Stats.1999, c. 478 (A.B.196), § 1. Amended by Stats.1999, c. 652 (S.B.240), § 19; Stats.2000, c. 808 (A.B.1358), § 88, eff. Sept. 28, 2000; Stats.2011, c. 227 (A.B.1400), § 4; Stats.2016, c. 474 (A.B.2882), § 21, eff. Jan. 1, 2017.)*

Cross References

Default in support order due to unemployment, proof that obligor is actively seeking employment, see Family Code § 4505.
Support defined for purposes of this Code, see Family Code § 150.

§ 17509. Information compare; obligor employment and earning withholding order

Once the statewide automated system is fully implemented, the Department of Child Support Services shall periodically compare Employment Development Department information collected under Division 1 (commencing with Section 100) of the Unemployment Insurance Code to child support obligor records and identify cases where the obligor is employed but there is no earning withholding order in effect. The department shall immediately notify local child support agencies in those cases. *(Added by Stats.1999, c. 652 (S.B.240), § 20.)*

Cross References

Judgment and order defined for purposes of this Code, see Family Code § 100.
Support defined for purposes of this Code, see Family Code § 150.

§ 17510. Workers' compensation notification project

To assist local agencies in child support enforcement activities, the department shall operate a workers' compensation notification project based on information received pursuant to Section 138.5 of the Labor Code or any other source of information. *(Added by Stats.1999, c. 478 (A.B.196), § 1.)*

Cross References

Child support obligations, workers' compensation notification project, see Labor Code § 138.5.
Identification by insurers of claimants owing past-due child support, reporting, exceptions, see Insurance Code § 13550.
Support defined for purposes of this Code, see Family Code § 150.
Workers' compensation, see Labor Code § 3200 et seq.

§ 17512. Employment and income information from employer or labor organization

(a) Upon receipt of a written request from a local child support agency enforcing the obligation of parents to support their children pursuant to Section 17400, or from an agency of another state enforcing support obligations pursuant to Section 654 of Title 42 of the United States Code, every employer, as specified in Section 5210, and every labor organization shall cooperate with and provide relevant employment and income information that they have in their possession to the local child support agency or other requesting agency for the purpose of establishing, modifying, or enforcing the support obligation. No employer or labor organization shall incur any liability for providing this information to the local child support agency or other requesting agency.

(b) Relevant employment and income information shall include, but not be limited to, all of the following:

(1) Whether a named person has or has not been employed by an employer or whether a named person has or has not been employed to the knowledge of the labor organization.

(2) The full name of the employee or member or the first and middle initial and last name of the employee or member.

(3) The employee's or member's last known residence address.

§ 17512

(4) The employee's or member's date of birth.

(5) The employee's or member's social security number.

(6) The dates of employment.

(7) All earnings paid to the employee or member and reported as W–2 compensation in the prior tax year and the employee's or member's current basic rate of pay.

(8) Other earnings, as specified in Section 5206, paid to the employee or member.

(9) Whether dependent health insurance coverage is available to the employee through employment or membership in the labor organization.

(c) The local child support agency or other agency shall notify the employer and labor organization of the local child support agency case file number in making a request pursuant to this section. The written request shall include at least three of the following elements regarding the person who is the subject of the inquiry: (A) first and last name and middle initial, if known; (B) social security number; (C) driver's license number; (D) birth date; (E) last known address; or (F) spouse's name.

(d) The local child support agency or other requesting agency shall send a notice that a request for this information has been made to the last known address of the person who is the subject of the inquiry.

(e) An employer or labor organization that fails to provide relevant employment information to the local child support agency or other requesting agency within 30 days of receiving a request pursuant to subdivision (a) may be assessed a civil penalty of a maximum of one thousand dollars ($1,000), plus attorneys' fees and costs. Proceedings to impose the civil penalty shall be commenced by the filing and service of an order to show cause.

(f) "Labor organization," for the purposes of this section means a labor organization as defined in Section 1117 of the Labor Code or any related benefit trust fund covered under the federal Employee Retirement Income Security Act of 1974 (Chapter 18 (commencing with Section 1001) of Title 29 of the United States Code).

(g) Any reference to the local child support agency in this section shall apply only when the local child support agency is otherwise ordered or required to act pursuant to existing law. Nothing in this section shall be deemed to mandate additional enforcement or collection duties upon the local child support agency beyond those imposed under existing law on the effective date of this section. *(Added by Stats.1999, c. 478 (A.B.196), § 1.)*

Cross References

Judgment and order defined for purposes of this Code, see Family Code § 100.
Person defined for purposes of this Code, see Family Code § 105.
Proceeding defined for purposes of this Code, see Family Code § 110.
References to husband, wife, spouses and married persons, persons included for purposes of this Code, see Family Code § 11.
State defined for purposes of this Code, see Family Code § 145.
Support defined for purposes of this Code, see Family Code § 150.

§ 17514. Child abduction records

(a) It is the intent of the Legislature to protect individual rights of privacy, and to facilitate and enhance the effectiveness of the child abduction and recovery programs, by ensuring the confidentiality of child abduction records, and to thereby encourage the full and frank disclosure of information relevant to all of the following:

(1) The establishment or maintenance of parent and child relationships and support obligations.

(2) The enforcement of the child support liability of absent parents.

(3) The enforcement of spousal support liability of the spouse or former spouse to the extent required by the state plan under Section 17400, and Chapter 6 (commencing with Section 4800) of Part 5 of Division 9.

(4) The location of absent parents.

(5) The location of parents and children abducted, concealed, or detained by them.

(b)(1) Except as provided in this subdivision, all files, applications, papers, documents, and records, established or maintained by a public entity for the purpose of locating an abducted child, locating a person who has abducted a child, or prosecution of a person who has abducted a child shall be confidential, and shall not be open to examination or released for disclosure for any purpose not directly connected with locating or recovering the abducted child or abducting person or prosecution of the abducting person.

(2) Except as provided in subdivision (c), a public entity shall not disclose any file, application, paper, document, or record described in this section, or the information contained therein.

(c)(1) All files, applications, papers, documents, and records as described in subdivision (b) shall be available and may be used by a public entity for all administrative, civil, or criminal investigations, actions, proceedings, or prosecution conducted in connection with the child abduction or prosecution of the abducting person.

(2) A document requested by a person who wrote, prepared, or furnished the document may be examined by or disclosed to that person or a designee.

(3) Public records subject to disclosure under Division 10 (commencing with Section 7920.000) of Title 1 of the Government Code may be released.

(4) After a noticed motion and a finding by the court, in a case in which child recovery or abduction prosecution actions are being taken, that release or disclosure is required by due process of law, the court may order a public entity that possesses an application, paper, document, or record described in this subdivision to make that item available to the defendant or other party for examination or copying, or to disclose to an appropriate person the contents of that item. Article 9 (commencing with Section 1040) of Chapter 4 of Division 8 of the Evidence Code shall not be applicable to proceedings under this part.

(5) To the extent not prohibited by federal law or regulation, information indicating the existence or imminent threat of a crime against a minor child, or location of a concealed or abducted child, or the location of the concealing or abducting person, may be disclosed to any appropriate law enforcement agency, or to any state or county child protective agency, or may be used in any judicial proceedings to prosecute that crime or to protect the child.

(6) Information may be released to any state or local agency for the purposes connected with establishing, modifying, and enforcing child support obligations, enforcing spousal support orders, or determining paternity as required by Part D (commencing with Section 651) of Subchapter IV of Chapter 7 of Title 42 of the United States Code and this article. *(Added by Stats.1999, c. 478 (A.B.196), § 1. Amended by Stats.2019, c. 115 (A.B.1817), § 154, eff. Jan. 1, 2020; Stats.2021, c. 615 (A.B.474), § 107, eff. Jan. 1, 2022, operative Jan. 1, 2023.)*

Cross References

Collection of child support, referral of child support delinquencies, see Revenue and Taxation Code § 19271.
County defined for purposes of this Code, see Family Code § 67.
Judgment and order defined for purposes of this Code, see Family Code § 100.
Minor defined for purposes of this Code, see Family Code § 6500.
Person defined for purposes of this Code, see Family Code § 105.
Privacy rights, confidentiality of records, see Family Code § 17212.
Proceeding defined for purposes of this Code, see Family Code § 110.
References to husband, wife, spouses and married persons, persons included for purposes of this Code, see Family Code § 11.
Spousal support defined for purposes of this Code, see Family Code § 142.
State defined for purposes of this Code, see Family Code § 145.
Support defined for purposes of this Code, see Family Code § 150.

§ 17516. Social service benefits use for support obligation

In no event shall public social service benefits, as defined in Section 10051 of the Welfare and Institutions Code, or benefits paid pursuant to Title XVI of the Social Security Act [1] be employed to satisfy a support obligation. *(Added by Stats.1999, c. 478 (A.B.196), § 1.)*

[1] See 42 U.S.C.A. § 1381 et seq.

Cross References

Support defined for purposes of this Code, see Family Code § 150.

§ 17518. Unemployment compensation benefits

(a) As authorized by subdivision (d) of Section 704.120 of the Code of Civil Procedure, the following actions shall be taken in order to enforce support obligations that are not being met. Whenever a support judgment or order has been rendered by a court of this state against an individual who is entitled to unemployment compensation benefits or unemployment compensation disability benefits, the local child support agency may file a certification of support judgment or support order with the Department of Child Support Services, verifying under penalty of perjury that there is or has been a judgment or an order for support with sums overdue thereunder. The department shall periodically present and keep current, by deletions and additions, a list of the certified support judgments and orders and shall periodically notify the Employment Development Department of individuals certified as owing support obligations.

(b) If the Employment Development Department determines that an individual who owes support may have a claim for unemployment compensation disability insurance benefits under a voluntary plan approved by the Employment Development Department in accordance with Chapter 6 (commencing with Section 3251) of Part 2 of Division 1 of the Unemployment Insurance Code, the Employment Development Department shall immediately notify the voluntary plan payer. When the department notifies the Employment Development Department of changes in an individual's support obligations, the Employment Development Department shall promptly notify the voluntary plan payer of these changes. The Employment Development Department shall maintain and keep current a record of individuals who owe support obligations who may have claims for unemployment compensation or unemployment compensation disability benefits.

(c) Notwithstanding any other law, the Employment Development Department shall withhold the amounts specified below from the unemployment compensation benefits or unemployment compensation disability benefits of individuals with unmet support obligations. The Employment Development Department shall forward the amounts to the Department of Child Support Services for distribution to the appropriate certifying county.

(d) Notwithstanding any other law, during the payment of unemployment compensation disability benefits to an individual, with respect to whom the Employment Development Department has notified a voluntary plan payer that the individual has a support obligation, the voluntary plan payer shall withhold the amounts specified below from the individual's unemployment compensation disability benefits and shall forward the amounts to the appropriate certifying county.

(e) The amounts withheld in subdivisions (c) and (d) shall be equal to 25 percent of each weekly unemployment compensation benefit payment or periodic unemployment compensation disability benefit payment, rounded down to the nearest whole dollar, which is due the individual identified on the certified list. However, the amount withheld may be reduced to a lower whole dollar amount through a written agreement between the individual and the local child support agency or through an order of the court.

(f) The department shall ensure that the appropriate certifying county shall resolve any claims for refunds in the amounts overwithheld by the Employment Development Department or voluntary plan payer.

(g) No later than the time of the first withholding, the individuals who are subject to the withholding shall be notified by the payer of benefits of all of the following:

(1) That the individual's unemployment compensation benefits or unemployment compensation disability benefits have been reduced by a court-ordered support judgment or order pursuant to this section.

(2) The address and telephone number of the local child support agency that submitted the certificate of support judgment or order.

(3) That the support order remains in effect even though the individual is unemployed or disabled unless it is modified by court order, and that if the amount withheld is less than the monthly support obligation, an arrearage will accrue.

(h) The individual may ask the appropriate court for an equitable division of the individual's unemployment compensation or unemployment compensation disability amounts withheld to take into account the needs of all the persons the individual is required to support.

(i) The Department of Child Support Services and the Employment Development Department shall enter into any agreements necessary to carry out this section.

(j) For purposes of this section, "support obligations" means the child and related spousal support obligations that are being enforced pursuant to a plan described in Section 454 of the Social Security Act and as that section may hereafter be amended. However, to the extent "related spousal support obligation" may not be collected from unemployment compensation under federal law, those obligations shall not be included in the definition of support obligations under this section. *(Added by Stats.1999, c. 478 (A.B.196), § 1. Amended by Stats.2000, c. 808 (A.B.1358), § 89, eff. Sept. 28, 2000; Stats.2019, c. 115 (A.B.1817), § 155, eff. Jan. 1, 2020.)*

Cross References

County defined for purposes of this Code, see Family Code § 67.
Judgment and order defined for purposes of this Code, see Family Code § 100.
Person defined for purposes of this Code, see Family Code § 105.
Spousal support defined for purposes of this Code, see Family Code § 142.
State defined for purposes of this Code, see Family Code § 145.
Support defined for purposes of this Code, see Family Code § 150.
Support order defined for purposes of this Code, see Family Code § 155.
Unemployment and disability compensation, individuals with claims for unemployment disability benefits who are certified as having support obligations, see Unemployment Insurance Code § 2630.
Unemployment compensation, generally, see Labor Code § 2010 et seq.
Unemployment insurance and compensation funds, child support judgments, see Code of Civil Procedure § 704.120.

§ 17520. License applicants; compliance with support orders; license issuance, renewal, and suspension; review

(a) As used in this section:

(1) "Applicant" means a person applying for issuance or renewal of a license.

(2) "Board" means an entity specified in Section 101 of the Business and Professions Code, the entities referred to in Sections 1000 and 3600 of the Business and Professions Code, the State Bar of California, the Department of Real Estate, the Department of Motor Vehicles, the Secretary of State, the Department of Fish and Wildlife, and any other state commission, department, committee, examiner, or agency that issues a license, certificate, credential, permit, registration, or any other authorization to engage in a business, occupation, or profession, or to the extent required by federal law or regulations, for recreational purposes. This term includes all boards, commissions, departments, committees, examin-

ers, entities, and agencies that issue a license, certificate, credential, permit, registration, or any other authorization to engage in a business, occupation, or profession. The failure to specifically name a particular board, commission, department, committee, examiner, entity, or agency that issues a license, certificate, credential, permit, registration, or any other authorization to engage in a business, occupation, or profession does not exclude that board, commission, department, committee, examiner, entity, or agency from this term.

(3) "Certified list" means a list provided by the local child support agency to the Department of Child Support Services in which the local child support agency verifies, under penalty of perjury, that the names contained therein are support obligors found to be out of compliance with a judgment or order for support in a case being enforced under Title IV–D of the federal Social Security Act.

(4) "Compliance with a judgment or order for support" means that, as set forth in a judgment or order for child or family support, the obligor is no more than 30 calendar days in arrears in making payments in full for current support, in making periodic payments in full, whether court ordered or by agreement with the local child support agency, on a support arrearage, or in making periodic payments in full, whether court ordered or by agreement with the local child support agency, on a judgment for reimbursement for public assistance, or has obtained a judicial finding that equitable estoppel as provided in statute or case law precludes enforcement of the order. The local child support agency is authorized to use this section to enforce orders for spousal support only when the local child support agency is also enforcing a related child support obligation owed to the obligee parent by the same obligor, pursuant to Sections 17400 and 17604.

(5) "License" includes membership in the State Bar of California, and a certificate, credential, permit, registration, or any other authorization issued by a board that allows a person to engage in a business, occupation, or profession, or to operate a commercial motor vehicle, including appointment and commission by the Secretary of State as a notary public. "License" also includes any driver's license issued by the Department of Motor Vehicles, any commercial fishing license issued by the Department of Fish and Wildlife, and to the extent required by federal law or regulations, any license used for recreational purposes. This term includes all licenses, certificates, credentials, permits, registrations, or any other authorization issued by a board that allows a person to engage in a business, occupation, or profession. The failure to specifically name a particular type of license, certificate, credential, permit, registration, or other authorization issued by a board that allows a person to engage in a business, occupation, or profession, does not exclude that license, certificate, credential, permit, registration, or other authorization from this term.

(6) "Licensee" means a person holding a license, certificate, credential, permit, registration, or other authorization issued by a board, to engage in a business, occupation, or profession, or a commercial driver's license as defined in Section 15210 of the Vehicle Code, including an appointment and commission by the Secretary of State as a notary public. "Licensee" also means a person holding a driver's license issued by the Department of Motor Vehicles, a person holding a commercial fishing license issued by the Department of Fish and Wildlife, and to the extent required by federal law or regulations, a person holding a license used for recreational purposes. This term includes all persons holding a license, certificate, credential, permit, registration, or any other authorization to engage in a business, occupation, or profession, and the failure to specifically name a particular type of license, certificate, credential, permit, registration, or other authorization issued by a board does not exclude that person from this term. For licenses issued to an entity that is not an individual person, "licensee" includes an individual who is either listed on the license or who qualifies for the license.

(b) The local child support agency shall maintain a list of those persons included in a case being enforced under Title IV–D of the federal Social Security Act against whom a support order or judgment has been rendered by, or registered in, a court of this state, and who are not in compliance with that order or judgment. The local child support agency shall submit a certified list with the names, social security numbers, individual taxpayer identification numbers, or other uniform identification numbers, and last known addresses of these persons and the name, address, and telephone number of the local child support agency who certified the list to the department. The local child support agency shall verify, under penalty of perjury, that the persons listed are subject to an order or judgment for the payment of support and that these persons are not in compliance with the order or judgment. The local child support agency shall submit to the department an updated certified list on a monthly basis.

(c) The department shall consolidate the certified lists received from the local child support agencies and, within 30 calendar days of receipt, shall provide a copy of the consolidated list to each board that is responsible for the regulation of licenses, as specified in this section.

(d) On or before November 1, 1992, or as soon thereafter as economically feasible, as determined by the department, all boards subject to this section shall implement procedures to accept and process the list provided by the department, in accordance with this section. Notwithstanding any other law, all boards shall collect social security numbers or individual taxpayer identification numbers from all applicants for the purposes of matching the names of the certified list provided by the department to applicants and licensees and of responding to requests for this information made by child support agencies.

(e)(1) Promptly after receiving the certified consolidated list from the department, and prior to the issuance or renewal of a license, each board shall determine whether the applicant is on the most recent certified consolidated list provided by the department. The board shall have the authority to withhold issuance or renewal of the license of an applicant on the list.

(2) If an applicant is on the list, the board shall immediately serve notice as specified in subdivision (f) on the applicant of the board's intent to withhold issuance or renewal of the license. The notice shall be made personally or by mail to the applicant's last known mailing address on file with the board. Service by mail shall be complete in accordance with Section 1013 of the Code of Civil Procedure.

(A) The board shall issue a temporary license valid for a period of 150 days to any applicant whose name is on the certified list if the applicant is otherwise eligible for a license.

(B) Except as provided in subparagraph (D), the 150–day time period for a temporary license shall not be extended. Except as provided in subparagraph (D), only one temporary license shall be issued during a regular license term and it shall coincide with the first 150 days of that license term. As this paragraph applies to commercial driver's licenses, "license term" shall be deemed to be 12 months from the date the application fee is received by the Department of Motor Vehicles. A license for the full or remainder of the license term shall be issued or renewed only upon compliance with this section.

(C) In the event that a license or application for a license or the renewal of a license is denied pursuant to this section, any funds paid by the applicant or licensee shall not be refunded by the board.

(D) This paragraph shall apply only in the case of a driver's license, other than a commercial driver's license. Upon the request of the local child support agency or by order of the court upon a showing of good cause, the board shall extend a 150–day temporary license for a period not to exceed 150 extra days.

(3)(A) The department may, when it is economically feasible for the department and the boards to do so as determined by the department, in cases where the department is aware that certain child support obligors listed on the certified lists have been out of compliance with a judgment or order for support for more than four months, provide a supplemental list of these obligors to each board with which the department has an interagency agreement to implement this paragraph. Upon request by the department, the licenses of these obligors shall be subject to suspension, provided that the licenses would not otherwise be eligible for renewal within six months from the date of the request by the department. The board shall have the authority to suspend the license of any licensee on this supplemental list.

(B) If a licensee is on a supplemental list, the board shall immediately serve notice as specified in subdivision (f) on the licensee that the license will be automatically suspended 150 days after notice is served, unless compliance with this section is achieved. The notice shall be made personally or by mail to the licensee's last known mailing address on file with the board. Service by mail shall be complete in accordance with Section 1013 of the Code of Civil Procedure.

(C) The 150-day notice period shall not be extended.

(D) In the event that any license is suspended pursuant to this section, any funds paid by the licensee shall not be refunded by the board.

(E) This paragraph shall not apply to licenses subject to annual renewal or annual fee.

(f) Notices shall be developed by each board in accordance with guidelines provided by the department and subject to approval by the department. The notice shall include the address and telephone number of the local child support agency that submitted the name on the certified list, and shall emphasize the necessity of obtaining a release from that local child support agency as a condition for the issuance, renewal, or continued valid status of a license or licenses.

(1) In the case of applicants not subject to paragraph (3) of subdivision (e), the notice shall inform the applicant that the board shall issue a temporary license, as provided in subparagraph (A) of paragraph (2) of subdivision (e), for 150 calendar days if the applicant is otherwise eligible and that upon expiration of that time period the license will be denied unless the board has received a release from the local child support agency that submitted the name on the certified list.

(2) In the case of licensees named on a supplemental list, the notice shall inform the licensee that the license will continue in its existing status for no more than 150 calendar days from the date of mailing or service of the notice and thereafter will be suspended indefinitely unless, during the 150-day notice period, the board has received a release from the local child support agency that submitted the name on the certified list. Additionally, the notice shall inform the licensee that any license suspended under this section will remain so until the expiration of the remaining license term, unless the board receives a release along with applications and fees, if applicable, to reinstate the license during the license term.

(3) The notice shall also inform the applicant or licensee that if an application is denied or a license is suspended pursuant to this section, any funds paid by the applicant or licensee shall not be refunded by the board. The Department of Child Support Services shall also develop a form that the applicant shall use to request a review by the local child support agency. A copy of this form shall be included with every notice sent pursuant to this subdivision.

(g)(1) Each local child support agency shall maintain review procedures consistent with this section to allow an applicant to have the underlying arrearage and any relevant defenses investigated, to provide an applicant information on the process of obtaining a modification of a support order, or to provide an applicant assistance in the establishment of a payment schedule on arrearages if the circumstances so warrant.

(2) It is the intent of the Legislature that a court or local child support agency, when determining an appropriate payment schedule for arrearages, base its decision on the facts of the particular case and the priority of payment of child support over other debts. The payment schedule shall also recognize that certain expenses may be essential to enable an obligor to be employed. Therefore, in reaching its decision, the court or the local child support agency shall consider both of these goals in setting a payment schedule for arrearages.

(h) If the applicant wishes to challenge the submission of their name on the certified list, the applicant shall make a timely written request for review to the local child support agency who certified the applicant's name. A request for review pursuant to this section shall be resolved in the same manner and timeframe provided for resolution of a complaint pursuant to Section 17800. The local child support agency shall immediately send a release to the appropriate board and the applicant, if any of the following conditions are met:

(1) The applicant is found to be in compliance or negotiates an agreement with the local child support agency for a payment schedule on arrearages or reimbursement.

(2) The applicant has submitted a request for review, but the local child support agency will be unable to complete the review and send notice of its findings to the applicant within the time specified in Section 17800.

(3) The applicant has filed and served a request for judicial review pursuant to this section, but a resolution of that review will not be made within 150 days of the date of service of notice pursuant to subdivision (f). This paragraph applies only if the delay in completing the judicial review process is not the result of the applicant's failure to act in a reasonable, timely, and diligent manner upon receiving the local child support agency's notice of findings.

(4) The applicant has obtained a judicial finding of compliance as defined in this section.

(i) An applicant is required to act with diligence in responding to notices from the board and the local child support agency with the recognition that the temporary license will lapse or the license suspension will go into effect after 150 days and that the local child support agency and, where appropriate, the court must have time to act within that period. An applicant's delay in acting, without good cause, which directly results in the inability of the local child support agency to complete a review of the applicant's request or the court to hear the request for judicial review within the 150-day period shall not constitute the diligence required under this section which would justify the issuance of a release.

(j) Except as otherwise provided in this section, the local child support agency shall not issue a release if the applicant is not in compliance with the judgment or order for support. The local child support agency shall notify the applicant, in writing, that the applicant may, by filing an order to show cause or notice of motion, request any or all of the following:

(1) Judicial review of the local child support agency's decision not to issue a release.

(2) A judicial determination of compliance.

(3) A modification of the support judgment or order.

The notice shall also contain the name and address of the court in which the applicant shall file the order to show cause or notice of motion and inform the applicant that their name shall remain on the certified list if the applicant does not timely request judicial review. The applicant shall comply with all statutes and rules of court regarding orders to show cause and notices of motion.

This section does not limit an applicant from filing an order to show cause or notice of motion to modify a support judgment or order or to fix a payment schedule on arrearages accruing under a support judgment or order or to obtain a court finding of compliance with a judgment or order for support.

(k) The request for judicial review of the local child support agency's decision shall state the grounds for which review is requested and judicial review shall be limited to those stated grounds. The court shall hold an evidentiary hearing within 20 calendar days of the filing of the request for review. Judicial review of the local child support agency's decision shall be limited to a determination of each of the following issues:

(1) Whether there is a support judgment, order, or payment schedule on arrearages or reimbursement.

(2) Whether the petitioner is the obligor covered by the support judgment or order.

(3) Whether the support obligor is or is not in compliance with the judgment or order of support.

(4)(A) The extent to which the needs of the obligor, taking into account the obligor's payment history and the current circumstances of both the obligor and the obligee, warrant a conditional release as described in this subdivision.

(B) The request for judicial review shall be served by the applicant upon the local child support agency that submitted the applicant's name on the certified list within seven calendar days of the filing of the petition. The court has the authority to uphold the action, unconditionally release the license, or conditionally release the license.

(C) If the judicial review results in a finding by the court that the obligor is in compliance with the judgment or order for support, the local child support agency shall immediately send a release in accordance with subdivision (*l*) to the appropriate board and the applicant. If the judicial review results in a finding by the court that the needs of the obligor warrant a conditional release, the court shall make findings of fact stating the basis for the release and the payment necessary to satisfy the unrestricted issuance or renewal of the license without prejudice to a later judicial determination of the amount of support arrearages, including interest, and shall specify payment terms, compliance with which are necessary to allow the release to remain in effect.

(*l*)(1) The department shall prescribe release forms for use by local child support agencies. When the obligor is in compliance, the local child support agency shall mail to the applicant and the appropriate board a release stating that the applicant is in compliance. The receipt of a release shall serve to notify the applicant and the board that, for the purposes of this section, the applicant is in compliance with the judgment or order for support. A board that has received a release from the local child support agency pursuant to this subdivision shall process the release within five business days of its receipt.

(2) When the local child support agency determines, subsequent to the issuance of a release, that the applicant is once again not in compliance with a judgment or order for support, or with the terms of repayment as described in this subdivision, the local child support agency may notify the board, the obligor, and the department in a format prescribed by the department that the obligor is not in compliance.

(3) The department may, when it is economically feasible for the department and the boards to develop an automated process for complying with this subdivision, notify the boards in a manner prescribed by the department, that the obligor is once again not in compliance. Upon receipt of this notice, the board shall immediately notify the obligor on a form prescribed by the department that the obligor's license will be suspended on a specific date, and this date shall be no longer than 30 days from the date the form is mailed. The obligor shall be further notified that the license will remain suspended until a new release is issued in accordance with subdivision (h). This section does not limit the obligor from seeking judicial review of suspension pursuant to the procedures described in subdivision (k).

(m) The department may enter into interagency agreements with the state agencies that have responsibility for the administration of boards necessary to implement this section, to the extent that it is cost effective to implement this section. These agreements shall provide for the receipt by the other state agencies and boards of federal funds to cover that portion of costs allowable in federal law and regulation and incurred by the state agencies and boards in implementing this section. Notwithstanding any other law, revenue generated by a board or state agency shall be used to fund the nonfederal share of costs incurred pursuant to this section. These agreements shall provide that boards shall reimburse the department for the nonfederal share of costs incurred by the department in implementing this section. The boards shall reimburse the department for the nonfederal share of costs incurred pursuant to this section from moneys collected from applicants and licensees.

(n) Notwithstanding any other law, in order for the boards subject to this section to be reimbursed for the costs incurred in administering its provisions, the boards may, with the approval of the appropriate department director, levy on all licensees and applicants a surcharge on any fee or fees collected pursuant to law; or, alternatively, with the approval of the appropriate department director, levy on the applicants or licensees named on a certified list or supplemental list, a special fee.

(*o*) The process described in subdivision (h) shall constitute the sole administrative remedy for contesting the issuance of a temporary license or the denial or suspension of a license under this section. The procedures specified in the administrative adjudication provisions of the Administrative Procedure Act (Chapter 4.5 (commencing with Section 11400) and Chapter 5 (commencing with Section 11500) of Part 1 of Division 3 of Title 2 of the Government Code) shall not apply to the denial, suspension, or failure to issue or renew a license or the issuance of a temporary license pursuant to this section.

(p) In furtherance of the public policy of increasing child support enforcement and collections, on or before November 1, 1995, the State Department of Social Services shall make a report to the Legislature and the Governor based on data collected by the boards and the district attorneys in a format prescribed by the State Department of Social Services. The report shall contain all of the following:

(1) The number of delinquent obligors certified by district attorneys under this section.

(2) The number of support obligors who also were applicants or licensees subject to this section.

(3) The number of new licenses and renewals that were delayed, temporary licenses issued, and licenses suspended subject to this section and the number of new licenses and renewals granted and licenses reinstated following board receipt of releases as provided by subdivision (h) by May 1, 1995.

(4) The costs incurred in the implementation and enforcement of this section.

(q) A board receiving an inquiry as to the licensed status of an applicant or licensee who has had a license denied or suspended under this section or has been granted a temporary license under this section shall respond only that the license was denied or suspended or the temporary license was issued pursuant to this section. Information collected pursuant to this section by a state agency, board, or department shall be subject to the Information Practices Act of 1977 (Chapter 1 (commencing with Section 1798) of Title 1.8 of Part 4 of Division 3 of the Civil Code).

(r) Any rules and regulations issued pursuant to this section by a state agency, board, or department may be adopted as emergency regulations in accordance with the rulemaking provisions of the Administrative Procedure Act (Chapter 3.5 (commencing with Section 11340) of Part 1 of Division 3 of Title 2 of the Government Code). The adoption of these regulations shall be deemed an emergency and necessary for the immediate preservation of the public peace, health, and safety, or general welfare. The regulations shall become effective immediately upon filing with the Secretary of State.

(s) The department and boards, as appropriate, shall adopt regulations necessary to implement this section.

(t) The Judicial Council shall develop the forms necessary to implement this section, except as provided in subdivisions (f) and (*l*).

(u) The release or other use of information received by a board pursuant to this section, except as authorized by this section, is punishable as a misdemeanor.

(v) The State Board of Equalization shall enter into interagency agreements with the department and the Franchise Tax Board that will require the department and the Franchise Tax Board to maximize the use of information collected by the State Board of Equalization, for child support enforcement purposes, to the extent it is cost effective and permitted by the Revenue and Taxation Code.

(w)(1) The suspension or revocation of a driver's license, including a commercial driver's license, under this section shall not subject the licensee to vehicle impoundment pursuant to Section 14602.6 of the Vehicle Code.

(2) Notwithstanding any other law, the suspension or revocation of a driver's license, including a commercial driver's license, under this section shall not subject the licensee to increased costs for vehicle liability insurance.

(x) If any provision of this section or the application thereof to any person or circumstance is held invalid, that invalidity shall not affect other provisions or applications of this section which can be given effect without the invalid provision or application, and to this end the provisions of this section are severable.

(y) All rights to administrative and judicial review afforded by this section to an applicant shall also be afforded to a licensee. *(Added by Stats.1999, c. 654 (A.B.370), § 3.5. Amended by Stats.2001, c. 755 (S.B.943), § 14, eff. Oct. 12, 2001; Stats.2013, c. 352 (A.B.1317), § 79, eff. Sept. 26, 2013, operative July 1, 2013; Stats.2014, c. 752 (S.B.1159), § 10, eff. Jan. 1, 2015; Stats.2018, c. 838 (S.B.695), § 7, eff. Jan. 1, 2019; Stats.2019, c. 115 (A.B.1817), § 156, eff. Jan. 1, 2020.)*

Cross References

Application for registration for admission to practice of law, use of federal tax identification number in lieu of social security number, see Business and Professions Code § 6060.6.
Architects, applications, individual tax identification number or other identification number acceptable in lieu of social security number, conditions, see Business and Professions Code § 5550.5.
Attorneys, enforcement of child support obligations, see Business and Professions Code § 6143.5.
Compliance with support orders, license qualifications, see Business and Professions Code § 29.5.
Driving privileges, records open to public inspection, timing of disclosures of suspensions and revocations, see Vehicle Code § 1808.
Family support defined for purposes of this Code, see Family Code § 92.
Franchise Tax Board, generally, see Government Code § 15700 et seq.
Franchise Tax Board, powers and duties, see Revenue and Taxation Code § 19501 et seq.
Judgment and order defined for purposes of this Code, see Family Code § 100.
Licensing, tax enforcement, furnishing of federal employer identification number, social security number and other information, see Business and Professions Code § 30.
Licensing of agents and broker-dealers, generally, see Corporations Code § 25210 et seq.
Misdemeanors, definition and penalties, see Penal Code §§ 17, 19 and 19.2.
Nursing home administrator program, additional application requirements, see Health and Safety Code § 1416.28.
Person defined for purposes of this Code, see Family Code § 105.
Petitioner defined for purposes of this Code, see Family Code § 126.
Spousal support defined for purposes of this Code, see Family Code § 142.
State defined for purposes of this Code, see Family Code § 145.
Support defined for purposes of this Code, see Family Code § 150.
Support order defined for purposes of this Code, see Family Code § 155.
Suspension of license for noncompliance with support order or judgment, see Business and Professions Code § 490.5.
Temporary real estate appraisers license, prohibition of renewal under this section, see Business and Professions Code § 11344.

Research References

Forms

West's California Judicial Council Forms FL-670, Notice of Motion for Judicial Review of License Denial (Governmental).

§ 17520.5. Denying, withholding, or suspending driver's license; support obligor at or below 70 percent median income

Section operative Jan. 1, 2025.

(a)(1) Notwithstanding any other law, the department shall not include in the list sent to the Department of Motor Vehicles pursuant to Section 17520, for the purpose of denying, withholding, or suspending a driver's license, the information of a support obligor found to be out of compliance with a judgment or order for support in a case being enforced under Title IV–D of the federal Social Security Act, if the annual household income of the support obligor is at or below 70 percent of the median income for the county in which the department or the local child support agency believes the support obligor resides, based on the most recent available data published by the Department of Housing and Community Development pursuant to Section 6932 of Title 25 of the California Code of Regulations or successor regulation thereto.

(2) Commencing January 1, 2027, this subdivision shall apply only with respect to noncommercial driver's licenses.

(b) This section shall be implemented to the extent allowed under federal law.

(c) This section shall become operative on January 1, 2025. *(Added by Stats.2022, c. 830 (S.B.1055), § 1, eff. Jan. 1, 2023, operative Jan. 1, 2025.)*

§ 17521. Order to show cause or notice of motion for judicial review of district attorney's decision; appropriate court

The order to show cause or notice of motion described in subdivision (j) of Section 17520 shall be filed and heard in the superior court. *(Added by Stats.1999, c. 653 (A.B.380), § 17. Amended by Stats.2002, c. 784 (S.B.1316), § 115.)*

Cross References

Judgment and order defined for purposes of this Code, see Family Code § 100.

§ 17522. Delinquent support obligors; collection or lien enforcement by levy

(a) Notwithstanding any other law, if a support obligor is delinquent in the payment of support for at least 30 days and the local child support agency is enforcing the support obligation pursuant to Section 17400, the local child support agency may collect the delinquency or enforce a lien by levy served on all persons having in their possession, or who will have in their possession or under their control, credits or personal property belonging to the delinquent support obligor, or who owe any debt to the obligor at the time they receive the notice of levy.

(b) A levy may be issued by a local child support agency for a support obligation that accrued under a court order or judgment if the obligor had notice of the accrued support arrearage as provided in this section, and did not make a timely request for review.

(c) The notice requirement shall be satisfied by the local child support agency sending a statement of support arrearages to the obligor at the obligor's last known address by first-class mail, postage prepaid. The notice shall advise the obligor of the amount of the support arrearage. The notice shall advise the obligor that the obligor may have the arrearage determination reviewed by administrative procedures and state how the review may be obtained. The

§ 17522

local child support agency shall conduct the review pursuant to this section in the same manner and timeframe provided for resolution of a complaint pursuant to Section 17800. The notice shall also advise the obligor of the right to seek a judicial determination of arrearages pursuant to Section 17526 and shall include a form to be filed with the court to request a judicial determination of arrearages. If the obligor requests an administrative review of the arrearage determination within 20 days from the date the notice was mailed to the obligor, the local child support agency may not issue the levy for a disputed amount of support until the administrative review procedure is completed.

(d) If the obligor requests a judicial determination of the arrearages within 20 days from the date the notice was mailed to the obligor, the local child support agency shall not issue the levy for a disputed amount of support until the judicial determination is complete.

(e) A person upon whom a levy has been served who possesses or controls any credits or personal property belonging to the delinquent support obligor or owing any debts to the delinquent support obligor at the time of receipt of the levy or coming into the person's possession or control within one year of receipt of the notice of levy, shall surrender the credits or personal property to the local child support agency or pay to the local child support agency the amount of any debt owing the delinquent support obligor within 10 days of service of the levy, and shall surrender the credits or personal property, or the amount of any debt owing to the delinquent support obligor coming into the person's possession or control within one year of receipt of the notice of levy, within 10 days of the date of coming into possession or control of the credits or personal property or the amount of any debt owing to the delinquent support obligor.

(f) A person who surrenders any credits or personal property or pays the debts owing the delinquent support obligor to the local child support agency pursuant to this section shall be discharged from any obligation or liability to the delinquent support obligor to the extent of the amount paid to the local child support agency as a result of the levy.

(g) When the levy is made on a deposit or credits or personal property in the possession or under the control of a bank, savings and loan association, or other financial institution as defined by Section 669A(d)(1) of Title 42 of the United States Code, the notice of levy may be delivered or mailed to a centralized location designated by the bank, savings and loan association, or other financial institution pursuant to Section 689.040 of the Code of Civil Procedure.

(h) A person who is served with a levy pursuant to this section and who fails or refuses to surrender any credits or other personal property or pay any debts owing to the delinquent support obligor shall be liable in their own person or estate to the local child support agency in an amount equal to the value of the credits or other personal property or in the amount of the levy, up to the amount specified in the levy.

(i) If an amount required to be paid pursuant to a levy under this section is not paid when due, the local child support agency may issue a warrant for enforcement of a lien and for the collection of any amount required to be paid to the local child support agency under this section. The warrant shall be directed to any sheriff, marshal, or the Department of the California Highway Patrol and shall have the same force and effect as a writ of execution. The warrant shall be levied and sale made pursuant to it in the manner and with the same force and effect as a levy and sale pursuant to a writ of execution. The local child support agency may pay or advance to the levying officer the same fees, commissions, and expenses for services under this section as are provided by law for similar services pursuant to a writ of execution, except for those fees and expenses for which a district attorney is exempt by law from paying. The local child support agency, and not the court, shall approve the fees for publication in a newspaper.

(j) The fees, commissions, expenses, and the reasonable costs associated with the sale of property levied upon by warrant or levy pursuant to this section, including, but not limited to, appraisers' fees, auctioneers' fees, and advertising fees are an obligation of the support obligor and may be collected from the obligor by virtue of the warrant or levy or in any other manner as though these items were support payments delinquent for at least 30 days. *(Added by Stats.1999, c. 478 (A.B.196), § 1. Amended by Stats.2001, c. 755 (S.B.943), § 15, eff. Oct. 12, 2001; Stats.2019, c. 115 (A.B.1817), § 157, eff. Jan. 1, 2020.)*

Cross References

Child support delinquency, statewide automated system for reporting administered by the department, see Family Code § 4701.
Default in support order due to unemployment, proof that obligor is actively seeking employment, see Family Code § 4505.
Enforcement of support judgments,
 Issue and levy of warrants by local child support agency, see Code of Civil Procedure § 689.020.
 Levy on property, see Code of Civil Procedure § 689.030.
Judgment and order defined for purposes of this Code, see Family Code § 100.
Person defined for purposes of this Code, see Family Code § 105.
Property defined for purposes of this Code, see Family Code § 113.
State defined for purposes of this Code, see Family Code § 145.
Support defined for purposes of this Code, see Family Code § 150.
Wage garnishment, withholding order for support, see Code of Civil Procedure § 706.030.

§ 17522.5. Issuance of levy or notice to withhold; liquidation of asset by person, financial institution, or securities intermediary in possession or control of financial asset; manner of liquidation and transfer of proceeds; value of financial assets exceeding total amount of support due; instructions for liquidation by obligor

(a) Notwithstanding Section 8112 of the Commercial Code and Section 700.130 of the Code of Civil Procedure, when a local child support agency pursuant to Section 17522, or the department pursuant to Section 17454 or 17500, issues a levy upon, or requires by notice any employer, person, political officer or entity, or depository institution to withhold the amount of, as applicable, a financial asset for the purpose of collecting a delinquent child support obligation, the person, financial institution, or securities intermediary (as defined in Section 8102 of the Commercial Code) in possession or control of the financial asset shall liquidate the financial asset in a commercially reasonable manner within 20 days of the issuance of the levy or the notice to withhold. Within five days of liquidation, the person, financial institution, or securities intermediary shall transfer to the State Disbursement Unit, established under Section 17309, the proceeds of the liquidation, less any reasonable commissions or fees, or both, which are charged in the normal course of business.

(b) If the value of the financial assets exceed the total amount of support due, the obligor may, within 10 days after the service of the levy or notice to withhold upon the person, financial institution, or securities intermediary, instruct the person, financial institution, or securities intermediary who possesses or controls the financial assets as to which financial assets are to be sold to satisfy the obligation for delinquent support. If the obligor does not provide instructions for liquidation, the person, financial institution, or securities intermediary who possesses or controls the financial assets shall liquidate the financial assets in a commercially reasonable manner and in an amount sufficient to cover the obligation for delinquent child support, and any reasonable commissions or fees, or both, which are charged in the normal course of business, beginning with the financial assets purchased most recently.

(c) For the purposes of this section, a financial asset shall include, but not be limited to, an uncertificated security, certificated security, or security entitlement (as defined in Section 8102 of the Commercial Code), security (as defined in Section 8103 of the Commercial Code), or a securities account (as defined in Section 8501 of the Commercial Code). *(Added by Stats.2003, c. 225 (A.B.1752), § 5, eff. Aug. 11, 2003. Amended by Stats.2004, c. 806 (A.B.2358), § 8; Stats.2016, c. 474 (A.B.2882), § 22, eff. Jan. 1, 2017.)*

Cross References

Franchise Tax Board,
    Generally, see Government Code § 15700 et seq.
    Powers and duties, see Revenue and Taxation Code § 19501 et seq.
Person defined for purposes of this Code, see Family Code § 105.
Support defined for purposes of this Code, see Family Code § 150.

§ 17523. Lien for child support against personal property; perfection; priority; enforcement

(a) Notwithstanding any other provision of law, if a support obligor is delinquent in the payment of support and the local child support agency is enforcing the support obligation pursuant to Section 17400 or 17402, a lien for child support shall arise against the personal property of the support obligor in either of the following circumstances:

(1) By operation of law for all amounts of overdue support, regardless of whether the amounts have been adjudicated or otherwise determined.

(2) When either a court having continuing jurisdiction or the local child support agency determines a specific amount of arrearages is owed by the support obligor.

(b) The lien for child support shall be perfected by filing a notice of child support lien with the Secretary of State pursuant to Section 697.510 of the Code of Civil Procedure. Once filed, the child support lien shall have the same priority, force, and effect as a judgment lien on personal property pursuant to Article 3 (commencing with Section 697.510) of Chapter 2 of Division 2 of Article 9 of the Code of Civil Procedure.

(c) For purposes of this section, the following definitions shall apply:

(1) "Notice of child support lien" means a document filed with the Secretary of State that substantially complies with the requirements of Section 697.530 of the Code of Civil Procedure.

(2) "Support obligor is delinquent in payment of support" means that the support obligor has failed to make payment equal to one month's support obligation.

(3) "Personal property" means that property that is subject to attachment by a judgment lien pursuant to Section 697.530 of the Code of Civil Procedure.

(d) Nothing in this section shall affect the priority of any of the following interests:

(1) State tax liens as set forth in Article 2 (commencing with Section 7170) of Division 7 of Title 1 of the Government Code.

(2) Liens or security interests as set forth in Article 3 (commencing with Section 697.510) of Chapter 2 of Division 2 of Article 9 of the Code of Civil Procedure.

(e) As between competing child support liens and state tax liens, a child support lien arising under this section shall have priority over a state tax lien if (1) the child support lien is filed with the Secretary of State, (2) the notice of child support lien is filed in an action or proceeding in which the obligor may become entitled to property or money judgment, or (3) the levy for child support on personal property is made, before a notice of state tax lien is filed with the Secretary of State pursuant to Section 7171 of the Government Code or filed in an action or proceeding in accordance with Section 7173 of the Government Code.

(f) A personal property lien for child support arising in another state may be enforced in the same manner and to the same extent as a personal property lien arising in this state. *(Added by Stats.1999, c. 980 (A.B.1671), § 15.)*

Cross References

Effect of,
    Liens generally, see Civil Code § 2888 et seq.
    Transfer of real property generally, see Civil Code § 1104 et seq.
Extinction of liens generally, see Civil Code § 2909 et seq.
Judgment and order defined for purposes of this Code, see Family Code § 100.
Priority of liens generally, see Civil Code § 2897 et seq.
Proceeding defined for purposes of this Code, see Family Code § 110.
Property defined for purposes of this Code, see Family Code § 113.
Real property defined, see Civil Code § 658.
State defined for purposes of this Code, see Family Code § 145.
Support defined for purposes of this Code, see Family Code § 150.

§ 17523.5. Lien for child support against real property; digitized or digital electronic record

(a)(1) Notwithstanding any other law, in connection with the duty of the department and the local child support agency to promptly and effectively collect and enforce child support obligations under Title IV–D, the transmission, filing, and recording of a lien record by departmental and local child support agency staff that arises pursuant to subdivision (a) of Section 4506 of this code or Section 697.320 of the Code of Civil Procedure against the real property of a support obligor in the form of a digital or a digitized electronic record shall be permitted and governed only by this section.

(2) A facsimile signature that complies with the requirements of paragraph (2) of subdivision (b) of Section 27201 of the Government Code shall be accepted on any document relating to a lien that is filed or recorded pursuant to this section.

(3) The department and the local child support agency may use the California Child Support Enforcement System to transmit, file, and record a lien record under this section.

(b) Nothing in this section shall be construed to require a county recorder to establish an electronic recording delivery system or to enter into a contract with an entity to implement this section.

(c) For purposes of this section, the following terms have the following meanings:

(1) "Digital electronic record" means a record containing information that is created, generated, sent, communicated, received, or stored by electronic means, but not created in original paper form.

(2) "Digitized electronic record" means a scanned image of the original paper document. *(Added by Stats.2007, c. 441 (S.B.892), § 2. Amended by Stats.2016, c. 474 (A.B.2882), § 23, eff. Jan. 1, 2017.)*

§ 17524. Statement of arrearages

(a) Upon making application to the local child support agency for child support enforcement services pursuant to Section 17400, every applicant shall be requested to give the local child support agency a statement of arrearages stating whether any support arrearages are owed. If the applicant alleges arrearages are owed, the statement shall be signed under penalty of perjury.

(b) For all cases opened by the district attorney or local child support agency after December 31, 1995, the local child support agency shall enforce only arrearages declared under penalty of perjury pursuant to subdivision (a), arrearages accrued after the case was opened, or arrearages determined by the court in the child support action. Arrearages may be determined by judgment, noticed motion, renewal of judgment, or registration of the support order.

(c) For all cases opened by the district attorney on or before December 31, 1995, the local child support agency shall enforce only arrearages that have been based upon a statement of arrearages signed under penalty of perjury or where the local child support agency has some other reasonable basis for believing the amount of claimed arrearages to be correct. *(Added by Stats.1999, c. 478 (A.B.196), § 1.)*

§ 17524

Cross References

Judgment and order defined for purposes of this Code, see Family Code § 100.
Support defined for purposes of this Code, see Family Code § 150.
Support order defined for purposes of this Code, see Family Code § 155.

Research References

Forms

West's California Judicial Council Forms FL–420, Declaration of Payment History (Governmental—Uniform Parentage Act).
West's California Judicial Council Forms FL–421, Payment History Attachment (Governmental—Uniform Parentage Act).

§ 17525. Notice of support delinquency; contents

(a) Whenever a state or local governmental agency issues a notice of support delinquency, the notice shall state the date upon which the amount of the delinquency was calculated, and shall notify the obligor that the amount calculated may, or may not, include accrued interest. This requirement shall not be imposed until the local child support agency has instituted the California Child Support Enforcement System implemented and maintained by the Department of Child Support Services pursuant to Section 17308. The notice shall further notify the obligor of the right to an administrative determination of arrears by requesting that the local child support agency review the arrears, but that payments on arrears continue to be due and payable unless and until the local child support agency notifies the obligor otherwise. A state agency shall not be required to suspend enforcement of any arrearages as a result of the obligor's request for an administrative determination of arrears, unless the agency receives notification of a suspension pursuant to subdivision (b) of Section 17526.

(b) For purposes of this section, "notice of support delinquency" means a notice issued to a support obligor that includes a specific statement of the amount of delinquent support due and payable.

(c) This section does not require a state or local entity to calculate the amount of a support delinquency, except as otherwise required by law. *(Added by Stats.1999, c. 654 (A.B.370), § 4. Amended by Stats.2000, c. 808 (A.B.1358), § 90, eff. Sept. 28, 2000; Stats.2001, c. 755 (S.B.943), § 16, eff. Oct. 12, 2001; Stats.2016, c. 474 (A.B.2882), § 24, eff. Jan. 1, 2017; Stats.2019, c. 115 (A.B.1817), § 158, eff. Jan. 1, 2020.)*

Cross References

Child support delinquency, statewide automated system for reporting administered by the department, see Family Code § 4701.
Default in support order due to unemployment, proof that obligor is actively seeking employment, see Family Code § 4505.
State defined for purposes of this Code, see Family Code § 145.
Support defined for purposes of this Code, see Family Code § 150.

§ 17526. Statement of arrearages; review

(a) Upon request of an obligor or obligee, the local child support agency shall review the amount of arrearages alleged in a statement of arrearages that may be submitted to the local child support agency by an applicant for child support enforcement services. The local child support agency shall complete the review in the same manner and pursuant to the same timeframes as a complaint submitted pursuant to Section 17800. In the review, the local child support agency shall consider all evidence and defenses submitted by either parent on the issues of the amount of support paid or owed.

(b) The local child support agency may, in its discretion, suspend enforcement or distribution of arrearages if it believes there is a substantial probability that the result of the administrative review will result in a finding that there are no arrearages.

(c) Any party to an action involving child support enforcement services of the local child support agency may request a judicial determination of arrearages. The party may request an administrative review of the alleged arrearages prior to requesting a judicial determination of arrearages. The local child support agency shall complete the review in the same manner and pursuant to the same timeframes specified in subdivision (a). Any motion to determine arrearages filed with the court shall include a monthly breakdown showing amounts ordered and amounts paid, in addition to any other relevant information.

(d) A county that submits a claim for reimbursement as a state-mandated local program of costs incurred with respect to the administrative review of alleged child support arrearages under this section shall be ineligible for state subventions or, to the extent permitted by federal law, state-administered federal subventions, for child support in the amount of any local costs under this section. *(Added by Stats.1999, c. 478 (A.B.196), § 1. Amended by Stats.2001, c. 755 (S.B.943), § 17, eff. Oct. 12, 2001; Stats.2002, c. 927 (A.B.3032), § 6.5.)*

Cross References

County defined for purposes of this Code, see Family Code § 67.
State defined for purposes of this Code, see Family Code § 145.
Support defined for purposes of this Code, see Family Code § 150.

Research References

Forms

West's California Judicial Council Forms FL–420, Declaration of Payment History (Governmental—Uniform Parentage Act).
West's California Judicial Council Forms FL–421, Payment History Attachment (Governmental—Uniform Parentage Act).
West's California Judicial Council Forms FL–626, Stipulation and Order Waiving Unassigned Arrears (Governmental) (Also Available in Chinese, Korean, Spanish, Tagalog, and Vietnamese).
West's California Judicial Council Forms FL–676, Request for Determination of Support Arrears (Also Available in Spanish).
West's California Judicial Council Forms FL–676–INFO, Information Sheet Request for Determination of Support Arrears.

§ 17528. Public Employees' Retirement System; withholding overdue support obligations

(a) As authorized by subdivision (c) of Section 704.110 of the Code of Civil Procedure, the following actions shall be taken in order to enforce support obligations that are not being met:

(1) Within 18 months of implementation of the California Child Support Enforcement System (CSE), or its replacement as prescribed by former Section 10815 of the Welfare and Institutions Code, and certification of CSE or its replacement by the United States Department of Health and Human Services, the department shall compile a file of all support judgments and orders that are being enforced by local child support agencies pursuant to Section 17400 that have sums overdue by at least 60 days or by an amount equal to 60 days of support.

(2) The file shall contain the name and social security number of the person who owes overdue support, the amount of overdue support as of the date the file is created, the name of the county in which the support obligation is being enforced by the local child support agency, and any other information that is deemed necessary by the department and the Public Employees' Retirement System.

(3) The department shall provide the certified file to the Public Employees' Retirement System for the purpose of matching the names in the file with members and beneficiaries of the Public Employees' Retirement System that are entitled to receive Public Employees' Retirement System benefits. The department and the Public Employees' Retirement System shall work cooperatively to develop an interface in order to match the names in their respective electronic data processing systems. The interface required to intercept benefits that are payable periodically shall be done as soon as it is technically feasible.

(4) The department shall update the certified file no less than on a monthly basis to add new cases within the local child support agencies or existing cases that become delinquent and to delete persons who are no longer delinquent. The department shall

provide the updated file no less than on a monthly basis to the Public Employees' Retirement System.

(5) Information contained in the certified file provided to the Public Employees' Retirement System by the department and the local child support agencies and information provided by the Public Employees' Retirement System to the department shall be used exclusively for child support enforcement purposes and may not be used for any other purpose.

(b) Notwithstanding any other law, the Public Employees' Retirement System shall withhold the amount certified from the benefits and refunds to be distributed to members with overdue support obligations or from benefits to be distributed to beneficiaries with overdue support obligations. If the benefits are payable periodically, the amount withheld pursuant to this section shall not exceed the amount permitted to be withheld for an earnings withholding order for support under Section 706.052 of the Code of Civil Procedure.

(c) The Public Employees' Retirement System shall forward the amounts withheld pursuant to subdivision (b) within 10 days of withholding to the department for distribution to the appropriate county.

(d) On an annual basis, the department shall notify individuals with overdue support obligations that PERS benefits or PERS contribution refunds may be intercepted for the purpose of enforcing family support obligations.

(e) No later than the time of the first withholding, the Public Employees' Retirement System shall send those persons subject to withholding the following:

(1) Notice that the person's benefits or retirement contribution refund have been reduced by payment on a support judgment pursuant to this section.

(2) A form developed by the department that the applicant shall use to request either a review by the local child support agency or a court hearing, as appropriate.

(f) The notice shall include the address and telephone number of the local child support agency that is enforcing the support obligation pursuant to Section 17400, and shall specify that the form requesting either a review by the local child support agency or a court hearing must be received by the local child support agency within 20 days of the date of the notice.

(g) The form shall include instructions that are designed to enable the member or beneficiary to obtain a review or a court hearing as appropriate on their own behalf. The form shall specify that if the member or beneficiary disputes the amount of support arrearages certified by the local child support agency pursuant to this section, the member or beneficiary may request a review by the local child support agency.

(h) The department shall develop procedures that are consistent with this section to be used by each local child support agency in conducting the requested review. The local child support agency shall complete the review in accordance with the procedures developed by the department and shall notify the member or beneficiary of the result of the review within 20 days of receiving the request for review. The notification of review results shall include a request for hearing form and shall inform the member or beneficiary that if the member or beneficiary returns the completed request for hearing form within 20 days of the date of the notice of review results, the local child support agency shall calendar the matter for court review. If the local child support agency cannot complete the review within 20 days, the local child support agency shall calendar the matter for hearing as specified in subdivision (k).

(i) The form specified in subdivision (g) shall also notify the member or beneficiary that the member or beneficiary may request a court hearing to claim an exemption of any benefit not payable periodically by returning the completed form to the local child support agency within 20 days. If the local child support agency receives a timely request for a hearing for a claim of exemption, the local child support agency shall calendar a court hearing. The amount of the exemption, if any, shall be determined by the court in accordance with the procedures set forth in Section 703.070 of the Code of Civil Procedure.

(j) If the local child support agency receives the form requesting either a review by the local child support agency or a court hearing within the 20 days specified in subdivision (f), the local child support agency shall not distribute the amount intercepted until the review by the local child support agency or the court hearing is completed. If the local child support agency determines that all or a portion of the member's or beneficiary's benefits were intercepted in error, or if the court determines that any amount of the benefits are exempt, the local child support agency shall refund any amount determined to be exempt or intercepted in excess of the correct amount to the member or beneficiary within 10 days of determination that a refund is due.

(k) A hearing properly requested pursuant to this section shall be calendared by the local child support agency. The hearing shall be held within 20 days from the date that the local child support agency receives the request for hearing. The local child support agency shall provide notice of the time and place for hearing by first-class mail no later than five days prior to the hearing.

(*l*) This section does not limit any existing rights of the member or beneficiary, including, but not limited to, the right to seek a determination of arrearages or other appropriate relief directly from the court. However, if the procedures of this section are not utilized by the member or beneficiary, the court may not require the local child support agency to refund any money that was distributed to the child support obligee prior to the local child support agency receiving notice of a court determination that a refund is due to the member or beneficiary.

(m) The Department of Child Support Services and the Public Employees' Retirement System shall enter into any agreement necessary to implement this section, which shall include provisions for the department to provide funding to the Public Employees' Retirement System to develop, implement, and maintain the intercept process described in this section.

(n) The Public Employees' Retirement System shall not assess service charges on members or beneficiaries in order to recover any administrative costs resulting from complying with this section. *(Added by Stats.1999, c. 478 (A.B.196), § 1. Amended by Stats.2016, c. 474 (A.B.2882), § 25, eff. Jan. 1, 2017; Stats.2019, c. 115 (A.B.1817), § 159, eff. Jan. 1, 2020.)*

Cross References

County defined for purposes of this Code, see Family Code § 67.
Department of Health Care Services, generally, see Health and Safety Code § 100100 et seq.
Family support defined for purposes of this Code, see Family Code § 92.
Judgment and order defined for purposes of this Code, see Family Code § 100.
Person defined for purposes of this Code, see Family Code § 105.
State defined for purposes of this Code, see Family Code § 145.
Support defined for purposes of this Code, see Family Code § 150.

§ 17530. Support enforcement action; allegation of error due to mistaken identity; administrative and judicial remedies; penalty

(a) Notwithstanding any other law, this section applies to any actions taken to enforce a judgment or order for support entered as a result of action filed by the local child support agency pursuant to Section 17400, 17402, or 17404, where it is alleged that the enforcement actions have been taken in error against a person who is not the support obligor named in the judgment or order.

(b) A person claiming that a support enforcement action has been taken against that person, or the person's wages or assets, in error, shall file a claim of mistaken identity with the local child support agency. The claim shall include verifiable information or documentation to establish that the person against whom the enforcement actions have been taken is not the person named in the support order or judgment. The local child support agency shall resolve a claim of mistaken identity submitted pursuant to this section in the same manner and timeframes provided for resolution of a complaint pursuant to Section 17800.

(c) If the local child support agency determines that a claim filed pursuant to this section is meritorious, or if the court enters an order pursuant to Section 17433, the agency shall immediately take the steps necessary to terminate all enforcement activities with respect to the claimant, to return to the claimant any assets seized, to terminate any levying activities or attachment or assignment orders, to release any license renewal or application being withheld pursuant to Section 17520, to return any sums paid by the claimant pursuant to the judgment or order, including sums paid to any federal, state, or local government, but excluding sums paid directly to the support obligee, and to ensure that all other enforcement agencies and entities cease further actions against the claimant. With respect to a claim filed under this section, the local child support agency shall also provide the claimant with a statement certifying that the claimant is not the support obligor named in the support order or judgment, which statement shall be prima facie evidence of the claimant's identity in any subsequent enforcement proceedings or actions with respect to that support order or judgment.

(d) If the local child support agency rejects a claim pursuant to this section, or if the agency, after finding a claim to be meritorious, fails to take any of the remedial steps provided in subdivision (c), the claimant may file an action with the superior court to establish the mistaken identity or to obtain the remedies described in subdivision (c), or both.

(e) Filing a false claim pursuant to this section shall be a misdemeanor. *(Added by Stats.1999, c. 653 (A.B.380), § 18, operative April 1, 2000. Amended by Stats.2001, c. 755 (S.B.943), § 18, eff. Oct. 12, 2001; Stats.2019, c. 115 (A.B.1817), § 160, eff. Jan. 1, 2020.)*

Cross References

False Claims Act, generally, see Government Code § 12650 et seq.
Judgment and order defined for purposes of this Code, see Family Code § 100.
Misdemeanors, definition and penalties, see Penal Code §§ 17, 19 and 19.2.
Person defined for purposes of this Code, see Family Code § 105.
Prima facie evidence, see Evidence Code § 602.
Proceeding defined for purposes of this Code, see Family Code § 110.
State defined for purposes of this Code, see Family Code § 145.
Support defined for purposes of this Code, see Family Code § 150.
Support order defined for purposes of this Code, see Family Code § 155.

§ 17531. Closure of a child support case; summary criminal history information in case; deletion or purging of file

When a local child support agency closes a child support case containing summary criminal history information, the local child support agency shall delete or purge from the file and destroy any documents or information concerning or arising from offenses for or of which the parent has been arrested, charged, or convicted, other than offenses related to the parent's having failed to provide support for minor children, no later than four years and four months, or any other timeframe that is consistent with federal regulations controlling child support records retention, after the date the local child support agency closes the case. *(Added by Stats.2000, c. 808 (A.B.1358), § 91, eff. Sept. 28, 2000.)*

Cross References

Local summary criminal history information, furnishing to authorized persons, see Penal Code § 13300.
Minor defined for purposes of this Code, see Family Code § 6500.
State summary criminal history information, see Penal Code § 11105.

Support defined for purposes of this Code, see Family Code § 150.

§ 17540. Payment of county claims for federal and state reimbursement; waiver of time limitation

(a)(1) Commencing July 1, 2000, the department shall pay only those county claims for federal or state reimbursement under this division which are filed with the department within nine months of the end of the calendar quarter in which the costs are paid. A claim filed after that time may only be paid if the claim falls within the exceptions set forth in federal law.

(2) The department may change the nine-month limitation specified in paragraph (1), as deemed necessary by the department to comply with federal changes which affect time limits for filing a claim.

(b)(1) The department may waive the time limit imposed by subdivision (a) if the department determines there was good cause for a county's failure to file a claim or claims within the time limit.

(2)(A) For purposes of this subdivision, "good cause" means circumstances which are beyond the county's control, including acts of God and documented action or inaction by the state or federal government.

(B) "Circumstances beyond the county's control" do not include neglect or failure on the part of the county or any of its offices, officers, or employees.

(C) A county shall request a waiver of the time limit imposed by this section for good cause in accordance with regulations adopted and promulgated by the department.

(3) The department's authority to waive the time limit under this subdivision shall be subject to the availability of funds and shall not apply to claims submitted more than 18 months after the end of the calendar quarter in which costs were paid. *(Added by Stats.2000, c. 808 (A.B.1358), § 92, eff. Sept. 28, 2000.)*

Cross References

County defined for purposes of this Code, see Family Code § 67.
County welfare department claims for reimbursement, waiver of time limits for good cause, see Welfare and Institutions Code § 10604.5.
State defined for purposes of this Code, see Family Code § 145.

§ 17550. Establishment of regulations by which the local child support agency may compromise parents' liability for public assistance debt in cases of separation or desertion of parent from child; conditions

(a) The Department of Child Support Services, in consultation with the State Department of Social Services, shall establish regulations by which the local child support agency, in any case of separation or desertion of a parent from a child that results in aid under Chapter 2 (commencing with Section 11200) of Part 3 of Division 9 of the Welfare and Institutions Code being granted to the child, may compromise the obligor parent or parents' liability for public assistance debt, including interest thereon, owed to the state where the child for whom public assistance was paid is residing with the obligor parent, and all of the following conditions are met:

(1) The obligor parent establishes one of the following:

(A) The child has been adjudged a dependent of the court under Section 300 of the Welfare and Institutions Code and the child has been reunified with the obligor parent pursuant to a court order.

(B) The child received public assistance while living with a guardian or relative caregiver and the child has been returned to the custody of the obligor parent, provided that the obligor parent for whom the debt compromise is being considered was the parent with whom the child resided prior to the child's placement with the guardian or relative caregiver.

(2) The obligor parent, for whom the debt compromise is being considered, has an income less than 250 percent of the current federal poverty level.

(3) The local child support agency, pursuant to regulations set forth by the department, has determined that the compromise is necessary for the child's support.

(b) Prior to compromising an obligor parent's liability for debt incurred for either AFDC–FC payments provided to a child pursuant to Section 11400 of the Welfare and Institutions Code, or incurred for CalWORKs payments provided on behalf of a child, the local child support agency shall consult with the county child welfare department.

(c) This section does not relieve an obligor, who has not been reunified with their child, of any liability for public assistance debt.

(d) For the purposes of this section, the following definitions apply:

(1) "Guardian" means the legal guardian of the child, who assumed care and control of the child while the child was in the guardian's control, and who is not a biological or adoptive parent.

(2) "Relative caregiver" means a relative as defined in subdivision (c) of Section 11362 of the Welfare and Institutions Code, who assumed primary responsibility for the child while the child was in the relative's care and control, and who is not a biological or adoptive parent.

(e) The department shall promulgate all necessary regulations pursuant to this section on or before October 1, 2002, including regulations that set forth guidelines to be used by the local child support agency when compromising public assistance debt. *(Added by Stats.2001, c. 463 (A.B.1449), § 2. Amended by Stats.2019, c. 115 (A.B.1817), § 161, eff. Jan, 1, 2020.)*

Implementation

For implementation relating to the availability of federal financial participation, see Stats.2001, c. 463 (A.B.1449), § 6.

Cross References

Administrative regulations and rulemaking, see Government Code § 11340 et seq.
County defined for purposes of this Code, see Family Code § 67.
Judgment and order defined for purposes of this Code, see Family Code § 100.
Juvenile court law, liability for costs of support, see Welfare and Institutions Code § 903.
State defined for purposes of this Code, see Family Code § 145.
Support defined for purposes of this Code, see Family Code § 150.

§ 17552. Regulations concerning determinations whether or not best interests of child or nonminor require case to be referred to local child support agency for child support services in situations resulting in foster care assistance, CalWORKs or Kin-GAP payments, or other specified aid; determination factors; review; nonminor dependents

(a)(1) The State Department of Social Services, in consultation with the Department of Child Support Services, shall promulgate regulations by which the county child welfare department, in any case of separation or desertion of a parent or parents from a child that results in foster care assistance payments under Section 11400 of, or a voluntary placement under Section 11401.1 of, or the payments for a minor child placed in the same home as a minor or nonminor dependent parent under Section 11401.4 of, the Welfare and Institutions Code, or CalWORKs payments to a caretaker relative of a child who comes within the jurisdiction of the juvenile court under Section 300, 601, or 602 of the Welfare and Institutions Code, who has been removed from the parental home and placed with the caretaker relative by court order, and who is under the supervision of the county child welfare agency or probation department under Section 11250 of, or Kin-GAP payments under Article 4.5 (commencing with Section 11360) or Article 4.7 (commencing with Section 11385) of, or aid under subdivision (c) of Section 10101 of, the Welfare and Institutions Code, shall determine whether it is in the best interests of the child or nonminor to have the case referred to the local child support agency for child support services. If reunification services are not offered or are terminated, the case may be referred to the local child support agency, unless the child's permanent plan is legal guardianship with a relative who is receiving Kin-GAP and the payment of support by the parent may compromise the stability of the current placement with the related guardian, or the permanent plan is transitional foster care for the nonminor under Section 11403 of the Welfare and Institutions Code. In making the determination, the department regulations shall provide the factors the county child welfare department shall consider, including:

(A) Whether the payment of support by the parent will pose a barrier to the proposed reunification, in that the payment of support will compromise the parent's ability to meet the requirements of the parent's reunification plan.

(B) Whether the payment of support by the parent will pose a barrier to the proposed reunification in that the payment of support will compromise the parent's current or future ability to meet the financial needs of the child.

(2) The department's regulations shall require the county welfare department, in making the determination pursuant to paragraph (1), to presume that the payment of support by the parent is likely to pose a barrier to the proposed reunification.

(b) The department regulations shall provide that, when the county child welfare department determines that it is not in the best interest of the child to seek a support order against the parent, the county child welfare department shall refrain from referring the case to the local child support agency. The regulations shall define those circumstances in which it is not in the best interest of the child to refer the case to the local child support agency. The regulations shall include the presumption described in paragraph (2) of subdivision (a) that the payment of support by the parent is likely to pose a barrier to the proposed reunification.

(c) The department regulations shall provide, when the county child welfare department determines that it is not in the child's best interest to have the case referred to the local child support agency, the county child welfare department shall review that determination periodically to coincide with the redetermination of AFDC–FC eligibility under Section 11401.5 of, or the CalWORKs eligibility under Section 11265 of, or Kin-GAP eligibility under Article 4.5 (commencing with Section 11360) or Article 4.7 (commencing with Section 11385) of Chapter 2 of Part 3 of Division 9 of, the Welfare and Institutions Code, and shall refer the child's case to the local child support agency upon a determination that, due to a change in the child's circumstances, it is no longer contrary to the child's best interest to have the case referred to the local child support agency.

* * *

(d) Notwithstanding any other law, a nonminor dependent, as described in subdivision (v) of Section 11400 of the Welfare and Institutions Code, who is over 19 years of age, is not a child for purposes of referral to the local child support agency for collection or enforcement of child support.

(e) Notwithstanding any other law, a minor or a nonminor dependent, as defined in subdivision (v) of Section 11400 of the Welfare and Institutions Code, who has a minor child placed in the same licensed or approved facility pursuant to Section 11401.4 of the Welfare and Institutions Code is not a parent for purposes of referral to the local child support agency for collection or enforcement of child support.

(f) The State Department of Social Services shall revise its regulations to implement the changes made by the act that added this subdivision on or before October 1, 2023. *(Added by Stats.2001, c. 463 (A.B.1449), § 3. Amended by Stats.2005, c. 198 (A.B.1743), § 1; Stats.2010, c. 559 (A.B.12), § 2; Stats.2011, c. 459 (A.B.212), § 1, eff.*

§ 17552   SUPPORT SERVICES

Oct. 4, 2011; Stats.2012, c. 846 (A.B.1712), § 2; Stats.2019, c. 115 (A.B.1817), § 162, eff. Jan. 1, 2020; Stats.2022, c. 755 (A.B.1686), § 2, eff. Jan. 1, 2023.)

Cross References

County defined for purposes of this Code, see Family Code § 67.
Department of Child Support Services, child support enforcement, public assistance application where parent absent or not established, see Family Code § 17415.
Establishment of Approved Relative Caregiver Funding Option Program, payment rate, conditions of participation, funds to be used, children under the jurisdiction of juvenile court, see Welfare and Institutions Code § 11461.3.
Judgment and order defined for purposes of this Code, see Family Code § 100.
Juvenile court law, liability for costs of support, see Welfare and Institutions Code § 903.
State defined for purposes of this Code, see Family Code § 145.
Support defined for purposes of this Code, see Family Code § 150.
Support order defined for purposes of this Code, see Family Code § 155.
Voluntary family reunification services, see Welfare and Institutions Code § 16507.4.

§ 17555. Appropriations in annual Budget Act for purpose of augmenting funding for collection responsibilities; requirements; legislative intent

(a) Any appropriation made available in the annual Budget Act for the purposes of augmenting funding for local child support agencies in the furtherance of their revenue collection responsibilities shall be subject to all of the following requirements:

(1) Each local child support agency shall submit to the department an early intervention plan with all components to take effect upon receipt of their additional allocation as a result of this proposal.

(2) Funds shall be distributed to counties based on their performance on the following two federal performance measures:

(A) Measure 3: Collections on Current Support.

(B) Measure 4: Cases with Collections on Arrears.

(3) A local child support agency shall be required to use and ensure that 100 percent of the new funds allocated are dedicated to maintaining caseworker staffing levels in order to stabilize child support collections.

(4) At the end of each fiscal year that this augmentation is in effect, the department shall provide a report on the cost-effectiveness of this augmentation, including an assessment of caseload changes over time.

(b) It is the intent of the Legislature to review the results of this augmentation and the level of related appropriation during the legislative budget review process. *(Added by Stats.2009–2010, 4th Ex.Sess., c. 4 (A.B.4), § 2, eff. July 28, 2009. Amended by Stats.2010, c. 725 (A.B.1612), § 3, eff. Oct. 19, 2010; Stats.2012, c. 728 (S.B.71), § 38.)*

§ 17556. Annual report

On or before March 1, 2019, and annually thereafter, the department shall submit a report to the Legislature providing information on the status of all of the following:

(a) Case-to-staff ratios for each local child support agency.

(b) Collections to families and recoupment collections to county, state, and federal governmental agencies.

(c) Cost avoidance benefits.

(d) The number of families served by the child support program. *(Added by Stats.2018, c. 35 (A.B.1811), § 2, eff. June 27, 2018.)*

§ 17560. Arrears collection enhancement process; development of program; acceptance of offers in compromise

Text of section as amended by Stats.2008, c. 759 (A.B.1279), § 16, eff. Sept. 30, 2008.

Section 17560 was added by Stats.2003, c. 225 (A.B.1752), § 6, eff. Aug. 11, 2003, amended by Stats.2005, c. 154 (S.B.1082), § 5, eff. Aug. 30, 2005; Stats.2006, c. 75 (A.B. 1808), § 8, eff. July 12, 2006, and repealed by its own terms, operative July 1, 2008. Therefore, this section was not in effect from July 1, 2008 until Sept. 30, 2008.

Stats.2008, c. 759 (A.B.1279), § 16, might be given effect as a new addition of this section; but see Government Code § 9609.

(a) The department shall establish and operate a statewide compromise of arrears program pursuant to which the department may accept offers in compromise of child support arrears and interest accrued thereon owed to the state for reimbursement of aid paid pursuant to Chapter 2 (commencing with Section 11200) of Part 3 of Division 9 of the Welfare and Institutions Code. The program shall operate uniformly across California and shall take into consideration the needs of the children subject to the child support order and the obligor's ability to pay.

(b) If the obligor owes current child support, the offer in compromise shall require the obligor to be in compliance with the current support order for a set period of time before any arrears and interest accrued thereon may be compromised.

(c) Absent a finding of good cause, or a determination by the director that it is in the best interest of the state to do otherwise, any offer in compromise entered into pursuant to this section shall be rescinded, all compromised liabilities shall be reestablished notwithstanding any statute of limitations that otherwise may be applicable, and no portion of the amount offered in compromise may be refunded, if either of the following occurs:

(1) The department or local child support agency determines that the obligor did any of the following acts regarding the offer in compromise:

(A) Concealed from the department or local child support agency any income, assets, or other property belonging to the obligor or any reasonably anticipated receipt of income, assets, or other property.

(B) Intentionally received, withheld, destroyed, mutilated, or falsified any information, document, or record, or intentionally made any false statement, relating to the financial conditions of the obligor.

(2) The obligor fails to comply with any of the terms and conditions of the offer in compromise.

(d) Pursuant to subdivision (k) of Section 17406, in no event may the administrator, director, or director's designee within the department, accept an offer in compromise of any child support arrears owed directly to the custodial party unless that party consents to the offer in compromise in writing and participates in the agreement. Prior to giving consent, the custodial party shall be provided with a clear written explanation of the rights with respect to child support arrears owed to the custodial party and the compromise thereof.

(e) Subject to the requirements of this section, the director shall delegate to the administrator of a local child support agency the authority to compromise an amount of child support arrears up to five thousand dollars ($5,000), and may delegate additional authority to compromise up to an amount determined by the director to support the effective administration of the offers in compromise program.

(f) For an amount to be compromised under this section, the following conditions shall exist:

(1)(A) The administrator, director or director's designee within the department determines that acceptance of an offer in compromise is in the best interest of the state and that the compromise amount equals or exceeds what the state can expect to collect for reimbursement of aid paid pursuant to Chapter 2 (commencing with Section 11200) of Part 3 of Division 9 of the Welfare and Institutions Code in the absence of the compromise, based on the obligor's ability to pay.

(B) Acceptance of an offer in compromise shall be deemed to be in the best interest of the state, absent a finding of good cause to the contrary, with regard to arrears that accrued as a result of a decrease in income when an obligor was a reservist or member of the National Guard, was activated to United States military service, and failed to modify the support order to reflect the reduction in income. Good cause to find that the compromise is not in the best interest of the state shall include circumstances in which the service member's failure to seek, or delay in seeking, the modification were not reasonable under the circumstances faced by the service member. The director, no later than 90 days after the effective date of the act adding this subparagraph, shall establish rules that compromise, at a minimum, the amount of support that would not have accrued had the order been modified to reflect the reduced income earned during the period of active military service.

(2) Any other terms and conditions that the director establishes that may include, but may not be limited to, paying current support in a timely manner, making lump-sum payments, and paying arrears in exchange for compromise of interest owed.

(3) The obligor shall provide evidence of income and assets, including, but not limited to, wage stubs, tax returns, and bank statements as necessary to establish all of the following:

(A) That the amount set forth in the offer in compromise of arrears owed is the most that can be expected to be paid or collected from the obligor's present assets or income.

(B) That the obligor does not have reasonable prospects of acquiring increased income or assets that would enable the obligor to satisfy a greater amount of the child support arrears than the amount offered, within a reasonable period of time.

(C) That the obligor has not withheld payment of child support in anticipation of the offers in compromise program.

(g) A determination by the administrator, director or the director's designee within the department that it would not be in the best interest of the state to accept or rescind an offer in compromise in satisfaction of child support arrears shall be final and not subject to the provisions of Chapter 5 (commencing with Section 17800) of Division 17, or subject to judicial review.

(h) Any offer in compromise entered into pursuant to this section shall be filed with the appropriate court. The local child support agency shall notify the court if the compromise is rescinded pursuant to subdivision (c).

(i) Any compromise of child support arrears pursuant to this section shall maximize to the greatest extent possible the state's share of the federal performance incentives paid pursuant to the Child Support Performance and Incentive Act of 1998 [1] and shall comply with federal law.

(j) The department shall ensure uniform application of this section across the state. *(Amended by Stats.2008, c. 759 (A.B.1279), § 16, eff. Sept. 30, 2008.)*

[1] Child Support Performance and Incentive Act of 1998 (Pub.L.105–200, July 16, 1998, 112 Stat. 645). Public law sections classified to U.S.C.A., see USCA–Tables.

§ 17561. Annual report on implementation of California Child Support Automation System; joint production by Office of the Chief Information Officer and Department of Child Support Services; contents

The Office of the Chief Information Officer and the Department of Child Support Services, beginning in 2010, shall jointly produce an annual report to be submitted on March 1, to the appropriate policy and fiscal committees of the Legislature on the ongoing implementation of the California Child Support Automation System (CCSAS), including all of the following components:

(a) A clear breakdown of funding elements for past, current, and future years.

(b) Descriptions of active functionalities and a description of their usefulness in child support collections by local child support agencies.

(c) A review of current considerations relative to federal law and policy.

(d) A policy narrative on future, planned changes to the CCSAS and how those changes will advance activities for workers, collections for the state, and payments for recipient families. *(Added by Stats.2009–2010, 4th Ex.Sess., c. 4 (A.B.4), § 3, eff. July 28, 2009.)*

ARTICLE 3. PROGRAM COMPLIANCE

Section
17600. Legislative findings and declarations; county reporting requirements.
17601. Performance data to be provided to Legislature.
17602. Performance standards for local agencies.
17604. Agency noncompliance with state plan; reduced federal funding.

§ 17600. Legislative findings and declarations; county reporting requirements

(a) The Legislature finds and declares all of the following:

(1) The Legislative Analyst has found that county child support enforcement programs provide a net increase in revenues to the state.

(2) The state has a fiscal interest in ensuring that county child support enforcement programs perform efficiently.

(3) The state does not provide information to counties on child support enforcement programs, based on common denominators that would facilitate comparison of program performance.

(4) Providing this information would allow county officials to monitor program performance and to make appropriate modifications to improve program efficiency.

(5) This information is required for effective management of the child support program.

(b) Except as provided in this subdivision commencing with the 1998–99 fiscal year, and for each fiscal year thereafter, each county that is participating in the state incentive program described in Section 17704 shall provide to the department, and the department shall compile from this county child support information, monthly and annually, all of the following performance-based data, as established by the federal incentive funding system, provided that the department may revise the data required by this paragraph in order to conform to the final federal incentive system data definitions:

(1) One of the following data relating to paternity establishment, as required by the department, provided that the department shall require all counties to report on the same measurement:

(A) The total number of children in the caseload governed by Part D (commencing with Section 451) of Title IV of the federal Social Security Act (42 U.S.C. Sec. 651 et seq.), as of the end of the federal fiscal year, who were born to unmarried parents for whom paternity was established or acknowledged, and the total number of children in that caseload, as of the end of the preceding federal fiscal year, who were born to unmarried parents.

(B) The total number of minor children who were born in the state to unmarried parents for whom paternity was established or acknowledged during a federal fiscal year, and the total number of children in the state born to unmarried parents during the preceding calendar year.

(2) The number of cases governed by Part D (commencing with Section 451) of Title IV of the federal Social Security Act (42 U.S.C. Sec. 651 et seq.) during the federal fiscal year and the total number of those cases with support orders.

§ 17600   SUPPORT SERVICES

(3) The total dollars collected during the federal fiscal year for current support in cases governed by Part D (commencing with Section 451) of Title IV of the federal Social Security Act (42 U.S.C. Sec. 651 et seq.) and the total number of dollars owing for current support during that federal fiscal year in cases governed by those provisions.

(4) The total number of cases for the federal fiscal year governed by Part D (commencing with Section 451) of Title IV of the federal Social Security Act (42 U.S.C. Sec. 651 et seq.) in which payment was being made toward child support arrearages and the total number of cases for that fiscal year governed by these federal provisions that had child support arrearages.

(5) The total number of dollars collected and expended during a federal fiscal year in cases governed by Part D (commencing with Section 451) of Title IV of the federal Social Security Act (42 U.S.C. Sec. 651 et seq.).

(6) The total amount of child support dollars collected during a federal fiscal year, and, if and when required by federal law, the amount of these collections broken down by collections distributed on behalf of current recipients of federal Temporary Assistance for Needy Families block grant funds or federal foster care funds, on behalf of former recipients of federal Temporary Assistance for Needy Families block grant funds or federal foster care funds, or on behalf of persons who have never been recipients of these federal funds.

(c) In addition to the information required by subdivision (b), the department shall collect, on a monthly basis, from each county that is participating in the state incentive program described in Section 17704, information on the local child support agency for each federal fiscal year, and shall report semiannually on all of the following performance measurements:

(1) The percentage of cases with collections of current support. This percentage shall be calculated by dividing the number of cases with an order for current support by the number of those cases with collections of current support. The number of cases with support collected shall include only the number of cases actually receiving a collection, not the number of payments received. Cases with a medical support order that do not have an order for current support may not be counted.

(2) The average amount collected per case for all cases with collections.

(3) The percentage of cases that had a support order established during the period. A support order shall be counted as established only when the appropriate court has issued an order for child support, including an order for temporary child support, or an order for medical support.

(4) The total cost of administering the local child support agency, including the federal, state, and county share of the costs, and the federal and state incentives received by each county. The total cost of administering the program shall be broken down by the following:

(A) The direct costs of the program, broken down further by total employee salaries and benefits, a list of the number of employees broken down into at least the following categories: attorneys, administrators, caseworkers, investigators, and clerical support; contractor costs; space charges; and payments to other county agencies. Employee salaries and numbers need only be reported in the annual report.

(B) The indirect costs, showing all overhead charges.

(5) In addition, the local child support agency shall report monthly on measurements developed by the department that provide data on the following:

(A) Locating obligors.

(B) Obtaining and enforcing medical support.

(C) Providing customer service.

(D) Any other measurements that the director determines to be an appropriate determination of a local child support agency's performance.

(6) A county may apply for an exemption from any or all of the reporting requirements of this subdivision for a fiscal year by submitting an application for the exemption to the department at least three months prior to the commencement of the fiscal year or quarter for which the exemption is sought. A county shall provide a separate justification for each data element under this subdivision for which the county is seeking an exemption and the cost to the county of providing the data. The department may not grant an exemption for more than one year. The department may grant a single exemption only if both of the following conditions are met:

(A) The county cannot compile the data being sought through its existing automated system or systems.

(B) The county cannot compile the data being sought through manual means or through an enhanced automated system or systems without significantly harming the child support collection efforts of the county.

(d) After implementation of the statewide automated system, in addition to the information required by subdivision (b), the Department of Child Support Services shall collect, on a monthly basis, from each county that is participating in the state incentive program described in Section 17704, information on the county child support enforcement program beginning with the 1998–99 fiscal year or a later fiscal year, as appropriate, and for each subsequent fiscal year, and shall report semiannually on all of the following measurements:

(1) For each of the following support collection categories, the number of cases with support collected shall include only the number of cases actually receiving a collection, not the number of payments received.

(A)(i) The number of cases with collections for current support.

(ii) The number of cases with arrears collections only.

(iii) The number of cases with both current support and arrears collections.

(B) For cases with current support only due:

(i) The number of cases in which the full amount of current support owed was collected.

(ii) The number of cases in which some amount of current support, but less than the full amount of support owed, was collected.

(iii) The number of cases in which no amount of support owed was collected.

(C) For cases in which arrears only were owed:

(i) The number of cases in which all arrears owed were collected.

(ii) The number of cases in which some amount of arrears, but less than the full amount of arrears owed, was collected.

(iii) The number of cases in which no amount of arrears owed was collected.

(D) For cases in which both current support and arrears are owed:

(i) The number of cases in which the full amount of current support and arrears owed was collected.

(ii) The number of cases in which some amount of current support and arrears, but less than the full amount of support owed, was collected.

(iii) The number of cases in which no amount of support owed was collected.

(E) The total number of cases in which an amount was due for current support only.

(F) The total number of cases in which an amount was due for both current support and arrears.

(G) The total number of cases in which an amount was due for arrears only.

(H) For cases with current support due, the number of cases without orders for medical support and the number of cases with an order for medical support.

(2) The number of alleged fathers or obligors who were served with a summons and complaint to establish paternity or a support order, and the number of alleged fathers or obligors for whom it is required that paternity or a support order be established. In order to be counted under this paragraph, the alleged father or obligor shall be successfully served with process. An alleged father shall be counted under this paragraph only once if served with process simultaneously for both a paternity and a support order proceeding for the same child or children. For purposes of this paragraph, a support order shall include a medical support order.

(3) The number of new asset seizures or successful initial collections on a wage assignment for purposes of child support collection. For purposes of this paragraph, a collection made on a wage assignment shall be counted only once for each wage assignment issued.

(4) The number of children requiring paternity establishment and the number of children for whom paternity has been established during the period. Paternity may only be established once for each child. A child for whom paternity is not at issue shall not be counted in the number of children for whom paternity has been established. For this purpose, paternity is not at issue if the parents were married and neither parent challenges paternity or a voluntary paternity declaration has been executed by the parents prior to the local child support agency obtaining the case and neither parent challenges paternity.

(5) The number of cases requiring that a support order be established and the number of cases that had a support order established during the period. A support order shall be counted as established only when the appropriate court has issued an order for child support, including an order for temporary child support, or an order for medical support.

(6) The total cost of administering the local child support agency, including the federal, state, and county share of the costs and the federal and state incentives received by each county. The total cost of administering the program shall be broken down by the following:

(A) The direct costs of the program, broken down further by total employee salaries and benefits, a list of the number of employees broken down into at least the following categories: attorneys, administrators, caseworkers, investigators, and clerical support; contractor costs; space charges; and payments to other county agencies. Employee salaries and numbers need only be reported in the annual report.

(B) The indirect costs, showing all overhead charges.

(7) The total child support collections due, broken down by current support, interest on arrears, and principal, and the total child support collections that have been collected, broken down by current support, interest on arrears, and principal.

(8) The actual case status for all cases in the county child support enforcement program. Each case shall be reported in one case status only. If a case falls within more than one status category, it shall be counted in the first status category of the list set forth below in which it qualifies. The following shall be the case status choices:

(A) No support order, location of obligor parent required.

(B) No support order, alleged obligor parent located and paternity required.

(C) No support order, location and paternity not at issue but support order must be established.

(D) Support order established with current support obligation and obligor is in compliance with support obligation.

(E) Support order established with current support obligation, obligor is in arrears, and location of obligor is necessary.

(F) Support order established with current support obligation, obligor is in arrears, and location of obligor's assets is necessary.

(G) Support order established with current support obligation, obligor is in arrears, and no location of obligor or obligor's assets is necessary.

(H) Support order established with current support obligation, obligor is in arrears, the obligor is located, but the local child support agency has established satisfactorily that the obligor has no income or assets and no ability to earn.

(I) Support order established with current support obligation and arrears, obligor is paying the current support and is paying some or all of the interest on the arrears, but is paying no principal.

(J) Support order established for arrears only and obligor is current in repayment obligation.

(K) Support order established for arrears only, obligor is not current in arrears repayment schedule, and location of obligor is required.

(L) Support order established for arrears only, obligor is not current in arrears repayment schedule, and location of obligor's assets is required.

(M) Support order established for arrears only, obligor is not current in arrears repayment schedule, and no location of obligor or obligor's assets is required.

(N) Support order established for arrears only, obligor is not current in arrears repayment, and the obligor is located, but the local child support agency has established satisfactorily that the obligor has no income or assets and no ability to earn.

(O) Support order established for arrears only and obligor is repaying some or all of the interest, but no principal.

(P) Other, if necessary, to be defined in the regulations promulgated under subdivision (e).

(e) Upon implementation of the statewide automated system, or at the time that the department determines that compliance with this subdivision is possible, whichever is earlier, each county that is participating in the state incentive program described in Section 17704 shall collect and report, and the department shall compile for each participating county, information on the county child support program in each fiscal year, all of the following data, in a manner that facilitates comparison of counties and the entire state, except that the department may eliminate or modify the requirement to report any data mandated to be reported pursuant to this subdivision if the department determines that the local child support agencies are unable to accurately collect and report the information or that collecting and reporting of the data by the local child support agencies will be onerous:

(1) The number of alleged obligors or fathers who receive CalWORKs benefits, CalFresh benefits, and Medi–Cal benefits.

(2) The number of obligors or alleged fathers who are in state prison or county jail.

(3) The number of obligors or alleged fathers who do not have a social security number.

(4) The number of obligors or alleged fathers whose address is unknown.

(5) The number of obligors or alleged fathers whose complete name, consisting of at least a first and last name, is not known by the local child support agency.

(6) The number of obligors or alleged fathers who filed a tax return with the Franchise Tax Board in the last year for which a data match is available.

§ 17600

(7) The number of obligors or alleged fathers who have no income reported to the Employment Development Department during the third quarter of the fiscal year.

(8) The number of obligors or alleged fathers who have income between one dollar ($1) and five hundred dollars ($500) reported to the Employment Development Department during the third quarter of the fiscal year.

(9) The number of obligors or alleged fathers who have income between five hundred one dollars ($501) and one thousand five hundred dollars ($1,500) reported to the Employment Development Department during the third quarter of the fiscal year.

(10) The number of obligors or alleged fathers who have income between one thousand five hundred one dollars ($1,501) and two thousand five hundred dollars ($2,500) reported to the Employment Development Department during the third quarter of the fiscal year.

(11) The number of obligors or alleged fathers who have income between two thousand five hundred one dollars ($2,501) and three thousand five hundred dollars ($3,500) reported to the Employment Development Department during the third quarter of the fiscal year.

(12) The number of obligors or alleged fathers who have income between three thousand five hundred one dollars ($3,501) and four thousand five hundred dollars ($4,500) reported to the Employment Development Department during the third quarter of the fiscal year.

(13) The number of obligors or alleged fathers who have income between four thousand five hundred one dollars ($4,501) and five thousand five hundred dollars ($5,500) reported to the Employment Development Department during the third quarter of the fiscal year.

(14) The number of obligors or alleged fathers who have income between five thousand five hundred one dollars ($5,501) and six thousand five hundred dollars ($6,500) reported to the Employment Development Department during the third quarter of the fiscal year.

(15) The number of obligors or alleged fathers who have income between six thousand five hundred one dollars ($6,501) and seven thousand five hundred dollars ($7,500) reported to the Employment Development Department during the third quarter of the fiscal year.

(16) The number of obligors or alleged fathers who have income between seven thousand five hundred one dollars ($7,501) and nine thousand dollars ($9,000) reported to the Employment Development Department during the third quarter of the fiscal year.

(17) The number of obligors or alleged fathers who have income exceeding nine thousand dollars ($9,000) reported to the Employment Development Department during the third quarter of the fiscal year.

(18) The number of obligors or alleged fathers who have two or more employers reporting earned income to the Employment Development Department during the third quarter of the fiscal year.

(19) The number of obligors or alleged fathers who receive unemployment benefits during the third quarter of the fiscal year.

(20) The number of obligors or alleged fathers who receive state disability benefits during the third quarter of the fiscal year.

(21) The number of obligors or alleged fathers who receive workers' compensation benefits during the third quarter of the fiscal year.

(22) The number of obligors or alleged fathers who receive Social Security Disability Insurance benefits during the third quarter of the fiscal year.

(23) The number of obligors or alleged fathers who receive Supplemental Security Income/State Supplementary Program for the Aged, Blind and Disabled benefits during the third quarter of the fiscal year.

(f) The department, in consultation with the Legislative Analyst's Office, the Judicial Council, the California Family Support Council, and child support advocates, shall develop regulations to ensure that all local child support agencies report the data required by this section uniformly and consistently throughout California.

(g) For each federal fiscal year, the department shall provide the information for all participating counties to each member of a county board of supervisors, county executive officer, local child support agency, and the appropriate policy committees and fiscal committees of the Legislature on or before June 30, of each fiscal year. The department shall provide data semiannually, based on the federal fiscal year, on or before December 31, of each year. The department shall present the information in a manner that facilitates comparison of county performance.

(h) For purposes of this section, "case" means a noncustodial parent, whether mother, father, or putative father, who is, or eventually may be, obligated under law for support of a child or children. For purposes of this definition, a noncustodial parent shall be counted once for each family that has a dependent child they may be obligated to support.

(i) This section shall be operative only for as long as Section 17704 requires participating counties to report data to the department. *(Added by Stats.1999, c. 478 (A.B.196), § 1. Amended by Stats.1999, c. 480 (S.B.542), § 20; Stats.2002, c. 927 (A.B.3032), § 7; Stats.2003, c. 308 (A.B.738), § 4; Stats.2004, c. 183 (A.B.3082), § 96; Stats.2011, c. 227 (A.B.1400), § 5; Stats.2019, c. 115 (A.B.1817), § 163, eff. Jan. 1, 2020.)*

Operative Effect

By its own terms, this section is operative only for as long as Family Code Section 17704 requires participating counties to report data to the department.

Cross References

County defined for purposes of this Code, see Family Code § 67.
Family support defined for purposes of this Code, see Family Code § 92.
Judgment and order defined for purposes of this Code, see Family Code § 100.
Minor defined for purposes of this Code, see Family Code § 6500.
Person defined for purposes of this Code, see Family Code § 105.
Proceeding defined for purposes of this Code, see Family Code § 110.
State defined for purposes of this Code, see Family Code § 145.
Support defined for purposes of this Code, see Family Code § 150.
Support order defined for purposes of this Code, see Family Code § 155.
Workers' compensation, see Labor Code § 3200 et seq.

§ 17601. Performance data to be provided to Legislature

The department shall provide to the Legislature actual performance data on child support collections within 60 days of the end of each quarter. This data shall include all comparative data for managing program performance currently provided to local child support agencies, including national, state, and local performance data, as available. The department shall prominently post the data on its Web site, and shall require all local child support agency Web sites to prominently post a link to the state Web site. The department shall update the Legislature during the annual budget subcommittee hearing process, commencing in 2008, on the state and local progress on child support federal performance measures and collections. *(Added by Stats.2007, c. 177 (S.B.84), § 1, eff. Aug. 24, 2007.)*

§ 17602. Performance standards for local agencies

(a) The department shall adopt the federal minimum standards as the baseline standard of performance for the local child support agencies and work in consultation with the local child support agencies to develop program performance targets on an annual federal fiscal year basis. The performance measures shall include, at a minimum, the federal performance measures and the state performance measures, as described in subdivision (c) of Section 17600. The program performance targets shall represent ongoing improvement in the performance measures for each local child support agency, as well as the department's statewide performance level.

(b) In determining the performance measures in subdivision (a), the department shall consider the total amount of uncollected child support arrearages that are realistically collectible. The director shall analyze, in consultation with local child support agencies and child support advocates, the current amount of uncollected child support arrearages statewide and in each county to determine the amount of child support that may realistically be collected. The director shall consider, in conducting the analysis, factors that may influence collections, including demographic factors such as welfare caseload, levels of poverty and unemployment, rates of incarceration of obligors, and age of delinquencies. The director shall use this analysis to establish program priorities as provided in paragraph (7) of subdivision (b) of Section 17306.

(c) The department shall use the performance-based data, and the criteria for that data, as set forth in Section 17600 to determine a local child support agency's performance measures for the quarter.

(d) The director shall adopt a three phase process to be used statewide when a local child support agency is out of compliance with the performance standards adopted pursuant to subdivision (a), or the director determines that the local child support agency is failing in a substantial manner to comply with any provision of the state plan, the provisions of this code, the requirements of federal law, the regulations of the department, or the cooperative agreement. The director shall adopt policies as to the implementation of each phase, including requirements for measurement of progress and improvement, which shall be met as part of the performance improvement plan specified in paragraphs (1) and (2), in order to avoid implementation of the next phase of compliance. The director shall not implement any of these phases until July 1, 2001, or until six months after a local child support agency has completed its transition from the office of the district attorney to the new county department of child support services, whichever is later. The phases shall include the following:

(1) Phase I: Development of a performance improvement plan that is prepared jointly by the local child support agency and the department, subject to the department's final approval. The plan shall provide performance expectations and goals for achieving compliance with the state plan and other state and federal laws and regulations that must be reviewed and assessed within specific timeframes in order to avoid execution of Phase II.

(2) Phase II: Onsite investigation, evaluation, and oversight of the local child support agency by the department. The director shall appoint program monitoring teams to make site visits, conduct educational and training sessions, and help the local child support agency identify and attack problem areas. The program monitoring teams shall evaluate all aspects of the functions and performance of the local child support agency, including compliance with state and federal laws and regulations. Based on these investigations and evaluations, the program monitoring team shall develop a final performance improvement plan and shall oversee implementation of all recommendations made in the plan. The local child support agency shall adhere to all recommendations made by the program monitoring team. The plan shall provide performance expectations and compliance goals that must be reviewed and assessed within specific timeframes in order to avoid execution of Phase III.

(3) Phase III: The director shall assume, either directly or through agreement with another entity, responsibility for the management of the child and spousal support enforcement program in the county until the local child support agency provides reasonable assurances to the director of its intention and ability to comply. During the period of state management responsibility, the director or an authorized representative shall have all of the powers and responsibilities of the local child support agency concerning the administration of the program. The local child support agency shall be responsible for providing any funds necessary for the continued operation of the program. If the local child support agency fails or refuses to provide these funds, including a sufficient amount to reimburse any and all costs incurred by the department in managing the program, the Controller may deduct an amount certified by the director as necessary for the continued operation of the program by the department from any state or federal funds payable to the county for any purpose.

(e) The director shall report in writing to the Legislature semiannually, beginning July 1, 2001, on the status of the state child support enforcement program. The director shall submit data semiannually to the Legislature, the Governor, and the public, on the progress of all local child support agencies in each performance measure, including identification of the local child support agencies that are out of compliance, the performance measures that they have failed to satisfy, and the performance improvement plan that is being taken for each. (Added by Stats.1999, c. 478 (A.B.196), § 1. Amended by Stats.1999, c. 480 (S.B.542), § 21; Stats.2002, c. 927 (A.B.3032), § 8; Stats.2003, c. 308 (A.B.738), § 5; Stats.2019, c. 115 (A.B.1817), § 164, eff. Jan. 1, 2020.)

Cross References

County defined for purposes of this Code, see Family Code § 67.
Judgment and order defined for purposes of this Code, see Family Code § 100.
Spousal support defined for purposes of this Code, see Family Code § 142.
State Controller, generally, see Government Code § 12400 et seq.
State defined for purposes of this Code, see Family Code § 145.
Support defined for purposes of this Code, see Family Code § 150.

§ 17604. Agency noncompliance with state plan; reduced federal funding

(a)(1) If at any time the director considers any public agency, that is required by law, by delegation of the department, or by cooperative agreement to perform functions relating to the state plan for securing child and spousal support and determining paternity, to be failing in a substantial manner to comply with any provision of the state plan, the director shall put that agency on written notice to that effect.

(2) The state plan concerning spousal support shall apply only to spousal support included in a child support order.

(3) In this chapter the term spousal support shall include support for a former spouse.

(b) After receiving notice, the public agency shall have 45 days to make a showing to the director of full compliance or set forth a compliance plan that the director finds to be satisfactory.

(c) If the director determines that there is a failure on the part of that public agency to comply with the provisions of the state plan, or to set forth a compliance plan that the director finds to be satisfactory, or if the state certifies to the director that the public agency is not in conformity with applicable merit system standards under Part 2.5 (commencing with Section 19800) of Division 5 of Title 2 of the Government Code, and that sanctions are necessary to secure compliance, the director shall withhold part or all of state and federal funds, including incentive funds, from that public agency until the public agency shall make a showing to the director of full compliance.

(d) After sanctions have been invoked pursuant to subdivision (c), if the director determines that there remains a failure on the part of the public agency to comply with the provisions of the state plan, the director may remove that public agency from performing any part or all of the functions relating to the state plan.

(e) In the event of any other audit or review that results in the reduction or modification of federal funding for the program under Part D (commencing with Section 652) of Subchapter IV of Title 42 of the United States Code, the sanction shall be assessed against those counties specifically cited in the federal findings in the amount cited in those findings.

§ 17604 SUPPORT SERVICES

(f) The department shall establish a process whereby any county assessed a portion of any sanction may appeal the department's decision.

(g) Nothing in this section shall be construed as relieving the board of supervisors of the responsibility to provide funds necessary for the continued operation of the state plan as required by law. (Added by Stats.1999, c. 478 (A.B.196), § 1. Amended by Stats.1999, c. 480 (S.B.542), § 21.5; Stats.2000, c. 808 (A.B.1358), § 93, eff. Sept. 28, 2000; Stats.2013, c. 427 (A.B.1062), § 1.)

Cross References

County defined for purposes of this Code, see Family Code § 67.
Judgment and order defined for purposes of this Code, see Family Code § 100.
References to husband, wife, spouses and married persons, persons included for purposes of this Code, see Family Code § 11.
Spousal support defined for purposes of this Code, see Family Code § 142.
State defined for purposes of this Code, see Family Code § 145.
State Personnel Board, generally, see Cal. Const. Art. 7, § 2 et seq.; Government Code § 18650 et seq.
Support defined for purposes of this Code, see Family Code § 150.
Support order defined for purposes of this Code, see Family Code § 155.

ARTICLE 4. PROGRAM COSTS

Section
17700. Repealed.
17701. Quality assurance and performance improvement program; minimum requirements; promulgation of regulations.
17702. Assessment of county and state compliance with child support laws and regulations; eligibility for state incentives.
17702.5. Child Support Collections Recovery Fund.
17703. Child Support Services Advance Fund; purpose; payments.
17704. State and federal child support incentives.
17705. Repealed.
17706. Counties with 10 best performance standards; additional incentives.
17708. Data submitted to department.
17710. Administrative expenditures.
17712. Child support commissioners and family law facilitators; Judicial Council costs.
17714. Excess funds.

§ 17700. Repealed by Stats.2002, c. 927 (A.B.3032), § 9

§ 17701. Quality assurance and performance improvement program; minimum requirements; promulgation of regulations

(a) There is established within California's child support program a quality assurance and performance improvement program, pursuant to which local child support agencies, in partnership with the Department of Child Support Services, shall monitor and measure program performance and compliance, and ensure the implementation of actions necessary to meet state and federal requirements and to continuously improve the quality of child support program services.

(b) Under the direction and oversight of the department, each local child support agency shall implement a quality assurance and performance improvement program that shall include, at a minimum, all of the following:

(1) An annual planning process that incorporates statewide standards and requirements, and establishes local performance goals that the department and local agency agree are appropriate.

(2) The inclusion of local performance goals and other performance-related measures in the local child support agency's Plan of Cooperation agreement with the department.

(3) Implementation of actions necessary to promote the delivery of enhanced program services and improved performance.

(4) An ongoing self-assessment process that evaluates progress in achieving performance improvement and compliance with program requirements.

(5) Regular and ongoing oversight by the department, including onsite reviews and the provision of technical assistance.

(c) The department shall promulgate regulations to implement this section. (Added by Stats.2003, c. 308 (A.B.738), § 6.)

Cross References

State defined for purposes of this Code, see Family Code § 145.
Support defined for purposes of this Code, see Family Code § 150.

§ 17702. Assessment of county and state compliance with child support laws and regulations; eligibility for state incentives

(a) The department shall assess, at least once every three years, each county's compliance with federal and state child support laws and regulations in effect for the time period being reviewed, using a statistically valid sample of cases. Counties found to be out of compliance shall be assessed annually, until they are found to be in compliance. The information for the assessment shall be based on reviews conducted and reports produced by either state or county staff, as determined by the department.

In addition, in order to meet federal self-assessment requirements, the department shall conduct an annual assessment of the state's compliance, using a statistically valid statewide sample of cases.

(b) A county shall be eligible for the state incentives under Section 17704 only if the department determines that the county is in compliance with all federal and state laws and regulations or if the county has a corrective action plan in place that has been certified by the department pursuant to this subdivision. If a county is determined not to be in compliance the county shall develop and submit a corrective action plan to the department. The department shall certify a corrective action plan if the department determines that the plan will put the county into compliance with federal and state laws and regulations. A county shall be eligible for state incentives under Section 17704 only for any quarter the county remains in compliance with a corrective action plan that has been certified by the department.

(c) Counties under a corrective action plan shall be assessed on a quarterly basis until the department determines that they are in compliance with federal and state child support program requirements. (Added by Stats.1999, c. 478 (A.B.196), § 1. Amended by Stats.2003, c. 308 (A.B.738), § 7.)

Cross References

County defined for purposes of this Code, see Family Code § 67.
Judgment and order defined for purposes of this Code, see Family Code § 100.
State defined for purposes of this Code, see Family Code § 145.
Support defined for purposes of this Code, see Family Code § 150.

§ 17702.5. Child Support Collections Recovery Fund

(a) The Child Support Collections Recovery Fund is hereby created in the State Treasury, and shall be administered by the department for the purposes specified in subdivision (c).

(b) Except as otherwise provided in this section, the fund shall consist of both of the following:

(1) All public moneys transferred by public agencies to the department for deposit into the fund, as permitted under Section 304.30 of Title 45 of the Code of Federal Regulations or any other applicable federal statutes.

(2) Any interest that accrues on amounts in the fund.

(c) Upon appropriation by the Legislature, all moneys in the fund shall be used to make payments or advances to local child support agencies of the federal share of administrative payments for costs incurred pursuant to this article.

(d) Upon repeal of this section, the Legislature intends that any moneys remaining in the fund shall be returned to the federal agency that provides federal financial participation to the department. *(Added by Stats.2001, c. 111 (A.B.429), § 7, eff. July 30, 2001.)*

Cross References

State defined for purposes of this Code, see Family Code § 145.
Support defined for purposes of this Code, see Family Code § 150.

§ 17703. Child Support Services Advance Fund; purpose; payments

(a) A revolving fund in the State Treasury is hereby created to be known as the Child Support Services Advance Fund. All moneys deposited into the fund are for the purpose of making a consolidated payment or advance to counties, state agencies, or other governmental entities, comprised of the state and federal share of costs associated with the programs administered by the Department of Child Support Services, inclusive of the payment of refunds. In addition, the fund may be used for the purpose of making a consolidated payment to a payee, comprised of the state and federal shares of local assistance costs associated with the programs administered by the Department of Child Support Services.

(b) Payments or advances of funds to counties, state agencies, or other governmental agencies and other payees doing business with the state that are properly chargeable to appropriations or other funds in the State Treasury, may be made by a Controller's warrant drawn against the Child Support Services Advance Fund. For every warrant so issued, a remittance advice shall be issued by the Department of Child Support Services to identify the purposes and amounts for which it was drawn.

(c) The amounts to be transferred to the Child Support Services Advance Fund at any time shall be determined by the department, and, upon order of the Controller, shall be transferred from the funds and appropriations otherwise properly chargeable.

(d) Refunds of amounts disbursed from the Child Support Services Advance Fund shall, on order of the Controller, be deposited in the Child Support Services Advance Fund, and, on order of the Controller, shall be transferred therefrom to the funds and appropriations from which those amounts were originally derived. Claims for amounts erroneously deposited into the Child Support Services Advance Fund shall be submitted by the department to the Controller who, if the claims are approved, shall draw a warrant in payment thereof against the Child Support Services Advance Fund.

(e) All amounts increasing the cash balance in the Child Support Services Advance Fund, that were derived from the cancellation of warrants issued therefrom, shall, on order of the Controller, be transferred to the appropriations from which the amounts were originally derived. *(Added by Stats.2000, c. 108 (A.B.2876), § 2, eff. July 10, 2000. Amended by Stats.2019, c. 115 (A.B.1817), § 165, eff. Jan. 1, 2020.)*

Cross References

County defined for purposes of this Code, see Family Code § 67.
Judgment and order defined for purposes of this Code, see Family Code § 100.
State Controller, generally, see Government Code § 12400 et seq.
State defined for purposes of this Code, see Family Code § 145.
Support defined for purposes of this Code, see Family Code § 150.

§ 17704. State and federal child support incentives

(a) For the 1998–99 fiscal year the department shall pay to each county a child support incentive payment. Every county shall receive the federal child support incentive. A county shall receive the state child support incentive if it elects to do both of the following:

(1) Comply with the reporting requirements of Section 17600 while federal financial participation is available for collecting and reporting data.

(2) Comply with federal and state child support laws and regulations, or has a corrective action plan certified by the department pursuant to Section 17702. The combined federal and state incentive payment shall be 13.6 percent of distributed collections. If the amount appropriated by the Legislature for the state incentives is less than the amount necessary to satisfy each county's actual incentives pursuant to this section, each county shall receive its proportional share of incentives.

(b)(1) Beginning July 1, 1999, the department shall pay to each county a child support incentive for child support collections. Every county shall receive the federal child support incentive. The combined federal and state incentive payments shall be 13.6 percent of distributed collections. In addition to the federal child support incentive, each county may also receive a state child support incentive. A county shall receive the state child support incentive if it elects to do both of the following:

(A) Comply with the reporting requirements of Section 17600 while federal financial participation is available for collecting and reporting data.

(B) Be in compliance with federal and state child support laws and regulations, or have a performance improvement plan certified by the department pursuant to Section 17702.

(2)(A) For purposes of paragraph (1), the federal incentive component shall be each county's share of the child support incentive payments that the state receives from the federal government, based on the county's collections.

(B)(i) Effective July 1, 1999, and annually thereafter, state funds appropriated for child support incentives shall first be used to fund the administrative costs incurred by local child support agencies in administering the child support program, excluding automation costs as set forth in Section 10085 of the Welfare and Institutions Code, after subtracting all federal financial participation for administrative costs and all federal child support incentives received by the state and passed on to the local child support agencies. The department shall allocate sufficient resources to each local child support agency to fully fund the remaining administrative costs of its budget as approved by the director pursuant to paragraph (9) of subdivision (b) of Section 17306, subject to the appropriation of funding in the annual Budget Act. No later than January 1, 2000, the department shall identify allowable administrative costs that may be claimed for reimbursement from the state, which shall be limited to reasonable amounts in relation to the scope of services and the total funds available. If the total amount of administrative costs claimed in any year exceeds the amount appropriated in the Budget Act, the amount provided to local child support agencies shall be reduced by the percentage necessary to ensure that projected General Fund expenditures do not exceed the amount authorized in the Budget Act.

(ii) Effective July 1, 2001, and annually thereafter, after allowable administrative costs are funded under clause (i), the department shall use any remaining unallocated incentive funds appropriated from the prior fiscal year which are hereby reappropriated to implement an incentive program that rewards up to 10 local child support agencies in each year, based on their performance or increase in performance on one or more of the federal performance standards set forth in Section 458 of the federal Social Security Act (42 U.S.C. Sec. 658), or state performance standards set forth in subdivision (a) of Section 17602, as determined by the department. The department shall determine the number of local agencies that receive state incentive funds under this program, subject to a maximum of 10 agencies and shall determine the amount received by each local agency based on the availability of funds and each local child support agency's proportional share based on the performance standard or standards used.

§ 17704 SUPPORT SERVICES

(iii) Any funds received pursuant to this subdivision shall be used only for child support enforcement activities.

(c) Each county shall continue to receive its federal child support incentive funding whether or not it elects to participate in the state child support incentive funding program.

(d) The department shall provide incentive funds pursuant to this section only during any fiscal year in which funding is provided for that purpose in the Budget Act. *(Added by Stats.1999, c. 478 (A.B.196), § 1. Amended by Stats.1999, c. 480 (S.B.542), § 23; Stats.2001, c. 111 (A.B.429), § 8, eff. July 30, 2001; Stats.2002, c. 927 (A.B.3032), § 10; Stats.2003, c. 308 (A.B.738), § 8.)*

Cross References

Automation costs, county interim systems, see Welfare and Institutions Code § 10085.
Child support enforcement, county reporting requirements, see Family Code § 17600.
Collection of child support, distribution of delinquencies collected, credits, see Revenue and Taxation Code § 19272.
County defined for purposes of this Code, see Family Code § 67.
Foster children and parent training fund, use of moneys, allocation, see Welfare and Institutions Code § 903.7.
State defined for purposes of this Code, see Family Code § 145.
State subventions, see Government Code § 7903.
Support defined for purposes of this Code, see Family Code § 150.

§ 17705. Repealed by Stats.2019, c. 497 (A.B.991), § 115, operative Jan. 1, 2021

§ 17706. Counties with 10 best performance standards; additional incentives

(a) It is the intent of the Legislature to encourage counties to elevate the visibility and significance of the child support enforcement program in the county. To advance this goal, effective July 1, 2000, the counties with the 10 best performance standards pursuant to clause (ii) of subparagraph (B) of paragraph (2) of subdivision (b) of Section 17704 shall receive an additional 5 percent of the state's share of those counties' collections that are used to reduce or repay aid that is paid pursuant to Article 6 (commencing with Section 11450) of Chapter 2 of Part 3 of Division 9 of the Welfare and Institutions Code. The counties shall use the increased recoupment for child support-related activities that may not be eligible for federal child support funding under Part D of Title IV of the Social Security Act, including, but not limited to, providing services to parents to help them better support their children financially, medically, and emotionally.

(b) The operation of subdivision (a) shall be suspended for the 2002–03, 2003–04, 2004–05, 2005–06, 2006–07, 2007–08, 2008–09, 2009–10, 2010–11, 2011–12, 2012–13, 2013–14, 2014–15, 2015–16, 2016–17, 2017–18, 2018–19, 2019–20, 2020–21, 2021–22, and 2022–23 fiscal years. *(Added by Stats.1999, c. 478 (A.B.196), § 1. Amended by Stats.1999, c. 480 (S.B.542), § 24; Stats.2001, c. 111 (A.B.429), § 9, eff. July 30, 2001; Stats.2002, c. 1022 (A.B.444), § 1, eff. Sept. 28, 2002; Stats.2003–2004, 1st Ex.Sess., c. 7 (S.B.24), § 1, eff. May 5, 2003; Stats.2006, c. 75 (A.B.1808), § 9, eff. July 12, 2006; Stats.2007, c. 177 (S.B.84), § 2, eff. Aug. 24, 2007; Stats.2008, c. 759 (A.B.1279), § 17, eff. Sept. 30, 2008; Stats.2009, c. 140 (A.B.1164), § 67; Stats.2012, c. 47 (S.B.1041), § 2, eff. June 27, 2012; Stats.2015, c. 20 (S.B.79), § 2, eff. June 24, 2015; Stats.2017, c. 24 (S.B.89), § 4, eff. June 27, 2017; Stats.2019, c. 27 (S.B.80), § 7, eff. June 27, 2019; Stats.2021, c. 85 (A.B.135), § 5, eff. July 16, 2021.)*

Cross References

County defined for purposes of this Code, see Family Code § 67.
State defined for purposes of this Code, see Family Code § 145.
Support defined for purposes of this Code, see Family Code § 150.

§ 17708. Data submitted to department

(a) This section shall apply to any county that elects to participate in the state incentive program described in Section 17704.

(b) Each participating county child support enforcement program shall provide the data required by Section 17600 to the department on a quarterly basis. The data shall be provided no later than 15 days after the end of each quarter.

(c) On and after July 1, 1998, a county shall be required to comply with the provisions of this section only during fiscal years in which funding is provided for that purpose in the Budget Act. *(Added by Stats.1999, c. 478 (A.B.196), § 1. Amended by Stats.2001, c. 755 (S.B.943), § 19, eff. Oct. 12, 2001.)*

Cross References

County defined for purposes of this Code, see Family Code § 67.
State defined for purposes of this Code, see Family Code § 145.
Support defined for purposes of this Code, see Family Code § 150.

§ 17710. Administrative expenditures

(a) Each county shall be responsible for any administrative expenditures for administering the child support program not covered by federal and state funds.

(b) Notwithstanding subdivision (a), effective July 1, 1991, to June 30, 1992, inclusive, counties shall pay the nonfederal share of the administrative costs of conducting the reviews required under former Section 15200.8 of the Welfare and Institutions Code from the savings counties will obtain as a result of the reduction in the maximum aid payments specified in Section 11450. Effective July 1, 1992, to June 30, 1993, inclusive, the state shall pay the nonfederal share of administrative costs of conducting the reviews required under former Section 15200.8 of the Welfare and Institutions Code. Funding for county costs after June 30, 1993, shall be subject to the availability of funds in the annual Budget Act. *(Added by Stats.1999, c. 478 (A.B.196), § 1. Amended by Stats.1999, c. 479 (A.B.150), § 1, eff. Sept. 27, 1999, operative Jan. 1, 2000; Stats.1999, c. 480 (S.B.542), § 24.5; Stats.2016, c. 474 (A.B.2882), § 26, eff. Jan. 1, 2017.)*

Cross References

County defined for purposes of this Code, see Family Code § 67.
Family support defined for purposes of this Code, see Family Code § 92.
State defined for purposes of this Code, see Family Code § 145.
State subventions, see Government Code § 7903.
Support defined for purposes of this Code, see Family Code § 150.

§ 17712. Child support commissioners and family law facilitators; Judicial Council costs

Notwithstanding subdivision (a) of Section 17708, and to the extent funds are appropriated by the annual Budget Act, funds shall be provided to the Judicial Council for the nonfederal share of costs for the costs of child support commissioners pursuant to Section 4251 and family law facilitators pursuant to Division 14 (commencing with Section 10000). The Judicial Council shall distribute the funds to the counties for the purpose of matching federal funds for the costs of child support commissioners and family law facilitators and related costs. Funds distributed pursuant to this section may also be used to offset the nonfederal share of costs incurred by the Judicial Council for performing the duties specified in Sections 4252 and 10010. *(Added by Stats.1999, c. 478 (A.B.196), § 1.)*

Cross References

County defined for purposes of this Code, see Family Code § 67.
Support defined for purposes of this Code, see Family Code § 150.

§ 17714. Excess funds

(a)(1) Any funds paid to a county pursuant to this chapter prior to June 30, 1999, which exceed the county's cost of administering the child support program of the local child support agency pursuant to Section 17400 to that date, hereafter referred to as "excess funds," shall be expended by the county only upon that program. All these excess funds shall be deposited by the county into a special fund established by the county for this purpose.

(2) Performance incentive funds shall include, but not be limited to, incentive funds paid pursuant to Section 17704, and performance incentive funds paid pursuant to Section 14124.93 of the Welfare and Institutions Code and all interest earned on deposits in the special fund. Performance incentive funds shall not include funds paid pursuant to Section 17706. Performance incentive funds shall be expended by the county only upon that program. All performance incentive funds shall be deposited by the county into a special fund established by the county for this purpose.

(b) All excess funds and performance incentive funds shall be expended by the county on the support enforcement program of the local child support agency within two fiscal years following the fiscal year of receipt of the funds by the county. Except as provided in subdivision (c), any excess funds or performance incentive funds paid pursuant to this chapter since July 1, 1992, that the department determines have not been spent within the required two-year period shall revert to the state General Fund, and shall be distributed by the department only to counties that have complied with this section. The formula for distribution shall be based on the number of CalWORKs cases within each county.

(c) A county that submits to the department a written plan approved by that county's local child support agency for the expenditure of excess funds or performance incentive funds shall be exempted from the requirements of subdivision (b), if the department determines that the expenditure will be cost-effective, will maximize federal funds, and the expenditure plan will require more than the time provided for in subdivision (b) to expend the funds. Once the department approves a plan pursuant to this subdivision, funds received by a county and designated for an expenditure in the plan shall not be expended by the county for any other purpose.

(d) Nothing in this section shall be construed to nullify the recovery and reversion to the General Fund of unspent incentive funds as provided in Section 6 of Chapter 479 of the Statutes of 1999. (Added by Stats.1999, c. 478, § 1. Amended by Stats.2000, c. 808 (A.B.1358), § 94, eff. Sept. 28, 2000; Stats.2001, c. 755 (S.B.943), § 20, eff. Oct. 12, 2001.)

Cross References

County defined for purposes of this Code, see Family Code § 67.
State defined for purposes of this Code, see Family Code § 145.
Support defined for purposes of this Code, see Family Code § 150.

CHAPTER 5. COMPLAINT RESOLUTION

Section
17800. Process; forms and procedures; complaint time limitations.
17801. State hearing.
17802. Repealed.
17803. Director's final decision; review in superior court; fees and costs.
17804. Time frames for process establishment and state hearing requirement implementation.

Cross References

Arrears collection enhancement process, development of program, requirements regarding acceptance of offers in compromise, see Family Code § 17560.

§ 17800. Process; forms and procedures; complaint time limitations

Each local child support agency shall maintain a complaint resolution process. The department shall specify by regulation, no later than July 1, 2001, uniform forms and procedures that each local child support agency shall use in resolving all complaints received from custodial and noncustodial parents. A complaint shall be made within 90 days after the custodial or noncustodial parent affected knew or should have known of the child support action complained of. The local child support agency shall provide a written resolution of the complaint within 30 days of the receipt of the complaint. The director of the local child support agency may extend the period for resolution of the complaint an additional 30 days in accordance with the regulations adopted pursuant to Section 17804. (Added by Stats.1999, c. 803 (A.B.472), § 2. Amended by Stats.2001, c. 755 (S.B.943), § 21, eff. Oct. 12, 2001.)

Cross References

Child support enforcement, collections, license applicants, see Family Code § 17520.
Child support enforcement, collections, statement of arrearages, see Family Code § 17526.
Enforcement of money judgments, wage garnishment, withholding order for support, see Code of Civil Procedure § 706.030.
Support defined for purposes of this Code, see Family Code § 150.

§ 17801. State hearing

(a) A custodial or noncustodial parent who is dissatisfied with the local child support agency's resolution of a complaint shall be accorded an opportunity for a state hearing when one or more of the following actions or failures to take action by the department or the local child support agency is claimed by the parent:

(1) An application for child support services has been denied or has not been acted upon within the required timeframe.

(2) The child support services case has been acted upon in violation of state or federal law or regulation or department letter ruling, or has not yet been acted upon within the required timeframe, including services for the establishment, modification, and enforcement of child support orders and child support accountings.

(3) Child support collections have not been distributed or have been distributed or disbursed incorrectly, or the amount of child support arrears, as calculated by the department or the local child support agency is inaccurate. The amount of the court order for support, including current support and arrears, is not subject to a state hearing under this section.

(4) The child support agency's decision to close a child support case.

(b) Prior to requesting a hearing pursuant to subdivision (a), the custodial or noncustodial parent shall exhaust the complaint resolution process required in Section 17800, unless the local child support agency has not, within the 30–day period required by that section, submitted a written resolution of the complaint. If the custodial or noncustodial parent does not receive that timely written resolution, the custodial parent may request a hearing pursuant to subdivision (a).

(c) A hearing shall be provided under subdivision (a) when the request for a hearing is made within 90 days after receiving the written notice of resolution required in Section 17800 or, if no written notice of resolution is provided within 30 days from the date the complaint was made, within 90 days after making the complaint.

(d)(1) A hearing under subdivision (a) shall be set to commence within 45 days after the request is received by the state hearing office, and at least 10 days prior to the hearing, all parties shall be given written notice of the time and place of the hearing. Unless the time period is waived by the complainant, the proposed hearing decision shall be rendered by the state hearing office within 75 days after the

§ 17801

request for a state hearing is received by the state hearing office. The department shall have 15 days from the date the proposed decision is rendered to act upon the decision. When a hearing is postponed, continued, or reopened with the consent of the complainant, the time for issuance of the decision, and action on the decision by the department, shall be extended for a period of time consistent with the postponement, continuance, or reopening.

(2) For purposes of this subdivision, the "state hearing office" refers to the division of the office or agency designated by the department to carry out state hearings, that conducts those state hearings.

(e) To the extent not inconsistent with this section, hearings under subdivision (a) shall be provided in the same manner in which hearings are provided in Sections 10950 to 10967 of the Welfare and Institutions Code and the State Department of Social Services' regulations implementing and interpreting those sections.

(f) Pendency of a state hearing shall not affect the obligation to comply with an existing child support order.

(g) A child support determination that is subject to the jurisdiction of the superior court and that is required by law to be addressed by motion, order to show cause, or appeal under this code shall not be subject to a state hearing under this section. The director shall, by regulation, specify and exclude from the subject matter jurisdiction of state hearings provided under subdivision (a), grievances arising from a child support case in the superior court that must, by law, be addressed by motion, order to show cause, or appeal under this code.

(h) The local child support agency shall comply with, and execute, every decision of the director rendered pursuant to this section.

(i) The director shall contract with the State Department of Social Services or the Office of Administrative Hearings for the provision of state hearings in accordance with this section.

(j) This section shall be implemented only to the extent that there is federal financial participation available at the child support funding rate set forth in Section 655(a)(2) of Title 42 of the United States Code. *(Added by Stats.1999, c. 803 (A.B.472), § 2. Amended by Stats.2002, c. 927 (A.B.3032), § 10.5; Stats.2016, c. 474 (A.B.2882), § 27, eff. Jan. 1, 2017; Stats.2019, c. 115 (A.B.1817), § 166, eff. Jan. 1, 2020.)*

Implementation

Implementation of this section, see subd. (j).

Cross References

Judgment and order defined for purposes of this Code, see Family Code § 100.
State defined for purposes of this Code, see Family Code § 145.
Support defined for purposes of this Code, see Family Code § 150.
Support order defined for purposes of this Code, see Family Code § 155.

§ 17802. Repealed by Stats.2016, c. 474 (A.B.2882), § 28, eff. Jan. 1, 2017

§ 17803. Director's final decision; review in superior court; fees and costs

The custodial or noncustodial parent, within one year after receiving notice of the director's final decision, may file a petition with the superior court, under Section 1094.5 of the Code of Civil Procedure, praying for a review of the entire proceedings in the matter, upon questions of law involved in the case. The review, if granted, shall be the exclusive remedy available to the custodial or noncustodial parent for review of the director's decision. The director shall be the sole respondent in the proceedings. A filing fee shall not be required for the filing of a petition pursuant to this section. Any such petition to the superior court shall be entitled to a preference in setting a date for hearing on the petition. A bond shall not be required in the case of any petition for review, nor in any appeal therefrom. The custodial or noncustodial parent shall be entitled to reasonable attorney's fees and costs, if the parent obtains a decision in their favor. *(Added by Stats.1999, c. 803 (A.B.472), § 2. Amended by Stats.2019, c. 115 (A.B.1817), § 167, eff. Jan. 1, 2020.)*

Cross References

Administrative proceedings, judicial review, see Government Code § 11523.
Proceeding defined for purposes of this Code, see Family Code § 110.
Respondent defined for purposes of this Code, see Family Code § 127.

§ 17804. Time frames for process establishment and state hearing requirement implementation

Each local child support agency shall establish the complaint resolution process specified in Section 17800. The department shall implement the state hearing requirements specified in Section 17801 no later than July 1, 2001. *(Added by Stats.1999, c. 803 (A.B.472), § 2. Amended by Stats.2001, c. 755 (S.B.943), § 22, eff. Oct. 12, 2001.)*

Cross References

Child support enforcement, complaint resolution, process and procedures, see Family Code § 17800.
State defined for purposes of this Code, see Family Code § 145.
Support defined for purposes of this Code, see Family Code § 150.

Division 20

PILOT PROJECTS

Part	Section
1. Family Law Pilot Projects	20000
2. Paternity Pilot Projects [Inoperative]	

Part 1

FAMILY LAW PILOT PROJECTS

Chapter	Section
1. General Provisions	20000
2. San Mateo County Pilot Project	20010
3. Santa Clara County Pilot Project	20030

CHAPTER 1. GENERAL PROVISIONS

Section
20000. Legislative findings and declarations.
20001. Authorization of pilot projects; superior courts of Santa Clara and San Mateo Counties.
20002. Duration of projects.
20003 to 20009. Inoperative.

§ 20000. Legislative findings and declarations

(a) The Legislature finds and declares the following:

(1) Child and spousal support are serious legal obligations. In addition, children are frequently left in limbo while their parents engage in protracted litigation concerning custody and visitation. The current system for obtaining child and spousal support orders is suffering because the family courts are unduly burdened with heavy

case loads and personnel insufficient to meet the needs of increased demands on the courts.

(2) There is a compelling state interest in the development of a child and spousal support system that is cost-effective and accessible to families with middle or low incomes.

(3) There is a compelling state interest in first implementing such a system on a small scale.

(4) There is a compelling state interest in the development of a speedy, conflict-reducing method of resolving custody and visitation disputes.

(b) Therefore, it is the intent of the Legislature in enacting this part to provide a means for experimenting with and evaluating procedural innovations with significant potential to improve the California child and spousal support systems, and the system for mediation, evaluation, and litigation of custody and visitation disputes. *(Added by Stats.1993, c. 219 (A.B.1500), § 210.)*

Cross References

Abandonment and neglect of children, see Penal Code § 270 et seq.
Child support, generally, see Family Code §§ 3500 et seq., 3900 et seq.
Court-ordered child support, see Family Code § 4000 et seq.
Dependent and neglected children, judgments and orders, see Welfare and Institutions Code § 360 et seq.
Domestic Violence Prevention Act, see Family Code § 6200 et seq.
Enforcement of child support orders, see Family Code § 4500 et seq.
Judgment and order defined for purposes of this Code, see Family Code § 100.
Juvenile court, detention of dependent children, see Welfare and Institutions Code § 367.
Limitations on parental control, see Welfare and Institutions Code § 361.
Minors,
  Age of majority, see Family Code § 6500 et seq.
  Civil actions, see Family Code § 6600 et seq.
  Contracts, see Family Code § 6700 et seq.
  Emancipation, see Family Code § 7000 et seq.
  Rights and liabilities, see Family Code § 6600 et seq.
Notice that parental rights may be terminated, see Welfare and Institutions Code § 294.
Parent and child relationship, generally, see Family Code § 7500 et seq.
Parental custody, generally, see Family Code §§ 3000 et seq., 3020 et seq.
Parental relationship, determination, see Family Code § 7600 et seq.
Removal of children from parental custody, see Welfare and Institutions Code § 360 et seq.
Spousal support defined for purposes of this Code, see Family Code § 142.
State defined for purposes of this Code, see Family Code § 145.
Support defined for purposes of this Code, see Family Code § 150.
Support order defined for purposes of this Code, see Family Code § 155.
Uniform Interstate Family Support Act, see Family Code § 5700.101 et seq.
Uniform Parentage Act, see Family Code § 7600 et seq.

§ 20001. Authorization of pilot projects; superior courts of Santa Clara and San Mateo Counties

The Superior Courts of the Counties of Santa Clara and San Mateo may conduct pilot projects pursuant to this part. Chapter 2 (commencing with Section 20010) shall govern the San Mateo County Pilot Project, and Chapter 3 (commencing with Section 20030) shall govern the Santa Clara County Pilot Project. *(Added by Stats.1993, c. 219 (A.B.1500), § 210.)*

Cross References

County defined for purposes of this Code, see Family Code § 67.

§ 20002. Duration of projects

The duration of the pilot projects shall be two years. *(Added by Stats.1993, c. 219 (A.B.1500), § 210.)*

§§ 20003 to 20009. Inoperative

CHAPTER 2. SAN MATEO COUNTY PILOT PROJECT

Section
20010. San Mateo County Pilot Project; hearings subject to project.
20011. Motions for temporary orders; time for hearing.
20012. Family Law Evaluator; duties.
20013. Family Law Evaluator; cost to parties.
20014. Unrepresented party; evaluator requirement notice; stamped pleadings service.
20015. Court hearing access; protocol adoption.
20016. Informational booklet; publication option.
20017. Family Law Evaluator; licensure as attorney.
20018. Temporary child support orders; compliance with uniform guidelines; basis in economic evidence.
20019. Child custody and visitation contested; mediation pursuant to § 3170.
20020. Contested proceedings; documents to be provided to the court.
20021. Contested proceedings; failure to provide documents; sanctions.
20022. Tax return; review by other party; examination.
20023. Children for whom services are to be provided by district attorney pursuant to Welfare and Institutions Code section; limited waiver.
20024. Repealed.
20025. Repealed.
20026. Pilot project; litigants served; savings and costs.

§ 20010. San Mateo County Pilot Project; hearings subject to project

The San Mateo County Pilot Project shall apply to hearings on motions for temporary child support, temporary spousal support, and temporary health insurance issuable in proceedings under this code, where at least one party is unrepresented by counsel. *(Added by Stats.1993, c. 219 (A.B.1500), § 210.)*

Cross References

County defined for purposes of this Code, see Family Code § 67.
Proceeding defined for purposes of this Code, see Family Code § 110.
Spousal support defined for purposes of this Code, see Family Code § 142.
Support defined for purposes of this Code, see Family Code § 150.

§ 20011. Motions for temporary orders; time for hearing

Motions for temporary orders under this chapter shall be heard as soon as practicable, consistent with the rules governing other civil actions. *(Added by Stats.1993, c. 219 (A.B.1500), § 210.)*

Cross References

Judgment and order defined for purposes of this Code, see Family Code § 100.

§ 20012. Family Law Evaluator; duties

The court shall appoint a Family Law Evaluator, who shall be available to assist parties. By local rule the superior court may designate the duties of the Family Law Evaluator, which may include, but are not limited to, the following:

(a) Requiring litigants in actions which involve temporary child support, temporary spousal support, and temporary maintenance of health insurance in which at least one litigant is unrepresented, to meet with the Family Law Evaluator prior to the support hearing.

(b) Preparing support schedules based on standardized formulae accessed through existing up-to-date computer technology.

(c) Drafting stipulations to include all issues agreed to by the parties.

(d) Prior to, or at, any hearing pursuant to this chapter, reviewing the paperwork by the court, advising the judge whether or not the matter is ready to proceed, and making a recommendation to the court regarding child support, spousal support, and health insurance.

(e) Assisting the clerk in maintaining records.

(f) Preparing a formal order consistent with the court's announced oral order, unless one of the parties is represented by an attorney.

(g) Assisting the court with research and any other responsibilities which will enable the court to be responsive to the litigants' needs. *(Added by Stats.1993, c. 219 (A.B.1500), § 210.)*

Cross References

Judgment and order defined for purposes of this Code, see Family Code § 100.
Spousal support defined for purposes of this Code, see Family Code § 142.
Support defined for purposes of this Code, see Family Code § 150.

§ 20013. Family Law Evaluator; cost to parties

The court shall provide the Family Law Evaluator at no cost to the parties. *(Added by Stats.1993, c. 219 (A.B.1500), § 210.)*

§ 20014. Unrepresented party; evaluator requirement notice; stamped pleadings service

The clerk shall stamp all moving papers in which a party is not represented by counsel with a notice of a requirement to see the Family Law Evaluator. The unrepresented party shall serve the stamped pleadings on the other party. *(Added by Stats.1993, c. 219 (A.B.1500), § 210.)*

§ 20015. Court hearing access; protocol adoption

The court shall adopt a protocol wherein all litigants, both unrepresented by counsel and represented by counsel, have ultimate access to a hearing before the court. *(Added by Stats.1993, c. 219 (A.B.1500), § 210.)*

§ 20016. Informational booklet; publication option

The court may elect to publish a low-cost booklet describing this program. *(Added by Stats.1993, c. 219 (A.B.1500), § 210.)*

§ 20017. Family Law Evaluator; licensure as attorney

The Family Law Evaluator shall be an attorney, licensed to practice in this state. *(Added by Stats.1993, c. 219 (A.B.1500), § 210.)*

Cross References

State defined for purposes of this Code, see Family Code § 145.

§ 20018. Temporary child support orders; compliance with uniform guidelines; basis in economic evidence

Orders for temporary support issued pursuant to this chapter shall comply with the statewide uniform guideline set forth in Article 2 (commencing with Section 4050) of Chapter 2 of Part 2 of Division 9 and shall be based on the economic evidence supplied by the parties or otherwise available to the court. *(Added by Stats.1993, c. 219 (A.B.1500), § 210.)*

Cross References

Judgment and order defined for purposes of this Code, see Family Code § 100.
Support defined for purposes of this Code, see Family Code § 150.

§ 20019. Child custody and visitation contested; mediation pursuant to § 3170

Where it appears from a party's application for an order under this chapter or otherwise in the proceedings that the custody of, or visitation with, a minor child is contested, the court shall set those issues for mediation pursuant to Section 3170. The pendency of the mediation proceedings shall not delay a hearing on any other matter for which a temporary order is required, including child support, and a separate hearing, if required, shall be scheduled respecting the custody and visitation issues following mediation in accordance with Section 3170. However, the court may grant a continuance for good cause shown. *(Added by Stats.1993, c. 219 (A.B.1500), § 210.)*

Cross References

Judgment and order defined for purposes of this Code, see Family Code § 100.
Minor defined for purposes of this Code, see Family Code § 6500.
Proceeding defined for purposes of this Code, see Family Code § 110.
Support defined for purposes of this Code, see Family Code § 150.

§ 20020. Contested proceedings; documents to be provided to the court

In a contested proceeding for temporary child or spousal support under this chapter, both the moving party and the responding party shall provide all of the following documents to the Family Law Evaluator, and to the court at the time of the hearing:

(a) Copies of the last two federal and state income tax returns filed.

(b) Paycheck stubs for all paychecks received in the four months immediately prior to the hearing. *(Added by Stats.1993, c. 219 (A.B.1500), § 210.)*

Cross References

Proceeding defined for purposes of this Code, see Family Code § 110.
Spousal support defined for purposes of this Code, see Family Code § 142.
State defined for purposes of this Code, see Family Code § 145.
Support defined for purposes of this Code, see Family Code § 150.

§ 20021. Contested proceedings; failure to provide documents; sanctions

A party who fails to submit documents to the court as required by Section 20020 may, in the court's discretion, not be granted the relief requested, or the court may impose evidentiary sanctions. *(Added by Stats.1993, c. 219 (A.B.1500), § 210.)*

§ 20022. Tax return; review by other party; examination

The tax return submitted pursuant to Section 20020 may be reviewed by the other party. A party may be examined by the other party as to the contents of the tax return. *(Added by Stats.1993, c. 219 (A.B.1500), § 210.)*

§ 20023. Children for whom services are to be provided by district attorney pursuant to Welfare and Institutions Code section; limited waiver

(a) Except as provided in subdivision (c):

(1) Nothing in this chapter shall be construed to apply to a child for whom services are provided or required to be provided by a district attorney pursuant to Section 11475.5 of the Welfare and Institutions Code.[1]

(2) The court shall not hear or enter any order under this chapter in a matter involving such a child.

(b) Any order entered contrary to the provisions of subdivision (a) is void and without legal effect.

(c) For purposes of enabling a custodial parent receiving assistance under Chapter 2 (commencing with Section 11200) of Part 3 of Division 9 of the Welfare and Institutions Code to participate in a pilot project authorized by this chapter, the district attorney, upon the request of the custodial parent, may execute a limited waiver of the obligation or representation under Section 11475.1 of the Welfare and Institutions Code. These limited waivers shall be signed by both the district attorney and custodial parent and shall only permit the custodial parent to participate in the proceedings under this chapter. It is not the intent of the Legislature in enacting this section to limit the duties of district attorneys with respect to seeking child support payments or to in any way limit or supersede other provisions of this code respecting temporary child support. *(Added by Stats.1993, c. 219 (A.B.1500), § 210.)*

¹ So in chaptered copy. See Welfare and Institutions Code § 11475.1.

Cross References

Judgment and order defined for purposes of this Code, see Family Code § 100.
Proceeding defined for purposes of this Code, see Family Code § 110.
Support defined for purposes of this Code, see Family Code § 150.

§ 20024. Repealed by Stats.2016, c. 86 (S.B.1171), § 133, eff. Jan. 1, 2017

§ 20025. Repealed by Stats.2004, c. 193 (S.B.111), § 18

§ 20026. Pilot project; litigants served; savings and costs

(a) It is estimated that under the pilot project authorized by this chapter, approximately 2,200 litigants will be served annually and that the following savings will occur:

(1) The program would save 520 hours, or 65 days, of court time per year.

(2) There would be a concomitant saving of time by litigants due to the expedited proceedings and, in addition, there would be a saving to litigants of wages that would otherwise be lost due to time off from work.

(b) The estimated costs of the pilot project are as follows:

(1) The salaries of the Family Law Evaluator and any staff necessary for the evaluator to carry out the evaluator's functions.

(2) The cost of a booklet, if any, describing the program.

(c) There would be no cost for the following:

(1) Computers, printers, or other equipment. This equipment is already available in the family law department.

(2) Training for the Family Law Evaluator or the evaluator's staff. They will be trained by already existing judicial personnel. *(Added by Stats.1993, c. 219 (A.B.1500), § 210. Amended by Stats.2019, c. 115 (A.B.1817), § 168, eff. Jan. 1, 2020.)*

Cross References

Proceeding defined for purposes of this Code, see Family Code § 110.

CHAPTER 3. SANTA CLARA COUNTY PILOT PROJECT

Section
20030. Santa Clara County Pilot Project.
20031. Pilot project; hearings subject to project.
20032. Contested proceedings; hearing date; duty and failure to provide documents to the court; notices; continuance.
20033. Income and Expense Declaration use; suspension.
20034. Attorney–Mediator; licensure and experience; duties; litigant hearing access.
20035. Temporary child support orders; compliance with uniform guidelines; basis in economic evidence.
20036. Pilot project proceedings; exemption; judicial order.
20037. Children for whom services are to be provided by district attorney pursuant to Welfare and Institutions Code § 11475.1; limited waiver.
20038. Mediation orientation class; mediation agreements; Early Resolution Project; extended evaluation; judicial settlement conference; trial.
20039. Repealed.
20040. Informational booklet; publication.
20041. Child-related programs; coordination by court.
20042. Repealed.
20043. Pilot project; litigants served; savings and costs; income.

§ 20030. Santa Clara County Pilot Project

The Superior Court of the County of Santa Clara may conduct a pilot project pursuant to this chapter. *(Added by Stats.1993, c. 219 (A.B.1500), § 210.)*

Cross References

County defined for purposes of this Code, see Family Code § 67.

§ 20031. Pilot project; hearings subject to project

The pilot project applies to all hearings, for temporary or permanent child or spousal support, modifications thereof, health insurance, custody, or visitation in a proceeding for dissolution of marriage, nullity of marriage, legal separation of the parties, exclusive custody, or pursuant to the Uniform Parentage Act (Part 3 (commencing with Section 7600) of Division 12). *(Added by Stats.1993, c. 219 (A.B.1500), § 210.)*

Cross References

Proceeding defined for purposes of this Code, see Family Code § 110.
Spousal support defined for purposes of this Code, see Family Code § 142.
Support defined for purposes of this Code, see Family Code § 150.

§ 20032. Contested proceedings; hearing date; duty and failure to provide documents to the court; notices; continuance

(a) Each and every hearing in a proceeding described in Section 20031 in which child or spousal support is at issue, including related contempt matters, shall be set by the clerk of the court for hearing within 30 days of filing.

(b) At any hearing in which child or spousal support is at issue, each party, both moving and responding, shall bring to the hearing, copies of the last two federal and state income tax returns filed by the party and pay stubs from the last four full months immediately preceding the hearing received by the party, and shall serve those documents on the opposing party at least five days in advance of the hearing date. Willful failure to comply with these requirements or any of the requirements of this pilot project may result in a citation for contempt under Title 5 (commencing with Section 1209) of Part 3 of the Code of Civil Procedure, or in the court's discretion, the court may refuse to grant relief requested or may impose evidentiary sanctions on a party who fails to submit these documents. The clerk shall cause to be placed on the face sheet of any moving papers for child or spousal support at the time of filing, a notice informing the parties of the requirements of this section. The notice shall also inform the parties that prior to the hearing, they must meet with the Attorney-Mediator pursuant to Section 20034. That meeting may occur in advance of the hearing dates by agreement of the parties, or on the day of the hearing.

(c) No continuance of any hearing involving child or spousal support shall be granted by a court without an order setting an interim support level unless the parties stipulate otherwise or the court finds good cause therefor. *(Added by Stats.1993, c. 219 (A.B.1500), § 210.)*

Cross References

Judgment and order defined for purposes of this Code, see Family Code § 100.
Proceeding defined for purposes of this Code, see Family Code § 110.
Spousal support defined for purposes of this Code, see Family Code § 142.
State defined for purposes of this Code, see Family Code § 145.
Support defined for purposes of this Code, see Family Code § 150.

§ 20033. Income and Expense Declaration use; suspension

The court may pass a local rule that suspends the use of the Income and Expense Declaration mandated by California Rule of Court 1285.50 ¹ in some or all proceedings during the pendency of the pilot project, provided that substitute forms are developed and adopted to solicit substantially the same information in a simplified format. The court may, notwithstanding the adoption of a local form, require the use of the Income and Expense Declaration

§ 20033

mandated by California Rule of Court 1285.50 [1] in appropriate cases on the motion of either party or on the court's own motion. *(Added by Stats.1993, c. 219 (A.B.1500), § 210.)*

[1] California Rules of Court, Rule 1285.50 was repealed eff. Jan. 1, 2003. See West's Judicial Council Forms Pamphlet for mandatory and optional forms adopted and approved by the Judicial Council.

Cross References

Income and expense declaration defined for purposes of this Code, see Family Code § 95.
Proceeding defined for purposes of this Code, see Family Code § 110.

§ 20034. Attorney–Mediator; licensure and experience; duties; litigant hearing access

(a) An attorney, known as an Attorney–Mediator, shall be hired to assist the court in resolving child and spousal support disputes, to develop community outreach programs, and to undertake other duties as assigned by the court.

(b) The Attorney–Mediator shall be an attorney, licensed to practice in this state, with mediation or litigation experience, or both, in the field of family law.

(c) By local rule, the superior court may designate the duties of the Attorney–Mediator, which may include, but are not limited to, the following:

(1) Meeting with litigants to mediate issues of child support, spousal support, and maintenance of health insurance. Actions in which one or both of the parties are unrepresented by counsel shall have priority.

(2) Preparing support schedules based on statutory guidelines accessed through existing up-to-date computer technology.

(3) Drafting stipulations to include all issues agreed to by the parties, which may include issues other than those specified in Section 20031.

(4) If the parties are unable to resolve issues with the assistance of the Attorney–Mediator, prior to or at the hearing, and at the request of the court, the Attorney–Mediator shall review the paperwork, examine documents, prepare support schedules, and advise the judge whether or not the matter is ready to proceed.

(5) Assisting the clerk in maintaining records.

(6) Preparing formal orders consistent with the court's announced order in cases where both parties are unrepresented.

(7) Serving as a special master to hearing proceedings and making findings to the court unless the individual has served as a mediator in that case.

(8) Assisting the court with research and any other responsibilities that will enable the court to be responsive to the litigants' needs.

(9) Developing programs for bar and community outreach through day and evening programs, video recordings, and other innovative means that will assist unrepresented and financially disadvantaged litigants in gaining meaningful access to family court. These programs shall specifically include information concerning underutilized legislation, such as expedited temporary support orders (Chapter 5 (commencing with Section 3620) of Part 1 of Division 9), modification of support orders (Article 3 (commencing with Section 3680) of Chapter 6 of Part 1 of Division 9), and preexisting, court-sponsored programs, such as supervised visitation and appointment of attorneys for children.

(d) The court shall develop a protocol wherein all litigants, both unrepresented by counsel and represented by counsel, have ultimate access to a hearing before the court. *(Added by Stats.1993, c. 219 (A.B.1500), § 210. Amended by Stats.2009, c. 88 (A.B.176), § 40; Stats.2019, c. 115 (A.B.1817), § 169, eff. Jan. 1, 2020.)*

Cross References

Judgment and order defined for purposes of this Code, see Family Code § 100.
Proceeding defined for purposes of this Code, see Family Code § 110.
Spousal support defined for purposes of this Code, see Family Code § 142.
State defined for purposes of this Code, see Family Code § 145.
Support defined for purposes of this Code, see Family Code § 150.
Support order defined for purposes of this Code, see Family Code § 155.

§ 20035. Temporary child support orders; compliance with uniform guidelines; basis in economic evidence

Orders for temporary support issued pursuant to this chapter shall comply with the statewide uniform guideline set forth in Article 2 (commencing with Section 4050) of Chapter 2 of Part 2 of Division 9 and shall be based on the economic evidence supplied by the parties or otherwise available to the court. *(Added by Stats.1993, c. 219 (A.B.1500), § 210.)*

Cross References

Judgment and order defined for purposes of this Code, see Family Code § 100.
Support defined for purposes of this Code, see Family Code § 150.

§ 20036. Pilot project proceedings; exemption; judicial order

Upon motion by either party or on the court's own motion, any proceeding that would otherwise fall within this pilot project may by judicial order be exempted from its requirements. *(Added by Stats.1993, c. 219 (A.B.1500), § 210.)*

Cross References

Judgment and order defined for purposes of this Code, see Family Code § 100.
Proceeding defined for purposes of this Code, see Family Code § 110.

§ 20037. Children for whom services are to be provided by district attorney pursuant to Welfare and Institutions Code § 11475.1; limited waiver

(a) Except as provided in subdivision (c):

(1) Nothing in this chapter shall be construed to apply to a child for whom services are provided or required to be provided by a district attorney pursuant to Section 11475.1 of the Welfare and Institutions Code.

(2) The court shall not hear or enter any order under this chapter in a matter involving such a child.

(b) Any order entered contrary to subdivision (a) is void and without legal effect.

(c) For purposes of enabling a custodial parent receiving assistance under Chapter 2 (commencing with Section 11200) of Part 3 of Division 9 of the Welfare and Institutions Code to participate in a pilot project authorized by this chapter, the district attorney, upon the request of the custodial parent, may execute a limited waiver of the obligation of representation under Section 11475.1 of the Welfare and Institutions Code. These limited waivers shall be signed by both the district attorney and custodial parent and shall only permit the custodial parent to participate in the proceedings under this chapter. It is not the intent of the Legislature in enacting this section to limit the duties of district attorneys with respect to seeking child support payments or to in any way limit or supersede other provisions of this code respecting temporary child support. *(Added by Stats.1993, c. 219 (A.B.1500), § 210.)*

Cross References

Judgment and order defined for purposes of this Code, see Family Code § 100.
Proceeding defined for purposes of this Code, see Family Code § 110.
Support defined for purposes of this Code, see Family Code § 150.

§ 20038. Mediation orientation class; mediation agreements; Early Resolution Project; extended evaluation; judicial settlement conference; trial

(a) In any case where either party has filed a motion regarding a custody or visitation dispute and has not yet scheduled an appointment for the mediation orientation class by the time of the hearing on the order to show cause, the court shall order all parties to go to

Family Court Services that day to schedule an appointment. The mediation orientation shall be scheduled within 14 days. Mediation orientation shall be conducted by Family Court Services and shall include general information on the effect of separation and dissolution on children and parents, the developmental and emotional needs of children in those circumstances, time-sharing considerations and various options concerning legal and physical custody of children, the effect of exposure to domestic violence and extreme conflict on children and parents, the nature of the mediation process and other Family Court Services procedures, and related community resources.

(b) After the mediation orientation, the parties may elect to utilize private mental health professionals, in which case the parties or the court may modify the fast track time guidelines provided for in this section.

(c) If, after orientation, either party requests mediation, and both parties complete Family Court Services mediation petitions, an appointment shall be scheduled within four weeks after both petitions are submitted and both parties shall attend the mediation as scheduled.

(d) At the mediation, if the parties agree to all of the issues regarding custody or visitation, the mediator shall memorialize the agreement in writing, and shall mail copies of the document to the attorneys and parents. Unless written objections to the agreement are sent to Family Court Services within 20 days of mailing the agreement, it will be submitted to the court and become a court order. A copy of the order shall be sent with proof of service to the parties and attorneys by the Family Court.

(e) If mediation is completed and there are remaining disputes, the mediator shall write a memorandum of any partial agreement and shall outline the remaining disputes which shall be sent to the attorneys and parties acting in propria persona. The mediator shall refer the parties to the Early Resolution Project. The parties shall meet and confer within 14 days of the referral to determine if a solution can be formulated. If there are remaining issues to be settled after the meeting, an early resolution judicial conference shall be scheduled within 30 days of the request of either party.

(f) At the early resolution conference, the judge may take stipulations resolving the issues of custody or visitation. The judge may also request the staff of Family Court Services to provide assessments and expedited evaluations to be held on the same day as the conference, in which case the judge, upon stipulation of the parties, may also order a hearing as soon as the same day on the issues. The judge may also order counseling, a mental health special master, psychological testing, or an extended evaluation by Family Court Services or a private evaluator on some or all issues.

(g) When the court at the early resolution judicial conference orders an extended evaluation, the parties shall complete all paperwork, submit deposits to Family Court Services, or both, within five days of the early resolution judicial conference. An evaluator shall be assigned to the case within 10 days thereafter.

(h) Evaluation shall be completed within 60 days of assignment to the evaluator, and the evaluator shall submit a report and recommendations which include a proposed order resolving all disputed issues. This report shall be served by certified mail on the attorneys of record, or on the parties if they are appearing in propria persona. If there are objections to the proposed order, the parties shall file written objections, meet with the evaluator within 30 days of service of the report, and serve a copy of the order on Family Court Services within the 30-day period. If a stipulation is reached, it shall be filed with the court. If a dispute remains, a judicial settlement conference shall be scheduled within 14 days of the meeting with the evaluator. Parties, counsel, and the evaluator shall be present at this judicial settlement conference. If there is no resolution at this settlement conference, a trial shall be set within 30 days from the settlement conference by the settlement conference judge. If no objections are filed, Family Court Services shall file the proposed order with the court, and it shall become the court's order.

(i) For good cause shown, all deadlines in this section may be altered by the court. *(Added by Stats.1993, c. 219 (A.B.1500), § 210.)*

Cross References

Domestic violence defined for purposes of this Code, see Family Code § 6211.
Judgment and order defined for purposes of this Code, see Family Code § 100.

§ 20039. Repealed by Stats.2016, c. 86 (S.B.1171), § 134, eff. Jan. 1, 2017

§ 20040. Informational booklet; publication

The court may elect to publish a low-cost booklet describing the program. *(Added by Stats.1993, c. 219 (A.B.1500), § 210.)*

§ 20041. Child-related programs; coordination by court

The court shall centralize, augment, and coordinate all presently existing programs under the court's supervision that relate to children, including, but not limited to, mental health special masters, appointment of attorneys for children, supervised visitation, and other supporting personnel. *(Added by Stats.1993, c. 219 (A.B.1500), § 210.)*

§ 20042. Repealed by Stats.2004, c. 193 (S.B.111), § 19

§ 20043. Pilot project; litigants served; savings and costs; income

(a) It is estimated for Santa Clara County's participation in the pilot project authorized by this chapter, that 4,000 litigants will be served annually, and that the following savings will occur:

(1) With an estimated 20 percent reduction in the use of court time over the current system, the county would save approximately 178 hours per year of court time, or approximately 22 workdays per year.

(2) With an estimated cost savings in incomes of judges, court reporters, clerks, bailiffs, and sheriffs, the project is expected to save approximately twenty thousand dollars ($20,000) per year. Cases involving child support obligations which the district attorney's office was required to handle in one participating county, for the 1989–90 fiscal year, number 2,461. The average time spent on a typical child support order is approximately five hours. There is a potential of 12,500 man-hours per year that could be saved, resulting in a savings of three hundred sixty-seven thousand eight hundred seventy-five dollars ($367,875) per year in attorney salaries alone. This does not take into consideration costs for documents, filing, and other district attorney personnel.

(3) The average savings personally to litigants who otherwise would require private representation would be from fifty dollars ($50) to two hundred fifty dollars ($250) per hour of court time and other preparation work.

(b) The satisfaction of participating parties will be determined by requiring the litigants using the pilot project to fill out a simple exit poll. The response of at least 70 percent of those questionnaires will be analyzed to decide whether the program has been deemed satisfactory by the participants.

(c) The estimated cost of the program is as follows:

(1) The estimated salary for an Attorney-Mediator is sixty thousand dollars ($60,000) to sixty-five thousand dollars ($65,000) per year, plus an additional 25 percent of salary to cover the costs of benefits for that position. In addition, there may be other costs connected with this position for support staff at the court.

(2) The costs of exit polling and any informational materials to be handed out to the public by the Attorney-Mediator is undetermined and cannot be estimated.

(d) The estimated income to cover the costs of this program will be as follows:

§ 20043   PILOT PROJECTS

(1) There are approximately 10,000 dissolution of marriage petitions filed in Santa Clara County each year. Of those cases, approximately one-third of them have responses filed. At the present time, it costs one hundred sixty-five dollars ($165) to have a petition for dissolution of marriage filed and one hundred twenty-seven dollars ($127) to have a response filed, for a cost differential of thirty-eight dollars ($38). By equalizing the response fee with the petition fee, income generated would be approximately one hundred twenty-five thousand four hundred dollars ($125,400) per year. This does not include the cost of fourteen dollars ($14) for each responsive declaration filed to a motion or order to show cause, the annual number of which is significantly greater than 3,300. It is estimated that an additional fifty thousand dollars ($50,000) per year could be generated by equalizing the responsive fees to a motion or order to show cause with the filing of those motions. These fees generated would more than offset the costs of the program.

(2) It is also anticipated that the Attorney-Mediator will develop public information and outreach programs which will be paid for by any excess revenue generated from the pilot project and ultimately will result in savings to the public and the court. The public will save by not having to pay attorneys for certain information regarding child support matters, and the court will save by not having to educate the public from the bench, thus expediting the handling of support and custody cases.

(e) The cost of computers, printers, and other equipment will be defrayed by contributions. *(Added by Stats.1993, c. 219 (A.B.1500), § 210.)*

Cross References

County defined for purposes of this Code, see Family Code § 67.
Judgment and order defined for purposes of this Code, see Family Code § 100.
Support defined for purposes of this Code, see Family Code § 150.
Support order defined for purposes of this Code, see Family Code § 155.

Part 2

PATERNITY PILOT PROJECTS [INOPERATIVE]

§§ 20100 to 20104. Inoperative

BUSINESS AND PROFESSIONS CODE

Division 2

HEALING ARTS

Cross References

Action against health care provider, periodic payments of future damages, see Code of Civil Procedure § 667.7.

Administration of the state correctional system, examination of staff for tuberculosis, see Penal Code § 6006.5.

Arbitration of medical malpractice, contract for medical services, see Code of Civil Procedure § 1295.

Classification as employee or independent contractor, factors considered, exceptions, court decisions, see Labor Code § 2775.

Commencement of actions based upon professional negligence, notice of intention, see Code of Civil Procedure § 364.

Compensation and expenses of members of boards and commissions created under this Division, see Business and Professions Code § 103.

Disability insurance, mental health and substance use disorder coverage, see Insurance Code § 10144.5.

Disclosure to patients, requirements for persons licensed under this Division, see Business and Professions Code § 680.5.

Employment of individuals by healing arts boards, see Business and Professions Code § 154.2.

Employment of medical personnel, health and physical development of pupils, psychological tests and other psychological activities, see Education Code § 49422.

Health care service provider, defined, see Health and Safety Code § 1375.8.

Liability insurance for health care providers rendering voluntary care at community or free clinics, see Government Code § 990.9.

Mental health and substance use disorder coverage, see Health and Safety Code § 1374.72.

Negligence actions against health care providers, claims for punitive damages, amended pleadings, see Code of Civil Procedure § 425.13.

Nonprofit corporations for medical services, formation, see Corporations Code § 10810.

Private postsecondary and vocational institutions, grounds for refusing to issue or renew approval to operate, see Education Code § 94830.

Professional corporations, licensed persons who may be shareholders, officers, directors or professional employees, conditions, see Corporations Code § 13401.5.

Provision of services via telehealth, licensed health care practitioner, applicable statutes and regulations, see Business and Professions Code § 686.

Review of administrative orders or decisions, stay, see Code of Civil Procedure § 1094.5.

Status of independent contractors engaged in business of massage, see Government Code § 51033.

Successful completion of pretrial diversion program, disclosure of arrest, see Penal Code § 1000.4.

Time of commencing civil actions, action against health care provider, see Code of Civil Procedure § 340.5.

Unlicensed persons who cause injury or damage to another person as result of providing goods or performing services for which a license is required, see Code of Civil Procedure § 1029.8.

Validity of state license in municipalities, healing arts professional license, local license taxes, see Business and Professions Code § 460.

CHAPTER 1. GENERAL PROVISIONS

Cross References

Actions against health care providers, statute of limitations, see Code of Civil Procedure § 340.5.

Health care provider, defined, see Business and Professions Code § 657.

Medical malpractice, arbitration, see Code of Civil Procedure § 1295.

Nonprofit professional corporation for licentiates under this Chapter, see Corporations Code § 10810.

Treble damages, costs, and attorneys' fees, liability of unlicensed persons who cause injury or damage to another person as result of providing goods or performing services for which license is required, see Code of Civil Procedure § 1029.8.

ARTICLE 15. SEXUAL ORIENTATION CHANGE EFFORTS

Section
865. Definitions.
865.1. Prohibited actions.
865.2. Unprofessional conduct of mental health provider; disciplinary action.

§ 865. Definitions

For the purposes of this article, the following terms shall have the following meanings:

(a) "Mental health provider" means a physician and surgeon specializing in the practice of psychiatry, a psychologist, a psychological assistant, intern, or trainee, a licensed marriage and family therapist, a registered associate marriage and family therapist, a marriage and family therapist trainee, a licensed educational psychologist, a credentialed school psychologist, a licensed clinical social worker, an associate clinical social worker, a licensed professional clinical counselor, a registered associate clinical counselor, a professional clinical counselor trainee, or any other person designated as a mental health professional under California law or regulation.

(b)(1) "Sexual orientation change efforts" means any practices by mental health providers that seek to change an individual's sexual orientation. This includes efforts to change behaviors or gender expressions, or to eliminate or reduce sexual or romantic attractions or feelings toward individuals of the same sex.

(2) "Sexual orientation change efforts" does not include psychotherapies that: (A) provide acceptance, support, and understanding of clients or the facilitation of clients' coping, social support, and identity exploration and development, including sexual orientation-neutral interventions to prevent or address unlawful conduct or unsafe sexual practices; and (B) do not seek to change sexual orientation. *(Added by Stats.2012, c. 835 (S.B.1172), § 2. Amended by Stats.2018, c. 703 (S.B.1491), § 3, eff. Jan. 1, 2019.)*

§ 865.1. Prohibited actions

Under no circumstances shall a mental health provider engage in sexual orientation change efforts with a patient under 18 years of age. *(Added by Stats.2012, c. 835 (S.B.1172), § 2.)*

§ 865.2. Unprofessional conduct of mental health provider; disciplinary action

Any sexual orientation change efforts attempted on a patient under 18 years of age by a mental health provider shall be considered unprofessional conduct and shall subject a mental health provider to discipline by the licensing entity for that mental health provider. *(Added by Stats.2012, c. 835 (S.B.1172), § 2.)*

CHAPTER 1.2. EXPEDITED LICENSURE PROCESS

Section
870. Expedited licensure process.

§ 870. Expedited licensure process

(a) The Medical Board of California, the Osteopathic Medical Board of California, the Board of Registered Nursing, and the Physician Assistant Board shall expedite the licensure process for an

§ 870

applicant who demonstrates that they intend to provide abortions, as defined in Section 123464 of the Health and Safety Code, within the scope of practice of their license.

(b) An applicant shall demonstrate their intent to provide abortions by providing a letter declaring the applicant's intention to provide abortions and a letter from an employer or health care entity indicating that the applicant has accepted employment or entered into a contract to provide abortions, the applicant's starting date, the location where the applicant will be providing abortions, and that the applicant will be providing abortions within the scope of practice of their license in accordance with Sections 2253, 2725.4, and 3502.4, as applicable.

(c) Nothing in this section shall be construed as changing existing licensure requirements. An applicant applying for expedited licensure under subdivision (a) shall meet all applicable statutory and regulatory licensure requirements. *(Added by Stats.2022, c. 560 (A.B.657), § 2, eff. Jan. 1, 2023.)*

CHAPTER 13. LICENSED MARRIAGE AND FAMILY THERAPISTS

Cross References

AIDS training in continuing education requirements, see Business and Professions Code § 32.
Authorization to disclose medical records to persons or organizations defending professional liability, see Civil Code § 56.105.
Authorization to view mental health records, see Health and Safety Code § 123115.
Board of Behavioral Sciences, board defined, see Business and Professions Code § 4990.02.
Chemical dependency and early intervention training, see Business and Professions Code § 29.
Child custody evaluator, see Family Code § 3110.5.
Consent by minor to medical treatment, mental health treatment or counseling services defined to include services provided by registered marriage and family therapist intern, see Family Code § 6924.
Consent to mental health treatment or counseling services by minors age 12 or older determined to meet maturity requirements, maturity determination made by professional person including marriage and family therapist or registered intern, see Health and Safety Code § 124260.
Conviction of crime, relationship to licensed activity, see Business and Professions Code § 490.
Criminal history record checks, see Business and Professions Code § 144.
Disability insurance written or issued for delivery outside of state, benefits provided within scope of practice of licensed marriage and family therapists, see Insurance Code § 10176.7.
Disclosure to patients, exception for persons licensed under this Chapter, see Business and Professions Code § 680.5.
Health care provider defined, see Health and Safety Code § 123105.
Human sexuality training, requirements as applied to this Chapter, see Business and Professions Code § 25.
Internet, dissemination of license status information by the Board under this chapter, see Business and Professions Code § 27.
Law enforcement collaboration, supervision, see Welfare and Institutions Code § 5848.7.
Medical treatment, consent by minor, mental health treatment or counseling services, see Family Code § 6924.
Noncompliance with support order or judgment, see Business and Professions Code § 490.5.
Patient access to health records,
  Definitions, see Health and Safety Code § 123105.
  Representative of minor, mental health records, see Health and Safety Code § 123115.
Psychological corporations, see Business and Professions Code § 2995.
Psychotherapist-patient privilege, see Evidence Code § 1010.
Self-insured employee welfare benefit plans written or issued for delivery outside state, selection of specified health care providers, see Insurance Code § 10177.8.
Settlement or arbitration award, reporting requirements, see Business and Professions Code § 802.
Telephone medical advice services, see Health and Safety Code § 1348.8.
Training for child abuse assessment and reporting, license requirements, see Business and Professions Code § 28.

Unprofessional conduct, prior sexual contact between psychotherapist and patient, failure to comply, see Business and Professions Code § 728.

ARTICLE 1. REGULATION

Section	
4980.	Necessity of license.
4980.01.	Construction with other laws; exemption of certain professionals and employees; status as health care practitioner.
4980.02.	Practice of marriage and family therapy; application of principles and methods.
4980.03.	Definitions.
4980.04.	Short title.
4980.05.	Exempt settings; exceptions.
4980.06.	Definitions; practice in nonexempt settings required; exceptions.
4980.08.	Licensed marriage and family therapist; marriage and family therapist; name change; construction of section.
4980.09.	Associate marriage and family therapist; registered associate marriage and family therapist; name change; construction of section.
4980.10.	Engaging in practice.
4980.30.	License requirement; fee.
4980.31.	Display of license in primary place of practice.
4980.32.	Notice to clients.
4980.34.	Legislative intent.
4980.35.	Obligation to provide complete and accurate application; duties of board.
4980.36.	Degree required by specified applicants; degree program requirements.
4980.37.	Degree required by specified applicants; degree program requirements.
4980.38.	Notification to students of design of degree program; certification of fulfillment of requirements.
4980.39.	Graduate study coursework in aging and long-term care; assessment, reporting, and treatment of elder and dependent adult abuse and neglect; program contents; minimum contact hours.
4980.395.	Applicants for marriage and family therapy licensure; completion of training or coursework; telehealth requirement.
4980.396.	Applicants for marriage and family therapy licensure; required coursework; applied experience; minimum number of hours; suicide risk assessment and intervention; proof of compliance.
4980.397.	Registrants or applicants for licensure; required examinations; time for California law and ethics examination; eligibility for clinical examination.
4980.398.	Passing scores required on specified examinations.
4980.399.	California law and ethics examination; participation prior to registration renewal; retaking examination; issuance of subsequent registration number; continuing education requirements.
4980.40.	Qualifications.
4980.41.	Eligibility to sit for licensing examinations; coursework or training.
4980.42.	Trainees' services.
4980.43.	Postdegree hours of supervised experience; requirements.
4980.43.1.	Supervision of trainees, associates, and applicants for licensure.
4980.43.2.	Direct supervisor contact.
4980.43.2.	Direct supervisor contact.

Section	
4980.43.3.	Trainee, associate, or applicant for licensure to perform services as employee or volunteer; setting for supervised experience; counseling or psychotherapy for applicants.
4980.43.4.	Location for provision of services by trainee, associate, or applicant for licensure; supervisor requirements; maximum number of supervisees; written oversight agreement.
4980.43.5.	Supervisors to maintain records; audits.
4980.44.	Unlicensed associate marriage and family therapists; requirements; notice to clients or patients; advertisements.
4980.46.	Fictitious business names.
4980.48.	Trainees; notice to clients and patients of unlicensed status; advertising.
4980.49.	Termination of therapy on or after Jan. 1, 2015; retention of health service records for specified time; records of minor clients or patients; format.
4980.50.	Examination; issuance or denial of license.
4980.54.	Continuing education requirements; hours; records; approved providers; subject matter.
4980.55.	Statements of experience, education, specialties, etc.
4980.57.	Licensees who began graduate study before January 1, 2004; required continuing education course.
4980.60.	Rules and regulations.
4980.70.	Additional personnel.
4980.72.	Reciprocity; conditions.
4980.74.	Applicants for licensure with education or experience gained outside California who do not qualify for reciprocity; acceptance of education or experience; qualification for licensure without taking clinical examination.
4980.76.	Foreign degrees; provision of comprehensive degree evaluation.
4980.78.	Applicants for licensure with education gained from out-of-state school who do not qualify for reciprocity; substantially equivalent education.
4980.81.	Reciprocity; applicants for licensure; education requirements.

§ 4980. Necessity of license

(a)(1) Many California families and many individual Californians are experiencing difficulty and distress, and are in need of wise, competent, caring, compassionate, and effective counseling in order to enable them to improve and maintain healthy family relationships.

(2) Healthy individuals and healthy families and healthy relationships are inherently beneficial and crucial to a healthy society, and are our most precious and valuable natural resource. Licensed marriage and family therapists provide a crucial support for the well-being of the people and the State of California.

(b) No person may engage in the practice of marriage and family therapy as defined by Section 4980.02, unless he or she holds a valid license as a marriage and family therapist, or unless he or she is specifically exempted from that requirement, nor may any person advertise himself or herself as performing the services of a marriage, family, child, domestic, or marital consultant, or in any way use these or any similar titles, including the letters "L.M.F.T." "M.F.T.," or "M.F.C.C.," or other name, word initial, or symbol in connection with or following his or her name to imply that he or she performs these services without a license as provided by this chapter. Persons licensed under Article 4 (commencing with Section 4996) of Chapter 14 of Division 2, or under Chapter 6.6 (commencing with Section 2900) may engage in such practice or advertise that they practice marriage and family therapy but may not advertise that they hold the marriage and family therapist's license. *(Added by Stats.1986, c. 1365, § 4. Amended by Stats.2000, c. 836 (S.B.1554), § 28; Stats. 2002, c. 1013 (S.B.2026), § 13; Stats.2014, c. 316 (S.B.1466), § 15, eff. Jan. 1, 2015.)*

Cross References

Advertise defined for purposes of this Chapter, see Business and Professions Code § 4980.03.
Authorization to view mental health records, see Health and Safety Code § 123115.
Child custody evaluator, prerequisites, see Family Code § 3110.5.
Inapplicability of article to educational psychologist, see Labor Code § 1703.6.
Privileged communications, see Evidence Code § 1010 et seq.
Specialized health care service plans, contracting with a telephonic medical advice service, appropriate licensing, registration and certification, see Health and Safety Code § 1348.8.
Unlicensed person, telephone directory advertising, see Business and Professions Code § 149.

§ 4980.01. Construction with other laws; exemption of certain professionals and employees; status as health care practitioner

(a) This chapter shall not be construed to constrict, limit, or withdraw the Medical Practice Act, the Social Work Licensing Law, the Nursing Practice Act, the Licensed Professional Clinical Counselor Act, or the Psychology Licensing Law.

(b) This chapter shall not apply to any priest, rabbi, or minister of the gospel of any religious denomination when performing counseling services as part of their pastoral or professional duties, or to any person who is admitted to practice law in the state, or a physician and surgeon who provides counseling services as part of their professional practice.

(c) This chapter shall not apply to an unlicensed or unregistered employee or volunteer working in a governmental entity, a school, a college, a university, or an institution that is both nonprofit and charitable if both of the following apply:

(1) The work of the employee or volunteer is performed under the oversight and direction of the entity.

(2)(A) On and after July 1, 2020, the employee or volunteer provides a client, prior to initiating psychotherapy services or as soon as practicably possible thereafter, a notice written in at least 12–point type that is in substantially the following form:

NOTICE TO CLIENTS

The (Name of office or unit) of the (Name of agency) receives and responds to complaints regarding the practice of psychotherapy by any unlicensed or unregistered practitioner providing services at (Name of agency). To file a complaint, contact (Telephone number, email address, internet website, or mailing address of agency).

The Board of Behavioral Sciences receives and responds to complaints regarding services provided by individuals licensed and registered by the board. If you have a complaint and are unsure if your practitioner is licensed or registered, please contact the Board of Behavioral Sciences at 916–574–7830 for assistance or utilize the board's online license verification feature by visiting www.bbs.ca.gov.

(B) The delivery of the notice described in subparagraph (A) to the client shall be documented.

(d) A marriage and family therapist licensed under this chapter is a licentiate for purposes of paragraph (2) of subdivision (a) of Section 805, and thus is a health care provider subject to the provisions of Section 2290.5 pursuant to subdivision (b) of that section.

(e) Notwithstanding subdivisions (b) and (c), all persons registered as associates or licensed under this chapter shall not be exempt from this chapter or the jurisdiction of the board. *(Added by Stats.1986, c. 1365, § 4. Amended by Stats.1993, c. 1054 (A.B.1885), § 1; Stats.*

§ 4980.01

2003, c. 20 (A.B.116), § 4; Stats.2007, c. 588 (S.B.1048), § 56; Stats.2011, c. 384 (S.B.363), § 1; Stats.2018, c. 743 (A.B.93), § 3, eff. Jan. 1, 2019; Stats.2019, c. 229 (A.B.630), § 1, eff. Jan. 1, 2020; Stats.2021, c. 647 (S.B.801), § 21, eff. Jan. 1, 2022; Stats.2021, c. 747 (A.B.690), § 1.5, eff. Jan. 1, 2022.)

Cross References

Board defined for purposes of this Chapter, see Business and Professions Code §§ 4980.03, 4990.02.
Board defined for purposes of this Code, see Business and Professions Code § 22.
Medical Practice Act, see Business and Professions Code § 2000 et seq.
Nursing Practice Act, see Business and Professions Code § 2700.
Social workers, see Business and Professions Code § 4990 et seq.

§ 4980.02. Practice of marriage and family therapy; application of principles and methods

(a) For the purposes of this chapter, the practice of marriage and family therapy shall mean the application of psychotherapeutic and family systems theories, principles, and methods in the delivery of services to individuals, couples, or groups in order to assess, evaluate, and treat relational issues, emotional disorders, behavioral problems, mental illness, alcohol and substance use, and to modify intrapersonal and interpersonal behaviors.

(b) The application of marriage and family therapy principles and methods includes, but is not limited to, all of the following:

(1) Assessment, evaluation, and prognosis.

(2) Treatment, planning, and evaluation.

(3) Individual, relationship, family, or group therapeutic interventions.

(4) Relational therapy.

(5) Psychotherapy.

(6) Client education.

(7) Clinical case management.

(8) Consultation.

(9) Supervision.

(10) Use, application, and integration of the coursework and training required by Sections 4980.36, 4980.37, and 4980.41, as applicable.

(c) The amendments to this section made by the act adding this subdivision¹ do not constitute a change in, but are declaratory of, existing law. It is the intent of the Legislature that these amendments shall not be construed to expand or constrict the existing scope of practice of a person licensed pursuant to this chapter. (Added by Stats.1986, c. 1365, § 4. Amended by Stats.1990, c. 1086 (S.B.2214), § 1; Stats.2002, c. 1013 (S.B.2026), § 14; Stats.2004, c. 204 (A.B. 2552), § 2; Stats.2009, c. 26 (S.B.33), § 2; Stats.2021, c. 647 (S.B.801), § 22, eff. Jan. 1, 2022.)

¹ Stats.2021, c. 647 (S.B.801).

§ 4980.03. Definitions

(a) "Board," as used in this chapter, means the Board of Behavioral Sciences.

(b) "Associate," as used in this chapter, means an unlicensed person who has earned a master's or doctoral degree qualifying the person for licensure and is registered with the board as an associate.

(c) "Trainee," as used in this chapter, means an unlicensed person who is currently enrolled in a master's or doctoral degree program, as specified in Sections 4980.36 and 4980.37, that is designed to qualify the person for licensure under this chapter, and who has completed no less than 12 semester units or 18 quarter units of coursework in any qualifying degree program.

(d) "Applicant for licensure," as used in this chapter, means an unlicensed person who has completed the required education and required hours of supervised experience for licensure.

(e) "Advertise," as used in this chapter, includes, but is not limited to, any public communication, as defined in subdivision (a) of Section 651, the issuance of any card, sign, or device to any person, or the causing, permitting, or allowing of any sign or marking on, or in, any building or structure, or in any newspaper or magazine or in any directory, or any printed matter whatsoever, with or without any limiting qualification. Signs within religious buildings or notices in church bulletins mailed to a congregation are not * * * advertising within the meaning of this chapter.

(f) "Experience," as used in this chapter, means experience in interpersonal relationships, psychotherapy, marriage and family therapy, direct clinical counseling, and nonclinical practice that satisfies the requirements for licensure as a marriage and family therapist.

(g) "Supervisor," as used in this chapter, means an individual who meets all of the following requirements:

(1) Has held an active license for at least two years within the five-year period immediately preceding any supervision as any of the following:

(A) A licensed professional clinical counselor, licensed marriage and family therapist, psychologist licensed pursuant to Chapter 6.6 (commencing with Section 2900), licensed clinical social worker, licensed educational psychologist, or equivalent out-of-state license. A licensed educational psychologist may only supervise the provision of educationally related mental health services that are consistent with the scope of practice of an educational psychologist, as specified in Section 4989.14.

(B) A physician and surgeon who is certified in psychiatry by the American Board of Psychiatry and Neurology or an out-of-state licensed physician and surgeon who is certified in psychiatry by the American Board of Psychiatry and Neurology.

(2) For at least two years within the five-year period immediately preceding any supervision, has practiced psychotherapy, provided psychological counseling pursuant to paragraph (5) of subdivision (a) of Section 4989.14, or provided direct clinical supervision of psychotherapy performed by marriage and family therapist trainees, associate marriage and family therapists, associate professional clinical counselors, or associate clinical social workers. Supervision of psychotherapy performed by a social work intern or a professional clinical counselor trainee shall be accepted if the supervision provided is substantially equivalent to the supervision required for registrants.

(3) Has received training in supervision as specified in this chapter and by regulation.

(4) Has not provided therapeutic services to the supervisee.

(5) Has and maintains a current and active license that is not under suspension or probation as one of the following:

(A) A marriage and family therapist, professional clinical counselor, clinical social worker, or licensed educational psychologist, issued by the board.

(B) A psychologist licensed pursuant to Chapter 6.6 (commencing with Section 2900).

(C) A physician and surgeon who is certified in psychiatry by the American Board of Psychiatry and Neurology.

(6) Is not a spouse, domestic partner, or relative of the supervisee.

(7) Does not currently have or previously had a personal, professional, or business relationship with the supervisee that undermines the authority or effectiveness of the supervision.

(h) "Client centered advocacy," as used in this chapter, includes, but is not limited to, researching, identifying, and accessing resources, or other activities, related to obtaining or providing services and supports for clients or groups of clients receiving psychotherapy or counseling services.

(i) "Accredited," as used in this chapter, means a school, college, or university accredited by either the Commission on Accreditation for Marriage and Family Therapy Education or a regional or national institutional accrediting agency that is recognized by the United States Department of Education.

(j) "Approved," as used in this chapter, means a school, college, or university that possessed unconditional approval by the Bureau for Private Postsecondary Education at the time of the applicant's graduation from the school, college, or university. *(Added by Stats.1986, c. 1365, § 4. Amended by Stats.1993, c. 1054 (A.B.1885), § 2; Stats.1996, c. 829 (A.B.3473), § 85; Stats.2000, c. 836 (S.B. 1554), § 29; Stats.2005, c. 658 (S.B.229), § 16; Stats.2007, c. 586 (A.B.234), § 1; Stats.2009, c. 26 (S.B.33), § 3; Stats.2011, c. 384 (S.B.363), § 2; Stats.2015, c. 262 (S.B.620), § 1, eff. Jan. 1, 2016; Stats.2018, c. 743 (A.B.93), § 4, eff. Jan. 1, 2019; Stats.2019, c. 321 (A.B.1651), § 1, eff. Jan. 1, 2020; Stats.2019, c. 380 (S.B.679), § 1.5, eff. Jan. 1, 2020; Stats.2021, c. 440 (A.B.462), § 1, eff. Jan. 1, 2022; Stats.2022, c. 511 (S.B.1495), § 27, eff. Jan. 1, 2023.)*

Cross References

Board defined for purposes of this Code, see Business and Professions Code § 22.

Child Abuse and Neglect Reporting Act, mandated reporter, see Penal Code § 11165.7.

Elder Abuse and Dependent Adult Civil Protection Act, health practitioner defined, see Welfare and Institutions Code § 15610.37.

Medical treatment, consent by minor, mental health treatment or counseling services, see Family Code § 6924.

Patient access to health records, representative of minor, mental health records, see Health and Safety Code § 123115.

Psychotherapist, psychotherapist-patient privilege, see Evidence Code § 1010.

§ 4980.04. Short title

This chapter shall be known and may be cited as the Licensed Marriage and Family Therapist Act. *(Added by Stats.2009, c. 308 (S.B.819), § 62. Amended by Stats.2012, c. 799 (S.B.1575), § 24.)*

§ 4980.05. Exempt settings; exceptions

The settings described in Section 4980.01 are exempt settings and do not fall under the jurisdiction of this chapter or the board except as specified in Section 4980.01, and with the following exceptions:

(a) Any individual working or volunteering in an exempt setting who is licensed or registered under this chapter shall fall under the jurisdiction of the board and is not exempt from this chapter.

(b) An entity that is licensed or certified by a government regulatory agency to provide health care services shall not be considered an exempt setting unless it directly meets the criteria described in Section 4980.01. *(Added by Stats.2021, c. 747 (A.B.690), § 2, eff. Jan. 1, 2022.)*

§ 4980.06. Definitions; practice in nonexempt settings required; exceptions

(a) For the purposes of this chapter, the following definitions apply:

(1) "Nonexempt setting" means any type of setting that does not qualify as an exempt setting, as specified in Section 4980.01.

(2) "Private practice" means a type of nonexempt setting that meets all of the following:

(A) The practice is owned by a health professional who is licensed under this division either independently or jointly with one or more other health professionals who are licensed under this division.

(B) The practice provides clinical mental health services, including psychotherapy, to clients.

(C) One or more licensed health professionals are responsible for the practice and for the services provided and set conditions of client payment or reimbursement for the provision of services.

(3) "Professional corporation" means a type of nonexempt setting and private practice that has been formed pursuant to Part 4 (commencing with Section 13400) of Division 3 of Title 1 of the Corporations Code.

(b) An active license or registration number shall be required to engage in the practice of marriage and family therapy, as defined in Section 4980.02, in nonexempt settings at all times with the following exceptions:

(1) A trainee may engage in the practice of marriage and family therapy in a nonexempt setting that is not a private practice or a professional corporation while they are gaining supervised experience that meets the requirements of this chapter under the jurisdiction and supervision of their school as specified in Section 4980.42.

(2) An applicant for registration as an associate may engage in the practice of marriage and family therapy in a nonexempt setting that is not a private practice or a professional corporation before the registration number is issued if they are in compliance with subdivision (b) of Section 4980.43 and are gaining supervised experience that meets the requirements of this chapter. *(Added by Stats.2021, c. 747 (A.B.690), § 3, eff. Jan. 1, 2022.)*

§ 4980.08. Licensed marriage and family therapist; marriage and family therapist; name change; construction of section

(a) The title "licensed marriage, family and child counselor" or "marriage, family and child counselor" is hereby renamed "licensed marriage and family therapist" or "marriage and family therapist," respectively. Any reference in any statute or regulation to a "licensed marriage, family and child counselor" or "marriage, family and child counselor" shall be deemed a reference to a "licensed marriage and family therapist" or "marriage and family therapist."

(b) Nothing in this section shall be construed to expand or constrict the scope of practice of a person licensed pursuant to this chapter.

(c) This section shall become operative July 1, 1999. *(Added by Stats.1998, c. 108 (A.B.1449), § 1, operative July 1, 1999.)*

§ 4980.09. Associate marriage and family therapist; registered associate marriage and family therapist; name change; construction of section

(a)(1) The title "marriage and family therapist intern" or "marriage and family therapist registered intern" is hereby renamed "associate marriage and family therapist" or "registered associate marriage and family therapist," respectively. Any reference in statute or regulation to a "marriage and family therapist intern" or "marriage and family therapist registered intern" shall be deemed a reference to an "associate marriage and family therapist" or "registered associate marriage and family therapist."

(2) Any reference in this chapter to the term "intern" means "associate." Any reference in statute or regulation to the abbreviation "MFTI" means an "AMFT."

(b) This section shall not be construed to expand or constrict the scope of practice of a person licensed or registered pursuant to this chapter. *(Added by Stats.2016, c. 489 (S.B.1478), § 28, eff. Jan. 1, 2017, operative Jan. 1, 2018. Amended by Stats.2017, c. 573 (S.B.800), § 4, eff. Jan. 1, 2018.)*

§ 4980.10. Engaging in practice

A person engages in the practice of marriage and family therapy when he or she performs or offers to perform or holds himself or herself out as able to perform this service for remuneration in any form, including donations. *(Added by Stats.1986, c. 1365, § 4. Amended by Stats.2002, c. 1013 (S.B.2026), § 15; Stats.2011, c. 148 (S.B.274), § 1, eff. Aug. 1, 2011.)*

§ 4980.30. License requirement; fee

Except as otherwise provided herein, a person desiring to practice and to advertise the performance of marriage and family therapy services shall apply to the board for a license, pay the license fee required by this chapter, and obtain a license from the board. *(Added by Stats.1986, c. 1365, § 4. Amended by Stats.2002, c. 1013 (S.B.2026), § 16; Stats.2009, c. 308 (S.B.819), § 63.)*

Cross References

Board defined for purposes of this Chapter, see Business and Professions Code §§ 4980.03, 4990.02.

Board defined for purposes of this Code, see Business and Professions Code § 22.

§ 4980.31. Display of license in primary place of practice

A licensee shall display his or her license in a conspicuous place in the licensee's primary place of practice. *(Added by Stats.1998, c. 879 (S.B.2238), § 4.)*

§ 4980.32. Notice to clients

(a) On and after July 1, 2020, a licensee or registrant shall provide a client with a notice written in at least 12–point type prior to initiating psychotherapy services, or as soon as practicably possible thereafter, that reads as follows:

NOTICE TO CLIENTS

The Board of Behavioral Sciences receives and responds to complaints regarding services provided within the scope of practice of marriage and family therapists. You may contact the board online at www.bbs.ca.gov, or by calling (916) 574–7830.

(b) Delivery of the notice required by this section to the client shall be documented. *(Added by Stats.2019, c. 229 (A.B.630), § 2, eff. Jan. 1, 2020. Amended by Stats.2021, c. 647 (S.B.801), § 23, eff. Jan. 1, 2022.)*

§ 4980.34. Legislative intent

It is the intent of the Legislature that the board employ its resources for each and all of the following functions:

(a) The licensing of marriage and family therapists, clinical social workers, professional clinical counselors, and educational psychologists.

(b) The development and administration of licensing examinations and examination procedures, as specified, consistent with prevailing standards for the validation and use of licensing and certification tests. Examinations shall measure knowledge and abilities demonstrably important to the safe, effective practice of the profession.

(c) Enforcement of laws designed to protect the public from incompetent, unethical, or unprofessional practitioners.

(d) Consumer education. *(Added by Stats.1986, c. 1365, § 4. Amended by Stats.1998, c. 589 (S.B.1983), § 10; Stats.2002, c. 1013 (S.B.2026), § 17; Stats.2003, c. 874 (S.B.363), § 6; Stats.2012, c. 799 (S.B.1575), § 25.)*

Cross References

Board defined for purposes of this Chapter, see Business and Professions Code §§ 4980.03, 4990.02.

Board defined for purposes of this Code, see Business and Professions Code § 22.

Statutory construction, legislative intent, see Code of Civil Procedure § 1859.

§ 4980.35. Obligation to provide complete and accurate application; duties of board

(a) The Legislature acknowledges that the basic obligation to provide a complete and accurate application for a marriage and family therapist license lies with the applicant. At the same time, the Legislature recognizes that an effort should be made by the board to ensure that persons who enter degree programs and supervisorial training settings that meet the requirements of this chapter are enabled to discern the requirements for licensing and to take the examination when they have completed their educational and experience requirements.

(b) In order that the board, the educational institutions, and the supervisors who monitor the education and experience of applicants may develop greater cooperation, the board shall do all of the following:

(1) Apply a portion of its limited resources specifically to the task of communicating information about its activities, the requirements and qualifications for licensure, and the practice of marriage and family therapy to the relevant educational institutions, supervisors, professional associations, applicants, trainees, associates, and the consuming public.

(2) Develop policies and procedures to assist educational institutions in meeting the curricula requirements of Sections 4980.36 and 4980.37 and any regulations adopted pursuant to those sections, so that those educational institutions may better provide assurance to their students that the curriculum offered to fulfill the educational requirements for licensure will meet those requirements at the time of the student's application for licensure.

(3) Notify applicants in the application procedure when applications are incomplete, inaccurate, or deficient, and inform applicants of any remediation, reconsideration, or appeal procedures that may be applicable.

(4) Undertake, or cause to be undertaken, further comprehensive review, in consultation with educational institutions, professional associations, supervisors, associates, and trainees, of the supervision of associates and trainees, which shall include, but not be limited to, the following, and shall propose regulations regarding the supervision of associates and trainees that may include, but not be limited to, the following:

(A) Supervisor qualifications.

(B) Continuing education requirements of supervisors.

(C) Registration or licensing of supervisors, or both.

(D) Responsibilities of supervisors in general.

(E) The board's authority in cases of noncompliance or negligence by supervisors.

(F) The associate's and trainee's need for guidance in selecting well-balanced and high-quality professional training opportunities within his or her community.

(G) The role of the supervisor in advising and encouraging his or her associate or trainee regarding the necessity or value and appropriateness of the associate or trainee engaging in personal psychotherapy, so as to enable the associate or trainee to become a more competent marriage and family therapist. *(Added by Stats. 1986, c. 1365, § 4. Amended by Stats.1993, c. 1054 (A.B.1885), § 3; Stats.2002, c. 1013 (S.B.2026), § 18; Stats.2009, c. 26 (S.B.33), § 4; Stats.2018, c. 743 (A.B.93), § 5, eff. Jan. 1, 2019.)*

Cross References

Board defined for purposes of this Chapter, see Business and Professions Code §§ 4980.03, 4990.02.

Board defined for purposes of this Code, see Business and Professions Code § 22.

§ 4980.36. Degree required by specified applicants; degree program requirements

(a) This section shall apply to the following:

(1) Applicants for licensure or registration who begin graduate study before August 1, 2012, and do not complete that study on or before December 31, 2018.

(2) Applicants for licensure or registration who begin graduate study before August 1, 2012, and who graduate from a degree program that meets the requirements of this section.

(3) Applicants for licensure or registration who begin graduate study on or after August 1, 2012.

(b) To qualify for a license or registration, applicants shall possess a doctoral or master's degree meeting the requirements of this section in marriage, family, and child counseling, marriage and family therapy, couple and family therapy, psychology, clinical psychology, counseling psychology, or either counseling or clinical mental health counseling with an emphasis in either marriage, family, and child counseling or marriage and family therapy. The degree shall be obtained from a school, college, or university approved by the Bureau for Private Postsecondary Education, or accredited by either the Commission on Accreditation for Marriage and Family Therapy Education, or a regional or national institutional accrediting agency that is recognized by the United States Department of Education. The board has the authority to make the final determination as to whether a degree meets all requirements, including, but not limited to, course requirements, regardless of accreditation or approval.

(c) A doctoral or master's degree program that qualifies for licensure or registration shall be a single, integrated program that does the following:

(1) Integrate all of the following throughout its curriculum:

(A) Marriage and family therapy principles.

(B) The principles of mental health recovery-oriented care and methods of service delivery in recovery-oriented practice environments, among others.

(C) An understanding of various cultures and the social and psychological implications of socioeconomic position, and an understanding of how poverty and social stress impact an individual's mental health and recovery.

(2) Allow for innovation and individuality in the education of marriage and family therapists.

(3) Encourage students to develop the personal qualities that are intimately related to effective practice, including, but not limited to, integrity, sensitivity, flexibility, insight, compassion, and personal presence.

(4) Permit an emphasis or specialization that may address any one or more of the unique and complex array of human problems, symptoms, and needs of Californians served by marriage and family therapists.

(5) Provide students with the opportunity to meet with various consumers and family members of consumers of mental health services to enhance understanding of their experience of mental illness, treatment, and recovery.

(d) The degree described in subdivision (b) shall contain no less than 60 semester or 90 quarter units of instruction that includes, but is not limited to, the following requirements:

(1) Both of the following:

(A) No less than 12 semester or 18 quarter units of coursework in theories, principles, and methods of a variety of psychotherapeutic orientations directly related to marriage and family therapy and marital and family systems approaches to treatment and how these theories can be applied therapeutically with individuals, couples, families, adults, including elder adults, children, adolescents, and groups to improve, restore, or maintain healthy relationships.

(B) Practicum that involves direct client contact, as follows:

(i) A minimum of six semester or nine quarter units of practicum in a supervised clinical placement that provides supervised fieldwork experience.

(ii) A minimum of 150 hours of face-to-face experience counseling individuals, couples, families, or groups.

(iii) A student must be enrolled in a practicum course while counseling clients, except as specified in subdivision (c) of Section 4980.42.

(iv) The practicum shall provide training in all of the following areas:

(I) Applied use of theory and psychotherapeutic techniques.

(II) Assessment, diagnosis, prognosis, and treatment planning.

(III) Treatment of individuals and premarital, couple, family, and child relationships, including trauma and abuse, dysfunctions, healthy functioning, health promotion, illness prevention, and working with families.

(IV) Professional writing, including documentation of services, treatment plans, and progress notes.

(V) How to connect people with resources that deliver the quality of services and support needed in the community.

(v) Educational institutions are encouraged to design the practicum required by this subparagraph to include marriage and family therapy experience in low income and multicultural mental health settings.

(vi) In addition to the 150 hours required in clause (ii), 75 hours of either of the following, or a combination thereof:

(I) Client centered advocacy, as defined in Section 4980.03.

(II) Face-to-face experience counseling individuals, couples, families, or groups.

(2) Instruction in all of the following:

(A) Diagnosis, assessment, prognosis, treatment planning, and treatment of mental disorders, including severe mental disorders, evidence-based practices, psychological testing, psychopharmacology, and promising mental health practices that are evaluated in peer-reviewed literature.

(B) Developmental issues from infancy to old age, including instruction in all of the following areas:

(i) The effects of developmental issues on individuals, couples, and family relationships.

(ii) The psychological, psychotherapeutic, and health implications of developmental issues and their effects.

(iii) Aging and its biological, social, cognitive, and psychological aspects. This coursework shall include instruction on the assessment and reporting of, as well as treatment related to, elder and dependent adult abuse and neglect.

(iv) A variety of cultural understandings of human development.

(v) The understanding of human behavior within the social context of socioeconomic status and other contextual issues affecting social position.

(vi) The understanding of human behavior within the social context of a representative variety of the cultures found within California.

(vii) The understanding of the impact that personal and social insecurity, social stress, low educational levels, inadequate housing, and malnutrition have on human development.

(C) The broad range of matters and life events that may arise within marriage and family relationships and within a variety of California cultures, including instruction in all of the following:

(i) A minimum of seven contact hours of training or coursework in child abuse assessment and reporting as specified in Section 28, and any regulations promulgated thereunder.

(ii) Spousal or partner abuse assessment, detection, intervention strategies, and same gender abuse dynamics.

(iii) Cultural factors relevant to abuse of partners and family members.

(iv) Childbirth, child rearing, parenting, and stepparenting.

(v) Marriage, divorce, and blended families.

(vi) Long-term care.

(vii) End-of-life and grief.

(viii) Poverty and deprivation.

(ix) Financial and social stress.

(x) Effects of trauma.

(xi) The psychological, psychotherapeutic, community, and health implications of the matters and life events described in clauses (i) to (x), inclusive.

(D) Cultural competency and sensitivity, including a familiarity with the racial, cultural, linguistic, and ethnic backgrounds of persons living in California.

(E) Multicultural development and cross-cultural interaction, including experiences of race, ethnicity, class, spirituality, sexual orientation, gender, and disability, and their incorporation into the psychotherapeutic process.

(F) The effects of socioeconomic status on treatment and available resources.

(G) Resilience, including the personal and community qualities that enable persons to cope with adversity, trauma, tragedy, threats, or other stresses.

(H) Human sexuality, including the study of physiological, psychological, and social cultural variables associated with sexual behavior and gender identity, and the assessment and treatment of psychosexual dysfunction.

(I) Substance use disorders, co-occurring disorders, and addiction, including, but not limited to, instruction in all of the following:

(i) The definition of substance use disorders, co-occurring disorders, and addiction. For purposes of this subparagraph, "co-occurring disorders" means a mental illness and substance abuse diagnosis occurring simultaneously in an individual.

(ii) Medical aspects of substance use disorders and co-occurring disorders.

(iii) The effects of psychoactive drug use.

(iv) Current theories of the etiology of substance abuse and addiction.

(v) The role of persons and systems that support or compound substance abuse and addiction.

(vi) Major approaches to identification, evaluation, and treatment of substance use disorders, co-occurring disorders, and addiction, including, but not limited to, best practices.

(vii) Legal aspects of substance abuse.

(viii) Populations at risk with regard to substance use disorders and co-occurring disorders.

(ix) Community resources offering screening, assessment, treatment, and follow up for the affected person and family.

(x) Recognition of substance use disorders, co-occurring disorders, and addiction, and appropriate referral.

(xi) The prevention of substance use disorders and addiction.

(J) California law and professional ethics for marriage and family therapists, including instruction in all of the following areas of study:

(i) Contemporary professional ethics and statutory, regulatory, and decisional laws that delineate the scope of practice of marriage and family therapy.

(ii) The therapeutic, clinical, and practical considerations involved in the legal and ethical practice of marriage and family therapy, including, but not limited to, family law.

(iii) The current legal patterns and trends in the mental health professions.

(iv) The psychotherapist-patient privilege, confidentiality, the patient dangerous to self or others, and the treatment of minors with and without parental consent.

(v) A recognition and exploration of the relationship between a practitioner's sense of self and human values and the practitioner's professional behavior and ethics.

(vi) The application of legal and ethical standards in different types of work settings.

(vii) Licensing law and licensing process.

(e) The degree described in subdivision (b) shall, in addition to meeting the requirements of subdivision (d), include instruction in case management, systems of care for the severely mentally ill, public and private services and supports available for the severely mentally ill, community resources for persons with mental illness and for victims of abuse, disaster and trauma response, advocacy for the severely mentally ill, and collaborative treatment. This instruction may be provided either in credit level coursework or through extension programs offered by the degree-granting institution.

(f) The changes made to law by this section are intended to improve the educational qualifications for licensure in order to better prepare future licentiates for practice, and are not intended to expand or restrict the scope of practice for marriage and family therapists. *(Added by Stats.2009, c. 26 (S.B.33), § 5. Amended by Stats.2011, c. 350 (S.B.943), § 26; Stats.2011, c. 384 (S.B.363), § 3.5; Stats.2013, c. 473 (S.B.821), § 21; Stats.2014, c. 316 (S.B.1466), § 16, eff. Jan. 1, 2015; Stats.2016, c. 489 (S.B.1478), § 29, eff. Jan. 1, 2017; Stats.2019, c. 456 (S.B.786), § 63, eff. Jan. 1, 2020; Stats.2021, c. 647 (S.B.801), § 24, eff. Jan. 1, 2022.)*

Cross References

Board defined for purposes of this Chapter, see Business and Professions Code §§ 4980.03, 4990.02.

Health facilities, licenses and permits, requirements for issuance, see Health and Safety Code § 1277.

Practice of marriage and family therapy, application of principles and methods, see Business and Professions Code § 4980.02.

Psychotherapist defined, see Evidence Code § 1010.

§ 4980.37. Degree required by specified applicants; degree program requirements

(a) This section shall apply to applicants for licensure or registration who began graduate study before August 1, 2012, and completed that study on or before December 31, 2018. Those applicants may alternatively qualify under paragraph (2) of subdivision (a) of Section 4980.36.

(b) To qualify for a license or registration, applicants shall possess a doctoral or master's degree in marriage, family, and child counseling, marriage and family therapy, couple and family therapy, psychology, clinical psychology, counseling psychology, or either counseling or clinical mental health counseling with an emphasis in either marriage, family, and child counseling or marriage and family therapy. The degree shall be obtained from a school, college, or university accredited by a regional or national institutional accrediting agency that is recognized by the United States Department of Education or approved by the Bureau for Private Postsecondary Education. The board has the authority to make the final determination as to whether a degree meets all requirements, including, but not limited to, course requirements, regardless of accreditation or approval. In order to qualify for licensure pursuant to this section, a doctoral or master's degree program shall be a single, integrated program primarily designed to train marriage and family therapists and shall contain no less than 48 semester units or 72 quarter units of instruction. This instruction shall include no less than 12 semester units or 18 quarter units of coursework in the areas of marriage, family, and child counseling, and marital and family systems approaches to treatment. The coursework shall include all of the following areas:

(1) The salient theories of a variety of psychotherapeutic orientations directly related to marriage and family therapy, and marital and family systems approaches to treatment.

(2) Theories of marriage and family therapy and how they can be utilized in order to intervene therapeutically with couples, families, adults, children, and groups.

(3) Developmental issues and life events from infancy to old age and their effect on individuals, couples, and family relationships. This may include coursework that focuses on specific family life events and the psychological, psychotherapeutic, and health implications that arise within couples and families, including, but not limited to, childbirth, child rearing, childhood, adolescence, adulthood, marriage, divorce, blended families, stepparenting, abuse and neglect of older and dependent adults, and geropsychology.

(4) A variety of approaches to the treatment of children.

The board shall, by regulation, set forth the subjects of instruction required in this subdivision.

(c)(1) In addition to the 12 semester or 18 quarter units of coursework specified in subdivision (b), the doctoral or master's degree program shall contain not less than six semester units or nine quarter units of supervised practicum in applied psychotherapeutic technique, assessments, diagnosis, prognosis, treatment planning, and treatment of premarital, couple, family, and child relationships, including dysfunctions, healthy functioning, health promotion, and illness prevention, in a supervised clinical placement that provides supervised fieldwork experience within the scope of practice of a marriage and family therapist.

(2) For applicants who enrolled in a degree program on or after January 1, 1995, the practicum shall include a minimum of 150 hours of face-to-face experience counseling individuals, couples, families, or groups.

(3) The practicum hours shall be considered as part of the 48 semester or 72 quarter unit requirement.

(d) As an alternative to meeting the qualifications specified in subdivision (b), the board shall accept as equivalent degrees those master's or doctoral degrees granted by educational institutions whose degree program is approved by the Commission on Accreditation for Marriage and Family Therapy Education.

(e) In order to provide an integrated course of study and appropriate professional training, while allowing for innovation and individuality in the education of marriage and family therapists, a degree program that meets the educational qualifications for licensure or registration under this section shall do all of the following:

(1) Provide an integrated course of study that trains students generally in the diagnosis, assessment, prognosis, treatment planning, and treatment of mental disorders.

(2) Prepare students to be familiar with the broad range of matters that may arise within marriage and family relationships.

(3) Train students specifically in the application of marriage and family relationship counseling principles and methods.

(4) Encourage students to develop those personal qualities that are intimately related to the counseling situation such as integrity, sensitivity, flexibility, insight, compassion, and personal presence.

(5) Teach students a variety of effective psychotherapeutic techniques and modalities that may be utilized to improve, restore, or maintain healthy individual, couple, and family relationships.

(6) Permit an emphasis or specialization that may address any one or more of the unique and complex array of human problems, symptoms, and needs of Californians served by marriage and family therapists.

(7) Prepare students to be familiar with cross-cultural mores and values, including a familiarity with the wide range of racial and ethnic backgrounds common among California's population, including, but not limited to, Blacks, Hispanics, Asians, and Native Americans.

(f) Educational institutions are encouraged to design the practicum required by this section to include marriage and family therapy experience in low income and multicultural mental health settings. *(Added by Stats.1986, c. 1365, § 4. Amended by Stats.1993, c. 1054 (A.B.1885), § 4; Stats.2002, c. 1013 (S.B.2026), § 19; Stats.2009, c. 26 (S.B.33), § 6; Stats.2010, c. 552 (A.B.2435), § 4; Stats.2011, c. 350 (S.B.943), § 27; Stats.2014, c. 316 (S.B.1466), § 17, eff. Jan. 1, 2015; Stats.2016, c. 489 (S.B.1478), § 30, eff. Jan, 1, 2017; Stats.2018, c. 703 (S.B.1491), § 29, eff. Jan. 1, 2019; Stats.2019, c. 456 (S.B.786), § 64, eff. Jan. 1, 2020; Stats.2021, c. 647 (S.B.801), § 25, eff. Jan. 1, 2022.)*

Cross References

Applicant defined for purposes of this Chapter, see Business and Professions Code § 4980.03.

Board defined for purposes of this Chapter, see Business and Professions Code §§ 4980.03, 4990.02.

Experience defined for purposes of this Chapter, see Business and Professions Code § 4980.03.

Health facilities, licenses and permits, requirements for issuance, see Health and Safety Code § 1277.

Practice of marriage and family therapy, application of principles and methods, see Business and Professions Code § 4980.02.

Psychotherapist defined, see Evidence Code § 1010.

§ 4980.38. Notification to students of design of degree program; certification of fulfillment of requirements

(a) Each educational institution preparing applicants to qualify for registration or licensure shall notify each of its students by means of its public documents or otherwise in writing that its degree program is designed to meet the requirements of Section 4980.36 or 4980.37, and shall certify to the board that it has so notified its students.

(b) An applicant for registration or licensure shall submit to the board a certification by the applicant's educational institution that the institution's required curriculum for graduation and any associated coursework completed by the applicant does one of the following:

(1) Meets all of the requirements set forth in Section 4980.36.

(2) Meets all of the requirements set forth in Section 4980.37 and paragraphs (4) and (5) of subdivision (a) of Section 4980.41. *(Added by Stats.1986, c. 1365, § 4. Amended by Stats.1987, c. 738, § 1; Stats.1993, c. 1054 (A.B.1885), § 5; Stats.2001, c. 435 (S.B.349), § 13; Stats.2002, c. 1013 (S.B.2026), § 20; Stats.2007, c. 588 (S.B.1048), § 57; Stats.2009, c. 26 (S.B.33), § 7.)*

Cross References

Board defined for purposes of this Chapter, see Business and Professions Code §§ 4980.03, 4990.02.

Board defined for purposes of this Code, see Business and Professions Code § 22.

§ 4980.39. Graduate study coursework in aging and long-term care; assessment, reporting, and treatment of elder and dependent adult abuse and neglect; program contents; minimum contact hours

(a) An applicant for licensure whose education qualifies him or her under Section 4980.37 shall complete, as a condition of licensure, a minimum of 10 contact hours of coursework in aging and long-term care, which may include, but is not limited to, the biological, social, and psychological aspects of aging. On and after January 1, 2012, this coursework shall include instruction on the assessment and reporting of, as well as treatment related to, elder and dependent adult abuse and neglect.

(b) Coursework taken in fulfillment of other educational requirements for licensure pursuant to this chapter, or in a separate course

§ 4980.39

of study, may, at the discretion of the board, fulfill the requirements of this section.

(c) In order to satisfy the coursework requirement of this section, the applicant shall submit to the board a certification from the chief academic officer of the educational institution from which the applicant graduated stating that the coursework required by this section is included within the institution's required curriculum for graduation, or within the coursework, that was completed by the applicant.

(d) The board shall not issue a license to the applicant until the applicant has met the requirements of this section. *(Added by Stats.2002, c. 541 (S.B.953), § 6. Amended by Stats.2009, c. 26 (S.B.33), § 8; Stats.2010, c. 552 (A.B.2435), § 5; Stats.2018, c. 703 (S.B.1491), § 30, eff. Jan. 1, 2019.)*

Cross References

Board defined for purposes of this Chapter, see Business and Professions Code §§ 4980.03, 4990.02.

Board defined for purposes of this Code, see Business and Professions Code § 22.

Clinical social workers, coursework in aging and long-term care, minimum number of hours required, see Business and Professions Code §§ 4996.25, 4996.26.

Gerontology and geriatric training for the healing arts, legislative intent concerning subject, see Business and Professions Code § 860.

Primary education model curriculum for lifelong health, aging, and financial preparedness, see Education Code § 51280 et seq.

Psychologists, coursework in aging and long-term care, minimum number of hours required, see Business and Professions Code §§ 2915.5, 2915.7.

Standards and guidelines for a curriculum in gerontology and geriatrics in higher education, see Education Code § 66085.

§ 4980.395. Applicants for marriage and family therapy licensure; completion of training or coursework; telehealth requirement

(a) On or after July 1, 2023, an applicant for licensure as a marriage and family therapist shall show, as part of the application, that they have completed a minimum of three hours of training or coursework in the provision of mental health services via telehealth, which shall include law and ethics related to telehealth. This requirement shall be met in one of the following ways:

(1) Obtained as part of their qualifying graduate degree program. To satisfy this requirement, the applicant shall submit to the board a written certification from the registrar or training director of the educational institution or program from which the applicant graduated stating that the coursework required by this section is included within the institution's curriculum required for graduation at the time the applicant graduated, or within the coursework that was completed by the applicant.

(2) Obtained by completing a continuing education course that meets the requirements of Section 4980.54. To satisfy this requirement, the applicant shall submit to the board a certification of completion.

(b) As a one-time requirement, a licensee before the time of their first renewal after July 1, 2023, or an applicant for reactivation or reinstatement to an active license status on or after July 1, 2023, shall have completed a minimum of three hours of training or coursework in the provision of mental health services via telehealth, which shall include law and ethics related to telehealth, using one of the methods specified in subdivision (a).

(c) Proof of compliance with subdivision (b) shall be certified under penalty of perjury that they are in compliance with this section and shall be retained for submission to the board upon request. *(Added by Stats.2022, c. 520 (A.B.1759), § 2, eff. Jan. 1, 2023.)*

§ 4980.396. Applicants for marriage and family therapy licensure; required coursework; applied experience; minimum number of hours; suicide risk assessment and intervention; proof of compliance

(a) On or after January 1, 2021, an applicant for licensure as a marriage and family therapist shall show, as part of the application, that * * * they have completed a minimum of six hours of coursework or applied experience under supervision in suicide risk assessment and intervention. This requirement shall be met in one of the following ways:

(1) Obtained as part of * * * their qualifying graduate degree program. To satisfy this requirement, the applicant shall submit to the board a written certification from the registrar or training director of the educational institution or program from which the applicant graduated stating that the coursework required by this section is included within the institution's curriculum required for graduation at the time the applicant graduated, or within the coursework that was completed by the applicant.

(2) Obtained as part of * * * their applied experience. Applied experience can be met in any of the following settings: practicum or associateship that meets the requirement of this chapter, formal postdoctoral placement that meets the requirements of Section 2911, or other qualifying supervised experience. To satisfy this requirement, the applicant shall submit to the board a written certification from the director of training for the program or primary supervisor where the qualifying experience has occurred stating that the training required by this section is included within the applied experience.

(3) By taking a continuing education course that meets the requirements of Section 4980.54. To satisfy this requirement, the applicant shall submit to the board a certification of completion.

(b) As a one-time requirement, a licensee prior to the time of * * * their first renewal after January 1, 2021, or an applicant for reactivation or reinstatement to an active license status on or after January 1, 2021, shall have completed a minimum of six hours of coursework or applied experience under supervision in suicide risk assessment and intervention, using one of the methods specified in subdivision (a).

* * * Proof of compliance with this section shall be certified under penalty of perjury that * * * they are in compliance with this section and shall be retained for submission to the board upon request. *(Added by Stats.2018, c. 527 (A.B.1436), § 1, eff. Jan. 1, 2019. Amended by Stats.2022, c. 511 (S.B.1495), § 28, eff. Jan. 1, 2023.)*

§ 4980.397. Registrants or applicants for licensure; required examinations; time for California law and ethics examination; eligibility for clinical examination

(a) A registrant or an applicant for licensure as a marriage and family therapist shall pass the following two examinations as prescribed by the board:

(1) A California law and ethics examination.

(2) A clinical examination.

(b) Upon registration with the board, an associate marriage and family therapist shall, within the first year of registration, take an examination on California law and ethics.

(c) A registrant or an applicant for licensure may take the clinical examination only upon meeting all of the following requirements:

(1) Completion of all required supervised work experience.

(2) Completion of all education requirements.

(3) Passage of the California law and ethics examination. *(Added by Stats.2011, c. 387 (S.B.704), § 2, operative Jan. 1, 2013. Amended by Stats.2012, c. 799 (S.B.1575), § 26, operative Jan. 1, 2014; Stats.2013, c. 473 (S.B.821), § 22, operative Jan. 1, 2016; Stats.2018, c. 743 (A.B.93), § 6, eff. Jan. 1, 2019.)*

§ 4980.398. Passing scores required on specified examinations

(a) Each applicant who had previously taken and passed the standard written examination but had not passed the clinical vignette examination shall also obtain a passing score on the clinical examination in order to be eligible for licensure.

(b) An applicant who had previously failed to obtain a passing score on the standard written examination shall obtain a passing score on the California law and ethics examination and the clinical examination.

(c) An applicant who had obtained eligibility for the standard written examination shall take the California law and ethics examination and the clinical examination.

(d) This section shall become operative on January 1, 2016. (Added by Stats.2011, c. 387 (S.B.704), § 3, operative Jan. 1, 2013. Amended by Stats.2012, c. 799 (S.B.1575), § 27, operative Jan. 1, 2014; Stats.2013, c. 473 (S.B.821), § 23, operative Jan. 1, 2016.)

§ 4980.399. California law and ethics examination; participation prior to registration renewal; retaking examination; issuance of subsequent registration number; continuing education requirements

(a) Except as provided in subdivision (a) of Section 4980.398, each applicant and registrant shall obtain a passing score on a board-administered California law and ethics examination in order to qualify for licensure.

(b) A registrant shall participate in a board-administered California law and ethics examination * * * before their registration renewal.

(c) If an applicant fails the California law and ethics examination, * * * they may retake the examination, upon payment of the required fees, without further application * * *.

(d) The board shall not issue a subsequent registration number unless the applicant has passed the California law and ethics examination.

* * * (e) A registrant * * * shall complete a minimum of three hours of continuing education on the subject of California law and ethics * * * during each renewal period * * * to be eligible to * * * renew their registration, regardless of whether they have passed the California law and ethics examination. * * * The coursework shall be * * * obtained from a board-accepted provider of continuing education * * *, as specified * * * in Section 4980.54. (Added by Stats.2011, c. 387 (S.B.704), § 4, operative Jan. 1, 2013. Amended by Stats.2012, c. 799 (S.B.1575), § 28, operative Jan. 1, 2014; Stats.2013, c. 473 (S.B.821), § 24, operative Jan. 1, 2016; Stats.2014, c. 316 (S.B.1466), § 18, eff. Jan. 1, 2015, operative Jan. 1, 2016; Stats.2015, c. 426 (S.B.800), § 38, eff. Jan. 1, 2016; Stats.2018, c. 743 (A.B.93), § 7, eff. Jan. 1, 2019; Stats.2022, c. 520 (A.B.1759), § 3, eff. Jan. 1, 2023.)

§ 4980.40. Qualifications

An applicant for licensure shall satisfy all of the following qualifications:

(a) Meet the educational requirements of Section 4980.36 or both Sections 4980.37 and 4980.41, as applicable.

(b) Be at least 18 years of age.

(c) Have at least two years of supervised experience as specified in this chapter and its corresponding regulations.

(d) Successfully pass a California law and ethics examination and a clinical examination. An applicant who has successfully passed a previously administered written examination may be subsequently required to take and pass another written examination.

(e) Not be subject to denial of licensure under Section 480. The board shall not issue a registration or license to any person who has been convicted of a crime in this or another state or in a territory of the United States that involves sexual abuse of children or who is required to register pursuant to Section 290 of the Penal Code or the equivalent in another state or territory, in accordance with Section 480. (Added by Stats.2011, c. 387 (S.B.704), § 6, operative Jan. 1, 2013. Amended by Stats.2012, c. 799 (S.B.1575), § 30, operative Jan. 1, 2014; Stats.2013, c. 473 (S.B.821), § 26, operative Jan. 1, 2016; Stats.2018, c. 743 (A.B.93), § 8, eff. Jan. 1, 2019; Stats.2021, c. 647 (S.B.801), § 26, eff. Jan. 1, 2022.)

Cross References

Board defined for purposes of this Chapter, see Business and Professions Code §§ 4980.03, 4990.02.

Board defined for purposes of this Code, see Business and Professions Code § 22.

Consent by minor to diagnosis or treatment of drug and alcohol abuse, professional person defined to include marriage and family therapist registered interns, see Family Code § 6929.

Consent to mental health treatment or counseling services by minors age 12 or older determined to meet maturity requirements, maturity determination made by professional person including marriage and family therapist registered intern working under supervision of licensed professional, see Health and Safety Code § 124260.

Criminal conviction, suspension or revocation of license, board authority, see Business and Professions Code § 490.

Health facilities, licenses and permits, requirements for issuance, see Health and Safety Code § 1277.

Medical treatment, consent by minor, mental health treatment or counseling services, see Family Code § 6924.

Patient access to health records, representative of minor, mental health records, see Health and Safety Code § 123115.

Practicing without license, registration, or certificate, offense punishable as a misdemeanor, see Business and Professions Code § 16240.

Psychotherapist-patient privilege, see Evidence Code § 1010.

Training for child abuse assessment and reporting, licensing prerequisites, see Business and Professions Code § 28.

Research References

Forms

West's California Code Forms, Business & Professions § 4980.40 Comment 1, Marriage and Family Therapist Intern.

§ 4980.41. Eligibility to sit for licensing examinations; coursework or training

(a) An applicant for licensure whose education qualifies him or her under Section 4980.37 shall complete the following coursework or training in order to be eligible to sit for the licensing examinations as specified in subdivision (d) of Section 4980.40:

(1) A two semester or three quarter unit course in California law and professional ethics for marriage and family therapists, which shall include, but not be limited to, the following areas of study:

(A) Contemporary professional ethics and statutory, regulatory, and decisional laws that delineate the profession's scope of practice.

(B) The therapeutic, clinical, and practical considerations involved in the legal and ethical practice of marriage and family therapy, including family law.

(C) The current legal patterns and trends in the mental health profession.

(D) The psychotherapist-patient privilege, confidentiality, the patient dangerous to self or others, and the treatment of minors with and without parental consent.

(E) A recognition and exploration of the relationship between a practitioner's sense of self and human values and his or her professional behavior and ethics.

This course may be considered as part of the 48 semester or 72 quarter unit requirements contained in Section 4980.37.

(2) A minimum of seven contact hours of training or coursework in child abuse assessment and reporting as specified in Section 28 and any regulations promulgated thereunder.

§ 4980.41

(3) A minimum of 10 contact hours of training or coursework in human sexuality as specified in Section 25, and any regulations promulgated thereunder. When coursework in a master's or doctor's degree program is acquired to satisfy this requirement, it shall be considered as part of the 48 semester or 72 quarter unit requirement contained in Section 4980.37.

(4) For persons who began graduate study on or after January 1, 1986, a master's or doctor's degree qualifying for licensure shall include specific instruction in alcoholism and other chemical substance dependency as specified by regulation. When coursework in a master's or doctor's degree program is acquired to satisfy this requirement, it shall be considered as part of the 48 semester or 72 quarter unit requirement contained in Section 4980.37. Coursework required under this paragraph may be satisfactory if taken either in fulfillment of other educational requirements for licensure or in a separate course. The applicant may satisfy this requirement by successfully completing this coursework from a master's or doctoral degree program at an accredited or approved institution, as described in subdivision (b) of Section 4980.37, or from a board-accepted provider of continuing education, as described in Section 4980.54.

(5) For persons who began graduate study during the period commencing on January 1, 1995, and ending on December 31, 2003, a master's or doctor's degree qualifying for licensure shall include coursework in spousal or partner abuse assessment, detection, and intervention. For persons who began graduate study on or after January 1, 2004, a master's or doctor's degree qualifying for licensure shall include a minimum of 15 contact hours of coursework in spousal or partner abuse assessment, detection, and intervention strategies, including knowledge of community resources, cultural factors, and same gender abuse dynamics. Coursework required under this paragraph may be satisfactory if taken either in fulfillment of other educational requirements for licensure or in a separate course. The applicant may satisfy this requirement by successfully completing this coursework from a master's or doctoral degree program at an accredited or approved institution, as described in subdivision (b) of Section 4980.37, or from a board-accepted provider of continuing education, as described in Section 4980.54.

(6) For persons who began graduate study on or after January 1, 2001, an applicant shall complete a minimum of a two semester or three quarter unit survey course in psychological testing. When coursework in a master's or doctor's degree program is acquired to satisfy this requirement, it may be considered as part of the 48 semester or 72 quarter unit requirement of Section 4980.37.

(7) For persons who began graduate study on or after January 1, 2001, an applicant shall complete a minimum of a two semester or three quarter unit survey course in psychopharmacology. When coursework in a master's or doctor's degree program is acquired to satisfy this requirement, it may be considered as part of the 48 semester or 72 quarter unit requirement of Section 4980.37.

(b) The requirements added by paragraphs (6) and (7) of subdivision (a) are intended to improve the educational qualifications for licensure in order to better prepare future licentiates for practice and are not intended in any way to expand or restrict the scope of practice for licensed marriage and family therapists. (Added by Stats.1986, c. 1365, § 4. Amended by Stats.1987, c. 738, § 3; Stats.1993, c. 1234 (A.B.890), § 9; Stats.1999, c. 406 (A.B.253), § 1; Stats.2001, c. 435 (S.B.349), § 14; Stats.2002, c. 481 (S.B.564), § 4; Stats.2003, c. 874 (S.B.363), § 8; Stats.2009, c. 26 (S.B.33), § 10; Stats.2013, c. 376 (A.B.428), § 1; Stats.2014, c. 316 (S.B.1466), § 19, eff. Jan. 1, 2015; Stats.2018, c. 703 (S.B.1491), § 31, eff. Jan. 1, 2019.)

Cross References

Board defined for purposes of this Chapter, see Business and Professions Code §§ 4980.03, 4990.02.
Board defined for purposes of this Code, see Business and Professions Code § 22.

Criminal conviction, suspension or revocation of license, board authority, see Business and Professions Code § 490.
Licentiate defined for purposes of this Code, see Business and Professions Code § 23.8.
Practice of marriage and family therapy, application of principles and methods, see Business and Professions Code § 4980.02.
Practicing without license, registration, or certificate, offense punishable as a misdemeanor, see Business and Professions Code § 16240.
Reciprocity, equivalent requirements, see Business and Professions Code § 4980.80.

§ 4980.42. Trainees' services

(a) Trainees performing services in any work setting specified in Section 4980.43.3 may perform those activities and services as a trainee, provided that the activities and services constitute part of the trainee's supervised course of study and that the person is designated by the title "trainee."

(b) Trainees subject to Section 4980.37 may gain hours of experience and counsel clients outside of the required practicum. This subdivision shall apply to hours of experience gained and client counseling provided on and after January 1, 2012.

(c) Trainees subject to Section 4980.36 may gain hours of experience outside of the required practicum but must be enrolled in a practicum course to counsel clients. Trainees subject to Section 4980.36 may counsel clients while not enrolled in a practicum course if the period of lapsed enrollment is less than 90 calendar days, and if that period is immediately preceded by enrollment in a practicum course and immediately followed by enrollment in a practicum course or completion of the degree program.

(d) All hours of experience gained pursuant to subdivisions (b) and (c) shall be subject to the other requirements of this chapter.

(e) All hours of experience gained as a trainee shall be coordinated between the school and the site where the hours are being accrued. The school shall approve each site and shall have a written agreement with each site that details each party's responsibilities, including the methods by which supervision shall be provided. The agreement shall provide for regular progress reports and evaluations of the student's performance at the site. If an applicant has gained hours of experience while enrolled in an institution other than the one that confers the qualifying degree, it shall be the applicant's responsibility to provide to the board satisfactory evidence that those hours of trainee experience were gained in compliance with this section. (Added by Stats.1993, c. 1054 (A.B.1885), § 8. Amended by Stats.2011, c. 350 (S.B.943), § 29; Stats.2011, c. 384 (S.B.363), § 4.5; Stats.2012, c. 50 (S.B.632), § 1, eff. July 3, 2012; Stats.2015, c. 262 (S.B.620), § 2, eff. Jan. 1, 2016; Stats.2018, c. 743 (A.B.93), § 9, eff. Jan. 1, 2019.)

Cross References

Board-defined for purposes of this Chapter, see Business and Professions Code §§ 4980.03, 4990.02.
Board defined for purposes of this Code, see Business and Professions Code § 22.
Criminal conviction, suspension or revocation of license, board authority, see Business and Professions Code § 490.
Practicing without license, registration, or certificate, offense punishable as a misdemeanor, see Business and Professions Code § 16240.
Trainees, see Business and Professions Code § 4980.03.

Research References

Forms

West's California Code Forms, Business & Professions § 4980.40 Comment 1, Marriage and Family Therapist Intern.

§ 4980.43. Postdegree hours of supervised experience; requirements

(a) Except as provided in subdivision (b), all applicants shall have an active associate registration with the board in order to gain postdegree hours of supervised experience.

(b)(1) Postdegree hours of experience gained before the issuance of an associate registration shall be credited toward licensure if all of the following apply:

(A) The registration applicant applies for the associate registration and the board receives the application within 90 days of the granting of the qualifying master's degree or doctoral degree.

(B) For applicants completing graduate study on or after January 1, 2020, the experience is obtained at a workplace that, prior to the registration applicant gaining supervised experience hours, requires completed Live Scan fingerprinting. The applicant shall provide the board with a copy of that completed State of California "Request for Live Scan Service" form with the application for licensure.

(C) The board subsequently grants the associate registration.

(2) The applicant shall not be employed or volunteer in a private practice or a professional corporation until the applicant has been issued an associate registration by the board.

(c) Supervised experience that is obtained for purposes of qualifying for licensure shall be related to the practice of marriage and family therapy and comply with the following:

(1) A minimum of 3,000 hours completed during a period of at least 104 weeks.

(2) A maximum of 40 hours in any seven consecutive days.

(3) A minimum of 1,700 hours obtained after the qualifying master's or doctoral degree was awarded.

(4) A maximum of 1,300 hours obtained prior to the award date of the qualifying master's or doctoral degree.

(5) A maximum of 750 hours of counseling and direct supervisor contact prior to the award date of the qualifying master's or doctoral degree.

(6) Hours of experience shall not be gained prior to completing either 12 semester units or 18 quarter units of graduate instruction.

(7) Hours of experience shall not have been gained more than six years prior to the date the application for licensure was received by the board, except that up to 500 hours of clinical experience gained in the supervised practicum required by subdivision (c) of Section 4980.37 and subparagraph (B) of paragraph (1) of subdivision (d) of Section 4980.36 shall be exempt from this six-year requirement.

(8) A minimum of 1,750 hours of direct clinical counseling with individuals, groups, couples, or families, that includes not less than 500 total hours of experience in diagnosing and treating couples, families, and children.

(9) A maximum of 1,200 hours gained under the supervision of a licensed educational psychologist providing educationally related mental health services that are consistent with the scope of practice of an educational psychologist, as specified in Section 4989.14.

(10) A maximum of 1,250 hours of nonclinical practice, consisting of direct supervisor contact, administering and evaluating psychological tests, writing clinical reports, writing progress or process notes, client-centered advocacy, and workshops, seminars, training sessions, or conferences directly related to marriage and family therapy that have been approved by the applicant's supervisor.

(11) It is anticipated and encouraged that hours of experience will include working with elders and dependent adults who have physical or mental limitations that restrict their ability to carry out normal activities or protect their rights.

This subdivision shall only apply to hours gained on and after January 1, 2010.

(d) An individual who submits an application for licensure between January 1, 2016, and December 31, 2020, may alternatively qualify under the experience requirements of this section that were in place on January 1, 2015. *(Added by Stats.1986, c. 1365, § 4. Amended by Stats.1987, c. 738, § 5; Stats.1989, c. 772, § 1; Stats. 1990, c. 1086 (S.B.2214), § 2; Stats.1992, c. 890 (S.B.1394), § 2;* Stats.1993, c. 1054 (A.B.1885), § 9; Stats.1994, c. 116 (S.B.133), § 1; Stats.1996, c. 739 (A.B.3073), § 1; Stats.1997, c. 196 (S.B.650), § 1; Stats.2000, c. 836 (S.B.1554), § 30; Stats.2002, c. 1013 (S.B.2026), § 22; Stats.2003, c. 607 (S.B.1077), § 14; Stats.2004, c. 204 (A.B. 2552), § 3; Stats.2005, c. 658 (S.B.229), § 18; Stats.2007, c. 586 (A.B.234), § 2; Stats.2009, c. 26 (S.B.33), § 11; Stats.2010, c. 552 (A.B.2435), § 6; Stats.2010, c. 653 (S.B.1489), § 38.5; Stats.2011, c. 384 (S.B.363), § 5; Stats.2012, c. 799 (S.B.1575), § 31; Stats.2013, c. 473 (S.B.821), § 27; Stats.2014, c. 316 (S.B.1466), § 20, eff. Jan. 1, 2015; Stats.2014, c. 435 (S.B.1012), § 1, eff. Jan. 1, 2015; Stats.2015, c. 50 (A.B.250), § 2, eff. Jan. 1, 2016; Stats.2015, c. 262 (S.B.620), § 3.5, eff. Jan. 1, 2016; Stats.2015, c. 426 (S.B.800), § 39, eff. Jan. 1, 2016; Stats.2016, c. 489 (S.B.1478), § 32, eff. Jan. 1, 2017; Stats.2018, c. 743 (A.B.93), § 10, eff. Jan. 1, 2019; Stats.2019, c. 321 (A.B.1651), § 2, eff. Jan. 1, 2020; Stats.2021, c. 747 (A.B.690), § 4, eff. Jan. 1, 2022.)

Cross References

Board defined for purposes of this Chapter, see Business and Professions Code §§ 4980.03, 4990.02.

Board defined for purposes of this Code, see Business and Professions Code § 22.

Consent by minor to diagnosis or treatment of drug and alcohol abuse, professional person defined to include marriage and family therapist registered interns, see Family Code § 6929.

Interns and trainees, see Business and Professions Code § 4980.03.

Licenses and permits, requirements for issuance, exemptions, waivers, see Health and Safety Code § 1277.

Professional licensure of personnel, exemption, waiver, see Welfare and Institutions Code § 5751.2.

Research References

Forms

West's California Code Forms, Business & Professions § 4980.03 Form 1, Marriage and Family Therapist Intern Registration Application Packet.

West's California Code Forms, Business & Professions § 4980 Form 1, Application Packet Mft.

§ 4980.43.1. Supervision of trainees, associates, and applicants for licensure

(a) All trainees, associates, and applicants for licensure shall be under the supervision of a supervisor at all times.

(b) As used in this chapter, the term "supervision" means responsibility for, and control of, the quality of mental health and related services provided by the supervisee. Consultation or peer discussion shall not be considered supervision and shall not qualify as supervised experience. Supervision includes, but is not limited to, all of the following:

(1) Ensuring the extent, kind, and quality of counseling performed is consistent with the education, training, and experience of the supervisee.

(2) Monitoring and evaluating the supervisee's assessment, diagnosis, and treatment decisions and providing regular feedback.

(3) Monitoring and evaluating the supervisee's ability to provide services at the site or sites where he or she is practicing and to the particular clientele being served.

(4) Monitoring and addressing clinical dynamics, including, but not limited to, countertransference-, intrapsychic-, interpersonal-, or trauma-related issues that may affect the supervisory or practitioner-patient relationship.

(5) Ensuring the supervisee's compliance with laws and regulations governing the practice of marriage and family therapy.

(6) Reviewing the supervisee's progress notes, process notes, and other patient treatment records, as deemed appropriate by the supervisor.

(7) With the client's written consent, providing direct observation or review of audio or video recordings of the supervisee's counseling

§ 4980.43.1

or therapy, as deemed appropriate by the supervisor. *(Added by Stats.2018, c. 743 (A.B.93), § 11, eff. Jan. 1, 2019.)*

§ 4980.43.2. Direct supervisor contact

Section operative until Jan. 1, 2026. See, also, § 4980.43.2 operative Jan. 1, 2026.

(a) Except for experience gained by attending workshops, seminars, training sessions, or conferences, as described in paragraph (10) of subdivision (c) of Section 4980.43, direct supervisor contact shall occur as follows:

(1) Supervision shall include at least one hour of direct supervisor contact in each week for which experience is credited in each work setting.

(2) A trainee shall receive an average of at least one hour of direct supervisor contact for every five hours of direct clinical counseling performed each week in each setting. For experience gained on or after January 1, 2009, no more than six hours of supervision, whether individual, triadic, or group, shall be credited during any single week.

(3) An associate gaining experience who performs more than 10 hours of direct clinical counseling in a week in any setting shall receive at least one additional hour of direct supervisor contact for that setting. For experience gained on or after January 1, 2009, no more than six hours of supervision, whether individual, triadic, or group, shall be credited during any single week.

(4) Of the 104 weeks of required supervision, 52 weeks shall be individual supervision, triadic supervision, or a combination of both.

(b)(1) For purposes of this chapter, "one hour of direct supervisor contact" means any of the following:

(A) Individual supervision, which means one hour of face-to-face contact between one supervisor and one supervisee.

(B) Triadic supervision, which means one hour of face-to-face contact between one supervisor and two supervisees.

(C) Group supervision, which means two hours of face-to-face contact between one supervisor and no more than eight supervisees. Segments of group supervision may be split into no less than one continuous hour. A supervisor shall ensure that the amount and degree of supervision is appropriate for each supervisee.

(2) For purposes of this subdivision, "face-to-face contact" means in-person contact, contact via two-way, real-time videoconferencing, or some combination of these.

* * * (c) The supervisor shall be responsible for ensuring compliance with federal and state laws relating to confidentiality of patient health information.

(d)(1) Within 60 days of the commencement of supervision, a supervisor shall conduct a meeting with the supervisee during which the supervisor shall assess the appropriateness of allowing the supervisee to receive supervision via two-way, real-time videoconferencing. This assessment of appropriateness shall include, but is not limited to, the abilities of the supervisee, the preferences of both the supervisee and supervisor, and the privacy of the locations of the supervisee and supervisor while supervision is conducted.

(2) The supervisor shall document the results of the assessment made pursuant to paragraph (1), and shall not utilize supervision via two-way, real-time videoconferencing if their assessment finds it is not appropriate.

(e) Direct supervisor contact shall occur within the same week as the hours claimed.

(f) Alternative supervision may be arranged during a supervisor's vacation or sick leave if the alternative supervision meets the requirements of this chapter.

(g) Notwithstanding any other law, once the required number of experience hours are gained, associates and applicants for licensure shall receive a minimum of one hour of direct supervisor contact per week for each practice setting in which direct clinical counseling is performed. Once the required number of experience hours are gained, further supervision for nonclinical practice, as defined in paragraph (10) of subdivision (c) of Section 4980.43, shall be at the supervisor's discretion.

(h) This section shall remain in effect only until January 1, 2026, and as of that date is repealed. *(Added by Stats.2018, c. 743 (A.B.93), § 12, eff. Jan. 1, 2019. Amended by Stats.2021, c. 747 (A.B.690), § 5, eff. Jan. 1, 2022; Stats.2022, c. 204 (A.B.1758), § 1, eff. Aug. 29, 2022.)*

Repeal

For repeal of this section, see its terms.

§ 4980.43.2. Direct supervisor contact

Section operative Jan. 1, 2026. See, also, § 4980.43.2 operative until Jan. 1, 2026.

(a) Except for experience gained by attending workshops, seminars, training sessions, or conferences, as described in paragraph (10) of subdivision (c) of Section 4980.43, direct supervisor contact shall occur as follows:

(1) Supervision shall include at least one hour of direct supervisor contact in each week for which experience is credited in each work setting.

(2) A trainee shall receive an average of at least one hour of direct supervisor contact for every five hours of direct clinical counseling performed each week in each setting. For experience gained on or after January 1, 2009, no more than six hours of supervision, whether individual, triadic, or group, shall be credited during any single week.

(3) An associate gaining experience who performs more than 10 hours of direct clinical counseling in a week in any setting shall receive at least one additional hour of direct supervisor contact for that setting. For experience gained on or after January 1, 2009, no more than six hours of supervision, whether individual, triadic, or group, shall be credited during any single week.

(4) Of the 104 weeks of required supervision, 52 weeks shall be individual supervision, triadic supervision, or a combination of both.

(b) For purposes of this chapter, "one hour of direct supervisor contact" means any of the following:

(1) Individual supervision, which means one hour of face-to-face contact between one supervisor and one supervisee.

(2) Triadic supervision, which means one hour of face-to-face contact between one supervisor and two supervisees.

(3) Group supervision, which means two hours of face-to-face contact between one supervisor and no more than eight supervisees. Segments of group supervision may be split into no less than one continuous hour. A supervisor shall ensure that the amount and degree of supervision is appropriate for each supervisee.

(c) Direct supervisor contact shall occur within the same week as the hours claimed.

(d) Alternative supervision may be arranged during a supervisor's vacation or sick leave if the alternative supervision meets the requirements of this chapter.

(e) Notwithstanding subdivision (b), a supervisee working in an exempt setting described in Section 4980.01 may obtain the required weekly direct supervisor contact via two-way, real-time videoconferencing. The supervisor shall be responsible for ensuring compliance with federal and state laws relating to confidentiality of patient health information.

(f) Notwithstanding any other law, once the required number of experience hours are gained, associates and applicants for licensure shall receive a minimum of one hour of direct supervisor contact per week for each practice setting in which direct clinical counseling is performed. Once the required number of experience hours are gained, further supervision for nonclinical practice, as defined in paragraph (10) of subdivision (c) of Section 4980.43, shall be at the supervisor's discretion.

(g) This section shall become operative on January 1, 2026. *(Added by Stats.2022, c. 204 (A.B.1758), § 2, eff. Aug. 29, 2022, operative Jan. 1, 2026.)*

§ 4980.43.3. Trainee, associate, or applicant for licensure to perform services as employee or volunteer; setting for supervised experience; counseling or psychotherapy for applicants

(a) A trainee, associate, or applicant for licensure shall only perform mental health and related services as an employee or volunteer, and not as an independent contractor. The requirements of this chapter regarding hours of experience and supervision shall apply equally to employees and volunteers. A trainee, associate, or applicant for licensure shall not perform any services or gain any experience within the scope of practice of the profession, as defined in Section 4980.02, as an independent contractor. While an associate may be either a paid employee or a volunteer, employers are encouraged to provide fair remuneration.

(1) If employed, an associate shall provide the board, upon application for licensure, with copies of the W–2 tax forms for each year of experience claimed.

(2) If volunteering, an associate shall provide the board, upon application for licensure, with a letter from the associate's employer verifying the associate's status as a volunteer during the dates the experience was gained.

(b)(1) A trainee shall not perform services in a private practice or a professional corporation. A trainee may be credited with supervised experience completed in a setting that meets all of the following:

(A) Is not a private practice or professional corporation.

(B) Lawfully and regularly provides mental health counseling or psychotherapy.

(C) Provides oversight to ensure that the trainee's work at the setting meets the experience and supervision requirements in this chapter and is within the scope of practice for the profession, as defined in Section 4980.02.

(2) Only experience gained in the position for which the trainee volunteers or is employed shall qualify as supervised experience.

(c)(1) An associate may be credited with supervised experience completed in any setting that meets both of the following:

(A) Lawfully and regularly provides mental health counseling or psychotherapy.

(B) Provides oversight to ensure that the associate's work at the setting meets the experience and supervision requirements in this chapter and is within the scope of practice for the profession, as defined in Section 4980.02.

(2) Only experience gained in the position for which the associate volunteers or is employed shall qualify as supervised experience.

(3) An applicant for registration as an associate shall not be employed or volunteer in a private practice or professional corporation until the applicant has been issued an associate registration by the board.

(d) Any experience obtained under the supervision of a spouse, relative, or domestic partner shall not be credited toward the required hours of supervised experience. Any experience obtained under the supervision of a supervisor with whom the applicant has had or currently has a personal, professional, or business relationship that undermines the authority or effectiveness of the supervision shall not be credited toward the required hours of supervised experience.

(e) A trainee, associate, or applicant for licensure shall not receive any remuneration from patients or clients and shall only be paid by their employer, if an employee.

(f) A trainee, associate, or applicant for licensure shall have no proprietary interest in their employer's business and shall not lease or rent space, pay for furnishings, equipment, or supplies, or in any other way pay for the obligations of their employer.

(g) A trainee, associate, or applicant for licensure who provides voluntary services in any lawful work setting and who only receives reimbursement for expenses actually incurred shall be considered an employee. The board may audit an applicant for licensure who receives reimbursement for expenses and the applicant for licensure shall have the burden of demonstrating that the payment received was for reimbursement of expenses actually incurred.

(h) A trainee, associate, or applicant for licensure who receives a stipend or educational loan repayment from a program designed to encourage demographically underrepresented groups to enter the profession or to improve recruitment and retention in underserved regions or settings shall be considered an employee. The board may audit an applicant who receives a stipend or educational loan repayment and the applicant shall have the burden of demonstrating that the payment received was for the specified purposes.

(i) An associate or a trainee may provide services via telehealth that are in the scope of practice outlined in this chapter.

(j) Each educational institution preparing applicants pursuant to this chapter shall consider requiring, and shall encourage, its students to undergo individual, marital, conjoint, family, or group counseling or psychotherapy, as appropriate. Each supervisor shall consider, advise, and encourage the supervisor's associates and trainees regarding the advisability of undertaking individual, marital, conjoint, family, or group counseling or psychotherapy, as appropriate. Insofar as it is deemed appropriate and is desired by the applicant, educational institutions and supervisors are encouraged to assist the applicant to locate counseling or psychotherapy at a reasonable cost.
(Added by Stats.2018, c. 743 (A.B.93), § 13, eff. Jan. 1, 2019. Amended by Stats.2021, c. 647 (S.B.801), § 27, eff. Jan. 1, 2022; Stats.2021, c. 747 (A.B.690), § 6.5, eff. Jan. 1, 2022.)

Cross References

Disability insurance, mental health and substance use disorder coverage, see Insurance Code § 10144.5.

Mental health and substance use disorder coverage, see Health and Safety Code § 1374.72.

§ 4980.43.4. Location for provision of services by trainee, associate, or applicant for licensure; supervisor requirements; maximum number of supervisees; written oversight agreement

(a) A trainee, associate, or applicant for licensure shall only perform mental health and related services at the places where their employer permits business to be conducted.

(b) An associate who is employed by or is volunteering in a private practice or a professional corporation shall be supervised by an individual who is both of the following:

(1) Is employed by or contracted by the associate's employer or is an owner of the private practice or professional corporation.

(2) Either provides psychotherapeutic services to clients for the associate's employer, or meets both of the following:

(A) The supervisor and the associate's employer have a written contract providing the supervisor the same access to the associate's clinical records provided to employees of that employer.

(B) The associate's clients authorize the release of their clinical records to the supervisor.

(c) Supervisors of supervisees in a nonexempt setting shall not serve as individual or triadic supervisors for more than six supervisees at any time. Supervisees may be registered as associate marriage and family therapists, associate professional clinical counselors, associate clinical social workers, or any combination of those registrations.

(d) A written oversight agreement, as specified by the board by regulation, shall be executed between the supervisor and employer when the supervisor is not employed by the supervisee's employer or is a volunteer. The supervisor shall evaluate the site or sites where the supervisee will be gaining experience to determine that the site or sites comply with the requirements of this chapter. *(Formerly § 4980.45, added by Stats.1986, c. 1365, § 4. Amended by Stats.1987, c. 738, § 7; Stats.1989, c. 772, § 2; Stats.1992, c. 890 (S.B.1394), § 3; Stats.1993, c. 1054 (A.B.1885), § 10; Stats.1994, c. 146 (A.B.3601), § 5; Stats.1999, c. 657 (A.B.1677), § 1; Stats.2001, c. 435 (S.B.349), § 15; Stats.2002, c. 1013 (S.B.2026), § 24; Stats.2007, c. 586 (A.B.234), § 3; Stats.2009, c. 307 (S.B.821), § 49; Stats.2011, c. 350 (S.B.943), § 30. Renumbered § 4980.43.4 and amended by Stats. 2018, c. 743 (A.B.93), § 16, eff. Jan. 1, 2019. Amended by Stats.2019, c. 456 (S.B.786), § 66, eff. Jan. 1, 2020; Stats.2021, c. 747 (A.B.690), § 7, eff. Jan. 1, 2022.)*

Cross References

Board defined for purposes of this Chapter, see Business and Professions Code §§ 4980.03, 4990.02.

Board defined for purposes of this Code, see Business and Professions Code § 22.

Interns, see Business and Professions Code § 4980.03.

§ 4980.43.5. Supervisors to maintain records; audits

The board may audit the records of any supervisor to verify the completion of the supervisor qualifications specified by this chapter and by regulation. A supervisor shall maintain records of completion of the required supervisor qualifications for seven years after termination of the supervision and shall make these records available to the board for auditing purposes upon request. *(Added by Stats.2018, c. 743 (A.B.93), § 14, eff. Jan. 1, 2019.)*

§ 4980.44. Unlicensed associate marriage and family therapists; requirements; notice to clients or patients; advertisements

An associate marriage and family therapist employed under this chapter shall comply with the following requirements:

(a) Inform each client or patient prior to performing any mental health and related services that the person is an unlicensed registered associate marriage and family therapist, provide the person's registration number and the name of the person's employer, and indicate whether the person is under the supervision of a licensed marriage and family therapist, licensed clinical social worker, licensed professional clinical counselor, psychologist licensed pursuant to Chapter 6.6 (commencing with Section 2900), licensed educational psychologist, or a licensed physician and surgeon certified in psychiatry by the American Board of Psychiatry and Neurology.

(b)(1) Any advertisement by or on behalf of a registered associate marriage and family therapist shall include, at a minimum, all of the following information:

(A) That the person is a registered associate marriage and family therapist.

(B) The associate's registration number.

(C) The name of the person's employer.

(D) That the person is supervised by a licensed person.

(2) The abbreviation "AMFT" shall not be used in an advertisement unless the title "registered associate marriage and family therapist" appears in the advertisement. *(Added by Stats.1995, c. 327 (A.B.610), § 3, operative Jan. 1, 1999. Amended by Stats.2000, c. 836 (S.B.1554), § 31; Stats.2001, c. 728 (S.B.724), § 37; Stats.2002, c. 1013 (S.B.2026), § 23; Stats.2003, c. 607 (S.B.1077), § 15; Stats. 2004, c. 204 (A.B.2552), § 4; Stats.2007, c. 588 (S.B.1048), § 59; Stats.2009, c. 26 (S.B.33), § 12; Stats.2010, c. 328 (S.B.1330), § 11; Stats.2011, c. 166 (A.B.956), § 1; Stats.2012, c. 799 (S.B.1575), § 32;* Stats.2015, c. 262 (S.B.620), § 4, eff. Jan. 1, 2016; Stats.2017, c. 573 (S.B.800), § 5, eff. Jan. 1, 2018; Stats.2018, c. 743 (A.B.93), § 15, eff. Jan. 1, 2019; Stats.2019, c. 321 (A.B.1651), § 3, eff. Jan. 1, 2020.)

Cross References

Board defined for purposes of this Chapter, see Business and Professions Code §§ 4980.03, 4990.02.

Board defined for purposes of this Code, see Business and Professions Code § 22.

Child Abuse and Neglect Reporting Act, mandated reporter, see Penal Code § 11165.7.

Health practitioner includes registered intern under this section, see Welfare and Institutions Code § 15610.37.

Interns, see Business and Professions Code § 4980.03.

Psychotherapist-patient privilege, see Evidence Code § 1010.

§ 4980.46. Fictitious business names

Any licensed marriage and family therapist who owns a business using a fictitious business name shall not use any name that is false, misleading, or deceptive, and shall inform the patient, prior to the commencement of treatment, of the name and license designation of the owner or owners of the practice. *(Added by Stats.1988, c. 864, § 1. Amended by Stats.2002, c. 1013 (S.B.2026), § 25; Stats.2021, c. 747 (A.B.690), § 8, eff. Jan. 1, 2022.)*

Research References

Forms

1 California Transactions Forms--Business Transactions § 5:4, Special Rules for Professionals.

§ 4980.48. Trainees; notice to clients and patients of unlicensed status; advertising

(a) A trainee shall, prior to performing any professional services, inform each client or patient that the trainee is an unlicensed marriage and family therapist trainee, provide the name of the trainee's employer, and indicate whether the trainee is under the supervision of a licensed marriage and family therapist, a licensed clinical social worker, a licensed professional clinical counselor, a licensed psychologist, a licensed physician certified in psychiatry by the American Board of Psychiatry and Neurology, or a licensed educational psychologist.

(b) Any person that advertises services performed by a trainee shall include the trainee's name, the supervisor's license designation or abbreviation, and the supervisor's license number.

(c) Any advertisement by or on behalf of a marriage and family therapist trainee shall include, at a minimum, all of the following information:

(1) That the trainee is a marriage and family therapist trainee.

(2) The name of the trainee's employer.

(3) That the trainee is supervised by a licensed person. *(Added by Stats.1989, c. 772, § 4. Amended by Stats.1993, c. 1054 (A.B.1885), § 12; Stats.2002, c. 1013 (S.B.2026), § 26; Stats.2009, c. 307 (S.B.821), § 50; Stats.2011, c. 166 (A.B.956), § 2; Stats.2012, c. 799 (S.B.1575), § 33; Stats.2019, c. 321 (A.B.1651), § 4, eff. Jan. 1, 2020.)*

Cross References

Board defined for purposes of this Chapter, see Business and Professions Code §§ 4980.03, 4990.02.

Board defined for purposes of this Code, see Business and Professions Code § 22.

Trainees, see Business and Professions Code § 4980.03.

§ 4980.49. Termination of therapy on or after Jan. 1, 2015; retention of health service records for specified time; records of minor clients or patients; format

(a) A marriage and family therapist shall retain a client's or patient's health service records for a minimum of seven years from the date therapy is terminated. If the client or patient is a minor, the client's or patient's health service records shall be retained for a minimum of seven years from the date the client or the patient reaches 18 years of age. Health service records may be retained in either a written or an electronic format.

(b) This section shall apply only to the records of a client or patient whose therapy is terminated on or after January 1, 2015. *(Added by Stats.2014, c. 312 (S.B.578), § 1, eff. Jan. 1, 2015.)*

§ 4980.50. Examination; issuance or denial of license

(a) Every applicant who meets the educational and experience requirements and applies for a license as a marriage and family therapist shall be examined by the board. The examinations shall be as set forth in subdivision (d) of Section 4980.40. The examinations shall be given at least twice a year at a time and place and under supervision as the board may determine. The board shall examine the candidate with regard to the candidate's knowledge and professional skills and judgment in the utilization of appropriate techniques and methods.

(b) The board shall not deny any applicant who has submitted a complete application for examination, admission to the licensure examinations required by this section if the applicant meets the educational and experience requirements of this chapter, and has not committed any acts or engaged in any conduct that would constitute grounds to deny licensure.

(c) The board shall not deny any applicant, whose application for licensure is complete, admission to the clinical examination, nor shall the board postpone or delay any applicant's clinical examination, solely upon the receipt by the board of a complaint alleging acts or conduct that would constitute grounds to deny licensure.

(d) If an applicant for examination who has passed the California law and ethics examination is the subject of a complaint or is under board investigation for acts or conduct that, if proven to be true, would constitute grounds for the board to deny licensure, the board shall permit the applicant to take the clinical examination for licensure, but may notify the applicant that licensure will not be granted pending completion of the investigation.

(e) Notwithstanding Section 135, the board may deny any applicant who has previously failed either the California law and ethics examination or the clinical examination permission to retake either examination pending completion of the investigation of any complaints against the applicant. Nothing in this section shall prohibit the board from denying an applicant admission to any examination or refusing to issue a license to any applicant when an accusation or statement of issues has been filed against the applicant pursuant to Sections 11503 and 11504 of the Government Code, respectively, or the applicant has been denied in accordance with subdivision (b) of Section 485.

(f) Notwithstanding any other provision of law, the board may destroy all examination materials two years following the date of an examination.

(g) An applicant for licensure shall not be eligible to participate in the clinical examination if the applicant fails to obtain a passing score on the clinical examination within seven years from their initial attempt, unless the applicant takes and obtains a passing score on the current version of the California law and ethics examination.

(h) A passing score on the clinical examination shall be accepted by the board for a period of seven years from the date the examination was taken.

(i) An applicant for licensure who has qualified pursuant to this chapter shall be issued a license as a marriage and family therapist in the form that the board deems appropriate. *(Added by Stats.2011, c. 387 (S.B.704), § 8, operative Jan. 1, 2013. Amended by Stats.2012, c. 799 (S.B.1575), § 35, operative Jan. 1, 2014; Stats.2012, c. 800 (S.B.1527), § 2, operative Jan. 1, 2014; Stats.2013, c. 473 (S.B.821),* § 29, *operative Jan. 1, 2016; Stats.2018, c. 743 (A.B.93), § 17, eff. Jan. 1, 2019; Stats.2019, c. 456 (S.B.786), § 67, eff. Jan. 1, 2020.)*

Cross References

Board defined for purposes of this Chapter, see Business and Professions Code §§ 4980.03, 4990.02.
Board defined for purposes of this Code, see Business and Professions Code § 22.
Health care service plans,
    Outstate contract, selection of California licensed clinical social worker, registered psychiatric-mental health nurse, advanced practice registered nurse, or marriage, family and child counselor, see Health and Safety Code § 1373.8.
    Prohibition on selection of licensed social worker or marriage or family therapist, see Health and Safety Code § 1373.
    Soliciting and advertising, applicability to pharmacies, see Health and Safety Code § 1395.
Life and disability insurance, mental health coverage in self-insured employee welfare benefit plan, see Insurance Code § 10177.
Medical reimbursement provisions of disability policies, selection of certificate holder or licensee, unenforceability of waiver of mental health services coverage, see Insurance Code § 10176.

§ 4980.54. Continuing education requirements; hours; records; approved providers; subject matter

(a) The Legislature recognizes that the education and experience requirements in this chapter constitute only minimal requirements to ensure that an applicant is prepared and qualified to take the licensure examinations as specified in subdivision (d) of Section 4980.40 and, if an applicant passes those examinations, to begin practice.

(b) In order to continuously improve the competence of licensed and registered marriage and family therapists and as a model for all psychotherapeutic professions, the Legislature encourages all licensees and registrants to regularly engage in continuing education related to the profession or scope of practice as defined in this chapter.

(c)(1) Except as provided in subdivision (e), the board shall not renew any license pursuant to this chapter unless the applicant certifies to the board, on a form prescribed by the board, that the applicant has completed not less than 36 hours of approved continuing education in or relevant to the field of marriage and family therapy in the preceding two years, as determined by the board.

(2) The board shall not renew any registration pursuant to this chapter unless the registrant certifies under penalty of perjury to the board, and on a form prescribed by the board, that they have completed not less than three hours of continuing education on the subject of California law and ethics during the preceding year.

(d) The board shall have the right to audit the records of any applicant to verify the completion of the continuing education requirement. Applicants shall maintain records of completion of required continuing education coursework for a minimum of two years and shall make these records available to the board for auditing purposes upon request.

(e) The board may establish exceptions from the continuing education requirements of this section for good cause, as defined by the board.

(f) The continuing education shall be obtained from one of the following sources:

(1) An accredited school or state-approved school that meets the requirements set forth in Section 4980.36 or 4980.37. Nothing in this paragraph shall be construed as requiring coursework to be offered as part of a regular degree program.

(2) Other continuing education providers, as specified by the board by regulation.

§ 4980.54

(g) The board shall establish, by regulation, a procedure for identifying acceptable providers of continuing education courses, and all providers of continuing education, as described in paragraphs (1) and (2) of subdivision (f), shall adhere to procedures established by the board. The board may revoke or deny the right of a provider to offer continuing education coursework pursuant to this section for failure to comply with this section or any regulation adopted pursuant to this section.

(h) Training, education, and coursework by approved providers shall incorporate one or more of the following:

(1) Aspects of the discipline that are fundamental to the understanding or the practice of marriage and family therapy.

(2) Aspects of the discipline of marriage and family therapy in which significant recent developments have occurred.

(3) Aspects of other disciplines that enhance the understanding or the practice of marriage and family therapy.

(i) A system of continuing education for licensed marriage and family therapists shall include courses directly related to the diagnosis, assessment, and treatment of the client population being served.

(j) The continuing education requirements of this section shall comply fully with the guidelines for mandatory continuing education established by the Department of Consumer Affairs pursuant to Section 166. *(Added by Stats.1986, c. 1365, § 4. Amended by Stats.1987, c. 738, § 9; Stats.1995, c. 839 (S.B.26), § 2; Stats.1997, c. 196 (S.B.650), § 2; Stats.2002, c. 1013 (S.B.2026), § 28; Stats.2003, c. 874 (S.B.363), § 10; Stats.2007, c. 588 (S.B.1048), § 60; Stats.2009, c. 26 (S.B.33), § 14; Stats.2015, c. 426 (S.B.800), § 40, eff. Jan. 1, 2016; Stats.2021, c. 647 (S.B.801), § 28, eff. Jan. 1, 2022; Stats.2022, c. 520 (A.B.1759), § 4, eff. Jan. 1, 2023.)*

Cross References

Board defined for purposes of this Chapter, see Business and Professions Code §§ 4980.03, 4990.02.

Board defined for purposes of this Code, see Business and Professions Code § 22.

Department defined for purposes of this Code, see Business and Professions Code § 23.

Inactive licenses, see Business and Professions Code § 4984.8.

Retired licenses, restoration requirements, continuing education hours, see Business and Professions Code § 4984.41.

Research References

Forms

West's California Code Forms, Business & Professions § 4980 Form 1, Application Packet Mft.

§ 4980.55. Statements of experience, education, specialties, etc.

As a model for all therapeutic professions, and to acknowledge respect and regard for the consuming public, all licensed marriage and family therapists are encouraged to provide to each client, at an appropriate time and within the context of the psychotherapeutic relationship, an accurate and informative statement of the therapist's experience, education, specialities, professional orientation, and any other information deemed appropriate by the licensee. *(Added by Stats.1986, c. 1365, § 4. Amended by Stats.2002, c. 1013 (S.B.2026), § 29; Stats.2014, c. 316 (S.B.1466), § 21, eff. Jan. 1, 2015.)*

Cross References

Experience defined for purposes of this Chapter, see Business and Professions Code § 4980.03.

§ 4980.57. Licensees who began graduate study before January 1, 2004; required continuing education course

(a) The board shall require a licensee who began graduate study prior to January 1, 2004, to take a continuing education course during his or her first renewal period after the operative date of this section in spousal or partner abuse assessment, detection, and intervention strategies, including community resources, cultural factors, and same gender abuse dynamics. On and after January 1, 2005, the course shall consist of not less than seven hours of training. Equivalent courses in spousal or partner abuse assessment, detection, and intervention strategies taken prior to the operative date of this section or proof of equivalent teaching or practice experience may be submitted to the board and at its discretion, may be accepted in satisfaction of this requirement.

(b) Continuing education courses taken pursuant to this section shall be applied to the 36 hours of approved continuing education required under subdivision (c) of Section 4980.54. *(Added by Stats.2002, c. 481 (S.B.564), § 5, operative Jan. 1, 2004. Amended by Stats.2003, c. 607 (S.B.1077), § 16, operative Jan. 1, 2004; Stats.2007, c. 588 (S.B.1048), § 61.)*

Cross References

Board defined for purposes of this Chapter, see Business and Professions Code §§ 4980.03, 4990.02.

Board defined for purposes of this Code, see Business and Professions Code § 22.

§ 4980.60. Rules and regulations

(a) The board may adopt those rules and regulations as may be necessary to enable it to carry into effect the provisions of this chapter. The adoption, amendment, or repeal of those rules and regulations shall be made in accordance with Chapter 3.5 (commencing with Section 11340) of Part 1 of Division 3 of Title 2 of the Government Code.

(b) The board may, by rules or regulations, adopt, amend, or repeal rules of advertising and professional conduct appropriate to the establishment and maintenance of a high standard of integrity in the profession, provided that the rules or regulations are not inconsistent with Section 4982. Every person who holds a license to practice marriage and family therapy shall be governed by the rules of professional conduct. *(Added by Stats.1986, c. 1365, § 4. Amended by Stats.2002, c. 1013 (S.B.2026), § 31.)*

Cross References

Administrative regulations and rulemaking, see Government Code § 11340 et seq.

Board defined for purposes of this Chapter, see Business and Professions Code §§ 4980.03, 4990.02.

Board defined for purposes of this Code, see Business and Professions Code § 22.

§ 4980.70. Additional personnel

Except as provided by Section 159.5, the board may employ whatever additional personnel is necessary to carry out the provisions of this chapter. *(Added by Stats.1986, c. 1365, § 4.)*

Cross References

Board defined for purposes of this Chapter, see Business and Professions Code §§ 4980.03, 4990.02.

Board defined for purposes of this Code, see Business and Professions Code § 22.

§ 4980.72. Reciprocity; conditions

The board may issue a license to a person who, at the time of submitting an application for a license pursuant to this chapter, holds a license in another jurisdiction of the United States as a marriage and family therapist at the highest level for independent clinical practice if all of the following requirements are met:

(a) The applicant's license in the other jurisdiction has been current, active, and unrestricted in that jurisdiction for at least two years immediately before the date the application was received by the board. The applicant shall disclose to the board for review any past restrictions or disciplinary action on an out-of-state license, and the board shall consider these actions in determining whether to issue a license to the applicant.

(b) The applicant's degree that qualified the person for the out-of-state license is a master's or doctoral degree that was obtained from an accredited or approved institution.

(c) The applicant complies with the fingerprint requirements established by Section 144.

(d) The applicant completes the coursework specified in paragraphs (1) and (2) from an accredited institution or an approved institution or from an acceptable provider of continuing education as specified in Section 4980.54. Undergraduate coursework shall not satisfy these requirements.

(1) A minimum of 12 hours of coursework in California law and professional ethics that includes, but is not limited to, instruction in advertising, scope of practice, scope of competence, treatment of minors, confidentiality, dangerous clients, psychotherapist-client privilege, recordkeeping, client access to records, state and federal laws relating to confidentiality of patient health information, dual relationships, child abuse, elder and dependent adult abuse, online therapy, insurance reimbursement, civil liability, disciplinary actions and unprofessional conduct, ethics complaints and ethical standards, termination of therapy, standards of care, relevant family law, therapist disclosures to clients, the application of legal and ethical standards in different types of work settings, and licensing law and the licensing process.

(2) At least one semester unit, or 15 hours, of instruction that includes an understanding of various California cultures and the social and psychological implications of socioeconomic position.

(e) The applicant obtains a minimum of seven contact hours of training or coursework in child abuse assessment and reporting, as specified in Section 28, and any regulations promulgated pursuant to that section.

(f) On or after January 1, 2021, the applicant shall show proof of completion of at least six hours of coursework or applied experience under supervision in suicide risk assessment and intervention using one of the methods specified in Section 4980.396.

(g) The applicant passes the board-administered California law and ethics examination specified in subdivision (d) of Section 4980.40. The clinical examination specified in subdivision (d) of Section 4980.40 shall be waived for an applicant qualifying under this section.

(h) This section was developed based on an examination of the licensure requirements for marriage and family therapists on a national level. This section shall not be construed to apply to any provisions under this division or Division 3 (commencing with Section 5000) other than this act. *(Added by Stats.2019, c. 380 (S.B.679), § 3, eff. Jan. 1, 2020.)*

Cross References

Applicant defined for purposes of this Chapter, see Business and Professions Code § 4980.03.
Board defined for purposes of this Chapter, see Business and Professions Code §§ 4980.03, 4990.02.
Experience defined for purposes of this Chapter, see Business and Professions Code § 4980.03.

§ 4980.74. Applicants for licensure with education or experience gained outside California who do not qualify for reciprocity; acceptance of education or experience; qualification for licensure without taking clinical examination

(a) This section applies to persons with education gained from an out-of-state school or experience gained outside of California who apply for licensure or registration and who do not qualify for a license under Section 4980.72.

(b) The board shall accept education gained from an out-of-state school for purposes of satisfying licensure or registration requirements if the education is substantially equivalent, as defined in Section 4980.78, and the applicant complies with Section 4980.76, if applicable. The applicant's degree title need not be identical to that required by Section 4980.36 or 4980.37.

(c) The board shall accept experience gained outside of California for purposes of satisfying licensure or registration requirements if the experience is substantially equivalent to the experience required by this chapter. If the applicant has fewer than 3,000 hours of qualifying supervised experience, the board shall accept as qualifying supervised experience the amount of time the applicant held an active license in good standing in another state or country as a marriage and family therapist at the highest level for independent clinical practice at a rate of 100 hours per month, up to a maximum of 1,200 hours.

(d) An applicant who obtained a license or registration in another state or country may qualify for licensure with the board without taking the clinical examination specified in Section 4980.40 if both of the following conditions are met:

(1) The applicant obtained a passing score on the clinical licensing examination set forth in regulation as accepted by the board.

(2) The applicant's license or registration in that state or country is active, in good standing at the time of the application, and is not revoked, suspended, surrendered, denied, or otherwise restricted or encumbered. *(Added by Stats.2009, c. 26 (S.B.33), § 16. Amended by Stats.2013, c. 551 (A.B.451), § 2; Stats.2016, c. 70 (A.B.1917), § 1, eff. Jan. 1, 2017; Stats.2019, c. 380 (S.B.679), § 4, eff. Jan. 1, 2020.)*

Cross References

Applicant defined for purposes of this Chapter, see Business and Professions Code § 4980.03.
Board defined for purposes of this Chapter, see Business and Professions Code §§ 4980.03, 4990.02.
Experience defined for purposes of this Chapter, see Business and Professions Code § 4980.03.

§ 4980.76. Foreign degrees; provision of comprehensive degree evaluation

An applicant for licensure or registration with a degree obtained from an educational institution outside the United States shall provide the board with a comprehensive evaluation of the degree performed by a foreign credential evaluation service that is a member of the National Association of Credential Evaluation Services (NACES), and shall provide any other documentation the board deems necessary. *(Added by Stats.2009, c. 26 (S.B.33), § 17.)*

Cross References

Applicant defined for purposes of this Chapter, see Business and Professions Code § 4980.03.
Board defined for purposes of this Chapter, see Business and Professions Code §§ 4980.03, 4990.02.

§ 4980.78. Applicants for licensure with education gained from out-of-state school who do not qualify for reciprocity; substantially equivalent education

(a) This section applies to persons with education gained from an out-of-state school who apply for licensure or registration and who do not qualify for a license under Section 4980.72.

(b) For purposes of Section 4980.74, education is substantially equivalent if all of the following requirements are met:

(1) The degree is obtained from an accredited institution or approved institution and consists of, at a minimum, the following:

(A)(i) For an applicant who obtained a degree within the timeline prescribed by subdivision (a) of Section 4980.36, the degree shall contain no less than 60 semester units or 90 quarter units of instruction.

§ 4980.78 BUSINESS AND PROFESSIONS CODE

(ii) Up to 12 semester units or 18 quarter units of instruction may be remediated, if missing from the degree. The remediation may occur while the applicant is registered as an associate.

(B) For an applicant who obtained a degree within the timeline prescribed by subdivision (a) of Section 4980.37, the degree shall contain no less than 48 semester units or 72 quarter units of instruction.

(C)(i) Six semester units or nine quarter units of supervised practicum, including, but not limited to, a minimum of 150 hours of face-to-face experience counseling individuals, couples, families, or groups, and an additional 75 hours of either face-to-face experience counseling individuals, couples, families, or groups or client centered advocacy, or a combination of face-to-face experience counseling individuals, couples, families, or groups and client centered advocacy.

(ii) An out-of-state applicant who holds a valid license in good standing in another state or country as a marriage and family therapist at the highest level for independent clinical practice is exempt from the practicum requirement specified in clause (i).

(D) Twelve semester units or 18 quarter units in the areas of marriage, family, and child counseling and marital and family systems approaches to treatment, as specified in subparagraph (A) of paragraph (1) of subdivision (d) of Section 4980.36.

(2) The applicant shall complete coursework in California law and ethics as follows:

(A) An applicant who completed a course in law and professional ethics for marriage and family therapists as specified in paragraph (8) of subdivision (a) of Section 4980.81, that did not contain instruction in California law and ethics, shall complete a 12-hour course in California law and professional ethics. The content of the course shall include, but not be limited to, advertising, scope of practice, scope of competence, treatment of minors, confidentiality, dangerous patients, psychotherapist-patient privilege, recordkeeping, patient access to records, state and federal laws relating to confidentiality of patient health information, dual relationships, child abuse, elder and dependent adult abuse, online therapy, insurance reimbursement, civil liability, disciplinary actions and unprofessional conduct, ethics complaints and ethical standards, termination of therapy, standards of care, relevant family law, therapist disclosures to patients, the application of legal and ethical standards in different types of work settings, and licensing law and licensing process. The coursework shall be from an accredited institution, an approved institution, or from a continuing education provider identified as acceptable by the board pursuant to Section 4980.54. This coursework shall be completed * * * before registration as an associate.

(B) An applicant who has not completed a course in law and professional ethics for marriage and family therapists as specified in paragraph (8) of subdivision (a) of Section 4980.81 shall complete this required coursework. The coursework shall contain content specific to California law and ethics. This coursework shall be completed before registration as an associate.

(3) The applicant completes the educational requirements specified in Section 4980.81 not already completed in the applicant's education. The coursework shall be from an accredited institution, an approved institution, or from a continuing education provider that is identified as acceptable by the board pursuant to Section 4980.54. Undergraduate courses shall not satisfy this requirement.

(4) The applicant completes the following coursework not already completed in the applicant's education from an accredited institution, an approved institution, or from a continuing education provider that is identified as acceptable by the board pursuant to Section 4980.54. Undergraduate courses shall not satisfy this requirement.

(A) At least three semester units, or 45 hours, of instruction regarding the principles of mental health recovery-oriented care and methods of service delivery in recovery-oriented practice environments, including structured meetings with various consumers and family members of consumers of mental health services to enhance understanding of their experience of mental illness, treatment, and recovery.

(B) At least one semester unit, or 15 hours, of instruction that includes an understanding of various California cultures and the social and psychological implications of socioeconomic position.

(5) An applicant may complete any units and course content requirements required under paragraphs (3) and (4) not already completed in the applicant's education while registered as an associate, unless otherwise specified.

(6) On and after January 1, 2021, an applicant for licensure shall show proof of completion of at least six hours of coursework or applied experience under supervision in suicide risk assessment and intervention using one of the methods specified in Section 4980.396.

(7) The applicant's degree title need not be identical to that required by subdivision (b) of Section 4980.36. *(Added by Stats.2009, c. 26 (S.B.33), § 18. Amended by Stats.2012, c. 799 (S.B.1575), § 36; Stats.2013, c. 551 (A.B.451), § 3; Stats.2014, c. 316 (S.B.1466), § 23, eff. Jan. 1, 2015; Stats.2014, c. 387 (A.B.2213), § 2.5, eff. Jan. 1, 2015; Stats.2016, c. 70 (A.B.1917), § 2, eff. Jan. 1, 2017; Stats.2016, c. 489 (S.B.1478), § 33, eff. Jan. 1, 2017; Stats.2018, c. 703 (S.B.1491), § 33, eff. Jan. 1, 2019; Stats.2018, c. 743 (A.B.93), § 18.5, eff. Jan. 1, 2019; Stats.2019, c. 380 (S.B.679), § 5, eff. Jan. 1, 2020.)*

Cross References

Applicant defined for purposes of this Chapter, see Business and Professions Code § 4980.03.
Experience defined for purposes of this Chapter, see Business and Professions Code § 4980.03.

§ 4980.81. Reciprocity; applicants for licensure; education requirements

This section applies to persons subject to Section 4980.78 who apply for licensure or registration.

(a)[1] For purposes of Section 4980.78, an applicant shall meet all of the following educational requirements:

(1) A minimum of two semester units of instruction in the diagnosis, assessment, prognosis, treatment planning, and treatment of mental disorders, including severe mental disorders, evidence-based practices, and promising mental health practices that are evaluated in peer-reviewed literature.

(2) At least one semester unit or 15 hours of instruction in psychological testing and at least one semester unit or 15 hours of instruction in psychopharmacology.

(3)(A) Developmental issues from infancy to old age, including demonstration of at least one semester unit, or 15 hours, of instruction that includes all of the following subjects:

(i) The effects of developmental issues on individuals, couples, and family relationships.

(ii) The psychological, psychotherapeutic, and health implications of developmental issues and their effects.

(iii) The understanding of the impact that personal and social insecurity, social stress, low educational levels, inadequate housing, and malnutrition have on human development.

(B) An applicant who is deficient in any of these subjects may remediate the coursework by completing three hours of instruction in each deficient subject.

(4)(A)[2] The broad range of matters and life events that may arise within marriage and family relationships and within a variety of California cultures, including instruction in all of the following:

(i) A minimum of seven contact hours of training or coursework in child abuse assessment and reporting as specified in Section 28 and any regulations promulgated under that section.

(ii) A minimum of 10 contact hours of coursework that includes all of the following:

(I) The assessment and reporting of, as well as treatment related to, elder and dependent adult abuse and neglect.

(II) Aging and its biological, social, cognitive, and psychological aspects.

(III) Long-term care.

(IV) End-of-life and grief.

(iii) A minimum of 15 contact hours of coursework in spousal or partner abuse assessment, detection, intervention strategies, and same-gender abuse dynamics.

(iv) Cultural factors relevant to abuse of partners and family members.

(v) Childbirth, child rearing, parenting, and stepparenting.

(vi) Marriage, divorce, and blended families.

(vii) Poverty and deprivation.

(viii) Financial and social stress.

(ix) Effects of trauma.

(x) The psychological, psychotherapeutic, community, and health implications of the matters and life events described in clauses (i) to (ix), inclusive.

(5) At least one semester unit, or 15 hours, of instruction in multicultural development and cross-cultural interaction, including experiences of race, ethnicity, class, spirituality, sexual orientation, gender, and disability, and their incorporation into the psychotherapeutic process.

(6) A minimum of 10 contact hours of training or coursework in human sexuality, as specified in Section 25 and any regulations promulgated under that section, including the study of physiological, psychological, and social cultural variables associated with sexual behavior and gender identity, and the assessment and treatment of psychosexual dysfunction.

(7) A minimum of 15 contact hours of coursework in substance use disorders, and a minimum of 15 contact hours of coursework in co-occurring disorders and addiction. The following subjects shall be included in this coursework:

(A) The definition of substance use disorders, co-occurring disorders, and addiction. For purposes of this subparagraph, "co-occurring disorders" means a mental illness and substance abuse diagnosis occurring simultaneously in an individual.

(B) Medical aspects of substance use disorders and co-occurring disorders.

(C) The effects of psychoactive drug use.

(D) Current theories of the etiology of substance abuse and addiction.

(E) The role of persons and systems that support or compound substance abuse and addiction.

(F) Major approaches to identification, evaluation, and treatment of substance use disorders, co-occurring disorders, and addiction, including, but not limited to, best practices.

(G) Legal aspects of substance abuse.

(H) Populations at risk with regard to substance use disorders and co-occurring disorders.

(I) Community resources offering screening, assessment, treatment, and followup for the affected person and family.

(J) Recognition of substance use disorders, co-occurring disorders, and addiction, and appropriate referral.

(K) The prevention of substance use disorders and addiction.

(8) A minimum of a two semester or three quarter unit course in law and professional ethics for marriage and family therapists, including instruction in all of the following subjects:

(A) Contemporary professional ethics and statutory, regulatory, and decisional laws that delineate the scope of practice of marriage and family therapy.

(B) The therapeutic, clinical, and practical considerations involved in the legal and ethical practice of marriage and family therapy, including, but not limited to, family law.

(C) The current legal patterns and trends in the mental health professions.

(D) The psychotherapist-patient privilege, confidentiality, the patient dangerous to self or others, and the treatment of minors with and without parental consent.

(E) A recognition and exploration of the relationship between a practitioner's sense of self and human values and their professional behavior and ethics.

(F) The application of legal and ethical standards in different types of work settings.

(G) Licensing law and licensing process. *(Added by Stats.2014, c. 387 (A.B.2213), § 5, eff. Jan. 1, 2015. Amended by Stats.2016, c. 489 (S.B.1478), § 35, eff. Jan. 1, 2017; Stats.2019, c. 380 (S.B.679), § 7, eff. Jan. 1, 2020; Stats.2019, c. 456 (S.B.786), § 68.5, eff. Jan. 1, 2020; Stats.2021, c. 647 (S.B.801), § 29, eff. Jan. 1, 2022.)*

¹ No subd. (b) in enrolled bill.
² No subd. (a)(4)(B) in enrolled bill.

ARTICLE 2. DENIAL, SUSPENSION AND REVOCATION

Section
4982.   Unprofessional conduct.
4982.05. Limitations period.
4982.1.   Mental illness or chemical dependency; grounds for refusal to license or register.
4982.15. Placing of license or registration on probation; circumstances.
4982.25. Denial of application or suspension or revocation of license or registration; grounds.
4982.26. Decision containing finding that licensee or registrant engaged in sexual contact with patient or former patient; order of revocation.
4982.3.   Procedure.

§ 4982. Unprofessional conduct

The board may deny a license or registration or may suspend or revoke the license or registration of a licensee or registrant if the licensee or registrant has been guilty of unprofessional conduct. Unprofessional conduct includes, but is not limited to, the following:

(a) The conviction of a crime substantially related to the qualifications, functions, or duties of a licensee or registrant under this chapter. The record of conviction shall be conclusive evidence only of the fact that the conviction occurred. The board may inquire into the circumstances surrounding the commission of the crime in order to fix the degree of discipline or to determine if the conviction is substantially related to the qualifications, functions, or duties of a licensee or registrant under this chapter. A conviction has the same meaning as defined in Section 7.5. The board may order any license or registration suspended or revoked, or may decline to issue a license or registration when the time for appeal has elapsed, or the judgment of conviction has been affirmed on appeal, or, when an order granting probation is made suspending the imposition of sentence. All actions pursuant to this subdivision shall be taken pursuant to Division 1.5 (commencing with Section 475).

(b) Securing a license or registration by fraud, deceit, or misrepresentation on any application for licensure or registration submitted to

§ 4982

the board, whether engaged in by an applicant for a license or registration, or by a licensee in support of any application for licensure or registration.

(c) Administering to themself any controlled substance or using of any of the dangerous drugs specified in Section 4022, or of any alcoholic beverage to the extent, or in a manner, as to be dangerous or injurious to the person applying for a registration or license or holding a registration or license under this chapter, or to any other person, or to the public, or, to the extent that the use impairs the ability of the person applying for or holding a registration or license to conduct with safety to the public the practice authorized by the registration or license. The board shall deny an application for a registration or license or revoke the license or registration of any person, other than one who is licensed as a physician and surgeon, who uses or offers to use drugs in the course of performing marriage and family therapy services.

(d) Gross negligence or incompetence in the performance of marriage and family therapy.

(e) Violating, attempting to violate, or conspiring to violate any of the provisions of this chapter or any regulation adopted by the board.

(f) Misrepresentation as to the type or status of a license or registration held by the licensee or registrant or otherwise misrepresenting or permitting misrepresentation of the licensee's or registrant's education, professional qualifications, or professional affiliations to any person or entity.

(g) Impersonation of another by any licensee, registrant, or applicant for a license or registration, or, in the case of a licensee or registrant, allowing any other person to use the licensee's or registrant's license or registration.

(h) Aiding or abetting, or employing, directly or indirectly, any unlicensed or unregistered person to engage in conduct for which a license or registration is required under this chapter.

(i) Intentionally or recklessly causing physical or emotional harm to any client.

(j) The commission of any dishonest, corrupt, or fraudulent act substantially related to the qualifications, functions, or duties of a licensee or registrant.

(k) Engaging in sexual relations with a client, or a former client within two years following termination of therapy, soliciting sexual relations with a client, or committing an act of sexual abuse, or sexual misconduct with a client, or committing an act punishable as a sexually related crime, if that act or solicitation is substantially related to the qualifications, functions, or duties of a marriage and family therapist.

(*l*) Performing, or holding oneself out as being able to perform, or offering to perform, or permitting any trainee, registered associate, or applicant for licensure under supervision to perform, any professional services beyond the scope of the license authorized by this chapter.

(m) Failure to maintain confidentiality, except as otherwise required or permitted by law, of all information that has been received from a client in confidence during the course of treatment and all information about the client that is obtained from tests or other means.

(n) Prior to the commencement of treatment, failing to disclose to the client or prospective client the fee to be charged for the professional services, or the basis upon which that fee will be computed.

(o) Paying, accepting, or soliciting any consideration, compensation, or remuneration, whether monetary or otherwise, for the referral of professional clients. All consideration, compensation, or remuneration shall be in relation to professional counseling services actually provided by the licensee. This subdivision does not prevent collaboration among two or more licensees in a case or cases.

However, a fee shall not be charged for that collaboration, except when disclosure of the fee has been made in compliance with subdivision (n).

(p) Advertising in a manner that is false, fraudulent, misleading, or deceptive, as defined in Section 651.

(q) Reproduction or description in public, or in any publication subject to general public distribution, of any psychological test or other assessment device, the value of which depends in whole or in part on the naivete of the subject, in ways that might invalidate the test or device.

(r) Any conduct in the supervision of any registered associate, trainee, or applicant for licensure by any licensee that violates this chapter or any rules or regulations adopted by the board.

(s) Performing or holding oneself out as being able to perform mental health services beyond the scope of one's competence, as established by one's education, training, or experience. This subdivision shall not be construed to expand the scope of the license authorized by this chapter.

(t) Permitting a trainee, registered associate, or applicant for licensure under one's supervision or control to perform, or permitting the trainee, registered associate, or applicant for licensure to hold themself out as competent to perform, mental health services beyond the trainee's, registered associate's, or applicant for licensure's level of education, training, or experience.

(u) The violation of any statute or regulation governing the gaining and supervision of experience required by this chapter.

(v) Failure to keep records consistent with sound clinical judgment, the standards of the profession, and the nature of the services being rendered.

(w) Failure to comply with the child abuse reporting requirements of Section 11166 of the Penal Code.

(x) Failure to comply with the elder and dependent adult abuse reporting requirements of Section 15630 of the Welfare and Institutions Code.

(y) Willful violation of Chapter 1 (commencing with Section 123100) of Part 1 of Division 106 of the Health and Safety Code.

(z) Failure to comply with Section 2290.5.

(aa)(1) Engaging in an act described in Section 261, 286, 287, or 289 of, or former Section 288a of, the Penal Code with a minor or an act described in Section 288 or 288.5 of the Penal Code regardless of whether the act occurred prior to or after the time the registration or license was issued by the board. An act described in this subdivision occurring prior to the effective date of this subdivision [1] shall constitute unprofessional conduct and shall subject the licensee to refusal, suspension, or revocation of a license under this section.

(2) The Legislature hereby finds and declares that protection of the public, and in particular minors, from sexual misconduct by a licensee is a compelling governmental interest, and that the ability to suspend or revoke a license for sexual conduct with a minor occurring prior to the effective date of this section is equally important to protecting the public as is the ability to refuse a license for sexual conduct with a minor occurring prior to the effective date of this section.

(ab) Engaging in any conduct that subverts or attempts to subvert any licensing examination or the administration of an examination as described in Section 123. (Added by Stats.1986, c. 1365, § 4. Amended by Stats.1987, c. 738, § 12; Stats.1989, c. 772, § 6; Stats.1992, c. 890 (S.B.1394), § 4; Stats.1993, c. 1054 (A.B.1885), § 13; Stats.1999, c. 657 (A.B.1677), § 3; Stats.2000, c. 135 (A.B. 2539), § 4; Stats.2001, c. 435 (S.B.349), § 16; Stats.2002, c. 1013 (S.B.2026), § 35; Stats.2003, c. 607 (S.B.1077), § 17; Stats.2007, c. 588 (S.B.1048), § 64; Stats.2008, c. 33 (S.B.797), § 8, eff. June 23, 2008; Stats.2009, c. 307 (S.B.821), § 51; Stats.2018, c. 423 (S.B.1494), § 1, eff. Jan. 1, 2019; Stats.2018, c. 743 (A.B.93), § 20, eff. Jan. 1,

2019; Stats.2019, c. 497 (A.B.991), § 8, eff. Jan. 1, 2020; Stats.2021, c. 647 (S.B.801), § 30, eff. Jan. 1, 2022.)

[1] Subd. (aa) was added by Stats.2008, c. 33 (S.B.797), § 8, eff. June 23, 2008.

Cross References

Board defined for purposes of this Chapter, see Business and Professions Code §§ 4980.03, 4990.02.

Board defined for purposes of this Code, see Business and Professions Code § 22.

Conviction defined for purposes of this Code, see Business and Professions Code § 7.5.

Denial of license,
 Additional grounds, generally, see Business and Professions Code § 480.
 Grounds, generally, see Business and Professions Code § 475.

Domestic violence, interagency death review teams, reporting procedures, see Penal Code § 11163.3.

Domestic violence multidisciplinary personnel team, disclosure and exchange of information following report of suspected domestic violence, privacy and confidentiality rights, see Penal Code § 13752.

Elder death review teams, confidentiality and disclosure of information, see Penal Code § 11174.8.

Human trafficking multidisciplinary personnel team, disclosure and exchange of information following report of human trafficking, privacy and confidentiality rights, see Penal Code § 13753.

Unprofessional conduct, prior sexual contact between psychotherapist and patient, failure to comply, see Business and Professions Code § 728.

§ 4982.05. Limitations period

(a) Except as provided in subdivisions (b), (c), and (e), any accusation filed against a licensee pursuant to Section 11503 of the Government Code shall be filed within three years from the date the board discovers the alleged act or omission that is the basis for disciplinary action, or within seven years from the date the alleged act or omission that is the basis for disciplinary action occurred, whichever occurs first.

(b) An accusation filed against a licensee pursuant to Section 11503 of the Government Code alleging the procurement of a license by fraud or misrepresentation is not subject to the limitations set forth in subdivision (a).

(c) The limitation provided for by subdivision (a) shall be tolled for the length of time required to obtain compliance when a report required to be filed by the licensee or registrant with the board pursuant to Article 11 (commencing with Section 800) of Chapter 1 is not filed in a timely fashion.

(d) If an alleged act or omission involves a minor, the seven-year limitations period provided for by subdivision (a) and the 10–year limitations period provided for by subdivision (e) shall be tolled until the minor reaches the age of majority.

(e) An accusation filed against a licensee pursuant to Section 11503 of the Government Code alleging sexual misconduct shall be filed within three years after the board discovers the act or omission alleged as the grounds for disciplinary action, or within 10 years after the act or omission alleged as the grounds for disciplinary action occurs, whichever occurs first. This subdivision shall apply to a complaint alleging sexual misconduct received by the board on and after January 1, 2002.

(f) The limitations period provided by subdivision (a) shall be tolled during any period if material evidence necessary for prosecuting or determining whether a disciplinary action would be appropriate is unavailable to the board due to an ongoing criminal investigation.

(g) For purposes of this section, "discovers" means the later of the occurrence of any of the following with respect to each act or omission alleged as the basis for disciplinary action:

(1) The date the board received a complaint or report describing the act or omission.

(2) The date, subsequent to the original complaint or report, on which the board became aware of any additional acts or omissions alleged as the basis for disciplinary action against the same individual.

(3) The date the board receives from the complainant a written release of information pertaining to the complainant's diagnosis and treatment. *(Added by Stats.1999, c. 459 (S.B.809), § 2. Amended by Stats.2001, c. 617 (A.B.1616), § 4; Stats.2002, c. 664 (A.B.3034), § 9; Stats.2005, c. 658 (S.B.229), § 19.)*

Cross References

Board defined for purposes of this Chapter, see Business and Professions Code §§ 4980.03, 4990.02.

Board defined for purposes of this Code, see Business and Professions Code § 22.

§ 4982.1. Mental illness or chemical dependency; grounds for refusal to license or register

The board may refuse to issue any registration or license whenever it appears that an applicant may be unable to practice his or her profession safely due to mental illness or chemical dependency. The procedures set forth in Article 12.5 (commencing with Section 820) of Chapter 1 shall apply to any denial of a license or registration pursuant to this section. *(Added by Stats.1992, c. 384 (S.B.1773), § 4.)*

Cross References

Board defined for purposes of this Chapter, see Business and Professions Code §§ 4980.03, 4990.02.

Board defined for purposes of this Code, see Business and Professions Code § 22.

Chemical dependency and early intervention training, see Business and Professions Code § 29.

§ 4982.15. Placing of license or registration on probation; circumstances

(a) The board may place a license or registration on probation under the following circumstances:

(1) In lieu of, or in addition to, any order of the board suspending or revoking the license or registration of any licensee or associate.

(2) Upon the issuance of a license to an individual who has been guilty of unprofessional conduct, but who had otherwise completed all education and training and experience required for licensure.

(3) As a condition upon the reissuance or reinstatement of any license that has been suspended or revoked by the board.

(b) The board may adopt regulations establishing a monitoring program to ensure compliance with any terms or conditions of probation imposed by the board pursuant to subdivision (a). The cost of probation or monitoring may be ordered to be paid by the licensee, registrant, or applicant.

(c) The board, in its discretion, may require any licensee or registrant who has been placed on probation, or whose license or registration has been suspended, to obtain additional professional training, and to pass an examination upon completion of that training, and to pay any necessary examination fee. The examination may be written, oral, or a practical or clinical examination. *(Formerly § 4982.2, added by Stats.1986, c. 1365, § 4. Renumbered § 4982.15 and amended by Stats.1994, c. 26 (A.B.1807), § 184, eff. March 30, 1994. Amended by Stats.2018, c. 743 (A.B.93), § 21, eff. Jan. 1, 2019.)*

Cross References

Board defined for purposes of this Chapter, see Business and Professions Code §§ 4980.03, 4990.02.

Board defined for purposes of this Code, see Business and Professions Code § 22.

Denial of license,
 Additional grounds, generally, see Business and Professions Code § 480.
 Grounds, generally, see Business and Professions Code § 475.

§ 4982.25. Denial of application or suspension or revocation of license or registration; grounds

The board may deny an application, or may suspend or revoke a license or registration issued under this chapter, for any of the following:

(a) Denial of licensure, revocation, suspension, restriction, or any other disciplinary action imposed by another state or territory or possession of the United States, or by any other governmental agency, on a license, certificate, or registration to practice marriage and family therapy, or any other healing art, shall constitute unprofessional conduct. A certified copy of the disciplinary action decision or judgment shall be conclusive evidence of that action.

(b) Revocation, suspension, or restriction by the board of a license, certificate, or registration to practice as a marriage and family therapist, clinical social worker, professional clinical counselor, or educational psychologist shall also constitute grounds for disciplinary action for unprofessional conduct against the licensee or registrant under this chapter. *(Added by Stats.1986, c. 1365, § 4. Amended by Stats.1987, c. 738, § 13; Stats.1992, c. 384 (S.B.1773), § 5; Stats.1998, c. 879 (S.B.2238), § 7; Stats.2002, c. 1013 (S.B.2026), § 37; Stats.2010, c. 653 (S.B.1489), § 41; Stats.2011, c. 350 (S.B.943), § 31.)*

Cross References

Board defined for purposes of this Chapter, see Business and Professions Code §§ 4980.03, 4990.02.
Board defined for purposes of this Code, see Business and Professions Code § 22.
Denial of license, generally,
   Additional grounds, see Business and Professions Code § 480.
   Grounds, see Business and Professions Code § 475.

§ 4982.26. Decision containing finding that licensee or registrant engaged in sexual contact with patient or former patient; order of revocation

The board shall revoke any license issued under this chapter upon a decision made in accordance with the procedures set forth in Chapter 5 (commencing with Section 11500) of Part 1 of Division 3 of Title 2 of the Government Code, that contains any finding of fact that the licensee or registrant engaged in any act of sexual contact, as defined in Section 729, when that act is with a patient, or with a former patient when the relationship was terminated primarily for the purpose of engaging in that act. The revocation shall not be stayed by the administrative law judge or the board. *(Added by Stats.1994, c. 1274 (S.B.2039), § 32. Amended by Stats.2005, c. 658 (S.B.229), § 20.)*

Cross References

Board defined for purposes of this Chapter, see Business and Professions Code §§ 4980.03, 4990.02.

§ 4982.3. Procedure

The proceedings conducted under this article shall be held in accordance with Chapter 5 (commencing with Section 11500) of Part 1 of Division 3 of Title 2 of the Government Code. *(Added by Stats.1986, c. 1365, § 4.)*

ARTICLE 3. PENALTIES

Section
4983. Violation; misdemeanor; punishment.
4983.1. Injunction.

§ 4983. Violation; misdemeanor; punishment

Any person who violates any of the provisions of this chapter is guilty of a misdemeanor punishable by imprisonment in the county jail not exceeding six months, or by a fine not exceeding two thousand five hundred dollars ($2,500), or by both. *(Added by Stats.1986, c. 1365, § 4.)*

Cross References

County defined for purposes of this Code, see Business and Professions Code § 17.
Misdemeanors, penalties and definition, see Penal Code §§ 17, 19, 19.2.

§ 4983.1. Injunction

In addition to other proceedings provided for in this chapter, whenever any person has engaged, or is about to engage, in any acts or practices which constitute, or will constitute, an offense against this chapter, the superior court in and for the county wherein the acts or practices take place, or are about to take place, may issue an injunction, or other appropriate order, restraining such conduct on application of the board, the Attorney General, or the district attorney of the county.

The proceedings under this section shall be governed by Chapter 3 (commencing with Section 525) of Title 7 of Part 2 of the Code of Civil Procedure. *(Added by Stats.1986, c. 1365, § 4.)*

Cross References

Attorney General, generally, see Government Code § 12500 et seq.
Board defined for purposes of this Chapter, see Business and Professions Code §§ 4980.03, 4990.02.
Board defined for purposes of this Code, see Business and Professions Code § 22.
County defined for purposes of this Code, see Business and Professions Code § 17.
Injunctions,
   Generally, see Code of Civil Procedure § 526.
   Under this Code, see Business and Professions Code § 125.5.
   Temporary restraining orders under this Code, see Business and Professions Code § 125.7.

ARTICLE 4. REVENUE

Section
4984. Expiration of licenses; renewal of unexpired licenses.
4984.01. Associate registration; duration of registration; renewal.
4984.1. Renewal of expired licenses.
4984.2. Renewal of suspended license; effect of renewal.
4984.3. Revoked license; reinstatement after expiration.
4984.4. Time limit for renewal after expiration; new license.
4984.41. Retired licenses; prohibited activities; renewal not required; restoration requirements; continuing education.
4984.5. Report and payment of revenue.
4984.7. Fees.
4984.72. Failed examination; time limits for retaking examination; necessity of new application.
4984.75. Additional fees.
4984.8. Inactive licenses.
4984.9. Written notice of name change; licensees or registrants.

§ 4984. Expiration of licenses; renewal of unexpired licenses

(a) Licenses issued under this chapter shall expire no more than 24 months after the issue date. The expiration date of the original license shall be set by the board.

(b) To renew an unexpired license, the licensee, on or before the expiration date of the license, shall do all of the following:

(1) Apply for a renewal on a form prescribed by the board.

(2) Pay a two-year renewal fee prescribed by the board.

(3) Certify compliance with the continuing education requirements set forth in Section 4980.54.

(4) Notify the board whether he or she has been convicted, as defined in Section 490, of a misdemeanor or felony, or whether any disciplinary action has been taken by any regulatory or licensing board in this or any other state, subsequent to the licensee's last renewal. *(Added by Stats.1986, c. 1365, § 4. Amended by Stats.2000, c. 836 (S.B.1554), § 35.)*

Cross References

Board defined for purposes of this Chapter, see Business and Professions Code §§ 4980.03, 4990.02.

Board defined for purposes of this Code, see Business and Professions Code § 22.

Felonies, definition and penalties, see Penal Code §§ 17, 18.

Misdemeanors, definition and penalties, see Penal Code §§ 17, 19, 19.2.

Renewal provisions under this Code, see Business and Professions Code §§ 152.5, 152.6.

§ 4984.01. Associate registration; duration of registration; renewal

(a) The associate marriage and family therapist registration shall expire one year from the last day of the month in which it was issued.

(b) To renew the registration, the registrant shall, on or before the expiration date of the registration, complete all of the following actions:

(1) Apply for renewal on a form prescribed by the board.

(2) Pay a renewal fee prescribed by the board.

(3) Participate in the California law and ethics examination pursuant to Section 4980.399 each year until successful completion of this examination.

(4) Notify the board whether * * * they have been convicted, as defined in Section 490, of a misdemeanor or felony, and whether any disciplinary action has been taken against * * * them by a regulatory or licensing board in this or any other state subsequent to the last renewal of the registration.

(5) Certify under penalty of perjury their compliance with the continuing education requirements set forth in Section 4980.54.

(c) An expired registration may be renewed by completing all of the actions described in paragraphs (1) to (5), inclusive, of subdivision (b).

(d) The registration may be renewed a maximum of five times. No registration shall be renewed or reinstated beyond six years from the last day of the month during which it was issued, regardless of whether it has been revoked. When no further renewals are possible, an applicant may apply for and obtain a subsequent associate registration number if the applicant meets the educational requirements for a subsequent associate registration number and has passed the California law and ethics examination. An applicant who is issued a subsequent associate registration number pursuant to this subdivision shall not be employed or volunteer in a private practice. *(Added by Stats.2011, c. 387 (S.B.704), § 10, operative Jan. 1, 2013. Amended by Stats.2012, c. 799 (S.B.1575), § 39, operative Jan. 1, 2014; Stats.2013, c. 473 (S.B.821), § 31, operative Jan. 1, 2016; Stats.2015, c. 426 (S.B.800), § 41, eff. Jan. 1, 2016; Stats.2018, c. 486 (A.B.2117), § 2, eff. Jan. 1, 2019; Stats.2018, c. 743 (A.B.93), § 22.5, eff. Jan. 1, 2019; Stats.2022, c. 520 (A.B.1759), § 5, eff. Jan. 1, 2023.)*

Cross References

Applicant defined for purposes of this Chapter, see Business and Professions Code § 4980.03.

Board defined for purposes of this Chapter, see Business and Professions Code §§ 4980.03, 4990.02.

Felonies, definition and penalties, see Penal Code §§ 17, 18.

Misdemeanors, definition and penalties, see Penal Code §§ 17, 19, 19.2.

§ 4984.1. Renewal of expired licenses

A licensee may renew a license at any time within three years after its expiration by completing all of the actions described in subdivision (b) of Section 4984 and paying any delinquency fees. *(Added by Stats.1986, c. 1365, § 4. Amended by Stats.1998, c. 879 (S.B.2238), § 8; Stats.2007, c. 588 (S.B.1048), § 66.)*

Cross References

Board defined for purposes of this Chapter, see Business and Professions Code §§ 4980.03, 4990.02.

Board defined for purposes of this Code, see Business and Professions Code § 22.

Renewal provisions under this Code, see Business and Professions Code §§ 152.5, 152.6.

§ 4984.2. Renewal of suspended license; effect of renewal

A suspended license is subject to expiration and shall be renewed as provided in this article, but such renewal does not entitle the licensee, while it remains suspended and until it is reinstated, to engage in the activity to which the license relates, or in any other activity or conduct in violation of the order or judgment by which it was suspended. *(Added by Stats.1986, c. 1365, § 4.)*

Cross References

Renewal provisions under this Code, see Business and Professions Code §§ 152.5, 152.6.

§ 4984.3. Revoked license; reinstatement after expiration

A revoked license is subject to expiration as provided in this article, but it may not be renewed. If it is reinstated after its expiration, the licensee shall, as a condition precedent to its reinstatement, pay a reinstatement fee in an amount equal to the renewal fee in effect on the last regular renewal date before the date on which it is reinstated, plus the delinquency fee, if any, accrued at the time of its revocation. *(Added by Stats.1986, c. 1365, § 4.)*

Cross References

Renewal provisions under this Code, see Business and Professions Code §§ 152.5, 152.6.

§ 4984.4. Time limit for renewal after expiration; new license

A license that is not renewed within three years after its expiration shall not be renewed, restored, reinstated, or reissued; however, the former licensee may apply for and obtain a new license if the following criteria are satisfied:

(a) No fact, circumstance, or condition exists that, if the license were issued, would constitute grounds for its revocation or suspension.

(b) He or she submits an application for licensure and the fee for that application.

(c) He or she takes and passes the current licensing examinations.

(d) He or she submits the fee for initial license issuance.

(e) He or she complies with the fingerprint requirements established by board regulation. *(Added by Stats.1986, c. 1365, § 4. Amended by Stats.1987, c. 738, § 14; Stats.1998, c. 879 (S.B.2238), § 9; Stats.2003, c. 874 (S.B.363), § 12; Stats.2007, c. 588 (S.B.1048), § 67; Stats.2012, c. 799 (S.B.1575), § 40; Stats.2017, c. 573 (S.B.800), § 7, eff. Jan. 1, 2018.)*

Cross References

Renewal provisions under this Code, see Business and Professions Code §§ 152.5, 152.6.

§ 4984.41. Retired licenses; prohibited activities; renewal not required; restoration requirements; continuing education

(a) The board shall issue, upon application and payment of the fee fixed by this chapter, a retired license to a marriage and family therapist who holds a license that is current and active or a license that is inactive, and whose license is not suspended, revoked, or

§ 4984.41

otherwise punitively restricted by the board or subject to disciplinary action under this chapter.

(b) The holder of a retired license issued pursuant to this section shall not engage in any activity for which an active marriage and family therapist license is required.

(c) The holder of a retired license shall not be required to renew that license.

(d) The holder of a retired license may apply to restore to active status his or her license to practice marriage and family therapy if that retired license was issued less than three years prior to the application date, and the applicant meets all of the following requirements:

(1) Has not committed an act or crime constituting grounds for denial of licensure.

(2) Pays the renewal fee required by this chapter.

(3) Completes the required continuing education as specified in Section 4980.54.

(4) Complies with the fingerprint submission requirements established by the board in regulation.

(e) An applicant requesting to restore his or her license pursuant to subdivision (d), whose license was issued in accordance with this section less than one year from the date of the application, shall complete 18 hours of continuing education as specified in Section 4980.54.

(f) An applicant requesting to restore his or her license pursuant to subdivision (d), whose license was issued in accordance with this section one or more years from the date of the application, shall complete 36 hours of continuing education as specified in Section 4980.54.

(g) The holder of a retired license may apply to restore to active status his or her license to practice marriage and family therapy if that retired license was issued three or more years prior to the application date, and the applicant meets all of the following requirements:

(1) Has not committed an act or crime constituting grounds for denial of licensure.

(2) Applies for licensure and pays the fee required by this chapter.

(3) Passes the examinations required for licensure.

(4) Complies with the fingerprint submission requirements established by the board in regulation. (Added by Stats.2010, c. 548 (A.B.2191), § 1. Amended by Stats.2013, c. 339 (A.B.404), § 1.)

Cross References

Applicant defined for purposes of this Chapter, see Business and Professions Code § 4980.03.
Board defined for purposes of this Chapter, see Business and Professions Code §§ 4980.03, 4990.02.

§ 4984.5. Report and payment of revenue

The board shall report each month to the Controller the amount and source of all revenue received pursuant to this chapter and at the same time pay the entire amount thereof into the State Treasury for credit to the Behavioral Sciences Fund. (Added by Stats.1986, c. 1365, § 4. Amended by Stats.1996, c. 829 (A.B.3473), § 87.)

Cross References

Board defined for purposes of this Chapter, see Business and Professions Code §§ 4980.03, 4990.02.
Board defined for purposes of this Code, see Business and Professions Code § 22.

State Controller, generally, see Government Code § 12402 et seq.

§ 4984.7. Fees

(a) The board shall assess the following fees relating to the licensure of marriage and family therapists:

(1) The application fee for an associate registration shall be one hundred fifty dollars ($150). The board may adopt regulations to set the fee at a higher amount, up to a maximum of three hundred dollars ($300).

(2) The annual renewal fee for an associate registration shall be one hundred fifty dollars ($150). The board may adopt regulations to set the fee at a higher amount, up to a maximum of three hundred dollars ($300).

(3) The fee for the application for licensure shall be two hundred fifty dollars ($250). The board may adopt regulations to set the fee at a higher amount, up to a maximum of five hundred dollars ($500).

(4)(A)(i) The fee for the clinical examination shall be two hundred fifty dollars ($250). The board may adopt regulations to set the fee at a higher amount, up to a maximum of five hundred dollars ($500).

(ii) The fee for the California law and ethics examination shall be one hundred fifty dollars ($150). The board may adopt regulations to set the fee at a higher amount, up to a maximum of three hundred dollars ($300).

(B) An applicant who fails to appear for an examination, after having been scheduled to take the examination, shall forfeit the examination fee.

(C) The amount of the examination fees shall be based on the actual cost to the board of developing, purchasing, and grading each examination and the actual cost to the board of administering each examination. The examination fees shall be adjusted periodically by regulation to reflect the actual costs incurred by the board.

(5) The fee for rescoring an examination shall be twenty dollars ($20).

(6) The fee for the issuance of an initial license shall be two hundred dollars ($200). The board may adopt regulations to set the fee at a higher amount, up to a maximum of four hundred dollars ($400).

(7) The fee for the two-year license renewal shall be two hundred dollars ($200). The board may adopt regulations to set the fee at a higher amount, up to a maximum of four hundred dollars ($400).

(8) The renewal delinquency fee shall be one-half of the fee for license renewal. A person who permits their license to expire is subject to the delinquency fee.

(9) The fee for issuance of a replacement registration, license, or certificate shall be twenty dollars ($20).

(10) The fee for issuance of a certificate or letter of good standing shall be twenty-five dollars ($25).

(11) The fee for issuance of a retired license shall be forty dollars ($40).

(b) This section shall become operative on January 1, 2021. (Added by Stats.2020, c. 359 (A.B.3330), § 9, eff. Jan. 1, 2021, operative Jan. 1, 2021. Amended by Stats.2021, c. 647 (S.B.801), § 31, eff. Jan. 1, 2022.)

Cross References

Agency with unencumbered funds, reduction of license or other fees, see Business and Professions Code § 128.5.
Board defined for purposes of this Chapter, see Business and Professions Code §§ 4980.03, 4990.02.

§ 4984.72. Failed examination; time limits for retaking examination; necessity of new application

(a) Effective January 1, 2016, an applicant who fails the clinical examination may, within one year from the notification date of that failure, retake the examination as regularly scheduled without further application upon payment of the fee for the examination. Thereafter, the applicant shall not be eligible for further examination until he or she files a new application, meets all requirements in effect on the date of application, and pays all required fees.

(b) This section shall become operative on January 1, 2016. *(Added by Stats.2011, c. 387 (S.B.704), § 14, operative Jan. 1, 2013. Amended by Stats.2012, c. 799 (S.B.1575), § 44, operative Jan. 1, 2014; Stats.2013, c. 473 (S.B.821), § 35, operative Jan. 1, 2016.)*

Cross References

Applicant defined for purposes of this Chapter, see Business and Professions Code § 4980.03.

§ 4984.75. Additional fees

(a) In addition to the fees charged pursuant to Section 4984.7 for the biennial renewal of a license pursuant to Section 4984, the board shall collect an additional fee of twenty dollars ($20) at the time of renewal. The board shall transfer this amount to the Controller who shall deposit the funds in the Mental Health Practitioner Education Fund.

(b) This section shall become operative on July 1, 2018. *(Added by Stats.2017, c. 557 (A.B.1188), § 4, eff. Oct. 7, 2017, operative July 1, 2018.)*

Cross References

Board defined for purposes of this Chapter, see Business and Professions Code §§ 4980.03, 4990.02.

Mental Health Practitioner Education Fund, see Health and Safety Code § 128458.

State Controller, generally, see Government Code § 12402 et seq.

§ 4984.8. Inactive licenses

(a) A licensee may apply to the board to request that his or her license be placed on inactive status.

(b) A licensee on inactive status shall be subject to this chapter and shall not engage in the practice of marriage and family therapy in this state.

(c) A licensee who holds an inactive license shall pay a biennial fee in the amount of one-half of the standard renewal fee and shall be exempt from continuing education requirements.

(d) A licensee on inactive status who has not committed an act or crime constituting grounds for denial of licensure may, upon request, restore his or her license to practice marriage and family therapy to active status.

(1) A licensee requesting to restore his or her license to active status between renewal cycles shall pay the remaining one-half of his or her renewal fee.

(2) A licensee requesting to restore his or her license to active status, whose license will expire less than one year from the date of the request, shall complete 18 hours of continuing education as specified in Section 4980.54.

(3) A licensee requesting to restore his or her license to active status, whose license will expire more than one year from the date of the request, shall complete 36 hours of continuing education as specified in Section 4980.54. *(Added by Stats.2007, c. 588 (S.B.1048), § 72. Amended by Stats.2010, c. 653 (S.B.1489), § 43.)*

Cross References

Board defined for purposes of this Chapter, see Business and Professions Code §§ 4980.03, 4990.02.

Board defined for purposes of this Code, see Business and Professions Code § 22.

§ 4984.9. Written notice of name change; licensees or registrants

A licensee or registrant shall give written notice to the board of a name change, giving both the old and new names. The written notice shall be submitted to the board within 30 days of the issuance of a new government-issued photographic identification. The licensee or registrant shall certify the information by signing a statement under penalty of perjury. A copy of both of the following documents evidencing the change shall be submitted with the notice:

(a) A current government-issued photographic identification.

(b) The legal document authorizing the name change, such as a court order or a marriage certificate. *(Added by Stats.1999, c. 655 (S.B.1308), § 85. Amended by Stats.2017, c. 573 (S.B.800), § 9, eff. Jan. 1, 2018.)*

Cross References

Board defined for purposes of this Chapter, see Business and Professions Code §§ 4980.03, 4990.02.

Board defined for purposes of this Code, see Business and Professions Code § 22.

ARTICLE 6. MARRIAGE AND FAMILY THERAPY CORPORATIONS

Section
4987.5. Definition.
4987.6. Unprofessional conduct.
4987.7. Name.
4987.8. Directors, shareholders, and officers; necessity of license.
4988.   Income for professional services not to accrue to disqualified shareholders.
4988.1. Scope of practice.
4988.2. Rules and regulations.

Cross References

Moscone-Knox Professional Corporation Act, see Corporations Code § 13400 et seq.

Psychotherapist-patient privilege, application to individuals and entities, see Evidence Code § 1014.

§ 4987.5. Definition

A marriage and family therapy corporation is a corporation that is authorized to render professional services, as defined in Section 13401 of the Corporations Code, so long as that corporation and its shareholders, officers, directors, and employees rendering professional services are in compliance with the Moscone-Knox Professional Corporation Act (Part 4 (commencing with Section 13400) of Division 3 of Title 1 of the Corporations Code), this article, and any other statute or regulation pertaining to that corporation and the conduct of its affairs. With respect to a marriage and family therapy corporation, the governmental agency referred to in the Moscone-Knox Professional Corporation Act is the Board of Behavioral Sciences. *(Added by Stats.1986, c. 1365, § 4. Amended by Stats.1996, c. 829 (A.B.3473), § 89; Stats.1999, c. 657 (A.B.1677), § 5; Stats.2002, c. 1013 (S.B.2026), § 41; Stats.2014, c. 316 (S.B.1466), § 24, eff. Jan. 1, 2015; Stats.2021, c. 647 (S.B.801), § 32, eff. Jan. 1, 2022.)*

Cross References

Board defined for purposes of this Chapter, see Business and Professions Code §§ 4980.03, 4990.02.

§ 4987.5

Board defined for purposes of this Code, see Business and Professions Code § 22.
Director defined for purposes of this Code, see Business and Professions Code § 23.5.
Moscone–Knox Professional Corporation Act, see Corporations Code § 13400 et seq.

Research References

Forms

1 California Transactions Forms--Business Entities § 1:12, Professional Corporations.
3A California Transactions Forms--Business Entities § 14:27, Rendering Professional Services.
3A California Transactions Forms--Business Entities § 15:2, Scope of Professional Corporation Act.

§ 4987.6. Unprofessional conduct

It shall constitute unprofessional conduct and a violation of this chapter for any person licensed under this chapter to violate, attempt to violate, directly or indirectly, or assist in or abet the violation of, or conspire to violate, any provision or term of this article, the Moscone–Knox Professional Corporation Act (Part 4 (commencing with Section 13400) of Division 3 of Title 1 of the Corporations Code), or any regulations duly adopted under those laws. *(Added by Stats.1999, c. 657 (A.B.1677), § 7.)*

§ 4987.7. Name

The name of a marriage and family therapy corporation shall contain one or more of the words "marriage," "family," or "child" together with one or more of the words "counseling," "counselor," "therapy," or "therapist," and wording or abbreviations denoting corporate existence. A marriage and family therapy corporation that conducts business under a fictitious business name shall not use any name that is false, misleading or deceptive, and shall inform the patient, prior to the commencement of treatment, that the business is conducted by a marriage and family therapy corporation. *(Formerly § 4987.8. Renumbered § 4987.7 and amended by Stats.1999, c. 657 (A.B.1677), § 9. Amended by Stats.2002, c. 1013 (S.B.2026), § 42; Stats.2004, c. 204 (A.B.2552), § 6.)*

§ 4987.8. Directors, shareholders, and officers; necessity of license

Except as provided in Section 13403 of the Corporations Code, each director, shareholder, and officer of a marriage and family therapy corporation shall be a licensed person as defined in the Moscone–Knox Professional Corporation Act. *(Formerly § 4987.9, added by Stats.1986, c. 1365, § 4. Amended by Stats.1988, c. 864, § 2. Renumbered § 4987.8 and amended by Stats.1999, c. 657 (A.B.1677), § 10. Amended by Stats.2002, c. 1013 (S.B.2026), § 43.)*

Cross References

Director defined or purposes of this Code, see Business and Professions Code § 23.5.
Moscone-Knox Professional Corporation Act, see Corporations Code § 13400 et seq.

§ 4988. Income for professional services not to accrue to disqualified shareholders

The income of a marriage and family therapy corporation attributable to professional services rendered while a shareholder is a disqualified person (as defined in the Moscone–Knox Professional Corporation Act) shall not in any manner accrue to the benefit of that shareholder or his or her shares in the marriage and family therapy corporation. *(Added by Stats.1986, c. 1365, § 4. Amended by Stats.2002, c. 1013 (S.B.2026), § 44.)*

Cross References

Moscone-Knox Professional Corporation Act, see Corporations Code § 13400 et seq.

§ 4988.1. Scope of practice

A marriage and family therapy corporation shall not do or fail to do any act the doing of which or the failure to do which would constitute unprofessional conduct under any statute, rule or regulation now or hereafter in effect. In the conduct of its practice, it shall observe and be bound by statutes, rules and regulations to the same extent as a person holding a license as a marriage and family therapist. *(Added by Stats.1986, c. 1365, § 4. Amended by Stats.1999, c. 657 (A.B.1677), § 11; Stats.2002, c. 1013 (S.B.2026), § 45.)*

§ 4988.2. Rules and regulations

The board may formulate and enforce rules and regulations to carry out the purposes and objectives of this article, including rules and regulations requiring (a) that the articles of incorporation or bylaws of a marriage and family therapy corporation shall include a provision whereby the capital stock of the corporation owned by a disqualified person (as defined in the Moscone–Knox Professional Corporation Act), or a deceased person, shall be sold to the corporation or to the remaining shareholders of the corporation within the time that rules and regulations may provide, and (b) that a marriage and family therapy corporation shall provide adequate security by insurance or otherwise for claims against it by its patients arising out of the rendering of professional services. *(Added by Stats.1986, c. 1365, § 4. Amended by Stats.1999, c. 657 (A.B.1677), § 12; Stats.2002, c. 1013 (S.B.2026), § 46.)*

Cross References

Administrative regulations and rulemaking, see Government Code § 11340 et seq.
Board defined for purposes of this Chapter, see Business and Professions Code §§ 4980.03, 4990.02.
Board defined for purposes of this Code, see Business and Professions Code § 22.
Moscone-Knox Professional Corporation Act, see Corporations Code § 13400 et seq.

ARTICLE 7. REVIEW

Section
4989. Powers and duties of board; date of review.

§ 4989. Powers and duties of board; date of review

The powers and duties of the board, as set forth in this chapter, shall be subject to the review required by Division 1.2 (commencing with Section 473). The review shall be performed as if this chapter were scheduled to become inoperative on July 1, 2005, and would be repealed as of January 1, 2006, as described in Section 473.1. *(Added by Stats.1994, c. 908 (S.B.2036), § 37. Amended by Stats.1998, c. 589 (S.B.1983), § 11.)*

Cross References

Board defined for purposes of this Chapter, see Business and Professions Code §§ 4980.03, 4990.02.
Board defined for purposes of this Code, see Business and Professions Code § 22.

CIVIL CODE

Division 1

PERSONS

Part 2

PERSONAL RIGHTS

Section
43.3. Breastfeeding; location.
43.4. Fraudulent promise to marry or cohabit not actionable.
43.5. Wrongs not actionable.
43.56. Foster parents; alienation of child's affection.
43.6. Immunity from liability; actions against parents on childbirth claims; defenses and damages in third party actions.
47. Privileged publication or broadcast.
48.7. Child abuse; prohibition against libel or slander action while charges pending; tolling of limitations; pleadings; demurrer; attorney fees and costs.
49. Personal relations, acts forbidden by.
52.4. Civil action for damages arising from gender violence.
52.45. Civil action for damages arising from sexual orientation violence.
52.5. Civil action for damages to victims of human trafficking.
52.6. Notice to be posted at specified businesses and establishments; slavery and human trafficking; location of posting; contents; languages; model notice; employee training; civil penalties; local ordinances.
52.65. Civil action for hotels in violation of sex trafficking activity.

Cross References

California Community Care Facilities Act, misuse of disclosed sex offender registration information, civil action, see Health and Safety Code § 1522.01.
Campaign advertising or communication, application of libel and slander provisions, see Elections Code § 20500.
Sex offenders, misuse of information disclosed to the public, see Penal Code §§ 290.4, 290.46.

§ 43.3. Breastfeeding; location

Notwithstanding any other provision of law, a mother may breastfeed her child in any location, public or private, except the private home or residence of another, where the mother and the child are otherwise authorized to be present. *(Added by Stats.1997, c. 59 (A.B.157), § 1.)*

Cross References

Reasonable accommodations for a lactating student to express breast milk, breast-feed an infant child, or address other needs related to breastfeeding, academic penalty against student for use of reasonable accommodations prohibited, requirement of a sink in new and existing facilities, complaint of noncompliance, implementation of requirements, see Education Code § 66271.9.
Right of applicant or recipient of aid to breastfeed child in county welfare department or other county office, see Welfare and Institutions Code § 11218.

§ 43.4. Fraudulent promise to marry or cohabit not actionable

A fraudulent promise to marry or to cohabit after marriage does not give rise to a cause of action for damages. *(Added by Stats.1959, c. 381, p. 2306, § 1.)*

Research References

Forms

West's California Code Forms, Civil § 43 Form 1, Complaint—False Imprisonment.

§ 43.5. Wrongs not actionable

No cause of action arises for:

(a) Alienation of affection.

(b) Criminal conversation.

(c) Seduction of a person over the age of legal consent.

(d) Breach of promise of marriage. *(Added by Stats.1939, c. 128, p. 1245, § 2.)*

Cross References

Inveiglement or enticement of unmarried female under 18, see Penal Code § 266.

§ 43.56. Foster parents; alienation of child's affection

No cause of action arises against a foster parent for alienation of affection of a foster child. *(Formerly § 43.55, added by Stats.1986, c. 1330, § 2, eff. Sept. 29, 1986. Amended by Stats.1988, c. 195, § 1, eff. June 16, 1988. Renumbered § 43.56 and amended by Stats.1990, c. 216 (S.B.2510), § 5.)*

§ 43.6. Immunity from liability; actions against parents on childbirth claims; defenses and damages in third party actions

(a) No cause of action arises against a parent of a child based upon the claim that the child should not have been conceived or, if conceived, should not have been allowed to have been born alive.

(b) The failure or refusal of a parent to prevent the live birth of his or her child shall not be a defense in any action against a third party, nor shall the failure or refusal be considered in awarding damages in any such action.

(c) As used in this section "conceived" means the fertilization of a human ovum by a human sperm. *(Added by Stats.1981, c. 331, § 1.)*

§ 47. Privileged publication or broadcast

A privileged publication or broadcast is one made:

(a) In the proper discharge of an official duty.

(b) In any (1) legislative proceeding, (2) judicial proceeding, (3) in any other official proceeding authorized by law, or (4) in the initiation or course of any other proceeding authorized by law and reviewable pursuant to Chapter 2 (commencing with Section 1084) of Title 1 of Part 3 of the Code of Civil Procedure, except as follows:

(1) An allegation or averment contained in any pleading or affidavit filed in an action for marital dissolution or legal separation made of or concerning a person by or against whom no affirmative relief is prayed in the action shall not be a privileged publication or broadcast as to the person making the allegation or averment within the meaning of this section unless the pleading is verified or affidavit

§ 47

sworn to, and is made without malice, by one having reasonable and probable cause for believing the truth of the allegation or averment and unless the allegation or averment is material and relevant to the issues in the action.

(2) This subdivision does not make privileged any communication made in furtherance of an act of intentional destruction or alteration of physical evidence undertaken for the purpose of depriving a party to litigation of the use of that evidence, whether or not the content of the communication is the subject of a subsequent publication or broadcast which is privileged pursuant to this section. As used in this paragraph, "physical evidence" means evidence specified in Section 250 of the Evidence Code or evidence that is property of any type specified in Chapter 14 (commencing with Section 2031.010) of Title 4 of Part 4 of the Code of Civil Procedure.

(3) This subdivision does not make privileged any communication made in a judicial proceeding knowingly concealing the existence of an insurance policy or policies.

(4) A recorded lis pendens is not a privileged publication unless it identifies an action previously filed with a court of competent jurisdiction which affects the title or right of possession of real property, as authorized or required by law.

(5) This subdivision does not make privileged any communication between a person and a law enforcement agency in which the person makes a false report that another person has committed, or is in the act of committing, a criminal act or is engaged in an activity requiring law enforcement intervention, knowing that the report is false, or with reckless disregard for the truth or falsity of the report.

(c) In a communication, without malice, to a person interested therein, (1) by one who is also interested, or (2) by one who stands in such a relation to the person interested as to afford a reasonable ground for supposing the motive for the communication to be innocent, or (3) who is requested by the person interested to give the information. This subdivision applies to and includes a communication concerning the job performance or qualifications of an applicant for employment, based upon credible evidence, made without malice, by a current or former employer of the applicant to, and upon request of, one whom the employer reasonably believes is a prospective employer of the applicant. This subdivision applies to and includes a complaint of sexual harassment by an employee, without malice, to an employer based upon credible evidence and communications between the employer and interested persons, without malice, regarding a complaint of sexual harassment. This subdivision authorizes a current or former employer, or the employer's agent, to answer, without malice, whether or not the employer would rehire a current or former employee and whether the decision to not rehire is based upon the employer's determination that the former employee engaged in sexual harassment. This subdivision does not apply to a communication concerning the speech or activities of an applicant for employment if the speech or activities are constitutionally protected, or otherwise protected by Section 527.3 of the Code of Civil Procedure or any other provision of law.

(d)(1) By a fair and true report in, or a communication to, a public journal, of (A) a judicial, (B) legislative, or (C) other public official proceeding, or (D) of anything said in the course thereof, or (E) of a verified charge or complaint made by any person to a public official, upon which complaint a warrant has been issued.

(2) Paragraph (1) does not make privileged any communication to a public journal that does any of the following:

(A) Violates Rule 5-120 of the State Bar Rules of Professional Conduct.

(B) Breaches a court order.

(C) Violates a requirement of confidentiality imposed by law.

(e) By a fair and true report of (1) the proceedings of a public meeting, if the meeting was lawfully convened for a lawful purpose and open to the public, or (2) the publication of the matter complained of was for the public benefit. *(Enacted in 1872. Amended by Code Am.1873–74, c. 612, p. 184, § 11; Stats.1895, c. 163, p. 167, § 1; Stats.1927, c. 866, p. 1881, § 1; Stats.1945, c. 1489, p. 2763, § 3; Stats.1979, c. 184, p. 403, § 1; Stats.1990, c. 1491 (A.B.3765), § 1; Stats.1991, c. 432 (A.B.529), § 1; Stats.1992, c. 615 (S.B.1804), § 1; Stats.1994, c. 364 (A.B.2778), § 1; Stats.1994, c. 700 (S.B.1457), § 2.5; Stats.1996, c. 1055 (S.B.1540), § 2; Stats.2002, c. 1029 (A.B.2868), § 1, eff. Sept. 28, 2002; Stats.2004, c. 182 (A.B. 3081), § 4, operative July 1, 2005; Stats.2018, c. 82 (A.B.2770), § 1, eff. Jan. 1, 2019; Stats.2020, c. 327 (A.B.1775), § 2, eff. Jan. 1, 2021.)*

Cross References

Alameda County Medical Center Hospital Authority, open sessions and peer review proceedings as official proceedings, see Health and Safety Code § 101850.

Arbitration and conciliation of international commercial disputes, immunity of arbitrators from civil liability, see Code of Civil Procedure § 1297.119.

Central Coast Hospital authority, powers of authority, see Health and Safety Code § 101661.

Claims subject to article governing false claims actions, applicability of section, see Government Code § 12654.

Contracts for Medi–Cal services and case management, County of Alameda health authority, open sessions and peer review proceedings as official proceedings, see Welfare and Institutions Code § 14087.35.

Contracts for Medi–Cal services and case management, special commission for Tulare and San Joaquin counties, peer review proceedings as official proceedings, see Welfare and Institutions Code § 14087.31.

Elder Abuse and Dependent Adult Civil Protection Act, mandated reporters of suspected financial abuse, see Welfare and Institutions Code §§ 15630.1, 15630.2.

Evidence of mitigating circumstances, see Code of Civil Procedure § 461.

Expulsion hearings, immunity of pupil witnesses, see Education Code § 48918.6.

Governmental access to financial records, authorized acts, see Government Code § 7480.

Kern County Hospital Authority, meetings, see Health and Safety Code § 101855.

Physician, surgeon, or doctor of podiatric medicine, complaints of professional competence or professional conduct subject to immunity, see Civil Code § 43.96.

Pleading and proof, see Code of Civil Procedure § 460.

Providing information indicating board licensee guilty of unprofessional conduct or impaired because of drug or alcohol abuse or mental illness, additional immunity, see Business and Professions Code § 2318.

Real property defined for purposes of this Code, see Civil Code § 658.

San Luis Obispo County Hospital Authority, open sessions as official proceedings, see Health and Safety Code § 101848.6.

San Luis Obispo County Hospital Authority, peer review proceedings as official proceedings, see Health and Safety Code § 101848.9.

Student expulsion hearings, privileged testimony, see Education Code § 48918.6.

Surplus line advisory organization, communications between interested persons, see Insurance Code § 1780.66.

Trade secrets, disclosure in official proceedings, see Civil Code § 3426.11.

Research References

Forms

2 California Transactions Forms--Business Transactions § 14:56, Characteristics of Arbitration, Definitions, and Distinctions.

West's California Code Forms, Civil § 45a Form 1, Complaint—Libel—Libelous on Its Face.

West's California Code Forms, Civil § 47 Form 1, Affirmative Defense—Defamation—Official Duty Privilege.

West's California Code Forms, Civil § 47 Form 2, Affirmative Defense—Defamation—Official Proceeding Privilege.

West's California Code Forms, Civil § 47 Form 5, Affirmative Defense—Defamation—Report of Public Meeting.

West's California Code Forms, Civil § 47 Form 8, Affirmative Defense—Defamation—Complaint of Sexual Harassment.

West's California Code Forms, Civil § 1788.30 Form 1, Complaint—Unfair Debt Collection Practices.

West's California Code Forms, Civil § 2924 Form 1, Notice—Of Default—Under Mortgage.

West's California Code Forms, Education § 48918 Form 1, Notice of Expulsion Hearing.

§ 48.7. Child abuse; prohibition against libel or slander action while charges pending; tolling of limitations; pleadings; demurrer; attorney fees and costs

(a) No person charged by indictment, information, or other accusatory pleading of child abuse may bring a civil libel or slander action against the minor, the parent or guardian of the minor, or any witness, based upon any statements made by the minor, parent or guardian, or witness which are reasonably believed to be in furtherance of the prosecution of the criminal charges while the charges are pending before a trial court. The charges are not pending within the meaning of this section after dismissal, after pronouncement of judgment, or during an appeal from a judgment.

Any applicable statute of limitations shall be tolled during the period that such charges are pending before a trial court.

(b) Whenever any complaint for libel or slander is filed which is subject to the provisions of this section, no responsive pleading shall be required to be filed until 30 days after the end of the period set forth in subdivision (a).

(c) Every complaint for libel or slander based on a statement that the plaintiff committed an act of child abuse shall state that the complaint is not barred by subdivision (a). A failure to include that statement shall be grounds for a demurrer.

(d) Whenever a demurrer against a complaint for libel or slander is sustained on the basis that the complaint was filed in violation of this section, attorney's fees and costs shall be awarded to the prevailing party.

(e) Whenever a prosecutor is informed by a minor, parent, guardian, or witness that a complaint against one of those persons has been filed which may be subject to the provisions of this section, the prosecutor shall provide that person with a copy of this section.

(f) As used in this section, child abuse has the meaning set forth in Section 11165 of the Penal Code. (Added by Stats.1981, c. 253, § 1.)

Cross References

Child abuse, see Penal Code §§ 273a, 273d.
Libel defined, see Civil Code § 45.
Slander defined, see Civil Code § 46.

Research References

Forms

West's California Code Forms, Civil § 48.7 Form 1, Allegation in Complaint for Defamation—Child Abuse.

§ 49. Personal relations, acts forbidden by

The rights of personal relations forbid:

(a) The abduction or enticement of a child from a parent, or from a guardian entitled to its custody;

(b) The seduction of a person under the age of legal consent;

(c) Any injury to a servant which affects his ability to serve his master, other than seduction, abduction or criminal conversation. (Enacted in 1872. Amended by Stats.1905, c. 70, p. 68, § 1; Stats.1939, c. 128, p. 1245, § 1; Stats.1939, c. 1103, p. 3037, § 5.)

Cross References

Abduction of minor, purpose of prostitution, see Penal Code § 267.
Custody of child, see Family Code § 3010.
Hormonal chemical treatment, see Penal Code § 645.
Inveiglement or enticement of unmarried female minor for purposes of prostitution, etc., see Penal Code § 266.
Kidnapping,
   Defined, see Penal Code § 207.
   Punishment for, see Penal Code § 208 et seq.
Limitation on action for seduction of person under age of consent, see Code of Civil Procedure § 340.

Wrongs not actionable, see Civil Code § 43.5.

Research References

Forms

22APT1 Am. Jur. Pl. & Pr. Forms Seduction § 2, Statutory References.
West's California Code Forms, Civil § 49 Form 1, Complaint—Abduction of Child.
West's California Code Forms, Civil § 49 Form 2, Complaint—By Employer—Injury to Domestic Employee.

§ 52.4. Civil action for damages arising from gender violence

(a) Any person who has been subjected to gender violence may bring a civil action for damages against any responsible party. The plaintiff may seek actual damages, compensatory damages, punitive damages, injunctive relief, any combination of those, or any other appropriate relief. A prevailing plaintiff may also be awarded attorney's fees and costs.

(b) An action brought pursuant to this section shall be commenced within three years of the act, or if the victim was a minor when the act occurred, within eight years after the date the plaintiff attains the age of majority or within three years after the date the plaintiff discovers or reasonably should have discovered the psychological injury or illness occurring after the age of majority that was caused by the act, whichever date occurs later.

(c) For purposes of this section, "gender violence" is a form of sex discrimination and means either of the following:

(1) One or more acts that would constitute a criminal offense under state law that has as an element the use, attempted use, or threatened use of physical force against the person or property of another, committed at least in part based on the gender of the victim, whether or not those acts have resulted in criminal complaints, charges, prosecution, or conviction.

(2) A physical intrusion or physical invasion of a sexual nature under coercive conditions, whether or not those acts have resulted in criminal complaints, charges, prosecution, or conviction.

(d) For purposes of this section, "gender" has the meaning set forth in Section 51.

(e) Notwithstanding any other laws that may establish the liability of an employer for the acts of an employee, this section does not establish any civil liability of a person because of his or her status as an employer, unless the employer personally committed an act of gender violence. (Added by Stats.2002, c. 842 (A.B.1928), § 2. Amended by Stats.2015, c. 202 (A.B.830), § 1, eff. Jan. 1, 2016.)

Cross References

Business of insurance, application of Unruh Civil Rights Act, see Insurance Code § 1861.03.

Research References

Forms

West's California Code Forms, Civil § 52.4 Form 1, Complaint—Gender Violence.
West's California Code Forms, Civil § 52.4 Form 2, Complaint—Gender Violence and Sexual Battery.
West's California Code Forms, Civil § 1708.5 Form 2, Complaint—Gender Violence and Sexual Battery.

§ 52.45. Civil action for damages arising from sexual orientation violence

(a) Any person who has been subjected to sexual orientation violence may bring a civil action for damages against any responsible party. The plaintiff may seek actual damages, compensatory damages, punitive damages, injunctive relief, any combination of those, or any other appropriate relief. A prevailing plaintiff may also be awarded attorney's fees and costs.

(b) An action brought pursuant to this section shall be commenced within three years of the act, or if the victim was a minor

§ 52.45

when the act occurred, within eight years after the date the plaintiff attains the age of majority or within three years after the date the plaintiff discovers or reasonably should have discovered the psychological injury or illness occurring after the age of majority that was caused by the act, whichever date occurs later.

(c) For purposes of this section, "sexual orientation violence" means one or more acts that would constitute a criminal offense under state law that has as an element the use, attempted use, or threatened use of physical force against the person or property of another, committed at least in part based on the sexual orientation of the victim, whether or not those acts have resulted in criminal complaints, charges, prosecution, or conviction.

(d) Notwithstanding any other laws that may establish the liability of an employer for the acts of an employee, this section does not establish any civil liability of a person because of his or her status as an employer, unless the employer personally committed an act of sexual orientation violence. *(Added by Stats.2015, c. 202 (A.B.830), § 2, eff. Jan. 1, 2016.)*

§ 52.5. Civil action for damages to victims of human trafficking

(a) A victim of human trafficking, as defined in Section 236.1 of the Penal Code, may bring a civil action for actual damages, compensatory damages, punitive damages, injunctive relief, any combination of those, or any other appropriate relief. A prevailing plaintiff may also be awarded attorney's fees and costs.

(b) In addition to the remedies specified in this section, in an action under subdivision (a), the plaintiff may be awarded up to three times his or her actual damages or ten thousand dollars ($10,000), whichever is greater. In addition, punitive damages may be awarded upon proof of the defendant's malice, oppression, fraud, or duress in committing the act of human trafficking.

(c) An action brought pursuant to this section shall be commenced within seven years of the date on which the trafficking victim was freed from the trafficking situation or, if the victim was a minor when the act of human trafficking against the victim occurred, within 10 years after the date the plaintiff attains the age of majority.

(d) If a person entitled to sue is under a disability at the time the cause of action accrues so that it is impossible or impracticable for him or her to bring an action, the time of the disability is not part of the time limited for the commencement of the action. Disability will toll the running of the statute of limitations for this action.

(1) Disability includes being a minor, lacking legal capacity to make decisions, imprisonment, or other incapacity or incompetence.

(2) The statute of limitations shall not run against a plaintiff who is a minor or who lacks the legal competence to make decisions simply because a guardian ad litem has been appointed. A guardian ad litem's failure to bring a plaintiff's action within the applicable limitation period will not prejudice the plaintiff's right to bring an action after his or her disability ceases.

(3) A defendant is estopped from asserting a defense of the statute of limitations when the expiration of the statute is due to conduct by the defendant inducing the plaintiff to delay the filing of the action, or due to threats made by the defendant causing the plaintiff duress.

(4) The suspension of the statute of limitations due to disability, lack of knowledge, or estoppel applies to all other related claims arising out of the trafficking situation.

(5) The running of the statute of limitations is postponed during the pendency of criminal proceedings against the victim.

(e) The running of the statute of limitations may be suspended if a person entitled to sue could not have reasonably discovered the cause of action due to circumstances resulting from the trafficking situation, such as psychological trauma, cultural and linguistic isolation, and the inability to access services.

CIVIL CODE

(f) A prevailing plaintiff may also be awarded reasonable attorney's fees and litigation costs including, but not limited to, expert witness fees and expenses as part of the costs.

(g) Restitution paid by the defendant to the victim shall be credited against a judgment, award, or settlement obtained pursuant to an action under this section. A judgment, award, or settlement obtained pursuant to an action under this section is subject to Section 13963 of the Government Code.

(h) A civil action filed under this section shall be stayed during the pendency of any criminal action arising out of the same occurrence in which the claimant is the victim. As used in this section, a "criminal action" includes investigation and prosecution, and is pending until a final adjudication in the trial court or dismissal. *(Added by Stats.2005, c. 240 (A.B.22), § 2. Amended by Stats.2014, c. 144 (A.B.1847), § 1, eff. Jan. 1, 2015; Stats.2015, c. 474 (A.B.15), § 1, eff. Jan. 1, 2016; Stats.2016, c. 86 (S.B.1171), § 18, eff. Jan. 1, 2017.)*

Cross References

Business of insurance, application of Unruh Civil Rights Act, see Insurance Code § 1861.03.
Department of Fair Employment and Housing functions, powers and duties, see Government Code § 12930.

Research References

Forms

West's California Code Forms, Civil § 52.5 Form 1, Complaint—Human Trafficking.
West's California Code Forms, Civil Procedure § 354.8 Form 1, Statute of Limitations—Crimes Against Humanity.

§ 52.6. Notice to be posted at specified businesses and establishments; slavery and human trafficking; location of posting; contents; languages; model notice; employee training; civil penalties; local ordinances

(a) Each of the following businesses and other establishments shall, upon the availability of the model notice described in subdivision (d), post a notice that complies with the requirements of this section in a conspicuous place near the public entrance of the establishment or in another conspicuous location in clear view of the public and employees where similar notices are customarily posted:

(1) On-sale general public premises licensees under the Alcoholic Beverage Control Act (Division 9 (commencing with Section 23000) of the Business and Professions Code).

(2) Adult or sexually oriented businesses, as defined in subdivision (a) of Section 318.5 of the Penal Code.

(3) Primary airports, as defined in Section 47102(16) of Title 49 of the United States Code.

(4) Intercity passenger rail or light rail stations.

(5) Bus stations.

(6) Truck stops. For purposes of this section, "truck stop" means a privately owned and operated facility that provides food, fuel, shower or other sanitary facilities, and lawful overnight truck parking.

(7) Emergency rooms within general acute care hospitals.

(8) Urgent care centers.

(9) Farm labor contractors, as defined in subdivision (b) of Section 1682 of the Labor Code.

(10) Privately operated job recruitment centers.

(11) Roadside rest areas.

(12) Businesses or establishments that offer massage or bodywork services for compensation and are not described in paragraph (1) of subdivision (b) of Section 4612 of the Business and Professions Code.

(13) Hotels, motels, and bed and breakfast inns, as defined in subdivision (b) of Section 24045.12 of the Business and Professions Code, not including personal residences.

(14) Hair, nail, electrolysis, and skin care, and other related businesses or establishments subject to regulation under Chapter 10 (commencing with Section 7301) of Division 3 of the Business and Professions Code.

(b) The notice to be posted pursuant to subdivision (a) shall be at least 8½ inches by 11 inches in size, written in a 16-point font, and shall state the following:

"If you or someone you know is being forced to engage in any activity and cannot leave-whether it is commercial sex, housework, farm work, construction, factory, retail, or restaurant work, or any other activity-text 233-733 (Be Free) or call the National Human Trafficking Hotline at 1-888-373-7888 or the California Coalition to Abolish Slavery and Trafficking (CAST) at 1-888-KEY-2-FRE(EDOM) or 1-888-539-2373 to access help and services.

Victims of slavery and human trafficking are protected under United States and California law.

The hotlines are:
· Available 24 hours a day, 7 days a week.
· Toll-free.
· Operated by nonprofit, nongovernmental organizations.
· Anonymous and confidential.
· Accessible in more than 160 languages.
· Able to provide help, referral to services, training, and general information."

(c) The notice to be posted pursuant to subdivision (a) shall be printed in English, Spanish, and in one other language that is the most widely spoken language in the county where the establishment is located and for which translation is mandated by the federal Voting Rights Act of 1965 (52 U.S.C. Sec. 10301 et seq.), as applicable. This section does not require a business or other establishment in a county where a language other than English or Spanish is the most widely spoken language to print the notice in more than one language in addition to English and Spanish.

(d)(1) On or before April 1, 2013, the Department of Justice shall develop a model notice that complies with the requirements of this section and make the model notice available for download on the department's internet website.

(2) On or before January 1, 2019, the Department of Justice shall revise and update the model notice to comply with the requirements of this section and make the updated model notice available for download on the department's internet website. A business or establishment required to post the model notice shall not be required to post the updated model notice until on and after January 1, 2019.

(e) On or before January 1, 2021, a business or other establishment that operates a facility described in paragraph (4) or (5) of subdivision (a) shall provide at least 20 minutes of training to its new and existing employees who may interact with, or come into contact with, a victim of human trafficking or who are likely to receive, in the course of their employment, a report from another employee about suspected human trafficking, in recognizing the signs of human trafficking and how to report those signs to the appropriate law enforcement agency.

(f) The employee training pursuant to subdivision (e) shall include, but not be limited to, all of the following:

(1) The definition of human trafficking, including sex trafficking and labor trafficking.

(2) Myths and misconceptions about human trafficking.

(3) Physical and mental signs to be aware of that may indicate that human trafficking is occurring.

(4) Guidance on how to identify individuals who are most at risk for human trafficking.

(5) Guidance on how to report human trafficking, including, but not limited to, national hotlines (1-888-373-7888 and text line 233733) and contact information for local law enforcement agencies that an employee may use to make a confidential report.

(6) Protocols for reporting human trafficking when on the job.

(g)(1) The human trafficking employee training pursuant to subdivision (e) may include, but shall not be limited to, information and material utilized in training Santa Clara County Valley Transportation Authority employees, private nonprofit organizations that represent the interests of human trafficking victims, and the Department of Justice.

(2) The failure to report human trafficking by an employee shall not, by itself, result in the liability of the business or other establishment that operates a facility described in paragraph (4) or (5) of subdivision (a) or of any other person or entity.

(h) A business or establishment that fails to comply with the requirements of this section is liable for a civil penalty of five hundred dollars ($500) for a first offense and one thousand dollars ($1,000) for each subsequent offense. A government entity identified in Section 17204 of the Business and Professions Code may bring an action to impose a civil penalty pursuant to this subdivision against a business or establishment if a local or state agency with authority to regulate that business or establishment has satisfied both of the following:

(1) Provided the business or establishment with reasonable notice of noncompliance, which informs the business or establishment that it is subject to a civil penalty if it does not correct the violation within 30 days from the date the notice is sent to the business or establishment.

(2) Verified that the violation was not corrected within the 30-day period described in paragraph (1).

(i) This section does not prevent a local governing body from adopting and enforcing a local ordinance, rule, or regulation to prevent slavery or human trafficking. If a local ordinance, rule, or regulation duplicates or supplements the requirements that this section imposes upon businesses and other establishments, this section does not supersede or preempt that local ordinance, rule, or regulation. (Added by Stats.2012, c. 515 (S.B.1193), § 1. Amended by Stats.2017, c. 547 (A.B.260), § 1, eff. Jan. 1, 2018; Stats.2017, c. 565 (S.B.225), § 1.5, eff. Jan. 1, 2018; Stats.2018, c. 812 (A.B.2034), § 1, eff. Jan. 1, 2019; Stats.2019, c. 57 (S.B.630), § 1, eff. Jan. 1, 2020; Stats.2020, c. 370 (S.B.1371), § 22, eff. Jan. 1, 2021; Stats.2022, c. 106 (A.B.1661), § 1, eff. Jan. 1, 2023.)

Research References

Forms

West's California Code Forms, Civil § 52.6 Form 1, Notice—Human Trafficking.

§ 52.65. Civil action for hotels in violation of sex trafficking activity

(a) A hotel is in violation of this section, and subject to civil penalties, if either or both of the following conditions are met:

(1) Sex trafficking activity occurred in the hotel, a supervisory employee of the hotel either knew of the nature of the activity, or acted in reckless disregard of the activity constituting sex trafficking activity within the hotel, and the supervisory employee of the hotel failed to inform law enforcement, the National Human Trafficking Hotline, or another appropriate victim service organization within 24 hours.

(2) An employee of the hotel was acting within the scope of employment and knowingly benefited, financially or by receiving anything of value, by participating in a venture that the employee knew or acted in reckless disregard of the activity constituting sex trafficking within the hotel.

(b) If there is reasonable cause to believe there has been a violation pursuant to subdivision (a), a city, county, or city and county

§ 52.65

attorney may bring a civil action for injunctive and other equitable relief against a hotel for violation of this section. A city, county, or city and county attorney who brings a civil action under this section may also seek civil penalties in the amount of one thousand dollars ($1,000) for the first violation in a calendar year, three thousand dollars ($3,000) for the second violation within the same calendar year, and five thousand dollars ($5,000) for the third and any subsequent violation within the same calendar year.

(c) The court may exercise its discretion to increase the amount of the civil penalty, not to exceed ten thousand dollars ($10,000), for any fourth or subsequent violation, considering all of the following factors:

(1) The defendant's culpability.

(2) The relationship between the harm and the penalty.

(3) The penalties imposed for similar conduct in similar statutes.

(4) The defendant's ability to pay.

(d) The lack of reporting of a sex trafficking case that occurs in a hotel shall not, by itself, without meeting the conditions in either paragraph (1) or (2) of subdivision (a), result in the liability of an employer of that establishment to the sex trafficking victim or victims in the case in question or to any other party.

(e) No liability for civil penalties shall arise under this section against a hotel employee.

(f) Violation of this section, by itself, shall not result in criminal liability against the hotel.

(g) Nothing in this section affects criminal or civil liability that may arise pursuant to other provisions of law.

(h) For the purposes of this section, the following terms shall have the following definitions:

(1) "Hotel" means a motel, or any other operator or management company that offers and accepts payment for rooms, sleeping accommodations, or board and lodging and retains the right of access to, and control of, a dwelling unit that is required to provide training and education regarding human trafficking awareness pursuant to Section 12950.3 of the Government Code.

(2) "Sex trafficking" means human trafficking for the purposes of engaging in a commercial sex act as set forth in subdivision (c) of Section 236.1 of the Penal Code.

(3) "Supervisory employee" means any individual, regardless of the job description or title, who has each of the following capabilities and qualifications:

(A) Holds authority, in the interest of the employer, to hire, transfer, suspend, lay off, recall, promote, discharge, assign, reward, or discipline other employees, or responsibility to direct them, or to adjust their grievances, or effectively to recommend this action, if, in connection with the foregoing, the exercise of this authority is not of a merely routine or clerical nature, but requires the use of independent judgment.

(B) Holds responsibility for duties that are not substantially similar to those of their subordinates. Employees whose duties are substantially similar to those of their subordinates shall not be considered to be supervisory employees.

(i) An action brought pursuant to this section shall be commenced within five years of the date when the violation of subdivision (a) occurred, or, if the victim of that sex trafficking activity was a minor when the violation occurred, within five years of the date the victim attains the age of majority. *(Added by Stats.2022, c. 760 (A.B.1788), § 1, eff. Jan. 1, 2023.)*

Division 2

PROPERTY

Part 1

PROPERTY IN GENERAL

Title 2

OWNERSHIP

CHAPTER 2. MODIFICATION OF OWNERSHIP

ARTICLE 1. INTERESTS IN PROPERTY

Section
682.1. Community property of spouses; subject to express declaration in transfer documents; application and operation of section.
683. Joint tenancy; definition; method of creation.
683.1. Joint tenancy; safe-deposit box.
683.2. Joint tenancy; severance; right of survivorship; applicable law.
685. Interest in common defined.
686. Interest in common; interests excluded.
687. Community property defined.

Cross References

Estates in real property, see Civil Code § 761 et seq.

§ 682.1. **Community property of spouses; subject to express declaration in transfer documents; application and operation of section**

(a)(1) Community property of spouses, when expressly declared in the transfer document to be community property with right of survivorship, and which may be accepted in writing on the face of the document by a statement signed or initialed by the grantees, shall, upon the death of one of the spouses, pass to the survivor, without administration, pursuant to the terms of the instrument, subject to the same procedures, as property held in joint tenancy. Prior to the death of either spouse, the right of survivorship may be terminated pursuant to the same procedures by which a joint tenancy may be severed.

(2) Part 1 (commencing with Section 5000) of Division 5 of the Probate Code and Chapter 2 (commencing with Section 13540), Chapter 3 (commencing with Section 13550), and Chapter 3.5 (commencing with Section 13560) of Part 2 of Division 8 of the Probate Code apply to this property.

(3) For the purposes of Chapter 3 (commencing with Section 13550) of Part 2 of Division 8 of the Probate Code, this property shall be treated as if it had passed without administration under Part 2 (commencing with Section 13500) of Division 8 of the Probate Code.

(b) This section does not apply to a joint account in a financial institution to which Part 2 (commencing with Section 5100) of Division 5 of the Probate Code applies.

(c) This section shall become operative on July 1, 2001, and shall apply to instruments created on or after that date. *(Added by Stats.2000, c. 645 (A.B.2913), § 1, operative July 1, 2001. Amended by Stats.2016, c. 50 (S.B.1005), § 8, eff. Jan. 1, 2017; Stats.2022, c. 29 (A.B.1716), § 1, eff. Jan. 1, 2023.)*

Cross References

Community property, presumptions as to property acquired by wife, see Family Code §§ 700, 760, 803.

Delivery,
  Co-owners, see Civil Code § 1827.
  Joint tenancy deposits, see Civil Code § 1828.
Husband and wife, methods of holding property, see Family Code § 750.
Insurance, transfer of interest between partners, see Insurance Code § 304.
Joinder, see Code of Civil Procedure § 378.
Nonprobate transfers, joint tenancy, severance, see Probate Code § 5601.
Partition, see Code of Civil Procedure § 872.010 et seq.
Partnership property, conveyance of realty, see Corporations Code § 15008.
Safe deposit boxes, see Financial Code § 1649.
Waste, actions, see Code of Civil Procedure § 732.

Research References

Forms

Asset Protection: Legal Planning, Strategies and Forms ¶ 4.04, Determining the Character of Property.
1A California Real Estate Forms (Miller & Starr) § 1:133 (2d ed.), Grant Deed.
1A California Real Estate Forms (Miller & Starr) § 1:134 (2d ed.), Interspousal Grant Deed.
1A California Real Estate Forms (Miller & Starr) § 1:135 (2d ed.), Quitclaim Deed.

§ 683. Joint tenancy; definition; method of creation

(a) A joint interest is one owned by two or more persons in equal shares, by a title created by a single will or transfer, when expressly declared in the will or transfer to be a joint tenancy, or by transfer from a sole owner to himself or herself and others, or from tenants in common or joint tenants to themselves or some of them, or to themselves or any of them and others, or from spouses, when holding title as community property or otherwise to themselves or to themselves and others or to one of them and to another or others, when expressly declared in the transfer to be a joint tenancy, or when granted or devised to executors or trustees as joint tenants. A joint tenancy in personal property may be created by a written transfer, instrument, or agreement.

(b) Provisions of this section do not apply to a joint account in a financial institution if Part 2 (commencing with Section 5100) of Division 5 of the Probate Code applies to such account. *(Enacted in 1872. Amended by Stats.1929, c. 93, p. 172, § 1; Stats.1931, c. 1051, p. 2205, § 1; Stats.1935, c. 234, p. 912, § 1; Stats.1955, c. 178, p. 645, § 1; Stats.1983, c. 92, § 1, operative July 1, 1984; Stats.1989, c. 397, § 1, operative July 1, 1990; Stats.1990, c. 79 (A.B.759), § 1, operative July 1, 1991; Stats.2016, c. 50 (S.B.1005), § 9, eff. Jan. 1, 2017.)*

Cross References

Cemetery plots, joint tenants of, see Health and Safety Code § 8625 et seq.
Corporate shares or other securities, transfers, see Corporations Code § 420.
Husband and wife may hold as joint tenants, see Family Code § 750.
Insurance, transfer of interest between partners, see Insurance Code § 304.
Joint tenancy deposits, delivery, see Civil Code § 1828.
Multiple party accounts, see Financial Code § 1402.
Partition, authorized persons, see Code of Civil Procedure § 872.210.
Partnership property, see Corporations Code § 16202 et seq.
Safe deposit boxes, notices, see Financial Code § 1649.
Simultaneous death of joint tenants, see Probate Code § 223.
Waste by joint tenant, see Code of Civil Procedure § 732.

Research References

Forms

1 California Transactions Forms--Estate Planning § 1:20, Joint Tenancy.
2 California Transactions Forms--Estate Planning § 10:19, Joint Tenancy Property.
5A¶ 1 Nichols Cyclopedia of Legal Forms Annotated § 111:3, Personal Property.
West's California Code Forms, Civil § 683 Form 1, Deed—Joint Tenancy—Sole Owner to Self and Others.

§ 683.1. Joint tenancy; safe-deposit box

No contract or other arrangement made after the effective date of this section between any person, firm, or corporation engaged in the business of renting safe-deposit boxes and the renter or renters of a safe-deposit box, shall create a joint tenancy in or otherwise establish ownership in any of the contents of such safe-deposit box. Any such contract or other arrangement purporting so to do shall be to such extent void and of no effect. *(Added by Stats.1949, c. 1597, p. 2845, § 1.)*

Cross References

Delivery,
  Co-owners, see Civil Code § 1827.
  Joint tenancy, see Civil Code § 1828.
Multiple party accounts, see Financial Code § 1402.
Ownership defined for purposes of this Code, see Civil Code § 654.
Partnership, see Corporations Code § 16101 et seq.
Safe deposit box in multiple names, see Financial Code § 1649.

Research References

Forms

1 California Transactions Forms--Estate Planning § 1:20, Joint Tenancy.
2 California Transactions Forms--Estate Planning § 10:19, Joint Tenancy Property.

§ 683.2. Joint tenancy; severance; right of survivorship; applicable law

(a) Subject to the limitations and requirements of this section, in addition to any other means by which a joint tenancy may be severed, a joint tenant may sever a joint tenancy in real property as to the joint tenant's interest without the joinder or consent of the other joint tenants by any of the following means:

(1) Execution and delivery of a deed that conveys legal title to the joint tenant's interest to a third person, whether or not pursuant to an agreement that requires the third person to reconvey legal title to the joint tenant.

(2) Execution of a written instrument that evidences the intent to sever the joint tenancy, including a deed that names the joint tenant as transferee, or of a written declaration that, as to the interest of the joint tenant, the joint tenancy is severed.

(b) Nothing in this section authorizes severance of a joint tenancy contrary to a written agreement of the joint tenants, but a severance contrary to a written agreement does not defeat the rights of a purchaser or encumbrancer for value in good faith and without knowledge of the written agreement.

(c) Severance of a joint tenancy of record by deed, written declaration, or other written instrument pursuant to subdivision (a) is not effective to terminate the right of survivorship of the other joint tenants as to the severing joint tenant's interest unless one of the following requirements is satisfied:

(1) Before the death of the severing joint tenant, the deed, written declaration, or other written instrument effecting the severance is recorded in the county where the real property is located.

(2) The deed, written declaration, or other written instrument effecting the severance is executed and acknowledged before a notary public by the severing joint tenant not earlier than three days before the death of that joint tenant and is recorded in the county where the real property is located not later than seven days after the death of the severing joint tenant.

(d) Nothing in subdivision (c) limits the manner or effect of:

(1) A written instrument executed by all the joint tenants that severs the joint tenancy.

(2) A severance made by or pursuant to a written agreement of all the joint tenants.

(3) A deed from a joint tenant to another joint tenant.

§ 683.2

(e) Subdivisions (a) and (b) apply to all joint tenancies in real property, whether the joint tenancy was created before, on, or after January 1, 1985, except that in the case of the death of a joint tenant before January 1, 1985, the validity of a severance under subdivisions (a) and (b) is determined by the law in effect at the time of death. Subdivisions (c) and (d) do not apply to or affect a severance made before January 1, 1986, of a joint tenancy. *(Added by Stats.1984, c. 519, § 1. Amended by Stats.1985, c. 157, § 1.)*

Cross References

Real property defined for purposes of this Code, see Civil Code § 658.

Research References

Forms

1 California Transactions Forms--Estate Planning § 1:15, Overview.
1 California Transactions Forms--Estate Planning § 1:21, Severing Joint Tenancies in Real Property.
1 California Transactions Forms--Estate Planning § 1:25, Joint Tenancy or Community Property Treatment of Property in Revocable Trust.
1 California Transactions Forms--Estate Planning § 1:77, Matters to Consider Regarding Property Distribution.
2 California Transactions Forms--Estate Planning § 10:19, Joint Tenancy Property.
4 California Transactions Forms--Estate Planning § 19:66, Determining Testator's Intent; Information Gathering.
4 California Transactions Forms--Estate Planning § 19:108, Special Precautions for Deathbed Wills.
4 California Transactions Forms--Estate Planning § 20:6, Property Passing Outside of Will.
West's California Code Forms, Civil § 683.2 Form 1, Deed—Severing Joint Tenancy—Joint Tenant to Others.

§ 685. Interest in common defined

INTEREST IN COMMON, WHAT. An interest in common is one owned by several persons, not in joint ownership or partnership. *(Enacted in 1872.)*

Cross References

Compulsory joinder, see Code of Civil Procedure § 389.
Depositary, delivery when owners in common cannot agree, see Civil Code § 1827.
Husband and wife, methods of holding property, see Family Code § 750.
Insurance, transfer of interest in insured property by one owner in common to another, see Insurance Code § 304.
Joinder, see Code of Civil Procedure §§ 378, 379.
Ownership defined for purposes of this Code, see Civil Code § 654.
Partition, see Code of Civil Procedure § 872.010 et seq.
Permissive joinder, see Code of Civil Procedure §§ 378, 379.
Safe deposit boxes, see Financial Code § 1649.
Waste, actions for, see Code of Civil Procedure § 732.

Research References

Forms

2 California Transactions Forms--Estate Planning § 10:6, Tenancy in Common.
West's California Code Forms, Civil § 685 Form 1, Deed—Tenants in Common.

§ 686. Interest in common; interests excluded

WHAT INTERESTS ARE IN COMMON. Every interest created in favor of several persons in their own right is an interest in common, unless acquired by them in partnership, for partnership purposes, or unless declared in its creation to be a joint interest, as provided in Section 683, or unless acquired as community property. *(Enacted in 1872.)*

Cross References

Sale of goods, see Commercial Code § 2105.

Research References

Forms

2 California Transactions Forms--Estate Planning § 10:6, Tenancy in Common.
4 California Transactions Forms--Estate Planning § 20:8, Class Devises.
West's California Code Forms, Civil § 685 Form 1, Deed—Tenants in Common.

§ 687. Community property defined

Community property is property that is community property under Part 2 (commencing with Section 760) of Division 4 of the Family Code. *(Enacted in 1872. Amended by Stats.1992, c. 163 (A.B.2641), § 6, operative Jan. 1, 1994.)*

Cross References

Community property generally, see Family Code §§ 63, 700, 751, 760, 803; Probate Code § 100.
Death of spouse, disposition of community property, see Probate Code § 6401 et seq.
Division of spousal property, see Family Code § 2500 et seq.
Interests of parties in community property, see Family Code § 751.
Separate property of spouse, see Family Code § 770 et seq.
Spousal liability, see Family Code § 910 et seq.

Research References

Forms

1 California Transactions Forms--Estate Planning § 1:22, Community Property.
1 California Transactions Forms--Estate Planning § 3:75, Community Property.
2 California Transactions Forms--Estate Planning § 10:10, Community Property.

ARTICLE 2. CONDITIONS OF OWNERSHIP

Section
710. Conditions in restraint of marriage.

§ 710. Conditions in restraint of marriage

Conditions imposing restraints upon marriage, except upon the marriage of a minor, are void; but this does not affect limitations where the intent was not to forbid marriage, but only to give the use until marriage. *(Enacted in 1872. Amended by Code Am.1873–74, c. 612, p. 218, § 101.)*

Cross References

Contract in restraint of marriage void, see Civil Code § 1669.

Research References

Forms

4 California Transactions Forms--Estate Planning § 19:4, Public Policy and Conditional Devises.
4 California Transactions Forms--Estate Planning § 20:13, Conditional Devises.

Division 3
OBLIGATIONS

Part 2
CONTRACTS

Cross References

Arbitration agreements, see Code of Civil Procedure § 1280 et seq.
Attachment, see Code of Civil Procedure § 484.010 et seq.
Commissions, rate agreed to in writing, presumption, see Insurance Code § 769.1.
Conditional sales contracts, motor vehicles, see Civil Code § 2981 et seq.
Estoppel, see Evidence Code § 623.
Forgery of contract, see Penal Code § 470.
Holidays, performance of obligation arising from contract, see Civil Code § 11; Code of Civil Procedure § 13 et seq.
Injunction, breach of contract, see Code of Civil Procedure § 526.
Joinder of actions, see Code of Civil Procedure §§ 427.10, 428.10.
Limitation of actions, contracts, see Code of Civil Procedure §§ 337, 339.
Marriage settlement contracts, see Family Code §§ 1500, 1610 et seq.
Obligations,
    Generally, see Civil Code § 1427 et seq.
    Arising from contract, see Civil Code § 1428; Code of Civil Procedure § 26.
    Imposed by law, see Civil Code § 1708 et seq.
Pledge, contract transferring personalty as security, see Commercial Code § 9102.
Restraint of trade, contracts, see Business and Professions Code § 16600 et seq.
Sales, see Commercial Code § 2204 et seq.
Separation agreements, see Family Code § 3580.
Specific performance, see Civil Code § 3384 et seq.
Statute of frauds, see Civil Code §§ 1623, 1624; Commercial Code § 2201.
Successive actions on same contract, see Code of Civil Procedure § 1047.
Transfer,
    Obligations, see Civil Code § 1457 et seq.
    Property, see Civil Code § 1044.
Waiver,
    Generally, see Civil Code §§ 3268, 3513, 3516.
    Offer of performance of obligation, see Civil Code § 1501.

Title 1
NATURE OF A CONTRACT

CHAPTER 3. CONSENT

Section
1590. Gifts in contemplation of marriage; recovery.

Cross References

Acquiescence in error as consent, see Civil Code § 3516.
Essential elements of contract, see Civil Code § 1550.

§ 1590. Gifts in contemplation of marriage; recovery

Where either party to a contemplated marriage in this State makes a gift of money or property to the other on the basis or assumption that the marriage will take place, in the event that the donee refuses to enter into the marriage as contemplated or that it is given up by mutual consent, the donor may recover such gift or such part of its value as may, under all of the circumstances of the case, be found by a court or jury to be just. (Added by Stats.1939, c. 128, p. 1245, § 3.)

Research References

Forms

1 California Transactions Forms--Estate Planning § 7:2, Types of Gifts.

Title 4
UNLAWFUL CONTRACTS

Section
1667. "Unlawfulness" defined.

Section
1668. Contracts contrary to policy of law.
1669. Restraint of marriage.
1670.5. Unconscionable contract or clause of contract; finding as matter of law; remedies.

§ 1667. "Unlawfulness" defined

That is not lawful which is:

1. Contrary to an express provision of law;

2. Contrary to the policy of express law, though not expressly prohibited; or,

3. Otherwise contrary to good morals. *(Enacted in 1872.)*

Cross References

Cannabis legislation, legislative intent, lawfulness of specified cannabis–related activities, see Civil Code § 1550.5.
Conditions to ownership of property, see Civil Code § 707 et seq.
Consent, element of contract, see Civil Code § 1565 et seq.
Consideration for contract, see Civil Code § 1605 et seq.
Contracts in restraint of trade, see Business and Professions Code § 16600 et seq.
Effect of illegal consideration, see Civil Code § 1608.
Grounds for rescission of contract, see Civil Code § 1689.
Illegal contracts,
    Between husband and wife, see Family Code § 1620.
    Capacity, see Civil Code §§ 1556, 1557.
    Construction of swimming pools, see Business and Professions Code § 7167 et seq.
    Dance studio lessons, see Civil Code § 1812.53.
    Franchise investments, see Corporations Code § 31000 et seq.
    Health studio services, see Civil Code § 1812.84.
    Persons in violation of pollution laws, see Government Code § 4477.
    Sale or lease of lots in subdivisions without report, see Business and Professions Code § 11018.2.
Impossible or unlawful conditions, see Civil Code § 1441.
Necessity of lawful consideration, see Civil Code § 1607.
Object of contract, see Civil Code § 1595 et seq.
Public educational employment, meeting and negotiating defined, see Government Code § 3540.1.
Retail installment sales, see Civil Code § 1801 et seq.
Rule against perpetuities, see Probate Code § 21200
Usury law,
    Generally, see Civil Code § 1916–1 et seq.
    Real property loans, see Business and Professions Code § 10242.

Research References

Forms

3 California Real Estate Forms (Miller & Starr) § 3:37 (2d ed.), Continuing Guaranty.
3 California Real Estate Forms (Miller & Starr) § 3:38 (2d ed.), Completion Guaranty.
3 California Real Estate Forms (Miller & Starr) § 3:57 (2d ed.), Loan Purchase and Sale Agreement.
4 California Real Estate Forms (Miller & Starr) § 4:5 (2d ed.), Construction Agreement—Cost Plus a Percentage Fee With a Guaranteed Maximum Price.
4 California Real Estate Forms (Miller & Starr) § 4:6 (2d ed.), Construction Contract—Commercial Project—Fixed Price.
1 California Transactions Forms--Business Transactions § 6:8, Void, Voidable, and Unenforceable.
1 California Transactions Forms--Business Transactions § 6:45, Illegality.
3 California Transactions Forms--Business Transactions § 17:21, Unlawfulness of Contract [Civ. Code, §1667].

§ 1667

West's California Code Forms, Civil § 1667 Form 1, Affirmative Defense—Unlawful Contract.

§ 1668. Contracts contrary to policy of law

All contracts which have for their object, directly or indirectly, to exempt anyone from responsibility for his own fraud, or willful injury to the person or property of another, or violation of law, whether willful or negligent, are against the policy of the law. *(Enacted in 1872.)*

Cross References

Cannabis legislation, legislative intent, lawfulness of specified cannabis–related activities, see Civil Code § 1550.5.
Enforcement of oral contract by reason of fraud, see Civil Code § 1623.
Essential elements of contract, see Civil Code § 1550.
Freedom from violence or intimidation, waiver of civil rights by contract, provisions of this section not abrogated, see Civil Code § 51.7.
Insurance contracts, claims against local public entities and employees, see Government Code § 990.
Invalid agreements of exoneration by common carrier, see Civil Code § 2175.
Kinds of fraud, see Civil Code § 1571 et seq.
Object of contract, see Civil Code § 1595 et seq.

Research References

Forms

1 California Transactions Forms--Business Transactions § 6:45, Illegality.
3 California Transactions Forms--Business Transactions § 17:21, Unlawfulness of Contract [Civ. Code, §1667].
3 California Transactions Forms--Business Transactions § 20:12, Validity of Indemnity Agreements Providing for Indemnification for Indemnitee's Own Negligence.
3 California Transactions Forms--Business Transactions § 21:9, Contractual Limits on Bailee's Liability.
West's California Code Forms, Civil § 1667 Form 1, Affirmative Defense—Unlawful Contract.
West's California Code Forms, Commercial § 2316 Form 13, Liquidation of Damages for Breach of Warranty.
West's California Code Forms, Commercial § 2719 Form 3, Alternate Form of Contractual Modification or Limitation of Remedies.
West's California Code Forms, Commercial § 2719 General Comment, Modification or Limitation of Noncontractual Remedies.

§ 1669. Restraint of marriage

Every contract in restraint of the marriage of any person, other than a minor, is void. *(Added by Stats.1977, c. 198, p. 718, § 1, operative July 1, 1978.)*

Cross References

Action to determine validity of marriage, see Family Code § 309.
Conditions in restraint of marriage, see Civil Code § 710.
Lack of cause of action for fraudulent promise to marry, see Civil Code § 43.4.
Marriage,
    Contract, see Family Code § 300 et seq.
    Minor, see Family Code § 302.
Minor defined, see Family Code § 6500.
Statute of frauds, see Civil Code § 1624.

Research References

Forms

1 California Transactions Forms--Business Transactions § 6:45, Illegality.

§ 1670.5. Unconscionable contract or clause of contract; finding as matter of law; remedies

(a) If the court as a matter of law finds the contract or any clause of the contract to have been unconscionable at the time it was made the court may refuse to enforce the contract, or it may enforce the remainder of the contract without the unconscionable clause, or it may so limit the application of any unconscionable clause as to avoid any unconscionable result.

(b) When it is claimed or appears to the court that the contract or any clause thereof may be unconscionable the parties shall be afforded a reasonable opportunity to present evidence as to its commercial setting, purpose, and effect to aid the court in making the determination. *(Added by Stats.1979, c. 819, p. 2827, § 3, eff. Sept. 19, 1979.)*

Cross References

Unconscionable loan contracts, violations and remedies, see Financial Code § 22302.

Research References

Forms

1 California Transactions Forms--Business Transactions § 1:72, Trend Toward Balance and Conciliation Between Parties.
1 California Transactions Forms--Business Transactions § 6:46, Unconscionability.
2 California Transactions Forms--Business Transactions § 12:21, Employment Contracts Generally.
2 California Transactions Forms--Business Transactions § 12:51, Disputes Included and Excluded from Arbitration.
West's California Code Forms, Commercial § 1304 Form 3, Standards of Good Faith—Statements by Agents or Employees.
West's California Code Forms, Commercial § 2302 General Comment, Unconscionable Contract or Clause.
West's California Code Forms, Commercial § 2714 Form 3, Clause Limiting Remedy for Breach of Warranty.
West's California Code Forms, Commercial § 2715 Form 2, Clauses Excluding Incidental and Consequential Damages of Buyer.
West's California Code Forms, Commercial § 2719 Form 3, Alternate Form of Contractual Modification or Limitation of Remedies.

Part 3

OBLIGATIONS IMPOSED BY LAW

Section
1714.1. Liability of parents and guardians for willful misconduct of minor.
1714.4. Knowingly assisting child support obligor escape, evade, or avoid paying court-ordered or court-approved child support; application to financial institutions.
1714.41. Knowingly assisting a child support obligor to escape, evade, or avoid paying child support; included actions.

§ 1714.1. Liability of parents and guardians for willful misconduct of minor

(a) Any act of willful misconduct of a minor that results in injury or death to another person or in any injury to the property of another shall be imputed to the parent or guardian having custody and control of the minor for all purposes of civil damages, and the parent or guardian having custody and control shall be jointly and severally liable with the minor for any damages resulting from the willful misconduct.

Subject to the provisions of subdivision (c), the joint and several liability of the parent or guardian having custody and control of a minor under this subdivision shall not exceed twenty-five thousand dollars ($25,000) for each tort of the minor, and in the case of injury to a person, imputed liability shall be further limited to medical, dental and hospital expenses incurred by the injured person, not to exceed twenty-five thousand dollars ($25,000). The liability imposed by this section is in addition to any liability now imposed by law.

(b) Any act of willful misconduct of a minor that results in the defacement of property of another with paint or a similar substance shall be imputed to the parent or guardian having custody and control of the minor for all purposes of civil damages, including court costs, and attorney's fees, to the prevailing party, and the parent or guardian having custody and control shall be jointly and severally liable with the minor for any damages resulting from the willful misconduct, not to exceed twenty-five thousand dollars ($25,000), except as provided in subdivision (c), for each tort of the minor.

(c) The amounts listed in subdivisions (a) and (b) shall be adjusted every two years by the Judicial Council to reflect any increases in the cost of living in California, as indicated by the annual average of the California Consumer Price Index. The Judicial Council shall round this adjusted amount up or down to the nearest hundred dollars. On or before July 1 of each odd-numbered year, the Judicial Council shall compute and publish the amounts listed in subdivisions (a) and (b), as adjusted according to this subdivision.

(d) The maximum liability imposed by this section is the maximum liability authorized under this section at the time that the act of willful misconduct by a minor was committed.

(e) Nothing in this section shall impose liability on an insurer for a loss caused by the willful act of the insured for purposes of Section 533 of the Insurance Code. An insurer shall not be liable for the conduct imputed to a parent or guardian by this section for any amount in excess of ten thousand dollars ($10,000). *(Added by Stats.1955, c. 820, p. 1438, § 1. Amended by Stats.1965, c. 407, p. 1719, § 1; Stats.1970, c. 640, p. 1258, § 1; Stats.1972, c. 442, p. 811, § 1; Stats.1974, c. 340, p. 670, § 1; Stats.1979, c. 127, p. 314, § 1; Stats.1983, c. 981, § 1; Stats.1994, c. 568 (A.B.308), § 1; Stats.1994, c. 909 (S.B.1779), § 1; Stats.2007, c. 738 (A.B.1248), § 2.)*

Cross References

Child abuse, prohibition against libel or slander action while charges pending, see Civil Code § 48.7.
Computer data access and fraud, offense of minor imputed to parent or legal guardian pursuant to this section, see Penal Code § 502.
Joint and several obligations, see Civil Code § 1430 et seq.
Juvenile court law,
    Criminal violation by minor, restitution hearing, citation ordering appearance by parents or guardians, see Welfare and Institutions Code § 739.5.
    Graffiti Removal and Damage Recovery Program, clean up, repair or replacement of property, restitution, see Welfare and Institutions Code § 742.16.
    Restitution, fine, or penalty assessment order, liability of parent or guardian, see Welfare and Institutions Code § 730.7.
Liability of parent or guardian for damage to school property by minor, see Education Code § 48904.
Minor defined, see Family Code § 6500.
Minor's liability for wrongs, see Family Code § 6600.
Motor vehicle accident, liability of parent, guardian or person signing application, see Vehicle Code §§ 17707, 17708.
Offenses against libraries by minors, liability of parents, see Education Code §§ 19910, 19911.
Petty theft of retail merchandise, inapplicability of this section, see Penal Code § 490.5.

Research References

Forms

19 Am. Jur. Pl. & Pr. Forms Parent and Child § 107, Introductory Comments.
1 California Transactions Forms--Family Law § 3:14, Fiscal Responsibility and Liability Issues.
West's California Code Forms, Civil § 1714.1 Form 1, Complaint—Against Parents for Minor's Tort—Property Damage.
West's California Judicial Council Forms CR-110, Order for Victim Restitution.
West's California Judicial Council Forms JV-790, Order for Victim Restitution.

§ 1714.4. Knowingly assisting child support obligor escape, evade, or avoid paying court-ordered or court-approved child support; application to financial institutions

(a) Any person or business entity that knowingly assists a child support obligor who has an unpaid child support obligation to escape, evade, or avoid paying court-ordered or court-approved child support shall be liable for three times the value of the assistance provided, such as the fair market value of the obligor's assets transferred or hidden. The maximum liability imposed by this section shall not exceed the entire child support obligation due. Any funds or assets collected pursuant to this section shall be paid to the child support obligee, and shall not reduce the amount of the unpaid child support obligation. Upon the satisfaction of the unpaid child support obligation, this section shall not apply.

(b) For purposes of this section, actions taken to knowingly assist a child support obligor to escape, evade, or avoid paying court-ordered or court-approved child support include, with actual knowledge of the child support obligation, helping to hide or transfer assets of the child support obligor.

(c) This section shall not apply to a financial institution unless the financial institution has actual knowledge of the child support obligation and, with that knowledge, knowingly assists the obligor to escape, evade, or avoid paying the child support obligation. However, a financial institution with knowledge of an asset transfer has no duty to inquire into the rightfulness of the transaction, nor shall it be deemed to have knowingly assisted an obligor to escape, evade, or avoid paying the child support obligation if that assistance is provided by an employee or agent of the financial institution acting outside the terms and conditions of employment or agency without the actual knowledge of the financial institution. *(Added by Stats.2006, c. 820 (A.B.2440), § 2.)*

§ 1714.41. Knowingly assisting a child support obligor to escape, evade, or avoid paying child support; included actions

(a) Any person or business entity that knowingly assists a child support obligor who has an unpaid child support obligation to escape, evade, or avoid paying court-ordered or court-approved child support shall be liable for three times the value of the assistance provided, such as the fair market value of the assets transferred or hidden, or the amount of the wages or other compensation paid to the child support obligor but not reported. The maximum liability imposed by this section shall not exceed the entire child support obligation due. Any funds or assets collected pursuant to this section shall be paid to the child support obligee, and shall not reduce the amount of the unpaid child support obligation. Upon the satisfaction of the unpaid child support obligation, this section shall not apply.

(b) For purposes of this section, actions taken to knowingly assist a child support obligor to escape, evade, or avoid paying court-ordered or court-approved child support include, but are not limited to, any of the following actions taken when the individual or entity knew or should have known of the child support obligation:

(1) Hiring or employing the child support obligor as an employee in a trade or business and failing to timely file a report of new employees with the California New Employee Registry maintained by the Employment Development Department.

(2) Engaging the child support obligor as a service provider and failing to timely file a report with the Employment Development Department as required by Section 1088.8 of the Unemployment Insurance Code.

(3) When engaged in a trade or business, paying wages or other forms of compensation for services rendered by a child support obligor that are not reported to the Employment Development Department as required, including, but not limited to, payment in cash or via barter or trade. *(Added by Stats.2006, c. 820 (A.B.2440), § 3.)*

Part 4

OBLIGATIONS ARISING FROM PARTICULAR TRANSACTIONS

Cross References

Personal property leases, see Commercial Code § 10101 et seq.

Privacy or confidentiality of information or material provided to Nationwide Multistate Licensing System & Registry, debt collector licensing, see Financial Code § 100016.

Secured transactions, general effectiveness of security agreement, see Commercial Code § 9201.

Title 1.81.45

THE PARENT'S ACCOUNTABILITY AND CHILD PROTECTION ACT

Section
1798.99.1. Age verification when selling products that are illegal to sell to minor; reasonable steps; products requiring age verification; penalties; application of section.

§ 1798.99.1. Age verification when selling products that are illegal to sell to minor; reasonable steps; products requiring age verification; penalties; application of section

(a)(1) A person or business that conducts business in California, and that seeks to sell any product or service in or into California that is illegal under state law to sell to a minor, as described in subdivisions (b) and (c), shall, notwithstanding any general term or condition, take reasonable steps to ensure that the purchaser is of legal age at the time of purchase or delivery, including, but not limited to, verifying the age of the purchaser.

(2) Reasonable steps as used in paragraph (1) for the purchase of items described in subdivision (b) include, but are not limited to, any of the following:

(A) Requiring the purchaser or recipient to input, scan, provide, or display a government-issued identification, provided that the person or business complies with all laws governing the retention, use, and disclosure of personally identifiable information, including, but not limited to, subdivision (a) of Section 1749.65, paragraphs (3) to (7), inclusive, of subdivision (b) of, and subdivisions (c) to (f), inclusive, of, Section 1798.90, paragraph (1) of subdivision (a) of Section 1798.90.1, Sections 1798.29, 1798.81.5, and 1798.82, and Sections 22575 to 22579, inclusive, of the Business and Professions Code.

(B) Requiring the purchaser to use a nonprepaid credit card for an online purchase.

(C) Implementing a system that restricts individuals with accounts designated as minor accounts from purchasing the products listed in subdivision (b).

(D) Shipping the product or service to an individual who is of legal age.

(3) Reasonable steps as used in paragraph (1) for the purchase of items described in subdivision (c) include, but are not limited to, any of the following:

(A) Requiring the purchaser or recipient to input, scan, provide, or display a government-issued identification, provided that the person or business complies with all laws governing the retention, use, and disclosure of personally identifiable information, including, but not limited to, subdivision (a) of Section 1749.65, paragraphs (3) to (7), inclusive, of subdivision (b) of, and subdivisions (c) to (f), inclusive, of, Section 1798.90, paragraph (1) of subdivision (a) of Section 1798.90.1, Sections 1798.29, 1798.81.5, and 1798.82, and Sections 22575 to 22579, inclusive, of the Business and Professions Code.

(B) Shipping the product or service to an individual who is of legal age.

(4) Reasonable steps as used in paragraph (1) shall not include consent obtained through the minor.

(5) A seller's reasonable and good faith reliance on bona fide evidence of the purchaser or recipient's age shall constitute an affirmative defense to any action under this subdivision.

(6) A person or business required to comply with this section shall not retain, use, or disclose any information it receives from a purchaser or recipient in an effort to verify age pursuant to this section for any purpose other than as required to comply with, or as needed to demonstrate compliance with, this section, California law, or a state or federal court order.

(b) Products or services that are illegal to sell to a minor under state law that are subject to subdivision (a) include all of the following:

(1) An aerosol container of paint that is capable of defacing property, as referenced in Section 594.1 of the Penal Code.

(2) Etching cream that is capable of defacing property, as referenced in Section 594.1 of the Penal Code.

(3) Dangerous fireworks, as referenced in Sections 12505 and 12689 of the Health and Safety Code.

(4) Tanning in an ultraviolet tanning device, as referenced in Sections 22702 and 22706 of the Business and Professions Code.

(5) Dietary supplement products containing ephedrine group alkaloids, as referenced in Section 110423.2 of the Health and Safety Code.

(6) Body branding, as referenced in Sections 119301 and 119302 of the Health and Safety Code.

(c) Products or services that are illegal to sell to a minor under state law that are subject to subdivision (a) include all of the following:

(1) Firearms or handguns, as referenced in Sections 16520, 16640, and 27505 of the Penal Code.

(2) A BB device, as referenced in Sections 16250 and 19910 of the Penal Code.

(3) Ammunition or reloaded ammunition, as referenced in Sections 16150 and 30300 of the Penal Code.

(4) Any tobacco, cigarette, cigarette papers, blunt wraps, any other preparation of tobacco, any other instrument or paraphernalia that is designed for the smoking or ingestion of tobacco, products prepared from tobacco, or any controlled substance, as referenced in Division 8.5 (commencing with Section 22950) of the Business and Professions Code, and Sections 308, 308.1, 308.2, and 308.3 of the Penal Code.

(5) Electronic cigarettes, as referenced in Section 119406 of the Health and Safety Code.

(6) A less lethal weapon, as referenced in Sections 16780 and 19405 of the Penal Code.

(d) In an action brought by a public prosecutor, a business or person that violates this section shall be subject to a civil penalty not exceeding seven thousand five hundred dollars ($7,500) for each violation.

(e) The provisions of this section do not apply to a business that is regulated by state or federal law providing greater protection to personal information or requiring greater age verification than provided by this section in regard to the subjects addressed by this section. Compliance with state or federal law shall be deemed compliance with this section with regard to those subjects. This subdivision does not relieve a business from a duty to comply with any other requirements of other state and federal law regarding the protection and privacy of personal information or age verification.

(f) For purposes of this section, a government-issued identification means any of the following:

(1) A document issued by a federal, state, county, or municipal government, or subdivision or agency thereof, including, but not limited to, an identification card or a valid motor vehicle operator's

license, including licenses or identification cards issued pursuant to Section 12801.9 of the Vehicle Code, that contains the name, date of birth, description, and picture of the person.

(2) A valid passport issued by the United States or by a foreign government.

(3) A valid identification card issued to a member of the United States Armed Forces that includes the date of birth and picture of the person.

(4) A valid consular identification document.

(5) An identification card issued by a federally recognized tribal government.

(g) This section shall become operative on January 1, 2020. *(Added by Stats.2018, c. 872 (A.B.2511), § 1, eff. Jan. 1, 2019, operative Jan. 1, 2020. Amended by Stats.2022, c. 482 (A.B.1766), § 1, eff. Jan. 1, 2023.)*

Title 1.81.46

ONLINE VIOLENCE PREVENTION ACT

Section
1798.99.20. Definitions.
1798.99.21. Social media platforms; mechanism for reporting violent posts.
1798.99.22. Person who is target of violent post; request for order requiring removal of post and related violent posts; costs and attorney's fees.
1798.99.23. Application of title.

§ 1798.99.20. Definitions

For purposes of this section:[1]

(a)(1) "Content" means statements or comments made by users and media that are created, posted, shared, or otherwise interacted with by users on an internet-based service or application.

(2) "Content" does not include media put on a service or application exclusively for the purpose of cloud storage, transmitting files, or file collaboration.

(b) "Social media platform" means a public or semipublic internet-based service or application that has users in California and that meets both of the following criteria:

(1)(A) A substantial function of the service or application is to connect users in order to allow users to interact socially with each other within the service or application.

(B) A service or application that provides email or direct messaging services shall not be considered to meet this criterion on the basis of that function alone.

(2) The service or application allows users to do all of the following:

(A) Construct a public or semipublic profile for purposes of signing into and using the service or application.

(B) Populate a list of other users with whom an individual shares a social connection within the system.

(C) Create or post content viewable by other users, including, but not limited to, on message boards, in chat rooms, or through a landing page or main feed that presents the user with content generated by other users.

(c) "Public or semipublic internet-based service or application" does not include a service or application used to facilitate communication with a business or enterprise among employees or affiliates of the business or enterprise, provided that access to the service or application is restricted to employees or affiliates of the business or enterprise using the service or application.

(d) "User" means a person with an account on a social media platform.

(e) "Violent post" means content on a social media platform that contains a true threat against a specific person that is not protected by the First Amendment to the United States Constitution. *(Added by Stats.2022, c. 881 (S.B.1056), § 1, eff. Jan. 1, 2023.)*

[1] So in enrolled bill; probably should be "title".

§ 1798.99.21. Social media platforms; mechanism for reporting violent posts

(a) A social media platform shall clearly and conspicuously state whether it has a mechanism for reporting violent posts that is available to users and nonusers of the platform.

(b) If the social media platform has a reporting mechanism, the statement required by this subdivision shall include a link to the reporting mechanism. *(Added by Stats.2022, c. 881 (S.B.1056), § 1, eff. Jan. 1, 2023.)*

§ 1798.99.22. Person who is target of violent post; request for order requiring removal of post and related violent posts; costs and attorney's fees

(a)(1)(A) A person who is the target of a violent post, or reasonably believes the person is the target of a violent post, may seek an order requiring the social media platform to remove the violent post and any related violent post the court determines shall be removed in the interests of justice.

(B)(i) A person may bring an action pursuant to this paragraph before 48 hours have passed since providing notice to a social media platform pursuant to paragraph (2), but the court shall not rule on the request for an order until 48 hours have passed from the provision of notice.

(ii) The court may dismiss an action described by clause (i) if the social media platform deletes the post before 48 hours have passed from the provision of notice.

(C) Except as provided in subparagraph (D), a person may bring an action pursuant to this paragraph at any time, and the court may rule on the request at any time, if the social media platform does not have a reporting mechanism described in Section 1798.99.21.

(D) A person shall not bring an action pursuant to this paragraph, nor shall a court issue an order requiring a social medial platform to remove a violent post or any related violent post, based upon content containing a true threat against a specific person if the date and time when the true threat that was threatened to occur has passed.

(2) If the social media platform has a reporting mechanism described in Section 1798.99.21, a person shall not bring an action pursuant to paragraph (1) until the person has notified the social media platform of the violent post and requested that it be removed through the reporting mechanism.

(b)(1) A court shall award court costs and reasonable attorney's fees to a prevailing plaintiff in an action brought pursuant to this section.

(2) Reasonable attorney's fees may be awarded to a prevailing defendant upon a finding by the court that the plaintiff's prosecution of the action was not in good faith. *(Added by Stats.2022, c. 881 (S.B.1056), § 1, eff. Jan. 1, 2023.)*

§ 1798.99.23. Application of title

This title does not apply to a social media platform with fewer than 1,000,000 discrete monthly users. *(Added by Stats.2022, c. 881 (S.B.1056), § 1, eff. Jan. 1, 2023.)*

Title 1.81.47

THE CALIFORNIA AGE–APPROPRIATE DESIGN CODE ACT

Section
1798.99.28. Short title.
1798.99.29. Legislative findings and declarations.
1798.99.30. Definitions.
1798.99.31. Business that provides an online service, product, or feature likely to be accessed by children; required actions; prohibited actions.
1798.99.32. California Children's Data Protection Working Group.
1798.99.33. Completion of Data Protection Impact Assessment; exception.
1798.99.35. Violations and penalties; business in substantial compliance.
1798.99.40. Application of title.

§ 1798.99.28. Short title

This title shall be known, and may be cited, as the California Age-Appropriate Design Code Act. *(Added by Stats.2022, c. 320 (A.B. 2273), § 2, eff. Jan. 1, 2023.)*

§ 1798.99.29. Legislative findings and declarations

The Legislature declares that children should be afforded protections not only by online products and services specifically directed at them but by all online products and services they are likely to access and makes the following findings:

(a) Businesses that develop and provide online services, products, or features that children are likely to access should consider the best interests of children when designing, developing, and providing that online service, product, or feature.

(b) If a conflict arises between commercial interests and the best interests of children, companies should prioritize the privacy, safety, and well-being of children over commercial interests. *(Added by Stats.2022, c. 320 (A.B.2273), § 2, eff. Jan. 1, 2023.)*

§ 1798.99.30. Definitions

(a) For purposes of this title, the definitions in Section 1798.140 shall apply unless otherwise specified in this title.

(b) For the purposes of this title:

(1) "Child" or "children," unless otherwise specified, means a consumer or consumers who are under 18 years of age.

(2) "Data Protection Impact Assessment" means a systematic survey to assess and mitigate risks that arise from the data management practices of the business to children who are reasonably likely to access the online service, product, or feature at issue that arises from the provision of that online service, product, or feature.

(3) "Default" means a preselected option adopted by the business for the online service, product, or feature.

(4) "Likely to be accessed by children" means it is reasonable to expect, based on the following indicators, that the online service, product, or feature would be accessed by children:

(A) The online service, product, or feature is directed to children as defined by the Children's Online Privacy Protection Act (15 U.S.C. Sec. 6501 et seq.).

(B) The online service, product, or feature is determined, based on competent and reliable evidence regarding audience composition, to be routinely accessed by a significant number of children.

(C) An online service, product, or feature with advertisements marketed to children.

(D) An online service, product, or feature that is substantially similar or the same as an online service, product, or feature subject to subparagraph (B).

(E) An online service, product, or feature that has design elements that are known to be of interest to children, including, but not limited to, games, cartoons, music, and celebrities who appeal to children.

(F) A significant amount of the audience of the online service, product, or feature is determined, based on internal company research, to be children.

(5) "Online service, product, or feature" does not mean any of the following:

(A) A broadband internet access service, as defined in Section 3100.

(B) A telecommunications service, as defined in Section 153 of Title 47 of the United States Code.

(C) The delivery or use of a physical product.

(6) "Profiling" means any form of automated processing of personal information that uses personal information to evaluate certain aspects relating to a natural person, including analyzing or predicting aspects concerning a natural person's performance at work, economic situation, health, personal preferences, interests, reliability, behavior, location, or movements. *(Added by Stats.2022, c. 320 (A.B.2273), § 2, eff. Jan. 1, 2023.)*

§ 1798.99.31. Business that provides an online service, product, or feature likely to be accessed by children; required actions; prohibited actions

Section operative July 1, 2024.

(a) A business that provides an online service, product, or feature likely to be accessed by children shall take all of the following actions:

(1)(A) Before any new online services, products, or features are offered to the public, complete a Data Protection Impact Assessment for any online service, product, or feature likely to be accessed by children and maintain documentation of this assessment as long as the online service, product, or feature is likely to be accessed by children. A business shall biennially review all Data Protection Impact Assessments.

(B) The Data Protection Impact Assessment required by this paragraph shall identify the purpose of the online service, product, or feature, how it uses children's personal information, and the risks of material detriment to children that arise from the data management practices of the business. The Data Protection Impact Assessment shall address, to the extent applicable, all of the following:

(i) Whether the design of the online product, service, or feature could harm children, including by exposing children to harmful, or potentially harmful, content on the online product, service, or feature.

(ii) Whether the design of the online product, service, or feature could lead to children experiencing or being targeted by harmful, or potentially harmful, contacts on the online product, service, or feature.

(iii) Whether the design of the online product, service, or feature could permit children to witness, participate in, or be subject to harmful, or potentially harmful, conduct on the online product, service, or feature.

(iv) Whether the design of the online product, service, or feature could allow children to be party to or exploited by a harmful, or potentially harmful, contact on the online product, service, or feature.

(v) Whether algorithms used by the online product, service, or feature could harm children.

(vi) Whether targeted advertising systems used by the online product, service, or feature could harm children.

(vii) Whether and how the online product, service, or feature uses system design features to increase, sustain, or extend use of the online product, service, or feature by children, including the automatic playing of media, rewards for time spent, and notifications.

(viii) Whether, how, and for what purpose the online product, service, or feature collects or processes sensitive personal information of children.

(2) Document any risk of material detriment to children that arises from the data management practices of the business identified in the Data Protection Impact Assessment required by paragraph (1) and create a timed plan to mitigate or eliminate the risk before the online service, product, or feature is accessed by children.

(3) Within three business days of a written request by the Attorney General, provide to the Attorney General a list of all Data Protection Impact Assessments the business has completed.

(4)(A) For any Data Protection Impact Assessment completed pursuant to paragraph (1), make the Data Protection Impact Assessment available, within five business days, to the Attorney General pursuant to a written request.

(B) Notwithstanding any other law, a Data Protection Impact Assessment is protected as confidential and shall be exempt from public disclosure, including under the California Public Records Act (Chapter 3.5 (commencing with Section 6250) of Division 7 of Title 1 of the Government Code).

(C) To the extent any information contained in a Data Protection Impact Assessment disclosed to the Attorney General includes information subject to attorney-client privilege or work product protection, disclosure pursuant to this paragraph shall not constitute a waiver of that privilege or protection.

(5) Estimate the age of child users with a reasonable level of certainty appropriate to the risks that arise from the data management practices of the business or apply the privacy and data protections afforded to children to all consumers.

(6) Configure all default privacy settings provided to children by the online service, product, or feature to settings that offer a high level of privacy, unless the business can demonstrate a compelling reason that a different setting is in the best interests of children.

(7) Provide any privacy information, terms of service, policies, and community standards concisely, prominently, and using clear language suited to the age of children likely to access that online service, product, or feature.

(8) If the online service, product, or feature allows the child's parent, guardian, or any other consumer to monitor the child's online activity or track the child's location, provide an obvious signal to the child when the child is being monitored or tracked.

(9) Enforce published terms, policies, and community standards established by the business, including, but not limited to, privacy policies and those concerning children.

(10) Provide prominent, accessible, and responsive tools to help children, or if applicable their parents or guardians, exercise their privacy rights and report concerns.

(b) A business that provides an online service, product, or feature likely to be accessed by children shall not take any of the following actions:

(1) Use the personal information of any child in a way that the business knows, or has reason to know, is materially detrimental to the physical health, mental health, or well-being of a child.

(2) Profile a child by default unless both of the following criteria are met:

(A) The business can demonstrate it has appropriate safeguards in place to protect children.

(B) Either of the following is true:

(i) Profiling is necessary to provide the online service, product, or feature requested and only with respect to the aspects of the online service, product, or feature with which the child is actively and knowingly engaged.

(ii) The business can demonstrate a compelling reason that profiling is in the best interests of children.

(3) Collect, sell, share, or retain any personal information that is not necessary to provide an online service, product, or feature with which a child is actively and knowingly engaged, or as described in paragraphs (1) to (4), inclusive, of subdivision (a) of Section 1798.145, unless the business can demonstrate a compelling reason that the collecting, selling, sharing, or retaining of the personal information is in the best interests of children likely to access the online service, product, or feature.

(4) If the end user is a child, use personal information for any reason other than a reason for which that personal information was collected, unless the business can demonstrate a compelling reason that use of the personal information is in the best interests of children.

(5) Collect, sell, or share any precise geolocation information of children by default unless the collection of that precise geolocation information is strictly necessary for the business to provide the service, product, or feature requested and then only for the limited time that the collection of precise geolocation information is necessary to provide the service, product, or feature.

(6) Collect any precise geolocation information of a child without providing an obvious sign to the child for the duration of that collection that precise geolocation information is being collected.

(7) Use dark patterns to lead or encourage children to provide personal information beyond what is reasonably expected to provide that online service, product, or feature to forego privacy protections, or to take any action that the business knows, or has reason to know, is materially detrimental to the child's physical health, mental health, or well-being.

(8) Use any personal information collected to estimate age or age range for any other purpose or retain that personal information longer than necessary to estimate age. Age assurance shall be proportionate to the risks and data practice of an online service, product, or feature.

(c)(1) A Data Protection Impact Assessment conducted by a business for the purpose of compliance with any other law complies with this section if the Data Protection Impact Assessment meets the requirements of this title.

(2) A single data protection impact assessment may contain multiple similar processing operations that present similar risks only if each relevant online service, product, or feature is addressed.

(d) This section shall become operative on July 1, 2024. *(Added by Stats.2022, c. 320 (A.B.2273), § 2, eff. Jan. 1, 2023, operative July 1, 2024.)*

§ 1798.99.32. California Children's Data Protection Working Group

(a) The California Children's Data Protection Working Group is hereby created to deliver a report to the Legislature, pursuant to subdivision (e), regarding best practices for the implementation of this title.

(b) Working Group members shall consist of Californians with expertise in at least two of the following areas:

(1) Children's data privacy.

(2) Physical health.

(3) Mental health and well-being.

(4) Computer science.

(5) Children's rights.

(c) The working group shall select a chair and a vice chair from among its members and shall consist of the following 10 members:

(1) Two appointees by the Governor.

(2) Two appointees by the President Pro Tempore of the Senate.

(3) Two appointees by the Speaker of the Assembly.

(4) Two appointees by the Attorney General.

(5) Two appointees by the California Privacy Protection Agency.

(d) The working group shall take input from a broad range of stakeholders, including from academia, consumer advocacy groups, and small, medium, and large businesses affected by data privacy policies and shall make recommendations to the Legislature on best practices regarding, at minimum, all of the following:

(1) Identifying online services, products, or features likely to be accessed by children.

(2) Evaluating and prioritizing the best interests of children with respect to their privacy, physical health, and mental health and well-being and evaluating how those interests may be furthered by the design, development, and implementation of an online service, product, or feature.

(3) Ensuring that age assurance methods used by businesses that provide online services, products, or features likely to be accessed by children are proportionate to the risks that arise from the data management practices of the business, privacy protective, and minimally invasive.

(4) Assessing and mitigating risks to children that arise from the use of an online service, product, or feature.

(5) Publishing privacy information, policies, and standards in concise, clear language suited for the age of children likely to access an online service, product, or feature.

(6) How the working group and the Department of Justice may leverage the substantial and growing expertise of the California Privacy Protection Agency in the long-term development of data privacy policies that affect the privacy, rights, and safety of children online.

(e) On or before January 1, 2024, and every two years thereafter, the working group shall submit, pursuant to Section 9795 of the Government Code, a report to the Legislature regarding the recommendations described in subdivision (d).

(f) The members of the working group shall serve without compensation but shall be reimbursed for all necessary expenses actually incurred in the performance of their duties.

(g) This section shall remain in effect until January 1, 2030, and as of that date is repealed. *(Added by Stats.2022, c. 320 (A.B.2273), § 2, eff. Jan. 1, 2023.)*

Repeal

For repeal of this section, see its terms.

§ 1798.99.33. Completion of Data Protection Impact Assessment; exception

(a) A business shall complete a Data Protection Impact Assessment on or before July 1, 2024, for any online service, product, or feature likely to be accessed by children offered to the public before July 1, 2024.

(b) This section does not apply to an online service, product, or feature that is not offered to the public on or after July 1, 2024. *(Added by Stats.2022, c. 320 (A.B.2273), § 2, eff. Jan. 1, 2023.)*

§ 1798.99.35. Violations and penalties; business in substantial compliance

(a) Any business that violates this title shall be subject to an injunction and liable for a civil penalty of not more than two thousand five hundred dollars ($2,500) per affected child for each negligent violation or not more than seven thousand five hundred dollars ($7,500) per affected child for each intentional violation, which shall be assessed and recovered only in a civil action brought in the name of the people of the State of California by the Attorney General.

(b) Any penalties, fees, and expenses recovered in an action brought under this title shall be deposited in the Consumer Privacy Fund, created within the General Fund pursuant to subdivision (a) of Section 1798.160, with the intent that they be used to fully offset costs incurred by the Attorney General in connection with this title.

(c)(1) If a business is in substantial compliance with the requirements of paragraphs (1) through (4), inclusive, of subdivision (a) of Section 1798.99.31, the Attorney General shall provide written notice to the business, before initiating an action under this title, identifying the specific provisions of this title that the Attorney General alleges have been or are being violated.

(2) If, within 90 days of the notice required by this subdivision, the business cures any noticed violation and provides the Attorney General a written statement that the alleged violations have been cured, and sufficient measures have been taken to prevent future violations, the business shall not be liable for a civil penalty for any violation cured pursuant to this subdivision.

(d) Nothing in this title shall be interpreted to serve as the basis for a private right of action under this title or any other law.

(e) The Attorney General may solicit broad public participation and adopt regulations to clarify the requirements of this title. *(Added by Stats.2022, c. 320 (A.B.2273), § 2, eff. Jan. 1, 2023.)*

§ 1798.99.40. Application of title

This title does not apply to the information or entities described in subdivision (c) of Section 1798.145. *(Added by Stats.2022, c. 320 (A.B.2273), § 2, eff. Jan. 1, 2023.)*

Title 2

CREDIT SALES

Cross References

Savings association, issuance of credit cards, application of this Title, see Financial Code § 7454.

Spanish language translation of contracts or agreements, necessity, exceptions, see Civil Code § 1632.

CHAPTER 2. CREDIT TRANSACTIONS REGARDING WOMEN

Section
1812.30. Denial of credit to person regardless of marital status; prohibition; conditions; reporting agency.
1812.31. Right of action; damages; individual and class suits.
1812.32. Injunction.
1812.33. Civil penalties; precedence of action; distribution of proceeds.
1812.34. Costs and attorney fees.
1812.35. Commencement of action; limitations.

§ 1812.30. Denial of credit to person regardless of marital status; prohibition; conditions; reporting agency

(a) No person, regardless of marital status, shall be denied credit in his or her own name if the earnings and other property over which he or she has management and control are such that a person of the opposite sex managing and controlling the same amount of earnings and other property would receive credit.

(b) No person, regardless of marital status, managing and controlling earnings and other property shall be offered credit on terms less favorable than those offered to a person of the opposite sex seeking the same type of credit and managing and controlling the same amount of earnings and other property.

(c) No unmarried person shall be denied credit if his or her earnings and other property are such that a married person managing and controlling the same amount of earnings and other property would receive credit.

(d) No unmarried person shall be offered credit on terms less favorable than those offered to a married person managing and controlling the same amount of earnings and other property.

(e) For accounts established after January 1, 1977 or for accounts in existence on January 1, 1977 where information on that account is received after January 1, 1977, a credit reporting agency which in its normal course of business receives information on joint credit accounts identifying the persons responsible for such accounts, or receives information which reflects the participation of both spouses, shall: (1) at the time such information is received file such information separately under the names of each person or spouse, or file such information in another manner which would enable either person or spouse to automatically gain access to the credit history without having in any way to list or refer to the name of the other person, and (2) provide access to all information about the account in the name of each person or spouse.

(f) For all accounts established prior to January 1, 1977, a credit reporting agency shall at any time upon the written or personal request of a person who is or has been married, verify the contractual liability, liability by operation of law, or authorized use by such person, of joint credit accounts appearing in the file of the person's spouse or former spouse, and, if applicable, shall file such information separately and thereafter continue to do so under the names of each person responsible for the joint account or in another manner which would enable either person responsible for the joint account to automatically gain access to the credit history without having in any way to list or refer to the name of the other person.

(g) For the purposes of this chapter "credit" means obtainment of money, property, labor, or services on a deferred-payment basis.

(h) For the purposes of this chapter, earnings shall include, but not be limited to, spousal, family, and child support payments, pensions, social security, disability or survivorship benefits. Spousal, family, and child support payments shall be considered in the same manner as earnings from salary, wages, or other sources where the payments are received pursuant to a written agreement or court decree to the extent that the reliability of such payments is established. The factors which a creditor may consider in evaluating the reliability of such payments are the length of time payments have been received; the regularity of receipt; and whether full or partial payments have been made.

(i) Nothing in this chapter shall be construed to prohibit a person from: (1) utilizing an evaluation of the reliability of earnings provided that such an evaluation is applied to persons without regard to their sex or marital status; or (2) inquiring into and utilizing an evaluation of the obligations for which community property is liable pursuant to the Family Code for the sole purpose of determining the creditor's rights and remedies with respect to the particular extension of credit, provided that such is done with respect to all applicants without regard to their sex; or (3) utilizing any other relevant factors or methods in determining whether to extend credit to an applicant provided that such factors or methods are applicable to all applicants without regard to their sex or marital status. For the purpose of this subdivision, the fact that an applicant is of childbearing age is not a relevant factor.

(j) Credit applications for the obtainment of money, goods, labor, or services shall clearly specify that the applicant, if married, may apply for a separate account. *(Added by Stats.1973, c. 999, p. 1987, § 1. Amended by Stats.1975, c. 332, p. 778, § 1; Stats.1976, c. 1361, p. 6203, § 1; Stats.1992, c. 163 (A.B.2641), § 11, operative Jan. 1, 1994.)*

Research References

Forms

West's California Code Forms, Civil § 1812.31 Form 1, Complaint—Wrongful Denial of Credit.
27A West's Legal Forms § 11:30, Charge Account and Installment Credit Agreements—State Notice Requirements.

§ 1812.31. Right of action; damages; individual and class suits

(a) Whoever violates Section 1812.30 shall be liable to the aggrieved person in an amount equal to the sum of any actual damages sustained by such person acting either in an individual capacity or as a representative of a class.

(b) Whoever violates Section 1812.30 shall be liable to the aggrieved person for punitive damages in an amount not greater than ten thousand dollars ($10,000), as determined by the court, in addition to any actual damages provided in subdivision (a); provided, however, that in pursuing the recovery allowed under this subdivision, the aggrieved person may proceed only in an individual capacity and not as a representative of a class.

(c) Notwithstanding subdivision (b), whoever violates Section 1812.30 may be liable for punitive damages in the case of a class action in such amount as the court may allow, except that as to each member of the class no minimum recovery shall be applicable, and the total recovery in such action shall not exceed the lesser of one hundred thousand dollars ($100,000) or one percent (1%) of the net worth of the creditor. In determining the amount of the award in any class action, the court shall consider, among other relevant factors, the amount of any actual damages awarded, the frequency and persistence of violations, the resources of the creditor, the number of persons adversely affected, and the extent to which the creditor's violation was intentional. *(Added by Stats.1973, c. 999, p. 1987, § 1. Amended by Stats.1975, c. 332, p. 779, § 2.)*

Research References

Forms

West's California Code Forms, Civil § 1812.31 Form 1, Complaint—Wrongful Denial of Credit.

§ 1812.32. Injunction

Any person, corporation, firm, partnership, joint stock company, or any other association or organization which violates or proposes to violate this chapter may be enjoined by any court of competent jurisdiction. Actions for injunction under this section may be prosecuted by the Attorney General or any district attorney, county counsel, city attorney, or city prosecutor in this state in the name of the people of the State of California or by any person denied credit or offered credit in violation of Section 1812.30. *(Added by Stats.1975, c. 332, p. 780, § 3.)*

Cross References

Attorney General, generally, see Government Code § 12500 et seq.

Research References

Forms

West's California Code Forms, Civil § 1812.31 Form 1, Complaint—Wrongful Denial of Credit.

§ 1812.33. Civil penalties; precedence of action; distribution of proceeds

(a) Any person who intentionally violates any injunction issued pursuant to this chapter shall be liable for a civil penalty not to exceed two thousand five hundred dollars ($2,500) for each day that such person violates the injunction.

§ 1812.33

(b) The civil penalty prescribed by this section shall be assessed and recovered in a civil action brought in the name of the people of the State of California by the Attorney General or by any district attorney, county counsel, or city attorney in any court of competent jurisdiction. An action brought pursuant to this section to recover such civil penalties shall take special precedence over all civil matters on the calendar of the court except those matters to which equal precedence on the calendar is granted by law.

(c) If such an action is brought by the Attorney General, one-half of the penalty collected pursuant to this section shall be paid to the treasurer of the county in which the judgment was entered, and one-half to the State Treasurer. If brought by a district attorney or county counsel, the entire amount of the penalty collected shall be paid to the treasurer of the county in which the judgment was entered. If brought by a city attorney or city prosecutor, one-half of the penalty shall be paid to the treasurer of the county in which the judgment was entered and one-half to the city. *(Added by Stats.1975, c. 332, p. 780, § 4.)*

Cross References

Attorney General, generally, see Government Code § 12500 et seq.
State Treasurer, generally, see Government Code § 12302 et seq.

§ 1812.34. Costs and attorney fees

Any person denied credit or offered credit in violation of Section 1812.30 who brings an action pursuant to Section 1812.31 or 1812.32 of this code may petition the court for award of costs and reasonable attorney's fees which the court shall award if the action is successful. *(Added by Stats.1975, c. 332, p. 781, § 5.)*

Research References

Forms

West's California Code Forms, Civil § 1812.31 Form 1, Complaint—Wrongful Denial of Credit.

§ 1812.35. Commencement of action; limitations

Any action commenced pursuant to Section 1812.31 shall be commenced within two years from the date on which the person is denied credit or is offered credit in violation of Section 1812.30. *(Added by Stats.1975, c. 332, p. 781, § 6.)*

Research References

Forms

West's California Code Forms, Civil § 1812.31 Form 1, Complaint—Wrongful Denial of Credit.

Title 5

HIRING

CHAPTER 2. HIRING OF REAL PROPERTY

Section
1941.5. Tenant protected by restraining order against non-tenant; change of locks on dwelling unit; definitions.
1941.6. Tenant protected by restraining order against another tenant; change of locks on dwelling unit; liability regarding person excluded; definitions.
1946.7. Victims of domestic violence, sexual assault, stalking, human trafficking, or abuse of elder or dependent adult; written notice to terminate tenancy; requirements of notice; landlord disclosure to third party; violations and remedies.

Cross References

Employee housing, termination or modification of tenancy or retaliatory employment actions, enforcement of tenants' rights, see Health and Safety Code §§ 17031.5, 17031.7.
Immigration or citizenship status irrelevant to issues of liability or remedy in specified proceedings, discovery, see Civil Code § 3339.10.

§ 1941.5. Tenant protected by restraining order against non-tenant; change of locks on dwelling unit; definitions

(a) This section shall apply if a person who is restrained from contact with the protected tenant under a court order or is named in a police report is not a tenant of the same dwelling unit as the protected tenant.

(b) A landlord shall change the locks of a protected tenant's dwelling unit upon written request of the protected tenant not later than 24 hours after the protected tenant gives the landlord a copy of a court order or police report, and shall give the protected tenant a key to the new locks.

(c)(1) If a landlord fails to change the locks within 24 hours, the protected tenant may change the locks without the landlord's permission, notwithstanding any provision in the lease to the contrary.

(2) If the protected tenant changes the locks pursuant to this subdivision, the protected tenant shall do all of the following:

(A) Change the locks in a workmanlike manner with locks of similar or better quality than the original lock.

(B) Notify the landlord within 24 hours that the locks have been changed.

(C) Provide the landlord with a key by any reasonable method agreed upon by the landlord and protected tenant.

(3) This subdivision shall apply to leases executed on or after the date the act that added this section takes effect.

(d) For the purposes of this section, the following definitions shall apply:

(1) "Court order" means a court order lawfully issued within the last 180 days pursuant to Section 527.6 of the Code of Civil Procedure, Part 3 (commencing with Section 6240), Part 4 (commencing with Section 6300), or Part 5 (commencing with Section 6400) of Division 10 of the Family Code, Section 136.2 of the Penal Code, or Section 213.5 of the Welfare and Institutions Code.

(2) "Locks" means any exterior lock that provides access to the dwelling.

(3) "Police report" means a written report, written within the last 180 days, by a peace officer employed by a state or local law enforcement agency acting in his or her official capacity, stating that the protected tenant or a household member has filed a report alleging that the protected tenant or the household member is a victim of domestic violence, sexual assault, or stalking.

(4) "Protected tenant" means a tenant who has obtained a court order or has a copy of a police report.

(5) "Tenant" means tenant, subtenant, lessee, or sublessee. *(Added by Stats.2010, c. 626 (S.B.782), § 2.)*

Cross References

Shelter crisis, emergency housing, homeless shelters, see Government Code § 8698.4.

§ 1941.6. Tenant protected by restraining order against another tenant; change of locks on dwelling unit; liability regarding person excluded; definitions

(a) This section shall apply if a person who is restrained from contact with a protected tenant under a court order is a tenant of the same dwelling unit as the protected tenant.

(b) A landlord shall change the locks of a protected tenant's dwelling unit upon written request of the protected tenant not later than 24 hours after the protected tenant gives the landlord a copy of a court order that excludes from the dwelling unit the restrained person referred to in subdivision (a). The landlord shall give the protected tenant a key to the new locks.

(c)(1) If a landlord fails to change the locks within 24 hours, the protected tenant may change the locks without the landlord's permission, notwithstanding any provision in the lease to the contrary.

(2) If the protected tenant changes the locks pursuant to this subdivision, the protected tenant shall do all of the following:

(A) Change the locks in a workmanlike manner with locks of similar or better quality than the original lock.

(B) Notify the landlord within 24 hours that the locks have been changed.

(C) Provide the landlord with a key by any reasonable method agreed upon by the landlord and protected tenant.

(3) This subdivision shall apply to leases executed on or after the date the act that added this section takes effect.

(d) Notwithstanding Section 789.3, if the locks are changed pursuant to this section, the landlord is not liable to a person excluded from the dwelling unit pursuant to this section.

(e) A person who has been excluded from a dwelling unit under this section remains liable under the lease with all other tenants of the dwelling unit for rent as provided in the lease.

(f) For the purposes of this section, the following definitions shall apply:

(1) "Court order" means a court order lawfully issued within the last 180 days pursuant to Section 527.6 of the Code of Civil Procedure, Part 3 (commencing with Section 6240), Part 4 (commencing with Section 6300), or Part 5 (commencing with Section 6400) of Division 10 of the Family Code, Section 136.2 of the Penal Code, or Section 213.5 of the Welfare and Institutions Code.

(2) "Locks" means any exterior lock that provides access to the dwelling.

(3) "Protected tenant" means a tenant who has obtained a court order.

(4) "Tenant" means tenant, subtenant, lessee, or sublessee. *(Added by Stats.2010, c. 626 (S.B.782), § 3.)*

Cross References

Shelter crisis, emergency housing, homeless shelters, see Government Code § 8698.4.

§ 1946.7. Victims of domestic violence, sexual assault, stalking, human trafficking, or abuse of elder or dependent adult; written notice to terminate tenancy; requirements of notice; landlord disclosure to third party; violations and remedies

(a) A tenant may notify the landlord that the tenant intends to terminate the tenancy if the tenant, a household member, or an immediate family member was the victim of an act that constitutes any of the following:

(1) Domestic violence as defined in Section 6211 of the Family Code.

(2) Sexual assault as defined in Section 261, 261.5, 286, 287, or 289 of the Penal Code.

(3) Stalking as defined in Section 1708.7.

(4) Human trafficking as defined in Section 236.1 of the Penal Code.

(5) Abuse of an elder or a dependent adult as defined in Section 15610.07 of the Welfare and Institutions Code.

(6) A crime that caused bodily injury or death.

(7) A crime that included the exhibition, drawing, brandishing, or use of a firearm or other deadly weapon or instrument.

(8) A crime that included the use of force against the victim or a threat of force against the victim.

(b) A notice to terminate a tenancy under this section shall be in writing, with one of the following attached to the notice:

(1) A copy of a temporary restraining order, emergency protective order, or protective order lawfully issued pursuant to Part 3 (commencing with Section 6240) or Part 4 (commencing with Section 6300) of Division 10 of the Family Code, Section 136.2 of the Penal Code, Section 527.6 of the Code of Civil Procedure, or Section 213.5 or 15657.03 of the Welfare and Institutions Code that protects the tenant, household member, or immediate family member from further domestic violence, sexual assault, stalking, human trafficking, abuse of an elder or a dependent adult, or any act or crime listed in subdivision (a).

(2) A copy of a written report by a peace officer employed by a state or local law enforcement agency acting in the peace officer's official capacity stating that the tenant, household member, or immediate family member has filed a report alleging that the tenant, the household member, or the immediate family member is a victim of an act or crime listed in subdivision (a).

(3)(A) Documentation from a qualified third party based on information received by that third party while acting in the third party's professional capacity to indicate that the tenant, household member, or immediate family member is seeking assistance for physical or mental injuries or abuse resulting from an act or crime listed in subdivision (a).

(B) The documentation shall contain, in substantially the same form, the following:

Tenant Statement and Qualified Third Party Statement under Civil Code Section 1946.7

Part I. Statement By Tenant
I, [insert name of tenant], state as follows:
I, or a member of my household or immediate family, have been a victim of:
[insert one or more of the following: domestic violence, sexual assault, stalking, human trafficking, elder abuse, dependent adult abuse, or a crime that caused bodily injury or death, a crime that included the exhibition, drawing, brandishing, or use of a firearm or other deadly weapon or instrument, or a crime that included the use of force against the victim or a threat of force against the victim.]
The most recent incident(s) happened on or about:
[insert date or dates.]
The incident(s) was/were committed by the following person(s), with these physical description(s), if known and safe to provide:
[if known and safe to provide, insert name(s) and physical description(s).]

_____   _____
(signature of tenant)   (date)

Part II. Qualified Third Party Statement
I, [insert name of qualified third party], state as follows:
My business address and phone number are:
[insert business address and phone number.]
Check and complete one of the following:
_____I meet the requirements for a sexual assault counselor provided in Section 1035.2 of the Evidence Code and I am either engaged in an office, hospital, institution, or center commonly known as a rape crisis center described in that section or employed by an organization providing the programs specified in Section 13835.2 of the Penal Code.
_____I meet the requirements for a domestic violence counselor provided in Section 1037.1 of the Evidence Code and I am employed, whether financially compensated or not, by a domestic violence victim service organization, as defined in that section.
_____I meet the requirements for a human trafficking caseworker provided in Section 1038.2 of the Evidence Code and I am employed, whether financially compensated or not, by an organization that provides programs specified in Section 18294 of the Welfare and Institutions Code or in Section 13835.2 of the Penal Code.
_____I meet the definition of "victim of violent crime advocate" provided in Section 1947.6 of the Civil Code and I am employed, whether financially compensated or not, by * * * an agency or organization that has a documented record of providing services to victims of violent crime or provides those services under the auspices or supervision of a court or a law enforcement or prosecution agency.
_____I am licensed by the State of California as a:
[insert one of the following: physician and surgeon, osteopathic physician and surgeon, registered nurse, psychiatrist, psychologist, licensed clinical social worker, licensed marriage and family therapist, or licensed professional clinical counselor.] and I am licensed by, and my license number is:

§ 1946.7

[insert name of state licensing entity and license number.]
The person who signed the Statement By Tenant above stated to me that the person, or a member of the person's household or immediate family, is a victim of: [insert one or more of the following: domestic violence, sexual assault, stalking, human trafficking, elder abuse, dependent adult abuse, or a crime that caused physical injury, emotional injury and the threat of physical injury, or death.]
The person further stated to me the incident(s) occurred on or about the date(s) stated above.
I understand that the person who made the Statement By Tenant may use this document as a basis for terminating a lease with the person's landlord.

_____   _____
(signature of qualified third party)   (date)

(C) The documentation may be signed by a person who meets the requirements for a sexual assault counselor, domestic violence counselor, a human trafficking caseworker, or a victim of violent crime advocate only if the documentation displays the letterhead of the office, hospital, institution, center, or organization, as appropriate, that engages or employs, whether financially compensated or not, this counselor, caseworker, or advocate.

(4) Any other form of documentation that reasonably verifies that the crime or act listed in subdivision (a) occurred.

(c) If the tenant is terminating tenancy pursuant to subdivision (a) because an immediate family member is a victim of an eligible act or crime listed in subdivision (a) and that tenant did not live in the same household as the immediate family member at the time of the act or crime, and no part of the act or crime occurred within the dwelling unit or within 1,000 feet of the dwelling unit of the tenant, the tenant shall attach to the notice and other documentation required by subdivision (b) a written statement stating all of the following:

(1) The tenant's immediate family member was a victim of an act or crime listed in subdivision (a).

(2) The tenant intends to relocate as a result of the tenant's immediate family member being a victim of an act or crime listed in subdivision (a).

(3) The tenant is relocating to increase the safety, physical well-being, emotional well-being, psychological well-being, or financial security of the tenant or of the tenant's immediate family member as a result of the act or crime.

(d) The notice to terminate the tenancy shall be given within 180 days of the date that any order described in paragraph (1) of subdivision (b) was issued, within 180 days of the date that any written report described in paragraph (2) of subdivision (b) was made, within 180 days of the date that an act or a crime described in * * * subdivision (a) occurred, or within the time period described in Section 1946.

(e) If notice to terminate the tenancy is provided to the landlord under this section, the tenant shall be responsible for payment of rent for no more than 14 calendar days following the giving of the notice, or for any shorter appropriate period as described in Section 1946 or the lease or rental agreement. The tenant shall be released without penalty from any further rent or other payment obligation to the landlord under the lease or rental agreement * * *. If the premises are relet to another party prior to the end of the obligation to pay rent, the rent owed under this subdivision shall be prorated.

(f) Notwithstanding any law, a landlord shall not, due to the termination, require a tenant who terminates a lease or rental agreement pursuant to this section to forfeit any security deposit money or advance rent paid * * *. A tenant who terminates a rental agreement pursuant to this section shall not be considered for any purpose, by reason of the termination, to have breached the lease or rental agreement. * * * In all other respects, the law governing the security deposit shall apply.

(g) This section does not relieve a tenant, other than the tenant who is, or who has a household member or immediate family member who is, a victim of an act or crime listed in subdivision (a) and members of that tenant's household, from their obligations under the lease or rental agreement.

(h) For purposes of this section, the following definitions apply:

(1) "Household member" means a member of the tenant's family who lives in the same * * * residential unit as the tenant.

(2) "Health practitioner" means a physician and surgeon, osteopathic physician and surgeon, psychiatrist, psychologist, registered nurse, licensed clinical social worker, licensed marriage and family therapist, * * * licensed professional clinical counselor, or a victim of violent crime advocate.

(3) "Immediate family member" means the parent, stepparent, spouse, child, child-in-law, stepchild, or sibling of the tenant, or any person living in the tenant's household at the time the crime or act listed in subdivision (a) occurred who has a relationship with the tenant that is substantially similar to that of a family member.

(4) "Qualified third party" means a health practitioner, domestic violence counselor, as defined in Section 1037.1 of the Evidence Code, a sexual assault counselor, as defined in Section 1035.2 of the Evidence Code, or a human trafficking caseworker, as defined in Section 1038.2 of the Evidence Code.

(5) "Victim of violent crime advocate" means a person who is employed, whether financially compensated or not, for the purpose of rendering advice or assistance to victims of violent crimes for * * * an agency or organization that has a documented record of providing services to victims of violent crime or provides those services under the auspices or supervision of a court or a law enforcement or prosecution agency.

(i)(1) A landlord shall not disclose any information provided by a tenant under this section to a third party unless the disclosure satisfies * * * one or more of the following:

(A) The tenant consents in writing to the disclosure.

(B) The disclosure is required by law or order of the court.

(2) A landlord's communication to a qualified third party who provides documentation under paragraph (3) of subdivision (b) to verify the contents of that documentation is not disclosure for purposes of this subdivision.

(j) An owner or an owner's agent shall not refuse to rent a dwelling unit to an otherwise qualified prospective tenant or refuse to continue to rent to an existing tenant solely on the basis that the tenant has previously exercised the tenant's rights under this section or has previously terminated a tenancy because of the circumstances described in subdivision (a).

(k) A landlord or agent of a landlord who violates this section shall be liable to the tenant in a civil action for both of the following:

(1) The actual damages sustained by the tenant.

(2)(A) Statutory damages of not less than one hundred dollars ($100) and not more than five thousand dollars ($5,000).

(B) Notwithstanding subparagraph (A), a landlord or agent of a landlord who violates this section shall not be liable for statutory damages if the tenant provided documentation of the crime or act to the landlord or the agent of the landlord pursuant to paragraph (4) of subdivision (b) only.

(*l*) The remedies provided by this section shall be in addition to any other remedy provided by law. *(Added by Stats.2008, c. 440 (A.B.2052), § 1, eff. Sept. 27, 2008. Amended by Stats.2011, c. 76 (A.B.588), § 1; Stats.2012, c. 516 (S.B.1403), § 1; Stats.2013, c. 130 (S.B.612), § 1; Stats.2015, c. 70 (A.B.418), § 1, eff. Jan. 1, 2016; Stats.2018, c. 423 (S.B.1494), § 6, eff. Jan. 1, 2019; Stats.2019, c. 497 (A.B.991), § 26, eff. Jan. 1, 2020; Stats.2020, c. 205 (S.B.1190), § 1, eff. Jan. 1, 2021; Stats.2021, c. 626 (A.B.1171), § 5, eff. Jan. 1, 2022; Stats.2022, c. 28 (S.B.1380), § 24, eff. Jan. 1, 2023; Stats.2022, c. 558 (S.B.1017), § 1, eff. Jan. 1, 2023.)*

Cross References

Informing crime victims of their rights, Victim Protections and Resources card, see Penal Code § 679.027.

CODE OF CIVIL PROCEDURE

Part 1

OF COURTS OF JUSTICE

Title 1

ORGANIZATION AND JURISDICTION

CHAPTER 1. COURTS OF JUSTICE IN GENERAL

Section
36. Motion for preference; party over 70 years of age; party under 14 years of age; medical reasons; interests of justice; time of trial.

Cross References

Courts in which judicial power is vested, see Cal. Const. Art. 6, § 1.
Courts of record, see Cal. Const. Art. 6, § 1.
District courts of appeal,
   Generally, see Cal. Const. Art. 6, §§ 1, 3, 10, 11.
   Jurisdiction in general, see Cal. Const. Art. 6, §§ 10, 11.
   Organization and government, see Cal. Const. Art. 6, § 4.
English language, use in courts, see Code of Civil Procedure § 185.
Incidental powers and duties of courts, see Code of Civil Procedure § 128 et seq.
Judicial council, see Government Code § 68500 et seq.
Judicial days, see Code of Civil Procedure § 133 et seq.
Jurisdiction, means to carry into effect, see Code of Civil Procedure § 187.
Justice courts,
   Generally, see Cal. Const. Art. 6, §§ 1, 5.
   Jurisdiction in general, see Code of Civil Procedure § 86; Cal. Const. Art. 6, § 5.
   Organization and government, see Government Code § 71600 et seq.
Municipal courts,
   Generally, see Cal. Const. Art. 6, §§ 1, 5.
   Jurisdiction in general, see Code of Civil Procedure § 86; Cal. Const. Art. 6, § 5.
   Organization and government of courts, general provisions, see Government Code § 68070 et seq.
Places of holding courts, see Government Code §§ 68100, 68115 et seq., 70311.
Publicity of court proceedings, see Code of Civil Procedure § 124.
Rules of court, see Cal. Const. Art. 6, § 6; Government Code § 68070 et seq.
Seals of courts, see Government Code § 68074 et seq.
Small claims courts, see Code of Civil Procedure § 116.110 et seq.
Superior courts,
   Generally, see Cal. Const. Art. 6, §§ 1, 10, 11.
   Jurisdiction in general, see Cal. Const. Art. 6, § 10.
   Organization and government, see Cal. Const. Art. 6, §§ 4, 16.
Supreme Court,
   Generally, see Cal. Const. Art. 6, § 2.
   Jurisdiction in general, see Cal. Const. Art. 6, §§ 10, 11.
   Organization and government, see Government Code § 68801 et seq.

§ 36. Motion for preference; party over 70 years of age; party under 14 years of age; medical reasons; interests of justice; time of trial

(a) A party to a civil action who is over 70 years of age may petition the court for a preference, which the court shall grant if the court makes both of the following findings:

(1) The party has a substantial interest in the action as a whole.

(2) The health of the party is such that a preference is necessary to prevent prejudicing the party's interest in the litigation.

(b) A civil action to recover damages for wrongful death or personal injury shall be entitled to preference upon the motion of any party to the action who is under 14 years of age unless the court finds that the party does not have a substantial interest in the case as a whole. A civil action subject to subdivision (a) shall be given preference over a case subject to this subdivision.

(c) Unless the court otherwise orders:

(1) A party may file and serve a motion for preference supported by a declaration of the moving party that all essential parties have been served with process or have appeared.

(2) At any time during the pendency of the action, a party who reaches 70 years of age may file and serve a motion for preference.

(d) In its discretion, the court may also grant a motion for preference that is accompanied by clear and convincing medical documentation that concludes that one of the parties suffers from an illness or condition raising substantial medical doubt of survival of that party beyond six months, and that satisfies the court that the interests of justice will be served by granting the preference.

(e) Notwithstanding any other provision of law, the court may in its discretion grant a motion for preference that is supported by a showing that satisfies the court that the interests of justice will be served by granting this preference.

(f) Upon the granting of such a motion for preference, the court shall set the matter for trial not more than 120 days from that date and there shall be no continuance beyond 120 days from the granting of the motion for preference except for physical disability of a party or a party's attorney, or upon a showing of good cause stated in the record. Any continuance shall be for no more than 15 days and no more than one continuance for physical disability may be granted to any party.

(g) Upon the granting of a motion for preference pursuant to subdivision (b), a party in an action based upon a health provider's alleged professional negligence, as defined in Section 364, shall receive a trial date not sooner than six months and not later than nine months from the date that the motion is granted. (Added by Stats.1979, c. 151, p. 348, § 2. Amended by Stats.1981, c. 215, § 1; Stats.1988, c. 1237, § 1; Stats.1989, c. 913, § 1; Stats.1990, c. 428 (A.B.3811), § 1; Stats.2008, c. 218 (A.B.1949), § 1.)

Cross References

Action, defined, see Code of Civil Procedure § 22.
Attorneys, State Bar Act, see Business and Professions Code § 6000.
Civil action, defined, see Code of Civil Procedure § 30.
Civil action, origin, see Code of Civil Procedure § 25.
Computation of time, see Code of Civil Procedure §§ 12, 12a, 12b; Government Code § 6800 et seq.
Kinds of actions, see Code of Civil Procedure § 24.
Kinds of injuries, see Code of Civil Procedure § 27.
Month, defined, see Code of Civil Procedure § 17.
Notice, actual and constructive, defined, see Civil Code § 18.
Precedence of actions for trial, see Penal Code § 1048.

Research References

Forms

West's California Code Forms, Civil Procedure § 36(a) Form 1, Preferences—Civil Cases—Notice of Motion for Preference by Party Exceeding Age 70.
West's California Code Forms, Civil Procedure § 36(a) Form 3, Preferences—Civil Cases—Order Granting Preference—Party Exceeding Age 70.

§ 36

West's California Code Forms, Civil Procedure § 36(e) Form 1, Preferences—Civil Cases—Order Denying Preference.

CHAPTER 6. GENERAL PROVISIONS RESPECTING COURTS OF JUSTICE

ARTICLE 2. INCIDENTAL POWERS AND DUTIES OF COURTS

Section
128. Powers of courts; contempt orders; execution of sentence; stay pending appeal; orders affecting county government.
128.5. Frivolous actions or delaying tactics; order for payment of expenses; punitive damages; sanctions.
128.7. Signature requirement for court papers; certification that specified conditions met; violations; sanctions; punitive damages.
129. Photographs, etc., taken in course of post mortem examination or autopsy; prohibition against reproduction or dissemination; exceptions; personal liability of coroner.
130. Deceased minor victims of criminal acts; sealing of autopsy report and associated evidence.

§ 128. Powers of courts; contempt orders; execution of sentence; stay pending appeal; orders affecting county government

(a) Every court shall have the power to do all of the following:

(1) To preserve and enforce order in its immediate presence.

(2) To enforce order in the proceedings before it, or before a person or persons empowered to conduct a judicial investigation under its authority.

(3) To provide for the orderly conduct of proceedings before it, or its officers.

(4) To compel obedience to its judgments, orders, and process, and to the orders of a judge out of court, in an action or proceeding pending therein.

(5) To control in furtherance of justice, the conduct of its ministerial officers, and of all other persons in any manner connected with a judicial proceeding before it, in every matter pertaining thereto.

(6) To compel the attendance of persons to testify in an action or proceeding pending therein, in the cases and manner provided in this code.

(7) To administer oaths in an action or proceeding pending therein, and in all other cases where it may be necessary in the exercise of its powers and duties.

(8) To amend and control its process and orders so as to make them conform to law and justice. An appellate court shall not reverse or vacate a duly entered judgment upon an agreement or stipulation of the parties unless the court finds both of the following:

(A) There is no reasonable possibility that the interests of nonparties or the public will be adversely affected by the reversal.

(B) The reasons of the parties for requesting reversal outweigh the erosion of public trust that may result from the nullification of a judgment and the risk that the availability of stipulated reversal will reduce the incentive for pretrial settlement.

(b) Notwithstanding Section 1211 or any other law, if an order of contempt is made affecting an attorney, his or her agent, investigator, or any person acting under the attorney's direction, in the preparation and conduct of any action or proceeding, the execution of any sentence shall be stayed pending the filing within three judicial days of a petition for extraordinary relief testing the lawfulness of the court's order, the violation of which is the basis of the contempt except for the conduct as may be proscribed by subdivision (b) of Section 6068 of the Business and Professions Code, relating to an attorney's duty to maintain respect due to the courts and judicial officers.

(c) Notwithstanding Section 1211 or any other law, if an order of contempt is made affecting a public safety employee acting within the scope of employment for reason of the employee's failure to comply with a duly issued subpoena or subpoena duces tecum, the execution of any sentence shall be stayed pending the filing within three judicial days of a petition for extraordinary relief testing the lawfulness of the court's order, a violation of which is the basis for the contempt.

As used in this subdivision, "public safety employee" includes any peace officer, firefighter, paramedic, or any other employee of a public law enforcement agency whose duty is either to maintain official records or to analyze or present evidence for investigative or prosecutorial purposes.

(d) Notwithstanding Section 1211 or any other law, if an order of contempt is made affecting the victim of a sexual assault, where the contempt consists of refusing to testify concerning that sexual assault, the execution of any sentence shall be stayed pending the filing within three judicial days of a petition for extraordinary relief testing the lawfulness of the court's order, a violation of which is the basis for the contempt.

As used in this subdivision, "sexual assault" means any act made punishable by Section 261, 262, 264.1, 285, 286, 287, 288, or 289 of, or former Section 288a of, the Penal Code.

(e) Notwithstanding Section 1211 or any other law, if an order of contempt is made affecting the victim of domestic violence, where the contempt consists of refusing to testify concerning that domestic violence, the execution of any sentence shall be stayed pending the filing within three judicial days of a petition for extraordinary relief testing the lawfulness of the court's order, a violation of which is the basis for the contempt.

As used in this subdivision, the term "domestic violence" means "domestic violence" as defined in Section 6211 of the Family Code.

(f) Notwithstanding Section 1211 or any other provision of law, no order of contempt shall be made affecting a county government or any member of its governing body acting pursuant to its constitutional or statutory authority unless the court finds, based on a review of evidence presented at a hearing conducted for this purpose, that either of the following conditions exist:

(1) That the county has the resources necessary to comply with the order of the court.

(2) That the county has the authority, without recourse to voter approval or without incurring additional indebtedness, to generate the additional resources necessary to comply with the order of the court, that compliance with the order of the court will not expose the county, any member of its governing body, or any other county officer to liability for failure to perform other constitutional or statutory duties, and that compliance with the order of the court will not deprive the county of resources necessary for its reasonable support and maintenance. *(Added by Stats.1987, c. 3, § 2, eff. March 11, 1987, operative March 11, 1989. Amended by Stats.1991, c. 866 (A.B.363), § 1; Stats.1992, c. 163 (A.B.2641), § 13; Stats.1992, c. 697 (S.B.1559), § 2; Stats.1993, c. 219 (A.B.1500), § 63.3; Stats.1999, c. 508 (A.B.1676), § 1; Stats.2018, c. 423 (S.B.1494), § 7, eff. Jan. 1, 2019.)*

Cross References

Action, defined, see Code of Civil Procedure § 22.
Acts or omissions contemptuous of court's authority, abuse of process, see Code of Civil Procedure § 1209.
Affirmation, see Code of Civil Procedure §§ 2093, 2097.
Attorneys, State Bar Act, see Business and Professions Code § 6000.
Computation of time, see Code of Civil Procedure §§ 12, 12a, 12b; Government Code § 6800 et seq.

Contempt for disobedience of subpoena, see Code of Civil Procedure §§ 1209, 1991 et seq.
Contempt in court's presence, see Code of Civil Procedure § 1211.
Control of conduct of proceedings, see Code of Civil Procedure § 177.
Correction of clerical mistakes in orders, see Code of Civil Procedure § 473.
Disobedience of order of referee, see Code of Civil Procedure § 708.140.
Extension of time for required acts, see Code of Civil Procedure §§ 473, 1054.
General jurisdiction, power and authority, see Probate Code § 800.
Health care decisions, superior court jurisdiction, see Probate Code § 4760.
Interference with process as contempt, see Code of Civil Procedure § 1209.
Oaths, see Code of Civil Procedure § 2093 et seq.
Official records and other official writings, see Evidence Code § 1280 et seq.
Peace officers, generally, Penal Code § 830 et seq.
Powers of attorney, superior court jurisdiction, see Probate Code § 4520.
Refusal of witness to be sworn, see Code of Civil Procedure § 1991.
Relief from judgment taken by neglect or inadvertence, see Code of Civil Procedure § 473.
Security required for breach of peace in court's presence, see Penal Code § 710.
Subpoena duces tecum, see Code of Civil Procedure § 1985.
Subpoena for appearance of witness before commissioner, see Code of Civil Procedure § 1985.5.
Subpoenas, in general, see Code of Civil Procedure § 1986.
Writ and process defined, see Code of Civil Procedure § 17.

Research References

Forms

West's California Code Forms, Civil Procedure § 128 Form 1, Powers of Courts—Order Reversing or Vacating Judgment Based Upon Stipulation of Parties.

West's California Code Forms, Civil Procedure § 1211 Form 1, Contempts—Declaration—Not in Court's Presence.

West's California Code Forms, Insurance § 11583 Form 1, Motion in Limine.

§ 128.5. Frivolous actions or delaying tactics; order for payment of expenses; punitive damages; sanctions

(a) A trial court may order a party, the party's attorney, or both, to pay the reasonable expenses, including attorney's fees, incurred by another party as a result of actions or tactics, made in bad faith, that are frivolous or solely intended to cause unnecessary delay. This section also applies to judicial arbitration proceedings under Chapter 2.5 (commencing with Section 1141.10) of Title 3 of Part 3.

(b) For purposes of this section:

(1) "Actions or tactics" include, but are not limited to, the making or opposing of motions or the filing and service of a complaint, cross-complaint, answer, or other responsive pleading. The mere filing of a complaint without service thereof on an opposing party does not constitute "actions or tactics" for purposes of this section.

(2) "Frivolous" means totally and completely without merit or for the sole purpose of harassing an opposing party.

(c) Expenses pursuant to this section shall not be imposed except on notice contained in a party's moving or responding papers or, on the court's own motion, after notice and opportunity to be heard. An order imposing expenses shall be in writing and shall recite in detail the action or tactic or circumstances justifying the order.

(d) In addition to any award pursuant to this section for an action or tactic described in subdivision (a), the court may assess punitive damages against the plaintiff on a determination by the court that the plaintiff's action was an action maintained by a person convicted of a felony against the person's victim, or the victim's heirs, relatives, estate, or personal representative, for injuries arising from the acts for which the person was convicted of a felony, and that the plaintiff is guilty of fraud, oppression, or malice in maintaining the action.

(e) This section shall not apply to disclosures and discovery requests, responses, objections, and motions.

(f) Sanctions ordered pursuant to this section shall be ordered pursuant to the following conditions and procedures:

(1) If, after notice and a reasonable opportunity to respond, the court issues an order pursuant to subdivision (a), the court may, subject to the conditions stated below, impose an appropriate sanction upon the party, the party's attorneys, or both, for an action or tactic described in subdivision (a). In determining what sanctions, if any, should be ordered, the court shall consider whether a party seeking sanctions has exercised due diligence.

(A) A motion for sanctions under this section shall be made separately from other motions or requests and shall describe the specific alleged action or tactic, made in bad faith, that is frivolous or solely intended to cause unnecessary delay.

(B) If the alleged action or tactic is the making or opposing of a written motion or the filing and service of a complaint, cross-complaint, answer, or other responsive pleading that can be withdrawn or appropriately corrected, a notice of motion shall be served as provided in Section 1010, but shall not be filed with or presented to the court, unless 21 days after service of the motion or any other period as the court may prescribe, the challenged action or tactic is not withdrawn or appropriately corrected.

(C) If warranted, the court may award to the party prevailing on the motion the reasonable expenses and attorney's fees incurred in presenting or opposing the motion. Absent exceptional circumstances, a law firm shall be held jointly responsible for violations committed by its partners, associates, and employees.

(D) If the alleged action or tactic is the making or opposing of a written motion or the filing and service of a complaint, cross-complaint, answer, or other responsive pleading that can be withdrawn or appropriately corrected, the court on its own motion may enter an order describing the specific action or tactic, made in bad faith, that is frivolous or solely intended to cause unnecessary delay, and direct an attorney, law firm, or party to show cause why it has made an action or tactic as defined in subdivision (b), unless, within 21 days of service of the order to show cause, the challenged action or tactic is withdrawn or appropriately corrected.

(2) An order for sanctions pursuant to this section shall be limited to what is sufficient to deter repetition of the action or tactic or comparable action or tactic by others similarly situated. Subject to the limitations in subparagraphs (A) and (B), the sanction may consist of, or include, directives of a nonmonetary nature, an order to pay a penalty into court, or, if imposed on motion and warranted for effective deterrence, an order directing payment to the movant of some or all of the reasonable attorney's fees and other expenses incurred as a direct result of the action or tactic described in subdivision (a).

(A) Monetary sanctions may not be awarded against a represented party for a violation of presenting a claim, defense, and other legal contentions that are warranted by existing law or by a nonfrivolous argument for the extension, modification, or reversal of existing law or the establishment of new law.

(B) Monetary sanctions may not be awarded on the court's motion unless the court issues its order to show cause before a voluntary dismissal or settlement of the claims made by or against the party that is, or whose attorneys are, to be sanctioned.

(g) A motion for sanctions brought by a party or a party's attorney primarily for an improper purpose, such as to harass or to cause unnecessary delay or needless increase in the cost of litigation, shall itself be subject to a motion for sanctions. It is the intent of the Legislature that courts shall vigorously use its sanction authority to deter the improper actions or tactics or comparable actions or tactics of others similarly situated.

(h) The liability imposed by this section is in addition to any other liability imposed by law for acts or omissions within the purview of this section.

(i) This section applies to actions or tactics that were part of a civil case filed on or after January 1, 2015. *(Added by Stats.1981, c. 762, § 1. Amended by Stats.1984, c. 355, § 1; Stats.1985, c. 296, § 1; Stats.1990, c. 887 (S.B.2766), § 1; Stats.1994, c. 1062 (A.B.3594), § 1;*

§ 128.5

Stats.2014, c. 425 (A.B.2494), § 1, eff. Jan. 1, 2015; Stats.2017, c. 169 (A.B.984), § 1, eff. Aug. 7, 2017.)

Cross References

Action, defined, see Code of Civil Procedure § 22.
Administrative adjudication, enforcement of orders and sanctions, attorney fees, see Government Code § 11455.30.
Arbitration, generally, see Code of Civil Procedure § 1281 et seq.
Attorney's fees and costs, generally, see Code of Civil Procedure § 1021.
Attorney's fees awarded against governmental agencies, see Family Code § 273.
Attorneys, State Bar Act, see Business and Professions Code § 6000.
Classes of judicial remedies, see Code of Civil Procedure § 21.
Consumer Credit Reporting Agencies Act, remedies, actions for actual and punitive damages, see Civil Code § 1785.31.
Counties, employment of legal counsel to assist assessor or sheriff, conflicts of interest, see Government Code § 31000.6.
Failure of plaintiffs to provide names of collateral source providers in personal injury or wrongful death actions against public entities, see Government Code § 985.
Felonies, definition and penalties, see Penal Code §§ 17, 18.
Fraud, actual or constructive, see Civil Code §§ 1572 to 1574.
Insurance, false and fraudulent claims, see Insurance Code § 1871.7.
Kinds of injuries, see Code of Civil Procedure § 27.
Legislative intent, construction of statutes, see Code of Civil Procedure § 1859.
Notice, actual and constructive, defined, see Civil Code § 18.
Oil Spill Response Trust Fund, designation of responsible party, see Government Code § 8670.51.1.
Peace officers, citizens' complaints against personnel, investigation, see Penal Code § 832.5.
Records relating to discharge of firearm, sexual assault, or dishonesty by peace officer or custodial officer available for public inspection, exceptions, see Penal Code § 832.7.
SLAPPback actions, procedures, see Code of Civil Procedure § 425.18.

Research References

Forms

2 California Transactions Forms--Business Transactions § 14:82, Availability of Sanctions.
2 California Transactions Forms--Business Transactions § 14:86, Matters to Consider in Drafting Arbitration Clauses.
1 Environmental Insurance Litigation: Practice Forms § 4:5 (2021 ed.), Sample Notice of Motion and Motion to Compel Further Responses and Production of Documents.
West's California Code Forms, Civil Procedure § 128.5 Form 1, Frivolous Actions or Delaying Tactics—Notice of Motion for Payment of Costs and Attorney's Fees.
West's California Code Forms, Civil Procedure § 128.5 Form 3, Frivolous Actions or Delaying Tactics—Order for Payment of Costs and Attorney's Fees.
West's California Code Forms, Civil Procedure § 128.5 Form 4, Frivolous Actions or Delaying Tactics—Notice of Motion for Order Assessing Punitive Damages.
West's California Code Forms, Civil Procedure § 128.7 Form 3, Frivolous Actions or Delaying Tactics—Order for Payment of Costs and Attorney's Fees.

§ 128.7. Signature requirement for court papers; certification that specified conditions met; violations; sanctions; punitive damages

(a) Every pleading, petition, written notice of motion, or other similar paper shall be signed by at least one attorney of record in the attorney's individual name, or, if the party is not represented by an attorney, shall be signed by the party. Each paper shall state the signer's address and telephone number, if any. Except when otherwise provided by law, pleadings need not be verified or accompanied by affidavit. An unsigned paper shall be stricken unless omission of the signature is corrected promptly after being called to the attention of the attorney or party.

(b) By presenting to the court, whether by signing, filing, submitting, or later advocating, a pleading, petition, written notice of motion, or other similar paper, an attorney or unrepresented party is certifying that to the best of the person's knowledge, information, and belief, formed after an inquiry reasonable under the circumstances, all of the following conditions are met:

(1) It is not being presented primarily for an improper purpose, such as to harass or to cause unnecessary delay or needless increase in the cost of litigation.

(2) The claims, defenses, and other legal contentions therein are warranted by existing law or by a nonfrivolous argument for the extension, modification, or reversal of existing law or the establishment of new law.

(3) The allegations and other factual contentions have evidentiary support or, if specifically so identified, are likely to have evidentiary support after a reasonable opportunity for further investigation or discovery.

(4) The denials of factual contentions are warranted on the evidence or, if specifically so identified, are reasonably based on a lack of information or belief.

(c) If, after notice and a reasonable opportunity to respond, the court determines that subdivision (b) has been violated, the court may, subject to the conditions stated below, impose an appropriate sanction upon the attorneys, law firms, or parties that have violated subdivision (b) or are responsible for the violation. In determining what sanctions, if any, should be ordered, the court shall consider whether a party seeking sanctions has exercised due diligence.

(1) A motion for sanctions under this section shall be made separately from other motions or requests and shall describe the specific conduct alleged to violate subdivision (b). Notice of motion shall be served as provided in Section 1010, but shall not be filed with or presented to the court unless, within 21 days after service of the motion, or any other period as the court may prescribe, the challenged paper, claim, defense, contention, allegation, or denial is not withdrawn or appropriately corrected. If warranted, the court may award to the party prevailing on the motion the reasonable expenses and attorney's fees incurred in presenting or opposing the motion. Absent exceptional circumstances, a law firm shall be held jointly responsible for violations committed by its partners, associates, and employees.

(2) On its own motion, the court may enter an order describing the specific conduct that appears to violate subdivision (b) and directing an attorney, law firm, or party to show cause why it has not violated subdivision (b), unless, within 21 days of service of the order to show cause, the challenged paper, claim, defense, contention, allegation, or denial is withdrawn or appropriately corrected.

(d) A sanction imposed for violation of subdivision (b) shall be limited to what is sufficient to deter repetition of this conduct or comparable conduct by others similarly situated. Subject to the limitations in paragraphs (1) and (2), the sanction may consist of, or include, directives of a nonmonetary nature, an order to pay a penalty into court, or, if imposed on motion and warranted for effective deterrence, an order directing payment to the movant of some or all of the reasonable attorney's fees and other expenses incurred as a direct result of the violation.

(1) Monetary sanctions may not be awarded against a represented party for a violation of paragraph (2) of subdivision (b).

(2) Monetary sanctions may not be awarded on the court's motion unless the court issues its order to show cause before a voluntary dismissal or settlement of the claims made by or against the party that is, or whose attorneys are, to be sanctioned.

(e) When imposing sanctions, the court shall describe the conduct determined to constitute a violation of this section and explain the basis for the sanction imposed.

(f) In addition to any award pursuant to this section for conduct described in subdivision (b), the court may assess punitive damages against the plaintiff upon a determination by the court that the plaintiff's action was an action maintained by a person convicted of a felony against the person's victim, or the victim's heirs, relatives, estate, or personal representative, for injuries arising from the acts for which the person was convicted of a felony, and that the plaintiff is guilty of fraud, oppression, or malice in maintaining the action.

(g) This section shall not apply to disclosures and discovery requests, responses, objections, and motions.

(h) A motion for sanctions brought by a party or a party's attorney primarily for an improper purpose, such as to harass or to cause unnecessary delay or needless increase in the cost of litigation, shall itself be subject to a motion for sanctions. It is the intent of the Legislature that courts shall vigorously use its sanctions authority to deter that improper conduct or comparable conduct by others similarly situated.

(i) This section shall apply to a complaint or petition filed on or after January 1, 1995, and any other pleading, written notice of motion, or other similar paper filed in that matter. (Added by Stats.1994, c. 1062 (A.B.3594), § 3. Amended by Stats.1998, c. 121 (S.B.1511), § 2; Stats.2002, c. 491 (S.B.2009), § 1; Stats.2005, c. 706 (A.B.1742), § 9.)

Application

For application of 2005 amendment, see Stats.2005, c. 706 (A.B.1742), § 41.

Cross References

Action, defined, see Code of Civil Procedure § 22.
Attorney's fees and costs, generally, see Code of Civil Procedure § 1021.
Attorneys, State Bar Act, see Business and Professions Code § 6000.
Computation of time, see Code of Civil Procedure §§ 12, 12a, 12b; Government Code § 6800 et seq.
Discovery, generally, see Code of Civil Procedure § 2016 et seq.
Effective date, conflicting measures, and amendment or repeal of initiative statutes, see Cal. Const. Art. 2, § 10.
Felonies, definition and penalties, see Penal Code §§ 17, 18.
Firefighters, refusal of rights, violation of chapter, see Government Code § 3260.
Fraud, actual or constructive, see Civil Code §§ 1572 to 1574.
Kinds of injuries, see Code of Civil Procedure § 27.
Notice, actual and constructive, defined, see Civil Code § 18.
Public safety officers, jurisdiction of courts for violations, remedies and sanctions, see Government Code § 3309.5.
Safe Drinking Water and Toxic Enforcement Act of 1986, enforcement, frivolous actions, see Health and Safety Code § 25249.7.

Research References

Forms

West's California Code Forms, Civil Procedure § 128.7 Form 1, Frivolous Actions or Delaying Tactics—Notice of Motion for Order Requiring Payment of Costs and Attorney's Fees.
West's California Code Forms, Civil Procedure § 128.7 Form 2, Frivolous Actions or Delaying Tactics—Declaration for Order Requiring Payment of Costs and Attorney's Fees.
West's California Code Forms, Civil Procedure § 128.7 Form 3, Frivolous Actions or Delaying Tactics—Order for Payment of Costs and Attorney's Fees.
West's California Code Forms, Civil Procedure § 128.7 Form 4, Frivolous Actions or Delaying Tactics—Order to Show Cause for Sanctions.

§ 129. Photographs, etc., taken in course of post mortem examination or autopsy; prohibition against reproduction or dissemination; exceptions; personal liability of coroner

(a) Notwithstanding any other law, a copy, reproduction, or facsimile of any kind of a photograph, negative, or print, including instant photographs and video recordings, of the body, or any portion of the body, of a deceased person, taken by or for the coroner at the scene of death or in the course of a post mortem examination or autopsy, shall not be made or disseminated except as follows:

(1) For use in a criminal action or proceeding in this state that relates to the death of that person.

(2) As a court of this state permits, by order after good cause has been shown and after written notification of the request for the court order has been served, at least five days before the order is made, upon the district attorney of the county in which the post mortem examination or autopsy has been made or caused to be made.

(3) For use or potential use in a civil action or proceeding in this state that relates to the death of that person, if either of the following applies:

(A) The coroner receives written authorization from a legal heir or representative of that person before the action is filed or while the action is pending. To verify the identity of the legal heir or representative, all of the following shall be provided to the coroner:

(i) A declaration under penalty of perjury that the individual is a legal heir or representative of the deceased person.

(ii) A valid form of identification.

(iii) A certified death certificate.

(B) A subpoena is issued by a party who is a legal heir or representative of the deceased person in a pending civil action.

(b) This section shall not apply to the making or dissemination of a copy, reproduction, or facsimile for use in the field of forensic pathology, in medical or scientific education or research, or by a coroner or any law enforcement agency in the United States for investigative purposes, including identification and identification confirmation.

(c) This section shall apply to a copy, reproduction, or facsimile, and to a photograph, negative, or print, regardless of when it was made.

(d) A coroner is not personally liable for monetary damages in a civil action for any act or omission in compliance with this section. (Added by Stats.1968, c. 6, 1st Ex.Sess., p. 37, § 1, eff. Sept. 25, 1969. Amended by Stats.1985, c. 304, § 1; Stats.2009, c. 88 (A.B.176), § 16; Stats.2013, c. 53 (A.B.957), § 1; Stats.2016, c. 467 (A.B.2427), § 1, eff. Jan. 1, 2017.)

Cross References

Action, defined, see Code of Civil Procedure § 22.
Attorneys, State Bar Act, see Business and Professions Code § 6000.
Computation of time, see Code of Civil Procedure §§ 12, 12a, 12b; Government Code § 6800 et seq.
District attorney, powers and duties, see Government Code § 26500 et seq.
Inspection of public records, exemptions from disclosure, see Government Code § 6276.34.
Kinds of actions, see Code of Civil Procedure § 24.
"State" and "United States" as including District of Columbia and territories, see Code of Civil Procedure § 17.

Research References

Forms

West's California Code Forms, Civil Procedure § 129 Form 1, Photographs—Notice of Motion for Order Permitting Reproduction of a Photograph of the Body of a Deceased Person Taken During a Coroner's Examination or Autopsy.

§ 130. Deceased minor victims of criminal acts; sealing of autopsy report and associated evidence

(a) Subject to the provisions of this section, when a child who is under 18 years of age is killed as a result of a criminal act and a person has been convicted and sentenced for the commission of that criminal act, or a person has been found to have committed that offense by the juvenile court and adjudged a ward of the juvenile court, upon the request of a qualifying family member of the deceased child, the autopsy report and evidence associated with the examination of the victim in the possession of a public agency, as defined in Section 7920.525 of the Government Code, shall be sealed and not disclosed, except that an autopsy report and evidence associated with the examination of the victim that has been sealed pursuant to this section may be disclosed, as follows:

(1) To law enforcement, prosecutorial agencies and experts hired by those agencies, public social service agencies, child death review teams, or the hospital that treated the child immediately prior to death, to be used solely for investigative, prosecutorial, or review purposes, and may not be disseminated further.

(2) To the defendant and the defense team in the course of criminal proceedings or related habeas proceedings, to be used solely for investigative, criminal defense, and review purposes, including review for the purpose of initiating any criminal proceeding or related habeas proceeding, and may not be disseminated further. The "defense team" includes, but is not limited to, all of the following: attorneys, investigators, experts, paralegals, support staff, interns, students, and state and privately funded legal assistance projects hired or consulted for the purposes of investigation, defense, appeal, or writ of habeas corpus on behalf of the person accused of killing the deceased child victim.

(3) To civil litigants in a cause of action related to the victim's death with a court order upon a showing of good cause and proper notice under Section 129, to be used solely to pursue the cause of action, and may not be disseminated further.

(b) Nothing in this section shall prohibit the use of autopsy reports and evidence in relation to court proceedings.

(c) Nothing in this section shall abrogate the rights of victims, their authorized representatives, or insurance carriers to request the release of information pursuant to Article 1 (commencing with Section 7923.600) of Chapter 1 of Part 5 of Division 10 of Title 1 of the Government Code. However, if a seal has been requested, an insurance carrier receiving items pursuant to a request under that article is prohibited from disclosing the requested items except as necessary in the normal course of business. An insurance carrier shall not, under any circumstances, disclose to the general public items received pursuant to Article 1 (commencing with Section 7923.600) of Chapter 1 of Part 5 of Division 10 of Title 1 of the Government Code.

(d) This section may not be invoked by a qualifying family member who has been charged with or convicted of any act in furtherance of the victim's death. Upon the filing of those charges against a qualifying family member, any seal maintained at the request of that qualifying family member under this section shall be removed.

(e) A coroner or medical examiner shall not be liable for damages in a civil action for any reasonable act or omission taken in good faith in compliance with this section.

(f) If sealing of the autopsy report has been requested by a qualifying family member and another qualifying family member opposes sealing, the opposing party may request a hearing in the superior court in the county with jurisdiction over the crime leading to the child's death for a determination of whether the sealing should be maintained. The opposing party shall notify all other qualifying family members, the medical examiner's office that conducted the autopsy, and the district attorney's office with jurisdiction over the crime at least 10 court days in advance of the hearing. At the hearing, the court shall consider the interests of all qualifying family members, the protection of the memory of the deceased child, any evidence that the qualifying family member requesting the seal was involved in the crime that resulted in the death of the child, the public interest in scrutiny of the autopsy report or the performance of the medical examiner, any impact that unsealing would have on pending investigations or pending litigation, and any other relevant factors. Official information in the possession of a public agency necessary to the determination of the hearing shall be received in camera upon a proper showing. In its discretion, the court may, to the extent allowable by law and with good cause shown, restrict the dissemination of an autopsy report or evidence associated with the examination of a victim. This section shall not apply if a public agency has independently determined that the autopsy report may not be disclosed pursuant to Article 1 (commencing with Section 7923.600) of Chapter 1 of Part 5 of Division 10 of Title 1 of the Government Code because it is an investigative file. In that instance, nothing in this section shall preclude the application of Part 5 (commencing with Section 7923.000) of Division 10 of Title 1 of the Government Code.

(g) If a seal has been maintained pursuant to this section, a qualifying family member, or a biological or adoptive aunt, uncle, sibling, first cousin, child, or grandparent of the deceased child may request that the seal be removed. The request to remove the seal shall be adjudicated pursuant to subdivision (f), with the party requesting the removal of the seal being the opposing party.

(h) Nothing in this section shall limit the public access to information contained in the death certificate including: name, age, gender, race, date, time and location of death, the name of a physician reporting a death in a hospital, the name of the certifying pathologist, date of certification, burial information, and cause of death.

(i) When a medical examiner declines a request to provide a copy of an autopsy report that has been sealed pursuant to this section, the examiner shall cite this section as the reason for declining to provide a copy of the report.

(j) For purposes of this section:

(1) A "child who is under 18 years of age" does not include any child who comes within either of the following descriptions:

(A) The child was a dependent child of the juvenile court pursuant to Section 300 of the Welfare and Institutions Code at the time of the child's death, or, pursuant to subdivision (b) of Section 10850.4 of the Welfare and Institutions Code, abuse or neglect is determined to have led to the child's death.

(B) The child was residing in a state or county juvenile facility, or a private facility under contract with the state or county for the placement of juveniles, as a ward of the juvenile court pursuant to Section 602 of the Welfare and Institutions Code at the time of the child's death.

(2) "Evidence associated with the examination of a victim" means any object, writing, diagram, recording, computer file, photograph, video, DVD, CD, film, digital device, or other item that was collected during, or serves to document, the autopsy of a deceased child.

(3) "Qualifying family member" means the biological or adoptive parent, spouse, or legal guardian.

(k) Nothing in this section shall limit the discovery provisions set forth in Chapter 10 (commencing with Section 1054) of Title 6 of the Penal Code.

(*l*) Nothing in this section shall be construed to limit the authority of the court to seal records or restrict the dissemination of an autopsy report or evidence associated with the examination of a victim under case law, other statutory law, or the rules of court.

(m) The provisions of this section are severable. If any provision of this section or its application is held invalid, that invalidity shall not affect other provisions or applications that can be given effect without the invalid provision or application. *(Added by Stats.2010, c. 302 (S.B.5), § 3, eff. Sept. 27, 2010. Amended by Stats.2021, c. 615 (A.B.474), § 55, eff. Jan. 1, 2022, operative Jan. 1, 2023.)*

Research References

Forms

West's California Code Forms, Civil Procedure § 130 Form 1, Photographs—Notice of Motion for Order Permitting Disclosure of Sealed Autopsy Report and Evidence Associated With the Examination of the Victim Related to a Deceased Child Victim.

Title 2

JUDICIAL OFFICERS

CHAPTER 3. DISQUALIFICATIONS OF JUDGES

Section
170. Duty to decide.
170.1. Grounds for disqualification.
170.2. Circumstances not constituting grounds for disqualification.
170.3. Proceedings; waiver; failure or refusal to withdraw.
170.4. Powers of disqualified judges.
170.5. Definitions.
170.6. Prejudice against party, attorney or interest thereof; motion and affidavit; assignment of another judge, court commissioner or referee; number of motions; continuance; cumulative remedy; severability.
170.7. Judge serving on appellate division; application of § 170.6.
170.8. No qualified judge; assignment of judge.
170.9. Acceptance of gifts; value limit; exceptions; adjustments; travel expenses.

Cross References

Unreasonable search and seizure, motion to return property or suppress evidence, see Penal Code § 1538.5.

§ 170. Duty to decide

A judge has a duty to decide any proceeding in which he or she is not disqualified. *(Added by Stats.1984, c. 1555, § 2.)*

Cross References

Action for refund of taxes by public agency, disqualification of judges, see Revenue and Taxation Code § 5161.
Affinity defined, see Code of Civil Procedure § 17.
Change of place of trial, see Code of Civil Procedure §§ 397, 398.
Definitions applicable to this section, see Code of Civil Procedure § 170.5.
Degree of consanguineous relationship, see Probate Code § 6402 et seq.
Disqualification of arbitrator, application of this section, see Code of Civil Procedure § 1141.18.
Disqualification of judge in probate proceedings, see Probate Code § 7060.
Eminent domain, see Code of Civil Procedure § 1230.010 et seq.; Cal. Const. Art. 1, § 19.
Judge as relative or partner of appraiser of estate, see Probate Code § 8923.
Juvenile court, disqualification of referee, reassignment of matter, see Welfare and Institutions Code § 247.5.
Juvenile court rules related to this section, see California Rules of Court, Rule 5.536.
Practice of law by judges, see Government Code § 68082.
Prejudice against party, attorney or interest thereof, cumulative remedy, see Code of Civil Procedure § 170.6.
Relationship between judge and receiver, see Code of Civil Procedure § 566.

Research References

Forms
West's California Code Forms, Civil Procedure § 1141.18 Form 9, Judicial Arbitration—Rule 3.816—Disclosure of Disqualifying Circumstances.
West's California Code Forms, Civil Procedure § 1141.22 Form 2, Judicial Arbitration—Rule 3.825—Declaration in Support of Motion to Vacate Judgment (Award of Arbitrator).

§ 170.1. Grounds for disqualification

(a) A judge shall be disqualified if any one or more of the following are true:

(1)(A) The judge has personal knowledge of disputed evidentiary facts concerning the proceeding.

(B) A judge shall be deemed to have personal knowledge within the meaning of this paragraph if the judge, or the spouse of the judge, or a person within the third degree of relationship to either of them, or the spouse of such a person is to the judge's knowledge likely to be a material witness in the proceeding.

(2)(A) The judge served as a lawyer in the proceeding, or in any other proceeding involving the same issues he or she served as a lawyer for a party in the present proceeding or gave advice to a party in the present proceeding upon a matter involved in the action or proceeding.

(B) A judge shall be deemed to have served as a lawyer in the proceeding if within the past two years:

(i) A party to the proceeding, or an officer, director, or trustee of a party, was a client of the judge when the judge was in the private practice of law or a client of a lawyer with whom the judge was associated in the private practice of law.

(ii) A lawyer in the proceeding was associated in the private practice of law with the judge.

(C) A judge who served as a lawyer for, or officer of, a public agency that is a party to the proceeding shall be deemed to have served as a lawyer in the proceeding if he or she personally advised or in any way represented the public agency concerning the factual or legal issues in the proceeding.

(3)(A) The judge has a financial interest in the subject matter in a proceeding or in a party to the proceeding.

(B) A judge shall be deemed to have a financial interest within the meaning of this paragraph if:

(i) A spouse or minor child living in the household has a financial interest.

(ii) The judge or the spouse of the judge is a fiduciary who has a financial interest.

(C) A judge has a duty to make reasonable efforts to inform himself or herself about his or her personal and fiduciary interests and those of his or her spouse and the personal financial interests of children living in the household.

(4) The judge, or the spouse of the judge, or a person within the third degree of relationship to either of them, or the spouse of such a person is a party to the proceeding or an officer, director, or trustee of a party.

(5) A lawyer or a spouse of a lawyer in the proceeding is the spouse, former spouse, child, sibling, or parent of the judge or the judge's spouse or if such a person is associated in the private practice of law with a lawyer in the proceeding.

(6)(A) For any reason:

(i) The judge believes his or her recusal would further the interests of justice.

(ii) The judge believes there is a substantial doubt as to his or her capacity to be impartial.

(iii) A person aware of the facts might reasonably entertain a doubt that the judge would be able to be impartial.

(B) Bias or prejudice toward a lawyer in the proceeding may be grounds for disqualification.

(7) By reason of permanent or temporary physical impairment, the judge is unable to properly perceive the evidence or is unable to properly conduct the proceeding.

(8)(A) The judge has a current arrangement concerning prospective employment or other compensated service as a dispute resolution neutral or is participating in, or, within the last two years has participated in, discussions regarding prospective employment or service as a dispute resolution neutral, or has been engaged in that employment or service, and any of the following applies:

(i) The arrangement is, or the prior employment or discussion was, with a party to the proceeding.

(ii) The matter before the judge includes issues relating to the enforcement of either an agreement to submit a dispute to an

§ 170.1

alternative dispute resolution process or an award or other final decision by a dispute resolution neutral.

(iii) The judge directs the parties to participate in an alternative dispute resolution process in which the dispute resolution neutral will be an individual or entity with whom the judge has the arrangement, has previously been employed or served, or is discussing or has discussed the employment or service.

(iv) The judge will select a dispute resolution neutral or entity to conduct an alternative dispute resolution process in the matter before the judge, and among those available for selection is an individual or entity with whom the judge has the arrangement, with whom the judge has previously been employed or served, or with whom the judge is discussing or has discussed the employment or service.

(B) For the purposes of this paragraph, all of the following apply:

(i) "Participating in discussions" or "has participated in discussion" means that the judge solicited or otherwise indicated an interest in accepting or negotiating possible employment or service as an alternative dispute resolution neutral, or responded to an unsolicited statement regarding, or an offer of, that employment or service by expressing an interest in that employment or service, making an inquiry regarding the employment or service, or encouraging the person making the statement or offer to provide additional information about that possible employment or service. If a judge's response to an unsolicited statement regarding, a question about, or offer of, prospective employment or other compensated service as a dispute resolution neutral is limited to responding negatively, declining the offer, or declining to discuss that employment or service, that response does not constitute participating in discussions.

(ii) "Party" includes the parent, subsidiary, or other legal affiliate of any entity that is a party and is involved in the transaction, contract, or facts that gave rise to the issues subject to the proceeding.

(iii) "Dispute resolution neutral" means an arbitrator, mediator, temporary judge appointed under Section 21 of Article VI of the California Constitution, referee appointed under Section 638 or 639, special master, neutral evaluator, settlement officer, or settlement facilitator.

(9)(A) The judge has received a contribution in excess of one thousand five hundred dollars ($1500) from a party or lawyer in the proceeding, and either of the following applies:

(i) The contribution was received in support of the judge's last election, if the last election was within the last six years.

(ii) The contribution was received in anticipation of an upcoming election.

(B) Notwithstanding subparagraph (A), the judge shall be disqualified based on a contribution of a lesser amount if subparagraph (A) of paragraph (6) applies.

(C) The judge shall disclose any contribution from a party or lawyer in a matter that is before the court that is required to be reported under subdivision (f) of Section 84211 of the Government Code, even if the amount would not require disqualification under this paragraph. The manner of disclosure shall be the same as that provided in Canon 3E of the Code of Judicial Ethics.

(D) Notwithstanding paragraph (1) of subdivision (b) of Section 170.3, the disqualification required under this paragraph may be waived by the party that did not make the contribution unless there are other circumstances that would prohibit a waiver pursuant to paragraph (2) of subdivision (b) of Section 170.3.

(b) A judge before whom a proceeding was tried or heard shall be disqualified from participating in any appellate review of that proceeding.

(c) At the request of a party or on its own motion an appellate court shall consider whether in the interests of justice it should direct that further proceedings be heard before a trial judge other than the judge whose judgment or order was reviewed by the appellate court. *(Added by Stats.1984, c. 1555, § 5. Amended by Stats.2002, c. 1094 (A.B.2504), § 1; Stats.2005, c. 332 (A.B.1322), § 1, eff. Sept. 22, 2005; Stats.2010, c. 686 (A.B.2487), § 1.)*

Cross References

Action defined, see Code of Civil Procedure § 22.
Affinity defined, see Code of Civil Procedure § 17.
Arbitration, generally, see Code of Civil Procedure § 1281 et seq.
Arbitration, neutral arbitrators, disclosure of information and disqualification, see Code of Civil Procedure § 1281.9.
Definitions applicable to this section, see Code of Civil Procedure § 170.5.
Disqualification of neutral arbitrator, see Code of Civil Procedure § 1281.91.
Each generation a degree, see Probate Code § 6402.
Judicial disqualification on relationship grounds, see Code of Civil Procedure § 170 et seq.
Witnesses, competency, judges, arbitrators or mediators as witnesses, see Evidence Code § 703.5.
Workers' compensation and insurance, selection of arbitrator, see Labor Code § 5271.

Research References

Forms

West's California Code Forms, Civil Procedure § 128.7 Form 4, Frivolous Actions or Delaying Tactics—Order to Show Cause for Sanctions.
West's California Code Forms, Civil Procedure § 170.1 Form 1, Judicial Officers—Objection to Judge on Ground of Disqualification.
West's California Code Forms, Civil Procedure § 170.3 Form 1, Judicial Officers—Stipulation of Parties and Attorneys Waiving Disqualification of Judge.
West's California Code Forms, Civil Procedure § 170.3 Form 5, Judicial Officers—Order Disqualifying Judge After Hearing.
West's California Code Forms, Civil Procedure § 1141.18 Form 9, Judicial Arbitration—Rule 3.816—Disclosure of Disqualifying Circumstances.
West's California Code Forms, Civil Procedure § 1141.18 Form 11, Judicial Arbitration—Demand for Disqualification of Arbitrator.
West's California Code Forms, Civil Procedure § 1281.6 Form 5, Arbitration—Declaration Disclosing Information Relating to Impartiality of Arbitrator.
West's California Code Forms, Civil Procedure § 1281.9 Form 1, Arbitration—Claims for Damages—Disclosure of Prior or Pending Arbitrated Cases.
West's California Code Forms, Civil Procedure § 1281.9 Form 5, Arbitration—Notice of Disqualification—Court-Appointed Arbitrator—Disqualification After Disclosure Statement—With Cause.
West's California Code Forms, Civil Procedure § 1281.9 Form 8, Arbitration—Demand for Disqualification of Arbitrator.
West's California Code Forms, Civil Procedure § 1297.121 Form 1, Arbitration and Conciliation—Declaration of Disclosure—Information Relating to Impartiality of Arbitrator or Conciliator.

§ 170.2. Circumstances not constituting grounds for disqualification

It shall not be grounds for disqualification that the judge:

(a) Is or is not a member of a racial, ethnic, religious, sexual or similar group and the proceeding involves the rights of such a group.

(b) Has in any capacity expressed a view on a legal or factual issue presented in the proceeding, except as provided in paragraph (2) of subdivision (a) of, or subdivision (b) or (c) of, Section 170.1.

(c) Has as a lawyer or public official participated in the drafting of laws or in the effort to pass or defeat laws, the meaning, effect or application of which is in issue in the proceeding unless the judge believes that his or her prior involvement was so well known as to raise a reasonable doubt in the public mind as to his or her capacity to be impartial. *(Added by Stats.1984, c. 1555, § 6.)*

Cross References

Definitions applicable to this section, see Code of Civil Procedure § 170.5.

§ 170.3. Proceedings; waiver; failure or refusal to withdraw

(a)(1) If a judge determines himself or herself to be disqualified, the judge shall notify the presiding judge of the court of his or her recusal and shall not further participate in the proceeding, except as provided in Section 170.4, unless his or her disqualification is waived by the parties as provided in subdivision (b).

(2) If the judge disqualifying himself or herself is the only judge or the presiding judge of the court, the notification shall be sent to the person having authority to assign another judge to replace the disqualified judge.

(b)(1) A judge who determines himself or herself to be disqualified after disclosing the basis for his or her disqualification on the record may ask the parties and their attorneys whether they wish to waive the disqualification, except where the basis for disqualification is as provided in paragraph (2). A waiver of disqualification shall recite the basis for the disqualification, and is effective only when signed by all parties and their attorneys and filed in the record.

(2) There shall be no waiver of disqualification if the basis therefor is either of the following:

(A) The judge has a personal bias or prejudice concerning a party.

(B) The judge served as an attorney in the matter in controversy, or the judge has been a material witness concerning that matter.

(3) The judge shall not seek to induce a waiver and shall avoid any effort to discover which lawyers or parties favored or opposed a waiver of disqualification.

(4) If grounds for disqualification are first learned of or arise after the judge has made one or more rulings in a proceeding, but before the judge has completed judicial action in a proceeding, the judge shall, unless the disqualification be waived, disqualify himself or herself, but in the absence of good cause the rulings he or she has made up to that time shall not be set aside by the judge who replaces the disqualified judge.

(c)(1) If a judge who should disqualify himself or herself refuses or fails to do so, any party may file with the clerk a written verified statement objecting to the hearing or trial before the judge and setting forth the facts constituting the grounds for disqualification of the judge. The statement shall be presented at the earliest practicable opportunity after discovery of the facts constituting the ground for disqualification. Copies of the statement shall be served on each party or his or her attorney who has appeared and shall be personally served on the judge alleged to be disqualified, or on his or her clerk, provided that the judge is present in the courthouse or in chambers.

(2) Without conceding his or her disqualification, a judge whose impartiality has been challenged by the filing of a written statement may request any other judge agreed upon by the parties to sit and act in his or her place.

(3) Within 10 days after the filing or service, whichever is later, the judge may file a consent to disqualification in which case the judge shall notify the presiding judge or the person authorized to appoint a replacement of his or her recusal as provided in subdivision (a), or the judge may file a written verified answer admitting or denying any or all of the allegations contained in the party's statement and setting forth any additional facts material or relevant to the question of disqualification. The clerk shall forthwith transmit a copy of the judge's answer to each party or his or her attorney who has appeared in the action.

(4) A judge who fails to file a consent or answer within the time allowed shall be deemed to have consented to his or her disqualification and the clerk shall notify the presiding judge or person authorized to appoint a replacement of the recusal as provided in subdivision (a).

(5) A judge who refuses to recuse himself or herself shall not pass upon his or her own disqualification or upon the sufficiency in law, fact, or otherwise, of the statement of disqualification filed by a party. In that case, the question of disqualification shall be heard and determined by another judge agreed upon by all the parties who have appeared or, in the event they are unable to agree within five days of notification of the judge's answer, by a judge selected by the chairperson of the Judicial Council, or if the chairperson is unable to act, the vice chairperson. The clerk shall notify the executive officer of the Judicial Council of the need for a selection. The selection shall be made as expeditiously as possible. No challenge pursuant to this subdivision or Section 170.6 may be made against the judge selected to decide the question of disqualification.

(6) The judge deciding the question of disqualification may decide the question on the basis of the statement of disqualification and answer and any written arguments as the judge requests, or the judge may set the matter for hearing as promptly as practicable. If a hearing is ordered, the judge shall permit the parties and the judge alleged to be disqualified to argue the question of disqualification and shall for good cause shown hear evidence on any disputed issue of fact. If the judge deciding the question of disqualification determines that the judge is disqualified, the judge hearing the question shall notify the presiding judge or the person having authority to appoint a replacement of the disqualified judge as provided in subdivision (a).

(d) The determination of the question of the disqualification of a judge is not an appealable order and may be reviewed only by a writ of mandate from the appropriate court of appeal sought only by the parties to the proceeding. The petition for the writ shall be filed and served within 10 days after service of written notice of entry of the court's order determining the question of disqualification. If the notice of entry is served by mail, that time shall be extended as provided in subdivision (a) of Section 1013. (Added by Stats.1984, c. 1555, § 7. Amended by Stats.1990, c. 910 (S.B.2316), § 1; Stats.2006, c. 567 (A.B.2303), § 4.)

Cross References

Action defined, see Code of Civil Procedure § 22.
Attorneys, State Bar Act, see Business and Professions Code § 6000.
Computation of time, see Code of Civil Procedure §§ 12, 12a, 12b; Government Code § 6800 et seq.
Definitions applicable to this section, see Code of Civil Procedure § 170.5.
Discovery, generally, see Code of Civil Procedure § 2016 et seq.
Judicial Council, see Government Code § 68500 et seq.
Mandamus, purpose of writ of mandate, courts which may issue writ and parties to whom issued, see Code of Civil Procedure § 1085.
Notice, actual and constructive, defined, see Civil Code § 18.
Writ and process defined, see Code of Civil Procedure § 17.

Research References

Forms
West's California Code Forms, Civil Procedure § 170.1 Form 1, Judicial Officers—Objection to Judge on Ground of Disqualification.
West's California Code Forms, Civil Procedure § 170.3 Form 5, Judicial Officers—Order Disqualifying Judge After Hearing.

§ 170.4. Powers of disqualified judges

(a) A disqualified judge, notwithstanding his or her disqualification may do any of the following:

(1) Take any action or issue any order necessary to maintain the jurisdiction of the court pending the assignment of a judge not disqualified.

(2) Request any other judge agreed upon by the parties to sit and act in his or her place.

(3) Hear and determine purely default matters.

(4) Issue an order for possession prior to judgment in eminent domain proceedings.

(5) Set proceedings for trial or hearing.

(6) Conduct settlement conferences.

(b) Notwithstanding paragraph (5) of subdivision (c) of Section 170.3, if a statement of disqualification is untimely filed or if on its face it discloses no legal grounds for disqualification, the trial judge against whom it was filed may order it stricken.

§ 170.4

(c)(1) If a statement of disqualification is filed after a trial or hearing has commenced by the start of voir dire, by the swearing of the first witness or by the submission of a motion for decision, the judge whose impartiality has been questioned may order the trial or hearing to continue, notwithstanding the filing of the statement of disqualification. The issue of disqualification shall be referred to another judge for decision as provided in subdivision (a) of Section 170.3, and if it is determined that the judge is disqualified, all orders and rulings of the judge found to be disqualified made after the filing of the statement shall be vacated.

(2) For the purposes of this subdivision, if (A) a proceeding is filed in a single judge court or has been assigned to a single judge for comprehensive disposition, and (B) the proceeding has been set for trial or hearing 30 or more days in advance before a judge whose name was known at the time, the trial or hearing shall be deemed to have commenced 10 days prior to the date scheduled for trial or hearing as to any grounds for disqualification known before that time.

(3) A party may file no more than one statement of disqualification against a judge unless facts suggesting new grounds for disqualification are first learned of or arise after the first statement of disqualification was filed. Repetitive statements of disqualification not alleging facts suggesting new grounds for disqualification shall be stricken by the judge against whom they are filed.

(d) Except as provided in this section, a disqualified judge shall have no power to act in any proceeding after his or her disqualification or after the filing of a statement of disqualification until the question of his or her disqualification has been determined. *(Added by Stats.1984, c. 1555, § 8.)*

Cross References
Action, defined, see Code of Civil Procedure § 22.
Computation of time, see Code of Civil Procedure §§ 12, 12a, 12b; Government Code § 6800 et seq.
Definitions applicable to this section, see Code of Civil Procedure § 170.5.
Eminent domain, generally, see Cal. Const. Art. 1, § 19; Code of Civil Procedure § 1240,010 et seq.; Government Code §§ 15850 et seq., 40404; Public Utilities Code § 619.

§ 170.5. Definitions

For the purposes of Sections 170 to 170.5, inclusive, the following definitions apply:

(a) "Judge" means judges of the superior courts, and court commissioners and referees.

(b) "Financial interest" means ownership of more than a 1 percent legal or equitable interest in a party, or a legal or equitable interest in a party of a fair market value in excess of one thousand five hundred dollars ($1,500), or a relationship as director, advisor or other active participant in the affairs of a party, except as follows:

(1) Ownership in a mutual or common investment fund that holds securities is not a "financial interest" in those securities unless the judge participates in the management of the fund.

(2) An office in an educational, religious, charitable, fraternal, or civic organization is not a "financial interest" in securities held by the organization.

(3) The proprietary interest of a policyholder in a mutual insurance company, or a depositor in a mutual savings association, or a similar proprietary interest, is a "financial interest" in the organization only if the outcome of the proceeding could substantially affect the value of the interest.

(c) "Officer of a public agency" does not include a Member of the Legislature or a state or local agency official acting in a legislative capacity.

(d) The third degree of relationship shall be calculated according to the civil law system.

(e) "Private practice of law" includes a fee for service, retainer, or salaried representation of private clients or public agencies, but excludes lawyers as full-time employees of public agencies or lawyers working exclusively for legal aid offices, public defender offices, or similar nonprofit entities whose clientele is by law restricted to the indigent.

(f) "Proceeding" means the action, case, cause, motion, or special proceeding to be tried or heard by the judge.

(g) "Fiduciary" includes any executor, trustee, guardian, or administrator. *(Added by Stats.1984, c. 1555, § 9. Amended by Stats.1998, c. 931 (S.B.2139), § 47, eff. Sept. 28, 1998; Stats.2002, c. 784 (S.B.1316), § 35.)*

Cross References
Action defined, see Code of Civil Procedure § 22.
Restrictions against private arbitration company from administering consumer arbitration or related services, presence of financial interest, see Code of Civil Procedure § 1281.92.
Special proceeding defined, see Code of Civil Procedure § 23.
State and United States as including District of Columbia and territories, see Code of Civil Procedure § 17.

§ 170.6. Prejudice against party, attorney or interest thereof; motion and affidavit; assignment of another judge, court commissioner or referee; number of motions; continuance; cumulative remedy; severability

(a)(1) A judge, court commissioner, or referee of a superior court of the State of California shall not try a civil or criminal action or special proceeding of any kind or character nor hear any matter therein that involves a contested issue of law or fact when it is established as provided in this section that the judge or court commissioner is prejudiced against a party or attorney or the interest of a party or attorney appearing in the action or proceeding.

(2) A party to, or an attorney appearing in, an action or proceeding may establish this prejudice by an oral or written motion without prior notice supported by affidavit or declaration under penalty of perjury, or an oral statement under oath, that the judge, court commissioner, or referee before whom the action or proceeding is pending, or to whom it is assigned, is prejudiced against a party or attorney, or the interest of the party or attorney, so that the party or attorney cannot, or believes that he or she cannot, have a fair and impartial trial or hearing before the judge, court commissioner, or referee. If the judge, other than a judge assigned to the case for all purposes, court commissioner, or referee assigned to, or who is scheduled to try, the cause or hear the matter is known at least 10 days before the date set for trial or hearing, the motion shall be made at least 5 days before that date. If directed to the trial of a cause with a master calendar, the motion shall be made to the judge supervising the master calendar not later than the time the cause is assigned for trial. If directed to the trial of a criminal cause that has been assigned to a judge for all purposes, the motion shall be made to the assigned judge or to the presiding judge by a party within 10 days after notice of the all purpose assignment, or if the party has not yet appeared in the action, then within 10 days after the appearance. If directed to the trial of a civil cause that has been assigned to a judge for all purposes, the motion shall be made to the assigned judge or to the presiding judge by a party within 15 days after notice of the all purpose assignment, or if the party has not yet appeared in the action, then within 15 days after the appearance. If the court in which the action is pending is authorized to have no more than one judge, and the motion claims that the duly elected or appointed judge of that court is prejudiced, the motion shall be made before the expiration of 30 days from the date of the first appearance in the action of the party who is making the motion or whose attorney is making the motion. In no event shall a judge, court commissioner, or referee entertain the motion if it is made after the drawing of the name of the first juror, or if there is no jury, after the making of an opening statement by counsel for plaintiff, or if there is no opening

statement by counsel for plaintiff, then after swearing in the first witness or the giving of any evidence or after trial of the cause has otherwise commenced. If the motion is directed to a hearing, other than the trial of a cause, the motion shall be made not later than the commencement of the hearing. In the case of trials or hearings not specifically provided for in this paragraph, the procedure specified herein shall be followed as nearly as possible. The fact that a judge, court commissioner, or referee has presided at, or acted in connection with, a pretrial conference or other hearing, proceeding, or motion prior to trial, and not involving a determination of contested fact issues relating to the merits, shall not preclude the later making of the motion provided for in this paragraph at the time and in the manner herein provided.

A motion under this paragraph may be made following reversal on appeal of a trial court's decision, or following reversal on appeal of a trial court's final judgment, if the trial judge in the prior proceeding is assigned to conduct a new trial on the matter. Notwithstanding paragraph (4), the party who filed the appeal that resulted in the reversal of a final judgment of a trial court may make a motion under this section regardless of whether that party or side has previously done so. The motion shall be made within 60 days after the party or the party's attorney has been notified of the assignment.

(3) A party to a civil action making that motion under this section shall serve notice on all parties no later than five days after making the motion.

(4) If the motion is duly presented, and the affidavit or declaration under penalty of perjury is duly filed or an oral statement under oath is duly made, thereupon and without any further act or proof, the judge supervising the master calendar, if any, shall assign some other judge, court commissioner, or referee to try the cause or hear the matter. In other cases, the trial of the cause or the hearing of the matter shall be assigned or transferred to another judge, court commissioner, or referee of the court in which the trial or matter is pending or, if there is no other judge, court commissioner, or referee of the court in which the trial or matter is pending, the Chair of the Judicial Council shall assign some other judge, court commissioner, or referee to try the cause or hear the matter as promptly as possible. Except as provided in this section, no party or attorney shall be permitted to make more than one such motion in any one action or special proceeding pursuant to this section. In actions or special proceedings where there may be more than one plaintiff or similar party or more than one defendant or similar party appearing in the action or special proceeding, only one motion for each side may be made in any one action or special proceeding.

(5) Unless required for the convenience of the court or unless good cause is shown, a continuance of the trial or hearing shall not be granted by reason of the making of a motion under this section. If a continuance is granted, the cause or matter shall be continued from day to day or for other limited periods upon the trial or other calendar and shall be reassigned or transferred for trial or hearing as promptly as possible.

(6) Any affidavit filed pursuant to this section shall be in substantially the following form:

(Here set forth court and cause)
State of California,   ss.   PEREMPTORY CHALLENGE
County of _____

_____, being duly sworn, deposes and says: That he or she is a party (or attorney for a party) to the within action (or special proceeding). That ____ the judge, court commissioner, or referee before whom the trial of the (or a hearing in the) action (or special proceeding) is pending (or to whom it is assigned) is prejudiced against the party (or his or her attorney) or the interest of the party (or his or her attorney) so that affiant cannot or believes that he or she cannot have a fair and impartial trial or hearing before the judge, court commissioner, or referee.

Subscribed and sworn to before me this _____ day of _____, 20___.
(Clerk or notary public or other officer administering oath)

(7) Any oral statement under oath or declaration under penalty of perjury made pursuant to this section shall include substantially the same contents as the affidavit above.

(b) Nothing in this section shall affect or limit Section 170 or Title 4 (commencing with Section 392) of Part 2, and this section shall be construed as cumulative thereto.

(c) If any provision of this section or the application to any person or circumstance is held invalid, that invalidity shall not affect other provisions or applications of the section that can be given effect without the invalid provision or application and, to this end, the provisions of this section are declared to be severable. (Added by Stats.1957, c. 1055, p. 2288, § 1. Amended by Stats.1959, c. 640, p. 2620, § 1; Stats.1961, c. 526, p. 1628, § 1; Stats.1965, c. 1442, p. 3375, § 1; Stats.1967, c. 1602, p. 3832, § 2; Stats.1976, c. 1071, p. 4815, § 1; Stats.1981, c. 192, § 1; Stats.1982, c. 1644, p. 6682, § 2; Stats.1985, c. 715, § 1; Stats.1989, c. 537, § 1; Stats.1998, c. 167 (A.B.1199), § 1; Stats.2002, c. 784 (S.B.1316), § 36; Stats.2003, c. 62 (S.B.600), § 22; Stats.2010, c. 131 (A.B.1894), § 1.)

Cross References

Action defined, see Code of Civil Procedure § 22.
Attorneys, State Bar Act, see Business and Professions Code § 6000.
Challenge, removal of action or proceeding from delay reduction program, see Government Code § 68607.5.
Classes of judicial remedies, see Code of Civil Procedure § 21.
Computation of time, see Code of Civil Procedure §§ 12, 12a, 12b; Government Code § 6800 et seq.
Disqualification of arbitrator, application of this section, see Code of Civil Procedure § 1141.18.
Disqualification of judges, see Code of Civil Procedure § 170.
Judicial Council, see Government Code § 68500 et seq.; Cal. Const. Art. 6, § 6.
Juvenile court, disqualification of referee, reassignment of matter, see Welfare and Institutions Code § 247.5.
Juvenile court law, parent or guardian, notice to appear, see Welfare and Institutions Code § 792.
Kinds of actions, see Code of Civil Procedure § 24.
Minimum time periods for certain actions, see Government Code § 68616.
Notice, actual and constructive, defined, see Civil Code § 18.
Oath defined, see Penal Code § 119.
Petition for coordination of cases, right to file peremptory challenge under this section limited upon grant of petition, see California Rules of Court, Rule 3.532.
Special proceeding, defined, see Code of Civil Procedure § 23.
"State" and "United States" as including District of Columbia and territories, see Code of Civil Procedure § 17.
Statement under oath, perjury, see Penal Code § 118 et seq.
Wards,
  Commencement of proceedings, notice, see Welfare and Institutions Code § 661.
  Commencement of proceedings, petition, see Welfare and Institutions Code § 656.
  Hearings, compulsory education violations, see Welfare and Institutions Code § 700.2.

Research References

Forms

California Practice Guide: Rutter Family Law Forms Form 5:23, Peremptory Challenge of Judge (CCP §170.6).
West's California Code Forms, Business & Professions § 475 Comment, Administrative Procedure Act.
West's California Code Forms, Civil Procedure § 170.6 Form 1, Judicial Officers—Declaration in Support of Motion to Disqualify Judge for Prejudice.
West's California Code Forms, Civil Procedure § 1141.18 Form 9, Judicial Arbitration—Rule 3.816—Disclosure of Disqualifying Circumstances.

§ 170.6

West's California Code Forms, Civil Procedure § 1141.22 Form 2, Judicial Arbitration—Rule 3.825—Declaration in Support of Motion to Vacate Judgment (Award of Arbitrator).

West's California Code Forms, Civil Procedure § 1281.9 Form 4, Arbitration—Notice of Disqualification—Court Appointed Arbitrator—Disqualification After Disclosure Statement—Without Cause.

West's California Judicial Council Forms JV–611, Child Habitually Truant §601(B) (Also Available in Spanish).

§ 170.7. Judge serving on appellate division; application of § 170.6

Section 170.6 does not apply to a judge designated or assigned to serve on the appellate division of a superior court in the judge's capacity as a judge of that division. *(Added by Stats.1963, c. 872, p. 2120, § 1. Amended by Stats.1998, c. 931 (S.B.2139), § 48, eff. Sept. 28, 1998.)*

§ 170.8. No qualified judge; assignment of judge

When there is no judge of a court qualified to hear an action or proceeding, the clerk shall forthwith notify the Chairman of the Judicial Council of that fact. The judge assigned by the Chairman of the Judicial Council shall hear the action or proceeding at the time fixed therefor or, if no time has been fixed or good cause appears for changing the time theretofore fixed, the judge shall fix a time for hearing in accordance with law and rules and hear the action or proceeding at the time so fixed. *(Added by Stats.1963, c. 872, p. 2120, § 2. Amended by Stats.1989, c. 1417, § 2.)*

Cross References

Action defined, see Code of Civil Procedure § 22.
Judicial Council, see Government Code § 68500 et seq.

§ 170.9. Acceptance of gifts; value limit; exceptions; adjustments; travel expenses

(a) A judge shall not accept gifts from a single source in a calendar year with a total value of more than two hundred fifty dollars ($250). This section shall not be construed to authorize the receipt of gifts that would otherwise be prohibited by the Code of Judicial Ethics adopted by the California Supreme Court or any other law.

(b) This section shall not prohibit or limit the following:

(1) Payments, advances, or reimbursements for travel and related lodging and subsistence permitted by subdivision (e).

(2) Wedding gifts and gifts exchanged between individuals on birthdays, holidays, and other similar occasions, if the gifts exchanged are not substantially disproportionate in value.

(3) A gift, bequest, favor, or loan from a person whose preexisting relationship with a judge would prevent the judge from hearing a case involving that person, under the Code of Judicial Ethics adopted by the California Supreme Court.

(c) For purposes of this section, "judge" includes all of the following:

(1) Judges of the superior courts.

(2) Justices of the courts of appeal and the Supreme Court.

(3) Subordinate judicial officers, as defined in Section 71601 of the Government Code.

(d) The gift limitation amounts in this section shall be adjusted biennially by the Commission on Judicial Performance to reflect changes in the Consumer Price Index, rounded to the nearest ten dollars ($10).

(e) Payments, advances, or reimbursements for travel, including actual transportation and related lodging and subsistence that is reasonably related to a judicial or governmental purpose, or to an issue of state, national, or international public policy, are not prohibited or limited by this section if any of the following apply:

(1) The travel is in connection with a speech, practice demonstration, or group or panel discussion given or participated in by the judge, the lodging and subsistence expenses are limited to the day immediately preceding, the day of, and the day immediately following the speech, demonstration, or discussion, and the travel is within the United States.

(2) The travel is provided by a government, a governmental agency or authority, a foreign government, a foreign bar association, an international service organization, a bona fide public or private educational institution, as defined in Section 203 of the Revenue and Taxation Code, or a nonprofit charitable or religious organization that is exempt from taxation under Section 501(c)(3) of the Internal Revenue Code,[1] or by a person domiciled outside the United States who substantially satisfies the requirements for tax-exempt status under Section 501(c)(3) of the Internal Revenue Code.

For purposes of this section, "foreign bar association" means an association of attorneys located outside the United States (A) that performs functions substantially equivalent to those performed by state or local bar associations in this state and (B) that permits membership by attorneys in that country representing various legal specialties and does not limit membership to attorneys generally representing one side or another in litigation. "International service organization" means a bona fide international service organization of which the judge is a member. A judge who accepts travel payments from an international service organization pursuant to this subdivision shall not preside over or participate in decisions affecting that organization, its state or local chapters, or its local members.

(3) The travel is provided by a state or local bar association or judges professional association in connection with testimony before a governmental body or attendance at any professional function hosted by the bar association or judges professional association, the lodging and subsistence expenses are limited to the day immediately preceding, the day of, and the day immediately following the professional function.

(f) Payments, advances, and reimbursements for travel not described in subdivision (e) are subject to the limit in subdivision (a).

(g) No judge shall accept any honorarium.

(h) "Honorarium" means a payment made in consideration for any speech given, article published, or attendance at a public or private conference, convention, meeting, social event, meal, or like gathering.

(i) "Honorarium" does not include earned income for personal services that are customarily provided in connection with the practice of a bona fide business, trade, or profession, such as teaching or writing for a publisher, and does not include fees or other things of value received pursuant to Section 94.5 of the Penal Code for performance of a marriage.

For purposes of this section, "teaching" shall include presentations to impart educational information to lawyers in events qualifying for credit under mandatory continuing legal education, to students in bona fide educational institutions, and to associations or groups of judges.

(j) Subdivisions (a) and (e) shall apply to all payments, advances, and reimbursements for travel and related lodging and subsistence.

(k) This section does not apply to any honorarium that is not used and, within 30 days after receipt, is either returned to the donor or delivered to the Controller for deposit in the General Fund without being claimed as a deduction from income for tax purposes.

(*l*) "Gift" means a payment to the extent that consideration of equal or greater value is not received and includes a rebate or discount in the price of anything of value unless the rebate or discount is made in the regular course of business to members of the public without regard to official status. A person, other than a defendant in a criminal action, who claims that a payment is not a gift by reason of receipt of consideration has the burden of proving that the consideration received is of equal or greater value. However, the term "gift" does not include any of the following:

(1) Informational material such as books, reports, pamphlets, calendars, periodicals, cassettes and discs, or free or reduced-price admission, tuition, or registration, for informational conferences or seminars. No payment for travel or reimbursement for any expenses shall be deemed "informational material."

(2) Gifts that are not used and, within 30 days after receipt, are returned to the donor or delivered to a charitable organization without being claimed as a charitable contribution for tax purposes.

(3) Gifts from a judge's spouse, child, parent, grandparent, grandchild, brother, sister, parent-in-law, brother-in-law, sister-in-law, nephew, niece, aunt, uncle, or first cousin or the spouse of any such person. However, a gift from any of those persons shall be considered a gift if the donor is acting as an agent or intermediary for a person not covered by this paragraph.

(4) Campaign contributions required to be reported under Chapter 4 (commencing with Section 84100) of Title 9 of the Government Code.

(5) Any devise or inheritance.

(6) Personalized plaques and trophies with an individual value of less than two hundred fifty dollars ($250).

(7) Admission to events hosted by state or local bar associations or judges professional associations, and provision of related food and beverages at those events, when attendance does not require "travel," as described in paragraph (3) of subdivision (e).

(m) The Commission on Judicial Performance shall enforce the prohibitions of this section with regard to judges of the superior courts and justices of the courts of appeal and the Supreme Court. With regard to subordinate judicial officers, consistent with Section 18.1 of Article VI of the California Constitution, the court employing the subordinate judicial officer shall exercise initial jurisdiction to enforce the prohibitions of this section, and the Commission on Judicial Performance shall exercise discretionary jurisdiction with respect to the enforcement of the prohibitions of this section. *(Added by Stats.1994, c. 1238 (A.B.3638), § 1. Amended by Stats. 1995, c. 378 (S.B.353), § 1; Stats.1996, c. 557 (S.B.1589), § 1; Stats.2002, c. 784 (S.B.1316), § 37; Stats.2010, c. 206 (A.B.2116), § 1; Stats.2011, c. 296 (A.B.1023), § 36.)*

[1] Internal Revenue Code sections are in Title 26 of the U.S.C.A.

Cross References

Action defined, see Code of Civil Procedure § 22.
Attorneys, State Bar Act, see Business and Professions Code § 6000.
Computation of time, see Code of Civil Procedure §§ 12, 12a, 12b; Government Code § 6800 et seq.
Holidays defined for purposes of this Code, see Code of Civil Procedure § 10.
Kinds of actions, see Code of Civil Procedure § 24.
"State" and "United States" as including District of Columbia and territories, see Code of Civil Procedure § 17.
State Controller, generally, see Government Code § 12402 et seq.
Travel payments, advances and reimbursements, see Government Code § 89506.

CHAPTER 4. INCIDENTAL POWERS AND DUTIES OF JUDICIAL OFFICERS

Section
177. Conduct of proceedings.
177.5. Money sanctions.
178. Punishment for contempt.
179. Taking and certifying acknowledgments, affidavits or depositions.

§ 177. Conduct of proceedings

A judicial officer shall have power:

(a) To preserve and enforce order in the officer's immediate presence, and in proceedings before the officer, when the officer is engaged in the performance of official duty.

(b) To compel obedience to the officer's lawful orders as provided in this code.

(c) To compel the attendance of persons to testify in a proceeding before the officer, in the cases and manner provided in this code.

(d) To administer oaths to persons in a proceeding pending before the officer, and in all other cases where it may be necessary in the exercise of the officer's powers and duties.

(e) To prohibit activities that threaten access to state courthouses and court proceedings, and to prohibit interruption of judicial administration, including protecting the privilege from civil arrest at courthouses and court proceedings. *(Enacted in 1872. Amended by Code Am.1880, c. 35, p. 42, § 1; Stats.2019, c. 787 (A.B.668), § 3, eff. Jan. 1, 2020.)*

Cross References

Acts or omissions contemptuous of court's authority, see Code of Civil Procedure § 1209.
Contempt for disobedience of subpoena, see Code of Civil Procedure §§ 1209, 1991 et seq.
Contempt in court's presence, see Code of Civil Procedure § 1211.
Incidental powers of the court, see Code of Civil Procedure § 166.
Judicial officer defined, see Elections Code § 327.
Oaths, see Code of Civil Procedure § 2093 et seq.
Refusal of witness to be sworn, see Code of Civil Procedure § 1991 et seq.
Security required for breach of peace in court's presence, see Penal Code § 710.
Subpoenas, in general, see Code of Civil Procedure § 1986.
Taking and certifying acknowledgments, affidavits or depositions, see Code of Civil Procedure § 179.
Witnesses,
  Attendance from outside state, see Code of Civil Procedure § 1989.
  Compelling attendance in election contests, see Elections Code § 16502.

§ 177.5. Money sanctions

A judicial officer shall have the power to impose reasonable money sanctions, not to exceed fifteen hundred dollars ($1,500), notwithstanding any other provision of law, payable to the court, for any violation of a lawful court order by a person, done without good cause or substantial justification. This power shall not apply to advocacy of counsel before the court. For the purposes of this section, the term "person" includes a witness, a party, a party's attorney, or both.

Sanctions pursuant to this section shall not be imposed except on notice contained in a party's moving or responding papers; or on the court's own motion, after notice and opportunity to be heard. An order imposing sanctions shall be in writing and shall recite in detail the conduct or circumstances justifying the order. *(Added by Stats.1982, c. 1564, p. 6173, § 1. Amended by Stats.2005, c. 75 (A.B.145), § 27, eff. July 19, 2005, operative Jan. 1, 2006.)*

Cross References

Application of Trial Court Trust Fund depositary requirements to fees and fines specified in this section, see Government Code § 68085.7.
Application of Trial Court Trust Fund provisions to fees and fines collected pursuant to this section, see Government Code § 68085.
Attorneys, State Bar Act, see Business and Professions Code § 6000.
Criminal actions, discussion of deliberation or verdict after discharge of jury, violations, see Code of Civil Procedure § 206.
Notice, actual and constructive, defined, see Civil Code § 18.
Organization and government of courts, collection of fees and fines pursuant to this section, deposits, see Government Code § 68085.1.

§ 177.5

Transfers of certain fees and fines specified in this section, effective date, see Government Code § 68085.5.

Research References

Forms

West's California Code Forms, Civil Procedure § 177.5 Form 1, Judicial Officers—Order for Payment of Money Sanctions.

§ 178. Punishment for contempt

For the effectual exercise of the powers conferred by the last section, a judicial officer may punish for contempt in the cases provided in this Code. *(Enacted in 1872. Amended by Code Am.1880, c. 35, p. 42, § 1.)*

Cross References

Abuse of process as contempt, see Code of Civil Procedure § 1209.
Contempt in court's presence, see Code of Civil Procedure § 1211.
Contemptuous acts and omissions, see Code of Civil Procedure § 1209.
Disobedience of subpoena, see Code of Civil Procedure §§ 1209, 1991 et seq.
Refusal of witness to be sworn, see Code of Civil Procedure § 1991 et seq.

§ 179. Taking and certifying acknowledgments, affidavits or depositions

Each of the justices of the Supreme Court and of any court of appeal and the judges of the superior courts, shall have power in any part of the state to take and certify:

(a) The proof and acknowledgment of a conveyance of real property, or of any other written instrument.

(b) The acknowledgment of satisfaction of a judgment of any court.

(c) An affidavit or deposition to be used in this state. *(Enacted in 1872. Amended by Code Am.1880, c. 35, p. 42, § 1; Stats.1933, c. 743, p. 1831, § 49; Stats.1953, c. 457, p. 1701, § 4; Stats.1967, c. 17, p. 828, § 11; Stats.1998, c. 931 (S.B.2139), § 49, eff. Sept. 28, 1998; Stats.2002, c. 784 (S.B.1316), § 38; Stats.2003, c. 62 (S.B.600), § 23.)*

Cross References

Affidavits, in general, see Code of Civil Procedure § 2009 et seq.
Conveyance of real property, proof and acknowledgment, see Civil Code § 1180 et seq.
Court commissioners, powers, see Code of Civil Procedure § 259.
Depositions, see Code of Civil Procedure § 2016 et seq.
Oaths, executive and judicial officers, power to administer and certify, see Government Code § 1225.
Officers before whom taken, see Code of Civil Procedure § 2012 et seq.
"Property" as including real and personal property, see Code of Civil Procedure § 17.
Real property as coextensive with lands, tenements, and hereditaments, see Code of Civil Procedure § 17.
Satisfaction of judgment, see Code of Civil Procedure § 724.010 et seq.
"State" and "United States" as including District of Columbia and territories, see Code of Civil Procedure § 17.

CHAPTER 5. MISCELLANEOUS PROVISIONS RESPECTING COURTS OF JUSTICE

Section
187. Jurisdiction; means to carry into effect; mode of proceeding.

§ 187. Jurisdiction; means to carry into effect; mode of proceeding

When jurisdiction is, by the Constitution or this Code, or by any other statute, conferred on a Court or judicial officer, all the means necessary to carry it into effect are also given; and in the exercise of this jurisdiction, if the course of proceeding be not specifically pointed out by this Code or the statute, any suitable process or mode of proceeding may be adopted which may appear most conformable to the spirit of this Code. *(Enacted in 1872. Amended by Code Am.1880, c. 35, p. 43, § 1.)*

Cross References

Jurisdiction of parties, time of acquisition, see Code of Civil Procedure § 410.50.
Partition of real and personal property, authority of court to carry out purposes of title, see Code of Civil Procedure § 872.120.

Title 3

PERSONS SPECIALLY INVESTED WITH POWERS OF A JUDICIAL NATURE

CHAPTER 2. COURT COMMISSIONERS

Section
259. Powers and duties.

§ 259. Powers and duties

Subject to the supervision of the court, every court commissioner shall have power to do all of the following:

(a) Hear and determine ex parte motions for orders and alternative writs and writs of habeas corpus in the superior court for which the court commissioner is appointed.

(b) Take proof and make and report findings thereon as to any matter of fact upon which information is required by the court. Any party to any contested proceeding may except to the report and the subsequent order of the court made thereon within five days after written notice of the court's action. A copy of the exceptions shall be filed and served upon opposing party or counsel within the five days. The party may argue any exceptions before the court on giving notice of motion for that purpose within 10 days from entry thereof. After a hearing before the court on the exceptions, the court may sustain, or set aside, or modify its order.

(c) Take and approve any bonds and undertakings in actions or proceedings, and determine objections to the bonds and undertakings.

(d) Act as temporary judge when otherwise qualified so to act and when appointed for that purpose, on stipulation of the parties litigant. While acting as temporary judge the commissioner shall receive no compensation therefor other than compensation as commissioner.

(e) Hear and report findings and conclusions to the court for approval, rejection, or change, all preliminary matters including motions or petitions for the custody and support of children, the allowance of temporary spousal support, costs and attorneys' fees, and issues of fact in contempt proceedings in proceedings for support, dissolution of marriage, nullity of marriage, or legal separation.

(f) Hear actions to establish paternity and to establish or enforce child and spousal support pursuant to subdivision (a) of Section 4251 of the Family Code.

(g) Hear, report on, and determine all uncontested actions and proceedings subject to the requirements of subdivision (d). *(Enacted in 1872. Amended by Code Am.1877–78, c. 154, p. 98, § 1; Code Am.1880, c. 35, p. 51, § 1; Stats.1980, c. 229, § 1; Stats.1982, c. 517, p. 2333, § 95; Stats.1989, c. 1105, § 5; Stats.1990, c. 411 (A.B.3973), § 5, eff. July 25, 1990; Stats.1992, c. 163 (A.B.2641), § 14, operative Jan. 1, 1994; Stats.1994, c. 1266 (A.B.3804), § 1; Stats.1996, c. 957 (A.B.1058), § 1; Stats.2004, c. 49 (S.B.1225), § 1.)*

Cross References

Action defined, see Code of Civil Procedure § 22.
Administration of oaths, see Code of Civil Procedure § 2093 et seq.

Affidavits, see Code of Civil Procedure § 2009 et seq.
Attorney's fees and costs, generally, see Code of Civil Procedure § 1021.
Attorneys, State Bar Act, see Business and Professions Code § 6000.
Bond and Undertaking Law, see Code of Civil Procedure § 995.010 et seq.
Classes of judicial remedies, see Code of Civil Procedure § 21.
Computation of time, see Code of Civil Procedure §§ 12, 12a, 12b; Government Code § 6800 et seq.
Decision of commissioner, see Code of Civil Procedure § 643 et seq.
Mortgage foreclosures, see Code of Civil Procedure § 726 et seq.
Notary fees, see Government Code § 8211.
Notice, actual and constructive, defined, see Civil Code § 18.
Official seals defined, see Code of Civil Procedure § 14.
Power of the Legislature to provide for court commissioners, see Cal. Const. Art. 6, § 22.
Proof and acknowledgment of instruments, see Civil Code § 1180 et seq.
References and trials by referees, see Code of Civil Procedure § 638 et seq.
Review of decision, see Code of Civil Procedure § 645.
Writ and process defined, see Code of Civil Procedure § 17.

Research References

Forms

West's California Code Forms, Civil Procedure § 259 Form 1, Notice of Motion for Modification or Disapproval of Court Commissioner's Report.
West's California Code Forms, Civil Procedure § 259 Form 3, Court Commissioners—Order Appointing Commissioner as Temporary Judge—Stipulation of Parties.

Title 5

PERSONS SPECIALLY INVESTED WITH MINISTERIAL POWERS RELATING TO COURTS OF JUSTICE

CHAPTER 1. ATTORNEYS AND COUNSELORS AT LAW

Section
284. Change or substitution; consent; order of court.
285.1. Withdrawal of attorneys of record in domestic relations proceedings; notice; contents; mailing and service.

Cross References

Attorneys, generally, see Business and Professions Code § 6000 et seq.
Circumstances where service on attorney is required, see Code of Civil Procedure § 1015.
Service of intervention on attorney, see Code of Civil Procedure § 387.

§ 284. Change or substitution; consent; order of court

The attorney in an action or special proceeding may be changed at any time before or after judgment or final determination, as follows:

1. Upon the consent of both client and attorney, filed with the clerk, or entered upon the minutes;

2. Upon the order of the court, upon the application of either client or attorney, after notice from one to the other. *(Enacted in 1872. Amended by Code Am.1873–74, c. 383, p. 289, § 26; Code Am.1880, c. 35, p. 57, § 1; Stats.1935, c. 560, p. 1647, § 1; Stats.1967, c. 161, p. 1246, § 1.)*

Cross References

Action defined, see Code of Civil Procedure § 22.
Attorney's fee fixed by court in mortgage foreclosure case, see Code of Civil Procedure § 730.

Attorneys,
  Generally, see Business and Professions Code § 6000 et seq.
  State Bar Act, see Business and Professions Code § 6000.
Compensation of attorneys, see Code of Civil Procedure § 1021 et seq.
Death or removal of attorney, see Code of Civil Procedure § 286.
Notice, actual and constructive, defined, see Civil Code § 18.
Special proceeding defined, see Code of Civil Procedure § 23.

Research References

Forms

West's California Code Forms, Civil Procedure § 284 Form 3, Attorneys—Notice of Motion for Substitution of Attorneys.
West's California Code Forms, Civil Procedure § 284 Form 9, Attorneys—Petition After Attorney-Client Fee Dispute Arbitration Award—Official Form.
West's California Code Forms, Civil Procedure § 284 Form 10, Attorneys—Information Regarding Rights After Attorney-Client Fee Dispute Arbitration Award—Official Form.
West's California Code Forms, Civil Procedure § 284 Form 11, Attorneys—Rejection of Award and Request for Trial After Attorney-Client Fee Arbitration (Alternative Dispute Resolution)—Official Form.
West's California Judicial Council Forms CIV–153, Order on Application to be Relieved as Attorney on Completion of Limited Scope Representation.
West's California Judicial Council Forms FL–958, Order on Completion of Limited Scope Representation.
West's California Judicial Council Forms MC–050, Substitution of Attorney—Civil (Without Court Order).
West's California Judicial Council Forms MC–051, Notice of Motion and Motion to be Relieved as Counsel—Civil.
West's California Judicial Council Forms MC–052, Declaration in Support of Attorney's Motion to be Relieved as Counsel—Civil.
West's California Judicial Council Forms MC–053, Order Granting Attorney's Motion to be Relieved as Counsel—Civil.

§ 285.1. Withdrawal of attorneys of record in domestic relations proceedings; notice; contents; mailing and service

An attorney of record for any party in any civil action or proceeding for dissolution of marriage, legal separation, or for a declaration of void or voidable marriage, or for the support, maintenance or custody of minor children may withdraw at any time subsequent to the time when any judgment in such action or proceeding, other than an interlocutory judgment, becomes final, and prior to service upon him of pleadings or motion papers in any proceeding then pending in said cause, by filing a notice of withdrawal. Such notice shall state (a) date of entry of final decree or judgment, (b) the last known address of such party, (c) that such attorney withdraws as attorney for such party. A copy of such notice shall be mailed to such party at his last known address and shall be served upon the adverse party. *(Added by Stats.1963, c. 1333, p. 2856, § 1. Amended by Stats.1969, c. 1608, p. 3344, § 10, operative Jan. 1, 1970.)*

Cross References

Action defined, see Code of Civil Procedure § 22.
Attorneys,
  Generally, see Business and Professions Code § 6000 et seq.
  State Bar Act, see Business and Professions Code § 6000.
Civil action defined, see Code of Civil Procedure § 30.
Civil action, origin, see Code of Civil Procedure § 25.
Kinds of actions, see Code of Civil Procedure § 24.
Notice, actual and constructive, defined, see Civil Code § 18.

Research References

Forms

California Practice Guide: Rutter Family Law Forms Form 14:10, Notice of Withdrawal of Attorney of Record.
West's California Judicial Council Forms FL–960, Notice of Withdrawal of Attorney of Record.

CODE OF CIVIL PROCEDURE

Part 2

OF CIVIL ACTIONS

Cross References

Arbitration of attorneys' fees, agreement to be bound by award of arbitrator, trial after arbitration in absence of agreement, see Business and Professions Code § 6204.

Eminent domain, rules of practice, see Code of Civil Procedure § 1230.040.

Forcible entry and detainer proceedings, applicability of this Part, see Code of Civil Procedure § 1177.

Produce dealers, rules of practice applicable, see Food and Agricultural Code § 56134.75.

Title 2

OF THE TIME OF COMMENCING CIVIL ACTIONS

Cross References

Arbitration of attorneys' fees, limitation of actions, judicial resolution of arbitration dispute, see Business and Professions Code § 6206.

CHAPTER 3. THE TIME OF COMMENCING ACTIONS OTHER THAN FOR THE RECOVERY OF REAL PROPERTY

Section
- 335. Periods of limitation.
- 335.1. Two years; actions for assault, battery, or injury to, or for death of, individual caused by wrongful act or neglect.
- 336. Five years; mesne profits.
- 336a. Six years; corporate obligations held by public; corporate mortgages, deeds of trust, etc.
- 337. Four years; written contract; exception; book account; account stated based upon account in writing; balance of mutual, open and current account in writing; rescission of written contract.
- 337a. "Book account" defined.
- 337.1. Four years; actions for damages from persons performing or furnishing design, specifications, surveying, planning, supervision or observation of construction or construction of improvement to realty.
- 337.15. Ten years; developer, contractor, architect, etc. of real property; latent deficiency in design, supervision, etc.; injury to property.
- 337.2. Four years; breach of written lease and abandonment of property.
- 337.5. Ten years; municipal general obligation bonds or coupons; judgments or decrees.
- 337.6. Municipal general obligation bonds or coupons; additional time.
- 338. Three years.
- 338.1. Five years; civil penalties or punitive damages for violations of certain hazardous waste, hazardous substance, and petroleum laws.
- 338.1. Five years; civil penalties or punitive damages for violations of certain hazardous waste, hazardous substance, and petroleum laws.
- 339. Two years; oral contract; certificate, abstract or guaranty of title; title insurance policy; sheriff; coroner; rescission of oral contract.
- 339.5. Two years; breach of unwritten lease and abandonment of property.

Section
- 340. One year; statutory penalty or forfeiture to individual and state; statutory forfeiture or penalty to state; libel, slander, false imprisonment, seduction, forged or raised checks, injury to animals by feeder or veterinarian; damages for seizure; action by good faith buyer.
- 340.1. Childhood sexual assault; certificates of merit executed by attorney; violations; failure to file; name designation of defendant; periods of limitation; presentation to government entity not required.
- 340.15. Action for damages suffered as result of domestic violence.
- 340.16. Action for damages suffered as result of sexual assault that occurred on or after plaintiff's 18th birthday.
- 340.2. Exposure to asbestos; actions for injury, illness or wrongful death.
- 340.3. Actions for damages against defendant arising from felony offense; limitation of actions; stay of judgment; restitution.
- 340.35. Causes of action involving sexual abuse of a minor; statutes of limitation.
- 340.4. Minors; action for personal injuries before or during birth; limitation of actions.
- 340.5. Action against health care provider; three years from injury or one year from discovery; exceptions; minors.
- 340.6. Attorneys; wrongful professional act or omission; tolling of period.
- 340.7. Dalkon Shield Claimants' Trust claims; tolling for bankruptcy of A.H. Robins Co.
- 340.8. Exposure to hazardous materials or toxic substances; time for commencement of action; injury or illness; wrongful death actions; definitions.
- 340.9. Northridge earthquake insurance claims.
- 340.10. "Terrorist victim" defined; statute of limitations for actions brought for injury or death to terrorist victim.
- 341. Six months; officer for seizure as tax collector; stock sold for delinquent assessment; vacation of act of trustees of dissolved corporation.
- 341.5. Actions challenging the constitutionality of state funding for municipalities, school districts, special districts, or local agencies; commencement.
- 341a. Ninety days; recovery or conversion of personal property, baggage, etc., left at hotel, hospital, boarding house, etc.
- 342. Actions against public entities.
- 343. Four years; relief not otherwise provided for.
- 344. Balance upon mutual, open and current account; accrual of cause.
- 345. Actions in name of state or county; applicability of chapter; support of patients at state or county hospitals; four year limit.
- 346. Action to redeem mortgage; effect of five years adverse possession.
- 347. Action to redeem mortgage; multiple mortgagors or persons claiming under mortgagor.
- 348. No limitation; action to recover deposit of money or property; effect of insolvency.
- 348.5. No limitation; action upon bonds or coupons issued by State of California.

Section
349.05. One hundred eighty days; underground trespass, use or occupancy by oil or gas well; conversion, taking or removal of oil, gas or other liquid; time of accrual; single cause of action; measure of damages; applicability to existing causes; definitions; exceptions.
349.1. Six months; contesting validity of formation, organization, consolidation, etc., of public entities.
349.2. Six months; contesting validity of authorization, issuance and sale of bonds by public entities.
349.4. Validation of formation, organization, consolidation, etc., of public entities; notice; effect of failure to file action within specified period.

Cross References

Effect of code on running of limitations, see Code of Civil Procedure § 9.

§ 335. Periods of limitation

The periods prescribed for the commencement of actions other than for the recovery of real property, are as follows: *(Enacted in 1872.)*

Cross References

Action defined, see Code of Civil Procedure § 22.
Classes of judicial remedies, see Code of Civil Procedure § 21.
Property as including real and personal property, see Code of Civil Procedure § 17.
Real property as coextensive with lands, tenements, and hereditaments, see Code of Civil Procedure § 17.
Running of limitations, see Code of Civil Procedure § 9.
Self-dealing transactions, public benefit corporations, limitations, see Corporations Code § 5233.
Special defenses not involving merits, see Code of Civil Procedure § 597.
Statute of limitations, pleading and proof, see Code of Civil Procedure § 458.
Time of commencing civil actions,
    Action defined, see Code of Civil Procedure § 363.
    Actions for damages against defendant arising from felony offense, limitation of actions, see Code of Civil Procedure § 340.3.
    Cause of action arising in another state or foreign country, see Code of Civil Procedure § 361.
    Computation of time, exclusion of certain disabilities, see Code of Civil Procedure § 328.
    Four year limitation, relief not otherwise provided for, see Code of Civil Procedure § 343.
    Reversal of judgment, limitation on new action, see Code of Civil Procedure § 355.
    Waiver of statute of limitations, see Code of Civil Procedure § 360.5.

Research References

Forms

West's California Code Forms, Civil Procedure § 352.1 Form 1, Statute of Limitations—Tolling—Imprisonment—Contract Actions.
West's California Code Forms, Civil Procedure § 352 Form 1, Statute of Limitations—Tolling—Contract Actions.

§ 335.1. Two years; actions for assault, battery, or injury to, or for death of, individual caused by wrongful act or neglect

Within two years: An action for assault, battery, or injury to, or for the death of, an individual caused by the wrongful act or neglect of another. *(Added by Stats.2002, c. 448 (S.B.688), § 2.)*

Cross References

Action defined, see Code of Civil Procedure § 22.
Classes of judicial remedies, see Code of Civil Procedure § 21.
Felonies, definition and penalties, see Penal Code §§ 16, 17, 18.
Kinds of injuries, see Code of Civil Procedure § 27.
Personal rights, wrongs not actionable, see Civil Code § 43.5.
Recovery for care and treatment of person injured or diseased by third party, see Government Code § 23004.1.

Time of commencing civil actions,
    Actions based upon professional negligence, notice, see Code of Civil Procedure § 364.
    Death of person entitled to bring action, see Code of Civil Procedure § 366.1 et seq.
    General limitations, see Code of Civil Procedure § 312 et seq.
    Recovery of real property, entry on real estate, sufficiency, see Code of Civil Procedure § 320.
    Reversal of judgment, see Code of Civil Procedure § 355.
    Terrorist victims, actions relating to injury or death, see Code of Civil Procedure § 340.10.

Research References

Forms

West's California Code Forms, Civil Procedure § 335.1 Form 1, Statutes of Limitation—Action for Assault, Battery, Injury, or Death on Another Due to Negligence—Two-Year Time Period.
West's California Code Forms, Civil Procedure § 340.10 Form 1, Statutes of Limitation—Action for Personal Injury or Wrongful Death of Another—Terrorist Victims of September 11, 2001 Attacks—Two-Year Time Period.

§ 336. Five years; mesne profits

Within five years:

(a) An action for mesne profits of real property.

(b) An action for violation of a restriction, as defined in Section 784 of the Civil Code. The period prescribed in this subdivision runs from the time the person seeking to enforce the restriction discovered or, through the exercise of reasonable diligence, should have discovered the violation. A failure to commence an action for violation of a restriction within the period prescribed in this subdivision does not waive the right to commence an action for any other violation of the restriction and does not, in itself, create an implication that the restriction is abandoned, obsolete, or otherwise unenforceable. This subdivision shall not bar commencement of an action for violation of a restriction before January 1, 2001, and until January 1, 2001, any other applicable statutory or common law limitation shall continue to apply to that action. *(Enacted in 1872. Amended by Code Am.1873–74, c. 383, p. 291, § 31; Stats.1953, c. 1153, p. 2652, § 1; Stats.1998, c. 14 (A.B.707), § 3.)*

Cross References

Action defined, see Code of Civil Procedure § 22.
Commencing actions other than for recovery of real property, three year limitation, see Code of Civil Procedure § 338.
Escheat proceedings in decedents' estates, appearances, see Code of Civil Procedure § 1423.
Hiring of real property, application of Chapter, see Civil Code § 1940.
Payment of earlier rent or installments, see Evidence Code § 636.
Property as including real and personal property, see Code of Civil Procedure § 17.
Real property as coextensive with lands, tenements, and hereditaments, see Code of Civil Procedure § 17.
Small claims court, jurisdiction, see Code of Civil Procedure § 116.220.
Statute of limitations, pleading and proof, see Code of Civil Procedure § 458.
Summary proceeding to obtain real property,
    Unlawful detainer defined, see Code of Civil Procedure § 1161 et seq.
    Writ of possession, see Code of Civil Procedure § 1166a.
Time of commencing civil actions, recovery of real property,
    Actions by people, see Code of Civil Procedure § 315.
    Computation of time, see Code of Civil Procedure § 328.
    Seizin within five years, see Code of Civil Procedure §§ 318, 319.

Research References

Forms

West's California Code Forms, Civil Procedure § 336 Form 1, Statutes of Limitation—Restrictions on Use of Real Property—Discovery of Violations.

§ 336a. Six years; corporate obligations held by public; corporate mortgages, deeds of trust, etc.

Within six years:

§ 336a

(a) An action upon any bonds, notes, or debentures issued by any corporation or pursuant to permit of the Commissioner of * * * Financial Protection and Innovation, or upon any coupons issued with the bonds, notes, or debentures, if those bonds, notes, or debentures shall have been issued to or held by the public.

(b) An action upon any mortgage, trust deed, or other agreement pursuant to which the bonds, notes, or debentures were issued. This section does not apply to bonds or other evidences of indebtedness of a public district or corporation. *(Added by Stats.1935, c. 614, p. 1740, § 1. Amended by Stats.2019, c. 143 (S.B.251), § 18, eff. Jan. 1, 2020; Stats.2020, c. 370 (S.B.1371), § 33, eff. Jan. 1, 2021; Stats.2022, c. 452 (S.B.1498), § 37, eff. Jan. 1, 2023.)*

Cross References

Action defined, see Code of Civil Procedure § 22.
Bond and Undertaking Law, bonds or undertakings given as security, see Code of Civil Procedure § 995.010 et seq.
Bonds and undertakings, definitions, construction, see Code of Civil Procedure § 995.110.
Disclosures on purchase money liens on residential property, limitation of actions, see Civil Code § 2967.
Obligation defined, see Code of Civil Procedure § 26.
Perfection of security interest in collateral, see Commercial Code §§ 9302, 9304 et seq., 9401, 9402.
Statute of frauds, see Civil Code § 1624.
Statute of limitations, pleading and proof, see Code of Civil Procedure § 458.
Time of commencing actions, principal and surety, see Code of Civil Procedure § 359.5.

§ 337. Four years; written contract; exception; book account; account stated based upon account in writing; balance of mutual, open and current account in writing; rescission of written contract

Within four years:

(a) An action upon any contract, obligation or liability founded upon an instrument in writing, except as provided in Section 336a; provided, that the time within which any action for a money judgment for the balance due upon an obligation for the payment of which a deed of trust or mortgage with power of sale upon real property or any interest therein was given as security, following the exercise of the power of sale in such deed of trust or mortgage, may be brought shall not extend beyond three months after the time of sale under such deed of trust or mortgage.

(b) An action to recover (1) upon a book account whether consisting of one or more entries; (2) upon an account stated based upon an account in writing, but the acknowledgment of the account stated need not be in writing; (3) a balance due upon a mutual, open and current account, the items of which are in writing; provided, however, that if an account stated is based upon an account of one item, the time shall begin to run from the date of the item, and if an account stated is based upon an account of more than one item, the time shall begin to run from the date of the last item.

(c) An action based upon the rescission of a contract in writing. The time begins to run from the date upon which the facts that entitle the aggrieved party to rescind occurred. Where the ground for rescission is fraud or mistake, the time shall not begin to run until the discovery by the aggrieved party of the facts constituting the fraud or mistake. Where the ground for rescission is misrepresentation under Section 359 of the Insurance Code, the time shall not begin to run until the representation becomes false.

(d) When the period in which an action must be commenced under this section has run, a person shall not bring suit or initiate an arbitration or other legal proceeding to collect the debt. The period in which an action may be commenced under this section shall only be extended pursuant to Section 360. *(Enacted in 1872. Amended by Code Am.1873–74, c. 383, p. 291, § 32; Stats.1906, c. 1, p. 5, § 1; Stats.1907, c. 323, p. 599, § 1; Stats.1917, c. 203, p. 299, § 1; Stats.1933, c. 790, p. 2116, § 1; Stats.1935, c. 614, p. 1740, § 2; Stats.1947, c. 809, p. 1923, § 1; Stats.1961, c. 589, p. 1735, § 6; Stats.2018, c. 247 (A.B.1526), § 2, eff. Jan. 1, 2019.)*

Cross References

Absence from state effecting limitation period, see Code of Civil Procedure § 351.
Acknowledgment or promise; payment on account, see Code of Civil Procedure § 360.
Action against attorney, see Code of Civil Procedure § 340.6.
Action defined, see Code of Civil Procedure § 22.
Action to redeem mortgage, see Code of Civil Procedure §§ 346, 347.
Balance upon mutual, open and current account, see Code of Civil Procedure § 344.
Bonds recorded before improvements completed, action against sureties, see Civil Code § 8610.
Book account, definition, see Code of Civil Procedure § 337a.
Concealment, ground for rescinding insurance contract, see Insurance Code §§ 331, 338.
Contracts,
 Generally, see Civil Code § 1549 et seq.
 Damages and interest, see Civil Code §§ 3300, 3287 and 3291.
 Fraud, see Civil Code §§ 1571 to 1574.
 Impairment of, see Cal. Const. Art. 1, § 9.
 Implied, see Civil Code § 1621.
 Interpretation, see Civil Code § 1635 et seq.
Discovery, generally, see Code of Civil Procedure § 2016 et seq.
Extinction of contracts, rescission, extinguishment, see Civil Code § 1688 et seq.
Extinguishment of lien by lapse of time, see Civil Code § 2911.
Fraud, actual or constructive, see Civil Code §§ 1572 to 1574.
Insurance, time for rescission, see Insurance Code § 650.
Liability of marital property, personal liability for debts incurred by spouse, statute of limitations, see Family Code § 914.
Limitation of action for deficiency judgment after foreclosure or trustee's sale, see Code of Civil Procedure § 580a.
Month defined, see Code of Civil Procedure § 17.
Obligation defined, see Code of Civil Procedure § 26.
Oral contracts, see Code of Civil Procedure § 339.
Payment bond for private works, invalidity of provisions limiting actions, see Civil Code § 8609.
Pleading and proof of statute of limitations, see Code of Civil Procedure § 458.
Processors of farm products, bond, see Food and Agricultural Code § 55435.
Property as including real and personal property, see Code of Civil Procedure § 17.
Real property as coextensive with lands, tenements, and hereditaments, see Code of Civil Procedure § 17.
Relief not otherwise provided, see Code of Civil Procedure § 343.

Research References

Forms

3 California Transactions Forms--Business Transactions § 19:42, Continuing Guaranty (Single Individual Guarantor).
3 California Transactions Forms--Business Transactions § 19:57, Continuing Guaranty (Multiple Individual Guarantors).
3 California Transactions Forms--Business Transactions § 19:73, Suretyship Waivers by Co-Borrowers (Single Lender).
4 California Transactions Forms--Business Transactions § 28:4, Availability of Remedies.
West's California Code Forms, Civil Procedure § 337.1 Form 1, Statutes of Limitation—Construction of Real Property—Personal Injury Caused by Patent Deficiency.
West's California Code Forms, Civil Procedure § 337 Form 1, Statutes of Limitation—Rescission of Written Contract—Discovery Fraud or Mistake.
West's California Code Forms, Commercial § 2725 General Comment, Statute of Limitations in Contracts of Sale.
West's California Code Forms, Commercial § 3118 General Comment, Statute of Limitations.

§ 337a. "Book account" defined

The term "book account" means a detailed statement which constitutes the principal record of one or more transactions between a debtor and a creditor arising out of a contract or some fiduciary relation, and shows the debits and credits in connection therewith, and against whom and in favor of whom entries are made, is entered in the regular course of business as conducted by such creditor or fiduciary, and is kept in a reasonably permanent form and manner and is (1) in a bound book, or (2) on a sheet or sheets fastened in a book or to backing but detachable therefrom, or (3) on a card or cards of a permanent character, or is kept in any other reasonably permanent form and manner. *(Added by Stats.1959, c. 1010, p. 3034, § 1.)*

Cross References

Action on contract based on book account, award of attorney's fees for the prevailing party, see Civil Code § 1717.5.

General rules of pleading, pleading accounts, see Code of Civil Procedure § 454.

§ 337.1. Four years; actions for damages from persons performing or furnishing design, specifications, surveying, planning, supervision or observation of construction or construction of improvement to realty

(a) Except as otherwise provided in this section, no action shall be brought to recover damages from any person performing or furnishing the design, specifications, surveying, planning, supervision or observation of construction or construction of an improvement to real property more than four years after the substantial completion of such improvement for any of the following:

(1) Any patent deficiency in the design, specifications, surveying, planning, supervision or observation of construction or construction of an improvement to, or survey of, real property;

(2) Injury to property, real or personal, arising out of any such patent deficiency; or

(3) Injury to the person or for wrongful death arising out of any such patent deficiency.

(b) If, by reason of such patent deficiency, an injury to property or the person or an injury causing wrongful death occurs during the fourth year after such substantial completion, an action in tort to recover damages for such an injury or wrongful death may be brought within one year after the date on which such injury occurred, irrespective of the date of death, but in no event may such an action be brought more than five years after the substantial completion of construction of such improvement.

(c) Nothing in this section shall be construed as extending the period prescribed by the laws of this state for the bringing of any action.

(d) The limitation prescribed by this section shall not be asserted by way of defense by any person in actual possession or the control, as owner, tenant or otherwise, of such an improvement at the time any deficiency in such an improvement constitutes the proximate cause of the injury or death for which it is proposed to bring an action.

(e) As used in this section, "patent deficiency" means a deficiency which is apparent by reasonable inspection.

(f) Subdivisions (a) and (b) shall not apply to any owner-occupied single-unit residence. *(Added by Stats.1967, c. 1326, p. 3157, § 1.)*

Cross References

Action defined, see Code of Civil Procedure § 22.
Classes of judicial remedies, see Code of Civil Procedure § 21.
Commencing civil actions, malpractice, see Code of Civil Procedure § 411.35.
General rules of pleading,
  Pleading accounts, see Code of Civil Procedure § 454.
  Statute of limitations, pleading and proof, see Code of Civil Procedure § 458.
Injury to property defined, see Code of Civil Procedure § 28.
Kinds of injuries, see Code of Civil Procedure § 27.
Limitation of action, tolling, see Civil Code § 937.
Professions and vocations generally, architect defined, see Business and Professions Code § 5500 et seq.

Property as including real and personal property, see Code of Civil Procedure § 17.
Real estate contract arbitration, other rights of action not limited, see Code of Civil Procedure § 1298.7.
Real property as coextensive with lands, tenements, and hereditaments, see Code of Civil Procedure § 17.
Regulation of buildings for human habitation, general provisions, see Health and Safety Code § 17910 et seq.
Relief of bidders, invalid contracts due to defective bidding processes, see Public Contract Code § 5110.
State and United States as including District of Columbia and territories, see Code of Civil Procedure § 17.
Time of commencing actions for the recovery of real property, seizing within five years, see Code of Civil Procedure § 319.

Research References

Forms

West's California Code Forms, Civil Procedure § 337.1 Form 1, Statutes of Limitation—Construction of Real Property—Personal Injury Caused by Patent Deficiency.
West's California Code Forms, Education, § 17406 Form 1, Complaint to Validate and Confirm Lease and Construction Services Agreement Using Competitive Solicitation Process.

§ 337.15. Ten years; developer, contractor, architect, etc. of real property; latent deficiency in design, supervision, etc.; injury to property

(a) No action may be brought to recover damages from any person, or the surety of a person, who develops real property or performs or furnishes the design, specifications, surveying, planning, supervision, testing, or observation of construction or construction of an improvement to real property more than 10 years after the substantial completion of the development or improvement for any of the following:

(1) Any latent deficiency in the design, specification, surveying, planning, supervision, or observation of construction or construction of an improvement to, or survey of, real property.

(2) Injury to property, real or personal, arising out of any such latent deficiency.

(b) As used in this section, "latent deficiency" means a deficiency which is not apparent by reasonable inspection.

(c) As used in this section, "action" includes an action for indemnity brought against a person arising out of that person's performance or furnishing of services or materials referred to in this section, except that a cross-complaint for indemnity may be filed pursuant to subdivision (b) of Section 428.10 in an action which has been brought within the time period set forth in subdivision (a) of this section.

(d) Nothing in this section shall be construed as extending the period prescribed by the laws of this state for bringing any action.

(e) The limitation prescribed by this section shall not be asserted by way of defense by any person in actual possession or the control, as owner, tenant or otherwise, of such an improvement, at the time any deficiency in the improvement constitutes the proximate cause for which it is proposed to bring an action.

(f) This section shall not apply to actions based on willful misconduct or fraudulent concealment.

(g) The 10-year period specified in subdivision (a) shall commence upon substantial completion of the improvement, but not later than the date of one of the following, whichever first occurs:

(1) The date of final inspection by the applicable public agency.

(2) The date of recordation of a valid notice of completion.

(3) The date of use or occupation of the improvement.

(4) One year after termination or cessation of work on the improvement.

§ 337.15

The date of substantial completion shall relate specifically to the performance or furnishing design, specifications, surveying, planning, supervision, testing, observation of construction or construction services by each profession or trade rendering services to the improvement. *(Added by Stats.1971, c. 1569, p. 3149, § 1. Amended by Stats.1979, c. 373, p. 1265, § 49; Stats.1979, c. 571, p. 1797, § 1; Stats.1980, c. 676, § 63; Stats.1981, c. 88, § 1.)*

Cross References

Action defined, see Code of Civil Procedure § 22.
Classes of judicial remedies, see Code of Civil Procedure § 21.
Commencing civil actions, malpractice, see Code of Civil Procedure § 411.35.
Injury to property defined, see Code of Civil Procedure § 28.
Kinds of injuries, see Code of Civil Procedure § 27.
Limitation of action, tolling, see Civil Code § 937.
Notice, actual and constructive, defined, see Civil Code § 18.
Professions and vocations generally, architect defined, see Business and Professions Code § 5500 et seq.
Property as including real and personal property, see Code of Civil Procedure § 17.
Real estate contract arbitration, other rights of action not limited, see Code of Civil Procedure § 1298.7.
Real property as coextensive with lands, tenements, and hereditaments, see Code of Civil Procedure § 17.
Regulation of buildings for human habitation, general provisions, see Health and Safety Code § 17910 et seq.
Relief of bidders, invalid contracts due to defective bidding processes, see Public Contract Code § 5110.
State and United States as including District of Columbia and territories, see Code of Civil Procedure § 17.
Statute of limitations, pleading and proof, see Code of Civil Procedure § 458.
Time of commencing actions for the recovery of real property, seizing within five years, see Code of Civil Procedure § 319.

Research References

Forms

West's California Code Forms, Civil Procedure § 337.1 Form 1, Statutes of Limitation—Construction of Real Property—Personal Injury Caused by Patent Deficiency.
West's California Code Forms, Civil Procedure § 337.15 Form 1, Statute of Limitations—Pleading—Real Property—Latent Design Deficiency—Fraudulent Concealment.

§ 337.2. Four years; breach of written lease and abandonment of property

Where a lease of real property is in writing, no action shall be brought under Section 1951.2 of the Civil Code more than four years after the breach of the lease and abandonment of the property, or more than four years after the termination of the right of the lessee to possession of the property, whichever is the earlier time. *(Added by Stats.1970, c. 89, p. 107, § 12, operative July 1, 1971.)*

Cross References

Action defined, see Code of Civil Procedure § 22.
Hiring of real property,
 Buildings for human occupancy, see Civil Code § 1941 et seq.
 Liquidated damages, see Civil Code § 1951.5.
 Renewal by continued possession and acceptance of rent, see Civil Code § 1945.
Liquidated damages, validity, see Civil Code § 1671.
Payment of earlier rent or installments, see Evidence Code § 636.
Property as including real and personal property, see Code of Civil Procedure § 17.
Real property as coextensive with lands, tenements, and hereditaments, see Code of Civil Procedure § 17.
Statute of limitations, pleading and proof, see Code of Civil Procedure § 458.
Summary proceedings to obtain real property,
 Unlawful detainer defined, see Code of Civil Procedure § 1161 et seq.
 Writ of possession, see Code of Civil Procedure § 1166a.

§ 337.5. Ten years; municipal general obligation bonds or coupons; judgments or decrees

Within 10 years:

(a) An action upon any general obligation bonds or coupons, not secured in whole or in part by a lien on real property, issued by any county, city and county, municipal corporation, district (including school districts), or other political subdivision of the State of California.

(b) An action upon a judgment or decree of any court of the United States or of any state within the United States. *(Added by Stats.1939, c. 724, p. 2255, § 1. Amended by Stats.1947, c. 626, p. 1634, § 1; Stats.1953, c. 1153, p. 2653, § 2; Stats.2010, c. 719 (S.B.856), § 7, eff. Oct. 19, 2010.)*

Cross References

Action defined, see Code of Civil Procedure § 22.
Bond and Undertaking Law, bonds or undertakings given as security, see Code of Civil Procedure § 995.010 et seq.
Bonds and undertakings, definitions, construction, see Code of Civil Procedure § 995.110 et seq.
Bonds, form of ballot for issuance of bonds by county government, see Government Code § 29902.
Bonds, purpose of bond issues, see Government Code § 29900 et seq.
Issuance of writ of possession or sale, see Code of Civil Procedure § 712.010 et seq.
Judgment defined, see Code of Civil Procedure § 577 et seq.
Obligation defined, see Code of Civil Procedure § 26.
Pleading and proof of statute of limitations, see Code of Civil Procedure § 458.
Property as including real and personal property, see Code of Civil Procedure § 17.
Public bonds and obligations, presentation and request for conversion, see Government Code § 5000 et seq.
Real property as coextensive with lands, tenements, and hereditaments, see Code of Civil Procedure § 17.
Registration of bonds, nonpayment for want of funds, see Government Code § 50630 et seq.
Renewal of judgments, period of enforceability, see Code of Civil Procedure § 683.110 et seq.
Satisfaction of judgment by payment in full or acceptance of lesser sum, see Code of Civil Procedure § 724.010 et seq.
Sister state and foreign money-judgments, definitions, see Code of Civil Procedure § 1710.01 et seq.
State and United States as including District of Columbia and territories, see Code of Civil Procedure § 17.
Time for issuance of writ of execution, see Code of Civil Procedure § 699.510.
Time of commencing actions,
 Death of party before expiration of limitation period, see Code of Civil Procedure §§ 366.1, 366.2, 377.20 et seq.
 Effect of absence from state on limitation period, see Code of Civil Procedure § 351.
Principal and surety, see Code of Civil Procedure § 359.5.

§ 337.6. Municipal general obligation bonds or coupons; additional time

Notwithstanding the provisions of Section 337.5 of this code actions may be brought on bonds or coupons as set forth in subsection 2 of said section, against which the statute of limitations ran on or after August 27, 1937; provided, such actions are brought on or before June 30, 1959. Upon presentation for payment they shall be registered and payment shall not be made thereon until the next fiscal year following presentation unless available funds are sufficient to first pay obligations which are due or will become due from the same fund during the fiscal year of presentation and during the next succeeding six months. Interest shall not be paid on bonds or coupons registered for the purpose of this section. *(Added by Stats.1949, c. 1282, p. 2265, § 1. Amended by Stats.1957, c. 719, p. 1925, § 1.)*

Cross References

Action defined, see Code of Civil Procedure § 22.
Bond and Undertaking Law, bonds or undertakings given as security, see Code of Civil Procedure § 995.010 et seq.
Classes of judicial remedies, see Code of Civil Procedure § 21.
Month defined, see Code of Civil Procedure § 17.
Obligation defined, see Code of Civil Procedure § 26.

Statute of limitations, pleading and proof, see Code of Civil Procedure § 458.

§ 338. Three years

Within three years:

(a) An action upon a liability created by statute, other than a penalty or forfeiture.

(b) An action for trespass upon or injury to real property.

(c)(1) An action for taking, detaining, or injuring goods or chattels, including an action for the specific recovery of personal property.

(2) The cause of action in the case of theft, as described in Section 484 of the Penal Code, of an article of historical, interpretive, scientific, or artistic significance is not deemed to have accrued until the discovery of the whereabouts of the article by the aggrieved party, the aggrieved party's agent, or the law enforcement agency that originally investigated the theft.

(3)(A) Notwithstanding paragraphs (1) and (2), an action for the specific recovery of a work of fine art brought against a museum, gallery, auctioneer, or dealer, in the case of an unlawful taking or theft, as described in Section 484 of the Penal Code, of a work of fine art, including a taking or theft by means of fraud or duress, shall be commenced within six years of the actual discovery by the claimant or the claimant's agent, of both of the following:

(i) The identity and the whereabouts of the work of fine art. In the case where there is a possibility of misidentification of the object of fine art in question, the identity can be satisfied by the identification of facts sufficient to determine that the work of fine art is likely to be the work of fine art that was unlawfully taken or stolen.

(ii) Information or facts that are sufficient to indicate that the claimant has a claim for a possessory interest in the work of fine art that was unlawfully taken or stolen.

(B) This paragraph shall apply to all pending and future actions commenced on or before December 31, 2017, including an action dismissed based on the expiration of statutes of limitations in effect prior to the date of enactment of this statute if the judgment in that action is not yet final or if the time for filing an appeal from a decision on that action has not expired, provided that the action concerns a work of fine art that was taken within 100 years prior to the date of enactment of this statute.

(C) For purposes of this paragraph:

(i) "Actual discovery," notwithstanding Section 19 of the Civil Code, does not include constructive knowledge imputed by law.

(ii) "Auctioneer" means an individual who is engaged in, or who by advertising or otherwise holds the individual out as being available to engage in, the calling for, the recognition of, and the acceptance of, offers for the purchase of goods at an auction as defined in subdivision (b) of Section 1812.601 of the Civil Code.

(iii) "Dealer" means a person who holds a valid seller's permit and who is actively and principally engaged in, or conducting the business of, selling works of fine art.

(iv) "Duress" means a threat of force, violence, danger, or retribution against an owner of the work of fine art in question, or the owner's family member, sufficient to coerce a reasonable person of ordinary susceptibilities to perform an act that otherwise would not have been performed or to acquiesce to an act to which the person would otherwise not have acquiesced.

(v) "Fine art" has the same meaning as defined in paragraph (1) of subdivision (d) of Section 982 of the Civil Code.

(vi) "Museum or gallery" shall include any public or private organization or foundation operating as a museum or gallery.

(4) Section 361 shall not apply to an action brought pursuant to paragraph (3).

(5) A party in an action to which paragraph (3) applies may raise all equitable and legal affirmative defenses and doctrines, including, without limitation, laches and unclean hands.

(d) An action for relief on the ground of fraud or mistake. The cause of action in that case is not deemed to have accrued until the discovery, by the aggrieved party, of the facts constituting the fraud or mistake.

(e) An action upon a bond of a public official except any cause of action based on fraud or embezzlement is not deemed to have accrued until the discovery, by the aggrieved party or the aggrieved party's agent, of the facts constituting the cause of action upon the bond.

(f)(1) An action against a notary public on the notary public's bond or in the notary public's official capacity except that a cause of action based on malfeasance or misfeasance is not deemed to have accrued until discovery, by the aggrieved party or the aggrieved party's agent, of the facts constituting the cause of action.

(2) Notwithstanding paragraph (1), an action based on malfeasance or misfeasance shall be commenced within one year from discovery, by the aggrieved party or the aggrieved party's agent, of the facts constituting the cause of action or within three years from the performance of the notarial act giving rise to the action, whichever is later.

(3) Notwithstanding paragraph (1), an action against a notary public on the notary public's bond or in the notary public's official capacity shall be commenced within six years.

(g) An action for slander of title to real property.

(h) An action commenced under Section 17536 of the Business and Professions Code. The cause of action in that case shall not be deemed to have accrued until the discovery by the aggrieved party, the Attorney General, the district attorney, the county counsel, the city prosecutor, or the city attorney of the facts constituting grounds for commencing the action.

(i) An action commenced under the Porter-Cologne Water Quality Control Act (Division 7 (commencing with Section 13000) of the Water Code). The cause of action in that case shall not be deemed to have accrued until the discovery by the State Water Resources Control Board or a regional water quality control board of the facts constituting grounds for commencing actions under their jurisdiction.

(j) An action to recover for physical damage to private property under Section 19 of Article I of the California Constitution.

(k) An action commenced under Division 26 (commencing with Section 39000) of the Health and Safety Code. These causes of action shall not be deemed to have accrued until the discovery by the State Air Resources Board or by a district, as defined in Section 39025 of the Health and Safety Code, of the facts constituting grounds for commencing the action under its jurisdiction.

(*l*) An action commenced under Section 1602, 1615, or 5650.1 of the Fish and Game Code. These causes of action shall not be deemed to have accrued until discovery by the agency bringing the action of the facts constituting the grounds for commencing the action.

(m) An action challenging the validity of the levy upon a parcel of a special tax levied by a local agency on a per parcel basis.

(n) An action commencing under Section 51.7 of the Civil Code.

(*o*) An action commenced under Section 4601.1 of the Public Resources Code, if the underlying violation is of Section 4571, 4581, or 4621 of the Public Resources Code, or of Section 1103.1 of Title 14 of the California Code of Regulations, and the underlying violation is related to the conversion of timberland to nonforestry-related agricultural uses. These causes of action shall not be deemed to have accrued until discovery by the Department of Forestry and Fire Protection.

§ 338

(p) An action for civil penalties commenced under Section 26038 of the Business and Professions Code. *(Enacted in 1872. Amended by Stats.1921, c. 183, p. 192, § 1; Stats.1933, c. 306, p. 878, § 1; Stats.1935, c. 581, p. 1673, § 1; Stats.1943, c. 1025, p. 2963, § 1; Stats.1949, c. 1540, p. 2734, § 1; Stats.1957, c. 649, p. 1849, § 1; Stats.1972, c. 823, p. 1470, § 2; Stats.1981, c. 247, § 1, eff. July 21, 1981; Stats.1981, c. 494, § 2; Stats.1982, c. 340, p. 1642, § 1; Stats.1987, c. 1200, § 1; Stats.1987, c. 1201, § 1; Stats.1988, c. 1186, § 1; Stats.1989, c. 467, § 1; Stats.1990, c. 669 (A.B.4049), § 1; Stats.1995, c. 238 (A.B.1174), § 1; Stats.1998, c. 342 (A.B.1933), § 1; Stats.2005, c. 123 (A.B.378), § 2; Stats.2005, c. 383 (S.B.1110), § 1.5; Stats.2006, c. 538 (S.B.1852), § 62; Stats.2010, c. 691 (A.B.2765), § 2; Stats.2015, c. 683 (S.B.798), § 1, eff. Jan. 1, 2016; Stats.2018, c. 796 (S.B.1453), § 1, eff. Jan. 1, 2019; Stats.2021, c. 264 (A.B.287), § 1, eff. Jan. 1, 2022.)*

Cross References

Action against directors or shareholders, see Code of Civil Procedure § 359.
Action against officer or person holding bond or covenant of indemnity, see Code of Civil Procedure § 1055.
Action against sureties on guardian's bond, see Probate Code § 2333.
Action defined, see Code of Civil Procedure § 22.
Action to recover property sold by guardian, see Probate Code § 2548.
Action to recover property sold by personal representative, see Probate Code § 10382.
Advertising, false or misleading statements, see Business and Professions Code § 17500 et seq.
Attorney General, generally, see Government Code § 12500 et seq.
Attorneys, State Bar Act, see Business and Professions Code § 6000.
Basic health care, third party liability, commencement of action, see Welfare and Institutions Code § 14124.72.
Bond and Undertaking Law, bonds or undertakings given as security, see Code of Civil Procedure § 995.010 et seq.
Bonds, clerk and treasurer, see Government Code § 36518 et seq.
Bonds and undertakings, preliminary provisions and definitions, officer, see Code of Civil Procedure § 995.160.
Bonds of employees, see Government Code § 31004.
Classes of judicial remedies, see Code of Civil Procedure § 21.
Commencing actions other than to recover real property,
    Actions in name of state or county, see Code of Civil Procedure § 345.
    Personal property left at hotel, hospital, etc., see Code of Civil Procedure § 341a.
Commencing actions to recover real property,
    Actions by people, see Code of Civil Procedure § 315.
    Seizin within five years, see Code of Civil Procedure §§ 318, 319.
Conservation, control, and utilization of water resources, see Water Code § 13000 et seq.
Construction defects in original construction intended to be sold as an individual dwelling unit, actions to recover for damages, limitations of actions, see Civil Code § 941.
Crimes against property, theft, see Penal Code § 484 et seq.
Definitions, personal representative, see Probate Code § 58.
Discovery, generally, see Code of Civil Procedure § 2016 et seq.
District attorney, powers and duties, see Government Code § 26500 et seq.
Draft element revision or draft amendment, submission, review and report, public comment period, adoption by legislative body, review by department and report to planning agency, review of action or failure to act, notification of violation, remedies, see Government Code § 65585.
Fire suppression and rescue or emergency medical costs, liability, collection, see Health and Safety Code § 13009.
Fraud, actual or constructive, see Civil Code §§ 1572 to 1574.
Fraudulent deceit, see Civil Code § 1709.
Guardianship and conservatorship, oath and bond, see Probate Code § 2300 et seq.
Indexes, official bonds, see Government Code § 27246 et seq.
Interests in property, absolute or qualified ownership, see Civil Code § 678 et seq.
Kinds of injuries, see Code of Civil Procedure § 27.
Notaries public,
    Appointment and commission, see Government Code § 8200 et seq.
    Bond, see Government Code § 8212 et seq.
Personal property as including money, goods, chattels, things in action, and evidences of debt, see Code of Civil Procedure § 17.
Prescribing official bonds, see Government Code § 24150 et seq.
Property as including real and personal property, see Code of Civil Procedure § 17.
Proscribed deceptive practices, see Civil Code § 1770.
Public officers and employees, filing official bonds, see Government Code § 1450 et seq.
Real property as coextensive with lands, tenements, and hereditaments, see Code of Civil Procedure § 17.
Regional centers for persons with developmental disabilities, time for commencing actions to recover the reasonable value of services provided, see Welfare and Institutions Code § 4659.12.
State and United States as including District of Columbia and territories, see Code of Civil Procedure § 17.
Statute of limitations, pleading and proof, see Code of Civil Procedure § 458.
Terms in writing intended as final expression of agreement, see Code of Civil Procedure § 1856.
Third party liability, injury to Medi-Cal recipient, see Welfare and Institutions Code § 14124.71.
Trespass by credible threat, see Penal Code § 601 et seq.

Research References

Forms

Asset Protection: Legal Planning, Strategies and Forms ¶ 3.06, Statute of Limitations.
Asset Protection: Legal Planning, Strategies and Forms ¶ 13.12, Protection of Artwork.
4 California Transactions Forms--Business Transactions § 28:4, Availability of Remedies.
5 California Transactions Forms--Business Transactions § 33:23, Relationship With Uniform Commercial Code.
1 California Transactions Forms--Estate Planning § 2:8, Conduct of Practitioner to Limit Tolling of Statute of Limitations.
West's California Code Forms, Civil Procedure § 338(a) Form 1, Statutes of Limitation—Liability Based on Statute—Action Challenging Validity of Tax.
West's California Code Forms, Civil Procedure § 338(d) Form 1, Statutes of Limitation—Action Based on Fraud or Mistake—Accrual—Discovery.
West's California Code Forms, Civil Procedure § 338(f) Form 1, Statutes of Limitation—Action Based on Malfeasance or Misfeasance of Notary Public—Accrual—Discovery.
West's California Code Forms, Commercial § 2725 General Comment, Statute of Limitations in Contracts of Sale.
West's California Code Forms, Government § 37101 Form 17, Mobile Home Rent Control Ordinance.

§ 338.1. Five years; civil penalties or punitive damages for violations of certain hazardous waste, hazardous substance, and petroleum laws

Section operative until Jan. 1, 2024. See, also, § 338.1 operative Jan. 1, 2024.

An action for civil penalties or punitive damages authorized under Chapter 6.5 (commencing with Section 25100), Chapter 6.67 (commencing with Section 25270), Chapter 6.7 (commencing with Section 25280), Chapter 6.8 (commencing with Section 25300), or Chapter 6.95 (commencing with Section 25500) of Division 20 of the Health and Safety Code shall be commenced within five years after the discovery by the agency bringing the action of the facts constituting the grounds for commencing the action. *(Added by Stats.1988, c. 1186, § 2. Amended by Stats.2009, c. 429 (A.B.305), § 1; Stats.2018, c. 141 (A.B.1980), § 1, eff. Jan. 1, 2019.)*

§ 338.1. Five years; civil penalties or punitive damages for violations of certain hazardous waste, hazardous substance, and petroleum laws

Section operative Jan. 1, 2024. See, also, § 338.1 operative until Jan. 1, 2024.

An action for civil penalties or punitive damages authorized under Chapter 6.5 (commencing with Section 25100), Chapter 6.67 (commencing with Section 25270), Chapter 6.7 (commencing with Section 25280), * * * or Chapter 6.95 (commencing with Section 25500) of Division 20 of, or Part 2 (commencing with Section 78000) of Division 45 of, the Health and Safety Code shall be commenced within five years after the discovery by the agency bringing the action of the facts constituting the grounds for commencing the action. *(Added by Stats.1988, c. 1186, § 2. Amended by Stats.2009, c. 429 (A.B.305), § 1; Stats.2018, c. 141 (A.B.1980), § 1, eff. Jan. 1, 2019; Stats.2022, c. 258 (A.B.2327), § 7, eff. Jan. 1, 2023, operative Jan. 1, 2024.)*

Cross References

Action defined, see Code of Civil Procedure § 22.
Discovery, generally, see Code of Civil Procedure § 2016 et seq.
Hazardous substance accounts,
  Short title, see Health and Safety Code § 25300 et seq.
  Time of commencing actions, see Health and safety Code § 25360.4.
Hazardous waste control, legislative findings, see Health and Safety Code § 25100 et seq.
Statute of limitations, pleading and proof, see Code of Civil Procedure § 458.
Underground storage of hazardous substances, legislation findings and declarations, see Health and Safety Code § 25280 et seq.

§ 339. Two years; oral contract; certificate, abstract or guaranty of title; title insurance policy; sheriff; coroner; rescission of oral contract

Within two years: 1. An action upon a contract, obligation or liability not founded upon an instrument of writing, except as provided in Section 2725 of the Commercial Code or subdivision 2 of Section 337 of this code; or an action founded upon a contract, obligation or liability, evidenced by a certificate, or abstract or guaranty of title of real property, or by a policy of title insurance; provided, that the cause of action upon a contract, obligation or liability evidenced by a certificate, or abstract or guaranty of title of real property or policy of title insurance shall not be deemed to have accrued until the discovery of the loss or damage suffered by the aggrieved party thereunder.

2. An action against a sheriff or coroner upon a liability incurred by the doing of an act in an official capacity and in virtue of office, or by the omission of an official duty including the nonpayment of money collected in the enforcement of a judgment.

3. An action based upon the rescission of a contract not in writing. The time begins to run from the date upon which the facts that entitle the aggrieved party to rescind occurred. Where the ground for rescission is fraud or mistake, the time does not begin to run until the discovery by the aggrieved party of the facts constituting the fraud or mistake. *(Enacted in 1872. Amended by Code Am.1873–74, c. 383, p. 291, § 33; Stats.1905, c. 258, p. 231, § 1; Stats.1906, c. 1, p. 5, § 2; Stats.1907, c. 323, p. 599, § 2; Stats.1913, c. 187, p. 332, § 1; Stats.1917, c. 203, p. 299, § 2; Stats.1961, c. 589, p. 1736, § 7; Stats.1980, c. 1307, § 1; Stats.1982, c. 497, p. 2154, § 31, operative July 1, 1983; Stats.1996, c. 872 (A.B.3472), § 11.)*

Cross References

Absence from state, effect on limitation period, see Code of Civil Procedure § 351.
Accrual of mutual account cause of action, see Code of Civil Procedure § 344.
Acknowledgment or promise, see Code of Civil Procedure § 360.
Action against attorney, see Code of Civil Procedure § 340.6.
Action defined, see Code of Civil Procedure § 22.
Action for breach of promise of marriage barred, see Civil Code § 43.5.
Contracts,
  Generally, see Civil Code § 1549 et seq.
  Damages and interest, see Civil Code §§ 3300, 3287, 3291.
  Fraud, see Civil Code §§ 1571 to 1574.
  Impairment of, see Cal. Const. Art. 1, § 9.
  Implied, see Civil Code § 1621.
  Interpretation, see Civil Code § 1635 et seq.
Death of party before expiration of limitation period, see Code of Civil Procedure §§ 366.1, 366.2, 377.20 et seq.
Disabilities of minority, see Code of Civil Procedure § 352.
Discovery, generally, see Code of Civil Procedure § 2016.010 et seq.
Fraud, actual or constructive, see Civil Code §§ 1572 to 1574.
General limitations for commencing civil actions, see Code of Civil Procedure § 312 et seq.
Instrument in writing, see Code of Civil Procedure § 337.
Liability of marital property, personal liability for debts incurred by spouse, statute of limitations, see Family Code § 914.
Mistake as ground of rescission, see Civil Code § 1689.
Obligation defined, see Code of Civil Procedure § 26.
Property as including real and personal property, see Code of Civil Procedure § 17.
Real property as coextensive with lands, tenements, and hereditaments, see Code of Civil Procedure § 17.
Sales, when seller may rescind, see Commercial Code § 2610.
Sheriff as including marshal, see Code of Civil Procedure § 17.
Statute of limitations in contracts for sale, see Commercial Code § 2725.

Research References

Forms

4 California Transactions Forms--Business Entities § 20:21, Right to Final Accounting.
West's California Code Forms, Civil Procedure § 339(3) Form 1, Statute of Limitations—Pleading—Rescission of Oral Contract—Fraud—Mistake.
West's California Code Forms, Commercial Div. 1 Intro., Division 1 General Provisions.

§ 339.5. Two years; breach of unwritten lease and abandonment of property

Where a lease of real property is not in writing, no action shall be brought under Section 1951.2 of the Civil Code more than two years after the breach of the lease and abandonment of the property, or more than two years after the termination of the right of the lessee to possession of the property, whichever is the earlier time. *(Added by Stats.1970, c. 89, p. 107, § 13, operative July 1, 1971.)*

Cross References

Action defined, see Code of Civil Procedure § 22.
General limitations for commencing civil actions, see Code of Civil Procedure § 312 et seq.
Property as including real and personal property, see Code of Civil Procedure § 17.
Real property as coextensive with lands, tenements, and hereditaments, see Code of Civil Procedure § 17.

§ 340. One year; statutory penalty or forfeiture to individual and state; statutory forfeiture or penalty to state; libel, slander, false imprisonment, seduction, forged or raised checks, injury to animals by feeder or veterinarian; damages for seizure; action by good faith buyer

Within one year:

(a) An action upon a statute for a penalty or forfeiture, if the action is given to an individual, or to an individual and the state, except if the statute imposing it prescribes a different limitation.

(b) An action upon a statute for a forfeiture or penalty to the people of this state.

(c) An action for libel, slander, false imprisonment, seduction of a person below the age of legal consent, or by a depositor against a bank for the payment of a forged or raised check, or a check that bears a forged or unauthorized endorsement, or against any person who boards or feeds an animal or fowl or who engages in the practice of veterinary medicine as defined in Section 4826 of the Business and Professions Code, for that person's neglect resulting in injury or death to an animal or fowl in the course of boarding or feeding the animal or fowl or in the course of the practice of veterinary medicine on that animal or fowl.

(d) An action against an officer to recover damages for the seizure of any property for a statutory forfeiture to the state, or for the detention of, or injury to property so seized, or for damages done to any person in making that seizure.

(e) An action by a good faith improver for relief under Chapter 10 (commencing with Section 871.1) of Title 10 of Part 2. The time begins to run from the date upon which the good faith improver discovers that the good faith improver is not the owner of the land upon which the improvements have been made. *(Enacted in 1872.*

§ 340

Amended by Code Am.1873–74, c. 383, p. 292, § 34; Code Am.1875–76, c. 29, p. 89, § 1; Stats.1905, c. 258, p. 232, § 2; Stats.1929, c. 518, p. 896, § 1; Stats.1939, c. 1103, p. 3036, § 1; Stats.1949, c. 863, p. 1637, § 1; Stats.1953, c. 1382, p. 2959, § 1; Stats.1963, c. 1681, p. 3284, § 2; Stats.1968, c. 150, p. 373, § 1; Stats.1973, c. 20, p. 32, § 1; Stats.1982, c. 517, p. 2334, § 97; Stats.2002, c. 448 (S.B.688), § 3.)

Cross References

Action barred for seduction of person over age of legal consent, see Civil Code § 43.5.
Action defined, see Code of Civil Procedure § 22.
Action for alienation of affections barred, see Civil Code § 43.5.
Administration of franchise and income tax laws, violations, statute of limitations, see Revenue and Taxation Code § 19704.
Banks, statement of account, correctness conclusively presumed after four years, see Financial Code § 1409.
Commencing actions for recovery of real property, entry on real estate, sufficiency, see Code of Civil Procedure § 320.
Contractors, judgment for amount of civil penalty, see Business and Professions Code § 7028.13.
Counties, recovery for care and treatment provided person injured or diseased by third person, see Government Code § 23004.1.
Death of party before expiration of limitation period, see Code of Civil Procedure §§ 366.1, 366.2, 377.20 et seq.
Directors or shareholders, actions against, see Code of Civil Procedure § 359.
Discovery, generally, see Code of Civil Procedure § 2016.010 et seq.
Employment regulation and supervision, action commenced by Division of Labor Standards Enforcement for collection of civil penalties, fees, or penalty fees that became final on or after Jan. 1, 2012, see Labor Code § 200.5.
Entry upon real estate, see Code of Civil Procedure § 320.
Estoppel and collateral estoppel, see Code of Civil Procedure § 1908; Evidence Code § 623.
Forfeiture of fishing nets when illegally used, see Fish and Game Code § 8630.
General limitations for commencing civil actions, see Code of Civil Procedure § 312 et seq.
Good faith improver of property owned by another, actions for relief fixed by subdivision 6 of this section, see Code of Civil Procedure § 871.3.
Injury to property defined, see Code of Civil Procedure § 28.
Kinds of injuries, see Code of Civil Procedure § 27.
Limitation of actions for sale of fine prints in violation of statutory regulations, see Civil Code § 1745.
Money or property deposited with bank, see Code of Civil Procedure § 348.
Occupational safety and health, enforcement of civil penalties, limitation of actions, see Labor Code § 6651.
Personal relations, seduction of person under age of consent, see Civil Code § 49.
Personal rights, wrongs not actionable, see Code of Civil Procedure § 43.5.
Property as including real and personal property, see Code of Civil Procedure § 17.
Public entities and employees, time of or presentation of claims, see Government Code §§ 911.2, 945.6.
Reversal of judgment, commencement of new action, see Code of Civil Procedure § 355.
State and United States as including District of Columbia and territories, see Code of Civil Procedure § 17.

Research References

Forms

West's California Code Forms, Civil Procedure § 340.1 Form 4, Statute of Limitations—Certificate of Merit—Plaintiff's Attorney—No Consultation—Statute of Limitations.
West's California Code Forms, Civil Procedure § 340.5 Form 1, Statute of Limitations—Pleading—Professional Negligence of Healthcare Provider—Reasonable.
West's California Code Forms, Civil Procedure § 340.7 Form 1, Statute of Limitations—Pleading—Dalkon Shield Claimants Trust Claims.
West's California Code Forms, Civil Procedure § 364 Form 1, Malpractice Actions—Notice of Intention to File Suit.
West's California Code Forms, Civil Procedure § 871.3 Form 1, Good Faith Improver—Complaint for Relief.

§ 340.1. Childhood sexual assault; certificates of merit executed by attorney; violations; failure to file; name designation of defendant; periods of limitation; presentation to government entity not required

(a) In an action for recovery of damages suffered as a result of childhood sexual assault, the time for commencement of the action shall be within 22 years of the date the plaintiff attains the age of majority or within five years of the date the plaintiff discovers or reasonably should have discovered that psychological injury or illness occurring after the age of majority was caused by the sexual assault, whichever period expires later, for any of the following actions:

(1) An action against any person for committing an act of childhood sexual assault.

(2) An action for liability against any person or entity who owed a duty of care to the plaintiff, if a wrongful or negligent act by that person or entity was a legal cause of the childhood sexual assault that resulted in the injury to the plaintiff.

(3) An action for liability against any person or entity if an intentional act by that person or entity was a legal cause of the childhood sexual assault that resulted in the injury to the plaintiff.

(b)(1) In an action described in subdivision (a), a person who is sexually assaulted and proves it was as the result of a cover up may recover up to treble damages against a defendant who is found to have covered up the sexual assault of a minor, unless prohibited by another law.

(2) For purposes of this subdivision, a "cover up" is a concerted effort to hide evidence relating to childhood sexual assault.

(c) An action described in paragraph (2) or (3) of subdivision (a) shall not be commenced on or after the plaintiff's 40th birthday unless the person or entity knew or had reason to know, or was otherwise on notice, of any misconduct that creates a risk of childhood sexual assault by an employee, volunteer, representative, or agent, or the person or entity failed to take reasonable steps or to implement reasonable safeguards to avoid acts of childhood sexual assault. For purposes of this subdivision, providing or requiring counseling is not sufficient, in and of itself, to constitute a reasonable step or reasonable safeguard. Nothing in this subdivision shall be construed to constitute a substantive change in negligence law.

(d) "Childhood sexual assault" as used in this section includes any act committed against the plaintiff that occurred when the plaintiff was under the age of 18 years and that would have been proscribed by Section 266j of the Penal Code; Section 285 of the Penal Code; paragraph (1) or (2) of subdivision (b), or of subdivision (c), of Section 286 of the Penal Code; subdivision (a) or (b) of Section 288 of the Penal Code; paragraph (1) or (2) of subdivision (b), or of subdivision (c), of Section 287 or of former Section 288a of the Penal Code; subdivision (h), (i), or (j) of Section 289 of the Penal Code; any sexual conduct as defined in paragraph (1) of subdivision (d) of Section 311.4 of the Penal Code; Section 647.6 of the Penal Code; or any prior laws of this state of similar effect at the time the act was committed. This subdivision does not limit the availability of causes of action permitted under subdivision (a), including causes of action against persons or entities other than the alleged perpetrator of the abuse.

(e) This section shall not be construed to alter the otherwise applicable burden of proof, as defined in Section 115 of the Evidence Code, that a plaintiff has in a civil action subject to this section.

(f) Every plaintiff 40 years of age or older at the time the action is filed shall file certificates of merit as specified in subdivision (g).

(g) Certificates of merit shall be executed by the attorney for the plaintiff and by a licensed mental health practitioner selected by the plaintiff declaring, respectively, as follows, setting forth the facts which support the declaration:

(1) That the attorney has reviewed the facts of the case, consulted with at least one mental health practitioner who the attorney reasonably believes is knowledgeable of the relevant facts and issues involved in the particular action, and concluded on the basis of that review and consultation that there is reasonable and meritorious cause for the filing of the action.

(2) That the mental health practitioner consulted is licensed to practice and practices in this state and is not a party to the action,

that the practitioner is not treating and has not treated the plaintiff, and that the practitioner has interviewed the plaintiff and is knowledgeable of the relevant facts and issues involved in the particular action, and has concluded, on the basis of the practitioner's knowledge of the facts and issues, that in the practitioner's professional opinion there is a reasonable basis to believe that the plaintiff had been subject to childhood sexual abuse.

(3) That the attorney was unable to obtain the consultation required by paragraph (1) because a statute of limitations would impair the action and that the certificates required by paragraphs (1) and (2) could not be obtained before the impairment of the action. If a certificate is executed pursuant to this paragraph, the certificates required by paragraphs (1) and (2) shall be filed within 60 days after filing the complaint.

(h) If certificates are required pursuant to subdivision (f), the attorney for the plaintiff shall execute a separate certificate of merit for each defendant named in the complaint.

(i) In any action subject to subdivision (f), a defendant shall not be served, and the duty to serve a defendant with process does not attach, until the court has reviewed the certificates of merit filed pursuant to subdivision (g) with respect to that defendant, and has found, in camera, based solely on those certificates of merit, that there is reasonable and meritorious cause for the filing of the action against that defendant. At that time, the duty to serve that defendant with process shall attach.

(j) A violation of this section may constitute unprofessional conduct and may be the grounds for discipline against the attorney.

(k) The failure to file certificates in accordance with this section shall be grounds for a demurrer pursuant to Section 430.10 or a motion to strike pursuant to Section 435.

(*l*) In any action subject to subdivision (f), a defendant shall be named by "Doe" designation in any pleadings or papers filed in the action until there has been a showing of corroborative fact as to the charging allegations against that defendant.

(m) At any time after the action is filed, the plaintiff may apply to the court for permission to amend the complaint to substitute the name of the defendant or defendants for the fictitious designation, as follows:

(1) The application shall be accompanied by a certificate of corroborative fact executed by the attorney for the plaintiff. The certificate shall declare that the attorney has discovered one or more facts corroborative of one or more of the charging allegations against a defendant or defendants, and shall set forth in clear and concise terms the nature and substance of the corroborative fact. If the corroborative fact is evidenced by the statement of a witness or the contents of a document, the certificate shall declare that the attorney has personal knowledge of the statement of the witness or of the contents of the document, and the identity and location of the witness or document shall be included in the certificate. For purposes of this section, a fact is corroborative of an allegation if it confirms or supports the allegation. The opinion of any mental health practitioner concerning the plaintiff shall not constitute a corroborative fact for purposes of this section.

(2) If the application to name a defendant is made before that defendant's appearance in the action, neither the application nor the certificate of corroborative fact by the attorney shall be served on the defendant or defendants, nor on any other party or their counsel of record.

(3) If the application to name a defendant is made after that defendant's appearance in the action, the application shall be served on all parties and proof of service provided to the court, but the certificate of corroborative fact by the attorney shall not be served on any party or their counsel of record.

(n) The court shall review the application and the certificate of corroborative fact in camera and, based solely on the certificate and any reasonable inferences to be drawn from the certificate, shall, if one or more facts corroborative of one or more of the charging allegations against a defendant has been shown, order that the complaint may be amended to substitute the name of the defendant or defendants.

(*o*) The court shall keep under seal and confidential from the public and all parties to the litigation, other than the plaintiff, any and all certificates of corroborative fact filed pursuant to subdivision (m).

(p) Upon the favorable conclusion of the litigation with respect to any defendant for whom a certificate of merit was filed or for whom a certificate of merit should have been filed pursuant to this section, the court may, upon the motion of a party or upon the court's own motion, verify compliance with this section by requiring the attorney for the plaintiff who was required by subdivision (g) to execute the certificate to reveal the name, address, and telephone number of the person or persons consulted with pursuant to subdivision (g) that were relied upon by the attorney in preparation of the certificate of merit. The name, address, and telephone number shall be disclosed to the trial judge in camera and in the absence of the moving party. If the court finds there has been a failure to comply with this section, the court may order a party, a party's attorney, or both, to pay any reasonable expenses, including attorney's fees, incurred by the defendant for whom a certificate of merit should have been filed.

(q) Notwithstanding any other * * * law, a claim for damages described in paragraphs (1) through (3), inclusive, of subdivision (a) that has not been litigated to finality and that would otherwise be barred as of January 1, 2020, because the applicable statute of limitations, claim presentation deadline, or any other time limit had expired, is revived, and these claims may be commenced within three years of January 1, 2020. A plaintiff shall have the later of the three-year time period under this subdivision or the time period under subdivision (a) as amended by the act that added this subdivision.

(r) The changes made to the time period under subdivision (a) as amended by the act that amended this subdivision in 2019 [1] apply to and revive any action commenced on or after the date of enactment of that act, and to any action filed before the date of enactment, and still pending on that date, including any action or causes of action that would have been barred by the laws in effect before the date of enactment.

(s) Notwithstanding any other law, including Chapter 1 of Part 3 of Division 3.6 of Title 1 of the Government Code (commencing with Section 900) and Chapter 2 of Part 3 of Division 3.6 of Title 1 of the Government Code (commencing with Section 910), a claim for damages described in paragraphs (1) through (3), inclusive, of subdivision (a), is not required to be presented to any government entity prior to the commencement of an action. (Added by Stats. 1986, c. 914, § 1. Amended by Stats.1990, c. 1578 (S.B.108), § 1; Stats.1994, c. 288 (A.B.2846), § 1; Stats.1998, c. 1032 (A.B.1651), § 1; Stats.1999, c. 120 (S.B.674), § 1; Stats.2002, c. 149 (S.B.1779), § 1; Stats.2018, c. 423 (S.B.1494), § 8, eff. Jan. 1, 2019; Stats.2019, c. 861 (A.B.218), § 1, eff. Jan. 1, 2020; Stats.2022, c. 444 (A.B.2959), § 1, eff. Jan. 1, 2023.)

[1] Stats.2019, c. 861 (A.B.218), § 1.

Validity

This section was held unconstitutional in the decision of Perez v. Roe 1 (App. 2 Dist. 2006) 52 Cal.Rptr.3d 762, 146 Cal.App.4th 171, as modified, review denied.

Cross References

Action defined, see Code of Civil Procedure § 22.
Attorney's fees and costs, generally, see Code of Civil Procedure § 1021.
Attorneys, State Bar Act, see Business and Professions Code § 6000.
Burden of proof, generally, see Evidence Code § 500 et seq.
Child abuse prevention coordinating council act, general provisions, see Welfare and Institutions Code § 18980 et seq.

§ 340.1 CODE OF CIVIL PROCEDURE

Civil action, origin, see Code of Civil Procedure § 25.
Civil action defined, see Code of Civil Procedure § 30.
Claims for money or damages against local public entities, exceptions, see Government Code § 905.
Classes of judicial remedies, see Code of Civil Procedure § 21.
Computation of time, see Code of Civil Procedure §§ 12, 12a, 12b; Government Code § 6800 et seq.
General limitations for commencing civil actions, see Code of Civil Procedure § 312 et seq.
Juvenile court law, general provisions, see Welfare and Institutions Code § 200 et seq.
Kinds of actions, see Code of Civil Procedure § 24.
Kinds of injuries, see Code of Civil Procedure § 27.
Legislative intent, construction of statutes, see Code of Civil Procedure § 1859.
Notice, actual and constructive, defined, see Civil Code § 18.
Office of child abuse prevention, legislative findings and declarations, see Welfare and Institutions Code § 18950 et seq.
Proof of service, see Code of Civil Procedure § 417.10 et seq.
Rape, abduction, carnal abuse of children, and seduction, see Penal Code § 261.
Seal defined, see Code of Civil Procedure § 14.
Service of process, generally, see Code of Civil Procedure § 410.10 et seq.
State and United States as including District of Columbia and territories, see Code of Civil Procedure § 17.
Writ and process defined, see Code of Civil Procedure § 17.

Research References

Forms

West's California Code Forms, Civil Procedure § 340.1 Form 1, Statute of Limitations—Pleading—Personal Injury Damages for Childhood Sexual Abuse.
West's California Code Forms, Civil Procedure § 340.1 Form 2, Statute of Limitations—Certificate of Merit—Plaintiff's Attorney.
West's California Code Forms, Civil Procedure § 340.1 Form 4, Statute of Limitations—Certificate of Merit—Plaintiff's Attorney—No Consultation—Statute of Limitations.
West's California Code Forms, Civil Procedure § 340.1 Form 5, Statute of Limitations—Certificate of Merit—Compliance—Notice of Motion for Order Requiring Disclosure of Consultant.
West's California Code Forms, Civil Procedure § 340.1 Form 7, Statute of Limitations—Certificate of Merit—Compliance—Notice of Motion for Order Awarding Sanctions for Noncompliance.
West's California Code Forms, Civil Procedure § 340.1 Form 9, Statute of Limitations—Childhood Sexual Abuse—Application to Amend Complaint—Substitution of Defendant's Name for Fictitious Designation.
West's California Code Forms, Civil Procedure § 340.1 Form 10, Statute of Limitations—Childhood Sexual Abuse—Certificate of Corroborative Fact—Substitution of Defendant's Name for Fictitious Designation.
West's California Code Forms, Civil Procedure § 340.1 Form 11, Statute of Limitations—Childhood Sexual Abuse—Order Allowing Amendment of Complaint—Substitution of Defendant's Name for Fictitious Designation.

§ 340.15. Action for damages suffered as result of domestic violence

(a) In any civil action for recovery of damages suffered as a result of domestic violence, the time for commencement of the action shall be the later of the following:

(1) Within three years from the date of the last act of domestic violence by the defendant against the plaintiff.

(2) Within three years from the date the plaintiff discovers or reasonably should have discovered that an injury or illness resulted from an act of domestic violence by the defendant against the plaintiff.

(b) As used in this section, "domestic violence" has the same meaning as defined in Section 6211 of the Family Code. *(Added by Stats.1995, c. 602 (S.B.924), § 1. Amended by Stats.1998, c. 123 (S.B.1939), § 1.)*

Cross References

Action defined, see Code of Civil Procedure § 22.
Civil action, origin, see Code of Civil Procedure § 25.
Civil action defined, see Code of Civil Procedure § 30.
Domestic violence, liability for tort of, see Civil Code § 1708.6.

General limitations for commencing civil actions, see Code of Civil Procedure § 312 et seq.
Kinds of actions, see Code of Civil Procedure § 24.
Kinds of injuries, see Code of Civil Procedure § 27.

Research References

Forms

West's California Code Forms, Civil Procedure § 340.15 Form 1, Statutes of Limitations—Pleading—Recovery of Damages—Domestic Violence.

§ 340.16. Action for damages suffered as result of sexual assault that occurred on or after plaintiff's 18th birthday

(a) In any civil action for recovery of damages suffered as a result of sexual assault, where the assault occurred on or after the plaintiff's 18th birthday, the time for commencement of the action shall be the later of the following:

(1) Within 10 years from the date of the last act, attempted act, or assault with the intent to commit an act, of sexual assault against the plaintiff.

(2) Within three years from the date the plaintiff discovers or reasonably should have discovered that an injury or illness resulted from an act, attempted act, or assault with the intent to commit an act, of sexual assault against the plaintiff.

(b)(1) As used in this section, "sexual assault" means any of the crimes described in Section 243.4, 261, * * * 264.1, 286, 287, or 289, or former * * * Sections 262 and 288a, of the Penal Code, assault with the intent to commit any of those crimes, or an attempt to commit any of those crimes.

(2) For the purpose of this section, it is not necessary that a criminal prosecution or other proceeding have been brought as a result of the sexual assault or, if a criminal prosecution or other proceeding was brought, that the prosecution or proceeding resulted in a conviction or adjudication. This subdivision does not limit the availability of causes of action permitted under subdivision (a), including causes of action against persons or entities other than the alleged person who committed the crime.

(3) This section applies to any action described in subdivision (a) that is based upon conduct that occurred on or after January 1, 2009, and is commenced on or after January 1, 2019 * * *, that would have been barred solely because the applicable statute of limitations has or had expired. Such claims are hereby revived and may be commenced until December 31, 2026. This subdivision does not revive any of the following claims:

(A) A claim that has been litigated to finality in a court of competent jurisdiction before January 1, 2023.

(B) A claim that has been compromised by a written settlement agreement between the parties entered into before January 1, 2023.

(c)(1) Notwithstanding any other law, any claim seeking to recover more than two hundred fifty thousand dollars ($250,000) in damages arising out of a sexual assault or other inappropriate contact, communication, or activity of a sexual nature by a physician occurring at a student health center between January 1, 1988, and January 1, 2017, that would otherwise be barred before January 1, 2020, solely because the applicable statute of limitations has or had expired, is hereby revived and, a cause of action may proceed if already pending in court on October 2, 2019, or, if not filed by that date, may be commenced between January 1, 2020, and December 31, 2020.

(2) This subdivision does not revive any of the following claims:

(A) A claim that has been litigated to finality in a court of competent jurisdiction before January 1, 2020.

(B) A claim that has been compromised by a written settlement agreement between the parties entered into before January 1, 2020.

(C) A claim brought against a public entity.

(3) An attorney representing a claimant seeking to recover under this subdivision shall file a declaration with the court under penalty of perjury stating that the attorney has reviewed the facts of the case and consulted with a mental health practitioner, and that the attorney has concluded on the basis of this review and consultation that it is the attorney's good faith belief that the claim value is more than two hundred fifty thousand dollars ($250,000). The declaration shall be filed upon filing the complaint, or for those claims already pending, by December 1, 2019.

(d)(1) Notwithstanding any other law, any claim seeking to recover damages arising out of a sexual assault or other inappropriate contact, communication, or activity of a sexual nature by a physician while employed by a medical clinic owned and operated by the University of California, Los Angeles, or a physician who held active privileges at a hospital owned and operated by the University of California, Los Angeles, at the time that the sexual assault or other inappropriate contact, communication, or activity of a sexual nature occurred, between January 1, 1983, and January 1, 2019, that would otherwise be barred before January 1, 2021, solely because the applicable statute of limitations has or had expired, is hereby revived, and a cause of action may proceed if already pending in court on January 1, 2021, or, if not filed by that date, may be commenced between January 1, 2021, and December 31, 2021.

(2) This subdivision does not revive either of the following claims:

(A) A claim that has been litigated to finality in a court of competent jurisdiction before January 1, 2021.

(B) A claim that has been compromised by a written settlement agreement between the parties entered into before January 1, 2021.

(e)(1) Notwithstanding any other law, any claim seeking to recover damages suffered as a result of a sexual assault that occurred on or after the plaintiff's 18th birthday that would otherwise be barred before January 1, 2023, solely because the applicable statute of limitations has or had expired, is hereby revived, and a cause of action may proceed if already pending in court on January 1, 2023, or, if not filed by that date, may be commenced between January 1, 2023, and December 31, 2023.

(2) This subdivision revives claims brought by a plaintiff who alleges all of the following:

(A) The plaintiff was sexually assaulted.

(B) One or more entities are legally responsible for damages arising out of the sexual assault.

(C) The entity or entities, including, but not limited to, their officers, directors, representatives, employees, or agents, engaged in a cover up or attempted a cover up of a previous instance or allegations of sexual assault by an alleged perpetrator of such abuse.

(3) Failure to allege a cover up as required by subparagraph (C) of paragraph (2) as to one entity does not affect revival of the plaintiff's claim or claims against any other entity.

(4) For purposes of this subdivision:

(A) "Cover up" means a concerted effort to hide evidence relating to a sexual assault that incentivizes individuals to remain silent or prevents information relating to a sexual assault from becoming public or being disclosed to the plaintiff, including, but not limited to, the use of nondisclosure agreements or confidentiality agreements.

(B) "Entity" means a sole proprietorship, partnership, limited liability company, corporation, association, or other legal entity.

(C) "Legally responsible" means that the entity or entities are liable under any theory of liability established by statute or common law, including, but not limited to, negligence, intentional torts, and vicarious liability.

(5) This subdivision revives any related claims, including, but not limited to, wrongful termination and sexual harassment, arising out of the sexual assault that is the basis for a claim pursuant to this subdivision.

(6) This subdivision does not revive either of the following claims:

(A) A claim that has been litigated to finality in a court of competent jurisdiction before January 1, 2023.

(B) A claim that has been compromised by a written settlement agreement between the parties entered into before January 1, 2023.

(7) This subdivision shall not be construed to alter the otherwise applicable burden of proof, as defined in Section 115 of the Evidence Code, that a plaintiff has in a civil action subject to this section.

(8) Nothing in this subdivision precludes a plaintiff from bringing an action for sexual assault pursuant to subdivisions (a) and (b). *(Added by Stats.2018, c. 939 (A.B.1619), § 1, eff. Jan. 1, 2019. Amended by Stats.2019, c. 462 (A.B.1510), § 1, eff. Oct. 2, 2019; Stats.2020, c. 246 (A.B.3092), § 1, eff. Jan. 1, 2021; Stats.2022, c. 442 (A.B.2777), § 3, eff. Jan. 1, 2023.)*

Research References

Forms

West's California Code Forms, Civil Procedure § 340.11 Form 1, Statute of Limitations—Action for Damages Suffered as a Result of Sexual Assault that Occurred on or After Plaintiff's 18th Birthday Three Year Ten Year Time Periods.

§ 340.2. Exposure to asbestos; actions for injury, illness or wrongful death

(a) In any civil action for injury or illness based upon exposure to asbestos, the time for the commencement of the action shall be the later of the following:

(1) Within one year after the date the plaintiff first suffered disability.

(2) Within one year after the date the plaintiff either knew, or through the exercise of reasonable diligence should have known, that such disability was caused or contributed to by such exposure.

(b) "Disability" as used in subdivision (a) means the loss of time from work as a result of such exposure which precludes the performance of the employee's regular occupation.

(c) In an action for the wrongful death of any plaintiff's decedent, based upon exposure to asbestos, the time for commencement of an action shall be the later of the following:

(1) Within one year from the date of the death of the plaintiff's decedent.

(2) Within one year from the date the death was caused or contributed to by such *Stats.1979, c. 513, p. 1689, § 1.)* the plaintiff first knew, or diligence should have known, that exposure. *(Added by*

Cross References

Action defined, see Code of Civil Procedure § 22.
Airborne asbestos monitoring in public schools, see Health and Safety Code § 24275.
Civil action, origin, see Code of Civil Procedure § 25.
Civil action defined, see Code of Civil Procedure § 30.
Classes of judicial remedies, see Code of Civil Procedure § 21.
General limitations for commencing civil actions, see Code of Civil Procedure § 312 et seq.
Kinds of actions, see Code of Civil Procedure § 24.
Kinds of injuries, see Code of Civil Procedure § 27.

Research References

Forms

West's California Code Forms, Civil Procedure § 340.2 Form 1, Statute of Limitations—Pleading—Asbestos Exposure—Reasonable Diligence.

§ 340.3. Actions for damages against defendant arising from felony offense; limitation of actions; stay of judgment; restitution

(a) Unless a longer period is prescribed for a specific action, in any action for damages against a defendant based upon the

§ 340.3

defendant's commission of a felony offense for which the defendant has been convicted, the time for commencement of the action shall be within one year after judgment is pronounced.

(b)(1) Notwithstanding subdivision (a), an action for damages against a defendant based upon the defendant's commission of a felony offense for which the defendant has been convicted may be commenced within 10 years of the date on which the defendant is discharged from parole if the conviction was for any offense specified in paragraph (1), except voluntary manslaughter, (2), (3), (4), (5), (6), (7), (9), (16), (17), (20), (22), (25), (34), or (35) of subdivision (c) of Section 1192.7 of the Penal Code.

(2) No civil action may be commenced pursuant to paragraph (1) if any of the following applies:

(A) The defendant has received either a certificate of rehabilitation as provided in Chapter 3.5 (commencing with Section 4852.01) of Title 6 of Part 3 of the Penal Code or a pardon as provided in Chapter 1 (commencing with Section 4800) or Chapter 3 (commencing with Section 4850) of Title 6 of Part 3 of the Penal Code.

(B) Following a conviction for murder or attempted murder, the defendant has been paroled based in whole or in part upon evidence presented to the Board of Prison Terms that the defendant committed the crime because he or she was the victim of intimate partner battering.

(C) The defendant was convicted of murder or attempted murder in the second degree in a trial at which substantial evidence was presented that the person committed the crime because he or she was a victim of intimate partner battering.

(D) The defendant was unlawfully imprisoned or restrained but has been released from prison after successfully prosecuting a writ of habeas corpus pursuant to Chapter 1 (commencing with Section 1473) of Title 12 of Part 2 of the Penal Code.

(c) If the sentence or judgment is stayed, the time for the commencement of the action shall be tolled until the stay is lifted. For purposes of this section, a judgment is not stayed if the judgment is appealed or the defendant is placed on probation.

(d)(1) Subdivision (b) shall apply to any action commenced before, on, or after the effective date of this section, including any action otherwise barred by a limitation of time in effect prior to the effective date of this section, thereby reviving those causes of action that had lapsed or expired under the law in effect prior to the effective date of this section.

(2) Paragraph (1) does not apply to either of the following:

(A) Any claim that has been litigated to finality on the merits in any court of competent jurisdiction prior to January 1, 2003. For purposes of this section, termination of a prior action on the basis of the statute of limitations does not constitute a claim that has been litigated to finality on the merits.

(B) Any written, compromised settlement agreement that has been entered into between a plaintiff and a defendant if the plaintiff was represented by an attorney who was admitted to practice law in this state at the time of the settlement, and the plaintiff signed the agreement.

(e) Any restitution paid by the defendant to the victim shall be credited against any judgment, award, or settlement obtained pursuant to this section. Any judgment, award, or settlement obtained pursuant to an action under this section shall be subject to the provisions of Section 13963 of the Government Code. *(Added by Stats.1983, c. 938, § 2, eff. Sept. 20, 1983. Amended by Stats.2002, c. 633 (S.B.1887), § 1, eff. Sept. 18, 2002; Stats.2005, c. 215 (A.B.220), § 1; Stats.2015, c. 465 (A.B.538), § 1, eff. Jan. 1, 2016.)*

Cross References

Action defined, see Code of Civil Procedure § 22.
Attorney's fees, action for damages arising from felony offense, see Code of Civil Procedure § 1021.4.
Attorneys, State Bar Act, see Business and Professions Code § 6000.
Civil action, origin, see Code of Civil Procedure § 25.
Civil action defined, see Code of Civil Procedure § 30.
Classes of judicial remedies, see Code of Civil Procedure § 21.
General limitations for commencing civil actions, see Code of Civil Procedure § 312 et seq.
Kinds of actions, see Code of Civil Procedure § 24.
Periods of limitation, see Code of Civil Procedure § 335.
Preference, action for damages incurred during felony, see Code of Civil Procedure § 37.
State and United States as including District of Columbia and territories, see Code of Civil Procedure § 17.

Research References

Forms

West's California Code Forms, Civil Procedure § 340.3 Form 1, Statute of Limitations—Pleading—Damages Arising from Felony Offense—Tolling—Stay of Judgment of Conviction.

§ 340.35. Causes of action involving sexual abuse of a minor; statutes of limitation

(a) This section shall apply if both of the following conditions are met:

(1) A complaint, information, or indictment was filed in a criminal case initiated pursuant to subdivision (f), (g), or (h) of Section 803 of the Penal Code.

(2) The case was dismissed or overturned pursuant to the United States Supreme Court's decision in Stogner v. California (2003) 156 L.Ed.2d 544.

(b) Unless a longer period is prescribed for a specific action, any action for damages against an individual for committing an act of childhood sexual abuse shall be commenced before January 1, 2006.

(c) This section shall apply to any action commenced before, on, or after the effective date of this section, including any action otherwise barred by a limitation of time in effect prior to the effective date of this section, thereby reviving those causes of action that had lapsed or expired under the law in effect prior to the effective date of this section.

(d) This section shall not apply to any of the following:

(1) Any claim against a person or entity other than the individual against whom a complaint, information, or indictment was filed as described in paragraph (1) of subdivision (a).

(2) Any claim that has been litigated to finality on the merits in any court of competent jurisdiction prior to the effective date of this section. For purposes of this section, termination of a prior action on the basis of the statute of limitations does not constitute a claim that has been "litigated to finality on the merits."

(3) Any written, compromised settlement agreement that has been entered into between a plaintiff and a defendant, if the plaintiff was represented by an attorney who was admitted to practice law in this state at the time of the settlement, and the plaintiff signed the agreement.

(e) Any restitution paid by the defendant to the victim shall be credited against any judgment, award, or settlement obtained pursuant to this section. Any judgment, award, or settlement obtained pursuant to an action under this section shall be subject to Section 13966.01 of the Government Code. *(Added by Stats.2004, c. 741 (S.B.1678), § 1.)*

Cross References

Action defined, see Code of Civil Procedure § 22.
Attorneys, State Bar Act, see Business and Professions Code § 6000.

State and United States as including District of Columbia and territories, see Code of Civil Procedure § 17.

§ 340.4. Minors; action for personal injuries before or during birth; limitation of actions

An action by or on behalf of a minor for personal injuries sustained before or in the course of his or her birth must be commenced within six years after the date of birth, and the time the minor is under any disability mentioned in Section 352 shall not be excluded in computing the time limited for the commencement of the action. *(Added by Stats.1992, c. 163 (A.B.2641), § 16, operative Jan. 1, 1994.)*

Cross References

Action defined, see Code of Civil Procedure § 22.
Classes of judicial remedies, see Code of Civil Procedure § 21.
Kinds of injuries, see Code of Civil Procedure § 27.

Research References

Forms

West's California Code Forms, Civil Procedure § 340.8 Form 1, Statutes of Limitation—Action for Personal Injury or Wrongful Death—Toxic Injuries—Two-Year Time Period.

§ 340.5. Action against health care provider; three years from injury or one year from discovery; exceptions; minors

In an action for injury or death against a health care provider based upon such person's alleged professional negligence, the time for the commencement of action shall be three years after the date of injury or one year after the plaintiff discovers, or through the use of reasonable diligence should have discovered, the injury, whichever occurs first. In no event shall the time for commencement of legal action exceed three years unless tolled for any of the following: (1) upon proof of fraud, (2) intentional concealment, or (3) the presence of a foreign body, which has no therapeutic or diagnostic purpose or effect, in the person of the injured person. Actions by a minor shall be commenced within three years from the date of the alleged wrongful act except that actions by a minor under the full age of six years shall be commenced within three years or prior to his eighth birthday whichever provides a longer period. Such time limitation shall be tolled for minors for any period during which parent or guardian and defendant's insurer or health care provider have committed fraud or collusion in the failure to bring an action on behalf of the injured minor for professional negligence.

For the purposes of this section:

(1) "Health care provider" means any person licensed or certified pursuant to Division 2 (commencing with Section 500) of the Business and Professions Code, or licensed pursuant to the Osteopathic Initiative Act, or the Chiropractic Initiative Act, or licensed pursuant to Chapter 2.5 (commencing with Section 1440) of Division 2 of the Health and Safety Code; and any clinic, health dispensary, or health facility, licensed pursuant to Division 2 (commencing with Section 1200) of the Health and Safety Code. "Health care provider" includes the legal representatives of a health care provider;

(2) "Professional negligence" means a negligent act or omission to act by a health care provider in the rendering of professional services, which act or omission is the proximate cause of a personal injury or wrongful death, provided that such services are within the scope of services for which the provider is licensed and which are not within any restriction imposed by the licensing agency or licensed hospital. *(Added by Stats.1970, c. 360, p. 772, § 1. Amended by Stats.1975, 2nd Ex.Sess., c. 1, p. 3969, § 25; Stats.1975, 2nd Ex.Sess., c. 2, p. 3991, § 1.192, eff. Sept. 24, 1975, operative Dec. 15, 1975.)*

Cross References

Action defined, see Code of Civil Procedure § 22.
Actions based upon professional negligence, see Code of Civil Procedure § 364 et seq.
Civil actions for abuse of elderly or dependent adults, negligence of health care providers, law governing, see Welfare and Institutions Code § 15657.2.
Classes of judicial remedies, see Code of Civil Procedure § 21.
Discovery, generally, see Code of Civil Procedure § 2016.010 et seq.
Fraud, actual or constructive, see Civil Code §§ 1572 to 1574.
General limitations for commencing civil actions, see Code of Civil Procedure § 312 et seq.
Health care service plans, standards, process for review of requests by health care service providers, see Health and Safety Code § 1367.01.
Health care service plans and managed care entities, duty of ordinary care, see Civil Code § 3428.
Kinds of injuries, see Code of Civil Procedure § 27.
Medical malpractice, see Code of Civil Procedure § 340.
Process for review of requests by health care service providers, see Insurance Code § 10123.135.

Research References

Forms

West's California Code Forms, Civil Procedure § 335.1 Form 1, Statutes of Limitation—Action for Assault, Battery, Injury, or Death on Another Due to Negligence—Two-Year Time Period.

West's California Code Forms, Civil Procedure § 340.5 Form 1, Statute of Limitations—Pleading—Professional Negligence of Healthcare Provider—Reasonable.

West's California Code Forms, Civil Procedure § 340.5 Form 2, Statute of Limitations—Pleading—Professional Negligence of Health Care Provider—Tolling—Fraud—Concealment—Foreign Body.

West's California Code Forms, Civil Procedure § 340.5 Form 3, Statute of Limitations—Pleading—Professional Negligence of Health Care Provider—Tolling—Fraud—Collusion.

West's California Code Forms, Civil Procedure § 352.1 Form 1, Statute of Limitations—Tolling—Imprisonment—Contract Actions.

West's California Code Forms, Civil Procedure § 364 Form 1, Malpractice Actions—Notice of Intention to File Suit.

§ 340.6. Attorneys; wrongful professional act or omission; tolling of period

(a) An action against an attorney for a wrongful act or omission, other than for actual fraud, arising in the performance of professional services shall be commenced within one year after the plaintiff discovers, or through the use of reasonable diligence should have discovered, the facts constituting the wrongful act or omission, or four years from the date of the wrongful act or omission, whichever occurs first. If the plaintiff is required to establish the plaintiff's factual innocence for an underlying criminal charge as an element of the plaintiff's claim, the action shall be commenced within two years after the plaintiff achieves postconviction exoneration in the form of a final judicial disposition of the criminal case. Except for a claim for which the plaintiff is required to establish the plaintiff's factual innocence, the time for commencement of legal action shall not exceed four years except that the period shall be tolled during the time that any of the following exist:

(1) The plaintiff has not sustained actual injury.

(2) The attorney continues to represent the plaintiff regarding the specific subject matter in which the alleged wrongful act or omission occurred.

(3) The attorney willfully conceals the facts constituting the wrongful act or omission when those facts are known to the attorney, except that this subdivision shall toll only the four-year limitation.

(4) The plaintiff is under a legal or physical disability that restricts the plaintiff's ability to commence legal action.

(5) A dispute between the lawyer and client concerning fees, costs, or both is pending resolution under Article 13 (commencing with Section 6200) of Chapter 4 of Division 3 of the Business and Professions Code. As used in this paragraph, "pending" means from the date a request for arbitration is filed until 30 days after receipt of notice of the award of the arbitrators, or receipt of notice that the arbitration is otherwise terminated, whichever occurs first.

(b) In an action based upon an instrument in writing, the effective date of which depends upon some act or event of the future, the

§ 340.6

period of limitations provided for by this section shall commence to run upon the occurrence of that act or event. *(Added by Stats.1977, c. 863, p. 2609, § 1. Amended by Stats.2009, c. 432 (A.B.316), § 2; Stats.2019, c. 13 (A.B.692), § 2, eff. Jan. 1, 2020.)*

Cross References

Action defined, see Code of Civil Procedure § 22.
Attorneys, State Bar Act, see Business and Professions Code § 6000.
Fraud, actual or constructive, see Civil Code §§ 1572 to 1574.
General limitations for commencing civil actions, see Code of Civil Procedure § 312 et seq.
Kinds of injuries, see Code of Civil Procedure § 27.
Legal malpractice actions, see Code of Civil Procedure § 339.
Professions and vocations, attorneys, general provisions, see Business and Professions Code § 6000 et seq.

Research References

Forms

1 California Transactions Forms--Estate Planning § 2:5, Necessity of Privity Between Estate Planner and Ultimate Beneficiary.
1 California Transactions Forms--Estate Planning § 2:7, Statute of Limitations; Tolling.
1 California Transactions Forms--Estate Planning § 2:8, Conduct of Practitioner to Limit Tolling of Statute of Limitations.
1 California Transactions Forms--Estate Planning § 2:46, Matters to Consider to Avoid Malpractice.
1 California Transactions Forms--Estate Planning § 2:56, Letter Terminating Attorney-Client Relationship.
West's California Code Forms, Civil Procedure § 340.6 Form 1, Statute of Limitations—Pleading—Professional Negligence of Attorney—Tolling—Legal Disability.
West's California Code Forms, Civil Procedure § 340.6 Form 2, Statute of Limitations—Pleading—Professional Negligence of Attorney—Tolling—Discovery of Facts.

§ 340.7. Dalkon Shield Claimants' Trust claims; tolling for bankruptcy of A.H. Robins Co.

(a) Notwithstanding Section 335.1, a civil action brought by, or on behalf of, a Dalkon Shield victim against the Dalkon Shield Claimants' Trust, shall be brought in accordance with the procedures established by A.H. Robins Company, Inc. Plan of Reorganization, and shall be brought within 15 years of the date on which the victim's injury occurred, except that the statute shall be tolled from August 21, 1985, the date on which the A.H. Robins Company filed for Chapter 11 Reorganization in Richmond, Virginia.

(b) This section applies regardless of when the action or claim shall have accrued or been filed and regardless of whether it might have lapsed or otherwise be barred by time under California law. However, this section shall only apply to victims who, prior to January 1, 1990, filed a civil action, a timely claim, or a claim that is declared to be timely under the sixth Amended and Restated Disclosure Statement filed pursuant to Section 1125 of the Federal Bankruptcy Code in re: A.H. Robins Company, Inc., dated March 28, 1988, U.S. Bankruptcy Court, Eastern District of Virginia (case number 85–01307–R). *(Added by Stats.1994, c. 107 (A.B.2855), § 1. Amended by Stats.2007, c. 130 (A.B.299), § 35; Stats.2008, c. 179 (S.B.1498), § 34.)*

Cross References

Action defined, see Code of Civil Procedure § 22.
Civil action, origin, see Code of Civil Procedure § 25.
Civil action defined, see Code of Civil Procedure § 30.
Kinds of actions, see Code of Civil Procedure § 24.
Kinds of injuries, see Code of Civil Procedure § 27.

§ 340.8. Exposure to hazardous materials or toxic substances; time for commencement of action; injury or illness; wrongful death actions; definitions

(a) In any civil action for injury or illness based upon exposure to a hazardous material or toxic substance, the time for commencement of the action shall be no later than either two years from the date of injury, or two years after the plaintiff becomes aware of, or reasonably should have become aware of, (1) an injury, (2) the physical cause of the injury, and (3) sufficient facts to put a reasonable person on inquiry notice that the injury was caused or contributed to by the wrongful act of another, whichever occurs later.

(b) In an action for the wrongful death of any plaintiff's decedent, based upon exposure to a hazardous material or toxic substance, the time for commencement of an action shall be no later than either (1) two years from the date of the death of the plaintiff's decedent, or (2) two years from the first date on which the plaintiff is aware of, or reasonably should have become aware of, the physical cause of the death and sufficient facts to put a reasonable person on inquiry notice that the death was caused or contributed to by the wrongful act of another, whichever occurs later.

(c) For purposes of this section:

(1) A "civil action for injury or illness based upon exposure to a hazardous material or toxic substance" does not include an action subject to Section 340.2 or 340.5.

(2) Media reports regarding the hazardous material or toxic substance contamination do not, in and of themselves, constitute sufficient facts to put a reasonable person on inquiry notice that the injury or death was caused or contributed to by the wrongful act of another.

(d) Nothing in this section shall be construed to limit, abrogate, or change the law in effect on the effective date of this section with respect to actions not based upon exposure to a hazardous material or toxic substance. *(Added by Stats.2003, c. 873 (S.B.331), § 1.)*

Cross References

Action defined, see Code of Civil Procedure § 22.
Civil action, origin, see Code of Civil Procedure § 25.
Civil action defined, see Code of Civil Procedure § 30.
Classes of judicial remedies, see Code of Civil Procedure § 21.
Kinds of actions, see Code of Civil Procedure § 24.
Kinds of injuries, see Code of Civil Procedure § 27.
Notice, actual and constructive, defined, see Civil Code § 18.

Research References

Forms

West's California Code Forms, Civil Procedure § 340.8 Form 1, Statutes of Limitation—Action for Personal Injury or Wrongful Death—Toxic Injuries—Two-Year Time Period.

§ 340.9. Northridge earthquake insurance claims

(a) Notwithstanding any other provision of law or contract, any insurance claim for damages arising out of the Northridge earthquake of 1994 which is barred as of the effective date of this section solely because the applicable statute of limitations has or had expired is hereby revived and a cause of action thereon may be commenced provided that the action is commenced within one year of the effective date of this section. This subdivision shall only apply to cases in which an insured contacted an insurer or an insurer's representative prior to January 1, 2000, regarding potential Northridge earthquake damage.

(b) Any action pursuant to this section commenced prior to, or within one year from, the effective date of this section shall not be barred based upon this limitations period.

(c) Nothing in this section shall be construed to alter the applicable limitations period of an action that is not time barred as of the effective date of this section.

(d) This section shall not apply to either of the following:

(1) Any claim that has been litigated to finality in any court of competent jurisdiction prior to the effective date of this section.

(2) Any written compromised settlement agreement which has been made between an insurer and its insured where the insured was represented by counsel admitted to the practice of law in California

at the time of the settlement, and who signed the agreement. *(Added by Stats.2000, c. 1090 (S.B.1899), § 1.)*

Cross References

Action defined, see Code of Civil Procedure § 22.

Research References

Forms

West's California Code Forms, Civil Procedure § 340.9 Form 1, Statutes of Limitation—Northridge Earthquake Insurance Claims—Revival of Barred Claims.

§ 340.10. "Terrorist victim" defined; statute of limitations for actions brought for injury or death to terrorist victim

(a) For purposes of this section, "terrorist victim" means any individual who died or was injured as a consequence of the terrorist-related aircraft crashes of September 11, 2001, including persons who were present at the World Trade Center in New York City, New York, the Pentagon in Arlington, Virginia, or at the site of the crash at Shanksville, Pennsylvania, or in the immediate aftermath of the terrorist-related aircraft crashes of September 11, 2001, including members of the flight crew and passengers on American Airlines Flight 11, American Airlines Flight 77, United Airlines Flight 175, and United Airlines Flight 93, and who suffered physical harm or death as a result of any of the crashes, as defined in Section 40101 of Title 49 of the United States Code and the related, applicable regulations, other than an individual identified by the Attorney General of the United States as a participant or conspirator in the terrorist-related aircraft crashes, or a representative or heir of such an individual.

(b) The statute of limitations for injury or death set forth in Section 335.1 shall apply to any action brought for injury to, or for the death of, any terrorist victim described in subdivision (a) and caused by the wrongful act or neglect of another, regardless of whether that action lapsed or was otherwise barred by time under California law predating the passage of this section and Section 335.1. *(Added by Stats.2002, c. 448 (S.B.688), § 4.)*

Cross References

Action defined, see Code of Civil Procedure § 22.
Attorney General, generally, see Government Code § 12500 et seq.
Attorneys, State Bar Act, see Business and Professions Code § 6000.
Classes of judicial remedies, see Code of Civil Procedure § 21.
Kinds of injuries, see Code of Civil Procedure § 27.
State and United States as including District of Columbia and territories, see Code of Civil Procedure § 17.

Research References

Forms

West's California Code Forms, Civil Procedure § 340.10 Form 1, Statutes of Limitation—Action for Personal Injury or Wrongful Death of Another—Terrorist Victims of September 11, 2001 Attacks—Two-Year Time Period.

§ 341. Six months; officer for seizure as tax collector; stock sold for delinquent assessment; vacation of act of trustees of dissolved corporation

Within six months:

An action against an officer, or officer de facto:

1. To recover any goods, wares, merchandise, or other property, seized by any such officer in his official capacity as tax collector, or to recover the price or value of any goods, wares, merchandise, or other personal property so seized, or for damages for the seizure, detention, sale of, or injury to any goods, wares, merchandise, or other personal property seized, or for damages done to any person or property in making any such seizure.

2. To recover stock sold for a delinquent assessment, as provided in section three hundred forty-seven of the Civil Code.[1]

3. To set aside or invalidate any action taken or performed by a majority of the trustees of any corporation heretofore or hereafter dissolved by operation of law, including the revivor of any such corporation. *(Enacted in 1872. Amended by Code Am.1873–74, c. 383, p. 292, § 35; Stats.1917, c. 217, p. 381, § 1.)*

[1] Now Corporations Code § 423.

Cross References

Action defined, see Code of Civil Procedure § 22.
Assessment of shares, see Corporations Code § 423.
Dissenting shareholders, action against corporation, limitation of six months, see Corporations Code § 1304.
General limitations for commencing civil actions, see Code of Civil Procedure § 312 et seq.
Kinds of injuries, see Code of Civil Procedure § 27.
Month defined, see Code of Civil Procedure § 17.
Personal property as including money, goods, chattels, things in action, and evidences of debt, see Code of Civil Procedure § 17.
Property as including real and personal property, see Code of Civil Procedure § 17.
Suit against sureties on contractor's bond on public work, six months' limitations, see Civil Code § 9558.
Taxpayer refund actions, see Revenue and Taxation Code § 5140 et seq.

§ 341.5. Actions challenging the constitutionality of state funding for municipalities, school districts, special districts, or local agencies; commencement

Notwithstanding any other provision of law, any action or proceeding in which a county, city, city and county, school district, special district, or any other local agency is a plaintiff or petitioner, that is brought against the State of California challenging the constitutionality of any statute relating to state funding for counties, cities, cities and counties, school districts, special districts, or other local agencies, shall be commenced within 90 days of the effective date of the statute at issue in the action. For purposes of this section, "State of California" means the State of California itself, or any of its agencies, departments, commissions, boards, or public officials. *(Added by Stats.1994, c. 155 (A.B.860), § 1, eff. July 11, 1994. Amended by Stats.1994, c. 156 (S.B.2127), § 1, eff. July 11, 1994.)*

Cross References

Action defined, see Code of Civil Procedure § 22.
Classes of judicial remedies, see Code of Civil Procedure § 21.
Computation of time, see Code of Civil Procedure §§ 12, 12a, 12b; Government Code § 6800 et seq.
State and United States as including District of Columbia and territories, see Code of Civil Procedure § 17.

§ 341a. Ninety days; recovery or conversion of personal property, baggage, etc., left at hotel, hospital, boarding house, etc.

All civil actions for the recovery or conversion of personal property, wearing apparel, trunks, valises or baggage alleged to have been left at a hotel, hospital, rest home, sanitarium, boarding house, lodging house, furnished apartment house, or furnished bungalow court, shall be begun within 90 days from and after the date of the departure of the owner of said personal property, wearing apparel, trunks, valises or baggage from said hotel, hospital, rest home, sanitarium, boarding house, lodging house, furnished apartment house, or furnished bungalow court. *(Added by Stats.1921, c. 152, p. 150, § 1. Amended by Stats.1927, c. 826, p. 1657, § 1; Stats.1943, c. 405, p. 1930, § 1.)*

Cross References

Action defined, see Code of Civil Procedure § 22.
Civil action, origin, see Code of Civil Procedure § 25.
Civil action defined, see Code of Civil Procedure § 30.
Claim and delivery of personal property, words and phrases defined, see Code of Civil Procedure § 511.010 et seq.
Classes of judicial remedies, see Code of Civil Procedure § 21.
Computation of time, see Code of Civil Procedure §§ 12, 12a, 12b; Government Code § 6800 et seq.

§ 341a

General limitations for commencing civil actions, see Code of Civil Procedure § 312 et seq.
Kinds of actions, see Code of Civil Procedure § 24.
Municipal incorporation annexation or consolidation, see Code of Civil Procedure § 349½.
Personal property as including money, goods, chattels, things in action, and evidences of debt, see Code of Civil Procedure § 17.
Property as including real and personal property, see Code of Civil Procedure § 17.
Refund actions, see Revenue and Taxation Code § 19384.
Sales or use tax refund, see Revenue and Taxation Code § 6933.
Three year limitation to commence actions other than for recovery of real property, see Code of Civil Procedure § 338.

§ 342. Actions against public entities

An action against a public entity upon a cause of action for which a claim is required to be presented in accordance with Chapter 1 (commencing with Section 900) and Chapter 2 (commencing with Section 910) of Part 3 of Division 3.6 of Title 1 of the Government Code must be commenced within the time provided in Section 945.6 of the Government Code. (Added by Stats.1963, c. 1715, p. 3394, § 4.)

Cross References

Action defined, see Code of Civil Procedure § 22.
Classes of judicial remedies, see Code of Civil Procedure § 21.
General limitations for commencing civil actions, see Code of Civil Procedure § 312 et seq.

§ 343. Four years; relief not otherwise provided for

An action for relief not hereinbefore provided for must be commenced within four years after the cause of action shall have accrued. (Enacted in 1872.)

Cross References

Action, as including special proceeding, see Code of Civil Procedure § 363.
Action defined, see Code of Civil Procedure § 22.
Administration of franchise and income tax laws, jeopardy assessments, due date, see Revenue and Taxation Code § 19083.
Allowance or rejection of claims in whole or part, see Probate Code § 9250.
Annulment of marriage, see Family Code § 2210 et seq.
Classes of judicial remedies, see Code of Civil Procedure § 21.
Community property, see Family Code §§ 700, 760, 803.
Corporations, action to recover shares sold for delinquent assessments, see Corporations Code § 423.
Death of party before expiration of limitation period, see Code of Civil Procedure §§ 366.1, 366.2, 377.20 et seq.
Definitions, personal representative, see Probate Code § 58.
Entry upon real estate, see Code of Civil Procedure § 320.
Financial institutions, actions to recover deposits, see Code of Civil Procedure § 348.
General limitations for commencing civil actions, see Code of Civil Procedure § 312 et seq.
Instrument in writing, four year limitation, see Code of Civil Procedure § 337.
Liens, extinguishment by lapse of time, see Civil Code § 2911.
Mailing notice of hearing, requirements, see Probate Code § 1220.
Personal representatives, action to recover property sold by, see Probate Code § 10382.
Public nuisance, lapse of time, see Civil Code § 3490.
Reversal on appeal, commencement of new action, see Code of Civil Procedure § 355.

Research References

Forms
4 California Transactions Forms--Business Entities § 20:21, Right to Final Accounting.

§ 344. Balance upon mutual, open and current account; accrual of cause

In an action brought to recover a balance due upon a mutual, open, and current account, where there have been reciprocal demands between the parties, the cause of action is deemed to have accrued from the time of the last item proved in the account on either side. (Enacted in 1872.)

Cross References

Action defined, see Code of Civil Procedure § 22.
Action to recover balance due upon mutual, open, and current account, see Code of Civil Procedure § 337.
General limitations for commencing civil actions, see Code of Civil Procedure § 312 et seq.

§ 345. Actions in name of state or county; applicability of chapter; support of patients at state or county hospitals; four year limit

The limitations prescribed in this chapter apply to actions brought in the name of the state or county or for the benefit of the state or county, in the same manner as to actions by private parties. Accounts for the support of patients at state or county hospitals are book accounts as defined in Section 337a, and actions on them may be commenced at any time within four years after the last date of service or the last date of payment. (Enacted in 1872. Amended by Stats.1905, c. 381, p. 487, § 1; Stats.1921, c. 475, p. 722, § 1; Stats.1943, c. 177, p. 1071, § 1; Stats.1984, c. 797, § 1.)

Cross References

Action defined, see Code of Civil Procedure § 22.
Actions by people in respect to real property, see Code of Civil Procedure § 315 et seq.
Classes of judicial remedies, see Code of Civil Procedure § 21.
General limitations for commencing civil actions, see Code of Civil Procedure § 312 et seq.
Limitation of § 349.05 inapplicable to actions by state, county or city, see Code of Civil Procedure § 349.05.
State and United States as including District of Columbia and territories, see Code of Civil Procedure § 17.

§ 346. Action to redeem mortgage; effect of five years adverse possession

An action to redeem a mortgage of real property, with or without an account of rents and profits, may be brought by the mortgagor or those claiming under him, against the mortgagee in possession, or those claiming under him, unless he or they have continuously maintained an adverse possession of the mortgaged premises for five years after breach of some condition of the mortgage. (Enacted in 1872, unpublished Act of 1872.)

Cross References

Action as including special proceeding, see Code of Civil Procedure § 363.
Action defined, see Code of Civil Procedure § 22.
Actions for foreclosure, mortgage or trust deed with power of sale, see Code of Civil Procedure § 725a.
General limitations for commencing civil actions, see Code of Civil Procedure § 312 et seq.
Property as including real and personal property, see Code of Civil Procedure § 17.
Real property as coextensive with lands, tenements, and hereditaments, see Code of Civil Procedure § 17.
Redemption from lien, see Civil Code § 2903.

§ 347. Action to redeem mortgage; multiple mortgagors or persons claiming under mortgagor

If there is more than one such mortgagor, or more than one person claiming under a mortgagor, some of whom are not entitled to maintain such an action under the provisions of this Chapter, any one of them who is entitled to maintain such an action may redeem therein a divided or undivided part of the mortgaged premises, according as his interest may appear and have an accounting, for a part of the rents and profits proportionate to his interest in the mortgaged premises, on payment of a part of the mortgage money, bearing the same proportion to the whole of such money as the value of his divided or undivided interest in the premises bears to the whole of such premises. (Enacted in 1872, unpublished Act of 1872.)

Cross References

Action defined, see Code of Civil Procedure § 22.
Actions for foreclosure, mortgage or trust deed with power of sale, see Code of Civil Procedure § 725a.
General limitations for commencing civil actions, see Code of Civil Procedure § 312 et seq.
Redemption from lien, see Civil Code § 2903.

§ 348. No limitation; action to recover deposit of money or property; effect of insolvency

To actions brought to recover money or other property deposited with any bank, banker, trust company, building and loan association, or savings and loan society or evidenced by a certificate issued by an industrial loan company or credit union there is no limitation.

This section shall not apply to banks, bankers, trust companies, building and loan associations, industrial loan companies, credit unions, and savings and loan societies which have become insolvent and are in process of liquidation and in such cases the statute of limitations shall be deemed to have commenced to run from the beginning of the process of liquidation; provided, however, nothing herein contained shall be construed so as to relieve any stockholder of any banking corporation or trust company from stockholders' liability as shall at any time, be provided by law. *(Added by Code Am.1873–74, c. 383, p. 293, § 36. Amended by Stats.1915, c. 411, p. 684, § 1; Stats.1917, c. 756, p. 1573, § 1; Stats.1955, c. 208, p. 677, § 1.)*

Cross References

Action by depositor against bank for payment of forged or raised check, see Code of Civil Procedure § 340.
Action defined, see Code of Civil Procedure § 22.
Classes of judicial remedies, see Code of Civil Procedure § 21.
General limitations for commencing civil actions, see Code of Civil Procedure § 312 et seq.
Property as including real and personal property, see Code of Civil Procedure § 17.
Writ and process defined, see Code of Civil Procedure § 17.

§ 348.5. No limitation; action upon bonds or coupons issued by State of California

An action upon any bonds or coupons issued by the State of California shall have no limitation. *(Added by Stats.2010, c. 719 (S.B.856), § 8, eff. Oct. 19, 2010.)*

§ 349.05. One hundred eighty days; underground trespass, use or occupancy by oil or gas well; conversion, taking or removal of oil, gas or other liquid; time of accrual; single cause of action; measure of damages; applicability to existing causes; definitions; exceptions

Within one hundred eighty days:

(a) An action to enjoin, abate, or for damages on account of, an underground trespass, use or occupancy, by means of a well drilled for oil or gas or both from a surface location on land other than real property in which the aggrieved party has some right, title or interest or in respect to which the aggrieved party has some right, title or interest.

(b) An action for conversion or for the taking or removing of oil, gas or other liquid, or fluids by means of any such well.

When any of said acts is by means of a new well the actual drilling of which is commenced after this section becomes effective, and such act was knowingly committed with actual intent to commit such act, the cause of action in such case shall not be deemed to have accrued until the discovery, by the aggrieved party, of the act or acts complained of; but in all other cases, and as to wells heretofore or hereafter drilled, the cause of action shall be deemed to have accrued ten days after the time when the well which is the subject of the cause of action was first placed on production.

Notwithstanding the continuing character of any such act, there shall be but one cause of action for any such act, and the cause of action shall accrue as aforesaid.

In all cases where oil or gas has been heretofore or is hereafter extracted from any existing or subsequently drilled well in this state, by a person without right but asserting a claim of right in good faith or acting under an honest mistake of law or fact, the measure of damages, if there be any right of recovery under existing law, shall be the value of the oil or gas at the time of extraction, without interest, after deducting all costs of development, operation and production, which costs shall include taxes and interest on all expenditures from the date thereof.

This section applies to causes of action existing when this section becomes effective. The time for commencement of existing causes of action which would be barred by this section within the first one hundred eighty days after this section becomes effective, shall be the said first one hundred eighty days.

Whenever the term "oil" is used in this section it shall be taken to include "petroleum," and the term "gas" shall mean natural gas coming from the earth.

The limitations prescribed by this section do not apply to rights of action or actions to be brought in the name of or for the benefit of the people of this State, or of any county, city and county, city or other political subdivision of this State. *(Formerly § 349¾, added by Stats.1935, c. 852, p. 2285, § 1. Renumbered § 349.05 and amended by Stats.2020, c. 370 (S.B.1371), § 34, eff. Jan. 1, 2021.)*

Cross References

Action defined, see Code of Civil Procedure § 22.
Classes of judicial remedies, see Code of Civil Procedure § 21.
Computation of time, see Code of Civil Procedure §§ 12, 12a, 12b; Government Code § 6800 et seq.
Discovery, generally, see Code of Civil Procedure § 2016.010 et seq.
General limitations for commencing civil actions, see Code of Civil Procedure § 312 et seq.
Property as including real and personal property, see Code of Civil Procedure § 17.
Real property as coextensive with lands, tenements, and hereditaments, see Code of Civil Procedure § 17.
Right of entry or occupation of surface lands under oil or gas lease, see Code of Civil Procedure § 772.010 et seq.
State and United States as including District of Columbia and territories, see Code of Civil Procedure § 17.
Trespass or injury to real property, see Code of Civil Procedure § 338.

§ 349.1. Six months; contesting validity of formation, organization, consolidation, etc., of public entities

The validity of any acts or proceedings taken under color of law for the formation, organization, incorporation, dissolution, consolidation, change of organization or reorganization of, or for any change in the territorial boundaries of, any city, county, city and county, special district, public corporation or other public entity, or improvement district within any of the foregoing, shall not be contested in any action unless such action shall have been brought within six months from the date of completion of said acts or proceedings. Unless an action is commenced within said period all said acts or proceedings shall be held valid and in every respect legal and incontestable.

This section shall not amend or repeal any existing statute prescribing a shorter period of limitation than that specified herein. *(Added by Stats.1957, c. 1344, p. 2675, § 1. Amended by Stats.1959, c. 1995, p. 4613, § 1; Stats.1965, c. 2044, p. 4767, § 3.5.)*

Cross References

Action defined, see Code of Civil Procedure § 22.
Formation of districts, contest of incorporation, effect of informality in proceedings, see Public Utilities Code § 11701.
General limitations for commencing civil actions, see Code of Civil Procedure § 312 et seq.

§ 349.2. Six months; contesting validity of authorization, issuance and sale of bonds by public entities

Where any acts or proceedings are taken under color of law by or on behalf of any city, county, city and county, special district, public corporation or other public entity for the authorization, sale or issuance of bonds:

(1) The validity of any such acts or proceedings for the authorization of bonds shall not be contested in any action unless such action shall have been brought within six months from the date of election authorizing said bonds, in cases where said bonds are required by law to be authorized at an election, or within six months from the date of adoption of a resolution or ordinance authorizing such bonds, in cases where bonds are not required by law to be authorized at an election;

(2) The validity of any such acts or proceedings for the sale of bonds (including all acts or proceedings taken prior thereto and providing for the issuance of such bonds) shall not be contested in any action unless such action shall have been brought within six months from the date of sale of said bonds;

(3) The validity of any such acts or proceedings for the issuance and delivery of, or payment for, bonds shall not be contested in any action unless such action shall have been brought within six months from the date of issuance and delivery of, or payment for, said bonds.

Unless an action is commenced within the applicable time hereinabove specified, said acts or proceedings for the authorization, sale or issuance of bonds shall be held valid and in every respect legal and incontestable.

This section shall not amend or repeal any existing statute prescribing a shorter period of limitation than that specified herein.

As used in this section, the term "bonds" means all instruments evidencing indebtedness incurred or to be incurred for any public purpose, all instruments evidencing the borrowing of money in anticipation of taxes, revenues or other income of a public body, all instruments payable from revenues or special funds, and all instruments funding or refunding any thereof or any indebtedness, but shall not include any special assessment bonds, special assessment refunding bonds, or bonds or other instruments issued to represent special assessments which are, directly or indirectly, secured by or payable from specific assessments levied against lands benefited, including bonds or other instruments issued under or pursuant to any statute, charter or ordinance providing for the improvement of streets, the opening and widening of streets, the provision for off-street parking, or the refunding of any of the same. *(Added by Stats.1957, c. 1345, p. 2675, § 1.)*

Cross References

Action defined, see Code of Civil Procedure § 22.
Bond and Undertaking Law, bonds or undertakings given as security, see Code of Civil Procedure § 995.010 et seq.
Bonds, form of ballot for issuance of bonds by county government, see Government Code § 29902.
General limitations for commencing civil actions, see Code of Civil Procedure § 312 et seq.
Month defined, see Code of Civil Procedure § 17.

§ 349.4. Validation of formation, organization, consolidation, etc., of public entities; notice; effect of failure to file action within specified period

All acts and proceedings heretofore or hereafter taken under color of law for the formation, organization or incorporation of, or for any change in the territorial boundaries of, any city, county, city and county, special district, public corporation or other public entity, or improvement district, annexed area or zone within any of the foregoing, and for the authorization, issuance, sale, or exchange of bonds of the entity or the territory thereof may be confirmed, validated, and declared legally effective in the manner provided in this section.

The legislative body of the entity may instruct its clerk or secretary to mail a notice to all owners of property within the entity, within the improvement district or zone, or within the annexed area, as the case may be, as their names and addresses appear on the last equalized county assessment roll, or as known to the clerk or secretary. Such notice shall include the name of the entity, the date the entity or the zone or improvement district therein was ordered formed or its territory changed by annexation or otherwise, as the case may be, the amount of bonds authorized, if any, and a statement that commencing with the date of mailing of said notice there shall be a 60-calendar-day period during which period any property owner may file an action contesting the validity of the formation of the entity, or of such improvement district or zone, or of such change of boundaries by annexation or otherwise, as the case may be, or the validity of the bond authorization, if any. The clerk or secretary shall make and file with the legislative body of the entity a certificate of mailing of the notices. The legislative body of the entity may order the clerk or secretary to include in such notice such other additional information that it deems pertinent.

If no action is filed during such 60-day period, the formation of the entity or of such improvement district or zone, or the change of boundaries by annexation or otherwise, as the case may be, and the bond authorization, if any, are valid and uncontestable. *(Added by Stats.1977, c. 7, p. 16, § 2, eff. March 4, 1977.)*

Cross References

Action defined, see Code of Civil Procedure § 22.
Bond and Undertaking Law, bonds or undertakings given as security, see Code of Civil Procedure § 995.010 et seq.
Bonds, form of ballot for issuance of bonds by county government, see Government Code § 29902.
General limitations for commencing civil actions, see Code of Civil Procedure § 312 et seq.
Notice, actual and constructive, defined, see Civil Code § 18.
Property as including real and personal property, see Code of Civil Procedure § 17.

Research References

Forms

West's California Code Forms, Civil Procedure § 352.1 Form 1, Statute of Limitations—Tolling—Imprisonment—Contract Actions.
West's California Code Forms, Civil Procedure § 352 Form 1, Statute of Limitations—Tolling—Contract Actions.

CHAPTER 4. GENERAL PROVISIONS AS TO THE TIME OF COMMENCING ACTIONS

Section
350. Action commenced with filing complaint.
351. Absence from state; effect on limitation period.
352. Disabilities of minority or lack of legal capacity to make decisions.
352.1. Disability of imprisonment.
352.5. Action against person under order for restitution as condition of probation; tolling.
353.1. Court assuming jurisdiction over attorney's practice; effect on limitation period.
354. Disability during war; effect on limitation period.
354.3. Recovery of Holocaust-era artwork from enumerated entities.
354.4. Armenian Genocide victims; insurance policy claims; waiver of statute of limitations.
354.45. Armenian Genocide victims; deposited and looted assets; waiver of statute of limitations.
354.5. Holocaust victims; insurance policy claims purchased in Europe; legal action to recover on claims.

OF CIVIL ACTIONS § 352.1

Section	
354.6.	Second World War slave or forced labor victims; heirs; actions for recovery of compensation; limitations.
354.7.	Braceros, heirs or beneficiaries of braceros; right of action for recovery of savings fund amounts; limitations; severability of provisions.
354.8.	Torture, genocide, war crime, extrajudicial killing, crimes against humanity; limitations; application; fees and costs; severability.
355.	Reversal of judgment; limitation on new action.
356.	Injunction against commencement of action; effect on limitation period.
357.	Disability; necessity of existence when right of action accrued.
358.	Coexisting disabilities; effect on limitation period.
359.	Corporate directors, stockholders or members; actions to recover penalty or forfeiture or enforce liability; inapplicability of title; limitation period.
359.5.	Principal and surety; performance bond; expiration of statute of limitations re obligations of principal; bar to action against principal or surety under bond.
360.	Acknowledgment or promise; payment on account; sufficiency to take case out of statute of limitations.
360.5.	Waiver of statute of limitations; effective period; renewal.
361.	Effect of limitation laws of other states.
362.	Exemption of existing causes of action.
363.	"Action" defined.

§ 350. Action commenced with filing complaint

An action is commenced, within the meaning of this Title, when the complaint is filed. *(Enacted in 1872.)*

Cross References

Action defined, see Code of Civil Procedure § 22.
Commencement of civil actions, see Code of Civil Procedure § 411.10 et seq.

§ 351. Absence from state; effect on limitation period

If, when the cause of action accrues against a person, he is out of the State, the action may be commenced within the term herein limited, after his return to the State, and if, after the cause of action accrues, he departs from the State, the time of his absence is not part of the time limited for the commencement of the action. *(Enacted in 1872.)*

Validity

This section was held unconstitutional, as violative of the commerce clause, with respect to residents who travel in the course of interstate commerce, in the decision of Filet Menu, Inc. v. Cheng (App. 2 Dist. 1999) 84 Cal.Rptr.2d 384, 71 Cal.App.4th 1276.

Cross References

Action defined, see Code of Civil Procedure § 22.
Motor vehicles, service of process in civil actions, see Vehicle Code § 17463.
Property taxation, limitation of actions, deeds by taxing agencies, see Revenue and Taxation Code § 177.
Sales and use taxes, actions, see Revenue and Taxation Code § 6711.

§ 352. Disabilities of minority or lack of legal capacity to make decisions

(a) If a person entitled to bring an action, mentioned in Chapter 3 (commencing with Section 335) is, at the time the cause of action accrued either under the age of majority or lacking the legal capacity to make decisions, the time of the disability is not part of the time limited for the commencement of the action.

(b) This section shall not apply to an action against a public entity or public employee upon a cause of action for which a claim is required to be presented in accordance with Chapter 1 (commencing with Section 900) or Chapter 2 (commencing with Section 910) of Part 3, or Chapter 3 (commencing with Section 950) of Part 4, of Division 3.6 of Title 1 of the Government Code. This subdivision shall not apply to any claim presented to a public entity prior to January 1, 1971. *(Enacted in 1872. Amended by Stats.1959, c. 192, p. 2085, § 1; Stats.1970, c. 104, p. 323, § 1, operative Jan. 1, 1971; Stats.1975, c. 1241, p. 3187, § 1.5; Stats.1986, c. 1161, § 1; Stats. 1994, c. 1083 (S.B.1445), § 4; Stats.2014, c. 144 (A.B.1847), § 4, eff. Jan. 1, 2015.)*

Cross References

Action defined, see Code of Civil Procedure § 22.
Community Care Facilities Act, claims against fund, procedure and period of limitations, see Health and Safety Code § 1527.6.
Guardianship and conservatorship,
  Recovery of property sold by guardian, see Probate Code § 2548.
  Suit against sureties, see Probate Code § 2333.
Limitations on claims against public entities required to be presented in accordance with chapters 1 and 2 of part 3, see Government Code § 945.6.
Probate proceedings, action to recover property sold by personal representative, see Probate Code § 10382.
Property taxation, limitation of actions, deeds by taxing agencies, see Revenue and Taxation Code § 177.
Real property, computation of time for certain disabilities, see Code of Civil Procedure § 328.
Unborn children, injuries suffered prior to or in course of birth, limitation of actions, see Code of Civil Procedure § 340.4.

Research References

Forms

Asset Protection: Legal Planning, Strategies and Forms ¶ 3.06, Statute of Limitations.
1 California Transactions Forms--Estate Planning § 2:5, Necessity of Privity Between Estate Planner and Ultimate Beneficiary.
West's California Code Forms, Civil Procedure § 340.4 Form 1, Statute of Limitations—Pleading—Damages Arising from Personal Injuries at Birth.
West's California Code Forms, Civil Procedure § 340.5 Form 1, Statute of Limitations—Pleading—Professional Negligence of Healthcare Provider—Reasonable.
West's California Code Forms, Civil Procedure § 340.6 Form 1, Statute of Limitations—Pleading—Professional Negligence of Attorney—Tolling—Legal Disability.
West's California Code Forms, Civil Procedure § 352 Form 1, Statute of Limitations—Tolling—Contract Actions.
West's California Code Forms, Civil Procedure § 366.2 Form 1, Statute of Limitations—Death of Persons—Defendants.

§ 352.1. Disability of imprisonment

(a) If a person entitled to bring an action, mentioned in Chapter 3 (commencing with Section 335), is, at the time the cause of action accrued, imprisoned on a criminal charge, or in execution under the sentence of a criminal court for a term less than for life, the time of that disability is not a part of the time limited for the commencement of the action, not to exceed two years.

(b) This section does not apply to an action against a public entity or public employee upon a cause of action for which a claim is required to be presented in accordance with Chapter 1 (commencing with Section 900) or Chapter 2 (commencing with Section 910) of Part 3, or Chapter 3 (commencing with Section 950) of Part 4, of Division 3.6 of Title 1 of the Government Code. This subdivision shall not apply to any claim presented to a public entity prior to January 1, 1971.

(c) This section does not apply to an action, other than an action to recover damages or that portion of an action that is for the recovery of damages, relating to the conditions of confinement, including an action brought by that person pursuant to Section 1983 of Title 42 of the United States Code. *(Added by Stats.1994, c. 1083 (S.B.1445), § 5.)*

§ 352.1

Cross References

Action defined, see Code of Civil Procedure § 22.
Property taxation, limitation of actions, deeds by taxing agencies, see Revenue and Taxation Code § 177.

Research References

Forms

West's California Code Forms, Civil Procedure § 340.5 Form 1, Statute of Limitations—Pleading—Professional Negligence of Healthcare Provider—Reasonable.

West's California Code Forms, Civil Procedure § 352.1 Form 1, Statute of Limitations—Tolling—Imprisonment—Contract Actions.

§ 352.5. Action against person under order for restitution as condition of probation; tolling

If, after a cause of action accrues against a person, that person comes under an order for restitution as a condition of probation with respect to the specific act or omission giving rise to such person's liability, the time during which the order is in effect is not a part of the time limited for the commencement of such an action based upon that act or omission. *(Added by Stats.1976, c. 282, p. 589, § 1.)*

Cross References

Action defined, see Code of Civil Procedure § 22.
Property taxation, limitation of actions, deeds by taxing agencies, see Revenue and Taxation Code § 177.

§ 353.1. Court assuming jurisdiction over attorney's practice; effect on limitation period

If a person entitled to bring an action or other proceeding, which action or other proceeding has not been filed or otherwise instituted, is represented by an attorney over whose practice a court of this state has assumed jurisdiction pursuant to Section 6180 or Section 6190 of the Business and Professions Code, and the application for the court to assume jurisdiction is filed prior to the expiration of the applicable statute of limitation or claim statute, the person shall have six months from the date of entry of the order assuming jurisdiction within which to file or otherwise institute the matter, if the applicable statute of limitation otherwise would have expired. *(Added by Stats.1983, c. 254, § 3.)*

Cross References

Action defined, see Code of Civil Procedure § 22.
Attorneys, State Bar Act, see Business and Professions Code § 6000.
Month defined, see Code of Civil Procedure § 17.
Property taxation, limitation of actions, deeds by taxing agencies, see Revenue and Taxation Code § 177.
State and United States as including District of Columbia and territories, see Code of Civil Procedure § 17.

§ 354. Disability during war; effect on limitation period

When a person is, by reason of the existence of a state of war, under a disability to commence an action, the time of the continuance of such disability is not part of the period limited for the commencement of the action whether such cause of action shall have accrued prior to or during the period of such disability. *(Enacted in 1872. Amended by Stats.1943, c. 151, p. 1043, § 1.)*

Cross References

Action defined, see Code of Civil Procedure § 22.
Property taxation, limitation of actions, deeds by taxing agencies, see Revenue and Taxation Code § 177.

§ 354.3. Recovery of Holocaust-era artwork from enumerated entities

(a) The following definitions govern the construction of this section:

(1) "Entity" means any museum or gallery that displays, exhibits, or sells any article of historical, interpretive, scientific, or artistic significance.

(2) "Holocaust-era artwork" means any article of artistic significance taken as a result of Nazi persecution during the period of 1929 to 1945, inclusive.

(b) Notwithstanding any other provision of law, any owner, or heir or beneficiary of an owner, of Holocaust-era artwork, may bring an action to recover Holocaust-era artwork from any entity described in paragraph (1) of subdivision (a). Subject to Section 410.10, that action may be brought in a superior court of this state, which court shall have jurisdiction over that action until its completion or resolution. Section 361 does not apply to this section.

(c) Any action brought under this section shall not be dismissed for failure to comply with the applicable statute of limitation, if the action is commenced on or before December 31, 2010. *(Added by Stats.2002, c. 332 (A.B.1758), § 2.)*

Validity

This section was held preempted by the foreign affairs doctrine in the decision of Von Saher v. Norton Simon Museum of Art at Pasadena, C.A.9 (Cal.)2010, 592 F.3d 954, certiorari denied 131 S.Ct. 3055, 564 U.S. 1037, 180 L.Ed.2d 885, on remand 862 F.Supp.2d 1044.

Cross References

Action defined, see Code of Civil Procedure § 22.
Holocaust Victim Compensation Relief Act, see Revenue and Taxation Code § 17155.
Property taxation, limitation of actions, deeds by taxing agencies, see Revenue and Taxation Code § 177.
State and United States as including District of Columbia and territories, see Code of Civil Procedure § 17.

Research References

Forms

West's California Code Forms, Civil Procedure § 354.3 Form 1, Statutes of Limitation—Holocaust Era Artwork—Claims Against Museums and Art Galleries.

§ 354.4. Armenian Genocide victims; insurance policy claims; waiver of statute of limitations

(a) The following definitions govern the construction of this section:

(1) "Armenian Genocide victim" means any person of Armenian or other ancestry living in the Ottoman Empire during the period of 1915 to 1923, inclusive, who died, was deported, or escaped to avoid persecution during that period.

(2) "Insurer" means an insurance provider doing business in the state, or whose contacts in the state satisfy the constitutional requirements for jurisdiction, that sold life, property, liability, health, annuities, dowry, educational, casualty, or any other insurance covering persons or property to persons in Europe or Asia at any time between 1875 and 1923.

(b) Notwithstanding any other provision of law, any Armenian Genocide victim, or heir or beneficiary of an Armenian Genocide victim, who resides in this state and has a claim arising out of an insurance policy or policies purchased or in effect in Europe or Asia between 1875 and 1923 from an insurer described in paragraph (2) of subdivision (a), may bring a legal action or may continue a pending legal action to recover on that claim in any court of competent jurisdiction in this state, which court shall be deemed the proper forum for that action until its completion or resolution.

(c) Any action, including any pending action brought by an Armenian Genocide victim or the heir or beneficiary of an Armenian Genocide victim, whether a resident or nonresident of this state, seeking benefits under the insurance policies issued or in effect between 1875 and 1923 shall not be dismissed for failure to comply with the applicable statute of limitation, provided the action is filed on or before December 31, 2016.

(d) The provisions of this section are severable. If any provision of this section or its application is held invalid, that invalidity shall not affect other provisions or applications that can be given effect without the invalid provision or application. *(Added by Stats.2000, c. 543 (S.B.1915), § 2, eff. Sept. 20, 2000. Amended by Stats.2011, c. 70 (A.B.173), § 1, eff. July 8, 2011.)*

Validity

For validity of this section, see Movsesian v. Victoria Versicherung AG, C.A.9 (Cal.)2012, 670 F.3d 1067, referred to 133 S.Ct. 404, 568 U.S. 809, 184 L.Ed.2d 19, certiorari denied 133 S.Ct. 2795, 569 U.S. 1029, 186 L.Ed.2d 860.

Cross References

Action defined, see Code of Civil Procedure § 22.
Property as including real and personal property, see Code of Civil Procedure § 17.
Property taxation, limitation of actions, deeds by taxing agencies, see Revenue and Taxation Code § 177.
State and United States as including District of Columbia and territories, see Code of Civil Procedure § 17.

§ 354.45. Armenian Genocide victims; deposited and looted assets; waiver of statute of limitations

(a) For purposes of this section, the following terms have the following meanings:

(1) "Armenian Genocide victim" means any person of Armenian or other ancestry living in the Ottoman Empire during the period of 1890 to 1923, inclusive, who died, was injured in person or property, was deported, or escaped to avoid persecution during that period.

(2) "Bank" means any banking or financial institution, including any institution that issued bonds, that conducted business in Ottoman Turkey at any time during the period of 1890 to 1923, inclusive.

(3) "Deposited assets" means any and all cash, securities, bonds, gold, jewels or jewelry, or any other tangible or intangible items of personal property, or any documents indicating ownership or possessory interests in real, personal, or intangible property, that were deposited with and held by a bank.

(4) "Looted assets" means any and all personal, commercial, real, and intangible property, including cash, securities, gold, jewelry, businesses, artwork, equipment, and intellectual property, that was taken from the ownership or control of an individual, organization, or entity, by theft, forced transfer, or exploitation, during the period of 1890 to 1923, inclusive, by any person, organization, or entity acting on behalf of, or in furtherance of the acts of, the Turkish Government, that were received by and deposited with a bank.

(b) Notwithstanding any other law, any Armenian Genocide victim, or heir or beneficiary of an Armenian Genocide victim, who resides in this state and has a claim arising out of a failure of a bank to pay or turn over deposited assets, or to turn over looted assets, may bring an action or may continue a pending action, to recover on that claim in any court of competent jurisdiction in this state, which court shall be deemed the proper forum for that action until its completion or resolution.

(c) Any action, including any pending action brought by an Armenian Genocide victim, or the heir or beneficiary of an Armenian Genocide victim, who resides in this state, seeking payment for, or the return of, deposited assets, or the return of looted assets, shall not be dismissed for failure to comply with the applicable statute of limitation, if the action is filed on or before December 31, 2016.

(d) The provisions of this section are severable. If any provision of this section or its application is held invalid, that invalidity shall not affect other provisions or applications that can be given effect without the invalid provision or application. *(Added by Stats.2006, c. 443 (S.B.1524), § 2.)*

Validity

This section was recognized as preempted for conflicting with the federal government's resolution of wartime claims arising out of World War I in the decision of Deirmenjian v. Deutsche Bank, A.G., C.D.Cal.2007, 526 F.Supp.2d 1068.

§ 354.5. Holocaust victims; insurance policy claims purchased in Europe; legal action to recover on claims

(a) The following definitions govern the construction of this section:

(1) "Holocaust victim" means any person who was persecuted during the period of 1929 to 1945, inclusive, by Nazi Germany, its allies, or sympathizers.

(2) "Related company" means any parent, subsidiary, reinsurer, successor in interest, managing general agent, or affiliate company of the insurer.

(3) "Insurer" means an insurance provider doing business in the state, or whose contacts in the state satisfy the constitutional requirements for jurisdiction, that sold life, property, liability, health, annuities, dowry, educational, casualty, or any other insurance covering persons or property to persons in Europe at any time before 1945, directly or through a related company, whether the sale of the insurance occurred before or after the insurer and the related company became related.

(b) Notwithstanding any other provision of law, any Holocaust victim, or heir or beneficiary of a Holocaust victim, who resides in this state and has a claim arising out of an insurance policy or policies purchased or in effect in Europe before 1945 from an insurer described in paragraph (3) of subdivision (a), may bring a legal action to recover on that claim in any superior court of the state for the county in which the plaintiff or one of the plaintiffs resides, which court shall be vested with jurisdiction over that action until its completion or resolution.

(c) Any action brought by a Holocaust victim or the heir or beneficiary of a Holocaust victim, whether a resident or nonresident of this state, seeking proceeds of the insurance policies issued or in effect before 1945 shall not be dismissed for failure to comply with the applicable statute of limitation, provided the action is commenced on or before December 31, 2010. *(Added by Stats.1998, c. 43 (A.B.1334), § 2, eff. May 22, 1998. Amended by Stats.1999, c. 827 (A.B.600), § 1, eff. Oct. 10, 1999.)*

Validity

This statute was held preempted by United States foreign policy favoring settlement of such claims by International Commission on Holocaust Era Insurance Claims, in the decision of Steinberg v. International Com'n on Holocaust Era Ins. Claims (App. 2 Dist. 2005) 34 Cal.Rptr.3d 944, 133 Cal.App.4th 689.

Cross References

Action defined, see Code of Civil Procedure § 22.
Evaluating archives of insurers, see Insurance Code § 12967.
Failure to pay Holocaust survivor claims, suspension of certificate of authority, see Insurance Code § 790.15.
German act regulating unresolved property claims compensation, Holocaust victim payments,
    Exclusion from income or resources for determining eligibility, see Welfare and Institutions Code § 11008.20.
    Items excluded from gross income, see Revenue and Taxation Code § 17155.
Holocaust Era Insurance Registry,
    Generally, see Insurance Code § 13800 et seq.
    Civil penalties, see Insurance Code § 13805.
    Disclosure requirements for insurers, see Insurance Code § 13804.
    Suspension of certificate of authority, see Insurance Code § 13805.

§ 354.5

Holocaust Victim Compensation Relief Act, see Revenue and Taxation Code § 17155.
Property as including real and personal property, see Code of Civil Procedure § 17.
Property taxation, limitation of actions, deeds by taxing agencies, see Revenue and Taxation Code § 177.
Recovery of Holocaust-era artwork from enumerated entities, see Code of Civil Procedure § 354.3.

Research References

Forms

West's California Code Forms, Civil Procedure § 354.5 Form 1, Statutes of Limitation—Holocaust Victims—Claims for Insurance Policy Proceeds.

§ 354.6. Second World War slave or forced labor victims; heirs; actions for recovery of compensation; limitations

(a) As used in this section:

(1) "Second World War slave labor victim" means any person taken from a concentration camp or ghetto or diverted from transportation to a concentration camp or from a ghetto to perform labor without pay for any period of time between 1929 and 1945, by the Nazi regime, its allies and sympathizers, or enterprises transacting business in any of the areas occupied by or under control of the Nazi regime or its allies and sympathizers.

(2) 'Second [1] World War forced labor victim" means any person who was a member of the civilian population conquered by the Nazi regime, its allies or sympathizers, or prisoner-of-war of the Nazi regime, its allies or sympathizers, forced to perform labor without pay for any period of time between 1929 and 1945, by the Nazi regime, its allies and sympathizers, or enterprises transacting business in any of the areas occupied by or under control of the Nazi regime or its allies and sympathizers.

(3) "Compensation" means the present value of wages and benefits that individuals should have been paid and damages for injuries sustained in connection with the labor performed. Present value shall be calculated on the basis of the market value of the services at the time they were performed, plus interest from the time the services were performed, compounded annually to date of full payment without diminution for wartime or postwar currency devaluation.

(b) Any Second World War slave labor victim, or heir of a Second World War slave labor victim, Second World War forced labor victim, or heir of a Second World War forced labor victim, may bring an action to recover compensation for labor performed as a Second World War slave labor victim or Second World War forced labor victim from any entity or successor in interest thereof, for whom that labor was performed, either directly or through a subsidiary or affiliate. That action may be brought in a superior court of this state, which court shall have jurisdiction over that action until its completion or resolution.

(c) Any action brought under this section shall not be dismissed for failure to comply with the applicable statute of limitation, if the action is commenced on or before December 31, 2010. *(Added by Stats.1999, c. 216 (S.B.1245), § 4, eff. July 28, 1999.)*

[1] Punctuation so in chaptered copy.

Validity

This statute was recognized as preempted by United States foreign policy favoring settlement of such claims by International Commission on Holocaust Era Insurance Claims, in the decision of Steinberg v. International Com'n on Holocaust Era Ins. Claims (App. 2 Dist. 2005) 34 Cal.Rptr.3d 944, 133 Cal.App.4th 689.

This section was held unconstitutional in the decision of In re World War II Era Japanese Forced Labor Litigation,

N.D.Cal.2001, 164 F.Supp.2d 1160, 108 A.L.R.5th 743, affirmed 317 F.3d 1005, amended and superseded on denial of rehearing 324 F.3d 692, 192 A.L.R. Fed. 657, certiorari denied 124 S.Ct. 105, 540 U.S. 820, 157 L.Ed.2d 39, certiorari denied 124 S.Ct. 132, 540 U.S. 820, 157 L.Ed.2d 39, certiorari denied 124 S.Ct. 133, 540 U.S. 821, 157 L.Ed.2d 39.

Cross References

Action defined, see Code of Civil Procedure § 22.
Classes of judicial remedies, see Code of Civil Procedure § 21.
Kinds of injuries, see Code of Civil Procedure § 27.
Property taxation, limitation of actions, deeds by taxing agencies, see Revenue and Taxation Code § 177.

Research References

Forms

West's California Code Forms, Civil Procedure § 354.6 Form 1, Statute of Limitations—Second World War Slave or Forced Labor Victims—Claims for Compensation.

§ 354.7. Braceros, heirs or beneficiaries of braceros; right of action for recovery of savings fund amounts; limitations; severability of provisions

(a) The following definitions govern the construction of this section:

(1) "Bracero" means any person who participated in the labor importation program known as the Bracero program between January 1, 1942, and January 1, 1950, pursuant to agreements between the United States and Mexico.

(2) "Savings fund" means funds withheld from the wages of braceros as savings to be paid to braceros upon their return to Mexico.

(b) Notwithstanding any other provision of law, any bracero, or heir or beneficiary of a bracero, who has a claim arising out of a failure to pay or turn over savings fund amounts may bring a legal action or may continue a pending legal action to recover on that claim in any court of competent jurisdiction in this state, which court shall be deemed a proper forum for that action until its completion or resolution.

(c) Notwithstanding any other provision of law, any action brought by a bracero, or heir or beneficiary of a bracero, arising out of a failure to pay or turn over savings fund amounts shall not be dismissed for failure to comply with the otherwise applicable statute of limitations, provided the action is filed on or before December 31, 2005.

(d) The provisions of this section are severable. If any provision of this section or its application is held invalid, that invalidity shall not affect other provisions or applications that can be given effect without the invalid provision or application. *(Added by Stats.2002, c. 1070 (A.B.2913), § 2, eff. Sept. 29, 2002.)*

Cross References

Action defined, see Code of Civil Procedure § 22.
Property taxation, limitation of actions, deeds by taxing agencies, see Revenue and Taxation Code § 177.
State and United States as including District of Columbia and territories, see Code of Civil Procedure § 17.
Statutes, construction and legislative intent, see Code of Civil Procedure §§ 1858, 1859.

Research References

Forms

West's California Code Forms, Civil Procedure § 354.7 Form 1, Statute of Limitations—Bracero Wage Claims (1942 to 1950).

§ 354.8. Torture, genocide, war crime, extrajudicial killing, crimes against humanity; limitations; application; fees and costs; severability

(a) Notwithstanding any other law, including, but not limited to Section 335.1, the following actions shall be commenced within 10 years:

(1) An action for assault, battery, or both, where the conduct constituting the assault or battery would also constitute any of the following:

(A) An act of torture, as described in Section 206 of the Penal Code.

(B) An act of genocide, as described in Section 1091(a) of Title 18 of the United States Code.

(C) A war crime, as defined in Section 2441 of Title 18 of the United States Code.

(D) An attempted extrajudicial killing, as defined in Section 3(a) of Public Law 102–256.

(E)(i) Crimes against humanity.

(ii) For purposes of this paragraph, "crimes against humanity" means any of the following acts as part of a widespread or systematic attack directed against a civil population, with knowledge of the attack:

(I) Murder.

(II) Extermination.

(III) Enslavement.

(IV) Forcible transfer of population.

(V) Arbitrary detention.

(VI) Rape, sexual slavery, enforced prostitution, forced pregnancy, enforced sterilization, or any other form of sexual violence of comparable gravity.

(VII) Persecution on political, race, national, ethnic, cultural, religious, or gender grounds.

(VIII) Enforced disappearance of persons.

(IX) Other inhuman acts of similar character intentionally causing great suffering, serious bodily injury, or serious mental injury.

(2) An action for wrongful death, where the death arises out of conduct constituting any of the acts described in paragraph (1), or where the death would constitute an extrajudicial killing, as defined in Section 3(a) of Public Law 102–256.

(3) An action for the taking of property in violation of international law, in which either of the following apply:

(A) That property, or any property exchanged for such property, is present in the United States in connection with a commercial activity carried on in the United States by a foreign state.

(B) That property, or any property exchanged for such property, is owned or operated by an agency or instrumentality of a foreign state and that agency or instrumentality is engaged in a commercial activity in the United States.

(4) An action seeking benefits under an insurance policy where the insurance claim arises out of any of the conduct described in paragraphs (1) to (3), inclusive.

(b) An action brought under this section shall not be dismissed for failure to comply with any previously applicable statute of limitations.

(c) Section 361 shall not apply to an action brought pursuant to this section if all or part of the unlawful act or acts out of which the action arises occurred in this state.

(d) A prevailing plaintiff may be awarded reasonable attorney's fees and litigation costs including, but not limited to, expert witness fees and expenses as part of the costs.

(e) This section shall apply to all actions commenced concerning an act described in paragraphs (1) to (4), inclusive, of subdivision (a), that occurs on or after January 1, 2016.

(f) The provisions of this section are severable. If any provision of this section or its application is held invalid, that invalidity shall not affect other provisions or applications that can be given effect without the invalid provision or application. *(Added by Stats.2015, c. 474 (A.B.15), § 2, eff. Jan. 1, 2016.)*

Research References

Forms

West's California Code Forms, Civil Procedure § 354.8 Form 1, Statute of Limitations—Crimes Against Humanity.

§ 355. Reversal of judgment; limitation on new action

If an action is commenced within the time prescribed therefor, and a judgment therein for the plaintiff be reversed on appeal other than on the merits, a new action may be commenced within one year after the reversal. *(Enacted in 1872. Amended by Stats.1992, c. 178 (S.B.1496), § 7.)*

Cross References

Action defined, see Code of Civil Procedure § 22.
Property taxation, limitation of actions, deeds by taxing agencies, see Revenue and Taxation Code § 177.

§ 356. Injunction against commencement of action; effect on limitation period

When the commencement of an action is stayed by injunction or statutory prohibition, the time of the continuance of the injunction or prohibition is not part of the time limited for the commencement of the action. *(Enacted in 1872.)*

Cross References

Action defined, see Code of Civil Procedure § 22.
Injunctions,
  Generally, see Code of Civil Procedure § 526.
  Preventive relief, see Civil Code § 3420 et seq.
Property taxation, limitation of actions, deeds by taxing agencies, see Revenue and Taxation Code § 177.

Research References

Forms

Asset Protection: Legal Planning, Strategies and Forms ¶ 3.06, Statute of Limitations.
Asset Protection: Legal Planning, Strategies and Forms ¶ 12.01, Overview.
West's California Code Forms, Civil Procedure § 340.5 Form 3, Statute of Limitations—Pleading—Professional Negligence of Health Care Provider—Tolling—Fraud—Collusion.

§ 357. Disability; necessity of existence when right of action accrued

No person can avail himself of a disability, unless it existed when his right of action accrued. *(Enacted in 1872.)*

Cross References

Action defined, see Code of Civil Procedure § 22.
Property taxation, limitation of actions, deeds by taxing agencies, see Revenue and Taxation Code § 177.

§ 358. Coexisting disabilities; effect on limitation period

When two or more disabilities coexist at the time the right of action accrues, the limitation does not attach until they are removed. *(Enacted in 1872.)*

Cross References

Action defined, see Code of Civil Procedure § 22.
Property taxation, limitation of actions, deeds by taxing agencies, see Revenue and Taxation Code § 177.

§ 359. Corporate directors, stockholders or members; actions to recover penalty or forfeiture or enforce liability; inapplicability of title; limitation period

This title does not affect actions against directors, shareholders, or members of a corporation, to recover a penalty or forfeiture imposed,

§ 359

or to enforce a liability created by law; but such actions must be brought within three years after the discovery by the aggrieved party of the facts upon which the penalty or forfeiture attached, or the liability was created. (Enacted in 1872. Amended by Stats.1978, c. 1305, p. 4265, § 1, operative Jan. 1, 1980.)

Cross References

Action defined, see Code of Civil Procedure § 22.
Classes of judicial remedies, see Code of Civil Procedure § 21.
Commencing actions other than to recover real property,
　One year limitation on selected actions, see Code of Civil Procedure § 340.
　Three year, see Code of Civil Procedure § 338.
Directors and management,
　Joint and several liability for directors, see Corporations Code § 316.
　Obligations of directors, officers, or other persons, see Corporations Code § 315.
Discovery, generally, see Code of Civil Procedure § 2016.010 et seq.
Minors, personal injuries before or during birth, see Code of Civil Procedure § 340.4.

§ 359.5. Principal and surety; performance bond; expiration of statute of limitations re obligations of principal; bar to action against principal or surety under bond

If the obligations under a surety bond are conditioned upon performance of the principal, the expiration of the statute of limitations with respect to the obligations of the principal, other than the obligations of the principal under the bond, shall also bar an action against the principal or surety under the bond, unless the terms of the bond provide otherwise. (Added by Stats.1982, c. 106, § 1.)

Cross References

Action defined, see Code of Civil Procedure § 22.
Bond and Undertaking Law, bonds or undertakings given as security, see Code of Civil Procedure § 995.010 et seq.
Obligation defined, see Code of Civil Procedure § 26.

Research References

Forms

3 California Real Estate Forms (Miller & Starr) § 3:37 (2d ed.), Continuing Guaranty.
3 California Real Estate Forms (Miller & Starr) § 3:38 (2d ed.), Completion Guaranty.
3 California Real Estate Forms (Miller & Starr) § 3:38.50 (2d ed.), "Bad Boy" Guaranty.
3 California Transactions Forms--Business Transactions § 19:58, Continuing Guaranty (Multiple Individual Guarantors)—Loan Secured by Deed of Trust.

§ 360. Acknowledgment or promise; payment on account; sufficiency to take case out of statute of limitations

No acknowledgment or promise is sufficient evidence of a new or continuing contract, by which to take the case out of the operation of this title, unless the same is contained in some writing, signed by the party to be charged thereby, provided that any payment on account of principal or interest due on a promissory note made by the party to be charged shall be deemed a sufficient acknowledgment or promise of a continuing contract to stop, from time to time as any such payment is made, the running of the time within which an action may be commenced upon the principal sum or upon any installment of principal or interest due on such note, and to start the running of a new period of time, but no such payment of itself shall revive a cause of action once barred. (Enacted in 1872. Amended by Stats.1947, c. 1108, p. 2547, § 1; Stats.1955, c. 417, p. 874, § 1.)

Cross References

Action defined, see Code of Civil Procedure § 22.

Research References

Forms

1 California Transactions Forms--Business Transactions § 6:42, Contracts Required to be in Writing.

3 California Transactions Forms--Business Transactions § 22:9, Waiver and Extinguishment.
1 California Transactions Forms--Family Law § 4:22, Statute of Frauds.

§ 360.5. Waiver of statute of limitations; effective period; renewal

No waiver shall bar a defense to any action that the action was not commenced within the time limited by this title unless the waiver is in writing and signed by the person obligated. No waiver executed prior to the expiration of the time limited for the commencement of the action by this title shall be effective for a period exceeding four years from the date of expiration of the time limited for commencement of the action by this title and no waiver executed after the expiration of such time shall be effective for a period exceeding four years from the date thereof, but any such waiver may be renewed for a further period of not exceeding four years from the expiration of the immediately preceding waiver. Such waivers may be made successively. The provisions of this section shall not be applicable to any acknowledgment, promise or any form of waiver which is in writing and signed by the person obligated and given to any county to secure repayment of indigent aid or the repayment of moneys fraudulently or illegally obtained from the county. (Added by Stats.1951, c. 1106, p. 2863, § 1. Amended by Stats.1953, c. 655, p. 1906, § 1.)

Cross References

Action defined, see Code of Civil Procedure § 22.
Ancient mortgages and deeds of trust, expiration date, see Civil Code § 882.020.

Research References

Forms

3 California Real Estate Forms (Miller & Starr) § 3:8 (2d ed.), Deed of Trust, Security Agreement, and Fixture Filing With Assignment of Rents and Agreements.
3 California Real Estate Forms (Miller & Starr) § 3:14 (2d ed.), Construction Deed of Trust, Security Agreement, and Fixture Filing With Assignment of Rents and Agreements.
3 California Transactions Forms--Business Transactions § 22:9, Waiver and Extinguishment.
West's California Code Forms, Civil Procedure § 360.5 Form 1, Statute of Limitations—Pleading—Waiver of Defense.

§ 361. Effect of limitation laws of other states

When a cause of action has arisen in another State, or in a foreign country, and by the laws thereof an action thereon cannot there be maintained against a person by reason of the lapse of time, an action thereon shall not be maintained against him in this State, except in favor of one who has been a citizen of this State, and who has held the cause of action from the time it accrued. (Enacted in 1872.)

Cross References

Action defined, see Code of Civil Procedure § 22.
Action for specific recovery of fine art against museum, gallery, auctioneer, or dealer, statute of limitations, inapplicability of this section, see Code of Civil Procedure § 338.
Recovery of Holocaust-era artwork from enumerated entities, see Code of Civil Procedure § 354.3.
State and United States as including District of Columbia and territories, see Code of Civil Procedure § 17.

Research References

Forms

West's California Code Forms, Civil Procedure § 361 Form 1, Statute of Limitations—Pleading—Other States Laws—Tolling—Resident Plaintiff.

§ 362. Exemption of existing causes of action

This Title does not extend to actions already commenced, nor to cases where the time prescribed in any existing statute for acquiring a right or barring a remedy has fully run, but the laws now in force are applicable to such actions and cases, and are repealed subject to the provisions of this section. *(Enacted in 1872.)*

Cross References

Action defined, see Code of Civil Procedure § 22.
Classes of judicial remedies, see Code of Civil Procedure § 21.
Effect of code on running of limitations, see Code of Civil Procedure § 9.

§ 363. "Action" defined

The word "action" as used in this Title is to be construed, whenever it is necessary so to do, as including a special proceeding of a civil nature. *(Enacted in 1872, unpublished Act of 1872.)*

Cross References

Special proceeding defined, see Code of Civil Procedure § 23.

Title 3

OF THE PARTIES TO CIVIL ACTIONS

CHAPTER 2. MARRIED PERSON

Section
370. Married persons.
371. Spouses sued together; defense by spouse.

§ 370. Married persons

A married person may be sued without his or her spouse being joined as a party, and may sue without his or her spouse being joined as a party in all actions. *(Enacted in 1872. Amended by Code Am.1873–74, c. 383, p. 293, § 37; Stats.1913, c. 130, p. 217, § 1; Stats.1921, c. 110, p. 102, § 1; Stats.1975, c. 1241, p. 3187, § 2.)*

Cross References

Community property, interests of spouses in, see Family Code §§ 700, 751, 760, 803.
Contracts, husband and wife may make, see Family Code § 721.
General personal rights, see Civil Code § 43.
Joinder of causes of action, when permitted, see Code of Civil Procedure § 427.10.
Libel and slander, see Cal. Const. Art. 1, § 2.
Separate property of married person, see Family Code §§ 770, 914.

§ 371. Spouses sued together; defense by spouse

If spouses are sued together, each may defend for his or her own right, but if one spouse neglects to defend, the other spouse may defend for that spouse's right also. *(Enacted in 1872. Amended by Stats.1975, c. 1241, p. 3187, § 3; Stats.2016, c. 50 (S.B.1005), § 15, eff. Jan. 1, 2017.)*

CHAPTER 3. DISABILITY OF PARTY

Section
372. Minors, persons who lack legal capacity to make decisions, or persons for whom conservator appointed; appearance by guardian, conservator or guardian ad litem; powers; disposition of moneys recovered; waiver of juvenile law rights.
372.5. Guardian ad litem; appointment under pseudonym; procedure.
373. Guardian ad litem; appointment procedure.
373.5. Guardian ad litem; persons not ascertained, not in being or unknown; powers; expenses.
374. Minor under age 12; appearance without counsel when accompanied by guardian ad litem; conditions.
374.5. Orders affecting minors; jurisdiction.
375. Disability of party; effect on action.

Section
376. Parents; injuries to child; failure of one parent to join as plaintiff; service on parent not joining; illegitimate child; ward; parties defendant; death of child or ward; damages; consolidation of injury and death action.

§ 372. Minors, persons who lack legal capacity to make decisions, or persons for whom conservator appointed; appearance by guardian, conservator or guardian ad litem; powers; disposition of moneys recovered; waiver of juvenile law rights

(a)(1) When a minor, a person who lacks legal capacity to make decisions, or a person for whom a conservator has been appointed is a party, that person shall appear either by a guardian or conservator of the estate or by a guardian ad litem appointed by the court in which the action or proceeding is pending, or by a judge thereof, in each case.

(2)(A) A guardian ad litem may be appointed in any case when it is deemed by the court in which the action or proceeding is prosecuted, or by a judge thereof, expedient to appoint a guardian ad litem to represent the minor, person * * * who lacks legal capacity to make decisions, or person for whom a conservator has been appointed, notwithstanding that the person may have a guardian or conservator of the estate and may have appeared by the guardian or conservator of the estate.

(B) If application is made for appointment of a guardian ad litem for a person described in paragraph (1), and that person has a guardian or conservator of the estate, the application may be granted only if all of the following occur:

(i) The applicant gives notice and a copy of the application to the guardian or conservator of the estate upon filing the application.

(ii) The application discloses the existence of a guardian or conservator of the estate.

(iii) The application sets forth the reasons why the guardian or conservator of the estate is inadequate to represent the interests of the proposed ward in the action.

(C) The guardian or conservator of the estate shall have five court days from receiving notice of the application to file any opposition to the application.

(3) The guardian or conservator of the estate or guardian ad litem so appearing for any minor, person who lacks legal capacity to make decisions, or person for whom a conservator has been appointed shall have power, with the approval of the court in which the action or proceeding is pending, to compromise the same, to agree to the order or judgment to be entered therein for or against the ward or conservatee, and to satisfy any judgment or order in favor of the ward or conservatee or release or discharge any claim of the ward or conservatee pursuant to that compromise. Money or other property to be paid or delivered pursuant to the order or judgment for the benefit of a minor, person lacking legal capacity to make decisions, or person for whom a conservator has been appointed shall be paid and delivered as provided in Chapter 4 (commencing with Section 3600) of Part 8 of Division 4 of the Probate Code.

(4) Where reference is made in this chapter to "a person * * * who lacks legal capacity to make decisions," the reference shall be deemed to include * * * all of the following:

(A) A person who lacks capacity to understand the nature or consequences of the action or proceeding.

(B) A person who lacks capacity to assist the person's attorney in the preparation of the case.

(C) A person for whom a conservator may be appointed * * * pursuant to Section 1801 of the Probate Code.

(5) Nothing in this section, or in any other provision of this code, the Civil Code, the Family Code, or the Probate Code is intended by

the Legislature to prohibit a minor from exercising an intelligent and knowing waiver of * * * the minor's constitutional rights in a proceeding under the Juvenile Court Law (Chapter 2 (commencing with Section 200) of Part 1 of Division 2 of the Welfare and Institutions Code).

(b)(1) Notwithstanding subdivision (a), a minor 12 years of age or older may appear in court without a guardian, counsel, or guardian ad litem, for the purpose of requesting or opposing a request for any of the following:

(A) An injunction or temporary restraining order or both to prohibit harassment pursuant to Section 527.6.

(B) An injunction or temporary restraining order or both against violence or a credible threat of violence in the workplace pursuant to Section 527.8.

(C) A protective order pursuant to Division 10 (commencing with Section 6200) of the Family Code.

(D) A protective order pursuant to Sections 7710 and 7720 of the Family Code.

The court may, either upon motion or in its own discretion, and after considering reasonable objections by the minor to the appointment of specific individuals, appoint a guardian ad litem to assist the minor in obtaining or opposing the order, provided that the appointment of the guardian ad litem does not delay the issuance or denial of the order being sought. In making the determination concerning the appointment of a particular guardian ad litem, the court shall consider whether the minor and the guardian have divergent interests.

(2) For purposes of this subdivision only, upon the issuance of an order pursuant to paragraph (1), if the minor initially appeared in court seeking an order without a guardian or guardian ad litem, and if the minor is residing with a parent or guardian, the court shall send a copy of the order to at least one parent or guardian designated by the minor, unless, in the discretion of the court, notification of a parent or guardian would be contrary to the best interest of the minor. The court is not required to send the order to more than one parent or guardian.

* * *

(c)(1) Notwithstanding subdivision (a), a minor may appear in court without a guardian ad litem in the following proceedings if the minor is a parent of the child who is the subject of the proceedings:

(A) Family court proceedings pursuant to Part 3 (commencing with Section 7600) of Division 12 of the Family Code.

(B) Dependency proceedings pursuant to Chapter 2 (commencing with Section 200) of Part 1 of Division 2 of the Welfare and Institutions Code.

(C) Guardianship proceedings for a minor child pursuant to Part 2 (commencing with Section 1500) of Division 4 of the Probate Code.

(D) Any other proceedings concerning child custody, visitation, or support.

(2) If the court finds that the minor parent is unable to understand the nature of the proceedings or to assist counsel in preparing the case, the court shall, upon its own motion or upon a motion by the minor parent or the minor parent's counsel, appoint a guardian ad litem.

(d) Before a court appoints a guardian ad litem pursuant to this chapter, a proposed guardian ad litem shall disclose both of the following to the court and all parties to the action or proceeding:

(1) Any known actual or potential conflicts of interest that would or might arise from the appointment.

(2) Any familial or affiliate relationship the proposed guardian ad litem has with any of the parties.

(e) If a guardian ad litem becomes aware that a potential conflict of interest has become an actual conflict of interest or that a new potential or actual conflict of interest exists, the guardian ad litem shall promptly disclose the conflict of interest to the court. *(Enacted in 1872. Amended by Code Am.1873–74, c. 383, p. 294, § 38; Code Am.1880, c. 68, p. 63, § 2; Stats.1913, c. 202, p. 350, § 1; Stats.1933, c. 744, p. 1837, § 1; Stats.1939, c. 313, p. 1599, § 1; Stats.1951, c. 1737, p. 4097, § 43; Stats.1953, c. 1315, p. 2873, § 1; Stats.1961, c. 721, p. 1962, § 1; Stats.1963, c. 127, p. 803, § 4; Stats.1967, c. 1259, p. 3046, § 1; Stats.1979, c. 730, p. 2476, § 19, operative Jan. 1, 1981; Stats.1994, c. 1269 (A.B.2208), § 2; Stats.1996, c. 727 (A.B.2155), § 2; Stats.1998, c. 706 (S.B.326), § 1, eff. Sept. 22, 1998; Stats.2008, c. 181 (S.B.1612), § 1; Stats.2014, c. 144 (A.B.1847), § 5, eff. Jan. 1, 2015; Stats.2022, c. 843 (S.B.1279), § 1, eff. Jan. 1, 2023.)*

Cross References

Action, guardian bringing and defending, see Probate Code § 2462.
Appointment of guardian ad litem for minor parent, see Welfare and Institutions Code § 326.7.
Appointment of guardians, see Probate Code § 1501 et seq.
Certificate of appointment, necessity of court seal, see Code of Civil Procedure § 153.
Compromise etc., in favor of minor, and deposits subject to withdrawal on court order, see Probate Code § 3600 et seq.
Compromise or covenant not to sue on minor's disputed claim, see Probate Code § 3500.
Department of mental health as guardian or administrator for estate of mentally disordered, see Welfare and Institutions Code § 7284.
Destruction of court records, notice, retention periods, see Government Code § 68152.
Divorce action on grounds of incurable insanity, guardian ad litem for defendant in, see Family Code § 2312.
Enforcement of minor's rights by guardian, see Family Code § 6601.
Injunctions, generally, see Code of Civil Procedure § 526.
Injunctions, preventive relief, see Civil Code § 3420 et seq.
Judicial Council, see Government Code § 68500 et seq.
Legislative intent, construction of statutes, see Code of Civil Procedure § 1859.
Protective orders and other domestic violence prevention orders, persons who may be granted order, see Family Code § 6301.
Tax refund action, see Revenue and Taxation Code §§ 5140, 5141 et seq.
Trust proceedings, appointment of guardian ad litem, exemption from this section, see Probate Code § 1003.
Workers' compensation proceedings, appointment of guardians in, see Labor Code §§ 5307.5, 5408.

Research References

Forms

7PT1 Am. Jur. Pl. & Pr. Forms Compromise and Settlement § 45, Statutory References.
3 California Transactions Forms--Business Transactions § 18:6, Capacity.
3 California Transactions Forms--Business Transactions § 18:16, Settlements that Require Court Approval.
West's California Code Forms, Civil Procedure § 372 Form 8, Parties—Notice of Motion for Order Appointing Guardian Ad Litem for Minor 12 Years or Older to Assist Minor in Obtaining Protective Order.
West's California Code Forms, Civil Procedure § 372 Form 10, Parties—Application for and Appointment of Guardian Ad Litem for Minor—Official Form.
West's California Code Forms, Probate § 2500–2507 Form 1, Petition by Guardian or Conservator to Approve Compromise of Disputed Personal Injury Claim of Minor or Incompetent Person—Judicial Council Form MC-350.
West's California Code Forms, Probate § 3500 Form 1, Petition by Parent to Compromise Disputed Personal Injury Claim of Minor Without a Guardian of the Estate—Judicial Council Form MC-350.
West's California Judicial Council Forms CIV-010, Application and Order for Appointment of Guardian Ad Litem—Civil.
West's California Judicial Council Forms MC-350, Petition for Approval of Compromise of Claim or Action or Disposition of Proceeds of Judgment for Minor or Person With a Disability.
West's California Judicial Council Forms MC-350(A-12b(5)), Additional Medical Service Providers Attachment to Petition for Approval of Compromise of Claim or Action or Disposition of Proceeds of Judgment.
West's California Judicial Council Forms MC-350EX, Petition for Expedited Approval of Compromise of Claim or Action or Disposition of Proceeds of Judgment for Minor or Person With a Disability.

West's California Judicial Council Forms MC–351, Order Approving Compromise of Disputed Claim or Pending Action or Disposition of Proceeds of Judgment for Minor or Person With a Disability.

West's California Judicial Council Forms MC–355, Order to Deposit Money Into Blocked Account.

West's California Judicial Council Forms MC–356, Acknowledgment of Receipt of Order and Funds for Deposit in Blocked Account.

§ 372.5. Guardian ad litem; appointment under pseudonym; procedure

(a) The court may appoint a guardian ad litem under a pseudonym pursuant to the requirements of this section.

(b) A person who applies for appointment as a guardian ad litem under a pseudonym shall, at the same time that the application is filed, file an ex parte request for leave to appear under a pseudonym. The ex parte request shall allege facts and circumstances establishing the guardian ad litem's overriding interest in preserving his or her anonymity.

(c) To permit an applicant for appointment as a guardian ad litem to appear under pseudonym, the court shall make each of the following findings:

(1) That the applicant has an overriding interest in preserving anonymity that supports permitting the applicant to appear under a pseudonym.

(2) That there is a substantial probability that the applicant's interest in preserving anonymity will be prejudiced if the applicant is not permitted to appear under a pseudonym.

(3) That permitting the applicant to appear under a pseudonym is narrowly tailored to serve the applicant's interest in preserving anonymity without unduly prejudicing the public's right of access or the ability of the other parties to prosecute, defend, or resolve the action.

(4) That there are no less restrictive means of protecting the applicant's interest in preserving his or her anonymity.

(d)(1) The court may make any further orders necessary to preserve the applicant's anonymity or to allow the other parties or financial institutions to know the applicant's identity to the extent necessary to prosecute, defend, or resolve the action.

(2) In addition to any other orders, the court may require a guardian ad litem who is permitted to appear under a pseudonym and is not represented by counsel to designate a mailing or electronic address for service of process and to consent to accept service of process under the pseudonym at that address for purposes of the action.

(e)(1) If a guardian ad litem is permitted to appear under a pseudonym, all court decisions, orders, petitions, and any documents filed with the court shall be written in a manner that protects the name and personal identifying information of the guardian ad litem from public disclosure, except to the extent the information is necessary for the parties to prosecute, defend, or resolve the action.

(2) For purposes of this subdivision, "personal identifying information" includes the guardian ad litem's name or any part thereof, his or her address or any part thereof, and the city or unincorporated area of the guardian ad litem's residence.

(f) The responsibility for excluding the name and personal identifying information of the guardian ad litem from documents filed with the court rests solely with the parties and their attorneys. This section does not require the court to review pleadings or other papers for compliance with this subdivision.

(g) After granting permission for a guardian ad litem to appear under a pseudonym pursuant to this section, the court shall retain discretion to reconsider its decision.

(h) This section does not affect the right of a plaintiff or petitioner to pursue litigation under a pseudonym in appropriate circumstances. (Added by Stats.2018, c. 817 (A.B.2185), § 1, eff. Jan. 1, 2019.)

§ 373. Guardian ad litem; appointment procedure

When a guardian ad litem is appointed, he or she shall be appointed as follows:

(a) If the minor is the plaintiff the appointment must be made before the summons is issued, upon the application of the minor, if the minor is 14 years of age or older, or, if under that age, upon the application of a relative or friend of the minor.

(b) If the minor is the defendant, upon the application of the minor, if the minor is 14 years of age or older, and the minor applies within 10 days after the service of the summons, or, if under that age or if the minor neglects to apply, then upon the application of a relative or friend of the minor, or of any other party to the action, or by the court on its own motion.

(c) If the person lacking legal competence to make decisions is a party to an action or proceeding, upon the application of a relative or friend of the person lacking legal competence to make decisions, or of any other party to the action or proceeding, or by the court on its own motion. *(Enacted in 1872. Amended by Code Am.1880, c. 68, p. 63, § 3; Stats.1933, c. 744, p. 1837, § 2; Stats.1971, c. 755, p. 1501, § 1; Stats.1980, c. 676, p. 1905, § 64; Stats.2014, c. 144 (A.B.1847), § 6, eff. Jan. 1, 2015.)*

Cross References

Appointment of guardians, see Probate Code § 1501 et seq.
Computation of time, see Code of Civil Procedure §§ 12, 12a; Government Code § 6800 et seq.
Enforcement of rights by minor, conduct of proceedings by guardian, see Family Code § 6601.
Guardians, notice of hearing, see Probate Code § 1460 et seq.
Guardianship and conservatorship, generally, see Probate Code § 1400 et seq.
Notice where personal representative and trustee are the same person, see Probate Code § 1208.
Service of summons on minors, wards and conservatees, see Code of Civil Procedure §§ 416.60, 416.70.
Service on guardians for wards, see Probate Code § 1210.
Trust proceedings, appointment of guardian ad litem, exemption from this section, see Probate Code § 1003.
Workers' compensation proceedings, appointment of guardians in, see Labor Code §§ 5307.5, 5408.

Research References

Forms

2 California Transactions Forms--Family Law § 6:11, Initiating Proceeding Under Uniform Parentage Act [Fam. Code, §§7600 to 7730].
West's California Code Forms, Civil Procedure § 116.410 Form 1, Small Claims Court—Order Appointing Guardian Ad Litem—Minor Under 14 Years.
West's California Code Forms, Civil Procedure § 373 Form 3, Parties—Petition for Appointment of Guardian Ad Litem—Application by Minor.
West's California Judicial Council Forms ADOPT–330, Request for Appointment of Confidential Intermediary.
West's California Judicial Council Forms FL–935, Application and Order for and Appointment of Guardian Ad Litem of Minor—Family Law.

§ 373.5. Guardian ad litem; persons not ascertained, not in being or unknown; powers; expenses

If under the terms of a written instrument, or otherwise, a person or persons of a designated class who are not ascertained or who are not in being, or a person or persons who are unknown, may be or may become legally or equitably interested in any property, real or personal, the court in which any action, petition or proceeding of any kind relative to or affecting the property is pending, may, upon the representation of any party thereto, or of any person interested, appoint a suitable person to appear and act therein as guardian ad litem of the person or persons not ascertained, not in being, or who are unknown; and the judgment, order or decree in the proceedings, made after the appointment, shall be conclusive upon all persons for whom the guardian ad litem was appointed.

§ 373.5

The guardian ad litem shall have power, with the approval of the court in which the action, petition or proceeding is pending, to compromise the same, to agree to the order or judgment to be entered therein for or against the persons for whom the guardian ad litem was appointed, and to satisfy any judgment or order in favor of the persons, or release, or discharge any claim of the persons pursuant to the compromise. The court shall have the same power with respect to the money or other property to be paid or delivered under such order or judgment as is provided in Section 372 of this code.

The reasonable expenses of the guardian ad litem, including compensation and counsel fees, shall be determined by the court and paid as it may order, either out of the property or by plaintiff or petitioner. If the expenses are to be paid by the plaintiff or petitioner, execution therefor may issue in the name of the guardian ad litem. *(Added by Stats.1949, c. 511, p. 869, § 1. Amended by Stats.1957, c. 976, p. 2217, § 1; Stats.1961, c. 435, p. 1503, § 1.)*

Cross References

Appointment of guardians, see Probate Code § 1501 et seq.
Eminent domain, unknown persons as defendants, see Code of Civil Procedure § 1250.220.
Instruments, construction and intent, see Code of Civil Procedure §§ 1858, 1859.
Quieting title, unknown persons as defendants, see Code of Civil Procedure § 762.010 et seq.
Trust proceedings, appointment of guardian ad litem, exemption from this section, see Probate Code § 1003.

§ 374. Minor under age 12; appearance without counsel when accompanied by guardian ad litem; conditions

(a) A minor under 12 years of age, accompanied by a duly appointed and acting guardian ad litem, shall be permitted to appear in court without counsel for the limited purpose of requesting or opposing a request for (1) an injunction or temporary restraining order or both to prohibit harassment pursuant to Section 527.6, (2) an injunction or temporary restraining order or both against violence or a credible threat of violence in the workplace pursuant to Section 527.8, (3) a protective order pursuant to Division 10 (commencing with Section 6200) of the Family Code, or (4) a protective order pursuant to Sections 7710 and 7720 of the Family Code.

(b) In making the determination concerning appointment of a particular guardian ad litem for purposes of this section, the court shall consider whether the minor and the guardian have divergent interests.

(c) The Judicial Council shall adopt forms by July 1, 1999, to implement this section. The forms shall be designed to facilitate the appointment of the guardian ad litem for purposes of this section. *(Added by Stats.1998, c. 706 (S.B.326), § 2, eff. Sept. 22, 1998.)*

Cross References

Counsel, right to, see Cal. Const. Art. 1, § 15, Cl. 3.
Injunctions, generally, see Code of Civil Procedure § 526.
Injunctions, preventive relief, see Civil Code § 3420 et seq.
Judicial Council, see Government Code § 68500 et seq.

§ 374.5. Orders affecting minors; jurisdiction

A proceeding initiated by or brought against a minor for any of the injunctions or orders described in paragraph (1) of subdivision (b) of Section 372 or subdivision (a) of Section 374 shall be heard in the court assigned to hear those matters; except that, if the minor bringing the action or against whom the action is brought has previously been adjudged a dependent child or a ward of the juvenile court, the matter shall be heard in the juvenile court having jurisdiction over the minor. *(Added by Stats.1998, c. 706 (S.B.326), § 3, eff. Sept. 22, 1998.)*

Cross References

Injunctions, generally, see Code of Civil Procedure § 526.
Injunctions, preventive relief, see Civil Code § 3420 et seq.

§ 375. Disability of party; effect on action

An action or proceeding does not abate by the disability of a party. The court, on motion, shall allow the action or proceeding to be continued by or against the party's representative. *(Added by Stats.1992, c. 178 (S.B.1496), § 17.)*

Research References

Forms
19 Am. Jur. Pl. & Pr. Forms Parties § 199, Statutory References.
19 Am. Jur. Pl. & Pr. Forms Parties § 248, Statutory References.
West's California Code Forms, Civil § 49 Form 1, Complaint—Abduction of Child.

§ 376. Parents; injuries to child; failure of one parent to join as plaintiff; service on parent not joining; illegitimate child; ward; parties defendant; death of child or ward; damages; consolidation of injury and death action

(a) The parents of a legitimate unmarried minor child, acting jointly, may maintain an action for injury to the child caused by the wrongful act or neglect of another. If either parent fails on demand to join as plaintiff in the action or is dead or cannot be found, then the other parent may maintain the action. The parent, if living, who does not join as plaintiff shall be joined as a defendant and, before trial or hearing of any question of fact, shall be served with summons either in the manner provided by law for the service of a summons in a civil action or by sending a copy of the summons and complaint by registered mail with proper postage prepaid addressed to that parent's last known address with request for a return receipt. If service is made by registered mail, the production of a return receipt purporting to be signed by the addressee creates a rebuttable presumption that the summons and complaint have been duly served. The presumption established by this section is a presumption affecting the burden of producing evidence. The respective rights of the parents to any award shall be determined by the court.

(b) A parent may maintain an action for such an injury to his or her illegitimate unmarried minor child if a guardian has not been appointed. Where a parent who does not have care, custody, or control of the child brings the action, the parent who has care, custody, or control of the child shall be served with the summons either in the manner provided by law for the serving of a summons in a civil action or by sending a copy of the summons and complaint by registered mail, with proper postage prepaid, addressed to the last known address of that parent, with request for a return receipt. If service is made by registered mail, the production of a return receipt purporting to be signed by the addressee creates a rebuttable presumption that the summons and complaint have been duly served. The presumption established by this section is a presumption affecting the burden of producing evidence. The respective rights of the parents to any award shall be determined by the court.

(c) The father of an illegitimate child who maintains an action under this section shall have acknowledged in writing prior to the child's injury, in the presence of a competent witness, that he is the father of the child, or, prior to the child's injury, have been judicially determined to be the father of the child.

(d) A parent of an illegitimate child who does not maintain an action under this section may be joined as a party thereto.

(e) A guardian may maintain an action for such an injury to his or her ward.

(f) An action under this section may be maintained against the person causing the injury. If any other person is responsible for the wrongful act or neglect, the action may also be maintained against the other person. The death of the child or ward does not abate the parents' or guardian's cause of action for the child's injury as to damages accruing before the child's death.

(g) In an action under this section, damages may be awarded that, under all of the circumstances of the case, may be just, except that:

(1) In an action maintained after the death of the child, the damages recoverable are as provided in Section 377.34.

(2) Where the person causing the injury is deceased, the damages recoverable in an action against the decedent's personal representative are as provided in Section 377.42.

(h) If an action arising out of the same wrongful act or neglect may be maintained pursuant to Section 377.60 for wrongful death of a child described in this section, the action authorized by this section may be consolidated therewith for trial as provided in Section 1048. (Enacted in 1872. Amended by Code Am.1873–74, c. 383, p. 294, § 39; Stats.1939, c. 425, p. 1759, § 1; Stats.1949, c. 1380, p. 2400, § 3; Stats.1961, c. 657, p. 1868, § 4; Stats.1969, c. 1611, p. 3378, § 4, operative July 1, 1970; Stats.1975, c. 1241, p. 3187, § 4; Stats.1992, c. 178 (S.B.1496), § 18.)

Cross References

Actions authorized by and against personal representative, see Probate Code § 9820 et seq.
Child custody, see Family Code § 3020 et seq.
Civil action defined, see Code of Civil Procedure § 30.
Hearsay rule, statement of minor child in parent's action for child's injury, see Evidence Code § 1226.
Physician-patient privilege, patient-litigant exception, see Evidence Code § 996.
Presumptions, see Evidence Code § 600 et seq.
Psychotherapist-patient privilege, patient-litigant exception, see Evidence Code § 1016.
Responsibility for willful acts and negligence, see Civil Code § 1714.
Survival of actions, generally, see Code of Civil Procedure §§ 377.20 et seq., 377.41.
Survival of actions for wrongful death, see Code of Civil Procedure § 377.20.
Unborn infants, limitation of actions for injuries suffered prior to or in course of birth, see Code of Civil Procedure § 340.4.
Writings, authentication and proof of, see Evidence Code § 1400 et seq.
Wrongful death of employee, action by personal representative, see Labor Code § 2803.

Research References

Forms

West's California Code Forms, Civil Procedure § 376 Form 3, Parties—Notice of Motion to Consolidate.

Title 4

OF THE PLACE OF TRIAL, RECLASSIFICATION, AND COORDINATION OF CIVIL ACTIONS

Cross References

Disciplinary actions by State Bar, venue, see Business and Professions Code § 6084.

CHAPTER 1. PLACE OF TRIAL

Section
395. Actions generally; proper court; waiver.
396b. Trial in court having jurisdiction of subject matter but not proper court; transfer; domestic relations cases; retention of cause for convenience of witnesses; time to file response upon denial of motion for transfer.
397. Change of place of trial; grounds.

Section
397.5. Proceedings related to continuation of marriage; transfer from county.
398. Transfer; proper court having jurisdiction.
399. Transfer; transmission of pleadings, papers, etc.; fees and costs; notice; jurisdiction of transferee court.
400. Petition for writ of mandate by party aggrieved.

Cross References

Disqualification of judge, rights under this Title not affected by, see Code of Civil Procedure § 170 et seq.
Proceedings to determine state's right to unclaimed property in federal custody, see Code of Civil Procedure § 1609.

§ 395. Actions generally; proper court; waiver

(a) Except as otherwise provided by law and subject to the power of the court to transfer actions or proceedings as provided in this title, the superior court in the county where the defendants or some of them reside at the commencement of the action is the proper court for the trial of the action. If the action is for injury to person or personal property or for death from wrongful act or negligence, the superior court in either the county where the injury occurs or the injury causing death occurs or the county where the defendants, or some of them reside at the commencement of the action, is a proper court for the trial of the action. In a proceeding for dissolution of marriage, the superior court in the county where either the petitioner or respondent has been a resident for three months next preceding the commencement of the proceeding is the proper court for the trial of the proceeding. In a proceeding for nullity of marriage or legal separation of the parties, the superior court in the county where either the petitioner or the respondent resides at the commencement of the proceeding is the proper court for the trial of the proceeding. In a proceeding to enforce an obligation of support under Section 3900 of the Family Code, the superior court in the county where the child resides is the proper court for the trial of the action. In a proceeding to establish and enforce a foreign judgment or court order for the support of a minor child, the superior court in the county where the child resides is the proper court for the trial of the action. Subject to subdivision (b), if a defendant has contracted to perform an obligation in a particular county, the superior court in the county where the obligation is to be performed, where the contract in fact was entered into, or where the defendant or any defendant resides at the commencement of the action is a proper court for the trial of an action founded on that obligation, and the county where the obligation is incurred is the county where it is to be performed, unless there is a special contract in writing to the contrary. If none of the defendants reside in the state or if they reside in the state and the county where they reside is unknown to the plaintiff, the action may be tried in the superior court in any county that the plaintiff may designate in his or her complaint, and, if the defendant is about to depart from the state, the action may be tried in the superior court in any county where either of the parties reside or service is made. If any person is improperly joined as a defendant or has been made a defendant solely for the purpose of having the action tried in the superior court in the county where he or she resides, his or her residence shall not be considered in determining the proper place for the trial of the action.

(b) Subject to the power of the court to transfer actions or proceedings as provided in this title, in an action arising from an offer or provision of goods, services, loans or extensions of credit intended primarily for personal, family or household use, other than an obligation described in Section 1812.10 or Section 2984.4 of the Civil Code, or an action arising from a transaction consummated as a proximate result of either an unsolicited telephone call made by a seller engaged in the business of consummating transactions of that kind or a telephone call or electronic transmission made by the buyer or lessee in response to a solicitation by the seller, the superior court in the county where the buyer or lessee in fact signed the contract,

§ 395

where the buyer or lessee resided at the time the contract was entered into, or where the buyer or lessee resides at the commencement of the action is the proper court for the trial of the action. In the superior court designated in this subdivision as the proper court, the proper court location for trial of a case is the location where the court tries that type of case that is nearest or most accessible to where the buyer or lessee resides, where the buyer or lessee in fact signed the contract, where the buyer or lessee resided at the time the contract was entered into, or where the buyer or lessee resides at the commencement of the action. Otherwise, any location of the superior court designated as the proper court in this subdivision is a proper court location for the trial. The court may specify by local rule the nearest or most accessible court location where the court tries that type of case.

(c) Any provision of an obligation described in subdivision (b) waiving that subdivision is void and unenforceable. *(Enacted in 1872. Amended by Stats.1907, c. 369, p. 700, § 3; Stats.1911, c. 421, p. 847, § 1; Stats.1933, c. 744, p. 1840, § 6; Stats.1939, c. 981, p. 2733, § 1; Stats.1951, c. 869, p. 2384, § 3; Stats.1955, c. 832, p. 1447, § 1; Stats.1969, c. 1608, p. 3344, § 11, operative Jan. 1, 1970; Stats.1970, c. 75, p. 88, § 1; Stats.1971, c. 1640, p. 3540, § 1; Stats.1972, c. 1117, § 1; Stats.1972, c. 1118, § 3; Stats.1972, c. 1119, § 3; Stats.1976, c. 610, p. 1460, § 1; Stats.1991, c. 228 (A.B.1889), § 3; Stats.1992, c. 163 (A.B.2641), § 17, operative Jan. 1, 1994; Stats.1994, c. 1269 (A.B.2208), § 2.4; Stats.1998, c. 473 (A.B.2134), § 1; Stats.1998, c. 931 (S.B.2139), § 62, eff. Sept. 28, 1998; Stats. 1998, c. 931 (S.B.2139), § 62.5, eff. Sept. 28, 1998, operative Jan. 1, 1999; Stats.2002, c. 806 (A.B.3027), § 8.)*

Cross References

Contracts,
   Generally, see Civil Code § 1549 et seq.
   Damages and interest, see Civil Code §§ 3287, 3291, 3300.
   Fraud, see Civil Code §§ 1571 to 1574.
   Impairment of, see Cal. Const. Art. 1, § 9.
   Implied, see Civil Code § 1621.
   Interpretation, see Civil Code § 1635 et seq.
Criminal actions,
   Change of venue, see Penal Code § 1033 et seq.
   Inferior court proceedings, see Penal Code §§ 1127, 1128.
Discovery prior to filing of claim, matters and methods available, see Code of Civil Procedure § 2035.010 et seq.
Dissolution of corporation, involuntary proceedings by directors or shareholders, see Corporations Code § 1806.
Divorce actions, residence requirements, see Family Code §§ 2320, 2321.
Eminent domain proceedings, see Code of Civil Procedure §§ 1250.010 et seq., 1250.110 et seq.
Escheat proceedings, venue, see Code of Civil Procedure § 1410.
Injury to persons, generally, see Code of Civil Procedure § 29.
Joinder of parties, see Code of Civil Procedure § 378.
Limited partnership, cancellation or amendment of certificate, see Corporations Code §§ 15902.02, 15902.03.
Obligation defined, see Code of Civil Procedure § 26.
Partition of real and personal property, venue, see Code of Civil Procedure § 872.110.
Residence, generally, see Government Code § 243.
Residence of minors, see Welfare and Institutions Code § 17.1.
Writings, authentication and proof of, see Evidence Code § 1400 et seq.

Research References

Forms

West's California Code Forms, Civil Procedure § 394 Form 3, Place of Trial—Order Transferring Case.
West's California Code Forms, Civil Procedure § 400 Form 1, Change of Venue—Petition for Writ of Mandate.
West's California Code Forms, Civil Procedure § 585.5 Form 1, Judgments—Default—Notice of Motion to Set Aside Default and Default Judgment and for Leave to Defend Action.
West's California Code Forms, Commercial § 1301 Form 6, Clause Selecting Applicable Forum.
West's California Code Forms, Corporations § 800 Form 5, Complaint for Breach of Contract (Alter Ego).

§ 396b. Trial in court having jurisdiction of subject matter but not proper court; transfer; domestic relations cases; retention of cause for convenience of witnesses; time to file response upon denial of motion for transfer

(a) Except as otherwise provided in Section 396a, if an action or proceeding is commenced in a court having jurisdiction of the subject matter thereof, other than the court designated as the proper court for the trial thereof, under this title, the action may, notwithstanding, be tried in the court where commenced, unless the defendant, at the time he or she answers, demurs, or moves to strike, or, at his or her option, without answering, demurring, or moving to strike and within the time otherwise allowed to respond to the complaint, files with the clerk, a notice of motion for an order transferring the action or proceeding to the proper court, together with proof of service, upon the adverse party, of a copy of those papers. Upon the hearing of the motion the court shall, if it appears that the action or proceeding was not commenced in the proper court, order the action or proceeding transferred to the proper court.

(b) In its discretion, the court may order the payment to the prevailing party of reasonable expenses and attorney's fees incurred in making or resisting the motion to transfer whether or not that party is otherwise entitled to recover his or her costs of action. In determining whether that order for expenses and fees shall be made, the court shall take into consideration (1) whether an offer to stipulate to change of venue was reasonably made and rejected, and (2) whether the motion or selection of venue was made in good faith given the facts and law the party making the motion or selecting the venue knew or should have known. As between the party and his or her attorney, those expenses and fees shall be the personal liability of the attorney not chargeable to the party. Sanctions shall not be imposed pursuant to this subdivision except on notice contained in a party's papers, or on the court's own noticed motion, and after opportunity to be heard.

(c) The court in a proceeding for dissolution of marriage or legal separation or under the Uniform Parentage Act (Part 3 (commencing with Section 7600) of Division 12 of the Family Code) may, prior to the determination of the motion to transfer, consider and determine motions for allowance of temporary spousal support, support of children, and counsel fees and costs, and motions to determine custody of and visitation with children, and may make all necessary and proper orders in connection therewith.

(d) In any case, if an answer is filed, the court may consider opposition to the motion to transfer, if any, and may retain the action in the county where commenced if it appears that the convenience of the witnesses or the ends of justice will thereby be promoted.

(e) If the motion to transfer is denied, the court shall allow the defendant time to move to strike, demur, or otherwise plead if the defendant has not previously filed a response. *(Added by Stats.1933, c. 744, p. 1842, § 8a. Amended by Stats.1939, c. 149, p. 1263, § 1; Stats.1951, c. 869, p. 2387, § 6; Stats.1969, c. 345, p. 720, § 1; Stats.1969, c. 1608, p. 3345, § 12; Stats.1969, c. 1609, p. 3360, § 28, operative Jan. 1, 1970; Stats.1974, c. 1369, p. 2964, § 2; Stats.1981, c. 122, p. 856, § 1; Stats.1982, c. 704, p. 2856, § 1; Stats.1983, c. 1167, § 1; Stats.1989, c. 1416, § 11; Stats.1989, c. 1417, § 3.5; Stats.1992, c. 163 (A.B.2641), § 18, operative Jan. 1, 1994; Stats.2005, c. 706 (A.B.1742), § 10.)*

Application

For application of 2005 amendment, see Stats.2005, c. 706 (A.B.1742), § 41.

Cross References

Attorney's fees and costs, generally, see Code of Civil Procedure § 1021.

Judgment on default, notice of motion to transfer, see Code of Civil Procedure § 585.
Judgments, jurisdiction necessary, see Code of Civil Procedure § 1917.
Motions and orders, see Code of Civil Procedure § 1003 et seq.
Notice, actual and constructive, defined, see Civil Code § 18.
Notices, and filing and service of papers, see Code of Civil Procedure § 1010 et seq.

Research References

Forms

West's California Code Forms, Civil Procedure § 396b Form 1, Place of Trial—Notice of Motion to Transfer Action Where Court Has Jurisdiction.

West's California Code Forms, Civil Procedure § 397 Form 2, Place of Trial—Notice of Motion for Change of Venue.

§ 397. Change of place of trial; grounds

The court may, on motion, change the place of trial in the following cases:

(a) When the court designated in the complaint is not the proper court.

(b) When there is reason to believe that an impartial trial cannot be had therein.

(c) When the convenience of witnesses and the ends of justice would be promoted by the change.

(d) When from any cause there is no judge of the court qualified to act.

(e) When a proceeding for dissolution of marriage has been filed in the county in which the petitioner has been a resident for three months next preceding the commencement of the proceeding, and the respondent at the time of the commencement of the proceeding is a resident of another county in this state, to the county of the respondent's residence when the ends of justice would be promoted by the change. If a motion to change the place of trial is made pursuant to this paragraph, the court may, prior to the determination of such motion, consider and determine motions for allowance of temporary spousal support, support of children, temporary restraining orders, attorneys' fees, and costs, and make all necessary and proper orders in connection therewith. (Enacted in 1872. Amended by Stats.1907, c. 369, p. 701, § 5; Stats.1933, c. 744, p. 1843, § 9; Stats.1955, c. 832, p. 1448, § 2; Stats.1969, c. 1608, p. 3346, § 13, operative Jan. 1, 1970; Stats.1992, c. 163 (A.B.2641), § 19, operative Jan. 1, 1994.)

Cross References

Attorney's fees and costs, generally, see Code of Civil Procedure § 1021.
Corporations, venue of actions against, see Code of Civil Procedure § 395.5.
Criminal cases, change of venue, see Penal Code § 1033 et seq.
Eminent domain proceedings, venue, see Code of Civil Procedure § 1250.020 et seq.
Grounds for disqualification of judges, see Code of Civil Procedure § 170.1.
Groundwater sustainability plan, action to determine validity of plan, see Water Code § 10726.6.
Guardianship proceedings, venue, see Probate Code § 2201.
Judges, disqualification, generally, see Code of Civil Procedure § 170 et seq.
Mandamus, see Code of Civil Procedure § 1085.
Methods for dissolution of marriage, see Family Code § 310.
Probate proceedings, transfer, see Probate Code § 7070 et seq.
Prohibition, see Code of Civil Procedure § 1102 et seq.
Residence requirement, dissolution of marriage, see Family Code § 2320 et seq.
Transfer of motion or order to show cause, see Code of Civil Procedure § 1006.
Venue, action or proceeding by local entity against state, change to Sacramento County, see Government Code § 955.3.

Research References

Forms

California Practice Guide: Rutter Family Law Forms Form 4:22, Request for Order to Transfer Venue.

West's California Code Forms, Civil Procedure § 397 Form 2, Place of Trial—Notice of Motion for Change of Venue.

West's California Code Forms, Civil Procedure § 400 Form 1, Change of Venue—Petition for Writ of Mandate.

§ 397.5. Proceedings related to continuation of marriage; transfer from county

In any proceeding for dissolution or nullity of marriage or legal separation of the parties under the Family Code, where it appears that both petitioner and respondent have moved from the county rendering the order, the court may, when the ends of justice and the convenience of the parties would be promoted by the change, order that the proceedings be transferred to the county of residence of either party. (Added by Stats.1971, c. 1210, p. 2328, § 7. Amended by Stats.1980, c. 234, p. 477, § 2; Stats.1994, c. 1269 (A.B.2208), § 2.6.)

Cross References

Enforcement proceedings, see Family Code § 290.
Modification of order for support of other party, see Family Code § 4330.
Residence requirements, dissolution of marriage, see Family Code § 2320 et seq.

§ 398. Transfer; proper court having jurisdiction

(a) If a court orders the transfer of an action or proceeding for a cause specified in subdivisions (b), (c), and (d) of Section 397, the action or proceeding shall be transferred to a court having jurisdiction of the subject matter of the action upon agreement of the parties by stipulation in writing, or in open court and entered in the minutes or docket. If the parties do not so agree, the action or proceeding shall be transferred to the nearest or most accessible court where the like objection or cause for making the order does not exist.

(b) If an action or proceeding is commenced in a court other than one designated as a proper court for the trial thereof by the provisions of this title, and the same is ordered transferred for that reason, the action or proceeding shall be transferred to a proper court upon agreement of the parties by stipulation in writing, or in open court and entered in the minutes or docket. If the parties do not so agree, the action or proceeding shall be transferred to a proper court in the county in which the action or proceeding was commenced which the defendant may designate or, if there is no proper court in that county, to a proper court, in a proper county, designated by the defendant. If the defendant does not designate the court as herein provided, or if the court orders the transfer of an action on its own motion as provided in this title, the action or proceeding shall be transferred to the proper court as determined by the court in which the action or proceeding is pending.

(c) The designation of the court by the defendant as provided for in subdivision (b), may be made in the notice of motion for change of venue or in open court and entered in the minutes or docket at the time the order for transfer is made. (Enacted in 1872. Amended by Stats.1881, c. 30, p. 23, § 2; Stats.1897, c. 124, p. 184, § 1; Stats.1925, c. 438, p. 948, § 1; Stats.1927, c. 744, p. 1406, § 2; Stats.1933, c. 744, p. 1843, § 10; Stats.2015, c. 303 (A.B.731), § 39, eff. Jan. 1, 2016.)

Cross References

Foreclosure of mechanic's liens, etc., transfer from municipal court, see Code of Civil Procedure § 86.
Notice, actual and constructive, defined, see Civil Code § 18.
Transfer for bias or prejudice of judge, see Code of Civil Procedure § 170 et seq.
Writings, authentication and proof of, see Evidence Code § 1400 et seq.

§ 399. Transfer; transmission of pleadings, papers, etc.; fees and costs; notice; jurisdiction of transferee court

(a) If an order is made transferring an action or proceeding under any provision of this title, the clerk shall, after expiration of the time within which a petition for writ of mandate could have been filed pursuant to Section 400, or if a writ petition is filed after judgment denying the writ becomes final, and upon payment of the costs and fees, transmit the pleadings and papers of the action or proceeding, or, if the pleadings are oral, a transcript of the pleadings, to the clerk of the court to which the action or proceeding is transferred. If the transfer is sought on any ground specified in subdivision (b), (c), (d), or (e) of Section 397, the costs and fees of the transfer, and of filing the papers in the court to which the transfer is ordered, shall be paid at the time the notice of motion is filed by the party making the motion for the transfer. If the transfer is sought solely, or is ordered, because the action or proceeding was commenced in a court other than that designated as proper by this title, those costs and fees, including any expenses and attorney's fees awarded to the defendant pursuant to Section 396b, shall be paid by the plaintiff before the transfer is made. If the defendant has paid those costs and fees at the time of filing a notice of motion, those costs and fees shall be repaid to the defendant, upon the making of the transfer order. If those costs and fees have not been paid by the plaintiff within five days after service of notice of the transfer order, any other party interested in the action or proceeding, whether named in the complaint as a party or not, may pay those costs and fees, and the clerk shall transmit the papers and pleadings of the action or proceeding as if those costs and fees had been originally paid by the plaintiff, and those costs and fees shall be a proper item of costs of the party paying them, recoverable by that party if that party prevails in the action. Otherwise, those costs and fees shall be offset against and deducted from the amount, if any, awarded the plaintiff if the plaintiff prevails against that party in the action. The cause of action shall not be further prosecuted in any court until those costs and fees are paid. If those costs and fees are not paid within 30 days after service of notice of the transfer order, if a copy of a petition for writ of mandate pursuant to Section 400 is filed in the trial court, or if an appeal is taken pursuant to Section 904.2, then, within 30 days after notice of finality of the order of transfer, the court on a duly noticed motion by any party may dismiss the action without prejudice to the cause on the condition that no other action on the cause may be commenced in another court before satisfaction of the court's order for costs and fees. If a petition for writ of mandate or appeal does not result in a stay of proceedings, the time for payment of those costs and fees shall be 60 days after service of the notice of the order.

(b) At the time of transmittal of the papers and pleadings, the clerk shall mail notice to all parties who have appeared in the action or special proceeding, stating the date on which the transmittal occurred. Promptly upon receipt of the papers and pleadings, the clerk of the court to which the action or proceeding is transferred shall mail notice to all parties who have appeared in the action or special proceeding, stating the date of the filing of the case and number assigned to the case in the court.

(c) The court to which an action or proceeding is transferred under this title shall have and exercise over the action or proceeding the like jurisdiction as if it had been originally commenced in that court, all prior proceedings being saved, and the court may require amendment of the pleadings, the filing and service of amended, additional, or supplemental pleadings, and the giving of notice, as may be necessary for the proper presentation and determination of the action or proceeding in the court.

(d) Notwithstanding subdivision (c), the court transferring jurisdiction of a family law action or proceeding pursuant to Section 398 shall, if another court has not assumed jurisdiction over the action or proceeding, retain jurisdiction to make orders designed to prevent:

(1) Immediate danger or irreparable harm to a party or to the children involved in the matter.

(2) Immediate loss or damage to property subject to disposition in the matter.

(e) By January 1, 2019, the Judicial Council shall, by rule of court, establish:

(1) The timeframe for a court to transfer jurisdiction over a family law action or proceeding.

(2) The timeframe for a court to assume jurisdiction over a family law action or proceeding. *(Enacted in 1872. Amended by Stats.1909, c. 723, p. 1097, § 1; Stats.1933, c. 744, p. 1844, § 11; Stats.1935, c. 722, p. 1949, § 3; Stats.1951, c. 869, p. 2388, § 7; Stats.1955, c. 832, p. 1449, § 3; Stats.1959, c. 1487, p. 3780, § 2; Stats.1961, c. 1059, p. 2747, § 1; Stats.1969, c. 345, p. 721, § 2; Stats.1974, c. 1369, p. 2965, § 3; Stats.1989, c. 1417, § 4; Stats.2007, c. 43 (S.B.649), § 4; Stats.2017, c. 316 (A.B.712), § 1, eff. Jan. 1, 2018.)*

Cross References

Attorney's fees and costs, generally, see Code of Civil Procedure § 1021.
Change of venue, transmission of transcript, fee, see Government Code § 26823.
Collection of fees, see Government Code §§ 26820, 72004.
Computation of time, see Code of Civil Procedure §§ 12, 12a; Government Code § 6800 et seq.
Guardianship proceedings, see Probate Code § 2211 et seq.
Mandamus, purpose of writ of mandate, courts which may issue writ and parties to whom issued, see Code of Civil Procedure § 1085.
Notice, actual and constructive, defined, see Civil Code § 18.
Probate proceedings, generally, see Probate Code § 1000 et seq.
Probate proceedings, retransfer to original court, conditions required, see Probate Code § 7072.
Special proceeding defined, see Code of Civil Procedure § 23.

Research References

Forms

West's California Code Forms, Civil Procedure § 399 Form 1, Place of Trial—Change of Venue—Notice of Motion to Dismiss for Failure to Pay Costs on Change of Venue.

§ 400. Petition for writ of mandate by party aggrieved

When an order is made by the superior court granting or denying a motion to change the place of trial, the party aggrieved by the order may, within 20 days after service of a written notice of the order, petition the court of appeal for the district in which the court granting or denying the motion is situated for a writ of mandate requiring trial of the case in the proper court. The superior court may, for good cause, and prior to the expiration of the initial 20-day period, extend the time for one additional period not to exceed 10 days. The petitioner shall file a copy of the petition in the trial court immediately after the petition is filed in the court of appeal. The court of appeal may stay all proceedings in the case, pending judgment on the petition becoming final. The clerk of the court of appeal shall file with the clerk of the trial court, a copy of any final order or final judgment immediately after the order or judgment becomes final. *(Added by Stats.1961, c. 1059, p. 2748, § 3. Amended by Stats.1963, c. 461, p. 1309, § 1; Stats.1967, c. 17, p. 828, § 12; Stats.1984, c. 145, § 1; Stats.1989, c. 1416, § 12; Stats.1998, c. 931 (S.B.2139), § 67, eff. Sept. 28, 1998; Stats.1999, c. 344 (S.B.210), § 10, eff. Sept. 7, 1999.)*

Cross References

Appeals in civil actions,
   Generally, see Code of Civil Procedure § 901 et seq.
   Computation of time, see Code of Civil Procedure §§ 12, 12a; Government Code § 6800 et seq.
Mandamus, purpose of writ of mandate, courts which may issue writ and parties to whom issued, see Code of Civil Procedure § 1085.
Notice, actual and constructive, defined, see Civil Code § 18.
Writ of mandate, see Code of Civil Procedure § 1084 et seq.

Research References

Forms

West's California Code Forms, Civil Procedure § 400 Form 1, Change of Venue—Petition for Writ of Mandate.

Title 4.5

RECORDING NOTICE OF CERTAIN ACTIONS

Cross References

Mechanics' liens, notice of pendency of proceedings to be recorded as provided in this title, see Civil Code § 8424.

Probate, proceedings affecting real property, notice of pendency of proceedings to be filed pursuant to civil action procedures, see Probate Code § 1004.
Recording,
   Constructive notice, conveyances or real property or estate for years, see Civil Code § 1213.
   Instruments or judgments, documents to be recorded and manner of recording, see Government Code § 27320 et seq., § 27280 et seq.
   Property transfers, place of recordation, see Civil Code § 1169.
Successor agency action directed by oversight board, challenge to action involving title to or an interest in real property, recording of notice of pendency of action, see Health and Safety Code § 34181.

CHAPTER 2. RECORDATION SERVICE AND FILING

Section
405.20. Place of recording; contents.
405.21. Prerequisites to recording.
405.22. Service.
405.23. Service upon adverse parties and owners; requirements; proof of service.
405.24. Constructive notice; time of recording; rights and interests relate back to date of recording.

§ 405.20. Place of recording; contents

A party to an action who asserts a real property claim may record a notice of pendency of action in which that real property claim is alleged. The notice may be recorded in the office of the recorder of each county in which all or part of the real property is situated. The notice shall contain the names of all parties to the action and a description of the property affected by the action. *(Added by Stats.1992, c. 883 (A.B.3620), § 2. Amended by Stats.2004, c. 227 (S.B.1102), § 10, eff. Aug. 16, 2004.)*

Cross References

Buildings in violation, notice to abate nuisance, instituting actions or proceedings, see Health and Safety Code § 17980.
Notice, actual and constructive, defined, see Civil Code § 18.
Recording,
   Constructive notice, conveyances or real property or estate for years, see Civil Code § 1213.
   Instruments or judgments, documents to be recorded and manner of recording, see Government Code § 27320 et seq., § 27280 et seq.
   Property transfers, place of recordation, see Civil Code § 1169.
Tax-deeded land, notice to state and last owner, neglected or abandoned plant or crop, see Food and Agricultural Code § 5577.

Research References

Forms

West's California Code Forms, Civil § 1013.5 Form 2, Notice—Lis Pendens—Action to Remove Improvements Erroneously Affixed to Land.

§ 405.21. Prerequisites to recording

An attorney of record in an action may sign a notice of pendency of action. Alternatively, a judge of the court in which an action that includes a real property claim is pending may, upon request of a party thereto, approve a notice of pendency of action. A notice of pendency of action shall not be recorded unless (a) it has been signed by the attorney of record, (b) it is signed by a party acting in propria persona and approved by a judge as provided in this section, or (c) the action is subject to Section 405.6. *(Added by Stats.1992, c. 883 (A.B.3620), § 2. Amended by Stats.1994, c. 146 (A.B.3601), § 20.)*

Cross References

Notice, actual and constructive, defined, see Civil Code § 18.

§ 405.22. Service

Except in actions subject to Section 405.6, the claimant shall, prior to recordation of the notice, cause a copy of the notice to be mailed, by registered or certified mail, return receipt requested, to all known addresses of the parties to whom the real property claim is adverse and to all owners of record of the real property affected by the real property claim as shown by the latest county assessment roll. If there is no known address for service on an adverse party or owner, then as to that party or owner a declaration under penalty of perjury to that effect may be recorded instead of the proof of service required above, and the service on that party or owner shall not be required. Immediately following recordation, a copy of the notice shall also be filed with the court in which the action is pending. Service shall also be made immediately and in the same manner upon each adverse party later joined in the action. *(Added by Stats.1992, c. 883 (A.B.3620), § 2. Amended by Stats.1996, c. 1159 (A.B.3471), § 9; Stats.2004, c. 227 (S.B.1102), § 11, eff. Aug. 16, 2004.)*

Cross References

Notice, actual and constructive, defined, see Civil Code § 18.
Recording,
   Constructive notice, conveyances or real property or estate for years, see Civil Code § 1213.
   Instruments or judgments, documents to be recorded and manner of recording, see Government Code § 27320 et seq., § 27280 et seq.
   Property transfers, place of recordation, see Civil Code § 1169.

§ 405.23. Service upon adverse parties and owners; requirements; proof of service

Any notice of pendency of action shall be void and invalid as to any adverse party or owner of record unless the requirements of Section 405.22 are met for that party or owner and a proof of service in the form and content specified in Section 1013a has been recorded with the notice of pendency of action. *(Added by Stats.1992, c. 883 (A.B.3620), § 2.)*

Cross References

Notice, actual and constructive, defined, see Civil Code § 18.

§ 405.24. Constructive notice; time of recording; rights and interests relate back to date of recording

From the time of recording the notice of pendency of action, a purchaser, encumbrancer, or other transferee of the real property described in the notice shall be deemed to have constructive notice of the pendency of the noticed action as it relates to the real property and only of its pendency against parties not fictitiously named. The rights and interest of the claimant in the property, as ultimately determined in the pending noticed action, shall relate back to the date of the recording of the notice. *(Added by Stats.1992, c. 883 (A.B.3620), § 2.)*

Cross References

Notice, actual and constructive, defined, see Civil Code § 18.
Recording,
   Constructive notice, conveyances or real property or estate for years, see Civil Code § 1213.
   Instruments or judgments, documents to be recorded and manner of recording, see Government Code § 27320 et seq., § 27280 et seq.
   Property transfers, place of recordation, see Civil Code § 1169.

CHAPTER 3. EXPUNGEMENT AND OTHER RELIEF

Section
405.30. Application to court for expungement; parties or nonparties with interest; evidence; burden of proof.
405.31. Pleading; real property claim.
405.32. Standard of proof.
405.33. Giving of an undertaking; conditional expungement of notice; fulfillment of condition; recovery; presumption.
405.34. Giving of undertaking as condition of maintaining notice; nonparties; evidence; compliance; recovery.

CODE OF CIVIL PROCEDURE

Section
405.35. Effective date and recording of order expunging notice of pendency.
405.36. Expungement of notice of pending action; subsequent notice as to affected property; recording.
405.37. Exoneration or modification of undertaking; conditional order.
405.38. Attorney's fees and costs.
405.39. Appeal of orders or other actions; review; writ of mandate; filing and service.

§ 405.30. Application to court for expungement; parties or nonparties with interest; evidence; burden of proof

At any time after notice of pendency of action has been recorded, any party, or any nonparty with an interest in the real property affected thereby, may apply to the court in which the action is pending to expunge the notice. However, a person who is not a party to the action shall obtain leave to intervene from the court at or before the time the party brings the motion to expunge the notice. Evidence or declarations may be filed with the motion to expunge the notice. The court may permit evidence to be received in the form of oral testimony, and may make any orders it deems just to provide for discovery by any party affected by a motion to expunge the notice. The claimant shall have the burden of proof under Sections 405.31 and 405.32. *(Added by Stats.1992, c. 883 (A.B.3620), § 2.)*

Cross References

Burden of proof, generally, see Evidence Code § 500 et seq.
Discovery, generally, see Code of Civil Procedure § 2016.010 et seq.
Notice, actual and constructive, defined, see Civil Code § 18.
Recording,
  Constructive notice, conveyances or real property or estate for years, see Civil Code § 1213.
  Instruments or judgments, documents to be recorded and manner of recording, see Government Code § 27320 et seq., § 27280 et seq.
Property transfers, place of recordation, see Civil Code § 1169.

Research References

Forms

West's California Code Forms, Civil Procedure § 405.30 Form 1, Commencement of Action—Notice of Pendency of Action—Notice of Motion to Expunge.

§ 405.31. Pleading; real property claim

In proceedings under this chapter, the court shall order the notice expunged if the court finds that the pleading on which the notice is based does not contain a real property claim. The court shall not order an undertaking to be given as a condition of expunging the notice where the court finds the pleading does not contain a real property claim. *(Added by Stats.1992, c. 883 (A.B.3620), § 2.)*

Cross References

Bond and Undertaking Law, bonds or undertakings given as security, see Code of Civil Procedure § 995.010 et seq.
Notice, actual and constructive, defined, see Civil Code § 18.

Research References

Forms

West's California Code Forms, Civil Procedure § 405.31 Form 1, Commencement of Action—Notice of Pendency of Action—Order Expunging Notice of Pendency of Action (No Undertaking).

§ 405.32. Standard of proof

In proceedings under this chapter, the court shall order that the notice be expunged if the court finds that the claimant has not established by a preponderance of the evidence the probable validity of the real property claim. The court shall not order an undertaking to be given as a condition of expunging the notice if the court finds the claimant has not established the probable validity of the real property claim. *(Added by Stats.1992, c. 883 (A.B.3620), § 2.)*

Cross References

Bond and Undertaking Law, bonds or undertakings given as security, see Code of Civil Procedure § 995.010 et seq.
Notice, actual and constructive, defined, see Civil Code § 18.

Research References

Forms

West's California Code Forms, Civil Procedure § 405.30 Form 1, Commencement of Action—Notice of Pendency of Action—Notice of Motion to Expunge.

§ 405.33. Giving of an undertaking; conditional expungement of notice; fulfillment of condition; recovery; presumption

In proceedings under this chapter, the court shall order that the notice be expunged if the court finds that the real property claim has probable validity, but adequate relief can be secured to the claimant by the giving of an undertaking. The expungement order shall be conditioned upon the giving of the undertaking of such nature and in such amount as will indemnify the claimant for all damages proximately resulting from the expungement which the claimant may incur if the claimant prevails upon the real property claim. In its order conditionally expunging the notice, the court shall set a return date for the moving party to show fulfillment of the condition, and if the moving party fails to show fulfillment of the condition on the return day, the court shall deny the motion to expunge without further notice or hearing. Recovery may be had on the undertaking pursuant to Section 996.440.

For purposes only of determining under this section whether the giving of an undertaking will secure adequate relief to the claimant, the presumption of Section 3387 of the Civil Code that real property is unique shall not apply, except in the case of real property improved with a single-family dwelling which the claimant intends to occupy. *(Added by Stats.1992, c. 883 (A.B.3620), § 2.)*

Cross References

Bond and Undertaking Law, bonds or undertakings given as security, see Code of Civil Procedure § 995.010 et seq.
Notice, actual and constructive, defined, see Civil Code § 18.
Presumptions, see Evidence Code § 600 et seq.

§ 405.34. Giving of undertaking as condition of maintaining notice; nonparties; evidence; compliance; recovery

Subject to the provisions of Sections 405.31 and 405.32, at any time after a notice of pendency of action has been recorded, and regardless of whether a motion to expunge has been filed, the court may, upon motion by any person with an interest in the property, require the claimant to give the moving party an undertaking as a condition of maintaining the notice in the record title. However, a person who is not a party to the action shall obtain leave to intervene from the court at or before the time the person moves to require an undertaking. The court may permit evidence to be received in the form of oral testimony and may make any orders it deems just to provide for discovery by any affected party. An undertaking required pursuant to this section shall be of such nature and in such amount as the court may determine to be just. In its order requiring an undertaking, the court shall set a return date for the claimant to show compliance and if the claimant fails to show compliance on the return date, the court shall order the notice of pendency of action expunged without further notice or hearing.

Recovery on an undertaking required pursuant to this section may be had in an amount not to exceed the undertaking, pursuant to Section 996.440, upon a showing (a) that the claimant did not prevail on the real property claim and (b) that the person seeking recovery suffered damages as a result of the maintenance of the notice. In assessing these damages, the court shall not consider the claimant's intent or the presence or absence of probable cause. *(Added by Stats.1992, c. 883 (A.B.3620), § 2.)*

Cross References

Bond and Undertaking Law, bonds or undertakings given as security, see Code of Civil Procedure § 995.010 et seq.
Notice, actual and constructive, defined, see Civil Code § 18.
Recording,
   Constructive notice, conveyances or real property or estate for years, see Civil Code § 1213.
   Instruments or judgments, documents to be recorded and manner of recording, see Government Code § 27320 et seq., § 27280 et seq.
   Property transfers, place of recordation, see Civil Code § 1169.

Research References

Forms

West's California Code Forms, Civil Procedure § 405.34 Form 1, Commencement of Action—Notice of Pendency of Action—Notice of Motion to Require Undertaking as Condition of Maintaining Notice.

§ 405.35. Effective date and recording of order expunging notice of pendency

No order expunging a notice of pendency of action shall be effective, nor shall it be recorded in the office of any county recorder, until the time within which a petition for writ of mandate may be filed pursuant to Section 405.39 has expired. No order expunging a notice of pendency of action shall be effective, nor shall it be recorded in the office of any county recorder, after a petition for writ of mandate has been timely filed pursuant to Section 405.39, until the proceeding commenced by the petition is finally adjudicated. This section imposes no duty on the county recorder to determine whether the requirements of this section or of any order expunging a notice of pendency of action have been met. *(Added by Stats.1992, c. 883 (A.B.3620), § 2.)*

Cross References

Discovery, generally, see Code of Civil Procedure § 2016.010 et seq.
Mandamus, purpose of writ of mandate, courts which may issue writ and parties to whom issued, see Code of Civil Procedure § 1085.
Notice, actual and constructive, defined, see Civil Code § 18.

§ 405.36. Expungement of notice of pending action; subsequent notice as to affected property; recording

Once a notice of pending action has been expunged, the claimant may not record another notice of pending action as to the affected property without leave of the court in which the action is pending. *(Added by Stats.1992, c. 883 (A.B.3620), § 2.)*

Cross References

Notice, actual and constructive, defined, see Civil Code § 18.
Recording,
   Constructive notice, conveyances or real property or estate for years, see Civil Code § 1213.
   Instruments or judgments, documents to be recorded and manner of recording, see Government Code § 27320 et seq., § 27280 et seq.
   Property transfers, place of recordation, see Civil Code § 1169.

§ 405.37. Exoneration or modification of undertaking; conditional order

After notice and hearing, for good cause and upon such terms as are just, the court may exonerate or modify any undertaking required by an order issued pursuant to Section 405.33 or 405.34 or pursuant to a stipulation made in lieu of such an order. An order of the court under this section may be made conditional upon the giving of a new undertaking under Section 405.33 or 405.34. *(Added by Stats.1992, c. 883 (A.B.3620), § 2.)*

Cross References

Bond and Undertaking Law, bonds or undertakings given as security, see Code of Civil Procedure § 995.010 et seq.

Notice, actual and constructive, defined, see Civil Code § 18.

§ 405.38. Attorney's fees and costs

The court shall direct that the party prevailing on any motion under this chapter be awarded the reasonable attorney's fees and costs of making or opposing the motion unless the court finds that the other party acted with substantial justification or that other circumstances make the imposition of attorney's fees and costs unjust. *(Added by Stats.1992, c. 883 (A.B.3620), § 2.)*

Cross References

Attorney's fees and costs, generally, see Code of Civil Procedure § 1021.

Research References

Forms

West's California Code Forms, Civil Procedure § 405.38 Form 1, Commencement of Action—Notice of Pendency of Action—Expungement—Notice of Motion for Award of Attorney's Fees and Costs.
West's California Code Forms, Civil Procedure § 405.38 Form 2, Commencement of Action—Notice of Pendency of Action—Expungement—Declaration for Award of Attorney's Fees and Costs.
West's California Code Forms, Civil Procedure § 405.38 Form 3, Commencement of Action—Notice of Pendency of Action—Expungement—Order for Award of Attorney's Fees and Costs.

§ 405.39. Appeal of orders or other actions; review; writ of mandate; filing and service

No order or other action of the court under this chapter shall be appealable. Any party aggrieved by an order made on a motion under this chapter may petition the proper reviewing court to review the order by writ of mandate. The petition for writ of mandate shall be filed and served within 20 days of service of written notice of the order by the court or any party. The court which issued the order may, within the initial 20-day period, extend the initial 20-day period for one additional period not to exceed 10 days. A copy of the petition for writ of mandate shall be delivered to the clerk of the court which issued the order with a request that it be placed in the court file. *(Added by Stats.1992, c. 883 (A.B.3620), § 2.)*

Cross References

Computation of time, see Code of Civil Procedure §§ 12, 12a; Government Code § 6800 et seq.
Mandamus, purpose of writ of mandate, courts which may issue writ and parties to whom issued, see Code of Civil Procedure § 1085.
Notice, actual and constructive, defined, see Civil Code § 18.

CHAPTER 4. WITHDRAWAL

Section
405.50. Notice of withdrawal; recording; acknowledgement.

§ 405.50. Notice of withdrawal; recording; acknowledgement

At any time after notice of pendency of an action has been recorded pursuant to this title or other law, the notice may be withdrawn by recording in the office of the recorder in which the notice of pendency was recorded a notice of withdrawal executed by the party who recorded the notice of pendency of action or by the party's successor in interest. The notice of withdrawal shall be acknowledged. *(Added by Stats.1992, c. 883 (A.B.3620), § 2.)*

Cross References

Notice, actual and constructive, defined, see Civil Code § 18.

CHAPTER 5. EFFECT OF WITHDRAWAL OR EXPUNGEMENT OF NOTICE

Section
405.60. Actual or constructive notice.

Section
405.61. Actual knowledge; nonfictitious parties; legislative intent.

§ 405.60. Actual or constructive notice

Upon the withdrawal of a notice of pendency of action pursuant to Section 405.50 or upon recordation of a certified copy of an order expunging a notice of pendency of action pursuant to this title, neither the notice nor any information derived from it, prior to the recording of a certified copy of the judgment or decree issued in the action, shall constitute actual or constructive notice of any of the matters contained, claimed, alleged, or contended therein, or of any of the matters related to the action, or create a duty of inquiry in any person thereafter dealing with the affected property. *(Added by Stats.1992, c. 883 (A.B.3620), § 2.)*

Cross References

Notice, actual and constructive, defined, see Civil Code § 18.
Recording,
    Constructive notice, conveyances or real property or estate for years, see Civil Code § 1213.
    Instruments or judgments, documents to be recorded and manner of recording, see Government Code § 27320 et seq., § 27280 et seq.
    Property transfers, place of recordation, see Civil Code § 1169.

§ 405.61. Actual knowledge; nonfictitious parties; legislative intent

Upon the withdrawal of a notice of pendency of action pursuant to Section 405.50 or upon recordation of a certified copy of an order expunging a notice of pendency of action pursuant to this title, no person except a nonfictitious party to the action at the time of recording of the notice of withdrawal or order, who thereafter becomes, by conveyance recorded prior to the recording of a certified copy of the judgment or decree issued in the action, a purchaser, transferee, mortgagee, or other encumbrancer for a valuable consideration of any interest in the real property subject to the action, shall be deemed to have actual knowledge of the action or any of the matters contained, claimed, or alleged therein, or of any of the matters related to the action, irrespective of whether that person possessed actual knowledge of the action or matter and irrespective of when or how the knowledge was obtained.

It is the intent of the Legislature that this section shall provide for the absolute and complete free transferability of real property after the expungement or withdrawal of a notice of pendency of action. *(Added by Stats.1992, c. 883 (A.B.3620), § 2.)*

Cross References

California Coastal Act, enforcement and penalties, notification of intent to record property violation, see Public Resources Code § 30812.
Legislative intent, construction of statutes, see Code of Civil Procedure § 1859.
Notice, actual and constructive, defined, see Civil Code § 18.
Recording,
    Constructive notice, conveyances or real property or estate for years, see Civil Code § 1213.
    Instruments or judgments, documents to be recorded and manner of recording, see Government Code § 27320 et seq., § 27280 et seq.
    Property transfers, place of recordation, see Civil Code § 1169.

Research References

Forms
West's California Code Forms, Civil § 1013.5 Form 2, Notice—Lis Pendens—Action to Remove Improvements Erroneously Affixed to Land.

Title 5

JURISDICTION AND SERVICE OF PROCESS

Cross References

Enforcement of support of spouse who has conservator, notice of hearing, see Probate Code § 3081.
Proration of estate taxes, notice of hearing, summons and copy of petition to persons interested, see Probate Code § 20122.
Proration of taxes on generation-skipping transfer, notice, summons and copy of petition to persons who may be directed to make payments, see Probate Code § 20222.

CHAPTER 3. SUMMONS

Section
412.20. Summons; formalities; contents.

Cross References

Contest of will, summons, see Probate Code § 8250.
Proceedings to determine state's right to unclaimed property in federal custody, see Code of Civil Procedure § 1609.

§ 412.20. Summons; formalities; contents

(a) Except as otherwise required by statute, a summons shall be directed to the defendant, signed by the clerk and issued under the seal of the court in which the action is pending, and it shall contain:

(1) The title of the court in which the action is pending.

(2) The names of the parties to the action.

(3) A direction that the defendant file with the court a written pleading in response to the complaint within 30 days after summons is served on him or her.

(4) A notice that, unless the defendant so responds, his or her default will be entered upon application by the plaintiff, and the plaintiff may apply to the court for the relief demanded in the complaint, which could result in garnishment of wages, taking of money or property, or other relief.

(5) The following statement in boldface type: "You may seek the advice of an attorney in any matter connected with the complaint or this summons. Such attorney should be consulted promptly so that your pleading may be filed or entered within the time required by this summons."

(6) The following introductory legend at the top of the summons above all other matter, in boldface type, in English and Spanish:

"Notice! You have been sued. The court may decide against you without your being heard unless you respond within 30 days. Read information below."

(b) Each county may, by ordinance, require that the legend contained in paragraph (6) of subdivision (a) be set forth in every summons issued out of the courts of that county in any additional foreign language, if the legend in the additional foreign language is set forth in the summons in the same manner as required in that paragraph.

(c) A summons in a form approved by the Judicial Council is deemed to comply with this section. *(Added by Stats.1969, c. 1610, p. 3363, § 3, operative July 1, 1970. Amended by Stats.1974, c. 363, p. 697, § 1; Stats.1989, c. 79, § 1, eff. June 30, 1989; Stats.1989, c. 1105, § 6.)*

Cross References

Adverse interests, etc., under public improvement assessments or bonds, action to determine, contents of summons, see Code of Civil Procedure § 801.6.
Computation of time, see Code of Civil Procedure §§ 12 and 12a; Government Code § 6800 et seq.
Conflicting claims to realty, summons, see Code of Civil Procedure § 763.010 et seq.
Destroyed land records, action to re-establish, form of summons, see Code of Civil Procedure § 751.05.
Dismissal for failure to serve summons, see Code of Civil Procedure § 583.250.
Eminent domain proceedings, see Code of Civil Procedure § 1250.120 et seq.
Forcible entry and detainer, complaint, see Code of Civil Procedure § 1166.
Foreign partnership, time for appearance, see Corporations Code § 15800.
Joint debtors, proceedings against, see Code of Civil Procedure § 989 et seq.
Judicial Council, see Government Code § 68500 et seq.

OF CIVIL ACTIONS

Notice, actual and constructive, defined, see Civil Code § 18.
Nullity, dissolution, and legal separation, temporary restraining order, contents, see Family Code § 2040.
Quiet title action by adverse possessor, contents of summons, see Code of Civil Procedure § 763.010.
Removal of children from state, temporary restraining order contained in summons, see Family Code § 7700.
Seal, documents to which affixed, see Code of Civil Procedure § 153.
Seal defined, see Code of Civil Procedure § 14.
Style of process, see Government Code § 100.
Tax title actions, see Revenue and Taxation Code § 3957.
Time not extended by reason of service of summons by mail, see Code of Civil Procedure § 413.20.
Trial court delay reduction act, time limitations, see Government Code § 68616.

Research References

Forms

West's California Code Forms, Civil Procedure § 412.20 Form 5, Summons—Family Law—Official Form.
West's California Code Forms, Civil Procedure § 412.20 Form 6, Summons—Complaint—Governmental—Official Form.
West's California Code Forms, Civil Procedure § 412.20 Form 8, Summons (Joinder)—Official Form.
West's California Code Forms, Civil Procedure § 412.20 Form 9, Summons (Uniform Parentage)—Official Form.
West's California Code Forms, Revenue and Taxation § 3950 Form 1, Action by Purchaser to Determine Adverse Claims to Tax Deed Property Purchased from State.
West's California Judicial Council Forms FL–110, Summons (Also Available in Arabic and Chinese).
West's California Judicial Council Forms SUM–100, Summons.
West's California Judicial Council Forms SUM–110, Summons—Cross-Complaint.
West's California Judicial Council Forms SUM–130, Summons—Unlawful Detainer—Eviction (Spanish Included).
West's California Judicial Council Forms SUM–145, Summons—Enforcement of State Housing Law.

Title 6

OF THE PLEADINGS IN CIVIL ACTIONS

CHAPTER 2. PLEADINGS DEMANDING RELIEF

ARTICLE 5. CONTENTS OF DOCUMENTS IN PARTICULAR ACTIONS OR PROCEEDINGS

Section
429.30. Infringement of rights in and to literary, artistic, or intellectual production; contents of complaint.

§ 429.30. Infringement of rights in and to literary, artistic, or intellectual production; contents of complaint

(a) As used in this section:

(1) "Complaint" includes a cross-complaint.

(2) "Plaintiff" includes the person filing a cross-complaint.

(b) If the complaint contains a demand for relief on account of the alleged infringement of the plaintiff's rights in and to a literary, artistic, or intellectual production, there shall be attached to the complaint a copy of the production as to which the infringement is claimed and a copy of the alleged infringing production. If, by reason of bulk or the nature of the production, it is not practicable to attach a copy to the complaint, that fact and the reasons why it is impracticable to attach a copy of the production to the complaint shall be alleged; and the court, in connection with any demurrer, motion, or other proceedings in the cause in which a knowledge of the contents of such production may be necessary or desirable, shall make such order for a view of the production not attached as will suit the convenience of the court to the end that the contents of such production may be deemed to be a part of the complaint to the same extent and with the same force as though such production had been capable of being and had been attached to the complaint. The attachment of any such production in accordance with the provisions of this section shall not be deemed a making public of the production within the meaning of Section 983 of the Civil Code. *(Added by Stats.1971, c. 244, p. 382, § 23, operative July 1, 1972.)*

Research References

Forms

West's California Code Forms, Civil § 980 Form 1, Complaint—Breach of Contract—Intellectual Property.
West's California Code Forms, Civil Procedure § 429.30 Form 2, Pleadings—Action for Infringement—Notice of Motion for Order Requiring Viewing of Artistic Production.

CHAPTER 7. GENERAL RULES OF PLEADING

Section
464. Supplemental pleadings.

Cross References

Criminal actions, rules of pleading, see Penal Code § 948 et seq.
Pleadings, in general, in civil actions, see Code of Civil Procedure § 420 et seq.
State license tax, action to collect, applicability of this chapter, see Business and Professions Code § 16222.
Variance, see Code of Civil Procedure § 469 et seq.

§ 464. Supplemental pleadings

(a) The plaintiff and defendant, respectively, may be allowed, on motion, to make a supplemental complaint or answer, alleging facts material to the case occurring after the former complaint or answer.

(b) The plaintiff and defendant, or petitioner and respondent, may, in any action in which the support of children is an issue, file a supplemental complaint seeking a judgment or order of paternity or support for a child of the mother and father of the child whose paternity and support are already in issue before the court. A supplemental complaint for paternity or child support may be filed without leave of court either before or after final judgment in the underlying action.

(c) Upon the filing of a supplemental complaint, the court clerk shall issue an amended or supplemental summons pursuant to Section 412.10. Service of the supplemental summons and complaint shall be made in the manner provided for the initial service of a summons by this code. *(Enacted in 1872. Amended by Stats.1994, c. 1269 (A.B.2208), § 2.8.)*

Cross References

Amendment of pleadings, see Code of Civil Procedure § 472 et seq.
Child support enforcement, supplemental complaint and judgment, see Family Code § 17428.
Compulsory joinder, conditions and indispensable persons, class actions, see Code of Civil Procedure § 389.
Dissolution of marriage and legal separation, supplemental complaint seeking order of paternity or child support, see Family Code § 2330.1.

Research References

Forms

West's California Code Forms, Civil Procedure § 464 Form 1, Pleadings—Notice of Motion for Leave to File Supplemental Complaint.
West's California Code Forms, Family § 2330, Comment Overview—Procedures.

CHAPTER 8. VARIANCE—MISTAKES IN PLEADINGS AND AMENDMENTS

Section
471.5. Amended complaint; filing; answer; time.

CODE OF CIVIL PROCEDURE

Section
472. Amendment without leave of court.
473. Amendments permitted by court; enlargement of time to answer or demur; continuance, costs; relief from judgment, etc., taken by mistake, inadvertence, surprise, or excusable neglect; vacating default judgment; compensatory costs and legal fees; penalties; clerical mistakes in judgment or order; relief
473.5. Motion to set aside default and for leave to defend action.
475. Errors, etc. not affecting substantial rights disregarded; reversal only for prejudicial error; presumptions.

Cross References

Application of this chapter to Juvenile Court Law, see Welfare and Institutions Code §§ 348, 678.

Dissolution of marriage, nunc pro tunc entry of judgment, showing that no relief under this chapter is to be asked, see Family Code § 2346.

State license tax, action to collect, applicability of this chapter, see Business and Professions Code § 16222.

§ 471.5. Amended complaint; filing; answer; time

(a) If the complaint is amended, a copy of the amendments shall be filed, or the court may, in its discretion, require the complaint as amended to be filed, and a copy of the amendments or amended complaint must be served upon the defendants affected thereby. The defendant shall answer the amendments, or the complaint as amended, within 30 days after service thereof, or such other time as the court may direct, and judgment by default may be entered upon failure to answer, as in other cases. For the purposes of this subdivision, "complaint" includes a cross-complaint, and "defendant" includes a person against whom a cross-complaint is filed.

(b) If the answer is amended, the adverse party has 10 days after service thereof, or such other time as the court may direct, in which to demur to the amended answer. *(Added by Stats.1972, c. 73, p. 94, § 2, eff. May 15, 1972, operative July 1, 1972.)*

Cross References

Answer, contents, see Code of Civil Procedure § 431.30.

Filing of pleadings subsequent to complaint, see Code of Civil Procedure § 465.

Pleadings, in general, see Code of Civil Procedure § 420 et seq.

§ 472. Amendment without leave of court

(a) A party may amend its pleading once without leave of the court at any time before the answer, demurrer, or motion to strike is filed, or after a demurrer or motion to strike is filed but before the demurrer or motion to strike is heard if the amended pleading is filed and served no later than the date for filing an opposition to the demurrer or motion to strike. A party may amend the pleading after the date for filing an opposition to the demurrer or motion to strike, upon stipulation by the parties. The time for responding to an amended pleading shall be computed from the date of service of the amended pleading.

(b) This section shall not apply to a special motion brought pursuant to Section 425.16. *(Enacted in 1872. Amended by Code Am.1873–74, c. 383, p. 302, § 59; Stats.1933, c. 744, p. 1850, § 31; Stats.1951, c. 1737, p. 4103, § 56, operative Jan. 1, 1952; Stats.1972, c. 73, p. 95, § 3; Stats.1977, c. 1257, § 13, eff. Jan. 3, 1977; Stats.1983, c. 142, § 4; Stats.2015, c. 418 (S.B.383), § 2, eff. Jan. 1, 2016; Stats.2017, c. 273 (A.B.644), § 3, eff. Jan. 1, 2018; Stats.2020, c. 36 (A.B.3364), § 19, eff. Jan. 1, 2021.)*

Cross References

Allegation of construction-related accessibility claim, statement of facts in complaint, verification by plaintiff, amendment of complaint, see Code of Civil Procedure § 425.50.

Answer, contents, see Code of Civil Procedure § 431.30.

Conversion from action for possession to action for damages, see Civil Code § 1952.3.

Demurrers, requisites, see Code of Civil Procedure § 430.30 et seq.

Filing fees, payment of additional fee portion for amending complaint or cross-complaint to an amount demanded in higher fee range, see Government Code § 70613.5.

Meeting prior to filing motion for judgment on the pleadings, resolution of claims, amended pleadings, see Code of Civil Procedure § 439.

Pleadings, generally, see Code of Civil Procedure § 420 et seq.

Research References

Forms

West's California Code Forms, Civil Procedure § 472 Form 1, Pleadings—Amendment of Pleadings—Caption and Allegation.

§ 473. Amendments permitted by court; enlargement of time to answer or demur; continuance, costs; relief from judgment, etc., taken by mistake, inadvertence, surprise, or excusable neglect; vacating default judgment; compensatory costs and legal fees; penalties; clerical mistakes in judgment or order; relief

(a)(1) The court may, in furtherance of justice, and on any terms as may be proper, allow a party to amend any pleading or proceeding by adding or striking out the name of any party, or by correcting a mistake in the name of a party, or a mistake in any other respect; and may, upon like terms, enlarge the time for answer or demurrer. The court may likewise, in its discretion, after notice to the adverse party, allow, upon any terms as may be just, an amendment to any pleading or proceeding in other particulars; and may upon like terms allow an answer to be made after the time limited by this code.

(2) When it appears to the satisfaction of the court that the amendment renders it necessary, the court may postpone the trial, and may, when the postponement will by the amendment be rendered necessary, require, as a condition to the amendment, the payment to the adverse party of any costs as may be just.

(b) The court may, upon any terms as may be just, relieve a party or his or her legal representative from a judgment, dismissal, order, or other proceeding taken against him or her through his or her mistake, inadvertence, surprise, or excusable neglect. Application for this relief shall be accompanied by a copy of the answer or other pleading proposed to be filed therein, otherwise the application shall not be granted, and shall be made within a reasonable time, in no case exceeding six months, after the judgment, dismissal, order, or proceeding was taken. However, in the case of a judgment, dismissal, order, or other proceeding determining the ownership or right to possession of real or personal property, without extending the six-month period, when a notice in writing is personally served within the State of California both upon the party against whom the judgment, dismissal, order, or other proceeding has been taken, and upon his or her attorney of record, if any, notifying that party and his or her attorney of record, if any, that the order, judgment, dismissal, or other proceeding was taken against him or her and that any rights the party has to apply for relief under the provisions of Section 473 of the Code of Civil Procedure shall expire 90 days after service of the notice, then the application shall be made within 90 days after service of the notice upon the defaulting party or his or her attorney of record, if any, whichever service shall be later. No affidavit or declaration of merits shall be required of the moving party. Notwithstanding any other requirements of this section, the court shall, whenever an application for relief is made no more than six months after entry of judgment, is in proper form, and is accompanied by an attorney's sworn affidavit attesting to his or her mistake, inadvertence, surprise, or neglect, vacate any (1) resulting default entered by the clerk against his or his client, and which will result in entry of a default judgment, or (2) resulting default judgment or dismissal entered against his or her client, unless the court finds that the default or dismissal was not in fact caused by the attorney's mistake, inadvertence, surprise, or neglect. The court shall, whenever relief is granted based on an attorney's affidavit of fault, direct the attorney to pay reasonable compensatory legal fees and costs to opposing counsel or parties. However, this section shall not lengthen the time within which an action shall be brought to trial pursuant to Section 583.310.

(c)(1) Whenever the court grants relief from a default, default judgment, or dismissal based on any of the provisions of this section, the court may do any of the following:

(A) Impose a penalty of no greater than one thousand dollars ($1,000) upon an offending attorney or party.

(B) Direct that an offending attorney pay an amount no greater than one thousand dollars ($1,000) to the State Bar Client Security Fund.

(C) Grant other relief as is appropriate.

(2) However, where the court grants relief from a default or default judgment pursuant to this section based upon the affidavit of the defaulting party's attorney attesting to the attorney's mistake, inadvertence, surprise, or neglect, the relief shall not be made conditional upon the attorney's payment of compensatory legal fees or costs or monetary penalties imposed by the court or upon compliance with other sanctions ordered by the court.

(d) The court may, upon motion of the injured party, or its own motion, correct clerical mistakes in its judgment or orders as entered, so as to conform to the judgment or order directed, and may, on motion of either party after notice to the other party, set aside any void judgment or order. *(Enacted in 1872. Amended by Code Am.1873–74, c. 383, p. 302, § 60; Code Am.1880, c. 14, p. 2, § 3; Stats.1917, c. 159, p. 242, § 1; Stats.1933, c. 744, p. 1851, § 34; Stats.1961, c. 722, p. 1965, § 1; Stats.1981, c. 122, p. 857, § 2; Stats.1988, c. 1131, § 1; Stats.1991, c. 1003 (S.B.882), § 1; Stats.1992, c. 427 (A.B.3355), § 16; Stats.1992, c. 876 (A.B.3296), § 4; Stats. 1996, c. 60 (S.B.52), § 1.)*

Cross References

Allegation of construction-related accessibility claim, statement of facts in complaint, verification by plaintiff, amendment of complaint, see Code of Civil Procedure § 425.50.
Attachment, see Code of Civil Procedure § 481.010 et seq.
Capitol area redevelopment, judgments determining validity of bonds, plans, documents, or proceedings subject to being reopened under this section, see Government Code § 8188.
Complaint, amendment of,
 Default judgment on failure to answer, see Code of Civil Procedure §§ 471.5, 586.
 Service of and answer required on amendment of, see Code of Civil Procedure § 471.5.
Conversion from action for possession to action for damages, see Civil Code § 1952.3.
County financial evaluation officer, see Government Code § 27750 et seq.
Death or disability of reporter, vacation of judgment, see Code of Civil Procedure § 914.
Dissolution and legal separation or nullification of marriage, relief from judgment, see Family Code § 2120 et seq.
Extension of time, see Code of Civil Procedure §§ 1054, 1054.1.
Filing and service of amendments, see Code of Civil Procedure § 471.5.
Grounds for demurrer, see Code of Civil Procedure § 430.10 et seq.
Industrial welfare commission, amendment of orders of, see Labor Code § 1182.
Limitation on reopening judgment determining validity of community redevelopment bonds, see Health and Safety Code § 33502.
Name of party, amendment to show correct, see Code of Civil Procedure § 474.
New parties, compulsory joinder, see Code of Civil Procedure § 389.
Nullification of marriage, relief from judgment, see Family Code § 2120 et seq.
Order or process of court, amendment, see Code of Civil Procedure § 128.
Parties, compulsory joinder, see Code of Civil Procedure § 389.
Pleadings, amendment, see Code of Civil Procedure §§ 399, 472, 472a, 472b.
Postponement, see Code of Civil Procedure § 594a.
Power of court to amend orders to make them conformable to law and justice, see Code of Civil Procedure § 128.
Public agencies, conclusiveness of judgments in actions to determine validity of agency's activity, see Code of Civil Procedure § 870.

Requirements for notices that demand payment of COVID-19 rental debts that came due during protected time period and transition time period, delivery of a declaration of COVID-19-related financial distress, filing of declaration with court, see Code of Civil Procedure § 1179.03.
Separation, relief from judgment, see Family Code § 2120 et seq.
Time for amendment of pleadings, extension of, see Code of Civil Procedure §§ 1054, 1054.1.
Trial, postponement on court's own motion, see Code of Civil Procedure § 594a.
Vacation of judgment,
 Based on findings or special verdict, and entry of other judgment, see Code of Civil Procedure § 663.
 Notice of intention to move for, see Code of Civil Procedure § 663a.
Variance, amendment of pleadings in case of, see Code of Civil Procedure §§ 469, 470.
Will contest, amendment of answer, see Probate Code § 8251.
Workers' compensation award, etc., amendment, see Labor Code §§ 5803, 5805.

Research References

Forms

California Practice Guide: Rutter Family Law Forms Form 16:1, Request for Order to Set Aside Judgment (Family Code § 2120 et seq.).
California Practice Guide: Rutter Family Law Forms Form 16:2, Request for Hearing and Application to Set Aside Support Order Under Family Code Section 3691.
California Practice Guide: Rutter Family Law Forms Form 16:3, Responsive Declaration to Application to Set Aside Support Order.
California Practice Guide: Rutter Family Law Forms Form 16:4, Order After Hearing on Motion to Set Aside Support Order.
2 California Real Estate Forms (Miller & Starr) § 2:18.30 (2d ed.), Office Lease—Medical.
2 California Transactions Forms--Business Transactions § 14:58, Offers to Compromise.
West's California Code Forms, Civil Procedure § 473 Form 4, Pleadings—Notice of Motion to Amend Pleading.
West's California Code Forms, Civil Procedure § 473 Form 7, Pleadings—Notice of Motion to Correct Judgment.
West's California Code Forms, Civil Procedure § 473 Form 9, Pleadings—Notice of Motion to Set Aside Default and Judgment Taken Thereon.
West's California Code Forms, Civil Procedure § 473 Form 11, Pleadings—Order Vacating Default and Permitting Filing of Answer.
West's California Code Forms, Civil Procedure § 473 Form 13, Pleadings—Order Vacating Default and Permitting Filing of Answer—Attorney Fault—Sanctions.
West's California Code Forms, Civil Procedure § 473 Form 14, Pleadings—Notice of Motion to Set Aside Void Judgment.
West's California Code Forms, Civil Procedure § 473 Form 16, Pleadings—Notice of Judgment or Order Determining Ownership of Real or Personal Property.
West's California Code Forms, Civil Procedure § 595.2 Form 1, Trial—Stipulation for Continuance—Order.
West's California Code Forms, Civil Procedure § 998 Form 1, Offer of Plaintiff to Compromise.
West's California Code Forms, Civil Procedure § 1008 Form 1, Motions and Orders—New Application for Order After Prior Refusal—Declaration Supporting New Application.
West's California Code Forms, Civil Procedure § 1141.22 Form 1, Judicial Arbitration—Rule 3.825—Notice of Motion to Vacate Judgment (Award of Arbitrator).
West's California Code Forms, Civil Procedure § 1285.4 Form 1, Arbitration—Petition to Confirm Award of Arbitrators.
West's California Code Forms, Family § 3690, Comment Overview—Relief from Order.
West's California Code Forms, Government § 911.4 Form 1, Application to Present Late Claim.
West's California Judicial Council Forms FL–280, Request for Hearing and Application to Cancel (Set Aside) Voluntary Declaration of Parentage or Paternity (Also Available in Spanish).
West's California Judicial Council Forms FL–281, Information Sheet for Completing Request for Hearing and Application to Cancel (Set Aside) Voluntary Declaration of Parentage or Paternity (Also Available in Spanish).
West's California Judicial Council Forms FL–285, Responsive Declaration to Application to Cancel (Set Aside) Voluntary Declaration of Parentage or Paternity (Also Available in Spanish).

§ 473 CODE OF CIVIL PROCEDURE

West's California Judicial Council Forms FL–290, Order After Hearing on Motion to Cancel (Set Aside) Voluntary Declaration of Parentage or Paternity (Also Available in Spanish).

West's California Judicial Council Forms SC–114, Request to Amend Party Name Before Hearing (Small Claims).

§ 473.5. Motion to set aside default and for leave to defend action

(a) When service of a summons has not resulted in actual notice to a party in time to defend the action and a default or default judgment has been entered against him or her in the action, he or she may serve and file a notice of motion to set aside the default or default judgment and for leave to defend the action. The notice of motion shall be served and filed within a reasonable time, but in no event exceeding the earlier of: (i) two years after entry of a default judgment against him or her; or (ii) 180 days after service on him or her of a written notice that the default or default judgment has been entered.

(b) A notice of motion to set aside a default or default judgment and for leave to defend the action shall designate as the time for making the motion a date prescribed by subdivision (b) of Section 1005, and it shall be accompanied by an affidavit showing under oath that the party's lack of actual notice in time to defend the action was not caused by his or her avoidance of service or inexcusable neglect. The party shall serve and file with the notice a copy of the answer, motion, or other pleading proposed to be filed in the action.

(c) Upon a finding by the court that the motion was made within the period permitted by subdivision (a) and that his or her lack of actual notice in time to defend the action was not caused by his or her avoidance of service or inexcusable neglect, it may set aside the default or default judgment on whatever terms as may be just and allow the party to defend the action. (Added by Stats.1969, c. 1610, p. 3373, § 23, operative July 1, 1970. Amended by Stats.1990, c. 1491 (A.B.3765), § 5.)

Cross References

Limitation on reopening judgment determining validity of community redevelopment bonds, see Health and Safety Code § 33502.

Private student loans, motion to set aside default judgment, see Civil Code § 1788.207.

Public agencies, conclusiveness of judgments in actions to determine validity of agency's activity, see Code of Civil Procedure § 870.

Time not extended by reason of service of summons by mail, see Code of Civil Procedure § 413.20.

Research References

Forms

3 California Transactions Forms—Business Entities § 13:68, Continued Existence of Dissolved Corporation.

West's California Code Forms, Civil Procedure § 473.5 Form 1, Pleadings—Notice of Motion to Set Aside Default and Judgment—No Actual Notice to Defendant.

§ 475. Errors, etc. not affecting substantial rights disregarded; reversal only for prejudicial error; presumptions

The court must, in every stage of an action, disregard any error, improper ruling, instruction, or defect, in the pleadings or proceedings which, in the opinion of said court, does not affect the substantial rights of the parties. No judgment, decision, or decree shall be reversed or affected by reason of any error, ruling, instruction, or defect, unless it shall appear from the record that such error, ruling, instruction, or defect was prejudicial, and also that by reason of such error, ruling, instruction, or defect, the said party complaining or appealing sustained and suffered substantial injury, and that a different result would have been probable if such error, ruling, instruction, or defect had not occurred or existed. There shall be no presumption that error is prejudicial, or that injury was done if error is shown. (Enacted in 1872. Amended by Stats.1897, c, 47, p. 44, § 1.)

Cross References

Matters reviewable on appeal, see Code of Civil Procedure § 906.

Miscarriage of justice resulting from error, new trial, see Cal. Const. Art. 6, § 13.

Questions determinable on appeal, see Code of Civil Procedure § 43.

Reversal for error, see Cal. Const. Art. 6, § 13; Code of Civil Procedure § 906; Penal Code §§ 960, 1258, 1404.

Title 7

OTHER PROVISIONAL REMEDIES IN CIVIL ACTIONS

CHAPTER 3. INJUNCTION

Section

527. Grants before judgment upon verified complaint or affidavits; service; notice; procedures; application; fees.

527.6. Harassment; temporary restraining order and order after hearing; procedure; allegations or threats of violence; support person; costs and attorney fees; punishment; confidentiality of information relating to minors.

527.85. Officers authorized to maintain order on school campus or facility; threat of violence made off school campus; temporary restraining order and order after hearing; violation of restraining order.

527.9. Relinquishment of firearms; persons subject to protective orders.

527.10. Addresses or locations of persons protected under court order; prohibition upon certain enjoined parties from acting to obtain such information.

529. Undertaking; objection; insufficiency; dissolution of injunction; exceptions.

Cross References

Abatement of nuisance, see Code of Civil Procedure § 731.

Administrators and executors, restraint, see Probate Code § 352.

Adult day health care centers, injunction against violations, see Health and Safety Code § 1595.5.

Advertising, injunctive relief, see Business and Professions Code § 17535.

Air pollution control violations, see Health and Safety Code § 42454.

Alcoholic beverage control, actions to enjoin, see Business and Professions Code § 23053.1.

Animals, generally, see Food and Agricultural Code §§ 16443, 17953, 18221, 20253, 23093, 24541, 24685, 24995, 26441, 27581.

Appeal from order granting or dissolving injunction, see Code of Civil Procedure §§ 904.1, 904.2.

Application of Chapter 3 to Chapter 2, see Code of Civil Procedure § 513.010.

Architecture or building design, injunction against unlawful practices, see Business and Professions Code § 5527.

Auctioneers, violations, injunction proceedings governed by this Chapter, see Civil Code § 1812.602.

Banks and banking,

   Adverse claimant to money on deposit, effect of restraining order, see Financial Code § 1450.

   Adverse claimant to property in safe deposit box, effect of restraining order, see Financial Code § 1650.

California Apiary Research Commission, actions and penalties, injunctive relief pursuant to this Chapter, see Food and Agricultural Code § 79693.

California Nursery Producers Commission, injunctive relief issued pursuant to this Chapter, see Food and Agricultural Code § 79514.

Cancer treatment, violations, see Health and Safety Code § 109355.

Clinics, licensing required, see Health and Safety Code § 1236.

Collective bargaining agreements, enforcement, see Labor Code § 1126.

Commencement of action, exclusion of time enjoined from limitation, see Code of Civil Procedure § 356.

Community Care Facilities Act, actions to enjoin violations of licensing provisions, see Health and Safety Code § 1541.

Community facilities, abatement of contamination, see Health and Safety Code § 5460.
Conduct of proceedings to enjoin waste of gas from wells, see Public Resources Code § 3311.
Contempt for disobeying injunction, see Code of Civil Procedure § 1209.
Cooperative bargaining associations, violations, consolidations of actions, see Food and Agricultural Code § 54405.
Escrow agents, see Financial Code § 17607.
Fish marketing, breach of contract, see Corporations Code § 13354.
Food, drugs and cosmetics, temporary or permanent injunction, see Health and Safety Code § 111900.
Food sanitation, abatement of public nuisance, see Health and Safety Code § 112050.
Forfeiture or penalty, specific relief unavailable to enforce, see Civil Code § 3369.
Franchise and income tax, restraining collection prohibited, see Revenue and Taxation Code § 19381.
Fraternal benefit societies, see Insurance Code §§ 11093, 11095, 11106.
Fruit, nut and vegetable standards, injunction, see Food and Agricultural Code § 43002.
Healing arts, licensed educational psychologists, injunctions to restrain prohibited conduct, see Business and Professions Code § 4989.64.
Health care service plans, see Health and Safety Code § 1392.
Health facilities injunction against violations, conformity to this Chapter, see Health and Safety Code § 1291.
Holidays, issuance of injunctions, see Code of Civil Procedure § 134.
Home health agencies, necessity of licensure, violation, see Health and Safety Code § 1740.
Household goods carriers, restraint, see Business and Professions Code §§ 19269, 19270.
Income tax, restraining assessment or collection prohibited, see Revenue and Taxation Code § 19381.
Injunction, violation of pawnbroker regulations, see Financial Code § 21302.
Injunction as preventive relief, see Civil Code § 3420 et seq.
Injury to property, see Code of Civil Procedure § 745.
Jurisdictional strikes, see Labor Code § 1116.
Livestock drugs, application of this Chapter to injunction proceedings for restraint of violations, see Food and Agricultural Code § 14390.
Mandamus, see Code of Civil Procedure § 1084 et seq.
Marketing of milk and milk products, see Food and Agricultural Code § 61573.
Marriage, family and child counselors, injunctions, proceedings, see Business and Professions Code § 4983.1.
Mental patient, injunction to prevent disclosure of confidential information, see Welfare and Institutions Code § 5330.
Milk and milk products, see Food and Agricultural Code § 32702.
Motor vehicle fuel tax, restraining collection prohibited, see Revenue and Taxation Code § 8146.
Ocean water intrusion, prevention, see Water Code §§ 2020, 2021.
Penalty, forfeiture, or penal law, specific relief unavailable to enforce, see Civil Code § 3369.
Personal representative, suspension of powers, see Probate Code § 9614.
Petroleum business regulations, actions to enjoin violations, see Business and Professions Code § 13611.
Pharmacy, actions to enjoin violations, see Business and Professions Code § 4339.
Physicians, prohibited acts, see Business and Professions Code § 2311.
Prescription lenses, injunction to restrain unlawful practices, see Business and Professions Code § 2545.
Preventive relief,
  Generally, see Civil Code § 3420 et seq.
  Limited by code, see Civil Code § 3274.
  Method of giving, see Civil Code § 3368.
Private duty nursing agencies, director authority to seek injunctive relief, see Health and Safety Code § 1743.33.
Private investigators, violation of injunction, see Business and Professions Code § 7561.1.
Private railroad car tax, restraining collection prohibited, see Revenue and Taxation Code § 11571.
Procedure on issuance of injunction to restrain waste of gas, see Public Resources Code § 3313.
Proceedings to enjoin violations of prepaid rental listing service regulations, see Business and Professions Code § 10167.14.
Processed pet food violations, injunctions, see Health and Safety Code § 113085.
Processors of farm products, see Food and Agricultural Code § 55921.
Produce dealer, see Food and Agricultural Code § 56651.
Producers' lien foreclosure, see Food and Agricultural Code § 55651 et seq.
Producers' marketing law, see Food and Agricultural Code § 60012.
Prohibition, see Code of Civil Procedure § 1102 et seq.
Psychologists' licensing, injunction against violation, application of this Chapter, see Business and Professions Code § 2971.
Public officers and employees, restrain removal from office, see Government Code § 1366.
Public utility, restraint, see Public Utilities Code § 2103.
Radioactive contamination, wastes, see Health and Safety Code § 114735.
Real estate licensing, injunctive relief, see Business and Professions Code § 10081.
Red Light Abatement Law, see Penal Code § 11225 et seq.
Sales and use taxes, restraining collection prohibited, see Revenue and Taxation Code § 6931.
Sherman Food, Drug, and Cosmetic Law, violations, authority to grant temporary or permanent injunction, see Health and Safety Code § 111910.
Speech-language pathologists, see Business and Professions Code § 2533.4.
Stabilization and marketing of fluid milk and fluid cream, see Food and Agricultural Code § 62403.
Stay of execution, see Code of Civil Procedure § 918.
Tanks and boilers, safety, see Labor Code §§ 7691, 7692.
Taxation, restraining collection prohibited, see Cal. Const. Art. 13, § 32.
Trade names and designations, violation of use, see Business and Professions Code § 14402.
Underground trespass, use or occupancy by oil and gas, see Code of Civil Procedure § 349¾.
Unfair trade practice, co-operative bargaining associations, see Food and Agricultural Code § 54431 et seq.
Unlawful release of confidential information or records on developmental disability services, see Welfare and Institutions Code § 4518.
Use fuel tax, restraining collection prohibited, see Revenue and Taxation Code § 9171.
Utilities, actions to enjoin or restrain unauthorized use of services, see Civil Code § 1882.4.
Water, diversion, see Water Code § 1052.
Water quality, cleanup or abatement, see Water Code § 13304.
Watermaster, injury by, see Water Code §§ 4160, 4161.
Weights and measures, see Business and Professions Code § 12012.1.

§ 527. Grants before judgment upon verified complaint or affidavits; service; notice; procedures; application; fees

(a) A preliminary injunction may be granted at any time before judgment upon a verified complaint, or upon affidavits if the complaint in the one case, or the affidavits in the other, show satisfactorily that sufficient grounds exist therefor. No preliminary injunction shall be granted without notice to the opposing party.

(b) A temporary restraining order or a preliminary injunction, or both, may be granted in a class action, in which one or more of the parties sues or defends for the benefit of numerous parties upon the same grounds as in other actions, whether or not the class has been certified.

(c) No temporary restraining order shall be granted without notice to the opposing party, unless both of the following requirements are satisfied:

(1) It appears from facts shown by affidavit or by the verified complaint that great or irreparable injury will result to the applicant before the matter can be heard on notice.

(2) The applicant or the applicant's attorney certifies one of the following to the court under oath:

(A) That within a reasonable time prior to the application the applicant informed the opposing party or the opposing party's attorney at what time and where the application would be made.

(B) That the applicant in good faith attempted but was unable to inform the opposing party and the opposing party's attorney, specifying the efforts made to contact them.

(C) That for reasons specified the applicant should not be required to so inform the opposing party or the opposing party's attorney.

(d) In case a temporary restraining order is granted without notice in the contingency specified in subdivision (c):

(1) The matter shall be made returnable on an order requiring cause to be shown why a preliminary injunction should not be granted, on the earliest day that the business of the court will admit of, but not later than 15 days or, if good cause appears to the court, 22 days from the date the temporary restraining order is issued.

(2) The party who obtained the temporary restraining order shall, within five days from the date the temporary restraining order is issued or two days prior to the hearing, whichever is earlier, serve on the opposing party a copy of the complaint if not previously served, the order to show cause stating the date, time, and place of the hearing, any affidavits to be used in the application, and a copy of the points and authorities in support of the application. The court may for good cause, on motion of the applicant or on its own motion, shorten the time required by this paragraph for service on the opposing party.

(3) When the matter first comes up for hearing, if the party who obtained the temporary restraining order is not ready to proceed, or if the party has failed to effect service as required by paragraph (2), the court shall dissolve the temporary restraining order.

(4) The opposing party is entitled to one continuance for a reasonable period of not less than 15 days or any shorter period requested by the opposing party, to enable the opposing party to meet the application for a preliminary injunction. If the opposing party obtains a continuance under this paragraph, the temporary restraining order shall remain in effect until the date of the continued hearing.

(5) Upon the filing of an affidavit by the applicant that the opposing party could not be served within the time required by paragraph (2), the court may reissue any temporary restraining order previously issued. The reissued order shall be made returnable as provided by paragraph (1), with the time for hearing measured from the date of reissuance. No fee shall be charged for reissuing the order.

(e) The opposing party may, in response to an order to show cause, present affidavits relating to the granting of the preliminary injunction, and if the affidavits are served on the applicant at least two days prior to the hearing, the applicant shall not be entitled to any continuance on account thereof. On the day the order is made returnable, the hearing shall take precedence over all other matters on the calendar of the day, except older matters of the same character, and matters to which special precedence may be given by law. When the cause is at issue it shall be set for trial at the earliest possible date and shall take precedence over all other cases, except older matters of the same character, and matters to which special precedence may be given by law.

(f) Notwithstanding failure to satisfy the time requirements of this section, the court may nonetheless hear the order to show cause why a preliminary injunction should not be granted if the moving and supporting papers are served within the time required by Section 1005 and one of the following conditions is satisfied:

(1) The order to show cause is issued without a temporary restraining order.

(2) The order to show cause is issued with a temporary restraining order, but is either not set for hearing within the time required by paragraph (1) of subdivision (d), or the party who obtained the temporary restraining order fails to effect service within the time required by paragraph (2) of subdivision (d).

(g) This section does not apply to an order issued under the Family Code.

(h) As used in this section:

(1) "Complaint" means a complaint or a cross-complaint.

(2) "Court" means the court in which the action is pending.
(Enacted in 1872. Amended by Stats.1895, c. 49, p. 51, § 1; Stats.1907, c. 272, p. 341, § 3; Stats.1911, c. 42, p. 59, § 1; Stats.1963, c. 878, p. 2125, § 2; Stats.1970, c. 488, p. 969, § 1; Stats.1977, c. 720, § 1; Stats.1978, c. 346, § 1; Stats.1979, c. 129, p. 316, § 1; Stats.1979, c. 795, p. 2707, § 7, operative July 1, 1980; Stats.1981, c. 182, p. 1100, § 1; Stats.1982, c. 812, p. 3100, § 1; Stats.1992, c. 163 (A.B.2641), § 23, operative Jan. 1, 1994; Stats.1993, c. 583 (A.B.284), § 1; Stats.1994, c. 587 (A.B.3600), § 5; Stats.1995, c. 796 (S.B.45), § 6; Stats.2000, c. 688 (A.B.1669), § 4.)

Cross References

Appointment of receiver to protect residents of residential care facilities for the elderly, divestment of possession and control of facility, powers and duties of receiver, duration of appointment, salary of receiver, see Health and Safety Code § 1569.482.

Appointment of receiver to temporarily operate community care facility, divestment of control and possession of facility, powers and duties of receiver, duration of appointment, salary, liability, application, see Health and Safety Code § 1546.2.

California Apiary Research Commission, actions and penalties, showing of irreparable harm or inadequate remedy at law not required for injunctive relief, see Food and Agricultural Code § 79693.

California Nursery Producers Commission, injunctive relief, showing of irreparable harm or inadequate remedy at law not required, see Food and Agricultural Code § 79514.

Civil actions for abuse of elderly or dependent adults, protective orders, see Welfare and Institutions Code § 15657.03.

Injunction defined, see Code of Civil Procedure § 525.

Marriage dissolution,
Ex parte protective orders, application, see Family Code §§ 6300 et seq., 6320 et seq.
Support, see Family Code §§ 3600 et seq., 4320.

Olive Oil Commission of California, civil actions and remedies, injunctive relief, showing of irreparable harm or inadequate remedy at law not required, see Food and Agricultural Code § 79883.

Proceedings to declare a minor child a dependent child, see Welfare and Institutions Code § 213.5.

Research References

Forms

West's California Code Forms, Civil § 798.88 Form 1, Petition—To Enjoin Continuing Violations of Mobile Home Park Rules.

West's California Code Forms, Civil Procedure § 527 Form 5, Injunction—Notice of Motion for Preliminary Injunction.

West's California Code Forms, Civil Procedure § 530 Form 1, Injunction—Notice of Motion for Preliminary Injunction Against Diversion of Water.

West's California Code Forms, Government § 38771 Form 5, Complaint for Abatement of Nuisance.

West's California Judicial Council Forms CD–200, Temporary Restraining Order.

West's California Judicial Council Forms CIV–025, Application and Order for Reissuance of Order to Show Cause and Temporary Restraining Order.

West's California Judicial Council Forms RC–200, Ex Parte Order Appointing Receiver and Order to Show Cause and Temporary Restraining Order—Rents, Issues, and Profits.

West's California Judicial Council Forms RC–210, Order Confirming Appointment of Receiver and Preliminary Injunction—Rents, Issues, and Profits.

West's California Judicial Council Forms RC–300, Order to Show Cause and Temporary Restraining Order—Rents, Issues, and Profits.

West's California Judicial Council Forms RC–310, Order Appointing Receiver After Hearing and Preliminary Injunction—Rents, Issues, and Profits.

§ 527.6. Harassment; temporary restraining order and order after hearing; procedure; allegations or threats of violence; support person; costs and attorney fees; punishment; confidentiality of information relating to minors

(a)(1) A person who has suffered harassment as defined in subdivision (b) may seek a temporary restraining order and an order after hearing prohibiting harassment as provided in this section.

(2) A minor, under 12 years of age, accompanied by a duly appointed and acting guardian ad litem, shall be permitted to appear in court without counsel for the limited purpose of requesting or

opposing a request for a temporary restraining order or order after hearing, or both, under this section as provided in Section 374.

(b) For purposes of this section, the following terms have the following meanings:

(1) "Course of conduct" is a pattern of conduct composed of a series of acts over a period of time, however short, evidencing a continuity of purpose, including following or stalking an individual, making harassing telephone calls to an individual, or sending harassing correspondence to an individual by any means, including, but not limited to, the use of public or private mails, interoffice mail, facsimile, or email. Constitutionally protected activity is not included within the meaning of "course of conduct."

(2) "Credible threat of violence" is a knowing and willful statement or course of conduct that would place a reasonable person in fear for the person's safety or the safety of the person's immediate family, and that serves no legitimate purpose.

(3) "Harassment" is unlawful violence, a credible threat of violence, or a knowing and willful course of conduct directed at a specific person that seriously alarms, annoys, or harasses the person, and that serves no legitimate purpose. The course of conduct must be that which would cause a reasonable person to suffer substantial emotional distress, and must actually cause substantial emotional distress to the petitioner.

(4) "Petitioner" means the person to be protected by the temporary restraining order and order after hearing and, if the court grants the petition, the protected person.

(5) "Respondent" means the person against whom the temporary restraining order and order after hearing are sought and, if the petition is granted, the restrained person.

(6) "Temporary restraining order" and "order after hearing" mean orders that include any of the following restraining orders, whether issued ex parte or after notice and hearing:

(A) An order enjoining a party from harassing, intimidating, molesting, attacking, striking, stalking, threatening, sexually assaulting, battering, abusing, telephoning, including, but not limited to, making annoying telephone calls, as described in Section 653m of the Penal Code, destroying personal property, contacting, either directly or indirectly, by mail or otherwise, or coming within a specified distance of, or disturbing the peace of, the petitioner. On a showing of good cause, in an order issued pursuant to this subparagraph in connection with an animal owned, possessed, leased, kept, or held by the petitioner, or residing in the residence or household of the petitioner, the court may do either or both of the following:

(i) Grant the petitioner exclusive care, possession, or control of the animal.

(ii) Order the respondent to stay away from the animal and refrain from taking, transferring, encumbering, concealing, molesting, attacking, striking, threatening, harming, or otherwise disposing of the animal.

(B) An order enjoining a party from specified behavior that the court determines is necessary to effectuate orders described in subparagraph (A).

(7) "Unlawful violence" is any assault or battery, or stalking as prohibited in Section 646.9 of the Penal Code, but does not include lawful acts of self-defense or defense of others.

(c) In the discretion of the court, on a showing of good cause, a temporary restraining order or order after hearing issued under this section may include other named family or household members.

(d) Upon filing a petition for orders under this section, the petitioner may obtain a temporary restraining order in accordance with Section 527, except to the extent this section provides an inconsistent rule. The temporary restraining order may include any of the restraining orders described in paragraph (6) of subdivision (b). A temporary restraining order may be issued with or without notice, based on a declaration that, to the satisfaction of the court, shows reasonable proof of harassment of the petitioner by the respondent, and that great or irreparable harm would result to the petitioner.

(e) A request for the issuance of a temporary restraining order without notice under this section shall be granted or denied on the same day that the petition is submitted to the court. If the petition is filed too late in the day to permit effective review, the order shall be granted or denied on the next day of judicial business in sufficient time for the order to be filed that day with the clerk of the court.

(f) A temporary restraining order issued under this section shall remain in effect, at the court's discretion, for a period not to exceed 21 days, or, if the court extends the time for hearing under subdivision (g), not to exceed 25 days, unless otherwise modified or terminated by the court.

(g) Within 21 days, or, if good cause appears to the court, 25 days from the date that a petition for a temporary order is granted or denied, a hearing shall be held on the petition. If a request for a temporary order is not made, the hearing shall be held within 21 days, or, if good cause appears to the court, 25 days, from the date that the petition is filed.

(h) The respondent may file a response that explains, excuses, justifies, or denies the alleged harassment, or may file a cross-petition under this section.

(i) At the hearing, the judge shall receive any testimony that is relevant, and may make an independent inquiry. If the judge finds by clear and convincing evidence that unlawful harassment exists, an order shall issue prohibiting the harassment.

(j)(1) In the discretion of the court, an order issued after notice and hearing under this section may have a duration of no more than five years, subject to termination or modification by further order of the court either on written stipulation filed with the court or on the motion of a party. The order may be renewed, upon the request of a party, for a duration of no more than five additional years, without a showing of any further harassment since the issuance of the original order, subject to termination or modification by further order of the court either on written stipulation filed with the court or on the motion of a party. A request for renewal may be brought any time within the three months before the order expires.

(2) The failure to state the expiration date on the face of the form creates an order with a duration of three years from the date of issuance.

(3) If an action is filed for the purpose of terminating or modifying a protective order before the expiration date specified in the order by a party other than the protected party, the party who is protected by the order shall be given notice, pursuant to subdivision (b) of Section 1005, of the proceeding by personal service or, if the protected party has satisfied the requirements of Chapter 3.1 (commencing with Section 6205) of Division 7 of Title 1 of the Government Code, by service on the Secretary of State. If the party who is protected by the order cannot be notified before the hearing for modification or termination of the protective order, the court shall deny the motion to modify or terminate the order without prejudice or continue the hearing until the party who is protected can be properly noticed and may, upon a showing of good cause, specify another method for service of process that is reasonably designed to afford actual notice to the protected party. The protected party may waive the protected party's right to notice if the protected party is physically present in court and does not challenge the sufficiency of the notice.

(k) This section does not preclude either party from representation by private counsel or from appearing on the party's own behalf.

(*l*) In a proceeding under this section, if there are allegations of unlawful violence or credible threats of violence, a support person may accompany a party in court and, if the party is not represented by an attorney, may sit with the party at the table that is generally reserved for the party and the party's attorney. The support person is present to provide moral and emotional support for a person who alleges they are a victim of violence. The support person is not present as a legal adviser and may not provide legal advice. The support person may assist the person who alleges they are a victim of violence in feeling more confident that they will not be injured or threatened by the other party during the proceedings if the person who alleges the person is a victim of violence and the other party are required to be present in close proximity. This subdivision does not preclude the court from exercising its discretion to remove the support person from the courtroom if the court believes the support person is prompting, swaying, or influencing the party assisted by the support person.

(m)(1) Except as provided in paragraph (2), upon the filing of a petition under this section, the respondent shall be personally served with a copy of the petition, temporary restraining order, if any, and notice of hearing of the petition. Service shall be made at least five days before the hearing. The court may for good cause, on motion of the petitioner or on its own motion, shorten the time for service on the respondent.

(2) If the court determines at the hearing that, after a diligent effort, the petitioner has been unable to accomplish personal service, and that there is reason to believe that the respondent is evading service or cannot be located, then the court may specify another method of service that is reasonably calculated to give actual notice to the respondent and may prescribe the manner in which proof of service shall be made.

(n) A notice of hearing under this section shall notify the respondent that if the respondent does not attend the hearing, the court may make orders against the respondent that could last up to five years.

(o) The respondent shall be entitled, as a matter of course, to one continuance, for a reasonable period, to respond to the petition.

(p)(1) Either party may request a continuance of the hearing, which the court shall grant on a showing of good cause. The request may be made in writing before or at the hearing, or orally at the hearing. The court may also grant a continuance on its own motion.

(2) If the court grants a continuance, any temporary restraining order that has been granted shall remain in effect until the end of the continued hearing, unless otherwise ordered by the court. In granting a continuance, the court may modify or terminate a temporary restraining order.

(q)(1) If a respondent named in a restraining order issued after a hearing has not been served personally with the order but has received actual notice of the existence and substance of the order through personal appearance in court to hear the terms of the order from the court, additional proof of service is not required for enforcement of the order.

(2) If the respondent named in a temporary restraining order is personally served with the order and notice of hearing with respect to a restraining order or protective order based on the temporary restraining order, but the respondent does not appear at the hearing, either personally or by an attorney, and the terms and conditions of the restraining order or protective order issued at the hearing are identical to the temporary restraining order, except for the duration of the order, the restraining order or protective order issued at the hearing may be served on the respondent by first-class mail sent to the respondent at the most current address for the respondent available to the court.

(3) The Judicial Council form for temporary orders issued pursuant to this subdivision shall contain a statement in substantially the following form:

"If you have been personally served with this temporary restraining order and notice of hearing, but you do not appear at the hearing either in person or by a lawyer, and a restraining order that is the same as this temporary restraining order except for the expiration date is issued at the hearing, a copy of the restraining order will be served on you by mail at the following address: ____.

If that address is not correct or you wish to verify that the temporary restraining order was converted to a restraining order at the hearing without substantive change and to find out the duration of that order, contact the clerk of the court."

(4) If information about a minor has been made confidential pursuant to subdivision (v), the notice shall identify the information, specifically, that has been made confidential and shall include a statement that disclosure or misuse of that information is punishable as a contempt of court.

(r)(1) Information on a temporary restraining order or order after hearing relating to civil harassment issued by a court pursuant to this section shall be transmitted to the Department of Justice in accordance with either paragraph (2) or (3).

(2) The court shall order the petitioner or the attorney for the petitioner to deliver a copy of an order issued under this section, or reissuance, extension, modification, or termination of the order, and any subsequent proof of service, by the close of the business day on which the order, reissuance, extension, modification, or termination was made, to a law enforcement agency having jurisdiction over the residence of the petitioner and to any additional law enforcement agencies within the court's discretion as are requested by the petitioner.

(3) Alternatively, the court or its designee shall transmit, within one business day, to law enforcement personnel all information required under subdivision (b) of Section 6380 of the Family Code regarding any order issued under this section, or a reissuance, extension, modification, or termination of the order, and any subsequent proof of service, by either one of the following methods:

(A) Transmitting a physical copy of the order or proof of service to a local law enforcement agency authorized by the Department of Justice to enter orders into the California Law Enforcement Telecommunications System (CLETS).

(B) With the approval of the Department of Justice, entering the order or proof of service into CLETS directly.

(4) Each appropriate law enforcement agency shall make available information as to the existence and current status of orders issued under this section to law enforcement officers responding to the scene of reported harassment.

(5) An order issued under this section shall, on request of the petitioner, be served on the respondent, whether or not the respondent has been taken into custody, by any law enforcement officer who is present at the scene of reported harassment involving the parties to the proceeding. The petitioner shall provide the officer with an endorsed copy of the order and a proof of service that the officer shall complete and send to the issuing court.

(6) Upon receiving information at the scene of an incident of harassment that a protective order has been issued under this section, or that a person who has been taken into custody is the subject of an order, if the protected person cannot produce a certified copy of the order, a law enforcement officer shall immediately attempt to verify the existence of the order.

(7) If the law enforcement officer determines that a protective order has been issued but not served, the officer shall immediately notify the respondent of the terms of the order and shall at that time also enforce the order. Verbal notice of the terms of the order shall constitute service of the order and is sufficient notice for purposes of this section and for purposes of Section 29825 of the Penal Code. Verbal notice shall include the information required pursuant to paragraph (4) of subdivision (q).

(s) The prevailing party in an action brought pursuant to this section may be awarded court costs and attorney's fees, if any.

(t) Willful disobedience of a temporary restraining order or order after hearing granted pursuant to this section is punishable pursuant to Section 273.6 of the Penal Code.

(u)(1) A person subject to a protective order issued pursuant to this section shall not own, possess, purchase, receive, or attempt to purchase or receive a firearm or ammunition while the protective order is in effect.

(2) The court shall order a person subject to a protective order issued pursuant to this section to relinquish any firearms the person owns or possesses pursuant to Section 527.9.

(3) A person who owns, possesses, purchases, or receives, or attempts to purchase or receive, a firearm or ammunition while the protective order is in effect is punishable pursuant to Section 29825 of the Penal Code.

(v)(1) A minor or the minor's legal guardian may petition the court to have information regarding the minor that was obtained in connection with a request for a protective order pursuant to this section, including, but not limited to, the minor's name, address, and the circumstances surrounding the request for a protective order with respect to that minor, be kept confidential.

(2) The court may order the information specified in paragraph (1) be kept confidential if the court expressly finds all of the following:

(A) The minor's right to privacy overcomes the right of public access to the information.

(B) There is a substantial probability that the minor's interest will be prejudiced if the information is not kept confidential.

(C) The order to keep the information confidential is narrowly tailored.

(D) No less restrictive means exist to protect the minor's privacy.

(3)(A) If the request is granted, except as provided in paragraph (4), information regarding the minor shall be maintained in a confidential case file and shall not become part of the public file in the proceeding or any other civil proceeding involving the parties. Except as provided in subparagraph (B), if the court determines that disclosure of confidential information has been made without a court order, the court may impose a sanction of up to one thousand dollars ($1,000). A minor who has alleged harassment, as defined in subdivision (b), shall not be sanctioned for disclosure of the confidential information. If the court imposes a sanction, the court shall first determine whether the person has or is reasonably likely to have the ability to pay.

(B) Confidential information may be disclosed without a court order only in the following circumstances:

(i) By the minor's legal guardian who petitioned to keep the information confidential pursuant to this subdivision or the protected party in an order pursuant to this division, provided that the disclosure is necessary to prevent harassment or is in the minor's best interest. A legal guardian or a protected party who makes a disclosure under this clause is subject to the sanction in subparagraph (A) only if the disclosure was malicious.

(ii) By a person to whom confidential information is disclosed, provided that the disclosure is necessary to prevent harassment or is in the best interest of the minor, no more information than necessary is disclosed, and a delay would be caused by first obtaining a court order to authorize the disclosure of the information. A person who makes a disclosure pursuant to this clause is subject to the sanction in subparagraph (A) if the person discloses the information in a manner that recklessly or maliciously disregards these requirements.

(4)(A) Confidential information shall be made available to both of the following:

(i) Law enforcement pursuant to subdivision (r), to the extent necessary and only for the purpose of enforcing the order.

(ii) The respondent to allow the respondent to comply with the order for confidentiality and to allow the respondent to comply with and respond to the protective order. A notice shall be provided to the respondent that identifies the specific information that has been made confidential and shall include a statement that disclosure is punishable by a monetary fine.

(B) At any time, the court on its own may authorize a disclosure of any portion of the confidential information to certain individuals or entities as necessary to prevent harassment, as defined under subdivision (b), including implementation of the protective order, or if it is in the best interest of the minor.

(C) The court may authorize a disclosure of any portion of the confidential information to any person that files a petition if necessary to prevent harassment, as defined under subdivision (b), or if it is in the best interest of the minor. The party who petitioned the court to keep the information confidential pursuant to this subdivision shall be served personally or by first-class mail with a copy of the petition and afforded an opportunity to object to the disclosure.

(w) This section does not apply to any action or proceeding covered by Title 1.6C (commencing with Section 1788) of Part 4 of Division 3 of the Civil Code or by Division 10 (commencing with Section 6200) of the Family Code. This section does not preclude a petitioner from using other existing civil remedies.

(x)(1) The Judicial Council shall develop forms, instructions, and rules relating to matters governed by this section. The petition and response forms shall be simple and concise, and their use by parties in actions brought pursuant to this section is mandatory.

(2) A temporary restraining order or order after hearing relating to civil harassment issued by a court pursuant to this section shall be issued on forms adopted by the Judicial Council and that have been approved by the Department of Justice pursuant to subdivision (i) of Section 6380 of the Family Code. However, the fact that an order issued by a court pursuant to this section was not issued on forms adopted by the Judicial Council and approved by the Department of Justice shall not, in and of itself, make the order unenforceable.

(y) There is no filing fee for a petition that alleges that a person has inflicted or threatened violence against the petitioner, stalked the petitioner, or acted or spoken in any other manner that has placed the petitioner in reasonable fear of violence, and that seeks a protective or restraining order restraining stalking, future violence, or threats of violence, in an action brought pursuant to this section. A fee shall not be paid for a subpoena filed in connection with a petition alleging these acts. A fee shall not be paid for filing a response to a petition alleging these acts.

(z)(1) Subject to paragraph (4) of subdivision (b) of Section 6103.2 of the Government Code, there shall not be a fee for the service of process by a sheriff or marshal of a protective or restraining order to be issued, if either of the following conditions apply:

(A) The protective or restraining order issued pursuant to this section is based upon stalking, as prohibited by Section 646.9 of the Penal Code.

(B) The protective or restraining order issued pursuant to this section is based upon unlawful violence or a credible threat of violence.

(2) The Judicial Council shall prepare and develop forms for persons who wish to avail themselves of the services described in this subdivision. *(Added by Stats.2013, c. 158 (A.B.499), § 2, operative July 1, 2014. Amended by Stats.2015, c. 401 (A.B.494), § 1, eff. Jan. 1, 2016; Stats.2015, c. 411 (A.B.1081), § 1.5, eff. Jan. 1, 2016; Stats. 2016, c. 86 (S.B.1171), § 24, eff. Jan. 1, 2017; Stats.2017, c. 384 (A.B.953), § 1, eff. Jan. 1, 2018; Stats.2019, c. 294 (A.B.925), § 1, eff. Jan. 1, 2020; Stats.2021, c. 156 (A.B.1143), § 1, eff. Jan. 1, 2022.)*

§ 527.6

Cross References

Acceptance of Judicial Council form, summons, order, or other notices by email, fax, or in-person delivery, fee, court fee waiver or exemption, see Government Code § 26666.5.

Arrest without warrant, see Penal Code § 836.

Court interpreter services provided in civil actions, reimbursement by Judicial Council, prioritization where funding is insufficient, see Evidence Code § 756.

Domestic violence support persons, presence at mediation proceedings, see Family Code §§ 3182, 6303.

Domestic violence victims, application for new and different license plates, conditions for issuance, see Vehicle Code § 4467.

Information transmittal to Department of Justice after issuance of order or injunction under this section, see Family Code § 6380.

Injunction defined, see Code of Civil Procedure § 525.

Orders or injunctions, sheriff or marshal providing service of process, payment of fee prohibited, notice of delivery, see Government Code § 6103.3.

Protective orders, fee waiver, see Family Code § 6222.

Sheriff or marshal, fees, charges, expenses, and prepayments for official services rendered, fee waiver, see Government Code § 6103.2.

Translations of court orders and domestic violence protective order forms issued pursuant to this section, see Code of Civil Procedure § 185.

Victims of domestic violence, sexual assault, or stalking, written notice to terminate tenancy, requirements, see Civil Code § 1946.7.

Violation of a restraining order under this section as an element of the tort of stalking, see Civil Code § 1708.7.

Violation of protective order under this section by possession of a firearm as a misdemeanor, see Penal Code § 273.6.

Violation of protective order under this section by possession of a firearm as a public offense, see Penal Code § 29825.

Research References

Forms

West's California Code Forms, Civil § 798.875 Form 1, Complaint—By Tenant for Injunction and Damages.

West's California Code Forms, Civil § 1708.7 Form 1, Complaint—Stalking.

West's California Code Forms, Civil Procedure § 425.10 Form 1, Pleadings—Complaint—Negligence Action.

West's California Code Forms, Civil Procedure § 430.10 Form 1, Pleadings—Demurrer.

West's California Code Forms, Civil Procedure § 527.6 Form 1, Injunction—Request for Civil Harassment Restraining Orders (Civil Harassment Prevention)—Official Form.

West's California Code Forms, Civil Procedure § 527.6 Form 10, Injunction—Request to Continue Court Hearing and to Reissue Temporary Restraining Order (CLETS-TCH) (Civil Harassment Prevention)—Official Form.

West's California Code Forms, Civil Procedure § 527.6 Form 15.1, Injunction—Request to Modify/Terminate Civil Harassment Restraining Order—Official Form.

West's California Code Forms, Civil Procedure § 527.6 Form 16, Injunction—Order to Show Cause (Workplace Violence) and Temporary Restraining Order (CLETS)—Official Form.

West's California Code Forms, Civil Procedure § 527.6 Form 18, Injunction—How Can I Respond to a Request for Civil Harassment Restraining Orders? (Civil Harassment Prevention)—Official Form.

West's California Judicial Council Forms CH–100, Request for Civil Harassment Restraining Orders (Also Available in Chinese, Korean, Spanish, and Vietnamese).

West's California Judicial Council Forms CH–100–INFO, Can a Civil Harassment Restraining Order Help Me?

West's California Judicial Council Forms CH–109, Notice of Court Hearing (Also Available in Chinese, Korean, Spanish, and Vietnamese).

West's California Judicial Council Forms CH–110, Temporary Restraining Order (CLETS-TCH) (Also Available in Chinese, Korean, Spanish, and Vietnamese).

West's California Judicial Council Forms CH–115, Request to Continue Court Hearing.

West's California Judicial Council Forms CH–115–INFO, How to Ask for a New Hearing Date.

West's California Judicial Council Forms CH–116, Order on Request to Continue Hearing.

West's California Judicial Council Forms CH–120, Response to Request for Civil Harassment Restraining Orders (Also Available in Chinese, Korean, Spanish, and Vietnamese).

West's California Judicial Council Forms CH–120–INFO, How Can I Respond to a Request for Civil Harassment Restraining Orders?

West's California Judicial Council Forms CH–130, Civil Harassment Restraining Order After Hearing (Clets-Cho) (Also Available in Chinese, Korean, Spanish, and Vietnamese).

West's California Judicial Council Forms CH–160, Request to Keep Minor's Information Confidential (Civil Harassment Prevention) (Also Available in Chinese, Korean, Spanish, and Vietnamese).

West's California Judicial Council Forms CH–160–INFO, Privacy Protection for a Minor (Person Under 18 Years Old) Civil Harassment Prevention.

West's California Judicial Council Forms CH–165, Order on Request to Keep Minor's Information Confidential (Also Available in Chinese, Korean, Spanish, and Vietnamese).

West's California Judicial Council Forms CH–170, Notice of Order Protecting Information of Minor (Civil Harassment Prevention) (Also Available in Chinese, Korean, Spanish, and Vietnamese).

West's California Judicial Council Forms CH–175, Cover Sheet for Confidential Information (Civil Harassment Prevention) (Also Available in Chinese, Korean, Spanish, and Vietnamese).

West's California Judicial Council Forms CH–176, Request for Release of Minor's Confidential Information.

West's California Judicial Council Forms CH–177, Notice of Request for Release of Minor's Confidential Information.

West's California Judicial Council Forms CH–178, Response to Request for Release of Minor's Confidential Information.

West's California Judicial Council Forms CH–179, Order on Request for Release of Minor's Confidential Information.

West's California Judicial Council Forms CH–200, Proof of Personal Service.

West's California Judicial Council Forms CH–250, Proof of Service of Response by Mail (Also Available in Chinese, Korean, Spanish, and Vietnamese).

West's California Judicial Council Forms CH–260, Proof of Service of Order After Hearing by Mail (Also Available in Chinese, Korean, Spanish, and Vietnamese).

West's California Judicial Council Forms CH–600, Request to Modify/Terminate Civil Harassment Restraining Order.

West's California Judicial Council Forms CH–610, Notice of Hearing on Request to Modify/Terminate Civil Harassment Restraining Order.

West's California Judicial Council Forms CH–620, Response to Request to Modify/Terminate Civil Harassment Restraining Order.

West's California Judicial Council Forms CH–630, Order on Request to Modify/Terminate Civil Harassment Restraining Order.

West's California Judicial Council Forms CH–700, Request to Renew Restraining Order (Also Available in Chinese, Korean, Spanish, and Vietnamese).

West's California Judicial Council Forms CH–710, Notice of Hearing to Renew Restraining Order (Also Available in Chinese, Korean, Spanish, and Vietnamese).

West's California Judicial Council Forms CH–720, Response to Request to Renew Restraining Order.

West's California Judicial Council Forms CH–730, Order Renewing Civil Harassment Restraining Order (CLETS) (Also Available in Chinese, Korean, Spanish, and Vietnamese).

§ 527.85. Officers authorized to maintain order on school campus or facility; threat of violence made off school campus; temporary restraining order and order after hearing; violation of restraining order

(a) Any chief administrative officer of a postsecondary educational institution, or an officer or employee designated by the chief administrative officer to maintain order on the school campus or facility, a student of which has suffered a credible threat of violence made off the school campus or facility from any individual which can reasonably be construed to be carried out or to have been carried out at the school campus or facility, may, with the written consent of the student, seek a temporary restraining order and an order after hearing on behalf of the student and, at the discretion of the court, any number of other students at the campus or facility who are similarly situated.

(b) For purposes of this section, the following definitions apply:

(1) "Chief administrative officer" means the principal, president, or highest ranking official of the postsecondary educational institution.

(2) "Course of conduct" means a pattern of conduct composed of a series of acts over a period of time, however short, evidencing a continuity of purpose, including any of the following:

(A) Following or stalking a student to or from school.

(B) Entering the school campus or facility.

(C) Following a student during school hours.

(D) Making telephone calls to a student.

(E) Sending correspondence to a student by any means, including, but not limited to, the use of the public or private mails, interoffice mail, facsimile, or computer email.

(3) "Credible threat of violence" means a knowing and willful statement or course of conduct that would place a reasonable person in fear for his or her safety, or the safety of his or her immediate family, and that serves no legitimate purpose.

(4) "Petitioner" means the chief administrative officer, or his or her designee, who petitions under subdivision (a) for a temporary restraining order and order after hearing.

(5) "Postsecondary educational institution" means a private institution of vocational, professional, or postsecondary education.

(6) "Respondent" means the person against whom the temporary restraining order and order after hearing are sought and, if the petition is granted, the restrained person.

(7) "Student" means an adult currently enrolled in or applying for admission to a postsecondary educational institution.

(8) "Temporary restraining order" and "order after hearing" mean orders that include any of the following restraining orders, whether issued ex parte, or after notice and hearing:

(A) An order enjoining a party from harassing, intimidating, molesting, attacking, striking, stalking, threatening, sexually assaulting, battering, abusing, telephoning, including, but not limited to, making annoying telephone calls as described in Section 653m of the Penal Code, destroying personal property, contacting, either directly or indirectly, by mail or otherwise, or coming within a specified distance of, or disturbing the peace of, the student.

(B) An order enjoining a party from specified behavior that the court determines is necessary to effectuate orders described in subparagraph (A).

(9) "Unlawful violence" means any assault or battery, or stalking as prohibited in Section 646.9 of the Penal Code, but shall not include lawful acts of self-defense or defense of others.

(c) This section does not permit a court to issue a temporary restraining order or order after hearing prohibiting speech or other activities that are constitutionally protected, or otherwise protected by Section 527.3 or any other provision of law.

(d) In the discretion of the court, on a showing of good cause, a temporary restraining order or order after hearing issued under this section may include other named family or household members of the student, or other students at the campus or facility.

(e) Upon filing a petition under this section, the petitioner may obtain a temporary restraining order in accordance with subdivision (a) of Section 527, if the petitioner also files a declaration that, to the satisfaction of the court, shows reasonable proof that a student has suffered a credible threat of violence made off the school campus or facility by the respondent, and that great or irreparable harm would result to the student. The temporary restraining order may include any of the protective orders described in paragraph (8) of subdivision (b).

(f) A request for the issuance of a temporary restraining order without notice under this section shall be granted or denied on the same day that the petition is submitted to the court, unless the petition is filed too late in the day to permit effective review, in which case the order shall be granted or denied on the next day of judicial business in sufficient time for the order to be filed that day with the clerk of the court.

(g) A temporary restraining order granted under this section shall remain in effect, at the court's discretion, for a period not to exceed 21 days, or if the court extends the time for hearing under subdivision (h), not to exceed 25 days, unless otherwise modified or terminated by the court.

(h) Within 21 days, or if good cause appears to the court, within 25 days, from the date that a petition for a temporary order is granted or denied, a hearing shall be held on the petition. If no request for temporary orders is made, the hearing shall be held within 21 days, or if good cause appears to the court, 25 days, from the date the petition is filed.

(i) The respondent may file a response that explains, excuses, justifies, or denies the alleged credible threats of violence.

(j) At the hearing, the judge shall receive any testimony that is relevant and may make an independent inquiry. Moreover, if the respondent is a current student of the entity requesting the order, the judge shall receive evidence concerning the decision of the postsecondary educational institution decision to retain, terminate, or otherwise discipline the respondent. If the judge finds by clear and convincing evidence that the respondent made a credible threat of violence off the school campus or facility, an order shall be issued prohibiting further threats of violence.

(k)(1) In the discretion of the court, an order issued after notice and hearing under this section may have a duration of not more than three years, subject to termination or modification by further order of the court either on written stipulation filed with the court or on the motion of a party. These orders may be renewed, upon the request of a party, for a duration of not more than three years, without a showing of any further violence or threats of violence since the issuance of the original order, subject to termination or modification by further order of the court either on written stipulation filed with the court or on the motion of a party. The request for renewal may be brought at any time within the three months before the expiration of the order.

(2) The failure to state the expiration date on the face of the form creates an order with a duration of three years from the date of issuance.

(3) If an action is filed for the purpose of terminating or modifying a protective order prior to the expiration date specified in the order by a party other than the protected party, the party who is protected by the order shall be given notice, pursuant to subdivision (b) of Section 1005, of the proceeding by personal service or, if the protected party has satisfied the requirements of Chapter 3.1 (commencing with Section 6205) of Division 7 of Title 1 of the Government Code, by service on the Secretary of State. If the party who is protected by the order cannot be notified prior to the hearing for modification or termination of the protective order, the court shall deny the motion to modify or terminate the order without prejudice or continue the hearing until the party who is protected can be properly noticed and may, upon a showing of good cause, specify another method for service of process that is reasonably designed to afford actual notice to the protected party. The protected party may waive his or her right to notice if he or she is physically present in court and does not challenge the sufficiency of the notice.

(*l*) This section does not preclude either party from representation by private counsel or from appearing on his or her own behalf.

(m) Upon filing of a petition under this section, the respondent shall be personally served with a copy of the petition, temporary restraining order, if any, and notice of hearing of the petition. Service shall be made at least five days before the hearing. The court may, for good cause, on motion of the petitioner or on its own motion, shorten the time for service on the respondent.

§ 527.85

(n) A notice of hearing under this section shall notify the respondent that if he or she does not attend the hearing, the court may make orders against him or her that could last up to three years.

(o) The respondent shall be entitled, as a matter of course, to one continuance, for a reasonable period, to respond to the petition.

(p)(1) Either party may request a continuance of the hearing, which the court shall grant on a showing of good cause. The request may be made in writing before or at the hearing or orally at the hearing. The court may also grant a continuance on its own motion.

(2) If the court grants a continuance, any temporary restraining order that has been granted shall remain in effect until the end of the continued hearing, unless otherwise ordered by the court. In granting a continuance, the court may modify or terminate a temporary restraining order.

(q)(1) If a respondent, named in an order issued under this section after a hearing, has not been served personally with the order but has received actual notice of the existence and substance of the order through personal appearance in court to hear the terms of the order from the court, no additional proof of service is required for enforcement of the order.

(2) If the respondent named in a temporary restraining order is personally served with the order and notice of hearing with respect to a restraining order or protective order based on the temporary restraining order, but the respondent does not appear at the hearing, either personally or by an attorney, and the terms and conditions of the restraining order or protective order issued at the hearing are identical to the temporary restraining order, except for the duration of the order, then the restraining order or protective order issued at the hearing may be served on the respondent by first-class mail sent to that person at the most current address for the respondent available to the court.

(3) The Judicial Council form for temporary orders issued pursuant to this subdivision shall contain a statement in substantially the following form:

"If you have been personally served with a temporary restraining order and notice of hearing, but you do not appear at the hearing either in person or by a lawyer, and a restraining order that is the same as this temporary restraining order except for the expiration date is issued at the hearing, a copy of the order will be served on you by mail at the following address:____

If that address is not correct or you wish to verify that the temporary restraining order was converted to a restraining order at the hearing without substantive change and to find out the duration of that order, contact the clerk of the court."

(r)(1) Information on a temporary restraining order or order after hearing relating to schoolsite violence issued by a court pursuant to this section shall be transmitted to the Department of Justice in accordance with either paragraph (2) or (3).

(2) The court shall order the petitioner or the attorney for the petitioner to deliver a copy of any order issued under this section, or a reissuance, extension, modification, or termination of the order, and any subsequent proof of service, by the close of the business day on which the order, reissuance, or termination of the order, and any proof of service, was made, to each law enforcement agency having jurisdiction over the residence of the petition and to any additional law enforcement agencies within the court's discretion as are requested by the petitioner.

(3) Alternatively, the court or its designee shall transmit, within one business day, to law enforcement personnel all information required under subdivision (b) of Section 6380 of the Family Code regarding any order issued under this section, or a reissuance, extension, modification, or termination of the order, and any subsequent proof of service, by either one of the following methods:

(A) Transmitting a physical copy of the order or proof of service to a local law enforcement agency authorized by the Department of Justice to enter orders into the California Law Enforcement Telecommunications System (CLETS).

(B) With the approval of the Department of Justice, entering the order of proof of service into CLETS directly.

(4) Each appropriate law enforcement agency shall make available information as to the existence and current status of these orders to law enforcement officers responding to the scene of reported unlawful violence or a credible threat of violence.

(5) At the request of the petitioner, an order issued under this section shall be served on the respondent, regardless of whether the respondent has been taken into custody, by any law enforcement officer who is present at the scene of reported unlawful violence or a credible threat of violence involving the parties to the proceedings. The petitioner shall provide the officer with an endorsed copy of the order and proof of service that the officer shall complete and send to the issuing court.

(6) Upon receiving information at the scene of an incident of unlawful violence or a credible threat of violence that a protective order has been issued under this section, or that a person who has been taken into custody is the subject of an order, if the petitioner or the protected person cannot produce an endorsed copy of the order, a law enforcement officer shall immediately attempt to verify the existence of the order.

(7) If the law enforcement officer determines that a protective order has been issued but not served, the officer shall immediately notify the respondent of the terms of the order and obtain the respondent's address. The law enforcement officer shall at that time also enforce the order, but may not arrest or take the respondent into custody for acts in violation of the order that were committed prior to the verbal notice of the terms and conditions of the order. The law enforcement officer's verbal notice of the terms of the order shall constitute service of the order and constitutes sufficient notice for the purposes of this section, and Section 29825 of the Penal Code. The petitioner shall mail an endorsed copy of the order to the respondent's mailing address provided to the law enforcement officer within one business day of the reported incident of unlawful violence or a credible threat of violence at which a verbal notice of the terms of the order was provided by a law enforcement officer.

(s)(1) A person subject to a protective order issued under this section shall not own, possess, purchase, receive, or attempt to purchase or receive a firearm or ammunition while the protective order is in effect.

(2) The court shall order a person subject to a protective order issued under this section to relinquish any firearms he or she owns or possesses pursuant to Section 527.9.

(3) Every person who owns, possesses, purchases, or receives, or attempts to purchase or receive a firearm or ammunition while the protective order is in effect is punishable pursuant to Section 29825 of the Penal Code.

(t) Any intentional disobedience of any temporary restraining order or order after hearing granted under this section is punishable pursuant to Section 273.6 of the Penal Code.

(u) This section shall not be construed as expanding, diminishing, altering, or modifying the duty, if any, of a postsecondary educational institution to provide a safe environment for students and other persons.

(v)(1) The Judicial Council shall develop forms, instructions, and rules relating to matters governed by this section. The forms for the petition and response shall be simple and concise, and their use by parties in actions brought pursuant to this section shall be mandatory.

(2) A temporary restraining order or order after hearing relating to unlawful violence or a credible threat of violence issued by a court pursuant to this section shall be issued on forms adopted by the Judicial Council that have been approved by the Department of Justice pursuant to subdivision (i) of Section 6380 of the Family Code. However, the fact that an order issued by a court pursuant to this section was not issued on forms adopted by the Judicial Council and approved by the Department of Justice shall not, in and of itself, make the order unenforceable.

(w) There is no filing fee for a petition that alleges that a person has threatened violence against a student of the petitioner, or stalked the student, or acted or spoken in any other manner that has placed the student in reasonable fear of violence, and that seeks a protective or restraining order restraining stalking or future threats of violence, in any action brought pursuant to this section. No fee shall be paid for a subpoena filed in connection with a petition alleging these acts. No fee shall be paid for filing a response to a petition alleging these acts.

(x)(1) Subject to paragraph (4) of subdivision (b) of Section 6103.2 of the Government Code, there shall be no fee for the service of process by a sheriff or marshal of a temporary restraining order or order after hearing to be issued pursuant to this section if either of the following conditions applies:

(A) The temporary restraining order or order after hearing issued pursuant to this section is based upon stalking, as prohibited by Section 646.9 of the Penal Code.

(B) The temporary restraining order or order after hearing issued pursuant to this section is based upon a credible threat of violence.

(2) The Judicial Council shall prepare and develop forms for persons who wish to avail themselves of the services described in this subdivision. *(Added by Stats.2009, c. 566 (S.B.188), § 1. Amended by Stats.2010, c. 178 (S.B.1115), § 22, operative Jan. 1, 2012; Stats.2010, c. 572 (A.B.1596), § 4, operative Jan. 1, 2012; Stats.2011, c. 285 (A.B.1402), § 3; Stats.2011, c. 101 (A.B.454), § 3; Stats.2012, c. 162 (S.B.1171), § 14; Stats.2015, c. 411 (A.B.1081), § 3, eff. Jan. 1, 2016.)*

Cross References

Acceptance of Judicial Council form, summons, order, or other notices by email, fax, or in-person delivery, fee, court fee waiver or exemption, see Government Code § 26666.5.
Injunction defined, see Code of Civil Procedure § 525.
Violation of protective order under this section by possession of a firearm as a misdemeanor, see Penal Code § 273.6.
Violation of protective order under this section by possession of a firearm as a public offense, see Penal Code § 29825.

Research References

Forms

West's California Judicial Council Forms SV-100, Petition for Private Postsecondary School Violence Restraining Orders.
West's California Judicial Council Forms SV-100-INFO, How Do I Get an Order to Prohibit Private Postsecondary School Violence?
West's California Judicial Council Forms SV-110, Temporary Restraining Order (Clets-Tsv).
West's California Judicial Council Forms SV-115, Request to Continue Court Hearing (Temporary Restraining Order) (Private Postsecondary School Violence Prevention).
West's California Judicial Council Forms SV-115-INFO, How to Ask for a New Hearing Date (Private Postsecondary School Violence Prevention).
West's California Judicial Council Forms SV-116, Order on Request to Continue Hearing (Temporary Restraining Order) (Clets-Tsv) (Private Postsecondary School Violence Prevention).
West's California Judicial Council Forms SV-120, Response to Petition for Private Postsecondary School Violence Restraining Orders.
West's California Judicial Council Forms SV-120-INFO, How Can I Respond to a Petition for Private Postsecondary School Violence Restraining Orders?
West's California Judicial Council Forms SV-130, Private Postsecondary School Violence Restraining Order After Hearing (Clets-Svo).
West's California Judicial Council Forms SV-200, Proof of Personal Service.
West's California Judicial Council Forms SV-250, Proof of Service of Response by Mail.
West's California Judicial Council Forms SV-260, Proof of Service of Order After Hearing by Mail.
West's California Judicial Council Forms SV-600, Request to Modify/Terminate Private Postsecondary School Violence Restraining Order.
West's California Judicial Council Forms SV-610, Notice of Hearing on Request to Modify/Terminate Private Postsecondary School Violence Restraining Order.
West's California Judicial Council Forms SV-620, Response to Request to Modify/Terminate Private Postsecondary School Violence Restraining Order.
West's California Judicial Council Forms SV-630, Order on Request to Modify/Terminate Private Postsecondary School Violence Restraining Order.
West's California Judicial Council Forms SV-700, Request to Renew Restraining Order.
West's California Judicial Council Forms SV-710, Notice of Hearing to Renew Restraining Order.
West's California Judicial Council Forms SV-720, Response to Request to Renew Restraining Order.
West's California Judicial Council Forms SV-730, Order Renewing Private Postsecondary School Violence Restraining Order.

§ 527.9. Relinquishment of firearms; persons subject to protective orders

(a) A person subject to a temporary restraining order or injunction issued pursuant to Section 527.6, 527.8, or 527.85 or subject to a restraining order issued pursuant to Section 136.2 of the Penal Code, or Section 15657.03 of the Welfare and Institutions Code, shall relinquish the firearm pursuant to this section.

(b) Upon the issuance of a protective order against a person pursuant to subdivision (a), the court shall order that person to relinquish any firearm in that person's immediate possession or control, or subject to that person's immediate possession or control, within 24 hours of being served with the order, either by surrendering the firearm to the control of local law enforcement officials, or by selling the firearm to a licensed gun dealer, as specified in Article 1 (commencing with Section 26700) and Article 2 (commencing with Section 26800) of Chapter 2 of Division 6 of Title 4 of Part 6 of the Penal Code. A person ordered to relinquish any firearm pursuant to this subdivision shall file with the court a receipt showing the firearm was surrendered to the local law enforcement agency or sold to a licensed gun dealer within 48 hours after receiving the order. In the event that it is necessary to continue the date of any hearing due to a request for a relinquishment order pursuant to this section, the court shall ensure that all applicable protective orders described in Section 6218 of the Family Code remain in effect or bifurcate the issues and grant the permanent restraining order pending the date of the hearing.

(c) A local law enforcement agency may charge the person subject to the order or injunction a fee for the storage of any firearm relinquished pursuant to this section. The fee shall not exceed the actual cost incurred by the local law enforcement agency for the storage of the firearm. For purposes of this subdivision, "actual cost" means expenses directly related to taking possession of a firearm, storing the firearm, and surrendering possession of the firearm to a licensed dealer as defined in Section 26700 of the Penal Code or to the person relinquishing the firearm.

(d) The restraining order requiring a person to relinquish a firearm pursuant to subdivision (b) shall state on its face that the respondent is prohibited from owning, possessing, purchasing, or receiving a firearm while the protective order is in effect and that the firearm shall be relinquished to the local law enforcement agency for that jurisdiction or sold to a licensed gun dealer, and that proof of surrender or sale shall be filed with the court within a specified period of receipt of the order. The order shall also state on its face the expiration date for relinquishment. Nothing in this section shall

§ 527.9

limit a respondent's right under existing law to petition the court at a later date for modification of the order.

(e) The restraining order requiring a person to relinquish a firearm pursuant to subdivision (b) shall prohibit the person from possessing or controlling any firearm for the duration of the order. At the expiration of the order, the local law enforcement agency shall return possession of any surrendered firearm to the respondent, within five days after the expiration of the relinquishment order, unless the local law enforcement agency determines that (1) the firearm has been stolen, (2) the respondent is prohibited from possessing a firearm because the respondent is in any prohibited class for the possession of firearms, as defined in Chapter 2 (commencing with Section 29800) and Chapter 3 (commencing with Section 29900) of Division 9 of Title 4 of Part 6 of the Penal Code and Sections 8100 and 8103 of the Welfare and Institutions Code, or (3) another successive restraining order is issued against the respondent under this section. If the local law enforcement agency determines that the respondent is the legal owner of any firearm deposited with the local law enforcement agency and is prohibited from possessing any firearm, the respondent shall be entitled to sell or transfer the firearm to a licensed dealer as defined in Section 26700 of the Penal Code. If the firearm has been stolen, the firearm shall be restored to the lawful owner upon his or her identification of the firearm and proof of ownership.

(f) The court may, as part of the relinquishment order, grant an exemption from the relinquishment requirements of this section for a particular firearm if the respondent can show that a particular firearm is necessary as a condition of continued employment and that the current employer is unable to reassign the respondent to another position where a firearm is unnecessary. If an exemption is granted pursuant to this subdivision, the order shall provide that the firearm shall be in the physical possession of the respondent only during scheduled work hours and during travel to and from his or her place of employment. In any case involving a peace officer who as a condition of employment and whose personal safety depends on the ability to carry a firearm, a court may allow the peace officer to continue to carry a firearm, either on duty or off duty, if the court finds by a preponderance of the evidence that the officer does not pose a threat of harm. Prior to making this finding, the court shall require a mandatory psychological evaluation of the peace officer and may require the peace officer to enter into counseling or other remedial treatment program to deal with any propensity for domestic violence.

(g) During the period of the relinquishment order, a respondent is entitled to make one sale of all firearms that are in the possession of a local law enforcement agency pursuant to this section. A licensed gun dealer, who presents a local law enforcement agency with a bill of sale indicating that all firearms owned by the respondent that are in the possession of the local law enforcement agency have been sold by the respondent to the licensed gun dealer, shall be given possession of those firearms, at the location where a respondent's firearms are stored, within five days of presenting the local law enforcement agency with a bill of sale. *(Added by Stats.2003, c. 498 (S.B.226), § 4. Amended by Stats.2006, c. 474 (A.B.2129), § 1; Stats.2010, c. 178 (S.B.1115), § 23, operative Jan. 1, 2012; Stats.2010, c. 572 (A.B.1596), § 5, operative Jan. 1, 2012; Stats.2011, c. 285 (A.B.1402), § 4.)*

Cross References

Domestic violence protective orders, requirement to relinquish firearms, see Penal Code § 136.2.
Injunction defined, see Code of Civil Procedure § 525.

Research References

Forms

West's California Code Forms, Civil Procedure § 527.6 Form 10, Injunction—Request to Continue Court Hearing and to Reissue Temporary Restraining Order (CLETS-TCH) (Civil Harassment Prevention)—Official Form.

West's California Code Forms, Civil Procedure § 527.6 Form 18, Injunction—How Can I Respond to a Request for Civil Harassment Restraining Orders? (Civil Harassment Prevention)—Official Form.
West's California Judicial Council Forms CH–100, Request for Civil Harassment Restraining Orders (Also Available in Chinese, Korean, Spanish, and Vietnamese).
West's California Judicial Council Forms CH–110, Temporary Restraining Order (CLETS-TCH) (Also Available in Chinese, Korean, Spanish, and Vietnamese).
West's California Judicial Council Forms CH–116, Order on Request to Continue Hearing.
West's California Judicial Council Forms CH–120, Response to Request for Civil Harassment Restraining Orders (Also Available in Chinese, Korean, Spanish, and Vietnamese).
West's California Judicial Council Forms CH–130, Civil Harassment Restraining Order After Hearing (Clets-Cho) (Also Available in Chinese, Korean, Spanish, and Vietnamese).
West's California Judicial Council Forms CH–800, Proof of Firearms Turned In, Sold, or Stored.
West's California Judicial Council Forms EA–100, Request for Elder or Dependent Adult Abuse Restraining Orders (Also Available in Chinese, Korean, Spanish, and Vietnamese).
West's California Judicial Council Forms EA–110, Temporary Restraining Order (Clets—Tea or Tef) (Also Available in Chinese, Korean, Spanish, and Vietnamese).
West's California Judicial Council Forms SV–100, Petition for Private Postsecondary School Violence Restraining Orders.
West's California Judicial Council Forms SV–110, Temporary Restraining Order (Clets-Tsv).
West's California Judicial Council Forms SV–120, Response to Petition for Private Postsecondary School Violence Restraining Orders.
West's California Judicial Council Forms SV–120–INFO, How Can I Respond to a Petition for Private Postsecondary School Violence Restraining Orders?
West's California Judicial Council Forms SV–130, Private Postsecondary School Violence Restraining Order After Hearing (Clets-Svo).
West's California Judicial Council Forms SV–800, Proof of Firearms Turned In, Sold, or Stored.
West's California Judicial Council Forms WV–100, Petition for Workplace Violence Restraining Orders.
West's California Judicial Council Forms WV–110, Temporary Restraining Order (Clets-Twh).
West's California Judicial Council Forms WV–115, Request to Continue Court Hearing (Temporary Restraining Order).
West's California Judicial Council Forms WV–120, Response to Petition for Workplace Violence Restraining Orders.
West's California Judicial Council Forms WV–120–INFO, How Can I Respond to a Petition for Workplace Violence Restraining Orders?
West's California Judicial Council Forms WV–130, Workplace Violence Restraining Order After Hearing (Clets- Who).
West's California Judicial Council Forms WV–800, Proof of Firearms Turned In, Sold, or Stored.

§ 527.10. Addresses or locations of persons protected under court order; prohibition upon certain enjoined parties from acting to obtain such information

(a) The court shall order that any party enjoined pursuant to Section 527.6, 527.8, or 527.85 be prohibited from taking any action to obtain the address or location of any protected person, unless there is good cause not to make that order.

(b) The Judicial Council shall develop forms necessary to effectuate this section. *(Added by Stats.2005, c. 472 (A.B.978), § 1. Amended by Stats.2010, c. 572 (A.B.1596), § 3, operative Jan. 1, 2012.)*

§ 529. Undertaking; objection; insufficiency; dissolution of injunction; exceptions

(a) On granting an injunction, the court or judge must require an undertaking on the part of the applicant to the effect that the applicant will pay to the party enjoined any damages, not exceeding an amount to be specified, the party may sustain by reason of the injunction, if the court finally decides that the applicant was not entitled to the injunction. Within five days after the service of the injunction, the person enjoined may object to the undertaking. If the court determines that the applicant's undertaking is insufficient and a sufficient undertaking is not filed within the time required by statute, the order granting the injunction must be dissolved.

(b) This section does not apply to any of the following persons:

(1) Either spouse against the other in a proceeding for legal separation or dissolution of marriage.

(2) The applicant for an order described in Division 10 (commencing with Section 6200) of the Family Code.

(3) A public entity or officer described in Section 995.220.

(4) An applicant requesting an injunction under subdivision (d) of Section 1708.85 of the Civil Code. *(Enacted in 1872. Amended by Code Am.1873–74, c. 624, p. 405, § 1; Code Am.1880, c. 64, p. 62, § 1; Stats.1907, c. 272, p. 342, § 4; Stats.1931, c. 140, p. 201, § 1; Stats.1933, c. 744, p. 1858, § 66; Stats.1979, c. 795, p. 2710, § 9, operative July 1, 1980; Stats.1982, c. 517, p. 2340, § 123; Stats.1992, c. 163 (A.B.2641), § 25, operative Jan. 1, 1994; Stats.1993, c. 219 (A.B.1500), § 63.7; Stats.2021, c. 518 (A.B.514), § 2, eff. Jan. 1, 2022.)*

Cross References

Adverse claim of, or denial of debt by third party, see Code of Civil Procedure § 708.180.
Bond and Undertaking Law, see Code of Civil Procedure § 995.010 et seq.
Claim and delivery undertaking, see Code of Civil Procedure § 515.010.
Corporate sureties, see Code of Civil Procedure § 995.120.
Court commissioners, power to take and approve bonds, see Code of Civil Procedure § 259.
Dismissal of actions, see Code of Civil Procedure § 581.
Enforcement of liability of surety by motion, see Code of Civil Procedure § 996.440.
Extension of time for filing undertaking, see Code of Civil Procedure §§ 1054, 1054.1, 995.050.
Form of undertaking, see Code of Civil Procedure § 995.320.
Injunction defined, see Code of Civil Procedure § 525.
Money deposit in lieu of undertaking, see Code of Civil Procedure § 995.710 et seq.
Parties exempt from giving bond, see Code of Civil Procedure § 995.220.
Sureties, see Code of Civil Procedure § 995.510 et seq.

Research References

Forms

West's California Code Forms, Civil § 52.1 Form 2, Order—Granting Preliminary Injunction for Violation of Civil Rights.
West's California Judicial Council Forms RC–200, Ex Parte Order Appointing Receiver and Order to Show Cause and Temporary Restraining Order—Rents, Issues, and Profits.
West's California Judicial Council Forms RC–210, Order Confirming Appointment of Receiver and Preliminary Injunction—Rents, Issues, and Profits.
West's California Judicial Council Forms RC–300, Order to Show Cause and Temporary Restraining Order—Rents, Issues, and Profits.
West's California Judicial Council Forms RC–310, Order Appointing Receiver After Hearing and Preliminary Injunction—Rents, Issues, and Profits.

CHAPTER 5. RECEIVERS

Section
564. Appointment; cases in which authorized; definitions.
565. Appointment upon dissolution of corporation.
566. Persons ineligible to appointment; consent; undertaking on ex parte application.
567. Oath and undertaking of receiver.
568. Powers.
568.1. Deposit of securities in securities depository.
568.2. Notification to court of order or notice to correct substandard or unsafe condition of rental housing.
568.3. Motion in receivership actions; who may file motion; conditions.
568.5. Sales; authority; manner; confirmation.

Section
568.6. Appointment for control and operation of Pacific Gas and Electric Company.
569. Interest bearing accounts; deposit of funds; conditions.
570. Unclaimed funds; publication of notice; payment to State Treasury; rights of owner; expense of notice.

Cross References

Receivership under this Chapter as a cause for disciplinary action against a contractor, see Business and Professions Code § 7113.5.
State license tax, action to collect, applicability of this Chapter, see Business and Professions Code § 16223.

§ 564. Appointment; cases in which authorized; definitions

(a) A receiver may be appointed, in the manner provided in this chapter, by the court in which an action or proceeding is pending in any case in which the court is empowered by law to appoint a receiver.

(b) A receiver may be appointed by the court in which an action or proceeding is pending, or by a judge of that court, in the following cases:

(1) In an action by a vendor to vacate a fraudulent purchase of property, or by a creditor to subject any property or fund to the creditor's claim, or between partners or others jointly owning or interested in any property or fund, on the application of the plaintiff, or of any party whose right to or interest in the property or fund, or the proceeds of the property or fund, is probable, and where it is shown that the property or fund is in danger of being lost, removed, or materially injured.

(2) In an action by a secured lender for the foreclosure of a deed of trust or mortgage and sale of property upon which there is a lien under a deed of trust or mortgage, where it appears that the property is in danger of being lost, removed, or materially injured, or that the condition of the deed of trust or mortgage has not been performed, and that the property is probably insufficient to discharge the deed of trust or mortgage debt.

(3) After judgment, to carry the judgment into effect.

(4) After judgment, to dispose of the property according to the judgment, or to preserve it during the pendency of an appeal, or pursuant to the Enforcement of Judgments Law (Title 9 (commencing with Section 680.010)), or after sale of real property pursuant to a decree of foreclosure, during the redemption period, to collect, expend, and disburse rents as directed by the court or otherwise provided by law.

(5) Where a corporation has been dissolved, as provided in Section 565.

(6) Where a corporation is insolvent, or in imminent danger of insolvency, or has forfeited its corporate rights.

(7) In an action of unlawful detainer.

(8) At the request of the Public Utilities Commission pursuant to Section 1825 or 1826 of the Public Utilities Code.

(9) In all other cases where necessary to preserve the property or rights of any party.

(10) At the request of the Office of Statewide Health Planning and Development, or the Attorney General, pursuant to Section 129173 of the Health and Safety Code.

(11) In an action by a secured lender for specific performance of an assignment of rents provision in a deed of trust, mortgage, or separate assignment document. The appointment may be continued after entry of a judgment for specific performance if appropriate to protect, operate, or maintain real property encumbered by a deed of trust or mortgage or to collect rents therefrom while a pending nonjudicial foreclosure under power of sale in a deed of trust or mortgage is being completed.

§ 564

(12) In a case brought by an assignee under an assignment of leases, rents, issues, or profits pursuant to subdivision (g) of Section 2938 of the Civil Code.

(c) A receiver may be appointed, in the manner provided in this chapter, including, but not limited to, Section 566, by the superior court in an action brought by a secured lender to enforce the rights provided in Section 2929.5 of the Civil Code, to enable the secured lender to enter and inspect the real property security for the purpose of determining the existence, location, nature, and magnitude of any past or present release or threatened release of any hazardous substance into, onto, beneath, or from the real property security. The secured lender shall not abuse the right of entry and inspection or use it to harass the borrower or tenant of the property. Except in case of an emergency, when the borrower or tenant of the property has abandoned the premises, or if it is impracticable to do so, the secured lender shall give the borrower or tenant of the property reasonable notice of the secured lender's intent to enter and shall enter only during the borrower's or tenant's normal business hours. Twenty-four hours' notice shall be presumed to be reasonable notice in the absence of evidence to the contrary.

(d) Any action by a secured lender to appoint a receiver pursuant to this section shall not constitute an action within the meaning of subdivision (a) of Section 726.

(e) For purposes of this section:

(1) "Borrower" means the trustor under a deed of trust, or a mortgagor under a mortgage, where the deed of trust or mortgage encumbers real property security and secures the performance of the trustor or mortgagor under a loan, extension of credit, guaranty, or other obligation. The term includes any successor in interest of the trustor or mortgagor to the real property security before the deed of trust or mortgage has been discharged, reconveyed, or foreclosed upon.

(2) "Hazardous substance" means any of the following:

(A) Any "hazardous substance" as defined in subdivision (h) of Section 25281 of the Health and Safety Code.

(B) Any "waste" as defined in subdivision (d) of Section 13050 of the Water Code.

(C) Petroleum including crude oil or any fraction thereof, natural gas, natural gas liquids, liquefied natural gas, or synthetic gas usable for fuel, or any mixture thereof.

(3) "Real property security" means any real property and improvements, other than a separate interest and any related interest in the common area of a residential common interest development, as the terms "separate interest," "common area," and "common interest development" are defined in Sections 4095, 4100, and 4185 of the Civil Code, or real property consisting of one acre or less that contains 1 to 15 dwelling units.

(4) "Release" means any spilling, leaking, pumping, pouring, emitting, emptying, discharging, injecting, escaping, leaching, dumping, or disposing into the environment, including continuing migration, of hazardous substances into, onto, or through soil, surface water, or groundwater.

(5) "Secured lender" means the beneficiary under a deed of trust against the real property security, or the mortgagee under a mortgage against the real property security, and any successor in interest of the beneficiary or mortgagee to the deed of trust or mortgage. *(Enacted in 1872. Amended by Stats.1919, c. 166, p. 251, § 1; Stats.1933, c. 744, p. 1867, § 85a; Stats.1941, c. 444, p. 1736, § 1; Stats.1980, c. 1078, p. 3438, § 1; Stats.1982, c. 497, p. 2155, § 34, operative July 1, 1983; Stats.1991, c. 1167 (A.B.1735), § 2; Stats.1992, c. 167 (A.B. 2750), § 2; Stats.1994, c. 414 (S.B.1705), § 2, eff. Sept. 1, 1994; Stats.1995, c. 384 (A.B.1110), § 1; Stats.1996, c. 1023 (S.B.1497), § 29, eff. Sept. 29, 1996; Stats.1996, c. 49 (S.B.947), § 4; Stats.1996, c. 1154 (A.B.3020), § 2, eff. Sept. 30, 1996; Stats.1996, c. 1154 (A.B.3020), § 2.1, eff. Sept. 30, 1996, operative Jan. 1, 1997; Stats.* 1998, c. 931 (S.B.2139), § 75, eff. Sept. 28, 1998; Stats.2001, c. 44 (S.B.562), § 4; Stats.2002, c. 999 (A.B.2481), § 3; Stats.2012, c. 181 (A.B.806), § 44, operative Jan. 1, 2014; Stats.2020, c. 27 (S.B.350), § 1, eff. Jan. 1, 2021.)

Cross References

Appeal of order appointing, see Code of Civil Procedure §§ 904.1, 904.2.
Appointment and qualification of receiver, see Code of Civil Procedure § 708.610.
Appointment of receiver to protect residents of residential care facilities for the elderly, divestment of possession and control of facility, powers and duties of receiver, duration of appointment, salary of receiver, see Health and Safety Code § 1569.482.
Appointment of receiver to temporarily operate community care facility, divestment of control and possession of facility, powers and duties of receiver, duration of appointment, salary, liability, application, see Health and Safety Code § 1546.2.
Attorney General, generally, see Government Code § 12500 et seq.
Dissolution of corporation,
  Involuntary proceedings, see Corporations Code § 1803.
  Proceedings by Attorney General, see Corporations Code § 1801.
Draft housing element or amendment, submission, review and report, adoption by legislative body, review by department and report to planning agency, review of action or failure to act, notification of violation, remedies, see Government Code § 65585.
Enforcement by receiver, see Family Code § 290.
Enforcement of judgment, see Code of Civil Procedure § 681.010.
Escheat proceedings, appointment of receiver, see Code of Civil Procedure § 1422.
Foreclosure of mortgages, see Code of Civil Procedure § 725a et seq.
Jurisdiction, actions to appoint a receiver, see Code of Civil Procedure § 86.
Perishable property under attachment, see Code of Civil Procedure § 488.700.
Searches and seizures, see Cal. Const. Art. 1, § 13.
Summary proceedings for obtaining possession of real property, see Code of Civil Procedure § 1159 et seq.
Uniform fraudulent conveyance act, see Civil Code § 3439 et seq.

Research References

Forms

21 Am. Jur. Pl. & Pr. Forms Receivers § 1, Introductory Comments.
3 California Real Estate Forms (Miller & Starr) § 3:8 (2d ed.), Deed of Trust, Security Agreement, and Fixture Filing With Assignment of Rents and Agreements.
3 California Real Estate Forms (Miller & Starr) § 3:10 (2d ed.), Environmental Certification, Agreement, and Indemnity of Borrower.
3 California Real Estate Forms (Miller & Starr) § 3:14 (2d ed.), Construction Deed of Trust, Security Agreement, and Fixture Filing With Assignment of Rents and Agreements.
3 California Real Estate Forms (Miller & Starr) § 3:21 (2d ed.), Deed of Trust, Assignment of Rents, Security Agreement and Fixture Filing—Conduit Loan.
3 California Real Estate Forms (Miller & Starr) § 3:30 (2d ed.), Environmental Indemnity—Conduit Loan.
West's California Code Forms, Civil Procedure § 564 Form 2, Receivers—Notice of Motion for Appointment of Receiver.
West's California Judicial Council Forms RC–200, Ex Parte Order Appointing Receiver and Order to Show Cause and Temporary Restraining Order—Rents, Issues, and Profits.
West's California Judicial Council Forms RC–210, Order Confirming Appointment of Receiver and Preliminary Injunction—Rents, Issues, and Profits.
West's California Judicial Council Forms RC–300, Order to Show Cause and Temporary Restraining Order—Rents, Issues, and Profits.
West's California Judicial Council Forms RC–310, Order Appointing Receiver After Hearing and Preliminary Injunction—Rents, Issues, and Profits.

§ 565. Appointment upon dissolution of corporation

Upon the dissolution of any corporation, the Superior Court of the county in which the corporation carries on its business or has its principal place of business, on application of any creditor of the corporation, or of any stockholder or member thereof, may appoint one or more persons to be receivers or trustees of the corporation, to take charge of the estate and effects thereof, and to collect the debts and property due and belonging to the corporation, and to pay the outstanding debts thereof, and to divide the moneys and other property that shall remain over among the stockholders or members. *(Enacted in 1872. Amended by Code Am.1880, c. 15, p. 4, § 7.)*

Cross References

Involuntary dissolution of corporation, see Corporations Code § 1800 et seq.
Orders winding up corporations, see Corporations Code § 1907.

§ 566. Persons ineligible to appointment; consent; undertaking on ex parte application

(a) No party, or attorney of a party, or person interested in an action, or related to any judge of the court by consanguinity or affinity within the third degree, can be appointed receiver therein without the written consent of the parties, filed with the clerk.

(b) If a receiver is appointed upon an ex parte application, the court, before making the order, must require from the applicant an undertaking in an amount to be fixed by the court, to the effect that the applicant will pay to the defendant all damages the defendant may sustain by reason of the appointment of the receiver and the entry by the receiver upon the duties, in case the applicant shall have procured the appointment wrongfully, maliciously, or without sufficient cause. *(Enacted in 1872. Amended by Code Am.1873–74, c. 383, p. 309, § 73; Stats.1897, c. 69, p. 60, § 1; Stats.1907, c. 374, p. 710, § 1; Stats.1982, c. 517, p. 2342, § 127.)*

Cross References

Deposit in lieu of undertaking, see Code of Civil Procedure § 995,710 et seq.
Household movers, abandonment of stored household goods or property, protection of property rights, appointment of receiver or bureau staff, see Business and Professions Code § 19269.1.
Involuntary dissolution of corporations, applicability of security provisions of this section, see Corporations Code § 1803.
Nonprofit mutual benefit corporations, security on appointment for receivership, see Corporations Code § 8513.
Nonprofit public benefit corporation, security on application for receivership, see Corporations Code § 6513.
Similar provision concerning judges, see Code of Civil Procedure § 170 et seq.

Research References

Forms

West's California Code Forms, Civil Procedure § 566 Form 2, Receivers—Oath of Receiver and Undertaking.

§ 567. Oath and undertaking of receiver

Before entering upon the duties of a receiver:

(a) The receiver must be sworn to perform the duties faithfully.

(b) The receiver shall give an undertaking to the State of California, in such sum as the court or judge may direct, to the effect that the receiver will faithfully discharge the duties of receiver in the action and obey the orders of the court therein. The receiver shall be allowed the cost of the undertaking. *(Enacted in 1872. Amended by Stats.1907, c. 374, p. 710, § 2; Stats.1982, c. 517, p. 2342, § 128.)*

Cross References

Falsity of oath, perjury, see Penal Code § 118.
Household movers, abandonment of stored household goods or property, protection of property rights, appointment of receiver or bureau staff, see Business and Professions Code § 19269.1.
Insufficient undertaking, see Code of Civil Procedure § 922.
Involuntary dissolution of corporations, applicability of security provisions of this section, see Corporations Code § 1803.
Nonprofit mutual benefit corporation, security on appointment for receivership, see Corporations Code § 8513.
Nonprofit public benefit corporation, security on application for receivership, see Corporations Code § 6513.

§ 568. Powers

The receiver has, under the control of the Court, power to bring and defend actions in his own name, as receiver; to take and keep possession of the property, to receive rents, collect debts, to compound for and compromise the same, to make transfers, and generally to do such acts respecting the property as the Court may authorize. *(Enacted in 1872.)*

Cross References

Household movers, abandonment of stored household goods or property, protection of property rights, appointment of receiver or bureau staff, see Business and Professions Code § 19269.1.

Research References

Forms

West's California Code Forms, Civil Procedure § 568 Form 6, Receivers—Order Granting Receiver's Petition for Instructions, etc.

§ 568.1. Deposit of securities in securities depository

Any securities in the hands of a receiver may, under the control of the court, be deposited by the receiver in a securities depository, as defined in Section 30004 of the Financial Code, which is licensed under Section 30200 of the Financial Code or exempted from licensing thereunder by Section 30005 or 30006 of the Financial Code, and such securities may be held by such securities depository in the manner authorized by Section 775 of the Financial Code. *(Added by Stats.1972, c. 1057, p. 1955, § 9.)*

Cross References

Deposit of securities in securities depository, authority, see Financial Code § 1612.
Securities depositories, see Financial Code § 30000 et seq.

§ 568.2. Notification to court of order or notice to correct substandard or unsafe condition of rental housing

(a) A receiver of real property containing rental housing shall notify the court of the existence of any order or notice to correct any substandard or unsafe condition, as defined in Section 17920.3 or 17920.10 of the Health and Safety Code, with which the receiver cannot comply within the time provided by the order or notice.

(b) The notice shall be filed within 30 days after the receiver's appointment or, if the substandard condition occurs subsequently, within 15 days of its occurrence.

(c) The notice shall inform the court of all of the following:

(1) The substandard conditions that exist.

(2) The threat or danger that the substandard conditions pose to any occupant of the property or the public.

(3) The approximate cost and time involved in abating the conditions. If more time is needed to approximate the cost, then the notice shall provide the date on which the approximate cost will be filed with the court and that date shall be within 10 days of the filing.

(4) Whether the receivership estate is likely to contain sufficient funds to abate the conditions.

(d) If the receivership estate does not contain sufficient funds to abate the conditions, the receiver shall request further instructions or orders from the court.

(e) The court, upon receipt of a notice pursuant to subdivision (d), shall consider appropriate orders or instructions to enable the receiver to correct the substandard conditions or to terminate or limit the period of receivership. *(Added by Stats.2001, c. 414 (A.B.472), § 1. Amended by Stats.2005, c. 595 (S.B.253), § 3.)*

§ 568.3. Motion in receivership actions; who may file motion; conditions

Any tenant of real property that is subject to receivership, a tenant association or organization, or any federal, state, or local enforcement agency, may file a motion in a receivership action for the purpose of seeking further instructions or orders from the court, if either of the following is true:

(a) Substandard conditions exist, as defined by Section 17920.3 or 17920.10 of the Health and Safety Code.

(b) A dispute or controversy exists concerning the powers or duties of the receiver affecting a tenant or the public. *(Added by Stats.2001, c. 414 (A.B.472), § 2. Amended by Stats.2005, c. 595 (S.B.253), § 4.)*

§ 568.5. Sales; authority; manner; confirmation

A receiver may, pursuant to an order of the court, sell real or personal property in the receiver's possession upon the notice and in the manner prescribed by Article 6 (commencing with Section 701.510) of Chapter 3 of Division 2 of Title 9. The sale is not final until confirmed by the court. *(Added by Stats.1939, c. 374, p. 1709, § 1. Amended by Stats.1982, c. 497, p. 2156, § 35, operative July 1, 1983.)*

Cross References
Execution of judgment, see Code of Civil Procedure § 699.010 et seq.
Exemption from corporate securities law, see Corporations Code § 25104.

§ 568.6. Appointment for control and operation of Pacific Gas and Electric Company

A receiver appointed at the request of the Public Utilities Commission pursuant to Section 1825 of the Public Utilities Code shall control and operate Pacific Gas and Electric Company upon such terms and conditions as the court prescribes. *(Added by Stats.2020, c. 27 (S.B.350), § 2, eff. Jan. 1, 2021.)*

§ 569. Interest bearing accounts; deposit of funds; conditions

Funds in the hands of a receiver may be deposited in one or more interest bearing accounts in the name and for the benefit of the receivership estate with one or more financial institutions, provided that all of the following conditions are satisfied:

(a) The deposits are fully guaranteed or insured under federal law.

(b) The financial institution in which the funds are deposited is not a party to the action in which the receiver was appointed.

(c) The receiver does not own 1 percent or more in value of the outstanding stock of the financial institution, is not an officer, director, or employee of the financial institution, and is not a sibling, whether by the whole or half-blood, spouse, aunt, uncle, nephew, niece, ancestor, or lineal descendant of an owner, officer, employee, or director. *(Enacted in 1872. Amended by Stats.1998, c. 932 (A.B.1094), § 16.)*

Cross References
Investment of,
  Estate money, see Probate Code § 9730 et seq.
  Guardianship funds, see Probate Code § 2403.

§ 570. Unclaimed funds; publication of notice; payment to State Treasury; rights of owner; expense of notice

A receiver having any funds in his hands belonging to a person whose whereabouts are unknown to him, shall, before receiving his discharge as such receiver, publish a notice, in one or more newspapers published in the county, at least once a week for four consecutive weeks, setting forth the name of the owner of any unclaimed funds, the last known place of residence or post office address of such owner and the amount of such unclaimed funds. Any funds remaining in his hands unclaimed for 30 days after the date of the last publication of such notice, shall be reported to the court, and upon order of the court, all such funds must be paid into the State Treasury accompanied with a copy of the order, which must set forth the facts required in the notice herein provided. Such funds shall be deemed to have been received by the State under Chapter 7 (commencing with Section 1500) of Title 10 of Part 3 of this code and may be recovered in the manner prescribed therein.

All costs and expenses connected with such advertising shall be paid out of the funds the whereabouts of whose owners are unknown. *(Added by Stats.1913, c. 87, p. 92, § 1. Amended by Stats.1915, c. 83, p. 107, § 1; Stats.1917, c. 138, p. 203, § 1; Stats.1963, c. 1762, p. 3516, § 1.)*

Cross References
Unclaimed Property Law, see Code of Civil Procedure § 1500 et seq.

CHAPTER 5A. UNDERTAKING OF PERSONS HANDLING PRIVATE PROPERTY OR FUNDS

Section
571. Provision of order of appointment.

§ 571. Provision of order of appointment

If a referee or commissioner is appointed by a court and the duties of the referee or commissioner will, or are reasonably anticipated to, involve the custody of personal property or the receipt or disbursement of moneys, the order of appointment shall provide that before entering upon the duties, the referee or commissioner shall execute an undertaking to the State of California, to the effect that the referee or commissioner will faithfully discharge the duties of referee or commissioner, as the case may be, and obey the orders of the court therein. The order of appointment shall specify the amount of the undertaking, but a failure to so specify shall not invalidate the order. *(Added by Stats.1963, c. 575, p. 1453, § 1. Amended by Stats.1977, c. 1257, § 16, eff. Jan. 3, 1977; Stats.1982, c. 517, p. 2343, § 129.)*

Cross References
Appointment and qualification of receiver, see Code of Civil Procedure § 708.610.
Approval and effect of bonds, see Code of Civil Procedure § 995.410 et seq.

Research References
Forms
West's California Code Forms, Civil Procedure § 571 Form 1, Undertaking of Persons Handling Private Property or Funds.

CHAPTER 6. DEPOSIT IN COURT

Section
572. Order for deposit; when authorized.
573. Deposit with court's treasury.
574. Order for deposit; enforcement.

§ 572. Order for deposit; when authorized

When it is admitted by the pleadings, or shown upon the examination of a party to the action, that he or she has in his or her possession, or under his or her control, any money or other thing capable of delivery, which, being the subject of litigation, is held by him or her as trustee for another party, or which belongs or which is due to another party or which should, under the circumstances of the case be held by the court pending final disposition of the action, the court may order the same, upon motion, to be deposited in court or delivered to such party, upon those conditions that may be just, subject to the further direction of the court. *(Enacted in 1872. Amended by Stats.1907, c. 375, p. 710, § 1; Stats.1986, c. 540, § 6.)*

Cross References

Custody of prisoners' property, see Government Code § 26640 et seq.
Deposit in lieu of undertaking, see Code of Civil Procedure § 995.710 et seq.
Eminent domain, deposit in treasury, see Code of Civil Procedure § 1255.070.
Property taxed in two or more counties, see Revenue and Taxation Code § 4988.
Receipts and warrants for money paid into court, withdrawn or paid out, see Government Code § 68084.
Surplus after payment of mortgage, see Code of Civil Procedure § 727.
Tender by defendant, see Code of Civil Procedure § 1025.

Research References

Forms

8B Am. Jur. Pl. & Pr. Forms Deposits in Court § 1, Introductory Comments.
West's California Code Forms, Civil Procedure § 572 Form 1, Deposit in Court—Notice of Motion for Deposit in Court or Delivery to Another Party.
West's California Code Forms, Civil Procedure § 572 Form 2, Deposit in Court—Declaration in Support of Motion for Deposit in Court or Delivery to Another Party.

§ 573. Deposit with court's treasury

Whenever money is paid into or deposited in the court under this chapter, it shall be deposited with the court's treasury as provided in Section 68084 of the Government Code. (Added by Stats.2005, c. 75 (A.B.145), § 35, eff. July 19, 2005, operative Jan. 1, 2006.)

Cross References

Eminent domain, service of order of possession, see Code of Civil Procedure § 1268.220.
Redeposit with treasurer, see Government Code § 68084.
Taxation of property in custodia legis, see Revenue and Taxation Code § 983.

§ 574. Order for deposit; enforcement

Whenever, in the exercise of its authority, a court has ordered the deposit or delivery of money, or other thing, and the order is disobeyed, the court, beside punishing the disobedience, may make an order requiring the sheriff or marshal to take the money, or thing, and deposit or deliver it in conformity with the direction of the court. (Enacted in 1872. Amended by Stats.1933, c. 744, p. 1868, § 87; Stats.1996, c. 872 (A.B.3472), § 15.)

Cross References

Deposit in lieu of undertaking, see Code of Civil Procedure § 995.710 et seq.
Liability of sheriff, see Government Code § 26680.

Title 7a

PRETRIAL CONFERENCES

Section
575. Promulgation of rules by Judicial Council.
575.1. Local rules; scope; purpose; promulgation.
575.2. Noncompliance with local rules; effects.
576. Amendment of pleadings or pretrial conference order.

§ 575. Promulgation of rules by Judicial Council

The Judicial Council may promulgate rules governing pretrial conferences, and the time, manner and nature thereof, in civil cases at issue, or in one or more classes thereof, in the superior courts. (Added by Stats.1955, c. 632, p. 1130, § 1. Amended by Stats.1977, c. 1257, § 17, eff. Jan. 3, 1977; Stats.1998, c. 931 (S.B.2139), § 76, eff. Sept. 28, 1998; Stats.2002, c. 784 (S.B.1316), § 61.)

Cross References

Authority of Judicial Council to adopt rules of practice and procedure, see Cal. Const. Art. 6, § 6.

§ 575.1. Local rules; scope; purpose; promulgation

(a) The presiding judge of each superior court may prepare, with the assistance of appropriate committees of the court, proposed local rules designed to expedite and facilitate the business of the court. The rules need not be limited to those actions on the civil active list, but may provide for the supervision and judicial management of actions from the date they are filed. Rules prepared pursuant to this section shall be submitted for consideration to the judges of the court and, upon approval by a majority of the judges, the judges shall have the proposed rules published and submitted to the local bar and others, as specified by the Judicial Council, for consideration and recommendations.

(b) After a majority of the judges have officially adopted the rules, they shall be filed with the Judicial Council as required by Section 68071 of the Government Code and as specified in rules adopted by the Judicial Council. The Judicial Council shall prescribe rules to ensure that a complete current set of local rules and amendments, for each county in the state, is made available for public examination in each county. The local rules shall also be published for general distribution in accordance with rules adopted by the Judicial Council. Each court shall make its local rules available for inspection and copying in every location of the court that generally accepts filing of papers. The court may impose a reasonable charge for copying the rules and may impose a reasonable page limit on copying. The rules shall be accompanied by a notice indicating where a full set of the rules may be purchased.

(c) If a judge of a court adopts a rule that applies solely to cases in that judge's courtroom, or a particular branch or district of a court adopts a rule that applies solely to cases in that particular branch or district of a court, the court shall publish these rules as part of the general publication of rules required by the California Rules of Court. The court shall organize the rules so that rules on a common subject, whether individual, branch, district, or courtwide appear sequentially. Individual judges' rules and branch and district rules are local rules of court for purposes of this section and for purposes of the adoption, publication, comment, and filing requirements set forth in the Judicial Council rules applicable to local court rules. (Added by Stats.1982, c. 1402, p. 5354, § 1. Amended by Stats.1989, c. 1416, § 19; Stats.1993, c. 925 (S.B.425), § 1; Stats.1993, c. 926 (A.B.2205), § 3.5; Stats.1998, c. 931 (S.B.2139), § 77, eff. Sept. 28, 1998; Stats.2003, c. 149 (S.B.79), § 9.)

Cross References

Dismissal for delay in prosecution, see Code of Civil Procedure § 583.150.

§ 575.2. Noncompliance with local rules; effects

(a) Local rules promulgated pursuant to Section 575.1 may provide that if any counsel, a party represented by counsel, or a party if in pro se, fails to comply with any of the requirements thereof, the court on motion of a party or on its own motion may strike out all or any part of any pleading of that party, or, dismiss the action or proceeding or any part thereof, or enter a judgment by default against that party, or impose other penalties of a lesser nature as otherwise provided by law, and may order that party or his or her counsel to pay to the moving party the reasonable expenses in making the motion, including reasonable attorney fees. No penalty may be imposed under this section without prior notice to, and an opportunity to be heard by, the party against whom the penalty is sought to be imposed.

(b) It is the intent of the Legislature that if a failure to comply with these rules is the responsibility of counsel and not of the party, any penalty shall be imposed on counsel and shall not adversely affect the party's cause of action or defense thereto. (Added by Stats.1982,

§ 575.2

c. 1402, p. 5354, § 2. Amended by Stats.2002, c. 806 (A.B.3027), § 14.)

Research References

Forms

West's California Code Forms, Civil Procedure § 177.5 Form 1, Judicial Officers—Order for Payment of Money Sanctions.

West's California Code Forms, Civil Procedure § 575 Form 8, Pretrial Conferences—Order Granting Sanctions—Rule 2.30.

§ 576. Amendment of pleadings or pretrial conference order

Any judge, at any time before or after commencement of trial, in the furtherance of justice, and upon such terms as may be proper, may allow the amendment of any pleading or pretrial conference order. *(Added by Stats.1963, c. 882, p. 2129, § 1.)*

Title 8

OF THE TRIAL AND JUDGMENT IN CIVIL ACTIONS

Cross References

Interpleader actions, trial under this title, see Code of Civil Procedure § 386.
Submission of controversy without action, see Code of Civil Procedure § 1138 et seq.

CHAPTER 1. JUDGMENT IN GENERAL

Section
580. Relief granted; no answer; limited civil case.
580a. Action for deficiency judgment after foreclosure or trustee's sale; complaint; appraisal; deficiency computed on basis of fair market value; limitation of actions; necessity of sale.
580b. Contract of sale; deed of trust or mortgage; credit transaction; chattel mortgage; no deficiency to be owed or collected and deficiency judgments prohibited; exception for liability of guarantor, pledgor, or other surety.
580c. Mortgage foreclosure or trustee's sale; liability for actual costs and reasonable fees.
580d. Real property or estate for years sold under power of sale; no deficiency to be owed or collected and deficiency judgments prohibited; exception for liability of guarantor, pledgor, or other surety.
580e. Deficiency collection and judgment following short sale with consent of trustee or mortgagee prohibited; circumstances; exception for fraud; non-application of section; waivers void and against public policy.
581. Dismissal; definitions.

Cross References

Adjudgment of items in judgment, see Code of Civil Procedure § 1911.
Adverse claim to real property, judgment in suit to determine, see Code of Civil Procedure § 760.010 et seq.
Adverse possession under judgment, see Code of Civil Procedure §§ 322, 323.
Agreed case, judgment on, see Code of Civil Procedure § 1138 et seq.
Arbitration, judgment on confirmation of award, see Code of Civil Procedure § 1287.4.
Attorneys, judgment in disciplinary proceedings, see Business and Professions Code § 6116.
Collusion, impeachment of judgment, see Code of Civil Procedure § 1916.
Common name of associates, effect of judgment in action under, see Code of Civil Procedure § 369.5.
Conclusiveness of judgment,
  Generally, see Code of Civil Procedure § 1908.
  Contempt, see Code of Civil Procedure § 1222.
Confession of judgment, see Code of Civil Procedure § 1132 et seq.
Contempt, disobedience of judgment, see Code of Civil Procedure § 1209.
Contempt proceedings, see Code of Civil Procedure § 1218 et seq.
Correcting clerical mistakes in judgment, etc., see Code of Civil Procedure § 473.
Costs, inclusion in judgment, see Code of Civil Procedure § 685.010.
Criminal actions, see Penal Code § 1191 et seq.
Debtor, transferring property to evade judgment, see Penal Code §§ 154, 155, 531.
Decedent, judgment entered against after death, see Probate Code § 9300 et seq.
Decedent's estates, debts, priority in payment, see Probate Code § 11420.
Declaratory relief, scope of judgment, see Code of Civil Procedure §§ 1060, 1062.
Default judgment, see Code of Civil Procedure §§ 585, 586.
Entry of judgment, manner, see Code of Civil Procedure § 664 et seq.
Estoppel of parties by judgment, see Code of Civil Procedure § 1908 et seq.
Evidence, admissibility, see Code of Civil Procedure § 1908.5; Evidence Code §§ 1300 et seq.
Execution of judgment, see Code of Civil Procedure § 699.010 et seq.
Fictitious name to designate defendant, entry of default judgment, see Code of Civil Procedure § 474.
Fine, judgment for as lien, see Code of Civil Procedure § 697.310 et seq.
Foreign state, effect of judgment, generally, see Code of Civil Procedure § 1913.
Impeachment for lack of jurisdiction, collusion or fraud, see Code of Civil Procedure § 1916.
Judicial notice, see Evidence Code §§ 451, 452.
Pleading judgments, see Code of Civil Procedure § 456.
Power of court to enforce, see Code of Civil Procedure § 128.
Presumption that judgment correctly determines rights of parties, see Evidence Code § 639.
Relief from judgment or order taken by mistake, inadvertence, surprise, or excusable neglect, see Code of Civil Procedure § 473.
Summary judgment, see Code of Civil Procedure § 437c.

§ 580. Relief granted; no answer; limited civil case

(a) The relief granted to the plaintiff, if there is no answer, cannot exceed that demanded in the complaint, in the statement required by Section 425.11, or in the statement provided for by Section 425.115; but in any other case, the court may grant the plaintiff any relief consistent with the case made by the complaint and embraced within the issue. The court may impose liability, regardless of whether the theory upon which liability is sought to be imposed involves legal or equitable principles.

(b) Notwithstanding subdivision (a), the following types of relief may not be granted in a limited civil case:

(1) Relief exceeding the maximum amount in controversy for a limited civil case as provided in Section 85, exclusive of attorney's fees, interest, and costs.

(2) A permanent injunction, except as otherwise authorized by statute.

(3) A determination of title to real property.

(4) Declaratory relief, except as authorized by Section 86. *(Enacted in 1872. Amended by Stats.1993, c. 456 (A.B.58), § 8; Stats.1995, c. 796 (S.B.45), § 9; Stats.1998, c. 931 (S.B.2139), § 78, eff. Sept. 28, 1998; Stats.2006, c. 86 (A.B.2126), § 1; Stats.2007, c. 43 (S.B.649), § 5.)*

Cross References

Appeal from superior court order on motion to vacate a bail forfeiture, see Penal Code § 1305.5.
Default judgment, see Code of Civil Procedure § 585 et seq.
Dissenting shareholders, judgment against corporation, see Corporations Code § 1305.
Enforcement of forfeiture, summary judgment, condition of relief from bail forfeitures, effect of dismissal of charge after default, appeal by surety or bondsman, appellate jurisdiction, demand for payment, limitations, see Penal Code § 1306.
Involuntary dissolution of corporation, see Corporations Code § 1804.
Judgment on cross-complaint, extent, see Code of Civil Procedure § 666.

Personal property, judgment for possession or value, see Code of Civil Procedure § 667.

Research References

Forms

3 California Real Estate Forms (Miller & Starr) § 3:8 (2d ed.), Deed of Trust, Security Agreement, and Fixture Filing With Assignment of Rents and Agreements.

3 California Real Estate Forms (Miller & Starr) § 3:14 (2d ed.), Construction Deed of Trust, Security Agreement, and Fixture Filing With Assignment of Rents and Agreements.

3 California Real Estate Forms (Miller & Starr) § 3:21 (2d ed.), Deed of Trust, Assignment of Rents, Security Agreement and Fixture Filing—Conduit Loan.

3 California Real Estate Forms (Miller & Starr) § 3:34 (2d ed.), Short Form Deed of Trust and Assignment of Rents.

3 California Real Estate Forms (Miller & Starr) § 3:35 (2d ed.), Long Form Deed of Trust and Assignment of Rents.

3 California Transactions Forms--Business Transactions § 19:42, Continuing Guaranty (Single Individual Guarantor).

3 California Transactions Forms--Business Transactions § 19:57, Continuing Guaranty (Multiple Individual Guarantors).

West's California Code Forms, Civil Procedure § 580 Comment, Judgment—Relief Granted—Default Proceeding.

§ 580a. Action for deficiency judgment after foreclosure or trustee's sale; complaint; appraisal; deficiency computed on basis of fair market value; limitation of actions; necessity of sale

Whenever a money judgment is sought for the balance due upon an obligation for the payment of which a deed of trust or mortgage with power of sale upon real property or any interest therein was given as security, following the exercise of the power of sale in such deed of trust or mortgage, the plaintiff shall set forth in his or her complaint the entire amount of the indebtedness which was secured by the deed of trust or mortgage at the time of sale, the amount for which the real property or interest therein was sold and the fair market value thereof at the date of sale and the date of that sale. Upon the application of either party made at least 10 days before the time of trial the court shall, and upon its own motion the court at any time may, appoint one of the probate referees provided for by law to appraise the property or the interest therein sold as of the time of sale. The referee shall file his or her appraisal with the clerk and that appraisal shall be admissible in evidence. The referee shall take and subscribe an oath to be attached to the appraisal that he or she has truly, honestly and impartially appraised the property to the best of his or her knowledge and ability. Any referee so appointed may be called and examined as a witness by any party or by the court itself. The court must fix the compensation of the referee in an amount as determined by the court to be reasonable, but those fees shall not exceed similar fees for similar services in the community where the services are rendered, which may be taxed and allowed in like manner as other costs. Before rendering any judgment the court shall find the fair market value of the real property, or interest therein sold, at the time of sale. The court may render judgment for not more than the amount by which the entire amount of the indebtedness due at the time of sale exceeded the fair market value of the real property or interest therein sold at the time of sale with interest thereon from the date of the sale; provided, however, that in no event shall the amount of the judgment, exclusive of interest after the date of sale, exceed the difference between the amount for which the property was sold and the entire amount of the indebtedness secured by the deed of trust or mortgage. Any such action must be brought within three months of the time of sale under the deed of trust or mortgage. No judgment shall be rendered in any such action until the real property or interest therein has first been sold pursuant to the terms of the deed of trust or mortgage, unless the real property or interest therein has become valueless. (Added by Stats.1933, c. 642, p. 1672, § 4. Reenacted by Stats.1935, c. 650, p. 1805, § 4. Amended by Stats.1968, c. 450, p. 1070, § 2; Stats.1970, c. 1282, p. 2320, § 1, eff. July 1, 1971; Stats.1982, c. 1535, p. 5965, § 1; Stats.1988, c. 1199, § 6, operative July 1, 1989.)

Cross References

Actions by state or nationally chartered banks or their subsidiaries for recovery of damages from borrowers who fraudulently induced original lender to make real estate loans, see Financial Code § 1612.

Actions taken by associations or federal associations for recovery of damages from borrowers who fraudulently induced original lender to make real estate loans, see Financial Code § 7460.

Application of section to judicial proceedings or actions taken prior to foreclosure on collateral and to those proceedings or actions taken to collect principal and interest due on a loan, see Health and Safety Code § 129172.

Attorney's authority to conduct sale under power of sale, see Civil Code § 2924a.

Foreclosure action by lender for damages based on borrower fraud shall not constitute a money judgment for deficiency, or a deficiency judgment, see Code of Civil Procedure § 726.

Inapplicability of this section to actions for rent skimming, see Civil Code § 891.

Invalidity of waiver of rights or privileges conferred by this section upon borrower, see Civil Code § 2953.

Judgment defined, see Code of Civil Procedure § 577.

Loggers and lumbermen's lien, foreclosure, see Civil Code § 3065a.

Mechanic's lien foreclosure, deficiency judgment, see Civil Code § 8466.

Power of sale by mortgagee, see Civil Code § 2932.

Probate referee, appointment, see Probate Code § 8900 et seq.

Restrictions, deficiency judgment in mortgage foreclosures, see Code of Civil Procedure § 726.

Undertaking to stay, deficiency on mortgage foreclosure, see Code of Civil Procedure § 917.4.

Waiver of suretyship rights or defenses, including those under this section, see Civil Code § 2856.

Research References

Forms

3 California Real Estate Forms (Miller & Starr) § 3:7 (2d ed.), Promissory Note.

3 California Real Estate Forms (Miller & Starr) § 3:8 (2d ed.), Deed of Trust, Security Agreement, and Fixture Filing With Assignment of Rents and Agreements.

3 California Real Estate Forms (Miller & Starr) § 3:9 (2d ed.), Assignment of Lessor's Interest in Leases and Seller's Interest in Contracts for Sale.

3 California Real Estate Forms (Miller & Starr) § 3:13 (2d ed.), Promissory Note Secured by Construction Deed of Trust.

3 California Real Estate Forms (Miller & Starr) § 3:14 (2d ed.), Construction Deed of Trust, Security Agreement, and Fixture Filing With Assignment of Rents and Agreements.

3 California Real Estate Forms (Miller & Starr) § 3:20 (2d ed.), Promissory Note—Conduit Loan.

3 California Real Estate Forms (Miller & Starr) § 3:22 (2d ed.), Assignment of Leases and Rents—Conduit Loans.

3 California Real Estate Forms (Miller & Starr) § 3:29 (2d ed.), Exceptions to Non Recourse Guaranty—Conduit Loan.

3 California Real Estate Forms (Miller & Starr) § 3:30 (2d ed.), Environmental Indemnity—Conduit Loan.

3 California Real Estate Forms (Miller & Starr) § 3:37 (2d ed.), Continuing Guaranty.

3 California Real Estate Forms (Miller & Starr) § 3:38 (2d ed.), Completion Guaranty.

3 California Real Estate Forms (Miller & Starr) § 3:38.50 (2d ed.), "Bad Boy" Guaranty.

3 California Real Estate Forms (Miller & Starr) § 3:40 (2d ed.), Assignment of Membership Interest.

3 California Real Estate Forms (Miller & Starr) § 3:77 (2d ed.), Loan Agreement—Line of Credit.

3 California Real Estate Forms (Miller & Starr) § 3:79 (2d ed.), Loan Agreement—Refinance (Multiple Borrowers).

3 California Real Estate Forms (Miller & Starr) § 3:79.50 (2d ed.), Limited Guaranty—Refinance (Multiple Borrowers).

3 California Real Estate Forms (Miller & Starr) § 3:101 (2d ed.), Payment Deferral Agreement.

4 California Transactions Forms--Business Entities § 21:18, Agreements to be Liable.

§ 580a

3 California Transactions Forms--Business Transactions § 19:13, Authority to Waive Suretyship Defenses.

3 California Transactions Forms--Business Transactions § 19:14, Language Required to Waive Defenses.

3 California Transactions Forms--Business Transactions § 19:42, Continuing Guaranty (Single Individual Guarantor).

3 California Transactions Forms--Business Transactions § 19:46, Limited Continuing Guaranty (Trust Guarantor)—Liability Limited to Specified Maximum Including Amount Paid Under Other Guarantees.

3 California Transactions Forms--Business Transactions § 19:57, Continuing Guaranty (Multiple Individual Guarantors).

3 California Transactions Forms--Business Transactions § 19:58, Continuing Guaranty (Multiple Individual Guarantors)—Loan Secured by Deed of Trust.

3 California Transactions Forms--Business Transactions § 19:59, Guaranty of Payment and Completion (Real Estate).

3 California Transactions Forms--Business Transactions § 19:62, Guaranty of Indebtedness by Subsidiary of Debtor.

3 California Transactions Forms--Business Transactions § 19:73, Suretyship Waivers by Co-Borrowers (Single Lender).

3 California Transactions Forms--Business Transactions § 20:42, Indemnity Agreement: Note and Deed of Trust.

5 California Transactions Forms--Business Transactions § 30:160, Mixed Collateral.

West's California Code Forms, Civil § 891 Form 1, Complaint—Rent Skimming—By Seller.

West's California Code Forms, Civil § 891 Form 2, Complaint—Rent Skimming—By Mortgagee or Beneficiary of Deed of Trust.

West's California Code Forms, Civil § 891 Form 3, Complaint—Rent Skimming—By Tenant.

West's California Code Forms, Civil Procedure § 580a Form 1, Judgment—Allegation in Complaint for Deficiency After Exercise of Power of Sale.

West's California Code Forms, Civil Procedure § 580a Form 2, Judgment—Application for Appointment of Appraiser—Complaint for Deficiency.

§ 580b. Contract of sale; deed of trust or mortgage; credit transaction; chattel mortgage; no deficiency to be owed or collected and deficiency judgments prohibited; exception for liability of guarantor, pledgor, or other surety

(a) Except as provided in subdivision (c), no deficiency shall be owed or collected, and no deficiency judgment shall lie, for any of the following:

(1) After a sale of real property or an estate for years therein for failure of the purchaser to complete his or her contract of sale.

(2) Under a deed of trust or mortgage given to the vendor to secure payment of the balance of the purchase price of that real property or estate for years therein.

(3) Under a deed of trust or mortgage on a dwelling for not more than four families given to a lender to secure repayment of a loan that was used to pay all or part of the purchase price of that dwelling, occupied entirely or in part by the purchaser. For purposes of subdivision (b), a loan described in this paragraph is a "purchase money loan."

(b) No deficiency shall be owed or collected, and no deficiency judgment shall lie, on a loan, refinance, or other credit transaction (collectively, a "credit transaction") that is used to refinance a purchase money loan, or subsequent refinances of a purchase money loan, except to the extent that in a credit transaction the lender or creditor advances new principal (hereafter "new advance") that is not applied to an obligation owed or to be owed under the purchase money loan, or to fees, costs, or related expenses of the credit transaction. A new credit transaction shall be deemed to be a purchase money loan except as to the principal amount of a new advance. For purposes of this section, any payment of principal shall be deemed to be applied first to the principal balance of the purchase money loan, and then to the principal balance of a new advance, and interest payments shall be applied to any interest due and owing. This subdivision applies only to credit transactions that are executed on or after January 1, 2013.

(c) The fact that no deficiency shall be owed or collected under the circumstances set forth in subdivisions (a) and (b) does not affect the liability that a guarantor, pledgor, or other surety might otherwise have with respect to the deficiency, or that might otherwise be satisfied in whole or in part from other collateral pledged to secure the obligation that is the subject of the deficiency.

(d) When both a chattel mortgage and a deed of trust or mortgage have been given to secure payment of the balance of the combined purchase price of both real and personal property, no deficiency judgment shall lie under any one thereof if no deficiency judgment would lie under the deed of trust or mortgage on the real property or estate for years therein. *(Added by Stats.1933, c. 642, p. 1673, § 5. Re-enacted and amended by Stats.1935, c. 650, p. 1806, § 5. Amended by Stats.1935, c. 680, p. 1869, § 1; Stats.1949, c. 1599, p. 2846, § 1; Stats.1963, c. 2158, p. 4500, § 1; Stats.1989, c. 698, § 12; Stats.2012, c. 64 (S.B.1069), § 1; Stats.2013, c. 65 (S.B.426), § 2; Stats.2014, c. 71 (S.B.1304), § 18, eff. Jan. 1, 2015.)*

Cross References

Actions by state or nationally chartered banks or their subsidiaries for recovery of damages from borrowers who fraudulently induced original lender to make real estate loans, see Financial Code § 551.

Actions taken by associations or federal associations for recovery of damages from borrowers who fraudulently induced original lender to make real estate loans, see Financial Code § 7460.

Application of section to judicial proceedings or actions taken prior to foreclosure on collateral and to those proceedings or actions taken to collect principal and interest due on a loan, see Health and Safety Code § 129172.

Foreclosure actions, action by lender for damages based on borrower fraud shall not constitute a money judgment for deficiency, or a deficiency judgment, see Code of Civil Procedure § 726.

Inapplicability of this section to actions for rent skimming, see Civil Code § 891.

Judgment defined, see Code of Civil Procedure § 577.

Shared appreciation loans for seniors subject to this section, see Civil Code § 1917.618.

Waiver of suretyship rights or defenses, including those under this section, see Civil Code § 2856.

Research References

Forms

3 California Real Estate Forms (Miller & Starr) § 3:7 (2d ed.), Promissory Note.

3 California Real Estate Forms (Miller & Starr) § 3:8 (2d ed.), Deed of Trust, Security Agreement, and Fixture Filing With Assignment of Rents and Agreements.

3 California Real Estate Forms (Miller & Starr) § 3:9 (2d ed.), Assignment of Lessor's Interest in Leases and Seller's Interest in Contracts for Sale.

3 California Real Estate Forms (Miller & Starr) § 3:13 (2d ed.), Promissory Note Secured by Construction Deed of Trust.

3 California Real Estate Forms (Miller & Starr) § 3:14 (2d ed.), Construction Deed of Trust, Security Agreement, and Fixture Filing With Assignment of Rents and Agreements.

3 California Real Estate Forms (Miller & Starr) § 3:20 (2d ed.), Promissory Note—Conduit Loan.

3 California Real Estate Forms (Miller & Starr) § 3:22 (2d ed.), Assignment of Leases and Rents—Conduit Loans.

3 California Real Estate Forms (Miller & Starr) § 3:29 (2d ed.), Exceptions to Non Recourse Guaranty—Conduit Loan.

3 California Real Estate Forms (Miller & Starr) § 3:30 (2d ed.), Environmental Indemnity—Conduit Loan.

3 California Real Estate Forms (Miller & Starr) § 3:37 (2d ed.), Continuing Guaranty.

3 California Real Estate Forms (Miller & Starr) § 3:38 (2d ed.), Completion Guaranty.

3 California Real Estate Forms (Miller & Starr) § 3:38.50 (2d ed.), "Bad Boy" Guaranty.

3 California Real Estate Forms (Miller & Starr) § 3:40 (2d ed.), Assignment of Membership Interest.

3 California Real Estate Forms (Miller & Starr) § 3:77 (2d ed.), Loan Agreement—Line of Credit.

3 California Real Estate Forms (Miller & Starr) § 3:79 (2d ed.), Loan Agreement—Refinance (Multiple Borrowers).

3 California Real Estate Forms (Miller & Starr) § 3:79.50 (2d ed.), Limited Guaranty—Refinance (Multiple Borrowers).

3 California Transactions Forms--Business Transactions § 19:13, Authority to Waive Suretyship Defenses.
3 California Transactions Forms--Business Transactions § 19:14, Language Required to Waive Defenses.
3 California Transactions Forms--Business Transactions § 19:42, Continuing Guaranty (Single Individual Guarantor).
3 California Transactions Forms--Business Transactions § 19:57, Continuing Guaranty (Multiple Individual Guarantors).
3 California Transactions Forms--Business Transactions § 19:58, Continuing Guaranty (Multiple Individual Guarantors)—Loan Secured by Deed of Trust.
3 California Transactions Forms--Business Transactions § 19:59, Guaranty of Payment and Completion (Real Estate).
3 California Transactions Forms--Business Transactions § 19:62, Guaranty of Indebtedness by Subsidiary of Debtor.
3 California Transactions Forms--Business Transactions § 19:73, Suretyship Waivers by Co-Borrowers (Single Lender).
5 California Transactions Forms--Business Transactions § 30:160, Mixed Collateral.
West's California Code Forms, Civil Procedure § 580a Form 1, Judgment—Allegation in Complaint for Deficiency After Exercise of Power of Sale.

§ 580c. Mortgage foreclosure or trustee's sale; liability for actual costs and reasonable fees

In all cases where existing deeds of trust or mortgages are judicially foreclosed, unless a different amount is set up in the mortgage or deed of trust, and in all cases of mortgages and deeds of trust executed after this act takes effect, the mortgagor or trustor may be required to pay only such amount as trustee's or attorney's fees for processing the judicial foreclosure as the court may find reasonable and also the actual cost of publishing, recording, mailing and posting notices, litigation guarantee, and litigation cost of suit. (Added by Stats.1933, c. 642, p. 1673, § 6. Re-enacted by Stats.1935, c. 650, p. 1806, § 6. Amended by Stats.1984, c. 1730, § 6.)

Cross References

Action on contract, award of attorney's fees and costs, see Civil Code § 1717.
Decree of foreclosure, court's discretion to award attorney fees and costs, see Civil Code § 2924d.

§ 580d. Real property or estate for years sold under power of sale; no deficiency to be owed or collected and deficiency judgments prohibited; exception for liability of guarantor, pledgor, or other surety

(a) Except as provided in subdivision (b), no deficiency shall be owed or collected, and no deficiency judgment shall be rendered for a deficiency on a note secured by a deed of trust or mortgage on real property or an estate for years therein executed in any case in which the real property or estate for years therein has been sold by the mortgagee or trustee under power of sale contained in the mortgage or deed of trust.

(b) The fact that no deficiency shall be owed or collected under the circumstances set forth in subdivision (a) does not affect the liability that a guarantor, pledgor, or other surety might otherwise have with respect to the deficiency, or that might otherwise be satisfied in whole or in part from other collateral pledged to secure the obligation that is the subject of the deficiency.

(c) This section does not apply to a deed of trust, mortgage, or other lien given to secure the payment of bonds or other evidences of indebtedness authorized or permitted to be issued by the Commissioner of * * * Financial Protection and Innovation or which is made by a public utility subject to the Public Utilities Act (Part 1 (commencing with Section 201) of Division 1 of the Public Utilities Code). (Added by Stats.1940, Ex.Sess., c. 29, p. 84, § 2. Amended by Stats.1989, c. 698, § 13; Stats.2013, c. 65 (S.B.426), § 3; Stats.2014, c. 71 (S.B.1304), § 19, eff. Jan. 1, 2015; Stats.2014, c. 401 (A.B.2763), § 14, eff. Jan. 1, 2015; Stats.2022, c. 452 (S.B.1498), § 38, eff. Jan. 1, 2023.)

Cross References

Actions by state or nationally chartered banks or their subsidiaries for recovery of damages from borrowers who fraudulently induced original lender to make real estate loans, see Financial Code § 551.
Actions taken by associations or federal associations for recovery of damages from borrowers who fraudulently induced original lender to make real estate loans, see Financial Code § 7460.
Application of section to judicial proceedings or actions taken prior to foreclosure on collateral and to those proceedings or actions taken to collect principal and interest due on a loan, see Health and Safety Code § 129172.
Attorney's authority to conduct sale under power of sale, see Civil Code § 2924a.
Deficiency in mechanics' lien foreclosure, see Civil Code § 8466.
Foreclosure action by lender for damages based on borrower fraud shall not constitute a money judgment for deficiency, or a deficiency judgment, see Code of Civil Procedure § 726.
Inapplicability of this section to actions for rent skimming, see Civil Code § 891.
Judgment defined, see Code of Civil Procedure § 577.
Mortgage or trust deed with power of sale, see Code of Civil Procedure §§ 725a, 726.
Power of sale by mortgagee, see Civil Code § 2932.
Waiver of guarantor rights and defenses, even though rights destroyed by operation of this section, see Civil Code § 2856.

Research References

Forms

3 California Real Estate Forms (Miller & Starr) § 3:7 (2d ed.), Promissory Note.
3 California Real Estate Forms (Miller & Starr) § 3:8 (2d ed.), Deed of Trust, Security Agreement, and Fixture Filing With Assignment of Rents and Agreements.
3 California Real Estate Forms (Miller & Starr) § 3:9 (2d ed.), Assignment of Lessor's Interest in Leases and Seller's Interest in Contracts for Sale.
3 California Real Estate Forms (Miller & Starr) § 3:13 (2d ed.), Promissory Note Secured by Construction Deed of Trust.
3 California Real Estate Forms (Miller & Starr) § 3:14 (2d ed.), Construction Deed of Trust, Security Agreement, and Fixture Filing With Assignment of Rents and Agreements.
3 California Real Estate Forms (Miller & Starr) § 3:20 (2d ed.), Promissory Note—Conduit Loan.
3 California Real Estate Forms (Miller & Starr) § 3:21 (2d ed.), Deed of Trust, Assignment of Rents, Security Agreement and Fixture Filing—Conduit Loan.
3 California Real Estate Forms (Miller & Starr) § 3:22 (2d ed.), Assignment of Leases and Rents—Conduit Loans.
3 California Real Estate Forms (Miller & Starr) § 3:29 (2d ed.), Exceptions to Non Recourse Guaranty—Conduit Loan.
3 California Real Estate Forms (Miller & Starr) § 3:30 (2d ed.), Environmental Indemnity—Conduit Loan.
3 California Real Estate Forms (Miller & Starr) § 3:36 (2d ed.), Contingent Interest Agreement.
3 California Real Estate Forms (Miller & Starr) § 3:37 (2d ed.), Continuing Guaranty.
3 California Real Estate Forms (Miller & Starr) § 3:38 (2d ed.), Completion Guaranty.
3 California Real Estate Forms (Miller & Starr) § 3:38.50 (2d ed.), "Bad Boy" Guaranty.
3 California Real Estate Forms (Miller & Starr) § 3:40 (2d ed.), Assignment of Membership Interest.
3 California Real Estate Forms (Miller & Starr) § 3:55 (2d ed.), Subordination, Nondisturbance, and Attornment Agreement.
3 California Real Estate Forms (Miller & Starr) § 3:66 (2d ed.), Deed in Lieu of Foreclosure—Transfer Agreement.
3 California Real Estate Forms (Miller & Starr) § 3:75 (2d ed.), Third-Party Waivers—Deed of Trust.
3 California Real Estate Forms (Miller & Starr) § 3:77 (2d ed.), Loan Agreement—Line of Credit.
3 California Real Estate Forms (Miller & Starr) § 3:79 (2d ed.), Loan Agreement—Refinance (Multiple Borrowers).
3 California Real Estate Forms (Miller & Starr) § 3:79.50 (2d ed.), Limited Guaranty—Refinance (Multiple Borrowers).
3 California Transactions Forms--Business Transactions § 19:13, Authority to Waive Suretyship Defenses.

§ 580d   CODE OF CIVIL PROCEDURE

3 California Transactions Forms--Business Transactions § 19:14, Language Required to Waive Defenses.
3 California Transactions Forms--Business Transactions § 19:42, Continuing Guaranty (Single Individual Guarantor).
3 California Transactions Forms--Business Transactions § 19:46, Limited Continuing Guaranty (Trust Guarantor)—Liability Limited to Specified Maximum Including Amount Paid Under Other Guarantees.
3 California Transactions Forms--Business Transactions § 19:57, Continuing Guaranty (Multiple Individual Guarantors).
3 California Transactions Forms--Business Transactions § 19:58, Continuing Guaranty (Multiple Individual Guarantors)—Loan Secured by Deed of Trust.
3 California Transactions Forms--Business Transactions § 19:59, Guaranty of Payment and Completion (Real Estate).
3 California Transactions Forms--Business Transactions § 19:62, Guaranty of Indebtedness by Subsidiary of Debtor.
3 California Transactions Forms--Business Transactions § 19:73, Suretyship Waivers by Co-Borrowers (Single Lender).
3 California Transactions Forms--Business Transactions § 20:42, Indemnity Agreement: Note and Deed of Trust.
4 California Transactions Forms--Business Transactions § 27:21, Subrogation.
5 California Transactions Forms--Business Transactions § 30:160, Mixed Collateral.
West's California Code Forms, Civil § 891 Form 1, Complaint—Rent Skimming—By Seller.
West's California Code Forms, Civil § 891 Form 2, Complaint—Rent Skimming—By Mortgagee or Beneficiary of Deed of Trust.
West's California Code Forms, Civil § 891 Form 3, Complaint—Rent Skimming—By Tenant.
West's California Code Forms, Commercial Div. 5 Intro., Division 5 Letters of Credit.

§ 580e. Deficiency collection and judgment following short sale with consent of trustee or mortgagee prohibited; circumstances; exception for fraud; non-application of section; waivers void and against public policy

(a)(1) No deficiency shall be owed or collected, and no deficiency judgment shall be requested or rendered for any deficiency upon a note secured solely by a deed of trust or mortgage for a dwelling of not more than four units, in any case in which the trustor or mortgagor sells the dwelling for a sale price less than the remaining amount of the indebtedness outstanding at the time of sale, in accordance with the written consent of the holder of the deed of trust or mortgage, provided that both of the following have occurred:

(A) Title has been voluntarily transferred to a buyer by grant deed or by other document of conveyance that has been recorded in the county where all or part of the real property is located.

(B) The proceeds of the sale have been tendered to the mortgagee, beneficiary, or the agent of the mortgagee or beneficiary, in accordance with the parties' agreement.

(2) In circumstances not described in paragraph (1), when a note is not secured solely by a deed of trust or mortgage for a dwelling of not more than four units, no judgment shall be rendered for any deficiency upon a note secured by a deed of trust or mortgage for a dwelling of not more than four units, if the trustor or mortgagor sells the dwelling for a sale price less than the remaining amount of the indebtedness outstanding at the time of sale, in accordance with the written consent of the holder of the deed of trust or mortgage. Following the sale, in accordance with the holder's written consent, the voluntary transfer of title to a buyer by grant deed or by other document of conveyance recorded in the county where all or part of the real property is located, and the tender to the mortgagee, beneficiary, or the agent of the mortgagee or beneficiary of the sale proceeds, as agreed, the rights, remedies, and obligations of any holder, beneficiary, mortgagee, trustor, mortgagor, obligor, obligee, or guarantor of the note, deed of trust, or mortgage, and with respect to any other property that secures the note, shall be treated and determined as if the dwelling had been sold through foreclosure under a power of sale contained in the deed of trust or mortgage for a price equal to the sale proceeds received by the holder, in the manner contemplated by Section 580d.

(b) A holder of a note shall not require the trustor, mortgagor, or maker of the note to pay any additional compensation, aside from the proceeds of the sale, in exchange for the written consent to the sale.

(c) If the trustor or mortgagor commits either fraud with respect to the sale of, or waste with respect to, the real property that secures the deed of trust or mortgage, this section shall not limit the ability of the holder of the deed of trust or mortgage to seek damages and use existing rights and remedies against the trustor or mortgagor or any third party for fraud or waste.

(d)(1) This section shall not apply if the trustor or mortgagor is a corporation, limited liability company, limited partnership, or political subdivision of the state.

(2) This section shall not apply to any deed of trust, mortgage, or other lien given to secure the payment of bonds or other evidence of indebtedness authorized, or permitted to be issued, by the Commissioner of * * * Financial Protection and Innovation, or that is made by a public utility subject to the Public Utilities Act (Part 1 (commencing with Section 201) of Division 1 of the Public Utilities Code).

(e) Any purported waiver of subdivision (a) or (b) shall be void and against public policy. *(Added by Stats.2010, c. 701 (S.B.931), § 1. Amended by Stats.2011, c. 82 (S.B.458), § 1, eff. July 15, 2011; Stats.2019, c. 143 (S.B.251), § 19, eff. Jan. 1, 2020; Stats.2022, c. 452 (S.B.1498), § 39, eff. Jan. 1, 2023.)*

Cross References

Judgment defined, see Code of Civil Procedure § 577.

§ 581. Dismissal; definitions

(a) As used in this section:

(1) "Action" means any civil action or special proceeding.

(2) "Complaint" means a complaint and a cross-complaint.

(3) "Court" means the court in which the action is pending.

(4) "Defendant" includes a cross-defendant.

(5) "Plaintiff" includes a cross-complainant.

(6) "Trial." A trial shall be deemed to actually commence at the beginning of the opening statement or argument of any party or his or her counsel, or if there is no opening statement, then at the time of the administering of the oath or affirmation to the first witness, or the introduction of any evidence.

(b) An action may be dismissed in any of the following instances:

(1) With or without prejudice, upon written request of the plaintiff to the clerk, filed with papers in the case, or by oral or written request to the court at any time before the actual commencement of trial, upon payment of the costs, if any.

(2) With or without prejudice, by any party upon the written consent of all other parties.

(3) By the court, without prejudice, when no party appears for trial following 30 days' notice of time and place of trial.

(4) By the court, without prejudice, when dismissal is made pursuant to the applicable provisions of Chapter 1.5 (commencing with Section 583.110).

(5) By the court, without prejudice, when either party fails to appear on the trial and the other party appears and asks for dismissal.

(c) A plaintiff may dismiss his or her complaint, or any cause of action asserted in it, in its entirety, or as to any defendant or defendants, with or without prejudice prior to the actual commencement of trial.

(d) Except as otherwise provided in subdivision (e), the court shall dismiss the complaint, or any cause of action asserted in it, in its entirety or as to any defendant, with prejudice, when upon the trial and before the final submission of the case, the plaintiff abandons it.

(e) After the actual commencement of trial, the court shall dismiss the complaint, or any causes of action asserted in it, in its entirety or as to any defendants, with prejudice, if the plaintiff requests a dismissal, unless all affected parties to the trial consent to dismissal without prejudice or by order of the court dismissing the same without prejudice on a showing of good cause.

(f) The court may dismiss the complaint as to that defendant when:

(1) Except where Section 597 applies, after a demurrer to the complaint is sustained without leave to amend and either party moves for dismissal.

(2) Except where Section 597 applies, after a demurrer to the complaint is sustained with leave to amend, the plaintiff fails to amend it within the time allowed by the court and either party moves for dismissal.

(3) After a motion to strike the whole of a complaint is granted without leave to amend and either party moves for dismissal.

(4) After a motion to strike the whole of a complaint or portion thereof is granted with leave to amend the plaintiff fails to amend it within the time allowed by the court and either party moves for dismissal.

(g) The court may dismiss without prejudice the complaint in whole, or as to that defendant, when dismissal is made under the applicable provisions of Chapter 1.5 (commencing with Section 583.110).

(h) The court may dismiss without prejudice the complaint in whole, or as to that defendant, when dismissal is made pursuant to Section 418.10.

(i) No dismissal of an action may be made or entered, or both, under paragraph (1) of subdivision (b) where affirmative relief has been sought by the cross-complaint of a defendant or if there is a motion pending for an order transferring the action to another court under the provisions of Section 396b.

(j) No dismissal may be made or entered, or both, under paragraph (1) or (2) of subdivision (b) except upon the written consent of the attorney for the party or parties applying therefor, or if consent of the attorney is not obtained, upon order of dismissal by the court after notice to the attorney.

(k) No action may be dismissed which has been determined to be a class action under the provisions of this code unless and until notice that the court deems adequate has been given and the court orders the dismissal.

(*l*) The court may dismiss, without prejudice, the complaint in whole, or as to that defendant when either party fails to appear at the trial and the other party appears and asks for the dismissal.

(m) The provisions of this section shall not be deemed to be an exclusive enumeration of the court's power to dismiss an action or dismiss a complaint as to a defendant. (Added by Stats.1986, c. 540, § 8. Amended by Stats.1987, c. 1080, § 3; Stats.1993, c. 456 (A.B.58), § 9.)

Cross References

Abandonment of eminent domain proceedings, dismissal, see Code of Civil Procedure § 1268.020.
Action commenced in superior court without jurisdiction, transfer of appeal or petition to court of appeal or Supreme Court having jurisdiction, see Code of Civil Procedure § 396.
Arbitration, proceedings to enforce, see Code of Civil Procedure § 1281.2.
Costs to defendant on dismissal, see Code of Civil Procedure § 1032.
Criminal proceedings, see Penal Code § 1381 et seq.
Delay in prosecution as ground for dismissal, see Code of Civil Procedure § 583.110 et seq.
Dismissal of an election contest, see Elections Code §§ 16403, 16602, 16800.
Dissolution of marriage, conditions for dismissal after interlocutory judgment, see Family Code § 2338.
Inconvenient forum, see Code of Civil Procedure §§ 410.30, 418.10.
Liability of principal and sureties on bond, see Code of Civil Procedure § 996.410 et seq.
Mechanics' liens, want of prosecution of action to foreclose, see Civil Code § 8462.
Medical malpractice, failure to give security, see Code of Civil Procedure § 1029.6.
Non-appearance of party for trial, see Code of Civil Procedure § 594.
Offer of settlement, costs after rejection, see Code of Civil Procedure § 998.
Order to bring in indispensable or conditionally necessary party, dismissal on failure to comply, see Code of Civil Procedure § 389.
Probationer, see Penal Code §§ 1203.3, 1203.4.
Security for costs, dismissal for failure to give, nonresident or foreign corporation, see Code of Civil Procedure § 1030.
Summary judgment, see Code of Civil Procedure § 437c.
Transfer of cases, failure to pay costs and fees, see Code of Civil Procedure § 399.
Variance between pleading and proof, see Code of Civil Procedure § 469 et seq.

Research References

Forms

19 Am. Jur. Pl. & Pr. Forms Parties § 236, Statutory References.
23B Am. Jur. Pl. & Pr. Forms Trial § 366, Introductory Comments.
3 California Transactions Forms--Business Transactions § 18:84, Dismissal of Pending Action.
West's California Code Forms, Civil Procedure § 581 Form 1, Judgments—Request for Dismissal—Official Form.
West's California Code Forms, Civil Procedure § 581 Form 4, Judgment—Notice to Attorney of Party's Motion for Leave to Dismiss Action.
West's California Code Forms, Civil Procedure § 581 Form 7, Judgment—Notice of Motion for Dismissal Upon Failure to Amend.
West's California Judicial Council Forms CIV–110, Request for Dismissal.
West's California Judicial Council Forms CIV–120, Notice of Entry of Dismissal and Proof of Service.
West's California Judicial Council Forms FL–618, Request for Dismissal (Governmental, UIFSA) (Also Available in Spanish).

CHAPTER 1.5. DISMISSAL FOR DELAY IN PROSECUTION

Cross References

Duration of child support orders notwithstanding this Chapter, see Family Code § 3601.

ARTICLE 1. DEFINITIONS AND GENERAL PROVISIONS

Section
583.161. Petition for separation or dissolution of marriage, nullity, or termination of domestic partnership, or petition filed under the Uniform Parentage Act; existence of child support, child custody, visitation, or spousal support orders, personal conduct restraining order, or bifurcated case; dismissal prohibited.

§ 583.161. Petition for separation or dissolution of marriage, nullity, or termination of domestic partnership, or petition filed under the Uniform Parentage Act; existence of child support, child custody, visitation, or spousal support orders, personal conduct restraining order, or bifurcated case; dismissal prohibited

A petition filed pursuant to Section 299, 2250, 2330, or 7600 of the Family Code shall not be dismissed pursuant to this chapter if any of the following conditions exist:

(a) An order for child support or an order regarding child custody or visitation has been issued in connection with the proceeding and the order has not been (1) terminated by the court or (2) terminated by operation of law pursuant to Sections 3022, 3900, 3901, 4007, and 4013 of the Family Code.

§ 583.161

(b) An order for spousal support has been issued in connection with the proceeding and the order has not been terminated by the court.

(c) A personal conduct restraining order has been issued pursuant to the Domestic Violence Prevention Act (Division 10 (commencing with Section 6200) of the Family Code) and the order has not been terminated by operation of law or by the court.

(d) An issue in the case has been bifurcated and one of the following has occurred:

(1) A separate trial has been conducted pursuant to Section 2337 of the Family Code.

(2) A separate trial has been conducted pursuant to the California Rules of Court. *(Added by Stats.1986, c. 366, § 2. Amended by Stats.1992, c. 163 (A.B.2641), § 26, operative Jan. 1, 1994; Stats.1993, c. 219 (A.B.1500), § 65; Stats.1994, c. 1269 (A.B.2208), § 3; Stats. 2013, c. 40 (A.B.522), § 1.)*

Cross References

Court defined for purposes of this Chapter, see Code of Civil Procedure § 583.110.

CHAPTER 3. ISSUES—THE MODE OF TRIAL AND POSTPONEMENTS

Section
594. Bringing issues to trial or hearing; absence of adversary; proof of notice.
595.4. Postponement; absence of evidence.
596. Postponement; deposition of witness.

Cross References

State license tax, action to collect, applicability of this chapter, see Business and Professions Code § 16222.

§ 594. Bringing issues to trial or hearing; absence of adversary; proof of notice

(a) In superior courts either party may bring an issue to trial or to a hearing, and, in the absence of the adverse party, unless the court, for good cause, otherwise directs, may proceed with the case and take a dismissal of the action, or a verdict, or judgment, as the case may require; provided, however, if the issue to be tried is an issue of fact, proof shall first be made to the satisfaction of the court that the adverse party has had 15 days' notice of such trial or five days' notice of the trial in an unlawful detainer action as specified in subdivision (b). If the adverse party has served notice of trial upon the party seeking the dismissal, verdict, or judgment at least five days prior to the trial, the adverse party shall be deemed to have had notice.

(b) The notice to the adverse party required by subdivision (a) shall be served by mail on all the parties by the clerk of the court not less than 20 days prior to the date set for trial. In an unlawful detainer action where notice is served by mail that service shall be mailed not less than 10 days prior to the date set for trial. If notice is not served by the clerk as required by this subdivision, it may be served by mail by any party on the adverse party not less than 15 days prior to the date set for trial, and in an unlawful detainer action where notice is served by mail that service shall be mailed not less than 10 days prior to the date set for trial. The time provisions of Section 1013 shall not serve to extend the notice of trial requirements under this subdivision for unlawful detainer actions. If notice is served by the clerk, proof thereof may be made by introduction into evidence of the clerk's certificate pursuant to subdivision (3) of Section 1013a or other competent evidence. If notice is served by a party, proof may be made by introduction into evidence of an affidavit or certificate pursuant to subdivision (1) or (2) of Section 1013a or other competent evidence. The provisions of this subdivision are exclusive. *(Enacted in 1872. Amended by Stats.1899, c. 6, p.*

5, § 1; *Stats.1933, c. 744, p. 1871, § 94; Stats.1935, c. 722, p. 1954, § 8; Stats.1951, c. 1737, p. 4113, § 86, operative Jan. 1, 1952; Stats.1969, c. 85, p. 205, § 1; Stats.1975, c. 1001, p. 2345, § 1; Stats.1976, c. 406, p. 1056, § 1; Stats.1977, c. 685, p. 2211, § 1; Stats.1977, c. 1257, p. 4761, § 19, eff. Oct. 3, 1977; Stats.1977, c. 1257, p. 4762, § 19.5, eff. Oct. 3, 1977, operative Jan. 1, 1978; Stats.1998, c. 931 (S.B.2139), § 81, eff. Sept. 28, 1998; Stats.2002, c. 784 (S.B.1316), § 62.)*

Cross References

Appearance, see Code of Civil Procedure § 1014.
Default judgment, see Code of Civil Procedure §§ 585, 586.
Dismissal of action, see Code of Civil Procedure § 581.
Dissenting shareholders, determination of issues, see Corporations Code § 1304.
Judgment defined, see Code of Civil Procedure § 577.
New trial, grounds, see Code of Civil Procedure § 657.
Notices,
  Requisites, see Code of Civil Procedure § 1010.
  Service, see Code of Civil Procedure § 1010 et seq.
Proof of service, see Code of Civil Procedure § 1013a.
Relief from judgment taken through mistake, inadvertence, surprise or excusable neglect, see Code of Civil Procedure § 473.

Research References

Forms
23B Am. Jur. Pl. & Pr. Forms Trial § 2, Introductory Comments.
West's California Code Forms, Civil Procedure § 595.2 Form 1, Trial—Stipulation for Continuance—Order.

§ 595.4. Postponement; absence of evidence

A motion to postpone a trial on the ground of the absence of evidence can only be made upon affidavit showing the materiality of the evidence expected to be obtained, and that due diligence has been used to procure it. The court may require the moving party, where application is made on account of the absence of a material witness, to state upon affidavit the evidence which he expects to obtain; and if the adverse party thereupon admits that such evidence would be given, and that it be considered as actually given on the trial, or offered and overruled as improper, the trial must not be postponed. *(Added by Stats.1965, c. 1989, p. 4517, § 2.)*

Cross References

Absence of judge, adjournments from day to day, see Code of Civil Procedure § 139.
Action for refund of taxes by public agency, continuance, see Revenue and Taxation Code § 5161.
Contempt proceedings, adjournment, see Code of Civil Procedure § 1217.
Costs imposed upon postponement, see Code of Civil Procedure § 1024.
Criminal trials, see Penal Code § 1050.
Extension of time where attorney or party is legislator, see Code of Civil Procedure §§ 595, 1054.1.
Mandamus proceedings, postponement for jury trial, see Code of Civil Procedure § 1090.
Refusal of continuance deemed excepted to, see Code of Civil Procedure § 647.

Research References

Forms
West's California Code Forms, Civil Procedure § 595.4 Form 1, Trial—Notice of Motion for Continuance for Lack of Evidence.

§ 596. Postponement; deposition of witness

The party obtaining a postponement of a trial, if required by the adverse party, must consent that the testimony of any witness of such adverse party, who is in attendance, be then taken by deposition before a judge or clerk of the court in which the case is pending, or before such notary public as the court may indicate, which must accordingly be done; and the testimony so taken may be read on the trial, with the same effect, and subject to the same objections, as if the witnesses were produced. *(Enacted in 1872. Amended by*

Stats.1933, c. 744, p. 1874, § 97; Stats.1951, c. 1737, p. 4114, § 87, operative Jan. 1, 1952.)

Cross References

Court commissioners may take depositions, see Code of Civil Procedure § 259.
Deposition defined, see Code of Civil Procedure § 2004.
Depositions, see Code of Civil Procedure § 2025 et seq.
Manner of taking deposition out of state, see Code of Civil Procedure § 2026.010.
Physical or mental examinations, see Code of Civil Procedure § 2032.010 et seq.
Taking of deposition, see Code of Civil Procedure § 2025.010 et seq.

CHAPTER 5. TRIAL BY THE COURT

Section
632. Statement of decision.
634. Omission or ambiguity brought to attention of trial court; inference.
635. Formal judgment or order; signature by presiding judge in absence of trial judge.

Cross References

Evidence in trial by court, applicability of code, see Evidence Code § 300.
Issues of fact, trial by court, see Code of Civil Procedure § 592; Evidence Code § 310.
Issues of law, trial by court, see Code of Civil Procedure § 591; Evidence Code § 310; Penal Code §§ 1124, 1126.
State license tax, action to collect, applicability of this chapter, see Business and Professions Code § 16222.

§ 632. Statement of decision

In superior courts, upon the trial of a question of fact by the court, written findings of fact and conclusions of law shall not be required. The court shall issue a statement of decision explaining the factual and legal basis for its decision as to each of the principal controverted issues at trial upon the request of any party appearing at the trial. The request must be made within 10 days after the court announces a tentative decision unless the trial is concluded within one calendar day or in less than eight hours over more than one day in which event the request must be made prior to the submission of the matter for decision. The request for a statement of decision shall specify those controverted issues as to which the party is requesting a statement of decision. After a party has requested the statement, any party may make proposals as to the content of the statement of decision.

The statement of decision shall be in writing, unless the parties appearing at trial agree otherwise; however, when the trial is concluded within one calendar day or in less than 8 hours over more than one day, the statement of decision may be made orally on the record in the presence of the parties. (Enacted in 1872. Amended by Code Am.1873–74, c. 383, p. 312, § 79; Stats.1933, c. 744, p. 1876, § 105; Stats.1951, c. 1737, p. 4116, § 92, operative Jan. 1, 1952; Stats.1959, c. 637, p. 2613, § 1; Stats.1968, c. 716, p. 1417, § 1, operative Jan. 1, 1969; Stats.1969, c. 339, p. 713, § 1; Stats.1975, c. 301, § 2; Stats.1977, c. 1257, p. 4763, § 22, eff. Jan. 3, 1977; Stats.1981, c. 900, p. 3425, § 1; Stats.1987, c. 207, § 1; Stats.1998, c. 931 (S.B.2139), § 84, eff. Sept. 28, 1998; Stats.2002, c. 784 (S.B.1316), § 64.)

Cross References

Actions by appellate courts, see Code of Civil Procedure § 43.
Appeal from trial courts, additional findings by reviewing court, see Code of Civil Procedure § 909; Cal. Const. Art. 6, § 11.
Attorneys' disciplinary proceedings, findings by board of governors, see Business and Professions Code § 6080.
Changing or adding to findings on motion for new trial, see Code of Civil Procedure § 662.
Decision in writing, supreme court and courts of appeal, see Cal. Const. Art. 6, § 14.
Election contests,
  General elections, findings and conclusions and entry of judgment, see Elections Code § 16603.
  Primary elections, findings and conclusions, see Elections Code § 16720.
Entry of judgment,
  Generally, see Code of Civil Procedure §§ 664, 668.
  Agreed statement of facts, see Code of Civil Procedure § 1138.
  Confession of judgment, see Code of Civil Procedure § 1134.
  Duty of clerk, see Code of Civil Procedure § 668.
  Notice, see Code of Civil Procedure § 664.5.
  Superior court judgment book, see Code of Civil Procedure § 668.
  Time, see Code of Civil Procedure § 664.
Immaterial variance, findings of fact, see Code of Civil Procedure § 470.
Industrial welfare commission, conclusiveness of findings, see Labor Code § 1187.
Judgment roll includes findings, see Code of Civil Procedure § 670.
Referee's decision, see Code of Civil Procedure §§ 644, 645.
Right to custody of minor child, statement of decision, see Family Code § 3022.3.
Special verdict, findings, see Code of Civil Procedure § 625.
Sterilization of developmentally disabled persons, written statement of decision required, see Probate Code § 1962.
Third party claims, findings not required, see Code of Civil Procedure § 720.400.
Workers' compensation proceedings,
  Conclusiveness of appeals board's findings, see Labor Code § 5953.
  Presumption of legality of appeals board's findings, see Labor Code § 5302.
  Time for filing findings, see Labor Code § 5313.

Research References

Forms

23B Am. Jur. Pl. & Pr. Forms Trial § 496, Introductory Comments.
California Practice Guide: Rutter Family Law Forms Form 13:3, Request for Statement of Decision.
West's California Code Forms, Civil Procedure § 632 Form 1, Trial—Request for Statement of Decision.
West's California Code Forms, Civil Procedure § 632 Form 3, Trial—Waiver of Statement of Decision.
West's California Code Forms, Civil Procedure § 632 Form 6, Trial—Notice of Motion for Order Deeming Statement of Decision Waived.
West's California Code Forms, Family § 3022, Comment Overview—Order for Custody.

§ 634. Omission or ambiguity brought to attention of trial court; inference

When a statement of decision does not resolve a controverted issue, or if the statement is ambiguous and the record shows that the omission or ambiguity was brought to the attention of the trial court either prior to entry of judgment or in conjunction with a motion under Section 657 or 663, it shall not be inferred on appeal or upon a motion under Section 657 or 663 that the trial court decided in favor of the prevailing party as to those facts or on that issue. (Enacted in 1872. Amended by Stats.1913, c. 58, p. 58, § 1; Stats.1933, c. 744, p. 1877, § 106; Stats.1959, c. 637, p. 2614, § 2; Stats.1963, c. 378, p. 1167, § 1; Stats.1968, c. 716, p. 1418, § 2, operative Jan. 1, 1969; Stats.1981, c. 900, p. 3425, § 2.)

Cross References

Judgment defined, see Code of Civil Procedure § 577.

Research References

Forms

West's California Code Forms, Civil Procedure § 632 Form 1, Trial—Request for Statement of Decision.

§ 635. Formal judgment or order; signature by presiding judge in absence of trial judge

In all cases where the decision of the court has been entered in its minutes, and when the judge who heard or tried the case is unavailable, the formal judgment or order conforming to the minutes may be signed by the presiding judge of the court or by a judge designated by the presiding judge. (Added by Stats.1965, c. 1942, p.

§ 635

4470, § 1. Amended by Stats.1981, c. 900, p. 3426, § 3; Stats.1992, c. 876 (A.B.3296), § 5.)

Cross References

Judgment defined, see Code of Civil Procedure § 577.

CHAPTER 6. OF REFERENCES AND TRIALS BY REFEREES

Section
638. Appointment of referee; agreement of parties.
639. Appointment of referee.
640. Selection of referees.
640.5. Judicial Council report on the practice and cost of referring discovery disputes to outside referees.
641. Objections to referee; grounds.
642. Objections to reference or to referee.
643. Written report; time; objections.
644. Effect of referee or commissioner's decision.

Cross References

Applicability of Evidence Code to this chapter, see Evidence Code § 300.
Costs occasioned by postponement, imposition by referee, see Code of Civil Procedure § 1024.
Default judgment, reference to take account or proof, see Code of Civil Procedure § 585.
Fees, see Code of Civil Procedure § 1023.
Issues of fact, see Code of Civil Procedure § 592.
Partition of real or personal property, referees, see Code of Civil Procedure §§ 872.030, 873.010 et seq.
Several referees, quorum and majority, see Code of Civil Procedure § 1053.
State license tax, action to collect, applicability of this chapter, see Business and Professions Code § 16222.
Unfair practices act proceedings, applicability of chapter, see Business and Professions Code § 17085.

§ 638. Appointment of referee; agreement of parties

A referee may be appointed upon the agreement of the parties filed with the clerk, or judge, or entered in the minutes, or upon the motion of a party to a written contract or lease that provides that any controversy arising therefrom shall be heard by a referee if the court finds a reference agreement exists between the parties:

(a) To hear and determine any or all of the issues in an action or proceeding, whether of fact or of law, and to report a statement of decision.

(b) To ascertain a fact necessary to enable the court to determine an action or proceeding.

(c) In any matter in which a referee is appointed pursuant to this section, a copy of the order shall be forwarded to the office of the presiding judge. The Judicial Council shall, by rule, collect information on the use of these referees. The Judicial Council shall also collect information on fees paid by the parties for the use of referees to the extent that information regarding those fees is reported to the court. The Judicial Council shall report thereon to the Legislature by July 1, 2003. This subdivision shall become inoperative on January 1, 2004. (Enacted in 1872. Amended by Stats.1933, c. 744, p. 1877, § 107; Stats.1951, c. 1737, p. 4117, § 93, operative Jan. 1, 1952; Stats.1982, c. 440, p. 1810, § 1; Stats.1984, c. 350, § 1; Stats.2000, c. 644 (A.B.2912), § 1; Stats.2001, c. 44 (S.B.562), § 5; Stats.2002, c. 1008 (A.B.3028), § 4.)

Cross References

Applicability of procedural provisions to all trial courts, exceptions, see Code of Civil Procedure § 34.
Court commissioners, see Code of Civil Procedure § 259.
Judgment roll as including finding of referee, see Code of Civil Procedure § 670.
Judgment upon failure to answer, reference, see Code of Civil Procedure § 585.

Judicial officers, grounds for disqualification, see Code of Civil Procedure § 170.1.
Proceedings supplemental to execution, see Code of Civil Procedure §§ 708.110, 708.170.
Three referees, authority of two to act, see Code of Civil Procedure § 1053.
Trial by court, reference, see Code of Civil Procedure § 636.

Research References

Forms

1 Alternative Dispute Resolution § 24:13 (4th ed.), Appointment.
1 Alternative Dispute Resolution § 24:14 (4th ed.), Private Judging Distinguished from Other Alternative Dispute Resolution Procedures.
21A Am. Jur. Pl. & Pr. Forms References § 1, Introductory Comments.
21A Am. Jur. Pl. & Pr. Forms References § 15, Introductory Comments.
3 California Real Estate Forms (Miller & Starr) § 3:55 (2d ed.), Subordination, Nondisturbance, and Attornment Agreement.
3 California Real Estate Forms (Miller & Starr) § 3:79 (2d ed.), Loan Agreement—Refinance (Multiple Borrowers).
3 California Real Estate Forms (Miller & Starr) § 3:79.50 (2d ed.), Limited Guaranty—Refinance (Multiple Borrowers).
3 California Real Estate Forms (Miller & Starr) § 3:80 (2d ed.), Loan Agreement—Consolidation (Multiple Borrowers).
2 California Transactions Forms--Business Transactions § 10:82, Agreement Between Production Company and Writer for Motion Picture.
2 California Transactions Forms--Business Transactions § 14:57, Choosing Arbitration.
3 California Transactions Forms--Business Transactions § 19:46, Limited Continuing Guaranty (Trust Guarantor)—Liability Limited to Specified Maximum Including Amount Paid Under Other Guarantees.
1 California Transactions Forms--Estate Planning § 1:54, Drafting Principles.
1 California Transactions Forms--Family Law § 2:73, Special Masters.
1 California Transactions Forms--Family Law § 3:16, Identifying Areas of Parental Decision Making and Participation.
1 California Transactions Forms--Family Law § 3:59, Basis for Modification of Physical Custody.
1 California Transactions Forms--Family Law § 3:87, Appointment of a Special Master.
2 California Transactions Forms--Family Law § 5:25, Special Master.
2 California Transactions Forms--Family Law § 5:30, Parenting Agreement Providing for Joint Legal and Joint Physical Custody Where Both Partners Are Biological Parents of Child.
2 California Transactions Forms--Family Law § 5:31, Parenting Agreement Providing for Joint Legal and Sole Physical Custody Where Both Partners Are Biological Parents of Child.
3 UCC Legal Forms § 9:927, Foreclosure Sale Agreement—Sample.
West's California Code Forms, Civil Procedure § 638 Form 1, Trial—Reference by Agreement of Parties.
West's California Code Forms, Civil Procedure § 638 Form 4, Trial—Order Appointing Referee (Alternative Dispute Resolution)—Official Form.
West's California Code Forms, Civil Procedure § 638 Form 5, Trial—Notice of Motion for Reference—Contract Cases.
West's California Judicial Council Forms ADR–109, Stipulation or Motion for Order Appointing Referee.
West's California Judicial Council Forms ADR–110, Order Appointing Referee.
26 West's Legal Forms § 2:85, Private Judging.

§ 639. Appointment of referee

(a) When the parties do not consent, the court may, upon the written motion of any party, or of its own motion, appoint a referee in the following cases pursuant to the provisions of subdivision (b) of Section 640:

(1) When the trial of an issue of fact requires the examination of a long account on either side; in which case the referees may be directed to hear and decide the whole issue, or report upon any specific question of fact involved therein.

(2) When the taking of an account is necessary for the information of the court before judgment, or for carrying a judgment or order into effect.

(3) When a question of fact, other than upon the pleadings, arises upon motion or otherwise, in any stage of the action.

(4) When it is necessary for the information of the court in a special proceeding.

(5) When the court in any pending action determines that it is necessary for the court to appoint a referee to hear and determine any and all discovery motions and disputes relevant to discovery in the action and to report findings and make a recommendation thereon.

(b) In a discovery matter, a motion to disqualify an appointed referee pursuant to Section 170.6 shall be made to the court by a party either:

(A) Within 10 days after notice of the appointment, or if the party has not yet appeared in the action, a motion shall be made within 10 days after the appearance, if a discovery referee has been appointed for all discovery purposes.

(B) At least five days before the date set for hearing, if the referee assigned is known at least 10 days before the date set for hearing and the discovery referee has been assigned only for limited discovery purposes.

(c) When a referee is appointed pursuant to paragraph (5) of subdivision (a), the order shall indicate whether the referee is being appointed for all discovery purposes in the action.

(d) All appointments of referees pursuant to this section shall be by written order and shall include the following:

(1) When the referee is appointed pursuant to paragraph (1), (2), (3), or (4) of subdivision (a), a statement of the reason the referee is being appointed.

(2) When the referee is appointed pursuant to paragraph (5) of subdivision (a), the exceptional circumstances requiring the reference, which must be specific to the circumstances of the particular case.

(3) The subject matter or matters included in the reference.

(4) The name, business address, and telephone number of the referee.

(5) The maximum hourly rate the referee may charge and, at the request of any party, the maximum number of hours for which the referee may charge. Upon the written application of any party or the referee, the court may, for good cause shown, modify the maximum number of hours subject to any findings as set forth in paragraph (6).

(6)(A) Either a finding that no party has established an economic inability to pay a pro rata share of the referee's fee or a finding that one or more parties has established an economic inability to pay a pro rata share of the referee's fees and that another party has agreed voluntarily to pay that additional share of the referee's fee. A court shall not appoint a referee at a cost to the parties if neither of these findings is made.

(B) In determining whether a party has established an inability to pay the referee's fees under subparagraph (A), the court shall consider only the ability of the party, not the party's counsel, to pay these fees. If a party is proceeding in forma pauperis, the party shall be deemed by the court to have an economic inability to pay the referee's fees. However, a determination of economic inability to pay the fees shall not be limited to parties that proceed in forma pauperis. For those parties who are not proceeding in forma pauperis, the court, in determining whether a party has established an inability to pay the fees, shall consider, among other things, the estimated cost of the referral and the impact of the proposed fees on the party's ability to proceed with the litigation.

(e) In any matter in which a referee is appointed pursuant to paragraph (5) of subdivision (a), a copy of the order appointing the referee shall be forwarded to the office of the presiding judge of the court. The Judicial Council shall, by rule, collect information on the use of these references and the reference fees charged to litigants, and shall report thereon to the Legislature by July 1, 2003. This subdivision shall become inoperative on January 1, 2004. *(Enacted in 1872. Amended by Stats.1933, c. 744, p. 1877, § 108; Stats.1951, c. 1737, p. 4117, § 94, operative Jan. 1, 1952; Stats.1977, c. 1257, p. 4764,* § 23, eff. Jan. 3, 1977; Stats.1981, c. 299, p. 1429, § 1; Stats.2000, c. 644 (A.B.2912), § 2; Stats.2000, c. 1011 (S.B.2153), § 1.5; Stats.2001, c. 362 (S.B.475), § 1.)

Cross References

Applicability of procedural provisions to all trial courts, exceptions, see Code of Civil Procedure § 34.

Corporate dissolution, court jurisdiction, see Corporations Code §§ 1806, 1904.

Judgment debtor, examination, see Code of Civil Procedure § 708.110.

Judgment defined, see Code of Civil Procedure § 577.

Judicial officers, grounds for disqualification, see Code of Civil Procedure § 170.1.

Mandamus, determination of damages by referee, see Code of Civil Procedure § 1095.

Research References

Forms

1 Alternative Dispute Resolution § 24:12 (4th ed.), Generally.

1 California Transactions Forms--Family Law § 2:73, Special Masters.

West's California Code Forms, Civil Procedure § 639 Form 1, Trial—Notice of Motion for Reference.

West's California Code Forms, Civil Procedure § 639 Form 3, Trial—Combined Order Appointing a Referee and for Payment of Referee's Fee.

§ 640. Selection of referees

(a) The court shall appoint as referee or referees the person or persons, not exceeding three, agreed upon by the parties.

(b) If the parties do not agree on the selection of the referee or referees, each party shall submit to the court up to three nominees for appointment as referee and the court shall appoint one or more referees, not exceeding three, from among the nominees against whom there is no legal objection. If no nominations are received from any of the parties, the court shall appoint one or more referees, not exceeding three, against whom there is no legal objection, or the court may appoint a court commissioner of the county where the cause is pending as a referee.

(c) Participation in the referee selection procedure pursuant to this section does not constitute a waiver of grounds for objection to the appointment of a referee under Section 641 or 641.2. *(Enacted in 1872. Amended by Stats.1913, c. 166, p. 246, § 1; Stats.1933, c. 744, p. 1877, § 109; Stats.1951, c. 1737, p. 4117, § 95, operative Jan. 1, 1952; Stats.1975, c. 1240, § 6, operative July 1, 1976; Stats.2000, c. 644 (A.B.2912), § 3.)*

Cross References

Applicability of procedural provisions to all trial courts, exceptions, see Code of Civil Procedure § 34.

Court commissioners, see Code of Civil Procedure § 259.

Eminent domain, see Cal. Const. Art. 1, § 19.

Two of three referees may act, see Code of Civil Procedure § 1053.

Research References

Forms

2 California Transactions Forms--Business Transactions § 10:82, Agreement Between Production Company and Writer for Motion Picture.

3 California Transactions Forms--Business Transactions § 19:46, Limited Continuing Guaranty (Trust Guarantor)—Liability Limited to Specified Maximum Including Amount Paid Under Other Guarantees.

§ 640.5. Judicial Council report on the practice and cost of referring discovery disputes to outside referees

It is the intent of the Legislature that the practice and cost of referring discovery disputes to outside referees be thoroughly reviewed. Therefore, in addition to the requirements of subdivision (e) of Section 639, the Judicial Council shall collect information from the trial courts on the use of referees in discovery matters pursuant to either Sections 638 and 639. The collected data shall include information on the number of referees, the cost to the parties, and the time spent by the discovery referee. The Judicial Council shall

§ 640.5

report thereon to the Legislature by July 1, 2003. *(Added by Stats.2001, c. 362 (S.B.475), § 2.)*

§ 641. Objections to referee; grounds

A party may object to the appointment of any person as referee, on one or more of the following grounds:

(a) A want of any of the qualifications prescribed by statute to render a person competent as a juror, except a requirement of residence within a particular county in the state.

(b) Consanguinity or affinity, within the third degree, to either party, or to an officer of a corporation which is a party, or to any judge of the court in which the appointment shall be made.

(c) Standing in the relation of guardian and ward, conservator and conservatee, master and servant, employer and clerk, or principal and agent, to either party; or being a member of the family of either party; or a partner in business with either party; or security on any bond or obligation for either party.

(d) Having served as a juror or been a witness on any trial between the same parties.

(e) Interest on the part of the person in the event of the action, or in the main question involved in the action.

(f) Having formed or expressed an unqualified opinion or belief as to the merits of the action.

(g) The existence of a state of mind in the potential referee evincing enmity against or bias toward either party. *(Enacted in 1872. Amended by Stats.1897, c. 69, p. 60, § 2; Stats.1907, c. 378, p. 714, § 1; Stats.1933, c. 744, p. 1878, § 110; Stats.1951, c. 1737, p. 4118, § 96, operative Jan. 1, 1952; Stats.1979, c. 730, p. 2477, § 22, operative Jan. 1, 1981; Stats.1997, c. 724 (A.B.1172), § 1; Stats.2000, c. 644 (A.B.2912), § 4.)*

Cross References

Applicability of procedural provisions to all trial courts, exceptions, see Code of Civil Procedure § 34.
Degrees of kindred, see Probate Code § 6402.
Jurors, qualifications, see Code of Civil Procedure § 198 et seq.
Workers' compensation proceedings, objection to reference on grounds specified in this section, see Labor Code § 5311.

§ 642. Objections to reference or to referee

Objections, if any, to a reference or to the referee or referees appointed by the court shall be made in writing, and must be heard and disposed of by the court, not by the referee. *(Added by Stats.2000, c. 644 (A.B.2912), § 7.)*

§ 643. Written report; time; objections

(a) Unless otherwise directed by the court, the referees or commissioner must report their statement of decision in writing to the court within 20 days after the hearing, if any, has been concluded and the matter has been submitted.

(b) A referee appointed pursuant to Section 638 shall report as agreed by the parties and approved by the court.

(c) A referee appointed pursuant to Section 639 shall file with the court a report that includes a recommendation on the merits of any disputed issue, a statement of the total hours spent and the total fees charged by the referee, and the referee's recommended allocation of payment. The referee shall serve the report on all parties. Any party may file an objection to the referee's report or recommendations within 10 days after the referee serves and files the report, or within another time as the court may direct. The objection shall be served on the referee and all other parties. Responses to the objections shall be filed with the court and served on the referee and all other parties within 10 days after the objection is served. The court shall review any objections to the report and any responses submitted to those objections and shall thereafter enter appropriate orders. Nothing in this section is intended to deprive the court of its power to change the terms of the referee's appointment or to modify or disregard the referee's recommendations, and this overriding power may be exercised at any time, either on the motion of any party for good cause shown or on the court's own motion. *(Enacted in 1872. Amended by Stats.1984, c. 350, § 2; Stats.2000, c. 644 (A.B.2912), § 8.)*

Cross References

Court commissioners, power to report conclusions, see Code of Civil Procedure § 259.
Evidence in proceeding conducted by referee, see Evidence Code § 300.
Review of decision, see Code of Civil Procedure § 645.
Two of three referees may act, see Code of Civil Procedure § 1053.

Research References

Forms

West's California Code Forms, Civil Procedure § 643 Form 1, Trial—Report of Referee.
West's California Judicial Council Forms ADR–111, Report of Referee.

§ 644. Effect of referee or commissioner's decision

(a) In the case of a consensual general reference pursuant to Section 638, the decision of the referee or commissioner upon the whole issue must stand as the decision of the court, and upon filing of the statement of decision with the clerk of the court, judgment may be entered thereon in the same manner as if the action had been tried by the court.

(b) In the case of all other references, the decision of the referee or commissioner is only advisory. The court may adopt the referee's recommendations, in whole or in part, after independently considering the referee's findings and any objections and responses thereto filed with the court. *(Enacted in 1872. Amended by Stats.1933, c. 744, p. 1878, § 111; Stats.1951, c. 1737, p. 4118, § 97, operative Jan. 1, 1952; Stats.1984, c. 350, § 3; Stats.2000, c. 644 (A.B.2912), § 9; Stats.2007, c. 263 (A.B.310), § 8.)*

Cross References

Applicability of procedural provisions to all trial courts, exceptions, see Code of Civil Procedure § 34.
Court commissioners, see Code of Civil Procedure § 259.
Finding of referee as part of judgment roll, see Code of Civil Procedure § 670.
Judgment, entry, see Code of Civil Procedure § 664.
Judgment defined, see Code of Civil Procedure § 577.

Research References

Forms

1 Alternative Dispute Resolution § 24:14 (4th ed.), Private Judging Distinguished from Other Alternative Dispute Resolution Procedures.
3 California Real Estate Forms (Miller & Starr) § 3:55 (2d ed.), Subordination, Nondisturbance, and Attornment Agreement.
West's California Code Forms, Probate § 9837 Form 4, [Proposed] Order for Instructions and Approval of Settlement Agreement [And Instructions to Distribute Estate Pursuant to Agreement] (Prob. Code §§ 9830, 9837, [11600, 11700] Code of Civil Procedure § 664.6).
West's California Code Forms, Probate § 17200(b)(6) Form 2, [Proposed] Order Approving Settlement Agreement [And Authorizing Distribution of Trust Pursuant to Agreement] Prob. Code § 17200(b)(6).

CHAPTER 7. PROVISIONS RELATING TO TRIALS IN GENERAL

Cross References

Mode of trial and postponements, see Code of Civil Procedure § 588 et seq.
State license tax, action to collect, applicability of this chapter, see Business and Professions Code § 16222.
Trial by court, see Code of Civil Procedure § 631 et seq.

Trial by jury, see Code of Civil Procedure § 607 et seq.

ARTICLE 1.5. VIEW BY TRIER OF FACT

Section
651. View; subject matter; personnel; procedure.

§ 651. View; subject matter; personnel; procedure

(a) On its own motion or on the motion of a party, where the court finds that such a view would be proper and would aid the trier of fact in its determination of the case, the court may order a view of any of the following:

(1) The property which is the subject of litigation.

(2) The place where any relevant event occurred.

(3) Any object, demonstration, or experiment, a view of which is relevant and admissible in evidence in the case and which cannot with reasonable convenience be viewed in the courtroom.

(b) On such occasion, the entire court, including the judge, jury, if any, court reporter, if any, and any necessary officers, shall proceed to the place, property, object, demonstration, or experiment to be viewed. The court shall be in session throughout the view. At the view, the court may permit testimony of witnesses. The proceedings at the view shall be recorded to the same extent as the proceedings in the courtroom. *(Added by Stats.1975, c. 301, § 3.)*

Cross References

Criminal cases, view by jury, see Penal Code § 1119.

Research References

Forms

West's California Code Forms, Civil Procedure § 651 Form 1, View by Trier of Fact—Notice of Motion.

ARTICLE 2. NEW TRIALS

Section
656. "New trial" defined.
657. Relief available on motion for new trial; causes; specification of grounds and reasons; new trial for insufficient evidence; manner of making and entering order; appeal.
657.1. Death or disability of court reporter or loss or destruction of notes.
658. Application; affidavits; minutes of court.
659. Notice of motion; filing and service, time; contents; extension of time.
659a. Supporting and counter-affidavits; time for service and filing; maximum extension of time.
660. Hearing; reference to pleadings, orders, depositions, documentary evidence, transcript, recollection of judge; attendance of reporter; precedence; time for ruling; automatic denial; determination; minute order.
661. Judge; designation and notice of time for argument; time for hearing by judge other than trial judge.
662. Cause tried by court; powers of judge on motion for new trial.
663. Setting aside judgment or decree; entry of new judgment; grounds.
663a. Notice of intention to move to set aside and vacate judgment; contents; power of court to rule; extension of time; filing deadlines; hearing; appeal of court order.

Cross References

Forcible entry and detainer proceedings, applicability of this Article, see Code of Civil Procedure § 1178.

§ 656. "New trial" defined

A new trial is a re-examination of an issue of fact in the same court after a trial and decision by a jury, court, or referee. *(Enacted in 1872. Amended by Stats.1907, c. 380, p. 717, § 1.)*

Cross References

Mandamus, motion for new trial, see Code of Civil Procedure § 1092.
New trial in criminal cases defined, see Penal Code § 1179.

Research References

Forms

West's California Code Forms, Fish and Game § 12157 Form 2, Notice of Motion to Vacate Order of Forfeiture.

§ 657. Relief available on motion for new trial; causes; specification of grounds and reasons; new trial for insufficient evidence; manner of making and entering order; appeal

The verdict may be vacated and any other decision may be modified or vacated, in whole or in part, and a new or further trial granted on all or part of the issues, on the application of the party aggrieved, for any of the following causes, materially affecting the substantial rights of such party:

1. Irregularity in the proceedings of the court, jury or adverse party, or any order of the court or abuse of discretion by which either party was prevented from having a fair trial.

2. Misconduct of the jury; and whenever any one or more of the jurors have been induced to assent to any general or special verdict, or to a finding on any question submitted to them by the court, by a resort to the determination of chance, such misconduct may be proved by the affidavit of any one of the jurors.

3. Accident or surprise, which ordinary prudence could not have guarded against.

4. Newly discovered evidence, material for the party making the application, which he could not, with reasonable diligence, have discovered and produced at the trial.

5. Excessive or inadequate damages.

6. Insufficiency of the evidence to justify the verdict or other decision, or the verdict or other decision is against law.

7. Error in law, occurring at the trial and excepted to by the party making the application.

When a new trial is granted, on all or part of the issues, the court shall specify the ground or grounds upon which it is granted and the court's reason or reasons for granting the new trial upon each ground stated.

A new trial shall not be granted upon the ground of insufficiency of the evidence to justify the verdict or other decision, nor upon the ground of excessive or inadequate damages, unless after weighing the evidence the court is convinced from the entire record, including reasonable inferences therefrom, that the court or jury clearly should have reached a different verdict or decision.

The order passing upon and determining the motion must be made and entered as provided in Section 660 and if the motion is granted must state the ground or grounds relied upon by the court, and may contain the specification of reasons. If an order granting such motion does not contain such specification of reasons, the court must, within 10 days after filing such order, prepare, sign and file such specification of reasons in writing with the clerk. The court shall not direct the attorney for a party to prepare either or both said order and said specification of reasons.

On appeal from an order granting a new trial the order shall be affirmed if it should have been granted upon any ground stated in the

§ 657

motion, whether or not specified in the order or specification of reasons, except that (a) the order shall not be affirmed upon the ground of the insufficiency of the evidence to justify the verdict or other decision, or upon the ground of excessive or inadequate damages, unless such ground is stated in the order granting the motion and (b) on appeal from an order granting a new trial upon the ground of the insufficiency of the evidence to justify the verdict or other decision, or upon the ground of excessive or inadequate damages, it shall be conclusively presumed that said order as to such ground was made only for the reasons specified in said order or said specification of reasons, and such order shall be reversed as to such ground only if there is no substantial basis in the record for any of such reasons. *(Enacted in 1872. Amended by Stats.1919, c. 100, p. 141, § 1; Stats.1929, c. 479, p. 841, § 2; Stats.1939, c. 713, p. 2234, § 1; Stats.1965, c. 1749, p. 3922, § 1; Stats.1967, c. 72, p. 970, § 1.)*

Cross References

Appealable judgments and orders,
   Municipal courts, see Code of Civil Procedure § 904.2.
   Superior courts, see Code of Civil Procedure § 904.1.
Application made on affidavits, see Code of Civil Procedure § 658.
Dismissal for delay in prosecution new trial, see Code of Civil Procedure § 583.110 et seq.
Effect of new trial in criminal cases, see Penal Code § 1180.
Findings of fact, inferences on appeal or motion under this section, see Code of Civil Procedure § 634.
Forcible entry and detainer, new trial procedure, see Code of Civil Procedure § 1178.
Grounds for new trial,
   Criminal cases, see Penal Code § 1181.
Lost or destroyed papers, see Code of Civil Procedure § 663.1.
Impossibility of obtaining record for appeal as ground for new trial, see Code of Civil Procedure § 914.
Inadequate or excessive damages as grounds for new trial, see Code of Civil Procedure § 662.5.
Judgment,
   Notwithstanding verdict, see Code of Civil Procedure § 629.
   On reopening case, see Code of Civil Procedure § 662.
Notes, loss or destruction, see Code of Civil Procedure § 914.
Power of judges to hear motions for new trial, see Code of Civil Procedure § 166.
Probate proceedings, new trials, see Probate Code § 7220.
Proceedings for writs, new trial procedure, see Code of Civil Procedure § 1110.
Reference to arbitration proceedings or award as an irregularity, see Code of Civil Procedure § 1141.25.
Reporters, death or disability, see Code of Civil Procedure § 914.
Weight of evidence generally, see Evidence Code § 410 et seq.
Works of improvement, new trials in enforcement proceedings, see Civil Code § 8056.
Writ of mandate, motion for new trial, see Code of Civil Procedure § 1092.
Youth Authority Act not to affect right to new trial, see Welfare and Institutions Code § 1739.

Research References

Forms

2 California Transactions Forms--Business Transactions § 14:50, Confidentiality of Mediation Process.
West's California Code Forms, Civil Procedure § 645 Form 1, Trial—Notice of Alternative Motion to Set Aside Report of Referee or for New Trial.
West's California Code Forms, Civil Procedure § 657 Form 1, New Trial—Notice of Intention to Move for New Trial.
West's California Code Forms, Civil Procedure § 657 Form 3, New Trial—Order Granting New Trial.
West's California Code Forms, Civil Procedure § 1008 Form 1, Motions and Orders—New Application for Order After Prior Refusal—Declaration Supporting New Application.
West's California Code Forms, Commercial § 1301 Form 8, Clause Providing for Mandatory Mediation.

§ 657.1. Death or disability of court reporter or loss or destruction of notes

A new trial may also be granted as provided in Section 914 of this code. *(Added by Stats.1968, c. 387, p. 821, § 1.)*

§ 658. Application; affidavits; minutes of court

When the application is made for a cause mentioned in the first, second, third and fourth subdivisions of Section 657, it must be made upon affidavits; otherwise it must be made on the minutes of the court. *(Enacted in 1872. Amended by Code Am.1873–74, c. 383, p. 314, § 84; Stats.1915, c. 107, p. 201, § 1; Stats.1983, c. 1167, § 9.)*

Cross References

Affidavits with defective title, validity, see Code of Civil Procedure § 1046.
Application in criminal procedure, see Penal Code § 1182.
Authority to take affidavits, see Code of Civil Procedure § 179.
Copy of affidavit as prima facie evidence, see Code of Civil Procedure § 2011.
Judgment notwithstanding verdict, see Code of Civil Procedure § 629.
Justice courts, statement of jurisdictional facts, see Code of Civil Procedure § 396a.
Powers and duties of court commissioners, see Code of Civil Procedure § 259.
Use of affidavits, see Code of Civil Procedure § 2009.

§ 659. Notice of motion; filing and service, time; contents; extension of time

(a) The party intending to move for a new trial shall file with the clerk and serve upon each adverse party a notice of his or her intention to move for a new trial, designating the grounds upon which the motion will be made and whether the same will be made upon affidavits or the minutes of the court, or both, either:

(1) After the decision is rendered and before the entry of judgment.

(2) Within 15 days of the date of mailing notice of entry of judgment by the clerk of the court pursuant to Section 664.5, or service upon him or her by any party of written notice of entry of judgment, or within 180 days after the entry of judgment, whichever is earliest; provided, that upon the filing of the first notice of intention to move for a new trial by a party, each other party shall have 15 days after the service of that notice upon him or her to file and serve a notice of intention to move for a new trial.

(b) That notice of intention to move for a new trial shall be deemed to be a motion for a new trial on all the grounds stated in the notice. The times specified in paragraphs (1) and (2) of subdivision (a) shall not be extended by order or stipulation or by those provisions of Section 1013 that extend the time for exercising a right or doing an act where service is by mail. *(Enacted in 1872. Amended by Code Am.1873–74, c. 383, p. 315, § 85; Stats.1907, c. 380, p. 717, § 2; Stats.1915, c. 107, p. 201, § 2; Stats.1923, c. 367, p. 751, § 1; Stats.1929, c. 479, p. 841, § 3; Stats.1951, c. 801, p. 2289, § 2, eff. Jan. 1, 1952; Stats.1959, c. 469, p. 2404, § 1; Stats.1961, c. 604, p. 1753, § 2; Stats.1965, c. 1890, p. 4359, § 1.5; Stats.1967, c. 169, p. 1266, § 1; Stats.1970, c. 621, p. 1232, § 1; Stats.2012, c. 83 (A.B.2106), § 1.)*

Cross References

Cause tried by court, applicability of this section, see Code of Civil Procedure § 662.
Commissioners, exceptions to report, see Code of Civil Procedure § 259.
Computation of time, see Code of Civil Procedure § 12.
Extensions of time,
   Generally, see Code of Civil Procedure §§ 1054, 1054.1.
   Holiday as last day for performance, see Code of Civil Procedure § 12a.
Judgment defined, see Code of Civil Procedure § 577.
Judgment notwithstanding verdict, alternative motion for new trial, see Code of Civil Procedure § 629.

Research References

Forms

West's California Code Forms, Civil Procedure § 657 Form 1, New Trial—Notice of Intention to Move for New Trial.

§ 659a. Supporting and counter-affidavits; time for service and filing; maximum extension of time

Within 10 days of filing the notice, the moving party shall serve upon all other parties and file any brief and accompanying documents, including affidavits in support of the motion. The other parties shall have 10 days after that service within which to serve upon the moving party and file any opposing briefs and accompanying documents, including counter-affidavits. The moving party shall have five days after that service to file any reply brief and accompanying documents. These deadlines may, for good cause shown by affidavit or by written stipulation of the parties, be extended by any judge for an additional period not to exceed 10 days. *(Added by Stats.1929, c. 479, p. 841, § 4. Amended by Stats.1933, c. 744, p. 1881, § 118; Stats.1935, c. 722, p. 1958, § 13; Stats.1989, c. 1416, § 20; Stats.2014, c. 93 (A.B.1659), § 2, eff. Jan. 1, 2015.)*

Cross References

Affidavits with defective title, validity, see Code of Civil Procedure § 1046.
Applicability of procedural provisions to all trial courts, exceptions, see Code of Civil Procedure § 34.
Authority to take affidavits, see Code of Civil Procedure § 179.
Computation of time, see Code of Civil Procedure § 12.
Copy of affidavit as prima facie evidence, see Code of Civil Procedure § 2011.
Holiday as last day for performance, extension of time, see Code of Civil Procedure § 12a.
Use of affidavits, see Code of Civil Procedure § 2009.

Research References

Forms

West's California Code Forms, Civil Procedure § 659a Form 1, New Trial—Counter Declaration Opposing Motion for New Trial.

§ 660. Hearing; reference to pleadings, orders, depositions, documentary evidence, transcript, recollection of judge; attendance of reporter; precedence; time for ruling; automatic denial; determination; minute order

(a) On the hearing of the motion, reference may be had in all cases to the pleadings and orders of the court on file, and when the motion is made on the minutes, reference may also be had to any depositions and documentary evidence offered at the trial and to the report of the proceedings on the trial taken by the phonographic reporter, or to any certified transcript of the report or if there be no such report or certified transcript, to proceedings occurring at the trial that are within the recollection of the judge; when the proceedings at the trial have been phonographically reported, but the reporter's notes have not been transcribed, the reporter shall, upon request of the court or either party, attend the hearing of the motion and read his or her notes, or such parts thereof as the court, or either party, may require.

(b) The hearing and determination of the motion for a new trial shall have precedence over all other matters except criminal cases, probate matters, and cases actually on trial, and it shall be the duty of the court to determine the motion at the earliest possible moment.

(c) Except as otherwise provided in Section 12a of this code, the power of the court to rule on a motion for a new trial shall expire 75 days after the mailing of notice of entry of judgment by the clerk of the court pursuant to Section 664.5 or 75 days after service on the moving party by any party of written notice of entry of judgment, whichever is earlier, or if that notice has not been given, 75 days after the filing of the first notice of intention to move for a new trial. If the motion is not determined within the 75-day period, or within that period as extended, the effect shall be a denial of the motion without further order of the court. A motion for a new trial is not determined within the meaning of this section until an order ruling on the motion is entered in the permanent minutes of the court or signed by the judge and filed with the clerk. The entry of a new trial order in the permanent minutes of the court shall constitute a determination of the motion even though that minute order, as entered, expressly directs that a written order be prepared, signed, and filed. The minute entry shall in all cases show the date on which the order is entered in the permanent minutes, but failure to comply with this direction shall not impair the validity or effectiveness of the order. *(Enacted in 1872. Amended by Code Am.1873–74, c. 383, p.* 317, § 86; Stats.1907, c. 380, p. 718, § 3; Stats.1915, c. 107, p. 202, § 3; Stats.1917, c. 156, p. 240, § 1; Stats.1923, c. 105, p. 233, § 1; Stats.1929, c. 479, p. 842, § 5; Stats.1933, c. 29, p. 305, § 5; Stats.1959, c. 468, p. 2403, § 1; Stats.1969, c. 87, p. 209, § 1; Stats.1970, c. 621, p. 1232, § 2; Stats.2018, c. 317 (A.B.2230), § 1, eff. Jan. 1, 2019.)*

Cross References

Appeal from an order granting a new trial, see Code of Civil Procedure § 904.1.
Appeal from an order on motion for new trial, see Code of Civil Procedure § 906.
Computation of time, see Code of Civil Procedure § 12.
Correction of clerical mistakes, vacation of void order, see Code of Civil Procedure § 473.
Jurisdiction of judges of superior, municipal and justice courts in chambers, see Code of Civil Procedure § 166.

Research References

Forms

West's California Code Forms, Civil Procedure § 657 Form 1, New Trial—Notice of Intention to Move for New Trial.
West's California Code Forms, Civil Procedure § 657 Form 3, New Trial—Order Granting New Trial.

§ 661. Judge; designation and notice of time for argument; time for hearing by judge other than trial judge

The motion for a new trial shall be heard and determined by the judge who presided at the trial; provided, however, that in case of the inability of such judge or if at the time noticed for hearing thereon he is absent from the county where the trial was had, the same shall be heard and determined by any other judge of the same court. Upon the expiration of the time to file counter affidavits the clerk forthwith shall call the motion to the attention of the judge who presided at the trial, or the judge acting in his place, as the case may be, and such judge thereupon shall designate the time for oral argument, if any, to be had on said motion. Five (5) days' notice by mail shall be given of such oral argument, if any, by the clerk to the respective parties. Such motion, if heard by a judge other than the trial judge shall be argued orally or shall be submitted without oral argument, as the judge may direct, not later than ten (10) days before the expiration of the time within which the court has power to pass on the same. *(Added by Stats.1929, c. 479, p. 842, § 6. Amended by Stats.1931, c. 768, p. 1608, § 1; Stats.1933, c. 744, p. 1881, § 119.)*

Cross References

Applicability of procedural provisions to all trial courts, exceptions, see Code of Civil Procedure § 34.
Case reserved for argument, bringing before court, see Code of Civil Procedure § 665.
Death or indisposition of judge during criminal trial, see Penal Code § 1053.
Disqualification of judges, grounds, proceedings, see Code of Civil Procedure § 170 et seq.
Judgment roll, see Code of Civil Procedure § 670.
Jurisdiction of judges of superior, municipal and justice courts in chambers, see Code of Civil Procedure § 166.
Relief from judgments taken by mistake, etc., see Code of Civil Procedure § 473.
Written notice of motion, time for service, see Code of Civil Procedure § 1005.

§ 662. Cause tried by court; powers of judge on motion for new trial

In ruling on such motion, in a cause tried without a jury, the court may, on such terms as may be just, change or add to the statement of decision, modify the judgment, in whole or in part, vacate the judgment, in whole or in part, and grant a new trial on all or part of the issues, or, in lieu of granting a new trial, may vacate and set aside the statement of decision and judgment and reopen the case for further proceedings and the introduction of additional evidence with the same effect as if the case had been reopened after the submission thereof and before a decision had been filed or judgment rendered.

§ 662

Any judgment thereafter entered shall be subject to the provisions of sections 657 and 659. *(Added by Stats.1929, c. 479, p. 843, § 7. Amended by Stats.1981, c. 900, p. 3426, § 4.)*

Cross References

Findings of fact, omission, ambiguity or conflict, see Code of Civil Procedure § 634.

Findings of fact and conclusions of law, waiver, judgment entry, see Code of Civil Procedure § 632.

Judgment defined, see Code of Civil Procedure § 577.

Jurisdiction of judges of superior, municipal or justice courts at chambers, see Code of Civil Procedure § 166.

Relief available on motion for new trial, see Code of Civil Procedure § 657.

Setting aside void judgment or order, see Code of Civil Procedure § 473.

Research References

Forms

West's California Code Forms, Civil Procedure § 663 Form 1, New Trial—Notice of Motion to Set Aside Judgment.

§ 663. Setting aside judgment or decree; entry of new judgment; grounds

A judgment or decree, when based upon a decision by the court, or the special verdict of a jury, may, upon motion of the party aggrieved, be set aside and vacated by the same court, and another and different judgment entered, for either of the following causes, materially affecting the substantial rights of the party and entitling the party to a different judgment:

1. Incorrect or erroneous legal basis for the decision, not consistent with or not supported by the facts; and in such case when the judgment is set aside, the statement of decision shall be amended and corrected.

2. A judgment or decree not consistent with or not supported by the special verdict. *(Added by Stats.1897, c. 67, p. 58, § 1. Amended by Stats.1933, c. 744, p. 1881, § 120; Stats.1981, c. 900, p. 3426, § 5.)*

Cross References

Applicability of procedural provisions to all trial courts, exceptions, see Code of Civil Procedure § 34.

Death or disability of reporter as ground for vacation of judgment, see Code of Civil Procedure § 914.

Decision, findings of fact and conclusions of law, waiver, see Code of Civil Procedure § 632.

Decisions appealable from superior court, see Code of Civil Procedure § 904.1.

Duties of phonographic reporters in superior court, see Code of Civil Procedure § 269.

Findings of fact, inferences on appeal or motion under this section, see Code of Civil Procedure § 634.

Judgment defined, see Code of Civil Procedure § 577.

Judgment notwithstanding verdict, alternative motion for new trial, see Code of Civil Procedure § 629.

Ordering judgment in accordance with motion for directed verdict, see Code of Civil Procedure § 630.

Power of judge to determine motion under this section at chambers, see Code of Civil Procedure § 166.

Setting aside void judgment or order, see Code of Civil Procedure § 473.

Research References

Forms

West's California Code Forms, Civil Procedure § 663 Form 1, New Trial—Notice of Motion to Set Aside Judgment.

§ 663a. Notice of intention to move to set aside and vacate judgment; contents; power of court to rule; extension of time; filing deadlines; hearing; appeal of court order

(a) A party intending to make a motion to set aside and vacate a judgment, as described in Section 663, shall file with the clerk and serve upon the adverse party a notice of his or her intention, designating the grounds upon which the motion will be made, and specifying the particulars in which the legal basis for the decision is not consistent with or supported by the facts, or in which the judgment or decree is not consistent with the special verdict, either:

(1) After the decision is rendered and before the entry of judgment.

(2) Within 15 days of the date of mailing of notice of entry of judgment by the clerk of the court pursuant to Section 664.5, or service upon him or her by any party of written notice of entry of judgment, or within 180 days after the entry of judgment, whichever is earliest.

(b) Except as otherwise provided in Section 12a, the power of the court to rule on a motion to set aside and vacate a judgment shall expire 75 days from the mailing of notice of entry of judgment by the clerk of the court pursuant to Section 664.5, or 75 days after service upon the moving party by any party of written notice of entry of the judgment, whichever is earlier, or if that notice has not been given, 75 days after the filing of the first notice of intention to move to set aside and vacate the judgment. If that motion is not determined within the 75–day period, or within that period as extended, the effect shall be a denial of the motion without further order of the court. A motion to set aside and vacate a judgment is not determined within the meaning of this section until an order ruling on the motion is entered in the permanent minutes of the court, or signed by the judge and filed with the clerk. The entry of an order to set aside and vacate the judgment in the permanent minutes of the court shall constitute a determination of the motion even though that minute order, as entered, expressly directs that a written order be prepared, signed, and filed. The minute entry shall, in all cases, show the date on which the order is entered in the permanent minutes, but failure to comply with this direction shall not impair the validity or effectiveness of the order.

(c) The provisions of Section 1013 extending the time for exercising a right or doing an act where service is by mail shall not apply to extend the times specified in paragraphs (1) and (2) of subdivision (a).

(d) The moving, opposing, and reply briefs and any accompanying documents shall be filed and served within the periods specified by Section 659a and the hearing on the motion shall be set in the same manner as the hearing on a motion for new trial under Section 660.

(e) An order of the court granting a motion may be reviewed on appeal in the same manner as a special order made after final judgment. *(Formerly § 663½, added by Stats.1897, c. 67, p. 59, § 1. Renumbered § 663a, and amended by Stats.1907, c. 380, p. 719, § 4. Amended by Stats.1915, c. 108, p. 203, § 1; Stats.1959, c. 469, p. 2404, § 2; Stats.1965, c. 1890, p. 4360, § 2; Stats.1967, c. 119, p. 1041, § 1; Stats.1967, c. 169, p. 1266, § 2; Stats.1983, c. 302, § 1; Stats.2012, c. 83 (A.B.2106), § 2; Stats.2014, c. 93 (A.B.1659), § 3, eff. Jan. 1, 2015; Stats.2018, c. 317 (A.B.2230), § 2, eff. Jan. 1, 2019.)*

Cross References

Computation of time for performance of act required by law, see Code of Civil Procedure § 12.

Decisions appealable from Superior Court, see Code of Civil Procedure § 904.1.

Judgment defined, see Code of Civil Procedure § 577.

Setting aside void judgment or order, see Code of Civil Procedure § 473.

Research References

Forms

West's California Code Forms, Civil Procedure § 663 Form 1, New Trial—Notice of Motion to Set Aside Judgment.

CHAPTER 8. THE MANNER OF GIVING AND ENTERING JUDGMENT

Section

664.6. Entry of judgment pursuant to terms of stipulation for settlement; signed writing; exceptions.

Section
669. Death of party after trial and submission to judge sitting without jury or after verdict and before judgment; rendition of judgment.
674. Abstract of judgment or decree; contents; amendment.

§ 664.6. Entry of judgment pursuant to terms of stipulation for settlement; signed writing; exceptions

(a) If parties to pending litigation stipulate, in a writing signed by the parties outside of the presence of the court or orally before the court, for settlement of the case, or part thereof, the court, upon motion, may enter judgment pursuant to the terms of the settlement. If requested by the parties, the court may retain jurisdiction over the parties to enforce the settlement until performance in full of the terms of the settlement.

(b) For purposes of this section, a writing is signed by a party if it is signed by any of the following:

(1) The party.

(2) An attorney who represents the party.

(3) If the party is an insurer, an agent who is authorized in writing by the insurer to sign on the insurer's behalf.

(c) Paragraphs (2) and (3) of subdivision (b) do not apply in a civil harassment action, an action brought pursuant to the Family Code, an action brought pursuant to the Probate Code, or a matter that is being adjudicated in a juvenile court or a dependency court.

(d) In addition to any available civil remedies, an attorney who signs a writing on behalf of a party pursuant to subdivision (b) without the party's express authorization shall, absent good cause, be subject to professional discipline. *(Added by Stats.1981, c. 904, p. 3437, § 2. Amended by Stats.1993, c. 768 (S.B.252), § 1; Stats.1994, c. 587 (A.B.3600), § 7; Stats.2020, c. 290 (A.B.2723), § 1, eff. Jan. 1, 2021.)*

Cross References

Judgment defined, see Code of Civil Procedure § 577.

Research References

Forms

California Practice Guide: Rutter Family Law Forms Form 13:2, Request for Order to Enforce Settlement (CCP § 664.6).
2 California Transactions Forms--Business Transactions § 14:51, Enforceability of Written Settlement Agreement Reached in Mediation.
2 California Transactions Forms--Business Transactions § 14:52, Enforceability of Oral Settlement Agreement Reached in Mediation.
3 California Transactions Forms--Business Transactions § 18:1, Definition, Nature, and Distinctions.
3 California Transactions Forms--Business Transactions § 18:9, Written or Oral Agreement.
3 California Transactions Forms--Business Transactions § 18:21, Admissibility of Settlement Offers and Negotiations.
3 California Transactions Forms--Business Transactions § 18:30, Enforcement of Settlement.
3 California Transactions Forms--Business Transactions § 18:51, Settlement Agreement for Contractual Claims—Cross-Complaints Filed and Settled—Agreement to Mediate and Arbitrate Future Disputes.
3 California Transactions Forms--Business Transactions § 18:51.30, Settlement Agreement Following Mediation of Disputes Subject to Pending Litigation.
West's California Code Forms, Civil Procedure § 664.6 Form 1, Judgment—Notice of Motion for Entry of Judgment Based Upon Stipulated Settlement.
West's California Code Forms, Civil Procedure § 664.6 Form 3, Judgment—Default—Stipulation—Court Trial—Official Form.
West's California Code Forms, Probate § 17200(b)(6) Form 1, Petition for Approval of Agreement [And for Authority to Distribute Trust Pursuant to Agreement] Prob. Code § 17200(B)(6).
West's California Judicial Council Forms JUD–100, Judgment.
West's California Judicial Council Forms UD–110, Judgment—Unlawful Detainer.
West's California Judicial Council Forms UD–115, Stipulation for Entry of Judgment.

§ 669. Death of party after trial and submission to judge sitting without jury or after verdict and before judgment; rendition of judgment

If a party dies after trial and submission of the case to a judge sitting without a jury for decision or after a verdict upon any issue of fact, and before judgment, the court may nevertheless render judgment thereon. *(Enacted in 1872. Amended by Stats.1965, c. 1636, p. 3730, § 1; Stats.1980, c. 124, p. 294, § 2.)*

Cross References

Dissolution of marriage, death of party after judgment, see Family Code § 2344.
Execution after death of party, see Code of Civil Procedure §§ 686.010, 686.020.
Judgment defined, see Code of Civil Procedure § 577.
Nonabatement of action on death or disability of party, substitution, see Code of Civil Procedure §§ 368.5, 375, 377.20 et seq.
Reversal of judgment, death of plaintiff before new action, see Code of Civil Procedure § 355.

§ 674. Abstract of judgment or decree; contents; amendment

(a) Except as otherwise provided in Section 4506 of the Family Code, an abstract of a judgment or decree requiring the payment of money shall be certified by the clerk of the court where the judgment or decree was entered and shall contain all of the following:

(1) The title of the court where the judgment or decree is entered and cause and number of the action.

(2) The date of entry of the judgment or decree and of any renewals of the judgment or decree and where entered in the records of the court.

(3) The name and last known address of the judgment debtor and the address at which the summons was either personally served or mailed to the judgment debtor or the judgment debtor's attorney of record.

(4) The name and address of the judgment creditor.

(5) The amount of the judgment or decree as entered or as last renewed.

(6) The last four digits of the social security number and driver's license number of the judgment debtor if they are known to the judgment creditor. If either or both of those sets of numbers are not known to the judgment creditor, that fact shall be indicated on the abstract of judgment.

(7) Whether a stay of enforcement has been ordered by the court and, if so, the date the stay ends.

(8) The date of issuance of the abstract.

(b) An abstract of judgment, recorded after January 1, 1979, that does not list the social security number and driver's license number of the judgment debtor, or either of them, as required by subdivision (a) or by Section 4506 of the Family Code, may be amended by the recording of a document entitled "Amendment to Abstract of Judgment." The Amendment to Abstract of Judgment shall contain all of the information required by this section or by Section 4506 of the Family Code, and shall set forth the date of recording and the book and page location in the records of the county recorder of the original abstract of judgment.

A recorded Amendment to Abstract of Judgment shall have priority as of the date of recordation of the original abstract of judgment, except as to any purchaser, encumbrancer, or lessee who obtained their interest after the recordation of the original abstract of judgment but prior to the recordation of the Amendment to Abstract of Judgment without actual notice of the original abstract of

§ 674

judgment. The purchaser, encumbrancer, or lessee without actual notice may assert as a defense against enforcement of the abstract of judgment the failure to comply with this section or Section 4506 of the Family Code regarding the contents of the original abstract of judgment notwithstanding the subsequent recordation of an Amendment to Abstract of Judgment. With respect to an abstract of judgment recorded between January 1, 1979, and July 10, 1985, the defense against enforcement for failure to comply with this section or Section 4506 of the Family Code may not be asserted by the holder of another abstract of judgment or involuntary lien, recorded without actual notice of the prior abstract, unless refusal to allow the defense would result in prejudice and substantial injury as used in Section 475. The recordation of an Amendment to Abstract of Judgment does not extend or otherwise alter the computation of time as provided in Section 697.310.

(c)(1) The abstract of judgment shall be certified in the name of the judgment debtor as listed on the judgment and may also include the additional name or names by which the judgment debtor is known as set forth in the affidavit of identity, as defined in Section 680.135, filed by the judgment creditor with the application for issuance of the abstract of judgment. Prior to the clerk of the court certifying an abstract of judgment containing any additional name or names by which the judgment debtor is known that are not listed on the judgment, the court shall approve the affidavit of identity. If the court determines, without a hearing or a notice, that the affidavit of identity states sufficient facts upon which the judgment creditor has identified the additional names of the judgment debtor, the court shall authorize the certification of the abstract of judgment with the additional name or names.

(2) The remedies provided in Section 697.410 apply to a recorded abstract of a money judgment based upon an affidavit of identity that appears to create a judgment lien on real property of a person who is not the judgment debtor. *(Enacted in 1872. Amended by Stats.1907, c. 381, p. 720, § 4; Stats.1923, c. 368, p. 752, § 3; Stats.1927, c. 493, p. 830, § 1; Stats.1933, c. 744, p. 1884, § 129; Stats.1935, c. 298, p. 1017, § 1; Stats.1947, c. 116, p. 638, § 1; Stats.1951, c. 1737, p. 4119, § 101, operative Jan. 1, 1952; Stats.1955, c. 781, p. 1380, § 1; Stats.1957, c. 43, p. 603, § 6; Stats.1973, c. 797, p. 1413, § 1; Stats.1974, c. 211, p. 405, § 1; Stats.1974, c. 1169, p. 2503, § 3; Stats.1976, c. 1000, p. 2368, § 1, operative July 1, 1977; Stats.1977, c. 1257, p. 4766, § 30, eff. Oct. 3, 1977; Stats.1978, c. 203, § 1; Stats.1980, c. 1281, p. 4326, § 2; Stats.1982, c. 517, p. 2344, § 131; Stats.1982, c. 497, p. 2157, § 39, operative July 1, 1983; Stats.1988, c. 153, § 6; Stats.1988, c. 1411, § 1; Stats.1992, c. 163 (A.B.2641), § 28, operative Jan. 1, 1994; Stats.2000, c. 639 (A.B.2405), § 1; Stats.2001, c. 159 (S.B.662), § 39; Stats.2007, c. 189 (S.B.644), § 1.)*

Cross References

Action on judgment against local public entity, time, see Government Code § 970.1.
Bond and Undertaking Law, see Code of Civil Procedure § 995.010 et seq.
Certification of abstract of judgment, notice of support judgment, see Family Code § 4506.
Death, disability or transfer of interest of a party, see Code of Civil Procedure §§ 368.5, 375, 377.20 et seq.
Documents to be recorded, see Government Code § 27280 et seq.
Judgment defined, see Code of Civil Procedure § 577.
Lien of judgment creditor of plaintiff, endorsement upon abstract of judgment, see Code of Civil Procedure § 708.460.
Limitation of action upon judgment, see Code of Civil Procedure § 337.5.
Order for deposit of assets to secure future child support payments, deposit of real property, certification of order as abstract of judgment, recordation, see Family Code § 4617.
Stay of enforcement, renewal of judgment, see Code of Civil Procedure § 683.210.

Venue for examination, see Code of Civil Procedure § 708.160.

Research References

Forms

West's California Judicial Council Forms CR–110, Order for Victim Restitution.

Title 9

ENFORCEMENT OF JUDGMENTS

Cross References

Agricultural chemical and seed lien, foreclosure in action to recover reasonable or agreed charges, see Food and Agricultural Code § 57586.
Bail upon being held to answer before indictment, justification of bail, judgment lien on bail forfeiture and summary judgment, see Penal Code § 1280.1.
Claims established by judgment,
    Execution liens, see Probate Code § 9303.
    Judgment for possession of trust property or for sale of trust property, see Probate Code § 19302.
    Judgments for possession or sale of property, see Probate Code § 9302.
    Money judgments against deceased settlor, trustee, or trust estate, see Probate Code § 19300.
Conviction of felony of theft or embezzlement of property, preliminary injunction, restitution, see Penal Code § 186.12.
Dairy cattle supply lien, foreclosure, enforcement of judgment, see Food and Agricultural Code § 57413.
Fair Practices of Equipment Manufacturers, Distributors, Wholesalers, and Dealers Act, right of foreclosure, enforcement of final judgment pursuant to this title, see Business and Professions Code § 22919.
Fine art works, sales, see Civil Code § 986.
Hearings and orders, enforcement of orders, see Probate Code § 1049.
Licenses to sell firearms, unlicensed persons, see Penal Code § 26500.
Local public entities, enforcement of judgments, applicability, see Government Code § 970.1.
Multiple felonies involving fraud or embezzlement, restitution, preservation and levy of defendant's property, see Penal Code § 186.11.
Municipal and justice courts, jurisdiction, see Code of Civil Procedure § 86.
New school facilities, voter-approved special taxes, collection of past due tax, see Education Code § 43048.
Oil Spill Response Trust Fund, payment of unenforced judgments, see Government Code § 8670.51.
Poultry and fish supply lien, foreclosure in action to recover reasonable or agreed charges, see Food and Agricultural Code § 57536.
School boards, payment of judgments, see Government Code § 970 et seq.
Secured party's rights on disposition of collateral, proceeds, see Commercial Code § 9306.
Secured transactions, secured party's rights on disposition of collateral and in proceeds, see Commercial Code § 9315.
Small claims courts, applicability of this Title, see Code of Civil Procedure § 116.110 et seq.
State or state agency, enforcement of money judgment against, law governing, see Government Code § 965.5.
Telephonic sellers, bond requirement, liability upon and enforcement of bond, see Business and Professions Code § 17511.12.
Trust property subject to execution lien, see Probate Code § 19303.

Division 1

DEFINITIONS AND GENERAL PROVISIONS

Cross References

Private Student Loan Collections Reform Act, violation of act, penalties, class actions, attorney's fees, exceptions, limitation of actions, see Civil Code § 1788.208.

CHAPTER 1. SHORT TITLE AND DEFINITIONS

Section
680.145. Child support.
680.365. Spousal support.

OF CIVIL ACTIONS

Cross References

Bonds given pursuant to this title subject to Bond and Undertaking Law (§ 995.010 et seq.), see Code of Civil Procedure § 720.710.

Dairy cattle supply lien, foreclosure, enforcement, surplus, attachment or temporary protective order, payments by others, and release, see Food and Agricultural Code § 57413.

Small claims courts, applicability of this Title, see Code of Civil Procedure § 116.110 et seq.

§ 680.145. Child support

"Child support" includes family support. *(Added by Stats.1992, c. 163 (A.B.2641), § 29, operative Jan. 1, 1994.)*

§ 680.365. Spousal support

"Spousal support" includes support for a former spouse. *(Added by Stats.1982, c. 1364, p. 5072, § 2, operative July 1, 1983.)*

CHAPTER 3. PERIOD FOR ENFORCEMENT AND RENEWAL OF JUDGMENTS

ARTICLE 1. PERIOD FOR ENFORCEMENT OF JUDGMENTS

Section
683.010. Entry of judgment.
683.020. Period of enforceability.
683.030. Period of enforceability; money judgments payable in installments.
683.040. Application more than 10 years after entry or renewal; affidavit.
683.050. Judgment creditor's right to bring action; limitations.

§ 683.010. Entry of judgment

Except as otherwise provided by statute or in the judgment, a judgment is enforceable under this title upon entry. *(Added by Stats.1982, c. 1364, p. 5073, § 2, operative July 1, 1983.)*

Research References

Forms

West's California Code Forms, Family § 290, Comment Overview—Enforcement of Judgments and Orders.

§ 683.020. Period of enforceability

Except as otherwise provided by statute, upon the expiration of 10 years after the date of entry of a money judgment or a judgment for possession or sale of property:

(a) The judgment may not be enforced.

(b) All enforcement procedures pursuant to the judgment or to a writ or order issued pursuant to the judgment shall cease.

(c) Any lien created by an enforcement procedure pursuant to the judgment is extinguished. *(Added by Stats.1982, c. 1364, p. 5073, § 2, operative July 1, 1983.)*

Cross References

Application for renewal of judgment, see Code of Civil Procedure § 683.130.
Limitation of actions, see Code of Civil Procedure § 708.230.
Money judgment defined for purposes of this Title, see Code of Civil Procedure § 680.270.
Property defined for purposes of this Title, see Code of Civil Procedure § 680.310.
Writ defined for purposes of this Title, see Code of Civil Procedure § 680.380.

§ 683.030. Period of enforceability; money judgments payable in installments

If a money judgment is payable in installments, the 10-year period of enforceability prescribed by Section 683.020 runs as to each installment from the date the installment becomes due and runs as to costs from the date the costs are added to the judgment pursuant to Section 685.090. *(Added by Stats.1982, c. 1364, p. 5073, § 2, operative July 1, 1983.)*

Cross References

Application for renewal of judgment, see Code of Civil Procedure § 683.130.
Costs defined for purposes of this Title, see Code of Civil Procedure § 680.150.
Money judgment defined for purposes of this Title, see Code of Civil Procedure § 680.270.

§ 683.040. Application more than 10 years after entry or renewal; affidavit

If the judgment creditor applies for a writ for the enforcement of a judgment and the application is made more than 10 years after the date the judgment was entered or renewed, the application shall be accompanied by an affidavit of a person having knowledge of the facts stating facts showing that the issuance of the writ sought in the application is not barred under this chapter. A copy of the affidavit shall be attached to the writ when issued. *(Added by Stats.1982, c. 1364, p. 5073, § 2, operative July 1, 1983.)*

Cross References

Judgment creditor defined for purposes of this Title, see Code of Civil Procedure § 680.240.
Person defined for purposes of this Title, see Code of Civil Procedure § 680.280.
Writ defined for purposes of this Title, see Code of Civil Procedure § 680.380.

§ 683.050. Judgment creditor's right to bring action; limitations

* * * (a) Except as provided in subdivision (b), nothing in this chapter limits any right the judgment creditor may have to bring an action on a judgment, but any such action shall be commenced within the period prescribed by Section 337.5.

(b) Notwithstanding subdivision (a), no action on a judgment may be brought on a judgment identified in subdivision (c) of Section 683.110. *(Added by Stats.1982, c. 1364, p. 5073, § 2, operative July 1, 1983. Amended by Stats.2022, c. 883 (S.B.1200), § 1, eff. Jan. 1, 2023.)*

Cross References

Judgment creditor defined for purposes of this Title, see Code of Civil Procedure § 680.240.

ARTICLE 2. RENEWAL OF JUDGMENTS

Section
683.110. Period of enforceability; extension; renewal of judgment.
683.120. Application for renewal; effect.
683.130. Application for renewal; time for filing.
683.140. Application for renewal; execution; contents.
683.150. Entry of renewal; amount of judgment as renewed.
683.160. Notice; service; filing proof of service.
683.170. Vacation of renewal.
683.180. Judgment liens; effect of renewal.
683.190. Liens other than judgment liens; effect of renewal.
683.200. Enforcement proceedings; continuance.
683.210. Stay of enforcement.
683.220. Application filing date; commencement of period for bringing action.

Cross References

Child, family or spousal support, application for renewal of judgment, see Family Code § 4502.
Destruction of court records, notice, retention periods, see Government Code § 68152.

Enforceability of judgment or order for possession or sale of property, see Family Code § 291.

§ 683.110. Period of enforceability; extension; renewal of judgment

(a) The period of enforceability of a money judgment or a judgment for possession or sale of property may be extended by renewal of the judgment as provided in this article.

(b) A judgment shall not be renewed under this article if the application for renewal is filed within five years from the time the judgment was previously renewed under this article.

(c) Notwithstanding subdivision (a), a judgment creditor may renew the period of enforceability of the following types of money judgments only once pursuant to subdivision (c) of Section 683.120:

(1) A judgment on a claim related to medical expenses if the principal amount of the money judgment remaining unsatisfied against a debtor is under two hundred thousand dollars ($200,000).

(2) A judgment on a claim related to personal debt if the principal amount of the money judgment remaining unsatisfied against a debtor is under fifty thousand dollars ($50,000).

(d) For purposes of this section, the following definitions apply:

(1) "Debtor" means a natural person from whom money is due or owing or alleged to be due or owing.

(2) "Due or owing" does not include debts incurred due to, or obtained by tortious or fraudulent conduct or judgments for unpaid wages, damages, or penalties owed to an employee.

(3) "Personal debt" means money due or owing or alleged to be due or owing from a natural person arising out of a transaction in which the money, property, insurance, or services which are the subject of the transaction are primarily for the debtor's personal, family, or household purposes. *(Added by Stats.1982, c. 1364, p. 5073, § 2, operative July 1, 1983. Amended by Stats.2022, c. 883 (S.B.1200), § 2, eff. Jan. 1, 2023.)*

Cross References

Money judgment defined for purposes of this Title, see Code of Civil Procedure § 680.270.
Property defined for purposes of this Title, see Code of Civil Procedure § 680.310.

Research References

Forms

West's California Code Forms, Civil Procedure § 683.140 Form 1, Enforcement of Judgments—Application for and Renewal of Judgment—Official Form.

§ 683.120. Application for renewal; effect

(a) The judgment creditor may renew a judgment by filing an application for renewal of the judgment with the court in which the judgment was entered.

(b) Except as otherwise provided in this article, the filing of the application renews the judgment in the amount determined under Section 683.150 and extends the period of enforceability of the judgment as renewed for a period of 10 years from the date the application is filed.

(c) Notwithstanding subdivisions (a) and (b), for a judgment identified in subdivision (c) of Section 683.110, a judgment creditor may renew the judgment only once. The filing of the application under this subdivision renews the judgment in the amount determined under Section 683.150 and extends the period of enforceability of the judgment as renewed for a period of five years from the date the application is filed. No application may be filed if the judgment was renewed on or before December 31, 2022.

(d) In the case of a money judgment payable in installments, for the purposes of enforcement and of any later renewal, the amount of the judgment as renewed shall be treated as a lump-sum money judgment entered on the date the application is filed. *(Added by Stats.1982, c. 1364, p. 5074, § 2, operative July 1, 1983. Amended by Stats.2022, c. 883 (S.B.1200), § 3, eff. Jan. 1, 2023.)*

Cross References

Court defined for purposes of this Title, see Code of Civil Procedure § 680.160.
Judgment creditor defined for purposes of this Title, see Code of Civil Procedure § 680.240.
Money judgment defined for purposes of this Title, see Code of Civil Procedure § 680.270.

§ 683.130. Application for renewal; time for filing

(a) In the case of a lump-sum money judgment or a judgment for possession or sale of property, the application for renewal of the judgment may be filed at any time before the expiration of the 10-year period of enforceability provided by Section 683.020 or, if the judgment is a renewed judgment, at any time before the expiration of the 10-year period of enforceability of the renewed judgment provided by Section 683.120.

(b) In the case of a money judgment payable in installments, the application for renewal of the judgment may be filed:

(1) If the judgment has not previously been renewed, at any time as to past due amounts that at the time of filing are not barred by the expiration of the 10-year period of enforceability provided by Sections 683.020 and 683.030.

(2) If the judgment has previously been renewed, within the time specified by subdivision (a) as to the amount of the judgment as previously renewed and, as to any past due amounts that became due and payable after the previous renewal, at any time before the expiration of the 10-year period of enforceability provided by Sections 683.020 and 683.030. *(Added by Stats.1982, c. 1364, p. 5074, § 2, operative July 1, 1983. Amended by Stats.1991, c. 110 (S.B.101), § 14; Stats.1992, c. 163 (A.B.2641), § 30, operative Jan. 1, 1994; Stats.1992, c. 718 (A.B.568), § 4; Stats.1993, c. 219 (A.B.1500), § 66; Stats.1993, c. 876 (S.B.1068), § 8, eff. Oct. 6, 1993; Stats.2000, c. 808 (A.B.1358), § 4, eff. Sept. 28, 2000.)*

Cross References

Money judgment defined for purposes of this Title, see Code of Civil Procedure § 680.270.
Property defined for purposes of this Title, see Code of Civil Procedure § 680.310.

Research References

Forms

West's California Code Forms, Civil Procedure § 683.140 Form 1, Enforcement of Judgments—Application for and Renewal of Judgment—Official Form.

§ 683.140. Application for renewal; execution; contents

The application for renewal of the judgment shall be executed under oath and shall include all of the following:

(a) The title of the court where the judgment is entered and the cause and number of the action.

(b) The date of entry of the judgment and of any renewals of the judgment and where entered in the records of the court.

(c) The name and address of the judgment creditor and the name and last known address of the judgment debtor. However, the judgment creditor shall omit the name of a judgment debtor from the application for a writ of execution if the liability of that judgment debtor has ceased with regard to the judgment, including either of the following occurrences:

(1) The judgment debtor has obtained a discharge of the judgment pursuant to Title 11 of the United States Code and notice thereof has been filed with the court.

(2) The judgment creditor files an acknowledgment of satisfaction of judgment with regard to the judgment debtor pursuant to Chapter 1 (commencing with Section 724.010) of Division 5.

(d) In the case of a money judgment, the information necessary to compute the amount of the judgment as renewed. In the case of a judgment for possession or sale of property, a description of the performance remaining due. *(Added by Stats.1982, c. 1364, p. 5074, § 2, operative July 1, 1983. Amended by Stats.2013, c. 176 (S.B.551), § 1.)*

Cross References

Court defined for purposes of this Title, see Code of Civil Procedure § 680.160.
Judgment creditor defined for purposes of this Title, see Code of Civil Procedure § 680.240.
Judgment debtor defined for purposes of this Title, see Code of Civil Procedure § 680.250.
Money judgment defined for purposes of this Title, see Code of Civil Procedure § 680.270.
Property defined for purposes of this Title, see Code of Civil Procedure § 680.310.

Research References

Forms

West's California Judicial Council Forms EJ-190, Application for and Renewal of Judgment.

§ 683.150. Entry of renewal; amount of judgment as renewed

(a) Upon the filing of the application, the court clerk shall enter the renewal of the judgment in the court records.

(b) The fee for filing an application for renewal of judgment is as provided in subdivision (b) of Section 70626 of the Government Code.

(c) In the case of a money judgment, the entry of renewal shall show the amount of the judgment as renewed. Except as provided in subdivisions (d) and (e), this amount is the amount required to satisfy the judgment on the date of the filing of the application for renewal and includes the fee for the filing of the application for renewal.

(d) In the case of a money judgment payable in installments not previously renewed, the amount of the judgment as renewed is the total of the past due installments, the costs added to the judgment pursuant to Section 685.090, and the accrued interest, which remains unsatisfied and is enforceable on the date of the filing of the application for renewal and includes the fee for the filing of the application for renewal.

(e) In the case of a money judgment payable in installments previously renewed, the amount of the judgment as renewed under the latest renewal is the total of the following which remains unsatisfied and is enforceable on the date of the filing of the application for the latest renewal:

(1) The amount of the judgment as renewed under the previous renewal.

(2) The past due installments that became due and payable after the previous renewal.

(3) The costs that have been added to the judgment pursuant to Section 685.090 after the previous renewal.

(4) The interest that has accrued on the amounts described in paragraphs (1), (2), and (3) since the last renewal.

(5) The fee for filing the application for renewal.

(f) In the case of a judgment for possession or sale of property, the entry of renewal shall describe the performance remaining due. *(Added by Stats.1982, c. 1364, p. 5074, § 2, operative July 1, 1983. Amended by Stats.2005, c. 75 (A.B.145), § 36, eff. July 19, 2005, operative Jan. 1, 2006.)*

Cross References

Costs defined for purposes of this Title, see Code of Civil Procedure § 680.150.
Court defined for purposes of this Title, see Code of Civil Procedure § 680.160.
Fees for miscellaneous services, see Government Code § 70626.
Money judgment defined for purposes of this Title, see Code of Civil Procedure § 680.270.
Organization and government of courts, collection of fees and fines pursuant to this section, deposits, see Government Code § 68085.1.
Property defined for purposes of this Title, see Code of Civil Procedure § 680.310.

§ 683.160. Notice; service; filing proof of service

(a) The judgment creditor shall serve a notice of renewal of the judgment on the judgment debtor. Service shall be made personally or by first-class mail and proof of service shall be filed with the court clerk. The notice shall be in a form prescribed by the Judicial Council and shall inform the judgment debtor that the judgment debtor has 60 days within which to make a motion to vacate or modify the renewal.

(b) Until proof of service is filed pursuant to subdivision (a), no writ may be issued, nor may any enforcement proceedings be commenced to enforce the judgment, except to the extent that the judgment would be enforceable had it not been renewed. *(Added by Stats.1982, c. 1364, p. 5074, § 2, operative July 1, 1983. Amended by Stats.1985, c. 41, § 4; Stats.1988, c. 900, § 5; Stats.2022, c. 883 (S.B.1200), § 4, eff. Jan. 1, 2023.)*

Cross References

Court defined for purposes of this Title, see Code of Civil Procedure § 680.160.
Judgment creditor defined for purposes of this Title, see Code of Civil Procedure § 680.240.
Judgment debtor defined for purposes of this Title, see Code of Civil Procedure § 680.250.
Writ defined for purposes of this Title, see Code of Civil Procedure § 680.380.

Research References

Forms

West's California Judicial Council Forms EJ-195, Notice of Renewal of Judgment.

§ 683.170. Vacation of renewal

(a) The renewal of a judgment pursuant to this article may be vacated on any ground that would be a defense to an action on the judgment, including the ground that the amount of the renewed judgment as entered pursuant to this article is incorrect, and shall be vacated if the application for renewal was filed within five years from the time the judgment was previously renewed under this article.

(b) Not later than 60 days after service of the notice of renewal pursuant to Section 683.160, the judgment debtor may apply by noticed motion under this section for an order of the court vacating the renewal of the judgment. The notice of motion shall be served on the judgment creditor. Service shall be made personally or by mail.

(c) Upon the hearing of the motion, the renewal may be ordered vacated upon any ground provided in subdivision (a), and another and different renewal may be entered, including, but not limited to, the renewal of the judgment in a different amount if the decision of the court is that the judgment creditor is entitled to renewal in a different amount. *(Added by Stats.1982, c. 1364, p. 5075, § 2, operative July 1, 1983. Amended by Stats.2022, c. 883 (S.B.1200), § 5, eff. Jan. 1, 2023.)*

Cross References

Court defined for purposes of this Title, see Code of Civil Procedure § 680.160.
Judgment creditor defined for purposes of this Title, see Code of Civil Procedure § 680.240.

§ 683.170

Judgment debtor defined for purposes of this Title, see Code of Civil Procedure § 680.250.

§ 683.180. Judgment liens; effect of renewal

(a) If a judgment lien on an interest in real property has been created pursuant to a money judgment and the judgment is renewed pursuant to this article, the duration of the judgment lien is extended until 10 years from the date of the filing of the application for renewal if, before the expiration of the judgment lien, a certified copy of the application for renewal is recorded with the county recorder of the county where the real property subject to the judgment lien is located.

(b) A judgment lien on an interest in real property that has been transferred subject to the lien is not extended pursuant to subdivision (a) if the transfer was recorded before the application for renewal was filed unless both of the following requirements are satisfied:

(1) A copy of the application for renewal is personally served on the transferee.

(2) Proof of such service is filed with the court clerk within 90 days after the filing of the application for renewal. *(Added by Stats.1982, c. 1364, p. 5076, § 2, operative July 1, 1983. Amended by Stats.1983, c. 155, § 9.5, eff. June 30, 1983, operative July 1, 1983.)*

Cross References

Court defined for purposes of this Title, see Code of Civil Procedure § 680.160.
Creation and duration of lien, see Code of Civil Procedure § 697.310.
Lien duration, see Code of Civil Procedure § 697.030.
Money judgment defined for purposes of this Title, see Code of Civil Procedure § 680.270.
Property defined for purposes of this Title, see Code of Civil Procedure § 680.310.
Real property defined for purposes of this Title, see Code of Civil Procedure § 680.320.

§ 683.190. Liens other than judgment liens; effect of renewal

If a lien (other than a judgment lien on an interest in real property or an execution lien) has been created by an enforcement procedure pursuant to a judgment and the judgment is renewed pursuant to this article, the duration of the lien is extended, subject to any other limitations on its duration under this title, until 10 years from the date of the filing of the application for renewal of the judgment if, before the expiration of the lien, a certified copy of the application for renewal is served on or filed with the same person and in the same manner as the notice or order that created the lien. *(Added by Stats.1982, c. 1364, p. 5076, § 2, operative July 1, 1983.)*

Cross References

Lien duration, see Code of Civil Procedure § 697.030.
Person defined for purposes of this Title, see Code of Civil Procedure § 680.280.
Property defined for purposes of this Title, see Code of Civil Procedure § 680.310.
Real property defined for purposes of this Title, see Code of Civil Procedure § 680.320.

§ 683.200. Enforcement proceedings; continuance

If a judgment is renewed pursuant to this article, any enforcement proceeding previously commenced pursuant to the judgment or to a writ or order issued pursuant to the judgment that would have ceased pursuant to Section 683.020 had the judgment not been renewed may be continued, subject to any other limitations provided in this title, if, before the expiration of the prior 10-year period of enforceability, a certified copy of the application for renewal of the judgment is filed with the levying officer, receiver, or other officer acting pursuant to such writ or order or, in other cases, is filed in the enforcement proceeding. *(Added by Stats.1982, c. 1364, p. 5076, § 2, operative July 1, 1983.)*

Cross References

Judgment creditor defined for purposes of this Title, see Code of Civil Procedure § 680.240.
Lien duration, see Code of Civil Procedure § 697.030.
Writ defined for purposes of this Title, see Code of Civil Procedure § 680.380.

§ 683.210. Stay of enforcement

A judgment may be renewed notwithstanding any stay of enforcement of the judgment, but the renewal of the judgment does not affect the stay of enforcement. *(Added by Stats.1982, c. 1364, p. 5076, § 2, operative July 1, 1983.)*

Validity

For validity of this section, see In re Lobherr, Bkrtcy. C.D.Cal.2002, 282 B.R. 912.

§ 683.220. Application filing date; commencement of period for bringing action

If a judgment is renewed pursuant to this article, the date of the filing of the application for renewal shall be deemed to be the date that the period for commencing an action on the renewed judgment commences to run under Section 337.5. *(Added by Stats.1982, c. 1364, p. 5076, § 2, operative July 1, 1983.)*

ARTICLE 3. APPLICATION OF CHAPTER

Section
683.310. Judgments under Family Code; application of chapter.
683.320. Money judgments against public entities.

§ 683.310. Judgments under Family Code; application of chapter

Except as otherwise provided in the Family Code, this chapter does not apply to a judgment or order made or entered pursuant to the Family Code. *(Added by Stats.1982, c. 1364, p. 5077, § 2, operative July 1, 1983. Amended by Stats.1991, c. 110 (S.B.101), § 15; Stats.1992, c. 163 (A.B.2641), § 31, operative Jan. 1, 1994; Stats.2000, c. 808 (A.B.1358), § 5, eff. Sept. 28, 2000.)*

§ 683.320. Money judgments against public entities

This chapter does not apply to a money judgment against a public entity that is subject to Section 965.5 or 970.1 of the Government Code. *(Added by Stats.1982, c. 1364, p. 5077, § 2, operative July 1, 1983.)*

Cross References

Money judgment defined for purposes of this Title, see Code of Civil Procedure § 680.270.

CHAPTER 5. INTEREST AND COSTS

Section
685.010. Rate of interest.
685.020. Interest; commencement of accrual.
685.030. Money judgments; satisfaction in full; accrual of interest; writ of execution.
685.040. Costs; attorney's fees.

Cross References

Salary increases, formula, rate of interest on unpaid salary or judicial retiree benefits, see Government Code § 68203.

§ 685.010. Rate of interest

(a) * * * (1) Except as provided in paragraph (2), interest accrues at the rate of 10 percent per annum on the principal amount of a money judgment remaining unsatisfied.

(2)(A) For judgments entered on or after January 1, 2023, or where an application for renewal of judgment is filed on or after January 1, 2023, interest accrues at the rate of 5 percent per annum on the principal amount of a money judgment remaining unsatisfied in the following cases:

(i) The principal amount of a money judgment of under two hundred thousand dollars ($200,000) remaining unsatisfied against a debtor for a claim related to medical expenses.

(ii) The principal amount of a money judgment of under fifty thousand dollars ($50,000) remaining unsatisfied against a debtor for a claim related to personal debt.

(B) The claims specified in subparagraph (A) include, but are not limited to, a claim based on any of the following transactions:

(i) An agreement governing the use of a credit card as defined in subdivision (a) of Section 1747.02 of the Civil Code.

(ii) A conditional sale contract as defined in subdivision (a) of Section 2981 of the Civil Code.

(iii) A deferred deposit transaction as defined in subdivision (a) of Section 23001 of the Financial Code.

(C) For purposes of this paragraph, the following definitions apply:

(i) "Debtor" means a natural person from whom money is due or owing or alleged to be due or owing.

(ii) "Due or owing" does not include debts incurred due to, or obtained by tortious or fraudulent conduct or judgments for unpaid wages, damages, or penalties owed to an employee.

(iii) "Personal debt" means money due or owing or alleged to be due or owing from a natural person arising out of a transaction in which the money, property, insurance, or services which are the subject of the transaction are primarily for the debtor's personal, family, or household purposes.

(b) The Legislature reserves the right to change the rate of interest provided in subdivision (a) at any time * * *, regardless of the date of entry of the judgment or the date any obligation upon which the judgment is based was incurred. A change in the rate of interest may be made applicable only to the interest that accrues after the operative date of the statute that changes the rate. *(Added by Stats.1982, c. 1364, p. 5080, § 2, operative July 1, 1983. Amended by Stats.2022, c. 883 (S.B.1200), § 6, eff. Jan. 1, 2023.)*

Cross References

Additional requirements for medicare supplement contracts, renewal or continuation provisions, see Health and Safety Code § 1358.17.
Amount of lien, see Code of Civil Procedure § 697.350.
Amount to satisfy judgment, see Code of Civil Procedure § 695.210.
Disability and life insurance, return, interest, see Insurance Code § 786.
Emergency physician fair pricing policies, reimbursement to patients of amount overpaid, including interest accrued pursuant to rate set forth in this section, see Health and Safety Code § 127458.
Interest on judgment, see Fish and Game Code § 8069.
Interest on unpaid progress payments, agency procedures on receipt of payment requests, see Public Contract Code § 10261.5.
Long-term care insurance, additional insurer obligations, interest on prepaid premiums, see Insurance Code § 10232.65.
Medicare supplement policies,
  Limit on funds submitted with application, see Insurance Code § 10192.185.
  Policy disclosures, see Insurance Code § 10192.17.
Money judgment defined for purposes of this Title, see Code of Civil Procedure § 680.270.
Offset of delinquent amounts due for services rendered to other public entities, notice, see Government Code § 907.
Patient reimbursement, see Health and Safety Code § 127440.
Priorities of judgment liens on real property, see Code of Civil Procedure § 697.380.
Salary increases, formula, rate of interest on unpaid salary or judicial retiree benefits, see Government Code § 68203.
Timely progress payments, payment requests, see Public Contract Code §§ 10853, 20104.50.

Unemployment compensation benefits, collection of penalty assessments, interest to accrue pursuant to this section, see Unemployment Insurance Code § 1900.

§ 685.020. Interest; commencement of accrual

(a) Except as provided in subdivision (b), interest commences to accrue on a money judgment on the date of entry of the judgment.

(b) Unless the judgment otherwise provides, if a money judgment is payable in installments, interest commences to accrue as to each installment on the date the installment becomes due. *(Added by Stats.1982, c. 1364, p. 5080, § 2, operative July 1, 1983. Amended by Stats.1983, c. 155, § 10, eff. June 30, 1983, operative July 1, 1983.)*

Cross References

Amount to satisfy judgment, see Code of Civil Procedure § 695.210.
Money judgment defined for purposes of this Title, see Code of Civil Procedure § 680.270.
Support order, see Family Code § 155.

§ 685.030. Money judgments; satisfaction in full; accrual of interest; writ of execution

(a) If a money judgment is satisfied in full pursuant to a writ under this title, interest ceases to accrue on the judgment:

(1) If the proceeds of collection are paid in a lump sum, on the date of levy.

(2) If the money judgment is satisfied pursuant to an earnings withholding order, on the date and in the manner provided in Section 706.024 or Section 706.028.

(3) In any other case, on the date the proceeds of sale or collection are actually received by the levying officer.

(b) If a money judgment is satisfied in full other than pursuant to a writ under this title, interest ceases to accrue on the date the judgment is satisfied in full.

(c) If a money judgment is partially satisfied pursuant to a writ under this title or is otherwise partially satisfied, interest ceases to accrue as to the part satisfied on the date the part is satisfied.

(d) For the purposes of subdivisions (b) and (c), the date a money judgment is satisfied in full or in part is the earliest of the following times:

(1) The date satisfaction is actually received by the judgment creditor.

(2) The date satisfaction is tendered to the judgment creditor or deposited in court for the judgment creditor.

(3) The date of any other performance that has the effect of satisfaction.

(e) The clerk of a court may enter in the Register of Actions a writ of execution on a money judgment as returned wholly satisfied when the judgment amount, as specified on the writ, is fully collected and only an interest deficit of no more than ten dollars ($10) exists, due to automation of the continual daily interest accrual calculation. *(Added by Stats.1982, c. 1364, p. 5080, § 2, operative July 1, 1983. Amended by Stats.1991, c. 1090 (A.B.1484), § 4.5; Stats.1992, c. 283 (S.B.1372), § 1, eff. July 21, 1992; Stats.1998, c. 931 (S.B.2139), § 88, eff. Sept. 28, 1998; Stats.2001, c. 812 (A.B.223), § 4.)*

Cross References

Amount to satisfy judgment, see Code of Civil Procedure § 695.210.
Contents of writ of execution, see Code of Civil Procedure § 699.520.
Court defined for purposes of this Title, see Code of Civil Procedure § 680.160.
Judgment creditor defined for purposes of this Title, see Code of Civil Procedure § 680.240.
Money judgment defined for purposes of this Title, see Code of Civil Procedure § 680.270.

§ 685.030

Writ defined for purposes of this Title, see Code of Civil Procedure § 680.380.

§ 685.040. Costs; attorney's fees

The judgment creditor is entitled to the reasonable and necessary costs of enforcing a judgment. Attorney's fees incurred in enforcing a judgment are not included in costs collectible under this title unless otherwise provided by law. Attorney's fees incurred in enforcing a judgment are included as costs collectible under this title if the underlying judgment includes an award of attorney's fees to the judgment creditor pursuant to subparagraph (A) of paragraph (10) of subdivision (a) of Section 1033.5. *(Added by Stats.1982, c. 1364, p. 5081, § 2, operative July 1, 1983. Amended by Stats.1992, c. 1348 (A.B.2616), § 3.)*

Cross References

Costs defined for purposes of this Title, see Code of Civil Procedure § 680.150.
Judgment creditor defined for purposes of this Title, see Code of Civil Procedure § 680.240.

Research References

Forms

Asset Protection: Legal Planning, Strategies and Forms ¶ 2.05, Damages.
West's California Judicial Council Forms MC–012, Memorandum of Costs After Judgment, Acknowledgment of Credit, and Declaration of Accrued Interest.

Division 2

ENFORCEMENT OF MONEY JUDGMENTS

Cross References

Private Student Loan Collections Reform Act, violation of act, penalties, class actions, attorney's fees, exceptions, limitation of actions, see Civil Code § 1788.208.

CHAPTER 1. GENERAL PROVISIONS

ARTICLE 1. PROPERTY SUBJECT TO ENFORCEMENT OF MONEY JUDGMENT

Section
695.010. Property subject to enforcement generally.
695.020. Community property.
695.030. Non-assignable and non-transferable property; interest in trust; cause of action for money or property.
695.035. Lessee's interest in real property; provisions in lease for termination or modification upon involuntary transfer or assignment.
695.040. Exempt property; release.
695.050. Money judgment against public entity.
695.060. License to engage in business, profession or activity.
695.070. Transfer or encumbrance of property subject to lien.

§ 695.010. Property subject to enforcement generally

(a) Except as otherwise provided by law, all property of the judgment debtor is subject to enforcement of a money judgment.

(b) If property of the judgment debtor was attached in the action but was transferred before entry of the money judgment in favor of the judgment creditor, the property is subject to enforcement of the money judgment so long as the attachment lien remains effective. *(Added by Stats.1982, c. 1364, p. 5103, § 2, operative July 1, 1983. Amended by Stats.1984, c. 538, § 17.)*

Cross References

Attachment, see Code of Civil Procedure § 481.010 et seq.

Exemptions from procedures for enforcement of a money judgment, see Code of Civil Procedure § 703.010 et seq.
Homesteads, see Code of Civil Procedure § 704.710 et seq.
Interests in personal property subject to attachment, proceeds, exemptions, fixtures, obligations on accounts receivable or chattel paper, see Code of Civil Procedure § 697.530.
Judgment creditor defined for purposes of this Title, see Code of Civil Procedure § 680.240.
Judgment debtor defined for purposes of this Title, see Code of Civil Procedure § 680.250.
Levy, how made, see Code of Civil Procedure § 699.510 et seq.
Levy of execution on earnings, see Code of Civil Procedure § 706.021.
Lien of officer levying execution, see Code of Civil Procedure § 687.050.
Misdemeanor, unlawful levy as, see Penal Code § 146.
Money judgment defined for purposes of this Title, see Code of Civil Procedure § 680.270.
Notice of execution sale, see Code of Civil Procedure § 701.530 et seq.
Property defined for purposes of this Title, see Code of Civil Procedure § 680.310.
Secured property, see Commercial Code § 9311.

Research References

Forms

Asset Protection: Legal Planning, Strategies and Forms ¶ 9.02, Charging Orders.
Asset Protection: Legal Planning, Strategies and Forms ¶ A.05, Appendix A.05 California (Opt Out State).
3 California Transactions Forms--Business Transactions § 22:14, Landlord's Lien.

§ 695.020. Community property

(a) Community property is subject to enforcement of a money judgment as provided in the Family Code.

(b) Unless the provision or context otherwise requires, if community property that is subject to enforcement of a money judgment is sought to be applied to the satisfaction of a money judgment:

(1) Any provision of this division that applies to the property of the judgment debtor or to obligations owed to the judgment debtor also applies to the community property interest of the spouse of the judgment debtor and to obligations owed to the other spouse that are community property.

(2) Any provision of this division that applies to property in the possession or under the control of the judgment debtor also applies to community property in the possession or under the control of the spouse of the judgment debtor. *(Added by Stats.1982, c. 1364, p. 5103, § 2, operative July 1, 1983. Amended by Stats.1983, c. 155, § 12, eff. June 30, 1983, operative July 1, 1983; Stats.1992, c. 163 (A.B.2641), § 33, operative Jan. 1, 1994.)*

Cross References

Judgment debtor defined for purposes of this Title, see Code of Civil Procedure § 680.250.
Money judgment defined for purposes of this Title, see Code of Civil Procedure § 680.270.
Property defined for purposes of this Title, see Code of Civil Procedure § 680.310.

§ 695.030. Non-assignable and non-transferable property; interest in trust; cause of action for money or property

(a) Except as otherwise provided by statute, property of the judgment debtor that is not assignable or transferable is not subject to enforcement of a money judgment.

(b) The following property is subject to enforcement of a money judgment:

(1) An interest in a trust, to the extent provided by law.

(2) A cause of action for money or property that is the subject of a pending action or special proceeding. *(Added by Stats.1982, c. 1364, p. 5103, § 2, operative July 1, 1983. Amended by Stats.1986, c. 820, § 17, operative July 1, 1987.)*

Cross References

Judgment debtor defined for purposes of this Title, see Code of Civil Procedure § 680.250.
Money judgment defined for purposes of this Title, see Code of Civil Procedure § 680.270.
Property defined for purposes of this Title, see Code of Civil Procedure § 680.310.

§ 695.035. Lessee's interest in real property; provisions in lease for termination or modification upon involuntary transfer or assignment

(a) A lessee's interest in real property may be applied to the satisfaction of a money judgment in any of the following circumstances:

(1) If the lessee has the right voluntarily to sublet the property or assign the interest in the lease.

(2) If the lessee has the right voluntarily to sublet the property or assign the interest in the lease subject to standards or conditions and the purchaser at the execution sale or other assignee agrees to comply with the standards or conditions that would have had to be complied with had the lessee voluntarily sublet the property or assigned the interest in the lease.

(3) If the lessee has the right voluntarily to sublet the property or assign the interest in the lease with the consent of the lessor, in which case the obligation of the lessor to consent to the assignment is subject to the same standard that would apply had the lessee voluntarily sublet the property or assigned the interest in the lease.

(4) In any other case, if the lessor consents in writing.

(b) A provision in a lease for the termination or modification of the lease upon an involuntary transfer or assignment of the lessee's interest is ineffective to the extent that such provision would prevent the application of the lessee's interest to the satisfaction of the money judgment under subdivision (a). *(Added by Stats.1982, c. 1364, p. 5104, § 2, operative July 1, 1983.)*

Cross References

Money judgment defined for purposes of this Title, see Code of Civil Procedure § 680.270.
Property defined for purposes of this Title, see Code of Civil Procedure § 680.310.
Real property defined for purposes of this Title, see Code of Civil Procedure § 680.320.

§ 695.040. Exempt property; release

Property that is not subject to enforcement of a money judgment may not be levied upon or in any other manner applied to the satisfaction of a money judgment. If property that is not subject to enforcement of a money judgment has been levied upon, the property may be released pursuant to the claim of exemption procedure provided in Article 2 (commencing with Section 703.510) of Chapter 4. *(Added by Stats.1982, c. 1364, p. 5104, § 2, operative July 1, 1983.)*

Cross References

Money judgment defined for purposes of this Title, see Code of Civil Procedure § 680.270.
Property defined for purposes of this Title, see Code of Civil Procedure § 680.310.

Research References

Forms

Asset Protection: Legal Planning, Strategies and Forms ¶ 3.07, Avoidable Preference Payments.

Asset Protection: Legal Planning, Strategies and Forms ¶ A.05, Appendix A.05 California (Opt Out State).

§ 695.050. Money judgment against public entity

A money judgment against a public entity is not enforceable under this division if the money judgment is subject to Chapter 1 (commencing with Section 965) of, or Article 1 (commencing with Section 970) of Chapter 2 of, Part 5 of Division 3.6 of Title 1 of the Government Code. *(Added by Stats.1982, c. 1364, p. 5104, § 2, operative July 1, 1983.)*

Cross References

Money judgment defined for purposes of this Title, see Code of Civil Procedure § 680.270.

§ 695.060. License to engage in business, profession or activity

Except as provided in Section 708.630, a license issued by a public entity to engage in any business, profession, or activity is not subject to enforcement of a money judgment. *(Added by Stats.1982, c. 1364, p. 5104, § 2, operative July 1, 1983.)*

Cross References

Money judgment defined for purposes of this Title, see Code of Civil Procedure § 680.270.

Research References

Forms

Asset Protection: Legal Planning, Strategies and Forms ¶ A.05, Appendix A.05 California (Opt Out State).

§ 695.070. Transfer or encumbrance of property subject to lien

(a) Notwithstanding the transfer or encumbrance of property subject to a lien created under this division, if the property remains subject to the lien after the transfer or encumbrance, the money judgment may be enforced against the property in the same manner and to the same extent as if it had not been transferred or encumbered.

(b) If the judgment debtor dies after the transfer of property that remains subject to a lien created under this division, the money judgment may be enforced against the property as provided in subdivision (a). *(Added by Stats.1982, c. 1364, p. 5104, § 2, operative July 1, 1983. Amended by Stats.1989, c. 1416, § 22.)*

Cross References

Judgment debtor defined for purposes of this Title, see Code of Civil Procedure § 680.250.
Money judgment defined for purposes of this Title, see Code of Civil Procedure § 680.270.
Property defined for purposes of this Title, see Code of Civil Procedure § 680.310.

ARTICLE 2. AMOUNT TO SATISFY MONEY JUDGMENT

Section
695.210. Amount required.
695.211. Interest accrual on arrearages; notice; statement of account; required contents.
695.215. Effect of payment on right to appeal.
695.220. Crediting of money received.
695.221. Crediting of money judgment for support.

§ 695.210. Amount required

The amount required to satisfy a money judgment is the total amount of the judgment as entered or renewed with the following additions and subtractions:

(a) The addition of costs added to the judgment pursuant to Section 685.090.

§ 695.210

(b) The addition of interest added to the judgment as it accrues pursuant to Sections 685.010 to 685.030, inclusive.

(c) The subtraction of the amount of any partial satisfactions of the judgment.

(d) The subtraction of the amount of any portion of the judgment that is no longer enforceable. *(Added by Stats.1982, c. 1364, p. 5105, § 2, operative July 1, 1983. Amended by Stats.1992, c. 848 (S.B.1614), § 8, eff. Sept. 22, 1992; Stats.1993, c. 876 (S.B.1068), § 9, eff. Oct. 6, 1993.)*

Cross References

Arrearage or arrearages, see Family Code § 5201.
Costs defined for purposes of this Title, see Code of Civil Procedure § 680.150.
Money judgment defined for purposes of this Title, see Code of Civil Procedure § 680.270.

§ 695.211. Interest accrual on arrearages; notice; statement of account; required contents

(a) Every money judgment or order for child support shall provide notice that interest on arrearages accrues at the legal rate.

(b) The notice provisions required by this section shall be incorporated in the appropriate Judicial Council forms.

(c) Upon implementation of the California Child Support Automation System prescribed in Chapter 4 (commencing with Section 10080) of Part 1 of Division 9 of the Welfare and Institutions Code and certification of the California Child Support Automation System by the United States Department of Health and Human Services, whenever a statement of account is issued by the local child support agency in any child support action, the statement shall include a statement of an amount of current support, arrears, and interest due. *(Added by Stats.1994, c. 959 (A.B.3072), § 1, eff. Sept. 28, 1994. Amended by Stats.2000, c. 808 (A.B.1358), § 10, eff. Sept. 28, 2000.)*

Cross References

Child support defined for purposes of this Title, see Code of Civil Procedure § 680.145.
Department of Health Care Services, generally, see Health and Safety Code § 100100 et seq.
Money judgment defined for purposes of this Title, see Code of Civil Procedure § 680.270.

§ 695.215. Effect of payment on right to appeal

Payment in satisfaction of a money judgment, including payment of a severable portion of the money judgment, interest thereon, and associated costs, does not constitute a waiver of the right to appeal, except to the extent that the payment is the product of compromise or is coupled with an agreement not to appeal. Payment in satisfaction of a severable portion of a money judgment, interest thereon, and associated costs, does not constitute a waiver of the right to appeal other portions of the money judgment. *(Added by Stats.2019, c. 48 (A.B.1361), § 1, eff. Jan. 1, 2020.)*

§ 695.220. Crediting of money received

Money received in satisfaction of a money judgment, except a money judgment for support, is to be credited as follows:

(a) The money is first to be credited against the amounts described in subdivision (b) of Section 685.050 that are collected by the levying officer.

(b) Any remaining money is next to be credited against any fee due the court pursuant to Section 6103.5 or 68511.3 of the Government Code, which are to be remitted to the court by the levying officer.

(c) Any remaining money is next to be credited against the accrued interest that remains unsatisfied.

(d) Any remaining money is to be credited against the principal amount of the judgment remaining unsatisfied. If the judgment is payable in installments, the remaining money is to be credited against the matured installments in the order in which they matured. *(Added by Stats.1982, c. 1364, p. 5105, § 2, operative July 1, 1983. Amended by Stats.1992, c. 848 (S.B.1614), § 9, eff. Sept. 22, 1992; Stats.1993, c. 158 (A.B.392), § 3.2, eff. July 21, 1993; Stats.1993, c. 876 (S.B.1068), § 10, eff. Oct. 6, 1993; Stats.1993, c. 909 (S.B.15), § 1; Stats.1994, c. 146 (A.B.3601), § 25; Stats.1994, c. 75 (A.B.1702), § 1, eff. May 20, 1994.)*

Cross References

Court defined for purposes of this Title, see Code of Civil Procedure § 680.160.
Judgment creditor defined for purposes of this Title, see Code of Civil Procedure § 680.240.
Money judgment defined for purposes of this Title, see Code of Civil Procedure § 680.270.
Principal amount of the judgment defined for purposes of this Title, see Code of Civil Procedure § 680.300.

§ 695.221. Crediting of money judgment for support

Satisfaction of a money judgment for support shall be credited as follows:

(a) The money shall first be credited against the current month's support.

(b) Any remaining money shall next be credited against the principal amount of the judgment remaining unsatisfied. If the judgment is payable in installments, the remaining money shall be credited against the matured installments in the order in which they matured.

(c) Any remaining money shall be credited against the accrued interest that remains unsatisfied.

(d) In cases enforced pursuant to Part D (commencing with Section 651) of Subchapter 4 of Chapter 7 of Title 42 of the United States Code, if a lump-sum payment is collected from a support obligor who has money judgments for support owing to more than one family, effective September 1, 2006, all support collected shall be distributed pursuant to guidelines developed by the Department of Child Support Services.

(e) Support collections received between January 1, 2009, and April 30, 2020, inclusive, shall be distributed by the Department of Child Support Services as follows:

(1) Notwithstanding subdivisions (a), (b), and (c), a collection received as a result of a federal tax refund offset shall first be credited against the principal amount of past due support that has been assigned to the state pursuant to Section 11477 of the Welfare and Institutions Code and federal law and then any interest due on that past due support, prior to the principal amount of any other past due support remaining unsatisfied and then any interest due on that past due support.

(2) The following shall be the order of distribution of child support collections through September 30, 2000, except for federal tax refund offset collections, for child support received for families and children who are former recipients of Aid to Families with Dependent Children (AFDC) program benefits or former recipients of Temporary Assistance for Needy Families (TANF) program benefits:

(A) The money shall first be credited against the current month's support.

(B) Any remaining money shall next be credited against interest that accrued on arrearages owed to the family or children since leaving the AFDC program or the TANF program and then the arrearages.

(C) Any remaining money shall next be credited against interest that accrued on arrearages owed during the time the family or children received benefits under the AFDC program or the TANF program and then the arrearages.

(D) Any remaining money shall next be credited against interest that accrued on arrearages owed to the family or children prior to receiving benefits from the AFDC program or the TANF program and then the arrearages.

(f) Support collections received on or after May 1, 2020, shall be distributed by the Department of Child Support Services in accordance with Section 657(a)(2)(B) of Title 42 of the United States Code, as amended by Section 7301(b)(1) of the federal Deficit Reduction Act of 2005, in such a manner as to distribute all support collections to families first to the maximum extent permitted by federal law. *(Added by Stats.2004, c. 305 (A.B.2669), § 2, operative Jan. 1, 2009. Amended by Stats.2021, c. 85 (A.B.135), § 1, eff. July 16, 2021.)*

Cross References

Allowable liens, see Labor Code § 4903.
Child support defined for purposes of this Title, see Code of Civil Procedure § 680.145.
Money judgment defined for purposes of this Title, see Code of Civil Procedure § 680.270.
Payments received from the federal government under specified federal acts or from specified agencies due to retirement or disability of noncustodial parent, see Family Code § 4504.
Principal amount of the judgment defined for purposes of this Title, see Code of Civil Procedure § 680.300.

CHAPTER 2. LIENS

Cross References

Community care facilities, appointment of receiver to temporarily operate facility, see Health and Safety Code § 1546.2.
Community care facilities, appointment of temporary manager, see Health and Safety Code § 1546.1.
Residential care facilities for the elderly, appointment of receiver to protect residents, see Health and Safety Code § 1569.482.
Residential care facilities for the elderly, appointment of temporary manager to protect residents, see Health and Safety Code § 1569.481.

ARTICLE 1. GENERAL PROVISIONS

Section
697.060. Creation of judgment liens.

§ 697.060. Creation of judgment liens

(a) An abstract or certified copy of a money judgment of a court of the United States that is enforceable in this state may be recorded to create a judgment lien on real property pursuant to Article 2 (commencing with Section 697.310).

(b) A notice of judgment lien based on a money judgment of a court of the United States that is enforceable in this state may be filed to create a judgment lien on personal property pursuant to Article 3 (commencing with Section 697.510). *(Added by Stats.1982, c. 1364, p. 5106, § 2, operative July 1, 1983.)*

Cross References

Court defined for purposes of this Title, see Code of Civil Procedure § 680.160.
Money judgment defined for purposes of this Title, see Code of Civil Procedure § 680.270.
Personal property defined for purposes of this Title, see Code of Civil Procedure § 680.290.
Property defined for purposes of this Title, see Code of Civil Procedure § 680.310.
Real property defined for purposes of this Title, see Code of Civil Procedure § 680.320.

ARTICLE 2. JUDGMENT LIEN ON REAL PROPERTY

Section
697.310. Creation and duration of lien generally.
697.320. Judgment for support payable in installments; judgment against health care provider requiring periodic payments; creation and duration.

§ 697.310. Creation and duration of lien generally

(a) Except as otherwise provided by statute, a judgment lien on real property is created under this section by recording an abstract of a money judgment with the county recorder.

(b) Unless the money judgment is satisfied or the judgment lien is released, subject to Section 683.180 (renewal of judgment), a judgment lien created under this section continues until 10 years from the date of entry of the judgment.

(c) The creation and duration of a judgment lien under a money judgment entered pursuant to Section 117 or 582.5 of this code or Section 16380 of the Vehicle Code or under a similar judgment is governed by this section, notwithstanding that the judgment may be payable in installments. *(Added by Stats.1982, c. 1364, p. 5106, § 2, operative July 1, 1983. Amended by Stats.1998, c. 931 (S.B.2139), § 90, eff. Sept. 28, 1998.)*

Cross References

Creation of judgment liens, see Code of Civil Procedure § 697.060.
Effect on liens of stay of enforcement of judgment, see Code of Civil Procedure § 697.040.
Money judgment defined for purposes of this Title, see Code of Civil Procedure § 680.270.
Property defined for purposes of this Title, see Code of Civil Procedure § 680.310.
Public utilities regulation, master meters in residential service, termination, damages, see Public Utilities Code §§ 777, 777.1, 10009.1, 12822.1, 16481.1.
Real property defined for purposes of this Title, see Code of Civil Procedure § 680.320.

§ 697.320. Judgment for support payable in installments; judgment against health care provider requiring periodic payments; creation and duration

(a) A judgment lien on real property is created under this section by recording an abstract, a notice of support judgment, an interstate lien form promulgated by the federal Secretary of Health and Human Services pursuant to Section 652(a)(11) of Title 42 of the United States Code, or a certified copy of either of the following money judgments with the county recorder:

(1) A judgment for child, family, or spousal support payable in installments.

(2) A judgment entered pursuant to Section 667.7 (judgment against health care provider requiring periodic payments).

(b) Unless the money judgment is satisfied or the judgment lien is released, a judgment lien created under paragraph (1) of subdivision (a) or by recording an interstate lien form, as described in subdivision (a), continues during the period the judgment remains enforceable. Unless the money judgment is satisfied or the judgment lien is released, a judgment lien created under paragraph (2) of subdivision (a) continues for a period of 10 years from the date of its creation. The duration of a judgment lien created under paragraph (2) of subdivision (a) may be extended any number of times by recording, during the time the judgment lien is in existence, a certified copy of the judgment in the manner provided in this section for the initial recording; this rerecording has the effect of extending the duration of the judgment lien created under paragraph (2) of subdivision (a) until 10 years from the date of the rerecording. *(Added by Stats.1982, c. 1364, p. 5107, § 2, operative July 1, 1983. Amended by Stats.1986, c. 946, § 2; Stats.1992, c. 163 (A.B.2641), § 34, operative Jan. 1, 1994; Stats.1993, c. 876 (S.B.1068), § 12, eff. Oct. 6, 1993; Stats.1997, c. 599 (A.B.573), § 3; Stats.2002, c. 927 (A.B.3032), § 1.5.)*

§ 697.320

Cross References

Abstracts and copies of judgments, satisfactions of judgment, see Government Code § 27248.

Enforcement of obligation pursuant to Title IV-D of the Social Security Act, see Family Code § 4506.2.

Lien for child support against real property, digitized or digital electronic record, see Family Code § 17523.5.

Money judgment defined for purposes of this Title, see Code of Civil Procedure § 680.270.

Property defined for purposes of this Title, see Code of Civil Procedure § 680.310.

Real property defined for purposes of this Title, see Code of Civil Procedure § 680.320.

Spousal support defined for purposes of this Title, see Code of Civil Procedure § 680.365.

Research References

Forms

West's California Judicial Council Forms FL–480, Abstract of Support Judgment.

CHAPTER 4. EXEMPTIONS

Explanatory Note

For a list of the amounts of exemptions as adjusted by the Judicial Council and required by Code of Civil Procedure § 703.150, which authorizes the Judicial Council to publish cost-of-living adjustments every three years, see the Judicial Council Form reproduced under Code of Civil Procedure § 703.150.

Cross References

Exemptions from levy,
  Adjustment for enforcing collection of debts to reflect changes in consumer price index, see Revenue and Taxation Code § 60633.
  Adjustments, see Revenue and Taxation Code §§ 7095, 55334.

Exemptions from levy for collection of debts under personal income or bank and corporation tax law, see Revenue and Taxation Code § 21017.

Release of levy or notice to withhold,
  Expense of sale exceeds liability, see Revenue and Taxation Code § 60632.
  Sale of seized property, see Revenue and Taxation Code § 7094.

Release of levy or notice to withhold on property, sale of seized property, see Revenue and Taxation Code § 55333.

Release of levy under franchise and income tax laws, sale of seized property only after notice of exemptions, see Revenue and Taxation Code § 21016.

ARTICLE 1. GENERAL PROVISIONS

Section

- 703.010. Application of exemptions.
- 703.020. Persons who may claim exemptions.
- 703.030. Claiming exemptions; time and manner; waiver; relief for failure to claim.
- 703.040. Prior waivers void.
- 703.050. Determination; judgments affected; levy of execution.
- 703.060. Power of state to repeal, alter, or add to exemptions.
- 703.070. Judgment for child, family, or spousal support.
- 703.080. Tracing exempt funds.
- 703.090. Levy on exempt property; recovery of collection costs.
- 703.100. Time for determination; circumstances considered.
- 703.110. Married judgment debtor; determination and application of exemption.
- 703.115. Exemption based upon need; consideration of property.
- 703.130. Federal bankruptcy exemptions; not authorized.
- 703.140. Federal bankruptcy; applicable exemptions.
- 703.150. Adjustment of exemption amounts; three-year intervals; increases; determination by Judicial

Section

  Council; publication of list; application of adjustments.

Cross References

Guardianship and conservatorship, support of spouse who has conservator, application of certain moneys and benefits to extent they are subject to wage assignment under this chapter, see Probate Code § 3088.

Notice of levy, see Code of Civil Procedure § 699.540.

§ 703.010. Application of exemptions

Except as otherwise provided by statute:

(a) The exemptions provided by this chapter or by any other statute apply to all procedures for enforcement of a money judgment.

(b) The exemptions provided by this chapter or by any other statute do not apply if the judgment to be enforced is for the foreclosure of a mortgage, deed of trust, or other lien or encumbrance on the property other than a lien created pursuant to this division or pursuant to Title 6.5 (commencing with Section 481.010) (attachment). (Added by Stats.1982, c. 1364, p. 5146, § 2, operative July 1, 1983.)

Cross References

Employee's bonds not subject to enforcement of a money judgment except in specified actions, see Labor Code § 404.

Foreclosure of liens, see Civil Code § 3052.

Foreclosure of mortgage,
  Action for, see Code of Civil Procedure § 726.
  Place of trial, see Code of Civil Procedure § 392.

Franchises, enforcement against, see Code of Civil Procedure § 708.910 et seq.

Money judgment defined for purposes of this Title, see Code of Civil Procedure § 680.270.

Preferred labor claims, see Code of Civil Procedure § 1204 et seq.

Property defined for purposes of this Title, see Code of Civil Procedure § 680.310.

Tools or implements used in commercial activity, see Code of Civil Procedure § 704.060.

Research References

Forms

Asset Protection: Legal Planning, Strategies and Forms ¶ A.05, Appendix A.05 California (Opt Out State).

3 California Transactions Forms--Business Transactions § 22:13, Innkeeper's Lien.

3 California Transactions Forms--Business Transactions § 22:14, Landlord's Lien.

4 California Transactions Forms--Business Transactions § 26:82, Exempt Deposits.

4 California Transactions Forms--Business Transactions § 26:83, Statutory Notice in Consumer Transactions.

4 California Transactions Forms--Business Transactions § 26:85, Notice of Setoff; Commercial Transaction.

§ 703.020. Persons who may claim exemptions

(a) The exemptions provided by this chapter apply only to property of a natural person.

(b) The exemptions provided in this chapter may be claimed by any of the following persons:

(1) In all cases, by the judgment debtor or a person acting on behalf of the judgment debtor.

(2) In the case of community property, by the spouse of the judgment debtor, whether or not the spouse is also a judgment debtor under the judgment.

(3) In the case of community property, by the domestic partner of the judgment debtor, as defined in Section 297 of the Family Code, whether or not the domestic partner is also a judgment debtor under the judgment. (Added by Stats.1982, c. 1364, p. 5146, § 2, operative July 1, 1983. Amended by Stats.2014, c. 415 (A.B.1945), § 1, eff. Jan. 1, 2015.)

Cross References

Judgment debtor defined for purposes of this Title, see Code of Civil Procedure § 680.250.

Person defined for purposes of this Title, see Code of Civil Procedure § 680.280.

Property defined for purposes of this Title, see Code of Civil Procedure § 680.310.

Research References

Forms

Asset Protection: Legal Planning, Strategies and Forms ¶ A.05, Appendix A.05 California (Opt Out State).

§ 703.030. Claiming exemptions; time and manner; waiver; relief for failure to claim

(a) An exemption for property that is described in this chapter or in any other statute as exempt may be claimed within the time and in the manner prescribed in the applicable enforcement procedure. If the exemption is not so claimed, the exemption is waived and the property is subject to enforcement of a money judgment.

(b) Except as otherwise specifically provided by statute, property that is described in this chapter or in any other statute as exempt without making a claim is not subject to any procedure for enforcement of a money judgment.

(c) Nothing in this section limits the authority of the court pursuant to Section 473 to relieve a person upon such terms as may be just from failure to claim an exemption within the time and in the manner prescribed in the applicable enforcement procedure. *(Added by Stats.1982, c. 1364, p. 5147, § 2, operative July 1, 1983.)*

Cross References

Court defined for purposes of this Title, see Code of Civil Procedure § 680.160.

Money judgment defined for purposes of this Title, see Code of Civil Procedure § 680.270.

Person defined for purposes of this Title, see Code of Civil Procedure § 680.280.

Property defined for purposes of this Title, see Code of Civil Procedure § 680.310.

§ 703.040. Prior waivers void

A purported contractual or other prior waiver of the exemptions provided by this chapter or by any other statute, other than a waiver by failure to claim an exemption required to be claimed or otherwise made at the time enforcement is sought, is against public policy and void. *(Added by Stats.1982, c. 1364, p. 5147, § 2, operative July 1, 1983.)*

§ 703.050. Determination; judgments affected; levy of execution

(a) The determination whether property is exempt or the amount of an exemption shall be made by application of the exemption statutes in effect (1) at the time the judgment creditor's lien on the property was created or (2) if the judgment creditor's lien on the property is the latest in a series of overlapping liens created when an earlier lien on the property in favor of the judgment creditor was in effect, at the time the earliest lien in the series of overlapping liens was created.

(b) This section applies to all judgments, whether based upon tort, contract, or other legal theory or cause of action that arose before or after the operative date of this section, and whether the judgment was entered before or after the operative date of this section.

(c) Notwithstanding subdivision (a), in the case of a levy of execution, the procedures to be followed in levying upon, selling, or releasing property, claiming, processing, opposing, and determining exemptions, and paying exemption proceeds, shall be governed by the law in effect at the time the levy of execution is made on the property. *(Added by Stats.1982, c. 1364, p. 5147, § 2, operative July 1, 1983.)*

Cross References

Judgment creditor defined for purposes of this Title, see Code of Civil Procedure § 680.240.

Property defined for purposes of this Title, see Code of Civil Procedure § 680.310.

§ 703.060. Power of state to repeal, alter, or add to exemptions

(a) The Legislature finds and declares that generally persons who enter into contracts do not do so in reliance on an assumption that the exemptions in effect at the time of the contract will govern enforcement of any judgment based on the contract, that liens imposed on property are imposed not as a matter of right but as a matter of privilege granted by statute for purposes of priority, that no vested rights with respect to exemptions are created by the making of a contract or imposition of a lien, that application of exemptions and exemption procedures in effect at the time of enforcement of a judgment is essential to the proper balance between the rights of judgment debtors and judgment creditors and has a minimal effect on the economic stability essential for the maintenance of private and public faith in commercial matters, and that it is the policy of the state to treat all judgment debtors equally with respect to exemptions and exemption procedures in effect at the time of enforcement of a money judgment. To this end, the Legislature reserves the right to repeal, alter, or add to the exemptions and the procedures therefor at any time and intends, unless otherwise provided by statute, that any repeals, alterations, or additions apply upon their operative date to enforcement of all money judgments, whether based upon tort, contract, or other legal theory or cause of action that arose before or after the operative date of the repeals, alterations, or additions, whether the judgment was entered before or after the operative date of the repeals, alterations, or additions.

(b) All contracts shall be deemed to have been made and all liens on property shall be deemed to have been created in recognition of the power of the state to repeal, alter, and add to statutes providing for liens and exemptions from the enforcement of money judgments. *(Added by Stats.1982, c. 1364, p. 5147, § 2, operative July 1, 1983.)*

Cross References

Judgment creditor defined for purposes of this Title, see Code of Civil Procedure § 680.240.

Judgment debtor defined for purposes of this Title, see Code of Civil Procedure § 680.250.

Money judgment defined for purposes of this Title, see Code of Civil Procedure § 680.270.

Person defined for purposes of this Title, see Code of Civil Procedure § 680.280.

Property defined for purposes of this Title, see Code of Civil Procedure § 680.310.

§ 703.070. Judgment for child, family, or spousal support

Except as otherwise provided by statute:

(a) The exemptions provided by this chapter or by any other statute apply to a judgment for child, family, or spousal support.

(b) If property is exempt without making a claim, the property is not subject to being applied to the satisfaction of a judgment for child, family, or spousal support.

(c) Except as provided in subdivision (b), if property sought to be applied to the satisfaction of a judgment for child, family, or spousal support is shown to be exempt under subdivision (a) in appropriate proceedings, the court shall, upon noticed motion of the judgment creditor, determine the extent to which the exempt property nevertheless shall be applied to the satisfaction of the judgment. In making this determination, the court shall take into account the needs of the judgment creditor, the needs of the judgment debtor and all the persons the judgment debtor is required to support, and all other relevant circumstances. The court shall effectuate its determination by an order specifying the extent to which the otherwise exempt property is to be applied to the satisfaction of the

§ 703.070

judgment. *(Added by Stats.1982, c. 1364, p. 5148, § 2, operative, July 1, 1983. Amended by Stats.1992, c. 163 (A.B.2641), § 37, operative Jan. 1, 1994.)*

Cross References

Court defined for purposes of this Title, see Code of Civil Procedure § 680.160.
Designation of assets subject to order, see Family Code § 4614.
Judgment creditor defined for purposes of this Title, see Code of Civil Procedure § 680.240.
Judgment debtor defined for purposes of this Title, see Code of Civil Procedure § 680.250.
Person defined for purposes of this Title, see Code of Civil Procedure § 680.280.
Property defined for purposes of this Title, see Code of Civil Procedure § 680.310.
Public Employees' Retirement System, withholding overdue support obligations, see Family Code § 17528.
Spousal support defined for purposes of this Title, see Code of Civil Procedure § 680.365.

§ 703.080. Tracing exempt funds

(a) Subject to any limitation provided in the particular exemption, a fund that is exempt remains exempt to the extent that it can be traced into deposit accounts or in the form of cash or its equivalent.

(b) The exemption claimant has the burden of tracing an exempt fund.

(c) The tracing of exempt funds in a deposit account shall be by application of the lowest intermediate balance principle unless the exemption claimant or the judgment creditor shows that some other method of tracing would better serve the interests of justice and equity under the circumstances of the case. *(Added by Stats.1982, c. 1364, p. 5148, § 2, operative July 1, 1983.)*

Cross References

Deposit account defined for purposes of this Title, see Code of Civil Procedure § 680.170.
Equity defined for purposes of this Title, see Code of Civil Procedure § 680.190.
Judgment creditor defined for purposes of this Title, see Code of Civil Procedure § 680.240.

Research References
Forms

Asset Protection: Legal Planning, Strategies and Forms ¶ 12.03, Exempt Property.
Asset Protection: Legal Planning, Strategies and Forms ¶ 13.03, Asset Protection Aspects of Retirement Plans.
Asset Protection: Legal Planning, Strategies and Forms ¶ A.05, Appendix A.05 California (Opt Out State).

§ 703.090. Levy on exempt property; recovery of collection costs

If a judgment creditor has failed to oppose a claim of exemption within the time allowed by Section 703.550 or if property has been determined by a court to be exempt, and the judgment creditor thereafter levies upon or otherwise seeks to apply the property toward the satisfaction of the same money judgment, the judgment creditor is not entitled to recover the subsequent costs of collection unless the property is applied to satisfaction of the judgment. *(Added by Stats.1982, c. 1364, p. 5149, § 2, operative July 1, 1983.)*

Cross References

Costs defined for purposes of this Title, see Code of Civil Procedure § 680.150.
Court defined for purposes of this Title, see Code of Civil Procedure § 680.160.
Judgment creditor defined for purposes of this Title, see Code of Civil Procedure § 680.240.
Money judgment defined for purposes of this Title, see Code of Civil Procedure § 680.270.
Property defined for purposes of this Title, see Code of Civil Procedure § 680.310.

§ 703.100. Time for determination; circumstances considered

(a) Subject to subdivision (b), the determination whether property is exempt shall be made under the circumstances existing at the earliest of the following times:

(1) The time of levy on the property.

(2) The time of the commencement of court proceedings for the application of the property to the satisfaction of the money judgment.

(3) The time a lien is created under Title 6.5 (commencing with Section 481.010) (attachment) or under this title.

(b) The court, in its discretion, may take into consideration any of the following changes that have occurred between the time of levy or commencement of enforcement proceedings or creation of the lien and the time of the hearing:

(1) A change in the use of the property if the exemption is based upon the use of property and if the property was used for the exempt purpose at the time of the levy or the commencement of enforcement proceedings or the creation of the lien but is used for a nonexempt purpose at the time of the hearing.

(2) A change in the value of the property if the exemption is based upon the value of property.

(3) A change in the financial circumstances of the judgment debtor and spouse and dependents of the judgment debtor if the exemption is based upon their needs. *(Added by Stats.1982, c. 1364, p. 5149, § 2, operative July 1, 1983.)*

Cross References

Court defined for purposes of this Title, see Code of Civil Procedure § 680.160.
Judgment debtor defined for purposes of this Title, see Code of Civil Procedure § 680.250.
Money judgment defined for purposes of this Title, see Code of Civil Procedure § 680.270.
Property defined for purposes of this Title, see Code of Civil Procedure § 680.310.

Research References
Forms

Asset Protection: Legal Planning, Strategies and Forms ¶ A.05, Appendix A.05 California (Opt Out State).

§ 703.110. Married judgment debtor; determination and application of exemption

If the judgment debtor is married:

(a) The exemptions provided by this chapter or by any other statute apply to all property that is subject to enforcement of a money judgment, including the interest of the spouse of the judgment debtor in community property. The fact that one or both spouses are judgment debtors under the judgment or that property sought to be applied to the satisfaction of the judgment is separate or community does not increase or reduce the number or amount of the exemptions. Where the property exempt under a particular exemption is limited to a specified maximum dollar amount, unless the exemption provision specifically provides otherwise, the two spouses together are entitled to one exemption limited to the specified maximum dollar amount, whether one or both of the spouses are judgment debtors under the judgment and whether the property sought to be applied to the satisfaction of the judgment is separate or community.

(b) If an exemption is required by statute to be applied first to property not before the court and then to property before the court, the application of the exemption to property not before the court shall be made to the community property and separate property of both spouses, whether or not such property is subject to enforcement of the money judgment.

(c) If the same exemption is claimed by the judgment debtor and the spouse of the judgment debtor for different property, and the property claimed by one spouse, but not both, is exempt, the exemption shall be applied as the spouses agree. If the spouses are unable to agree, the exemption shall be applied as directed by the court in its discretion. *(Added by Stats.1982, c. 1364, p. 5149, § 2, operative July 1, 1983. Amended by Stats.1983, c. 155, § 14.7, eff. June 30, 1983, operative July 1, 1983.)*

Cross References

Court defined for purposes of this Title, see Code of Civil Procedure § 680.160.

Judgment debtor defined for purposes of this Title, see Code of Civil Procedure § 680.250.

Money judgment defined for purposes of this Title, see Code of Civil Procedure § 680.270.

Property defined for purposes of this Title, see Code of Civil Procedure § 680.310.

Research References

Forms

Asset Protection: Legal Planning, Strategies and Forms ¶ A.05, Appendix A.05 California (Opt Out State).

§ 703.115. Exemption based upon need; consideration of property

In determining an exemption based upon the needs of the judgment debtor and the spouse and dependents of the judgment debtor or an exemption based upon the needs of the judgment debtor and the family of the judgment debtor, the court shall take into account all property of the judgment debtor and, to the extent the judgment debtor has a spouse and dependents or family, all property of such spouse and dependents or family, including community property and separate property of the spouse, whether or not such property is subject to enforcement of the money judgment. *(Added by Stats.1983, c. 155, § 15, eff. June 30, 1983, operative July 1, 1983.)*

Cross References

Court defined for purposes of this Title, see Code of Civil Procedure § 680.160.

Judgment debtor defined for purposes of this Title, see Code of Civil Procedure § 680.250.

Money judgment defined for purposes of this Title, see Code of Civil Procedure § 680.270.

Property defined for purposes of this Title, see Code of Civil Procedure § 680.310.

Research References

Forms

Asset Protection: Legal Planning, Strategies and Forms ¶ A.05, Appendix A.05 California (Opt Out State).

§ 703.130. Federal bankruptcy exemptions; not authorized

Pursuant to the authority of paragraph (2) of subsection (b) of Section 522 of Title 11 of the United States Code, the exemptions set forth in subsection (d) of Section 522 of Title 11 of the United States Code (Bankruptcy) are not authorized in this state. *(Added by Stats.1984, c. 218, § 1.5. Amended by Stats.2009, c. 500 (A.B.1059), § 14.)*

Research References

Forms

Asset Protection: Legal Planning, Strategies and Forms ¶ A.05, Appendix A.05 California (Opt Out State).

§ 703.140. Federal bankruptcy; applicable exemptions

(a) In a case under Title 11 of the United States Code, all of the exemptions provided by this chapter, including the homestead exemption, other than the provisions of subdivision (b) are applicable regardless of whether there is a money judgment against the debtor or whether a money judgment is being enforced by execution sale or any other procedure, but the exemptions provided by subdivision (b) may be elected in lieu of all other exemptions provided by this chapter, as follows:

(1) If spouses are joined in the petition, they jointly may elect to utilize the applicable exemption provisions of this chapter other than the provisions of subdivision (b), or to utilize the applicable exemptions set forth in subdivision (b), but not both.

(2)(A) If the petition is filed individually, and not jointly, for a spouse, the exemptions provided by this chapter other than provisions of subdivision (b) are applicable, except that, if both of the spouses effectively waive in writing the right to claim, during the period the case commenced by filing the petition is pending, the exemptions provided by the applicable exemption provisions of this chapter, other than subdivision (b), in any case commenced by filing a petition for either of them under Title 11 of the United States Code, then they may elect to instead utilize the applicable exemptions set forth in subdivision (b).

(B) Notwithstanding subparagraph (A), a waiver is not required from a debtor who is living separate and apart from their spouse as of the date the petition commencing the case under Title 11 of the United States Code is filed, unless, on the petition date, the debtor and the debtor's spouse shared an ownership interest in property that could be exempted as a homestead under Article 4 of this chapter.

(3) If the petition is filed for an unmarried person, that person may elect to utilize the applicable exemption provisions of this chapter other than subdivision (b), or to utilize the applicable exemptions set forth in subdivision (b), but not both.

(b) The following exemptions may be elected as provided in subdivision (a):

(1) The debtor's aggregate interest, not to exceed twenty-nine thousand two hundred seventy-five dollars ($29,275) in value, in real property or personal property that the debtor or a dependent of the debtor uses as a residence, in a cooperative that owns property that the debtor or a dependent of the debtor uses as a residence.

(2) The debtor's interest, not to exceed seven thousand five hundred * * * dollars ($7,500) in value, in one or more motor vehicles.

(3) The debtor's interest, not to exceed seven hundred twenty-five dollars ($725) in value in any particular item, in household furnishings, household goods, wearing apparel, appliances, books, animals, crops, or musical instruments, that are held primarily for the personal, family, or household use of the debtor or a dependent of the debtor.

(4) The debtor's aggregate interest, not to exceed one thousand seven hundred fifty dollars ($1,750) in value, in jewelry held primarily for the personal, family, or household use of the debtor or a dependent of the debtor.

(5) The debtor's aggregate interest, not to exceed one thousand five hundred fifty dollars ($1,550) in value, plus any unused amount of the exemption provided under paragraph (1), in any property.

(6) The debtor's aggregate interest, not to exceed eight thousand seven hundred twenty-five dollars ($8,725) in value, in any implements, professional books, or tools of the trade of the debtor or the trade of a dependent of the debtor.

(7) Any unmatured life insurance contract owned by the debtor, other than a credit life insurance contract.

(8) The debtor's aggregate interest, not to exceed fifteen thousand six hundred fifty dollars ($15,650) in value, in any accrued dividend or interest under, or loan value of, any unmatured life insurance contract owned by the debtor under which the insured is the debtor or an individual of whom the debtor is a dependent.

(9) Professionally prescribed health aids for the debtor, the debtor's spouse, or a dependent of the debtor, including vehicles

§ 703.140

converted for use by the debtor, the debtor's spouse, or a dependent of the debtor, who has a disability. Conversion of a vehicle for use by a person who has a disability includes altering the interior, installing steering, a wheelchair lift, or motorized steps, or modifying the operation of the vehicle.

(10) The debtor's right to receive any of the following:

(A) A social security benefit, unemployment compensation, or a local public assistance benefit.

(B) A veterans' benefit.

(C) A disability, illness, or unemployment benefit.

(D) Alimony, support, or separate maintenance, to the extent reasonably necessary for the support of the debtor and any dependent of the debtor.

(E) A payment under a stock bonus, pension, profit-sharing, annuity, or similar plan or contract on account of illness, disability, death, age, or length of service, to the extent reasonably necessary for the support of the debtor and any dependent of the debtor, unless all of the following apply:

(i) That plan or contract was established by or under the auspices of an insider that employed the debtor at the time the debtor's rights under the plan or contract arose.

(ii) The payment is on account of age or length of service.

(iii) That plan or contract does not qualify under Section 401(a), 403(a), 403(b), 408, or 408A of the Internal Revenue Code of 1986.[1]

(F) The aggregate interest, not to exceed seven thousand five hundred dollars ($7,500), in vacation credits or accrued, or unused, vacation pay, sick leave, family leave, or wages, as defined in Section 200 of the Labor Code.

(11) The debtor's right to receive, or property that is traceable to, any of the following:

(A) An award under a crime victim's reparation law.

(B) A payment under a settlement agreement arising out of or regarding the debtor's employment, to the extent reasonably necessary for the support of the debtor, the debtor's spouse, or a dependent of the debtor.

(C) A payment on account of the wrongful death of an individual of whom the debtor was a dependent, to the extent reasonably necessary for the support of the debtor and any dependent of the debtor.

(D) A payment under a life insurance contract that insured the life of an individual of whom the debtor was a spouse or dependent on the date of that individual's death, to the extent reasonably necessary for the support of the debtor and any dependent of the debtor.

(E) A payment, not to exceed twenty-nine thousand two hundred seventy-five dollars ($29,275) on account of personal bodily injury of the debtor, the debtor's spouse, or an individual of whom the debtor is a dependent.

(F) A payment in compensation of loss of future earnings of the debtor or an individual of whom the debtor is or was a spouse or dependent, to the extent reasonably necessary for the support of the debtor and * * * the debtor's spouse or a dependent of the debtor.

(12) Money held in an account owned by the judgment debtor and established pursuant to the Golden State Scholarshare Trust Act (Article 19 (commencing with Section 69980) of Chapter 2 of Part 42 of Division 5 of Title 3 of the Education Code), subject to the following limits:

(A) The amount exempted for contributions to an account during the 365-day period prior to the date of filing of the debtor's petition for bankruptcy, in the aggregate during this period, shall not exceed the amount of the annual gift tax exclusion under Section 2503(b) of the Internal Revenue Code of 1986, as amended, in effect at the time of the * * * filing of the debtor's petition for bankruptcy.

(B) The amount exempted for contributions to an account during the period commencing 730 days prior to and ending 366 days prior to the date of filing of the debtor's petition for bankruptcy, in the aggregate during this period, shall not exceed the amount of the annual gift tax exclusion under Section 2503(b) of the Internal Revenue Code of 1986, as amended, in effect at the time of the * * * filing of the debtor's petition for bankruptcy.

(C) For the purposes of this paragraph, "account" includes all accounts having the same beneficiary.

(D) This paragraph is not subject to the requirements of Section 703.150.

(c) In a case under Title 11 of the United States Code, the value of the property claimed as exempt and the debtor's exemptions provided by this chapter with respect to such property shall be determined as of the date the bankruptcy petition is filed. In a case where the debtor's equity in a residence is less than or equal to the amount of the debtor's allowed homestead exemption as of the date the bankruptcy petition is filed, any appreciation in the value of the debtor's interest in the property during the pendency of the case is exempt. (Added by Stats.1984, c. 218, § 2. Amended by Stats.1993, c. 1111 (S.B.651), § 1, eff. Oct. 11, 1993; Stats.1995, c. 196 (S.B.832), § 1, eff. July 31, 1995; Stats.1999, c. 98 (S.B.469), § 1; Stats.2000, c. 135 (A.B.2539), § 15; Stats.2001, c. 42 (A.B.1704), § 1; Stats.2003, c. 379 (A.B.182), § 3; Stats.2012, c. 678 (A.B.929), § 1; Stats.2016, c. 50 (S.B.1005), § 16, eff. Jan. 1, 2017; Stats.2020, c. 81 (S.B.898), § 1, eff. Jan. 1, 2021; Stats.2021, c. 124 (A.B.938), § 10, eff. Jan. 1, 2022; Stats.2022, c. 25 (S.B.956), § 1, eff. Jan. 1, 2023; Stats.2022, c. 716 (S.B.1099), § 2.5, eff. Jan. 1, 2023.)

[1] Internal Revenue Code sections are in Title 26 of the U.S.C.A.

Explanatory Note

For a list of the amounts of exemptions as adjusted by the Judicial Council and required by Code of Civil Procedure § 703.150, which authorizes the Judicial Council to publish cost-of-living adjustments every three years, see the Judicial Council Form reproduced under Code of Civil Procedure § 703.150.

Cross References

Judgment defined for purposes of this Title, see Code of Civil Procedure § 680.230.

Money judgment defined for purposes of this Title, see Code of Civil Procedure § 680.270.

Person defined for purposes of this Title, see Code of Civil Procedure § 680.280.

Personal property defined for purposes of this Title, see Code of Civil Procedure § 680.290.

Property defined for purposes of this Title, see Code of Civil Procedure § 680.310.

Real property defined for purposes of this Title, see Code of Civil Procedure § 680.320.

Security defined for purposes of this Title, see Code of Civil Procedure § 680.345.

Research References

Forms

Asset Protection: Legal Planning, Strategies and Forms ¶ 12.03, Exempt Property.

Asset Protection: Legal Planning, Strategies and Forms ¶ 13.03, Asset Protection Aspects of Retirement Plans.

Asset Protection: Legal Planning, Strategies and Forms ¶ A.05, Appendix A.05 California (Opt Out State).

West's California Judicial Council Forms EJ–156, Current Dollar Amounts of Exemptions from Enforcement of Judgments.

§ 703.150. Adjustment of exemption amounts; three-year intervals; increases; determination by Judicial Council; publication of list; application of adjustments

(a) On April 1, 2004, and at each three-year interval ending on April 1 thereafter, the dollar amounts of exemptions provided in subdivision (b) of Section 703.140 in effect immediately before that date shall be adjusted as provided in subdivision (e).

(b) On April 1, 2007, and at each three-year interval ending on April 1 thereafter, the dollar amounts of exemptions provided in Article 3 (commencing with Section 704.010) in effect immediately before that date shall be adjusted as provided in subdivision (e).

(c) On April 1, 2022, and at each three-year interval ending on April 1 thereafter, the dollar amount set forth in paragraph (7) of subdivision (b) of Section 699.730 in effect immediately before that date shall be adjusted as provided in subdivision (e).

(d) On April 1, 2013, and at each three-year interval ending on April 1 thereafter, the Judicial Council shall submit to the Legislature the amount by which the dollar amounts of exemptions provided in subdivision (a) of Section 704.730 in effect immediately before that date may be increased as provided in subdivision (e). Those increases shall not take effect unless they are approved by the Legislature.

(e) The Judicial Council shall determine the amount of the adjustment based on the change in the annual California Consumer Price Index for All Urban Consumers, published by the Department of Industrial Relations, Division of Labor Statistics, for the most recent three-year period ending on December 31 preceding the adjustment, with each adjusted amount rounded to the nearest twenty-five dollars ($25).

(f) Beginning April 1, 2004, the Judicial Council shall publish a list of the current dollar amounts of exemptions provided in subdivision (b) of Section 703.140 and in Article 3 (commencing with Section 704.010), and the dollar amount set forth in paragraph (7) of subdivision (b) of Section 699.730, together with the date of the next scheduled adjustment. In any year that the Legislature votes to increase the exemptions provided in subdivision (a) of Section 704.730, the Judicial Council shall publish a list of current dollar amounts of exemptions.

(g) Adjustments made under subdivision (a) do not apply with respect to cases commenced before the date of the adjustment, subject to any contrary rule applicable under the federal Bankruptcy Code. The applicability of adjustments made under subdivisions (b), (c), and (d) is governed by Section 703.050. *(Added by Stats.2003, c. 379 (A.B.182), § 4. Amended by Stats.2009, c. 499 (A.B.1046), § 1; Stats.2010, c. 212 (A.B.2767), § 1; Stats.2012, c. 678 (A.B.929), § 2; Stats.2020, c. 218 (A.B.2463), § 2, eff. Jan. 1, 2021.)*

OFFICIAL FORMS
CURRENT DOLLAR AMOUNTS OF EXEMPTIONS FROM ENFORCEMENT OF JUDGMENTS
Code of Civil Procedure sections 703.140(b) and 704.010 et seq.

EXEMPTIONS UNDER SECTION 703.140(b)

The following lists the current dollar amounts of exemptions from enforcement of judgment under Code of Civil Procedure section 703.140(b) used in a case under title 11 of the United States Code (bankruptcy).

These amounts are effective April 1, 2022. Unless otherwise provided by statute after that date, they will be adjusted at each three-year interval, ending on March 31. The amount of the adjustment to the prior amounts is based on the change in the annual California Consumer Price Index for All Urban Consumers for the most recent three-year period ending on the preceding December 31, with each adjusted amount rounded to the nearest $25. (See Code Civ. Proc., § 703.150(e).)

Code Civ. Proc., § 703.140(b)	Type of Property	Amount of Exemption
(1)	The debtor's aggregate interest in real property or personal property that the debtor or a dependent of the debtor uses as a residence, or in a cooperative that owns property that the debtor or a dependent of the debtor uses as a residence	$31,950
(2)	The debtor's interest in one or more motor vehicles	$6,375
(3)	The debtor's interest in household furnishings, household goods, wearing apparel, appliances, books, animals, crops, or musical instruments, that are held primarily for the personal, family, or household use of the debtor or a dependent of the debtor (value is of any particular item)	$800
(4)	The debtor's aggregate interest in jewelry held primarily for the personal, family, or household use of the debtor or a dependent of the debtor	$1,900
(5)	The debtor's aggregate interest, plus any unused amount of the exemption provided under paragraph (1), in any property	$1,700
(6)	The debtor's aggregate interest in any implements, professional books, or tools of the trade of the debtor or the trade of a dependent of the debtor	$9,525
(8)	The debtor's aggregate interest in any accrued dividend or interest under, or loan value of, any unmatured life insurance contract owned by the debtor under which the insured is the debtor or an individual of whom the debtor is a dependent	$17,075
(11)(D)	The debtor's right to receive, or property traceable to, a payment on account of personal bodily injury of the debtor or an	

§ 703.150

Code Civ. Proc., § 703.140(b)	Type of Property	Amount of Exemption
	individual of whom the debtor is a dependent	$31,950

EXEMPTIONS UNDER SECTION 704.010 et seq.

The following lists the current dollar amounts of exemptions from enforcement of judgment under title 9, division 2, chapter 4, article 3 (commencing with section 704.010) of the Code of Civil Procedure.

The amount of the automatic exemption for a deposit account under section 704.220(a) is effective July 1, 2021, and unless otherwise provided by statute after that date, will be adjusted annually effective July 1 by the Department of Social Services under Welfare and Institutions Code section 11453 to reflect the minimum basic standard of care for a family of four as established by § 11452.*

Code Civ. Proc. Section	Type of Property	Amount of Exemption
704.010	Motor vehicle (any combination of aggregate equity, proceeds of execution sale, and proceeds of insurance or other indemnification for loss, damage, or destruction)	$ 3,625
704.030	Material to be applied to repair or maintenance of residence	$ 3,825
704.040	Jewelry, heirlooms, art	$ 9,525
704.060	Personal property used in debtor's or debtor's spouse's trade, business, or profession (amount of exemption for commercial motor vehicle not to exceed $4,850)	$ 9,525
704.060	Personal property used in debtor's and spouse's common trade, business, or profession (amount of exemption for commercial motor vehicle not to exceed $9,700)	$19,050
704.080	Deposit account with direct payment of social security or public benefits (exemption without claim, section 704.080(b)) [2]	
	• Public benefits, one depositor is designated payee	$ 1,900
	• Social security benefits, one depositor is designated payee	$ 3,825
	• Public benefits, two or more depositors are designated payees [3]	$ 2,825
	• Social security benefits, two or more depositors are designated payees [3]	$ 5,725
704.090	Inmate trust account	$ 1,900
	Inmate trust account (restitution fine or order)	$ 325 [4]

Code Civ. Proc. Section	Type of Property	Amount of Exemption
704.100	Aggregate loan value of unmatured life insurance policies	$15,250

[1] This exemption does not preclude or reduce other exemptions for deposit accounts. However, if the exemption amount for the deposit account applicable under other automatic exemptions—such as those applicable for direct deposit of social security benefits or public benefits—is greater under the other exemptions, then those apply instead of this one. (Code Civ. Proc., § 704.220(b).)

[2] The amount of a deposit account with direct deposited funds that exceeds exemption amounts shown is also exempt to the extent it consists of payments of public benefits or social security benefits. (Code Civ. Proc., § 704.080(c).)

[3] If only one joint payee is a beneficiary of the payment, the exemption is in the amount available to a single designated payee. (Code Civ. Proc., § 704.080(b)(3) and (4).)

[4] This amount is not subject to adjustments under Code Civ. Proc., § 703.150.

Cross References

Exempt property,
  Funds in trust, see Code of Civil Procedure § 704.090.
  Jewelry, heirlooms, and works of art, see Code of Civil Procedure § 704.040.
  Life insurance policies, see Code of Civil Procedure § 704.100.
  Personal property necessary to and used in exercise of trade, business or profession, see Code of Civil Procedure § 704.060.
Material for repair or improvement of residence, see Code of Civil Procedure § 704.030.
Service of judgment debtor, see Code of Civil Procedure § 700.010.

Research References

Forms

Asset Protection: Legal Planning, Strategies and Forms ¶ A.05, Appendix A.05 California (Opt Out State).

West's California Code Forms, Civil Procedure § 700.010 Form 1, Enforcement of Judgments—Exemptions from the Enforcement of Judgments—Information Sheet—Official Form.

West's California Judicial Council Forms EJ–156, Current Dollar Amounts of Exemptions from Enforcement of Judgments.

CHAPTER 5. WAGE GARNISHMENT

Cross References

Release of levy under franchise and income tax laws, sale of seized property only after notice of exemptions, see Revenue and Taxation Code § 21016.
Willfully false return, name as prima facie evidence of signature, see Revenue and Taxation Code § 19705.

ARTICLE 1. SHORT TITLE; DEFINITIONS

Section
706.010. Short title.
706.011. Definitions.

Cross References

Enforcement of money judgment against interest in trust, see Code of Civil Procedure § 709.010.

§ 706.010. Short title

This chapter shall be known and may be cited as the "Wage Garnishment Law." *(Added by Stats.1982, c. 1364, p. 5172, § 2, operative July 1, 1983.)*

Cross References

Earnings of public officer or employee, see Code of Civil Procedure § 708.720.

Interest as beneficiary of trust subject to satisfaction of money judgment, see Code of Civil Procedure § 709.010.

Research References

Forms

2B Am. Jur. Pl. & Pr. Forms Attachment and Garnishment § 2, Statutory References.

2B Am. Jur. Pl. & Pr. Forms Attachment and Garnishment § 214, Statutory References.

3 California Transactions Forms--Business Transactions § 16:88, Assignment of Wages or Salary (General).

3 California Transactions Forms--Business Transactions § 16:94, Assignor's Revocation of Assignment of Wages or Salary.

3 California Transactions Forms--Estate Planning § 18:36, Disclaimers as Protective Device.

§ 706.011. Definitions

As used in this chapter:

(a) "Disposable earnings" means the portion of an individual's earnings that remains after deducting all amounts required to be withheld by law.

(b) "Earnings" means compensation payable by an employer to an employee for personal services performed by such employee, whether denominated as wages, salary, commission, bonus, or otherwise.

(c) "Earnings withholding order for elder or dependent adult financial abuse" means an earnings withholding order, made pursuant to Article 5 (commencing with Section 706.100) and based on a money judgment in an action for elder or adult dependent financial abuse under Section 15657.5 of the Welfare and Institutions Code.

(d) "Earnings assignment order for support" means an order, made pursuant to Chapter 8 (commencing with Section 5200) of Part 5 of Division 9 of the Family Code or Section 3088 of the Probate Code, which requires an employer to withhold earnings for support.

(e) "Employee" means a public officer and any individual who performs services subject to the right of the employer to control both what shall be done and how it shall be done.

(f) "Employer" means a person for whom an individual performs services as an employee.

(g) "Judgment creditor," as applied to the state, means the specific state agency seeking to collect a judgment or tax liability.

(h) "Judgment debtor" includes a person from whom the state is seeking to collect a tax liability under Article 4 (commencing with Section 706.070), whether or not a judgment has been obtained on such tax liability.

(i) "Person" includes an individual, a corporation, a partnership or other unincorporated association, a limited liability company, and a public entity. (Added by Stats.1982, c. 1364, p. 5172, § 2, operative July 1, 1983. Amended by Stats.1990, c. 1493 (A.B.3974), § 30.5; Stats.1992, c. 163 (A.B.2641), § 45, operative Jan. 1, 1994; Stats.1994, c. 1010 (S.B.2053), § 61; Stats.2010, c. 64 (A.B.2619), § 1, operative Jan. 1, 2012; Stats.2012, c. 474 (A.B.1775), § 1, operative July 1, 2013.)

Cross References

Definitions, employer, see Family Code § 5210.

Judgment creditor defined for purposes of this Title, see Code of Civil Procedure § 680.240.

Judgment debtor defined for purposes of this Title, see Code of Civil Procedure § 680.250.

Levy of feepayer's assets held by another, notice to financial institution, continued withholding, see Revenue and Taxation Code § 46406.

Notice of levy,
 Continued withholding, see Revenue and Taxation Code §§ 7855, 8957, 30315, 32387, 41123.5, 43444.2, 55205.
 Order to withhold from credits or personal property the amount of tax, payment, see Revenue and Taxation Code § 60407.
 Transmittal of amount withheld, see Revenue and Taxation Code § 45605.

Notice of levy to require withholding of fees, interest or penalties due, see Revenue and Taxation Code § 50136.

Notice to withhold, notice of levy, see Revenue and Taxation Code § 40155.

Notice to withhold and transmit amounts due, amount required to be withheld, see Revenue and Taxation Code § 18671.

Person defined for purposes of this Title, see Code of Civil Procedure § 680.280.

Security for tax, notice of levy, generally, see Revenue and Taxation Code § 6703.

Security for tax, notice of levy, withholding requirements, see Revenue and Taxation Code § 38503.

Wage assignment for support of conservatee, see Probate Code § 3088.

Research References

Forms

Asset Protection: Legal Planning, Strategies and Forms ¶ A.05, Appendix A.05 California (Opt Out State).

ARTICLE 2. GENERAL PROVISIONS

Section
706.020. Application of chapter.
706.021. Procedure for levy of execution upon employee earnings.
706.022. "Withholding period" defined; amount withheld; employer liability for amounts withheld and paid prior to service of order.
706.023. Multiple earnings withholding orders; earnings withholding orders for elder or dependent adult financial abuse.
706.024. Amount required to satisfy earnings withholding order; discretionary notice; accrual of interest.
706.025. Payments to levying officer.
706.026. Levying officer; receipt, accounting, and payment of amounts received; electronic filing.
706.027. Notice of satisfaction of judgment.
706.028. Final earnings withholding order for costs and interest.
706.029. Service of order creating lien; duration.
706.030. Withholding order for support; operation with earnings withholding order.
706.031. Earnings assignment order for support; operation with earnings withholding order.
706.032. Termination of earnings withholding orders.
706.033. Return of writ before earnings withholding order terminates; supplemental return on writ.
706.034. Deduction from employee earnings for payments made in accordance with earnings withholding order.

§ 706.020. Application of chapter

Except for an earning assignment order for support, the earnings of an employee shall not be required to be withheld by an employer for payment of a debt by means of any judicial procedure other than pursuant to this chapter. (Added by Stats.1982, c. 1364, p. 5173, § 2, operative July 1, 1983. Amended by Stats.1992, c. 163 (A.B.2641), § 46, operative Jan. 1, 1994.)

Cross References

Earnings defined for purposes of this Chapter, see Code of Civil Procedure § 706.011.

Employee defined for purposes of this Chapter, see Code of Civil Procedure § 706.011.

Employer defined for purposes of this Chapter, see Code of Civil Procedure § 706.011.

§ 706.021. Procedure for levy of execution upon employee earnings

Notwithstanding any other provision of this title, a levy of execution upon the earnings of an employee shall be made by service of an earnings withholding order upon the employer in accordance

§ 706.021

with this chapter. *(Added by Stats.1982, c. 1364, p. 5173, § 2, operative July 1, 1983.)*

Cross References

Assignment of right to payments, service of notice, factors considered, and amount assigned, see Code of Civil Procedure § 708.510.
Earnings defined for purposes of this Chapter, see Code of Civil Procedure § 706.011.
Employee defined for purposes of this Chapter, see Code of Civil Procedure § 706.011.
Employer defined for purposes of this Chapter, see Code of Civil Procedure § 706.011.
Service of withholding order, creation of lien on earnings of judgment debtor, see Code of Civil Procedure § 706.029.

§ 706.022. "Withholding period" defined; amount withheld; employer liability for amounts withheld and paid prior to service of order

(a) As used in this section, "withholding period" means the period which commences on the 10th day after service of an earnings withholding order upon the employer and which continues until the earliest of the following dates:

(1) The date the employer has withheld the full amount required to satisfy the order.

(2) The date of termination specified in a court order served on the employer.

(3) The date of termination specified in a notice of termination served on the employer by the levying officer.

(4) The date of termination of a dormant or suspended earnings withholding order as determined pursuant to Section 706.032.

(b) Except as otherwise provided by statute, an employer shall withhold the amounts required by an earnings withholding order from all earnings of the employee payable for any pay period of the employee which ends during the withholding period.

(c) An employer is not liable for any amounts withheld and paid over to the levying officer pursuant to an earnings withholding order prior to service upon the employer pursuant to paragraph (2) or (3) of subdivision (a). *(Added by Stats.1982, c. 1364, p. 5173, § 2, operative July 1, 1983. Amended by Stats.1989, c. 263, § 1; Stats.1992, c. 283 (S.B.1372), § 5, eff. July 21, 1992.)*

Cross References

Court defined for purposes of this Title, see Code of Civil Procedure § 680.160.
Deferment or acceleration of payment of earnings to alter rights of judgment creditor, liability, see Code of Civil Procedure § 706.153.
Earnings defined for purposes of this Chapter, see Code of Civil Procedure § 706.011.
Employee defined for purposes of this Chapter, see Code of Civil Procedure § 706.011.
Employer defined for purposes of this Chapter, see Code of Civil Procedure § 706.011.
Jeopardy withholding order for taxes, see Code of Civil Procedure § 706.078.
Judgment creditor defined for purposes of this Title, see Code of Civil Procedure § 680.240.
Satisfaction of judgment prior to termination of order, see Code of Civil Procedure § 706.027.
Service of withholding order, see Code of Civil Procedure § 706.101.

Research References

Forms

3 California Transactions Forms--Business Transactions § 16:94, Assignor's Revocation of Assignment of Wages or Salary.
West's California Judicial Council Forms WG-002, Earnings Withholding Order.

§ 706.023. Multiple earnings withholding orders; earnings withholding orders for elder or dependent adult financial abuse

Except as otherwise provided in this chapter:

(a) An employer shall comply with the first earnings withholding order served upon the employer.

(b) If the employer is served with two or more earnings withholding orders on the same day, the employer shall comply with the order issued pursuant to the judgment first entered. If two or more orders served on the same day are based on judgments entered upon the same day, the employer shall comply with whichever one of the orders the employer selects.

(c) If an earnings withholding order is served while an employer is required to comply with another earnings withholding order with respect to the earnings of the same employee, the subsequent order is ineffective and the employer shall not withhold earnings pursuant to the subsequent order, except as provided in subdivision (d).

(d) Notwithstanding any other provisions of this section, a withholding order for elder or dependent adult financial abuse has priority over any other earning withholding order except for a withholding order for support under Section 706.030 and a withholding order for taxes under Section 706.072.

(1) An employer upon whom a withholding order for elder or dependent adult financial abuse is served shall withhold and pay over earnings of the employee pursuant to that order notwithstanding the requirements of another earnings withholding order except as provided in paragraph (2).

(2) An employer shall not withhold earnings of an employee pursuant to an earnings withholding order for elder or dependent adult financial abuse if a withholding order for support or for taxes is in effect or if a prior withholding order for elder or dependent adult financial abuse is in effect. In that case, the subsequent withholding order for elder or dependent financial abuse is ineffective.

(3) When an employer is required to cease withholding earnings pursuant to a prior earnings withholding order, the employer shall notify the levying officer who served the prior earnings withholding order that a supervening earnings withholding order for elder or dependent financial abuse is in effect. *(Added by Stats.1982, c. 1364, p. 5173, § 2, operative July 1, 1983. Amended by Stats.2010, c. 64 (A.B.2619), § 2, operative Jan. 1, 2012.)*

Cross References

Duration of lien, see Code of Civil Procedure § 706.029.
Earnings defined for purposes of this Chapter, see Code of Civil Procedure § 706.011.
Employee defined for purposes of this Chapter, see Code of Civil Procedure § 706.011.
Employer defined for purposes of this Chapter, see Code of Civil Procedure § 706.011.
Priority of support order, see Code of Civil Procedure §§ 706.030, 706.077.

Research References

Forms

West's California Judicial Council Forms WG-030, Earnings Withholding Order for Elder or Dependent Adult Financial Abuse.

§ 706.024. Amount required to satisfy earnings withholding order; discretionary notice; accrual of interest

(a) The amount required to satisfy an earnings withholding order is the total amount required to satisfy the writ of execution on the date the order is issued, with the following additions and subtractions:

(1) The addition of the statutory fee for service of the order and any other statutory fees for performing duties under the order.

(2) The addition of costs added to the order pursuant to Section 685.090.

(3) The subtraction of the amount of any partial satisfactions.

(4) The addition of daily interest accruing after issuance of the order, as adjusted for partial satisfactions.

(b) From time to time the levying officer, in the levying officer's discretion, may give written notice to the employer of the amount required to satisfy the earnings withholding order and the employer shall determine the total amount to withhold based upon the levying officer's notice, notwithstanding a different amount stated in the order originally served on the employer.

(c) If the full amount required to satisfy the earnings withholding order as stated in the order or in the levying officer's notice under subdivision (b) is withheld from the judgment debtor's earnings, interest ceases to accrue on that amount. *(Added by Stats.1992, c. 283 (S.B.1372), § 6, eff. July 21, 1992.)*

Cross References

Costs defined for purposes of this Title, see Code of Civil Procedure § 680.150.
Earnings defined for purposes of this Chapter, see Code of Civil Procedure § 706.011.
Employer defined for purposes of this Chapter, see Code of Civil Procedure § 706.011.
Judgment creditor defined for purposes of this Title, see Code of Civil Procedure § 680.240.
Judgment debtor defined for purposes of this Chapter, see Code of Civil Procedure § 706.011.
Judgment debtor defined for purposes of this Title, see Code of Civil Procedure § 680.250.
Writ defined for purposes of this Title, see Code of Civil Procedure § 680.380.

§ 706.025. Payments to levying officer

(a) Except as provided in subdivision (b), the amount required to be withheld pursuant to an earnings withholding order shall be paid monthly to the levying officer not later than the 15th day of each month. The initial monthly payment shall include all amounts required to be withheld from the earnings of the employee during the preceding calendar month up to the close of the employee's pay period ending closest to the last day of that month, and thereafter each monthly payment shall include amounts withheld from the employee's earnings for services rendered in the interim up to the close of the employee's pay period ending closest to the last day of the preceding calendar month.

(b) The employer may elect to pay the amounts withheld to the levying officer more frequently than monthly. If the employer so elects, payment of the amount withheld from the employee's earnings for each pay period shall be made not later than 10 days after the close of the pay period. *(Added by Stats.1982, c. 1364, p. 5173, § 2, operative July 1, 1983.)*

Cross References

Duties of employer, see Code of Civil Procedure §§ 706.104, 706.126.
Earnings defined for purposes of this Chapter, see Code of Civil Procedure § 706.011.
Employee defined for purposes of this Chapter, see Code of Civil Procedure § 706.011.
Employer defined for purposes of this Chapter, see Code of Civil Procedure § 706.011.
Judgment creditor defined for purposes of this Title, see Code of Civil Procedure § 680.240.

§ 706.026. Levying officer; receipt, accounting, and payment of amounts received; electronic filing

(a) The levying officer shall receive and account for all amounts paid by the employer pursuant to Section 706.025 and shall pay the amounts so received over to the person entitled thereto at least once every 30 days.

(b) At least once every two years, the levying officer shall file an accounting with the court, as provided by Section 699.560, for all amounts collected under the earnings withholding order, including costs and interest added to the amount due. Subject to the limitations in subdivision (c) of Section 263, the levying officer may electronically file the accounting with the court, pursuant to Chapter 2 (commencing with Section 263) of Title 4 of Part 1. *(Added by Stats.1982, c. 1364, p. 5174, § 2, operative July 1, 1983. Amended by Stats.1992, c. 283 (S.B.1372), § 7, eff. July 21, 1992; Stats.2010, c. 680 (A.B.2394), § 12.)*

Cross References

Costs defined for purposes of this Title, see Code of Civil Procedure § 680.150.
Court defined for purposes of this Title, see Code of Civil Procedure § 680.160.
Earnings defined for purposes of this Chapter, see Code of Civil Procedure § 706.011.
Employer defined for purposes of this Chapter, see Code of Civil Procedure § 706.011.
Judgment creditor defined for purposes of this Title, see Code of Civil Procedure § 680.240.
Person defined for purposes of this Chapter, see Code of Civil Procedure § 706.011.
Person defined for purposes of this Title, see Code of Civil Procedure § 680.280.

§ 706.027. Notice of satisfaction of judgment

If the judgment pursuant to which the earnings withholding order is issued is satisfied before the order otherwise terminates pursuant to Section 706.022, the judgment creditor shall promptly notify the levying officer who shall promptly terminate the order by serving a notice of termination on the employer. *(Added by Stats.1982, c. 1364, p. 5174, § 2, operative July 1, 1983.)*

Cross References

Earnings defined for purposes of this Chapter, see Code of Civil Procedure § 706.011.
Employer defined for purposes of this Chapter, see Code of Civil Procedure § 706.011.
Jeopardy withholding order for taxes, see Code of Civil Procedure § 706.078.
Judgment creditor defined for purposes of this Chapter, see Code of Civil Procedure § 706.011.
Judgment creditor defined for purposes of this Title, see Code of Civil Procedure § 680.240.

Research References

Forms

3 California Transactions Forms--Business Transactions § 16:94, Assignor's Revocation of Assignment of Wages or Salary.

§ 706.028. Final earnings withholding order for costs and interest

(a) "Final earnings withholding order for costs and interest" means an earnings withholding order for the collection only of unsatisfied costs and interest, which is issued after an earlier earnings withholding order has been returned satisfied.

(b) After the amount stated as owing in a prior earnings withholding order is paid, the judgment creditor may obtain a final earnings withholding order for costs and interest to collect amounts of costs and interest that were not collected under the prior earnings withholding order.

(c) A final earnings withholding order for costs and interest shall be enforced in the same manner as other earnings withholding orders.

(d) Satisfaction of the amount stated as owing in a final earnings withholding order for costs and interest is equivalent to satisfaction of the money judgment. For this purpose, interest ceases to accrue on the date of issuance of the final earnings withholding order and no additional costs may be added after that date, except for the statutory fee for service of the order and any other statutory fees for performing duties under the order. *(Added by Stats.1992, c. 283 (S.B.1372), § 9, eff. July 21, 1992.)*

Cross References

Costs defined for purposes of this Title, see Code of Civil Procedure § 680.150.
Earnings defined for purposes of this Chapter, see Code of Civil Procedure § 706.011.

§ 706.028

Judgment creditor defined for purposes of this Chapter, see Code of Civil Procedure § 706.011.
Judgment creditor defined for purposes of this Title, see Code of Civil Procedure § 680.240.
Money judgment defined for purposes of this Title, see Code of Civil Procedure § 680.270.

§ 706.029. Service of order creating lien; duration

Service of an earnings withholding order creates a lien upon the earnings of the judgment debtor that are required to be withheld pursuant to the order and upon all property of the employer subject to the enforcement of a money judgment in the amount required to be withheld pursuant to such order. The lien continues for a period of one year from the date the earnings of the judgment debtor become payable unless the amount required to be withheld pursuant to the order is paid as required by law. *(Added by Stats.1982, c. 1364, p. 5174, § 2, operative July 1, 1983.)*

Cross References

Earnings defined for purposes of this Chapter, see Code of Civil Procedure § 706.011.
Employer defined for purposes of this Chapter, see Code of Civil Procedure § 706.011.
Judgment debtor defined for purposes of this Chapter, see Code of Civil Procedure § 706.011.
Judgment debtor defined for purposes of this Title, see Code of Civil Procedure § 680.250.
Lien on earnings, service of order, see Family Code § 5242.
Money judgment defined for purposes of this Title, see Code of Civil Procedure § 680.270.
Property defined for purposes of this Title, see Code of Civil Procedure § 680.310.

Research References

Forms

2B Am. Jur. Pl. & Pr. Forms Attachment and Garnishment § 240, Statutory References.

§ 706.030. Withholding order for support; operation with earnings withholding order

(a) A "withholding order for support" is an earnings withholding order issued on a writ of execution to collect delinquent amounts payable under a judgment for the support of a child, or spouse or former spouse, of the judgment debtor. A withholding order for support shall be denoted as such on its face.

(b) The local child support agency may issue a withholding order for support on a notice of levy pursuant to Section 17522 of the Family Code to collect a support obligation.

(1) When the local child support agency issues a withholding order for support, a reference in this chapter to a levying officer is deemed to mean the local child support agency who issues the withholding order for support.

(2) Service of a withholding order for support issued by the local child support agency may be made by first-class mail or in any other manner described in Section 706.101. Service of a withholding order for support issued by the local child support agency is complete when it is received by the employer or a person described in paragraph (1) or (2) of subdivision (a) of Section 706.101, or if service is by first-class mail, service is complete as specified in Section 1013.

(3) The local child support agency shall serve upon the employer the withholding order for support, a copy of the order, and a notice informing the support obligor of the effect of the order and of his or her right to hearings and remedies provided in this chapter and in the Family Code. The notice shall be accompanied by the forms necessary to obtain an administrative review and a judicial hearing and instructions on how to file the forms. Within 10 days from the date of service, the employer shall deliver to the support obligor a copy of the withholding order for support, the forms to obtain an administrative review and judicial hearing, and the notice. If the support obligor is no longer employed by the employer and the employer does not owe the support obligor any earnings, the employer shall inform the local child support agency that the support obligor is no longer employed by the employer.

(4) An employer who fails to comply with paragraph (3) shall be subject to a civil penalty of five hundred dollars ($500) for each occurrence.

(5) The local child support agency shall provide for an administrative review to reconsider or modify the amount to be withheld for arrearages pursuant to the withholding order for support, if the support obligor requests a review at any time after service of the withholding order. The local child support agency shall provide the review in the same manner and timeframes provided for resolution of a complaint pursuant to Section 17800 of the Family Code. The local child support agency shall notify the employer if the review results in any modifications to the withholding order for support. If the local child support agency cannot complete the administrative review within 30 calendar days of receipt of the complaint, the local child support agency shall notify the employer to suspend withholding any disputed amount pending the completion of the review and the determination by the local child support agency.

(6) Nothing in this section prohibits the support obligor from seeking a judicial determination of arrearages pursuant to subdivision (c) of Section 17256 of the Family Code or from filing a motion for equitable division of earnings pursuant to Section 706.052 either prior to or after the administrative review provided by this section. Within five business days after receiving notice of the obligor having filed for judicial relief pursuant to this section, the local child support agency shall notify the employer to suspend withholding any disputed amount pending a determination by the court. The employer shall then adjust the withholding within not more than nine days of receiving the notice from the local child support agency.

(c) Notwithstanding any other provision of this chapter:

(1) An employer shall continue to withhold pursuant to a withholding order for support until the earliest of the dates specified in paragraph (1), (2), or (3) of subdivision (a) of Section 706.022, except that a withholding order for support shall automatically terminate one year after the employment of the employee by the employer terminates.

(2) A withholding order for support has priority over any other earnings withholding order. An employer upon whom a withholding order for support is served shall withhold and pay over earnings of the employee pursuant to that order notwithstanding the requirements of another earnings withholding order.

(3) Subject to paragraph (2) and to Article 3 (commencing with Section 706.050), an employer shall withhold earnings pursuant to both a withholding order for support and another earnings withholding order simultaneously.

(4) An employer who willfully fails to withhold and forward support pursuant to a valid earnings withholding order for support issued and served upon the employer pursuant to this chapter is liable to the support obligee, as defined in Section 5214 of the Family Code, for the amount of support not withheld, forwarded, or otherwise paid to the support obligee.

(5) Notwithstanding any other provision of law, an employer shall send all earnings withheld pursuant to a withholding order for support to the levying officer or the State Disbursement Unit as described in Section 17309 of the Family Code within the time period specified by federal law.

(6) Once the State Disbursement Unit as described in Section 17309 of the Family Code is operational, all support payments made pursuant to an earnings withholding order shall be made to that unit.

(7) Earnings withheld pursuant to an earnings withholding order for support shall be credited toward satisfaction of a support judgment as specified in Section 695.221. *(Added by Stats.1982, c.*

1364, p. 5174, § 2, operative July 1, 1983. Amended by Stats.1992, c. 283 (S.B.1372), § 10, eff. July 21, 1992; Stats.1997, c. 599 (A.B.573), § 5; Stats.2000, c. 808 (A.B.1358), § 17, eff. Sept. 28, 2000; Stats. 2001, c. 755 (S.B.943), § 1, eff. Oct. 12, 2001; Stats.2003, c. 387 (A.B.739), § 1.)

Cross References

Child support defined for purposes of this Title, see Code of Civil Procedure § 680.145.
Court defined for purposes of this Title, see Code of Civil Procedure § 680.160.
Earnings defined for purposes of this Chapter, see Code of Civil Procedure § 706.011.
Earnings exemption, withholding order for support, see Code of Civil Procedure § 706.052.
Employee defined for purposes of this Chapter, see Code of Civil Procedure § 706.011.
Employer defined for purposes of this Chapter, see Code of Civil Procedure § 706.011.
Enforcement of support orders without prior court approval, see Family Code § 5100.
Judgment creditor defined for purposes of this Title, see Code of Civil Procedure § 680.240.
Judgment debtor defined for purposes of this Chapter, see Code of Civil Procedure § 706.011.
Judgment debtor defined for purposes of this Title, see Code of Civil Procedure § 680.250.
Maximum amount of earnings subject to levy, see Code of Civil Procedure § 706.050.
Multiple earnings withholding orders, priorities, see Code of Civil Procedure § 706.023.
Person defined for purposes of this Chapter, see Code of Civil Procedure § 706.011.
Person defined for purposes of this Title, see Code of Civil Procedure § 680.280.
Writ defined for purposes of this Title, see Code of Civil Procedure § 680.380.

Research References

Forms

West's California Judicial Council Forms WG–004, Earnings Withholding Order for Support.

§ 706.031. Earnings assignment order for support; operation with earnings withholding order

(a) Nothing in this chapter affects an earnings assignment order for support.

(b) An earnings assignment order for support shall be given priority over any earnings withholding order. An employer upon whom an earnings assignment order for support is served shall withhold and pay over the earnings of the employee pursuant to the assignment order notwithstanding the requirements of any earnings withholding order. When an employer is required to cease withholding earnings pursuant to an earnings withholding order, the employer shall notify the levying officer who served the earnings withholding order that a supervening earnings assignment order for support is in effect.

(c) Subject to subdivisions (b), (d), and (e), an employer shall withhold earnings of an employee pursuant to both an earnings assignment order for support and an earnings withholding order.

(d) The employer shall withhold pursuant to an earnings withholding order only to the extent that the sum of the amount withheld pursuant to any earnings assignment order for support and the amount withheld pursuant to the earnings withholding order does not exceed the amount that may be withheld under Article 3 (commencing with Section 706.050).

(e) The employer shall withhold pursuant to an earnings withholding order for taxes only to the extent that the sum of the amount withheld pursuant to any earnings assignment order for support and the amount withheld pursuant to the earnings withholding order for taxes does not exceed the amount that may be withheld under Article 4 (commencing with Section 706.070). (Added by Stats.1982, c. 1364, p. 5175, § 2, operative July 1, 1983. Amended by Stats.1992, c. 163 (A.B.2641), § 47, operative Jan. 1, 1994.)

Cross References

Earnings assignment order for support defined for purposes of this Chapter, see Code of Civil Procedure § 706.011.
Earnings defined for purposes of this Chapter, see Code of Civil Procedure § 706.011.
Employee defined for purposes of this Chapter, see Code of Civil Procedure § 706.011.
Employer defined for purposes of this Chapter, see Code of Civil Procedure § 706.011.
Judgment creditor defined for purposes of this Title, see Code of Civil Procedure § 680.240.
Maximum amount of earnings subject to levy, see Code of Civil Procedure § 706.050.
Priority of order, see Family Code § 5243.

Research References

Forms

West's California Judicial Council Forms FL–435, Earnings Assignment Order for Spousal or Partner Support.

§ 706.032. Termination of earnings withholding orders

(a) Except as otherwise provided by statute:

(1) If withholding under an earnings withholding order ceases because the judgment debtor's employment has terminated, the earnings withholding order terminates at the conclusion of a continuous 180-day period during which no amounts are withheld under the order.

(2) If withholding under an earnings withholding order ceases because the judgment debtor's earnings are subject to an order or assignment with higher priority, the earnings withholding order terminates at the conclusion of a continuous two-year period during which no amounts are withheld under the order.

(b) If an earnings withholding order has terminated pursuant to subdivision (a), the employer shall return the order to the levying officer along with a statement of the reasons for returning the order. (Added by Stats.1992, c. 283 (S.B.1372), § 11, eff. July 21, 1992.)

Cross References

Earnings defined for purposes of this Chapter, see Code of Civil Procedure § 706.011.
Employer defined for purposes of this Chapter, see Code of Civil Procedure § 706.011.
Judgment creditor defined for purposes of this Title, see Code of Civil Procedure § 680.240.
Judgment debtor defined for purposes of this Chapter, see Code of Civil Procedure § 706.011.
Judgment debtor defined for purposes of this Title, see Code of Civil Procedure § 680.250.

Research References

Forms

3 California Transactions Forms--Business Transactions § 16:94, Assignor's Revocation of Assignment of Wages or Salary.

§ 706.033. Return of writ before earnings withholding order terminates; supplemental return on writ

If the writ is returned before the earnings withholding order terminates, on termination of the earnings withholding order the levying officer shall make a supplemental return on the writ. The supplemental return shall contain the same information as an original return pursuant to Section 699.560. (Added by Stats.1992, c. 283 (S.B.1372), § 12, eff. July 21, 1992.)

§ 706.033

Cross References

Earnings defined for purposes of this Chapter, see Code of Civil Procedure § 706.011.

Judgment creditor defined for purposes of this Title, see Code of Civil Procedure § 680.240.

Writ defined for purposes of this Title, see Code of Civil Procedure § 680.380.

§ 706.034. Deduction from employee earnings for payments made in accordance with earnings withholding order

The employer may deduct from the earnings of the employee the sum of one dollar and fifty cents ($1.50) for each payment made in accordance with an earnings withholding order issued pursuant to this chapter. *(Added by Stats.1997, c. 137 (A.B.519), § 1. Amended by Stats.2004, c. 520 (A.B.2530), § 1.)*

Cross References

Earnings defined for purposes of this Chapter, see Code of Civil Procedure § 706.011.

Employee defined for purposes of this Chapter, see Code of Civil Procedure § 706.011.

Employer defined for purposes of this Chapter, see Code of Civil Procedure § 706.011.

ARTICLE 3. RESTRICTIONS ON EARNINGS WITHHOLDING

Section
706.050. Maximum amount of disposable earnings of an individual judgment debtor subject to levy.
706.050. Maximum amount of disposable earnings of an individual judgment debtor subject to levy.
706.051. Amount necessary for support of judgment debtor or family; exemption.
706.052. Disposable earnings and earnings withheld pursuant to earning assignment order for support; exemption; equitable division of earnings by court.

§ 706.050. Maximum amount of disposable earnings of an individual judgment debtor subject to levy

Section operative until Sept. 1, 2023. See, also, § 706.050 operative Sept. 1, 2023.

(a) Except as otherwise provided in this chapter, the maximum amount of disposable earnings of an individual judgment debtor for any workweek that is subject to levy under an earnings withholding order shall not exceed the lesser of the following:

(1) Twenty-five percent of the individual's disposable earnings for that week.

(2) Fifty percent of the amount by which the individual's disposable earnings for that week exceed 40 times the state minimum hourly wage in effect at the time the earnings are payable. If a judgment debtor works in a location where the local minimum hourly wage is greater than the state minimum hourly wage, the local minimum hourly wage in effect at the time the earnings are payable shall be used for the calculation made pursuant to this paragraph.

(b) For any pay period other than weekly, the following multipliers shall be used to determine the maximum amount of disposable earnings subject to levy under an earnings withholding order that is proportional in effect to the calculation described in paragraph (2) of subdivision (a), except as specified in paragraph (1):

(1) For a daily pay period, the amounts shall be identical to the amounts described in subdivision (a).

(2) For a biweekly pay period, multiply the applicable hourly minimum wage by 80 work hours.

(3) For a semimonthly pay period, multiply the applicable hourly minimum wage by 86⅔ work hours.

(4) For a monthly pay period, multiply the applicable hourly minimum wage by 173⅓ work hours.

(c) This section shall become inoperative on September 1, 2023, and, as of January 1, 2024, is repealed, unless a later enacted statute that becomes operative on * * * or before January 1, 2024, deletes or extends the dates on which it becomes inoperative and is repealed. *(Added by Stats.2015, c. 800 (S.B.501), § 2, eff. Jan. 1, 2016, operative July 1, 2016. Amended by Stats.2022, c. 849 (S.B.1477), § 1, eff. Jan. 1, 2023.)*

Inoperative Date and Repeal

For inoperative date and repeal of this section, see its terms.

Cross References

Amount to be withheld, statement in earnings withholding order, see Code of Civil Procedure § 706.125.

Earnings defined for purposes of this Chapter, see Code of Civil Procedure § 706.011.

Enforcement of money judgment, exempt property, paid earnings, withholding order, wage assignment for support, see Code of Civil Procedure § 704.070.

Enforcement of money judgment against interest in trust, see Code of Civil Procedure § 709.010.

Issuance of withholding order by state for state tax liability, see Code of Civil Procedure § 706.074.

Judgment debtor defined for purposes of this Chapter, see Code of Civil Procedure § 706.011.

Judgment debtor defined for purposes of this Title, see Code of Civil Procedure § 680.250.

Notice to employee of earnings withholding order, see Code of Civil Procedure § 706.122.

Research References

Forms

Asset Protection: Legal Planning, Strategies and Forms ¶ A.05, Appendix A.05 California (Opt Out State).

§ 706.050. Maximum amount of disposable earnings of an individual judgment debtor subject to levy

Section operative Sept. 1, 2023. See, also, § 706.050 operative until Sept. 1, 2023.

(a) Except as otherwise provided in this chapter, the maximum amount of disposable earnings of an individual judgment debtor for any workweek that is subject to levy under an earnings withholding order shall not exceed the lesser of the following:

(1) Twenty percent of the individual's disposable earnings for that week.

(2) Forty percent of the amount by which the individual's disposable earnings for that week exceed 48 times the state minimum hourly wage in effect at the time the earnings are payable. If a judgment debtor works in a location where the local minimum hourly wage is greater than the state minimum hourly wage, the local minimum hourly wage in effect at the time the earnings are payable shall be used for the calculation made pursuant to this paragraph.

(b) For any pay period other than weekly, the following multipliers shall be used to determine the maximum amount of disposable earnings subject to levy under an earnings withholding order that is proportional in effect to the calculation described in paragraph (2) of subdivision (a), except as specified in paragraph (1):

(1) For a daily pay period, the amounts shall be identical to the amounts described in subdivision (a).

(2) For a biweekly pay period, multiply the applicable hourly minimum wage by 96 work hours.

(3) For a semimonthly pay period, multiply the applicable hourly minimum wage by 104 work hours.

(4) For a monthly pay period, multiply the applicable hourly minimum wage by 208 work hours.

(c) This section shall become operative on September 1, 2023. *(Added by Stats.2022, c. 849 (S.B.1477), § 2, eff. Jan. 1, 2023, operative Sept. 1, 2023.)*

Cross References

Amount to be withheld, statement in earnings withholding order, see Code of Civil Procedure § 706.125.
Earnings defined for purposes of this Chapter, see Code of Civil Procedure § 706.011.
Enforcement of money judgment, exempt property, paid earnings, withholding order, wage assignment for support, see Code of Civil Procedure § 704.070.
Enforcement of money judgment against interest in trust, see Code of Civil Procedure § 709.010.
Issuance of withholding order by state for state tax liability, see Code of Civil Procedure § 706.074.
Judgment debtor defined for purposes of this Chapter, see Code of Civil Procedure § 706.011.
Judgment debtor defined for purposes of this Title, see Code of Civil Procedure § 680.250.
Notice to employee of earnings withholding order, see Code of Civil Procedure § 706.122.

§ 706.051. Amount necessary for support of judgment debtor or family; exemption

(a) For the purposes of this section, "family of the judgment debtor" includes the spouse or former spouse of the judgment debtor.

(b) Except as provided in subdivision (c), the portion of the judgment debtor's earnings that the judgment debtor proves is necessary for the support of the judgment debtor or the judgment debtor's family supported in whole or in part by the judgment debtor is exempt from levy under this chapter.

(c) The exemption provided in subdivision (b) is not available if any of the following exceptions applies:

(1) The debt was incurred pursuant to an order or award for the payment of attorney's fees under Section 2030, 3121, or 3557 of the Family Code.

(2) The debt was incurred for personal services rendered by an employee or former employee of the judgment debtor.

(3) The order is a withholding order for support under Section 706.030.

(4) The order is one governed by Article 4 (commencing with Section 706.070) (state tax order). *(Added by Stats.1982, c. 1364, p. 5175, § 2, operative July 1, 1983. Amended by Stats.2011, c. 694 (A.B.1388), § 1.)*

Cross References

Claim of exemption, grounds, procedures, see Code of Civil Procedure § 706.105.
Earnings defined for purposes of this Chapter, see Code of Civil Procedure § 706.011.
Employee defined for purposes of this Chapter, see Code of Civil Procedure § 706.011.
Enforcement of money judgment against interest in trust, see Code of Civil Procedure § 709.010.
Judgment debtor defined for purposes of this Chapter, see Code of Civil Procedure § 706.011.
Judgment debtor defined for purposes of this Title, see Code of Civil Procedure § 680.250.
Persons eligible to proceed without paying court fees and costs, see Government Code § 68632.

Research References

Forms

West's California Judicial Council Forms WG-026, Claim of Exemption and Financial Declaration (State Tax Liability).

§ 706.052. Disposable earnings and earnings withheld pursuant to earning assignment order for support; exemption; equitable division of earnings by court

(a) Except as provided in subdivision (b), one-half of the disposable earnings (as defined by Section 1672 of Title 15 of the United States Code) of the judgment debtor, plus any amount withheld from the judgment debtor's earnings pursuant to any earnings assignment order for support, is exempt from levy under this chapter where the earnings withholding order is a withholding order for support under Section 706.030.

(b) Except as provided in subdivision (c), upon motion of any interested party, the court shall make an equitable division of the judgment debtor's earnings that takes into account the needs of all the persons the judgment debtor is required to support and shall effectuate such division by an order determining the amount to be withheld from the judgment debtor's earnings pursuant to the withholding order for support.

(c) An order made under subdivision (b) may not authorize the withholding of an amount in excess of the amount that may be withheld for support under federal law under Section 1673 of Title 15 of the United States Code. *(Added by Stats.1982, c. 1364, p. 5176, § 2, operative July 1, 1983. Amended by Stats.1992, c. 163 (A.B.2641), § 48, operative Jan. 1, 1994.)*

Cross References

Application for health insurance coverage assignment, see Family Code § 3761.
Court defined for purposes of this Title, see Code of Civil Procedure § 680.160.
Earnings assignment order for support defined for purposes of this Chapter, see Code of Civil Procedure § 706.011.
Earnings defined for purposes of this Chapter, see Code of Civil Procedure § 706.011.
Enforcement of money judgment against interest in trust, see Code of Civil Procedure § 709.010.
Forms, adoption by Judicial Council, see Family Code § 3772.
Judgment debtor defined for purposes of this Chapter, see Code of Civil Procedure § 706.011.
Judgment debtor defined for purposes of this Title, see Code of Civil Procedure § 680.250.
Maximum amount of earnings subject to levy, see Code of Civil Procedure § 706.050.
Person defined for purposes of this Chapter, see Code of Civil Procedure § 706.011.
Person defined for purposes of this Title, see Code of Civil Procedure § 680.280.
Public Employees' Retirement System, withholding overdue support obligations, see Family Code § 17528.

Research References

Forms

West's California Judicial Council Forms FL-460, Qualified Domestic Relations Order for Support (Earnings Assignment Order for Support).
West's California Judicial Council Forms WG-004, Earnings Withholding Order for Support.
West's California Judicial Council Forms WG-030, Earnings Withholding Order for Elder or Dependent Adult Financial Abuse.

ARTICLE 5. PROCEDURE FOR EARNINGS WITHHOLDING ORDERS AND EXEMPTION CLAIMS

Section
706.100. Practice and procedure in proceedings under this chapter; rules.
706.101. Service of order by delivery; earnings withholding order.
706.102. Issuance of earnings withholding order where writ of execution issued and time for levy on property under writ not yet expired.
706.103. Service of documents by levying officer on employer.
706.104. Delivery of copy of order, notice of earnings withholding, copy of form for claim of exemption, and copy of form to provide financial statement; completion of employer return.

CODE OF CIVIL PROCEDURE

Section
706.105. Claim of exemption under Section 706.051.
706.106. Findings in court proceedings.
706.108. Earnings withholding order; service and filing requirements; duties of levying officer.
706.109. Earnings withholding order; issuance against spouse of judgment debtor.

§ 706.100. Practice and procedure in proceedings under this chapter; rules

Notwithstanding any other provision of law, the Judicial Council may provide by rule for the practice and procedure in proceedings under this chapter except for the state's administrative hearings provided by Article 4 (commencing with Section 706.070). *(Added by Stats.1982, c. 1364, p. 5181, § 2, operative July 1, 1983.)*

Cross References

Forms prescribed by state, see Code of Civil Procedure § 706.081.

Research References

Forms

Asset Protection: Legal Planning, Strategies and Forms ¶ A.05, Appendix A.05 California (Opt Out State).

§ 706.101. Service of order by delivery; earnings withholding order

(a) An earnings withholding order shall be served by the levying officer upon the employer by delivery of the order to any of the following:

(1) The managing agent or person in charge, at the time of service, of the branch or office where the employee works or the office from which the employee is paid. In the case of a state employee, the office from which the employee is paid does not include the Controller's office unless the employee works directly for the Controller's office.

(2) Any person to whom a copy of the summons and of the complaint may be delivered to make service on the employer under Article 4 (commencing with Section 416.10) of Chapter 4 of Title 5.

(b) Service of an earnings withholding order shall be made by personal delivery as provided in Section 415.10 or 415.20 or by delivery by first-class mail, postage prepaid. When service is made by first-class mail, service is complete at the time of receipt of the earnings withholding order, as indicated in the employer's return, or the date of mailing if the date of receipt is not indicated on the employer's return. If the levying officer attempts service by first-class mail under this subdivision and does not receive the employer's return within 15 days from the date of mailing, the levying officer shall make service as provided in Article 3 (commencing with Section 415.10) of Chapter 4 of Title 5. For purposes of this section, "employer's return" refers to the Judicial Council-issued form specified by Section 706.126.

(c) The state may issue an earnings withholding order directly, without the use of a levying officer, for purposes of collecting overpayments of unemployment compensation or disability benefits pursuant to Article 4 (commencing with Section 1375) of Chapter 5 of Part 1 of, and Article 5 (commencing with Section 2735) of Chapter 2 of Part 2 of, Division 1 of the Unemployment Insurance Code. The earnings withholding order shall be served by registered or certified mail, postage prepaid, with return receipt requested. Service is deemed complete at the time the return receipt is executed by, or on behalf of, the recipient. If the state does not receive a return receipt within 15 days from the date of deposit in the mail of the withholding order, the state shall refer the earnings withholding order to a levying officer for service in accordance with subdivision (b).

(d) Except as provided in subdivision (b) or (c), service of any notice or document under this chapter may be made by first-class mail, postage prepaid. If service is made on the employer after the employer's return has been received by the levying officer, the service shall be made by first-class mail, postage prepaid, on the person designated in the employer's return to receive notices and at the address indicated in the employer's return, whether or not that address is within the county. This subdivision does not preclude service by personal delivery (1) on the employer before the employer's return has been received by the levying officer or (2) on the person designated in the employer's return after its receipt.

(e) Notwithstanding subdivision (b), if the judgment creditor so requests, the levying officer shall make service of the earnings withholding order by personal delivery as provided in Section 415.10 or 415.20. *(Added by Stats.1982, c. 1364, p. 5181, § 2.2, operative July 1, 1983. Amended by Stats.1984, c. 538, § 28; Stats.1989, c. 1416, § 24; Stats.2002, c. 890 (A.B.2929), § 1; Stats.2010, c. 680 (A.B. 2394), § 13.)*

Cross References

Delivery by first class mail, see Code of Civil Procedure § 415.20.
Earnings defined for purposes of this Chapter, see Code of Civil Procedure § 706.011.
Employee defined for purposes of this Chapter, see Code of Civil Procedure § 706.011.
Employer defined for purposes of this Chapter, see Code of Civil Procedure § 706.011.
Fees for service of earnings withholding order, see Government Code § 26750.
Judgment creditor defined for purposes of this Chapter, see Code of Civil Procedure § 706.011.
Judgment creditor defined for purposes of this Title, see Code of Civil Procedure § 680.240.
Person defined for purposes of this Chapter, see Code of Civil Procedure § 706.011.
Person defined for purposes of this Title, see Code of Civil Procedure § 680.280.
Personal delivery, see Code of Civil Procedure § 415.10.
Service of earnings withholding orders, electronic transmission or other electronic technology, see Revenue and Taxation Code § 19264.
Service of order, notice or document for taxes, see Code of Civil Procedure § 706.080.
State Controller, generally, see Government Code § 12402 et seq.
Unemployment compensation, generally, see Labor Code § 2010 et seq.

Research References

Forms

2B Am. Jur. Pl. & Pr. Forms Attachment and Garnishment § 240, Statutory References.

§ 706.102. Issuance of earnings withholding order where writ of execution issued and time for levy on property under writ not yet expired

(a) If a writ of execution has been issued to the county where the judgment debtor's employer is to be served and the time specified in subdivision (b) of Section 699.530 for levy on property under the writ has not expired, a judgment creditor may apply for the issuance of an earnings withholding order by filing an application with a levying officer in such county who shall promptly issue an earnings withholding order.

(b) This section does not apply where the earnings withholding order is a withholding order for taxes. *(Added by Stats.1982, c. 1364, p. 5182, § 2, operative July 1, 1983.)*

Cross References

Earnings defined for purposes of this Chapter, see Code of Civil Procedure § 706.011.
Employer defined for purposes of this Chapter, see Code of Civil Procedure § 706.011.
Judgment creditor defined for purposes of this Chapter, see Code of Civil Procedure § 706.011.
Judgment creditor defined for purposes of this Title, see Code of Civil Procedure § 680.240.

Judgment debtor defined for purposes of this Chapter, see Code of Civil Procedure § 706.011.
Judgment debtor defined for purposes of this Title, see Code of Civil Procedure § 680.250.
Levy on property under writ, see Code of Civil Procedure § 699.530.
Property defined for purposes of this Title, see Code of Civil Procedure § 680.310.
Writ defined for purposes of this Title, see Code of Civil Procedure § 680.380.

§ 706.103. Service of documents by levying officer on employer

(a) The levying officer shall serve upon the designated employer all of the following:

(1) The original and one copy of the earnings withholding order.

(2) The form for the employer's return.

(3) The notice to employee of earnings withholding order.

(4) A copy of the form that the judgment debtor may use to make a claim of exemption.

(5) A copy of the form the judgment debtor may use to provide a financial statement.

(b) At the time the levying officer makes service pursuant to subdivision (a), the levying officer shall provide the employer with a copy of the employer's instructions referred to in Section 706.127. The Judicial Council may adopt rules prescribing the circumstances when compliance with this subdivision is not required.

(c) No earnings withholding order shall be served upon the employer after the time specified in subdivision (b) of Section 699.530. *(Added by Stats.1982, c. 1364, p. 5182, § 2, operative July 1, 1983. Amended by Stats.2013, c. 64 (S.B.233), § 5.)*

Cross References

Earnings defined for purposes of this Chapter, see Code of Civil Procedure § 706.011.
Employee defined for purposes of this Chapter, see Code of Civil Procedure § 706.011.
Employer defined for purposes of this Chapter, see Code of Civil Procedure § 706.011.
Judgment creditor defined for purposes of this Title, see Code of Civil Procedure § 680.240.

Research References

Forms

2B Am. Jur. Pl. & Pr. Forms Attachment and Garnishment § 240, Statutory References.

§ 706.104. Delivery of copy of order, notice of earnings withholding, copy of form for claim of exemption, and copy of form to provide financial statement; completion of employer return

Any employer who is served with an earnings withholding order shall:

(a) Deliver to the judgment debtor a copy of the earnings withholding order, the notice to employee of earnings withholding, a copy of the form that the judgment debtor may use to make a claim of exemption, and a copy of the form the judgment debtor may use to provide a financial statement within 10 days from the date of service. If the judgment debtor is no longer employed by the employer and the employer does not owe the employee any earnings, the employer is not required to make such delivery. The employer is not subject to any civil liability for failure to comply with this subdivision. Nothing in this subdivision limits the power of a court to hold the employer in contempt of court for failure to comply with this subdivision.

(b) Complete the employer's return on the form provided by the levying officer and mail it by first-class mail, postage prepaid, to the levying officer within 15 days from the date of service. If the earnings withholding order is ineffective, the employer shall state in the employer's return that the order will not be complied with for this reason and shall return the order to the levying officer with the employer's return. *(Added by Stats.1982, c. 1364, p. 5182, § 2, operative July 1, 1983. Amended by Stats.2013, c. 64 (S.B.233), § 6.)*

Cross References

Court defined for purposes of this Title, see Code of Civil Procedure § 680.160.
Earnings defined for purposes of this Chapter, see Code of Civil Procedure § 706.011.
Employee defined for purposes of this Chapter, see Code of Civil Procedure § 706.011.
Employer defined for purposes of this Chapter, see Code of Civil Procedure § 706.011.
Judgment creditor defined for purposes of this Title, see Code of Civil Procedure § 680.240.
Judgment debtor defined for purposes of this Chapter, see Code of Civil Procedure § 706.011.
Judgment debtor defined for purposes of this Title, see Code of Civil Procedure § 680.250.

Research References

Forms

2B Am. Jur. Pl. & Pr. Forms Attachment and Garnishment § 240, Statutory References.
2B Am. Jur. Pl. & Pr. Forms Attachment and Garnishment § 287, Statutory References.

§ 706.105. Claim of exemption under Section 706.051

(a) A judgment debtor may claim an exemption under Section 706.051 under either of the following circumstances:

(1) No prior hearing has been held with respect to the earnings withholding order.

(2) There has been a material change in circumstances since the time of the last prior hearing on the earnings withholding order.

(b) A claim of exemption shall be made by filing with the levying officer an original and one copy of (1) the judgment debtor's claim of exemption and (2) the judgment debtor's financial statement.

(c) Upon filing of the claim of exemption, the levying officer shall promptly send to the judgment creditor, at the address stated in the application for the earnings withholding order, by first-class mail, postage prepaid, all of the following:

(1) A copy of the claim of exemption.

(2) A copy of the financial statement.

(3) A notice of claim of exemption. The notice shall state that the claim of exemption has been filed and that the earnings withholding order will be terminated, or modified to reflect the amount of earnings claimed to be exempt in the claim of exemption, unless a notice of opposition to the claim of exemption is filed with the levying officer by the judgment creditor within 10 days after the date of the mailing of the notice of claim of exemption.

(d) A judgment creditor who desires to contest a claim of exemption shall, within 10 days after the date of the mailing of the notice of claim of exemption, file with the levying officer a notice of opposition to the claim of exemption.

(e) If a notice of opposition to the claim of exemption is filed with the levying officer within the 10–day period, the judgment creditor is entitled to a hearing on the claim of exemption. If the judgment creditor desires a hearing on the claim of exemption, the judgment creditor shall file a notice of motion for an order determining the claim of exemption with the court within 10 days after the date the levying officer mailed the notice of claim of exemption. If the notice of motion is so filed, the hearing on the motion shall be held not later than 30 days from the date the notice of motion was filed unless continued by the court for good cause. At the time prescribed by subdivision (b) of Section 1005, the judgment creditor shall give written notice of the hearing to the levying officer and shall serve a notice of the hearing and a copy of the notice of opposition to the claim of exemption on the judgment debtor and, if the claim of

§ 706.105

exemption so requested, on the attorney for the judgment debtor. Service is deemed made when the notice of the hearing and a copy of the notice of opposition to the claim of exemption are deposited in the mail, postage prepaid, addressed to the judgment debtor at the address stated in the claim of exemption and, if service on the attorney for the judgment debtor was requested in the claim of exemption, to the attorney at the address stated in the claim of exemption. The judgment creditor shall file proof of the service with the court. After receiving the notice of the hearing and before the date set for the hearing, the levying officer shall file the claim of exemption and the notice of opposition to the claim of exemption with the court.

(f) If the levying officer does not receive a notice of opposition to the claim of exemption within the 10-day period after the date of mailing of the notice of claim of exemption and a notice of the hearing not later than 10 days after the filing of the notice of opposition to the claim of exemption, the levying officer shall serve on the employer one of the following:

(1) A notice that the earnings withholding order has been terminated if all of the judgment debtor's earnings were claimed to be exempt.

(2) A modified earnings withholding order that reflects the amount of earnings claimed to be exempt in the claim of exemption if only a portion of the judgment debtor's earnings was claimed to be exempt.

(g) If, after hearing, the court orders that the earnings withholding order be modified or terminated, the clerk shall promptly transmit a certified copy of the order to the levying officer who shall promptly serve on the employer of the judgment debtor (1) a copy of the modified earnings withholding order or (2) a notice that the earnings withholding order has been terminated. The court may order that the earnings withholding order be terminated as of a date that precedes the date of hearing. If the court determines that any amount withheld pursuant to the earnings withholding order shall be paid to the judgment debtor, the court shall make an order directing the person who holds that amount to pay it promptly to the judgment debtor.

(h) If the earnings withholding order is terminated by the court, unless the court otherwise orders or unless there is a material change of circumstances since the time of the last prior hearing on the earnings withholding order, the judgment creditor may not apply for another earnings withholding order directed to the same employer with respect to the same judgment debtor for a period of 100 days following the date of service of the earnings withholding order or 60 days after the date of the termination of the order, whichever is later.

(i) If an employer has withheld and paid over amounts pursuant to an earnings withholding order after the date of termination of the order but prior to the receipt of notice of its termination, the judgment debtor may recover those amounts only from the levying officer if the levying officer still holds those amounts or, if those amounts have been paid over to the judgment creditor, from the judgment creditor. If the employer has withheld amounts pursuant to an earnings withholding order after termination of the order but has not paid over those amounts to the levying officer, the employer shall promptly pay those amounts to the judgment debtor.

(j) An appeal lies from any court order under this section denying a claim of exemption or modifying or terminating an earnings withholding order. An appeal by the judgment creditor from an order modifying or terminating the earnings withholding order does not stay the order from which the appeal is taken. Notwithstanding the appeal, until the order modifying or terminating the earnings withholding order is set aside or modified, the order allowing the claim of exemption in whole or in part shall be given the same effect as if the appeal had not been taken.

(k) This section does not apply to a withholding order for support or a withholding order for taxes. *(Added by Stats.1982, c. 1364, p. 5183, § 2, operative July 1, 1983. Amended by Stats.1989, c. 693, § 3; Stats.1998, c. 931 (S.B.2139), § 94, eff. Sept. 28, 1998.)*

Cross References

Court defined for purposes of this Title, see Code of Civil Procedure § 680.160.
Earnings defined for purposes of this Chapter, see Code of Civil Procedure § 706.011.
Employer defined for purposes of this Chapter, see Code of Civil Procedure § 706.011.
Judgment creditor defined for purposes of this Chapter, see Code of Civil Procedure § 706.011.
Judgment creditor defined for purposes of this Title, see Code of Civil Procedure § 680.240.
Judgment debtor defined for purposes of this Chapter, see Code of Civil Procedure § 706.011.
Judgment debtor defined for purposes of this Title, see Code of Civil Procedure § 680.250.
Maximum amount of earnings subject to levy, see Code of Civil Procedure § 706.050.
Person defined for purposes of this Chapter, see Code of Civil Procedure § 706.011.
Person defined for purposes of this Title, see Code of Civil Procedure § 680.280.
Service of earnings withholding orders, electronic transmission or other electronic technology, see Revenue and Taxation Code § 19264.

Research References

Forms

2B Am. Jur. Pl. & Pr. Forms Attachment and Garnishment § 287, Statutory References.
West's California Judicial Council Forms WG–008, Notice of Filing of Claim of Exemption.
West's California Judicial Council Forms WG–011, Order Determining Claim of Exemption.
West's California Judicial Council Forms WG–012, Notice of Termination or Modification of Earnings Withholding Order.

§ 706.106. Findings in court proceedings

No findings are required in court proceedings under this chapter. *(Added by Stats.1982, c. 1364, p. 5185, § 2, operative July 1, 1983.)*

Cross References

Court defined for purposes of this Title, see Code of Civil Procedure § 680.160.

§ 706.108. Earnings withholding order; service and filing requirements; duties of levying officer

(a) If a writ of execution has been issued to the county where the judgment debtor's employer is to be served and the time specified in subdivision (b) of Section 699.530 for levy on property under the writ has not expired, a judgment creditor may deliver an application for issuance of an earnings withholding order to a registered process server who may then issue an earnings withholding order.

(b) If the registered process server has issued the earnings withholding order, the registered process server, before serving the earnings withholding order, shall cause to be deposited with the levying officer a copy of the writ of execution, the application for issuance of an earnings withholding order, a copy of the earnings withholding order, and the fee, as provided by Section 26750 of the Government Code.

(c) A registered process server may serve an earnings withholding order on an employer whether the earnings withholding order was issued by a levying officer or by a registered process server, but no earnings withholding order may be served after the time specified in subdivision (b) of Section 699.530. In performing this function, the registered process server shall serve upon the designated employer all of the following:

(1) The original and one copy of the earnings withholding order.

(2) The form for the employer's return.

(3) The notice to the employee of the earnings withholding order.

(4) A copy of the form that the judgment debtor may use to make a claim of exemption.

(5) A copy of the form the judgment debtor may use to provide a financial statement.

(6) A copy of the employer's instructions referred to in Section 706.127, except as otherwise prescribed in rules adopted by the Judicial Council.

(d) Within five court days after service under this section, all of the following shall be filed with the levying officer:

(1) The writ of execution, if it is not already in the hands of the levying officer.

(2) Proof of service on the employer of the papers listed in subdivision (c).

(3) Instructions in writing, as required by the provisions of Section 687.010.

(e) If the fee provided by Section 26750 of the Government Code has been paid, the levying officer shall perform all other duties required by this chapter as if the levying officer had served the earnings withholding order. If the registered process server does not comply with subdivisions (b), where applicable, and (d), the service of the earnings withholding order is ineffective and the levying officer shall not be required to perform any duties under the order, and may terminate the order and release any withheld earnings to the judgment debtor.

(f) The fee for services of a registered process server under this section is a recoverable cost pursuant to Section 1033.5. *(Added by Stats.1984, c. 538, § 29. Amended by Stats.1987, c. 1080, § 6; Stats.2002, c. 197 (A.B.2493), § 4; Stats.2009, c. 54 (S.B.544), § 6; Stats.2013, c. 64 (S.B.233), § 7; Stats.2016, c. 102 (A.B.2211), § 3, eff. Jan. 1, 2017.)*

Cross References

Earnings defined for purposes of this Chapter, see Code of Civil Procedure § 706.011.
Employee defined for purposes of this Chapter, see Code of Civil Procedure § 706.011.
Employer defined for purposes of this Chapter, see Code of Civil Procedure § 706.011.
Judgment creditor defined for purposes of this Chapter, see Code of Civil Procedure § 706.011.
Judgment creditor defined for purposes of this Title, see Code of Civil Procedure § 680.240.
Judgment debtor defined for purposes of this Chapter, see Code of Civil Procedure § 706.011.
Judgment debtor defined for purposes of this Title, see Code of Civil Procedure § 680.250.
Levy on property under writ, see Code of Civil Procedure § 699.530.
Property defined for purposes of this Title, see Code of Civil Procedure § 680.310.
Registered process server defined for purposes of this Title, see Code of Civil Procedure § 680.330.
Writ defined for purposes of this Title, see Code of Civil Procedure § 680.380.

Research References

Forms

West's California Judicial Council Forms WG-002, Earnings Withholding Order.
West's California Judicial Council Forms WG-004, Earnings Withholding Order for Support.
West's California Judicial Council Forms WG-030, Earnings Withholding Order for Elder or Dependent Adult Financial Abuse.

§ 706.109. Earnings withholding order; issuance against spouse of judgment debtor

An earnings withholding order may not be issued against the earnings of the spouse of the judgment debtor except by court order upon noticed motion. *(Added by Stats.1984, c. 1671, § 20.)*

Cross References

Court defined for purposes of this Title, see Code of Civil Procedure § 680.160.
Earnings defined for purposes of this Chapter, see Code of Civil Procedure § 706.011.
Judgment debtor defined for purposes of this Chapter, see Code of Civil Procedure § 706.011.
Judgment debtor defined for purposes of this Title, see Code of Civil Procedure § 680.250.

CHAPTER 6. MISCELLANEOUS CREDITORS' REMEDIES

ARTICLE 2. EXAMINATION PROCEEDINGS

Section
708.110. Order for examination; service; contents.
708.120. Orders where property in possession or control of third party.
708.130. Witnesses; privilege.
708.140. Proceedings conducted by referee or temporary judge.
708.150. Order for examination in case of corporation, partnership, etc.
708.160. Venue for examination.
708.170. Failure to appear after service of order; improper service.
708.180. Adverse claim of, or denial of debt by third party.
708.190. Intervention of third party.
708.200. Protective orders.
708.205. Order for satisfaction of money judgment or forbidding transfer or payment.

§ 708.110. Order for examination; service; contents

(a) The judgment creditor may apply to the proper court for an order requiring the judgment debtor to appear before the court, or before a referee appointed by the court, at a time and place specified in the order, to furnish information to aid in enforcement of the money judgment.

(b) If the judgment creditor has not caused the judgment debtor to be examined under this section during the preceding 120 days, the court shall make the order upon ex parte application of the judgment creditor.

(c) If the judgment creditor has caused the judgment debtor to be examined under this section during the preceding 120 days, the court shall make the order if the judgment creditor by affidavit or otherwise shows good cause for the order. The application shall be made on noticed motion if the court so directs or a court rule so requires. Otherwise, it may be made ex parte.

(d) The judgment creditor shall personally serve a copy of the order on the judgment debtor not less than 10 days before the date set for the examination. Service shall be made in the manner specified in Section 415.10. Service of the order creates a lien on the personal property of the judgment debtor for a period of one year from the date of the order unless extended or sooner terminated by the court.

(e) The order shall contain the following statement in 14-point boldface type if printed or in capital letters if typed: "NOTICE TO JUDGMENT DEBTOR. If you fail to appear at the time and place specified in this order, you may be subject to arrest and punishment for contempt of court and the court may make an order requiring you to pay the reasonable attorney's fees incurred by the judgment creditor in this proceeding." *(Added by Stats.1982, c. 1364, p. 5190, § 2, operative July 1, 1983. Amended by Stats.1984, c. 538, § 30; Stats.1993, c. 793 (A.B.504), § 1.)*

§ 708.110

Cross References

Court defined for purposes of this Title, see Code of Civil Procedure § 680.160.
Depositions, costs, record of testimony, see Code of Civil Procedure § 2025.510.
Filing fees, generally, see Government Code § 70617.
Judgment creditor defined for purposes of this Title, see Code of Civil Procedure § 680.240.
Judgment debtor defined for purposes of this Title, see Code of Civil Procedure § 680.250.
Money judgment defined for purposes of this Title, see Code of Civil Procedure § 680.270.
Personal property defined for purposes of this Title, see Code of Civil Procedure § 680.290.
Property defined for purposes of this Title, see Code of Civil Procedure § 680.310.
Venue for examination, see Code of Civil Procedure § 708.160.

Research References

Forms

Asset Protection: Legal Planning, Strategies and Forms ¶ 12.01, Overview.
3 California Transactions Forms—Business Transactions § 22:2, Types of Liens.
West's California Code Forms, Civil Procedure § 708.110 Form 1, Enforcement of Judgments—Application and Order for Appearance and Examination (Attachment—Enforcement of Judgment)—Official Form.
West's California Judicial Council Forms AT–138, Application and Order for Appearance and Examination.
West's California Judicial Council Forms EJ–125, Application and Order for Appearance and Examination.

§ 708.120. Orders where property in possession or control of third party

(a) Upon ex parte application by a judgment creditor who has a money judgment and proof by the judgment creditor by affidavit or otherwise to the satisfaction of the proper court that a third person has possession or control of property in which the judgment debtor has an interest or is indebted to the judgment debtor in an amount exceeding two hundred fifty dollars ($250), the court shall make an order directing the third person to appear before the court, or before a referee appointed by the court, at a time and place specified in the order, to answer concerning such property or debt. The affidavit in support of the judgment creditor's application may be based on the affiant's information and belief.

(b) Not less than 10 days prior to the date set for the examination, a copy of the order shall be:

(1) Served personally on the third person.

(2) Served personally or by mail on the judgment debtor.

(c) If the property in the third person's possession or control in which the judgment debtor has an interest or the debt owed by the third person to the judgment debtor is described in the affidavit or application for an order under subdivision (a) in a manner reasonably adequate to permit it to be identified, service of the order on the third person creates a lien on the judgment debtor's interest in the property or on the debt for a period of one year from the date of the order unless extended or sooner terminated by the court.

(d) The judgment debtor may claim that all or any portion of the property or debt is exempt from enforcement of a money judgment by application to the court on noticed motion, filed with the court and personally served on the judgment creditor not later than three days before the date set for the examination. The judgment debtor shall execute an affidavit in support of the application that includes all of the matters set forth in subdivision (b) of Section 703.520. If a claim of exemption is made pursuant to this section, a notice of opposition to the claim of exemption is not required. The court shall determine any claim of exemption made pursuant to this section. Failure of the judgment debtor to make a claim of exemption does not preclude the judgment debtor from later claiming the exemption unless the property or debt is described in the order in a manner reasonably adequate to permit it to be identified and the judgment debtor receives notice of the examination proceeding at least 10 days before the date set for the examination.

(e) An order made pursuant to subdivision (a) shall contain the following statements in 14–point boldface type if printed or in capital letters if typed:

(1) "NOTICE TO PERSON SERVED. If you fail to appear at the time and place specified in this order, you may be subject to arrest and punishment for contempt of court and the court may make an order requiring you to pay the reasonable attorney's fees incurred by the judgment creditor in this proceeding."

(2) "NOTICE TO JUDGMENT DEBTOR. The person in whose favor the judgment was entered in this action claims that the person to be examined pursuant to this order has possession or control of property which is yours or owes you a debt. This property or debt is as follows: (Description of property or debt). If you claim that all or any portion of this property or debt is exempt from enforcement of the money judgment, you must file your exemption claim in writing with the court and personally serve a copy on the judgment creditor not later than three days before the date set for the examination. You must appear at the time and place set for this examination to establish your claim of exemption or your exemption may be waived."

(f) An order made pursuant to subdivision (a) is not effective unless, at the time it is served on the third person, the person serving the order tenders to the third person fees for the mileage necessary to be traveled from the third person's residence to the place of examination. The mileage fees shall be in the same amount generally provided for witnesses when legally required to attend civil proceedings in the court where the examination proceeding is to be conducted. *(Added by Stats.1982, c. 1364, p. 5191, § 2, operative July 1, 1983. Amended by Stats.1995, c. 576 (A.B.1225), § 3.6.)*

Cross References

Court defined for purposes of this Title, see Code of Civil Procedure § 680.160.
Judgment creditor defined for purposes of this Title, see Code of Civil Procedure § 680.240.
Judgment debtor defined for purposes of this Title, see Code of Civil Procedure § 680.250.
Money judgment defined for purposes of this Title, see Code of Civil Procedure § 680.270.
Order applying property toward satisfaction of judgment, see Code of Civil Procedure § 708.205.
Order for satisfaction of money judgment, see Code of Civil Procedure § 708.205.
Person defined for purposes of this Title, see Code of Civil Procedure § 680.280.
Property defined for purposes of this Title, see Code of Civil Procedure § 680.310.
Third party in debt to or in possession of property of judgment debtor, action by judgment creditor, see Code of Civil Procedure § 708.210.
Venue for examination, see Code of Civil Procedure § 708.160.

Research References

Forms

3 California Transactions Forms—Business Transactions § 22:2, Types of Liens.
West's California Code Forms, Civil Procedure § 708.110 Form 1, Enforcement of Judgments—Application and Order for Appearance and Examination (Attachment—Enforcement of Judgment)—Official Form.
West's California Judicial Council Forms AT–138, Application and Order for Appearance and Examination.
West's California Judicial Council Forms EJ–125, Application and Order for Appearance and Examination.

§ 708.130. Witnesses; privilege

(a) Witnesses may be required to appear and testify before the court or referee in an examination proceeding under this article in the same manner as upon the trial of an issue.

(b) The privilege prescribed by Article 4 (commencing with Section 970) of Chapter 4 of Division 8 of the Evidence Code does not apply in an examination proceeding under this article. *(Added by Stats.1982, c. 1364, p. 5192, § 2, operative July 1, 1983.)*

Cross References

Court defined for purposes of this Title, see Code of Civil Procedure § 680.160.

Means of production of evidence, generally, see Code of Civil Procedure § 1985 et seq.

Residency requirements for attendance of witnesses, see Code of Civil Procedure § 1989.

Rights and duties of witnesses, see Code of Civil Procedure §§ 2064, 2065.

§ 708.140. Proceedings conducted by referee or temporary judge

(a) The examination proceedings authorized by this article may be conducted by a referee appointed by the court. The referee may issue, modify, or vacate an order authorized by Section 708.205, may make a protective order authorized by Section 708.200, and may issue a warrant authorized by Section 708.170, and has the same power as the court to grant adjournments, to preserve order, and to subpoena witnesses to attend the examination, but only the court that ordered the reference has power to do the following:

(1) Punish for contempt for disobeying an order of the referee.

(2) Make an award of attorney's fees pursuant to Section 708.170.

(3) Determine a contested claim of exemption or determine a third-party claim under Section 708.180.

(b) Only a member of the State Bar of California is eligible for appointment as a referee pursuant to this article. A person who was duly appointed as a referee prior to July 1, 1983, pursuant to the law in operation at the time of appointment, and who is available to perform the duties of a referee on July 1, 1983, shall be exempt from the requirements of this subdivision.

(c) Nothing in subdivision (a) limits the power of a court to appoint a temporary judge pursuant to Section 21 of Article VI of the California Constitution. *(Added by Stats.1982, c. 1364, p. 5192, § 2, operative July 1, 1983. Amended by Stats.1983, c. 155, § 19, eff. June 30, 1983, operative July 1, 1983.)*

Cross References

Contempts, see Code of Civil Procedure § 1209 et seq.

Court defined for purposes of this Title, see Code of Civil Procedure § 680.160.

Order by referee forbidding transfer of interest, see Code of Civil Procedure § 708.240.

Person defined for purposes of this Title, see Code of Civil Procedure § 680.280.

§ 708.150. Order for examination in case of corporation, partnership, etc.

(a)(1) If a corporation, partnership, association, trust, limited liability company, or other organization is served with an order to appear for an examination, it shall designate to appear and be examined one or more officers, directors, managing agents, or other persons who are familiar with its property and debts.

(2) If a corporation, partnership, association, trust, limited liability company, or other organization served with an order to appear for an examination fails to designate a person to appear pursuant to paragraph (1), the order to appear for an examination shall be deemed to have been made to and served upon the individuals designated in the manner described in paragraph (2) of subdivision (c).

(b) If the order to appear for an examination requires the appearance of a specified individual, the specified individual shall appear for the examination and may be accompanied by one or more officers, directors, managing agents, or other persons familiar with the property and debts of the corporation, partnership, association, trust, limited liability company, or other organization.

(c) If the order to appear for the examination does not require the appearance of a specified individual, the order shall advise the corporation, partnership, association, trust, limited liability company, or other organization of all of the following:

(1) The organization's duty to make a designation under paragraph (1) of subdivision (a).

(2) That the organization's failure to make a designation under paragraph (1) of subdivision (a) shall result in the order to appear for the examination to be deemed to have been made to, and require the appearance of, the following:

(A) If the organization is a corporation registered with the Secretary of State, a natural person named as the chief financial officer in the corporation's most recent filing with the Secretary of State. If no one is so named, a natural person named as the chief executive officer in the corporation's most recent filing with the Secretary of State. If no one is so named, a natural person named as the secretary in the corporation's most recent filing with the Secretary of State.

(B) If the organization is a limited liability company registered with the Secretary of State, the first natural person named as a manager or member in the limited liability company's most recent filing with the Secretary of State.

(C) If the organization is a limited partnership registered with the Secretary of State, the first natural person named as a general partner in the limited partnership's most recent filing with the Secretary of State.

(D) If the organization is not registered with the Secretary of State or the organization's filings with the Secretary of State do not identify a natural person as described in subparagraph (A), (B), or (C), a natural person identified by the judgment creditor as being familiar with the property and debts of the organization, together with an affidavit or declaration signed by the judgment creditor that sets forth the factual basis for the identification of the individual. The affidavit or declaration shall be served on the organization together with the order.

(3) That service of an order to appear for an examination upon an organization by any method permitted under this code or the Corporations Code, including service on the agent of the organization for service of process, shall be deemed effective service of the order to appear upon the individuals identified under subparagraphs (A), (B), (C), and (D) of paragraph (2).

(d) A corporation, partnership, association, trust, limited liability company, or other organization, whether or not a party, may appear at an examination through any authorized officer, director, or employee, whether or not the person is an attorney.

(e) The powers of the court under Section 708.170 extend to natural persons ordered to appear and served pursuant to this section.

(f) This section shall be strictly construed and its requirements may not be varied by local rule or otherwise. *(Added by Stats.1982, c. 1364, p. 5192, § 2, operative July 1, 1983. Amended by Stats.1984, c. 538, § 30.5; Stats.2020, c. 36 (A.B.3364), § 24, eff. Jan. 1, 2021; Stats.2021, c. 30 (A.B.1580), § 1, eff. Jan. 1, 2022.)*

Cross References

Person defined for purposes of this Title, see Code of Civil Procedure § 680.280.

Property defined for purposes of this Title, see Code of Civil Procedure § 680.310.

§ 708.160. Venue for examination

(a) Except as otherwise provided in this section, the proper court for examination of a person under this article is the court in which the money judgment is entered.

(b) A person sought to be examined may not be required to attend an examination before a court located outside the county in which the person resides or has a place of business unless the distance from the person's place of residence or place of business to the place of examination is less than 150 miles.

(c) If a person sought to be examined does not reside or have a place of business in the county where the judgment is entered, the superior court in the county where the person resides or has a place of business is a proper court for examination of the person.

(d) If the judgment creditor seeks an examination of a person before a court other than the court in which the judgment is entered, the judgment creditor shall file an application that shall include all of the following:

(1) An abstract of judgment in the form prescribed by Section 674.

(2) An affidavit in support of the application stating the place of residence or place of business of the person sought to be examined.

(3) Any necessary affidavit or showing for the examination as required by Section 708.110 or 708.120.

(4) The filing fee for a motion as provided in subdivision (a) of Section 70617 of the Government Code. *(Added by Stats.1982, c. 1364, p. 5193, § 2, operative July 1, 1983. Amended by Stats.2005, c. 75 (A.B.145), § 38, eff. July 19, 2005, operative Jan. 1, 2006.)*

Cross References

Application of Trial Court Trust Fund provisions to fees and fines collected pursuant to this section, see Government Code § 68085.

Court defined for purposes of this Title, see Code of Civil Procedure § 680.160.

Deposit of fees or fines collected pursuant to this section in the Trial Court Trust Fund, effect of prior agreements or practices, long-term revenue allocation schedule proposal, see Government Code § 68085.5.

Fees for miscellaneous services, see Government Code § 70626.

Filing fee for first paper in civil action, documents included, see Government Code § 70611.

Filing fees, generally, see Government Code § 70617.

Judgment creditor defined for purposes of this Title, see Code of Civil Procedure § 680.240.

Money judgment defined for purposes of this Title, see Code of Civil Procedure § 680.270.

Organization and government of courts, collection of fees and fines pursuant to this section, deposits, see Government Code § 68085.1.

Person defined for purposes of this Title, see Code of Civil Procedure § 680.280.

§ 708.170. Failure to appear after service of order; improper service

(a) If an order requiring a person to appear for an examination was served by a sheriff, marshal, a person specially appointed by the court in the order, or a registered process server, and the person fails to appear:

(1) The court may do either of the following:

(A) Pursuant to a warrant, have the person brought before the court to answer for the failure to appear and may punish the person for contempt.

(B) Issue a warrant for the arrest of the person who failed to appear as required by the court order, pursuant to Section 1993.

(2) If the person's failure to appear is without good cause, the judgment creditor shall be awarded reasonable attorney's fees incurred in the examination proceeding. Attorney's fees awarded against the judgment debtor shall be added to and become part of the principal amount of the judgment.

(b) A person who willfully makes an improper service of an order for an examination which subsequently results in the arrest pursuant to subdivision (a) of the person who fails to appear is guilty of a misdemeanor. *(Added by Stats.1982, c. 1364, p. 5193, § 2, operative July 1, 1983. Amended by Stats.1996, c. 872 (A.B.3472), § 17; Stats.2006, c. 277 (A.B.2369), § 2.)*

Cross References

Court defined for purposes of this Title, see Code of Civil Procedure § 680.160.

Judgment creditor defined for purposes of this Title, see Code of Civil Procedure § 680.240.

Judgment debtor defined for purposes of this Title, see Code of Civil Procedure § 680.250.

Misdemeanors, definition and penalties, see Penal Code §§ 17, 19, 19.2.

Person defined for purposes of this Title, see Code of Civil Procedure § 680.280.

Principal amount of the judgment defined for purposes of this Title, see Code of Civil Procedure § 680.300.

Proceedings by referee or temporary judge, see Code of Civil Procedure § 708.140.

Registered process server defined for purposes of this Title, see Code of Civil Procedure § 680.330.

Review, stay of execution, satisfaction of judgment, see Labor Code § 98.2.

Serving or executing bench warrant arising out of order of appearance, see Government Code § 26744.

Research References

Forms

West's California Judicial Council Forms AT–138, Application and Order for Appearance and Examination.

West's California Judicial Council Forms EJ–125, Application and Order for Appearance and Examination.

West's California Judicial Council Forms SC–134, Application and Order to Produce Statement of Assets and to Appear for Examination.

§ 708.180. Adverse claim of, or denial of debt by third party

(a) Subject to subdivision (b), if a third person examined pursuant to Section 708.120 claims an interest in the property adverse to the judgment debtor or denies the debt, the court may, if the judgment creditor so requests, determine the interests in the property or the existence of the debt. The determination is conclusive as to the parties to the proceeding and the third person, and an appeal may be taken from the determination. The court may grant a continuance for a reasonable time for discovery proceedings, the production of evidence, or other preparation for the hearing.

(b) The court may not make the determination provided in subdivision (a) if the third person's claim is made in good faith and any of the following conditions is satisfied:

(1) The court would not be a proper court for the trial of an independent civil action (including a creditor's suit) for the determination of the interests in the property or the existence of the debt, and the third person objects to the determination of the matter under subdivision (a).

(2) At the time an order for examination pursuant to Section 708.120 is served on the third person a civil action (including a creditor's suit) is pending with respect to the interests in the property or the existence of the debt.

(3) The court determines that the interests in the property or the existence of the debt should be determined in a creditor's suit.

(c) Upon application of the judgment creditor made ex parte, the court may make an order forbidding transfer of the property to the judgment debtor or payment of the debt to the judgment debtor until the interests in the property or the existence of the debt is determined pursuant to subdivision (a) or until a creditor's suit may be commenced and an order obtained pursuant to Section 708.240. An undertaking may be required in the discretion of the court. The court may modify or vacate the order at any time with or without a hearing on such terms as are just.

(d) Upon application of the judgment creditor upon noticed motion, the court may, if it determines that the judgment debtor probably owns an interest in the property or that the debt probably is owed to the judgment debtor, make an order forbidding the transfer or other disposition of the property to any person or forbidding payment of the debt until the interests in the property or the existence of the debt is determined pursuant to subdivision (a) or until a creditor's suit may be commenced and an order obtained pursuant to Section 708.240. The court shall require the judgment creditor to furnish an undertaking as provided in Section 529. The court may modify or vacate the order at any time after notice and hearing on such terms as are just. *(Added by Stats.1982, c. 1364, p. 5194, § 2, operative July 1, 1983. Amended by Stats.1998, c. 931 (S.B.2139), § 95, eff. Sept. 28, 1998.)*

Cross References

Court defined for purposes of this Title, see Code of Civil Procedure § 680.160.
Judgment creditor defined for purposes of this Title, see Code of Civil Procedure § 680.240.
Judgment debtor defined for purposes of this Title, see Code of Civil Procedure § 680.250.
Order for satisfaction of money judgment, see Code of Civil Procedure § 708.205.
Person defined for purposes of this Title, see Code of Civil Procedure § 680.280.
Property defined for purposes of this Title, see Code of Civil Procedure § 680.310.

§ 708.190. Intervention of third party

The court may permit a person claiming an interest in the property or debt sought to be applied in an examination proceeding to intervene in the proceeding and may determine the person's rights in the property or debt pursuant to Section 708.180. *(Added by Stats.1982, c. 1364, p. 5195, § 2, operative July 1, 1983.)*

Cross References

Court defined for purposes of this Title, see Code of Civil Procedure § 680.160.
Person defined for purposes of this Title, see Code of Civil Procedure § 680.280.
Property defined for purposes of this Title, see Code of Civil Procedure § 680.310.

§ 708.200. Protective orders

In any proceeding under this article, the court may, on motion of the person to be examined or on its own motion, make such protective orders as justice may require. *(Added by Stats.1982, c. 1364, p. 5195, § 2, operative July 1, 1983.)*

Cross References

Court defined for purposes of this Title, see Code of Civil Procedure § 680.160.
Person defined for purposes of this Title, see Code of Civil Procedure § 680.280.
Proceedings by referee or temporary judge, see Code of Civil Procedure § 708.140.

§ 708.205. Order for satisfaction of money judgment or forbidding transfer or payment

(a) Except as provided in subdivision (b), at the conclusion of a proceeding pursuant to this article, the court may order the judgment debtor's interest in the property in the possession or under the control of the judgment debtor or the third person or a debt owed by the third person to the judgment debtor to be applied toward the satisfaction of the money judgment if the property is not exempt from enforcement of a money judgment. Such an order creates a lien on the property or debt.

(b) If a third person examined pursuant to Section 708.120 claims an interest in the property adverse to the judgment debtor or denies the debt and the court does not determine the matter as provided in subdivision (a) of Section 708.180, the court may not order the property or debt to be applied toward the satisfaction of the money judgment but may make an order pursuant to subdivision (c) or (d) of Section 708.180 forbidding transfer or payment to the extent authorized by that section. *(Added by Stats.1982, c. 1364, p. 5195, § 2, operative July 1, 1983.)*

Cross References

Court defined for purposes of this Title, see Code of Civil Procedure § 680.160.
Judgment debtor defined for purposes of this Title, see Code of Civil Procedure § 680.250.
Money judgment defined for purposes of this Title, see Code of Civil Procedure § 680.270.
Person defined for purposes of this Title, see Code of Civil Procedure § 680.280.
Proceedings by referee or temporary judge, see Code of Civil Procedure § 708.140.
Property defined for purposes of this Title, see Code of Civil Procedure § 680.310.
Receiver, appointment in proceedings in aid of enforcement of judgments, see Code of Civil Procedure § 564.

Research References

Forms
3 California Transactions Forms--Business Transactions § 22:2, Types of Liens.

Title 13

APPEALS IN CIVIL ACTIONS

CHAPTER 1. APPEALS IN GENERAL

Section
904.1. Appealable judgments and orders.

Cross References

Eminent domain proceedings, rules of practice, see Code of Civil Procedure § 1230.040.
Forcible entry and detainer proceedings, applicability of this Title, see Code of Civil Procedure § 1178.
State license tax, action to collect, applicability of this chapter, see Business and Professions Code § 16222.

§ 904.1. Appealable judgments and orders

(a) An appeal, other than in a limited civil case, is to the court of appeal. An appeal, other than in a limited civil case, may be taken from any of the following:

(1) From a judgment, except an interlocutory judgment, other than as provided in paragraphs (8), (9), and (11), or a judgment of contempt that is made final and conclusive by Section 1222.

(2) From an order made after a judgment made appealable by paragraph (1).

(3) From an order granting a motion to quash service of summons or granting a motion to stay the action on the ground of inconvenient forum, or from a written order of dismissal under Section 581d following an order granting a motion to dismiss the action on the ground of inconvenient forum.

(4) From an order granting a new trial or denying a motion for judgment notwithstanding the verdict.

(5) From an order discharging or refusing to discharge an attachment or granting a right to attach order.

(6) From an order granting or dissolving an injunction, or refusing to grant or dissolve an injunction.

§ 904.1

(7) From an order appointing a receiver.

(8) From an interlocutory judgment, order, or decree, made or entered in an action to redeem real or personal property from a mortgage thereof, or a lien thereon, determining the right to redeem and directing an accounting.

(9) From an interlocutory judgment in an action for partition determining the rights and interests of the respective parties and directing partition to be made.

(10) From an order made appealable by the Probate Code or the Family Code.

(11) From an interlocutory judgment directing payment of monetary sanctions by a party or an attorney for a party if the amount exceeds five thousand dollars ($5,000).

(12) From an order directing payment of monetary sanctions by a party or an attorney for a party if the amount exceeds five thousand dollars ($5,000).

(13) From an order granting or denying a special motion to strike under Section 425.16.

(14) From a final order or judgment in a bifurcated proceeding regarding child custody or visitation rights.

(b) Sanction orders or judgments of five thousand dollars ($5,000) or less against a party or an attorney for a party may be reviewed on an appeal by that party after entry of final judgment in the main action, or, at the discretion of the court of appeal, may be reviewed upon petition for an extraordinary writ. *(Added by Stats.1968, c. 385, p. 812, § 2. Amended by Stats.1969, c. 1611, p. 3394, § 21, operative July 1, 1970; Stats.1971, c. 1210, p. 2328, § 8; Stats.1978, c. 395, § 1, eff. July 11, 1978; Stats.1982, c. 931, p. 3387, § 1; Stats.1982, c. 1198, p. 4323, § 63.2, operative July 1, 1983; Stats.1983, c. 1159, § 12, operative July 1, 1984; Stats.1984, c. 29, § 2; Stats.1988, c. 678, § 2; Stats.1988, c. 1199, § 7; Stats.1988, c. 1447, § 1; Stats.1989, c. 1416, § 25; Stats.1992, c. 163 (A.B.2641), § 54, operative Jan. 1, 1994; Stats.1993, c. 456 (A.B.58), § 12; Stats.1998, c. 931 (S.B.2139), § 100, eff. Sept. 28, 1998; Stats.1999, c. 960 (A.B.1675), § 2, eff. Oct. 10, 1999; Stats.2006, c. 567 (A.B.2303), § 8; Stats.2007, c. 43 (S.B.649), § 9; Stats.2017, c. 41 (A.B.369), § 1, eff. Jan. 1, 2018.)*

Cross References

Appeal from superior court order on motion to vacate a bail forfeiture, see Penal Code § 1305.5.
Appeals from order in arbitration, see Code of Civil Procedure §§ 1294, 1294.2.
Appeals from Superior Courts in civil actions, generally, see Code of Civil Procedure § 901 et seq.
Appeals from Superior Courts in criminal cases generally, see Penal Code § 1235 et seq.
Applicability of appeal provisions of Part 2, see Civil Code § 8056.
Conclusiveness of contempt judgment or order, see Code of Civil Procedure § 1222.
Disposition of community estate, revision on appeal, dissolution of marriage, see Family Code § 2555.
Election contest, appeal from judgment, see Elections Code § 16900.
Enforcement of forfeiture, summary judgment, condition of relief from bail forfeitures, effect of dismissal of charge after default, appeal by surety or bondsman, appellate jurisdiction, demand for payment, limitations, see Penal Code § 1306.
Findings of fact on appeal, see Code of Civil Procedure § 909.
Identification of person appearing in chain of title, appealability of decree determining, see Code of Civil Procedure § 770.070.
Interlocutory judgment in trial of certain special defenses, appealability, see Code of Civil Procedure § 597.
Judgment notwithstanding the verdict, see Code of Civil Procedure § 629.
Jurisdiction, Supreme Court, courts of appeal, superior courts, see Cal. Const. Art. 6, §§ 10, 11.
Juvenile court appeals, see Welfare and Institutions Code § 800.
Legislative findings and declarations regarding California Anti-SLAPP Law, exemptions for certain actions, application of appeal provisions in this section, see Code of Civil Procedure § 425.17.
Matters reviewable on appeal from judgment, see Code of Civil Procedure § 906.
Newspaper, establishment of standing as paper of general circulation, appeal, see Government Code § 6026.
Order defined, see Code of Civil Procedure § 1003.
Parties aggrieved as entitled to appeal, see Code of Civil Procedure § 902.
Partition before distribution reviewable on appeal from order for distribution, see Probate Code § 11956.
Petition for writ of mandate by party aggrieved by order granting or denying motion for change of place of trial, see Code of Civil Procedure § 400.
Procuring or offering false or forged instrument for record, violations, punishment, see Penal Code § 115.
Setting aside or vacating judgment, appealability of order, see Code of Civil Procedure § 663a.
SLAPPback actions, procedures, see Code of Civil Procedure § 425.18.
Submission of controversy without action, appealability of judgment, see Code of Civil Procedure § 1140.
Supreme Court and District Courts of Appeal, powers in appealed cases, see Code of Civil Procedure § 43.
Writs of review, mandate and prohibition, applicability of appeal provisions of Part 2, see Code of Civil Procedure § 1110.

Research References

Forms

2 Environmental Insurance Litigation: Practice Forms § 9:25 (2021 ed.), Opening Brief of Plaintiffs and Appellants in Stonelight Tile, Inc. v. California Insurance Guarantee Association.
West's California Code Forms, Civil Procedure § 425.16 Form 1, Pleadings—Notice of Motion to Strike Complaint Infringing on Party's Right of Petition or Free Speech.
West's California Code Forms, Civil Procedure § 904.1 Form 1, Appeals—Civil Case Information Sheet—Official Form.

CHAPTER 2. STAY OF ENFORCEMENT AND OTHER PROCEEDINGS

Section
916. Stay on perfection of appeal; release from levy; proceeding upon matters not affected by appeal.
917.1. Appeal from money judgment; undertaking to stay enforcement; subrogation; costs awarded by trial court.
917.7. Appeal; stay of proceedings as to judgment or order affecting custody.
917.75. Perfecting of an appeal; stay of enforcement.

§ 916. Stay on perfection of appeal; release from levy; proceeding upon matters not affected by appeal

(a) Except as provided in Sections 917.1 to 917.9, inclusive, and in Section 116.810, the perfecting of an appeal stays proceedings in the trial court upon the judgment or order appealed from or upon the matters embraced therein or affected thereby, including enforcement of the judgment or order, but the trial court may proceed upon any other matter embraced in the action and not affected by the judgment or order.

(b) When there is a stay of proceedings other than the enforcement of the judgment, the trial court shall have jurisdiction of proceedings related to the enforcement of the judgment as well as any other matter embraced in the action and not affected by the judgment or order appealed from. *(Added by Stats.1968, c. 385, p. 816, § 2. Amended by Stats.1975, c. 266, p. 673, § 5; Stats.1982, c. 497, p. 2165, § 64, operative July 1, 1983; Stats.1990, c. 1305 (S.B.2627), § 8.)*

Cross References

Appeal from mandate commanding delivery of water for irrigation, no stay, bond for expenses, see Code of Civil Procedure § 1110a.
Attachment,
   Application to quash, release of property, see Code of Civil Procedure §§ 485.240, 492.050.
   Deposit in lieu of undertaking, see Code of Civil Procedure § 995.710 et seq.

Procedure, generally, see Code of Civil Procedure § 484.010 et seq.
Undertakings, see Code of Civil Procedure §§ 489.010, 489.060, 489.130, 489.210 et seq., 489.310, 489.320, 489.410, 489.420.
Computation of time, holidays, see Code of Civil Procedure § 12a.
Family allowance, stay of payments and undertaking pending appeal, see Probate Code § 6545.
Forcible entry and detainer, stay on appeal, see Code of Civil Procedure § 1176.
Lien of judgment as affected by stay on appeal, see Code of Civil Procedure § 697.040.
Receiver to preserve property during pendency of appeal, see Code of Civil Procedure § 564.
Stay of proceedings, use of affidavits in, see Code of Civil Procedure § 2009.
Undertaking, objections to, determination of insufficiency, see Code of Civil Procedure § 922.
Undertakings or bonds,
　Affidavits of sureties, see Code of Civil Procedure § 995.520.
　Deposit in lieu of, see Code of Civil Procedure § 995.710 et seq.
　Extension of time, see Code of Civil Procedure §§ 1054, 1054.1, 995.050.
　Form, see Code of Civil Procedure § 995.320.

Research References

Forms

2 Am. Jur. Pl. & Pr. Forms Appeal and Error § 1, Introductory Comments.

§ 917.1. Appeal from money judgment; undertaking to stay enforcement; subrogation; costs awarded by trial court

(a) Unless an undertaking is given, the perfecting of an appeal shall not stay enforcement of the judgment or order in the trial court if the judgment or order is for any of the following:

(1) Money or the payment of money, whether consisting of a special fund or not, and whether payable by the appellant or another party to the action.

(2) Costs awarded pursuant to Section 998 which otherwise would not have been awarded as costs pursuant to Section 1033.5.

(3) Costs awarded pursuant to Section 1141.21 which otherwise would not have been awarded as costs pursuant to Section 1033.5.

(b) The undertaking shall be on condition that if the judgment or order or any part of it is affirmed or the appeal is withdrawn or dismissed, the party ordered to pay shall pay the amount of the judgment or order, or the part of it as to which the judgment or order is affirmed, as entered after the receipt of the remittitur, together with any interest which may have accrued pending the appeal and entry of the remittitur, and costs which may be awarded against the appellant on appeal. This section shall not apply in cases where the money to be paid is in the actual or constructive custody of the court; and such cases shall be governed, instead, by the provisions of Section 917.2. The undertaking shall be for double the amount of the judgment or order unless given by an admitted surety insurer in which event it shall be for one and one-half times the amount of the judgment or order. The liability on the undertaking may be enforced if the party ordered to pay does not make the payment within 30 days after the filing of the remittitur from the reviewing court.

(c) If a surety on the undertaking pays the judgment, either with or without action, after the judgment is affirmed, the surety is substituted to the rights of the creditor and is entitled to control, enforce, and satisfy the judgment, in all respects as if the surety had recovered the judgment.

(d) Costs awarded by the trial court under Chapter 6 (commencing with Section 1021) of Title 14 shall be included in the amount of the judgment or order for the purpose of applying paragraph (1) of subdivision (a) and subdivision (b). However, no undertaking shall be required pursuant to this section solely for costs awarded under Chapter 6 (commencing with Section 1021) of Title 14. *(Added by Stats.1968, c. 385, p. 816, § 2. Amended by Stats.1972, c. 546, p. 936, § 1; Stats.1981, c. 196, p. 1120, § 1; Stats.1982, c. 517, p. 2354, § 155; Stats.1986, c. 1174, § 1; Stats.1993, c. 456 (A.B.58), § 13.)*

Validity

This section was held preempted by the federal procedural rule prohibiting unsecured stays in the case of Leuzinger v. County of Lake, N.D.Cal.2008, 253 F.R.D. 469.

Cross References

Bond and Undertaking Law, see Code of Civil Procedure § 995.010 et seq.
Repayment of surety by principal, see Code of Civil Procedure § 882.
Surety's rights, see Civil Code §§ 2848, 2849.
Undertakings or bonds,
　Affidavits of sureties, see Code of Civil Procedure § 995.520.
　Deposit in lieu of, see Code of Civil Procedure § 995.710 et seq.
　Extension of time, see Code of Civil Procedure §§ 1054, 1054.1, 995.050.
　Form, see Code of Civil Procedure § 995.320.
　Limitations on amount of recovery, see Code of Civil Procedure §§ 917.5, 996.470.
　Necessity of sureties, see Code of Civil Procedure §§ 995.310.
　Qualification of sureties, see Code of Civil Procedure §§ 995.120, 995.520.
　State or officers of state exempt, see Code of Civil Procedure § 995.220.

Research References

Forms

West's California Code Forms, Civil Procedure § 917.1 Form 1, Appeals—Notice of Motion for Judgment Against Sureties on Appeal Bond.

§ 917.7. Appeal; stay of proceedings as to judgment or order affecting custody

The perfecting of an appeal shall not stay proceedings as to those provisions of a judgment or order which award, change, or otherwise affect the custody, including the right of visitation, of a minor child in any civil action, in an action filed under the Juvenile Court Law, or in a special proceeding, or the provisions of a judgment or order for the temporary exclusion of a party from a dwelling, as provided in the Family Code. However, the trial court may in its discretion stay execution of these provisions pending review on appeal or for any other period or periods that it may deem appropriate. Further, in the absence of a writ or order of a reviewing court providing otherwise, the provisions of the judgment or order allowing, or eliminating restrictions against, removal of the minor child from the state are stayed by operation of law for a period of seven calendar days from the entry of the judgment or order by a juvenile court in a dependency hearing, or for a period of 30 calendar days from the entry of judgment or order by any other trial court. The periods during which these provisions allowing, or eliminating restrictions against, removal of the minor child from the state are stayed, are subject to further stays as ordered by the trial court or by the juvenile court pursuant to this section. An order directing the return of a child to a sister state or country, including any order effectuating that return, made in a proceeding brought pursuant to the Uniform Child Custody Jurisdiction and Enforcement Act (Part 3 (commencing with Section 3400) of Division 8 of the Family Code), the Parental Kidnapping Prevention Act of 1980 (28 U.S.C. Sec. 1738A), or the Hague Convention on the Civil Aspects of International Child Abduction (implemented pursuant to the International Child Abduction Remedies Act (22 U.S.C. Secs. 9001–9011)) is not a judgment or order which awards, changes, or otherwise affects the custody of a minor child within the meaning of this section, and therefore is not subject to the automatic stay provisions of this section. *(Added by Stats.1968, c. 385, p. 818, § 2. Amended by Stats.1971, c. 1210, p. 2328, § 9; Stats.1981, c. 714, p. 2596, § 70; Stats.1992, c. 163 (A.B.2641), § 55, operative Jan. 1, 1994; Stats.1993, c. 219 (A.B.1500), § 69.5; Stats.1999, c. 346 (S.B.518), § 1; Stats.2001, c. 48 (S.B.1151), § 1; Stats.2021, c. 124 (A.B.938), § 13, eff. Jan. 1, 2022.)*

Cross References

Appeals, stay of judgment or order, acts of fiduciaries directed by court, guardianship proceedings, undertaking required by court, see Probate Code § 1310.

§ 917.7

Custody of children, see Family Code §§ 3000 et seq., 3020 et seq.

Research References

Forms

West's California Code Forms, Civil Procedure § 917.7 Form 1, Appeals—Custody of Minor—Notice of Motion for Stay of Proceedings.

West's California Code Forms, Civil Procedure § 917.7 Form 2, Appeals—Order Staying Change of Custody of Minor.

§ 917.75. Perfecting of an appeal; stay of enforcement

The perfecting of an appeal shall not stay enforcement of the judgment or order of the trial court awarding attorney's fees or costs, or both, if the judgment or order appealed from was rendered in a proceeding under the Family Code, unless an undertaking is given in a sum and upon conditions fixed by the trial court. *(Added by Stats.2014, c. 95 (A.B.2154), § 1, eff. Jan. 1, 2015.)*

Title 14

OF MISCELLANEOUS PROVISIONS

CHAPTER 4. MOTIONS AND ORDERS

Section
1003. Order and motion defined.
1004. Motions; court in which made.
1005. Written notice for motions; service and filing of moving and supporting papers.
1005.5. Making and pendency of motion.
1006. Transfer of motion or order to show cause.
1008. Application to reconsider and modify or revoke prior order; affidavit; noncompliance; revocation of order; contempt; appeal.

§ 1003. Order and motion defined

Every direction of a court or judge, made or entered in writing, and not included in a judgment, is denominated an order. An application for an order is a motion. *(Enacted in 1872. Amended by Stats.1933, c. 744, p. 1897, § 173; Stats.1951, c. 1737, p. 4132, § 131, operative Jan. 1, 1952.)*

Cross References

Action on uncontested motions at chambers, see Code of Civil Procedure § 166.
Affidavit in support of motion, see Code of Civil Procedure § 2009.
Amendment of orders, powers of courts, see Code of Civil Procedure § 128.
Conclusiveness of order, see Code of Civil Procedure § 1908 et seq.
Court commissioners, power to hear and determine ex parte motions for orders, see Code of Civil Procedure § 259.
Disobedience of order as contempt, see Code of Civil Procedure §§ 1209, 1211, 1212; Penal Code § 166.
Disobedience of order by attorney, cause for disbarment or suspension, see Business and Professions Code § 6103.
Enforcement of order, see Code of Civil Procedure §§ 128, 177.
Motion and order in special proceedings defined, see Code of Civil Procedure § 1064.
Order as evidence, see Code of Civil Procedure § 1908.5.
Order deemed excepted to, see Code of Civil Procedure § 647.
Orders constituting part of judgment roll, see Code of Civil Procedure § 670.
Pleading judgment or order, see Code of Civil Procedure §§ 456, 1908.5.
Probate proceedings, jurisdictional facts not needed in orders and decrees, see Probate Code § 1047.
Relief from order taken through mistake, etc., see Code of Civil Procedure § 473.

Review of order, see Code of Civil Procedure § 901.

Research References

Forms

West's California Code Forms, Corporations § 317 Form 1, Defendants' Notice of Application to Court for Indemnity.

§ 1004. Motions; court in which made

Except as provided in section 166 of this code, motions must be made in the court in which the action is pending. *(Enacted in 1872. Amended by Code Am.1880, c. 23, p. 12, § 1; Stats.1933, c. 744, p. 1897, § 174.)*

Cross References

Court commissioners, see Code of Civil Procedure § 259.
Supreme court and district courts of appeal, see Code of Civil Procedure § 165.

§ 1005. Written notice for motions; service and filing of moving and supporting papers

(a) Written notice shall be given, as prescribed in subdivisions (b) and (c), for the following motions:

(1) Notice of Application and Hearing for Writ of Attachment under Section 484.040.

(2) Notice of Application and Hearing for Claim and Delivery under Section 512.030.

(3) Notice of Hearing for Claim of Exemption under Section 706.105.

(4) Motion to Quash Summons pursuant to subdivision (b) of Section 418.10.

(5) Motion for Determination of Good Faith Settlement pursuant to Section 877.6.

(6) Hearing for Discovery of Peace Officer Personnel Records in a civil action pursuant to Section 1043 of the Evidence Code.

(7) Notice of Hearing of Third-Party Claim pursuant to Section 720.320.

(8) Motion for an Order to Attend Deposition more than 150 miles from deponent's residence pursuant to Section 2025.260.

(9) Notice of Hearing of Application for Relief pursuant to Section 946.6 of the Government Code.

(10) Motion to Set Aside Default or Default Judgment and for Leave to Defend Actions pursuant to Section 473.5.

(11) Motion to Expunge Notice of Pendency of Action pursuant to Section 405.30.

(12) Motion to Set Aside Default and for Leave to Amend pursuant to Section 585.5.

(13) Any other proceeding under this code in which notice is required, and no other time or method is prescribed by law or by court or judge.

(b) Unless otherwise ordered or specifically provided by law, all moving and supporting papers shall be served and filed at least 16 court days before the hearing. The moving and supporting papers served shall be a copy of the papers filed or to be filed with the court. However, if the notice is served by mail, the required 16-day period of notice before the hearing shall be increased by five calendar days if the place of mailing and the place of address are within the State of California, 10 calendar days if either the place of mailing or the place of address is outside the State of California but within the United States, 12 calendar days if the place of address is the Secretary of State's address confidentiality program (Chapter 3.1 (commencing with Section 6205) of Division 7 of Title 1 of the Government Code), and 20 calendar days if either the place of mailing or the place of address is outside the United States, and if the notice is served by facsimile transmission, express mail, or another method of delivery providing for overnight delivery, the required 16-day period of notice before the hearing shall be increased by two calendar days. Section 1013, which extends the time within which a right may be exercised or an act may be done, does not apply to a notice of motion, papers opposing a motion, or reply papers governed by this section. All papers opposing a motion so noticed shall be filed with the court and a copy served on each party at least nine court days, and all reply papers at least five court days before the hearing.

The court, or a judge thereof, may prescribe a shorter time.

(c) Notwithstanding any other provision of this section, all papers opposing a motion and all reply papers shall be served by personal delivery, facsimile transmission, express mail, or other means consistent with Sections 1010, 1011, 1012, and 1013, and reasonably calculated to ensure delivery to the other party or parties not later than the close of the next business day after the time the opposing papers or reply papers, as applicable, are filed. This subdivision applies to the service of opposition and reply papers regarding motions for summary judgment or summary adjudication, in addition to the motions listed in subdivision (a).

The court, or a judge thereof, may prescribe a shorter time. (Enacted in 1872. Amended by Code Am.1880, c. 23, p. 13, § 2; Stats.1907, c. 326, p. 601, § 1; Stats.1919, c. 195, p. 289, § 1; Stats.1933, c. 744, p. 1897, § 175; Stats.1935, c. 658, p. 1816, § 1; Stats.1935, c. 722, p. 1966, § 27; Stats.1951, c. 1737, p. 4132, § 132, operative Jan. 1, 1952; Stats.1963, c. 878, p. 2126, § 3; Stats.1980, c. 196, p. 418, § 1; Stats.1981, c. 197, p. 1121, § 1; Stats.1984, c. 352, § 2; Stats.1986, c. 246, § 1; Stats.1989, c. 693, § 6; Stats.1990, c. 1491 (A.B.3765), § 7; Stats.1991, c. 1090 (A.B.1484), § 5; Stats.1992, c. 339 (S.B.1409), § 2; Stats.1993, c. 456 (A.B.58), § 14.5; Stats.1997, c. 571 (A.B.1088), § 1.3; Stats.1998, c. 932 (A.B.1094), § 18; Stats.1999, c. 43 (A.B.1132), § 1; Stats.2002, c. 806 (A.B.3027), § 16; Stats.2004, c. 182 (A.B.3081), § 13; Stats.2004, c. 171 (A.B.3078), § 3; Stats.2005, c. 294 (A.B.333), § 3; Stats.2019, c. 585 (A.B.1600), § 1, eff. Jan. 1, 2020; Stats.2022, c. 686 (A.B.1726), § 1, eff. Jan. 1, 2023.)

Cross References

Extension of time, service of notice by mail, see Code of Civil Procedure § 1013.
Filing fees, generally, see Government Code § 70617.
Judgment on default, notice of motion to strike, see Code of Civil Procedure § 585.
Proof of service, see Code of Civil Procedure § 2009.
Service, manner of, see Code of Civil Procedure § 1010 et seq.
Termination or modification of protective order prior to the specified expiration date by a party other than the protected party, notice of proceedings, see Code of Civil Procedure §§ 527.6, 527.8, 527.85; Family Code § 6345; Welfare and Institutions Code §§ 213.5, 15657.03.
Trial Court Delay Reduction Act, minimum time periods for certain actions, see Government Code § 68616.
Written notice, see Code of Civil Procedure § 1010.

Research References

Forms

California Practice Guide: Rutter Family Law Forms Form 5:15, Stipulation Waiving Time for Hearing, Acknowledgment of Service of Notice of Request for Order and Order Thereon.
West's California Code Forms, Civil Procedure § 527 Form 3, Injunction—Temporary Restraining Order and Order to Show Cause.
West's California Code Forms, Civil Procedure § 527 Form 5, Injunction—Notice of Motion for Preliminary Injunction.
West's California Code Forms, Government § 946.6 Form 1, Petition for Order Seeking Relief from Claims Statute—Action Against Local Public Entity.
West's California Judicial Council Forms App-025, Appellant Motion to Use a Settled Statement (Unlimited Civil Case).
West's California Judicial Council Forms FL-320, Responsive Declaration to Request for Order (Also Available in Spanish).

West's California Judicial Council Forms FL-685, Response to Governmental Notice of Motion or Order to Show Cause.

§ 1005.5. Making and pendency of motion

A motion upon all the grounds stated in the written notice thereof is deemed to have been made and to be pending before the court for all purposes, upon the due service and filing of the notice of motion, but this shall not deprive a party of a hearing of the motion to which he is otherwise entitled. Procedure upon a motion for new trial shall be as otherwise provided. (Added by Stats.1953, c. 909, p. 2265, § 1.)

Cross References

New trial, see Code of Civil Procedure § 659.
Service, manner of, see Code of Civil Procedure § 1010 et seq.

Research References

Forms

7PT1 Am. Jur. Pl. & Pr. Forms Compromise and Settlement § 111, Motion—For Judgment in Accordance With Settlement Agreement in Pending Action.
7PT1 Am. Jur. Pl. & Pr. Forms Compromise and Settlement § 112, Notice of Motion—For Entry of Judgment in Accordance With Settlement Agreement in Pending Action.

§ 1006. Transfer of motion or order to show cause

When a notice of motion is given, or an order to show cause is made returnable before a judge out of court, and at the time fixed for the motion, or on the return day of the order, the judge is unable to hear the parties, the matter may be transferred by his order to some other judge, before whom it might originally have been brought. (Enacted in 1872. Amended by Stats.1933, c. 744, p. 1897, § 176; Stats.1951, c. 1737, p. 4132, § 133, operative Jan. 1, 1952.)

§ 1008. Application to reconsider and modify or revoke prior order; affidavit; noncompliance; revocation of order; contempt; appeal

(a) When an application for an order has been made to a judge, or to a court, and refused in whole or in part, or granted, or granted conditionally, or on terms, any party affected by the order may, within 10 days after service upon the party of written notice of entry of the order and based upon new or different facts, circumstances, or law, make application to the same judge or court that made the order, to reconsider the matter and modify, amend, or revoke the prior order. The party making the application shall state by affidavit what application was made before, when and to what judge, what order or decisions were made, and what new or different facts, circumstances, or law are claimed to be shown.

(b) A party who originally made an application for an order which was refused in whole or part, or granted conditionally or on terms, may make a subsequent application for the same order upon new or different facts, circumstances, or law, in which case it shall be shown by affidavit what application was made before, when and to what judge, what order or decisions were made, and what new or different facts, circumstances, or law are claimed to be shown. For a failure to comply with this subdivision, any order made on a subsequent application may be revoked or set aside on ex parte motion.

(c) If a court at any time determines that there has been a change of law that warrants it to reconsider a prior order it entered, it may do so on its own motion and enter a different order.

(d) A violation of this section may be punished as a contempt and with sanctions as allowed by Section 128.7. In addition, an order made contrary to this section may be revoked by the judge or commissioner who made it, or vacated by a judge of the court in which the action or proceeding is pending.

(e) This section specifies the court's jurisdiction with regard to applications for reconsideration of its orders and renewals of previous motions, and applies to all applications to reconsider any order of a judge or court, or for the renewal of a previous motion,

§ 1008 CODE OF CIVIL PROCEDURE

whether the order deciding the previous matter or motion is interim or final. No application to reconsider any order or for the renewal of a previous motion may be considered by any judge or court unless made according to this section.

(f) For the purposes of this section, an alleged new or different law shall not include a later enacted statute without a retroactive application.

(g) An order denying a motion for reconsideration made pursuant to subdivision (a) is not separately appealable. However, if the order that was the subject of a motion for reconsideration is appealable, the denial of the motion for reconsideration is reviewable as part of an appeal from that order.

(h) This section applies to all applications for interim orders. (Added by Stats.1978, c. 631, § 2. Amended by Stats.1992, c. 460 (S.B.1805), § 4; Stats.1998, c. 200 (S.B.1556), § 2; Stats.2011, c. 78 (A.B.1067), § 1.)

Cross References

Contempt, punishment for, see Code of Civil Procedure § 1218 et seq.

Research References

Forms

1 Environmental Insurance Litigation: Practice Forms § 1:14 (2021 ed.), Insurer's Notice of Motion and Motion for Reconsideration (With Supporting Memorandum and Declaration) (Owned Property Exclusion and Absence of Third Party Property Damage).

West's California Code Forms, Civil Procedure § 437c Form 1, Summary Judgment—Notice of Motion for Summary Judgment or Summary Adjudication—By Plaintiff.

West's California Code Forms, Civil Procedure § 473 Form 9, Pleadings—Notice of Motion to Set Aside Default and Judgment Taken Thereon.

West's California Code Forms, Civil Procedure § 473 Form 11, Pleadings—Order Vacating Default and Permitting Filing of Answer.

West's California Code Forms, Civil Procedure § 1008 Form 1, Motions and Orders—New Application for Order After Prior Refusal—Declaration Supporting New Application.

West's California Code Forms, Civil Procedure § 1008 Form 2, Motions and Orders—Application to Set Aside Order Obtained Without Prior Refusal Disclosure.

CHAPTER 5. NOTICES, AND FILING AND SERVICE OF PAPERS

Section
1010.6. Electronic service of documents; local rules for electronic filing; uniform rules.
1013. Service by mail, Express Mail or facsimile transmission; procedure; completion of service; extension of time; electronic service permitted.
1013a. Service by mail; proof.
1013b. Proof of electronic service.
1015. Service; nonresident party; service on clerk or attorney.
1016. Service; process to bring party into contempt; inapplicability of certain sections.

Cross References

Arbitration, service under this chapter, see Code of Civil Procedure §§ 1290.4, 1290.8.
Blood tests to determine paternity, genetic test results, see Family Code § 7552.5.
Preventive relief, modification or dissolution of final injunction, see Civil Code § 3424.
Punitive damages, service of statement, see Code of Civil Procedure § 425.115.
Records destroyed in fire or calamity, proceedings for restoration, see Code of Civil Procedure §§ 1953.02, 1953.03.

Settlement offers in eminent domain proceedings, service pursuant to this chapter, see Code of Civil Procedure § 1250.410.

§ 1010.6. Electronic service of documents; local rules for electronic filing; uniform rules

(a) A document may be served electronically in an action filed with the court as provided in this section, in accordance with rules adopted pursuant to subdivision (h).

(1) For purposes of this section:

(A) "Electronic service" means service of a document, on a * * * person, by either electronic transmission or electronic notification. Electronic service may be performed directly by a * * * person, * * * including a party * * *, by a person's agent, including the * * * person's attorney, or through an electronic filing service provider, and by a court.

(B) "Electronic transmission" means the transmission of a document by electronic means to the electronic service address at or through which a * * * person * * * receives electronic service.

(C) "Electronic notification" means the notification of the * * * person that a document is served by sending an electronic message to the electronic address at or through which the * * * person * * * receives electronic service, specifying the exact name of the document served, and providing a hyperlink at which the served document may be viewed and downloaded.

(D) "Electronic filing" means the electronic transmission to a court of a document presented for filing in electronic form. For purposes of this section, this definition of electronic filing concerns the activity of filing and does not include the processing and review of the document and its entry into the court's records, which are necessary for a document to be officially filed.

(2) If a document is required to be served by certified or registered mail, electronic service of the document is not authorized.

* * *

(3)(A) If a document may be served by mail, express mail, overnight delivery, or facsimile transmission, electronic service of that document is deemed complete at the time of the electronic transmission of the document or at the time that the electronic notification of service of the document is sent.

(B) Any period of notice, or any right or duty to do any act or make any response within any period or on a date certain after the service of the document, which time period or date is prescribed by statute or rule of court, shall be extended after service by electronic means by two court days, but the extension shall not apply to extend the time for filing any of the following:

(i) A notice of intention to move for new trial.

(ii) A notice of intention to move to vacate judgment under Section 663a.

(iii) A notice of appeal.

(C) This extension applies in the absence of a specific exception provided by any other statute or rule of court.

(4) Any document that is served electronically between 12:00 a.m. and 11:59:59 p.m. on a court day shall be deemed served on that court day. Any document that is served electronically on a noncourt day shall be deemed served on the next court day.

(5) Confidential or sealed records shall be electronically served through encrypted methods to ensure that the documents are not improperly disclosed.

(b)(1) This subdivision applies to mandatory electronic service. The court may order electronic service on a person represented by counsel who has appeared in an action or proceeding.

* * * (2) A person represented by counsel, who has appeared in an action or proceeding, shall accept electronic service of a notice or

692

document that may be served by mail, express mail, overnight delivery, or facsimile transmission.

(3) Before first serving a represented person electronically, the * * * person effecting service shall confirm * * * the appropriate electronic service address for the counsel being served.

(4) A person represented by counsel shall, upon the request of any person who has appeared in an action or proceeding and who provides an electronic service address, electronically serve the requesting person with any notice or document that may be served by mail, express mail, overnight delivery, or facsimile transmission.

(c)(1) This subdivision applies to electronic service by consent of an unrepresented person in a civil action.

(2) An unrepresented party may consent to receive electronic service.

* * * (3) Express consent to electronic service may be * * * given by either * * * of the following:

(i) Serving a notice on all * * * parties and filing the notice with the court * * *.

(ii) Manifesting affirmative consent through electronic means with the court or the court's electronic filing service provider, and concurrently providing the party's electronic address with that consent for the purpose of receiving electronic service. The act of electronic filing shall not be construed as express consent.

* * * (4) A person who has provided express consent to accept service electronically may withdraw consent at any time by completing and filing with the court the appropriate Judicial Council form. * * *

(5) Consent, or the withdrawal of consent, to receive electronic service may only be completed by a * * * person entitled to service * * *.

(d) On and after July 1, 2024, in any action in which a party or other person * * * is subject to mandatory electronic service under subdivision (b) or has consented to electronic service under * * * subdivision (c) * * *, the court shall electronically transmit, to * * * a person subject to mandatory electronic service or who consented to electronic service, any document issued by the court that the court is required to transmit, deliver, or serve. The electronic service of documents by the court shall have the same legal effect as service by mail, except as provided in paragraph * * * (3) of subdivision (a).

(e) A trial court may adopt local rules permitting electronic filing of documents, subject to rules adopted by the Judicial Council pursuant to subdivision (h) and the following conditions:

(1) A document that is filed electronically shall have the same legal effect as an original paper document.

(2)(A) When a document to be filed requires the signature of any person, not under penalty of perjury, the document shall be deemed to have been signed by that person if filed electronically and if either of the following conditions is satisfied:

(i) The filer is the signer.

(ii) The person has signed the document pursuant to the procedure set forth in the California Rules of Court.

(B) When a document to be filed requires the signature, under penalty of perjury, of any person, the document shall be deemed to have been signed by that person if filed electronically and if either of the following conditions is satisfied:

(i) The person has signed a printed form of the document before, or on the same day as, the date of filing. The attorney or other person filing the document represents, by the act of filing, that the declarant has complied with this section. The attorney or other person filing the document shall maintain the printed form of the document bearing the original signature until final disposition of the case, as defined in subdivision (c) of Section 68151 of the Government Code, and make it available for review and copying upon the request of the court or any party to the action or proceeding in which it is filed.

(ii) The person has signed the document using a computer or other technology pursuant to the procedure set forth in a rule of court adopted by the Judicial Council by January 1, 2019.

(3) Any document received electronically by the court between 12:00 a.m. and 11:59:59 p.m. on a court day shall be deemed filed on that court day. Any document that is received electronically on a noncourt day shall be deemed filed on the next court day.

(4)(A) Whichever of a court, an electronic filing service provider, or an electronic filing manager is the first to receive a document submitted for electronic filing shall promptly send a confirmation of receipt of the document indicating the date and time of receipt to the party or person who submitted the document.

(B) If a document received by the court under subparagraph (A) complies with filing requirements and all required filing fees have been paid, the court shall promptly send confirmation that the document has been filed to the party or person who submitted the document.

(C) If the clerk of the court does not file a document received by the court under subparagraph (A) because the document does not comply with applicable filing requirements or the required filing fee has not been paid, the court shall promptly send notice of the rejection of the document for filing to the party or person who submitted the document. The notice of rejection shall state the reasons that the document was rejected for filing and include the date the clerk of the court sent the notice.

(D) If the court utilizes an electronic filing service provider or electronic filing manager to send the notice of rejection described in subparagraph (C), the electronic filing service provider or electronic filing manager shall promptly send the notice of rejection to the party or person who submitted the document. A notice of rejection sent pursuant to this subparagraph shall include the date the electronic filing service provider or electronic filing manager sent the notice.

(E) If the clerk of the court does not file a complaint or cross complaint because the complaint or cross complaint does not comply with applicable filing requirements or the required filing fee has not been paid, any statute of limitations applicable to the causes of action alleged in the complaint or cross complaint shall be tolled for the period beginning on the date on which the court received the document and as shown on the confirmation of receipt described in subparagraph (A), through the later of either the date on which the clerk of the court sent the notice of rejection described in subparagraph (C) or the date on which the electronic filing service provider or electronic filing manager sent the notice of rejection as described in subparagraph (D), plus one additional day if the complaint or cross complaint is subsequently submitted in a form that corrects the errors which caused the document to be rejected. The party filing the complaint or cross complaint shall not make any change to the complaint or cross complaint other than those required to correct the errors which caused the document to be rejected.

(5) Upon electronic filing of a complaint, petition, or other document that must be served with a summons, a trial court, upon request of the party filing the action, shall issue a summons with the court seal and the case number. The court shall keep the summons in its records and shall electronically transmit a copy of the summons to the requesting party. Personal service of a printed form of the electronic summons shall have the same legal effect as personal service of an original summons. * * *

(6) The court shall permit a party or attorney to file an application for waiver of court fees and costs, in lieu of requiring the payment of the filing fee, as part of the process involving the electronic filing of a document. The court shall consider and determine the application in accordance with Article 6 (commencing with Section 68630) of Chapter 2 of Title 8 of the Government Code and shall not require the party or attorney to submit any documentation other than that set

forth in Article 6 (commencing with Section 68630) of Chapter 2 of Title 8 of the Government Code. The court, an electronic filing service provider, or an electronic filing manager shall waive any fees charged to a party <u>or the party's attorney</u> if the party has been granted a waiver of court fees pursuant to Section 68631 <u>of the Government Code or if the party is indigent or being represented by the public defender or court-appointed counsel</u>. The electronic filing manager or electronic filing service provider shall not seek payment from the court of any fee waived by the court. This section does not require the court to waive a filing fee that is not otherwise waivable.

(7) If a party electronically files a filing that is exempt from the payment of filing fees under any other law, including a filing described in Section 212 of the Welfare and Institutions Code or Section 6103.9, subdivision (b) of Section 70617, or Section 70672 of the Government Code, the party shall not be required to pay any court fees associated with the electronic filing. An electronic filing service provider or an electronic filing manager shall not seek payment of these fees from the court.

(8) A fee, if any, charged by the court, an electronic filing service provider, or an electronic filing manager to process a payment for filing fees and other court fees shall not exceed the costs incurred in processing the payment.

(9) The court shall not charge fees for electronic filing and service of documents that are more than the court's actual cost of electronic filing and service of the documents.

* * * <u>(f)</u>(1) Except as provided in paragraph (2), if a trial court adopts rules conforming to subdivision <u>(e)</u>, it may provide by order, subject to the requirements and conditions stated in paragraphs (2) to (4), inclusive, of subdivision <u>(g)</u>, and the rules adopted by the Judicial Council under subdivision <u>(i)</u>, that all parties to an action file * * * documents electronically in a class action, a consolidated action, a group of actions, a coordinated action, or an action that is deemed complex under Judicial Council rules, provided that the trial court's order does not cause undue hardship or significant prejudice to any party in the action.

<u>(2) Unrepresented persons are exempt from any mandatory electronic filing imposed pursuant to this subdivision.</u>

<u>(g)</u> A trial court may, by local rule, require electronic filing * * * in civil actions, subject to the requirements and conditions stated in subdivision <u>(e)</u>, the rules adopted by the Judicial Council under subdivision <u>(i)</u>, and the following conditions:

(1) The court shall have the ability to maintain the official court record in electronic format for all cases where electronic filing is required.

(2) The court and the parties shall have access to more than one electronic filing service provider capable of electronically filing documents with the court or to electronic filing access directly through the court. Any fees charged by an electronic filing service provider shall be reasonable. An electronic filing manager or an electronic filing service provider shall waive any fees charged if the court deems a waiver appropriate, including in instances where a party has received a fee waiver.

(3) The court shall have a procedure for the filing of nonelectronic documents in order to prevent the program from causing undue hardship or significant prejudice to any party in an action, including, but not limited to, unrepresented parties. The Judicial Council shall make a form available to allow a party to seek an exemption from mandatory electronic filing and service on the grounds provided in this paragraph.

(4) Unrepresented persons are exempt from mandatory electronic filing * * * <u>imposed pursuant to this subdivision</u>.

(5) Until January 1, 2021, a local child support agency, as defined in subdivision (h) of Section 17000 of the Family Code, is exempt from a trial court's mandatory electronic filing and service requirements, unless the Department of Child Support Services and the local child support agency determine it has the capacity and functionality to comply with the trial court's mandatory electronic filing and service requirements.

<u>(h)</u> The Judicial Council shall adopt uniform rules for the electronic filing and service of documents in the trial courts of the state, which shall include statewide policies on vendor contracts, privacy, and access to public records, and rules relating to the integrity of electronic service. These rules shall conform to the conditions set forth in this section, as amended from time to time.

<u>(i)</u> The Judicial Council shall adopt uniform rules to permit the mandatory electronic filing and service of documents for specified civil actions in the trial courts of the state, which shall include statewide policies on vendor contracts, privacy, access to public records, unrepresented parties, parties with fee waivers, hardships, reasonable exceptions to electronic filing, and rules relating to the integrity of electronic service. These rules shall conform to the conditions set forth in this section, as amended from time to time.

<u>(j)</u>(1) Any system for the electronic filing and service of documents, including any information technology applications, internet websites and web-based applications, used by an electronic service provider or any other vendor or contractor that provides an electronic filing and service system to a trial court, regardless of the case management system used by the trial court, shall satisfy both of the following requirements:

(A) The system shall be accessible to individuals with disabilities, including parties and attorneys with disabilities, in accordance with Section 508 of the federal Rehabilitation Act of 1973 (29 U.S.C. Sec. 794d), as amended, the regulations implementing that act set forth in Part 1194 of Title 36 of the Code of Federal Regulations and Appendices A, C, and D of that part, and the federal Americans with Disabilities Act of 1990 (42 U.S.C. Sec. 12101 et seq.).

(B) The system shall comply with the Web Content Accessibility Guidelines 2.0 at a Level AA success criteria.

(2) Commencing on June 27, 2017, the vendor or contractor shall provide an accommodation to an individual with a disability in accordance with subparagraph (D) of paragraph (3).

(3) A trial court that contracts with an entity for the provision of a system for electronic filing and service of documents shall require the entity, in the trial court's contract with the entity, to do all of the following:

(A) Test and verify that the entity's system complies with this subdivision and provide the verification to the Judicial Council no later than June 30, 2019.

(B) Respond to, and resolve, any complaints regarding the accessibility of the system that are brought to the attention of the entity.

(C) Designate a lead individual to whom any complaints concerning accessibility may be addressed and post the individual's name and contact information on the entity's internet website.

(D) Provide to an individual with a disability, upon request, an accommodation to enable the individual to file and serve documents electronically at no additional charge for any time period that the entity is not compliant with paragraph (1). Exempting an individual with a disability from mandatory electronic filing and service of documents shall not be deemed an accommodation unless the person chooses that as an accommodation. The vendor or contractor shall clearly state <u>on</u> its internet website that an individual with a disability may request an accommodation and the process for submitting a request for an accommodation.

(4) A trial court that provides electronic filing and service of documents directly to the public shall comply with this subdivision to the same extent as a vendor or contractor that provides electronic filing and services to a trial court.

(5)(A) The Judicial Council shall submit four reports to the appropriate committees of the Legislature relating to the trial courts that have implemented a system of electronic filing and service of documents. The first report is due by June 30, 2018; the second report is due by December 31, 2019; the third report is due by December 31, 2021; and the fourth report is due by December 31, 2023.

(B) The Judicial Council's reports shall include all of the following information:

(i) The name of each court that has implemented a system of electronic filing and service of documents.

(ii) A description of the system of electronic filing and service.

(iii) The name of the entity or entities providing the system.

(iv) A statement as to whether the system complies with this subdivision and, if the system is not fully compliant, a description of the actions that have been taken to make the system compliant.

(6) An entity that contracts with a trial court to provide a system for electronic filing and service of documents shall cooperate with the Judicial Council by providing all information, and by permitting all testing, necessary for the Judicial Council to prepare its reports to the Legislature in a complete and timely manner. *(Added by Stats.1999, c. 514 (S.B.367), § 1. Amended by Stats.2001, c. 824 (A.B.1700), § 10.5; Stats.2005, c. 300 (A.B.496), § 5; Stats.2010, c. 156 (S.B. 1274), § 1; Stats.2011, c. 296 (A.B.1023), § 40; Stats.2012, c. 320 (A.B.2073), § 1; Stats.2016, c. 461 (A.B.2244), § 1, eff. Jan. 1, 2017; Stats.2017, c. 17 (A.B.103), § 5, eff. June 27, 2017; Stats.2017, c. 319 (A.B.976), § 2, eff. Jan. 1, 2018; Stats.2018, c. 504 (A.B.3248), § 1, eff. Jan. 1, 2019; Stats.2020, c. 112 (S.B.1146), § 2, eff. Sept. 18, 2020; Stats.2020, c. 215 (A.B.2165), § 1.5, eff. Jan. 1, 2021; Stats.2021, c. 124 (A.B.938), § 14, eff. Jan. 1, 2022; Stats.2021, c. 214 (S.B.241), § 7, eff. Jan. 1, 2022; Stats.2022, c. 215 (A.B.2961), § 1, eff. Jan. 1, 2023.)*

Cross References

Claims against public entities, manner and presentation and of giving notice, electronic submissions, see Government Code § 915.2.

Juvenile court law, electronic filing and service, conditions, see Welfare and Institutions Code § 212.5.

Service of complaint filed for investigation, see Government Code § 12962.

Research References

Forms

West's California Judicial Council Forms EFS–006, Withdrawal of Consent to Electronic Service (Electronic Filing and Service).

§ 1013. Service by mail, Express Mail or facsimile transmission; procedure; completion of service; extension of time; electronic service permitted

(a) In case of service by mail, the notice or other paper shall be deposited in a post office, mailbox, subpost office, substation, or mail chute, or other like facility regularly maintained by the United States Postal Service, in a sealed envelope, with postage paid, addressed to the person on whom it is to be served, at the office address as last given by that person on any document filed in the cause and served on the party making service by mail; otherwise at that party's place of residence. Service is complete at the time of the deposit, but any period of notice and any right or duty to do any act or make any response within any period or on a date certain after service of the document, which time period or date is prescribed by statute or rule of court, shall be extended five calendar days, upon service by mail, if the place of address and the place of mailing is within the State of California, 10 calendar days if either the place of mailing or the place of address is outside the State of California but within the United States, <u>12 calendar days if the place of address is the Secretary of State's address confidentiality program (Chapter 3.1 (commencing with Section 6205) of Division 7 of Title 1 of the Government Code),</u> and 20 calendar days if either the place of mailing or the place of address is outside the United States, but the extension shall not apply to extend the time for filing notice of intention to move for new trial, notice of intention to move to vacate judgment pursuant to Section 663a, or notice of appeal. This extension applies in the absence of a specific exception provided for by this section or other statute or rule of court.

(b) The copy of the notice or other paper served by mail pursuant to this chapter shall bear a notation of the date and place of mailing or be accompanied by an unsigned copy of the affidavit or certificate of mailing.

(c) In case of service by Express Mail, the notice or other paper <u>shall</u> be deposited in a post office, mailbox, subpost office, substation, or mail chute, or other like facility regularly maintained by the United States Postal Service for receipt of Express Mail, in a sealed envelope, with Express Mail postage paid, addressed to the person on whom it is to be served, at the office address as last given by that person on any document filed in the cause and served on the party making service by Express Mail; otherwise at that party's place of residence. In case of service by another method of delivery providing for overnight delivery, the notice or other paper <u>shall</u> be deposited in a box or other facility regularly maintained by the express service carrier, or delivered to an authorized courier or driver authorized by the express service carrier to receive documents, in an envelope or package designated by the express service carrier with delivery fees paid or provided for, addressed to the person on whom it is to be served, at the office address as last given by that person on any document filed in the cause and served on the party making service; otherwise at that party's place of residence. Service is complete at the time of the deposit, but any period of notice and any right or duty to do any act or make any response within any period or on a date certain after service of the document served by Express Mail or other method of delivery providing for overnight delivery shall be extended by two court days. The extension shall not apply to extend the time for filing notice of intention to move for new trial, notice of intention to move to vacate judgment pursuant to Section 663a, or notice of appeal. This extension applies in the absence of a specific exception provided for by this section or other statute or rule of court.

(d) The copy of the notice or other paper served by Express Mail or another means of delivery providing for overnight delivery pursuant to this chapter shall bear a notation of the date and place of deposit or be accompanied by an unsigned copy of the affidavit or certificate of deposit.

(e) Service by facsimile transmission shall be permitted only where the parties agree and a written confirmation of that agreement is made. The Judicial Council may adopt rules implementing the service of documents by facsimile transmission and may provide a form for the confirmation of the agreement required by this subdivision. In case of service by facsimile transmission, the notice or other paper <u>shall</u> be transmitted to a facsimile machine maintained by the person on whom it is served at the facsimile machine telephone number as last given by that person on any document which * * * <u>they have</u> filed in the cause and served on the party making the service. Service is complete at the time of transmission, but any period of notice and any right or duty to do any act or make any response within any period or on a date certain after service of the document, which time period or date is prescribed by statute or rule of court, shall be extended, after service by facsimile transmission, by two court days, but the extension shall not apply to extend the time for filing notice of intention to move for new trial, notice of intention to move to vacate judgment pursuant to Section 663a, or notice of appeal. This extension applies in the absence of a specific exception provided for by this section or other statute or rule of court.

(f) The copy of the notice or other paper served by facsimile transmission pursuant to this chapter shall bear a notation of the date and place of transmission and the facsimile telephone number to

§ 1013

which transmitted, or to be accompanied by an unsigned copy of the affidavit or certificate of transmission which shall contain the facsimile telephone number to which the notice or other paper was transmitted.

(g) Electronic service shall be permitted pursuant to Section 1010.6 and the rules on electronic service in the California Rules of Court.

(h) Subdivisions (b), (d), and (f) are directory. *(Enacted in 1872. Amended by Code Am.1873–74, c. 383, p. 343, § 138; Stats.1907, c. 327, p. 602, § 3; Stats.1929, c. 480, p. 845, § 1; Stats.1931, c. 739, p. 1534, § 2; Stats.1949, c. 456, p. 800, § 3; Stats.1967, c. 169, p. 1267, § 6; Stats.1968, c. 166, p. 390, § 1; Stats.1974, c. 281, p. 544, § 1; Stats.1974, c. 282, § 1, eff. May 28, 1974; Stats.1974, c. 282, § 2, eff. May 28, 1974, operative Jan. 1, 1975; Stats.1980, c. 196, § 2; Stats.1992, c. 339 (S.B.1409), § 4; Stats.1995, c. 576 (A.B.1225), § 3.8; Stats.2001, c. 812 (A.B.223), § 8; Stats.2010, c. 156 (S.B.1274), § 2; Stats.2022, c. 686 (A.B.1726), § 2, eff. Jan. 1, 2023.)*

Cross References

Alcoholic beverage control notices, service by mail, applicability of this section, see Business and Professions Code § 25760.
Attachment, levy procedures, property in safe-deposit box, see Code of Civil Procedure § 488.460.
Cancellation of certain property insurance policies, time frame for delivery of notice, see Insurance Code § 677.4.
Child support assigned to county, local child support agency providing child support enforcement services, notice regarding where payments should be directed, see Family Code § 4204.
Child, support obligations,
   Default judgment, see Family Code § 17430.
   Procedure in actions, see Family Code § 17404.
Cigarette tax, notice of deficiency determination, application of this section, see Revenue and Taxation Code § 30206.
Civil discovery act, service of notice or other papers, allowed methods, see Code of Civil Procedure § 2016.050.
Computation of time, in general, see Code of Civil Procedure § 12.
Contractors, citation or civil penalty, notice, see Labor Code § 1023.
Employment of minors, judgment, see Labor Code § 1289.
Enforcement of money judgments, execution, property in safe-deposit box, see Code of Civil Procedure § 700.150.
Holidays, extension, see Code of Civil Procedure § 12a et seq.
Industrial homework, authority of division to confiscate articles and materials, see Labor Code § 2664.
Intercounty support obligations, registration by local child support agency of support order made in another county, notice, see Family Code § 5601.
Judgment creditor, costs of enforcing judgment, applicability of this section, see Code of Civil Procedure § 685.070.
Lien of state for taxes due, see Government Code § 12419.4.
Payment of less than minimum wage, hearing, notice of decision, see Labor Code § 1197.1.
Payment of wages, hearing on citation or assessment of civil penalty, service of decision on parties, see Labor Code § 226.5.
Proceedings for judge recusal, or when judge fails or refuses to withdraw, see Code of Civil Procedure § 170.3.
Property insurance,
   Cancellation notice grounds, rate and coverage changes, see Insurance Code § 676.2.
   Notice of nonrenewal or conditional renewal, see Insurance Code § 678.1.
   Requirements of notice of cancellation, see Insurance Code § 677.2.
Public works,
   Deposits of penalties or forfeitures withheld from contract payment, see Labor Code § 1771.6.
   Review of wage and penalty assessments, hearing procedure, see Labor Code § 1742.
   Violations, civil wage and penalty assessments, service, see Labor Code § 1741.
Service of summons by mail, section inapplicable, see Code of Civil Procedure § 413.20.
Simultaneous exchange of expert witness information, method of exchange, form and contents, see Code of Civil Procedure § 2034.260.
State civil service, service by mail governed by this section, see Government Code § 18575.
Support, earnings assignment order, service of order on employer, see Family Code § 5232.
Trial Court Delay Reduction Act, minimum time periods for certain actions, see Government Code § 68616.
Unemployment insurance contributions and reports, notices by mail respecting these matters, with certain exceptions, to be made pursuant to this section, see Unemployment Insurance Code § 1206.
Workers' compensation policies, nonrenewal notices, requirements, see Insurance Code § 11664.
Written notice of motion, time for giving, see Code of Civil Procedure § 1005.

Research References

Forms

2A California Real Estate Forms (Miller & Starr) § 2:34 (2d ed.), Sublease—Shared Office Space.
2 California Real Estate Forms (Miller & Starr) § 2:17 (2d ed.), Office Lease—Mixed Use Building.
West's California Code Forms, Civil § 827 Form 1, Notice—To Tenant Changing Terms of Lease.
West's California Code Forms, Civil Procedure § 998 Form 1, Offer of Plaintiff to Compromise.
West's California Code Forms, Civil Procedure § 1013 Form 3, Notices—Proof of Service by First-Class Mail (Civil)—Official Form.
West's California Code Forms, Education § 44944 Form 4, Notice of Hearing.
West's California Code Forms, Government § 913 Form 1, Notice of Action Taken.
West's California Code Forms, Government § 3520 Form 1, Judicial Review.
West's California Code Forms, Government § 3542 Form 1, Petition for Writ of Mandate.
West's California Code Forms, Government § 11509 Form 1, Notice of Hearing.
West's California Judicial Council Forms FL–334, Declaration Regarding Address Verification—Postjudgment Request to Modify a Child Custody, Visitation, or Child Support Order.
West's California Judicial Council Forms FL–335, Proof of Service by Mail.
West's California Judicial Council Forms FL–335–INFO, Information Sheet for Proof of Service by Mail.
West's California Judicial Council Forms FL–686, Proof of Service by Mail.
West's California Judicial Council Forms POS–030, Proof of Service by First-Class Mail—Civil (Proof of Service)/Information Sheet for Proof of Service by First-Class Mail—Civil.
West's California Judicial Council Forms POS–040, Proof of Service—Civil.

§ 1013a. Service by mail; proof

Proof of service by mail may be made by one of the following methods:

(1) An affidavit setting forth the exact title of the document served and filed in the cause, showing the name and residence or business address of the person making the service, showing that he or she is a resident of or employed in the county where the mailing occurs, that he or she is over the age of 18 years and not a party to the cause, and showing the date and place of deposit in the mail, the name and address of the person served as shown on the envelope, and also showing that the envelope was sealed and deposited in the mail with the postage thereon fully prepaid.

(2) A certificate setting forth the exact title of the document served and filed in the cause, showing the name and business address of the person making the service, showing that he or she is an active member of the State Bar of California and is not a party to the cause, and showing the date and place of deposit in the mail, the name and address of the person served as shown on the envelope, and also showing that the envelope was sealed and deposited in the mail with the postage thereon fully prepaid.

(3) An affidavit setting forth the exact title of the document served and filed in the cause, showing (A) the name and residence or business address of the person making the service, (B) that he or she is a resident of, or employed in, the county where the mailing occurs, (C) that he or she is over the age of 18 years and not a party to the cause, (D) that he or she is readily familiar with the business' practice for collection and processing of correspondence for mailing with the United States Postal Service, (E) that the correspondence would be deposited with the United States Postal Service that same day in the ordinary course of business, (F) the name and address of the person

served as shown on the envelope, and the date and place of business where the correspondence was placed for deposit in the United States Postal Service, and (G) that the envelope was sealed and placed for collection and mailing on that date following ordinary business practices. Service made pursuant to this paragraph, upon motion of a party served, shall be presumed invalid if the postal cancellation date or postage meter date on the envelope is more than one day after the date of deposit for mailing contained in the affidavit.

(4) In case of service by the clerk of a court of record, a certificate by that clerk setting forth the exact title of the document served and filed in the cause, showing the name of the clerk and the name of the court of which he or she is the clerk, and that he or she is not a party to the cause, and showing the date and place of deposit in the mail, the name and address of the person served as shown on the envelope, and also showing that the envelope was sealed and deposited in the mail with the postage thereon fully prepaid. This form of proof is sufficient for service of process in which the clerk or deputy clerk signing the certificate places the document for collection and mailing on the date shown thereon, so as to cause it to be mailed in an envelope so sealed and so addressed on that date following standard court practices. Service made pursuant to this paragraph, upon motion of a party served and a finding of good cause by the court, shall be deemed to have occurred on the date of postage cancellation or postage meter imprint as shown on the envelope if that date is more than one day after the date of deposit for mailing contained in the certificate. *(Added by Stats.1931, c. 739, p. 1534, § 3. Amended by Stats.1953, c. 1110, p. 2606, § 1; Stats.1955, c. 779, p. 1379, § 1; Stats.1959, c. 345, p. 2268, § 1; Stats.1972, c. 601, p. 1065, § 3; Stats.1972, c. 1083, p. 2019, § 1; Stats.1973, c. 302, p. 718, § 1; Stats.1974, c. 282, p. 546, § 3, eff. May 28, 1974; Stats.1980, c. 196, p. 419, § 3; Stats.1987, c. 190, § 1; Stats.1988, c. 160, § 18; Stats.1995, c. 576 (A.B.1225), § 4.)*

Cross References

Affidavit to prove service, see Code of Civil Procedure § 2009.
Claims against public entities, notice, mailing manner, see Government Code § 915.2.
Dishonored checks, liability, demands for payment, stop payments, notice, see Civil Code § 1719.

Research References

Forms

West's California Code Forms, Civil Procedure § 595.2 Form 1, Trial—Stipulation for Continuance—Order.
West's California Code Forms, Corporations § 317 Form 1, Defendants' Notice of Application to Court for Indemnity.
West's California Code Forms, Government § 913 Form 1, Notice of Action Taken.
West's California Code Forms, Probate § 1211 Form 1, Notice of Hearing (Probate)—Judicial Council Form DE-120.
West's California Judicial Council Forms DAL-012, Proof of Service—Disability Access Litigation.
West's California Judicial Council Forms FL-334, Declaration Regarding Address Verification—Postjudgment Request to Modify a Child Custody, Visitation, or Child Support Order.
West's California Judicial Council Forms FL-335, Proof of Service by Mail.
West's California Judicial Council Forms FL-335-INFO, Information Sheet for Proof of Service by Mail.
West's California Judicial Council Forms FL-686, Proof of Service by Mail.
West's California Judicial Council Forms JV-310, Proof of Service Under Section 366.26 of the Welfare and Institutions Code (Also Available in Spanish).
West's California Judicial Council Forms POS-030, Proof of Service by First-Class Mail—Civil (Proof of Service)/Information Sheet for Proof of Service by First-Class Mail—Civil.
West's California Judicial Council Forms POS-040, Proof of Service—Civil.

§ 1013b. Proof of electronic service

(a) Proof of electronic service may be made by any of the following methods:

(1) An affidavit setting forth the exact title of the document served and filed in the cause, showing the name and residence or business address of the person making the service, showing that * * * the person is a resident of or employed in the county where the electronic service occurs, and that * * * the person is over * * * 18 years of age.

(2) A certificate setting forth the exact title of the document served and filed in the cause, showing the name and business address of the person making the service, and showing that * * * the person is an active member of the State Bar of California.

(3) An affidavit setting forth the exact title of the document served and filed in the cause, showing all of the following:

(A) The name and residence or business address of the person making the service.

(B) * * * That the person is a resident of, or employed in, the county where the electronic service occurs.

(C) * * * That the person is over * * * 18 years * * * of age.

(D) * * * That the person is readily familiar with the business' practice for filing electronically * * *.

(E) That the document would be electronically served that same day in the ordinary course of business following ordinary business practices.

(4) In case of service by the clerk of a court of record, a certificate by that clerk setting forth the exact title of the document served and filed in the cause, showing the name of the clerk and the name of the court of which * * * they are the clerk.

(b) Proof of electronic service shall include all of the following:

(1) The electronic service address and the residence or business address of the person making the electronic service.

(2) The date of electronic service.

(3) The name and electronic service address of the person served.

(4) A statement that the document was served electronically.

(c) Proof of electronic service shall be signed as provided in subparagraph (B) of paragraph (2) of subdivision (e) of Section 1010.6.

(d) Proof of electronic service may be in electronic form and may be filed electronically with the court. *(Added by Stats.2017, c. 319 (A.B.976), § 4, eff. Jan. 1, 2018. Amended by Stats.2018, c. 776 (A.B.3250), § 8, eff. Jan. 1, 2019; Stats.2022, c. 215 (A.B.2961), § 2, eff. Jan. 1, 2023.)*

Cross References

Claims against public entities, manner and presentation and of giving notice, electronic submissions, see Government Code § 915.2.

§ 1015. Service; nonresident party; service on clerk or attorney

When a plaintiff or a defendant, who has appeared, resides out of the state, and has no attorney in the action or proceeding, the service may be made on the clerk of the court, for that party. But in all cases where a party has an attorney in the action or proceeding, the service of papers, when required, must be upon the attorney instead of the party, except service of subpoenas, of writs, and other process issued in the suit, and of papers to bring the party into contempt. If the sole attorney for a party is removed or suspended from practice, then the party has no attorney within the meaning of this section. If the party's sole attorney has no known office in this state, notices and papers may be served by leaving a copy thereof with the clerk of the court, unless the attorney has filed in the cause an address of a place at which notices and papers may be served on the attorney, in which event they may be served at that place. *(Enacted in 1872. Amended by Stats.1907, c. 327, p. 602, § 4; Stats.1933, c. 744, p. 1899, § 179; Stats.1951, c. 1737, p. 4133, § 136, operative Jan. 1, 1952; Stats.2007, c. 263 (A.B.310), § 12.)*

Cross References

Attorney,
  Authority of, see Code of Civil Procedure § 283.
  Duties of, see Business and Professions Code § 6068.
  Manner of service on, see Code of Civil Procedure § 1011.
Owners and operators of watercraft, service on nonresidents, see Harbors and Navigation Code § 600 et seq.

§ 1015

Subpoena, service of, see Code of Civil Procedure § 1987.
Wharf, service of notice as to construction of, see Harbors and Navigation Code § 4005.

§ 1016. Service; process to bring party into contempt; inapplicability of certain sections

The foregoing provisions of this Chapter do not apply to the service of a summons or other process, or of any paper to bring a party into contempt. *(Enacted in 1872.)*

Cross References

Warrant, service and return of in contempt, see Code of Civil Procedure §§ 1212, 1216.

Part 3

OF SPECIAL PROCEEDINGS OF A CIVIL NATURE

Cross References

Arbitration of attorneys' fees, see Business and Professions Code § 6203.
Regional centers for persons with developmental disabilities, actions against third parties, disputes regarding amount of regional center or department's lien to recover costs of services provided, see Welfare and Institutions Code § 4659.16.

Title 3

OF SUMMARY PROCEEDINGS

Chapter	Section
6. COVID–19 Rental Housing Recovery Act	1179.08

CHAPTER 4. SUMMARY PROCEEDINGS FOR OBTAINING POSSESSION OF REAL PROPERTY IN CERTAIN CASES

Section

1161.3. Termination of lease prohibited based upon acts of domestic violence, sexual assault, stalking, human trafficking, or abuse of elder or dependent adult; documentation; exceptions; limitation of landlord liability to other tenants; disclosure to third parties; forms.

Cross References

Deposition notice, date of deposition, see Code of Civil Procedure § 2025.270.
Employee housing, eviction of tenants, application of Health and Safety Code provision, see Health and Safety Code § 17031.6.
Form and content of demand, see Code of Civil Procedure § 2031.030.
Immigration or citizenship status irrelevant to issues of liability or remedy in specified proceedings, discovery, see Civil Code § 3339.10.
Mobilehome parks, termination of tenancy, application of law, see Civil Code § 798.60.
Nuisance caused by illegal conduct involving unlawful weapons or ammunition purpose, unlawful detainer action, see Civil Code § 3485.
Requests for admission, admissions without leave of court, time to request, earlier requests with leave of court, see Code of Civil Procedure § 2033.020.
Response to inspection demand, time to respond, see Code of Civil Procedure § 2031.260.
Response to requests for admission, time to respond, see Code of Civil Procedure § 2033.250.
Time to make demand, inspection prior to time allowed, see Code of Civil Procedure § 2031.020.
Time to respond, shortening of time, copies to all parties, see Code of Civil Procedure § 2030.260.
Time to submit interrogatories, motion to submit at earlier time, see Code of Civil Procedure § 2030.020.

Unlawful detainer actions to abate nuisance caused by illegal conduct involving controlled substance purpose, procedures, see Civil Code § 3486.

§ 1161.3. Termination of lease prohibited based upon acts of domestic violence, sexual assault, stalking, human trafficking, or abuse of elder or dependent adult; documentation; exceptions; limitation of landlord liability to other tenants; disclosure to third parties; forms

(a) For purposes of this section:

* * * (1) "Abuse or violence" means domestic violence as defined in Section 6211 of the Family Code, sexual assault as defined in Section 1219, stalking as defined in Section 1708.7 of the Civil Code or Section 646.9 of the Penal Code, human trafficking as defined in Section 236.1 of the Penal Code, * * * abuse of an elder or a dependent adult as defined in Section 15610.07 of the Welfare and Institutions Code, * * * or any act described in paragraphs (6) to (8), inclusive, * * * of subdivision (a) of Section 1946.7 of the Civil Code.

* * *

<u>(2) "Documentation evidencing abuse or violence against the tenant, the tenant's immediate family member, or the tenant's household member"</u> means any of the following:

(A) A temporary restraining order, emergency protective order, or protective order lawfully issued within the last 180 days pursuant to Section 527.6, Part 3 (commencing with Section 6240), Part 4 (commencing with Section 6300), or Part 5 (commencing with Section 6400) of Division 10 of the Family Code, Section 136.2 of the Penal Code, or Section 213.5 or 15657.03 of the Welfare and Institutions Code that protects the tenant * * *, <u>the tenant's immediate family member, or the tenant's household member</u> from * * * abuse * * * <u>or violence</u>.

(B) A copy of a written report, written within the last 180 days, by a peace officer employed by a state or local law enforcement agency acting in * * * the officer's official capacity, stating that the tenant * * *, <u>the tenant's immediate family member, or the tenant's</u> household member has filed a report alleging that * * * <u>they are a</u> victim of * * * abuse * * * <u>or violence</u>.

(C)<u>(i)</u> Documentation from a qualified third party based on information received by that third party while acting in * * * <u>their</u> professional capacity to indicate that the tenant * * *, <u>the tenant's immediate family member, or the tenant's</u> household member is seeking assistance for physical or mental injuries or abuse resulting from an act of * * * abuse or violence, * * * <u>which shall contain, in substantially the same form, the following</u>:

* * *

Tenant Statement and Qualified Third Party Statement under Code of Civil Procedure Section 1161.3

Part I. Statement By Tenant

I, [insert name of tenant], state as follows:

I, my immediate family member, or a member of my household, have been a victim of:

[insert one or more of the following: domestic violence, sexual assault, stalking, human trafficking, elder abuse, * * * dependent adult abuse, a crime that caused bodily injury or death, a crime that included the exhibition, drawing, brandishing, or use of a firearm or other deadly weapon or instrument, or a crime that included the use or threat of force against the victim.]

The most recent incident(s) happened on or about:
[insert date or dates.]

The incident(s) was/were committed by the following person(s), with these physical description(s), if known and safe to provide:
[if known and safe to provide, insert name(s) and physical description(s).]

_____ _____
(signature of tenant)   (date)

Part II.   Qualified Third Party Statement

I, [insert name of qualified third party], state as follows:

My business address and phone number are:
[insert business address and phone number.]

Check and complete one of the following:

_____I meet the requirements for a sexual assault counselor provided in Section 1035.2 of the Evidence Code and I am either engaged in an office, hospital, institution, or center commonly known as a rape crisis center described in that section or employed by an organization providing the programs specified in Section 13835.2 of the Penal Code.

_____I meet the requirements for a domestic violence counselor provided in Section 1037.1 of the Evidence Code and I am employed, whether financially compensated or not, by a domestic violence victim service organization, as defined in that section.

_____I meet the requirements for a human trafficking caseworker provided in Section 1038.2 of the Evidence Code and I am employed, whether financially compensated or not, by an organization that provides programs specified in Section 18294 of the Welfare and Institutions Code or in Section 13835.2 of the Penal Code.

_____I meet the definition of "victim of violent crime advocate" provided in Section 1946.7 of the Civil Code and I am employed, whether financially compensated or not, by an agency or organization that has a documented record of providing services to victims of violent crime or provides those services under the auspices or supervision of a court or a law enforcement or prosecution agency.

_____I am licensed by the State of California as a:
[insert one of the following: physician and surgeon, osteopathic physician and surgeon, registered nurse, psychiatrist, psychologist, licensed clinical social worker, licensed marriage and family therapist, or licensed professional clinical counselor.] and I am licensed by, and my license number is:

[insert name of state licensing entity and license number.]

The person who signed the Statement By Tenant above stated to me that * * *they, * * *a member of * * *their immediate family, or a member of their household * * *is a victim of:
[insert one or more of the following: domestic violence, sexual assault, stalking, human trafficking, elder abuse, * * *dependent adult abuse, a crime that caused bodily injury or death, a crime that included the exhibition, drawing, brandishing, or use of a firearm or other deadly weapon or instrument, or a crime that included the use or threat of force against the victim.]
The person further stated to me the incident(s) occurred on or about the date(s) stated above.

_____ _____
(signature of qualified third party)   (date)

(ii) The documentation may be signed by a person who meets the requirements for a sexual assault counselor, domestic violence counselor, * * * a human trafficking caseworker, or a victim of violent crime advocate only if the documentation displays the letterhead of the office, hospital, institution, center, or organization, as appropriate, that engages or employs, whether financially compensated or not, this counselor * * *, caseworker, or advocate.

* * *

(D) Any other form of documentation or evidence that reasonably verifies that the abuse or violence occurred.

(3) "Health practitioner" means a physician and surgeon, osteopathic physician and surgeon, psychiatrist, psychologist, registered nurse, licensed clinical social worker, licensed marriage and family therapist, or licensed professional clinical counselor.

(4) "Immediate family member" has the same meaning as defined in Section 1946.7 of the Civil Code.

(5) "Perpetrator of abuse or violence" means any of the following:

(A) The person against whom an order described in subparagraph (A) of paragraph (1) of subdivision (a) has been issued.

(B) The person who was named or referred to as causing the abuse or violence in the report described in subparagraph (B) of paragraph (1) of subdivision (a).

(C) The person who was named or referred to as causing the abuse or violence in the documentation described in subparagraph (C) of paragraph (1) of subdivision (a).

(D) The person who was named or referred to as causing the abuse or violence in the documentation described in subparagraph (D) of paragraph (1) of subdivision (a).

(6) "Qualified third party" means a health practitioner, domestic violence counselor, as defined in Section 1037.1 of the Evidence Code, a sexual assault counselor, as defined in Section 1035.2 of the Evidence Code, a human trafficking caseworker, as defined in Section 1038.2 of the Evidence Code, or a victim of violent crime advocate.

(7) "Tenant" means tenant, subtenant, lessee, or sublessee.

(8) "Tenant in residence" means a tenant who is currently residing in the unit and has full physical and legal access to the unit.

(9) "Victim of violent crime advocate" has the same meaning as defined in Section 1946.7 of the Civil Code.

(b)(1) A landlord shall not terminate a tenancy or fail to renew a tenancy based on an act of abuse or violence against a tenant, a tenant's immediate family member, or a tenant's household member if the landlord has received documentation evidencing abuse or violence against the tenant, the tenant's immediate family member, or the tenant's household member.

(2) Notwithstanding paragraph (1), a landlord may terminate a tenancy or fail to renew a tenancy based on an act of abuse or violence against a tenant, a tenant's immediate family member, or a tenant's household member even after receiving documentation of abuse or violence against the tenant, the tenant's immediate family member, or the tenant's household member if either of the following apply:

§ 1161.3

(A) The perpetrator of abuse or violence is a tenant in residence of the same dwelling unit as the tenant, the tenant's immediate family member, or household member.

(B) Both of the following apply:

(i) The perpetrator of abuse or violence's words or actions have threatened the physical safety of other tenants, guests, invitees, or licensees.

(ii) After expiration of a three-day notice requiring the tenant not to voluntarily permit or consent to the presence of the perpetrator of abuse or violence on the premises, the tenant continues to do so.

(c) Notwithstanding any provision in a lease to the contrary, a landlord shall not be liable to any other tenants for any action that arises due to the landlord's compliance with this section.

(d) A violation of subdivision (b) by the landlord shall be an affirmative defense to a cause of action for unlawful detainer that is based on an act of abuse or violence against a tenant, a tenant's immediate family member, or a tenant's household member as follows:

(1) If the perpetrator of the abuse or violence is not a tenant in residence of the same dwelling unit as the tenant, the tenant's immediate family member, or household member, then the defendant shall have a complete defense as to that cause of action, unless each clause of subparagraph (B) of paragraph (2) of subdivision (b) applies.

(2) If the perpetrator of the abuse or violence is a tenant in residence of the same dwelling unit as the tenant, the tenant's immediate family member, or household member, the court shall proceed in accordance with Section 1174.27.

(e)(1) A landlord shall not disclose any information provided by a tenant under this section to a third party unless either of the following is true:

(A) The tenant has consented in writing to the disclosure.

(B) The disclosure is required by law or court order.

(2) A landlord's communication with the qualified third party who provides documentation in order to verify the contents of that documentation is not a disclosure for purposes of this subdivision.

* * *

(f) The Judicial Council shall * * * review its forms that may be used by a party to assert in the responsive pleading the grounds set forth in this section as an affirmative defense to an unlawful detainer action and, by January 1, 2024, make any changes to those forms that the Judicial Council deems necessary to conform them to this section. (Added by Stats.2010, c. 626 (S.B.782), § 4. Amended by Stats.2012, c. 516 (S.B.1403), § 2; Stats.2013, c. 130 (S.B.612), § 3; Stats.2018, c. 190 (A.B.2413), § 2, eff. Jan. 1, 2019; Stats.2022, c. 558 (S.B.1017), § 2, eff. Jan. 1, 2023.)

Cross References

Informing crime victims of their rights, Victim Protections and Resources card, see Penal Code § 679.027.

Title 5

OF CONTEMPTS

Section
1209. Acts or omissions constituting; stay of sentence pending appeal.
1209.5. Noncompliance with order for care or support of child.
1210. Re-entry after ejectment; alias process after conviction; undertaking for appeal.
1211. Summary punishment; order; affidavit or statement of facts; compliance by filing of form.

Section
1211.5. Affidavit or statement of facts; rules for construction, amendment and review.
1212. Warrant of attachment; issuance; order to show cause; warrant of commitment.
1213. Warrant of attachment; endorsement for undertaking.
1214. Warrant of attachment; execution.
1215. Discharge on undertaking.
1216. Warrant of attachment; undertaking; return.
1217. Trial.
1218. Determination of guilt; punishment; restrictions on enforcement of orders by party in contempt; action for contempt of domestic violence prevention order.
1218.5. Child, family, or spousal support; contempt for failure to pay; separate counts; limitation of actions.
1219. Imprisonment to compel performance of acts; exemptions; definitions.
1219.5. Minors under 16 years of age; refusal to take oath; referral to probation officer; meeting with victim advocate; placement outside minor's home; sanctions.
1220. Nonappearance; alias warrant; enforcement of undertaking; damages.
1221. Illness for excuse for not bringing in prisoner; unnecessary restraint.
1222. Conclusiveness of judgments and orders.

Cross References

Committees of the State Bar, contempt for disobedience of subpoena, see Business and Professions Code §§ 6050, 6051.
Criminal contempt of court, see Penal Code §§ 166, 166.5.
Disobedience to referee's order, see Code of Civil Procedure § 708.140.
Estate administration, removal of personal representative for contempt, see Probate Code § 8505.
Legislative contempts, see Government Code § 9406 et seq.
Military courts, contempt, see Military and Veterans Code § 468.
Public Utilities Commission, power to punish for contempt, see Cal. Const. Art 12, § 6.
Punishment,
  Judicial officer, see Code of Civil Procedure § 178.
  Mitigating circumstance in subsequent criminal proceeding, see Penal Code § 658.
Officers authorized to take proof of instruments, see Civil Code § 1201.
Unauthorized practice of law, contempt proceedings to conform with this title, see Business and Professions Code § 6127.
Witness, arrest for failure to attend legislature, see Government Code § 9409.
Witnesses, punishment for contempt, see Code of Civil Procedure § 1991 et seq.
Workers Compensation Appeals Board, service of process in proceedings for contempt, see Labor Code § 134.

§ 1209. Acts or omissions constituting; stay of sentence pending appeal

(a) The following acts or omissions in respect to a court of justice, or proceedings therein, are contempts of the authority of the court:

(1) Disorderly, contemptuous, or insolent behavior toward the judge while holding the court, tending to interrupt the due course of a trial or other judicial proceeding.

(2) A breach of the peace, boisterous conduct, or violent disturbance, tending to interrupt the due course of a trial or other judicial proceeding.

(3) Misbehavior in office, or other willful neglect or violation of duty by an attorney, counsel, clerk, sheriff, coroner, or other person, appointed or elected to perform a judicial or ministerial service.

(4) Abuse of the process or proceedings of the court, or falsely pretending to act under authority of an order or process of the court.

(5) Disobedience of any lawful judgment, order, or process of the court.

(6) Willful disobedience by a juror of a court admonishment related to the prohibition on any form of communication or research about the case, including all forms of electronic or wireless communication or research.

(7) Rescuing any person or property in the custody of an officer by virtue of an order or process of that court.

(8) Unlawfully detaining a witness or party to an action while going to, remaining at, or returning from the court where the action is on the calendar for trial.

(9) Any other unlawful interference with the process or proceedings of a court.

(10) Disobedience of a subpoena duly served, or refusing to be sworn or answer as a witness.

(11) When summoned as a juror in a court, neglecting to attend or serve as a juror, or improperly conversing with a party to an action to be tried at the court, or with any other person, in relation to the merits of the action, or receiving a communication from a party or other person in respect to the action, without immediately disclosing the communication to the court.

(12) Disobedience by an inferior tribunal or judicial officer of the lawful judgment, order, or process of a superior court, or proceeding in an action or special proceeding contrary to law, after the action or special proceeding is removed from the jurisdiction of the inferior tribunal or judicial officer.

(b) A speech or publication reflecting upon or concerning a court or an officer thereof shall not be treated or punished as a contempt of the court unless made in the immediate presence of the court while in session and in such a manner as to actually interfere with its proceedings.

(c) Notwithstanding Section 1211 or any other law, if an order of contempt is made affecting an attorney, his or her agent, investigator, or any person acting under the attorney's direction, in the preparation and conduct of an action or proceeding, the execution of any sentence shall be stayed pending the filing within three judicial days of a petition for extraordinary relief testing the lawfulness of the court's order, the violation of which is the basis of the contempt, except for conduct proscribed by subdivision (b) of Section 6068 of the Business and Professions Code, relating to an attorney's duty to maintain respect due to the courts and judicial officers.

(d) Notwithstanding Section 1211 or any other law, if an order of contempt is made affecting a public safety employee acting within the scope of employment for reason of the employee's failure to comply with a duly issued subpoena or subpoena duces tecum, the execution of any sentence shall be stayed pending the filing within three judicial days of a petition for extraordinary relief testing the lawfulness of the court's order, a violation of which is the basis for the contempt.

As used in this subdivision, "public safety employee" includes any peace officer, firefighter, paramedic, or any other employee of a public law enforcement agency whose duty is either to maintain official records or to analyze or present evidence for investigative or prosecutorial purposes. *(Enacted in 1872. Amended by Stats.1891, c. 9, p. 6, § 1; Stats.1907, c. 255, p. 319, § 1; Stats.1939, c. 979, p. 2731, § 1; Stats.1975, c. 836, p. 1896, § 2; Stats.1982, c. 510, p. 2286, § 2; Stats.2011, c. 181 (A.B.141), § 3.)*

Cross References

Attorneys,
    Acts or omissions constituting contempt, see Business and Professions Code § 6127.
    Disciplinary authority of courts, see Business and Professions Code § 6100 et seq.
    Duties toward court, see Business and Professions Code § 6068.
    Unlawful practice, see Business and Professions Code § 6125 et seq.
Citation, refusal to obey citation, see Probate Code § 8870.
Disobedience of order of appearance before workmen's compensation appeals board, see Labor Code § 132.
Disobedience to subpoena, board of governors and bar committees, see Business and Professions Code §§ 6050, 6051.
Disobedience to subpoena or refusal to be sworn or to answer or subscribe affidavit or deposition, see Code of Civil Procedure § 1991 et seq.
Employer's failure to report injury as ordered, see Labor Code § 3760.
Failure, upon subsequent application for order, to reveal facts of prior application, see Code of Civil Procedure § 1008.
Failure to appear at custody and control hearing, see Family Code § 7883.
Jurors, failure to attend, see Code of Civil Procedure § 209.
Misdemeanor, contempts constituting, see Penal Code § 166.
Newsman's refusal to disclose news source, see Evidence Code § 1070.
Noncompliance of personal representative with order to attend or answer at hearing, see Probate Code § 8500.
Power of courts, see Code of Civil Procedure § 128.
Power of judicial officers, see Code of Civil Procedure §§ 177, 178.
Privileged information, failure to disclose, see Evidence Code § 914.
Proof of instruments, power of officer to punish for contempt, see Civil Code § 1201.
Re-entry upon property after dispossession, see Code of Civil Procedure § 1210.
Refusal to,
    Be sworn, depositions, see Code of Civil Procedure § 1991.1.
    Make discovery, see Code of Civil Procedure §§ 2031.010 et seq. and 2036.210 et seq.
    Submit to examination or answer interrogatories, see Probate Code § 8870.
Supplemental proceedings, disobedience of referee's orders, see Code of Civil Procedure § 708.140.
Violation of court's prohibition against operation of aircraft,
    Generally, see Public Utilities Code § 21408.
    Failure to obey order of appearance before state water resources control board, see Water Code § 1097.
Warrant for absent witness, see Code of Civil Procedure § 1993.

Research References

Forms

West's California Code Forms, Civil Procedure § 1211 Form 1, Contempts—Declaration—Not in Court's Presence.
West's California Judicial Council Forms FL-411, Affidavit of Facts Constituting Contempt (Financial and Injunctive Orders).
West's California Judicial Council Forms FL-415, Findings and Order Regarding Contempt (Domestic Violence Prevention—Uniform Parentage—Governmental).

§ 1209.5. Noncompliance with order for care or support of child

When a court of competent jurisdiction makes an order compelling a parent to furnish support or necessary food, clothing, shelter, medical attendance, or other remedial care for his or her child, proof that the order was made, filed, and served on the parent or proof that the parent was present in court at the time the order was pronounced and proof that the parent did not comply with the order is prima facie evidence of a contempt of court. *(Added by Stats.1955, c. 1359, p. 2444, § 1. Amended by Stats.1961, c. 1307, p. 3087, § 1, eff. July 10, 1961; Stats.1992, c. 163 (A.B.2641), § 57, operative Jan. 1, 1994.)*

Cross References

Child support, see Family Code §§ 3028, 3651 et seq., 4001 et seq.
Custody of children, see Family Code §§ 3000 et seq., 3020 et seq.
Prima facie evidence, see Evidence Code § 602.
Proof defined, see Evidence Code § 190.

§ 1210. Re-entry after ejectment; alias process after conviction; undertaking for appeal

Every person dispossessed or ejected from any real property by the judgment or process of any court of competent jurisdiction, who, not having right so to do, reenters into or upon or takes possession of the real property, or induces or procures any person not having right so to do, or aids or abets such a person therein, is guilty of a contempt of the court by which the judgment was rendered or from which the process issued. Upon a conviction for contempt the court must immediately issue an alias process, directed to the proper officer, and requiring the officer to restore possession to the party entitled under

§ 1210

the original judgment or process, or to the party's lessee, grantee, or successor in interest. No appeal from the order directing the issuance of an alias writ of possession stays the execution of the writ, unless an undertaking is executed on the part of the appellant to the effect that the appellant will not commit or suffer to be committed any waste on the property, and if the order is affirmed, or the appeal dismissed, the appellant will pay the value of the use and occupation of the property from the time of the unlawful reentry until the delivery of the possession of the property, pursuant to the judgment or order, not exceeding a sum to be fixed by the judge of the court by which the order for the alias writ was made. *(Enacted in 1872. Amended by Stats.1893, c. 198, p. 281, § 1; Stats.1907, c. 255, p. 320, § 2; Stats.1982, c. 517, p. 2362, § 179.)*

Cross References

Possessory action for real property, see Civil Code §§ 793, 3375.
Re-entry,
   How effected, see Civil Code §§ 790, 791.
   Transferability of right, see Civil Code § 1046.
Undertaking, form, see Code of Civil Procedure § 995.320.

§ 1211. Summary punishment; order; affidavit or statement of facts; compliance by filing of form

(a) When a contempt is committed in the immediate view and presence of the court, or of the judge at chambers, it may be punished summarily; for which an order must be made, reciting the facts as occurring in such immediate view and presence, adjudging that the person proceeded against is thereby guilty of a contempt, and that he or she be punished as therein prescribed.

When the contempt is not committed in the immediate view and presence of the court, or of the judge at chambers, an affidavit shall be presented to the court or judge of the facts constituting the contempt, or a statement of the facts by the referees or arbitrators, or other judicial officers.

(b) In family law matters, filing of the Judicial Council form entitled "Order to Show Cause and Affidavit for Contempt (Family Law)" shall constitute compliance with this section. *(Enacted in 1872. Amended by Stats.1933, c. 745, p. 1906, § 11; Stats.1951, c. 1737, p. 4141, § 162, operative Jan. 1, 1952; Stats.1995, c. 904 (A.B.965), § 1; Stats.2001, c. 754 (A.B.1697), § 1.)*

Cross References

Automatic stay of sentence for certain individuals, see Code of Civil Procedure § 128.
Depositions, disobedience to subpoena or refusal to be sworn, see Code of Civil Procedure § 1991 et seq.

Research References

Forms

West's California Code Forms, Civil Procedure § 1211 Form 1, Contempts—Declaration—Not in Court's Presence.
West's California Judicial Council Forms FL–411, Affidavit of Facts Constituting Contempt (Financial and Injunctive Orders).

§ 1211.5. Affidavit or statement of facts; rules for construction, amendment and review

At all stages of all proceedings, the affidavit or statement of facts, as the case may be, required by Section 1211 shall be construed, amended, and reviewed according to the followings [1] rules:

(a) If no objection is made to the sufficiency of such affidavit or statement during the hearing on the charges contained therein, jurisdiction of the subject matter shall not depend on the averments of such affidavit or statement, but may be established by the facts found by the trial court to have been proved at such hearing, and the court shall cause the affidavit or statement to be amended to conform to proof.

(b) The court may order or permit amendment of such affidavit or statement for any defect or insufficiency at any stage of the proceedings, and the trial of the person accused of contempt shall continue as if the affidavit or statement had been originally filed as amended, unless substantial rights of such person accused would be prejudiced thereby, in which event a reasonable postponement, not longer than the ends of justice require, may be granted.

(c) No such affidavit or statement is insufficient, nor can the trial, order, judgment, or other proceeding thereon be affected by reason of any defect or imperfection in matter of form which does not prejudice a substantial right of the person accused on the merits. No order or judgment of conviction of contempt shall be set aside, nor new trial granted, for any error as to any matter of pleading in such affidavit or statement, unless, after an examination of the entire cause, including the evidence, the court shall be of the opinion that the error complained of has resulted in a miscarriage of justice. *(Added by Stats.1970, c. 1264, p. 2282, § 1.)*

[1] So in chaptered copy.

Cross References

Affidavit defined, see Code of Civil Procedure § 2003.

Research References

Forms

West's California Judicial Council Forms FL–410, Order to Show Cause and Affidavit for Contempt.
West's California Judicial Council Forms FL–411, Affidavit of Facts Constituting Contempt (Financial and Injunctive Orders).
West's California Judicial Council Forms FL–412, Affidavit of Facts Constituting Contempt (Domestic Violence/Custody and Visitation).

§ 1212. Warrant of attachment; issuance; order to show cause; warrant of commitment

When the contempt is not committed in the immediate view and presence of the court or judge, a warrant of attachment may be issued to bring the person charged to answer, or, without a previous arrest, a warrant of commitment may, upon notice, or upon an order to show cause, be granted; and no warrant of commitment can be issued without such previous attachment to answer, or such notice or order to show cause. *(Enacted in 1872. Amended by Stats.1933, c. 745, p. 1906, § 12; Stats.1951, c. 1737, p. 4141, § 163, operative Jan. 1, 1952.)*

Cross References

Notice defined, see Civil Code §§ 18, 19.
Searches and seizures, see Cal. Const. Art. 1, § 13.
Service and notice, see Code of Civil Procedure § 1010 et seq.

§ 1213. Warrant of attachment; endorsement for undertaking

Whenever a warrant of attachment is issued pursuant to this title the court or judge must direct, by an endorsement on the warrant, that the person charged may give an undertaking for the person's appearance in an amount to be specified in such endorsement. *(Enacted in 1872. Amended by Stats.1933, c. 745, p. 1906, § 13; Stats.1951, c. 1737, p. 4142, § 164, operative Jan. 1, 1952; Stats.1982, c. 517, p. 2362, § 179.5.)*

Cross References

Discharge on undertaking, see Code of Civil Procedure § 1215.
Surety,
   Defined, see Code of Civil Procedure § 995.185; Civil Code § 2787.
   Law governing, see Code of Civil Procedure § 995.320.

§ 1214. Warrant of attachment; execution

Upon executing the warrant of attachment, the officer executing the warrant must keep the person in custody, bring him before the court or judge, and detain him until an order be made in the premises, unless the person arrested entitle himself to be discharged, as provided in the next section. *(Enacted in 1872. Amended by Stats.1933, c. 745, p. 1906, § 14; Stats.1951, c. 1737, p. 4142, § 165, operative Jan. 1, 1952.)*

Cross References

Searches and seizures, see Cal. Const. Art. 1, § 13.

§ 1215. Discharge on undertaking

The person arrested must be discharged from the arrest upon executing and delivering to the officer, at any time before the return day of the warrant, an undertaking to the effect that the person arrested will appear on the return of the warrant and abide the order of the court or judge thereupon. *(Enacted in 1872. Amended by Stats.1933, c. 745, p. 1907, § 15; Stats.1951, c. 1737, p. 4142, § 166, operative Jan. 1, 1952; Stats.1982, c. 517, p. 2362, § 180.)*

Cross References

Surety,
  Defined, see Code of Civil Procedure § 995.185; Civil Code § 2787.
  Law governing, see Code of Civil Procedure § 995.320.

§ 1216. Warrant of attachment; undertaking; return

The officer must return the warrant of arrest and undertaking, if any, received by him from the person arrested, by the return day specified therein. *(Enacted in 1872.)*

§ 1217. Trial

When the person arrested has been brought up or appeared, the court or judge must proceed to investigate the charge, and must hear any answer which the person arrested may make to the same, and may examine witnesses for or against him, for which an adjournment may be had from time to time if necessary. *(Enacted in 1872. Amended by Stats.1933, c. 745, p. 1907, § 16; Stats.1951, c. 1737, p. 4142, § 167, operative Jan. 1, 1952.)*

§ 1218. Determination of guilt; punishment; restrictions on enforcement of orders by party in contempt; action for contempt of domestic violence prevention order

(a) Upon the answer and evidence taken, the court or judge shall determine whether the person proceeded against is guilty of the contempt charged, and if it be adjudged that the person is guilty of the contempt, a fine may be imposed on the person not exceeding one thousand dollars ($1,000), payable to the court, or the person may be imprisoned not exceeding five days, or both. In addition, a person who is subject to a court order as a party to the action, or any agent of this person, who is adjudged guilty of contempt for violating that court order may be ordered to pay to the party initiating the contempt proceeding the reasonable attorney's fees and costs incurred by this party in connection with the contempt proceeding.

(b) Any party, who is in contempt of a court order or judgment in a dissolution of marriage, dissolution of domestic partnership, or legal separation action, shall not be permitted to enforce such an order or judgment, by way of execution or otherwise, either in the same action or by way of a separate action, against the other party. This restriction shall not affect nor apply to the enforcement of child or spousal support orders.

(c)(1) In any court action in which a party is found in contempt of court for failure to comply with a court order pursuant to the Family Code, the court shall, subject to the sentencing option provided in paragraph (2), order the following:

(A) Upon a first finding of contempt, the court shall order the contemner to perform community service of up to 120 hours, or to be imprisoned up to 120 hours, for each count of contempt.

(B) Upon the second finding of contempt, the court shall order the contemner to perform community service of up to 120 hours, in addition to ordering imprisonment of the contemner up to 120 hours, for each count of contempt.

(C) Upon the third or any subsequent finding of contempt, the court shall order that the contemner serve a term of imprisonment of up to 240 hours and perform community service of up to 240 hours, for each count of contempt. The court shall also order the contemner to pay an administrative fee, not to exceed the actual cost of the contemner's administration and supervision, while assigned to a community service program pursuant to this paragraph.

(D) The court shall take parties' employment schedules into consideration when ordering either community service or imprisonment, or both.

(2) In lieu of an order of imprisonment, community service, or both, as set forth in paragraph (1), the court may grant probation or a conditional sentence for a period not to exceed one year upon a first finding of contempt, a period not to exceed two years upon a second finding of contempt, and a period not to exceed three years upon a third or any subsequent finding of contempt.

(3) For purposes of this subdivision, "probation" and "conditional sentence" shall have the meanings set forth in subdivision (a) of Section 1203 of the Penal Code.

(d) Pursuant to Section 1211 and this section, a district attorney or city attorney may initiate and pursue a court action for contempt against a party for failing to comply with a court order entered pursuant to the Domestic Violence Protection Act (Division 10 (commencing with Section 6200) of the Family Code). Any attorney's fees and costs ordered by the court pursuant to subdivision (a) against a party who is adjudged guilty of contempt under this subdivision shall be paid to the Office of Emergency Services' account established for the purpose of funding domestic violence shelter service providers pursuant to subdivision (f) of Section 13823.15 of the Penal Code. *(Enacted in 1872. Amended by Stats.1933, c. 745, p. 1907, § 17; Stats.1951, c. 1737, p. 4142, § 168, operative Jan. 1, 1952; Stats.1968, c. 938, p. 1788, § 2; Stats.1977, c. 1257, p. 4770, § 39, eff. Jan. 3, 1977; Stats.1983, c. 1092, § 72, eff. Sept. 27, 1983, operative Jan. 1, 1984; Stats.1988, c. 969, § 2; Stats.1993, c. 745 (S.B.788), § 1; Stats.1993, c. 746 (A.B.934), § 1; Stats.1994, c. 368 (A.B.2911), § 1; Stats.1994, c. 1269 (A.B.2208), § 3.3; Stats.1995, c. 576 (A.B.1225), § 5.5; Stats.2000, c. 808 (A.B.1358), § 20, eff. Sept. 28, 2000; Stats.2005, c. 75 (A.B.145), § 44, eff. July 19, 2005, operative Jan. 1, 2006; Stats.2005, c. 631 (S.B.720), § 1; Stats.2010, c. 618 (A.B.2791), § 3; Stats.2013, c. 352 (A.B.1317), § 56, eff. Sept. 26, 2013, operative July 1, 2013; Stats.2020, c. 283 (A.B.2338), § 1, eff. Jan. 1, 2021.)*

Cross References

Application of Trial Court Trust Fund depositary requirements to fees and fines specified in this section, see Government Code § 68085.7.
Organization and government of courts, collection of fees and fines pursuant to this section, deposits, see Government Code § 68085.1.
Personal representative, commitment for contempt, see Probate Code § 8505.
Proof of instruments, authority of officer to punish for contempt, see Civil Code § 1201.
Punishment for contempt, see Code of Civil Procedure § 178.
Transfers of certain fees and fines specified in this section, effective date, see Government Code § 68085.5.
Witnesses, punishment for contempt, see Code of Civil Procedure § 1991.

Research References

Forms

Asset Protection: Legal Planning, Strategies and Forms ¶ 7.01, Introduction.
West's California Code Forms, Civil Procedure § 1218 Form 1, Contempts—Order Holding Party in Contempt.
West's California Code Forms, Civil Procedure § 1218 Form 2, Contempts—Notice of Motion for Order Awarding Attorney's Fees.
West's California Code Forms, Civil Procedure § 1218 Form 4, Contempts—Order Awarding Attorney's Fees.
West's California Judicial Council Forms FL–415, Findings and Order Regarding Contempt (Domestic Violence Prevention—Uniform Parentage—Governmental).

§ 1218.5. Child, family, or spousal support; contempt for failure to pay; separate counts; limitation of actions

(a) If the contempt alleged is for failure to pay child, family, or spousal support, each month for which payment has not been made

§ 1218.5

in full may be alleged as a separate count of contempt and punishment imposed for each count proven.

(b) If the contempt alleged is the failure to pay child, family, or spousal support, the period of limitations for commencing a contempt action is three years from the date that the payment was due. If the action before the court is enforcement of another order under the Family Code, the period of limitations for commencing a contempt action is two years from the time that the alleged contempt occurred. *(Added by Stats.1994, c. 1269 (A.B.2208), § 3.5.)*

§ 1219. Imprisonment to compel performance of acts; exemptions; definitions

(a) Except as provided in subdivisions (b) and (c), if the contempt consists of the omission to perform an act which is yet in the power of the person to perform, he or she may be imprisoned until he or she has performed it, and in that case the act shall be specified in the warrant of commitment.

(b) Notwithstanding any other law, a court shall not imprison or otherwise confine or place in custody the victim of a sexual assault or domestic violence crime for contempt if the contempt consists of refusing to testify concerning that sexual assault or domestic violence crime. Before finding a victim of a domestic violence crime in contempt as described in this section, the court may refer the victim for consultation with a domestic violence counselor. All communications between the victim and the domestic violence counselor that occur as a result of that referral shall remain confidential under Section 1037.2 of the Evidence Code.

(c) Notwithstanding any other law, a court shall not imprison, hold in physical confinement, or otherwise confine or place in custody a minor for contempt if the contempt consists of the minor's failure to comply with a court order pursuant to subdivision (b) of Section 601 of, or Section 727 of, the Welfare and Institutions Code, if the minor was adjudged a ward of the court on the ground that he or she is a person described in subdivision (b) of Section 601 of the Welfare and Institutions Code. Upon a finding of contempt of court, the court may issue any other lawful order, as necessary, to secure the minor's attendance at school.

(d) As used in this section, the following terms have the following meanings:

(1) "Sexual assault" means any act made punishable by Section 261, 262, 264.1, 285, 286, 287, 288, or 289 of, or former Section 288a of, the Penal Code.

(2) "Domestic violence" means "domestic violence" as defined in Section 6211 of the Family Code.

(3) "Domestic violence counselor" means "domestic violence counselor" as defined in subdivision (a) of Section 1037.1 of the Evidence Code.

(4) "Physical confinement" has the same meaning as defined in subdivision (d) of Section 726 of the Welfare and Institutions Code. *(Enacted in 1872. Amended by Stats.1980, c. 676, § 68; Stats.1984, c. 1644, § 2; Stats.1991, c. 866 (A.B.363), § 4; Stats.1992, c. 163 (A.B.2641), § 58, operative Jan. 1, 1994; Stats.1993, c. 219 (A.B.1500), § 69.7; Stats.2008, c. 49 (S.B.1356), § 1; Stats.2009, c. 35 (S.B.174), § 3; Stats.2012, c. 510 (A.B.2051), § 1; Stats.2014, c. 70 (S.B.1296), § 1, eff. Jan. 1, 2015; Stats.2018, c. 423 (S.B.1494), § 9, eff. Jan. 1, 2019.)*

Cross References

Compulsion of personal representative to obey order requiring answering of questions, see Probate Code §§ 8500, 8505.
Dismissal as bar to prosecution, exceptions, see Penal Code § 1387.
Lease not to be terminated based on domestic or sexual assault against tenant, landlord's liability for compliance, see Code of Civil Procedure § 1161.3.

Searches and seizures, see Cal. Const. Art. 1, § 13.

§ 1219.5. Minors under 16 years of age; refusal to take oath; referral to probation officer; meeting with victim advocate; placement outside minor's home; sanctions

(a) Except as provided in subdivision (d), in any case in which a contempt consists of the refusal of a minor under 16 years of age to take the oath or to testify, before imposing any sanction for the contempt, the court shall first refer the matter to the probation officer in charge of matters coming before the juvenile court for a report and recommendation as to the appropriateness of the imposition of a sanction. The probation officer shall prepare and file the report and recommendation within the time directed by the court. In making the report and recommendation, the probation officer shall consider factors such as the maturity of the minor, the reasons for the minor's refusal to take the oath or to testify, the probability that available sanctions will affect the decision of the minor not to take the oath or not to testify, the potential impact on the minor of his or her testimony, the potential impact on the pending litigation of the minor's unavailability as a witness, and the appropriateness of the various available sanctions in the minor's case. The court shall consider the report and recommendation in imposing a sanction in the case.

(b) A victim of a sex crime who is subject to subdivision (a) shall meet with a victim advocate, as defined in Section 679.04 of the Penal Code, unless the court, for good cause, finds that it is not in the best interest of the victim.

(c) In any case in which the court orders the minor to be placed outside of his or her home, the placement shall be in the least restrictive setting available. Except as provided in subdivision (e), the court shall not order the minor to be placed in a secure facility unless other placements have been made and the minor has fled the custody and control of the person under the control of whom he or she has been placed or has persistently refused to obey the reasonable and proper orders or directions of the person under the control of whom he or she has been placed.

(d) The court may impose a sanction for contempt prior to receipt of the report and recommendation required by subdivision (a) if the court enters a finding, supported by specific facts stated on the record, that the minor would be likely to flee if released before the receipt of the report and recommendation.

(e) The court may order the minor placed in a secure facility without first attempting the nonsecure placement required by subdivision (c) if the court enters a finding, supported by specific facts stated on the record, that the minor would be likely to flee if released to nonsecure placement as a prerequisite to secure confinement. *(Added by Stats.1984, c. 1643, § 1. Amended by Stats.2012, c. 223 (S.B.1248), § 1.)*

§ 1220. Nonappearance; alias warrant; enforcement of undertaking; damages

When the warrant of arrest has been returned served, if the person arrested does not appear on the return day, the court or judge may issue another warrant of arrest or may order the undertaking to be enforced, or both. If the undertaking is enforced, the measure of damages is the extent of the loss or injury sustained by the aggrieved party by reason of the misconduct for which the warrant was issued. *(Enacted in 1872. Amended by Stats.1933, c. 745, p. 1907, § 18; Stats.1951, c. 1737, p. 2143, § 169, operative Jan. 1, 1952; Stats.1982, c. 517, p. 2362, § 181.)*

Cross References

Costs, see Code of Civil Procedure § 1021 et seq.

§ 1221. Illness for excuse for not bringing in prisoner; unnecessary restraint

Whenever, by the provisions of this title, an officer is required to keep a person arrested on a warrant of attachment in custody, and to bring him before a court or judge, the inability, from illness or otherwise, of the person to attend, is a sufficient excuse for not bringing him up; and the officer must not confine a person arrested upon the warrant in a prison, or otherwise restrain him of personal liberty, except so far as may be necessary to secure his personal attendance. *(Enacted in 1872. Amended by Stats.1933, c. 745, p. 1907, § 19; Stats.1951, c. 1737, p. 4143, § 170, operative Jan. 1, 1952.)*

Cross References

Searches and seizures, see Cal. Const. Art. 1, § 13.

§ 1222. Conclusiveness of judgments and orders

The judgment and orders of the court or judge, made in cases of contempt, are final and conclusive. *(Enacted in 1872. Amended by Stats.1933, c. 745, p. 1908, § 20; Stats.1951, c. 1737, p. 4143, § 171, operative Jan. 1, 1952.)*

Cross References

Appeal of judgment of contempt made final and conclusive by this section prohibited, see Code of Civil Procedure § 904.1.
Conclusiveness of judgment or order, see Code of Civil Procedure § 1908.
Municipal and justice courts, appeal prohibited from judgment of contempt made final and conclusive by this section, see Code of Civil Procedure § 904.2.

Research References

Forms

West's California Code Forms, Civil Procedure § 1219 Form 1, Contempts—Judgment of Contempt and Commitment to Compel Act.

Title 8

CHANGE OF NAMES

Section
1275. Jurisdiction.
1276. Application or petition; venue; contents; petitions for minors.
1277. Orders to show cause; publication or posting; petitions for minors; exemptions; service of notice.
1277.5. Petition for change of name to conform petitioner's name to petitioner's gender identity; objections; minors; exemptions; hearings.
1278. Hearings; orders without hearings.
1278.5. Petitions relating to minors; absence of consent of both parents.
1279.5. Name change; common law right; state prisoners; parolees and probationers; registered sex offenders.
1279.6. Trade or business; doing business or providing services; prohibitions.

Cross References

Marriage, change of name, see Family Code § 306.5.
Registered domestic partnership, change of name, see Family Code § 298.6.
Revision of birth records to reflect change of sex, petition, procedure, see Health and Safety Code § 103435.

§ 1275. Jurisdiction

Applications for change of names must be determined by the Superior Courts. *(Enacted in 1872. Amended by Code Am.1880, c. 113, p. 117, § 1; Stats.1983, c. 486, § 1.)*

Cross References

Deed to show change of name, see Civil Code § 1096.

Research References

Forms

18A Am. Jur. Pl. & Pr. Forms Name § 3, Statutory References.
West's California Judicial Council Forms NC–100, Petition for Change of Name.
West's California Judicial Council Forms NC–110, Attachment to Petition for Change of Name.
West's California Judicial Council Forms NC–110G, Supplemental Attachment to Petition for Change of Name (Declaration of Guardian).
West's California Judicial Council Forms NC–200, Petition for Change of Name, Recognition of Change of Gender, and Issuance of New Birth Certificate.
West's California Judicial Council Forms NC–225, Order to Show Cause for Change of Name to Conform to Gender Identity (Same as Nc-125).
West's California Judicial Council Forms NC–500, Petition for Recognition of Minor's Change of Gender and Issuance of New Birth Certificate.
West's California Judicial Council Forms NC–510G, Supplemental Attachment to Petition for Change of Name (Declaration of Guardian).

§ 1276. Application or petition; venue; contents; petitions for minors

(a)(1) All applications for change of names shall be made to the superior court of the county where the person whose name is proposed to be changed resides, except as specified in subdivision (e) or (g), either (A) by petition signed by the person or, if the person is under 18 years of age, by one of the person's parents, by any guardian of the person, or as specified in subdivision (e), or, if both parents are deceased and there is no guardian of the person, then by some near relative or friend of the person, or (B) as provided in Section 7638 of the Family Code.

(2) The petition or pleading shall specify the place of birth and residence of the person, the person's present name, the name proposed, and the reason for the change of name.

(b) In a proceeding for a change of name commenced by the filing of a petition, if the person whose name is to be changed is under 18 years of age, the petition shall, if neither parent of the person has signed the petition, name, as far as known to the person proposing the name change, the parents of the person and their place of residence, if living, or, if neither parent is living, near relatives of the person, and their place of residence.

(c) In a proceeding for a change of name commenced by the filing of a petition, if the person whose name is proposed to be changed is under 18 years of age and the petition is signed by only one parent, the petition shall specify the address, if known, of the other parent if living. If the petition is signed by a guardian, the petition shall specify the name and address, if known, of the parent or parents, if living, or the grandparents, if the addresses of both parents are unknown or if both parents are deceased, of the person whose name is proposed to be changed.

(d) In a proceeding for a change of name commenced by the filing of a petition, if the person whose name is proposed to be changed is 12 years of age or older, has been relinquished to an adoption agency by the person's parent or parents, and has not been legally adopted, the petition shall be signed by the person and the adoption agency to which the person was relinquished. The near relatives of the person and their place of residence shall not be included in the petition unless they are known to the person whose name is proposed to be changed.

(e) All petitions for the change of the name of a minor submitted by a guardian appointed by the juvenile court or the probate court, by a court-appointed dependency attorney appointed as guardian ad litem pursuant to rules adopted under Section 326.5 of the Welfare and Institutions Code, or by an attorney for a minor who is alleged or adjudged to be a person described in Section 601 or 602 of the Welfare and Institutions Code shall be made in the court having

§ 1276   CODE OF CIVIL PROCEDURE

jurisdiction over the minor. All petitions for the change of name of a nonminor dependent may be made in the juvenile court.

(f) If the petition is signed by a guardian, the petition shall specify relevant information regarding the guardianship, the likelihood that the child will remain under the guardian's care until the child reaches the age of majority, and information suggesting that the child will not likely be returned to the custody of the child's parents.

(g)(1) On or after January 1, 2023, an application for a change of name may be made to a superior court for a person whose name is proposed to be changed, even if the person does not reside within the State of California, if the person is seeking to change their name on at least one of the following documents:

(A) A birth certificate that was issued within this state to the person whose name is proposed to be changed.

(B) A birth certificate that was issued within this state to the legal child of the person whose name is proposed to be changed.

(C) A marriage license and certificate or a confidential marriage license and certificate that was issued within this state to the person whose name is proposed to be changed.

(2) For the purposes of this subdivision, the superior court in the county where the birth under subparagraph (A) or (B) of paragraph (1) occurred or marriage under subparagraph (C) of paragraph (1) was entered shall be a proper venue for the proceeding. The name change shall be adjudicated in accordance with California law. (Enacted in 1872. Amended by Code Am.1877–78, c. 413, p. 110, § 1; Code Am.1880, c. 113, p. 117, § 2; Stats.1885, c. 128, p. 112, § 1; Stats.1929, c. 710, p. 1260, § 1; Stats.1945, c. 842, p. 1540, § 1; Stats.1961, c. 1817, p. 3864, § 1; Stats.1970, c. 651, p. 1276, § 1; Stats.1971, c. 1748, p. 3748, § 30; Stats.1975, c. 1241, p. 3192, § 9; Stats.1989, c. 1105, § 9; Stats.1992, c. 163 (A.B.2641), § 59, operative Jan. 1, 1994; Stats.2000, c. 111 (A.B.2155), § 1; Stats.2006, c. 567 (A.B.2303), § 10; Stats.2018, c. 776 (A.B.3250), § 9, eff. Jan. 1, 2019; Stats.2021, c. 401 (A.B.1578), § 7, eff. Jan. 1, 2022; Stats.2021, c. 577 (A.B.218), § 1.5, eff. Jan. 1, 2022.)

Cross References

Corporations, adoption of new name, see Corporations Code §§ 201, 909.

§ 1277. Orders to show cause; publication or posting; petitions for minors; exemptions; service of notice

(a)(1) If a proceeding for a change of name is commenced by the filing of a petition, except as provided in subdivisions (b), (c), (d), and (f), or Section 1277.5, the court shall thereupon make an order reciting the filing of the petition, the name of the person by whom it is filed, and the name proposed. The order shall direct all persons interested in the matter to appear before the court at a time and place specified, which shall be not less than 6 weeks nor more than 12 weeks from the time of making the order, unless the court orders a different time, to show cause why the application for change of name should not be granted. The order shall direct all persons interested in the matter to make known any objection that they may have to the granting of the petition for change of name by filing a written objection, which includes the reasons for the objection, with the court at least two court days before the matter is scheduled to be heard and by appearing in court at the hearing to show cause why the petition for change of name should not be granted. The order shall state that, if no written objection is timely filed, the court may grant the petition without a hearing.

(2)(A) A copy of the order to show cause shall be published pursuant to Section 6064 of the Government Code in a newspaper of general circulation to be designated in the order published in the county. If a newspaper of general circulation is not published in the county, a copy of the order to show cause shall be posted by the clerk of the court in three of the most public places in the county in which the court is located, for a like period. Proof shall be made to the satisfaction of the court of this publication or posting at the time of the hearing of the application.

(B)(i) On or after January 1, 2023, if the person whose name is proposed to be changed does not live in the county where the petition is filed, pursuant to subdivision (g) of Section 1276, the copy of the order to show cause shall be published pursuant to Section 6064 of the Government Code in a newspaper of general circulation published in the county of the person's residence. If a newspaper of general circulation is not published in the county of the person's residence, a copy of the order to show cause shall be posted by the clerk of the court in the county of the person's residence or a similarly situated local official in three of the most public places in the county of the person's residence, for a like period. If the place where the person seeking the name change lives does not have counties, publication shall be made according to the requirements of this paragraph in the local subdivision or territory of the person's residence. Proof shall be made to the satisfaction of the court of this publication or posting at the time of the hearing of the application.

(ii) If the person is unable to publish or post a copy of the order to show cause pursuant to clause (i), the court may allow an alternate method of publication or posting or may waive this requirement after sufficient evidence of diligent efforts to publish or post a copy of the order has been submitted to the satisfaction of the court.

(3) Four weekly publications shall be sufficient publication of the order to show cause. If the order is published in a daily newspaper, publication once a week for four successive weeks shall be sufficient.

(4) If a petition has been filed for a minor by a parent and the other parent, if living, does not join in consenting thereto, the petitioner shall cause, not less than 30 days before the hearing, to be served notice of the time and place of the hearing or a copy of the order to show cause on the other parent pursuant to Section 413.10, 414.10, 415.10, or 415.40. If notice of the hearing cannot reasonably be accomplished pursuant to Section 415.10 or 415.40, the court may order that notice be given in a manner that the court determines is reasonably calculated to give actual notice to the nonconsenting parent. In that case, if the court determines that notice by publication is reasonably calculated to give actual notice to the nonconsenting parent, the court may determine that publication of the order to show cause pursuant to this subdivision is sufficient notice to the nonconsenting parent.

(b)(1) If the petition for a change of name alleges a reason or circumstance described in paragraph (2), and the petitioner has established that the petitioner is an active participant in the address confidentiality program created pursuant to Chapter 3.1 (commencing with Section 6205) of Division 7 of Title 1 of the Government Code, and that the name the petitioner is seeking to acquire is on file with the Secretary of State, the action for a change of name is exempt from the requirement for publication of the order to show cause under subdivision (a), and the petition and the order of the court shall, in lieu of reciting the proposed name, indicate that the proposed name is confidential and is on file with the Secretary of State pursuant to the provisions of the address confidentiality program.

(2) The procedure described in paragraph (1) applies to petitions alleging any of the following reasons or circumstances:

(A) To avoid domestic violence, as defined in Section 6211 of the Family Code.

(B) To avoid stalking, as defined in Section 646.9 of the Penal Code.

(C) To avoid sexual assault, as defined in Section 1036.2 of the Evidence Code.

(D) To avoid human trafficking, as defined in Section 236.1 of the Penal Code.

(3) For any petition under this subdivision, the current legal name of the petitioner shall be kept confidential by the court and shall not

be published or posted in the court's calendars, indexes, or register of actions, as required by Article 7 (commencing with Section 69840) of Chapter 5 of Title 8 of the Government Code, or by any means or in any public forum, including a hardcopy or an electronic copy, or any other type of public media or display.

(4) Notwithstanding paragraph (3), the court may, at the request of the petitioner, issue an order reciting the name of the petitioner at the time of the filing of the petition and the new legal name of the petitioner as a result of the court's granting of the petition.

(5) A petitioner may request that the court file the petition and any other papers associated with the proceeding under seal. The court may consider the request at the same time as the petition for name change, and may grant the request in any case in which the court finds that all of the following factors apply:

(A) There exists an overriding interest that overcomes the right of public access to the record.

(B) The overriding interest supports sealing the record.

(C) A substantial probability exists that the overriding interest will be prejudiced if the record is not sealed.

(D) The proposed order to seal the records is narrowly tailored.

(E) No less restrictive means exist to achieve the overriding interest.

(c) If the petition is filed for a minor or nonminor dependent who is under the jurisdiction of the juvenile court, the action for a change of name is exempt from the requirement for publication of the order to show cause under subdivision (a).

(d) A proceeding for a change of name for a witness participating in the state Witness Relocation and Assistance Program established by Title 7.5 (commencing with Section 14020) of Part 4 of the Penal Code who has been approved for the change of name by the program is exempt from the requirement for publication of the order to show cause under subdivision (a).

(e) If an application for change of name is brought as part of an action under the Uniform Parentage Act (Part 3 (commencing with Section 7600) of Division 12 of the Family Code), whether as part of a petition or cross-complaint or as a separate order to show cause in a pending action thereunder, service of the application shall be made upon all other parties to the action in a like manner as prescribed for the service of a summons, as set forth in Article 3 (commencing with Section 415.10) of Chapter 4 of Title 5 of Part 2. Upon the setting of a hearing on the issue, notice of the hearing shall be given to all parties in the action in a like manner and within the time limits prescribed generally for the type of hearing (whether trial or order to show cause) at which the issue of the change of name is to be decided.

(f) If a guardian files a petition to change the name of the guardian's minor ward pursuant to Section 1276:

(1) The guardian shall provide notice of the hearing to any living parent of the minor by personal service at least 30 days before the hearing.

(2) If either or both parents are deceased or cannot be located, the guardian shall cause, not less than 30 days before the hearing, to be served a notice of the time and place of the hearing or a copy of the order to show cause on the child's grandparents, if living, pursuant to Section 413.10, 414.10, 415.10, or 415.40. *(Added by Stats.2017, c. 853 (S.B.179), § 4, eff. Jan. 1, 2018, operative Sept. 1, 2018. Amended by Stats.2018, c. 776 (A.B.3250), § 10, eff. Jan. 1, 2019; Stats.2018, c. 818 (A.B.2201), § 1, eff. Jan. 1, 2019; Stats.2021, c. 401 (A.B.1578), § 8, eff. Jan. 1, 2022; Stats.2021, c. 577 (A.B.218), § 2.5, eff. Jan. 1, 2022.)*

Cross References

Computation of time, see Code of Civil Procedure §§ 12 and 12a; Government Code § 6800 et seq.

Fees for change of name proceeding, action filed on behalf of minor, see Government Code § 70635.

Notice, actual and constructive, defined, see Civil Code § 18.

Persons upon whom summons may be served, see Code of Civil Procedure § 416.10 et seq.

Victims of domestic violence, sexual assault, and stalking, confidentiality of name changes, see Government Code § 6206.4.

Witness defined for purposes of this Code, see Code of Civil Procedure § 1878.

Research References

Forms

West's California Judicial Council Forms NC-120, Order to Show Cause for Change of Name.

West's California Judicial Council Forms NC-121, Proof of Service of Order to Show Cause.

West's California Judicial Council Forms NC-400, Confidential Cover Sheet—Name Change Proceeding Under Address Confidentiality Program (Safe at Home).

West's California Judicial Council Forms NC-400-INFO, Information Sheet for Name Change Proceedings Under Address Confidentiality Program (Safe at Home).

West's California Judicial Council Forms NC-410, Application to File Documents Under Seal in Name Change Proceeding Under Address Confidentiality Program (Safe at Home).

West's California Judicial Council Forms NC-420, Declaration in Support of Publication to File Documents Under Seal in Name Change Proceeding Under Address Confidentiality Program (Safe at Home).

West's California Judicial Council Forms NC-425, Order on Application to File Documents Under Seal in Name Change Proceeding Under Address Confidentiality Program (Safe at Home).

West's California Judicial Council Forms NC-520, Order to Show Cause for Recognition of Minor's Change of Gender and Issuance of New Birth Certificate.

§ 1277.5. Petition for change of name to conform petitioner's name to petitioner's gender identity; objections; minors; exemptions; hearings

(a)(1) If a proceeding for a change of name to conform the petitioner's name to the petitioner's gender identity is commenced by the filing of a petition, the court shall thereupon make an order reciting the filing of the petition, the name of the person by whom it is filed, and the name proposed. The order shall direct all persons interested in the matter to make known any objection to the change of name by filing a written objection, which includes any reasons for the objection, within six weeks of the making of the order, and shall state that if no objection showing good cause to oppose the name change is timely filed, the court shall, without hearing, enter the order that the change of name is granted.

(2) If a petition is filed to change the name of a minor to conform to gender identity that does not include the signatures of both living parents, the petition and the order to show cause made in accordance with paragraph (1) shall be served on the parent who did not sign the petition, pursuant to Section 413.10, 414.10, 415.10, or 415.40, within 30 days from the date on which the order is made by the court. If service cannot reasonably be accomplished pursuant to Section 415.10 or 415.40, the court may order that service be accomplished in a manner that the court determines is reasonably calculated to give actual notice to the parent who did not sign the petition.

(b) The proceeding for a change of name to conform the petitioner's name to the petitioner's gender identity is exempt from any requirement for publication.

(c) A hearing date shall not be set in the proceeding unless an objection is timely filed and shows good cause for opposing the name change. Objections based solely on concerns that the proposed change is not the petitioner's actual gender identity or gender assigned at birth shall not constitute good cause. At the hearing, the court may examine under oath any of the petitioners, remonstrants, or other persons touching the petition or application, and may make an order changing the name or dismissing the petition or application as the court may deem right and proper. *(Added by Stats.2017, c. 853*

§ 1277.5

(S.B.179), § 5, eff. Jan. 1, 2018, operative Sept. 1, 2018. Amended by Stats.2018, c. 776 (A.B.3250), § 11, eff. Jan. 1, 2019.)

Research References

Forms

West's California Judicial Council Forms NC–125, Order to Show Cause for Change of Name to Conform to Gender Identity (Same as Nc–225).

West's California Judicial Council Forms NC–150, Notice of Hearing on Petition.

§ 1278. Hearings; orders without hearings

(a)(1) Except as provided in subdivisions (c) and (d), the petition or application shall be heard at the time designated by the court, only if objections are filed by a person who can, in those objections, show to the court good cause against the change of name. At the hearing, the court may examine on oath any of the petitioners, remonstrants, or other persons touching the petition or application, and may make an order changing the name, or dismissing the petition or application, as the court may deem right and proper.

(2) If no objection is filed at least two court days before the date set for hearing, the court may, without hearing, enter the order that the change of name is granted.

(b) If the provisions of subdivision (b) of Section 1277 apply, the court shall not disclose the proposed name unless the court finds by clear and convincing evidence that the allegations of domestic violence, stalking, or sexual assault in the petition are false.

(c) If the application for a change of name is brought as part of an action under the Uniform Parentage Act (Part 3 (commencing with Section 7600) of Division 12 of the Family Code), the hearing on the issue of the change of name shall be conducted pursuant to statutes and rules of court governing those proceedings, whether the hearing is conducted upon an order to show cause or upon trial.

(d) If the petition for a change of name is filed by a guardian on behalf of a minor ward, the court shall first find that the ward is likely to remain in the guardian's care until the age of majority and that the ward is not likely to be returned to the custody of the parents. Upon making those findings, the court shall consider the petition and may grant the petition only if it finds that the proposed name change is in the best interest of the child.

(e) This section shall become operative on September 1, 2018. *(Added by Stats.2017, c. 853 (S.B.179), § 7, eff. Jan. 1, 2018, operative Sept. 1, 2018.)*

Cross References

Computation of time, see Code of Civil Procedure §§ 12 and 12a; Government Code § 6800 et seq.

Research References

Forms

West's California Judicial Council Forms NC–130, Decree Changing Name.

West's California Judicial Council Forms NC–130G, Decree Changing Name.

West's California Judicial Council Forms NC–230, Decree Changing Name and Order Recognizing Change of Gender and for Issuance of New Birth Certificate.

West's California Judicial Council Forms NC–400, Confidential Cover Sheet—Name Change Proceeding Under Address Confidentiality Program (Safe at Home).

§ 1278.5. Petitions relating to minors; absence of consent of both parents

In any proceeding pursuant to this title in which a petition has been filed to change the name of a minor, and both parents, if living, do not join in consent, the court may deny the petition in whole or in part if it finds that any portion of the proposed name change is not in the best interest of the child. *(Added by Stats.1996, c. 1061 (S.B.1033), § 2. Amended by Stats.2006, c. 567 (A.B.2303), § 13.)*

§ 1279.5. Name change; common law right; state prisoners; parolees and probationers; registered sex offenders

(a) Except as provided in subdivision (e) or (f), this title does not abrogate the common law right of a person to change his or her name.

(b) A person under the jurisdiction of the Department of Corrections and Rehabilitation or sentenced to county jail has the right to petition the court to obtain a name or gender change pursuant to this title or Article 7 (commencing with Section 103425) of Chapter 11 of Part 1 of Division 102 of the Health and Safety Code.

(c) A person under the jurisdiction of the Department of Corrections and Rehabilitation shall provide a copy of the petition for a name change to the department, in a manner prescribed by the department, at the time the petition is filed. A person sentenced to county jail shall provide a copy of the petition for name change to the sheriff's department, in a manner prescribed by the department, at the time the petition is filed.

(d) In all documentation of a person under the jurisdiction of the Department of Corrections and Rehabilitation or imprisoned within a county jail, the new name of a person who obtains a name change shall be used, and prior names shall be listed as an alias.

(e) Notwithstanding any other law, a court shall deny a petition for a name change pursuant to this title made by a person who is required to register as a sex offender under Section 290 of the Penal Code, unless the court determines that it is in the best interest of justice to grant the petition and that doing so will not adversely affect the public safety. If a petition for a name change is granted for an individual required to register as a sex offender, the individual shall, within five working days, notify the chief of police of the city in which he or she is domiciled, or the sheriff of the county if he or she is domiciled in an unincorporated area, and additionally with the chief of police of a campus of a University of California or California State University if he or she is domiciled upon the campus or in any of its facilities.

(f) For the purpose of this section, the court shall use the California Law Enforcement Telecommunications System (CLETS) and Criminal Justice Information System (CJIS) to determine whether or not an applicant for a name change is required to register as a sex offender pursuant to Section 290 of the Penal Code. Each person applying for a name change shall declare under penalty of perjury that he or she is not required to register as a sex offender pursuant to Section 290 of the Penal Code. If a court is not equipped with CLETS or CJIS, the clerk of the court shall contact an appropriate local law enforcement agency, which shall determine whether or not the petitioner is required to register as a sex offender pursuant to Section 290 of the Penal Code.

(g) This section shall become operative on September 1, 2018. *(Added by Stats.2017, c. 856 (S.B.310), § 3, eff. Jan. 1, 2018, operative Sept. 1, 2018.)*

Cross References

Computation of time, see Code of Civil Procedure §§ 12 and 12a; Government Code § 6800 et seq.

Department of Corrections, generally, see Penal Code § 5000 et seq.

§ 1279.6. Trade or business; doing business or providing services; prohibitions

No person engaged in a trade or business of any kind or in the provision of a service of any kind shall do any of the following:

(a) Refuse to do business with a person, or refuse to provide the service to a person, regardless of the person's marital status, because he or she has chosen to use or regularly uses his or her birth name, former name, or name adopted upon solemnization of marriage or registration of domestic partnership.

(b) Impose, as a condition of doing business with a person, or as a condition of providing the service to a person, a requirement that the person, regardless of his or her marital status, use a name other than his or her birth name, former name, or name adopted upon solemnization of marriage or registration of domestic partnership, if the person has chosen to use or regularly uses that name. *(Added by Stats.1992, c. 163 (A.B.2641), § 63, operative Jan. 1, 1994. Amended by Stats.2007, c. 567 (A.B.102), § 3.)*

Title 11

MONEY JUDGMENTS OF OTHER JURISDICTIONS

CHAPTER 1. SISTER STATE MONEY JUDGMENTS

Section
1710.10. Definitions.
1710.15. Application for entry; statement; contents.
1710.20. Filing of application; place.
1710.25. Entry of judgment; accrued interest.
1710.30. Notice of entry; procedure; fee.
1710.35. Effect of entry; enforcement.
1710.40. Vacation of judgment; motion; entry of another and different judgment; filing.
1710.45. Writ of execution or enforcement; resident and nonresident debtors; sale or distribution of property.
1710.50. Stay of enforcement.
1710.55. Restrictions on entry of judgment.
1710.60. Right of action to enforce judgment; exception.
1710.65. Right of action for other than payment of money.

§ 1710.10. Definitions

As used in this chapter:

(a) "Judgment creditor" means the person or persons who can bring an action to enforce a sister state judgment.

(b) "Judgment debtor" means the person or persons against whom an action to enforce a sister state judgment can be brought.

(c) "Sister state judgment" means that part of any judgment, decree, or order of a court of a state of the United States, other than California, which requires the payment of money, but does not include a support order as defined in Section 155 of the Family Code. *(Added by Stats.1974, c. 211, p. 405, § 3. Amended by Stats.1992, c. 163 (A.B.2641), § 64, operative Jan. 1, 1994.)*

Research References

Forms

West's California Code Forms, Civil Procedure § 1710.40 Form 1, Sister State Money Judgment—Notice of Motion to Vacate Judgment.

West's California Code Forms, Civil Procedure § 1710.40 Form 2, Sister State Money Judgment—Order Vacating Judgment.

West's California Code Forms, Civil Procedure § 1713.3 Form 1, Foreign Money—Judgments—Complaint.

West's California Code Forms, Civil Procedure § 1720 Form 3, Foreign-Country Money Judgments—Complaint.

§ 1710.15. Application for entry; statement; contents

(a) A judgment creditor may apply for the entry of a judgment based on a sister state judgment by filing an application pursuant to Section 1710.20.

(b) The application shall be executed under oath and shall include all of the following:

(1) A statement that an action in this state on the sister state judgment is not barred by the applicable statute of limitations.

(2) A statement, based on the applicant's information and belief, that no stay of enforcement of the sister state judgment is currently in effect in the sister state.

(3) A statement of the amount remaining unpaid under the sister state judgment and, if accrued interest on the sister state judgment is to be included in the California judgment, a statement of the amount of interest accrued on the sister state judgment (computed at the rate of interest applicable to the judgment under the law of the sister state), a statement of the rate of interest applicable to the judgment under the law of the sister state, and a citation to the law of the sister state establishing the rate of interest.

(4) A statement that no action based on the sister state judgment is currently pending in any court in this state and that no judgment based on the sister state judgment has previously been entered in any proceeding in this state.

(5) Where the judgment debtor is an individual, a statement setting forth the name and last known residence address of the judgment debtor. Where the judgment debtor is a corporation, a statement of the corporation's name, place of incorporation, and whether the corporation, if foreign, has qualified to do business in this state under the provisions of Chapter 21 (commencing with Section 2100) of Division 1 of Title 1 of the Corporations Code. Where the judgment debtor is a partnership, a statement of the name of the partnership, whether it is a foreign partnership, and, if it is a foreign partnership, whether it has filed a statement pursuant to Section 15800 of the Corporations Code designating an agent for service of process. Except for facts which are matters of public record in this state, the statements required by this paragraph may be made on the basis of the judgment creditor's information and belief.

(6) A statement setting forth the name and address of the judgment creditor.

(c) A properly authenticated copy of the sister state judgment shall be attached to the application. *(Added by Stats.1974, c. 211, p. 406, § 3. Amended by Stats.1977, c. 232, p. 1029, § 1; Stats.1982, c. 150, p. 495, § 4; Stats.1984, c. 311, § 2; Stats.1985, c. 106, § 11.)*

Cross References

Judgment creditor defined for purposes of this Chapter, see Code of Civil Procedure § 1710.10.
Judgment debtor defined for purposes of this Chapter, see Code of Civil Procedure § 1710.10.
Recording,
  Constructive notice, conveyances of real property or estate for years, see Civil Code § 1213.
  Instruments or judgments, documents to be recorded and manner of recording, see Government Code § 27320 et seq., § 27280 et seq.
  Property transfers, place of recordation, see Civil Code § 1169.
Sister state judgment defined for purposes of this Chapter, see Code of Civil Procedure § 1710.10.

Research References

Forms

West's California Code Forms, Civil Procedure § 1710.45 Form 1, Sister State Money Judgment—Ex Parte Application for Order Directing Immediate Issuance of Writ of Execution—Order.

West's California Judicial Council Forms EJ–105, Application for Entry of Judgment on Sister-State Judgment.

§ 1710.20. Filing of application; place

(a) An application for entry of a judgment based on a sister state judgment shall be filed in a superior court.

(b) Subject to the power of the court to transfer proceedings under this chapter pursuant to Title 4 (commencing with Section 392) of Part 2, the proper county for the filing of an application is any of the following:

(1) The county in which any judgment debtor resides.

(2) If no judgment debtor is a resident, any county in this state.

(c) A case in which the sister state judgment amounts to twenty-five thousand dollars ($25,000) or less is a limited civil case. *(Added by Stats.1974, c. 211, p. 406, § 3. Amended by Stats.1984, c. 311, § 3;*

§ 1710.20

Stats.1988, c. 54, § 1; Stats.1998, c. 931 (S.B.2139), § 125, eff. Sept. 28, 1998; Stats.2002, c. 784 (S.B.1316), § 86.)

Cross References

Judgment debtor defined for purposes of this Chapter, see Code of Civil Procedure § 1710.10.
Sister state judgment defined for purposes of this Chapter, see Code of Civil Procedure § 1710.10.

Research References

Forms

West's California Judicial Council Forms EJ-105, Application for Entry of Judgment on Sister-State Judgment.

§ 1710.25. Entry of judgment; accrued interest

(a) Upon the filing of the application, the clerk shall enter a judgment based upon the application for the total of the following amounts as shown therein:

(1) The amount remaining unpaid under the sister state judgment.

(2) The amount of interest accrued on the sister state judgment (computed at the rate of interest applicable to the judgment under the law of the sister state).

(3) The amount of the fee for filing the application for entry of the sister state judgment.

(b) Entry shall be made in the same manner as entry of an original judgment of the court. From the time of entry, interest shall accrue on the judgment so entered at the rate of interest applicable to a judgment entered in this state. *(Added by Stats.1974, c. 211, p. 406, § 3. Amended by Stats.1977, c. 232, p. 1030, § 2; Stats.1982, c. 150, p. 495, § 5; Stats.1984, c. 311, § 4.)*

Cross References

Sister state judgment defined for purposes of this Chapter, see Code of Civil Procedure § 1710.10.

§ 1710.30. Notice of entry; procedure; fee

(a) Notice of entry of judgment shall be served promptly by the judgment creditor upon the judgment debtor in the manner provided for service of summons by Article 3 (commencing with Section 415.10) of Chapter 4 of Title 5 of Part 2. Notice shall be in a form prescribed by the Judicial Council and shall inform the judgment debtor that the judgment debtor has 30 days within which to make a motion to vacate the judgment.

(b) The fee for service of the notice of entry of judgment under this section is an item of costs recoverable in the same manner as statutory fees for service of a writ as provided in Chapter 5 (commencing with Section 685.010) of Division 1 of Title 9 of Part 2, but such fee may not exceed the amount allowed to a public officer or employee in this state for such service. *(Added by Stats.1974, c. 211, p. 406, § 3. Amended by Stats.1977, c. 232, p. 1030, § 3; Stats.1982, c. 497, p. 2173, § 79, operative July 1, 1983.)*

Cross References

Computation of time, see Code of Civil Procedure §§ 12 and 12a; Government Code § 6800 et seq.
Judgment creditor defined for purposes of this Chapter, see Code of Civil Procedure § 1710.10.
Judgment debtor defined for purposes of this Chapter, see Code of Civil Procedure § 1710.10.
Judicial Council, see Government Code § 68500 et seq.
Notice, actual and constructive, defined, see Civil Code § 18.

Persons upon whom summons may be served, see Code of Civil Procedure § 416.10 et seq.

Research References

Forms

West's California Judicial Council Forms EJ-110, Notice of Entry of Judgment on Sister-State Judgment.

§ 1710.35. Effect of entry; enforcement

Except as otherwise provided in this chapter, a judgment entered pursuant to this chapter shall have the same effect as an original money judgment of the court and may be enforced or satisfied in like manner. *(Added by Stats.1974, c. 211, p. 407, § 3. Amended by Stats.1984, c. 311, § 5.)*

§ 1710.40. Vacation of judgment; motion; entry of another and different judgment; filing

(a) A judgment entered pursuant to this chapter may be vacated on any ground which would be a defense to an action in this state on the sister state judgment, including the ground that the amount of interest accrued on the sister state judgment and included in the judgment entered pursuant to this chapter is incorrect.

(b) Not later than 30 days after service of notice of entry of judgment pursuant to Section 1710.30, proof of which has been made in the manner provided by Article 5 (commencing with Section 417.10) of Chapter 4 of Title 5 of Part 2, the judgment debtor, on written notice to the judgment creditor, may make a motion to vacate the judgment under this section.

(c) Upon the hearing of the motion to vacate the judgment under this section, the judgment may be vacated upon any ground provided in subdivision (a) and another and different judgment entered, including, but not limited to, another and different judgment for the judgment creditor if the decision of the court is that the judgment creditor is entitled to such different judgment. The decision of the court on the motion to vacate the judgment shall be given and filed with the clerk of court in the manner provided in Sections 632, 634, and 635, except that the court is not required to make any written findings and conclusions if the amount of the judgment as entered under Section 1710.25 does not exceed one thousand dollars ($1,000). *(Added by Stats.1974, c. 211, p. 407, § 3. Amended by Stats.1977, c. 232, p. 1031, § 4.)*

Cross References

Computation of time, see Code of Civil Procedure §§ 12 and 12a; Government Code § 6800 et seq.
Judgment creditor defined for purposes of this Chapter, see Code of Civil Procedure § 1710.10.
Judgment debtor defined for purposes of this Chapter, see Code of Civil Procedure § 1710.10.
Notice, actual and constructive, defined, see Civil Code § 18.
Sister state judgment defined for purposes of this Chapter, see Code of Civil Procedure § 1710.10.

Research References

Forms

West's California Code Forms, Civil Procedure § 1710.40 Form 1, Sister State Money Judgment—Notice of Motion to Vacate Judgment.
West's California Code Forms, Civil Procedure § 1710.40 Form 2, Sister State Money Judgment—Order Vacating Judgment.
West's California Judicial Council Forms EJ-110, Notice of Entry of Judgment on Sister-State Judgment.

§ 1710.45. Writ of execution or enforcement; resident and nonresident debtors; sale or distribution of property

(a) Except as otherwise provided in this section, a writ of execution on a judgment entered pursuant to this chapter shall not issue, nor may the judgment be enforced by other means, until at least 30 days after the judgment creditor serves notice of entry of the judgment upon the judgment debtor, proof of which has been made in the manner provided by Article 5 (commencing with Section 417.10) of Chapter 4 of Title 5 of Part 2.

(b) A writ of execution may be issued, or other enforcement sought, before service of the notice of entry of judgment if the judgment debtor is any of the following:

(1) An individual who does not reside in this state.

(2) A foreign corporation not qualified to do business in this state under the provisions of Chapter 21 (commencing with Section 2100) of Division 1 of Title 1 of the Corporations Code.

(3) A foreign partnership which has not filed a statement pursuant to Section 15700 of the Corporations Code designating an agent for service of process.

(c) The court may order that a writ of execution be issued, or may permit enforcement by other means, before service of the notice of entry of judgment if the court finds upon an ex parte showing that great or irreparable injury would result to the judgment creditor if issuance of the writ or enforcement were delayed as provided in subdivision (a).

(d) Property levied upon pursuant to a writ issued under subdivision (b) or (c) or otherwise sought to be applied to the satisfaction of the judgment shall not be sold or distributed before 30 days after the judgment creditor serves notice of entry of the judgment upon the judgment debtor, proof of which has been made in the manner provided by Article 5 (commencing with Section 417.10) of Chapter 4 of Title 5 of Part 2. However, if property levied upon is perishable, it may be sold in order to prevent its destruction or loss of value, but the proceeds of the sale shall not be distributed to the judgment creditor before the date sale of nonperishable property is permissible. *(Added by Stats.1974, c. 211, p. 407, § 3. Amended by Stats.1976, c. 641, p. 1508, § 1.2, eff. Jan. 1, 1977; Stats.1982, c. 497, p. 2174, § 80, operative July 1, 1983.)*

Cross References

Computation of time, see Code of Civil Procedure §§ 12 and 12a; Government Code § 6800 et seq.
Judgment creditor defined for purposes of this Chapter, see Code of Civil Procedure § 1710.10.
Judgment debtor defined for purposes of this Chapter, see Code of Civil Procedure § 1710.10.
Notice, actual and constructive, defined, see Civil Code § 18.

Research References

Forms

West's California Code Forms, Civil Procedure § 1710.45 Form 1, Sister State Money Judgment—Ex Parte Application for Order Directing Immediate Issuance of Writ of Execution—Order.
West's California Judicial Council Forms EJ–110, Notice of Entry of Judgment on Sister-State Judgment.

§ 1710.50. Stay of enforcement

(a) The court shall grant a stay of enforcement where:

(1) An appeal from the sister state judgment is pending or may be taken in the state which originally rendered the judgment. Under this paragraph, enforcement shall be stayed until the proceedings on appeal have been concluded or the time for appeal has expired.

(2) A stay of enforcement of the sister state judgment has been granted in the sister state. Under this paragraph, enforcement shall be stayed until the sister state stay of enforcement expires or is vacated.

(3) The judgment debtor has made a motion to vacate pursuant to Section 1710.40. Under this paragraph, enforcement shall be stayed until the judgment debtor's motion to vacate is determined.

(4) Any other circumstance exists where the interests of justice require a stay of enforcement.

(b) The court may grant a stay of enforcement under this section on its own motion, on ex parte motion, or on noticed motion.

(c) The court shall grant a stay of enforcement under this section on such terms and conditions as are just including but not limited to the following:

(1) The court may require an undertaking in an amount it determines to be just, but the amount of the undertaking shall not exceed double the amount of the judgment creditor's claim.

(2) If a writ of execution has been issued, the court may order that it remain in effect.

(3) If property of the judgment debtor has been levied upon under a writ of execution, the court may order the levying officer to retain possession of the property capable of physical possession and to maintain the levy on other property. *(Added by Stats.1974, c. 211, p. 408, § 3.)*

Cross References

Judgment creditor defined for purposes of this Chapter, see Code of Civil Procedure § 1710.10.
Judgment debtor defined for purposes of this Chapter, see Code of Civil Procedure § 1710.10.
Sister state judgment defined for purposes of this Chapter, see Code of Civil Procedure § 1710.10.

Research References

Forms

West's California Code Forms, Civil Procedure § 1710.50 Form 1, Sister State Money Judgment—Notice of Motion to Stay Enforcement.
West's California Code Forms, Civil Procedure § 1710.50 Form 2, Sister State Money Judgment—Order Staying Enforcement.

§ 1710.55. Restrictions on entry of judgment

No judgment based on a sister state judgment may be entered pursuant to this chapter in any of the following cases:

(a) A stay of enforcement of the sister state judgment is currently in effect in the sister state.

(b) An action based on the sister state judgment is currently pending in any court in this state.

(c) A judgment based on the sister state judgment has previously been entered in any proceeding in this state. *(Added by Stats.1974, c. 211, p. 408, § 3.)*

Cross References

Sister state judgment defined for purposes of this Chapter, see Code of Civil Procedure § 1710.10.

Research References

Forms

West's California Code Forms, Civil Procedure § 1710.40 Form 1, Sister State Money Judgment—Notice of Motion to Vacate Judgment.

§ 1710.60. Right of action to enforce judgment; exception

(a) Except as provided in subdivision (b), nothing in this chapter affects any right a judgment creditor may have to bring an action to enforce a sister state judgment.

(b) No action to enforce a sister state judgment may be brought where a judgment based on such sister state judgment has previously been entered pursuant to this chapter. *(Added by Stats.1974, c. 211, p. 408, § 3.)*

Cross References

Judgment creditor defined for purposes of this Chapter, see Code of Civil Procedure § 1710.10.

§ 1710.60

Sister state judgment defined for purposes of this Chapter, see Code of Civil Procedure § 1710.10.

Research References

Forms

West's California Code Forms, Civil Procedure § 1710.40 Form 2, Sister State Money Judgment—Order Vacating Judgment.

§ 1710.65. Right of action for other than payment of money

The entry of a judgment based on a sister state judgment pursuant to this chapter does not limit the right of the judgment creditor to bring an action based on the part of a judgment of a sister state which does not require the payment of money, nor does the bringing of such an action limit the right of the judgment creditor to obtain entry of judgment based on the sister state judgment pursuant to this chapter. *(Added by Stats.1974, c. 211, p. 408, § 3.)*

Cross References

Judgment creditor defined for purposes of this Chapter, see Code of Civil Procedure § 1710.10.

Sister state judgment defined for purposes of this Chapter, see Code of Civil Procedure § 1710.10.

CHAPTER 2. FOREIGN–COUNTRY MONEY JUDGMENTS

Section
1713. Short title.
1714. Definitions.
1715. Applicability.
1716. Standards for recognition; mandatory and permissible reasons for refusal.
1717. Refusal for lack of personal jurisdiction; permissible reasons.
1718. Procedure for recognition of foreign-country judgment.
1719. Effect of recognition of foreign-country judgment.
1720. Stay of proceedings pending appeal of foreign-county judgment.
1721. Statute of limitations.
1722. Uniformity of interpretation.
1723. Saving clause.
1724. Effective date; continuing application of former law.

§ 1713. Short title

This chapter may be cited as the Uniform Foreign–Country Money Judgments Recognition Act. *(Added by Stats.2007, c. 212 (S.B.639), § 2.)*

§ 1714. Definitions

As used in this chapter:

(a) "Foreign country" means a government other than any of the following:

(1) The United States.

(2) A state, district, commonwealth, territory, or insular possession of the United States.

(3) A federally recognized Indian nation, tribe, pueblo, band, or Alaska Native village.

(4) Any other government with regard to which the decision in this state as to whether to recognize a judgment of that government's courts is initially subject to determination under the Full Faith and Credit Clause of the United States Constitution.

(b) "Foreign–country judgment" means a judgment of a court of a foreign country. *(Added by Stats.2007, c. 212 (S.B.639), § 2. Amended by Stats.2014, c. 243 (S.B.406), § 2, eff. Jan. 1, 2015; Stats.2017, c. 168 (A.B.905), § 3, eff. Jan. 1, 2018.)*

§ 1715. Applicability

(a) Except as otherwise provided in subdivision (b), this chapter applies to a foreign-country judgment to the extent that the judgment both:

(1) Grants or denies recovery of a sum of money.

(2) Under the law of the foreign country where rendered, is final, conclusive, and enforceable.

(b) This chapter does not apply to a foreign-country judgment, even if the judgment grants or denies recovery of a sum of money, to the extent that the judgment is any of the following:

(1) A judgment for taxes.

(2) A fine or other penalty.

(3)(A) A judgment for divorce, support, or maintenance, or other judgment rendered in connection with domestic relations.

(B) A judgment for divorce, support, or maintenance, or other judgment rendered in connection with domestic relations may be recognized by a court of this state pursuant to Section 1723.

(c) A party seeking recognition of a foreign-country judgment has the burden of establishing that the foreign-country judgment is entitled to recognition under this chapter. *(Added by Stats.2007, c. 212 (S.B.639), § 2.)*

Cross References

Foreign judgment defined for purposes of this Chapter, see Code of Civil Procedure § 1714.

Research References

Forms

West's California Code Forms, Civil Procedure § 1713.3 Form 1, Foreign Money—Judgments—Complaint.

§ 1716. Standards for recognition; mandatory and permissible reasons for refusal

(a) Except as otherwise provided in subdivisions (b), (c), (d), and (f), a court of this state shall recognize a foreign-country judgment to which this chapter applies.

(b) A court of this state shall not recognize a foreign-country judgment if any of the following apply:

(1) The judgment was rendered under a judicial system that does not provide impartial tribunals or procedures compatible with the requirements of due process of law.

(2) The foreign court did not have personal jurisdiction over the defendant.

(3) The foreign court did not have jurisdiction over the subject matter.

(c)(1) A court of this state shall not recognize a foreign-country judgment if any of the following apply:

(A) The defendant in the proceeding in the foreign court did not receive notice of the proceeding in sufficient time to enable the defendant to defend.

(B) The judgment was obtained by fraud that deprived the losing party of an adequate opportunity to present its case.

(C) The judgment or the cause of action or claim for relief on which the judgment is based is repugnant to the public policy of this state or of the United States.

(D) The proceeding in the foreign court was contrary to an agreement between the parties under which the dispute in question was to be determined otherwise than by proceedings in that foreign court.

(E) In the case of jurisdiction based only on personal service, the foreign court was a seriously inconvenient forum for the trial of the action.

(F) The judgment was rendered in circumstances that raise substantial doubt about the integrity of the rendering court with respect to the judgment.

(G) The specific proceeding in the foreign court leading to the judgment was not compatible with the requirements of due process of law.

(2) Notwithstanding an applicable ground for nonrecognition under paragraph (1), the court may nonetheless recognize a foreign-country judgment if the party seeking recognition of the judgment demonstrates good reason to recognize the judgment that outweighs the ground for nonrecognition.

(d) A court of this state is not required to recognize a foreign-country judgment if the judgment conflicts with another final and conclusive judgment.

(e) If the party seeking recognition of a foreign-country judgment has met its burden of establishing recognition of the foreign-country judgment pursuant to subdivision (c) of Section 1715, a party resisting recognition of a foreign-country judgment has the burden of establishing that a ground for nonrecognition stated in subdivision (b), (c), or (d) exists.

(f) A court of this state shall not recognize a foreign-country judgment for defamation if that judgment is not recognizable under Section 4102 of Title 28 of the United States Code. *(Added by Stats.2007, c. 212 (S.B.639), § 2. Amended by Stats.2009, c. 579 (S.B.320), § 1; Stats.2017, c. 168 (A.B.905), § 5, eff. Jan. 1, 2018.)*

Cross References

Foreign judgment defined for purposes of this Chapter, see Code of Civil Procedure § 1714.

§ 1717. Refusal for lack of personal jurisdiction; permissible reasons

(a) For the purpose of paragraph (2) of subdivision (b) of Section 1716, a foreign court lacks personal jurisdiction over a defendant if either of the following conditions is met:

(1) The foreign court lacks a basis for exercising personal jurisdiction that would be sufficient according to the standards governing personal jurisdiction in this state.

(2) The foreign court lacks personal jurisdiction under its own law.

(b) A foreign-country judgment shall not be refused recognition for lack of personal jurisdiction under paragraph (1) of subdivision (a) if any of the following apply:

(1) The defendant was served with process personally in the foreign country.

(2) The defendant voluntarily appeared in the proceeding, other than for the purpose of protecting property seized or threatened with seizure in the proceeding or of contesting the jurisdiction of the court over the defendant.

(3) The defendant, before the commencement of the proceeding, had agreed to submit to the jurisdiction of the foreign court with respect to the subject matter involved.

(4) The defendant was domiciled in the foreign country when the proceeding was instituted or was a corporation or other form of business organization that had its principal place of business in, or was organized under the laws of, the foreign country.

(5) The defendant had a business office in the foreign country and the proceeding in the foreign court involved a cause of action or claim for relief arising out of business done by the defendant through that office in the foreign country.

(6) The defendant operated a motor vehicle or airplane in the foreign country and the proceeding involved a cause of action or claim for relief arising out of that operation.

(c) The list of bases for personal jurisdiction in subdivision (b) is not exclusive. The courts of this state may recognize bases of personal jurisdiction other than those listed in subdivision (b) as sufficient for the purposes of paragraph (1) of subdivision (a). *(Added by Stats.2007, c. 212 (S.B.639), § 2. Amended by Stats.2009, c. 579 (S.B.320), § 2; Stats.2017, c. 168 (A.B.905), § 6, eff. Jan. 1, 2018.)*

Cross References

Foreign judgment defined for purposes of this Chapter, see Code of Civil Procedure § 1714.

Research References

Forms

Asset Protection: Legal Planning, Strategies and Forms ¶ 2.05, Damages.
West's California Code Forms, Civil Procedure § 1280 Form 1, Arbitration—Contract Clause Providing for Arbitration.

§ 1718. Procedure for recognition of foreign-country judgment

(a) If recognition of a foreign-country judgment is sought as an original matter, the issue of recognition shall be raised by filing an action seeking recognition of the foreign-country judgment.

(b) If recognition of a foreign-country judgment is sought in a pending action, the issue of recognition may be raised by counter-claim, cross-claim, or affirmative defense. *(Added by Stats.2007, c. 212 (S.B.639), § 2.)*

§ 1719. Effect of recognition of foreign-country judgment

If the court in a proceeding under Section 1718 finds that the foreign-country judgment is entitled to recognition under this chapter then, to the extent that the foreign-country judgment grants or denies recovery of a sum of money, the foreign-country judgment is both of the following:

(a) Conclusive between the parties to the same extent as the judgment of a sister state entitled to full faith and credit in this state would be conclusive.

(b) Enforceable in the same manner and to the same extent as a judgment rendered in this state. *(Added by Stats.2007, c. 212 (S.B.639), § 2.)*

§ 1720. Stay of proceedings pending appeal of foreign-county judgment

If a party establishes that an appeal from a foreign-country judgment is pending or will be taken in the foreign country, the court may stay any proceedings with regard to the foreign-country judgment until the appeal is concluded, the time for appeal expires, or the appellant has had sufficient time to prosecute the appeal and has failed to do so. *(Added by Stats.2007, c. 212 (S.B.639), § 2.)*

Cross References

Foreign judgment defined for purposes of this Chapter, see Code of Civil Procedure § 1714.

§ 1721. Statute of limitations

An action to recognize a foreign-country judgment shall be commenced within the earlier of the time during which the foreign-country judgment is effective in the foreign country or 10 years from the date that the foreign-country judgment became effective in the foreign country. *(Added by Stats.2007, c. 212 (S.B.639), § 2.)*

§ 1722. Uniformity of interpretation

In applying and construing this uniform act, consideration shall be given to the need to promote uniformity of the law with respect to its subject matter among states that enact it. *(Added by Stats.2007, c. 212 (S.B.639), § 2.)*

§ 1723. Saving clause

This chapter does not prevent the recognition under principles of comity or otherwise of a foreign-country judgment not within the scope of this chapter. *(Added by Stats.2007, c. 212 (S.B.639), § 2.)*

Cross References

Foreign judgment defined for purposes of this Chapter, see Code of Civil Procedure § 1714.

§ 1724. Effective date; continuing application of former law

(a) This chapter applies to all actions commenced on or after the effective date of this chapter in which the issue of recognition of a foreign-country judgment is raised.

(b) The former Uniform Foreign Money–Judgments Recognition Act (Chapter 2 (commencing with Section 1713) of Title 11 of Part 3) applies to all actions commenced before the effective date of this chapter in which the issue of recognition of a foreign-country judgment is raised. *(Added by Stats.2007, c. 212 (S.B.639), § 2.)*

Title 11.7

RECOVERY OF PREFERENCES AND EXEMPT PROPERTY IN AN ASSIGNMENT FOR THE BENEFIT OF CREDITORS

Section
1800. Recovery of preferences.
1801. Assignments for benefit of creditors; exempt property.
1802. Notice of assignment to parties in interest; claims filing deadline; list of parties in interest.

§ 1800. Recovery of preferences

(a) As used in this section, the following terms have the following meanings:

(1) "Insolvent" means:

(A) With reference to a person other than a partnership, a financial condition such that the sum of the person's debts is greater than all of the person's property, at a fair valuation, exclusive of both of the following:

(i) Property transferred, concealed, or removed with intent to hinder, delay, or defraud the person's creditors.

(ii) Property that is exempt from property of the estate pursuant to the election of the person made pursuant to Section 1801.

(B) With reference to a partnership, financial condition such that the sum of the partnership's debts are greater than the aggregate of, at a fair valuation, both of the following:

(i) All of the partnership's property, exclusive of property of the kind specified in clause (i) of subparagraph (A).

(ii) The sum of the excess of the value of each general partner's separate property, exclusive of property of the kind specified in clause (ii) of subparagraph (A), over the partner's separate debts.

(2) "Inventory" means personal property leased or furnished, held for sale or lease, or to be furnished under a contract for service, raw materials, work in process, or materials used or consumed in a business, including farm products such as crops or livestock, held for sale or lease.

(3) "Insider" means:

(A) If the assignor is an individual, any of the following:

(i) A relative of the assignor or of a general partner of the assignor.

(ii) A partnership in which the assignor is a general partner.

(iii) A general partner of the assignor.

(iv) A corporation of which the assignor is a director, officer, or person in control.

(B) If the assignor is a corporation, any of the following:

(i) A director of the assignor.

(ii) An officer of the assignor.

(iii) A person in control of the assignor.

(iv) A partnership in which the assignor is a general partner.

(v) A general partner of the assignor.

(vi) A relative of a general partner, director, officer, or person in control of the assignor.

(C) If the assignor is a partnership, any of the following:

(i) A general partner in the assignor.

(ii) A relative of a general partner in, general partner of, or person in control of the assignor.

(iii) A partnership in which the assignor is a general partner.

(iv) A general partner of the assignor.

(v) A person in control of the assignor.

(D) An affiliate of the assignor or an insider of an affiliate as if the affiliate were the assignor.

(E) A managing agent of the assignor.

As used in this paragraph, the following terms have the following meanings:

"Relative" means an individual related by affinity or consanguinity within the third degree as determined by the common law, or an individual in a step or adoptive relationship within the third degree.

An "affiliate" means a person that directly or indirectly owns, controls, or holds, with power to vote, 20 percent or more of the outstanding voting securities of the assignor, or 20 percent or more of whose outstanding voting securities are directly or indirectly owned, controlled, or held with power to vote by the assignor, excluding securities held in a fiduciary or agency capacity without sole discretionary power to vote, or held solely to secure a debt if the holder has not in fact exercised the power to vote, or a person who operates the business of the assignor under a lease or operating agreement or whose business is operated by the assignor under a lease or operating agreement.

(4) "Judicial lien" means a lien obtained by judgment, levy, sequestration, or other legal or equitable process or proceeding.

(5) "New value" means money or money's worth in goods, services, or new credit, or release by a transferee of property previously transferred to the transferee in a transaction that is neither void nor voidable by the assignor or the assignee under any applicable law, but does not include an obligation substituted for an existing obligation.

(6) "Receivable" means a right to payment, whether or not the right has been earned by performance.

(7) "Security agreement" means an agreement that creates or provides for a security interest.

(8) "Security interest" means a lien created by an agreement.

(9) "Statutory lien" means a lien arising solely by force of a statute on specified circumstances or conditions, or lien of distress for rent, whether or not statutory, but does not include a security interest or judicial lien, whether or not the interest or lien is provided by or is dependent on a statute and whether or not the interest or lien is made fully effective by statute.

(10) "Transfer" means every mode, direct or indirect, absolute or conditional, voluntary or involuntary, or disposing of or parting with property or with an interest in property, including retention of title as a security interest.

(b) Except as provided in subdivision (c), the assignee of any general assignment for the benefit of creditors, as defined in Section 493.010, may recover any transfer of property of the assignor that is all of the following:

(1) To or for the benefit of a creditor.

(2) For or on account of an antecedent debt owed by the assignor before the transfer was made.

(3) Made while the assignor was insolvent.

(4) Made on or within 90 days before the date of the making of the assignment or made between 90 days and one year before the date of making the assignment if the creditor, at the time of the transfer, was an insider and had reasonable cause to believe the debtor was insolvent at the time of the transfer.

(5) Enables the creditor to receive more than another creditor of the same class.

(c) The assignee may not recover under this section a transfer as follows:

(1) To the extent that the transfer was both of the following:

(A) Intended by the assignor and the creditor to or for whose benefit the transfer was made to be a contemporaneous exchange for new value given to the assignor.

(B) In fact a substantially contemporaneous exchange.

(2) To the extent that the transfer was all of the following:

(A) In payment of a debt incurred in the ordinary course of business or financial affairs of the assignor and the transferee.

(B) Made in the ordinary course of business or financial affairs of the assignor and the transferee.

(C) Made according to ordinary business terms.

(3) Of a security interest in property acquired by the assignor that meets both of the following:

(A) To the extent the security interest secures new value that was all of the following:

(i) Given at or after the signing of a security agreement that contains a description of the property as collateral.

(ii) Given by or on behalf of the secured party under the agreement.

(iii) Given to enable the assignor to acquire the property.

(iv) In fact used by the assignor to acquire the property.

(B) That is perfected within 20 days after the security interest attaches.

(4) To or for the benefit of a creditor, to the extent that, after the transfer, the creditor gave new value to or for the benefit of the assignor that meets both of the following:

(A) Not secured by an otherwise unavoidable security interest.

(B) On account of which new value the assignor did not make an otherwise unavoidable transfer to or for the benefit of the creditor.

(5) Of a perfected security interest in inventory or a receivable or the proceeds of either, except to the extent that the aggregate of all the transfers to the transferee caused a reduction, as of the date of the making of the assignment and to the prejudice of other creditors holding unsecured claims, of any amount by which the debt secured by the security interest exceeded the value of all security interest for the debt on the later of the following:

(A) Ninety days before the date of the making of the assignment.

(B) The date on which new value was first given under the security agreement creating the security interest.

(6) That is the fixing of a statutory lien.

(7) That is payment to a claimant, as defined in Section 8004 of the Civil Code, in exchange for the claimant's waiver or release of any potential or asserted claim of lien, stop payment notice, or right to recover on a payment bond, or any combination thereof.

(8) To the extent that the transfer was a bona fide payment of a debt to a spouse, former spouse, or child of the debtor, for alimony to, maintenance for, or support of, the spouse or child, in connection with a separation agreement, divorce decree, or other order of a court of record, or a determination made in accordance with state or territorial law by a governmental unit, or property settlement agreement; but not to the extent that either of the following occurs:

(A) The debt is assigned to another entity voluntarily, by operation of law or otherwise, in which case the assignee may not recover that portion of the transfer that is assigned to the state or any political subdivision of the state pursuant to Part D of Title IV of the Social Security Act (42 U.S.C. Sec. 601 et seq.) and passed on to the spouse, former spouse, or child of the debtor.

(B) The debt includes a liability designated as alimony, maintenance, or support, unless the liability is actually in the nature of alimony, maintenance, or support.

(d) An assignee of any general assignment for the benefit of creditors, as defined in Section 493.010, may avoid a transfer of property of the assignor transferred to secure reimbursement of a surety that furnished a bond or other obligation to dissolve a judicial lien that would have been avoidable by the assignee under subdivision (b). The liability of the surety under the bond or obligation shall be discharged to the extent of the value of the property recovered by the assignee or the amount paid to the assignee.

(e)(1) For the purposes of this section:

(A) A transfer of real property other than fixtures, but including the interest of a seller or purchaser under a contract for the sale of real property, is perfected when a bona fide purchaser of the property from the debtor, against whom applicable law permits the transfer to be perfected, cannot acquire an interest that is superior to the interest of the transferee.

(B) A transfer of a fixture or property other than real property is perfected when a creditor on a simple contract cannot acquire a judicial lien that is superior to the interest of the transferee.

(2) For the purposes of this section, except as provided in paragraph (3), a transfer is made at any of the following times:

(A) At the time the transfer takes effect between the transferor and the transferee, if the transfer is perfected at, or within 10 days after, the time, except as provided in subparagraph (B) of paragraph (3) of subdivision (c).

(B) At the time the transfer is perfected, if the transfer is perfected after the 10 days.

(C) Immediately before the date of making the assignment if the transfer is not perfected at the later of:

(i) The making of the assignment.

(ii) Ten days after the transfer takes effect between the transferor and the transferee.

(3) For the purposes of this section, a transfer is not made until the assignor has acquired rights in the property transferred.

(f) For the purposes of this section, the assignor is presumed to have been insolvent on and during the 90 days immediately preceding the date of making the assignment.

(g) An action by an assignee under this section must be commenced within one year after making the assignment. *(Added by Stats.1979, c. 394, p. 1467, § 5, eff. July 27, 1979, operative Oct. 1, 1979. Amended by Stats.1980, c. 135, § 6; Stats.1982, c. 35, p. 64, § 3, eff. Feb. 17, 1982; Stats.1982, c. 497, p. 2175, § 81.5, operative July 1, 1983; Stats.1992, c. 1348 (A.B.2616), § 7; Stats.1995, c. 152 (A.B.1156), § 1; Stats.1999, c. 202 (S.B.219), § 2; Stats.2006, c. 538 (S.B.1852), § 75; Stats.2010, c. 697 (S.B.189), § 26, operative July 1, 2012.)*

§ 1800

Cross References

Computation of time, see Code of Civil Procedure §§ 12 and 12a; Government Code § 6800 et seq.
Contracts, generally, see Civil Code § 1549 et seq.
Contracts, interpretation, see Civil Code § 1635 et seq.
Notice, actual and constructive, defined, see Civil Code § 18.
Recording,
  Constructive notice, conveyances of real property or estate for years, see Civil Code § 1213.
  Instruments or judgments, documents to be recorded and manner of recording, see Government Code § 27320 et seq., § 27280 et seq.
  Property transfers, place of recordation, see Civil Code § 1169.

Research References

Forms

3 California Transactions Forms--Business Transactions § 16:66, Debtor's Right to Transfer Property by Assignment.

§ 1801. Assignments for benefit of creditors; exempt property

In any general assignment for the benefit of creditors (as defined in Section 493.010), the assignor, if an individual, may choose to retain as exempt property either the property which is otherwise exempt under Chapter 4 (commencing with Section 703.010) of Division 2 of Title 9 of Part 2 or, in the alternative, the following property:

(a) The assignor's aggregate interest, not to exceed seven thousand five hundred dollars ($7,500) in value, in real property or personal property that the assignor or a dependent of the assignor uses as a residence, in a cooperative that owns property that the assignor or a dependent of the assignor uses as a residence, or in a burial plot for the assignor or a dependent of the assignor.

(b) The assignor's interest, not to exceed one thousand two hundred dollars ($1,200) in value, in one motor vehicle.

(c) The assignor's interest, not to exceed two hundred dollars ($200) in value in any particular item, in household furnishings, household goods, wearing apparel, appliances, books, animals, crops, or musical instruments, that are held primarily for the personal, family, or household use of the assignor or a dependent of the assignor.

(d) The assignor's aggregate interest, not to exceed five hundred dollars ($500) in value, in jewelry held primarily for the personal, family, or household use of the assignor or a dependent of the assignor.

(e) The assignor's aggregate interest, not to exceed in value four hundred dollars ($400) plus any unused amount of the exemption provided under subdivision (a), in any property.

(f) The assignor's aggregate interest, not to exceed seven hundred fifty dollars ($750) in value, in any implements, professional books, or tools, of the trade of the assignor or the trade of a dependent of the assignor.

(g) Any unmatured life insurance contract owned by the assignor, other than a credit life insurance contract.

(h) The assignor's aggregate interest, not to exceed in value four thousand dollars ($4,000) in any accrued dividend or interest under, or loan value of, any unmatured life insurance contract owned by the assignor under which the insured is the assignor or an individual of whom the assignor is a dependent.

(i) Professionally prescribed health aids for the assignor or a dependent of the assignor.

(j) The assignor's right to receive any of the following:

(1) A social security benefit, unemployment compensation, or a local public assistance benefit except that this paragraph does not preclude the application of Section 1255.7 of the Unemployment Insurance Code.

(2) A veterans' benefit.

(3) A disability, illness, or unemployment benefit except that this paragraph does not preclude the application of Section 1255.7 of the Unemployment Insurance Code.

(4) Alimony, support, or separate maintenance, to the extent reasonably necessary for the support of the assignor and any dependent of the assignor.

(5) A payment under a stock bonus, pension, profit sharing, annuity, or similar plan or contract on account of illness, disability, death, age, or length of service, to the extent reasonably necessary for the support of the assignor and any dependent of the assignor, unless:

(i) The plan or contract was established by or under the auspices of an employer of which the assignor was a partner, officer, director or controlling person at the time the assignor's rights under the plan or contract arose;

(ii) The payment is on account of age or length of service; and

(iii) Such plan or contract does not qualify under Section 401(a), 403(a), 403(b), 408, or 409 of the Internal Revenue Code of 1954 (26 U.S.C. 401(a), 403(a), 403(b), 408, or 409).[1]

(k) The assignor's right to receive, or property that is traceable to any of the following:

(1) An award under a crime victim's reparation law.

(2) A payment on account of the wrongful death of an individual of whom the assignor was a dependent, to the extent reasonably necessary for the support of the assignor and any dependent of the assignor.

(3) A payment under a life insurance contract that insured the life of an individual of whom the assignor was a dependent on the date of such individual's death, to the extent reasonably necessary for the support of the assignor and any dependent of the assignor.

(4) A payment, not to exceed seven thousand five hundred dollars ($7,500), on account of personal bodily injury, as compensation for pain and suffering or actual pecuniary loss (other than loss of future earnings), of the assignor or an individual of whom the assignor is a dependent.

(5) A payment in compensation of loss of future earnings of the assignor or an individual of whom the assignor is or was a dependent, to the extent reasonably necessary for the support of the assignor and any dependent of the assignor.

In this section, "dependent" includes spouse, whether or not actually dependent, "assignor" means each spouse, if the assignment is made by a married couple, and "value" means fair market value as of the date of the making of the assignment. *(Added by Stats.1982, c. 497, p. 2178, § 82, operative July 1, 1983. Amended by Stats.1983, c. 155, § 23, eff. June 30, 1983, operative July 1, 1983.)*

[1] 26 U.S.C.A. §§ 401(a), 403(a), 403(b), 408, 409.

Cross References

Contracts, generally, see Civil Code § 1549 et seq.
Contracts, interpretation, see Civil Code § 1635 et seq.
Unemployment compensation, generally, see Labor Code § 2010 et seq.

Research References

Forms

3 California Transactions Forms--Business Transactions § 16:66, Debtor's Right to Transfer Property by Assignment.

§ 1802. Notice of assignment to parties in interest; claims filing deadline; list of parties in interest

(a) In any general assignment for the benefit of creditors, as defined in Section 493.010, the assignee shall, within 30 days after the assignment has been accepted in writing, give written notice of the assignment to the assignor's creditors, equityholders, and other parties in interest as set forth on the list provided by the assignor pursuant to subdivision (c).

MISCELLANEOUS PROVISIONS

(b) In the notice given pursuant to subdivision (a), the assignee shall establish a date by which creditors must file their claims to be able to share in the distribution of proceeds of the liquidation of the assignor's assets. That date shall be not less than 150 days and not greater than 180 days after the date of the first giving of the written notice to creditors and parties in interest.

(c) The assignor shall provide to the assignee at the time of the making of the assignment a list of creditors, equityholders, and other parties in interest, signed under penalty of perjury, which shall include the names, addresses, cities, states, and ZIP Codes for each person together with the amount of that person's anticipated claim in the assignment proceedings. *(Added by Stats.1992, c. 1348 (A.B. 2616), § 8.)*

Cross References

Computation of time, see Code of Civil Procedure §§ 12 and 12a; Government Code § 6800 et seq.

Notice, actual and constructive, defined, see Civil Code § 18.

Research References

Forms

3 California Transactions Forms--Business Transactions § 16:67, Requirements for Valid Assignment for Benefit of Creditors.

3 California Transactions Forms--Business Transactions § 16:68, Form Drafting Principles.

3 California Transactions Forms--Business Transactions § 16:73, Assignment by Individual Debtor.

3 California Transactions Forms--Business Transactions § 16:79, Assignor's Schedule of Debts and Creditors.

Part 4
MISCELLANEOUS PROVISIONS

Title 2
OF THE KINDS AND DEGREES OF EVIDENCE

CHAPTER 3. WRITINGS
ARTICLE 2. PUBLIC WRITINGS

Section
1913. Judicial record; foreign state; effect; enforcement; authority of guardian, etc.

§ 1913. Judicial record; foreign state; effect; enforcement; authority of guardian, etc.

(a) Subject to subdivision (b), the effect of a judicial record of a sister state is the same in this state as in the state where it was made, except that it can only be enforced in this state by an action or special proceeding.

(b) The authority of a guardian, conservator, or committee, or of a personal representative, does not extend beyond the jurisdiction of the government under which that person was invested with authority, except to the extent expressly authorized by Article 4 (commencing with Section 2011) of Chapter 8 of Part 3 of Division 4 of the Probate Code or another statute. *(Enacted in 1872. Amended by Stats.1979, c. 730, p. 2482, § 34, operative Jan. 1, 1981; Stats.1988, c. 1199, § 13, operative July 1, 1989; Stats.2014, c. 553 (S.B.940), § 1, eff. Jan. 1, 2015, operative Jan. 1, 2016.)*

Cross References

Disputable presumptions, see Evidence Code §§ 639, 645, 666.

Effect of Uniform Divorce Recognition Act, see Family Code § 2090 et seq.

Enforcement of judgments in general, see Code of Civil Procedure § 681.010.

Judgments in general not effectual until entered, see Code of Civil Procedure § 664.

Local probate of foreign wills, see Probate Code §§ 12510, 12511.

Pleading judgments in general, see Code of Civil Procedure § 456.

Privileged publication of judicial proceeding, see Civil Code § 47.

Satisfaction of mortgages by foreign executors, administrators and guardians, see Civil Code § 2939.5.

Research References

Forms

15A Am. Jur. Pl. & Pr. Forms Judgments § 464, Statutory References.

15A Am. Jur. Pl. & Pr. Forms Judgments § 494, Statutory References.

Title 3
OF THE PRODUCTION OF EVIDENCE

Cross References

Inspector General, books, papers, records, and correspondence as public records, exemption from public records and discovery provisions, see Penal Code § 6126.3.

CHAPTER 2. MEANS OF PRODUCTION

Section
1985. "Subpoena" defined; affidavit for subpoena duces tecum; issuance of subpoena in blank.
1985.1. Agreement to appear at time other than specified in subpoena.
1985.2. Subpoenas; civil trials, attendance of witnesses; notice.
1985.3. Subpoena duces tecum; personal records of consumer.
1985.4. Application of procedures in § 1985.3; subpoena duces tecum for records exempt from public disclosure under Public Records Act and maintained by state or local agency.
1985.5. Subpena for attendance before officer or commissioner out of court; alternative requirement.
1985.6. Employment records; subpoena duces tecum or production of records; notice and service; motion to quash or modify subpoena.
1986.5. Witness fees and mileage for persons required to give depositions; fees for production of business records.
1987. Subpoena; notice to produce party or agent; method of service; production of books, documents, and electronically stored information.
1987.1. Subpoena; motion and order to quash; other orders.
1987.2. Award of reasonable expenses and reasonable attorney's fees incurred in making or opposing motion; failure to provide lost, damaged, altered, or overwritten electronically stored information; award of reasonable expenses and attorney's fees in making a motion in an action arising from free speech rights on the Internet.

Section	
1987.3.	Service of subpoena duces tecum upon custodian of records or other qualified witness under Evidence Code section 1560.
1987.5.	Subpoena duces tecum; conditions to validity; original affidavit; deposition subpoenas for production of business records.
1988.	Subpoena; service; witness concealed.
1990.	Person present; compelling to testify.

Cross References

Corporate investigations, see Corporations Code § 25531.
Escrow agents, hearings, see Financial Code § 17611.

§ 1985. "Subpoena" defined; affidavit for subpoena duces tecum; issuance of subpoena in blank

(a) The process by which the attendance of a witness is required is the subpoena. It is a writ or order directed to a person and requiring the person's attendance at a particular time and place to testify as a witness. It may also require a witness to bring any books, documents, electronically stored information, or other things under the witness's control which the witness is bound by law to produce in evidence. When a county recorder is using the microfilm system for recording, and a witness is subpoenaed to present a record, the witness shall be deemed to have complied with the subpoena if the witness produces a certified copy thereof.

(b) A copy of an affidavit shall be served with a subpoena duces tecum issued before trial, showing good cause for the production of the matters and things described in the subpoena, specifying the exact matters or things desired to be produced, setting forth in full detail the materiality thereof to the issues involved in the case, and stating that the witness has the desired matters or things in his or her possession or under his or her control.

(c) The clerk, or a judge, shall issue a subpoena or subpoena duces tecum signed and sealed but otherwise in blank to a party requesting it, who shall fill it in before service. An attorney at law who is the attorney of record in an action or proceeding, may sign and issue a subpoena to require attendance before the court in which the action or proceeding is pending or at the trial of an issue therein, or upon the taking of a deposition in an action or proceeding pending therein; the subpoena in such a case need not be sealed. An attorney at law who is the attorney of record in an action or proceeding, may sign and issue a subpoena duces tecum to require production of the matters or things described in the subpoena. *(Enacted in 1872. Amended by Stats.1933, c. 567, p. 1479, § 1; Stats.1961, c. 496, p. 1590, § 1; Stats.1967, c. 431, p. 1645, § 1; Stats.1968, c. 95, p. 305, § 1; Stats.1979, c. 458, p. 1607, § 1; Stats.1982, c. 452, § 1; Stats.1986, c. 603, § 3; Stats.1990, c. 511 (S.B.163), § 1, eff. Aug. 13, 1990; Stats.2012, c. 72 (S.B.1574), § 1.)*

Cross References

Account, delivery of copy after demand, see Code of Civil Procedure § 454.
Accused in criminal proceedings, right to subpoena, see Cal. Const. Art. 1, § 15; Penal Code § 1326.
Administrative proceedings, issuance of subpoena by state agency or administrative law judge, see Government Code § 11450.05 et seq.
Affidavit, copy required to be served at time of service of subpoena duces tecum, see Code of Civil Procedure § 1987.5.
Attendance of witnesses from without state in criminal cases, see Penal Code § 1334 et seq.
Attorney general, issuance of subpoena, see Government Code §§ 12550, 12560.
Compelling attendance of witnesses in criminal proceedings, see Penal Code § 1326 et seq.
Definition, see Penal Code § 1326.
Depositions, see Code of Civil Procedure §§ 2020.010 et seq., 2025.010 et seq., 2026.010, 2027.010, 2028.010 et seq.
Duty of subpoenaed witness to attend, see Code of Civil Procedure § 2064.
Election contests, subpoenas for witnesses, see Elections Code § 16502.
Form of subpoena in criminal proceedings, see Penal Code § 1327.
Habeas corpus proceedings, see Penal Code §§ 1484, 1489, 1503.
Inspection of writings, photographs, objects, or tangible things, see Code of Civil Procedure § 2031.010 et seq.
Insurance commissioner, see Insurance Code §§ 1042, 12924.
Legislature and committees thereof, attendance of witnesses, see Government Code § 9401 et seq.
Military courts, issuance of subpoenas, see Military and Veterans Code § 460 et seq.
Person present without subpoena, obligation to testify, see Code of Civil Procedure § 1990.
Sheriff oversight board, subpoenas, office of the inspector general, see Government Code § 25303.7.
Unfair trade practices, see Business and Professions Code § 17083.
Witness defined for purposes of this Code, see Code of Civil Procedure § 1878.

Research References

Forms

West's California Code Forms, Business & Professions § 475 Comment, Administrative Procedure Act.
West's California Code Forms, Civil Procedure § 1282.6 Form 2, Arbitration—Subpena Duces Tecum.
West's California Code Forms, Civil Procedure § 1985 Form 4, Evidence—Notice of Motion to Quash Service of Subpena Duces Tecum.
West's California Judicial Council Forms SUBP–001, Civil Subpena for Personal Appearance at Trial or Hearing.
West's California Judicial Council Forms SUBP–002, Civil Subpena (Duces Tecum) for Personal Appearance and Production of Documents, Electronically Stored Information, and Things at Trial or Hearing and Declaration.

§ 1985.1. Agreement to appear at time other than specified in subpoena

Any person who is subpoenaed to appear at a session of court, or at the trial of an issue therein, may, in lieu of appearance at the time specified in the subpoena, agree with the party at whose request the subpoena was issued to appear at another time or upon such notice as may be agreed upon. Any failure to appear pursuant to such agreement may be punished as a contempt by the court issuing the subpoena. The facts establishing or disproving such agreement and the failure to appear may be proved by an affidavit of any person having personal knowledge of the facts. *(Added by Stats.1969, c. 140, p. 385, § 1.)*

Cross References

Notice, actual and constructive, defined, see Civil Code § 18.
Sheriff oversight board, subpoenas, office of the inspector general, see Government Code § 25303.7.

§ 1985.2. Subpoenas; civil trials, attendance of witnesses; notice

Any subpoena which requires the attendance of a witness at any civil trial shall contain the following notice in a type face designed to call attention to the notice:

Contact the attorney requesting this subpoena, listed above, before the date on which you are required to be in court, if you have any question about the time or date for you to appear, or if you want to be certain that your presence in court is required. *(Added by Stats.1978, c. 431, p. 1494, § 1, operative July 1, 1979.)*

Cross References

Notice, actual and constructive, defined, see Civil Code § 18.
Sheriff oversight board, subpoenas, office of the inspector general, see Government Code § 25303.7.
Witness defined for purposes of this Code, see Code of Civil Procedure § 1878.

§ 1985.3. Subpoena duces tecum; personal records of consumer

(a) For purposes of this section, the following definitions apply:

(1) "Personal records" means the original, any copy of books, documents, other writings, or electronically stored information pertaining to a consumer and which are maintained by any "witness" which is a physician, dentist, ophthalmologist, optometrist, chiropractor, physical therapist, acupuncturist, podiatrist, veterinarian, veteri-

nary hospital, veterinary clinic, pharmacist, pharmacy, hospital, medical center, clinic, radiology or MRI center, clinical or diagnostic laboratory, state or national bank, state or federal association (as defined in Section 5102 of the Financial Code), state or federal credit union, trust company, anyone authorized by this state to make or arrange loans that are secured by real property, security brokerage firm, insurance company, title insurance company, underwritten title company, escrow agent licensed pursuant to Division 6 (commencing with Section 17000) of the Financial Code or exempt from licensure pursuant to Section 17006 of the Financial Code, attorney, accountant, institution of the Farm Credit System, as specified in Section 2002 of Title 12 of the United States Code, or telephone corporation which is a public utility, as defined in Section 216 of the Public Utilities Code, or psychotherapist, as defined in Section 1010 of the Evidence Code, or a private or public preschool, elementary school, secondary school, or postsecondary school as described in Section 76244 of the Education Code.

(2) "Consumer" means any individual, partnership of five or fewer persons, association, or trust which has transacted business with, or has used the services of, the witness or for whom the witness has acted as agent or fiduciary.

(3) "Subpoenaing party" means the person or persons causing a subpoena duces tecum to be issued or served in connection with any civil action or proceeding pursuant to this code, but shall not include the state or local agencies described in Section 7465 of the Government Code, or any entity provided for under Article VI of the California Constitution in any proceeding maintained before an adjudicative body of that entity pursuant to Chapter 4 (commencing with Section 6000) of Division 3 of the Business and Professions Code.

(4) "Deposition officer" means a person who meets the qualifications specified in Section 2020.420.

(b) Prior to the date called for in the subpoena duces tecum for the production of personal records, the subpoenaing party shall serve or cause to be served on the consumer whose records are being sought a copy of the subpoena duces tecum, of the affidavit supporting the issuance of the subpoena, if any, and of the notice described in subdivision (e), and proof of service as indicated in paragraph (1) of subdivision (c). This service shall be made as follows:

(1) To the consumer personally, or at his or her last known address, or in accordance with Chapter 5 (commencing with Section 1010) of Title 14 of Part 3, or, if he or she is a party, to his or her attorney of record. If the consumer is a minor, service shall be made on the minor's parent, guardian, conservator, or similar fiduciary, or if one of them cannot be located with reasonable diligence, then service shall be made on any person having the care or control of the minor or with whom the minor resides or by whom the minor is employed, and on the minor if the minor is at least 12 years of age.

(2) Not less than 10 days prior to the date for production specified in the subpoena duces tecum, plus the additional time provided by Section 1013 if service is by mail.

(3) At least five days prior to service upon the custodian of the records, plus the additional time provided by Section 1013 if service is by mail.

(c) Prior to the production of the records, the subpoenaing party shall do either of the following:

(1) Serve or cause to be served upon the witness a proof of personal service or of service by mail attesting to compliance with subdivision (b).

(2) Furnish the witness a written authorization to release the records signed by the consumer or by his or her attorney of record. The witness may presume that any attorney purporting to sign the authorization on behalf of the consumer acted with the consent of the consumer, and that any objection to release of records is waived.

(d) A subpoena duces tecum for the production of personal records shall be served in sufficient time to allow the witness a reasonable time, as provided in Section 2020.410, to locate and produce the records or copies thereof.

(e) Every copy of the subpoena duces tecum and affidavit, if any, served on a consumer or his or her attorney in accordance with subdivision (b) shall be accompanied by a notice, in a typeface designed to call attention to the notice, indicating that (1) records about the consumer are being sought from the witness named on the subpoena; (2) if the consumer objects to the witness furnishing the records to the party seeking the records, the consumer must file papers with the court or serve a written objection as provided in subdivision (g) prior to the date specified for production on the subpoena; and (3) if the party who is seeking the records will not agree in writing to cancel or limit the subpoena, an attorney should be consulted about the consumer's interest in protecting his or her rights of privacy. If a notice of taking of deposition is also served, that other notice may be set forth in a single document with the notice required by this subdivision.

(f) A subpoena duces tecum for personal records maintained by a telephone corporation which is a public utility, as defined in Section 216 of the Public Utilities Code, shall not be valid or effective unless it includes a consent to release, signed by the consumer whose records are requested, as required by Section 2891 of the Public Utilities Code.

(g) Any consumer whose personal records are sought by a subpoena duces tecum and who is a party to the civil action in which this subpoena duces tecum is served may, prior to the date for production, bring a motion under Section 1987.1 to quash or modify the subpoena duces tecum. Notice of the bringing of that motion shall be given to the witness and deposition officer at least five days prior to production. The failure to provide notice to the deposition officer shall not invalidate the motion to quash or modify the subpoena duces tecum but may be raised by the deposition officer as an affirmative defense in any action for liability for improper release of records.

Any other consumer or nonparty whose personal records are sought by a subpoena duces tecum may, prior to the date of production, serve on the subpoenaing party, the witness, and the deposition officer, a written objection that cites the specific grounds on which production of the personal records should be prohibited.

No witness or deposition officer shall be required to produce personal records after receipt of notice that the motion has been brought by a consumer, or after receipt of a written objection from a nonparty consumer, except upon order of the court in which the action is pending or by agreement of the parties, witnesses, and consumers affected.

The party requesting a consumer's personal records may bring a motion under Section 1987.1 to enforce the subpoena within 20 days of service of the written objection. The motion shall be accompanied by a declaration showing a reasonable and good faith attempt at informal resolution of the dispute between the party requesting the personal records and the consumer or the consumer's attorney.

(h) Upon good cause shown and provided that the rights of witnesses and consumers are preserved, a subpoenaing party shall be entitled to obtain an order shortening the time for service of a subpoena duces tecum or waiving the requirements of subdivision (b) where due diligence by the subpoenaing party has been shown.

(i) Nothing contained in this section shall be construed to apply to any subpoena duces tecum which does not request the records of any particular consumer or consumers and which requires a custodian of records to delete all information which would in any way identify any consumer whose records are to be produced.

(j) This section shall not apply to proceedings conducted under Division 1 (commencing with Section 50), Division 4 (commencing

§ 1985.3

with Section 3200), Division 4.5 (commencing with Section 6100), or Division 4.7 (commencing with Section 6200), of the Labor Code.

(k) Failure to comply with this section shall be sufficient basis for the witness to refuse to produce the personal records sought by a subpoena duces tecum.

(*l*) If the subpoenaing party is the consumer, and the consumer is the only subject of the subpoenaed records, notice to the consumer, and delivery of the other documents specified in subdivision (b) to the consumer, is not required under this section. (Added by Stats.1980, c. 976, p. 3101, § 1, operative July 1, 1981. Amended by Stats.1981, c. 227, p. 1152, § 1, eff. July 20, 1981, operative July 1, 1981; Stats.1981, c. 1014, p. 3912, § 1; Stats.1982, c. 666, § 1; Stats.1984, c. 603, § 1; Stats.1985, c. 983, § 1, eff. Sept. 26, 1985; Stats.1986, c. 248, § 21; Stats.1986, c. 605, § 1; Stats.1986, c. 1209, § 2; Stats.1987, c. 20, § 1; Stats.1987, c. 149, § 1, eff. July 10, 1987; Stats.1987, c. 1080, § 10; Stats.1987, c. 1492, § 2; Stats.1988, c. 184, § 1; Stats.1990, c. 1220 (A.B.2980), § 1; Stats.1996, c. 679 (S.B.1821), § 1; Stats.1997, c. 442 (A.B.758), § 10; Stats.1998, c. 932 (A.B.1094), § 19; Stats. 1999, c. 444 (A.B.794), § 1; Stats.2004, c. 182 (A.B.3081), § 18, operative July 1, 2005; Stats.2005, c. 300 (A.B.496), § 6; Stats.2012, c. 72 (S.B.1574), § 2.)

Cross References

Computation of time, see Code of Civil Procedure §§ 12 and 12a; Government Code § 6800 et seq.

Date of deposition, see Code of Civil Procedure § 2025.270.

Depositions, see Code of Civil Procedure §§ 2020.010 et seq., 2025.010 et seq., 2026.010, 2027.010, 2028.010 et seq.

Notice to parties to the action, subpoenaing party duties, consumer or employee records, see Code of Civil Procedure § 2025.240.

Proof of service, see Code of Civil Procedure § 417.10 et seq.

Recording,
Constructive notice, conveyances of real property or estate for years, see Civil Code § 1213.
Instruments or judgments, documents to be recorded and manner of recording, see Government Code § 27320 et seq., § 27280 et seq.
Property transfers, place of recordation, see Civil Code § 1169.

Sheriff oversight board, subpoenas, office of the inspector general, see Government Code § 25303.7.

Subpoena, motion and order to quash, other orders, see Code of Civil Procedure § 1987.1.

Witness defined for purposes of this Code, see Code of Civil Procedure § 1878.

Research References

Forms

West's California Code Forms, Business & Professions § 475 Comment, Administrative Procedure Act.

West's California Code Forms, Civil Procedure § 1985.3 Form 1, Evidence—Subpena—Notice to Consumer or Employee and Objection—Official Form.

West's California Code Forms, Civil Procedure § 1985.3 Form 3, Evidence—Subpena of Consumer Records—Proof of Service.

West's California Code Forms, Civil Procedure § 1985.3 Form 5, Evidence—Subpena of Consumer Records—Notice of Motion to Quash or Modify Subpena Duces Tecum.

West's California Code Forms, Civil Procedure § 1985.3 Form 8, Evidence—Subpena of Consumer Records—Notice of Motion to Enforce Subpena Duces Tecum Against Nonparty Consumer.

West's California Judicial Council Forms SUBP–025, Notice to Consumer or Employee and Objection.

§ 1985.4. Application of procedures in § 1985.3; subpoena duces tecum for records exempt from public disclosure under Public Records Act and maintained by state or local agency

The procedures set forth in Section 1985.3 are applicable to a subpoena duces tecum for records containing "personal information," as defined in Section 1798.3 of the Civil Code that are otherwise exempt from public disclosure under a provision listed in Section 7920.505 of the Government Code that are maintained by a state or local agency as defined in Section 7920.510 or 7920.540 of the Government Code. For the purposes of this section, "witness" means a state or local agency as defined in Section 7920.510 or 7920.540 of the Government Code and "consumer" means any employee of any state or local agency as defined in Section 7920.510 or 7920.540 of the Government Code, or any other natural person. Nothing in this section shall pertain to personnel records as defined in Section 832.8 of the Penal Code. (Added by Stats.1984, c. 437, § 1. Amended by Stats.1988, c. 441, § 1; Stats.2021, c. 615 (A.B.474), § 57, eff. Jan. 1, 2022, operative Jan. 1, 2023.)

Cross References

Sheriff oversight board, subpoenas, office of the inspector general, see Government Code § 25303.7.

Witness defined for purposes of this Code, see Code of Civil Procedure § 1878.

Research References

Forms

West's California Code Forms, Business & Professions § 475 Comment, Administrative Procedure Act.

§ 1985.5. Subpena for attendance before officer or commissioner out of court; alternative requirement

If a subpena requires the attendance of a witness before an officer or commissioner out of court, it shall, for a refusal to be sworn, or to answer as a witness, or to subscribe an affidavit or deposition when required, also require the witness to attend a session of the court issuing the subpena at a time and place thereof to be fixed by said officer or commissioner. (Added by Stats.1941, c. 405, p. 1690, § 1.)

Cross References

Administrative adjudication, issuance of subpoenas by agency, see Government Code § 11510.05 et seq.

Depositions, see Code of Civil Procedure §§ 2020.010 et seq., 2025.010 et seq., 2026.010, 2027.010, 2028.010 et seq.

Witness defined for purposes of this Code, see Code of Civil Procedure § 1878.

§ 1985.6. Employment records; subpoena duces tecum or production of records; notice and service; motion to quash or modify subpoena

(a) For purposes of this section, the following terms have the following meanings:

(1) "Deposition officer" means a person who meets the qualifications specified in Section 2020.420.

(2) "Employee" means any individual who is or has been employed by a witness subject to a subpoena duces tecum. "Employee" also means any individual who is or has been represented by a labor organization that is a witness subject to a subpoena duces tecum.

(3) "Employment records" means the original or any copy of books, documents, other writings, or electronically stored information pertaining to the employment of any employee maintained by the current or former employer of the employee, or by any labor organization that has represented or currently represents the employee.

(4) "Labor organization" has the meaning set forth in Section 1117 of the Labor Code.

(5) "Subpoenaing party" means the person or persons causing a subpoena duces tecum to be issued or served in connection with any civil action or proceeding, but does not include the state or local agencies described in Section 7465 of the Government Code, or any entity provided for under Article VI of the California Constitution in any proceeding maintained before an adjudicative body of that entity pursuant to Chapter 4 (commencing with Section 6000) of Division 3 of the Business and Professions Code.

(b) Prior to the date called for in the subpoena duces tecum of the production of employment records, the subpoenaing party shall serve or cause to be served on the employee whose records are being sought a copy of: the subpoena duces tecum; the affidavit supporting the issuance of the subpoena, if any; the notice described in subdivision (e); and proof of service as provided in paragraph (1) of subdivision (c). This service shall be made as follows:

(1) To the employee personally, or at his or her last known address, or in accordance with Chapter 5 (commencing with Section 1010) of Title 14 of Part 2, or, if he or she is a party, to his or her attorney of record. If the employee is a minor, service shall be made on the minor's parent, guardian, conservator, or similar fiduciary, or if one of them cannot be located with reasonable diligence, then service shall be made on any person having the care or control of the minor, or with whom the minor resides, and on the minor if the minor is at least 12 years of age.

(2) Not less than 10 days prior to the date for production specified in the subpoena duces tecum, plus the additional time provided by Section 1013 if service is by mail.

(3) At least five days prior to service upon the custodian of the employment records, plus the additional time provided by Section 1013 if service is by mail.

(c) Prior to the production of the records, the subpoenaing party shall either:

(1) Serve or cause to be served upon the witness a proof of personal service or of service by mail attesting to compliance with subdivision (b).

(2) Furnish the witness a written authorization to release the records signed by the employee or by his or her attorney of record. The witness may presume that the attorney purporting to sign the authorization on behalf of the employee acted with the consent of the employee, and that any objection to the release of records is waived.

(d) A subpoena duces tecum for the production of employment records shall be served in sufficient time to allow the witness a reasonable time, as provided in Section 2020.410, to locate and produce the records or copies thereof.

(e) Every copy of the subpoena duces tecum and affidavit served on an employee or his or her attorney in accordance with subdivision (b) shall be accompanied by a notice, in a typeface designed to call attention to the notice, indicating that (1) employment records about the employee are being sought from the witness named on the subpoena; (2) the employment records may be protected by a right of privacy; (3) if the employee objects to the witness furnishing the records to the party seeking the records, the employee shall file papers with the court prior to the date specified for production on the subpoena; and (4) if the subpoenaing party does not agree in writing to cancel or limit the subpoena, an attorney should be consulted about the employee's interest in protecting his or her rights of privacy. If a notice of taking of deposition is also served, that other notice may be set forth in a single document with the notice required by this subdivision.

(f)(1) Any employee whose employment records are sought by a subpoena duces tecum may, prior to the date for production, bring a motion under Section 1987.1 to quash or modify the subpoena duces tecum. Notice of the bringing of that motion shall be given to the witness and the deposition officer at least five days prior to production. The failure to provide notice to the deposition officer does not invalidate the motion to quash or modify the subpoena duces tecum but may be raised by the deposition officer as an affirmative defense in any action for liability for improper release of records.

(2) Any nonparty employee whose employment records are sought by a subpoena duces tecum may, prior to the date of production, serve on the subpoenaing party, the deposition officer, and the witness a written objection that cites the specific grounds on which production of the employment records should be prohibited.

(3) No witness or deposition officer shall be required to produce employment records after receipt of notice that the motion has been brought by an employee, or after receipt of a written objection from a nonparty employee, except upon order of the court in which the action is pending or by agreement of the parties, witnesses, and employees affected.

(4) The party requesting an employee's employment records may bring a motion under subdivision (c) of Section 1987 to enforce the subpoena within 20 days of service of the written objection. The motion shall be accompanied by a declaration showing a reasonable and good faith attempt at informal resolution of the dispute between the party requesting the employment records and the employee or the employee's attorney.

(g) Upon good cause shown and provided that the rights of witnesses and employees are preserved, a subpoenaing party shall be entitled to obtain an order shortening the time for service of a subpoena duces tecum or waiving the requirements of subdivision (b) if due diligence by the subpoenaing party has been shown.

(h) This section may not be construed to apply to any subpoena duces tecum that does not request the records of any particular employee or employees and that requires a custodian of records to delete all information that would in any way identify any employee whose records are to be produced.

(i) This section does not apply to proceedings conducted under Division 1 (commencing with Section 50), Division 4 (commencing with Section 3200), Division 4.5 (commencing with Section 6100), or Division 4.7 (commencing with Section 6200), of the Labor Code.

(j) Failure to comply with this section shall be sufficient basis for the witness to refuse to produce the employment records sought by subpoena duces tecum.

(k) If the subpoenaing party is the employee, and the employee is the only subject of the subpoenaed records, notice to the employee, and delivery of the other documents specified in subdivision (b) to the employee, are not required under this section. *(Added by Stats.1995, c. 299 (A.B.617), § 1. Amended by Stats.1996, c. 679 (S.B.1821), § 2; Stats.1997, c. 442 (A.B.758), § 11; Stats.1998, c. 932 (A.B.1094), § 20; Stats.1999, c. 444 (A.B.794), § 2; Stats.2004, c. 182 (A.B.3081), § 19, operative July 1, 2005; Stats.2004, c. 101 (S.B.1465), § 1; Stats.2005, c. 22 (S.B.1108), § 20; Stats.2005, c. 294 (A.B.333), § 5; Stats.2005, c. 300 (A.B.496), § 7.5; Stats.2006, c. 538 (S.B.1852), § 76; Stats.2012, c. 72 (S.B.1574), § 3.)*

Cross References

Computation of time, see Code of Civil Procedure §§ 12 and 12a; Government Code § 6800 et seq.
Contents of subpoena, necessity of affidavit or declaration showing good cause, see Code of Civil Procedure § 2020.510.
Date of deposition, see Code of Civil Procedure § 2025.270.
Depositions, see Code of Civil Procedure §§ 2020.010 et seq., 2025.010 et seq., 2026.010, 2027.010, 2028.010 et seq.
Notice, actual and constructive, defined, see Civil Code § 18.
Notice to parties to the action, subpoenaing party duties, consumer or employee records, see Code of Civil Procedure § 2025.240.
Proof of service, see Code of Civil Procedure § 417.10 et seq.
Recording,
   Constructive notice, conveyances of real property or estate for years, see Civil Code § 1213.
   Instruments or judgments, documents to be recorded and manner of recording, see Government Code § 27320 et seq., § 27280 et seq.
   Property transfers, place of recordation, see Civil Code § 1169.
Subpoena, motion and order to quash, other orders, see Code of Civil Procedure § 1987.1.
Witness defined for purposes of this Code, see Code of Civil Procedure § 1878.

Research References

Forms

West's California Code Forms, Business & Professions § 475 Comment, Administrative Procedure Act.
West's California Code Forms, Civil Procedure § 1985.6 Form 3, Evidence—Subpena of Employee Records—Proof of Service.
West's California Code Forms, Civil Procedure § 1985.6 Form 5, Evidence—Subpena of Employee Records—Notice of Motion to Quash or Modify Subpena Duces Tecum.

§ 1985.6

West's California Code Forms, Civil Procedure § 1985.6 Form 8, Evidence—Subpena of Employee Records—Notice of Motion to Enforce Subpena Duces Tecum Against Nonparty Employee.

West's California Judicial Council Forms SUBP–025, Notice to Consumer or Employee and Objection.

§ 1986.5. Witness fees and mileage for persons required to give depositions; fees for production of business records

Any person who is subpoenaed and required to give a deposition shall be entitled to receive the same witness fees and mileage as if the subpoena required him or her to attend and testify before a court in which the action or proceeding is pending. Notwithstanding this requirement, the only fees owed to a witness who is required to produce business records under Section 1560 of the Evidence Code pursuant to a subpoena duces tecum, but who is not required to personally attend a deposition away from his or her place of business, shall be those prescribed in Section 1563 of the Evidence Code. (Added by Stats.1961, c. 1386, p. 3159, § 1. Amended by Stats.1986, c. 603, § 4.)

Cross References

Depositions, see Code of Civil Procedure §§ 2020.010 et seq., 2025.010 et seq., 2026.010, 2027.010, 2028.010 et seq.

Witness defined for purposes of this Code, see Code of Civil Procedure § 1878.

§ 1987. Subpoena; notice to produce party or agent; method of service; production of books, documents, and electronically stored information

(a) Except as provided in Sections 68097.1 to 68097.8, inclusive, of the Government Code, the service of a subpoena is made by delivering a copy, or a ticket containing its substance, to the witness personally, giving or offering to the witness at the same time, if demanded by him or her, the fees to which he or she is entitled for travel to and from the place designated, and one day's attendance there. The service shall be made so as to allow the witness a reasonable time for preparation and travel to the place of attendance. The service may be made by any person. If service is to be made on a minor, service shall be made on the minor's parent, guardian, conservator, or similar fiduciary, or if one of those persons cannot be located with reasonable diligence, service shall be made on any person having the care or control of the minor or with whom the minor resides or by whom the minor is employed, and on the minor if the minor is 12 years of age or older. If the minor is alleged to come within the description of Section 300, 601, or 602 of the Welfare and Institutions Code and the minor is not in the custody of a parent or guardian, regardless of the age of the minor, service also shall be made upon the designated agent for service of process at the county child welfare department or the probation department under whose jurisdiction the minor has been placed.

(b) In the case of the production of a party to the record of any civil action or proceeding or of a person for whose immediate benefit an action or proceeding is prosecuted or defended or of anyone who is an officer, director, or managing agent of any such party or person, the service of a subpoena upon any such witness is not required if written notice requesting the witness to attend before a court, or at a trial of an issue therein, with the time and place thereof, is served upon the attorney of that party or person. The notice shall be served at least 10 days before the time required for attendance unless the court prescribes a shorter time. If entitled thereto, the witness, upon demand, shall be paid witness fees and mileage before being required to testify. The giving of the notice shall have the same effect as service of a subpoena on the witness, and the parties shall have those rights and the court may make those orders, including the imposition of sanctions, as in the case of a subpoena for attendance before the court.

(c) If the notice specified in subdivision (b) is served at least 20 days before the time required for attendance, or within any shorter period of time as the court may order, it may include a request that the party or person bring with him or her books, documents, electronically stored information, or other things. The notice shall state the exact materials or things desired and that the party or person has them in his or her possession or under his or her control. Within five days thereafter, or any other time period as the court may allow, the party or person of whom the request is made may serve written objections to the request or any part thereof, with a statement of grounds. Thereafter, upon noticed motion of the requesting party, accompanied by a showing of good cause and of materiality of the items to the issues, the court may order production of items to which objection was made, unless the objecting party or person establishes good cause for nonproduction or production under limitations or conditions. The procedure of this subdivision is alternative to the procedure provided by Sections 1985 and 1987.5 in the cases herein provided for, and no subpoena duces tecum shall be required.

Subject to this subdivision, the notice provided in this subdivision shall have the same effect as is provided in subdivision (b) as to a notice for attendance of that party or person. (Enacted in 1872. Amended by Stats.1963, c. 1485, p. 3049, § 3; Stats.1968, c. 933, p. 1783, § 1; Stats.1969, c. 311, p. 678, § 1; Stats.1969, c. 1034, p. 2013, § 1.5; Stats.1981, c. 184, p. 1105, § 2; Stats.1986, c. 605, § 2; Stats.1989, c. 1416, § 28; Stats.2002, c. 1008 (A.B.3028), § 6; Stats.2012, c. 72 (S.B.1574), § 5.)

Cross References

Administrative adjudication, service of subpoenas by agency, see Government Code § 11450.05 et seq.

Computation of time, see Code of Civil Procedure §§ 12 and 12a; Government Code § 6800 et seq.

Concealment of witness, see Code of Civil Procedure § 1988.

Copy of supporting affidavit required to be served with subpoena, see Code of Civil Procedure § 1987.5.

Criminal proceedings, service in, see Penal Code § 1328.

Legislator's privilege, see Cal. Const. Art. 4, § 14.

Notice, actual and constructive, defined, see Civil Code § 18.

Process servers, compensation, see Code of Civil Procedure § 1033.5.

Service of legislative subpoena, see Government Code § 9403.

Sheriff oversight board, subpoenas, office of the inspector general, see Government Code § 25303.7.

Sheriff, duty to serve process, see Government Code § 26608.

Sheriff's fee for service, see Government Code § 26743.

State civil service, investigations and hearing, process and delivery of subpoenas and subpoenas duces tecum in accordance with this section, see Government Code § 18672.

Witness defined for purposes of this Code, see Code of Civil Procedure § 1878.

Witness fees and mileage,
  Amount, see Government Code § 68093.
  Demand for advance payment, see Labor Code § 131.

Research References

Forms

California Practice Guide: Rutter Family Law Forms Form 11:19, Notice to Compel Attendance of Party and to Bring Books, Documents or Other Things.

1 Environmental Insurance Litigation: Practice Forms § 6:12 (2021 ed.), Trial Management Order: Shell Coverage Litigation.

West's California Code Forms, Business & Professions § 475 Comment, Administrative Procedure Act.

West's California Code Forms, Civil Procedure § 1987 Form 1, Notice to Attorney in Lieu of Service of Subpena.

West's California Code Forms, Civil Procedure § 1987 Form 2, Evidence—Notice to Appear—Party.

West's California Code Forms, Civil Procedure § 1987 Form 3, Evidence—Objection to Request for Witness.

West's California Code Forms, Civil Procedure § 1987 Form 4, Evidence—Notice of Motion to Produce Requested Material.

West's California Judicial Council Forms SUBP–001, Civil Subpena for Personal Appearance at Trial or Hearing.

§ 1987.1. Subpoena; motion and order to quash; other orders

(a) If a subpoena requires the attendance of a witness or the production of books, documents, electronically stored information, or other things before a court, or at the trial of an issue therein, or at the taking of a deposition, the court, upon motion reasonably made by any person described in subdivision (b), or upon the court's own motion after giving counsel notice and an opportunity to be heard, may make an order quashing the subpoena entirely, modifying it, or directing compliance with it upon those terms or conditions as the court shall declare, including protective orders. In addition, the court may make any other order as may be appropriate to protect the person from unreasonable or oppressive demands, including unreasonable violations of the right of privacy of the person.

(b) The following persons may make a motion pursuant to subdivision (a):

(1) A party.

(2) A witness.

(3) A consumer described in Section 1985.3.

(4) An employee described in Section 1985.6.

(5) A person whose personally identifying information, as defined in subdivision (b) of Section 1798.79.8 of the Civil Code, is sought in connection with an underlying action involving that person's exercise of free speech rights.

(c) Nothing in this section shall require any person to move to quash, modify, or condition any subpoena duces tecum of personal records of any consumer served under paragraph (1) of subdivision (b) of Section 1985.3 or employment records of any employee served under paragraph (1) of subdivision (b) of Section 1985.6. *(Added by Stats.1976, c. 1168, p. 5249, § 1. Amended by Stats.1980, c. 976, p. 3102, § 2, operative July 1, 1981; Stats.1997, c. 442 (A.B.758), § 12; Stats.2007, c. 113 (A.B.1126), § 3; Stats.2008, c. 742 (A.B.2433), § 1; Stats.2012, c. 72 (S.B.1574), § 6.)*

Cross References

Depositions, see Code of Civil Procedure §§ 2020.010 et seq., 2025.010 et seq., 2026.010, 2027.010, 2028.010 et seq.

Notice, actual and constructive, defined, see Civil Code § 18.

Witness defined for purposes of this Code, see Code of Civil Procedure § 1878.

Research References

Forms

West's California Code Forms, Civil Procedure § 1985.3 Form 5, Evidence—Subpena of Consumer Records—Notice of Motion to Quash or Modify Subpena Duces Tecum.

West's California Code Forms, Civil Procedure § 1985.3 Form 8, Evidence—Subpena of Consumer Records—Notice of Motion to Enforce Subpena Duces Tecum Against Nonparty Consumer.

West's California Code Forms, Civil Procedure § 1985.6 Form 5, Evidence—Subpena of Employee Records—Notice of Motion to Quash or Modify Subpena Duces Tecum.

West's California Code Forms, Civil Procedure § 1985.6 Form 8, Evidence—Subpena of Employee Records—Notice of Motion to Enforce Subpena Duces Tecum Against Nonparty Employee.

West's California Code Forms, Civil Procedure § 1987.1 Form 1, Evidence—Notice of Motion to Quash or Modify or Direct Compliance—Subpena.

§ 1987.2. Award of reasonable expenses and reasonable attorney's fees incurred in making or opposing motion; failure to provide lost, damaged, altered, or overwritten electronically stored information; award of reasonable expenses and attorney's fees in making a motion in an action arising from free speech rights on the Internet

(a) Except as specified in subdivision (c), in making an order pursuant to motion made under subdivision (c) of Section 1987 or under Section 1987.1, the court may in its discretion award the amount of the reasonable expenses incurred in making or opposing the motion, including reasonable attorney's fees, if the court finds the motion was made or opposed in bad faith or without substantial justification or that one or more of the requirements of the subpoena was oppressive.

(b)(1) Notwithstanding subdivision (a), absent exceptional circumstances, the court shall not impose sanctions on a subpoenaed person or the attorney of a subpoenaed person for failure to provide electronically stored information that has been lost, damaged, altered, or overwritten as the result of the routine, good faith operation of an electronic information system.

(2) This subdivision shall not be construed to alter any obligation to preserve discoverable information.

(c) If a motion is filed under Section 1987.1 for an order to quash or modify a subpoena from a court of this state for personally identifying information, as defined in subdivision (b) of Section 1798.79.8 of the Civil Code, for use in an action pending in another state, territory, or district of the United States, or in a foreign nation, and that subpoena has been served on any Internet service provider, or on the provider of any other interactive computer service, as defined in Section 230(f)(2) of Title 47 of the United States Code, if the moving party prevails, and if the underlying action arises from the moving party's exercise of free speech rights on the Internet and the respondent has failed to make a prima facie showing of a cause of action, the court shall award the amount of the reasonable expenses incurred in making the motion, including reasonable attorney's fees. *(Added by Stats.1976, c. 1168, p. 5249, § 2. Amended by Stats.2008, c. 742 (A.B.2433), § 2; Stats.2012, c. 72 (S.B.1574), § 7.)*

Cross References

Attorney's fees and costs, generally, see Code of Civil Procedure § 1021.

Research References

Forms

West's California Code Forms, Civil Procedure § 1987.1 Form 1, Evidence—Notice of Motion to Quash or Modify or Direct Compliance—Subpena.

West's California Code Forms, Civil Procedure § 1987.1 Form 2, Evidence—Order Quashing, Modifying or Directing Compliance With Subpena—Fees.

§ 1987.3. Service of subpoena duces tecum upon custodian of records or other qualified witness under Evidence Code section 1560

When a subpoena duces tecum is served upon a custodian of records or other qualified witness as provided in Article 4 (commencing with Section 1560) of Chapter 2 of Division 11 of the Evidence Code, and his personal attendance is not required by the terms of the subpoena, Section 1989 shall not apply. *(Added by Stats.1970, c. 590, p. 1171, § 1.)*

Cross References

Witness defined for purposes of this Code, see Code of Civil Procedure § 1878.

§ 1987.5. Subpoena duces tecum; conditions to validity; original affidavit; deposition subpoenas for production of business records

The service of a subpoena duces tecum is invalid unless at the time of such service a copy of the affidavit upon which the subpoena is based is served on the person served with the subpoena. In the case of a subpoena duces tecum which requires appearance and the production of matters and things at the taking of a deposition, the subpoena shall not be valid unless a copy of the affidavit upon which the subpoena is based and the designation of the materials to be produced, as set forth in the subpoena, is attached to the notice of taking the deposition served upon each party or its attorney as provided in Chapter 3 (commencing with Section 2002) and in Title 4 (commencing with Section 2016.010). If matters and things are produced pursuant to a subpoena duces tecum in violation of this

§ 1987.5

section, any other party to the action may file a motion for, and the court may grant, an order providing appropriate relief, including, but not limited to, exclusion of the evidence affected by the violation, a retaking of the deposition notwithstanding any other limitation on discovery proceedings, or a continuance. The party causing the subpoena to be served shall retain the original affidavit until final judgment in the action, and shall file the affidavit with the court only upon reasonable request by any party or witness affected thereby. This section does not apply to deposition subpoenas commanding only the production of business records for copying under Article 4 (commencing with Section 2020.410) of Chapter 6 of Title 4. *(Added by Stats.1951, c. 1413, p. 3368, § 1. Amended by Stats.1968, c. 95, p. 1783, § 2; Stats.1981, c. 189, p. 1114, § 1; Stats.1982, c. 452, § 2; Stats.1985, c. 1239, § 1; Stats.1993, c. 926 (A.B.2205), § 7; Stats. 2004, c. 182 (A.B.3081), § 20, operative July 1, 2005.)*

Cross References

Affidavit for subpoena duces tecum, see Code of Civil Procedure § 1985.
Depositions, see Code of Civil Procedure §§ 2020.010 et seq., 2025.010 et seq., 2026.010, 2027.010, 2028.010 et seq.
Discovery, generally, see Code of Civil Procedure § 2016.010 et seq.
Notice, actual and constructive, defined, see Civil Code § 18.
Witness defined for purposes of this Code, see Code of Civil Procedure § 1878.

Research References

Forms

West's California Code Forms, Civil Procedure § 1985 Form 3, Evidence— Declaration for Issuance of Subpena Duces Tecum.

§ 1988. Subpoena; service; witness concealed

If a witness is concealed in a building or vessel, so as to prevent the service of a subpoena upon him, any Court or Judge, or any officer issuing the subpoena, may, upon proof by affidavit of the concealment, and of the materiality of the witness, make an order that the Sheriff of the county serve the subpoena; and the Sheriff must serve it accordingly, and for that purpose may break into the building or vessel where the witness is concealed. *(Enacted in 1872.)*

Cross References

Issuance of subpoena by state agency or administrative law judge, see Government Code § 11450.05 et seq.
Sheriff oversight board, subpoenas, office of the inspector general, see Government Code § 25303.7.
Sheriff's fee for service, see Government Code § 26743.
State civil service, investigations and hearing, process and delivery of subpoenas and subpoenas duces tecum in accordance with this section, see Government Code § 18672.
Witness defined for purposes of this Code, see Code of Civil Procedure § 1878.

Research References

Forms

West's California Code Forms, Business & Professions § 475 Comment, Administrative Procedure Act.
West's California Code Forms, Civil Procedure § 1988 Form 1, Evidence— Declaration of Concealment of Witness to Avoid Service of Subpena and Order.

§ 1990. Person present; compelling to testify

A person present in Court, or before a judicial officer, may be required to testify in the same manner as if he were in attendance upon a subpoena issued by such Court or officer. *(Enacted in 1872.)*

Cross References

Accused cannot be compelled to testify, see Cal. Const. Art. 1, § 15; Evidence Code §§ 930, 940.
Adverse party, calling as witness, see Evidence Code § 776.
Issuance of subpoena, see Code of Civil Procedure § 1986.

Refusal to be sworn or to testify as contempt, see Code of Civil Procedure § 1209.

Title 4

CIVIL DISCOVERY ACT

Cross References

Actions on policies containing liability provisions, uninsured/underinsured motorist coverage, see Insurance Code § 11580.2.
Arbitration, depositions, see Code of Civil Procedure § 1283.
Community colleges, classified employees, hearings or investigation by hearing officer, see Education Code § 88131.
Community colleges, evaluations and discipline, administrative law judge's conduct of proceedings, see Education Code § 87679.
Community colleges, evaluations and discipline, arbitration proceedings, scope of discovery, see Education Code § 87675.
Contracting by local agencies, resolution of construction claims, procedures, see Public Contract Code § 20104.4.
Elementary and secondary education, classified employees, see Education Code § 45312.
Fish, generally, dams, conduits, and screens, dams and obstructions, depositions, see Fish and Game Code § 5934.
Fish and Game Commission, other regulatory powers, depositions, compelling attendance of witnesses and production of documents, see Fish and Game Code § 309.
New motor vehicle board, oaths, depositions, certification of official acts, subpoenas, discovery, see Vehicle Code § 3050.1.
Occupational safety and health, appeal proceedings, depositions, see Labor Code § 6613.
Oil and gas, geothermal resources, depositions, see Public Resources Code § 3769.
Oil and gas conservation, appeals and review, depositions, see Public Resources Code § 3357.
Petitions for transfer of property belonging to decedent or other person, commencement of discovery, see Probate Code § 851.1.
Prevention of dissipation or secreting of property, filing complaint, notice, see Penal Code § 186.12.
Probate Code, rules of practice, commencement of discovery, see Probate Code § 1000.
Proceedings concerning trusts, commencement of discovery, see Probate Code § 17201.1.
Regulation of public utilities, hearings and judicial review, see Public Utilities Code § 1794.
State departments and agencies, administrative adjudication, depositions, see Government Code § 11511.
State departments and agencies, investigations and hearings, deposition, see Government Code § 11189.
Summary judgment, continuances to allow more discovery, see Code of Civil Procedure § 437c.
Time-limited demands, construction with Civil Discovery Act, see Code of Civil Procedure § 999.4.
The Trial Court Delay Reduction Act, minimum time periods for certain actions, see Government Code § 68616.
Water, witnesses and production of evidence, depositions, see Water Code § 1100.
Workers' compensation and insurance, compensation proceedings, depositions, see Labor Code § 5710.

Disposition of Existing Law

Note. In 2004, California's Civil Discovery Act was reorganized on recommendation of the Law Revision Commission. In connection with that reform, the Commission prepared a disposition table, showing the disposition of each provision, which is set out below. See also *Civil Discovery: Nonsubstantive Reform*, 33 Cal. L. Revision Comm'n Reports 789, 1073–1087 (2003). This table shows the disposition of Article 3 (commencing with Section 2016) of Chapter 3 of Title 3 of Part 4 of the Code of Civil Procedure. Unless otherwise indicated, all dispositions are to the Code of Civil Procedure.

Existing Provision	Corresponding New Provision
2016(a)	2016.010
2016(b)	2016.020
2016(c)	2016.070
2017(a)	2017.010

MISCELLANEOUS PROVISIONS

Existing Provision	Corresponding New Provision
2017(b)	2017.210
2017(c), 1st ¶	2017.020(a)
2017(c), 2d ¶	2017.020(b)
2017(d), 1st ¶	2017.220(a)
2017(d), 2d ¶	2017.220(b)
2017(e)(1), 1st snt.	2017.730(a)
2017(e)(1), 2d snt.	2017.730(b)
2017(e)(2)	2017.730(c)
2017(e)(3), 1st & 2d snt.	2017.730(d)
2017(e)(3), 3d snt.	2017.730(e)
2017(e)(4)	2017.720(a)
2017(e)(5), 1st–4th snt.	2017.740(a)
2017(e)(5), 5th–7th snt.	2017.740(b)
2017(e)(6)	2017.710
2017(e)(7)	2017.720(b)
2017(e)(8)	2017.720(c)
2018(a)	2018.020
2018(b)	2018.030(b)
2018(c)	2018.030(a)
2018(d), 1st & 2d snt.	2018.040
2018(d), 3d snt.	2018.050
2018(d), 4th snt.	2018.060
2018(e), 1st snt.	2018.070(a)-(b)
2018(e), 2d snt.	2018.070(c)
2018(f), 1st ¶	2018.080
2018(f), 2d ¶	2018.010
2019(a)	2019.010
2019(b), intro. clause	2019.030(a), intro. clause
2019(b)(1)	2019.030(a)(1)
2019(b)(2)	2019.030(a)(2)
2019(b), next-to-last ¶	2019.030(b)
2019(b), last ¶	2019.030(c)
2019(c), 1st snt.	2019.020(a)
2019(c), 2d snt.	2019.020(b)
2019(d)	2019.210
2019(e)	2016.050
2020(a), 1st snt.	2020.010(a)
2020(a), 2d snt.	2020.010(b)
2020(a), 3d snt. (including items (1)-(3))	2020.020
2020(a), last ¶	2020.030
2020(b), 1st snt.	2020.210(a)
2020(b), 2d snt.	2020.210(b)
2020(c)	2020.310
2020(d)(1), 1st snt.	2020.410(a)-(b)
2020(d)(1), 2d–4th snt.	2020.410(c)
2020(d)(2)	2020.410(d)
2020(d)(3)	2020.420
2020(d)(4), 1st snt.	2020.430(a), (e)
2020(d)(4), 2d snt.	2020.430(b)
2020(d)(4), 3d & 4th snt.	2020.430(c)
2020(d)(4), 5th & 6th snt.	2020.430(d)
2020(d)(5)	2020.440
2020(d)(6)	2020.430(f)
2020(e), 1st snt.	2020.510(a)
2020(e), 2d snt.	2020.510(b)
2020(e), 2d ¶	2020.510(c)
2020(f), 1st snt.	2020.220(a)
2020(f), 2d snt.	2020.220(b)
2020(f), 2d ¶	2020.230(a)
2020(f), 3d ¶	2020.230(b)
2020(g)	2020.220(c)
2020(h)	2020.240
2021	2016.030
2023(a)(1)-(8) & (9), 1st snt.	2023.010
2023(a)(9), 2d snt.	2023.020
2023(b), intro. clause	2023.030, intro. clause
2023(b)(1)	2023.030(a)
2023(b)(2)	2023.030(b)
2023(b)(3)	2023.030(c)
2023(b)(4)	2023.030(d)
2023(b)(5)	2023.030(e)
2023(c)	2023.040
2024(a), 1st snt.	2024.020(a)
	Not continued (redundant).
2024(a), 2d snt.	See 2016.060.
2024(a), 3d snt.	2024.010
2024(a), 4th snt.	2024.020(b)
2024(b)	2024.040(a)
2024(c)	2024.040(b)
2024(d)	2024.030
2024(e), 1st ¶	2024.050(a)
2024(e), 2d ¶ (including items (1)-(4))	2024.050(b)
2024(e), last ¶	2024.050(c)
2024(f)	2024.060
2024(g)	2016.060
2025(a)	2025.010
2025(b)	2025.210
2025(c), 1st snt.	2025.220(a), intro. clause
2025(c), 2d snt.	2025.220(b)
2025(c), 3d & 4th snt.	2025.240(a)
2025(c), 2d ¶	2025.240(b)
2025(d), intro. clause	2025.220(a), intro. clause
2025(d)(1)	2025.220(a)(1)
2025(d)(2)	2025.220(a)(2)
2025(d)(3)	2025.220(a)(3)
2025(d)(4)	2025.220(a)(4)
2025(d)(5)	2025.220(a)(5)
2025(d)(6), 1st ¶	2025.220(a)(6)
2025(d)(6), 2d ¶, 1st snt.	2025.230
2025(d)(6), 2d ¶, 2d snt.	Not continued (redundant). See 2020.310(e), 2020.510(a)(1).
2025(d)(6), 3d ¶	2025.240(c)
2025(e)(1)	2025.250(a)
2025(e)(2), 1st snt.	2025.250(b)
2025(e)(2), 2d & 3d snt.	2025.250(c)
2025(e)(3), 1st ¶	2025.260(a)
2025(e)(3), 2d ¶ (including items (A)-(F))	2025.260(b)
2025(e)(3), next-to-last ¶	2025.260(c)
2025(e)(3), last ¶	2025.260(d)
2025(f), 1st & 2d snt.	2025.270(a)
2025(f), 3d snt.	2025.270(b)
2025(f), 2d ¶	2025.270(c)
2025(g), 1st snt.	2025.410(a)
2025(g), 2d & 3d snt.	2025.410(b)
2025(g), 2d ¶	2025.410(c)
2025(g), 3d ¶	2025.410(d)
2025(h)(1)	2025.280(a)
2025(h)(2)	2025.280(b)
2025(h)(3), 1st snt.	2025.310(a)
2025(h)(3), 2d & 3d snt.	2025.310(b)
2025(h)(3), 4th snt.	2025.310(c)
2025(i), 1st ¶	2025.420(a)
2025(i), 2d ¶ (including items (1)-(15))	2025.420(b)
2025(i), next-to-last ¶	2025.420(c)
2025(i), last ¶	2025.420(d)
2025(j)(1)	2025.430
2025(j)(2), 1st ¶	2025.440(a)
2025(j)(2), 2d ¶	2025.440(b)
2025(j)(3), 1st snt.	2025.450(a)

CODE OF CIVIL PROCEDURE

Existing Provision	Corresponding New Provision
2025(j)(3), 2d snt.	2025.450(b)
2025(j)(3), 3d & 4th snt.	2025.450(c)
2025(j)(3), 2d ¶	2025.450(d)
2025(k), intro. clause	2025.320, intro. clause
2025(k)(1)	2025.320(a)
2025(k)(2)	2025.320(b)
2025(k)(3)	2025.320(c)
2025(k)(4)	2025.320(d)
2025(k)(5)	2025.320(e)
2025(*l*)(1), 1st snt.	2025.330(a)
2025(*l*)(1), 2d snt.	2025.330(b)
2025(*l*)(1), 3d–5th snt.	2025.330(c)
2025(*l*)(1), 6th snt.	2025.330(d)
2025(*l*)(2), intro. clause	2025.340, intro. clause
2025(*l*)(2)(A)	2025.340(a)
2025(*l*)(2)(B), 1st & 2d snt.	2025.340(b)
2025(*l*)(2)(B), 3d snt.	2025.340(c)
2025(*l*)(2)(B), 4th–6th snt.	2025.340(d)
2025(*l*)(2)(B), 7th & 8th snt.	2025.340(e)
2025(*l*)(2)(B), 9th & 10th snt.	2025.340(f)
2025(*l*)(2)(C)	2025.340(g)
2025(*l*)(2)(D)	2025.340(h)
2025(*l*)(2)(E)	2025.340(i)
2025(*l*)(2)(F)	2025.340(j)
2025(*l*)(2)(G)	2025.340(k)
2025(*l*)(2)(H)	2025.340(*l*)
2025(*l*)(2)(I)	2025.340(m)
2025(*l*)(3)	2025.330(e)
2025(m)(1)	2025.460(a)
2025(m)(2)	2025.460(b)
2025(m)(3)	2025.460(c)
2025(m)(4)	2025.460(d)
2025(n), 1st & 2d snt.	2025.470
2025(n), 3d & 4th snt.	2025.420(b)(16)
2025(n), 2d ¶	2025.470
2025(o), 1st snt.	2025.480(a)
2025(o), 2d snt.	2025.480(b)
2025(o), 3d & 4th snt.	2025.480(c)
2025(o), 5th & 6th snt.	2025.480(d)
2025(o), 7th snt.	2025.480(e)
2025(o), 2d ¶	2025.480(f)
2025(o), 3d ¶	2025.480(g)
2025(p), 1st snt.	2025.510(a)
2025(p), 2d snt.	2025.510(b)
2025(p), 3d snt.	2025.510(c)
2025(p), 4th snt.	2025.510(d)
2025(p), 5th & 6th snt.	2025.510(e)
2025(p), 7th snt.	2025.510(f)
2025(p), 2d ¶	2025.510(g)
2025(q)(1), 1st snt.	2025.520(a)
2025(q)(1), 2d snt.	2025.520(b)
2025(q)(1), 2d ¶, 1st & 2d snt.	2025.520(c)
2025(q)(1), 2d ¶, 3d snt.	2025.520(d)
2025(q)(1), 3d ¶, 1st & 2d snt.	2025.520(e)
2025(q)(1), 3d ¶, 3d snt.	2025.520(f)
2025(q)(1), 3d ¶, 4th snt.	2025.520(g)
2025(q)(1), 4th ¶	2025.520(h)
2025(q)(2), 1st snt.	2025.530(a)
2025(q)(2), 2d snt.	2025.530(b)
2025(q)(2), 2d ¶, 1st snt.	2025.530(c)
2025(q)(2), 2d ¶, 2d snt.	2025.530(d)
2025(q)(2), 2d ¶, 3d snt.	2025.530(e)
2025(q)(2), 3d ¶	2025.530(f)
2025(r)(1)	2025.540(a)
2025(r)(2)	2025.540(b)
2025(s)(1), 1st ¶	2025.550(a)
2025(s)(1), 2d ¶	2025.550(b)
2025(s)(2), 1st ¶	2025.560(a)
2025(s)(2), 2d ¶	2025.560(b)
2025(s)(2), 3d ¶	2025.560(c)
2025(t), 1st snt.	2025.610(a)
2025(t), 2d snt.	2025.610(b)
2025(t), 3d snt.	2025.610(c)
2025(t), 4th snt.	2025.610(d)
2025(u), intro. clause	2025.620, intro. clause
2025(u)(1)	2025.620(a)
2025(u)(2)	2025.620(b)
2025(u)(3)	2025.620(c)
2025(u)(4)	2025.620(d)
2025(u)(5)	2025.620(e)
2025(u)(6)	2025.620(f)
2025(u)(7)	2025.620(g)
2025(v)	2025.320(f)
2025.5(a)	2025.570(a)
2025.5(b), 1st snt.	2025.570(b)
2025.5(b), 2d snt.	2025.570(c)
2025.5(c)	2025.570(d)
2026(a)	2026.010(a)
2026(b)(1)	2026.010(b)
2026(b)(2)	2026.010(c)
2026(c), 1st snt.	2026.010(d)
2026(c), 2d snt.	2026.010(e)
2026(c), 3d–7th snt.	2026.010(f)
2027(a)	2027.010(a)
2027(b)(1)	2027.010(b)
2027(b)(2)	2027.010(c)
2027(c), 1st ¶	2027.010(d)
2027(c), 2d ¶	2027.010(e)
2028(a)	2028.010
2028(b)	2028.020
2028(c), 1st ¶	2028.030(a)
2028(c), 2d ¶	2028.030(b)
2028(c), 3d ¶	2028.030(c)
2028(c), 4th ¶	2028.030(d)
2028(c), 5th ¶	2028.030(e)
2028(d)(1), 1st & 2d snt.	2028.040(a)
2028(d)(1), 3d–5th snt.	2028.040(b)
2028(d)(1), 2d ¶	2028.040(c)
2028(d)(2), 1st & 2d snt.	2028.050(a)
2028(d)(2), 3d–5th snt.	2028.050(b)
2028(d)(2), 2d ¶	2028.050(c)
2028(e), 1st snt.	2028.060(a)
2028(e), 2d snt.	2028.060(b)
2028(f)	2028.070
2028(g)	2028.080
2029	2029.010
2030(a)	2030.010(a)
2030(b), 1st snt.	2030.020(a)
2030(b), 2d snt.	2030.020(b)
2030(b), 3d snt.	2030.020(c)
2030(c)(1), 1st snt.	2030.030(a)
2030(c)(1), 2d & 3d snt.	2030.030(b)
2030(c)(1), 4th snt.	2030.030(c)
2030(c)(2), 1st ¶ (including items (A)-(C))	2030.040(a)
2030(c)(2), last ¶	2030.040(b)
2030(c)(3)	2030.050
2030(c)(4), 1st snt.	2030.060(a)
2030(c)(4), 2d snt.	2030.060(b)
2030(c)(4), 3d snt.	2030.060(c)
2030(c)(5), 1st & 2d snt.	2030.060(d)
2030(c)(5), 3d snt.	2030.060(e)
2030(c)(5), 4th snt.	2030.060(f)
2030(c)(6)	2030.010(b)

MISCELLANEOUS PROVISIONS

Existing Provision	Corresponding New Provision
2030(c)(7)	2030.060(g)
2030(c)(8), 1st snt.	2030.070(a)-(b)
2030(c)(8), 2d snt.	2030.070(c)
2030(d)	2030.080
2030(e), 1st ¶	2030.090(a)
2030(e), 2d ¶ (including items (1)-(7))	2030.090(b)
2030(e), next-to-last ¶	2030.090(c)
2030(e), last ¶	2030.090(d)
2030(f), 1st snt.	2030.210(a)
2030(f), 2d snt.	2030.210(b)
2030(f), 3d snt.	2030.210(c)
2030(f)(1), 1st snt.	2030.220(a)
2030(f)(1), 2d snt.	2030.220(b)
2030(f)(1), 3d snt.	2030.220(c)
2030(f)(2)	2030.230
2030(f)(3), 1st snt.	2030.240(a)
2030(f)(3), 2d-4th snt.	2030.240(b)
2030(g), 1st snt.	2030.250(a)
2030(g), 2d & 3d snt.	2030.250(b)
2030(g), 4th snt.	2030.250(c)
2030(h), 1st & 2d snt.	2030.260(a)
2030(h), 3d snt.	2030.260(b)
2030(i), 1st snt.	2030.270(a)
2030(i), 2d snt.	2030.270(b)
2030(i), 3d snt.	2030.270(c)
2030(j), 1st snt.	2030.280(a)
2030(j), 2d & 3d snt.	2030.280(b)
2030(k), 1st ¶	2030.290(a)
2030(k), 2d ¶, 1st snt.	2030.290(b)
2030(k), 2d ¶, 2d-4th snt.	2030.290(c)
2030(*l*), 1st snt.	2030.300(a)
2030(*l*), 2d snt.	2030.300(b)
2030(*l*), 2d ¶	2030.300(c)
2030(*l*), 3d ¶	2030.300(d)
2030(*l*), 4th ¶	2030.300(e)
2030(m), 1st ¶	2030.310(a)
2030(m), 2d ¶, 1st & 2d snt.	2030.310(b)
2030(m), 2d ¶, 3d snt.	2030.310(c)
2030(m), 3d ¶	2030.310(d)
2030(n)	2030.410
2031(a), intro. ¶	2031.010(a)
2031(a)(1)	2031.010(b)
2031(a)(2)	2031.010(c)
2031(a)(3)	2031.010(d)
2031(b), 1st snt.	2031.020(a)
2031(b), 2d snt.	2031.020(b)
2031(b), 3d snt.	2031.020(c)
2031(c), 1st snt.	2031.030(a)
2031(c), 2d snt.	2031.030(b)
2031(c), 3d snt. (including items (1)-(4))	2031.030(c)
2031(d)	2031.040
2031(e), 1st snt.	2031.050(a)-(b)
2031(e), 2d snt.	2031.050(c)
2031(f), 1st ¶	2031.060(a)
2031(f), 2d ¶ (including items (1)-(6))	2031.060(b)
2031(f), next-to-last ¶	2031.060(c)
2031(f), last ¶	2031.060(d)
2031(g), 1st ¶	2031.210(a)
2031(g), 2d ¶, 1st snt.	2031.210(b)
2031(g), 2d ¶, 2d snt.	2031.210(c)
2031(g)(1), 1st ¶	2031.220
2031(g)(1), 2d ¶, 1st snt.	2031.280(a)
2031(g)(1), 2d ¶, 2d snt.	2031.280(b)
2031(g)(2)	2031.230
2031(g)(3), 1st snt.	2031.240(a)
2031(g)(3), 2d-4th snt.	2031.240(b)
2031(h), 1st snt.	2031.250(a)
2031(h), 2d & 3d snt.	2031.250(b)
2031(h), 4th snt.	2031.250(c)
2031(i)	2031.260
2031(j), 1st snt.	2031.270(a)
2031(j), 2d snt.	2031.270(b)
2031(j), 3d snt.	2031.270(c)
2031(k), 1st snt.	2031.290(a)
2031(k), 2d & 3d snt.	2031.290(b)
2031(*l*), 1st ¶	2031.300, intro. cl. & (a)
2031(*l*), 2d ¶, 1st snt.	2031.300(b)
2031(*l*), 2d ¶, 2d-4th snt.	2031.300(c)
2031(m), 1st snt.	2031.310(a)
2031(m), 2d snt.	2031.310(b)
2031(m), 2d ¶	2031.310(c)
2031(m), 3d ¶	2031.310(d)
2031(m), 4th ¶	2031.310(e)
2031(n), 1st ¶	2031.320(a)
2031(n), 2d ¶	2031.320(b)
2031(n), 3d ¶	2031.320(c)
2031.1	2017.310
2031.2	2017.320
2031.5, 1st snt.	2031.510(a)
2031.5, 2d & 3d snt.	2031.510(b)
2032(a)	2032.020
2032(b), 1st snt.	2032.020(b)
2032(b), 2d snt.	2032.020(c)
2032(b), 3d snt.	2032.010(a)
2032(c)(1)	2032.210
2032(c)(2), 1st snt.	2032.220(a)
2032(c)(2), 2d snt.	2032.220(b)
2032(c)(2), 3d snt.	2032.220(c)
2032(c)(3)	2032.220(d)
2032(c)(4)	2032.220(e)
2032(c)(5), 1st snt.	2032.230(a)
2032(c)(5), 2d snt.	2032.230(b)
2032(c)(6), 1st ¶	2032.240(a)
2032(c)(6), 2d ¶, 1st snt.	2032.240(b)
2032(c)(6), 2d ¶, 2d snt.	2032.240(c)
2032(c)(6), 3d ¶	2032.240(d)
2032(c)(7), 1st ¶	2032.250(a)
2032(c)(7), 2d ¶	2032.250(b)
2032(c)(8), 1st snt.	2032.260(a)
2032(c)(8), 2d snt.	2032.260(b)
2032(d), 1st snt.	2032.310(a)
2032(d), 2d & 3d snt.	2032.310(b)
2032(d), 4th snt.	2032.310(c)
2032(d), 2d ¶, 1st snt.	2032.320(a)
2032(d), 2d ¶, 2d snt.	2032.320(b)-(c)
2032(d), 2d ¶, 3d snt.	2032.320(d)
2032(d), 2d ¶, 4th snt.	2032.320(e)
	Not continued (redundant).
2032(e)	See 2016.030.
2032(f), 1st ¶	2032.410
2032(f), 2d ¶	2032.420
2032(g)(1), 1st snt.	2032.510(a)
2032(g)(1), 2d snt.	2032.510(b)
2032(g)(1), 3d snt.	2032.510(c)
2032(g)(1), 2d ¶, 1st snt.	2032.510(d)
2032(g)(1), 2d ¶, 2d snt.	2032.510(e)
2032(g)(1), 3d ¶	2032.510(f)
2032(g)(1), 4th ¶	2032.520
2032(g)(2), 1st snt.	2032.530(a)
2032(g)(2), 2d snt.	2032.530(b)
2032(h), 1st snt.	2032.610(a)

CODE OF CIVIL PROCEDURE

Existing Provision	Corresponding New Provision
2032(h), 2d snt.	2032.610(b)
2032(h), 3d snt.	2032.610(c)
2032(h), 2d ¶	2032.620(a)
2032(h), 3d ¶	2032.620(b)
2032(h), 4th ¶	2032.620(c)
2032(i)	2032.630
2032(j), 1st ¶	2032.640
2032(j), 2d ¶	2032.650(a)
2032(j), 3d ¶	2032.650(b)
2032(j), 4th ¶	2032.650(c)
2032(k)	2032.010(b)
2033(a)	2033.010
2033(b), 1st snt.	2033.020(a)
2033(b), 2d snt.	2033.020(b)
2033(b), 3d snt.	2033.020(c)
2033(c)(1), 1st snt.	2033.030(a)
2033(c)(1), 2d snt.	2033.030(b)
2033(c)(1), 2d ¶	2033.030(c)
2033(c)(2), 1st ¶	2033.040(a)
2033(c)(2), 2d ¶	2033.040(b)
2033(c)(3)	2033.050
2033(c)(4), 1st snt.	2033.060(a)
2033(c)(4), 2d snt.	2033.060(b)
2033(c)(4), 3d snt.	2033.060(c)
2033(c)(5), 1st & 2d snt.	2033.060(d)
2033(c)(5), 3d snt.	2033.060(e)
2033(c)(5), 4th snt.	2033.060(f)
2033(c)(6)	2033.060(g)
2033(c)(7)	2033.060(h)
2033(d)	2033.070
2033(e), 1st ¶	2033.080(a)
2033(e), 2d ¶ (including items (1)-(5))	2033.080(b)
2033(e), next-to-last ¶	2033.080(c)
2033(e), last ¶	2033.080(d)
2033(f), intro. ¶, 1st snt.	2033.210(a)
2033(f), intro. ¶, 2d snt.	2033.210(b)
2033(f), intro. ¶, 3d snt.	2033.210(c)
2033(f), intro. ¶, 4th snt.	2033.210(d)
2033(f)(1), 1st snt.	2033.220(a)
2033(f)(1), 2d snt.	2033.220(b)
2033(f)(1), 3d snt.	2033.220(c)
2033(f)(2), 1st snt.	2033.230(a)
2033(f)(2), 2d–4th snt.	2033.230(b)
2033(g), 1st snt.	2033.240(a)
2033(g), 2d & 3d snt.	2033.240(b)
2033(g), 4th snt.	2033.240(c)
2033(h)	2033.250
2033(i), 1st snt.	2033.260(a)
2033(i), 2d snt.	2033.260(b)
2033(i), 3d snt.	2033.260(c)
2033(i), 4th snt.	2033.260(d)
2033(j), 1st snt.	2033.270(a)
2033(j), 2d & 3d snt.	2033.270(b)
2033(k), 1st ¶	2033.280(a)
2033(k), 2d ¶, 1st snt.	2033.280(b)
2033(k), 2d ¶, 2d & 3d snt.	2033.280(c)
2033(l), 1st snt.	2033.290(a)
2033(l), 2d snt.	2033.290(b)
2033(l), 2d ¶	2033.290(c)
2033(l), 3d ¶	2033.290(d)
2033(l), 4th ¶	2033.290(e)
2033(m), 1st snt.	2033.300(a)
2033(m), 2d snt.	2033.300(b)
2033(m), 3d snt.	2033.300(c)
2033(n), 1st snt.	2033.410(a)
2033(n), 2d & 3d snt.	2033.410(b)
2033(o), 1st snt.	2033.420(a)
2033(o), 2d snt.	2033.420(b)
2033.5(a), 1st snt.	2033.710
2033.5(a), 2d snt.	2033.740(a)
2033.5(b), 1st snt.	2033.730(a)
2033.5(b), 2d snt., 1st clause	2033.730(b)
2033.5(b), 2d snt., 2d clause	2033.740(b)
2033.5(c)	2033.740(c)
2033.5(d)	2033.720(a)
2033.5(e)	2033.720(b)
2033.5(f)	Not continued (obsolete)
2034(a), intro. clause	2034.210, intro. clause
2034(a)(1)	2034.210(a)
2034(a)(2)	2034.210(b)
2034(a)(3)	2034.210(c)
2034(a), last ¶	2034.010
2034(b)	2034.220
2034(c), 1st ¶	2034.230(a)
2034(c), 2d ¶	2034.230(b)
2034(d)	2034.240
2034(e), 1st ¶	2034.250(a)
2034(e), 2d ¶ (including items (1)-(6))	2034.250(b)
2034(e), next-to-last ¶	2034.250(c)
2034(e), last ¶	2034.250(d)
2034(f), intro. ¶	2034.260(a)
2034(f)(1) (including items (A) and (B))	2034.260(b)
2034(f)(2) (including items (A)-(E))	2034.260(c)
2034(g)	2034.270
2034(h), 1st snt.	2034.280(a)
2034(h), 2d snt.	2034.280(b)
2034(h), 3d snt.	2034.280(c)
2034(i), intro. ¶	2034.410
2034(i)(1)	2034.420
2034(i)(2), 1st ¶, 1st snt.	2034.430(a)-(b)
2034(i)(2), 1st ¶, 2d snt.	2034.430(c)
2034(i)(2), 1st ¶, 3d snt.	2034.430(d)
2034(i)(2), 1st ¶, 4th snt.	2034.430(e)
2034(i)(2), 1st ¶, 5th snt.	2034.430(f)
2034(i)(2), 2d ¶, 1st snt.	2034.450(a)
2034(i)(2), 2d ¶, 2d snt.	2034.450(b)
2034(i)(2), 2d ¶, 3d snt.	2034.450(c)
2034(i)(2), 2d ¶, 4th snt.	2034.440
2034(i)(3), 1st snt.	2034.460(a)
2034(i)(3), 2d snt.	2034.460(b)
2034(i)(4), 1st ¶, 1st & 3d snt.	2034.470(a)
2034(i)(4), 1st ¶, 2d & 4th snt.	2034.470(b)
2034(i)(4), 2d ¶, 1st & 2d snt.	2034.470(c)-(d)
2034(i)(4), 2d ¶, 3d snt.	2034.470(e)
2034(i)(4), 3d ¶	2034.470(f)
2034(i)(4), 4th ¶	2034.470(g)
2034(j)	2034.300
2034(k), 1st ¶, 1st snt.	2034.610(a)
2034(k), 1st ¶, 2d & 3d snt.	2034.610(b)
2034(k), 1st ¶, 4th snt.	2034.610(c)
2034(k), 1st ¶, 5th snt.	2034.290(c)
2034(k), 1st ¶, 6th snt.	2034.620, intro. cl. & (a)-(c)
2034(k), 1st ¶, 7th snt.	2034.620(d)
2034(k), 2d ¶	2034.630
2034(l), 1st snt.	2034.710(a)
2034(l), 2d & 3d snt.	2034.710(b)
2034(l), 4th snt.	2034.710(c)
2034(l), 2d ¶, 1st snt.	2034.720, intro. cl. & (a)-(c)
2034(l), 2d ¶, 2d snt.	2034.720(d)
2034(l), 3d ¶	2034.730

MISCELLANEOUS PROVISIONS

Existing Provision	Corresponding New Provision
2034(m)	2034.310
2034(n), 1st snt.	2034.290(a)
2034(n), 2d & 3d snt.	2034.290(b)
2035(a), 1st snt.	2035.010(a)
2035(a), 2d snt.	2035.010(b)
2035(b)	2035.020
2035(c)	2035.030(a)
2035(d), 1st ¶ (including items (1)-(9))	2035.030(b)
2035(d), last ¶	2035.030(c)
2035(e), 1st & 2d snt.	2035.040(a)
2035(e), 3d & 4th snt.	2035.040(b)
2035(e), 5th snt.	2035.040(c)
2035(e), 2d ¶, 1st snt.	2035.040(d)
2035(e), 2d ¶, 2d & 3d snt.	2035.040(e)
2035(f), 1st snt.	2035.050(a)
2035(f), 2d snt.	2035.050(b)
2035(f), 3d snt.	2035.050(c)
2035(g)	2035.060
2036(a)	2036.010
2036(b)	2036.020
2036(c)	2036.030(a)
2036(d)	2036.030(b)
2036(e), 1st snt.	2036.040(a)
2036(e), 2d snt.	2036.040(b)
2036(e), 3d snt.	2036.040(c)
2036(f)	2036.050

DERIVATION TABLE

This table shows the derivation by section number of the subject matter of Part 4, added by Stats.2004, c. 182 (A.B.3081), § 23, operative July 1, 2005. This part was derived from Article 3 (commencing with Code of Civil Procedure § 2016) of Chapter 3 of Title 3 of Part 4 of the Code of Civil Procedure. Section references are to the Code of Civil Procedure.

New	Old
2016.010	2016(a)
2016.020	2016(b)
2016.030	2021
2016.040	(none)
2016.050	2019(e)
2016.060	2024(g)
2016.070	2016(c)
2017.010	2017(a)
2017.020	2017(c)
2017.210	2017(b)
2017.220	2017(d)
2017.310	2031.1
2017.320	2031.2
2017.710	2017(e)(6)
2017.720	2017(e)(4), (e)(7), (e)(8)
2017.730	2017(e)(1), (e)(2), (e)(3)
2017.740	2017(e)(5)
2018.010	2018(f)
2018.020	2018(a)
2018.030	2018(b), (c)
2018.040	2018(d)
2018.050	2018(d)
2018.060	2018(d)
2018.070	2018(e)
2018.080	2018(f)
2019.010	2019(a)
2019.020	2019(c)
2019.030	2019(b)
2019.210	2019(d)
2020.010	2020(a)
2020.020	2020(a)
2020.030	2020(a)
2020.210	2020(b)
2020.220	2020(f), (g)
2020.230	2020(f)
2020.240	2020(h)
2020.310	2020(c)
2020.410	2020(d)(1), (d)(2)
2020.420	2020(d)(3)
2020.430	2020(d)(4), (d)(6)
2020.440	2020(d)(5)
2020.510	2020(e)
2023.010	2023(a)
2023.020	2023(a)
2023.030	2023(b)
2023.040	2023(c)
2024.010	2024(a)
2024.020	2024(a)
2024.030	2024(d)
2024.040	2024(b), (c)
2024.050	2024(e)
2024.060	2024(f)
2025.010	2025(a)
2025.210	2025(b)
2025.220	2025(c), (d)
2025.230	2025(d)
2025.240	2025(c), (d)
2025.250	2025(e)(1), (e)(2)
2025.260	2025(e)(3)
2025.270	2025(f)
2025.280	2025(h)(1), (h)(2)
2025.310	2025(h)(3)
2025.320	2025(k)(v)
2025.330	2025(*l*)(1), (*l*)(3)
2025.340	2025(*l*)(2)
2025.410	2025(g)
2025.420	2025(i), (n)
2025.430	2025(j)(1)
2025.440	2025(j)(2)
2025.450	2025(j)(3)
2025.460	2025(m)
2025.470	2025(n)
2025.480	2025(*o*)
2025.510	2025(p)
2025.520	2025(q)(1)
2025.530	2025(q)(2)
2025.540	2025(r)
2025.550	2025(s)(1)
2025.560	2025(s)(2)
2025.570	2025.5
2025.610	2025(t)
2025.620	2025(u)
2026.010	2026
2027.010	2027
2028.010	2028(a)
2028.020	2028(b)
2028.030	2028(c)
2028.040	2028(d)(1)
2028.050	2028(d)(2)
2028.060	2028(e)
2028.070	2028(f)
2028.080	2028(g)
2029.010	2029
2030.010	2030(a), (c)(b)
2030.020	2030(b)
2030.030	2030(c)(1)
2030.040	2030(c)(2)
2030.050	2030(c)(3)
2030.060	2030(c)(4), (c)(5), (c)(7)
2030.070	2030(c)(8)

CODE OF CIVIL PROCEDURE

New	Old
2030.080	2030(d)
2030.090	2030(e)
2030.210	2030(f)
2030.220	2030(f)(1)
2030.230	2030(f)(2)
2030.240	2030(f)(3)
2030.250	2030(g)
2030.260	2030(h)
2030.270	2030(i)
2030.280	2030(j)
2030.290	2030(k)
2030.300	2030(*l*)
2030.310	2030(m)
2030.410	2030(n)
2031.010	2031(a)
2031.020	2031(b)
2031.030	2031(c)
2031.040	2031(d)
2031.050	2031(e)
2031.060	2031(f)
2031.210	2031(g)
2031.220	2031(g)(1)
2031.230	2031(g)(2)
2031.240	2031(g)(3)
2031.250	2031(h)
2031.260	2031(i)
2031.270	2031(j)
2031.280	2031(g)(1)
2031.290	2031(k)
2031.300	2031(*l*)
2031.310	2031(m)
2031.320	2031(n)
2031.510	2031.5
2032.010	2032(b), (k)
2032.020	2032(a), (b)
2032.210	2032(c)(1)
2032.220	2032(c)(2) to (c)(4)
2032.230	2032(c)(5)
2032.240	2032(c)(6)
2032.250	2032(c)(7)
2032.260	2032(c)(8)
2032.310	2032(d)
2032.320	2032(d)
2032.410	2032(f)
2032.420	2032(f)
2032.510	2032(g)(1)
2032.520	2032(g)(1)
2032.530	2032(g)(2)
2032.610	2032(h)
2032.620	2032(h)
2032.630	2032(i)
2032.640	2032(j)
2032.650	2032(j)
2033.010	2033(a)
2033.020	2033(b)
2033.030	2033(c)(1)
2033.040	2033(c)(2)
2033.050	2033(c)(3)
2033.060	2033(c)(4) to (c)(7)
2033.070	2033(d)
2033.080	2033(e)
2033.210	2033(f)
2033.220	2033(f)(1)
2033.230	2033(f)(2)
2033.240	2033(g)
2033.250	2033(h)
2033.260	2033(i)
2033.270	2033(j)

New	Old
2033.280	2033(k)
2033.290	2033(*l*)
2033.300	2033(m)
2033.410	2033(n)
2033.420	2033(o)
2033.710	2033.5(a)
2033.720	2033.5(d), (e)
2033.730	2033.5(b)
2033.740	2033.5(a) to (c)
2034.010	2034(a)
2034.210	2034(a)
2034.220	2034(b)
2034.230	2034(c)
2034.240	2034(d)
2034.250	2034(e)
2034.260	2034(f)
2034.270	2034(g)
2034.280	2034(h)
2034.290	2034(k), (n)
2034.300	2034(j)
2034.310	2034(m)
2034.410	2034(i)
2034.420	2034(i)(1)
2034.430	2034(i)(2)
2034.440	2034(i)(2)
2034.450	2034(i)(2)
2034.460	2034(i)(3)
2034.470	2034(i)(4)
2034.610	2034(k)
2034.620	2034(k)
2034.630	2034(k)
2034.710	2034(*l*)
2034.720	2034(*l*)
2034.730	2034(*l*)
2035.010	2035(a)
2035.020	2035(b)
2035.030	2035(c), (d)
2035.040	2035(e)
2035.050	2035(f)
2035.060	2035(g)
2036.010	2036(a)
2036.020	2036(b)
2036.030	2036(c), (d)
2036.040	2036(e)
2036.050	2036(f)

CHAPTER 1. GENERAL PROVISIONS

Section
2016.010. Short title.
2016.020. Definitions.
2016.030. Stipulation to modify discovery; requirements.
2016.040. Meet and confer declaration; requirements.
2016.050. Service of notice or other papers; allowed methods.
2016.060. Saturday, Sunday or holiday as last day to act.
2016.070. Application to enforcement of money judgments.
2016.080. Informal discovery conferences.
2016.090. Initial disclosures; application of section.

Cross References
Attorneys prohibited from disclosing identifying information of a victim or witness, violations, see Welfare and Institutions Code § 6603.3.

§ 2016.010. Short title

This title may be cited as the "Civil Discovery Act." *(Added by Stats.2004, c. 182 (A.B.3081), § 23, operative July 1, 2005.)*

Cross References

Filing fees, generally, see Government Code § 70617.

Written interrogatories to judgment debtor, see Code of Civil Procedure § 708.010 et seq.

Research References

Forms

8A Am. Jur. Pl. & Pr. Forms Depositions and Discovery § 1, Introductory Comments.

2 California Transactions Forms--Business Transactions § 8:78.10, Retention and Preservation of E-Communications Records.

West's California Code Forms, Civil Procedure § 2016.010 Comment, New Discovery Act.

West's California Code Forms, Civil Procedure § 2017.730 Form 1, Evidence—Discovery—Notice of Motion for Order Allowing Use of Electronic Technology in Complex Cases.

West's California Code Forms, Civil Procedure § 2020.310 Form 1, Evidence—Discovery—Deposition Subpena for Personal Appearance—Proof of Service—Official Form.

West's California Code Forms, Civil Procedure § 2024.060 Form 1, Evidence—Discovery—Written Agreement Extending Time for Completion of Discovery.

West's California Code Forms, Civil Procedure § 2025.210 Form 1, Evidence—Discovery—Notice of Motion for Leave of Court to Take Deposition Upon Oral Examination Within Twenty Days After Service of Summons on Defendant—Order Shortening Time.

West's California Code Forms, Civil Procedure § 2026.010 Form 1, Evidence—Discovery—Notice of Motion for Commission for Deposition of Out of State Witness.

West's California Code Forms, Civil Procedure § 2027.010 Form 1, Evidence—Discovery—Notice of Motion for Issuance of Commission or Letters Rogatory.

West's California Code Forms, Civil Procedure § 2028.020 Form 1, Evidence—Discovery—Notice of Taking Deposition by Written Questions.

West's California Code Forms, Civil Procedure § 2030.010 Comment, —New Discovery Act.

West's California Code Forms, Civil Procedure § 2030.020 Form 1, Evidence—Discovery—Notice of Motion for Leave to Serve Interrogatories Within Ten Days—Order Shortening Time.

West's California Code Forms, Civil Procedure § 2031.010 Form 1, Evidence—Discovery—Demand for Inspection.

West's California Code Forms, Civil Procedure § 2031.510 Form 1, Evidence—Discovery—Declaration of Disclosure—Nonprivileged Relevant Written Evidence—State Land Patents or Grants—Validity or Boundary Dispute.

West's California Code Forms, Civil Procedure § 2032.220 Form 1, Evidence—Discovery—Demand for Physical Examination of Plaintiff.

West's California Code Forms, Civil Procedure § 2033.020 Form 1, Evidence—Discovery—Request for Admissions—Truth of Facts—Genuineness of Documents—Official Form.

West's California Code Forms, Civil Procedure § 2033.710 Form 1, Evidence—Discovery—Form Interrogatories—Official Form.

West's California Code Forms, Civil Procedure § 2034.230 Form 1, Evidence—Discovery—Demand for Simultaneous Exchange of Information Concerning Expert Witnesses—Simultaneous Production of Discoverable Expert's Reports.

West's California Code Forms, Civil Procedure § 2035.030 Form 1, Evidence—Discovery—Petition to Perpetuate Testimony Before Action.

West's California Code Forms, Civil Procedure § 2036.030 Form 1, Evidence—Discovery—Notice of Motion for Leave to Conduct Discovery to Perpetuate Testimony Pending Appeal.

§ 2016.020. Definitions

As used in this title:

(a) "Action" includes a civil action and a special proceeding of a civil nature.

(b) "Court" means the trial court in which the action is pending, unless otherwise specified.

(c) "Document" and "writing" mean a writing, as defined in Section 250 of the Evidence Code.

(d) "Electronic" means relating to technology having electrical, digital, magnetic, wireless, optical, electromagnetic, or similar capabilities.

(e) "Electronically stored information" means information that is stored in an electronic medium. *(Added by Stats.2004, c. 182 (A.B.3081), § 23, operative July 1, 2005. Amended by Stats.2009, c. 5 (A.B.5), § 3, eff. June 29, 2009.)*

Cross References

Means of production of electronically stored information, see Code of Civil Procedure § 1985.8.

Research References

Forms

2 California Transactions Forms--Business Transactions § 8:78.10, Retention and Preservation of E-Communications Records.

§ 2016.030. Stipulation to modify discovery; requirements

Unless the court orders otherwise, the parties may by written stipulation modify the procedures provided by this title for any method of discovery permitted under Section 2019.010. *(Added by Stats.2004, c. 182 (A.B.3081), § 23, operative July 1, 2005.)*

Cross References

Court defined for purposes of this Title, see Code of Civil Procedure § 2016.020.

Research References

Forms

West's California Code Forms, Civil Procedure § 2032.320 Form 1, Evidence—Discovery—Stipulation for Physical Examination.

§ 2016.040. Meet and confer declaration; requirements

A meet and confer declaration in support of a motion shall state facts showing a reasonable and good faith attempt at an informal resolution of each issue presented by the motion. *(Added by Stats.2004, c. 182 (A.B.3081), § 23, operative July 1, 2005.)*

§ 2016.050. Service of notice or other papers; allowed methods

Sections 1011 and 1013 apply to any method of discovery or service of a motion provided for in this title. *(Added by Stats.2004, c. 182 (A.B.3081), § 23, operative July 1, 2005. Amended by Stats.2017, c. 64 (S.B.543), § 2, eff. Jan. 1, 2018.)*

§ 2016.060. Saturday, Sunday or holiday as last day to act

When the last day to perform or complete any act provided for in this title falls on a Saturday, Sunday, or holiday as specified in Section 10, the time limit is extended until the next court day closer to the trial date. *(Added by Stats.2004, c. 182 (A.B.3081), § 23.5, operative July 1, 2005.)*

Cross References

Court defined for purposes of this Title, see Code of Civil Procedure § 2016.020.

§ 2016.070. Application to enforcement of money judgments

This title applies to discovery in aid of enforcement of a money judgment only to the extent provided in Article 1 (commencing with Section 708.010) of Chapter 6 of Title 9 of Part 2. *(Added by Stats.2004, c. 182 (A.B.3081), § 23, operative July 1, 2005.)*

§ 2016.080. Informal discovery conferences

(a) If an informal resolution is not reached by the parties, as described in Section 2016.040, the court may conduct an informal discovery conference upon request by a party or on the court's own motion for the purpose of discussing discovery matters in dispute between the parties.

(b) If a party requests an informal discovery conference, the party shall file a declaration described in Section 2016.040 with the court. Any party may file a response to a declaration filed pursuant to this subdivision. If a court is in session and does not grant, deny, or

§ 2016.080

schedule the party's request within 10 calendar days after the initial request, the request shall be deemed denied.

(c)(1) If a court grants or orders an informal discovery conference, the court may schedule and hold the conference no later than 30 calendar days after the court granted the request or issued its order, and before the discovery cutoff date.

(2) If an informal discovery conference is granted or ordered, the court may toll the deadline for filing a discovery motion or make any other appropriate discovery order.

(d) If an informal discovery conference is not held within 30 calendar days from the date the court granted the request, the request for an informal discovery conference shall be deemed denied, and any tolling period previously ordered by the court shall continue to apply to that action.

(e) The outcome of an informal discovery conference does not bar a party from filing a discovery motion or prejudice the disposition of a discovery motion.

(f) This section does not prevent the parties from stipulating to the timing of discovery proceedings as described in Section 2024.060.

(g) This section shall remain in effect only until January 1, 2023, and as of that date is repealed, unless a later enacted statute that is enacted before January 1, 2023, deletes or extends that date. *(Added by Stats.2017, c. 189 (A.B.383), § 1, eff. Jan. 1, 2018. Amended by Stats.2018, c. 92 (S.B.1289), § 44, eff. Jan. 1, 2019.)*

Repeal

For repeal of this section, see its terms.

§ 2016.090. Initial disclosures; application of section

(a) The following shall apply only to a civil action upon an order of the court following stipulation by all parties to the action:

(1) Within 45 days of the order of the court, a party shall, without awaiting a discovery request, provide to the other parties an initial disclosure that includes all of the following information:

(A) The names, addresses, telephone numbers, and email addresses of all persons likely to have discoverable information, along with the subjects of that information, that the disclosing party may use to support its claims or defenses, unless the use would be solely for impeachment.

(B) A copy, or a description by category and location, of all documents, electronically stored information, and tangible things that the disclosing party has in its possession, custody, or control and may use to support its claims or defenses, unless the use would be solely for impeachment.

(C) Any agreement under which an insurance company may be liable to satisfy, in whole or in part, a judgment entered in the action or to indemnify or reimburse for payments made to satisfy the judgment.

(D) Any agreement under which a person, as defined in Section 175 of the Evidence Code, may be liable to satisfy, in whole or in part, a judgment entered in the action or to indemnify or reimburse for payments made to satisfy the judgment. Only those provisions of an agreement that are material to the terms of the insurance, indemnification, or reimbursement are required to be included in the initial disclosure. Material provisions include, but are not limited to, the identities of parties to the agreement and the nature and limits of the coverage.

(2) A party shall make its initial disclosures based on the information then reasonably available to it. A party is not excused from making its initial disclosures because it has not fully investigated the case, because it challenges the sufficiency of another party's disclosures, or because another party has not made its disclosures.

(3) A party that has made its initial disclosures, as described in paragraph (1), or that has responded to another party's discovery request, shall supplement or correct a disclosure or response in the following situations:

(A) In a timely manner if the party learns that in some material respect the disclosure or response is incomplete or incorrect and the additional or corrective information has not otherwise been made known to the other parties during the disclosure or discovery process.

(B) As ordered by the court.

(4) A party's obligations under this section may be enforced by a court on its own motion or the motion of a party to compel disclosure.

(5) A party's disclosures under this section shall be verified under penalty of perjury as being true and correct to the best of the party's knowledge.

(b) Notwithstanding subdivision (a), this section does not apply to the following actions:

(1) An unlawful detainer action, as defined in Section 1161.

(2) An action in the small claims division of a court, as defined in Section 116.210. *(Added by Stats.2019, c. 836 (S.B.17), § 1, eff. Jan. 1, 2020.)*

CHAPTER 2. SCOPE OF DISCOVERY

ARTICLE 1. GENERAL PROVISIONS

Section
2017.010. Persons entitled to discovery; matters discoverable.
2017.020. Judicial limits upon discovery; order; sanctions; exceptions.

§ 2017.010. Persons entitled to discovery; matters discoverable

Unless otherwise limited by order of the court in accordance with this title, any party may obtain discovery regarding any matter, not privileged, that is relevant to the subject matter involved in the pending action or to the determination of any motion made in that action, if the matter either is itself admissible in evidence or appears reasonably calculated to lead to the discovery of admissible evidence. Discovery may relate to the claim or defense of the party seeking discovery or of any other party to the action. Discovery may be obtained of the identity and location of persons having knowledge of any discoverable matter, as well as of the existence, description, nature, custody, condition, and location of any document, electronically stored information, tangible thing, or land or other property. *(Added by Stats.2004, c. 182 (A.B.3081), § 23, operative July 1, 2005. Amended by Stats.2012, c. 72 (S.B.1574), § 8.)*

Cross References

Abuse of discovery, sanctions, see Code of Civil Procedure § 2023.010 et seq.
Action defined for purposes of this Title, see Code of Civil Procedure § 2016.020.
Administrative adjudication, see Government Code § 11450.05 et seq.
Arbitration proceedings, see Code of Civil Procedure § 1283 et seq.
Attorneys, depositions in disciplinary proceedings, see Business and Professions Code § 6115.
Authority of court to take and certify deposition, see Code of Civil Procedure § 179.
Costs, see Code of Civil Procedure § 1033.5.
Court defined for purposes of this Title, see Code of Civil Procedure § 2016.020.
Criminal proceedings, see Penal Code § 1335 et seq.
Destruction of depositions, see Code of Civil Procedure § 1952.
Discovery, generally, see Code of Civil Procedure § 2016.010 et seq.
Document defined for purposes of this Title, see Code of Civil Procedure § 2016.020.
Examination of witnesses, general rules, see Evidence Code § 760 et seq.
Impeachment of witnesses, see Evidence Code §§ 770, 785 et seq., 1235, 1324.
Prisoners, see Penal Code §§ 2622, 2623.
Privileged communications, see Evidence Code § 911 et seq.

Refusal to obey subpoena as contempt, see Code of Civil Procedure § 2031.010 et seq.

Study made by in-hospital staff committee, discovery, see Evidence Code § 1156.

Unfair trade practices act proceedings, authority to take depositions, see Business and Professions Code § 17083.

Research References

Forms

West's California Code Forms, Civil Procedure § 2030.010 Comment, —New Discovery Act.

§ 2017.020. Judicial limits upon discovery; order; sanctions; exceptions

(a) The court shall limit the scope of discovery if it determines that the burden, expense, or intrusiveness of that discovery clearly outweighs the likelihood that the information sought will lead to the discovery of admissible evidence. The court may make this determination pursuant to a motion for protective order by a party or other affected person. This motion shall be accompanied by a meet and confer declaration under Section 2016.040.

(b) The court shall impose a monetary sanction under Chapter 7 (commencing with Section 2023.010) against any party, person, or attorney who unsuccessfully makes or opposes a motion for a protective order, unless it finds that the one subject to the sanction acted with substantial justification or that other circumstances make the imposition of the sanction unjust.

(c)(1) Notwithstanding subdivision (b), or any other section of this title, absent exceptional circumstances, the court shall not impose sanctions on a party or any attorney of a party for failure to provide electronically stored information that has been lost, damaged, altered, or overwritten as the result of the routine, good faith operation of an electronic information system.

(2) This subdivision shall not be construed to alter any obligation to preserve discoverable information. *(Added by Stats.2004, c. 182 (A.B.3081), § 23, operative July 1, 2005. Amended by Stats.2012, c. 72 (S.B.1574), § 9.)*

Cross References

Court defined for purposes of this Title, see Code of Civil Procedure § 2016.020.

Discovery, generally, see Code of Civil Procedure § 2016.010 et seq.

ARTICLE 2. SCOPE OF DISCOVERY IN SPECIFIC CONTEXTS

Section
2017.210. Insurance carriers; nature, limits or disputes regarding coverage.
2017.220. Sexual harassment, assault or battery allegations; monetary sanctions.

§ 2017.210. Insurance carriers; nature, limits or disputes regarding coverage

A party may obtain discovery of the existence and contents of any agreement under which any insurance carrier may be liable to satisfy in whole or in part a judgment that may be entered in the action or to indemnify or reimburse for payments made to satisfy the judgment. This discovery may include the identity of the carrier and the nature and limits of the coverage. A party may also obtain discovery as to whether that insurance carrier is disputing the agreement's coverage of the claim involved in the action, but not as to the nature and substance of that dispute. Information concerning the insurance agreement is not by reason of disclosure admissible in evidence at trial. *(Added by Stats.2004, c. 182 (A.B.3081), § 23, operative July 1, 2005.)*

Cross References

Action defined for purposes of this Title, see Code of Civil Procedure § 2016.020.

Discovery, generally, see Code of Civil Procedure § 2016.010 et seq.

§ 2017.220. Sexual harassment, assault or battery allegations; monetary sanctions

(a) In any civil action alleging conduct that constitutes sexual harassment, sexual assault, or sexual battery, any party seeking discovery concerning the plaintiff's sexual conduct with individuals other than the alleged perpetrator shall establish specific facts showing that there is good cause for that discovery, and that the matter sought to be discovered is relevant to the subject matter of the action and reasonably calculated to lead to the discovery of admissible evidence. This showing shall be made by a noticed motion, accompanied by a meet and confer declaration under Section 2016.040, and shall not be made or considered by the court at an ex parte hearing.

(b) The court shall impose a monetary sanction under Chapter 7 (commencing with Section 2023.010) against any party, person, or attorney who unsuccessfully makes or opposes a motion for discovery under subdivision (a), unless it finds that the one subject to the sanction acted with substantial justification or that other circumstances make the imposition of the sanction unjust. *(Added by Stats.2004, c. 182 (A.B.3081), § 23, operative July 1, 2005.)*

Cross References

Action defined for purposes of this Title, see Code of Civil Procedure § 2016.020.

Court defined for purposes of this Title, see Code of Civil Procedure § 2016.020.

Discovery, generally, see Code of Civil Procedure § 2016.010 et seq.

ARTICLE 3. VIOLATION OF THE ELDER ABUSE AND DEPENDENT ADULT CIVIL PROTECTION ACT

Section
2017.310. Confidential settlement agreements; recognition or enforcement by court; sealing or redacting defendant's name; enforcement of nondisclosure provisions.
2017.320. Evidence subject to pre-existing protective order; evidence of abuse excluded from protection; use in subsequent proceedings; standard of proof; judicial authority to seal or redact.

§ 2017.310. Confidential settlement agreements; recognition or enforcement by court; sealing or redacting defendant's name; enforcement of nondisclosure provisions

(a) Notwithstanding any other provision of law, it is the policy of the State of California that confidential settlement agreements are disfavored in any civil action the factual foundation for which establishes a cause of action for a violation of the Elder Abuse and Dependent Adult Civil Protection Act (Chapter 11(commencing with Section 15600) of Part 3 of Division 9 of the Welfare and Institutions Code).

(b) Provisions of a confidential settlement agreement described in subdivision (a) may not be recognized or enforced by the court absent a showing of any of the following:

(1) The information is privileged under existing law.

(2) The information is not evidence of abuse of an elder or dependent adult, as described in Sections 15610.30, 15610.57, and 15610.63 of the Welfare and Institutions Code.

(3) The party seeking to uphold the confidentiality of the information has demonstrated that there is a substantial probability that prejudice will result from the disclosure and that the party's interest in the information cannot be adequately protected through redaction.

§ 2017.310

(c) Nothing in paragraph (1), (2), or (3) of subdivision (b) permits the sealing or redacting of a defendant's name in any information made available to the public.

(d) Except as expressly provided in this section, nothing in this section is intended to alter, modify, or amend existing law.

(e) Nothing in this section may be deemed to prohibit the entry or enforcement of that part of a confidentiality agreement, settlement agreement, or stipulated agreement between the parties that requires the nondisclosure of the amount of any money paid in a settlement of a claim.

(f) Nothing in this section applies to or affects an action for professional negligence against a health care provider. *(Added by Stats.2004, c. 182 (A.B.3081), § 23, operative July 1, 2005.)*

Cross References

Action defined for purposes of this Title, see Code of Civil Procedure § 2016.020.
Court defined for purposes of this Title, see Code of Civil Procedure § 2016.020.
Fundamental rights of residents of residential care facilities, see Health and Safety Code § 1569.261 et seq.

§ 2017.320. Evidence subject to pre-existing protective order; evidence of abuse excluded from protection; use in subsequent proceedings; standard of proof; judicial authority to seal or redact

(a) In any civil action the factual foundation for which establishes a cause of action for a violation of the Elder Abuse and Dependent Adult Civil Protection Act (Chapter 11 (commencing with Section 15600) of Part 3 of Division 9 of the Welfare and Institutions Code), any information that is acquired through discovery and is protected from disclosure by a stipulated protective order shall remain subject to the protective order, except for information that is evidence of abuse of an elder or dependent adult as described in Sections 15610.30, 15610.57, and 15610.63 of the Welfare and Institutions Code.

(b) In that instance, after redacting information in the document that is not evidence of abuse of an elder or dependent adult as described in Sections 15610.30, 15610.57, and 15610.63 of the Welfare and Institutions Code, a party may file that particularized information with the court. The party proposing to file the information shall offer to meet and confer with the party from whom the information was obtained at least one week prior to filing that information with the court.

(c) The filing party shall give concurrent notice of the filing with the court and its basis to the party from whom the information was obtained.

(d) Any filed information submitted to the court shall remain confidential under any protective order for 30 days after the filing and shall be part of the public court record thereafter, unless an affected party petitions the court and shows good cause for a court protective order.

(e) The burden of showing good cause shall be on the party seeking the court protective order.

(f) A stipulated protective order may not be recognized or enforced by the court to prevent disclosure of information filed with the court pursuant to subdivision (b), absent a showing of any of the following:

(1) The information is privileged under existing law.

(2) The information is not evidence of abuse of an elder or dependent adult as described in Sections 15610.30, 15610.57, and 15610.63 of the Welfare and Institutions Code.

(3) The party seeking to uphold the confidentiality of the information has demonstrated that there is a substantial probability that prejudice will result from the disclosure and that the party's interest in the information cannot be adequately protected through redaction.

(g) If the court denies the petition for a court protective order, it shall redact any part of the filed information it finds is not evidence of abuse of an elder or dependent adult, as described in Sections 15610.30, 15610.57, and 15610.63 of the Welfare and Institutions Code. Nothing in this subdivision or in paragraph (1), (2), or (3) of subdivision (f) permits the sealing or redacting of a defendant's name in any information made available to the public.

(h) Nothing in this section applies to or affects an action for professional negligence against a health care provider. *(Added by Stats.2004, c. 182 (A.B.3081), § 23, operative July 1, 2005.)*

Cross References

Action defined for purposes of this Title, see Code of Civil Procedure § 2016.020.
Computation of time, see Code of Civil Procedure §§ 12 and 12a; Government Code § 6800 et seq.
Court defined for purposes of this Title, see Code of Civil Procedure § 2016.020.
Discovery, generally, see Code of Civil Procedure § 2016.010 et seq.
Document defined for purposes of this Title, see Code of Civil Procedure § 2016.020.
Notice, actual and constructive, defined, see Civil Code § 18.

CHAPTER 4. ATTORNEY WORK PRODUCT

Section
2018.010. "Client" defined.
2018.020. Policy of the state.
2018.030. Writings and written documentation.
2018.040. Restatement of existing law.
2018.050. Participation in crime or fraud.
2018.060. In camera hearings.
2018.070. Disciplinary proceedings.
2018.080. Breach of duty; actions against attorney by client or former client.

Cross References

Arbitration of attorneys' fees, disclosure of attorney-client communication or attorney's work product, limitation, see Business and Professions Code § 6202.
Beer price posting and marketing regulations, bringing defendant or witness and books and records into court, see Business and Professions Code § 25009.
Criminal procedure, search warrants, see Penal Code § 1524.
Records of medical or dental study of in-hospital staff committee, see Evidence Code § 1156.
Records of medical or psychiatric studies of quality assurance committees, see Evidence Code § 1156.1.
Unfair trade practices, information excluded in criminal prosecution, see Business and Professions Code § 17086.

§ 2018.010. "Client" defined

For purposes of this chapter, "client" means a "client" as defined in Section 951 of the Evidence Code. *(Added by Stats.2004, c. 182 (A.B.3081), § 23, operative July 1, 2005.)*

Cross References

Administrative adjudication, see Government Code § 11511.
Arbitration proceedings, see Code of Civil Procedure § 1283 et seq.
Attorneys, depositions in disciplinary proceedings, see Business and Professions Code § 6115.
Executive department, employment of outside counsel and consent from Attorney General, written notification, see Government Code § 11045.
Privileged communications, see Evidence Code § 911 et seq.
Refusal to obey subpoena as contempt, see Code of Civil Procedure § 2031.
Untimely response to a demand for inspection, objection on the basis of attorney work product, relief from waiver of objection under certain conditions, see Code of Civil Procedure § 2031.300.

§ 2018.020. Policy of the state

It is the policy of the state to do both of the following:

(a) Preserve the rights of attorneys to prepare cases for trial with that degree of privacy necessary to encourage them to prepare their cases thoroughly and to investigate not only the favorable but the unfavorable aspects of those cases.

(b) Prevent attorneys from taking undue advantage of their adversary's industry and efforts. *(Added by Stats.2004, c. 182 (A.B.3081), § 23, operative July 1, 2005.)*

§ 2018.030. Writings and written documentation

(a) A writing that reflects an attorney's impressions, conclusions, opinions, or legal research or theories is not discoverable under any circumstances.

(b) The work product of an attorney, other than a writing described in subdivision (a), is not discoverable unless the court determines that denial of discovery will unfairly prejudice the party seeking discovery in preparing that party's claim or defense or will result in an injustice. *(Added by Stats.2004, c. 182 (A.B.3081), § 23, operative July 1, 2005.)*

Cross References

Court defined for purposes of this Title, see Code of Civil Procedure § 2016.020.
Criminal procedure, search warrants, see Penal Code § 1054.6.
Discovery, generally, see Code of Civil Procedure § 2016.010 et seq.
Writing defined for purposes of this Title, see Code of Civil Procedure § 2016.020.

Research References

Forms

West's California Code Forms, Civil Procedure § 2016.010 Comment, New Discovery Act.
West's California Code Forms, Civil Procedure § 2030.010 Comment, —New Discovery Act.

§ 2018.040. Restatement of existing law

This chapter is intended to be a restatement of existing law relating to protection of work product. It is not intended to expand or reduce the extent to which work product is discoverable under existing law in any action. *(Added by Stats.2004, c. 182 (A.B.3081), § 23, operative July 1, 2005.)*

Cross References

Action defined for purposes of this Title, see Code of Civil Procedure § 2016.020.

§ 2018.050. Participation in crime or fraud

Notwithstanding Section 2018.040, when a lawyer is suspected of knowingly participating in a crime or fraud, there is no protection of work product under this chapter in any official investigation by a law enforcement agency or proceeding or action brought by a public prosecutor in the name of the people of the State of California if the services of the lawyer were sought or obtained to enable or aid anyone to commit or plan to commit a crime or fraud. *(Added by Stats.2004, c. 182 (A.B.3081), § 23, operative July 1, 2005.)*

Cross References

Action defined for purposes of this Title, see Code of Civil Procedure § 2016.020.
Fraud, actual or constructive, see Civil Code §§ 1572 to 1574.

§ 2018.060. In camera hearings

Nothing in this chapter is intended to limit an attorney's ability to request an in camera hearing as provided for in People v. Superior Court (Laff) (2001) 25 Cal.4th 703.[1] *(Added by Stats.2004, c. 182 (A.B.3081), § 23, operative July 1, 2005.)*

[1] 107 Cal.Rptr.2d 328.

Cross References

Court defined for purposes of this Title, see Code of Civil Procedure § 2016.020.

§ 2018.070. Disciplinary proceedings

(a) The State Bar may discover the work product of an attorney against whom disciplinary charges are pending when it is relevant to issues of breach of duty by the lawyer and requisite client approval has been granted.

(b) Where requested and for good cause, discovery under this section shall be subject to a protective order to ensure the confidentiality of the work product except for its use by the State Bar in disciplinary investigations and its consideration under seal in State Bar Court proceedings.

(c) For purposes of this chapter, whenever a client has initiated a complaint against an attorney, the requisite client approval shall be deemed to have been granted. *(Added by Stats.2004, c. 182 (A.B.3081), § 23, operative July 1, 2005.)*

Cross References

Client defined for purposes of this Chapter, see Code of Civil Procedure § 2018.010.
Court defined for purposes of this Title, see Code of Civil Procedure § 2016.020.
Discovery, generally, see Code of Civil Procedure § 2016.010 et seq.

§ 2018.080. Breach of duty; actions against attorney by client or former client

In an action between an attorney and a client or a former client of the attorney, no work product privilege under this chapter exists if the work product is relevant to an issue of breach by the attorney of a duty to the client arising out of the attorney-client relationship. *(Added by Stats.2004, c. 182 (A.B.3081), § 23, operative July 1, 2005.)*

Cross References

Action defined for purposes of this Title, see Code of Civil Procedure § 2016.020.
Client defined for purposes of this Chapter, see Code of Civil Procedure § 2018.010.

CHAPTER 5. METHODS AND SEQUENCE OF DISCOVERY

ARTICLE 1. GENERAL PROVISIONS

Section
2019.010. Approved methods.
2019.020. Sequence and timing; discretion of parties; court order.
2019.030. Court–imposed restrictions; motion; monetary sanction.
2019.040. Application of discovery methods and procedures to electronically stored information.

§ 2019.010. Approved methods

Any party may obtain discovery by one or more of the following methods:

(a) Oral and written depositions.

(b) Interrogatories to a party.

(c) Inspections of documents, things, and places.

(d) Physical and mental examinations.

(e) Requests for admissions.

§ 2019.010

(f) Simultaneous exchanges of expert trial witness information. *(Added by Stats.2004, c. 182 (A.B.3081), § 23, operative July 1, 2005.)*

Cross References

Depositions, see Code of Civil Procedure §§ 2020.010 et seq., 2025.010 et seq., 2026.010, 2027.010, 2028.010 et seq.
Discovery, generally, see Code of Civil Procedure § 2016.010 et seq.
Document defined for purposes of this Title, see Code of Civil Procedure § 2016.020.
Service by mail, extensions of time by place of address, see Code of Civil Procedure § 1013.
Witness defined for purposes of this Code, see Code of Civil Procedure § 1878.

§ 2019.020. Sequence and timing; discretion of parties; court order

(a) Except as otherwise provided by a rule of the Judicial Council, a local court rule, or a local uniform written policy, the methods of discovery may be used in any sequence, and the fact that a party is conducting discovery, whether by deposition or another method, shall not operate to delay the discovery of any other party.

(b) Notwithstanding subdivision (a), on motion and for good cause shown, the court may establish the sequence and timing of discovery for the convenience of parties and witnesses and in the interests of justice. *(Added by Stats.2004, c. 182 (A.B.3081), § 23, operative July 1, 2005.)*

Cross References

Court defined for purposes of this Title, see Code of Civil Procedure § 2016.020.
Depositions, see Code of Civil Procedure §§ 2020.010 et seq., 2025.010 et seq., 2026.010, 2027.010, 2028.010 et seq.
Discovery, generally, see Code of Civil Procedure § 2016.010 et seq.
Judicial Council, see Government Code § 68500 et seq.
Witness defined for purposes of this Code, see Code of Civil Procedure § 1878.

§ 2019.030. Court–imposed restrictions; motion; monetary sanction

(a) The court shall restrict the frequency or extent of use of a discovery method provided in Section 2019.010 if it determines either of the following:

(1) The discovery sought is unreasonably cumulative or duplicative, or is obtainable from some other source that is more convenient, less burdensome, or less expensive.

(2) The selected method of discovery is unduly burdensome or expensive, taking into account the needs of the case, the amount in controversy, and the importance of the issues at stake in the litigation.

(b) The court may make these determinations pursuant to a motion for a protective order by a party or other affected person. This motion shall be accompanied by a meet and confer declaration under Section 2016.040.

(c) The court shall impose a monetary sanction under Chapter 7 (commencing with Section 2023.010) against any party, person, or attorney who unsuccessfully makes or opposes a motion for a protective order, unless it finds that the one subject to the sanction acted with substantial justification or that other circumstances make the imposition of the sanction unjust. *(Added by Stats.2004, c. 182 (A.B.3081), § 23, operative July 1, 2005.)*

Cross References

Court defined for purposes of this Title, see Code of Civil Procedure § 2016.020.
Discovery, generally, see Code of Civil Procedure § 2016.010 et seq.

§ 2019.040. Application of discovery methods and procedures to electronically stored information

(a) When any method of discovery permits the production, inspection, copying, testing, or sampling of documents or tangible things, that method shall also permit the production, inspection, copying, testing, or sampling of electronically stored information.

(b) All procedures available under this title to compel, prevent, or limit the production, inspection, copying, testing, or sampling of documents or tangible things shall be available to compel, prevent, or limit the production, inspection, copying, testing, or sampling of electronically stored information. *(Added by Stats.2012, c. 72 (S.B. 1574), § 14.)*

ARTICLE 2. METHODS AND SEQUENCE OF DISCOVERY IN SPECIFIC CONTEXTS

Section
2019.210. Misappropriation of trade secrets.

§ 2019.210. Misappropriation of trade secrets

In any action alleging the misappropriation of a trade secret under the Uniform Trade Secrets Act (Title 5 (commencing with Section 3426) of Part 1 of Division 4 of the Civil Code), before commencing discovery relating to the trade secret, the party alleging the misappropriation shall identify the trade secret with reasonable particularity subject to any orders that may be appropriate under Section 3426.5 of the Civil Code. *(Added by Stats.2004, c. 182 (A.B.3081), § 23, operative July 1, 2005.)*

Cross References

Action defined for purposes of this Title, see Code of Civil Procedure § 2016.020.
Discovery, generally, see Code of Civil Procedure § 2016.010 et seq.

CHAPTER 6. NONPARTY DISCOVERY

Cross References

Powers of probate referee, subpoenas, see Probate Code § 451.
Powers of probate referee, subpoenas to compel production, see Probate Code § 452.

ARTICLE 1. GENERAL PROVISIONS

Section
2020.010. Persons within the state; approved methods.
2020.020. Deposition subpoena; scope of authority.
2020.030. Application of Evidence Code provisions to deposition subpoena.

§ 2020.010. Persons within the state; approved methods

(a) Any of the following methods may be used to obtain discovery within the state from a person who is not a party to the action in which the discovery is sought:

(1) An oral deposition under Chapter 9 (commencing with Section 2025.010).

(2) A written deposition under Chapter 11 (commencing with Section 2028.010).

(3) A deposition for production of business records and things under Article 4 (commencing with Section 2020.410) or Article 5 (commencing with Section 2020.510).

(b) Except as provided in subdivision (a) of Section 2025.280, the process by which a nonparty is required to provide discovery is a deposition subpoena. *(Added by Stats.2004, c. 182 (A.B.3081), § 23, operative July 1, 2005.)*

Cross References

Action defined for purposes of this Title, see Code of Civil Procedure § 2016.020.
Administrative adjudication, see Government Code § 11511.
Arbitration proceedings, see Code of Civil Procedure § 1283 et seq.

MISCELLANEOUS PROVISIONS § 2020.220

Attorneys, depositions in disciplinary proceedings, see Business and Professions Code § 6115.
Authority of court to take and certify deposition, see Code of Civil Procedure § 179.
Costs, see Code of Civil Procedure § 1033.5.
Criminal proceedings, see Penal Code § 1335 et seq.
Depositions, see Code of Civil Procedure § 2025.010 et seq., § 2026.010, § 2027.010, § 2028.010 et seq.
Destruction of depositions, see Code of Civil Procedure § 1952.
Discovery, generally, see Code of Civil Procedure § 2016.010 et seq.
Dismissal of action, see Code of Civil Procedure § 581 et seq.
Examination of witnesses, general rules, see Evidence Code § 760 et seq.
Examination of witnesses on commission, see Penal Code § 1349 et seq.
Impeachment of witnesses, see Evidence Code §§ 770, 785 et seq., 1235, 1324.
Means of production, deposition officers and employment records, subpoenas, see Code of Civil Procedure § 1985.6.
Monetary sanctions, see Code of Civil Procedure § 2023.050.
Prisoners, see Penal Code §§ 2622, 2623.
Privileged communications, see Evidence Code § 911 et seq.
Production of business records, see Evidence Code § 1560 et seq.
Production of evidence, means of production, see Code of Civil Procedure § 1985 et seq.
Refusal to obey subpoena as contempt, see Code of Civil Procedure § 2031.010 et seq.
Study made by in-hospital staff committee, discovery, see Evidence Code § 1156.
Unfair trade practices act proceedings, authority to take depositions, see Business and Professions Code § 17083.
Violation of court order as contempt, see Code of Civil Procedure § 1209.

Research References

Forms

West's California Judicial Council Forms SUBP–025, Notice to Consumer or Employee and Objection.

§ 2020.020. Deposition subpoena; scope of authority

A deposition subpoena may command any of the following:

(a) Only the attendance and the testimony of the deponent, under Article 3 (commencing with Section 2020.310).

(b) Only the production of business records for copying, under Article 4 (commencing with Section 2020.410).

(c) The attendance and the testimony of the deponent, as well as the production of business records, other documents, electronically stored information, and tangible things, under Article 5 (commencing with Section 2020.510). *(Added by Stats.2004, c. 182 (A.B.3081), § 23, operative July 1, 2005. Amended by Stats.2012, c. 72 (S.B.1574), § 15.)*

Cross References

Depositions, see Code of Civil Procedure §§ 2020.010 et seq., 2025.010 et seq., 2026.010, 2027.010, 2028.010 et seq.
Document defined for purposes of this Title, see Code of Civil Procedure § 2016.020.
Recording,
Constructive notice, conveyances of real property or estate for years, see Civil Code § 1213.
Instruments or judgments, documents to be recorded and manner of recording, see Government Code § 27320 et seq., § 27280 et seq.
Property transfers, place of recordation, see Civil Code § 1169.

§ 2020.030. Application of Evidence Code provisions to deposition subpoena

Except as modified in this chapter, the provisions of Chapter 2 (commencing with Section 1985) of Title 3 of Part 4 of this code, and of Article 4 (commencing with Section 1560) of Chapter 2 of Division 11 of the Evidence Code, apply to a deposition subpoena. *(Added by Stats.2004, c. 182 (A.B.3081), § 23, operative July 1, 2005.)*

Cross References

Depositions, see Code of Civil Procedure §§ 2020.010 et seq., 2025.010 et seq., 2026.010, 2027.010, 2028.010 et seq.

ARTICLE 2. PROCEDURES APPLICABLE TO ALL TYPES OF DEPOSITION SUBPOENAS

Section
2020.210. Issuance by court clerk; alternative method of issuance.
2020.220. Service of deposition subpoena; timing; persons authorized to serve; scope of subpoena authority; subpoena of electronically stored information.
2020.230. Personal attendance of deponent; witness and mileage fees; custodian of records.
2020.240. Failure to obey subpoena; contempt; punishment; compliance.

§ 2020.210. Issuance by court clerk; alternative method of issuance

(a) The clerk of the court in which the action is pending shall issue a deposition subpoena signed and sealed, but otherwise in blank, to a party requesting it, who shall fill it in before service.

(b) Instead of a court-issued deposition subpoena, an attorney of record for any party may sign and issue a deposition subpoena. A deposition subpoena issued under this subdivision need not be sealed. A copy may be served on the nonparty, and the attorney may retain the original. *(Added by Stats.2004, c. 182 (A.B.3081), § 23, operative July 1, 2005.)*

Cross References

Action defined for purposes of this Title, see Code of Civil Procedure § 2016.020.
Court defined for purposes of this Title, see Code of Civil Procedure § 2016.020.
Depositions, see Code of Civil Procedure §§ 2020.010 et seq., 2025.010 et seq., 2026.010, 2027.010, 2028.010 et seq.

§ 2020.220. Service of deposition subpoena; timing; persons authorized to serve; scope of subpoena authority; subpoena of electronically stored information

(a) Subject to subdivision (c) of Section 2020.410, service of a deposition subpoena shall be effected a sufficient time in advance of the deposition to provide the deponent a reasonable opportunity to locate and produce any designated business records, documents, electronically stored information, and tangible things, as described in Article 4 (commencing with Section 2020.410), and, where personal attendance is commanded, a reasonable time to travel to the place of deposition.

(b) Any person may serve the subpoena by personal delivery of a copy of it as follows:

(1) If the deponent is a natural person, to that person.

(2) If the deponent is an organization, to any officer, director, custodian of records, or to any agent or employee authorized by the organization to accept service of a subpoena.

(c) Personal service of any deposition subpoena is effective to require all of the following of any deponent who is a resident of California at the time of service:

(1) Personal attendance and testimony, if the subpoena so specifies.

(2) Any specified production, inspection, testing, and sampling.

(3) The deponent's attendance at a court session to consider any issue arising out of the deponent's refusal to be sworn, or to answer any question, or to produce specified items, or to permit inspection

§ 2020.220

or photocopying, if the subpoena so specifies, or specified testing and sampling of the items produced.

(d) Unless the subpoenaing party and the subpoenaed person otherwise agree or the court otherwise orders, the following shall apply:

(1) If a subpoena requiring production of electronically stored information does not specify a form or forms for producing a type of electronically stored information, the person subpoenaed shall produce the information in the form or forms in which it is ordinarily maintained or in a form that is reasonably usable.

(2) A subpoenaed person need not produce the same electronically stored information in more than one form.

(e) The subpoenaed person opposing the production, inspection, copying, testing, or sampling of electronically stored information on the basis that the information is from a source that is not reasonably accessible because of undue burden or expense shall bear the burden of demonstrating that the information is from a source that is not reasonably accessible because of undue burden or expense.

(f) If the person from whom discovery of electronically stored information is subpoenaed establishes that the information is from a source that is not reasonably accessible because of undue burden or expense, the court may nonetheless order discovery if the subpoenaing party shows good cause, subject to any limitations imposed under subdivision (i).

(g) If the court finds good cause for the production of electronically stored information from a source that is not reasonably accessible, the court may set conditions for the discovery of the electronically stored information, including allocation of the expense of discovery.

(h) If necessary, the subpoenaed person, at the reasonable expense of the subpoenaing party, shall, through detection devices, translate any data compilations included in the subpoena into a reasonably usable form.

(i) The court shall limit the frequency or extent of discovery of electronically stored information, even from a source that is reasonably accessible, if the court determines that any of the following conditions exists:

(1) It is possible to obtain the information from some other source that is more convenient, less burdensome, or less expensive.

(2) The discovery sought is unreasonably cumulative or duplicative.

(3) The party seeking discovery has had ample opportunity by discovery in the action to obtain the information sought.

(4) The likely burden or expense of the proposed discovery outweighs the likely benefit, taking into account the amount in controversy, the resources of the parties, the importance of the issues in the litigation, and the importance of the requested discovery in resolving the issues.

(j) If a subpoenaed person notifies the subpoenaing party that electronically stored information produced pursuant to a subpoena is subject to a claim of privilege or of protection as attorney work product, as described in Section 2031.285, the provisions of Section 2031.285 shall apply.

(k) A party serving a subpoena requiring the production of electronically stored information shall take reasonable steps to avoid imposing undue burden or expense on a person subject to the subpoena.

(l) An order of the court requiring compliance with a subpoena issued under this section shall protect a person who is neither a party nor a party's officer from undue burden or expense resulting from compliance.

(m)(1) Absent exceptional circumstances, the court shall not impose sanctions on a subpoenaed person or any attorney of a subpoenaed person for failure to provide electronically stored information that has been lost, damaged, altered, or overwritten as the result of the routine, good faith operation of an electronic information system.

(2) The subdivision shall not be construed to alter any obligation to preserve discoverable information. *(Added by Stats.2004, c. 182 (A.B.3081), § 23, operative July 1, 2005. Amended by Stats.2012, c. 72 (S.B.1574), § 16.)*

Cross References

Court defined for purposes of this Title, see Code of Civil Procedure § 2016.020.
Depositions, see Code of Civil Procedure §§ 2020.010 et seq., 2025.010 et seq., 2026.010, 2027.010, 2028.010 et seq.
Document defined for purposes of this Title, see Code of Civil Procedure § 2016.020.
Recording,
  Constructive notice, conveyances of real property or estate for years, see Civil Code § 1213.
  Instruments or judgments, documents to be recorded and manner of recording, see Government Code § 27320 et seq., § 27280 et seq.
Property transfers, place of recordation, see Civil Code § 1169.

§ 2020.230. Personal attendance of deponent; witness and mileage fees; custodian of records

(a) If a deposition subpoena requires the personal attendance of the deponent, under Article 3 (commencing with Section 2020.310) or Article 5 (commencing with Section 2020.510), the party noticing the deposition shall pay to the deponent in cash or by check the same witness fee and mileage required by Chapter 1 (commencing with Section 68070) of Title 8 of the Government Code for attendance and testimony before the court in which the action is pending. This payment, whether or not demanded by the deponent, shall be made, at the option of the party noticing the deposition, either at the time of service of the deposition subpoena, or at the time the deponent attends for the taking of testimony.

(b) Service of a deposition subpoena that does not require the personal attendance of a custodian of records or other qualified person, under Article 4 (commencing with Section 2020.410), shall be accompanied, whether or not demanded by the deponent, by a payment in cash or by check of the witness fee required by paragraph (6) of subdivision (b) of Section 1563 of the Evidence Code. *(Added by Stats.2004, c. 182 (A.B.3081), § 23, operative July 1, 2005.)*

Cross References

Action defined for purposes of this Title, see Code of Civil Procedure § 2016.020.
Court defined for purposes of this Title, see Code of Civil Procedure § 2016.020.
Depositions, see Code of Civil Procedure §§ 2020.010 et seq., 2025.010 et seq., 2026.010, 2027.010, 2028.010 et seq.
Witness defined for purposes of this Code, see Code of Civil Procedure § 1878.

§ 2020.240. Failure to obey subpoena; contempt; punishment; compliance

A deponent who disobeys a deposition subpoena in any manner described in subdivision (c) of Section 2020.220 may be punished for contempt under Chapter 7 (commencing with Section 2023.010) without the necessity of a prior order of court directing compliance by the witness. The deponent is also subject to the forfeiture and the payment of damages set forth in Section 1992. *(Added by Stats.2004, c. 182 (A.B.3081), § 23, operative July 1, 2005.)*

Cross References

Court defined for purposes of this Title, see Code of Civil Procedure § 2016.020.
Depositions, see Code of Civil Procedure §§ 2020.010 et seq., 2025.010 et seq., 2026.010, 2027.010, 2028.010 et seq.
Production of business records, compliance with subpoena duces tecum for business records, see Evidence Code § 1560.

MISCELLANEOUS PROVISIONS § 2020.420

Witness defined for purposes of this Code, see Code of Civil Procedure § 1878.

ARTICLE 3. SUBPOENA COMMANDING ONLY ATTENDANCE AND TESTIMONY OF THE DEPONENT

Section
2020.310. Contents of subpoena; summarization of enumerated topics; recordation at hearing; visual displays; necessity of attendance by agents or employees of deponent.

§ 2020.310. Contents of subpoena; summarization of enumerated topics; recordation at hearing; visual displays; necessity of attendance by agents or employees of deponent

The following rules apply to a deposition subpoena that commands only the attendance and the testimony of the deponent:

(a) The subpoena shall specify the time when and the place where the deponent is commanded to attend the deposition.

(b) The subpoena shall set forth a summary of all of the following:

(1) The nature of a deposition.

(2) The rights and duties of the deponent.

(3) The penalties for disobedience of a deposition subpoena, as described in Section 2020.240.

(c) If the deposition will be recorded using audio or video technology by, or at the direction of, the noticing party under Section 2025.340, the subpoena shall state that it will be recorded in that manner.

(d) If the deposition testimony will be conducted using instant visual display, the subpoena shall state that it will be conducted in that manner.

(e) If the deponent is an organization, the subpoena shall describe with reasonable particularity the matters on which examination is requested. The subpoena shall also advise the organization of its duty to make the designation of employees or agents who will attend the deposition, as described in Section 2025.230. *(Added by Stats. 2004, c. 182 (A.B.3081), § 23, operative July 1, 2005.)*

Cross References

Depositions, see Code of Civil Procedure §§ 2020.010 et seq., 2025.010 et seq., 2026.010, 2027.010, 2028.010 et seq.

Research References

Forms

West's California Judicial Council Forms SUBP-015, Deposition Subpena for Personal Appearance.

West's California Judicial Council Forms SUBP-040, Deposition Subpena for Personal Appearance in Action Pending Outside California.

ARTICLE 4. SUBPOENA COMMANDING ONLY PRODUCTION OF BUSINESS RECORDS FOR COPYING

Section
2020.410. Specificity of requests; production of business records and electronically stored information; certification by custodian; personal records pertaining to consumers.
2020.420. Professional photocopier services; qualifications; objections.
2020.430. Delivery for copying; requirements; time to deliver; application of Evidence Code concerning inspection of records.
2020.440. Distribution of copies to parties; deposition officer duties; additional copies.

§ 2020.410. Specificity of requests; production of business records and electronically stored information; certification by custodian; personal records pertaining to consumers

(a) A deposition subpoena that commands only the production of business records for copying shall designate the business records to be produced either by specifically describing each individual item or by reasonably particularizing each category of item, and shall specify the form in which any electronically stored information is to be produced, if a particular form is desired.

(b) Notwithstanding subdivision (a), specific information identifiable only to the deponent's records system, like a policy number or the date when a consumer interacted with the witness, is not required.

(c) A deposition subpoena that commands only the production of business records for copying need not be accompanied by an affidavit or declaration showing good cause for the production of the business records designated in it. It shall be directed to the custodian of those records or another person qualified to certify the records. It shall command compliance in accordance with Section 2020.430 on a date that is no earlier than 20 days after the issuance, or 15 days after the service, of the deposition subpoena, whichever date is later.

(d) If, under Section 1985.3 or 1985.6, the one to whom the deposition subpoena is directed is a witness, and the business records described in the deposition subpoena are personal records pertaining to a consumer, the service of the deposition subpoena shall be accompanied either by a copy of the proof of service of the notice to the consumer described in subdivision (e) of Section 1985.3, or subdivision (b) of Section 1985.6, as applicable, or by the consumer's written authorization to release personal records described in paragraph (2) of subdivision (c) of Section 1985.3, or paragraph (2) of subdivision (c) of Section 1985.6, as applicable. *(Added by Stats.2004, c. 182 (A.B.3081), § 23, operative July 1, 2005. Amended by Stats.2012, c. 72 (S.B.1574), § 17.)*

Cross References

Computation of time, see Code of Civil Procedure §§ 12 and 12a; Government Code § 6800 et seq.
Depositions, see Code of Civil Procedure §§ 2020.010 et seq., 2025.010 et seq., 2026.010, 2027.010, 2028.010 et seq.
Monetary sanctions, see Code of Civil Procedure § 2023.050.
Notice, actual and constructive, defined, see Civil Code § 18.
Proof of service, see Code of Civil Procedure § 417.10 et seq.
Witness defined for purposes of this Code, see Code of Civil Procedure § 1878.

Research References

Forms

West's California Code Forms, Civil Procedure § 2020.410 Form 1, Evidence—Discovery—Deposition Subpena for Production of Business Records—Proof of Service—Official Form.
West's California Judicial Council Forms SUBP-010, Deposition Subpena for Production of Business Records.
West's California Judicial Council Forms SUBP-035, Subpena for Production of Business Records in Action Pending Outside California.

§ 2020.420. Professional photocopier services; qualifications; objections

The officer for a deposition seeking discovery only of business records for copying under this article shall be a professional photocopier registered under Chapter 20 (commencing with Section 22450) of Division 8 of the Business and Professions Code, or a person exempted from the registration requirements of that chapter under Section 22451 of the Business and Professions Code. This deposition officer shall not be financially interested in the action, or a relative or employee of any attorney of the parties. Any objection to the qualifications of the deposition officer is waived unless made before the date of production or as soon thereafter as the ground for that objection becomes known or could be discovered by reasonable

§ 2020.420

diligence. *(Added by Stats.2004, c. 182 (A.B.3081), § 23, operative July 1, 2005.)*

Cross References

Action defined for purposes of this Title, see Code of Civil Procedure § 2016.020.

Depositions, see Code of Civil Procedure §§ 2020.010 et seq., 2025.010 et seq., 2026.010, 2027.010, 2028.010 et seq.

Discovery, generally, see Code of Civil Procedure § 2016.010 et seq.

Production of business records, compliance with subpoena duces tecum for business records, see Evidence Code § 1560.

§ 2020.430. Delivery for copying; requirements; time to deliver; application of Evidence Code concerning inspection of records

(a) Except as provided in subdivision (e), if a deposition subpoena commands only the production of business records for copying, the custodian of the records or other qualified person shall, in person, by messenger, or by mail, deliver both of the following only to the deposition officer specified in the subpoena:

(1) A true, legible, and durable copy of the records.

(2) An affidavit in compliance with Section 1561 of the Evidence Code.

(b) If the delivery required by subdivision (a) is made to the office of the deposition officer, the records shall be enclosed, sealed, and directed as described in subdivision (c) of Section 1560 of the Evidence Code.

(c) If the delivery required by subdivision (a) is made at the office of the business whose records are the subject of the deposition subpoena, the custodian of those records or other qualified person shall do one of the following:

(1) Permit the deposition officer specified in the deposition subpoena to make a copy of the originals of the designated business records during normal business hours, as defined in subdivision (e) of Section 1560 of the Evidence Code.

(2) Deliver to the deposition officer a true, legible, and durable copy of the records on receipt of payment in cash or by check, by or on behalf of the party serving the deposition subpoena, of the reasonable costs of preparing that copy, together with an itemized statement of the cost of preparation, as determined under subdivision (b) of Section 1563 of the Evidence Code. This copy need not be delivered in a sealed envelope.

(d) Unless the parties, and if the records are those of a consumer as defined in Section 1985.3 or 1985.6, the consumer, stipulate to an earlier date, the custodian of the records shall not deliver to the deposition officer the records that are the subject of the deposition subpoena prior to the date and time specified in the deposition subpoena. The following legend shall appear in boldface type on the deposition subpoena immediately following the date and time specified for production: "Do not release the requested records to the deposition officer prior to the date and time stated above."

(e) This section does not apply if the subpoena directs the deponent to make the records available for inspection or copying by the subpoenaing party's attorney or a representative of that attorney at the witness' business address under subdivision (e) of Section 1560 of the Evidence Code.

(f) The provisions of Section 1562 of the Evidence Code concerning the admissibility of the affidavit of the custodian or other qualified person apply to a deposition subpoena served under this article. *(Added by Stats.2004, c. 182 (A.B.3081), § 23, operative July 1, 2005.)*

Cross References

Depositions, see Code of Civil Procedure §§ 2020.010 et seq., 2025.010 et seq., 2026.010, 2027.010, 2028.010 et seq.

Witness defined for purposes of this Code, see Code of Civil Procedure § 1878.

§ 2020.440. Distribution of copies to parties; deposition officer duties; additional copies

Promptly on or after the deposition date and after the receipt or the making of a copy of business records under this article, the deposition officer shall provide that copy to the party at whose instance the deposition subpoena was served, and a copy of those records to any other party to the action who then or subsequently, within a period of six months following the settlement of the case, notifies the deposition officer that the party desires to purchase a copy of those records. *(Added by Stats.2004, c. 182 (A.B.3081), § 23, operative July 1, 2005.)*

Cross References

Action defined for purposes of this Title, see Code of Civil Procedure § 2016.020.

Depositions, see Code of Civil Procedure §§ 2020.010 et seq., 2025.010 et seq., 2026.010, 2027.010, 2028.010 et seq.

Research References

Forms

West's California Judicial Council Forms SUBP–010, Deposition Subpena for Production of Business Records.

West's California Judicial Council Forms SUBP–035, Subpena for Production of Business Records in Action Pending Outside California.

ARTICLE 5. SUBPOENA COMMANDING BOTH PRODUCTION OF BUSINESS RECORDS AND ATTENDANCE AND TESTIMONY OF THE DEPONENT

Section

2020.510. Contents of subpoena; necessity of affidavit or declaration showing good cause; personal records pertaining to consumers; employment records pertaining to employees.

§ 2020.510. Contents of subpoena; necessity of affidavit or declaration showing good cause; personal records pertaining to consumers; employment records pertaining to employees

(a) A deposition subpoena that commands the attendance and the testimony of the deponent, as well as the production of business records, documents, electronically stored information, and tangible things, shall:

(1) Comply with the requirements of Section 2020.310.

(2) Designate the business records, documents, electronically stored information, and tangible things to be produced either by specifically describing each individual item or by reasonably particularizing each category of item.

(3) Specify any testing or sampling that is being sought.

(4) Specify the form in which any electronically stored information is to be produced, if a particular form is desired.

(b) A deposition subpoena under subdivision (a) need not be accompanied by an affidavit or declaration showing good cause for the production of the documents and things designated.

(c) If, as described in Section 1985.3, the person to whom the deposition subpoena is directed is a witness, and the business records described in the deposition subpoena are personal records pertaining to a consumer, the service of the deposition subpoena shall be accompanied either by a copy of the proof of service of the notice to the consumer described in subdivision (e) of Section 1985.3, or by the consumer's written authorization to release personal records described in paragraph (2) of subdivision (c) of Section 1985.3.

(d) If, as described in Section 1985.6, the person to whom the deposition subpoena is directed is a witness and the business records described in the deposition subpoena are employment records pertaining to an employee, the service of the deposition subpoena shall be accompanied either by a copy of the proof of service of the notice to the employee described in subdivision (e) of Section 1985.6, or by the employee's written authorization to release personal records described in paragraph (2) of subdivision (c) of Section 1985.6. *(Added by Stats.2004, c. 182 (A.B.3081), § 23, operative July 1, 2005. Amended by Stats.2007, c. 113 (A.B.1126), § 4; Stats.2012, c. 72 (S.B.1574), § 18.)*

Cross References

Depositions, see Code of Civil Procedure §§ 2020.010 et seq., 2025.010 et seq., 2026.010, 2027.010, 2028.010 et seq.
Document defined for purposes of this Title, see Code of Civil Procedure § 2016.020.
Monetary sanctions, see Code of Civil Procedure § 2023.050.
Notice, actual and constructive, defined, see Civil Code § 18.
Proof of service, see Code of Civil Procedure § 417.10 et seq.
Recording,
  Constructive notice, conveyances of real property or estate for years, see Civil Code § 1213.
  Instruments or judgments, documents to be recorded and manner of recording, see Government Code § 27320 et seq., § 27280 et seq.
  Property transfers, place of recordation, see Civil Code § 1169.
Witness defined for purposes of this Code, see Code of Civil Procedure § 1878.

Research References

Forms

West's California Judicial Council Forms SUBP–020, Deposition Subpena for Personal Appearance and Production of Documents and Things.
West's California Judicial Council Forms SUBP–045, Deposition Subpena for Personal Appearance and Production of Documents, Electronically Stored Information, and Things in Action Pending Outside California.

CHAPTER 7. SANCTIONS

Section
2023.010. Conduct subject to sanctions.
2023.020. Monetary sanctions for failure to confer.
2023.030. Monetary sanctions; issue sanctions; evidence sanctions; terminating sanctions; contempt sanctions; electronically stored information sanctions.
2023.040. Requests for sanctions; form and supporting documents.
2023.050. Monetary sanctions; failure to respond in good faith to document request; production of requested documents within 7 days of motion to compel; failure to meet and confer.

§ 2023.010. Conduct subject to sanctions

Misuses of the discovery process include, but are not limited to, the following:

(a) Persisting, over objection and without substantial justification, in an attempt to obtain information or materials that are outside the scope of permissible discovery.

(b) Using a discovery method in a manner that does not comply with its specified procedures.

(c) Employing a discovery method in a manner or to an extent that causes unwarranted annoyance, embarrassment, or oppression, or undue burden and expense.

(d) Failing to respond or to submit to an authorized method of discovery.

(e) Making, without substantial justification, an unmeritorious objection to discovery.

(f) Making an evasive response to discovery.

(g) Disobeying a court order to provide discovery.

(h) Making or opposing, unsuccessfully and without substantial justification, a motion to compel or to limit discovery.

(i) Failing to confer in person, by telephone, or by letter with an opposing party or attorney in a reasonable and good faith attempt to resolve informally any dispute concerning discovery, if the section governing a particular discovery motion requires the filing of a declaration stating facts showing that an attempt at informal resolution has been made. *(Added by Stats.2004, c. 182 (A.B.3081), § 23, operative July 1, 2005.)*

Cross References

Court defined for purposes of this Title, see Code of Civil Procedure § 2016.020.
Discovery, generally, see Code of Civil Procedure § 2016.010 et seq.
Dismissal of action, see now Code of Civil Procedure § 399
Examination of witnesses on commission, see Penal Code § 1349 et seq.
Motion to compel answers or produce documents or items, authority to impose monetary sanctions under this section against a party, person or attorney, see Code of Civil Procedure § 2025.480.
Untimely response to a demand for inspection, authority to impose monetary sanctions under this section against a party, person or attorney, see Code of Civil Procedure § 2031.300.
Violation of court order as contempt, see Code of Civil Procedure § 1209.

Research References

Forms

West's California Code Forms, Civil Procedure § 93 Form 3, Economic Litigation for Limited Civil Cases—Notice of Motion for Order Compelling Response to Case Questionnaire.
West's California Code Forms, Civil Procedure § 93 Form 5, Economic Litigation for Limited Civil Cases—Order Compelling Response to Case Questionnaire.

§ 2023.020. Monetary sanctions for failure to confer

Notwithstanding the outcome of the particular discovery motion, the court shall impose a monetary sanction ordering that any party or attorney who fails to confer as required pay the reasonable expenses, including attorney's fees, incurred by anyone as a result of that conduct. *(Added by Stats.2004, c. 182 (A.B.3081), § 23, operative July 1, 2005.)*

Cross References

Attorney's fees and costs, generally, see Code of Civil Procedure § 1021.
Court defined for purposes of this Title, see Code of Civil Procedure § 2016.020.
Discovery, generally, see Code of Civil Procedure § 2016.010 et seq.

§ 2023.030. Monetary sanctions; issue sanctions; evidence sanctions; terminating sanctions; contempt sanctions; electronically stored information sanctions

To the extent authorized by the chapter governing any particular discovery method or any other provision of this title, the court, after notice to any affected party, person, or attorney, and after opportunity for hearing, may impose the following sanctions against anyone engaging in conduct that is a misuse of the discovery process:

(a) The court may impose a monetary sanction ordering that one engaging in the misuse of the discovery process, or any attorney advising that conduct, or both pay the reasonable expenses, including attorney's fees, incurred by anyone as a result of that conduct. The court may also impose this sanction on one unsuccessfully asserting that another has engaged in the misuse of the discovery process, or on any attorney who advised that assertion, or on both. If a monetary sanction is authorized by any provision of this title, the court shall impose that sanction unless it finds that the one subject to the sanction acted with substantial justification or that other circumstances make the imposition of the sanction unjust.

(b) The court may impose an issue sanction ordering that designated facts shall be taken as established in the action in accordance with the claim of the party adversely affected by the misuse of the discovery process. The court may also impose an issue sanction by an order prohibiting any party engaging in the misuse of the discovery process from supporting or opposing designated claims or defenses.

(c) The court may impose an evidence sanction by an order prohibiting any party engaging in the misuse of the discovery process from introducing designated matters in evidence.

(d) The court may impose a terminating sanction by one of the following orders:

(1) An order striking out the pleadings or parts of the pleadings of any party engaging in the misuse of the discovery process.

(2) An order staying further proceedings by that party until an order for discovery is obeyed.

(3) An order dismissing the action, or any part of the action, of that party.

(4) An order rendering a judgment by default against that party.

(e) The court may impose a contempt sanction by an order treating the misuse of the discovery process as a contempt of court.

(f)(1) Notwithstanding subdivision (a), or any other section of this title, absent exceptional circumstances, the court shall not impose sanctions on a party or any attorney of a party for failure to provide electronically stored information that has been lost, damaged, altered, or overwritten as the result of the routine, good faith operation of an electronic information system.

(2) This subdivision shall not be construed to alter any obligation to preserve discoverable information. *(Added by Stats.2004, c. 182 (A.B.3081), § 23, operative July 1, 2005. Amended by Stats.2012, c. 72 (S.B.1574), § 19.)*

Cross References

Action defined for purposes of this Title, see Code of Civil Procedure § 2016.020.
Attorney's fees and costs, generally, see Code of Civil Procedure § 1021.
Court defined for purposes of this Title, see Code of Civil Procedure § 2016.020.
Discovery, generally, see Code of Civil Procedure § 2016.010 et seq.
Notice, actual and constructive, defined, see Civil Code § 18.

Research References

Forms

Asset Protection: Legal Planning, Strategies and Forms ¶ 12.04, Discharge.

§ 2023.040. Requests for sanctions; form and supporting documents

A request for a sanction shall, in the notice of motion, identify every person, party, and attorney against whom the sanction is sought, and specify the type of sanction sought. The notice of motion shall be supported by a memorandum of points and authorities, and accompanied by a declaration setting forth facts supporting the amount of any monetary sanction sought. *(Added by Stats.2004, c. 182 (A.B.3081), § 23, operative July 1, 2005.)*

Cross References

Notice, actual and constructive, defined, see Civil Code § 18.

§ 2023.050. Monetary sanctions; failure to respond in good faith to document request; production of requested documents within 7 days of motion to compel; failure to meet and confer

(a) Notwithstanding any other law, and in addition to any other sanctions imposed pursuant to this chapter, a court shall impose a two hundred and fifty dollar ($250) sanction, payable to the requesting party, upon a party, person, or attorney if, upon reviewing a request for a sanction made pursuant to Section 2023.040, the court finds any of the following:

(1) The party, person, or attorney did not respond in good faith to a request for the production of documents made pursuant to Section 2020.010, 2020.410, 2020.510, or 2025.210, or to an inspection demand made pursuant to Section 2031.010.

(2) The party, person, or attorney produced requested documents within seven days before the court was scheduled to hear a motion to compel production of the records pursuant to Section 2025.450, 2025.480, or 2031.320 that is filed by the requesting party as a result of the other party, person, or attorney's failure to respond in good faith.

(3) The party, person, or attorney failed to confer in person, by telephone, letter, or other means of communication in writing, as defined in Section 250 of the Evidence Code, with the party or attorney requesting the documents in a reasonable and good faith attempt to resolve informally any dispute concerning the request.

(b) Notwithstanding paragraph (3) of subdivision (*o*) of Section 6068 of the Business and Professions Code, the court may, in its discretion, require an attorney who is sanctioned pursuant to subdivision (a) to report the sanction, in writing, to the State Bar within 30 days of the imposition of the sanction.

(c) The court may excuse the imposition of the sanction required by subdivision (a) if the court makes written findings that the one subject to the sanction acted with substantial justification or that other circumstances make the imposition of the sanction unjust.

(d) Sanctions pursuant to this section shall be imposed only after notice to the party, person, or attorney against whom the sanction is proposed to be imposed and opportunity for that party, person, or attorney to be heard.

(e) For purposes of this section, there is a rebuttable presumption that a natural person acted in good faith if that person was not represented by an attorney in the action at the time the conduct that is sanctionable under subdivision (a) occurred. This presumption may only be overcome by clear and convincing evidence. *(Added by Stats.2019, c. 836 (S.B.17), § 2, eff. Jan. 1, 2020.)*

CHAPTER 8. TIME FOR COMPLETION OF DISCOVERY

Section
2024.010. Completion date.
2024.020. Discovery cutoff.
2024.030. Expert witnesses; time to complete discovery; motions prior to trial.
2024.040. Application to arbitration proceedings; application to summary proceedings to obtain possession of real property or eminent domain.
2024.050. Motions to complete discovery closer to initial trial date; reopening of discovery; discretion of court; monetary sanctions.
2024.060. Agreements to extend time or reopen discovery; written agreement.

§ 2024.010. Completion date

As used in this chapter, discovery is considered completed on the day a response is due or on the day a deposition begins. *(Added by Stats.2004, c. 182 (A.B.3081), § 23, operative July 1, 2005.)*

Cross References

Depositions, see Code of Civil Procedure §§ 2020.010 et seq., 2025.010 et seq., 2026.010, 2027.010, 2028.010 et seq.
Discovery, generally, see Code of Civil Procedure § 2016.010 et seq.

Expert witnesses, exchange of information by parties, see Code of Civil Procedure § 2034.

§ 2024.020. Discovery cutoff

(a) Except as otherwise provided in this chapter, any party shall be entitled as a matter of right to complete discovery proceedings on or before the 30th day, and to have motions concerning discovery heard on or before the 15th day, before the date initially set for the trial of the action.

(b) Except as provided in Section 2024.050, a continuance or postponement of the trial date does not operate to reopen discovery proceedings. *(Added by Stats.2004, c. 182 (A.B.3081), § 23, operative July 1, 2005.)*

Cross References

Action defined for purposes of this Title, see Code of Civil Procedure § 2016.020.
Discovery, generally, see Code of Civil Procedure § 2016.010 et seq.

§ 2024.030. Expert witnesses; time to complete discovery; motions prior to trial

Any party shall be entitled as a matter of right to complete discovery proceedings pertaining to a witness identified under Chapter 18 (commencing with Section 2034.010) on or before the 15th day, and to have motions concerning that discovery heard on or before the 10th day, before the date initially set for the trial of the action. *(Added by Stats.2004, c. 182 (A.B.3081), § 23, operative July 1, 2005.)*

Cross References

Action defined for purposes of this Title, see Code of Civil Procedure § 2016.020.
Discovery, generally, see Code of Civil Procedure § 2016.010 et seq.
Witness defined for purposes of this Code, see Code of Civil Procedure § 1878.

§ 2024.040. Application to arbitration proceedings; application to summary proceedings to obtain possession of real property or eminent domain

(a) The time limit on completing discovery in an action to be arbitrated under Chapter 2.5 (commencing with Section 1141.10) of Title 3 of Part 3 is subject to Judicial Council Rule. After an award in a case ordered to judicial arbitration, completion of discovery is limited by Section 1141.24.

(b) This chapter does not apply to either of the following:

(1) Summary proceedings for obtaining possession of real property governed by Chapter 4 (commencing with Section 1159) of Title 3 of Part 3. Except as provided in Sections 2024.050 and 2024.060, discovery in these proceedings shall be completed on or before the fifth day before the date set for trial.

(2) Eminent domain proceedings governed by Title 7 (commencing with Section 1230.010) of Part 3. *(Added by Stats.2004, c. 182 (A.B.3081), § 23, operative July 1, 2005. Amended by Stats.2012, c. 162 (S.B.1171), § 17.)*

Cross References

Action defined for purposes of this Title, see Code of Civil Procedure § 2016.020.
Arbitration, generally, see Code of Civil Procedure § 1280 et seq.
Discovery, generally, see Code of Civil Procedure § 2016.010 et seq.
Eminent domain, generally, see Cal. Const. Art. 1, § 19; Code of Civil Procedure § 1240.010 et seq.; Government Code §§ 15850 et seq., 40404; Public Utilities Code § 619.

Judicial Council, see Government Code § 68500 et seq.

§ 2024.050. Motions to complete discovery closer to initial trial date; reopening of discovery; discretion of court; monetary sanctions

(a) On motion of any party, the court may grant leave to complete discovery proceedings, or to have a motion concerning discovery heard, closer to the initial trial date, or to reopen discovery after a new trial date has been set. This motion shall be accompanied by a meet and confer declaration under Section 2016.040.

(b) In exercising its discretion to grant or deny this motion, the court shall take into consideration any matter relevant to the leave requested, including, but not limited to, the following:

(1) The necessity and the reasons for the discovery.

(2) The diligence or lack of diligence of the party seeking the discovery or the hearing of a discovery motion, and the reasons that the discovery was not completed or that the discovery motion was not heard earlier.

(3) Any likelihood that permitting the discovery or hearing the discovery motion will prevent the case from going to trial on the date set, or otherwise interfere with the trial calendar, or result in prejudice to any other party.

(4) The length of time that has elapsed between any date previously set, and the date presently set, for the trial of the action.

(c) The court shall impose a monetary sanction under Chapter 7 (commencing with Section 2023.010) against any party, person, or attorney who unsuccessfully makes or opposes a motion to extend or to reopen discovery, unless it finds that the one subject to the sanction acted with substantial justification or that other circumstances make the imposition of the sanction unjust. *(Added by Stats.2004, c. 182 (A.B.3081), § 23, operative July 1, 2005.)*

Cross References

Action defined for purposes of this Title, see Code of Civil Procedure § 2016.020.
Court defined for purposes of this Title, see Code of Civil Procedure § 2016.020.
Discovery, generally, see Code of Civil Procedure § 2016.010 et seq.

Research References

Forms

West's California Code Forms, Civil Procedure § 2024.050 Form 1, Evidence—Discovery—Notice of Motion for Order Permitting Discovery Motion to be Heard Less Than Fifteen Days Prior to Trial Date.

§ 2024.060. Agreements to extend time or reopen discovery; written agreement

Parties to an action may, with the consent of any party affected by it, enter into an agreement to extend the time for the completion of discovery proceedings or for the hearing of motions concerning discovery, or to reopen discovery after a new date for trial of the action has been set. This agreement may be informal, but it shall be confirmed in a writing that specifies the extended date. In no event shall this agreement require a court to grant a continuance or postponement of the trial of the action. *(Added by Stats.2004, c. 182 (A.B.3081), § 23, operative July 1, 2005.)*

Cross References

Action defined for purposes of this Title, see Code of Civil Procedure § 2016.020.
Court defined for purposes of this Title, see Code of Civil Procedure § 2016.020.
Discovery, generally, see Code of Civil Procedure § 2016.010 et seq.

§ 2024.060

Writing defined for purposes of this Title, see Code of Civil Procedure § 2016.020.

CHAPTER 9. ORAL DEPOSITION INSIDE CALIFORNIA

Cross References

Subpoenas for taking depositions of peace officers and others, see Government Code § 68097.6.

ARTICLE 1. GENERAL PROVISIONS

Section
2025.010. Persons and entities within the state subject to deposition.

§ 2025.010. Persons and entities within the state subject to deposition

Any party may obtain discovery within the scope delimited by Chapter 2 (commencing with Section 2017.010), and subject to the restrictions set forth in Chapter 5 (commencing with Section 2019.010), by taking in California the oral deposition of any person, including any party to the action. The person deposed may be a natural person, an organization such as a public or private corporation, a partnership, an association, or a governmental agency. *(Added by Stats.2004, c. 182 (A.B.3081), § 23, operative July 1, 2005. Amended by Stats.2016, c. 86 (S.B.1171), § 41, eff. Jan. 1, 2017.)*

Cross References

Abuse of discovery, sanctions, see Code of Civil Procedure § 2023.010 et seq.
Action defined for purposes of this Title, see Code of Civil Procedure § 2016.020.
Acts constituting waiver of notice, see Code of Civil Procedure § 2004.
Administrative adjudication, see Government Code § 11511.
Arbitration proceedings, see Code of Civil Procedure § 1283 et seq.
Attorneys' work products, discovery, see Code of Civil Procedure § 2018.020 et seq.
Beer pricing and marketing enforcement action; protection of witnesses against self-incrimination, see Business and Professions Code § 25009.
Costs, see Code of Civil Procedure § 1033.5.
Depositions, see Code of Civil Procedure § 2020.010 et seq., § 2026.010, § 2027.010, § 2028.010 et seq.
Discovery, generally, see Code of Civil Procedure § 2016.010 et seq.
Elementary and secondary education certificated employees, disclosures by parties in a dismissal or suspension proceeding, see Education Code § 44944.05.
Frequency or extent of discovery, restrictions, see Code of Civil Procedure § 2019.030.
Judges and justices, power to take depositions, see Code of Civil Procedure § 179.
Notice of motion, see Code of Civil Procedure § 1005.
Oath to witness, form, see Code of Civil Procedure § 2094.
Personal records, subpoena, see Code of Civil Procedure § 1985.3.
Personal service, see Code of Civil Procedure § 1011.
Postponement, reasons for, see Code of Civil Procedure § 595.
Refusal to make discovery, see Code of Civil Procedure § 2031.010 et seq.
Violation of court order as contempt, see Code of Civil Procedure § 1209.

ARTICLE 2. DEPOSITION NOTICE

Section
2025.210. Service of notice; time allowed.
2025.220. Contents of deposition notice; copy of deposition subpoena as notice of deposition.
2025.230. Contents of deposition notice; deponent not a natural person.
2025.240. Notice to parties to the action; subpoenaing party duties; consumer or employee records.
2025.250. Location of deposition; mileage restrictions.
2025.260. Location of deposition; exemption from mileage restrictions; order of court.
2025.270. Date of deposition.
2025.280. Service of notice upon party deponents; production of documents and electronically stored information for inspection and copying.
2025.290. Time limits of depositions.
2025.295. Health of deponent; additional time allowed.

§ 2025.210. Service of notice; time allowed

Subject to Sections 2025.270 and 2025.610, an oral deposition may be taken as follows:

(a) The defendant may serve a deposition notice without leave of court at any time after that defendant has been served or has appeared in the action, whichever occurs first.

(b) The plaintiff may serve a deposition notice without leave of court on any date that is 20 days after the service of the summons on, or appearance by, any defendant. On motion with or without notice, the court, for good cause shown, may grant to a plaintiff leave to serve a deposition notice on an earlier date. *(Added by Stats.2004, c. 182 (A.B.3081), § 23, operative July 1, 2005.)*

Cross References

Action defined for purposes of this Title, see Code of Civil Procedure § 2016.020.
Computation of time, see Code of Civil Procedure §§ 12 and 12a; Government Code § 6800 et seq.
Court defined for purposes of this Title, see Code of Civil Procedure § 2016.020.
Depositions, see Code of Civil Procedure §§ 2020.010 et seq., 2025.010 et seq., 2026.010, 2027.010, 2028.010 et seq.
Monetary sanctions, see Code of Civil Procedure § 2023.050.
Notice, actual and constructive, defined, see Civil Code § 18.
Persons upon whom summons may be served, see Code of Civil Procedure § 416.10 et seq.

Research References

Forms

West's California Code Forms, Civil Procedure § 2025.210 Form 1, Evidence—Discovery—Notice of Motion for Leave of Court to Take Deposition Upon Oral Examination Within Twenty Days After Service of Summons on Defendant—Order Shortening Time.

§ 2025.220. Contents of deposition notice; copy of deposition subpoena as notice of deposition

(a) A party desiring to take the oral deposition of any person shall give notice in writing. The deposition notice shall state all of the following, in at least 12–point type:

(1) The address where the deposition will be taken.

(2) The date of the deposition, selected under Section 2025.270, and the time it will commence.

(3) The name of each deponent, and the address and telephone number, if known, of any deponent who is not a party to the action. If the name of the deponent is not known, the deposition notice shall set forth instead a general description sufficient to identify the person or particular class to which the person belongs.

(4) The specification with reasonable particularity of any materials or category of materials, including any electronically stored information, to be produced by the deponent.

(5) Any intention by the party noticing the deposition to record the testimony by audio or video technology, in addition to recording the testimony by the stenographic method as required by Section 2025.330 and any intention to record the testimony by stenographic method through the instant visual display of the testimony. If the deposition will be conducted using instant visual display, a copy of the deposition notice shall also be given to the deposition officer.

Any offer to provide the instant visual display of the testimony or to provide rough draft transcripts to any party which is accepted prior to, or offered at, the deposition shall also be made by the deposition officer at the deposition to all parties in attendance. Any party or attorney requesting the provision of the instant visual display of the testimony, or rough draft transcripts, shall pay the reasonable cost of those services, which may be no greater than the costs charged to any other party or attorney.

(6) Any intention to reserve the right to use at trial a video recording of the deposition testimony of a treating or consulting physician or of an expert witness under subdivision (d) of Section 2025.620. In this event, the operator of the video camera shall be a person who is authorized to administer an oath, and shall not be financially interested in the action or be a relative or employee of any attorney of any of the parties.

(7) The form in which any electronically stored information is to be produced, if a particular form is desired.

(8)(A) A statement disclosing the existence of a contract, if any is known to the noticing party, between the noticing party or a third party who is financing all or part of the action and either of the following for any service beyond the noticed deposition:

(i) The deposition officer.

(ii) The entity providing the services of the deposition officer.

(B) A statement disclosing that the party noticing the deposition, or a third party financing all or part of the action, directed his or her attorney to use a particular officer or entity to provide services for the deposition, if applicable.

(b) Notwithstanding subdivision (a), where under Article 4 (commencing with Section 2020.410) only the production by a nonparty of business records for copying is desired, a copy of the deposition subpoena shall serve as the notice of deposition. *(Added by Stats.2004, c. 182 (A.B.3081), § 23, operative July 1, 2005. Amended by Stats.2012, c. 72 (S.B.1574), § 20; Stats.2015, c. 346 (A.B.1197), § 2, eff. Jan. 1, 2016; Stats.2018, c. 268 (A.B.3019), § 1, eff. Jan. 1, 2019.)*

Cross References

Action defined for purposes of this Title, see Code of Civil Procedure § 2016.020.
Attorney's fees and costs, generally, see Code of Civil Procedure § 1021.
Deposition of expert witness, production of materials, see Code of Civil Procedure § 2034.415.
Depositions, see Code of Civil Procedure §§ 2020.010 et seq., 2025.010 et seq., 2026.010, 2027.010, 2028.010 et seq.
Notice, actual and constructive, defined, see Civil Code § 18.
Witness defined for purposes of this Code, see Code of Civil Procedure § 1878.
Writing defined for purposes of this Title, see Code of Civil Procedure § 2016.020.

Research References

Forms

West's California Judicial Council Forms SUBP–015, Deposition Subpena for Personal Appearance.
West's California Judicial Council Forms SUBP–020, Deposition Subpena for Personal Appearance and Production of Documents and Things.
West's California Judicial Council Forms SUBP–040, Deposition Subpena for Personal Appearance in Action Pending Outside California.
West's California Judicial Council Forms SUBP–045, Deposition Subpena for Personal Appearance and Production of Documents, Electronically Stored Information, and Things in Action Pending Outside California.

§ 2025.230. Contents of deposition notice; deponent not a natural person

If the deponent named is not a natural person, the deposition notice shall describe with reasonable particularity the matters on which examination is requested. In that event, the deponent shall designate and produce at the deposition those of its officers, directors, managing agents, employees, or agents who are most qualified to testify on its behalf as to those matters to the extent of any information known or reasonably available to the deponent. *(Added by Stats.2004, c. 182 (A.B.3081), § 23, operative July 1, 2005.)*

Cross References

Depositions, see Code of Civil Procedure §§ 2020.010 et seq., 2025.010 et seq., 2026.010, 2027.010, 2028.010 et seq.
Notice, actual and constructive, defined, see Civil Code § 18.
Time limits of depositions, see Code of Civil Procedure § 2025.290.

Research References

Forms

West's California Judicial Council Forms SUBP–015, Deposition Subpena for Personal Appearance.
West's California Judicial Council Forms SUBP–020, Deposition Subpena for Personal Appearance and Production of Documents and Things.
West's California Judicial Council Forms SUBP–040, Deposition Subpena for Personal Appearance in Action Pending Outside California.
West's California Judicial Council Forms SUBP–045, Deposition Subpena for Personal Appearance and Production of Documents, Electronically Stored Information, and Things in Action Pending Outside California.

§ 2025.240. Notice to parties to the action; subpoenaing party duties; consumer or employee records

(a) The party who prepares a notice of deposition shall give the notice to every other party who has appeared in the action. The deposition notice, or the accompanying proof of service, shall list all the parties or attorneys for parties on whom it is served.

(b) If, as defined in subdivision (a) of Section 1985.3 or subdivision (a) of Section 1985.6, the party giving notice of the deposition is a subpoenaing party, and the deponent is a witness commanded by a deposition subpoena to produce personal records of a consumer or employment records of an employee, the subpoenaing party shall serve on that consumer or employee all of the following:

(1) A notice of the deposition.

(2) The notice of privacy rights specified in subdivision (e) of Section 1985.3 or in subdivision (e) of Section 1985.6.

(3) A copy of the deposition subpoena.

(c) If the attendance of the deponent is to be compelled by service of a deposition subpoena under Chapter 6 (commencing with Section 2020.010), an identical copy of that subpoena shall be served with the deposition notice. *(Added by Stats.2004, c. 182 (A.B.3081), § 23, operative July 1, 2005. Amended by Stats.2007, c. 113 (A.B.1126), § 5.)*

Cross References

Action defined for purposes of this Title, see Code of Civil Procedure § 2016.020.
Depositions, see Code of Civil Procedure §§ 2020.010 et seq., 2025.010 et seq., 2026.010, 2027.010, 2028.010 et seq.
Notice, actual and constructive, defined, see Civil Code § 18.
Proof of service, see Code of Civil Procedure § 417.10 et seq.
Witness defined for purposes of this Code, see Code of Civil Procedure § 1878.

§ 2025.250. Location of deposition; mileage restrictions

(a) Unless the court orders otherwise under Section 2025.260, the deposition of a natural person, whether or not a party to the action, shall be taken at a place that is, at the option of the party giving notice of the deposition, either within 75 miles of the deponent's residence, or within the county where the action is pending and within 150 miles of the deponent's residence.

(b) The deposition of an organization that is a party to the action shall be taken at a place that is, at the option of the party giving notice of the deposition, either within 75 miles of the organization's principal executive or business office in California, or within the county where the action is pending and within 150 miles of that office.

(c) Unless the organization consents to a more distant place, the deposition of any other organization shall be taken within 75 miles of the organization's principal executive or business office in California.

(d) If an organization has not designated a principal executive or business office in California, the deposition shall be taken at a place that is, at the option of the party giving notice of the deposition, either within the county where the action is pending, or within 75 miles of any executive or business office in California of the organization. *(Added by Stats.2004, c. 182 (A.B.3081), § 23, operative July 1, 2005. Amended by Stats.2005, c. 294 (A.B.333), § 7.)*

Cross References

Action defined for purposes of this Title, see Code of Civil Procedure § 2016.020.

Court defined for purposes of this Title, see Code of Civil Procedure § 2016.020.

Depositions, see Code of Civil Procedure §§ 2020.010 et seq., 2025.010 et seq., 2026.010, 2027.010, 2028.010 et seq.

Notice, actual and constructive, defined, see Civil Code § 18.

Research References

Forms

West's California Judicial Council Forms SUBP–015, Deposition Subpena for Personal Appearance.

West's California Judicial Council Forms SUBP–020, Deposition Subpena for Personal Appearance and Production of Documents and Things.

West's California Judicial Council Forms SUBP–040, Deposition Subpena for Personal Appearance in Action Pending Outside California.

West's California Judicial Council Forms SUBP–045, Deposition Subpena for Personal Appearance and Production of Documents, Electronically Stored Information, and Things in Action Pending Outside California.

§ 2025.260. Location of deposition; exemption from mileage restrictions; order of court

(a) A party desiring to take the deposition of a natural person who is a party to the action or an officer, director, managing agent, or employee of a party may make a motion for an order that the deponent attend for deposition at a place that is more distant than that permitted under Section 2025.250. This motion shall be accompanied by a meet and confer declaration under Section 2016.040.

(b) In exercising its discretion to grant or deny this motion, the court shall take into consideration any factor tending to show whether the interests of justice will be served by requiring the deponent's attendance at that more distant place, including, but not limited to, the following:

(1) Whether the moving party selected the forum.

(2) Whether the deponent will be present to testify at the trial of the action.

(3) The convenience of the deponent.

(4) The feasibility of conducting the deposition by written questions under Chapter 11 (commencing with Section 2028.010), or of using a discovery method other than a deposition.

(5) The number of depositions sought to be taken at a place more distant than that permitted under Section 2025.250.

(6) The expense to the parties of requiring the deposition to be taken within the distance permitted under Section 2025.250.

(7) The whereabouts of the deponent at the time for which the deposition is scheduled.

(c) The order may be conditioned on the advancement by the moving party of the reasonable expenses and costs to the deponent for travel to the place of deposition.

(d) The court shall impose a monetary sanction under Chapter 7 (commencing with Section 2023.010) against any party, person, or attorney who unsuccessfully makes or opposes a motion to increase the travel limits for a party deponent, unless it finds that the one subject to the sanction acted with substantial justification or that other circumstances make the imposition of the sanction unjust. *(Added by Stats.2004, c. 182 (A.B.3081), § 23, operative July 1, 2005.)*

Cross References

Action defined for purposes of this Title, see Code of Civil Procedure § 2016.020.

Actions on policies containing liability provisions, uninsured motorist/underinsured motorist coverage, see Insurance Code § 11580.2.

Court defined for purposes of this Title, see Code of Civil Procedure § 2016.020.

Depositions, see Code of Civil Procedure §§ 2020.010 et seq., 2025.010 et seq., 2026.010, 2027.010, 2028.010 et seq.

Discovery, generally, see Code of Civil Procedure § 2016.010 et seq.

Research References

Forms

West's California Code Forms, Civil Procedure § 2025.260 Form 1, Evidence—Discovery—Notice of Motion to Take Deposition of Party at a Place More Than 150 Miles from Deponent's Place of Residence.

§ 2025.270. Date of deposition

(a) An oral deposition shall be scheduled for a date at least 10 days after service of the deposition notice.

(b) Notwithstanding subdivision (a), in an unlawful detainer action or other proceeding under Chapter 4 (commencing with Section 1159) of Title 3 of Part 3, an oral deposition shall be scheduled for a date at least five days after service of the deposition notice, but not later than five days before trial.

(c) Notwithstanding subdivisions (a) and (b), if, as defined in Section 1985.3 or 1985.6, the party giving notice of the deposition is a subpoenaing party, and the deponent is a witness commanded by a deposition subpoena to produce personal records of a consumer or employment records of an employee, the deposition shall be scheduled for a date at least 20 days after issuance of that subpoena.

(d) On motion or ex parte application of any party or deponent, for good cause shown, the court may shorten or extend the time for scheduling a deposition, or may stay its taking until the determination of a motion for a protective order under Section 2025.420. *(Added by Stats.2004, c. 182 (A.B.3081), § 23, operative July 1, 2005. Amended by Stats.2007, c. 113 (A.B.1126), § 6.)*

Cross References

Action defined for purposes of this Title, see Code of Civil Procedure § 2016.020.

Computation of time, see Code of Civil Procedure §§ 12 and 12a; Government Code § 6800 et seq.

Court defined for purposes of this Title, see Code of Civil Procedure § 2016.020.

Depositions, see Code of Civil Procedure §§ 2020.010 et seq., 2025.010 et seq., 2026.010, 2027.010, 2028.010 et seq.

Notice, actual and constructive, defined, see Civil Code § 18.

Witness defined for purposes of this Code, see Code of Civil Procedure § 1878.

Research References

Forms

West's California Code Forms, Civil Procedure § 2025.270 Form 1, Evidence—Discovery—Notice of Motion to Extend Time for Scheduling Deposition.

West's California Code Forms, Civil Procedure § 2025.270 Form 3, Evidence—Discovery—Notice of Motion for Order Shortening Time for Notice of Scheduling Deposition.

West's California Code Forms, Civil Procedure § 2025.270 Form 4, Evidence—Discovery—Declaration for Order Shortening Time for Notice of Scheduling Deposition.

West's California Code Forms, Civil Procedure § 2025.270 Form 5, Evidence—Discovery—Stipulation to Take Deposition.

§ 2025.280. Service of notice upon party deponents; production of documents and electronically stored information for inspection and copying

(a) The service of a deposition notice under Section 2025.240 is effective to require any deponent who is a party to the action or an officer, director, managing agent, or employee of a party to attend and to testify, as well as to produce any document, electronically stored information, or tangible thing for inspection and copying.

(b) The attendance and testimony of any other deponent, as well as the production by the deponent of any document, electronically stored information, or tangible thing for inspection and copying, requires the service on the deponent of a deposition subpoena under Chapter 6 (commencing with Section 2020.010).

(c) A deponent required by notice or subpoena to produce electronically stored information shall provide a means of gaining direct access to, or a translation into a reasonably usable form of, any electronically stored information that is password protected or otherwise inaccessible. *(Added by Stats.2004, c. 182 (A.B.3081), § 23, operative July 1, 2005. Amended by Stats.2012, c. 72 (S.B.1574), § 21; Stats.2016, c. 467 (A.B.2427), § 2, eff. Jan. 1, 2017.)*

Cross References

Action defined for purposes of this Title, see Code of Civil Procedure § 2016.020.
Actions on policies containing liability provisions, uninsured motorist/underinsured motorist coverage, see Insurance Code § 11580.2.
Depositions, see Code of Civil Procedure §§ 2020.010 et seq., 2025.010 et seq., 2026.010, 2027.010, 2028.010 et seq.
Document defined for purposes of this Title, see Code of Civil Procedure § 2016.020.
Notice, actual and constructive, defined, see Civil Code § 18.

§ 2025.290. Time limits of depositions

(a) Except as provided in subdivision (b), or by any court order, including a case management order, a deposition examination of the witness by all counsel, other than the witness' counsel of record, shall be limited to seven hours of total testimony. The court shall allow additional time, beyond any limits imposed by this section, if needed to fairly examine the deponent or if the deponent, another person, or any other circumstance impedes or delays the examination.

(b) This section shall not apply under any of the following circumstances:

(1) If the parties have stipulated that this section will not apply to a specific deposition or to the entire proceeding.

(2) To any deposition of a witness designated as an expert pursuant to Sections 2034.210 to 2034.310, inclusive.

(3) To any case designated as complex by the court pursuant to Rule 3.400 of the California Rules of Court, unless a licensed physician attests in a declaration served on the parties that the deponent suffers from an illness or condition that raises substantial medical doubt of survival of the deponent beyond six months, in which case the deposition examination of the witness by all counsel, other than the witness' counsel of record, shall be limited to two days of no more than seven hours of total testimony each day, or 14 hours of total testimony.

(4) To any case brought by an employee or applicant for employment against an employer for acts or omissions arising out of or relating to the employment relationship.

(5) To any deposition of a person who is designated as the most qualified person to be deposed under Section 2025.230.

(6) To any party who appeared in the action after the deposition has concluded, in which case the new party may notice another deposition subject to the requirements of this section.

(c) It is the intent of the Legislature that any exclusions made by this section shall not be construed to create any presumption or any substantive change to existing law relating to the appropriate time limit for depositions falling within the exclusion. Nothing in this section shall be construed to affect the existing right of any party to move for a protective order or the court's discretion to make any order that justice requires to limit a deposition in order to protect any party, deponent, or other natural person or organization from unwarranted annoyance, embarrassment, oppression, undue burden, or expense. *(Added by Stats.2012, c. 346 (A.B.1875), § 1.)*

Research References

Forms

West's California Code Forms, Civil Procedure § 2025.220 Form 1, Evidence—Discovery—Notice of Taking of Oral Deposition.

§ 2025.295. Health of deponent; additional time allowed

(a) Notwithstanding Section 2025.290, in any civil action for injury or illness that results in mesothelioma or silicosis, a deposition examination of the plaintiff by all counsel, other than the plaintiff's counsel of record, shall be limited to seven hours of total testimony if a licensed physician attests in a declaration served on the parties that the deponent suffers from mesothelioma or silicosis, raising substantial medical doubt of the survival of the deponent beyond six months.

(b) Notwithstanding the presumptive time limit in subdivision (a), upon request by a defendant, a court may, in its discretion, grant one of the following up to:

(1) An additional three hours of deposition testimony for no more than 10 hours of total deposition conducted by the defendants if there are more than 10 defendants appearing at the deposition.

(2) An additional seven hours of deposition testimony for no more than 14 hours of total deposition conducted by the defendants if there are more than 20 defendants appearing at the deposition.

(c) The court may grant the additional time provided for in paragraphs (1) and (2) of subdivision (b) only if it finds that an extension, in the instant case, is in the interest of fairness, which includes consideration of the number of defendants appearing at the deposition, and determines that the health of the deponent does not appear to be endangered by the grant of additional time. *(Added by Stats.2019, c. 212 (S.B.645), § 1, eff. Jan. 1, 2020.)*

ARTICLE 3. CONDUCT OF DEPOSITION

Section
2025.310. Attendance via remote means.
2025.320. Deposition officers; officer qualifications and requirements; conflict of interest; objections; civil penalty for violations.
2025.330. Oath or affirmation; stenographic record; electronic recording; examination subject to Evidence Code provisions; questions submitted to deposition officer for answer by deponent in lieu of party participation.
2025.340. Recordation by audio or video technology; procedural requirements; submission at hearing with stenographic transcript.

§ 2025.310. Attendance via remote means

(a) At the election of the deponent or the deposing party, the deposition officer may attend the deposition at a different location than the deponent via remote means. A deponent is not required to be physically present with the deposition officer when being sworn in at the time of the deposition.

(b) Subject to Section 2025.420, any party or attorney of record may, but is not required to, be physically present at the deposition at the location of the deponent. <u>If a party or attorney of record elects</u>

to be physically present at the location of the deponent, all physically present participants in the deposition shall comply with local health and safety ordinances, rules, and orders.

(c) The procedures to implement this section shall be established by court order in the specific action or proceeding or by the California Rules of Court.

(d) An exercise of the authority granted by subdivision (a) or (b) does not waive any other provision of this title, including, but not limited to, provisions regarding the time, place, or manner in which a deposition shall be conducted.

(e) This section does not alter or amend who may lawfully serve as a deposition officer pursuant to this title or who otherwise may administer oaths pursuant to Sections 2093 and 2094 of this code or Section 8201 of the Government Code. *(Added by Stats.2004, c. 182 (A.B.3081), § 23, operative July 1, 2005. Amended by Stats.2020, c. 112 (S.B.1146), § 3, eff. Sept. 18, 2020; Stats.2022, c. 92 (S.B.1037), § 1, eff. Jan. 1, 2023.)*

Cross References

Action defined for purposes of this Title, see Code of Civil Procedure § 2016.020.
Court defined for purposes of this Title, see Code of Civil Procedure § 2016.020.
Depositions, see Code of Civil Procedure §§ 2020.010 et seq., 2025.010 et seq., 2026.010, 2027.010, 2028.010 et seq.

§ 2025.320. Deposition officers; officer qualifications and requirements; conflict of interest; objections; civil penalty for violations

Except as provided in Section 2020.420, the deposition shall be conducted under the supervision of an officer who is authorized to administer an oath and is subject to all of the following requirements:

(a) The officer shall not be financially interested in the action and shall not be a relative or employee of any attorney of the parties, or of any of the parties.

(b) Services and products offered or provided by the deposition officer or the entity providing the services of the deposition officer to any party or to any party's attorney or third party who is financing all or part of the action shall be offered to all parties or their attorneys attending the deposition. No service or product may be offered or provided by the deposition officer or by the entity providing the services of the deposition officer to any party or any party's attorney or third party who is financing all or part of the action unless the service or product is offered or provided to all parties or their attorneys attending the deposition. All services and products offered or provided shall be made available at the same time to all parties or their attorneys.

(c) The deposition officer or the entity providing the services of the deposition officer shall not provide to any party or any party's attorney or third party who is financing all or part of the action any service or product consisting of the deposition officer's notations or comments regarding the demeanor of any witness, attorney, or party present at the deposition. The deposition officer or entity providing the services of the deposition officer shall not collect any personal identifying information about the witness as a service or product to be provided to any party or third party who is financing all or part of the action.

(d) Upon the request of any party or any party's attorney attending a deposition, any party or any party's attorney attending the deposition shall enter in the record of the deposition all services and products made available to that party or party's attorney or third party who is financing all or part of the action by the deposition officer or by the entity providing the services of the deposition officer. A party in the action who is not represented by an attorney shall be informed by the noticing party or the party's attorney that the unrepresented party may request this statement.

(e) Any objection to the qualifications of the deposition officer is waived unless made before the deposition begins or as soon thereafter as the ground for that objection becomes known or could be discovered by reasonable diligence.

(f) Violation of this section by any person may result in a civil penalty of up to five thousand dollars ($5,000) imposed by a court of competent jurisdiction. *(Added by Stats.2004, c. 182 (A.B.3081), § 23, operative July 1, 2005.)*

Cross References

Action defined for purposes of this Title, see Code of Civil Procedure § 2016.020.
Court defined for purposes of this Title, see Code of Civil Procedure § 2016.020.
Department of Fair Employment and Housing, enforcement and hearing procedures, deposition, see Government Code § 12963.3.
Depositions, see Code of Civil Procedure §§ 2020.010 et seq., 2025.010 et seq., 2026.010, 2027.010, 2028.010 et seq.
Licensed shorthand reporters and shorthand reporting corporations, specific violations, applicability of section, civil fine, attorney's fees, see Business and Professions Code § 8050.
Witness defined for purposes of this Code, see Code of Civil Procedure § 1878.

§ 2025.330. Oath or affirmation; stenographic record; electronic recording; examination subject to Evidence Code provisions; questions submitted to deposition officer for answer by deponent in lieu of party participation

(a) The deposition officer shall put the deponent under oath or affirmation.

(b) Unless the parties agree or the court orders otherwise, the testimony, as well as any stated objections, shall be taken stenographically. If taken stenographically, it shall be by a person certified pursuant to Article 3 (commencing with Section 8020) of Chapter 13 of Division 3 of the Business and Professions Code.

(c) The party noticing the deposition may also record the testimony by audio or video technology if the notice of deposition stated an intention also to record the testimony by either of those methods, or if all the parties agree that the testimony may also be recorded by either of those methods. Any other party, at that party's expense, may make an audio or video record of the deposition, provided that the other party promptly, and in no event less than three calendar days before the date for which the deposition is scheduled, serves a written notice of this intention to make an audio or video record of the deposition testimony on the party or attorney who noticed the deposition, on all other parties or attorneys on whom the deposition notice was served under Section 2025.240, and on any deponent whose attendance is being compelled by a deposition subpoena under Chapter 6 (commencing with Section 2020.010). If this notice is given three calendar days before the deposition date, it shall be made by personal service under Section 1011.

(d) Examination and cross-examination of the deponent shall proceed as permitted at trial under the provisions of the Evidence Code.

(e) In lieu of participating in the oral examination, parties may transmit written questions in a sealed envelope to the party taking the deposition for delivery to the deposition officer, who shall unseal the envelope and propound them to the deponent after the oral examination has been completed. *(Added by Stats.2004, c. 182 (A.B.3081), § 23, operative July 1, 2005. Amended by Stats.2005, c. 294 (A.B.333), § 8.)*

Cross References

Computation of time, see Code of Civil Procedure §§ 12 and 121; Government Code § 6800 et seq.
Court defined for purposes of this Title, see Code of Civil Procedure § 2016.020.
Depositions, see Code of Civil Procedure §§ 2020.010 et seq., 2025.010 et seq., 2026.010, 2027.010, 2028.010 et seq.

MISCELLANEOUS PROVISIONS

Notice, actual and constructive, defined, see Civil Code § 18.

§ 2025.340. Recordation by audio or video technology; procedural requirements; submission at hearing with stenographic transcript

If a deposition is being recorded by means of audio or video technology by, or at the direction of, any party, the following procedure shall be observed:

(a) The area used for recording the deponent's oral testimony shall be suitably large, adequately lighted, and reasonably quiet.

(b) The operator of the recording equipment shall be competent to set up, operate, and monitor the equipment in the manner prescribed in this section. Except as provided in subdivision (c), the operator may be an employee of the attorney taking the deposition unless the operator is also the deposition officer.

(c) If a video recording of deposition testimony is to be used under subdivision (d) of Section 2025.620, the operator of the recording equipment shall be a person who is authorized to administer an oath, and shall not be financially interested in the action or be a relative or employee of any attorney of any of the parties, unless all parties attending the deposition agree on the record to waive these qualifications and restrictions.

(d) Services and products offered or provided by the deposition officer or the entity providing the services of the deposition officer to any party or to any party's attorney or third party who is financing all or part of the action shall be offered or provided to all parties or their attorneys attending the deposition. No service or product may be offered or provided by the deposition officer or by the entity providing the services of the deposition officer to any party or any party's attorney or third party who is financing all or part of the action unless the service or product is offered or provided to all parties or their attorneys attending the deposition. All services and products offered or provided shall be made available at the same time to all parties or their attorneys.

(e) The deposition officer or the entity providing the services of the deposition officer shall not provide to any party or any other person or entity any service or product consisting of the deposition officer's notations or comments regarding the demeanor of any witness, attorney, or party present at the deposition. The deposition officer or the entity providing the services of the deposition officer shall not collect any personal identifying information about the witness as a service or product to be provided to any party or third party who is financing all or part of the action.

(f) Upon the request of any party or any party's attorney attending a deposition, any party or any party's attorney attending the deposition shall enter in the record of the deposition all services and products made available to that party or party's attorney or third party who is financing all or part of the action by the deposition officer or by the entity providing the services of the deposition officer. A party in the action who is not represented by an attorney shall be informed by the noticing party that the unrepresented party may request this statement.

(g) The operator shall not distort the appearance or the demeanor of participants in the deposition by the use of camera or sound recording techniques.

(h) The deposition shall begin with an oral or written statement on camera or on the audio recording that includes the operator's name and business address, the name and business address of the operator's employer, the date, time, and place of the deposition, the caption of the case, the name of the deponent, a specification of the party on whose behalf the deposition is being taken, and any stipulations by the parties.

(i) Counsel for the parties shall identify themselves on camera or on the audio recording.

(j) The oath shall be administered to the deponent on camera or on the audio recording.

(k) If the length of a deposition requires the use of more than one unit of tape or electronic storage, the end of each unit and the beginning of each succeeding unit shall be announced on camera or on the audio recording.

(*l*) At the conclusion of a deposition, a statement shall be made on camera or on the audio recording that the deposition is ended and shall set forth any stipulations made by counsel concerning the custody of the audio or video recording and the exhibits, or concerning other pertinent matters.

(m) A party intending to offer an audio or video recording of a deposition in evidence under Section 2025.620 shall notify the court and all parties in writing of that intent and of the parts of the deposition to be offered. That notice shall be given within sufficient time for objections to be made and ruled on by the judge to whom the case is assigned for trial or hearing, and for any editing of the recording. Objections to all or part of the deposition shall be made in writing. The court may permit further designations of testimony and objections as justice may require. With respect to those portions of an audio or video record of deposition testimony that are not designated by any party or that are ruled to be objectionable, the court may order that the party offering the recording of the deposition at the trial or hearing suppress those portions, or that an edited version of the deposition recording be prepared for use at the trial or hearing. The original audio or video record of the deposition shall be preserved unaltered. If no stenographic record of the deposition testimony has previously been made, the party offering an audio or video recording of that testimony under Section 2025.620 shall accompany that offer with a stenographic transcript prepared from that recording. *(Added by Stats.2004, c. 182 (A.B.3081), § 23, operative July 1, 2005.)*

Cross References

Action defined for purposes of this Title, see Code of Civil Procedure § 2016.020.
Court defined for purposes of this Title, see Code of Civil Procedure § 2016.020.
Depositions, see Code of Civil Procedure §§ 2020.010 et seq., 2025.010 et seq., 2026.010, 2027.010, 2028.010 et seq.
Notice, actual and constructive, defined, see Civil Code § 18.
Witness defined for purposes of this Code, see Code of Civil Procedure § 1878.
Writing defined for purposes of this Title, see Code of Civil Procedure § 2016.020.

Research References

Forms

West's California Code Forms, Civil Procedure § 2025.340 Form 1, Evidence—Discovery—Notice of Taking of Oral Deposition—Instant Visual Display.

ARTICLE 4. OBJECTIONS, SANCTIONS, PROTECTIVE ORDERS, MOTIONS TO COMPEL, AND SUSPENSION OF DEPOSITIONS

Section
2025.410. Defective notice; time to object; waiver; motion to stay; meet and confer declaration; monetary sanctions; electronically stored information sanctions.
2025.420. Protective orders; authority and action by court; burden of demonstrating inaccessibility of information; court order and conditions for discovery; monetary sanctions; electronically stored information sanctions.
2025.430. Failure to attend by party giving notice; sanctions; exceptions.

CODE OF CIVIL PROCEDURE

Section
2025.440. Failure to attend by deponent; defective service; monetary sanctions; sanction where service is effective; refusal to give oath.
2025.450. Failure of party deponent to appear or produce documents, electronically stored information, or items; contents of motion to compel; burden of demonstrating inaccessibility of electronic information; court order and conditions for discovery; monetary sanctions; issue, evidence, or terminating sanction; electronically stored information sanctions.
2025.460. Privileged or protected information; objection to disclosure; waiver; identification of inaccessible electronically stored information; adjournment.
2025.470. Suspension of testimony; authority of deposition officer.
2025.480. Motion to compel answers or produce documents, electronically stored information, or items; procedural requirements; burden of demonstrating inaccessibility of electronic information; court order and conditions of discovery; monetary sanctions; contempt of court; electronically stored information sanctions.

§ 2025.410. Defective notice; time to object; waiver; motion to stay; meet and confer declaration; monetary sanctions; electronically stored information sanctions

(a) Any party served with a deposition notice that does not comply with Article 2 (commencing with Section 2025.210) waives any error or irregularity unless that party promptly serves a written objection specifying that error or irregularity at least three calendar days prior to the date for which the deposition is scheduled, on the party seeking to take the deposition and any other attorney or party on whom the deposition notice was served.

(b) If an objection is made three calendar days before the deposition date, the objecting party shall make personal service of that objection pursuant to Section 1011 on the party who gave notice of the deposition. Any deposition taken after the service of a written objection shall not be used against the objecting party under Section 2025.620 if the party did not attend the deposition and if the court determines that the objection was a valid one.

(c) In addition to serving this written objection, a party may also move for an order staying the taking of the deposition and quashing the deposition notice. This motion shall be accompanied by a meet and confer declaration under Section 2016.040. The taking of the deposition is stayed pending the determination of this motion.

(d) The court shall impose a monetary sanction under Chapter 7 (commencing with Section 2023.010) against any party, person, or attorney who unsuccessfully makes or opposes a motion to quash a deposition notice, unless it finds that the one subject to the sanction acted with substantial justification or that other circumstances make the imposition of the sanction unjust.

(e)(1) Notwithstanding subdivision (d), absent exceptional circumstances, the court shall not impose sanctions on any party, person, or attorney for failure to provide electronically stored information that has been lost, damaged, altered, or overwritten as the result of the routine, good faith operation of an electronic information system.

(2) This subdivision shall not be construed to alter any obligation to preserve discoverable information. (Added by Stats.2004, c. 182 (A.B.3081), § 23, operative July 1, 2005. Amended by Stats.2012, c. 72 (S.B.1574), § 22.)

Cross References

Computation of time, see Code of Civil Procedure §§ 12 and 12a; Government Code § 6800 et seq.

Court defined for purposes of this Title, see Code of Civil Procedure § 2016.020.
Depositions, see Code of Civil Procedure §§ 2020.010 et seq., 2025.010 et seq., 2026.010, 2027.010, 2028.010 et seq.
Notice, actual and constructive, defined, see Civil Code § 18.

Research References

Forms

West's California Code Forms, Civil Procedure § 2025.410 Form 1, Evidence—Discovery—Notice of Motion for Order Staying the Taking of a Deposition and Quashing the Deposition Notice.
West's California Code Forms, Civil Procedure § 2025.460 Form 1, Evidence—Discovery—Objection to Notice of Taking Deposition.

§ 2025.420. Protective orders; authority and action by court; burden of demonstrating inaccessibility of information; court order and conditions for discovery; monetary sanctions; electronically stored information sanctions

(a) Before, during, or after a deposition, any party, any deponent, or any other affected natural person or organization may promptly move for a protective order. The motion shall be accompanied by a meet and confer declaration under Section 2016.040.

(b) The court, for good cause shown, may make any order that justice requires to protect any party, deponent, or other natural person or organization from unwarranted annoyance, embarrassment, or oppression, or undue burden and expense. This protective order may include, but is not limited to, one or more of the following directions:

(1) That the deposition not be taken at all.

(2) That the deposition be taken at a different time.

(3) That a video recording of the deposition testimony of a treating or consulting physician or of any expert witness, intended for possible use at trial under subdivision (d) of Section 2025.620, be postponed until the moving party has had an adequate opportunity to prepare, by discovery deposition of the deponent, or other means, for cross-examination.

(4) That the deposition be taken at a place other than that specified in the deposition notice, if it is within a distance permitted by Sections 2025.250 and 2025.260.

(5) That the deposition be taken only on certain specified terms and conditions.

(6) That the deponent's testimony be taken by written, instead of oral, examination.

(7) That the method of discovery be interrogatories to a party instead of an oral deposition.

(8) That the testimony be recorded in a manner different from that specified in the deposition notice.

(9) That certain matters not be inquired into.

(10) That the scope of the examination be limited to certain matters.

(11) That all or certain of the writings or tangible things designated in the deposition notice not be produced, inspected, copied, tested, or sampled, or that conditions be set for the production of electronically stored information designated in the deposition notice.

(12) That designated persons, other than the parties to the action and their officers and counsel, be excluded from attending the deposition.

(13) That a trade secret or other confidential research, development, or commercial information not be disclosed or be disclosed only to specified persons or only in a specified way.

(14) That the parties simultaneously file specified documents enclosed in sealed envelopes to be opened as directed by the court.

(15) That the deposition be sealed and thereafter opened only on order of the court.

(16) That examination of the deponent be terminated. If an order terminates the examination, the deposition shall not thereafter be resumed, except on order of the court.

(c) The party, deponent, or any other affected natural person or organization that seeks a protective order regarding the production, inspection, copying, testing, or sampling of electronically stored information on the basis that the information is from a source that is not reasonably accessible because of undue burden or expense shall bear the burden of demonstrating that the information is from a source that is not reasonably accessible because of undue burden or expense.

(d) If the party or affected person from whom discovery of electronically stored information is sought establishes that the information is from a source that is not reasonably accessible because of undue burden or expense, the court may nonetheless order discovery if the demanding party shows good cause, subject to any limitations imposed under subdivision (f).

(e) If the court finds good cause for the production of electronically stored information from a source that is not reasonably accessible, the court may set conditions for the discovery of the electronically stored information, including allocation of the expense of discovery.

(f) The court shall limit the frequency or extent of discovery of electronically stored information, even from a source that is reasonably accessible, if the court determines that any of the following conditions exist:

(1) It is possible to obtain the information from some other source that is more convenient, less burdensome, or less expensive.

(2) The discovery sought is unreasonably cumulative or duplicative.

(3) The party seeking discovery has had ample opportunity by discovery in the action to obtain the information sought.

(4) The likely burden or expense of the proposed discovery outweighs the likely benefit, taking into account the amount in controversy, the resources of the parties, the importance of the issues in the litigation, and the importance of the requested discovery in resolving the issues.

(g) If the motion for a protective order is denied in whole or in part, the court may order that the deponent provide or permit the discovery against which protection was sought on those terms and conditions that are just.

(h) The court shall impose a monetary sanction under Chapter 7 (commencing with Section 2023.010) against any party, person, or attorney who unsuccessfully makes or opposes a motion for a protective order, unless it finds that the one subject to the sanction acted with substantial justification or that other circumstances make the imposition of the sanction unjust.

(i)(1) Notwithstanding subdivision (h), absent exceptional circumstances, the court shall not impose sanctions on any party, deponent, or other affected natural person or organization or any of their attorneys for failure to provide electronically stored information that has been lost, damaged, altered, or overwritten as the result of the routine, good faith operation of an electronic information system.

(2) This subdivision shall not be construed to alter any obligation to preserve discoverable information. *(Added by Stats.2004, c. 182 (A.B.3081), § 23, operative July 1, 2005. Amended by Stats.2012, c. 72 (S.B.1574), § 23.)*

Cross References

Action defined for purposes of this Title, see Code of Civil Procedure § 2016.020.
Attendance via remote means, conduct of deposition, see Code of Civil Procedure § 2025.310.
Court defined for purposes of this Title, see Code of Civil Procedure § 2016.020.
Deposition notice, date of deposition, see Code of Civil Procedure § 2025.270.
Depositions, see Code of Civil Procedure §§ 2020.010 et seq., 2025.010 et seq., 2026.010, 2027.010, 2028.010 et seq.
Discovery, generally, see Code of Civil Procedure § 2016.010 et seq.
Document defined for purposes of this Title, see Code of Civil Procedure § 2016.020.
Notice, actual and constructive, defined, see Civil Code § 18.
Witness defined for purposes of this Code, see Code of Civil Procedure § 1878.
Writing defined for purposes of this Title, see Code of Civil Procedure § 2016.020.

Research References

Forms

West's California Code Forms, Civil Procedure § 2025.420 Form 1, Evidence—Discovery—Notice of Motion for Protective Order Requiring that Deposition Not be Taken.
West's California Code Forms, Civil Procedure § 2025.420 Form 4, Evidence—Discovery—Notice of Motion to Limit Pending Deposition.
West's California Code Forms, Civil Procedure § 2025.470 Form 1, Evidence—Discovery—Stipulation to Suspend Taking of Testimony.

§ 2025.430. Failure to attend by party giving notice; sanctions; exceptions

If the party giving notice of a deposition fails to attend or proceed with it, the court shall impose a monetary sanction under Chapter 7 (commencing with Section 2023.010) against that party, or the attorney for that party, or both, and in favor of any party attending in person or by attorney, unless it finds that the one subject to the sanction acted with substantial justification or that other circumstances make the imposition of the sanction unjust. *(Added by Stats.2004, c. 182 (A.B.3081), § 23, operative July 1, 2005.)*

Cross References

Court defined for purposes of this Title, see Code of Civil Procedure § 2016.020.
Depositions, see Code of Civil Procedure §§ 2020.010 et seq., 2025.010 et seq., 2026.010, 2027.010, 2028.010 et seq.
Notice, actual and constructive, defined, see Civil Code § 18.

§ 2025.440. Failure to attend by deponent; defective service; monetary sanctions; sanction where service is effective; refusal to give oath

(a) If a deponent does not appear for a deposition because the party giving notice of the deposition failed to serve a required deposition subpoena, the court shall impose a monetary sanction under Chapter 7 (commencing with Section 2023.010) against that party, or the attorney for that party, or both, in favor of any other party who, in person or by attorney, attended at the time and place specified in the deposition notice in the expectation that the deponent's testimony would be taken, unless the court finds that the one subject to the sanction acted with substantial justification or that other circumstances make the imposition of the sanction unjust.

(b) If a deponent on whom a deposition subpoena has been served fails to attend a deposition or refuses to be sworn as a witness, the court may impose on the deponent the sanctions described in Section 2020.240. *(Added by Stats.2004, c. 182 (A.B.3081), § 23, operative July 1, 2005.)*

Cross References

Court defined for purposes of this Title, see Code of Civil Procedure § 2016.020.
Depositions, see Code of Civil Procedure §§ 2020.010 et seq., 2025.010 et seq., 2026.010, 2027.010, 2028.010 et seq.
Notice, actual and constructive, defined, see Civil Code § 18.
Witness defined for purposes of this Code, see Code of Civil Procedure § 1878.

Research References

Forms

West's California Code Forms, Civil Procedure § 2025.440 Form 1, Evidence—Discovery—Notice of Motion for Order for Expenses—Failure to Appear or Serve Subpena.

§ 2025.450. Failure of party deponent to appear or produce documents, electronically stored information, or items; contents of motion to compel; burden of demonstrating inaccessibility of electronic information; court order and conditions for discovery; monetary sanctions; issue, evidence, or terminating sanction; electronically stored information sanctions

(a) If, after service of a deposition notice, a party to the action or an officer, director, managing agent, or employee of a party, or a person designated by an organization that is a party under Section 2025.230, without having served a valid objection under Section 2025.410, fails to appear for examination, or to proceed with it, or to produce for inspection any document, electronically stored information, or tangible thing described in the deposition notice, the party giving the notice may move for an order compelling the deponent's attendance and testimony, and the production for inspection of any document, electronically stored information, or tangible thing described in the deposition notice.

(b) A motion under subdivision (a) shall comply with both of the following:

(1) The motion shall set forth specific facts showing good cause justifying the production for inspection of any document, electronically stored information, or tangible thing described in the deposition notice.

(2) The motion shall be accompanied by a meet and confer declaration under Section 2016.040, or, when the deponent fails to attend the deposition and produce the documents, electronically stored information, or things described in the deposition notice, by a declaration stating that the petitioner has contacted the deponent to inquire about the nonappearance.

(c) In a motion under subdivision (a) relating to the production of electronically stored information, the party or party-affiliated deponent objecting to or opposing the production, inspection, copying, testing, or sampling of electronically stored information on the basis that the information is from a source that is not reasonably accessible because of the undue burden or expense shall bear the burden of demonstrating that the information is from a source that is not reasonably accessible because of undue burden or expense.

(d) If the party or party-affiliated deponent from whom discovery of electronically stored information is sought establishes that the information is from a source that is not reasonably accessible because of the undue burden or expense, the court may nonetheless order discovery if the demanding party shows good cause, subject to any limitations imposed under subdivision (f).

(e) If the court finds good cause for the production of electronically stored information from a source that is not reasonably accessible, the court may set conditions for the discovery of the electronically stored information, including allocation of the expense of discovery.

(f) The court shall limit the frequency or extent of discovery of electronically stored information, even from a source that is reasonably accessible, if the court determines that any of the following conditions exists:

(1) It is possible to obtain the information from some other source that is more convenient, less burdensome, or less expensive.

(2) The discovery sought is unreasonably cumulative or duplicative.

(3) The party seeking discovery has had ample opportunity by discovery in the action to obtain the information sought.

(4) The likely burden or expense of the proposed discovery outweighs the likely benefit, taking into account the amount in controversy, the resources of the parties, the importance of the issues in the litigation, and the importance of the requested discovery in resolving the issues.

(g)(1) If a motion under subdivision (a) is granted, the court shall impose a monetary sanction under Chapter 7 (commencing with Section 2023.010) in favor of the party who noticed the deposition and against the deponent or the party with whom the deponent is affiliated, unless the court finds that the one subject to the sanction acted with substantial justification or that other circumstances make the imposition of the sanction unjust.

(2) On motion of any other party who, in person or by attorney, attended at the time and place specified in the deposition notice in the expectation that the deponent's testimony would be taken, the court shall impose a monetary sanction under Chapter 7 (commencing with Section 2023.010) in favor of that party and against the deponent or the party with whom the deponent is affiliated, unless the court finds that the one subject to the sanction acted with substantial justification or that other circumstances make the imposition of the sanction unjust.

(h) If that party or party-affiliated deponent then fails to obey an order compelling attendance, testimony, and production, the court may make those orders that are just, including the imposition of an issue sanction, an evidence sanction, or a terminating sanction under Chapter 7 (commencing with Section 2023.010) against that party deponent or against the party with whom the deponent is affiliated. In lieu of, or in addition to, this sanction, the court may impose a monetary sanction under Chapter 7 (commencing with Section 2023.010) against that deponent or against the party with whom that party deponent is affiliated, and in favor of any party who, in person or by attorney, attended in the expectation that the deponent's testimony would be taken pursuant to that order.

(i)(1) Notwithstanding subdivisions (g) and (h), absent exceptional circumstances, the court shall not impose sanctions on a party or any attorney of a party for failure to provide electronically stored information that has been lost, damaged, altered, or overwritten as the result of the routine, good faith operation of an electronic information system.

(2) This subdivision shall not be construed to alter any obligation to preserve discoverable information. *(Added by Stats.2004, c. 182 (A.B.3081), § 23, operative July 1, 2005. Amended by Stats.2012, c. 72 (S.B.1574), § 24.)*

Cross References

Action defined for purposes of this Title, see Code of Civil Procedure § 2016.020.
Court defined for purposes of this Title, see Code of Civil Procedure § 2016.020.
Depositions, see Code of Civil Procedure §§ 2020.010 et seq., 2025.010 et seq., 2026.010, 2027.010, 2028.010 et seq.
Document defined for purposes of this Title, see Code of Civil Procedure § 2016.020.
Monetary sanctions, see Code of Civil Procedure § 2023.050.
Notice, actual and constructive, defined, see Civil Code § 18.

§ 2025.460. Privileged or protected information; objection to disclosure; waiver; identification of inaccessible electronically stored information; adjournment

(a) The protection of information from discovery on the ground that it is privileged or that it is a protected work product under Chapter 4 (commencing with Section 2018.010) is waived unless a specific objection to its disclosure is timely made during the deposition.

(b) Errors and irregularities of any kind occurring at the oral examination that might be cured if promptly presented are waived unless a specific objection to them is timely made during the deposition. These errors and irregularities include, but are not limited to, those relating to the manner of taking the deposition, to the oath or affirmation administered, to the conduct of a party, attorney, deponent, or deposition officer, or to the form of any question or answer. Unless the objecting party demands that the taking of the deposition be suspended to permit a motion for a protective order under Sections 2025.420 and 2025.470, the deposition shall proceed subject to the objection.

(c) Objections to the competency of the deponent, or to the relevancy, materiality, or admissibility at trial of the testimony or of the materials produced are unnecessary and are not waived by failure to make them before or during the deposition.

(d) If a deponent objects to the production of electronically stored information on the grounds that it is from a source that is not reasonably accessible because of undue burden or expense and that the deponent will not search the source in the absence of an agreement with the deposing party or court order, the deponent shall identify in its objection the types or categories of sources of electronically stored information that it asserts are not reasonably accessible. By objecting and identifying information of a type or category of source or sources that are not reasonably accessible, the deponent preserves any objections it may have relating to that electronically stored information.

(e) If a deponent fails to answer any question or to produce any document, electronically stored information, or tangible thing under the deponent's control that is specified in the deposition notice or a deposition subpoena, the party seeking that answer or production may adjourn the deposition or complete the examination on other matters without waiving the right at a later time to move for an order compelling that answer or production under Section 2025.480.

(f) Notwithstanding subdivision (a), if a deponent notifies the party that took a deposition that electronically stored information produced pursuant to the deposition notice or subpoena is subject to a claim of privilege or of protection as attorney work product, as described in Section 2031.285, the provisions of Section 2031.285 shall apply. *(Added by Stats.2004, c. 182 (A.B.3081), § 23, operative July 1, 2005. Amended by Stats.2012, c. 72 (S.B.1574), § 25.)*

Cross References

Depositions, see Code of Civil Procedure §§ 2020.010 et seq., 2025.010 et seq., 2026.010, 2027.010, 2028.010 et seq.

Discovery, generally, see Code of Civil Procedure § 2016.010 et seq.

Document defined for purposes of this Title, see Code of Civil Procedure § 2016.020.

Notice, actual and constructive, defined, see Civil Code § 18.

§ 2025.470. Suspension of testimony; authority of deposition officer

The deposition officer may not suspend the taking of testimony without the stipulation of all parties present unless any party attending the deposition, including the deponent, demands that the deposition officer suspend taking the testimony to enable that party or deponent to move for a protective order under Section 2025.420 on the ground that the examination is being conducted in bad faith or in a manner that unreasonably annoys, embarrasses, or oppresses that deponent or party. *(Added by Stats.2004, c. 182 (A.B.3081), § 23, operative July 1, 2005.)*

Cross References

Depositions, see Code of Civil Procedure §§ 2020.010 et seq., 2025.010 et seq., 2026.010, 2027.010, 2028.010 et seq.

§ 2025.480. Motion to compel answers or produce documents, electronically stored information, or items; procedural requirements; burden of demonstrating inaccessibility of electronic information; court order and conditions of discovery; monetary sanctions; contempt of court; electronically stored information sanctions

(a) If a deponent fails to answer any question or to produce any document, electronically stored information, or tangible thing under the deponent's control that is specified in the deposition notice or a deposition subpoena, the party seeking discovery may move the court for an order compelling that answer or production.

(b) This motion shall be made no later than 60 days after the completion of the record of the deposition, and shall be accompanied by a meet and confer declaration under Section 2016.040.

(c) Notice of this motion shall be given to all parties and to the deponent either orally at the examination, or by subsequent service in writing. If the notice of the motion is given orally, the deposition officer shall direct the deponent to attend a session of the court at the time specified in the notice.

(d) In a motion under subdivision (a) relating to the production of electronically stored information, the deponent objecting to or opposing the production, inspection, copying, testing, or sampling of electronically stored information on the basis that the information is from a source that is not reasonably accessible because of the undue burden or expense shall bear the burden of demonstrating that the information is from a source that is not reasonably accessible because of undue burden or expense.

(e) If the deponent from whom discovery of electronically stored information is sought establishes that the information is from a source that is not reasonably accessible because of the undue burden or expense, the court may nonetheless order discovery if the deposing party shows good cause, subject to any limitations imposed under subdivision (g).

(f) If the court finds good cause for the production of electronically stored information from a source that is not reasonably accessible, the court may set conditions for the discovery of the electronically stored information, including allocation of the expense of discovery.

(g) The court shall limit the frequency or extent of discovery of electronically stored information, even from a source that is reasonably accessible, if the court determines that any of the following conditions exists:

(1) It is possible to obtain the information from some other source that is more convenient, less burdensome, or less expensive.

(2) The discovery sought is unreasonably cumulative or duplicative.

(3) The party seeking discovery has had ample opportunity by discovery in the action to obtain the information sought.

(4) The likely burden or expense of the proposed discovery outweighs the likely benefit, taking into account the amount in controversy, the resources of the parties, the importance of the issues in the litigation, and the importance of the requested discovery in resolving the issues.

(h) Not less than five days prior to the hearing on this motion, the moving party shall lodge with the court a certified copy of any parts of the stenographic transcript of the deposition that are relevant to the motion. If a deposition is recorded by audio or video technology, the moving party is required to lodge a certified copy of a transcript of any parts of the deposition that are relevant to the motion.

(i) If the court determines that the answer or production sought is subject to discovery, it shall order that the answer be given or the production be made on the resumption of the deposition.

(j) The court shall impose a monetary sanction under Chapter 7 (commencing with Section 2023.010) against any party, person, or attorney who unsuccessfully makes or opposes a motion to compel an answer or production, unless it finds that the one subject to the sanction acted with substantial justification or that other circumstances make the imposition of the sanction unjust.

(k) If a deponent fails to obey an order entered under this section, the failure may be considered a contempt of court. In addition, if the disobedient deponent is a party to the action or an officer, director, managing agent, or employee of a party, the court may make those orders that are just against the disobedient party, or against the party with whom the disobedient deponent is affiliated, including the imposition of an issue sanction, an evidence sanction, or a terminating sanction under Chapter 7 (commencing with Section 2023.010). In lieu of or in addition to this sanction, the court may impose a monetary sanction under Chapter 7 (commencing with Section 2023.010) against that party deponent or against any party with whom the deponent is affiliated.

§ 2025.480   CODE OF CIVIL PROCEDURE

(*l*)(1) Notwithstanding subdivisions (j) and (k), absent exceptional circumstances, the court shall not impose sanctions on a deponent or any attorney of a deponent for failure to provide electronically stored information that has been lost, damaged, altered, or overwritten as the result of the routine, good faith operation of an electronic information system.

(2) This subdivision shall not be construed to alter any obligation to preserve discoverable information. *(Added by Stats.2004, c. 182 (A.B.3081), § 23, operative July 1, 2005. Amended by Stats.2005, c. 22 (S.B.1108), § 21; Stats.2012, c. 72 (S.B.1574), § 26.)*

Cross References

Action defined for purposes of this Title, see Code of Civil Procedure § 2016.020.
Computation of time, see Code of Civil Procedure §§ 12 and 12a; Government Code § 6800 et seq.
Court defined for purposes of this Title, see Code of Civil Procedure § 2016.020.
Depositions, see Code of Civil Procedure §§ 2020.010 et seq., 2025.010 et seq., 2026.010, 2027.010, 2028.010 et seq.
Discovery, generally, see Code of Civil Procedure § 2016.010 et seq.
Document defined for purposes of this Title, see Code of Civil Procedure § 2016.020.
Monetary sanctions, see Code of Civil Procedure § 2023.050.
Notice, actual and constructive, defined, see Civil Code § 18.
Writing defined for purposes of this Title, see Code of Civil Procedure § 2016.020.

Research References

Forms

West's California Code Forms, Civil Procedure § 2025.480 Form 1, Evidence—Discovery—Notice of Motion for Order Compelling Answers or Production.
West's California Code Forms, Civil Procedure § 2025.480 Form 4, Evidence—Discovery—Notice of Motion for Order to Strike Pleadings and to Award Monetary Sanctions.

ARTICLE 5. TRANSCRIPT OR RECORDING

Section
2025.510. Transcription of testimony; payment of cost; distribution of original and copies; record retention; audio or video recordings; official record.
2025.520. Reading and correction of transcript; signed approval; change of form or substance of an answer; waiver; suppression motions.
2025.530. Depositions without stenographic transcription; review of recording; change of form or substance of an answer; signed approval; suppression motions.
2025.540. Certification of deposition record; rough draft transcripts.
2025.550. Original certified transcript; transmittal and custody; record retention.
2025.560. Audio or video recording of deposition; transmittal and custody of electronic media; distribution of copies; recording retention.
2025.570. Third–party request where original in possession of deposition officer; availability; notice to parties and deponent; protective orders.

§ 2025.510. Transcription of testimony; payment of cost; distribution of original and copies; record retention; audio or video recordings; official record

(a) Unless the parties agree otherwise, the testimony at a deposition recorded by stenographic means shall be transcribed.

(b) The party noticing the deposition shall bear the cost of the transcription, unless the court, on motion and for good cause shown, orders that the cost be borne or shared by another party.

(c) Notwithstanding subdivision (b) of Section 2025.320, any other party or the deponent, at the expense of that party or deponent, may obtain a copy of the transcript.

(d) If the deposition officer receives a request from a party for an original or a copy of the deposition transcript, or any portion thereof, and the full or partial transcript will be available to that party prior to the time the original or copy would be available to any other party, the deposition officer shall immediately notify all other parties attending the deposition of the request, and shall, upon request by any party other than the party making the original request, make that copy of the full or partial deposition transcript available to all parties at the same time.

(e) Stenographic notes of depositions shall be retained by the reporter for a period of not less than eight years from the date of the deposition, where no transcript is produced, and not less than one year from the date on which the transcript is produced. The notes may be either on paper or electronic media, as long as it allows for satisfactory production of a transcript at any time during the periods specified.

(f) At the request of any other party to the action, including a party who did not attend the taking of the deposition testimony, any party who records or causes the recording of that testimony by means of audio or video technology shall promptly do both of the following:

(1) Permit that other party to hear the audio recording or to view the video recording.

(2) Furnish a copy of the audio or video recording to that other party on receipt of payment of the reasonable cost of making that copy of the recording.

(g) If the testimony at the deposition is recorded both stenographically and by audio or video technology, the stenographic transcript shall be the official record of that testimony for the purpose of the trial and any subsequent hearing or appeal.

(h)(1) The requesting attorney or party appearing in propria persona shall timely pay the deposition officer or the entity providing the services of the deposition officer for the transcription or copy of the transcription described in subdivision (b) or (c), and any other deposition product or service that is requested either orally or in writing.

(2) This subdivision shall apply unless responsibility for the payment is otherwise provided by law or unless the deposition officer or entity is notified in writing at the time the services or products are requested that the party or another identified person will be responsible for payment.

(3) This subdivision does not prohibit or supersede an agreement between an attorney and a party allocating responsibility for the payment of deposition costs to the party.

(4) Nothing in the case of Serrano v. Stefan Merli Plastering Co., Inc. (2008) 162 Cal.App.4th 1014 shall be construed to alter the standards by which a court acquires personal jurisdiction over a nonparty to an action.

(5) The requesting attorney or party appearing in propria persona, upon the written request of a deposition officer who has obtained a final judgment for payment of services provided pursuant to this subdivision, shall provide to the deposition officer an address that can be used to effectuate service for the purpose of Section 708.110 in the manner specified in Section 415.10.

(i) For purposes of this section, "deposition product or service" means any product or service provided in connection with a deposition that qualifies as shorthand reporting, as described in Section 8017 of the Business and Professions Code, and any product or service derived from that shorthand reporting. *(Added by Stats.2004, c. 182 (A.B.3081), § 23, operative July 1, 2005. Amended by Stats.2007, c. 115 (A.B.1211), § 1; Stats.2012, c. 125 (A.B.2372), § 1; Stats.2014, c. 913 (A.B.2747), § 12, eff. Jan. 1, 2015.)*

Cross References

Action defined for purposes of this Title, see Code of Civil Procedure § 2016.020.

Court defined for purposes of this Title, see Code of Civil Procedure § 2016.020.

Depositions, see Code of Civil Procedure §§ 2020.010 et seq., 2025.010 et seq., 2026.010, 2027.010, 2028.010 et seq.

Licensed shorthand reporters and shorthand reporting corporations, specific violations, applicability of section, civil fine, attorney's fees, see Business and Professions Code § 8050.

§ 2025.520. Reading and correction of transcript; signed approval; change of form or substance of an answer; waiver; suppression motions

(a) If the deposition testimony is stenographically recorded, the deposition officer shall send written notice to the deponent and to all parties attending the deposition when the original transcript of the testimony for each session of the deposition is available for reading, correcting, and signing, unless the deponent and the attending parties agree on the record that the reading, correcting, and signing of the transcript of the testimony will be waived or that the reading, correcting, and signing of a transcript of the testimony will take place after the entire deposition has been concluded or at some other specific time.

(b) For 30 days following each notice under subdivision (a), unless the attending parties and the deponent agree on the record or otherwise in writing to a longer or shorter time period, the deponent may change the form or the substance of the answer to a question, and may either approve the transcript of the deposition by signing it, or refuse to approve the transcript by not signing it.

(c) Alternatively, within this same period, the deponent may change the form or the substance of the answer to any question and may approve or refuse to approve the transcript by means of a letter to the deposition officer signed by the deponent which is mailed by certified or registered mail with return receipt requested. A copy of that letter shall be sent by first-class mail to all parties attending the deposition.

(d) For good cause shown, the court may shorten the 30-day period for making changes, approving, or refusing to approve the transcript.

(e) The deposition officer shall indicate on the original of the transcript, if the deponent has not already done so at the office of the deposition officer, any action taken by the deponent and indicate on the original of the transcript, the deponent's approval of, or failure or refusal to approve, the transcript. The deposition officer shall also notify in writing the parties attending the deposition of any changes which the deponent timely made in person.

(f) If the deponent fails or refuses to approve the transcript within the allotted period, the deposition shall be given the same effect as though it had been approved, subject to any changes timely made by the deponent.

(g) Notwithstanding subdivision (f), on a seasonable motion to suppress the deposition, accompanied by a meet and confer declaration under Section 2016.040, the court may determine that the reasons given for the failure or refusal to approve the transcript require rejection of the deposition in whole or in part.

(h) The court shall impose a monetary sanction under Chapter 7 (commencing with Section 2023.010) against any party, person, or attorney who unsuccessfully makes or opposes a motion to suppress a deposition under this section, unless the court finds that the one subject to the sanction acted with substantial justification or that other circumstances make the imposition of the sanction unjust. (Added by Stats.2004, c. 182 (A.B.3081), § 23, operative July 1, 2005.)

Cross References

Action defined for purposes of this Title, see Code of Civil Procedure § 2016.020.

Computation of time, see Code of Civil Procedure §§ 12 and 12a; Government Code § 6800 et seq.

Court defined for purposes of this Title, see Code of Civil Procedure § 2016.020.

Depositions, see Code of Civil Procedure §§ 2020.010 et seq., 2025.010 et seq., 2026.010, 2027.010, 2028.010 et seq.

Notice, actual and constructive, defined, see Civil Code § 18.

Writing defined for purposes of this Title, see Code of Civil Procedure § 2016.020.

§ 2025.530. Depositions without stenographic transcription; review of recording; change of form or substance of an answer; signed approval; suppression motions

(a) If there is no stenographic transcription of the deposition, the deposition officer shall send written notice to the deponent and to all parties attending the deposition that the audio or video recording made by, or at the direction of, any party, is available for review, unless the deponent and all these parties agree on the record to waive the hearing or viewing of the audio or video recording of the testimony.

(b) For 30 days following a notice under subdivision (a), the deponent, either in person or by signed letter to the deposition officer, may change the substance of the answer to any question.

(c) The deposition officer shall set forth in a writing to accompany the recording any changes made by the deponent, as well as either the deponent's signature identifying the deposition as the deponent's own, or a statement of the deponent's failure to supply the signature, or to contact the officer within the period prescribed by subdivision (b).

(d) When a deponent fails to contact the officer within the period prescribed by subdivision (b), or expressly refuses by a signature to identify the deposition as the deponent's own, the deposition shall be given the same effect as though signed.

(e) Notwithstanding subdivision (d), on a reasonable motion to suppress the deposition, accompanied by a meet and confer declaration under Section 2016.040, the court may determine that the reasons given for the refusal to sign require rejection of the deposition in whole or in part.

(f) The court shall impose a monetary sanction under Chapter 7 (commencing with Section 2023.010) against any party, person, or attorney who unsuccessfully makes or opposes a motion to suppress a deposition under this section, unless it finds that the one subject to the sanction acted with substantial justification or that other circumstances make the imposition of the sanction unjust. (Added by Stats.2004, c. 182 (A.B.3081), § 23, operative July 1, 2005.)

Cross References

Computation of time, see Code of Civil Procedure §§ 12 and 12a; Government Code § 6800 et seq.

Court defined for purposes of this Title, see Code of Civil Procedure § 2016.020.

Depositions, see Code of Civil Procedure §§ 2020.010 et seq., 2025.010 et seq., 2026.010, 2027.010, 2028.010 et seq.

Notice, actual and constructive, defined, see Civil Code § 18.

Writing defined for purposes of this Title, see Code of Civil Procedure § 2016.020.

§ 2025.540. Certification of deposition record; rough draft transcripts

(a) The deposition officer shall certify on the transcript of the deposition, or in a writing accompanying an audio or video record of deposition testimony, as described in Section 2025.530, that the deponent was duly sworn and that the transcript or recording is a true record of the testimony given.

(b) When prepared as a rough draft transcript, the transcript of the deposition may not be certified and may not be used, cited, or transcribed as the certified transcript of the deposition proceedings. The rough draft transcript may not be cited or used in any way or at

§ 2025.540

any time to rebut or contradict the certified transcript of deposition proceedings as provided by the deposition officer. *(Added by Stats.2004, c. 182 (A.B.3081), § 23, operative July 1, 2005.)*

Cross References

Depositions, see Code of Civil Procedure §§ 2020.010 et seq., 2025.010 et seq., 2026.010, 2027.010, 2028.010 et seq.

Writing defined for purposes of this Title, see Code of Civil Procedure § 2016.020.

§ 2025.550. Original certified transcript; transmittal and custody; record retention

(a) The certified transcript of a deposition shall not be filed with the court. Instead, the deposition officer shall securely seal that transcript in an envelope or package endorsed with the title of the action and marked: "Deposition of (here insert name of deponent)," and shall promptly transmit it to the attorney for the party who noticed the deposition. This attorney shall store it under conditions that will protect it against loss, destruction, or tampering.

(b) The attorney to whom the transcript of a deposition is transmitted shall retain custody of it until six months after final disposition of the action. At that time, the transcript may be destroyed, unless the court, on motion of any party and for good cause shown, orders that the transcript be preserved for a longer period. *(Added by Stats.2004, c. 182 (A.B.3081), § 23, operative July 1, 2005.)*

Cross References

Action defined for purposes of this Title, see Code of Civil Procedure § 2016.020.

Court defined for purposes of this Title, see Code of Civil Procedure § 2016.020.

Depositions, see Code of Civil Procedure §§ 2020.010 et seq., 2025.010 et seq., 2026.010, 2027.010, 2028.010 et seq.

§ 2025.560. Audio or video recording of deposition; transmittal and custody of electronic media; distribution of copies; recording retention

(a) An audio or video recording of deposition testimony made by, or at the direction of, any party, including a certified recording made by an operator qualified under subdivisions (b) to (f), inclusive, of Section 2025.340, shall not be filed with the court. Instead, the operator shall retain custody of that recording and shall store it under conditions that will protect it against loss, destruction, or tampering, and preserve as far as practicable the quality of the recording and the integrity of the testimony and images it contains.

(b) At the request of any party to the action, including a party who did not attend the taking of the deposition testimony, or at the request of the deponent, that operator shall promptly do both of the following:

(1) Permit the one making the request to hear or to view the recording on receipt of payment of a reasonable charge for providing the facilities for hearing or viewing the recording.

(2) Furnish a copy of the audio or video recording to the one making the request on receipt of payment of the reasonable cost of making that copy of the recording.

(c) The attorney or operator who has custody of an audio or video recording of deposition testimony made by, or at the direction of, any party, shall retain custody of it until six months after final disposition of the action. At that time, the audio or video recording may be destroyed or erased, unless the court, on motion of any party and for good cause shown, orders that the recording be preserved for a longer period. *(Added by Stats.2004, c. 182 (A.B.3081), § 23, operative July 1, 2005. Amended by Stats.2009, c. 88 (A.B.176), § 18.)*

Cross References

Action defined for purposes of this Title, see Code of Civil Procedure § 2016.020.

Court defined for purposes of this Title, see Code of Civil Procedure § 2016.020.

Depositions, see Code of Civil Procedure §§ 2020.010 et seq., 2025.010 et seq., 2026.010, 2027.010, 2028.010 et seq.

§ 2025.570. Third–party request where original in possession of deposition officer; availability; notice to parties and deponent; protective orders

(a) Notwithstanding subdivision (b) of Section 2025.320, unless the court issues an order to the contrary, a copy of the transcript of the deposition testimony made by, or at the direction of, any party, or an audio or video recording of the deposition testimony, if still in the possession of the deposition officer, shall be made available by the deposition officer to any person requesting a copy, on payment of a reasonable charge set by the deposition officer.

(b) If a copy is requested from the deposition officer, the deposition officer shall mail a notice to all parties attending the deposition and to the deponent at the deponent's last known address advising them of all of the following:

(1) The copy is being sought.

(2) The name of the person requesting the copy.

(3) The right to seek a protective order under Section 2025.420.

(c) If a protective order is not served on the deposition officer within 30 days of the mailing of the notice, the deposition officer shall make the copy available to the person requesting the copy.

(d) This section shall apply only to recorded testimony taken at depositions occurring on or after January 1, 1998. *(Added by Stats.2004, c. 182 (A.B.3081), § 23, operative July 1, 2005.)*

Cross References

Computation of time, see Code of Civil Procedure §§ 12 and 12a; Government Code § 6800 et seq.

Court defined for purposes of this Title, see Code of Civil Procedure § 2016.020.

Depositions, see Code of Civil Procedure §§ 2020.010 et seq., 2025.010 et seq., 2026.010, 2027.010, 2028.010 et seq.

Notice, actual and constructive, defined, see Civil Code § 18.

ARTICLE 6. POST–DEPOSITION PROCEDURES

Section
2025.610. Subsequent deposition of deponents; restrictions; exceptions.
2025.620. Use of deposition at trial or other hearings; procedural requirements; permitted uses; submission of total or partial testimony.

§ 2025.610. Subsequent deposition of deponents; restrictions; exceptions

(a) Once any party has taken the deposition of any natural person, including that of a party to the action, neither the party who gave, nor any other party who has been served with a deposition notice pursuant to Section 2025.240 may take a subsequent deposition of that deponent.

(b) Notwithstanding subdivision (a), for good cause shown, the court may grant leave to take a subsequent deposition, and the parties, with the consent of any deponent who is not a party, may stipulate that a subsequent deposition be taken.

(c) This section does not preclude taking one subsequent deposition of a natural person who has previously been examined under either or both of the following circumstances:

(1) The person was examined as a result of that person's designation to testify on behalf of an organization under Section 2025.230.

(2) The person was examined pursuant to a court order under Section 485.230, for the limited purpose of discovering pursuant to

Section 485.230 the identity, location, and value of property in which the deponent has an interest.

(d) This section does not authorize the taking of more than one subsequent deposition for the limited purpose of Section 485.230. *(Added by Stats.2004, c. 182 (A.B.3081), § 23, operative July 1, 2005.)*

Cross References

Action defined for purposes of this Title, see Code of Civil Procedure § 2016.020.
Court defined for purposes of this Title, see Code of Civil Procedure § 2016.020.
Depositions, see Code of Civil Procedure §§ 2020.010 et seq., 2025.010 et seq., 2026.010, 2027.010, 2028.010 et seq.
Notice, actual and constructive, defined, see Civil Code § 18.

§ 2025.620. Use of deposition at trial or other hearings; procedural requirements; permitted uses; submission of total or partial testimony

At the trial or any other hearing in the action, any part or all of a deposition may be used against any party who was present or represented at the taking of the deposition, or who had due notice of the deposition and did not serve a valid objection under Section 2025.410, so far as admissible under the rules of evidence applied as though the deponent were then present and testifying as a witness, in accordance with the following provisions:

(a) Any party may use a deposition for the purpose of contradicting or impeaching the testimony of the deponent as a witness, or for any other purpose permitted by the Evidence Code.

(b) An adverse party may use for any purpose, a deposition of a party to the action, or of anyone who at the time of taking the deposition was an officer, director, managing agent, employee, agent, or designee under Section 2025.230 of a party. It is not ground for objection to the use of a deposition of a party under this subdivision by an adverse party that the deponent is available to testify, has testified, or will testify at the trial or other hearing.

(c) Any party may use for any purpose the deposition of any person or organization, including that of any party to the action, if the court finds any of the following:

(1) The deponent resides more than 150 miles from the place of the trial or other hearing.

(2) The deponent, without the procurement or wrongdoing of the proponent of the deposition for the purpose of preventing testimony in open court, is any of the following:

(A) Exempted or precluded on the ground of privilege from testifying concerning the matter to which the deponent's testimony is relevant.

(B) Disqualified from testifying.

(C) Dead or unable to attend or testify because of existing physical or mental illness or infirmity.

(D) Absent from the trial or other hearing and the court is unable to compel the deponent's attendance by its process.

(E) Absent from the trial or other hearing and the proponent of the deposition has exercised reasonable diligence but has been unable to procure the deponent's attendance by the court's process.

(3) Exceptional circumstances exist that make it desirable to allow the use of any deposition in the interests of justice and with due regard to the importance of presenting the testimony of witnesses orally in open court.

(d) Any party may use a video recording of the deposition testimony of a treating or consulting physician or of any expert witness even though the deponent is available to testify if the deposition notice under Section 2025.220 reserved the right to use the deposition at trial, and if that party has complied with subdivision (m) of Section 2025.340.

(e) Subject to the requirements of this chapter, a party may offer in evidence all or any part of a deposition, and if the party introduces only part of the deposition, any other party may introduce any other parts that are relevant to the parts introduced.

(f) Substitution of parties does not affect the right to use depositions previously taken.

(g) When an action has been brought in any court of the United States or of any state, and another action involving the same subject matter is subsequently brought between the same parties or their representatives or successors in interest, all depositions lawfully taken and duly filed in the initial action may be used in the subsequent action as if originally taken in that subsequent action. A deposition previously taken may also be used as permitted by the Evidence Code. *(Added by Stats.2004, c. 182 (A.B.3081), § 23, operative July 1, 2005.)*

Cross References

Action defined for purposes of this Title, see Code of Civil Procedure § 2016.020.
Court defined for purposes of this Title, see Code of Civil Procedure § 2016.020.
Depositions, see Code of Civil Procedure §§ 2020.010 et seq., 2025.010 et seq., 2026.010, 2027.010, 2028.010 et seq.
Notice, actual and constructive, defined, see Civil Code § 18.
Witness defined for purposes of this Code, see Code of Civil Procedure § 1878.

Research References

Forms

West's California Judicial Council Forms SUBP–015, Deposition Subpena for Personal Appearance.
West's California Judicial Council Forms SUBP–020, Deposition Subpena for Personal Appearance and Production of Documents and Things.
West's California Judicial Council Forms SUBP–040, Deposition Subpena for Personal Appearance in Action Pending Outside California.
West's California Judicial Council Forms SUBP–045, Deposition Subpena for Personal Appearance and Production of Documents, Electronically Stored Information, and Things in Action Pending Outside California.

CHAPTER 10. ORAL DEPOSITION OUTSIDE CALIFORNIA

Section
2026.010. Depositions in another state of the United States.
2027.010. Depositions in a foreign nation.

§ 2026.010. Depositions in another state of the United States

(a) Any party may obtain discovery by taking an oral deposition, as described in Section 2025.010, in another state of the United States, or in a territory or an insular possession subject to its jurisdiction. Except as modified in this section, the procedures for taking oral depositions in California set forth in Chapter 9 (commencing with Section 2025.010) apply to an oral deposition taken in another state of the United States, or in a territory or an insular possession subject to its jurisdiction.

(b) If a deponent is a party to the action or an officer, director, managing agent, or employee of a party, the service of the deposition notice is effective to compel that deponent to attend and to testify, as well as to produce any document, electronically stored information, or tangible thing for inspection, copying, testing, or sampling. The deposition notice shall specify a place in the state, territory, or insular possession of the United States that is within 75 miles of the residence or a business office of a deponent.

(c) If the deponent is not a party to the action or an officer, director, managing agent, or employee of a party, a party serving a deposition notice under this section shall use any process and procedures required and available under the laws of the state, territory, or insular possession where the deposition is to be taken to compel the deponent to attend and to testify, as well as to produce

§ 2026.010

any document, electronically stored information, or tangible thing for inspection, copying, testing, sampling, and any related activity.

(d) A deposition taken under this section shall be conducted in either of the following ways:

(1) Under the supervision of a person who is authorized to administer oaths by the laws of the United States or those of the place where the examination is to be held, and who is not otherwise disqualified under Section 2025.320 and subdivisions (b) to (f), inclusive, of Section 2025.340.

(2) Before a person appointed by the court.

(e) An appointment under subdivision (d) is effective to authorize that person to administer oaths and to take testimony.

(f) On request, the clerk of the court shall issue a commission authorizing the deposition in another state or place. The commission shall request that process issue in the place where the examination is to be held, requiring attendance and enforcing the obligations of the deponents to produce documents and electronically stored information and answer questions. The commission shall be issued by the clerk to any party in any action pending in its venue without a noticed motion or court order. The commission may contain terms that are required by the foreign jurisdiction to initiate the process. If a court order is required by the foreign jurisdiction, an order for a commission may be obtained by ex parte application. (Added by Stats.2004, c. 182 (A.B.3081), § 23, operative July 1, 2005. Amended by Stats.2012, c. 72 (S.B.1574), § 27.)

Cross References

Action defined for purposes of this Title, see Code of Civil Procedure § 2016.020.

Acts constituting waiver of notice, see Code of Civil Procedure § 2004.

Beer pricing and marketing enforcement action, protection of witnesses against self-incrimination, see Business and Professions Code § 25009.

Court defined for purposes of this Title, see Code of Civil Procedure § 2016.020.

Default as waiver of notice of deposition proceedings, see Code of Civil Procedure § 2004.

Depositions, see Code of Civil Procedure § 2020.010 et seq., § 2025.010 et seq., § 2027.010, § 2028.010 et seq.

Discovery, generally, see Code of Civil Procedure § 2016.010 et seq.

Document defined for purposes of this Title, see Code of Civil Procedure § 2016.020.

Notice, actual and constructive, defined, see Civil Code § 18.

Officers, authorized to administer oaths, see Code of Civil Procedure § 2093.

Production of business records, compliance with subpoena duces tecum for business records, see Evidence Code § 1560.

Superior court fees for miscellaneous services, see Government Code § 70626.

Research References

Forms

West's California Code Forms, Civil Procedure § 2026.010 Form 1, Evidence—Discovery—Notice of Motion for Commission for Deposition of Out of State Witness.

West's California Judicial Council Forms DISC–030, Commission to Take Deposition Outside California.

§ 2027.010. Depositions in a foreign nation

(a) Any party may obtain discovery by taking an oral deposition, as described in Section 2025.010, in a foreign nation. Except as modified in this section, the procedures for taking oral depositions in California set forth in Chapter 9 (commencing with Section 2025.010) apply to an oral deposition taken in a foreign nation.

(b) If a deponent is a party to the action or an officer, director, managing agent, or employee of a party, the service of the deposition notice is effective to compel the deponent to attend and to testify, as well as to produce any document, electronically stored information, or tangible thing for inspection, copying, testing, or sampling.

(c) If a deponent is not a party to the action or an officer, director, managing agent or employee of a party, a party serving a deposition notice under this section shall use any process and procedures required and available under the laws of the foreign nation where the deposition is to be taken to compel the deponent to attend and to testify, as well as to produce any document, electronically stored information, or tangible thing for inspection, copying, testing, sampling, and any related activity.

(d) A deposition taken under this section shall be conducted under the supervision of any of the following:

(1) A person who is authorized to administer oaths or their equivalent by the laws of the United States or of the foreign nation, and who is not otherwise disqualified under Section 2025.320 and subdivisions (b) to (f), inclusive, of Section 2025.340.

(2) A person or officer appointed by commission or under letters rogatory.

(3) Any person agreed to by all the parties.

(e) On motion of the party seeking to take an oral deposition in a foreign nation, the court in which the action is pending shall issue a commission, letters rogatory, or a letter of request, if it determines that one is necessary or convenient. The commission, letters rogatory, or letter of request may include any terms and directions that are just and appropriate. The deposition officer may be designated by name or by descriptive title in the deposition notice and in the commission. Letters rogatory or a letter of request may be addressed: "To the Appropriate Judicial Authority in [name of foreign nation]." (Added by Stats.2004, c. 182 (A.B.3081), § 23, operative July 1, 2005. Amended by Stats.2012, c. 72 (S.B.1574), § 28.)

Cross References

Action defined for purposes of this Title, see Code of Civil Procedure § 2016.020.

Court defined for purposes of this Title, see Code of Civil Procedure § 2016.020.

Depositions, see Code of Civil Procedure § 2020.010 et seq., § 2025.010 et seq., § 2026.010, § 2028.010 et seq.

Discovery, generally, see Code of Civil Procedure § 2016.010 et seq.

Document defined for purposes of this Title, see Code of Civil Procedure § 2016.020.

Notice, actual and constructive, defined, see Civil Code § 18.

State departments, investigations and hearings, order to compel witness to answer interrogatories or to attend and testify or produce papers required by subpoena, see Government Code § 11187.

Research References

Forms

West's California Code Forms, Civil Procedure § 2027.010 Form 1, Evidence—Discovery—Notice of Motion for Issuance of Commission or Letters Rogatory.

CHAPTER 11. DEPOSITION BY WRITTEN QUESTIONS

Section
2028.010. Procedures applicable.
2028.020. Notice requirements.
2028.030. Attachment of questions to notice; cross questions; redirect and recross questions.
2028.040. Objection to form of question; service; time to serve; meet and confer declaration; court action.
2028.050. Protection of privileged or attorney work product; time to object; meet and confer declaration; court action.
2028.060. Questions on direct examination; copy for prior study by deponent.
2028.070. Orders for protection of parties and deponents; additional court remedies.
2028.080. Duty of officer before whom deposition is taken.

§ 2028.010. Procedures applicable

Any party may obtain discovery by taking a deposition by written questions instead of by oral examination. Except as modified in this chapter, the procedures for taking oral depositions set forth in Chapters 9 (commencing with Section 2025.010) and 10 (commencing with Section 2026.010) apply to written depositions. *(Added by Stats.2004, c. 182 (A.B.3081), § 23, operative July 1, 2005.)*

Cross References

Acts constituting waiver of notice, see Code of Civil Procedure § 2004.
Depositions, see Code of Civil Procedure §§ 2020.010 et seq., 2025.010 et seq., 2026.010, 2027.010.
Discovery, generally, see Code of Civil Procedure § 2016.010 et seq.
Notice of motion, see Code of Civil Procedure § 1005.
Violation of court order as contempt, see Code of Civil Procedure § 1209.

§ 2028.020. Notice requirements

The notice of a written deposition shall comply with Sections 2025.220 and 2025.230, and with subdivision (c) of Section 2020.240,[1] except as follows:

(a) The name or descriptive title, as well as the address, of the deposition officer shall be stated.

(b) The date, time, and place for commencement of the deposition may be left to future determination by the deposition officer. *(Added by Stats.2004, c. 182 (A.B.3081), § 23, operative July 1, 2005.)*

[1] So in chaptered copy; probably should refer to Section 2025.240.

Cross References

Depositions, see Code of Civil Procedure §§ 2020.010 et seq., 2025.010 et seq., 2026.010, 2027.010, 2028.010 et seq.
Notice, actual and constructive, defined, see Civil Code § 18.

§ 2028.030. Attachment of questions to notice; cross questions; redirect and recross questions

(a) The questions to be propounded to the deponent by direct examination shall accompany the notice of a written deposition.

(b) Within 30 days after the deposition notice and questions are served, a party shall serve any cross questions on all other parties entitled to notice of the deposition.

(c) Within 15 days after being served with cross questions, a party shall serve any redirect questions on all other parties entitled to notice of the deposition.

(d) Within 15 days after being served with redirect questions, a party shall serve any recross questions on all other parties entitled to notice of the deposition.

(e) The court may, for good cause shown, extend or shorten the time periods for the interchange of cross, redirect, and recross questions. *(Added by Stats.2004, c. 182 (A.B.3081), § 23, operative July 1, 2005.)*

Cross References

Computation of time, see Code of Civil Procedure §§ 12 and 12a; Government Code § 6800 et seq.
Court defined for purposes of this Title, see Code of Civil Procedure § 2016.020.
Depositions, see Code of Civil Procedure §§ 2020.010 et seq., 2025.010 et seq., 2026.010, 2027.010, 2028.010 et seq.
Notice, actual and constructive, defined, see Civil Code § 18.

§ 2028.040. Objection to form of question; service; time to serve; meet and confer declaration; court action

(a) A party who objects to the form of any question shall serve a specific objection to that question on all parties entitled to notice of the deposition within 15 days after service of the question. A party who fails to timely serve an objection to the form of a question waives it.

(b) The objecting party shall promptly move the court to sustain the objection. This motion shall be accompanied by a meet and confer declaration under Section 2016.040. Unless the court has sustained that objection, the deposition officer shall propound to the deponent that question subject to that objection as to its form.

(c) The court shall impose a monetary sanction under Chapter 7 (commencing with Section 2023.010) against any party, person, or attorney who unsuccessfully makes or opposes a motion to sustain an objection, unless it finds that the one subject to the sanction acted with substantial justification or that other circumstances make the imposition of the sanction unjust. *(Added by Stats.2004, c. 182 (A.B.3081), § 23, operative July 1, 2005.)*

Cross References

Computation of time, see Code of Civil Procedure §§ 12 and 12a; Government Code § 6800 et seq.
Court defined for purposes of this Title, see Code of Civil Procedure § 2016.020.
Depositions, see Code of Civil Procedure §§ 2020.010 et seq., 2025.010 et seq., 2026.010, 2027.010, 2028.010 et seq.
Notice, actual and constructive, defined, see Civil Code § 18.

§ 2028.050. Protection of privileged or attorney work product; time to object; meet and confer declaration; court action

(a) A party who objects to any question on the ground that it calls for information that is privileged or is protected work product under Chapter 4 (commencing with Section 2018.010) shall serve a specific objection to that question on all parties entitled to notice of the deposition within 15 days after service of the question. A party who fails to timely serve that objection waives it.

(b) The party propounding any question to which an objection is made on those grounds may then move the court for an order overruling that objection. This motion shall be accompanied by a meet and confer declaration under Section 2016.040. The deposition officer shall not propound to the deponent any question to which a written objection on those grounds has been served unless the court has overruled that objection.

(c) The court shall impose a monetary sanction under Chapter 7 (commencing with Section 2023.010) against any party, person, or attorney who unsuccessfully makes or opposes a motion to overrule an objection, unless it finds that the one subject to the sanction acted with substantial justification or that other circumstances make the imposition of the sanction unjust. *(Added by Stats.2004, c. 182 (A.B.3081), § 23, operative July 1, 2005.)*

Cross References

Computation of time, see Code of Civil Procedure §§ 12 and 12a; Government Code § 6800 et seq.
Court defined for purposes of this Title, see Code of Civil Procedure § 2016.020.
Depositions, see Code of Civil Procedure §§ 2020.010 et seq., 2025.010 et seq., 2026.010, 2027.010, 2028.010 et seq.
Notice, actual and constructive, defined, see Civil Code § 18.

§ 2028.060. Questions on direct examination; copy for prior study by deponent

(a) The party taking a written deposition may forward to the deponent a copy of the questions on direct examination for study prior to the deposition.

(b) No party or attorney shall permit the deponent to preview the form or the substance of any cross, redirect, or recross questions. *(Added by Stats.2004, c. 182 (A.B.3081), § 23, operative July 1, 2005.)*

Cross References

Depositions, see Code of Civil Procedure §§ 2020.010 et seq., 2025.010 et seq., 2026.010, 2027.010, 2028.010 et seq.

§ 2028.070. Orders for protection of parties and deponents; additional court remedies

In addition to any appropriate order listed in Section 2025.420, the court may order any of the following:

§ 2028.070

(a) That the deponent's testimony be taken by oral, instead of written, examination.

(b) That one or more of the parties receiving notice of the written deposition be permitted to attend in person or by attorney and to propound questions to the deponent by oral examination.

(c) That objections under Sections 2028.040 and 2028.050 be sustained or overruled.

(d) That the deposition be taken before an officer other than the one named or described in the deposition notice. *(Added by Stats.2004, c. 182 (A.B.3081), § 23, operative July 1, 2005.)*

Cross References

Court defined for purposes of this Title, see Code of Civil Procedure § 2016.020.
Depositions, see Code of Civil Procedure §§ 2020.010 et seq., 2025.010 et seq., 2026.010, 2027.010, 2028.010 et seq.
Notice, actual and constructive, defined, see Civil Code § 18.

Research References

Forms

West's California Code Forms, Civil Procedure § 2028.070 Form 1, Evidence—Discovery—Notice of Motion for Protective Order Requiring that Deposition be Taken by Oral Examination.

§ 2028.080. Duty of officer before whom deposition is taken

The party taking a written deposition shall deliver to the officer designated in the deposition notice a copy of that notice and of all questions served under Section 2028.030. The deposition officer shall proceed promptly to propound the questions and to take and record the testimony of the deponent in response to the questions. *(Added by Stats.2004, c. 182 (A.B.3081), § 23, operative July 1, 2005.)*

Cross References

Depositions, see Code of Civil Procedure §§ 2020.010 et seq., 2025.010 et seq., 2026.010, 2027.010, 2028.010 et seq.
Notice, actual and constructive, defined, see Civil Code § 18.

CHAPTER 12. DISCOVERY IN ACTION PENDING OUTSIDE CALIFORNIA

ARTICLE 1. INTERSTATE AND INTERNATIONAL DEPOSITIONS AND DISCOVERY ACT

Section
2029.100. Short title.
2029.200. Definitions.
2029.300. Issuance of subpoena.
2029.350. Foreign subpoenas; issuance of subpoena under this article.
2029.390. Judicial Council; development of forms.
2029.400. Service of subpoena.
2029.500. Deposition, production, and inspection; applicable laws and rules.
2029.600. Application to court.
2029.610. Fees; assignment of case number; requirements for filed documents.
2029.620. Subsequent petitions.
2029.630. Application of requirements of Code of Civil Procedure § 1005.
2029.640. Witnesses in state; necessity of subpoena.
2029.650. Writ petition.
2029.700. Uniformity of application and construction.
2029.800. Application to pending actions.
2029.900. Operative date.

Operative Effect

For operative effect of this Article, see Code of Civil Procedure § 2029.900.

§ 2029.100. Short title

This article may be cited as the Interstate and International Depositions and Discovery Act. *(Added by Stats.2008, c. 231 (A.B.2193), § 3, operative Jan. 1, 2010.)*

Operative Effect

For operative effect of this Article, see Code of Civil Procedure § 2029.900.

Research References

Forms

West's California Judicial Council Forms SUBP-030, Application for Discovery Subpena in Action Pending Outside California.
West's California Judicial Council Forms SUBP-035, Subpena for Production of Business Records in Action Pending Outside California.
West's California Judicial Council Forms SUBP-040, Deposition Subpena for Personal Appearance in Action Pending Outside California.
West's California Judicial Council Forms SUBP-045, Deposition Subpena for Personal Appearance and Production of Documents, Electronically Stored Information, and Things in Action Pending Outside California.
West's California Judicial Council Forms SUBP-050, Subpena for Inspection of Premises in Action Pending Outside California.

§ 2029.200. Definitions

In this article:

(a) "Foreign jurisdiction" means either of the following:

(1) A state other than this state.

(2) A foreign nation.

(b) "Foreign penal civil action" means a civil action authorized by the law of a state other than this state in which the sole purpose is to punish an offense against the public justice of that state.

(c) "Foreign subpoena" means a subpoena issued under authority of a court of record of a foreign jurisdiction.

(d) "Person" means an individual, corporation, business trust, estate, trust, partnership, limited liability company, association, joint venture, public corporation, government, or governmental subdivision, agency, or instrumentality, or any other legal or commercial entity.

(e) "State" means a state of the United States, the District of Columbia, Puerto Rico, the Virgin Islands, a federally recognized Indian tribe, or any territory or insular possession subject to the jurisdiction of the United States.

(f) "Subpoena" means a document, however denominated, issued under authority of a court of record requiring a person to do any of the following:

(1) Attend and give testimony at a deposition.

(2) Produce and permit inspection, copying, testing, or sampling of designated books, documents, records, electronically stored information, or tangible things in the possession, custody, or control of the person.

(3) Permit inspection of premises under the control of the person. *(Added by Stats.2008, c. 231 (A.B.2193), § 3, operative Jan. 1, 2010. Amended by Stats.2012, c. 72 (S.B.1574), § 29; Stats.2022, c. 628 (A.B.2091), § 3, eff. Sept. 27, 2022.)*

Operative Effect

For operative effect of this Article, see Code of Civil Procedure § 2029.900.

Cross References

Prohibition on disclosure of medical information related to individual seeking or obtaining an abortion in response to subpoena or request, criteria, disclosure to law enforcement, see Civil Code § 56.108.

Reproductive Privacy Act, disclosure of information in foreign penal civil action, see Health and Safety Code § 123466.

§ 2029.300. Issuance of subpoena

(a) To request issuance of a subpoena under this section, a party shall submit the original or a true and correct copy of a foreign subpoena to the clerk of the superior court in the county in which discovery is sought to be conducted in this state. A request for the issuance of a subpoena under this section does not constitute making an appearance in the courts of this state.

(b) In addition to submitting a foreign subpoena under subdivision (a), a party seeking discovery shall do both of the following:

(1) Submit an application requesting that the superior court issue a subpoena with the same terms as the foreign subpoena. The application shall be on a form prescribed by the Judicial Council pursuant to Section 2029.390. No civil case cover sheet is required.

(2) Pay the fee specified in Section 70626 of the Government Code.

(c) When a party submits a foreign subpoena to the clerk of the superior court in accordance with subdivision (a), and satisfies the requirements of subdivision (b), the clerk shall promptly issue a subpoena for service upon the person to which the foreign subpoena is directed.

(d) A subpoena issued under this section shall satisfy all of the following conditions:

(1) It shall incorporate the terms used in the foreign subpoena.

(2) It shall contain or be accompanied by the names, addresses, and telephone numbers of all counsel of record in the proceeding to which the subpoena relates and of any party not represented by counsel.

(3) It shall bear the caption and case number of the out-of-state case to which it relates.

(4) It shall state the name of the court that issues it.

(5) It shall be on a form prescribed by the Judicial Council pursuant to Section 2029.390.

(e) Notwithstanding subdivision (a), a subpoena shall not be issued pursuant to this section in any of the following circumstances:

(1) If the foreign subpoena is based on a violation of another state's laws that interfere with a person's right to allow a child to receive gender-affirming health care or gender-affirming mental health care. For the purpose of this paragraph, "gender-affirming health care" and "gender-affirming mental health care" shall have the same meaning as provided in Section 16010.2 of the Welfare and Institutions Code.

(2) If the submitted foreign subpoena relates to a foreign penal civil action and would require disclosure of information related to sensitive services. For purposes of this paragraph, "sensitive services" has the same meaning as defined in Section 791.02 of the Insurance Code. *(Added by Stats.2008, c. 231 (A.B.2193), § 3, operative Jan. 1, 2010. Amended by Stats.2022, c. 628 (A.B.2091), § 4, eff. Sept. 27, 2022; Stats.2022, c. 810 (S.B.107), § 2.5, eff. Jan. 1, 2023.)*

Operative Effect

For operative effect of this Article, see Code of Civil Procedure § 2029.900.

§ 2029.350. Foreign subpoenas; issuance of subpoena under this article

(a) Notwithstanding Sections 1986 and 2029.300, if a party to a proceeding pending in a foreign jurisdiction retains an attorney licensed to practice in this state, who is an active member of the State Bar, and that attorney receives the original or a true and correct copy of a foreign subpoena, the attorney may issue a subpoena under this article.

(b)(1) Notwithstanding subdivision (a), an authorized attorney shall not issue a subpoena pursuant to subdivision (a) if the foreign subpoena is based on a violation of another state's laws that interfere with a person's right to allow a child to receive gender-affirming health care or gender-affirming mental health care.

(2) For the purpose of this subdivision, "gender-affirming health care" and "gender-affirming mental health care" shall have the same meaning as provided in Section 16010.2 of the Welfare and Institutions Code.

(c) Notwithstanding subdivision (a), an attorney shall not issue a subpoena under this article based on a foreign subpoena that relates to a foreign penal civil action and that would require disclosure of information related to sensitive services. For purposes of this subdivision, "sensitive services" has the same meaning as defined in Section 791.02 of the Insurance Code.

(d) A subpoena issued under this section shall satisfy all of the following conditions:

(1) It shall incorporate the terms used in the foreign subpoena.

(2) It shall contain or be accompanied by the names, addresses, and telephone numbers of all counsel of record in the proceeding to which the subpoena relates and of any party not represented by counsel.

(3) It shall bear the caption and case number of the out-of-state case to which it relates.

(4) It shall state the name of the superior court of the county in which the discovery is to be conducted.

(5) It shall be on a form prescribed by the Judicial Council pursuant to Section 2029.390. *(Added by Stats.2008, c. 231 (A.B. 2193), § 3, operative Jan. 1, 2010. Amended by Stats.2022, c. 628 (A.B.2091), § 5, eff. Sept. 27, 2022; Stats.2022, c. 810 (S.B.107), § 3.5, eff. Jan. 1, 2023.)*

Operative Effect

For operative effect of this Article, see Code of Civil Procedure § 2029.900.

§ 2029.390. Judicial Council; development of forms

On or before January 1, 2010, the Judicial Council shall do all of the following:

(a) Prepare an application form to be used for purposes of Section 2029.300.

(b) Prepare one or more new subpoena forms that include clear instructions for use in issuance of a subpoena under Section 2029.300 or 2029.350. Alternatively, the Judicial Council may modify one or more existing subpoena forms to include clear instructions for use in issuance of a subpoena under Section 2029.300 or 2029.350. *(Added by Stats.2008, c. 231 (A.B.2193), § 3.)*

Operative Effect

For operative effect of this Article, see Code of Civil Procedure § 2029.900.

§ 2029.400. Service of subpoena

A subpoena issued under this article shall be personally served in compliance with the law of this state, including, without limitation,

§ 2029.400

Section 1985. *(Added by Stats.2008, c. 231 (A.B.2193), § 3, operative Jan. 1, 2010.)*

Operative Effect

For operative effect of this Article, see Code of Civil Procedure § 2029.900.

§ 2029.500. Deposition, production, and inspection; applicable laws and rules

Titles 3 (commencing with Section 1985) and 4 (commencing with Section 2016.010) of Part 4, and any other law or court rule of this state governing a deposition, a production of documents or other tangible items, or an inspection of premises, including any law or court rule governing payment of court costs or sanctions, apply to discovery under this article. *(Added by Stats.2008, c. 231 (A.B.2193), § 3, operative Jan. 1, 2010.)*

Operative Effect

For operative effect of this Article, see Code of Civil Procedure § 2029.900.

§ 2029.600. Application to court

(a) If a dispute arises relating to discovery under this article, any request for a protective order or to enforce, quash, or modify a subpoena, or for other relief may be filed in the superior court in the county in which discovery is to be conducted and, if so filed, shall comply with the applicable rules or statutes of this state.

(b) A request for relief pursuant to this section shall be referred to as a petition notwithstanding any statute under which a request for the same relief would be referred to as a motion or by another term if it was brought in a proceeding pending in this state.

(c) A petition for relief pursuant to this section shall be accompanied by a civil case cover sheet. *(Added by Stats.2008, c. 231 (A.B.2193), § 3, operative Jan. 1, 2010.)*

Operative Effect

For operative effect of this Article, see Code of Civil Procedure § 2029.900.

§ 2029.610. Fees; assignment of case number; requirements for filed documents

(a) On filing a petition under Section 2029.600, a petitioner who is a party to the out-of-state proceeding shall pay a first appearance fee as specified in Section 70611 of the Government Code. A petitioner who is not a party to the out-of-state proceeding shall pay the fee specified in subdivision (c) of Section 70626 of the Government Code.

(b) The court in which the petition is filed shall assign it a case number.

(c) On responding to a petition under Section 2029.600, a party to the out-of-state proceeding shall pay a first appearance fee as specified in Section 70612 of the Government Code. A person who is not a party to the out-of-state proceeding may file a response without paying a fee.

(d) Any petition, response, or other document filed under this section shall satisfy all of the following conditions:

(1) It shall bear the caption and case number of the out-of-state case to which it relates.

(2) The first page shall state the name of the court in which the document is filed.

(3) The first page shall state the case number assigned by the court under subdivision (b).

(4) The first page shall state whether or not the person filing the document is a party to the out-of-state case. *(Added by Stats.2008, c. 231 (A.B.2193), § 3, operative Jan. 1, 2010. Amended by Stats.2011, c. 308 (S.B.647), § 4.)*

Operative Effect

For operative effect of this Article, see Code of Civil Procedure § 2029.900.

§ 2029.620. Subsequent petitions

(a) If a petition has been filed under Section 2029.600 and another dispute later arises relating to discovery being conducted in the same county for purposes of the same out-of-state proceeding, the deponent or other disputant may file a petition for appropriate relief in the same superior court as the previous petition.

(b) The first page of the petition shall clearly indicate that it is not the first petition filed in that court that relates to the out-of-state case.

(c)(1) If the petitioner in the new dispute is a party to the out-of-state case who previously paid a first appearance fee under this article, the petitioner shall pay a motion fee as specified in subdivision (a) of Section 70617 of the Government Code. If the petitioner in the new dispute is a party to the out-of-state case but has not previously paid a first appearance fee under this article, the petitioner shall pay a first appearance fee as specified in Section 70611 of the Government Code.

(2) If the petitioner in the new dispute is not a party to the out-of-state case, the petitioner shall pay the fee specified in subdivision (c) of Section 70626 of the Government Code, unless the petitioner previously paid that fee. If the petitioner previously paid the fee specified in subdivision (c) of Section 70626 of the Government Code, the petitioner shall pay a motion fee as specified in subdivision (a) of Section 70617 of the Government Code.

(d) If a person responding to the new petition is not a party to the out-of-state case, or is a party who previously paid a first appearance fee under this article, that person does not have to pay a fee for responding. If a person responding to the new petition is a party to the out-of-state case but has not previously paid a first appearance fee under this article, that person shall pay a first appearance fee as specified in Section 70612 of the Government Code.

(e) Any petition, response, or other document filed under this section shall satisfy all of the following conditions:

(1) It shall bear the caption and case number of the out-of-state case to which it relates.

(2) The first page shall state the name of the court in which the document is filed.

(3) The first page shall state the same case number that the court assigned to the first petition relating to the out-of-state case.

(4) The first page shall state whether or not the person filing the document is a party to the out-of-state case.

(f) A petition for relief pursuant to this section shall be accompanied by a civil case cover sheet. *(Added by Stats.2008, c. 231 (A.B.2193), § 3, operative Jan. 1, 2010. Amended by Stats.2011, c. 308 (S.B.647), § 5.)*

Operative Effect

For operative effect of this Article, see Code of Civil Procedure § 2029.900.

§ 2029.630. Application of requirements of Code of Civil Procedure § 1005

A petition under Section 2029.600 or Section 2029.620 is subject to the requirements of Section 1005 relating to notice and to filing and service of papers. *(Added by Stats.2008, c. 231 (A.B.2193), § 3, operative Jan. 1, 2010.)*

Operative Effect

For operative effect of this Article, see Code of Civil Procedure § 2029.900.

§ 2029.640. Witnesses in state; necessity of subpoena

If a party to a proceeding pending in a foreign jurisdiction seeks discovery from a witness in this state by properly issued notice or by agreement, it is not necessary for that party to obtain a subpoena under this article to be able to seek relief under Section 2029.600 or 2029.620. The deponent or any other party may also seek relief under Section 2029.600 or 2029.620 in those circumstances, regardless of whether the deponent was subpoenaed under this article. (Added by Stats.2008, c. 231 (A.B.2193), § 3, operative Jan. 1, 2010.)

Operative Effect

For operative effect of this Article, see Code of Civil Procedure § 2029.900.

§ 2029.650. Writ petition

(a) If a superior court issues an order granting, denying, or otherwise resolving a petition under Section 2029.600 or 2029.620, a person aggrieved by the order may petition the appropriate court of appeal for an extraordinary writ. No order or other action of a court under this article is appealable in this state.

(b) Pending its decision on the writ petition, the court of appeal may stay the order of the superior court, the discovery that is the subject of that order, or both. (Added by Stats.2008, c. 231 (A.B.2193), § 3, operative Jan. 1, 2010.)

Operative Effect

For operative effect of this Article, see Code of Civil Procedure § 2029.900.

§ 2029.700. Uniformity of application and construction

(a) Sections 2029.100, 2029.200, 2029.300, 2029.400, 2029.500, 2029.600, 2029.800, 2029.900, and this section, collectively, constitute and may be referred to as the "California version of the Uniform Interstate Depositions and Discovery Act."

(b) In applying and construing this uniform act, consideration shall be given to the need to promote uniformity of the law with respect to its subject matter among the states that enact it. (Added by Stats.2008, c. 231 (A.B.2193), § 3, operative Jan. 1, 2010.)

Operative Effect

For operative effect of this Article, see Code of Civil Procedure § 2029.900.

§ 2029.800. Application to pending actions

This article applies to requests for discovery in cases pending on or after the operative date of this section. (Added by Stats.2008, c. 231 (A.B.2193), § 3, operative Jan. 1, 2010.)

Operative Effect

For operative effect of this Article, see Code of Civil Procedure § 2029.900.

§ 2029.900. Operative date

Section 2029.390 is operative on January 1, 2009. The remainder of this article is operative on January 1, 2010. (Added by Stats.2008, c. 231 (A.B.2193), § 3, operative Jan. 1, 2010.)

Research References

Forms

West's California Judicial Council Forms SUBP–030, Application for Discovery Subpoena in Action Pending Outside California.

West's California Judicial Council Forms SUBP–035, Subpena for Production of Business Records in Action Pending Outside California.
West's California Judicial Council Forms SUBP–040, Deposition Subpena for Personal Appearance in Action Pending Outside California.
West's California Judicial Council Forms SUBP–045, Deposition Subpena for Personal Appearance and Production of Documents, Electronically Stored Information, and Things in Action Pending Outside California.
West's California Judicial Council Forms SUBP–050, Subpena for Inspection of Premises in Action Pending Outside California.

CHAPTER 13. WRITTEN INTERROGATORIES

Cross References

New motor vehicle board, oaths, depositions, certification of official acts, subpoenas, discovery, see Vehicle Code § 3050.1.

ARTICLE 1. PROPOUNDING INTERROGATORIES

Section
2030.010. Scope of discovery; restrictions.
2030.020. Time to submit interrogatories; motion to submit at earlier time.
2030.030. Special interrogatories; official form interrogatories; restriction on number allowed; numbers in excess of amount allowed.
2030.040. Special interrogatories with supporting declaration; exception to number restrictions; burden of proof; protective order.
2030.050. Special interrogatories exceeding numeric restriction; Declaration for Additional Discovery; form and contents.
2030.060. Form of interrogatories; content requirements.
2030.070. Supplemental interrogatories; restriction on number permitted; exception.
2030.080. Service of documents.
2030.090. Protective orders; persons entitled to protection; time to file; meet and confer; authorized court action; monetary sanctions.

§ 2030.010. Scope of discovery; restrictions

(a) Any party may obtain discovery within the scope delimited by Chapter 2 (commencing with Section 2017.010), and subject to the restrictions set forth in Chapter 5 (commencing with Section 2019.010), by propounding to any other party to the action written interrogatories to be answered under oath.

(b) An interrogatory may relate to whether another party is making a certain contention, or to the facts, witnesses, and writings on which a contention is based. An interrogatory is not objectionable because an answer to it involves an opinion or contention that relates to fact or the application of law to fact, or would be based on information obtained or legal theories developed in anticipation of litigation or in preparation for trial. (Added by Stats.2004, c. 182 (A.B.3081), § 23, operative July 1, 2005. Amended by Stats.2015, c. 303 (A.B.731), § 42, eff. Jan. 1, 2016.)

Cross References

Abuse of discovery, sanctions, see Code of Civil Procedure §§ 2019.010, 2019.030.
Action defined for purposes of this Title, see Code of Civil Procedure § 2016.020.
Discovery, generally, see Code of Civil Procedure § 2016.010 et seq.
Dismissal of action, see Code of Civil Procedure § 581 et seq.
Examination of witnesses on commission, see Penal Code § 1349 et seq.
Privileges, see Evidence Code § 900 et seq.
Violation of court order as contempt, see Code of Civil Procedure § 1209.
Witness defined for purposes of this Code, see Code of Civil Procedure § 1878.

Writing defined for purposes of this Title, see Code of Civil Procedure § 2016.020.

Research References

Forms

West's California Code Forms, Civil § 1940 Form 4, Interrogatories—Unlawful Detainer.

West's California Judicial Council Forms CR-200, Form Interrogatories—Crime Victim Restitution.

West's California Judicial Council Forms DISC-001, Form Interrogatories—General.

West's California Judicial Council Forms DISC-002, Form Interrogatories—Employment Law.

West's California Judicial Council Forms DISC-003, Form Interrogatories—Unlawful Detainer.

West's California Judicial Council Forms DISC-004, Form Interrogatories—Limited Civil Cases (Economic Litigation).

West's California Judicial Council Forms DISC-005, Form Interrogatories—Construction Litigation.

West's California Judicial Council Forms FL-145, Form Interrogatories—Family Law.

West's California Judicial Council Forms UD-106, Form Interrogatories—Unlawful Detainer.

§ 2030.020. Time to submit interrogatories; motion to submit at earlier time

(a) A defendant may propound interrogatories to a party to the action without leave of court at any time.

(b) A plaintiff may propound interrogatories to a party without leave of court at any time that is 10 days after the service of the summons on, or appearance by, that party, whichever occurs first.

(c) Notwithstanding subdivision (b), in an unlawful detainer action or other proceeding under Chapter 4 (commencing with Section 1159) of Title 3 of Part 3, a plaintiff may propound interrogatories to a party without leave of court at any time that is five days after service of the summons on, or appearance by, that party, whichever occurs first.

(d) Notwithstanding subdivisions (b) and (c), on motion with or without notice, the court, for good cause shown, may grant leave to a plaintiff to propound interrogatories at an earlier time. *(Added by Stats.2004, c. 182 (A.B.3081), § 23, operative July 1, 2005. Amended by Stats.2007, c. 113 (A.B.1126), § 7.)*

Cross References

Action defined for purposes of this Title, see Code of Civil Procedure § 2016.020.

Computation of time, see Code of Civil Procedure §§ 12 and 12a; Government Code § 6800 et seq.

Court defined for purposes of this Title, see Code of Civil Procedure § 2016.020.

Notice, actual and constructive, defined, see Civil Code § 18.

Persons upon whom summons may be served, see Code of Civil Procedure § 416.10 et seq.

Research References

Forms

West's California Code Forms, Civil Procedure § 2030.020 Form 1, Evidence—Discovery—Notice of Motion for Leave to Serve Interrogatories Within Ten Days—Order Shortening Time.

§ 2030.030. Special interrogatories; official form interrogatories; restriction on number allowed; numbers in excess of amount allowed

(a) A party may propound to another party either or both of the following:

(1) Thirty-five specially prepared interrogatories that are relevant to the subject matter of the pending action.

(2) Any additional number of official form interrogatories, as described in Chapter 17 (commencing with Section 2033.710), that are relevant to the subject matter of the pending action.

(b) Except as provided in Section 2030.070, no party shall, as a matter of right, propound to any other party more than 35 specially prepared interrogatories. If the initial set of interrogatories does not exhaust this limit, the balance may be propounded in subsequent sets.

(c) Unless a declaration as described in Section 2030.050 has been made, a party need only respond to the first 35 specially prepared interrogatories served, if that party states an objection to the balance, under Section 2030.240, on the ground that the limit has been exceeded. *(Added by Stats.2004, c. 182 (A.B.3081), § 23, operative July 1, 2005.)*

Cross References

Action defined for purposes of this Title, see Code of Civil Procedure § 2016.020.

§ 2030.040. Special interrogatories with supporting declaration; exception to number restrictions; burden of proof; protective order

(a) Subject to the right of the responding party to seek a protective order under Section 2030.090, any party who attaches a supporting declaration as described in Section 2030.050 may propound a greater number of specially prepared interrogatories to another party if this greater number is warranted because of any of the following:

(1) The complexity or the quantity of the existing and potential issues in the particular case.

(2) The financial burden on a party entailed in conducting the discovery by oral deposition.

(3) The expedience of using this method of discovery to provide to the responding party the opportunity to conduct an inquiry, investigation, or search of files or records to supply the information sought.

(b) If the responding party seeks a protective order on the ground that the number of specially prepared interrogatories is unwarranted, the propounding party shall have the burden of justifying the number of these interrogatories. *(Added by Stats.2004, c. 182 (A.B.3081), § 23, operative July 1, 2005.)*

Cross References

Depositions, see Code of Civil Procedure §§ 2020.010 et seq., 2025.010 et seq., 2026.010, 2027.010, 2028.010 et seq.

Discovery, generally, see Code of Civil Procedure § 2016.010 et seq.

§ 2030.050. Special interrogatories exceeding numeric restriction; Declaration for Additional Discovery; form and contents

Any party who is propounding or has propounded more than 35 specially prepared interrogatories to any other party shall attach to each set of those interrogatories a declaration containing substantially the following:

DECLARATION FOR ADDITIONAL DISCOVERY

I, _____, declare:

1. I am (a party to this action or proceeding appearing in propria persona) (presently the attorney for _____, a party to this action or proceeding).

2. I am propounding to _____ the attached set of interrogatories.

3. This set of interrogatories will cause the total number of specially prepared interrogatories propounded to the party to whom they are directed to exceed the number of specially prepared interrogatories permitted by Section 2030.030 of the Code of Civil Procedure.

4. I have previously propounded a total of _____ interrogatories to this party, of which _____ interrogatories were not official form interrogatories.

5. This set of interrogatories contains a total of _____ specially prepared interrogatories.

6. I am familiar with the issues and the previous discovery conducted by all of the parties in the case.

7. I have personally examined each of the questions in this set of interrogatories.

8. This number of questions is warranted under Section 2030.040 of the Code of Civil Procedure because _____. (Here state each factor described in Section 2030.040 that is relied on, as well as the reasons why any factor relied on is applicable to the instant lawsuit.)

9. None of the questions in this set of interrogatories is being propounded for any improper purpose, such as to harass the party, or the attorney for the party, to whom it is directed, or to cause unnecessary delay or needless increase in the cost of litigation.

I declare under penalty of perjury under the laws of California that the foregoing is true and correct, and that this declaration was executed on _____.

_____
(Signature)

Attorney for _____

(Added by Stats.2004, c. 182 (A.B.3081), § 23, operative July 1, 2005. Amended by Stats.2005, c. 22 (S.B.1108), § 22.)

Cross References

Action defined for purposes of this Title, see Code of Civil Procedure § 2016.020.

Attorney's fees and costs, generally, see Code of Civil Procedure § 1021.

Discovery, generally, see Code of Civil Procedure § 2016.010 et seq.

§ 2030.060. Form of interrogatories; content requirements

(a) A party propounding interrogatories shall number each set of interrogatories consecutively.

(b) In the first paragraph immediately below the title of the case, there shall appear the identity of the propounding party, the set number, and the identity of the responding party.

(c) Each interrogatory in a set shall be separately set forth and identified by number or letter.

(d) Each interrogatory shall be full and complete in and of itself. No preface or instruction shall be included with a set of interrogatories unless it has been approved under Chapter 17 (commencing with Section 2033.710).

(e) Any term specially defined in a set of interrogatories shall be typed with all letters capitalized wherever that term appears.

(f) No specially prepared interrogatory shall contain subparts, or a compound, conjunctive, or disjunctive question.

(g) An interrogatory may not be made a continuing one so as to impose on the party responding to it a duty to supplement an answer to it that was initially correct and complete with later acquired information. *(Added by Stats.2004, c. 182 (A.B.3081), § 23, operative July 1, 2005.)*

§ 2030.070. Supplemental interrogatories; restriction on number permitted; exception

(a) In addition to the number of interrogatories permitted by Sections 2030.030 and 2030.040, a party may propound a supplemental interrogatory to elicit any later acquired information bearing on all answers previously made by any party in response to interrogatories.

(b) A party may propound a supplemental interrogatory twice before the initial setting of a trial date, and, subject to the time limits on discovery proceedings and motions provided in Chapter 8 (commencing with Section 2024.010), once after the initial setting of a trial date.

(c) Notwithstanding subdivisions (a) and (b), on motion, for good cause shown, the court may grant leave to a party to propound an additional number of supplemental interrogatories. *(Added by Stats.2004, c. 182 (A.B.3081), § 23, operative July 1, 2005.)*

Cross References

Court defined for purposes of this Title, see Code of Civil Procedure § 2016.020.

Discovery, generally, see Code of Civil Procedure § 2016.010 et seq.

§ 2030.080. Service of documents

(a) The party propounding interrogatories shall serve a copy of them on the party to whom the interrogatories are directed.

(b) The propounding party shall also serve a copy of the interrogatories on all other parties who have appeared in the action. On motion, with or without notice, the court may relieve the party from this requirement on its determination that service on all other parties would be unduly expensive or burdensome. *(Added by Stats.2004, c. 182 (A.B.3081), § 23, operative July 1, 2005.)*

Cross References

Action defined for purposes of this Title, see Code of Civil Procedure § 2016.020.

Court defined for purposes of this Title, see Code of Civil Procedure § 2016.020.

Notice, actual and constructive, defined, see Civil Code § 18.

§ 2030.090. Protective orders; persons entitled to protection; time to file; meet and confer; authorized court action; monetary sanctions

(a) When interrogatories have been propounded, the responding party, and any other party or affected natural person or organization may promptly move for a protective order. This motion shall be accompanied by a meet and confer declaration under Section 2016.040.

(b) The court, for good cause shown, may make any order that justice requires to protect any party or other natural person or organization from unwarranted annoyance, embarrassment, or oppression, or undue burden and expense. This protective order may include, but is not limited to, one or more of the following directions:

(1) That the set of interrogatories, or particular interrogatories in the set, need not be answered.

(2) That, contrary to the representations made in a declaration submitted under Section 2030.050, the number of specially prepared interrogatories is unwarranted.

(3) That the time specified in Section 2030.260 to respond to the set of interrogatories, or to particular interrogatories in the set, be extended.

(4) That the response be made only on specified terms and conditions.

(5) That the method of discovery be an oral deposition instead of interrogatories to a party.

(6) That a trade secret or other confidential research, development, or commercial information not be disclosed or be disclosed only in a certain way.

(7) That some or all of the answers to interrogatories be sealed and thereafter opened only on order of the court.

(c) If the motion for a protective order is denied in whole or in part, the court may order that the party provide or permit the discovery against which protection was sought on terms and conditions that are just.

(d) The court shall impose a monetary sanction under Chapter 7 (commencing with Section 2023.010) against any party, person, or

§ 2030.090

attorney who unsuccessfully makes or opposes a motion for a protective order under this section, unless it finds that the one subject to the sanction acted with substantial justification or that other circumstances make the imposition of the sanction unjust. *(Added by Stats.2004, c. 182 (A.B.3081), § 23, operative July 1, 2005.)*

Cross References

Court defined for purposes of this Title, see Code of Civil Procedure § 2016.020.

Depositions, see Code of Civil Procedure §§ 2020.010 et seq., 2025.010 et seq., 2026.010, 2027.010, 2028.010 et seq.

Discovery, generally, see Code of Civil Procedure § 2016.010 et seq.

Research References

Forms

West's California Code Forms, Civil Procedure § 2030.090 Form 1, Evidence—Discovery—Notice of Motion for Protective Order—Interrogatories.

West's California Code Forms, Civil Procedure § 2030.090 Form 5, Evidence—Discovery—Notice of Motion for Order Substituting an Oral Deposition for Interrogatories to a Party.

ARTICLE 2. RESPONSE TO INTERROGATORIES

Section

2030.210. Mode of response; required contents.
2030.220. Answers in response; contents and form; obligations of responding party.
2030.230. Answers supplemented by attached documents; specificity of references to attachments; examination and inspection by responding party.
2030.240. Partial objection to form of interrogatory; response; statement of claim of privilege or work product.
2030.250. Signature upon response; oath; officers or agents of an entity; responses containing objections.
2030.260. Time to respond; shortening of time; copies to all parties.
2030.270. Time to respond; extension of time by agreement.
2030.280. Custody of interrogatories, responses and supporting documents; originals; record retention.
2030.290. Untimely responses; waiver of rights; exception; motions to compel; monetary sanctions.
2030.300. Motion to compel further response; meet and confer declaration; time to serve motion; monetary sanctions; failure to obey court order.
2030.310. Amended answers to interrogatories; use at trial; motion to bind original answer; meet and confer; court order; monetary sanctions.

§ 2030.210. Mode of response; required contents

(a) The party to whom interrogatories have been propounded shall respond in writing under oath separately to each interrogatory by any of the following:

(1) An answer containing the information sought to be discovered.

(2) An exercise of the party's option to produce writings.

(3) An objection to the particular interrogatory.

(b) In the first paragraph of the response immediately below the title of the case, there shall appear the identity of the responding party, the set number, and the identity of the propounding party.

(c) Each answer, exercise of option, or objection in the response shall bear the same identifying number or letter and be in the same sequence as the corresponding interrogatory. The text of that interrogatory need not be repeated, except as provided in paragraph (6) of subdivision (d).

(d) In order to facilitate the discovery process:

(1) Except as provided in paragraph (5), upon request by the responding party, the propounding party shall provide the interrogatories in an electronic format to the responding party within three court days of the request.

(2) Except as provided in paragraph (5), upon request by the propounding party after receipt of the responses to the interrogatories, the responding party shall provide the responses in an electronic format to the propounding party within three court days of the request.

(3) A party may provide the interrogatories or responses to the interrogatories requested pursuant to paragraphs (1) and (2) in any format agreed upon by the parties. If the parties are unable to agree on a format, the interrogatories or responses to interrogatories shall be provided in plain text format.

(4) A party may transmit the interrogatories or responses to the interrogatories requested pursuant to paragraphs (1) and (2) by any method agreed upon by the parties. If the parties are unable to agree on a method of transmission, the interrogatories or responses to interrogatories shall be transmitted by electronic mail to an email address provided by the requesting party.

(5) If the interrogatories or responses to interrogatories were not created in an electronic format, a party is not required to create the interrogatories or response to interrogatories in an electronic format for the purpose of transmission to the requesting party.

(6) A responding party who has requested and received the interrogatories in an electronic format pursuant to paragraph (1) shall include the text of the interrogatory immediately preceding the response. *(Added by Stats.2004, c. 182 (A.B.3081), § 23, operative July 1, 2005. Amended by Stats.2019, c. 190 (A.B.1349), § 1, eff. Jan. 1, 2020.)*

Cross References

Writing defined for purposes of this Title, see Code of Civil Procedure § 2016.020.

Research References

Forms

West's California Code Forms, Corporations § 800 Form 6, Interrogatories to Defendants—Alter Ego.

§ 2030.220. Answers in response; contents and form; obligations of responding party

(a) Each answer in a response to interrogatories shall be as complete and straightforward as the information reasonably available to the responding party permits.

(b) If an interrogatory cannot be answered completely, it shall be answered to the extent possible.

(c) If the responding party does not have personal knowledge sufficient to respond fully to an interrogatory, that party shall so state, but shall make a reasonable and good faith effort to obtain the information by inquiry to other natural persons or organizations, except where the information is equally available to the propounding party. *(Added by Stats.2004, c. 182 (A.B.3081), § 23, operative July 1, 2005.)*

§ 2030.230. Answers supplemented by attached documents; specificity of references to attachments; examination and inspection by responding party

If the answer to an interrogatory would necessitate the preparation or the making of a compilation, abstract, audit, or summary of or from the documents of the party to whom the interrogatory is directed, and if the burden or expense of preparing or making it would be substantially the same for the party propounding the interrogatory as for the responding party, it is a sufficient answer to that interrogatory to refer to this section and to specify the writings from which the answer may be derived or ascertained. This specification shall be in sufficient detail to permit the propounding party to locate and to identify, as readily as the responding party can, the documents from which the answer may be ascertained. The responding party shall then afford to the propounding party a reasonable opportunity to examine, audit, or inspect these documents and to make copies, compilations, abstracts, or summaries of them. *(Added by Stats.2004, c. 182 (A.B.3081), § 23, operative July 1, 2005.)*

Cross References

Document defined for purposes of this Title, see Code of Civil Procedure § 2016.020.

Writing defined for purposes of this Title, see Code of Civil Procedure § 2016.020.

§ 2030.240. Partial objection to form of interrogatory; response; statement of claim of privilege or work product

(a) If only a part of an interrogatory is objectionable, the remainder of the interrogatory shall be answered.

(b) If an objection is made to an interrogatory or to a part of an interrogatory, the specific ground for the objection shall be set forth clearly in the response. If an objection is based on a claim of privilege, the particular privilege invoked shall be clearly stated. If an objection is based on a claim that the information sought is protected work product under Chapter 4 (commencing with Section 2018.010), that claim shall be expressly asserted. *(Added by Stats. 2004, c. 182 (A.B.3081), § 23, operative July 1, 2005.)*

§ 2030.250. Signature upon response; oath; officers or agents of an entity; responses containing objections

(a) The party to whom the interrogatories are directed shall sign the response under oath unless the response contains only objections.

(b) If that party is a public or private corporation, or a partnership, association, or governmental agency, one of its officers or agents shall sign the response under oath on behalf of that party. If the officer or agent signing the response on behalf of that party is an attorney acting in that capacity for the party, that party waives any lawyer-client privilege and any protection for work product under Chapter 4 (commencing with Section 2018.010) during any subsequent discovery from that attorney concerning the identity of the sources of the information contained in the response.

(c) The attorney for the responding party shall sign any responses that contain an objection. *(Added by Stats.2004, c. 182 (A.B.3081), § 23, operative July 1, 2005.)*

Cross References

Discovery, generally, see Code of Civil Procedure § 2016.010 et seq.

§ 2030.260. Time to respond; shortening of time; copies to all parties

(a) Within 30 days after service of interrogatories, the party to whom the interrogatories are propounded shall serve the original of the response to them on the propounding party, unless on motion of the propounding party the court has shortened the time for response, or unless on motion of the responding party the court has extended the time for response.

(b) Notwithstanding subdivision (a), in an unlawful detainer action or other proceeding under Chapter 4 (commencing with Section 1159) of Title 3 of Part 3, the party to whom the interrogatories are propounded shall have five days from the date of service to respond, unless on motion of the propounding party the court has shortened the time for response, or unless on motion of the responding party the court has extended the time for response.

(c) The party to whom the interrogatories are propounded shall also serve a copy of the response on all other parties who have appeared in the action. On motion, with or without notice, the court may relieve the party from this requirement on its determination that service on all other parties would be unduly expensive or burdensome. *(Added by Stats.2004, c. 182 (A.B.3081), § 23, operative July 1, 2005. Amended by Stats.2007, c. 113 (A.B.1126), § 8.)*

Cross References

Action defined for purposes of this Title, see Code of Civil Procedure § 2016.020.

Computation of time, see Code of Civil Procedure §§ 12 and 12a; Government Code § 6800 et seq.

Court defined for purposes of this Title, see Code of Civil Procedure § 2016.020.

Notice, actual and constructive, defined, see Civil Code § 18.

Research References

Forms

West's California Code Forms, Civil Procedure § 2030.060 Form 1, Evidence—Discovery—Written Interrogatories.

West's California Code Forms, Civil Procedure § 2030.260 Form 1, Evidence—Discovery—Notice of Motion for Order Enlarging Time to Answer Interrogatories.

§ 2030.270. Time to respond; extension of time by agreement

(a) The party propounding interrogatories and the responding party may agree to extend the time for service of a response to a set of interrogatories, or to particular interrogatories in a set, to a date beyond that provided in Section 2030.260.

(b) This agreement may be informal, but it shall be confirmed in a writing that specifies the extended date for service of a response.

(c) Unless this agreement expressly states otherwise, it is effective to preserve to the responding party the right to respond to any interrogatory to which the agreement applies in any manner specified in Sections 2030.210, 2030.220, 2030.230, and 2030.240. *(Added by Stats.2004, c. 182 (A.B.3081), § 23, operative July 1, 2005.)*

Cross References

Writing defined for purposes of this Title, see Code of Civil Procedure § 2016.020.

§ 2030.280. Custody of interrogatories, responses and supporting documents; originals; record retention

(a) The interrogatories and the response thereto shall not be filed with the court.

(b) The propounding party shall retain both the original of the interrogatories, with the original proof of service affixed to them, and the original of the sworn response until six months after final disposition of the action. At that time, both originals may be destroyed, unless the court on motion of any party and for good cause shown orders that the originals be preserved for a longer period. *(Added by Stats.2004, c. 182 (A.B.3081), § 23, operative July 1, 2005.)*

Cross References

Action defined for purposes of this Title, see Code of Civil Procedure § 2016.020.

Court defined for purposes of this Title, see Code of Civil Procedure § 2016.020.

Proof of service, see Code of Civil Procedure § 417.10 et seq.

§ 2030.290. Untimely responses; waiver of rights; exception; motions to compel; monetary sanctions

If a party to whom interrogatories are directed fails to serve a timely response, the following rules apply:

(a) The party to whom the interrogatories are directed waives any right to exercise the option to produce writings under Section 2030.230, as well as any objection to the interrogatories, including one based on privilege or on the protection for work product under Chapter 4 (commencing with Section 2018.010). The court, on motion, may relieve that party from this waiver on its determination that both of the following conditions are satisfied:

§ 2030.290

(1) The party has subsequently served a response that is in substantial compliance with Sections 2030.210, 2030.220, 2030.230, and 2030.240.

(2) The party's failure to serve a timely response was the result of mistake, inadvertence, or excusable neglect.

(b) The party propounding the interrogatories may move for an order compelling response to the interrogatories.

(c) The court shall impose a monetary sanction under Chapter 7 (commencing with Section 2023.010) against any party, person, or attorney who unsuccessfully makes or opposes a motion to compel a response to interrogatories, unless it finds that the one subject to the sanction acted with substantial justification or that other circumstances make the imposition of the sanction unjust. If a party then fails to obey an order compelling answers, the court may make those orders that are just, including the imposition of an issue sanction, an evidence sanction, or a terminating sanction under Chapter 7 (commencing with Section 2023.010). In lieu of or in addition to that sanction, the court may impose a monetary sanction under Chapter 7 (commencing with Section 2023.010). *(Added by Stats. 2004, c. 182 (A.B.3081), § 23, operative July 1, 2005.)*

Cross References

Court defined for purposes of this Title, see Code of Civil Procedure § 2016.020.

Writing defined for purposes of this Title, see Code of Civil Procedure § 2016.020.

Research References

Forms

West's California Code Forms, Civil Procedure § 2030.290 Form 1, Evidence—Discovery—Notice of Motion for Order Compelling Further Response to Interrogatories.

§ 2030.300. Motion to compel further response; meet and confer declaration; time to serve motion; monetary sanctions; failure to obey court order

(a) On receipt of a response to interrogatories, the propounding party may move for an order compelling a further response if the propounding party deems that any of the following apply:

(1) An answer to a particular interrogatory is evasive or incomplete.

(2) An exercise of the option to produce documents under Section 2030.230 is unwarranted or the required specification of those documents is inadequate.

(3) An objection to an interrogatory is without merit or too general.

(b)(1) A motion under subdivision (a) shall be accompanied by a meet and confer declaration under Section 2016.040.

(2) In lieu of a separate statement required under the California Rules of Court, the court may allow the moving party to submit a concise outline of the discovery request and each response in dispute.

(c) Unless notice of this motion is given within 45 days of the service of the verified response, or any supplemental verified response, or on or before any specific later date to which the propounding party and the responding party have agreed in writing, the propounding party waives any right to compel a further response to the interrogatories.

(d) The court shall impose a monetary sanction under Chapter 7 (commencing with Section 2023.010) against any party, person, or attorney who unsuccessfully makes or opposes a motion to compel a further response to interrogatories, unless it finds that the one subject to the sanction acted with substantial justification or that other circumstances make the imposition of the sanction unjust.

(e) If a party then fails to obey an order compelling further response to interrogatories, the court may make those orders that are just, including the imposition of an issue sanction, an evidence sanction, or a terminating sanction under Chapter 7 (commencing with Section 2023.010). In lieu of, or in addition to, that sanction, the court may impose a monetary sanction under Chapter 7 (commencing with Section 2023.010). *(Added by Stats.2004, c. 182 (A.B.3081), § 23, operative July 1, 2005. Amended by Stats.2013, c. 18 (A.B.1183), § 1; Stats.2018, c. 317 (A.B.2230), § 3, eff. Jan. 1, 2019, operative Jan. 1, 2020.)*

Cross References

Computation of time, see Code of Civil Procedure §§ 12 and 12a; Government Code § 6800 et seq.

Court defined for purposes of this Title, see Code of Civil Procedure § 2016.020.

Document defined for purposes of this Title, see Code of Civil Procedure § 2016.020.

Notice, actual and constructive, defined, see Civil Code § 18.

Writing defined for purposes of this Title, see Code of Civil Procedure § 2016.020.

§ 2030.310. Amended answers to interrogatories; use at trial; motion to bind original answer; meet and confer; court order; monetary sanctions

(a) Without leave of court, a party may serve an amended answer to any interrogatory that contains information subsequently discovered, inadvertently omitted, or mistakenly stated in the initial interrogatory. At the trial of the action, the propounding party or any other party may use the initial answer under Section 2030.410, and the responding party may then use the amended answer.

(b) The party who propounded an interrogatory to which an amended answer has been served may move for an order that the initial answer to that interrogatory be deemed binding on the responding party for the purpose of the pending action. This motion shall be accompanied by a meet and confer declaration under Section 2016.040.

(c) The court shall grant a motion under subdivision (b) if it determines that all of the following conditions are satisfied:

(1) The initial failure of the responding party to answer the interrogatory correctly has substantially prejudiced the party who propounded the interrogatory.

(2) The responding party has failed to show substantial justification for the initial answer to that interrogatory.

(3) The prejudice to the propounding party cannot be cured either by a continuance to permit further discovery or by the use of the initial answer under Section 2030.410.

(d) The court shall impose a monetary sanction under Chapter 7 (commencing with Section 2023.010) against any party, person, or attorney who unsuccessfully makes or opposes a motion to deem binding an initial answer to an interrogatory, unless it finds that the one subject to the sanction acted with substantial justification or that other circumstances make the imposition of the sanction unjust. *(Added by Stats.2004, c. 182 (A.B.3081), § 23, operative July 1, 2005.)*

Cross References

Action defined for purposes of this Title, see Code of Civil Procedure § 2016.020.

Court defined for purposes of this Title, see Code of Civil Procedure § 2016.020.

Discovery, generally, see Code of Civil Procedure § 2016.010 et seq.

ARTICLE 3. USE OF INTERROGATORY ANSWER

Section

2030.410. Trial or hearing in which respondent is a party.

§ 2030.410. Trial or hearing in which respondent is a party

At the trial or any other hearing in the action, so far as admissible under the rules of evidence, the propounding party or any party other than the responding party may use any answer or part of an answer to an interrogatory only against the responding party. It is not ground for objection to the use of an answer to an interrogatory that the responding party is available to testify, has testified, or will testify at the trial or other hearing. *(Added by Stats.2004, c. 182 (A.B.3081), § 23, operative July 1, 2005.)*

Cross References
Action defined for purposes of this Title, see Code of Civil Procedure § 2016.020.

Research References
Forms
West's California Code Forms, Civil § 1940 Form 4, Interrogatories—Unlawful Detainer.
West's California Judicial Council Forms CR-200, Form Interrogatories—Crime Victim Restitution.
West's California Judicial Council Forms DISC-001, Form Interrogatories—General.
West's California Judicial Council Forms DISC-002, Form Interrogatories—Employment Law.
West's California Judicial Council Forms DISC-003, Form Interrogatories—Unlawful Detainer.
West's California Judicial Council Forms DISC-004, Form Interrogatories—Limited Civil Cases (Economic Litigation).
West's California Judicial Council Forms DISC-005, Form Interrogatories—Construction Litigation.
West's California Judicial Council Forms FL-145, Form Interrogatories—Family Law.
West's California Judicial Council Forms UD-106, Form Interrogatories—Unlawful Detainer.

CHAPTER 14. INSPECTION, COPYING, TESTING, SAMPLING, AND PRODUCTION OF DOCUMENTS, ELECTRONICALLY STORED INFORMATION, TANGIBLE THINGS, LAND, AND OTHER PROPERTY

Cross References
Long-term health facilities, quality assurance log, discoverability or admissibility, see Health and Safety Code § 1424.1.
Privileged publication or broadcast, see Civil Code § 47.

ARTICLE 1. INSPECTION DEMAND

Section
2031.010. Persons subject to demand; scope of demand; entrance on land or property; electronically stored information.
2031.020. Time to make demand; inspection, copying, testing, or sampling prior to time allowed.
2031.030. Form and content of demand.
2031.040. Service of documents.
2031.050. Supplemental demands; limitations and restrictions; court order.
2031.060. Protective order; time to demand; meet and confer; authorized court action; electronically stored information; monetary sanctions.

§ 2031.010. Persons subject to demand; scope of demand; entrance on land or property; electronically stored information

(a) Any party may obtain discovery within the scope delimited by Chapter 2 (commencing with Section 2017.010), and subject to the restrictions set forth in Chapter 5 (commencing with Section 2019.010), by inspecting, copying, testing, or sampling documents, tangible things, land or other property, and electronically stored information in the possession, custody, or control of any other party to the action.

(b) A party may demand that any other party produce and permit the party making the demand, or someone acting on the demanding party's behalf, to inspect and to copy a document that is in the possession, custody, or control of the party on whom the demand is made.

(c) A party may demand that any other party produce and permit the party making the demand, or someone acting on the demanding party's behalf, to inspect and to photograph, test, or sample any tangible things that are in the possession, custody, or control of the party on whom the demand is made.

(d) A party may demand that any other party allow the party making the demand, or someone acting on the demanding party's behalf, to enter on any land or other property that is in the possession, custody, or control of the party on whom the demand is made, and to inspect and to measure, survey, photograph, test, or sample the land or other property, or any designated object or operation on it.

(e) A party may demand that any other party produce and permit the party making the demand, or someone acting on the demanding party's behalf, to inspect, copy, test, or sample electronically stored information in the possession, custody, or control of the party on whom demand is made. *(Added by Stats.2004, c. 182 (A.B.3081), § 23, operative July 1, 2005. Amended by Stats.2009, c. 5 (A.B.5), § 4, eff. June 29, 2009; Stats.2016, c. 86 (S.B.1171), § 42, eff. Jan. 1, 2017.)*

Cross References
Abuse of discovery, sanctions, see Code of Civil Procedure § 2023.
Action defined for purposes of this Title, see Code of Civil Procedure § 2016.020.
Acts constituting waiver of notice, see Code of Civil Procedure § 2004.
Discovery, generally, see Code of Civil Procedure § 2016.010 et seq.
Dismissal of action, see Code of Civil Procedure § 581 et seq.
Document defined for purposes of this Title, see Code of Civil Procedure § 2016.020.
Examination of witnesses on commission, see Penal Code § 1349 et seq.
Frequency or extent of discovery, restrictions, see Code of Civil Procedure § 2019.030.
Monetary sanctions, see Code of Civil Procedure § 2023.050.
Privileges, see Evidence Code § 900 et seq.
Subpoena, issuance for attendance of witnesses, see Code of Civil Procedure § 1985 et seq.
Violation of court order as contempt, see Code of Civil Procedure § 1209.

§ 2031.020. Time to make demand; inspection, copying, testing, or sampling prior to time allowed

(a) A defendant may make a demand for inspection, copying, testing, or sampling without leave of court at any time.

(b) A plaintiff may make a demand for inspection, copying, testing, or sampling without leave of court at any time that is 10 days after the service of the summons on, or appearance by, the party to whom the demand is directed, whichever occurs first.

(c) Notwithstanding subdivision (b), in an unlawful detainer action or other proceeding under Chapter 4 (commencing with Section 1159) of Title 3 of Part 3, a plaintiff may make a demand for inspection, copying, testing, or sampling without leave of court at any time that is five days after service of the summons on, or appearance by, the party to whom the demand is directed, whichever occurs first.

(d) Notwithstanding subdivisions (b) and (c), on motion with or without notice, the court, for good cause shown, may grant leave to a plaintiff to make a demand for inspection, copying, testing, or sampling at an earlier time. *(Added by Stats.2004, c. 182 (A.B.3081), § 23, operative July 1, 2005. Amended by Stats.2007, c. 113 (A.B. 1126), § 9; Stats.2009, c. 5 (A.B.5), § 5, eff. June 29, 2009.)*

§ 2031.020

Cross References

Action defined for purposes of this Title, see Code of Civil Procedure § 2016.020.
Computation of time, see Code of Civil Procedure §§ 12 and 12a; Government Code § 6800 et seq.
Court defined for purposes of this Title, see Code of Civil Procedure § 2016.020.
Notice, actual and constructive, defined, see Civil Code § 18.
Persons upon whom summons may be served, see Code of Civil Procedure § 416.10 et seq.

§ 2031.030. Form and content of demand

(a)(1) A party demanding inspection, copying, testing, or sampling shall number each set of demands consecutively.

(2) A party demanding inspection, copying, testing, or sampling of electronically stored information may specify the form or forms in which each type of electronically stored information is to be produced.

(b) In the first paragraph immediately below the title of the case, there shall appear the identity of the demanding party, the set number, and the identity of the responding party.

(c) Each demand in a set shall be separately set forth, identified by number or letter, and shall do all of the following:

(1) Designate the documents, tangible things, land or other property, or electronically stored information to be inspected, copied, tested, or sampled either by specifically describing each individual item or by reasonably particularizing each category of item.

(2) Specify a reasonable time for the inspection, copying, testing, or sampling that is at least 30 days after service of the demand, unless the court for good cause shown has granted leave to specify an earlier date. In an unlawful detainer action or other proceeding under Chapter 4 (commencing with Section 1159) of Title 3 of Part 3, the demand shall specify a reasonable time for the inspection, copying, testing, or sampling that is at least five days after service of the demand, unless the court, for good cause shown, has granted leave to specify an earlier date.

(3) Specify a reasonable place for making the inspection, copying, testing, or sampling, and performing any related activity.

(4) Specify any inspection, copying, testing, sampling, or related activity that is being demanded, as well as the manner in which that activity will be performed, and whether that activity will permanently alter or destroy the item involved. *(Added by Stats.2004, c. 182 (A.B.3081), § 23, operative July 1, 2005. Amended by Stats.2007, c. 113 (A.B.1126), § 10; Stats.2009, c. 5 (A.B.5), § 6, eff. June 29, 2009.)*

Cross References

Action defined for purposes of this Title, see Code of Civil Procedure § 2016.020.
Computation of time, see Code of Civil Procedure §§ 12 and 12a; Government Code § 6800 et seq.
Court defined for purposes of this Title, see Code of Civil Procedure § 2016.020.
Document defined for purposes of this Title, see Code of Civil Procedure § 2016.020.
Inspection demand, response, content and form, see Code of Civil Procedure § 2031.210.

§ 2031.040. Service of documents

The party making a demand for inspection, copying, testing, or sampling shall serve a copy of the demand on the party to whom it is directed and on all other parties who have appeared in the action. *(Added by Stats.2004, c. 182 (A.B.3081), § 23, operative July 1, 2005. Amended by Stats.2009, c. 5 (A.B.5), § 7, eff. June 29, 2009.)*

Cross References

Action defined for purposes of this Title, see Code of Civil Procedure § 2016.020.

§ 2031.050. Supplemental demands; limitations and restrictions; court order

(a) In addition to the demands for inspection, copying, testing, or sampling permitted by this chapter, a party may propound a supplemental demand to inspect, copy, test, or sample any later acquired or discovered documents, tangible things, land or other property, or electronically stored information in the possession, custody, or control of the party on whom the demand is made.

(b) A party may propound a supplemental demand for inspection, copying, testing, or sampling twice before the initial setting of a trial date, and, subject to the time limits on discovery proceedings and motions provided in Chapter 8 (commencing with Section 2024.010), once after the initial setting of a trial date.

(c) Notwithstanding subdivisions (a) and (b), on motion, for good cause shown, the court may grant leave to a party to propound an additional number of supplemental demands for inspection, copying, testing, or sampling. *(Added by Stats.2004, c. 182 (A.B.3081), § 23, operative July 1, 2005. Amended by Stats.2009, c. 5 (A.B.5), § 8, eff. June 29, 2009.)*

Cross References

Court defined for purposes of this Title, see Code of Civil Procedure § 2016.020.
Discovery, generally, see Code of Civil Procedure § 2016.010 et seq.
Document defined for purposes of this Title, see Code of Civil Procedure § 2016.020.

§ 2031.060. Protective order; time to demand; meet and confer; authorized court action; electronically stored information; monetary sanctions

(a) When an inspection, copying, testing, or sampling of documents, tangible things, places, or electronically stored information has been demanded, the party to whom the demand has been directed, and any other party or affected person, may promptly move for a protective order. This motion shall be accompanied by a meet and confer declaration under Section 2016.040.

(b) The court, for good cause shown, may make any order that justice requires to protect any party or other person from unwarranted annoyance, embarrassment, or oppression, or undue burden and expense. This protective order may include, but is not limited to, one or more of the following directions:

(1) That all or some of the items or categories of items in the demand need not be produced or made available at all.

(2) That the time specified in Section 2031.260 to respond to the set of demands, or to a particular item or category in the set, be extended.

(3) That the place of production be other than that specified in the demand.

(4) That the inspection, copying, testing, or sampling be made only on specified terms and conditions.

(5) That a trade secret or other confidential research, development, or commercial information not be disclosed, or be disclosed only to specified persons or only in a specified way.

(6) That the items produced be sealed and thereafter opened only on order of the court.

(c) The party or affected person who seeks a protective order regarding the production, inspection, copying, testing, or sampling of electronically stored information on the basis that the information is from a source that is not reasonably accessible because of undue burden or expense shall bear the burden of demonstrating that the information is from a source that is not reasonably accessible because of undue burden or expense.

(d) If the party or affected person from whom discovery of electronically stored information is sought establishes that the information is from a source that is not reasonably accessible because of undue burden or expense, the court may nonetheless order discovery if the demanding party shows good cause, subject to any limitations imposed under subdivision (f).

(e) If the court finds good cause for the production of electronically stored information from a source that is not reasonably accessible, the court may set conditions for the discovery of the electronically stored information, including allocation of the expense of discovery.

(f) The court shall limit the frequency or extent of discovery of electronically stored information, even from a source that is reasonably accessible, if the court determines that any of the following conditions exist:

(1) It is possible to obtain the information from some other source that is more convenient, less burdensome, or less expensive.

(2) The discovery sought is unreasonably cumulative or duplicative.

(3) The party seeking discovery has had ample opportunity by discovery in the action to obtain the information sought.

(4) The likely burden or expense of the proposed discovery outweighs the likely benefit, taking into account the amount in controversy, the resources of the parties, the importance of the issues in the litigation, and the importance of the requested discovery in resolving the issues.

(g) If the motion for a protective order is denied in whole or in part, the court may order that the party to whom the demand was directed provide or permit the discovery against which protection was sought on terms and conditions that are just.

(h) Except as provided in subdivision (i), the court shall impose a monetary sanction under Chapter 7 (commencing with Section 2023.010) against any party, person, or attorney who unsuccessfully makes or opposes a motion for a protective order, unless it finds that the one subject to the sanction acted with substantial justification or that other circumstances make the imposition of the sanction unjust.

(i)(1) Notwithstanding subdivision (h), absent exceptional circumstances, the court shall not impose sanctions on a party or any attorney of a party for failure to provide electronically stored information that has been lost, damaged, altered, or overwritten as the result of the routine, good faith operation of an electronic information system.

(2) This subdivision shall not be construed to alter any obligation to preserve discoverable information. *(Added by Stats.2004, c. 182 (A.B.3081), § 23, operative July 1, 2005. Amended by Stats.2009, c. 5 (A.B.5), § 9, eff. June 29, 2009; Stats.2021, c. 124 (A.B.938), § 15, eff. Jan. 1, 2022.)*

Cross References

Court defined for purposes of this Title, see Code of Civil Procedure § 2016.020.
Discovery, generally, see Code of Civil Procedure § 2016.010 et seq.
Document defined for purposes of this Title, see Code of Civil Procedure § 2016.020.

Research References

Forms

2 California Transactions Forms--Business Transactions § 8:78.10, Retention and Preservation of E-Communications Records.
West's California Code Forms, Civil Procedure § 2031.060 Form 1, Evidence—Discovery—Notice of Motion for Protective Order Sealing Items Produced.

ARTICLE 2. RESPONSE TO INSPECTION DEMAND

Section
2031.210. Content and form of response.
2031.220. Statement of compliance in full or in part.
2031.230. Statement of inability to comply; contents.
2031.240. Partial objection to demand; statement of compliance or representation of inability to comply; privilege log.
2031.250. Signatures; oath; officers or agents; responses with objections.
2031.260. Time to respond.
2031.270. Extension of time to respond; agreement of the parties.
2031.280. Production of documents; form; data translation.
2031.285. Electronically stored information; privileged information or attorney work product.
2031.290. Original demand, response and service documents; custody of documents; record retention.
2031.300. Untimely responses; waiver; motion to compel response; monetary sanctions.
2031.310. Motion to compel further response; form and content; time to bring motion; electronically stored information; monetary sanctions; failure to obey court order.
2031.320. Failure to produce items for inspection, copying, testing, or sampling; order compelling compliance; monetary sanctions; failure to obey court order.

§ 2031.210. Content and form of response

(a) The party to whom a demand for inspection, copying, testing, or sampling has been directed shall respond separately to each item or category of item by any of the following:

(1) A statement that the party will comply with the particular demand for inspection, copying, testing, or sampling by the date set for the inspection, copying, testing, or sampling pursuant to paragraph (2) of subdivision (c) of Section 2031.030 and any related activities.

(2) A representation that the party lacks the ability to comply with the demand for inspection, copying, testing, or sampling of a particular item or category of item.

(3) An objection to the particular demand for inspection, copying, testing, or sampling.

(b) In the first paragraph of the response immediately below the title of the case, there shall appear the identity of the responding party, the set number, and the identity of the demanding party.

(c) Each statement of compliance, each representation, and each objection in the response shall bear the same number and be in the same sequence as the corresponding item or category in the demand, but the text of that item or category need not be repeated.

(d) If a party objects to the discovery of electronically stored information on the grounds that it is from a source that is not reasonably accessible because of undue burden or expense and that the responding party will not search the source in the absence of an agreement with the demanding party or court order, the responding party shall identify in its response the types or categories of sources of electronically stored information that it asserts are not reasonably accessible. By objecting and identifying information of a type or category of source or sources that are not reasonably accessible, the responding party preserves any objections it may have relating to that electronically stored information. *(Added by Stats.2004, c. 182 (A.B.3081), § 23, operative July 1, 2005. Amended by Stats.2007, c. 738 (A.B.1248), § 7; Stats.2009, c. 5 (A.B.5), § 10, eff. June 29, 2009.)*

§ 2031.220. Statement of compliance in full or in part

A statement that the party to whom a demand for inspection, copying, testing, or sampling has been directed will comply with the particular demand shall state that the production, inspection, copying, testing, or sampling, and related activity demanded, will be allowed either in whole or in part, and that all documents or things in the demanded category that are in the possession, custody, or control of that party and to which no objection is being made will be included in the production. *(Added by Stats.2004, c. 182 (A.B.3081), § 23, operative July 1, 2005. Amended by Stats.2009, c. 5 (A.B.5), § 11, eff. June 29, 2009.)*

Cross References

Document defined for purposes of this Title, see Code of Civil Procedure § 2016.020.

§ 2031.230. Statement of inability to comply; contents

A representation of inability to comply with the particular demand for inspection, copying, testing, or sampling shall affirm that a diligent search and a reasonable inquiry has been made in an effort to comply with that demand. This statement shall also specify whether the inability to comply is because the particular item or category has never existed, has been destroyed, has been lost, misplaced, or stolen, or has never been, or is no longer, in the possession, custody, or control of the responding party. The statement shall set forth the name and address of any natural person or organization known or believed by that party to have possession, custody, or control of that item or category of item. *(Added by Stats.2004, c. 182 (A.B.3081), § 23, operative July 1, 2005. Amended by Stats.2009, c. 5 (A.B.5), § 12, eff. June 29, 2009.)*

§ 2031.240. Partial objection to demand; statement of compliance or representation of inability to comply; privilege log

(a) If only part of an item or category of item in a demand for inspection, copying, testing, or sampling is objectionable, the response shall contain a statement of compliance, or a representation of inability to comply with respect to the remainder of that item or category.

(b) If the responding party objects to the demand for inspection, copying, testing, or sampling of an item or category of item, the response shall do both of the following:

(1) Identify with particularity any document, tangible thing, land, or electronically stored information falling within any category of item in the demand to which an objection is being made.

(2) Set forth clearly the extent of, and the specific ground for, the objection. If an objection is based on a claim of privilege, the particular privilege invoked shall be stated. If an objection is based on a claim that the information sought is protected work product under Chapter 4 (commencing with Section 2018.010), that claim shall be expressly asserted.

(c)(1) If an objection is based on a claim of privilege or a claim that the information sought is protected work product, the response shall provide sufficient factual information for other parties to evaluate the merits of that claim, including, if necessary, a privilege log.

(2) It is the intent of the Legislature to codify the concept of a privilege log as that term is used in California case law. Nothing in this subdivision shall be construed to constitute a substantive change in case law. *(Added by Stats.2004, c. 182 (A.B.3081), § 23, operative July 1, 2005. Amended by Stats.2009, c. 5 (A.B.5), § 13, eff. June 29, 2009; Stats.2012, c. 232 (A.B.1354), § 1.)*

Cross References

Document defined for purposes of this Title, see Code of Civil Procedure § 2016.020.

Research References

Forms

West's California Code Forms, Civil Procedure § 2031.210 Form 1, Evidence—Discovery—Response to Inspection Demand.

§ 2031.250. Signatures; oath; officers or agents; responses with objections

(a) The party to whom the demand for inspection, copying, testing, or sampling is directed shall sign the response under oath unless the response contains only objections.

(b) If that party is a public or private corporation or a partnership or association or governmental agency, one of its officers or agents shall sign the response under oath on behalf of that party. If the officer or agent signing the response on behalf of that party is an attorney acting in that capacity for a party, that party waives any lawyer-client privilege and any protection for work product under Chapter 4 (commencing with Section 2018.010) during any subsequent discovery from that attorney concerning the identity of the sources of the information contained in the response.

(c) The attorney for the responding party shall sign any responses that contain an objection. *(Added by Stats.2004, c. 182 (A.B.3081), § 23, operative July 1, 2005. Amended by Stats.2009, c. 5 (A.B.5), § 14, eff. June 29, 2009.)*

Cross References

Discovery, generally, see Code of Civil Procedure § 2016.010 et seq.

§ 2031.260. Time to respond

(a) Within 30 days after service of a demand for inspection, copying, testing, or sampling, the party to whom the demand is directed shall serve the original of the response to it on the party making the demand, and a copy of the response on all other parties who have appeared in the action, unless on motion of the party making the demand, the court has shortened the time for response, or unless on motion of the party to whom the demand has been directed, the court has extended the time for response.

(b) Notwithstanding subdivision (a), in an unlawful detainer action or other proceeding under Chapter 4 (commencing with Section 1159) of Title 3 of Part 3, the party to whom a demand for inspection, copying, testing, or sampling is directed shall have at least five days from the date of service of the demand to respond, unless on motion of the party making the demand, the court has shortened the time for the response, or unless on motion of the party to whom the demand has been directed, the court has extended the time for response. *(Added by Stats.2004, c. 182 (A.B.3081), § 23, operative July 1, 2005. Amended by Stats.2007, c. 113 (A.B.1126), § 11; Stats.2009, c. 5 (A.B.5), § 15, eff. June 29, 2009.)*

Cross References

Action defined for purposes of this Title, see Code of Civil Procedure § 2016.020.

Computation of time, see Code of Civil Procedure §§ 12 and 12a; Government Code § 6800 et seq.

Court defined for purposes of this Title, see Code of Civil Procedure § 2016.020.

§ 2031.270. Extension of time to respond; agreement of the parties

(a) The party demanding inspection, copying, testing, or sampling and the responding party may agree to extend the date for the inspection, copying, testing, or sampling or the time for service of a response to a set of demands, or to particular items or categories of items in a set, to a date or dates beyond those provided in Sections 2031.030, 2031.210, 2031.260, and 2031.280.

(b) This agreement may be informal, but it shall be confirmed in a writing that specifies the extended date for inspection, copying, testing, or sampling, or for the service of a response.

(c) Unless this agreement expressly states otherwise, it is effective to preserve to the responding party the right to respond to any item or category of item in the demand to which the agreement applies in any manner specified in Sections 2031.210, 2031.220, 2031.230, 2031.240, and 2031.280. *(Added by Stats.2004, c. 182 (A.B.3081), § 23, operative July 1, 2005. Amended by Stats.2007, c. 738 (A.B. 1248), § 8; Stats.2009, c. 5 (A.B.5), § 16, eff. June 29, 2009.)*

Cross References

Writing defined for purposes of this Title, see Code of Civil Procedure § 2016.020.

§ 2031.280. Production of documents; form; data translation

(a) Any documents or category of documents produced in response to a demand for inspection, copying, testing, or sampling shall be identified with the specific request number to which the documents respond.

(b) The documents shall be produced on the date specified in the demand pursuant to paragraph (2) of subdivision (c) of Section 2031.030, unless an objection has been made to that date. If the date for inspection has been extended pursuant to Section 2031.270, the documents shall be produced on the date agreed to pursuant to that section.

(c) If a party responding to a demand for production of electronically stored information objects to a specified form for producing the information, or if no form is specified in the demand, the responding party shall state in its response the form in which it intends to produce each type of information.

(d) Unless the parties otherwise agree or the court otherwise orders, the following shall apply:

(1) If a demand for production does not specify a form or forms for producing a type of electronically stored information, the responding party shall produce the information in the form or forms in which it is ordinarily maintained or in a form that is reasonably usable.

(2) A party need not produce the same electronically stored information in more than one form.

(e) If necessary, the responding party at the reasonable expense of the demanding party shall, through detection devices, translate any data compilations included in the demand into reasonably usable form. *(Added by Stats.2004, c. 182 (A.B.3081), § 23, operative July 1, 2005. Amended by Stats.2007, c. 738 (A.B.1248), § 9; Stats.2009, c. 5 (A.B.5), § 17, eff. June 29, 2009; Stats.2019, c. 208 (S.B.370), § 1, eff. Jan. 1, 2020.)*

Cross References

Document defined for purposes of this Title, see Code of Civil Procedure § 2016.020.

§ 2031.285. Electronically stored information; privileged information or attorney work product

(a) If electronically stored information produced in discovery is subject to a claim of privilege or of protection as attorney work product, the party making the claim may notify any party that received the information of the claim and the basis for the claim.

(b) After being notified of a claim of privilege or of protection under subdivision (a), a party that received the information shall immediately sequester the information and either return the specified information and any copies that may exist or present the information to the court conditionally under seal for a determination of the claim.

(c)(1) Prior to the resolution of the motion brought under subdivision (d), a party shall be precluded from using or disclosing the specified information until the claim of privilege is resolved.

(2) A party who received and disclosed the information before being notified of a claim of privilege or of protection under subdivision (a) shall, after that notification, immediately take reasonable steps to retrieve the information.

(d)(1) If the receiving party contests the legitimacy of a claim of privilege or protection, he or she may seek a determination of the claim from the court by making a motion within 30 days of receiving the claim and presenting the information to the court conditionally under seal.

(2) Until the legitimacy of the claim of privilege or protection is resolved, the receiving party shall preserve the information and keep it confidential and shall be precluded from using the information in any manner. *(Added by Stats.2009, c. 5 (A.B.5), § 18, eff. June 29, 2009.)*

Cross References

Means of production of electronically stored information, see Code of Civil Procedure § 1985.8.

Privileged or protected information, objection to disclosure, electronically stored information, see Code of Civil Procedure § 2025.460.

§ 2031.290. Original demand, response and service documents; custody of documents; record retention

(a) The demand for inspection, copying, testing, or sampling, and the response to it, shall not be filed with the court.

(b) The party demanding an inspection, copying, testing, or sampling shall retain both the original of the demand, with the original proof of service affixed to it, and the original of the sworn response until six months after final disposition of the action. At that time, both originals may be destroyed, unless the court, on motion of any party and for good cause shown, orders that the originals be preserved for a longer period. *(Added by Stats.2004, c. 182 (A.B.3081), § 23, operative July 1, 2005. Amended by Stats.2009, c. 5 (A.B.5), § 19, eff. June 29, 2009.)*

Cross References

Action defined for purposes of this Title, see Code of Civil Procedure § 2016.020.

Court defined for purposes of this Title, see Code of Civil Procedure § 2016.020.

Proof of service, see Code of Civil Procedure § 417.10 et seq.

§ 2031.300. Untimely responses; waiver; motion to compel response; monetary sanctions

If a party to whom a demand for inspection, copying, testing, or sampling is directed fails to serve a timely response to it, the following rules shall apply:

(a) The party to whom the demand for inspection, copying, testing, or sampling is directed waives any objection to the demand, including one based on privilege or on the protection for work product under Chapter 4 (commencing with Section 2018.010). The court, on motion, may relieve that party from this waiver on its determination that both of the following conditions are satisfied:

(1) The party has subsequently served a response that is in substantial compliance with Sections 2031.210, 2031.220, 2031.230, 2031.240, and 2031.280.

(2) The party's failure to serve a timely response was the result of mistake, inadvertence, or excusable neglect.

(b) The party making the demand may move for an order compelling response to the demand.

(c) Except as provided in subdivision (d), the court shall impose a monetary sanction under Chapter 7 (commencing with Section 2023.010) against any party, person, or attorney who unsuccessfully

§ 2031.300

makes or opposes a motion to compel a response to a demand for inspection, copying, testing, or sampling, unless it finds that the one subject to the sanction acted with substantial justification or that other circumstances make the imposition of the sanction unjust. If a party then fails to obey the order compelling a response, the court may make those orders that are just, including the imposition of an issue sanction, an evidence sanction, or a terminating sanction under Chapter 7 (commencing with Section 2023.010). In lieu of or in addition to this sanction, the court may impose a monetary sanction under Chapter 7 (commencing with Section 2023.010).

(d)(1) Notwithstanding subdivision (c), absent exceptional circumstances, the court shall not impose sanctions on a party or any attorney of a party for failure to provide electronically stored information that has been lost, damaged, altered, or overwritten as a result of the routine, good faith operation of an electronic information system.

(2) This subdivision shall not be construed to alter any obligation to preserve discoverable information. *(Added by Stats.2004, c. 182 (A.B.3081), § 23, operative July 1, 2005. Amended by Stats.2005, c. 22 (S.B.1108), § 23; Stats.2009, c. 5 (A.B.5), § 20, eff. June 29, 2009.)*

Cross References

Court defined for purposes of this Title, see Code of Civil Procedure § 2016.020.

§ 2031.310. Motion to compel further response; form and content; time to bring motion; electronically stored information; monetary sanctions; failure to obey court order

(a) On receipt of a response to a demand for inspection, copying, testing, or sampling, the demanding party may move for an order compelling further response to the demand if the demanding party deems that any of the following apply:

(1) A statement of compliance with the demand is incomplete.

(2) A representation of inability to comply is inadequate, incomplete, or evasive.

(3) An objection in the response is without merit or too general.

(b) A motion under subdivision (a) shall comply with each of the following:

(1) The motion shall set forth specific facts showing good cause justifying the discovery sought by the demand.

(2) The motion shall be accompanied by a meet and confer declaration under Section 2016.040.

(3) In lieu of a separate statement required under the California Rules of Court, the court may allow the moving party to submit a concise outline of the discovery request and each response in dispute.

(c) Unless notice of this motion is given within 45 days of the service of the verified response, or any supplemental verified response, or on or before any specific later date to which the demanding party and the responding party have agreed in writing, the demanding party waives any right to compel a further response to the demand.

(d) In a motion under subdivision (a) relating to the production of electronically stored information, the party or affected person objecting to or opposing the production, inspection, copying, testing, or sampling of electronically stored information on the basis that the information is from a source that is not reasonably accessible because of the undue burden or expense shall bear the burden of demonstrating that the information is from a source that is not reasonably accessible because of undue burden or expense.

(e) If the party or affected person from whom discovery of electronically stored information is sought establishes that the information is from a source that is not reasonably accessible because of the undue burden or expense, the court may nonetheless order discovery if the demanding party shows good cause, subject to any limitations imposed under subdivision (g).

(f) If the court finds good cause for the production of electronically stored information from a source that is not reasonably accessible, the court may set conditions for the discovery of the electronically stored information, including allocation of the expense of discovery.

(g) The court shall limit the frequency or extent of discovery of electronically stored information, even from a source that is reasonably accessible, if the court determines that any of the following conditions exists:

(1) It is possible to obtain the information from some other source that is more convenient, less burdensome, or less expensive.

(2) The discovery sought is unreasonably cumulative or duplicative.

(3) The party seeking discovery has had ample opportunity by discovery in the action to obtain the information sought.

(4) The likely burden or expense of the proposed discovery outweighs the likely benefit, taking into account the amount in controversy, the resources of the parties, the importance of the issues in the litigation, and the importance of the requested discovery in resolving the issues.

(h) Except as provided in subdivision (j), the court shall impose a monetary sanction under Chapter 7 (commencing with Section 2023.010) against any party, person, or attorney who unsuccessfully makes or opposes a motion to compel further response to a demand, unless it finds that the one subject to the sanction acted with substantial justification or that other circumstances make the imposition of the sanction unjust.

(i) Except as provided in subdivision (j), if a party fails to obey an order compelling further response, the court may make those orders that are just, including the imposition of an issue sanction, an evidence sanction, or a terminating sanction under Chapter 7 (commencing with Section 2023.010). In lieu of, or in addition to, that sanction, the court may impose a monetary sanction under Chapter 7 (commencing with Section 2023.010).

(j)(1) Notwithstanding subdivisions (h) and (i), absent exceptional circumstances, the court shall not impose sanctions on a party or any attorney of a party for failure to provide electronically stored information that has been lost, damaged, altered, or overwritten as the result of the routine, good faith operation of an electronic information system.

(2) This subdivision shall not be construed to alter any obligation to preserve discoverable information. *(Added by Stats.2004, c. 182 (A.B.3081), § 23, operative July 1, 2005. Amended by Stats.2009, c. 5 (A.B.5), § 21, eff. June 29, 2009; Stats.2013, c. 18 (A.B.1183), § 2; Stats.2018, c. 317 (A.B.2230), § 4, eff. Jan. 1, 2019, operative Jan. 1, 2020.)*

Cross References

Computation of time, see Code of Civil Procedure §§ 12 and 12a; Government Code § 6800 et seq.
Court defined for purposes of this Title, see Code of Civil Procedure § 2016.020.
Discovery, generally, see Code of Civil Procedure § 2016.010 et seq.
Notice, actual and constructive, defined, see Civil Code § 18.
Writing defined for purposes of this Title, see Code of Civil Procedure § 2016.020.

Research References

Forms

West's California Code Forms, Civil Procedure § 2031.310 Form 1, Evidence—Discovery—Notice of Motion for Order Compelling Further Response to Inspection Demand.

§ 2031.320. Failure to produce items for inspection, copying, testing, or sampling; order compelling compliance; monetary sanctions; failure to obey court order

(a) If a party filing a response to a demand for inspection, testing, or sampling under Sections 2031.210, 2031.220, 2031.230, 2031.240, and 2031.280 thereafter fails to permit the inspection, copying, testing, or sampling in accordance with that party's statement of compliance, the demanding party may move for an order compelling compliance.

(b) Except as provided in subdivision (d), the court shall impose a monetary sanction under Chapter 7 (commencing with Section 2023.010) against any party, person, or attorney who unsuccessfully makes or opposes a motion to compel compliance with a demand, unless it finds that the one subject to the sanction acted with substantial justification or that other circumstances make the imposition of the sanction unjust.

(c) Except as provided in subdivision (d), if a party then fails to obey an order compelling inspection, copying, testing, or sampling, the court may make those orders that are just, including the imposition of an issue sanction, an evidence sanction, or a terminating sanction under Chapter 7 (commencing with Section 2023.010). In lieu of or in addition to that sanction, the court may impose a monetary sanction under Chapter 7 (commencing with Section 2023.010).

(d)(1) Notwithstanding subdivisions (b) and (c), absent exceptional circumstances, the court shall not impose sanctions on a party or any attorney of a party for failure to provide electronically stored information that has been lost, damaged, altered, or overwritten as the result of the routine, good faith operation of an electronic information system.

(2) This subdivision shall not be construed to alter any obligation to preserve discoverable information. *(Added by Stats.2004, c. 182 (A.B.3081), § 23, operative July 1, 2005. Amended by Stats.2009, c. 5 (A.B.5), § 22, eff. June 29, 2009.)*

Cross References

Court defined for purposes of this Title, see Code of Civil Procedure § 2016.020.
Monetary sanctions, see Code of Civil Procedure § 2023.050.

ARTICLE 3. INSPECTION AND PRODUCTION OF DOCUMENTS AND OTHER PROPERTY IN SPECIFIC CONTEXTS

Section
2031.510. Land patented or granted by the state; time to disclose.

§ 2031.510. Land patented or granted by the state; time to disclose

(a) In any action, regardless of who is the moving party, where the boundary of land patented or otherwise granted by the state is in dispute, or the validity of any state patent or grant dated before 1950 is in dispute, all parties shall have the duty to disclose to all opposing parties all nonprivileged relevant written evidence then known and available, including evidence against interest, relating to the above issues.

(b) This evidence shall be disclosed within 120 days after the filing with the court of proof of service upon all named defendants. Thereafter, the parties shall have the continuing duty to make all subsequently discovered relevant and nonprivileged written evidence available to the opposing parties. *(Added by Stats.2004, c. 182 (A.B.3081), § 23, operative July 1, 2005.)*

Cross References

Action defined for purposes of this Title, see Code of Civil Procedure § 2016.020.

Computation of time, see Code of Civil Procedure §§ 12 and 12a; Government Code § 6800 et seq.
Court defined for purposes of this Title, see Code of Civil Procedure § 2016.020.
Proof of service, see Code of Civil Procedure § 417.10 et seq.

CHAPTER 15. PHYSICAL OR MENTAL EXAMINATION

Cross References

Right to custody of minor child, child custody evaluator, education, experience, and training, see Family Code § 3110.5.

ARTICLE 1. GENERAL PROVISIONS

Section
2032.010. Application to genetic testing statutes; disclosure of certifying experts in professional negligence actions.
2032.020. Persons subject to discovery; restrictions; qualifications of examining physicians and psychologists.

§ 2032.010. Application to genetic testing statutes; disclosure of certifying experts in professional negligence actions

(a) This chapter does not affect genetic testing under Chapter 2 (commencing with Section 7550) of Part 2 of Division 12 of the Family Code.

(b) This chapter does not require the disclosure of the identity of an expert consulted by an attorney in order to make the certification required in an action for professional negligence under Section 411.35. *(Added by Stats.2004, c. 182 (A.B.3081), § 23, operative July 1, 2005. Amended by Stats.2018, c. 876 (A.B.2684), § 2, eff. Jan. 1, 2019.)*

Cross References

Action defined for purposes of this Title, see Code of Civil Procedure § 2016.020.
Blood tests, paternity, see Family Code § 7550 et seq.
Expert witnesses, exchange of information by parties, see Code of Civil Procedure § 2016.
Frequency or extent of discovery, restrictions, see Code of Civil Procedure § 2019.030.
Violation of court order as contempt, see Code of Civil Procedure § 1209.

§ 2032.020. Persons subject to discovery; restrictions; qualifications of examining physicians and psychologists

(a) Any party may obtain discovery, subject to the restrictions set forth in Chapter 5 (commencing with Section 2019.010), by means of a physical or mental examination of (1) a party to the action, (2) an agent of any party, or (3) a natural person in the custody or under the legal control of a party, in any action in which the mental or physical condition (including the blood group) of that party or other person is in controversy in the action.

(b) A physical examination conducted under this chapter shall be performed only by a licensed physician or other appropriate licensed health care practitioner.

(c)(1) A mental examination conducted under this chapter shall be performed only by a licensed physician, or by a licensed clinical psychologist who holds a doctoral degree in psychology and has had at least five years of postgraduate experience in the diagnosis of emotional and mental disorders.

(2) If an action involves allegations of sexual abuse of a minor, including any act listed in paragraphs (1) to (3), inclusive, of subdivision (a) of Section 1002, and the examinee is less than 15 years of age, the licensed physician or clinical psychologist shall have expertise in child abuse and trauma. *(Added by Stats.2004, c. 182*

§ 2032.020

(A.B.3081), § 23, operative July 1, 2005. Amended by Stats.2017, c. 133 (S.B.755), § 1, eff. Jan. 1, 2018.)

Cross References

Action defined for purposes of this Title, see Code of Civil Procedure § 2016.020.

Actions involving allegations of sexual abuse of a minor, mental examination of child, duration, see Code of Civil Procedure § 2032.340.

Discovery, generally, see Code of Civil Procedure § 2016.010 et seq.

Referral of conservatee for assessment to determine if conservatee has treatable mental illness and is unwilling or unable to accept voluntary treatment, see Welfare and Institutions Code § 5350.5.

ARTICLE 2. PHYSICAL EXAMINATION OF PERSONAL INJURY PLAINTIFF

Section
2032.210. Definitions.
2032.220. Number of examinations; conditions upon examination; time to demand; form and content of demand; service upon parties.
2032.230. Statement of compliance, partial compliance or refusal to comply; time to respond; shortened or extended time by court.
2032.240. Untimely response to demand; waiver; order compelling response and compliance; monetary sanctions; failure to obey court order.
2032.250. Motion to compel compliance; meet and confer declaration; monetary sanctions.
2032.260. Original demand, response and service documents; custody; record retention.

§ 2032.210. Definitions

As used in this article, "plaintiff" includes a cross-complainant, and "defendant" includes a cross-defendant. *(Added by Stats.2004, c. 182 (A.B.3081), § 23, operative July 1, 2005.)*

§ 2032.220. Number of examinations; conditions upon examination; time to demand; form and content of demand; service upon parties

(a) In any case in which a plaintiff is seeking recovery for personal injuries, any defendant may demand one physical examination of the plaintiff, if both of the following conditions are satisfied:

(1) The examination does not include any diagnostic test or procedure that is painful, protracted, or intrusive.

(2) The examination is conducted at a location within 75 miles of the residence of the examinee.

(b) A defendant may make a demand under this article without leave of court after that defendant has been served or has appeared in the action, whichever occurs first.

(c) A demand under subdivision (a) shall specify the time, place, manner, conditions, scope, and nature of the examination, as well as the identity and the specialty, if any, of the physician who will perform the examination.

(d) A physical examination demanded under subdivision (a) shall be scheduled for a date that is at least 30 days after service of the demand. On motion of the party demanding the examination, the court may shorten this time.

(e) The defendant shall serve a copy of the demand under subdivision (a) on the plaintiff and on all other parties who have appeared in the action. *(Added by Stats.2004, c. 182 (A.B.3081), § 23, operative July 1, 2005.)*

Cross References

Action defined for purposes of this Title, see Code of Civil Procedure § 2016.020.

Computation of time, see Code of Civil Procedure §§ 12 and 12a; Government Code § 6800 et seq.

Court defined for purposes of this Title, see Code of Civil Procedure § 2016.020.

Plaintiff and defendant defined for purposes of this Article, see Code of Civil Procedure § 2032.210.

Research References

Forms

West's California Code Forms, Civil Procedure § 2032.320 Form 1, Evidence—Discovery—Stipulation for Physical Examination.

§ 2032.230. Statement of compliance, partial compliance or refusal to comply; time to respond; shortened or extended time by court

(a) The plaintiff to whom a demand for a physical examination under this article is directed shall respond to the demand by a written statement that the examinee will comply with the demand as stated, will comply with the demand as specifically modified by the plaintiff, or will refuse, for reasons specified in the response, to submit to the demanded physical examination.

(b) Within 20 days after service of the demand the plaintiff to whom the demand is directed shall serve the original of the response to it on the defendant making the demand, and a copy of the response on all other parties who have appeared in the action. On motion of the defendant making the demand, the court may shorten the time for response. On motion of the plaintiff to whom the demand is directed, the court may extend the time for response. *(Added by Stats.2004, c. 182 (A.B.3081), § 23, operative July 1, 2005.)*

Cross References

Action defined for purposes of this Title, see Code of Civil Procedure § 2016.020.

Computation of time, see Code of Civil Procedure §§ 12 and 12a; Government Code § 6800 et seq.

Court defined for purposes of this Title, see Code of Civil Procedure § 2016.020.

Plaintiff and defendant defined for purposes of this Article, see Code of Civil Procedure § 2032.210.

§ 2032.240. Untimely response to demand; waiver; order compelling response and compliance; monetary sanctions; failure to obey court order

(a) If a plaintiff to whom a demand for a physical examination under this article is directed fails to serve a timely response to it, that plaintiff waives any objection to the demand. The court, on motion, may relieve that plaintiff from this waiver on its determination that both of the following conditions are satisfied:

(1) The plaintiff has subsequently served a response that is in substantial compliance with Section 2032.230.

(2) The plaintiff's failure to serve a timely response was the result of mistake, inadvertence, or excusable neglect.

(b) The defendant may move for an order compelling response and compliance with a demand for a physical examination.

(c) The court shall impose a monetary sanction under Chapter 7 (commencing with Section 2023.010) against any party, person, or attorney who unsuccessfully makes or opposes a motion to compel response and compliance with a demand for a physical examination, unless it finds that the one subject to the sanction acted with substantial justification or that other circumstances make the imposition of the sanction unjust.

(d) If a plaintiff then fails to obey the order compelling response and compliance, the court may make those orders that are just, including the imposition of an issue sanction, an evidence sanction, or a terminating sanction under Chapter 7 (commencing with Section 2023.010). In lieu of or in addition to that sanction the court may impose a monetary sanction under Chapter 7 (commencing with

Section 2023.010). *(Added by Stats.2004, c. 182 (A.B.3081), § 23, operative July 1, 2005.)*

Cross References

Court defined for purposes of this Title, see Code of Civil Procedure § 2016.020.

Plaintiff and defendant defined for purposes of this Article, see Code of Civil Procedure § 2032.210.

§ 2032.250. Motion to compel compliance; meet and confer declaration; monetary sanctions

(a) If a defendant who has demanded a physical examination under this article, on receipt of the plaintiff's response to that demand, deems that any modification of the demand, or any refusal to submit to the physical examination is unwarranted, that defendant may move for an order compelling compliance with the demand. This motion shall be accompanied by a meet and confer declaration under Section 2016.040.

(b) The court shall impose a monetary sanction under Chapter 7 (commencing with Section 2023.010) against any party, person, or attorney who unsuccessfully makes or opposes a motion to compel compliance with a demand for a physical examination, unless it finds that the one subject to the sanction acted with substantial justification or that other circumstances make the imposition of the sanction unjust. *(Added by Stats.2004, c. 182 (A.B.3081), § 23, operative July 1, 2005.)*

Cross References

Court defined for purposes of this Title, see Code of Civil Procedure § 2016.020.

Plaintiff and defendant defined for purposes of this Article, see Code of Civil Procedure § 2032.210.

Research References

Forms

West's California Code Forms, Civil Procedure § 2032.250 Form 1, Evidence—Discovery—Notice of Motion for Order Compelling Compliance With Demand for Physical Examination of Plaintiff.

§ 2032.260. Original demand, response and service documents; custody; record retention

(a) The demand for a physical examination under this article and the response to it shall not be filed with the court.

(b) The defendant shall retain both the original of the demand, with the original proof of service affixed to it, and the original response until six months after final disposition of the action. At that time, the original may be destroyed, unless the court, on motion of any party and for good cause shown, orders that the originals be preserved for a longer period. *(Added by Stats.2004, c. 182 (A.B. 3081), § 23, operative July 1, 2005.)*

Cross References

Action defined for purposes of this Title, see Code of Civil Procedure § 2016.020.

Court defined for purposes of this Title, see Code of Civil Procedure § 2016.020.

Plaintiff and defendant defined for purposes of this Article, see Code of Civil Procedure § 2032.210.

Proof of service, see Code of Civil Procedure § 417.10 et seq.

ARTICLE 3. MOTION FOR PHYSICAL OR MENTAL EXAMINATION

Section

2032.310. Other forms of examination by leave of court; form and contents of notice of motion; parties served.

2032.320. Standard of proof; exceptional circumstances; stipulation of parties; form and content of order; mileage limitations.

2032.340. Actions involving allegations of sexual abuse of a minor; mental examination of child; duration.

§ 2032.310. Other forms of examination by leave of court; form and contents of notice of motion; parties served

(a) If any party desires to obtain discovery by a physical examination other than that described in Article 2 (commencing with Section 2032.210), or by a mental examination, the party shall obtain leave of court.

(b) A motion for an examination under subdivision (a) shall specify the time, place, manner, conditions, scope, and nature of the examination, as well as the identity and the specialty, if any, of the person or persons who will perform the examination. The motion shall be accompanied by a meet and confer declaration under Section 2016.040.

(c) Notice of the motion shall be served on the person to be examined and on all parties who have appeared in the action. *(Added by Stats.2004, c. 182 (A.B.3081), § 23, operative July 1, 2005.)*

Cross References

Action defined for purposes of this Title, see Code of Civil Procedure § 2016.020.

Court defined for purposes of this Title, see Code of Civil Procedure § 2016.020.

Discovery, generally, see Code of Civil Procedure § 2016.010 et seq.

Notice, actual and constructive, defined, see Civil Code § 18.

§ 2032.320. Standard of proof; exceptional circumstances; stipulation of parties; form and content of order; mileage limitations

(a) The court shall grant a motion for a physical or mental examination under Section 2032.310 only for good cause shown.

(b) If a party stipulates as provided in subdivision (c), the court shall not order a mental examination of a person for whose personal injuries a recovery is being sought except on a showing of exceptional circumstances.

(c) A stipulation by a party under this subdivision shall include both of the following:

(1) A stipulation that no claim is being made for mental and emotional distress over and above that usually associated with the physical injuries claimed.

(2) A stipulation that no expert testimony regarding this usual mental and emotional distress will be presented at trial in support of the claim for damages.

(d) An order granting a physical or mental examination shall specify the person or persons who may perform the examination, as well as the time, place, manner, diagnostic tests and procedures, conditions, scope, and nature of the examination.

(e) If the place of the examination is more than 75 miles from the residence of the person to be examined, an order to submit to it shall be entered only if both of the following conditions are satisfied:

(1) The court determines that there is good cause for the travel involved.

(2) The order is conditioned on the advancement by the moving party of the reasonable expenses and costs to the examinee for travel to the place of examination. *(Added by Stats.2004, c. 182 (A.B.3081), § 23, operative July 1, 2005.)*

§ 2032.320

Cross References

Court defined for purposes of this Title, see Code of Civil Procedure § 2016.020.

§ 2032.340. Actions involving allegations of sexual abuse of a minor; mental examination of child; duration

(a) If any action involving allegations of sexual abuse of a minor, including any act listed in paragraphs (1) to (3), inclusive, of subdivision (a) of Section 1002, the mental examination of a child less than 15 years of age shall not exceed three hours, inclusive of breaks.

(b) Notwithstanding subdivision (a), the court may grant an extension of the three-hour limit for good cause. *(Added by Stats.2017, c. 133 (S.B.755), § 2, eff. Jan. 1, 2018.)*

Cross References

Actions involving allegations of sexual abuse of a minor, mental examination of child, qualifications of examining physicians and psychologists, see Code of Civil Procedure § 2032.020.

ARTICLE 4. FAILURE TO SUBMIT TO OR PRODUCE ANOTHER FOR PHYSICAL OR MENTAL EXAMINATION

Section
2032.410. Failure of party to submit to examination; availability of sanctions.
2032.420. Failure of nonparty to submit to examination; availability of sanctions.

§ 2032.410. Failure of party to submit to examination; availability of sanctions

If a party is required to submit to a physical or mental examination under Articles 2 (commencing with Section 2032.210) or 3 (commencing with Section 2032.310), or under Section 2016.030, but fails to do so, the court, on motion of the party entitled to the examination, may make those orders that are just, including the imposition of an issue sanction, an evidence sanction, or a terminating sanction under Chapter 7 (commencing with Section 2023.010). In lieu of or in addition to that sanction, the court may, on motion of the party, impose a monetary sanction under Chapter 7 (commencing with Section 2023.010). *(Added by Stats.2004, c. 182 (A.B.3081), § 23, operative July 1, 2005.)*

Cross References

Court defined for purposes of this Title, see Code of Civil Procedure § 2016.020.

§ 2032.420. Failure of nonparty to submit to examination; availability of sanctions

If a party is required to produce another for a physical or mental examination under Articles 2 (commencing with Section 2032.210) or 3 (commencing with Section 2032.310), or under Section 2032.030, but fails to do so, the court, on motion of the party entitled to the examination, may make those orders that are just, including the imposition of an issue sanction, an evidence sanction, or a terminating sanction under Chapter 7 (commencing with Section 2023.010), unless the party failing to comply demonstrates an inability to produce that person for examination. In lieu of or in addition to that sanction, the court may impose a monetary sanction under Chapter 7 (commencing with Section 2023.010). *(Added by Stats.2004, c. 182 (A.B.3081), § 23, operative July 1, 2005.)*

Cross References

Court defined for purposes of this Title, see Code of Civil Procedure § 2016.020.

ARTICLE 5. CONDUCT OF EXAMINATION

Section
2032.510. Attendance of attorney or attorney's representative at examination; use of stenographic or audio technology recording; rights of attendee to monitor; authorization of attorney's representative; suspension of examination; monetary sanctions.
2032.520. X-ray examinations.
2032.530. Recording mental examination by audio technology.

§ 2032.510. Attendance of attorney or attorney's representative at examination; use of stenographic or audio technology recording; rights of attendee to monitor; authorization of attorney's representative; suspension of examination; monetary sanctions

(a) The attorney for the examinee or for a party producing the examinee, or that attorney's representative, shall be permitted to attend and observe any physical examination conducted for discovery purposes, and to record stenographically or by audio technology any words spoken to or by the examinee during any phase of the examination.

(b) The observer under subdivision (a) may monitor the examination, but shall not participate in or disrupt it.

(c) If an attorney's representative is to serve as the observer, the representative shall be authorized to so act by a writing subscribed by the attorney which identifies the representative.

(d) If in the judgment of the observer the examiner becomes abusive to the examinee or undertakes to engage in unauthorized diagnostic tests and procedures, the observer may suspend it to enable the party being examined or producing the examinee to make a motion for a protective order.

(e) If the observer begins to participate in or disrupt the examination, the person conducting the physical examination may suspend the examination to enable the party at whose instance it is being conducted to move for a protective order.

(f) The court shall impose a monetary sanction under Chapter 7 (commencing with Section 2023.010) against any party, person, or attorney who unsuccessfully makes or opposes a motion for a protective order under this section, unless it finds that the one subject to the sanction acted with substantial justification or that other circumstances make the imposition of the sanction unjust. *(Added by Stats.2004, c. 182 (A.B.3081), § 23, operative July 1, 2005. Amended by Stats.2005, c. 294 (A.B.333), § 10.)*

Cross References

Court defined for purposes of this Title, see Code of Civil Procedure § 2016.020.
Discovery, generally, see Code of Civil Procedure § 2016.010 et seq.
Writing defined for purposes of this Title, see Code of Civil Procedure § 2016.020.

§ 2032.520. X-ray examinations

If an examinee submits or authorizes access to X-rays of any area of his or her body for inspection by the examining physician, no additional X-rays of that area may be taken by the examining physician except with consent of the examinee or on order of the court for good cause shown. *(Added by Stats.2004, c. 182 (A.B.3081), § 23, operative July 1, 2005.)*

Cross References

Court defined for purposes of this Title, see Code of Civil Procedure § 2016.020.

§ 2032.530. Recording mental examination by audio technology

(a) The examiner and examinee shall have the right to record a mental examination by audio technology.

(b) Nothing in this title shall be construed to alter, amend, or affect existing case law with respect to the presence of the attorney for the examinee or other persons during the examination by agreement or court order. *(Added by Stats.2004, c. 182 (A.B.3081),*

§ 23, operative July 1, 2005. Amended by Stats.2005, c. 294 (A.B.333), § 11.)

Cross References

Court defined for purposes of this Title, see Code of Civil Procedure § 2016.020.

ARTICLE 6. REPORTS OF EXAMINATION

Section

2032.610. Demand for copy of examination records; right to demand; time to deliver documents; waiver of work product protection.

2032.620. Untimely delivery of requested documents; motion to compel; meet and confer declaration; monetary sanction; failure to obey court order.

2032.630. Waiver of work product privilege in pending and subsequent actions.

2032.640. Exchange of documents and reports related to condition; exchange of follow-up or late reports.

2032.650. Failure to deliver or exchange reports; motion to compel delivery; meet and confer; monetary sanctions; failure to obey court order.

§ 2032.610. Demand for copy of examination records; right to demand; time to deliver documents; waiver of work product protection

(a) If a party submits to, or produces another for, a physical or mental examination in compliance with a demand under Article 2 (commencing with Section 2032.210), an order of court under Article 3 (commencing with Section 2032.310), or an agreement under Section 2016.030, that party has the option of making a written demand that the party at whose instance the examination was made deliver both of the following to the demanding party:

(1) A copy of a detailed written report setting out the history, examinations, findings, including the results of all tests made, diagnoses, prognoses, and conclusions of the examiner.

(2) A copy of reports of all earlier examinations of the same condition of the examinee made by that or any other examiner.

(b) If the option under subdivision (a) is exercised, a copy of the requested reports shall be delivered within 30 days after service of the demand, or within 15 days of trial, whichever is earlier.

(c) In the circumstances described in subdivision (a), the protection for work product under Chapter 4 (commencing with Section 2018.010) is waived, both for the examiner's writings and reports and to the taking of the examiner's testimony. *(Added by Stats.2004, c. 182 (A.B.3081), § 23, operative July 1, 2005.)*

Cross References

Computation of time, see Code of Civil Procedure §§ 12 and 12a; Government Code § 6800 et seq.

Court defined for purposes of this Title, see Code of Civil Procedure § 2016.020.

Writing defined for purposes of this Title, see Code of Civil Procedure § 2016.020.

Research References

Forms

West's California Code Forms, Civil Procedure § 2032.610 Form 1, Evidence—Discovery—Demand for Copy of Examiner's Report.

§ 2032.620. Untimely delivery of requested documents; motion to compel; meet and confer declaration; monetary sanction; failure to obey court order

(a) If the party at whose instance an examination was made fails to make a timely delivery of the reports demanded under Section 2032.610, the demanding party may move for an order compelling their delivery. This motion shall be accompanied by a meet and confer declaration under Section 2016.040.

(b) The court shall impose a monetary sanction under Chapter 7 (commencing with Section 2023.010) against any party, person, or attorney who unsuccessfully makes or opposes a motion to compel delivery of medical reports under this section, unless it finds that the one subject to the sanction acted with substantial justification or that other circumstances make the imposition of the sanction unjust.

(c) If a party then fails to obey an order compelling delivery of demanded medical reports, the court may make those orders that are just, including the imposition of an issue sanction, an evidence sanction, or a terminating sanction under Chapter 7 (commencing with Section 2023.010). In lieu of or in addition to those sanctions, the court may impose a monetary sanction under Chapter 7 (commencing with Section 2023.010). The court shall exclude at trial the testimony of any examiner whose report has not been provided by a party. *(Added by Stats.2004, c. 182 (A.B.3081), § 23, operative July 1, 2005.)*

Cross References

Court defined for purposes of this Title, see Code of Civil Procedure § 2016.020.

Research References

Forms

West's California Code Forms, Civil Procedure § 2032.620 Form 1, Evidence—Discovery—Notice of Motion for Order Compelling Delivery of Examination Report.

§ 2032.630. Waiver of work product privilege in pending and subsequent actions

By demanding and obtaining a report of a physical or mental examination under Section 2032.610 or 2032.620, or by taking the deposition of the examiner, other than under Article 3 (commencing with Section 2034.410) of Chapter 18, the party who submitted to, or produced another for, a physical or mental examination waives in the pending action, and in any other action involving the same controversy, any privilege, as well as any protection for work product under Chapter 4 (commencing with Section 2018.010), that the party or other examinee may have regarding reports and writings as well as the testimony of every other physician, psychologist, or licensed health care practitioner who has examined or may thereafter examine the party or other examinee in respect of the same physical or mental condition. *(Added by Stats.2004, c. 182 (A.B.3081), § 23, operative July 1, 2005.)*

Cross References

Action defined for purposes of this Title, see Code of Civil Procedure § 2016.020.

Depositions, see Code of Civil Procedure §§ 2020.010 et seq., 2025.010 et seq., 2026.010, 2027.010, 2028.010 et seq.

Writing defined for purposes of this Title, see Code of Civil Procedure § 2016.020.

§ 2032.640. Exchange of documents and reports related to condition; exchange of follow-up or late reports

A party receiving a demand for a report under Section 2032.610 is entitled at the time of compliance to receive in exchange a copy of any existing written report of any examination of the same condition by any other physician, psychologist, or licensed health care practitioner. In addition, that party is entitled to receive promptly any later report of any previous or subsequent examination of the same condition, by any physician, psychologist, or licensed health care practitioner. *(Added by Stats.2004, c. 182 (A.B.3081), § 23, operative July 1, 2005.)*

§ 2032.650. Failure to deliver or exchange reports; motion to compel delivery; meet and confer; monetary sanctions; failure to obey court order

(a) If a party who has demanded and received delivery of medical reports under Section 2032.610 fails to deliver existing or later reports of previous or subsequent examinations under Section 2032.640, a party who has complied with Section 2032.610 may move for an order compelling delivery of medical reports. This motion shall be accompanied by a meet and confer declaration under Section 2016.040.

(b) The court shall impose a monetary sanction under Chapter 7 (commencing with Section 2023.010) against any party, person, or attorney who unsuccessfully makes or opposes a motion to compel delivery of medical reports under this section, unless it finds that the one subject to the sanction acted with substantial justification or that other circumstances make the imposition of the sanction unjust.

(c) If a party then fails to obey an order compelling delivery of medical reports, the court may make those orders that are just, including the imposition of an issue sanction, an evidence sanction, or a terminating sanction under Chapter 7 (commencing with Section 2023.010). In lieu of or in addition to the sanction, the court may impose a monetary sanction under Chapter 7 (commencing with Section 2023.010). The court shall exclude at trial the testimony of any health care practitioner whose report has not been provided by a party ordered to do so by the court. *(Added by Stats.2004, c. 182 (A.B.3081), § 23, operative July 1, 2005.)*

Cross References

Court defined for purposes of this Title, see Code of Civil Procedure § 2016.020.

CHAPTER 16. REQUESTS FOR ADMISSION

ARTICLE 1. REQUESTS FOR ADMISSION

Section
2033.010. Persons subject to admission requests; restrictions; scope of requests.
2033.020. Admissions without leave of court; time to request; earlier requests with leave of court.
2033.030. Number of admission requests; limitations; requests exceeding numeric limitation; exception.
2033.040. Exemption from numeric limitations; nature and complexity of issues; protective order; burden of proof.
2033.050. Admissions exceeding numeric restrictions; Declaration for Additional Discovery; form and content.
2033.060. Form and content of request for admissions.
2033.070. Service of documents.
2033.080. Motion for protective order; meet and confer declaration; standard of proof; scope of order; monetary sanctions.

§ 2033.010. Persons subject to admission requests; restrictions; scope of requests

Any party may obtain discovery within the scope delimited by Chapter 2 (commencing with Section 2017.010), and subject to the restrictions set forth in Chapter 5 (commencing with Section 2019.010), by a written request that any other party to the action admit the genuineness of specified documents, or the truth of specified matters of fact, opinion relating to fact, or application of law to fact. A request for admission may relate to a matter that is in controversy between the parties. *(Added by Stats.2004, c. 182 (A.B.3081), § 23, operative July 1, 2005. Amended by Stats.2016, c. 86 (S.B.1171), § 43, eff. Jan. 1, 2017.)*

Cross References

Action defined for purposes of this Title, see Code of Civil Procedure § 2016.020.
Discovery, generally, see Code of Civil Procedure § 2016.010 et seq.
Document defined for purposes of this Title, see Code of Civil Procedure § 2016.020.
Expenses on refusal to admit, see Code of Civil Procedure § 2016.
Privileges, see Evidence Code § 900 et seq.

Research References

Forms

West's California Judicial Council Forms DISC–020, Request for Admission.

§ 2033.020. Admissions without leave of court; time to request; earlier requests with leave of court

(a) A defendant may make requests for admission by a party without leave of court at any time.

(b) A plaintiff may make requests for admission by a party without leave of court at any time that is 10 days after the service of the summons on, or appearance by, that party, whichever occurs first.

(c) Notwithstanding subdivision (b), in an unlawful detainer action or other proceeding under Chapter 4 (commencing with Section 1159) of Title 3 of Part 3, a plaintiff may make requests for admission by a party without leave of court at any time that is five days after service of the summons on, or appearance by, that party, whichever occurs first.

(d) Notwithstanding subdivisions (b) and (c), on motion with or without notice, the court, for good cause shown, may grant leave to a plaintiff to make requests for admission at an earlier time. *(Added by Stats.2004, c. 182 (A.B.3081), § 23, operative July 1, 2005. Amended by Stats.2007, c. 113 (A.B.1126), § 12.)*

Cross References

Action defined for purposes of this Title, see Code of Civil Procedure § 2016.020.
Computation of time, see Code of Civil Procedure §§ 12 and 12a; Government Code § 6800 et seq.
Court defined for purposes of this Title, see Code of Civil Procedure § 2016.020.
Notice, actual and constructive, defined, see Civil Code § 18.
Persons upon whom summons may be served, see Code of Civil Procedure § 416.10 et seq.

Research References

Forms

West's California Code Forms, Civil Procedure § 2033.020 Form 1, Evidence—Discovery—Request for Admissions—Truth of Facts—Genuineness of Documents—Official Form.
West's California Code Forms, Civil Procedure § 2033.020 Form 2, Evidence—Discovery—Ex Parte Application to Serve Request for Admissions Within Ten Days After Service of Summons—Order.

§ 2033.030. Number of admission requests; limitations; requests exceeding numeric limitation; exception

(a) No party shall request, as a matter of right, that any other party admit more than 35 matters that do not relate to the genuineness of documents. If the initial set of admission requests does not exhaust this limit, the balance may be requested in subsequent sets.

(b) Unless a declaration as described in Section 2033.050 has been made, a party need only respond to the first 35 admission requests served that do not relate to the genuineness of documents, if that party states an objection to the balance under Section 2033.230 on the ground that the limit has been exceeded.

(c) The number of requests for admission of the genuineness of documents is not limited except as justice requires to protect the responding party from unwarranted annoyance, embarrassment, oppression, or undue burden and expense. *(Added by Stats.2004, c. 182 (A.B.3081), § 23, operative July 1, 2005.)*

Cross References

Document defined for purposes of this Title, see Code of Civil Procedure § 2016.020.

§ 2033.040. Exemption from numeric limitations; nature and complexity of issues; protective order; burden of proof

(a) Subject to the right of the responding party to seek a protective order under Section 2033.080, any party who attaches a supporting declaration as described in Section 2033.050 may request a greater number of admissions by another party if the greater number is warranted by the complexity or the quantity of the existing and potential issues in the particular case.

(b) If the responding party seeks a protective order on the ground that the number of requests for admission is unwarranted, the propounding party shall have the burden of justifying the number of requests for admission. *(Added by Stats.2004, c. 182 (A.B.3081), § 23, operative July 1, 2005.)*

§ 2033.050. Admissions exceeding numeric restrictions; Declaration for Additional Discovery; form and content

Any party who is requesting or who has already requested more than 35 admissions not relating to the genuineness of documents by any other party shall attach to each set of requests for admissions a declaration containing substantially the following words:

DECLARATION FOR ADDITIONAL DISCOVERY

I, _____, declare:

1. I am (a party to this action or proceeding appearing in propria persona) (presently the attorney for _____, a party to this action or proceeding).

2. I am propounding to _____ the attached set of requests for admission.

3. This set of requests for admission will cause the total number of requests propounded to the party to whom they are directed to exceed the number of requests permitted by Section 2033.030 of the Code of Civil Procedure.

4. I have previously propounded a total of _____ requests for admission to this party.

5. This set of requests for admission contains a total of _____ requests.

6. I am familiar with the issues and the previous discovery conducted by all of the parties in this case.

7. I have personally examined each of the requests in this set of requests for admission.

8. This number of requests for admission is warranted under Section 2033.040 of the Code of Civil Procedure because _____. (Here state the reasons why the complexity or the quantity of issues in the instant lawsuit warrant this number of requests for admission.)

9. None of the requests in this set of requests is being propounded for any improper purpose, such as to harass the party, or the attorney for the party, to whom it is directed, or to cause unnecessary delay or needless increase in the cost of litigation.

I declare under penalty of perjury under the laws of California that the foregoing is true and correct, and that this declaration was executed on _____

_____
(Signature)

Attorney for _____

(Added by Stats.2004, c. 182 (A.B.3081), § 23, operative July 1, 2005.)

Cross References

Action defined for purposes of this Title, see Code of Civil Procedure § 2016.020.
Attorney's fees and costs, generally, see Code of Civil Procedure § 1021.
Discovery, generally, see Code of Civil Procedure § 2016.010 et seq.
Document defined for purposes of this Title, see Code of Civil Procedure § 2016.020.

Research References

Forms

West's California Code Forms, Civil Procedure § 2033.050 Form 1, Evidence—Discovery—Declaration for Additional Discovery.

§ 2033.060. Form and content of request for admissions

(a) A party requesting admissions shall number each set of requests consecutively.

(b) In the first paragraph immediately below the title of the case, there shall appear the identity of the party requesting the admissions, the set number, and the identity of the responding party.

(c) Each request for admission in a set shall be separately set forth and identified by letter or number.

(d) Each request for admission shall be full and complete in and of itself. No preface or instruction shall be included with a set of admission requests unless it has been approved under Chapter 17 (commencing with Section 2033.710).

(e) Any term specially defined in a request for admission shall be typed with all letters capitalized whenever the term appears.

(f) No request for admission shall contain subparts, or a compound, conjunctive, or disjunctive request unless it has been approved under Chapter 17 (commencing with Section 2033.710).

(g) A party requesting an admission of the genuineness of any documents shall attach copies of those documents to the requests, and shall make the original of those documents available for inspection on demand by the party to whom the requests for admission are directed.

(h) No party shall combine in a single document requests for admission with any other method of discovery. *(Added by Stats.2004, c. 182 (A.B.3081), § 23, operative July 1, 2005.)*

Cross References

Discovery, generally, see Code of Civil Procedure § 2016.010 et seq.
Document defined for purposes of this Title, see Code of Civil Procedure § 2016.020.

§ 2033.070. Service of documents

The party requesting admissions shall serve a copy of them on the party to whom they are directed and on all other parties who have appeared in the action. *(Added by Stats.2004, c. 182 (A.B.3081), § 23, operative July 1, 2005.)*

Cross References

Action defined for purposes of this Title, see Code of Civil Procedure § 2016.020.

§ 2033.080. Motion for protective order; meet and confer declaration; standard of proof; scope of order; monetary sanctions

(a) When requests for admission have been made, the responding party may promptly move for a protective order. This motion shall be accompanied by a meet and confer declaration under Section 2016.040.

(b) The court, for good cause shown, may make any order that justice requires to protect any party from unwarranted annoyance, embarrassment, oppression, or undue burden and expense. This protective order may include, but is not limited to, one or more of the following directions:

§ 2033.080

(1) That the set of admission requests, or particular requests in the set, need not be answered at all.

(2) That, contrary to the representations made in a declaration submitted under Section 2033.050, the number of admission requests is unwarranted.

(3) That the time specified in Section 2033.250 to respond to the set of admission requests, or to particular requests in the set, be extended.

(4) That a trade secret or other confidential research, development, or commercial information not be admitted or be admitted only in a certain way.

(5) That some or all of the answers to requests for admission be sealed and thereafter opened only on order of the court.

(c) If the motion for a protective order is denied in whole or in part, the court may order that the responding party provide or permit the discovery against which protection was sought on terms and conditions that are just.

(d) The court shall impose a monetary sanction under Chapter 7 (commencing with Section 2023.010) against any party, person, or attorney who unsuccessfully makes or opposes a motion for a protective order under this section, unless it finds that the one subject to the sanction acted with substantial justification or that other circumstances make the imposition of the sanction unjust. *(Added by Stats.2004, c. 182 (A.B.3081), § 23, operative July 1, 2005.)*

Cross References

Court defined for purposes of this Title, see Code of Civil Procedure § 2016.020.

Discovery, generally, see Code of Civil Procedure § 2016.010 et seq.

ARTICLE 2. RESPONSE TO REQUESTS FOR ADMISSION

Section

2033.210. Written response; oath; form and contents.
2033.220. Scope of response; statement of reasonable inquiry into matters where respondent lacks information or knowledge.
2033.230. Partial objection to requested admission; grounds for objection.
2033.240. Signatures; oath; employees or agents; responses that contain objections.
2033.250. Time to respond.
2033.260. Extension of time by agreement; writing; notice to all parties.
2033.270. Original requests, admissions and proof of service; custody; document retention.
2033.280. Untimely response; waiver; relief from waiver; motion for court order; monetary sanctions.
2033.290. Motion to compel further response; meet and confer declaration; time to bring motion; monetary sanctions; failure to obey court order.
2033.300. Withdrawal of or amendment to admission; authority and discretion of court.

§ 2033.210. Written response; oath; form and contents

(a) The party to whom requests for admission have been directed shall respond in writing under oath separately to each request.

(b) Each response shall answer the substance of the requested admission, or set forth an objection to the particular request.

(c) In the first paragraph of the response immediately below the title of the case, there shall appear the identity of the responding party, the set number, and the identity of the requesting party.

(d) Each answer or objection in the response shall bear the same identifying number or letter and be in the same sequence as the corresponding request. The text of that request need not be repeated, except as provided in paragraph (6) of subdivision (e).

(e) In order to facilitate the discovery process:

(1) Except as provided in paragraph (5), upon request by the responding party, the propounding party shall provide the requests for admission in an electronic format to the responding party within three court days of the request.

(2) Except as provided in paragraph (5), upon request by the propounding party after receipt of the responses to the requests for admission, the responding party shall provide the responses in an electronic format to the propounding party within three court days of the request.

(3) A party may provide the requests for admission or responses to the requests for admission requested pursuant to paragraphs (1) and (2) in any format agreed upon by the parties. If the parties are unable to agree on a format, the requests for admission or responses to the requests for admission shall be provided in plain text format.

(4) A party may transmit the requests for admission or responses to the requests for admission requested pursuant to paragraphs (1) and (2) by any method agreed upon by the parties. If the parties are unable to agree on a method of transmission, the requests for admission or responses to the requests for admission shall be transmitted by electronic mail to an email address provided by the requesting party.

(5) If the requests for admission or responses to the requests for admission were not created in an electronic format, a party is not required to create the requests for admission or responses in an electronic format for the purpose of transmission to the requesting party.

(6) A responding party who has requested and received requests for admission in an electronic format pursuant to paragraph (1) shall include the text of the request immediately preceding the response. *(Added by Stats.2004, c. 182 (A.B.3081), § 23, operative July 1, 2005. Amended by Stats.2019, c. 190 (A.B.1349), § 2, eff. Jan. 1, 2020.)*

Cross References

Writing defined for purposes of this Title, see Code of Civil Procedure § 2016.020.

§ 2033.220. Scope of response; statement of reasonable inquiry into matters where respondent lacks information or knowledge

(a) Each answer in a response to requests for admission shall be as complete and straightforward as the information reasonably available to the responding party permits.

(b) Each answer shall:

(1) Admit so much of the matter involved in the request as is true, either as expressed in the request itself or as reasonably and clearly qualified by the responding party.

(2) Deny so much of the matter involved in the request as is untrue.

(3) Specify so much of the matter involved in the request as to the truth of which the responding party lacks sufficient information or knowledge.

(c) If a responding party gives lack of information or knowledge as a reason for a failure to admit all or part of a request for admission, that party shall state in the answer that a reasonable inquiry concerning the matter in the particular request has been made, and that the information known or readily obtainable is insufficient to enable that party to admit the matter. *(Added by Stats.2004, c. 182 (A.B.3081), § 23, operative July 1, 2005. Amended by Stats.2005, c. 22 (S.B.1108), § 24.)*

§ 2033.230. Partial objection to requested admission; grounds for objection

(a) If only a part of a request for admission is objectionable, the remainder of the request shall be answered.

(b) If an objection is made to a request or to a part of a request, the specific ground for the objection shall be set forth clearly in the response. If an objection is based on a claim of privilege, the particular privilege invoked shall be clearly stated. If an objection is based on a claim that the matter as to which an admission is requested is protected work product under Chapter 4 (commencing with Section 2018.010), that claim shall be expressly asserted. *(Added by Stats.2004, c. 182 (A.B.3081), § 23, operative July 1, 2005.)*

Research References

Forms

West's California Code Forms, Civil Procedure § 2033.230 Form 1, Evidence—Discovery—Notice of Motion for Protective Order Sealing Answers to Requests for Admissions.

§ 2033.240. Signatures; oath; employees or agents; responses that contain objections

(a) The party to whom the requests for admission are directed shall sign the response under oath, unless the response contains only objections.

(b) If that party is a public or private corporation, or a partnership or association or governmental agency, one of its officers or agents shall sign the response under oath on behalf of that party. If the officer or agent signing the response on behalf of that party is an attorney acting in that capacity for the party, that party waives any lawyer-client privilege and any protection for work product under Chapter 4 (commencing with Section 2018.010) during any subsequent discovery from that attorney concerning the identity of the sources of the information contained in the response.

(c) The attorney for the responding party shall sign any response that contains an objection. *(Added by Stats.2004, c. 182 (A.B.3081), § 23, operative July 1, 2005.)*

Cross References

Discovery, generally, see Code of Civil Procedure § 2016.010 et seq.

§ 2033.250. Time to respond

(a) Within 30 days after service of requests for admission, the party to whom the requests are directed shall serve the original of the response to them on the requesting party, and a copy of the response on all other parties who have appeared, unless on motion of the requesting party the court has shortened the time for response, or unless on motion of the responding party the court has extended the time for response.

(b) Notwithstanding subdivision (a), in an unlawful detainer action or other proceeding under Chapter 4 (commencing with Section 1159) of Title 3 of Part 3, the party to whom the request is directed shall have at least five days from the date of service to respond, unless on motion of the requesting party the court has shortened the time for response, or unless on motion of the responding party the court has extended the time for response. *(Added by Stats.2004, c. 182 (A.B.3081), § 23, operative July 1, 2005. Amended by Stats.2007, c. 113 (A.B.1126), § 13.)*

Cross References

Action defined for purposes of this Title, see Code of Civil Procedure § 2016.020.
Computation of time, see Code of Civil Procedure §§ 12 and 12a; Government Code § 6800 et seq.
Court defined for purposes of this Title, see Code of Civil Procedure § 2016.020.

Research References

Forms

West's California Code Forms, Civil Procedure § 2033.250 Form 1, Evidence—Discovery—Notice of Motion for Order Shortening Time to Respond to Request for Admissions.
West's California Code Forms, Civil Procedure § 2033.250 Form 2, Evidence—Discovery—Order Shortening Time for Response to Request for Admissions.
West's California Code Forms, Civil Procedure § 2033.250 Form 3, Evidence—Discovery—Notice of Motion for Order Extending Time to Respond to Request for Admissions.

§ 2033.260. Extension of time by agreement; writing; notice to all parties

(a) The party requesting admissions and the responding party may agree to extend the time for service of a response to a set of admission requests, or to particular requests in a set, to a date beyond that provided in Section 2033.250.

(b) This agreement may be informal, but it shall be confirmed in a writing that specifies the extended date for service of a response.

(c) Unless this agreement expressly states otherwise, it is effective to preserve to the responding party the right to respond to any request for admission to which the agreement applies in any manner specified in Sections 2033.210, 2033.220, and 2033.230.

(d) Notice of this agreement shall be given by the responding party to all other parties who were served with a copy of the request. *(Added by Stats.2004, c. 182 (A.B.3081), § 23, operative July 1, 2005.)*

Cross References

Notice, actual and constructive, defined, see Civil Code § 18.
Writing defined for purposes of this Title, see Code of Civil Procedure § 2016.020.

§ 2033.270. Original requests, admissions and proof of service; custody; document retention

(a) The requests for admission and the response to them shall not be filed with the court.

(b) The party requesting admissions shall retain both the original of the requests for admission, with the original proof of service affixed to them, and the original of the sworn response until six months after final disposition of the action. At that time, both originals may be destroyed, unless the court, on motion of any party and for good cause shown, orders that the originals be preserved for a longer period. *(Added by Stats.2004, c. 182 (A.B.3081), § 23, operative July 1, 2005.)*

Cross References

Action defined for purposes of this Title, see Code of Civil Procedure § 2016.020.
Court defined for purposes of this Title, see Code of Civil Procedure § 2016.020.
Proof of service, see Code of Civil Procedure § 417.10 et seq.

§ 2033.280. Untimely response; waiver; relief from waiver; motion for court order; monetary sanctions

If a party to whom requests for admission are directed fails to serve a timely response, the following rules apply:

(a) The party to whom the requests for admission are directed waives any objection to the requests, including one based on privilege or on the protection for work product under Chapter 4 (commencing with Section 2018.010). The court, on motion, may relieve that party from this waiver on its determination that both of the following conditions are satisfied:

§ 2033.280

(1) The party has subsequently served a response that is in substantial compliance with Sections 2033.210, 2033.220, and 2033.230.

(2) The party's failure to serve a timely response was the result of mistake, inadvertence, or excusable neglect.

(b) The requesting party may move for an order that the genuineness of any documents and the truth of any matters specified in the requests be deemed admitted, as well as for a monetary sanction under Chapter 7 (commencing with Section 2023.010).

(c) The court shall make this order, unless it finds that the party to whom the requests for admission have been directed has served, before the hearing on the motion, a proposed response to the requests for admission that is in substantial compliance with Section 2033.220. It is mandatory that the court impose a monetary sanction under Chapter 7 (commencing with Section 2023.010) on the party or attorney, or both, whose failure to serve a timely response to requests for admission necessitated this motion. *(Added by Stats.2004, c. 182 (A.B.3081), § 23, operative July 1, 2005. Amended by Stats.2005, c. 294 (A.B.333), § 12.)*

Cross References

Court defined for purposes of this Title, see Code of Civil Procedure § 2016.020.
Document defined for purposes of this Title, see Code of Civil Procedure § 2016.020.

§ 2033.290. Motion to compel further response; meet and confer declaration; time to bring motion; monetary sanctions; failure to obey court order

(a) On receipt of a response to requests for admissions, the party requesting admissions may move for an order compelling a further response if that party deems that either or both of the following apply:

(1) An answer to a particular request is evasive or incomplete.

(2) An objection to a particular request is without merit or too general.

(b)(1) A motion under subdivision (a) shall be accompanied by a meet and confer declaration under Section 2016.040.

(2) In lieu of a separate statement required under the California Rules of Court, the court may allow the moving party to submit a concise outline of the discovery request and each response in dispute.

(c) Unless notice of this motion is given within 45 days of the service of the verified response, or any supplemental verified response, or any specific later date to which the requesting party and the responding party have agreed in writing, the requesting party waives any right to compel further response to the requests for admission.

(d) The court shall impose a monetary sanction under Chapter 7 (commencing with Section 2023.010) against any party, person, or attorney who unsuccessfully makes or opposes a motion to compel further response, unless it finds that the one subject to the sanction acted with substantial justification or that other circumstances make the imposition of the sanction unjust.

(e) If a party then fails to obey an order compelling further response to requests for admission, the court may order that the matters involved in the requests be deemed admitted. In lieu of, or in addition to, this order, the court may impose a monetary sanction under Chapter 7 (commencing with Section 2023.010). *(Added by Stats.2004, c. 182 (A.B.3081), § 23, operative July 1, 2005. Amended by Stats.2013, c. 18 (A.B.1183), § 3; Stats.2018, c. 317 (A.B.2230), § 5, eff. Jan. 1, 2019, operative Jan. 1, 2020.)*

Cross References

Computation of time, see Code of Civil Procedure §§ 12 and 12a; Government Code § 6800 et seq.
Court defined for purposes of this Title, see Code of Civil Procedure § 2016.020.
Notice, actual and constructive, defined, see Civil Code § 18.
Writing defined for purposes of this Title, see Code of Civil Procedure § 2016.020.

Research References

Forms

West's California Code Forms, Civil Procedure § 2033.290 Form 1, Evidence—Discovery—Notice of Motion for Order Compelling Further Response to Request for Admissions.

§ 2033.300. Withdrawal of or amendment to admission; authority and discretion of court

(a) A party may withdraw or amend an admission made in response to a request for admission only on leave of court granted after notice to all parties.

(b) The court may permit withdrawal or amendment of an admission only if it determines that the admission was the result of mistake, inadvertence, or excusable neglect, and that the party who obtained the admission will not be substantially prejudiced in maintaining that party's action or defense on the merits.

(c) The court may impose conditions on the granting of the motion that are just, including, but not limited to, the following:

(1) An order that the party who obtained the admission be permitted to pursue additional discovery related to the matter involved in the withdrawn or amended admission.

(2) An order that the costs of any additional discovery be borne in whole or in part by the party withdrawing or amending the admission. *(Added by Stats.2004, c. 182 (A.B.3081), § 23, operative July 1, 2005.)*

Cross References

Action defined for purposes of this Title, see Code of Civil Procedure § 2016.020.
Court defined for purposes of this Title, see Code of Civil Procedure § 2016.020.
Discovery, generally, see Code of Civil Procedure § 2016.010 et seq.
Notice, actual and constructive, defined, see Civil Code § 18.

ARTICLE 3. EFFECT OF ADMISSION

Section
2033.410. Conclusiveness of admission; application to other proceedings.
2033.420. Failure to admit genuineness of document or truth of any matter; binding effect; reasonable expenses and attorneys fees.

§ 2033.410. Conclusiveness of admission; application to other proceedings

(a) Any matter admitted in response to a request for admission is conclusively established against the party making the admission in the pending action, unless the court has permitted withdrawal or amendment of that admission under Section 2033.300.

(b) Notwithstanding subdivision (a), any admission made by a party under this section is binding only on that party and is made for the purpose of the pending action only. It is not an admission by that party for any other purpose, and it shall not be used in any manner against that party in any other proceeding. *(Added by Stats.2004, c. 182 (A.B.3081), § 23, operative July 1, 2005.)*

Cross References

Action defined for purposes of this Title, see Code of Civil Procedure § 2016.020.

§ 2033.420. Failure to admit genuineness of document or truth of any matter; binding effect; reasonable expenses and attorneys fees

(a) If a party fails to admit the genuineness of any document or the truth of any matter when requested to do so under this chapter, and if the party requesting that admission thereafter proves the genuineness of that document or the truth of that matter, the party requesting the admission may move the court for an order requiring the party to whom the request was directed to pay the reasonable expenses incurred in making that proof, including reasonable attorney's fees.

(b) The court shall make this order unless it finds any of the following:

(1) An objection to the request was sustained or a response to it was waived under Section 2033.290.

(2) The admission sought was of no substantial importance.

(3) The party failing to make the admission had reasonable ground to believe that that party would prevail on the matter.

(4) There was other good reason for the failure to admit. *(Added by Stats.2004, c. 182 (A.B.3081), § 23, operative July 1, 2005.)*

Cross References

Attorney's fees and costs, generally, see Code of Civil Procedure § 1021.
Court defined for purposes of this Title, see Code of Civil Procedure § 2016.020.
Document defined for purposes of this Title, see Code of Civil Procedure § 2016.020.

Research References

Forms

West's California Code Forms, Civil Procedure § 2033.420 Form 1, Evidence—Discovery—Order Granting Reasonable Expenses.
West's California Judicial Council Forms DISC–020, Request for Admission.

CHAPTER 17. FORM INTERROGATORIES AND REQUESTS FOR ADMISSION

Section
2033.710. Interrogatories and requests for admission of the genuineness of documents or truths; Judicial Council official forms.
2033.720. Interrogatories for use by a victim who has not received complete payment under certain restitution orders; Judicial Council official forms.
2033.730. Advisory committee to assist with form development; use of nontechnical language.
2033.740. Optional use of forms; rules and regulations.

§ 2033.710. Interrogatories and requests for admission of the genuineness of documents or truths; Judicial Council official forms

The Judicial Council shall develop and approve official form interrogatories and requests for admission of the genuineness of any relevant documents or of the truth of any relevant matters of fact for use in any civil action in a state court based on personal injury, property damage, wrongful death, unlawful detainer, breach of contract, family law, or fraud and for any other civil actions the Judicial Council deems appropriate. *(Added by Stats.2004, c. 182 (A.B.3081), § 23, operative July 1, 2005.)*

Cross References

Action defined for purposes of this Title, see Code of Civil Procedure § 2016.020.
Contracts, generally, see Civil Code § 1549 et seq.
Contracts, interpretation, see Civil Code § 1635 et seq.
Court defined for purposes of this Title, see Code of Civil Procedure § 2016.020.
Document defined for purposes of this Title, see Code of Civil Procedure § 2016.020.
Fraud, actual or constructive, see Civil Code §§ 1572 to 1574.
Judicial Council, see Government Code § 68500 et seq.

Research References

Forms

West's California Code Forms, Civil § 1940 Form 4, Interrogatories—Unlawful Detainer.
West's California Judicial Council Forms CR–200, Form Interrogatories—Crime Victim Restitution.
West's California Judicial Council Forms DISC–001, Form Interrogatories—General.
West's California Judicial Council Forms DISC–002, Form Interrogatories—Employment Law.
West's California Judicial Council Forms DISC–003, Form Interrogatories—Unlawful Detainer.
West's California Judicial Council Forms DISC–004, Form Interrogatories—Limited Civil Cases (Economic Litigation).
West's California Judicial Council Forms DISC–005, Form Interrogatories—Construction Litigation.
West's California Judicial Council Forms DISC–020, Request for Admission.
West's California Judicial Council Forms FL–145, Form Interrogatories—Family Law.
West's California Judicial Council Forms UD–106, Form Interrogatories—Unlawful Detainer.

§ 2033.720. Interrogatories for use by a victim who has not received complete payment under certain restitution orders; Judicial Council official forms

(a) The Judicial Council shall develop and approve official form interrogatories for use by a victim who has not received complete payment of a restitution order made pursuant to Section 1202.4 of the Penal Code.

(b) Notwithstanding whether a victim initiates or maintains an action to satisfy the unpaid restitution order, a victim may propound the form interrogatories approved pursuant to this section once each calendar year. The defendant subject to the restitution order shall, in responding to the interrogatories propounded, provide current information regarding the nature, extent, and location of any assets, income, and liabilities in which the defendant claims a present or future interest. *(Added by Stats.2004, c. 182 (A.B.3081), § 23, operative July 1, 2005.)*

Cross References

Action defined for purposes of this Title, see Code of Civil Procedure § 2016.020.
Judicial Council, see Government Code § 68500 et seq.

§ 2033.730. Advisory committee to assist with form development; use of nontechnical language

(a) In developing the form interrogatories and requests for admission required by Sections 2033.710 and 2033.720, the Judicial Council shall consult with a representative advisory committee which shall include, but not be limited to, representatives of all of the following:

(1) The plaintiff's bar.

(2) The defense bar.

(3) The public interest bar.

(4) Court administrators.

(5) The public.

(b) The form interrogatories and requests for admission shall be drafted in nontechnical language. *(Added by Stats.2004, c. 182 (A.B.3081), § 23, operative July 1, 2005.)*

§ 2033.730

Cross References

Court defined for purposes of this Title, see Code of Civil Procedure § 2016.020.
Judicial Council, see Government Code § 68500 et seq.

§ 2033.740. Optional use of forms; rules and regulations

(a) Use of the form interrogatories and requests for admission approved by the Judicial Council shall be optional.

(b) The form interrogatories and requests for admission shall be made available through the office of the clerk of the appropriate trial court.

(c) The Judicial Council shall promulgate any necessary rules to govern the use of the form interrogatories and requests for admission. *(Added by Stats.2004, c. 182 (A.B.3081), § 23, operative July 1, 2005.)*

Cross References

Court defined for purposes of this Title, see Code of Civil Procedure § 2016.020.
Judicial Council, see Government Code § 68500 et seq.

CHAPTER 18. SIMULTANEOUS EXCHANGE OF EXPERT WITNESS INFORMATION

ARTICLE 1. GENERAL PROVISIONS

Section
2034.010. Application to eminent domain proceedings.

§ 2034.010. Application to eminent domain proceedings

This chapter does not apply to exchanges of lists of experts and valuation data in eminent domain proceedings under Chapter 7 (commencing with Section 1258.010) of Title 7 of Part 3. *(Added by Stats.2004, c. 182 (A.B.3081), § 23, operative July 1, 2005.)*

Cross References

Eminent domain, generally, see Cal. Const. Art. 1, § 19; Code of Civil Procedure § 1240.010 et seq.; Government Code §§ 15850 et seq., 40404; Public Utilities Code § 619.

ARTICLE 2. DEMAND FOR EXCHANGE OF EXPERT WITNESS INFORMATION

Section
2034.210. Simultaneous exchange of information; time to issue demand; discoverable reports and writings supporting opinion.
2034.220. Persons authorized to issue demand; time to make demand.
2034.230. Written demand; form and contents of demand.
2034.240. Service of documents.
2034.250. Protective orders; motion; meet and confer declaration; standard of proof; scope of order; monetary sanctions.
2034.260. Method of exchange; form and contents; expert witness declaration; form and contents.
2034.270. Production of reports and writings; time and place to exchange.
2034.280. Supplemental expert witness lists.
2034.290. Original demand for exchange of information, responses and proof of service; custody of documents; record retention; time to file with court.
2034.300. Exclusion of expert opinions; failure of party to comply with certain conditions.
2034.310. Experts not designated on party's list; testimony at trial; permissible conditions.

§ 2034.210. Simultaneous exchange of information; time to issue demand; discoverable reports and writings supporting opinion

After the setting of the initial trial date for the action, any party may obtain discovery by demanding that all parties simultaneously exchange information concerning each other's expert trial witnesses to the following extent:

(a) Any party may demand a mutual and simultaneous exchange by all parties of a list containing the name and address of any natural person, including one who is a party, whose oral or deposition testimony in the form of an expert opinion any party expects to offer in evidence at the trial.

(b) If any expert designated by a party under subdivision (a) is a party or an employee of a party, or has been retained by a party for the purpose of forming and expressing an opinion in anticipation of the litigation or in preparation for the trial of the action, the designation of that witness shall include or be accompanied by an expert witness declaration under Section 2034.260.

(c) Any party may also include a demand for the mutual and simultaneous production for inspection and copying of all discoverable reports and writings, if any, made by any expert described in subdivision (b) in the course of preparing that expert's opinion. *(Added by Stats.2004, c. 182 (A.B.3081), § 23, operative July 1, 2005.)*

Cross References

Action defined for purposes of this Title, see Code of Civil Procedure § 2016.020.
Deposition of expert witness, production of materials, see Code of Civil Procedure § 2034.415.
Depositions, see Code of Civil Procedure §§ 2020.010 et seq., 2025.010 et seq., 2026.010, 2027.010, 2028.010 et seq.
Discovery, generally, see Code of Civil Procedure § 2016.010 et seq.
Time limits of depositions, see Code of Civil Procedure § 2025.290.
Witness defined for purposes of this Code, see Code of Civil Procedure § 1878.
Writing defined for purposes of this Title, see Code of Civil Procedure § 2016.020.

Research References

Forms

West's California Code Forms, Civil Procedure § 2034.230 Form 1, Evidence—Discovery—Demand for Simultaneous Exchange of Information Concerning Expert Witnesses—Simultaneous Production of Discoverable Expert's Reports.

§ 2034.220. Persons authorized to issue demand; time to make demand

Any party may make a demand for an exchange of information concerning expert trial witnesses without leave of court. A party shall make this demand no later than the 10th day after the initial trial date has been set, or 70 days before that trial date, whichever is closer to the trial date. *(Added by Stats.2004, c. 182 (A.B.3081), § 23, operative July 1, 2005.)*

Cross References

Computation of time, see Code of Civil Procedure §§ 12 and 12a; Government Code § 6800 et seq.
Court defined for purposes of this Title, see Code of Civil Procedure § 2016.020.
Witness defined for purposes of this Code, see Code of Civil Procedure § 1878.

§ 2034.230. Written demand; form and contents of demand

(a) A demand for an exchange of information concerning expert trial witnesses shall be in writing and shall identify, below the title of the case, the party making the demand. The demand shall state that it is being made under this chapter.

(b) The demand shall specify the date for the exchange of lists of expert trial witnesses, expert witness declarations, and any demanded production of writings. The specified date of exchange shall be 50 days before the initial trial date, or 20 days after service of the demand, whichever is closer to the trial date, unless the court, on motion and a showing of good cause, orders an earlier or later date of exchange. *(Added by Stats.2004, c. 182 (A.B.3081), § 23, operative July 1, 2005.)*

Cross References

Computation of time, see Code of Civil Procedure §§ 12 and 12a; Government Code § 6800 et seq.

Court defined for purposes of this Title, see Code of Civil Procedure § 2016.020.

Witness defined for purposes of this Code, see Code of Civil Procedure § 1878.

Writing defined for purposes of this Title, see Code of Civil Procedure § 2016.020.

Research References

Forms

West's California Code Forms, Civil Procedure § 2034.230 Form 1, Evidence—Discovery—Demand for Simultaneous Exchange of Information Concerning Expert Witnesses—Simultaneous Production of Discoverable Expert's Reports.

West's California Code Forms, Civil Procedure § 2034.230 Form 2, Evidence—Discovery—Notice of Motion for Order Permitting Service of Demand Less Than Fifty Days Before Trial.

West's California Code Forms, Civil Procedure § 2034.230 Form 3, Evidence—Discovery—Order Permitting Service of Demand Less Than Fifty Days Before Trial.

§ 2034.240. Service of documents

The party demanding an exchange of information concerning expert trial witnesses shall serve the demand on all parties who have appeared in the action. *(Added by Stats.2004, c. 182 (A.B.3081), § 23, operative July 1, 2005.)*

Cross References

Action defined for purposes of this Title, see Code of Civil Procedure § 2016.020.

Witness defined for purposes of this Code, see Code of Civil Procedure § 1878.

§ 2034.250. Protective orders; motion; meet and confer declaration; standard of proof; scope of order; monetary sanctions

(a) A party who has been served with a demand to exchange information concerning expert trial witnesses may promptly move for a protective order. This motion shall be accompanied by a meet and confer declaration under Section 2016.040.

(b) The court, for good cause shown, may make any order that justice requires to protect any party from unwarranted annoyance, embarrassment, oppression, or undue burden and expense. The protective order may include, but is not limited to, one or more of the following directions:

(1) That the demand be quashed because it was not timely served.

(2) That the date of exchange be earlier or later than that specified in the demand.

(3) That the exchange be made only on specified terms and conditions.

(4) That the production and exchange of any reports and writings of experts be made at a different place or at a different time than specified in the demand.

(5) That some or all of the parties be divided into sides on the basis of their identity of interest in the issues in the action, and that the designation of any experts as described in subdivision (b) of Section 2034.210 be made by any side so created.

(6) That a party or a side reduce the list of employed or retained experts designated by that party or side under subdivision (b) of Section 2034.210.

(c) If the motion for a protective order is denied in whole or in part, the court may order that the parties against whom the motion is brought, provide or permit the discovery against which the protection was sought on those terms and conditions that are just.

(d) The court shall impose a monetary sanction under Chapter 7 (commencing with Section 2023.010) against any party, person, or attorney who unsuccessfully makes or opposes a motion for a protective order under this section, unless it finds that the one subject to the sanction acted with substantial justification or that other circumstances make the imposition of the sanction unjust. *(Added by Stats.2004, c. 182 (A.B.3081), § 23, operative July 1, 2005.)*

Cross References

Action defined for purposes of this Title, see Code of Civil Procedure § 2016.020.

Court defined for purposes of this Title, see Code of Civil Procedure § 2016.020.

Discovery, generally, see Code of Civil Procedure § 2016.010 et seq.

Witness defined for purposes of this Code, see Code of Civil Procedure § 1878.

Writing defined for purposes of this Title, see Code of Civil Procedure § 2016.020.

Research References

Forms

West's California Code Forms, Civil Procedure § 2034.250 Form 1, Evidence—Discovery—Notice of Motion for Protective Order Changing Date of Exchange.

§ 2034.260. Method of exchange; form and contents; expert witness declaration; form and contents

(a) All parties who have appeared in the action shall exchange information concerning expert witnesses in writing on or before the date of exchange specified in the demand. The exchange of information may occur at a meeting of the attorneys for the parties involved or by serving the information on the other party by any method specified in Section 1011 or 1013, on or before the date of exchange.

(b) The exchange of expert witness information shall include either of the following:

(1) A list setting forth the name and address of a person whose expert opinion that party expects to offer in evidence at the trial.

(2) A statement that the party does not presently intend to offer the testimony of an expert witness.

(c) If a witness on the list is an expert as described in subdivision (b) of Section 2034.210, the exchange shall also include or be accompanied by an expert witness declaration signed only by the attorney for the party designating the expert, or by that party if that party has no attorney. This declaration shall be under penalty of perjury and shall contain all of the following:

(1) A brief narrative statement of the qualifications of each expert.

(2) A brief narrative statement of the general substance of the testimony that the expert is expected to give.

(3) A representation that the expert has agreed to testify at the trial.

(4) A representation that the expert will be sufficiently familiar with the pending action to submit to a meaningful oral deposition concerning the specific testimony, including an opinion and its basis, that the expert is expected to give at trial.

(5) A statement of the expert's hourly and daily fee for providing deposition testimony and for consulting with the retaining attorney. *(Added by Stats.2004, c. 182 (A.B.3081), § 23, operative July 1, 2005. Amended by Stats.2017, c. 64 (S.B.543), § 3, eff. Jan. 1, 2018; Stats.2018, c. 92 (S.B.1289), § 45, eff. Jan. 1, 2019.)*

Cross References

Action defined for purposes of this Title, see Code of Civil Procedure § 2016.020.

Attorney's fees and costs, generally, see Code of Civil Procedure § 1021.

§ 2034.260

Depositions, see Code of Civil Procedure §§ 2020.010 et seq., 2025.010 et seq., 2026.010, 2027.010, 2028.010 et seq.
Witness defined for purposes of this Code, see Code of Civil Procedure § 1878.
Writing defined for purposes of this Title, see Code of Civil Procedure § 2016.020.

Research References

Forms

West's California Code Forms, Civil Procedure § 2034.260 Form 1, Evidence—Discovery—Written Exchange of Expert Witness Information.
West's California Code Forms, Civil Procedure § 2034.260 Form 2, Evidence—Discovery—Expert Witness Declaration.

§ 2034.270. Production of reports and writings; time and place to exchange

If a demand for an exchange of information concerning expert trial witnesses includes a demand for production of reports and writings as described in subdivision (c) of Section 2034.210, all parties shall produce and exchange, at the place and on the date specified in the demand, all discoverable reports and writings, if any, made by any designated expert described in subdivision (b) of Section 2034.210. *(Added by Stats.2004, c. 182 (A.B.3081), § 23, operative July 1, 2005.)*

Cross References

Witness defined for purposes of this Code, see Code of Civil Procedure § 1878.
Writing defined for purposes of this Title, see Code of Civil Procedure § 2016.020.

§ 2034.280. Supplemental expert witness lists

(a) Within 20 days after the exchange described in Section 2034.260, any party who engaged in the exchange may submit a supplemental expert witness list containing the name and address of any experts who will express an opinion on a subject to be covered by an expert designated by an adverse party to the exchange, if the party supplementing an expert witness list has not previously retained an expert to testify on that subject.

(b) This supplemental list shall be accompanied by an expert witness declaration under subdivision (c) of Section 2034.260 concerning those additional experts, and by all discoverable reports and writings, if any, made by those additional experts.

(c) The party shall also make those experts available immediately for a deposition under Article 3 (commencing with Section 2034.410), which deposition may be taken even though the time limit for discovery under Chapter 8 (commencing with Section 2024.010) has expired. *(Added by Stats.2004, c. 182 (A.B.3081), § 23, operative July 1, 2005.)*

Cross References

Computation of time, see Code of Civil Procedure §§ 12 and 12a; Government Code § 6800 et seq.
Depositions, see Code of Civil Procedure §§ 2020.010 et seq., 2025.010 et seq., 2026.010, 2027.010, 2028.010 et seq.
Discovery, generally, see Code of Civil Procedure § 2016.010 et seq.
Witness defined for purposes of this Code, see Code of Civil Procedure § 1878.
Writing defined for purposes of this Title, see Code of Civil Procedure § 2016.020.

§ 2034.290. Original demand for exchange of information, responses and proof of service; custody of documents; record retention; time to file with court

(a) A demand for an exchange of information concerning expert trial witnesses, and any expert witness lists and declarations exchanged shall not be filed with the court.

(b) The party demanding the exchange shall retain both the original of the demand, with the original proof of service affixed, and the original of all expert witness lists and declarations exchanged in response to the demand until six months after final disposition of the action. At that time, all originals may be destroyed unless the court, on motion of any party and for good cause shown, orders that the originals be preserved for a longer period.

(c) Notwithstanding subdivisions (a) and (b), a demand for exchange of information concerning expert trial witnesses, and all expert witness lists and declarations exchanged in response to it, shall be lodged with the court when their contents become relevant to an issue in any pending matter in the action. *(Added by Stats.2004, c. 182 (A.B.3081), § 23, operative July 1, 2005.)*

Cross References

Action defined for purposes of this Title, see Code of Civil Procedure § 2016.020.
Court defined for purposes of this Title, see Code of Civil Procedure § 2016.020.
Proof of service, see Code of Civil Procedure § 417.10 et seq.
Witness defined for purposes of this Code, see Code of Civil Procedure § 1878.

§ 2034.300. Exclusion of expert opinions; failure of party to comply with certain conditions

Except as provided in Section 2034.310 and in Articles 4 (commencing with Section 2034.610) and 5 (commencing with Section 2034.710), on objection of any party who has made a complete and timely compliance with Section 2034.260, the trial court shall exclude from evidence the expert opinion of any witness that is offered by any party who has unreasonably failed to do any of the following:

(a) List that witness as an expert under Section 2034.260.

(b) Submit an expert witness declaration.

(c) Produce reports and writings of expert witnesses under Section 2034.270.

(d) Make that expert available for a deposition under Article 3 (commencing with Section 2034.410). *(Added by Stats.2004, c. 182 (A.B.3081), § 23, operative July 1, 2005.)*

Cross References

Court defined for purposes of this Title, see Code of Civil Procedure § 2016.020.
Depositions, see Code of Civil Procedure §§ 2020.010 et seq., 2025.010 et seq., 2026.010, 2027.010, 2028.010 et seq.
Witness defined for purposes of this Code, see Code of Civil Procedure § 1878.
Writing defined for purposes of this Title, see Code of Civil Procedure § 2016.020.

§ 2034.310. Experts not designated on party's list; testimony at trial; permissible conditions

A party may call as a witness at trial an expert not previously designated by that party if either of the following conditions is satisfied:

(a) That expert has been designated by another party and has thereafter been deposed under Article 3 (commencing with Section 2034.410).

(b) That expert is called as a witness to impeach the testimony of an expert witness offered by any other party at the trial. This impeachment may include testimony to the falsity or nonexistence of any fact used as the foundation for any opinion by any other party's expert witness, but may not include testimony that contradicts the opinion. *(Added by Stats.2004, c. 182 (A.B.3081), § 23, operative July 1, 2005.)*

Cross References

Time limits of depositions, see Code of Civil Procedure § 2025.290.
Witness defined for purposes of this Code, see Code of Civil Procedure § 1878.

ARTICLE 3. DEPOSITION OF EXPERT WITNESS

Section
2034.410. Persons permitted to depose experts; procedural requirements.

MISCELLANEOUS PROVISIONS § 2034.450

Section
2034.415. Production of materials.
2034.420. Location of deposition; mileage limitations; exception.
2034.430. Application of section to certain designated experts; payment of fees; fees for delay caused by tardy counsel; daily fee; application to certain worker compensation claims.
2034.440. Fees for preparation and travel.
2034.450. Tender of fees; deposition conducted beyond anticipated length of time; time to tender additional fee amount.
2034.460. Production of expert at deposition; proper service of notice and prepayment of fees; proper service without tender of fees.
2034.470. Reasonableness of expert fees; order setting compensation of expert; service of notice; meet and confer declaration; determination by court; monetary sanctions.

§ 2034.410. Persons permitted to depose experts; procedural requirements

On receipt of an expert witness list from a party, any other party may take the deposition of any person on the list. The procedures for taking oral and written depositions set forth in Chapters 9 (commencing with Section 2025.010), 10 (commencing with Section 2026.010), and 11 (commencing with Section 2028.010) apply to a deposition of a listed trial expert witness except as provided in this article. *(Added by Stats.2004, c. 182 (A.B.3081), § 23, operative July 1, 2005.)*

Cross References

Depositions, see Code of Civil Procedure §§ 2020.010 et seq., 2025.010 et seq., 2026.010, 2027.010, 2028.010 et seq.
Witness defined for purposes of this Code, see Code of Civil Procedure § 1878.

§ 2034.415. Production of materials

An expert described in subdivision (b) of Section 2034.210 whose deposition is noticed pursuant to Section 2025.220 shall, no later than three business days before his or her deposition, produce any materials or category of materials, including any electronically stored information, called for by the deposition notice. *(Added by Stats. 2016, c. 467 (A.B.2427), § 3, eff. Jan. 1, 2017.)*

§ 2034.420. Location of deposition; mileage limitations; exception

The deposition of any expert described in subdivision (b) of Section 2034.210 shall be taken at a place that is within 75 miles of the courthouse where the action is pending. On motion for a protective order by the party designating an expert witness, and on a showing of exceptional hardship, the court may order that the deposition be taken at a more distant place from the courthouse. *(Added by Stats.2004, c. 182 (A.B.3081), § 23, operative July 1, 2005. Amended by Stats.2008, c. 303 (A.B.2619), § 1.)*

Cross References

Action defined for purposes of this Title, see Code of Civil Procedure § 2016.020.
Court defined for purposes of this Title, see Code of Civil Procedure § 2016.020.
Depositions, see Code of Civil Procedure §§ 2020.010 et seq., 2025.010 et seq., 2026.010, 2027.010, 2028.010 et seq.
Witness defined for purposes of this Code, see Code of Civil Procedure § 1878.

§ 2034.430. Application of section to certain designated experts; payment of fees; fees for delay caused by tardy counsel; daily fee; application to certain worker compensation claims

(a) Except as provided in subdivision (f), this section applies to an expert witness, other than a party or an employee of a party, who is any of the following:

(1) An expert described in subdivision (b) of Section 2034.210.

(2) A treating physician and surgeon or other treating health care practitioner who is to be asked during the deposition to express opinion testimony, including opinion or factual testimony regarding the past or present diagnosis or prognosis made by the practitioner or the reasons for a particular treatment decision made by the practitioner, but not including testimony requiring only the reading of words and symbols contained in the relevant medical record or, if those words and symbols are not legible to the deponent, the approximation by the deponent of what those words or symbols are.

(3) An architect, professional engineer, or licensed land surveyor who was involved with the original project design or survey for which that person is asked to express an opinion within the person's expertise and relevant to the action or proceeding.

(b) A party desiring to depose an expert witness described in subdivision (a) shall pay the expert's reasonable and customary hourly or daily fee for any time spent at the deposition from the time noticed in the deposition subpoena, or from the time of the arrival of the expert witness should that time be later than the time noticed in the deposition subpoena, until the time the expert witness is dismissed from the deposition, regardless of whether the expert is actually deposed by any party attending the deposition.

(c) If any counsel representing the expert or a nonnoticing party is late to the deposition, the expert's reasonable and customary hourly or daily fee for the time period determined from the time noticed in the deposition subpoena until the counsel's late arrival, shall be paid by that tardy counsel.

(d) Notwithstanding subdivision (c), the hourly or daily fee charged to the tardy counsel shall not exceed the fee charged to the party who retained the expert, except where the expert donated services to a charitable or other nonprofit organization.

(e) A daily fee shall only be charged for a full day of attendance at a deposition or where the expert was required by the deposing party to be available for a full day and the expert necessarily had to forgo all business that the expert would otherwise have conducted that day but for the request that the expert be available all day for the scheduled deposition.

(f) In a worker's compensation case arising under Division 4 (commencing with Section 3201) or Division 4.5 (commencing with Section 6100) of the Labor Code, a party desiring to depose any expert on another party's expert witness list shall pay the fee under this section. *(Added by Stats.2004, c. 182 (A.B.3081), § 23, operative July 1, 2005. Amended by Stats.2008, c. 303 (A.B.2619), § 2.)*

Cross References

Action defined for purposes of this Title, see Code of Civil Procedure § 2016.020.
Depositions, see Code of Civil Procedure §§ 2020.010 et seq., 2025.010 et seq., 2026.010, 2027.010, 2028.010 et seq.
Witness defined for purposes of this Code, see Code of Civil Procedure § 1878.

§ 2034.440. Fees for preparation and travel

The party designating an expert is responsible for any fee charged by the expert for preparing for a deposition and for traveling to the place of the deposition, as well as for any travel expenses of the expert. *(Added by Stats.2004, c. 182 (A.B.3081), § 23, operative July 1, 2005.)*

Cross References

Depositions, see Code of Civil Procedure §§ 2020.010 et seq., 2025.010 et seq., 2026.010, 2027.010, 2028.010 et seq.

§ 2034.450. Tender of fees; deposition conducted beyond anticipated length of time; time to tender additional fee amount

(a) The party taking the deposition of an expert witness shall either accompany the service of the deposition notice with a tender

§ 2034.450

of the expert's fee based on the anticipated length of the deposition, or tender that fee at the commencement of the deposition.

(b) The expert's fee shall be delivered to the attorney for the party designating the expert.

(c) If the deposition of the expert takes longer than anticipated, the party giving notice of the deposition shall pay the balance of the expert's fee within five days of receipt of an itemized statement from the expert. *(Added by Stats.2004, c. 182 (A.B.3081), § 23, operative July 1, 2005.)*

Cross References

Attorney's fees and costs, generally, see Code of Civil Procedure § 1021.
Computation of time, see Code of Civil Procedure §§ 12 and 12a; Government Code § 6800 et seq.
Depositions, see Code of Civil Procedure §§ 2020.010 et seq., 2025.010 et seq., 2026.010, 2027.010, 2028.010 et seq.
Notice, actual and constructive, defined, see Civil Code § 18.
Witness defined for purposes of this Code, see Code of Civil Procedure § 1878.

§ 2034.460. Production of expert at deposition; proper service of notice and prepayment of fees; proper service without tender of fees

(a) The service of a proper deposition notice accompanied by the tender of the expert witness fee described in Section 2034.430 is effective to require the party employing or retaining the expert to produce the expert for the deposition.

(b) If the party noticing the deposition fails to tender the expert's fee under Section 2034.430, the expert shall not be deposed at that time unless the parties stipulate otherwise. *(Added by Stats.2004, c. 182 (A.B.3081), § 23, operative July 1, 2005.)*

Cross References

Depositions, see Code of Civil Procedure §§ 2020.010 et seq., 2025.010 et seq., 2026.010, 2027.010, 2028.010 et seq.
Notice, actual and constructive, defined, see Civil Code § 18.
Witness defined for purposes of this Code, see Code of Civil Procedure § 1878.

§ 2034.470. Reasonableness of expert fees; order setting compensation of expert; service of notice; meet and confer declaration; determination by court; monetary sanctions

(a) If a party desiring to take the deposition of an expert witness under this article deems that the hourly or daily fee of that expert for providing deposition testimony is unreasonable, that party may move for an order setting the compensation of that expert. Notice of this motion shall also be given to the expert.

(b) A motion under subdivision (a) shall be accompanied by a meet and confer declaration under Section 2016.040. In any attempt at an informal resolution under Section 2016.040, either the party or the expert shall provide the other with all of the following:

(1) Proof of the ordinary and customary fee actually charged and received by that expert for similar services provided outside the subject litigation.

(2) The total number of times the presently demanded fee has ever been charged and received by that expert.

(3) The frequency and regularity with which the presently demanded fee has been charged and received by that expert within the two-year period preceding the hearing on the motion.

(c) In addition to any other facts or evidence, the expert or the party designating the expert shall provide, and the court's determination as to the reasonableness of the fee shall be based on, proof of the ordinary and customary fee actually charged and received by that expert for similar services provided outside the subject litigation.

(d) In an action filed after January 1, 1994, the expert or the party designating the expert shall also provide, and the court's determination as to the reasonableness of the fee shall also be based on, both of the following:

(1) The total number of times the presently demanded fee has ever been charged and received by that expert.

(2) The frequency and regularity with which the presently demanded fee has been charged and received by that expert within the two-year period preceding the hearing on the motion.

(e) The court may also consider the ordinary and customary fees charged by similar experts for similar services within the relevant community and any other factors the court deems necessary or appropriate to make its determination.

(f) Upon a determination that the fee demanded by that expert is unreasonable, and based upon the evidence and factors considered, the court shall set the fee of the expert providing testimony.

(g) The court shall impose a monetary sanction under Chapter 7 (commencing with Section 2023.010) against any party, person, or attorney who unsuccessfully makes or opposes a motion to set the expert witness fee, unless it finds that the one subject to the sanction acted with substantial justification or that other circumstances make the imposition of the sanction unjust. *(Added by Stats.2004, c. 182 (A.B.3081), § 23, operative July 1, 2005.)*

Cross References

Action defined for purposes of this Title, see Code of Civil Procedure § 2016.020.
Attorney's fees and costs, generally, see Code of Civil Procedure § 1021.
Court defined for purposes of this Title, see Code of Civil Procedure § 2016.020.
Depositions, see Code of Civil Procedure §§ 2020.010 et seq., 2025.010 et seq., 2026.010, 2027.010, 2028.010 et seq.
Notice, actual and constructive, defined, see Civil Code § 18.
Witness defined for purposes of this Code, see Code of Civil Procedure § 1878.

ARTICLE 4. MOTION TO AUGMENT OR AMEND EXPERT WITNESS LIST OR DECLARATION

Section
2034.610. Scope of judicial authority where exchange of information was timely; time to complete additional discovery; meet and confer declaration.
2034.620. Expert witness lists; court authority upon satisfaction of certain conditions.
2034.630. Monetary sanctions; exception.

§ 2034.610. Scope of judicial authority where exchange of information was timely; time to complete additional discovery; meet and confer declaration

(a) On motion of any party who has engaged in a timely exchange of expert witness information, the court may grant leave to do either or both of the following:

(1) Augment that party's expert witness list and declaration by adding the name and address of any expert witness whom that party has subsequently retained.

(2) Amend that party's expert witness declaration with respect to the general substance of the testimony that an expert previously designated is expected to give.

(b) A motion under subdivision (a) shall be made at a sufficient time in advance of the time limit for the completion of discovery under Chapter 8 (commencing with Section 2024.010) to permit the deposition of any expert to whom the motion relates to be taken within that time limit. Under exceptional circumstances, the court may permit the motion to be made at a later time.

(c) The motion shall be accompanied by a meet and confer declaration under Section 2016.040. *(Added by Stats.2004, c. 182 (A.B.3081), § 23, operative July 1, 2005.)*

MISCELLANEOUS PROVISIONS § 2034.720

Cross References

Court defined for purposes of this Title, see Code of Civil Procedure § 2016.020.
Depositions, see Code of Civil Procedure §§ 2020.010 et seq., 2025.010 et seq., 2026.010, 2027.010, 2028.010 et seq.
Discovery, generally, see Code of Civil Procedure § 2016.010 et seq.
Witness defined for purposes of this Code, see Code of Civil Procedure § 1878.

§ 2034.620. Expert witness lists; court authority upon satisfaction of certain conditions

The court shall grant leave to augment or amend an expert witness list or declaration only if all of the following conditions are satisfied:

(a) The court has taken into account the extent to which the opposing party has relied on the list of expert witnesses.

(b) The court has determined that any party opposing the motion will not be prejudiced in maintaining that party's action or defense on the merits.

(c) The court has determined either of the following:

(1) The moving party would not in the exercise of reasonable diligence have determined to call that expert witness or have decided to offer the different or additional testimony of that expert witness.

(2) The moving party failed to determine to call that expert witness, or to offer the different or additional testimony of that expert witness as a result of mistake, inadvertence, surprise, or excusable neglect, and the moving party has done both of the following:

(A) Sought leave to augment or amend promptly after deciding to call the expert witness or to offer the different or additional testimony.

(B) Promptly thereafter served a copy of the proposed expert witness information concerning the expert or the testimony described in Section 2034.260 on all other parties who have appeared in the action.

(d) Leave to augment or amend is conditioned on the moving party making the expert available immediately for a deposition under Article 3 (commencing with Section 2034.410), and on any other terms as may be just, including, but not limited to, leave to any party opposing the motion to designate additional expert witnesses or to elicit additional opinions from those previously designated, a continuance of the trial for a reasonable period of time, and the awarding of costs and litigation expenses to any party opposing the motion. *(Added by Stats.2004, c. 182 (A.B.3081), § 23, operative July 1, 2005.)*

Cross References

Action defined for purposes of this Title, see Code of Civil Procedure § 2016.020.
Court defined for purposes of this Title, see Code of Civil Procedure § 2016.020.
Depositions, see Code of Civil Procedure §§ 2020.010 et seq., 2025.010 et seq., 2026.010, 2027.010, 2028.010 et seq.
Witness defined for purposes of this Code, see Code of Civil Procedure § 1878.

§ 2034.630. Monetary sanctions; exception

The court shall impose a monetary sanction under Chapter 7 (commencing with Section 2023.010) against any party, person, or attorney who unsuccessfully makes or opposes a motion to augment or amend expert witness information, unless it finds that the one subject to the sanction acted with substantial justification or that other circumstances make the imposition of the sanction unjust. *(Added by Stats.2004, c. 182 (A.B.3081), § 23, operative July 1, 2005.)*

Cross References

Court defined for purposes of this Title, see Code of Civil Procedure § 2016.020.
Witness defined for purposes of this Code, see Code of Civil Procedure § 1878.

ARTICLE 5. MOTION TO SUBMIT TARDY EXPERT WITNESS INFORMATION

Section
2034.710. Untimely response to demand for witness information; court authority to extend time; time to complete discovery; meet and confer declaration.
2034.720. Scope of judicial authority to grant tardy filing of list; satisfaction of certain conditions.
2034.730. Monetary sanctions; exception.

§ 2034.710. Untimely response to demand for witness information; court authority to extend time; time to complete discovery; meet and confer declaration

(a) On motion of any party who has failed to submit expert witness information on the date specified in a demand for that exchange, the court may grant leave to submit that information on a later date.

(b) A motion under subdivision (a) shall be made a sufficient time in advance of the time limit for the completion of discovery under Chapter 8 (commencing with Section 2024.010) to permit the deposition of any expert to whom the motion relates to be taken within that time limit. Under exceptional circumstances, the court may permit the motion to be made at a later time.

(c) The motion shall be accompanied by a meet and confer declaration under Section 2016.040. *(Added by Stats.2004, c. 182 (A.B.3081), § 23, operative July 1, 2005.)*

Cross References

Court defined for purposes of this Title, see Code of Civil Procedure § 2016.020.
Depositions, see Code of Civil Procedure §§ 2020.010 et seq., 2025.010 et seq., 2026.010, 2027.010, 2028.010 et seq.
Discovery, generally, see Code of Civil Procedure § 2016.010 et seq.
Witness defined for purposes of this Code, see Code of Civil Procedure § 1878.

§ 2034.720. Scope of judicial authority to grant tardy filing of list; satisfaction of certain conditions

The court shall grant leave to submit tardy expert witness information only if all of the following conditions are satisfied:

(a) The court has taken into account the extent to which the opposing party has relied on the absence of a list of expert witnesses.

(b) The court has determined that any party opposing the motion will not be prejudiced in maintaining that party's action or defense on the merits.

(c) The court has determined that the moving party did all of the following:

(1) Failed to submit the information as the result of mistake, inadvertence, surprise, or excusable neglect.

(2) Sought leave to submit the information promptly after learning of the mistake, inadvertence, surprise, or excusable neglect.

(3) Promptly thereafter served a copy of the proposed expert witness information described in Section 2034.260 on all other parties who have appeared in the action.

(d) The order is conditioned on the moving party making the expert available immediately for a deposition under Article 3 (commencing with Section 2034.410), and on any other terms as may be just, including, but not limited to, leave to any party opposing the motion to designate additional expert witnesses or to elicit additional opinions from those previously designated, a continuance of the trial for a reasonable period of time, and the awarding of costs and litigation expenses to any party opposing the motion. *(Added by Stats.2004, c. 182 (A.B.3081), § 23, operative July 1, 2005.)*

§ 2034.720

Cross References

Action defined for purposes of this Title, see Code of Civil Procedure § 2016.020.

Court defined for purposes of this Title, see Code of Civil Procedure § 2016.020.

Depositions, see Code of Civil Procedure §§ 2020.010 et seq., 2025.010 et seq., 2026.010, 2027.010, 2028.010 et seq.

Witness defined for purposes of this Code, see Code of Civil Procedure § 1878.

§ 2034.730. Monetary sanctions; exception

The court shall impose a monetary sanction under Chapter 7 (commencing with Section 2023.010) against any party, person, or attorney who unsuccessfully makes or opposes a motion to submit tardy expert witness information, unless it finds that the one subject to the sanction acted with substantial justification or that other circumstances make the imposition of the sanction unjust. *(Added by Stats.2004, c. 182 (A.B.3081), § 23, operative July 1, 2005.)*

Cross References

Court defined for purposes of this Title, see Code of Civil Procedure § 2016.020.

Witness defined for purposes of this Code, see Code of Civil Procedure § 1878.

CHAPTER 19. PERPETUATION OF TESTIMONY OR PRESERVATION OF EVIDENCE BEFORE FILING ACTION

Section
2035.010. Persons permitted to obtain discovery; restrictions.
2035.020. Methods available.
2035.030. Filing of verified petition; content and form of petition; court order.
2035.040. Service of notice; form and contents; time; service by publication; appointment of counsel for absent party; payment of attorney's fees.
2035.050. Authority to issue order; considerations; contents of order.
2035.060. Use of deposition to perpetuate testimony in subsequent actions; requirements.

§ 2035.010. Persons permitted to obtain discovery; restrictions

(a) One who expects to be a party or expects a successor in interest to be a party to an action that may be cognizable in a court of the state, whether as a plaintiff, or as a defendant, or in any other capacity, may obtain discovery within the scope delimited by Chapter 2 (commencing with Section 2017.010), and subject to the restrictions set forth in Chapter 5 (commencing with Section 2019.010), for the purpose of perpetuating that person's own testimony or that of another natural person or organization, or of preserving evidence for use in the event an action is subsequently filed.

(b) One shall not employ the procedures of this chapter for purposes of either ascertaining the possible existence of a cause of action or a defense to it, or of identifying those who might be made parties to an action not yet filed. *(Added by Stats.2004, c. 182 (A.B.3081), § 23, operative July 1, 2005. Amended by Stats.2005, c. 294 (A.B.333), § 13; Stats.2016, c. 86 (S.B.1171), § 44, eff. Jan. 1, 2017.)*

Cross References

Action defined for purposes of this Title, see Code of Civil Procedure § 2016.020.

Court defined for purposes of this Title, see Code of Civil Procedure § 2016.020.

Discovery, generally, see Code of Civil Procedure § 2016.010 et seq.

§ 2035.020. Methods available

The methods available for discovery conducted for the purposes set forth in Section 2035.010 are all of the following:

(a) Oral and written depositions.

(b) Inspections of documents, things, and places.

(c) Physical and mental examinations. *(Added by Stats.2004, c. 182 (A.B.3081), § 23, operative July 1, 2005.)*

Cross References

Depositions, see Code of Civil Procedure §§ 2020.010 et seq., 2025.010 et seq., 2026.010, 2027.010, 2028.010 et seq.

Discovery, generally, see Code of Civil Procedure § 2016.010 et seq.

Document defined for purposes of this Title, see Code of Civil Procedure § 2016.020.

§ 2035.030. Filing of verified petition; content and form of petition; court order

(a) One who desires to perpetuate testimony or preserve evidence for the purposes set forth in Section 2035.010 shall file a verified petition in the superior court of the county of the residence of at least one expected adverse party, or, if no expected adverse party is a resident of the State of California, in the superior court of a county where the action or proceeding may be filed.

(b) The petition shall be titled in the name of the one who desires the perpetuation of testimony or the preservation of evidence. The petition shall set forth all of the following:

(1) The expectation that the petitioner or the petitioner's successor in interest will be a party to an action cognizable in a court of the State of California.

(2) The present inability of the petitioner and, if applicable, the petitioner's successor in interest either to bring that action or to cause it to be brought.

(3) The subject matter of the expected action and the petitioner's involvement. A copy of any written instrument the validity or construction of which may be called into question, or which is connected with the subject matter of the proposed discovery, shall be attached to the petition.

(4) The particular discovery methods described in Section 2035.020 that the petitioner desires to employ.

(5) The facts that the petitioner desires to establish by the proposed discovery.

(6) The reasons for desiring to perpetuate or preserve these facts before an action has been filed.

(7) The name or a description of those whom the petitioner expects to be adverse parties so far as known.

(8) The name and address of those from whom the discovery is to be sought.

(9) The substance of the information expected to be elicited from each of those from whom discovery is being sought.

(c) The petition shall request the court to enter an order authorizing the petitioner to engage in discovery by the described methods for the purpose of perpetuating the described testimony or preserving the described evidence. *(Added by Stats.2004, c. 182 (A.B.3081), § 23, operative July 1, 2005. Amended by Stats.2005, c. 294 (A.B.333), § 14.)*

Cross References

Action defined for purposes of this Title, see Code of Civil Procedure § 2016.020.

Court defined for purposes of this Title, see Code of Civil Procedure § 2016.020.

Discovery, generally, see Code of Civil Procedure § 2016.010 et seq.

Instruments, construction and intent, see Code of Civil Procedure §§ 1858, 1859.

Research References

Forms

West's California Code Forms, Civil Procedure § 2035.030 Form 1, Evidence—Discovery—Petition to Perpetuate Testimony Before Action.

§ 2035.040. Service of notice; form and contents; time; service by publication; appointment of counsel for absent party; payment of attorney's fees

(a) The petitioner shall cause service of a notice of the petition under Section 2035.030 to be made on each natural person or organization named in the petition as an expected adverse party. This service shall be made in the same manner provided for the service of a summons.

(b) The service of the notice shall be accompanied by a copy of the petition. The notice shall state that the petitioner will apply to the court at a time and place specified in the notice for the order requested in the petition.

(c) This service shall be effected at least 20 days prior to the date specified in the notice for the hearing on the petition.

(d) If after the exercise of due diligence, the petitioner is unable to cause service to be made on any expected adverse party named in the petition, the court in which the petition is filed shall make an order for service by publication.

(e) If any expected adverse party served by publication does not appear at the hearing, the court shall appoint an attorney to represent that party for all purposes, including the cross-examination of any person whose testimony is taken by deposition. The court shall order that the petitioner pay the reasonable fees and expenses of any attorney so appointed. *(Added by Stats.2004, c. 182 (A.B. 3081), § 23, operative July 1, 2005.)*

Cross References

Attorney's fees and costs, generally, see Code of Civil Procedure § 1021.
Computation of time, see Code of Civil Procedure §§ 12 and 12a; Government Code § 6800 et seq.
Court defined for purposes of this Title, see Code of Civil Procedure § 2016.020.
Depositions, see Code of Civil Procedure §§ 2020.010 et seq., 2025.010 et seq., 2026.010, 2027.010, 2028.010 et seq.
Notice, actual and constructive, defined, see Civil Code § 18.
Persons upon whom summons may be served, see Code of Civil Procedure § 416.10 et seq.

§ 2035.050. Authority to issue order; considerations; contents of order

(a) If the court determines that all or part of the discovery requested under this chapter may prevent a failure or delay of justice, it shall make an order authorizing that discovery. In determining whether to authorize discovery by a petitioner who expects a successor in interest to be a party to an action, the court shall consider, in addition to other appropriate factors, whether the requested discovery could be conducted by the petitioner's successor in interest, instead of by the petitioner.

(b) The order shall identify any witness whose deposition may be taken, and any documents, things, or places that may be inspected, and any person whose physical or mental condition may be examined.

(c) Any authorized depositions, inspections, and physical or mental examinations shall then be conducted in accordance with the provisions of this title relating to those methods of discovery in actions that have been filed. *(Added by Stats.2004, c. 182 (A.B.3081), § 23, operative July 1, 2005. Amended by Stats.2005, c. 294 (A.B.333), § 15.)*

Cross References

Action defined for purposes of this Title, see Code of Civil Procedure § 2016.020.
Court defined for purposes of this Title, see Code of Civil Procedure § 2016.020.
Depositions, see Code of Civil Procedure §§ 2020.010 et seq., 2025.010 et seq., 2026.010, 2027.010, 2028.010 et seq.
Discovery, generally, see Code of Civil Procedure § 2016.010 et seq.
Document defined for purposes of this Title, see Code of Civil Procedure § 2016.020.
Witness defined for purposes of this Code, see Code of Civil Procedure § 1878.

§ 2035.060. Use of deposition to perpetuate testimony in subsequent actions; requirements

If a deposition to perpetuate testimony has been taken either under the provisions of this chapter, or under comparable provisions of the laws of the state in which it was taken, or the federal courts, or a foreign nation in which it was taken, that deposition may be used, in any action involving the same subject matter that is brought in a court of the State of California, in accordance with Section 2025.620 against any party, or the successor in interest of any party, named in the petition as an expected adverse party. *(Added by Stats.2004, c. 182 (A.B.3081), § 23, operative July 1, 2005. Amended by Stats.2005, c. 294 (A.B.333), § 16.)*

Cross References

Action defined for purposes of this Title, see Code of Civil Procedure § 2016.020.
Court defined for purposes of this Title, see Code of Civil Procedure § 2016.020.
Depositions, see Code of Civil Procedure §§ 2020.010 et seq., 2025.010 et seq., 2026.010, 2027.010, 2028.010 et seq.

CHAPTER 20. PERPETUATION OF TESTIMONY OR PRESERVATION OF INFORMATION PENDING APPEAL

Section
2036.010. Persons permitted to obtain discovery; scope of use.
2036.020. Methods available.
2036.030. Motion to obtain discovery; notice and service of motion; form and contents.
2036.040. Determination of necessity in the event of further proceedings; order; contents; compliance with discovery provisions.
2036.050. Use of deposition at subsequent proceedings; scope of use.

§ 2036.010. Persons permitted to obtain discovery; scope of use

If an appeal has been taken from a judgment entered by a court of the state, or if the time for taking an appeal has not expired, a party may obtain discovery within the scope delimited by Chapter 2 (commencing with Section 2017.010), and subject to the restrictions set forth in Chapter 5 (commencing with Section 2019.010), for purposes of perpetuating testimony or preserving information for use in the event of further proceedings in that court. *(Added by Stats.2004, c. 182 (A.B.3081), § 23, operative July 1, 2005. Amended by Stats.2016, c. 86 (S.B.1171), § 45, eff. Jan. 1, 2017.)*

Cross References

Court defined for purposes of this Title, see Code of Civil Procedure § 2016.020.
Discovery, generally, see Code of Civil Procedure § 2016.010 et seq.

§ 2036.020. Methods available

The methods available for discovery for the purpose set forth in Section 2036.010 are all of the following:

(a) Oral and written depositions.

§ 2036.020

(b) Inspections of documents, things, and places.

(c) Physical and mental examinations. *(Added by Stats.2004, c. 182 (A.B.3081), § 23, operative July 1, 2005.)*

Cross References

Depositions, see Code of Civil Procedure §§ 2020.010 et seq., 2025.010 et seq., 2026.010, 2027.010, 2028.010 et seq.
Discovery, generally, see Code of Civil Procedure § 2016.010 et seq.
Document defined for purposes of this Title, see Code of Civil Procedure § 2016.020.

§ 2036.030. Motion to obtain discovery; notice and service of motion; form and contents

(a) A party who desires to obtain discovery pending appeal shall obtain leave of the court that entered the judgment. This motion shall be made on the same notice to and service of parties as is required for discovery sought in an action pending in that court.

(b) The motion for leave to conduct discovery pending appeal shall set forth all of the following:

(1) The names and addresses of the natural persons or organizations from whom the discovery is being sought.

(2) The particular discovery methods described in Section 2036.020 for which authorization is being sought.

(3) The reasons for perpetuating testimony or preserving evidence. *(Added by Stats.2004, c. 182 (A.B.3081), § 23, operative July 1, 2005.)*

Cross References

Action defined for purposes of this Title, see Code of Civil Procedure § 2016.020.
Court defined for purposes of this Title, see Code of Civil Procedure § 2016.020.
Discovery, generally, see Code of Civil Procedure § 2016.010 et seq.
Notice, actual and constructive, defined, see Civil Code § 18.

Research References

Forms

West's California Code Forms, Civil Procedure § 2036.030 Form 1, Evidence—Discovery—Notice of Motion for Leave to Conduct Discovery to Perpetuate Testimony Pending Appeal.

§ 2036.040. Determination of necessity in the event of further proceedings; order; contents; compliance with discovery provisions

(a) If the court determines that all or part of the discovery requested under this chapter may prevent a failure or delay of justice in the event of further proceedings in the action in that court, it shall make an order authorizing that discovery.

(b) The order shall identify any witness whose deposition may be taken, and any documents, things, or places that may be inspected, and any person whose physical or mental condition may be examined.

(c) Any authorized depositions, inspections, and physical and mental examinations shall then be conducted in accordance with the provisions of this title relating to these methods of discovery in a pending action. *(Added by Stats.2004, c. 182 (A.B.3081), § 23, operative July 1, 2005.)*

Cross References

Action defined for purposes of this Title, see Code of Civil Procedure § 2016.020.
Court defined for purposes of this Title, see Code of Civil Procedure § 2016.020.

Depositions, see Code of Civil Procedure §§ 2020.010 et seq., 2025.010 et seq., 2026.010, 2027.010, 2028.010 et seq.
Discovery, generally, see Code of Civil Procedure § 2016.010 et seq.
Document defined for purposes of this Title, see Code of Civil Procedure § 2016.020.
Witness defined for purposes of this Code, see Code of Civil Procedure § 1878.

§ 2036.050. Use of deposition at subsequent proceedings; scope of use

If a deposition to perpetuate testimony has been taken under the provisions of this chapter, it may be used in any later proceeding in accordance with Section 2025.620. *(Added by Stats.2004, c. 182 (A.B.3081), § 23, operative July 1, 2005.)*

Cross References

Depositions, see Code of Civil Procedure §§ 2020.010 et seq., 2025.010 et seq., 2026.010, 2027.010, 2028.010 et seq.

Research References

Forms

West's California Code Forms, Civil Procedure § 2016.010 Comment, New Discovery Act.
West's California Code Forms, Civil Procedure § 2017.730 Form 1, Evidence—Discovery—Notice of Motion for Order Allowing Use of Electronic Technology in Complex Cases.
West's California Code Forms, Civil Procedure § 2020.310 Form 1, Evidence—Discovery—Deposition Subpena for Personal Appearance—Proof of Service—Official Form.
West's California Code Forms, Civil Procedure § 2024.060 Form 1, Evidence—Discovery—Written Agreement Extending Time for Completion of Discovery.
West's California Code Forms, Civil Procedure § 2025.210 Form 1, Evidence—Discovery—Notice of Motion for Leave of Court to Take Deposition Upon Oral Examination Within Twenty Days After Service of Summons on Defendant—Order Shortening Time.
West's California Code Forms, Civil Procedure § 2026.010 Form 1, Evidence—Discovery—Notice of Motion for Commission for Deposition of Out of State Witness.
West's California Code Forms, Civil Procedure § 2027.010 Form 1, Evidence—Discovery—Notice of Motion for Issuance of Commission or Letters Rogatory.
West's California Code Forms, Civil Procedure § 2028.020 Form 1, Evidence—Discovery—Notice of Taking Deposition by Written Questions.
West's California Code Forms, Civil Procedure § 2030.020 Form 1, Evidence—Discovery—Notice of Motion for Leave to Serve Interrogatories Within Ten Days—Order Shortening Time.
West's California Code Forms, Civil Procedure § 2031.010 Form 1, Evidence—Discovery—Demand for Inspection.
West's California Code Forms, Civil Procedure § 2031.510 Form 1, Evidence—Discovery—Declaration of Disclosure—Nonprivileged Relevant Written Evidence—State Land Patents or Grants—Validity or Boundary Dispute.
West's California Code Forms, Civil Procedure § 2032.220 Form 1, Evidence—Discovery—Demand for Physical Examination of Plaintiff.
West's California Code Forms, Civil Procedure § 2033.020 Form 1, Evidence—Discovery—Request for Admissions—Truth of Facts—Genuineness of Documents—Official Form.
West's California Code Forms, Civil Procedure § 2033.710 Form 1, Evidence—Discovery—Form Interrogatories—Official Form.
West's California Code Forms, Civil Procedure § 2034.230 Form 1, Evidence—Discovery—Demand for Simultaneous Exchange of Information Concerning Expert Witnesses—Simultaneous Production of Discoverable Expert's Reports.
West's California Code Forms, Civil Procedure § 2035.030 Form 1, Evidence—Discovery—Petition to Perpetuate Testimony Before Action.
West's California Code Forms, Civil Procedure § 2036.030 Form 1, Evidence—Discovery—Notice of Motion for Leave to Conduct Discovery to Perpetuate Testimony Pending Appeal.

EDUCATION CODE

Title 1

GENERAL EDUCATION CODE PROVISIONS

Division 1

GENERAL EDUCATION CODE PROVISIONS

Part 13

STATE TEACHERS' RETIREMENT SYSTEM

Cross References

Agreements for social security coverage, see Government Code § 22200 et seq.
Apportionment of funds, see Cal. Const. Art. 9, § 6.
Construction, effect on charter provisions concerning school employees, see Education Code §§ 44850, 87419.
Construction to preserve judicial rights and remedies, see Education Code §§ 44849, 87418.
Contributions made in carrying out contracts with governmental units, see Education Code § 33117.
County Employees Retirement Law of 1937, see Government Code § 31450 et seq.
County superintendents, retirement system contributions and benefits, see Education Code § 1204.
Deposits of public pension and retirement funds, see Government Code § 7520 et seq.
Exchange position, effect of acceptance on teacher's rights, see Education Code §§ 44854, 87423.
Exchange teachers, see Education Code §§ 44854, 44855, 87423, 87424.
Failure to present district system warrants on time, see Education Code §§ 42661, 85271.
Joint district salary retirement plans, see Education Code § 24900 et seq.
Public employees' retirement system, see Government Code § 20000 et seq.
Public pension and retirement plans, see Government Code § 7500 et seq.
Retiree benefit funds, see Education Code § 1350.
Retirement of employees of school districts as having effect of dismissal, see Education Code §§ 44907, 87467.
Teacher-assistant with temporary certificate, see Education Code § 44926.
Termination of school district employees, effect on retirement rights, see Education Code §§ 44956, 87744.
Waiver of provisions of code permissible except provisions of this Part, see Education Code § 33050.

CHAPTER 12. COMMUNITY PROPERTY

Section
22650. Marriage dissolution or legal separation; rights of nonmember spouses and nonmember registered domestic partners; termination or separation of domestic partnership.
22651. Nonmember spouse; treatment of domestic partner as nonmember spouse.
22652. Court orders; division of contributions and service credits; community property rights.
22653. Status of nonmember spouse; limitation of rights and benefits.
22655. Retirement allowance or retirement annuity; community property rights of nonmember spouse; rights upon death.
22656. Judgments or orders; conditions for binding effect.
22657. Nonmember spouse; applicable statutory provisions.
22658. Accounts of nonmember spouse; administration; separation.
22659. Information from nonmember spouse.

Section
22660. Beneficiary of nonmember spouse; modification of allowance.
22661. Accumulated retirement contributions; nonmember spouse's right to refund; lump-sum payment; mode of deposit and notice.
22662. Accumulated retirement contributions refunded to members; redeposit by nonmember spouse.
22663. Additional service credit; purchase by nonmember spouse.
22664. Service retirement allowance for nonmember spouse; conditions for retirement for service; limitations; calculation of allowance; increases; nonmember spouse of member subject to the California Public Employees' Pension Reform Act of 2013.
22665. Service credit awarded in judgment or court order; calculation of retirement or disability allowance.
22666. Terminable interest doctrine; legislative intent.

Cross References

Community property, see Family Code §§ 65, 760.
Division of accumulated community property contributions and service credit, see Family Code § 2610.

§ 22650. Marriage dissolution or legal separation; rights of nonmember spouses and nonmember registered domestic partners; termination or separation of domestic partnership

(a) This chapter establishes the power of a court in a dissolution of marriage or legal separation action with respect to community property rights in accounts with the plan under this part and establishes and defines the rights of nonmember spouses and nonmember registered domestic partners in the plan under this part.

(b) For purposes of this chapter, the termination, dissolution, or nullity of a registered domestic partnership, or the legal separation of partners in a registered domestic partnership, as provided in Section 299 of the Family Code, shall be treated in the same manner as a dissolution of marriage or legal separation of a member and his or her spouse. *(Added by Stats.1993, c. 893 (A.B.1796), § 2. Amended by Stats.1996, c. 634 (S.B.2041), § 118; Stats.1998, c. 965 (A.B.2765), § 59; Stats.2004, c. 912 (A.B.2233), § 6; Stats.2005, c. 418 (S.B.973), § 4.)*

Cross References

Community property, see Family Code §§ 65, 760.
State teachers' retirement system cash balance plan, community property, dissolution or legal separation and rights of registered domestic partners, see Education Code § 27400.

Research References

Forms

5¶ 2 Nichols Cyclopedia of Legal Forms Annotated § 100:4, Dissolution or Termination of Marital Relationship, Generally.

§ 22651. Nonmember spouse; treatment of domestic partner as nonmember spouse

(a) For purposes of this chapter and Section 23300, "nonmember spouse" means a member's spouse or former spouse, and also includes a member's registered domestic partner or former registered domestic partner, who is being or has been awarded a community

§ 22651

property interest in the service credit, accumulated retirement contributions, accumulated Defined Benefit Supplement account balance, or benefits of the member under this part.

(b) For purposes of this chapter and Section 23300, a member's registered domestic partner or former registered domestic partner who is being or has been awarded a community property interest in the service credit, accumulated retirement contributions, accumulated Defined Benefit Supplement account balance, or benefits of the member under this part shall be treated in the same manner as a nonmember spouse.

(c) A nonmember spouse shall not be considered a member based upon his or her receipt of any of the following being awarded to the nonmember spouse as a result of legal separation or dissolution of marriage:

(1) A separate account of service credit and accumulated retirement contributions, a retirement allowance, or an interest in the member's retirement allowance under the Defined Benefit Program.

(2) A separate account based on the member's Defined Benefit Supplement account balance, a retirement benefit, or an interest in the member's retirement benefit under the Defined Benefit Supplement Program. *(Added by Stats.1993, c. 893 (A.B.1796), § 2. Amended by Stats.1996, c. 634 (S.B.2041), § 119; Stats.1998, c. 965 (A.B.2765), § 60; Stats.2000, c. 74 (A.B.1509), § 33; Stats.2000, c. 1021 (A.B.2700), § 18; Stats.2004, c. 912 (A.B.2233), § 7; Stats.2005, c. 418 (S.B.973), § 5.)*

Cross References
Community property, see Family Code §§ 65, 760.

§ 22652. Court orders; division of contributions and service credits; community property rights

(a) Upon the legal separation or dissolution of marriage of a member, other than a retired member, the court shall include in the judgment or a court order the date on which the parties separated.

(b) The court may order in the judgment or court order that the member's accumulated retirement contributions and service credit under the Defined Benefit Program, or the member's Defined Benefit Supplement account balance, or both, under this part that are attributable to periods of service during the marriage be divided into two separate and distinct accounts in the name of the member and the nonmember spouse, respectively. Any service credit and accumulated retirement contributions under the Defined Benefit Program and any accumulated Defined Benefit Supplement account balance under this part that are not explicitly awarded by the judgment or court order shall be deemed the exclusive property of the member under the Defined Benefit Program or the Defined Benefit Supplement Program, as applicable.

(c) The determination of the court of community property rights pursuant to this section shall be consistent with this chapter and shall address the rights of the nonmember spouse under this part, including, but not limited to, the following:

(1) The right to a retirement allowance under the Defined Benefit Program and, if applicable, a retirement benefit under the Defined Benefit Supplement Program.

(2) The right to a refund of accumulated retirement contributions under the Defined Benefit Program and the return of the accumulated Defined Benefit Supplement account balance that were awarded to the nonmember spouse.

(3) The right to redeposit all or a portion of accumulated retirement contributions previously refunded to the member which the member is eligible to redeposit pursuant to Sections 23200 to 23203, inclusive, and shall specify the shares of the redeposit amount awarded to the member and the nonmember spouse.

(4) The right to purchase additional service credit that the member is eligible to purchase pursuant to Sections 22800 to 22810, inclusive, and shall specify the shares of the additional service credit awarded to the member and the nonmember spouse. *(Added by Stats.1993, c. 893 (A.B.1796), § 2. Amended by Stats.1998, c. 965 (A.B.2765), § 61; Stats.2000, c. 74 (A.B.1509), § 34; Stats.2000, c. 1020 (A.B.820), § 1, operative July 1, 2001; Stats.2000, c. 1021 (A.B.2700), § 19.5.)*

Cross References
Community property, see Family Code §§ 65, 760.

§ 22653. Status of nonmember spouse; limitation of rights and benefits

(a) The nonmember spouse who is awarded a separate account under this part pursuant to Section 22652 is not a member of the Defined Benefit Program based on that award. The nonmember spouse is entitled only to rights and benefits based on that award explicitly established by this chapter.

(b) This section shall not be construed to limit any right arising from the account of a nonmember spouse under this part that exists because the nonmember spouse is or was employed to perform creditable service subject to coverage by the Defined Benefit Program. *(Added by Stats.1993, c. 893 (A.B.1796), § 2. Amended by Stats.1996, c. 634 (S.B.2041), § 120; Stats.1998, c. 965 (A.B.2765), § 62.)*

§ 22655. Retirement allowance or retirement annuity; community property rights of nonmember spouse; rights upon death

(a) Upon the legal separation or dissolution of marriage of a retired member, the court may include in the judgment or court order a determination of the community property rights of the parties in the retired member's retirement allowance and, if applicable, retirement benefit under this part consistent with this section. Upon election under subparagraph (B) of paragraph (3) of subdivision (a) of Section 2610 of the Family Code, the court order awarding the nonmember spouse a community property share in the retirement allowance or retirement benefit, or both, of a retired member shall be consistent with this section.

(b) If the court does not award the entire retirement allowance or retirement benefit under this part to the retired member and the retired member is receiving a retirement allowance that has not been modified pursuant to Section 24300 or 24300.1, a single life annuity pursuant to Section 25011 or 25018, or a member only annuity described in paragraph (1) of subdivision (a) of Sections 25011.1 and 25018.1, the court shall require only that the system pay the nonmember spouse, by separate warrant, his or her community property share of the retired member's retirement allowance or retirement benefit, or both, under this part.

(c) If the court does not award the entire retirement allowance or retirement benefit under this part to the retired member and the retired member is receiving an allowance that has been actuarially modified pursuant to Section 24300 or 24300.1, or a joint and survivor annuity pursuant to Section 25011, 25011.1, 25018, or 25018.1, the court shall order only one of the following:

(1) The retired member shall maintain the retirement allowance or joint and survivor annuity, or both, under this part without change.

(2) The retired member shall cancel the option that modified the retirement allowance under this part pursuant to Section 24322 and elect a new joint and survivor option or designate a new beneficiary or both, and the system shall pay the nonmember spouse, by separate warrant, his or her community property share of the retirement allowance payable to the retired member, the option beneficiary, or both.

(3) The retired member shall cancel the joint and survivor annuity under which the retirement benefit is being paid pursuant to Section 24324, and elect a new joint and survivor annuity or designate a new annuity beneficiary or both, based on the actuarial equivalent of the

member's canceled annuity, and the system shall pay the nonmember spouse, by separate warrant, his or her community property share of the retirement benefit payable to the retired member, the annuity beneficiary, or both.

(4) The retired member shall take the action specified in both paragraphs (2) and (3).

(5) The retired member shall cancel the option that modified the retirement allowance under this part pursuant to Section 24322 and elect an unmodified retirement allowance and the system shall pay the nonmember spouse, by separate warrant, his or her community property share of the retired member's retirement allowance under this part.

(6) The retired member shall cancel, pursuant to Section 24324, the joint and survivor annuity under which the retirement benefit is being paid, and elect a single life annuity, and the system shall pay the nonmember spouse, by separate warrant, his or her community property share of the retirement benefit payable to the retired member.

(7) The retired member shall take the action specified in both paragraphs (5) and (6).

(d) If the option beneficiary or annuity beneficiary or both under this part, other than the nonmember spouse, predeceases the retired member, the court shall order the retired member to designate a new option beneficiary pursuant to Section 24323, or a new annuity beneficiary pursuant to Section 24324 and shall order the system to pay the nonmember spouse, by separate warrant, his or her share of the community property interest in the retirement allowance or retirement benefit payable to the retired member or the new option beneficiary or annuity beneficiary or each of them.

(e) The right of the nonmember spouse to receive his or her community property share of the retired member's retirement allowance or retirement benefit or both under this section shall terminate upon the death of the nonmember spouse. However, the nonmember spouse may designate a beneficiary under the Defined Benefit Program and a payee under the Defined Benefit Supplement Program to receive his or her community property share of the retired member's accumulated retirement contributions and accumulated Defined Benefit Supplement account balance under this part in the event that there are remaining accumulated retirement contributions and a balance of credits in the member's Defined Benefit Supplement account to be paid upon the death of the nonmember spouse. *(Added by Stats.1993, c. 893 (A.B.1796), § 2. Amended by Stats.1994, c. 1269 (A.B.2208), § 5; Stats.1996, c. 634 (S.B.2041), § 122; Stats.1998, c. 965 (A.B.2765), § 63; Stats.2000, c. 74 (A.B.1509), § 35; Stats.2000, c. 1021 (A.B.2700), § 20; Stats.2006, c. 655 (S.B.1466), § 9; Stats.2014, c. 755 (S.B.1220), § 16, eff. Jan. 1, 2015.)*

Cross References

Community property, see Family Code §§ 65, 760.

§ 22656. Judgments or orders; conditions for binding effect

No judgment or court order issued pursuant to this chapter is binding on the system with respect to the Defined Benefit Program or the Defined Benefit Supplement Program until the system has been joined as a party to the action and has been served with a certified copy of the judgment or court order. *(Added by Stats.1993, c. 893 (A.B.1796), § 2. Amended by Stats.1996, c. 634 (S.B.2041), § 122.5; Stats.1998, c. 965 (A.B.2765), § 64; Stats.2000, c. 74 (A.B.1509), § 36; Stats.2000, c. 1021 (A.B.2700), § 21.)*

§ 22657. Nonmember spouse; applicable statutory provisions

(a) The following provisions shall apply to a nonmember spouse as if he or she were a member under this part: Sections 22107, 22306, 22906, and 23802, subdivisions (a) and (b) of Section 24600, and Sections 24601, 24602, 24603, 24605, 24606, 24607, 24608, 24611, 24612, 24613, 24616, 24617, 25009, 25010, 25011, 25011.1, 25013, 25020, 25021, and 25022.

(b) Notwithstanding subdivision (a), this section shall not be construed to establish any right for the nonmember spouse under this part that is not explicitly established in Sections 22650 to 22655, inclusive, and Sections 22658 to 22665, inclusive. *(Added by Stats.1993, c. 893 (A.B.1796), § 2. Amended by Stats.1996, c. 634 (S.B.2041), § 123; Stats.1998, c. 965 (A.B.2765), § 65; Stats.2002, c. 375 (A.B.2982), § 5; Stats.2006, c. 655 (S.B.1466), § 10.)*

§ 22658. Accounts of nonmember spouse; administration; separation

(a) A separate account awarded to a nonmember spouse pursuant to Section 22652 shall be administered independently of the member's account.

(b) An accumulated Defined Benefit Supplement account balance, accumulated retirement contributions, service credit, and final compensation attributable to a separate account of a nonmember spouse under this part shall not be combined in any way or for any purpose with the accumulated Defined Benefit Supplement account balance, accumulated retirement contributions, service credit, and final compensation of any other separate account of the nonmember spouse.

(c) An accumulated Defined Benefit Supplement account balance, accumulated retirement contributions, service credit, and final compensation attributable to the separate account of a nonmember spouse shall not be combined in any way or for any purpose with the accumulated Defined Benefit Supplement account balance, accumulated retirement contributions, service credit, and final compensation of an account that exists under this part because the nonmember spouse is employed or has been employed to perform creditable service subject to coverage under the Defined Benefit Program or the Defined Benefit Supplement Program. *(Added by Stats.1993, c. 893 (A.B.1796), § 2. Amended by Stats.1996, c. 634 (S.B.2041), § 123.5; Stats.1998, c. 965 (A.B.2765), § 66; Stats.2000, c. 74 (A.B.1509), § 37.)*

§ 22659. Information from nonmember spouse

Upon being awarded a separate account or an interest in the retirement allowance or retirement benefit of a retired member under this part, a nonmember spouse shall provide the system with proof of his or her date of birth, social security number, and any other information requested by the system, in the form and manner requested by the system. *(Added by Stats.1993, c. 893 (A.B.1796), § 2. Amended by Stats.1996, c. 634 (S.B.2041), § 124; Stats.1998, c. 965 (A.B.2765), § 67; Stats.2000, c. 74 (A.B.1509), § 38; Stats.2000, c. 1021 (A.B.2700), § 22.)*

§ 22660. Beneficiary of nonmember spouse; modification of allowance

(a) The nonmember spouse who is awarded a separate account under this part shall have the right to designate, pursuant to Sections 23300 to 23304, inclusive, a beneficiary or beneficiaries to receive the accumulated retirement contributions under the Defined Benefit Program and to designate a payee to receive the remaining balance of payments for a period-certain annuity, or the accumulated Defined Benefit Supplement account balance under the Defined Benefit Supplement Program remaining in the separate account of the nonmember spouse on his or her date of death, and any accrued allowance or accrued benefit under the Defined Benefit Supplement Program that is attributable to the separate account of the nonmember spouse and that is unpaid on the date of the death of the nonmember spouse.

(b) This section shall not be construed to provide the nonmember spouse with any right to elect to modify a retirement allowance under Section 24300 or 24300.1, or to elect a joint and survivor annuity under the Defined Benefit Supplement Program. *(Added by Stats.*

§ 22660

1993, c. 893 (A.B.1796), § 2. Amended by Stats.1998, c. 965 (A.B.2765), § 68; Stats.2000, c. 74 (A.B.1509), § 39; Stats.2000, c. 1021 (A.B.2700), § 23; Stats.2001, c. 159 (S.B.662), § 59; Stats.2006, c. 655 (S.B.1466), § 11; Stats.2017, c. 298 (A.B.1325), § 3, eff. Jan. 1, 2018.)

Cross References

Death of nonmember spouse, remaining balance of payments, payments made to payee designated pursuant to this section, see Education Code § 25022.5.

State Teachers' Retirement System, service retirement allowance for nonmember spouse, see Education Code § 22664.

§ 22661. Accumulated retirement contributions; nonmember spouse's right to refund; lump-sum payment; mode of deposit and notice

(a) The nonmember spouse who is awarded a separate account under this part shall have the right to a refund of the accumulated retirement contributions in the account under the Defined Benefit Program, and a return of the Defined Benefit Supplement account balance, of the nonmember spouse under this part.

(b) The nonmember spouse shall file an application on a form provided by the system to obtain a refund or lump-sum payment.

(c) Except as provided in subdivision (i), the refund of accumulated retirement contributions in the account under the Defined Benefit Program and the return of the accumulated Defined Benefit Supplement account balance under this part are effective when the system deposits in the United States mail an initial warrant drawn in favor of the nonmember spouse and addressed to the latest address for the nonmember spouse on file with the system.

(d) Except as provided in subdivision (i), if the nonmember spouse has elected on a form provided by the system to transfer all or a specified portion of the accumulated retirement contributions or accumulated Defined Benefit Supplement account balance that are eligible for direct trustee-to-trustee transfer to the trustee of a qualified plan under Section 402 of the Internal Revenue Code of 1986 (26 U.S.C. Sec. 402), deposit in the United States mail of a notice that the requested transfer has been made constitutes a refund of the nonmember spouse's accumulated retirement contributions as defined in Section 22161.5 or the return of the accumulated Defined Benefit Supplement account balance. This subdivision shall not apply to a nonmember domestic partner, consistent with Section 402 of the Internal Revenue Code.

(e) The nonmember spouse is deemed to have permanently waived all rights and benefits pertaining to the service credit, accumulated retirement contributions, and accumulated Defined Benefit Supplement account balance under this part when the refund and lump-sum payment become effective.

(f) The nonmember spouse may not cancel a refund or lump-sum payment under this part after it is effective.

(g) The nonmember spouse shall not have a right to elect to redeposit the refunded accumulated retirement contributions under this part after the refund is effective, to redeposit under Section 22662 or purchase additional service credit under Section 22663 after the refund becomes effective, or to redeposit the accumulated Defined Benefit Supplement account balance after the lump-sum payment becomes effective.

(h) If the total service credit in the separate account of the nonmember spouse under the Defined Benefit Program, including service credit purchased under Sections 22662 and 22663, is less than two and one-half years, the system shall refund the accumulated retirement contributions in the account.

(i) The mode of deposit described in subdivision (c) and the mode of notice described in subdivision (d) are subject to Section 22337. (Added by Stats.1993, c. 893 (A.B.1796), § 2. Amended by Stats.1994, c. 933 (A.B.3171), § 38, eff. Sept. 28, 1994; Stats.1996, c. 634 (S.B.2041), § 125; Stats.1998, c. 965 (A.B.2765), § 69; Stats.2000, c. 74 (A.B.1509), § 40; Stats.2000, c. 1021 (A.B.2700), § 24; Stats.2004, c. 912 (A.B.2233), § 8; Stats.2007, c. 513 (A.B.1432), § 1; Stats.2009, c. 304 (S.B.634), § 4; Stats.2013, c. 459 (A.B.989), § 3.)

Cross References

State teachers' retirement system, registered domestic partner of member included as spouse, see Education Code §§ 22007.5, 22171.

State teachers' retirement system cash balance plan, registered domestic partner of member included as spouse, see Education Code §§ 26002.5, 26140.

§ 22662. Accumulated retirement contributions refunded to members; redeposit by nonmember spouse

The nonmember spouse who is awarded a separate account under the Defined Benefit Program may redeposit accumulated retirement contributions previously refunded to the member in accordance with the determination of the court pursuant to Section 22652.

(a) The nonmember spouse may redeposit under the Defined Benefit Program only those accumulated retirement contributions that were previously refunded to the member and in which the court has determined the nonmember spouse has a community property interest.

(b) The nonmember spouse shall inform the system in writing of his or her intent to redeposit within 180 days after the judgment or court order that specifies the redeposit rights of the nonmember spouse is entered. Except as provided in subdivision (g), the nonmember spouse's election to redeposit shall be made on a form provided by the system within 30 days after the system mails an election form and the billing.

(c) If the nonmember spouse elects to redeposit under the Defined Benefit Program, he or she shall repay all or a portion of the member's refunded accumulated retirement contributions that were awarded to the nonmember spouse and shall pay regular interest from the date of the refund to the date payment of the redeposit is completed.

(d) All payments shall be received by the system before the effective date of the nonmember spouse's retirement under this part. If any payment due because of the election is not received at the system's headquarters office within 120 days of its due date, the election shall be canceled and any payments made under the election shall be returned to the nonmember spouse.

(e) The right of the nonmember spouse to redeposit shall be subject to Section 23203.

(f) The member shall not have a right to redeposit the share of the nonmember spouse in the previously refunded accumulated retirement contributions under this part whether or not the nonmember spouse elects to redeposit. However, any accumulated retirement contributions previously refunded under this part and not explicitly awarded to the nonmember spouse under this part by the judgment or court order shall be deemed the exclusive property of the member.

(g) The measurement of time within which the election to redeposit described in subdivision (b) shall be made is subject to Section 22337. (Added by Stats.1993, c. 893 (A.B.1796), § 2. Amended by Stats.1996, c. 634 (S.B.2041), § 126; Stats.1998, c. 965 (A.B.2765), § 70; Stats.2000, c. 74 (A.B.1509), § 41; Stats.2000, c. 1020 (A.B.820), § 2, operative July 1, 2001; Stats.2000, c. 1021 (A.B.2700), § 25.5; Stats.2005, c. 351 (A.B.224), § 7; Stats.2013, c. 558 (A.B.1379), § 8; Stats.2013, c. 459 (A.B.989), § 4; Stats.2014, c. 755 (S.B.1220), § 17, eff. Jan. 1, 2015.)

Cross References

Community property, see Family Code §§ 65, 760.

Computation of time,

    Generally, see Code of Civil Procedure §§ 12, 12a; Government Code § 6800 et seq.

Time in which any act provided by the Education Code is to be done, see Education Code § 9.
Continuation of statutes relating to subjects covered by provisions of this Code, see Education Code § 3.

§ 22663. Additional service credit; purchase by nonmember spouse

The nonmember spouse who is awarded a separate account under this part has the right to purchase additional service credit in accordance with the determination of the court pursuant to Section 22652.

(a) The nonmember spouse may purchase only the service credit that the court, pursuant to Section 22652, has determined to be the community property interest of the nonmember spouse.

(b) The nonmember spouse shall inform the system in writing of his or her intent to purchase additional service credit within 180 days after the date the judgment or court order addressing the right of the nonmember spouse to purchase additional service credit is entered. Except as provided in subdivision (f), the nonmember spouse shall elect to purchase additional service credit on a form provided by the system within 30 days after the system mails an election form and billing.

(c) If the nonmember spouse elects to purchase additional service credit, he or she shall pay, prior to retirement under this part, all contributions with respect to the additional service at the contribution rate for additional service credit in effect at the time of election and regular interest from July 1 of the year following the year upon which contributions are based.

(1)(A) The nonmember spouse shall purchase additional service credit by paying the required contributions and interest in one lump sum, or in not more than 120 monthly installments, provided that no installment, except the final installment, is less than twenty-five dollars ($25). Regular interest shall be charged on the monthly, unpaid balance if the nonmember spouse pays in installments.

(B) If any payment due, because of the election, is not received at the system's headquarters office within 120 days of its due date, the election shall be canceled and any payments made under the election shall be returned to the nonmember spouse.

(2) The contributions shall be based on the member's compensation earnable in the most recent school year during which the member was employed, preceding the date of separation established by the court pursuant to Section 22652.

(3) All payments of contributions and interest shall be received by the system before the effective date of the retirement of the nonmember spouse.

(d) The nonmember spouse does not have a right to purchase additional service credit under this part after the effective date of a refund of the accumulated retirement contributions in the separate account of the nonmember spouse.

(e) The member does not have a right to purchase the community property interest of the nonmember spouse of additional service credit under this part whether or not the nonmember spouse elects to purchase the additional service credit. However, any additional service credit eligible for purchase that is not explicitly awarded to the nonmember spouse by the judgment or court order shall be deemed the exclusive property of the member.

(f) The measurement of time within which the election to purchase additional service credit described in subdivision (b) shall be made is subject to Section 22337. *(Added by Stats.1993, c. 893 (A.B.1796), § 2. Amended by Stats.1996, c. 634 (S.B.2041), § 127; Stats.1998, c. 965 (A.B.2765), § 71; Stats.2003, c. 859 (S.B.627), § 7; Stats.2004, c. 912 (A.B.2233), § 9; Stats.2005, c. 351 (A.B.224), § 8; Stats.2013, c. 558 (A.B.1379), § 9; Stats.2013, c. 459 (A.B.989), § 5; Stats.2014, c. 755 (S.B.1220), § 18, eff. Jan. 1, 2015.)*

Cross References

Community property, see Family Code §§ 65, 760.
Computation of time,
  Generally, see Code of Civil Procedure §§ 12, 12a; Government Code § 6800 et seq.
  Time in which any act provided by the Education Code is to be done, see Education Code § 9.
Continuation of statutes relating to subjects covered by provisions of this Code, see Education Code § 3.

§ 22664. Service retirement allowance for nonmember spouse; conditions for retirement for service; limitations; calculation of allowance; increases; nonmember spouse of member subject to the California Public Employees' Pension Reform Act of 2013

The nonmember spouse who is awarded a separate account shall have the right to a service retirement allowance and, if applicable, a retirement benefit under this part.

(a) The nonmember spouse shall be eligible to retire for service under this part if the following conditions are satisfied:

(1) The member had at least five years of credited service during the period of marriage, at least one year of which had been performed subsequent to the most recent refund to the member of accumulated retirement contributions. The credited service may include service credited to the account of the member as of the date of the dissolution or legal separation, previously refunded service, out-of-state service, and permissive service credit that the member is eligible to purchase at the time of the dissolution or legal separation.

(2) The nonmember spouse has at least two and one-half years of credited service in his or her separate account.

(3) The nonmember spouse has attained 55 years of age or more.

(b) A service retirement allowance of a nonmember spouse under this part shall become effective upon a date designated by the nonmember spouse, provided:

(1) The requirements of subdivision (a) are satisfied.

(2) The nonmember spouse has filed an application for service retirement on a properly executed form provided by the system, that is executed no earlier than six months before the effective date of the retirement allowance.

(3) The effective date is no earlier than the first day of the month that the application is received at the system's headquarters office and the effective date is after the date the judgment or court order pursuant to Section 22652 was entered.

(c)(1) Upon service retirement at normal retirement age under this part, the nonmember spouse shall receive a retirement allowance that shall consist of an annual allowance payable in monthly installments equal to 2 percent of final compensation for each year of credited service.

(2) If the nonmember spouse's retirement is effective at less than normal retirement age and between early retirement age under this part and normal retirement age, the retirement allowance shall be reduced by one-half of 1 percent for each full month, or fraction of a month, that will elapse until the nonmember spouse would have reached normal retirement age.

(3) If the nonmember spouse's service retirement is effective at an age greater than normal retirement age and is effective on or after January 1, 1999, the percentage of final compensation for each year of credited service shall be determined pursuant to the following table:

Age at Retirement	Percentage
60¼	2.033
60½	2.067
60¾	2.10
61	2.133
61¼	2.167
61½	2.20

§ 22664

61¾	2.233
62	2.267
62¼	2.30
62½	2.333
62¾	2.367
63 and over	2.40

(4) In computing the retirement allowance of the nonmember spouse, the age of the nonmember spouse on the last day of the month that the retirement allowance begins to accrue shall be used.

(5) Final compensation, for purposes of calculating the service retirement allowance of the nonmember spouse under this subdivision, shall be calculated according to the definition of final compensation in Section 22134, 22134.5, or 22135, whichever is applicable, and shall be based on the member's compensation earnable up to the date the parties separated, as established in the judgment or court order pursuant to Section 22652. The nonmember spouse shall not be entitled to use any other calculation of final compensation.

(d) Upon service retirement under this part, the nonmember spouse shall receive a retirement benefit based on an amount equal to the balance of credits in the nonmember spouse's Defined Benefit Supplement account on the date the retirement benefit becomes payable.

(1) A retirement benefit shall be a lump-sum payment, or an annuity payable in monthly installments, or a combination of both a lump-sum payment and an annuity, as elected by the nonmember spouse on the application for a retirement benefit. A retirement benefit paid as an annuity under this chapter shall be subject to Sections 22660, 25011, and 25011.1.

(2) Upon distribution of the entire retirement benefit in a lump-sum payment, no other benefit shall be payable to the nonmember spouse or the nonmember spouse's beneficiary under the Defined Benefit Supplement Program.

(e) If the member is or was receiving a disability allowance under this part with an effective date before or on the date the parties separated as established in the judgment or court order pursuant to Section 22652, or at any time applies for and receives a disability allowance with an effective date that is before or coincides with the date the parties separated as established in the judgment or court order pursuant to Section 22652, the nonmember spouse shall not be eligible to retire until after the disability allowance of the member terminates. If the member who is or was receiving a disability allowance returns to employment to perform creditable service subject to coverage under the Defined Benefit Program or has his or her allowance terminated under Section 24015, the nonmember spouse may not be paid a retirement allowance until at least six months after termination of the disability allowance and the return of the member to employment to perform creditable service subject to coverage under the Defined Benefit Program, or the termination of the disability allowance and the employment or self-employment of the member in any capacity, notwithstanding Section 22132. If at the end of the six-month period, the member has not had a recurrence of the original disability or has not had his or her earnings fall below the amounts described in Section 24015, the nonmember spouse may be paid a retirement allowance if all other eligibility requirements are met.

(1) The retirement allowance of the nonmember spouse under this subdivision shall be calculated as follows: the disability allowance the member was receiving, exclusive of the portion for dependent children, shall be divided between the share of the member and the share of the nonmember spouse. The share of the nonmember spouse shall be the amount obtained by multiplying the disability allowance, exclusive of the portion for dependent children, by the years of service credited to the separate account of the nonmember spouse, including service projected to the date of separation, and dividing by the projected service of the member. The nonmember spouse's retirement allowance shall be the lesser of the share of the nonmember spouse under this subdivision or the retirement allowance under subdivision (c).

(2) The share of the member shall be the total disability allowance reduced by the share of the nonmember spouse. The share of the member shall be considered the disability allowance of the member for purposes of Section 24213.

(f) The nonmember spouse who receives a retirement allowance is not a retired member under this part. However, the allowance of the nonmember spouse shall be increased by application of the improvement factor and shall be eligible for the application of supplemental increases and other benefit maintenance provisions under this part, including, but not limited to, Sections 24412 and 24415 based on the same criteria used for the application of these benefit maintenance increases to the service retirement allowances of members.

(g) Paragraphs (1) to (3), inclusive, of subdivision (c) shall not apply to a nonmember spouse of a member subject to the California Public Employees' Pension Reform Act of 2013. For a person who is a nonmember spouse of a member subject to the California Public Employees' Pension Reform Act of 2013 and is awarded a separate account, the retirement allowance shall equal the percentage of final compensation for each year of credited service that is equal to the percentage specified in Section 24202.6 based on the age of the nonmember spouse on the effective date of the allowance. (Added by Stats.1993, c. 893 (A.B.1796), § 2. Amended by Stats.1996, c. 634 (S.B.2041), § 128; Stats.1998, c. 965 (A.B.2765), § 72.5; Stats.1999, c. 939 (S.B.1074), § 43; Stats.2000, c. 74 (A.B.1509), § 42; Stats. 2000, c. 1021 (A.B.2700), § 26; Stats.2001, c. 803 (S.B.501), § 6; Stats.2002, c. 375 (A.B.2982), § 6; Stats.2006, c. 655 (S.B.1466), § 12; Stats.2008, c. 751 (A.B.1389), § 4, eff. Sept. 30, 2008; Stats.2013, c. 558 (A.B.1379), § 10; Stats.2013, c. 559 (A.B.1381), § 13, operative Jan. 1, 2013; Stats.2014, c. 755 (S.B.1220), § 19, eff. Jan. 1, 2015; Stats.2016, c. 218 (S.B.1352), § 15, eff. Jan. 1, 2017.)

§ 22665. Service credit awarded in judgment or court order; calculation of retirement or disability allowance

The system shall include the service credit awarded to a nonmember spouse in the judgment or court order to determine the eligibility of a member for a retirement or disability allowance under this part. That portion of awarded service credit based on previously refunded accumulated retirement contributions or on permissive service credit may not be used by the member for eligibility requirements until the member has redeposited or purchased his or her portion of the service credit. The member's service retirement allowance shall be calculated based on the service credit in the member's account on the effective date of service retirement. (Added by Stats.1993, c. 893 (A.B.1796), § 2. Amended by Stats.1996, c. 634 (S.B.2041), § 129; Stats.1998, c. 965 (A.B.2765), § 73; Stats.2000, c. 74 (A.B.1509), § 43.)

§ 22666. Terminable interest doctrine; legislative intent

It is the intent of the Legislature to abolish any remaining application of the terminable interest doctrine in California relating to the division of public retirement benefits of a member in the event of dissolution of marriage or death if the division is made under this chapter. (Added by Stats.1993, c. 893 (A.B.1796), § 2.)

Cross References

Statutes,
   Construction and legislative intent, see Code of Civil Procedure §§ 1858 and 1859.
   Liberal construction of Education Code, see Education Code § 3.
   Rules of construction and definition for the Education Code, see Education Code § 10.

Title 2

ELEMENTARY AND SECONDARY EDUCATION

Cross References

Service on board or commission by public secondary school pupil, see Education Code § 54.

Division 4

INSTRUCTION AND SERVICES

Part 27

PUPILS

Cross References

Employment agencies, employment of minors, notification required to be given to jobseekers, see Civil Code § 1812.509.
Employment of minors under 16, see Labor Code § 1290.
Job listing services, illegal employment, minors, see Civil Code § 1812.521.
Permits and certificates for employment of minors, see Labor Code § 1299.

CHAPTER 6. PUPIL RIGHTS AND RESPONSIBILITIES

Cross References

Waiver of provisions of code permissible except provisions of this Chapter, see Education Code § 33050.

ARTICLE 6. ATHLETIC PROGRAMS

Section
49024. Activity Supervisor Clearance Certificates; requirement for noncertificated candidates to work with pupils in pupil activity programs; exceptions; temporary certificates.

§ 49024. Activity Supervisor Clearance Certificates; requirement for noncertificated candidates to work with pupils in pupil activity programs; exceptions; temporary certificates

(a) Prior to assuming a paid or volunteer position to work with pupils in a pupil activity program sponsored by a school district, all noncertificated candidates shall obtain an Activity Supervisor Clearance Certificate from the Commission on Teacher Credentialing pursuant to subdivision (f) of Section 44258.7.

(b) A pupil activity program sponsored by a school district includes, but is not limited to, scholastic programs, interscholastic programs, and extracurricular activities sponsored by a school district or school booster club, including, but not limited to, cheer team, drill team, dance team, and marching band.

(c) Volunteer supervisors for breakfast, lunch, or other nutritional periods pursuant to Sections 44814 and 44815, and nonteaching volunteer aides, as defined in Section 35021, under the immediate supervision and direction of certificated personnel of the district, shall not be required to obtain an Activity Supervisor Clearance Certificate. For purposes of this section, a nonteaching volunteer aide includes a parent volunteering in a classroom or on a field trip or a community member providing noninstructional services.

(d) Candidates may be issued a temporary certificate in accordance with Sections 44332 and 44332.5 while the application is being processed.

(e) This section does not apply to a candidate who is required by the school district to clear a Department of Justice and Federal Bureau of Investigation criminal background check prior to beginning the paid or volunteer activities described in subdivision (a).

(f) This section shall become operative on July 1, 2010. *(Added by Stats.2009, c. 379 (A.B.1025), § 3, operative July 1, 2010. Amended by Stats.2010, c. 52 (A.B.346), § 2, eff. July 9, 2010.)*

Cross References

Non-certificated applicants for employment, employees, or candidates assuming a paid or volunteer position in multiple districts, duties regarding fingerprints, criminal history, and maintenance of a list of persons eligible for employment, see Education Code § 45125.01.
Teacher certificates and credentials, submission of fingerprint images and related information for state and federal criminal history records search, see Education Code § 44346.5.

CHAPTER 11. INTERSTATE COMPACT ON EDUCATIONAL OPPORTUNITY FOR MILITARY CHILDREN

Section
49700. Legislative findings and declarations.
49700.5. Ratification of compact.
49701. Provisions of compact.
49702. Acceptance of nonstate funding.
49703. Procedures for training and implementation.

§ 49700. Legislative findings and declarations

The Legislature finds and declares that the purpose of the Interstate Compact on Educational Opportunity for Military Children is to remove barriers to educational success imposed on children of military families due to the frequent moves and deployment of their parents by doing all of the following:

(a) Facilitating the timely enrollment of children of military families and ensuring that they are not placed at a disadvantage due to difficulty in the transfer of educational records from the previous school district or variations in entrance or age requirements.

(b) Facilitating the pupil placement process through which children of military families are not disadvantaged by variations in attendance requirements, scheduling, sequencing, grading, course content, or assessment.

(c) Facilitating the qualification and eligibility of children of military families for enrollment, educational programs, and participation in extracurricular academic, athletic, and social activities.

(d) Facilitating the on-time graduation of children of military families.

(e) Providing for the promulgation and enforcement of administrative rules implementing the provisions of the compact.

(f) Providing for the uniform collection and sharing of information between and among member states, schools, and military families pursuant to the compact.

(g) Promoting coordination between the compact and other compacts affecting military children.

(h) Promoting flexibility and cooperation between the educational system, parents, and the pupil in order to achieve educational success for the pupil. *(Added by Stats.2009, c. 237 (A.B.343), § 1.)*

§ 49700.5. Ratification of compact

The Legislature of the State of California hereby ratifies the Interstate Compact on Educational Opportunity for Military Chil-

§ 49700.5

dren as set forth in Section 49701. *(Added by Stats.2009, c. 237 (A.B.343), § 1.)*

§ 49701. Provisions of compact

The provisions of the Interstate Compact on Educational Opportunity for Military Children are as follows:

Article I. Purpose

It is the purpose of this compact to remove barriers to educational success imposed on children of military families because of frequent moves and deployment of their parents by:

(A) Facilitating the timely enrollment of children of military families and ensuring that they are not placed at a disadvantage due to difficulty in the transfer of education records from the previous school district(s) or variations in entrance/age requirements.

(B) Facilitating the student placement process through which children of military families are not disadvantaged by variations in attendance requirements, scheduling, sequencing, grading, course content, or assessment.

(C) Facilitating the qualification and eligibility for enrollment, educational programs, and participation in extracurricular academic, athletic, and social activities.

(D) Facilitating the on-time graduation of children of military families.

(E) Providing for the promulgation and enforcement of administrative rules implementing the provisions of this compact.

(F) Providing for the uniform collection and sharing of information between and among member states, schools, and military families under this compact.

(G) Promoting coordination between this compact and other compacts affecting military children.

(H) Promoting flexibility and cooperation between the educational system, parents and the student in order to achieve educational success for the student.

Article II. Definitions

As used in this compact, unless the context clearly requires a different construction:

(A) "Active duty" means: full-time duty status in the active uniformed service of the United States, including members of the National Guard and Reserve on active duty orders pursuant to 10 U.S.C. Sections 1209 and 1211.

(B) "Children of military families" means: a school-aged child or children, enrolled in Kindergarten through Twelfth (12th) grade, in the household of an active duty member.

(C) "Compact commissioner" means: the voting representative of each compacting state appointed pursuant to Article VIII of this compact.

(D) "Deployment" means: the period one (1) month prior to the service members' departure from their home station on military orders though six (6) months after return to their home station.

(E) "Educational records" means: those official records, files, and data directly related to a student and maintained by the school or local education agency, including, but not limited to, records encompassing all the material kept in the student's cumulative folder such as general identifying data, records of attendance and of academic work completed, records of achievement and results of evaluative tests, health data, disciplinary status, test protocols, and individualized education programs.

(F) "Extracurricular activities" means: a voluntary activity sponsored by the school or local education agency or an organization sanctioned by the local education agency. Extracurricular activities include, but are not limited to, preparation for and involvement in public performances, contests, athletic competitions, demonstrations, displays, and club activities.

(G) "Interstate Commission on Educational Opportunity for Military Children" means: the commission that is created under Article IX of this compact, which is generally referred to as Interstate Commission.

(H) "Local education agency" means: a public authority legally constituted by the state as an administrative agency to provide control of and direction for Kindergarten through Twelfth (12th) grade public educational institutions.

(I) "Member state" means: a state that has enacted this compact.

(J) "Military installation" means: a base, camp, post, station, yard, center, homeport facility for any ship, or other activity under the jurisdiction of the Department of Defense, including any leased facility, which is located within any of the several states, the District of Columbia, the Commonwealth of Puerto Rico, the U.S. Virgin Islands, Guam, American Samoa, the Northern Marianas Islands, and any other U.S. Territory. Such term does not include any facility used primarily for civil works, rivers and harbors projects, or flood control projects.

(K) "Non-member state" means: a state that has not enacted this compact.

(L) "Receiving state" means: the state to which a child of a military family is sent, brought, or caused to be sent or brought.

(M) "Rule" means: a written statement by the Interstate Commission promulgated pursuant to Article XII of this compact that is of general applicability, implements, interprets, or prescribes a policy or provision of the Compact, or an organizational, procedural, or practice requirement of the Interstate Commission, and has the force and effect of statutory law in a member state, and includes the amendment, repeal, or suspension of an existing rule.

(N) "Sending state" means: the state from which a child of a military family is sent, brought, or caused to be sent or brought.

(O) "State" means: a state of the United States, the District of Columbia, the Commonwealth of Puerto Rico, the U.S. Virgin Islands, Guam, American Samoa, the Northern Marianas Islands, and any other U.S. Territory.

(P) "Student" means: the child of a military family for whom the local education agency receives public funding and who is formally enrolled in Kindergarten through Twelfth (12th) grade.

(Q) "Transition" means: 1) the formal and physical process of transferring from school to school or 2) the period of time in which a student moves from one school in the sending state to another school in the receiving state.

(R) "Uniformed service(s)" means: the U.S. Army, Navy, Air Force, Marine Corps, or Coast Guard, as well as the Commissioned Corps of the National Oceanic and Atmospheric Administration and the U.S. Public Health Services.

(S) "Veteran" means: a person who served in the uniformed services and who was discharged or released therefrom under conditions other than dishonorable.

Article III. Applicability

(A) Except as otherwise provided in Section B, this compact shall apply to the children of:

(1) Active duty members of the uniformed services as defined in this compact, including members of the National Guard and Military Reserve on active duty orders pursuant to 10 U.S.C. Sections 1209 and 1211;

(2) Members or veterans of the uniformed services who are severely injured and medically discharged or retired for a period of one (1) year after medical discharge or retirement; and

(3) Members of the uniformed services who die on active duty or as a result of injuries sustained on active duty for a period of one (1) year after death.

(B) The provisions of this interstate compact shall only apply to local education agencies as defined in this compact.

(C) The provisions of this compact shall not apply to the children of:

(1) Inactive members of the National Guard and Military Reserve;

(2) Members of the uniformed services now retired, except as provided in Section A;

(3) Veterans of the uniformed services, except as provided in Section A; and

(4) Other U.S. Dept. of Defense personnel and other federal agency civilian and contract employees not defined as active duty members of the uniformed services.

Article IV. Educational Records and Enrollment

(A) Unofficial or "hand-carried" education records—In the event that official education records cannot be released to the parents for the purpose of transfer, the custodian of the records in the sending state shall prepare and furnish to the parent a complete set of unofficial educational records containing uniform information as determined by the Interstate Commission to the extent feasible. Upon receipt of the unofficial education records by a school in the receiving state, the school shall enroll and appropriately place the student based on the information provided in the unofficial records pending validation by the official records, as quickly as possible.

(B) Official education records/transcripts—Simultaneous with the enrollment and conditional placement of the student, the school in the receiving state shall request the student's official education record from the school in the sending state. Upon receipt of this request, the school in the sending state will process and furnish the official education records to the school in the receiving state within ten (10) days or within such time as is reasonably determined under the rules promulgated by the Interstate Commission to the extent practicable in each case.

(C) Immunizations—Compacting states shall give thirty (30) days from the date of enrollment or within such time as is reasonably determined under the rules promulgated by the Interstate Commission, for students to obtain any immunization(s) required by the receiving state. For a series of immunizations, initial vaccinations must be obtained within thirty (30) days or within such time as is reasonably determined under the rules promulgated by the Interstate Commission.

(D) Kindergarten and First (1st) grade entrance age—Students shall be allowed to continue their enrollment at grade level in the receiving state commensurate with their grade level (including Kindergarten) from a local education agency in the sending state at the time of transition, regardless of age. A student that has satisfactorily completed the prerequisite grade level in the local education agency in the sending state shall be eligible for enrollment in the next highest grade level in the receiving state, regardless of age. A student transferring after the start of the school year in the receiving state shall enter the school in the receiving state on his or her validated level from an accredited school in the sending state.

Article V. Placement and Attendance

(A) Course placement—When the student transfers before or during the school year, the receiving state school shall initially honor placement of the student in educational courses based on the student's enrollment in the sending state school and/or educational assessments conducted at the school in the sending state if the courses are offered and there is space available, as determined by the school district. Course placement includes, but is not limited to, Honors, International Baccalaureate, Advanced Placement, vocational, technical and career pathways courses. Continuing the student's academic program from the previous school and promoting placement in academically and career challenging courses should be paramount when considering placement. This does not preclude the school in the receiving state from performing subsequent evaluations to ensure appropriate placement and continued enrollment of the student in the course(s).

(B) Educational program placement—The receiving state school shall initially honor placement of the student in educational programs based on current educational assessments conducted at the school in the sending state or participation/placement in like programs in the sending state, provided that the program exists in the school and there is space available, as determined by the school district. Such programs include, but are not limited to: 1) gifted and talented programs; and 2) English as a second language (ESL). This does not preclude the school in the receiving state from performing subsequent evaluations to ensure appropriate placement of the student.

(C) Special education services—1) In compliance with the federal requirements of the Individuals with Disabilities Education Act (IDEA), 20 U.S.C.A. Section 1400 et seq., the receiving state shall initially provide comparable services to a student with disabilities based on his/her current Individualized Education Program (IEP); and 2) In compliance with the requirements of Section 504 of the Rehabilitation Act, 29 U.S.C.A. Section 794, and with Title II of the Americans with Disabilities Act, 42 U.S.C.A. Sections 12131–12165, the receiving state shall make reasonable accommodations and modifications to address the needs of incoming students with disabilities, subject to an existing Section 504 or Title II Plan, to provide the student with equal access to education. This does not preclude the school in the receiving state from performing subsequent evaluations to ensure appropriate placement of the student.

(D) Placement flexibility—Local education agency administrative officials shall have flexibility in waiving course/program prerequisites, or other preconditions for placement in courses/programs offered under the jurisdiction of the local education agency.

(E) Absence as related to deployment activities—A student whose parent or legal guardian is an active duty member of the uniformed services, as defined by the compact, and has been called to duty for, is on leave from, or immediately returned from deployment to a combat zone or combat support posting, shall be granted additional excused absences at the discretion of the local education agency superintendent to visit with his or her parent or legal guardian relative to such leave or deployment of the parent or guardian.

Article VI. Eligibility

(A) Eligibility for enrollment

(1) Special power of attorney, relative to the guardianship of a child of a military family and executed under applicable law, shall be sufficient for the purposes of enrollment and all other actions requiring parental participation and consent.

(2) A local education agency shall be prohibited from charging local tuition to a transitioning military child placed in the care of a noncustodial parent or other person standing in loco parentis who lives in a jurisdiction other than that of the custodial parent.

(3) A transitioning military child, placed in the care of a noncustodial parent or other person standing in loco parentis, who lives in a jurisdiction other than that of the custodial parent, may continue to attend the school in which he/she was enrolled while residing with the custodial parent.

(B) Eligibility for extracurricular participation—State and local education agencies shall facilitate the opportunity for transitioning military children's inclusion in extracurricular activities, regardless of application deadlines, to the extent they are otherwise qualified and space is available, as determined by the school district.

§ 49701

Article VII. Graduation

In order to facilitate the on-time graduation of children of military families, states and local education agencies shall incorporate the following procedures:

(A) Waiver requirements—Local education agency administrative officials shall use best efforts to waive specific courses required for graduation if similar coursework has been satisfactorily completed in another local education agency or shall provide reasonable justification for denial. Should a waiver not be granted to a student who would qualify to graduate from the sending school, the local education agency shall use best efforts to provide an alternative means of acquiring required coursework so that graduation may occur on time.

(B) Exit exams—States shall accept: 1) exit or end-of-course exams required for graduation from the sending state; or 2) national norm-referenced achievement tests; or 3) alternative testing, in lieu of testing requirements for graduation in the receiving state; or 4) in California, the passage of the exit examination adopted pursuant to Section 60850 is required for the student to graduate if the diploma is to be issued by a California public school, as long as it is a requirement in California. In the event the above alternatives cannot be accommodated by the receiving state for a student transferring in his or her Senior year, then the provisions of Section C of this Article shall apply.

(C) Transfers during Senior year—Should a military student transferring at the beginning or during his or her Senior year be ineligible to graduate from the receiving local education agency after all alternatives have been considered, the sending and receiving local education agencies shall make best efforts to ensure the receipt of a diploma from the sending local education agency, if the student meets the graduation requirements of the sending local education agency. In the event that one of the states in question is not a member of this compact, the member state shall use best efforts to facilitate the on-time graduation of the student in accordance with Sections A and B of this Article.

Article VIII. State Coordination

(A)(1) Each member state shall, through the creation of a State Council or use of an existing body or board, provide for the coordination among its agencies of government, local education agencies and military installations concerning the state's participation in, and compliance with, this compact and Interstate Commission activities. While each member state may determine the membership of its own State Council, its membership must include at least: the state superintendent of education, superintendent of a school district with a high concentration of military children, representative from a military installation, one representative each from the legislative and executive branches of government, and other offices and stakeholder groups the State Council deems appropriate. A member state that does not have a school district deemed to contain a high concentration of military children may appoint a superintendent from another school district to represent local education agencies on the State Council.

(2) In California, members of the State Council shall include all of the following:

(a) The State Superintendent of Public Instruction or his or her designee.

(b) A school district superintendent or his or her designee from a school district with a high concentration of military children, selected by the State Superintendent of Public Instruction.

(c) A representative from a military installation.

(d) A member of the Senate appointed by the Senate Committee on Rules, or his or her designee, who represents a legislative district with a high concentration of military children.

(e) A member of the Assembly appointed by the Speaker of the Assembly, or his or her designee, who represents a legislative district with a high concentration of military children.

(f) The President of the State Board of Education or his or her designee.

(g) Any other persons appointed by the State Superintendent of Public Instruction.

(B) The State Council of each member state shall appoint or designate a military family education liaison to assist military families and the state in facilitating the implementation of this compact.

(C)(1) The compact commissioner responsible for the administration and management of the state's participation in the compact shall be appointed by the Governor or as otherwise determined by each member state.

(2) In California, the State Superintendent of Public Instruction shall appoint the compact commissioner.

(D) The compact commissioner and the military family education liaison designated herein shall be ex-officio members of the State Council, unless either is already a full voting member of the State Council.

Article IX. Interstate Commission on Educational Opportunity for Military Children

The member states hereby create the "Interstate Commission on Educational Opportunity for Military Children." The activities of the Interstate Commission are the formation of public policy and are a discretionary state function. The Interstate Commission shall:

(A) Be a body corporate and joint agency of the member states and shall have all the responsibilities, powers and duties set forth herein, and such additional powers as may be conferred upon it by a subsequent concurrent action of the respective legislatures of the member states in accordance with the terms of this compact.

(B) Consist of one Interstate Commission voting representative from each member state, who shall be that state's compact commissioner.

(1) Each member state represented at a meeting of the Interstate Commission is entitled to one vote.

(2) A majority of the total member states shall constitute a quorum for the transaction of business, unless a larger quorum is required by the bylaws of the Interstate Commission.

(3) A representative shall not delegate a vote to another member state. In the event the compact commissioner is unable to attend a meeting of the Interstate Commission, the Governor or State Council may delegate voting authority to another person from their state for a specified meeting.

(4) The bylaws may provide for meetings of the Interstate Commission to be conducted by telecommunication or electronic communication.

(C) Consist of ex-officio, nonvoting representatives who are members of interested organizations. Such ex-officio members, as defined in the bylaws, may include, but not be limited to, members of the representative organizations of military family advocates, local education agency officials, parent and teacher groups, the U.S. Department of Defense, the Education Commission of the States, the Interstate Agreement on the Qualification of Educational Personnel and other interstate compacts affecting the education of children of military members.

(D) Meet at least once each calendar year. The chairperson may call additional meetings and, upon the request of a simple majority of the member states, shall call additional meetings.

(E) Establish an executive committee, whose members shall include the officers of the Interstate Commission and such other members of the Interstate Commission as determined by the bylaws.

Members of the executive committee shall serve a one year term. Members of the executive committee shall be entitled to one vote each. The executive committee shall have the power to act on behalf of the Interstate Commission, with the exception of rulemaking, during periods when the Interstate Commission is not in session. The executive committee shall oversee the day-to-day activities of the administration of the compact, including enforcement and compliance with the provisions of the compact, its bylaws and rules, and other such duties as deemed necessary. The U.S. Dept. of Defense shall serve as an ex-officio, nonvoting member of the executive committee.

(F) Establish bylaws and rules that provide for conditions and procedures under which the Interstate Commission shall make its information and official records available to the public for inspection or copying. The Interstate Commission may exempt from disclosure information or official records to the extent they would adversely affect personal privacy rights or proprietary interests.

(G) Public notice shall be given by the Interstate Commission of all meetings, and all meetings shall be open to the public, except as set forth in the rules or as otherwise provided in the compact. The Interstate Commission and its committees may close a meeting, or portion thereof, where it determines by two-thirds vote that an open meeting would be likely to:

(1) Relate solely to the Interstate Commission's internal personnel practices and procedures;

(2) Disclose matters specifically exempted from disclosure by federal and state statute;

(3) Disclose trade secrets or commercial or financial information which is privileged or confidential;

(4) Involve accusing a person of a crime, or formally censuring a person;

(5) Disclose information of a personal nature where disclosure would constitute a clearly unwarranted invasion of personal privacy;

(6) Disclose investigative records compiled for law enforcement purposes; or

(7) Specifically relate to the Interstate Commission's participation in a civil action or other legal proceeding.

(H) For a meeting, or portion of a meeting, closed pursuant to this provision, the Interstate Commission's legal counsel or designee shall certify that the meeting may be closed and shall reference each relevant exemptible provision. The Interstate Commission shall keep minutes which shall fully and clearly describe all matters discussed in a meeting and shall provide a full and accurate summary of actions taken, and the reasons therefor, including a description of the views expressed and the record of a roll call vote. All documents considered in connection with an action shall be identified in such minutes. All minutes and documents of a closed meeting shall remain under seal, subject to release by a majority vote of the Interstate Commission.

(I) The Interstate Commission shall collect standardized data concerning the educational transition of the children of military families under this compact as directed through its rules which shall specify the data to be collected, the means of collection and data exchange and reporting requirements. Such methods of data collection, exchange and reporting shall, in so far as is reasonably possible, conform to current technology and coordinate its information functions with the appropriate custodian of records as identified in the bylaws and rules.

(J) The Interstate Commission shall create a process that permits military officials, education officials and parents to inform the Interstate Commission if and when there are alleged violations of the compact or its rules or when issues subject to the jurisdiction of the compact or its rules are not addressed by the state or local education agency. This section shall not be construed to create a private right of action against the Interstate Commission or any member state.

Article X. Powers and Duties of the Interstate Commission

The Interstate Commission shall have the following powers:

(A) To provide for dispute resolution among member states.

(B) To promulgate rules and take all necessary actions to effect the goals, purposes, and obligations as specifically set forth in Articles IV, V, VI, and VII of this compact. The rules shall have the force and effect of statutory law and shall be binding in the compact states to the extent and in the manner provided in this compact.

(C) To issue, upon request of a member state, advisory opinions concerning the meaning or interpretation of the interstate compact, its bylaws, rules, and actions.

(D) To enforce compliance with the compact provisions, the rules promulgated by the Interstate Commission, and the bylaws, using all necessary and proper means, including, but not limited to, the use of judicial process.

(E) To establish and maintain offices which shall be located within one or more of the member states.

(F) To purchase and maintain insurance and bonds.

(G) To borrow, accept, hire, or contract for services of personnel.

(H) To establish and appoint committees including, but not limited to, an executive committee as required by Article IX, Section E, which shall have the power to act on behalf of the Interstate Commission in carrying out its powers and duties hereunder.

(I) To elect or appoint such officers, attorneys, employees, agents, or consultants, and to fix their compensation, define their duties and determine their qualifications, and to establish the Interstate Commission's personnel policies and programs relating to conflicts of interest, rates of compensation, and qualifications of personnel.

(J) To accept any and all donations and grants of money, equipment, supplies, materials, and services, and to receive, utilize, and dispose of it.

(K) To lease, purchase, accept contributions or donations of, or otherwise to own, hold, improve or use any property, real, personal, or mixed.

(L) To sell, convey, mortgage, pledge, lease, exchange, abandon, or otherwise dispose of any property, real, personal, or mixed.

(M) To establish a budget and make expenditures.

(N) To adopt a seal and bylaws governing the management and operation of the Interstate Commission.

(O) To report annually to the legislatures, governors, judiciary, and state councils of the member states concerning the activities of the Interstate Commission during the preceding year. Such reports shall also include any recommendations that may have been adopted by the Interstate Commission.

(P) To coordinate education, training, and public awareness regarding the compact, its implementation and operation for officials and parents involved in such activity.

(Q) To establish uniform standards for the reporting, collecting, and exchanging of data.

(R) To maintain corporate books and records in accordance with the bylaws.

(S) To perform such functions as may be necessary or appropriate to achieve the purposes of this compact.

(T) To provide for the uniform collection and sharing of information between and among member states, schools, and military families under this compact.

Article XI. Organization and Operation
of the Interstate Commission

(A) The Interstate Commission shall, by a majority of the members present and voting, within 12 months after the first

Interstate Commission meeting, adopt bylaws to govern its conduct as may be necessary or appropriate to carry out the purposes of the compact, including, but not limited to:

(1) Establishing the fiscal year of the Interstate Commission;

(2) Establishing an executive committee, and such other committees as may be necessary;

(3) Providing for the establishment of committees and for governing any general or specific delegation of authority or function of the Interstate Commission;

(4) Providing reasonable procedures for calling and conducting meetings of the Interstate Commission, and ensuring reasonable notice of each such meeting;

(5) Establishing the titles and responsibilities of the officers and staff of the Interstate Commission;

(6) Providing a mechanism for concluding the operations of the Interstate Commission and the return of surplus funds that may exist upon the termination of the compact after the payment and reserving of all of its debts and obligations.

(7) Providing "start up" rules for initial administration of the compact.

(B) The Interstate Commission shall, by a majority of the members, elect annually from among its members a chairperson, a vice-chairperson, and a treasurer, each of whom shall have such authority and duties as may be specified in the bylaws. The chairperson or, in the chairperson's absence or disability, the vice-chairperson, shall preside at all meetings of the Interstate Commission. The officers so elected shall serve without compensation or remuneration from the Interstate Commission; provided that, subject to the availability of budgeted funds, the officers shall be reimbursed for ordinary and necessary costs and expenses incurred by them in the performance of their responsibilities as officers of the Interstate Commission.

(C) Executive Committee, Officers and Personnel

(1) The executive committee shall have such authority and duties as may be set forth in the bylaws, including, but not limited to:

(a) Managing the affairs of the Interstate Commission in a manner consistent with the bylaws and purposes of the Interstate Commission;

(b) Overseeing an organizational structure within, and appropriate procedures for the Interstate Commission to provide for the creation of rules, operating procedures, and administrative and technical support functions; and

(c) Planning, implementing, and coordinating communications and activities with other state, federal and local government organizations in order to advance the goals of the Interstate Commission.

(2) The executive committee may, subject to the approval of the Interstate Commission, appoint or retain an executive director for such period, upon such terms and conditions and for such compensation, as the Interstate Commission may deem appropriate. The executive director shall serve as secretary to the Interstate Commission, but shall not be a Member of the Interstate Commission. The executive director shall hire and supervise such other persons as may be authorized by the Interstate Commission.

(D) The Interstate Commission's executive director and its employees shall be immune from suit and liability, either personally or in their official capacity, for a claim for damage to or loss of property or personal injury or other civil liability caused or arising out of or relating to an actual or alleged act, error, or omission that occurred, or that such person had a reasonable basis for believing occurred, within the scope of Interstate Commission employment, duties, or responsibilities; provided, that such person shall not be protected from suit or liability for damage, loss, injury, or liability caused by the intentional or willful and wanton misconduct of such person.

(1) The liability of the Interstate Commission's executive director and employees or Interstate Commission representatives, acting within the scope of such person's employment or duties for acts, errors, or omissions occurring within such person's state, may not exceed the limits of liability set forth under the Constitution and laws of that state for state officials, employees, and agents. The Interstate Commission is considered to be an instrumentality of the states for the purposes of any such action. Nothing in this subsection shall be construed to protect such person from suit or liability for damage, loss, injury, or liability caused by the intentional or willful and wanton misconduct of such person.

(2) The Interstate Commission shall defend the executive director and its employees and, subject to the approval of the Attorney General or other appropriate legal counsel of the member state represented by an Interstate Commission representative, shall defend such Interstate Commission representative in any civil action seeking to impose liability arising out of an actual or alleged act, error or omission that occurred within the scope of Interstate Commission employment, duties or responsibilities, or that the defendant had a reasonable basis for believing occurred within the scope of Interstate Commission employment, duties, or responsibilities, provided that the actual or alleged act, error, or omission did not result from intentional or willful and wanton misconduct on the part of such person.

(3) To the extent not covered by the state involved, member state, or the Interstate Commission, the representatives or employees of the Interstate Commission shall be held harmless in the amount of a settlement or judgment, including attorney's fees and costs, obtained against such persons arising out of an actual or alleged act, error, or omission that occurred within the scope of Interstate Commission employment, duties, or responsibilities, or that such persons had a reasonable basis for believing occurred within the scope of Interstate Commission employment, duties, or responsibilities, provided that the actual or alleged act, error, or omission did not result from intentional or willful and wanton misconduct on the part of such persons.

Article XII. Rulemaking Functions of the Interstate Commission

(A) Rulemaking Authority—The Interstate Commission shall promulgate reasonable rules in order to effectively and efficiently achieve the purposes of this compact, as specifically set forth in Articles IV, V, VI, and VII. Notwithstanding the foregoing, in the event the Interstate Commission exercises its rulemaking authority in a manner that is beyond the scope of the specific matters set forth in Articles IV, V, VI, and VII of this Act, or the powers granted hereunder, then such an action by the Interstate Commission shall be invalid and have no force or effect.

(B) Rulemaking Procedure—Rules shall be made pursuant to a rulemaking process that substantially conforms to the "Model State Administrative Procedure Act," of 1981, Uniform Laws Annotated, Vol. 15, p.1 (2000) as amended, as may be appropriate to the operations of the Interstate Commission.

(C) Not later than thirty (30) days after a rule is promulgated, any person may file a petition for judicial review of the rule; provided, that the filing of such a petition shall not stay or otherwise prevent the rule from becoming effective unless the court finds that the petitioner has a substantial likelihood of success. The court shall give deference to the actions of the Interstate Commission consistent with applicable law and shall not find the rule to be unlawful if the rule represents a reasonable exercise of the Interstate Commission's authority.

(D) If a majority of the legislatures of the compacting states rejects a Rule by enactment of a statute or resolution in the same manner used to adopt the compact, then such rule shall have no further force and effect in any compacting state.

Article XIII. Oversight, Enforcement, and Dispute Resolution

(A) Oversight

(1) The executive, legislative and judicial branches of state government in each member state shall enforce this compact, and shall take all actions necessary and appropriate to effectuate the compact's purposes and intent. The provisions of this compact and the rules promulgated hereunder shall have standing as statutory law.

(2) All courts shall take judicial notice of the compact and the rules in any judicial or administrative proceeding in a member state pertaining to the subject matter of this compact which may affect the powers, responsibilities or actions of the Interstate Commission.

(3) The Interstate Commission shall be entitled to receive all service of process in any such proceeding, and shall have standing to intervene in the proceeding for all purposes. Failure to provide service of process to the Interstate Commission shall render a judgment or order void as to the Interstate Commission, this compact or promulgated rules.

(B) Default, Technical Assistance, Suspension and Termination - If the Interstate Commission determines that a member state has defaulted in the performance of its obligations or responsibilities under this compact, or the bylaws or promulgated rules, the Interstate Commission shall:

(1) Provide written notice, to the defaulting state and other member states, of the nature of the default, the means of curing the default and any action taken by the Interstate Commission. The Interstate Commission shall specify the conditions by which the defaulting state must cure its default.

(2) Provide remedial training and specific technical assistance regarding the default.

(3) If the defaulting state fails to cure the default, the defaulting state shall be terminated from the compact upon an affirmative vote of a majority of the member states and all rights, privileges and benefits conferred by this compact shall be terminated from the effective date of termination. A cure of the default does not relieve the offending state of obligations or liabilities incurred during the period of the default.

(4) Suspension or termination of membership in the compact shall be imposed only after all other means of securing compliance have been exhausted. Notice of intent to suspend or terminate shall be given by the Interstate Commission to the Governor, the majority and minority leaders of the defaulting state's legislature, and each of the member states.

(5) The state which has been suspended or terminated is responsible for all assessments, obligations and liabilities incurred through the effective date of suspension or termination including obligations, the performance of which extends beyond the effective date of suspension or termination.

(6) The Interstate Commission shall not bear any costs relating to any state that has been found to be in default or which has been suspended or terminated from the compact, unless otherwise mutually agreed upon in writing between the Interstate Commission and the defaulting state.

(7) The defaulting state may appeal the action of the Interstate Commission by petitioning the U.S. District Court for the District of Columbia or the federal district where the Interstate Commission has its principal offices. The prevailing party shall be awarded all costs of such litigation including reasonable attorney's fees.

(C) Dispute Resolution

(1) The Interstate Commission shall attempt, upon the request of a member state, to resolve disputes which are subject to the compact and which may arise among member states and between member and nonmember states.

(2) The Interstate Commission shall promulgate a rule providing for both mediation and binding dispute resolution for disputes as appropriate.

(D) Enforcement

(1) The Interstate Commission, in the reasonable exercise of its discretion, shall enforce the provisions and rules of this compact.

(2) The Interstate Commission may, by majority vote of the members, initiate legal action in the United States District Court for the District of Columbia or, at the discretion of the Interstate Commission, in the federal district where the Interstate Commission has its principal offices, to enforce compliance with the provisions of the compact or its promulgated rules and bylaws against a member state in default. The relief sought may include both injunctive relief and damages. In the event judicial enforcement is necessary, the prevailing party shall be awarded all costs of such litigation including reasonable attorney's fees.

(3) The remedies herein shall not be the exclusive remedies of the Interstate Commission. The Interstate Commission may avail itself of any other remedies available under state law or the regulation of a profession.

Article XIV. Financing of the Interstate Commission

(A) The Interstate Commission shall pay, or provide for the payment of, the reasonable expenses of its establishment, organization and ongoing activities.

(B) The Interstate Commission may levy on and collect an annual assessment from each member state to cover the cost of the operations and activities of the Interstate Commission and its staff which must be in a total amount sufficient to cover the Interstate Commission's annual budget as approved each year. The aggregate annual assessment amount shall be allocated based upon a formula to be determined by the Interstate Commission, which shall promulgate a rule binding upon all member states.

(C) The Interstate Commission shall not incur obligations of any kind prior to securing the funds adequate to meet the same; nor shall the Interstate Commission pledge the credit of any of the member states, except by and with the authority of the member state.

(D) The Interstate Commission shall keep accurate accounts of all receipts and disbursements. The receipts and disbursements of the Interstate Commission shall be subject to the audit and accounting procedures established under its bylaws. However, all receipts and disbursements of funds handled by the Interstate Commission shall be audited yearly by a certified or licensed public accountant, and the report of the audit shall be included in and become part of the annual report of the Interstate Commission.

Article XV. Member, States, Effective Date and Amendment

(A) Any state is eligible to become a member state.

(B) The compact shall become effective and binding upon legislative enactment of the compact into law by no less than ten (10) of the states. The effective date shall be no earlier than December 1, 2007. Thereafter it shall become effective and binding as to any other member state upon enactment of the compact into law by that state. The governors of non-member states or their designees shall be invited to participate in the activities of the Interstate Commission on a nonvoting basis prior to adoption of the compact by all states.

(C) The Interstate Commission may propose amendments to the compact for enactment by the member states. No amendment shall become effective and binding upon the Interstate Commission and the member states unless and until it is enacted into law by unanimous consent of the member states.

Article XVI. Withdrawal and Dissolution

(A) Withdrawal

(1) Once effective, the compact shall continue in force and remain binding upon each and every member state; provided that a member state may withdraw from the compact by specifically repealing the statute which enacted the compact into law.

(2) Withdrawal from this compact shall be by the enactment of a statute repealing the same, but shall not take effect until one (1) year after the effective date of such statute and until written notice of the withdrawal has been given by the withdrawing state to the Governor of each other member jurisdiction.

(3) The withdrawing state shall immediately notify the chairperson of the Interstate Commission in writing upon the introduction of legislation repealing this compact in the withdrawing state. The Interstate Commission shall notify the other member states of the withdrawing state's intent to withdraw within sixty (60) days of its receipt thereof.

(4) The withdrawing state is responsible for all assessments, obligations and liabilities incurred through the effective date of withdrawal, including obligations, the performance of which extend beyond the effective date of withdrawal.

(5) Reinstatement following withdrawal of a member state shall occur upon the withdrawing state reenacting the compact or upon such later date as determined by the Interstate Commission.

(B) Dissolution of Compact

(1) This compact shall dissolve effective upon the date of the withdrawal or default of the member state which reduces the membership in the compact to one (1) member state.

(2) Upon the dissolution of this compact, the compact becomes null and void and shall be of no further force or effect, and the business and affairs of the Interstate Commission shall be concluded and surplus funds shall be distributed in accordance with the bylaws.

Article XVII. Severability and Construction

(A) The provisions of this compact shall be severable, and if any phrase, clause, sentence or provision is deemed unenforceable, the remaining provisions of the compact shall be enforceable.

(B) The provisions of this compact shall be liberally construed to effectuate its purposes.

(C) Nothing in this compact shall be construed to prohibit the applicability of other interstate compacts to which the states are members.

Article XVIII. Binding Effect of Compact and Other Laws

(A) Other Laws

(1) Nothing herein prevents the enforcement of any other law of a member state that is not inconsistent with this compact.

(2) All member states' laws conflicting with this compact are superseded to the extent of the conflict.

(B) Binding Effect of the Compact

(1) All lawful actions of the Interstate Commission, including all rules and bylaws promulgated by the Interstate Commission, are binding upon the member states.

(2) All agreements between the Interstate Commission and the member states are binding in accordance with their terms.

(3) In the event any provision of this compact exceeds the constitutional limits imposed on the legislature of any member state, such provision shall be ineffective to the extent of the conflict with the constitutional provision in question in that member state. *(Added by Stats.2009, c. 237 (A.B.343), § 1. Amended by Stats.2010, c. 328 (S.B.1330), § 44; Stats.2011, c. 347 (S.B.942), § 23.)*

Cross References

Pupils who are children of military families, change of residence, see Education Code § 48204.6.

Research References

Forms

West's California Code Forms, Education § 48205 Form 1, Request for Excused Absence for Justifiable Reasons.
West's California Code Forms, Education § 48980 Form 1, Notice to Parents and Guardians Regarding Statutory Rights.

§ 49702. Acceptance of nonstate funding

Notwithstanding any other provision of law, the Superintendent may accept nonstate funding to offset the cost of the annual assessment required by Section (B) of Article XIV of the Interstate Compact on Educational Opportunity for Military Children. These moneys shall be available, upon appropriation by the Legislature, for that purpose. *(Added by Stats.2009, c. 237 (A.B.343), § 1.)*

§ 49703. Procedures for training and implementation

The Superintendent may develop procedures for the training of employees of local educational agencies in the implementation of the Interstate Compact on Educational Opportunity for Military Children as part of the process developed pursuant to Article 4.5 (commencing with Section 51250) of Chapter 2 of Part 28. *(Added by Stats.2009, c. 237 (A.B.343), § 1.)*

Title 3

POSTSECONDARY EDUCATION

Division 7

COMMUNITY COLLEGES

Part 47

STUDENTS

CHAPTER 1. GENERAL PROVISIONS

ARTICLE 1.5. STUDENT HOUSING

Section
76010. Current and former homeless and foster youth; priority housing; plan to ensure access to housing resources during and between academic terms.
76011. Community college campus shower facilities; allowing use by homeless enrolled students.

§ 76010. Current and former homeless and foster youth; priority housing; plan to ensure access to housing resources during and between academic terms

(a) In order to ensure that current and former homeless youth and current and former foster youth who are students at the campuses of the California Community Colleges have stable housing, each campus of the California Community Colleges that maintains student housing facilities is requested to give priority for housing to current and former homeless youth and current and former foster youth. In addition, each campus of the California Community Colleges that maintains student housing facilities open for occupation during school breaks, or on a year-round basis, is requested to give first priority to current and former homeless youth and current and former foster youth for residence in the housing facilities that are open for uninterrupted year-round occupation and provide this housing to current and former homeless youth and current and former foster youth at no extra cost during academic or campus breaks, and next give priority to current and former homeless youth and current and former foster youth for housing that is open for occupation during the most days in the calendar year.

(b) In addition, each campus of the California Community Colleges is requested to develop a plan to ensure that current and former homeless youth and current and former foster youth can access housing resources as needed during and between academic terms, including during academic and campus breaks, regardless of whether the campus maintains student housing facilities.

(c) As used in this section, a "homeless youth" means a student under 25 years of age, who has been verified, in the case of a former homeless youth, at any time during the 24 months immediately preceding the receipt of his or her application for admission by a campus of the California Community Colleges, as a homeless child or youth, as defined in subsection (2) of Section 725 of the federal McKinney–Vento Homeless Assistance Act (42 U.S.C. Sec. 11434a(2)), by at least one of the following:

(1) A homeless services provider, as defined in paragraph (3) of subdivision (d) of Section 103577 of the Health and Safety Code.

(2) The director, or his or her designee, of a federal TRIO program or a Gaining Early Awareness and Readiness for Undergraduate Programs program.

(3) A financial aid administrator.

(d) For purposes of this section, a student who is verified as a former homeless youth pursuant to subdivision (c) shall retain that status for a period of six years from the date of admission. *(Added by Stats.2009, c. 391 (A.B.1393), § 1. Amended by Stats.2015, c. 571 (A.B.1228), § 2, eff. Jan. 1, 2016.)*

§ 76011. Community college campus shower facilities; allowing use by homeless enrolled students

(a) If a community college campus has shower facilities for student use on campus, the governing board of the community college district shall grant access to those facilities to any homeless student who is enrolled in coursework, has paid enrollment fees, and is in good standing with the community college district without requiring the student to enroll in additional courses.

(b) The governing board shall determine a plan of action to implement subdivision (a) that includes, but is not limited to, all of the following:

(1) Hours of operation for the shower facilities, consistent with subdivision (c).

(2) The minimum number of units a student must be enrolled in to use the facilities.

(3) A plan of action if hours of operation conflict with an intercollegiate athletic program.

(4) A definition of homeless student that is based on the definition of homeless youth specified in the McKinney–Vento Homeless Assistance Act (42 U.S.C. Sec. 11434a(2)), but also reflects the age of the homeless student population at the community college campus.

(c) Hours of operation shall be consistent with hours of operation of the facilities in which the showers are located, shall be set at a minimum of two hours per weekday, and shall not conflict with the intercollegiate athletic program of the campus. *(Added by Stats. 2016, c. 407 (A.B.1995), § 1, eff. Jan. 1, 2017.)*

Division 8

CALIFORNIA STATE UNIVERSITY

Cross References

Property taxation, exemptions, personal property used in management and control of state colleges, see Revenue and Taxation Code § 202.5.
Trustees, creation of, see Education Code § 66600.

Part 55

CALIFORNIA STATE UNIVERSITY

CHAPTER 8. HOUSING AND AUXILIARY SERVICES

ARTICLE 1. HOUSING

Section
90001.5. Current and former homeless and foster youth; priority housing; plan to ensure access to housing resources during and between academic terms.

Cross References

State university system, see Education Code §§ 66600 et seq., 89000 et seq.
Student housing sites, use for other purpose, see Government Code § 15861.
Trustees of the California State University and Colleges,
  Generally, see Education Code §§ 66600 et seq., 89000 et seq.
  Powers, see Education Code § 89030 et seq.
University of California Dormitory Revenue Bond Act of 1947, see Education Code § 92400 et seq.

§ 90001.5. Current and former homeless and foster youth; priority housing; plan to ensure access to housing resources during and between academic terms

(a) In order to ensure that current and former homeless youth and current and former foster youth who are students at campuses of the California State University have stable housing, each campus of the California State University that maintains student housing facilities shall give priority to current and former homeless youth and current and former foster youth. In addition, each campus of the California State University that maintains student housing facilities open for occupation during school breaks, or on a year-round basis, shall first give priority to current and former homeless youth and current and former foster youth for residence in the housing facilities that are open for uninterrupted year-round occupation and provide this housing to current and former homeless youth and current and former foster youth at no extra cost during academic or campus breaks, and next give priority to current and former homeless youth and current and former foster youth for housing that is open for occupation during the most days in the calendar year.

(b) In addition, each campus of the California State University is requested to develop a plan to ensure that current and former homeless youth and current and former foster youth can access housing resources as needed during and between academic terms, including during academic and campus breaks, regardless of whether the campus maintains student housing facilities.

(c) As used in this section, a "homeless youth" means a student under 25 years of age, who has been verified, in the case of a former homeless youth, at any time during the 24 months immediately preceding the receipt of his or her application for admission by a campus of the California State University, as a homeless child or youth, as defined in subsection (2) of Section 725 of the federal McKinney–Vento Homeless Assistance Act (42 U.S.C. Sec. 11434a(2)), by at least one of the following:

(1) A homeless services provider, as defined in paragraph (3) of subdivision (d) of Section 103577 of the Health and Safety Code.

§ 90001.5

(2) The director, or his or her designee, of a federal TRIO program or a Gaining Early Awareness and Readiness for Undergraduate Programs program.

(3) A financial aid administrator.

(d) For purposes of this section, a student who is verified as a former homeless youth pursuant to subdivision (c) shall retain that status for a period of six years from the date of admission. *(Added by Stats.2009, c. 391 (A.B.1393), § 2. Amended by Stats.2015, c. 571 (A.B.1228), § 3, eff. Jan. 1, 2016.)*

Division 9

UNIVERSITY OF CALIFORNIA

Part 57

UNIVERSITY OF CALIFORNIA

CHAPTER 6. MISCELLANEOUS PROVISIONS

ARTICLE 6.5. HOUSING

Section
92660. Current and former homeless and foster youth; priority housing; plan to ensure access to housing resources during and between academic terms.

§ 92660. Current and former homeless and foster youth; priority housing; plan to ensure access to housing resources during and between academic terms

(a) In order to ensure that current and former homeless youth and current and former foster youth who are students at campuses of the University of California have stable housing, each campus of the University of California that maintains student housing facilities shall give priority to current and former homeless youth and current and former foster youth. In addition, each campus of the University of California that maintains student housing facilities open for occupation during school breaks, or on a year-round basis, shall first give priority to current and former homeless youth and current and former foster youth for residence in the housing facilities for which they are eligible that are open for uninterrupted year-round occupation and provide this housing to current and former homeless youth and current and former foster youth at no extra cost during academic or campus breaks, and next give priority to current or former homeless youth and current and former foster youth for residence in the housing facilities for which they are eligible that are open for occupation during the most days in the calendar year.

(b) In addition, a campus of the University of California is requested to develop a plan to ensure that current and former homeless youth and current and former foster youth can access housing resources as needed during and between academic terms, including during academic and campus breaks, regardless of whether the campus maintains student housing facilities.

(c) As used in this section, a "homeless youth" means a student under 25 years of age, who has been verified, in the case of a former homeless youth, at any time during the 24 months immediately preceding the receipt of his or her application for admission by a campus of the University of California, as a homeless child or youth, as defined in subsection (2) of Section 725 of the federal McKinney–Vento Homeless Assistance Act (42 U.S.C. Sec. 11434a(2)), by at least one of the following:

(1) A homeless services provider, as defined in paragraph (3) of subdivision (d) of Section 103577 of the Health and Safety Code.

(2) The director, or his or her designee, of a federal TRIO program or a Gaining Early Awareness and Readiness for Undergraduate Programs program.

(3) A financial aid administrator.

(d) For purposes of this section, a student who is verified as a former homeless youth pursuant to subdivision (c) shall retain that status for a period of six years from the date of admission.

(e) This section shall not apply to the University of California except to the extent that the Regents of the University of California, by appropriate resolution, make this section applicable. *(Added by Stats.2009, c. 391 (A.B.1393), § 3. Amended by Stats.2015, c. 571 (A.B.1228), § 4, eff. Jan. 1, 2016.)*

EVIDENCE CODE

Division 5

BURDEN OF PROOF; BURDEN OF PRODUCING EVIDENCE; PRESUMPTIONS AND INFERENCES

CHAPTER 3. PRESUMPTIONS AND INFERENCES

ARTICLE 4. PRESUMPTIONS AFFECTING THE BURDEN OF PROOF

Section
663. Ceremonial marriage.

§ 663. Ceremonial marriage

A ceremonial marriage is presumed to be valid. *(Stats.1965, c. 299, § 2, operative Jan. 1, 1967.)*

Cross References

Authentication of marriage, see Family Code § 306.
Marriage relation, see Family Code § 720.

Division 8

PRIVILEGES

Cross References

Gambling control, applicant, licensee, or registrant communication or publication subject to privilege, see Business and Professions Code § 19828.

CHAPTER 4. PARTICULAR PRIVILEGES

Cross References

Domestic violence multidisciplinary personnel team, disclosure and exchange of information following report of suspected domestic violence, privacy and confidentiality rights, see Penal Code § 13752.
Human trafficking multidisciplinary personnel team, disclosure and exchange of information following report of human trafficking, privacy and confidentiality rights, see Penal Code § 13753.
Welfare-to-Work activities, disclosure between team members of information related to CalWORKs clients, see Welfare and Institutions Code § 11325.93.

ARTICLE 3. LAWYER–CLIENT PRIVILEGE

Section
950. Lawyer.
951. Client.
952. Confidential communication between client and lawyer.
953. Holder of the privilege.
954. Lawyer-client privilege.
955. When lawyer required to claim privilege.
956. Exception: Crime or fraud; applicability to legal services for lawful cannabis-related activities.
956.5. Exception: Prevention of criminal act likely to result in death or substantial bodily harm.
957. Exception: Parties claiming through deceased client.
958. Exception: Breach of duty arising out of lawyer-client relationship.
959. Exception: Lawyer as attesting witness.
960. Exception: Intention of deceased client concerning writing affecting property interest.
961. Exception: Validity of writing affecting property interest.
962. Exception: Joint clients.

Cross References

Arbitration of attorneys' fees, disclosure of attorney-client communication or attorney's work product, see Business and Professions Code § 6202.
Child Abuse and Neglect Reporting Act, public or private postsecondary institutions, mandated reporters, effect on lawyer-client privilege, see Penal Code § 11165.7.
County patients' rights advocates, whistleblower protections, see Welfare and Institutions Code § 5525.
Domestic violence, interagency death review teams, confidentiality, disclosure, see Penal Code § 11163.3.
Elder death review teams, confidentiality and disclosure of information, see Penal Code § 11174.8.
Victims' Legal Resource Center, confidential records, see Penal Code § 13897.2.

§ 950. Lawyer

As used in this article, "lawyer" means a person authorized, or reasonably believed by the client to be authorized, to practice law in any state or nation. *(Stats.1965, c. 299, § 2, operative Jan. 1, 1967.)*

Cross References

Admission to the practice of law, see Business and Professions Code § 6060 et seq.
Definitions,
  Client, see Evidence Code § 951.
  Person, see Evidence Code § 175.
  State, see Evidence Code § 220.
Physician-patient privilege, see Evidence Code § 990.
Psychotherapist-patient privilege, see Evidence Code § 1010.
Subsequent administration, appointment of personal representative, priority, notice of hearing, see Probate Code § 12252.
Unauthorized persons practicing law, authority of court to obtain jurisdiction over practice and appoint qualified counsel, see Business and Professions Code § 6126.3.

Research References

Forms
3A California Transactions Forms--Business Entities § 15:56, Employment Agreement for Employee-Shareholder.
1 Environmental Insurance Litigation: Practice Forms § 2:16 (2021 ed.), Sample Memorandum in Opposition to Plaintiff Insured's Motion to Compel Further Responses and Production of Documents (Drafting History; General Interpretive Material; Communications Among Insurers; Underwriting and Claims Manuals; Promotional, Advertising or Marketing Materials; Lobbying Materials; Reinsurance Information).

§ 950   EVIDENCE CODE

West's California Code Forms, Government § 54954 Form 1, Ordinance Fixing Time and Place for Holding Regular Meetings.

3 Environmental Insurance Litigation: Practice Forms Appendix A (2021 ed.), Spring 2021 Survey.

§ 951. Client

As used in this article, "client" means a person who, directly or through an authorized representative, consults a lawyer for the purpose of retaining the lawyer or securing legal service or advice from him in his professional capacity, and includes an incompetent (a) who himself so consults the lawyer or (b) whose guardian or conservator so consults the lawyer in behalf of the incompetent. *(Stats.1965, c. 299, § 2, operative Jan. 1, 1967.)*

Cross References

Definitions,
  Lawyer, see Evidence Code § 950.
  Person, see Evidence Code § 175.
Physician-patient privilege, see Evidence Code § 991.
Psychotherapist-patient privilege, see Evidence Code § 1011.

§ 952. Confidential communication between client and lawyer

As used in this article, "confidential communication between client and lawyer" means information transmitted between a client and his or her lawyer in the course of that relationship and in confidence by a means which, so far as the client is aware, discloses the information to no third persons other than those who are present to further the interest of the client in the consultation or those to whom disclosure is reasonably necessary for the transmission of the information or the accomplishment of the purpose for which the lawyer is consulted, and includes a legal opinion formed and the advice given by the lawyer in the course of that relationship. *(Stats.1965, c. 299, § 2, operative Jan. 1, 1967. Amended by Stats.1967, c. 650, p. 2006, § 3; Stats.1994, c. 186 (A.B.2662), § 1; Stats.1994, c. 587 (A.B.3600), § 9; Stats.2002, c. 72 (S.B.2061), § 3.)*

Cross References

Definitions,
  Client, see Evidence Code § 951.
  Lawyer, see Evidence Code § 950.
  Person, see Evidence Code § 175.
Disclosure to third person, when privileged, see Evidence Code § 912.
Eavesdropping on or recording confidential communications, see Penal Code § 632.
Electronic communications, presumption that certain communications are confidential, privileged character of electronic communications, see Evidence Code § 917.
Executive department, employment of outside counsel and consent from Attorney General, written notification, see Government Code § 11045.
Juvenile court law, wards, duties of appointed counsel, see Welfare and Institutions Code § 634.3.
Physician-patient privilege, see Evidence Code § 992.
Psychotherapist-patient privilege, see Evidence Code § 1012.
Unauthorized persons practicing law, authority of court to obtain jurisdiction over practice and appoint qualified counsel, see Business and Professions Code § 6126.3.
Written fee contract as confidential communication, see Business and Professions Code § 6149.

Research References

Forms

1 California Transactions Forms--Business Transactions § 6:51, Attorney-Client Privilege.
4 California Transactions Forms--Estate Planning § 19:57, Maintaining Confidentiality.
1 California Transactions Forms--Family Law § 1:132, Signature by Attorneys.
1 California Transactions Forms--Family Law § 4:128, Signature by Attorneys.
1 Environmental Insurance Litigation: Practice Forms § 2:14 (2021 ed.), Sample Notice of Motion and Motion to Compel Production of Documents (Insurers Attacking Policyholders' Claims of Attorney Work Product and Attorney Client Privilege).
1 Environmental Insurance Litigation: Practice Forms § 4:8 (2021 ed.), Opposition to Motion to Compel Production of Documents.

§ 953. Holder of the privilege

As used in this article, "holder of the privilege" means:

(a) The client, if the client has no guardian or conservator.

(b)(1) A guardian or conservator of the client, if the client has a guardian or conservator, except as provided in paragraph (2).

(2) If the guardian or conservator has an actual or apparent conflict of interest with the client, then the guardian or conservator does not hold the privilege.

(c) The personal representative of the client if the client is dead, including a personal representative appointed pursuant to Section 12252 of the Probate Code.

(d) A successor, assign, trustee in dissolution, or any similar representative of a firm, association, organization, partnership, business trust, corporation, or public entity that is no longer in existence. *(Stats.1965, c. 299, § 2, operative Jan. 1, 1967. Amended by Stats.2009, c. 8 (A.B.1163), § 1; Stats.2018, c. 475 (A.B.1290), § 1, eff. Jan. 1, 2019.)*

Cross References

Definitions,
  Client, see Evidence Code § 951.
  Public entity, see Evidence Code § 200.
Similar provisions,
  Physician-patient privilege, see Evidence Code § 993.
  Psychotherapist-patient privilege, see Evidence Code § 1013.

Research References

Forms

West's California Code Forms, Probate § 2584 Form 1, Order Authorizing Conservator to Make Gifts.

§ 954. Lawyer-client privilege

Subject to Section 912 and except as otherwise provided in this article, the client, whether or not a party, has a privilege to refuse to disclose, and to prevent another from disclosing, a confidential communication between client and lawyer if the privilege is claimed by:

(a) The holder of the privilege;

(b) A person who is authorized to claim the privilege by the holder of the privilege; or

(c) The person who was the lawyer at the time of the confidential communication, but such person may not claim the privilege if there is no holder of the privilege in existence or if he is otherwise instructed by a person authorized to permit disclosure.

The relationship of attorney and client shall exist between a law corporation as defined in Article 10 (commencing with Section 6160) of Chapter 4 of Division 3 of the Business and Professions Code and the persons to whom it renders professional services, as well as between such persons and members of the State Bar employed by such corporation to render services to such persons. The word "persons" as used in this subdivision includes partnerships, corporations, limited liability companies, associations and other groups and entities. *(Stats.1965, c. 299, § 2, operative Jan. 1, 1967. Amended by Stats.1968, c. 1375, p. 2695, § 2; Stats.1994, c. 1010 (S.B.2053), § 104.)*

Cross References

Custody of minor child, duties and rights of private counsel, see Family Code § 3151.
Definitions,
  Client, see Evidence Code § 951.
  Confidential communication between client and lawyer, see Evidence Code § 952.
  Holder of the privilege, see Evidence Code § 953.

Lawyer, see Evidence Code § 950.
Person, see Evidence Code § 175.
Eavesdropping on privileged communications prohibited, see Penal Code §§ 632, 636.
General provisions relating to privileges, see Evidence Code § 911 et seq.
Similar provisions,
   Physician-patient privilege, see Evidence Code § 994.
   Psychotherapist-patient privilege, see Evidence Code § 1014.

Research References

Forms

1 California Transactions Forms--Business Transactions § 6:51, Attorney-Client Privilege.
4 California Transactions Forms--Estate Planning § 19:57, Maintaining Confidentiality.
1 Environmental Insurance Litigation: Practice Forms § 4:8 (2021 ed.), Opposition to Motion to Compel Production of Documents.

§ 955. When lawyer required to claim privilege

The lawyer who received or made a communication subject to the privilege under this article shall claim the privilege whenever he is present when the communication is sought to be disclosed and is authorized to claim the privilege under subdivision (c) of Section 954. *(Stats.1965, c. 299, § 2, operative Jan. 1, 1967.)*

Cross References

Duty of lawyer to maintain confidence, see Business and Professions Code § 6068.
Lawyer defined, see Evidence Code § 950.
Similar provisions,
   Physician-patient privilege, see Evidence Code § 995.
   Psychotherapist-patient privilege, see Evidence Code § 1015.

Research References

Forms

1 California Transactions Forms--Business Transactions § 6:51, Attorney-Client Privilege.

§ 956. Exception: Crime or fraud; applicability to legal services for lawful cannabis–related activities

(a) There is no privilege under this article if the services of the lawyer were sought or obtained to enable or aid anyone to commit or plan to commit a crime or a fraud.

(b) This exception to the privilege granted by this article shall not apply to legal services rendered in compliance with state and local laws on medicinal cannabis or adult-use cannabis, and confidential communications provided for the purpose of rendering those services are confidential communications between client and lawyer, as defined in Section 952, provided the lawyer also advises the client on conflicts with respect to federal law. *(Stats.1965, c. 299, § 2, operative Jan. 1, 1967. Amended by Stats.2017, c. 530 (A.B.1159), § 2, eff. Jan. 1, 2018.)*

Cross References

Lawyer defined, see Evidence Code § 950.
Similar provisions,
   Marital communications privilege, see Evidence Code § 981.
   Physician-patient privilege, see Evidence Code § 997.
   Psychotherapist-patient privilege, see Evidence Code § 1018.

§ 956.5. Exception: Prevention of criminal act likely to result in death or substantial bodily harm

There is no privilege under this article if the lawyer reasonably believes that disclosure of any confidential communication relating to representation of a client is necessary to prevent a criminal act that the lawyer reasonably believes is likely to result in the death of, or substantial bodily harm to, an individual. *(Added by Stats.1993, c. 982 (S.B.645), § 8. Amended by Stats.2003, c. 765 (A.B.1101), § 2, operative July 1, 2004; Stats.2004, c. 183 (A.B.3082), § 94.)*

Cross References

Client defined for purposes of this Article, see Evidence Code § 951.
Lawyer defined for purposes of this Article, see Evidence Code § 950.

§ 957. Exception: Parties claiming through deceased client

There is no privilege under this article as to a communication relevant to an issue between parties all of whom claim through a deceased client, regardless of whether the claims are by testate or intestate succession, nonprobate transfer, or inter vivos transaction. *(Stats.1965, c. 299, § 2, operative Jan. 1, 1967. Amended by Stats. 2009, c. 8 (A.B.1163), § 2.)*

Cross References

Client defined, see Evidence Code § 951.
Similar provisions,
   Marital communications privilege, see Evidence Code § 984.
   Physician-patient privilege, see Evidence Code § 1000.
   Psychotherapist-patient privilege, see Evidence Code § 1019.

Research References

Forms

4 California Transactions Forms--Estate Planning § 19:57, Maintaining Confidentiality.

§ 958. Exception: Breach of duty arising out of lawyer-client relationship

There is no privilege under this article as to a communication relevant to an issue of breach, by the lawyer or by the client, of a duty arising out of the lawyer-client relationship. *(Stats.1965, c. 299, § 2, operative Jan. 1, 1967.)*

Cross References

Definitions,
   Client, see Evidence Code § 951.
   Lawyer, see Evidence Code § 950.
Similar provisions,
   Physician-patient privilege, see Evidence Code § 1001.
   Psychotherapist-patient privilege, see Evidence Code § 1020.

Research References

Forms

Asset Protection: Legal Planning, Strategies and Forms ¶ 12.01, Overview.

§ 959. Exception: Lawyer as attesting witness

There is no privilege under this article as to a communication relevant to an issue concerning the intention or competence of a client executing an attested document of which the lawyer is an attesting witness, or concerning the execution or attestation of such a document. *(Stats.1965, c. 299, § 2, operative Jan. 1, 1967.)*

Cross References

Authentication of writing by subscribing witness, see Evidence Code § 1411 et seq.
Definitions,
   Client, see Evidence Code § 951.
   Lawyer, see Evidence Code § 950.
Opinion as to sanity by subscribing witness, see Evidence Code § 870.

§ 960. Exception: Intention of deceased client concerning writing affecting property interest

There is no privilege under this article as to a communication relevant to an issue concerning the intention of a client, now deceased, with respect to a deed of conveyance, will, or other writing, executed by the client, purporting to affect an interest in property. *(Stats.1965, c. 299, § 2, operative Jan. 1, 1967.)*

Cross References

Definitions,
   Client, see Evidence Code § 951.

Property, see Evidence Code § 185.
Writing, see Evidence Code § 250.
Similar provisions,
Physician-patient privilege, see Evidence Code § 1002.
Psychotherapist-patient privilege, see Evidence Code § 1021.

§ 961. Exception: Validity of writing affecting property interest

There is no privilege under this article as to a communication relevant to an issue concerning the validity of a deed of conveyance, will, or other writing, executed by a client, now deceased, purporting to affect an interest in property. *(Stats.1965, c. 299, § 2, operative Jan. 1, 1967.)*

Cross References

Definitions,
Client, see Evidence Code § 951.
Property, see Evidence Code § 185.
Writing, see Evidence Code § 250.
Similar provisions,
Physician-patient privilege, see Evidence Code § 1003.
Psychotherapist-patient privilege, see Evidence Code § 1022.

§ 962. Exception: Joint clients

Where two or more clients have retained or consulted a lawyer upon a matter of common interest, none of them, nor the successor in interest of any of them, may claim a privilege under this article as to a communication made in the course of that relationship when such communication is offered in a civil proceeding between one of such clients (or his successor in interest) and another of such clients (or his successor in interest). *(Stats.1965, c. 299, § 2, operative Jan. 1, 1967.)*

Cross References

Definitions,
Civil proceeding, see Evidence Code § 902.
Client, see Evidence Code § 951.
Lawyer, see Evidence Code § 950.
Waiver of privilege by joint holder, see Evidence Code § 912.

Research References

Forms

3A California Transactions Forms--Business Entities § 15:56, Employment Agreement for Employee-Shareholder.
4 California Transactions Forms--Business Entities § 20:13, Fiduciary Obligations of Attorney for Dissolved Partnership.
4 California Transactions Forms--Estate Planning § 20:4, Separate and Community Property.
1 Environmental Insurance Litigation: Practice Forms § 4:8 (2021 ed.), Opposition to Motion to Compel Production of Documents.
West's California Code Forms, Government § 54954 Form 1, Ordinance Fixing Time and Place for Holding Regular Meetings.

ARTICLE 4. PRIVILEGE NOT TO TESTIFY AGAINST SPOUSE

Section
970. Spouse's privilege not to testify against spouse; exceptions.
971. Privilege not to be called as a witness against spouse.
972. Exceptions to privilege.
973. Waiver of privilege.

Cross References

Privilege for confidential marital communications, see Evidence Code § 980 et seq.

§ 970. Spouse's privilege not to testify against spouse; exceptions

Except as otherwise provided by statute, a married person has a privilege not to testify against his spouse in any proceeding. *(Stats.1965, c. 299, § 2, operative Jan. 1, 1967.)*

Cross References

Abandonment or nonsupport of wife or child, see Penal Code § 270e.
General provisions relating to privileges, see Evidence Code § 911.
Privilege of witnesses in examination proceedings, see Code of Civil Procedure § 708.130.
Proceeding defined, see Evidence Code § 901.
Prostitution, placing wife in house of, see Penal Code § 266g.
Venereal disease control violations, see Health and Safety Code § 120595.

Research References

Forms

1 California Transactions Forms--Family Law § 4:14, Domestic Violence and Restraining Orders.

§ 971. Privilege not to be called as a witness against spouse

Except as otherwise provided by statute, a married person whose spouse is a party to a proceeding has a privilege not to be called as a witness by an adverse party to that proceeding without the prior express consent of the spouse having the privilege under this section unless the party calling the spouse does so in good faith without knowledge of the marital relationship. *(Stats.1965, c. 299, § 2, operative Jan. 1, 1967.)*

Cross References

Privilege not to be called as a witness and not to testify, see Evidence Code § 930.
Proceeding defined, see Evidence Code § 901.

Research References

Forms

1 California Transactions Forms--Family Law § 4:14, Domestic Violence and Restraining Orders.

§ 972. Exceptions to privilege

A married person does not have a privilege under this article in:

(a) A proceeding brought by or on behalf of one spouse against the other spouse.

(b) A proceeding to commit or otherwise place his or her spouse or his or her spouse's property, or both, under the control of another because of the spouse's alleged mental or physical condition.

(c) A proceeding brought by or on behalf of a spouse to establish his or her competence.

(d) A proceeding under the Juvenile Court Law, Chapter 2 (commencing with Section 200) of Part 1 of Division 2 of the Welfare and Institutions Code.

(e) A criminal proceeding in which one spouse is charged with:

(1) A crime against the person or property of the other spouse or of a child, parent, relative, or cohabitant of either, whether committed before or during marriage.

(2) A crime against the person or property of a third person committed in the course of committing a crime against the person or property of the other spouse, whether committed before or during marriage.

(3) Bigamy.

(4) A crime defined by Section 270 or 270a of the Penal Code.

(f) A proceeding resulting from a criminal act which occurred prior to legal marriage of the spouses to each other regarding knowledge acquired prior to that marriage if prior to the legal marriage the witness spouse was aware that his or her spouse had been arrested for or had been formally charged with the crime or crimes about which the spouse is called to testify.

(g) A proceeding brought against the spouse by a former spouse so long as the property and debts of the marriage have not been adjudicated, or in order to establish, modify, or enforce a child, family or spousal support obligation arising from the marriage to the former spouse; in a proceeding brought against a spouse by the other parent in order to establish, modify, or enforce a child support obligation for a child of a nonmarital relationship of the spouse; or in a proceeding brought against a spouse by the guardian of a child of that spouse in order to establish, modify, or enforce a child support obligation of the spouse. The married person does not have a privilege under this subdivision to refuse to provide information relating to the issues of income, expenses, assets, debts, and employment of either spouse, but may assert the privilege as otherwise provided in this article if other information is requested by the former spouse, guardian, or other parent of the child.

Any person demanding the otherwise privileged information made available by this subdivision, who also has an obligation to support the child for whom an order to establish,[1] modify, or enforce child support is sought, waives his or her marital privilege to the same extent as the spouse as provided in this subdivision. *(Stats.1965, c. 299, § 2, operative Jan. 1, 1967. Amended by Stats.1975, c. 71, p. 132, § 2; Stats.1982, c. 256, p. 833, § 1; Stats.1983, c. 244, § 1; Stats.1986, c. 769, § 1, eff. Sept. 15, 1986; Stats.1989, c. 1359, § 9.7.)*

[1] So in chaptered copy.

Cross References

Definitions,
 Criminal proceeding, see Evidence Code § 903.
 Person, see Evidence Code § 175.
 Proceeding, see Evidence Code § 901.
 Property, see Evidence Code § 185.
Similar provisions,
 Marital communications privilege, see Evidence Code § 982 et seq.
 Physician-patient privilege, see Evidence Code § 1004 et seq.
 Psychotherapist-patient privilege, see Evidence Code § 1024 et seq.

§ 973. Waiver of privilege

(a) Unless erroneously compelled to do so, a married person who testifies in a proceeding to which his spouse is a party, or who testifies against his spouse in any proceeding, does not have a privilege under this article in the proceeding in which such testimony is given.

(b) There is no privilege under this article in a civil proceeding brought or defended by a married person for the immediate benefit of his spouse or of himself and his spouse. *(Stats.1965, c. 299, § 2, operative Jan. 1, 1967.)*

Cross References

Definitions,
 Civil proceeding, see Evidence Code § 902.
 Proceeding, see Evidence Code § 901.
Waiver of privilege, generally, see Evidence Code § 912.

ARTICLE 5. PRIVILEGE FOR CONFIDENTIAL MARITAL COMMUNICATIONS

Section
980. Confidential spousal communication privilege.
981. Exception: Crime or fraud.
982. Commitment or similar proceedings.
983. Competency proceedings.
984. Proceeding between spouses.
985. Criminal proceedings.
986. Juvenile court proceedings.
987. Communication offered by spouse who is criminal defendant.

Cross References

Privilege not to testify against spouse, see Evidence Code § 970 et seq.

§ 980. Confidential spousal communication privilege

Subject to Section 912 and except as otherwise provided in this article, a spouse (or his or her guardian or conservator when he or she has a guardian or conservator), whether or not a party, has a privilege during the marital or domestic partnership relationship and afterwards to refuse to disclose, and to prevent another from disclosing, a communication if he or she claims the privilege and the communication was made in confidence between him or her and the other spouse while they were spouses. *(Stats.1965, c. 299, § 2, operative Jan. 1, 1967. Amended by Stats.2016, c. 86 (S.B.1171), § 125, eff. Jan. 1, 2017; Stats.2016, c. 50 (S.B.1005), § 34, eff. Jan. 1, 2017.)*

Cross References

General provisions relating to privileges, see Evidence Code § 910.
Overhearing and recording confidential communication, see Penal Code § 632.
Presumption that communication confidential, see Evidence Code § 917.
Privilege inapplicable in prosecutions for,
 Abandonment or nonsupport of wife or child, see Penal Code § 270e.
 Venereal disease control, see Health and Safety Code § 120595.
Privilege of spouse not to be called as witness, see Evidence Code § 971.
Privilege of spouse not to testify, see Evidence Code § 970.

Research References

Forms

1 California Transactions Forms--Family Law § 4:14, Domestic Violence and Restraining Orders.

§ 981. Exception: Crime or fraud

There is no privilege under this article if the communication was made, in whole or in part, to enable or aid anyone to commit or plan to commit a crime or a fraud. *(Stats.1965, c. 299, § 2, operative Jan. 1, 1967.)*

Cross References

Similar provisions,
 Lawyer-client privilege, see Evidence Code § 956.
 Physician-patient privilege, see Evidence Code § 997.
 Psychotherapist-patient privilege, see Evidence Code § 1018.

§ 982. Commitment or similar proceedings

There is no privilege under this article in a proceeding to commit either spouse or otherwise place him or his property, or both, under the control of another because of his alleged mental or physical condition. *(Stats.1965, c. 299, § 2, operative Jan. 1, 1967.)*

Cross References

Proceeding defined, see Evidence Code § 901.
Similar provisions,
 Marital testimonial privilege, see Evidence Code § 972.
 Physician-patient privilege, see Evidence Code § 1004.
 Psychotherapist-patient privilege, see Evidence Code § 1024.

§ 983. Competency proceedings

There is no privilege under this article in a proceeding brought by or on behalf of either spouse to establish his competence. *(Stats. 1965, c. 299, § 2, operative Jan. 1, 1967.)*

Cross References

Proceeding defined, see Evidence Code § 901.
Similar provisions,
 Marital testimonial privilege, see Evidence Code § 972.
 Physician-patient privilege, see Evidence Code § 1005.
 Psychotherapist-patient privilege, see Evidence Code § 1025.

§ 984. Proceeding between spouses

There is no privilege under this article in:

(a) A proceeding brought by or on behalf of one spouse against the other spouse.

(b) A proceeding between a surviving spouse and a person who claims through the deceased spouse, regardless of whether such claim

§ 984

is by testate or intestate succession or by inter vivos transaction. *(Stats.1965, c. 299, § 2, operative Jan. 1, 1967.)*

Cross References

Proceeding defined, see Evidence Code § 901.
Similar provisions,
 Lawyer-client privilege, see Evidence Code § 957.
 Marital testimonial privilege, see Evidence Code § 972.
 Physician-patient privilege, see Evidence Code § 1000.
 Psychotherapist-patient privilege, see Evidence Code § 1019.

§ 985. Criminal proceedings

There is no privilege under this article in a criminal proceeding in which one spouse is charged with:

(a) A crime committed at any time against the person or property of the other spouse or of a child of either.

(b) A crime committed at any time against the person or property of a third person committed in the course of committing a crime against the person or property of the other spouse.

(c) Bigamy.

(d) A crime defined by Section 270 or 270a of the Penal Code. *(Stats.1965, c. 299, § 2, operative Jan. 1, 1967. Amended by Stats. 1975, c. 71, p. 133, § 3.)*

Cross References

Definitions,
 Criminal proceeding, see Evidence Code § 903.
 Person, see Evidence Code § 175.
 Property, see Evidence Code § 185.
Similar provision, marital testimonial privilege, see Evidence Code § 972.

§ 986. Juvenile court proceedings

There is no privilege under this article in a proceeding under the Juvenile Court Law, Chapter 2 (commencing with Section 200) of Part 1 of Division 2 of the Welfare and Institutions Code. *(Stats. 1965, c. 299, § 2, operative Jan. 1, 1967. Amended by Stats.1982, c. 256, p. 833, § 2.)*

Cross References

Similar provision, marital testimonial privilege, see Evidence Code § 972.

§ 987. Communication offered by spouse who is criminal defendant

There is no privilege under this article in a criminal proceeding in which the communication is offered in evidence by a defendant who is one of the spouses between whom the communication was made. *(Stats.1965, c. 299, § 2, operative Jan. 1, 1967.)*

Cross References

Criminal proceeding defined, see Evidence Code § 903.

ARTICLE 7. PSYCHOTHERAPIST–PATIENT PRIVILEGE

Section
1010. Psychotherapist.
1010.5. Privileged communication between patient and educational psychologist.
1011. Patient.
1012. Confidential communication between patient and psychotherapist.
1013. Holder of the privilege.
1014. Psychotherapist-patient privilege; application to individuals and entities.
1015. When psychotherapist required to claim privilege.
1016. Exception: Patient-litigant exception.
1017. Exception: Psychotherapist appointed by court or board of prison terms.
1018. Exception: Crime or tort.

Section
1019. Exception: Parties claiming through deceased patient.
1020. Exception: Breach of duty arising out of psychotherapist-patient relationship.
1021. Exception: Intention of deceased patient concerning writing affecting property interest.
1022. Exception: Validity of writing affecting property interest.
1023. Exception: Proceeding to determine sanity of criminal defendant.
1024. Exception: Patient dangerous to himself or others.
1025. Exception: Proceeding to establish competence.
1026. Exception: Required report.
1027. Exception: Child under 16 victim of crime.

Cross References

Confidential information and records, disclosure, consent, comprehensive assessment, see Welfare and Institutions Code § 4514.
Coroners, subpoenas for privileged communications of deceased persons, see Government Code § 27491.8.
Elder death review teams, confidentiality and disclosure of information, see Penal Code § 11174.8.
Physician-patient privilege, see Evidence Code § 990 et seq.
Psychologists, confidential relations and communications, privilege, see Business and Professions Code § 2918.
Reports of injuries, domestic violence, see Penal Code § 11163.3.
Services for the developmentally disabled, confidential information and records, see Welfare and Institutions Code § 4514.

§ 1010. Psychotherapist

As used in this article, "psychotherapist" means a person who is, or is reasonably believed by the patient to be:

(a) A person authorized to practice medicine in any state or nation who devotes, or is reasonably believed by the patient to devote, a substantial portion of their time to the practice of psychiatry.

(b) A person licensed as a psychologist under Chapter 6.6 (commencing with Section 2900) of Division 2 of the Business and Professions Code.

(c) A person licensed as a clinical social worker under Chapter 14 (commencing with Section 4991) of Division 2 of the Business and Professions Code, when they are engaged in applied psychotherapy of a nonmedical nature.

(d) A person who is serving as a school psychologist and holds a credential authorizing that service issued by the state.

(e) A person licensed as a marriage and family therapist under Chapter 13 (commencing with Section 4980) of Division 2 of the Business and Professions Code.

(f) A person registered as a registered psychological associate who is under the supervision of a licensed psychologist as required by Section 2913 of the Business and Professions Code, or a person registered as an associate marriage and family therapist who is under the supervision of a licensed marriage and family therapist, a licensed clinical social worker, a licensed professional clinical counselor, a licensed psychologist, or a licensed physician and surgeon certified in psychiatry, as specified in Section 4980.44 of the Business and Professions Code.

(g) A person registered as an associate clinical social worker who is under supervision as specified in Section 4996.23 of the Business and Professions Code.

(h) A psychological intern as defined in Section 2911 of the Business and Professions Code who is under the primary supervision of a licensed psychologist.

(i) A trainee, as defined in subdivision (c) of Section 4980.03 of the Business and Professions Code, who is fulfilling their supervised practicum required by subparagraph (B) of paragraph (1) of subdivision (d) of Section 4980.36 of, or subdivision (c) of Section 4980.37 of, the Business and Professions Code and is supervised by a licensed psychologist, a board certified psychiatrist, a licensed clinical social worker, a licensed marriage and family therapist, or a licensed professional clinical counselor.

(j) A person licensed as a registered nurse pursuant to Chapter 6 (commencing with Section 2700) of Division 2 of the Business and Professions Code, who possesses a master's degree in psychiatric-mental health nursing and is listed as a psychiatric-mental health nurse by the Board of Registered Nursing.

(k) An advanced practice registered nurse who is certified as a clinical nurse specialist pursuant to Article 9 (commencing with Section 2838) of Chapter 6 of Division 2 of the Business and Professions Code and who participates in expert clinical practice in the specialty of psychiatric-mental health nursing.

(*l*) A person rendering mental health treatment or counseling services as authorized pursuant to Section 6924 of the Family Code.

(m) A person licensed as a professional clinical counselor under Chapter 16 (commencing with Section 4999.10) of Division 2 of the Business and Professions Code.

(n) A person registered as an associate professional clinical counselor who is under the supervision of a licensed professional clinical counselor, a licensed marriage and family therapist, a licensed clinical social worker, a licensed psychologist, or a licensed physician and surgeon certified in psychiatry, as specified in Sections 4999.42 to 4999.48, inclusive, of the Business and Professions Code.

(*o*) A clinical counselor trainee, as defined in subdivision (g) of Section 4999.12 of the Business and Professions Code, who is fulfilling their supervised practicum required by paragraph (3) of subdivision (c) of Section 4999.32 of, or paragraph (3) of subdivision (c) of Section 4999.33 of, the Business and Professions Code, and is supervised by a licensed psychologist, a board-certified psychiatrist, a licensed clinical social worker, a licensed marriage and family therapist, or a licensed professional clinical counselor. *(Stats.1965, c. 299, § 2, operative Jan. 1, 1967. Amended by Stats.1967, c. 1677, p. 4211, § 3; Stats.1970, c. 1396, p. 2624, § 1.5; Stats.1970, c. 1397, p. 2626, § 1.5; Stats.1972, c. 888, p. 1584, § 1; Stats.1974, c. 546, p. 1359, § 16; Stats.1983, c. 928, § 8; Stats.1987, c. 724, § 1; Stats. 1988, c. 488, § 1; Stats.1989, c. 1104, § 37; Stats.1990, c. 662 (A.B.3613), § 1; Stats.1992, c. 308 (A.B.3035), § 2; Stats.1994, c. 1270 (A.B.2659), § 1; Stats.2001, c. 142 (S.B.716), § 1; Stats.2001, c. 420 (A.B.1253), § 1, eff. Oct. 2, 2001; Stats.2001, c. 420 (A.B.1253), § 1.5, eff. Oct. 2, 2001, operative Jan. 1, 2002; Stats.2009, c. 26 (S.B.33), § 21; Stats.2011, c. 381 (S.B.146), § 21; Stats.2015, c. 529 (A.B.1374), § 4, eff. Jan. 1, 2016; Stats.2016, c. 86 (S.B.1171), § 126, eff. Jan. 1, 2017; Stats.2017, c. 573 (S.B.800), § 75, eff. Jan. 1, 2018; Stats.2018, c. 389 (A.B.2296), § 10, eff. Jan. 1, 2019; Stats.2021, c. 647 (S.B.801), § 74, eff. Jan. 1, 2022.)*

Cross References

Counseling services, information of personal nature disclosed by pupil, parent or guardian during counseling, confidentiality, see Education Code § 72621.

Definitions,
  Patient, see Evidence Code § 1011.
  State, see Evidence Code § 220.
Disclosure of medical information,
  Necessity, see Civil Code § 56.10.
  Patient's participation in outpatient treatment with psychotherapist, see Civil Code § 56.104.
  To specified persons involved with patient's care or health care payments, see Civil Code § 56.1007.
Duty to warn of threatened violent behavior of patient, immunity from monetary liability, see Civil Code § 43.92.
Educational counseling, confidentiality of pupil information, see Education Code § 49602.
Elder abuse and dependent adult civil protection, mandated reporters, Welfare and Institutions Code § 15630.

Firearms, possession, purchase or receipt by person receiving inpatient treatment for a mental disorder or who has communicated a threat of physical violence to a psychotherapist, see Welfare and Institutions Code § 8100.
Independent adoptions, advice of birth parents' rights, role of counselor, see Family Code § 8801.5.
Involuntary treatment, confidential information and records, see Welfare and Institutions Code § 5328.
Psychologists, confidential relations and communications, privilege, see Business and Professions Code § 2918.
Reports of injuries, domestic violence, see Penal Code § 11163,3.
Services for the developmentally disabled, confidential information and records, see Welfare and Institutions Code § 4514.
Similar provisions,
  Lawyer-client privilege, see Evidence Code § 950.
  Physician-patient privilege, see Evidence Code § 990.
Subpoena duces tecum, see Code of Civil Procedure § 1985.3.

Research References

Forms

1 California Transactions Forms--Family Law § 3:16, Identifying Areas of Parental Decision Making and Participation.

§ 1010.5. Privileged communication between patient and educational psychologist

A communication between a patient and an educational psychologist, licensed under Chapter 13.5 (commencing with Section 4989.10) of Division 2 of the Business and Professions Code, shall be privileged to the same extent, and subject to the same limitations, as a communication between a patient and a psychotherapist described in subdivisions (c), (d), and (e) of Section 1010. *(Added by Stats.1985, c. 545, § 1. Amended by Stats.2020, c. 370 (S.B.1371), § 113, eff. Jan. 1, 2021.)*

Cross References

Patient defined for purposes of this Article, see Evidence Code § 1011.
Psychotherapist defined for purposes of this Article, see Evidence Code § 1010.

§ 1011. Patient

As used in this article, "patient" means a person who consults a psychotherapist or submits to an examination by a psychotherapist for the purpose of securing a diagnosis or preventive, palliative, or curative treatment of his mental or emotional condition or who submits to an examination of his mental or emotional condition for the purpose of scientific research on mental or emotional problems. *(Stats.1965, c. 299, § 2, operative Jan. 1, 1967.)*

Cross References

Psychotherapist defined for purposes of this Article, see Evidence Code § 1010.
Similar provisions,
  Lawyer-client privilege, see Evidence Code § 951.
  Physician-patient privilege, see Evidence Code § 991.

§ 1012. Confidential communication between patient and psychotherapist

As used in this article, "confidential communication between patient and psychotherapist" means information, including information obtained by an examination of the patient, transmitted between a patient and his psychotherapist in the course of that relationship and in confidence by a means which, so far as the patient is aware, discloses the information to no third persons other than those who are present to further the interest of the patient in the consultation, or those to whom disclosure is reasonably necessary for the transmission of the information or the accomplishment of the purpose for which the psychotherapist is consulted, and includes a diagnosis made and the advice given by the psychotherapist in the course of that relationship. *(Stats.1965, c. 299, § 2, operative Jan. 1, 1967. Amended by Stats.1967, c. 650, p. 2006, § 5; Stats.1970, c. 1396, p. 2625, § 2; Stats.1970, c. 1397, p. 2627, § 2.)*

§ 1012

Cross References

Definitions,
  Patient, see Evidence Code § 1011.
  Psychotherapist, see Evidence Code § 1010.
Disclosure to third person, when privileged, see Evidence Code § 912.
Presumption that communication was confidential, see Evidence Code § 917.
Similar provisions,
  Lawyer-client privilege, see Evidence Code § 952.
  Physician-patient privilege, see Evidence Code § 992.

§ 1013. Holder of the privilege

As used in this article, "holder of the privilege" means:

(a) The patient when he has no guardian or conservator.

(b) A guardian or conservator of the patient when the patient has a guardian or conservator.

(c) The personal representative of the patient if the patient is dead. (Stats.1965, c. 299, § 2, operative Jan. 1, 1967.)

Cross References

Patient defined, see Evidence Code § 1011.
Similar provisions,
  Lawyer-client privilege, see Evidence Code § 953.
  Physician-patient privilege, see Evidence Code § 993.

§ 1014. Psychotherapist-patient privilege; application to individuals and entities

Subject to Section 912 and except as otherwise provided in this article, the patient, whether or not a party, has a privilege to refuse to disclose, and to prevent another from disclosing, a confidential communication between patient and psychotherapist if the privilege is claimed by:

(a) The holder of the privilege.

(b) A person who is authorized to claim the privilege by the holder of the privilege.

(c) The person who was the psychotherapist at the time of the confidential communication, but the person may not claim the privilege if there is no holder of the privilege in existence or if he or she is otherwise instructed by a person authorized to permit disclosure.

The relationship of a psychotherapist and patient shall exist between a psychological corporation as defined in Article 9 (commencing with Section 2995) of Chapter 6.6 of Division 2 of the Business and Professions Code, a marriage and family therapist corporation as defined in Article 6 (commencing with Section 4987.5) of Chapter 13 of Division 2 of the Business and Professions Code, a licensed clinical social workers corporation as defined in Article 5 (commencing with Section 4998) of Chapter 14 of Division 2 of the Business and Professions Code, or a professional clinical counselor corporation as defined in Article 7 (commencing with Section 4999.123) of Chapter 16 of Division 2 of the Business and Professions Code, and the patient to whom it renders professional services, as well as between those patients and psychotherapists employed by those corporations to render services to those patients. The word "persons" as used in this subdivision includes partnerships, corporations, limited liability companies, associations, and other groups and entities. (Stats.1965, c. 299, § 2, operative Jan. 1, 1967. Amended by Stats.1969, c. 1436, p. 2943, § 1; Stats.1972, c. 1286, p. 2569, § 6; Stats.1989, c. 1104, § 38; Stats.1990, c. 605 (S.B.2245), § 1; Stats. 1994, c. 1010 (S.B.2053), § 106; Stats.2002, c. 1013 (S.B.2026), § 78; Stats.2011, c. 381 (S.B.146), § 22.)

Cross References

Child sex abuse allegations, child custody evaluation, investigation or assessment, see Family Code § 3118.
Confidential communication between patient and psychotherapist defined for purposes of this Article, see Evidence Code § 1012.

Holder of the privilege defined for purposes of this Article, see Evidence Code § 1013.
Patient defined for purposes of this Article, see Evidence Code § 1011.
Privilege inapplicable in prosecution for violation of venereal disease control regulations, see Health and Safety Code § 120595.
Psychotherapist defined for purposes of this Article, see Evidence Code § 1010.
Similar provisions,
  Lawyer-client privilege, see Evidence Code § 954.
  Physician-patient privilege, see Evidence Code § 994.

§ 1015. When psychotherapist required to claim privilege

The psychotherapist who received or made a communication subject to the privilege under this article shall claim the privilege whenever he is present when the communication is sought to be disclosed and is authorized to claim the privilege under subdivision (c) of Section 1014. (Stats.1965, c. 299, § 2, operative Jan. 1, 1967.)

Cross References

Duty to maintain confidence, physician, see Business and Professions Code § 2225.
Juvenile court law, disclosure of information by members of child and family team, instructions to counties on confidentiality protections, see Welfare and Institutions Code § 832.
Psychotherapist defined, see Evidence Code § 1010.
Similar provisions,
  Lawyer-client privilege, see Evidence Code § 955.
  Physician-patient privilege, see Evidence Code § 995.

§ 1016. Exception: Patient-litigant exception

There is no privilege under this article as to a communication relevant to an issue concerning the mental or emotional condition of the patient if such issue has been tendered by:

(a) The patient;

(b) Any party claiming through or under the patient;

(c) Any party claiming as a beneficiary of the patient through a contract to which the patient is or was a party; or

(d) The plaintiff in an action brought under Section 376 or 377 of the Code of Civil Procedure for damages for the injury or death of the patient. (Stats.1965, c. 299, § 2, operative Jan. 1, 1967.)

Cross References

Patient defined, see Evidence Code § 1011.
Similar provision, physician-patient privilege, see Evidence Code § 996.

§ 1017. Exception: Psychotherapist appointed by court or board of prison terms

(a) There is no privilege under this article if the psychotherapist is appointed by order of a court to examine the patient, but this exception does not apply where the psychotherapist is appointed by order of the court upon the request of the lawyer for the defendant in a criminal proceeding in order to provide the lawyer with information needed so that he or she may advise the defendant whether to enter or withdraw a plea based on insanity or to present a defense based on his or her mental or emotional condition.

(b) There is no privilege under this article if the psychotherapist is appointed by the Board of Prison Terms to examine a patient pursuant to the provisions of Article 4 (commencing with Section 2960) of Chapter 7 of Title 1 of Part 3 of the Penal Code. (Stats.1965, c. 299, § 2, operative Jan. 1, 1967. Amended by Stats. 1967, c. 650, p. 2007, § 6; Stats.1987, c. 687, § 1.)

Cross References

Definitions,
  Criminal proceeding, see Evidence Code § 903.
  Patient, see Evidence Code § 1011.
  Psychotherapist, see Evidence Code § 1010.

§ 1018. Exception: Crime or tort

There is no privilege under this article if the services of the psychotherapist were sought or obtained to enable or aid anyone to commit or plan to commit a crime or a tort or to escape detection or apprehension after the commission of a crime or a tort. *(Stats.1965, c. 299, § 2, operative Jan. 1, 1967.)*

Cross References
Psychotherapist defined, see Evidence Code § 1010.
Similar provisions,
  Lawyer-client privilege, see Evidence Code § 956.
  Marital communications privilege, see Evidence Code § 981.
  Physician-patient privilege, see Evidence Code § 997.

§ 1019. Exception: Parties claiming through deceased patient

There is no privilege under this article as to a communication relevant to an issue between parties all of whom claim through a deceased patient, regardless of whether the claims are by testate or intestate succession or by inter vivos transaction. *(Stats.1965, c. 299, § 2, operative Jan. 1, 1967.)*

Cross References
Patient defined, see Evidence Code § 1011.
Similar provisions,
  Lawyer-client privilege, see Evidence Code § 957.
  Marital communications privilege, see Evidence Code § 984.
  Physician-patient privilege, see Evidence Code § 1000.

§ 1020. Exception: Breach of duty arising out of psychotherapist-patient relationship

There is no privilege under this article as to a communication relevant to an issue of breach, by the psychotherapist or by the patient, of a duty arising out of the psychotherapist-patient relationship. *(Stats.1965, c. 299, § 2, operative Jan. 1, 1967.)*

Cross References
Definitions,
  Patient, see Evidence Code § 1011.
  Psychotherapist, see Evidence Code § 1010.
Similar provisions,
  Lawyer-client privilege, see Evidence Code § 958.
  Physician-patient privilege, see Evidence Code § 1001.

§ 1021. Exception: Intention of deceased patient concerning writing affecting property interest

There is no privilege under this article as to a communication relevant to an issue concerning the intention of a patient, now deceased, with respect to a deed of conveyance, will, or other writing, executed by the patient, purporting to affect an interest in property. *(Stats.1965, c. 299, § 2, operative Jan. 1, 1967.)*

Cross References
Definitions,
  Patient, see Evidence Code § 1011.
  Property, see Evidence Code § 185.
  Writing, see Evidence Code § 250.
Similar provisions,
  Lawyer-client privilege, see Evidence Code § 960.
  Physician-patient privilege, see Evidence Code § 1002.

§ 1022. Exception: Validity of writing affecting property interest

There is no privilege under this article as to a communication relevant to an issue concerning the validity of a deed of conveyance, will, or other writing, executed by a patient, now deceased, purporting to affect an interest in property. *(Stats.1965, c. 299, § 2, operative Jan. 1, 1967.)*

Cross References
Definitions,
  Patient, see Evidence Code § 1011.
  Property, see Evidence Code § 185.
  Writing, see Evidence Code § 250.
Similar provisions,
  Lawyer-client privilege, see Evidence Code § 961.
  Physician-patient privilege, see Evidence Code § 1003.

§ 1023. Exception: Proceeding to determine sanity of criminal defendant

There is no privilege under this article in a proceeding under Chapter 6 (commencing with Section 1367) of Title 10 of Part 2 of the Penal Code initiated at the request of the defendant in a criminal action to determine his sanity. *(Stats.1965, c. 299, § 2, operative Jan. 1, 1967.)*

Cross References
Criminal action defined, see Evidence Code § 130.

§ 1024. Exception: Patient dangerous to himself or others

There is no privilege under this article if the psychotherapist has reasonable cause to believe that the patient is in such mental or emotional condition as to be dangerous to himself or to the person or property of another and that disclosure of the communication is necessary to prevent the threatened danger. *(Stats.1965, c. 299, § 2, operative Jan. 1, 1967.)*

Cross References
Definitions,
  Patient, see Evidence Code § 1011.
  Property, see Evidence Code § 185.
  Psychotherapist, see Evidence Code § 1010.
Similar provisions,
  Marital communications privilege, see Evidence Code § 982.
  Marital testimonial privilege, see Evidence Code § 972.
  Physician-patient privilege, see Evidence Code § 1004.

§ 1025. Exception: Proceeding to establish competence

There is no privilege under this article in a proceeding brought by or on behalf of the patient to establish his competence. *(Stats.1965, c. 299, § 2, operative Jan. 1, 1967.)*

Cross References
Definitions,
  Patient, see Evidence Code § 1011.
  Proceeding, see Evidence Code § 901.
Similar provisions,
  Marital communications privilege, see Evidence Code § 983.
  Marital testimonial privilege, see Evidence Code § 972.
  Physician-patient privilege, see Evidence Code § 1005.

§ 1026. Exception: Required report

There is no privilege under this article as to information that the psychotherapist or the patient is required to report to a public employee or as to information required to be recorded in a public office, if such report or record is open to public inspection. *(Stats.1965, c. 299, § 2, operative Jan. 1, 1967.)*

Cross References
Definitions,
  Patient, see Evidence Code § 1011.
  Proceeding, see Evidence Code § 901.
  Psychotherapist, see Evidence Code § 1010.
  Public employee, see Evidence Code § 195.
  Statute, see Evidence Code § 230.
Similar provision, physician-patient privilege, see Evidence Code § 1006.

§ 1027. Exception: Child under 16 victim of crime

There is no privilege under this article if all of the following circumstances exist:

(a) The patient is a child under the age of 16.

§ 1027

(b) The psychotherapist has reasonable cause to believe that the patient has been the victim of a crime and that disclosure of the communication is in the best interest of the child. *(Added by Stats.1970, c. 1397, p. 2627, § 3.)*

Cross References

Patient defined for purposes of this Article, see Evidence Code § 1011.
Psychotherapist defined for purposes of this Article, see Evidence Code § 1010.

ARTICLE 8.7. DOMESTIC VIOLENCE COUNSELOR–VICTIM PRIVILEGE

Section
1037. Victim.
1037.1. Domestic violence counselor; qualifications; domestic violence victim service organization.
1037.2. Confidential communication; compulsion of disclosure by court; claim of privilege.
1037.3. Child abuse; reporting.
1037.4. Holder of the privilege.
1037.5. Privilege of refusal to disclose communication; claimants.
1037.6. Claim of privilege by counselor.
1037.7. Domestic violence.
1037.8. Notice; limitations on confidential communications.

Cross References

Sexual assaults or domestic violence on campus grounds or related facilities, procedures or protocols for treatment of victims, counselor qualifications and confidentiality requirements, see Education Code § 67385.

§ 1037. Victim

As used in this article, "victim" means any person who suffers domestic violence, as defined in Section 1037.7. *(Added by Stats. 1986, c. 854, § 1.)*

Cross References

Domestic violence defined for purposes of this Article, see Evidence Code § 1037.7.

§ 1037.1. Domestic violence counselor; qualifications; domestic violence victim service organization

(a)(1) As used in this article, "domestic violence counselor" means a person who is employed by a domestic violence victim service organization, as defined in this article, whether financially compensated or not, for the purpose of rendering advice or assistance to victims of domestic violence and who has at least 40 hours of training as specified in paragraph (2).

(2) The 40 hours of training shall be supervised by an individual who qualifies as a counselor under paragraph (1), and who has at least one year of experience counseling domestic violence victims for the domestic violence victim service organization. The training shall include, but need not be limited to, the following areas: history of domestic violence, civil and criminal law as it relates to domestic violence, the domestic violence victim-counselor privilege and other laws that protect the confidentiality of victim records and information, societal attitudes towards domestic violence, peer counseling techniques, housing, public assistance and other financial resources available to meet the financial needs of domestic violence victims, and referral services available to domestic violence victims.

(3) A domestic violence counselor who has been employed by the domestic violence victim service organization for a period of less than six months shall be supervised by a domestic violence counselor who has at least one year of experience counseling domestic violence victims for the domestic violence victim service organization.

(b) As used in this article, "domestic violence victim service organization" means either of the following:

(1) A nongovernmental organization or entity that provides shelter, programs, or services to victims of domestic violence and their children, including, but not limited to, either of the following:

(A) Domestic violence shelter-based programs, as described in Section 18294 of the Welfare and Institutions Code.

(B) Other programs with the primary mission to provide services to victims of domestic violence whether or not that program exists in an agency that provides additional services.

(2) Programs on the campus of a public or private institution of higher education with the primary mission to provide support or advocacy services to victims of domestic violence. *(Added by Stats.1986, c. 854, § 1. Amended by Stats.1990, c. 1342 (S.B.2501), § 2; Stats.2007, c. 206 (S.B.407), § 2; Stats.2017, c. 178 (S.B.331), § 1, eff. Jan. 1, 2018.)*

Cross References

Comprehensive Statewide Domestic Violence Program, staff and volunteers meeting requirements of this section, see Penal Code § 13823.15.
Domestic violence defined for purposes of this Article, see Evidence Code § 1037.7.
Domestic violence education, prevention, and services for the gay, lesbian, bisexual, and transgendered community, staff and volunteers meeting requirements of this section, see Penal Code § 13823.17.
Domestic violence shelter-based programs,
 Generally, see Welfare and Institutions Code § 18290 et seq.
 Meeting requirements, see Welfare and institutions code § 18290.
 Services to be provided, see Welfare and Institutions Code § 18294.
Reports of injuries, domestic violence, see Penal Code § 11163.3.
Rights of victims and witnesses, domestic violence or abuse counselors, presence at law enforcement interviews, see Penal Code § 679.05.
Victim defined for purposes of this Article, see Evidence Code § 1037.

§ 1037.2. Confidential communication; compulsion of disclosure by court; claim of privilege

(a) As used in this article, "confidential communication" means any information, including, but not limited to, written or oral communication, transmitted between the victim and the counselor in the course of their relationship and in confidence by a means which, so far as the victim is aware, discloses the information to no third persons other than those who are present to further the interests of the victim in the consultation or those to whom disclosures are reasonably necessary for the transmission of the information or an accomplishment of the purposes for which the domestic violence counselor is consulted. The term includes all information regarding the facts and circumstances involving all incidences of domestic violence, as well as all information about the children of the victim or abuser and the relationship of the victim with the abuser.

(b) The court may compel disclosure of information received by a domestic violence counselor which constitutes relevant evidence of the facts and circumstances involving a crime allegedly perpetrated against the victim or another household member and which is the subject of a criminal proceeding, if the court determines that the probative value of the information outweighs the effect of disclosure of the information on the victim, the counseling relationship, and the counseling services. The court may compel disclosure if the victim is either dead or not the complaining witness in a criminal action against the perpetrator. The court may also compel disclosure in proceedings related to child abuse if the court determines that the probative value of the evidence outweighs the effect of the disclosure on the victim, the counseling relationship, and the counseling services.

(c) When a court rules on a claim of privilege under this article, it may require the person from whom disclosure is sought or the person authorized to claim the privilege, or both, to disclose the information in chambers out of the presence and hearing of all persons except the person authorized to claim the privilege and such other persons as the person authorized to claim the privilege consents to have present. If the judge determines that the information is privileged and shall not be disclosed, neither he nor she nor any other person may disclose, without the consent of a person authorized to permit disclosure, any information disclosed in the course of the proceedings in chambers.

(d) If the court determines that information shall be disclosed, the court shall so order and inform the defendant in the criminal action. If the court finds there is a reasonable likelihood that any information is subject to disclosure pursuant to the balancing test provided in this section, the procedure specified in subdivisions (1), (2), and (3) of Section 1035.4 shall be followed. *(Added by Stats.1986, c. 854, § 1. Amended by Stats.2007, c. 206 (S.B.407), § 3.)*

Cross References

Contempt powers, exemption of sexual assault and domestic violence victims who refuse to testify, confidential communications between victim and counselor, see Code of Civil Procedure § 1219.
Criminal proceeding defined for purposes of this Division, see Evidence Code § 903.
Domestic violence counselor defined for purposes of this Article, see Evidence Code § 1037.1.
Domestic violence defined for purposes of this Article, see Evidence Code § 1037.7.
Victim defined for purposes of this Article, see Evidence Code § 1037.

§ 1037.3. Child abuse; reporting

Nothing in this article shall be construed to limit any obligation to report instances of child abuse as required by Section 11166 of the Penal Code. *(Added by Stats.1986, c. 854, § 1.)*

§ 1037.4. Holder of the privilege

As used in this article, "holder of the privilege" means:

(a) The victim when he or she has no guardian or conservator.

(b) A guardian or conservator of the victim when the victim has a guardian or conservator, unless the guardian or conservator is accused of perpetrating domestic violence against the victim. *(Added by Stats.1986, c. 854, § 1. Amended by Stats.2007, c. 206 (S.B.407), § 4.)*

Cross References

Domestic violence defined for purposes of this Article, see Evidence Code § 1037.7.
Victim defined for purposes of this Article, see Evidence Code § 1037.

§ 1037.5. Privilege of refusal to disclose communication; claimants

A victim of domestic violence, whether or not a party to the action, has a privilege to refuse to disclose, and to prevent another from disclosing, a confidential communication between the victim and a domestic violence counselor in any proceeding specified in Section 901 if the privilege is claimed by any of the following persons:

(a) The holder of the privilege.

(b) A person who is authorized to claim the privilege by the holder of the privilege.

(c) The person who was the domestic violence counselor at the time of the confidential communication. However, that person may not claim the privilege if there is no holder of the privilege in existence or if he or she is otherwise instructed by a person authorized to permit disclosure. *(Added by Stats.1986, c. 854, § 1. Amended by Stats.2007, c. 206 (S.B.407), § 5.)*

Cross References

Confidential communication defined for purposes of this Article, see Evidence Code § 1037.2.
Domestic violence counselor defined for purposes of this Article, see Evidence Code § 1037.1.
Domestic violence defined for purposes of this Article, see Evidence Code § 1037.7.
Holder of the privilege defined for purposes of this Article, see Evidence Code § 1037.4.
Victim defined for purposes of this Article, see Evidence Code § 1037.
Waiver of right to claim privilege under this section, see Evidence Code § 912.

§ 1037.6. Claim of privilege by counselor

The domestic violence counselor who received or made a communication subject to the privilege granted by this article shall claim the privilege whenever he or she is present when the communication is sought to be disclosed and he or she is authorized to claim the privilege under subdivision (c) of Section 1037.5. *(Added by Stats.1986, c. 854, § 1.)*

Cross References

Domestic violence counselor defined for purposes of this Article, see Evidence Code § 1037.1.
Domestic violence defined for purposes of this Article, see Evidence Code § 1037.6.

§ 1037.7. Domestic violence

As used in this article, "domestic violence" means "domestic violence" as defined in Section 6211 of the Family Code. *(Added by Stats.1993, c. 219 (A.B.1500), § 77.4.)*

§ 1037.8. Notice; limitations on confidential communications

A domestic violence counselor shall inform a domestic violence victim of any applicable limitations on confidentiality of communications between the victim and the domestic violence counselor. This information may be given orally. *(Added by Stats.2002, c. 629 (S.B.1735), § 1.)*

Cross References

Domestic violence counselor defined for purposes of this Article, see Evidence Code § 1037.1.
Domestic violence defined for the purposes of this Article, see Evidence Code § 1037.7.
Victim defined for purposes of this Article, see Evidence Code § 1037.

Division 10

HEARSAY EVIDENCE

Cross References

Admissibility of hearsay evidence in criminal actions, see Penal Code § 686.
Official writings affecting property, see Evidence Code § 1600 et seq.
Official writings and recorded writings, see Evidence Code §§ 1450 et seq., 1530 et seq., 1600.
Part of transaction proved, admissibility of whole, see Evidence Code § 356.
Photographic copies of writings, see Evidence Code §§ 1550, 1551.
Preliminary determinations on admissibility of evidence, see Evidence Code § 400 et seq.
Production of business records, see Evidence Code § 1560 et seq.

CHAPTER 2. EXCEPTIONS TO THE HEARSAY RULE

ARTICLE 11. FAMILY HISTORY

Section
1310. Statement concerning declarant's own family history.

EVIDENCE CODE

Section
1311. Statement concerning family history of another.
1312. Entries in family records and the like.
1313. Reputation in family concerning family history.
1314. Reputation in community concerning family history.
1315. Church records concerning family history.
1316. Marriage, baptismal and similar certificates.

§ 1310. Statement concerning declarant's own family history

(a) Subject to subdivision (b), evidence of a statement by a declarant who is unavailable as a witness concerning his own birth, marriage, divorce, a parent and child relationship, relationship by blood or marriage, race, ancestry, or other similar fact of his family history is not made inadmissible by the hearsay rule, even though the declarant had no means of acquiring personal knowledge of the matter declared.

(b) Evidence of a statement is inadmissible under this section if the statement was made under circumstances such as to indicate its lack of trustworthiness. *(Stats.1965, c. 299, § 2, operative Jan. 1, 1967. Amended by Stats.1975, c. 1244, p. 3202, § 15.)*

Cross References

Administrative proceedings to establish birth, see Health and Safety Code § 102575 et seq.
Birth, marriage, or death, court proceedings to establish, see Health and Safety Code § 103450 et seq.
Definitions,
　Declarant, see Evidence Code § 135.
　Evidence, see Evidence Code § 140.
　Statement, see Evidence Code § 225.
　Unavailable as a witness, see Evidence Code § 240.
Federal Missing Persons Act, findings, see Evidence Code § 1282 et seq.
Hearsay rule, see Evidence Code § 1200.
Presumption that ceremonial marriage is valid, see Evidence Code § 663.
Trustworthiness requirement, similar provisions, see Evidence Code §§ 1252, 1260, 1311, 1323.
Vital statistics records, see Evidence Code § 1281.

§ 1311. Statement concerning family history of another

(a) Subject to subdivision (b), evidence of a statement concerning the birth, marriage, divorce, death, parent and child relationship, race, ancestry, relationship by blood or marriage, or other similar fact of the family history of a person other than the declarant is not made inadmissible by the hearsay rule if the declarant is unavailable as a witness and:

(1) The declarant was related to the other by blood or marriage; or

(2) The declarant was otherwise so intimately associated with the other's family as to be likely to have had accurate information concerning the matter declared and made the statement (i) upon information received from the other or from a person related by blood or marriage to the other or (ii) upon repute in the other's family.

(b) Evidence of a statement is inadmissible under this section if the statement was made under circumstances such as to indicate its lack of trustworthiness. *(Stats.1965, c. 299, § 2, operative Jan. 1, 1967. Amended by Stats.1975, c. 1244, p. 3202, § 16.)*

Cross References

Definitions,
　Declarant, see Evidence Code § 135.
　Evidence, see Evidence Code § 140.
　Statement, see Evidence Code § 225.
　Unavailable as a witness, see Evidence Code § 240.
Hearsay rule, see Evidence Code § 1200.
Official records, generally, see Evidence Code § 1280.
Trustworthiness requirement, similar provisions, see Evidence Code §§ 1252, 1260, 1310, 1323.
Vital statistics records, see Evidence Code § 1281.

§ 1312. Entries in family records and the like

Evidence of entries in family Bibles or other family books or charts, engravings on rings, family portraits, engravings on urns, crypts, or tombstones, and the like, is not made inadmissible by the hearsay rule when offered to prove the birth, marriage, divorce, death, parent and child relationship, race, ancestry, relationship by blood or marriage, or other similar fact of the family history of a member of the family by blood or marriage. *(Stats.1965, c. 299, § 2, operative Jan. 1, 1967. Amended by Stats.1975, c. 1244, p. 3202, § 17.)*

Cross References

Definitions,
　Evidence, see Evidence Code § 140.
　Proof, see Evidence Code § 190.
Hearsay rule, see Evidence Code § 1200.

§ 1313. Reputation in family concerning family history

Evidence of reputation among members of a family is not made inadmissible by the hearsay rule if the reputation concerns the birth, marriage, divorce, death, parent and child relationship, race, ancestry, relationship by blood or marriage, or other similar fact of the family history of a member of the family by blood or marriage. *(Stats.1965, c. 299, § 2, operative Jan. 1, 1967. Amended by Stats. 1975, c. 1244, p. 3202, § 18.)*

Cross References

Definition, evidence, see Evidence Code § 140.
Hearsay rule, see Evidence Code § 1200.

§ 1314. Reputation in community concerning family history

Evidence of reputation in a community concerning the date or fact of birth, marriage, divorce, or death of a person resident in the community at the time of the reputation is not made inadmissible by the hearsay rule. *(Stats.1965, c. 299, § 2, operative Jan. 1, 1967.)*

Cross References

Definition, evidence, see Evidence Code § 140.
Hearsay rule, see Evidence Code § 1200.

§ 1315. Church records concerning family history

Evidence of a statement concerning a person's birth, marriage, divorce, death, parent and child relationship, race, ancestry, relationship by blood or marriage, or other similar fact of family history which is contained in a writing made as a record of a church, religious denomination, or religious society is not made inadmissible by the hearsay rule if:

(a) The statement is contained in a writing made as a record of an act, condition, or event that would be admissible as evidence of such act, condition, or event under Section 1271; and

(b) The statement is of a kind customarily recorded in connection with the act, condition, or event recorded in the writing. *(Stats.1965, c. 299, § 2, operative Jan. 1, 1967. Amended by Stats.1975, c. 1244, p. 3203, § 19.)*

Cross References

Church records acceptable to establish birth, see Health and Safety Code § 102580.
Definitions,
　Evidence, see Evidence Code § 140.
　Statement, see Evidence Code § 225.
　Writing, see Evidence Code § 250.
Hearsay rule, see Evidence Code § 1200.
Presumption of genuineness of writing more than 30 years old, see Evidence Code § 643.

Translating foreign language of instrument, see Evidence Code § 753.

§ 1316. Marriage, baptismal and similar certificates

Evidence of a statement concerning a person's birth, marriage, divorce, death, parent and child relationship, race, ancestry, relationship by blood or marriage, or other similar fact of family history is not made inadmissible by the hearsay rule if the statement is contained in a certificate that the maker thereof performed a marriage or other ceremony or administered a sacrament and:

(a) The maker was a clergyman, civil officer, or other person authorized to perform the acts reported in the certificate by law or by the rules, regulations, or requirements of a church, religious denomination, or religious society; and

(b) The certificate was issued by the maker at the time and place of the ceremony or sacrament or within a reasonable time thereafter. (Stats.1965, c. 299, § 2, operative Jan. 1, 1967. Amended by Stats. 1975, c. 1244, p. 3203, § 20.)

Cross References

Baptismal certificates acceptable to establish birth, see Health and Safety Code § 102580.
Definitions,
  Evidence, see Evidence Code § 140.
  Law, see Evidence Code § 160.
  Statement, see Evidence Code § 225.
Hearsay rule, see Evidence Code § 1200.

ARTICLE 17. PHYSICAL ABUSE

Section
1370. Threat of infliction of injury.
1380. Elder and dependent adults; statements by victims of abuse.
1390. Statements against parties involved in causing unavailability of declarant as witness.

§ 1370. Threat of infliction of injury

(a) Evidence of a statement by a declarant is not made inadmissible by the hearsay rule if all of the following conditions are met:

(1) The statement purports to narrate, describe, or explain the infliction or threat of physical injury upon the declarant.

(2) The declarant is unavailable as a witness pursuant to Section 240.

(3) The statement was made at or near the time of the infliction or threat of physical injury. Evidence of statements made more than five years before the filing of the current action or proceeding shall be inadmissible under this section.

(4) The statement was made under circumstances that would indicate its trustworthiness.

(5) The statement was made in writing, was electronically recorded, or made to a physician, nurse, paramedic, or to a law enforcement official.

(b) For purposes of paragraph (4) of subdivision (a), circumstances relevant to the issue of trustworthiness include, but are not limited to, the following:

(1) Whether the statement was made in contemplation of pending or anticipated litigation in which the declarant was interested.

(2) Whether the declarant has a bias or motive for fabricating the statement, and the extent of any bias or motive.

(3) Whether the statement is corroborated by evidence other than statements that are admissible only pursuant to this section.

(c) A statement is admissible pursuant to this section only if the proponent of the statement makes known to the adverse party the intention to offer the statement and the particulars of the statement sufficiently in advance of the proceedings in order to provide the adverse party with a fair opportunity to prepare to meet the statement. (Added by Stats.1996, c. 416 (A.B.2068), § 2, eff. Sept. 4, 1996. Amended by Stats.2000, c. 1001 (S.B.1944), § 2.)

§ 1380. Elder and dependent adults; statements by victims of abuse

(a) In a criminal proceeding charging a violation, or attempted violation, of Section 368 of the Penal Code, evidence of a statement made by a declarant is not made inadmissible by the hearsay rule if the declarant is unavailable as a witness, as defined in subdivisions (a) and (b) of Section 240, and all of the following are true:

(1) The party offering the statement has made a showing of particularized guarantees of trustworthiness regarding the statement, the statement was made under circumstances which indicate its trustworthiness, and the statement was not the result of promise, inducement, threat, or coercion. In making its determination, the court may consider only the circumstances that surround the making of the statement and that render the declarant particularly worthy of belief.

(2) There is no evidence that the unavailability of the declarant was caused by, aided by, solicited by, or procured on behalf of, the party who is offering the statement.

(3) The entire statement has been memorialized in a videotape recording made by a law enforcement official, prior to the death or disabling of the declarant.

(4) The statement was made by the victim of the alleged violation.

(5) The statement is supported by corroborative evidence.

(6) The victim of the alleged violation is an individual who meets both of the following requirements:

(A) Was 65 years of age or older or was a dependent adult when the alleged violation or attempted violation occurred.

(B) At the time of any criminal proceeding, including, but not limited to, a preliminary hearing or trial, regarding the alleged violation or attempted violation, is either deceased or suffers from the infirmities of aging as manifested by advanced age or organic brain damage, or other physical, mental, or emotional dysfunction, to the extent that the ability of the person to provide adequately for the person's own care or protection is impaired.

(b) If the prosecution intends to offer a statement pursuant to this section, the prosecution shall serve a written notice upon the defendant at least 10 days prior to the hearing or trial at which the prosecution intends to offer the statement, unless the prosecution shows good cause for the failure to provide that notice. In the event that good cause is shown, the defendant shall be entitled to a reasonable continuance of the hearing or trial.

(c) If the statement is offered during trial, the court's determination as to the availability of the victim as a witness shall be made out of the presence of the jury. If the defendant elects to testify at the hearing on a motion brought pursuant to this section, the court shall exclude from the examination every person except the clerk, the court reporter, the bailiff, the prosecutor, the investigating officer, the defendant and his or her counsel, an investigator for the defendant, and the officer having custody of the defendant. Notwithstanding any other provision of law, the defendant's testimony at the hearing shall not be admissible in any other proceeding except the hearing brought on the motion pursuant to this section. If a transcript is made of the defendant's testimony, it shall be sealed and transmitted to the clerk of the court in which the action is pending. (Added by Stats.1999, c. 383 (A.B.526), § 1.)

Validity

This section was held unconstitutional on its face as violating the Confrontation Clause in the decision of People v. Pirwani (App. 6 Dist. 2004) 14 Cal.Rptr.3d 673, 119 Cal. App.4th 770.

§ 1390. Statements against parties involved in causing unavailability of declarant as witness

(a) Evidence of a statement is not made inadmissible by the hearsay rule if the statement is offered against a party that has engaged, or aided and abetted, in the wrongdoing that was intended to, and did, procure the unavailability of the declarant as a witness.

(b)(1) The party seeking to introduce a statement pursuant to subdivision (a) shall establish, by a preponderance of the evidence, that the elements of subdivision (a) have been met at a foundational hearing.

(2) The hearsay evidence that is the subject of the foundational hearing is admissible at the foundational hearing. However, a finding that the elements of subdivision (a) have been met shall not be based solely on the unconfronted hearsay statement of the unavailable declarant, and shall be supported by independent corroborative evidence.

(3) The foundational hearing shall be conducted outside the presence of the jury. However, if the hearing is conducted after a jury trial has begun, the judge presiding at the hearing may consider evidence already presented to the jury in deciding whether the elements of subdivision (a) have been met.

(4) In deciding whether or not to admit the statement, the judge may take into account whether it is trustworthy and reliable.

(c) This section shall apply to any civil, criminal, or juvenile case or proceeding initiated or pending as of January 1, 2011. *(Added by Stats.2010, c. 537 (A.B.1723), § 2. Amended by Stats.2011, c. 296 (A.B.1023), § 90; Stats.2015, c. 55 (A.B.593), § 1, eff. Jan. 1, 2016.)*

Division 11

WRITINGS

Cross References

Ancient writings and dispositive instruments as hearsay evidence, see Evidence Code §§ 1330, 1331.
Bank collection items, see Commercial Code § 4201 et seq.
Business records, see Evidence Code § 1270 et seq.
Church records and certificates, see Evidence Code §§ 1315, 1316.
Commercial, scientific, and similar publications as hearsay evidence, see Evidence Code §§ 1340, 1341.
Court records, judicial notice, see Evidence Code §§ 451, 452.
Definition, writing, see Commercial Code § 1201; Corporations Code § 8; Evidence Code § 250; Insurance Code § 8.
Documents of title, see Commercial Code § 7101 et seq.
Examination of witness about writing, see Evidence Code § 768.
Family records as hearsay evidence, see Evidence Code § 1312.
Inspection of writings, see Evidence Code §§ 768, 771.
Investment securities, see Commercial Code § 8101 et seq.
Judgments as hearsay evidence, see Evidence Code § 1300 et seq.
Letters of credit, see Commercial Code § 5101 et seq.
Negotiable bills of lading, see Commercial Code §§ 7104, 7301 et seq.
Negotiable instruments, see Commercial Code § 3101 et seq.
Official records, see Evidence Code § 1280 et seq.
Part of transaction proved, admissibility of whole, see Evidence Code § 356.
Preliminary determinations on admissibility of evidence, see Evidence Code § 400 et seq.
Presumptions relating to,
  Authenticity of ancient writings affecting property interest, see Evidence Code § 643.
  Book containing reports of cases, see Evidence Code § 645.
  Book published by public authority, see Evidence Code § 644.
  Letter mailed was received, see Evidence Code § 641.
  Writing truly dated, see Evidence Code § 640.
Private writings, see Code of Civil Procedure § 1929 et seq.
Privileges, exceptions relating to dispositive instruments, see Evidence Code §§ 960, 961, 1002, 1003, 1021, 1022.
Public utilities, documents or records, admissibility or use as basis for testimony, see Public Utilities Code § 1710.
Recorded memory, see Evidence Code § 1237.
Refreshing recollection with writing, see Evidence Code § 771.
Sales, contracts in writing, see Commercial Code § 2201 et seq.
Scientific and professional treatises, use in cross-examination, see Evidence Code § 721.
Secured transactions, see Commercial Code § 9101 et seq.
Subscribing witnesses, see Evidence Code § 870.
Translators of writings, see Evidence Code §§ 750, 751, 753.
Warehouse receipts, see Commercial Code §§ 7104, 7201 et seq.
Wills, proof of, see Probate Code § 8220 et seq.

CHAPTER 2. SECONDARY EVIDENCE OF WRITINGS

ARTICLE 1. PROOF OF THE CONTENT OF A WRITING

Section
1520. Content of writing; proof.
1521. Secondary evidence rule.
1522. Additional grounds for exclusion of secondary evidence.
1523. Oral testimony of the content of a writing; admissibility.

Cross References

Criminal procedure, proof of the content of a writing in preliminary examinations, see Penal Code § 872.5.

§ 1520. Content of writing; proof

The content of a writing may be proved by an otherwise admissible original. *(Added by Stats.1998, c. 100 (S.B.177), § 2, operative Jan. 1, 1999.)*

§ 1521. Secondary evidence rule

(a) The content of a writing may be proved by otherwise admissible secondary evidence. The court shall exclude secondary evidence of the content of writing if the court determines either of the following:

(1) A genuine dispute exists concerning material terms of the writing and justice requires the exclusion.

(2) Admission of the secondary evidence would be unfair.

(b) Nothing in this section makes admissible oral testimony to prove the content of a writing if the testimony is inadmissible under Section 1523 (oral testimony of the content of a writing).

(c) Nothing in this section excuses compliance with Section 1401 (authentication).

(d) This section shall be known as the "Secondary Evidence Rule." *(Added by Stats.1998, c. 100 (S.B.177), § 2, operative Jan. 1, 1999.)*

§ 1522. Additional grounds for exclusion of secondary evidence

(a) In addition to the grounds for exclusion authorized by Section 1521, in a criminal action the court shall exclude secondary evidence of the content of a writing if the court determines that the original is in the proponent's possession, custody, or control, and the proponent has not made the original reasonably available for inspection at or before trial. This section does not apply to any of the following:

(1) A duplicate as defined in Section 260.

(2) A writing that is not closely related to the controlling issues in the action.

(3) A copy of a writing in the custody of a public entity.

(4) A copy of a writing that is recorded in the public records, if the record or a certified copy of it is made evidence of the writing by statute.

(b) In a criminal action, a request to exclude secondary evidence of the content of a writing, under this section or any other law, shall not be made in the presence of the jury. *(Added by Stats.1998, c. 100 (S.B.177), § 2, operative Jan. 1, 1999.)*

§ 1523. Oral testimony of the content of a writing; admissibility

(a) Except as otherwise provided by statute, oral testimony is not admissible to prove the content of a writing.

(b) Oral testimony of the content of a writing is not made inadmissible by subdivision (a) if the proponent does not have possession or control of a copy of the writing and the original is lost or has been destroyed without fraudulent intent on the part of the proponent of the evidence.

(c) Oral testimony of the content of a writing is not made inadmissible by subdivision (a) if the proponent does not have possession or control of the original or a copy of the writing and either of the following conditions is satisfied:

(1) Neither the writing nor a copy of the writing was reasonably procurable by the proponent by use of the court's process or by other available means.

(2) The writing is not closely related to the controlling issues and it would be inexpedient to require its production.

(d) Oral testimony of the content of a writing is not made inadmissible by subdivision (a) if the writing consists of numerous accounts or other writings that cannot be examined in court without great loss of time, and the evidence sought from them is only the general result of the whole. *(Added by Stats.1998, c. 100 (S.B.177), § 2, operative Jan. 1, 1999.)*

ARTICLE 2. OFFICIAL WRITINGS AND RECORDED WRITINGS

Section
1530. Copy of writing in official custody.
1531. Certification of copy for evidence.
1532. Official record of recorded writing.

§ 1530. Copy of writing in official custody

(a) A purported copy of a writing in the custody of a public entity, or of an entry in such a writing, is prima facie evidence of the existence and content of such writing or entry if:

(1) The copy purports to be published by the authority of the nation or state, or public entity therein in which the writing is kept;

(2) The office in which the writing is kept is within the United States or within the Panama Canal Zone, the Trust Territory of the Pacific Islands, or the Ryukyu Islands, and the copy is attested or certified as a correct copy of the writing or entry by a public employee, or a deputy of a public employee, having the legal custody of the writing; or

(3) The office in which the writing is kept is not within the United States or any other place described in paragraph (2) and the copy is attested as a correct copy of the writing or entry by a person having authority to make attestation. The attestation must be accompanied by a final statement certifying the genuineness of the signature and the official position of (i) the person who attested the copy as a correct copy or (ii) any foreign official who has certified either the genuineness of the signature and official position of the person attesting the copy or the genuineness of the signature and official position of another foreign official who has executed a similar certificate in a chain of such certificates beginning with a certificate of the genuineness of the signature and official position of the person attesting the copy. Except as provided in the next sentence, the final statement may be made only by a secretary of an embassy or legation, consul general, consul, vice consul, or consular agent of the United States, or a diplomatic or consular official of the foreign country assigned or accredited to the United States. Prior to January 1, 1971, the final statement may also be made by a secretary of an embassy or legation, consul general, consul, vice consul, consular agent, or other officer in the foreign service of the United States stationed in the nation in which the writing is kept, authenticated by the seal of his office. If reasonable opportunity has been given to all parties to investigate the authenticity and accuracy of the documents, the court may, for good cause shown, (i) admit an attested copy without the final statement or (ii) permit the writing or entry in foreign custody to be evidenced by an attested summary with or without a final statement.

(b) The presumptions established by this section are presumptions affecting the burden of producing evidence. *(Stats.1965, c. 299, § 2, operative Jan. 1, 1967. Amended by Stats.1970, c. 41, p. 60, § 1, eff. April 3, 1970.)*

Cross References

Attestation or certification of writing, see Evidence Code § 1531.
Authentication,
  Means of authenticating writings, see Evidence Code § 1410 et seq.
  Requirement, see Evidence Code § 1400 et seq.
Authority to prepare certified copy of motor vehicle department record, see Vehicle Code § 1813.
Books published by public authority, presumption, see Evidence Code § 644.
Conveyance pursuant to legal process, certified copy, see Evidence Code § 1603.
Criminal conviction records, admissibility of electronically digitized copies, see Evidence Code § 452.5.
Definitions,
  Burden of producing evidence, see Evidence Code § 110.
  Evidence, see Evidence Code § 140.
  Presumption, see Evidence Code § 600.
  Public employee, see Evidence Code § 195.
  Public entity, see Evidence Code § 200.
  State, see Evidence Code § 220.
  Writing, see Evidence Code § 250.
Official seals and signatures presumed genuine, see Evidence Code § 1452 et seq.
Out of state acknowledgments, see Civil Code § 1189.
Photostatic copy of vital statistic as prima facie evidence, see Health and Safety Code § 103550.
Presumptions affecting,
  Acknowledged writings and official writings, see Evidence Code § 1450 et seq.
  Burden of producing evidence, effect of, see Evidence Code § 604.
Prima facie evidence, effect of, see Evidence Code § 602.
Spanish title papers, copies as evidence, see Evidence Code § 1605.

Research References

Forms
9A Am. Jur. Pl. & Pr. Forms Evidence § 110, Introductory Comments.

§ 1531. Certification of copy for evidence

For the purpose of evidence, whenever a copy of a writing is attested or certified, the attestation or certificate must state in substance that the copy is a correct copy of the original, or of a specified part thereof, as the case may be. *(Stats.1965, c. 299, § 2, operative Jan. 1, 1967.)*

Cross References

Abstract of judgment, contents, see Code of Civil Procedure § 674.
Action for judgment proving instrument, see Civil Code § 1203.
Court's seal, documents to which seal must be or need not be affixed, see Code of Civil Procedure § 153.
Definitions,
  Evidence, see Evidence Code § 140.
  Writing, see Evidence Code § 250.
Letters of administration, contents, see Probate Code § 8405.
Letters of guardianship, form, see Probate Code § 2311.

§ 1531

Prima facie evidence, see Evidence Code § 602.
Seals, method of affixing, see Civil Code § 1628.

§ 1532. Official record of recorded writing

(a) The official record of a writing is prima facie evidence of the existence and content of the original recorded writing if:

(1) The record is in fact a record of an office of a public entity; and

(2) A statute authorized such a writing to be recorded in that office.

(b) The presumption established by this section is a presumption affecting the burden of producing evidence. *(Stats.1965, c. 299, § 2, operative Jan. 1, 1967.)*

Cross References

Definitions,
 Burden of producing evidence, see Evidence Code § 110.
 Evidence, see Evidence Code § 140.
 Presumption, see Evidence Code § 600.
 Public entity, see Evidence Code § 200.
 Statute, see Evidence Code § 230.
 Writing, see Evidence Code § 250.
Presumption affecting the burden of producing evidence, effect of, see Evidence Code § 604.
Prima facie evidence, effect of, see Evidence Code § 602.
Proof of content of writing, see Evidence Code § 1520 et seq.
Record destroyed by calamity, see Evidence Code § 1601.
Record of document affecting property, see Evidence Code § 1600.

Research References

Forms

9A Am. Jur. Pl. & Pr. Forms Evidence § 110, Introductory Comments.

ARTICLE 3. PHOTOGRAPHIC COPIES AND PRINTED REPRESENTATIONS OF WRITINGS

Section
1550. Photographic copies made as business records.
1550. Types of evidence as writing admissible as the writing itself.
1550.1. Admissibility of reproductions of files, records, writings, photographs, and fingerprints.
1551. Photographic copies where original destroyed or lost.
1552. Printed representation of computer-generated information.
1553. Printed representation of video or digital images.

§ 1550. Photographic copies made as business records

Section prior to amendment by Stats.2002, c. 124 (A.B. 2033), § 1. See, also, section as amended by Stats.2002, c. 124 (A.B.2033), § 1.

A nonerasable optical image reproduction provided that additions, deletions, or changes to the original document are not permitted by the technology, a photostatic, microfilm, microcard, miniature photographic, or other photographic copy or reproduction, or an enlargement thereof, of a writing is as admissible as the writing itself if the copy or reproduction was made and preserved as a part of the records of a business (as defined by Section 1270) in the regular course of that business. The introduction of the copy, reproduction, or enlargement does not preclude admission of the original writing if it is still in existence. A court may require the introduction of a hard copy printout of the document. *(Stats.1965, c. 299, § 2, operative Jan. 1, 1967. Amended by Stats.1992, c. 876 (A.B.3296), § 10.)*

Cross References

Definition, writing, see Evidence Code § 250.

Payments by check, presumptions based on copies produced in accordance with this section, see Evidence Code § 670.

Research References

Forms

4 California Transactions Forms--Business Transactions § 26:28, Presumption of Payment by Check [Ev C §670].

§ 1550. Types of evidence as writing admissible as the writing itself

Section as amended by Stats.2002, c. 124 (A.B.2033), § 1. See, also, section prior to amendment by Stats.2002, c. 124 (A.B.2033), § 1.

(a) If made and preserved as a part of the records of a business, as defined in Section 1270, in the regular course of that business, the following types of evidence of a writing are as admissible as the writing itself:

(1) A nonerasable optical image reproduction or any other reproduction of a public record by a trusted system, as defined in Section 12168.7 of the Government Code, if additions, deletions, or changes to the original document are not permitted by the technology.

(2) A photostatic copy or reproduction.

(3) A microfilm, microcard, or miniature photographic copy, reprint, or enlargement.

(4) Any other photographic copy or reproduction, or an enlargement thereof.

(b) The introduction of evidence of a writing pursuant to subdivision (a) does not preclude admission of the original writing if it is still in existence. A court may require the introduction of a hard copy printout of the document. *(Stats.1965, c. 299, § 2, operative Jan. 1, 1967. Amended by Stats.1992, c. 876 (A.B.3296), § 10; Stats.2002, c. 124 (A.B.2033), § 1, operative contingent.)*

Operative Effect

Stats.2002, c. 124 (A.B.2033), § 2, provides that this act shall become operative on the date the Secretary of State adopts uniform standards for storing and recording permanent and nonpermanent documents in electronic media as required by Government Code § 12168.7.

Cross References

Definition, writing, see Evidence Code § 250.
Payments by check, presumptions based on copies produced in accordance with this section, see Evidence Code § 670.

Research References

Forms

4 California Transactions Forms--Business Transactions § 26:28, Presumption of Payment by Check [Ev C §670].

§ 1550.1. Admissibility of reproductions of files, records, writings, photographs, and fingerprints

Reproductions of files, records, writings, photographs, fingerprints or other instruments in the official custody of a criminal justice agency that were microphotographed or otherwise reproduced in a manner that conforms with the provisions of Section 11106.1, 11106.2, or 11106.3 of the Penal Code shall be admissible to the same extent and under the same circumstances as the original file, record, writing or other instrument would be admissible. *(Added by Stats.2004, c. 65 (A.B.883), § 1.)*

§ 1551. Photographic copies where original destroyed or lost

A print, whether enlarged or not, from a photographic film (including a photographic plate, microphotographic film, photostatic negative, or similar reproduction) of an original writing destroyed or lost after such film was taken or a reproduction from an electronic recording of video images on magnetic surfaces is admissible as the original writing itself if, at the time of the taking of such film or electronic recording, the person under whose direction and control it was taken attached thereto, or to the sealed container in which it was placed and has been kept, or incorporated in the film or electronic recording, a certification complying with the provisions of Section 1531 and stating the date on which, and the fact that, it was so taken under his direction and control. *(Stats.1965, c. 299, § 2, operative Jan. 1, 1967. Amended by Stats.1969, c. 646, p. 1298, § 1.)*

Cross References

Certified copy of public record of writing, see Evidence Code § 1530 et seq.
Certified copy of public writing, prima facie evidence, see Evidence Code § 1532.
Copy of vital statistic as prima facie evidence, see Health and Safety Code § 103550.
Definition, writing, see Evidence Code § 250.
Photographic copy of will, admissibility, see Probate Code § 8202.
Proof of content of writing, see Evidence Code § 1520 et seq.
Record of instrument where previous record lost or destroyed, see Government Code § 27329.

§ 1552. Printed representation of computer-generated information

(a) A printed representation of computer information or a computer program is presumed to be an accurate representation of the computer information or computer program that it purports to represent. This presumption is a presumption affecting the burden of producing evidence. If a party to an action introduces evidence that a printed representation of computer information or computer program is inaccurate or unreliable, the party introducing the printed representation into evidence has the burden of proving, by a preponderance of evidence, that the printed representation is an accurate representation of the existence and content of the computer information or computer program that it purports to represent.

(b) Subdivision (a) applies to the printed representation of computer-generated information stored by an automated traffic enforcement system.

(c) Subdivision (a) shall not apply to computer-generated official records certified in accordance with Section 452.5 or 1530. *(Added by Stats.1998, c. 100 (S.B.177), § 4, operative Jan. 1, 1999. Amended by Stats.2012, c. 735 (S.B.1303), § 1.)*

Cross References

Offenses, automated traffic enforcement system, requirements, use of printed representation as evidence, confidentiality and retention of records, review of alleged violation by registered owner, manufacturers and suppliers, duties and contract limitations, see Vehicle Code § 21455.5.
Procedure, certain violations recorded by automated traffic enforcement system, notice to appear, contents, notice of nonliability, form, dismissal, see Vehicle Code § 40518.

§ 1553. Printed representation of video or digital images

(a) A printed representation of images stored on a video or digital medium is presumed to be an accurate representation of the images it purports to represent. This presumption is a presumption affecting the burden of producing evidence. If a party to an action introduces evidence that a printed representation of images stored on a video or digital medium is inaccurate or unreliable, the party introducing the printed representation into evidence has the burden of proving, by a preponderance of evidence, that the printed representation is an accurate representation of the existence and content of the images that it purports to represent.

(b) Subdivision (a) applies to the printed representation of video or photographic images stored by an automated traffic enforcement system. *(Added by Stats.1998, c. 100 (S.B.177), § 5, operative Jan. 1, 1999. Amended by Stats.2012, c. 735 (S.B.1303), § 2.)*

Cross References

Offenses, automated traffic enforcement system, requirements, use of printed representation as evidence, confidentiality and retention of records, review of alleged violation by registered owner, manufacturers and suppliers, duties and contract limitations, see Vehicle Code § 21455.5.
Procedure, certain violations recorded by automated traffic enforcement system, notice to appear, contents, notice of nonliability, form, dismissal, see Vehicle Code § 40518.

ARTICLE 4. PRODUCTION OF BUSINESS RECORDS

Section
1560. Compliance with subpoena duces tecum or search warrant for business records.
1561. Affidavit accompanying records.
1562. Admissibility of affidavit and copy of records.
1563. One witness and mileage fee.
1564. Personal attendance of custodian and production of original records.
1565. Service of more than one subpoena duces tecum.
1566. Applicability of article.
1567. Employee income and benefit information; forms completed by employer; support modification or termination proceedings.

§ 1560. Compliance with subpoena duces tecum or search warrant for business records

(a) As used in this article:

(1) "Business" includes every kind of business described in Section 1270.

(2) "Record" includes every kind of record maintained by a business.

(b) Except as provided in Section 1564, when a subpoena duces tecum is served upon the custodian of records or other qualified witness of a business in an action in which the business is neither a party nor the place where any cause of action is alleged to have arisen, and the subpoena requires the production of all or any part of the records of the business, it is sufficient compliance therewith if the custodian or other qualified witness delivers by mail or otherwise a true, legible, and durable copy of all of the records described in the subpoena to the clerk of the court or to another person described in subdivision (d) of Section 2026.010 of the Code of Civil Procedure, together with the affidavit described in Section 1561, within one of the following time periods:

(1) In any criminal action, five days after the receipt of the subpoena.

(2) In any civil action, within 15 days after the receipt of the subpoena.

(3) Within the time agreed upon by the party who served the subpoena and the custodian or other qualified witness.

(c) The copy of the records shall be separately enclosed in an inner envelope or wrapper, sealed, with the title and number of the action, name of witness, and date of subpoena clearly inscribed thereon; the sealed envelope or wrapper shall then be enclosed in an outer envelope or wrapper, sealed, and directed as follows:

(1) If the subpoena directs attendance in court, to the clerk of the court.

(2) If the subpoena directs attendance at a deposition, to the officer before whom the deposition is to be taken, at the place designated in the subpoena for the taking of the deposition or at the officer's place of business.

(3) In other cases, to the officer, body, or tribunal conducting the hearing, at a like address.

(d) Unless the parties to the proceeding otherwise agree, or unless the sealed envelope or wrapper is returned to a witness who is to appear personally, the copy of the records shall remain sealed and shall be opened only at the time of trial, deposition, or other hearing, upon the direction of the judge, officer, body, or tribunal conducting the proceeding, in the presence of all parties who have appeared in person or by counsel at the trial, deposition, or hearing. Records that are original documents and that are not introduced in evidence or required as part of the record shall be returned to the person or entity from whom received. Records that are copies may be destroyed.

(e) As an alternative to the procedures described in subdivisions (b), (c), and (d), the subpoenaing party in a civil action may direct the witness to make the records available for inspection or copying by the party's attorney, the attorney's representative, or deposition officer as described in Section 2020.420 of the Code of Civil Procedure, at the witness' business address under reasonable conditions during normal business hours. Normal business hours, as used in this subdivision, means those hours that the business of the witness is normally open for business to the public. When provided with at least five business days' advance notice by the party's attorney, attorney's representative, or deposition officer, the witness shall designate a time period of not less than six continuous hours on a date certain for copying of records subject to the subpoena by the party's attorney, attorney's representative, or deposition officer. It shall be the responsibility of the attorney's representative to deliver any copy of the records as directed in the subpoena. Disobedience to the deposition subpoena issued pursuant to this subdivision is punishable as provided in Section 2020.240 of the Code of Civil Procedure.

(f) If a search warrant for business records is served upon the custodian of records or other qualified witness of a business in compliance with Section 1524 of the Penal Code regarding a criminal investigation in which the business is neither a party nor the place where any crime is alleged to have occurred, and the search warrant provides that the warrant will be deemed executed if the business causes the delivery of records described in the warrant to the law enforcement agency ordered to execute the warrant, it is sufficient compliance therewith if the custodian or other qualified witness delivers by mail or otherwise a true, legible, and durable copy of all of the records described in the search warrant to the law enforcement agency ordered to execute the search warrant, together with the affidavit described in Section 1561, within five days after the receipt of the search warrant or within such other time as is set forth in the warrant. This subdivision does not abridge or limit the scope of search warrant procedures set forth in Chapter 3 (commencing with Section 1523) of Title 12 of Part 2 of the Penal Code or invalidate otherwise duly executed search warrants. *(Stats.1965, c. 299, § 2, operative Jan. 1, 1967. Amended by Stats.1969, c. 199, p. 484, § 2; Stats.1982, c. 452, p. 1824, § 2.5; Stats.1984, c. 481, § 2; Stats.1986, c. 603, § 6; Stats.1991, c. 1090 (A.B.1484), § 14; Stats.1997, c. 442 (A.B.758), § 16; Stats.1999, c. 444 (A.B.794), § 4; Stats.2000, c. 287 (S.B.1955), § 1; Stats.2004, c. 182 (A.B.3081), § 32, operative July 1, 2005; Stats.2004, c. 162 (A.B.1249), § 1; Stats.2005, c. 294 (A.B.333), § 18; Stats.2006, c. 538 (S.B.1852), § 155; Stats.2016, c. 85 (S.B. 1087), § 1, eff. Jan. 1, 2017.)*

Cross References

Attendance of witnesses, persons authorized to issue subpoenas, see Penal Code § 1326.
Definitions,
  Action, see Evidence Code § 105.
  Hearing, see Evidence Code § 145.
  Public entity, see Evidence Code § 200.
Professional photocopiers, see Business and Professions Code § 22450 et seq.
Subpoena duces tecum, see Code of Civil Procedure § 1985 et seq.; Penal Code § 1326 et seq.

Research References

Forms
25B Am. Jur. Pl. & Pr. Forms Witnesses § 1, Introductory Comments.

§ 1561. Affidavit accompanying records

(a) The records shall be accompanied by the affidavit of the custodian or other qualified witness, stating in substance each of the following:

(1) The affiant is the duly authorized custodian of the records or other qualified witness and has authority to certify the records.

(2) The copy is a true copy of all the records described in the subpoena duces tecum or search warrant, or pursuant to subdivision (e) of Section 1560, the records were delivered to the attorney, the attorney's representative, or deposition officer for copying at the custodian's or witness' place of business, as the case may be.

(3) The records were prepared by the personnel of the business in the ordinary course of business at or near the time of the act, condition, or event.

(4) The identity of the records.

(5) A description of the mode of preparation of the records.

(b) If the business has none of the records described, or only part thereof, the custodian or other qualified witness shall so state in the affidavit, and deliver the affidavit and those records that are available in one of the manners provided in Section 1560.

(c) If the records described in the subpoena were delivered to the attorney or his or her representative or deposition officer for copying at the custodian's or witness' place of business, in addition to the affidavit required by subdivision (a), the records shall be accompanied by an affidavit by the attorney or his or her representative or deposition officer stating that the copy is a true copy of all the records delivered to the attorney or his or her representative or deposition officer for copying. *(Stats.1965, c. 299, § 2, operative Jan. 1, 1967. Amended by Stats.1969, c. 199, p. 484, § 3; Stats.1986, c. 603, § 7; Stats.1987, c. 19, § 2, eff. May 12, 1987; Stats.1996, c. 146 (A.B.3001), § 1; Stats.1999, c. 444 (A.B.794), § 5; Stats.2016, c. 85 (S.B.1087), § 2, eff. Jan. 1, 2017.)*

Cross References

Production of or access to electronic communication information, warrant requirements, see Penal Code § 1546.1.
State civil service, investigations and hearing, process and delivery of subpoenas and subpoenas duces tecum in accordance with this section, see Government Code § 18672.

Research References

Forms
California Practice Guide: Rutter Family Law Forms Form 11:17, Declaration of Custodian of Records (Evidence Code §1561(A)).
West's California Code Forms, Business & Professions § 475 Comment, Administrative Procedure Act.

§ 1562. Admissibility of affidavit and copy of records

If the original records would be admissible in evidence if the custodian or other qualified witness had been present and testified to the matters stated in the affidavit, and if the requirements of Section 1271 have been met, the copy of the records is admissible in evidence. The affidavit is admissible as evidence of the matters stated therein pursuant to Section 1561 and the matters so stated are presumed true. When more than one person has knowledge of the facts, more than one affidavit may be made. The presumption established by this section is a presumption affecting the burden of producing evidence. *(Stats.1965, c. 299, § 2, operative Jan. 1, 1967. Amended by Stats.1989, c. 1416, § 31; Stats.1996, c. 146 (A.B.3001), § 2.)*

Cross References

Definitions,
  Burden of proof, see Evidence Code § 115.
  Presumption, see Evidence Code § 600.
Presumption affecting the burden of proof, effect of, see Evidence Code § 606.
Production of or access to electronic communication information, warrant requirements, see Penal Code § 1546.1.
Proof of content of writing, see Evidence Code § 1250 et seq.

§ 1563. One witness and mileage fee

(a) This article does not require tender or payment of more than one witness fee and one mileage fee or other charge, to a witness or witness' business, unless there is an agreement to the contrary between the witness and the requesting party.

(b) All reasonable costs incurred in a civil proceeding by a witness who is not a party with respect to the production of all or any part of business records requested pursuant to a subpoena duces tecum shall be charged against the party serving the subpoena duces tecum.

(1) "Reasonable costs," as used in this section, includes, but is not limited to, the following specific costs: ten cents ($0.10) per page for standard reproduction of documents of a size 8 ½ by 14 inches or less; twenty cents ($0.20) per page for copying of documents from microfilm; actual costs for the reproduction of oversize documents or the reproduction of documents requiring special processing which are made in response to a subpoena; reasonable clerical costs incurred in locating and making the records available to be billed at the maximum rate of twenty-four dollars ($24) per hour per person, computed on the basis of six dollars ($6) per quarter hour or fraction thereof; actual postage charges; and the actual cost, if any, charged to the witness by a third person for the retrieval and return of records held offsite by that third person.

(2) The requesting party, or the requesting party's deposition officer, shall not be required to pay the reasonable costs or any estimate thereof before the records are available for delivery pursuant to the subpoena, but the witness may demand payment of costs pursuant to this section simultaneous with actual delivery of the subpoenaed records, and until payment is made, the witness is under no obligation to deliver the records.

(3) The witness shall submit an itemized statement for the costs to the requesting party, or the requesting party's deposition officer, setting forth the reproduction and clerical costs incurred by the witness. If the costs exceed those authorized in paragraph (1), or if the witness refuses to produce an itemized statement of costs as required by paragraph (3), upon demand by the requesting party, or the requesting party's deposition officer, the witness shall furnish a statement setting forth the actions taken by the witness in justification of the costs.

(4) The requesting party may petition the court in which the action is pending to recover from the witness all or a part of the costs paid to the witness, or to reduce all or a part of the costs charged by the witness, pursuant to this subdivision, on the grounds that those costs were excessive. Upon the filing of the petition the court shall issue an order to show cause and from the time the order is served on the witness the court has jurisdiction over the witness. The court may hear testimony on the order to show cause and if it finds that the costs demanded and collected, or charged but not collected, exceed the amount authorized by this subdivision, it shall order the witness to remit to the requesting party, or reduce its charge to the requesting party by an amount equal to, the amount of the excess. If the court finds the costs were excessive and charged in bad faith by the witness, the court shall order the witness to remit the full amount of the costs demanded and collected, or excuse the requesting party from any payment of costs charged but not collected, and the court shall also order the witness to pay the requesting party the amount of the reasonable expenses incurred in obtaining the order, including attorney's fees. If the court finds the costs were not excessive, the court shall order the requesting party to pay the witness the amount of the reasonable expenses incurred in defending the petition, including attorney's fees.

(5) If a subpoena is served to compel the production of business records and is subsequently withdrawn, or is quashed, modified, or limited on a motion made other than by the witness, the witness shall be entitled to reimbursement pursuant to paragraph (1) for all reasonable costs incurred in compliance with the subpoena to the time that the requesting party has notified the witness that the subpoena has been withdrawn or quashed, modified, or limited. If the subpoena is withdrawn or quashed, if those costs are not paid within 30 days after demand therefor, the witness may file a motion in the court in which the action is pending for an order requiring payment, and the court shall award the payment of expenses and attorney's fees in the manner set forth in paragraph (4).

(6) If records requested pursuant to a subpoena duces tecum are delivered to the attorney, the attorney's representative, or the deposition officer for inspection or photocopying at the witness' place of business, the only fee for complying with the subpoena shall not exceed fifteen dollars ($15), plus the actual cost, if any, charged to the witness by a third person for retrieval and return of records held offsite by that third person. If the records are retrieved from microfilm, the reasonable costs, as defined in paragraph (1), applies.

(c) If the personal attendance of the custodian of a record or other qualified witness is required pursuant to Section 1564, in a civil proceeding, he or she shall be entitled to the same witness fees and mileage permitted in a case where the subpoena requires the witness to attend and testify before a court in which the action or proceeding is pending and to any additional costs incurred as provided by subdivision (b). *(Stats.1965, c. 299, § 2, operative Jan. 1, 1967. Amended by Stats.1972, c. 396, p. 719, § 1; Stats.1981, c. 1014, p. 3913, § 2; Stats.1982, c. 452, p. 1825, § 3; Stats.1986, c. 603, § 8; Stats.1987, c. 19, § 3, eff. May 12, 1987; Stats.1997, c. 442 (A.B.758), § 17; Stats.1999, c. 444 (A.B.794), § 6; Stats.2016, c. 85 (S.B.1087), § 3, eff. Jan. 1, 2017.)*

Fees and Charges

Commissioner's authority to increase or decrease fees, and schedule of fees and charges, see Insurance Code § 12978.

§ 1564. Personal attendance of custodian and production of original records

The personal attendance of the custodian or other qualified witness and the production of the original records is not required unless, at the discretion of the requesting party, the subpoena duces tecum contains a clause which reads:

"The personal attendance of the custodian or other qualified witness and the production of the original records are required by this subpoena. The procedure authorized pursuant to subdivision (b) of Section 1560, and Sections 1561 and 1562, of the Evidence Code will not be deemed sufficient compliance with this subpoena." *(Stats.1965, c. 299, § 2, operative Jan. 1, 1967. Amended by Stats. 1984, c. 603, § 2; Stats.1986, c. 603, § 9; Stats.1987, c. 19, § 4, eff. May 12, 1987.)*

§ 1565. Service of more than one subpoena duces tecum

If more than one subpoena duces tecum is served upon the custodian of records or other qualified witness and the personal attendance of the custodian or other qualified witness is required pursuant to Section 1564, the witness shall be deemed to be the witness of the party serving the first such subpoena duces tecum. *(Stats.1965, c. 299, § 2, operative Jan. 1, 1967. Amended by Stats. 1969, c. 199, p. 485, § 4.)*

§ 1566. Applicability of article

This article applies in any proceeding in which testimony can be compelled. *(Stats.1965, c. 299, § 2, operative Jan. 1, 1967.)*

§ 1567. Employee income and benefit information; forms completed by employer; support modification or termination proceedings

A completed form described in Section 3664 of the Family Code for income and benefit information provided by the employer may be admissible in a proceeding for modification or termination of an order for child, family, or spousal support if both of the following requirements are met:

(a) The completed form complies with Sections 1561 and 1562.

§ 1567 EVIDENCE CODE

(b) A copy of the completed form and notice was served on the employee named therein pursuant to Section 3664 of the Family Code. *(Added by Stats.1995, c. 506 (A.B.413), § 1.)*

GOVERNMENT CODE

Title 2

GOVERNMENT OF THE STATE OF CALIFORNIA

Division 3

EXECUTIVE DEPARTMENT

Cross References

Attorneys, general provisions, see Business and Professions Code § 6001.
Grant to City of Santa Cruz of property known as Lighthouse Field State Beach, see Public Resources Code § 5003.19.
Old Sacramento State Historic Park, fair market value requirements for sale, see Public Resources Code § 5003.16.

Part 2.8

* * * CIVIL RIGHTS DEPARTMENT

Cross References

Applicability of Private Attorneys General Act on employees in construction industry subject to valid collective bargaining agreement, arbitration, see Labor Code § 2699.6.
Commission on human relations, creation, see Government Code § 50262.
Community Redevelopment Law, state policy of antidiscrimination, see Health and Safety Code §§ 33039, 33050, 33337.
Deeds, leases or contracts, see Health and Safety Code §§ 33337, 33435, 33436.
Legislative Employee Whistleblower Protection Act, see Government Code § 9149.30 et seq.
Local tenant preference policy, purpose, see Government Code § 7061.
Mandated reporter defined, see Penal Code § 11165.7.
Planning and zoning, contents of housing element, rezoning, see Government Code § 65583.
Planning and Zoning Law, prohibition of discrimination, see Government Code § 65008.
Public social services, see Welfare and Institutions Code § 10000 et seq.
Racial, national or ethnic restrictions in deeds, invalidity, see Civil Code § 782.
Requirement to approve or disapprove proposed changes, see Civil Code § 4765.
Retaliation prohibited against advocates or employees opposing or filing complaints about practices, fine for violation, see Government Code § 9149.40.
Unlawful to disclose individual's HIV status, see Health and Safety Code § 120990.
Unruh Civil Rights Act, see Civil Code § 51 et seq.
Waiver of rights, forums or procedures, prohibited practices, see Labor Code § 432.6.

CHAPTER 6. DISCRIMINATION PROHIBITED

ARTICLE 1. UNLAWFUL PRACTICES, GENERALLY

Section
12945. Pregnancy, childbirth, or related medical condition; actions constituting unlawful employment practice.
12945.2. Family care and medical leave; definitions; conditions; unlawful employment practices.
12947. Child care services for employees or members; not an unlawful practice.

§ 12945. Pregnancy, childbirth, or related medical condition; actions constituting unlawful employment practice

(a) In addition to the provisions that govern pregnancy, childbirth, or a related medical condition in Sections 12926 and 12940, each of the following shall be an unlawful employment practice, unless based upon a bona fide occupational qualification:

(1) For an employer to refuse to allow an employee disabled by pregnancy, childbirth, or a related medical condition to take a leave for a reasonable period of time not to exceed four months and thereafter return to work, as set forth in the council's regulations. The employee shall be entitled to utilize any accrued vacation leave during this period of time. Reasonable period of time means that period during which the employee is disabled on account of pregnancy, childbirth, or a related medical condition.

An employer may require an employee who plans to take a leave pursuant to this subdivision to give the employer reasonable notice of the date the leave shall commence and the estimated duration of the leave.

(2)(A) For an employer to refuse to maintain and pay for coverage for an eligible employee who takes leave pursuant to paragraph (1) under a group health plan, as defined in Section 5000(b)(1) of the Internal Revenue Code [1] of 1986, for the duration of the leave, not to exceed four months over the course of a 12–month period, commencing on the date the leave taken under paragraph (1) begins, at the level and under the conditions that coverage would have been provided if the employee had continued in employment continuously for the duration of the leave. Nothing in this paragraph shall preclude an employer from maintaining and paying for coverage under a group health plan beyond four months. An employer may recover from the employee the premium that the employer paid as required under this subdivision for maintaining coverage for the employee under the group health plan if both of the following conditions occur:

(i) The employee fails to return from leave after the period of leave to which the employee is entitled has expired.

(ii) The employee's failure to return from leave is for a reason other than one of the following:

(I) The employee taking leave under the Moore-Brown-Roberti Family Rights Act (Sections 12945.2 and 19702.3 of the Government Code).

(II) The continuation, recurrence, or onset of a health condition that entitles the employee to leave under paragraph (1) or other circumstance beyond the control of the employee.

(B) If the employer is a state agency, the collective bargaining agreement shall govern with respect to the continued receipt by an eligible employee of the health care coverage specified in subparagraph (A).

(3)(A) For an employer to refuse to provide reasonable accommodation for an employee for a condition related to pregnancy, childbirth, or a related medical condition, if the employee so requests, with the advice of the employee's health care provider.

(B) For an employer who has a policy, practice, or collective bargaining agreement requiring or authorizing the transfer of temporarily disabled employees to less strenuous or hazardous positions for the duration of the disability to refuse to transfer a pregnant employee who so requests.

(C) For an employer to refuse to temporarily transfer a pregnant employee to a less strenuous or hazardous position for the duration of the pregnancy if the employee so requests, with the advice of the

§ 12945

employee's physician, where that transfer can be reasonably accommodated. However, no employer shall be required by this section to create additional employment that the employer would not otherwise have created, nor shall the employer be required to discharge any employee, transfer any employee with more seniority, or promote any employee who is not qualified to perform the job.

(4) For an employer to interfere with, restrain, or deny the exercise of, or the attempt to exercise, any right provided under this section.

(b) This section shall not be construed to affect any other provision of law relating to sex discrimination or pregnancy, or in any way to diminish the coverage of pregnancy, childbirth, or a medical condition related to pregnancy or childbirth under any other provision of this part, including subdivision (a) of Section 12940. (Added by Stats.1980, c. 992, § 4. Amended by Stats.1990, c. 15 (S.B.1027), § 2; Stats.1992, c. 907 (A.B.2865), § 1; Stats.1999, c. 591 (A.B.1670), § 9; Stats.2004, c. 647 (A.B.2870), § 5; Stats.2011, c. 510 (S.B.299), § 1; Stats.2011, c. 678 (A.B.592), § 1.5; Stats.2017, c. 799 (A.B.1556), § 10, eff. Jan. 1, 2018; Stats.2022, c. 48 (S.B.189), § 39, eff. June 30, 2022.)

[1] Internal Revenue Code sections are in Title 25 of the U.S.C.A.

Cross References

Commission defined for purposes of this Part, see Government Code § 12925.
Credit for uncompensated leave of absence for illness, conditions, see Government Code § 31646.
Medical condition defined for purposes of this Part, see Government Code § 12926.
Reasonable accommodation defined for purposes of this Part, see Government Code § 12926.
Sex defined for purposes of this Part, see Government Code § 12926.

Research References

Forms

4A West's Federal Forms § 58:51, Complaint for Declaratory and Injunctive Relief Challenging Statute Limiting Use of Arbitration.

§ 12945.2. Family care and medical leave; definitions; conditions; unlawful employment practices

(a) It shall be an unlawful employment practice for any employer, as defined in paragraph (4) of subdivision (b), to refuse to grant a request by any employee with more than 12 months of service with the employer, and who has at least 1,250 hours of service with the employer during the previous 12-month period or who meets the requirements of subdivision (r), to take up to a total of 12 workweeks in any 12-month period for family care and medical leave. Family care and medical leave requested pursuant to this subdivision shall not be deemed to have been granted unless the employer provides the employee, upon granting the leave request, a guarantee of employment in the same or a comparable position upon the termination of the leave. The council shall adopt a regulation specifying the elements of a reasonable request.

(b) For purposes of this section:

(1) "Child" means a biological, adopted, or foster child, a stepchild, a legal ward, a child of a domestic partner, or a person to whom the employee stands in loco parentis.

(2) "Designated person" means any individual related by blood or whose association with the employee is the equivalent of a family relationship. The designated person may be identified by the employee at the time the employee requests the leave. An employer may limit an employee to one designated person per 12-month period for family care and medical leave.

(3) "Domestic partner" has the same meaning as defined in Section 297 of the Family Code.

(4) "Employer" means either of the following:

(A) Any person who directly employs five or more persons to perform services for a wage or salary.

(B) The state, and any political or civil subdivision of the state and cities.

(5) "Family care and medical leave" means any of the following:

(A) Leave for reason of the birth of a child of the employee or the placement of a child with an employee in connection with the adoption or foster care of the child by the employee.

(B) Leave to care for a child, parent, grandparent, grandchild, sibling, spouse, * * * domestic partner, or designated person who has a serious health condition.

(C) Leave because of an employee's own serious health condition that makes the employee unable to perform the functions of the position of that employee, except for leave taken for disability on account of pregnancy, childbirth, or related medical conditions.

(D) Leave because of a qualifying exigency related to the covered active duty or call to covered active duty of an employee's spouse, domestic partner, child, or parent in the Armed Forces of the United States, as specified in Section 3302.2 of the Unemployment Insurance Code.

(6) "Employment in the same or a comparable position" means employment in a position that has the same or similar duties and pay that can be performed at the same or similar geographic location as the position held prior to the leave.

(7) "FMLA" means the federal Family and Medical Leave Act of 1993 (P.L. 103-3).[1]

(8) "Grandchild" means a child of the employee's child.

(9) "Grandparent" means a parent of the employee's parent.

(10) "Health care provider" means any of the following:

(A) An individual holding either a physician's and surgeon's certificate issued pursuant to Article 4 (commencing with Section 2080) of Chapter 5 of Division 2 of the Business and Professions Code, an osteopathic physician's and surgeon's certificate issued pursuant to Article 4.5 (commencing with Section 2099.5) of Chapter 5 of Division 2 of the Business and Professions Code, or an individual duly licensed as a physician, surgeon, or osteopathic physician or surgeon in another state or jurisdiction, who directly treats or supervises the treatment of the serious health condition.

(B) Any other person determined by the United States Secretary of Labor to be capable of providing health care services under the FMLA.

(11) "Parent" means a biological, foster, or adoptive parent, a parent-in-law, a stepparent, a legal guardian, or other person who stood in loco parentis to the employee when the employee was a child.

(12) "Parent-in-law" means the parent of a spouse or domestic partner.

(13) "Serious health condition" means an illness, injury, impairment, or physical or mental condition that involves either of the following:

(A) Inpatient care in a hospital, hospice, or residential health care facility.

(B) Continuing treatment or continuing supervision by a health care provider.

(14) "Sibling" means a person related to another person by blood, adoption, or affinity through a common legal or biological parent.

(c) An employer shall not be required to pay an employee for any leave taken pursuant to subdivision (a), except as required by subdivision (d).

(d) An employee taking a leave permitted by subdivision (a) may elect, or an employer may require the employee, to substitute, for leave allowed under subdivision (a), any of the employee's accrued vacation leave or other accrued time off during this period or any other paid or unpaid time off negotiated with the employer. If an employee takes a leave because of the employee's own serious health condition, the employee may also elect, or the employer may also require the employee, to substitute accrued sick leave during the period of the leave. However, an employee shall not use sick leave during a period of leave in connection with the birth, adoption, or foster care of a child, or to care for a child, parent, grandparent, grandchild, sibling, spouse, * * * domestic partner, or designated person with a serious health condition, unless mutually agreed to by the employer and the employee.

(e)(1) During any period that an eligible employee takes leave pursuant to subdivision (a) or takes leave that qualifies as leave taken under the FMLA, the employer shall maintain and pay for coverage under a "group health plan," as defined in Section 5000(b)(1) of the Internal Revenue Code,[2] for the duration of the leave, not to exceed 12 workweeks in a 12-month period, commencing on the date leave taken under the FMLA commences, at the level and under the conditions coverage would have been provided if the employee had continued in employment continuously for the duration of the leave. Nothing in the preceding sentence shall preclude an employer from maintaining and paying for coverage under a "group health plan" beyond 12 workweeks. An employer may recover the premium that the employer paid as required by this subdivision for maintaining coverage for the employee under the group health plan if both of the following conditions occur:

(A) The employee fails to return from leave after the period of leave to which the employee is entitled has expired.

(B) The employee's failure to return from leave is for a reason other than the continuation, recurrence, or onset of a serious health condition that entitles the employee to leave under subdivision (a) or other circumstances beyond the control of the employee.

(2) Any employee taking leave pursuant to subdivision (a) shall continue to be entitled to participate in employee health plans for any period during which coverage is not provided by the employer under paragraph (1), employee benefit plans, including life insurance or short-term or long-term disability or accident insurance, pension and retirement plans, and supplemental unemployment benefit plans to the same extent and under the same conditions as apply to an unpaid leave taken for any purpose other than those described in subdivision (a). In the absence of these conditions an employee shall continue to be entitled to participate in these plans and, in the case of health and welfare employee benefit plans, including life insurance or short-term or long-term disability or accident insurance, or other similar plans, the employer may, at the employer's discretion, require the employee to pay premiums, at the group rate, during the period of leave not covered by any accrued vacation leave, or other accrued time off, or any paid or unpaid time off negotiated with the employer, as a condition of continued coverage during the leave period. However, the nonpayment of premiums by an employee shall not constitute a break in service, for purposes of longevity, seniority under any collective bargaining agreement, or any employee benefit plan.

For purposes of pension and retirement plans, an employer shall not be required to make plan payments for an employee during the leave period, and the leave period shall not be required to be counted for purposes of time accrued under the plan. However, an employee covered by a pension plan may continue to make contributions in accordance with the terms of the plan during the period of the leave.

(f) During a family care and medical leave period, the employee shall retain employee status with the employer, and the leave shall not constitute a break in service, for purposes of longevity, seniority under any collective bargaining agreement, or any employee benefit plan. An employee returning from leave shall return with no less seniority than the employee had when the leave commenced, for purposes of layoff, recall, promotion, job assignment, and seniority-related benefits such as vacation.

(g) If the employee's need for a leave pursuant to this section is foreseeable, the employee shall provide the employer with reasonable advance notice of the need for the leave.

(h) If the employee's need for leave pursuant to this section is foreseeable due to a planned medical treatment or supervision, the employee shall make a reasonable effort to schedule the treatment or supervision to avoid disruption to the operations of the employer, subject to the approval of the health care provider of the individual requiring the treatment or supervision.

(i)(1) An employer may require that an employee's request for leave to care for a child, parent, grandparent, grandchild, sibling, spouse, * * * domestic partner, or designated person who has a serious health condition be supported by a certification issued by the health care provider of the individual requiring care. That certification shall be sufficient if it includes all of the following:

(A) The date on which the serious health condition commenced.

(B) The probable duration of the condition.

(C) An estimate of the amount of time that the health care provider believes the employee needs to care for the individual requiring the care.

(D) A statement that the serious health condition warrants the participation of a family member to provide care during a period of the treatment or supervision of the individual requiring care.

(2) Upon expiration of the time estimated by the health care provider in subparagraph (C) of paragraph (1), the employer may require the employee to obtain recertification, in accordance with the procedure provided in paragraph (1), if additional leave is required.

(j)(1) An employer may require that an employee's request for leave because of the employee's own serious health condition be supported by a certification issued by the employee's health care provider. That certification shall be sufficient if it includes all of the following:

(A) The date on which the serious health condition commenced.

(B) The probable duration of the condition.

(C) A statement that, due to the serious health condition, the employee is unable to perform the function of the employee's position.

(2) The employer may require that the employee obtain subsequent recertification regarding the employee's serious health condition on a reasonable basis, in accordance with the procedure provided in paragraph (1), if additional leave is required.

(3)(A) In any case in which the employer has reason to doubt the validity of the certification provided pursuant to this section, the employer may require, at the employer's expense, that the employee obtain the opinion of a second health care provider, designated or approved by the employer, concerning any information certified under paragraph (1).

(B) The health care provider designated or approved under subparagraph (A) shall not be employed on a regular basis by the employer.

(C) In any case in which the second opinion described in subparagraph (A) differs from the opinion in the original certification, the employer may require, at the employer's expense, that the employee obtain the opinion of a third health care provider, designated or approved jointly by the employer and the employee, concerning the information certified under paragraph (1).

(D) The opinion of the third health care provider concerning the information certified under paragraph (1) shall be considered to be final and shall be binding on the employer and the employee.

(4) As a condition of an employee's return from leave taken because of the employee's own serious health condition, the employer may have a uniformly applied practice or policy that requires the employee to obtain certification from the employee's health care

§ 12945.2

provider that the employee is able to resume work. Nothing in this paragraph shall supersede a valid collective bargaining agreement that governs the return to work of that employee.

(k) It shall be an unlawful employment practice for an employer to refuse to hire, or to discharge, fine, suspend, expel, or discriminate against, any individual because of any of the following:

(1) An individual's exercise of the right to family care and medical leave provided by subdivision (a).

(2) An individual's giving information or testimony as to the individual's own family care and medical leave, or another person's family care and medical leave, in any inquiry or proceeding related to rights guaranteed under this section.

(*l*) This section shall not be construed to require any changes in existing collective bargaining agreements during the life of the contract, or until January 1, 1993, whichever occurs first.

(m) The amendments made to this section by Chapter 827 of the Statutes of 1993 shall not be construed to require any changes in existing collective bargaining agreements during the life of the contract, or until February 5, 1994, whichever occurs first.

(n) This section shall be construed as separate and distinct from Section 12945.

(*o*) Leave provided for pursuant to this section may be taken in one or more periods. The 12-month period during which 12 workweeks of leave may be taken under this section shall run concurrently with the 12-month period under the FMLA, and shall commence the date leave taken under the FMLA commences.

(p) Leave taken by an employee pursuant to this section shall run concurrently with leave taken pursuant to the FMLA, except for any leave taken under the FMLA for disability on account of pregnancy, childbirth, or related medical conditions. The aggregate amount of leave taken under this section or the FMLA, or both, except for leave taken for disability on account of pregnancy, childbirth, or related medical conditions, shall not exceed 12 workweeks in a 12-month period. An employee is entitled to take, in addition to the leave provided for under this section and the FMLA, the leave provided for in Section 12945, if the employee is otherwise qualified for that leave.

(q) It shall be an unlawful employment practice for an employer to interfere with, restrain, or deny the exercise of, or the attempt to exercise, any right provided under this section.

(r)(1) An employee employed by an air carrier as a flight deck or cabin crew member meets the eligibility requirements specified in subdivision (a) if all of the following requirements are met:

(A) The employee has 12 months or more of service with the employer.

(B) The employee has worked or been paid for 60 percent of the applicable monthly guarantee, or the equivalent annualized over the preceding 12-month period.

(C) The employee has worked or been paid for a minimum of 504 hours during the preceding 12-month period.

(2) As used in this subdivision, the term "applicable monthly guarantee" means both of the following:

(A) For employees described in this subdivision other than employees on reserve status, the minimum number of hours for which an employer has agreed to schedule those employees for any given month.

(B) For employees described in this subdivision who are on reserve status, the number of hours for which an employer has agreed to pay those employees on reserve status for any given month, as established in the collective bargaining agreement or, if none exists, in the employer's policies.

(3) The department may provide, by regulation, a method for calculating the leave described in subdivision (a) with respect to employees described in this subdivision. *(Added by Stats.2020, c. 86 (S.B.1383), § 2, eff. Jan. 1, 2021, operative Jan. 1, 2021. Amended by Stats.2021, c. 327 (A.B.1033), § 1, eff. Jan. 1, 2022; Stats.2021, c. 401 (A.B.1578), § 17, eff. Jan. 1, 2022; Stats.2022, c. 748 (A.B.1041), § 1, eff. Jan. 1, 2023.)*

[1] For public law sections classified to the U.S.C.A., see USCA–Tables.

[2] Internal Revenue Code sections are in Title 26 of the U.S.C.A.

Cross References

Commission defined for purposes of this Part, see Government Code § 12925.
Employee defined for purposes of this Part, see Government Code § 12926.
Employer defined for purposes of this Part, see Government Code §§ 12926, 12926.2.
General occupations, sick leave, see Labor Code § 233.
Medical condition defined for purposes of this Part, see Government Code § 12926.
Organ and bone marrow donation, paid leaves of absence, leave not to be taken concurrently with leave taken pursuant to this section, see Labor Code § 1510.
Person defined for purposes of this Part, see Government Code § 12925.
Police officers, firefighters, sheriff's officers, and other personnel, leave of absence with salary in lieu of temporary disability or maintenance payments, see Labor Code § 4850.
State teachers' retirement system, credit for services in various teaching positions, see Education Code § 22803.

Research References

Forms

3A California Transactions Forms--Business Entities § 15:56, Employment Agreement for Employee-Shareholder.

§ 12947. Child care services for employees or members; not an unlawful practice

It shall not be an unlawful practice under this part for an employer or labor organization to provide or make financial provision for child care services of a custodial or other nature for its employees or members who are responsible for minor children. *(Added by Stats.1980, c. 992, § 4.)*

Cross References

Employee defined for purposes of this Part, see Government Code § 12926.
Employer defined for purposes of this Part, see Government Code §§ 12926, 12926.2.
Labor organization defined for purposes of this Part, see Government Code § 12926.

Division 5

PERSONNEL

Cross References

Board of Pilot Commissioners, appointment of additional personnel, see Harbors and Navigation Code § 1156.
Employment training panel, establishment of panel, see Unemployment Insurance Code § 10202.
Housing and home finance, bond and loan insurance, application of laws governing personnel management, see Health and Safety Code § 51637.
Industrial development financing, exemption from this division, see Government Code § 91543.
Industrial welfare commission, employment of personnel, see Labor Code § 73.
Occupational Safety and Health Standards Board, personnel, see Labor Code § 145.
State compensation insurance fund, coverage of public employers, laws applicable, see Insurance Code § 11873.
State Personnel Board, generally, see Government Code § 18650 et seq.

Succession of State Department of Public Health to duties, powers, etc. of former State Department of Alcohol and Drug Programs relating to the Office of Problem and Pathological Gambling, references to former department, deposit and use of fees, continuation of agreements, availability of unexpended funds, transfer of property, positions, and employees, continuation of regulations and lawfully commenced proceedings, see Health and Safety Code § 131055.2.

Part 2

STATE CIVIL SERVICE

Cross References

Acupuncture, administrative personnel, executive officer, see Business and Professions Code § 4934.
Aid and medical assistance, family planning, officers and employees, departmental transfer, see Welfare and Institutions Code § 14507.
Automotive repair, personnel, see Business and Professions Code § 9882.1.
Bigamy, incest, and the crime against nature, public entity employees, officers, or agents, see Penal Code § 289.6.
Board of Behavioral Sciences, personnel, see Business and Professions Code § 4990.06.
Board of Dental Examiners, transferred civil service employees, retention of positions, status, and rights, see Business and Professions Code § 160.5.
Bureau of Livestock Identification, chief, administration of bureau, appointment, see Food and Agricultural Code § 20402.
Bureau of Narcotic Enforcement, agents and employees of attorney general, see Health and Safety Code § 11450.
California African–American Museum, board of directors, see Food and Agricultural Code § 4104.
California Bay–Delta Authority, staff and administrative support, status of positions transferred from the authority, see Water Code § 79442.
California Commission on Disability Access, hiring, compliance with this Act, see Government Code § 14985.8.
California Conservation Corps, employment of staff, see Public Resources Code § 14301.
California deferred deposit transactions, enforcement, transition provisions, see Financial Code § 23073.
Cessation of coverage and operation of Federal Temporary High Risk Pool, transfer of civil service employees to California Health Benefit Exchange, see Insurance Code § 12739.61.
Commission on Health and Safety and Workers' Compensation, personnel of the commission, see Labor Code § 76.
Commission on teacher credentialing, personnel, see Education Code § 44221.
Department of Alcoholic Beverage Control, civil service personnel, see Business and Professions Code § 23054.
Department of Child Support Services, staff, see Family Code § 17314.
Department of Consumer Affairs, investigators, inspectors and deputies, see Business and Professions Code § 155.
Department of Corrections and Rehabilitation, transfer of officers or employees of predecessor entities or continuing entities who are engaged in the performance of a function specified in reorganization plan and are serving in state civil service, see Government Code § 12838.12.
Department of Pesticide Regulation, officers and employees of Department of Food and Agriculture, transfer to department, status and rights, see Food and Agricultural Code § 11458.
Department of Resources Recycling and Recovery, transfer of employees from California Integrated Waste Management Board and Department of Conservation, status, position and rights of persons transferred, see Public Resources Code § 40401.
Department of Social Services, employees, civil service, see Welfare and Institutions Code § 10555.
Department of Toxic Substances, officers and employees of state Department of Health Care Services, transfer to department, see Health and Safety Code § 58006.
Dissolution or termination of Managed Risk Medical Insurance Board, transfer of employees to State Department of Health Care Services or California Health Benefit Exchange, see Insurance Code § 12739.78.
Division of resource conservation, civil service, transfer and status of personnel, see Public Resources Code § 9069.
Duties, powers, purposes, responsibilities and jurisdiction of the Department of Toxic Substances Control, see Health and Safety Code § 58004.5.
Integrated Waste Management Board, appointment of staff, see Public Resources Code § 40431.
Occupational Safety and Health Appeals Board, personnel, see Labor Code § 148.2.
Office of environmental health hazard assessment, officers and employees of state Department of Health Care Services, transfer to office, see Health and Safety Code § 59006.
Officers and employees of Department of Corporations, transfer to Department of Managed Care, see Health and Safety Code § 1341.11.
Physical Therapy Board of California, employment of executive officer exempt from provisions of State Civil Service Act, see Business and Professions Code § 2607.5.
Professional foresters, staff personnel, executive officer, civil service, see Public Resources Code § 760.5.
Public health, general powers of the department, transfer of positions and employees, see Health and Safety Code § 131055.
San Diego River Conservancy, staffing, see Public Resources Code § 32641.
State acquisition of goods and services, federal surplus personal property, transfer of officers and employees, see Public Contract Code § 10383.7.
State Administration of Health Care Services and Medical Assistance, transfer of officers and employees, see Welfare and Institutions Code § 10724.
State Bar, laws applicable, see Business and Professions Code § 6001.
State personnel board, meetings, see Government Code § 18653.
Succession of State Department of Health Care Services to duties, powers, etc. of former State Department of Alcohol and Drug Programs, references to former department, continuation of agreements, availability of unexpended funds, transfer of property, positions, and employees, continuation of regulations and lawfully commenced proceedings, see Health and Safety Code § 11751.
Transfer of services and responsibilities from Public Safety Communications Division to the Office of Emergency Services, transfer of employees and property, see Government Code § 15280.
Unemployment compensation, employment for older workers, formulation of policies, see Unemployment Insurance Code § 2074.
Workers' compensation administrative law judges, eligible lists, qualifications, see Labor Code § 123.5.
Yacht and ship brokers, director, powers, see Harbors and Navigation Code § 703.

CHAPTER 10. PROHIBITIONS AND OFFENSES

ARTICLE 2. DISCRIMINATION

Section
19702.3. Family care leave; exercise of rights; giving information or testimony in inquiry.

Cross References

Discriminatory rejection of probationer, prohibited, see Government Code § 19173.
Forms, use by state agencies of approved employment or occupational licensing or registration forms as subject to enforcement under this Article, see Government Code § 18720.5.

§ 19702.3. Family care leave; exercise of rights; giving information or testimony in inquiry

(a) An appointing authority shall not refuse to hire, and shall not discharge, suspend, expel, or discriminate against, any individual because of any of the following:

(1) An individual's exercise of the right to family care leave provided by subdivision (a) of Section 12945.2.

(2) An individual's giving information or testimony as to his or her own family care leave, or another person's family care leave, in any inquiry or proceeding related to rights guaranteed under Section 12945.2.

(b) This section shall not be construed to require any changes in existing collective bargaining agreements during the life of the contract, or until January 1, 1993, whichever occurs first. *(Added by Stats.1991, c. 462 (A.B.77), § 5. Amended by Stats.1994, c. 1232 (A.B.3619), § 1.)*

§ 19702.3

Cross References

Citation of this section as Moore-Brown-Roberti Family Rights Act, see Government Code § 12945.1.

Organ and bone marrow donation, paid leaves of absence, leave not to be taken concurrently with leave taken pursuant to this section, see Labor Code § 1510.

Pregnancy, childbirth or related medical condition, actions constituting unlawful employment practice, employees taking leave under this section, see Government Code § 12945.

Research References

Forms

3A California Transactions Forms--Business Entities § 15:56, Employment Agreement for Employee-Shareholder.

Title 3

GOVERNMENT OF COUNTIES

Cross References

Local agency public construction act, public works contracts, generally, see Public Contract Code § 20120.

Division 2

OFFICERS

Part 3

OTHER OFFICERS

CHAPTER 3. COUNTY CLERK

ARTICLE 2. FEES

Section
26840. Marriage license; disposition of fees.
26840.1. Marriage certificate.
26840.2. Marriage license; issuance outside of normal business hours; additional fee.
26840.3. Increase of fees for support of family conciliation court and mediation services.
26840.7. Marriage license; additional fee upon issuance; use of fee.
26840.8. Marriage authorization; additional fee upon filing; use of fee.
26840.10. Alameda County Board of Supervisors; domestic violence; fee increase for marriage and confidential marriage licenses; collection.
26840.11. Solano County Board of Supervisors; domestic violence; fee increase for marriage and confidential marriage licenses; collection; preliminary and followup reports.
26861. Performance of marriage.

Cross References

County officers' fees, see Government Code § 24350 et seq.
Fees, generally, see Government Code § 6100 et seq.

§ 26840. Marriage license; disposition of fees

The fee for issuing a marriage license is ten dollars ($10), to be collected at the time it is issued. One dollar ($1) of this fee shall be paid to the county recorder, one dollar ($1) of this fee shall be paid to the county clerk, and one dollar ($1) of this fee shall be paid to the State Registrar of Vital Statistics and seven dollars ($7) of this fee shall be disposed of pursuant to the provisions of Section 54 of Chapter 120, Statutes of 1966, First Extraordinary Session. In counties where the salary of the county recorder is the sole compensation allowed by law, this fee shall be paid to the county treasurer who shall credit one dollar ($1) to the county recorder and shall pay one dollar ($1) to the State Registrar of Vital Statistics.

The fee provided by this section is in full for all services of the clerk and recorder in connection with the issuance of a marriage license and the filing of a certificate of registry of marriage. *(Added by Stats.1947, c. 424, p. 1148, § 1. Amended by Stats.1947, c. 1303, p. 2840, § 1; Stats.1966, 1st Ex.Sess., c. 120, p. 604, § 39; Stats.1967, c. 1500, p. 3509, § 6, operative Jan. 1, 1968; Stats.1979, c. 139, p. 327, § 3.)*

Cross References

Annual adjustments, fees and charges for record search or issuance of certificates, permits, registrations or other documents, see Health and Safety Code § 100430.

Authentication of marriage, generally, see Family Code § 306.

California Department of Health Care Services, fees or charges for issuance and renewal of documents, marriage license fee, see Health and Safety Code § 100435.

Certificate of registry, see Health and Safety Code §§ 103125, 103175.

Domestic Violence Shelter-Based Programs Act, additional marriage license fees, deposit into domestic violence shelter-based programs special fund, see Welfare and Institutions Code § 18305.

Marriage license,
 Filing with county recorder, see Family Code § 423.
 Necessity of, see Family Code § 350.
 Registering, see Health and Safety Code § 103150.

References to "spouse" and "marriage" as including domestic partners and partnerships, see Government Code § 20065.5.

§ 26840.1. Marriage certificate

(a) The fee for filing a marriage certificate pursuant to Part 4 (commencing with Section 500) of Division 3 of the Family Code is fourteen dollars ($14), to be collected at the time an authorization for the performance of the marriage is issued or a blank authorization form is obtained from the county clerk pursuant to Part 4 (commencing with Section 500) of Division 3 of the Family Code. Four dollars ($4) of the fee shall be paid to the State Registrar of Vital Statistics. One dollar ($1) of the fee shall be paid to the county treasurer and shall be used to defray any local costs incurred pursuant to Part 4 (commencing with Section 500) of Division 3 of the Family Code.

(b) Notwithstanding subdivision (a), in addition to the amount authorized by subdivision (a) the county clerk may impose an additional amount, not to exceed three dollars ($3), if he or she determines that the additional amount is necessary to defray local costs. *(Added by Stats.1971, c. 1244, p. 2444, § 2. Amended by Stats.1979, c. 139, p. 327, § 4; Stats.1981, c. 872, p. 3336, § 3; Stats.1992, c. 163 (A.B.2641), § 81, operative Jan. 1, 1994.)*

Cross References

Application of Trial Court Trust Fund depositary provision to specified fees and fines, see Government Code § 68085.7.

Confidential marriage, issuance of confidential marriage license upon request of notary public, fees, see Family Code § 503.

Confidential marriage, issuance of license, see Family Code § 501.

Deposit of fees or fines collected pursuant to this section in the Trial Court Trust Fund, effect of prior agreements or practices, long-term revenue allocation schedule proposal, see Government Code § 68085.5.

References to "spouse" and "marriage" as including domestic partners and partnerships, see Government Code § 20065.5.

§ 26840.2. Marriage license; issuance outside of normal business hours; additional fee

Whenever the board of supervisors of a county makes provision by ordinance for the issuance of marriage licenses outside of the normal business hours, the board may establish a fee, in addition to that provided in Section 26840, not to exceed five dollars ($5), which shall be paid to the county treasury. (Added by Stats.1971, c. 1527, p. 3019, § 1. Amended by Stats.1981, c. 199, p. 1123, § 1.)

Cross References

References to "spouse" and "marriage" as including domestic partners and partnerships, see Government Code § 20065.5.

§ 26840.3. Increase of fees for support of family conciliation court and mediation services

(a) For the support of the family conciliation court or for conciliation and mediation services provided pursuant to Chapter 11 (commencing with Section 3160) of Part 2 of Division 8 of the Family Code, to provide all space costs and indirect overhead costs from other sources, the board of supervisors in any county may increase:

(1) The fee for issuing a marriage license, by an amount not to exceed five dollars ($5).

(2) The fee for issuing a marriage certificate pursuant to Part 4 (commencing with Section 500) of Division 3 of the Family Code, by an amount not to exceed five dollars ($5).

(b) The county shall distribute the moneys received under subdivision (a) to the court to be used exclusively to pay the costs of maintaining the family conciliation court or conciliation and mediation services provided pursuant to Chapter 11 (commencing with Section 3160) of Part 2 of Division 8 of the Family Code. (Added by Stats.1976, c. 1356, p. 6180, § 1. Amended by Stats.1977, c. 786, p. 2430, § 1; Stats.1980, c. 48, p. 134, § 6, eff. March 27, 1980; Stats.1982, c. 1071, p. 3855, § 2; Stats.1983, c. 1277, § 2; Stats.1992, c. 163 (A.B.2641), § 82; Stats.1992, c. 696 (A.B.1344), § 19, eff. Sept. 15, 1992; Stats.1993, c. 219 (A.B.1500), § 214; Stats.2005, c. 75 (A.B.145), § 83, eff. July 19, 2005, operative Jan. 1, 2006.)

Cross References

Confidential marriage, issuance of license, see Family Code § 501.

References to "spouse" and "marriage" as including domestic partners and partnerships, see Government Code § 20065.5.

§ 26840.7. Marriage license; additional fee upon issuance; use of fee

In addition to the fee prescribed by Section 26840 and as authorized by Section 26840.3, the county clerk shall collect a fee of twenty-three dollars ($23) at the time of issuance of the license. The fee shall be disposed of by the clerk pursuant to Chapter 5 (commencing with Section 18290) of Part 6 of Division 9 of the Welfare and Institutions Code. Of this amount, four dollars ($4) shall be used, to the extent feasible, to develop or expand domestic violence shelter-based programs to target underserved areas and populations. (Added by Stats.1980, c. 146, p. 339, § 1, eff. June 4, 1980. Amended by Stats.1982, c. 522, p. 2450, § 1; Stats.1984, c. 112, § 1; Stats.1992, c. 916 (S.B.5), § 1; Stats.1993, c. 420 (S.B.5), § 1; Stats.2006, c. 857 (A.B.2084), § 1.)

§ 26840.8. Marriage authorization; additional fee upon filing; use of fee

In addition to the fee prescribed by Section 26840.1 and as authorized by Section 26840.3, the person issuing an authorization for the performance of a marriage pursuant to Part 4 (commencing with Section 500) of Division 3 of the Family Code or the county clerk, upon providing a blank authorization form pursuant to Part 4 (commencing with Section 500) of Division 3 of the Family Code, shall collect a fee of twenty-three dollars ($23) at the time of providing the authorization. The fee shall be disposed of pursuant to Chapter 5 (commencing with Section 18290) of Part 6 of Division 9 of the Welfare and Institutions Code. Of this amount, four dollars ($4) shall be used, to the extent feasible, to develop or expand domestic violence shelter-based programs to target underserved areas and populations. (Added by Stats.1980, c. 146, p. 339, § 1.5, eff. June 4, 1980. Amended by Stats.1981, c. 872, p. 3337, § 4; Stats.1982, c. 449, p. 1819, § 2; Stats.1982, c. 522, p. 2450, § 2.5; Stats.1984, c. 112, § 2; Stats.1992, c. 163 (A.B.2641), § 83, operative Jan. 1, 1994; Stats.1992, c. 916 (S.B.5), § 2; Stats.1993, c. 420 (S.B.5), § 2; Stats.2006, c. 857 (A.B.2084), § 2.)

Cross References

References to "spouse" and "marriage" as including domestic partners and partnerships, see Government Code § 20065.5.

§ 26840.10. Alameda County Board of Supervisors; domestic violence; fee increase for marriage and confidential marriage licenses; collection

(a) The Alameda County Board of Supervisors, upon making findings and declarations for the need for governmental oversight and coordination of the multiple agencies dealing with domestic violence, may authorize an increase in the fees for marriage licenses and confidential marriage licenses, up to a maximum increase of two dollars ($2).

(b) Effective July 1 of each year, the Alameda County Board of Supervisors may authorize an increase in these fees by an amount equal to the increase in the Consumer Price Index for the San Francisco metropolitan area for the preceding calendar year, rounded to the nearest half-dollar ($0.50). The fees shall be allocated pursuant to Section 18309 of the Welfare and Institutions Code.

(c) In addition to the fee prescribed by Section 26840.1, in Alameda County, the person issuing authorization for the performance of a marriage or confidential marriage, or the county clerk upon providing a blank authorization form pursuant to Part 4 (commencing with Section 500) of Division 3 of the Family Code, shall collect the fees specified in subdivisions (a) and (b), at the time of providing the authorization.

(d) This section shall become operative on January 1, 2015. (Added by Stats.2009, c. 215 (A.B.73), § 3, operative Jan. 1, 2015.)

Cross References

References to "spouse" and "marriage" as including domestic partners and partnerships, see Government Code § 20065.5.

§ 26840.11. Solano County Board of Supervisors; domestic violence; fee increase for marriage and confidential marriage licenses; collection; preliminary and followup reports

(a) The Solano County Board of Supervisors, upon making findings and declarations for the need for governmental oversight and coordination of the multiple agencies dealing with domestic violence, may authorize an increase in the fees for marriage licenses and confidential marriage licenses, up to a maximum increase of two dollars ($2).

(b) Effective July 1 of each year, the Solano County Board of Supervisors may authorize an increase in these fees by an amount equal to the increase in the Consumer Price Index for the San Francisco metropolitan area for the preceding calendar year, rounded to the nearest one-half dollar ($0.50). The fees shall be allocated pursuant to Section 18309.5 of the Welfare and Institutions Code.

(c) In addition to the fee prescribed by Section 26840.1, in Solano County, the person issuing authorization for the performance of a marriage or confidential marriage, or the county clerk upon provid-

§ 26840.11

ing a blank authorization form pursuant to Part 4 (commencing with Section 500) of Division 3 of the Family Code, shall collect the fees specified in subdivisions (a) and (b), at the time of providing the authorization.

(d) The Solano County Board of Supervisors shall submit to the Assembly and Senate Committees on Judiciary, no later than July 1, 2009, a preliminary report and a followup report no later than July 1, 2014, containing the following information:

(1) The annual amounts of funds received and expended from fee increases for the purpose of governmental oversight and coordination of domestic violence prevention, intervention, and prosecution efforts in the county.

(2) Outcomes achieved as a result of the activities associated with the implementation of this section. *(Added by Stats.2004, c. 830 (A.B.2010), § 3. Amended by Stats.2009, c. 356 (S.B.635), § 1; Stats.2010, c. 520 (S.B.1222), § 1; Stats.2011, c. 120 (S.B.154), § 1.)*

Cross References

References to "spouse" and "marriage" as including domestic partners and partnerships, see Government Code § 20065.5.

§ 26861. Performance of marriage

A fee of fifteen dollars ($15) may be charged for performing a marriage ceremony pursuant to Section 401 of the Family Code, which shall be paid into the county treasury. *(Added by Stats.1973, c. 979, p. 1885, § 3. Amended by Stats.1974, c. 974, p. 2023, § 1; Stats.1979, c. 139, p. 328, § 11; Stats.1992, c. 163 (A.B.2641), § 85, operative Jan. 1, 1994.)*

Cross References

References to "spouse" and "marriage" as including domestic partners and partnerships, see Government Code § 20065.5.

Division 4

EMPLOYEES

Part 3

RETIREMENT SYSTEMS

CHAPTER 4. COUNTY PEACE OFFICERS RETIREMENT LAW

Cross References

Disability retirement, death or illness related to exposure to biological agents, see Government Code § 31720.9.

ARTICLE 7. BENEFITS

Section
32056. Death or disability in performance of duty; payment of pension to family; amounts; effect of remarriage of beneficiary.

§ 32056. Death or disability in performance of duty; payment of pension to family; amounts; effect of remarriage of beneficiary

Whenever any member or pensioner is killed, or dies as a result of any injury received during the performance of his duty, or from sickness caused by the discharge of such duty, or after retirement for service connected disability, an annual pension shall be paid in equal monthly installments to his widow or widower in an amount equal to one-half of his terminal salary, not to exceed two hundred fifty dollars ($250) a month. The pension shall be paid to the widow or widower during her or his lifetime or until he or she remarries. Thereafter, or if there is no widow or widower entitled to receive the pension, it shall be paid to such of his children, through their guardian, as are under eighteen years of age, to be equally divided among them in the following amounts:

For one child	$ 50
For two children	$ 75
For three or more children	$100

A widow or widower of a pensioner is not entitled to a pension unless she or he was married to the deceased pensioner at least five years prior to the date of his retirement. If the widow, widower, child, or children marry, the pension paid to the person so marrying shall cease. *(Added by Stats.1947, c. 424, p. 1294, § 1. Amended by Stats.1947, c. 1483, p. 3071, § 8; Stats.1949, c. 1367, p. 2378, § 1.)*

Cross References

Member defined for purposes of this Chapter, see Government Code § 31907.
Pensioner defined for purposes of this Chapter, see Government Code § 31906.
Terminal salary defined for purposes of this Chapter, see Government Code § 31905.

CHAPTER 5. COUNTY FIRE SERVICE RETIREMENT LAW

Cross References

Disability retirement, death or illness related to exposure to biological agents, see Government Code § 31720.9.

ARTICLE 6. BENEFITS

Section
32355. Payment of pension to family of member from death in performance of duty; amounts; conditions; effect of remarriage of beneficiary.

§ 32355. Payment of pension to family of member from death in performance of duty; amounts; conditions; effect of remarriage of beneficiary

Whenever any member is killed, or dies, as a result of any injury received during the performance of his duty, or from sickness caused by the discharge of such duty, or after retirement for service connected disability, an annual pension shall be paid in equal monthly installments to his widow, or child, or children, in an amount equal to one-half of his terminal salary, not to exceed two hundred fifty dollars ($250) a month. The pension shall be paid to the widow, during her lifetime or until she remarries. Thereafter, or if there is no widow qualified to receive the pension, it shall be paid to such of his children, through their guardian, as are under eighteen years of age, to be equally divided among them in the following amounts:

For one child	$ 50
For two children	$ 75
For three or more children	$100

A widow of a pensioner is not entitled to a pension unless she was married to the deceased pensioner at least five years prior to the date of his retirement. If the widow, widower, child, or children marry, the pension paid to the person so marrying shall cease. If a member is subject to the provisions of Section 32341 and does not exercise the option provided for therein, the amount shall not exceed one hundred fifty dollars ($150) per month. *(Added by Stats.1947, c. 424, p. 1305, § 1. Amended by Stats.1949, c. 1367, p. 2379, § 3; Stats.1949, c. 1369, p. 2384, § 13.)*

Cross References

Member defined for purposes of this Chapter, see Government Code § 32209.

Title 5

LOCAL AGENCIES

Cross References
Local Agency Allocation Law, see Government Code § 15500 et seq.

Division 1

CITIES AND COUNTIES

Part 1

POWERS AND DUTIES COMMON TO CITIES AND COUNTIES

CHAPTER 4. POLICE OFFICERS' PENSION FUND AND FIREMEN'S PENSION FUND

ARTICLE 3. PENSIONS AND DEATH BENEFITS

Section
50880. Marriage of surviving spouse or child receiving pension.

§ 50880. Marriage of surviving spouse or child receiving pension

If the surviving spouse or a child marries, the pension to such person ceases. *(Added by Stats.1949, c. 81, p. 275, § 1. Amended by Stats.1976, c. 1436, p. 6435, § 29.)*

Title 8

THE ORGANIZATION AND GOVERNMENT OF COURTS

Cross References
Authority to increase or decrease fees or charges, see Government Code § 54985.

CHAPTER 2. THE JUDICIAL COUNCIL

Cross References
Actions by or against a city or county, assignment of judges, see Code of Civil Procedure § 394.
Court unable to hear criminal case within 30 days, see Penal Code § 1050.
Death or inability of trial judge in criminal proceedings, see Penal Code § 1053.
Designation of judges, appellate department of superior court, see Code of Civil Procedure § 77.
Disqualification of judges, see Code of Civil Procedure § 170.
Distribution of business by presiding judges of superior courts, see Government Code § 69508.
Indictment or information against superior court judge, see Penal Code § 1029.
Judge's Retirement Law,
   Disregard of assignment by Judicial Council, see Government Code § 75028.
   Retired judges, assignment by chairman of Judicial Council, see Government Code § 68543.5.
Rules of court,
   Adoption, effective date, see Government Code § 68072.
   Appellate procedure, see Code of Civil Procedure § 901 et seq.; Penal Code § 1247k.
   Authority to make, restrictions, see Government Code § 68070.
   Filing, public examination, see Government Code § 68071.
Trial by temporary judge, see Cal. Const. Art. 6, § 21.

ARTICLE 3. COORDINATED EDUCATIONAL PROGRAMS FOR THE JUDICIARY

Section
68551. Institutes and seminars; purpose; scope; expenses.
68552. Publication and distribution of educational materials.
68553. Family law training.
68553.5. Juvenile delinquency proceedings; mental health and developmental disability issues.
68554. Leave of absence for study; compensation, service toward retirement, and term of office.
68555. Domestic violence training programs.

§ 68551. Institutes and seminars; purpose; scope; expenses

The Judicial Council is authorized to conduct institutes and seminars from time to time, either regionally or on a statewide basis, for the purpose of orienting judges to new judicial assignments, keeping them informed concerning new developments in the law and promoting uniformity in judicial procedure. Such institutes and seminars shall include, without being limited thereto, consideration of juvenile court proceedings, sentencing practices in criminal cases and the handling of traffic cases. Actual and necessary expenses incurred by superior and municipal court judges at any such institute or seminar shall be a charge against the county to the extent that funds are available therefor. *(Added by Stats.1965, c. 412, p. 1727, § 2, eff. May 29, 1965. Amended by Stats.1998, c. 931 (S.B.2139), § 246, eff. Sept. 28, 1998.)*

Cross References
Annual sentencing institutes for trial judges, see Penal Code § 1170.5.

§ 68552. Publication and distribution of educational materials

In carrying out its duties under this article, the Judicial Council may publish and distribute manuals, guides, checklists and other materials designed to assist the judiciary. *(Added by Stats.1965, c. 412, p. 1727, § 2, eff. May 29, 1965.)*

§ 68553. Family law training

(a) The Judicial Council shall establish judicial training programs for judges, referees, commissioners, mediators, and others who are deemed appropriate who perform duties in family law matters.

(b) The training shall include a family law session in any orientation session conducted for newly appointed or elected judges and an annual training session in family law.

(c) The training shall include instruction in all aspects of family law, including effects of gender, gender identity, and sexual orientation on family law proceedings, the economic effects of dissolution on the involved parties, and, on and after July 1, 1994, the effects of allegations of child abuse or neglect made during family law proceedings. *(Added by Stats.1987, c. 1134, § 2. Amended by Stats.1994, c. 688 (A.B.2845), § 2; Stats.2013, c. 300 (A.B.868), § 1.)*

§ 68553.5. Juvenile delinquency proceedings; mental health and developmental disability issues

To the extent resources are available, the Judicial Council shall provide education on mental health and developmental disability issues affecting juveniles in delinquency proceedings pursuant to Section 602 of the Welfare and Institutions Code to judicial officers and, as appropriate, to other public officers and entities that may be involved in the arrest, evaluation, prosecution, defense, disposition, and postdisposition or placement phases of delinquency proceedings. The education shall include, to the extent possible, using available resources, information on the early identification of mental illness or developmental disability in delinquency proceedings, on statutory and case law providing for the assessment or evaluation of minors with mental health problems or developmental disabilities, on specialized adjudication or disposition procedures, such as mental health courts, that may apply to these minors, and on appropriate programs, services, and placements for minors with mental health problems or developmental disabilities, including information on the benefits and detriments of placing minors with mental health problems or developmental disabilities in secure juvenile justice facilities, such as the Department of the Youth Authority. *(Added by Stats.2005, c. 265 (S.B.570), § 2.)*

Cross References

Children's Mental Health Services Act, see Welfare and Institutions Code § 5850 et seq.
Mental health evaluations, recommendations, and dispositional procedures for minors, see Welfare and Institutions Code § 710 et seq.

§ 68554. Leave of absence for study; compensation, service toward retirement, and term of office

Notwithstanding subdivisions (f) and (g) of Section 1770, the Judicial Council may grant any judge a leave of absence for a period not to exceed one year for the purpose of permitting study which will benefit the administration of justice and the individual's performance of judicial duties, upon a finding that the absence will not work to the detriment of the court. During a study leave, the judge shall receive no compensation, nor shall the period of absence count as service toward retirement, but the time of leave shall not toll the term of office. *(Added by Stats.1992, c. 1199 (A.B.2409), § 4, eff. Sept. 30, 1992.)*

§ 68555. Domestic violence training programs

The Judicial Council shall establish judicial training programs for individuals who perform duties in domestic violence matters, including, but not limited to, judges, referees, commissioners, mediators, and others as deemed appropriate by the Judicial Council. The training programs shall include a domestic violence session in any orientation session conducted for newly appointed or elected judges and an annual training session in domestic violence. The training programs shall include instruction in all aspects of domestic violence, including, but not limited to, the detriment to children of residing with a person who perpetrates domestic violence and that domestic violence can occur without a party seeking or obtaining a restraining order, without a substantiated child protective services finding, and without other documented evidence of abuse. *(Added by Stats.1996, c. 695 (A.B.2819), § 1. Amended by Stats.2018, c. 941 (A.B.2044), § 5, eff. Jan. 1, 2019.)*

HEALTH AND SAFETY CODE

Division 2

LICENSING PROVISIONS

Cross References

Attorneys, fee agreements, limitations, see Business and Professions Code § 6146.
Confidentiality of medical information, see Civil Code § 56.05.
Disclosure of medical records to law enforcement agencies, see Penal Code § 1545 et seq.
Employment of certified polysomnographic technologist by clinic or health facility, see Business and Professions Code § 3578.
Grant or renewal of staff privileges for certain medical professionals, see Business and Professions Code § 805.5.
Health care providers,
  Claims for punitive damages, see Code of Civil Procedure § 425.13.
  Noneconomic losses, limitation, see Civil Code § 3333.2.
  Notice of intention, see Code of Civil Procedure § 364.
  Professional negligence or malpractice, exemption from liability, see Civil Code § 1714.8.
Immunity from liability of clinic, health dispensary or health facility licensed under this division for professional negligence due to unsolicited referral from tests by multiphasic screening unit, see Civil Code § 43.9.
Judgments, action against health care provider, see Code of Civil Procedure § 667.7.
Life and disability insurance, sale, lease, or transfer of list of contracted health care providers and their reimbursement rates, see Insurance Code § 10178.3.
Medi–Cal benefits program, assisted living demonstration project, see Welfare and Institutions Code § 14132.26.
Personal rights, information to be provided to a complainant, see Civil Code § 43.96.
Pharmacy,
  Exemptions, see Business and Professions Code § 4057.
  Facilities, licensed clinics, see Business and Professions Code § 4027.
  Records and hours, violation, see Business and Professions Code § 4081.
Privately owned and operated detention facilities, facilities exempt from prohibition, see Penal Code § 9502.
Psychologists, refusal to comply with request for medical records of patient, see Business and Professions Code § 2969.
Sale, lease, or transfer of list of contracted health care providers and their reimbursement rates, disclosures and other requirements, see Labor Code § 4609.
Sale of list of contracted health care providers and their reimbursement rates, see Business and Professions Code § 511.1.

CHAPTER 2. HEALTH FACILITIES

Cross References

Aid and medical assistance, reimbursement requests, see Welfare and Institutions Code § 14045.
Attorney General, authorization to inspect business locations of Medi–Cal providers, see Government Code § 12528.1.
Contracts with state departments to provide or administer certain programs exempt from the requirements of this Chapter, see Government Code § 30029.3.
Legal and civil rights of persons involuntarily detained, authorized disclosure of confidential information and records, see Welfare and Institutions Code § 5328.15.
Legislative findings, definitions, PPE stockpile, distribution, guidelines, establishment of the Personal Protective Equipment Advisory Committee, see Health and Safety Code § 131021.
Medical foster homes for veterans, license application procedure, see Health and Safety Code § 1568.24.
Revocation of previous license issued under this chapter, exclusion from medical foster home for veterans, see Health and Safety Code § 1568.296.
Standards for the collection, processing, storage, or distribution of human milk collected from a mother for exclusive use by her own child, see Health and Safety Code § 1648.

ARTICLE 1. GENERAL

Section
1254.4. Irreversible cessation of all brain function; patient declared dead; period of accommodation for next of kin; continuation of cardiopulmonary support; written statement; special religious or cultural practices; considerations; right of action prohibited.
1254.6. Sudden infant death syndrome; hospitals to provide free of charge information upon discharge of infant.
1255.7. Safe-surrender sites; surrender of physical custody of minor 72 hours old or younger by parent or legal custodian; duties of personnel; actions of child protective services; return of child.
1256.2. Differing standards of obstetrical care based on source of payment and ability to pay not allowed; written policy statement; posting written notices; unprofessional conduct to deny or threaten to withhold pain management services.
1257.9. Training for hospital staff on hospital policies and recommendations that promote breast-feeding.
1258. Sterilization for contraceptive purposes; prohibition against nonmedical qualifications; exceptions.
1259.5. Spousal or partner abuse detection; policies and procedures.
1261. Visitation rights of domestic partners, domestic partner's children, and domestic partner of patient's parent or child.
1264. Prenatal screening ultrasound to detect congenital heart defects; necessity of sonographer; supervision; qualifications; policies and procedures.

Cross References

Certificate of authority, suspension or revocation for noncompliance with this chapter, see Health and Safety Code § 1793.21.
Confidential information, use, see Welfare and Institutions Code § 5328.15.
Confidential information and records on developmentally disability services, see Welfare and Institutions Code § 4514.
Evidence in personal injury action against health care provider, see Civil Code § 3333.1.
Failure of health facility to obtain certificate of need, denial of Medi–Cal payments, see Welfare and Institutions Code § 14105.6.
Funeral Directors and Embalmers Laws, exemption from provision of this chapter, see Business and Professions Code § 7609.
Hospital building used as health facility, see Health and Safety Code § 129725.
Immunity from liability of clinic, health dispensary or health facility for professional negligence due to unsolicited referral from tests by multiphasic screening unit, see Civil Code § 43.9.
Incidental medical services, see Health and Safety Code § 1507.
Medical malpractice insurance, explanation of rates, see Insurance Code § 11587.
Projects requiring a certificate of need, see Health and Safety Code § 127170.
Provisional license, see Health and Safety Code § 1437.
Special fee charged to health facilities, see Health and Safety Code § 127280.
Standardized procedures, see Business and Professions Code § 2725.

§ 1254.4. Irreversible cessation of all brain function; patient declared dead; period of accommodation for next of kin; continuation of cardiopulmonary support; written statement; special religious or cultural practices; considerations; right of action prohibited

(a) A general acute care hospital shall adopt a policy for providing family or next of kin with a reasonably brief period of accommodation, as described in subdivision (b), from the time that a patient is declared dead by reason of irreversible cessation of all functions of the entire brain, including the brain stem, in accordance with Section 7180, through discontinuation of cardiopulmonary support for the patient. During this reasonably brief period of accommodation, a hospital is required to continue only previously ordered cardiopulmonary support. No other medical intervention is required.

(b) For purposes of this section, a "reasonably brief period" means an amount of time afforded to gather family or next of kin at the patient's bedside.

(c)(1) A hospital subject to this section shall provide the patient's legally recognized health care decisionmaker, if any, or the patient's family or next of kin, if available, with a written statement of the policy described in subdivision (a), upon request, but no later than shortly after the treating physician has determined that the potential for brain death is imminent.

(2) If the patient's legally recognized health care decisionmaker, family, or next of kin voices any special religious or cultural practices and concerns of the patient or the patient's family surrounding the issue of death by reason of irreversible cessation of all functions of the entire brain of the patient, the hospital shall make reasonable efforts to accommodate those religious and cultural practices and concerns.

(d) For purposes of this section, in determining what is reasonable, a hospital shall consider the needs of other patients and prospective patients in urgent need of care.

(e) There shall be no private right of action to sue pursuant to this section. *(Added by Stats.2008, c. 465 (A.B.2565), § 1.)*

§ 1254.6. Sudden infant death syndrome; hospitals to provide free of charge information upon discharge of infant

(a) A hospital shall provide, free of charge, information and instructional materials regarding sudden infant death syndrome, as described in Section 1596.847, explaining the medical effects upon infants and young children and emphasizing measures that may reduce the risk.

(b) The information and materials described in subdivision (a) shall be provided to parents or guardians of each newborn, upon discharge from the hospital. In the event of home birth attended by a licensed midwife, the midwife shall provide the information and instructional materials to the parents or guardians of the newborn.

(c) To the maximum extent practicable, the materials provided to parents or guardians of each newborn shall substantially reflect the information contained in materials approved by the state department for public circulation. The state department shall make available to hospitals, free of charge, information in camera-ready typesetting format. Nothing in this section prohibits a hospital from obtaining free and suitable information from any other public or private agency. *(Added by Stats.1997, c. 263 (A.B.757), § 2.)*

§ 1255.7. Safe-surrender sites; surrender of physical custody of minor 72 hours old or younger by parent or legal custodian; duties of personnel; actions of child protective services; return of child

(a)(1) For purposes of this section, "safe-surrender site" means either of the following:

(A) A location designated by the board of supervisors of a county or by a local fire agency, upon the approval of the appropriate local governing body of the agency, to be responsible for accepting physical custody of a minor child who is 72 hours old or younger from a parent or individual who has lawful custody of the child and who surrenders the child pursuant to Section 271.5 of the Penal Code. Before designating a location as a safe-surrender site pursuant to this subdivision, the designating entity shall consult with the governing body of a city, if the site is within the city limits, and with representatives of a fire department and a child welfare agency that may provide services to a child who is surrendered at the site, if that location is selected.

(B) A location within a public or private hospital that is designated by that hospital to be responsible for accepting physical custody of a minor child who is 72 hours old or younger from a parent or individual who has lawful custody of the child and who surrenders the child pursuant to Section 271.5 of the Penal Code.

(2) For purposes of this section, "parent" means a birth parent of a minor child who is 72 hours old or younger.

(3) For purposes of this section, "personnel" means a person who is an officer or employee of a safe-surrender site or who has staff privileges at the site.

(4) A hospital and a safe-surrender site designated by the county board of supervisors or by a local fire agency, upon the approval of the appropriate local governing body of the agency, shall post a sign displaying a statewide logo that has been adopted by the State Department of Social Services that notifies the public of the location where a minor child 72 hours old or younger may be safely surrendered pursuant to this section.

(b) Personnel on duty at a safe-surrender site shall accept physical custody of a minor child 72 hours old or younger pursuant to this section if a parent or other individual having lawful custody of the child voluntarily surrenders physical custody of the child to personnel who are on duty at the safe-surrender site. Safe-surrender site personnel shall ensure that a qualified person does all of the following:

(1) Places a coded, confidential ankle bracelet on the child.

(2) Provides, or makes a good faith effort to provide, to the parent or other individual surrendering the child a copy of a unique, coded, confidential ankle bracelet identification in order to facilitate reclaiming the child pursuant to subdivision (f). However, possession of the ankle bracelet identification, in and of itself, does not establish parentage or a right to custody of the child.

(3) Provides, or makes a good faith effort to provide, to the parent or other individual surrendering the child a medical information questionnaire, which may be declined, voluntarily filled out and returned at the time the child is surrendered, or later filled out and mailed in the envelope provided for this purpose. This medical information questionnaire shall not require identifying information about the child or the parent or individual surrendering the child, other than the identification code provided in the ankle bracelet placed on the child. Every questionnaire provided pursuant to this section shall begin with the following notice in no less than 12–point type:

"NOTICE: THE BABY YOU HAVE BROUGHT IN TODAY MAY HAVE SERIOUS MEDICAL NEEDS IN THE FUTURE THAT WE DON'T KNOW ABOUT TODAY. SOME ILLNESSES, INCLUDING CANCER, ARE BEST TREATED WHEN WE KNOW ABOUT FAMILY MEDICAL HISTORIES. IN ADDITION, SOMETIMES RELATIVES ARE NEEDED FOR LIFE-SAVING TREATMENTS. TO MAKE SURE THIS BABY WILL HAVE A HEALTHY FUTURE, YOUR ASSISTANCE IN COMPLETING THIS QUESTIONNAIRE FULLY IS ESSENTIAL. THANK YOU."

(c) Personnel of a safe-surrender site that has physical custody of a minor child pursuant to this section shall ensure that a medical screening examination and any necessary medical care is provided to the minor child. Notwithstanding any other provision of law, the consent of the parent or other relative shall not be required to provide that care to the minor child.

(d)(1) As soon as possible, but in no event later than 48 hours after the physical custody of a child has been accepted pursuant to this section, personnel of the safe-surrender site that has physical custody of the child shall notify child protective services or a county agency providing child welfare services pursuant to Section 16501 of the Welfare and Institutions Code, that the safe-surrender site has physical custody of the child pursuant to this section. In addition, medical information pertinent to the child's health, including, but not limited to, information obtained pursuant to the medical information questionnaire described in paragraph (3) of subdivision (b) that has been received by or is in the possession of the safe-surrender site shall be provided to that child protective services or county agency.

(2) Any personal identifying information that pertains to a parent or individual who surrenders a child that is obtained pursuant to the medical information questionnaire is confidential and shall be exempt from disclosure by the child protective services or county agency under the California Public Records Act (Division 10 (commencing with Section 7920.000) of Title 1 of the Government Code). Personal identifying information that pertains to a parent or individual who surrenders a child shall be redacted from any medical information provided to child protective services or the county agency providing child welfare services.

(e) Child protective services or the county agency providing child welfare services pursuant to Section 16501 of the Welfare and Institutions Code shall assume temporary custody of the child pursuant to Section 300 of the Welfare and Institutions Code immediately upon receipt of notice under subdivision (d). Child protective services or the county agency providing child welfare services pursuant to Section 16501 of the Welfare and Institutions Code shall immediately investigate the circumstances of the case and file a petition pursuant to Section 311 of the Welfare and Institutions Code. Child protective services or the county agency providing child welfare services pursuant to Section 16501 of the Welfare and Institutions Code shall immediately notify the State Department of Social Services of each child to whom this subdivision applies upon taking temporary custody of the child pursuant to Section 300 of the Welfare and Institutions Code. As soon as possible, but no later than 24 hours after temporary custody is assumed, child protective services or the county agency providing child welfare services pursuant to Section 16501 of the Welfare and Institutions Code shall report all known identifying information concerning the child, except personal identifying information pertaining to the parent or individual who surrendered the child, to the California Missing Children Clearinghouse and to the National Crime Information Center.

(f) If, prior to the filing of a petition under subdivision (e), a parent or individual who has voluntarily surrendered a child pursuant to this section requests that the safe-surrender site that has physical custody of the child pursuant to this section return the child and the safe-surrender site still has custody of the child, personnel of the safe-surrender site shall either return the child to the parent or individual or contact a child protective agency if any personnel at the safe-surrender site knows or reasonably suspects that the child has been the victim of child abuse or neglect. The voluntary surrender of a child pursuant to this section is not in and of itself a sufficient basis for reporting child abuse or neglect. The terms "child abuse," "child protective agency," "mandated reporter," "neglect," and "reasonably suspects" shall be given the same meanings as in Article 2.5 (commencing with Section 11164) of Title 1 of Part 4 of the Penal Code.

(g) Subsequent to the filing of a petition under subdivision (e), if, within 14 days of the voluntary surrender described in this section, the parent or individual who surrendered custody returns to claim physical custody of the child, the child welfare agency shall verify the identity of the parent or individual, conduct an assessment of that person's circumstances and ability to parent, and request that the juvenile court dismiss the petition for dependency and order the release of the child, if the child welfare agency determines that none of the conditions described in subdivisions (a) to (d), inclusive, of Section 319 of the Welfare and Institutions Code currently exist.

(h) A safe-surrender site, or the personnel of a safe-surrender site, shall not have liability of any kind for a surrendered child prior to taking actual physical custody of the child. A safe-surrender site, or personnel of the safe-surrender site, that accepts custody of a surrendered child pursuant to this section shall not be subject to civil, criminal, or administrative liability for accepting the child and caring for the child in the good faith belief that action is required or authorized by this section, including, but not limited to, instances where the child is older than 72 hours or the parent or individual surrendering the child did not have lawful physical custody of the child. A safe-surrender site, or the personnel of a safe-surrender site, shall not be subject to civil, criminal, or administrative liability for a surrendered child prior to the time that the site or its personnel know, or should know, that the child has been surrendered. This subdivision does not confer immunity from liability for personal injury or wrongful death, including, but not limited to, injury resulting from medical malpractice.

(i)(1) In order to encourage assistance to persons who voluntarily surrender physical custody of a child pursuant to this section or Section 271.5 of the Penal Code, no person who, without compensation and in good faith, provides assistance for the purpose of effecting the safe surrender of a minor 72 hours old or younger shall be civilly liable for injury to or death of the minor child as a result of the person's acts or omissions. This immunity does not apply to an act or omission constituting gross negligence, recklessness, or willful misconduct.

(2) For purposes of this section, "assistance" means transporting the minor child to the safe-surrender site as a person with lawful custody, or transporting or accompanying the parent or person with lawful custody at the request of that parent or person to effect the safe surrender, or performing any other act in good faith for the purpose of effecting the safe surrender of the minor.

(j) For purposes of this section, "lawful custody" means physical custody of a minor 72 hours old or younger accepted by a person from a parent of the minor, who the person believes in good faith is the parent of the minor, with the specific intent and promise of effecting the safe surrender of the minor.

(k) Any identifying information that pertains to a parent or individual who surrenders a child pursuant to this section, that is obtained as a result of the questionnaire described in paragraph (3) of subdivision (b) or in any other manner, is confidential, shall be exempt from disclosure under the California Public Records Act (Division 10 (commencing with Section 7920.000) of Title 1 of the Government Code), and shall not be disclosed by any personnel of a safe-surrender site that accepts custody of a child pursuant to this section. *(Added by Stats.2000, c. 824 (S.B.1368), § 1. Amended by Stats.2003, c. 150 (S.B.139), § 1; Stats.2004, c. 103 (S.B.1413), § 1; Stats.2005, c. 625 (S.B.116), § 1; Stats.2010, c. 567 (A.B.1048), § 1; Stats.2021, c. 615 (A.B.474), § 220, eff. Jan. 1, 2022, operative Jan. 1, 2023.)*

Cross References

Authorized comprehensive sexual health education, course offerings criteria, see Education Code § 51933.
Delinquents and wards of the juvenile court,
  Child welfare services, reunification of family, hearing, see Welfare and Institutions Code § 361.5.
  Children subject to jurisdiction, see Welfare and Institutions Code § 300.
  Exceptions to release or detention, see Welfare and Institutions Code § 309.
Inspection of public records, exemptions from disclosure, safe surrender site, information regarding parent or individual surrendering a child, see Government Code § 6276.38.
Notice to counties of process for voluntarily surrendering physical custody of a child, see Welfare and Institutions Code § 14005.24.
Removal of child from parental custody, search for relative and furnishing identifying information, see Welfare and Institutions Code § 361.3.

Sex education classes, course criteria, advising pupils of the content of this section, see Education Code § 51933.

§ 1256.2. Differing standards of obstetrical care based on source of payment and ability to pay not allowed; written policy statement; posting written notices; unprofessional conduct to deny or threaten to withhold pain management services

(a)(1) No general acute care hospital may promulgate policies or implement practices that determine differing standards of obstetrical care based upon a patient's source of payment or ability to pay for medical services.

(2) Each hospital holding an obstetrical services permit shall provide the licensing and certification division of the department with a written policy statement reflecting paragraph (1) and shall post written notices of this policy in the obstetrical admitting areas of the hospital by July 1, 1999. Notices posted pursuant to this section shall be posted in the predominant language or languages spoken in the hospital's service area.

(b) It shall constitute unprofessional conduct within the meaning of the Medical Practice Act, Chapter 5 (commencing with Section 2000) of Division 2 of the Business and Professions Code, for a physician or surgeon to deny, or threaten to withhold pain management services from a woman in active labor, based upon that patient's source of payment, or ability to pay for medical services. *(Added by Stats.1998, c. 652 (A.B.1397), § 2.)*

Cross References

General acute care hospital defined for purposes of this Chapter, see Health and Safety Code § 1250.

§ 1257.9. Training for hospital staff on hospital policies and recommendations that promote breast-feeding

(a)(1) The department shall recommend training for general acute care hospitals, as defined in subdivision (a) of Section 1250, and special hospitals, as defined in subdivision (f) of Section 1250, that is intended to improve breast-feeding rates among mothers and infants. This recommended training should be designed for general acute care hospitals that provide maternity care and have exclusive patient breast-feeding rates in the lowest 25 percent, according to the data published yearly by the State Department of Public Health, when ranked from highest to lowest rates. The training offered shall include a minimum of eight hours of training provided to appropriate administrative and supervisory staff on hospital policies and recommendations that promote exclusive breast-feeding. Hospitals that meet the minimum criteria for exclusive breast-feeding rates prescribed in the most current Healthy People Guidelines of the United States Department of Health and Human Services shall be excluded from the training requirements recommended by this paragraph.

(2) The department shall notify the hospital director or other person in charge of a hospital to which paragraph (1) applies, that the eight-hour model training course developed pursuant to subdivision (b) of Section 123360, is available, upon request, to the hospital.

(b) The recommendations provided for in this section are advisory only. Nothing in this section shall require a hospital to comply with the training recommended by this section. Section 1290 shall not apply to this section, nor shall meeting the recommendations of this section be a condition of licensure. *(Added by Stats.2007, c. 460 (S.B.22), § 2.)*

Cross References

General acute care hospital defined for purposes of this Chapter, see Health and Safety Code § 1250.

§ 1258. Sterilization for contraceptive purposes; prohibition against nonmedical qualifications; exceptions

No health facility which permits sterilization operations for contraceptive purposes to be performed therein, nor the medical staff of such health facility, shall require the individual upon whom such a sterilization operation is to be performed to meet any special nonmedical qualifications, which are not imposed on individuals seeking other types of operations in the health facility. Such prohibited nonmedical qualifications shall include, but not be limited to, age, marital status, and number of natural children.

Nothing in this section shall prohibit requirements relating to the physical or mental condition of the individual or affect the right of the attending physician to counsel or advise his patient as to whether or not sterilization is appropriate. This section shall not affect existing law with respect to individuals below the age of majority. *(Added by Stats.1974, c. 755, p. 1670, § 1.)*

Cross References

Health facility defined for purposes of this Chapter, see Health and Safety Code § 1250.
Similar provisions, see Health and Safety Code §§ 1232, 1459, 32128.10.

§ 1259.5. Spousal or partner abuse detection; policies and procedures

By January 1, 1995, each general acute care hospital, acute psychiatric hospital, special hospital, psychiatric health facility, and chemical dependency recovery hospital shall establish written policies and procedures to screen patients routinely for the purpose of detecting spousal or partner abuse. The policies shall include guidelines on all of the following:

(a) Identifying, through routine screening, spousal or partner abuse among patients.

(b) Documenting patient injuries or illnesses attributable to spousal or partner abuse.

(c) Educating appropriate hospital staff about the criteria for identifying, and the procedures for handling, patients whose injuries or illnesses are attributable to spousal or partner abuse.

(d) Advising patients exhibiting signs of spousal or partner abuse of crisis intervention services that are available either through the hospital facility or through community-based crisis intervention and counseling services.

(e) Providing to patients who exhibit signs of spousal or partner abuse information on domestic violence and a referral list, to be updated periodically, of private and public community agencies that provide, or arrange for, evaluation of and care for persons experiencing spousal or partner abuse, including, but not limited to, hot lines, local * * * domestic violence shelter-based programs, legal services, and information about temporary restraining orders. *(Added by Stats.1993, c. 1234 (A.B.890), § 13. Amended by Stats.1994, c. 146 (A.B.3601), § 95; Stats.2022, c. 197 (S.B.1493), § 10, eff. Jan. 1, 2023.)*

Cross References

Acute psychiatric hospital defined for purposes of this Chapter, see Health and Safety Code § 1250.
General acute care hospital defined for purposes of this Chapter, see Health and Safety Code § 1250.
Health facility defined for purposes of this Chapter, see Health and Safety Code § 1250.
Special hospital defined for purposes of this Chapter, see Health and Safety Code § 1250.

§ 1261. Visitation rights of domestic partners, domestic partner's children, and domestic partner of patient's parent or child

(a) A health facility shall allow a patient's domestic partner, the children of the patient's domestic partner, and the domestic partner of the patient's parent or child to visit, unless one of the following is met:

(1) No visitors are allowed.

(2) The facility reasonably determines that the presence of a particular visitor would endanger the health or safety of a patient,

member of the health facility staff, or other visitor to the health facility, or would significantly disrupt the operations of a facility.

(3) The patient has indicated to health facility staff that the patient does not want this person to visit.

(b) This section may not be construed to prohibit a health facility from otherwise establishing reasonable restrictions upon visitation, including restrictions upon the hours of visitation and number of visitors.

(c) For purposes of this section, "domestic partner" has the same meaning as that term is used in Section 297 of the Family Code. *(Added by Stats.1999, c. 588 (A.B.26), § 4.)*

Cross References

Health facility defined for purposes of this Chapter, see Health and Safety Code § 1250.

§ 1264. Prenatal screening ultrasound to detect congenital heart defects; necessity of sonographer; supervision; qualifications; policies and procedures

(a) Any health facility licensed under Section 1250 that provides prenatal screening ultrasound to detect congenital heart defects shall require that the ultrasound be performed by a sonographer who is nationally certified in obstetrical ultrasound by the American Registry for Diagnostic Medical Sonography (ARDMS), nationally certified in cardiac sonography by Cardiovascular Credentialing International (CCI), or credentialed in sonography by the American Registry of Radiologic Technologists (ARRT).

(b) For purposes of this section, the following shall apply:

(1) A sonographer is also known as an "ultrasound technologist" or "sonologist."

(2) "Sonographer" means any nonphysician who is qualified by national certification or academic or clinical experience to perform diagnostic medical ultrasound, with a subspecialty in obstetrical ultrasound.

(c)(1) Any sonographer who is certified as required in subdivision (a) or otherwise meets the requirements of this section, shall, in performing a prenatal ultrasound to detect congenital heart defects, perform the work under the supervision of a licensed physician and surgeon.

(2) For purposes of this section, licensed physician and surgeon means any physician and surgeon, licensed pursuant to Chapter 5 (commencing with Section 2000) of Division 2 of the Business and Professions Code.

(d) Any person with a minimum of two years of full-time work experience in this state as a sonographer in prenatal ultrasound and has obtained, or is in the process of obtaining, 30 continuing medical education credits over a three-year period in ultrasound shall be deemed to be in compliance with the requirements of this section.

(e) A health facility shall develop policies and procedures to implement the requirements of this section.

(f) This section and policies and procedures adopted pursuant to this section shall not prohibit any physician and surgeon licensed pursuant to Chapter 5 (commencing with Section 2000) of Division 2 of the Business and Professions Code from performing a prenatal ultrasound nor in any other way limit the ability of a licensed physician and surgeon to practice medicine in a manner consistent with that license.

(g) This section and policies and procedures adopted pursuant to this section shall not apply to any physician and surgeon, sonologist, certified nurse-midwife, or nurse practitioner who performs limited prenatal ultrasounds for the purpose of obtaining an amniotic fluid index, fetal position, a biophysical profile or dating a pregnancy prior to 20 weeks gestation.

(h) Article 4 (commencing with Section 1235) and any other provision relating to criminal sanctions for violations of this chapter shall not apply to any person who violates this section or any regulation adopted pursuant to this section.

(i) This section shall become operative on July 1, 2006. *(Added by Stats.2004, c. 770 (A.B.3044), § 2, operative July 1, 2006.)*

Cross References

Health facility defined for purposes of this Chapter, see Health and Safety Code § 1250.

CHAPTER 3. CALIFORNIA COMMUNITY CARE FACILITIES ACT

Cross References

Adult Day Health Care Act,
  Generally, see Health and Safety Code § 1570 et seq.
  Independent program, see Health and Safety Code § 1585.2.
AFDC-FC, children placed in for-profit child care institutions, see Welfare and Institutions Code § 11402.6.
Aid for adoption of children,
  Adoption assistance, see Welfare and Institutions Code § 16121.
  Reimbursement, see Welfare and Institutions Code § 16122.
Alcohol and drug-exposed and HIV positive children, placement of children in prospective adoptive homes, see Welfare and Institutions Code § 16135.30.
Certificate of authority for continuing care contracts, suspension or revocation, see Health and Safety Code § 1793.21 et seq.
Children who are consumers of regional center services and are also AFDC-FC or AAP recipients, findings and declarations, see Welfare and Institutions Code § 11464.
Children with special health care needs, legislative findings, declarations, and intent, see Welfare and Institutions Code § 17700.
Community crisis homes, licensure, facility program plan, urgent action necessary to protect a consumer residing in a community crisis home, rescindment of certificate of program approval, see Welfare and Institutions Code § 4698.
Community living facilities, funding of specified services for children who are both AFDC-FC or AAP recipients and regional center consumers, see Welfare and Institutions Code § 4684.
Community residential treatment system, programs to serve children and adolescents, see Welfare and Institutions Code § 5672.
County adoption agencies, license, see Welfare and Institutions Code § 16100.
Dependent children under jurisdiction of juvenile court, placement in family home or private institution, see Welfare and Institutions Code § 362.
Determination of capacity of specialized foster care home, see Welfare and Institutions Code § 17732.2.
Development of performance standards and outcome measures for providers of out-of-home care placements made under AFDC-FC program and for effective and efficient administration of the program, see Welfare and Institutions Code § 11467.
Establishment of medical foster home program by United States Department of Veterans Affairs facility, exemption from licensure or regulation under this act, requirements, see Military and Veterans Code § 1851.
Evidence in personal injury action against health care provider, see Civil Code § 3333.1.
Foster care,
  Children placed in public child care institutions, see Welfare and Institutions Code § 11402.5.
  County placement of children, see Welfare and Institutions Code § 17736.
  Specialized care home, number of foster children in home, see Welfare and Institutions Code § 17732.
Foster Child Ombudsman Program, functions, confidentiality of complaints, see Welfare and Institutions Code § 16164.
Habeas corpus hearing, right of adult admitted or committed to community care facility, see Welfare and Institutions Code § 4800.
Immunity from liability of clinic, health dispensary or health facility for professional negligence due to unsolicited referral from tests by multiphasic screening unit, see Civil Code § 43.9.

HEALTH AND SAFETY CODE

Implementation of pilot project to test the effectiveness of providing enhanced behavioral supports in homelike community settings, approval of enhanced behavioral supports homes, licensure as an adult residential facility or a group home, urgent action necessary to protect a consumer residing in an enhanced behavioral supports home, facility program plan, see Welfare and Institutions Code § 4684.81.

Juvenile case file inspection, see Welfare and Institutions Code § 827.

Legal and civil rights of persons involuntarily detained, authorized disclosure of confidential information and records, see Welfare and Institutions Code § 5328.15.

License under this Chapter not required of a county that provides agency adoption program services, see Government Code § 30029.3.

Licensing, adult day care facilities, disclosure of corporate or business information by applicant for license, see Health and Safety Code § 1575.1.

Licensure of enhanced behavioral supports home as adult residential facility or a group home, placement of dual agency clients, see Health and Safety Code § 1567.62.

Medical foster homes for veterans, license application procedure, see Health and Safety Code § 1568.24.

Napa and Riverside counties, community care facilities, see Welfare and Institutions Code § 5673.

Nonminor dependents, opening of separate court file, access to file, see Welfare and Institutions Code § 362.5.

Parental custody, right of specified entities to file petition, see Family Code § 7840.

Programs for seriously emotionally disturbed children and court wards and dependents, program standards, see Welfare and Institutions Code § 4094.

Reference to certain hospitals or private mental institutions if applicable to community care facility to mean this chapter, see Welfare and Institutions Code §§ 22, 23.

Revocation of previous license issued under this chapter, exclusion from medical foster home for veterans, see Health and Safety Code § 1568.296.

Services for the developmentally disabled, confidential information and records, see Welfare and Institutions Code § 4514.

State university and colleges, child development centers, see Education Code § 89400 et seq.

ARTICLE 3. REGULATIONS

Section
1530.6. Persons providing residential foster care; authority to give same legal consent as parent; exceptions; rules and regulations.

§ 1530.6. Persons providing residential foster care; authority to give same legal consent as parent; exceptions; rules and regulations

(a) Notwithstanding any other law, persons licensed or approved pursuant to this chapter to provide residential foster care to a child either placed with them pursuant to order of the juvenile court or voluntarily placed with them by the person or persons having legal custody of the child, may give the same legal consent for that child as a parent except for the following:

(1) Marriage.

(2) Entry into the Armed Forces.

(3) Medical and dental treatment, except that consent may be given for ordinary medical and dental treatment for the child, including, but not limited to, immunizations, physical examinations, and X-rays.

(4) Educational decisions that are required to be made by a child's educational rights holder.

(5) If the child is voluntarily placed by the parent or parents, those items as are agreed to in writing by the parties to the placement.

(b) To this effect, the department shall prescribe rules and regulations to carry out the intent of this section.

(c) This section does not apply to any situation in which a juvenile court order expressly reserves the right to consent to those activities to the court. *(Added by Stats.1977, c. 391, § 1, eff. Aug. 27, 1977. Amended by Stats.1992, c. 865 (A.B.2691), § 1; Stats.2017, c. 732 (A.B.404), § 24, eff. Jan. 1, 2018.)*

Cross References

Children who are exposed to alcohol or drugs or who are HIV positive, placement, see Welfare and Institutions Code § 16525.30.

Department or state department defined for purposes of this Chapter, see Health and Safety Code § 1502.

Immunization information systems, see Health and Safety Code § 120440.

Division 8
CEMETERIES

Cross References

Abandonment of cemeteries, see Health and Safety Code § 8825 et seq.

Application of definitions contained in Chapter 1 (commencing with Health and Safety Code § 7000) of Part 1 of Division 7 of the Health and Safety Code to this Chapter, see Health and Safety Code § 7000.

Part 3
PRIVATE CEMETERIES

Cross References

Administration and enforcement of this part by cemetery board, see Business and Professions Code § 7614.6.

Exemption of cemeteries from taxation, see Cal. Const. Art. 13, § 3; Revenue and Taxation Code § 204.

CHAPTER 4. PROPERTY RIGHTS

ARTICLE 1. GENERAL PROVISIONS

Section
8601. Spouse's vested right of interment.
8602. Divestment of right of interment; written consent; divorce.

Cross References

Abandonment of cemeteries, see Health and Safety Code § 8825 et seq.

§ 8601. Spouse's vested right of interment

The spouse of an owner of any plot containing more than one interment space has a vested right of interment of his remains in the plot and any person thereafter becoming the spouse of the owner has a vested right of interment of his remains in the plot if more than one interment space is unoccupied at the time the person becomes the spouse of the owner. *(Stats.1939, c. 60, p. 706, § 8601. Amended by Stats.1939, c. 339, p. 1677.)*

Cross References

Interment defined for purposes of this Division, see Health and Safety Code § 7009.

Owner defined for purposes of this Division, see Health and Safety Code § 7023.

Plot defined for purposes of this Division, see Health and Safety Code § 7022.

Remains defined for purposes of this Division, see Health and Safety Code § 7001.
Vested right of interment, see Health and Safety Code § 8675 et seq.

§ 8602. Divestment of right of interment; written consent; divorce

No conveyance or other action of the owner without the written consent or joinder of the spouse of the owner divests the spouse of a vested right of interment, except that a final decree of divorce between them terminates the vested right of interment unless otherwise provided in the decree. *(Stats.1939, c. 60, p. 706, § 8602. Amended by Stats.1939, c. 339, p. 1677.)*

Cross References

Final decree of divorce, see Family Code § 2339 et seq.
Interment defined for purposes of this Division, see Health and Safety Code § 7009.
Owner defined for purposes of this Division, see Health and Safety Code § 7023.
Waiver of right of interment, see Health and Safety Code §§ 8653, 8675.

Division 102
VITAL RECORDS AND HEALTH STATISTICS

Cross References

Address confidentiality for reproductive health care service providers, employees, volunteers, and patients, request that state and local agencies use address designated by secretary of state, modifying or maintaining public record with respect to birth, fetal death, death or marriage information, see Government Code § 6215.5.
Address confidentiality for victims of domestic violence and stalking, use of substitute address by state and local agencies, see Government Code § 6207.
Application of definitions contained in chapter 1 (commencing with Health and Safety Code § 7000) of part 1 of division 7 to this division, see Health and Safety Code § 7000.
Funeral directors and embalmers, refusal to surrender human remains, see Business and Professions Code § 7706.

Part 1
VITAL RECORDS

Cross References

Certificate of registry of marriage, preparation and filing, see Family Code § 359.
Confidentiality of medical information, exemptions from disclosure and use limitations, see Civil Code § 56.30.
Failure of registrars to perform duties required by this Part, offense, see Health and Safety Code § 103790.

CHAPTER 5. CERTIFICATES OF BIRTH FOLLOWING ADOPTION, LEGITIMATION, COURT DETERMINATION OF PARENTAGE, AND ACKNOWLEDGMENT

ARTICLE 1. ADOPTION

Section
102625. Report of adoption; completion and forwarding by clerk of court.
102630. Out of state births; forwarding report to place of birth.
102635. Establishment of new birth certificate.
102640. New certificate not established upon request of adopting parent.
102645. Contents; form.
102650. Single-parent adoption; contents of certificate.
102660. Inclusion of name of deceased adopting parent.
102670. Preparation of additional amended record; fee.
102675. Amended certificate; deletions.
102680. Effect on prior certificate.
102685. Transmittal or sealing of local registrar's copies of original birth certificate.
102690. Child born in state and having no original birth record; report as court order delayed birth registration.
102695. Birth outside United States, Territories of United States or Canada; report as court order delayed birth registration.
102700. Filing court report of adoption with original birth record.
102705. Availability of records and information upon court order.
102710. Certified copy of amended record; cost.

§ 102625. Report of adoption; completion and forwarding by clerk of court

The clerk of the court shall complete a report upon a form provided for that purpose and forward the report to the State Registrar within five days after a decree of adoption has been entered declaring a child legally adopted by any court in the state. The report shall be forwarded within five days after an interlocutory decree of adoption becomes a final decree of adoption, and not earlier. *(Added by Stats.1995, c. 415 (S.B.1360), § 4.)*

Cross References

Annual adjustment of fees and charges, see Health and Safety Code § 100430.
Computation of time, see Code of Civil Procedure §§ 12 and 12a; Government Code § 6800 et seq.
Name of child, effect of adoption, see Family Code § 8618.
New birth certificate for adopted child, contents, see Family Code § 8615.

§ 102630. Out of state births; forwarding report to place of birth

The court reports of adoption that are received by the State Registrar for births that occurred in another state, the District of Columbia, in any territory of the United States, or Canada shall be transmitted to the registration authority of the place of birth. *(Added by Stats.1995, c. 415 (S.B.1360), § 4.)*

§ 102635. Establishment of new birth certificate

A new birth certificate shall be established by the State Registrar upon receipt of either of the following:

(a) A report of adoption from any court of record that has jurisdiction of the child in this state, another state, the District of Columbia, in any territory of the United States, or in any foreign country, for any child born in California and whose certificate of birth is on file in the office of the State Registrar.

(b) A readoption order issued pursuant to Section 8919 of the Family Code. *(Added by Stats.1995, c. 415 (S.B.1360), § 4. Amended by Stats.2006, c. 809 (S.B.1393), § 2.)*

Cross References

Certificate of adoption, name of child, see Family Code § 8614.

§ 102640. New certificate not established upon request of adopting parent

When requested by the adopting parent or parents, a new certificate shall not be established by the State Registrar. *(Added by Stats.1995, c. 415 (S.B.1360), § 4.)*

847

§ 102645. Contents; form

The new birth certificate shall bear the name of the child as shown in the report of adoption, the names and ages of his or her adopting parents, the date and place of birth, and no reference shall be made in the new birth certificate to the adoption of the child. The new certificate shall be identical with a birth certificate registered for the birth of a child of natural parents, except, when requested by the adopting parents, the new birth certificate shall not include the specific name and address of the hospital or other facility where the birth occurred, the color and race of the parents, or both. *(Added by Stats.1995, c. 415 (S.B.1360), § 4.)*

§ 102650. Single-parent adoption; contents of certificate

Notwithstanding other provisions in this article, when a child is adopted by an unmarried man or woman, the new certificate shall, if the adopting parent so requests, reflect the fact that it is a single-parent adoption. *(Added by Stats.1995, c. 415 (S.B.1360), § 4.)*

§ 102660. Inclusion of name of deceased adopting parent

If both adopting parents were in the home at the time of the initial placement of the child for adoption the newly amended birth record may include the names of both adopting parents despite the death of one of the adopting parents, upon receipt of an order from the court granting the adoption that directs under the authority of Section 8615 of the Family Code that the names of both adopting parents shall be included on the newly amended birth record. *(Added by Stats.1995, c. 415 (S.B.1360), § 4.)*

§ 102670. Preparation of additional amended record; fee

Notwithstanding any other provision of law, an adopting parent who has adopted a child for whom an amended record has already been prepared under authority of this article may have another amended record prepared for the child, upon application, furnishing a copy of the court order made in an action brought pursuant to Section 8615 of the Family Code, and payment of the required fee. *(Added by Stats.1995, c. 415 (S.B.1360), § 4.)*

Cross References

Annual adjustment of fees and charges, see Health and Safety Code § 100430.
Fee, see Health and Safety Code § 103705.

§ 102675. Amended certificate; deletions

At any time after the issuance of a new birth certificate another amended certificate may be issued, at the request of the adopting parents, that omits any or all of the following:

(a) The specific name and address of the hospital or other facility where the birth occurred.

(b) The city and county of birth.

(c) The color and race of the parents. *(Added by Stats.1995, c. 415 (S.B.1360), § 4.)*

§ 102680. Effect on prior certificate

The new birth certificate shall supplant any birth certificate previously registered for the child and shall be the only birth certificate open to public inspection. *(Added by Stats.1995, c. 415 (S.B.1360), § 4.)*

§ 102685. Transmittal or sealing of local registrar's copies of original birth certificate

When a new birth certificate is established under this article, the State Registrar shall inform the local registrar and the county recorder whose records contain copies of the original certificate, who shall forward the copies to the State Registrar for filing with the original certificate, if it is practical for him or her to do so. If it is impractical for him or her to forward the copy to the State Registrar, he or she shall effectually seal a cover over the copy in a manner as not to deface or destroy the copy and forward a verified statement of his or her action to the State Registrar. Thereafter the information contained in the record shall be available only as provided in this article. *(Added by Stats.1995, c. 415 (S.B.1360), § 4.)*

Cross References

Failure of registrars to perform duty, offense, see Health and Safety Code § 103790.

§ 102690. Child born in state and having no original birth record; report as court order delayed birth registration

For court reports of adoptions received from any court of record of this State, another state, the District of Columbia, or in any territory of the United States, that has jurisdiction of a child born in this State and for whom no original record of birth is on file in the Office of the State Registrar the court report of adoption shall constitute a court order delayed birth registration; provided, the court report contains a statement of the date and place of birth. *(Added by Stats.1995, c. 415 (S.B.1360), § 4.)*

§ 102695. Birth outside United States, Territories of United States or Canada; report as court order delayed birth registration

A court report of adoption received from any court of record in this State, wherein the birth occurred outside the United States, the Territories of the United States, or Canada shall constitute a court order delayed registration of birth; provided, the court report contains a statement of the date and place of birth. *(Added by Stats.1995, c. 415 (S.B.1360), § 4.)*

§ 102700. Filing court report of adoption with original birth record

The court report of adoption shall be filed with the original record of birth, that shall remain as a part of the records of the State Registrar. *(Added by Stats.1995, c. 415 (S.B.1360), § 4.)*

§ 102705. Availability of records and information upon court order

All records and information specified in this article, other than the newly issued birth certificate, shall be available only upon the order of the superior court of the county of residence of the adopted child or the superior court of the county granting the order of adoption.

No such order shall be granted by the superior court unless a verified petition setting forth facts showing the necessity of the order has been presented to the court and good and compelling cause is shown for the granting of the order. The clerk of the superior court shall send a copy of the petition to the State Department of Social Services and the department shall send a copy of all records and information it has concerning the adopted person with the name and address of the natural parents removed to the court. The court must review these records before making an order and the order should so state. If the petition is by or on behalf of an adopted child who has attained majority, these facts shall be given great weight, but the granting of any petition is solely within the sound discretion of the court.

The name and address of the natural parents shall be given to the petitioner only if he or she can demonstrate that the name and address, or either of them, are necessary to assist him or her in establishing a legal right. *(Added by Stats.1995, c. 415 (S.B.1360), § 4.)*

Cross References

Courts of record, see Cal. Const. Art. 6, § 1.

§ 102710. Certified copy of amended record; cost

The State Registrar shall furnish a certified copy of the newly amended record of birth prepared under authority of this article to the registrant without additional cost. *(Added by Stats.1995, c. 415 (S.B.1360), § 4.)*

ARTICLE 2. ADJUDICATION OF FACTS OF PARENTAGE

Section
102725. Establishment of new birth certificate.
102730. Records and information; availability only on order of court.
102735. Certified copy of amended record; cost.

Cross References

Determination of father and child relationship, order for issuance of new birth certificate, see Family Code § 7639.

§ 102725. Establishment of new birth certificate

Whenever the existence or nonexistence of the parent and child relationship has been determined by a court of this state or a court of another state, and upon receipt of a certified copy of the court order, application, and payment of the required fee, the State Registrar shall establish a new birth certificate for the child in the manner prescribed in Article 1 (commencing with Section 102625), if the original record of birth is on file in the office of the State Registrar. *(Added by Stats.1995, c. 415 (S.B.1360), § 4.)*

Cross References

Affidavits in uncontested proceedings to establish record of birth, see Code of Civil Procedure § 2009 et seq.
Annual adjustment of fees and charges, see Health and Safety Code § 100430.
Determination of parent and child relationship, new birth certificate, see Family Code §§ 7636, 7639.

§ 102730. Records and information; availability only on order of court

All records and information specified in this article, other than the newly issued birth certificate, shall be available only upon order of a court of record. *(Added by Stats.1995, c. 415 (S.B.1360), § 4.)*

§ 102735. Certified copy of amended record; cost

The State Registrar shall furnish a certified copy of the newly amended record of birth prepared under authority of this article to the registrant without additional cost. *(Added by Stats.1995, c. 415 (S.B.1360), § 4.)*

ARTICLE 3. ACKNOWLEDGEMENT OF PATERNITY

Section
102750. Affidavit of parents.
102755. Establishment of new birth certificate.
102760. Records and information; availability only on order of court.
102765. Certified copy of amended record; cost.

§ 102750. Affidavit of parents

Whenever the mother and the other genetic parent or intended parent acknowledges parentage of a child by affidavit, and in the absence of conflicting information on the originally registered certificate of live birth, an application including the affidavits may be filed with the office of the State Registrar upon a form provided for that purpose. *(Added by Stats.1995, c. 415 (S.B.1360), § 4. Amended by Stats.2019, c. 539 (A.B.785), § 7, eff. Jan. 1, 2020.)*

Cross References

Annual adjustment of fees and charges, see Health and Safety Code § 100430.

§ 102755. Establishment of new birth certificate

Upon receipt of the application and payment of the required fee, and in the absence of conflicting information on the originally registered certificate of live birth, the State Registrar shall review the application for acceptance for filing, and if accepted shall establish a new birth certificate for the child in the manner prescribed in Article 1 (commencing with Section 102625), if the original record of birth is on file in the office of the State Registrar. *(Added by Stats.1995, c. 415 (S.B.1360), § 4.)*

Cross References

Fee, see Health and Safety Code § 103715.

§ 102760. Records and information; availability only on order of court

All records and information specified in this article, other than the newly issued birth certificate, shall be available only upon order of a court of record. *(Added by Stats.1995, c. 415 (S.B.1360), § 4.)*

Cross References

Inspection of public records, other exemptions from disclosure, see Government Code § 6276.34.

§ 102765. Certified copy of amended record; cost

The State Registrar shall furnish a certified copy of the new record of birth prepared under authority of this article to the registrant with additional cost. *(Added by Stats.1995, c. 415 (S.B.1360), § 4.)*

ARTICLE 4. VOLUNTARY DECLARATION OF PARENTAGE

Section
102766. Addition of voluntary declaration of parentage signatory's name to birth certificate; application; review.
102767. Removal of voluntary declaration of parentage signatory's name from birth certificate following rescission; application.
102768. Availability of records.
102769. Certified copy; provision to registrant.

§ 102766. Addition of voluntary declaration of parentage signatory's name to birth certificate; application; review

(a) When a voluntary declaration of parentage is filed with the Department of Child Support Services pursuant to subdivision (d) of Section 7571 of the Family Code, an application may be submitted to the State Registrar requesting that the signatory's name be added to the child's birth certificate.

(b) Upon receipt of the application and payment of the required fee, the State Registrar shall review the application for acceptance for filing and, if accepted, shall establish a new birth certificate for the child in the manner prescribed in Article 1 (commencing with Section 102625), if the original record of birth is on file in the office of the State Registrar. *(Added by Stats.1996, c. 1062 (A.B.1832), § 19.5. Amended by Stats.1998, c. 858 (A.B.2169), § 7; Stats.2018, c. 876 (A.B.2684), § 73, eff. Jan. 1, 2019; Stats.2019, c. 539 (A.B.785), § 8, eff. Jan. 1, 2020.)*

§ 102767. Removal of voluntary declaration of parentage signatory's name from birth certificate following rescission; application

(a) When a voluntary declaration of parentage is rescinded pursuant to Section 7575 of the Family Code, an application may be submitted to the State Registrar requesting that the signatory's name be removed from the child's birth certificate.

(b) Upon receipt of the application and payment of the required fee, the State Registrar shall establish a new birth certificate for the child in the manner prescribed in Article 1 (commencing with Section 102625), if the original record of birth is on file in the office of the State Registrar. *(Added by Stats.1996, c. 1062 (A.B.1832), § 19.5. Amended by Stats.2018, c. 876 (A.B.2684), § 74, eff. Jan. 1, 2019.)*

§ 102768. Availability of records

All records and information specified in this article, other than the newly established certificate, shall be available only to those persons specified in subdivision (i) of Section 7571 of the Family Code or upon order of a court of record. *(Added by Stats.1996, c. 1062 (A.B.1832), § 19.5. Amended by Stats.2019, c. 539 (A.B.785), § 9, eff. Jan. 1, 2020.)*

§ 102769. Certified copy; provision to registrant

The State Registrar shall furnish a certified copy of the new record of birth prepared under authority of this article to the registrant without additional cost. *(Added by Stats.1996, c. 1062 (A.B.1832), § 19.5.)*

CHAPTER 9. MARRIAGE REGISTRATION

ARTICLE 1. GENERAL PROVISIONS

Section
103125. Forms.

§ 103125. Forms

The forms for the marriage license shall be prescribed by the State Registrar. *(Added by Stats.1995, c. 415 (S.B.1360), § 4. Amended by Stats.2006, c. 816 (A.B.1102), § 45, operative Jan. 1, 2008.)*

Operative Effect

For operative effect of Stats.2006, c. 816 (A.B.1102), see § 56 of that act.

ARTICLE 2. DUTY OF REGISTERING

Section
103150. Required registration.

§ 103150. Required registration

Each marriage that is performed shall be registered by the person performing the ceremony as provided by Chapter 2 (commencing with Section 420) of Part 3 of Division 3 of the Family Code. *(Added by Stats.1995, c. 415 (S.B.1360), § 4.)*

Cross References

Duty to furnish information, see Health and Safety Code § 102135.
Failure to file marriage license by person solemnizing marriage, penalty, see Penal Code § 360.
Filing certificate of registry, see Family Code § 359.
Issuance of marriage certificate by person solemnizing marriage, requirement, see Family Code § 422.
Local registrar's copy of certificate, see Health and Safety Code § 102330.
Necessity of certificate, see Family Code § 306.
Return of endorsed marriage license to local registrar, see Family Code § 423.

ARTICLE 3. CONTENT OF CERTIFICATE OF REGISTRY OF MARRIAGE

Section
103175. Division into three sections; items.
103180. Religious societies or denominations; marriages not solemnized by clergy; License and Certificate of Non–Clergy Marriage.

§ 103175. Division into three sections; items

(a) The marriage license shall contain as nearly as can be ascertained all of the following and other items as the State Registrar may designate:

(1) The first section shall include the personal data of each party married, including the date of birth, full given name at birth or by court order, birthplace, mailing address, names and birthplaces of each party's parents, last names at birth of each party's parents, the number of previous marriages, marital status, the name used prior to the intended marriage by each party at the time of the marriage license application, if the name is different from the name given at birth or by court order, and the new name, if any, selected by each party for intended use upon solemnization of the marriage.

(2) The second section shall include the signatures of parties married, license to marry, county and date of issuance of license, and the marriage license number.

(3) The third section shall include the certification of one person performing the ceremony, that shall show his or her official position including the denomination if he or she is a clergy or clergyperson, and the printed name, signature, and mailing address of at least one, and no more than two, witnesses to the marriage ceremony. The person performing the marriage ceremony shall also type or print his or her name and mailing address on the marriage license.

(b) The marriage license shall not contain any reference to the race or color of parties married. *(Added by Stats.1995, c. 415 (S.B.1360), § 4. Amended by Stats.1996, c. 1023 (S.B.1497), § 304.5, eff. Sept. 29, 1996; Stats.2006, c. 816 (A.B.1102), § 46, operative Jan. 1, 2008; Stats.2007, c. 567 (A.B.102), § 10, operative Jan. 1, 2009.)*

Cross References

Certificate of registry and marriage license, address information, see Family Code § 351.5.
Determination of correctness of facts stated in license, see Family Code § 354.
Failure to fill out and deliver certificate, see Health and Safety Code § 103785.
Issuance and filing of certificate of registry, see Family Code § 359.
Marriage license and certificate of registry, mailing address of applicant, witness, or person solemnizing, see Family Code § 351.6.
Statement of person solemnizing marriage, see Family Code § 422.

§ 103180. Religious societies or denominations; marriages not solemnized by clergy; License and Certificate of Non–Clergy Marriage

(a) Sections 103150 and 103175 do not apply to marriages entered into pursuant to Section 307 of the Family Code. Subdivisions (b) and (c) govern the registration and the content of the License and Certificate of Non–Clergy Marriage of those marriages.

(b) Each marriage entered into pursuant to Section 307 of the Family Code shall be registered by the parties entering into the marriage or by a witness who signed under paragraph (2) of subdivision (a) of Section 307 within 10 days after the ceremony with the local registrar of marriages for the county in which the License and Certificate of Non–Clergy Marriage was issued.

(c) The License and Certificate of Non–Clergy Marriage entered into pursuant to Section 307 of the Family Code shall contain as nearly as can be ascertained the following:

(1) The personal data of each party married, including the date of birth, full given name at birth or by court order, birthplace, mailing address, names and birthplaces of each party's parents, last names at birth of each party's parents, the number of previous marriages, marital status, the name used prior to the intended marriage by each party at the time of the marriage license application, if the name is different from the name given at birth or by court order, and the new name, if any, selected by each party for intended use upon solemnization of the marriage.

(2) The license to marry.

(3) The county and date of issuance of the license.

(4) The marriage license number.

(5) The certification of the parties entering into the marriage, that shall show the following:

(A) The fact, time, and place of entering into the marriage.

(B) The printed name, signature, and mailing address of two witnesses to the marriage ceremony.

(C) The religious society or denomination of the parties married, and that the marriage was entered into in accordance with the rules and customs of that religious society or denomination.

(6) The signatures of the parties married.

(7) Any other items that the State Registrar shall designate.

(d) The License and Certificate of Non–Clergy Marriage shall not contain any reference to the race or color of parties married or to a person performing or solemnizing the marriage. *(Added by Stats. 1995, c. 415 (S.B.1360), § 4. Amended by Stats.2006, c. 816 (A.B.1102), § 47, operative Jan. 1, 2008; Stats.2007, c. 567 (A.B.102), § 11, operative Jan. 1, 2009.)*

Cross References

Computation of time, see Code of Civil Procedure §§ 12 and 12a; Government Code § 6800 et seq.

Marriage license and certificate of registry, mailing address of applicant, witness, or person solemnizing, see Family Code § 351.6.

CHAPTER 10. FINAL DECREES OF DISSOLUTION OF MARRIAGE, OR LEGAL SEPARATION

Section
103200. Judgments of dissolution, legal separation, declaration of nullity; copies to state registrar.
103205. Index of decrees.

§ 103200. Judgments of dissolution, legal separation, declaration of nullity; copies to state registrar

The clerk of the court of each county shall send a copy of every judgment of dissolution of marriage, of legal separation, and of declaration of nullity to the State Registrar monthly. If a judgment of dissolution of marriage is vacated, the clerk of the court shall send a copy of the order or dismissal to the State Registrar. *(Added by Stats.1995, c. 415 (S.B.1360), § 4. Amended by Stats.2006, c. 816 (A.B.1102), § 48, operative Jan. 1, 2008.)*

Operative Effect

For operative effect of Stats.2006, c. 816 (A.B.1102), see § 56 of that act.

Cross References

Dissolution of marriage and legal separation, annual report to Judicial Council by superior court clerks on number of judgements, see Family Code § 2348.

§ 103205. Index of decrees

The State Registrar shall maintain a comprehensive and continuous index of all decrees received under Section 103200. *(Added by Stats.1995, c. 415 (S.B.1360), § 4.)*

CHAPTER 11. AMENDMENT OF RECORDS

ARTICLE 7. REVISION OF BIRTH AND MARRIAGE RECORDS TO REFLECT CHANGE OF GENDER AND SEX IDENTIFIER

Section
103425. Petition for recognition of change of gender and sex identifier; order for new birth certificate, marriage license and certificate, confidential marriage license and certificate, or birth certificate of petitioner's child.
103426. New birth certificate, marriage license and certificate, or confidential marriage license and certificate issued without court order; affidavit of request for change of gender and sex identifier to conform to person's gender identity; fee; name change.
103430. Petition for recognition of change of gender and sex identifier; affidavit of petitioner; grant of petition without hearing; order for new administrative documents.
103431. Order for new birth certificate, marriage license and certificate, confidential marriage license and certificate, or birth certificate of petitioner's child; filing with State Registrar.
103435. Single petition for change of name, recognition of change in gender and sex identifier, and issuance new birth certificate, marriage license and certificate, confidential marriage license and certificate, or birth certificate of petitioner's child; procedure.
103440. New birth certificate, marriage license and certificate, or confidential marriage license and certificate; effect; inspection; filing; availability of information.
103443. Transmittal of certified copy of birth certificate or confidential marriage certificate to registrant.
103445. Operative date of article.

Operative Effect

For operative effect of Article 7, see Health and Safety Code § 103445.

Explanatory Note

Another Article 7, added as "Revision of Birth Records to Reflect Change of Gender" by Stats.1995, c. 415 (S.B.1360), § 4, relating to similar subject matter, was repealed by Stats.2021, c. 577 (A.B.218), § 7, operative Jan. 1, 2023.

§ 103425. Petition for recognition of change of gender and sex identifier; order for new birth certificate, marriage license and certificate, confidential marriage license and certificate, or birth certificate of petitioner's child

(a) A person may file a petition with the superior court in any county seeking a judgment recognizing the change of gender and sex identifier to female, male, or nonbinary.

(b) If requested, the judgment shall include an order that a new birth certificate be prepared for the person reflecting the change of gender and sex identifier and any change of name accomplished by an order of a court of this state, another state, the District of Columbia, any territory of the United States, or any foreign court.

(c) Subject to the requirements of Section 103430, if requested, the judgment shall include an order that a new marriage license and certificate or confidential marriage license and certificate be prepared for the person reflecting the change to the designation of the person as bride, groom, or having neither box checked on the marriage license and certificate or confidential marriage license and certificate and any change of name accomplished by an order of a court of this state, another state, the District of Columbia, any territory of the United States, or any foreign court.

(d) Subject to the requirements of Section 103430, if requested, the judgment shall include an order that a new birth certificate be prepared for the person's child or children reflecting the change to the designation of the person as mother, father, or parent and any change of name of the petitioner accomplished by an order of a court of this state, another state, the District of Columbia, or any territory of the United States, or foreign court.

(e) A petition seeking a judgment recognizing the change of gender and sex identifier to female, male, or nonbinary may be made to a superior court within this state, even if the person whose gender

§ 103425

and sex identifier is proposed to be changed does not reside within the State of California, if the person is seeking to change the designation to reflect their gender on at least one of the following documents:

(1) A birth certificate that was issued within this state to the person whose gender and sex identifier is proposed to be changed.

(2) A birth certificate that was issued within this state to the legal child of the person whose gender and sex identifier is proposed to be changed.

(3) A marriage license and certificate or confidential marriage license and certificate that was issued within this state to the person whose gender and sex identifier is proposed to be changed. *(Added by Stats.2021, c. 577 (A.B.218), § 8, eff. Jan. 1, 2022, operative Jan. 1, 2023.)*

Operative Effect

For operative effect of Article 7, see Health and Safety Code § 103445.

Research References

Forms

West's California Judicial Council Forms NC–300, Petition for Recognition of Change of Gender and for Issuance of New Birth Certificate.

West's California Judicial Council Forms NC–330, Order Recognizing Change of Gender and for Issuance of New Birth Certificate.

§ 103426. New birth certificate, marriage license and certificate, or confidential marriage license and certificate issued without court order; affidavit of request for change of gender and sex identifier to conform to person's gender identity; fee; name change

(a) The State Registrar shall issue a new birth certificate reflecting a change of gender and sex identifier to female, male, or nonbinary without a court order for any person who has a birth certificate issued by this state who submits directly to the State Registrar an application to change the gender and sex identifier on the birth certificate and an affidavit attesting under penalty of perjury that the request for a change of gender and sex identifier to female, male, or nonbinary is to conform the person's legal gender and sex identifier to the person's gender identity and is not made for any fraudulent purpose. Upon receipt of the documentation and the fee prescribed by Section 103725, the State Registrar shall establish a new birth certificate reflecting the gender and sex identifier stated in the application and any change in name, if accompanied by a certified copy of the court order for a change of name.

(b)(1) The State Registrar shall issue a new birth certificate for the minor child or children who have a birth certificate issued by this state without a court order when a parent submits directly to the State Registrar all of the following:

(A) An application for a new birth certificate for their minor child or children reflecting the change of the designation of the petitioner as mother, father, or parent, and, if applicable, any change of name of the parent.

(B) A copy of at least one of the following documents:

(i) A certified copy of the court-ordered change of gender, including a certified English translation, if applicable.

(ii) The parent's new birth certificate reflecting a change of gender and sex identifier.

(iii) A government-issued identity document reflecting the parent's change of gender and sex identifier.

(iv) An affidavit attesting under penalty of perjury that the request for a change of the designation of the petitioner as mother, father, or parent is to conform to the person's gender identity and is not made for any fraudulent purpose.

(C) The fee prescribed by Section 103725.

(D) If applicable, a certified copy of the court-ordered change of name, including a certified English translation, if applicable.

(2) The new birth certificate shall reflect the change of the designation of the parent whose gender and sex identifier has been changed as mother, father, or parent, and, if applicable, any change of name that the parent has legally obtained.

(c)(1) The State Registrar shall issue a new birth certificate for an adult child who has a birth certificate issued by this state without a court order when the parent submits directly to the State Registrar all of the following:

(A) An application for a new birth certificate for their adult child reflecting the change of the designation of the petitioner as mother, father, or parent, and, if applicable, any change of name of the parent.

(B) A copy of at least one of the following documents:

(i) A certified copy of the court-ordered change of gender, including a certified English translation, if applicable.

(ii) The parent's new birth certificate reflecting a change of gender and sex identifier.

(iii) A government-issued identity document reflecting the parent's change of gender and sex identifier.

(iv) An affidavit attesting under penalty of perjury that the request for a change of the designation of the petitioner as mother, father, or parent is to conform to the person's gender identity and is not made for any fraudulent purpose.

(C) A notarized letter from the adult child stipulating to the change to the adult child's birth certificate.

(D) The fee prescribed by Section 103725.

(E) If applicable, a certified copy of the court-ordered change of name, including a certified English translation, if applicable.

(2) The notarized letter from the adult child shall be accepted if it contains substantially the following language: "I, (adult child's full name), stipulate to an issuance of a new birth certificate for me that reflects my parent's legal gender and name."

(3) The new birth certificate shall reflect the change of the designation of the parent whose gender and sex identifier has been changed as mother, father, or parent, and, if applicable, any change of name that the parent has legally obtained.

(d)(1) The county clerk shall issue a new confidential marriage license and certificate for a person who has a confidential marriage license and certificate that was issued from their county without a court order when the person submits directly to the county clerk all of the following:

(A) An application from the spouse who has legally changed their gender and sex identifier for a new confidential marriage license and certificate reflecting the change to the designation of the person as bride, groom, or having neither box checked on the confidential marriage license and certificate, and, if applicable, any change of name of the spouse.

(B) A copy of at least one of the following documents:

(i) A certified copy of the court-ordered change of gender, including a certified English translation, if applicable.

(ii) The spouse's new birth certificate reflecting a change of gender and sex identifier.

(iii) A government-issued identity document reflecting the spouse's change of gender and sex identifier.

(iv) An affidavit attesting under penalty of perjury that the request for a change of the designation of the petitioner as bride, groom, or having neither box checked on the marriage license and certificate is to conform to the person's gender identity and is not made for any fraudulent purpose.

(C) A notarized letter from the spouse who is not requesting the new confidential marriage license and certificate stipulating to the change in the confidential marriage license and certificate.

(D) The fee established by the county clerk, not to exceed the amount of the fee for any other confidential marriage license and certificate issued by the county clerk and not to exceed the reasonable cost to provide the confidential marriage license and certificate.

(E) If applicable, a certified copy of the court-ordered change of name, including a certified English translation, if applicable.

(2) The notarized letter from the spouse who is not requesting the new confidential marriage license and certificate shall be accepted if it contains substantially the following language: "I, (spouse's full name), stipulate to an issuance of a new confidential marriage license and certificate for me that reflects my spouse's legal gender and name."

(3) The new confidential marriage license and certificate shall reflect the change to the designation of the person as bride, groom, or having neither box checked on the confidential marriage license and certificate, and, if applicable, any change of name that the spouse has legally obtained.

(4) For purposes of this section, a court-ordered change of gender or name shall include a change of gender or name accomplished by an order of a court of this state, another state, the District of Columbia, any territory of the United States, or any foreign court.

(e)(1) The State Registrar shall issue a new marriage license and certificate for a person who has a marriage license and certificate without a court order if the person submits directly to the State Registrar all of the following:

(A) An application from the spouse who has legally changed their gender and sex identifier for a new marriage license and certificate reflecting the change to the designation of the person as bride, groom, or having neither box checked on the marriage license and certificate, and, if applicable, any change of name of the spouse.

(B) A copy of at least one of the following documents:

(i) A certified copy of the court-ordered change of gender, including a certified English translation, if applicable.

(ii) The spouse's new birth certificate reflecting a change of gender and sex identifier.

(iii) A government-issued identity document reflecting the spouse's change of gender and sex identifier.

(iv) An affidavit attesting under penalty of perjury that the request for a change of the designation of the petitioner as bride, groom, or having neither box checked on the marriage license and certificate is to conform to the person's gender identity and is not made for any fraudulent purpose.

(C) A notarized letter from the spouse who is not requesting the new marriage license and certificate stipulating to the change in the marriage license and certificate.

(D) If applicable, a certified copy of the court-ordered change of name, including a certified English translation, if applicable.

(E) The fee prescribed by Section 103725.

(2) The notarized letter from the spouse who is not requesting the new marriage license and certificate shall be accepted if it contains substantially the following language: "I, (spouse's full name), stipulate to an issuance of a new marriage license and certificate for me that reflects my spouse's legal gender and name."

(3) The new marriage license and certificate shall reflect the change to the designation of the person as bride, groom, or having neither box checked on the marriage license and certificate, and, if applicable, any change of name that the spouse has legally obtained.

(4) For purposes of this section, a court-ordered change of gender or name shall include a change of gender or name accomplished by an order of a court of this state, another state, the District of Columbia, any territory of the United States, or any foreign court.
(Added by Stats.2021, c. 577 (A.B.218), § 8, eff. Jan. 1, 2022, operative Jan. 1, 2023.)

Operative Effect

For operative effect of Article 7, see Health and Safety Code § 103445.

§ 103430. Petition for recognition of change of gender and sex identifier; affidavit of petitioner; grant of petition without hearing; order for new administrative documents

(a) A petition for a court order to recognize a change in the petitioner's gender and sex identifier as female, male, or nonbinary and to direct the issuance of new administrative documents to reflect those changes shall be accompanied by an affidavit from the petitioner and a certified copy of the court order changing the petitioner's name, if applicable. The petitioner's affidavit shall be accepted as conclusive proof of gender change if it contains substantially the following language: "I, (petitioner's full name), hereby attest under penalty of perjury that the request for a change in gender to (female, male, or nonbinary) is to conform my legal gender to my gender identity and is not for any fraudulent purpose."

(b)(1) If the person whose gender is to be changed is under 18 years of age, the petition shall be signed either (A) by at least one of the minor's parents, any guardian of the minor, or a person specified in subdivision (c); or (B) if both parents are deceased and there is no guardian of the minor, by either a near relative or friend of the minor. The affidavit pursuant to subdivision (a) may be signed by the minor.

(2) If the person whose gender is to be changed requests in their petition the issuance of a new marriage license and certificate or confidential marriage license and certificate pursuant to subdivision (c) of Section 103425, the petition shall be signed by the spouse who shares the marriage license and certificate or confidential marriage license and certificate that would be changed by granting the petition if the spouse is living and capable of signing the petition, or, if not signed by the spouse who shares the marriage license and certificate or confidential marriage license and certificate, and the spouse is living and capable, notice must be given to that nonsigning spouse as provided in subdivision (f).

(3) If the person whose gender is to be changed requests in their petition the issuance of a new birth certificate for their adult child pursuant to subdivision (d) of Section 103425, the petition shall be signed by the child whose birth certificate would be changed by granting the petition if the child is 18 years of age or older. A petition that requests a new birth certificate for an adult child pursuant to subdivision (d) of Section 103425 that does not include the signature of the adult child shall not be granted with respect to the new birth certificate for that child if the child is living and capable of providing a signature.

(4) If the person whose gender is to be changed requests in their petition the issuance of a new birth certificate for their minor child pursuant to subdivision (d) of Section 103425, the petition need not include the signature of the petitioner's child if the child is under 18 years of age.

(c) * * * A petition to recognize a change of the gender of a minor signed by a guardian appointed by the juvenile court or the probate court, by a court-appointed dependency attorney appointed as guardian ad litem pursuant to rules adopted under Section 326.5 of the Welfare and Institutions Code, or by an attorney for a minor who is alleged or adjudged to be a person described in Section 601 or 602 of the Welfare and Institutions Code shall be made in the court having jurisdiction over the minor. All petitions to recognize a change of the gender of a nonminor dependent may be made in the juvenile court.

§ 103430

* * *

(d)(1) If the petition is signed by a guardian, the petition shall specify relevant information regarding the guardianship, the likelihood that the child will remain under the guardian's care until the child reaches the age of majority, and information suggesting that the child will not likely be returned to the custody of the child's parents.

(2) Before granting a petition in accordance with this subdivision, the court shall first find that the ward is likely to remain in the guardian's care until the age of majority and that the ward is not likely to be returned to the custody of the parents.

(e)(1) If a petition * * * to * * * <u>recognize a change of gender of a minor</u> does not include the signature * * * of * * * <u>all living parents</u>, then upon receipt of the petition, the court shall thereupon make an order directing the <u>parent or</u> * * * <u>parents who did not sign</u> the petition to show cause why the petition for a court order to recognize a change in the minor's gender and sex identifier to female, male, or nonbinary should not be granted by filing a written objection, which includes any reasons for the objection, within six weeks of the making of the order, and shall state that if no objection showing good cause to oppose the gender recognition is timely filed, the court shall, without hearing, enter the order that the gender and sex identifier recognition is granted.

(2) <u>If a petition to recognize a change of gender of a minor is filed by a person specified in subdivision (c) and all parents are deceased or cannot be located, then upon receipt of the petition, the court shall thereupon make an order directing the living grandparents to show cause why the petition for a court order to recognize a change in the minor's gender and sex identifier to female, male, or nonbinary should not be granted by filing a written objection, which includes any reasons for the objection, within six weeks of the making of the order, and shall state that if no objection showing good cause to oppose the gender recognition is timely filed, the court shall, without hearing, enter the order that the gender and sex identifier recognition is granted.</u>

(3) If a petition pursuant to this section does not include any signature required by paragraph (2) of subdivision (b), then upon receipt of the petition, the court shall thereupon make an order reciting the filing of the petition, the proposed changes to the petitioner's marriage license and certificate or confidential marriage license and certificate, and the name of the person by whom it is filed. The order shall direct the spouse of the petitioner who appears on the marriage license and certificate or confidential marriage license and certificate to make known any objection to the changes requested on the marriage license and certificate or confidential marriage license and certificate by filing a written objection, which includes any reasons why the requested changes would be fraudulent, within six weeks of the making of the order, and shall state that if no objection showing good cause to oppose the changes to the marriage license and certificate or confidential marriage license and certificate is timely filed, the court shall, without hearing, enter the order that the gender and sex identifier recognition is granted.

(f) * * * <u>If the court makes an</u> order to show cause * * * in accordance with subdivision (e)<u>, the petition and the order to show cause</u> shall be served on the required person or persons who did not sign the petition, pursuant to Section 413.10, 414.10, 415.10, or 415.40 of the Code of Civil Procedure, within * * * <u>four weeks</u> from the date on which the order is made by the court. If service cannot reasonably be accomplished pursuant to Section 415.10 or 415.40 of the Code of Civil Procedure, the court may order that service be accomplished in a manner that the court determines is reasonably calculated to give actual notice to the person who did not sign the petition.

(g) If no service is required on any party pursuant to this section, the court shall grant the petition without a hearing if no written objection is timely filed within six weeks of the filing of the petition.

(h) The court shall grant the petition without a hearing, unless a timely objection showing good cause is filed. If an objection showing good cause is timely filed, the court may set a hearing at a time designated by the court. Objections based solely on concerns over the petitioner's actual gender identity or gender assigned at birth shall not constitute good cause.

(1) If a timely objection showing good cause is filed by anyone other than a parent who objects to changes to their minor child's birth certificate, at the hearing, the court may examine under oath the petitioner and any other person having knowledge of the facts relevant to the petition. At the conclusion of the hearing, the court shall grant the petition if the court determines that the petition is not made for any fraudulent purpose.

(2) If the objection was timely filed by a parent who objects to changes to their minor child's birth certificate, after holding a hearing on the matter, the court may deny the petition if the court finds that the change of gender and sex identifier is not in the best interest of the minor. At the hearing, the court may examine under oath the minor and any other person having knowledge of the facts relevant to the petition.

(i) This section shall become operative January 1, 2023. *(Added by Stats.2021, c. 577 (A.B.218), § 8.5, eff. Jan. 1, 2022, operative Jan. 1, 2023. Amended by Stats.2022, c. 40 (A.B.421), § 1, eff. June 23, 2022, operative Jan. 1, 2023.)*

Operative Effect

For operative effect of Article 7, see Health and Safety Code § 103445.

Research References

Forms

West's California Judicial Council Forms NC–200, Petition for Change of Name, Recognition of Change of Gender, and Issuance of New Birth Certificate.

West's California Judicial Council Forms NC–230, Decree Changing Name and Order Recognizing Change of Gender and for Issuance of New Birth Certificate.

West's California Judicial Council Forms NC–300, Petition for Recognition of Change of Gender and for Issuance of New Birth Certificate.

West's California Judicial Council Forms NC–330, Order Recognizing Change of Gender and for Issuance of New Birth Certificate.

West's California Judicial Council Forms NC–500, Petition for Recognition of Minor's Change of Gender and Issuance of New Birth Certificate.

West's California Judicial Council Forms NC–530G, Order Recognizing Change of Gender and for Issuance of New Birth Certificate (By Guardian or Dependency Attorney).

§ 103431. Order for new birth certificate, marriage license and certificate, confidential marriage license and certificate, or birth certificate of petitioner's child; filing with State Registrar

(a)(1) If a judgment pursuant to Section 103430 includes an order for a new birth certificate for the petitioner and if the petitioner has a birth certificate issued by this state, a certified copy of the judgment of the court ordering the new birth certificate, shall, within 30 days from the date of the judgment, be filed by the petitioner with the State Registrar. Upon receipt thereof, together with the application and the fee prescribed by Section 103725, the State Registrar shall establish a new birth certificate for the petitioner.

(2) The new birth certificate shall reflect the gender of the petitioner, as specified in the judgment of the court, and shall reflect any change of name, as specified in the court order, as prescribed by Section 103425. No reference shall be made in the new birth certificate, nor shall its form in any way indicate, that it is not the original birth certificate of the petitioner.

(b)(1)(A) If a judgment pursuant to Section 103430 includes an order for a new marriage license and certificate, and the original marriage license and certificate was confidential and issued within this state, a certified copy of the judgment of the court ordering the new confidential marriage license and certificate shall, within 30 days from the date of the judgment, be filed by the petitioner with the county clerk in the county where the confidential marriage license and certificate was issued, along with the application and the fee established by the county clerk, not to exceed the fee for any other confidential marriage license and certificate issued by the county clerk and not to exceed the reasonable cost to provide the confidential marriage license and certificate. Upon receipt of the copy of the judgment, the application, and the fee, the county clerk shall issue a confidential marriage license and certificate for the petitioner.

(B) If a judgment pursuant to Section 103430 includes an order for a new marriage license and certificate, and the original marriage license and certificate was not confidential and issued within this state, a certified copy of the judgment of the court ordering the new marriage license and certificate shall, within 30 days from the date of the judgment, be filed by the petitioner with the State Registrar, along with the application and the fee prescribed by Section 103725. Upon receipt of the copy of the judgment, the application, and the fee, the State Registrar shall establish a new marriage license and certificate for the petitioner.

(2) If a new marriage license and certificate or confidential marriage license and certificate is requested under subdivision (c) of Section 103425, the new marriage license and certificate or new confidential marriage license and certificate shall reflect any change in the designation of the person as bride, groom, or having neither box checked as requested, and shall reflect any change of name, as specified in the court order, as prescribed by Section 103425. If the "New Names" section of the original marriage license and certificate or original confidential marriage license and certificate that refers to the person whose gender and sex identifier was changed pursuant to Section 103430 does not match any change of name, as specified in the court order, then the "New Names" section for that person shall be left blank on the new marriage license and certificate or new confidential marriage license and certificate of marriage. A new marriage license and certificate or new confidential marriage license and certificate issued pursuant to this article shall not entitle the parties to the marriage to change their names using the procedures in Section 306.5 of the Family Code at the time of the issuance of the new marriage license and certificate or confidential marriage license and certificate. Notwithstanding Sections 103235 and 103255, reference shall not be made in the new marriage license and certificate or new confidential marriage license and certificate, and its form shall not in any way indicate, that it is not the original marriage license and certificate or original confidential marriage license and certificate of the petitioner.

(c)(1) If a judgment pursuant to Section 103430 includes an order for a new birth certificate for the petitioner's child and if the petitioner's child has a birth certificate issued by this state, a certified copy of the judgment of the court ordering the new birth certificate, shall, within 30 days from the date of the judgment, be filed by the petitioner with the State Registrar. Upon receipt thereof, together with the application and the fee prescribed by Section 103725, the State Registrar shall establish a new birth certificate for the petitioner's child.

(2) If a new birth certificate is requested under subdivision (d) of Section 103425, the new birth certificate for the petitioner's child shall reflect the change of the designation of the petitioner as mother, father, or parent and, if applicable, any change of name of the petitioner, as specified in the court order and as prescribed by Section 103425. Reference shall not be made in the new birth certificate, and its form shall not in any way indicate, that it is not the original birth certificate of the petitioner's child. (Added by Stats. 2021, c. 577 (A.B.218), § 8, eff. Jan. 1, 2022, operative Jan. 1, 2023.)

Operative Effect

For operative effect of Article 7, see Health and Safety Code § 103445.

§ 103435. Single petition for change of name, recognition of change in gender and sex identifier, and issuance new birth certificate, marriage license and certificate, confidential marriage license and certificate, or birth certificate of petitioner's child; procedure

(a) In lieu of separate proceedings, a single petition may be filed with the superior court to change the petitioner's name and recognize the change to the petitioner's gender and sex identifier and, if requested, to order the issuance of a new birth certificate, marriage license and certificate, confidential marriage license and certificate, or birth certificate of the petitioner's child. With respect to a single petition, the court shall comply with both of the following:

(1) The procedure set forth in Title 8 (commencing with Section 1275) of Part 3 of the Code of Civil Procedure; however, the order to show cause shall not include the petition to recognize the change of gender and sex identifier.

(2) The procedure set forth in Section 103430 if there is a request for a new marriage license and certificate, confidential marriage license and certificate, or for a new birth certificate for any child of the petitioner.

(b)(1) A certified copy of the judgment of the court issued pursuant to this section shall, within 30 days, be filed by the petitioner with the Secretary of State.

(2) A certified copy of the judgment of the court issued pursuant to this section shall, within 30 days, be filed by the petitioner with the State Registrar, if any of the following conditions are met:

(A) The judgment includes an order for a new birth certificate and the petitioner has a birth certificate issued by this state.

(B) The judgment includes an order for a new marriage license and certificate and the original marriage license and certificate was issued within this state.

(C) The judgment includes an order for a new birth certificate for the petitioner's child and the petitioner's child has a birth certificate issued by this state.

(3) If the judgment issued pursuant to this section includes an order for a new marriage license and certificate, and the original marriage license and certificate was confidential and issued within this state, a certified copy of the judgment of the court shall, within 30 days, be filed by the petitioner with the county clerk in the county where the confidential marriage license and certificate was issued.

(c) Upon receipt of a certified copy of a judgment of the court issued pursuant to this section, together with the application and the fee prescribed by Section 103725, the State Registrar shall establish a new birth certificate or marriage license and certificate as provided in this article.

(d) Upon receipt of a certified copy of a judgment of the court issued pursuant to this section, together with the application and the fee established by the county clerk, not to exceed the fee for any other confidential marriage license and certificate issued by the county clerk and not to exceed the reasonable cost to provide the confidential marriage license and certificate, the county clerk shall issue a new confidential marriage license and certificate as provided in this article. (Added by Stats.2021, c. 577 (A.B.218), § 8, eff. Jan. 1, 2022, operative Jan. 1, 2023.)

Operative Effect

For operative effect of Article 7, see Health and Safety Code § 103445.

Research References

Forms

West's California Judicial Council Forms NC–200, Petition for Change of Name, Recognition of Change of Gender, and Issuance of New Birth Certificate.

§ 103435   HEALTH AND SAFETY CODE

West's California Judicial Council Forms NC–230, Decree Changing Name and Order Recognizing Change of Gender and for Issuance of New Birth Certificate.

West's California Judicial Council Forms NC–300, Petition for Recognition of Change of Gender and for Issuance of New Birth Certificate.

West's California Judicial Council Forms NC–330, Order Recognizing Change of Gender and for Issuance of New Birth Certificate.

West's California Judicial Council Forms NC–500, Petition for Recognition of Minor's Change of Gender and Issuance of New Birth Certificate.

West's California Judicial Council Forms NC–530G, Order Recognizing Change of Gender and for Issuance of New Birth Certificate (By Guardian or Dependency Attorney).

§ 103440. New birth certificate, marriage license and certificate, or confidential marriage license and certificate; effect; inspection; filing; availability of information

(a) The new birth certificate, marriage license and certificate, or confidential marriage license and certificate established pursuant to this article shall supplant any birth certificate, marriage license and certificate, or confidential marriage license and certificate previously registered for the registrant. The new birth certificate or new marriage license and certificate shall be the only birth certificate or marriage license and certificate open to public inspection. The application and supporting affidavit filed pursuant to subdivision (a) of Section 103426 and the applications, supporting affidavits, and stipulations filed pursuant to subdivisions (b) and (c) of Section 103426 shall be filed with the original record of birth, which shall remain as a part of the records of the State Registrar. The applications, supporting affidavits, and stipulations filed pursuant to subdivision (d) of Section 103426 for a confidential marriage license and certificate shall be filed with the original confidential record of marriage, which shall remain as a part of the records of the county clerk. The applications, supporting affidavits, and stipulations filed pursuant to subdivision (e) of Section 103426 for a marriage license and certificate shall be filed with the original record of marriage, which shall remain as a part of the records of the State Registrar. All records and information specified in this article, other than the newly issued birth certificate or marriage license and certificate, shall be available only upon written request of the registrant or an order of a court of record. Nothing in this section changes the confidentiality of or access to a confidential marriage certificate.

(b) When a new birth certificate or a new marriage license and certificate is established under this article, the State Registrar shall transmit copies of the newly established birth certificate or marriage license and certificate for filing to the local registrar and the county recorder whose records contain copies of the original certificate, who shall forward the copies of the original certificate to the State Registrar for filing with the original certificate, if it is practical for the local registrar or the county recorder to do so. If it is impractical for the local registrar or the county recorder to forward the copy to the State Registrar, the local registrar or the county recorder shall effectually seal a cover over the copy of the original certificate in a manner as not to deface or destroy the copy and forward a verified statement of the action to the State Registrar. Thereafter the information contained in the record shall be available only upon written request of the registrant or on order of a court of record.

(c) When a new confidential marriage license and certificate is ordered under this article, the county clerk shall effectually seal a cover over the original certificate in a manner as not to deface or destroy the copy, issue a new confidential marriage license and certificate, and file the new confidential marriage license and certificate in its place. Thereafter the information contained in the record shall be available only upon written request of the registrant or on order of a court of record. *(Added by Stats.2021, c. 577 (A.B.218), § 8, eff. Jan. 1, 2022, operative Jan. 1, 2023.)*

Operative Effect

For operative effect of Article 7, see Health and Safety Code § 103445.

Research References

Forms

West's California Judicial Council Forms NC–300, Petition for Recognition of Change of Gender and for Issuance of New Birth Certificate.

West's California Judicial Council Forms NC–330, Order Recognizing Change of Gender and for Issuance of New Birth Certificate.

§ 103443. Transmittal of certified copy of birth certificate or confidential marriage certificate to registrant

(a) The State Registrar shall transmit a certified copy of a birth certificate newly established under this article to the registrant without additional charge.

(b) The county clerk shall transmit a copy of a confidential marriage certificate newly established under this article to the registrant without additional charge. *(Added by Stats.2021, c. 577 (A.B.218), § 8, eff. Jan. 1, 2022, operative Jan. 1, 2023.)*

Operative Effect

For operative effect of Article 7, see Health and Safety Code § 103445.

§ 103445. Operative date of article

This article shall become operative on January 1, 2023. *(Added by Stats.2021, c. 577 (A.B.218), § 8, eff. Jan. 1, 2022, operative Jan. 1, 2023.)*

CHAPTER 12. COURT PROCEEDINGS TO ESTABLISH RECORD OF BIRTH, DEATH OR MARRIAGE

Section
103450. Filing petition; venue; mass fatalities incidents.
103451. Mass fatalities incident.
103455. Verification; contents.
103460. Time and place of birth unknown; contents of petition; verification of known facts.
103465. Hearing; continuance.
103466. Filing petition for determination of death in mass fatalities incident; timing and notice of hearing.
103470. Filing fee; hearings in counties having more than one superior court judge.
103475. Order of court.
103480. Time and place of birth unknown; evidence; order of court.
103485. Form of order; effective date; presumption.
103490. Transmittal of certified copies; mass fatalities incident.

§ 103450. Filing petition; venue; mass fatalities incidents

(a) A verified petition may be filed by any beneficially interested person with the clerk of the superior court in and for (1) the county in which the birth, death, or marriage is alleged to have occurred, (2) the county of residence of the person whose birth or marriage it is sought to establish, or (3) the county in which the person was domiciled at the date of death for an order to judicially establish the fact of, and the time and place of, a birth, death, or marriage that is not registered or for which a certified copy is not obtainable.

(b) In the event of a mass fatalities incident, a verified petition may be filed by a coroner, medical examiner, or any beneficially interested person with the clerk of the superior court in and for (1) the county in which the death is alleged to have occurred, or (2) the county in which the person was domiciled at the date of death for an order to judicially establish the fact of, and the time and place of, a death that is not registered or for which a certified copy of the death certificate is not obtainable.

(c) In the event of a mass fatalities incident, a single verified petition with respect to all persons who died may be filed by a coroner or medical examiner with the clerk of the superior court in and for the county in which the mass fatalities incident occurred for an order to judicially establish the fact of, and the time and place of, each person's death that is not registered or for which a certified copy of the death certificate is not obtainable. *(Added by Stats.1995, c. 415 (S.B.1360), § 4. Amended by Stats.2002, c. 717 (A.B.1872), § 1.)*

Cross References

Action to test validity of marriage pursuant to this section, see Family Code § 309.
Affidavits, use in uncontested proceedings to establish record of birth, see Code of Civil Procedure § 2009.
Annual adjustment of fees and charges, see Health and Safety Code § 100430.
Establishment of fact of death, see Probate Code § 200 et seq.
Intercountry adoptions, adoptions finalized in foreign country, readoption of child in state, state-issued birth certificate, see Family Code § 8919.
Person not heard from in five years presumed dead, see Evidence Code § 667.
Place of trial, generally, see Code of Civil Procedure § 392 et seq.
Verification of pleadings, see Code of Civil Procedure § 446.

Research References

Forms

West's California Judicial Council Forms BMD–001, Petition to Establish Fact, Time, and Place of Birth.
West's California Judicial Council Forms BMD–001A, Declaration in Support of Petition to Establish Fact, Time, and Place of Birth.
West's California Judicial Council Forms BMD–002, Petition to Establish Fact, Time, and Place of Marriage.
West's California Judicial Council Forms BMD–002A, Declaration in Support of Petition to Establish Fact, Time, and Place of Marriage.
West's California Judicial Council Forms BMD–003, Petition to Establish Fact, Date, and Place of Death.
West's California Judicial Council Forms BMD–003A, Declaration in Support of Petition to Establish Fact, Date, and Place of Death.

§ 103451. Mass fatalities incident

(a) For purposes of this chapter, "mass fatalities incident" means a situation in which any of the following conditions exist:

(1) There are more dead bodies than can be handled using local resources.

(2) Numerous persons are known to have died, but no bodies were recovered from the site of the incident.

(3) Numerous persons are known to have died, but the recovery and identification of the bodies of those persons is impracticable or impossible.

(b) The county coroner or medical examiner may make the determination that a condition described in subdivision (a) exists. *(Added by Stats.2002, c. 717 (A.B.1872), § 2.)*

§ 103455. Verification; contents

The petition shall be verified and shall contain all the facts necessary to enable the court to determine the fact of and the time and place of the birth, death, or marriage upon the proofs adduced in behalf of the petitioner at the hearing. *(Added by Stats.1995, c. 415 (S.B.1360), § 4.)*

Cross References

Family history, admissibility of evidence, see Evidence Code § 1310 et seq.
Verification of pleadings, see Code of Civil Procedure § 446.

§ 103460. Time and place of birth unknown; contents of petition; verification of known facts

If the time and place of birth are not known, the petition shall contain all of the facts known to the petitioner or otherwise available and a statement of the probable time and place of birth as accurately as the circumstances permit. The petition shall be verified as to the known facts only. *(Added by Stats.1995, c. 415 (S.B.1360), § 4.)*

§ 103465. Hearing; continuance

Upon the filing of the petition a hearing shall be fixed by the clerk and at the convenience of the court set at a time not less than five nor more than 10 days after the filing of the petition. The hearing may be held in chambers. The court, for good cause, may continue the hearing beyond the 10–day period. *(Added by Stats.1995, c. 415 (S.B.1360), § 4.)*

Cross References

Computation of time, see Code of Civil Procedure §§ 12 and 12a; Government Code § 6800 et seq.
Hearing in chambers, see Code of Civil Procedure § 166.

§ 103466. Filing petition for determination of death in mass fatalities incident; timing and notice of hearing

Notwithstanding Section 103465, upon the filing of a petition for a determination of the fact of death in the event of a mass fatalities incident, the clerk shall set a hearing no later than 15 days from the date the petition was filed. The petitioner shall make a reasonable effort to provide notice of the hearing to the known heirs of the deceased up to the second degree of relationship. Failure to provide the notice specified in this section shall not invalidate the judicial proceedings regarding the determination of the fact of death. *(Added by Stats.2002, c. 717 (A.B.1872), § 3.)*

Cross References

Computation of time, see Code of Civil Procedure §§ 12 and 12a; Government Code § 6800 et seq.
Notice, actual and constructive, defined, see Civil Code § 18.

§ 103470. Filing fee; hearings in counties having more than one superior court judge

The fee for filing the petition is two hundred five dollars ($205). This fee shall be distributed as provided in Section 68085.4 of the Government Code. The petition may be heard by any judge hearing probate matters, or if a probate department has been designated for hearing probate matters, the matter shall be assigned to the probate department for hearing. *(Added by Stats.1995, c. 415 (S.B.1360), § 4. Amended by Stats.2005, c. 75 (A.B.145), § 144, eff. July 19, 2005, operative Jan. 1, 2006; Stats.2008, c. 311 (S.B.1407), § 26; Stats.2009–2010, 4th Ex.Sess., c. 22 (S.B.13), § 28, eff. July 28, 2009.)*

Cross References

Certain fees to be deposited into bank account, distribution and transmittal, see Government Code § 68085.4.
County fees, authority to increase or decrease fees or charges, application to this section, see Government Code § 54985.
Deposit of fees or fines collected pursuant to this section in the Trial Court Trust Fund, effect of prior agreements or practices, long-term revenue allocation schedule proposal, see Government Code § 68085.5.
Organization and government of courts, collection of fees and fines pursuant to this section, deposits, see Government Code § 68085.1.
Superior court filing fees, distribution to county law library funds, see Business and Professions Code § 6321.

§ 103475. Order of court

If, upon the hearing, the allegations of the petition are established to the satisfaction of the court, the court may make an order determining that the birth, death, or marriage did in fact occur at the time and place shown by the proofs adduced at the hearing. *(Added by Stats.1995, c. 415 (S.B.1360), § 4.)*

Cross References

Inspection of public records, other exemptions from disclosure, see Government Code § 6276.06.

§ 103480. Time and place of birth unknown; evidence; order of court

If the time and place of birth are not known, the court shall receive and consider evidence and testimony as may be available and from

§ 103480

the facts adduced may, by order, fix the time and place that the court finds to be a probable time and place of birth of the person in relation to whom the petition has been filed, as the time and place of birth. The time and place so fixed shall thereafter for all purposes be the time and place of birth of the person. (Added by Stats.1995, c. 415 (S.B.1360), § 4.)

§ 103485. Form of order; effective date; presumption

The order shall be made in the form and upon the blank prescribed and furnished by the State Registrar and shall become effective upon a filing of a certified copy with the State Registrar.

Every order determining the date of birth made pursuant to this chapter shall establish a presumption that the matter contained therein is a true and accurate statement of the time of birth. The presumption established by this section is a presumption affecting the burden of proof. (Added by Stats.1995, c. 415 (S.B.1360), § 4.)

Cross References

Presumptions, see Evidence Code § 600 et seq.

§ 103490. Transmittal of certified copies; mass fatalities incident

(a) The State Registrar shall send certified copies of the court order delayed certificate to the local registrar and the county recorder within the area in which the event occurred and in whose offices copies of records of the year of occurrence of the event are on file. However, if the event occurred outside the state, a certified copy shall be sent only to the county recorder of the county in which the petitioner resides.

(b) In the event of a mass fatalities incident, the State Registrar, without delay, shall send certified copies of the court order delayed death certificate to the local registrar and the county recorder of the county in which the incident occurred and in whose offices copies of records of the year of occurrence of the incident are on file. The State Registrar, without delay, also shall send a certified copy of the court order delayed death certificate to the spouse or next of kin of the decedent, if there is no spouse, provided the spouse or next of kin's name and address information are included in the court order or on the application form submitted by the spouse, next of kin, coroner, or medical examiner. However, if the incident occurred outside the state, a certified copy shall be sent only to the county recorder of the county in which the decedent was domiciled at the date of death. (Added by Stats.1995, c. 415 (S.B.1360), § 4. Amended by Stats.2002, c. 717 (A.B.1872), § 4.)

Research References

Forms

West's California Judicial Council Forms BMD–001, Petition to Establish Fact, Time, and Place of Birth.

West's California Judicial Council Forms BMD–001A, Declaration in Support of Petition to Establish Fact, Time, and Place of Birth.

West's California Judicial Council Forms BMD–002, Petition to Establish Fact, Time, and Place of Marriage.

West's California Judicial Council Forms BMD–002A, Declaration in Support of Petition to Establish Fact, Time, and Place of Marriage.

West's California Judicial Council Forms BMD–003, Petition to Establish Fact, Date, and Place of Death.

West's California Judicial Council Forms BMD–003A, Declaration in Support of Petition to Establish Fact, Date, and Place of Death.

CHAPTER 15. FEES OF STATE AND LOCAL REGISTRARS

ARTICLE 2. FEE FOR CERTIFIED COPY OR SEARCH OF RECORDS

Section
103626. Contra Costa County Board of Supervisors; domestic violence; fee increase for certified copies of marriage certificates, birth certificates, fetal death records, and death records; additional fees.
103627. Alameda County and City of Berkeley; fee increase for certified copies of marriage, birth, and death records; additional fees.
103628. Solano County Board of Supervisors; domestic violence; fee increase for certified copies of marriage certificates, birth certificates, fetal death records, and death records; additional fees.

§ 103626. Contra Costa County Board of Supervisors; domestic violence; fee increase for certified copies of marriage certificates, birth certificates, fetal death records, and death records; additional fees

(a) The Contra Costa County Board of Supervisors, upon making findings and declarations supporting the need for governmental oversight and coordination of the multiple agencies dealing with domestic violence, may authorize an increase in the fees for certified copies of marriage certificates, birth certificates, fetal death records, and death records, up to a maximum increase of four dollars ($4).

(b) Effective July 1 of each year, the Contra Costa County Board of Supervisors may authorize an increase in these fees by an amount equal to the increase in the Consumer Price Index for the San Francisco metropolitan area for the preceding calendar year, rounded to the nearest half-dollar. The fees shall be disposed of pursuant to the provisions of Section 18308 of the Welfare and Institutions Code.

(c) In addition to the fees prescribed by subdivisions (a) and (b) of this section, any applicant for a certified copy of a birth certificate, a fetal death record, or death record in Contra Costa County shall pay an additional fee to the local registrar, county recorder, or county clerk as established by the Contra Costa County Board of Supervisors. (Added by Stats.2001, c. 90 (S.B.425), § 3. Amended by Stats.2006, c. 635 (S.B.968), § 2.)

Cross References

Contra Costa County Board of Supervisors, depositing fees collected pursuant to this section into special fund, use of proceeds, see Welfare and Institutions Code § 18308.

§ 103627. Alameda County and City of Berkeley; fee increase for certified copies of marriage, birth, and death records; additional fees

(a)(1) The Alameda County Board of Supervisors, upon making findings and declarations supporting the need for governmental oversight and coordination of the multiple agencies dealing with domestic violence, may authorize an increase in the fees for certified copies of marriage certificates, birth certificates, fetal death records, and death records, up to a maximum increase of two dollars ($2).

(2) The City Council of the City of Berkeley, upon making findings and declarations supporting the need for governmental oversight and coordination of the multiple agencies dealing with domestic violence, may authorize an increase in the fees for certified copies of birth certificates, fetal death records, and death records, up to a maximum increase of two dollars ($2).

(b) Effective July 1 of each year, the Alameda County Board of Supervisors and the City Council of the City of Berkeley may authorize an increase in these fees by an amount equal to the increase in the Consumer Price Index for the San Francisco metropolitan area for the preceding calendar year, rounded to the nearest half-dollar ($0.50). The fees shall be disposed of pursuant to the provisions of Section 18309 of the Welfare and Institutions Code.

(c) In addition to the fees prescribed by subdivisions (a) and (b), any applicant for a certified copy of a birth certificate, a fetal death record, or death record in Alameda County or in the City of Berkeley shall pay an additional fee to the local registrar, county recorder, or county clerk, as applicable, as established by the Alameda County Board of Supervisors or the City Council of the City of Berkeley. *(Added by Stats.2004, c. 830 (A.B.2010), § 4. Amended by Stats.2005, c. 545 (A.B.1712), § 1; Stats.2009, c. 215 (A.B.73), § 4.)*

§ 103628. Solano County Board of Supervisors; domestic violence; fee increase for certified copies of marriage certificates, birth certificates, fetal death records, and death records; additional fees

(a) The Solano County Board of Supervisors, upon making findings and declarations for the need for governmental oversight and coordination of the multiple agencies dealing with domestic violence, may authorize an increase in the fees for certified copies of marriage certificates, birth certificates, fetal death records, and death records, up to a maximum increase of two dollars ($2).

(b) Effective July 1 of each year, the Solano County Board of Supervisors may authorize an increase in these fees by an amount equal to the increase in the Consumer Price Index for the San Francisco metropolitan area for the preceding calendar year, rounded to the nearest one-half dollar ($0.50). The fees shall be allocated pursuant to Section 18309.5 of the Welfare and Institutions Code.

(c) In addition to the fees prescribed by subdivisions (a) and (b), any applicant for a certified copy of a birth certificate, a fetal death record, or death record in Solano County shall pay an additional fee to the local registrar, county recorder, or county clerk as established by the Solano County Board of Supervisors. *(Added by Stats.2004, c. 830 (A.B.2010), § 5. Amended by Stats.2009, c. 356 (S.B.635), § 3; Stats.2010, c. 520 (S.B.1222), § 2; Stats.2011, c. 120 (S.B.154), § 2.)*

Cross References

Solano County Board of Supervisors, depositing fees collected pursuant to this section into special fund, use of proceeds, see Welfare and Institutions Code § 18309.5.

INSURANCE CODE

Division 1

GENERAL RULES GOVERNING INSURANCE

Cross References

Interpretation of provisions, see Insurance Code § 37.

Writing defined for purposes of this Code, see Insurance Code § 8.

Part 1

THE CONTRACT

Cross References

Admitted defined for purposes of this Code, see Insurance Code § 24.
City defined for purposes of this Code, see Insurance Code § 15.
Commissioner defined for purposes of this Code, see Insurance Code § 20.
County defined for purposes of this Code, see Insurance Code § 14.
Department or division defined for purposes of this Code, see Insurance Code § 14.
Domestic defined for purposes of this Code, see Insurance Code § 26.
Foreign defined for purposes of this Code, see Insurance Code § 27.
Group as designation of insurance coverage, see Insurance Code § 42.
Lien, mortgage, mortgagor, and mortgagee defined for purposes of this Code, see Insurance Code § 29.
Notice, method required and affidavit for purposes of this Code, see Insurance Code § 38.
Person defined for purposes of this Code, see Insurance Code § 19.
Policy defined, generally, see Insurance Code § 380.
Transact, as applied to insurance, defined for purposes of this Code, see Insurance Code § 35.

CHAPTER 4. THE POLICY

ARTICLE 1. DEFINITION AND SCOPE

Section
381.5. Domestic partners; coverage.

§ 381.5. Domestic partners; coverage

(a) Every policy issued, amended, delivered, or renewed in this state shall provide coverage for the registered domestic partner of an insured or policyholder that is equal to, and subject to the same terms and conditions as, the coverage provided to a spouse of an insured or policyholder. A policy may not offer or provide coverage for a registered domestic partner if it is not equal to the coverage provided for the spouse of an insured or policyholder. This subdivision applies to all forms of insurance regulated by this code.

(b) A policy subject to this section that is issued, amended, delivered, or renewed in this state on or after January 1, 2005, shall be deemed to provide coverage for registered domestic partners that is equal to the coverage provided to a spouse of an insured or policyholder.

(c) It is the intent of the Legislature that, for purposes of this section, "terms," "conditions," and "coverage" do not include instances of differential treatment of domestic partners and spouses under federal law. *(Added by Stats.2004, c. 488 (A.B.2208), § 3.)*

Division 3

THE INSURANCE COMMISSIONER

Cross References

Admitted defined for purposes of this Code, see Insurance Code § 24.
City defined for purposes of this Code, see Insurance Code § 15.
Commissioner defined for purposes of this Code, see Insurance Code § 20.
County defined for purposes of this Code, see Insurance Code § 14.
Department or division defined for purposes of this Code, see Insurance Code § 21.
Domestic defined for purposes of this Code, see Insurance Code § 26.
Foreign defined for purposes of this Code, see Insurance Code § 27.
"Group" as designation of insurance coverage, see Insurance Code § 42.
Lien, mortgage, mortgagor, and mortgagee defined for purposes of this Code, see Insurance Code § 29.
Notice, method required and affidavit for purposes of this Code, see Insurance Code § 38.
Person defined for purposes of this Code, see Insurance Code § 19.
Policy defined, generally, see Insurance Code § 380.
"Transact", as applied to insurance, defined for purposes of this Code, see Insurance Code § 35.
Writing defined for purposes of this Code, see Insurance Code § 8.

CHAPTER 2. POWERS AND DUTIES

ARTICLE 8. INSURANCE PAYMENT INTERCEPT PROGRAM

Section
13550. Identification by insurers of claimants owing past-due child support; reporting; exceptions; withholding from disability insurance payment; notice by department and compliance.
13551. Immunity from liability for parties releasing information, withholding payments, or making disbursements; claimants owing past-due child support.
13552. Use of data identifying claimants owing past-due child support; compliance with privacy protection laws.
13553. Use of central reporting organization to identify and report claimants owing past-due child support; notification of Department of Child Support Services.
13554. "Central reporting organization" defined.
13555. Operative date of article.

Operative Effect

For operative effect of Article 8, see Insurance Code § 13555.

§ 13550. Identification by insurers of claimants owing past-due child support; reporting; exceptions; withholding from disability insurance payment; notice by department and compliance

(a) An insurer shall cooperate with the Department of Child Support Services to identify claimants who are also obligors who owe past-due child support and report those claimants to the Department of Child Support Services.

§ 13550

(b) An insurer shall identify and report a claimant to the Department of Child Support Services if the claim seeks an economic benefit for an obligor who owes past-due child support.

(1) An "economic benefit" under a life insurance policy, disability income insurance policy, or annuity means a payment totaling at least one thousand dollars ($1,000) in which an individual is paid as the payee or copayee for any of the following:

(A) A claim by a beneficiary under a life insurance policy.

(B) A payment of the cash surrender value of a life insurance policy or annuity.

(C) A payment to an annuitant.

(D) A payment from a disability income insurance policy.

(E) A loan against the cash value or surrender value of an insurance policy or annuity, excluding loans for premium payments.

(2) An "economic benefit" under a property and casualty insurance policy means a payment totaling at least one thousand dollars ($1,000) under a liability insurance policy or underinsured motorist policy issued by an insurance company authorized to do business in this state. An "economic benefit" under a property and casualty insurance policy does not include payments to replace or repair lost or damaged property.

(c) Notwithstanding subdivision (b), and except as provided in subdivision (h), a claimant with any of following economic benefits shall not be reported:

(1) Payments resulting from an accelerated death benefit.

(2) A claim for benefits assigned to be paid to a health care provider or facility for actual medical expenses owed by the insured that are not otherwise paid or reimbursed, or a payment made after the claimant provides proof of the amount actually paid by the claimant to a health care provider if the amount is at least as much as the insurance payment, but not any amounts billed but not paid.

(3) A claim for benefits to be paid under a limited benefit insurance policy that provides one of the following:

(A) Coverage for one or more specified diseases or illnesses.

(B) Dental or vision benefits.

(C) Hospital indemnity or other fixed indemnity coverage.

(D) Accident only coverage.

(4) A claim for benefits that are the result of a state of emergency, as defined in Section 8558 of the Government Code.

(5) A claim for benefits under a workers' compensation policy, except as provided in Section 17510 of the Family Code and Section 138.5 of the Labor Code.

(d) An insurer in California subject to the requirements of this article shall identify and report a claimant to the Department of Child Support Services if either of the following apply:

(1) A payment is made to the owner of a life policy or annuity that was issued to the owner while residing or located in California.

(2) A beneficiary making a claim resides or is located in California.

(e) Withholding from a qualifying disability insurance payment made to an obligor who owes past-due child support shall be limited to 50 percent of the claim for benefits.

(f)(1) If an insurer identifies a claimant as an obligor who owes past-due child support and reports the claimant to the Department of Child Support Services, the Department of Child Support Services shall provide the insurer with either of the following to secure the payment of the amount of past-due child support:

(A) A notice of child support lien.

(B) An income-withholding order.

(2) Upon receiving notice from the Department of Child Support Services that a reported insurance claim is payable to an obligor with a child support delinquency, an insurer shall comply with the requirements of the notice.

(3) Notwithstanding paragraph (2), this section does not require an insurer to comply with a notice from the Department of Child Support Services on a reported insurance claim payable to an obligor with a child support delinquency if the notice is received after the insurer has paid the claim.

(g) For the purposes of this section, "insurer" includes a fraternal benefit society.

(h) This section does not prohibit an insurer from cooperating voluntarily with the Department of Child Support Services to identify claimants who are also obligors who owe past-due child support and report those claimants to the Department of Child Support Services. *(Added by Stats.2018, c. 439 (A.B.2802), § 1, eff. Jan. 1, 2019, operative Jan. 1, 2020. Amended by Stats.2019, c. 201 (A.B.1813), § 14, eff. Jan. 1, 2020; Stats.2020, c. 184 (S.B.1255), § 47, eff. Jan. 1, 2021.)*

Operative Effect

For operative effect of Article 8, see Insurance Code § 13555.

§ 13551. Immunity from liability for parties releasing information, withholding payments, or making disbursements; claimants owing past-due child support

Notwithstanding any other law, an insurer or insurance company, its directors, agents, and employees, an insured individual on whose behalf the company makes a payment, and a central reporting organization and its respective employees and agents authorized by an insurer to act on its behalf who, in good faith, release information in accordance with this article, withhold amounts from payment based on the latest information supplied by the Department of Child Support Services pursuant to Section 13550, or make disbursements in accordance with Section 13550 shall be in compliance with this section and any applicable fair claim settlement act, and shall be immune from any liability to the claimant or other interested party arising from the payment. *(Added by Stats.2018, c. 439 (A.B.2802), § 1, eff. Jan. 1, 2019, operative Jan. 1, 2020.)*

Operative Effect

For operative effect of Article 8, see Insurance Code § 13555.

§ 13552. Use of data identifying claimants owing past-due child support; compliance with privacy protection laws

(a) Data obtained pursuant to this article shall only be used for the purpose of identifying claimants who are also obligors who owe past-due child support. If the Department of Child Support Services does not identify an obligor in the data obtained pursuant to this article with a child support obligor, the Department of Child Support Services shall not maintain that data and shall immediately destroy that data.

(b) An insurer that provides, attempts to provide, or in any way accesses data pursuant to this article shall comply with all applicable state and federal laws for the protection of the privacy and the security of that data, including, but not limited to, the Insurance Information and Privacy Protection Act (Article 6.6 (commencing with Section 791) of Chapter 1 of Part 2 of Division 1), the Information Practices Act of 1977 (Chapter 1 (commencing with Section 1798) of Title 1.8 of Part 4 of Division 3 of the Civil Code), and the federal Health Insurance Portability and Accountability Act of 1996 (Public Law 104–191).[1]

(c) The Department of Child Support Services shall consider any information received from an insurer as confidential. That information shall be used or disclosed only for the purpose of collecting past-due child support.

(d) Information provided by the Department of Child Support Services to an insurer, or its designated agent, for the purpose of identifying claimants who are also obligors shall not be used by the insurer or its agent for any other purpose, and shall not be disclosed to any person except to the extent necessary to identify and report a claimant who owes past-due child support. This subdivision does not apply to information contained in a child support lien or an income-withholding order received from the Department of Child Support Services after the insurer has identified and reported a claimant.

(e) This section does not prohibit the Department of Child Support Services from disclosing aggregate data that does not reveal personally identifying information. *(Added by Stats.2018, c. 439 (A.B.2802), § 1, eff. Jan. 1, 2019, operative Jan. 1, 2020.)*

[1] For public law sections classified to the U.S.C.A., see USCA–Tables.

Operative Effect

For operative effect of Article 8, see Insurance Code § 13555.

§ 13553. Use of central reporting organization to identify and report claimants owing past-due child support; notification of Department of Child Support Services

(a) An insurer may satisfy its obligation to identify and report a claimant who owes past-due child support through the use of a central reporting organization. If an insurer does not use a central reporting organization to automate the process, the insurer shall determine if the claimant owes past-due child support before paying a claim.

(b) For claims involving periodic payments after the insurer has determined that benefits will be paid, the insurer shall only determine if the claimant owes past-due child support before the initial payment and either 12 months thereafter, or the insurer may provide a copy of the settlement to the Department of Child Support Services.

(c) If a central reporting organization identifies a claimant who is also an obligor, the central reporting organization shall notify the Department of Child Support Services, and the Department of Child Support Services shall follow the requirements of subdivision (e) of Section 13550. *(Added by Stats.2018, c. 439 (A.B.2802), § 1, eff. Jan. 1, 2019, operative Jan. 1, 2020.)*

Operative Effect

For operative effect of Article 8, see Insurance Code § 13555.

§ 13554. "Central reporting organization" defined

For the purposes of this article, "central reporting organization" means a third-party service that automates the claims identifying process or provides interactive lookups. *(Added by Stats.2018, c. 439 (A.B.2802), § 1, eff. Jan. 1, 2019, operative Jan. 1, 2020.)*

Operative Effect

For operative effect of Article 8, see Insurance Code § 13555.

§ 13555. Operative date of article

This article shall become operative on January 1, 2020. *(Added by Stats.2018, c. 439 (A.B.2802), § 1, eff. Jan. 1, 2019, operative Jan. 1, 2020.)*

PENAL CODE

Part 1

OF CRIMES AND PUNISHMENTS

Title 5

OF CRIMES BY AND AGAINST THE EXECUTIVE POWER OF THE STATE

Section
70.5. Commissioner of civil marriages; acceptance of fees or gratuities.

Cross References

Applicability of this Title to administrative and ministerial officers, see Penal Code § 77.

Exclusion from office, franchise or privilege, see Code of Civil Procedure § 809.

Executive department, generally, see Cal. Const. Art. 5, § 1 et seq.; Government Code § 11000 et seq.

Financial institutions, bribery of officer, director or employee to procure loan or extension of credit, see Penal Code § 639.

Local agencies, abuse of office or position defined, see Government Code § 53243.4.

Militia,
  Disobedience of orders, see Military and Veterans Code § 364.
  Failure to enroll, see Military and Veterans Code § 124.
  Firing blank cartridges upon mob or unlawful assemblage, see Military and Veterans Code § 367.
  Military forces, discrimination against personnel, see Military and Veterans Code § 394.
  Right of way while parading or performing military duty, see Military and Veterans Code § 396.

Privilege and confidentiality as to communications to public officers, see Evidence Code §§ 1040, 1041; Insurance Code §§ 1433, 12919; Labor Code § 6412; Revenue and Taxation Code §§ 408, 833, 7056; Welfare and Institutions Code § 10850.

Public officers,
  Divulging confidential information, see Government Code § 11183.
  Willful omission to perform duty, see Government Code § 1222.

Public officers and employees interest in official contracts, violations, see Government Code § 1090.

Public utility districts, unlawful interest of officers in contracts, see Public Utilities Code § 16043.

San Francisco Bay Area Rapid Transit District, prohibited interests of officers, see Public Utilities Code § 28816.

Unemployment compensation, divulging confidential information, see Unemployment Insurance Code § 2111.

§ 70.5. Commissioner of civil marriages; acceptance of fees or gratuities

Every commissioner of civil marriages or every deputy commissioner of civil marriages who accepts any money or other thing of value for performing any marriage pursuant to Section 401 of the Family Code, including any money or thing of value voluntarily tendered by the persons about to be married or who have been married by the commissioner of civil marriages or deputy commissioner of civil marriages, other than a fee expressly imposed by law for performance of a marriage, whether the acceptance occurs before or after performance of the marriage and whether or not performance of the marriage is conditioned on the giving of such money or the thing of value by the persons being married, is guilty of a misdemeanor.

It is not a necessary element of the offense described by this section that the acceptance of the money or other thing of value be committed with intent to commit extortion or with other criminal intent.

This section does not apply to the request or acceptance by any retired commissioner of civil marriages of a fee for the performance of a marriage.

This section is inapplicable to the acceptance of a fee for the performance of a marriage on Saturday, Sunday, or a legal holiday. (Added by Stats.1973, c. 979, p. 1885, § 4. Amended by Stats.1981, c. 327, p. 1469, § 1; Stats.1987, c. 753, § 1; Stats.1992, c. 163 (A.B.2641), § 100, operative Jan. 1, 1994.)

Title 7

OF CRIMES AGAINST PUBLIC JUSTICE

CHAPTER 1. BRIBERY AND CORRUPTION

Section
94.5. Judges or commissioners; acceptance of fees or gratuities for performing marriage; exceptions.

Cross References

Conviction of crime as disqualification for peace officer, felonies, guilty pleas, see Government Code § 1029.

§ 94.5. Judges or commissioners; acceptance of fees or gratuities for performing marriage; exceptions

Every judge, justice, commissioner, or assistant commissioner of a court of this state who accepts any money or other thing of value for performing any marriage, including any money or thing of value voluntarily tendered by the persons about to be married or who have been married by such judge, justice, commissioner, or assistant commissioner, whether the acceptance occurs before or after performance of the marriage and whether or not performance of the marriage is conditioned on the giving of such money or the thing of value by the persons being married, is guilty of a misdemeanor.

It is not a necessary element of the offense described by this section that the acceptance of the money or other thing of value be committed with intent to commit extortion or with other criminal intent.

This section does not apply to the request for or acceptance of a fee expressly imposed by law for performance of a marriage or to the request or acceptance by any retired judge, retired justice, or retired commissioner of a fee for the performance of a marriage. For the purposes of this section, a retired judge or retired justice sitting on assignment in court shall not be deemed to be a retired judge or retired justice.

This section does not apply to an acceptance of a fee for performing a marriage on Saturday, Sunday, or a legal holiday. (Added by Stats.1959, c. 1589, p. 3919, § 1. Amended by Stats.1971, c. 642, p. 1264, § 2; Stats.1971, c. 671, p. 1327, § 2.5; Stats.1973, c. 927, p. 1717, § 2; Stats.1977, c. 1257, p. 4432, § 117, eff. Jan. 3, 1977; Stats.1978, c. 305, p. 633, § 1; Stats.1987, c. 753, § 2.)

Cross References

Persons authorized to solemnize marriage, see Family Code § 400.

§ 94.5

Punishment, misdemeanor, see Penal Code §§ 19, 19.2, 19.4.

CHAPTER 6. FALSIFYING EVIDENCE, AND BRIBING, INFLUENCING, INTIMIDATING OR THREATENING WITNESSES

Section

136.2. Protective orders available in response to good cause belief of harm to, intimidation of, or dissuasion of victim or witness; hearings; findings and consent of law enforcement required; transmission of orders and modified orders; effect of emergency protective orders; restrictions on firearms possession; forms; electronic monitoring.

136.3. Addresses or locations of persons protected under court order; prohibition upon certain enjoined parties from acting to obtain such information.

Cross References

Compounding or concealing crimes, see Penal Code § 153.
Conviction of crime as disqualification for peace officer, felonies, guilty pleas, see Government Code § 1029.
Evidence, generally, see Evidence Code § 140; Penal Code § 1102.
Felony and misdemeanor defined, see Penal Code § 17.
Perjury and subornation of perjury, see Penal Code § 118 et seq.
Witnesses, see Penal Code § 1321 et seq.; Code of Civil Procedure § 1878 et seq.

§ 136.2. Protective orders available in response to good cause belief of harm to, intimidation of, or dissuasion of victim or witness; hearings; findings and consent of law enforcement required; transmission of orders and modified orders; effect of emergency protective orders; restrictions on firearms possession; forms; electronic monitoring

(a)(1) Upon a good cause belief that harm to, or intimidation or dissuasion of, a victim or witness has occurred or is reasonably likely to occur, a court with jurisdiction over a criminal matter may issue orders, including, but not limited to, the following:

(A) An order issued pursuant to Section 6320 of the Family Code.

(B) An order that a defendant shall not violate any provision of Section 136.1.

(C) An order that a person before the court other than a defendant, including, but not limited to, a subpoenaed witness or other person entering the courtroom of the court, shall not violate any provision of Section 136.1.

(D) An order that a person described in this section shall have no communication whatsoever with a specified witness or a victim, except through an attorney under reasonable restrictions that the court may impose.

(E) An order calling for a hearing to determine if an order described in subparagraphs (A) to (D), inclusive, should be issued.

(F)(i) An order that a particular law enforcement agency within the jurisdiction of the court provide protection for a victim, witness, or both, or for immediate family members of a victim or a witness who reside in the same household as the victim or witness or within reasonable proximity of the victim's or witness' household, as determined by the court. The order shall not be made without the consent of the law enforcement agency except for limited and specified periods of time and upon an express finding by the court of a clear and present danger of harm to the victim or witness or immediate family members of the victim or witness.

(ii) For purposes of this paragraph, "immediate family members" include the spouse, children, or parents of the victim or witness.

(G)(i) An order protecting a victim or witness of violent crime from all contact by the defendant, or contact, with the intent to annoy, harass, threaten, or commit acts of violence, by the defendant.

The court or its designee shall transmit orders made under this paragraph to law enforcement personnel within one business day of the issuance, modification, extension, or termination of the order, pursuant to subdivision (a) of Section 6380 of the Family Code. It is the responsibility of the court to transmit the modification, extension, or termination orders made under this paragraph to the same agency that entered the original protective order into the California Restraining and Protective Order System.

(ii)(I) If a court does not issue an order pursuant to clause (i) when the defendant is charged with a crime involving domestic violence as defined in Section 13700 of this code or in Section 6211 of the Family Code, the court, on its own motion, shall consider issuing a protective order upon a good cause belief that harm to, or intimidation or dissuasion of, a victim or witness has occurred or is reasonably likely to occur, that provides as follows:

(ia) The defendant shall not own, possess, purchase, receive, or attempt to purchase or receive, a firearm while the protective order is in effect.

(ib) The defendant shall relinquish ownership or possession of any firearms, pursuant to Section 527.9 of the Code of Civil Procedure.

(II) Every person who owns, possesses, purchases, or receives, or attempts to purchase or receive, a firearm while this protective order is in effect is punishable pursuant to Section 29825.

(iii) An order issued, modified, extended, or terminated by a court pursuant to this subparagraph shall be issued on forms adopted by the Judicial Council of California that have been approved by the Department of Justice pursuant to subdivision (i) of Section 6380 of the Family Code. However, the fact that an order issued by a court pursuant to this section was not issued on forms adopted by the Judicial Council and approved by the Department of Justice shall not, in and of itself, make the order unenforceable.

(iv) A protective order issued under this subparagraph may require the defendant to be placed on electronic monitoring if the local government, with the concurrence of the county sheriff or the chief probation officer with jurisdiction, adopts a policy to authorize electronic monitoring of defendants and specifies the agency with jurisdiction for this purpose. If the court determines that the defendant has the ability to pay for the monitoring program, the court shall order the defendant to pay for the monitoring. If the court determines that the defendant does not have the ability to pay for the electronic monitoring, the court may order electronic monitoring to be paid for by the local government that adopted the policy to authorize electronic monitoring. The duration of electronic monitoring shall not exceed one year from the date the order is issued. The electronic monitoring shall not be in place if the protective order is not in place.

(2) For purposes of this subdivision, a minor who was not a victim of, but who was physically present at the time of, an act of domestic violence, is a witness and is deemed to have suffered harm within the meaning of paragraph (1).

(b) A person violating an order made pursuant to subparagraphs (A) to (G), inclusive, of paragraph (1) of subdivision (a) may be punished for any substantive offense described in Section 136.1, or for a contempt of the court making the order. A finding of contempt shall not be a bar to prosecution for a violation of Section 136.1. However, a person held in contempt shall be entitled to credit for punishment imposed therein against a sentence imposed upon conviction of an offense described in Section 136.1. A conviction or acquittal for a substantive offense under Section 136.1 shall be a bar to a subsequent punishment for contempt arising out of the same act.

(c)(1)(A) Notwithstanding subdivision (e), an emergency protective order issued pursuant to Chapter 2 (commencing with Section 6250) of Part 3 of Division 10 of the Family Code or Section 646.91 shall have precedence in enforcement over any other restraining or protective order, provided the emergency protective order meets all of the following requirements:

(i) The emergency protective order is issued to protect one or more individuals who are already protected persons under another restraining or protective order.

(ii) The emergency protective order restrains the individual who is the restrained person in the other restraining or protective order specified in clause (i).

(iii) The provisions of the emergency protective order are more restrictive in relation to the restrained person than are the provisions of the other restraining or protective order specified in clause (i).

(B) An emergency protective order that meets the requirements of subparagraph (A) shall have precedence in enforcement over the provisions of any other restraining or protective order only with respect to those provisions of the emergency protective order that are more restrictive in relation to the restrained person.

(2) Except as described in paragraph (1), a no-contact order, as described in Section 6320 of the Family Code, shall have precedence in enforcement over any other restraining or protective order.

(d)(1) A person subject to a protective order issued under this section shall not own, possess, purchase, or receive, or attempt to purchase or receive, a firearm while the protective order is in effect.

(2) The court shall order a person subject to a protective order issued under this section to relinquish ownership or possession of any firearms, pursuant to Section 527.9 of the Code of Civil Procedure.

(3) A person who owns, possesses, purchases, or receives, or attempts to purchase or receive, a firearm while the protective order is in effect is punishable pursuant to Section 29825.

(e)(1) When the defendant is charged with a crime involving domestic violence, as defined in Section 13700 of this code or in Section 6211 of the Family Code, or a violation of Section 261, 261.5, or former Section 262, or a crime that requires the defendant to register pursuant to subdivision (c) of Section 290, including, but not limited to, commercial sexual exploitation of a minor in violation of Section 236.1, the court shall consider issuing the above-described orders on its own motion. All interested parties shall receive a copy of those orders. In order to facilitate this, the court's records of all criminal cases involving domestic violence or a violation of Section 261, 261.5, or former Section 262, or a crime that requires the defendant to register pursuant to subdivision (c) of Section 290, including, but not limited to, commercial sexual exploitation of a minor in violation of Section 236.1, shall be marked to clearly alert the court to this issue.

(2) When a complaint, information, or indictment charging a crime involving domestic violence, as defined in Section 13700 or in Section 6211 of the Family Code, or a violation of Section 261, 261.5, or former Section 262, or a crime that requires the defendant to register pursuant to subdivision (c) of Section 290, including, but not limited to, commercial sexual exploitation of a minor in violation of Section 236.1, has been issued, except as described in subdivision (c), a restraining order or protective order against the defendant issued by the criminal court in that case has precedence in enforcement over a civil court order against the defendant.

(3) Custody and visitation with respect to the defendant and the defendant's minor children may be ordered by a family or juvenile court consistent with the protocol established pursuant to subdivision (f), but if ordered after a criminal protective order has been issued pursuant to this section, the custody and visitation order shall make reference to, and, if there is not an emergency protective order that has precedence in enforcement pursuant to paragraph (1) of subdivision (c), or a no-contact order, as described in Section 6320 of the Family Code, acknowledge the precedence of enforcement of, an appropriate criminal protective order. On or before July 1, 2014, the Judicial Council shall modify the criminal and civil court forms consistent with this subdivision.

(f) On or before January 1, 2003, the Judicial Council shall promulgate a protocol, for adoption by each local court in substantially similar terms, to provide for the timely coordination of all orders against the same defendant and in favor of the same named victim or victims. The protocol shall include, but shall not be limited to, mechanisms for ensuring appropriate communication and information sharing between criminal, family, and juvenile courts concerning orders and cases that involve the same parties, and shall permit a family or juvenile court order to coexist with a criminal court protective order subject to the following conditions:

(1) An order that permits contact between the restrained person and the person's children shall provide for the safe exchange of the children and shall not contain language, either printed or handwritten, that violates a "no-contact order" issued by a criminal court.

(2) The safety of all parties shall be the courts' paramount concern. The family or juvenile court shall specify the time, day, place, and manner of transfer of the child, as provided in Section 3100 of the Family Code.

(g) On or before January 1, 2003, the Judicial Council shall modify the criminal and civil court protective order forms consistent with this section.

(h)(1) When a complaint, information, or indictment charging a crime involving domestic violence, as defined in Section 13700 or in Section 6211 of the Family Code, has been filed, the court may consider, in determining whether good cause exists to issue an order under subparagraph (A) of paragraph (1) of subdivision (a), the underlying nature of the offense charged, and the information provided to the court pursuant to Section 273.75.

(2) When a complaint, information, or indictment charging a violation of Section 261, 261.5, or former Section 262, or a crime that requires the defendant to register pursuant to subdivision (c) of Section 290, including, but not limited to, commercial sexual exploitation of a minor in violation of Section 236.1, has been filed, the court may consider, in determining whether good cause exists to issue an order under paragraph (1) of subdivision (a), the underlying nature of the offense charged, the defendant's relationship to the victim, the likelihood of continuing harm to the victim, any current restraining order or protective order issued by a civil or criminal court involving the defendant, and the defendant's criminal history, including, but not limited to, prior convictions for a violation of Section 261, 261.5, or former Section 262, a crime that requires the defendant to register pursuant to subdivision (c) of Section 290, including, but not limited to, commercial sexual exploitation of a minor in violation of Section 236.1, any other forms of violence, or a weapons offense.

(i)(1) When a criminal defendant has been convicted of a crime involving domestic violence as defined in Section 13700 or in Section 6211 of the Family Code, a violation of subdivision (a), (b), or (c) of Section 236.1 prohibiting human trafficking, Section 261, 261.5, former Section 262, subdivision (a) of Section 266h, or subdivision (a) of Section 266i, a violation of Section 186.22, or a crime that requires the defendant to register pursuant to subdivision (c) of Section 290, the court, at the time of sentencing, shall consider issuing an order restraining the defendant from any contact with a victim of the crime. The order may be valid for up to 10 years, as determined by the court. This protective order may be issued by the court regardless of whether the defendant is sentenced to the state prison or a county jail or subject to mandatory supervision, or whether imposition of sentence is suspended and the defendant is placed on probation. It is the intent of the Legislature in enacting this subdivision that the duration of a restraining order issued by the court be based upon the seriousness of the facts before the court, the probability of future violations, and the safety of a victim and the victim's immediate family.

(2) When a criminal defendant has been convicted of a crime involving domestic violence as defined in Section 13700 or in Section 6211 of the Family Code, a violation of Section 261, 261.5, or former Section 262, a violation of Section 186.22, or a crime that requires the

§ 136.2

defendant to register pursuant to subdivision (c) of Section 290, the court, at the time of sentencing, shall consider issuing an order restraining the defendant from any contact with a percipient witness to the crime if it can be established by clear and convincing evidence that the witness has been harassed, as defined in paragraph (3) of subdivision (b) of Section 527.6 of the Code of Civil Procedure, by the defendant.

(3) An order under this subdivision may include provisions for electronic monitoring if the local government, upon receiving the concurrence of the county sheriff or the chief probation officer with jurisdiction, adopts a policy authorizing electronic monitoring of defendants and specifies the agency with jurisdiction for this purpose. If the court determines that the defendant has the ability to pay for the monitoring program, the court shall order the defendant to pay for the monitoring. If the court determines that the defendant does not have the ability to pay for the electronic monitoring, the court may order the electronic monitoring to be paid for by the local government that adopted the policy authorizing electronic monitoring. The duration of the electronic monitoring shall not exceed one year from the date the order is issued.

(j) For purposes of this section, "local government" means the county that has jurisdiction over the protective order. (Added by Stats.1980, c. 686, p. 2077, § 2.2. Amended by Stats.1988, c. 182, § 1, eff. June 15, 1988; Stats.1989, c. 1378, § 1; Stats.1990, c. 935 (A.B.3593), § 6; Stats.1996, c. 904 (A.B.2224), § 2; Stats.1997, c. 48 (A.B.340), § 1; Stats.1997, c. 847 (A.B.45), § 1.5; Stats.1998, c. 187 (A.B.1531), § 2; Stats.1999, c. 83 (S.B.966), § 136; Stats.1999, c. 661 (A.B.825), § 9; Stats.2001, c. 698 (A.B.160), § 4; Stats.2003, c. 498 (S.B.226), § 6; Stats.2005, c. 132 (A.B.112), § 1; Stats.2005, c. 465 (A.B.118), § 2; Stats.2005, c. 631 (S.B.720), § 3; Stats.2005, c. 702 (A.B.1288), § 1.7; Stats.2008, c. 86 (A.B.1771), § 1; Stats.2010, c. 178 (S.B.1115), § 42, operative Jan. 1, 2012; Stats.2011, c. 155 (S.B.723), § 1; Stats.2012, c. 162 (S.B.1171), § 121; Stats.2012, c. 513 (A.B.2467), § 2; Stats.2013, c. 76 (A.B.383), § 145; Stats.2013, c. 291 (A.B.307), § 1; Stats.2013, c. 263 (A.B.176), § 4, operative July 1, 2014; Stats.2013, c. 291 (A.B.307), § 1.5, operative July 1, 2014; Stats.2014, c. 71 (S.B.1304), § 115, eff. Jan. 1, 2015; Stats.2014, c. 638 (S.B.910), § 1, eff. Jan. 1, 2015; Stats.2014, c. 665 (A.B.1498), § 1, eff. Jan. 1, 2015; Stats.2014, c. 673 (A.B.1850), § 1.3, eff. Jan. 1, 2015; Stats.2015, c. 60 (S.B.307), § 1, eff. Jan. 1, 2016; Stats.2016, c. 86 (S.B.1171), § 220, eff. Jan. 1, 2017; Stats.2017, c. 270 (A.B.264), § 1, eff. Jan. 1, 2018; Stats.2018, c. 805 (A.B.1735), § 1, eff. Jan. 1, 2019; Stats.2019, c. 256 (S.B.781), § 6, eff. Jan. 1, 2020; Stats.2021, c. 626 (A.B.1171), § 14, eff. Jan. 1, 2022; Stats.2022, c. 87 (S.B.382), § 1, eff. Jan. 1, 2023.)

Cross References

Domestic violence prevention orders, transfer of children where visitation has been ordered, see Family Code § 3100.

Identification of persons eligible for automatic conviction record relief, granting of relief, notice to court, conditions for relief, see Penal Code § 1203.425.

Interstate enforcement of domestic violence protection orders, more than one order issued, precedence of emergency protective order, see Family Code § 6405.

Issuance of protective, stay-away orders under this section in appropriate domestic violence cases, see Penal Code § 13710.

Lease not to be terminated based on domestic or sexual assault against tenant, landlord's liability for compliance, form for affirmative defense to unlawful detainer action, see Code of Civil Procedure § 1161.3.

Participation in California Conservation Camp program as incarcerated individual hand crew member or participation as member of county incarcerated individual hand crew, petition for relief, dismissal of accusations or information and release from penalties and disabilities, see Penal Code § 1203.4b.

Proceedings before trial, presence of defendant and counsel, exception, see Penal Code § 977.

Protective orders and other domestic violence protection orders, more than one order issued, precedence of emergency protective order, see Family Code § 6383.

Relinquishment of firearms, persons subject to restraining orders, see Code of Civil Procedure § 527.9.

Tenant protected by restraining order against another tenant, change of locks on dwelling unit, definitions, see Civil Code § 1941.6.

Uniform Recognition and Enforcement of Canadian Domestic Violence Protection Orders Act, multiple protective orders, priority of enforcement, see Family Code § 6457.

Victims of domestic violence, sexual assault, or stalking, written notice to terminate tenancy, requirements, see Civil Code § 1946.7.

Research References

Forms

West's California Code Forms, Family § 6300, Comment Overview—Protective Orders.

West's California Judicial Council Forms CR–160, Criminal Protective Order—Domestic Violence (Clets—Cpo) (Also Available in Spanish).

West's California Judicial Council Forms CR–161, Criminal Protective Order—Other Than Domestic Violence (Clets—Cpo).

West's California Judicial Council Forms CR–162, Order to Surrender Firearms in Domestic Violence Case (Clets—Cpo).

West's California Judicial Council Forms CR–165, Notice of Termination of Protective Order in Criminal Proceeding (CLETS-CANCEL).

West's California Judicial Council Forms JV–200, Custody Order—Juvenile—Final Judgment (Also Available in Spanish).

West's California Judicial Council Forms JV–205, Visitation Order—Juvenile (Also Available in Spanish).

West's California Judicial Council Forms JV–245, Request for Restraining Order—Juvenile (Also Available in Chinese, Korean, Spanish, and Vietnamese).

West's California Judicial Council Forms JV–250, Notice of Hearing and Temporary Restraining Order—Juvenile (Also Available in Chinese, Korean, Spanish, and Vietnamese).

West's California Judicial Council Forms JV–255, Restraining Order—Juvenile (Clets—Juv) (Also Available in Chinese, Korean, Spanish, and Vietnamese).

§ 136.3. Addresses or locations of persons protected under court order; prohibition upon certain enjoined parties from acting to obtain such information

(a) The court shall order that any party enjoined pursuant to Section 136.2 be prohibited from taking any action to obtain the address or location of a protected party or a protected party's family members, caretakers, or guardian, unless there is good cause not to make that order.

(b) The Judicial Council shall promulgate forms necessary to effectuate this section. (Added by Stats.2005, c. 472 (A.B.978), § 4.)

CHAPTER 7. OTHER OFFENSES AGAINST PUBLIC JUSTICE

Section
166. Contempt of court; conduct constituting.
166.5. Contempt of court; order for child, spousal, or family support; suspension of proceedings; conditions.

Cross References

Conviction of crime as disqualification for peace officer, felonies, guilty pleas, see Government Code § 1029.

Municipal and justice courts, willful failure of judge to keep accounts, see Government Code § 71382.

Oil and gas districts, failure to comply with orders or subpoenas or refusal to testify, see Public Resources Code § 3359.

§ 166. Contempt of court; conduct constituting

(a) Except as provided in subdivisions (b), (c), and (d), a person guilty of any of the following contempts of court is guilty of a misdemeanor:

(1) Disorderly, contemptuous, or insolent behavior committed during the sitting of a court of justice, in the immediate view and presence of the court, and directly tending to interrupt its proceedings or to impair the respect due to its authority.

(2) Behavior specified in paragraph (1) that is committed in the presence of a referee, while actually engaged in a trial or hearing, pursuant to the order of a court, or in the presence of a jury while actually sitting for the trial of a cause, or upon an inquest or other proceeding authorized by law.

(3) A breach of the peace, noise, or other disturbance directly tending to interrupt the proceedings of the court.

(4) Willful disobedience of the terms, as written, of a process or court order or out-of-state court order, lawfully issued by a court, including orders pending trial.

(5) Resistance willfully offered by a person to the lawful order or process of a court.

(6) The contumacious and unlawful refusal of a person to be sworn as a witness or, when so sworn, the like refusal to answer a material question.

(7) The publication of a false or grossly inaccurate report of the proceedings of a court.

(8) Presenting to a court having power to pass sentence upon a prisoner under conviction, or to a member of the court, an affidavit, testimony, or representation of any kind, verbal or written, in aggravation or mitigation of the punishment to be imposed upon the prisoner, except as provided in this code.

(9) Willful disobedience of the terms of an injunction that restrains the activities of a criminal street gang or any of its members, lawfully issued by a court, including an order pending trial.

(b)(1) A person who is guilty of contempt of court under paragraph (4) of subdivision (a) by willfully contacting a victim by telephone or mail, social media, electronic communication, or electronic communication device, or directly, and who has been previously convicted of a violation of Section 646.9 shall be punished by imprisonment in a county jail for not more than one year, by a fine of no more than five thousand dollars ($5,000), or by both that fine and imprisonment.

(2) For the purposes of sentencing under this subdivision, each contact shall constitute a separate violation of this subdivision.

(3) The present incarceration of a person who makes contact with a victim in violation of paragraph (1) is not a defense to a violation of this subdivision.

(4) For purposes of this subdivision, the following definitions shall apply:

(A) "Social media" has the same definition as in Section 632.01.

(B) "Electronic communication" has the same definition as in Section 646.9.

(C) "Electronic communication device" has the same definition as in Section 646.9.

(c)(1) Notwithstanding paragraph (4) of subdivision (a), a willful and knowing violation of a protective order or stay-away court order described as follows shall constitute contempt of court, a misdemeanor, punishable by imprisonment in a county jail for not more than one year, by a fine of not more than one thousand dollars ($1,000), or by both that imprisonment and fine:

(A) An order issued pursuant to Section 136.2.

(B) An order issued pursuant to paragraph (2) of subdivision (a) of Section 1203.097.

(C) An order issued after a conviction in a criminal proceeding involving elder or dependent adult abuse, as defined in Section 368.

(D) An order issued pursuant to Section 1201.3.

(E) An order described in paragraph (3).

(F) An order issued pursuant to subdivision (j) of Section 273.5.

(2) If a violation of paragraph (1) results in a physical injury, the person shall be imprisoned in a county jail for at least 48 hours, whether a fine or imprisonment is imposed, or the sentence is suspended.

(3) Paragraphs (1) and (2) apply to the following court orders:

(A) An order issued pursuant to Section 6320 or 6389 of the Family Code.

(B) An order excluding one party from the family dwelling or from the dwelling of the other.

(C) An order enjoining a party from specified behavior that the court determined was necessary to effectuate the orders described in paragraph (1).

(4) A second or subsequent conviction for a violation of an order described in paragraph (1) occurring within seven years of a prior conviction for a violation of any of those orders and involving an act of violence or "a credible threat" of violence, as provided in subdivision (c) of Section 139, is punishable by imprisonment in a county jail not to exceed one year, or in the state prison for 16 months or two or three years.

(5) The prosecuting agency of each county shall have the primary responsibility for the enforcement of the orders described in paragraph (1).

(d)(1) A person who owns, possesses, purchases, or receives a firearm knowing that person is prohibited from doing so by the provisions of a protective order as defined in Section 136.2 of this code, Section 6218 of the Family Code, or Section 527.6 or 527.8 of the Code of Civil Procedure, shall be punished under Section 29825.

(2) A person subject to a protective order described in paragraph (1) shall not be prosecuted under this section for owning, possessing, purchasing, or receiving a firearm to the extent that firearm is granted an exemption pursuant to subdivision (h) of Section 6389 of the Family Code.

(e)(1) If probation is granted upon conviction of a violation of subdivision (c), the court shall impose probation consistent with Section 1203.097.

(2) If probation is granted upon conviction of a violation of subdivision (c), the conditions of probation may include, in lieu of a fine, one or both of the following requirements:

(A) That the defendant make payments to a domestic violence shelter-based program up to a maximum of one thousand dollars ($1,000).

(B) That the defendant provide restitution to reimburse the victim for reasonable costs of counseling and other reasonable expenses that the court finds are the direct result of the defendant's offense.

(3) For an order to pay a fine, make payments to a domestic violence shelter-based program, or pay restitution as a condition of probation under this subdivision or subdivision (c), the court shall make a determination of the defendant's ability to pay. An order to make payments to a domestic violence shelter-based program, shall not be made if it would impair the ability of the defendant to pay direct restitution to the victim or court-ordered child support.

(4) If the injury to a married person is caused, in whole or in part, by the criminal acts of the person's spouse in violation of subdivision (c), the community property shall not be used to discharge the liability of the offending spouse for restitution to the injured spouse required by Section 1203.04, as operative on or before August 2, 1995, or Section 1202.4, or to a shelter for costs with regard to the injured spouse and dependents required by this subdivision, until all separate property of the offending spouse is exhausted.

(5) A person violating an order described in subdivision (c) may be punished for any substantive offenses described under Section 136.1 or 646.9. A finding of contempt shall not be a bar to prosecution for a violation of Section 136.1 or 646.9. However, a person held in contempt for a violation of subdivision (c) shall be entitled to credit for any punishment imposed as a result of that violation against a sentence imposed upon conviction of an offense

§ 166

described in Section 136.1 or 646.9. A conviction or acquittal for a substantive offense under Section 136.1 or 646.9 shall be a bar to a subsequent punishment for contempt arising out of the same act. *(Enacted in 1872. Amended by Stats.1993, c. 345 (A.B.303), § 1; Stats.1993, c. 583 (S.B.850), § 4; Stats.1996, c. 904 (A.B.2244), § 3; Stats.1996, c. 1077 (A.B.2898), § 13.1; Stats.1999, c. 662 (S.B.218), § 7; Stats.2002, c. 830 (A.B.2695), § 1; Stats.2008, c. 152 (A.B.1424), § 1; Stats.2009, c. 140 (A.B.1164), § 139; Stats.2010, c. 178 (S.B. 1115), § 44, operative Jan. 1, 2012; Stats.2010, c. 677 (A.B.2632), § 1; Stats.2011, c. 285 (A.B.1402), § 9; Stats.2011, c. 296 (A.B.1023), § 199; Stats.2011, c. 181 (A.B.141), § 4; Stats.2013, c. 76 (A.B.383), § 145.3; Stats.2013, c. 291 (A.B.307), § 2; Stats.2014, c. 99 (A.B. 2683), § 1, eff. Jan. 1, 2015; Stats.2015, c. 279 (S.B.352), § 1, eff. Jan. 1, 2016; Stats.2016, c. 342 (S.B.883), § 1, eff. Jan. 1, 2017; Stats.2021, c. 704 (A.B.764), § 1, eff. Jan. 1, 2022.)*

Cross References

Application of Trial Court Trust Fund provisions to fees and fines collected pursuant to this section, see Government Code § 68085.

Attorneys,
    Acts or omissions constituting contempt, see Business and Professions Code § 6127.
    Disciplinary authority of courts, see Business and Professions Code § 6100 et seq.
    Duties toward court, see Business and Professions Code § 6068.
    Unlawful practice, see Business and Professions Code § 6125 et seq.

Contempt,
    Generally, see Code of Civil Procedure § 1209 et seq.
    Acts or omissions constituting, see Code of Civil Procedure § 1209.
    Administrative agencies, see Government Code §§ 11455.10, 11455.20.
    Disobedience of order regarding appearance before workers' compensation judge, see Labor Code § 132.
    Employer's failure to report injury as ordered, see Labor Code § 3760.
    Estates of decedents, see Probate Code §§ 8870, 8873.
    Examination proceedings, disobedience of referee's orders, see Code of Civil Procedure § 708.140.
    Failure, upon subsequent application for order, to reveal facts of prior application, see Code of Civil Procedure § 1008.
    Grand jury, see Penal Code § 939.5.
    Juvenile court, see Welfare and Institutions Code § 213.
    Legislature, offense, see Government Code § 9412.
    Noncompliance of personal representative with order to attend or answer at hearing, see Probate Code § 8505.
    Punishment by judicial officer, see Code of Civil Procedure § 178.
    Punishment by officers authorized to take proof of instruments, see Civil Code § 1201.
    Refusal to submit to examination or answer interrogatories, see Probate Code § 8870.
    State department hearing, see Government Code § 11189.
    Subpoenaing body for disobedience of subpoena, see Business and Professions Code §§ 6050, 6051.
    Violation of order prohibiting harassment of minor victim of sexual offense, see Penal Code § 1201.3.

Corporate records, refusal to produce, see Corporations Code § 1603.

Definitions,
    Action, see Code of Civil Procedure § 20 et seq.; Commercial Code § 1201.
    Civil action, see Code of Civil Procedure § 30.
    Judgment, see Code of Civil Procedure §§ 577, 1064.
    Misdemeanor, see Penal Code § 17.
    Order, see Code of Civil Procedure §§ 1003, 1064.
    Principals, see Penal Code § 31.
    Process, see Penal Code § 7; Code of Civil Procedure § 17; Government Code §§ 22, 26660.
    Published, see Government Code § 6004.
    Willfully, see Penal Code § 7.
    Witness, see Code of Civil Procedure § 1878.

Due process, see Cal. Const. Art. 1, § 15.

Jurors' failure to attend,
    Generally, see Code of Civil Procedure § 209.
    Alternate jurors, see Penal Code § 1089.

Newsmen, immunity from citation for contempt, see Evidence Code § 1070.

Offenses also punishable as contempt, see Penal Code § 657.

Organization and government of courts, collection of fees and fines pursuant to this section, deposits, see Government Code § 68085.1.

Powers,
    Court martial or military authority to punish for contempt, preservation, see Penal Code § 11.
    Courts, see Code of Civil Procedure §§ 128, 178.

Prison or state prison defined for purposes of this Code, see Penal Code § 6081.

Probation, see Penal Code § 1202.7 et seq.

Public utilities, punishment for contempt of commission, see Cal. Const. Art. 12, § 6; Public Utilities Code §§ 728.5, 1793, 2100, 2113.

Punishments,
    Determination, see Penal Code § 13.
    Maximum confinement, see Penal Code § 19.2.
    Mitigation in certain cases, see Penal Code §§ 658, 1204.

Receipt of person committed by civil process, sheriff's duty, see Penal Code § 4016.

Resistance to commission of public offense, see Penal Code § 692 et seq.

Resistance to process, see Penal Code §§ 723, 724.

Resisting, delaying or obstructing officer, see Penal Code § 148.

Searches and seizures, see Cal. Const. Art. 1, § 13.

Self-incrimination, immunity from contempt prosecution, see Penal Code § 1324.1.

Transfers of certain fees and fines specified in this section, effective date, see Government Code § 68085.5.

Witnesses,
    Attendance outside state, see Penal Code § 1334 et seq.
    Compelling attendance, see Code of Civil Procedure § 128; Military and Veterans Code § 460; Penal Code § 1326 et seq.
    Conditional examination, see Penal Code § 1335 et seq.
    Confidential or privileged information, failure to disclose, see Evidence Code § 914.
    Failure to appear, department of water resources, see Water Code § 1097.
    Legislature or legislative committees, see Government Code § 9400 et seq.
    Oath, see Evidence Code § 710.
    Preventing or dissuading from attending, see Penal Code § 136.1.
    Refusal to be sworn, see Penal Code §§ 1331, 1331.5; Code of Civil Procedure § 1991 et seq.
    Rights and duties, see Code of Civil Procedure §§ 2064, 2065.
    Subpoenas, disobedience, see Penal Code §§ 1331, 1331.5, 1564; Code of Civil Procedure § 1991 et seq.

Research References

Forms

Asset Protection: Legal Planning, Strategies and Forms ¶ 7.01, Introduction.

West's California Judicial Council Forms CR-160, Criminal Protective Order—Domestic Violence (Clets—Cpo) (Also Available in Spanish).

West's California Judicial Council Forms CR-162, Order to Surrender Firearms in Domestic Violence Case (Clets—Cpo).

West's California Judicial Council Forms CR-165, Notice of Termination of Protective Order in Criminal Proceeding (CLETS-CANCEL).

§ 166.5. Contempt of court; order for child, spousal, or family support; suspension of proceedings; conditions

(a) After arrest and before plea or trial or after conviction or plea of guilty and before sentence under paragraph (4) of subdivision (a) of Section 166, for willful disobedience of any order for child, spousal, or family support issued pursuant to Division 9 (commencing with Section 3500) of the Family Code or Section 17400 of the Family Code, the court may suspend proceedings or sentence therein if:

(1) The defendant appears before the court and affirms his or her obligation to pay to the person having custody of the child, or the spouse, that sum per month as shall have been previously fixed by the court in order to provide for the minor child or the spouse.

(2) The defendant provides a bond or other undertaking with sufficient sureties to the people of the State of California in a sum as the court may fix to secure the defendant's performance of his or her support obligations and that bond or undertaking is valid and binding for two years, or any lesser time that the court shall fix.

(b) Upon the failure of the defendant to comply with the conditions imposed by the court in subdivision (a), the defendant may be ordered to appear before the court and show cause why further proceedings should not be had in the action or why sentence should not be imposed, whereupon the court may proceed with the action, or pass sentence, or for good cause shown may modify the order and take a new bond or undertaking and further suspend proceedings or sentence for a like period. *(Added by Stats.1999, c. 653 (A.B.380), § 20.)*

Title 9

OF CRIMES AGAINST THE PERSON INVOLVING SEXUAL ASSAULT, AND CRIMES AGAINST PUBLIC DECENCY AND GOOD MORALS

CHAPTER 2. ABANDONMENT AND NEGLECT OF CHILDREN

Section
- 270. Failure to provide; parent; punishment; effect of custody; evidence; applicability of section; artificial insemination; treatment by spiritual means.
- 270.1. Parent or guardian of chronic truant; failure to reasonably supervise and encourage school attendance deemed misdemeanor; punishment; deferred entry of judgment program; funding; punishment under other provisions; declaration of eligibility or ineligibility for program.
- 270.5. Duty to accept minor into parent's home or provide alternative shelter; request of child protection agency; lawful excuse.
- 270.6. Willful violation of court order to pay spousal support; punishment.
- 270a. Failure to provide support for spouse; punishment.
- 270b. Undertaking to provide support; suspension of proceedings or sentence; proceedings on breach of undertaking.
- 270c. Failure of adult child to provide for indigent parent.
- 270d. Fine; disposition.
- 270e. Evidence of marriage, domestic partnership, or parenthood; confidential communications; competency of spouse as witness; proof of willfulness.
- 270f. Report by parent of failure to support; investigation and action by district attorney.
- 270g. Review of reports.
- 270h. Support order included in order granting probation; issuance of execution; assignment of wages.
- 271. Desertion of child under 14 with intent to abandon; punishment.
- 271a. Abandonment or failure to maintain child under 14; false representation that child is orphan; punishment.
- 271.5. Safe-surrender sites; parents or other individuals surrendering custody of baby.
- 272. Contributing to delinquency of persons under 18 years; persuading, luring, or transporting minors 12 years of age or younger.
- 273. Paying or receiving money or thing of value to parent for placement for, or consent to, adoption of child.
- 273a. Willful harm or injury to child; endangering person or health; punishment; conditions of probation.
- 273ab. Assault resulting in death, comatose state, or paralysis of child under 8; imprisonment.
- 273b. Children under 16; placement in courtroom or vehicle with adult offender; restriction.
- 273c. Prosecution instituted by society for prevention of cruelty to children; fines, penalties and forfeitures payable to society.
- 273d. Corporal punishment or injury of child; felony; punishment; enhancement for prior conviction; conditions of probation.

Section
- 273e. Places of questionable repute; minors not to deliver messages, etc., or enter.
- 273f. Sending minors to immoral places.
- 273g. Degrading, immoral, or vicious practices or habitual drunkenness in presence of children.
- 273h. Sentence to work on public roads; payment of earnings to wife or to guardian of children, etc.
- 273i. Publication of information describing or depicting child or relating to child with intent that information be used to commit crime against child; punishment; definitions; injunction.
- 273j. Notification of public safety agency of death of child; notification of law enforcement of missing child; penalties.
- 273.1. Treatment programs for child abusers convicted of specified sections.
- 273.4. Female genital mutilation; additional punishment.
- 273.5. Willful infliction of corporal injury; violation; punishment.
- 273.6. Intentional and knowing violation of court order to prevent harassment, disturbing the peace, or threats or acts of violence; penalties.
- 273.65. Intentional and knowing violations of restraining and protective orders relating to minors adjudged to be dependent children of the juvenile court; offense; penalties.
- 273.7. Malicious disclosure of location of trafficking shelter or domestic violence shelter; misdemeanor; definitions; exemption for attorney-client communications.
- 273.75. Criminal history search; prior restraining orders.

§ 270. Failure to provide; parent; punishment; effect of custody; evidence; applicability of section; artificial insemination; treatment by spiritual means

If a parent of a minor child willfully omits, without lawful excuse, to furnish necessary clothing, food, shelter or medical attendance, or other remedial care for his or her child, he or she is guilty of a misdemeanor punishable by a fine not exceeding two thousand dollars ($2,000), or by imprisonment in the county jail not exceeding one year, or by both such fine and imprisonment. If a court of competent jurisdiction has made a final adjudication in either a civil or a criminal action that a person is the parent of a minor child and the person has notice of such adjudication and he or she then willfully omits, without lawful excuse, to furnish necessary clothing, food, shelter, medical attendance or other remedial care for his or her child, this conduct is punishable by imprisonment in the county jail not exceeding one year or in a state prison for a determinate term of one year and one day, or by a fine not exceeding two thousand dollars ($2,000), or by both such fine and imprisonment. This statute shall not be construed so as to relieve such parent from the criminal liability defined herein for such omission merely because the other parent of such child is legally entitled to the custody of such child nor because the other parent of such child or any other person or organization voluntarily or involuntarily furnishes such necessary food, clothing, shelter or medical attendance or other remedial care for such child or undertakes to do so.

Proof of abandonment or desertion of a child by such parent, or the omission by such parent to furnish necessary food, clothing, shelter or medical attendance or other remedial care for his or her child is prima facie evidence that such abandonment or desertion or omission to furnish necessary food, clothing, shelter or medical attendance or other remedial care is willful and without lawful excuse.

The court, in determining the ability of the parent to support his or her child, shall consider all income, including social insurance benefits and gifts.

The provisions of this section are applicable whether the parents of such child are or were ever married or divorced, and regardless of any decree made in any divorce action relative to alimony or to the support of the child. A child conceived but not yet born is to be deemed an existing person insofar as this section is concerned.

The husband of a woman who bears a child as a result of artificial insemination shall be considered the father of that child for the purpose of this section, if he consented in writing to the artificial insemination.

If a parent provides a minor with treatment by spiritual means through prayer alone in accordance with the tenets and practices of a recognized church or religious denomination, by a duly accredited practitioner thereof, such treatment shall constitute "other remedial care", as used in this section. (Enacted in 1872. Amended by Stats.1905, c. 568, p. 758, § 1; Stats.1909, c. 159, p. 258, § 1; Stats.1915, c. 374, p. 572, § 1; Stats.1917, c. 168, p. 252, § 1; Stats.1921, c. 911, p. 1723, § 1; Stats.1923, c. 284, p. 592, § 1; Stats.1925, c. 325, p. 544, § 1; Stats.1931, c. 696, p. 1438, § 1; Stats.1939, c. 1001, p. 2783, § 1; Stats.1955, c. 753, p. 1247, § 1; Stats.1957, c. 139, p. 742, § 32; Stats.1957, c. 1855, p. 3255, § 1; Stats.1965, c. 496, p. 1805, § 1; Stats.1968, c. 235, p. 546, § 2; Stats.1971, c. 1587, p. 3202, § 1; Stats.1974, c. 893, p. 1892, § 1; Stats.1976, c. 673, p. 1661, § 1; Stats.1983, c. 1092, § 259, eff. Sept. 27, 1983, operative Jan. 1, 1984; Stats.1984, c. 1432, § 1.)

Cross References

Abandonment or failure to maintain child under fourteen, see Penal Code § 271a.
Action for exclusive custody of children, see Family Code § 3120.
Adoption, legal relation of parent and child, see Family Code § 8616.
California parent locator service and central registry, California child support automation system, see Family Code § 17506.
Child support obligations, agency agreement with noncustodial parent, see Family Code § 17416.
Commitment to county industrial farm or camp, see Penal Code § 4116.
Contempt, willful disobedience of court order, see Penal Code § 166.
Contributing to delinquency of minors, see Penal Code § 272.
Desertion of child under fourteen with intent to abandon, see Penal Code § 271.
Effect of judgment determining parent and child relationship, see Family Code § 7636.
Felony and misdemeanor defined, see Penal Code § 17.
Foundling registration, see Health and Safety Code § 102500 et seq.
Jurisdiction for violation of this section, see Penal Code § 777a.
Minors, definition, see Family Code § 6500.
Necessaries,
   Minors' liability, see Family Code § 6712.
   Parents' liability, see Family Code § 3950.
Non-liability of parent for support furnished child, see Family Code § 3951.
Order for support of children, see Family Code § 4001.
Payment of fine to spouse or to guardian of child, see Penal Code § 270d.
Presumption of legitimacy, see Family Code § 7611 et seq.
Prima facie evidence, see Evidence Code § 602.
Prison or state prison defined for purposes of this Code, see Penal Code § 6081.
Privilege not to testify against spouse, exception in case of crime defined by this section, see Evidence Code § 972.
Privileges for confidential marital communications, criminal proceedings, see Evidence Code § 985.
Probation officers, additional power, receipt, deposit and disbursement of money, see Welfare and Institutions Code § 276.
Proceeding to declare minor ward of juvenile court, see Welfare and Institutions Code § 650 et seq.
Remedy when parent dies without providing for support of child, see Family Code § 3952.
Sentence to work on public roads, payment of earnings to wife or to guardian of children, see Penal Code § 273h.
Societies for prevention of cruelty to children, see Corporations Code §§ 10400 et seq., 14500 et seq.
State and local agency cooperation with local child support agencies, information on location of children or parents, etc., see Family Code § 17505.
Support and education of children, see Family Code § 3900 et seq.
Undertaking to provide support, see Penal Code § 270b.

Uniform act on blood tests to determine paternity, applicability, see Family Code § 7556.
Uniform Interstate Family Support Act, see Family Code § 5700.101 et seq.
Victim compensation, requirements, persons and derivative victims, see Government Code § 13955.
Willfully, definition, see Penal Code § 7.
Witnesses, husband and wife competent, see Penal Code § 270e.

Research References

Forms
West's California Code Forms, Family § 7630, Comment Overview—Determining Parent and Child Relationship.

§ 270.1. Parent or guardian of chronic truant; failure to reasonably supervise and encourage school attendance deemed misdemeanor; punishment; deferred entry of judgment program; funding; punishment under other provisions; declaration of eligibility or ineligibility for program

(a) A parent or guardian of a pupil of six years of age or more who is in kindergarten or any of grades 1 to 8, inclusive, and who is subject to compulsory full-time education or compulsory continuation education, whose child is a chronic truant as defined in Section 48263.6 of the Education Code, who has failed to reasonably supervise and encourage the pupil's school attendance, and who has been offered language accessible support services to address the pupil's truancy, is guilty of a misdemeanor punishable by a fine not exceeding two thousand dollars ($2,000), or by imprisonment in a county jail not exceeding one year, or by both that fine and imprisonment. A parent or guardian guilty of a misdemeanor under this subdivision may participate in the deferred entry of judgment program defined in subdivision (b).

(b) A superior court may establish a deferred entry of judgment program that includes the components listed in paragraphs (1) to (7), inclusive, to adjudicate cases involving parents or guardians of elementary school pupils who are chronic truants as defined in Section 48263.6 of the Education Code:

(1) A dedicated court calendar.

(2) Leadership by a judge of the superior court in that county.

(3) Meetings, scheduled and held periodically, with school district representatives designated by the chronic truant's school district of enrollment. Those representatives may include school psychologists, school counselors, teachers, school administrators, or other educational service providers deemed appropriate by the school district.

(4) Service referrals for parents or guardians, as appropriate to each case that may include, but are not limited to, all of the following:

(A) Case management.

(B) Mental and physical health services.

(C) Parenting classes and support.

(D) Substance abuse treatment.

(E) Child care and housing.

(5) A clear statement that, in lieu of trial, the court may grant deferred entry of judgment with respect to the current crime or crimes charged if the defendant pleads guilty to each charge and waives time for the pronouncement of judgment and that, upon the defendant's compliance with the terms and conditions set forth by the court and agreed to by the defendant upon the entry of his or her plea, and upon the motion of the prosecuting attorney, the court will dismiss the charge or charges against the defendant and the same procedures specified for successful completion of a drug diversion program or a deferred entry of judgment program pursuant to Section 851.90 and the provisions of Section 1203.4 shall apply.

(6) A clear statement that failure to comply with any condition under the program may result in the prosecuting attorney or the court making a motion for entry of judgment, whereupon the court

will render a finding of guilty to the charge or charges pled, enter judgment, and schedule a sentencing hearing as otherwise provided in this code.

(7) An explanation of criminal record retention and disposition resulting from participation in the deferred entry of judgment program and the defendant's rights relative to answering questions about his or her arrest and deferred entry of judgment following successful completion of the program.

(c) Funding for the deferred entry of judgment program pursuant to this section shall be derived solely from nonstate sources.

(d) A parent or guardian of an elementary school pupil who is a chronic truant, as defined in Section 48263.6 of the Education Code, may not be punished for a violation of both this section and the provisions of Section 272 that involve criminal liability for parents and guardians of truant children.

(e) If any district attorney chooses to charge a defendant with a violation of subdivision (a) and the defendant is found by the prosecuting attorney to be eligible or ineligible for deferred entry of judgment, the prosecuting attorney shall file with the court a declaration in writing, or state for the record, the grounds upon which that determination is based. *(Added by Stats.2010, c. 647 (S.B.1317), § 2.)*

Cross References
Compulsory Education Law, violations, notice of outcome of each truancy-related referral, see Education Code § 48297.

§ 270.5. Duty to accept minor into parent's home or provide alternative shelter; request of child protection agency; lawful excuse

(a) Every parent who refuses, without lawful excuse, to accept his or her minor child into the parent's home, or, failing to do so, to provide alternative shelter, upon being requested to do so by a child protective agency and after being informed of the duty imposed by this statute to do so, is guilty of a misdemeanor and shall be punished by a fine of not more than five hundred dollars ($500).

(b) For purposes of this section, "child protective agency" means a police or sheriff's department, a county probation department, or a county welfare department.

(c) For purposes of this section, "lawful excuse" shall include, but not be limited to, a reasonable fear that the minor child's presence in the home will endanger the safety of the parent or other persons residing in the home. *(Added by Stats.1984, c. 1616, § 1.)*

Cross References
Adoption, legal relation of parent and child, see Family Code § 8616.
Duty of support, see Family Code § 3900 et seq.
Misdemeanors, definition and penalties, see Penal Code §§ 17, 19 and 19.2.
Non-liability of parent for support furnished child, see Family Code § 3951.

§ 270.6. Willful violation of court order to pay spousal support; punishment

If a court of competent jurisdiction has made a temporary or permanent order awarding spousal support that a person must pay, the person has notice of that order, and he or she then leaves the state with the intent to willfully omit, without lawful excuse, to furnish the spousal support, he or she is punishable by imprisonment in a county jail for a period not exceeding one year, a fine not exceeding two thousand dollars ($2,000), or both that imprisonment and fine. *(Added by Stats.2002, c. 410 (S.B.1399), § 1.)*

§ 270a. Failure to provide support for spouse; punishment

Every individual who has sufficient ability to provide for his or her spouse's support, or who is able to earn the means of such spouse's support, who willfully abandons and leaves his or her spouse in a destitute condition, or who refuses or neglects to provide such spouse with necessary food, clothing, shelter, or medical attendance, unless by such spouse's conduct the individual was justified in abandoning such spouse, is guilty of a misdemeanor. *(Added by Stats.1907, c. 74, p. 91, § 1. Amended by Stats.1909, c. 159, p. 258, § 2; Stats.1957, c. 139, p. 743, § 33; Stats.1957, c. 1855, p. 3255, § 2; Stats.1976, c. 1170, p. 5250, § 1.)*

Cross References
Commitment to county industrial farm or camp, see Penal Code § 4116.
Definitions,
  Neglect, see Penal Code § 7.
  Willfully, see Penal Code § 7.
Labor on public works or ways by persons confined in county jail, see Penal Code § 4017.
Misdemeanor defined, see Penal Code § 17.
Mutual obligations of husband and wife, see Family Code § 720.
Order for support of other party, see Family Code § 4330.
Payment of fine to spouse, see Penal Code § 270d.
Privilege not to testify against spouse, exception in case of crime defined by this section, see Evidence Code § 972.
Privileges for confidential marital communications, criminal proceedings, see Evidence Code § 985.
Probation officers, authority to receive and disburse money payable to wife, child, etc., after claimed violation of this section, see Welfare and Institutions Code § 276.
Punishment for misdemeanor, see Penal Code §§ 19, 19.2.
Residence, determining place of, see Government Code § 244.
Sentence to work on public roads, payment of earnings to wife, see Penal Code § 273h.
Separate property of married person, liability of, see Family Code §§ 913, 914.
Support,
  Children, see Family Code § 3900 et seq.
  During separation, see Family Code § 3580.
  Spouse, see Family Code § 4300 et seq.
Uniform Interstate Family Support Act, see Family Code § 5700.101 et seq.
Support order included in order granting probation, issuance of execution, assignment of wages, see Penal Code § 270h.
Witnesses, husband and wife competent, see Penal Code § 270e.

§ 270b. Undertaking to provide support; suspension of proceedings or sentence; proceedings on breach of undertaking

After arrest and before plea or trial, or after conviction or plea of guilty and before sentence under either Section 270 or 270a, if the defendant shall appear before the court and enter into an undertaking with sufficient sureties to the people of the State of California in such penal sum as the court may fix, to be approved by the court, and conditioned that the defendant will pay to the person having custody of such child or to such spouse, such sum per month as may be fixed by the court in order to thereby provide such minor child or such spouse as the case may be, with necessary food, shelter, clothing, medical attendance, or other remedial care, then the court may suspend proceedings or sentence therein; and such undertaking is valid and binding for two years, or such lesser time which the court shall fix; and upon the failure of defendant to comply with such undertaking, the defendant may be ordered to appear before the court and show cause why further proceedings should not be had in such action or why sentence should not be imposed, whereupon the court may proceed with such action, or pass sentence, or for good cause shown may modify the order and take a new undertaking and further suspend proceedings or sentence for a like period. *(Added by Stats.1907, c. 74, p. 92, § 2. Amended by Stats.1909, c. 159, p. 259, § 3; Stats.1931, c. 645, p. 1386, § 1; Stats.1976, c. 1170, p. 5250, § 2.)*

Cross References
Bond or undertaking, sufficiency, form, sureties, see Code of Civil Procedure § 995.320.
Sentence to work on public roads, payment of earnings to wife, see Penal Code § 273h.

§ 270c. Failure of adult child to provide for indigent parent

Except as provided in Chapter 2 (commencing with Section 4410) of Part 4 of Division 9 of the Family Code, every adult child who, having the ability so to do, fails to provide necessary food, clothing,

§ 270c

shelter, or medical attendance for an indigent parent, is guilty of a misdemeanor. *(Added by Stats.1909, c. 113, p. 166, § 1. Amended by Stats.1955, c. 613, p. 1103, § 3; Stats.1992, c. 163 (A.B.2641), § 102, operative Jan. 1, 1994.)*

Cross References

Aid to indigent persons, charge against responsible relative or relatives, see Welfare and Institutions Code § 17300.
Duty of adult children to support parents, see Family Code § 4400.
Effect of adoption, see Family Code §§ 8616, 8617.
Medical care of prisoner in county jail, payment, see Penal Code § 4011.
Misdemeanor defined, see Penal Code § 17.
Probation officers, authority to receive and disburse money payable to wife, child, etc., after claimed violation of this section, see Welfare and Institutions Code § 276.
Punishment for misdemeanor, see Penal Code §§ 19, 19.2.
Supplementary program for aged, blind and disabled, relative's liability for recipient's support, see Welfare and Institutions Code § 12350.

§ 270d. Fine; disposition

In any case where there is a conviction and sentence under the provisions of either Section 270 or Section 270a, should a fine be imposed, such fine shall be directed by the court to be paid in whole or in part to the spouse of the defendant or guardian or custodian of the child or children of such defendant, except as follows:

If the children are receiving public assistance, all fines, penalties or forfeitures imposed and all funds collected from the defendant shall be paid to the county department. Money so paid shall be applied first to support for the calendar month following its receipt by the county department and any balance remaining shall be applied to future needs, or be treated as reimbursement for past support furnished from public assistance funds. *(Added by Stats.1911, c. 379, p. 687, § 1. Amended by Stats.1963, c. 834, p. 2033, § 2; Stats.1974, c. 893, p. 1893, § 2.)*

Cross References

Fines,
Discharge on payment, see Penal Code § 1457.
Distribution in municipal or justice courts, see Penal Code § 1463.
Excessive imposition prohibited, see Cal. Const. Art. 1, § 17.
Payment, see Penal Code § 1205.
Prosecutions by society for prevention of cruelty to children, disposition of fines, see Penal Code § 273c.

§ 270e. Evidence of marriage, domestic partnership, or parenthood; confidential communications; competency of spouse as witness; proof of willfulness

No other evidence shall be required to prove marriage or registered domestic partnership of spouses, or that a person is the lawful father or mother of a child or children, than is or shall be required to prove such facts in a civil action. In all prosecutions under either Section 270a or 270 of this code, Sections 970, 971, and 980 of the Evidence Code do not apply, and both spouses or domestic partners shall be competent to testify to any and all relevant matters, including the fact of marriage or registered domestic partnership and the parentage of a child or children. Proof of the abandonment and nonsupport of a spouse, or of the omission to furnish necessary food, clothing, shelter, or of medical attendance for a child or children is prima facie evidence that such abandonment and nonsupport or omission to furnish necessary food, clothing, shelter, or medical attendance is willful. In any prosecution under Section 270, it shall be competent for the people to prove nonaccess of husband to wife or any other fact establishing nonpaternity of a husband. In any prosecution pursuant to Section 270, the final establishment of paternity or nonpaternity in another proceeding shall be admissible as evidence of paternity or nonpaternity. *(Added by Stats.1911, c. 379, c. 688, § 1. Amended by Stats.1955, c. 948, p. 1834, § 1; Stats.1957, c. 1855, p. 3256, § 3; Stats.1965, c. 299, p. 1367, § 138, operative Jan. 1, 1967; Stats.1976, c. 1170, p. 5250, § 3; Stats.2016, c. 50 (S.B.1005), § 68, eff. Jan. 1, 2017.)*

Cross References

Marital communications, privilege, see Evidence Code § 980 et seq.
Marriage, proof of consent and solemnization, see Family Code § 305.
Privilege not to testify against spouse, see Evidence Code §§ 970, 972.
Proof of fact of marriage, see Evidence Code § 1314.
Statute making one fact prima facie evidence of another fact as establishing rebuttable presumption, see Evidence Code § 602.
Uniform act on blood tests to determine paternity, applicability, see Family Code § 7556.
Uniform Interstate Family Support Act, see Family Code § 5700.101 et seq.
Witness, definition, see Code of Civil Procedure § 1878.

§ 270f. Report by parent of failure to support; investigation and action by district attorney

Where, under the provisions of this chapter, a report is filed by a parent of a child with the district attorney averring:

(1) That the other parent has failed to provide necessary support and

(2) That neither the child in need of assistance nor another on his behalf is receiving public assistance, the district attorney shall immediately investigate the verity of such report and determine the defaulting parent's location and financial ability to provide the needed support, and upon a finding that the report is true shall immediately take all steps necessary to obtain support for the child in need of assistance. *(Added by Stats.1965, c. 496, p. 1806, § 2. Amended by Stats.1974, c. 893, p. 1893, § 3.)*

§ 270g. Review of reports

A review of each report filed with the district attorney under Section 270f shall be made at 90-day intervals unless the support payments have been legally terminated, the parties involved are permanently located beyond county jurisdiction, or the defaulting parent is complying with the provisions of this chapter. *(Added by Stats.1965, c. 496, p. 1806, § 3. Amended by Stats.1974, c. 893, p. 1894, § 4.)*

Cross References

Misdemeanor defined, see Penal Code § 17.

§ 270h. Support order included in order granting probation; issuance of execution; assignment of wages

In any case where there is a conviction under either Section 270 or 270a and there is an order granting probation which includes an order for support, the court may:

(a) Issue an execution on the order for the support payments that accrue during the time the probation order is in effect, in the same manner as on a judgment in a civil action for support payments. This remedy shall apply only when there is no existing civil order of this state or a foreign court order that has been reduced to a judgment of this state for support of the same person or persons included in the probation support order.

(b) Issue an earnings assignment order for support pursuant to Chapter 8 (commencing with Section 5200) of Part 5 of Division 9 of the Family Code as a condition of probation. This remedy shall apply only when there is no existing civil order for support of the same person or persons included in the probation support order upon which an assignment order has been entered pursuant to Chapter 8 (commencing with Section 5200) of Part 5 of Division 9 of the Family Code or pursuant to former Chapter 5 (commencing with Section 4390) of Title 1.5 of Part 5 of Division 4 of the Civil Code.

These remedies are in addition to any other remedies available to the court. *(Added by Stats.1969, c. 1202, p. 2342, § 1. Amended by Stats.1971, c. 1587, p. 3203, § 2; Stats.1991, c. 1091 (A.B.1487), § 118; Stats.1992, c. 163 (A.B.2641), § 103, operative Jan. 1, 1994.)*

Cross References

Additional power of probation officer, receipt, deposit and disbursement of money, see Welfare and Institutions Code § 276.
Contempt, willful disobedience of court order, see Penal Code § 166.
Cumulative nature of support duties, see Family Code § 4402.
Enforcement of judgment in civil actions, see Code of Civil Procedure § 683.010 et seq.
Payment of fine to spouse or to guardian of child, see Penal Code § 270d.
Probation, see Penal Code § 1202.7 et seq.
Support of spouse living separate by agreement, see Family Code § 4302.
Undertaking to provide support, see Penal Code § 270b.
Uniform Interstate Family Support Act, remedies cumulative, see Family Code § 5700.104.

§ 271. Desertion of child under 14 with intent to abandon; punishment

Every parent of any child under the age of 14 years, and every person to whom any such child has been confided for nurture, or education, who deserts such child in any place whatever with intent to abandon it, is punishable by imprisonment pursuant to subdivision (h) of Section 1170 or in the county jail not exceeding one year or by fine not exceeding one thousand dollars ($1,000) or by both. (Enacted in 1872. Amended by Stats.1909, c. 190, p. 297, § 1; Stats.1945, c. 250, p. 713, § 1; Stats.1983, c. 1092, § 260, eff. Sept. 27, 1983, operative Jan. 1, 1984; Stats.2011, c. 15 (A.B.109), § 306, eff. April 4, 2011, operative Oct. 1, 2011.)

Cross References

Contributing to delinquency of minors, see Penal Code § 272.
Failure to provide for minor child, see Penal Code § 270.
Manifestation of intent, see Penal Code § 21.
Misdemeanor defined, see Penal Code § 17.
Presumption of relinquishment of services and custody of child by abandonment, see Family Code § 7504.
Proceedings to declare person free from custody and control of parents, procedure, see Family Code § 7840 et seq.
Sentence to work on public roads, see Penal Code § 273h.
Substitution of one child for another, see Penal Code § 157.

§ 271a. Abandonment or failure to maintain child under 14; false representation that child is orphan; punishment

Every person who knowingly and willfully abandons, or who, having ability so to do, fails or refuses to maintain his or her minor child under the age of 14 years, or who falsely, knowing the same to be false, represents to any manager, officer or agent of any orphan asylum or charitable institution for the care of orphans, that any child for whose admission into that asylum or institution application has been made is an orphan, is punishable by imprisonment pursuant to subdivision (h) of Section 1170, or in the county jail not exceeding one year, or by fine not exceeding one thousand dollars ($1,000), or by both. (Added by Stats.1905, c. 568, p. 758, § 2. Amended by Stats.1909, c. 190, p. 297, § 2; Stats.1983, c. 1092, § 261, eff. Sept. 27, 1983, operative Jan. 1, 1984; Stats.2011, c. 15 (A.B.109), § 307, eff. April 4, 2011, operative Oct. 1, 2011.)

Cross References

Adoption, see Family Code § 8500 et seq.
Definitions,
   Knowingly, see Penal Code § 7.
   Misdemeanor, see Penal Code § 17.
   Willfully, see Penal Code § 7.
Duty of support, see Family Code § 3900 et seq.
Effect of adoption, see Family Code §§ 8616, 8617.
False pretenses regarding birth of child to intercept inheritance, see Penal Code § 156.
Presumption of relinquishment of services and custody of child by abandonment, see Family Code § 7504.
Proceedings to declare a person free from custody and control of parents, procedure, see Family Code § 7840 et seq.
Remedy when parent dies without providing for support of child, see Family Code § 3952.
Sentence to work on public roads, see Penal Code § 273h.

Unauthorized placement for adoption, see Family Code § 8609.
Uniform Interstate Family Support Act, see Family Code § 5700.101 et seq.

§ 271.5. Safe-surrender sites; parents or other individuals surrendering custody of baby

(a) No parent or other individual having lawful custody of a minor child 72 hours old or younger may be prosecuted for a violation of Section 270, 270.5, 271, or 271a if he or she voluntarily surrenders physical custody of the child to personnel on duty at a safe-surrender site.

(b) For purposes of this section, "safe-surrender site" has the same meaning as defined in paragraph (1) of subdivision (a) of Section 1255.7 of the Health and Safety Code.

(c)(1) For purposes of this section, "lawful custody" has the same meaning as defined in subdivision (j) of Section 1255.7 of the Health and Safety Code.

(2) For purposes of this section, "personnel" has the same meaning as defined in paragraph (3) of subdivision (a) of Section 1255.7 of the Health and Safety Code. (Added by Stats.2000, c. 824 (S.B.1368), § 2. Amended by Stats.2003, c. 150 (S.B.139), § 2; Stats.2004, c. 103 (S.B.1413), § 2; Stats.2005, c. 279 (S.B.1107), § 3; Stats.2005, c. 625 (S.B.116), § 2; Stats.2007, c. 130 (A.B.299), § 186.)

Cross References

Comprehensive sexual health and HIV/AIDS prevention education, authority of school districts, see Education Code § 51933.
Health facilities, safe-surrender sites, see Health and Safety Code § 1255.7.
Sex education classes, course criteria, advising pupils of the content of this section, see Education Code § 51933.

§ 272. Contributing to delinquency of persons under 18 years; persuading, luring, or transporting minors 12 years of age or younger

(a)(1) Every person who commits any act or omits the performance of any duty, which act or omission causes or tends to cause or encourage any person under the age of 18 years to come within the provisions of Section 300, 601, or 602 of the Welfare and Institutions Code or which act or omission contributes thereto, or any person who, by any act or omission, or by threats, commands, or persuasion, induces or endeavors to induce any person under the age of 18 years or any ward or dependent child of the juvenile court to fail or refuse to conform to a lawful order of the juvenile court, or to do or to perform any act or to follow any course of conduct or to so live as would cause or manifestly tend to cause that person to become or to remain a person within the provisions of Section 300, 601, or 602 of the Welfare and Institutions Code, is guilty of a misdemeanor and upon conviction thereof shall be punished by a fine not exceeding two thousand five hundred dollars ($2,500), or by imprisonment in the county jail for not more than one year, or by both fine and imprisonment in a county jail, or may be released on probation for a period not exceeding five years.

(2) For purposes of this subdivision, a parent or legal guardian to any person under the age of 18 years shall have the duty to exercise reasonable care, supervision, protection, and control over their minor child.

(b)(1) An adult stranger who is 21 years of age or older, who knowingly contacts or communicates with a minor who is under 14 years of age, who knew or reasonably should have known that the minor is under 14 years of age, for the purpose of persuading and luring, or transporting, or attempting to persuade and lure, or transport, that minor away from the minor's home or from any location known by the minor's parent, legal guardian, or custodian, to be a place where the minor is located, for any purpose, without the express consent of the minor's parent or legal guardian, and with the intent to avoid the consent of the minor's parent or legal guardian, is guilty of an infraction or a misdemeanor, subject to subdivision (d) of Section 17.

(2) This subdivision shall not apply in an emergency situation.

(3) As used in this subdivision, the following terms are defined to mean:

(A) "Emergency situation" means a situation where the minor is threatened with imminent bodily harm, emotional harm, or psychological harm.

(B) "Contact" or "communication" includes, but is not limited to, the use of a telephone or the Internet, as defined in Section 17538 of the Business and Professions Code.

(C) "Stranger" means a person of casual acquaintance with whom no substantial relationship exists, or an individual with whom a relationship has been established or promoted for the primary purpose of victimization, as defined in subdivision (e) of Section 6600 of the Welfare and Institutions Code.

(D) "Express consent" means oral or written permission that is positive, direct, and unequivocal, requiring no inference or implication to supply its meaning.

(4) This section shall not be interpreted to criminalize acts of persons contacting minors within the scope and course of their employment, or status as a volunteer of a recognized civic or charitable organization.

(5) This section is intended to protect minors and to help parents and legal guardians exercise reasonable care, supervision, protection, and control over minor children. *(Added by Stats.1961, c. 1616, p. 3503, § 3. Amended by Stats.1972, c. 579, p. 1005, § 34; Stats.1976, c. 1068, p. 4740, § 1; Stats.1976, c. 1125, p. 5037, § 16; Stats.1979, c. 373, p. 1349, § 237; Stats.1988, c. 1256, § 2, eff. Sept. 26, 1988; Stats.2000, c. 621 (A.B.2021), § 1; Stats.2001, c. 159 (S.B.662), § 161; Stats.2005, c. 461 (A.B.33), § 1.)*

Cross References

Absence of pupil from school without permission, see Education Code § 48613.
Alcohol provided to minors, prohibition and punishment, see Business and Professions Code § 25658.
California work opportunity and responsibility to kids act, prosecution for contributing to delinquency of minor, see Welfare and Institutions Code § 11481.
Community care facilities, residence in facility within one mile of elementary school by person convicted of sex offense against minor prohibited, see Health and Safety Code § 1564.
Compulsory Education Law, violations, notice of outcome of each truancy-related referral, see Education Code § 48297.
Controlled substances, use or employment of minors in transporting or selling, see Health and Safety Code §§ 11353, 11354, 11361.
Conviction as ground for revocation of,
   County teaching certificate, see Education Code § 44435.
   Teaching credential, see Education Code § 44424.
Distribution or exhibition of harmful matter to minors, see Penal Code § 313.1.
Employment agencies, sending minors to places adversely affecting health, safety, welfare or morals, see Civil Code §§ 1812.521, 1812.523.
Employment or use of minor to perform prohibited acts, see Penal Code § 311.4.
Forfeiture of property used in committing telecommunications or computer crimes, application to minors, see Penal Code § 502.01.
Juvenile court, see Welfare and Institutions Code § 245 et seq.
Lewd or lascivious acts with child under fourteen, see Penal Code §§ 288, 288.1.
Minors not permitted to deliver messages or enter places of questionable repute, see Penal Code §§ 273e, 273f.
Misdemeanor defined, see Penal Code § 17.
Parent or guardian of chronic truant, failure to reasonably supervise and encourage school attendance deemed misdemeanor, deferred entry of judgment program, see Penal Code § 270.1.
Photographs of minors that are harmful matter, preservation of and access to evidence, application to actions under this section, see Penal Code § 1417.8.
Pleadings and proceedings before trial, see Penal Code § 976 et seq.
Prosecution for contributing to delinquency of minor, see Welfare and Institutions Code § 11481.
Sex offenders, mandatory registration, see Penal Code § 290 et seq.
Sex offense as including violation of this section, see Education Code §§ 44010, 87010.
Statutory rape, see Penal Code § 261 et seq.

Research References

Forms

1 California Transactions Forms--Family Law § 3:14, Fiscal Responsibility and Liability Issues.

§ 273. Paying or receiving money or thing of value to parent for placement for, or consent to, adoption of child

(a) It is a misdemeanor for any person or agency to pay, offer to pay, or to receive money or anything of value for the placement for adoption or for the consent to an adoption of a child. This subdivision shall not apply to any fee paid for adoption services provided by the State Department of Social Services, a licensed adoption agency, adoption services providers, as defined in Section 8502 of the Family Code, or an attorney providing adoption legal services.

(b) This section shall not make it unlawful to pay or receive the maternity-connected medical or hospital and necessary living expenses of the mother preceding and during confinement as an act of charity, as long as the payment is not contingent upon placement of the child for adoption, consent to the adoption, or cooperation in the completion of the adoption.

(c) It is a misdemeanor punishable by imprisonment in a county jail not exceeding one year or by a fine not exceeding two thousand five hundred dollars ($2,500) for any parent to obtain the financial benefits set forth in subdivision (b) with the intent to receive those financial benefits where there is an intent to do either of the following:

(1) Not complete the adoption.

(2) Not consent to the adoption.

(d) It is a misdemeanor punishable by imprisonment in a county jail not exceeding one year or by a fine not exceeding two thousand five hundred dollars ($2,500) for any parent to obtain the financial benefits set forth in subdivision (b) from two or more prospective adopting families or persons, if either parent does both of the following:

(1) Knowingly fails to disclose to those families or persons that there are other prospective adopting families or persons interested in adopting the child, with knowledge that there is an obligation to disclose that information.

(2) Knowingly accepts the financial benefits set forth in subdivision (b) if the aggregate amount exceeds the reasonable maternity-connected medical or hospital and necessary living expenses of the mother preceding and during the pregnancy.

(e) Any person who has been convicted previously of an offense described in subdivision (c) or (d), who is separately tried and convicted of a subsequent violation of subdivision (c) or (d), is guilty of a public offense punishable by imprisonment in a county jail or in the state prison.

(f) Nothing in this section shall be construed to prohibit the prosecution of any person for a misdemeanor or felony pursuant to Section 487 or any other provision of law in lieu of prosecution pursuant to this section. *(Added by Stats.1967, c. 1088, p. 2723, § 1. Amended by Stats.1990, c. 1492 (A.B.4288), § 1; Stats.1993, c. 377 (S.B.244), § 1; Stats.1997, c. 185 (S.B.122), § 1.)*

Cross References

Adoption consent by birth parents, see Family Code §§ 8603 to 8606.
Child witnesses, contemporaneous examination and cross-examination by closed-circuit television, see Penal Code § 1347.

Children, refusal to grant approval of placement in violation of state law, see Family Code § 7910.
Felonies, definition and penalties, see Penal Code §§ 17, 18.
Misdemeanors, definition and penalties, see Penal Code §§ 17, 19 and 19.2.
Prison or state prison defined for purposes of this Code, see Penal Code § 6081.
Refusal to grant approval of placement in violation of state law, see Family Code § 7910.

Research References
Forms
2 California Transactions Forms--Family Law § 6:2, Governing Law.
2 California Transactions Forms--Family Law § 6:20, Financial Assistance to Birth Parents.

§ 273a. Willful harm or injury to child; endangering person or health; punishment; conditions of probation

(a) Any person who, under circumstances or conditions likely to produce great bodily harm or death, willfully causes or permits any child to suffer, or inflicts thereon unjustifiable physical pain or mental suffering, or having the care or custody of any child, willfully causes or permits the person or health of that child to be injured, or willfully causes or permits that child to be placed in a situation where his or her person or health is endangered, shall be punished by imprisonment in a county jail not exceeding one year, or in the state prison for two, four, or six years.

(b) Any person who, under circumstances or conditions other than those likely to produce great bodily harm or death, willfully causes or permits any child to suffer, or inflicts thereon unjustifiable physical pain or mental suffering, or having the care or custody of any child, willfully causes or permits the person or health of that child to be injured, or willfully causes or permits that child to be placed in a situation where his or her person or health may be endangered, is guilty of a misdemeanor.

(c) If a person is convicted of violating this section and probation is granted, the court shall require the following minimum conditions of probation:

(1) A mandatory minimum period of probation of 48 months.

(2) A criminal court protective order protecting the victim from further acts of violence or threats, and, if appropriate, residence exclusion or stay-away conditions.

(3)(A) Successful completion of no less than one year of a child abuser's treatment counseling program approved by the probation department. The defendant shall be ordered to begin participation in the program immediately upon the grant of probation. The counseling program shall meet the criteria specified in Section 273.1. The defendant shall produce documentation of program enrollment to the court within 30 days of enrollment, along with quarterly progress reports.

(B) The terms of probation for offenders shall not be lifted until all reasonable fees due to the counseling program have been paid in full, but in no case shall probation be extended beyond the term provided in subdivision (a) of Section 1203.1. If the court finds that the defendant does not have the ability to pay the fees based on the defendant's changed circumstances, the court may reduce or waive the fees.

(4) If the offense was committed while the defendant was under the influence of drugs or alcohol, the defendant shall abstain from the use of drugs or alcohol during the period of probation and shall be subject to random drug testing by his or her probation officer.

(5) The court may waive any of the above minimum conditions of probation upon a finding that the condition would not be in the best interests of justice. The court shall state on the record its reasons for any waiver. *(Added by Stats.1905, c. 568, p. 759, § 5. Amended by Stats.1963, c. 783, p. 1811, § 1; Stats.1965, c. 697, p. 2091, § 1; Stats.1976, c. 1139, p. 5108, § 165, operative July 1, 1977; Stats.1980, c. 1117, p. 3590, § 4; Stats.1984, c. 1423, § 2, eff. Sept. 26, 1984;* Stats.1993, c. 1253 (A.B.897), § 1; Stats.1994, c. 1263 (A.B.1328), § 3; Stats.1996, c. 1090 (A.B.3215), § 1; Stats.1997, c. 134 (A.B.273), § 1.)

Cross References

Advertising placement of children for adoption, see Family Code § 8609.
Calendar, priorities, see Penal Code § 1048.
Child abusers, prosecution efforts, selection criteria, see Penal Code § 999t.
Child day care, forfeiture of license by operation of law, see Health and Safety Code § 1596.858.
Child welfare services, security procedures for county employees having frequent contact with children, see Welfare and Institutions Code § 16501.
Child witnesses, precautions for comfort, support, and protection, see Penal Code § 868.8.
Community care facilities, forfeiture of license by operation by law, see Health and Safety Code § 1524.
Community care facilities, licenses or special permits, fingerprinting, nonexemption, see Health and Safety Code § 1522.
Conviction as ground for revocation of,
  County teaching certificate, see Education Code § 44435.
  Teaching credential, see Education Code § 44424.
Conviction for violation of this section, restitution fine imposition, child abuse prevention purposes, see Penal Code § 294.
Corporal punishment or injury, infliction upon child, see Penal Code § 273d.
Counties and cities, persons convicted of Penal Code offenses, supervisory or disciplinary authority over minors, see Public Resources Code § 5164.
Criminal record information of individuals in contact with child day care facility clients, see Health and Safety Code § 1596.871.
Custody and visitation, child support, and disclosure of information, see Family Code § 3030.
Disclosure of records, exemption at request of victim, see Government Code § 6254.
Dismissal of complaint if preliminary examination continued over ten court days after arraignment, exception where prosecuting attorney has schedule conflict, see Penal Code § 859b.
Drug endangered children, law enforcement and social services agencies' response, development of policies and standards for narcotic crime scenes, see Penal Code § 13879.80 et seq.
Drugs, unlawful use of minor as agent, see Business and Professions Code § 4336.
Employments dangerous or injurious to minors, determination, see Labor Code § 1296.
Examination of victims of sexual crimes, see Penal Code § 1346 et seq.
Female genital mutilation, additional punishment for violation of this section, see Penal Code § 273.4.
Freedom from parental custody and control, see Family Code § 7800 et seq.
Home health aides, grounds for disciplinary action, see Health and Safety Code § 1736.5.
Injuries as result of assaultive or abusive conduct, reporting requirements by health facilities, clinics, or physician's offices, see Penal Code § 11160.
Jurisdiction of juvenile court in cases of cruelty, see Welfare and Institutions Code § 300.
Leading questions, child under ten years of age, see Evidence Code § 767.
Leaving a child unsupervised inside a motor vehicle, prosecution, see Vehicle Code § 15620.
Misdemeanor,
  Definition, see Penal Code § 17.
  Punishment, see Penal Code §§ 19, 19.2.
Multiple violations, local jurisdiction of offenses, see Penal Code § 784.7.
Nurse assistants, grounds for disciplinary action, see Health and Safety Code § 1337.9.
Occupations prohibited to minors under 16, see Labor Code § 1308.
Prison or state prison defined for purposes of this Code, see Penal Code § 6081.
Public social services, eligibility for supportive services following fraud conviction, see Welfare and Institutions Code § 12305.81.
Public social services, services for children, family reunification, see Welfare and Institutions Code § 16507.
Remedy for parental abuse, see Family Code § 7507.
Report of physician or surgeon treating apparent victim, see Penal Code § 11165 et seq.
Residential care facilities for persons with chronic life-threatening illness, criminal records of applicants or persons in frequent contact with residents, see Health and Safety Code § 1568.09.

§ 273a

Residential care facilities for persons with chronic life-threatening illness, forfeiture of license, see Health and Safety Code § 1568.061.
Residential care facilities for the elderly, criminal records of individuals in contact with clients, see Health and Safety Code § 1569.17.
Residential care facilities for the elderly, renewal application, forfeiture of license by operation of law, see Health and Safety Code § 1569.19.
Sentencing for driving while under the influence, minor in vehicle, enhanced punishment, see Vehicle Code § 23572.
Societies for prevention of cruelty to children, generally, see Corporations Code §§ 10400 et seq., 14500 et seq.
Statements describing an act or attempted act of child abuse or neglect, criminal prosecutions, requirements, see Evidence Code § 1360.
Violent crime information center, online missing persons registry, historic database, see Penal Code § 14203.
Willful harm or injury resulting in death of child, sentence enhancement, see Penal Code § 12022.95.
Willfully, definition, see Penal Code § 7.

§ 273ab. Assault resulting in death, comatose state, or paralysis of child under 8; imprisonment

(a) Any person, having the care or custody of a child who is under eight years of age, who assaults the child by means of force that to a reasonable person would be likely to produce great bodily injury, resulting in the child's death, shall be punished by imprisonment in the state prison for 25 years to life. Nothing in this section shall be construed as affecting the applicability of subdivision (a) of Section 187 or Section 189.

(b) Any person, having the care or custody of a child who is under eight years of age, who assaults the child by means of force that to a reasonable person would be likely to produce great bodily injury, resulting in the child becoming comatose due to brain injury or suffering paralysis of a permanent nature, shall be punished by imprisonment in the state prison for life with the possibility of parole. As used in this subdivision, "paralysis" means a major or complete loss of motor function resulting from injury to the nervous system or to a muscular mechanism. *(Added by Stats.1993–94, 1st Ex.Sess., c. 47 (A.B.27), § 1, eff. Nov. 30, 1994. Amended by Stats.1996, c. 460 (A.B.2258), § 2; Stats.2010, c. 300 (A.B.1280), § 1.)*

Cross References

Child abusers, prosecution efforts, selection criteria, see Penal Code § 999t.
Child day cares, fingerprints and criminal records, exemption not to be granted for offense specified in this section, see Health and Safety Code § 1596.871.
Community care facilities, fingerprints and criminal records, exemption not to be granted for offense specified in this section, see Health and Safety Code § 1522.
Prison or state prison defined for purposes of this Code, see Penal Code § 6081.
Public social services, services for children, family reunification, see Welfare and Institutions Code § 16507.
Residential care facilities for persons with chronic life-threatening illness, fingerprints and criminal records, exemption not to be granted for offense specified in this section, see Health and Safety Code § 1568.09.
Residential care facilities for the elderly, fingerprints and criminal records, exemption not to be granted for offense specified in this section, see Health and Safety Code § 1569.17.

§ 273b. Children under 16; placement in courtroom or vehicle with adult offender; restriction

No child under the age of 16 years shall be placed in any courtroom, or in any vehicle for transportation to any place, in company with adults charged with or convicted of crime, except in the presence of a proper official. *(Added by Stats.1905, c. 568, p. 760, § 6. Amended by Stats.1941, c. 106, p. 1081, § 8; Stats.1987, c. 828, § 13.5.)*

Cross References

Children of female inmates, community treatment programs, see Penal Code § 3410 et seq.
Contributing to delinquency of minors, see Penal Code § 272.
Detaining persons under eighteen, see Welfare and Institutions Code §§ 207, 208.
Jurisdiction of juvenile court, see Welfare and Institutions Code § 300 et seq.

§ 273c. Prosecution instituted by society for prevention of cruelty to children; fines, penalties and forfeitures payable to society

All fines, penalties, and forfeitures imposed and collected under the provisions of Sections 270, 271, 271a, 273a, and 273b, or under the provisions of any law relating to, or affecting, children, in every case where the prosecution is instituted or conducted by a society incorporated under the laws of this state for the prevention of cruelty to children, inure to such society in aid of the purposes for which it is incorporated. *(Added by Stats.1905, c. 568, p. 760, § 7. Amended by Stats.1987, c. 828, § 14.)*

Cross References

Fines,
 Discharge on payment, see Penal Code § 1457.
 Distribution in municipal or justice courts, see Penal Code § 1463.
 Excessive imposition prohibited, see Cal. Const. Art. 1, § 17.
 Payment, see Penal Code § 1205.
Societies for prevention of cruelty to children, generally, see Corporations Code §§ 10400 et seq., 14500 et seq.

§ 273d. Corporal punishment or injury of child; felony; punishment; enhancement for prior conviction; conditions of probation

(a) Any person who willfully inflicts upon a child any cruel or inhuman corporal punishment or an injury resulting in a traumatic condition is guilty of a felony and shall be punished by imprisonment pursuant to subdivision (h) of Section 1170 for two, four, or six years, or in a county jail for not more than one year, by a fine of up to six thousand dollars ($6,000), or by both that imprisonment and fine.

(b) Any person who is found guilty of violating subdivision (a) shall receive a four-year enhancement for a prior conviction of that offense provided that no additional term shall be imposed under this subdivision for any prison term or term imposed under the provisions of subdivision (h) of Section 1170 served prior to a period of 10 years in which the defendant remained free of both the commission of an offense that results in a felony conviction and prison custody or custody in a county jail under the provisions of subdivision (h) of Section 1170.

(c) If a person is convicted of violating this section and probation is granted, the court shall require the following minimum conditions of probation:

(1) A mandatory minimum period of probation of 36 months.

(2) A criminal court protective order protecting the victim from further acts of violence or threats, and, if appropriate, residence exclusion or stay-away conditions.

(3)(A) Successful completion of no less than one year of a child abuser's treatment counseling program. The defendant shall be ordered to begin participation in the program immediately upon the grant of probation. The counseling program shall meet the criteria specified in Section 273.1. The defendant shall produce documentation of program enrollment to the court within 30 days of enrollment, along with quarterly progress reports.

(B) The terms of probation for offenders shall not be lifted until all reasonable fees due to the counseling program have been paid in full, but in no case shall probation be extended beyond the term provided in subdivision (a) of Section 1203.1. If the court finds that the defendant does not have the ability to pay the fees based on the defendant's changed circumstances, the court may reduce or waive the fees.

(4) If the offense was committed while the defendant was under the influence of drugs or alcohol, the defendant shall abstain from the use of drugs or alcohol during the period of probation and shall be subject to random drug testing by his or her probation officer.

(5) The court may waive any of the above minimum conditions of probation upon a finding that the condition would not be in the best interests of justice. The court shall state on the record its reasons for any waiver. *(Added by Stats.1945, c. 1312, p. 2462, § 1. Amended by Stats.1957, c. 1342, p. 2673, § 1; Stats.1965, c. 1271, p. 3146, § 4; Stats.1976, c. 1139, p. 5109, § 166, operative July 1, 1977; Stats.1977, c. 908, p. 2780, § 1; Stats.1977, c. 912, p. 2786, § 2; Stats.1980, c. 1117, p. 3590, § 5; Stats.1984, c. 1423, § 3, eff. Sept. 26, 1984; Stats.1987, c. 415, § 1; Stats.1993, c. 607 (S.B.529), § 1; Stats.1996, c. 1090 (A.B.3215), § 2; Stats.1997, c. 134 (A.B.273), § 2; Stats.1999, c. 662 (S.B.218), § 8; Stats.2004, c. 229 (S.B.1104), § 14, eff. Aug. 16, 2004; Stats.2011, c. 15 (A.B.109), § 312, eff. April 4, 2011, operative Oct. 1, 2011; Stats.2011–2012, 1st Ex.Sess., c. 12 (A.B.17), § 8, eff. Sept. 21, 2011, operative Oct. 1, 2011.)*

Cross References

Battery on school or park property or hospital grounds, punishment, see Penal Code § 243.2.
Calendar, priorities, see Penal Code § 1048.
Child abusers, prosecution efforts, selection criteria, see Penal Code § 999t.
Child day care, forfeiture of license by operation of law, see Health and Safety Code § 1596.858.
Child witnesses, contemporaneous examination and cross-examination by closed-circuit television, see Penal Code § 1347.
Child witnesses, precautions for comfort, support, and protection, see Penal Code § 868.8.
Community care facilities, forfeiture of license by operation by law, see Health and Safety Code § 1524.
Community care facilities, licenses or special permits, fingerprinting, nonexemption, see Health and Safety Code § 1522.
Conviction for violation of this section, restitution fine imposition, child abuse prevention purposes, see Penal Code § 294.
Counties and cities, persons convicted of Penal Code offenses, supervisory or disciplinary authority over minors, see Public Resources Code § 5164.
Custody and visitation, child support, and disclosure of information, see Family Code § 3030.
Definitions,
　Assault, see Penal Code § 240.
　Battery, see Penal Code § 242.
　Felony, see Penal Code § 17.
　Willfully, see Penal Code § 7.
Disclosure of records, exemption at request of victim, see Government Code § 6254.
Dismissal of complaint if preliminary examination continued over ten court days after arraignment, exception where prosecuting attorney has schedule conflict, see Penal Code § 859b.
Evidence of defendant's other acts of domestic violence, see Evidence Code § 1109.
Examination of victims of sexual crimes, see Penal Code § 1346 et seq.
Fine authorized in addition to punishment, see Penal Code § 672.
Injuries as result of assaultive or abusive conduct, reporting requirements by health facilities, clinics, or physician's offices, see Penal Code § 11160.
Jurisdiction of juvenile court in cases of cruelty, see Welfare and Institutions Code § 300.
Leading questions, child under ten years of age, see Evidence Code § 767.
Lewd or lascivious acts with child under fourteen, see Penal Code §§ 288, 288.1.
Prison or state prison defined for purposes of this Code, see Penal Code § 6081.
Public social services, services for children, family reunification, see Welfare and Institutions Code § 16507.
Remedy for parental abuse, see Family Code § 7507.
Residential care facilities for persons with chronic life–threatening illness, forfeiture of license, see Health and Safety Code § 1568.061.
Residential care facilities for the elderly, renewal application, forfeiture of license by operation of law, see Health and Safety Code § 1569.19.
Societies for prevention of cruelty to children, generally, see Corporations Code §§ 10400 et seq., 14500 et seq.
Statements describing an act or attempted act of child abuse or neglect, criminal prosecutions, requirements, see Evidence Code § 1360.
Violent crime information center, online missing persons registry, historic database, see Penal Code § 14203.

Willful cruelty or unjustifiable punishment of child, see Penal Code § 273a.

§ 273e. Places of questionable repute; minors not to deliver messages, etc., or enter

Every telephone, special delivery company or association, and every other corporation or person engaged in the delivery of packages, letters, notes, messages, or other matter, and every manager, superintendent, or other agent of such person, corporation, or association, who sends any minor in the employ or under the control of any such person, corporation, association, or agent, to the keeper of any house of prostitution, variety theater, or other place of questionable repute, or to any person connected with, or any inmate of, such house, theater, or other place, or who permits such minor to enter such house, theater, or other place, is guilty of a misdemeanor. *(Added by Stats.1905, c. 568, p. 760, § 9.)*

Cross References

Admitting or keeping minors in house of prostitution, see Penal Code § 309.
Allowing minors to gamble in drinking place, see Penal Code § 336.
Contributing to delinquency of minors, see Penal Code § 272.
Definitions,
　Minors, see Family Code § 6500.
　Misdemeanor, see Penal Code § 17.
Employment agency, sending applicant to place adversely affecting health, safety, welfare or morals, see Civil Code §§ 1812.521, 1812.523.
Employment of minors as messengers, see Labor Code § 1297.
Jurisdiction of juvenile court, see Welfare and Institutions Code § 300 et seq.
Places of illegal gambling or prostitution, prevailing upon person to visit, see Penal Code § 318.
Punishment for misdemeanor, see Penal Code §§ 19, 19.2.

§ 273f. Sending minors to immoral places

Any person, whether as parent, guardian, employer, or otherwise, and any firm or corporation, who as employer or otherwise, shall send, direct, or cause to be sent or directed to any saloon, gambling house, house of prostitution, or other immoral place, any minor, is guilty of a misdemeanor. *(Added by Stats.1907, c. 294, p. 565, § 2. Amended by Stats.1972, c. 579, p. 1006, § 35.)*

Cross References

Abduction of female under eighteen for purpose of prostitution, see Penal Code § 267.
Admitting or keeping minors in house of prostitution, see Penal Code § 309.
Alcohol provided to minors, prohibition and punishment, see Business and Professions Code § 25658.
Allowing minors to gamble in drinking place, see Penal Code § 336.
Contributing to delinquency of minors, see Penal Code § 272.
Conviction as ground for revocation of,
　County teaching certificate, see Education Code § 44435.
　Teaching credential, see Education Code § 44424.
Employment agency, sending applicant to place adversely affecting health, safety, welfare or morals, see Civil Code §§ 1812.521, 1812.523.
Employment of minors as messengers, see Labor Code § 1297.
Jurisdiction of juvenile court, see Welfare and Institutions Code § 300 et seq.
Misdemeanor,
　Definition, see Penal Code § 17.
　Punishment, see Penal Code §§ 19, 19.2.
Places of illegal gambling or prostitution, prevailing upon person to visit, see Penal Code § 318.
Prizefights and cockfights, exclusion of minors under 16, see Penal Code § 310.

§ 273g. Degrading, immoral, or vicious practices or habitual drunkenness in presence of children

Any person who in the presence of any child indulges in any degrading, lewd, immoral or vicious habits or practices, or who is habitually drunk in the presence of any child in his care, custody or control, is guilty of a misdemeanor. *(Added by Stats.1907, c. 413, p. 756, § 1.)*

§ 273g PENAL CODE

Validity

This section was held unconstitutional in the decision of People v. Perreault (Super. 1960), 5 Cal.Rptr. 849, 182 Cal.App.2d Supp. 843.

Cross References

Annoying or molesting child under eighteen, see Penal Code § 647.6.
Contributing to delinquency of minors, see Penal Code § 272.
Conviction as ground for revocation of,
   County teaching certificate, see Education Code § 44435.
   Teaching credential, see Education Code § 44424.
Indecent exposure, see Penal Code § 314.
Lewd or lascivious acts upon the body of a child under fourteen, see Penal Code §§ 288, 288.1.
Misdemeanor,
   Definition, see Penal Code § 17.
   Punishment, see Penal Code §§ 19, 19.2.
Voluntary intoxication no excuse for crime, see Penal Code § 22.

§ 273h. Sentence to work on public roads; payment of earnings to wife or to guardian of children, etc.

In all prosecutions under the provisions of either section 270, section 270a, section 270b, section 271 or section 271a, of this code, where a conviction is had and sentence of imprisonment in the county jail or in the city jail is imposed, the court may direct that the person so convicted shall be compelled to work upon the public roads or highways, or any other public work, in the county or in the city where such conviction is had, during the term of such sentence. And it shall be the duty of the board of supervisors of the county where such person is imprisoned in the county jail, and of the city council of the city where such person is imprisoned in the city jail, where such conviction and sentence are had and where such work is performed by a person under sentence to the county jail or to the city jail, to allow and order the payment out of any funds available, to the wife or to the guardian, or to the custodian of a child or children, or to an organization, or to an individual, appointed by the court as trustee, at the end of each calendar month, for the support of such wife or children, a sum not to exceed two dollars for each day's work of such person so imprisoned. *(Added by Stats.1911, c. 379, p. 688, § 1. Amended by Stats.1927, c. 243, p. 433, § 1.)*

Cross References

County jails, work by prisoners, see Penal Code §§ 4017, 4018.
Employment of prisoners, see Penal Code § 2700 et seq.
Fines, payment, see Penal Code § 1205.
Labor on public works, authority to require, see Penal Code § 4017.
Payment of fine to spouse or to guardian of child, see Penal Code § 270d.
Prosecutions by society for prevention of cruelty to children, disposition of fines, see Penal Code § 273c.
Working of prisoners on public property, see Government Code § 25359.

§ 273i. Publication of information describing or depicting child or relating to child with intent that information be used to commit crime against child; punishment; definitions; injunction

(a) Any person who publishes information describing or depicting a child, the physical appearance of a child, the location of a child, or locations where children may be found with the intent that another person imminently use the information to commit a crime against a child and the information is likely to aid in the imminent commission of a crime against a child, is guilty of a misdemeanor, punishable by imprisonment in a county jail for not more than one year, a fine of not more than one thousand dollars ($1,000), or by both a fine and imprisonment.

(b) For purposes of this section, "publishes" means making the information available to another person through any medium, including, but not limited to, the Internet, the World Wide Web, or e-mail.

(c) For purposes of this section, "child" means a person who is 14 years of age or younger.

(d) For purposes of this section, "information" includes, but is not limited to, an image, film, filmstrip, photograph, negative, slide, photocopy, videotape, video laser disc, or any other computer-generated image.

(e) Any parent or legal guardian of a child about whom information is published in violation of subdivision (a) may seek a preliminary injunction enjoining any further publication of that information. *(Added by Stats.2008, c. 423 (A.B.534), § 1.)*

§ 273j. Notification of public safety agency of death of child; notification of law enforcement of missing child; penalties

(a)(1) Any parent or guardian having the care, custody, or control of a child under 14 years of age who knows or should have known that the child has died shall notify a public safety agency, as defined in Section 53102 of the Government Code, within 24 hours of the time that the parent or guardian knew or should have known that the child has died.

(2) This subdivision shall not apply when a child is otherwise under the immediate care of a physician at the time of death, or if a public safety agency, a coroner, or a medical examiner is otherwise aware of the death.

(b)(1) Any parent or guardian having the care, custody, or control of a child under 14 years of age shall notify law enforcement within 24 hours of the time that the parent or guardian knows or should have known that the child is a missing person and there is evidence that the child is a person at risk, as those terms are defined in Section 14215.

(2) This subdivision shall not apply if law enforcement is otherwise aware that the child is a missing person.

(c) A violation of this section is a misdemeanor punishable by imprisonment in a county jail for not more than one year, or by a fine not exceeding one thousand dollars ($1,000), or by both that fine and imprisonment.

(d) Nothing in this section shall preclude prosecution under any other provision of law. *(Added by Stats.2012, c. 805 (A.B.1432), § 2. Amended by Stats.2014, c. 437 (S.B.1066), § 8, eff. Jan. 1, 2015.)*

§ 273.1. Treatment programs for child abusers convicted of specified sections

(a) Any treatment program to which a child abuser convicted of a violation of Section 273a or 273d is referred as a condition of probation shall meet the following criteria:

(1) Substantial expertise and experience in the treatment of victims of child abuse and the families in which abuse and violence have occurred.

(2) Staff providing direct service are therapists licensed to practice in this state or are under the direct supervision of a therapist licensed to practice in this state.

(3) Utilization of a treatment regimen designed to specifically address the offense, including methods of preventing and breaking the cycle of family violence, anger management, and parenting education that focuses, among other things, on means of identifying the developmental and emotional needs of the child.

(4) Utilization of group and individual therapy and counseling, with groups no larger than 12 persons.

(5) Capability of identifying substance abuse and either treating the abuse or referring the offender to a substance abuse program, to the extent that the court has not already done so.

(6) Entry into a written agreement with the defendant that includes an outline of the components of the program, the attendance requirements, a requirement to attend group session free of chemical influence, and a statement that the defendant may be removed from the program if it is determined that the defendant is not benefiting from the program or is disruptive to the program.

(7) The program may include, on the recommendation of the treatment counselor, family counseling. However, no child victim shall be compelled or required to participate in the program, including family counseling, and no program may condition a defendant's enrollment on participation by the child victim. The treatment counselor shall privately advise the child victim that his or her participation is voluntary.

(b) If the program finds that the defendant is unsuitable, the program shall immediately contact the probation department or the court. The probation department or court shall either recalendar the case for hearing or refer the defendant to an appropriate alternative child abuser's treatment counseling program.

(c) Upon request by the child abuser's treatment counseling program, the court shall provide the defendant's arrest report, prior incidents of violence, and treatment history to the program.

(d) The child abuser's treatment counseling program shall provide the probation department and the court with periodic progress reports at least every three months that include attendance, fee payment history, and program compliance. The program shall submit a final evaluation that includes the program's evaluation of the defendant's progress, and recommendation for either successful or unsuccessful termination of the program.

(e) The defendant shall pay for the full costs of the treatment program, including any drug testing. However, the court may waive any portion or all of that financial responsibility upon a finding of an inability to pay. Upon the request of the defendant, the court shall hold a hearing to determine the defendant's ability to pay for the treatment program. At the hearing the court may consider all relevant information, but shall consider the impact of the costs of the treatment program on the defendant's ability to provide food, clothing, and shelter for the child injured by a violation of Section 273a or 273d. If the court finds that the defendant is unable to pay for any portion of the costs of the treatment program, its reasons for that finding shall be stated on the record. In the event of this finding, the program fees or a portion thereof shall be waived.

(f) All programs accepting referrals of child abusers pursuant to this section shall accept offenders for whom fees have been partially or fully waived. However, the court shall require each qualifying program to serve no more than its proportionate share of those offenders who have been granted fee waivers, and require all qualifying programs to share equally in the cost of serving those offenders with fee waivers. *(Added by Stats.1996, c. 1090 (A.B.3215), § 3. Amended by Stats.1997, c. 17 (S.B.947), § 95.)*

§ 273.4. Female genital mutilation; additional punishment

(a) If the act constituting a felony violation of subdivision (a) of Section 273a was female genital mutilation, as defined in subdivision (b), the defendant shall be punished by an additional term of imprisonment in the state prison for one year, in addition and consecutive to the punishment prescribed by Section 273a.

(b) "Female genital mutilation" means the excision or infibulation of the labia majora, labia minora, clitoris, or vulva, performed for nonmedical purposes.

(c) Nothing in this section shall preclude prosecution under Section 203, 205, or 206 or any other provision of law. *(Added by Stats.1996, c. 790 (A.B.2125), § 4. Amended by Stats.2011, c. 15 (A.B.109), § 308, eff. April 4, 2011, operative Oct. 1, 2011; Stats.2011, c. 39 (A.B.117), § 12, eff. June 30, 2011, operative Oct. 1, 2011.)*

Cross References

Discharge, discrimination, or retaliation by employees against domestic violence or sexual assault victims prohibited, see Labor Code § 230.
Employment, right of employees to take time off due to domestic violence or sexual assault, see Labor Code § 230.1.
Felonies, definition and penalties, see Penal Code §§ 17, 18.

Informational activities relating to the prohibition and ramifications of this section, information directed towards new immigrant populations that traditionally practice female genital mutilation and toward the medical community, see Health and Safety Code § 124170.
Prison or state prison defined for purposes of this Code, see Penal Code § 6081.

§ 273.5. Willful infliction of corporal injury; violation; punishment

(a) Any person who willfully inflicts corporal injury resulting in a traumatic condition upon a victim described in subdivision (b) is guilty of a felony, and upon conviction thereof shall be punished by imprisonment in the state prison for two, three, or four years, or in a county jail for not more than one year, or by a fine of up to six thousand dollars ($6,000), or by both that fine and imprisonment.

(b) Subdivision (a) shall apply if the victim is or was one or more of the following:

(1) The offender's spouse or former spouse.

(2) The offender's cohabitant or former cohabitant.

(3) The offender's fiancé or fiancée, or someone with whom the offender has, or previously had, an engagement or dating relationship, as defined in paragraph (10) of subdivision (f) of Section 243.

(4) The mother or father of the offender's child.

(c) Holding oneself out to be the spouse of the person with whom one is cohabiting is not necessary to constitute cohabitation as the term is used in this section.

(d) As used in this section, "traumatic condition" means a condition of the body, such as a wound, or external or internal injury, including, but not limited to, injury as a result of strangulation or suffocation, whether of a minor or serious nature, caused by a physical force. For purposes of this section, "strangulation" and "suffocation" include impeding the normal breathing or circulation of the blood of a person by applying pressure on the throat or neck.

(e) For the purpose of this section, a person shall be considered the father or mother of another person's child if the alleged male parent is presumed the natural father under Sections 7611 and 7612 of the Family Code.

(f)(1) Any person convicted of violating this section for acts occurring within seven years of a previous conviction under subdivision (a), or subdivision (d) of Section 243, or Section 243.4, 244, 244.5, or 245, shall be punished by imprisonment in a county jail for not more than one year, or by imprisonment in the state prison for two, four, or five years, or by both imprisonment and a fine of up to ten thousand dollars ($10,000).

(2) Any person convicted of a violation of this section for acts occurring within seven years of a previous conviction under subdivision (e) of Section 243 shall be punished by imprisonment in the state prison for two, three, or four years, or in a county jail for not more than one year, or by a fine of up to ten thousand dollars ($10,000), or by both that imprisonment and fine.

(g) If probation is granted to any person convicted under subdivision (a), the court shall impose probation consistent with the provisions of Section 1203.097.

(h) If probation is granted, or the execution or imposition of a sentence is suspended, for any defendant convicted under subdivision (a) who has been convicted of any prior offense specified in subdivision (f), the court shall impose one of the following conditions of probation:

(1) If the defendant has suffered one prior conviction within the previous seven years for a violation of any offense specified in subdivision (f), it shall be a condition of probation, in addition to the provisions contained in Section 1203.097, that * * * the defendant be imprisoned in a county jail for not less than 15 days.

§ 273.5

(2) If the defendant has suffered two or more prior convictions within the previous seven years for a violation of any offense specified in subdivision (f), it shall be a condition of probation, in addition to the provisions contained in Section 1203.097, that * * * the defendant be imprisoned in a county jail for not less than 60 days.

(3) The court, upon a showing of good cause, may find that the mandatory imprisonment required by this subdivision shall not be imposed and shall state on the record its reasons for finding good cause.

(i) If probation is granted upon conviction of a violation of subdivision (a), the conditions of probation may include, consistent with the terms of probation imposed pursuant to Section 1203.097, in lieu of a fine, one or both of the following requirements:

(1) That the defendant make payments to a * * * domestic violence shelter-based program, up to a maximum of five thousand dollars ($5,000), pursuant to Section 1203.097.

(2)(A) That the defendant reimburse the victim for reasonable costs of counseling and other reasonable expenses that the court finds are the direct result of the defendant's offense.

(B) For any order to pay a fine, make payments to a * * * domestic violence shelter-based program, or pay restitution as a condition of probation under this subdivision, the court shall make a determination of the defendant's ability to pay. An order to make payments to a * * * domestic violence shelter-based program shall not be made if it would impair the ability of the defendant to pay direct restitution to the victim or court-ordered child support. If the injury to a person who is married or in a registered domestic partnership is caused in whole or in part by the criminal acts of * * * their spouse or domestic partner in violation of this section, the community property may not be used to discharge the liability of the offending spouse or domestic partner for restitution to the injured spouse or domestic partner, required by Section 1203.04, as operative on or before August 2, 1995, or Section 1202.4, or to a shelter for costs with regard to the injured spouse or domestic partner and dependents, required by this section, until all separate property of the offending spouse or domestic partner is exhausted.

(j) Upon conviction under subdivision (a), the sentencing court shall also consider issuing an order restraining the defendant from any contact with the victim, which may be valid for up to 10 years, as determined by the court. It is the intent of the Legislature that the length of any restraining order be based upon the seriousness of the facts before the court, the probability of future violations, and the safety of the victim and * * * their immediate family. This protective order may be issued by the court whether the defendant is sentenced to state prison or county jail, or if imposition of sentence is suspended and the defendant is placed on probation.

(k) If a peace officer makes an arrest for a violation of this section, the peace officer is not required to inform the victim of * * * their right to make a citizen's arrest pursuant to subdivision (b) of Section 836. (Added by Stats.1977, c. 912, p. 2786, § 3. Amended by Stats.1980, c. 1117, p. 3589, § 3; Stats.1985, c. 563, § 1; Stats.1987, c. 415, § 2; Stats.1988, c. 576, § 1, eff. Aug. 26, 1988; Stats.1990, c. 680 (A.B.2632), § 1; Stats.1992, c. 163 (A.B.2641), § 104; Stats.1992, c. 183 (S.B.1545), § 1; Stats.1992, c. 184 (A.B.2439), § 3; Stats.1993, c. 219 (A.B.1500), § 216.4; Stats.1993–94, 1st Ex.Sess., c. 28 (A.B.93), § 2, eff. Nov. 30, 1994; Stats.1996, c. 1075 (S.B.1444), § 15; Stats.1996, c. 1077 (A.B.2898), § 16; Stats.1999, c. 660 (S.B.563), § 2; Stats.1999, c. 662 (S.B.218), § 9.5; Stats.2000, c. 287 (S.B.1955), § 5; Stats.2003, c. 262 (A.B.134), § 1; Stats.2007, c. 582 (A.B.289), § 1; Stats.2011, c. 129 (S.B.430), § 2; Stats.2012, c. 867 (S.B.1144), § 16; Stats.2013, c. 763 (A.B.16), § 1; Stats.2014, c. 71 (S.B.1304), § 117, eff. Jan. 1, 2015; Stats.2016, c. 50 (S.B.1005), § 69, eff. Jan. 1, 2017; Stats.2022, c. 197 (S.B.1493), § 13, eff. Jan. 1, 2023.)

Cross References

Arrests under this section, unscheduled bail amounts or release on own recognizance, see Penal Code § 1270.1.

Assault defined, see Penal Code § 240.

Battery defined, see Penal Code § 242.

Community care facilities, criminal record clearances, see Health and Safety Code § 1522.

Conditions preventing deferral of sentencing from being offered, see Penal Code § 1001.98.

Counties and cities, persons convicted of Penal Code offenses, supervisory or disciplinary authority over minors, see Public Resources Code § 5164.

Criminal record information of individuals in contact with child day care facility clients, see Health and Safety Code § 1596.871.

Domestic violence crimes, fees upon fine, penalty, or forfeiture imposed and collected by courts, determination by court of ability to pay, use of moneys collected, see Penal Code § 1463.27.

Evidence that victim or witness to serious felony, assault, domestic violence, extortion, human trafficking, sexual battery, or stalking was engaged in act of prostitution, inadmissibility in separate prostitution prosecution, see Evidence Code § 1162.

Felonies, definition and penalties, see Penal Code §§ 17, 18.

Home health aides, grounds for disciplinary action, see Health and Safety Code § 1736.5.

Identification of persons eligible for automatic conviction record relief, granting of relief, notice to court, conditions for relief, see Penal Code § 1203.425.

Injuries as result of assaultive or abusive conduct, reporting requirements by health facilities, clinics, or physician's offices, see Penal Code § 11160.

Intimate partner battering, abuse and domestic violence, expert testimony, see Evidence Code § 1107.

Misdemeanors, release procedures, exception for crimes specified in § 1270.1 and crimes defined in this section, see Penal Code § 853.6.

Multiple violations, local jurisdiction of offenses, see Penal Code § 784.7.

Nurse assistants, grounds for disciplinary action, see Health and Safety Code § 1337.9.

Offer of diversion to misdemeanor defendant, dismissal of action, reinstitution of criminal proceedings, charged offenses not eligible for diversion, see Penal Code § 1001.95.

Participation in California Conservation Camp program as incarcerated individual hand crew member or participation as member of county incarcerated individual hand crew, petition for relief, dismissal of accusations or information and release from penalties and disabilities, see Penal Code § 1203.4b.

Powers and duties of youth authority, release of information to victim or next of kin, see Welfare and Institutions Code § 1764.2.

Presumption against persons perpetrating domestic violence, custody of children, see Family Code § 3044.

Prison or state prison defined for purposes of this Code, see Penal Code § 6081.

Public housing authority, access to criminal history for convictions under this section, see Penal Code § 11105.03.

Rape defined, see Penal Code § 261.

Rape of spouse defined, see Penal Code § 262.

Residential care facilities for persons with chronic life-threatening illness, criminal records of applicants or persons in frequent contact with residents, see Health and Safety Code § 1568.09.

Residential care facilities for the elderly, criminal records of individuals in contact with clients, see Health and Safety Code § 1569.17.

Senior and Disability Justice Act, see Penal Code § 368.6.

Sexual battery defined, see Penal Code § 243.4.

Spousal rape or infliction of corporal injury, use of videotape to preserve testimony, see Penal Code § 1346.1.

Sufficiency of penetration, see Penal Code § 263.

Victim or witness to serious felony, assault, domestic violence, extortion, human trafficking, sexual battery, or stalking, exclusion from arrest for specified offenses related to reported crime, see Penal Code § 647.3.

Violent crime information center, online missing persons registry, historic database, see Penal Code § 14203.

Research References

Forms

West's California Judicial Council Forms CR–160, Criminal Protective Order—Domestic Violence (Clets—Cpo) (Also Available in Spanish).

West's California Judicial Council Forms CR–165, Notice of Termination of Protective Order in Criminal Proceeding (CLETS-CANCEL).

§ 273.6. Intentional and knowing violation of court order to prevent harassment, disturbing the peace, or threats or acts of violence; penalties

(a) Any intentional and knowing violation of a protective order, as defined in Section 6218 of the Family Code, or of an order issued pursuant to Section 527.6, 527.8, or 527.85 of the Code of Civil Procedure, or Section 15657.03 of the Welfare and Institutions Code, is a misdemeanor punishable by a fine of not more than one thousand dollars ($1,000), or by imprisonment in a county jail for not more than one year, or by both that fine and imprisonment.

(b) In the event of a violation of subdivision (a) that results in physical injury, the person shall be punished by a fine of not more than two thousand dollars ($2,000), or by imprisonment in a county jail for not less than 30 days nor more than one year, or by both that fine and imprisonment. However, if the person is imprisoned in a county jail for at least 48 hours, the court may, in the interest of justice and for reasons stated on the record, reduce or eliminate the 30-day minimum imprisonment required by this subdivision. In determining whether to reduce or eliminate the minimum imprisonment pursuant to this subdivision, the court shall consider the seriousness of the facts before the court, whether there are additional allegations of a violation of the order during the pendency of the case before the court, the probability of future violations, the safety of the victim, and whether the defendant has successfully completed or is making progress with counseling.

(c) Subdivisions (a) and (b) shall apply to the following court orders:

(1) Any order issued pursuant to Section 6320 or 6389 of the Family Code.

(2) An order excluding one party from the family dwelling or from the dwelling of the other.

(3) An order enjoining a party from specified behavior that the court determined was necessary to effectuate the order described in subdivision (a).

(4) Any order issued by another state that is recognized under Part 5 (commencing with Section 6400) of Division 10 of the Family Code.

(d) A subsequent conviction for a violation of an order described in subdivision (a), occurring within seven years of a prior conviction for a violation of an order described in subdivision (a) and involving an act of violence or "a credible threat" of violence, as defined in subdivision (c) of Section 139, is punishable by imprisonment in a county jail not to exceed one year, or pursuant to subdivision (h) of Section 1170.

(e) In the event of a subsequent conviction for a violation of an order described in subdivision (a) for an act occurring within one year of a prior conviction for a violation of an order described in subdivision (a) that results in physical injury to a victim, the person shall be punished by a fine of not more than two thousand dollars ($2,000), or by imprisonment in a county jail for not less than six months nor more than one year, by both that fine and imprisonment, or by imprisonment pursuant to subdivision (h) of Section 1170. However, if the person is imprisoned in a county jail for at least 30 days, the court may, in the interest of justice and for reasons stated in the record, reduce or eliminate the six-month minimum imprisonment required by this subdivision. In determining whether to reduce or eliminate the minimum imprisonment pursuant to this subdivision, the court shall consider the seriousness of the facts before the court, whether there are additional allegations of a violation of the order during the pendency of the case before the court, the probability of future violations, the safety of the victim, and whether the defendant has successfully completed or is making progress with counseling.

(f) The prosecuting agency of each county shall have the primary responsibility for the enforcement of orders described in subdivisions (a), (b), (d), and (e).

(g)(1) Every person who owns, possesses, purchases, or receives a firearm knowing * * * they are prohibited from doing so by the provisions of a protective order as defined in Section 136.2 of this code, Section 6218 of the Family Code, or Section 527.6, 527.8, or 527.85 of the Code of Civil Procedure, or Section 15657.03 of the Welfare and Institutions Code, shall be punished under Section 29825.

(2) Every person subject to a protective order described in paragraph (1) shall not be prosecuted under this section for owning, possessing, purchasing, or receiving a firearm to the extent that firearm is granted an exemption pursuant to subdivision (f) of Section 527.9 of the Code of Civil Procedure, or subdivision (h) of Section 6389 of the Family Code.

(h) If probation is granted upon conviction of a violation of subdivision (a), (b), (c), (d), or (e), the court shall impose probation consistent with Section 1203.097, and the conditions of probation may include, in lieu of a fine, one or both of the following requirements:

(1) That the defendant make payments to a * * * domestic violence shelter-based program or to a shelter for abused elder persons or dependent adults, up to a maximum of five thousand dollars ($5,000), pursuant to Section 1203.097.

(2) That the defendant reimburse the victim for reasonable costs of counseling and other reasonable expenses that the court finds are the direct result of the defendant's offense.

(i) For any order to pay a fine, make payments to a * * * domestic violence shelter-based program, or pay restitution as a condition of probation under subdivision (e), the court shall make a determination of the defendant's ability to pay. In no event shall any order to make payments to a * * * domestic violence shelter-based program be made if it would impair the ability of the defendant to pay direct restitution to the victim or court-ordered child support. Where the injury to a married person is caused in whole or in part by the criminal acts of * * * their spouse in violation of this section, the community property may not be used to discharge the liability of the offending spouse for restitution to the injured spouse, required by Section 1203.04, as operative on or before August 2, 1995, or Section 1202.4, or to a shelter for costs with regard to the injured spouse and dependents, required by this section, until all separate property of the offending spouse is exhausted. (Added by Stats.1979, c. 795, p. 2713, § 12, operative July 1, 1980. Amended by Stats.1981, c. 182, p. 1104, § 5; Stats.1982, c. 423, p. 1775, § 2; Stats.1983, c. 1092, § 262, eff. Sept. 27, 1983, operative Jan. 1, 1984; Stats.1985, c. 1387, § 1; Stats.1986, c. 10, § 1, eff. Feb. 28, 1986; Stats.1988, c. 674, § 1, eff. Aug. 27, 1988; Stats.1989, c. 1105, § 12; Stats.1990, c. 411 (A.B. 3973), § 8, eff. July 25, 1990; Stats.1992, c. 163 (A.B.2641), § 105; Stats.1992, c. 184 (A.B.2439), § 4; Stats.1992, c. 1209 (A.B.2762), §§ 1, 2; Stats.1993, c. 219 (A.B.1500), § 216.5; Stats.1993, c. 583 (A.B.284), § 5; Stats.1993–94, 1st Ex.Sess., c. 28 (A.B.93), § 3, eff. Nov. 30, 1994; Stats.1993–94, 1st Ex.Sess., c. 29 (A.B.68), § 3.5, eff. Nov. 30, 1994; Stats.1994, c. 873 (S.B.739), § 2.3; Stats.1996, c. 904 (A.B.2224), § 5; Stats.1996, c. 1077 (A.B.2898), § 17.1; Stats.1999, c. 561 (A.B.59), § 5; Stats.1999, c. 662 (S.B.218), § 12.5; Stats.2001, c. 816 (A.B.731), § 4; Stats.2003, c. 498 (S.B.226), § 7; Stats.2009, c. 566 (S.B.188), § 2; Stats.2010, c. 709 (S.B.1062), § 10; Stats.2010, c. 178 (S.B.1115), § 55, operative Jan. 1, 2012; Stats.2011, c. 285 (A.B.1402), § 13; Stats.2011, c. 15 (A.B.109), § 310, eff. April 4, 2011, operative Jan. 1, 2012; Stats.2013, c. 76 (A.B.383), § 145.7; Stats. 2022, c. 197 (S.B.1493), § 14, eff. Jan. 1, 2023.)

Cross References

Arraignment or plea and sentencing in certain misdemeanors, presence of defendant, see Penal Code § 977.

§ 273.6

Authority to compromise misdemeanors for which victim has civil action, exceptions, see Penal Code § 1377.

Civil actions for abuse of elderly or dependent adults, protective orders, see Welfare and Institutions Code § 15657.03.

Conditions preventing deferral of sentencing from being offered, see Penal Code § 1001.98.

Duration of temporary restraining order, enforceability, violation, and punishment, see Family Code § 233.

Employees subject to unlawful violence or threat of violence at the workplace, temporary restraining order and injunction, see Code of Civil Procedure § 527.8.

Harassment, temporary restraining order and injunction, see Code of Civil Procedure § 527.6.

Misdemeanors, definition and penalties, see Penal Code §§ 17, 19 and 19.2.

Misdemeanors, release procedures, exception for crimes specified in § 1270.1 and crimes defined in this section, see Penal Code § 853.6.

Officers authorized to maintain order on school campus or facility, threat of violence made off school campus, temporary restraining order and injunction, violation of restraining order, see Code of Civil Procedure § 527.85.

Protective orders and other domestic violence prevention orders, enforceability of domestic violence restraining order registry, see Family Code § 6381.

Public housing authority, access to criminal history for convictions under this section, see Penal Code § 11105.03.

Schools and school districts, employees, revocation of credential where criminal conviction or probation terms prohibit association with minors, see Education Code § 44423.6.

Service of protective orders and other domestic violence prevention orders, see Family Code § 6383.

Violent felonies and specified acts, bail and hearings, threats against victim or witness, see Penal Code § 1270.1.

Willful and knowing violation of protective orders and other domestic violence prevention orders, penalty, see Family Code § 6388.

§ 273.65. Intentional and knowing violations of restraining and protective orders relating to minors adjudged to be dependent children of the juvenile court; offense; penalties

(a) Any intentional and knowing violation of a protective order issued pursuant to Section 213.5, 304, or 362.4 of the Welfare and Institutions Code is a misdemeanor punishable by a fine of not more than one thousand dollars ($1,000), or by imprisonment in a county jail for not more than one year, or by both the fine and imprisonment.

(b) In the event of a violation of subdivision (a) which results in physical injury, the person shall be punished by a fine of not more than two thousand dollars ($2,000), or by imprisonment in a county jail for not less than 30 days nor more than one year, or by both the fine and imprisonment. However, if the person is imprisoned in a county jail for at least 48 hours, the court may, in the interests of justice and for reasons stated on the record, reduce or eliminate the 30-day minimum imprisonment required by this subdivision. In determining whether to reduce or eliminate the minimum imprisonment pursuant to this subdivision, the court shall consider the seriousness of the facts before the court, whether there are additional allegations of a violation of the order during the pendency of the case before the court, the probability of future violations, the safety of the victim, and whether the defendant has successfully completed or is making progress with counseling.

(c) Subdivisions (a) and (b) shall apply to the following court orders:

(1) An order enjoining any party from molesting, attacking, striking, threatening, sexually assaulting, battering, harassing, contacting repeatedly by mail with the intent to harass, or disturbing the peace of the other party, or other named family and household members.

(2) An order excluding one party from the family dwelling or from the dwelling of the other.

(3) An order enjoining a party from specified behavior which the court determined was necessary to effectuate the order under subdivision (a).

(d) A subsequent conviction for a violation of an order described in subdivision (a), occurring within seven years of a prior conviction for a violation of an order described in subdivision (a) and involving an act of violence or "a credible threat" of violence, as defined in subdivision (c) of Section 139, is punishable by imprisonment in a county jail not to exceed one year, or pursuant to subdivision (h) of Section 1170.

(e) In the event of a subsequent conviction for a violation of an order described in subdivision (a) for an act occurring within one year of a prior conviction for a violation of an order described in subdivision (a) which results in physical injury to the same victim, the person shall be punished by a fine of not more than two thousand dollars ($2,000), or by imprisonment in a county jail for not less than six months nor more than one year, by both that fine and imprisonment, or by imprisonment pursuant to subdivision (h) of Section 1170. However, if the person is imprisoned in a county jail for at least 30 days, the court may, in the interests of justice and for reasons stated in the record, reduce or eliminate the six-month minimum imprisonment required by this subdivision. In determining whether to reduce or eliminate the minimum imprisonment pursuant to this subdivision, the court shall consider the seriousness of the facts before the court, whether there are additional allegations of a violation of the order during the pendency of the case before the court, the probability of future violations, the safety of the victim, and whether the defendant has successfully completed or is making progress with counseling.

(f) The prosecuting agency of each county shall have the primary responsibility for the enforcement of orders issued pursuant to subdivisions (a), (b), (d), and (e).

(g) The court may order a person convicted under this section to undergo counseling, and, if appropriate, to complete a batterer's treatment program.

(h) If probation is granted upon conviction of a violation of subdivision (a), (b), or (c), the conditions of probation may include, in lieu of a fine, one or both of the following requirements:

(1) That the defendant make payments to a * * * <u>domestic violence shelter-based program</u>, up to a maximum of five thousand dollars ($5,000), pursuant to Section 1203.097.

(2) That the defendant reimburse the victim for reasonable costs of counseling and other reasonable expenses that the court finds are the direct result of the defendant's offense.

(i) For any order to pay a fine, make payments to a * * * <u>domestic violence shelter-based program</u>, or pay restitution as a condition of probation under subdivision (e), the court shall make a determination of the defendant's ability to pay. In no event shall any order to make payments to a * * * <u>domestic violence shelter-based program</u> be made if it would impair the ability of the defendant to pay direct restitution to the victim or court-ordered child support. (Added by Stats.1996, c. 1139 (A.B.2647), § 2. Amended by Stats. 2011, c. 15 (A.B.109), § 311, eff. April 4, 2011, operative Oct. 1, 2011; Stats.2022, c. 197 (S.B.1493), § 15, eff. Jan. 1, 2023.)

Cross References

Misdemeanors, definition and penalties, see Penal Code §§ 17, 19 and 19.2.

Proceedings to declare a minor child a dependent child, ex parte orders, see Welfare and Institutions Code § 213.5.

§ 273.7. Malicious disclosure of location of trafficking shelter or domestic violence shelter; misdemeanor; definitions; exemption for attorney-client communications

(a) A person who maliciously publishes, disseminates, or otherwise discloses the location of a trafficking shelter or domestic violence shelter or a place designated as a trafficking shelter or domestic violence shelter, without the authorization of that trafficking shelter or domestic violence shelter, is guilty of a misdemeanor.

(b) For purposes of this section, the following definitions apply:

(1) "Domestic violence shelter" means a confidential location that provides emergency housing on a 24–hour basis for victims of sexual assault, spousal abuse, or both, and their families.

(2) "Trafficking shelter" means a confidential location that provides emergency housing on a 24–hour basis for victims of human trafficking, including any person who is a victim under Section 236.1.

(3) Sexual assault, spousal abuse, or both, include, but are not limited to, those crimes described in Sections 240, 242, 243.4, 261, 261.5, 264.1, 266, 266a, 266b, 266c, 266f, 273.5, 273.6, 285, 288, and 289.

(c) This section does not apply to confidential communications between an attorney and their client. (Added by Stats.1988, c. 840, § 1. Amended by Stats.1994, c. 1188 (S.B.59), § 4; Stats.2005, c. 240 (A.B.22), § 9; Stats.2006, c. 538 (S.B.1852), § 499; Stats.2021, c. 626 (A.B.1171), § 24, eff. Jan. 1, 2022.)

Cross References

Misdemeanors, definition and penalties, see Penal Code §§ 17, 19 and 19.2.

§ 273.75. Criminal history search; prior restraining orders

(a) On any charge involving acts of domestic violence as defined in subdivisions (a) and (b) of Section 13700 of the Penal Code or Sections 6203 and 6211 of the Family Code, the district attorney or prosecuting city attorney shall perform or cause to be performed, by accessing the electronic databases enumerated in subdivision (b), a thorough investigation of the defendant's history, including, but not limited to, prior convictions for domestic violence, other forms of violence or weapons offenses and any current protective or restraining order issued by any civil or criminal court. This information shall be presented for consideration by the court (1) when setting bond or when releasing a defendant on his or her own recognizance at the arraignment, if the defendant is in custody, (2) upon consideration of any plea agreement, and (3) when issuing a protective order pursuant to Section 136.2 of the Penal Code, in accordance with subdivision (h) of that section. In determining bail or release upon a plea agreement, the court shall consider the safety of the victim, the victim's children, and any other person who may be in danger if the defendant is released.

(b) For purposes of this section, the district attorney or prosecuting city attorney shall search or cause to be searched the following databases, when readily available and reasonably accessible:

(1) The California Sex and Arson Registry (CSAR).

(2) The Supervised Release File.

(3) State summary criminal history information maintained by the Department of Justice pursuant to Section 11105 of the Penal Code.

(4) The Federal Bureau of Investigation's nationwide database.

(5) Locally maintained criminal history records or databases.

However, a record or database need not be searched if the information available in that record or database can be obtained as a result of a search conducted in another record or database.

(c) If the investigation required by this section reveals a current civil protective or restraining order or a protective or restraining order issued by another criminal court and involving the same or related parties, and if a protective or restraining order is issued in the current criminal proceeding, the district attorney or prosecuting city attorney shall send relevant information regarding the contents of the order issued in the current criminal proceeding, and any information regarding a conviction of the defendant, to the other court immediately after the order has been issued. When requested, the information described in this subdivision may be sent to the appropriate family, juvenile, or civil court. When requested, and upon a showing of a compelling need, the information described in this section may be sent to a court in another state. (Added by Stats.2001, c. 572 (S.B.66), § 4. Amended by Stats.2008, c. 86 (A.B.1771), § 2; Stats.2014, c. 54 (S.B.1461), § 10, eff. Jan. 1, 2015.)

CHAPTER 2.5. SPOUSAL ABUSERS

Section
273.8. Legislative findings.
273.81. Spousal abuser prosecution program; appropriation, allocation, and award of funds; guidelines for grant awards; matching funds.
273.82. Enhanced prosecution efforts and resources.
273.83. Individuals subject to spousal abuser prosecution effort; selection of cases.
273.84. Policies; pretrial release, sentence, and reduction of time between arrest and disposition of charge.
273.85. Adherence to selection criteria; quarterly submission of information.
273.86. Characterization of defendant as spousal abuser.
273.87. Use of federal funds; implementation of chapter.
273.88. Administrative costs; limit.

§ 273.8. Legislative findings

The Legislature hereby finds that spousal abusers present a clear and present danger to the mental and physical well-being of the citizens of the State of California. The Legislature further finds that the concept of vertical prosecution, in which a specially trained deputy district attorney, deputy city attorney, or prosecution unit is assigned to a case after arraignment and continuing to its completion, is a proven way of demonstrably increasing the likelihood of convicting spousal abusers and ensuring appropriate sentences for those offenders. In enacting this chapter, the Legislature intends to support increased efforts by district attorneys' and city attorneys' offices to prosecute spousal abusers through organizational and operational techniques that have already proven their effectiveness in selected cities and counties in this and other states. (Added by Stats.1985, c. 1122, § 1. Amended by Stats.1994, c. 599 (A.B.801), § 2, eff. Sept. 16, 1994.)

§ 273.81. Spousal abuser prosecution program; appropriation, allocation, and award of funds; guidelines for grant awards; matching funds

(a) There is hereby established in the Department of Justice a program of financial and technical assistance for district attorneys' or city attorneys' offices, designated the Spousal Abuser Prosecution Program. All funds appropriated to the Department of Justice for the purposes of this chapter shall be administered and disbursed by the Attorney General, and shall to the greatest extent feasible, be coordinated or consolidated with any federal or local funds that may be made available for these purposes.

The Department of Justice shall establish guidelines for the provision of grant awards to proposed and existing programs prior to the allocation of funds under this chapter. These guidelines shall contain the criteria for the selection of agencies to receive funding and the terms and conditions upon which the Department of Justice is prepared to offer grants pursuant to statutory authority. The guidelines shall not constitute rules, regulations, orders, or standards of general application.

(b) The Attorney General may allocate and award funds to cities or counties, or both, in which spousal abuser prosecution units are established or are proposed to be established in substantial compliance with the policies and criteria set forth in this chapter.

(c) The allocation and award of funds shall be made upon application executed by the county's district attorney or by the city's attorney and approved by the county board of supervisors or by the city council. Funds disbursed under this chapter shall not supplant local funds that would, in the absence of the California Spousal Abuser Prosecution Program, be made available to support the prosecution of spousal abuser cases. Local grant awards made under this program shall not be subject to review as specified in Section 10295 of the Public Contract Code.

(d) Local government recipients shall provide 20 percent matching funds for every grant awarded under this program. *(Added by Stats.1985, c. 1122, § 1. Amended by Stats.1987, c. 828, § 15; Stats.1994, c. 599 (A.B.801), § 3, eff. Sept. 16, 1994.)*

Cross References

Attorney General, generally, see Government Code § 12500 et seq.

§ 273.82. Enhanced prosecution efforts and resources

Spousal abuser prosecution units receiving funds under this chapter shall concentrate enhanced prosecution efforts and resources upon individuals identified under selection criteria set forth in Section 273.83. Enhanced prosecution efforts and resources shall include, but not be limited to, all of the following:

(a)(1) Vertical prosecutorial representation, whereby the prosecutor who, or prosecution unit that, makes all major court appearances on that particular case through its conclusion, including bail evaluation, preliminary hearing, significant law and motion litigation, trial, and sentencing.

(2) Vertical counselor representation, whereby a trained domestic violence counselor maintains liaison from initial court appearances through the case's conclusion, including the sentencing phase.

(b) The assignment of highly qualified investigators and prosecutors to spousal abuser cases. "Highly qualified" for the purposes of this chapter means any of the following:

(1) Individuals with one year of experience in the investigation and prosecution of felonies.

(2) Individuals with at least two years of experience in the investigation and prosecution of misdemeanors.

(3) Individuals who have attended a program providing domestic violence training as approved by the Office of Emergency Services or the Department of Justice.

(c) A significant reduction of caseloads for investigators and prosecutors assigned to spousal abuser cases.

(d) Coordination with local rape victim counseling centers, spousal abuse services programs, and victim-witness assistance programs. That coordination shall include, but not be limited to: referrals of individuals to receive client services; participation in local training programs; membership and participation in local task forces established to improve communication between criminal justice system agencies and community service agencies; and cooperating with individuals serving as liaison representatives of local rape victim counseling centers, spousal abuse victim programs, and victim-witness assistance programs. *(Added by Stats.1985, c. 1122, § 1. Amended by Stats.1987, c. 828, § 16; Stats.1994, c. 599 (A.B.801), § 4, eff. Sept. 16, 1994; Stats.2003, c. 229 (A.B.1757), § 2.4; Stats.2010, c. 618 (A.B.2791), § 191; Stats.2013, c. 352 (A.B.1317), § 403, eff. Sept. 26, 2013, operative July 1, 2013.)*

Cross References

Felonies, definition and penalties, see Penal Code §§ 17, 18.
Misdemeanors, definition and penalties, see Penal Code §§ 17, 19 and 19.2.

§ 273.83. Individuals subject to spousal abuser prosecution effort; selection of cases

(a) An individual shall be the subject of a spousal abuser prosecution effort who is under arrest for any act or omission described in subdivisions (a) and (b) of Section 13700.

(b) In applying the spousal abuser selection criteria set forth in subdivision (a), a district attorney or city attorney shall not reject cases for filing exclusively on the basis that there is a family or personal relationship between the victim and the alleged offender.

(c) In exercising the prosecutorial discretion granted by Section 273.85, the district attorney or city attorney shall consider the number and seriousness of the offenses currently charged against the defendant. *(Added by Stats.1985, c. 1122, § 1. Amended by Stats.1994, c. 599 (A.B.801), § 5, eff. Sept. 16, 1994.)*

§ 273.84. Policies; pretrial release, sentence, and reduction of time between arrest and disposition of charge

Each district attorney's or city attorney's office establishing a spousal abuser prosecution unit and receiving state support under this chapter shall adopt and pursue the following policies for spousal abuser cases:

(a) All reasonable prosecutorial efforts shall be made to resist the pretrial release of a charged defendant meeting spousal abuser selection criteria.

(b) All reasonable prosecutorial efforts shall be made to persuade the court to impose the most severe authorized sentence upon a person convicted after prosecution as a spousal abuser. In the prosecution of an intrafamily sexual abuse case, discretion may be exercised as to the type and nature of sentence recommended to the court.

(c) All reasonable prosecutorial efforts shall be made to reduce the time between arrest and disposition of charge against an individual meeting spousal abuser criteria. *(Added by Stats.1985, c. 1122, § 1. Amended by Stats.1994, c. 599 (A.B.801), § 6, eff. Sept. 16, 1994; Stats.2000, c. 135 (A.B.2539), § 131.)*

§ 273.85. Adherence to selection criteria; quarterly submission of information

(a) The selection criteria set forth in Section 273.84 shall be adhered to for each spousal abuser case unless, in the reasonable exercise of prosecutor's discretion, extraordinary circumstances require departure from those policies in order to promote the general purposes and intent of this chapter.

(b) Each district attorney's and city attorney's office establishing a spousal abuser prosecution unit and receiving state support under this chapter shall submit the following information, on a quarterly basis, to the Department of Justice:

(1) The number of spousal abuser cases referred to the district attorney's or city attorney's office for possible filing.

(2) The number of spousal abuser cases filed for prosecution.

(3) The number of spousal abuser cases taken to trial.

(4) The number of spousal abuser cases tried that resulted in conviction. *(Added by Stats.1985, c. 1122, § 1. Amended by Stats.1994, c. 599 (A.B.801), § 7, eff. Sept. 16, 1994.)*

§ 273.86. Characterization of defendant as spousal abuser

The characterization of a defendant as a "spousal abuser" as defined by this chapter shall not be communicated to the trier of fact. *(Added by Stats.1985, c. 1122, § 1.)*

§ 273.87. Use of federal funds; implementation of chapter

The Department of Justice is encouraged to utilize Federal Victims of Crimes Act (VOCA) funds or any other federal funds that may become available in order to implement this chapter. *(Added by Stats.1985, c. 1122, § 1. Amended by Stats.1994, c. 599 (A.B.801), § 8, eff. Sept. 16, 1994.)*

§ 273.88. Administrative costs; limit

Administrative costs incurred by the Department of Justice pursuant to the Spousal Abuser Prosecution Program shall not exceed 5 percent of the total funds allocated for the program. *(Added by Stats.1994, c. 599 (A.B.801), § 9, eff. Sept. 16, 1994.)*

CHAPTER 4. CHILD ABDUCTION

Section
277. Definitions.

Section

Section	
278.	Noncustodial persons; detainment or concealment of child from legal custodian; punishment.
278.5.	Deprivation of custody of child or right to visitation; punishment.
278.6.	Sentencing; relevant factors and circumstances; aggravation; mitigation; expenses and costs in recovering child.
278.7.	Exception; belief of bodily injury or emotional harm; report by person taking or concealing child; confidentiality.
279.	Jurisdiction; persons not residents or present in state at time of offense.
279.1.	Continuation of offenses.
279.5.	Bail; considerations.
279.6.	Protective custody; circumstances; procedures; conflicting custodial orders; court hearing and enforcement.
280.	Violations of specified adoption proceedings; punishment.

§ 277. Definitions

The following definitions apply for the purposes of this chapter:

(a) "Child" means a person under the age of 18 years.

(b) "Court order" or "custody order" means a custody determination decree, judgment, or order issued by a court of competent jurisdiction, whether permanent or temporary, initial or modified, that affects the custody or visitation of a child, issued in the context of a custody proceeding. An order, once made, shall continue in effect until it expires, is modified, is rescinded, or terminates by operation of law.

(c) "Custody proceeding" means a proceeding in which a custody determination is an issue, including, but not limited to, an action for dissolution or separation, dependency, guardianship, termination of parental rights, adoption, paternity, except actions under Section 11350 or 11350.1 of the Welfare and Institutions Code, or protection from domestic violence proceedings, including an emergency protective order pursuant to Part 3 (commencing with Section 6240) of Division 10 of the Family Code.

(d) "Lawful custodian" means a person, guardian, or public agency having a right to custody of a child.

(e) A "right to custody" means the right to the physical care, custody, and control of a child pursuant to a custody order as defined in subdivision (b) or, in the absence of a court order, by operation of law, or pursuant to the Uniform Parentage Act contained in Part 3 (commencing with Section 7600) of Division 12 of the Family Code. Whenever a public agency takes protective custody or jurisdiction of the care, custody, control, or conduct of a child by statutory authority or court order, that agency is a lawful custodian of the child and has a right to physical custody of the child. In any subsequent placement of the child, the public agency continues to be a lawful custodian with a right to physical custody of the child until the public agency's right of custody is terminated by an order of a court of competent jurisdiction or by operation of law.

(f) In the absence of a court order to the contrary, a parent loses his or her right to custody of the child to the other parent if the parent having the right to custody is dead, is unable or refuses to take the custody, or has abandoned his or her family. A natural parent whose parental rights have been terminated by court order is no longer a lawful custodian and no longer has a right to physical custody.

(g) "Keeps" or "withholds" means retains physical possession of a child whether or not the child resists or objects.

(h) "Visitation" means the time for access to the child allotted to any person by court order.

(i) "Person" includes, but is not limited to, a parent or an agent of a parent.

(j) "Domestic violence" means domestic violence as defined in Section 6211 of the Family Code.

(k) "Abduct" means take, entice away, keep, withhold, or conceal.
(Added by Stats.1996, c. 988 (A.B.2936), § 9.)

§ 278. Noncustodial persons; detainment or concealment of child from legal custodian; punishment

Every person, not having a right to custody, who maliciously takes, entices away, keeps, withholds, or conceals any child with the intent to detain or conceal that child from a lawful custodian shall be punished by imprisonment in a county jail not exceeding one year, a fine not exceeding one thousand dollars ($1,000), or both that fine and imprisonment, or by imprisonment pursuant to subdivision (h) of Section 1170 for two, three, or four years, a fine not exceeding ten thousand dollars ($10,000), or both that fine and imprisonment.
(Added by Stats.1996, c. 988 (A.B.2936), § 9. Amended by Stats.2011, c. 15 (A.B.109), § 313, eff. April 4, 2011, operative Oct. 1, 2011.)

Cross References

Child defined for purposes of this Chapter, see Penal Code § 277.
Contributing to delinquency of minors, see Penal Code § 272.
Conviction as ground for revocation of,
  County teaching certificate, see Education Code § 44435.
  Teaching credential, see Education Code § 44424.
Felony,
  Definition, see Penal Code § 17.
  Punishment, see Penal Code § 18.
Fine authorized in addition to imprisonment, see Penal Code § 672.
Guardianship, conservatorship, and other protective proceedings, see Probate Code § 1400 et seq.
Jurisdiction, see Penal Code § 784.5.
Keeps or withholds defined for purposes of this Chapter, see Penal Code § 277.
Kidnapping,
  Generally, see Penal Code § 207 et seq.
  Persons under fourteen years of age, punishment, see Penal Code § 208.
  Persons under fourteen years of age to commit sexual felony offenses, punishment, see Penal Code § 667.8.
Lawful custodian defined for purposes of this Chapter, see Penal Code § 277.
Maliciously defined, see Penal Code § 7.
Minors, defined, see Family Code § 6500.
Offenses for which no fine prescribed, punishment, see Penal Code § 672.
Person defined for purposes of this Chapter, see Penal Code § 277.
Persons liable to punishment, see Penal Code § 27.
Right to custody defined for purposes of this Chapter, see Penal Code § 277.
Substitution of one child for another, see Penal Code § 157.
Victim compensation, requirements, persons and derivative victims, see Government Code § 13955.

Research References

Forms

1 California Transactions Forms--Family Law § 3:9, Statutory Custody Definitions.

§ 278.5. Deprivation of custody of child or right to visitation; punishment

(a) Every person who takes, entices away, keeps, withholds, or conceals a child and maliciously deprives a lawful custodian of a right to custody, or a person of a right to visitation, shall be punished by imprisonment in a county jail not exceeding one year, a fine not exceeding one thousand dollars ($1,000), or both that fine and imprisonment, or by imprisonment pursuant to subdivision (h) of Section 1170 for 16 months, or two or three years, a fine not exceeding ten thousand dollars ($10,000), or both that fine and imprisonment.

(b) Nothing contained in this section limits the court's contempt power.

§ 278.5

(c) A custody order obtained after the taking, enticing away, keeping, withholding, or concealing of a child does not constitute a defense to a crime charged under this section. *(Added by Stats.1996, c. 988 (A.B.2936), § 9. Amended by Stats.2011, c. 15 (A.B.109), § 314, eff. April 4, 2011, operative Oct. 1, 2011.)*

Cross References

Child defined for purposes of this Chapter, see Penal Code § 277.
Court order or custody order defined for purposes of this Chapter, see Penal Code § 277.
Duration of temporary restraining order, enforceability, violation, and punishment, see Family Code § 233.
Jurisdiction, see Penal Code § 784.5.
Keeps or withholds defined for purposes of this Chapter, see Penal Code § 277.
Kidnapping persons under fourteen years of age, punishment, see Penal Code § 208.
Kidnapping persons under fourteen years of age to commit sexual felony offenses, punishment, see Penal Code § 667.8.
Lawful custodian defined for purposes of this Chapter, see Penal Code § 277.
Person defined for purposes of this Chapter, see Penal Code § 277.
Right to custody defined for purposes of this Chapter, see Penal Code § 277.
Victim compensation, requirements, persons and derivative victims, see Government Code § 13955.
Visitation defined for purposes of this Chapter, see Penal Code § 277.

Research References

Forms

1 California Transactions Forms--Family Law § 3:9, Statutory Custody Definitions.

§ 278.6. Sentencing; relevant factors and circumstances; aggravation; mitigation; expenses and costs in recovering child

(a) At the sentencing hearing following a conviction for a violation of Section 278 or 278.5, or both, the court shall consider any relevant factors and circumstances in aggravation, including, but not limited to, all of the following:

(1) The child was exposed to a substantial risk of physical injury or illness.

(2) The defendant inflicted or threatened to inflict physical harm on a parent or lawful custodian of the child or on the child at the time of or during the abduction.

(3) The defendant harmed or abandoned the child during the abduction.

(4) The child was taken, enticed away, kept, withheld, or concealed outside the United States.

(5) The child has not been returned to the lawful custodian.

(6) The defendant previously abducted or threatened to abduct the child.

(7) The defendant substantially altered the appearance or the name of the child.

(8) The defendant denied the child appropriate education during the abduction.

(9) The length of the abduction.

(10) The age of the child.

(b) At the sentencing hearing following a conviction for a violation of Section 278 or 278.5, or both, the court shall consider any relevant factors and circumstances in mitigation, including, but not limited to, both of the following:

(1) The defendant returned the child unharmed and prior to arrest or issuance of a warrant for arrest, whichever is first.

(2) The defendant provided information and assistance leading to the child's safe return.

(c) In addition to any other penalties provided for a violation of Section 278 or 278.5, a court shall order the defendant to pay restitution to the district attorney for any costs incurred in locating and returning the child as provided in Section 3134 of the Family Code, and to the victim for those expenses and costs reasonably incurred by, or on behalf of, the victim in locating and recovering the child. An award made pursuant to this section shall constitute a final judgment and shall be enforceable as such. *(Added by Stats.1996, c. 988 (A.B.2936), § 9.)*

Cross References

Abduct defined for purposes of this Chapter, see Penal Code § 277.
Child defined for purposes of this Chapter, see Penal Code § 277.
Lawful custodian defined for purposes of this Chapter, see Penal Code § 277.

§ 278.7. Exception; belief of bodily injury or emotional harm; report by person taking or concealing child; confidentiality

(a) Section 278.5 does not apply to a person with a right to custody of a child who, with a good faith and reasonable belief that the child, if left with the other person, will suffer immediate bodily injury or emotional harm, takes, entices away, keeps, withholds, or conceals that child.

(b) Section 278.5 does not apply to a person with a right to custody of a child who has been a victim of domestic violence who, with a good faith and reasonable belief that the child, if left with the other person, will suffer immediate bodily injury or emotional harm, takes, entices away, keeps, withholds, or conceals that child. "Emotional harm" includes having a parent who has committed domestic violence against the parent who is taking, enticing away, keeping, withholding, or concealing the child.

(c) The person who takes, entices away, keeps, withholds, or conceals a child shall do all of the following:

(1) Within a reasonable time from the taking, enticing away, keeping, withholding, or concealing, make a report to the office of the district attorney of the county where the child resided before the action. The report shall include the name of the person, the current address and telephone number of the child and the person, and the reasons the child was taken, enticed away, kept, withheld, or concealed.

(2) Within a reasonable time from the taking, enticing away, keeping, withholding, or concealing, commence a custody proceeding in a court of competent jurisdiction consistent with the federal Parental Kidnapping Prevention Act (Section 1738A, Title 28, United States Code) or the Uniform Child Custody Jurisdiction Act (Part 3 (commencing with Section 3400) of Division 8 of the Family Code).

(3) Inform the district attorney's office of any change of address or telephone number of the person and the child.

(d) For the purposes of this article, a reasonable time within which to make a report to the district attorney's office is at least 10 days and a reasonable time to commence a custody proceeding is at least 30 days. This section shall not preclude a person from making a report to the district attorney's office or commencing a custody proceeding earlier than those specified times.

(e) The address and telephone number of the person and the child provided pursuant to this section shall remain confidential unless released pursuant to state law or by a court order that contains appropriate safeguards to ensure the safety of the person and the child. *(Added by Stats.1996, c. 988 (A.B.2936), § 9.)*

Cross References

Child defined for purposes of this Chapter, see Penal Code § 277.
Court order or custody order defined for purposes of this Chapter, see Penal Code § 277.
Custody proceeding defined for purposes of this Chapter, see Penal Code § 277.
Domestic violence defined for purposes of this Chapter, see Penal Code § 277.
Keeps or withholds defined for purposes of this Chapter, see Penal Code § 277.
Person defined for purposes of this Chapter, see Penal Code § 277.

Right to custody defined for purposes of this Chapter, see Penal Code § 277.

§ 279. Jurisdiction; persons not residents or present in state at time of offense

A violation of Section 278 or 278.5 by a person who was not a resident of, or present in, this state at the time of the alleged offense is punishable in this state, whether the intent to commit the offense is formed within or outside of this state, if any of the following apply:

(a) The child was a resident of, or present in, this state at the time the child was taken, enticed away, kept, withheld, or concealed.

(b) The child thereafter is found in this state.

(c) A lawful custodian or a person with a right to visitation is a resident of this state at the time the child was taken, enticed away, kept, withheld, or concealed. *(Added by Stats.1996, c. 988 (A.B. 2936), § 9.)*

Cross References

Child defined for purposes of this Chapter, see Penal Code § 277.
Lawful custodian defined for purposes of this Chapter, see Penal Code § 277.
Person defined for purposes of this Chapter, see Penal Code § 277.
Visitation defined for purposes of this Chapter, see Penal Code § 277.

§ 279.1. Continuation of offenses

The offenses enumerated in Sections 278 and 278.5 are continuous in nature, and continue for as long as the minor child is concealed or detained. *(Added by Stats.1996, c. 988 (A.B.2936), § 9.)*

Cross References

Child defined for purposes of this Chapter, see Penal Code § 277.

§ 279.5. Bail; considerations

When a person is arrested for an alleged violation of Section 278 or 278.5, the court, in setting bail, shall take into consideration whether the child has been returned to the lawful custodian, and if not, shall consider whether there is an increased risk that the child may not be returned, or the defendant may flee the jurisdiction, or, by flight or concealment, evade the authority of the court. *(Added by Stats.1996, c. 988 (A.B.2936), § 9.)*

Cross References

Child defined for purposes of this Chapter, see Penal Code § 277.
Lawful custodian defined for purposes of this Chapter, see Penal Code § 277.
Person defined for purposes of this Chapter, see Penal Code § 277.

§ 279.6. Protective custody; circumstances; procedures; conflicting custodial orders; court hearing and enforcement

(a) A law enforcement officer may take a child into protective custody under any of the following circumstances:

(1) It reasonably appears to the officer that a person is likely to conceal the child, flee the jurisdiction with the child, or, by flight or concealment, evade the authority of the court.

(2) There is no lawful custodian available to take custody of the child.

(3) There are conflicting custody orders or conflicting claims to custody and the parties cannot agree which party should take custody of the child.

(4) The child is an abducted child.

(b) When a law enforcement officer takes a child into protective custody pursuant to this section, the officer shall do one of the following:

(1) Release the child to the lawful custodian of the child, unless it reasonably appears that the release would cause the child to be endangered, abducted, or removed from the jurisdiction.

(2) Obtain an emergency protective order pursuant to Part 3 (commencing with Section 6240) of Division 10 of the Family Code ordering placement of the child with an interim custodian who agrees in writing to accept interim custody.

(3) Release the child to the social services agency responsible for arranging shelter or foster care.

(4) Return the child as ordered by a court of competent jurisdiction.

(c) Upon the arrest of a person for a violation of Section 278 or 278.5, a law enforcement officer shall take possession of an abducted child who is found in the company of, or under the control of, the arrested person and deliver the child as directed in subdivision (b).

(d) Notwithstanding any other law, when a person is arrested for an alleged violation of Section 278 or 278.5, the court shall, at the time of the arraignment or thereafter, order that the child shall be returned to the lawful custodian by or on a specific date, or that the person show cause on that date why the child has not been returned as ordered. If conflicting custodial orders exist within this state, or between this state and a foreign state, the court shall set a hearing within five court days to determine which court has jurisdiction under the laws of this state and determine which state has subject matter jurisdiction to issue a custodial order under the laws of this state, the Uniform Child Custody Jurisdiction Act (Part 3 (commencing with Section 3400) of Division 8 of the Family Code), or federal law, if applicable. At the conclusion of the hearing, or if the child has not been returned as ordered by the court at the time of arraignment, the court shall enter an order as to which custody order is valid and is to be enforced. If the child has not been returned at the conclusion of the hearing, the court shall set a date within a reasonable time by which the child shall be returned to the lawful custodian, and order the defendant to comply by this date, or to show cause on that date why he or she has not returned the child as directed. The court shall only enforce its order, or any subsequent orders for the return of the child, under subdivision (a) of Section 1219 of the Code of Civil Procedure, to ensure that the child is promptly placed with the lawful custodian. An order adverse to either the prosecution or defense is reviewable by a writ of mandate or prohibition addressed to the appropriate court. *(Added by Stats.1996, c. 988 (A.B.2936), § 9.)*

Cross References

Child defined for purposes of this Chapter, see Penal Code § 277.
Court order or custody order defined for purposes of this Chapter, see Penal Code § 277.
Lawful custodian defined for purposes of this Chapter, see Penal Code § 277.
Mandamus, purpose of writ of mandate, courts which may issue writ and parties to whom issued, see Code of Civil Procedure § 1085.
Person defined for purposes of this Chapter, see Penal Code § 277.
Uniform Child Custody Jurisdiction and Enforcement Act, effect on authority of district attorney or arresting agency, see Family Code § 3135.

§ 280. Violations of specified adoption proceedings; punishment

Every person who willfully causes or permits the removal or concealment of any child in violation of Section 8713, 8803, or 8910 of the Family Code shall be punished as follows:

(a) By imprisonment in a county jail for not more than one year if the child is concealed within the county in which the adoption proceeding is pending or in which the child has been placed for adoption, or is removed from that county to a place within this state.

(b) By imprisonment pursuant to subdivision (h) of Section 1170, or by imprisonment in a county jail for not more than one year, if the child is removed from that county to a place outside of this state. *(Added by Stats.1996, c. 988 (A.B.2936), § 9. Amended by Stats.2011, c. 15 (A.B.109), § 315, eff. April 4, 2011, operative Oct. 1, 2011.)*

Cross References

Agency adoptions, removal of child from county in which placed, concealment of child, violation, see Family Code § 8713.
Child defined for purposes of this Chapter, see Penal Code § 277.
Felony, punishment, see Penal Code § 18.

Independent adoptions, concealment or removal of child from county, see Family Code § 8803.
Intercountry adoptions, removal of child from county or concealment of child, see Family Code § 8910.
Person defined for purposes of this Chapter, see Penal Code § 277.

Research References

Forms
2 California Transactions Forms--Family Law § 6:2, Governing Law.
2 California Transactions Forms--Family Law § 6:90, Adoptive Placement Agreement.

CHAPTER 5. BIGAMY, INCEST, AND THE CRIME AGAINST NATURE

Section
281. "Bigamy" defined; evidence necessary to support proof.
282. Bigamy; exceptions.
283. Bigamy; punishment.
284. Marrying or entering into registered domestic partnership with another's spouse; scienter; punishment.
285. Incest.

Cross References

Admissibility of certain out-of-court statements of minors under the age of 12, see Evidence Code § 1228.
Attendance during testimony of prosecuting witness to support person, see Penal Code § 868.5.
Formation of the trial jury and the calendar of issues for trial, see Penal Code § 1048.
Home health aides, grounds for disciplinary action, see Health and Safety Code § 1736.5.
Kidnapping victims to commit felony sexual offenses, sentence enhancements, see Penal Code § 667.8.
Medroxyprogesterone acetate (MPA treatment) or equivalent for sex offenses, see Penal Code § 645.
Nurse assistants, grounds for disciplinary action, see Health and Safety Code § 1337.9.
Permit a leading question to be asked of a child under 10 years of age, see Evidence Code § 767.
Repeat sexual offenders, see Penal Code § 999i.
Use of videotape to preserve testimony at preliminary hearing, procedure, see Penal Code § 1346.

§ 281. "Bigamy" defined; evidence necessary to support proof

(a) Every person having a spouse living, who marries or enters into a registered domestic partnership with any other person, except in the cases specified in Section 282, is guilty of bigamy.

(b) Upon a trial for bigamy, it is not necessary to prove either of the marriages or registered domestic partnerships by the register, certificate, or other record evidence thereof, but the marriages or registered domestic partnerships may be proved by evidence which is admissible to prove a marriage or registered domestic partnership in other cases; and when the second marriage or registered domestic partnership took place out of this state, proof of that fact, accompanied with proof of cohabitation thereafter in this state, is sufficient to sustain the charge. *(Enacted in 1872. Amended by Stats.1987, c. 828, § 17; Stats.1989, c. 897, § 18; Stats.2016, c. 50 (S.B.1005), § 70, eff. Jan. 1, 2017.)*

Cross References

Annulment of marriage, causes for, see Family Code § 2210.
Jurisdiction, see Penal Code § 785.
Marital privilege exceptions, see Evidence Code §§ 972, 984.
Marriage defined, see Family Code § 300.
Marrying husband or wife of another, see Penal Code § 284.
Privilege not to testify against spouse, see Evidence Code § 970 et seq.
Proof of consent and solemnization of marriage, see Family Code § 305.
Reputation in community concerning marriage date, see Evidence Code § 1314.

Statements for purposes of medical diagnosis or treatment in sexual assault prosecutions, see Evidence Code § 1253.
Validity of bigamous and polygamous marriages, see Family Code § 2201.

§ 282. Bigamy; exceptions

Section 281 does not extend to any of the following:

(a) To any person by reason of any former marriage or former registered domestic partnership whose spouse by such marriage or registered domestic partnership has been absent for five successive years without being known to such person within that time to be living.

(b) To any person by reason of any former marriage, or any former registered domestic partnership, which has been pronounced void, annulled, or dissolved by the judgment of a competent court. *(Enacted in 1872. Amended by Stats.1987, c. 828, § 18; Stats.2016, c. 50 (S.B.1005), § 71, eff. Jan. 1, 2017.)*

§ 283. Bigamy; punishment

Bigamy is punishable by a fine not exceeding ten thousand dollars ($10,000) or by imprisonment in a county jail not exceeding one year or in the state prison. *(Enacted in 1872. Amended by Stats.1905, c. 272, p. 245, § 1; Stats.1949, c. 1252, p. 2205, § 1; Stats.1976, c. 1139, p. 5110, § 172, operative July 1, 1977; Stats.1983, c. 1092, § 264, eff. Sept. 27, 1983, operative Jan. 1, 1984.)*

Cross References

Felony and misdemeanor, defined, see Penal Code § 17.
Jurisdiction, see Penal Code § 785.
Prison or state prison defined for purposes of this Code, see Penal Code § 6081.
Punishment for felony, see Penal Code § 18.

§ 284. Marrying or entering into registered domestic partnership with another's spouse; scienter; punishment

Every person who knowingly and willfully marries or enters into a registered domestic partnership with the spouse of another, in any case in which such spouse would be punishable under the provisions of this chapter, is punishable by a fine not less than five thousand dollars ($5,000), or by imprisonment pursuant to subdivision (h) of Section 1170. *(Enacted in 1872. Amended by Stats.1905, c. 272, p. 245, § 2; Stats.1976, c. 1139, p. 5110, § 173, operative July 1, 1977; Stats.2011, c. 15 (A.B.109), § 316, eff. April 4, 2011, operative Oct. 1, 2011; Stats.2016, c. 50 (S.B.1005), § 72, eff. Jan. 1, 2017.)*

Cross References

Alternate sentences, see Penal Code § 18.
Bigamy, see Penal Code § 281 et seq.
Entry of final judgment of divorce after death of one of the parties not a defense to criminal action, see Family Code § 2344.
Felony and misdemeanor defined, see Penal Code § 17.
Knowingly defined, see Penal Code § 7.
Punishment for felony, see Penal Code § 18.
Willfully defined, see Penal Code § 7.

§ 285. Incest

Persons being within the degrees of consanguinity within which marriages are declared by law to be incestuous and void, who intermarry with each other, or who being 14 years of age or older, commit fornication or adultery with each other, are punishable by imprisonment in the state prison. *(Enacted in 1872. Amended by Stats.1921, c. 101, p. 96, § 1; Stats.1976, c. 1139, p. 5110, § 174, operative July 1, 1977; Stats.2005, c. 477 (S.B.33), § 1.)*

Cross References

Accomplices, corroboration of testimony, see Penal Code § 1111.
Calendar, priorities, see Penal Code § 1048.
Conviction as ground for revocation of,
  County teaching certificate, see Education Code § 44435.
  Teaching credential, see Education Code § 44424.

Discharge, discrimination, or retaliation by employees against domestic violence or sexual assault victims prohibited, see Labor Code § 230.
Dismissal of complaint if preliminary examination continued over ten court days after arraignment, exception for offenses where prosecuting attorney has schedule conflict, see Penal Code § 859b.
Elder abuse and dependent adult civil protection act, physical abuse, see Welfare and Institutions Code § 15610.63.
Employment, right of employees to take time off due to domestic violence or sexual assault, see Labor Code § 230.1.
Examination of victims of sexual crimes, see Penal Code § 1346 et seq.
Felony defined, see Penal Code § 17.
Grants to child sexual exploitation and child sexual abuse victim counseling centers, and grants to sexual assault services programs operating rape victim centers and prevention programs, see Penal Code § 13837.
Hearsay statements by complaining witness, admissibility, see Evidence Code § 1228.
Husband and wife, privilege not to testify against spouse, see Evidence Code § 970 et seq.
Incestuous and void marriages, see Family Code §§ 2200, 2201.
Injuries as result of assaultive or abusive conduct, reporting requirements by health facilities, clinics, or physician's offices, see Penal Code § 11160.
Jurisdiction, see Penal Code § 785.
Prison or state prison defined for purposes of this Code, see Penal Code § 6081.
Psychiatric or psychological examination of witnesses, see Penal Code § 1112.
Restitution for costs of medical or psychological treatment of minor victim, see Penal Code § 1203.1g.
Sex offenders, mandatory registration, see Penal Code § 290 et seq.
Sex offense as including violation of this section, see Education Code §§ 44010, 87010.
Sexual offenses, evidence of sexual conduct of complaining witness, procedure for admissibility, treatment of resealed affidavits, see Evidence Code § 782.
Solemnizing incestuous marriages, punishment, see Penal Code § 359.
State prison sentence, victim under age of 18 years, visitation,
  Generally, see Penal Code § 1202.05.
  Power of Director of Corrections, see Penal Code § 5054.2.
Summoning law enforcement assistance or emergency assistance, lease or rental agreement provisions prohibiting or limiting right void, see Civil Code § 1946.8.
Summoning law enforcement assistance or emergency assistance by victim of abuse, victim of crime, or individual in emergency, local agency ordinance, etc. limiting right prohibited, see Government Code § 53165.
Witness or victim name and address revealed by imprisoned offender with intent that another prisoner initiate harassing correspondence, see Penal Code § 136.7.

CHAPTER 12. OTHER INJURIES TO PERSONS

Section
359. Solemnizing marriages; incestuous or forbidden marriages; punishment.
360. Solemnizing marriages; presentment of license; authorization; false returns; misdemeanor.

Cross References

Advertising abortions, see Business and Professions Code § 601.
Alcoholic beverages,
  Excise taxes, willful evasion as felony, see Revenue and Taxation Code § 32552.
  Minors, employment in on-sale and off-sale premises, see Business and Professions Code § 25663.
  Minors, false evidence of age and identity, see Business and Professions Code § 25661.
  Minors, possession by as misdemeanor, see Business and Professions Code § 25662.
  Minors, selling to or furnishing, see Business and Professions Code § 25658.
Conspiracies in restraint of trade, see Business and Professions Code § 16755.
Container brands, violation of provisions, see Business and Professions Code § 14436.
Contractors, failure to obtain required asbestos certificate, see Business and Professions Code § 7028.1.
Contracts for dance studios, see Civil Code § 1812.63.
Contriving to have person adjudged to have a developmental disability, see Welfare and Institutions Code § 6511.
Controlled substances users, violation of provisions, see Health and Safety Code § 11550.
Corporate Securities Law violations, see Corporations Code § 25540.
Discrimination in recruitment or apprenticeship program, see Labor Code § 3073.6.
Drinking water, failure of employer to furnish, see Labor Code § 2441.
Drugs or devices,
  Dangerous drugs, see Business and Professions Code § 4022.
  Manufacturing, compounding, selling or dispensing by unregistered person, see Business and Professions Code § 4051.
  Refusal to cooperate under Sherman Food, Drug, and Cosmetic Laws, see Health and Safety Code § 110160.
Employees,
  Bonds and photographs, see Labor Code § 400 et seq.
  Compelling or coercing to purchase from employer, see Labor Code § 450.
  Influencing or interfering with political affiliations by employee, see Labor Code § 1101.
  Minimum wages and maximum hours, violations, see Labor Code § 1197 et seq.
  Preventing former employee from obtaining reemployment by misrepresentation, see Labor Code § 1050 et seq.
  Solicitation by misrepresentation, see Labor Code § 970.
Employment agencies, violations, penalties, see Civil Code § 1812.523.
Employment applications, violations of provisions, see Labor Code § 433.
Employment of minors,
  Hours of labor, violations, see Labor Code §§ 1308.5, 1391 et seq.
  Occupational restrictions, violations, see Labor Code §§ 1303, 1308, 1308.5, 1309.
Fair Packaging and Labeling Act violations, see Business and Professions Code § 12615.5.
Farm labor contractors, violation of provisions, see Labor Code § 1698.1 et seq.
Hazardous Substances Act, violations, see Health and Safety Code § 108295.
Hours of labor,
  Pharmacies, violations of provisions, see Labor Code § 853.
  Railroads, violations of provisions, see Labor Code §§ 605, 606.
  Smelters and underground workings, violations of provisions, see Labor Code § 752.
Household goods carriers, violations, see Business and Professions Code § 19277 et seq.
Indemnification of private citizens, see Government Code § 13959 et seq.
Industrial homework, violations of provisions, see Labor Code § 2667.
Intimidating voters, see Elections Code § 18540 et seq.
Minors,
  Dangerous drugs, use as agent or furnishing, see Business and Professions Code § 4336.
  Using to transport or sell controlled substances, see Health and Safety Code §§ 11353, 11354, 11361.
Occupational safety and health, see Labor Code § 6300 et seq.
Petroleum, filling containers in conformity with labels, see Business and Professions Code § 13486.
Petroleum tank vehicles, necessity of tag, plate, or label provisions, see Business and Professions Code § 13500.
Prenatal syphilis tests, violations, see Health and Safety Code § 120715.
Public utility corporations, failure or refusal to furnish statements to employees leaving employ, see Labor Code §§ 1055, 1056.
Real property sales contract, see Civil Code § 2985 et seq.
Trade names,
  Defacing or concealing, see Business and Professions Code § 14404.
  Use of container bearing name of another, see Business and Professions Code §§ 14403, 14405.
Unfair trade practices, see Business and Professions Code § 17000 et seq.
Union card, unauthorized use, see Labor Code § 1017.
Union employees, false representations as to employment in manufacture, production or sale by employer, see Labor Code § 1012.
Wages in general, violations of provisions, see Labor Code §§ 215, 216, 222, 225.

§ 359. Solemnizing marriages; incestuous or forbidden marriages; punishment

Every person authorized to solemnize marriage, who willfully and knowingly solemnizes any incestuous or other marriage forbidden by law, is punishable by fine of not less than one hundred nor more than one thousand dollars, or by imprisonment in the County Jail not less than three months nor more than one year, or by both. *(Enacted in 1872.)*

§ 359

Cross References

Definitions,
  Bigamy, see Penal Code § 281; Family Code § 2201.
  Incestuous marriage, see Family Code § 2200.
  Knowingly, see Penal Code § 7.
  Marriage, see Family Code § 300.
  Misdemeanor, see Penal Code § 17.
  Willfully, see Penal Code § 7.
Jurisdiction over offenses of incest or bigamy, see Penal Code § 785.
Persons authorized to solemnize marriage, see Family Code § 400.
Punishment for crime of incest, see Penal Code § 285.

§ 360. Solemnizing marriages; presentment of license; authorization; false returns; misdemeanor

Every person authorized to solemnize any marriage, who solemnizes a marriage without first being presented with the marriage license, as required by Section 421 of the Family Code; or who solemnizes a marriage pursuant to Part 4 (commencing with Section 500) of Division 3 of the Family Code without the authorization required by that part; or who willfully makes a false return of any marriage or pretended marriage to the recorder or clerk and every person who willfully makes a false record of any marriage return, is guilty of a misdemeanor. *(Enacted in 1872. Amended by Stats.1905, c. 510, p. 669, § 1; Stats.1981, c. 872, p. 3337, § 5; Stats.1992, c. 163 (A.B.2641), § 109; Stats.1992, c. 318 (A.B.1101), § 14; Stats.1993, c. 219 (A.B.1500), § 217; Stats.2001, c. 39 (A.B.1323), § 11.)*

Cross References

Authentication of marriage, generally, see Family Code § 306 et seq.
License, necessity for, see Family Code § 350.
Misdemeanors, definition and penalties, see Penal Code §§ 17, 19, 19.2.
Persons authorized to solemnize marriage, see Family Code § 400.
Solemnization of marriage, proof, see Family Code § 305.
Willfully defined, see Penal Code § 7.

Research References

Forms
West's California Code Forms, Family § 350 Form 1, California Marriage License, Registration and Ceremony Information.

Title 13

OF CRIMES AGAINST PROPERTY

Cross References

Crimes under this title, civil resolution in lieu of criminal complaint, prosecutor's discretion, see Code of Civil Procedure § 33.

CHAPTER 5. LARCENY [THEFT]

Section
487i. Public housing authority program; fraud.

Cross References

Child care and development services, persons convicted of specified crimes, penalties for placement in positions of fiscal responsibility or control, see Education Code § 8406.9.
Home health aides, grounds for disciplinary action, see Health and Safety Code § 1736.5.
Nurse assistants, grounds for disciplinary action, see Health and Safety Code § 1337.9.
Offenses under this chapter, restitution for misappropriation of escrow funds, see Financial Code § 17414.
Securities, unlawful advertising, see Financial Code § 565.

§ 487i. Public housing authority program; fraud

Any person who defrauds a housing program of a public housing authority of more than four hundred dollars ($400) is guilty of grand theft. *(Added by Stats.2008, c. 105 (A.B.2827), § 1.)*

Cross References

Grand theft defined, see Penal Code § 487.
Theft defined, see Penal Code § 484.

CHAPTER 8. FALSE PERSONATION AND CHEATS

Section
528. Marriage under false personation.

Cross References

Aid to needy, disclosure of confidential information, see Welfare and Institutions Code § 10850.
Air Force, unauthorized wearing of uniform, see Military and Veterans Code § 422.
Banks,
  Extension of credit as felony, see Financial Code § 1367.
  False statements in records and reports as felony, see Financial Code § 754.
  Purchase of property or interest in property from subject person, see Financial Code § 1329.
Birth of child, false pretenses to intercept inheritance, see Penal Code § 156.
Bucket Shop Law, violations as felony, see Corporations Code § 29100 et seq.
Coal, sale or exchange under false name, see Business and Professions Code §§ 17532, 17534.
Conspiracy to obtain money or property by false pretenses, see Penal Code § 182.
Dentistry, practice without license, see Business and Professions Code § 1701.
Employment agencies,
  Operating without license, see Civil Code § 1812.523.
  Publication of false or misleading advertisements, see Civil Code § 1812.508.
Evidence of false pretenses, necessity of note or memorandum or corroboration, see Penal Code § 532.
False or misleading statements in general, see Business and Professions Code §§ 17500, 17534.
Finance lenders, violation of regulatory provisions, see Financial Code § 22713.
Home furnishings, engaging in business without license, see Business and Professions Code § 19049.
Impersonating an officer, see Penal Code §§ 146a, 538d.
Individual activity without license, see Business and Professions Code §§ 7028, 7028.5.
Insurance,
  False or fraudulent claims, see Penal Code § 550.
  Misrepresentation of policies, see Insurance Code § 780 et seq.
  Theft of premium by agent, broker, solicitor, etc., see Insurance Code § 1730.
Marriage license application, see Family Code §§ 300, 306, 350 et seq.
National Guard, unauthorized wearing of uniform, see Military and Veterans Code § 422.
Navy, unauthorized wearing of uniform, see Military and Veterans Code § 422.
Nursery stock, sale without license, see Food and Agricultural Code § 6721 et seq.
Nursing,
  Impersonation or pretense of being professional nurse, see Business and Professions Code §§ 2796, 2799.
  Misrepresentation or impersonation connected with license application or examination, see Business and Professions Code §§ 2797, 2799.
Optometry,
  Practice under false or assumed name, see Business and Professions Code § 3078.
  Unlawful advertising, see Business and Professions Code § 3102.
Physicians and surgeons,
  False or assumed name, acting under, see Business and Professions Code § 2285.
  Unauthorized use of word "doctor" or "physician", see Business and Professions Code § 2054.
Posing as kidnapper or claiming ability to obtain release of victim, see Penal Code § 210.
Premium coupons, unlawful issuance, see Business and Professions Code §§ 17701, 17702.
Private investigators, unauthorized use of different names, see Business and Professions Code § 7532.
Public assistance, disclosure of confidential information, see Welfare and Institutions Code § 10850.
Rape by false personation of spouse, see Penal Code § 261.

OF CRIMES AND PUNISHMENTS

Real estate, untrue statements respecting, see Business and Professions Code § 17530.
Sale of goods, falsely using name of other dealer, manufacturer or producer, see Penal Code § 351a.
Secondhand or used merchandise, offenses in connection with sale, see Business and Professions Code §§ 17531, 17534.
Structural pest control, unlicensed operations, see Business and Professions Code § 8550 et seq.
Telegraphic or telephonic message, representing another to obtain, see Penal Code § 637.1.
Theft, taking by false or fraudulent representation or pretense, see Penal Code § 484.
Uniforms, unauthorized wearing, see Military and Veterans Code § 422.
Untrue statements respecting real estate, see Business and Professions Code § 17530.
Veterans,
  Misuse of badges and insignia, see Military and Veterans Code § 1820.
  Misuse of solicited funds, see Military and Veterans Code § 1802.
  Unlawful solicitation for, see Military and Veterans Code § 1801.
Voter signatures or other information collected for initiative, referendum or recall petitions, prohibition on sending or making information available outside of United States, see Elections Code § 2188.5.
Water storage districts, false statements respecting right to vote, see Water Code § 41012.
Weights and measures,
  Adding substance to increase weight, see Business and Professions Code § 12022.
  False markings, see Business and Professions Code § 12021.
  False weight or measure, unlawful use, see Business and Professions Code § 12020.
  Inspection, refusal to permit, see Business and Professions Code § 12018.
  Instruments or devices, unlawful use, see Business and Professions Code §§ 12508, 12510, 12512, 12515.
  Refusal to exhibit commodity to sealer, see Business and Professions Code § 12025.
  Sale by gross weight or measure, see Business and Professions Code § 12023.
  Sale of meat, fish, dressed fowl or rabbits by weight, violations, see Business and Professions Code § 12024.5.
  Sealers, hindering or obstructing, see Business and Professions Code § 12016.
  Sealers, sealing or condemning instruments without testing, see Business and Professions Code § 12014.
  Sealers, unlawful sale of instruments, see Business and Professions Code § 12514.
  Short quantity sales, see Business and Professions Code § 12024.
  Tolerances and specifications, sales at variance from standard, see Business and Professions Code § 12107.

§ 528. Marriage under false personation

Every person who falsely personates another, and in such assumed character marries or pretends to marry, or to sustain the marriage relation towards another, with or without the connivance of such other, is guilty of a felony. *(Enacted in 1872.)*

Cross References

Evidence of false pretenses, inapplicability of provision to marrying under false personation, see Penal Code § 532.
Person and personal identifying information defined for purposes of this Chapter, see Penal Code § 530.55.
Procuring illicit sexual intercourse by false pretenses, see Penal Code § 266.
Punishment for felony when not otherwise prescribed, see Penal Code § 18.

Title 15

MISCELLANEOUS CRIMES

CHAPTER 1.5. INVASION OF PRIVACY

Section
633.6. Domestic violence restraining order; permission to record prohibited communications by perpetrator.

Cross References

Family law proceedings, evidence collected by eavesdropping, see Family Code § 2022.

§ 633.6. Domestic violence restraining order; permission to record prohibited communications by perpetrator

(a) Notwithstanding the provisions of this chapter, and in accordance with federal law, upon the request of a victim of domestic violence who is seeking a domestic violence restraining order, a judge issuing the order may include a provision in the order that permits the victim to record any prohibited communication made to him or her by the perpetrator.

(b) Notwithstanding the provisions of this chapter, and in accordance with federal law, a victim of domestic violence who is seeking a domestic violence restraining order from a court, and who reasonably believes that a confidential communication made to him or her by the perpetrator may contain evidence germane to that restraining order, may record that communication for the exclusive purpose and use of providing that evidence to the court.

(c) The Judicial Council shall amend its domestic violence prevention application and order forms to incorporate the provisions of this section. *(Added by Stats.1999, c. 367 (A.B.207), § 1. Amended by Stats.2017, c. 191 (A.B.413), § 2, eff. Jan. 1, 2018.)*

CHAPTER 2. OF OTHER AND MISCELLANEOUS OFFENSES

Section
646.9. Stalking.
646.91. Stalking; emergency protective orders; issuance; expiration; service; filing; enforcement; liability; scope of section; punishment.
646.91a. Addresses or locations of persons protected under court order; prohibition upon certain enjoined parties from acting to obtain such information.
646.92. Notification to victim or witness of release of person convicted of stalking or domestic violence.
646.93. Telephone number available to public and victims for bail status inquiries; notification of victim of bail hearing; additional conditions of release.
646.94. Parolee convicted of stalking; specialized parole supervision program; specialized services.

Cross References

Aeronautics, punishment for violations, see Public Utilities Code §§ 21019, 21407.6.
Agricultural producers marketing law, offenses, see Food and Agricultural Code §§ 60014, 60015.
Agricultural seeds, violation of code provisions, see Food and Agricultural Code § 52481 et seq.
Air pollution, rules and regulations, violations, penalties, see Health and Safety Code § 42400 et seq.
Alcoholic beverages,
  Felonies, punishment not otherwise specified, see Business and Professions Code § 25618.
  Misdemeanors, punishment not otherwise specified, see Business and Professions Code § 25617.
Food,
  Sanitation, violations, see Health and Safety Code §§ 112130, 113940.
  Violations, see Health and Safety Code § 111825.
Forests, prohibited acts, see Public Resources Code § 4021.
Health facilities, violation of provisions, see Health and Safety Code § 1290.
Housing, violations, see Health and Safety Code § 17995 et seq.
Industrial loan companies, violation of provisions, see Financial Code § 18435.
Milk and dairy products, violations of marketing provisions, see Food and Agricultural Code § 61571 et seq.
Mobilehome parks, violations, see Health and Safety Code § 18700.
Motor vehicles,
  Felony, see Vehicle Code § 42000.
  Misdemeanors, see Vehicle Code §§ 40000.5 et seq., 42001 et seq.

Owner's responsibility, violations, see Vehicle Code § 40001.
Reckless driving, see Vehicle Code §§ 23103, 23104.
Rules of the road, violations, exceptions, see Vehicle Code §§ 21000 et seq., 40000.1 et seq.
Size, weight and loading violations, see Vehicle Code §§ 2803, 40000.23.
Unlicensed drivers, see Vehicle Code §§ 12500, 14600 et seq., 40000.11.
Water,
Distribution, violation of rules, see Water Code § 35424.
Diversion or unauthorized use, see Water Code §§ 4175, 4177.
Misuse, see Water Code § 31029.
Water wells,
Noncompliance with requirements, see Water Code § 13754.
Registration violations, see Water Code §§ 75640, 75641.

§ 646.9. Stalking

(a) Any person who willfully, maliciously, and repeatedly follows or willfully and maliciously harasses another person and who makes a credible threat with the intent to place that person in reasonable fear for his or her safety, or the safety of his or her immediate family is guilty of the crime of stalking, punishable by imprisonment in a county jail for not more than one year, or by a fine of not more than one thousand dollars ($1,000), or by both that fine and imprisonment, or by imprisonment in the state prison.

(b) Any person who violates subdivision (a) when there is a temporary restraining order, injunction, or any other court order in effect prohibiting the behavior described in subdivision (a) against the same party, shall be punished by imprisonment in the state prison for two, three, or four years.

(c)(1) Every person who, after having been convicted of a felony under Section 273.5, 273.6, or 422, commits a violation of subdivision (a) shall be punished by imprisonment in a county jail for not more than one year, or by a fine of not more than one thousand dollars ($1,000), or by both that fine and imprisonment, or by imprisonment in the state prison for two, three, or five years.

(2) Every person who, after having been convicted of a felony under subdivision (a), commits a violation of this section shall be punished by imprisonment in the state prison for two, three, or five years.

(d) In addition to the penalties provided in this section, the sentencing court may order a person convicted of a felony under this section to register as a sex offender pursuant to Section 290.006.

(e) For the purposes of this section, "harasses" means engages in a knowing and willful course of conduct directed at a specific person that seriously alarms, annoys, torments, or terrorizes the person, and that serves no legitimate purpose.

(f) For the purposes of this section, "course of conduct" means two or more acts occurring over a period of time, however short, evidencing a continuity of purpose. Constitutionally protected activity is not included within the meaning of "course of conduct."

(g) For the purposes of this section, "credible threat" means a verbal or written threat, including that performed through the use of an electronic communication device, or a threat implied by a pattern of conduct or a combination of verbal, written, or electronically communicated statements and conduct, made with the intent to place the person that is the target of the threat in reasonable fear for his or her safety or the safety of his or her family, and made with the apparent ability to carry out the threat so as to cause the person who is the target of the threat to reasonably fear for his or her safety or the safety of his or her family. It is not necessary to prove that the defendant had the intent to actually carry out the threat. The present incarceration of a person making the threat shall not be a bar to prosecution under this section. Constitutionally protected activity is not included within the meaning of "credible threat."

(h) For purposes of this section, the term "electronic communication device" includes, but is not limited to, telephones, cellular phones, computers, video recorders, fax machines, or pagers. "Electronic communication" has the same meaning as the term defined in Subsection 12 of Section 2510 of Title 18 of the United States Code.

(i) This section shall not apply to conduct that occurs during labor picketing.

(j) If probation is granted, or the execution or imposition of a sentence is suspended, for any person convicted under this section, it shall be a condition of probation that the person participate in counseling, as designated by the court. However, the court, upon a showing of good cause, may find that the counseling requirement shall not be imposed.

(k)(1) The sentencing court also shall consider issuing an order restraining the defendant from any contact with the victim, that may be valid for up to 10 years, as determined by the court. It is the intent of the Legislature that the length of any restraining order be based upon the seriousness of the facts before the court, the probability of future violations, and the safety of the victim and his or her immediate family.

(2) This protective order may be issued by the court whether the defendant is sentenced to state prison, county jail, or if imposition of sentence is suspended and the defendant is placed on probation.

(*l*) For purposes of this section, "immediate family" means any spouse, parent, child, any person related by consanguinity or affinity within the second degree, or any other person who regularly resides in the household, or who, within the prior six months, regularly resided in the household.

(m) The court shall consider whether the defendant would benefit from treatment pursuant to Section 2684. If it is determined to be appropriate, the court shall recommend that the Department of Corrections and Rehabilitation make a certification as provided in Section 2684. Upon the certification, the defendant shall be evaluated and transferred to the appropriate hospital for treatment pursuant to Section 2684. (*Added by Stats.1990, c. 1527 (S.B.2184), § 1. Amended by Stats.1992, c. 627 (S.B.1342), § 1; Stats.1993, c. 581 (A.B.1178), § 1; Stats.1993–94, 1st Ex.Sess., c.12 (A.B.95), § 1; Stats.1994, c. 931, § 1.5; Stats.1995, c. 438 (A.B.985), § 2; Stats.1998, c. 825 (S.B.1796), § 4; Stats.1998, c. 826 (A.B.2351), § 1; Stats.2000, c. 669 (A.B.2425), § 1; Stats.2002, c. 832 (S.B.1320), § 1; Stats.2007, c. 579 (S.B.172), § 39, eff. Oct. 13, 2007; Stats.2007, c. 582 (A.B.289), § 2.5.*)

Cross References

Arrests under this section, unscheduled bail amounts or release on own recognizance, see Penal Code § 1270.1.
Attendance during testimony of prosecuting witness for support, see Penal Code § 868.5.
Community college applicants previously expelled or undergoing expulsion procedures in another district for specified offenses, hearing to determine if applicant poses danger to physical safety of students and employees, see Education Code § 76038.
Department of Corrections and Rehabilitation, generally, see Penal Code § 5000 et seq.
Domestic violence victims, application for new and different license plates, see Vehicle Code § 4467.
Employers with 25 or more employees, victims of domestic violence, sexual assault, or stalking, employer prohibited from discharging or discriminating against employee for taking time off for specific purposes, see Labor Code § 230.1.
Evidence that victim or witness to this offense was engaged in act of prostitution, inadmissibility in prostitution prosecution, see Evidence Code § 1162.
Felonies, definition and penalties, see Penal Code §§ 17, 18.
Identification of persons eligible for automatic conviction record relief, granting of relief, notice to court, conditions for relief, see Penal Code § 1203.425.
Lease not to be terminated based on domestic or sexual assault against tenant, landlord's liability for compliance, form for affirmative defense to unlawful detainer action, see Code of Civil Procedure § 1161.3.

Legal actions by victims of domestic violence, sexual assault, or stalking, employer prohibited from discharging or discriminating against employee for taking time off or due to employee's status as a victim, see Labor Code § 230.

Misdemeanors, release procedures, exception for crimes specified in section 1270.1 and crimes defined in this section, see Penal Code § 853.6.

Multiple violations, local jurisdiction of offenses, see Penal Code § 784.7.

Name changes, exemptions to publication provisions, see Code of Civil Procedure § 1277.

Offer of diversion to misdemeanor defendant, dismissal of action, reinstitution of criminal proceedings, charged offenses not eligible for diversion, see Penal Code § 1001.95.

Officers authorized to maintain order on school campus or facility, threat of violence made off school campus, temporary restraining order and injunction, violation of restraining order, see Code of Civil Procedure § 527.85.

Participation in California Conservation Camp program as incarcerated individual hand crew member or participation as member of county incarcerated individual hand crew, petition for relief, dismissal of accusations or information and release from penalties and disabilities, see Penal Code § 1203.4b.

Presumption against persons perpetrating domestic violence, custody of children, see Family Code § 3044.

Prison or state prison defined for purposes of this Code, see Penal Code § 6081.

Summoning law enforcement assistance or emergency assistance, lease or rental agreement provisions prohibiting or limiting right void, see Civil Code § 1946.8.

Summoning law enforcement assistance or emergency assistance by victim of abuse, victim of crime, or individual in emergency, local agency ordinance, etc. limiting right prohibited, see Government Code § 53165.

Witnesses who are minors or persons with a disability in certain criminal proceedings, precautions and protection, see Penal Code § 868.8.

Research References

Forms

California Practice Guide: Rutter Family Law Forms Form 1:32, Glossary of Common Family Law Terms, Phrases and Concepts (Enclosure to Form 1:31).

West's California Judicial Council Forms CR–160, Criminal Protective Order—Domestic Violence (Clets–Cpo) (Also Available in Spanish).

West's California Judicial Council Forms CR–161, Criminal Protective Order—Other Than Domestic Violence (Clets–Cpo).

West's California Judicial Council Forms CR–165, Notice of Termination of Protective Order in Criminal Proceeding (CLETS-CANCEL).

§ 646.91. Stalking; emergency protective orders; issuance; expiration; service; filing; enforcement; liability; scope of section; punishment

(a) Notwithstanding any other law, a judicial officer may issue an ex parte emergency protective order if a peace officer, as defined in Section 830.1, 830.2, 830.32, or subdivision (a) of Section 830.33, asserts reasonable grounds to believe that a person is in immediate and present danger of stalking based upon the person's allegation that he or she has been willfully, maliciously, and repeatedly followed or harassed by another person who has made a credible threat with the intent of placing the person who is the target of the threat in reasonable fear for his or her safety, or the safety of his or her immediate family, within the meaning of Section 646.9.

(b) A peace officer who requests an emergency protective order shall reduce the order to writing and sign it.

(c) An emergency protective order shall include all of the following:

(1) A statement of the grounds asserted for the order.

(2) The date and time the order expires.

(3) The address of the superior court for the district or county in which the protected party resides.

(4) The following statements, which shall be printed in English and Spanish:

(A) "To the protected person: This order will last until the date and time noted above. If you wish to seek continuing protection, you will have to apply for an order from the court at the address noted above. You may seek the advice of an attorney as to any matter connected with your application for any future court orders. The attorney should be consulted promptly so that the attorney may assist you in making your application."

(B) "To the restrained person: This order will last until the date and time noted above. The protected party may, however, obtain a more permanent restraining order from the court. You may seek the advice of an attorney as to any matter connected with the application. The attorney should be consulted promptly so that the attorney may assist you in responding to the application. You may not own, possess, purchase, or receive, or attempt to purchase or receive, a firearm while this order is in effect."

(d) An emergency protective order may be issued under this section only if the judicial officer finds both of the following:

(1) That reasonable grounds have been asserted to believe that an immediate and present danger of stalking, as defined in Section 646.9, exists.

(2) That an emergency protective order is necessary to prevent the occurrence or reoccurrence of the stalking activity.

(e) An emergency protective order may include either of the following specific orders as appropriate:

(1) A harassment protective order as described in Section 527.6 of the Code of Civil Procedure.

(2) A workplace violence protective order as described in Section 527.8 of the Code of Civil Procedure.

(f) An emergency protective order shall be issued without prejudice to any person.

(g) An emergency protective order expires at the earlier of the following times:

(1) The close of judicial business on the fifth court day following the day of its issuance.

(2) The seventh calendar day following the day of its issuance.

(h) A peace officer who requests an emergency protective order shall do all of the following:

(1) Serve the order on the restrained person, if the restrained person can reasonably be located.

(2) Give a copy of the order to the protected person, or, if the protected person is a minor child, to a parent or guardian of the protected child if the parent or guardian can reasonably be located, or to a person having temporary custody of the child.

(3) File a copy of the order with the court as soon as practicable after issuance.

(4) Have the order entered into the computer database system for protective and restraining orders maintained by the Department of Justice.

(i) A peace officer shall use every reasonable means to enforce an emergency protective order.

(j) A peace officer who acts in good faith to enforce an emergency protective order is not civilly or criminally liable.

(k) A peace officer described in subdivision (a) or (b) of Section 830.32 who requests an emergency protective order pursuant to this section shall also notify the sheriff or police chief of the city in whose jurisdiction the peace officer's college or school is located after issuance of the order.

(*l*) "Judicial officer," as used in this section, means a judge, commissioner, or referee.

(m) A person subject to an emergency protective order under this section shall not own, possess, purchase, or receive a firearm while the order is in effect.

§ 646.91

(n) Nothing in this section shall be construed to permit a court to issue an emergency protective order prohibiting speech or other activities that are constitutionally protected or protected by the laws of this state or by the United States or activities occurring during a labor dispute, as defined by Section 527.3 of the Code of Civil Procedure, including, but not limited to, picketing and hand billing.

(o) The Judicial Council shall develop forms, instructions, and rules for the scheduling of hearings and other procedures established pursuant to this section.

(p) Any intentional disobedience of any emergency protective order granted under this section is punishable pursuant to Section 166. Nothing in this subdivision shall be construed to prevent punishment under Section 646.9, in lieu of punishment under this section, if a violation of Section 646.9 is also pled and proven. *(Added by Stats.1997, c. 169 (A.B.350), § 2. Amended by Stats.1999, c. 659 (S.B.355), § 2; Stats.2003, c. 495 (A.B.1290), § 1; Stats.2013, c. 145 (A.B.238), § 3; Stats.2014, c. 71 (S.B.1304), § 124, eff. Jan. 1, 2015; Stats.2014, c. 559 (S.B.1154), § 1, eff. Jan. 1, 2015.)*

Cross References

Domestic violence prevention, emergency protective orders, precedence over other restraining or protective orders for enforcement purposes, see Penal Code § 136.2.
Officer to inform that order may be sought, request for person in immediate and present danger, see Family Code § 6275.

Research References

Forms

West's California Code Forms, Family § 6274, Comment Overview—Stalking.
West's California Judicial Council Forms EPO-001, Emergency Protective Order (CLETS-EPO) (Also Available in Chinese, Korean, Spanish, and Vietnamese).

§ 646.91a. Addresses or locations of persons protected under court order; prohibition upon certain enjoined parties from acting to obtain such information

(a) The court shall order that any party enjoined pursuant to Section 646.91 be prohibited from taking any action to obtain the address or location of a protected party or a protected party's family members, caretakers, or guardian, unless there is good cause not to make that order.

(b) The Judicial Council shall promulgate forms necessary to effectuate this section. *(Formerly § 646.91A, added by Stats.2005, c. 472 (A.B.978), § 5. Renumbered § 646.91a and amended by Stats.2006, c. 901 (S.B.1422), § 6.1.)*

§ 646.92. Notification to victim or witness of release of person convicted of stalking or domestic violence

(a)(1) The Department of Corrections and Rehabilitation, county sheriff, or director of the local department of corrections shall give notice not less than 15 days prior to the release from the state prison or a county jail of any person who is convicted of violating Section 646.9 or convicted of a felony offense involving domestic violence, as defined in Section 6211 of the Family Code, or any change in the parole status or relevant change in the parole location of the convicted person, or if the convicted person absconds from supervision while on parole, to any person the court identifies as a victim of the offense, a family member of the victim, or a witness to the offense by telephone, electronic mail, or certified mail at his or her last known address, upon request and using the method of communication selected by the requesting party, if that method is available. A victim, family member, or witness shall keep the department or county sheriff informed of his or her current contact information to be entitled to receive notice. A victim may designate another person for the purpose of receiving notification. The department, county sheriff, or director of the local department of corrections, shall make reasonable attempts to locate a person who has requested notification but whose contact information is incorrect or not current. However, the duty to keep the department or county sheriff informed of current contact information shall remain with the victim.

(2) Following notification by the department pursuant to Section 3058.61, in the event the victim had not originally requested notification under this section, the sheriff or the chief of police, as appropriate, shall make an attempt to advise the victim or, if the victim is a minor, the parent or guardian of the victim, of the victim's right to notification under this section.

(b) All information relating to any person who receives notice under this section shall remain confidential and shall not be made available to the person convicted of violating this section.

(c) For purposes of this section, "release" includes a release from the state prison or a county jail because time has been served, a release from the state prison or a county jail to parole or probation supervision, or an escape from an institution or reentry facility.

(d) The department or county sheriff shall give notice of an escape from an institution or reentry facility of any person convicted of violating Section 646.9 or convicted of a felony offense involving domestic violence, as defined in Section 6211 of the Family Code, to the notice recipients described in subdivision (a).

(e) Substantial compliance satisfies the notification requirements of subdivision (a). *(Added by Stats.1995, c. 438 (A.B.985), § 3. Amended by Stats.2000, c. 561 (S.B.580), § 1; Stats.2011, c. 364 (S.B.852), § 1, eff. Sept. 29, 2011.)*

Cross References

Department of Corrections and Rehabilitation, generally, see Penal Code § 5000 et seq.
Felonies, definition and penalties, see Penal Code §§ 17, 18.
Prison or state prison defined for purposes of this Code, see Penal Code § 6081.

§ 646.93. Telephone number available to public and victims for bail status inquiries; notification of victim of bail hearing; additional conditions of release

(a)(1) In those counties where the arrestee is initially incarcerated in a jail operated by the county sheriff, the sheriff shall designate a telephone number that shall be available to the public to inquire about bail status or to determine if the person arrested has been released and if not yet released, the scheduled release date, if known. This subdivision does not require a county sheriff or jail administrator to establish a new telephone number but shall require that the information contained on the victim resource card, as defined in Section 264.2, specify the phone number that a victim should call to obtain this information. This subdivision shall not require the county sheriff or municipal police departments to produce new victim resource cards containing a designated phone number for the public to inquire about the bail or custody status of a person who has been arrested until their existing supply of victim resource cards has been exhausted.

(2) In those counties where the arrestee is initially incarcerated in an incarceration facility other than a jail operated by the county sheriff and in those counties that do not operate a Victim Notification (VNE) system, a telephone number shall be available to the public to inquire about bail status or to determine if the person arrested has been released and if not yet released, the scheduled release date, if known. This subdivision does not require a municipal police agency or jail administrator to establish a new telephone number but shall require that the information contained on the victim resource card, as defined in Section 264.2, specify the phone number that a victim should call to obtain this information. This subdivision shall not require the county sheriff or municipal police departments to produce new victim resource cards containing a designated phone number for the public to inquire about the bail or custody status of a person who has been arrested until their existing supply of victim resource cards has been exhausted.

(3) If an arrestee is transferred to another incarceration facility and is no longer in the custody of the initial arresting agency, the transfer date and new incarceration location shall be made available through the telephone number designated by the arresting agency.

(4) The resource card provided to victims pursuant to Section 264.2 shall list the designated telephone numbers to which this section refers.

(b) Any request to lower bail shall be heard in open court in accordance with Section 1270.1. In addition, the prosecutor shall make all reasonable efforts to notify the victim or victims of the bail hearing. The victims may be present at the hearing and shall be permitted to address the court on the issue of bail.

(c) Unless good cause is shown not to impose the following conditions, the judge shall impose as additional conditions of release on bail that:

(1) The defendant shall not initiate contact in person, by telephone, or any other means with the alleged victims.

(2) The defendant shall not knowingly go within 100 yards of the alleged victims, their residence, or place of employment.

(3) The defendant shall not possess any firearms or other deadly or dangerous weapons.

(4) The defendant shall obey all laws.

(5) The defendant, upon request at the time of his or her appearance in court, shall provide the court with an address where he or she is residing or will reside, a business address and telephone number if employed, and a residence telephone number if the defendant's residence has a telephone.

A showing by declaration that any of these conditions are violated shall, unless good cause is shown, result in the issuance of a no-bail warrant. *(Added by Stats.1999, c. 703 (A.B.1284), § 3. Amended by Stats.2000, c. 669 (A.B.2425), § 2; Stats.2001, c. 854 (S.B.205), § 35.)*

§ 646.94. Parolee convicted of stalking; specialized parole supervision program; specialized services

(a) Contingent upon a Budget Act appropriation, the Department of Corrections shall ensure that any parolee convicted of violating Section 646.9 on or after January 1, 2002, who is deemed to pose a high risk of committing a repeat stalking offense be placed on an intensive and specialized parole supervision program for a period not to exceed the period of parole.

(b)(1) The program shall include referral to specialized services, for example substance abuse treatment, for offenders needing those specialized services.

(2) Parolees participating in this program shall be required to participate in relapse prevention classes as a condition of parole.

(3) Parole agents may conduct group counseling sessions as part of the program.

(4) The department may include other appropriate offenders in the treatment program if doing so facilitates the effectiveness of the treatment program.

(c) The program shall be established with the assistance and supervision of the staff of the department primarily by obtaining the services of mental health providers specializing in the treatment of stalking patients. Each parolee placed into this program shall be required to participate in clinical counseling programs aimed at reducing the likelihood that the parolee will commit or attempt to commit acts of violence or stalk their victim.

(d) The department may require persons subject to this section to pay some or all of the costs associated with this treatment, subject to the person's ability to pay. "Ability to pay" means the overall capability of the person to reimburse the costs, or a portion of the costs, of providing mental health treatment, and shall include, but shall not be limited to, consideration of all of the following factors:

(1) Present financial position.

(2) Reasonably discernible future financial position.

(3) Likelihood that the person shall be able to obtain employment after the date of parole.

(4) Any other factor or factors that may bear upon the person's financial capability to reimburse the department for the costs.

(e) For purposes of this section, a mental health provider specializing in the treatment of stalking patients shall meet all of the following requirements:

(1) Be a licensed clinical social worker, as defined in Article 4 (commencing with Section 4996) of Chapter 14 of Division 2 of the Business and Professions Code, a clinical psychologist, as defined in Section 1316.5 of the Health and Safety Code, or a physician and surgeon engaged in the practice of psychiatry.

(2) Have clinical experience in the area of assessment and treatment of stalking patients.

(3) Have two letters of reference from professionals who can attest to the applicant's experience in counseling stalking patients.

(f) The program shall target parolees convicted of violating Section 646.9 who meet the following conditions:

(1) The offender has been subject to a clinical assessment.

(2) A review of the offender's criminal history indicates that the offender poses a high risk of committing further acts of stalking or acts of violence against his or her victim or other persons upon his or her release on parole.

(3) The parolee, based on his or her clinical assessment, may be amenable to treatment.

(g) On or before January 1, 2006, the Department of Corrections shall evaluate the intensive and specialized parole supervision program and make a report to the Legislature regarding the results of the program, including, but not limited to, the recidivism rate for repeat stalking related offenses committed by persons placed into the program and a cost-benefit analysis of the program.

(h) This section shall become operative upon the appropriation of sufficient funds in the Budget Act to implement this section. *(Added by Stats.2000, c. 669 (A.B.2425), § 3. Amended by Stats.2001, c. 159 (S.B.662), § 163.)*

Cross References

Department of Corrections and Rehabilitation, generally, see Penal Code § 5000 et seq.

Title 17

RIGHTS OF VICTIMS AND WITNESSES OF CRIME

Section
679.05. Right to have domestic violence or abuse advocates present at interviews with law enforcement authorities; notice.
679.10. Victim of qualifying criminal activity under Immigration and Nationality Act provision; copy of police report; certification of victim helpfulness; use of Form I-918 Supplement B.

§ 679.05. Right to have domestic violence or abuse advocates present at interviews with law enforcement authorities; notice

(a) A victim of domestic violence or abuse, as defined in Sections 6203 or 6211 of the Family Code, or Section 13700 of the Penal Code, has the right to have a domestic violence advocate and a support person of the victim's choosing present at any interview by law enforcement authorities, prosecutors, or defense attorneys.

§ 679.05

However, the support person may be excluded from an interview by law enforcement or the prosecutor if the law enforcement authority or the prosecutor determines that the presence of that individual would be detrimental to the purpose of the interview. As used in this section, "domestic violence advocate" means either a person employed by a program specified in Section 13835.2 for the purpose of rendering advice or assistance to victims of domestic violence, or a domestic violence counselor, as defined in Section 1037.1 of the Evidence Code. Prior to being present at any interview conducted by law enforcement authorities, prosecutors, or defense attorneys, a domestic violence advocate shall advise the victim of any applicable limitations on the confidentiality of communications between the victim and the domestic violence advocate.

(b)(1) Prior to the commencement of the initial interview by law enforcement authorities or the prosecutor pertaining to any criminal action arising out of a domestic violence incident, a victim of domestic violence or abuse, as defined in Section 6203 or 6211 of the Family Code, or Section 13700 of this code, shall be notified orally or in writing by the attending law enforcement authority or prosecutor that the victim has the right to have a domestic violence advocate and a support person of the victim's choosing present at the interview or contact. This subdivision applies to investigators and agents employed or retained by law enforcement or the prosecutor.

(2) At the time the victim is advised of his or her rights pursuant to paragraph (1), the attending law enforcement authority or prosecutor shall also advise the victim of the right to have a domestic violence advocate and a support person present at any interview by the defense attorney or investigators or agents employed by the defense attorney.

(c) An initial investigation by law enforcement to determine whether a crime has been committed and the identity of the suspects shall not constitute a law enforcement interview for purposes of this section. *(Added by Stats.2004, c. 159 (S.B.1441), § 1. Amended by Stats.2005, c. 279 (S.B.1107), § 6; Stats.2005, c. 22 (S.B.1108), § 149; Stats.2007, c. 206 (S.B.407), § 6.)*

Cross References

Crime defined for purposes of this Chapter, see Penal Code § 679.01.
Victim defined for purposes of this Chapter, see Penal Code § 679.01.

§ 679.10. Victim of qualifying criminal activity under Immigration and Nationality Act provision; copy of police report; certification of victim helpfulness; use of Form I–918 Supplement B

(a) For purposes of this section, a "certifying entity" is any of the following:

(1) A state or local law enforcement agency, including, without limitation, the police department of the University of California, a California State University campus, or the police department of a school district, established pursuant to Section 38000 of the Education Code.

(2) A prosecutor.

(3) A judge.

(4) Any other authority that has responsibility for the detection or investigation or prosecution of a qualifying crime or criminal activity.

(5) Agencies that have criminal detection or investigative jurisdiction in their respective areas of expertise, including, but not limited to, child protective services, the * * * Civil Rights Department, and the Department of Industrial Relations.

(b) For purposes of this section, a "certifying official" is any of the following:

(1) The head of the certifying entity.

(2) A person in a supervisory role who has been specifically designated by the head of the certifying entity to issue Form I–918 Supplement B certifications on behalf of that agency.

(3) A judge.

(4) Any other certifying official defined under Section 214.14 (a)(2) of Title 8 of the Code of Federal Regulations.

(c) "Qualifying criminal activity" has the same meaning as qualifying criminal activity pursuant to Section 101(a)(15)(U)(iii) of the federal Immigration and Nationality Act which includes, but is not limited to, the following crimes:

(1) Rape.
(2) Torture.
(3) Human trafficking.
(4) Incest.
(5) Domestic violence.
(6) Sexual assault.
(7) Abusive sexual conduct.
(8) Prostitution.
(9) Sexual exploitation.
(10) Female genital mutilation.
(11) Being held hostage.
(12) Peonage.
(13) Perjury.
(14) Involuntary servitude.
(15) Slavery.
(16) Kidnapping.
(17) Abduction.
(18) Unlawful criminal restraint.
(19) False imprisonment.
(20) Blackmail.
(21) Extortion.
(22) Manslaughter.
(23) Murder.
(24) Felonious assault.
(25) Witness tampering.
(26) Obstruction of justice.
(27) Fraud in foreign labor contracting.
(28) Stalking.

(d) A "qualifying crime" includes criminal offenses for which the nature and elements of the offenses are substantially similar to the criminal activity described in subdivision (c), and the attempt, conspiracy, or solicitation to commit any of those offenses.

(e) A "representative fully accredited by the United States Department of Justice" is a person who is approved by the United States Department of Justice to represent individuals before the Board of Immigration Appeals, the immigration courts, or the Department of Homeland Security. The representative shall be a person who works for a specific nonprofit, religious, charitable, social service, or similar organization that has been recognized by the United States Department of Justice to represent those individuals and whose accreditation is in good standing.

(f) Upon the request of a victim, licensed attorney representing the victim, or representative fully accredited by the United States Department of Justice authorized to represent the victim in immigration proceedings, a state or local law enforcement agency with whom the victim had filed a police report shall provide a copy of the police report within seven days of the request.

(g) Upon the request of the victim, victim's family member, licensed attorney representing the victim, or representative fully accredited by the United States Department of Justice authorized to represent the victim in immigration proceedings, a certifying official from a certifying entity shall certify victim helpfulness on the Form I–

918 Supplement B certification, when the victim was a victim of a qualifying criminal activity and has been helpful, is being helpful, or is likely to be helpful to the detection or investigation or prosecution of that qualifying criminal activity.

(h) For purposes of determining helpfulness pursuant to subdivision (g), there is a rebuttable presumption that a victim is helpful, has been helpful, or is likely to be helpful to the detection or investigation or prosecution of that qualifying criminal activity, if the victim has not refused or failed to provide information and assistance reasonably requested by law enforcement.

(i) The certifying official shall fully complete and sign the Form I–918 Supplement B certification and, regarding victim helpfulness, include specific details about the nature of the crime investigated or prosecuted and a detailed description of the victim's helpfulness or likely helpfulness to the detection or investigation or prosecution of the criminal activity.

(j) A certifying entity shall process a Form I–918 Supplement B certification within 30 days of request, unless the noncitizen is in removal proceedings, in which case the certification shall be processed within 7 days of the first business day following the day the request was received.

(k)(1) A current investigation, the filing of charges, closing of a case, and a prosecution or conviction are not required for the victim to request and obtain the Form I–918 Supplement B certification from a certifying official.

(2) A certifying official shall not refuse to complete the Form I–918 Supplement B certification or to otherwise certify that a victim has been helpful, solely because a case has already been prosecuted or otherwise closed, or because the time for commencing a criminal action has expired.

(*l*) A certifying official may only withdraw the certification if the victim refuses to provide information and assistance when reasonably requested.

(m) A certifying entity is prohibited from disclosing the immigration status of a victim or person requesting the Form I–918 Supplement B certification, except to comply with federal law or legal process, or if authorized by the victim or person requesting the Form I–918 Supplement B certification.

(n) A certifying entity that receives a request for a Form I–918 Supplement B certification shall report to the Legislature, on or before January 1, 2017, and annually thereafter, the number of victims that requested Form I–918 Supplement B certifications from the entity, the number of those certification forms that were signed, and the number that were denied. A report pursuant to this subdivision shall comply with Section 9795 of the Government Code. *(Added by Stats.2015, c. 721 (S.B.674), § 1, eff. Jan. 1, 2016. Amended by Stats.2016, c. 86 (S.B.1171), § 227, eff. Jan. 1, 2017; Stats.2019, c. 576 (A.B.917), § 1, eff. Jan. 1, 2020; Stats.2020, c. 187 (A.B.2426), § 1, eff. Jan. 1, 2021; Stats.2022, c. 48 (S.B.189), § 72, eff. June 30, 2022.)*

Part 2

OF CRIMINAL PROCEDURE

Title 6

PLEADINGS AND PROCEEDINGS BEFORE TRIAL

CHAPTER 2.4. CHILD ABUSERS

Section
999q. Legislative findings; intent.
999r. Child abuser prosecution program; establishment; funds; grant awards.
999s. Enhanced prosecution efforts and resources.
999t. Subjects of child abuser prosecution efforts; selection criteria; application of criteria; considerations in exercising prosecutorial discretion.
999u. Policies for child abuser cases.
999v. Departure from selection criteria under extraordinary circumstances; quarterly reports.
999w. Characterization of defendant as "child abuser"; communication to trier of fact prohibited.
999x. Use of federal funds.
999y. Annual report to Legislature; evaluation of the Child Abuser Prosecution Program; outcome measures.

§ 999q. Legislative findings; intent

The Legislature hereby finds that child abusers present a clear and present danger to the mental health and physical well-being of the citizens of the State of California, especially of its children. The Legislature further finds that the concept of vertical prosecution, in which a specially trained deputy district attorney or prosecution unit is assigned to a case from its filing to its completion, is a proven way of demonstrably increasing the likelihood of convicting child abusers and ensuring appropriate sentences for such offenders. In enacting this chapter, the Legislature intends to support increased efforts by district attorneys' offices to prosecute child abusers through organizational and operational techniques that have already proven their effectiveness in selected counties in this and other states, as demonstrated by the California Career Criminal Prosecution Program, the California Gang Violence Suppression Program, and the Repeat Sexual Offender Prosecution Program. *(Added by Stats.1985, c. 1097, § 1.)*

Cross References

Words and phrases, "county", see Penal Code § 691.

§ 999r. Child abuser prosecution program; establishment; funds; grant awards

(a) There is hereby established in the Office of Emergency Services a program of financial and technical assistance for district attorneys' offices, designated the Child Abuser Prosecution Program. All funds appropriated to the agency for the purposes of this chapter shall be administered and disbursed by the executive director of that agency or agencies, and shall to the greatest extent feasible, be coordinated or consolidated with any federal or local funds that may be made available for these purposes.

The Office of Emergency Services shall establish guidelines for the provision of grant awards to proposed and existing programs prior to the allocation of funds under this chapter. These guidelines shall contain the criteria for the selection of agencies to receive funding and the terms and conditions upon which the agency is prepared to offer grants pursuant to statutory authority. The guidelines shall not constitute rules, regulations, orders, or standards of general application. The guidelines shall be submitted to the appropriate policy committees of the Legislature prior to their adoption.

(b) The Director of Emergency Services is authorized to allocate and award funds to counties in which child abuser offender prosecution units are established or are proposed to be established in substantial compliance with the policies and criteria set forth below in Sections 999s, 999t, and 999u.

§ 999r

(c) The allocation and award of funds shall be made upon application executed by the county's district attorney and approved by its board of supervisors. Funds disbursed under this chapter shall not supplant local funds that would, in the absence of the California Child Abuser Prosecution Program, be made available to support the prosecution of child abuser felony cases. Local grant awards made under this program shall not be subject to review as specified in Section 14780 of the Government Code. *(Added by Stats.1985, c. 1097, § 1. Amended by Stats.2003, c. 229 (A.B.1757), § 7; Stats. 2010, c. 618 (A.B.2791), § 198; Stats.2013, c. 352 (A.B.1317), § 411, eff. Sept. 26, 2013, operative July 1, 2013.)*

Cross References

Felonies, definition and penalties, see Penal Code §§ 17, 18.
Words and phrases,
  County, see Penal Code § 691.
  Felony case, see Penal Code § 691.

§ 999s. Enhanced prosecution efforts and resources

Child abuser prosecution units receiving funds under this chapter shall concentrate enhanced prosecution efforts and resources upon individuals identified under selection criteria set forth in Section 999t. Enhanced prosecution efforts and resources shall include, but not be limited to:

(a) Vertical prosecutorial representation, whereby the prosecutor who, or prosecution unit which, makes the initial filing or appearance in a case performs all subsequent court appearances on that particular case through its conclusion, including the sentencing phase.

(b) The assignment of highly qualified investigators and prosecutors to child abuser cases. "Highly qualified" for the purposes of this chapter means: (1) individuals with one year of experience in the investigation and prosecution of felonies or specifically the felonies listed in subdivision (a) of Section 999*l* or 999t; or (2) individuals whom the district attorney has selected to receive training as set forth in Section 13836; or (3) individuals who have attended a program providing equivalent training as approved by the Office of Emergency Services.

(c) A significant reduction of caseloads for investigators and prosecutors assigned to child abuser cases.

(d) Coordination with local rape victim counseling centers, child abuse services programs, and victim witness assistance programs. That coordination shall include, but not be limited to: referrals of individuals to receive client services; participation in local training programs; membership and participation in local task forces established to improve communication between criminal justice system agencies and community service agencies; and cooperating with individuals serving as liaison representatives of child abuse and child sexual abuse programs, local rape victim counseling centers and victim witness assistance programs. *(Added by Stats.1985, c. 1097, § 1. Amended by Stats.2003, c. 229 (A.B.1757), § 8; Stats.2010, c. 618 (A.B.2791), § 199; Stats.2013, c. 352 (A.B.1317), § 412, eff. Sept. 26, 2013, operative July 1, 2013.)*

Cross References

Felonies, definition and penalties, see Penal Code §§ 17, 18.

§ 999t. Subjects of child abuser prosecution efforts; selection criteria; application of criteria; considerations in exercising prosecutorial discretion

(a) An individual may be the subject of a child abuser prosecution effort who is under arrest for the sexual assault of a child, as defined in Section 11165, or a violation of subdivision (a) or (b) of Section 273a, or a violation of Section 273ab, or 273d, or a violation of Section 288.2 when committed in conjunction with any other violation listed in this subdivision.

(b) In applying the child abuser selection criteria set forth above: (1) a district attorney may elect to limit child abuser prosecution efforts to persons arrested for any one or more of the offenses described in subdivision (a) if crime statistics demonstrate that the incidence of such one or more offenses presents a particularly serious problem in the county; (2) a district attorney shall not reject cases for filing exclusively on the basis that there is a family or personal relationship between the victim and the alleged offender.

(c) In exercising the prosecutorial discretion granted by Section 999v, the district attorney shall consider the character, the background, and the prior criminal background of the defendant. *(Added by Stats.1985, c. 1097, § 1. Amended by Stats.1993, c. 589, § 118; Stats.2001, c. 210 (A.B.929), § 1.)*

Cross References

Arrest defined, see Penal Code § 834.
Words and phrases, "county", see Penal Code § 691.

§ 999u. Policies for child abuser cases

Each district attorney's office establishing a child abuser prosecution unit and receiving state support under this chapter shall adopt and pursue the following policies for child abuser cases:

(a) Except as provided in subdivision (b), all reasonable prosecutorial efforts will be made to resist the pretrial release of a charged defendant meeting child abuser selection criteria.

(b) Nothing in this chapter shall be construed to limit the application of diversion programs authorized by law. All reasonable efforts shall be made to utilize diversion alternatives in appropriate cases.

(c) All reasonable prosecutorial efforts will be made to reduce the time between arrest and disposition of charge against an individual meeting child abuser criteria. *(Added by Stats.1985, c. 1097, § 1.)*

Cross References

Arrest defined, see Penal Code § 834.

§ 999v. Departure from selection criteria under extraordinary circumstances; quarterly reports

(a) The selection criteria set forth in Section 999t shall be adhered to for each child abuser case unless, in the reasonable exercise of prosecutor's discretion, extraordinary circumstances require departure from those policies in order to promote the general purposes and intent of this chapter.

(b) Each district attorney's office establishing a child abuser prosecution unit and receiving state support under this chapter shall submit the following information, on a quarterly basis, to the Office of Emergency Services:

(1) The number of child abuser cases referred to the district attorney's office for possible filing.

(2) The number of child abuser cases filed for felony prosecution.

(3) The number of sexual assault cases taken to trial.

(4) The number of child abuser cases tried which resulted in conviction. *(Added by Stats.1985, c. 1097, § 1. Amended by Stats.2003, c. 229 (A.B.1757), § 9; Stats.2010, c. 618 (A.B.2791), § 200; Stats.2013, c. 352 (A.B.1317), § 413, eff. Sept. 26, 2013, operative July 1, 2013.)*

Cross References

Felonies, definition and penalties, see Penal Code §§ 17, 18.

§ 999w. Characterization of defendant as "child abuser"; communication to trier of fact prohibited

The characterization of a defendant as a "child abuser" as defined by this chapter shall not be communicated to the trier of fact. *(Added by Stats.1985, c. 1097, § 1.)*

§ 999x. Use of federal funds

The Office of Emergency Services is encouraged to utilize any federal funds which may become available in order to implement the provisions of this chapter. *(Added by Stats.1985, c. 1097, § 1. Amended by Stats.2003, c. 229 (A.B.1757), § 10; Stats.2010, c. 618 (A.B.2791), § 201; Stats.2013, c. 352 (A.B.1317), § 414, eff. Sept. 26, 2013, operative July 1, 2013.)*

§ 999y. Annual report to Legislature; evaluation of the Child Abuser Prosecution Program; outcome measures

The Office of Emergency Services shall report annually to the Legislature concerning the program established by this chapter. The office shall prepare and submit to the Legislature on or before December 15, 2002, and within six months of the completion of subsequent funding cycles for this program, an evaluation of the Child Abuser Prosecution Program. This evaluation shall identify outcome measures to determine the effectiveness of the programs established under this chapter, which shall include, but not be limited to, both of the following, to the extent that data is available:

(a) Child abuse conviction rates of Child Abuser Prosecution Program units compared to those of nonfunded counties.

(b) Quantification of the annual per capita costs of the Child Abuser Prosecution Program compared to the costs of prosecuting child abuse crimes in nonfunded counties. *(Added by Stats.1985, c. 1097, § 1. Amended by Stats.2001, c. 210 (A.B.929), § 2; Stats.2003, c. 229 (A.B.1757), § 11; Stats.2010, c. 618 (A.B.2791), § 202; Stats.2013, c. 352 (A.B.1317), § 415, eff. Sept. 26, 2013, operative July 1, 2013.)*

Cross References

Words and phrases, "county", see Penal Code § 691.

CHAPTER 2.65. CHILD ABUSE AND NEGLECT COUNSELING

Section

1000.12. Legislative intent; referral to counseling or psychological treatment in lieu of prosecution; deferral of judgment in lieu of trial; dismissal of charges; eligibility standards.

1000.17. Administrative cost of referral and expense of counseling; payment.

§ 1000.12. Legislative intent; referral to counseling or psychological treatment in lieu of prosecution; deferral of judgment in lieu of trial; dismissal of charges; eligibility standards

(a) It is the intent of the Legislature that nothing in this chapter deprive a prosecuting attorney of the ability to prosecute any person who is suspected of committing any crime in which a minor is a victim of an act of physical abuse or neglect to the fullest extent of the law, if the prosecuting attorney so chooses.

(b) In lieu of prosecuting a person suspected of committing any crime, involving a minor victim, of an act of physical abuse or neglect, the prosecuting attorney may refer that person to the county department in charge of public social services or the probation department for counseling or psychological treatment and such other services as the department deems necessary. The prosecuting attorney shall seek the advice of the county department in charge of public social services or the probation department in determining whether or not to make the referral.

(c) This section shall not apply to any person who is charged with sexual abuse or molestation of a minor victim, or any sexual offense involving force, violence, duress, menace, or fear of immediate and unlawful bodily injury on the minor victim or another person. *(Added by Stats.1983, c. 804, § 2. Amended by Stats.1985, c. 1262,*

§ 1; Stats.1993–94, 1st Ex.Sess., c. 49 (S.B.38), § 1; Stats.1995, c. 935 (S.B.816), § 3; Stats.2005, c. 477 (S.B.33), § 3.)

Cross References

Child abuse reporting, see Penal Code § 11165 et seq.
Cruelty to children, see Penal Code §§ 273a, 273d.
Words and phrases,
   County, see Penal Code § 691.
   Prosecuting attorney, see Penal Code § 691.

§ 1000.17. Administrative cost of referral and expense of counseling; payment

If the person is referred pursuant to this chapter he or she shall be responsible for paying the administrative cost of the referral and the expense of such counseling as determined by the county department responsible for public social services or the probation department. The administrative cost of the referral shall not exceed one hundred dollars ($100) for any person referred pursuant to this chapter for an offense punishable as a felony and shall not exceed fifty dollars ($50) for any person referred pursuant to the chapter for an offense punishable as a misdemeanor. The department shall take into consideration the ability of the referred party to pay and no such person shall be denied counseling services because of his or her inability to pay. *(Added by Stats.1983, c. 804, § 2.)*

Cross References

Felony, classification and punishment, see Penal Code §§ 17, 18.
Misdemeanors, definition and penalties, see Penal Code §§ 17, 19 and 19.2.
Words and phrases,
   County, see Penal Code § 691.
   Misdemeanor, see Penal Code § 691.

CHAPTER 2.9E. PRIMARY CAREGIVER DIVERSION

Section

1001.83. Pretrial diversion program for primary caregivers; contents of program; requirements to take part in program; reports of progress; reinstatement of criminal proceedings if unsatisfactory progress or conviction of other crime; dismissal of criminal charges and sealing of arrest record upon successful completion of diversion.

§ 1001.83. Pretrial diversion program for primary caregivers; contents of program; requirements to take part in program; reports of progress; reinstatement of criminal proceedings if unsatisfactory progress or conviction of other crime; dismissal of criminal charges and sealing of arrest record upon successful completion of diversion

(a) The presiding judge of the superior court, or a judge designated by the presiding judge, in consultation with the presiding juvenile court judge and criminal court judges, and together with the prosecuting entity and the public defender or the contracted criminal defense office that provides the services of a public defender, may agree in writing to establish and conduct a pretrial diversion program for primary caregivers, pursuant to the provisions of this chapter, wherein criminal proceedings are suspended without a plea of guilty for a period of not less than 6 months and not more than 24 months. If the defendant is also participating in juvenile court proceedings, the juvenile and criminal courts shall not duplicate efforts.

(b) The program described in this section may include, but not be limited to, all of the following components:

(1) Parenting classes.

(2) Family and individual counseling.

(3) Mental health screening, education, and treatment.

(4) Family case management services.

(5) Drug and alcohol treatment.

§ 1001.83

(6) Domestic violence education and prevention.

(7) Physical and sexual abuse counseling.

(8) Anger management.

(9) Vocational and educational services.

(10) Job training and placement.

(11) Affordable and safe housing assistance.

(12) Financial literacy courses.

(c) The defendant may be referred to supportive services and classes in already existing diversion programs and county outpatient services. Before approving a proposed treatment program, the court shall consider the request of the defense, the request of the prosecution, the needs of the defendant and the dependent child or children, and the interests of the community. The programming may be procured using public or private funds. A referral may be made to a county agency, existing collaborative court, or assisted outpatient treatment or services, if the entity agrees to provide the required programming.

(d) On an accusatory pleading alleging the commission of a misdemeanor or felony offense, the court may, after considering the positions of the defense and prosecution, grant pretrial diversion to a defendant pursuant to this section if the defendant meets all of the following requirements:

(1) The defendant is a custodial parent or legal guardian of a minor child under 18 years of age, presently resides in the same household as that child, presently provides care or financial support for that minor child either alone or with the assistance of other household members, and the defendant's absence in the child's life would be detrimental to the child.

(2) The defendant has been advised of and waived the right to a speedy trial and a speedy preliminary hearing.

(3) The defendant has been informed of and agrees to comply with the requirements of the program.

(4) The court is satisfied that the defendant will not pose an unreasonable risk of danger to public safety, as defined in Section 1170.18, or to the minor child in their custody, if allowed to remain in the community. The court may consider the positions of the prosecuting entity and defense counsel, the defendant's violence and criminal history, the recency of the defendant's criminal history, the defendant's history of behavior towards minors, the risk of the dependent minor's exposure to or involvement in criminal activity, the current charged offense, child welfare history involving the defendant, and any other factors that the court deems appropriate.

(5) The defendant is not being placed into a diversion program, pursuant to this section, for any serious felony as described in Section 1192.7 or 1192.8 or violent felony as described in subdivision (c) of Section 667.5.

(6) The defendant is not being placed into a diversion program pursuant to this section for a crime alleged to have been committed against a person for whom the defendant is the primary caregiver.

(e) The provider of the pretrial diversion services in which the defendant has been placed shall provide regular reports to the court, the defense, and the prosecutor on the defendant's progress in the programming.

(f)(1) If it appears to the prosecuting attorney, the court, pretrial services, or the probation department that the defendant is performing unsatisfactorily in the assigned program, or if the defendant is, subsequent to entering the program, convicted of a felony or any offense that reflects a propensity for violence, the prosecuting attorney or the probation department may make a motion to reinstate criminal proceedings. The court may also reinstate criminal proceedings on its own motion.

(2) After notice to the defendant, the court shall hold a hearing to determine whether to reinstate criminal proceedings.

(3) If the court finds that the defendant is not performing satisfactorily in the assigned program, or the court finds that the defendant has been convicted of a crime as indicated in paragraph (1), the court may end the diversion program and order the resumption of criminal proceedings.

(g) If the defendant has performed satisfactorily in diversion, at the end of the period of diversion, the court shall dismiss the defendant's criminal charges that were the subject of the criminal proceedings at the time of the initial diversion. A court may conclude that the defendant has performed satisfactorily if the defendant has substantially complied with the requirements of diversion, and has avoided significant new violations of law. If the court dismisses the charges, the clerk of the court shall file a record with the Department of Justice indicating the disposition of the case diverted pursuant to this section. Upon successful completion of diversion, if the court dismisses the charges, the arrest upon which the diversion was based shall be deemed never to have occurred, and the court shall order access to the record of the arrest restricted in accordance with Section 1001.9, except as specified in subdivision (i). The defendant who successfully completes diversion may indicate in response to any question concerning the defendant's prior criminal record that they were not arrested or diverted for the offense, except as specified in subdivision (i).

(h) A record pertaining to an arrest resulting in successful completion of diversion, or any record generated as a result of the defendant's application for or participation in diversion, shall not, without the defendant's consent, be used in any way that could result in the denial of any employment, benefit, license, or certificate.

(i) The defendant shall be advised that, regardless of the defendant's completion of diversion, both of the following apply:

(1) The arrest upon which the diversion was based may be disclosed by the Department of Justice to any peace officer application request and that, notwithstanding subdivision (h), this section does not relieve the defendant of the obligation to disclose the arrest in response to any direct question contained in any questionnaire or application for a position as a peace officer, as defined in Section 830.

(2) An order to seal records pertaining to an arrest made pursuant to this section has no effect on a criminal justice agency's ability to access and use those sealed records and information regarding sealed arrests, as described in Section 851.92. *(Added by Stats.2019, c. 593 (S.B.394), § 1, eff. Jan. 1, 2020.)*

Title 12

OF SPECIAL PROCEEDINGS OF A CRIMINAL NATURE

CHAPTER 1. OF THE WRIT OF HABEAS CORPUS

Section
1473.5. Circumstances under which writ of habeas corpus may be prosecuted relating to evidence of intimate partner battering and its effects; limitation to violent felonies; expert testimony; grounds for denial; legislative intent.

Cross References

Actions for damages against defendant arising from felony offense, limitation of actions, stay of judgment, restitution, see Code of Civil Procedure § 340.3.

§ 1473.5. Circumstances under which writ of habeas corpus may be prosecuted relating to evidence of intimate partner battering and its effects; limitation to violent felonies; expert testimony; grounds for denial; legislative intent

(a) A writ of habeas corpus also may be prosecuted on the basis that competent and substantial expert testimony relating to intimate partner battering and its effects, within the meaning of Section 1107 of the Evidence Code, was not presented to the trier of fact at the trial court proceedings and is of such substance that, had the competent and substantial expert testimony been presented, there is a reasonable probability, sufficient to undermine confidence in the judgment of conviction or sentence, that the result of the proceedings would have been different. Sections 1260 to 1262, inclusive, apply to the prosecution of a writ of habeas corpus pursuant to this section. As used in this section, "trial court proceedings" means those court proceedings that occur from the time the accusatory pleading is filed until and including judgment and sentence.

(b) This section is limited to violent felonies as specified in subdivision (c) of Section 667.5 that were committed before August 29, 1996, and that resulted in judgments of conviction or sentence after a plea or trial as to which expert testimony admissible pursuant to Section 1107 of the Evidence Code may be probative on the issue of culpability.

(c) A showing that expert testimony relating to intimate partner battering and its effects was presented to the trier of fact is not a bar to granting a petition under this section if that expert testimony was not competent or substantial. The burden of proof is on the petitioner to establish a sufficient showing that competent and substantial expert testimony, of a nature which would be competent using prevailing understanding of intimate partner battering and its effects, was not presented to the trier of fact, and had that evidence been presented, there is a reasonable probability that the result of the proceedings would have been different.

(d) If a petitioner for habeas corpus under this section has previously filed a petition for writ of habeas corpus, it is grounds for denial of the new petition if a court determined on the merits in the prior petition that the omission of expert testimony relating to battered women's syndrome or intimate partner battering and its effects at trial was not prejudicial and did not entitle the petitioner to the writ of habeas corpus.

(e) For purposes of this section, the changes that become effective on January 1, 2005, are not intended to expand the uses or applicability of expert testimony on battering and its effects that were in effect immediately prior to that date in criminal cases. (Added by Stats.2001, c. 858 (S.B.799), § 1. Amended by Stats.2003, c. 136 (S.B.784), § 1; Stats.2004, c. 609 (S.B.1385), § 2; Stats.2008, c. 146 (A.B.2306), § 1; Stats.2012, c. 803 (A.B.593), § 1.)

Cross References

Accusatory pleading defined for purposes of this Part, see Penal Code § 691.
Felonies, definition and penalties, see Penal Code §§ 17, 18.

Part 4
PREVENTION OF CRIMES AND APPREHENSION OF CRIMINALS

Title 5
LAW ENFORCEMENT RESPONSE TO DOMESTIC VIOLENCE

Cross References

License plates, application for new and different plates by domestic violence victims, conditions for issuance, see Vehicle Code § 4467.

CHAPTER 1. GENERAL PROVISIONS

Section
13700. Definitions.
13701. Written policies and standards; development, adoption, and implementation; availability to public; consultations with experts.
13702. Written policies and standards for dispatchers' response to domestic calls.

§ 13700. Definitions

As used in this title:

(a) "Abuse" means intentionally or recklessly causing or attempting to cause bodily injury, or placing another person in reasonable apprehension of imminent serious bodily injury to himself or herself, or another.

(b) "Domestic violence" means abuse committed against an adult or a minor who is a spouse, former spouse, cohabitant, former cohabitant, or person with whom the suspect has had a child or is having or has had a dating or engagement relationship. For purposes of this subdivision, "cohabitant" means two unrelated adult persons living together for a substantial period of time, resulting in some permanency of relationship. Factors that may determine whether persons are cohabiting include, but are not limited to, (1) sexual relations between the parties while sharing the same living quarters, (2) sharing of income or expenses, (3) joint use or ownership of property, (4) whether the parties hold themselves out as spouses, (5) the continuity of the relationship, and (6) the length of the relationship.

(c) "Officer" means any officer or employee of a local police department or sheriff's office, and any peace officer of the Department of the California Highway Patrol, the Department of Parks and Recreation, the University of California Police Department, or the California State University and College Police Departments, as defined in Section 830.2, a peace officer of the Department of General Services of the City of Los Angeles, as defined in subdivision (c) of Section 830.31, a housing authority patrol officer, as defined in subdivision (d) of Section 830.31, a peace officer as defined in subdivisions (a) and (b) of Section 830.32, or a peace officer as defined in subdivision (a) of Section 830.33.

(d) "Victim" means a person who is a victim of domestic violence. (Added by Stats.1984, c. 1609, § 3. Amended by Stats.1992, c. 1136 (S.B.1541), § 9; Stats.1993, c. 1229 (A.B.224), § 3; Stats.1993, c. 1230 (A.B.2250), § 1.5; Gov.Reorg.Plan No. 1 of 1995, § 57, eff. July 12, 1995; Stats.1996, c. 305 (A.B.3103), § 58; Stats.1999, c. 659 (S.B.355), § 5; Stats.2002, c. 534 (A.B.2826), § 2; Stats.2004, c. 250 (S.B.1391), § 3; Stats.2014, c. 559 (S.B.1154), § 2, eff. Jan. 1, 2015; Stats.2016, c. 50 (S.B.1005), § 75, eff. Jan. 1, 2017.)

Cross References

Additional and consecutive terms, enhancement for infliction of great bodily injury in instances involving domestic violence, see Penal Code § 12022.7.
Authority to compromise misdemeanors for which victim has civil action, see Penal Code § 1377.
Criminal history, use when setting bond or considering plea agreement, see Penal Code § 273.75.
Criminal proceedings, child witnesses, precautions, see Penal Code § 868.8.
Department of General Services, generally, see Government Code § 14600 et seq.

§ 13700

Domestic violence, liability for tort of, see Civil Code § 1708.6.
Domestic violence protective orders, requirement to relinquish firearms, see Penal Code § 136.2.
Evidence of defendant's other acts of domestic violence, see Evidence Code § 1109.
Offer of diversion to misdemeanor defendant, charged offenses not eligible for diversion, see Penal Code § 1001.95.
Physicians or surgeons reporting duties, contents of medical records, referral to domestic violence services, see Penal Code § 11161.
Prosecution of spousal abusers, see Penal Code § 273.83.
Public housing authority, access to criminal history for convictions under this section, see Penal Code § 11105.03.
Rights of victims and witnesses, domestic violence or abuse counselors, presence at law enforcement interviews, see Penal Code § 679.05.
Senior and Disability Justice Act, see Penal Code § 368.6.

Research References

Forms

West's California Code Forms, Civil § 1708.6 Form 1, Complaint—Domestic Violence.

§ 13701. Written policies and standards; development, adoption, and implementation; availability to public; consultations with experts

(a) Every law enforcement agency in this state shall develop, adopt, and implement written policies and standards for officers' responses to domestic violence calls by January 1, 1986. These policies shall reflect that domestic violence is alleged criminal conduct. Further, they shall reflect existing policy that a request for assistance in a situation involving domestic violence is the same as any other request for assistance where violence has occurred.

(b) The written policies shall encourage the arrest of domestic violence offenders if there is probable cause that an offense has been committed. These policies also shall require the arrest of an offender, absent exigent circumstances, if there is probable cause that a protective order issued under Chapter 4 (commencing with Section 2040) of Part 1 of Division 6, Division 10 (commencing with Section 6200), or Chapter 6 (commencing with Section 7700) of Part 3 of Division 12, of the Family Code, or Section 136.2 of this code, or by a court of any other state, a commonwealth, territory, or insular possession subject to the jurisdiction of the United States, a military tribunal, or a tribe has been violated. These policies shall discourage, when appropriate, but not prohibit, dual arrests. Peace officers shall make reasonable efforts to identify the dominant aggressor in any incident. The dominant aggressor is the person determined to be the most significant, rather than the first, aggressor. In identifying the dominant aggressor, an officer shall consider the intent of the law to protect victims of domestic violence from continuing abuse, the threats creating fear of physical injury, the history of domestic violence between the persons involved, and whether either person acted in self-defense. Notwithstanding subdivision (d), law enforcement agencies shall develop these policies with the input of local domestic violence agencies.

(c) These existing local policies and those developed shall be in writing and shall be available to the public upon request and shall include specific standards for the following:

(1) Felony arrests.

(2) Misdemeanor arrests.

(3) Use of citizen arrests.

(4) Verification and enforcement of temporary restraining orders when (A) the suspect is present and (B) the suspect has fled.

(5) Verification and enforcement of stay-away orders.

(6) Cite and release policies.

(7) Emergency assistance to victims, such as medical care, transportation to a shelter or to a hospital for treatment when necessary, and police standbys for removing personal property and assistance in safe passage out of the victim's residence.

(8) Assisting victims in pursuing criminal options, such as giving the victim the report number and directing the victim to the proper investigation unit.

(9) Furnishing written notice to victims at the scene, including, but not limited to, all of the following information:

(A) A statement informing the victim that despite official restraint of the person alleged to have committed domestic violence, the restrained person may be released at any time.

(B) A statement that, "For further information about a shelter you may contact _____."

(C) A statement that, "For information about other services in the community, where available, you may contact _____."

(D) A statement that, "For information about the California Victims' Compensation Program, you may contact 1–800–777–9229."

(E) A statement informing the victim of domestic violence that the victim may ask the district attorney to file a criminal complaint.

(F) A statement informing the victim of the right to go to the superior court and file a petition requesting any of the following orders for relief:

(i) An order restraining the attacker from abusing the victim and other family members.

(ii) An order directing the attacker to leave the household.

(iii) An order preventing the attacker from entering the residence, school, business, or place of employment of the victim.

(iv) An order awarding the victim or the other parent custody of or visitation with a minor child or children.

(v) An order restraining the attacker from molesting or interfering with minor children in the custody of the victim.

(vi) An order directing the party not granted custody to pay support of minor children, if that party has a legal obligation to do so.

(vii) An order directing the defendant to make specified debit payments coming due while the order is in effect.

(viii) An order directing that either or both parties participate in counseling.

(G) A statement informing the victim of the right to file a civil suit for losses suffered as a result of the abuse, including medical expenses, loss of earnings, and other expenses for injuries sustained and damage to property, and any other related expenses incurred by the victim or any agency that shelters the victim.

(H) In the case of an alleged violation of subdivision (e) of Section 243 or Section 261, 261.5, 273.5, 286, 287, or 289, or former Section 262 or 288a, a "Victims of Domestic Violence" card which shall include, but is not limited to, the following information:

(i) The names and phone numbers of or local county hotlines for, or both the phone numbers of and local county hotlines for, local shelters for victims of domestic violence and rape victim counseling centers within the county, including those centers specified in Section 13837, and their 24-hour counseling service telephone numbers.

(ii) A simple statement on the proper procedures for a victim to follow after a sexual assault.

(iii) A statement that sexual assault by a person who is known to the victim, including sexual assault by a person who is the spouse of the victim, is a crime.

(iv) A statement that domestic violence or assault by a person who is known to the victim, including domestic violence or assault by a person who is the spouse of the victim, is a crime.

(I) A statement informing the victim that strangulation may cause internal injuries and encouraging the victim to seek medical attention.

(10) Writing of reports.

(d) In the development of these policies and standards, each local department is encouraged to consult with domestic violence experts, such as the staff of the local shelter for victims of domestic violence and their children. Departments may use the response guidelines developed by the commission in developing local policies. *(Added by Stats.1984, c. 1609, § 3. Amended by Stats.1985, c. 668, § 1; Stats.1990, c. 1692 (A.B.4237), § 3; Stats.1991, c. 999 (S.B.835), § 2; Stats.1995, c. 246 (S.B.591), § 4; Stats.1998, c. 698 (A.B.1201), § 2; Stats.1998, c. 701 (A.B.2172), § 2; Stats.1998, c. 702 (A.B.2177), § 3.3; Stats.1999, c. 661 (A.B.825), § 11; Stats.2000, c. 1001 (S.B.1944), § 5; Stats.2013, c. 28 (S.B.71), § 47, eff. June 27, 2013; Stats.2013, c. 161 (A.B.81), § 1, eff. Aug. 27, 2013; Stats.2014, c. 71 (S.B.1304), § 133, eff. Jan. 1, 2015; Stats.2017, c. 331 (S.B.40), § 1, eff. Jan. 1, 2018; Stats.2018, c. 423 (S.B.1494), § 119, eff. Jan. 1, 2019; Stats.2021, c. 626 (A.B.1171), § 68, eff. Jan. 1, 2022.)*

Cross References

Abuse defined for purposes of this Title, see Penal Code § 13700.
Counseling information for sexual assault victims, see Penal Code § 264.2.
Domestic violence defined for purposes of this Title, see Penal Code § 13700.
Felonies, definition and penalties, see Penal Code §§ 17, 18.
Misdemeanors, definition and penalties, see Penal Code §§ 17, 19, 19.2.
Officer defined for purposes of this Title, see Penal Code § 13700.
Victim defined for purposes of this Title, see Penal Code § 13700.

§ 13702. Written policies and standards for dispatchers' response to domestic calls

Every law enforcement agency in this state shall develop, adopt, and implement written policies and standards for dispatchers' response to domestic violence calls by July 1, 1991. These policies shall reflect that calls reporting threatened, imminent, or ongoing domestic violence, and the violation of any protection order, including orders issued pursuant to Section 136.2, and restraining orders, shall be ranked among the highest priority calls. Dispatchers are not required to verify the validity of the protective order before responding to the request for assistance. *(Added by Stats.1990, c. 1692 (A.B.4237) § 4.)*

Cross References

Domestic violence defined for purposes of this Title, see Penal Code § 13700.

CHAPTER 2. RESTRAINING ORDERS

Section
13710. Record of orders; enforceability of terms and conditions; service to party to be restrained.
13711. Protection order; application for or issuance; pamphlet to person to be protected; contents.

§ 13710. Record of orders; enforceability of terms and conditions; service to party to be restrained

(a)(1) Law enforcement agencies shall maintain a complete and systematic record of all protection orders with respect to domestic violence incidents, including orders which have not yet been served, issued pursuant to Section 136.2, restraining orders, and proofs of service in effect. This shall be used to inform law enforcement officers responding to domestic violence calls of the existence, terms, and effective dates of protection orders in effect.

(2) The police department of a community college or school district described in subdivision (a) or (b) of Section 830.32 shall notify the sheriff or police chief of the city in whose jurisdiction the department is located of any protection order served by the department pursuant to this section.

(b) The terms and conditions of the protection order remain enforceable, notwithstanding the acts of the parties, and may be changed only by order of the court.

(c) Upon request, law enforcement agencies shall serve the party to be restrained at the scene of a domestic violence incident or at any time the party is in custody. *(Added by Stats.1984, c. 1609, § 3. Amended by Stats.1986, c. 1183, § 2, eff. Sept. 26, 1986; Stats.1990, c. 1692 (A.B.4237), § 5; Stats.1999, c. 659 (S.B.355), § 6; Stats.2013, c. 28 (S.B.71), § 48, eff. June 27, 2013; Stats.2013, c. 161 (A.B.81), § 2, eff. Aug. 27, 2013.)*

Cross References

Domestic violence defined for purposes of this Title, see Penal Code § 13700.
Officer defined for purposes of this Title, see Penal Code § 13700.

§ 13711. Protection order; application for or issuance; pamphlet to person to be protected; contents

Whenever a protection order with respect to domestic violence incidents, including orders issued pursuant to Section 136.2 and restraining orders, is applied for or issued, it shall be the responsibility of the clerk of the superior court to distribute a pamphlet to the person who is to be protected by the order that includes the following:

(a) Information as specified in subdivision (i) of Section 13701.

(b) Notice that it is the responsibility of the victim to request notification of an inmate's release.

(c) Notice that the terms and conditions of the protection order remain enforceable, notwithstanding any acts of the parties, and may be changed only by order of the court.

(d) Notice that the protection order is enforceable in any state, in a commonwealth, territory, or insular possession subject to the jurisdiction of the United States, or on a reservation, and general information about agencies in other jurisdictions that may be contacted regarding enforcement of a protective order issued by a court of this state. *(Added by Stats.1990, c. 1692 (A.B.4237) § 6. Amended by Stats.1998, c. 702 (A.B.2177), § 4; Stats.1999, c. 661 (A.B.825), § 12.)*

Cross References

Domestic violence defined for purposes of this Title, see Penal Code § 13700.
Victim defined for purposes of this Title, see Penal Code § 13700.

CHAPTER 4. DATA COLLECTION

Section
13730. Recordation system for domestic violence calls; annual report; incident report form.
13731. Domestic violence data regional clearinghouse; San Diego Association of Governments.
13732. Legislative findings and declarations regarding the connection between domestic violence and child abuse.

§ 13730. Recordation system for domestic violence calls; annual report; incident report form

(a) Each law enforcement agency shall develop a system, by January 1, 1986, for recording all domestic violence-related calls for assistance made to the department, including whether weapons are involved, or whether the incident involved strangulation or suffocation. All domestic violence-related calls for assistance shall be supported with a written incident report, as described in subdivision (c), identifying the domestic violence incident. Monthly, the total number of domestic violence calls received and the numbers of those cases involving weapons or strangulation or suffocation shall be compiled by each law enforcement agency and submitted to the Attorney General.

(b) The Attorney General shall report annually to the Governor, the Legislature, and the public the total number of domestic violence-related calls received by California law enforcement agencies, the number of cases involving weapons, the number of cases involving strangulation or suffocation, and a breakdown of calls received by agency, city, and county.

(c) Each law enforcement agency shall develop an incident report form that includes a domestic violence identification code by January 1, 1986. In all incidents of domestic violence, a report shall be written and shall be identified on the face of the report as a domestic violence incident. The report shall include at least all of the following:

(1) A notation of whether the officer or officers who responded to the domestic violence call observed any signs that the alleged abuser was under the influence of alcohol or a controlled substance.

(2) A notation of whether the officer or officers who responded to the domestic violence call determined if any law enforcement agency had previously responded to a domestic violence call at the same address involving the same alleged abuser or victim.

(3) A notation of whether the officer or officers who responded to the domestic violence call found it necessary, for the protection of the peace officer or other persons present, to inquire of the victim, the alleged abuser, or both, whether a firearm or other deadly weapon was present at the location, and, if there is an inquiry, whether that inquiry disclosed the presence of a firearm or other deadly weapon. Any firearm or other deadly weapon discovered by an officer at the scene of a domestic violence incident shall be subject to confiscation pursuant to Division 4 (commencing with Section 18250) of Title 2 of Part 6.

(4) A notation of whether there were indications that the incident involved strangulation or suffocation. This includes whether any witness or victim reported any incident of strangulation or suffocation, whether any victim reported symptoms of strangulation or suffocation, or whether the officer observed any signs of strangulation or suffocation. *(Added by Stats.1984, c. 1609, § 3. Amended by Stats.1993, c. 1230 (A.B.2250), § 2; Stats.1995, c. 965 (S.B.132), § 2; Stats.2001, c. 483 (A.B.469), § 1; Stats.2010, c. 178 (S.B.1115), § 94, operative Jan. 1, 2012; Stats.2013, c. 28 (S.B.71), § 49, eff. June 27, 2013; Stats.2013, c. 161 (A.B.81), § 3, eff. Aug. 27, 2013; Stats.2017, c. 331 (S.B.40), § 2, eff. Jan. 1, 2018.)*

Cross References

Attorney General, generally, see Government Code § 12500 et seq.
Domestic violence defined for purposes of this Title, see Penal Code § 13700.
Officer defined for purposes of this Title, see Penal Code § 13700.
Protective orders and other domestic violence prevention orders, registration and enforcement of orders, generally, see Family Code § 6380 et seq.
Victim defined for purposes of this Title, see Penal Code § 13700.

§ 13731. Domestic violence data regional clearinghouse; San Diego Association of Governments

(a) The San Diego Association of Governments may serve as the regional clearinghouse for criminal justice data involving domestic violence. The association may obtain monthly crime statistics from all law enforcement agencies in San Diego County. These law enforcement agencies may include their domestic violence supplements in the monthly crime reports that are supplied to the association. The association may obtain client-based data regarding clients or victims of domestic violence who seek protection in San Diego County shelters.

(b) Contingent upon the appropriation of funds therefor, the association shall do all of the following:

(1) Create a standardized, uniform intake form, to be referred to as a Compilation of Research and Evaluation Intake Instrument, also known as C.O.R.E., for use in San Diego County's domestic violence shelters. This form shall be completed and ready to use in the field for data collection purposes not later than March 31, 1997. The C.O.R.E. intake form shall be standardized to compile the same information from all clients for all shelters.

(2) Collect and analyze the standardized, uniform intake form in order to compile information including, but not limited to, victim sociodemographic characteristics, descriptions of domestic violence incidents pertaining to each victim and services needed by domestic violence shelter clients within San Diego County.

(3) Use the collected client-based data to describe the nature and scope of violence from the perspective of domestic violence shelter clients and to determine the service needs of clients and what gaps in service delivery exist, so that resources can be appropriately targeted and allocated. All data supplied to the association shall be stripped of any information regarding the personal identity of an individual to protect the privacy of domestic violence shelter clients.

(4) Establish an advisory committee in order to facilitate the research effort and to assess the value of the research project. The advisory committee shall consist of representation from the shelters, as well as members of the San Diego County Domestic Violence Council, local justice administrators, and the principal investigator. The advisory committee shall meet at least four times before April 30, 1999, to review the progress of the research, including research methodology, data collection instruments, preliminary analyses, and work product as they are drafted. Advisory committee members shall evaluate the final research product in terms of applicability and utility of findings and recommendations. *(Added by Stats.1996, c. 375 (A.B.2448), § 2. Amended by Stats.2001, c. 745 (S.B.1191), § 163, eff. Oct. 12, 2001.)*

Cross References

Victim defined for purposes of this Title, see Penal Code § 13700.

§ 13732. Legislative findings and declarations regarding the connection between domestic violence and child abuse

(a) The Legislature finds and declares that a substantial body of research demonstrates a strong connection between domestic violence and child abuse. However, despite this connection, child abuse and domestic violence services and agencies often fail to coordinate appropriately at the local level. It is the intent of the Legislature in enacting this section to improve preventative and supportive services to families experiencing violence in order to prevent further abuse of children and the victims of domestic violence. It is the further intent of this section that child protective services agencies develop a protocol which clearly sets forth the criteria for a child protective services response to a domestic violence related incident in a home in which a child resides.

(b) Commencing January 1, 2003, child protective services agencies, law enforcement, prosecution, child abuse and domestic violence experts, and community-based organizations serving abused children and victims of domestic violence shall develop, in collaboration with one another, protocols as to how law enforcement and child welfare agencies will cooperate in their response to incidents of domestic violence in homes in which a child resides. The requirements of this section shall not apply to counties where protocols consistent with this section already have been developed. *(Added by Stats.2002, c. 187 (S.B.1745), § 3.)*

Cross References

Abuse defined for purposes of this Title, see Penal Code § 13700.
Victim defined for purposes of this Title, see Penal Code § 13700.

Title 5.3

FAMILY JUSTICE CENTERS AND MULTIDISCIPLINARY TEAMS

CHAPTER 1. FAMILY JUSTICE CENTERS

Section
13750. Establishment of family justice centers; definitions.

Section
13751. Mandatory training programs.

§ 13750. Establishment of family justice centers; definitions

(a) A city, county, city and county, or community-based nonprofit organization may each establish a multiagency, multidisciplinary family justice center to assist victims of domestic violence, sexual assault, elder or dependent adult abuse, and human trafficking, to ensure that victims of abuse are able to access all needed services in one location in order to enhance victim safety, increase offender accountability, and improve access to services for victims of domestic violence, sexual assault, elder or dependent adult abuse, and human trafficking.

(b) For purposes of this title, the following terms have the following meanings:

(1) "Abuse" has the same meaning as set forth in Section 6203 of the Family Code.

(2) "Domestic violence" has the same meaning as set forth in Section 6211 of the Family Code.

(3) "Sexual assault" means an act or attempt made punishable by Section 220, 261, 261.5, 264.1, 266c, 269, 285, 286, 287, 288, 288.5, 289, or 647.6, or former Section 262 or 288a.

(4) "Elder or dependent adult abuse" means an act made punishable by Section 368.

(5) "Human trafficking" has the same meaning as set forth in Section 236.1.

(c) For purposes of this title, family justice centers shall be defined as multiagency, multidisciplinary service centers where public and private agencies assign staff members on a full-time or part-time basis in order to provide services to victims of domestic violence, sexual assault, elder or dependent adult abuse, or human trafficking from one location in order to reduce the number of times victims must tell their story, reduce the number of places victims must go for help, and increase access to services and support for victims and their children. Staff members at a family justice center may be comprised of, but are not limited to, the following:

(1) Law enforcement personnel.

(2) Medical personnel.

(3) District attorneys and city attorneys.

(4) Victim-witness program personnel.

(5) Domestic violence shelter service staff.

(6) Community-based rape crisis, domestic violence, and human trafficking advocates.

(7) Social service agency staff members.

(8) Child welfare agency social workers.

(9) County health department staff.

(10) City or county welfare and public assistance workers.

(11) Nonprofit agency counseling professionals.

(12) Civil legal service providers.

(13) Supervised volunteers from partner agencies.

(14) Other professionals providing services.

(d) This section does not abrogate existing laws regarding privacy or information sharing. Family justice center staff members shall comply with the laws governing their respective professions.

(e) Victims of crime shall not be denied services on the grounds of criminal history. A criminal history search shall not be conducted of a victim at a family justice center without the victim's written consent unless the criminal history search is pursuant to a criminal investigation.

(f) Victims of crime shall not be required to participate in the criminal justice system or cooperate with law enforcement in order to receive counseling, medical care, or other services at a family justice center.

(g)(1) Each family justice center shall consult with community-based domestic violence, sexual assault, elder or dependent adult abuse, and human trafficking agencies in partnership with survivors of violence and abuse and their advocates in the operations process of the family justice center, and shall establish procedures for the ongoing input, feedback, and evaluation of the family justice center by survivors of violence and abuse and community-based crime victim service providers and advocates.

(2) Each family justice center shall develop policies and procedures, in collaboration with local community-based crime victim service providers and local survivors of violence and abuse, to ensure coordinated services are provided to victims and to enhance the safety of victims and professionals at the family justice center who participate in affiliated survivor-centered support or advocacy groups. Each family justice center shall maintain a formal client feedback, complaint, and input process to address client concerns about services provided or the conduct of any family justice center professionals, agency partners, or volunteers providing services in the family justice center.

<u>(3) Each family justice center shall provide clients with educational materials relating to gun violence restraining orders, domestic violence restraining orders, and other legal avenues of protection for victims and their families, if appropriate.</u>

(h)(1) Each family justice center shall maintain a client consent policy and shall be in compliance with all state and federal laws protecting the confidentiality of the types of information and documents that may be in a victim's file, including, but not limited to, medical, legal, and victim counselor records. Each family justice center shall have a designated privacy officer to develop and oversee privacy policies and procedures consistent with state and federal privacy laws and the Fair Information Practice Principles promulgated by the United States Department of Homeland Security. At no time shall a victim be required to sign a client consent form to share information in order to access services.

(2) Each family justice center is required to obtain informed, written, reasonably time limited, consent from the victim before sharing information obtained from the victim with any staff member or agency partner, except as provided in paragraphs (3) and (4).

(3) A family justice center is not required to obtain consent from the victim before sharing information obtained from the victim with any staff member or agency partner if the person is a mandated reporter, a peace officer, or a member of the prosecution team and is required to report or disclose specific information or incidents. These persons shall inform the victim that they may share information obtained from the victim without the victim's consent.

(4) Each family justice center is required to inform the victim that information shared with staff members or partner agencies at a family justice center may be shared with law enforcement professionals without the victim's consent if there is a mandatory duty to report, or the client is a danger to themselves or others. Each family justice center shall obtain written acknowledgment that the victim has been informed of this policy.

(5) Consent by a victim for sharing information within a family justice center pursuant to this section shall not be construed as a universal waiver of any existing evidentiary privilege that makes confidential any communications or documents between the victim and any service provider, including, but not limited to, any lawyer, advocate, sexual assault or domestic violence counselor as defined in Section 1035.2 or 1037.1 of the Evidence Code, human trafficking caseworker as defined in Section 1038.2 of the Evidence Code, therapist, doctor, or nurse. Any oral or written communication or any document authorized by the victim to be shared for the purposes

of enhancing safety and providing more effective and efficient services to the victim of domestic violence, sexual assault, elder or dependent adult abuse, or human trafficking shall not be disclosed to any third party, unless that third-party disclosure is authorized by the victim, or required by other state or federal law or by court order.

(i) An individual staff member, volunteer, or agency that has victim information governed by this section shall not be required to disclose that information unless the victim has consented to the disclosure or it is otherwise required by other state or federal law or by court order.

(j) A disclosure of information consented to by the victim in a family justice center, made for the purposes of clinical assessment, risk assessment, safety planning, or service delivery, shall not be deemed a waiver of any privilege or confidentiality provision contained in Sections 2263, 2918, 4982, and 6068 of the Business and Professions Code, the lawyer-client privilege protected by Article 3 (commencing with Section 950) of Chapter 4 of Division 8 of the Evidence Code, the physician-patient privilege protected by Article 6 (commencing with Section 990) of Chapter 4 of Division 8 of the Evidence Code, the psychotherapist-patient privilege protected by Article 7 (commencing with Section 1010) of Chapter 4 of Division 8 of the Evidence Code, the sexual assault counselor-victim privilege protected by Article 8.5 (commencing with Section 1035) of Chapter 4 of Division 8 of the Evidence Code, or the domestic violence counselor-victim privilege protected by Article 8.7 (commencing with Section 1037) of Chapter 4 of Division 8 of the Evidence Code. *(Added by Stats.2014, c. 85 (A.B.1623), § 1, eff. Jan. 1, 2015. Amended by Stats.2018, c. 423 (S.B.1494), § 120, eff. Jan. 1, 2019; Stats.2021, c. 626 (A.B.1171), § 69, eff. Jan. 1, 2022; Stats.2022, c. 20 (A.B.2137), § 1, eff. Jan. 1, 2023.)*

§ 13751. Mandatory training programs

Each family justice center established pursuant to subdivision (a) of Section 13750 shall maintain a formal training program with mandatory training for all staff members, volunteers, and agency professionals of not less than eight hours per year on subjects, including, but not limited to, privileges and confidentiality, information sharing, risk assessment, safety planning, victim advocacy, and high-risk case response. *(Added by Stats.2014, c. 85 (A.B.1623), § 1, eff. Jan. 1, 2015.)*

CHAPTER 2. MULTIDISCIPLINARY TEAMS

Section
13752. Domestic violence multidisciplinary personnel team; provision of a broad range of services related to domestic violence; members; disclosure and exchange of information following report of suspected domestic violence; privacy and confidentiality rights.
13753. Human trafficking multidisciplinary personnel team; provision of a broad range of services related to human trafficking; members; disclosure and exchange of information following report of suspected human trafficking; privacy and confidentiality rights.

§ 13752. Domestic violence multidisciplinary personnel team; provision of a broad range of services related to domestic violence; members; disclosure and exchange of information following report of suspected domestic violence; privacy and confidentiality rights

(a) Notwithstanding any other law, a city, county, city and county, or community-based nonprofit organization may establish a domestic violence multidisciplinary personnel team consisting of two or more persons who are trained in the prevention, identification, management, or treatment of domestic violence cases and who are qualified to provide a broad range of services related to domestic violence.

(b) A domestic violence multidisciplinary team may include, but need not be limited to, any of the following:

(1) Law enforcement personnel.

(2) Medical personnel.

(3) Psychiatrists, psychologists, marriage and family therapists, or other trained counseling personnel.

(4) District attorneys and city attorneys.

(5) Victim–witness program personnel.

(6) Sexual assault counselors, as defined in Section 1035.2 of the Evidence Code.

(7) Domestic violence counselors, as defined in Section 1037.1 of the Evidence Code.

(8) Social service agency staff members.

(9) Child welfare agency social workers.

(10) County health department staff.

(11) City or county welfare and public assistance workers.

(12) Nonprofit agency counseling professionals.

(13) Civil legal service providers.

(14) Human trafficking caseworkers, as defined in Section 1038.2 of the Evidence Code.

(c)(1) Notwithstanding any other law, following a report of suspected domestic violence, members of a domestic violence multidisciplinary personnel team engaged in the prevention, identification, and treatment of domestic violence may disclose to and exchange with one another information and writings that relate to any incident of domestic violence that may also be designated as confidential under state law if the member of the team having that information or writing reasonably believes it is generally relevant to the prevention, identification, or treatment of domestic violence. Any discussion relative to the disclosure or exchange of the information or writings during a team meeting is confidential, and testimony concerning that discussion is not admissible in any criminal, civil, or juvenile court proceeding unless required by law.

(2) Disclosure and exchange of information pursuant to this section may occur telephonically or electronically if there is adequate verification of the identity of the domestic violence multidisciplinary personnel who are involved in that disclosure or exchange of information.

(3) Disclosure and exchange of information pursuant to this section shall not be made to anyone other than members of the domestic violence multidisciplinary personnel team and those qualified to receive information as set forth in subdivision (d).

(d) The domestic violence multidisciplinary personnel team may designate persons qualified pursuant to subdivision (b) to be a member of the team for a particular case. A person designated as a team member pursuant to this subdivision may receive and disclose relevant information and records, subject to the confidentiality provisions of subdivision (g).

(e)(1) The sharing of information permitted under subdivision (c) shall be governed by protocols developed in each county describing how and what information may be shared by the domestic violence multidisciplinary team to ensure that confidential information gathered by the team is not disclosed in violation of state or federal law. A copy of the protocols shall be distributed to each participating agency and to persons in those agencies who participate in the domestic violence multidisciplinary team.

(2) Members of the team that have confidential information obtained from an individual shall not disclose that information to and with one another unless the member has obtained that individual's informed, written, reasonably time-limited consent to the disclosure, in accordance with all applicable state and federal confidentiality laws, or it is otherwise required by other state or federal law or by court order. Before that consent is obtained, a member of the team is required to inform the individual that the information may be shared with law enforcement professionals or other entities without that individual's consent if required by law.

(3) A disclosure of information consented to by an individual shall not be deemed a waiver of any privilege or confidentiality provision, including those contained in Sections 2263, 2918, 4982, and 6068 of the Business and Professions Code and in Chapter 4 of Division 8 of the Evidence Code.

(f) Every member of the domestic violence multidisciplinary personnel team who receives information or records regarding children or families in his or her capacity as a member of the team shall be under the same privacy and confidentiality obligations and subject to the same confidentiality penalties as the person disclosing or providing the information or records. The information or records obtained shall be maintained in a manner that ensures the maximum protection of privacy and confidentiality rights.

(g) This section shall not be construed to restrict guarantees of confidentiality provided under state or federal law.

(h) Information and records communicated or provided to the team members by providers and agencies, as well as information and records created in the course of a domestic violence investigation, shall be deemed private and confidential and shall be protected from discovery and disclosure by applicable statutory and common law protections, except where disclosure is required by law. Existing civil and criminal penalties shall apply to the inappropriate disclosure of information held by the team members. *(Added by Stats.2018, c. 802 (A.B.998), § 3, eff. Jan. 1, 2019.)*

§ 13753. Human trafficking multidisciplinary personnel team; provision of a broad range of services related to human trafficking; members; disclosure and exchange of information following report of suspected human trafficking; privacy and confidentiality rights

(a) Notwithstanding any other law, a city, county, city and county, or community-based nonprofit organization may establish a human trafficking multidisciplinary personnel team consisting of two or more persons who are trained in the prevention, identification, management, or treatment of human trafficking cases and who are qualified to provide a broad range of services related to human trafficking.

(b) A human trafficking multidisciplinary team may include, but need not be limited to, any of the following:

(1) Law enforcement personnel.

(2) Medical personnel.

(3) Psychiatrists, psychologists, marriage and family therapists, or other trained counseling personnel.

(4) District attorneys and city attorneys.

(5) Victim–witness program personnel.

(6) Sexual assault counselors, as defined in Section 1035.2 of the Evidence Code.

(7) Domestic violence counselors, as defined in Section 1037.1 of the Evidence Code.

(8) Social service agency staff members.

(9) Child welfare agency social workers.

(10) County health department staff.

(11) City or county welfare and public assistance workers.

(12) Nonprofit agency counseling professionals.

(13) Civil legal service providers.

(14) Human trafficking caseworkers, as defined in Section 1038.2 of the Evidence Code.

(c)(1) Notwithstanding any other law, following a report of suspected human trafficking, members of a human trafficking multidisciplinary personnel team engaged in the prevention, identification, and treatment of human trafficking may disclose to and exchange with one another information and writings that relate to any incident of human trafficking that may also be designated as confidential under state law if the member of the team having that information or writing reasonably believes it is generally relevant to the prevention, identification, or treatment of human trafficking. Any discussion relative to the disclosure or exchange of the information or writings during a team meeting is confidential, and testimony concerning that discussion is not admissible in any criminal, civil, or juvenile court proceeding unless required by law.

(2) Disclosure and exchange of information pursuant to this section may occur telephonically or electronically if there is adequate verification of the identity of the human trafficking multidisciplinary personnel who are involved in that disclosure or exchange of information.

(3) Disclosure and exchange of information pursuant to this section shall not be made to anyone other than members of the human trafficking multidisciplinary personnel team and those qualified to receive information as set forth in subdivision (d).

(d) The human trafficking multidisciplinary personnel team may designate persons qualified pursuant to subdivision (b) to be a member of the team for a particular case. A person designated as a team member pursuant to this subdivision may receive and disclose relevant information and records, subject to the confidentiality provisions of subdivision (g).

(e)(1) The sharing of information permitted under subdivision (c) shall be governed by protocols developed in each county describing how and what information may be shared by the human trafficking multidisciplinary team to ensure that confidential information gathered by the team is not disclosed in violation of state or federal law. A copy of the protocols shall be distributed to each participating agency and to persons in those agencies who participate in the human trafficking multidisciplinary team.

(2) Members of the team that have confidential information obtained from an individual shall not disclose that information to and with one another unless the member has obtained that individual's informed, written, reasonably time-limited consent to the disclosure, in accordance with all applicable state and federal confidentiality laws, or it is otherwise required by other state or federal law or by court order. Before such consent is obtained, a member of the team is required to inform the individual that the information may be shared with law enforcement professionals or other entities without that individual's consent if required by law.

(3) A disclosure of information consented to by an individual shall not be deemed a waiver of any privilege or confidentiality provision, including those contained in Sections 2263, 2918, 4982, and 6068 of the Business and Professions Code and in Chapter 4 of Division 8 of the Evidence Code.

§ 13753

(f) Every member of the human trafficking multidisciplinary personnel team who receives information or records regarding children or families in his or her capacity as a member of the team shall be under the same privacy and confidentiality obligations and subject to the same confidentiality penalties as the person disclosing or providing the information or records. The information or records obtained shall be maintained in a manner that ensures the maximum protection of privacy and confidentiality rights.

(g) This section shall not be construed to restrict guarantees of confidentiality provided under state or federal law.

(h) Information and records communicated or provided to the team members by providers and agencies, as well as information and records created in the course of a domestic violence investigation, shall be deemed private and confidential and shall be protected from discovery and disclosure by applicable statutory and common law protections, except where disclosure is required by law. Existing civil and criminal penalties shall apply to the inappropriate disclosure of information held by the team members. (Added by Stats.2018, c. 802 (A.B.998), § 3, eff. Jan. 1, 2019.)

Title 6

CALIFORNIA COUNCIL ON CRIMINAL JUSTICE

CHAPTER 3. CRIMINAL JUSTICE PLANNING

Section
13823.3. Local domestic violence programs; expenditure of funds.
13823.4. Family Violence Prevention Program; funding; information and materials.

Cross References

Governor's mentoring partnership, legislative goal to give every California youth access to quality mentoring relationships, sustaining and growing efforts of state agencies departments in support of mentoring and identifying opportunities for increased private sector investment, see Welfare and Institutions Code § 2100 et seq.

State advisory groups for Runaway and Homeless Youth, see Welfare and Institutions Code § 1785.

§ 13823.3. Local domestic violence programs; expenditure of funds

The Office of Emergency Services may expend funds for local domestic violence programs, subject to the availability of funds therefor. (Added by Stats.1984, c. 412, § 1. Amended by Stats.2010, c. 618 (A.B.2791), § 220; Stats.2013, c. 352 (A.B.1317), § 431, eff. Sept. 26, 2013, operative July 1, 2013.)

Cross References

Agency defined for purposes of this Title, see Penal Code § 13800.

§ 13823.4. Family Violence Prevention Program; funding; information and materials

(a) The Legislature finds the problem of family violence to be of serious and increasing magnitude. The Legislature also finds that acts of family violence often result in other crimes and social problems.

(b) There is in the Office of Emergency Services, a Family Violence Prevention Program. This program shall provide financial and technical assistance to local domestic and family violence centers in implementing family violence prevention programs.

The goals and functions of the program shall include all of the following:

(1) Promotion of community involvement through public education geared specifically toward reaching and educating the friends and neighbors of members of violent families.

(2) Development and dissemination of model protocols for the training of criminal justice system personnel in domestic violence intervention and prevention.

(3) Increasing citizen involvement in family violence prevention.

(4) Identification and testing of family violence prevention models.

(5) Replication of successful models, as appropriate, through the state.

(6) Identification and testing of domestic violence model protocols and intervention systems in major service delivery institutions.

(7) Development of informational materials and seminars to enable emulation or adaptation of the models by other communities.

(8) Provision of domestic violence prevention education and skills to students in schools.

(c) The Director of Emergency Services shall allocate funds to local centers meeting the criteria for funding that shall be established by the Office of Emergency Services in consultation with practitioners and experts in the field of family violence prevention. All centers receiving funds pursuant to this section shall have had an ongoing recognized program, supported by either public or private funds, dealing with an aspect of family violence, for at least two years prior to the date specified for submission of applications for funding pursuant to this section. All centers funded pursuant to this section shall utilize volunteers to the greatest extent possible.

The centers may seek, receive, and make use of any funds which may be available from all public and private sources to augment any state funds received pursuant to this section. Sixty percent of the state funds received pursuant to this section shall be used to develop and implement model program protocols and materials. Forty percent of the state funds received pursuant to this section shall be allocated to programs to disseminate model program protocols and materials. Dissemination shall include training for domestic violence agencies in California. Each of the programs funded under this section shall focus on no more than two targeted areas. These targeted model areas shall be determined by the Office of Emergency Services in consultation with practitioners and experts in the field of domestic violence, using the domestic violence model priorities survey of the California Alliance Against Domestic Violence.

Centers receiving funding shall provide matching funds of at least 10 percent of the funds received pursuant to this section.

(d) The Office of Emergency Services shall develop and disseminate throughout the state information and materials concerning family violence prevention, including, but not limited to, a procedures manual on prevention models. The Office of Emergency Services shall also establish a resource center for the collection, retention, and distribution of educational materials related to family violence and its prevention. (Added by Stats.1985, c. 250, § 1, eff. July 26, 1985. Amended by Stats.1988, c. 1371, § 3; Stats.2003, c. 229 (A.B.1757), § 35; Stats.2010, c. 618 (A.B.2791), § 221; Stats.2013, c. 352 (A.B.1317), § 432, eff. Sept. 26, 2013, operative July 1, 2013.)

Cross References

Domestic violence and sexual assault awareness license plate program, see Vehicle Code § 5156.5.

Part 6

CONTROL OF DEADLY WEAPONS

Cross References

Persons engaged in the manufacture, distribution, importation, transportation, sale, lease, or transfer of firearms and precursor parts, legislative findings and declarations, see Business and Professions Code § 22949.60.

Title 4

FIREARMS

Division 9

SPECIAL FIREARM RULES RELATING TO PARTICULAR PERSONS

CHAPTER 2. PERSON CONVICTED OF SPECIFIED OFFENSE, ADDICTED TO NARCOTIC, OR SUBJECT TO COURT ORDER

Cross References

Certificate of eligibility requirement for agents or employees who handle, sell, or deliver firearm precursor parts, prohibition against specified agents or employees handling firearm precursor parts, see Penal Code § 30447.

Criminal procedure, sealing of arrest records where arrest did not result in conviction, effect of successful petition, see Penal Code § 851.91.

Firearm or ammunition ownership, possession, purchase, or receipt, relinquishment order, see Family Code § 6389.

Members of the military, mental health problems stemming from service, probation or dismissal of action, release from penalties and disabilities, exceptions, see Penal Code § 1170.9.

Person prohibited from owning or possessing firearm also prohibited from owning or possessing firearm precursor part, penalties, exemptions, see Penal Code § 30405.

Prohibited persons, attempt to acquire or report acquisition or ownership of firearm, notice to local law enforcement agency, see Penal Code § 29880.

Relinquishment of firearms, persons subject to protective order, see Code of Civil Procedure § 527.9.

ARTICLE 1. PROHIBITIONS ON FIREARM ACCESS

Section

29825. Persons restricted from purchasing, receiving, owning, or possessing firearm by temporary restraining order, injunction, or protective order; punishment for violation; probation; notice of restriction on protective order.

§ 29825. Persons restricted from purchasing, receiving, owning, or possessing firearm by temporary restraining order, injunction, or protective order; punishment for violation; probation; notice of restriction on protective order

(a) A person who purchases or receives, or attempts to purchase or receive, a firearm knowing that the person is prohibited from doing so in any jurisdiction by a temporary restraining order or injunction issued pursuant to Section 527.6, 527.8, or 527.85 of the Code of Civil Procedure, a protective order as defined in Section 6218 of the Family Code, a protective order issued pursuant to Section 136.2 or 646.91 of this code, a protective order issued pursuant to Section 15657.03 of the Welfare and Institutions Code, or by a valid order issued by an out-of-state jurisdiction that is similar or equivalent to a temporary restraining order, injunction, or protective order specified in this subdivision, that includes a prohibition from owning or possessing a firearm, is guilty of a public offense, punishable by imprisonment in a county jail not exceeding one year or in the state prison, by a fine not exceeding one thousand dollars ($1,000), or by both that imprisonment and fine.

(b) A person who owns or possesses a firearm knowing that the person is prohibited from doing so in any jurisdiction by a temporary restraining order or injunction issued pursuant to Section 527.6, 527.8, or 527.85 of the Code of Civil Procedure, a protective order as defined in Section 6218 of the Family Code, a protective order issued pursuant to Section 136.2 or 646.91 of this code, a protective order issued pursuant to Section 15657.03 of the Welfare and Institutions Code, or by a valid order issued by an out-of-state jurisdiction that is similar or equivalent to a temporary restraining order, injunction, or protective order specified in this subdivision, that includes a prohibition from owning or possessing a firearm, is guilty of a public offense, punishable by imprisonment in a county jail not exceeding one year, by a fine not exceeding one thousand dollars ($1,000), or by both that imprisonment and fine.

(c) If probation is granted upon conviction of a violation of this section, the court shall impose probation consistent with Section 1203.097.

(d) The Judicial Council shall provide notice on all protective orders issued within the state that the respondent is prohibited from owning, possessing, purchasing, receiving, or attempting to purchase or receive a firearm while the protective order is in effect. The order shall also state that a firearm owned or possessed by the person shall be relinquished to the local law enforcement agency for that jurisdiction, sold to a licensed firearms dealer, or transferred to a licensed firearms dealer pursuant to Section 29830 for the duration of the period that the protective order is in effect, and that proof of surrender or sale shall be filed within a specified time of receipt of the order. The order shall state the penalties for a violation of the prohibition. The order shall also state on its face the expiration date for relinquishment. *(Added by Stats.2010, c. 711 (S.B.1080), § 6.77, operative Jan. 1, 2012. Amended by Stats.2013, c. 739 (A.B.539), § 3; Stats.2019, c. 726 (A.B.164), § 1, eff. Jan. 1, 2020.)*

Cross References

Contempt of court, conduct constituting, see Penal Code § 166.

Elder Abuse and Dependent Adult Civil Protection Act, protective orders, see Welfare and Institutions Code § 15657.03.

Employees subject to unlawful violence or threat of violence at the workplace, temporary restraining order, injunction, see Code of Civil Procedure § 527.8.

Firearm defined for purposes of this Part, see Penal Code § 16520.

Firearm or ammunition ownership, possession, purchase, or receipt, relinquishment order, see Family Code § 6389.

Harassment, temporary restraining order and injunction, see Code of Civil Procedure § 527.6.

Officers authorized to maintain order on school campus or facility, threat of violence made off school campus, temporary restraining order and injunction, violation of restraining order, see Code of Civil Procedure § 527.85.

Proof of protective orders, purchase or receipt of firearm, see Family Code § 6385.

Research References

Forms

West's California Judicial Council Forms JV–250, Notice of Hearing and Temporary Restraining Order—Juvenile (Also Available in Chinese, Korean, Spanish, and Vietnamese).

West's California Judicial Council Forms JV–255, Restraining Order—Juvenile (Clets—Juv) (Also Available in Chinese, Korean, Spanish, and Vietnamese).

PROBATE CODE
Division 2
GENERAL PROVISIONS

Part 3
CONTRACTUAL ARRANGEMENTS RELATING TO RIGHTS AT DEATH

CHAPTER 1. SURVIVING SPOUSE'S WAIVER OF RIGHTS

Section
140. Waiver.
141. Rights which may be waived.
142. Requirement of writing; enforceability; defenses.
143. Enforceability.
144. Enforceability under certain circumstances.
145. Waiver of "all rights".
146. Agreement; requirements.
147. Waiver, agreement or property settlement; validity; validity or effect of premarital property agreement; right to dispose of community or quasi-community property.

Cross References
Application of old and new law, see Probate Code § 3.
Surviving spouse, defined, see Probate Code § 78.

§ 140. Waiver

As used in this chapter, "waiver" means a waiver by the surviving spouse of any of the rights listed in subdivision (a) of Section 141, whether signed before or during marriage. *(Stats.1990, c. 79 (A.B.759), § 14, operative July 1, 1991.)*

Cross References
Surviving spouse, defined, see Probate Code § 78.

Research References
Forms
1 California Transactions Forms--Estate Planning § 6:28, Exceptions to Omitted Spouse Statute.
1 California Transactions Forms--Estate Planning § 6:99, Omitted Spouse Made Valid Agreement Waiving Right to Share in Decedent's Estate.
2 California Transactions Forms--Estate Planning § 11:49, Introduction and Definition [Prob C § 140].
2 California Transactions Forms--Estate Planning § 11:50, Rights of Surviving Spouse that May be Waived [Prob C § 141].
2 California Transactions Forms--Estate Planning § 11:51, Requirements.
2 California Transactions Forms--Estate Planning § 11:52, Enforceability Under Probate Code § 143.
2 California Transactions Forms--Estate Planning § 11:53, Enforceability Under Probate Code § 144.
4 California Transactions Forms--Estate Planning § 19:15, Waiver of Family Protection.

§ 141. Rights which may be waived

(a) The right of a surviving spouse to any of the following may be waived in whole or in part by a waiver under this chapter:

(1) Property that would pass from the decedent by intestate succession.

(2) Property that would pass from the decedent by testamentary disposition in a will executed before the waiver.

(3) A probate homestead.

(4) The right to have exempt property set aside.

(5) Family allowance.

(6) The right to have an estate set aside under Chapter 6 (commencing with Section 6600) of Part 3 of Division 6.

(7) The right to elect to take community or quasi-community property against the decedent's will.

(8) The right to take the statutory share of an omitted spouse.

(9) The right to be appointed as the personal representative of the decedent's estate.

(10) An interest in property that is the subject of a nonprobate transfer on death under Part 1 (commencing with Section 5000) of Division 5.

(b) Nothing in this chapter affects or limits the waiver or manner of waiver of rights other than those referred to in subdivision (a), including, but not limited to, the right to property that would pass from the decedent to the surviving spouse by nonprobate transfer upon the death of the decedent, such as the survivorship interest under a joint tenancy, a Totten trust account, or a pay-on-death account. *(Stats.1990, c. 79 (A.B.759), § 14, operative July 1, 1991. Amended by Stats.1992, c. 51 (A.B.1719), § 2.)*

Cross References
Appointment of personal representative, generally, see Probate Code § 8400 et seq.
Community property, generally, see Family Code §§ 65, 760.
Community property, defined, see Probate Code § 28.
Disposition of estate without administration, passage of property to surviving spouse, see Probate Code § 13500 et seq.
Estate administration, generally, see Probate Code § 7000 et seq.
Family allowance defined, see Probate Code § 38.
Intestate succession, generally, see Probate Code § 6400 et seq.
Pay-on-death account, defined, see Probate Code § 55.
Personal representative and general personal representative, defined, see Probate Code § 58.
Probate homestead, defined, see Probate Code § 60.
Quasi-community property, defined, see Probate Code § 66.
Surviving spouse, defined, see Probate Code § 78.
Totten trust account, defined, see Probate Code § 80.

Research References
Forms
1 California Transactions Forms--Estate Planning § 1:26, Quasi-Community Property; Separate Property.
2 California Transactions Forms--Estate Planning § 11:50, Rights of Surviving Spouse that May be Waived [Prob C § 141].
2 California Transactions Forms--Estate Planning § 11:53, Enforceability Under Probate Code § 144.
2 California Transactions Forms--Estate Planning § 11:62, Matters to Include in Spousal Waiver.
2 California Transactions Forms--Estate Planning § 11:72, Spousal Waiver.
4 California Transactions Forms--Estate Planning § 19:15, Waiver of Family Protection.
1 California Transactions Forms--Family Law § 1:27, Complete Agreement.
West's California Code Forms, Family § 1611 Form 1, Premarital Agreement.

§ 142. Requirement of writing; enforceability; defenses

(a) A waiver under this chapter shall be in writing and shall be signed by the surviving spouse.

§ 142

(b) Subject to subdivision (c), a waiver under this chapter is enforceable only if it satisfies the requirements of subdivision (a) and is enforceable under either Section 143 or Section 144.

(c) Enforcement of the waiver against the surviving spouse is subject to the same defenses as enforcement of a contract, except that:

(1) Lack of consideration is not a defense to enforcement of the waiver.

(2) A minor intending to marry may make a waiver under this chapter as if married, but the waiver becomes effective only upon the marriage. *(Stats.1990, c. 79 (A.B.759), § 14, operative July 1, 1991.)*

Cross References

Minors, defined, see Family Code § 6500.
Surviving spouse, defined, see Probate Code § 78.

Research References

Forms

1 California Transactions Forms--Estate Planning § 6:28, Exceptions to Omitted Spouse Statute.
2 California Transactions Forms--Estate Planning § 11:51, Requirements.
4 California Transactions Forms--Estate Planning § 19:15, Waiver of Family Protection.

§ 143. Enforceability

(a) Subject to Section 142, a waiver is enforceable under this section unless the surviving spouse proves either of the following:

(1) A fair and reasonable disclosure of the property or financial obligations of the decedent was not provided to the surviving spouse prior to the signing of the waiver unless the surviving spouse waived such a fair and reasonable disclosure after advice by independent legal counsel.

(2) The surviving spouse was not represented by independent legal counsel at the time of signing of the waiver.

(b) Subdivision (b) of Section 721 of the Family Code does not apply if the waiver is enforceable under this section. *(Stats.1990, c. 79 (A.B.759), § 14, operative July 1, 1991. Amended by Stats.1992, c. 163 (A.B.2641), § 120, operative Jan. 1, 1994.)*

Cross References

Rights and obligations during marriage, contracts with each other and third parties, see Family Code § 721.
Surviving spouse, defined, see Probate Code § 78.

Research References

Forms

2 California Transactions Forms--Estate Planning § 11:51, Requirements.
2 California Transactions Forms--Estate Planning § 11:52, Enforceability Under Probate Code § 143.
4 California Transactions Forms--Estate Planning § 19:15, Waiver of Family Protection.

§ 144. Enforceability under certain circumstances

(a) Except as provided in subdivision (b), subject to Section 142, a waiver is enforceable under this section if the court determines either of the following:

(1) The waiver at the time of signing made a fair and reasonable disposition of the rights of the surviving spouse.

(2) The surviving spouse had, or reasonably should have had, an adequate knowledge of the property and financial obligations of the decedent and the decedent did not violate the duty imposed by subdivision (b) of Section 721 of the Family Code.

(b) If, after considering all relevant facts and circumstances, the court finds that enforcement of the waiver pursuant to subdivision (a) would be unconscionable under the circumstances existing at the time enforcement is sought, the court may refuse to enforce the waiver, enforce the remainder of the waiver without the unconscionable provisions, or limit the application of the unconscionable provisions to avoid an unconscionable result.

(c) Except as provided in paragraph (2) of subdivision (a), subdivision (b) of Section 721 of the Family Code does not apply if the waiver is enforceable under this section. *(Stats.1990, c. 79 (A.B.759), § 14, operative July 1, 1991. Amended by Stats.1992, c. 163 (A.B.2641), § 121, operative Jan. 1, 1994.)*

Cross References

Rights and obligations during marriage, contracts with each other and third parties, see Family Code § 721.
Surviving spouse, defined, see Probate Code § 78.

Research References

Forms

2 California Transactions Forms--Estate Planning § 11:51, Requirements.
2 California Transactions Forms--Estate Planning § 11:52, Enforceability Under Probate Code § 143.
2 California Transactions Forms--Estate Planning § 11:53, Enforceability Under Probate Code § 144.
4 California Transactions Forms--Estate Planning § 19:15, Waiver of Family Protection.

§ 145. Waiver of "all rights"

Unless the waiver or property settlement provides to the contrary, a waiver under this chapter of "all rights" (or equivalent language) in the property or estate of a present or prospective spouse, or a complete property settlement entered into after or in anticipation of separation or dissolution or annulment of marriage, is a waiver by the spouse of the rights described in subdivision (a) of Section 141. *(Stats.1990, c. 79 (A.B.759), § 14, operative July 1, 1991.)*

Research References

Forms

2 California Transactions Forms--Estate Planning § 11:50, Rights of Surviving Spouse that May be Waived [Prob C § 141].
4 California Transactions Forms--Estate Planning § 19:15, Waiver of Family Protection.

§ 146. Agreement; requirements

(a) As used in this section, "agreement" means a written agreement signed by each spouse or prospective spouse altering, amending, or revoking a waiver under this chapter.

(b) Except as provided in subdivisions (c) and (d) of Section 147, unless the waiver specifically otherwise provides, a waiver under this chapter may not be altered, amended, or revoked except by a subsequent written agreement signed by each spouse or prospective spouse.

(c) Subject to subdivision (d), the agreement is enforceable only if it satisfies the requirements of subdivision (b) and is enforceable under either subdivision (e) or subdivision (f).

(d) Enforcement of the agreement against a party to the agreement is subject to the same defenses as enforcement of any other contract, except that:

(1) Lack of consideration is not a defense to enforcement of the agreement.

(2) A minor intending to marry may enter into the agreement as if married, but the agreement becomes effective only upon the marriage.

(e) Subject to subdivision (d), an agreement is enforceable under this subdivision unless the party to the agreement against whom enforcement is sought proves either of the following:

(1) A fair and reasonable disclosure of the property or financial obligations of the other spouse was not provided to the spouse against whom enforcement is sought prior to the signing of the agreement unless the spouse against whom enforcement is sought waived such a fair and reasonable disclosure after advice by independent legal counsel.

(2) The spouse against whom enforcement is sought was not represented by independent legal counsel at the time of signing of the agreement.

(f) Subject to subdivisions (d) and (g), an agreement is enforceable under this subdivision if the court determines that the agreement at the time of signing made a fair and reasonable disposition of the rights of the spouses.

(g) If, after considering all relevant facts and circumstances, the court finds that enforcement of the agreement pursuant to subdivision (f) would be unconscionable under the circumstances existing at the time enforcement is sought, the court may refuse to enforce the agreement, enforce the remainder of the agreement without the unconscionable provisions, or limit the application of the unconscionable provisions to avoid an unconscionable result.

(h) Subdivision (b) of Section 721 of the Family Code does not apply if the agreement is enforceable under this section. *(Stats.1990, c. 79 (A.B.759), § 14, operative July 1, 1991. Amended by Stats.1992, c. 163 (A.B.2641), § 122, operative Jan. 1, 1994.)*

Cross References

Minors, defined, see Family Code § 6500.
Rights and obligations during marriage, contracts with each other and third parties, see Family Code § 721.

Research References

Forms

2 California Transactions Forms--Estate Planning § 11:54, Revocation and Amendment of Waiver by Agreement.

2 California Transactions Forms--Estate Planning § 11:63, Matters to Include in Agreement Revoking Spousal Waiver.

§ 147. Waiver, agreement or property settlement; validity; validity or effect of premarital property agreement; right to dispose of community or quasi-community property

(a) Subject to subdivisions (c) and (d), a waiver, agreement, or property settlement made after December 31, 1984, is invalid insofar as it affects the rights listed in subdivision (a) of Section 141 unless it satisfies the requirements of this chapter.

(b) Nothing in this chapter affects the validity or effect of any waiver, agreement, or property settlement made prior to January 1, 1985, and the validity and effect of such waiver, agreement, or property settlement shall continue to be determined by the law applicable to the waiver, agreement, or settlement prior to January 1, 1985.

(c) Nothing in this chapter affects the validity or effect of any premarital property agreement, whether made prior to, on, or after January 1, 1985, insofar as the premarital property agreement affects the rights listed in subdivision (a) of Section 141, and the validity and effect of such premarital property agreement shall be determined by the law otherwise applicable to the premarital property agreement. Nothing in this subdivision limits the enforceability under this chapter of a waiver made under this chapter by a person intending to marry that is otherwise enforceable under this chapter.

(d) Nothing in this chapter limits any right one spouse otherwise has to revoke a consent or election to disposition of his or her half of the community or quasi-community property under the will of the other spouse. *(Stats.1990, c. 79 (A.B.759), § 14, operative July 1, 1991.)*

Cross References

Community property, generally, see Family Code §§ 65, 760.
Community property, defined, see Probate Code § 28.
Quasi-community property, defined, see Probate Code § 66.

Research References

Forms

2 California Transactions Forms--Estate Planning § 11:54, Revocation and Amendment of Waiver by Agreement.

Division 3

GENERAL PROVISIONS OF A PROCEDURAL NATURE

Part 3

APPEALS

Cross References

Nonprobate transfer to trustee named in decedent's will, appealable orders, see Probate Code § 6327.

CHAPTER 1. GENERAL

Section
1301.5. Conservatorships; appealable orders.

§ 1301.5. Conservatorships; appealable orders

The following rules apply with respect to the California Conservatorship Jurisdiction Act (Chapter 8 (commencing with Section 1980) of Part 3 of Division 4):

(a)(1) An appeal may be taken from an order assessing expenses against a party under Section 1997 if the amount exceeds five thousand dollars ($5,000).

(2) An order under Section 1997 assessing expenses of five thousand dollars ($5,000) or less against a party may be reviewed on an appeal by that party after entry of a final judgment or an appealable order in the conservatorship proceeding. At the discretion of the court of appeal, that type of order may also be reviewed upon petition for an extraordinary writ.

(b) An appeal may be taken from an order under Section 2001 denying a petition to transfer a conservatorship to another state.

(c) An appeal may be taken from a final order under Section 2002 accepting a transfer and appointing a conservator in this state.

(d) Notwithstanding any other law, an appeal may not be taken from either of the following until the court enters a final order under Section 2002 accepting the proposed transfer and appointing a conservator in this state:

(1) An order under Section 2002 determining whether or how to conform a conservatorship to the law of this state.

(2) An order that is made pursuant to a court review under Sections 1851.1 and 2002. *(Added by Stats.2014, c. 553 (S.B.940), § 3, eff. Jan. 1, 2015, operative Jan. 1, 2016.)*

Division 4

GUARDIANSHIP, CONSERVATORSHIP, AND OTHER PROTECTIVE PROCEEDINGS

Cross References

Application of guardianship and conservatorship law, see Health and Safety Code § 416.1.
Cancellation and voter file maintenance, mentally incompetent persons, review under Probate Code of capability to complete affidavit, see Elections Code § 2209.
Conservatorship and guardianship for developmentally disabled,
    Evaluation report, see Health and Safety Code § 416.8.
    Fiduciary powers and duties, see Health and Safety Code § 416.16.
Conservatorship for gravely disabled persons, appointment, procedure, see Welfare and Institutions Code § 5350.
Enforcement of money judgments, property in guardianship or conservatorship estate, see Code of Civil Procedure § 709.030.
Human experimentation, informed consent, see Health and Safety Code § 24175.
Judicial determination of incapacity, conservatorship, see Civil Code § 40.
Mentally incompetent persons, disqualification from voting, see Elections Code § 2208.
Persons with intellectual disabilities, cost of determining fitness of person for admission to home, see Welfare and Institutions Code § 6717.
Public defender, duties, probate proceedings, see Government Code § 27706.

Statutory construction, generally, see Cal. Const. Art. 4, § 19; Code of Civil Procedure §§ 1858, 1859; Government Code § 9603 et seq.

§ 1400. Guardianship–Conservatorship Law

The portion of this division consisting of Part 1 (commencing with Section 1400), Part 2 (commencing with Section 1500), Part 3 (commencing with Section 1800), and Part 4 (commencing with Section 2100) may be cited as the Guardianship-Conservatorship Law. *(Stats.1990, c. 79 (A.B.759), § 14, operative July 1, 1991.)*

Cross References

Professional fiduciaries, suspension, revocation or other adverse action, see Business and Professions Code § 6584.
Property in guardianship or conservatorship, see Code of Civil Procedure § 709.030.

Research References

Forms

24B Am. Jur. Pl. & Pr. Forms Veterans and Veterans' Laws § 85, Statutory References.
2 California Transactions Forms--Family Law § 6:2, Governing Law.

§ 1401. Application of definitions

Unless the provision or context otherwise requires, the definitions in this chapter govern the construction of this division. *(Stats.1990, c. 79 (A.B.759), § 14, operative July 1, 1991.)*

§ 1403. Absentee

"Absentee" means either of the following:

(a) A member of a uniformed service covered by United States Code, Title 37, Chapter 10, who is determined thereunder by the secretary concerned, or by the authorized delegate thereof, to be in missing status as missing status is defined therein.

(b) An employee of the United States government or an agency thereof covered by United States Code, Title 5, Chapter 55, Subchapter VII, who is determined thereunder by the head of the department or agency concerned, or by the authorized delegate thereof, to be in missing status as missing status is defined therein. *(Stats.1990, c. 79 (A.B.759), § 14, operative July 1, 1991.)*

Cross References

Absentee principal, application of this section, see Civil Code § 2357.
Conservator of estate of absentee, appointment, see Probate Code § 1803.
Personal property of absentees, see Probate Code § 3700 et seq.
Review of conservatorship, inapplicability of chapter to absentees, see Probate Code § 1850.
Secretary concerned, defined, see Probate Code § 1440.
Special provisions applicable where proposed conservatee is an absentee, see Probate Code § 1840 et seq.
Spouse of absentee, appointment as conservator of the estate, see Probate Code § 1813.

Research References

Forms

West's California Code Forms, Probate § 1820 Form 1, Attachment Requesting Special Orders Regarding a Major Neurocognitive Disorder.

§ 1418. Court

"Court," when used in connection with matters in the guardianship or conservatorship proceeding, means the court in which such

Part 1

DEFINITIONS AND GENERAL PROVISIONS

Cross References

Freedom from parental custody and control, stay of proceedings and effect upon jurisdiction under these provisions, see Family Code § 7807.
Termination of parental rights of father, filing of petition, stay of proceedings affecting a child pending final determination of parental rights, see Family Code § 7662.

CHAPTER 1. SHORT TITLE AND DEFINITIONS

Section
1400.   Guardianship–Conservatorship Law.
1401.   Application of definitions.
1403.   Absentee.
1418.   Court.
1419.   Court investigator.
1419.5. Custodial parent.
1420.   Developmental disability.
1424.   Interested person.
1430.   Petition.
1431.   Proceedings to establish a limited conservatorship.
1440.   Secretary concerned.
1446.   Single-premium deferred annuity.
1449.   Indian child custody proceedings; definitions; membership in more than one tribe.

Cross References

Application of division to guardianship and conservatorship appointments for developmentally disabled persons, see Health and Safety Code § 416.1.
Application of old and new law, see Probate Code § 3.
Inapplicability of certain notice provisions, see Probate Code § 1200.
Public defender, duty to represent persons not financially able to employ counsel in proceedings under this division, see Government Code § 27706.
Public guardians, see Government Code § 27430 et seq.

proceeding is pending. *(Stats.1990, c. 79 (A.B.759), § 14, operative July 1, 1991.)*

§ 1419. Court investigator

"Court investigator" means the person referred to in Section 1454. *(Stats.1990, c. 79 (A.B.759), § 14, operative July 1, 1991.)*

§ 1419.5. Custodial parent

"Custodial parent" means the parent who either (a) has been awarded sole legal and physical custody of the child in another proceeding, or (b) with whom the child resides if there is currently no operative custody order. If the child resides with both parents, then they are jointly the custodial parent. *(Added by Stats.1993, c. 978 (S.B.305), § 1.)*

Cross References
Child, defined, see Probate Code § 26.

§ 1420. Developmental disability

"Developmental disability" means a disability that originates before an individual attains 18 years of age, continues, or can be expected to continue, indefinitely, and constitutes a substantial handicap for the individual. As defined by the Director of Developmental Services, in consultation with the Superintendent of Public Instruction, this term includes intellectual disability, cerebral palsy, epilepsy, and autism. This term also includes handicapping conditions found to be closely related to intellectual disability or to require treatment similar to that required for individuals with an intellectual disability, but does not include other handicapping conditions that are solely physical in nature. *(Stats.1990, c. 79 (A.B.759), § 14, operative July 1, 1991. Amended by Stats.2012, c. 448 (A.B.2370), § 44; Stats.2012, c. 457 (S.B.1381), § 44.)*

Cross References
Conservatorship and guardianship for developmentally disabled persons, see Health and Safety Code § 416 et seq.
Services for the developmentally disabled, see Welfare and Institutions Code § 4500 et seq.
Sterilization of adults with developmental disabilities, petition by limited conservator, see Probate Code § 1952.

Research References
Forms
West's California Code Forms, Probate § 1952 Form 1, Allegations for Petition for Authority to Consent to Sterilization of Developmentally Disabled Adult.

§ 1424. Interested person

"Interested person" includes, but is not limited to:

(a) Any interested state, local, or federal entity or agency.

(b) Any interested public officer or employee of this state or of a local public entity of this state or of the federal government. *(Stats.1990, c. 79 (A.B.759), § 14, operative July 1, 1991.)*

Cross References
Interested person, defined, see Probate Code § 48.

§ 1430. Petition

"Petition" includes an application or request in the nature of a petition. *(Stats.1990, c. 79 (A.B.759), § 14, operative July 1, 1991.)*

§ 1431. Proceedings to establish a limited conservatorship

"Proceedings to establish a limited conservatorship" include proceedings to modify or revoke the powers or duties of a limited conservator. *(Stats.1990, c. 79 (A.B.759), § 14, operative July 1, 1991.)*

§ 1440. Secretary concerned

"Secretary concerned" has the same meaning as provided in United States Code, Title 37, Section 101. *(Stats.1990, c. 79 (A.B.759), § 14, operative July 1, 1991.)*

§ 1446. Single-premium deferred annuity

"Single-premium deferred annuity" means an annuity offered by an admitted life insurer for the payment of a one-time lump-sum premium and for which the insurer neither assesses any initial charges or administrative fees against the premium paid nor exacts or assesses any penalty for withdrawal of any funds by the annuitant after a period of five years. *(Stats.1990, c. 79 (A.B.759), § 14, operative July 1, 1991.)*

§ 1449. Indian child custody proceedings; definitions; membership in more than one tribe

(a) As used in this division, unless the context otherwise requires, the terms "Indian," "Indian child," "Indian child's tribe," "Indian custodian," "Indian tribe," "reservation," and "tribal court" shall be defined as provided in Section 1903 of the Indian Child Welfare Act (25 U.S.C. Sec. 1901 et seq.).

(b) When used in connection with an Indian child custody proceeding, the terms "extended family member" and "parent" shall be defined as provided in Section 1903 of the Indian Child Welfare Act (25 U.S.C. Sec. 1901 et seq.).

(c) "Indian child custody proceeding" means a "child custody proceeding" within the meaning of Section 1903 of the Indian Child Welfare Act (25 U.S.C. Sec. 1901 et seq.), including a voluntary or involuntary proceeding that may result in an Indian child's temporary or long-term foster care or guardianship placement if the parent or Indian custodian cannot have the child returned upon demand, termination of parental rights or adoptive placement.

(d) When an Indian child is a member of more than one tribe or is eligible for membership in more than one tribe, the court shall make a determination, in writing together with the reasons for it, as to which tribe is the Indian child's tribe for purposes of the Indian child custody proceeding. The court shall make that determination as follows:

(1) If the Indian child is or becomes a member of only one tribe, that tribe shall be designated as the Indian child's tribe, even though the child is eligible for membership in another tribe.

(2) If an Indian child is or becomes a member of more than one tribe, or is not a member of any tribe but is eligible for membership in more than one tribe, the tribe with which the child has the more significant contacts shall be designated as the Indian child's tribe. In determining which tribe the child has the more significant contacts with, the court shall consider, among other things, the following factors:

(A) The length of residence on or near the reservation of each tribe and frequency of contact with each tribe.

(B) The child's participation in activities of each tribe.

(C) The child's fluency in the language of each tribe.

(D) Whether there has been a previous adjudication with respect to the child by a court of one of the tribes.

(E) The residence on or near one of the tribes' reservations by the child parents, Indian custodian, or extended family members.

(F) Tribal membership of custodial parent or Indian custodian.

(G) Interest asserted by each tribe in response to the notice specified in Section 1460.2.

(H) The child's self-identification.

(3) If an Indian child becomes a member of a tribe other than the one designated by the court as the Indian child's tribe under paragraph (2), actions taken based on the court's determination prior

to the child's becoming a tribal member shall continue to be valid. *(Added by Stats.2006, c. 838 (S.B.678), § 16.)*

Research References

Forms

West's California Code Forms, Probate § 1459.5 Comment, Application of Federal Law to Proceedings Involving Children of Indian Ancestry.
West's California Judicial Council Forms GC–210(CA), Child Information Attachment to Probate Guardianship Petition.
West's California Judicial Council Forms ICWA–030, Notice of Child Custody Proceeding for Indian Child (Also Available in Spanish).
West's California Judicial Council Forms ICWA–030(A), Attachment to Notice of Child Custody Proceeding for Indian Child (Also Available in Spanish).

CHAPTER 2. GENERAL PROVISIONS

Section
1452. Trial by jury.
1453. Motion for new trial.
1454. Court investigator; appointment; qualifications.
1455. Petitions for instructions, or grant of power or authority; persons authorized to file.
1456. Court-appointed attorneys, examiners and investigators; educational requirements.
1456.2. Continuing education requirements; compliance by public conservator.
1456.5. Compliance with filing requirements.
1457. Nonprofessional conservators and guardians; educational program and training.
1458. Judicial Council; legislative report.
1459. Legislative findings and declarations; children of Indian ancestry.
1459.5. Application of federal law to proceedings involving children of Indian ancestry.

§ 1452. Trial by jury

Except as otherwise specifically provided in this division, there is no right to trial by jury in proceedings under this division. *(Stats. 1990, c. 79 (A.B.759), § 14, operative July 1, 1991.)*

Cross References

Establishment of conservatorship, trial by jury, see Probate Code § 1827.
Jury trial, generally, see Code of Civil Procedure § 592; Cal. Const. Art. 1, § 16.
Termination of conservatorship, trial by jury, see Probate Code § 1863.

§ 1453. Motion for new trial

A motion for a new trial may be made only in cases in which, under the provisions of this division, a right to jury trial is expressly granted, whether or not the case was tried by a jury. *(Stats.1990, c. 79 (A.B.759), § 14, operative July 1, 1991.)*

Cross References

Appeals, see Probate Code § 1300 et seq.
Jury trial, conservatorship,
 Establishment, see Probate Code § 1827.
 Termination, see Probate Code § 1863.
New trials, generally, see Code of Civil Procedure § 656 et seq.

§ 1454. Court investigator; appointment; qualifications

(a) The court shall appoint a court investigator when one is required for the purposes of a proceeding under this division. The person appointed as the court investigator shall be an officer or special appointee of the court with no personal or other beneficial interest in the proceeding.

(b) The person appointed as the court investigator shall have the following qualifications:

(1) The training or experience, or both, necessary (i) to make the investigations required under this division, (ii) to communicate with, assess, and deal with persons who are or may be the subject of proceedings under this division, and (iii) to perform the other duties required of a court investigator.

(2) A demonstrated sufficient knowledge of law so as to be able to inform conservatees and proposed conservatees of the nature and effect of a conservatorship proceeding and of their rights, to answer their questions, and to inform conservators concerning their powers and duties. *(Stats.1990, c. 79 (A.B.759), § 14, operative July 1, 1991.)*

Research References

Forms

1 California Transactions Forms--Estate Planning § 1:4, Loss of Due Process Inherent in Probate Avoidance.
West's California Code Forms, Probate § 1454 Form 1, Order Appointing Court Investigator—Judicial Council Form GC-330.
West's California Code Forms, Probate § 4765 Form 1, Petition to Enforce Duties of Attorney-In-Fact for Health Care.
West's California Judicial Council Forms GC–330, Order Appointing Court Investigator.
West's California Judicial Council Forms GC–331, Order Appointing Court Investigator (Review and Successor Conservator Investigations).
West's California Judicial Council Forms GC–332, Order Setting Biennial Review Investigation and Directing Status Report Before Review.

§ 1455. Petitions for instructions, or grant of power or authority; persons authorized to file

Any petition for instructions or to grant a guardian or a conservator any power or authority under this division, which may be filed by a guardian or conservator, may also be filed by a person who petitions for the appointment of a guardian or conservator, including, but not limited to, a person who petitions under Section 2002 for transfer of conservatorship. *(Added by Stats.1996, c. 563 (S.B.392), § 5. Amended by Stats.2014, c. 553 (S.B.940), § 4, eff. Jan. 1, 2015, operative Jan. 1, 2016.)*

§ 1456. Court-appointed attorneys, examiners and investigators; educational requirements

(a) In addition to any other requirements that are part of the judicial branch education program, on or before January 1, 2008, the Judicial Council shall adopt a rule of court that shall do all of the following:

(1) Specifies the qualifications of a court-employed staff attorney, examiner, and investigator, and any attorney appointed pursuant to Sections 1470 and 1471.

(2) Specifies the number of hours of education in classes related to conservatorships or guardianships that a judge who is regularly assigned to hear probate matters shall complete, upon assuming the probate assignment, and then over a three-year period on an ongoing basis.

(3) Specifies the number of hours of education in classes related to conservatorships or guardianships that a court-employed staff attorney, examiner, and investigator, and any attorney appointed pursuant to Sections 1470 and 1471 shall complete each year.

(4) Specifies the particular subject matter that shall be included in the education required each year. <u>The subject matter shall, at a minimum, include the less restrictive alternatives to conservatorship set forth in Section 1800.3.</u>

(5) Specifies reporting requirements to ensure compliance with this section.

(b) In formulating the rule required by this section, the Judicial Council shall consult with interested parties, including, but not limited to, the California Judges Association, the California Association of Superior Court Investigators, the California Public Defenders Association, the County Counsels' Association of California, the State Bar of California, the National Guardianship Association, the

Professional Fiduciary Association of California, the California Association of Public Administrators, Public Guardians and Public Conservators, a disability rights organization, the State Council on Developmental Disabilities, the State Department of Developmental Services, the California Department of Aging, and the Association of Professional Geriatric Care Managers. *(Added by Stats.2006, c. 493 (A.B.1363), § 3. Amended by Stats.2007, c. 553 (A.B.1727), § 2; Stats.2022, c. 894 (A.B.1663), § 3, eff. Jan. 1, 2023.)*

Research References
Forms

West's California Judicial Council Forms GC–010, Certification of Attorney Qualifications.

§ 1456.2. Continuing education requirements; compliance by public conservator

On or before January 1, 2010, the public conservator shall comply with the continuing education requirements that are established by the California State Association of Public Administrators, Public Guardians, and Public Conservators. *(Added by Stats.2008, c. 237 (A.B.2343), § 2.)*

§ 1456.5. Compliance with filing requirements

Each court shall ensure compliance with the requirements of filing the inventory and appraisal and the accountings required by this division. Courts may comply with this section in either of the following ways:

(a) By placing on the court's calendar, at the time of the appointment of the guardian or conservator and at the time of approval of each accounting, a future hearing date to enable the court to confirm timely compliance with these requirements.

(b) By establishing and maintaining internal procedures to generate an order for appearance and consideration of appropriate sanctions or other actions if the guardian or conservator fails to comply with the requirements of this section. *(Added by Stats.2007, c. 553 (A.B.1727), § 3.)*

§ 1457. Nonprofessional conservators and guardians; educational program and training

In order to assist relatives and friends who may seek appointment as a nonprofessional conservator or guardian the Judicial Council shall, on or before January 1, 2008, develop a short educational program of no more than three hours that is user-friendly and shall make that program available free of charge to each proposed conservator and guardian and each court-appointed conservator and guardian who is not required to be licensed as a professional conservator or guardian pursuant to Chapter 6 (commencing with Section 6500) of Division 3 of the Business and Professions Code. The program may be available by video presentation or Internet access. *(Added by Stats.2006, c. 493 (A.B.1363), § 4. Amended by Stats.2007, c. 553 (A.B.1727), § 4.)*

§ 1458. Judicial Council; legislative report

(a) On or before January 1, 2024, the Judicial Council shall report to the Legislature the findings of a study measuring court effectiveness in conservatorship cases, including the effectiveness of protecting the legal rights and best interests of a conservatee. The report shall include all of the following, with respect to the courts chosen for evaluation pursuant to subdivision (b):

(1) Caseload statistics from the 2018–19 fiscal year, for both temporary and general probate conservatorships, including, at a minimum, all of the following:

(A) The number of petitions filed requesting appointment of a conservator, the number of those petitions granted, and the number denied, with cases in which a professional fiduciary was appointed presented separately from cases in which a nonprofessional conservator was appointed.

(B) The number of conservatorships under court supervision at the end of the fiscal year in which a court investigation was conducted, with cases in which a professional fiduciary was appointed presented separately from cases in which a nonprofessional conservator was appointed.

(C) The number of conservatorships under court supervision at the end of the fiscal year in which a court review hearing was held, with cases in which a professional fiduciary was appointed presented separately from cases in which a nonprofessional conservator was appointed.

(D) The number of petitions or objections filed by or on behalf of a conservatee challenging a conservator's action, failure to act, accounting, or compensation; the number of those petitions that were granted; and the number of petitions that were denied, with cases in which a professional fiduciary was appointed presented separately from cases in which a nonprofessional conservator was appointed.

(E) The number of conservatorships under court supervision in which accountings due, and the number of accountings received after they were due, or not received at all, with cases in which a professional fiduciary was appointed presented separately from cases in which a nonprofessional conservator was appointed.

(F) The number of conservatorships of the estate, or of the person and the estate, under court supervision in which bond was not required of the conservator, with cases in which a professional fiduciary was appointed presented separately from cases in which a nonprofessional conservator was appointed.

(2) An analysis of compliance with statutory timeframes in the 2018–19 fiscal year.

(3) A description of any operational differences between courts that affect the processing of conservatorship cases, including timeframes and steps taken to protect the legal rights and best interests of conservatees.

(b) The Judicial Council shall select at least three courts for the evaluation required by this section, including one small court, one medium-sized court, and one large court.

(c) The report shall include recommendations for statewide performance measures to be collected, best practices that serve to protect the legal rights of conservatees, and staffing needs to meet case processing requirements.

(d) The report shall be submitted pursuant to Section 9795 of the Government Code.

(e) This section shall remain in effect only until January 1, 2026, and as of that date is repealed. *(Added by Stats.2021, c. 417 (A.B.1194), § 4, eff. Jan. 1, 2022.)*

Repeal

For repeal of this section, see its terms.

§ 1459. Legislative findings and declarations; children of Indian ancestry

(a) The Legislature finds and declares the following:

(1) There is no resource that is more vital to the continued existence and integrity of recognized Indian tribes than their children, and the State of California has an interest in protecting Indian children who are members of, or are eligible for membership in, an Indian tribe. The state is committed to protecting the essential tribal relations and best interest of an Indian child by promoting practices, in accordance with the Indian Child Welfare Act (25 U.S.C. Sec. 1901 et seq.) and other applicable law, designed to prevent the child's involuntary out-of-home placement and, whenever such placement is necessary or ordered, by placing the child, whenever possible, in a placement that reflects the unique values of the child's tribal culture and is best able to assist the child in

establishing, developing, and maintaining a political, cultural, and social relationship with the child's tribe and tribal community.

(2) It is in the interest of an Indian child that the child's membership in the child's Indian tribe and connection to the tribal community be encouraged and protected, regardless of whether or not the child is in the physical custody of an Indian parent or Indian custodian at the commencement of a child custody proceeding, the parental rights of the child's parents have been terminated, or where the child has resided or been domiciled.

(b) In all Indian child custody proceedings, as defined in the federal Indian Child Welfare Act, the court shall consider all of the findings contained in subdivision (a), strive to promote the stability and security of Indian tribes and families, comply with the federal Indian Child Welfare Act, and seek to protect the best interest of the child. Whenever an Indian child is removed from a foster care home or institution, guardianship, or adoptive placement for the purpose of further foster care, guardianship, or adoptive placement, placement of the child shall be in accordance with the Indian Child Welfare Act.

(c) A determination by an Indian tribe that an unmarried person, who is under the age of 18 years, is either (1) a member of an Indian tribe or (2) eligible for membership in an Indian tribe and a biological child of a member of an Indian tribe shall constitute a significant political affiliation with the tribe and shall require the application of the federal Indian Child Welfare Act to the proceedings.

(d) In any case in which this code or other applicable state or federal law provides a higher standard of protection to the rights of the parent or Indian custodian of an Indian child, or the Indian child's tribe, than the rights provided under the Indian Child Welfare Act, the court shall apply the higher state or federal standard.

(e) Any Indian child, the Indian child's tribe, or the parent or Indian custodian from whose custody the child has been removed, may petition the court to invalidate an action in an Indian child custody proceeding for foster care or guardianship placement or termination of parental rights if the action violated Sections 1911, 1912, and 1913 of the Indian Child Welfare Act. *(Added by Stats.2006, c. 838 (S.B.678), § 17.)*

Research References

Forms

West's California Code Forms, Probate § 1459 Comment, Guardianships for Children of Indian Ancestry.

§ 1459.5. Application of federal law to proceedings involving children of Indian ancestry

(a) The Indian Child Welfare Act (25 U.S.C. Sec. 1901 et seq.) shall apply to the following guardianship or conservatorship proceedings under this division when the proposed ward or conservatee is an Indian child:

(1) In any case in which the petition is a petition for guardianship of the person and the proposed guardian is not the natural parent or Indian custodian of the proposed ward, unless the proposed guardian has been nominated by the natural parents pursuant to Section 1500 and the parents retain the right to have custody of the child returned to them upon demand.

(2) To a proceeding to have an Indian child declared free from the custody and control of one or both parents brought in a guardianship proceeding.

(3) In any case in which the petition is a petition for conservatorship of the person of a minor whose marriage has been dissolved, the proposed conservator is seeking physical custody of the minor, the proposed conservator is not the natural parent or Indian custodian of the proposed conservatee and the natural parent or Indian custodian does not retain the right to have custody of the child returned to them upon demand.

(b) When the Indian Child Welfare Act applies to a proceeding under this division, the court shall apply Sections 224.3 to 224.6, inclusive, and Sections 305.5, 361.31, and 361.7 of the Welfare and Institutions Code, and the following rules from the California Rules of Court, as they read on January 1, 2005:

(1) Paragraph (7) of subdivision (b) of Rule 1410.

(2) Subdivision (i) of Rule 1412.

(c) In the provisions cited in subdivision (b), references to social workers, probation officers, county welfare department, or probation department shall be construed as meaning the party seeking a foster care placement, guardianship, or adoption. *(Added by Stats.2006, c. 838 (S.B.678), § 18.)*

Research References

Forms

West's California Code Forms, Probate § 1459.5 Comment, Application of Federal Law to Proceedings Involving Children of Indian Ancestry.

West's California Judicial Council Forms GC–210(CA), Child Information Attachment to Probate Guardianship Petition.

West's California Judicial Council Forms ICWA–020, Parental Notification of Indian Status (Also Available in Spanish).

West's California Judicial Council Forms ICWA–030, Notice of Child Custody Proceeding for Indian Child (Also Available in Spanish).

West's California Judicial Council Forms ICWA–030(A), Attachment to Notice of Child Custody Proceeding for Indian Child (Also Available in Spanish).

West's California Judicial Council Forms ICWA–040, Notice of Designation of Tribal Representative in a Court Proceeding Involving an Indian Child.

West's California Judicial Council Forms ICWA–050, Notice of Petition and Petition to Transfer Case Involving an Indian Child to Tribal Jurisdiction.

West's California Judicial Council Forms ICWA–060, Order on Petition to Transfer Case Involving an Indian Child to Tribal Jurisdiction.

CHAPTER 3. NOTICES

Section
1460. Notice of time and place; delivery; posting; special notice; dispensation.
1460.1. Children under 12 years of age; exceptions to notice requirements.
1460.2. Knowledge that proposed ward or conservatee may be a child of Indian ancestry; notice to interested parties; requirements; time; proof.
1461. Notice to director; conditions; certificate; limitations.
1461.4. Regional center for developmentally disabled; notice of hearing and copy of petition; report and recommendation.
1461.5. Veterans Administration; notice of hearing on petition, report, account or inventory; time; conditions.
1461.7. Time and place of hearing on petition, report, or account; copies.
1467. Service by mail deemed complete.
1469. References to § 1220 deemed references to this chapter.

Cross References

Notice of hearing on the petition, conservatorships, modification or vacation of orders for application of community property for support and maintenance, see Probate Code § 3088.

§ 1460. Notice of time and place; delivery; posting; special notice; dispensation

(a) Subject to Sections 1202 and 1203, if notice of hearing is required under this division but the applicable provision does not fix the manner of giving notice of hearing, the notice of the time and place of the hearing shall be given at least 15 days before the day of the hearing as provided in this section.

(b) Subject to subdivision (e), the petitioner, who includes, for purposes of this section, a person filing a petition, report, or account, shall cause the notice of hearing to be delivered pursuant to Section 1215, to each of the following persons:

(1) The guardian or conservator.

(2) The ward or the conservatee.

(3) The spouse of the ward or conservatee, if the ward or conservatee has a spouse, or the domestic partner of the conservatee, if the conservatee has a domestic partner.

(4) Any person who has requested special notice of the matter, as provided in Section 2700.

(5) For any hearing on a petition to terminate a guardianship, to accept the resignation of a guardian, or to remove a guardian, the persons described in subdivision (c) of Section 1510.

(6) For any hearing to consider terminating a conservatorship, to accept the resignation of a conservator, or to remove a conservator, the persons described in subdivision (b) of Section 1821.

(c) The clerk of the court shall cause the notice of the hearing to be posted as provided in Section 1230 if the posting is required by subdivision (c) of Section 2543.

(d) Except as provided in subdivision (e), this section does not excuse compliance with the requirements for notice to a person who has requested special notice pursuant to Chapter 10 (commencing with Section 2700) of Part 4.

(e) The court, for good cause, may dispense with the notice otherwise required to be given to a person as provided in this section. (Stats.1990, c. 79 (A.B.759), § 14, operative July 1, 1991. Amended by Stats.1994, c. 806 (A.B.3686), § 8; Stats.1996, c. 862 (A.B.2751), § 5; Stats.2001, c. 893 (A.B.25), § 14; Stats.2017, c. 319 (A.B.976), § 26, eff. Jan. 1, 2018; Stats.2021, c. 417 (A.B.1194), § 5, eff. Jan. 1, 2022.)

Cross References

Account of guardian or conservator, notice of hearing, see Probate Code § 2621.

Computation of time, see Code of Civil Procedure §§ 12 and 12a; Government Code § 6800 et seq.

Definitions,
  Court, see Probate Code § 1418.
  Domestic partner, see Probate Code § 37.
  Interested person, see Probate Code § 1424.
  Petition, see Probate Code § 1430.

Guardians and conservators, removal or resignation, see Probate Code § 2650 et seq.

Notice,
  Mailing, see Probate Code § 1215 et seq.
  Posting, see Probate Code § 1230.
  Proof of giving notice, see Probate Code § 1260 et seq.
  Special notice, see Probate Code § 1250 et seq.
  This code, generally, see Probate Code § 1200 et seq.

Notice of conservatee's death, see Probate Code § 2361.

Notice of hearing on the petition,
  Borrowing money and giving security, see Probate Code § 2551.
  Change of venue, see Probate Code § 2214.
  Compelling guardian or conservator to pay support or debts, see Probate Code § 2404.
  Compensation of guardian, conservator, and attorney, see Probate Code § 2640 et seq.
  Compromise of claims and actions, extension, renewal or modification of obligations, see Probate Code § 2500.
  Contingent fee contract with attorney, see Probate Code § 2644.
  Conveyance or transfer of property claimed to belong to ward or conservatee or other person, see Probate Code § 851.
  Court ordered medical treatment, see Probate Code § 2357.
  Dedication or conveyance of real property or easement with or without consideration, see Probate Code § 2556.
  Determination of capacity of conservatee to marry, see Probate Code § 1901.
  Disposition of remaining balance of money or property paid or delivered pursuant to compromise or judgment for minor or incompetent person, see Probate Code § 3602.
  Estate management, limitation of powers of guardian or conservator, see Probate Code § 2450.
  Exchange of property, see Probate Code § 2557.
  Guardianship or conservatorship of the estate, instructions from or confirmation by court, see Probate Code § 2403.
  Guardianship or conservatorship of the person, instructions from or confirmation by court, see Probate Code § 2359.
  Guardianship or conservatorship of the person, order for care, custody, control and education of ward or conservatee, see Probate Code § 2351.
  Independent exercise of powers, order granting, see Probate Code § 2592.
  Independent exercise of powers, withdrawal or subsequent limitation of powers, see Probate Code § 2593.
  Investments of proceeds of sale and other money of the estate, see Probate Code § 2570.
  Leases, see Probate Code § 2553.
  Reduction in amount of bond of guardian or conservator, see Probate Code § 2329.
  Residence of ward or conservatee, notice according to this section, see Probate Code § 2352.
  Resignation of guardian or conservator, see Probate Code § 2660.
  Substituted judgment, see Probate Code § 2581.
  Support and maintenance of ward or conservatee and dependents by guardian or conservator of the estate, see Probate Code § 2421 et seq.
  Termination of guardianship, see Probate Code § 1601.

Notice to specified persons,
  Director of Developmental Services, see Probate Code §§ 1461, 2611, 2621.
  Director of Social Services, see Probate Code § 1542.
  Director of State Hospitals, see Probate Code §§ 1461, 2611, 2621.

Professional fiduciary as guardian or conservator, court authorization of periodic payments, contents of petition, see Probate Code § 2643.1.

Service of process,
  Generally, see Code of Civil Procedure § 413.10 et seq.
  Mail, see Code of Civil Procedure §§ 415.30, 1012 et seq.
  Personal delivery, see Code of Civil Procedure § 415.10.
  Proof of service, see Code of Civil Procedure § 417.10 et seq.
  Publication, see Code of Civil Procedure § 415.50.

Vacancy in office of guardian or conservator, appointment of successor, notice and hearing, see Probate Code § 2670.

Research References

Forms

West's California Code Forms, Probate § 277(c) Form 1, Petition for Order Authorizing Personal Representative to Disclaim.

West's California Code Forms, Probate § 851 Form 1, Notice of Hearing on Petition to Determine Claim to Property—Judicial Council Form DE-115/GC-015.

West's California Code Forms, Probate § 1460–1461 Form 1, Notice of Hearing (Guardianship or Conservatorship)—Judicial Council Form GC-020.

West's California Code Forms, Probate § 1460–1461 Form 2, Order Dispensing With Notice—Judicial Council Form GC-021.

West's California Code Forms, Probate § 1861 Form 1, Petition for Termination of Conservatorship.

West's California Code Forms, Probate § 1874 Form 1, Petition for Order Authorizing Conservatee to Enter Into Transaction.

West's California Code Forms, Probate § 2213 Form 1, Petition for Order for Transfer of Proceedings.

West's California Code Forms, Probate § 2329 Form 1, Petition for Reduction of Bond.

West's California Code Forms, Probate § 2361 Form 1, Notice of the Conservatee's Death—Judicial Council Form GC-399.

West's California Code Forms, Probate § 2403 Form 1, Petition for Instructions (Or Confirmation).

West's California Code Forms, Probate § 2404 Form 1, Petition to Compel Payment of Support.

West's California Code Forms, Probate § 2404 Form 3, Petition by Creditor to Compel Payment of Debt.

West's California Code Forms, Probate § 2421 Form 1, Petition for Allowance.

West's California Code Forms, Probate § 2423 Form 1, Petition for Payment of Surplus Income to Relatives of Conservatee.

West's California Code Forms, Probate § 2450 Form 1, Petition to Withdraw or Limit Independent Powers of Guardian or Conservator.

West's California Code Forms, Probate § 2456 Form 1, Petition for Order Conditioning Withdrawal of Deposits in Financial Institution on Prior Authorization of the Court.

§ 1460

West's California Code Forms, Probate § 2459(e) Form 1, Petition for Authorization for Guardian to Effect or Maintain in Force Contract Under Insurance Code Section 10112.

West's California Code Forms, Probate § 2500–2507 Form 1, Petition by Guardian or Conservator to Approve Compromise of Disputed Personal Injury Claim of Minor or Incompetent Person—Judicial Council Form MC-350.

West's California Code Forms, Probate § 2551 Form 1, Petition to Borrow Money and Encumber Real Property.

West's California Code Forms, Probate § 2553 Form 1, Petition to Lease Real Property.

West's California Code Forms, Probate § 2580 Form 1, Petition for Authority to Make Gifts.

West's California Code Forms, Probate § 2620 Form 1, [First/Second, Etc] Account for Guardianship or Conservatorship Estate and Petition for Settlement of Account [And for Compensation].

West's California Code Forms, Probate § 2630 Form 2, Order Settling Final Account of Guardian or Conservator.

West's California Code Forms, Probate § 2640 Form 1, Petition for Fees.

West's California Code Forms, Probate § 2651 Form 1, Petition for Removal of Guardian or Conservator.

West's California Code Forms, Probate § 3080 Form 1, Petition for Support; for Injunctive Orders; for Determination of the Character of Property; for an Accounting; for Employment of Counsel; and for Attorney Fees and Costs.

West's California Judicial Council Forms DE–115, Notice of Hearing on Petition to Determine Claim to Property.

West's California Judicial Council Forms GC–015, Notice of Hearing on Petition to Determine Claim to Property.

West's California Judicial Council Forms GC–020, Notice of Hearing—Guardianship or Conservatorship.

West's California Judicial Council Forms GC–020(C), Clerk's Certificate of Posting Notice of Hearing—Guardianship or Conservatorship.

West's California Judicial Council Forms GC–020(P), Proof of Personal Service of Notice of Hearing—Guardianship or Conservatorship.

West's California Judicial Council Forms GC–021, Order Dispensing With Notice.

West's California Judicial Council Forms GC–255, Petition for Termination of Guardianship.

§ 1460.1. Children under 12 years of age; exceptions to notice requirements

Notwithstanding any other provision of this division, no notice is required to be given to any child under the age of 12 years if the court determines either of the following:

(a) Notice was properly given to a parent, guardian, or other person having legal custody of the minor, with whom the minor resides.

(b) The petition is brought by a parent, guardian, or other person having legal custody of the minor, with whom the minor resides.

(Added by Stats.1997, c. 724 (A.B.1172), § 9.)

Cross References

Child, defined, see Probate Code § 26.

Research References

Forms

West's California Code Forms, Probate § 1460–1461 Form 1, Notice of Hearing (Guardianship or Conservatorship)—Judicial Council Form GC-020.

§ 1460.2. Knowledge that proposed ward or conservatee may be a child of Indian ancestry; notice to interested parties; requirements; time; proof

(a) If the court or petitioner knows or has reason to know that the proposed ward or conservatee may be an Indian child, notice shall comply with subdivision (b) in any case in which the Indian Child Welfare Act (25 U.S.C. Sec. 1901 et seq.) applies, as specified in Section 1459.5.

(b) Any notice sent under this section shall be sent to the minor's parent or legal guardian, Indian custodian, if any, and the Indian child's tribe, and shall comply with all of the following requirements:

(1) Notice shall be sent by registered or certified mail with return receipt requested. Additional notice by first-class mail is recommended, but not required.

(2) Notice to the tribe shall be to the tribal chairperson, unless the tribe has designated another agent for service.

(3) Notice shall be sent to all tribes of which the child may be a member or eligible for membership until the court makes a determination as to which tribe is the Indian child's tribe in accordance with subdivision (d) of Section 1449, after which notice need only be sent to the tribe determined to be the Indian child's tribe.

(4) Notice, to the extent required by federal law, shall be sent to the Secretary of the Interior's designated agent, the Sacramento Area Director, Bureau of Indian Affairs. If the identity or location of the Indian child's tribe is known, a copy of the notice shall also be sent directly to the Secretary of the Interior, unless the Secretary of the Interior has waived the notice in writing and the person responsible for giving notice under this section has filed proof of the waiver with the court.

(5) The notice shall include all of the following information:

(A) The name, birthdate, and birthplace of the Indian child, if known.

(B) The name of any Indian tribe in which the child is a member or may be eligible for membership, if known.

(C) All names known of the Indian child's biological parents, grandparents and great-grandparents or Indian custodians, including maiden, married, and former names or aliases, as well as their current and former addresses, birthdates, places of birth and death, tribal enrollment numbers, and any other identifying information, if known.

(D) A copy of the petition.

(E) A copy of the child's birth certificate, if available.

(F) The location, mailing address, and telephone number of the court and all parties notified pursuant to this section.

(G) A statement of the following:

(i) The absolute right of the child's parents, Indian custodians, and tribe to intervene in the proceeding.

(ii) The right of the child's parents, Indian custodians, and tribe to petition the court to transfer the proceeding to the tribal court of the Indian child's tribe, absent objection by either parent and subject to declination by the tribal court.

(iii) The right of the child's parents, Indian custodians, and tribe to, upon request, be granted up to an additional 20 days from the receipt of the notice to prepare for the proceeding.

(iv) The potential legal consequences of the proceedings on the future custodial rights of the child's parents or Indian custodians.

(v) That if the parents or Indian custodians are unable to afford counsel, counsel shall be appointed to represent the parents or Indian custodians pursuant to Section 1912 of the Indian Child Welfare Act (25 U.S.C. Sec. 1901 et seq.).

(vi) That the information contained in the notice, petition, pleading, and other court documents is confidential, so any person or entity notified shall maintain the confidentiality of the information contained in the notice concerning the particular proceeding and not reveal it to anyone who does not need the information in order to exercise the tribe's rights under the Indian Child Welfare Act (25 U.S.C. Sec. 1901 et seq.).

(c) Notice shall be sent whenever it is known or there is reason to know that an Indian child is involved, and for every hearing thereafter, including, but not limited to, the hearing at which a final adoption order is to be granted. After a tribe acknowledges that the child is a member or eligible for membership in the tribe, or after the Indian child's tribe intervenes in a proceeding, the information set out in subparagraphs (C), (D), (E), and (G) of paragraph (5) of subdivision (b) need not be included with the notice.

(d) Proof of the notice, including copies of notices sent and all return receipts and responses received, shall be filed with the court in advance of the hearing except as permitted under subdivision (e).

(e) No proceeding shall be held until at least 10 days after receipt of notice by the parent, Indian custodian, the tribe or the Bureau of Indian Affairs. The parent, Indian custodian, or the tribe shall, upon request, be granted up to 20 additional days to prepare for the proceeding. Nothing herein shall be construed as limiting the rights of the parent, Indian custodian, or tribe to 10 days' notice when a lengthier notice period is required by statute.

(f) With respect to giving notice to Indian tribes, a party shall be subject to court sanctions if that person knowingly and willfully falsifies or conceals a material fact concerning whether the child is an Indian child, or counsels a party to do so.

(g) The inclusion of contact information of any adult or child that would otherwise be required to be included in the notification pursuant to this section, shall not be required if that person is at risk of harm as a result of domestic violence, child abuse, sexual abuse, or stalking. *(Added by Stats.2006, c. 838 (S.B.678), § 19.)*

Research References

Forms

West's California Code Forms, Probate § 1459.5 Comment, Application of Federal Law to Proceedings Involving Children of Indian Ancestry.
West's California Judicial Council Forms ICWA–030, Notice of Child Custody Proceeding for Indian Child (Also Available in Spanish).
West's California Judicial Council Forms ICWA–030(A), Attachment to Notice of Child Custody Proceeding for Indian Child (Also Available in Spanish).

§ 1461. Notice to director; conditions; certificate; limitations

(a) As used in this section, "director" means:

(1) The Director of State Hospitals when the state hospital referred to in subdivision (b) is under the jurisdiction of the State Department of State Hospitals.

(2) The Director of Developmental Services when the state hospital referred to in subdivision (b) is under the jurisdiction of the State Department of Developmental Services.

(b) Notice of the time and place of hearing on the petition, report, or account, and a copy of the petition, report, or account, shall be delivered pursuant to Section 1215 to the director at the director's office in Sacramento or to the electronic address designated by the director for receipt of notice pursuant to this code, at least 15 days before the hearing if both of the following conditions exist:

(1) The ward or conservatee is or has been during the guardianship or conservatorship proceeding a patient in, or on leave from, a state hospital under the jurisdiction of the State Department of State Hospitals or the State Department of Developmental Services.

(2) The petition, report, or account is filed under any one or more of the following provisions: Section 1510, 1820, 1861, 2212, 2403, 2421, 2422, or 2423; Article 7 (commencing with Section 2540) of Chapter 6 of Part 4; Section 2580, 2592, or 2620; Chapter 9.5 (commencing with Section 2670) of Part 4; Section 3080 or 3088; or Chapter 3 (commencing with Section 3100) of Part 6. Notice under this section is not required in the case of an account pursuant to Section 2620 if the total guardianship or conservatorship assets are less than one thousand five hundred dollars ($1,500) and the gross annual income, exclusive of any public assistance income, is less than six thousand dollars ($6,000), and the ward or conservatee is not a patient in, or on leave or on outpatient status from, a state hospital at the time of the filing of the petition.

(c) If the ward or conservatee has been discharged from the state hospital, the director, upon ascertaining the facts, may file with the court a certificate stating that the ward or conservatee is not indebted to the state and waive the giving of further notices under this section. Upon the filing of the certificate of the director, compliance with this section thereafter is not required unless the certificate is revoked by the director and notice of the revocation is filed with the court.

(d) The statute of limitations does not run against any claim of the State Department of State Hospitals or the State Department of Developmental Services against the estate of the ward or conservatee for board, care, maintenance, or transportation with respect to an account that is settled without giving the notice required by this section. *(Stats.1990, c. 79 (A.B.759), § 14, operative July 1, 1991. Amended by Stats.2012, c. 440 (A.B.1488), § 39, eff. Sept. 22, 2012; Stats.2017, c. 319 (A.B.976), § 27, eff. Jan. 1, 2018.)*

Cross References

Appointment of guardian, notice of hearing, see Probate Code § 1511.
Computation of time, see Code of Civil Procedure §§ 12 and 12a; Government Code § 6800 et seq.
Definitions,
  Court, see Probate Code § 1418.
  Petition, see Probate Code § 1430.
Establishment of conservatorship, mailing of notice of hearing, see Probate Code § 1822.
Inventory and appraisement procedures when unrevoked certificate is on file with court, see Probate Code § 2611.
Notice,
  Mailing, see Probate Code § 1215 et seq.
  Posting, see Probate Code § 1230.
  Proof of giving notice, see Probate Code § 1260 et seq.
  Special notice, see Probate Code § 1250 et seq.
  This code, generally, see Probate Code § 1200 et seq.
Notice to,
  Director of Social Services, see Probate Code § 1542.
  Director of State Hospitals, see Probate Code §§ 2611, 2621.
  Interested persons, request for special notice, see Probate Code § 2700.
Service of process,
  Generally, see Code of Civil Procedure § 413.10 et seq.
  Mail, see Code of Civil Procedure §§ 415.30, 1012 et seq.
  Personal delivery, see Code of Civil Procedure § 415.10.
  Proof of service, see Code of Civil Procedure § 417.10 et seq.
  Publication, see Code of Civil Procedure § 415.50.

Research References

Forms

West's California Code Forms, Probate § 2620 Form 1, [First/Second, Etc] Account for Guardianship or Conservatorship Estate and Petition for Settlement of Account [And for Compensation].

§ 1461.4. Regional center for developmentally disabled; notice of hearing and copy of petition; report and recommendation

(a) The petitioner shall deliver pursuant to Section 1215 a notice of the hearing and a copy of the petition to the director of the regional center for the developmentally disabled at least 30 days before the day of the hearing on a petition for appointment in any case in which all of the following conditions exist:

(1) The proposed ward or conservatee has developmental disabilities.

(2) The proposed guardian or conservator is not the natural parent of the proposed ward or conservatee.

(3) The proposed guardian or conservator is a provider of board and care, treatment, habilitation, or other services to persons with developmental disabilities or is a spouse or employee of a provider.

(4) The proposed guardian or conservator is not a public entity.

(b) The regional center shall file a written report and recommendation with the court regarding the suitability of the petitioners to meet the needs of the proposed ward or conservatee in any case described in subdivision (a). *(Stats.1990, c. 79 (A.B.759), § 14, operative July 1, 1991. Amended by Stats.2017, c. 319 (A.B.976), § 28, eff. Jan. 1, 2018.)*

§ 1461.4

Cross References

Computation of time, see Code of Civil Procedure §§ 12 and 12a; Government Code § 6800 et seq.

Notice,
- Mailing, see Probate Code § 1215 et seq.
- Posting, see Probate Code § 1230.
- Proof of giving notice, see Probate Code § 1260 et seq.
- Special notice, see Probate Code § 1250 et seq.
- This code, generally, see Probate Code § 1200 et seq.

Service of process,
- Generally, see Code of Civil Procedure § 413.10 et seq.
- Mail, see Code of Civil Procedure §§ 415.30, 1012 et seq.
- Personal delivery, see Code of Civil Procedure § 415.10.
- Proof of service, see Code of Civil Procedure § 417.10 et seq.
- Publication, see Code of Civil Procedure § 415.50.

§ 1461.5. Veterans Administration; notice of hearing on petition, report, account or inventory; time; conditions

Notice of the time and place of hearing on a petition, report, or account, and a notice of the filing of an inventory, together with a copy of the petition, report, inventory, or account, shall be delivered pursuant to Section 1215 to the office of the Veterans Administration having jurisdiction over the area in which the court is located at least 15 days before the hearing, or within 15 days after the inventory is filed, if both of the following conditions exist:

(a) The guardianship or conservatorship estate consists or will consist wholly or in part of any of the following:

(1) Money received from the Veterans Administration.

(2) Revenue or profit from such money or from property acquired wholly or in part from such money.

(3) Property acquired wholly or in part with such money or from such property.

(b) The petition, report, inventory, or account is filed under any one or more of the following provisions: Section 1510, 1601, 1820, 1861, 1874, 2422, or 2423; Article 7 (commencing with Section 2540) of Chapter 6 of Part 4; Section 2570, 2571, 2580, 2592, 2610, 2613, or 2620; Chapter 8 (commencing with Section 2640) of Part 4; Chapter 9.5 (commencing with Section 2670) of Part 4; Section 3080 or 3088; or Chapter 3 (commencing with Section 3100) of Part 6. *(Stats.1990, c. 79 (A.B.759), § 14, operative July 1, 1991. Amended by Stats.2017, c. 319 (A.B.976), § 29, eff. Jan. 1, 2018.)*

Cross References

Appointment of guardian, notice of hearing, see Probate Code § 1511.
Computation of time, see Code of Civil Procedure §§ 12 and 12a; Government Code § 6800 et seq.
Establishment of conservatorship, notice of hearing, mailing, see Probate Code § 1822.

Research References

Forms

West's California Code Forms, Probate § 1510 Form 1, Petition for Appointment of Guardian of Estate of Minor—Judicial Council Form GC-210.

§ 1461.7. Time and place of hearing on petition, report, or account; copies

Unless the court for good cause dispenses with such notice, notice of the time and place of the hearing on a petition, report, or account, together with a copy of the petition, report, or account, shall be given to the same persons who are required to be given notice under Section 2581 for the period and in the manner provided in this chapter if both of the following conditions exist:

(a) A conservator of the estate has been appointed under Article 5 (commencing with Section 1845) of Chapter 1 of Part 3 for a person who is missing and whose whereabouts is unknown.

(b) The petition, report, or account is filed in the conservatorship proceeding under any one or more of the following provisions:

(1) Section 1861 or 2423.

(2) Article 7 (commencing with Section 2540) of Chapter 6 of Part 4.

(3) Section 2570, 2571, 2580, 2592, or 2620.

(4) Chapter 8 (commencing with Section 2640) of Part 4.

(5) Chapter 9.5 (commencing with Section 2670) of Part 4.

(6) Chapter 3 (commencing with Section 3100) of Part 6. *(Stats.1990, c. 79 (A.B.759), § 14, operative July 1, 1991.)*

§ 1467. Service by mail deemed complete

If service is made by mail pursuant to this division in the manner authorized in Section 415.30 of the Code of Civil Procedure, the service is complete on the date a written acknowledgment of receipt is executed. *(Stats.1990, c. 79 (A.B.759), § 14, operative July 1, 1991.)*

Cross References

Notice,
- Mailing, see Probate Code § 1215 et seq.
- Posting, see Probate Code § 1230.
- Proof of giving notice, see Probate Code § 1260 et seq.
- Special notice, see Probate Code § 1250 et seq.
- This code, generally, see Probate Code § 1200 et seq.

Service of process, mail, see Code of Civil Procedure §§ 415.30, 1012 et seq.
Service of process, proof of service, see Code of Civil Procedure § 417.10 et seq.

§ 1469. References to § 1220 deemed references to this chapter

Where a provision of this division applies the provisions of this code applicable to personal representatives to proceedings under this division, a reference to Section 1220 in the provisions applicable to personal representatives shall be deemed to be a reference to this chapter. *(Stats.1990, c. 79 (A.B.759), § 14, operative July 1, 1991.)*

Cross References

Appointment of personal representative, generally, see Probate Code § 8400 et seq.
Personal representative and general personal representative, defined, see Probate Code § 58.

Research References

Forms

West's California Judicial Council Forms GC–020, Notice of Hearing—Guardianship or Conservatorship.
West's California Judicial Council Forms GC–020(P), Proof of Personal Service of Notice of Hearing—Guardianship or Conservatorship.

CHAPTER 4. APPOINTMENT OF LEGAL COUNSEL

Section
1470. Discretionary appointment; compensation and expenses; source for payment.
1471. Mandatory appointment; proceedings.
1472. Mandatory appointment; compensation and expenses; determination by court; source for payment.
1474. Matters involving children of Indian ancestry.

§ 1470. Discretionary appointment; compensation and expenses; source for payment

(a) The court may appoint private legal counsel for a ward, a proposed ward, a conservatee, or a proposed conservatee in any proceeding under this division if the court determines the person is not otherwise represented by legal counsel and that the appointment would be helpful to the resolution of the matter or is necessary to protect the person's interests.

(b) If a person is furnished legal counsel under this section, the court shall, upon conclusion of the matter, fix a reasonable sum for compensation and expenses of counsel. The sum may, in the discretion of the court, include compensation for services rendered, and expenses incurred, before the date of the order appointing counsel.

(c) The court shall order the sum fixed under subdivision (b) to be paid:

(1) If the person for whom legal counsel is appointed is an adult, from the estate of that person.

(2) If the person for whom legal counsel is appointed is a minor, by a parent or the parents of the minor or from the minor's estate, or any combination thereof, in any proportions the court deems just.

(3) If a ward or proposed ward is furnished legal counsel for a guardianship proceeding, upon its own motion or that of a party, the court shall determine whether a parent or parents of the ward or proposed ward or the estate of the ward or proposed ward is financially unable to pay all or a portion of the cost of counsel appointed pursuant to this section. Any portion of the cost of that counsel that the court finds the parent or parents or the estate of the ward or proposed ward is unable to pay shall be paid by the county. The Judicial Council shall adopt guidelines to assist in determining financial eligibility for county payment of counsel appointed by the court pursuant to this chapter.

(d) The court may make an order under subdivision (c) requiring payment by a parent or parents of the minor only after the parent or parents, as the case may be, have been given notice and the opportunity to be heard on whether the order would be just under the circumstances of the particular case. *(Stats.1990, c. 79 (A.B.759), § 14, operative July 1, 1991. Amended by Stats.1992, c. 572 (S.B. 1455), § 1.5; Stats.2007, c. 719 (S.B.241), § 1.)*

Cross References

Child custody, private counsel, see Family Code § 3150 et seq.
Conservatorships and other protective proceedings, educational requirements for court-appointed attorneys and other staff members, see Probate Code § 1456.
Minors, see Family Code § 6500.
Parent, defined, see Probate Code § 54.
Public defender, duty to represent persons not financially able to employ counsel, see Government Code § 27706.

Research References

Forms

1 California Transactions Forms--Estate Planning § 1:4, Loss of Due Process Inherent in Probate Avoidance.
West's California Judicial Council Forms GC–005, Application for Appointment of Counsel.
West's California Judicial Council Forms GC–006, Order Appointing Legal Counsel.
West's California Judicial Council Forms GC–010, Certification of Attorney Qualifications.

§ 1471. Mandatory appointment; proceedings

(a) If a conservatee, proposed conservatee, or person alleged to lack legal capacity is * * * not represented by legal counsel and * * * does not plan to retain counsel, whether or not that person lacks or appears to lack legal capacity, the court shall, at or before the time of the hearing, appoint the public defender or private counsel to represent the person in the following proceedings under this division:

(1) A proceeding to establish or transfer a conservatorship or to appoint a proposed conservator.

(2) A proceeding to terminate the conservatorship.

(3) A proceeding to remove the conservator.

(4) A proceeding for a court order affecting the legal capacity of the conservatee.

(5) A proceeding to obtain an order authorizing removal of a temporary conservatee from the temporary conservatee's place of residence.

* * *

(b) In a proceeding to establish a limited conservatorship, if the proposed limited conservatee has not retained legal counsel and does not plan to retain legal counsel, the court shall immediately appoint the public defender or private counsel to represent the proposed limited conservatee. The proposed limited conservatee shall pay the cost for that legal service if they are able. This subdivision applies irrespective of any medical or psychological inability to attend the hearing on the part of the proposed limited conservatee as allowed in Section 1825.

(c) If a conservatee, proposed conservatee, or person alleged to lack legal capacity expresses a preference for a particular attorney to represent them, the court shall allow representation by the preferred attorney, even if the attorney is not on the court's list of a court-appointed attorneys, and the attorney shall provide zealous representation as provided in subdivision (d). However, an attorney who cannot provide zealous advocacy or who has a conflict of interest with respect to the representation of the conservatee, proposed conservatee, or person alleged to lack legal capacity shall be disqualified.

(d) The role of legal counsel of a conservatee, proposed conservatee, or a person alleged to lack legal capacity is that of a zealous, independent advocate representing the wishes of their client, consistent with the duties set forth in Section 6068 of the Business and Professions Code and the California Rules of Professional Conduct.

(e) In an appeal or writ proceeding arising out of a proceeding described in this section, if a conservatee or proposed conservatee is not represented by legal counsel, the reviewing court shall appoint legal counsel to represent the conservatee or proposed conservatee before the court. *(Stats.1990, c. 79 (A.B.759), § 14, operative July 1, 1991. Amended by Stats.2014, c. 553 (S.B.940), § 5, eff. Jan. 1, 2015, operative Jan. 1, 2016; Stats.2021, c. 417 (A.B.1194), § 6, eff. Jan. 1, 2022; Stats.2022, c. 420 (A.B.2960), § 32, eff. Jan. 1, 2023.)*

Cross References

Authorization of medical treatment for adult without conservator, appointment of counsel, see Probate Code § 3205.
Community property, transactions, representation of counsel, see Probate Code § 3140.
Conservatorships and other protective proceedings, educational requirements for court-appointed attorneys and other staff members, see Probate Code § 1456.
Counsel, right to, see Cal. Const. Art. 1, § 15.
Court investigator,
  Appointment and qualifications, see Probate Code § 1454.
  Defined, see Probate Code § 1419.
  Duties and report, see Probate Code §§ 1826, 1894.
Court ordered medical treatment, duty of attorney, see Probate Code § 2357.
Duty of public defender to represent persons not financially able to employ counsel, see Government Code § 27706.
Establishment of conservatorship, see Probate Code § 1800 et seq.
Guardians and conservators, removal or resignation, see Probate Code § 2650 et seq.
Legal capacity of conservatee, see Probate Code § 1870 et seq.
Limited conservatorship,
  Establishment, developmentally disabled adults, see Probate Code §§ 1801, 1828.5, 1830.
  Proceedings to establish, defined, see Probate Code § 1431.
Periodic review of conservatorship, notification of counsel, see Probate Code § 1852.
Referral of conservatee for assessment to determine if conservatee has treatable mental illness and is unwilling or unable to accept voluntary treatment, counsel, see Welfare and Institutions Code § 5350.5.
Removal of temporary conservatee from place of residence, see Probate Code §§ 2253, 2254.

§ 1471 PROBATE CODE

Termination of conservatorship, see Probate Code § 1860 et seq.

Research References

Forms

West's California Code Forms, Probate § 3204 Form 2, Medical Declaration of Patient's Physician.

West's California Judicial Council Forms GC–005, Application for Appointment of Counsel.

West's California Judicial Council Forms GC–006, Order Appointing Legal Counsel.

West's California Judicial Council Forms GC–010, Certification of Attorney Qualifications.

§ 1472. Mandatory appointment; compensation and expenses; determination by court; source for payment

(a) If a person is furnished legal counsel under Section 1471:

(1) The court shall, upon conclusion of the matter, fix a reasonable sum for compensation and expenses of counsel and shall make a determination of the person's ability to pay all or a portion of that sum. The sum may, in the discretion of the court, include compensation for services rendered, and expenses incurred, before the date of the order appointing counsel.

(2) If the court determines that the person has the ability to pay all or a portion of the sum, the court shall order the conservator of the estate or, if none, the person, to pay in any installments and in any manner the court determines to be reasonable and compatible with the person's financial ability.

(3) In a proceeding under Chapter 3 (commencing with Section 3100) of Part 6 for court authorization of a proposed transaction involving community property, the court may order payment out of the proceeds of the transaction.

(4) If a conservator is not appointed for the person furnished legal counsel, the order for payment may be enforced in the same manner as a money judgment.

(b) If the court determines that a person furnished private counsel under Section 1471 lacks the ability to pay all or a portion of the sum determined under paragraph (1) of subdivision (a), the county shall pay the sum to the private counsel to the extent the court determines the person is unable to pay.

(c) The payment ordered by the court under subdivision (a) shall be made to the county if the public defender has been appointed or if private counsel has been appointed to perform the duties of the public defender and the county has compensated that counsel. In the case of other court-appointed counsel, the payment shall be made to that counsel. *(Stats.1990, c. 79 (A.B.759), § 14, operative July 1, 1991. Amended by Stats.1992, c. 572 (S.B.1455), § 2.)*

Cross References

Authorization of medical treatment for adult without conservator, application of this section, see Probate Code § 3205.
Community property, see Family Code §§ 65, 760.
Community property, defined, see Probate Code § 28.
Counsel, right to, see Cal. Const. Art. 1, § 15.
Court ordered medical treatment, duty of attorney, see Probate Code § 2357.
Enforcement of judgment in civil actions, see Code of Civil Procedure § 683.010 et seq.
Periodic review of conservatorship, see Probate Code § 1852.
Transaction involving community property, compensation of appointed legal counsel, see Probate Code § 3140.

§ 1474. Matters involving children of Indian ancestry

If an Indian custodian or biological parent of an Indian child lacks the financial ability to retain counsel and requests the appointment of counsel in proceedings described in Section 1459.5, the provisions of subsection (b) of Section 1912 of the Indian Child Welfare Act (25 U.S.C. Sec. 1901 et seq.) and Section 23.13 of Title 25 of the Code of Federal Regulations are applicable. *(Added by Stats.2006, c. 838 (S.B.678), § 20.)*

Research References

Forms

West's California Code Forms, Probate § 1459.5 Comment, Application of Federal Law to Proceedings Involving Children of Indian Ancestry.

CHAPTER 5. TRANSITIONAL PROVISIONS

Section
1488. Nomination by adult of guardian for such adult deemed nomination of conservator.
1489. Appointment of guardian by parent or other person for a minor; effect.
1490. References in statutes.

§ 1488. Nomination by adult of guardian for such adult deemed nomination of conservator

If before January 1, 1981, an adult has in a signed writing nominated a person to serve as guardian if a guardian is in the future appointed for such adult, such nomination shall be deemed to be a nomination of a conservator. This section applies whether or not the signed writing was executed in the same manner as a witnessed will so long as the person signing the writing had at the time the writing was signed sufficient capacity to form an intelligent preference. *(Stats. 1990, c. 79 (A.B.759), § 14, operative July 1, 1991.)*

§ 1489. Appointment of guardian by parent or other person for a minor; effect

If, before January 1, 1981, a parent or other person has in a signed writing appointed a person to serve as the guardian of the person or estate or both of a minor, or as the guardian of the property the minor receives from or by designation of the person making the appointment, such appointment shall be deemed to be a nomination of a guardian if the requirements of Section 1500 or 1501 are satisfied and, in such case, shall be given the same effect it would have under Section 1500 or 1501, as the case may be, if made on or after January 1, 1981. This section applies whether or not the signed writing is a will or deed so long as the person signing the writing had at the time the writing was signed sufficient capacity to form an intelligent preference. *(Stats.1990, c. 79 (A.B.759), § 14, operative July 1, 1991.)*

§ 1490. References in statutes

Except as set forth in Section 1510.1, when used in any statute of this state with reference to an adult or to the person of a married minor, "guardian" means the conservator of that adult or the conservator of the person in the case of the married minor. *(Stats.1990, c. 79 (A.B.759), § 14, operative July 1, 1991. Amended by Stats.2015, c. 694 (A.B.900), § 2, eff. Jan. 1, 2016; Stats.2016, c. 86 (S.B.1171), § 244, eff. Jan. 1, 2017.)*

Part 2

GUARDIANSHIP

Cross References

Delinquents and wards of the juvenile court, custody of child, see Welfare and Institutions Code § 304.
Freedom from parental custody and control, stay of proceedings and effect upon jurisdiction under these provisions, see Family Code § 7807.
Juvenile case file inspection, confidentiality, release, probation reports, destruction of records, and liability, see Welfare and Institutions Code § 827.
Juvenile court law, guardianships resulting from selection or implementation of a permanent plan, see Welfare and Institutions Code § 366.4.
Termination of parental rights of father, filing of petition, stay of proceedings affecting a child pending final determination of parental rights, see Family Code § 7662.

CHAPTER 1. ESTABLISHMENT OF GUARDIANSHIP

ARTICLE 1. NOMINATION OF GUARDIAN

Section
1500. Nomination of guardian of person or estate or both by parent.
1500.1. Consent by Indian child's parent; requirements.
1501. Nomination of guardian for property received by minor.
1502. Manner of nomination; time effective; subsequent legal incapacity or death of nominator.

Cross References

Right to custody of minor child, nomination of guardian by parent, see Family Code § 3043.

§ 1500. Nomination of guardian of person or estate or both by parent

Subject to Section 1502, a parent may nominate a guardian of the person or estate, or both, of a minor child in either of the following cases:

(a) Where the other parent nominates, or consents in writing to the nomination of, the same guardian for the same child.

(b) Where, at the time the petition for appointment of the guardian is filed, either (1) the other parent is dead or lacks legal capacity to consent to the nomination or (2) the consent of the other parent would not be required for an adoption of the child. *(Stats.1990, c. 79 (A.B.759), § 14, operative July 1, 1991.)*

Cross References

Additional powers of guardian nominated by will, see Probate Code § 2108.
Appointment of guardian, see Probate Code § 1514.
Bond of nominated guardian, see Probate Code § 2324.
Capacity of trust company to act as guardian or conservator of estate, see Probate Code § 300.
Child, defined, see Probate Code § 26.
Consent of parent to adoption of child, see Family Code § 8604 et seq.
Joint guardians for one ward, see Probate Code § 2105.
Manner of nomination, see Probate Code § 1502.
Nonrelative guardianships, see Probate Code § 1540 et seq.
Notice of hearing, see Probate Code § 1511.
One guardian for several wards, see Probate Code § 2106.
Parent, defined, see Probate Code § 54.
Petition for appointment, contents, see Probate Code § 1510.
Powers and duties,
  Guardian of estate, see Probate Code § 2400 et seq.
  Guardian of person, see Probate Code § 2350 et seq.
Transitional provision, appointment of guardian deemed to be nomination of guardian, see Probate Code § 1489.

Research References

Forms

1 California Transactions Forms--Estate Planning § 6:15, Minors' Capacity to Take Devised Property.
1 California Transactions Forms--Estate Planning § 6:16, Guardian of Person.
1 California Transactions Forms--Estate Planning § 6:17, Guardian of Estate or of Property.
1 California Transactions Forms--Estate Planning § 6:53, Matters to Consider in Drafting Gifts to Minors.
1 California Transactions Forms--Estate Planning § 6:73, Appointment of Guardian of Person of Minor Child and Statement of Desire that Same Person be Appointed Guardian of Minor's Estate.
1 California Transactions Forms--Estate Planning § 6:74, Appointment of Guardian of Person and Estate of Minor Children.
1 California Transactions Forms--Estate Planning § 6:77, Use of Child's Estate by Guardian of Person.
4 California Transactions Forms--Estate Planning § 19:93, Nomination of Guardian.
4 California Transactions Forms--Estate Planning § 19:94, Appointment of Guardian of Person.
4 California Transactions Forms--Estate Planning § 19:95, Appointment of Guardian of Estate.
2 California Transactions Forms--Family Law § 5:3, Rights of Nonparents Generally.
2 California Transactions Forms--Family Law § 5:4, Rights of De Facto Parents.
West's California Code Forms, Family § 7500, Comment Overview—Rights of Parents.
West's California Code Forms, Probate § 1500–1502 Form 1, Nomination of Guardian.
West's California Code Forms, Probate § 1500–1502 Form 2, Probate Guardianship Pamphlet—Judicial Council Form GC-205.
West's California Code Forms, Probate § 1510 Form 1, Petition for Appointment of Guardian of Estate of Minor—Judicial Council Form GC-210.
West's California Code Forms, Probate § 1510 Form 2, Consent of Guardian, Nomination and Waiver of Notice—Judicial Council Form GC-211.
West's California Code Forms, Probate § 1514 Form 1, Order Appointing Guardian of Minor—Judicial Council Form GC-240.
West's California Code Forms, Probate § 2651 Form 1, Petition for Removal of Guardian or Conservator.
West's California Judicial Council Forms GC–211, Consent of Proposed Guardian, Nomination of Guardian, and Consent to Appointment of Guardian and Waiver of Notice.

§ 1500.1. Consent by Indian child's parent; requirements

(a) Notwithstanding any other section in this part, and in accordance with Section 1913 of the Indian Child Welfare Act (25 U.S.C. Sec. 1901 et seq.), consent to nomination of a guardian of the person or of a guardian of the person and the estate given by an Indian child's parent is not valid unless both of the following occur:

(1) The consent is executed in writing at least 10 days after the child's birth and recorded before a judge.

(2) The judge certifies that the terms and consequences of the consent were fully explained in detail in English and were fully understood by the parent or that they were interpreted into a language that the parent understood.

(b) The parent of an Indian child may withdraw his or her consent to guardianship for any reason at any time prior to the issuance of letters of guardianship and the child shall be returned to the parent. *(Added by Stats.2006, c. 838 (S.B.678), § 21.)*

Research References

Forms

West's California Code Forms, Probate § 1459.5 Comment, Application of Federal Law to Proceedings Involving Children of Indian Ancestry.
West's California Code Forms, Probate § 1811 Form 1, Nomination of Conservator by Spouse/Domestic Partner or Parent.

§ 1501. Nomination of guardian for property received by minor

Subject to Section 1502, a parent or any other person may nominate a guardian for property that a minor receives from or by designation of the nominator (whether before, at the time of, or after the nomination) including, but not limited to, property received by the minor by virtue of a gift, deed, trust, will, succession, insurance, or benefits of any kind. *(Stats.1990, c. 79 (A.B.759), § 14, operative July 1, 1991.)*

Cross References

Appointment of guardian, see Probate Code § 1514.
Bond of nominated guardian, see Probate Code § 2324.
California Uniform Transfers to Minors Act, see Probate Code § 3900.
Duties of trustees, see Probate Code § 16000 et seq.
Guardian, powers and duties,
  Nominated in will, see Probate Code § 2108.
  Particular property appointed, see Probate Code § 2109.
Notice of hearing, see Probate Code § 1511.
Petition for appointment, contents, see Probate Code § 1510.
Transitional provision, appointment of guardian deemed to be nomination of guardian, see Probate Code § 1489.

§ 1501

Trustees, powers, see Probate Code § 16200 et seq.

Research References

Forms

1 California Transactions Forms--Estate Planning § 6:16, Guardian of Person.

1 California Transactions Forms--Estate Planning § 6:17, Guardian of Estate or of Property.

1 California Transactions Forms--Estate Planning § 6:73, Appointment of Guardian of Person of Minor Child and Statement of Desire that Same Person be Appointed Guardian of Minor's Estate.

1 California Transactions Forms--Estate Planning § 6:75, Appointment of Guardian of Specific Property.

West's California Code Forms, Probate § 1500–1502 Form 1, Nomination of Guardian.

West's California Code Forms, Probate § 1510 Form 1, Petition for Appointment of Guardian of Estate of Minor—Judicial Council Form GC-210.

West's California Code Forms, Probate § 1510 Form 2, Consent of Guardian, Nomination and Waiver of Notice—Judicial Council Form GC-211.

West's California Code Forms, Probate § 1514 Form 1, Order Appointing Guardian of Minor—Judicial Council Form GC-240.

West's California Code Forms, Probate § 2651 Form 1, Petition for Removal of Guardian or Conservator.

§ 1502. Manner of nomination; time effective; subsequent legal incapacity or death of nominator

(a) A nomination of a guardian under this article may be made in the petition for the appointment of the guardian or at the hearing on the petition or in a writing signed either before or after the petition for the appointment of the guardian is filed.

(b) The nomination of a guardian under this article is effective when made except that a writing nominating a guardian under this article may provide that the nomination becomes effective only upon the occurrence of such specified condition or conditions as are stated in the writing, including but not limited to such conditions as the subsequent legal incapacity or death of the person making the nomination.

(c) Unless the writing making the nomination expressly otherwise provides, a nomination made under this article remains effective notwithstanding the subsequent legal incapacity or death of the person making the nomination. *(Stats.1990, c. 79 (A.B.759), § 14, operative July 1, 1991.)*

Cross References

Petition for appointment, see Probate Code § 1510.

Research References

Forms

1 California Transactions Forms--Estate Planning § 6:16, Guardian of Person.

1 California Transactions Forms--Estate Planning § 6:17, Guardian of Estate or of Property.

1 California Transactions Forms--Estate Planning § 6:73, Appointment of Guardian of Person of Minor Child and Statement of Desire that Same Person be Appointed Guardian of Minor's Estate.

1 California Transactions Forms--Estate Planning § 6:74, Appointment of Guardian of Person and Estate of Minor Children.

1 California Transactions Forms--Estate Planning § 6:77, Use of Child's Estate by Guardian of Person.

4 California Transactions Forms--Estate Planning § 19:93, Nomination of Guardian.

West's California Code Forms, Probate § 1500–1502 Form 1, Nomination of Guardian.

West's California Judicial Council Forms GC–211, Consent of Proposed Guardian, Nomination of Guardian, and Consent to Appointment of Guardian and Waiver of Notice.

ARTICLE 2. APPOINTMENT OF GUARDIAN GENERALLY

Section

1510. Petition for appointment; contents.

1510.1. Appointment of guardian for unmarried individual between 18 and 21 years of age; findings regarding special immigrant juvenile status; rights as an adult; adoption of rules and forms for implementation.

1511. Notice of hearing.

1512. Amendment of petition to disclose newly discovered proceeding affecting custody.

1513. Investigation; filing of report and recommendation concerning proposed guardianship; contents of report; confidentiality; application of section.

1513.1. Assessments.

1513.2. Status report; form; contents; confidentiality.

1514. Appointment of guardian.

1514.5. Information available for probate guardianship proceeding and guardianship investigator regarding best interest of child; confidentiality.

1515. No guardian of person for married minor.

1516. Petitions for guardianship of the person; delivery of notice of hearing and copy of petition; screening of guardians; application of section.

1516.5. Proceeding to have child declared free from custody and control of one or both parents.

1517. Guardianships resulting from selection and implementation of a permanent plan; application of part; administration of funds for benefit of child.

Cross References

Aid to Families with Dependent Children—Foster Care, child whose nonrelated guardianship was ordered in probate court pursuant to this Article, eligibility of nonminor for continued benefits, see Welfare and Institutions Code § 11405.

§ 1510. Petition for appointment; contents

(a) A relative or other person on behalf of the minor, or the minor if 12 years of age or older, may file a petition for the appointment of a guardian of the minor. A relative may file a petition for the appointment of a guardian under this section regardless of the relative's immigration status.

(b) The petition shall request that a guardian of the person or estate of the minor, or both, be appointed, shall specify the name and address of the proposed guardian and the name and date of birth of the proposed ward, and shall state that the appointment is necessary or convenient.

(c) The petition shall set forth, so far as is known to the petitioner, the names and addresses of all of the following:

(1) The parents of the proposed ward.

(2) The person having legal custody of the proposed ward and, if that person does not have the care of the proposed ward, the person having the care of the proposed ward.

(3) The relatives of the proposed ward within the second degree.

(4) In the case of a guardianship of the estate, the spouse of the proposed ward.

(5) Any person nominated as guardian for the proposed ward under Section 1500 or 1501.

(6) In the case of a guardianship of the person involving an Indian child, any Indian custodian and the Indian child's tribe.

(d) If the petitioner or proposed guardian is a professional fiduciary, as described in Section 2340, who is required to be licensed under the Professional Fiduciaries Act (Chapter 6 (commencing with Section 6500) of Division 3 of the Business and Professions Code), the petition shall include the following:

(1) The petitioner's or proposed guardian's proposed hourly fee schedule or another statement of his or her proposed compensation from the estate of the proposed ward for services performed as a guardian. The petitioner's or proposed guardian's provision of a

proposed hourly fee schedule or another statement of his or her proposed compensation, as required by this paragraph, shall not preclude a court from later reducing the petitioner's or proposed guardian's fees or other compensation.

(2) Unless a petition for appointment of a temporary guardian that contains the statements required by this paragraph is filed together with a petition for appointment of a guardian, both of the following:

(A) A statement of the petitioner's or proposed guardian's license information.

(B) A statement explaining who engaged the petitioner or proposed guardian or how the petitioner or proposed guardian was engaged to file the petition for appointment of a guardian or to agree to accept the appointment as guardian and what prior relationship the petitioner or proposed guardian had with the proposed ward or the proposed ward's family or friends.

(e) If the proposed ward is a patient in or on leave of absence from a state institution under the jurisdiction of the State Department of State Hospitals or the State Department of Developmental Services and that fact is known to the petitioner or proposed guardian, the petition shall state that fact and name the institution.

(f) The petition shall state, so far as is known to the petitioner or proposed guardian, whether or not the proposed ward is receiving or is entitled to receive benefits from the Veterans Administration and the estimated amount of the monthly benefit payable by the Veterans Administration for the proposed ward.

(g) If the petitioner or proposed guardian has knowledge of any pending adoption, juvenile court, marriage dissolution, domestic relations, custody, or other similar proceeding affecting the proposed ward, the petition shall disclose the pending proceeding.

(h) If the petitioners or proposed guardians have accepted or intend to accept physical care or custody of the child with intent to adopt, whether formed at the time of placement or formed subsequent to placement, the petitioners or proposed guardians shall so state in the guardianship petition, whether or not an adoption petition has been filed.

(i) If the proposed ward is or becomes the subject of an adoption petition, the court shall order the guardianship petition consolidated with the adoption petition, and the consolidated case shall be heard and decided in the court in which the adoption is pending.

(j) If the proposed ward is or may be an Indian child, the petition shall state that fact. *(Stats.1990, c. 79 (A.B.759), § 14, operative July 1, 1991. Amended by Stats.1992, c. 1064 (S.B.1445), § 1; Stats.2006, c. 838 (S.B.678), § 22; Stats.2008, c. 534 (S.B.1726), § 12; Stats.2012, c. 440 (A.B.1488), § 40, eff. Sept. 22, 2012; Stats.2012, c. 845 (S.B.1064), § 2; Stats.2013, c. 248 (A.B.1339), § 1.)*

Cross References

Adoption, see Family Code § 8500 et seq.
Appointment of guardian to fill vacancy, see Probate Code § 2670 et seq.
Appointment of legal counsel for proposed ward, see Probate Code § 1470.
Child, defined, see Probate Code § 26.
Custody of children, see Family Code § 3000 et seq.
Guardianship proceedings, exclusive jurisdiction, consolidation of guardianship and adoption proceedings, see Probate Code § 2205.
Independent exercise of powers, see Probate Code § 2592.
Joint guardians for one ward, see Probate Code § 2105.
Jurisdiction and venue, see Probate Code § 2200 et seq.
Juvenile court law, see Welfare and Institutions Code § 200 et seq.
Marriage dissolution, see Family Code § 2300 et seq.
Nonprofit charitable corporation as guardian, see Probate Code § 2104.
Notice to directors, see Probate Code §§ 1461, 1542.
Notice to Veterans Administration, see Probate Code § 1461.5.
One guardian for several wards, see Probate Code § 2106.
Parent, defined, see Probate Code § 54.
Petition,
  Clerk to set petition for hearing, see Probate Code § 1041.
  Nonrelative guardianships, see Probate Code §§ 1541, 1542.
Petitions and other papers, see Probate Code § 1020 et seq.
Professional fiduciary as guardian or conservator, submission of new proposed hourly fee schedule or statement of compensation on or after one year from original submission, see Probate Code § 2614.8.
Service of summons on minors, wards and conservatees, see Code of Civil Procedure §§ 416.60, 416.70.
Temporary guardian or conservator, see Probate Code § 2250 et seq.

Research References

Forms

1 California Transactions Forms--Estate Planning § 6:16, Guardian of Person.
2 California Transactions Forms--Family Law § 6:41, Initiating the Adoption.
2 California Transactions Forms--Family Law § 6:47, Matters to Consider in Drafting Petition for Independent Adoption of Unmarried Minor.
2 California Transactions Forms--Family Law § 6:108, Petition for Stepparent Adoption.
West's California Code Forms, Family § 7500, Comment Overview—Rights of Parents.
West's California Code Forms, Probate § 1459.5 Comment, Application of Federal Law to Proceedings Involving Children of Indian Ancestry.
West's California Code Forms, Probate § 1460–1461 Form 1, Notice of Hearing (Guardianship or Conservatorship)—Judicial Council Form GC-020.
West's California Code Forms, Probate § 1510 Form 1, Petition for Appointment of Guardian of Estate of Minor—Judicial Council Form GC-210.
West's California Code Forms, Probate § 1510 Form 3, Declaration Under Uniform Child Custody Jurisdiction and Enforcement Act (UCCJEA)-Judicial Council Form FL-105/GC-120.
West's California Code Forms, Probate § 2357 Form 1, Petition for Order Directing Medical Treatment for Ward or Conservatee.
West's California Judicial Council Forms FL–105, Declaration Under Uniform Child Custody Jurisdiction and Enforcement Act (UCCJEA) (Also Available in Spanish).
West's California Judicial Council Forms FL–105(A), Attachment to Declaration Under Uniform Child Custody Jurisdiction and Enforcement Act (UCCJEA).
West's California Judicial Council Forms GC–120, Declaration Under Uniform Child Custody Jurisdiction and Enforcement Act (UCCJEA) (Also Available in Spanish).
West's California Judicial Council Forms GC–120(A), Attachment to Declaration Under Uniform Child Custody Jurisdiction and Enforcement Act (UCCJEA).
West's California Judicial Council Forms GC–210, Petition for Appointment of Guardian of Minor.
West's California Judicial Council Forms GC–210(CA), Child Information Attachment to Probate Guardianship Petition.
West's California Judicial Council Forms GC–210(P), Petition for Appointment of Guardian of the Person.
West's California Judicial Council Forms GC–210(PE), Petition to Extend Guardianship of the Person.

§ 1510.1. Appointment of guardian for unmarried individual between 18 and 21 years of age; findings regarding special immigrant juvenile status; rights as an adult; adoption of rules and forms for implementation

(a)(1) With the consent of the proposed ward, the court may appoint a guardian of the person for an unmarried individual who is 18 years of age or older, but who has not yet attained 21 years of age, in connection with a petition to make the necessary findings regarding special immigrant juvenile status pursuant to subdivision (b) of Section 155 of the Code of Civil Procedure.

(2) A petition for guardianship of the person of a proposed ward who is 18 years of age or older, but who has not yet attained 21 years of age, may be filed by a parent, relative, or any other person on behalf of the proposed ward, or the proposed ward.

(b)(1) At the request of, or with the consent of, the ward, the court may extend an existing guardianship of the person for a ward past 18 years of age, for purposes of allowing the ward to complete the application process with the United States Citizenship and Immigration Services for classification as a special immigrant juvenile pursuant to Section 1101(a)(27)(J) of Title 8 of the United States Code.

§ 1510.1

(2) A relative or any other person on behalf of a ward, or the ward, may file a petition to extend the guardianship of the person for a period of time not to extend beyond the ward reaching 21 years of age.

(c) This section does not authorize the guardian to abrogate any of the rights that a person who has attained 18 years of age may have as an adult under state law, including, but not limited to, decisions regarding the ward's medical treatment, education, or residence, without the ward's express consent.

(d) For purposes of this division, the terms "child," "minor," and "ward" include an unmarried individual who is younger than 21 years of age and who, pursuant to this section, consents to the appointment of a guardian or extension of a guardianship after he or she attains 18 years of age.

(e) The Judicial Council shall, by July 1, 2016, adopt any rules and forms needed to implement this section. *(Added by Stats.2015, c. 694 (A.B.900), § 3, eff. Jan. 1, 2016. Amended by Stats.2016, c. 86 (S.B.1171), § 245, eff. Jan. 1, 2017; Stats.2018, c. 209 (A.B.2090), § 1, eff. Jan. 1, 2019.)*

Research References

Forms

West's California Judicial Council Forms GC–210, Petition for Appointment of Guardian of Minor.

West's California Judicial Council Forms GC–210(P), Petition for Appointment of Guardian of the Person.

West's California Judicial Council Forms GC–210(PE), Petition to Extend Guardianship of the Person.

West's California Judicial Council Forms GC–240, Order Appointing Guardian or Extending Guardianship of the Person.

§ 1511. Notice of hearing

(a) Except as provided in subdivisions (f) and (g), at least 15 days before the hearing on the petition for the appointment of a guardian, notice of the time and place of the hearing shall be given as provided in subdivisions (b), (c), (d), and (e) of this section. The notice shall be accompanied by a copy of the petition and shall include a copy of the form required by Section 68511.1 of the Government Code. The court shall not shorten the time for giving the notice of hearing under this section.

(b) Notice shall be served in the manner provided in Section 415.10 or 415.30 of the Code of Civil Procedure, or in any manner authorized by the court, on all of the following persons:

(1) The proposed ward if 12 years of age or older.

(2) Any person having legal custody of the proposed ward, or serving as guardian of the estate of the proposed ward.

(3) The parents of the proposed ward.

(4) Any person nominated as a guardian for the proposed ward under Section 1500 or 1501.

(c) Notice shall be delivered pursuant to Section 1215 to the addresses stated in the petition, or in any manner authorized by the court, to all of the following:

(1) The spouse named in the petition.

(2) The relatives named in the petition, except that if the petition is for the appointment of a guardian of the estate only the court may dispense with the giving of notice to any one or more or all of the relatives.

(3) The person having the care of the proposed ward if other than the person having legal custody of the proposed ward.

(d) If notice is required by Section 1461 or 1542 to be given to the Director of State Hospitals or the Director of Developmental Services or the Director of Social Services, notice shall be delivered pursuant to Section 1215 as required.

(e) If the petition states that the proposed ward is receiving or is entitled to receive benefits from the Veterans Administration, notice shall be delivered pursuant to Section 1215 to the office of the Veterans Administration referred to in Section 1461.5.

(f) Unless the court orders otherwise, notice shall not be given to any of the following:

(1) The parents or other relatives of a proposed ward who has been relinquished to a licensed adoption agency.

(2) The parents of a proposed ward who has been judicially declared free from their custody and control.

(g) Notice need not be given to any person if the court so orders upon a determination of either of the following:

(1) The person cannot with reasonable diligence be given the notice.

(2) The giving of the notice would be contrary to the interest of justice.

(h) Before the appointment of a guardian is made, proof shall be made to the court that each person entitled to notice under this section either:

(1) Has been given notice as required by this section.

(2) Has not been given notice as required by this section because the person cannot with reasonable diligence be given the notice or because the giving of notice to that person would be contrary to the interest of justice.

(i) If notice is required by Section 1460.2 to be given to an Indian custodian or tribe, notice shall be mailed as required. *(Stats.1990, c. 79 (A.B.759), § 14, operative July 1, 1991. Amended by Stats.1992, c. 1064 (S.B.1445), § 2; Stats.1996, c. 563 (S.B.392), § 6; Stats.2006, c. 838 (S.B.678), § 23; Stats.2012, c. 440 (A.B.1488), § 41, eff. Sept. 22, 2012; Stats.2017, c. 319 (A.B.976), § 30, eff. Jan. 1, 2018; Stats.2021, c. 578 (A.B.260), § 2, eff. Jan. 1, 2022.)*

Cross References

Computation of time, see Code of Civil Procedure §§ 12 and 12a; Government Code § 6800 et seq.

Developmental services, director, see Welfare and Institutions Code § 4404 et seq.

Freedom from parental custody and control,
   Generally, see Family Code § 7800 et seq.
   Appointment of guardian, see Family Code § 7893.

Hearings and orders, see Probate Code § 1040 et seq.

Mailing, completion of service, see Probate Code § 1467.

Mental health, director, see Welfare and Institutions Code §§ 4004, 4005.

Notices,
   Generally, see Probate Code § 1200 et seq.
   Filing and service of papers, see Code of Civil Procedure § 1010 et seq.
   Mailing, see Probate Code § 1215 et seq.
   Petition for removal of guardian or conservator, see Probate Code § 2652.
   Posting, see Probate Code § 1230.
   Residence of ward or conservatee, notice according to this section, see Probate Code § 2352.
   Special notice, see Probate Code § 1250 et seq.

Parent, defined, see Probate Code § 54.

Proof of giving of notice, see Probate Code § 1260 et seq.

Relinquishment of child to licensed adoption agency, see Family Code § 8700 et seq.

Request for special notice of proceedings by guardian, see Probate Code § 2700.

Service of process,
   Generally, see Code of Civil Procedure § 413.10 et seq.
   Mail, see Code of Civil Procedure §§ 415.30, 1012 et seq.
   Personal delivery, see Code of Civil Procedure § 415.10.
   Proof of service, see Code of Civil Procedure § 417.10 et seq.
   Publication, see Code of Civil Procedure § 415.50.

Social services, director, see Welfare and Institutions Code § 10552.

Termination or modification of guardianship under the Probate Code, see Welfare and Institutions Code § 728.

Research References

Forms

13 Am. Jur. Pl. & Pr. Forms Guardian and Ward § 91, Statutory References.

West's California Code Forms, Probate § 1459.5 Comment, Application of Federal Law to Proceedings Involving Children of Indian Ancestry.

West's California Code Forms, Probate § 1460–1461 Form 2, Order Dispensing With Notice—Judicial Council Form GC–021.

West's California Code Forms, Probate § 1510 Form 1, Petition for Appointment of Guardian of Estate of Minor—Judicial Council Form GC–210.

West's California Code Forms, Probate § 2352 Form 1, Change of Residence Notice—Judicial Council Form GC–080.

West's California Judicial Council Forms GC–020, Notice of Hearing—Guardianship or Conservatorship.

West's California Judicial Council Forms GC–020(P), Proof of Personal Service of Notice of Hearing—Guardianship or Conservatorship.

West's California Judicial Council Forms GC–505, Forms You Need to Ask the Court to Appoint a Guardian of the Person (Also Available in Spanish).

West's California Judicial Council Forms GC–510, What is Proof of Service in a Guardianship? (Also Available in Spanish).

§ 1512. Amendment of petition to disclose newly discovered proceeding affecting custody

Within 10 days after the petitioner in the guardianship proceeding becomes aware of any proceeding not disclosed in the guardianship petition affecting the custody of the proposed ward (including any adoption, juvenile court, marriage dissolution, domestic relations, or other similar proceeding affecting the proposed ward), the petitioner shall amend the guardianship petition to disclose the other proceeding. (Stats.1990, c. 79 (A.B.759), § 14, operative July 1, 1991.)

Cross References

Adoption, see Family Code § 8500 et seq.
Computation of time, see Code of Civil Procedure §§ 12 and 12a; Government Code § 6800 et seq.
Custody of children, see Family Code § 3000 et seq.
Juvenile court law, see Welfare and Institutions Code § 200 et seq.
Marriage dissolution, see Family Code § 2300 et seq.

Research References

Forms

West's California Judicial Council Forms FL–105, Declaration Under Uniform Child Custody Jurisdiction and Enforcement Act (UCCJEA) (Also Available in Spanish).

West's California Judicial Council Forms FL–105(A), Attachment to Declaration Under Uniform Child Custody Jurisdiction and Enforcement Act (UCCJEA).

West's California Judicial Council Forms GC–120, Declaration Under Uniform Child Custody Jurisdiction and Enforcement Act (UCCJEA) (Also Available in Spanish).

West's California Judicial Council Forms GC–120(A), Attachment to Declaration Under Uniform Child Custody Jurisdiction and Enforcement Act (UCCJEA).

§ 1513. Investigation; filing of report and recommendation concerning proposed guardianship; contents of report; confidentiality; application of section

(a) Unless waived by the court for good cause, a court investigator, probation officer, or domestic relations investigator shall make an investigation and file with the court a report and recommendation concerning each proposed guardianship of the person or guardianship of the estate. Investigations where the proposed guardian is a relative shall be made by a court investigator. Investigations where the proposed guardian is a nonrelative shall be made by the county agency designated to investigate potential dependency. The report of the investigation for a guardianship of the person shall include, but need not be limited to, a discussion of all of the following:

(1) A social history of the proposed guardian.

(2) A social history of the proposed ward, including, to the extent feasible, an assessment of any identified developmental, emotional, psychological, or educational needs of the proposed ward and the capability of the proposed guardian to meet those needs.

(3) The relationship of the proposed ward to the proposed guardian, including the duration and character of the relationship, the circumstances under which the proposed guardian took physical custody of the proposed ward, and a statement of the proposed ward's wishes concerning the proposed guardianship, unless the proposed ward's developmental, physical, or emotional condition prevents the proposed ward from forming or stating their wishes concerning the proposed guardianship.

(4) The duration of the guardianship anticipated by the parents and the proposed guardian and the plans of each parent and the proposed guardian to provide a stable and permanent home for the child. The court may waive this requirement when no parent is available.

(b) If the proposed ward is or may be described by Section 300 of the Welfare and Institutions Code, the court may refer the matter, in writing, to the local child welfare agency to initiate an investigation pursuant to Section 329 of the Welfare and Institutions Code. The referral shall include a summary of the reasons for the referral and may include a copy of the petition under Section 1510, the investigator's report filed pursuant to subdivision (a), and any other material information.

(1) Pursuant to the timeline in Section 329 of the Welfare and Institutions Code, the child welfare agency shall report the findings and conclusions of its investigation, any decision made as a result, and the reasons for the decision to the probate court.

(2) The probate court shall not hear and determine the petition to appoint a guardian of the minor until the child welfare agency has completed its investigation and has submitted the report to the probate court.

(3) Notwithstanding paragraph (2), pending completion of the child welfare investigation, the probate court may take any reasonable steps it deems appropriate to protect the child's safety, including, but not limited to, appointing a temporary guardian or issuing a temporary restraining order.

(4) If the child welfare agency has not, within three weeks of the referral, notified the probate court that it has commenced juvenile dependency proceedings, the probate court or counsel appointed pursuant to Section 1470 to represent the minor may apply to the juvenile court, pursuant to Section 331 of the Welfare and Institutions Code, for an order directing the agency to commence juvenile dependency proceedings.

(5) If the juvenile court commences dependency proceedings, the guardianship proceedings shall be stayed in accordance with Section 304 of the Welfare and Institutions Code. This section does not affect the applicability of Section 16504 or 16506 of the Welfare and Institutions Code. If the juvenile court does not commence dependency proceedings, the probate court shall retain jurisdiction to hear and determine the guardianship petition.

(c) Before ruling on the petition for guardianship, the court shall read and consider all reports submitted pursuant to this section and shall affirm that it has done so in the minutes or on the record. A person who reports to the court pursuant to this section may be called and examined by any party to the proceeding.

(d) All reports authorized by this section are confidential and shall only be made available to persons who have been served in the proceedings or their attorneys. The clerk of the court shall make provisions to limit access to the reports exclusively to persons entitled to receipt. The reports shall be made available to all parties entitled to receipt no less than three court days before the hearing on the guardianship petition.

§ 1513

(e) For the purpose of writing either report authorized by this section, the person making the investigation and report shall have access to the proposed ward's school records, probation records, and public and private social services records, and to an oral or written summary of the proposed ward's medical records and psychological records prepared by any physician, psychologist, or psychiatrist who made or who is maintaining those records. The physician, psychologist, or psychiatrist shall be available to clarify information regarding these records pursuant to the investigator's responsibility to gather and provide information for the court.

(f) This section does not apply to guardianships resulting from a permanency plan for a dependent child pursuant to Section 366.26 of the Welfare and Institutions Code.

(g) For purposes of this section, a "relative" means a person who is a spouse, parent, stepparent, brother, sister, stepbrother, stepsister, half-brother, half-sister, uncle, aunt, niece, nephew, first cousin, or any person denoted by the prefix "grand" or "great," or the spouse of any of these persons, even after the marriage has been terminated by death or dissolution.

(h) In an Indian child custody proceeding, any person making an investigation and report shall consult with the Indian child's tribe and include in the report information provided by the tribe.

(i) It is the intent of the Legislature that the guardianship laws in this code and the juvenile court laws in the Welfare and Institutions Code operate together as a cohesive statutory structure that ensures all cases referred by the probate court for a child welfare investigation are subject to review by the juvenile court without limiting the probate court's ability to take immediate action to protect the child while the child welfare investigation and juvenile court review are pending. The purpose of this statutory structure is to ensure the protection of every child's health, safety, and welfare and to provide due process to every child, parent, and family.

(j) On or before January 1, 2023, the Judicial Council shall adopt, amend, or revise any rules or forms necessary to implement this section. (Stats.1990, c. 79 (A.B.759), § 14, operative July 1, 1991. Amended by Stats.1992, c. 572 (S.B.1455), § 3; Stats.1993, c. 59 (S.B.443), § 16, eff. June 30, 1993; Stats.1996, c. 563 (S.B.392), § 7; Stats.2002, c. 784 (S.B.1316), § 576; Stats.2006, c. 838 (S.B.678), § 24; Stats.2012, c. 638 (A.B.1757), § 14; Stats.2021, c. 578 (A.B. 260), § 3, eff. Jan. 1, 2022.)

Cross References

Appointment of legal counsel for proposed ward, see Probate Code § 1470 et seq.
Child Abuse and Neglect Reporting Act, notice to child protection agencies or district attorneys, see Penal Code § 11170.
Court investigator,
   Appointment, see Probate Code § 1454.
   Defined, see Probate Code § 1419.
Custody investigation and report, court appointed investigator, see Family Code § 3111.
Inspection of public records, exemptions from disclosure, "guardian" to "guardianship," see Government Code § 6276.22.
Parent, defined, see Probate Code § 54.
Report in case of certain nonrelative guardianships, see Probate Code § 1543.
Waiver of court fees and costs, initial fee waiver, see Government Code § 68631.

Research References

Forms

West's California Code Forms, Probate § 1459.5 Comment, Application of Federal Law to Proceedings Involving Children of Indian Ancestry.
West's California Code Forms, Probate § 1514.5 Comment, Confidential Information from Family Law Court.
West's California Code Forms, Probate § 1516 Form 1, Confidential Guardianship Screening Report—Judicial Council Form GC-212.

§ 1513.1. Assessments

(a) Each court or county shall assess (1) the parent, parents, or other person charged with the support and maintenance of the ward or proposed ward, and (2) the guardian, proposed guardian, or the estate of the ward or proposed ward, for court or county expenses incurred for any investigation or review conducted by the court investigator, probation officer, or domestic relations investigator. Subject to Section 68631 of the Government Code, the court may order reimbursement to the court or to the county in the amount of the assessment, unless the court finds that all or any part of the assessment would impose a hardship on the ward or the ward's estate. A county may waive any or all of an assessment against the guardianship on the basis of hardship. There shall be a rebuttable presumption that the assessment would impose a hardship if the ward is receiving Medi–Cal benefits.

(b) Any amount chargeable as state-mandated local costs incurred by a county for the cost of the investigation or review shall be reduced by any assessments actually collected by the county pursuant to subdivision (a) during that fiscal year. (Stats.1990, c. 79 (A.B.759), § 14, operative July 1, 1991. Amended by Stats.1991, c. 82 (S.B.896), § 4, eff. June 30, 1991, operative July 1, 1991; Stats.1996, c. 563 (S.B.392), § 8; Stats.2002, c. 1008 (A.B.3028), § 27; Stats.2003, c. 62 (S.B.600), § 242; Stats.2014, c. 913 (A.B.2747), § 27.5, eff. Jan. 1, 2015.)

Cross References

Organization and government of courts, collection of fees and fines pursuant to this section, deposits, see Government Code § 68085.1.
Parent, defined, see Probate Code § 54.
Presumptions, see Evidence Code § 600 et seq.

§ 1513.2. Status report; form; contents; confidentiality

(a) To the extent resources are available, the court shall implement procedures, as described in this section, to ensure that every guardian annually completes and returns to the court a status report, including the statement described in subdivision (b). A guardian who willfully submits any material information required by the form which he or she knows to be false shall be guilty of a misdemeanor. Not later than one month before the date the status report is required to be returned, the clerk of the court shall deliver a notice pursuant to Section 1215 to the guardian informing the guardian that he or she is required to complete and return the status report to the court. The clerk shall enclose with the letter a blank status report form for the guardian to complete and return. If the status report is not completed and returned as required, or if the court finds, after a status report has been completed and returned, that further information is needed, the court shall attempt to obtain the information required in the report from the guardian or other sources. If the court is unable to obtain this information within 30 days after the date the status report is due, the court shall either order the guardian to make himself or herself available to the investigator for purposes of investigation of the guardianship, or to show cause why the guardian should not be removed.

(b) The Judicial Council shall develop a form for the status report. The form shall include the following statement: "A guardian who willfully submits any material information required by this form which he or she knows to be false is guilty of a misdemeanor." The form shall request information the Judicial Council deems necessary to determine the status of the guardianship, including, but not limited to, the following:

(1) The guardian's present address and electronic address.

(2) The name and birth date of the child under guardianship.

(3) The name of the school in which the child is enrolled, if any.

(4) If the child is not in the guardian's home, the name, relationship, address, electronic address, and telephone number of the person or persons with whom the child resides.

(5) If the child is not in the guardian's home, why the child was moved.

(c) The report authorized by this section is confidential and shall only be made available to persons who have been served in the proceedings or their attorneys. The clerk of the court shall implement procedures for the limitation of the report exclusively to persons entitled to its receipt. *(Added by Stats.2002, c. 1115 (A.B.3036), § 2. Amended by Stats.2017, c. 319 (A.B.976), § 31, eff. Jan. 1, 2018.)*

Research References

Forms

West's California Code Forms, Probate § 1513.2 Form 1, Confidential Guardianship Status Report—Judicial Council Form GC 251.

West's California Code Forms, Probate § 1514 Form 1, Order Appointing Guardian of Minor—Judicial Council Form GC-240.

West's California Code Forms, Probate § 1516 Form 1, Confidential Guardianship Screening Report—Judicial Council Form GC-212.

West's California Judicial Council Forms GC–251, Confidential Guardianship Status Report.

§ 1514. Appointment of guardian

(a) Upon hearing of the petition, if it appears necessary or convenient, the court may appoint a guardian of the person or estate of the proposed ward or both.

(b)(1) In appointing a guardian of the person, the court is governed by Chapter 1 (commencing with Section 3020) and Chapter 2 (commencing with Section 3040) of Part 2 of Division 8 of the Family Code, relating to custody of a minor.

(2) Except as provided in Section 2105, a minor's parent may not be appointed as a guardian of the person of the minor.

(c) The court shall appoint a guardian nominated under Section 1500 insofar as the nomination relates to the guardianship of the estate unless the court determines that the nominee is unsuitable. If the nominee is a relative, the nominee's immigration status alone shall not constitute unsuitability.

(d) The court shall appoint the person nominated under Section 1501 as guardian of the property covered by the nomination unless the court determines that the nominee is unsuitable. If the person so appointed is appointed only as guardian of the property covered by the nomination, the letters of guardianship shall so indicate.

(e) Subject to subdivisions (c) and (d), in appointing a guardian of the estate:

(1) The court is to be guided by what appears to be in the best interest of the proposed ward, taking into account the proposed guardian's ability to manage and to preserve the estate as well as the proposed guardian's concern for and interest in the welfare of the proposed ward.

(2) If the proposed ward is of sufficient age to form an intelligent preference as to the person to be appointed as guardian, the court shall give consideration to that preference in determining the person to be so appointed. *(Stats.1990, c. 79 (A.B.759), § 14, operative July 1, 1991. Amended by Stats.1992, c. 163 (A.B.2641), § 123, operative Jan. 1, 1994; Stats.2011, c. 102 (A.B.458), § 1; Stats.2012, c. 845 (S.B.1064), § 3.)*

Cross References

Action, guardian or conservator bringing and defending, see Probate Code § 2462.

Action for exclusive custody of children, see Family Code § 3120.

Appealable orders, see Probate Code § 1300 et seq.

Appointment of guardian to fill vacancy, see Probate Code § 2670.

Appointment of legal counsel for proposed ward, see Probate Code § 1470.

Authority of guardian does not extend beyond jurisdiction of Government under which that person was invested with authority, see Code of Civil Procedure § 1913.

Capacity of trust company to act as guardian or conservator of estate, see Probate Code §§ 300, 301.

Child custody, order of preference, see Family Code § 3040.

Conservatorship and guardianship for developmentally disabled persons, see Health and Safety Code § 416 et seq.

Conservatorship for gravely disabled persons, see Welfare and Institutions Code § 5350 et seq.

Enforcement of minor's rights by guardian, see Family Code § 6601.

Hearings and orders, generally, see Probate Code § 1040 et seq.

Nonprofit charitable corporation as guardian, see Probate Code § 2104.

Powers and duties of guardian or conservator,
  Generally, see Probate Code § 2350 et seq.
  Guardian for particular property, see Probate Code § 2109.
  Guardian nominated by will, see Probate Code § 2108.

Public guardian, see Government Code § 27430 et seq.

Removal of guardian for insolvency or bankruptcy, see Probate Code § 2650.

Temporary guardians, appointment, see Probate Code § 2250.

Research References

Forms

1 California Transactions Forms--Estate Planning § 6:17, Guardian of Estate or of Property.

4 California Transactions Forms--Estate Planning § 19:95, Appointment of Guardian of Estate.

West's California Code Forms, Probate § 1510 Form 1, Petition for Appointment of Guardian of Estate of Minor—Judicial Council Form GC-210.

West's California Code Forms, Probate § 1514 Form 1, Order Appointing Guardian of Minor—Judicial Council Form GC-240.

West's California Judicial Council Forms GC–240, Order Appointing Guardian or Extending Guardianship of the Person.

§ 1514.5. Information available for probate guardianship proceeding and guardianship investigator regarding best interest of child; confidentiality

Notwithstanding any other provision of law, except provisions of law governing the retention and storage of data, a family law court shall, upon request from the court in any county hearing a probate guardianship matter proceeding before the court pursuant to this part, provide to the court all available information the court deems necessary to make a determination regarding the best interest of a child, as described in Section 3011 of the Family Code, who is the subject of the proceeding. The information shall also be released to a guardianship investigator, as provided in subdivision (a) of Section 1513, acting within the scope of his or her duties in that proceeding. Any information released pursuant to this section that is confidential pursuant to any other provision of law shall remain confidential and may not be released, except to the extent necessary to comply with this section. No records shared pursuant to this section may be disclosed to any party in a case unless the party requests the agency or court that originates the record to release these records and the request is granted. In counties that provide confidential family law mediation, or confidential dependency mediation, those mediations are not covered by this section. *(Added by Stats.2004, c. 574 (A.B.2228), § 2.)*

Cross References

Child custody evaluations, availability of report, see Family Code § 3111.

Information available for juvenile court proceedings regarding best interest of child, see Welfare and Institutions Code § 204.

Research References

Forms

1 California Transactions Forms--Estate Planning § 6:16, Guardian of Person.

West's California Code Forms, Probate § 1514,5 Comment, Confidential Information from Family Law Court.

§ 1515. No guardian of person for married minor

Notwithstanding any other provision of this part, no guardian of the person may be appointed for a minor who is married or whose

§ 1515

marriage has been dissolved. This section does not apply in the case of a minor whose marriage has been adjudged a nullity. *(Stats.1990, c. 79 (A.B.759), § 14, operative July 1, 1991.)*

Cross References

Action to test validity of marriage, see Family Code § 309.
Dissolution of marriage, defined, see Probate Code § 36.
Minors, see Family Code § 6500.
Termination of guardianship by majority, death, adoption or marriage of ward, see Probate Code § 1600.

Research References

Forms

1 California Transactions Forms--Estate Planning § 6:16, Guardian of Person.

§ 1516. Petitions for guardianship of the person; delivery of notice of hearing and copy of petition; screening of guardians; application of section

(a) In each case involving a petition for guardianship of the person, the petitioner shall deliver pursuant to Section 1215 a notice of the hearing and a copy of the petition, at least 15 days before the hearing, to the local agency designated by the board of supervisors to investigate guardianships for the court. The local social services agency providing child protection services shall screen the name of the guardian for prior referrals of neglect or abuse of minors. The results of this screening shall be provided to the court.

(b) This section does not apply to guardianships resulting from a permanency plan for a dependent child pursuant to Section 366.25 of the Welfare and Institutions Code. *(Stats.1990, c. 79 (A.B.759), § 14, operative July 1, 1991. Amended by Stats.2017, c. 319 (A.B.976), § 32, eff. Jan. 1, 2018.)*

Cross References

Computation of time, see Code of Civil Procedure §§ 12 and 12a; Government Code § 6800 et seq.
Notice,
   Mailing, see Probate Code § 1215 et seq.
   Posting, see Probate Code § 1230.
   Proof of giving notice, see Probate Code § 1260 et seq.
   Special notice, see Probate Code § 1250 et seq.
   This code, generally, see Probate Code § 1200 et seq.
Service of process,
   Generally, see Code of Civil Procedure § 413.10 et seq.
   Mail, see Code of Civil Procedure §§ 415.30, 1012 et seq.
   Personal delivery, see Code of Civil Procedure § 415.10.
   Proof of service, see Code of Civil Procedure § 417.10 et seq.
   Publication, see Code of Civil Procedure § 415.50.

Research References

Forms

West's California Code Forms, Probate § 1516 Form 1, Confidential Guardianship Screening Report—Judicial Council Form GC–212.
West's California Judicial Council Forms GC–212, Confidential Guardian Screening Form.

§ 1516.5. Proceeding to have child declared free from custody and control of one or both parents

(a) A proceeding to have a child declared free from the custody and control of one or both parents may be brought in accordance with the procedures specified in Part 4 (commencing with Section 7800) of Division 12 of the Family Code within an existing guardianship proceeding, in an adoption action, or in a separate action filed for that purpose, if all of the following requirements are satisfied:

(1) One or both parents do not have the legal custody of the child.

(2) The child has been in the physical custody of the guardian for a period of not less than two years.

(3) The court finds that the child would benefit from being adopted by his or her guardian. In making this determination, the court shall consider all factors relating to the best interest of the child, including, but not limited to, the nature and extent of the relationship between all of the following:

(A) The child and the birth parent.

(B) The child and the guardian, including family members of the guardian.

(C) The child and any siblings or half siblings.

(b) The court shall appoint a court investigator or other qualified professional to investigate all factors enumerated in subdivision (a). The findings of the investigator or professional regarding those issues shall be included in the written report required pursuant to Section 7851 of the Family Code.

(c) The rights of the parent, including the rights to notice and counsel provided in Part 4 (commencing with Section 7800) of Division 12 of the Family Code, shall apply to actions brought pursuant to this section.

(d) This section does not apply to any child who is a dependent of the juvenile court or to any Indian child. *(Added by Stats.2003, c. 251 (S.B.182), § 11, Amended by Stats.2006, c. 838 (S.B.678), § 25; Stats.2010, c. 588 (A.B.2020), § 9.)*

Research References

Forms

2 California Transactions Forms--Family Law § 6:10, Initiating Proceeding Under Fam. Code, §§ 7800 et seq.
2 California Transactions Forms--Family Law § 6:107, Adoption Without Consent of Noncustodial Parent.
West's California Code Forms, Probate § 1459.5 Comment, Application of Federal Law to Proceedings Involving Children of Indian Ancestry.
West's California Code Forms, Probate § 1510 Form 1, Petition for Appointment of Guardian of Estate of Minor—Judicial Council Form GC-210.

§ 1517. Guardianships resulting from selection and implementation of a permanent plan; application of part; administration of funds for benefit of child

(a) This part does not apply to guardianships resulting from the selection and implementation of a permanent plan pursuant to Section 366.26 of the Welfare and Institutions Code. For those minors, Section 366.26 of the Welfare and Institutions Code and Division 3 (commencing with Rule 5.500) of Title Five of the California Rules of Court specify the exclusive procedures for establishing, modifying, and terminating legal guardianships. If no specific provision of the Welfare and Institutions Code or the California Rules of Court is applicable, the provisions applicable to the administration of estates under Part 4 (commencing with Section 2100) govern so far as they are applicable to like situations.

(b) This chapter shall not be construed to prevent a court that assumes jurisdiction of a minor child pursuant to Section 300 of the Welfare and Institutions Code, or a probate court, as appropriate, from issuing orders or making appointments, on motion of the child's counsel, consistent with Division 2 of the Welfare and Institutions Code or Divisions 4 to 6, inclusive, of the Probate Code necessary to ensure the appropriate administration of funds for the benefit of the child. Orders or appointments regarding those funds may continue after the court's jurisdiction is terminated pursuant to Section 391 of the Welfare and Institutions Code. *(Added by Stats.1991, c. 82 (S.B.896), § 6, eff. June 30, 1991, operative July 1, 1991. Amended by Stats.2008, c. 166 (A.B.3051), § 2.)*

ARTICLE 3. NONRELATIVE GUARDIANSHIPS

Section
1540. Application of article.
1541. Petition for guardianship; additional contents.
1542. Notice of hearing and copy of petition to director and local agency.

Section
1543. Suitability of proposed guardian for guardianship; report; confidentiality.

Cross References

Child Abuse and Neglect Reporting Act, notice to child protection agencies or district attorneys, see Penal Code § 11170.

§ 1540. Application of article

This article does not apply in any of the following cases:

(a) Where the petition is for guardianship of the estate exclusively.

(b) Where the proposed guardian is a relative of the proposed ward.

(c) Where the Director of Developmental Services is appointed guardian pursuant to Article 7.5 (commencing with Section 416) of Chapter 2 of Part 1 of Division 1 of the Health and Safety Code.

(d) Where the director of the department designated by the board of supervisors to provide social services is appointed guardian.

(e) Where the public guardian is appointed guardian.

(f) Where the guardianship results from a permanency plan for a dependent child pursuant to Section 366.25 of the Welfare and Institutions Code. *(Stats.1990, c. 79 (A.B.759), § 14, operative July 1, 1991.)*

Cross References

Director of Developmental Services, see Welfare and Institutions Code § 4404 et seq.
Public guardian, see Government Code § 27430 et seq.
Public guardian, generally, see Probate Code § 2900 et seq.

§ 1541. Petition for guardianship; additional contents

In addition to the other required contents of the petition for appointment of a guardian, the petition shall include both of the following:

(a) A statement by the proposed guardian that, upon request by an agency referred to in Section 1543 for information relating to the investigation referred to in that section, the proposed guardian will promptly submit the information required.

(b) A disclosure of any petition for adoption by the proposed guardian of the minor who is the subject of the guardianship petition regardless of when or where filed.

(c) A statement whether or not the home of the proposed guardian is a licensed foster family home, a certified family home of a licensed foster family agency, or a resource family home approved by a county or a licensed foster family agency. *(Stats.1990, c. 79 (A.B.759), § 14, operative July 1, 1991. Amended by Stats.2016, c. 612 (A.B.1997), § 58, eff. Jan. 1, 2017.)*

Cross References

Disclosure of proceedings affecting custody, see Probate Code §§ 1510, 1512.

Research References

Forms

3 California Transactions Forms--Estate Planning § 13:60, Revocation by Settlor.

§ 1542. Notice of hearing and copy of petition to director and local agency

In each case involving a petition for guardianship of the person, the petitioner shall deliver pursuant to Section 1215 a notice of the hearing and a copy of the petition, at least 15 days before the hearing, to the Director of Social Services at the director's office in Sacramento and to the local agency designated by the board of supervisors to investigate guardianships for the court. *(Stats.1990, c. 79 (A.B.759), § 14, operative July 1, 1991. Amended by Stats.2017, c. 319 (A.B.976), § 33, eff. Jan. 1, 2018.)*

Cross References

Completion of mailing, see Probate Code § 1467.
Computation of time, see Code of Civil Procedure §§ 12 and 12a; Government Code § 6800 et seq.
Director of Social Services, see Welfare and Institutions Code § 10552.
Notice,
  Mailing, see Probate Code § 1215 et seq.
  Posting, see Probate Code § 1230.
  Proof of giving notice, see Probate Code § 1260 et seq.
  Special notice, see Probate Code § 1250 et seq.
  This code, generally, see Probate Code § 1200 et seq.
Service of process,
  Generally, see Code of Civil Procedure § 413.10 et seq.
  Mail, see Code of Civil Procedure §§ 415.30, 1012 et seq.
  Personal delivery, see Code of Civil Procedure § 415.10.
  Proof of service, see Code of Civil Procedure § 417.10 et seq.
  Publication, see Code of Civil Procedure § 415.50.

§ 1543. Suitability of proposed guardian for guardianship; report; confidentiality

(a) If the petition as filed or as amended states that an adoption petition has been filed, a report with respect to the suitability of the proposed guardian for guardianship shall be filed with the court by the agency investigating the adoption. In other cases, the local agency designated by the board of supervisors to provide public social services shall file a report with the court with respect to the proposed guardian of the same character required to be made with regard to an applicant for foster family home licensure, or, on and after January 1, 2020, resource family approval, as described in Section 16519.5 of the Welfare and Institutions Code.

(b) The report filed with the court pursuant to this section is confidential. The report may be considered by the court and shall be made available only to the persons who have been served in the proceeding and the persons who have appeared in the proceeding or their attorneys. The report may be received in evidence upon stipulation of counsel for all of those persons who are present at the hearing or, if a person is present at the hearing but is not represented by counsel, upon consent of that person. *(Stats.1990, c. 79 (A.B.759), § 14, operative July 1, 1991. Amended by Stats.2016, c. 612 (A.B.1997), § 59, eff. Jan. 1, 2017.)*

Cross References

Appointment of legal counsel, see Probate Code § 1470.
Inspection of public records, exemptions from disclosure, "guardian" to "guardianship", see Government Code § 6276.22.
Investigation and report, see Probate Code § 1513.
Licensure foster family home, see Health and Safety Code § 1502 et seq.

CHAPTER 2. TERMINATION

Section
1600. Majority, death, adoption, or emancipation of ward.
1601. Court order; notice.
1602. Visitation.

§ 1600. Majority, death, adoption, or emancipation of ward

(a) A guardianship of the person or estate or both terminates when the ward attains majority unless, pursuant to Section 1510.1, the ward requests the extension of, or consents to the extension of, the guardianship of the person until the ward attains 21 years of age.

(b) A guardianship of the person terminates upon the death of the ward, the adoption of the ward, or upon the emancipation of the ward under Section 7002 of the Family Code.

(c) A guardianship of the estate terminates upon the death of the ward, except as provided by Section 2467 and Article 4 (commencing with Section 2630) of Chapter 7 of Part 4, and except as otherwise provided by law. *(Stats.1990, c. 79 (A.B.759), § 14, operative July 1, 1991. Amended by Stats.1996, c. 862 (A.B.2751), § 6; Stats.2015, c.*

694 (A.B.900), § 4, eff. Jan. 1, 2016; Stats.2018, c. 73 (A.B.2113), § 1, eff. Jan. 1, 2019.)

Cross References

Age of majority, see Family Code § 6500 et seq.
Allowance of disbursements after termination of guardianship, allowance of expenses for care of estate after death of ward, see Probate Code § 2623.
Care of estate after death of ward, see Probate Code § 2467.
Conservatorship,
  Comparable provisions, see Probate Code § 1860.
  Filing petition during minority to become effective upon attaining age of majority, see Probate Code § 1820.
Disposition of assets after death of ward, see Probate Code § 2631.
Marriage of ward, consent of guardian of ward under age of 18, see Family Code § 302.
Married minors, conservatorships, see Probate Code § 1800.3.
Restriction on appointment of guardian of married minor, see Probate Code § 1515.
Settlement of accounts with guardian, ward reaching majority, see Probate Code § 2627.

Research References

Forms

1 California Transactions Forms--Estate Planning § 1:29, Options Involving Gifts to Minors.
1 California Transactions Forms--Estate Planning § 6:16, Guardian of Person.
1 California Transactions Forms--Estate Planning § 6:17, Guardian of Estate or of Property.
West's California Code Forms, Probate § 1601 Form 1, Petition for Termination of Guardianship—Judicial Council Form GC-255.
West's California Judicial Council Forms GC–255, Petition for Termination of Guardianship.

§ 1601. Court order; notice

Upon petition of the guardian, a parent, the minor ward, or, in the case of an Indian child custody proceeding, an Indian custodian or the ward's tribe, the court may make an order terminating the guardianship if the court determines that it is in the ward's best interest to terminate the guardianship. Upon petition of a ward who is 18 years of age or older, the court shall make an order terminating the guardianship. Notice of the hearing on the petition shall be given for the period and in the manner provided in Chapter 3 (commencing with Section 1460) of Part 1. *(Stats.1990, c. 79 (A.B.759), § 14, operative July 1, 1991. Amended by Stats.2002, c. 1118 (A.B.1938), § 6; Stats.2006, c. 838 (S.B.678), § 26; Stats.2015, c. 694 (A.B.900), § 5, eff. Jan. 1, 2016.)*

Cross References

Allowance of disbursements after termination, see Probate Code § 2623.
Appealable orders, see Probate Code § 1300 et seq.
Notice to Veterans Administration, see Probate Code § 1461.5.
Order for permanent plan of adoption or legal guardianship, termination of guardianship, see Welfare and Institutions Code § 366.3.
Parent, defined, see Probate Code § 54.
Request for special notice, see Probate Code § 2700.
Termination of proceedings upon,
  Exhaustion of estate, see Probate Code § 2626.
  Transfer of all assets to foreign guardian, see Probate Code § 2808.
Termination or modification of guardianship under the Probate Code, see Welfare and Institutions Code § 728.

Research References

Forms

1 California Transactions Forms--Estate Planning § 6:16, Guardian of Person.
1 California Transactions Forms--Estate Planning § 6:17, Guardian of Estate or of Property.
West's California Code Forms, Probate § 1601 Form 1, Petition for Termination of Guardianship—Judicial Council Form GC-255.
West's California Code Forms, Probate § 2626 Form 1, Ex Parte Petition for Final Discharge and Order—Judicial Council Form DE-295/GC-395.
West's California Judicial Council Forms GC–255, Petition for Termination of Guardianship.
West's California Judicial Council Forms GC–260, Order Terminating Guardianship.

§ 1602. Visitation

(a) The Legislature hereby finds and declares that guardians perform a critical and important role in the lives of minors, frequently assuming a parental role and caring for a child when the child's parent or parents are unable or unwilling to do so.

(b) Upon making a determination that a guardianship should be terminated pursuant to Section 1601, the court may consider whether continued visitation between the ward and the guardian is in the ward's best interest. As part of the order of termination, the court shall have jurisdiction to issue an order providing for ongoing visitation between a former guardian and his or her former minor ward after the termination of the guardianship. The order granting or denying visitation may not be modified unless the court determines, based upon evidence presented, that there has been a significant change of circumstances since the court issued the order and that modification of the order is in the best interest of the child.

(c) A copy of the visitation order shall be filed in any court proceeding relating to custody of the minor. If a prior order has not been filed, and a proceeding is not pending relating to the custody of the minor in the court of any county, the visitation order may be used as the sole basis for opening a file in the court of the county in which the custodial parent resides. While a parent of the child has custody of the child, proceedings for modification of the visitation order shall be determined in a proceeding under the Family Code. *(Added by Stats.2004, c. 301 (A.B.2292), § 2.)*

Research References

Forms

West's California Code Forms, Probate § 1601 Form 1, Petition for Termination of Guardianship—Judicial Council Form GC-255.
West's California Code Forms, Probate § 1601 Form 2, Order Terminating Guardianship—Judicial Council Form GC-260.
West's California Judicial Council Forms GC–260, Order Terminating Guardianship.

CHAPTER 3. PERMANENT AND STABLE HOME

Section
1610. Legislative findings and declarations.
1611. Petitions without merit or intended to harass or annoy guardian.

§ 1610. Legislative findings and declarations

(a) The Legislature finds and declares that it is in the best interests of children to be raised in a permanent, safe, stable, and loving environment.

(b) Unwarranted petitions, applications, or motions other than discovery motions after the guardianship has been established create an environment that can be harmful to children and are inconsistent with the goals of permanency, safety, and stability. *(Added by Stats.2002, c. 1118 (A.B.1938), § 7. Amended by Stats.2006, c. 493 (A.B.1363), § 6.)*

§ 1611. Petitions without merit or intended to harass or annoy guardian

If a person files a petition for visitation, termination of the guardianship, or instruction to the guardian that is unmeritorious, or intended to harass or annoy the guardian, and the person has previously filed pleadings in the guardianship proceedings that were unmeritorious, or intended to harass or annoy the guardian, this petition shall be grounds for the court to determine that the person is a vexatious litigant for the purposes of Title 3a (commencing with Section 391) of Part 2 of the Code of Civil Procedure. For these purposes, the term "new litigation" shall include petitions for visitation, termination of the guardianship, or instruction to the guardian. *(Added by Stats.2002, c. 1118 (A.B.1938), § 7.)*

Part 3

CONSERVATORSHIP

Cross References

California Community Care Facilities Act, placement agencies, see Health and Safety Code § 1536.1.
Residential care facilities for the elderly, placement agencies, see Health and Safety Code § 1569.47.

CHAPTER 1. ESTABLISHMENT OF CONSERVATORSHIP

ARTICLE 1. PERSONS FOR WHOM CONSERVATOR MAY BE APPOINTED

Section
1800. Purpose of chapter.
1800.3. Conservatorship for adults and married minors.
1801. Conservator of person or estate or person and estate; limited conservator; appointment; standard of proof.
1802. Appointment upon request of proposed conservatee; good cause.
1803. Conservator of estate of absentee; appointment.
1804. Missing persons; appointment of conservator of estate.

Cross References

Application of old and new law, see Probate Code § 3.
Placement agency defined to include conservator,
   Community care facilities, see Health and Safety Code § 1536.1.
   Residential care facilities for the elderly, see Health and Safety Code § 1569.47.

§ 1800. Purpose of chapter

It is the intent of the Legislature in enacting this chapter to do the following:

(a) Protect the rights of persons who are placed under conservatorship.

(b) Provide that an assessment of the needs of the person is performed in order to determine the appropriateness and extent of a conservatorship and to set goals for increasing the conservatee's functional abilities to whatever extent possible.

(c) Provide that the health and psychosocial needs of the proposed conservatee are met.

(d) Provide that community-based services are used to the greatest extent in order to allow the conservatee to remain as independent and in the least restrictive setting as possible.

(e) Provide that the periodic review of the conservatorship by the court investigator shall consider the best interests and expressed wishes of the conservatee; whether the conservatee has regained or could regain abilities and capacity with or without supports; and whether the conservatee continues to need a conservatorship.

(f) Ensure that the conservatee's basic needs for physical health, food, clothing, and shelter are met.

(g) Provide for the proper management and protection of the conservatee's real and personal property.

(h) Ensure, to the greatest possible extent, that the conservatee is able to understand, make, and communicate their own, informed, choices while under conservatorship. *(Stats.1990, c. 79 (A.B.759),* § 14, operative July 1, 1991. *Amended by Stats.2022, c. 894 (A.B. 1663), § 4, eff. Jan. 1, 2023.)*

Cross References

Conservatorship and guardianship for developmentally disabled persons, see Health and Safety Code § 416 et seq.
Conservatorship for gravely disabled persons, see Welfare and Institutions Code § 5350 et seq.
Legislative intent, construction of statutes, see Code of Civil Procedure § 1859.
Public guardian, see Probate Code § 2900 et seq.; Government Code § 27430 et seq.
Residential care facilities for the elderly, definitions, see 22 Cal. Code of Regs. § 87101.
Temporary guardians, appointment, see Probate Code § 2250.

§ 1800.3. Conservatorship for adults and married minors

(a) If the need therefor is established to the satisfaction of the court and the other requirements of this chapter are satisfied, the court may appoint:

(1) A conservator of the person or estate of an adult, or both.

(2) A conservator of the person of a minor who is married or whose marriage has been dissolved.

(b) A conservatorship of the person or of the estate shall not be granted by the court unless the court makes an express finding that the granting of the conservatorship is the least restrictive alternative needed for the protection of the conservatee.

(c) In determining whether a conservatorship is the least restrictive alternative available, and whether to grant or deny a conservatorship petition, the court shall consider the person's abilities and capacities with current and possible supports, including, but not limited to, supported decisionmaking agreements, as defined in Section 21001 of the Welfare and Institutions Code, powers of attorney, designation of a health care surrogate as set forth in Section 4711, and advance health care directives.

(d) If the court becomes aware that the proposed conservatee has a developmental disability, and the proposed conservator is not seeking authority to act under Section 2356.5, the court shall deem the proceeding to be seeking a limited conservatorship. *(Stats.1990, c. 79 (A.B.759), § 14, operative July 1, 1991. Amended by Stats.1997, c. 663 (S.B.628), § 1; Stats.2007, c. 553 (A.B.1727), § 6; Stats.2022, c. 894 (A.B.1663), § 5, eff. Jan. 1, 2023.)*

Cross References

Capacity of conservatee to marry, see Probate Code §§ 1900, 1901.
Court-appointed attorneys, examiners and investigators, educational requirements, see Probate Code § 1456.
Dissolution of marriage, defined, see Probate Code § 36.

§ 1801. Conservator of person or estate or person and estate; limited conservator; appointment; standard of proof

Subject to Section 1800.3:

(a) A conservator of the person may be appointed for a person who is unable to provide properly for his or her personal needs for physical health, food, clothing, or shelter, except as provided for the person as described in subdivision (b) or (c) of Section 1828.5.

(b) A conservator of the estate may be appointed for a person who is substantially unable to manage his or her own financial resources or resist fraud or undue influence, except as provided for that person as described in subdivision (b) or (c) of Section 1828.5. Substantial inability may not be proved solely by isolated incidents of negligence or improvidence.

(c) A conservator of the person and estate may be appointed for a person described in subdivisions (a) and (b).

(d) A limited conservator of the person or of the estate, or both, may be appointed for a developmentally disabled adult. A limited conservatorship may be utilized only as necessary to promote and protect the well-being of the individual, shall be designed to

§ 1801

encourage the development of maximum self-reliance and independence of the individual, and shall be ordered only to the extent necessitated by the individual's proven mental and adaptive limitations. The conservatee of the limited conservator shall not be presumed to be incompetent and shall retain all legal and civil rights except those which by court order have been designated as legal disabilities and have been specifically granted to the limited conservator. The intent of the Legislature, as expressed in Section 4501 of the Welfare and Institutions Code, that developmentally disabled citizens of this state receive services resulting in more independent, productive, and normal lives is the underlying mandate of this division in its application to adults alleged to be developmentally disabled.

(e) The standard of proof for the appointment of a conservator pursuant to this section shall be clear and convincing evidence. (Stats.1990, c. 79 (A.B.759), § 14, operative July 1, 1991. Amended by Stats.1995, c. 842 (S.B.730), § 7.)

Cross References

Conservatorship for gravely disabled persons, see Welfare and Institutions Code § 5350 et seq.
Contracts, fraud, see Civil Code §§ 1571 to 1574.
Developmental disability, defined, see Probate Code § 1420.
Developmentally disabled adult,
  Contents of order appointing conservator or limited conservator, see Probate Code § 1830.
  Duties of court at hearing to appoint limited conservator, see Probate Code § 1828.5.
Developmentally disabled persons, guardianship and conservatorship, see Health and Safety Code § 416 et seq.; Welfare and Institutions Code § 4825.
Legal capacity of conservatee, see Probate Code § 1870 et seq.
Statutes, construction and legislative intent, see Code of Civil Procedure §§ 1858 and 1859.
Termination of limited conservatorship, see Probate Code § 1860.5.

Research References

Forms

2 California Transactions Forms--Business Transactions § 15:3.50, Ethical Considerations.
1 California Transactions Forms--Estate Planning § 1:2, Probate System.
1 California Transactions Forms--Estate Planning § 1:6, Revocable Living Trust as Centerpiece.
1 California Transactions Forms--Estate Planning § 2:17, Definitions of Capacity.
2 California Transactions Forms--Estate Planning § 8:8, Ethical Considerations.
West's California Code Forms, Probate § 1820 Form 1, Attachment Requesting Special Orders Regarding a Major Neurocognitive Disorder.
West's California Judicial Council Forms GC-335, Capacity Declaration—Conservatorship.
West's California Judicial Council Forms GC-336, Ex Parte Order Authorizing Disclosure of (Proposed) Conservatee's Health Information to Court Investigator—HIPAA.

§ 1802. Appointment upon request of proposed conservatee; good cause

Subject to Section 1800.3, a conservator of the person or estate, or both, may be appointed for a person who voluntarily requests the appointment and who, to the satisfaction of the court, establishes good cause for the appointment. (Stats.1990, c. 79 (A.B.759), § 14, operative July 1, 1991.)

Research References

Forms

West's California Code Forms, Probate § 1820 Form 1, Attachment Requesting Special Orders Regarding a Major Neurocognitive Disorder.

§ 1803. Conservator of estate of absentee; appointment

A conservator of the estate may be appointed for a person who is an absentee as defined in Section 1403. (Stats.1990, c. 79 (A.B.759), § 14, operative July 1, 1991.)

Cross References

Special provisions applicable where proposed conservatee is an absentee, see Probate Code § 1840 et seq.

Research References

Forms

West's California Code Forms, Probate § 1820 Form 1, Attachment Requesting Special Orders Regarding a Major Neurocognitive Disorder.

§ 1804. Missing persons; appointment of conservator of estate

Subject to Section 1800.3, a conservator of the estate may be appointed for a person who is missing and whose whereabouts is unknown. (Stats.1990, c. 79 (A.B.759), § 14, operative July 1, 1991.)

Cross References

Administration of estates of missing persons presumed dead, see Probate Code § 12400 et seq.
Death of persons not heard from in five years, presumption, see Evidence Code § 667.
Federal Missing Persons Act, findings under, see Evidence Code §§ 1282, 1283.
Property of absent federal personnel, see Probate Code § 3700 et seq.
Special conservatorship provisions where proposed conservatee is a missing person, see Probate Code § 1845 et seq.

Research References

Forms

West's California Code Forms, Probate § 1820 Form 1, Attachment Requesting Special Orders Regarding a Major Neurocognitive Disorder.

ARTICLE 2. ORDER OF PREFERENCE FOR APPOINTMENT OF CONSERVATOR

Section
1810. Nomination by proposed conservatee.
1811. Nomination by spouse or relative of proposed conservatee.
1812. Order of preference for appointment as conservator; regional centers as designee of Director of Developmental Services.
1813. Appointment of spouse; conditions; consultation with counsel and report by counsel; disclosure of specified matters.
1813.1. Domestic partner of proposed conservatee.

§ 1810. Nomination by proposed conservatee

If the proposed conservatee has sufficient capacity at the time to form an intelligent preference, the proposed conservatee may nominate a conservator in the petition or in a writing signed either before or after the petition is filed. The court shall appoint the nominee as conservator unless the court finds that the appointment of the nominee is not in the best interests of the proposed conservatee. (Stats.1990, c. 79 (A.B.759), § 14, operative July 1, 1991.)

Cross References

Nomination by means of durable power of attorney, see Probate Code § 4126.
Petition,
  Contents, see Probate Code § 1821.
  Defined, see Probate Code § 1430.

Research References

Forms

1 California Transactions Forms--Estate Planning § 1:16, Compared to Conservatorship.
1 California Transactions Forms--Estate Planning § 1:94, Nomination of Conservator.
West's California Code Forms, Probate § 1810 Form 1, Nomination of Conservator by Proposed Conservatee.

West's California Code Forms, Probate § 4126 Form 1, Power of Attorney—Provision Nominating Conservator.

West's California Judicial Council Forms GC–314, Confidential Conservator Screening Form.

§ 1811. Nomination by spouse or relative of proposed conservatee

(a) Subject to Sections 1813 and 1813.1, the spouse, domestic partner, or an adult child, parent, brother, or sister of the proposed conservatee may nominate a conservator in the petition or at the hearing on the petition.

(b) Subject to Sections 1813 and 1813.1, the spouse, domestic partner, or a parent of the proposed conservatee may nominate a conservator in a writing signed either before or after the petition is filed and that nomination remains effective notwithstanding the subsequent legal incapacity or death of the spouse, domestic partner, or parent. *(Stats.1990, c. 79 (A.B.759), § 14, operative July 1, 1991. Amended by Stats.2000, c. 17 (A.B.1491), § 3; Stats.2001, c. 893 (A.B.25), § 15; Stats.2014, c. 913 (A.B.2747), § 28, eff. Jan. 1, 2015.)*

Cross References

Dissolution of marriage,
  Generally, see Family Code § 2300 et seq.
  Methods, see Family Code § 310.
Domestic partner, defined, see Probate Code § 37.
Guardianship, subsequent legal incapacity or death of nominator, see Probate Code § 1502.
Parent, defined, see Probate Code § 54.

Research References

Forms

West's California Judicial Council Forms GC–314, Confidential Conservator Screening Form.

§ 1812. Order of preference for appointment as conservator; regional centers as designee of Director of Developmental Services

(a) Subject to Sections 1810, 1813, and 1813.1, the selection of a conservator of the person or estate, or both, is solely in the discretion of the court and, in making the selection, the court is to be guided by what appears to be for the best interests of the proposed conservatee.

(b) Subject to Sections 1810, 1813, and 1813.1, of persons equally qualified in the opinion of the court to appointment as conservator of the person or estate or both, preference is to be given in the following order:

(1) The conservatee or proposed conservatee's stated preference, including preferences expressed by speech, sign language, alternative or augmentative communication, actions, facial expressions, and other spoken and nonspoken methods of communication.

(2) The prior conservator's preference, if known, if the selection of a successor conservator is being made pursuant to the provisions of Article 2 (commencing with Section 2680) of Chapter 9.5 of Part 4 and the prior conservator is a person described in paragraphs (3) to (6), inclusive, unless either of the following apply:

(A) The reason for the appointment of a successor conservator is due to the prior conservator's removal pursuant to the provisions of Article 1 (commencing with Section 2650) of Chapter 9 of Part 4.

(B) The prior conservator or prior conservator's preference for a successor conservator has been found criminally, civilly, or administratively liable for abuse, neglect, mistreatment, coercion, or fraud with respect to the conservatee or any elder or dependent adult.

(3) The spouse or domestic partner of the proposed conservatee or the person nominated by the spouse or domestic partner pursuant to Section 1811.

(4) An adult child of the proposed conservatee or the person nominated by the child pursuant to Section 1811.

(5) A parent of the proposed conservatee or the person nominated by the parent pursuant to Section 1811.

(6) A * * * sibling of the proposed conservatee or the person nominated by the brother or sister pursuant to Section 1811.

(7) Any other person or entity eligible for appointment as a conservator under this code or, if there is no person or entity willing to act as a conservator, under the Welfare and Institutions Code.

(c) The preference for any nominee for appointment under paragraphs (4), (5), and (6) of subdivision (b) is subordinate to the preference for any other parent, child, * * * or sibling in that class.

(d) For any conservatorship petition filed on or after January 1, 2023, a regional center, as provided in Chapter 5 (commencing with Section 4620) of Division 4.5 of the Welfare and Institutions Code, or any employee or agent acting on a regional center's behalf, shall not act as a conservator, but may act as the designee of the Director of Developmental Services, subject to Section 416.19 of the Health and Safety Code. *(Stats.1990, c. 79 (A.B.759), § 14, operative July 1, 1991. Amended by Stats.2001, c. 893 (A.B.25), § 16; Stats.2014, c. 913 (A.B.2747), § 29, eff. Jan. 1, 2015; Stats.2022, c. 894 (A.B.1663), § 6, eff. Jan. 1, 2023.)*

Cross References

Appointment of conservator to fill vacancy, see Probate Code § 2680 et seq.
Appointment of director as guardian or conservator, request for adjudication of incompetency, see Health and Safety Code § 416.9.
Child, defined, see Probate Code § 26.
Conservatorship for gravely disabled persons, appointment, procedure, see Welfare and Institutions Code § 5350 et seq.
Domestic partner, defined, see Probate Code § 37.
Nonprofit charitable corporation as guardian, see Probate Code § 2104.
Parent, defined, see Probate Code § 54.
Public guardian, see Probate Code § 2900 et seq.; Government Code § 27430 et seq.
Temporary guardians, appointment, see Probate Code § 2250.

Research References

Forms

West's California Code Forms, Probate § 1820 Form 1, Attachment Requesting Special Orders Regarding a Major Neurocognitive Disorder.

§ 1813. Appointment of spouse; conditions; consultation with counsel and report by counsel; disclosure of specified matters

(a)(1) The spouse of a proposed conservatee may not petition for the appointment of a conservator for a spouse or be appointed as conservator of the person or estate of the proposed conservatee unless the petitioner alleges in the petition for appointment as conservator, and the court finds, that the spouse is not a party to any action or proceeding against the proposed conservatee for legal separation of the parties, dissolution of marriage, or adjudication of nullity of their marriage. However, if the court finds by clear and convincing evidence that the appointment of the spouse, who is a party to an action or proceeding against the proposed conservatee for legal separation of the parties, dissolution of marriage, or adjudication of nullity of their marriage, or has obtained a judgment in any of these proceedings, is in the best interests of the proposed conservatee, the court may appoint the spouse.

(2) Prior to making this appointment, the court shall appoint counsel to consult with and advise the conservatee, and to report to the court his or her findings concerning the suitability of appointing the spouse as conservator.

(b) The spouse of a conservatee shall disclose to the conservator, or if the spouse is the conservator, shall disclose to the court, the filing of any action or proceeding against the conservatee for legal separation of the parties, dissolution of marriage, or adjudication of nullity of the marriage, within 10 days of the filing of the action or proceeding by filing a notice with the court and serving the notice according to the notice procedures under this title. The court may, upon receipt of the notice, set the matter for hearing on an order to

§ 1813

show cause why the appointment of the spouse as conservator, if the spouse is the conservator, should not be terminated and a new conservator appointed by the court. (Stats.1990, c. 79 (A.B.759), § 14, operative July 1, 1991. Amended by Stats.2000, c. 17 (A.B.1491), § 4; Stats.2001, c. 159 (S.B.662), § 165; Stats.2014, c. 913 (A.B. 2747), § 30, eff. Jan. 1, 2015.)

Cross References

Computation of time, see Code of Civil Procedure §§ 12 and 12a; Government Code § 6800 et seq.
Dissolution of marriage,
   Generally, see Family Code §§ 310, 2300 et seq.
   Defined, see Probate Code § 36.
Notice,
   Mailing, see Probate Code § 1215 et seq.
   Posting, see Probate Code § 1230.
   Proof of giving notice, see Probate Code § 1260 et seq.
   Special notice, see Probate Code § 1250 et seq.
   This code, generally, see Probate Code § 1200 et seq.
   This division, generally, see Probate Code § 1460 et seq.
Service of process,
   Generally, see Code of Civil Procedure § 413.10 et seq.
   Mail, see Code of Civil Procedure §§ 415.30, 1012 et seq.
   Personal delivery, see Code of Civil Procedure § 415.10.
   Proof of service, see Code of Civil Procedure § 417.10 et seq.
   Publication, see Code of Civil Procedure § 415.50.

§ 1813.1. Domestic partner of proposed conservatee

(a)(1) The domestic partner of a proposed conservatee may not petition for the appointment of a conservator for a domestic partner or be appointed as conservator of the person or estate of the proposed conservatee unless the petitioner alleges in the petition for appointment as conservator, and the court finds, that the domestic partner has not terminated and is not intending to terminate the domestic partnership as provided in Section 299 of the Family Code. However, if the court finds by clear and convincing evidence that the appointment of a domestic partner who has terminated or is intending to terminate the domestic partnership is in the best interests of the proposed conservatee, the court may appoint the domestic partner.

(2) Prior to making this appointment, the court shall appoint counsel to consult with and advise the conservatee, and to report to the court his or her findings concerning the suitability of appointing the domestic partner as conservator.

(b) The domestic partner of a conservatee shall disclose to the conservator, or if the domestic partner is the conservator, shall notify the court, of the termination of a domestic partnership as provided in Section 299 of the Family Code within 10 days of its occurrence. The court may, upon receipt of the notice, set the matter for hearing on an order to show cause why the appointment of the domestic partner as conservator, if the domestic partner is the conservator, should not be terminated and a new conservator appointed by the court. (Added by Stats.2001, c. 893 (A.B.25), § 16.5.)

Cross References

Domestic partner, defined, see Probate Code § 37.

Research References

Forms

West's California Code Forms, Probate § 1820 Form 1, Attachment Requesting Special Orders Regarding a Major Neurocognitive Disorder.
West's California Code Forms, Probate § 1830 Form 1, Order Appointing Probate Conservator (Probate Conservatorship)—Judicial Council Form GC-340.

ARTICLE 3. ESTABLISHMENT OF CONSERVATORSHIP

Section
1820. Petition; filing; persons authorized.

Section
1821. Contents of petition; supplemental information; form.
1822. Notice of hearing.
1823. Citation to proposed conservatee; contents.
1824. Service of citation and petition upon proposed conservatee.
1825. Attendance of proposed conservatee at hearing; exceptions; inability to attend; affidavit.
1826. Court investigator; duties; report; distribution; confidentiality.
1827. Law and procedure applicable to hearing.
1827.5. Assessment of proposed limited or general conservatee.
1828. Information to proposed conservatee by court.
1828.5. Limited conservator for developmentally disabled adult; appointment; hearing.
1829. Persons who may support or oppose petition.
1830. Order appointing conservator or limited conservator for developmentally disabled adult; contents.
1834. Acknowledgment of receipt by conservator; statement of duties and liabilities; conservatorship information.
1835. Conservator's rights, duties, limitations and responsibilities; dissemination of information by superior court; failure to provide information.
1835.5. Conservatee's rights; dissemination of information by superior court.
1836. Conservatorship alternatives program; establishment; purpose; staff; operation.

Cross References

Application of old and new law, see Probate Code § 3.
Limited conservatee, capacity to give informed consent for medical treatment, order of court, see Probate Code § 1890.
Proof of status of proposed conservatee, attendance at hearing not required, see Probate Code § 1844.
Special provisions applicable where proposed conservatee is a missing person, see Probate Code §§ 1845, 1848.
Special provisions applicable where proposed conservatee is an absentee, see Probate Code § 1840 et seq.

§ 1820. Petition; filing; persons authorized

(a) A petition for the appointment of a conservator may be filed by any of the following:

(1) The proposed conservatee.

(2) The spouse or domestic partner of the proposed conservatee.

(3) A relative of the proposed conservatee.

(4) Any interested state or local entity or agency of this state or any interested public officer or employee of this state or of a local public entity of this state.

(5) Any other interested person or friend of the proposed conservatee.

(b) If the proposed conservatee is a minor, the petition may be filed during his or her minority so that the appointment of a conservator may be made effective immediately upon the minor's attaining the age of majority. An existing guardian of the minor may be appointed as conservator under this part upon the minor's attaining the age of majority, whether or not the guardian's accounts have been settled.

(c) A creditor of the proposed conservatee may not file a petition for appointment of a conservator unless the creditor is a person described in paragraph (2), (3), or (4) of subdivision (a). (Stats.1990, c. 79 (A.B.759), § 14, operative July 1, 1991. Amended by Stats.2001, c. 893 (A.B.25), § 17.)

Cross References

Age of majority, see Family Code § 6500 et seq.
Appointment of legal counsel for proposed conservatee, see Probate Code § 1471.
Domestic partner, defined, see Probate Code § 37.
Interested person, defined, see Probate Code § 1424.
Notice to Veterans Administration, see Probate Code § 1461.5.

Research References

Forms

1 California Transactions Forms--Estate Planning § 1:2, Probate System.
West's California Code Forms, Probate § 1820 Form 1, Attachment Requesting Special Orders Regarding a Major Neurocognitive Disorder.
West's California Code Forms, Probate § 1952 Form 1, Allegations for Petition for Authority to Consent to Sterilization of Developmentally Disabled Adult.
West's California Judicial Council Forms GC-310, Petition for Appointment of Probate Conservator.

§ 1821. Contents of petition; supplemental information; form

(a)(1) The petition shall request that a conservator be appointed for the person or estate, or both, shall specify the name, address, and telephone number of the proposed conservator and the name, address, and telephone number of the proposed conservatee, and state the reasons why a conservatorship is necessary. Unless the petitioner or proposed conservator is a bank or other entity authorized to conduct the business of a trust company, the petitioner or proposed conservator shall also file supplemental information as to why the appointment of a conservator is required. The supplemental information to be submitted shall include a brief statement of facts addressed to each of the following categories:

(A) The inability of the proposed conservatee to properly provide for * * * their own needs for physical health, food, clothing, or shelter.

(B) The location and nature of the proposed conservatee's residence and the ability of the proposed conservatee to live in the residence while under conservatorship.

(C) Alternatives to conservatorship considered by the petitioner or proposed conservator and reasons why those alternatives are not * * * suitable, alternatives tried by the petitioner or proposed conservators, if any, including details as to the length and duration of attempted alternatives and the reasons why those alternatives do not meet the conservatee's needs. Those alternatives include, but are not limited to, all of the following:

(i) Supported decisionmaking agreements, as defined in Section 21001 of the Welfare and Institutions Code.

(ii) Powers of Attorney set forth in Division 4.5 (commencing with Section 4000).

(iii) Advanced Health Care Directives set forth in Chapter 1 (commencing with Section 4670) of Part 2 of Division 4.7.

(iv) Designations of a health care surrogate as set forth in Section 4711.

(D) Health or social services provided to the proposed conservatee during the year immediately preceding the filing of the petition, when the petitioner or proposed conservator has information as to those services.

(E) The substantial inability of the proposed conservatee to * * * manage * * * their own financial resources, or to resist fraud or undue influence.

(2) The facts required to address the categories set forth in * * * subparagraphs (A) to (E), inclusive, of paragraph (1) shall be set forth by the petitioner or proposed conservator if * * * the proposed conservator has knowledge of the facts or by the declarations or affidavits of other persons having knowledge of those facts.

(3) If any of the categories set forth in * * * subparagraphs (A) to (E), inclusive, of paragraph (1) are not applicable to the proposed conservatorship, the petitioner or proposed conservator shall so indicate and state on the supplemental information form the reasons therefor.

(4) The Judicial Council shall develop a supplemental information form for the information required pursuant to * * * subparagraphs (A) to (E), inclusive, of paragraph (1) after consultation with individuals or organizations approved by the Judicial Council, who represent public conservators, court investigators, the State Bar, specialists with experience in performing assessments and coordinating community-based services, and legal services for the elderly and disabled.

(5) The supplemental information form shall be separate and distinct from the form for the petition. The supplemental information shall be confidential and shall be made available only to parties, persons given notice of the petition who have requested this supplemental information or who have appeared in the proceedings, their attorneys, and the court. The court shall have discretion at any other time to release the supplemental information to other persons if it would serve the interests of the conservatee. The clerk of the court shall make provision for limiting disclosure of the supplemental information exclusively to persons entitled thereto under this section.

(b) The petition shall set forth, so far as they are known to the petitioner or proposed conservator, the names and addresses of the spouse or domestic partner, and of the relatives of the proposed conservatee within the second degree. If no spouse or domestic partner of the proposed conservatee or relatives of the proposed conservatee within the second degree are known to the petitioner or proposed conservator, the petition shall set forth, so far as they are known to the petitioner or proposed conservator, the names and addresses of the following persons who, for the purposes of Section 1822, shall all be deemed to be relatives:

(1) A spouse or domestic partner of a predeceased parent of a proposed conservatee.

(2) The children of a predeceased spouse or domestic partner of a proposed conservatee.

(3) The siblings of the proposed conservatee's parents, if any, but if none, then the natural and adoptive children of the proposed conservatee's parents' siblings.

(4) The natural and adoptive children of the proposed conservatee's siblings.

(c) If the petitioner or proposed conservator is a professional fiduciary, as described in Section 2340, who is required to be licensed under the Professional Fiduciaries Act (Chapter 6 (commencing with Section 6500) of Division 3 of the Business and Professions Code), the petition shall include the following:

(1) The petitioner's or proposed conservator's proposed hourly fee schedule or another statement of * * * their proposed compensation from the estate of the proposed conservatee for services performed as a conservator. The petitioner's or proposed conservator's provision of a proposed hourly fee schedule or another statement of * * * their proposed compensation, as required by this paragraph, shall not preclude a court from later reducing the petitioner's or proposed conservator's fees or other compensation.

(2) Unless a petition for appointment of a temporary conservator that contains the statements required by this paragraph is filed together with a petition for appointment of a conservator, both of the following:

(A) A statement of the petitioner's or proposed conservator's license information.

(B) A statement explaining who engaged the petitioner or proposed conservator or how the petitioner or proposed conservator was engaged to file the petition for appointment of a conservator or to agree to accept the appointment as conservator and what prior relationship the petitioner or proposed conservator had with the

§ 1821

proposed conservatee or the proposed conservatee's family or friends.

(d) If the petition is filed by a person other than the proposed conservatee, the petition shall include a declaration of due diligence showing both of the following:

(1) Either the efforts to find the proposed conservatee's relatives or why it was not feasible to contact any of them.

(2) Either the preferences of the proposed conservatee concerning the appointment of a conservator and the appointment of the proposed conservator or why it was not feasible to ascertain those preferences.

(e) If the petition is filed by a person other than the proposed conservatee, the petition shall state whether or not the petitioner is a creditor or debtor, or the agent of a creditor or debtor, of the proposed conservatee.

(f) If the proposed conservatee is a patient in, or on leave of absence from, a state institution under the jurisdiction of the State Department of State Hospitals or the State Department of Developmental Services and that fact is known to the petitioner or proposed conservator, the petition shall state that fact and name the institution.

(g) The petition shall state, so far as is known to the petitioner or proposed conservator, whether or not the proposed conservatee is receiving, or is entitled to receive, benefits from the Veterans Administration and the estimated amount of the monthly benefit payable by the Veterans Administration for the proposed conservatee.

(h) The petition may include an application for any order or orders authorized under this division, including, but not limited to, orders under Chapter 4 (commencing with Section 1870).

(i) The petition may include a further statement that the proposed conservatee is not willing to attend the hearing on the petition, does not wish to contest the establishment of the conservatorship, and does not object to the proposed conservator or prefer that another person act as conservator.

(j)(1) In the case of an allegedly developmentally disabled adult, the petition shall set forth the following:

(A) The nature and degree of the alleged disability, the specific duties and powers requested by or for the limited conservator, and the limitations of civil and legal rights requested to be included in the court's order of appointment.

(B) Whether or not the proposed limited conservatee is, or is alleged to be, developmentally disabled.

(2) Reports submitted pursuant to Section 416.8 of the Health and Safety Code meet the requirements of this section, and conservatorships filed pursuant to Article 7.5 (commencing with Section 416) of Chapter 2 of Part 1 of Division 1 of the Health and Safety Code are exempt from providing the supplemental information required by this section, as long as the guidelines adopted by the State Department of Developmental Services for regional centers are publicly accessible via the department's internet website and require the same information that is required pursuant to this section.

(k) The petition shall state, so far as is known to the petitioner, whether or not the proposed conservatee is a member of a federally recognized Indian tribe. If so, the petition shall state the name of the tribe, the state in which the tribe is located, whether the proposed conservatee resides on tribal land, and whether the proposed conservatee is known to own property on tribal land. For the purposes of this subdivision, "tribal land" means land that is, with respect to a specific Indian tribe and the members of that tribe, "Indian country" as defined in Section 1151 of Title 18 of the United States Code. *(Stats.1990, c. 79 (A.B.759), § 14, operative July 1, 1991. Amended by Stats.1991, c. 82 (S.B.896), § 8, eff. June 30, 1991, operative July 1, 1991; Stats.2001, c. 893 (A.B.25), § 18; Stats.2002, c. 784 (S.B.1316), § 577; Stats.2008, c. 293 (A.B.1340), § 1; Stats.2012,* c. 440 (A.B.1488), § 42, eff. Sept. 22, 2012; Stats.2013, c. 248 (A.B.1339), § 2; Stats.2014, c. 553 (S.B.940), § 6, eff. Jan. 1, 2015, operative Jan. 1, 2016; Stats.2022, c. 420 (A.B.2960), § 33, eff. Jan. 1, 2023; Stats.2022, c. 894 (A.B.1663), § 7, eff. Jan. 1, 2023.)

Cross References

Additional contents of petition for conservatorship of absentee, see Probate Code §§ 1813, 1841.
Attendance of proposed conservatee at hearing, see Probate Code § 1825.
Child, defined, see Probate Code § 26.
Conservators for gravely disabled persons, petition, see Welfare and Institutions Code § 5352.
Contracts, fraud, see Civil Code §§ 1571 to 1574.
Department of Developmental Services, see Welfare and Institutions Code § 4400 et seq.
Department of State Hospitals, see Welfare and Institutions Code § 4000 et seq.
Developmental disability, defined, see Probate Code § 1420.
Developmentally disabled adult,
  Contents of order appointing conservator or limited conservator, see Probate Code § 1830.
  Duties of court at hearing to appoint limited conservator, see Probate Code § 1828.5.
Developmentally disabled persons, guardianship and conservatorship, see Health and Safety Code § 416 et seq.; Welfare and Institutions Code § 4825.
Domestic partner, defined, see Probate Code § 37.
Independent exercise of powers, guardians and conservators,
  Order granting, see Probate Code § 2592.
  Withdrawal or subsequent limitation of powers, see Probate Code § 2593.
Inspection of public records, exemptions from disclosure, "conservatee" to "conservatorship", see Government Code § 6276.12.
Jurisdiction and venue, see Probate Code § 2200 et seq.
Legal capacity of conservatee, see Probate Code § 1870 et seq.
Parent, defined, see Probate Code § 54.
Predeceased spouse, defined, see Probate Code § 59.
Professional fiduciary as guardian or conservator, submission of new proposed hourly fee schedule or statement of compensation on or after one year from original submission, see Probate Code § 2614.8.
Termination of limited conservatorship, see Probate Code § 1860.5.
Transfer of conservatorship to state, investigation and report, duties of investigator, see Probate Code § 1851.1.
Trust company, defined, see Probate Code § 83.

Research References

Forms

West's California Code Forms, Probate § 1460–1461 Form 1, Notice of Hearing (Guardianship or Conservatorship)—Judicial Council Form GC-020.
West's California Code Forms, Probate § 1820 Form 1, Attachment Requesting Special Orders Regarding a Major Neurocognitive Disorder.
West's California Code Forms, Probate § 1821 Form 1, Confidential Supplemental Information—Judicial Council Form GC-312.
West's California Code Forms, Probate § 1861 Form 1, Petition for Termination of Conservatorship.
West's California Code Forms, Probate § 1952 Form 1, Allegations for Petition for Authority to Consent to Sterilization of Developmentally Disabled Adult.
West's California Code Forms, Probate § 2357 Form 1, Petition for Order Directing Medical Treatment for Ward or Conservatee.
West's California Code Forms, Probate § 2580 Form 1, Petition for Authority to Make Gifts.
West's California Judicial Council Forms GC–085, Petition to Fix Residence Outside the State of California.
West's California Judicial Council Forms GC–210(A–PF), Professional Fiduciary Attachment to Petition for Appointment of Guardian or Conservator.
West's California Judicial Council Forms GC–310, Petition for Appointment of Probate Conservator.
West's California Judicial Council Forms GC–310(A–PF), Professional Fiduciary Attachment to Petition for Appointment of Guardian or Conservator.
West's California Judicial Council Forms GC–312, Confidential Supplemental Information.

West's California Judicial Council Forms GC–336, Ex Parte Order Authorizing Disclosure of (Proposed) Conservatee's Health Information to Court Investigator—HIPAA.

§ 1822. Notice of hearing

(a) At least 15 days before the hearing on the petition for appointment of a conservator, notice of the time and place of the hearing shall be given as provided in this section. The notice shall be accompanied by a copy of the petition. The court shall not shorten the time for giving the notice of hearing under this section.

(b) Notice shall be delivered pursuant to Section 1215 to the following persons:

(1) The spouse, if any, or registered domestic partner, if any, of the proposed conservatee at the address stated in the petition.

(2) The relatives named in the petition at their addresses stated in the petition.

(c) If notice is required by Section 1461 to be given to the Director of State Hospitals or the Director of Developmental Services, notice shall be delivered pursuant to Section 1215 as required.

(d) If the petition states that the proposed conservatee is receiving or is entitled to receive benefits from the Veterans Administration, notice shall be mailed to the Office of the Veterans Administration referred to in Section 1461.5.

(e) If the proposed conservatee is a person with developmental disabilities, at least 30 days before the day of the hearing on the petition, the petitioner shall deliver pursuant to Section 1215 a notice of the hearing and a copy of the petition to the regional center identified in Section 1827.5.

(f) If the petition states that the petitioner and the proposed conservator have no prior relationship with the proposed conservatee and are not nominated by a family member, friend, or other person with a relationship to the proposed conservatee, notice shall be delivered pursuant to Section 1215 to the public guardian of the county in which the petition is filed. *(Stats.1990, c. 79 (A.B.759), § 14, operative July 1, 1991. Amended by Stats.1991, c. 82 (S.B.896), § 10, eff. June 30, 1991, operative July 1, 1991; Stats.2001, c. 893 (A.B.25), § 19; Stats.2006, c. 493 (A.B.1363), § 7; Stats.2008, c. 293 (A.B.1340), § 2; Stats.2012, c. 440 (A.B.1488), § 43, eff. Sept. 22, 2012; Stats.2017, c. 319 (A.B.976), § 34, eff. Jan. 1, 2018.)*

Cross References

Computation of time, see Code of Civil Procedure §§ 12 and 12a; Government Code § 6800 et seq.
Domestic partner, defined, see Probate Code § 37.
Limited conservator for developmentally disabled adult, appointment, see Probate Code § 1828.5.
Mailing, completion, see Probate Code § 1467.
Notice,
  Mailing, see Probate Code § 1215 et seq.
  Missing persons, petition for appointment of conservator, see Probate Code § 1847.
  Posting, see Probate Code § 1230.
  Proof of giving notice, see Probate Code § 1260 et seq.
  Special notice, see Probate Code § 1250 et seq.
  This code, generally, see Probate Code § 1200 et seq.
  This division, generally, see Probate Code § 1460 et seq.
Residence of ward or conservatee, notice according to this section, see Probate Code § 2352.
Service of process,
  Generally, see Code of Civil Procedure § 413.10 et seq.
  Mail, see Code of Civil Procedure §§ 415.30, 1012 et seq.
  Personal delivery, see Code of Civil Procedure § 415.10.
  Proof of service, see Code of Civil Procedure § 417.10 et seq.
  Publication, see Code of Civil Procedure § 415.50.
Termination of conservatorship, notice of hearing, see Probate Code § 1862.

Research References

Forms

1 California Transactions Forms--Estate Planning § 1:2, Probate System.

West's California Code Forms, Probate § 1460–1461 Form 2, Order Dispensing With Notice—Judicial Council Form GC-021.
West's California Code Forms, Probate § 1820 Form 1, Attachment Requesting Special Orders Regarding a Major Neurocognitive Disorder.
West's California Code Forms, Probate § 1830 Form 1, Order Appointing Probate Conservator (Probate Conservatorship)—Judicial Council Form GC-340.
West's California Code Forms, Probate § 1850 Comment, Periodic Court Review of Conservatorship.
West's California Code Forms, Probate § 2001 Form 1, Transfer of Conservatorship of the Person to Another State—Judicial Council Form GC-363.
West's California Code Forms, Probate § 2001 Form 2, Provisional Order for Transfer.
West's California Code Forms, Probate § 2001 Form 3, Transfer of Conservatorship of the Person and Estate to Another State.
West's California Code Forms, Probate § 2352 Form 1, Change of Residence Notice—Judicial Council Form GC-080.
West's California Judicial Council Forms GC–020, Notice of Hearing—Guardianship or Conservatorship.
West's California Judicial Council Forms GC–020(P), Proof of Personal Service of Notice of Hearing—Guardianship or Conservatorship.

§ 1823. Citation to proposed conservatee; contents

(a) If the petition is filed by a person other than the proposed conservatee, the clerk shall issue a citation directed to the proposed conservatee setting forth the time and place of hearing.

(b) The citation shall state the legal standards by which the need for a conservatorship is adjudged as stated in Section 1801 and shall state the substance of all of the following:

(1) The proposed conservatee may be adjudged unable to provide for personal needs or to manage financial resources and, by reason thereof, a conservator may be appointed for the person or estate, or both.

(2) Such adjudication may affect or transfer to the conservator the proposed conservatee's right to contract, in whole or in part, to manage and control property, to give informed consent for medical treatment, and to fix a residence.

(3)(A) The proposed conservatee may be disqualified from voting pursuant to Section 2208 of the Elections Code if * * * the proposed conservatee is incapable of communicating, with or without reasonable accommodations, a desire to participate in the voting process.

(B) The proposed conservatee shall not be disqualified from voting on the basis that * * * the proposed conservatee does, or would need to do, any of the following to complete an affidavit of voter registration:

(i) Signs the affidavit of voter registration with a mark or a cross pursuant to subdivision (b) of Section 2150 of the Elections Code.

(ii) Signs the affidavit of voter registration by means of a signature stamp pursuant to Section 354.5 of the Elections Code.

(iii) Completes the affidavit of voter registration with the assistance of another person pursuant to subdivision (d) of Section 2150 of the Elections Code.

(iv) Completes the affidavit of voter registration with reasonable accommodations.

(4) The court or a court investigator shall explain the nature, purpose, and effect of the proceeding to the proposed conservatee and shall answer questions concerning the explanation.

(5) The proposed conservatee has the right to appear at the hearing and to oppose the petition, and in the case of an alleged developmentally disabled adult, to oppose the petition in part, by objecting to any or all of the requested duties or powers of the limited conservator.

(6) The proposed conservatee has the right to choose and be represented by legal counsel and has the right to have legal counsel appointed by the court if * * * not otherwise represented by legal counsel.

§ 1823

(7) The proposed conservatee has the right to a jury trial, if desired. (Stats.1990, c. 79 (A.B.759), § 14, operative July 1, 1991. Amended by Stats.2014, c. 591 (A.B.1311), § 4, eff. Jan. 1, 2015; Stats.2015, c. 736 (S.B.589), § 8, eff. Jan. 1, 2016; Stats.2022, c. 420 (A.B.2960), § 34, eff. Jan. 1, 2023.)

Cross References

Appointment of legal counsel for proposed conservatee, see Probate Code § 1470 et seq.
Counsel, right to, see Cal. Const. Art. 1, § 15.
Court investigator, see Probate Code § 1419.
Developmental disability, defined, see Probate Code § 1420.
Disqualification from voting, see Elections Code § 2208 et seq.
Informed consent for medical treatment, capacity of conservatee to give, see Probate Code § 1880 et seq.
Jury trial, see Cal. Const. Art. 1, § 16.
Legal capacity of conservatee, see Probate Code § 1870 et seq.
Limited conservator, powers and duties, see Probate Code § 2351.5.

Research References

Forms

West's California Code Forms, Probate § 1820 Form 1, Attachment Requesting Special Orders Regarding a Major Neurocognitive Disorder.
West's California Code Forms, Probate § 1823 Form 1, Citation for Conservatorship and Proof of Service—Judicial Council Form GC-320.
West's California Judicial Council Forms GC–320, Citation for Conservatorship.

§ 1824. Service of citation and petition upon proposed conservatee

The citation and a copy of the petition shall be served on the proposed conservatee at least 15 days before the hearing. Service shall be made in the manner provided in Section 415.10 or 415.30 of the Code of Civil Procedure or in such manner as may be authorized by the court. If the proposed conservatee is outside this state, service may also be made in the manner provided in Section 415.40 of the Code of Civil Procedure. (Stats.1990, c. 79 (A.B.759), § 14, operative July 1, 1991.)

Cross References

Citation not required to proposed conservatee who is an absentee, see Probate Code § 1843.
Computation of time, see Code of Civil Procedure §§ 12 and 12a; Government Code § 6800 et seq.
Notice,
  Mailing, see Probate Code § 1215 et seq.
  Posting, see Probate Code § 1230.
  Proof of giving notice, see Probate Code § 1260 et seq.
  Special notice, see Probate Code § 1250 et seq.
  This code, generally, see Probate Code § 1200 et seq.
  This division, generally, see Probate Code § 1460 et seq.
Service of process,
  Generally, see Code of Civil Procedure § 413.10 et seq.
  Mail, see Code of Civil Procedure §§ 415.30, 1012 et seq.
  Personal delivery, see Code of Civil Procedure § 415.10.
  Proof of service, see Code of Civil Procedure § 417.10 et seq.
  Publication, see Code of Civil Procedure § 415.50.

Research References

Forms

West's California Code Forms, Probate § 1823 Form 1, Citation for Conservatorship and Proof of Service—Judicial Council Form GC-320.

§ 1825. Attendance of proposed conservatee at hearing; exceptions; inability to attend; affidavit

(a) The proposed conservatee shall be produced at the hearing except in the following cases:

(1) Where the proposed conservatee is out of the state when served and is not the petitioner.

(2) Where the proposed conservatee is unable to attend the hearing by reason of medical inability.

(3) Where the court investigator has reported to the court that the proposed conservatee has expressly communicated that the proposed conservatee (i) is not willing to attend the hearing, (ii) does not wish to contest the establishment of the conservatorship, and (iii) does not object to the proposed conservator or prefer that another person act as conservator, and the court makes an order that the proposed conservatee need not attend the hearing.

(b) If the proposed conservatee is unable to attend the hearing because of medical inability, such inability shall be established (1) by the affidavit or certificate of a licensed medical practitioner or (2) if the proposed conservatee is an adherent of a religion whose tenets and practices call for reliance on prayer alone for healing and is under treatment by an accredited practitioner of that religion, by the affidavit of the practitioner. The affidavit or certificate is evidence only of the proposed conservatee's inability to attend the hearing and shall not be considered in determining the issue of need for the establishment of a conservatorship.

(c) Emotional or psychological instability is not good cause for the absence of the proposed conservatee from the hearing unless, by reason of such instability, attendance at the hearing is likely to cause serious and immediate physiological damage to the proposed conservatee. (Stats.1990, c. 79 (A.B.759), § 14, operative July 1, 1991.)

Cross References

Absentees, proof of status of proposed conservatee, attendance at hearing not required, see Probate Code § 1844.
Affidavits, see Code of Civil Procedure §§ 2003, 2009 et seq.
Conservatorship and guardianship for developmentally disabled persons, affidavit or certificate, see Health and Safety Code § 416.7.
Court investigator, defined, see Probate Code § 1419.
Transfer of conservatorship to state, investigation and report, duties of investigator, see Probate Code § 1851.1.

Research References

Forms

West's California Code Forms, Probate § 1820 Form 1, Attachment Requesting Special Orders Regarding a Major Neurocognitive Disorder.
West's California Code Forms, Probate § 1891 Form 1, Petition for Exclusive Authority to Give Consent for Medical Treatment (Probate Conservatorship)—Judicial Council Form GC-380.
West's California Judicial Council Forms GC–333, Ex Parte Application for Order Authorizing Completion of Capacity Declaration—HIPAA.
West's California Judicial Council Forms GC–334, Ex Parte Order Re: Completion of Capacity Declaration—HIPAA.
West's California Judicial Council Forms GC–335, Capacity Declaration—Conservatorship.

§ 1826. Court investigator; duties; report; distribution; confidentiality

(a) Regardless of whether the proposed conservatee attends the hearing, the court investigator shall do all of the following:

(1) Conduct the following interviews:

(A) The proposed conservatee personally.

(B) All petitioners and all proposed conservators who are not petitioners.

(C) The proposed conservatee's spouse or registered domestic partner and relatives within the first degree. If the proposed conservatee does not have a spouse, registered domestic partner, or relatives within the first degree, to the greatest extent possible, the proposed conservatee's relatives within the second degree.

(D) To the greatest extent practical and taking into account the proposed conservatee's wishes, the proposed conservatee's relatives within the second degree not required to be interviewed under subparagraph (C), neighbors, and, if known, close friends.

(2) Inform the proposed conservatee of the contents of the petition and citation, of the nature, purpose, and effect of the proceeding, and of the right of the proposed conservatee to oppose

the petition, to attend the hearing on the petition, to have the matter of the establishment of the conservatorship tried by jury, to be represented by legal counsel, and to have legal counsel appointed by the court if * * * not otherwise represented by legal counsel.

(3) Determine if it appears that the proposed conservatee is unable to attend the hearing and, if able to attend, whether the proposed conservatee is willing to attend the hearing.

(4) Review the allegations of the petition as to why the appointment of the conservator is required and, in making the determination, do the following:

(A) Refer to the supplemental information form submitted by the petitioner and consider the facts set forth in the form that address each of the categories specified in * * * subparagraphs (A) to (E), inclusive, of paragraph (1) of subdivision (a) of Section 1821, as well as the medical reports received pursuant to paragraph (9).

(B) Determine, to the extent practicable or possible, whether the court investigator believes the proposed conservatee suffers from any of the mental function deficits listed in subdivision (a) of Section 811 that significantly impairs the proposed conservatee's ability to understand and appreciate the consequences of the proposed conservatee's actions in connection with any of the functions described in subdivision (a) or (b) of Section 1801 and describe the observations that support that belief, including information in the medical reports received pursuant to paragraph (9).

(5) Determine if the proposed conservatee wishes to oppose the establishment of the conservatorship.

(6) Determine if the proposed conservatee objects to the proposed conservator or prefers another person to act as conservator.

(7) Determine if the proposed conservatee wishes to be represented by legal counsel and, if so, whether the proposed conservatee has retained legal counsel and, if not, whether the proposed conservatee plans to retain legal counsel.

* * *

(8)(A) Determine if the proposed conservatee is incapable of communicating, with or without reasonable accommodations, a desire to participate in the voting process, and may be disqualified from voting pursuant to Section 2208 of the Elections Code.

(B) The proposed conservatee shall not be disqualified from voting on the basis that the proposed conservatee does, or would need to do, any of the following to complete an affidavit of voter registration:

(i) Signs the affidavit of voter registration with a mark or a cross pursuant to subdivision (b) of Section 2150 of the Elections Code.

(ii) Signs the affidavit of voter registration by means of a signature stamp pursuant to Section 354.5 of the Elections Code.

(iii) Completes the affidavit of voter registration with the assistance of another person pursuant to subdivision (d) of Section 2150 of the Elections Code.

(iv) Completes the affidavit of voter registration with reasonable accommodations.

(9) Gather and review relevant medical reports regarding the proposed conservatee from the proposed conservatee's primary care physician and other relevant mental and physical health care providers.

(10) Report to the court in writing, at least five days before the hearing, concerning all of the foregoing, including the proposed conservatee's express communications concerning both of the following:

(A) Representation by legal counsel.

(B) If the proposed conservatee is not willing to attend the hearing, does not wish to contest the establishment of the conservatorship, and does not object to the proposed conservator or prefers that another person act as conservator.

(11) Deliver pursuant to Section 1215, at least five days before the hearing, a copy of the report referred to in paragraph (10) to all of the following:

(A) The attorney, if any, for the petitioner.

(B) The attorney, if any, for the proposed conservatee.

(C) The proposed conservatee.

(D) The spouse, registered domestic partner, and relatives within the first degree of the proposed conservatee who are required to be named in the petition for appointment of the conservator, unless the court determines that the delivery will harm the conservatee.

(E) Any other persons as the court orders.

(b) The court investigator has discretion to release the report required by this section to the public conservator, interested public agencies, and the long-term care ombudsperson.

(c)(1) The report required by this section is confidential and shall be made available only to parties, persons described in paragraph (11) of subdivision (a), persons given notice of the petition who have requested this report or who have appeared in the proceedings, their attorneys, and the court. The court has discretion at any other time to release the report, if it would serve the interests of the conservatee. The clerk of the court shall provide for the limitation of the report exclusively to persons entitled to its receipt.

(2) Notwithstanding paragraph (1), confidential medical information and confidential information from the California Law Enforcement Telecommunications System (CLETS) shall be placed in a separate attachment to the report and shall be made available only to the proposed conservatee and the proposed conservatee's attorney.

(d) This section does not apply to a proposed conservatee who has personally executed the petition for conservatorship, or a proposed conservatee who has nominated their own conservator, if the proposed conservatee attends the hearing.

(e) If the court investigator has performed an investigation within the preceding six months and furnished a report thereon to the court, the court may order, upon good cause shown, that another investigation is not necessary or that a more limited investigation may be performed.

(f) An investigation by the court investigator related to a temporary conservatorship also may be a part of the investigation for the general petition for conservatorship, but the court investigator shall make a second visit to the proposed conservatee and the report required by this section shall include the effect of the temporary conservatorship on the proposed conservatee.

(g) The Judicial Council shall, on or before January 1, 2023, update the rules of court and Judicial Council forms as necessary to implement this section.

(h)(1) A superior court shall not be required to perform any duties imposed pursuant to the amendments to this section enacted by Chapter 493 of the Statutes of 2006 until the Legislature makes an appropriation identified for this purpose.

(2) A superior court shall not be required to perform any duties imposed pursuant to the amendments to this section enacted by the measure that added this paragraph until the Legislature makes an appropriation identified for this purpose. *(Stats.1990, c. 79 (A.B. 759), § 14, operative July 1, 1991. Amended by Stats.1998, c. 581 (A.B.2801), § 21; Stats.2002, c. 784 (S.B.1316), § 578; Stats.2006, c. 493 (A.B.1363), § 8, operative July 1, 2007; Stats.2007, c. 553 (A.B.1727), § 7; Stats.2011, c. 10 (S.B.78), § 12, eff. March 24, 2011; Stats.2014, c. 591 (A.B.1311), § 5, eff. Jan. 1, 2015; Stats.2015, c. 736 (S.B.589), § 9, eff. Jan. 1, 2016; Stats.2017, c. 319 (A.B.976), § 35, eff. Jan. 1, 2018; Stats.2021, c. 417 (A.B.1194), § 7, eff. Jan. 1, 2022; Stats.2022, c. 420 (A.B.2960), § 35, eff. Jan. 1, 2023.)*

Cross References

Appointment of legal counsel, see Probate Code § 1470 et seq.

§ 1826

Citation, contents, see Probate Code § 1823.
Conservatorship for gravely disabled persons, appointment, procedure, see Welfare and Institutions Code § 5350.
Court investigator,
 Appointment, see Probate Code § 1454.
 Defined, see Probate Code § 1419.
Guardianship and conservatorship, interested person, defined, see Probate Code § 1424.
Inspection of public records, exemptions from disclosure, "conservatee" to "conservatorship", see Government Code § 6276.12.
Waiver of court fees and costs, initial fee waiver, see Government Code § 68631.

Research References

Forms

West's California Code Forms, Probate § 1454 Form 1, Order Appointing Court Investigator—Judicial Council Form GC-330.
West's California Code Forms, Probate § 1826 Comment, Duties of Court Investigator.
West's California Judicial Council Forms GC-330, Order Appointing Court Investigator.
West's California Judicial Council Forms GC-336, Ex Parte Order Authorizing Disclosure of (Proposed) Conservatee's Health Information to Court Investigator—HIPAA.

§ 1827. Law and procedure applicable to hearing

The court shall hear and determine the matter of the establishment of the conservatorship according to the law and procedure relating to the trial of civil actions, including trial by jury if demanded by the proposed conservatee. (Stats.1990, c. 79 (A.B.759), § 14, operative July 1, 1991. Amended by Stats.2000, c. 17 (A.B.1491), § 4.2.)

Cross References

Civil action defined, see Code of Civil Procedure § 30.
Counsel, right to, see Cal. Const. Art. 1, § 15.
Depositions and discovery, see Code of Civil Procedure § 2016 et seq.
Execution of judgment in civil actions, generally, see Code of Civil Procedure § 683.010 et seq.
Filing decisions in writing in civil actions, see Code of Civil Procedure § 632.
Jury trial, see Cal. Const. Art. 1, § 16; Probate Code § 825.
Rules of practice in civil actions,
 Generally, see Code of Civil Procedure § 307 et seq.; Probate Code § 1000 et seq.
Trial by court, see Code of Civil Procedure § 631 et seq.

Research References

Forms

West's California Code Forms, Probate § 1820 Form 1, Attachment Requesting Special Orders Regarding a Major Neurocognitive Disorder.

§ 1827.5. Assessment of proposed limited or general conservatee

(a) In the case of any proceeding to establish a limited conservatorship for a person with developmental disabilities, within 30 days after the filing of a petition for limited conservatorship, a proposed limited conservatee, with his or her consent, shall be assessed at a regional center as provided in Chapter 5 (commencing with Section 4620) of Division 4.5 of the Welfare and Institutions Code. The regional center shall submit a written report of its findings and recommendations to the court.

(b) In the case of any proceeding to establish a general conservatorship for a person with developmental disabilities, the regional center, with the consent of the proposed conservatee, may prepare an assessment as provided in Chapter 5 (commencing with Section 4620) of Division 4.5 of the Welfare and Institutions Code. If an assessment is prepared, the regional center shall submit its findings and recommendations to the court.

(c)(1) A report prepared under subdivision (a) or (b) shall include a description of the specific areas, nature, and degree of disability of the proposed conservatee or proposed limited conservatee. The findings and recommendations of the regional center are not binding upon the court.

(2) In a proceeding where the petitioner is a provider of board and care, treatment, habilitation, or other services to persons with developmental disabilities or a spouse or employee of a provider, is not the natural parent of the proposed conservatee or proposed limited conservatee, and is not a public entity, the regional center shall include a recommendation in its report concerning the suitability of the petitioners to meet the needs of the proposed conservatee or proposed limited conservatee.

(d) At least five days before the hearing on the petition, the regional center shall deliver pursuant to Section 1215 a copy of the report described in subdivision (a) to all of the following:

(1) The proposed limited conservatee.

(2) The attorney, if any, for the proposed limited conservatee.

(3) If the petitioner is not the proposed limited conservatee, the attorney for the petitioner or the petitioner if the petitioner does not have an attorney.

(4) Any other persons as the court orders.

(e) The report referred to in subdivisions (a) and (b) shall be confidential and shall be made available only to parties listed in subdivision (d) unless the court, in its discretion, determines that the release of the report would serve the interests of the conservatee who is developmentally disabled. The clerk of the court shall limit disclosure of the report exclusively to persons entitled under this section. (Stats.1990, c. 79 (A.B.759), § 14, operative July 1, 1991. Amended by Stats.1991, c. 82 (S.B.896), § 12, eff. June 30, 1991, operative July 1, 1991; Stats.2002, c. 784 (S.B.1316), § 579; Stats. 2017, c. 319 (A.B.976), § 36, eff. Jan. 1, 2018.)

Cross References

Computation of time, see Code of Civil Procedure §§ 12 and 12a; Government Code § 6800 et seq.
Developmentally disabled persons, evaluation report, see Health and Safety Code § 416.8.
Inspection of public records, exemptions from disclosure, "conservatee" to "conservatorship", see Government Code § 6276.12.
Notice of hearing to regional center, see Probate Code § 1822.
Services for the developmentally disabled, confidential information and records, disclosure, see Welfare and Institutions Code § 4514.

Research References

Forms

West's California Code Forms, Probate § 1820 Form 1, Attachment Requesting Special Orders Regarding a Major Neurocognitive Disorder.

§ 1828. Information to proposed conservatee by court

(a) Except as provided in subdivision (c), before the establishment of a conservatorship of the person or estate, or both, the court shall inform the proposed conservatee of all of the following:

(1) The nature and purpose of the proceeding.

(2) The establishment of a conservatorship is a legal adjudication of the proposed conservatee's inability to properly provide for * * * the proposed conservatee's personal needs or to manage the conservatee's own financial resources, or both, depending on the allegations made and the determinations requested in the petition, and the effect of such an adjudication on the proposed conservatee's basic rights.

(3)(A) The proposed conservatee may be disqualified from voting pursuant to Section 2208 of the Elections Code if * * * the proposed conservatee is incapable of communicating, with or without reasonable accommodations, a desire to participate in the voting process.

(B) The proposed conservatee shall not be disqualified from voting on the basis that * * * the proposed conservatee does, or would need to do, any of the following to complete an affidavit of voter registration:

(i) Signs the affidavit of voter registration with a mark or a cross pursuant to subdivision (b) of Section 2150 of the Elections Code.

(ii) Signs the affidavit of voter registration by means of a signature stamp pursuant to Section 354.5 of the Elections Code.

(iii) Completes the affidavit of voter registration with the assistance of another person pursuant to subdivision (d) of Section 2150 of the Elections Code.

(iv) Completes the affidavit of voter registration with reasonable accommodations.

(4) The identity of the proposed conservator.

(5) The nature and effect on the proposed conservatee's basic rights of any order requested under Chapter 4 (commencing with Section 1870), and in the case of an allegedly developmentally disabled adult, the specific effects of each limitation requested in such order.

(6) The proposed conservatee has the right to oppose the proceeding, to have the matter of the establishment of the conservatorship tried by jury, to be represented by legal counsel if the proposed conservatee so chooses, and to have legal counsel appointed by the court if * * * not otherwise represented by legal counsel.

(b) After the court so informs the proposed conservatee and before the establishment of the conservatorship, the court shall consult the proposed conservatee to determine the proposed conservatee's opinion concerning all of the following:

(1) The establishment of the conservatorship.

(2) The appointment of the proposed conservator.

(3) Any order requested under Chapter 4 (commencing with Section 1870), and in the case of an allegedly developmentally disabled adult, of each limitation requested in that order.

(c) This section does not apply where both of the following conditions are satisfied:

(1) The proposed conservatee is absent from the hearing and is not required to attend the hearing under subdivision (a) of Section 1825.

(2) Any showing required by Section 1825 has been made. *(Stats.1990, c. 79 (A.B.759), § 14, operative July 1, 1991. Amended by Stats.2014, c. 591 (A.B.1311), § 6, eff. Jan. 1, 2015; Stats.2015, c. 736 (S.B.589), § 10, eff. Jan. 1, 2016; Stats.2016, c. 86 (S.B.1171), § 246, eff. Jan. 1, 2017; Stats.2022, c. 420 (A.B.2960), § 36, eff. Jan. 1, 2023.)*

Cross References

Appointment of legal counsel for proposed conservatee, see Probate Code § 1471.
Counsel, right to, see Cal. Const. Art. 1, § 15.
Disqualification from voting, see Probate Code § 1910; Elections Code § 2208 et seq.

Research References

Forms

West's California Code Forms, Probate § 1820 Form 1, Attachment Requesting Special Orders Regarding a Major Neurocognitive Disorder.

§ 1828.5. Limited conservator for developmentally disabled adult; appointment; hearing

(a) At the hearing on the petition for appointment of a limited conservator for an allegedly developmentally disabled adult, the court shall do each of the following:

(1) Inquire into the nature and extent of the general intellectual functioning of the individual alleged to be developmentally disabled.

(2) Evaluate the extent of the impairment of his or her adaptive behavior.

(3) Ascertain his or her capacity to care for himself or herself and his or her property.

(4) Inquire into the qualifications, abilities, and capabilities of the person seeking appointment as limited conservator.

(5) If a report by the regional center, in accordance with Section 1827.5, has not been filed in court because the proposed limited conservatee withheld his or her consent to assessment by the regional center, the court shall determine the reason for withholding such consent.

(b) If the court finds that the proposed limited conservatee possesses the capacity to care for himself or herself and to manage his or her property as a reasonably prudent person, the court shall dismiss the petition for appointment of a limited conservator.

(c) If the court finds that the proposed limited conservatee lacks the capacity to perform some, but not all, of the tasks necessary to provide properly for his or her own personal needs for physical health, food, clothing, or shelter, or to manage his or her own financial resources, the court shall appoint a limited conservator for the person or the estate or the person and the estate.

(d) If the court finds that the proposed limited conservatee lacks the capacity to perform all of the tasks necessary to provide properly for his or her own personal needs for physical health, food, clothing, or shelter, or to manage his or her own financial resources, the court shall appoint either a conservator or a limited conservator for the person or the estate, or the person and the estate.

(e) The court shall define the powers and duties of the limited conservator so as to permit the developmentally disabled adult to care for himself or herself or to manage his or her financial resources commensurate with his or her ability to do so.

(f) Prior to the appointment of a limited conservator for the person or estate or person and estate of a developmentally disabled adult, the court shall inform the proposed limited conservatee of the nature and purpose of the limited conservatorship proceeding, that the appointment of a limited conservator for his or her person or estate or person and estate will result in the transfer of certain rights set forth in the petition and the effect of such transfer, the identity of the person who has been nominated as his or her limited conservator, that he or she has a right to oppose such proceeding, and that he or she has a right to have the matter tried by jury. After communicating such information to the person and prior to the appointment of a limited conservator, the court shall consult the person to determine his or her opinion concerning the appointment. *(Stats.1990, c. 79 (A.B.759), § 14, operative July 1, 1991.)*

Cross References

Developmental disability, defined, see Probate Code § 1420.
Developmentally disabled adult,
 Authorization for appointment of limited conservator, see Probate Code § 1801.
 Contents of order appointing conservator or limited conservator, see Probate Code § 1830.
Developmentally disabled persons,
 Application of this division, see Health and Safety Code § 416.1 et seq.
 Guardianships and conservatorships for those in state hospitals, see Welfare and Institutions Code § 4825.
Limited conservator, powers and duties, see Probate Code § 2351.5.
Regional centers for persons with developmental disabilities, see Welfare and Institutions Code § 4620 et seq.

Research References

Forms

1 California Transactions Forms--Estate Planning § 2:17, Definitions of Capacity.
West's California Code Forms, Probate § 1820 Form 1, Attachment Requesting Special Orders Regarding a Major Neurocognitive Disorder.

§ 1829. Persons who may support or oppose petition

Any of the following persons may appear at the hearing to support or oppose the petition:

(a) The proposed conservatee.

(b) The spouse or registered domestic partner of the proposed conservatee.

(c) A relative of the proposed conservatee.

(d) Any interested person or friend of the proposed conservatee. (Stats.1990, c. 79 (A.B.759), § 14, operative July 1, 1991. Amended by Stats.2001, c. 893 (A.B.25), § 20; Stats.2006, c. 493 (A.B.1363), § 9.)

Cross References
Domestic partner, defined, see Probate Code § 37.
Interested person, defined, see Probate Code § 1424.

Research References
Forms

West's California Code Forms, Probate § 1829 Comment, Opposing or Supporting Petition.

§ 1830. Order appointing conservator or limited conservator for developmentally disabled adult; contents

(a) The order appointing the conservator shall contain, among other things, the names, addresses, and telephone numbers of:

(1) The conservator.

(2) The conservatee's attorney, if any.

(3) The court investigator, if any.

(b) In the case of a limited conservator for a developmentally disabled adult, any order the court issues shall include the findings of the court specified in Section 1828.5. The order shall specify the powers granted to and duties imposed upon the limited conservator, which powers and duties shall not exceed the powers and duties applicable to a conservator under this code. The order shall also specify all of the following:

(1) The properties of the limited conservatee to which the limited conservator is entitled to possession and management, giving a description of the properties that will be sufficient to identify them.

(2) The debts, rentals, wages, or other claims due to the limited conservatee which the limited conservator is entitled to collect, or file suit with respect to, if necessary, and thereafter to possess and manage.

(3) The contractual or other obligations which the limited conservator may incur on behalf of the limited conservatee.

(4) The claims against the limited conservatee which the limited conservator may pay, compromise, or defend, if necessary.

(5) Any other powers, limitations, or duties with respect to the care of the limited conservatee or the management of the property specified in this subdivision by the limited conservator which the court shall specifically and expressly grant.

(c) An information notice of the rights of conservatees shall be attached to the order. The conservator shall deliver pursuant to Section 1215 the order and the attached information notice to the conservatee and the conservatee's relatives, as set forth in subdivision (b) of Section 1821, within 30 days of the issuance of the order. By January 1, 2008, the Judicial Council shall develop the notice required by this subdivision. (Stats.1990, c. 79 (A.B.759), § 14, operative July 1, 1991. Amended by Stats.2006, c. 493 (A.B.1363), § 10; Stats.2007, c. 553 (A.B.1727), § 8; Stats.2017, c. 319 (A.B.976), § 37, eff. Jan. 1, 2018.)

Cross References
Appealable orders, see Probate Code § 1300 et seq.
Contracts,
  Generally, see Civil Code § 1549 et seq.
  Interpretation, see Civil Code § 1635 et seq.
Court investigator, defined, see Probate Code § 1419.
Developmental disability, defined, see Probate Code § 1420.
Limited conservator, powers and duties, see Probate Code § 2351.5.
Order of appointment, additional conditions, see Probate Code §§ 2358, 2402.

Powers and duties of conservators, see Probate Code §§ 2350 et seq., 2400 et seq.

Research References
Forms

West's California Code Forms, Probate § 1820 Form 1, Attachment Requesting Special Orders Regarding a Major Neurocognitive Disorder.
West's California Code Forms, Probate § 10831 Form 2, Order Fixing and Allowing Compensation.
West's California Judicial Council Forms GC–340, Order Appointing Probate Conservator.
West's California Judicial Council Forms GC–341, Notice of Conservatee's Rights (Also Available in Spanish).

§ 1834. Acknowledgment of receipt by conservator; statement of duties and liabilities; conservatorship information

(a) Before letters are issued in a conservatorship that originates in this state or a conservatorship that is transferred to this state under Chapter 8 (commencing with Section 1980), the conservator (other than a trust company or a public conservator) shall file an acknowledgment of receipt of (1) a statement of duties and liabilities of the office of conservator, and (2) a copy of the conservatorship information required under Section 1835. The acknowledgment and the statement shall be in the form prescribed by the Judicial Council.

(b) The court may by local rules require the acknowledgment of receipt to include the conservator's birth date and driver's license number, if any, provided that the court ensures their confidentiality.

(c) The statement of duties and liabilities prescribed by the Judicial Council shall not supersede the law on which the statement is based. (Added by Stats.1991, c. 1019 (S.B.1022), § 1. Amended by Stats.1994, c. 806 (A.B.3686), § 9; Stats.2014, c. 553 (S.B.940), § 7, eff. Jan. 1, 2015, operative Jan. 1, 2016.)

Cross References
Inspection of public records, exemptions from disclosure, "conservatee" to "conservatorship", see Government Code § 6276.12.
Letters, defined, see Probate Code § 52.

Research References
Forms

West's California Code Forms, Probate § 1834 Form 1, Duties of Conservator and Acknowledgment of Receipt of Handbook (Probate Conservatorship)—Judicial Council Form GC-348.
West's California Judicial Council Forms GC–348, Duties of Conservator and Acknowledgment of Receipt of Handbook for Conservators (Also Available in Spanish).
West's California Judicial Council Forms GC–350, Letters of Conservatorship.

§ 1835. Conservator's rights, duties, limitations and responsibilities; dissemination of information by superior court; failure to provide information

(a) Every superior court shall provide all * * * conservators with written information concerning a conservator's rights, duties, limitations, and responsibilities under this division.

(b) The information to be provided shall include, but need not be limited to, the following:

(1) The rights, duties, limitations, and responsibilities of a conservator.

(2) The rights of a conservatee.

(3) How to assess the needs and preferences of the conservatee.

(4) How to use community-based services to meet the needs of the conservatee.

(5) How to ensure that the conservatee is provided with the least restrictive possible environment.

(6) The court procedures and processes relevant to conservatorships.

(7) The procedures for inventory and appraisal, and the filing of accounts.

(8) Procedures to petition to terminate or modify the conservatorship.

(9) The conservator's obligations pursuant to Section 2113.

(c) An information package shall be developed by the Judicial Council, after consultation with the following organizations or individuals:

(1) The California State Association of Public Administrators, Public Guardians, and Public Conservators, or other comparable organizations.

(2) The State Bar.

(3) Individuals or organizations, approved by the Judicial Council, who represent court investigators, specialists with experience in performing assessments and coordinating community-based services, and legal services programs for the elderly.

(d) The failure of any court or any employee or agent thereof, to provide information to a conservator as required by this section does not:

(1) Relieve the conservator of any of the conservator's duties as required by this division.

(2) Make the court or the employee or agent thereof, liable, in either a personal or official capacity, for damages to a conservatee, conservator, the conservatorship of a person or an estate, or any other person or entity.

(e) The information package shall be made available to individual courts. The Judicial Council shall periodically update the information package when changes in the law warrant revision. The revisions shall be provided to individual courts.

(f) To cover the costs of providing the written information required by this section, a court may charge each private conservator a fee of twenty dollars ($20) which shall be distributed to the court in which it was collected. *(Stats.1990, c. 79 (A.B.759), § 14, operative July 1, 1991. Amended by Stats.1991, c. 1019 (S.B.1022), § 2; Stats.2005, c. 75 (A.B.145), § 147, eff. July 19, 2005, operative Jan. 1, 2006; Stats.2022, c. 894 (A.B.1663), § 8, eff. Jan. 1, 2023.)*

Cross References

Deposit of fees or fines collected pursuant to this section in the Trial Court Trust Fund, effect of prior agreements or practices, long-term revenue allocation schedule proposal, see Government Code § 68085.5.
Organization and government of courts, collection of fees and fines pursuant to this section, deposits, see Government Code § 68085.1.
Public guardian, generally, see Probate Code § 2900 et seq.

Research References

Forms

West's California Code Forms, Probate § 1834 Form 1, Duties of Conservator and Acknowledgment of Receipt of Handbook (Probate Conservatorship)—Judicial Council Form GC-348.
West's California Judicial Council Forms GC-362, Conservatorship Registrant'S Acknowledgment of Receipt of Handbook for Conservators.

§ 1835.5. Conservatee's rights; dissemination of information by superior court

(a) Within 30 days of the establishment of a conservatorship under this division, and annually thereafter, the superior court shall provide information to a conservatee under its jurisdiction, written in plain language, with a list of the conservatee's rights within the conservatorship.

(b) The information to be provided shall include, but need not be limited to, all of the following:

(1) The name and contact information of the conservator.

(2) A description of the conservatorship, including the rights the conservatee retains under the conservatorship.

(3) The role, duties, and contact information, including name, telephone number, address, and email address, of the court investigator and the court alternatives program.

(4) The person to petition to end or change the conservatorship and contact information for the person to contact to begin that process.

(5) A personalized list of rights that the conservatee retains, even under the conservatorship, including the rights to do all of the following:

(A) Directly receive and control their own salary.

(B) Make or change their will.

(C) Get married.

(D) Receive mail.

(E) Have visits from family and friends.

(F) Have a lawyer.

(G) Ask a judge to change conservators.

(H) Ask a judge to end the conservatorship.

(I) Vote, unless expressly withheld by the court.

(J) Control personal spending money if a judge permits an allowance to be paid directly to the conservatee.

(K) Make their own health care decisions.

(L) Enter into business transactions to provide for the conservatee's basic needs and those of their children.

(M) Participate in other activities the court allows when the conservator is appointed, or when the court order later grants that right at the conservatee's request.

(6) The personalized list of rights in paragraph (5) shall state which rights, if any, were expressly withheld by the court. *(Added by Stats.2022, c. 894 (A.B.1663), § 9, eff. Jan. 1, 2023.)*

§ 1836. Conservatorship alternatives program; establishment; purpose; staff; operation

(a) Upon appropriation by the Legislature, the Judicial Council shall establish a conservatorship alternatives program within each self-help center in every state Superior Court.

(b) The purposes of the conservatorship alternatives program are:

(1) To provide information relating to less restrictive alternatives to conservatorship, including, but not limited to, supported decision-making agreements, as defined in Section 21001 of the Welfare and Institutions Code, to interested individuals.

(2) To educate interested individuals on less restrictive alternatives to conservatorship that may be appropriate, and to provide assistance in considering and implementing those alternatives.

(c) Each court's conservatorship alternatives program shall include staff who provide information and resources to interested individuals about less restrictive alternatives to conservatorship.

(d) The conservatorship alternatives program shall operate as follows:

(1) Any interested individual who contacts a superior court self-help center to inquire about conservatorship proceedings or to request documents to petition for a conservatorship shall be advised of the conservatorship alternatives program.

(2) The conservatorship alternatives program shall be a component of each superior court's self-help center.

(3) Conservatorship alternatives program staff shall be trained in less restrictive alternatives to conservatorship and shall be available to meet, through in-person or remote means, with interested individuals to provide education and resources on supported decisionmaking agreements and other less restrictive alternatives to

§ 1836   PROBATE CODE

conservatorship, and to provide resources to assist people who wish to implement or establish those alternatives.

(4) Conservatorship alternatives program staff shall be able to provide the following to interested individuals:

(A) Practical resources, information, and documents to establish and implement alternatives to conservatorship, including powers of attorney, advance health care directives, and supported decisionmaking agreements.

(B) Technical support and education on these alternatives, including assistance in filling out any associated paperwork and in understanding these alternatives.

(5) Interactions or communication with the CAP Program shall not be used as evidence of incapacity or introduced for any other reason in a conservatorship proceeding under this division unless introduced by the conservatee or proposed conservatee. *(Added by Stats.2022, c. 894 (A.B.1663), § 10, eff. Jan. 1, 2023.)*

ARTICLE 4. SPECIAL PROVISIONS APPLICABLE WHERE PROPOSED CONSERVATEE IS AN ABSENTEE

Section
1840. Appointment of conservator for absentee; procedure.
1841. Petition; additional contents.
1842. Notice of hearing.
1843. Citation to proposed conservatee not required; notice to absentee conservatee not required.
1844. Proof of status of proposed conservatee; attendance at hearing not required.

Cross References

Application of old and new law, see Probate Code § 3.

§ 1840. Appointment of conservator for absentee; procedure

Except as otherwise provided in this article, a conservator for an absentee (Section 1403) shall be appointed as provided in Article 3 (commencing with Section 1820) of this chapter or Article 3 (commencing with Section 2001) of Chapter 8. *(Stats.1990, c. 79 (A.B.759), § 14, operative July 1, 1991. Amended by Stats.2014, c. 553 (S.B.940), § 8, eff. Jan. 1, 2015, operative Jan. 1, 2016.)*

Cross References

Absentee, defined, see Probate Code § 1403.
Condition for appointment of spouse of absentee as conservator, see Probate Code § 1813.
Conservator of estate, appointment for absentee, see Probate Code § 1803.
Termination of conservatorship of absentee, see Probate Code § 1864.

§ 1841. Petition; additional contents

In addition to the other required contents of the petition, if the proposed conservatee is an absentee:

(a) The petition, and any notice required by Section 1822 or 2002, or any other law, shall set forth the last known military rank or grade and the social security account number of the proposed conservatee.

(b) The petition shall state whether the absentee's spouse has commenced any action or proceeding against the absentee for judicial or legal separation, dissolution of marriage, annulment, or adjudication of nullity of their marriage. *(Stats.1990, c. 79 (A.B.759), § 14, operative July 1, 1991. Amended by Stats.2014, c. 553 (S.B.940), § 9, eff. Jan. 1, 2015, operative Jan. 1, 2016.)*

Cross References

Absentee, defined, see Probate Code § 1403.
Condition for appointment of spouse of absentee as conservator, see Probate Code § 1813.
Contents of petition, see Probate Code § 1821.

Dissolution of marriage, defined, see Probate Code § 36.

§ 1842. Notice of hearing

In addition to the persons and entities to whom notice of hearing is required under Section 1822 or 2002, if the proposed conservatee is an absentee, a copy of the petition and notice of the time and place of the hearing shall be delivered pursuant to Section 1215 at least 15 days before the hearing to the secretary concerned or to the head of the United States department or agency concerned, as the case may be. In that case, notice shall also be published pursuant to Section 6061 of the Government Code in a newspaper of general circulation in the county in which the hearing will be held. *(Stats.1990, c. 79 (A.B.759), § 14, operative July 1, 1991. Amended by Stats.2014, c. 553 (S.B.940), § 10, eff. Jan. 1, 2015, operative Jan. 1, 2016; Stats.2017, c. 319 (A.B.976), § 38, eff. Jan. 1, 2018.)*

Cross References

Computation of time, see Code of Civil Procedure §§ 12 and 12a; Government Code § 6800 et seq.
Definitions,
   Absentee, see Probate Code § 1403.
   Secretary concerned, see Probate Code § 1440.
Mailing, completion, see Probate Code § 1467.
Newspaper of general circulation, establishment of standing, see Government Code § 6020 et seq.
Notice,
   Mailing, see Probate Code § 1215 et seq.
   Posting, see Probate Code § 1230.
   Proof of giving notice, see Probate Code § 1260 et seq.
   Special notice, see Probate Code § 1250 et seq.
   This code, generally, see Probate Code § 1200 et seq.
   This division, generally, see Probate Code § 1460 et seq.
Service of process,
   Generally, see Code of Civil Procedure § 413.10 et seq.
   Mail, see Code of Civil Procedure §§ 415.30, 1012 et seq.
   Personal delivery, see Code of Civil Procedure § 415.10.
   Proof of service, see Code of Civil Procedure § 417.10 et seq.
   Publication, see Code of Civil Procedure § 415.50.

§ 1843. Citation to proposed conservatee not required; notice to absentee conservatee not required

(a) No citation is required under Section 1823 to the proposed conservatee if the proposed conservatee is an absentee.

(b) No notice is required under Section 2002 to the proposed conservatee if the proposed conservatee is an absentee. *(Stats.1990, c. 79 (A.B.759), § 14, operative July 1, 1991. Amended by Stats.2014, c. 553 (S.B.940), § 11, eff. Jan. 1, 2015, operative Jan. 1, 2016.)*

§ 1844. Proof of status of proposed conservatee; attendance at hearing not required

(a) In a proceeding to appoint a conservator for an absentee under Article 3 (commencing with Section 1820) of this chapter or Article 3 (commencing with Section 2001) of Chapter 8, an official written report or record complying with Section 1283 of the Evidence Code that a proposed conservatee is an absentee shall be received as evidence of that fact and the court shall not determine the status of the proposed conservatee inconsistent with the status determined as shown by the written report or record.

(b) The inability of the proposed conservatee to attend the hearing is established by the official written report or record referred to in subdivision (a). *(Stats.1990, c. 79 (A.B.759), § 14, operative July 1, 1991. Amended by Stats.2014, c. 553 (S.B.940), § 12, eff. Jan. 1, 2015, operative Jan. 1, 2016.)*

Cross References

Absentee, defined, see Probate Code § 1403.

Attendance of proposed conservatee at hearing, generally, see Probate Code § 1825.

ARTICLE 5. SPECIAL PROVISIONS APPLICABLE WHERE PROPOSED CONSERVATEE IS A MISSING PERSON

Section
1845. Appointment of conservator.
1846. Contents of petition for conservatorship of missing person's estate.
1847. Notice; petition for appointment of conservator.
1848. Appointment of conservator; acts not required.
1849. Appointment of conservator; conditions.
1849.5. Application of article.

Cross References

Application of old and new law, see Probate Code § 3.
Appointment of conservator authorized, see Probate Code § 1804.
Death of persons not heard from in five years, presumption, see Evidence Code § 667.
Personal property of absent federal personnel, see Probate Code § 3700 et seq.
Persons to whom notice of time and place of hearing on petition, report or account if conservator of estate appointed under this Article, see Probate Code § 1461.7.

§ 1845. Appointment of conservator

(a) Except as otherwise provided in this article, a conservator of the estate of a person who is missing and whose whereabouts is unknown shall be appointed as provided in Article 3 (commencing with Section 1820) of this chapter or Article 3 (commencing with Section 2001) of Chapter 8.

(b) This article does not apply where the proposed conservatee is an absentee as defined in Section 1403. *(Stats.1990, c. 79 (A.B.759), § 14, operative July 1, 1991. Amended by Stats.2014, c. 553 (S.B.940), § 13, eff. Jan. 1, 2015, operative Jan. 1, 2016.)*

§ 1846. Contents of petition for conservatorship of missing person's estate

In addition to the other required contents of the petition, if the proposed conservatee is a person who is missing and whose whereabouts is unknown, the petition shall state all of the following:

(a) The proposed conservatee owns or is entitled to the possession of real or personal property located in this state. In a proceeding to transfer a conservatorship of a missing person to this state under Article 3 (commencing with Section 2001) of Chapter 8, this requirement is also satisfied if the petition states that the proposed conservatee owns or is entitled to the possession of personal property that is to be relocated to this state upon approval of the transfer.

(b) The time and circumstance of the person's disappearance and that the missing person has not been heard from by the persons most likely to hear (naming them and their relationship to the missing person) since the time of disappearance and that the whereabouts of the missing person is unknown to those persons and to the petitioner.

(c) The last known residence of the missing person.

(d) A description of any search or inquiry made concerning the whereabouts of the missing person.

(e) A description of the estate of the proposed conservatee which requires attention, supervision, and care. *(Stats.1990, c. 79 (A.B. 759), § 14, operative July 1, 1991. Amended by Stats.2014, c. 553 (S.B.940), § 14, eff. Jan. 1, 2015, operative Jan. 1, 2016.)*

Cross References

Missing persons presumed dead, estate administration, see Probate Code § 12400 et seq.

§ 1847. Notice; petition for appointment of conservator

In addition to the persons and entities to whom notice of hearing is required under Section 1822 or 2002, if the proposed conservatee is a person who is missing and whose whereabouts is unknown:

(a) A copy of the petition for appointment of a conservator and notice of the time and place of the hearing on the petition shall be delivered pursuant to Section 1215 at least 15 days before the hearing to the proposed conservatee at the last known address of the proposed conservatee.

(b) Notice of the time and place of the hearing shall also be published pursuant to Section 6061 of the Government Code in a newspaper of general circulation in the county in which the proposed conservatee was last known to reside if the proposed conservatee's last known address is in this state.

(c) Pursuant to Section 1202, the court may require that further or additional notice of the hearing be given. *(Stats.1990, c. 79 (A.B.759), § 14, operative July 1, 1991. Amended by Stats.2014, c. 553 (S.B.940), § 15, eff. Jan. 1, 2015, operative Jan. 1, 2016; Stats.2017, c. 319 (A.B.976), § 39, eff. Jan. 1, 2018.)*

Cross References

Computation of time, see Code of Civil Procedure §§ 12 and 12a; Government Code § 6800 et seq.
Publication, generally, see Government Code § 6000 et seq.

§ 1848. Appointment of conservator; acts not required

(a) In a proceeding under Article 3 (commencing with Section 1820) to appoint a conservator of the estate of a person who is missing and whose whereabouts is unknown, the following acts are not required:

(1) Issuance of a citation to the proposed conservatee pursuant to Section 1823.

(2) Service of a citation and petition pursuant to Section 1824.

(3) Production of the proposed conservatee at the hearing pursuant to Section 1825.

(4) Performance of the duties of the court investigator pursuant to Section 1826.

(5) Performance of any other act that depends upon knowledge of the location of the proposed conservatee.

(b) In a proceeding to transfer a conservatorship of a missing person to this state under Article 3 (commencing with Section 2001) of Chapter 8, the following acts are not required:

(1) Notice to the proposed conservatee pursuant to Section 2002.

(2) Production of the proposed conservatee at the hearings pursuant to Section 2002.

(3) Performance of the duties of the court investigator pursuant to Section 1851.1.

(4) Performance of any other act that depends upon knowledge of the location of the proposed conservatee. *(Stats.1990, c. 79 (A.B. 759), § 14, operative July 1, 1991. Amended by Stats.2014, c. 553 (S.B.940), § 16, eff. Jan. 1, 2015, operative Jan. 1, 2016.)*

Cross References

Notice,
  Mailing, see Probate Code § 1215 et seq.
  Posting, see Probate Code § 1230.
  Proof of giving notice, see Probate Code § 1260 et seq.
  Special notice, see Probate Code § 1250 et seq.
  This code, generally, see Probate Code § 1200 et seq.
  This division, generally, see Probate Code § 1460 et seq.
Service of process,
  Generally, see Code of Civil Procedure § 413.10 et seq.
  Mail, see Code of Civil Procedure §§ 415.30, 1012 et seq.
  Personal delivery, see Code of Civil Procedure § 415.10.
  Proof of service, see Code of Civil Procedure § 417.10 et seq.
  Publication, see Code of Civil Procedure § 415.50.

§ 1849. Appointment of conservator; conditions

A conservator of the estate of a person who is missing and whose whereabouts is unknown may be appointed only if the court finds all of the following:

(a) The proposed conservatee owns or is entitled to the possession of real or personal property located in this state. In a proceeding to transfer a conservatorship of a missing person to this state under Article 3 (commencing with Section 2001) of Chapter 8, this requirement is also satisfied if the court finds that the proposed conservatee owns or is entitled to the possession of personal property that is to be relocated to this state upon approval of the transfer.

(b) The proposed conservatee remains missing and his or her whereabouts remains unknown.

(c) The estate of the proposed conservatee requires attention, supervision, and care. *(Stats.1990, c. 79 (A.B.759), § 14, operative July 1, 1991. Amended by Stats.2014, c. 553 (S.B.940), § 17, eff. Jan. 1, 2015, operative Jan. 1, 2016.)*

§ 1849.5. Application of article

(a) A petition may be filed under this article regardless of when the proposed conservatee became missing or how long the proposed conservatee has been missing.

(b) If a trustee was appointed pursuant to former Section 262, repealed by Chapter 201 of the Statutes of 1983, the provisions of former Sections 260 to 272, inclusive, repealed by Chapter 201 of the Statutes of 1983, continue to apply to the case after December 31, 1983, unless, upon a petition filed under this article after December 31, 1983, the trustee is replaced by a conservator. *(Stats.1990, c. 79 (A.B.759), § 14, operative July 1, 1991.)*

CHAPTER 2. PERIODIC REVIEW OF CONSERVATORSHIP

Section
1850. Review of conservatorship; application.
1850.5. Limited conservatorship for developmentally disabled adult; judicial review.
1851. Court investigator; visitation of conservatee, conservator, or others; findings; recommendation.
1851.1. Transfer of conservatorship to state; investigation and report; duties of investigator.
1851.2. Coordination.
1851.5. Court investigators; assessments.
1851.6. Court investigator; prior investigation.
1852. Notification of counsel; representation of conservatee at hearing.
1853. Failure to locate conservatee; termination of conservatorship; discharge of conservator; petition to appoint new conservator.

Cross References

Application of old and new law, see Probate Code § 3.
Cancellation and voter file maintenance, mentally incompetent persons, review under Probate Code of capability to complete affidavit, see Elections Code § 2209.
Conservatorship for gravely disabled persons, appointment, procedure, see Welfare and Institutions Code § 5350.

§ 1850. Review of conservatorship; application

(a) Except as provided in subdivision (e), each conservatorship established pursuant to this part shall be reviewed by the court as follows:

(1) Six months after the initial appointment of the conservator, the court investigator shall visit the conservatee, conduct an investigation as provided in subdivision (a) of Section 1851, and report to the court regarding the appropriateness of the conservatorship and whether the conservator is acting in the best interests of the conservatee regarding the conservatee's placement, quality of care, including physical and mental health treatment, and finances. In response to the investigator's report, the court may take appropriate action including, but not limited to, ordering a hearing or ordering the conservator to submit an accounting pursuant to subdivision (a) of Section 2620.

(2) One year after the initial appointment of the conservator and annually thereafter, the court investigator shall, as provided in Section 1851, visit the conservatee, conduct an investigation, including, when possible, discussing with the conservatee less restrictive alternatives to conservatorship as set forth in Section 1800.3, and report the findings of the investigation to the court, including whether the conservator or conservatee wishes to modify or terminate the conservatorship and whether less restrictive alternatives could be tried. On receipt of the investigator's report, the court shall, if indicated by the report, consider promptly terminating or modifying the conservatorship at a hearing pursuant to Section 1860.5 or 1863 and take any other appropriate action.

(b) At any time, the court may, on its own motion or upon request by any interested person, take appropriate action including, but not limited to, ordering a review of the conservatorship at a noticed hearing or ordering the conservator to submit an accounting pursuant to Section 2620.

(c) Notice of a review hearing pursuant to this section shall be given to the persons, for the period and in the manner provided in Chapter 3 (commencing with Section 1460) of Part 1.

(d) This chapter does not apply to either of the following:

(1) A conservatorship for an absentee as defined in Section 1403.

(2) A conservatorship of the estate for a nonresident of this state where the conservatee is not present in this state.

(e)(1) A superior court shall not be required to perform any duties imposed pursuant to the amendments to this section enacted by Chapter 493 of the Statutes of 2006 until the Legislature makes an appropriation identified for this purpose.

(2) A superior court shall not be required to perform any duties imposed pursuant to the measure that added this paragraph until the Legislature makes an appropriation identified for this purpose. *(Stats.1990, c. 79 (A.B.759), § 14, operative July 1, 1991. Amended by Stats.2006, c. 492 (S.B.1716), § 3; Stats.2006, c. 493 (A.B.1363), § 11.5, operative July 1, 2007; Stats.2011, c. 10 (S.B.78), § 13, eff. March 24, 2011; Stats.2021, c. 417 (A.B.1194), § 8, eff. Jan. 1, 2022; Stats.2022, c. 894 (A.B.1663), § 11, eff. Jan. 1, 2023.)*

Research References

Forms

West's California Code Forms, Probate § 1454 Form 2, Order Appointing Court Investigator—Judicial Council Form GC-331.
West's California Code Forms, Probate § 1454 Form 3, Order Setting Biennial Review Investigation and Directing Status Report Before Review—Judicial Council Form GC-332.
West's California Code Forms, Probate § 1850 Comment, Periodic Court Review of Conservatorship.
West's California Judicial Council Forms GC–331, Order Appointing Court Investigator (Review and Successor Conservator Investigations).
West's California Judicial Council Forms GC–332, Order Setting Biennial Review Investigation and Directing Status Report Before Review.

§ 1850.5. Limited conservatorship for developmentally disabled adult; judicial review

(a) Notwithstanding Section 1850, each limited conservatorship for a developmentally disabled adult, as defined in subdivision (d) of Section 1801, shall be reviewed by the court one year after the appointment of the conservator and biennially thereafter.

(b) The court may, on its own motion or upon request by any interested person, take appropriate action, including, but not limited to, ordering a review of the limited conservatorship at a noticed hearing, at any time.

(c) At any review pursuant to this section, the court shall consider terminating the limited conservatorship, as provided in Section 1860.5.

(d) Notice of a review hearing pursuant to this section shall be given to the persons, for the period and in the manner provided in subdivision (d) of Section 1860.5.

(e)(1) A superior court shall not be required to perform any duties imposed by this section until the Legislature makes an appropriation identified for this purpose.

(2) A superior court shall not be required to perform any duties imposed pursuant to the amendments to this section enacted by the measure that added this paragraph until the Legislature makes an appropriation identified for this purpose. *(Added by Stats.2006, c. 493 (A.B.1363), § 11.7, operative July 1, 2007. Amended by Stats. 2011, c. 10 (S.B.78), § 14, eff. March 24, 2011; Stats.2021, c. 417 (A.B.1194), § 9, eff. Jan. 1, 2022.)*

Research References

Forms

West's California Code Forms, Probate § 1850 Comment, Periodic Court Review of Conservatorship.

§ 1851. Court investigator; visitation of conservatee, conservator, or others; findings; recommendation

(a)(1) If court review is required pursuant to Section 1850 or 1850.5, the court investigator shall, without prior notice to the conservator except as ordered by the court for necessity or to prevent harm to the conservatee, visit the conservatee. The court investigator shall inform the conservatee personally that the conservatee is under a conservatorship and shall give the name of the conservator to the conservatee. The court investigator shall determine all of the following:

(A) If the conservatee wishes the court to terminate the conservatorship.

(B) If the conservatee wishes the court to remove the conservator and appoint a successor conservator.

(C) If both of the following are true:

(i) The conservatee still meets the criteria for appointment of a conservator of the person under subdivision (a) of Section 1801, a conservator of the estate under subdivision (b) of Section 1801, or both.

(ii) The conservatorship remains the least restrictive alternative needed for the protection of the conservatee, as required by subdivision (b) of Section 1800.3.

(D) If the conservator is acting in the best interests of the conservatee. In determining if the conservator is acting in the best interests of the conservatee, the court investigator's evaluation shall include an examination of the conservatee's placement, the quality of care, including physical and mental health treatment, and the conservatee's finances. To the extent practicable, the investigator shall review the accounting with a conservatee who has sufficient capacity. To the greatest extent possible, the court investigator shall interview individuals set forth in paragraph (1) of subdivision (a) of Section 1826, in order to determine if the conservator is acting in the best interests of the conservatee.

(E)(i) If the conservatee is incapable of communicating, with or without reasonable accommodations, a desire to participate in the voting process and may be disqualified from voting pursuant to Section 2208 or 2209 of the Elections Code.

(ii) The conservatee shall not be disqualified from voting on the basis that the conservatee does, or would need to do, any of the following to complete an affidavit of voter registration:

(I) Signs the affidavit of voter registration with a mark or a cross pursuant to subdivision (b) of Section 2150 of the Elections Code.

(II) Signs the affidavit of voter registration by means of a signature stamp pursuant to Section 354.5 of the Elections Code.

(III) Completes the affidavit of voter registration with the assistance of another person pursuant to subdivision (d) of Section 2150 of the Elections Code.

(IV) Completes the affidavit of voter registration with reasonable accommodations.

(2) If the court investigator determines that the conservatee still meets the criteria for appointment of a conservator under Section 1801, the investigator shall determine if the terms of the appointment order should be modified to reduce or expand the conservator's powers and duties to ensure that the conservatorship is the least restrictive alternative needed for the conservatee's protection.

(3) Upon request of the court investigator, the conservator shall make available to the court investigator during the investigation for inspection and copying all books and records, including receipts and any expenditures, of the conservatorship.

(b)(1) The findings of the court investigator, including the facts upon which the findings are based, shall be certified in writing to the court not less than 15 days before the date of review. A copy of the report shall be delivered pursuant to Section 1215 to the conservatee, the conservator, and the attorneys of record for the conservator and conservatee at the same time it is certified to the court. A copy of the report, modified as set forth in paragraph (2), also shall be delivered pursuant to Section 1215 to the conservatee's spouse or registered domestic partner and the conservatee's relatives in the first degree, or, if there are no such relatives, to the next closest relative, unless the court determines that the delivery will harm the conservatee.

(2) Confidential medical information and confidential information from the California Law Enforcement Telecommunications System shall be in a separate attachment to the report and shall not be provided in copies sent to the conservatee's spouse or registered domestic partner and the conservatee's relatives in the first degree, or, if there are no such relatives, to the next closest relative.

(c) In the case of a limited conservatee, the court investigator shall recommend whether to continue, modify, or terminate the limited conservatorship.

(d) The court investigator may personally visit the conservator and any other persons necessary to determine if the conservator is acting in the best interests of the conservatee.

(e) The report required by this section shall be confidential and shall be made available only to parties, persons described in subdivision (b), persons given notice of the petition who have requested the report or who have appeared in the proceeding, their attorneys, and the court. The court shall have discretion at any other time to release the report if it would serve the interests of the conservatee. The clerk of the court shall limit disclosure of the report exclusively to persons entitled to the report under this section.

(f)(1) A superior court is not required to perform any duties imposed pursuant to the amendments to this section enacted by Chapter 493 of the Statutes of 2006 until the Legislature makes an appropriation identified for this purpose.

(2) A superior court shall not be required to perform any duties imposed pursuant to the amendments to this section enacted by the measure that added this paragraph until the Legislature makes an appropriation identified for this purpose. *(Stats.1990, c. 79 (A.B. 759), § 14, operative July 1, 1991. Amended by Stats.1991, c. 82 (S.B.896), § 16, eff. June 30, 1991, operative July 1, 1991; Stats.2002, c. 784 (S.B.1316), § 580; Stats.2002, c. 1008 (A.B.3028), § 28; Stats. 2006, c. 492 (S.B.1716), § 4; Stats.2006, c. 493 (A.B.1363), § 12.5, operative July 1, 2007; Stats.2007, c. 553 (A.B.1727), § 9; Stats.2011, c. 10 (S.B.78), § 15, eff. March 24, 2011; Stats.2014, c. 591 (A.B.*

§ 1851   PROBATE CODE

1311), § 7, eff. Jan. 1, 2015; Stats.2015, c. 736 (S.B.589), § 11, eff. Jan. 1, 2016; Stats.2016, c. 86 (S.B.1171), § 247, eff. Jan. 1, 2017; Stats.2017, c. 319 (A.B.976), § 40, eff. Jan. 1, 2018; Stats.2021, c. 417 (A.B.1194), § 10, eff. Jan. 1, 2022.)

Cross References

Affidavit of voter registration, see Elections Code §§ 2102, 2150 et seq., 3400 et seq.

Completion of affidavit of voter registration, report concerning capability of conservatee, see Elections Code § 2209.

Court investigator,
  Defined, see Probate Code § 1419.
  Qualifications, see Probate Code § 1454.

Disqualification from voting, see Elections Code § 2208.

Inspection of public records, exemptions from disclosure, "conservatee" to "conservatorship", see Government Code § 6276.12.

Termination of conservatorship, see Probate Code § 1860 et seq.

Waiver of court fees and costs, initial fee waiver, see Government Code § 68631.

Research References

Forms

West's California Code Forms, Probate § 1454 Form 1, Order Appointing Court Investigator—Judicial Council Form GC-330.

West's California Code Forms, Probate § 1454 Form 2, Order Appointing Court Investigator—Judicial Council Form GC-331.

West's California Judicial Council Forms GC–331, Order Appointing Court Investigator (Review and Successor Conservator Investigations).

§ 1851.1. Transfer of conservatorship to state; investigation and report; duties of investigator

(a) When a court issues an order provisionally granting a petition under Section 2002, the investigator appointed under Section 2002 shall promptly commence an investigation under this section.

(b) In conducting an investigation and preparing a report under this section, the court investigator shall do all of the following:

(1) Comply with the requirements of Section 1851.

(2) Conduct an interview of the conservator.

(3) Conduct an interview of the conservatee's spouse or registered domestic partner, if any.

(4) Inform the conservatee of the nature, purpose, and effect of the conservatorship.

(5) Inform the conservatee and all other persons entitled to notice under subdivision (b) of Section 2002 of the right to seek termination of the conservatorship.

(6) Determine whether the conservatee objects to the conservator or prefers another person to act as conservator.

(7) Inform the conservatee of the right to attend the hearing under subdivision (c).

(8) Determine whether it appears that the conservatee is unable to attend the hearing and, if able to attend, whether the conservatee is willing to attend the hearing.

(9) Inform the conservatee of the right to be represented by legal counsel if the conservatee so chooses, and to have legal counsel appointed by the court if the conservatee is unable to retain legal counsel.

(10) Determine whether the conservatee wishes to be represented by legal counsel and, if so, whether the conservatee has retained legal counsel and, if not, the name of an attorney the conservatee wishes to retain.

(11) If the conservatee has not retained legal counsel, determine whether the conservatee desires the court to appoint legal counsel.

(12) Determine whether the appointment of legal counsel would be helpful to the resolution of the matter or is necessary to protect the interests of the conservatee when the conservatee does not plan to retain legal counsel and has not requested the appointment of legal counsel by the court.

(13) Consider each of the categories specified in paragraphs (1) to (5), inclusive, of subdivision (a) of Section 1821.

(14) Consider, to the extent practicable, whether the investigator believes the conservatee suffers from any of the mental function deficits listed in subdivision (a) of Section 811 that significantly impairs the conservatee's ability to understand and appreciate the consequences of the conservatee's actions in connection with any of the functions described in subdivision (a) or (b) of Section 1801 and identify the observations that support that belief.

(c) The court shall review the conservatorship as provided in Section 2002. The conservatee shall attend the hearing unless the conservatee's attendance is excused under Section 1825. The court may take appropriate action in response to the court investigator's report under this section.

(d) The court investigator's report under this section shall be confidential as provided in Section 1851.

(e) Except as provided in paragraph (2) of subdivision (a) of Section 1850, the court shall review the conservatorship again one year after the review conducted pursuant to subdivision (c), and annually thereafter, in the manner specified in Section 1850.

(f) The first time that the need for a conservatorship is challenged by any interested person or raised on the court's own motion after a transfer under Section 2002, whether in a review pursuant to this section or in a petition to terminate the conservatorship under Chapter 3 (commencing with Section 1860), the court shall presume that there is no need for a conservatorship. This presumption is rebuttable, but can only be overcome by clear and convincing evidence. The court shall make an express finding on whether continuation of the conservatorship is the least restrictive alternative needed for the protection of the conservatee.

(g)(1) If a duty described in this section is the same as a duty imposed pursuant to the amendments to Sections 1826, 1850, 1851, 2250, 2253, and 2620 and the addition of Sections 2250.4 and 2250.6 enacted by Chapter 493 of the Statutes of 2006, and the addition of Section 1051 enacted by Chapter 492 of the Statutes of 2006, a superior court shall not be required to perform that duty until the Legislature makes an appropriation identified for this purpose.

(2) If a duty described in this section is the same as a duty imposed pursuant to the amendments to Sections 1826, 1850, 1851, 2250, 2250.4, 2250.6, 2253, and 2620 enacted by the measure that added this paragraph, a superior court shall not be required to perform that duty until the Legislature makes an appropriation identified for this purpose. (Added by Stats.2014, c. 553 (S.B.940), § 18, eff. Jan. 1, 2015, operative Jan. 1, 2016. Amended by Stats.2021, c. 417 (A.B. 1194), § 11, eff. Jan. 1, 2022.)

Cross References

Conservatorships, appealable orders, see Probate Code § 1301.5.

§ 1851.2. Coordination

Each court shall coordinate investigations with the filing of accountings, so that investigators may review accountings before visiting conservatees, if feasible. (Added by Stats.2007, c. 553 (A.B.1727), § 10.)

§ 1851.5. Court investigators; assessments

Each court shall assess each conservatee in the county for any investigation or review conducted by a court investigator with respect to that person. Subject to Section 68631 of the Government Code, the court may order reimbursement to the court for the amount of the assessment, unless the court finds that all or any part of the assessment would impose a hardship on conservatee or the conservatee's estate. There shall be a rebuttable presumption that the assessment would impose a hardship if the conservatee is receiving

Medi–Cal benefits. *(Stats.1990, c. 79 (A.B.759), § 14, operative July 1, 1991. Amended by Stats.1991, c. 82 (S.B.896), § 18, eff. June 30, 1991, operative July 1, 1991; Stats.1996, c. 563 (S.B.392), § 9; Stats.2002, c. 1008 (A.B.3028), § 29; Stats.2014, c. 913 (A.B.2747), § 30.5, eff. Jan. 1, 2015.)*

Cross References

Medi–Cal Act, see Welfare and Institutions Code § 14000 et seq.
Organization and government of courts, collection of fees and fines pursuant to this section, deposits, see Government Code § 68085.1.

§ 1851.6. Court investigator; prior investigation

(a) Any interested person, as defined in Section 48 or any person entitled to receive notice pursuant to Section 1822, if they have personal knowledge of a conservatee, may petition the court to investigate an allegation of abuse, as defined by Section 15610.07 of the Welfare and Institutions Code, of the conservatee by a conservator. The court shall investigate all such allegations that establish a prima facie case of abuse. If the court investigator has performed an investigation within the preceding six months and reported the results of that investigation to the court, the court may order, upon good cause shown, that a new investigation is not necessary or that a more limited investigation is sufficient.

(b) A superior court shall not be required to perform any duties imposed pursuant to this section until the Legislature makes an appropriation identified for this purpose. *(Added by Stats.2021, c. 417 (A.B.1194), § 12, eff. Jan. 1, 2022.)*

§ 1852. Notification of counsel; representation of conservatee at hearing

If the conservatee wishes to petition the court for termination of the conservatorship or for removal of the existing conservator or for the making, modification, or revocation of a court order under Chapter 4 (commencing with Section 1870) or for restoration of the right to register to vote, or if, based on information contained in the court investigator's report or obtained from any other source, the court determines that a trial or hearing for termination of the conservatorship or removal of the existing conservator is in the best interests of the conservatee, the court shall notify the attorney of record for the conservatee, if any, or shall appoint the public defender or private counsel under Section 1471, to file the petition and represent the conservatee at the trial or hearing and, if such appointment is made, Section 1472 applies. *(Stats.1990, c. 79 (A.B.759), § 14, operative July 1, 1991.)*

Cross References

Counsel, right to, see Cal. Const. Art. 1, § 15.
Guardians and conservators, removal or resignation, see Probate Code § 2650 et seq.
Removal of guardian or conservator, petition, see Probate Code § 2651.
Representation of persons not financially able to employ counsel, by public defender, see Government Code § 27706.
Restoration of right to register to vote, see Probate Code § 1865.
Termination of conservatorship, petition, see Probate Code § 1861.

§ 1853. Failure to locate conservatee; termination of conservatorship; discharge of conservator; petition to appoint new conservator

(a) If the court investigator is unable to locate the conservatee, the court shall order the court investigator to serve notice upon the conservator of the person, or upon the conservator of the estate if there is no conservator of the person, in the manner provided in Section 415.10 or 415.30 of the Code of Civil Procedure or in such other manner as is ordered by the court, to make the conservatee available for the purposes of Section 1851 to the court investigator within 15 days of the receipt of such notice or to show cause why the conservatorship should not be terminated.

(b) If the conservatee is not made available within the time prescribed, unless good cause is shown for not doing so, the court shall make such a finding and shall enter judgment terminating the conservatorship and, in case of a conservatorship of the estate, shall order the conservator to file an account and to surrender the estate to the person legally entitled thereto. At the hearing, or thereafter on further notice and hearing, the conservator may be discharged and the bond given by the conservator may be exonerated upon the settlement and approval of the conservator's final account by the court.

(c) Termination of the conservatorship under this section does not preclude institution of new proceedings for the appointment of a conservator. Nothing in this section limits the power of a court to appoint a temporary conservator under Chapter 3 (commencing with Section 2250) of Part 4. *(Stats.1990, c. 79 (A.B.759), § 14, operative July 1, 1991.)*

Cross References

Accounts on termination of conservatorship, see Probate Code § 2630 et seq.
Appointment to fill vacancy, see Probate Code § 2670.
Computation of time, see Code of Civil Procedure §§ 12 and 12a; Government Code § 6800 et seq.
Court investigator, defined, see Probate Code § 1419.
Notice,
    Mailing, see Probate Code § 1215 et seq.
    Posting, see Probate Code § 1230.
    Proof of giving notice, see Probate Code § 1260 et seq.
    Special notice, see Probate Code § 1250 et seq.
    This code, generally, see Probate Code § 1200 et seq.
    This division, generally, see Probate Code § 1460 et seq.
Representation of persons not financially able to employ counsel by public defender, see Government Code § 27706.
Service of process,
    Generally, see Code of Civil Procedure § 413.10 et seq.
    Mail, see Code of Civil Procedure §§ 415.30, 1012 et seq.
    Personal delivery, see Code of Civil Procedure § 415.10.
    Proof of service, see Code of Civil Procedure § 417.10 et seq.
    Publication, see Code of Civil Procedure § 415.50.
Temporary guardians and conservators, generally, see Probate Code § 2250 et seq.

CHAPTER 3. TERMINATION

Section	
1860.	Death of conservatee or order of court; continuation of conservatorship of married minor upon marriage dissolution or nullity.
1860.5.	Limited conservatorship.
1861.	Petition; persons authorized to file; contents.
1861.5.	Conditions for appointment of counsel and setting of hearing.
1862.	Notice of hearing.
1863.	Hearing and judgment.
1864.	Conservatorship of absentee; petition; filing; order.
1865.	Restoration of right to register to vote; notice to county elections official.

Cross References

Application of old and new law, see Probate Code § 3.

§ 1860. Death of conservatee or order of court; continuation of conservatorship of married minor upon marriage dissolution or nullity

(a) A conservatorship continues until terminated by the death of the conservatee or by order of the court pursuant to Section 1863, subject to Section 2467 and Article 4 (commencing with Section 2630) of Chapter 7 of Part 4, and except as otherwise provided by law.

(b) At a hearing under Section 1850 or a hearing on a petition to terminate a conservatorship under Section 1861, the court shall proceed as provided in Section 1863.

§ 1860

(c) If a conservatorship is established for the person of a married minor, the conservatorship does not terminate automatically if the marriage is dissolved or is adjudged a nullity.

(d) This section does not apply to limited conservatorships.

(e) A superior court shall not be required to perform any duties imposed pursuant to the amendments to this section enacted by the measure that added this subdivision until the Legislature makes an appropriation identified for this purpose. *(Stats.1990, c. 79 (A.B. 759), § 14, operative July 1, 1991. Amended by Stats.2018, c. 126 (A.B.2236), § 1, eff. Jan. 1, 2019; Stats.2021, c. 417 (A.B.1194), § 13, eff. Jan. 1, 2022.)*

Cross References

Allowance for, care of estate after conservatee's death, disbursements after termination of conservatorship, see Probate Code § 2623.
Disposition of assets after death of conservatee, see Probate Code § 2631.
Dissolution,
   Generally, see Family Code § 2300 et seq.
   Defined, see Probate Code § 36.
No guardian of person for married minor, see Probate Code § 1515.
Termination of proceeding upon,
   Exhaustion of estate, see Probate Code § 2626.
   Transfer of all assets to foreign guardian or conservator, see Probate Code § 2808.

Research References

Forms

1 California Transactions Forms--Estate Planning § 1:2, Probate System.
West's California Code Forms, Probate § 1861 Form 1, Petition for Termination of Conservatorship.

§ 1860.5. Limited conservatorship

(a) A limited conservatorship continues until the authority of the conservator is terminated by one of the following:

(1) The death of the limited conservator.

(2) The death of the limited conservatee.

(3) An order appointing a conservator of the former limited conservatee.

(4) An order of the court terminating the limited conservatorship.

(b) A petition for the termination of a limited conservatorship may be filed by any of the following:

(1) The limited conservator.

(2) The limited conservatee.

(3) Any relative or friend of the limited conservatee.

(c) The petition shall state facts showing that the limited conservatorship is no longer required.

(d) Notice of a hearing pursuant to Section 1850.5 or on a petition filed pursuant to this section shall be given to the same persons and in the same manner as provided for a petition for the appointment of a limited conservator.

(1) If a petition is filed and the limited conservator is not the petitioner, or has not joined in the petition, the limited conservator shall be served with a notice of the time and place of the hearing accompanied by a copy of the petition at least five days prior to the hearing. This service shall be made in the same manner provided for in Section 415.10 or 415.30 of the Code of Civil Procedure or in another manner authorized by the court. If the limited conservator cannot, with reasonable diligence, be so served with notice, the court may dispense with notice.

(2) If the court sets a hearing pursuant to Section 1850.5 to consider termination of a limited conservatorship and no petition is filed, the court shall order the limited conservator to give notice of the hearing as provided in this subdivision and to appear at the hearing and show cause why the limited conservatorship should not be terminated.

(e)(1) The limited conservatee shall be produced at the hearing except in the following cases:

(A) When the limited conservatee is out of the state and is not the petitioner.

(B) When the limited conservatee is unable to attend the hearing by reason of medical inability.

(C) When the court investigator has reported to the court that the limited conservatee has expressly communicated that the limited conservatee (i) is not willing to attend the hearing, (ii) does not wish to contest the continuation of the limited conservatorship, and (iii) does not object to the current limited conservator or prefer that another person act as limited conservator, and the court makes an order that the limited conservatee need not attend the hearing.

(2) If the limited conservatee is unable to attend the hearing because of medical inability, that inability shall be established by the affidavit or certificate of a licensed medical practitioner or, if the conservatee is an adherent of a religion whose tenets and practices call for reliance on prayer alone for healing and is under treatment by an accredited practitioner of that religion, by the affidavit of the practitioner. The affidavit or certificate is evidence only of the limited conservatee's inability to attend the hearing and shall not be considered in determining the issue of need for the continuation of the limited conservatorship.

(3) Emotional or psychological instability is not good cause for the absence of the conservatee from the hearing unless, by reason of that instability, attendance at the hearing is likely to cause serious and immediate physiological damage to the conservatee.

(f) The limited conservator or any relative or friend of the limited conservatee may appear and support or oppose termination of the limited conservatorship. The court shall hear and determine the matter according to the laws and procedures relating to the trial of civil actions, including trial by jury if demanded. If the court terminates the limited conservatorship, the limited conservator may, either at the hearing or thereafter on further notice and hearing, be discharged and the bond exonerated upon the settlement and approval of the final account by the court.

(g)(1) The court shall order the termination of the limited conservatorship unless the court finds, on the record and by clear and convincing evidence, that the limited conservatee still meets the criteria for appointment of a limited conservator under Section 1801 and a limited conservatorship remains the least restrictive alternative needed for the limited conservatee's protection.

(2) If the petition for termination is uncontested and states facts showing that both the limited conservator and limited conservatee wish to terminate the limited conservatorship, and the conservatorship is no longer the least restrictive alternative for the limited conservatee's protection, the court may terminate the limited conservatorship without an evidentiary hearing.

(h) If the court determines, by clear and convincing evidence, that the limited conservatee meets the criteria for appointment of a limited conservator under Section 1801, the court shall determine whether to modify the powers granted to the limited conservator to ensure that the limited conservatorship remains the least restrictive alternative needed for the limited conservatee's protection. If the court modifies any powers granted to the limited conservator, new letters shall issue. *(Stats.1990, c. 79 (A.B.759), § 14, operative July 1, 1991. Amended by Stats.2021, c. 417 (A.B.1194), § 14, eff. Jan. 1, 2022; Stats.2022, c. 894 (A.B.1663), § 12, eff. Jan. 1, 2023.)*

Cross References

Accounts, see Probate Code § 2620 et seq.
Bonds of guardians and conservators, see Probate Code § 2320 et seq.
Jury trial, see Cal. Const. Art. 1, § 16.
Notice,
   Mailing, see Probate Code § 1215 et seq.
   Posting, see Probate Code § 1230.

Proof of giving notice, see Probate Code § 1260 et seq.
Special notice, see Probate Code § 1250 et seq.
This code, generally, see Probate Code § 1200 et seq.
This division, generally, see Probate Code § 1460 et seq.
Powers and duties of limited conservator, see Probate Code § 2351.5.
Service of process,
  Generally, see Code of Civil Procedure § 413.10 et seq.
  Mail, see Code of Civil Procedure §§ 415.30, 1012 et seq.
  Personal delivery, see Code of Civil Procedure § 415.10.
  Proof of service, see Code of Civil Procedure § 417.10 et seq.
  Publication, see Code of Civil Procedure § 415.50.

§ 1861. Petition; persons authorized to file; contents

(a) A petition for the termination of the conservatorship may be filed by any of the following:

(1) The conservator.

(2) The conservatee.

(3) The spouse, or domestic partner, or any relative or friend of the conservatee or other interested person.

(b) The petition shall state facts showing that the conservatorship is no longer required. *(Stats.1990, c. 79 (A.B.759), § 14, operative July 1, 1991. Amended by Stats.2001, c. 893 (A.B.25), § 21.)*

Cross References

Domestic partner, defined, see Probate Code § 37.
Interested person, defined, see Probate Code § 1424.
Persons who may petition where conservatee is an absentee, see Probate Code § 1864.

Research References

Forms

West's California Code Forms, Probate § 1861 Form 1, Petition for Termination of Conservatorship.

§ 1861.5. Conditions for appointment of counsel and setting of hearing

Upon the receipt of a communication from the conservatee that the conservatee wishes to terminate the conservatorship, a court shall appoint counsel for the conservatee and set a hearing for the termination of the conservatorship when either of the following conditions apply:

(a) There has not been a hearing for the termination of the conservatorship within the 12 months preceding the communication from the conservatee.

(b) The court believes there is good cause to set a hearing for the termination of the conservatorship. *(Added by Stats.2022, c. 894 (A.B.1663), § 13, eff. Jan. 1, 2023.)*

§ 1862. Notice of hearing

(a) Notice of the hearing to consider the termination of the conservatorship shall be given for the period and in the manner provided in Chapter 3 (commencing with Section 1460) of Part 1.

(b) If the court sets a hearing pursuant to paragraph (2) of subdivision (a) of Section 1850 and no petition is filed, the court shall order the conservator to give notice of the hearing as provided in subdivision (a), and to appear at the hearing and show cause why the conservatorship should not be terminated. *(Stats.1990, c. 79 (A.B. 759), § 14, operative July 1, 1991. Amended by Stats.2021, c. 417 (A.B.1194), § 15, eff. Jan. 1, 2022.)*

Cross References

Notice to,
  Director of State Hospitals or Director of Developmental Services, see Probate Code § 1461.
Persons requesting special notice, see Probate Code § 2700 et seq.

Service by mail, completion, see Probate Code § 1467.

Research References

Forms

West's California Code Forms, Probate § 1861 Form 1, Petition for Termination of Conservatorship.

§ 1863. Hearing and judgment

(a) The court shall hear and determine the matter according to the law and procedure relating to the trial of civil actions, including trial by jury if demanded by the conservatee. The conservator, the conservatee, the spouse or domestic partner, or any relative or friend of the conservatee or other interested person may appear and support or oppose the termination of the conservatorship.

(b)(1) The conservatee shall be produced at the hearing except in the following cases:

(A) When the conservatee is out of the state and is not the petitioner.

(B) When the conservatee is unable to attend the hearing by reason of medical inability.

(C) When the court investigator has reported to the court that the conservatee has expressly communicated that the conservatee (i) is not willing to attend the hearing, (ii) does not wish to contest the continuation of the conservatorship, and (iii) does not object to the current conservator or prefer that another person act as conservator, and the court makes an order that the conservatee need not attend the hearing.

(2) If the conservatee is unable to attend the hearing because of medical inability, that inability shall be established by the affidavit or certificate of a licensed medical practitioner or, if the conservatee is an adherent of a religion whose tenets and practices call for reliance on prayer alone for healing and is under treatment by an accredited practitioner of that religion, by the affidavit of the practitioner. The affidavit or certificate is evidence only of the conservatee's inability to attend the hearing and shall not be considered in determining the issue of need for the continuation of the conservatorship.

(3) Emotional or psychological instability is not good cause for the absence of the conservatee from the hearing unless, by reason of that instability, attendance at the hearing is likely to cause serious and immediate physiological damage to the conservatee.

(c) Unless the court determines, on the record and by clear and convincing evidence, that (1) the conservatee still meets the criteria for appointment of a conservator of the person under subdivision (a) of Section 1801, a conservator of the estate under subdivision (b) of Section 1801, or both; and (2) a conservatorship remains the least restrictive alternative needed for the conservatee's protection, as required by subdivision (b) of Section 1800.3, the court shall enter judgment terminating the conservatorship.

(d) If the court determines, by clear and convincing evidence, that the conservatee meets the criteria for appointment of a conservator of the person under subdivision (a) of Section 1801, a conservator of the estate under subdivision (b) of Section 1801, or both, the court shall determine whether to modify the existing powers of the conservator to ensure that the conservatorship remains the least restrictive alternative needed for the conservatee's protection and shall order the conservatorship to continue accordingly. If the court modifies the existing powers of the conservator, new letters shall issue.

(e) At the hearing, or thereafter on further notice and hearing, the conservator may be discharged and the bond given by the conservator may be exonerated upon the settlement and approval of the conservator's final account by the court.

(f) This section does not apply to limited conservatorships.

§ 1863

(g) Termination of conservatorship does not preclude a new proceeding for appointment of a conservator on the same or other grounds.

(h) If a petition for termination pursuant to Section 1861 is uncontested and states facts showing that both the conservator and conservatee wish to terminate the conservatorship and the conservatorship is no longer the least restrictive alternative for the conservatee's protection, the court may terminate the conservatorship without an evidentiary hearing. *(Stats.1990, c. 79 (A.B.759), § 14, operative July 1, 1991. Amended by Stats.2000, c. 17 (A.B.1491), § 4.4; Stats.2001, c. 893 (A.B.25), § 22; Stats.2021, c. 417 (A.B.1194), § 16, eff. Jan. 1, 2022; Stats.2022, c. 894 (A.B.1663), § 14, eff. Jan. 1, 2023.)*

Cross References

Bonds of conservators, see Probate Code § 2320 et seq.
Domestic partner, defined, see Probate Code § 37.
Establishment of conservatorship, see Probate Code § 1820 et seq.
Interested person, defined, see Probate Code § 1424.
Jurisdiction of court after termination of conservatorship, see Probate Code § 2630.
Termination of court order affecting legal capacity, see Probate Code § 1896.

Research References

Forms

1 California Transactions Forms--Estate Planning § 1:4, Loss of Due Process Inherent in Probate Avoidance.
West's California Code Forms, Probate § 1861 Form 1, Petition for Termination of Conservatorship.

§ 1864. Conservatorship of absentee; petition; filing; order

(a) In the case of the conservatorship of an absentee as defined in Section 1403, the petition to terminate the conservatorship may also be filed by any officer or agency of this state or of the United States or the authorized delegate thereof.

(b) If the petition states and the court determines that the absentee has returned to the controllable jurisdiction of the military department or civilian department or agency concerned, or is deceased, as determined under 37 United States Code, Section 556, or 5 United States Code, Section 5566, as the case may be, the court shall order the conservatorship terminated. An official written report or record of such military department or civilian department or agency that the absentee has returned to such controllable jurisdiction or is deceased shall be received as evidence of such fact. *(Stats.1990, c. 79 (A.B.759), § 14, operative July 1, 1991.)*

Cross References

Newspapers, publications and official advertising, see Government Code § 6000 et seq.
Official records and other official writings, see Evidence Code § 1280 et seq.
Record by federal employee as evidence, see Evidence Code § 1283.

§ 1865. Restoration of right to register to vote; notice to county elections official

If the conservatee has been disqualified from voting pursuant to Section 2208 or 2209 of the Elections Code, upon termination of the conservatorship, the court shall notify the county elections official of the county of residence of the former conservatee that the former conservatee's right to register to vote is restored. *(Stats.1990, c. 79 (A.B.759), § 14, operative July 1, 1991. Amended by Stats.1994, c. 923 (S.B.1546), § 160; Stats.2002, c. 221 (S.B.1019), § 80.)*

Cross References

Disqualification from voting, see Probate Code § 1910.

CHAPTER 4. LEGAL CAPACITY OF CONSERVATEE

Cross References

Modification or revocation of court order, petition by conservatee, periodic review of conservatorship, see Probate Code § 1852.

Periodic review of conservatorship, court investigator's findings, modification or revocation of order, see Probate Code § 1851.
Request for special notice, see Probate Code § 2700.

ARTICLE 1. CAPACITY TO BIND OR OBLIGATE CONSERVATORSHIP ESTATE

Section
1870. Transaction.
1871. Rights not limited by this article.
1872. Effect of conservatorship or limited conservatorship.
1873. Court order; authority of conservatee; limitations and conditions; termination; continuation.
1874. Petition for order; person authorized to file.
1875. Transactions affecting real property; persons acting in good faith.
1876. Applicability of other law.

Cross References

Application of old and new law, see Probate Code § 3.

§ 1870. Transaction

As used in this article, unless the context otherwise requires, "transaction" includes, but is not limited to, making a contract, sale, transfer, or conveyance, incurring a debt or encumbering property, making a gift, delegating a power, and waiving a right. *(Stats.1990, c. 79 (A.B.759), § 14, operative July 1, 1991.)*

Cross References

Transaction, provisions common to guardianships and conservators, see Probate Code § 2111.

Research References

Forms

West's California Code Forms, Probate § 1874 Form 1, Petition for Order Authorizing Conservatee to Enter Into Transaction.
West's California Code Forms, Probate § 2404 Form 3, Petition by Creditor to Compel Payment of Debt.

§ 1871. Rights not limited by this article

Nothing in this article shall be construed to deny a conservatee any of the following:

(a) The right to control an allowance provided under Section 2421.

(b) The right to control wages or salary to the extent provided in Section 2601.

(c) The right to make a will.

(d) The right to enter into transactions to the extent reasonable to provide the necessaries of life to the conservatee and the spouse and minor children of the conservatee and to provide the basic living expenses, as defined in Section 297 of the Family Code, to the domestic partner of the conservatee. *(Stats.1990, c. 79 (A.B.759), § 14, operative July 1, 1991. Amended by Stats.2001, c. 893 (A.B.25), § 23.)*

Cross References

Domestic partner, defined, see Probate Code § 37.
Judicial determination of incapacity, conservatorship, see Civil Code § 40.

Research References

Forms

1 California Transactions Forms--Estate Planning § 1:32, Testamentary Capacity.

4 California Transactions Forms--Estate Planning § 19:32, Persons Who May Make Will.

§ 1872. Effect of conservatorship or limited conservatorship

(a) Except as otherwise provided in this article, the appointment of a conservator of the estate is an adjudication that the conservatee lacks the legal capacity to enter into or make any transaction that binds or obligates the conservatorship estate.

(b) Except as otherwise provided in the order of the court appointing a limited conservator, the appointment does not limit the legal capacity of the limited conservatee to enter into transactions or types of transactions. *(Stats.1990, c. 79 (A.B.759), § 14, operative July 1, 1991.)*

Cross References

Legal capacity with respect to community property, see Probate Code § 3012.

Research References

Forms

West's California Code Forms, Probate § 1874 Form 1, Petition for Order Authorizing Conservatee to Enter Into Transaction.

§ 1873. Court order; authority of conservatee; limitations and conditions; termination; continuation

(a) In the order appointing the conservator or upon a petition filed under Section 1874, the court may, by order, authorize the conservatee, subject to Section 1876, to enter into transactions or types of transactions as may be appropriate in the circumstances of the particular conservatee and conservatorship estate. The court, by order, may modify the legal capacity a conservatee would otherwise have under Section 1872 by broadening or restricting the power of the conservatee to enter into transactions or types of transactions as may be appropriate in the circumstances of the particular conservatee and conservatorship estate.

(b) In an order made under this section, the court may include limitations or conditions on the exercise of the authority granted to the conservatee as the court determines to be appropriate including, but not limited to, the following:

(1) A requirement that for specific types of transactions or for all transactions authorized by the order, the conservatee obtain prior approval of the transaction by the court or conservator before exercising the authority granted by the order.

(2) A provision that the conservator has the right to avoid any transaction made by the conservatee pursuant to the authority of the order if the transaction is not one into which a reasonably prudent person might enter.

(c) The court, in its discretion, may provide in the order that, unless extended by subsequent order of the court, the order or specific provisions of the order terminate at a time specified in the order.

(d) An order under this section continues in effect until the earliest of the following times:

(1) The time specified in the order, if any.

(2) The time the order is modified or revoked.

(3) The time the conservatorship of the estate is terminated.

(e) An order under this section may be modified or revoked upon petition filed by the conservator, conservatee, the spouse or domestic partner of the conservatee, or any relative or friend of the conservatee, or any interested person. Notice of the hearing on the petition shall be given for the period and in the manner provided in Chapter 3 (commencing with Section 1460) of Part 1. *(Stats.1990, c. 79 (A.B.759), § 14, operative July 1, 1991. Amended by Stats.2001, c. 893 (A.B.25), § 24.)*

Cross References

Definitions,
  Interested person, see Probate Code § 1424.
  Transaction, see Probate Code § 1870.
Domestic partner, defined, see Probate Code § 37.
Judicial determination of incapacity, conservatorship, see Civil Code § 40.
Termination, see Probate Code § 1860 et seq.

Research References

Forms

West's California Code Forms, Probate § 1874 Form 1, Petition for Order Authorizing Conservatee to Enter Into Transaction.
West's California Judicial Council Forms GC–331, Order Appointing Court Investigator (Review and Successor Conservator Investigations).

§ 1874. Petition for order; person authorized to file

(a) After a conservator has been appointed, a petition requesting an order under Section 1873 may be filed by any of the following:

(1) The conservator.

(2) The conservatee.

(3) The spouse, domestic partner, or any relative or friend of the conservatee.

(b) Notice of the hearing on the petition shall be given for the period and in the manner provided in Chapter 3 (commencing with Section 1460) of Part 1. *(Stats.1990, c. 79 (A.B.759), § 14, operative July 1, 1991. Amended by Stats.2001, c. 893 (A.B.25), § 25.)*

Cross References

Domestic partner, defined, see Probate Code § 37.
Judicial determination of incapacity, conservatorship, see Civil Code § 40.

Research References

Forms

West's California Code Forms, Probate § 1874 Form 1, Petition for Order Authorizing Conservatee to Enter Into Transaction.

§ 1875. Transactions affecting real property; persons acting in good faith

A transaction that affects real property of the conservatorship estate, entered into by a person acting in good faith and for a valuable consideration and without knowledge of the establishment of the conservatorship, is not affected by any provision of this article or any order made under this article unless a notice of the establishment of the conservatorship or temporary conservatorship has been recorded prior to the transaction in the county in which the property is located. *(Stats.1990, c. 79 (A.B.759), § 14, operative July 1, 1991. Amended by Stats.1991, c. 82 (S.B.896), § 20, eff. June 30, 1991, operative July 1, 1991.)*

Cross References

Comparable provision, real property, see Probate Code § 3074.
Judicial determination of incapacity, conservatorship, see Civil Code § 40.
Mode of recording, see Civil Code § 1169 et seq.
Real property, defined, see Probate Code § 68.

Research References

Forms

West's California Code Forms, Probate § 1874 Form 1, Petition for Order Authorizing Conservatee to Enter Into Transaction.

§ 1876. Applicability of other law

The provisions of this article relating to the legal capacity of a conservatee to bind or obligate the conservatorship estate, and the provisions of any order of the court broadening such capacity, do not displace but are supplemented by general principles of law and equity relating to transactions including, but not limited to, capacity to contract, joinder or consent requirements, estoppel, fraud, misrepre-

§ 1876

sentation, duress, coercion, mistake, or other validating or invalidating cause. *(Stats.1990, c. 79 (A.B.759), § 14, operative July 1, 1991.)*

Cross References

Consent, see Civil Code § 1565 et seq.
Contracts, generally, see Civil Code § 1549 et seq.
Contracts, fraud, see Civil Code §§ 1571 to 1574.
Duress, see Civil Code § 1569.
Judicial determination of incapacity, conservatorship, see Civil Code § 40.
Mistake, see Civil Code § 1576 et seq.
Persons capable of contracting, see Civil Code §§ 1556, 1557.

Research References

Forms

West's California Code Forms, Probate § 2404 Form 3, Petition by Creditor to Compel Payment of Debt.

ARTICLE 2. CAPACITY TO GIVE INFORMED CONSENT FOR MEDICAL TREATMENT

Section
1880. Determination by court; order.
1881. Inability of conservatee to give informed medical consent; judicial determination; factors.
1890. Order; inclusion in order appointing conservator; limited conservatee; physician's declaration.
1891. Petition for order; modification or revocation; contents.
1892. Notice of hearing.
1893. Attendance of conservatee at hearing.
1894. Court investigator; duties; report.
1895. Hearing, appearances; information to conservatee.
1896. Order; termination.
1897. Duration of order.
1898. Modification or revocation of order.

Cross References

Application of old and new law, see Probate Code § 3.

§ 1880. Determination by court; order

If the court determines that there is no form of medical treatment for which the conservatee has the capacity to give an informed consent, the court shall (1) adjudge that the conservatee lacks the capacity to give informed consent for medical treatment and (2) by order give the conservator of the person the powers specified in Section 2355. If an order is made under this section, the letters shall include a statement that the conservator has the powers specified in Section 2355. *(Stats.1990, c. 79 (A.B.759), § 14, operative July 1, 1991.)*

Cross References

Court ordered medical treatment, see Probate Code § 2357.
Duration of order, see Probate Code § 1897.
Legal and civil rights of persons involuntarily detained under Lanterman–Petris–Short Act, see Welfare and Institutions Code § 5325 et seq.
Letters, defined, see Probate Code § 52.
Letters of conservatorship, see Probate Code § 2310 et seq.
Modification or revocation of order, see Probate Code § 1898.
Petition for order, modification or revocation of order, see Probate Code § 1891.
Termination of order, see Probate Code § 1896.

Research References

Forms

West's California Code Forms, Probate § 1891 Form 1, Petition for Exclusive Authority to Give Consent for Medical Treatment (Probate Conservatorship)—Judicial Council Form GC-380.
West's California Judicial Council Forms GC-331, Order Appointing Court Investigator (Review and Successor Conservator Investigations).

West's California Judicial Council Forms GC-380, Petition for Exclusive Authority to Give Consent for Medical Treatment.
West's California Judicial Council Forms GC-385, Order Authorizing Conservator to Give Consent for Medical Treatment.

§ 1881. Inability of conservatee to give informed medical consent; judicial determination; factors

(a) A conservatee shall be deemed unable to give informed consent to any form of medical treatment pursuant to Section 1880 if, for all medical treatments, the conservatee is unable to respond knowingly and intelligently to queries about medical treatment or is unable to participate in a treatment decision by means of a rational thought process.

(b) In order for a court to determine that a conservatee is unable to respond knowingly and intelligently to queries about his or her medical treatment or is unable to participate in treatment decisions by means of a rational thought process, a court shall do both of the following:

(1) Determine that, for all medical treatments, the conservatee is unable to understand at least one of the following items of minimum basic medical treatment information:

(A) The nature and seriousness of any illness, disorder, or defect that the conservatee has or may develop.

(B) The nature of any medical treatment that is being or may be recommended by the conservatee's health care providers.

(C) The probable degree and duration of any benefits and risks of any medical intervention that is being or may be recommended by the conservatee's health care providers, and the consequences of lack of treatment.

(D) The nature, risks, and benefits of any reasonable alternatives.

(2) Determine that one or more of the mental functions of the conservatee described in subdivision (a) of Section 811 is impaired and that there is a link between the deficit or deficits and the conservatee's inability to give informed consent.

(c) A deficit in the mental functions listed in subdivision (a) of Section 811 may be considered only if the deficit by itself, or in combination with one or more other mental function deficits, significantly impairs the conservatee's ability to understand the consequences of his or her decisions regarding medical care.

(d) In determining whether a conservatee's mental functioning is so severely impaired that the conservatee lacks the capacity to give informed consent to any form of medical treatment, the court may take into consideration the frequency, severity, and duration of periods of impairment.

(e) In the interest of minimizing unnecessary expense to the parties to a proceeding, paragraph (2) of subdivision (b) shall not apply to a petition pursuant to Section 1880 wherein the conservatee, after notice by the court of his or her right to object which, at least, shall include an interview by a court investigator pursuant to Section 1826 prior to the hearing on the petition, does not object to the proposed finding of incapacity, or waives any objections. *(Added by Stats.1995, c. 842 (S.B.730), § 8. Amended by Stats.1996, c. 178 (S.B.1650), § 8.)*

Cross References

Health care decisions, generally, see Probate Code § 4600 et seq.

Research References

Forms

West's California Code Forms, Probate § 1825 Form 1, Capacity Declaration—Conservatorship—Judicial Council Form GC-335.
West's California Code Forms, Probate § 1891 Form 1, Petition for Exclusive Authority to Give Consent for Medical Treatment (Probate Conservatorship)—Judicial Council Form GC-380.

West's California Judicial Council Forms GC–335, Capacity Declaration—Conservatorship.

§ 1890. Order; inclusion in order appointing conservator; limited conservatee; physician's declaration

(a) An order of the court under Section 1880 may be included in the order of appointment of the conservator if the order was requested in the petition for the appointment of the conservator or the transfer petition under Section 2002 or, except in the case of a limited conservator, may be made subsequently upon a petition made, noticed, and heard by the court in the manner provided in this article.

(b) In the case of a petition filed under this chapter requesting that the court make an order under this chapter or that the court modify or revoke an order made under this chapter, when the order applies to a limited conservatee, the order may only be made upon a petition made, noticed, and heard by the court in the manner provided by Article 3 (commencing with Section 1820) of Chapter 1.

(c) No court order under Section 1880, whether issued as part of an order granting the original petition for appointment of a conservator or issued subsequent thereto, may be granted unless supported by a declaration, filed at or before the hearing on the request, executed by a licensed physician, or a licensed psychologist within the scope of his or her licensure, and stating that the proposed conservatee or the conservatee, as the case may be, lacks the capacity to give an informed consent for any form of medical treatment and the reasons therefor. Nothing in this section shall be construed to expand the scope of practice of psychologists as set forth in the Business and Professions Code. *(Stats.1990, c. 79 (A.B.759), § 14, operative July 1, 1991. Amended by Stats.1992, c. 572 (S.B.1455), § 4; Stats.1996, c. 563 (S.B.392), § 10; Stats.1997, c. 724 (A.B.1172), § 10; Stats.2014, c. 553 (S.B.940), § 19, eff. Jan. 1, 2015, operative Jan. 1, 2016.)*

Research References

Forms

West's California Code Forms, Probate § 1825 Form 1, Capacity Declaration—Conservatorship—Judicial Council Form GC-335.

West's California Code Forms, Probate § 1891 Form 1, Petition for Exclusive Authority to Give Consent for Medical Treatment (Probate Conservatorship)—Judicial Council Form GC-380.

West's California Judicial Council Forms GC–333, Ex Parte Application for Order Authorizing Completion of Capacity Declaration—HIPAA.

West's California Judicial Council Forms GC–334, Ex Parte Order Re: Completion of Capacity Declaration—HIPAA.

§ 1891. Petition for order; modification or revocation; contents

(a) A petition may be filed under this article requesting that the court make an order under Section 1880 or that the court modify or revoke an order made under Section 1880. The petition shall state facts showing that the order requested is appropriate.

(b) The petition may be filed by any of the following:

(1) The conservator.

(2) The conservatee.

(3) The spouse, domestic partner, or any relative or friend of the conservatee.

(c) The petition shall set forth, so far as they are known to the petitioner, the names and addresses of the spouse or domestic partner and of the relatives of the conservatee within the second degree. *(Stats.1990, c. 79 (A.B.759), § 14, operative July 1, 1991. Amended by Stats.2001, c. 893 (A.B.25), § 26.)*

Cross References

Domestic partner, defined, see Probate Code § 37.

Research References

Forms

West's California Code Forms, Probate § 1891 Form 1, Petition for Exclusive Authority to Give Consent for Medical Treatment (Probate Conservatorship)—Judicial Council Form GC-380.

§ 1892. Notice of hearing

Notice of the hearing on the petition shall be given for the period and in the manner provided in Chapter 3 (commencing with Section 1460) of Part 1. *(Stats.1990, c. 79 (A.B.759), § 14, operative July 1, 1991.)*

Cross References

Mailing, completion, see Probate Code § 1467.

Research References

Forms

West's California Code Forms, Probate § 1891 Form 1, Petition for Exclusive Authority to Give Consent for Medical Treatment (Probate Conservatorship)—Judicial Council Form GC-380.

§ 1893. Attendance of conservatee at hearing

The conservatee shall be produced at the hearing except in the following cases:

(a) Where the conservatee is out of state when served and is not the petitioner.

(b) Where the conservatee is unable to attend the hearing by reason of medical inability established (1) by the affidavit or certificate of a licensed medical practitioner or (2) if the conservatee is an adherent of a religion whose tenets and practices call for reliance on prayer alone for healing and is under treatment by an accredited practitioner of that religion, by the affidavit of the practitioner. The affidavit or certificate is evidence only of the conservatee's inability to attend the hearing and shall not be considered in determining the issue of the legal capacity of the conservatee. Emotional or psychological instability is not good cause for the absence of the conservatee from the hearing unless, by reason of such instability, attendance at the hearing is likely to cause serious and immediate physiological damage to the conservatee.

(c) Where the court investigator has reported to the court that the conservatee has expressly communicated that the conservatee (1) is not willing to attend the hearing and (2) does not wish to contest the petition, and the court makes an order that the conservatee need not attend the hearing. *(Stats.1990, c. 79 (A.B.759), § 14, operative July 1, 1991.)*

Cross References

Affidavits, see Code of Civil Procedure §§ 2003, 2009 et seq.
Capacity determinations, generally, see Probate Code § 3200 et seq.
Court investigator, see Probate Code §§ 1419, 1454.
Information given to conservatee prior to granting petition, see Probate Code § 1895.

Research References

Forms

West's California Code Forms, Probate § 1891 Form 1, Petition for Exclusive Authority to Give Consent for Medical Treatment (Probate Conservatorship)—Judicial Council Form GC-380.

West's California Code Forms, Probate § 2356.5 Form 1, Attachment Requesting Special Orders Regarding Dementia—Judicial Council Form GC-313.

West's California Judicial Council Forms GC–333, Ex Parte Application for Order Authorizing Completion of Capacity Declaration—HIPAA.

§ 1893

West's California Judicial Council Forms GC–334, Ex Parte Order Re: Completion of Capacity Declaration—HIPAA.

§ 1894. Court investigator; duties; report

If the petition alleges that the conservatee is not willing to attend the hearing or upon receipt of an affidavit or certificate attesting to the medical inability of the conservatee to attend the hearing, the court investigator shall do all of the following:

(a) Interview the conservatee personally.

(b) Inform the conservatee of the contents of the petition, of the nature, purpose, and effect of the proceeding, and of the right of the conservatee to oppose the petition, attend the hearing, * * * be represented by legal counsel, and to have legal counsel appointed by the court if not otherwise represented by legal counsel.

(c) Determine whether it appears that the conservatee is unable to attend the hearing and, if able to attend, whether the conservatee is willing to attend the hearing.

(d) Determine whether the conservatee wishes to contest the petition.

(e) Determine whether the conservatee wishes to be represented by legal counsel and, if so, whether the conservatee has retained legal counsel and, if not, whether the * * * conservatee plans to retain legal counsel.

* * *

(f) Report to the court in writing, at least five days before the hearing, concerning all of the foregoing, including the conservatee's express communications concerning both (1) representation by legal counsel and (2) whether the conservatee is not willing to attend the hearing and does not wish to contest the petition. *(Stats.1990, c. 79 (A.B.759), § 14, operative July 1, 1991. Amended by Stats.2022, c. 420 (A.B.2960), § 37, eff. Jan. 1, 2023.)*

Cross References

Court investigator, see Probate Code §§ 1419, 1454.

Research References

Forms

West's California Code Forms, Probate § 1454 Form 1, Order Appointing Court Investigator—Judicial Council Form GC-330.

West's California Judicial Council Forms GC–330, Order Appointing Court Investigator.

§ 1895. Hearing, appearances; information to conservatee

(a) The conservatee, the spouse, the domestic partner, a relative, or a friend of the conservatee, the conservator, or any other interested person may appear at the hearing to support or oppose the petition.

(b) Except where the conservatee is absent from the hearing and is not required to attend the hearing under the provisions of Section 1893 and any showing required by Section 1893 has been made, the court shall inform, * * * before granting the petition, * * * the conservatee of all of the following:

(1) The nature and purpose of the proceeding.

(2) The nature and effect on the conservatee's basic rights of the order requested.

(3) The conservatee has the right to oppose the petition, to be represented by legal counsel if the conservatee so chooses, and to have legal counsel appointed by the court if * * * not otherwise represented by legal counsel.

(c) After the court informs the conservatee of the matters listed in subdivision (b) and * * * before granting the petition, the court shall consult the conservatee to determine the conservatee's opinion concerning the order requested in the petition. *(Stats.1990, c. 79 (A.B.759), § 14, operative July 1, 1991. Amended by Stats.2001, c. 893 (A.B.25), § 27; Stats.2022, c. 420 (A.B.2960), § 38, eff. Jan. 1, 2023.)*

Cross References

Appointment of legal counsel, see Probate Code § 1470 et seq.
Domestic partner, defined, see Probate Code § 37.
Interested person, see Probate Code § 1424.

§ 1896. Order; termination

(a) If the court determines that the order requested in the petition is proper, the court shall make the order.

(b) The court, in its discretion, may provide in the order that, unless extended by subsequent order of the court, the order or specific provisions of the order terminate at a time specified in the order. *(Stats.1990, c. 79 (A.B.759), § 14, operative July 1, 1991.)*

Research References

Forms

West's California Code Forms, Probate § 1896 Form 1, Order Authorizing Conservator to Give Consent for Medical Treatment—Judicial Council Form GC-385.

§ 1897. Duration of order

An order of the court under Section 1880 continues in effect until the earliest of the following times:

(1) The time specified in the order, if any.

(2) The time the order is modified or revoked.

(3) The time the conservatorship is terminated. *(Stats.1990, c. 79 (A.B.759), § 14, operative July 1, 1991.)*

Cross References

Termination of conservatorship, see Probate Code § 1860 et seq.

Research References

Forms

West's California Code Forms, Probate § 1896 Form 1, Order Authorizing Conservator to Give Consent for Medical Treatment—Judicial Council Form GC-385.

§ 1898. Modification or revocation of order

An order of the court under Section 1880 may be modified or revoked upon a petition made, noticed, and heard by the court in the manner provided in this article. *(Stats.1990, c. 79 (A.B.759), § 14, operative July 1, 1991.)*

Research References

Forms

West's California Code Forms, Probate § 1896 Form 1, Order Authorizing Conservator to Give Consent for Medical Treatment—Judicial Council Form GC-385.

ARTICLE 3. CAPACITY OF CONSERVATEE TO MARRY

Section
1900. Appointment of conservator; effect.
1901. Determination of capacity; order; law governing; filing of petition; notice of hearing.

§ 1900. Appointment of conservator; effect

The appointment of a conservator of the person or estate or both does not affect the capacity of the conservatee to marry or to enter into a registered domestic partnership. *(Stats.1990, c. 79 (A.B.759), § 14, operative July 1, 1991. Amended by Stats.2005, c. 418 (S.B.973), § 26.)*

§ 1901. Determination of capacity; order; law governing; filing of petition; notice of hearing

(a) The court may by order determine whether the conservatee has the capacity to enter into a valid marriage, as provided in Part 1 (commencing with Section 300) of Division 3 of the Family Code, or to enter into a registered domestic partnership, as provided in Section 297 of the Family Code, at the time the order is made.

(b) A petition for an order under this section may be filed by the conservator of the person or estate or both, the conservatee, any relative or friend of the conservatee, or any interested person.

(c) Notice of the hearing on the petition shall be given for the period and in the manner provided in Chapter 3 (commencing with Section 1460) of Part 1. *(Stats.1990, c. 79 (A.B.759), § 14, operative July 1, 1991. Amended by Stats.1992, c. 163 (A.B.2641), § 124, operative Jan. 1, 1994; Stats.2005, c. 418 (S.B.973), § 27.)*

Cross References

Action to test validity of marriage, see Family Code § 309.
Authorization of conservator to commence annulment proceedings, see Family Code § 2211.
Capacity determinations, generally, see Probate Code § 3200 et seq.
Hearings and orders, see Probate Code § 1040 et seq.
Interested person, defined, see Probate Code § 1424.
Petitions and other papers, see Probate Code § 1020 et seq.
Proceeding to have marriage adjudged a nullity, see Family Code § 2210 et seq.
Rules of practice, see Probate Code § 1000 et seq.

Research References

Forms

West's California Judicial Council Forms GC–331, Order Appointing Court Investigator (Review and Successor Conservator Investigations).

CHAPTER 5. DISQUALIFICATION FROM VOTING

Section
1910. Disqualification by order of court; exceptions.

§ 1910. Disqualification by order of court; exceptions

(a) If the court determines the conservatee is incapable of communicating, with or without reasonable accommodations, a desire to participate in the voting process, the court shall by order disqualify the conservatee from voting pursuant to Section 2208 or 2209 of the Elections Code.

(b) The conservatee shall not be disqualified from voting on the basis that he or she does, or would need to do, any of the following to complete an affidavit of voter registration:

(1) Signs the affidavit of voter registration with a mark or a cross pursuant to subdivision (b) of Section 2150 of the Elections Code.

(2) Signs the affidavit of voter registration by means of a signature stamp pursuant to Section 354.5 of the Elections Code.

(3) Completes the affidavit of voter registration with the assistance of another person pursuant to subdivision (d) of Section 2150 of the Elections Code.

(4) Completes the affidavit of voter registration with reasonable accommodations. *(Stats.1990, c. 79 (A.B.759), § 14, operative July 1, 1991. Amended by Stats.1994, c. 923 (S.B.1546), § 161; Stats.2014, c. 591 (A.B.1311), § 8, eff. Jan. 1, 2015; Stats.2015, c. 736 (S.B.589), § 12, eff. Jan. 1, 2016.)*

Cross References

Final judgment or order, see Probate Code § 2103.
Hearings and orders, see Probate Code § 1040 et seq.
Petitions and other papers, see Probate Code § 1020 et seq.
Restoration of right to vote, see Probate Code § 1865.

Research References

Forms

West's California Judicial Council Forms GC–335, Capacity Declaration—Conservatorship.

CHAPTER 6. STERILIZATION

Section
1950. Persons with developmental disabilities; legislative intent.
1951. Persons with ability to consent to sterilization; definitions.
1952. Appointment of limited conservator to consent to sterilization of developmentally disabled adults; petition; contents.
1953. Hearing on petition; service of notice and copy of petition.
1954. Appointment of counsel; presumption.
1954.5. Appointment of facilitator; duties; considerations.
1955. Investigation; preparation of written report by appropriate regional center; examination of person named in petition; reports; confidentiality; use of examiners as expert witnesses.
1956. Presence of person named in petition at hearing.
1957. Consideration of views of person for whom sterilization is proposed.
1958. Authorization for conservator to consent to sterilization of person named in petition; findings required by court beyond a reasonable doubt.
1959. Vulnerability of developmentally disabled person to unlawful sexual conduct by others; not a consideration in sterilization determination.
1960. Assurance by court of adequate representation by existing conservator or appointment of limited conservator.
1961. Sterilization procedure not to include hysterectomy or castration unless medically indicated.
1962. Court order granting petition; written statement of findings; appeal.
1963. Payment of costs and fees.
1964. Expiration of consent to sterilization; termination of conservatorship upon completion of sterilization.
1965. Stay of court order pending appeal.
1966. Denial of first petition; filing of subsequent petitions on showing of material change in circumstances.
1967. Immunity from liability; exception; civil liability for petitioner who seeks sterilization when person named in petition is capable of consent.
1968. Unavoidable sterilization as part of other medical treatment.
1969. Right of persons with developmental disabilities to consent to sterilization without court order.

§ 1950. Persons with developmental disabilities; legislative intent

The Legislature recognizes that the right to exercise choice over matters of procreation is fundamental and may not be denied to an individual on the basis of disability. This chapter is enacted for the benefit of those persons with developmental disabilities who, despite those disabilities, are capable of engaging in sexual activity yet who, because of those disabilities, are unable to give the informed, voluntary consent necessary to their fully exercising the right to procreative choice, which includes the right to choose sterilization.

However, the Legislature further recognizes that the power to sterilize is subject to abuse and, historically, has been abused. It is the intent of the Legislature that no individual shall be sterilized

§ 1950

solely by reason of a developmental disability and that no individual who knowingly opposes sterilization be sterilized involuntarily. It is further the intent of the Legislature that this chapter shall be applied in accord with the overall intent of Division 4.5 (commencing with Section 4500) of the Welfare and Institutions Code that persons with developmental disabilities be provided with those services needed to enable them to live more normal, independent, and productive lives, including assistance and training that might obviate the need for sterilization. (Stats.1990, c. 79 (A.B.759), § 14, operative July 1, 1991.)

Cross References

Statutes, construction and legislative intent, see Code of Civil Procedure §§ 1858 and 1859.

Research References

Forms

West's California Code Forms, Probate § 1952 Form 1, Allegations for Petition for Authority to Consent to Sterilization of Developmentally Disabled Adult.

§ 1951. Persons with ability to consent to sterilization; definitions

(a) No person who has the ability to consent to his or her sterilization shall be sterilized pursuant to this chapter.

(b) For the purposes of this chapter, the following terms have the meanings given:

(1) "Consent to sterilization" means making a voluntary decision to undergo sterilization after being fully informed about, and after fully understanding the nature and consequences of, sterilization.

(2) "Voluntary" means performed while competent to make the decision, and as a matter of free choice and will and not in response to coercion, duress, or undue influence.

(3) "Fully understanding the nature and consequences of sterilization," includes, but is not limited to, the ability to understand each of the following:

(A) That the individual is free to withhold or withdraw consent to the procedure at any time before the sterilization without affecting the right to future care or treatment and without loss or withdrawal of any publicly funded program benefits to which the individual might be otherwise entitled.

(B) Available alternative methods of family planning and birth control.

(C) That the sterilization procedure is considered to be irreversible.

(D) The specific sterilization procedure to be performed.

(E) The discomforts and risks that may accompany or follow the performing of the procedure, including an explanation of the type and possible effects of any anesthetic to be used.

(F) The benefits or advantages that may be expected as a result of the sterilization.

(G) The approximate length of the hospital stay.

(H) The approximate length of time for recovery.

(c) The court shall appoint a facilitator or interpreter if such a person's assistance would enable the person named in the petition to understand any of these factors. (Stats.1990, c. 79 (A.B.759), § 14, operative July 1, 1991.)

Research References

Forms

West's California Code Forms, Probate § 1952 Form 1, Allegations for Petition for Authority to Consent to Sterilization of Developmentally Disabled Adult.

§ 1952. Appointment of limited conservator to consent to sterilization of developmentally disabled adults; petition; contents

The conservator of an adult, or any person authorized to file a petition for the appointment of a conservator under paragraphs (2) to (5), inclusive, of subdivision (a) of Section 1820, may file a petition under this chapter for appointment of a limited conservator authorized to consent to the sterilization of an adult with a developmental disability. The content of the petition under this chapter shall conform to the provisions of Section 1821 and in addition allege that the person for whom sterilization is proposed has a developmental disability as defined in Section 1420 and shall allege specific reasons why court-authorized sterilization is deemed necessary. A petition under this chapter shall be considered separately from any contemporaneous petition for appointment of a conservator under this division. (Stats.1990, c. 79 (A.B.759), § 14, operative July 1, 1991.)

Research References

Forms

West's California Code Forms, Probate § 1952 Form 1, Allegations for Petition for Authority to Consent to Sterilization of Developmentally Disabled Adult.

§ 1953. Hearing on petition; service of notice and copy of petition

At least 90 days before the hearing on the petition under this chapter, notice of the time and place of the hearing and a copy of the petition shall be served on the person named in the petition and, if the petitioner is not the conservator of the person, on the conservator, if any. Service shall be made in the manner provided in Section 415.10 or Section 415.30 of the Code of Civil Procedure or in such manner as may be authorized by the court. (Stats.1990, c. 79 (A.B.759), § 14, operative July 1, 1991.)

Cross References

Computation of time, see Code of Civil Procedure §§ 12 and 12a; Government Code § 6800 et seq.
Notice of hearing,
  Generally, see Probate Code §§ 1200 et seq., 1460 et seq.
  Mailing, see Probate Code § 1215 et seq.
  Posting, see Probate Code § 1230.
  Proof of giving notice, see Probate Code § 1260 et seq.
  Special notice, see Probate Code §§ 1250 and 2700 et seq.
Service of process,
  Generally, see Code of Civil Procedure § 413.10 et seq.
  Mail, see Code of Civil Procedure §§ 415.30, 1012 et seq.
  Personal delivery, see Code of Civil Procedure § 415.10.
  Proof of service, see Code of Civil Procedure § 417.10 et seq.
  Publication, see Code of Civil Procedure § 415.50.

Research References

Forms

West's California Code Forms, Probate § 1952 Form 1, Allegations for Petition for Authority to Consent to Sterilization of Developmentally Disabled Adult.

§ 1954. Appointment of counsel; presumption

In any proceeding under this chapter, if the person named in the petition for court authorization to consent to sterilization has not retained legal counsel and does not plan to retain legal counsel, the court shall immediately appoint the public defender or private counsel to represent the individual for whom sterilization is proposed. Counsel shall undertake the representation with the presumption that the individual opposes the petition. (Stats.1990, c. 79 (A.B.759), § 14, operative July 1, 1991.)

Cross References

Counsel, right to, see Cal. Const. Art. 1, § 15.

Presumptions, see Evidence Code § 600 et seq.

Research References

Forms

West's California Code Forms, Probate § 1952 Form 1, Allegations for Petition for Authority to Consent to Sterilization of Developmentally Disabled Adult.

§ 1954.5. Appointment of facilitator; duties; considerations

(a) The court shall appoint a facilitator for the person named in the petition, who shall assist the person named in the petition to do all of the following:

(1) Understand the nature of the proceedings.

(2) Understand the evaluation process required by Section 1955.

(3) Communicate his or her views.

(4) Participate as fully as possible in the proceedings.

(b) All of the following factors shall be considered by the court in appointing a facilitator:

(1) The preference of the person named in the petition.

(2) The proposed facilitator's personal knowledge of the person named in the petition.

(3) The proposed facilitator's ability to communicate with the person named in the petition, when that person is nonverbal, has limited verbal skills, or relies on alternative modes of communication.

(4) The proposed facilitator's knowledge of the developmental disabilities service system.

(c) The petitioner may not be appointed as the facilitator. (Stats.1990, c. 79 (A.B.759), § 14, operative July 1, 1991.)

Research References

Forms

West's California Code Forms, Probate § 1952 Form 1, Allegations for Petition for Authority to Consent to Sterilization of Developmentally Disabled Adult.

§ 1955. Investigation; preparation of written report by appropriate regional center; examination of person named in petition; reports; confidentiality; use of examiners as expert witnesses

(a) The court shall request the director of the appropriate regional center for the developmentally disabled to coordinate an investigation and prepare and file a written report thereon. The appropriate regional center for purposes of this section is (1) the regional center of which the person named in the petition is a client, (2) if the individual named in the petition is not a client of any regional center, the regional center responsible for the area in which the individual is then living, or (3) such other regional center as may be in the best interests of the individual. The report shall be based upon comprehensive medical, psychological, and sociosexual evaluations of the individual conducted pursuant to subdivisions (b) and (c), and shall address, but shall not be limited to, each of the factors listed in Section 1958. A copy of the report shall be provided to each of the parties at least 15 days prior to the hearing.

(b) Prior to the hearing on the issue of sterilization, the person who is proposed to be sterilized shall be personally examined by two physicians, one of whom shall be a surgeon competent to perform the procedure, and one psychologist or clinical social worker, each of whom has been mutually agreed to by the petitioner and counsel for the person named in the petition or, if agreement is not reached, appointed by the court from a panel of qualified professionals. At the request of counsel for the person named in the petition, the court shall appoint one additional psychologist, clinical social worker, or physician named by counsel. Any psychologist or clinical social worker and, to the extent feasible, any physicians conducting an examination shall have had experience with persons who have developmental disabilities. To the extent feasible, each of the examiners shall also have knowledge and experience relating to sociosexual skills and behavior. The examinations shall be at county expense subject to Section 1963.

(c) The examiners shall consider all available alternatives to sterilization and shall recommend sterilization only if no suitable alternative is available. Each examiner shall prepare a written, comprehensive report containing all relevant aspects of the person's medical, psychological, family, and sociosexual conditions. Each examiner shall address those factors specified in Section 1958 related to his or her particular area of expertise. In considering the factors in subdivision (a) of, and paragraph (1) of subdivision (d) of, Section 1958, each examiner shall include information regarding the intensity, extent, and recentness of the person's education and training, if any, regarding human sexuality, including birth control methods and parenting skills, and in addition, shall consider whether the individual would benefit from training provided by persons competent in education and training of persons with comparable intellectual impairments. If an examiner recommends against sterilization, the examiner shall set forth in his or her report available alternatives, including, as warranted, recommendations for sex education, parent training, or training in the use of alternative methods of contraception. Copies of each report shall be furnished at least 30 days prior to the hearing on the petition to the person or persons who filed the petition, the conservator, if any, and counsel for the person proposed to be sterilized, the regional center responsible for the investigation and report required under this section, and such other persons as the court may direct. The court may receive these reports in evidence.

(d) The contents of the reports prepared pursuant to this section shall be confidential. Upon judgment in the action or the proceeding becoming final, the court shall order the contents of the reports sealed.

(e) Regional centers for the developmentally disabled shall compile and maintain lists of persons competent to perform the examinations required by this section. These lists shall be provided to the court. If the person named in the petition resides at a state hospital or other residential care facility, no person conducting an examination pursuant to subdivision (b) shall be an employee of the facility.

(f) Any party to the proceedings has the right to submit additional reports from qualified experts.

(g) Any person who has written a report received in evidence may be subpoenaed and questioned by any party to the proceedings or by the court and when so called is subject to all rules of evidence including those of legal objections as to the qualification of expert witnesses.

(h) No regional center or person acting in his or her capacity as a regional center employee may file a petition under Section 1952. (Stats.1990, c. 79 (A.B.759), § 14, operative July 1, 1991.)

Cross References

Sterilization of disabled, confidentiality of evaluation report, see Government Code § 6276.42.

Research References

Forms

West's California Code Forms, Probate § 1952 Form 1, Allegations for Petition for Authority to Consent to Sterilization of Developmentally Disabled Adult.

§ 1956. Presence of person named in petition at hearing

The person to whom the petition applies shall be present at the hearing except for reason of medical inability. Emotional or psychological instability is not good cause for the absence of the proposed conservatee from the hearing unless, by reason of the instability, attendance at the hearing is likely to cause serious and immediate physiological damage to the proposed conservatee. (Stats.1990, c. 79 (A.B.759), § 14, operative July 1, 1991.)

Research References

Forms

West's California Code Forms, Probate § 1952 Form 1, Allegations for Petition for Authority to Consent to Sterilization of Developmentally Disabled Adult.

§ 1957. Consideration of views of person for whom sterilization is proposed

To the greatest extent possible, the court shall elicit and take into account the views of the individual for whom sterilization is proposed in determining whether sterilization is to be authorized. *(Stats.1990, c. 79 (A.B.759), § 14, operative July 1, 1991.)*

§ 1958. Authorization for conservator to consent to sterilization of person named in petition; findings required by court beyond a reasonable doubt

The court may authorize the conservator of a person proposed to be sterilized to consent to the sterilization of that person only if the court finds that the petitioner has established all of the following beyond a reasonable doubt:

(a) The person named in the petition is incapable of giving consent to sterilization, as defined in Section 1951, and the incapacity is in all likelihood permanent.

(b) Based on reasonable medical evidence, the individual is fertile and capable of procreation.

(c) The individual is capable of engaging in, and is likely to engage in sexual activity at the present or in the near future under circumstances likely to result in pregnancy.

(d) Either of the following:

(1) The nature and extent of the individual's disability as determined by empirical evidence and not solely on the basis of any standardized test, renders him or her permanently incapable of caring for a child, even with appropriate training and reasonable assistance.

(2) Due to a medical condition, pregnancy or childbirth would pose a substantially elevated risk to the life of the individual to such a degree that, in the absence of other appropriate methods of contraception, sterilization would be deemed medically necessary for an otherwise nondisabled woman under similar circumstances.

(e) All less invasive contraceptive methods including supervision are unworkable even with training and assistance, inapplicable, or medically contraindicated. Isolation and segregation shall not be considered as less invasive means of contraception.

(f) The proposed method of sterilization entails the least invasion of the body of the individual.

(g) The current state of scientific and medical knowledge does not suggest either (1) that a reversible sterilization procedure or other less drastic contraceptive method will shortly be available, or (2) that science is on the threshold of an advance in the treatment of the individual's disability.

(h) The person named in the petition has not made a knowing objection to his or her sterilization. For purposes of this subdivision, an individual may be found to have knowingly objected to his or her sterilization notwithstanding his or her inability to give consent to sterilization as defined in Section 1951. In the case of persons who are nonverbal, have limited verbal ability to communicate, or who rely on alternative modes of communication, the court shall ensure that adequate effort has been made to elicit the actual views of the individual by the facilitator appointed pursuant to Section 1954.5, or by any other person with experience in communicating with developmentally disabled persons who communicate using similar means. *(Stats.1990, c. 79 (A.B.759), § 14, operative July 1, 1991.)*

Cross References

Capacity determinations, generally, see Probate Code § 3200 et seq.

Hearings and orders, see Probate Code § 1040 et seq.
Petitions and other papers, see Probate Code § 1020 et seq.
Rules of practice, see Probate Code § 1000 et seq.

Research References

Forms

West's California Code Forms, Probate § 1952 Form 1, Allegations for Petition for Authority to Consent to Sterilization of Developmentally Disabled Adult.

§ 1959. Vulnerability of developmentally disabled person to unlawful sexual conduct by others; not a consideration in sterilization determination

The fact that, due to the nature or severity of his or her disability, a person for whom an authorization to consent to sterilization is sought may be vulnerable to sexual conduct by others that would be deemed unlawful, shall not be considered by the court in determining whether sterilization is to be authorized under this chapter. *(Stats.1990, c. 79 (A.B.759), § 14, operative July 1, 1991.)*

Research References

Forms

West's California Code Forms, Probate § 1952 Form 1, Allegations for Petition for Authority to Consent to Sterilization of Developmentally Disabled Adult.

§ 1960. Assurance by court of adequate representation by existing conservator or appointment of limited conservator

If the person named in the petition already has a conservator, the court may authorize that person to consent to sterilization or may appoint another person as limited conservator under the provisions of this chapter. The court shall ensure that the person or agency designated as conservator under this chapter is capable of adequately representing and safeguarding the interests of the conservatee. *(Stats.1990, c. 79 (A.B.759), § 14, operative July 1, 1991.)*

§ 1961. Sterilization procedure not to include hysterectomy or castration unless medically indicated

A sterilization procedure authorized under this chapter shall not include hysterectomy or castration. However, if the report prepared under Section 1955 indicates that hysterectomy or castration is a medically necessary treatment, regardless of the need for sterilization, the court shall proceed pursuant to Section 2357. *(Stats.1990, c. 79 (A.B.759), § 14, operative July 1, 1991.)*

Research References

Forms

West's California Code Forms, Probate § 1952 Form 1, Allegations for Petition for Authority to Consent to Sterilization of Developmentally Disabled Adult.

§ 1962. Court order granting petition; written statement of findings; appeal

(a) Any court order granting a petition under this chapter shall be accompanied by a written statement of decision pursuant to Section 632 of the Code of Civil Procedure detailing the factual and legal bases for the court's determination on each of the findings required under Section 1958.

(b) When a judgment authorizing the conservator of a person to consent to the sterilization is rendered, an appeal is automatically taken by the person proposed to be sterilized without any action by that person, or by his or her counsel. The Judicial Council shall provide by rule for notice of and procedure for the appeal. The appeal shall have precedence over other cases in the court in which the appeal is pending. *(Stats.1990, c. 79 (A.B.759), § 14, operative July 1, 1991.)*

Cross References

Appeals, generally, see Code of Civil Procedure § 901 et seq.
Effect of final orders, see Probate Code § 2103.
Hearings and orders, see Probate Code § 1040 et seq.
Petitions and other papers, see Probate Code § 1020 et seq.
Rules of practice, see Probate Code § 1000 et seq.

Research References

Forms

West's California Code Forms, Probate § 1952 Form 1, Allegations for Petition for Authority to Consent to Sterilization of Developmentally Disabled Adult.

§ 1963. Payment of costs and fees

(a) At the conclusion of the hearing, the court, after inquiring into financial ability, may make an order based upon their ability that any one or more of the following persons pay court costs and fees in whole or in part as in the opinion of the court is proper and in any installments and manner which is both reasonable and compatible with ability to pay:

(1) The person to whom the petition applies.

(2) The petitioner.

(3) Any person liable for the support and maintenance of the person to whom the petition applies.

(b) An order under subdivision (a) may be enforced in the same manner as a money judgment.

(c) For the purposes of this section, court costs and fees include the costs of any examination or investigation ordered by the court, expert witnesses' fees, and the costs and fees of the court-appointed public defender or private counsel representing the person to whom the petition applies.

(d) Any fees and costs not ordered to be paid by persons under subdivision (a) are a charge against and paid out of the treasury of the county on order of the court. (Stats.1990, c. 79 (A.B.759), § 14, operative July 1, 1991.)

Cross References

Costs, see Probate Code § 1002.
Effect of final orders, see Probate Code § 2103.
Enforcement of orders, see Probate Code § 1049.
Hearings and orders, see Probate Code § 1040 et seq.
Petitions and other papers, see Probate Code § 1020 et seq.
Rules of practice, see Probate Code § 1000 et seq.

§ 1964. Expiration of consent to sterilization; termination of conservatorship upon completion of sterilization

An order of the court authorizing a conservator to consent to sterilization which is upheld on appeal automatically expires in one year from the final determination on appeal unless earlier terminated by the court. A conservatorship established for the sole purpose of authorizing a conservator to consent to sterilization under this chapter shall automatically terminate upon completion of the sterilization procedure or upon expiration of the court's order authorizing the conservator to consent to sterilization, whichever occurs first. If, upon the expiration of the court's order under this chapter, the person named as conservator determines that the conservatorship is still required for the purpose of this chapter, he or she may petition the court for reappointment as conservator for a succeeding six-month period upon a showing of good cause as to why any sterilization authorized by the court has not been completed. (Stats.1990, c. 79 (A.B.759), § 14, operative July 1, 1991.)

§ 1965. Stay of court order pending appeal

Any court order made pursuant to this chapter granting authority to consent to sterilization shall be stayed pending a final determination on appeal. (Stats.1990, c. 79 (A.B.759), § 14, operative July 1, 1991.)

Cross References

Appeals, generally, see Code of Civil Procedure § 901 et seq.

§ 1966. Denial of first petition; filing of subsequent petitions on showing of material change in circumstances

After the filing of a first petition for sterilization pursuant to this chapter and a determination by the court that any one or more of the conditions required in Section 1958 has not been proven beyond a reasonable doubt, and that therefore authorization for the proposed sterilization should not be given by the court, a subsequent petition may be filed only on the showing of a material change in circumstances. (Stats.1990, c. 79 (A.B.759), § 14, operative July 1, 1991.)

§ 1967. Immunity from liability; exception; civil liability for petitioner who seeks sterilization when person named in petition is capable of consent

(a) The sterilization of a person in accordance with this chapter does not render the petitioner or any person participating in the conservatorship proceedings or sterilization liable, either civilly or criminally, except for any injury caused by negligent or willful misconduct in the performance of the sterilization.

(b) Notwithstanding the provisions of subdivision (a), any individual who petitions for authorization to consent to sterilization knowing that the person to whom the petition relates is capable of giving consent to sterilization as defined in Section 1951 is guilty of a misdemeanor, and may be civilly liable to the person concerning whom sterilization was sought. (Stats.1990, c. 79 (A.B.759), § 14, operative July 1, 1991.)

Cross References

Misdemeanors, definition and penalties, see Penal Code §§ 17, 19 and 19.2.

§ 1968. Unavoidable sterilization as part of other medical treatment

This chapter does not prohibit medical treatment or surgery required for other medical reasons and in which sterilization is an unavoidable or medically probable consequence, but is not the object of the treatment or surgery. (Stats.1990, c. 79 (A.B.759), § 14, operative July 1, 1991.)

§ 1969. Right of persons with developmental disabilities to consent to sterilization without court order

Nothing in this chapter shall infringe on the right of persons with developmental disabilities who are capable of giving consent to sterilization to give that consent without the necessity of a court order or substitute decisionmaker. (Stats.1990, c. 79 (A.B.759), § 14, operative July 1, 1991.)

CHAPTER 7. UNWARRANTED PETITIONS

Section
1970. Legislative findings; vexatious litigants.

§ 1970. Legislative findings; vexatious litigants

(a) The Legislature finds that unwarranted petitions, applications, or motions other than discovery motions after a conservatorship has been established create an environment that can be harmful to the conservatee and are inconsistent with the goal of protecting the conservatee.

(b) Notwithstanding Section 391 of the Code of Civil Procedure, if a person other than the conservatee files a petition for termination of the conservatorship, or instruction to the conservator, that is unmeritorious or intended to harass or annoy the conservator, and the person has previously filed pleadings in the conservatorship proceedings that were unmeritorious or intended to harass or annoy the conservator, the petition shall be grounds for the court to determine that the person is a vexatious litigant for the purposes of

Title 3A (commencing with Section 391) of Part 2 of the Code of Civil Procedure. For these purposes, the term "new litigation" shall include petitions for visitation, termination of the conservatorship, or instruction to the conservator. *(Added by Stats.2008, c. 293 (A.B. 1340), § 3.)*

CHAPTER 8. INTERSTATE JURISDICTION, TRANSFER, AND RECOGNITION: CALIFORNIA CONSERVATORSHIP JURISDICTION ACT

Cross References

Acknowledgment of receipt by conservator, statement of duties and liabilities, conservatorship information, see Probate Code § 1834.

Jurisdiction and venue, determination of state jurisdiction, see Probate Code § 2200.

ARTICLE 1. GENERAL PROVISIONS

Section
1980. Legislative intent; short title.
1981. Application of chapter.
1982. Definitions.
1983. International application of chapter.
1984. Communication between courts.
1985. Cooperation between courts.
1986. Taking testimony in another state.

§ 1980. Legislative intent; short title

(a) By enacting this chapter, it is the Legislature's intent to enact a modified version of the Uniform Adult Guardianship and Protective Proceedings Jurisdiction Act.

(b) This chapter may be cited as the "California Conservatorship Jurisdiction Act." *(Added by Stats.2014, c. 553 (S.B.940), § 20, eff. Jan. 1, 2015, operative Jan. 1, 2016.)*

§ 1981. Application of chapter

(a)(1) This chapter does not apply to a minor, regardless of whether the minor is or was married.

(2) This chapter does not apply to any proceeding in which a person is appointed to provide personal care or property administration for a minor, including, but not limited to, a guardianship under Part 2 (commencing with Section 1500).

(b) This chapter does not apply to any proceeding in which a person is involuntarily committed to a mental health facility or subjected to other involuntary mental health care, including, but not limited to, any of the following proceedings or any proceeding that is similar in substance:

(1) A proceeding under Sections 1026 to 1027, inclusive, of the Penal Code.

(2) A proceeding under Chapter 6 (commencing with Section 1367) of Title 10 of Part 2 of the Penal Code.

(3) A proceeding under Article 4 (commencing with Section 2960) of Chapter 7 of Title 1 of Part 3 of the Penal Code.

(4) A proceeding under Article 6 (commencing with Section 1800) of Chapter 1 of Division 2.5 of the Welfare and Institutions Code.

(5) A proceeding under Part 1 (commencing with Section 5000) of Division 5 of the Welfare and Institutions Code, which is also known as the Lanterman–Petris–Short Act.

(6) A proceeding under Article 2 (commencing with Section 6500) of Chapter 2 of Part 2 of Division 6 of the Welfare and Institutions Code.

(7) A proceeding under Article 4 (commencing with Section 6600) of Chapter 2 of Part 2 of Division 6 of the Welfare and Institutions Code.

(c) Article 3 (commencing with Section 2001) does not apply to an adult with a developmental disability, or to any proceeding in which a person is appointed to provide personal care or property administration for an adult with a developmental disability, including, but not limited to, the following types of proceedings:

(1) A proceeding under Article 7.5 (commencing with Section 416) of Chapter 2 of Part 1 of Division 1 of the Health and Safety Code.

(2) A limited conservatorship under subdivision (d) of Section 1801.

(3) A proceeding under Section 4825 of the Welfare and Institutions Code.

(4) A proceeding under Article 2 (commencing with Section 6500) of Chapter 2 of Part 2 of Division 6 of the Welfare and Institutions Code.

(d) Application of this chapter to a conservatee with major neurocognitive disorder is subject to the express limitations of Sections 2002 and 2016, as well as the other requirements of this chapter. *(Added by Stats.2014, c. 553 (S.B.940), § 20, eff. Jan. 1, 2015, operative Jan. 1, 2016. Amended by Stats.2017, c. 122 (S.B.413), § 4, eff. Jan. 1, 2018.)*

Research References

Forms

West's California Code Forms, Probate § 1980–1981 Comment:.

§ 1982. Definitions

In this chapter:

(a) "Adult" means an individual who has attained 18 years of age.

(b) "Conservatee" means an adult for whom a conservator of the estate, a conservator of the person, or a conservator of the person and estate has been appointed.

(c) "Conservator" means a person appointed by the court to serve as a conservator of the estate, a conservator of the person, or a conservator of the person and estate.

(d) "Conservator of the estate" means a person appointed by the court to administer the property of an adult, including, but not limited to, a person appointed for that purpose under subdivision (b) of Section 1801.

(e) "Conservator of the person" means a person appointed by the court to make decisions regarding the person of an adult, including, but not limited to, a person appointed for that purpose under subdivision (a) of Section 1801.

(f) "Conservator of the person and estate" means a person appointed by the court to make decisions regarding the person of an adult and to administer the property of that adult, including, but not limited to, a person appointed for those purposes under subdivision (c) of Section 1801.

(g) "Conservatorship order" means an order appointing a conservator of the estate, a conservator of the person, or a conservator of the person and estate in a conservatorship proceeding.

(h) "Conservatorship proceeding" means a judicial proceeding in which an order for the appointment of a conservator of the estate, a conservator of the person, or a conservator of the person and estate is sought or has been issued.

(i) "Party" means the conservatee, proposed conservatee, petitioner, conservator, proposed conservator, or any other person allowed by the court to participate in a conservatorship proceeding.

(j) "Person" means an individual, corporation, business trust, estate, trust, partnership, limited liability company, association, joint venture, public corporation, government or governmental subdivision, agency, or instrumentality, or any other legal or commercial entity.

(k) "Proposed conservatee" means an adult for whom a conservatorship order is sought.

(*l*) "Record" means information that is inscribed on a tangible medium or that is stored in an electronic or other medium and is retrievable in perceivable form.

(m) Notwithstanding Section 74, "state" means a state of the United States, the District of Columbia, Puerto Rico, the United States Virgin Islands, a federally recognized Indian tribe, or any territory or insular possession subject to the jurisdiction of the United States. *(Added by Stats.2014, c. 553 (S.B.940), § 20, eff. Jan. 1, 2015, operative Jan. 1, 2016.)*

§ 1983. International application of chapter

A court of this state may treat a foreign country as if it were a state for the purpose of applying this article and Articles 2, 3, and 5. *(Added by Stats.2014, c. 553 (S.B.940), § 20, eff. Jan. 1, 2015, operative Jan. 1, 2016.)*

§ 1984. Communication between courts

(a) A court of this state may communicate with a court in another state concerning a proceeding arising under this chapter. The court may allow the parties to participate in the communication. Except as otherwise provided in subdivision (b), the court shall make a record of the communication. The record may be limited to the fact that the communication occurred.

(b) Courts may communicate concerning schedules, calendars, court records, and other administrative matters without making a record. *(Added by Stats.2014, c. 553 (S.B.940), § 20, eff. Jan. 1, 2015, operative Jan. 1, 2016.)*

§ 1985. Cooperation between courts

(a) In a conservatorship proceeding in this state, a court of this state may request the appropriate court of another state to do any of the following:

(1) Hold an evidentiary hearing.

(2) Order a person in that state to produce evidence or give testimony pursuant to procedures of that state.

(3) Order that an evaluation or assessment be made of the proposed conservatee.

(4) Order any appropriate investigation of a person involved in a proceeding.

(5) Forward to the court of this state a certified copy of the transcript or other record of a hearing under paragraph (1) or any other proceeding, any evidence otherwise produced under paragraph (2), and any evaluation or assessment prepared in compliance with an order under paragraph (3) or (4).

(6) Issue any order necessary to ensure the appearance in the proceeding of a person whose presence is necessary for the court to make a determination, including the conservatee or the proposed conservatee.

(7) Issue an order authorizing the release of medical, financial, criminal, or other relevant information in that state, including protected health information as defined in Section 160.103 of Title 45 of the Code of Federal Regulations.

(b) If a court of another state in which a conservatorship proceeding is pending requests assistance of the kind provided in subdivision (a), a court of this state has jurisdiction for the limited purpose of granting the request or making reasonable efforts to comply with the request.

(c) Travel and other necessary and reasonable expenses incurred under subdivisions (a) and (b) may be assessed against the parties according to the law of this state. *(Added by Stats.2014, c. 553 (S.B.940), § 20, eff. Jan. 1, 2015, operative Jan. 1, 2016.)*

§ 1986. Taking testimony in another state

(a) In a conservatorship proceeding, in addition to other procedures that may be available, testimony of a witness who is located in another state may be offered by deposition or other means allowable in this state for testimony taken in another state. The court on its own motion may order that the testimony of a witness be taken in another state and may prescribe the manner in which and the terms upon which the testimony is to be taken.

(b) In a conservatorship proceeding, a court in this state may permit a witness located in another state to be deposed or to testify by telephone or audiovisual or other electronic means. A court of this state shall cooperate with the court of the other state in designating an appropriate location for the deposition or testimony. *(Added by Stats.2014, c. 553 (S.B.940), § 20, eff. Jan. 1, 2015, operative Jan. 1, 2016.)*

ARTICLE 2. JURISDICTION

Section
1991. Definitions; significant connection factors.
1992. Exclusive basis.
1993. Jurisdiction.
1994. Special jurisdiction.
1995. Exclusive and continuing jurisdiction.
1996. Appropriate forum.
1997. Jurisdiction declined by reason of conduct.
1998. Notice of proceeding.
1999. Proceedings in more than one state.

§ 1991. Definitions; significant connection factors

(a) In this article:

(1) "Emergency" means a circumstance that likely will result in substantial harm to a proposed conservatee's health, safety, or welfare, and for which the appointment of a conservator of the person is necessary because no other person has authority and is willing to act on behalf of the proposed conservatee.

(2) "Home state" means the state in which the proposed conservatee was physically present, including any period of temporary absence, for at least six consecutive months immediately before the filing of a petition for a conservatorship order, or, if none, the state in which the proposed conservatee was physically present, including any period of temporary absence, for at least six consecutive months ending within the six months prior to the filing of the petition.

(3) "Significant–connection state" means a state, other than the home state, with which a proposed conservatee has a significant connection other than mere physical presence and in which substantial evidence concerning the proposed conservatee is available.

(b) In determining under Section 1993 and subdivision (e) of Section 2001 whether a proposed conservatee has a significant connection with a particular state, the court shall consider all of the following:

(1) The location of the proposed conservatee's family and other persons required to be notified of the conservatorship proceeding.

(2) The length of time the proposed conservatee at any time was physically present in the state and the duration of any absence.

(3) The location of the proposed conservatee's property.

(4) The extent to which the proposed conservatee has ties to the state such as voting registration, state or local tax return filing, vehicle registration, driver's license, social relationship, and receipt of services. *(Added by Stats.2014, c. 553 (S.B.940), § 20, eff. Jan. 1, 2015, operative Jan. 1, 2016.)*

§ 1992. Exclusive basis

For a conservatorship proceeding governed by this article, this article provides the exclusive basis for determining whether the courts of this state, as opposed to the courts of another state, have jurisdiction to appoint a conservator of the person, a conservator of the estate, or a conservator of the person and estate. *(Added by Stats.2014, c. 553 (S.B.940), § 20, eff. Jan. 1, 2015, operative Jan. 1, 2016.)*

§ 1993. Jurisdiction

(a) A court of this state has jurisdiction to appoint a conservator for a proposed conservatee if this state is the proposed conservatee's home state.

(b) A court of this state has jurisdiction to appoint a conservator for a proposed conservatee if, on the date the petition is filed, this state is a significant-connection state and the proposed conservatee does not have a home state.

(c) A court of this state has jurisdiction to appoint a conservator for a proposed conservatee if, on the date the petition is filed, this state is a significant-connection state and a court of the proposed conservatee's home state has expressly declined to exercise jurisdiction because this state is a more appropriate forum.

(d) A court of this state has jurisdiction to appoint a conservator for a proposed conservatee if both of the following conditions are satisfied:

(1) On the date the petition is filed, this state is a significant-connection state, the proposed conservatee has a home state, and a conservatorship petition is not pending in a court of the home state or another significant-connection state.

(2) Before the court makes the appointment, no conservatorship petition is filed in the proposed conservatee's home state, no objection to the court's jurisdiction is filed by a person required to be notified of the proceeding, and the court in this state concludes that it is an appropriate forum under the factors set forth in Section 1996.

(e) A court of this state has jurisdiction to appoint a conservator for a proposed conservatee if all of the following conditions are satisfied:

(1) This state does not have jurisdiction under subdivision (a), (b), (c), or (d).

(2) The proposed conservatee's home state and all significant-connection states have expressly declined to exercise jurisdiction because this state is the more appropriate forum.

(3) Jurisdiction in this state is consistent with the constitutions of this state and the United States.

(f) A court of this state has jurisdiction to appoint a conservator for a proposed conservatee if the requirements for special jurisdiction under Section 1994 are met. *(Added by Stats.2014, c. 553 (S.B.940), § 20, eff. Jan. 1, 2015, operative Jan. 1, 2016. Amended by Stats.2019, c. 497 (A.B.991), § 211, eff. Jan. 1, 2020.)*

Research References

Forms

West's California Code Forms, Probate § 1991–1999 Comment.

West's California Judicial Council Forms GC–366, Petition for Orders Accepting Transfer (California Conservatorship Jurisdiction Act).

West's California Judicial Council Forms GC–367, Provisional Order Accepting Transfer (California Conservatorship Jurisdiction Act).

West's California Judicial Council Forms GC–368, Final Order Accepting Transfer (California Conservatorship Jurisdiction Act).

§ 1994. Special jurisdiction

(a) A court of this state lacking jurisdiction under subdivisions (a) to (e), inclusive, of Section 1993 has special jurisdiction to do any of the following:

(1) Appoint a temporary conservator of the person in an emergency for a proposed conservatee who is physically present in this state. In making an appointment under this paragraph, a court shall follow the procedures specified in Chapter 3 (commencing with Section 2250) of Part 4. The temporary conservatorship shall terminate in accordance with Section 2257.

(2) Appoint a conservator of the estate with respect to real or tangible personal property located in this state.

(3) Appoint a conservator of the person, conservator of the estate, or conservator of the person and estate for a proposed conservatee for whom a provisional order to transfer a proceeding from another state has been issued under procedures similar to Section 2001. In making an appointment under this paragraph, a court shall follow the procedures specified in Chapter 3 (commencing with Section 2250) of Part 4. The temporary conservatorship shall terminate in accordance with Section 2257.

(b) If a petition for the appointment of a conservator of the person in an emergency is brought in this state and this state was not the home state of the proposed conservatee on the date the petition was filed, the court shall dismiss the proceeding at the request of the court of the home state, if any, whether dismissal is requested before or after the emergency appointment of a temporary conservator of the person. *(Added by Stats.2014, c. 553 (S.B.940), § 20, eff. Jan. 1, 2015, operative Jan. 1, 2016.)*

Research References

Forms

West's California Code Forms, Probate § 1991–1999 Comment.

West's California Judicial Council Forms GC–366, Petition for Orders Accepting Transfer (California Conservatorship Jurisdiction Act).

West's California Judicial Council Forms GC–367, Provisional Order Accepting Transfer (California Conservatorship Jurisdiction Act).

West's California Judicial Council Forms GC–368, Final Order Accepting Transfer (California Conservatorship Jurisdiction Act).

§ 1995. Exclusive and continuing jurisdiction

Except as otherwise provided in Section 1994, a court that has appointed a conservator consistent with this chapter has exclusive and continuing jurisdiction over the proceeding until it is terminated by the court or the appointment expires by its own terms. *(Added by Stats.2014, c. 553 (S.B.940), § 20, eff. Jan. 1, 2015, operative Jan. 1, 2016.)*

§ 1996. Appropriate forum

(a)(1) A court of this state having jurisdiction under Section 1993 to appoint a conservator may decline to exercise its jurisdiction if it determines at any time that a court of another state is a more appropriate forum.

(2) The issue of appropriate forum may be raised upon petition of any interested person, the court's own motion, or the request of another court.

(3) The petitioner, or, if there is no petitioner, the court in this state, shall give notice of the petition, motion, or request to the same persons and in the same manner as for a petition for a conservatorship under Section 1801. The notice shall state the basis for the petition, motion, or request, and shall inform the recipients of the date, time, and place of the hearing under paragraph (4). The notice shall also advise the recipients that they have a right to object to the petition, motion, or request. The notice to the potential conservatee shall inform the potential conservatee of the right to be represented by legal counsel if the potential conservatee so chooses, and to have legal counsel appointed by the court if the potential conservatee is unable to retain legal counsel.

(4) The court shall hold a hearing on the petition, motion, or request.

(b) If a court of this state declines to exercise its jurisdiction under subdivision (a), it shall grant the petition, motion, or request, and either dismiss or stay any conservatorship proceeding pending in this state. The court's order shall be based on evidence presented to the court. The order shall be in a record and shall expressly state that the court declines to exercise its jurisdiction because a court of another state is a more appropriate forum. The court may impose any condition the court considers just and proper, including the condition that a petition for the appointment of a conservator of the person, conservator of the estate, or conservator of the person and estate be filed promptly in another state.

(c) In determining whether it is an appropriate forum, the court shall consider all relevant factors, including all of the following:

(1) Any expressed preference of the proposed conservatee.

(2) Whether abuse, neglect, or exploitation of the proposed conservatee has occurred or is likely to occur and which state could best protect the proposed conservatee from the abuse, neglect, or exploitation.

(3) The length of time the proposed conservatee was physically present in or was a legal resident of this or another state.

(4) The location of the proposed conservatee's family, friends, and other persons required to be notified of the conservatorship proceeding.

(5) The distance of the proposed conservatee from the court in each state.

(6) The financial circumstances of the estate of the proposed conservatee.

(7) The nature and location of the evidence.

(8) The ability of the court in each state to decide the issue expeditiously and the procedures necessary to present evidence.

(9) The familiarity of the court of each state with the facts and issues in the proceeding.

(10) If an appointment were made, the court's ability to monitor the conduct of the conservator. *(Added by Stats.2014, c. 553 (S.B.940), § 20, eff. Jan. 1, 2015, operative Jan. 1, 2016.)*

Research References

Forms

West's California Code Forms, Probate § 1991–1999 Comment.

§ 1997. Jurisdiction declined by reason of conduct

(a) If at any time a court of this state determines that it acquired jurisdiction to appoint a conservator because of unjustifiable conduct, the court may do any of the following:

(1) Decline to exercise jurisdiction.

(2) Exercise jurisdiction for the limited purpose of fashioning an appropriate remedy to ensure the health, safety, and welfare of the conservatee or proposed conservatee or the protection of the property of the conservatee or proposed conservatee or to prevent a repetition of the unjustifiable conduct, including staying the proceeding until a petition for the appointment of a conservator of the person, conservator of the estate, or conservator of the person and estate is filed in a court of another state having jurisdiction.

(3) Continue to exercise jurisdiction after considering all of the following:

(A) The extent to which the conservatee or proposed conservatee and all persons required to be notified of the proceedings have acquiesced in the exercise of the court's jurisdiction.

(B) Whether it is a more appropriate forum than the court of any other state under the factors set forth in subdivision (c) of Section 1996.

(C) Whether the court of any other state would have jurisdiction under factual circumstances in substantial conformity with the jurisdictional standards of Section 1993.

(b) If a court of this state determines that it acquired jurisdiction to appoint a conservator because a party seeking to invoke its jurisdiction engaged in unjustifiable conduct, it may assess against that party necessary and reasonable expenses, including attorney's fees, investigative fees, court costs, communication expenses, medical examination expenses, witness fees and expenses, and travel expenses. The court may not assess fees, costs, or expenses of any kind against this state or a governmental subdivision, agency, or instrumentality of this state unless authorized by law other than this chapter. *(Added by Stats.2014, c. 553 (S.B.940), § 20, eff. Jan. 1, 2015, operative Jan. 1, 2016.)*

Cross References

Conservatorships, appealable orders, see Probate Code § 1301.5.

Research References

Forms

West's California Code Forms, Probate § 1991–1999 Comment.

§ 1998. Notice of proceeding

If a petition for the appointment of a conservator of the person, conservator of the estate, or conservator of the person and estate is brought in this state and this state was not the home state of the proposed conservatee on the date the petition was filed, in addition to complying with the notice requirements of this state, the petitioner shall give notice of the petition or of a hearing on the petition to those persons who would be entitled to notice of the petition or of a hearing on the petition if a proceeding were brought in the home state of the proposed conservatee. The notice shall be given in the same manner as notice is required to be given in this state. *(Added by Stats.2014, c. 553 (S.B.940), § 20, eff. Jan. 1, 2015, operative Jan. 1, 2016.)*

§ 1999. Proceedings in more than one state

Except for a petition for the appointment of a conservator under paragraph (1) or paragraph (2) of subdivision (a) of Section 1994, if a petition for the appointment of a conservator is filed in this state and in another state and neither petition has been dismissed or withdrawn, the following rules apply:

(a) If the court in this state has jurisdiction under Section 1993, it may proceed with the case unless a court in another state acquires jurisdiction under provisions similar to Section 1993 before the appointment.

(b) If the court in this state does not have jurisdiction under Section 1993, whether at the time the petition is filed or at any time before the appointment, the court shall stay the proceeding and communicate with the court in the other state. If the court in the other state has jurisdiction, the court in this state shall dismiss the petition unless the court in the other state determines that the court in this state is a more appropriate forum. *(Added by Stats.2014, c. 553 (S.B.940), § 20, eff. Jan. 1, 2015, operative Jan. 1, 2016.)*

Research References

Forms

West's California Code Forms, Probate § 1991–1999 Comment.

ARTICLE 3. TRANSFER OF CONSERVATORSHIP

Section
2001. Transfer of conservatorship to another state.
2002. Accepting conservatorship transferred from another state.
2003. Transfer involving court of California tribe.

Cross References

Appointment of conservator for absentee, procedure, see Probate Code § 1840.

Powers and duties of guardian or conservator of the person, residence of ward or conservatee, see Probate Code § 2352.

Proof of status of proposed conservatee, attendance at hearing not required, see Probate Code § 1844.
Removal of property of nonresident, petition not required for conservatorship transferred pursuant to this Article, see Probate Code § 3800.
Special provisions applicable where proposed conservatee is a missing person,
  Appointment of conservator, see Probate Code § 1845.
  Appointment of conservator, acts not required, see Probate Code § 1848.
  Appointment of conservator, conditions, see Probate Code § 1849.
  Contents of petition for conservatorship of missing person's estate, see Probate Code § 1846.

§ 2001. Transfer of conservatorship to another state

(a) A conservator appointed in this state may petition the court to transfer the conservatorship to another state.

(b) The petitioner shall give notice of a hearing on a petition under subdivision (a) to the persons that would be entitled to notice of a hearing on a petition in this state for the appointment of a conservator.

(c) The court shall hold a hearing on a petition filed pursuant to subdivision (a).

(d) The court shall issue an order provisionally granting a petition to transfer a conservatorship of the person, and shall direct the conservator of the person to petition for acceptance of the conservatorship in the other state, if the court is satisfied that the conservatorship will be accepted by the court in the other state and the court finds all of the following:

(1) The conservatee is physically present in or is reasonably expected to move permanently to the other state.

(2) An objection to the transfer has not been made or, if an objection has been made, the court determines that the transfer would not be contrary to the interests of the conservatee.

(3) Plans for care and services for the conservatee in the other state are reasonable and sufficient.

(e) The court shall issue a provisional order granting a petition to transfer a conservatorship of the estate, and shall direct the conservator of the estate to petition for acceptance of the conservatorship in the other state, if the court is satisfied that the conservatorship will be accepted by the court of the other state and the court finds all of the following:

(1) The conservatee is physically present in or is reasonably expected to move permanently to the other state, or the conservatee has a significant connection to the other state considering the factors in subdivision (b) of Section 1991.

(2) An objection to the transfer has not been made or, if an objection has been made, the court determines that the transfer would not be contrary to the interests of the conservatee.

(3) Adequate arrangements will be made for management of the conservatee's property.

(f) The court shall issue a provisional order granting a petition to transfer a conservatorship of the person and estate, and shall direct the conservator to petition for acceptance of the conservatorship in the other state, if the requirements of subdivision (d) and the requirements of subdivision (e) are both satisfied.

(g) The court shall issue a final order confirming the transfer and terminating the conservatorship upon its receipt of both of the following:

(1) A provisional order accepting the proceeding from the court to which the proceeding is to be transferred which is issued under provisions similar to Section 2002.

(2) The documents required to terminate a conservatorship in this state, including, but not limited to, any required accounting. *(Added by Stats.2014, c. 553 (S.B.940), § 20, eff. Jan. 1, 2015, operative Jan. 1, 2016.)*

Cross References

Conservatorships, appealable orders, see Probate Code § 1301.5.
Oath and bond, necessity before appointment, see Probate Code § 2300.

Research References

Forms

West's California Code Forms, Probate § 2001 Form 1, Transfer of Conservatorship of the Person to Another State—Judicial Council Form GC-363.
West's California Code Forms, Probate § 2001 Form 2, Provisional Order for Transfer.
West's California Code Forms, Probate § 2001 Form 3, Transfer of Conservatorship of the Person and Estate to Another State.
West's California Judicial Council Forms GC-363, Petition to Transfer Orders (California Conservatorship Jurisdiction Act).
West's California Judicial Council Forms GC-364, Provisional Order for Transfer (California Conservatorship Jurisdiction Act).
West's California Judicial Council Forms GC-365, Final Order Confirming Transfer (California Conservatorship Jurisdiction Act).

§ 2002. Accepting conservatorship transferred from another state

(a)(1) To confirm transfer of a conservatorship transferred to this state under provisions similar to Section 2001, the conservator shall petition the court in this state to accept the conservatorship.

(2) The petition shall include a certified copy of the other state's provisional order of transfer.

(3) On the first page of the petition, the petitioner shall state that the conservatorship does not fall within the limitations of Section 1981. The body of the petition shall allege facts showing that this chapter applies and the requirements for transfer of the conservatorship are satisfied.

(4) The petition shall specify any modifications necessary to conform the conservatorship to the law of this state, and the terms of a proposed final order accepting the conservatorship.

(5) A petition for the appointment of a temporary conservator under Section 1994 and Chapter 3 (commencing with Section 2250) of Part 4 may be filed while a petition under this section is pending. The petition for the appointment of a temporary conservator shall request the appointment of a temporary conservator eligible for appointment in this state, and shall be limited to powers authorized for a temporary conservator in this state. For purposes of Chapter 3 (commencing with Section 2250) of Part 4, the court shall treat a petition under this section as the equivalent of a petition for a general conservatorship.

(b) The petitioner shall give notice of a hearing on a petition under subdivision (a) to those persons that would be entitled to notice if the petition were a petition for the appointment of a conservator in both the transferring state and this state. The petitioner shall also give notice to any attorney of record for the conservatee in the transferring state and to any attorney appointed or appearing for the conservatee in this state. The petitioner shall give the notice in the same manner that notice of a petition for the appointment of a conservator is required to be given in this state, except that notice to the conservatee shall be given by mailing the petition instead of by personal service of a citation.

(c) Any person entitled to notice under subdivision (b) may object to the petition on one or more of the following grounds:

(1) Transfer of the proceeding would be contrary to the interests of the conservatee.

(2) Under the law of the transferring state, the conservator is ineligible for appointment in this state.

(3) Under the law of this state, the conservator is ineligible for appointment in this state, and the transfer petition does not identify a replacement who is willing and eligible to serve in this state.

(4) This chapter is inapplicable under Section 1981.

(d) Promptly after the filing of a petition under subdivision (a), the court shall appoint an investigator under Section 1454. The investigator shall promptly commence a preliminary investigation of the conservatorship, which focuses on the matters described in subdivision (f).

(e) The court shall hold a hearing on a petition filed pursuant to subdivision (a).

(f) The court shall issue an order provisionally granting a petition filed under subdivision (a) unless any of the following occurs:

(1) The court determines that transfer of the proceeding would be contrary to the interests of the conservatee.

(2) The court determines that, under the law of the transferring state, the conservator is ineligible for appointment in this state.

(3) The court determines that, under the law of this state, the conservator is ineligible for appointment in this state, and the transfer petition does not identify a replacement who is willing and eligible to serve in this state.

(4) The court determines that this chapter is inapplicable under Section 1981.

(g) If the court issues an order provisionally granting the petition, the investigator shall promptly commence an investigation under Section 1851.1.

(h)(1) Not later than 60 days after issuance of an order provisionally granting the petition, the court shall determine whether the conservatorship needs to be modified to conform to the law of this state. The court may take any action necessary to achieve compliance with the law of this state, including, but not limited to, striking or modifying any conservator powers that are not permitted under the law of this state.

(2) At the same time that it makes the determination required by paragraph (1), the court shall review the conservatorship as provided in Section 1851.1.

(3) The conformity determination and the review required by this subdivision shall occur at a hearing, which shall be noticed as provided in subdivision (b).

(i)(1) The court shall issue a final order accepting the proceeding and appointing the conservator in this state upon completion of the conformity determination and review required by subdivision (h), or upon its receipt from the court from which the proceeding is being transferred of a final order issued under provisions similar to Section 2001 transferring the proceeding to this state, whichever occurs later. In appointing a conservator under this paragraph, the court shall comply with Section 1830.

(2) A transfer to this state does not become effective unless and until the court issues a final order under paragraph (1). A conservator may not take action in this state pursuant to a transfer petition unless and until the transfer becomes effective and all of the following steps have occurred:

(A) The conservator has taken an oath in accordance with Section 2300.

(B) The conservator has filed the required bond, if any.

(C) The court has provided the information required by Section 1835 to the conservator.

(D) The conservator has filed an acknowledgment of receipt as required by Section 1834.

(E) The clerk of the court has issued the letters of conservatorship.

(3) Paragraph (2) does not preclude a person who has been appointed as a temporary conservator pursuant to Chapter 3 (commencing with Section 2250) from taking action in this state pursuant to the order establishing the temporary conservatorship.

(4) When a transfer to this state becomes effective, the conservatorship is subject to the law of this state and shall thereafter be treated as a conservatorship under the law of this state. If a law of this state, including, but not limited to, Section 2356.5, mandates compliance with special requirements to exercise a particular conservatorship power or take a particular step, the conservator of a transferred conservatorship may not exercise that power or take that step without first complying with those special requirements.

(j) Except as otherwise provided by Section 1851.1, Chapter 3 (commencing with Section 1860), Chapter 9 (commencing with Section 2650) of Part 4, and other law, when the court grants a petition under this section, the court shall recognize a conservatorship order from the other state, including the determination of the conservatee's incapacity and the appointment of the conservator.

(k) The denial by a court of this state of a petition to accept a conservatorship transferred from another state does not affect the ability of the conservator to seek appointment as conservator in this state under Chapter 1 (commencing with Section 1800) of Part 3 if the court has jurisdiction to make an appointment other than by reason of the provisional order of transfer. *(Added by Stats.2014, c. 553 (S.B.940), § 20, eff. Jan. 1, 2015, operative Jan. 1, 2016.)*

Cross References

Capacity to give informed consent for medical treatment, inclusion in transfer petition, see Probate Code § 1890.
Citation to proposed conservatee not required, notice to absentee conservatee not required, see Probate Code § 1843.
Conservatorships, appealable orders, see Probate Code § 1301.5.
Establishment of conservatorship,
    Notice of hearing, see Probate Code § 1842.
    Petition, additional contents, see Probate Code § 1841.
Oath and bond, necessity before appointment, see Probate Code § 2300.
Petitions for instructions, or grant of power or authority, persons authorized to file, see Probate Code § 1455.
Special provisions applicable where proposed conservatee is a missing person, Appointment of conservator, acts not required, see Probate Code § 1848.
Notice, petition for appointment of conservator, see Probate Code § 1847.
Transfer of conservatorship to state, investigation and report, duties of investigator, see Probate Code § 1851.1.

Research References

Forms

West's California Judicial Council Forms GC–366, Petition for Orders Accepting Transfer (California Conservatorship Jurisdiction Act).
West's California Judicial Council Forms GC–367, Provisional Order Accepting Transfer (California Conservatorship Jurisdiction Act).
West's California Judicial Council Forms GC–368, Final Order Accepting Transfer (California Conservatorship Jurisdiction Act).

§ 2003. Transfer involving court of California tribe

If a conservatorship is transferred under this article from a court of this state to the court of a California tribe or from the court of a California tribe to a court of this state, the order that provisionally grants the transfer may expressly provide that specified powers of the conservator will not be transferred. Jurisdiction over the specified powers will be retained by the transferring state and will not be included in the powers that are granted to the conservator in the state that accepts the transfer. *(Added by Stats.2014, c. 553 (S.B.940), § 20, eff. Jan. 1, 2015, operative Jan. 1, 2016.)*

ARTICLE 4. REGISTRATION AND RECOGNITION OF ORDERS FROM OTHER STATES

Section	
2011.	Registration of order of conservatorship of person.
2012.	Registration of order of conservatorship of estate.
2013.	Registration of order of conservatorship of person and estate.
2014.	Notice of intent to register conservatorship.
2015.	Court to provide written information to conservator regarding rights, duties, etc.
2016.	Effect of registration.

Section

2017. Third parties; actions in good faith reliance on conservatorship order.
2018. Recording copies of registration documents; reasonable fee.
2019. Registration of California tribal orders.

Cross References

Conservatorships, appealable orders, see Probate Code § 1301.5.
Fee for registering conservatorship, see Government Code § 70663.
Powers and duties of guardian or conservator of the person, court approval of transaction or matter, provisions inapplicable to this Article, see Probate Code § 2505.

§ 2011. Registration of order of conservatorship of person

If a conservator of the person has been appointed in another state and a petition for the appointment of a conservator of the person is not pending in this state, the conservator of the person appointed in the other state, after providing notice pursuant to Section 2014, may register the conservatorship order in this state by filing certified copies of the order and letters of office, and proof of notice as required herein, together with a cover sheet approved by the Judicial Council, in the superior court of any appropriate county of this state. *(Added by Stats.2014, c. 553 (S.B.940), § 20, eff. Jan. 1, 2015, operative Jan. 1, 2016.)*

Research References

Forms

West's California Code Forms, Probate § 2011-2013 Form 1, Conservatorship Registration Cover Sheet and Attestation of Conservatee's Non Residence in California.

West's California Code Forms, Probate § 2356.5 Form 1, Attachment Requesting Special Orders Regarding Dementia—Judicial Council Form GC-313.

West's California Judicial Council Forms GC-360, Conservatorship Registration Cover Sheet and Attestation of Conservatee's Non-Residence in California.

§ 2012. Registration of order of conservatorship of estate

If a conservator of the estate has been appointed in another state and a petition for a conservatorship of the estate is not pending in this state, the conservator appointed in the other state, after providing notice pursuant to Section 2014, may register the conservatorship order in this state by filing certified copies of the order and letters of office and of any bond, and proof of notice as required herein, together with a cover sheet approved by the Judicial Council, in the superior court of any county of this state in which property belonging to the conservatee is located. *(Added by Stats.2014, c. 553 (S.B.940), § 20, eff. Jan. 1, 2015, operative Jan. 1, 2016.)*

§ 2013. Registration of order of conservatorship of person and estate

If a conservator of the person and estate has been appointed in another state and a petition for a conservatorship of the person, conservatorship of the estate, or conservatorship of the person and estate is not pending in this state, the conservator appointed in the other state, after providing notice pursuant to Section 2014, may register the conservatorship order in this state by filing certified copies of the order and letters of office and of any bond, and proof of notice as required herein, together with a cover sheet approved by the Judicial Council, in the superior court of any appropriate county of this state. *(Added by Stats.2014, c. 553 (S.B.940), § 20, eff. Jan. 1, 2015, operative Jan. 1, 2016.)*

Research References

Forms

West's California Judicial Council Forms GC-360, Conservatorship Registration Cover Sheet and Attestation of Conservatee's Non-Residence in California.

§ 2014. Notice of intent to register conservatorship

(a) At least 15 days before registering a conservatorship in this state, the conservator shall provide notice of an intent to register to all of the following:

(1) The court supervising the conservatorship.

(2) Every person who would be entitled to notice of a petition for the appointment of a conservator in the state where the conservatorship is being supervised.

(3) Every person who would be entitled to notice of a petition for the appointment of a conservator in this state.

(b) Each notice provided pursuant to subdivision (a) shall comply with all of the following:

(1) The notice shall prominently state that when a conservator acts pursuant to this article, the conservator is subject to the law of this state governing the action, including, but not limited to, all applicable procedures, and is not authorized to take any action prohibited by the law of this state.

(2) The notice shall explain that if a conservatorship is registered pursuant to this article, and the conservator later proposes to take a specific action pursuant to this article, which, under the law of this state, requires court approval or other action in court, the conservator will be required to notify the recipient of the request for court approval or other court action, and the recipient will have an opportunity to object or otherwise participate at that time, in the same manner as other persons are entitled to object or otherwise participate under the law of this state.

(3) The notice shall advise the recipient that information about a conservator's rights, duties, limitations, and responsibilities under the law of this state is available, free of charge, on an Internet Web site maintained by the Judicial Council. The notice shall explain specifically how to locate that information on the Judicial Council's Internet Web site.

(c) Except as provided in subdivision (c) of Section 2023, each notice provided pursuant to subdivision (a) shall also prominently state that the registration is effective only while the conservatee resides in another jurisdiction and does not authorize the conservator to take any action while the conservatee is residing in this state. *(Added by Stats.2014, c. 553 (S.B.940), § 20, eff. Jan. 1, 2015, operative Jan. 1, 2016.)*

Research References

Forms

West's California Judicial Council Forms GC-361, Notice of Intent to Register Conservatorship.

§ 2015. Court to provide written information to conservator regarding rights, duties, etc.

Upon registration of a conservatorship pursuant to this article, the court shall provide the conservator with written information concerning a conservator's rights, duties, limitations, and responsibilities in this state, as specified in Section 1835. To cover the costs of providing that information, a court may charge the conservator the fee specified in Section 1835, which shall be distributed as specified in that section. The conservator shall file an acknowledgment of receipt of the written information, on a form prescribed by the Judicial Council. *(Added by Stats.2014, c. 553 (S.B.940), § 20, eff. Jan. 1, 2015, operative Jan. 1, 2016.)*

Research References

Forms

West's California Judicial Council Forms GC-362, Conservatorship Registrant'S Acknowledgment of Receipt of Handbook for Conservators.

§ 2016. Effect of registration

(a) Upon registration of a conservatorship order from another state and the filing by the conservator of an acknowledgment of receipt of the written information required by Section 2015, the conservator may, while the conservatee resides out of this state, exercise in any county of this state all powers authorized in the order of appointment except as prohibited under the laws of this state, including maintaining actions and proceedings in this state and, if the conservator is not a resident of this state, subject to any conditions imposed upon nonresident parties. When acting pursuant to registration, the conservator is subject to the law of this state governing the action, including, but not limited to, all applicable procedures, and is not authorized to take any action prohibited by the law of this state. If a law of this state, including, but not limited to, Section 2352, 2352.5, 2355, 2356.5, 2540, 2543, 2545, or 2591.5, or Article 2 (commencing with Section 1880) of Chapter 4 of Part 4, mandates compliance with special requirements to exercise a particular conservatorship power or take a particular step, the conservator of a registered conservatorship may not exercise that power or take that step without first complying with those special requirements.

(b)(1) When subdivision (a) requires a conservator to comply with a law of this state that makes it necessary to obtain court approval or take other action in court, the conservator shall seek that approval or proceed as needed in an appropriate court of this state. In handling the matter, that court shall communicate and cooperate with the court that is supervising the conservatorship, in accordance with Sections 1984 and 1985.

(2) In addition to providing any other notice required by law, the conservator shall provide notice of a court proceeding under paragraph (1) to all of the following:

(A) The court supervising the conservatorship.

(B) Every person who would be entitled to notice of a petition for the appointment of a conservator in the state where the conservatorship is being supervised.

(C) Every person who would be entitled to notice of a petition for the appointment of a conservator in this state.

(3) Any person entitled to notice under paragraph (2) may raise an objection or otherwise participate in the proceeding in the same manner as other persons are allowed to do under the law of this state.

(c) Subdivision (a) applies only when the conservatee resides out of this state. When the conservatee resides in this state, a conservator may not exercise any powers pursuant to a registration under this article.

(d) A court of this state may grant any relief available under this chapter and other law of this state to enforce a registered order. *(Added by Stats.2014, c. 553 (S.B.940), § 20, eff. Jan. 1, 2015, operative Jan. 1, 2016.)*

Research References
Forms

West's California Code Forms, Probate § 2356.5 Form 1, Attachment Requesting Special Orders Regarding Dementia—Judicial Council Form GC-313.

§ 2017. Third parties; actions in good faith reliance on conservatorship order

(a) A third person who acts in good faith reliance on a conservatorship order registered under this article is not liable to any person for so acting if all of the following requirements are satisfied:

(1) The conservator presents to the third person a file-stamped copy of the registration documents required by Section 2011, 2012, or 2013, including, but not limited to, the certified copy of the conservatorship order.

(2) Each of the registration documents, including, but not limited to, the conservatorship order and the file-stamped cover sheet, appears on its face to be valid.

(3) The conservator presents to the third person a form approved by the Judicial Council, in which the conservator attests that the conservatee does not reside in this state and the conservator promises to promptly notify the third person if the conservatee becomes a resident of this state. The form shall also prominently state that the registration is effective only while the conservatee resides in another jurisdiction and does not authorize the conservator to take any action while the conservatee is residing in this state.

(4) The third person has not received any actual notice that the conservatee is residing in this state.

(b) Nothing in this section is intended to create an implication that a third person is liable for acting in reliance on a conservatorship order registered under this article under circumstances where the requirements of subdivision (a) are not satisfied. Nothing in this section affects any immunity that may otherwise exist apart from this section. *(Added by Stats.2014, c. 553 (S.B.940), § 20, eff. Jan. 1, 2015, operative Jan. 1, 2016.)*

Research References
Forms

West's California Judicial Council Forms GC-360, Conservatorship Registration Cover Sheet and Attestation of Conservatee's Non-Residence in California.

§ 2018. Recording copies of registration documents; reasonable fee

(a) A file-stamped copy of the registration documents required by Section 2011, 2012, or 2013 may be recorded in the office of any county recorder in this state.

(b) A county recorder may charge a reasonable fee for recordation under subdivision (a). *(Added by Stats.2014, c. 553 (S.B.940), § 20, eff. Jan. 1, 2015, operative Jan. 1, 2016.)*

§ 2019. Registration of California tribal orders

Notwithstanding any other provision of this article:

(a) A conservatorship order of a court of a California tribe can be registered under Section 2011, 2012, or 2013, regardless of whether the conservatee resides in California.

(b) The effect of a conservatorship order of a court of a California tribe that is registered under Section 2011, 2012, or 2013 is not contingent on whether the conservatee resides in California.

(c) Paragraphs (3) and (4) of subdivision (a) of Section 2017 do not apply to a conservatorship order of a court of a California tribe. *(Added by Stats.2014, c. 553 (S.B.940), § 20, eff. Jan. 1, 2015, operative Jan. 1, 2016.)*

ARTICLE 5. MISCELLANEOUS PROVISIONS

Section
2021. Uniformity of application and construction.
2022. Relation to Electronic Signatures in Global and National Commerce Act.
2023. Development of court rules and forms.
2024. Transitional provisions.

§ 2021. Uniformity of application and construction

In applying and construing this uniform act, consideration shall be given to the need to promote uniformity of the law with respect to its subject matter among states that enact it, consistent with the need to protect individual civil rights and in accordance with due process. *(Added by Stats.2014, c. 553 (S.B.940), § 20, eff. Jan. 1, 2015, operative Jan. 1, 2016.)*

§ 2022. Relation to Electronic Signatures in Global and National Commerce Act

This chapter modifies, limits, and supersedes the federal Electronic Signatures in Global and National Commerce Act (Title 15 (commencing with Section 7001) of the United States Code), but does not

§ 2022

modify, limit, or supersede subdivision (c) of Section 101 of that act, which is codified as subdivision (c) of Section 7001 of Title 15 of the United States Code, or authorize electronic delivery of any of the notices described in subdivision (b) of Section 103 of that act, which is codified as subdivision (b) of Section 7003 of Title 15 of the United States Code. *(Added by Stats.2014, c. 553 (S.B.940), § 20, eff. Jan. 1, 2015, operative Jan. 1, 2016.)*

§ 2023. Development of court rules and forms

(a) On or before January 1, 2016, the Judicial Council shall develop court rules and forms as necessary for the implementation of this chapter.

(b) The materials developed pursuant to this section shall include, but not be limited to, all of the following:

(1) A cover sheet for registration of a conservatorship under Section 2011, 2012, or 2013. The cover sheet shall explain that a proceeding may not be registered under Section 2011, 2012, or 2013 if the proceeding relates to a minor. The cover sheet shall further explain that a proceeding in which a person is subjected to involuntary mental health care may not be registered under Section 2011, 2012, or 2013. The cover sheet shall require the conservator to initial each of these explanations. The cover sheet shall also prominently state that when a conservator acts pursuant to registration, the conservator is subject to the law of this state governing the action, including, but not limited to, all applicable procedures, and is not authorized to take any action prohibited by the law of this state. Except as provided in subdivision (c), the cover sheet shall also prominently state that the registration is effective only while the conservatee resides in another jurisdiction and does not authorize the conservator to take any action while the conservatee is residing in this state. Directly beneath these statements, the cover sheet shall include a signature box in which the conservator attests to these matters.

(2) The form required by paragraph (3) of subdivision (a) of Section 2017. If the Judicial Council deems it advisable, this form may be included in the civil cover sheet developed under paragraph (1).

(3) A form for providing notice of intent to register a proceeding under Section 2011, 2012, or 2013.

(4) A form for a conservator to acknowledge receipt of the written information required by Section 2015.

(c) The materials prepared pursuant to this section shall be consistent with Section 2019. *(Added by Stats.2014, c. 553 (S.B.940), § 20, eff. Jan. 1, 2015, operative Jan. 1, 2015.)*

Research References

Forms

West's California Judicial Council Forms GC–360, Conservatorship Registration Cover Sheet and Attestation of Conservatee's Non-Residence in California.

West's California Judicial Council Forms GC–362, Conservatorship Registrant'S Acknowledgment of Receipt of Handbook for Conservators.

§ 2024. Transitional provisions

(a) This chapter applies to conservatorship proceedings begun on or after January 1, 2016.

(b) Articles 1, 3, and 4 and Sections 2021 and 2022 apply to proceedings begun before January 1, 2016, regardless of whether a conservatorship order has been issued. *(Added by Stats.2014, c. 553 (S.B.940), § 20, eff. Jan. 1, 2015, operative Jan. 1, 2016.)*

ARTICLE 6. FEDERALLY RECOGNIZED INDIAN TRIBE

Section
2031. Definitions.
2032. Application of Article 2.
2033. Proposed conservatees who are tribal members; dismissal of petition; factors considered.

§ 2031. Definitions

For the purposes of this chapter:

(a) "California tribe" means an Indian tribe with jurisdiction that has tribal land located in California.

(b) "Indian tribe with jurisdiction" means a federally recognized Indian tribe that has a court system that exercises jurisdiction over proceedings that are substantially equivalent to conservatorship proceedings.

(c) "Tribal land" means land that is, with respect to a specific Indian tribe and the members of that tribe, "Indian country" as defined in Section 1151 of Title 18 of the United States Code. *(Added by Stats.2014, c. 553 (S.B.940), § 20, eff. Jan. 1, 2015, operative Jan. 1, 2016.)*

§ 2032. Application of Article 2

Article 2 (commencing with Section 1991) does not apply to a proposed conservatee who is a member of an Indian tribe with jurisdiction. *(Added by Stats.2014, c. 553 (S.B.940), § 20, eff. Jan. 1, 2015, operative Jan. 1, 2016.)*

§ 2033. Proposed conservatees who are tribal members; dismissal of petition; factors considered

(a) If a petition for the appointment of a conservator has been filed in a court of this state and a conservator has not yet been appointed, any person entitled to notice of a hearing on the petition may move to dismiss the petition on the grounds that the proposed conservatee is a member of an Indian tribe with jurisdiction. The petition shall state the name of the Indian tribe.

(b) If, after communicating with the named tribe, the court of this state finds that the proposed conservatee is a member of an Indian tribe with jurisdiction, it may grant the motion to dismiss if it finds that there is good cause to do so. If the motion is granted, the court may impose any condition the court considers just and proper, including the condition that a petition for the appointment of a conservator be filed promptly in the tribal court.

(c) In determining whether there is good cause to grant the motion, the court may consider all relevant factors, including, but not limited to, the following:

(1) Any expressed preference of the proposed conservatee.

(2) Whether abuse, neglect, or exploitation of the proposed conservatee has occurred or is likely to occur and which state could best protect the proposed conservatee from the abuse, neglect, or exploitation.

(3) The length of time the proposed conservatee was physically present in or was a legal resident of this or another state.

(4) The location of the proposed conservatee's family, friends, and other persons required to be notified of the conservatorship proceeding.

(5) The distance of the proposed conservatee from the court in each state.

(6) The financial circumstances of the estate of the proposed conservatee.

(7) The nature and location of the evidence.

(8) The ability of the court in each state to decide the issue expeditiously and the procedures necessary to present evidence.

(9) The familiarity of the court of each state with the facts and issues in the proceeding.

(10) If an appointment were made, the court's ability to monitor the conduct of the conservator.

(11) The timing of the motion, taking into account the parties' and court's expenditure of time and resources.

(d) Notwithstanding subdivision (b), the court shall not grant a motion to dismiss pursuant to this section if the tribal court expressly declines to exercise its jurisdiction with regard to the proposed conservatee. *(Added by Stats.2014, c. 553 (S.B.940), § 20, eff. Jan. 1, 2015, operative Jan. 1, 2016.)*

Part 4

PROVISIONS COMMON TO GUARDIANSHIP AND CONSERVATORSHIP

Cross References

Freedom from parental custody and control, stay of proceedings and effect upon jurisdiction under these provisions, see Family Code § 7807.
Juvenile court law, guardianships resulting from selection or implementation of a permanent plan, see Welfare and Institutions Code § 366.4.
Termination of parental rights of father, filing of petition, stay of proceedings affecting a child pending final determination of parental rights, see Family Code § 7662.

CHAPTER 1. GENERAL PROVISIONS

Section
2100. Law governing.
2101. Fiduciary relationship; trust law.
2102. Control by court.
2103. Final judgment or order.
2104. Nonprofit charitable corporation; appointment.
2104.1. Non-profit charitable corporation not incorporated in California; appointment; requirements.
2105. Joint guardians or conservators; appointment.
2105.5. Multiple guardians or conservators; liability for breach of another guardian or conservator.
2106. One guardian or conservator for several wards or conservatees; appointment.
2107. Person or estate of nonresident; guardian or conservator; powers and duties.
2108. Powers granted guardian nominated by will.
2109. Guardian for particular property; powers and duties.
2110. Personal liability.
2111. Transaction.
2111.5. Court official's or employee's with responsibilities related to guardians or conservators; prohibitions against purchasing, leasing, or renting property from estate.
2112. Conservatee abuse; penalty; report.
2113. Balance of conflicting interests; preferences of conservatee.

§ 2100. Law governing

Guardianships and conservatorships are governed by Division 3 (commencing with Section 1000), except to the extent otherwise expressly provided by statute, and by this division. If no specific provision of this division is applicable, the provisions applicable to administration of estates of decedents govern so far as they are applicable to like situations. *(Stats.1990, c. 79 (A.B.759), § 14, operative July 1, 1991.)*

Cross References

Estate administration, generally, see Probate Code § 7000 et seq.
Final orders, effect of, see Probate Code § 2103.
Notice, general provisions, see Probate Code § 1200 et seq.
Notice of hearing, see Probate Code § 1460 et seq.
Petitions and other papers, see Probate Code § 1020 et seq.
Special notice to persons requesting, see Probate Code § 2700 et seq.

Trial by jury, see Probate Code § 1452.

Research References
Forms
West's California Judicial Council Forms DE–295, Ex Parte Petition for Final Discharge and Order.
West's California Judicial Council Forms GC–395, Ex Parte Petition for Final Discharge and Order.

§ 2101. Fiduciary relationship; trust law

The relationship of guardian and ward and of conservator and conservatee is a fiduciary relationship that is governed by the law of trusts, except as provided in this division. *(Stats.1990, c. 79 (A.B.759), § 14, operative July 1, 1991. Amended by Stats.1993, c. 293 (A.B.21), § 2.)*

Cross References

Duties of trustees, see Probate Code § 16000 et seq.
Fiduciary, defined, see Probate Code § 39.

§ 2102. Control by court

A guardian or conservator is subject to the regulation and control of the court in the performance of the duties of the office. *(Stats.1990, c. 79 (A.B.759), § 14, operative July 1, 1991.)*

Cross References

Court, defined, see Probate Code § 1418.
Instructions from or confirmation by court, see Probate Code §§ 2359, 2403.

§ 2103. Final judgment or order

(a) When a judgment or order made pursuant to this division becomes final, it releases the guardian or conservator and the sureties from all claims of the ward or conservatee and of any persons affected thereby based upon any act or omission directly authorized, approved, or confirmed in the judgment or order. For the purposes of this section, "order" includes an order settling an account of the guardian or conservator, whether an intermediate or final account.

(b) This section does not apply where the judgment or order is obtained by fraud or conspiracy or by misrepresentation contained in the petition or account or in the judgment or order as to any material fact. For the purposes of this subdivision, misrepresentation includes, but is not limited to, the omission of a material fact. *(Stats.1990, c. 79 (A.B.759), § 14, operative July 1, 1991.)*

Cross References

Appealable orders, see Probate Code § 1300 et seq.
Claims of heirs or devisees, release, see Probate Code § 7250.
Fraud, see Civil Code § 1571 et seq.
Reversal of order appointing guardian or conservator, see Probate Code § 1311.

§ 2104. Nonprofit charitable corporation; appointment

(a) A nonprofit charitable corporation may be appointed as a guardian or conservator of the person or estate, or both, if all of the following requirements are met:

(1) The corporation is incorporated in this state.

(2) The articles of incorporation specifically authorize the corporation to accept appointments as guardian or conservator, as the case may be.

(3) The corporation has been providing, at the time of appointment, care, counseling, or financial assistance to the proposed ward or conservatee under the supervision of a registered social worker certified by the Board of Behavioral Science Examiners of this state.

(b) The petition for appointment of a nonprofit charitable corporation described in this section as a guardian or conservator shall include in the caption the name of a responsible corporate officer who shall act for the corporation for the purposes of this division. If,

§ 2104

for any reason, the officer so named ceases to act as the responsible corporate officer for the purposes of this division, the corporation shall file with the court a notice containing (1) the name of the successor responsible corporate officer and (2) the date the successor becomes the responsible corporate officer.

(c) If a nonprofit charitable corporation described in this section is appointed as a guardian or conservator:

(1) The corporation's compensation as guardian or conservator shall be allowed only for services actually rendered.

(2) Any fee allowed for an attorney for the corporation shall be for services actually rendered. *(Stats.1990, c. 79 (A.B.759), § 14, operative July 1, 1991. Amended by Stats.2001, c. 351 (A.B.479), § 1.)*

Cross References

Attorney's fees and costs, generally, see Code of Civil Procedure § 1021.
Board of Behavioral Sciences, see Business and Professions Code § 4990.
Compensation of guardian, conservator, and attorney, see Probate Code § 2640 et seq.

Research References

Forms

1 California Transactions Forms--Estate Planning § 6:16, Guardian of Person.
West's California Code Forms, Probate § 1820 Form 1, Attachment Requesting Special Orders Regarding a Major Neurocognitive Disorder.
West's California Judicial Council Forms GC–314, Confidential Conservator Screening Form.

§ 2104.1. Non-profit charitable corporation not incorporated in California; appointment; requirements

A nonprofit charitable corporation not incorporated in this state may be appointed as the guardian of a minor if all of the following requirements are met:

(a) The articles of incorporation specifically authorize the non-profit charitable corporation to accept appointments as a guardian.

(b) The nonprofit charitable corporation is contracted by the federal Department of Health and Human Services, Office of Refugee Resettlement, or its successor federal government entity, to provide care and custody of the minor.

(c) The petition for guardianship is filed in connection with a petition to make the necessary findings regarding special immigrant juvenile status pursuant to subdivision (b) of Section 155 of the Code of Civil Procedure.

(d) The nonprofit charitable corporation is licensed by this state to provide care for minors.

(e) The nonprofit charitable corporation complies with all of the requirements of Section 2104, except for paragraphs (1) and (2) of subdivision (a) of Section 2104. *(Added by Stats.2018, c. 103 (A.B.2642), § 2, eff. Jan. 1, 2019. Amended by Stats.2021, c. 528 (A.B.829), § 2, eff. Jan. 1, 2022.)*

§ 2105. Joint guardians or conservators; appointment

(a) The court, in its discretion, may appoint for a ward or conservatee:

(1) Two or more joint guardians or conservators of the person.

(2) Two or more joint guardians or conservators of the estate.

(3) Two or more joint guardians or conservators of the person and estate.

(b) When joint guardians or conservators are appointed, each shall qualify in the same manner as a sole guardian or conservator.

(c) Subject to subdivisions (d) and (e):

(1) Where there are two guardians or conservators, both must concur to exercise a power.

(2) Where there are more than two guardians or conservators, a majority must concur to exercise a power.

(d) If one of the joint guardians or conservators dies or is removed or resigns, the powers and duties continue in the remaining joint guardians or conservators until further appointment is made by the court.

(e) Where joint guardians or conservators have been appointed and one or more are (1) absent from the state and unable to act, (2) otherwise unable to act, or (3) legally disqualified from serving, the court may, by order made with or without notice, authorize the remaining joint guardians or conservators to act as to all matters embraced within its order.

(f) If a custodial parent has been diagnosed as having a terminal condition, as evidenced by a declaration executed by a licensed physician, the court, in its discretion, may appoint the custodial parent and a person nominated by the custodial parent as joint guardians of the person of the minor. However, this appointment shall not be made over the objection of a noncustodial parent without a finding that the noncustodial parent's custody would be detrimental to the minor, as provided in Section 3041 of the Family Code. It is the intent of the Legislature in enacting the amendments to this subdivision adopted during the 1995–96 Regular Session for a parent with a terminal condition to be able to make arrangements for the joint care, custody, and control of his or her minor children so as to minimize the emotional stress of, and disruption for, the minor children whenever the parent is incapacitated or upon the parent's death, and to avoid the need to provide a temporary guardian or place the minor children in foster care, pending appointment of a guardian, as might otherwise be required.

"Terminal condition," for purposes of this subdivision, means an incurable and irreversible condition that, without the administration of life-sustaining treatment, will, within reasonable medical judgment, result in death. *(Stats.1990, c. 79 (A.B.759), § 14, operative July 1, 1991. Amended by Stats.1993, c. 978 (S.B.305), § 2; Stats.1995, c. 278 (A.B.1104), § 1; Stats.1999, c. 658 (A.B.891), § 11, operative July 1, 2000.)*

Cross References

Appointment of guardian, parent not to be appointed as guardian of minor except as provided in this section, see Probate Code § 1514.
Guardians and conservators, removal or resignation, see Probate Code § 2650 et seq.
Joint personal representatives, death or disqualification of one or all, see Probate Code §§ 8521, 8522, 9630.
Parent, defined, see Probate Code § 54.
Personal representatives, breach of fiduciary duty committed by another representative, see Probate Code § 9631.
Powers and duties, see Probate Code § 2350 et seq.
Removal or resignation, see Probate Code § 2650 et seq.
Temporary guardians and conservators, generally, see Probate Code § 2250 et seq.
Termination of guardianship as affected by death of guardian, see Probate Code § 2632.
Vacancy in office of cotrustee, see Probate Code § 15621.

Research References

Forms

4 California Transactions Forms--Estate Planning § 19:93, Nomination of Guardian.

§ 2105.5. Multiple guardians or conservators; liability for breach of another guardian or conservator

(a) Except as provided in subdivision (b), where there is more than one guardian or conservator of the estate, one guardian or conservator is not liable for a breach of fiduciary duty committed by another guardian or conservator.

(b) Where there is more than one guardian or conservator of the estate, one guardian or conservator is liable for a breach of fiduciary duty committed by another guardian or conservator of the same estate under any of the following circumstances:

(1) Where the guardian or conservator participates in a breach of fiduciary duty committed by the other guardian or conservator.

(2) Where the guardian or conservator improperly delegates the administration of the estate to the other guardian or conservator.

(3) Where the guardian or conservator approves, knowingly acquiesces in, or conceals a breach of fiduciary duty committed by the other guardian or conservator.

(4) Where the guardian or conservator negligently enables the other guardian or conservator to commit a breach of fiduciary duty.

(5) Where the guardian or conservator knows or has information from which the guardian or conservator reasonably should have known of the breach of fiduciary duty by the other guardian or conservator and fails to take reasonable steps to compel the other guardian or conservator to redress the breach.

(c) The liability of a guardian or conservator for a breach of fiduciary duty committed by another guardian or conservator that occurred before July 1, 1988, is governed by prior law and not by this section. *(Stats.1990, c. 79 (A.B.759), § 14, operative July 1, 1991.)*

Cross References

Fiduciary, defined, see Probate Code § 39.

§ 2106. One guardian or conservator for several wards or conservatees; appointment

(a) The court, in its discretion, may appoint one guardian or conservator for several wards or conservatees.

(b) The appointment of one guardian or conservator for several wards or conservatees may be requested in the initial petition filed in the proceeding or may be requested subsequently upon a petition filed in the same proceeding and noticed and heard with respect to the newly proposed ward or conservatee in the same manner as an initial petition for appointment of a guardian or conservator. *(Stats.1990, c. 79 (A.B.759), § 14, operative July 1, 1991.)*

§ 2107. Person or estate of nonresident; guardian or conservator; powers and duties

(a) Unless limited by court order, when a court of this state appoints a guardian or conservator of the person of a nonresident, the appointee has the same powers and duties as a guardian or conservator of the person of a resident while the nonresident is in this state.

(b) When a court of this state appoints a guardian or conservator of the estate of a nonresident, the appointee has, with respect to the property of the nonresident within this state, the same powers and duties as a guardian or conservator of the estate of a resident. The responsibility of such a guardian or conservator with regard to inventory, accounting, and disposal of the estate is confined to the property that comes into the hands of the guardian or conservator in this state. *(Stats.1990, c. 79 (A.B.759), § 14, operative July 1, 1991. Amended by Stats.2014, c. 553 (S.B.940), § 21, eff. Jan. 1, 2015, operative Jan. 1, 2016.)*

Cross References

Inventory and accounts, see Probate Code § 2600 et seq.
Powers and duties of guardian or conservator, see Probate Code § 2350 et seq.

§ 2108. Powers granted guardian nominated by will

(a) Except to the extent the court for good cause determines otherwise, if a guardian of the person is nominated as provided in Article 1 (commencing with Section 1500) of Chapter 1 of Part 2 and is appointed by the court, the guardian shall be granted in the order of appointment, to the extent provided in the nomination, the same authority with respect to the person of the ward as a parent having legal custody of a child and may exercise such authority without notice, hearing, or court authorization, instructions, approval, or confirmation in the same manner as if such authority were exercised by a parent having legal custody of a child.

(b) Except to the extent the court for good cause determines otherwise and subject to Sections 2593, 2594, and 2595, if a guardian of the estate is nominated under Section 1500 or a guardian for property is nominated under Section 1501 and the guardian is appointed by the court, the guardian shall be granted in the order of appointment, to the extent provided in the nomination, the right to exercise any one or more of the powers listed in Section 2591 without notice, hearing, or court authorization, instructions, approval, or confirmation in the same manner as if such authority were granted by order of the court under Section 2590. In the case of a guardian nominated under Section 1501, such additional authority shall be limited to the property covered by the nomination.

(c) The terms of any order made under this section shall be included in the letters. *(Stats.1990, c. 79 (A.B.759), § 14, operative July 1, 1991.)*

Cross References

Bond of nominated guardian, see Probate Code § 2324.
Child, defined, see Probate Code § 26.
Custody of minors, see Family Code § 3020 et seq.
Letters, defined, see Probate Code § 52.

Research References

Forms

1 California Transactions Forms--Estate Planning § 6:16, Guardian of Person.
1 California Transactions Forms--Estate Planning § 6:17, Guardian of Estate or of Property.
1 California Transactions Forms--Estate Planning § 6:73, Appointment of Guardian of Person of Minor Child and Statement of Desire that Same Person be Appointed Guardian of Minor's Estate.
1 California Transactions Forms--Estate Planning § 6:74, Appointment of Guardian of Person and Estate of Minor Children.
4 California Transactions Forms--Estate Planning § 19:93, Nomination of Guardian.
4 California Transactions Forms--Estate Planning § 19:141, Additional Powers Granted to Guardian of Minor's Person [Prob C § 2108(A)].
4 California Transactions Forms--Estate Planning § 19:142, Additional Powers Granted to Guardian of Minor's Estate [Prob C § 2108(B)].

§ 2109. Guardian for particular property; powers and duties

(a) Subject to Section 2108, a guardian appointed under subdivision (d) of Section 1514 for particular property upon a nomination made under Section 1501 has, with respect to that property, the same powers and duties as a guardian of the estate. The responsibility of such a guardian with regard to inventory, accounting, and disposal of the estate is confined to the property covered by the nomination.

(b) When a guardian is appointed under subdivision (d) of Section 1514 for particular property upon a nomination made under Section 1501 and there is a guardian of the estate appointed under any other provision of Part 2 (commencing with Section 1500):

(1) The guardian appointed for the property covered by the nomination manages and controls that property and the guardian of the estate manages and controls the balance of the guardianship estate.

(2) Either guardian may petition under Section 2403 to the court in which the guardianship of the estate proceeding is pending for instructions concerning how the duties that are imposed by law upon the guardian of the estate are to be allocated between the two guardians. *(Stats.1990, c. 79 (A.B.759), § 14, operative July 1, 1991.)*

Cross References

Inventory and accounts, see Probate Code § 2600 et seq.

Powers and duties of guardian of the estate, see Probate Code § 2400 et seq.

§ 2110. Personal liability

Unless otherwise provided in the instrument or in this division, a guardian or conservator is not personally liable on an instrument, including but not limited to a note, mortgage, deed of trust, or other contract, properly entered into in the guardian's or conservator's fiduciary capacity in the course of the guardianship or conservatorship unless the guardian or conservator fails to reveal the guardian's or conservator's representative capacity or identify the guardianship or conservatorship estate in the instrument. *(Stats.1990, c. 79 (A.B.759), § 14, operative July 1, 1991.)*

Cross References

Instrument, defined, see Probate Code § 45.
Trustees, liability to beneficiaries, see Probate Code § 16400 et seq.

§ 2111. Transaction

(a) As used in this section, "transaction" means any of the following:

(1) A conveyance or lease of real property of the guardianship or conservatorship estate.

(2) The creation of a mortgage or deed of trust on real property of the guardianship or conservatorship estate.

(3) A transfer of personal property of the guardianship or conservatorship estate.

(4) The creation of a security interest or other lien in personal property of the guardianship or conservatorship estate.

(b) Whenever the court authorizes or directs a transaction, the transaction shall be carried out by the guardian or conservator of the estate in accordance with the terms of the order.

(c) A conveyance, lease, or mortgage of, or deed of trust on, real property executed by a guardian or conservator shall set forth therein that it is made by authority of the order authorizing or directing the transaction and shall give the date of the order. A certified copy of the order shall be recorded in the office of the county recorder in each county in which any portion of the real property is located.

(d) A transaction carried out by a guardian or conservator in accordance with an order authorizing or directing the transaction has the same effect as if the ward or conservatee had carried out the transaction while having legal capacity to do so. *(Stats.1990, c. 79 (A.B.759), § 14, operative July 1, 1991.)*

Cross References

Borrowing money and mortgaging property by personal representative, see Probate Code § 9800 et seq.
Contracts, interpretation, see Civil Code § 1635 et seq.
Exchange of property, see Probate Code § 2557.
Execution of conveyance or transfer, effective order, see Probate Code § 857.
Leases, see Probate Code § 2553 et seq.; Civil Code § 1940 et seq.
Liens, see Civil Code § 2872 et seq.
Mechanics liens, see Civil Code § 8400.
Mortgages, see Civil Code § 2920 et seq.
Orders, see Probate Code § 1047 et seq.
Real property, defined, see Probate Code § 68.
Transaction, legal capacity of conservatee, see Probate Code § 1870.
Transfer, defined, see Civil Code § 3439.01.
Transfer of interest by death of insured, see Insurance Code § 303.
Transfer of personal property, generally, see Commercial Code §§ 2101 et seq., 2401 et seq.
Transfer of real property,
  Effect, see Civil Code § 1104 et seq.
  Method, see Civil Code § 1091 et seq.
  Recording, see Civil Code § 1169 et seq.

Research References

Forms

West's California Code Forms, Probate § 2500–2507 Form 2, Order Approving Compromise or Other Modification of Claim—Judicial Council Form MC-351.
West's California Code Forms, Probate § 2551 Form 2, Order Authorizing Guardian or Conservator to Borrow Money and to Encumber Real Property.
West's California Code Forms, Probate § 2553 Form 2, Order Authorizing Lease of Real Property.

§ 2111.5. Court official's or employee's with responsibilities related to guardians or conservators; prohibitions against purchasing, leasing, or renting property from estate

(a) Except as provided in subdivision (b), every court official or employee who has duties or responsibilities related to the appointment of a guardian or conservator, or the processing of any document related to a guardian or conservator, and every person who is related by blood or marriage to a court official or employee who has these duties, is prohibited from purchasing, leasing, or renting any real or personal property from the estate of the ward or conservatee whom the guardian or conservator represents. For purposes of this subdivision, a "person related by blood or marriage" means any of the following:

(1) A person's spouse or domestic partner.

(2) Relatives within the second degree of lineal or collateral consanguinity of a person or a person's spouse.

(b) A person described in subdivision (a) is not prohibited from purchasing real or personal property from the estate of the ward or conservatee whom the guardian or conservator represents where the purchase is made under terms and conditions of a public sale of the property.

(c) A violation of this section shall result in the rescission of the purchase, lease, or rental of the property. Any losses incurred by the estate of the ward or conservatee because the property was sold or leased at less than fair market value shall be deemed as charges against the guardian or conservator under the provisions of Sections 2401.3 and 2401.5. The court shall assess a civil penalty equal to three times the charges against the guardian, conservator, or other person in violation of this section, and may assess punitive damages as it deems proper. If the estate does not incur losses as a result of the violation, the court shall order the guardian, conservator, or other person in violation of this section to pay a fine of up to five thousand dollars ($5,000) for each violation. The fines and penalties provided in this section are in addition to any other rights and remedies provided by law. *(Added by Stats.2000, c. 565 (A.B.1950), § 3. Amended by Stats.2001, c. 893 (A.B.25), § 28.)*

Cross References

Domestic partner, defined, see Probate Code § 37.

§ 2112. Conservatee abuse; penalty; report

(a)(1) In addition to other remedies available under statutory or common law, if the court finds that a conservator who is a professional fiduciary licensed by the Professional Fiduciaries Bureau has abused a conservatee, the conservator shall be liable for a civil penalty of up to ten thousand dollars ($10,000) for each separate act of abuse, payable to the estate of the conservatee.

(2) In addition to other remedies available under statutory or common law, if the court finds that a conservator who is not a professional fiduciary licensed by the Professional Fiduciaries Bureau has abused a conservatee, the conservator shall be liable for a civil penalty of up to one thousand dollars ($1,000) for each separate act of abuse, payable to the estate of the conservatee.

(b) If the court finds that a professional fiduciary has abused a conservatee, or if the court imposes a penalty on the professional fiduciary, including, but not limited to, surcharging, punishing for contempt, suspending, or removing the professional fiduciary as a conservator for cause, the court shall report that finding or penalty to the Professional Fiduciaries Bureau. If the court reports an action taken under this section, the court shall provide the bureau, at no charge, with access to the information, including confidential information, regarding its investigation of the professional fiduciary contained in court records. The bureau shall maintain the confidentiality of the information, as required by paragraph (4) of subdivision (a) of Section 6580 of the Business and Professions Code or any other applicable state or federal law.

(c) For purposes of this section, the following definitions apply:

(1) "Abused" means that the conservator engaged in an act described in Section 15610.07 of the Welfare and Institutions Code.

(2) "Professional fiduciary" has the same meaning as defined in Section 6501 of the Business and Professions Code.

(d) A superior court shall not be required to perform any duties imposed pursuant to this section until the Legislature makes an appropriation identified for this purpose. *(Added by Stats.2021, c. 417 (A.B.1194), § 17, eff. Jan. 1, 2022.)*

§ 2113. Balance of conflicting interests; preferences of conservatee

A conservator shall accommodate the desires of the conservatee, except to the extent that doing so would violate the conservator's fiduciary duties to the conservatee or impose an unreasonable expense on the conservatorship estate. To the greatest extent possible, the conservator shall support the conservatee to maximize their autonomy, support the conservatee in making decisions, and, on a regular basis, inform the conservatee of decisions made on their behalf. In determining the desires of the conservatee, the conservator shall consider stated or previously expressed preferences, including preferences expressed by speech, sign language, alternative or augmentative communication, actions, facial expressions, and other spoken and nonspoken methods of communication. *(Added by Stats.2006, c. 493 (A.B.1363), § 13. Amended by Stats.2022, c. 894 (A.B.1663), § 15, eff. Jan. 1, 2023.)*

Cross References

Conservator's rights, duties, limitations and responsibilities, dissemination of information by superior court, failure to provide information, see Probate Code § 1835.

CHAPTER 2. JURISDICTION AND VENUE

ARTICLE 1. JURISDICTION AND VENUE

Section
2200. Superior court jurisdiction; determination of state jurisdiction.
2201. Residents; venue.
2202. Nonresidents; venue.
2203. Priority of court; proceedings instituted in several counties.
2204. Custody or visitation proceedings pending in more than one court; determination of venue; communications between the courts.
2205. Exclusive jurisdiction; consolidation of guardianship and adoption proceedings.

Cross References

Application of old and new law, see Probate Code § 3.
Trusts, judicial proceedings, generally, see Probate Code § 17000 et seq.

§ 2200. Superior court jurisdiction; determination of state jurisdiction

(a) The superior court has jurisdiction of guardianship and conservatorship proceedings.

(b) Chapter 8 (commencing with Section 1980) of Part 3 governs which state has jurisdiction of a conservatorship proceeding. *(Stats. 1990, c. 79 (A.B.759), § 14, operative July 1, 1991. Amended by Stats.2014, c. 553 (S.B.940), § 22, eff. Jan. 1, 2015, operative Jan. 1, 2016.)*

Cross References

Jurisdiction necessary for judgment, see Code of Civil Procedure § 1917.
Jurisdictional limitation on guardian's or conservator's authority, see Code of Civil Procedure § 1913.
Superior courts,
  Generally, see Cal. Const. Art. 6, § 4.
  Jurisdiction, see Cal. Const. Art. 6, §§ 10, 11.
Trusts, judicial proceedings, generally, see Probate Code § 17000 et seq.

§ 2201. Residents; venue

The proper county for the commencement of a guardianship or conservatorship proceeding for a resident of this state is either of the following:

(a) The county in which the proposed ward or proposed conservatee resides.

(b) Such other county as may be in the best interests of the proposed ward or proposed conservatee. *(Stats.1990, c. 79 (A.B. 759), § 14, operative July 1, 1991.)*

Cross References

Change of venue, see Probate Code § 2210 et seq.
Place of trial, see Code of Civil Procedure § 395 et seq.
Probate proceedings, jurisdiction and venue, see Probate Code § 7050 et seq.
Residence,
  Determination of place of residence, see Government Code § 244.
  Effect of absence from state on official business, see Government Code § 245.
Voting residence, see Cal. Const. Art. 2, § 3; Elections Code § 349.

Research References

Forms

West's California Code Forms, Probate § 1510 Form 3, Declaration Under Uniform Child Custody Jurisdiction and Enforcement Act (UCCJEA)-Judicial Council Form FL-105/GC-120.

§ 2202. Nonresidents; venue

(a) The proper county for the commencement of a proceeding for the guardianship or conservatorship of the person of a nonresident of this state is either of the following:

(1) The county in which the proposed ward or conservatee is temporarily living.

(2) Such other county as may be in the best interests of the proposed ward or proposed conservatee.

(b) The proper county for the commencement of a proceeding for the guardianship or conservatorship of the estate for a nonresident of this state is any of the following:

(1) The county in which the proposed ward or proposed conservatee is temporarily living.

(2) Any county in which the proposed ward or proposed conservatee has property.

(3) Such other county as may be in the best interests of the proposed ward or proposed conservatee. *(Stats.1990, c. 79 (A.B. 759), § 14, operative July 1, 1991.)*

Cross References

Change of venue, see Probate Code § 2210 et seq.

Place of trial, see Code of Civil Procedure § 395 et seq.

§ 2203. Priority of court; proceedings instituted in several counties

(a) If proceedings for the guardianship or conservatorship of the estate are commenced in more than one county, the guardianship or conservatorship of the estate first granted, including a temporary guardianship or conservatorship of the estate, governs and extends to all the property of the ward or conservatee within this state and the other proceeding shall be dismissed.

(b) If proceedings for the guardianship or conservatorship of the person are commenced in more than one county, the guardianship or conservatorship of the person first granted, including a temporary guardianship or conservatorship of the person, governs and the other proceeding shall be dismissed.

(c) If a proceeding for the guardianship or conservatorship of the person is commenced in one county and a proceeding for the guardianship or conservatorship of the estate is commenced in a different county, the court first granting the guardianship or conservatorship, whether of the person or of the estate, may find that it is in the best interests of the ward or conservatee that the guardianship or conservatorship of both the person and the estate be maintained in that county or in such other county as the court shall determine. Thereupon, the guardianship or conservatorship proceeding in the court of the county found by the court to be in the best interests of the ward or conservatee shall govern and shall extend to all property of the ward or conservatee within this state, and the other proceeding shall be dismissed. *(Stats.1990, c. 79 (A.B.759), § 14, operative July 1, 1991.)*

Cross References

Jurisdictional limitation on guardian's or conservator's authority, see Code of Civil Procedure § 1913.

Temporary guardians and conservators, generally, see Probate Code § 2250 et seq.

Trusts, judicial proceedings, generally, see Probate Code § 17000 et seq.

§ 2204. Custody or visitation proceedings pending in more than one court; determination of venue; communications between the courts

(a) If a proceeding for the guardianship of the person of the minor is filed in one county and a custody or visitation proceeding has already been filed in one or more other counties, the following shall apply:

(1) If the guardianship proceeding is filed in a county where the proposed ward and the proposed guardian have resided for six or more consecutive months immediately prior to the commencement of the proceeding, or, in the case of a minor less than six months of age, since the minor's birth, the court in that county is the proper court to hear and determine the guardianship proceeding, unless that court determines that the best interests of the minor require that the proceeding be transferred to one of the other courts. A period of temporary absence no longer than 30 days from the county of the minor or the proposed guardian shall not be considered an interruption of the six-month period.

(2) If the guardianship proceeding is filed in a county where the proposed ward and the proposed guardian have resided for less than six consecutive months immediately prior to the commencement of the proceeding, or, in the case of a minor less than six months of age, a period less than the minor's life, the court shall transfer the case to one of the other courts, unless the court determines that the best interests of the minor require that the guardianship proceeding be maintained in the court where it was filed.

(3) If a petitioner or respondent in a custody or visitation proceeding who is an authorized petitioner under Section 2212 petitions the court where the guardianship proceeding is filed for transfer of the guardianship proceeding to the court where the custody or visitation proceeding is on file at any time before the appointment of a guardian, including a temporary guardian, the provisions of this subdivision shall apply to the court's determination of the petition for transfer. Except as provided in this paragraph, the petition for transfer shall be determined as provided in Sections 2212 to 2217, inclusive.

(b) The following shall apply concerning communications between the courts:

(1) The court where the guardianship proceeding is commenced shall communicate concerning the proceedings with each court where a custody or visitation proceeding is on file prior to making a determination authorized in subdivision (a), including a determination of a petition to transfer.

(2) If a petitioner or respondent, who is authorized to petition to transfer under Section 2212, petitions the court where the guardianship proceeding is filed for transfer of the guardianship after the appointment of a guardian, including a temporary guardian, the court in the guardianship proceeding may communicate with each court where a custody or visitation proceeding is on file before determining the petition for transfer.

(3) If the court in the guardianship proceeding appoints a guardian of the person of the minor, including a temporary guardian, the court shall transmit a copy of the order appointing a guardian to each court where a custody or visitation proceeding is on file, and each of those courts shall file the order in the case file for its custody or visitation proceeding.

(4) The provisions of subdivisions (b) to (e), inclusive, of Section 3410 of the Family Code shall apply to communications between courts under this subdivision.

(5) The Judicial Council shall, on or before January 1, 2013, adopt rules of court to implement the provisions of this subdivision.

(c) For purposes of this section, "custody or visitation proceeding" means a proceeding described in Section 3021 of the Family Code that relates to the rights to custody or visitation of the minor under Part 2 (commencing with Section 3020) of Division 8 of the Family Code. *(Added by Stats.2011, c. 102 (A.B.458), § 2. Amended by Stats.2012, c. 207 (A.B.2683), § 1.)*

§ 2205. Exclusive jurisdiction; consolidation of guardianship and adoption proceedings

(a) Except as provided in Section 304 of the Welfare and Institutions Code, and subject to the provisions specified in subdivision (b), upon the filing of an order appointing a guardian of the person of a minor in a guardianship proceeding, including an order appointing a temporary guardian of the person of the minor, the court in the guardianship proceeding shall have exclusive jurisdiction to determine all issues of custody or visitation of the minor until the guardianship proceeding is terminated.

(b) This section is subject to the provisions of Sections 1510 of this code, and 8714, 8714.5, and 8802 of the Family Code, relating to consolidation of guardianship and adoption proceedings and the court where the consolidated case is to be heard and decided. *(Added by Stats.2011, c. 102 (A.B.458), § 3.)*

ARTICLE 2. CHANGE OF VENUE

Section
2210. Definitions.
2211. Transfer of proceedings.
2212. Petition for transfer; persons authorized to file.
2213. Petition for transfer; contents.
2214. Notice of hearing.
2215. Hearing and order.
2216. Transfer of proceedings; fees.

Section
2217. Transferred guardianship or conservatorship; notice of receipt; compliance; review; hearing by transferring court.

§ 2210. Definitions

As used in this article:

(a) "Guardian or conservator" includes a proposed guardian or proposed conservator.

(b) "Ward or conservatee" includes a proposed ward or proposed conservatee. *(Stats.1990, c. 79 (A.B.759), § 14, operative July 1, 1991.)*

Research References

Forms

West's California Code Forms, Probate § 2213 Form 1, Petition for Order for Transfer of Proceedings.

§ 2211. Transfer of proceedings

The court in which a guardianship or conservatorship proceeding is pending may, upon petition therefor, transfer the proceeding to another county within this state. *(Stats.1990, c. 79 (A.B.759), § 14, operative July 1, 1991.)*

Cross References

Civil actions, change of place of trial, generally, see Code of Civil Procedure § 397 et seq.
Probate proceedings, transfer to another county, see Probate Code § 7070 et seq.

§ 2212. Petition for transfer; persons authorized to file

The petition for transfer may be filed only by one or more of the following:

(a) The guardian or conservator.

(b) The ward or conservatee.

(c) The spouse of the ward or the spouse or domestic partner of the conservatee.

(d) A relative or friend of the ward or conservatee.

(e) Any other interested person. *(Stats.1990, c. 79 (A.B.759), § 14, operative July 1, 1991. Amended by Stats.2001, c. 893 (A.B.25), § 29.)*

Cross References

Domestic partner, defined, see Probate Code § 37.
Guardian or conservator, defined, see Probate Code § 2210.
Interested person, see Probate Code § 1424.
Ward or conservatee, defined, see Probate Code § 2210.

Research References

Forms

West's California Code Forms, Probate § 2213 Form 1, Petition for Order for Transfer of Proceedings.

§ 2213. Petition for transfer; contents

The petition for transfer shall set forth all of the following:

(a) The county to which the proceeding is to be transferred.

(b) The name and address of the ward or conservatee.

(c) A brief description of the character, value, and location of the property of the ward or conservatee.

(d) The reasons for the transfer.

(e) The names and addresses, so far as they are known to the petitioner, of the spouse and of the relatives of the ward within the second degree, or of the spouse or domestic partner of and of the relatives of the conservatee within the second degree.

(f) The name and address of the guardian or conservator if other than the petitioner. *(Stats.1990, c. 79 (A.B.759), § 14, operative July 1, 1991. Amended by Stats.2001, c. 893 (A.B.25), § 30.)*

Cross References

Domestic partner, defined, see Probate Code § 37.

Research References

Forms

West's California Code Forms, Probate § 2213 Form 1, Petition for Order for Transfer of Proceedings.

§ 2214. Notice of hearing

Notice of the hearing shall be given for the period and in the manner provided in Chapter 3 (commencing with Section 1460) of Part 1. In addition, the petitioner shall deliver pursuant to Section 1215 a notice of the time and place of the hearing and a copy of the petition to all persons required to be listed in the petition at least 15 days before the date set for the hearing. *(Stats.1990, c. 79 (A.B.759), § 14, operative July 1, 1991. Amended by Stats.2017, c. 319 (A.B.976), § 41, eff. Jan. 1, 2018.)*

Cross References

Computation of time, see Code of Civil Procedure §§ 12 and 12a; Government Code § 6800 et seq.
Mailing, completion, see Probate Code § 1467.
Notice,
    Mailing, see Probate Code § 1215 et seq.
    Posting, see Probate Code § 1230.
    Proof of giving notice, see Probate Code § 1260 et seq.
    Special notice, see Probate Code § 1250 et seq.
    This code, generally, see Probate Code § 1200 et seq.
    This division, generally, see Probate Code § 1460 et seq.
    To directors, see Probate Code § 1461.
Request for special notice, see Probate Code § 2700 et seq.
Service of process,
    Generally, see Code of Civil Procedure § 413.10 et seq.
    Mail, see Code of Civil Procedure §§ 415.30, 1012 et seq.
    Personal delivery, see Code of Civil Procedure § 415.10.
    Proof of service, see Code of Civil Procedure § 417.10 et seq.
    Publication, see Code of Civil Procedure § 415.50.

Research References

Forms

West's California Code Forms, Probate § 2213 Form 1, Petition for Order for Transfer of Proceedings.

§ 2215. Hearing and order

(a) Any of the following persons may appear at the hearing to support or oppose the petition and may file written objections to the petition:

(1) Any person required to be listed in the petition.

(2) Any creditor of the ward or conservatee or of the estate.

(3) Any other interested person.

(b)(1) If the court determines that the transfer requested in the petition will be for the best interests of the ward or conservatee, it shall make an order transferring the proceeding to the other county.

(2) In those cases in which the court has approved a change of residence of the conservatee, it shall be presumed to be in the best interests of the conservatee to transfer the proceedings if the ward or conservatee has moved his or her residence to another county within the state in which any person set forth in subdivision (b) of Section 1821 also resides. The presumption that the transfer is in the best interests of the ward or conservatee, may be rebutted by clear and convincing evidence that the transfer will harm the ward or conservatee. *(Stats.1990, c. 79 (A.B.759), § 14, operative July 1, 1991. Amended by Stats.2006, c. 493 (A.B.1363), § 14.)*

§ 2215

Cross References

Interested person, defined, see Probate Code § 1424.

Research References

Forms

West's California Code Forms, Probate § 2213 Form 1, Petition for Order for Transfer of Proceedings.

West's California Code Forms, Probate § 2215 Form 1, Order Transferring Proceedings.

§ 2216. Transfer of proceedings; fees

(a) Upon the order of transfer, the clerk shall transmit to the clerk of the court to which the proceeding is transferred a certified or exemplified copy of the order, together with all papers in the proceeding on file with the clerk.

(b) The clerk of the court from which the removal is made shall receive no fee therefor but shall be paid out of the estate all expenses incurred by the clerk in the removal. The clerk of the court to which the proceeding is transferred is entitled to such fees as are payable on the filing of a like original proceeding. *(Stats.1990, c. 79 (A.B.759), § 14, operative July 1, 1991.)*

Cross References

Civil actions, transfer of cases, transmission of papers, fees and costs, see Code of Civil Procedure § 399.

Research References

Forms

West's California Code Forms, Probate § 2213 Form 1, Petition for Order for Transfer of Proceedings.

West's California Code Forms, Probate § 2215 Form 1, Order Transferring Proceedings.

§ 2217. Transferred guardianship or conservatorship; notice of receipt; compliance; review; hearing by transferring court

(a) When an order has been made transferring venue to another county, the court transferring the matter shall set a hearing within two months to confirm receipt of the notification described in subdivision (b). If the notification has not been made, the transferring court shall make reasonable inquiry into the status of the matter.

(b) When a court receives the file of a transferred guardianship or conservatorship, the court:

(1) Shall send written notification of the receipt to the court that transferred the matter.

(2) Shall take proper action pursuant to ensure compliance by the guardian or conservator with the matters provided in Section 1456.5.

(3) If the case is a conservatorship, may conduct a review, including an investigation, as described in Sections 1851 to 1853, inclusive. *(Added by Stats.2007, c. 553 (A.B.1727), § 11.)*

CHAPTER 3. TEMPORARY GUARDIANS AND CONSERVATORS

Section
2250. Petition for appointment.
2250.2. Petition for appointment of a temporary conservator.
2250.4. Hearing on appointment of temporary conservatee.
2250.6. Investigation and interview relative to proposed temporary conservatee.
2250.8. Appointment of temporary conservatorship in instances of gravely disabled persons.
2251. Issuance of letters.
2252. Powers and duties.
2253. Change of residence of conservatee; request; duties of court investigator.

Section
2254. Removal of conservatee from residence in emergency; medical treatment; removal to health facility with consent of conservatee.
2255. Inventory and appraisement of estate.
2256. Settlement and allowance of accounts.
2257. Termination of powers; time.
2258. Suspension, removal, resignation and discharge.

Cross References

Application of old and new law, see Probate Code § 3.

§ 2250. Petition for appointment

(a) On or after the filing of a petition for appointment of a guardian or conservator, any person entitled to petition for appointment of the guardian or conservator may file a petition for appointment of:

(1) A temporary guardian of the person or estate, or both.

(2) A temporary conservator of the person or estate, or both.

(b) The petition shall state facts that establish good cause for appointment of the temporary guardian or temporary conservator. The court, upon that petition or other showing as it may require, may appoint a temporary guardian of the person or estate, or both, or a temporary conservator of the person or estate, or both, to serve pending the final determination of the court upon the petition for the appointment of the guardian or conservator.

(c) If the petitioner, proposed guardian, or proposed conservator is a professional fiduciary, as described in Section 2340, who is required to be licensed under the Professional Fiduciaries Act (Chapter 6 (commencing with Section 6500) of Division 3 of the Business and Professions Code), the petition for appointment of a temporary guardian or temporary conservator shall include the following:

(1) The petitioner's, proposed guardian's, or proposed conservator's proposed hourly fee schedule or another statement of their proposed compensation from the estate of the proposed ward or proposed conservatee for services performed as a guardian or conservator. The petitioner's, proposed guardian's, or proposed conservator's provision of a proposed hourly fee schedule or another statement of their proposed compensation, as required by this paragraph, shall not preclude a court from later reducing the petitioner's, proposed guardian's, or proposed conservator's fees or other compensation.

(2) Unless a petition for appointment of a guardian or conservator that contains the statements required by this paragraph is filed together with a petition for appointment of a temporary guardian or temporary conservator, both of the following:

(A) A statement of the petitioner's, proposed guardian's, or proposed conservator's registration or license information.

(B) A statement explaining who engaged the petitioner, proposed guardian, or proposed conservator or how the petitioner, proposed guardian, or proposed conservator was engaged to file the petition for appointment of a temporary guardian or temporary conservator or to agree to accept the appointment as temporary guardian or temporary conservator and what prior relationship the petitioner, proposed guardian, or proposed conservator had with the proposed ward or proposed conservatee or the proposed ward's or proposed conservatee's family or friends.

(d) If the petition is filed by a party other than the proposed conservatee, the petition shall include a declaration of due diligence showing both of the following:

(1) Either the efforts to find the proposed conservatee's relatives named in the petition for appointment of a general conservator or why it was not feasible to contact any of them.

(2) Either the preferences of the proposed conservatee concerning the appointment of a temporary conservator and the appointment of the proposed temporary conservator or why it was not feasible to ascertain those preferences.

(e) Unless the court for good cause otherwise orders, at least five court days before the hearing on the petition, notice of the hearing shall be given as follows:

(1) Notice of the hearing shall be personally delivered to the proposed ward if the proposed ward is 12 years of age or older, to the parent or parents of the proposed ward, and to any person having a valid visitation order with the proposed ward that was effective at the time of the filing of the petition. Notice of the hearing shall not be delivered to the proposed ward if the proposed ward is under 12 years of age. In a proceeding for temporary guardianship of the person, evidence that a custodial parent has died or become incapacitated, and that the petitioner or proposed guardian is the nominee of the custodial parent, may constitute good cause for the court to order that this notice not be delivered.

(2) Notice of the hearing shall be personally delivered to the proposed conservatee, and notice of the hearing shall be delivered pursuant to Section 1215 on the persons required to be named in the petition for appointment of conservator. If the petition states that the petitioner and the proposed conservator have no prior relationship with the proposed conservatee and have not been nominated by a family member, friend, or other person with a relationship to the proposed conservatee, notice of hearing shall be delivered pursuant to Section 1215 on the public guardian of the county in which the petition is filed.

(3) A copy of the petition for temporary appointment shall be delivered pursuant to Section 1215 with the notice of hearing.

(f) If a temporary guardianship is granted ex parte and the hearing on the general guardianship petition is not to be held within 30 days of the granting of the temporary guardianship, the court shall set a hearing within 30 days to reconsider the temporary guardianship. Notice of the hearing for reconsideration of the temporary guardianship shall be provided pursuant to Section 1511, except that the court may for good cause shorten the time for the notice of the hearing.

(g) Visitation orders with the proposed ward granted before the filing of a petition for temporary guardianship shall remain in effect, unless for good cause the court orders otherwise.

(h)(1) If a temporary conservatorship is granted ex parte, and a petition to terminate the temporary conservatorship is filed more than 15 days before the first hearing on the general petition for appointment of conservator, the court shall set a hearing within 15 days of the filing of the petition for termination of the temporary conservatorship to reconsider the temporary conservatorship. Unless the court otherwise orders, notice of the hearing on the petition to terminate the temporary conservatorship shall be given at least 10 days before the hearing.

(2) If a petition to terminate the temporary conservatorship is filed within 15 days before the first hearing on the general petition for appointment of a conservator, the court shall set the hearing at the same time that the hearing on the general petition is set. Unless the court otherwise orders, notice of the hearing on the petition to terminate the temporary conservatorship pursuant to this section shall be given at least five court days before the hearing.

(i) If the court suspends powers of the guardian or conservator under Section 2334 or 2654 or under any other provision of this division, the court may appoint a temporary guardian or conservator to exercise those powers until the powers are restored to the guardian or conservator or a new guardian or conservator is appointed.

(j) If for any reason a vacancy occurs in the office of guardian or conservator, the court, on a petition filed under subdivision (a) or on its own motion, may appoint a temporary guardian or conservator to exercise the powers of the guardian or conservator until a new guardian or conservator is appointed.

(k) A superior court shall not be required to perform any duties imposed pursuant to the amendments to this section enacted by Chapter 493 of the Statutes of 2006 until the Legislature makes an appropriation identified for this purpose. *(Stats.1990, c. 79 (A.B. 759), § 14, operative July 1, 1991. Amended by Stats.1993, c. 978 (S.B.305), § 3; Stats.1995, c. 730 (A.B.1466), § 3; Stats.2006, c. 493 (A.B.1363), § 15, operative July 1, 2007; Stats.2007, c. 553 (A.B.1727), § 12; Stats.2008, c. 293 (A.B.1340), § 4; Stats.2011, c. 10 (S.B.78), § 16, eff. March 24, 2011; Stats.2013, c. 248 (A.B.1339), § 3; Stats.2017, c. 319 (A.B.976), § 42, eff. Jan. 1, 2018; Stats.2021, c. 417 (A.B.1194), § 18, eff. Jan. 1, 2022.)*

Cross References

Action for exclusive custody of children, see Family Code § 3120.
Computation of time, see Code of Civil Procedure §§ 12 and 12a; Government Code § 6800 et seq.
Elder Abuse and Dependent Adult Civil Protection Act, victim's refusal or withdrawal of consent, see Welfare and Institutions Code § 15636.
Elder or dependent adults as abuse victims, appointment of conservator or guardian, see Welfare and Institutions Code § 15650.
Parent, defined, see Probate Code § 54.
Petition for appointment,
  Conservator, see Probate Code § 1820.
  Guardian, see Probate Code § 1510.
Professional fiduciary as guardian or conservator, submission of new proposed hourly fee schedule or statement of compensation on or after one year from original submission, see Probate Code § 2614.8.
Relationship of guardian and ward, generally, see Probate Code § 2101.
Temporary guardian or conservator pending appeal, see Probate Code § 1310.

Research References

Forms

West's California Code Forms, Probate § 2250 Form 1, Petition for Appointment of Temporary Guardian—Judicial Council Form GC-110.
West's California Code Forms, Probate § 2250 Form 1.6, Petition for Appointment of Temporary Conservator—Judicial Council Form GC-111.
West's California Judicial Council Forms GC-110, Petition for Appointment of Temporary Guardian.
West's California Judicial Council Forms GC-110(P), Petition for Appointment of Temporary Guardian of the Person.
West's California Judicial Council Forms GC-111, Petition for Appointment of Temporary Conservator.
West's California Judicial Council Forms GC-112, Ex Parte Application for Good Cause Exception to Notice of Hearing on Petition for Appointment of Temporary Conservator.
West's California Judicial Council Forms GC-112(A-1), Declaration in Support of Ex Parte Application for Good Cause Exception to Notice of Hearing on Petition for Appointment of Temporary Conservator.
West's California Judicial Council Forms GC-112(A-2), Declaration Continuation Page.
West's California Judicial Council Forms GC-115, Order on Ex Parte Application for Good Cause Exception to Notice of Hearing on Petition for Appointment of Temporary Conservator.
West's California Judicial Council Forms GC-140, Order Appointing Temporary Guardian.
West's California Judicial Council Forms GC-141, Order Appointing Temporary Conservator.
West's California Judicial Council Forms GC-150, Letters of Temporary Guardianship or Conservatorship.

§ 2250.2. Petition for appointment of a temporary conservator

(a) On or after the filing of a petition for appointment of a conservator, any person entitled to petition for appointment of the conservator may file a petition for appointment of a temporary conservator of the person or estate or both.

(b) The petition shall state facts that establish good cause for appointment of the temporary conservator. The court, upon that petition or any other showing as it may require, may appoint a temporary conservator of the person or estate or both, to serve

§ 2250.2

pending the final determination of the court upon the petition for the appointment of the conservator.

(c) Unless the court for good cause otherwise orders, not less than five days before the appointment of the temporary conservator, notice of the proposed appointment shall be personally delivered to the proposed conservatee.

(d) If the court suspends powers of the conservator under Section 2334 or 2654 or under any other provision of this division, the court may appoint a temporary conservator to exercise those powers until the powers are restored to the conservator or a new conservator is appointed.

(e) If for any reason a vacancy occurs in the office of conservator, the court, on a petition filed under subdivision (a) or on its own motion, may appoint a temporary conservator to exercise the powers of the conservator until a new conservator is appointed.

(f) This section shall only apply to proceedings under Chapter 3 (commencing with Section 5350) of Part 1 of Division 5 of the Welfare and Institutions Code. *(Added by Stats.2006, c. 493 (A.B. 1363), § 15.5, operative July 1, 2007. Amended by Stats.2007, c. 553 (A.B.1727), § 12.5.)*

Research References

Forms

West's California Code Forms, Probate § 2250 Form 1, Petition for Appointment of Temporary Guardian—Judicial Council Form GC-110.

§ 2250.4. Hearing on appointment of temporary conservatee

The proposed temporary conservatee shall attend the hearing except in the following cases:

(a) If the proposed temporary conservatee is out of the state when served and is not the petitioner.

(b) If the proposed temporary conservatee is unable to attend the hearing by reason of medical inability.

(c) If the court investigator has visited the proposed conservatee prior to the hearing and the court investigator has reported to the court that the proposed temporary conservatee has expressly communicated that all of the following apply:

(1) The proposed conservatee is not willing to attend the hearing.

(2) The proposed conservatee does not wish to contest the establishment of the temporary conservatorship.

(3) The proposed conservatee does not object to the proposed temporary conservator or prefer that another person act as temporary conservator.

(d) If the court determines that the proposed conservatee is unable or unwilling to attend the hearing, and holding the hearing in the absence of the proposed conservatee is necessary to protect the conservatee from substantial harm.

(e) A superior court shall not be required to perform any duties imposed by this section until the Legislature makes an appropriation identified for this purpose. *(Added by Stats.2006, c. 493 (A.B.1363), § 16, operative July 1, 2007. Amended by Stats.2011, c. 10 (S.B.78), § 17, eff. March 24, 2011.)*

Research References

Forms

West's California Code Forms, Probate § 2250 Form 1, Petition for Appointment of Temporary Guardian—Judicial Council Form GC-110.

West's California Code Forms, Probate § 2250 Form 1.6, Petition for Appointment of Temporary Conservator—Judicial Council Form GC-111.

§ 2250.6. Investigation and interview relative to proposed temporary conservatee

(a) Regardless of whether the proposed temporary conservatee attends the hearing, the court investigator shall do all of the following * * * before the hearing, unless it is not feasible to do so, in which case the court investigator shall comply with the requirements set forth in subdivision (b):

(1) Interview the proposed conservatee personally. The court investigator also shall do all of the following:

(A) Interview the petitioner and the proposed conservator, if different from the petitioner.

(B) To the greatest extent possible, interview the proposed conservatee's spouse or registered domestic partner, relatives within the first degree, neighbors, and, if known, close friends.

(C) To the extent possible, interview the proposed conservatee's relatives within the second degree as set forth in subdivision (b) of Section 1821, before the hearing.

(2) Inform the proposed conservatee of the contents of the citation, of the nature, purpose, and effect of the temporary conservatorship, and of the right of the proposed conservatee to oppose the petition, to attend the hearing, to have the matter of the establishment of the conservatorship tried by jury, to be represented by legal counsel, and to have legal counsel appointed by the court * * *.

(3) Determine whether it appears that the proposed conservatee is unable to attend the hearing and, if able to attend, whether the proposed conservatee is willing to attend the hearing.

(4) Determine whether the proposed conservatee wishes to oppose the establishment of the conservatorship.

(5) Determine whether the proposed conservatee objects to the proposed conservator or prefers another person to act as conservator.

(6) Report to the court, in writing, concerning all of the foregoing.

(b) If not feasible before the hearing, the court investigator shall do all of the following within two court days after the hearing:

(1) Interview the conservatee personally. The court investigator also shall do all of the following:

(A) Interview the petitioner and the proposed conservator, if different from the petitioner.

(B) To the greatest extent possible, interview the proposed conservatee's spouse or registered domestic partner, relatives within the first degree, neighbors, and, if known, close friends.

(C) To the extent possible, interview the proposed conservatee's relatives within the second degree as set forth in subdivision (b) of Section 1821.

(2) Inform the conservatee of the nature, purpose, and effect of the temporary conservatorship, as well as the right of the conservatee to oppose the petition to appoint a general conservator, to attend the hearing, to have the matter of the establishment of the conservatorship tried by jury, to be represented by legal counsel, and to have legal counsel appointed by the court if * * * not otherwise represented by legal counsel.

(c) If the investigator does not visit the conservatee until after the hearing at which a temporary conservator was appointed, and the conservatee objects to the appointment of the temporary conservator, or requests * * * appointment of legal counsel, the court investigator shall report this information promptly, and in no event more than three court days later, to the court. Upon receipt of that information, the court may proceed with appointment of * * * legal counsel as provided in Chapter 4 (commencing with Section 1470) of Part 1.

(d) If it appears to the court investigator that the temporary conservatorship is inappropriate, the court investigator shall immediately, and in no event more than two court days later, provide a written report to the court so the court can consider taking appropriate action on its own motion.

(e) A superior court shall not be required to perform any duties imposed by this section until the Legislature makes an appropriation identified for this purpose. *(Added by Stats.2006, c. 493 (A.B.1363), § 17, operative July 1, 2007. Amended by Stats.2007, c. 553 (A.B. 1727), § 13; Stats.2011, c. 10 (S.B.78), § 18, eff. March 24, 2011; Stats.2021, c. 417 (A.B.1194), § 19, eff. Jan. 1, 2022; Stats.2022, c. 420 (A.B.2960), § 39, eff. Jan. 1, 2023.)*

Research References

Forms

West's California Code Forms, Probate § 2250 Form 1, Petition for Appointment of Temporary Guardian—Judicial Council Form GC-110.

West's California Judicial Council Forms GC-330, Order Appointing Court Investigator.

§ 2250.8. Appointment of temporary conservatorship in instances of gravely disabled persons

Sections 2250, 2250.4, and 2250.6 shall not apply to proceedings under Chapter 3 (commencing with Section 5350) of Part 1 of Division 5 of the Welfare and Institutions Code. *(Added by Stats.2006, c. 493 (A.B.1363), § 17.5.)*

Research References

Forms

West's California Code Forms, Probate § 2250 Form 1, Petition for Appointment of Temporary Guardian—Judicial Council Form GC-110.

§ 2251. Issuance of letters

A temporary guardian or temporary conservator shall be issued letters of temporary guardianship or conservatorship upon taking the oath and filing the bond as in the case of a guardian or conservator. The letters shall indicate the termination date of the temporary appointment. *(Stats.1990, c. 79 (A.B.759), § 14, operative July 1, 1991.)*

Cross References

Letters of conservatorship or guardianship, generally, see Probate Code § 2310 et seq.
Oaths, affirmation in lieu of, see Code of Civil Procedure § 2015.6.
Oaths, letters, and bond, generally, see Probate Code § 2300 et seq.
Oaths, officers authorized to administer, see Government Code § 1225.
Termination date, see Probate Code § 2257.

Research References

Forms

West's California Code Forms, Probate § 1820 Form 1, Attachment Requesting Special Orders Regarding a Major Neurocognitive Disorder.

§ 2252. Powers and duties

(a) Except as otherwise provided in subdivisions (b) and (c), a temporary guardian or temporary conservator has only those powers and duties of a guardian or conservator that are necessary to provide for the temporary care, maintenance, and support of the ward or conservatee and that are necessary to conserve and protect the property of the ward or conservatee from loss or injury.

(b) Unless the court otherwise orders:

(1) A temporary guardian of the person has the powers and duties specified in Section 2353 (medical treatment).

(2) A temporary conservator of the person has the powers and duties specified in Section 2354 (medical treatment).

(3) A temporary guardian of the estate or temporary conservator of the estate may marshal assets and establish accounts at financial institutions.

(c) The temporary guardian or temporary conservator has the additional powers and duties as may be ordered by the court (1) in the order of appointment or (2) by subsequent order made with or without notice as the court may require. Notwithstanding subdivision (e), those additional powers and duties may include relief granted pursuant to Article 10 (commencing with Section 2580) of Chapter 6 if this relief is not requested in a petition for the appointment of a temporary conservator but is requested in a separate petition.

(d) The terms of any order made under subdivision (b) or (c) shall be included in the letters of temporary guardianship or conservatorship.

(e) A temporary conservator is not permitted to sell or relinquish, on the conservatee's behalf, any lease or estate in real or personal property used as or within the conservatee's place of residence without the specific approval of the court. This approval may be granted only if the conservatee has been served with notice of the hearing, the notice to be personally delivered to the temporary conservatee unless the court for good cause otherwise orders, and only if the court finds that the conservatee will be unable to return to the residence and exercise dominion over it and that the action is necessary to avert irreparable harm to the conservatee. The temporary conservator is not permitted to sell or relinquish on the conservatee's behalf any estate or interest in other real or personal property without specific approval of the court, which may be granted only upon a finding that the action is necessary to avert irreparable harm to the conservatee. A finding of irreparable harm as to real property may be based upon a reasonable showing that the real property is vacant, that it cannot reasonably be rented, and that it is impossible or impractical to obtain fire or liability insurance on the property. *(Stats.1990, c. 79 (A.B.759), § 14, operative July 1, 1991. Amended by Stats.1994, c. 806 (A.B.3686), § 10; Stats.1996, c. 563 (S.B.392), § 11.)*

Cross References

Account defined, see Probate Code § 21
Court ordered medical treatment, see Probate Code § 2357.
Custody, services and earnings of minors, see Family Code §§ 7500, 7503.
Determination of place of residence, see Government Code § 244.
Financial institution, defined, see Probate Code § 40.
Notice,
  Mailing, see Probate Code § 1215 et seq.
  Posting, see Probate Code § 1230.
  Proof of giving notice, see Probate Code § 1260 et seq.
  Special notice, see Probate Code § 1250 et seq.
  This code, generally, see Probate Code § 1200 et seq.
  This division, generally, see Probate Code § 1460 et seq.
Real property, defined, see Probate Code § 68.
Service of process,
  Generally, see Code of Civil Procedure § 413.10 et seq.
  Mail, see Code of Civil Procedure §§ 415.30, 1012 et seq.
  Personal delivery, see Code of Civil Procedure § 415.10.
  Proof of service, see Code of Civil Procedure § 417.10 et seq.
  Publication, see Code of Civil Procedure § 415.50.

Research References

Forms

West's California Code Forms, Probate § 2357 Form 1, Petition for Order Directing Medical Treatment for Ward or Conservatee.

§ 2253. Change of residence of conservatee; request; duties of court investigator

(a) If a temporary conservator of the person proposes to fix the residence of the conservatee at a place other than that where the conservatee resided before the commencement of the proceedings, that power shall be requested of the court in writing, unless the change of residence is required of the conservatee by a prior court order. The request shall be filed with the petition for temporary conservatorship or, if a temporary conservatorship has already been established, separately. The request shall specify in detail the place to which the temporary conservator proposes to move the conservatee, the precise reasons that the petitioner or temporary conservator has concluded that the conservatee will suffer irreparable harm if the change of residence is not permitted, and why no means less restrictive of the conservatee's liberty will suffice to prevent that harm.

§ 2253

(b) The court investigator shall do all of the following:

(1) Interview the conservatee personally.

(2) Inform the conservatee of the nature, purpose, and effect of the request made under subdivision (a), and of the right of the conservatee to oppose the request, attend the hearing, be represented by legal counsel, and to have legal counsel appointed by the court if * * * not otherwise represented by legal counsel.

(3) Determine whether the conservatee is unable to attend the hearing because of medical inability and, if able to attend, whether the conservatee is willing to attend the hearing.

(4) Determine whether the conservatee wishes to oppose the request.

(5) Determine whether the conservatee wishes to be represented by legal counsel at the hearing and, if so, whether the conservatee has retained legal counsel and, if not, whether the conservatee plans to retain legal * * * counsel.

* * *

(6) Determine, by considering, among other things, the medical information received pursuant to paragraph (7), whether the proposed change of place of residence is required to prevent irreparable harm to the conservatee and whether no means less restrictive of the conservatee's liberty will suffice to prevent that harm.

(7) Gather and review relevant medical reports regarding the proposed conservatee from the proposed conservatee's primary care physician and other relevant mental and physical health care providers.

(8) Report to the court in writing, at least two days before the hearing, concerning all of the foregoing, including the conservatee's express communications concerning representation by legal counsel and whether the conservatee is not willing to attend the hearing and does not wish to oppose the request.

(c) Within seven days of the date of filing of a temporary conservator's request to remove the conservatee from the conservatee's previous place of residence, the court shall hold a hearing on the request.

(d) The conservatee shall be present at the hearing except in the following cases:

(1) Where the conservatee is unable to attend the hearing by reason of medical inability. Emotional or psychological instability is not good cause for the absence of the conservatee from the hearing unless, by reason of that instability, attendance at the hearing is likely to cause serious and immediate physiological damage to the conservatee.

(2) Where the court investigator has reported to the court that the conservatee has expressly communicated that the conservatee is not willing to attend the hearing and does not wish to oppose the request, and the court makes an order that the conservatee need not attend the hearing.

(e) If the conservatee is unable to attend the hearing because of medical inability, that inability shall be established (1) by the affidavit or certificate of a licensed medical practitioner or (2) if the conservatee is an adherent of a religion whose tenets and practices call for reliance on prayer alone for healing and is under treatment by an accredited practitioner of that religion, by the affidavit of the practitioner. The affidavit or certificate is evidence only of the conservatee's inability to attend the hearing and shall not be considered in determining the issue of need for the establishment of a conservatorship.

(f) At the hearing, the conservatee has the right to be represented by counsel and the right to confront and cross-examine any witness presented by₂ or on behalf of₂ the temporary conservator and to present evidence on their own behalf.

(g) The court may approve the request to remove the conservatee from the previous place of residence only if the court finds (1) that change of residence is required to prevent irreparable harm to the conservatee and (2) that no means less restrictive of the conservatee's liberty will suffice to prevent that harm. If an order is made authorizing the temporary conservator to remove the conservatee from the previous place of residence, the order shall specify the specific place wherein the temporary conservator is authorized to place the conservatee. The temporary conservator may not be authorized to remove the conservatee from this state unless it is additionally shown that the removal is required to permit the performance of specified nonpsychiatric medical treatment, consented to by the conservatee, which is essential to the conservatee's physical survival. A temporary conservator who willfully removes a temporary conservatee from this state without authorization of the court is guilty of a felony.

(h) Subject to subdivision (e) of Section 2252, the court shall also order the temporary conservator to take all reasonable steps to preserve the status quo concerning the conservatee's previous place of residence.

(i)(1) The report required by this section shall be confidential and shall be made available only to parties, their attorneys, and the court. The clerk of the court shall limit disclosure of the report exclusively to persons entitled to the report pursuant to this section.

(2) Notwithstanding paragraph (1), confidential medical information and confidential information from the California Law Enforcement Telecommunications System (CLETS) shall be placed in a separate attachment to the report and shall not be made available to the petitioner or proposed temporary conservator if the request is filed with the petition, the temporary conservatee's spouse or registered domestic partner, and the conservatee's relatives in the first degree or, if there are no such relatives, to the next closest relative.

(j)(1) A superior court shall not be required to perform any duties imposed pursuant to the amendments to this section enacted by Chapter 493 of the Statutes of 2006 until the Legislature makes an appropriation identified for this purpose.

(2) A superior court shall not be required to perform any duties imposed pursuant to the amendments to this section enacted by the measure that added this paragraph until the Legislature makes an appropriation identified for this purpose. (Stats.1990, c. 79 (A.B. 759), § 14, operative July 1, 1991. Amended by Stats.2006, c. 493 (A.B.1363), § 18, operative July 1, 2007; Stats.2011, c. 10 (S.B.78), § 19, eff. March 24, 2011; Stats.2021, c. 417 (A.B.1194), § 20, eff. Jan. 1, 2022; Stats.2022, c. 420 (A.B.2960), § 40, eff. Jan. 1, 2023.)

Cross References

Affidavits, generally, see Code of Civil Procedure §§ 2003, 2009 et seq.
Appointment of legal counsel, see Probate Code § 1470 et seq.
Counsel, right to, see Cal. Const. Art. 1, § 15.
Court investigator, see Probate Code §§ 1419, 1454.
Determination of place of residence, see Government Code § 244.
Felonies, definition and penalties, see Penal Code §§ 17, 18.

Research References

Forms

West's California Code Forms, Probate § 1454 Form 1, Order Appointing Court Investigator—Judicial Council Form GC-330.
West's California Code Forms, Probate § 2215 Form 1, Order Transferring Proceedings.
West's California Code Forms, Probate § 2253 Form 1, Request for Change of Residence of Temporary Conservatee.
West's California Judicial Council Forms GC–330, Order Appointing Court Investigator.

§ 2254. Removal of conservatee from residence in emergency; medical treatment; removal to health facility with consent of conservatee

(a) Notwithstanding Section 2253, a temporary conservator may remove a temporary conservatee from the temporary conservatee's place of residence without court authorization if an emergency exists. For the purposes of this section, an emergency exists if the temporary conservatee's place of residence is unfit for habitation or if the temporary conservator determines in good faith based upon medical advice that the case is an emergency case in which removal from the place of residence is required (1) to provide medical treatment needed to alleviate severe pain or (2) to diagnose or treat a medical condition which, if not immediately diagnosed and treated, will lead to serious disability or death.

(b) No later than one judicial day after the emergency removal of the temporary conservatee, the temporary conservator shall file a written request pursuant to Section 2253 for authorization to fix the residence of the temporary conservatee at a place other than the temporary conservatee's previous place of residence.

(c) Nothing in this chapter prevents a temporary conservator from removing a temporary conservatee from the place of residence to a health facility for treatment without court authorization when the temporary conservatee has given informed consent to the removal.

(d) Nothing in this chapter prevents a temporary conservator from removing a temporary conservatee without court authorization from one health facility where the conservatee is receiving medical care to another health facility where the conservatee will receive medical care. *(Stats.1990, c. 79 (A.B.759), § 14, operative July 1, 1991.)*

Cross References

Authorization of medical treatment for adult without conservator, see Probate Code § 3200 et seq.
Capacity of conservatee to give informed consent for medical treatment, see Probate Code § 1880 et seq.
Computation of time, see Code of Civil Procedure §§ 12 and 12a; Government Code § 6800 et seq.
Determination of place of residence, see Government Code § 244.
Powers and duties of guardian or conservator of the person, medical treatment of conservatee not adjudicated to lack capacity to give informed consent, see Probate Code § 2354.

Research References

Forms

West's California Code Forms, Probate § 2253 Form 1, Request for Change of Residence of Temporary Conservatee.
West's California Judicial Council Forms GC–140, Order Appointing Temporary Guardian.
West's California Judicial Council Forms GC–141, Order Appointing Temporary Conservator.

§ 2255. Inventory and appraisement of estate

(a) Except as provided in subdivision (b), an inventory and appraisal of the estate shall be filed by the temporary guardian or temporary conservator of the estate as required by Article 2 (commencing with Section 2610) of Chapter 7.

(b) A temporary guardian or temporary conservator of the estate may inventory the estate in the final account, without the necessity for an appraisal of the estate, if the final account is filed within 90 days after the appointment of the temporary guardian or temporary conservator. *(Stats.1990, c. 79 (A.B.759), § 14, operative July 1, 1991.)*

§ 2256. Settlement and allowance of accounts

(a) Except as provided in subdivision (b), the temporary guardian or temporary conservator of the estate shall present his or her account to the court for settlement and allowance within 90 days after the appointment of a guardian or conservator of the estate or within such other time as the court may fix.

(b) If the temporary guardian or temporary conservator of the estate is appointed guardian or conservator of the estate, the guardian or conservator may account for the administration as temporary guardian or temporary conservator in his or her first regular account.

(c) Accounts are subject to Sections 2621 to 2626, inclusive, Sections 2630 to 2633, inclusive, and Sections 2640 to 2642, inclusive. *(Stats.1990, c. 79 (A.B.759), § 14, operative July 1, 1991.)*

§ 2257. Termination of powers; time

(a) Except as provided in subdivision (b), the powers of a temporary guardian or temporary conservator terminate, except for the rendering of the account, at the earliest of the following times:

(1) The time the temporary guardian or conservator acquires notice that a guardian or conservator is appointed and qualified.

(2) Thirty days after the appointment of the temporary guardian or temporary conservator or such earlier time as the court may specify in the order of appointment.

(b) With or without notice as the court may require, the court may for good cause order that the time for the termination of the powers of the temporary guardian or temporary conservator be extended or shortened pending final determination by the court of the petition for appointment of a guardian or conservator or pending the final decision on appeal therefrom or for other cause. The order which extends the time for termination shall fix the time when the powers of the temporary guardian or temporary conservator terminate except for the rendering of the account. *(Stats.1990, c. 79 (A.B.759), § 14, operative July 1, 1991. Amended by Stats.2007, c. 553 (A.B.1727), § 14.)*

Cross References

Temporary guardian or conservator pending appeal, see Probate Code § 1310.
Termination date to be stated in letters, see Probate Code § 2251.

§ 2258. Suspension, removal, resignation and discharge

A temporary guardian or temporary conservator is subject to the provisions of this division governing the suspension, removal, resignation, and discharge of a guardian or conservator. *(Stats.1990, c. 79 (A.B.759), § 14, operative July 1, 1991.)*

Cross References

Guardians and conservators, removal or resignation, see Probate Code § 2650 et seq.

CHAPTER 4. OATH, LETTERS, AND BOND

Cross References

Oaths,
  Affirmation in lieu of, see Code of Civil Procedure § 2015.6.
  Officers authorized to administer, see Government Code § 1225.
Sureties on bond, see Code of Civil Procedure § 995.520.
Trust company acting as guardian or conservator, oath, see Financial Code § 1607.

ARTICLE 1. REQUIREMENT OF OATH AND BOND

Section
2300. Oath and bond; necessity before appointment.

Cross References

Application of old and new law, see Probate Code § 3.
Oaths,
  Affirmation in lieu of, see Code of Civil Procedure § 2015.6.
  Officers authorized to administer, see Government Code § 1225.

§ 2300. Oath and bond; necessity before appointment

Before the appointment of a guardian or conservator is effective, including, but not limited to, the appointment of a conservator under Section 2002, the guardian or conservator shall:

(a) Take an oath to perform the duties of the office according to law. The oath obligates the guardian or conservator to comply with the law of this state, as well as other applicable law, at all times, in

§ 2300

any location within or without the state. If the conservator petitions for transfer of the conservatorship to another state pursuant to Section 2001, the conservator shall continue to comply with the law of this state until the court issues a final order confirming the transfer and terminating the conservatorship pursuant to Section 2001. The oath shall be attached to or endorsed upon the letters.

(b) File the required bond if a bond is required. *(Stats.1990, c. 79 (A.B.759), § 14, operative July 1, 1991. Amended by Stats.2014, c. 553 (S.B.940), § 23, eff. Jan. 1, 2015, operative Jan. 1, 2016.)*

Cross References

Additional bond when required, see Probate Code § 2330.
Filing bond with clerk, see Code of Civil Procedure § 995.340.
Letters, defined, see Probate Code § 52.
Oath and bond,
   Personal representative, see Probate Code § 8403.
   Temporary guardian or conservator, see Probate Code § 2251.
Oath as including affirmation or declaration, see Code of Civil Procedure § 17.
Oaths, affirmation in lieu of, see Code of Civil Procedure § 2015.6.
Oaths, officers authorized to administer, see Government Code § 1225.
Principal and sureties, liability on bond, see Code of Civil Procedure § 996.460 et seq.

Research References

Forms

1 California Transactions Forms--Estate Planning § 1:2, Probate System.
1 California Transactions Forms--Estate Planning § 1:29, Options Involving Gifts to Minors.
West's California Code Forms, Probate § 1510 Form 1, Petition for Appointment of Guardian of Estate of Minor—Judicial Council Form GC-210.
West's California Judicial Council Forms JV-330, Letters of Guardianship (Juvenile) (Also Available in Chinese, Korean, Spanish, Vietnamese).

ARTICLE 2. LETTERS

Section
2310. Issuance; evidence of appointment; warning.
2311. Form.
2313. Recording of letters.

Cross References

Application of old and new law, see Probate Code § 3.

§ 2310. Issuance; evidence of appointment; warning

(a) The appointment, the taking of the oath, and the filing of the bond, if required, shall thereafter be evidenced by the issuance of letters by the clerk of the court.

(b) The order appointing a guardian or conservator shall state in capital letters on the first page of the order, in at least 12–point type, the following: "WARNING: THIS APPOINTMENT IS NOT EFFECTIVE UNTIL LETTERS HAVE ISSUED." *(Stats.1990, c. 79 (A.B.759), § 14, operative July 1, 1991. Amended by Stats.1996, c. 862 (A.B.2751), § 7.)*

Cross References

Additional conditions in order of appointment, inclusion in letters, see Probate Code § 2358.
Filing bond with court, see Code of Civil Procedure § 995.340.
Letters, defined, see Probate Code § 52.
Letters of temporary guardianship or conservatorship, see Probate Code §§ 2251, 2252.
Oaths, affirmation in lieu of, see Code of Civil Procedure § 2015.6.
Oaths, officers authorized to administer, see Government Code § 1225.

Research References

Forms

West's California Code Forms, Probate § 1514 Form 1, Order Appointing Guardian of Minor—Judicial Council Form GC-240.
West's California Judicial Council Forms GC-240, Order Appointing Guardian or Extending Guardianship of the Person.

West's California Judicial Council Forms GC-250, Letters of Guardianship.
West's California Judicial Council Forms JV-330, Letters of Guardianship (Juvenile) (Also Available in Chinese, Korean, Spanish, Vietnamese).

§ 2311. Form

Except as otherwise required by the order of appointment, the letters of guardianship or conservatorship shall be in substantially the same form as letters of administration. *(Stats.1990, c. 79 (A.B.759), § 14, operative July 1, 1991.)*

Cross References

Letters of administration, see Probate Code § 8405.
Letters of temporary guardianship or conservatorship, see Probate Code §§ 2251, 2252.
Oath, attachment to or endorsement upon letters, see Probate Code § 2300.

Research References

Forms

West's California Judicial Council Forms GC-250, Letters of Guardianship.

§ 2313. Recording of letters

Except in temporary conservatorships, a conservator of the estate shall record a certified copy of the letters with the county recorder's office in each county in which the conservatee owns an interest in real property, including a security interest. The conservator shall record the letters as soon as practicable after they are issued, but no later than 90 days after the conservator is appointed. A temporary conservator of the estate may record the letters if the conservator deems it appropriate. *(Added by Stats.1991, c. 1019 (S.B.1022), § 3.)*

Cross References

Letters, defined, see Probate Code § 52.
Real property, defined, see Probate Code § 68.

Research References

Forms

West's California Code Forms, Probate § 2310 Form 1, Letters of Conservatorship—Judicial Council Form GC-350.

ARTICLE 3. BONDS OF GUARDIANS AND CONSERVATORS

Section
2320. Necessity; amount.
2320.1. Bond in lesser amount than required; ex parte applications for order increasing the amount of the bond.
2320.2. Additional bond required by court.
2321. Waiver of bond.
2322. Guardian or conservator of person; necessity of court order.
2323. Estate consisting solely of public benefits.
2324. Nominated guardian.
2325. Bond of nonprofit charitable corporation.
2326. Joint guardians or conservators.
2327. Separate bond for each ward or conservatee.
2328. Deposit of property subject to court control.
2329. Reduction in the amount of bond.
2330. Additional bond on real property transactions.
2333. Suit against sureties on bond; limitation period.
2334. Petition to require bond or objection to sufficiency of bond; suspension of powers.
2335. Substitution of surety.

Cross References

Application of old and new law, see Probate Code § 3.

Bond and Undertaking Law, see Code of Civil Procedure § 995.010 et seq.

§ 2320. Necessity; amount

(a) Except as otherwise provided by statute, every person appointed as guardian or conservator shall, before letters are issued, give a bond approved by the court.

(b) The bond shall be for the benefit of the ward or conservatee and all persons interested in the guardianship or conservatorship estate and shall be conditioned upon the faithful execution of the duties of the office, according to law, by the guardian or conservator.

(c) Except as otherwise provided by statute, unless the court increases or decreases the amount upon a showing of good cause, the amount of a bond given by an admitted surety insurer shall be the sum of all of the following:

(1) The value of the personal property of the estate.

(2) The probable annual gross income of all of the property of the estate.

(3) The sum of the probable annual gross payments from the following:

(A) Part 3 (commencing with Section 11000) of, Part 4 (commencing with Section 16000) of, or Part 5 (commencing with Section 17000) of, Division 9 of the Welfare and Institutions Code.

(B) Subchapter II (commencing with Section 401) of, or Part A of Subchapter XVI (commencing with Section 1382) of, Chapter 7 of Title 42 of the United States Code.

(C) Any other public entitlements of the ward or conservatee.

(4) On or after January 1, 2008, a reasonable amount for the cost of recovery to collect on the bond, including attorney's fees and costs. The attorney's fees and costs incurred in a successful action for surcharge against a conservator or guardian for breach of his or her duty under this code shall be a surcharge against the conservator or guardian and, if unpaid, shall be recovered against the surety on the bond. The Judicial Council shall, on or before January 1, 2008, adopt a rule of court to implement this paragraph.

(d) If the bond is given by personal sureties, the amount of the bond shall be twice the amount required for a bond given by an admitted surety insurer.

(e) The Bond and Undertaking Law (Chapter 2 (commencing with Section 995.010) of Title 14 of Part 2 of the Code of Civil Procedure) applies to a bond given under this article, except to the extent inconsistent with this article. *(Stats.1990, c. 79 (A.B.759), § 14, operative July 1, 1991. Amended by Stats.2006, c. 493 (A.B.1363), § 19; Stats.2007, c. 553 (A.B.1727), § 15.)*

Cross References

Additional bond on real property transactions, see Probate Code § 2330.
Additional conditions in order of appointment, liability of surety, see Probate Code §§ 2358, 2402.
Bond, approval of individual sureties, see Code of Civil Procedure § 996.010.
Bond of nominated guardian, see Probate Code § 2324.
Cost of surety bond as an allowable expense of guardian or conservator, see Probate Code § 2623.
Estate consisting solely of public benefits, bond, see Probate Code § 2323.
Guardian or conservator of person only, bond, see Probate Code § 2322.
Letters, defined, see Probate Code § 52.
Limitation of actions against sureties upon bond, see Probate Code § 2333.
Principal and sureties, liability on bond, see Code of Civil Procedure § 996.470.
Reduction in amount of bond,
   Generally, see Probate Code § 2329.
   Deposit of money or other property subject to court control, see Probate Code § 2328.
Separate bonds, single bond or combination, several wards or conservatees, see Probate Code § 2327.
Sureties on bond, see Code of Civil Procedure § 995.520.
Suretyship, generally, see Civil Code § 2787 et seq.

Trust company acting as guardian or conservator, oath, see Probate Code § 301; Financial Code § 1607.

Research References

Forms

1 California Transactions Forms--Estate Planning § 1:29, Options Involving Gifts to Minors.
1 California Transactions Forms--Estate Planning § 6:16, Guardian of Person.
1 California Transactions Forms--Estate Planning § 6:73, Appointment of Guardian of Person of Minor Child and Statement of Desire that Same Person be Appointed Guardian of Minor's Estate.
4 California Transactions Forms--Estate Planning § 19:95, Appointment of Guardian of Estate.
West's California Code Forms, Probate § 1510 Form 1, Petition for Appointment of Guardian of Estate of Minor—Judicial Council Form GC-210.
West's California Code Forms, Probate § 1820 Form 1, Attachment Requesting Special Orders Regarding a Major Neurocognitive Disorder.
West's California Code Forms, Probate § 2329 Form 1, Petition for Reduction of Bond.

§ 2320.1. Bond in lesser amount than required; ex parte applications for order increasing the amount of the bond

When the conservator or guardian has knowledge of facts from which the guardian or conservator knows or should know that the bond posted is less than the amount required under Section 2320, the conservator or guardian, and the attorney, if any, shall make an ex parte application for an order increasing the bond to the amount required under Section 2320. *(Added by Stats.2001, c. 359 (S.B.140), § 1.)*

§ 2320.2. Additional bond required by court

If additional bond is required by the court when the account is heard, the order approving the account and related matters, including fees, is not effective and the court shall not file the order until the additional bond is filed. *(Added by Stats.2001, c. 359 (S.B.140), § 2.)*

§ 2321. Waiver of bond

(a) Notwithstanding any other provision of law, the court in a conservatorship proceeding may not waive the filing of a bond or reduce the amount of bond required, without a good cause determination by the court which shall include a determination by the court that the conservatee will not suffer harm as a result of the waiver or reduction of the bond. Good cause may not be established merely by the conservator having filed a bond in another or prior proceeding.

(b) In a conservatorship proceeding, where the conservatee, having sufficient capacity to do so, has waived the filing of a bond, the court in its discretion may permit the filing of a bond in an amount less than would otherwise be required under Section 2320. *(Added by Stats.1979, c. 726, p. 2335, § 3, operative Jan. 1, 1981. Amended by Stats.2001, c. 563 (A.B.1286), § 4; Stats.2006, c. 493 (A.B.1363), § 20.)*

Cross References

Legal capacity of conservatee, see Probate Code § 1870 et seq.

Research References

Forms

West's California Code Forms, Probate § 1820 Form 1, Attachment Requesting Special Orders Regarding a Major Neurocognitive Disorder.
West's California Code Forms, Probate § 2329 Form 1, Petition for Reduction of Bond.

§ 2322. Guardian or conservator of person; necessity of court order

One appointed only as guardian of the person or conservator of the person need not file a bond unless required by the court. *(Stats.1990, c. 79 (A.B.759), § 14, operative July 1, 1991.)*

§ 2322 PROBATE CODE

Research References

Forms

1 California Transactions Forms--Estate Planning § 6:16, Guardian of Person.
1 California Transactions Forms--Estate Planning § 6:73, Appointment of Guardian of Person of Minor Child and Statement of Desire that Same Person be Appointed Guardian of Minor's Estate.
West's California Code Forms, Probate § 1510 Form 1, Petition for Appointment of Guardian of Estate of Minor—Judicial Council Form GC-210.
West's California Code Forms, Probate § 2329 Form 1, Petition for Reduction of Bond.

§ 2323. Estate consisting solely of public benefits

(a) The court may dispense with the requirement of a bond if it appears likely that the estate will satisfy the conditions of subdivision (a) of Section 2628 for its duration.

(b) If at any time it appears that the estate does not satisfy the conditions of subdivision (a) of Section 2628, the court shall require the filing of a bond unless the court determines that good cause exists, as provided in Section 2321. *(Stats.1990, c. 79 (A.B.759), § 14, operative July 1, 1991. Amended by Stats.2008, c. 293 (A.B. 1340), § 5.)*

Research References

Forms

West's California Code Forms, Probate § 1510 Form 1, Petition for Appointment of Guardian of Estate of Minor—Judicial Council Form GC-210.

§ 2324. Nominated guardian

If the person making the nomination has waived the filing of the bond, a guardian nominated under Section 1500 or 1501 need not file a bond unless required by the court. *(Stats.1990, c. 79 (A.B.759), § 14, operative July 1, 1991.)*

Cross References

Nomination of guardian, see Probate Code § 1500 et seq.

Research References

Forms

1 California Transactions Forms--Estate Planning § 6:16, Guardian of Person.
1 California Transactions Forms--Estate Planning § 6:73, Appointment of Guardian of Person of Minor Child and Statement of Desire that Same Person be Appointed Guardian of Minor's Estate.
4 California Transactions Forms--Estate Planning § 19:95, Appointment of Guardian of Estate.
West's California Code Forms, Probate § 1510 Form 1, Petition for Appointment of Guardian of Estate of Minor—Judicial Council Form GC-210.

§ 2325. Bond of nonprofit charitable corporation

The surety on the bond of a nonprofit charitable corporation described in Section 2104 shall be an admitted surety insurer. *(Stats.1990, c. 79 (A.B.759), § 14, operative July 1, 1991.)*

Cross References

Cost of surety bond as an allowable expense, see Probate Code § 2623.
Suretyship, see Civil Code § 2787 et seq.

§ 2326. Joint guardians or conservators

(a) If joint guardians or conservators are appointed, the court may order that separate bonds or a joint bond or a combination thereof be furnished.

(b) If a joint bond is furnished, the liability on the bond is joint and several. *(Stats.1990, c. 79 (A.B.759), § 14, operative July 1, 1991.)*

Cross References

Bonds by several personal representatives, see Probate Code § 8480.
Joint guardians or conservators, see Probate Code § 2105.
Joint or several obligations, see Civil Code § 1430 et seq.

§ 2327. Separate bond for each ward or conservatee

(a) In a conservatorship proceeding, the court shall order a separate bond for each conservatee, except where the assets of the conservatees are commingled in which case a combined bond that covers all assets may be provided.

(b) If a guardianship proceeding involves more than one ward, the court may order separate bonds, or a single bond which is for the benefit of two or more wards in that proceeding, or a combination thereof. *(Added by Stats.1990, c. 79 (A.B.759), § 14, operative July 1, 1991. Amended by Stats.2001, c. 563 (A.B.1286), § 5.)*

Cross References

One guardian or conservator for several wards or conservatees, see Probate Code § 2106.

§ 2328. Deposit of property subject to court control

(a) In any proceeding to determine the amount of the bond of the guardian or conservator (whether at the time of appointment or subsequently), if the estate includes property which has been or will be deposited with a trust company or financial institution pursuant to Sections 2453 to 2456, inclusive, upon the condition that the property, including any earnings thereon, will not be withdrawn except on authorization of the court, the court, in its discretion, with or without notice, may so order and may do either of the following:

(1) Exclude the property deposited in determining the amount of the required bond or reduce the amount of the bond to be required in respect to the property deposited to such an amount as the court determines is reasonable.

(2) If a bond has already been furnished or the amount fixed, reduce the amount to such an amount as the court determines is reasonable.

(b) The petitioner for letters, or the proposed guardian or conservator in advance of appointment of a guardian or conservator, may do any one or more of the following:

(1) Deliver personal property in the person's possession to a trust company.

(2) Deliver money in the person's possession for deposit in an insured account in a financial institution in this state.

(3) Allow a trust company to retain personal property already in its possession.

(4) Allow a financial institution in this state to retain money already invested in an insured account in a financial institution.

(c) In the cases described in subdivision (b), the petitioner or proposed guardian or conservator shall obtain and file with the court a written receipt including the agreement of the trust company or financial institution that the property deposited, including any earnings thereon, shall not be allowed to be withdrawn except upon authorization of the court.

(d) In receiving and retaining property on deposit pursuant to subdivisions (b) and (c), the trust company or financial institution is protected to the same extent as though it received the property on deposit from a person to whom letters had been issued. *(Stats.1990, c. 79 (A.B.759), § 14, operative July 1, 1991.)*

Cross References

Account defined, see Probate Code § 21.
Banks, see Financial Code § 99 et seq.
Capacity of trust company to act as guardian of estate of ward, see Probate Code § 300.
Court ordered deposits, see Financial Code §§ 1586, 7000.
Deposits in bank and savings accounts, see Probate Code § 2453.
Deposits withdrawable only on court order, see Probate Code § 2456.
Financial institution, defined, see Probate Code § 40.
Letters, defined, see Probate Code § 52.

Management or disposition of community property where spouse lacks legal capacity, bond of petitioner, see Probate Code § 3150.
Personal property, deposit with trust company, see Probate Code § 2454.
Savings associations, see Financial Code § 5000.
Trust companies, see Financial Code § 1550 et seq.
Trust company, defined, see Probate Code § 83.

Research References

Forms

West's California Code Forms, Probate § 2329 Form 1, Petition for Reduction of Bond.
West's California Code Forms, Probate § 2456 Form 1, Petition for Order Conditioning Withdrawal of Deposits in Financial Institution on Prior Authorization of the Court.

§ 2329. Reduction in the amount of bond

(a) If a guardian or conservator moves the court for reduction in the amount of the bond, the motion shall include an affidavit setting forth the condition of the estate.

(b) Except upon a showing of good cause, the amount of the bond shall not be reduced below the amount determined pursuant to Section 2320.

(c) Nothing in this section limits the authority of the court to reduce the amount of the bond with or without notice under Section 2328. *(Stats.1990, c. 79 (A.B.759), § 14, operative July 1, 1991.)*

Cross References

Affidavits, see Code of Civil Procedure § 2009 et seq.
Bond in excessive amount, recover on, see Code of Civil Procedure § 996.470.

Research References

Forms

West's California Code Forms, Probate § 2329 Form 1, Petition for Reduction of Bond.

§ 2330. Additional bond on real property transactions

Upon the confirmation of the sale of any real property of the estate, or upon the authorization of the borrowing of money secured by a mortgage or deed of trust on real property of the estate, the guardian or conservator shall furnish an additional bond as is required by the court in order to make the sum of the bonds furnished by the guardian or conservator equal to the amount determined pursuant to Section 2320, taking into account the proceeds of the sale or mortgage or deed of trust, unless the court makes an express finding stating the reason why the bond should not be increased. If a bond or additional bond is required under this section, the order confirming the sale of real property of the estate or authorizing the borrowing of money secured by a mortgage or deed of trust on real property of the estate is not effective and the court shall not file the order until the additional bond is filed. *(Stats.1990, c. 79 (A.B.759), § 14, operative July 1, 1991. Amended by Stats.2001, c. 359 (S.B.140), § 3.)*

Cross References

Additional bond on realty sales by administrator, see Probate Code § 8482.
Cost of bond, see Probate Code § 2623.
Filing of bonds, see Code of Civil Procedure § 995.340.
Limitation of actions on bonds, see Probate Code § 2333.
Mortgages, generally, see Civil Code § 2920 et seq.
Real property, defined, see Probate Code § 68.
Sales of real or personal property, see Probate Code § 2540 et seq.

Research References

Forms

West's California Code Forms, Probate § 2540 Form 2, Order Confirming Sale of Real Property and Other Property (Probate)—Judicial Council Form DE-265, GC-065.

West's California Code Forms, Probate § 2551 Form 2, Order Authorizing Guardian or Conservator to Borrow Money and to Encumber Real Property.

§ 2333. Suit against sureties on bond; limitation period

(a) In case of a breach of a condition of the bond, an action may be brought against the sureties on the bond for the use and benefit of the ward or conservatee or of any person interested in the estate.

(b) No action may be maintained against the sureties on the bond unless commenced within four years from the discharge or removal of the guardian or conservator or within four years from the date the order surcharging the guardian or conservator becomes final, whichever is later.

(c) In any case, and notwithstanding subdivision (b) of Section 2103, no action may be maintained against the sureties on the bond unless the action commences within six years from the date the judgment under Section 2103 or the later of the orders under subdivision (b) of this section becomes final. *(Stats.1990, c. 79 (A.B.759), § 14, operative July 1, 1991. Amended by Stats.1990, c. 710 (S.B.1775), § 7, operative July 1, 1991; Stats.1993, c. 794 (A.B.516), § 1; Stats.1994, c. 806 (A.B.3686), § 11.)*

Cross References

Actions on bonds, see Code of Civil Procedure § 996.460 et seq.; Probate Code § 9822.
Guardianship and conservatorship, interested person, defined, see Probate Code § 1424.
Nature of surety's liability, see Code of Civil Procedure § 996.460 et seq.
Periods of limitation, generally, see Code of Civil Procedure § 335 et seq.
Removal of guardian or conservator, see Probate Code § 2650 et seq.
Suretyship, see Civil Code § 2787 et seq.

§ 2334. Petition to require bond or objection to sufficiency of bond; suspension of powers

Where a petition is filed requesting an order that a guardian or conservator be required to give a bond where no bond was originally required, or an objection is made to the sufficiency of the bond, and the petition or affidavit supporting the objection alleges facts showing that the guardian or conservator is failing to use ordinary care and diligence in the management of the estate, the court, by order, may suspend the powers of the guardian or conservator until the matter can be heard and determined. *(Stats.1990, c. 79 (A.B.759), § 14, operative July 1, 1991.)*

Cross References

Accounts on removal of guardian or conservator, see Probate Code § 2630.
Executors and administrators, insufficiency of sureties, see Code of Civil Procedure § 996.010.
Removal of guardian or conservator, see Probate Code § 2650 et seq.
Suspension of powers of guardian or conservator upon petition for removal, see Probate Code § 2654.
Temporary guardian or conservator, appointment by court upon suspension of powers of the guardian or conservator, see Probate Code § 2250.

§ 2335. Substitution of surety

A guardian or conservator who applies for a substitution and release of a surety shall file an account with the application. The court shall not order a substitution unless the account is approved. *(Stats.1990, c. 79 (A.B.759), § 14, operative July 1, 1991.)*

Cross References

Accounts, see Probate Code § 2620 et seq.
Application for release of surety, see Code of Civil Procedure §§ 996.110, 996.130.

Research References

Forms

West's California Code Forms, Probate § 1510 Form 1, Petition for Appointment of Guardian of Estate of Minor—Judicial Council Form GC-210.

ARTICLE 4. PROFESSIONAL FIDUCIARIES

Section
2340. Appointment of professional fiduciaries; licensing requirements.

Section	
2341.	Operative date.

§ 2340. Appointment of professional fiduciaries; licensing requirements

A superior court may not appoint a person to carry out the duties of a professional fiduciary, or permit a person to continue those duties, unless he or she holds a valid, unexpired, unsuspended license as a professional fiduciary under Chapter 6 (commencing with Section 6500) of Division 3 of the Business and Professions Code, is exempt from the definition of "professional fiduciary" under Section 6501 of the Business and Professions Code, or is exempt from the licensing requirements of Section 6530 of the Business and Professions Code. *(Added by Stats.2006, c. 491 (S.B.1550), § 5, operative July 1, 2008. Amended by Stats.2008, c. 293 (A.B.1340), § 6.)*

Cross References

Petition for appointment as guardian, contents of petition, see Probate Code § 1510.
Petition for temporary guardian or conservator, contents of petition, see Probate Code § 2250.
Petition to appoint a conservator, contents of petition, see Probate Code § 1821.
Professional fiduciary as guardian or conservator, court authorization of periodic payments, contents of petition, see Probate Code § 2643.1.
Professional fiduciary as guardian or conservator, proposed hourly fee schedule or proposed compensation filing requirement, see Probate Code § 2614.7.

Research References

Forms

West's California Code Forms, Probate § 1820 Form 1, Attachment Requesting Special Orders Regarding a Major Neurocognitive Disorder.
West's California Code Forms, Probate § 2250 Form 1, Petition for Appointment of Temporary Guardian—Judicial Council Form GC-110.

§ 2341. Operative date

This article shall become operative on July 1, 2008. *(Added by Stats.2006, c. 491 (S.B.1550), § 5, operative July 1, 2008.)*

Research References

Forms

West's California Code Forms, Probate § 1820 Form 1, Attachment Requesting Special Orders Regarding a Major Neurocognitive Disorder.
West's California Code Forms, Probate § 2250 Form 1, Petition for Appointment of Temporary Guardian—Judicial Council Form GC-110.

CHAPTER 5. POWERS AND DUTIES OF GUARDIAN OR CONSERVATOR OF THE PERSON

Section	
2350.	Definitions.
2351.	Care, custody, control and education.
2351.5.	Limited conservator; modification of powers; notice; hearing.
2352.	Residence of ward or conservatee.
2352.5.	Presumption relating to residence of conservatee; level of care determination; conservatees with developmental disabilities.
2353.	Medical treatment of ward.
2354.	Medical treatment of conservatee not adjudicated to lack capacity to give informed consent.
2355.	Medical treatment of conservatee adjudicated to lack capacity to make health care decisions.
2356.	Limitations on application of chapter.
2356.5.	Major neurocognitive disorder; legislative findings, declarations, and intent; placement in secured facility; administration of medication; procedures.
2357.	Court ordered medical treatment.
2358.	Additional conditions in order of appointment.
2359.	Petitions of guardian, conservator, ward or conservatee; approval of purchase, lease, or rental of property from estate; violations of section.
2360.	Photograph of conservatee.
2361.	Notice of conservatee's death.

Cross References

Application of old and new law, see Probate Code § 3.

§ 2350. Definitions

As used in this chapter:

(a) "Conservator" means the conservator of the person.

(b) "Guardian" means the guardian of the person.

(c) "Residence" does not include a regional center established pursuant to Chapter 5 (commencing with Section 4620) of Division 4.5 of the Welfare and Institutions Code. *(Stats.1990, c. 79 (A.B.759), § 14, operative July 1, 1991. Amended by Stats.2008, c. 293 (A.B.1340), § 7.)*

Cross References

Nonresident ward or conservatee, powers and duties of guardian or conservator, see Probate Code § 2107.

Research References

Forms

2 California Transactions Forms--Estate Planning § 8:22, Authority of Attorney-In-Fact.
2 California Transactions Forms--Estate Planning § 8:76, Statutory Limitations on Agent's Authority.

§ 2351. Care, custody, control and education

(a) Subject to subdivision (b), the guardian or conservator, but not a limited conservator, has the care, custody, and control of, and has charge of the education of, the ward or conservatee. This control shall not extend to personal rights retained by the conservatee, including, but not limited to, the right to receive visitors, telephone calls, and personal mail, unless specifically limited by court order. The court may issue an order that specifically grants the conservator the power to enforce the conservatee's rights to receive visitors, telephone calls, and personal mail, or that directs the conservator to allow those visitors, telephone calls, and personal mail.

(b) Where the court determines that it is appropriate in the circumstances of the particular conservatee, the court, in its discretion, may limit the powers and duties that the conservator would otherwise have under subdivision (a) by an order stating either of the following:

(1) The specific powers that the conservator does not have with respect to the conservatee's person and reserving the powers so specified to the conservatee.

(2) The specific powers and duties the conservator has with respect to the conservatee's person and reserving to the conservatee all other rights with respect to the conservatee's person that the conservator otherwise would have under subdivision (a).

(c) An order under this section (1) may be included in the order appointing a conservator of the person or (2) may be made, modified, or revoked upon a petition subsequently filed, notice of the hearing on the petition having been given for the period and in the manner provided in Chapter 3 (commencing with Section 1460) of Part 1.

(d) The guardian or conservator, in exercising his or her powers, may not hire or refer any business to an entity in which he or she has a financial interest except upon authorization of the court. Prior to authorization from the court, the guardian or conservator shall disclose to the court in writing his or her financial interest in the entity. For the purposes of this subdivision, "financial interest" shall mean (1) an ownership interest in a sole proprietorship, a partnership, or a closely held corporation, or (2) an ownership interest of greater than 1 percent of the outstanding shares in a publicly traded corporation, or (3) being an officer or a director of a corporation. This subdivision shall apply only to conservators and guardians required to register with the Statewide Registry under Chapter 13 (commencing with Section 2850). *(Stats.1990, c. 79 (A.B.759), § 14, operative July 1, 1991. Amended by Stats.2000, c. 565 (A.B.1950), § 4; Stats.2013, c. 127 (A.B.937), § 1; Stats.2015, c. 92 (A.B.1085), § 2, eff. Jan. 1, 2016.)*

Cross References

Additional powers of guardian nominated by will, see Probate Code § 2108.

Research References

Forms

1 California Transactions Forms--Estate Planning § 6:16, Guardian of Person.
West's California Code Forms, Probate § 1488 Form 1, Petition to Convert Guardianship to Conservatorship.
West's California Judicial Council Forms JV–330, Letters of Guardianship (Juvenile) (Also Available in Chinese, Korean, Spanish, Vietnamese).

§ 2351.5. Limited conservator; modification of powers; notice; hearing

(a) Subject to subdivision (b):

(1) The limited conservator has the care, custody, and control of the limited conservatee.

(2) The limited conservator shall secure for the limited conservatee those habilitation or treatment, training, education, medical and psychological services, and social and vocational opportunity as appropriate and as will assist the limited conservatee in the development of maximum self-reliance and independence.

(b) A limited conservator does not have any of the following powers or controls over the limited conservatee unless those powers or controls are specifically requested in the petition for appointment of a limited conservator and granted by the court in its order appointing the limited conservator:

(1) To fix the residence or specific dwelling of the limited conservatee.

(2) Access to the confidential records and papers of the limited conservatee.

(3) To consent or withhold consent to the marriage of, or the entrance into a registered domestic partnership by, the limited conservatee.

(4) The right of the limited conservatee to contract.

(5) The power of the limited conservatee to give or withhold medical consent.

(6) The limited conservatee's right to control his or her own social and sexual contacts and relationships.

(7) Decisions concerning the education of the limited conservatee.

(c) Any limited conservator, the limited conservatee, or any relative or friend of the limited conservatee may apply by petition to the superior court of the county in which the proceedings are pending to have the limited conservatorship modified by the elimination or addition of any of the powers which must be specifically granted to the limited conservator pursuant to subdivision (b). The petition shall state the facts alleged to establish that the limited conservatorship should be modified. The granting or elimination of those powers is discretionary with the court. Notice of the hearing on the petition shall be given for the period and in the manner provided in Chapter 3 (commencing with Section 1460) of Part 1.

(d) The limited conservator or any relative or friend of the limited conservatee may appear and oppose the petition. The court shall hear and determine the matter according to the laws and procedures relating to the trial of civil actions, including trial by jury if demanded. If any of the powers which must be specifically granted to the limited conservator pursuant to subdivision (b) are granted or eliminated, new letters of limited conservatorship shall be issued reflecting the change in the limited conservator's powers. *(Stats. 1990, c. 79 (A.B.759), § 14, operative July 1, 1991. Amended by Stats.2005, c. 418 (S.B.973), § 28.)*

Cross References

Capacity of conservatee to give informed consent for medical treatment, see Probate Code § 1880 et seq.
Capacity of conservatee to marry, see Probate Code §§ 1900, 1901.
Determination of place of residence, see Government Code § 244.
Letters, generally, see Probate Code § 2310 et seq.
Marriage, generally, see Family Code § 300 et seq.
Persons capable of contracting, see Civil Code §§ 1556, 1557.

Research References

Forms

West's California Code Forms, Probate § 1488 Form 1, Petition to Convert Guardianship to Conservatorship.

§ 2352. Residence of ward or conservatee

(a) The guardian may establish the residence of the ward at any place within this state without the permission of the court. The guardian shall select the least restrictive appropriate residence that is available and necessary to meet the needs of the ward, and that is in the best interests of the ward.

(b) The conservator may establish the residence of the conservatee at any place within this state without the permission of the court. The conservator shall select the least restrictive appropriate residence, as described in Section 2352.5, that is available and necessary to meet the needs of the conservatee, and that is in the best interests of the conservatee.

(c) If permission of the court is first obtained, a guardian or conservator may establish the residence of a ward or conservatee at a place not within this state. Notice of the hearing on the petition to establish the residence of the ward or conservatee out of state, together with a copy of the petition, shall be given in the manner required by subdivision (a) of Section 1460 to all persons entitled to notice under subdivision (b) of Section 1511 or subdivision (b) of Section 1822.

(d)(1) An order under subdivision (c) relating to a ward shall require the guardian either to return the ward to this state, or to cause a guardianship proceeding or its equivalent to be commenced in the place of the new residence, when the ward has resided in the place of new residence for a period of four months or a longer or shorter period specified in the order.

(2) An order under subdivision (c) relating to a conservatee shall require the conservator to do one of the following when the conservatee has resided in the other state for a period of four months or a longer or shorter period specified in the order:

(A) Return the conservatee to this state.

(B) Petition for transfer of the conservatorship to the other state under Article 3 (commencing with Section 2001) of Chapter 8 of Part 3 and corresponding law of the other state.

(C) Cause a conservatorship proceeding or its equivalent to be commenced in the other state.

(e)(1) The guardian or conservator shall file a notice of change of residence with the court within 30 days of the date of the change. The guardian or conservator shall include in the notice of change of residence a declaration stating that the ward's or conservatee's change of residence is consistent with the standard described in subdivision (b).

(2) The guardian or conservator shall deliver pursuant to Section 1215 a copy of the notice to all persons entitled to notice under subdivision (b) of Section 1511 or subdivision (b) of Section 1822 and shall file proof of delivery of the notice with the court. The court

§ 2352

may, for good cause, waive the delivery requirement pursuant to this paragraph in order to prevent harm to the conservatee or ward.

(3) If the guardian or conservator proposes to remove the ward or conservatee from his or her personal residence, except as provided by subdivision (c), the guardian or conservator shall deliver pursuant to Section 1215 a notice of his or her intention to change the residence of the ward or conservatee to all persons entitled to notice under subdivision (b) of Section 1511 and subdivision (b) of Section 1822. In the absence of an emergency, that notice shall be delivered at least 15 days before the proposed removal of the ward or conservatee from his or her personal residence. If the notice is delivered less than 15 days before the proposed removal of the ward or conservatee, the guardian or conservator shall set forth the basis for the emergency in the notice. The guardian or conservator shall file proof of delivery of that notice with the court.

(f) This section does not apply where the court has made an order under Section 2351 pursuant to which the conservatee retains the right to establish his or her own residence.

(g) As used in this section, "guardian" or "conservator" includes a proposed guardian or proposed conservator and "ward" or "conservatee" includes a proposed ward or proposed conservatee.

(h) This section does not apply to a person with developmental disabilities for whom the Director of Developmental Services or a regional center, established pursuant to Chapter 5 (commencing with Section 4620) of Division 4.5 of the Welfare and Institutions Code, acts as the conservator. *(Stats.1990, c. 79 (A.B.759), § 14, operative July 1, 1991. Amended by Stats.2006, c. 490 (S.B.1116), § 1; Stats.2008, c. 293 (A.B.1340), § 8; Stats.2014, c. 553 (S.B.940), § 24, eff. Jan. 1, 2015, operative Jan. 1, 2016; Stats.2017, c. 319 (A.B.976), § 43, eff. Jan. 1, 2018.)*

Cross References

Determination of place of residence, see Government Code § 244.
Notice,
  Mailing, see Probate Code § 1215 et seq.
  Posting, see Probate Code § 1230.
  Proof of giving notice, see Probate Code § 1260 et seq.
  Special notice, see Probate Code § 1250 et seq.
  This code, generally, see Probate Code § 1200 et seq.
  This division, generally, see Probate Code § 1460 et seq.
Request for special notice, see Probate Code § 2700 et seq.
Service of process,
  Generally, see Code of Civil Procedure § 413.10 et seq.
  Mail, see Code of Civil Procedure §§ 415.30, 1012 et seq.
  Personal delivery, see Code of Civil Procedure § 415.10.
  Proof of service, see Code of Civil Procedure § 417.10 et seq.
  Publication, see Code of Civil Procedure § 415.50.

Research References

Forms

1 California Transactions Forms--Estate Planning § 6:16, Guardian of Person.
West's California Code Forms, Probate § 2352 Form 1, Change of Residence Notice—Judicial Council Form GC-080.
West's California Code Forms, Probate § 2352 Form 3, Order Fixing Residence Outside the State of California—Judicial Council Form GC-090.
West's California Judicial Council Forms GC–079, Pre-Move Notice of Proposed Change of Personal Residence of Conservatee or Ward.
West's California Judicial Council Forms GC–080, Change of Residence Notice.
West's California Judicial Council Forms GC–085, Petition to Fix Residence Outside the State of California.
West's California Judicial Council Forms GC–090, Order Fixing Residence Outside the State of California.
West's California Judicial Council Forms JV–330, Letters of Guardianship (Juvenile) (Also Available in Chinese, Korean, Spanish, Vietnamese).

§ 2352.5. Presumption relating to residence of conservatee; level of care determination; conservatees with developmental disabilities

(a) It shall be presumed that the personal residence of the conservatee at the time of commencement of the proceeding is the least restrictive appropriate residence for the conservatee. In any hearing to determine if removal of the conservatee from the conservatee's personal residence is appropriate, that presumption may be overcome by clear and convincing evidence.

(b) Upon appointment, the conservator shall determine the appropriate level of care for the conservatee.

(1) That determination shall include an evaluation of the level of care existing at the time of commencement of the proceeding and the measures that would be necessary to keep the conservatee in their personal residence.

(2) If the conservatee is living at a location other than the conservatee's personal residence at the commencement of the proceeding, that determination shall either include a plan to return the conservatee to their personal residence or an explanation of the limitations or restrictions on a return of the conservatee to their personal residence in the foreseeable future.

(c) The determination made by the conservator pursuant to subdivision (b) shall be in writing, signed under penalty of perjury, and submitted to the court within 60 days of appointment as conservator.

(d) The conservator shall evaluate the conservatee's placement and level of care if there is a material change in circumstances affecting the conservatee's needs for placement and care.

(e)(1) This section shall not apply to a conservatee with developmental disabilities for whom the Director of Developmental Services or a regional center for the developmentally disabled, established pursuant to Chapter 5 (commencing with Section 4620) of Division 4.5 of the Welfare and Institutions Code, acts as the conservator and who receives services from a regional center pursuant to the Lanterman Developmental Disabilities Act (Division 4.5 (commencing with Section 4500) of the Welfare and Institutions Code).

(2) Services, including residential placement, for a conservatee described in paragraph (1) who is a consumer, as defined in Section 4512 of the Welfare and Institutions Code, shall be identified, delivered, and evaluated consistent with the individual program plan process described in Article 2 (commencing with Section 4640) of Chapter 5 of Division 4.5 of the Welfare and Institutions Code. *(Added by Stats.2006, c. 490 (S.B.1116), § 2. Amended by Stats.2007, c. 130 (A.B.299), § 195; Stats.2019, c. 847 (S.B.303), § 1, eff. Jan. 1, 2020.)*

Research References

Forms

West's California Code Forms, Probate § 2352 Form 1, Change of Residence Notice—Judicial Council Form GC-080.
West's California Judicial Council Forms GC–355, Determination of Conservatee's Appropriate Level of Care.

§ 2353. Medical treatment of ward

(a) Subject to subdivision (b), the guardian has the same right as a parent having legal custody of a child to give consent to medical treatment performed upon the ward and to require the ward to receive medical treatment.

(b) Except as provided in subdivision (c), if the ward is 14 years of age or older, no surgery may be performed upon the ward without either (1) the consent of both the ward and the guardian or (2) a court order obtained pursuant to Section 2357 specifically authorizing such treatment.

(c) The guardian may consent to surgery to be performed upon the ward, and may require the ward to receive the surgery, in any case where the guardian determines in good faith based upon medical advice that the case is an emergency case in which the ward faces loss of life or serious bodily injury if the surgery is not performed. In such a case, the consent of the guardian alone is sufficient and no person is liable because the surgery is performed upon the ward without the ward's consent.

(d) Nothing in this section requires the consent of the guardian for medical or surgical treatment for the ward in any case where the ward alone may consent to such treatment under other provisions of law. *(Stats.1990, c. 79 (A.B.759), § 14, operative July 1, 1991.)*

Cross References

Additional powers of guardian nominated by will, see Probate Code § 2108.
Caregiver, authorization for medical or dental care of minor, see Family Code § 6550.
Consent by,
   Director of regional center, see Welfare and Institutions Code § 4655.
   Medical director of state hospital, see Welfare and Institutions Code § 7518.
Medical treatment for adult without conservator, authorization, see Probate Code § 3200 et seq.
Minors, caregivers, authorization affidavits, see Family Code § 6550.

Research References

Forms

1 California Transactions Forms--Estate Planning § 6:16, Guardian of Person.
West's California Code Forms, Family § 6550, Comment Overview—Authorization Affidavits.
West's California Code Forms, Probate § 2357 Form 1, Petition for Order Directing Medical Treatment for Ward or Conservatee.
West's California Judicial Council Forms JV–330, Letters of Guardianship (Juvenile) (Also Available in Chinese, Korean, Spanish, Vietnamese).

§ 2354. Medical treatment of conservatee not adjudicated to lack capacity to give informed consent

(a) If the conservatee has not been adjudicated to lack the capacity to give informed consent for medical treatment, the conservatee may consent to his or her medical treatment. The conservator may also give consent to the medical treatment, but the consent of the conservator is not required if the conservatee has the capacity to give informed consent to the medical treatment, and the consent of the conservator alone is not sufficient under this subdivision if the conservatee objects to the medical treatment.

(b) The conservator may require the conservatee to receive medical treatment, whether or not the conservatee consents to the treatment, if a court order specifically authorizing the medical treatment has been obtained pursuant to Section 2357.

(c) The conservator may consent to medical treatment to be performed upon the conservatee, and may require the conservatee to receive the medical treatment, in any case where the conservator determines in good faith based upon medical advice that the case is an emergency case in which the medical treatment is required because (1) the treatment is required for the alleviation of severe pain or (2) the conservatee has a medical condition which, if not immediately diagnosed and treated, will lead to serious disability or death. In such a case, the consent of the conservator alone is sufficient and no person is liable because the medical treatment is performed upon the conservatee without the conservatee's consent. *(Stats.1990, c. 79 (A.B.759), § 14, operative July 1, 1991.)*

Cross References

Adjudication of lack of capacity to give informed consent for medical treatment, see Probate Code § 1880.
Consent by,
   Director of regional center, see Welfare and Institutions Code § 4655.
   Medical director of state hospital, see Welfare and Institutions Code § 7518.
Gravely disabled persons, medical treatment of conservatee, see Welfare and Institutions Code § 5358.2.
Human experimentation, informed consent, see Health and Safety Code § 24175.
Medical treatment for adult without conservator, authorization, see Probate Code § 3200 et seq.

Research References

Forms

West's California Code Forms, Probate § 2357 Form 1, Petition for Order Directing Medical Treatment for Ward or Conservatee.

§ 2355. Medical treatment of conservatee adjudicated to lack capacity to make health care decisions

(a) If the conservatee has been adjudicated to lack the capacity to make health care decisions, the conservator has the exclusive authority to make health care decisions for the conservatee that the conservator in good faith based on medical advice determines to be necessary. The conservator shall make health care decisions for the conservatee in accordance with the conservatee's individual health care instructions, if any, and other wishes to the extent known to the conservator. Otherwise, the conservator shall make the decision in accordance with the conservator's determination of the conservatee's best interest. In determining the conservatee's best interest, the conservator shall consider the conservatee's personal values to the extent known to the conservator. The conservator may require the conservatee to receive the health care, whether or not the conservatee objects. In this case, the health care decision of the conservator alone is sufficient and no person is liable because the health care is administered to the conservatee without the conservatee's consent. For the purposes of this subdivision, "health care" and "health care decision" have the meanings provided in Sections 4615 and 4617, respectively.

(b) If prior to the establishment of the conservatorship the conservatee was an adherent of a religion whose tenets and practices call for reliance on prayer alone for healing, the treatment required by the conservator under the provisions of this section shall be by an accredited practitioner of that religion. *(Stats.1990, c. 79 (A.B.759), § 14, operative July 1, 1991. Amended by Stats.1999, c. 658 (A.B.891), § 12, operative July 1, 2000.)*

Cross References

Adjudication of lack of capacity to give informed consent for medical treatment, see Probate Code § 1880.
Consent by,
   Director of regional center, see Welfare and Institutions Code § 4655.
   Medical director of state hospital, see Welfare and Institutions Code § 7518.
Court ordered medical treatment, see Probate Code § 2357.
Gravely disabled persons, medical treatment of conservatee, see Welfare and Institutions Code § 5358.2.
Health care decisions, generally, see Probate Code § 4600 et seq.
Human experimentation, informed consent, see Health and Safety Code § 24175.

Research References

Forms

2 California Transactions Forms--Estate Planning § 8:77, Withholding or Withdrawing Medical Treatment.
West's California Code Forms, Probate § 1891 Form 1, Petition for Exclusive Authority to Give Consent for Medical Treatment (Probate Conservatorship)—Judicial Council Form GC-380.
West's California Code Forms, Probate § 2357 Form 1, Petition for Order Directing Medical Treatment for Ward or Conservatee.
West's California Judicial Council Forms GC–380, Petition for Exclusive Authority to Give Consent for Medical Treatment.
West's California Judicial Council Forms GC–385, Order Authorizing Conservator to Give Consent for Medical Treatment.

§ 2356. Limitations on application of chapter

(a) A ward or conservatee shall not be placed in a mental health treatment facility under this division against his or her will. Involuntary civil placement of a ward or conservatee in a mental health treatment facility may be obtained only pursuant to Chapter 2 (commencing with Section 5150) or Chapter 3 (commencing with Section 5350) of Part 1 of Division 5 of the Welfare and Institutions Code. Nothing in this subdivision precludes the placing of a ward in a state hospital under Section 6000 of the Welfare and Institutions Code upon application of the guardian as provided in that section.

(b) An experimental drug as defined in Section 111515 of the Health and Safety Code shall not be prescribed for or administered to a ward or conservatee under this division. An experimental drug may be prescribed for or administered to a ward or conservatee only as provided in Article 4 (commencing with Section 111515) of Chapter 6 of Part 5 of Division 104 of the Health and Safety Code.

§ 2356

(c) Convulsive treatment as defined in Section 5325 of the Welfare and Institutions Code shall not be performed on a ward or conservatee under this division. Convulsive treatment may be performed on a ward or conservatee only as provided in Article 7 (commencing with Section 5325) of Chapter 2 of Part 1 of Division 5 of the Welfare and Institutions Code.

(d) A minor shall not be sterilized under this division.

(e) This chapter is subject to a valid and effective advance health care directive under the Health Care Decisions Law (Division 4.7 (commencing with Section 4600)). *(Stats.1990, c. 79 (A.B.759), § 14, operative July 1, 1991. Amended by Stats.1990, c. 710 (S.B.1775), § 8, operative July 1, 1991; Stats.1996, c. 1023 (S.B.1497), § 398, eff. Sept. 29, 1996; Stats.1999, c. 658 (A.B.891), § 13, operative July 1, 2000; Stats.2014, c. 442 (S.B.1465), § 12, eff. Sept. 18, 2014; Stats.2015, c. 117 (A.B.468), § 1, eff. Jan. 1, 2016.)*

Cross References

Health care decisions, generally, see Probate Code § 4600 et seq.
Medical experiments, informed consent, see Health and Safety Code § 24175.
Minors, caregivers, authorization affidavits, see Family Code § 6550.

Research References

Forms

2 California Transactions Forms--Estate Planning § 8:76, Statutory Limitations on Agent's Authority.

West's California Code Forms, Probate § 2357 Form 1, Petition for Order Directing Medical Treatment for Ward or Conservatee.

West's California Code Forms, Probate § 2651 Form 1, Petition for Removal of Guardian or Conservator.

§ 2356.5. Major neurocognitive disorder; legislative findings, declarations, and intent; placement in secured facility; administration of medication; procedures

(a) The Legislature hereby finds and declares all of the following:

(1) That a person with a major neurocognitive disorder, as defined in the last published edition of the * * * Diagnostic and Statistical Manual of Mental Disorders, * * * should have a conservatorship to serve * * * the person's unique and special needs.

(2) That, by adding powers to the probate conservatorship for people with major neurocognitive disorders, their unique and special needs can be met. This will reduce costs to the conservatee and the family of the conservatee, reduce costly administration by state and county government, and safeguard the basic dignity and rights of the conservatee.

(3) That it is the intent of the Legislature to recognize that the administration of psychotropic medications has been, and can be, abused by caregivers and, therefore, granting powers to a conservator to authorize these medications for the treatment of major neurocognitive disorders requires the protections specified in this section.

(b) Notwithstanding any other law, a conservator may authorize the placement of a conservatee in a secured perimeter residential care facility for the elderly operated pursuant to Section 1569.698 of the Health and Safety Code, and that has a care plan that meets the requirements of Section 87705 of Title 22 of the California Code of Regulations, upon a court's finding, by clear and convincing evidence, of all of the following:

(1) The conservatee has a major neurocognitive disorder, as defined in the last published edition of the * * * Diagnostic and Statistical Manual of Mental Disorders. * * *

(2) The conservatee lacks the capacity to give informed consent to this placement and has at least one mental function deficit pursuant to subdivision (a) of Section 811, and this deficit significantly impairs the person's ability to understand and appreciate the consequences of * * * their actions pursuant to subdivision (b) of Section 811.

(3) The conservatee needs, or would benefit from, a restricted and secure environment, as demonstrated by evidence presented by the physician or psychologist referred to in paragraph (3) of subdivision (f).

(4) The court finds that the proposed placement in a locked facility is the least restrictive placement appropriate to the needs of the conservatee.

(c) Notwithstanding any other law, a conservator of a person may authorize the administration of medications appropriate for the care and treatment of a major neurocognitive disorder, upon a court's finding, by clear and convincing evidence, of all of the following:

(1) The conservatee has a major neurocognitive disorder, as defined in the last published edition of the * * * Diagnostic and Statistical Manual of Mental Disorders. * * *

(2) The conservatee lacks the capacity to give informed consent to the administration of medications appropriate to the care of a major neurocognitive disorder, * * * has at least one mental function deficit pursuant to subdivision (a) of Section 811, and this deficit or deficits significantly impairs the person's ability to understand and appreciate the consequences of * * * their actions pursuant to subdivision (b) of Section 811.

(3) The conservatee needs, or would benefit from, appropriate medication, as demonstrated by evidence presented by the physician or psychologist referred to in paragraph (3) of subdivision (f).

(d) Pursuant to subdivision (b) of Section 2355, in the case of a person who is an adherent of a religion whose tenets and practices call for a reliance on prayer alone for healing, the treatment required by the conservator under subdivision (c) shall be by an accredited practitioner of that religion in lieu of the administration of medications.

(e) A conservatee who is to be placed in a facility pursuant to this section shall not be placed in a mental health rehabilitation center as described in Section 5675 of the Welfare and Institutions Code, or in an institution for mental disease as described in Section 5900 of the Welfare and Institutions Code.

(f) A petition for authority to act under this section is governed by Section 2357, except as follows:

(1) The conservatee shall be represented by an attorney pursuant to Chapter 4 (commencing with Section 1470) of Part 1. Upon granting or denying authority to a conservator under this section, the court shall discharge the attorney or order the continuation of the legal representation, consistent with the standard set forth in subdivision (a) of Section 1470.

(2) The conservatee shall be produced at the hearing, unless excused pursuant to Section 1893.

(3) The petition shall be supported by a declaration of a licensed physician, or a licensed psychologist within the scope of * * * their licensure, regarding each of the findings required to be made under this section for any power requested, except that the psychologist has at least two years of experience in diagnosing major neurocognitive disorders.

(4) The petition may be filed by any of the persons designated in Section 1891.

(g) The court investigator shall annually investigate and report to the court * * * pursuant to Sections 1850 and 1851 if the conservator is authorized to act under this section. In addition to the other matters provided in Section 1851, the conservatee shall be specifically advised by the investigator that the conservatee has the right to object to the conservator's powers granted under this section, and the report shall also include whether powers granted under this section are warranted. If the conservatee objects to the conservator's powers granted under this section, or the investigator determines that some change in the powers granted under this section is warranted, the court shall provide a copy of the report to the attorney of record for the conservatee. If an attorney has not been appointed for the conservatee, one shall be appointed pursuant to Chapter 4 (commencing with Section 1470) of Part 1. The attorney shall, within 30 days after receiving this report, do either of the following:

(1) File a petition with the court regarding the status of the conservatee.

(2) File a written report with the court stating that the attorney has met with the conservatee and determined that the petition would be inappropriate.

(h) A petition to terminate authority granted under this section shall be governed by Section 2359.

(i) This section <u>does</u> not * * * affect a conservatorship of the estate of a person who has <u>a</u> major neurocognitive disorder.

(j) This section does not affect the laws that would otherwise apply in emergency situations.

(k) This section does not affect current law regarding the power of a probate court to fix the residence of a conservatee or to authorize medical treatment for a conservatee who has not been determined to have a major neurocognitive disorder. *(Added by Stats.1996, c. 910 (S.B.1481), § 1. Amended by Stats.1997, c. 724 (A.B.1172), § 13; Stats.2003, c. 32 (A.B.167), § 2; Stats.2014, c. 913 (A.B.2747), § 31, eff. Jan, 1, 2015; Stats.2015, c. 197 (A.B.436), § 1, eff. Jan. 1, 2016; Stats.2017, c. 122 (S.B.413), § 5, eff. Jan. 1, 2018; Stats.2018, c. 92 (S.B.1289), § 171, eff. Jan. 1, 2019; Stats.2022, c. 420 (A.B.2960), § 41, eff. Jan. 1, 2023.)*

Cross References

Capacity determinations, generally, see Probate Code § 3200 et seq.
Conservatorship for adults and married minors, see Probate Code § 1800.3.
Counsel, right to, see Cal. Const. Art. 1, § 15.
Due process, generally, see Cal. Const. Art. 1, § 7.
Health care decisions, generally, see Probate Code § 4600 et seq.
Legislative intent, construction of statutes, see Code of Civil Procedure § 1859.

Research References

Forms

West's California Code Forms, Probate § 1891 Form 1, Petition for Exclusive Authority to Give Consent for Medical Treatment (Probate Conservatorship)—Judicial Council Form GC-380.

West's California Code Forms, Probate § 2356.5 Form 1, Attachment Requesting Special Orders Regarding Dementia—Judicial Council Form GC-313.

West's California Judicial Council Forms GC-313, Attachment Requesting Special Orders Regarding Dementia.

West's California Judicial Council Forms GC-331, Order Appointing Court Investigator (Review and Successor Conservator Investigations).

West's California Judicial Council Forms GC-333, Ex Parte Application for Order Authorizing Completion of Capacity Declaration—HIPAA.

West's California Judicial Council Forms GC-334, Ex Parte Order Re: Completion of Capacity Declaration—HIPAA.

West's California Judicial Council Forms GC-335, Capacity Declaration—Conservatorship.

West's California Judicial Council Forms GC-335A, Dementia Attachment to Capacity Declaration—Conservatorship.

West's California Judicial Council Forms GC-385, Order Authorizing Conservator to Give Consent for Medical Treatment.

§ 2357. Court ordered medical treatment

(a) As used in this section:

(1) "Guardian or conservator" includes a temporary guardian of the person or a temporary conservator of the person.

(2) "Ward or conservatee" includes a person for whom a temporary guardian of the person or temporary conservator of the person has been appointed.

(b) If the ward or conservatee requires medical treatment for an existing or continuing medical condition which is not authorized to be performed upon the ward or conservatee under Section 2252, 2353, 2354, or 2355, and the ward or conservatee is unable to give an informed consent to this medical treatment, the guardian or conservator may petition the court under this section for an order authorizing the medical treatment and authorizing the guardian or conservator to consent on behalf of the ward or conservatee to the medical treatment.

(c) The petition shall state, or set forth by medical affidavit attached thereto, all of the following so far as is known to the petitioner at the time the petition is filed:

(1) The nature of the medical condition of the ward or conservatee which requires treatment.

(2) The recommended course of medical treatment which is considered to be medically appropriate.

(3) The threat to the health of the ward or conservatee if authorization to consent to the recommended course of treatment is delayed or denied by the court.

(4) The predictable or probable outcome of the recommended course of treatment.

(5) The medically available alternatives, if any, to the course of treatment recommended.

(6) The efforts made to obtain an informed consent from the ward or conservatee.

(7) The name and addresses, so far as they are known to the petitioner, of the persons specified in subdivision (c) of Section 1510 in a guardianship proceeding or subdivision (b) of Section 1821 in a conservatorship proceeding.

(d) Upon the filing of the petition, unless an attorney is already appointed the court shall appoint the public defender or private counsel under Section 1471, to consult with and represent the ward or conservatee at the hearing on the petition and, if that appointment is made, Section 1472 applies.

(e) Notice of the petition shall be given as follows:

(1) Not less than 15 days before the hearing, notice of the time and place of the hearing, and a copy of the petition shall be personally served on the ward, if 12 years of age or older, or the conservatee, and on the attorney for the ward or conservatee.

(2) Not less than 15 days before the hearing, notice of the time and place of the hearing, and a copy of the petition shall be delivered pursuant to Section 1215 to the following persons:

(A) The spouse or domestic partner, if any, of the proposed conservatee at the address stated in the petition.

(B) The relatives named in the petition at their addresses stated in the petition.

(f) For good cause, the court may shorten or waive notice of the hearing as provided by this section. In determining the period of notice to be required, the court shall take into account both of the following:

(1) The existing medical facts and circumstances set forth in the petition or in a medical affidavit attached to the petition or in a medical affidavit presented to the court.

(2) The desirability, where the condition of the ward or conservatee permits, of giving adequate notice to all interested persons.

(g) Notwithstanding subdivisions (e) and (f), the matter may be submitted for the determination of the court upon proper and sufficient medical affidavits or declarations if the attorney for the petitioner and the attorney for the ward or conservatee so stipulate and further stipulate that there remains no issue of fact to be determined.

(h) The court may make an order authorizing the recommended course of medical treatment of the ward or conservatee and authorizing the guardian or conservator to consent on behalf of the ward or conservatee to the recommended course of medical treatment for the ward or conservatee if the court determines from the evidence all of the following:

(1) The existing or continuing medical condition of the ward or conservatee requires the recommended course of medical treatment.

(2) If untreated, there is a probability that the condition will become life-endangering or result in a serious threat to the physical or mental health of the ward or conservatee.

(3) The ward or conservatee is unable to give an informed consent to the recommended course of treatment.

(i) Upon petition of the ward or conservatee or other interested person, the court may order that the guardian or conservator obtain or consent to, or obtain and consent to, specified medical treatment to be performed upon the ward or conservatee. Notice of the hearing on the petition under this subdivision shall be given for the period and in the manner provided in Chapter 3 (commencing with Section 1460) of Part 1. *(Stats.1990, c. 79 (A.B.759), § 14, operative July 1, 1991. Amended by Stats.1990, c. 710 (S.B.1775), § 9, operative July 1, 1991; Stats.1999, c. 175 (A.B.239), § 2; Stats.2000, c. 135 (A.B.2539), § 143; Stats.2001, c. 893 (A.B.25), § 31; Stats.2017, c. 319 (A.B.976), § 44, eff. Jan. 1, 2018.)*

Cross References

Adjudication of lack of capacity to give informed consent for medical treatment, see Probate Code § 1880.
Affidavits, see Code of Civil Procedure §§ 2003, 2009 et seq.
Computation of time, see Code of Civil Procedure §§ 12 and 12a; Government Code § 6800 et seq.
Counsel, right to, see Cal. Const. Art. 1, § 15, Cl. 3.
Domestic partner, defined, see Probate Code § 37.
Effect of court authorization, see Probate Code § 2103.
Interested person, defined, see Probate Code § 1424.
Medical treatment,
   Conservatee not adjudicated to lack capacity to give informed consent, see Probate Code § 2354.
   Ward, see Probate Code § 2353.
Temporary guardians and conservators, generally, see Probate Code § 2250 et seq.

Research References

Forms

West's California Code Forms, Probate § 2356.5 Form 1, Attachment Requesting Special Orders Regarding Dementia—Judicial Council Form GC-313.
West's California Code Forms, Probate § 2357 Form 1, Petition for Order Directing Medical Treatment for Ward or Conservatee.
West's California Code Forms, Probate § 3204 Form 2, Medical Declaration of Patient's Physician.

§ 2358. Additional conditions in order of appointment

When a guardian or conservator is appointed, the court may, with the consent of the guardian or conservator, insert in the order of appointment conditions not otherwise obligatory providing for the care, treatment, education, and welfare of the ward or conservatee. Any such conditions shall be included in the letters. The performance of such conditions is a part of the duties of the guardian or conservator for the faithful performance of which the guardian or conservator and the sureties on the bond are responsible. *(Stats. 1990, c. 79 (A.B.759), § 14, operative July 1, 1991.)*

Cross References

Additional powers of guardian nominated by will, see Probate Code § 2108.
Guardian or conservator, liability not limited to amount of bond, see Code of Civil Procedure § 996.470.
Letters, defined, see Probate Code § 52.
Nature of surety's liability, see Code of Civil Procedure § 996.470.
Suit against sureties on bond, see Probate Code § 2333.

Research References

Forms

West's California Code Forms, Probate § 1514 Form 1, Order Appointing Guardian of Minor—Judicial Council Form GC-240.

§ 2359. Petitions of guardian, conservator, ward or conservatee; approval of purchase, lease, or rental of property from estate; violations of section

(a) Upon petition of the guardian or conservator or ward or conservatee or other interested person, the court may authorize and instruct the guardian or conservator or approve and confirm the acts of the guardian or conservator.

(b) Notice of the hearing on the petition shall be given for the period and in the manner provided in Chapter 3 (commencing with Section 1460) of Part 1.

(c)(1) When a guardian or conservator petitions for the approval of a purchase, lease, or rental of real or personal property from the estate of a ward or conservatee, the guardian or conservator shall provide a statement disclosing the family or affiliate relationship between the guardian and conservator and the purchaser, lessee, or renter of the property, and the family or affiliate relationship between the guardian or conservator and any agent hired by the guardian or conservator.

(2) For the purposes of this subdivision, "family" means a person's spouse, domestic partner, or relatives within the second degree of lineal or collateral consanguinity of a person or a person's spouse. For the purposes of this subdivision, "affiliate" means an entity that is under the direct control, indirect control, or common control of the guardian or conservator.

(3) A violation of this section shall result in the rescission of the purchase, lease, or rental of the property. Any losses incurred by the estate of the ward or conservatee because the property was sold or leased at less than fair market value shall be deemed as charges against the guardian or conservator under the provisions of Sections 2401.3 and 2401.5. The court shall assess a civil penalty equal to three times the charges against the guardian, conservator, or other person in violation of this section, and may assess punitive damages as it deems proper. If the estate does not incur losses as a result of the violation, the court shall order the guardian, conservator, or other person in violation of this section to pay a fine of up to five thousand dollars ($5,000) for each violation. The fines and penalties provided in this section are in addition to any other rights and remedies provided by law. *(Stats.1990, c. 79 (A.B.759), § 14, operative July 1, 1991. Amended by Stats.2000, c. 565 (A.B.1950), § 5; Stats.2001, c. 893 (A.B.25), § 32.)*

Cross References

Domestic partner, defined, see Probate Code § 37.
Effect of court authorization, approval or confirmation, see Probate Code § 2103.
Guardianship and conservatorship, interested person, defined, see Probate Code § 1424.

Research References

Forms

West's California Code Forms, Probate § 2403 Form 1, Petition for Instructions (Or Confirmation).

§ 2360. Photograph of conservatee

Upon the establishment of a conservatorship by the court and annually thereafter, the conservator shall ensure that a clear photograph of the conservatee is taken and preserved for the purpose of identifying the conservatee if he or she becomes missing. *(Added by Stats.2010, c. 97 (A.B.2493), § 1.)*

§ 2361. Notice of conservatee's death

A conservator shall provide notice of a conservatee's death by delivering pursuant to Section 1215 a copy of the notice to all persons entitled to notice under Section 1460 and by filing a proof of delivery with the court, unless otherwise ordered by the court. *(Added by Stats.2015, c. 92 (A.B.1085), § 3, eff. Jan. 1, 2016. Amended by Stats.2017, c. 319 (A.B.976), § 45, eff. Jan. 1, 2018.)*

Research References

Forms

West's California Code Forms, Probate § 2361 Form 1, Notice of the Conservatee's Death—Judicial Council Form GC-399.

GUARDIANSHIP—CONSERVATORSHIP LAW § 2401

West's California Judicial Council Forms GC-399, Notice of Conservatee's Death.

CHAPTER 6. POWERS AND DUTIES OF GUARDIAN OR CONSERVATOR OF THE ESTATE

Cross References

Conservatorship for gravely disabled persons, general and special powers, see Welfare and Institutions Code § 5357.

Court-ordered termination of guardianship over minor's estate where sole asset is money, deposit of funds with county treasurer, see Probate Code § 3412.

Court-orders relating to minors and persons with a disability who are paid money or property but lack guardianship or conservatorship over the estate, order to deposit with county treasurer the remaining balances of money paid or to be paid, see Probate Code § 3611.

Court-orders relating to minors having monetary estates but no guardian, order to deposit funds with county treasurer, see Probate Code § 3413.

ARTICLE 1. DEFINITIONS AND GENERAL PROVISIONS

Section
2400. Definitions.
2401. Management and control of estate; ordinary care and diligence.
2401.1. Real property located in foreign jurisdiction; guardian or conservator use of ordinary care and diligence in determination of ownership.
2401.3. Breach of fiduciary duty; liability.
2401.5. Breach of fiduciary duty; interest liability calculation; excuse from liability.
2401.6. Surcharge; offset against future fees prohibited.
2401.7. Breach of fiduciary duty; additional remedies.
2402. Additional conditions in order of appointment.
2403. Instructions from or confirmation by court; petitions for approval or purchase, lease, or rental of property from estate.
2404. Order compelling guardian or conservator to pay support or debts.
2405. Summary determination of disputes.
2406. Submission of dispute to arbitration.
2407. Application of chapter to community property.
2408. Construction with other laws.
2410. Uniform standards of conduct.

Cross References

Application of old and new law, see Probate Code § 3.

§ 2400. Definitions

As used in this chapter:

(a) "Conservator" means the conservator of the estate, or the limited conservator of the estate to the extent that the powers and duties of the limited conservator are specifically and expressly provided by the order appointing the limited conservator.

(b) "Estate" means all of the conservatee's or ward's personal property, wherever located, and real property located in this state.

(c) "Guardian" means the guardian of the estate. *(Stats.1990, c. 79 (A.B.759), § 14, operative July 1, 1991. Amended by Stats.2008, c. 52 (A.B.2014), § 2.)*

Cross References

Appointment of limited conservator, see Probate Code §§ 1801, 1828.5.

Order appointing limited conservator for developmentally disabled adult, see Probate Code § 1830.

Research References

Forms

2 California Transactions Forms--Estate Planning § 8:22, Authority of Attorney-In-Fact.

§ 2401. Management and control of estate; ordinary care and diligence

(a) The guardian or conservator, or limited conservator to the extent specifically and expressly provided in the appointing court's order, has the management and control of the estate and, in managing and controlling the estate, shall use ordinary care and diligence. What constitutes use of ordinary care and diligence is determined by all the circumstances of the particular estate.

(b) The guardian or conservator:

(1) Shall exercise a power to the extent that ordinary care and diligence requires that the power be exercised.

(2) Shall not exercise a power to the extent that ordinary care and diligence requires that the power not be exercised.

(c) Notwithstanding any other law, a guardian or conservator who is not a trust company, or an employee of that guardian or conservator, in exercising their powers, may not hire or refer any business to an entity in which the guardian or conservator or an employee has a financial interest. For the purposes of this subdivision, "financial interest" shall mean (1) an ownership interest in a sole proprietorship, a partnership, or a closely held corporation, or (2) an ownership interest of greater than 1 percent of the outstanding shares in a publicly held corporation, or (3) being an officer or a director of a corporation.

(d) Subdivision (c) does not prohibit a professional fiduciary appointed as a guardian or conservator from hiring and compensating individuals as employees, with court approval.

(e)(1) Notwithstanding any other law, a guardian or conservator who is a trust company, in exercising its powers may not, except upon authorization of the court, invest in securities of the trust company or an affiliate or subsidiary, or other securities from which the trust company or affiliate or subsidiary receives a financial benefit or in a mutual fund, other than a mutual fund authorized in paragraph (5) of subdivision (a) of Section 2574, registered under the Investment Company Act of 1940 (Subchapter 1 (commencing with Sec. 80a–1) of Chapter 2D of Title 15 of the United States Code), to which the trust company or its affiliate provides services, including, but not limited to, services as an investment adviser, sponsor, distributor, custodian, agent, registrar, administrator, servicer, or manager, and for which the trust company or its affiliate receives compensation.

(2) Before authorization from the court, the guardian or conservator shall disclose to the court in writing the trust company's financial interest. *(Stats.1990, c. 79 (A.B.759), § 14, operative July 1, 1991. Amended by Stats.2000, c. 565 (A.B.1950), § 6; Stats.2006, c. 493 (A.B.1363), § 21; Stats.2021, c. 417 (A.B.1194), § 21, eff. Jan. 1, 2022.)*

Cross References

Community property, management and control, see Probate Code § 3051.
Inventory and accounting by guardian or conservator, generally, see Probate Code § 2600 et seq.
Review of sales, purchases and other transactions upon accounting, see Probate Code § 2625.

Research References

Forms

1 California Transactions Forms--Estate Planning § 1:2, Probate System.
1 California Transactions Forms--Estate Planning § 6:17, Guardian of Estate or of Property.

1 California Transactions Forms--Estate Planning § 6:73, Appointment of Guardian of Person of Minor Child and Statement of Desire that Same Person be Appointed Guardian of Minor's Estate.

1 California Transactions Forms--Estate Planning § 6:74, Appointment of Guardian of Person and Estate of Minor Children.

§ 2401.1. Real property located in foreign jurisdiction; guardian or conservator use of ordinary care and diligence in determination of ownership

The guardian or conservator shall use ordinary care and diligence to determine whether the ward or conservatee owns real property in a foreign jurisdiction and to preserve and protect that property. What constitutes use of ordinary care and diligence shall be determined by all the facts and circumstances known, or that become known, to the guardian or conservator, the value of the real property located in the foreign jurisdiction, and the needs of the ward or conservatee. The guardian or conservator, except as provided in subdivision (a) of Section 1061 and in Section 1062, is not charged with, and shall have no duty to inventory or account for the real property located in a foreign jurisdiction, but the guardian or conservator shall, when presenting the inventory and appraisal and accounting to the court, include the schedule set forth in subdivision (h) of Section 1063. *(Added by Stats.2008, c. 52 (A.B.2014), § 3.)*

§ 2401.3. Breach of fiduciary duty; liability

(a) If the guardian or conservator breaches a fiduciary duty, the guardian or conservator is chargeable with any of the following that is appropriate under the circumstances:

(1) Any loss or depreciation in value of the estate resulting from the breach of duty, with interest.

(2) Any profit made by the guardian or conservator through the breach of duty, with interest.

(3) Any profit that would have accrued to the estate if the loss of profit is the result of the breach of duty.

(b) If the guardian or conservator has acted reasonably and in good faith under the circumstances as known to the guardian or conservator, the court, in its discretion, may excuse the guardian or conservator in whole or in part from liability under subdivision (a) if it would be equitable to do so. *(Stats.1990, c. 79 (A.B.759), § 14, operative July 1, 1991.)*

Cross References

Fiduciary, defined, see Probate Code § 39.

§ 2401.5. Breach of fiduciary duty; interest liability calculation; excuse from liability

(a) If the guardian or conservator is liable for interest pursuant to Section 2401.3, the guardian or conservator is liable for the greater of the following amounts:

(1) The amount of interest that accrues at the legal rate on judgments.

(2) The amount of interest actually received.

(b) If the guardian or conservator has acted reasonably and in good faith under the circumstances as known to the guardian or conservator, the court, in its discretion, may excuse the guardian or conservator in whole or in part from liability under subdivision (a) if it would be equitable to do so. *(Stats.1990, c. 79 (A.B.759), § 14, operative July 1, 1991. Amended by Stats.1998, c. 77 (S.B.1841), § 2.)*

Cross References

Personal representatives, duties and liabilities, interest and excuse, see Probate Code § 9602.

Trustees, measure of liability, interest and excuse, see Probate Code § 16441.

§ 2401.6. Surcharge; offset against future fees prohibited

Any surcharge that a guardian or conservator incurs under the provisions of Sections 2401.3 or 2401.5 may not be paid by or offset against future fees or wages to be provided by the estate to the guardian or conservator. *(Added by Stats.2000, c. 565 (A.B.1950), § 7.)*

§ 2401.7. Breach of fiduciary duty; additional remedies

The provisions of Sections 2401.3 and 2401.5 for liability of a guardian or conservator for breach of a fiduciary duty do not prevent resort to any other remedy available against the guardian or conservator under the statutory or common law. *(Stats.1990, c. 79 (A.B.759), § 14, operative July 1, 1991.)*

§ 2402. Additional conditions in order of appointment

When a guardian or conservator is appointed, the court may, with the consent of the guardian or conservator, insert in the order of appointment conditions not otherwise obligatory providing for the care and custody of the property of the ward or conservatee. Any such conditions shall be included in the letters. The performance of such conditions is a part of the duties of the guardian or conservator for the faithful performance of which the guardian or conservator and the sureties on the bond are responsible. *(Stats.1990, c. 79 (A.B.759), § 14, operative July 1, 1991.)*

Cross References

Bonds of guardians or conservators, see Probate Code § 2320 et seq.
Letters, generally, see Probate Code § 2310 et seq.
Letters, defined, see Probate Code § 52.
Nature of surety's liability, see Code of Civil Procedure § 996.470.

Research References

Forms

West's California Code Forms, Probate § 1514 Form 1, Order Appointing Guardian of Minor—Judicial Council Form GC-240.

§ 2403. Instructions from or confirmation by court; petitions for approval or purchase, lease, or rental of property from estate

(a) Upon petition of the guardian or conservator, the ward or conservatee, a creditor, or other interested person, the court may authorize and instruct the guardian or conservator, or approve and confirm the acts of the guardian or conservator, in the administration, management, investment, disposition, care, protection, operation, or preservation of the estate, or the incurring or payment of costs, fees, or expenses in connection therewith.

(b) Notice of the hearing on the petition shall be given for the period and in the manner provided in Chapter 3 (commencing with Section 1460) of Part 1.

(c)(1) When a guardian or conservator petitions for the approval of a purchase, lease, or rental of real or personal property from the estate of a ward or conservatee, the guardian or conservator shall provide a statement disclosing the family or affiliate relationship between the guardian and conservator and the purchaser, lessee, or renter of the property, and the family or affiliate relationship between the guardian or conservator and any agent hired by the guardian or conservator.

(2) For the purposes of this subdivision, "family" means a person's spouse, domestic partner, or relatives within the second degree of lineal or collateral consanguinity of a person or a person's spouse. For the purposes of this subdivision, "affiliate" means an entity that is under the direct control, indirect control, or common control of the guardian or conservator.

(3) A violation of this section shall result in the rescission of the purchase, lease, or rental of the property. Any losses incurred by the estate of the ward or conservatee because the property was sold or leased at less than fair market value shall be deemed as charges against the guardian or conservator under the provisions of Sections 2401.3 and 2401.5. The court shall assess a civil penalty equal to three times the charges against the guardian, conservator, or other person in violation of this section, and may assess punitive damages

as it deems proper. If the estate does not incur losses as a result of the violation, the court shall order the guardian, conservator, or other person in violation of this section to pay a fine of up to five thousand dollars ($5,000) for each violation. The fines and penalties provided in this section are in addition to any other rights and remedies provided by law. *(Stats.1990, c. 79 (A.B.759), § 14, operative July 1, 1991. Amended by Stats.2000, c. 565 (A.B.1950), § 8; Stats.2001, c. 893 (A.B.25), § 33.)*

Cross References

Compensation of guardian, conservator, and attorney, see Probate Code § 2640 et seq.
Domestic partner, defined, see Probate Code § 37.
Guardian for particular property and guardian of the estate, allocation of powers and duties, see Probate Code § 2109.
Interested person, defined, see Probate Code § 1424.
Payment of debts and expenses, guardian or conservator of the estate, petition for instructions, see Probate Code §§ 2430, 2431, 2500.
Support, maintenance and education of ward or conservatee, see Probate Code § 2420.

Research References

Forms

3 California Transactions Forms--Business Transactions § 18:16, Settlements that Require Court Approval.
West's California Code Forms, Probate § 2403 Form 1, Petition for Instructions (Or Confirmation).
West's California Code Forms, Probate § 2404 Form 3, Petition by Creditor to Compel Payment of Debt.
West's California Code Forms, Probate § 2500–2507 Form 1, Petition by Guardian or Conservator to Approve Compromise of Disputed Personal Injury Claim of Minor or Incompetent Person—Judicial Council Form MC-350.

§ 2404. Order compelling guardian or conservator to pay support or debts

(a) If the guardian or conservator fails, neglects, or refuses to furnish comfortable and suitable support, maintenance, or education for the ward or conservatee as required by this division, or to pay a debt, expense, or charge lawfully due and payable by the ward or conservatee or the estate as provided in this division, the court shall, upon petition or upon its own motion, order the guardian or conservator to do so from the estate.

(b) The petition may be filed by the ward or conservatee or by the creditor or any other interested person. Notice of the hearing on the petition shall be given for the period and in the manner provided in Chapter 3 (commencing with Section 1460) of Part 1. *(Stats.1990, c. 79 (A.B.759), § 14, operative July 1, 1991.)*

Cross References

Guardianship and conservatorship, interested person, defined, see Probate Code § 1424.

Research References

Forms

West's California Code Forms, Probate § 2403 Form 1, Petition for Instructions (Or Confirmation).
West's California Code Forms, Probate § 2404 Form 1, Petition to Compel Payment of Support.
West's California Code Forms, Probate § 2404 Form 3, Petition by Creditor to Compel Payment of Debt.

§ 2405. Summary determination of disputes

If there is a dispute relating to the estate between the guardian or conservator and a third person, the guardian or conservator, or the limited conservator to the extent specifically and expressly provided in the order appointing the limited conservator, may do either of the following:

(a) Enter into an agreement in writing with the third person to refer the dispute to a temporary judge designated in the agreement.

The agreement shall be filed with the clerk, who shall thereupon, with the approval of the court, enter an order referring the matter to the designated person. The temporary judge shall proceed promptly to hear and determine the matter in controversy by summary procedure, without any pleadings, discovery, or jury trial. The decision of the temporary judge is subject to Section 632 of the Code of Civil Procedure. Judgment shall be entered on the decision and is as valid and effective as if rendered by a judge of the court in an action against the guardian or conservator or the third person commenced by ordinary process.

(b) Enter into an agreement in writing with the third person that a judge of the court, pursuant to the agreement and with the written consent of the judge, both filed with the clerk within the time for bringing an independent action on the matter in dispute, may hear and determine the dispute pursuant to the procedure provided in subdivision (a). *(Stats.1990, c. 79 (A.B.759), § 14, operative July 1, 1991.)*

§ 2406. Submission of dispute to arbitration

If there is a dispute relating to the estate between the guardian or conservator and a third person, the guardian or conservator may enter into an agreement in writing with the third person to submit the dispute to arbitration under Title 9 (commencing with Section 1280) of Part 3 of the Code of Civil Procedure. The agreement is not effective unless it has first been approved by the court and a copy of the approved agreement is filed with the court. *(Stats.1990, c. 79 (A.B.759), § 14, operative July 1, 1991.)*

Cross References

Appeals from order in arbitration, see Code of Civil Procedure §§ 1294, 1294.2.
Arbitration, generally, see Code of Civil Procedure § 1281 et seq.

§ 2407. Application of chapter to community property

This chapter applies to property owned by spouses as community property only to the extent authorized by Part 6 (commencing with Section 3000). *(Stats.1990, c. 79 (A.B.759), § 14, operative July 1, 1991. Amended by Stats.2016, c. 50 (S.B.1005), § 82, eff. Jan. 1, 2017.)*

Cross References

Community property, generally, see Family Code §§ 65, 760.
Community property, succession as to, see Probate Code §§ 100, 6101, 6401.
Definitions, community property, see Probate Code §§ 28 and 3002; Civil Code § 687.

§ 2408. Construction with other laws

Nothing in this chapter limits or restricts any authority granted to a guardian or conservator pursuant to Article 11 (commencing with Section 2590) to administer the estate under that article. *(Stats.1990, c. 79 (A.B.759), § 14, operative July 1, 1991.)*

§ 2410. Uniform standards of conduct

On or before January 1, 2008, the Judicial Council, in consultation with the California Judges Association, the California Association of Superior Court Investigators, the California State Association of Public Administrators, Public Guardians, and Public Conservators, the State Bar of California, the National Guardianship Association, and the Association of Professional Geriatric Care Managers, shall adopt a rule of court that shall require uniform standards of conduct for actions that conservators and guardians may take under this chapter on behalf of conservatees and wards to ensure that the estate of conservatees or wards are maintained and conserved as appropriate and to prevent risk of loss or harm to the conservatees or wards. This rule shall include at a minimum standards for determining the fees that may be charged to conservatees or wards and standards for asset management. *(Added by Stats.2006, c. 493 (A.B.1363), § 22.)*

ARTICLE 2. SUPPORT AND MAINTENANCE OF WARD OR CONSERVATEE AND DEPENDENTS

Section
2420. Support, maintenance and education.
2421. Allowance for ward or conservatee.
2422. Order authorizing support notwithstanding third party liability.
2423. Payment of surplus income to relatives of conservatee.

Cross References

Application of old and new law, see Probate Code § 3.

§ 2420. Support, maintenance and education

(a) Subject to Section 2422, the guardian or conservator shall apply the income from the estate, so far as necessary, to the comfortable and suitable support, maintenance, and education of the ward or conservatee (including care, treatment, and support of a ward or conservatee who is a patient in a state hospital under the jurisdiction of the State Department of State Hospitals or the State Department of Developmental Services) and of those legally entitled to support, maintenance, or education from the ward or conservatee, taking into account the value of the estate and the condition of life of the persons required to be furnished such support, maintenance, or education.

(b) If the income from the estate is insufficient for the purpose described in subdivision (a), the guardian or conservator may sell or give a security interest in or other lien on any personal property of the estate, or sell or mortgage or give a deed of trust on any real property of the estate, as provided in this part.

(c) When the amount paid by the guardian or conservator for the purpose described in subdivision (a) satisfies the standard set out in that subdivision, and the payments are supported by proper vouchers or other proof satisfactory to the court, the guardian or conservator shall be allowed credit for such payments when the accounts of the guardian or conservator are settled.

(d) Nothing in this section requires the guardian or conservator to obtain court authorization before making the payments authorized by this section, but nothing in this section dispenses with the need to obtain any court authorization otherwise required for a particular transaction.

(e) Nothing in this section precludes the guardian or conservator from seeking court authorization or instructions or approval and confirmation pursuant to Section 2403. *(Stats.1990, c. 79 (A.B.759), § 14, operative July 1, 1991. Amended by Stats.2012, c. 440 (A.B. 1488), § 44, eff. Sept. 22, 2012.)*

Cross References

Authority to exchange property, see Probate Code § 2557.
Borrowing money and giving security, see Probate Code § 2551.
Duty to support and maintain ward or conservatee in state hospital, see Welfare and Institutions Code §§ 7275, 7279.
Instructions from or confirmation by court, see Probate Code § 2403.
Mentally disordered in state institutions, care and maintenance by guardian or conservator, see Welfare and Institutions Code §§ 7275, 7278, 7281, 7282.
Order authorizing support from estate where third party liable for support, see Probate Code § 2422.
Payment or settlement of debts by guardian or conservator, see Probate Code §§ 2430, 2500.
Powers and duties of guardians or conservators of the person generally, see Probate Code § 2350 et seq.
Review on settlement of accounts, see Probate Code § 2625.
Sale of estate property, see Probate Code § 2541.

Research References

Forms
1 California Transactions Forms--Estate Planning § 1:29, Options Involving Gifts to Minors.

1 California Transactions Forms--Estate Planning § 6:17, Guardian of Estate or of Property.
West's California Code Forms, Probate § 2404 Form 1, Petition to Compel Payment of Support.

§ 2421. Allowance for ward or conservatee

(a) Upon petition of the guardian or conservator or the ward or conservatee, the court may authorize the guardian or conservator to pay to the ward or conservatee out of the estate a reasonable allowance for the personal use of the ward or conservatee. The allowance shall be in such amount as the court may determine to be for the best interests of the ward or conservatee.

(b) Notice of the hearing on the petition shall be given for the period and in the manner provided in Chapter 3 (commencing with Section 1460) of Part 1.

(c) The guardian or conservator is not required to account for such allowance other than to establish that it has been paid to the ward or conservatee. The funds so paid are subject to the sole control of the ward or conservatee. *(Stats.1990, c. 79 (A.B.759), § 14, operative July 1, 1991.)*

Cross References

Right of conservatee to control allowance, legal capacity, see Probate Code § 1871.
Wages of ward or conservatee, see Probate Code § 2601.

Research References

Forms
West's California Code Forms, Probate § 2403 Form 1, Petition for Instructions (Or Confirmation).
West's California Code Forms, Probate § 2421 Form 1, Petition for Allowance.

§ 2422. Order authorizing support notwithstanding third party liability

(a) Upon petition of the guardian or conservator, the ward or conservatee, or any other interested person, the court may for good cause order the ward or conservatee to be wholly or partially supported, maintained, or educated out of the estate notwithstanding the existence of a third party legally obligated to provide such support, maintenance, or education. Such order may be made for a limited period of time. If not so limited, it continues in effect until modified or revoked.

(b) Notice of the hearing on the petition shall be given for the period and in the manner provided in Chapter 3 (commencing with Section 1460) of Part 1. *(Stats.1990, c. 79 (A.B.759), § 14, operative July 1, 1991.)*

Cross References

Guardianship and conservatorship, interested person, defined, see Probate Code § 1424.
Notice to,
    Director of State Hospitals or Director of Developmental Services, see Probate Code § 1461.
    Veterans Administration, see Probate Code § 1461.5.
Use of income from the estate for support, see Probate Code § 2420.

Research References

Forms
West's California Code Forms, Probate § 2403 Form 1, Petition for Instructions (Or Confirmation).

§ 2423. Payment of surplus income to relatives of conservatee

(a) Upon petition of the conservator, the conservatee, the spouse or domestic partner of the conservatee, or a relative within the second degree of the conservatee, the court may by order authorize or direct the conservator to pay and distribute surplus income of the estate or any part of the surplus income (not used for the support, maintenance, and education of the conservatee and of those legally entitled to support, maintenance, or education from the conservatee) to the spouse or domestic partner of the conservatee and to relatives within the second degree of the conservatee whom the conservatee would, in the judgment of the court, have aided but for the existence of the conservatorship. The court in ordering payments under this section may impose conditions if the court determines that the conservatee would have imposed the conditions if the conservatee had the capacity to act.

(b) The granting of the order and the amounts and proportions of the payments are discretionary with the court, but the court shall consider all of the following:

(1) The amount of surplus income available after adequate provision has been made for the comfortable and suitable support, maintenance, and education of the conservatee and of those legally entitled to support, maintenance, or education from the conservatee.

(2) The circumstances and condition of life to which the conservatee and the spouse or domestic partner and relatives have been accustomed.

(3) The amount that the conservatee would in the judgment of the court have allowed the spouse or domestic partner and relatives but for the existence of the conservatorship.

(c) Notice of the hearing on the petition shall be given for the period and in the manner provided in Chapter 3 (commencing with Section 1460) of Part 1. (Stats.1990, c. 79 (A.B.759), § 14, operative July 1, 1991. Amended by Stats.2001, c. 893 (A.B.25), § 34.)

Cross References

Domestic partner, defined, see Probate Code § 37.
Notice to,
 Directors, see Probate Code § 1461.
 Veterans Administration, see Probate Code § 1461.5.
Support of ward's dependents, see Probate Code §§ 2420, 2541.

Research References

Forms

West's California Code Forms, Probate § 2403 Form 1, Petition for Instructions (Or Confirmation).
West's California Code Forms, Probate § 2423 Form 1, Petition for Payment of Surplus Income to Relatives of Conservatee.
West's California Code Forms, Probate § 2423 Form 2, Order Directing Payment of Surplus Income to Relatives of Conservatee.

ARTICLE 3. PAYMENT OF DEBTS AND EXPENSES

Section
2430. Payments from principal and income; debts and expenses.
2431. Wage claims; priority.

Cross References

Application of old and new law, see Probate Code § 3.

§ 2430. Payments from principal and income; debts and expenses

(a) Subject to subdivisions (b) and (c), the guardian or conservator shall pay the following from any principal and income of the estate:

(1) The debts incurred by the ward or conservatee before creation of the guardianship or conservatorship, giving priority to the debts described in Section 2431 to the extent required by that section.

(2) The debts incurred by the ward or conservatee during the guardianship or conservatorship to provide the necessaries of life to the ward or conservatee, and to the spouse and minor children of the ward or conservatee, to the extent the debt is reasonable. Also, the debts reasonably incurred by the conservatee during the conservatorship to provide the basic living expenses, as defined in Section 297 of the Family Code, to the domestic partner of the conservatee. The guardian or conservator may deduct the amount of any payments for these debts from any allowance otherwise payable to the ward or conservatee.

(3) In the case of a conservatorship, any other debt incurred by the conservatee during the conservatorship only if the debt satisfies the requirements of any order made under Chapter 4 (commencing with Section 1870) of Part 3.

(4) The reasonable expenses incurred in the collection, care, and administration of the estate, but court authorization is required for payment of compensation to any of the following:

(A) The guardian or conservator of the person or estate or both.

(B) An attorney for the guardian or conservator of the person or estate or both.

(C) An attorney for the ward or conservatee.

(D) An attorney for the estate.

(E) The public guardian for the costs and fee under Section 2902.

(b) The payments provided for by paragraph (3) of subdivision (a) are not required to be made to the extent the payments would impair the ability to provide the necessaries of life to the conservatee and the spouse and minor children of the conservatee and to provide the basic living expenses, as defined in Section 297 of the Family Code, of the domestic partner of the conservatee.

(c) The guardian or conservator may petition the court under Section 2403 for instructions when there is doubt whether a debt should be paid under this section. (Stats.1990, c. 79 (A.B.759), § 14, operative July 1, 1991. Amended by Stats.2001, c. 893 (A.B.25), § 35.)

Cross References

Allowance for ward or conservatee, see Probate Code § 2421.
Attorney's fees and costs, generally, see Code of Civil Procedure § 1021.
Capacity of conservatee to bind or obligate conservatorship estate, see Probate Code § 1870 et seq.
Compensation and expenses of guardian or conservator or attorney, see Probate Code §§ 2623, 2640 et seq.
Compromise and settlement of claims, see Probate Code § 2500.
Domestic partner, defined, see Probate Code § 37.
Order compelling payment of debts, see Probate Code § 2404.
Review on settlement of accounts, see Probate Code § 2625.

Research References

Forms

1 California Transactions Forms--Estate Planning § 6:17, Guardian of Estate or of Property.
West's California Code Forms, Probate § 2403 Form 1, Petition for Instructions (Or Confirmation).
West's California Code Forms, Probate § 2404 Form 3, Petition by Creditor to Compel Payment of Debt.
West's California Code Forms, Probate § 2540 Form 1, Report of Sale and Petition for Order Confirming Sale of Real Property (Probate)—Judicial Council Form DE-260, GC-060.

§ 2431. Wage claims; priority

(a) Subject to subdivision (d), the guardian or conservator may petition the court under Section 2403 for instructions when there is doubt whether a wage claim should be paid under this section.

(b) The guardian or conservator shall promptly pay wage claims for work done or services rendered for the ward or conservatee within 30 days prior to the date the petition for appointment of the guardian or conservator was filed. The payments made pursuant to this subdivision shall not exceed nine hundred dollars ($900) to each claimant. If there is insufficient money to pay all the claims described in this subdivision up to nine hundred dollars ($900), the money available shall be distributed among such claimants in proportion to the amount of their respective claims.

(c) After the payments referred to in subdivision (b) have been made, the guardian or conservator shall pay wage claims for work done or services rendered for the ward or conservatee within 90 days prior to the date the petition for appointment of the guardian or conservator was filed, excluding the claims described in subdivision (b). The payments made pursuant to this subdivision shall not exceed one thousand one hundred dollars ($1,100) to each claimant. If there is insufficient money to pay all the claims described in this subdivision up to one thousand one hundred dollars ($1,100), the money available shall be distributed among such claimants in proportion to the amounts of their respective claims.

(d) The guardian or conservator may require sworn claims to be presented. If there is reasonable cause to believe that the claim is not valid, the guardian or conservator may refuse to pay the claim in whole or in part but shall pay any part thereof that is not disputed without prejudice to the claimant's rights as to the balance of the claim. The guardian or conservator shall withhold sufficient money to cover the disputed portion until the claimant has had a reasonable opportunity to establish the validity of the claim by bringing an action, either in the claimant's own name or through an assignee, against the guardian or conservator.

(e) If the guardian or conservator neglects or refuses to pay all or any portion of a claim which is not in dispute, the court shall order the guardian or conservator to do so upon the informal application of any wage claimant or the assignee or legal representative of such claimant. *(Stats.1990, c. 79 (A.B.759), § 14, operative July 1, 1991.)*

Cross References

Assignment of wages by minor, written consent of guardian required, see Labor Code § 300.
Instructions from or confirmation by court, see Probate Code § 2403.
Order compelling payment of debts, see Probate Code § 2404.
Payment of wages or debts,
 Generally, see Labor Code § 200 et seq.
 Claims in decedent's estates, see Probate Code § 11401 et seq.

Research References

Forms
West's California Code Forms, Probate § 2403 Form 1, Petition for Instructions (Or Confirmation).
West's California Code Forms, Probate § 2540 Form 1, Report of Sale and Petition for Order Confirming Sale of Real Property (Probate)—Judicial Council Form DE-260, GC-060.

ARTICLE 4. ESTATE MANAGEMENT POWERS GENERALLY

Section
2450. Extent of court supervision.
2451. Collection of debts and benefits.
2451.5. Powers of guardian or conservator.
2452. Checks, warrants and drafts.
2453. Financial institution insured account.
2453.5. Deposit of estate money in trust company department; interest rate.
2454. Deposit of personal property with trust company.
2455. Deposit of securities in securities depository.
2456. Deposits withdrawable only upon court authorization.
2457. Maintenance of home of ward or conservatee and dependents.
2458. Voting rights with respect to corporate shares, memberships or property.
2459. Life insurance, medical, retirement and other plans and benefits.
2460. Liability and casualty insurance.
2461. Taxes and tax returns.
2462. Representation in actions and proceedings.
2463. Partition actions.
2464. Acceptance of deed in lieu of foreclosure or trustee's sale.
2465. Abandonment of valueless property.
2466. Advances by guardian or conservator.

Section
2467. Care of estate pending delivery to personal representative.
2468. Disabled attorney; petition for appointment; notice and hearing; contents; compensation; termination.
2469. Incapacitated professional fiduciary; petition for appointment; termination; notice and hearing; compensation; duties of professional fiduciary practice administrator; extension; creation or revision of forms for implementation.

Cross References

Application of old and new law, see Probate Code § 3.

§ 2450. Extent of court supervision

(a) Unless this article specifically provides a proceeding to obtain court authorization or requires court authorization, the powers and duties set forth in this article may be exercised or performed by the guardian or conservator without court authorization, instruction, approval, or confirmation. Nothing in this subdivision precludes the guardian or conservator from seeking court authorization, instructions, approval, or confirmation pursuant to Section 2403.

(b) Upon petition of the ward or conservatee, a creditor, or any other interested person, or upon the court's own motion, the court may limit the authority of the guardian or conservator under subdivision (a) as to a particular power or duty or as to particular powers or duties. Notice of the hearing on a petition under this subdivision shall be given for the period and in the manner provided in Chapter 3 (commencing with Section 1460) of Part 1. *(Stats.1990, c. 79 (A.B.759), § 14, operative July 1, 1991.)*

Cross References

Administration of decedent's estate, extent of court supervision, see Probate Code §§ 10500, 10501.
Extension, renewal or modifications of obligations, see Probate Code § 2500 et seq.
Guardianship and conservatorship, interested person, defined, see Probate Code § 1424.
Request for special notice, see Probate Code § 2700 et seq.

§ 2451. Collection of debts and benefits

The guardian or conservator may collect debts and benefits due to the ward or conservatee and the estate. *(Stats.1990, c. 79 (A.B.759), § 14, operative July 1, 1991.)*

Cross References

Review on settlement of accounts, see Probate Code § 2625.

Research References

Forms
1 California Transactions Forms--Estate Planning § 6:17, Guardian of Estate or of Property.

§ 2451.5. Powers of guardian or conservator

The guardian or conservator may do any of the following:

(a) Contract for the guardianship or conservatorship, perform outstanding contracts, and, thereby, bind the estate.

(b) Purchase tangible personal property.

(c) Subject to the provisions of Chapter 8 (commencing with Section 2640), employ an attorney to advise and represent the guardian or conservator in all matters, including the conservatorship proceeding and all other actions or proceedings.

(d) Employ and pay the expense of accountants, investment advisers, agents, depositaries, and employees.

(e) Operate for a period of 45 days after the issuance of the letters of guardianship or conservatorship, at the risk of the estate, a business, farm, or enterprise constituting an asset of the estate. (Added by Stats.2007, c. 553 (A.B.1727), § 16.)

§ 2452. Checks, warrants and drafts

(a) The guardian or conservator may endorse and cash or deposit any checks, warrants, or drafts payable to the ward or conservatee which constitute property of the estate.

(b) If it appears likely that the estate will satisfy the conditions of subdivision (b) of Section 2628, the court may order that the guardian or conservator be the designated payee for public assistance payments received pursuant to Part 3 (commencing with Section 11000) or Part 4 (commencing with Section 16000) of Division 9 of the Welfare and Institutions Code. (Stats.1990, c. 79 (A.B.759), § 14, operative July 1, 1991.)

Cross References

Draft or check, defined, see Commercial Code § 3104.
Indorsements, see Commercial Code § 3204 et seq.

§ 2453. Financial institution insured account

The guardian or conservator may deposit money belonging to the estate in an insured account in a financial institution in this state. Unless otherwise provided by court order, the money deposited under this section may be withdrawn without order of court. (Stats.1990, c. 79 (A.B.759), § 14, operative July 1, 1991.)

Cross References

Account defined, see Probate Code § 21.
Deposit of estate funds and assets with trust company, see Financial Code § 1586.
Deposits of money or property subject to court control, use in determining amount of bond, see Probate Code § 2328.
Deposits withdrawable only upon court order, see Probate Code § 2456.
Financial institution, defined, see Probate Code § 40.
Investments requiring court authorization, see Probate Code § 2570.
Prior court authorization not required, see Probate Code § 2450.

Research References

Forms

West's California Code Forms, Probate § 2456 Form 1, Petition for Order Conditioning Withdrawal of Deposits in Financial Institution on Prior Authorization of the Court.

§ 2453.5. Deposit of estate money in trust company department; interest rate

(a) Subject to subdivision (b), where a trust company is a guardian or conservator and in the exercise of reasonable judgment deposits money of the estate in an account in any department of the corporation or association of which it is a part, it is chargeable with interest thereon at the rate of interest prevailing among banks of the locality on such deposits.

(b) Where it is to the advantage of the estate, the amount of cash that is reasonably necessary for orderly administration of the estate may be deposited in a checking account that does not bear interest which is maintained in a department of the corporation or association of which the trust company is a party. (Stats.1990, c. 79 (A.B.759), § 14, operative July 1, 1991.)

Cross References

Trust company, defined, see Probate Code § 83.

§ 2454. Deposit of personal property with trust company

The guardian or conservator may deposit personal property of the estate with a trust company for safekeeping. Unless otherwise provided by court order, the personal property may be withdrawn without order of court. (Stats.1990, c. 79 (A.B.759), § 14, operative July 1, 1991.)

Cross References

Deposits,
   Estate funds and assets in trust company by guardian, reduction of bond, see Financial Code § 1586.
   Withdrawable only upon court order, see Probate Code § 2456.
Trust companies,
   Generally, see Financial Code § 1550 et seq.
   Capacity to act as guardian, see Probate Code § 300.
   Definitions, see Financial Code §§ 107, 109; Probate Code § 83.

§ 2455. Deposit of securities in securities depository

(a) A trust company serving as guardian or conservator may deposit securities that constitute all or part of the estate in a securities depository as provided in Section 775 of the Financial Code.

(b) If the securities have been deposited with a trust company pursuant to Section 2328 or Section 2454, the trust company may deposit the securities in a securities depository as provided in Section 775 of the Financial Code.

(c) The securities depository may hold securities deposited with it in the manner authorized by Section 775 of the Financial Code. (Stats.1990, c. 79 (A.B.759), § 14, operative July 1, 1991.)

Cross References

Security, defined, see Probate Code § 70.
Trust company,
   Definition, see Probate Code § 83.
   Deposit of securities held under court order in securities depository, see Financial Code § 1606.

§ 2456. Deposits withdrawable only upon court authorization

(a) Upon application of the guardian or conservator, the court may, with or without notice, order that money or other personal property be deposited pursuant to Section 2453 or 2454, and be subject to withdrawal only upon authorization of the court.

(b) The guardian or conservator shall deliver a copy of the court order to the financial institution or trust company at the time the deposit is made.

(c) No financial institution or trust company accepting a deposit pursuant to Section 2453 or 2454 is on notice of the existence of an order that the money or other property is subject to withdrawal only upon authorization of the court unless it has actual notice of the order. (Stats.1990, c. 79 (A.B.759), § 14, operative July 1, 1991.)

Cross References

Deposit of estate funds with trust company, see Financial Code § 1586.
Deposit of money, generally, see Probate Code § 2453.
Deposit of personal property, generally, see Probate Code § 2454.
Financial institution, defined, see Probate Code § 40.
Money or property paid or delivered pursuant to compromise or judgment for minor or incompetent person, disposition of remaining balance, see Probate Code § 3602.
Request for special notice, see Probate Code § 2700 et seq.
Trust company, defined, see Probate Code § 83.

Research References

Forms

West's California Code Forms, Probate § 2456 Form 1, Petition for Order Conditioning Withdrawal of Deposits in Financial Institution on Prior Authorization of the Court.
West's California Code Forms, Probate § 3600 Comment, Disposition of Compromise or Judgment Amount on Behalf of an Incompetent Person Without a Conservator of the Estate.

§ 2457. Maintenance of home of ward or conservatee and dependents

The guardian or conservator may maintain in good condition and repair the home or other dwelling of either or both of the following:

(a) The ward or conservatee.

§ 2457

(b) The persons legally entitled to such maintenance and repair from the ward or conservatee. *(Stats.1990, c. 79 (A.B.759), § 14, operative July 1, 1991.)*

Cross References

Order compelling guardian or conservator to furnish support and maintenance, see Probate Code § 2404.

Research References

Forms

1 California Transactions Forms--Estate Planning § 6:17, Guardian of Estate or of Property.

§ 2458. Voting rights with respect to corporate shares, memberships or property

With respect to a share of stock of a domestic or foreign corporation held in the estate, a membership in a nonprofit corporation held in the estate, or other property held in the estate, a guardian or conservator may do any one or more of the following:

(a) Vote in person, and give proxies to exercise, any voting rights with respect to the share, membership, or other property.

(b) Waive notice of a meeting or give consent to the holding of a meeting.

(c) Authorize, ratify, approve, or confirm any action which could be taken by shareholders, members, or property owners. *(Stats.1990, c. 79 (A.B.759), § 14, operative July 1, 1991.)*

Cross References

By-law provisions governing use of proxies, see Corporations Code § 212.
Persons entitled to vote, record date, see Corporations Code § 701.
Proxies, revocation, see Corporations Code § 705.
Shareholders' meetings, notice, see Corporations Code § 601.

§ 2459. Life insurance, medical, retirement and other plans and benefits

(a) The guardian or conservator may obtain, continue, renew, modify, terminate, or otherwise deal in any of the following for the purpose of providing protection to the ward or conservatee or a person legally entitled to support from the ward or conservatee:

(1) Medical, hospital, and other health care policies, plans, or benefits.

(2) Disability policies, plans, or benefits.

(b) The conservator may continue in force any of the following in which the conservatee, or a person legally entitled to support, maintenance, or education from the conservatee, has or will have an interest:

(1) Life insurance policies, plans, or benefits.

(2) Annuity policies, plans, or benefits.

(3) Mutual fund and other dividend reinvestment plans.

(4) Retirement, profit-sharing, and employee welfare plans or benefits.

(c) The right to elect benefit or payment options, to terminate, to change beneficiaries or ownership, to assign rights, to borrow, or to receive cash value in return for a surrender of rights, or to take similar actions under any of the policies, plans, or benefits described in subdivision (b) may be exercised by the conservator only after authorization or direction by order of the court, except as permitted in Section 2544.5. To obtain such an order, the conservator or other interested person shall petition under Article 10 (commencing with Section 2580).

(d) Notwithstanding subdivision (c), unless the court otherwise orders, the conservator without authorization of the court may borrow on the loan value of an insurance policy to pay the current premiums to keep the policy in force if the conservatee followed that practice prior to the establishment of the conservatorship.

(e) The guardian may give the consent provided in Section 10112 of the Insurance Code without authorization of the court, but the guardian may use funds of the guardianship estate to effect or maintain in force a contract entered into by the ward under Section 10112 of the Insurance Code only after authorization by order of the court. To obtain such an order, the guardian, the ward, or any other interested person shall file a petition showing that it is in the best interest of the ward or of the guardianship estate to do so. Notice of the hearing on the petition shall be given for the period and in the manner provided in Chapter 3 (commencing with Section 1460) of Part 1.

(f) Nothing in this section limits the power of the guardian or conservator to make investments as otherwise authorized by this division. *(Stats.1990, c. 79 (A.B.759), § 14, operative July 1, 1991. Amended by Stats.1996, c. 86 (A.B.2146), § 1.)*

Cross References

Guardianship and conservatorship, interested person, defined, see Probate Code § 1424.
Investments, see Probate Code § 2570 et seq.
Life and disability insurance for minors, see Insurance Code § 10112.
Request for special notice, see Probate Code § 2700 et seq.

Research References

Forms

West's California Code Forms, Probate § 2459(c) Form 1, Petition for Authorization for Conservator to Take Actions Regarding Insurance and Other Policies and Plans.

West's California Code Forms, Probate § 2459(e) Form 1, Petition for Authorization for Guardian to Effect or Maintain in Force Contract Under Insurance Code Section 10112.

§ 2460. Liability and casualty insurance

The guardian or conservator may insure:

(a) Property of the estate against loss or damage.

(b) The ward or conservatee, the guardian or conservator, and all or any part of the estate against liability to third persons. *(Stats. 1990, c. 79 (A.B.759), § 14, operative July 1, 1991.)*

Cross References

Liability insurance, see Insurance Code §§ 108, 11550 et seq.

§ 2461. Taxes and tax returns

(a) The guardian or conservator may prepare, execute, and file tax returns for the ward or conservatee and for the estate and may exercise options and elections and claim exemptions for the ward or conservatee and for the estate under the applicable tax laws.

(b) Notwithstanding Section 2502, the guardian or conservator may pay, contest, and compromise taxes, penalties, and assessments upon the property of the estate and income and other taxes payable or claimed to be payable by the ward or conservatee or the estate. *(Stats.1990, c. 79 (A.B.759), § 14, operative July 1, 1991.)*

Cross References

Property tax refund, action to recover, see Revenue and Taxation Code § 5140.

§ 2462. Representation in actions and proceedings

Subject to Section 2463, unless another person is appointed for that purpose, the guardian or conservator may:

(a) Commence and maintain actions and proceedings for the benefit of the ward or conservatee or the estate.

(b) Defend actions and proceedings against the ward or conservatee, the guardian or conservator, or the estate.

(c) File a petition commencing a case under Title 11 of the United States Code (Bankruptcy) on behalf of the ward or conservatee. *(Stats.1990, c. 79 (A.B.759), § 14, operative July 1, 1991.)*

Cross References

Compromise of claims and actions, see Probate Code § 2500 et seq.
Election of guardian or conservator of surviving spouse to have property administered in probate, see Probate Code § 13502 et seq.

§ 2463. Partition actions

(a) The guardian or conservator may bring an action against the other cotenants for partition of any property in which the ward or conservatee has an undivided interest if the court has first made an order authorizing the guardian or conservator to do so. The court may make * * * the order ex parte on a petition filed by the guardian or conservator.

(b) The guardian or conservator may consent and agree, without an action, to a partition of the property and to the part to be set off to the estate, and may execute deeds or conveyances to the owners of the remaining interests of the parts to which they may be respectively entitled, if the court has made an order under Article 5 (commencing with Section 2500) authorizing the guardian or conservator to do so.

(c) If the ward or conservatee, or the guardian or conservator * * * in that capacity, is made a defendant in a partition action, the guardian or conservator may defend the action without authorization of the court.

(d) If the subject property is the conservatee's present or former personal residence, the powers granted pursuant to subdivisions (a) and (b) of this section are subject to the requirements of Sections 2352.5, 2540, 2541, and 2541.5, which govern the sale and partition of a conservatee's personal residence. *(Stats.1990, c. 79 (A.B.759), § 14, operative July 1, 1991. Amended by Stats.2022, c. 91 (S.B.1005), § 1, eff. Jan. 1, 2023.)*

Cross References

Actions for partition against personal representative, see Probate Code § 9823.
Consent to appointment of referee in partition action, see Code of Civil Procedure § 873.040.
Conveyance or transfer of property, generally, see Probate Code § 2111.
Instructions from or confirmation by court, see Probate Code § 2403.
Partition, generally, see Code of Civil Procedure § 872.010 et seq.
Partition of decedents' estates before distribution, generally, see Probate Code § 11950.
Recording,
  Constructive notice, conveyances of real property or estate for years, see Civil Code § 1213.
  Instruments or judgments, documents to be recorded and manner of recording, see Government Code §§ 27320 et seq., 27280 et seq.
Property transfers, place of recordation, see Civil Code § 1169.

§ 2464. Acceptance of deed in lieu of foreclosure or trustee's sale

(a) If it is to the advantage of the estate to accept a deed to property which is subject to a mortgage or deed of trust in lieu of foreclosure of the mortgage or sale under the deed of trust, the guardian or conservator may, after authorization by order of the court and upon such terms and conditions as may be imposed by the court, accept a deed conveying the property to the ward or conservatee.

(b) To obtain an order under this section, the guardian or conservator shall file a petition showing the advantage to the estate of accepting the deed. Notice of the hearing on the petition shall be given for the period and in the manner provided in Chapter 3 (commencing with Section 1460) of Part 1.

(c) The court shall make an order under this section only if the advantage to the estate of accepting the deed is shown by clear and convincing evidence. *(Stats.1990, c. 79 (A.B.759), § 14, operative July 1, 1991.)*

Cross References

Appealable orders, see Probate Code § 1300 et seq.
Mortgages, generally, see Civil Code § 2920 et seq.
Trustees, powers, see Probate Code § 16200 et seq.

Research References

Forms

West's California Code Forms, Probate § 2403 Form 1, Petition for Instructions (Or Confirmation).

§ 2465. Abandonment of valueless property

The guardian or conservator may dispose of or abandon valueless property. *(Stats.1990, c. 79 (A.B.759), § 14, operative July 1, 1991.)*

§ 2466. Advances by guardian or conservator

The guardian or conservator may advance the guardian's or conservator's own funds for the benefit of the ward or conservatee or the estate and may reimburse the advance out of the income and principal of the estate first available. With court authorization or approval, interest on the amount advanced may be allowed at the legal rate payable on judgments. *(Stats.1990, c. 79 (A.B.759), § 14, operative July 1, 1991.)*

Cross References

Instructions from or confirmation by court, see Probate Code § 2403.
Legal rate of interest, see Cal. Const. Art. 15, § 1; Civil Code § 1916–1 et seq.

Research References

Forms

West's California Code Forms, Probate § 2403 Form 1, Petition for Instructions (Or Confirmation).

§ 2467. Care of estate pending delivery to personal representative

(a) The guardian or conservator continues to have the duty of custody and conservation of the estate after the death of the ward or conservatee pending the delivery thereof to the personal representative of the ward's or conservatee's estate or other disposition according to law.

(b) The guardian or conservator has such powers as are granted to a guardian or conservator under this division as are necessary for the performance of the duty imposed by subdivision (a). *(Stats.1990, c. 79 (A.B.759), § 14, operative July 1, 1991.)*

Cross References

Disposition of assets upon death of ward or conservatee, see Probate Code § 2631.
Personal representative and general personal representative, defined, see Probate Code § 58.
Review on settlement of accounts, see Probate Code § 2625.
Termination of conservatorship upon death of conservatee or by order of the court, see Probate Code § 1860.
Termination of conservatorship, death of conservatee or court order, see Probate Code § 1860.
Termination of guardianship upon majority, death, adoption or emancipation of ward, see Probate Code § 1600.

Research References

Forms

1 California Transactions Forms--Estate Planning § 1:2, Probate System.
West's California Code Forms, Probate § 1601 Form 1, Petition for Termination of Guardianship—Judicial Council Form GC-255.

§ 2468. Disabled attorney; petition for appointment; notice and hearing; contents; compensation; termination

(a) The conservator of the estate of a disabled attorney who was engaged in the practice of law at the time of his or her disability, or other person interested in the estate, may bring a petition seeking the appointment of an active member of the State Bar of California to take control of the files and assets of the practice of the disabled member.

(b) The petition may be filed and heard on such notice that the court determines is in the best interests of the persons interested in

§ 2468

the estate of the disabled member. If the petition alleges that the immediate appointment of a practice administrator is required to safeguard the interests of the estate, the court may dispense with notice provided that the conservator is the petitioner or has joined in the petition or has otherwise waived notice of hearing on the petition.

(c) The petition shall indicate the powers sought for the practice administrator from the list of powers set forth in Section 6185 of the Business and Professions Code. These powers shall be specifically listed in the order appointing the practice administrator.

(d) The petition shall allege the value of the assets that are to come under the control of the practice administrator, including but not limited by the amount of funds in all accounts used by the disabled member. The court shall require the filing of a surety bond in the amount of the value of the personal property to be filed with the court by the practice administrator. No action may be taken by the practice administrator unless a bond has been duly filed with the court.

(e) The practice administrator shall not be the attorney representing the conservator.

(f) The court shall appoint the attorney nominated by the disabled member in a writing, including but not limited to the disabled member's will, unless the court concludes that the appointment of the nominated person would be contrary to the best interests of the estate or would create a conflict of interest with any of the clients of the disabled member.

(g) The practice administrator shall be compensated only upon order of the court making the appointment for his or her reasonable and necessary services. The law practice shall be the source of the compensation for the practice administrator unless the assets are insufficient, in which case, the compensation of the practice administrator shall be charged against the assets of the estate as a cost of administration. The practice administrator shall also be entitled to reimbursement of his or her costs.

(h) Upon conclusion of the services of the practice administrator, the practice administrator shall render an accounting and petition for its approval by the superior court making the appointment. Upon settlement of the accounting, the practice administrator shall be discharged and the surety on his or her bond exonerated.

(i) If the court appointing the practice administrator determines upon petition that the disabled attorney has recovered his or her capacity to resume his or her law practice, the appointment of a practice administrator shall forthwith terminate and the disabled attorney shall be restored to his or her practice.

(j) For purposes of this section, the person appointed to take control of the practice of the disabled member shall be referred to as the "practice administrator" and the conservatee shall be referred to as the "disabled member." *(Added by Stats.1998, c. 682 (A.B.2069), § 4.)*

Cross References

Guardianship and conservatorship, interested person, defined, see Probate Code § 1424.
Incapacity to attend to law practice, jurisdiction of courts, see Business and Professions Code § 6185.

Research References

Forms

West's California Code Forms, Probate § 2468 Form 1, Petition for Appointment of State Bar Member to Take Control of Disabled Attorney's Practice.

West's California Code Forms, Probate § 2468 Form 2, Order for Appointment of State Bar Member to Take Control of Disabled Attorney's Practice.

§ 2469. Incapacitated professional fiduciary; petition for appointment; termination; notice and hearing; compensation; duties of professional fiduciary practice administrator; extension; creation or revision of forms for implementation

(a) Commencing January 1, 2024, when a professional fiduciary becomes incapacitated and a vacancy exists, the incapacitated fiduciary's conservator, agent under a power of attorney for asset management, trustee, or interested person may petition for the appointment of one or more individuals qualified to act as a professional fiduciary under the Professional Fiduciaries Act (Chapter 6 (commencing with Section 6500) of Division 3 of the Business and Professions Code) as a professional fiduciary practice administrator to take control of the incapacitated professional fiduciary's files and to be appointed as temporary successor as to those matters for which a vacancy exists as a result of the professional fiduciary's incapacity.

(b) The petition shall request an order appointing a professional fiduciary practice administrator as temporary successor, with all of the powers and duties held by the incapacitated fiduciary, in each matter in which the incapacitated fiduciary was acting in a representative capacity, including guardianships of the estate, conservatorships of the person and the estate, decedent's estates, court-supervised trusts, and non-court-supervised trusts.

(c) The court shall require the professional fiduciary practice administrator to file a surety bond in each matter in which the professional fiduciary practice administrator is appointed temporary successor, in the amount currently required of the incapacitated fiduciary or in another amount as the court deems appropriate.

(d) The court may appoint as the professional fiduciary practice administrator the professional fiduciary nominated by the incapacitated fiduciary in a writing, including, but not limited to, the incapacitated fiduciary's will or trust, or in the absence thereof, the person nominated by the person having legal standing to act on behalf of the incapacitated professional fiduciary. The court shall not make the appointment if the court concludes that the appointment of the nominated person would be contrary to the best interests of, or would create a conflict of interest with, any interested party in a matter in which the incapacitated fiduciary was acting in a fiduciary capacity.

(e) The appointment of the professional fiduciary practice administrator as temporary successor shall terminate, in each of the matters in which the professional fiduciary practice administrator was appointed as temporary successor, 45 days after the entry of the order appointing the professional fiduciary practice administrator, or earlier if another person is appointed.

(f) Notice of the hearing on the petition for appointment of a professional fiduciary practice administrator as temporary successor shall be given to all persons entitled to notice in each of the matters which are the subject of the petition. The court may dispense with notice if the petition alleges that the immediate appointment of a professional fiduciary practice administrator is required to safeguard the interests of an individual or an asset in a matter in which the incapacitated fiduciary was acting in a representative capacity.

(g) The professional fiduciary practice administrator shall be compensated for services provided and reimbursement of costs incurred in each matter solely from the assets of that matter subject to the provisions of the applicable document or as determined by the court, and in no event more than the incapacitated fiduciary would have been paid.

(h) The professional fiduciary practice administrator appointed in a given matter shall do all of the following:

(1) File a copy of the order appointing the professional fiduciary practice administrator as temporary successor in each of the matters in which the court appoints the professional fiduciary practice administrator as temporary successor.

(2) Take control and review all files and writings maintained by the incapacitated fiduciary for matters in which the incapacitated fiduciary was acting in a representative capacity.

(3) Within 15 days after the entry of the order appointing the professional fiduciary practice administrator as temporary successor, provide written notice to all interested parties as to each matter in which the incapacitated fiduciary was acting in a representative capacity who can be reasonably ascertained and located to inform those parties of the appointment of the professional fiduciary practice administrator as temporary successor. The notice shall advise the interested parties of the necessity and process for the appointment of a permanent successor, which shall include the following:

(A) The right of the parties to petition the court for the appointment of a permanent successor.

(B) The right of any interested party to nominate an individual to act as permanent successor, and then the obligation of the professional fiduciary practice administrator to petition for the appointment of the individual nominated, provided an interested party provides the professional fiduciary practice administrator with the name of their nominee within 15 days after the date notice was given.

(C) The ability of the professional fiduciary practice administrator, in the event none of the interested parties act within the time prescribed, under subparagraph (A) or (B), to petition the court for appointment of a permanent successor.

(4) Upon the court's appointment of a permanent successor, the professional fiduciary practice administrator shall file an account and report on behalf of the incapacitated fiduciary for any period of time the incapacitated fiduciary would have been required to account, as well as for the period of time the professional fiduciary practice administrator served as temporary successor. As part of that account and report, the professional fiduciary practice administrator may request compensation both on behalf of the incapacitated fiduciary, for services rendered prior to their incapacity, and on their own behalf for services rendered after the incapacitated fiduciary's incapacity, as temporary successor, subject to any limitation on fees and costs that existed for the incapacitated fiduciary, and may request discharge and exoneration of bond. The account filed for the period during which the matter was administered by the now incapacitated fiduciary may be verified on information and belief.

(5) Comply with any other obligations imposed by the court.

(i) Each of the time periods prescribed in this section may be extended by the court if the court determines that good cause exists, and if the court determines that the extension is in the best interest of the minor, the conservatee, the decedent's estate, or the current income beneficiaries under a trust, as applicable.

(j) For purposes of this section, the following definitions apply:

(1) "Incapacitated" means that the person is unable to fulfill their duties as a professional fiduciary because of either temporary or permanent disability, incapacity, or absence.

(2) "Professional fiduciary practice administrator" means the person or persons appointed pursuant to this section to take over the responsibilities from the incapacitated fiduciary.

(3) "Vacancy" means that the instrument under which the incapacitated fiduciary was acting does not name a successor to fill the vacancy, the instrument under which the incapacitated fiduciary was acting does not provide a nonjudicial method to fill the vacancy, and a cofiduciary, authorized to act solely, was not acting with the incapacitated fiduciary.

(k) This section does not limit the authority granted to the court under subdivision (j) of Section 2250, Section 8523, and subdivision (e) of Section 15642.

(*l*) The Judicial Council shall create or revise any forms or rules necessary to implement this section no later than January 1, 2024. *(Added by Stats.2022, c. 612 (S.B.1024), § 4, eff. Jan. 1, 2023.)*

ARTICLE 5. COMPROMISE OF CLAIMS AND ACTIONS; EXTENSION, RENEWAL, OR MODIFICATION OF OBLIGATIONS

Section
2500. Authority.
2501. Matters relating to real property.
2502. Compromise in excess of specified amount.
2503. Compromise of claim of ward or conservatee against guardian or conservator.
2504. Support, wrongful death and personal injury claims.
2505. Court approval of transaction or matter; exemptions.
2506. Petition for approval of court in guardianship or conservatorship proceeding.
2507. Application of another statute to the compromise, settlement, etc.

Cross References

Application of old and new law, see Probate Code § 3.

§ 2500. Authority

(a) Unless this article or some other applicable statute requires court authorization or approval, if it is to the advantage of the estate, the guardian or conservator may do any of the following without court authorization, instruction, approval, or confirmation:

(1) Compromise or settle a claim, action, or proceeding by or for the benefit of, or against, the ward or conservatee, the guardian or conservator, or the estate, including the giving of a covenant not to sue.

(2) Extend, renew, or in any manner modify the terms of an obligation owing to or running in favor of the ward or conservatee or the estate.

(b) Nothing in this section precludes the guardian or conservator from seeking court authorization, instructions, approval, or confirmation pursuant to Section 2403.

(c) Upon petition of the ward or conservatee, a creditor, or any interested person, or upon the court's own motion, the court may limit the authority of the guardian or conservator under subdivision (a). Notice of the hearing on the petition shall be given for the period and in the manner provided in Chapter 3 (commencing with Section 1460) of Part 1. *(Stats.1990, c. 79 (A.B.759), § 14, operative July 1, 1991.)*

Cross References

Filing and payment of claims, see Probate Code § 9150 et seq.
Guardianship and conservatorship, interested person, defined, see Probate Code § 1424.
Representation in actions and proceedings, see Probate Code §§ 2462, 2463.
Request for special notice, see Probate Code § 2700 et seq.
Review on settlement of accounts, see Probate Code § 2625.

Research References

Forms

3 California Transactions Forms--Business Transactions § 18:16, Settlements that Require Court Approval.
West's California Code Forms, Probate § 2500–2507 Form 1, Petition by Guardian or Conservator to Approve Compromise of Disputed Personal Injury Claim of Minor or Incompetent Person—Judicial Council Form MC-350.
West's California Code Forms, Probate § 3500 Form 1, Petition by Parent to Compromise Disputed Personal Injury Claim of Minor Without a Guardian of the Estate—Judicial Council Form MC-350.

§ 2500

West's California Code Forms, Probate § 3500 Form 2, Order Authorizing Parent to Compromise Claim of Minor Without Guardian—Judicial Council Form MC-351.

West's California Code Forms, Probate § 3600 Comment, Disposition of Compromise or Judgment Amount on Behalf of an Incompetent Person Without a Conservator of the Estate.

§ 2501. Matters relating to real property

(a) Except as provided in subdivision (b), court approval is required for a compromise, settlement, extension, renewal, or modification which affects any of the following:

(1) Title to real property.

(2) An interest in real property or a lien or encumbrance on real property.

(3) An option to purchase real property or an interest in real property.

(b) If it is to the advantage of the estate, the guardian or conservator without prior court approval may extend, renew, or modify a lease of real property in either of the following cases:

(1) Where under the lease as extended, renewed, or modified the rental does not exceed five thousand dollars ($5,000) a month and the term does not exceed two years.

(2) Where the lease is from month to month, regardless of the amount of the rental.

(c) For the purposes of subdivision (b), if the lease as extended, renewed, or modified gives the lessee the right to extend the term of the lease, the length of the term shall be considered as though the right to extend had been exercised. *(Stats.1990, c. 79 (A.B.759), § 14, operative July 1, 1991. Amended by Stats.1990, c. 710 (S.B. 1775), § 10, operative July 1, 1991.)*

Cross References

Acceptance of deed in lieu of foreclosure, see Probate Code § 2464.
Court authorized to approve transaction or matter, see Probate Code § 2505.
Leases authorized without court permission, see Probate Code § 2555.
Life and disability insurance, insurance of minors, see Insurance Code § 10112.
Real property, defined, see Probate Code § 68.

Research References

Forms

3 California Transactions Forms--Business Transactions § 18:16, Settlements that Require Court Approval.
West's California Code Forms, Probate § 2403 Form 1, Petition for Instructions (Or Confirmation).
West's California Code Forms, Probate § 2500–2507 Form 1, Petition by Guardian or Conservator to Approve Compromise of Disputed Personal Injury Claim of Minor or Incompetent Person—Judicial Council Form MC-350.

§ 2502. Compromise in excess of specified amount

Court approval is required for a compromise or settlement of a matter when the transaction requires the transfer or encumbrance of property of the estate, or the creation of an unsecured liability of the estate, or both, in an amount or value in excess of twenty-five thousand dollars ($25,000). *(Stats.1990, c. 79 (A.B.759), § 14, operative July 1, 1991.)*

Cross References

Court authorized to approve transaction or matter, see Probate Code § 2505.
Life and disability insurance, insurance of minors, see Insurance Code § 10112.

Research References

Forms

3 California Transactions Forms--Business Transactions § 18:16, Settlements that Require Court Approval.
West's California Code Forms, Probate § 2403 Form 1, Petition for Instructions (Or Confirmation).

West's California Code Forms, Probate § 2500–2507 Form 1, Petition by Guardian or Conservator to Approve Compromise of Disputed Personal Injury Claim of Minor or Incompetent Person—Judicial Council Form MC-350.

§ 2503. Compromise of claim of ward or conservatee against guardian or conservator

Court approval is required for any of the following:

(a) A compromise or settlement of a claim by the ward or conservatee against the guardian or conservator or against the attorney for the guardian or conservator, whether or not the claim arises out of the administration of the estate.

(b) An extension, renewal, or modification of the terms of a debt or similar obligation of the guardian or conservator, or of the attorney for the guardian or conservator, owing to or running in favor of the ward or conservatee or the estate. *(Stats.1990, c. 79 (A.B.759), § 14, operative July 1, 1991.)*

Cross References

Appealable orders, see Probate Code § 1300 et seq.
Court authorized to approve transaction or matter, see Probate Code § 2505.
Life and disability insurance, insurance of minors, see Insurance Code § 10112.

Research References

Forms

3 California Transactions Forms--Business Transactions § 18:16, Settlements that Require Court Approval.
West's California Code Forms, Probate § 2500–2507 Form 1, Petition by Guardian or Conservator to Approve Compromise of Disputed Personal Injury Claim of Minor or Incompetent Person—Judicial Council Form MC-350.

§ 2504. Support, wrongful death and personal injury claims

Court approval is required for the compromise or settlement of any of the following:

(a) A claim for the support, maintenance, or education of (1) the ward or conservatee, or (2) a person whom the ward or conservatee is legally obligated to support, maintain, or educate, against any other person (including, but not limited to, the spouse or parent of the ward or the spouse, domestic partner, parent, or adult child of the conservatee).

(b) A claim of the ward or conservatee for wrongful death.

(c) A claim of the ward or conservatee for physical or nonphysical harm to the person. *(Stats.1990, c. 79 (A.B.759), § 14, operative July 1, 1991. Amended by Stats.2001, c. 893 (A.B.25), § 36.)*

Cross References

Appealable orders, see Probate Code § 1300 et seq.
Domestic partner, defined, see Probate Code § 37.
Life and disability insurance, insurance of minors, see Insurance Code § 10112.
Parent, defined, see Probate Code § 54.
Pending actions and proceedings, compromise, see Code of Civil Procedure § 372.
Support and maintenance of ward or conservatee and dependents, see Probate Code § 2420 et seq.
Wrongful death, see Code of Civil Procedure § 377.60 et seq.

Research References

Forms

3 California Transactions Forms--Business Transactions § 18:16, Settlements that Require Court Approval.
West's California Code Forms, Probate § 2500–2507 Form 1, Petition by Guardian or Conservator to Approve Compromise of Disputed Personal Injury Claim of Minor or Incompetent Person—Judicial Council Form MC-350.

§ 2505. Court approval of transaction or matter; exemptions

(a) Subject to subdivision (c), where the claim or matter is the subject of a pending action or proceeding, the court approval required by this article shall be obtained from the court in which the action or proceeding is pending.

(b) Where the claim or matter is not the subject of a pending action or proceeding, the court approval required by this article shall be obtained from one of the following:

(1) The court in which the guardianship or conservatorship proceeding is pending.

(2) The superior court of the county where the ward or conservatee or guardian or conservator resides at the time the petition for approval is filed.

(3) The superior court of any county where a suit on the claim or matter properly could be brought.

(c) Where the claim or matter is the subject of a pending action or proceeding that is not brought in a court of this state, court approval required by this article shall be obtained from either of the following:

(1) The court in which the action or proceeding is pending.

(2) The court in which the guardianship or conservatorship proceeding is pending.

(d)(1) Subdivisions (a), (b), and (c) do not apply to a conservatorship that is registered in this state pursuant to Article 4 (commencing with Section 2011) of Chapter 8 of Part 3.

(2) Except as provided in paragraph (3), when a conservatorship is registered in this state pursuant to Article 4 (commencing with Section 2011) of Chapter 8 of Part 3, the court approval required by this article shall be obtained in accordance with Section 2016.

(3) Notwithstanding Section 2016, when a conservatorship is registered in this state pursuant to Article 4 (commencing with Section 2011) of Chapter 8 of Part 3, and the claim or matter in question is the subject of a pending action or proceeding that is not brought in a court of this state, the court approval required by this article may be obtained from the court in which the action or proceeding is pending. (Stats.1990, c. 79 (A.B.759), § 14, operative July 1, 1991. Amended by Stats.2014, c. 553 (S.B.940), § 25, eff. Jan. 1, 2015, operative Jan. 1, 2016.)

Cross References

Life and disability insurance, insurance of minors, see Insurance Code § 10112.

Research References

Forms

West's California Code Forms, Probate § 2500–2507 Form 1, Petition by Guardian or Conservator to Approve Compromise of Disputed Personal Injury Claim of Minor or Incompetent Person—Judicial Council Form MC-350.

§ 2506. Petition for approval of court in guardianship or conservatorship proceeding

Where approval of the court in which the guardianship or conservatorship proceeding is pending is required under this article, the guardian or conservator shall file a petition with the court showing the advantage of the compromise, settlement, extension, renewal, or modification to the ward or conservatee and the estate. Notice of the hearing on the petition shall be given for the period and in the manner provided in Chapter 3 (commencing with Section 1460) of Part 1. (Stats.1990, c. 79 (A.B.759), § 14, operative July 1, 1991.)

Research References

Forms

West's California Code Forms, Probate § 2500–2507 Form 1, Petition by Guardian or Conservator to Approve Compromise of Disputed Personal Injury Claim of Minor or Incompetent Person—Judicial Council Form MC-350.

§ 2507. Application of another statute to the compromise, settlement, etc.

Notwithstanding Sections 2500 to 2506, inclusive:

(a) Whenever another statute requires, provides a procedure for, or dispenses with court approval of a compromise, settlement, extension, renewal, or modification, the provisions of that statute govern any case to which that statute applies.

(b) Whenever another statute provides that a compromise or settlement of an administrative proceeding is not valid unless approved in such proceeding, the approval is governed by that statute, and approval in the guardianship or conservatorship proceeding is not required. (Stats.1990, c. 79 (A.B.759), § 14, operative July 1, 1991.)

Cross References

Life and disability insurance, insurance of minors, see Insurance Code § 10112.

Research References

Forms

West's California Code Forms, Probate § 2500–2507 Form 1, Petition by Guardian or Conservator to Approve Compromise of Disputed Personal Injury Claim of Minor or Incompetent Person—Judicial Council Form MC-350.

ARTICLE 7. SALES

Section
2540. Court supervision; exceptions; personal residence.
2541. Purpose.
2541.5. Court authorization.
2542. Terms of sales.
2543. Manner of sale.
2544. Sale of securities.
2544.5. Sale of mutual funds held without beneficiary designation.
2545. Sale or other disposition of tangible personal property.
2547. Disposition of proceeds of sale.
2548. Recovery of property sold; limitation of action.

Cross References

Application of old and new law, see Probate Code § 3.

§ 2540. Court supervision; exceptions; personal residence

(a) Except as otherwise provided in Sections 2544 and 2545, and except for the sale of a conservatee's present or former personal residence as set forth in subdivision (b), sales of real or personal property of the estate under this article are subject to authorization, confirmation, or direction of the court, as provided in this article.

(b) In seeking authorization to sell a conservatee's present or former personal residence, <u>consent and agree to partition of a conservatee's present or former personal residence, or bring an action for partition of a conservatee's present or former personal residence,</u> the conservator shall notify the court that the present or former personal residence is proposed to be sold <u>or partitioned</u> and that the conservator has discussed the proposed sale <u>or partition</u> with the conservatee. The conservator shall inform the court whether the conservatee supports or is opposed to the proposed sale <u>or partition</u> and shall describe the circumstances that necessitate the proposed sale <u>or partition</u>, including whether the conservatee has the ability to live in the personal residence and why other alternatives, including, but not limited to, in-home care services, are not available. The court, in its discretion, may require the court investigator to discuss the proposed sale <u>or partition</u> with the conservatee.

(c) Notice under subdivision (b) shall be provided to the court before the conservator commits any significant resources to the proposed sale <u>or partition</u> of the residence, unless the conservator

§ 2540

can establish that either the conservatee has the capacity to consent and unequivocally consents to the sale or partition, or there are exigent circumstances that require the conservator to commit resources to the sale or partition prior to court approval. (Stats.1990, c. 79 (A.B.759), § 14, operative July 1, 1991. Amended by Stats.2006, c. 490 (S.B.1116), § 3; Stats.2019, c. 847 (S.B.303), § 2, eff. Jan. 1, 2020; Stats.2022, c. 91 (S.B.1005), § 2, eff. Jan. 1, 2023.)

Cross References
Exchanges of property, see Probate Code § 2557.

Research References
Forms
West's California Code Forms, Probate § 2540 Form 1, Report of Sale and Petition for Order Confirming Sale of Real Property (Probate)—Judicial Council Form DE-260, GC-060.
West's California Judicial Council Forms DE-260, Report of Sale and Petition for Order Confirming Sale of Real Property.

§ 2541. Purpose

The guardian or conservator may sell real or personal property of the estate, consent and agree to partition of real or personal property of the estate, or bring an action for partition of real or personal property of the estate, in any of the following cases:

(a) If the income of the estate is insufficient for the comfortable and suitable support, maintenance, and education of the ward or conservatee (including care, treatment, and support of the ward or conservatee if a patient in a state hospital under the jurisdiction of the State Department of State Hospitals or the State Department of Developmental Services) or of those legally entitled to support, maintenance, or education from the ward or conservatee.

(b) If the sale or partition is necessary to pay the debts referred to in Sections 2430 and 2431.

(c) If the sale or partition is for the advantage, benefit, and best interest of (1) the ward or conservatee, (2) the estate, or (3) the ward or conservatee and those legally entitled to support, maintenance, or education from the ward or conservatee. (Stats.1990, c. 79 (A.B. 759), § 14, operative July 1, 1991. Amended by Stats.2012, c. 440 (A.B.1488), § 45, eff. Sept. 22, 2012; Stats.2022, c. 91 (S.B.1005), § 3, eff. Jan. 1, 2023.)

Cross References
Borrowing money and giving security, see Probate Code § 2551.
County aid and relief to indigents, termination and recovery of assistance, see Welfare and Institutions Code § 17403.
Disposition of proceeds of sale, see Probate Code § 2547.
Sale or encumbrance of property when income is insufficient for support, see Probate Code § 2420.
State Department of Developmental Services, see Welfare and Institutions Code § 4400 et seq.
State Department of State Hospitals, see Welfare and Institutions Code § 4000 et seq.
Tangible personal property, sale or other disposition, see Probate Code § 2545.

Research References
Forms
West's California Code Forms, Probate § 2540 Form 1, Report of Sale and Petition for Order Confirming Sale of Real Property (Probate)—Judicial Council Form DE-260, GC-060.
West's California Code Forms, Probate § 2551 Form 1, Petition to Borrow Money and Encumber Real Property.

§ 2541.5. Court authorization

Notwithstanding Section 2541, the court may authorize a conservator to sell a conservatee's present or former personal residence, consent and agree to partition of a conservatee's present or former personal residence, or bring an action for partition of a conservatee's present or former personal residence, only if the court finds by clear and convincing evidence that the conservator demonstrated a compelling need to sell or partition the personal residence for the benefit of the conservatee. (Added by Stats.2019, c. 847 (S.B.303), § 3, eff. Jan. 1, 2020. Amended by Stats.2022, c. 91 (S.B.1005), § 4, eff. Jan. 1, 2023.)

Research References
Forms
West's California Code Forms, Probate § 2540 Form 1, Report of Sale and Petition for Order Confirming Sale of Real Property (Probate)—Judicial Council Form DE-260, GC-060.

§ 2542. Terms of sales

(a) All sales shall be for cash or for part cash and part deferred payments. Except as otherwise provided in Sections 2544 and 2545, the terms of sale are subject to the approval of the court.

(b) If real property is sold for part deferred payments, the guardian or conservator shall take the note of the purchaser for the unpaid portion of the purchase money, with a mortgage or deed of trust on the property to secure payment of the note. The mortgage or deed of trust shall be subject only to encumbrances existing at the date of sale and such other encumbrances as the court may approve.

(c) If real or personal property of the estate sold for part deferred payments consists of an undivided interest, a joint tenancy interest, or any other interest less than the entire ownership, and the owner or owners of the remaining interests in the property join in the sale, the note and deed of trust or mortgage may be made to the ward or conservatee and the other owner or owners. (Stats.1990, c. 79 (A.B.759), § 14, operative July 1, 1991.)

Cross References
Interests in property, see Civil Code § 678 et seq.
Joint tenancy, see Civil Code § 683.
Mortgages, see Civil Code § 2920 et seq.
Real property, defined, see Probate Code § 68.
Sales by personal representatives, see Probate Code §§ 10257, 10315.
Transfers of real property, see Civil Code § 1091 et seq.

Research References
Forms
13 Am. Jur. Pl. & Pr. Forms Guardian and Ward § 406, Statutory References.
West's California Code Forms, Probate § 2540 Form 1, Report of Sale and Petition for Order Confirming Sale of Real Property (Probate)—Judicial Council Form DE-260, GC-060.
West's California Code Forms, Probate § 2542 Form 1, Notice of Private Sale by Guardian or Conservator of Real Property.

§ 2543. Manner of sale

(a) If estate property is required or permitted to be sold, the guardian or conservator may:

(1) Use discretion as to which property to sell first.

(2) Sell the entire interest of the estate in the property or any lesser interest therein.

(3) Sell the property either at public auction or private sale.

(b) Subject to Section 1469, unless otherwise specifically provided in this article, all proceedings concerning sales by guardians or conservators, publishing and posting notice of sale, reappraisal for sale, minimum offer price for the property, reselling the property, report of sale and petition for confirmation of sale, and notice and hearing of that petition, making orders authorizing sales, rejecting or confirming sales and reports of sales, ordering and making conveyances of property sold, and allowance of commissions, shall conform, as nearly as may be, to the provisions of this code concerning sales by a personal representative, including, but not limited to, Articles 6 (commencing with Section 10300), 7 (commencing with Section 10350), 8 (commencing with Section 10360), and 9 (commencing with Section 10380) of Chapter 18 of Part 5 of Division 7. The provisions concerning sales by a personal representative as described in the

Independent Administration of Estates Act, Part 6 (commencing with Section 10400) of Division 7 shall not apply to this subdivision.

(c) Notwithstanding Section 10309, if the last appraisal of the conservatee's personal residence was conducted more than six months prior to the confirmation hearing, a new appraisal shall be required prior to the confirmation hearing, unless the court finds that it is in the best interests of the conservatee to rely on an appraisal of the personal residence that was conducted not more than one year prior to the confirmation hearing.

(d) The clerk of the court shall cause notice to be posted pursuant to subdivision (b) only in the following cases:

(1) If posting of notice of hearing is required on a petition for the confirmation of a sale of real or personal property of the estate.

(2) If posting of notice of a sale governed by Section 10250 (sales of personal property) is required or authorized.

(3) If posting of notice is ordered by the court. *(Stats.1990, c. 79 (A.B.759), § 14, operative July 1, 1991. Amended by Stats.2006, c. 490 (S.B.1116), § 4; Stats.2007, c. 553 (A.B.1727), § 17.)*

Cross References

Administration of decedents' estates, abatement, see Probate Code § 21400 et seq.
Conveyance by guardian or conservator, see Probate Code § 2111.
Notice,
 Mailing, see Probate Code § 1215 et seq.
 Posting, see Probate Code § 1230.
 Proof of giving notice, see Probate Code § 1260 et seq.
 Special notice, see Probate Code § 1250 et seq.
 This code, generally, see Probate Code § 1200 et seq.
 This division, generally, see Probate Code § 1460 et seq.
Notice to,
 Directors, see Probate Code § 1461.
 Veterans Administration, see Probate Code § 1461.5.
Personal representative and general personal representative, defined, see Probate Code § 58.
Service of process,
 Generally, see Code of Civil Procedure § 413.10 et seq.
 Mail, see Code of Civil Procedure §§ 415.30, 1012 et seq.
 Personal delivery, see Code of Civil Procedure § 415.10.
 Proof of service, see Code of Civil Procedure § 417.10 et seq.
 Publication, see Code of Civil Procedure § 415.50.

Research References

Forms

West's California Code Forms, Probate § 2540 Form 1, Report of Sale and Petition for Order Confirming Sale of Real Property (Probate)—Judicial Council Form DE-260, GC-060.
West's California Code Forms, Probate § 2542 Form 1, Notice of Private Sale by Guardian or Conservator of Real Property.
West's California Judicial Council Forms DE-265, Order Confirming Sale of Real Property.
West's California Judicial Council Forms GC-020(C), Clerk's Certificate of Posting Notice of Hearing—Guardianship or Conservatorship.
West's California Judicial Council Forms GC-065, Order Confirming Sale of Real Property.

§ 2544. Sale of securities

(a) Except as specifically limited by order of the court, subject to Section 2541, the guardian or conservator may sell securities without authorization, confirmation, or direction of the court if any of the following conditions is satisfied:

(1) The securities are to be sold on an established stock or bond exchange.

(2) The securities to be sold are securities designated as a national market system security on an interdealer quotation system or subsystem thereof, by the National Association of Securities Dealers, Inc., sold through a broker-dealer registered under the Securities Exchange Act of 1934 during the regular course of business of the broker-dealer.

(3) The securities are to be directly redeemed by the issuer thereof.

(b) Section 2543 does not apply to sales under this section. *(Stats.1990, c. 79 (A.B.759), § 14, operative July 1, 1991. Amended by Stats.1996, c. 86 (A.B.2146), § 2.)*

Cross References

Court supervision, see Probate Code § 2540.
Investment in government obligations, stocks, bonds and securities, see Probate Code § 2574.
Security, defined, see Probate Code § 70.

Research References

Forms

West's California Code Forms, Probate § 2540 Form 1, Report of Sale and Petition for Order Confirming Sale of Real Property (Probate)—Judicial Council Form DE-260, GC-060.

§ 2544.5. Sale of mutual funds held without beneficiary designation

Except as specifically limited by the court, subject to Section 2541, the guardian or conservator may sell mutual funds held without designation of a beneficiary without authorization, confirmation, or direction of the court. Section 2543 does not apply to sales under this section. *(Added by Stats.1996, c. 86 (A.B.2146), § 2.5.)*

Research References

Forms

West's California Code Forms, Probate § 2540 Form 1, Report of Sale and Petition for Order Confirming Sale of Real Property (Probate)—Judicial Council Form DE-260, GC-060.

§ 2545. Sale or other disposition of tangible personal property

(a) Subject to subdivisions (b) and (c) and to Section 2541, the guardian or conservator may sell or exchange tangible personal property of the estate without authorization, confirmation, or direction of the court.

(b) The aggregate of the sales or exchanges made during any calendar year under this section may not exceed five thousand dollars ($5,000).

(c) A sale or exchange of personal effects or of furniture or furnishings used for personal, family, or household purposes may be made under this section only if:

(1) In the case of a guardianship, the ward is under the age of 14 or, if 14 years of age or over, consents to the sale or exchange.

(2) In the case of a conservatorship, the conservatee either (i) consents to the sale or exchange or (ii) the conservatee does not have legal capacity to give such consent.

(d) Failure of the guardian or conservator to observe the limitations of subdivision (b) or (c) does not invalidate the title of, or impose any liability upon, a third person who acts in good faith and without actual notice of the lack of authority of the guardian or conservator.

(e) Subdivision (b) of Section 2543 does not apply to sales under this section. *(Stats.1990, c. 79 (A.B.759), § 14, operative July 1, 1991.)*

Cross References

Court supervision, see Probate Code § 2540.
Legal capacity of conservatee, see Probate Code § 1870 et seq.

Research References

Forms

West's California Code Forms, Probate § 2540 Form 1, Report of Sale and Petition for Order Confirming Sale of Real Property (Probate)—Judicial Council Form DE-260, GC-060.

§ 2547. Disposition of proceeds of sale

The guardian or conservator shall apply the proceeds of the sale to the purposes for which it was made, as far as necessary, and the residue, if any, shall be managed as the other property of the estate. *(Stats.1990, c. 79 (A.B.759), § 14, operative July 1, 1991.)*

Cross References

Investment of proceeds of sales, see Probate Code § 2570.
Purposes for which sale can be made, see Probate Code § 2541.

§ 2548. Recovery of property sold; limitation of action

No action for the recovery of any property sold by a guardian or conservator may be maintained by the ward or conservatee or by any person claiming under the ward or conservatee unless commenced within the later of the following times:

(a) Three years after the termination of the guardianship or conservatorship.

(b) When a legal disability to sue exists by reason of minority or otherwise at the time the cause of action accrues, within three years after the removal thereof. *(Stats.1990, c. 79 (A.B.759), § 14, operative July 1, 1991.)*

Cross References

Administration of decedents' estates, limitation of actions, see Probate Code § 10382.
Disabilities as affecting computation of time, generally, see Code of Civil Procedure §§ 328, 352, 357, 358.
Limitations on actions, generally, see Code of Civil Procedure § 312 et seq.
Minors defined, see Family Code § 6500.
Three year statute of limitations, see Code of Civil Procedure § 338.

ARTICLE 8. NOTES, MORTGAGES, LEASES, CONVEYANCES, AND EXCHANGES

Section	
2550.	Court supervision.
2551.	Borrowing money and giving security.
2552.	Refinancing, improving or repairing property.
2552.5.	Leases; length of term.
2553.	Leases; necessity for court order.
2554.	Leases; terms and conditions.
2555.	Leases; authorized without court permission.
2556.	Dedication or conveyance of real property or easement with or without consideration.
2557.	Exchange of property.

Cross References

Application of old and new law, see Probate Code § 3.
Mortgages in administration of estates, see Probate Code § 9800 et seq.

§ 2550. Court supervision

Except as otherwise provided by statute, a guardian or conservator may borrow money, lend money, give security, lease, convey, or exchange property of the estate, or engage in any other transaction under this article only after authorization by order of the court. Such an order may be obtained in the manner provided in this article. *(Stats.1990, c. 79 (A.B.759), § 14, operative July 1, 1991. Amended by Stats.1992, c. 572 (S.B.1455), § 5.)*

Cross References

Exchanges of certain tangible personal property without court authorization, see Probate Code § 2545.

§ 2551. Borrowing money and giving security

(a) In any case described in Section 2541 or Section 2552, the guardian or conservator, after authorization by order of the court, may borrow money upon a note, either unsecured or to be secured by a security interest or other lien on the personal property of the estate or any part thereof or to be secured by a mortgage or deed of trust on the real property of the estate or any part thereof. The guardian or conservator shall apply the money to the purpose specified in the order.

(b) To obtain an order under this section, the guardian or conservator, the ward or conservatee, or any other interested person may file a petition with the court. The petition shall state the purpose for which the order is sought, the necessity for or advantage to accrue from the order, the amount of money proposed to be borrowed, the rate of interest to be paid, the length of time the note is to run, and a general description of the property proposed to be mortgaged or subjected to a deed of trust or other lien. Notice of the hearing on the petition shall be given for the period and in the manner provided in Chapter 3 (commencing with Section 1460) of Part 1.

(c) The court may require such additional proof of the fairness and feasibility of the transaction as the court determines is necessary. If the required showing is made, the court may make an order authorizing the transaction.

The court in its order may do any one or more of the following:

(1) Order that the amount specified in the petition, or a lesser amount, be borrowed.

(2) Prescribe the maximum rate of interest and the period of the loan.

(3) Require that the interest and the whole or any part of the principal be paid from time to time out of the estate or any part thereof.

(4) Require that the personal property used as security or any buildings on real property to be mortgaged or subjected to the deed of trust be insured for the further security of the lender and that the premiums be paid out of the estate.

(5) Specify the purpose for which the money to be borrowed is to be applied.

(6) Prescribe such other terms and conditions concerning the transaction as the court determines to be to the advantage of the estate.

(d) The note and the mortgage or deed of trust, if any, shall be signed by the guardian or conservator.

(e) Jurisdiction of the court to administer the estate of the ward or conservatee is effectual to vest the court with jurisdiction to make the order for the note and for the security interest, lien, mortgage, or deed of trust. This jurisdiction shall conclusively inure to the benefit of the owner of the security interest or lien, mortgagee named in the mortgage, or the trustee and beneficiary named in the deed of trust, and their heirs and assigns. No omission, error, or irregularity in the proceedings shall impair or invalidate the proceedings or the note, security interest, lien, mortgage, or deed of trust given pursuant to an order under this section.

(f) Upon any foreclosure or sale under a security interest, lien, mortgage, or deed of trust described in subdivision (a), if the proceeds of the sale of the encumbered property are insufficient to pay the note, the security interest, lien, mortgage, or deed of trust, and the costs or expenses of sale, no judgment or claim for any deficiency may be had or allowed against the ward or conservatee or the estate. *(Stats.1990, c. 79 (A.B.759), § 14, operative July 1, 1991.)*

Cross References

Borrowing money or mortgaging property, see Probate Code § 9800 et seq.
Deficiency judgment, see Code of Civil Procedure §§ 580a, 726.
Foreclosure,
   Actions for foreclosure of trust deeds and mortgages, see Code of Civil Procedure § 725a et seq.
   Authority for, see Civil Code § 2931.
Interested person, defined, see Probate Code § 1424.

Liens,
  Generally, see Civil Code § 2872 et seq.
  Mortgages, generally, see Civil Code § 2920 et seq.
Mortgage not a personal obligation, see Civil Code § 2928.
Real property, defined, see Probate Code § 68.

Research References

Forms

West's California Code Forms, Probate § 2551 Form 1, Petition to Borrow Money and Encumber Real Property.

West's California Code Forms, Probate § 2551 Form 2, Order Authorizing Guardian or Conservator to Borrow Money and to Encumber Real Property.

§ 2552. Refinancing, improving or repairing property

(a) The guardian or conservator may give a security interest or other lien upon the personal property of the estate or any part thereof or a mortgage or deed of trust upon the real property of the estate or any part thereof, after authorization by order of the court as provided in Section 2551, for any of the following purposes:

(1) To pay, reduce, extend, or renew a security interest, lien, mortgage, or deed of trust already existing on property of the estate.

(2) To improve, use, operate, or preserve the property proposed to be mortgaged or subjected to a deed of trust, or some part thereof.

(b) If property of the estate consists of an undivided interest in real or personal property, or any other interest therein less than the entire ownership, upon a showing that it would be to the advantage of the estate to borrow money to improve, use, operate, or preserve the property jointly with the owners of the other interests therein, or to pay, reduce, extend, or renew a security interest, lien, mortgage, or deed of trust already existing on all of the property, the guardian or conservator, after authorization by order of the court as provided in Section 2551, may join with the owners of the other interests in the borrowing of money and the execution of a joint and several note and such security interest, lien, mortgage, or deed of trust as may be required to secure the payment of the note. The note may be for such sum as is required for the purpose.

(c) No omission, error, or irregularity in the proceedings under this section shall impair or invalidate the proceedings or the note, security interest, lien, mortgage, or deed of trust given pursuant to an order made under this section. (Stats.1990, c. 79 (A.B.759), § 14, operative July 1, 1991.)

Cross References

Instructions from or confirmation by court, see Probate Code § 2403.
Interests in property, see Civil Code § 678 et seq.
Liens,
  Generally, see Civil Code § 2872 et seq.
  Mortgages, generally, see Civil Code § 2920 et seq.
Mechanics liens, see Civil Code § 8400.
Real property, defined, see Probate Code § 68.

Research References

Forms

West's California Code Forms, Probate § 2551 Form 1, Petition to Borrow Money and Encumber Real Property.

§ 2552.5. Leases; length of term

For the purpose of this article, if a lease gives the lessee the right to extend the term of the lease, the length of the term shall be considered as though the right to extend had been exercised. (Stats.1990, c. 79 (A.B.759), § 14, operative July 1, 1991.)

§ 2553. Leases; necessity for court order

(a) Except as provided in Section 2555, leases may be executed by the guardian or conservator with respect to the property of the estate only after authorization by order of the court.

(b) To obtain an order under this section, the guardian or conservator or any interested person may file a petition with the court. The petition shall state (1) a general description of the property proposed to be leased, (2) the term, rental, and general conditions of the proposed lease, and (3) the advantage to the estate to accrue from giving the lease. If the lease is proposed to be for a term longer than 10 years, the petition shall also state facts showing the need for the longer lease and its advantage to the estate. Notice of the hearing on the petition shall be given for the period and in the manner provided in Chapter 3 (commencing with Section 1460) of Part 1.

(c) At the hearing, the court shall entertain and consider any other offer made in good faith at the hearing to lease the same property on more favorable terms. If the court is satisfied that it will be to the advantage of the estate, the court shall make an order authorizing the guardian or conservator to make the lease to the person and on the terms and conditions stated in the order. The court shall not make an order authorizing the guardian or conservator to make the lease to any person other than the lessee named in the petition unless the offer made at the hearing is acceptable to the guardian or conservator.

(d) Jurisdiction of the court to administer the estate of the ward or conservatee is effectual to vest the court with jurisdiction to make the order for the lease. This jurisdiction shall conclusively inure to the benefit of the lessee and the lessee's heirs and assigns. No omission, error, or irregularity in the proceedings shall impair or invalidate the proceedings or the lease made pursuant to an order made under this article. (Stats.1990, c. 79 (A.B.759), § 14, operative July 1, 1991.)

Cross References

Interested person, defined, see Probate Code § 1424.
Leases by personal representatives, see Probate Code § 9942.
Orders, see Probate Code § 1047 et seq.

Research References

Forms

West's California Code Forms, Probate § 2553 Form 1, Petition to Lease Real Property.

§ 2554. Leases; terms and conditions

(a) An order authorizing the execution of a lease shall set forth the minimum rental or royalty or both and the period of the lease, which shall be for such time as the court may authorize.

(b) The order may authorize other terms and conditions, including, with respect to a lease for the purpose of exploration for or production or removal of minerals, oil, gas, or other hydrocarbon substances, or geothermal energy, any one or more of the following:

(1) A provision for the payment of rental and royalty to a depositary.

(2) A provision for the appointment of a common agent to represent the interests of all the lessors.

(3) A provision for the payment of a compensatory royalty in lieu of rental and in lieu of drilling and producing operations on the land covered by the lease.

(4) A provision empowering the lessee to enter into any agreement authorized by Section 3301 of the Public Resources Code with respect to the land covered by the lease.

(5) A provision for a community oil lease or pooling or unitization by the lessee.

(c) If the lease covers additional property owned by other persons or an undivided or other interest of the ward or conservatee less than the entire ownership in the property, the order may authorize the lease to provide for division of rental and royalty in the proportion that the land or interest of each owner bears to the total area of the land or total interests covered by such lease.

§ 2554

(d) If the lease is for the purpose of exploration for or production or removal of minerals, oil, gas, or other hydrocarbon substances, or geothermal energy, the court may authorize that the lease be for a fixed period and any of the following:

(1) So long thereafter as minerals, oil, gas, or other hydrocarbon substances or geothermal energy are produced in paying quantities from the property leased or mining or drilling operations are conducted thereon.

(2) If the lease provides for the payment of a compensatory royalty, so long thereafter as such compensatory royalty is paid.

(3) If the land covered by the lease is included in an agreement authorized by Section 3301 of the Public Resources Code, so long thereafter as oil, gas, or other hydrocarbon substances are produced in paying quantities from any of the lands included in any such agreement or drilling operations are conducted thereon. *(Stats.1990, c. 79 (A.B.759), § 14, operative July 1, 1991.)*

Cross References

Lease of property in administration of estates, see Probate Code § 9945.
Oil, gas and mineral leases,
  Generally, see Public Resources Code § 6801 et seq.
  Duration, see Civil Code § 718.
Recordation and constructive notice, oil and gas leases, see Civil Code § 1219.

Research References

Forms

West's California Code Forms, Probate § 2553 Form 1, Petition to Lease Real Property.

§ 2555. Leases; authorized without court permission

If it is to the advantage of the estate, the guardian or conservator may lease, as lessor, real property of the estate without authorization of the court in either of the following cases:

(a) Where the rental does not exceed five thousand dollars ($5,000) a month and the term does not exceed two years.

(b) Where the lease is from month to month, regardless of the amount of the rental. *(Stats.1990, c. 79 (A.B.759), § 14, operative July 1, 1991. Amended by Stats.1990, c. 710 (S.B.1775), § 11, operative July 1, 1991.)*

Cross References

Effect of court authorization or approval, see Probate Code § 2103.
Hiring of real property, see Civil Code § 1940 et seq.
Instructions from or confirmation by court, see Probate Code § 2403.
Modification, extension, or renewal of leases, see Probate Code § 2501.
Real property, defined, see Probate Code § 68.

Research References

Forms

West's California Code Forms, Probate § 2553 Form 1, Petition to Lease Real Property.

§ 2556. Dedication or conveyance of real property or easement with or without consideration

(a) If it is for the advantage, benefit, and best interests of the estate and those interested therein, the guardian or conservator, after authorization by order of the court, may do any of the following either with or without consideration:

(1) Dedicate or convey real property of the estate for any purpose to any of the following:

(A) This state or any public entity in this state.

(B) The United States or any agency or instrumentality of the United States.

(2) Dedicate or convey an easement over any real property of the estate to any person for any purpose.

(3) Convey, release, or relinquish to this state or any public entity in this state any access rights to any street, highway, or freeway from any real property of the estate.

(4) Consent as a lienholder to a dedication, conveyance, release, or relinquishment under paragraph (1), (2), or (3) by the owner of property subject to the lien.

(b) To obtain an order under this section, the guardian or conservator or any other interested person shall file a petition with the court. Notice of the hearing on the petition shall be given for the period and in the manner provided in Chapter 3 (commencing with Section 1460) of Part 1. *(Stats.1990, c. 79 (A.B.759), § 14, operative July 1, 1991.)*

Cross References

Community property, court authorization, see Probate Code §§ 3101, 3102.
Dedication of real property for public purposes, see Government Code § 7050.
Easements, generally, see Civil Code § 801 et seq.
Interested person, defined, see Probate Code § 1424.
Liens, generally, see Civil Code § 2872 et seq.
Personal representatives, similar provisions relating to, see Probate Code § 9900.
Power of legislative body to acquire easements for public interest, see Streets and Highways Code § 10102.
Real property, defined, see Probate Code § 68.

§ 2557. Exchange of property

(a) Whenever it is for the advantage, benefit, and best interests of the ward or conservatee and those legally entitled to support, maintenance, or education from the ward or conservatee, the guardian or conservator, after authorization by order of the court, may exchange any property of the estate for other property upon such terms and conditions as may be prescribed by the court. The terms and conditions prescribed by the court may include the payment or receipt of part cash by the guardian or conservator.

(b) To obtain an order under this section, the guardian or conservator or any interested person shall file a petition containing all of the following:

(1) A description of the property.

(2) The terms and conditions of the proposed exchange.

(3) A showing that the proposed exchange is for the advantage, benefit, and best interests of the ward or conservatee and those legally entitled to support, maintenance, or education from the ward or conservatee.

(c) Except as provided in subdivision (d), notice of the hearing on the petition shall be given for the period and in the manner provided in Chapter 3 (commencing with Section 1460) of Part 1.

(d) If the petition is for authorization to exchange stocks, bonds, or other securities as defined in Section 10200 for different stocks, bonds, or other securities, the court, upon a showing of good cause, may order that the notice be given for a shorter period or be dispensed with.

(e) After authorization by order of the court, the guardian or conservator may execute the conveyance or transfer to the person with whom the exchange is made to effectuate the exchange.

(f) No omission, error, or irregularity in the proceedings under this section shall impair or invalidate the proceedings or the exchange made pursuant to an order made under this section. *(Stats.1990, c. 79 (A.B.759), § 14, operative July 1, 1991.)*

Cross References

Conveyance by guardian or conservator, see Probate Code § 2111.
Disposition or sale of tangible personal property, see Probate Code § 2545.
Exchange of property by personal representative, see Probate Code § 9920.
Interested person, defined, see Probate Code § 1424.

Security, defined, see Probate Code § 70.

Research References

Forms

13 Am. Jur. Pl. & Pr. Forms Guardian and Ward § 395, Statutory References.

ARTICLE 9. INVESTMENTS AND PURCHASE OF PROPERTY

Section
2570. Authority; petition; hearing; order.
2571. Purchase of home for ward, conservatee or dependents.
2572. Purchase of real property; order.
2573. Investment in governmental bonds; order.
2574. Investment of funds; federal and state obligations; stocks, bonds and securities.

Cross References

Application of old and new law, see Probate Code § 3.

§ 2570. Authority; petition; hearing; order

(a) The guardian or conservator, after authorization by order of the court, may invest the proceeds of sales and any other money of the estate as provided in the order.

(b) To obtain an order of the court authorizing a transaction under subdivision (a) of this section, the guardian or conservator, the ward or conservatee, or any other interested person may file a petition with the court.

(c) Notice of the hearing on the petition shall be given for the period and in the manner provided in Chapter 3 (commencing with Section 1460) of Part 1. The court may order that the notice be dispensed with.

(d) The court may require such proof of the fairness and feasibility of the transaction as the court determines is necessary.

(e) If the required showing is made, the court may make an order authorizing the transaction and may prescribe in the order the terms and conditions upon which the transaction shall be made. *(Stats. 1990, c. 79 (A.B.759), § 14, operative July 1, 1991.)*

Cross References

Deposits in bank and savings accounts, see Probate Code § 2453.
Disposition of proceeds of sale, see Probate Code § 2547.
Interested persons, defined, see Probate Code § 1424.

§ 2571. Purchase of home for ward, conservatee or dependents

When authorized by order of the court under Section 2570, the guardian or conservator may purchase:

(a) Real property in this state as a home for the ward or conservatee if such purchase is for the advantage, benefit, and best interest of the ward or conservatee.

(b) Real property as a home for those legally entitled to support and maintenance from the ward or conservatee if such purchase is for the advantage, benefit, and best interest of the ward or conservatee and of those legally entitled to support and maintenance from the ward or conservatee. *(Stats.1990, c. 79 (A.B.759), § 14, operative July 1, 1991.)*

Cross References

Order authorizing purchase of real property, see Probate Code § 2572.

Real property, defined, see Probate Code § 68.

Research References

Forms

West's California Code Forms, Probate § 2572 Form 1, Petition for Authority to Purchase Real Property.

§ 2572. Purchase of real property; order

An order authorizing the guardian or conservator to purchase real property may authorize the guardian or conservator to join with the spouse of the ward or the spouse or domestic partner of the conservatee or with any other person or persons in the purchase of the real property, or an interest, equity, or estate therein, in severalty, in common, in community, or in joint tenancy, for cash or upon a credit or for part cash and part credit. When the court authorizes the purchase of real property, the court may order the guardian or conservator to execute all necessary instruments and commitments to complete the transaction. *(Stats.1990, c. 79 (A.B.759), § 14, operative July 1, 1991. Amended by Stats.2001, c. 893 (A.B.25), § 37.)*

Cross References

Community property, see Probate Code § 3020 et seq.
Domestic partner, defined, see Probate Code § 37.
Instrument, defined, see Probate Code § 45.
Interests in property, see Civil Code § 678 et seq.
Real property, defined, see Probate Code § 68.

Research References

Forms

West's California Code Forms, Probate § 2572 Form 1, Petition for Authority to Purchase Real Property.
West's California Code Forms, Probate § 2572 Form 2, Order Authorizing Purchase of Real Property.

§ 2573. Investment in governmental bonds; order

An order authorizing investment in bonds issued by any state or of any city, county, city and county, political subdivision, public corporation, district, or special district of any state may authorize the guardian or conservator to select from among bonds issued by any such issuer, without specifying any particular issuer or issue of bonds, if the type of issuer is designated in general terms and the order specifies as to such bonds a minimum quality rating as shown in a recognized investment service, a minimum interest coupon rate, a minimum yield to maturity, and the date of maturity within a five-year range. *(Stats.1990, c. 79 (A.B.759), § 14, operative July 1, 1991.)*

Cross References

Sales of stocks, bonds and securities, see Probate Code § 2544.

§ 2574. Investment of funds; federal and state obligations; stocks, bonds and securities

(a) Subject to subdivision (b), the guardian or conservator, without authorization of the court, may invest funds of the estate pursuant to this section in:

(1) Direct obligations of the United States, or of the State of California, maturing not later than five years from the date of making the investment.

(2) United States Treasury bonds redeemable at par value on the death of the holder for payment of federal estate taxes, regardless of maturity date.

(3) Securities listed on an established stock or bond exchange in the United States which are purchased on such exchange.

(4) Eligible securities for the investment of surplus state moneys as provided for in Section 16430 of the Government Code.

(5) An interest in a money market mutual fund registered under the Investment Company Act of 1940 (15 U.S.C. Sec. 80a–1, et seq.) or an investment vehicle authorized for the collective investment of

§ 2574

trust funds pursuant to Section 9.18 of Part 9 of Title 12 of the Code of Federal Regulations, the portfolios of which are limited to United States government obligations maturing not later than five years from the date of investment and to repurchase agreements fully collateralized by United States government obligations.

(6) Units of a common trust fund described in Section 1585 of the Financial Code. The common trust fund shall have as its objective investment primarily in short-term fixed income obligations and shall be permitted to value investments at cost pursuant to regulations of the appropriate regulatory authority.

(b) In making and retaining investments made under this section, the guardian or conservator shall take into consideration the circumstances of the estate, indicated cash needs, and, if reasonably ascertainable, the date of the prospective termination of the guardianship or conservatorship.

(c) This section shall not limit the authority of the guardian or conservator to seek court authorization for any investment, or to make other investments with court authorization, as provided in this division. *(Stats.1990, c. 79 (A.B.759), § 14, operative July 1, 1991. Amended by Stats.2014, c. 71 (S.B.1304), § 136, eff. Jan. 1, 2015.)*

Cross References

Administration of decedents' estates, court order for sale of securities, see Probate Code § 10200.
Court authorization, see Probate Code § 2570.
Effect of court authorization or approval, see Probate Code § 2103.
Sales of stocks, bonds and securities, see Probate Code § 2544.
Security, defined, see Probate Code § 70.

ARTICLE 10. SUBSTITUTED JUDGMENT

Section
2580. Petition to authorize proposed action.
2581. Notice of hearing of petition.
2582. Consent or lack of capacity of conservatee; adequate provision for conservatee and dependents.
2583. Proposed actions by court; relevant circumstances.
2584. Determination and order.
2585. No duty to propose action.
2586. Production of conservatee's will and other relevant estate plan documents; safekeeping of documents by custodian appointed by the court.

Cross References

Application of old and new law, see Probate Code § 3.
Fee for filing petition and opposition papers concerning internal affairs of certain trusts or first accounts of trustees of certain testamentary trusts, see Government Code § 70652.
Powers of appointment, generally, see Probate Code § 600 et seq.

§ 2580. Petition to authorize proposed action

(a) The conservator or other interested person may file a petition under this article for an order of the court authorizing or requiring the conservator to take a proposed action for any one or more of the following purposes:

(1) Benefiting the conservatee or the estate.

(2) Minimizing current or prospective taxes or expenses of administration of the conservatorship estate or of the estate upon the death of the conservatee.

(3) Providing gifts for any purposes, and to any charities, relatives (including the other spouse or domestic partner), friends, or other objects of bounty, as would be likely beneficiaries of gifts from the conservatee.

(b) The action proposed in the petition may include, but is not limited to, the following:

(1) Making gifts of principal or income, or both, of the estate, outright or in trust.

(2) Conveying or releasing the conservatee's contingent and expectant interests in property, including marital property rights and any right of survivorship incident to joint tenancy or tenancy by the entirety.

(3) Exercising or releasing the conservatee's powers as donee of a power of appointment.

(4) Entering into contracts.

(5) Creating for the benefit of the conservatee or others, revocable or irrevocable trusts of the property of the estate, which trusts may extend beyond the conservatee's disability or life. A special needs trust for money paid pursuant to a compromise or judgment for a conservatee may be established only under Chapter 4 (commencing with Section 3600) of Part 8, and not under this article.

(6) Transferring to a trust created by the conservator or conservatee any property unintentionally omitted from the trust.

(7) Exercising options of the conservatee to purchase or exchange securities or other property.

(8) Exercising the rights of the conservatee to elect benefit or payment options, to terminate, to change beneficiaries or ownership, to assign rights, to borrow, or to receive cash value in return for a surrender of rights under any of the following:

(A) Life insurance policies, plans, or benefits.

(B) Annuity policies, plans, or benefits.

(C) Mutual fund and other dividend investment plans.

(D) Retirement, profit sharing, and employee welfare plans and benefits.

(9) Exercising the right of the conservatee to elect to take under or against a will.

(10) Exercising the right of the conservatee to disclaim any interest that may be disclaimed under Part 8 (commencing with Section 260) of Division 2.

(11) Exercising the right of the conservatee (A) to revoke or modify a revocable trust or (B) to surrender the right to revoke or modify a revocable trust, but the court shall not authorize or require the conservator to exercise the right to revoke or modify a revocable trust if the instrument governing the trust (A) evidences an intent to reserve the right of revocation or modification exclusively to the conservatee, (B) provides expressly that a conservator may not revoke or modify the trust, or (C) otherwise evidences an intent that would be inconsistent with authorizing or requiring the conservator to exercise the right to revoke or modify the trust.

(12) Making an election referred to in Section 13502 or an election and agreement referred to in Section 13503.

(13) Making a will.

(14) Making or revoking a revocable transfer on death deed. *(Stats.1990, c. 79 (A.B.759), § 14, operative July 1, 1991. Amended by Stats.1992, c. 355 (A.B.3328), § 1; Stats.1992, c. 572 (S.B.1455), § 6.5; Stats.1995, c. 730 (A.B.1466), § 4; Stats.1999, c; 175 (A.B. 239), § 3; Stats.2001, c. 893 (A.B.25), § 38; Stats.2015, c. 293 (A.B.139), § 7, eff. Jan. 1, 2016.)*

Cross References

Contracts, generally, see Civil Code § 1549 et seq.
Destruction of court records, notice, retention periods, see Government Code § 68152.
Disclaimer of testamentary and other interests on behalf of ward or conservatee, see Probate Code § 276.
Domestic partner, defined, see Probate Code § 37.
Election of benefit or payment options, etc., of certain policies or plans, authority of guardian or conservator, see Probate Code § 2459.
Election of guardian or conservator of surviving spouse to have property administered in probate, see Probate Code § 13502 et seq.

Exchange of securities, see Probate Code § 2557.
Gifts, generally, see Civil Code § 1146 et seq.
Instrument, defined, see Probate Code § 45.
Interested person, defined, see Probate Code § 1424.
Interests in property, see Civil Code § 678 et seq.
Joint tenancy, see Civil Code § 683.
Payment of surplus income to relatives of conservatee, see Probate Code § 2423.
Proration of estate taxes, see Probate Code § 20100 et seq.
Proration of generation-skipping transfer tax, see Probate Code § 20200 et seq.
Security, defined, see Probate Code § 70.
Transfers of property, generally, see Civil Code § 1039 et seq.
Trusts, creation, validity, modification, and termination, see Probate Code § 15200 et seq.

Research References
Forms

Asset Protection: Legal Planning, Strategies and Forms ¶ 14.05, Planning Strategies for the Elderly and the Disabled.
1 California Transactions Forms--Estate Planning § 2:21, Execution of Documents Under Durable Power of Attorney; Substituted Judgment.
1 California Transactions Forms--Estate Planning § 2:27, Exceptions to Limitations on Transfers to Drafters and Others.
3 California Transactions Forms--Estate Planning § 12:22, Trustee's Removal.
3 California Transactions Forms--Estate Planning § 13:11, Conservator's Right to Revoke.
3 California Transactions Forms--Estate Planning § 13:49, Exercise of Settlor's Rights and Powers to Amend, Revoke, or Terminate Trust by Others.
3 California Transactions Forms--Estate Planning § 17:2, Types of Special Needs Trusts.
3 California Transactions Forms--Estate Planning § 17:41, Types of Special Needs Trusts Requiring Payback Provisions (Self-Settled Trusts Established on or After October 1, 1993).
4 California Transactions Forms--Estate Planning § 19:32, Persons Who May Make Will.
4 California Transactions Forms--Estate Planning § 19:36, Overview.
4 California Transactions Forms--Estate Planning § 19:37, Testator's Signature or Acknowledgment.
4 California Transactions Forms--Estate Planning § 21:5, Valid Will Requirements.
4 California Transactions Forms--Estate Planning § 21:13, Matters to Consider in Drafting Testamentary Trust.
4 California Transactions Forms--Estate Planning § 22:2, Formal Witnessed Codicils.
4 California Transactions Forms--Estate Planning § 22:39, Provision for Signature Per Substituted Judgment Order.
4 California Transactions Forms--Estate Planning § 22:40, Attestation Provision for Signature Per Substituted Judgment Order.
West's California Code Forms, Probate § 277(c) Form 1, Petition for Order Authorizing Personal Representative to Disclaim.
West's California Code Forms, Probate § 2423 Form 1, Petition for Payment of Surplus Income to Relatives of Conservatee.
West's California Code Forms, Probate § 2580 Form 1, Petition for Authority to Make Gifts.
West's California Code Forms, Probate § 3121 Form 1, Petition for Order Authorizing Proposed Transaction and Joinder of Conservator.
West's California Code Forms, Probate § 3144 Form 1, Order Authorizing Transaction.

§ 2581. Notice of hearing of petition

Notice of the hearing of the petition shall be given, regardless of age, for the period and in the manner provided in Chapter 3 (commencing with Section 1460) or Part 1 to all of the following:

(a) The persons required to be given notice under Chapter 3 (commencing with Section 1460) of Part 1.

(b) The persons required to be named in a petition for the appointment of a conservator.

(c) So far as is known to the petitioner, beneficiaries under any document executed by the conservatee which may have testamentary effect unless the court for good cause dispenses with such notice.

(d) So far as is known to the petitioner, the persons who, if the conservatee were to die immediately, would be the conservatee's heirs under the laws of intestate succession unless the court for good cause dispenses with such notice.

(e) Such other persons as the court may order. *(Stats.1990, c. 79 (A.B.759), § 14, operative July 1, 1991. Amended by Stats.1996, c. 862 (A.B.2751), § 8.)*

Cross References
Beneficiary defined, see Probate Code § 24
Contents of petition for appointment of conservator, see Probate Code § 1821.
Notice to directors, see Probate Code § 1461.
Request for special notice, see Probate Code § 2700 et seq.
Succession, generally, see Probate Code § 250.

Research References
Forms

West's California Code Forms, Probate § 2580 Form 1, Petition for Authority to Make Gifts.
West's California Code Forms, Probate § 3121 Form 1, Petition for Order Authorizing Proposed Transaction and Joinder of Conservator.

§ 2582. Consent or lack of capacity of conservatee; adequate provision for conservatee and dependents

The court may make an order authorizing or requiring the proposed action under this article only if the court determines all of the following:

(a) The conservatee either (1) is not opposed to the proposed action or (2) if opposed to the proposed action, lacks legal capacity for the proposed action.

(b) Either the proposed action will have no adverse effect on the estate or the estate remaining after the proposed action is taken will be adequate to provide for the needs of the conservatee and for the support of those legally entitled to support, maintenance, and education from the conservatee, taking into account the age, physical condition, standards of living, and all other relevant circumstances of the conservatee and those legally entitled to support, maintenance, and education from the conservatee. *(Stats.1990, c. 79 (A.B.759), § 14, operative July 1, 1991.)*

Cross References
Legal capacity of conservatee, see Probate Code § 1870 et seq.

Research References
Forms

West's California Code Forms, Probate § 2580 Form 1, Petition for Authority to Make Gifts.

§ 2583. Proposed actions by court; relevant circumstances

In determining whether to authorize or require a proposed action under this article, the court shall take into consideration all the relevant circumstances, which may include, but are not limited to, the following:

(a) Whether the conservatee has legal capacity for the proposed transaction and, if not, the probability of the conservatee's recovery of legal capacity.

(b) The past donative declarations, practices, and conduct of the conservatee.

(c) The traits of the conservatee.

(d) The relationship and intimacy of the prospective donees with the conservatee, their standards of living, and the extent to which they would be natural objects of the conservatee's bounty by any objective test based on such relationship, intimacy, and standards of living.

(e) The wishes of the conservatee.

(f) Any known estate plan of the conservatee (including, but not limited to, the conservatee's will, any trust of which the conservatee is the settlor or beneficiary, any power of appointment created by or

§ 2583 PROBATE CODE

exercisable by the conservatee, and any contract, transfer, or joint ownership arrangement with provisions for payment or transfer of benefits or interests at the conservatee's death to another or others which the conservatee may have originated).

(g) The manner in which the estate would devolve upon the conservatee's death, giving consideration to the age and the mental and physical condition of the conservatee, the prospective devisees or heirs of the conservatee, and the prospective donees.

(h) The value, liquidity, and productiveness of the estate.

(i) The minimization of current or prospective income, estate, inheritance, or other taxes or expenses of administration.

(j) Changes of tax laws and other laws which would likely have motivated the conservatee to alter the conservatee's estate plan.

(k) The likelihood from all the circumstances that the conservatee as a reasonably prudent person would take the proposed action if the conservatee had the capacity to do so.

(*l*) Whether any beneficiary is the spouse or domestic partner of the conservatee.

(m) Whether a beneficiary has committed physical abuse, neglect, false imprisonment, or financial abuse against the conservatee after the conservatee was substantially unable to manage his or her financial resources, or resist fraud or undue influence, and the conservatee's disability persisted throughout the time of the hearing on the proposed substituted judgment. *(Stats.1990, c. 79 (A.B.759), § 14, operative July 1, 1991. Amended by Stats.1992, c. 871 (A.B. 2975), § 6; Stats.1993, c. 293 (A.B.21), § 3; Stats.1998, c. 935 (S.B.1715), § 5; Stats.2010, c. 620 (S.B.105), § 2; Stats.2011, c. 308 (S.B.647), § 10.)*

Cross References

Beneficiary defined, see Probate Code § 24
Devisee, defined, see Probate Code § 34.
Legal capacity of conservatee, see Probate Code § 1870 et seq.
Powers of appointment, generally, see Probate Code § 600 et seq.
Presumption of fraud or undue influence with respect to wills and trusts, enumeration of certain donative transfers subject to the presumption, see Probate Code § 21380.
Production of conservatee's will and other relevant estate plan documents, see Probate Code § 2586.
Proration of estate taxes, see Probate Code § 20100 et seq.
Proration of generation-skipping transfer tax, see Probate Code § 20200 et seq.

Research References

Forms

4 California Transactions Forms--Estate Planning § 19:32, Persons Who May Make Will.
West's California Code Forms, Probate § 2580 Form 1, Petition for Authority to Make Gifts.

§ 2584. Determination and order

After hearing, the court, in its discretion, may approve, modify and approve, or disapprove the proposed action and may authorize or direct the conservator to transfer or dispose of assets or take other action as provided in the court's order. *(Stats.1990, c. 79 (A.B.759), § 14, operative July 1, 1991.)*

Cross References

Appealable orders, see Probate Code § 1300 et seq.

Research References

Forms

West's California Code Forms, Probate § 2584 Form 1, Order Authorizing Conservator to Make Gifts.

§ 2585. No duty to propose action

Nothing in this article imposes any duty on the conservator to propose any action under this article, and the conservator is not liable for failure to propose any action under this article. *(Stats.1990, c. 79 (A.B.759), § 14, operative July 1, 1991.)*

Research References

Forms

West's California Code Forms, Probate § 2580 Form 1, Petition for Authority to Make Gifts.

§ 2586. Production of conservatee's will and other relevant estate plan documents; safekeeping of documents by custodian appointed by the court

(a) As used in this section, "estate plan of the conservatee" includes, but is not limited to, the conservatee's will, any trust of which the conservatee is the settlor or beneficiary, any power of appointment created by or exercisable by the conservatee, and any contract, transfer, or joint ownership arrangement with provisions for payment or transfer of benefits or interests at the conservatee's death to another or others which the conservatee may have originated.

(b) Notwithstanding Article 3 (commencing with Section 950) of Chapter 4 of Division 8 of the Evidence Code (lawyer-client privilege), the court, in its discretion, may order that any person having possession of any document constituting all or part of the estate plan of the conservatee shall deliver the document to the court for examination by the court, and, in the discretion of the court, by the attorneys for the persons who have appeared in the proceedings under this article, in connection with the petition filed under this article.

(c) Unless the court otherwise orders, no person who examines any document produced pursuant to an order under this section shall disclose the contents of the document to any other person. If that disclosure is made, the court may adjudge the person making the disclosure to be in contempt of court.

(d) For good cause, the court may order that a document constituting all or part of the estate plan of the conservatee, whether or not produced pursuant to an order under this section, shall be delivered for safekeeping to the custodian designated by the court. The court may impose those conditions it determines are appropriate for holding and safeguarding the document. The court may authorize the conservator to take any action a depositor may take under Part 15 (commencing with Section 700) of Division 2. *(Stats.1990, c. 79 (A.B.759), § 14, operative July 1, 1991. Amended by Stats.1993, c. 519 (A.B.209), § 5.)*

Cross References

Appealable orders, see Probate Code § 1300 et seq.
Appointment of legal counsel, see Probate Code § 1470 et seq.
Contempt of court, generally, see Code of Civil Procedure § 1209 et seq.
Contracts, generally, see Civil Code § 1549 et seq.
Inspection of public records, exemptions from disclosure, "conservatee" to "conservatorship", see Government Code § 6276.12.
Interests in property, generally, see Civil Code § 678 et seq.
Powers of appointment, generally, see Probate Code § 600 et seq.
Transfers of property, generally, see Civil Code § 1039 et seq.
Wills, generally, see Probate Code § 6100 et seq.

Research References

Forms

West's California Code Forms, Probate § 2580 Form 1, Petition for Authority to Make Gifts.
West's California Code Forms, Probate § 2584 Form 1, Order Authorizing Conservator to Make Gifts.
West's California Code Forms, Probate § 3144 Form 1, Order Authorizing Transaction.

ARTICLE 11. INDEPENDENT EXERCISE OF POWERS

Section
2590. Independent exercise of powers; order granting authority.

Section
2591. Powers that may be granted.
2591.5. Sale of personal residence; best interests of conservatee.
2592. Petition.
2593. Withdrawal or subsequent limitation of powers.
2594. Letters; contents; requirements for new letters.
2595. Effect of article.

Cross References

Application of old and new law, see Probate Code § 3.
Conservatorship for gravely disabled persons, general and special powers, see Welfare and Institutions Code § 5357.

§ 2590. Independent exercise of powers; order granting authority

(a) The court may, in its discretion, make an order granting the guardian or conservator any one or more or all of the powers specified in Section 2591 if the court determines that, under the circumstances of the particular guardianship or conservatorship, it would be to the advantage, benefit, and best interest of the estate to do so. Subject only to the requirements, conditions, or limitations as are specifically and expressly provided, either directly or by reference, in the order granting the power or powers, and if consistent with Section 2591, the guardian or conservator may exercise the granted power or powers without notice, hearing, or court authorization, instructions, approval, or confirmation in the same manner as the ward or conservatee could do if possessed of legal capacity.

(b) The guardian or conservator does not have a power specified in Section 2591 without authorization by a court under this article or other express provisions of this code. *(Stats.1990, c. 79 (A.B.759), § 14, operative July 1, 1991. Amended by Stats.2006, c. 490 (S.B. 1116), § 5; Stats.2007, c. 553 (A.B.1727), § 18.)*

Cross References

Additional powers of guardian nominated by will, see Probate Code § 2108.
Appointment of legal counsel, see Probate Code § 1470 et seq.
Request for special notice, see Probate Code § 2700 et seq.

Research References

Forms

West's California Code Forms, Probate § 2450 Form 1, Petition to Withdraw or Limit Independent Powers of Guardian or Conservator.
West's California Code Forms, Probate § 2540 Form 1, Report of Sale and Petition for Order Confirming Sale of Real Property (Probate)—Judicial Council Form DE-260, GC-060.
West's California Judicial Council Forms GC–240, Order Appointing Guardian or Extending Guardianship of the Person.

§ 2591. Powers that may be granted

The powers referred to in Section 2590 are:

(a) The power to operate, for a period longer than 45 days, at the risk of the estate a business, farm, or enterprise constituting an asset of the estate.

(b) The power to grant and take options.

(c)(1) The power to sell at public or private sale real or personal property of the estate without confirmation of the court of the sale, other than the personal residence of a conservatee.

(2) The power to sell at public or private sale the personal residence of the conservatee as described in Section 2591.5 without confirmation of the court of the sale. The power granted pursuant to this paragraph is subject to the requirements of Sections 2352.5, 2540, 2541, and 2541.5.

(3) For purposes of this subdivision, authority to sell property includes authority to contract for the sale and fulfill the terms and conditions of the contract, including conveyance of the property.

(d) The power to create by grant or otherwise easements and servitudes.

(e) The power to borrow money.

(f) The power to give security for the repayment of a loan.

(g) The power to purchase real or personal property.

(h) The power to alter, improve, raze, replace, and rebuild property of the estate.

(i) The power to let or lease property of the estate, or extend, renew, or modify a lease of real property, for which the monthly rental or lease term exceeds the maximum specified in Sections 2501 and 2555 for any purpose (including exploration for and removal of gas, oil, and other minerals and natural resources) and for any period, including a term commencing at a future time.

(j) The power to lend money on adequate security.

(k) The power to exchange property of the estate.

(*l*) The power to sell property of the estate on credit if any unpaid portion of the selling price is adequately secured.

(m) The power to commence and maintain an action for partition. The power granted pursuant to this subdivision is subject to the requirements of Sections 2352.5, 2540, 2541, and 2541.5.

(n) The power to exercise stock rights and stock options.

(o) The power to participate in and become subject to and to consent to the provisions of a voting trust and of a reorganization, consolidation, merger, dissolution, liquidation, or other modification or adjustment affecting estate property.

(p) The power to pay, collect, compromise, or otherwise adjust claims, debts, or demands upon the guardianship or conservatorship described in subdivision (a) of Section 2501, Section 2502 or 2504, or to arbitrate any dispute described in Section 2406. *(Stats.1990, c. 79 (A.B.759), § 14, operative July 1, 1991. Amended by Stats.2006, c. 490 (S.B.1116), § 6; Stats.2007, c. 553 (A.B.1727), § 19; Stats.2019, c. 847 (S.B.303), § 4, eff. Jan. 1, 2020; Stats.2022, c. 91 (S.B.1005), § 5, eff. Jan. 1, 2023.)*

Cross References

Conservatorship for gravely disabled persons, recommendations of officer providing conservatorship investigation, see Welfare and Institutions Code § 5360.
Easements and servitudes, see Civil Code § 801 et seq.
Voting of corporate shares, see Corporations Code § 700 et seq.

Research References

Forms

1 California Transactions Forms--Estate Planning § 6:17, Guardian of Estate or of Property.
1 California Transactions Forms--Estate Planning § 6:74, Appointment of Guardian of Person and Estate of Minor Children.
4 California Transactions Forms--Estate Planning § 19:93, Nomination of Guardian.
4 California Transactions Forms--Estate Planning § 19:142, Additional Powers Granted to Guardian of Minor's Estate [Prob C § 2108(B)].
4 California Transactions Forms--Estate Planning § 21:16, Married Person's Will With Contingent Testamentary Trust for Children.
West's California Code Forms, Probate § 2450 Form 1, Petition to Withdraw or Limit Independent Powers of Guardian or Conservator.

§ 2591.5. Sale of personal residence; best interests of conservatee

(a) Notwithstanding any other provisions of this article, a conservator seeking an order under Section 2590 authorizing a sale of the conservatee's personal residence shall demonstrate to the court that the terms of sale, including the price for which the property is to be sold, the commissions to be paid from the estate, estimated capital gains income and tax consequences, and impact on access to governmental benefits, are in all respects in the best interests of the conservatee.

(b) A conservator authorized to sell the conservatee's personal residence pursuant to Section 2590 shall comply with the provisions of Section 10309 concerning appraisal or new appraisal of the

§ 2591.5

property for sale and sale at a minimum offer price. Notwithstanding Section 10309, if the last appraisal of the conservatee's personal residence was conducted more than six months prior to the proposed sale of the property, a new appraisal shall be required prior to the sale of the property, unless the court finds that it is in the best interests of the conservatee to rely on an appraisal of the personal residence that was conducted not more than one year prior to the proposed sale of the property. For purposes of this section, the date of sale is the date of the contract for sale of the property.

(c) Within 15 days of the close of escrow, the conservator shall serve a copy of the final escrow settlement statement on all persons entitled to notice of the petition for appointment for a conservator and all persons who have filed and served a request for special notice and shall file a copy of the final escrow statement along with a proof of service with the court. (Added by Stats.2006, c. 490 (S.B.1116), § 7. Amended by Stats.2007, c. 553 (A.B.1727), § 20; Stats.2019, c. 847 (S.B.303), § 5, eff. Jan. 1, 2020.)

Research References

Forms

West's California Code Forms, Probate § 2540 Form 1, Report of Sale and Petition for Order Confirming Sale of Real Property (Probate)—Judicial Council Form DE-260, GC-060.

§ 2592. Petition

(a) The guardian or conservator may apply by petition for an order under Section 2590.

(b) The application for the order may be included in the petition for the appointment of the guardian or conservator. In such case, the notice of hearing on the petition shall include a statement that the petition includes an application for the grant of one or more powers under this article and shall list the specific power or powers applied for.

(c) If the application for the order is made by petition filed after the filing of the petition for the appointment of the guardian or conservator, notice of the hearing on the petition shall be given for the period and in the manner provided in Chapter 3 (commencing with Section 1460) of Part 1. (Stats.1990, c. 79 (A.B.759), § 14, operative July 1, 1991.)

Cross References

Notice to,
   Directors, see Probate Code § 1461.
   Veterans Administration, see Probate Code § 1461.5.

§ 2593. Withdrawal or subsequent limitation of powers

(a) The court, on its own motion or on petition of any interested person, when it appears to be for the best interests of the ward or conservatee or the estate, may withdraw any or all of the powers previously granted pursuant to this article or may impose restrictions, conditions, and limitations on the exercise of such powers by the guardian or conservator.

(b) Notice of the hearing on a petition under this section shall be given for the period and in the manner provided in Chapter 3 (commencing with Section 1460) of Part 1. (Stats.1990, c. 79 (A.B.759), § 14, operative July 1, 1991.)

Cross References

Interested person, defined, see Probate Code § 1424.
Powers granted guardian nominated by will, see Probate Code § 2108.

Research References

Forms

West's California Code Forms, Probate § 2450 Form 1, Petition to Withdraw or Limit Independent Powers of Guardian or Conservator.

§ 2594. Letters; contents; requirements for new letters

(a) When a power or powers are granted pursuant to this article, the letters of guardianship or conservatorship shall state the power or powers so granted and the restrictions, conditions, or limitations, if any, prescribed in the order and shall refer to this article.

(b) When a power or powers are granted by a subsequent order, new letters shall be issued in the form described in subdivision (a).

(c) If the powers are withdrawn, or if the powers are restricted, conditioned, or limited by a subsequent order after they are granted, new letters shall be issued accordingly. (Stats.1990, c. 79 (A.B.759), § 14, operative July 1, 1991.)

Cross References

Letters of guardianship or conservatorship, see Probate Code § 2310 et seq.
Powers granted guardian nominated by will, see Probate Code § 2108.

Research References

Forms

West's California Code Forms, Probate § 2450 Form 2, Order Withdrawing or Limiting Independent Powers of Guardian or Conservator.

§ 2595. Effect of article

(a) The grant of a power or powers pursuant to this article does not affect the right of the guardian or conservator to petition the court as provided in Section 2403 or to petition the court under other provisions of this code, as to a particular transaction or matter, in the same manner as if the power or powers had not been granted pursuant to this article.

(b) Where authority exists under other provisions of law, either general or specific, for the guardian or conservator to do any act or to enter into any transaction described in Section 2591, the guardian or conservator may proceed under such other provisions of law and is not required to obtain authority under this article. (Stats.1990, c. 79 (A.B.759), § 14, operative July 1, 1991.)

CHAPTER 7. INVENTORY AND ACCOUNTS

ARTICLE 1. DEFINITIONS AND GENERAL PROVISIONS

Section
2600. Definitions.
2601. Wages of ward or conservatee.

Cross References

Application of old and new law, see Probate Code § 3.

§ 2600. Definitions

As used in this chapter, unless the context otherwise requires:

(a) "Conservator" means (1) the conservator of the estate or (2) the limited conservator of the estate to the extent that the powers and duties of the limited conservator are specifically and expressly provided by the order appointing the limited conservator.

(b) "Estate" means all of the conservatee's or ward's personal property, wherever located, and real property located in this state.

(c) "Guardian" means the guardian of the estate. (Stats.1990, c. 79 (A.B.759), § 14, operative July 1, 1991. Amended by Stats.2008, c. 52 (A.B.2014), § 4.)

Cross References

Order appointing limited conservator for developmentally disabled adult, see Probate Code § 1830.

§ 2601. Wages of ward or conservatee

(a) Unless otherwise ordered by the court, if the ward or conservatee is employed at any time during the continuance of the guardianship or conservatorship:

(1) The wages or salaries for such employment are not a part of the estate and the guardian or conservator is not accountable for such wages or salaries.

(2) The wages or salaries for such employment shall be paid to the ward or conservatee and are subject to his or her control to the same extent as if the guardianship or conservatorship did not exist.

(b) Any court order referred to in subdivision (a) is binding upon the employer only after notice of the order has been received by the employer. *(Stats.1990, c. 79 (A.B.759), § 14, operative July 1, 1991.)*

Cross References

Allowance for ward or conservatee, see Probate Code § 2421.
Payment of earnings to minor, see Family Code § 7503.
Payment of wages, generally, see Labor Code § 200 et seq.
Right of conservatee to control wages or salary, legal capacity, see Probate Code § 1871.

ARTICLE 2. INVENTORY AND APPRAISAL OF ESTATE

Section
2610. Filing inventory and appraisal.
2611. Copy to directors of state hospitals or developmental services.
2612. Copy to county assessor.
2613. Subsequently discovered or acquired property; supplemental inventory and appraisement.
2614. Objections to appraisals.
2614.5. Failure to file inventory and appraisal; removal of guardian or conservator.
2614.7. Professional fiduciary as guardian or conservator; proposed hourly fee schedule or proposed compensation filing requirement.
2614.8. Professional fiduciary as guardian or conservator; submission of new proposed hourly fee schedule or statement of compensation on or after one year from original submission.
2615. Failure to file inventory; liability; damages; bond.

Cross References

Application of old and new law, see Probate Code § 3.

§ 2610. Filing inventory and appraisal

(a) Within 90 days after appointment, or within any further time as the court for reasonable cause upon ex parte petition of the guardian or conservator may allow, the guardian or conservator shall file with the clerk of the court and deliver pursuant to Section 1215 to the conservatee and to the attorneys of record for the ward or conservatee, along with notice of how to file an objection, an inventory and appraisal of the estate, made as of the date of the appointment of the guardian or conservator. A copy of this inventory and appraisal, along with notice of how to file an objection, also shall be delivered to the conservatee's spouse or registered domestic partner, the conservatee's relatives in the first degree, and, if there are no such relatives, to the next closest relative, unless the court determines that the delivery will result in harm to the conservatee.

(b) The guardian or conservator shall take and subscribe to an oath that the inventory contains a true statement of all of the estate of the ward or conservatee of which the guardian or conservator has possession or knowledge. The oath shall be endorsed upon or annexed to the inventory.

(c) The property described in the inventory shall be appraised in the manner provided for the inventory and appraisal of estates of decedents. The guardian or conservator may appraise the assets that a personal representative could appraise under Section 8901.

(d) If a conservatorship is initiated pursuant to the Lanterman-Petris-Short Act (Part 1 (commencing with Section 5000) of Division 5 of the Welfare and Institutions Code), and no sale of the estate will occur:

(1) The inventory and appraisal required by subdivision (a) shall be filed within 90 days after appointment of the conservator.

(2) The property described in the inventory may be appraised by the conservator and need not be appraised by a probate referee.

(e) By January 1, 2008, the Judicial Council shall develop a form to effectuate the notice required in subdivision (a). *(Stats.1990, c. 79 (A.B.759), § 14, operative July 1, 1991. Amended by Stats.2006, c. 493 (A.B.1363), § 23; Stats.2017, c. 319 (A.B.976), § 46, eff. Jan. 1, 2018.)*

Cross References

Affirmation in lieu of oath, see Code of Civil Procedure § 2015.6.
Appraisement of decedent's estates, manner of, see Probate Code § 8901.
Declaration under penalty of perjury, see Code of Civil Procedure § 2015.5.
Inventory and appraisal, generally, see Probate Code § 8800 et seq.
Inventory and appraisement by,
   Guardian for particular property, see Probate Code § 2109.
   Guardian or conservator for nonresident, see Probate Code § 2107.
   Temporary guardian or conservator, see Probate Code § 2255.
Oaths,
   Affirmation in lieu of, see Code of Civil Procedure § 2015.6.
Letters and bond, generally, see Probate Code § 2300 et seq.
Officers authorized to administer, see Government Code § 1225.
Personal representative and general personal representative, defined, see Probate Code § 58.
Professional fiduciary as guardian or conservator, proposed hourly fee schedule or proposed compensation filing requirement, see Probate Code § 2614.7.

Research References

Forms

1 California Transactions Forms--Estate Planning § 1:2, Probate System.
West's California Code Forms, Probate § 2610 Form 1, Inventory and Appraisal—Judicial Council Form DE–160, GC–040.
West's California Judicial Council Forms DE–160, Inventory and Appraisal.
West's California Judicial Council Forms GC–042, Notice of Filing of Inventory and Appraisal and How to Object to the Inventory or the Appraised Value of Property.

§ 2611. Copy to directors of state hospitals or developmental services

If the ward or conservatee is or has been during the guardianship or conservatorship a patient in a state hospital under the jurisdiction of the State Department of State Hospitals or the State Department of Developmental Services, the guardian or conservator shall deliver pursuant to Section 1215 a copy of the inventory and appraisal filed under Section 2610 to the director of the appropriate department at the director's office in Sacramento not later than 15 days after the inventory and appraisal is filed with the court. Compliance with this section is not required if an unrevoked certificate described in subdivision (c) of Section 1461 is on file with the court with respect to the ward or conservatee. *(Stats.1990, c. 79 (A.B.759), § 14, operative July 1, 1991. Amended by Stats.2012, c. 440 (A.B.1488), § 46, eff. Sept. 22, 2012; Stats.2017, c. 319 (A.B.976), § 47, eff. Jan. 1, 2018.)*

Cross References

Department of Developmental Services, see Welfare and Institutions Code § 4400 et seq.
Department of State Hospitals, see Welfare and Institutions Code § 4000 et seq.
Mailing, completion, see Probate Code § 1467.

§ 2612. Copy to county assessor

If a timely request is made, the clerk of court shall deliver pursuant to Section 1215 a copy of the inventory and appraisal filed under Section 2610 to the county assessor. *(Stats.1990, c. 79 (A.B.759), § 14, operative July 1, 1991. Amended by Stats.2017, c. 319 (A.B.976), § 48, eff. Jan. 1, 2018.)*

§ 2612

Cross References

County assessor, see Government Code § 24000.

§ 2613. Subsequently discovered or acquired property; supplemental inventory and appraisement

Whenever any property of the ward or conservatee is discovered that was not included in the inventory, or whenever any other property is received by the ward or conservatee or by the guardian or conservator on behalf of the ward or conservatee (other than by the actions of the guardian or conservator in the investment and management of the estate), the guardian or conservator shall file a supplemental inventory and appraisal for that property and like proceedings shall be followed with respect thereto as in the case of an original inventory, but the appraisal shall be made as of the date the property was so discovered or received. *(Stats.1990, c. 79 (A.B.759), § 14, operative July 1, 1991.)*

Research References

Forms

West's California Code Forms, Probate § 2610 Form 1, Inventory and Appraisal—Judicial Council Form DE-160, GC-040.
West's California Judicial Council Forms GC–400(AP), Additional Property Received During Period of Account—Standard and Simplified Accounts.
West's California Judicial Council Forms GC–405(AP), Additional Property Received During Period of Account— Standard and Simplified Accounts.

§ 2614. Objections to appraisals

(a) Within 30 days after the inventory and appraisal is filed, the guardian or conservator or any creditor or other interested person may file written objections to any or all appraisals. The clerk shall set the objections for hearing not less than 15 days after their filing.

(b) Notice of the hearing, together with a copy of the objections, shall be given for the period and in the manner provided in Chapter 3 (commencing with Section 1460) of Part 1. If the appraisal was made by a probate referee, the person objecting shall also deliver pursuant to Section 1215 notice of the hearing and a copy of the objection to the probate referee at least 15 days before the time set for the hearing.

(c) The court shall determine the objections and may fix the true value of any asset to which objection has been filed. For the purpose of this subdivision, the court may cause an independent appraisal or appraisals to be made by at least one additional appraiser at the expense of the estate or, if the objecting party is not the guardian or conservator and the objection is rejected by the court, the court may assess the cost of any additional appraisal or appraisals against the objecting party. *(Stats.1990, c. 79 (A.B.759), § 14, operative July 1, 1991. Amended by Stats.2017, c. 319 (A.B.976), § 49, eff. Jan. 1, 2018.)*

Cross References

Computation of time, see Code of Civil Procedure §§ 12 and 12a; Government Code § 6800 et seq.
Interested person, defined, see Probate Code § 1424.
Mailing, completion, see Probate Code § 1467.
Notice,
  Mailing, see Probate Code § 1215 et seq.
  Posting, see Probate Code § 1230.
  Proof of giving notice, see Probate Code § 1260 et seq.
  Special notice, see Probate Code § 1250 et seq.
  This code, generally, see Probate Code § 1200 et seq.
  This division, generally, see Probate Code § 1460 et seq.
Probate referees,
  Appointment and duties, see Probate Code § 400 et seq.
  Authority and powers, see Probate Code § 450 et seq.
Service of process,
  Generally, see Code of Civil Procedure § 413.10 et seq.
  Mail, see Code of Civil Procedure §§ 415.30, 1012 et seq.
  Personal delivery, see Code of Civil Procedure § 415.10.
  Proof of service, see Code of Civil Procedure § 417.10 et seq.
  Publication, see Code of Civil Procedure § 415.50.

Research References

Forms

West's California Code Forms, Probate § 2610 Form 1, Inventory and Appraisal—Judicial Council Form DE-160, GC-040.
West's California Judicial Council Forms GC–042, Notice of Filing of Inventory and Appraisal and How to Object to the Inventory or the Appraised Value of Property.
West's California Judicial Council Forms GC–045, Objections to Inventory and Appraisal of Conservator or Guardian.

§ 2614.5. Failure to file inventory and appraisal; removal of guardian or conservator

(a) If the guardian or conservator fails to file an inventory and appraisal within the time allowed by law or by court order, upon request of the ward or conservatee, the spouse of the ward or the spouse or domestic partner of the conservatee, any relative or friend of the ward or conservatee, or any interested person, the court shall order the guardian or conservator to file the inventory and appraisal within the time prescribed in the order or to show cause why the guardian or conservator should not be removed. The person who requested the order shall serve it upon the guardian or conservator in the manner provided in Section 415.10 or 415.30 of the Code of Civil Procedure or in a manner as is ordered by the court.

(b) If the guardian or conservator fails to file the inventory and appraisal as required by the order within the time prescribed in the order, unless good cause is shown for not doing so, the court, on its own motion or on petition, may remove the guardian or conservator, revoke the letters of guardianship or conservatorship, and enter judgment accordingly, and order the guardian or conservator to file an account and to surrender the estate to the person legally entitled thereto.

(c) The procedure provided in this section is optional and does not preclude the use of any other remedy or sanction when an inventory and appraisal is not timely filed. *(Stats.1990, c. 79 (A.B.759), § 14, operative July 1, 1991. Amended by Stats.2001, c. 893 (A.B.25), § 39.)*

Cross References

Domestic partner, defined, see Probate Code § 37.
Guardians and conservators, removal or resignation, see Probate Code § 2650 et seq.
Interested person, defined, see Probate Code § 1424.

Research References

Forms

West's California Code Forms, Probate § 2610 Form 1, Inventory and Appraisal—Judicial Council Form DE-160, GC-040.

§ 2614.7. Professional fiduciary as guardian or conservator; proposed hourly fee schedule or proposed compensation filing requirement

If a guardian or conservator of the person or estate, or both, is a professional fiduciary, as described in Section 2340, who is required to be licensed under the Professional Fiduciaries Act (Chapter 6 (commencing with Section 6500) of Division 3 of the Business and Professions Code), the guardian or conservator shall file, concurrently with the inventory and appraisal required by Section 2610, a proposed hourly fee schedule or another statement of his or her proposed compensation from the estate of the ward or conservatee for services performed as a guardian or conservator. The filing of a proposed hourly fee schedule or another statement of the guardian's or conservator's proposed compensation, as required by this section, shall not preclude a court from later reducing the guardian's, conservator's, or his or her attorney's fees or other compensation. *(Added by Stats.2013, c. 248 (A.B.1339), § 4.)*

GUARDIANSHIP—CONSERVATORSHIP LAW § 2617

Cross References

Professional fiduciary as guardian or conservator, court authorization of periodic payments, contents of petition, see Probate Code § 2643.1.

Research References

Forms

West's California Code Forms, Probate § 2610 Form 1, Inventory and Appraisal—Judicial Council Form DE-160, GC-040.
West's California Code Forms, Probate § 2640 Form 1, Petition for Fees.

§ 2614.8. Professional fiduciary as guardian or conservator; submission of new proposed hourly fee schedule or statement of compensation on or after one year from original submission

At any time on or after one year from the submission of an hourly fee schedule or another statement of proposed compensation under this section or under Section 1510, 1821, 2250, or 2614.7, a guardian or conservator who is a professional fiduciary may submit a new proposed hourly fee schedule or another statement of his or her proposed compensation from the estate of the proposed ward or proposed conservatee. The submittal of a new hourly fee schedule or another statement of the guardian's or conservator's proposed compensation, as authorized by this section, shall not preclude a court from later reducing the guardian's or conservator's hourly fees or other compensation, or his or her attorney's fees or other compensation. *(Added by Stats.2013, c. 248 (A.B.1339), § 5.)*

Research References

Forms

West's California Code Forms, Probate § 2610 Form 1, Inventory and Appraisal—Judicial Council Form DE-160, GC-040.

§ 2615. Failure to file inventory; liability; damages; bond

If a guardian or conservator fails to file any inventory required by this article within the time prescribed by law or by court order, the guardian or conservator is liable for damages for any injury to the estate, or to any interested person, directly resulting from the failure timely to file the inventory. Damages awarded pursuant to this section are a personal liability of the guardian or conservator and a liability on the bond, if any. *(Stats.1990, c. 79 (A.B.759), § 14, operative July 1, 1991.)*

Cross References

Bonds of guardians and conservators, see Probate Code § 2320 et seq.
Interested person, defined, see Probate Code § 1424.
Principal and sureties, liability on bond, see Code of Civil Procedure § 996.460.
Removal of guardian or conservator for failure to file inventory, see Probate Code § 2650.

Research References

Forms

West's California Code Forms, Probate § 2610 Form 1, Inventory and Appraisal—Judicial Council Form DE-160, GC-040.

ARTICLE 2.5. EXAMINATION CONCERNING ASSETS OF ESTATE

Section
2616. Examination concerning assets of estate.
2617. Interrogatories; answers.
2618. Witnesses; truth or falsity of allegations; disclosure of personal knowledge; payment of person's expenses.
2619. Account of property and guardian's or conservator's actions; citation.

Cross References

Conveyances or transfers of property claimed to belong to decedent or other person, see Probate Code § 850 et seq.

§ 2616. Examination concerning assets of estate

(a) A petition may be filed under this article by any one or more of the following:

(1) The guardian or conservator.

(2) The ward or conservatee.

(3) A creditor or other interested person, including persons having only an expectancy or prospective interest in the estate.

(b) Upon the filing of a petition under this article, the court may order that a citation be issued to a person to answer interrogatories, or to appear before the court and be examined under oath, or both, concerning any of the following allegations made in the petition:

(1) The person has wrongfully taken, concealed, or disposed of property of the ward or conservatee.

(2) The person has knowledge or possession of any of the following:

(A) A deed, conveyance, bond, contract, or other writing that contains evidence of or tends to disclose the right, title, interest, or claim of the ward or conservatee to property.

(B) An instrument in writing belonging to the ward or conservatee.

(3) The person asserts a claim against the ward or conservatee or the estate.

(4) The estate asserts a claim against the person.

(c) If the citation requires the person to appear before the court, the court and the petitioner may examine the person under oath upon the matters recited in the petition. The citation may include a requirement for this person to produce documents and other personal property specified in the citation.

(d) Disobedience of a citation issued pursuant to this section may be punished as a contempt of the court issuing the citation. *(Stats.1990, c. 79 (A.B.759), § 14, operative July 1, 1991. Amended by Stats.1994, c. 806 (A.B.3686), § 18.)*

Cross References

Examination or interrogatories in court, see Probate Code § 8870 et seq.
Instrument, defined, see Probate Code § 45.
Newspapers, publications and official advertising, see Government Code § 6000 et seq.
Oaths,
  Affirmation in lieu of, see Code of Civil Procedure § 2015.6.
  Letters and bond, generally, see Probate Code § 2300 et seq.
  Officers authorized to administer, see Government Code § 1225.
Official records and other official writings, see Evidence Code § 1280 et seq.
Production of conservatee's will or other document, see Probate Code § 2586.
Recording,
  Constructive notice, conveyance of real property or estate for years, see Civil Code § 1213.
  Instruments or judgments, documents to be recorded and manner of recording, see Government Code §§ 27280 et seq., 27320 et seq.
Property transfers, place of recordation, see Civil Code § 1169.

Research References

Forms

West's California Code Forms, Probate § 2610 Form 1, Inventory and Appraisal—Judicial Council Form DE-160, GC-040.
West's California Judicial Council Forms DE-160, Inventory and Appraisal.

§ 2617. Interrogatories; answers

Interrogatories may be put to a person cited to answer interrogatories under Section 2616. The interrogatories and answers shall be in writing. The answers shall be signed under penalty of perjury by the

§ 2617

person cited. The interrogatories and answers shall be filed with the court. *(Stats.1990, c. 79 (A.B.759), § 14, operative July 1, 1991.)*

§ 2618. Witnesses; truth or falsity of allegations; disclosure of personal knowledge; payment of person's expenses

(a) At an examination, witnesses may be produced and examined on either side.

(b) If upon the examination it appears that the allegations of the petition are true, the court may order the person to disclose the person's knowledge of the facts.

(c) If upon the examination it appears that the allegations of the petition are not true, the person's necessary expenses, including reasonable attorney's fees, shall be charged against the petitioner or allowed out of the estate, in the discretion of the court. *(Stats.1990, c. 79 (A.B.759), § 14, operative July 1, 1991.)*

Cross References
Attorney's fees and costs, generally, see Code of Civil Procedure § 1021.
Estate attorney, compensation, amount, see Probate Code § 10810 et seq.

§ 2619. Account of property and guardian's or conservator's actions; citation

(a) On petition of the guardian or conservator, the court may issue a citation to a person who has possession or control of property in the estate of the ward or conservatee to appear before the court and make an account under oath of the property and the person's actions with respect to the property.

(b) Disobedience of a citation issued pursuant to this section may be punished as a contempt of the court issuing the citation. *(Stats.1990, c. 79 (A.B.759), § 14, operative July 1, 1991.)*

Cross References
Oaths,
  Affirmation in lieu of, see Code of Civil Procedure § 2015.6.
  Letters and bond, generally, see Probate Code § 2300 et seq.
  Officers authorized to administer, see Government Code § 1225.

ARTICLE 3. ACCOUNTS

Section
2620. Periodic accounting of guardian or conservator; final court accounting; filing of original account statements.
2620.1. Guidelines to be developed.
2620.2. Failure to file account; notice; citation; contempt; removal.
2621. Notice of hearing.
2622. Objections to account.
2622.5. Objections or opposition to objections without reasonable cause or in bad faith; payment of costs and expenses; personal liability.
2623. Compensation and expenses of guardian or conservator.
2625. Review of sales, purchases and other transactions.
2626. Termination of proceeding upon exhaustion of estate.
2627. Settlement of accounts and release by ward; discharge of guardian.
2628. Public benefit payments; procedure; conditions.

Cross References
Application of old and new law, see Probate Code § 3.

§ 2620. Periodic accounting of guardian or conservator; final court accounting; filing of original account statements

(a) At the expiration of one year from the time of appointment and thereafter not less frequently than biennially, unless otherwise ordered by the court to be more frequent, the guardian or conservator shall present the accounting of the assets of the estate of the ward or conservatee to the court for settlement and allowance in the manner provided in Chapter 4 (commencing with Section 1060) of Part 1 of Division 3. By January 1, 2008, the Judicial Council, in consultation with the California Judges Association, the California Association of Superior Court Investigators, the California State Association of Public Administrators, Public Guardians, and Public Conservators, the State Bar of California, and the California Society of Certified Public Accountants, shall develop a standard accounting form, a simplified accounting form, and rules for when the simplified accounting form may be used. After January 1, 2008, all accountings submitted pursuant to this section shall be submitted on the Judicial Council form.

(b) The final court accounting of the guardian or conservator following the death of the ward or conservatee shall include a court accounting for the period that ended on the date of death and a separate accounting for the period subsequent to the date of death.

(c) Along with each court accounting, the guardian or conservator shall file supporting documents, as provided in this section.

(1) For purposes of this subdivision, the term "account statement" shall include any original account statement or verified electronic statement from any institution, as defined in Section 2890, or any financial institution, as defined in Section 2892, in which money or other assets of the estate are held or deposited. A court may also accept a computer-generated printout of an original verified electronic statement if the guardian or conservator verifies that the statement was received in electronic form and printed without alteration. A verification shall be executed by the guardian or conservator pursuant to Section 2015.5 of the Code of Civil Procedure.

(2) The filing shall include all account statements showing the account balance as of the closing date of the accounting period of the court accounting. If the court accounting is the first court accounting of the guardianship or conservatorship, the guardian or conservator shall provide to the court all account statements showing the account balance immediately preceding the date the conservator or guardian was appointed and all account statements showing the account balance as of the closing date of the first court accounting.

(3) The filing shall include the original closing escrow statement received showing the charges and credits for any sale of real property of the estate.

(4) If the ward or conservatee is in a residential care facility or a long-term care facility, the filing shall include the original bill statements for the facility.

(5) This subdivision shall not apply to the public guardian if the money belonging to the estate is pooled with money belonging to other estates pursuant to Section 2940 and Article 3 (commencing with Section 7640) of Chapter 4 of Part 1 of Division 7. Nothing in this section shall affect any other duty or responsibility of the public guardian with regard to managing money belonging to the estate or filing accountings with the court.

(6) If any document to be filed or lodged with the court under this section contains the ward's or conservatee's social security number or any other personal information regarding the ward or conservatee that would not ordinarily be disclosed in a court accounting, an inventory and appraisal, or other nonconfidential pleadings filed in the action, the account statement or other document shall be attached to a separate affidavit describing the character of the document, captioned "CONFIDENTIAL FINANCIAL STATEMENT" in capital letters. Except as otherwise ordered by the court, the clerk of the court shall keep the document confidential except to the court and subject to disclosure only upon an order of the court. The guardian or conservator may redact the ward's or conservatee's social security number from any document lodged with the court under this section.

(7) Courts may provide by local rule that the court shall retain all documents lodged with it under this subdivision until the court's determination of the guardian's or conservator's account has become final, at which time the supporting documents shall be returned to the depositing guardian or conservator or delivered to any successor appointed by the court.

(d) Each accounting is subject to random or discretionary, full or partial review by the court. The review may include consideration of any information necessary to determine the accuracy of the accounting. If the accounting has any material error, the court shall make an express finding as to the severity of the error and what further action is appropriate in response to the error, if any. Among the actions available to the court is immediate suspension of the guardian or conservator without further notice or proceedings and appointment of a temporary guardian or conservator or removal of the guardian or conservator pursuant to Section 2650 and appointment of a temporary guardian or conservator.

(e) The guardian or conservator shall make available for inspection and copying, upon reasonable notice, to any person designated by the court to verify the accuracy of the accounting, all books and records, including receipts for any expenditures, of the guardianship or conservatorship.

(f) A superior court shall not be required to perform any duties imposed pursuant to the amendments to this section enacted by Chapter 493 of the Statutes of 2006 until the Legislature makes an appropriation identified for this purpose. *(Added by Stats.1996, c. 862 (A.B.2751), § 10, operative July 1, 1997. Amended by Stats.1998, c. 581 (A.B.2801), § 22; Stats.2000, c. 565 (A.B.1950), § 9; Stats. 2001, c. 232 (A.B.1517), § 1; Stats.2001, c. 563 (A.B.1286), § 6; Stats.2006, c. 493 (A.B.1363), § 24, operative July 1, 2007; Stats.2008, c. 293 (A.B.1340), § 9; Stats.2009, c. 54 (S.B.544), § 8; Stats.2011, c. 10 (S.B.78), § 20, eff. March 24, 2011; Stats.2020, c. 221 (A.B.2844), § 1, eff. Jan. 1, 2021; Stats.2021, c. 417 (A.B.1194), § 22, eff. Jan. 1, 2022.)*

Cross References

Account defined, see Probate Code § 21
Accounting for deceased or incapacitated personal representative, see Probate Code § 10953.
Accounting upon removal of guardian or conservator, see Probate Code § 2653.
Appointment of legal counsel, see Probate Code § 1470 et seq.
Compensation of guardian, conservator, and attorney, see Probate Code § 2640 et seq.
Financial institution, defined, see Probate Code § 40.
Joint guardians or conservators, see Probate Code § 2105.
Professional fiduciary as guardian or conservator, court authorization of periodic payments, contents of petition, see Probate Code § 2643.1.
Public guardian, generally, see Probate Code § 2900 et seq.
Settlement of accounts upon, termination of guardianship or conservatorship, see Probate Code § 2630.

Research References

Forms

1 California Transactions Forms--Estate Planning § 1:2, Probate System.
1 California Transactions Forms--Estate Planning § 6:16, Guardian of Person.
West's California Code Forms, Probate § 1064 Form 1, Petition for Approval of Account and for Compensation.
West's California Code Forms, Probate § 2620 Form 1, [First/Second, Etc] Account for Guardianship or Conservatorship Estate and Petition for Settlement of Account [And for Compensation].
West's California Code Forms, Probate § 2630 Form 2, Order Settling Final Account of Guardian or Conservator.
West's California Judicial Council Forms GC-400(A)(1), Schedule A, Receipts, Dividends-Standard Account.
West's California Judicial Council Forms GC-400(A)(2), Schedule A, Receipts, Interest—Standard Account.
West's California Judicial Council Forms GC-400(A)(3), Schedule A, Receipts, Pensions, Annuities, and Other Regular Periodic Payments—Standard Account.
West's California Judicial Council Forms GC-400(A)(4), Schedule A, Receipts, Rent—Standard Account.
West's California Judicial Council Forms GC-400(A)(5), Schedule A, Receipts, Social Security, Veterans' Benefits, Other Public Benefits—Standard Account.
West's California Judicial Council Forms GC-400(A)(6), Schedule A, Receipts, Other Receipts—Standard Account.
West's California Judicial Council Forms GC-400(A)(C), Schedules a and C, Receipts and Disbursements Worksheet—Standard Account.
West's California Judicial Council Forms GC-400(AP), Additional Property Received During Period of Account—Standard and Simplified Accounts.
West's California Judicial Council Forms GC-400(B), Schedule B, Gains on Sales—Standard and Simplified Accounts.
West's California Judicial Council Forms GC-400(C)(1), Schedule C, Disbursements, Conservatee's Caregiver Expenses—Standard Account.
West's California Judicial Council Forms GC-400(C)(2), Schedule C, Disbursements, Conservatee's Residential or Long-Term Care Facility Living Expenses—Standard Account.
West's California Judicial Council Forms GC-400(C)(3), Schedule C, Disbursements, Ward's Education Expenses—Standard Account.
West's California Judicial Council Forms GC-400(C)(4), Schedule C, Disbursements, Fiduciary and Attorney Fees—Standard Account.
West's California Judicial Council Forms GC-400(C)(5), Schedule C, Disbursements, General Administration Expenses—Standard Account.
West's California Judicial Council Forms GC-400(C)(6), Schedule C, Disbursements, Investment Expenses—Standard Account.
West's California Judicial Council Forms GC-400(C)(7), Schedule C, Disbursements, Living Expenses—Standard Account.
West's California Judicial Council Forms GC-400(C)(8), Schedule C, Disbursements, Medical Expenses—Standard Account.
West's California Judicial Council Forms GC-400(C)(9), Schedule C, Disbursements, Property Sale Expenses—Standard Account.
West's California Judicial Council Forms GC-400(C)(10), Schedule C, Disbursements, Rental Property Expenses—Standard Account.
West's California Judicial Council Forms GC-400(C)(11), Schedule C, Disbursements, Other Expenses—Standard Account.
West's California Judicial Council Forms GC-400(D), Schedule D, Losses on Sales—Standard and Simplified Accounts.
West's California Judicial Council Forms GC-400(DIST), Distributions to Conservatee or Ward—Standard and Simplified Accounts.
West's California Judicial Council Forms GC-400(E)(1), Cash Assets on Hand at End of Account Period—Standard and Simplified Accounts.
West's California Judicial Council Forms GC-400(E)(2), Non-Cash Assets on Hand at End of Account Period—Standard and Simplified Accounts.
West's California Judicial Council Forms GC-400(F), Schedule F, Changes in Form of Assets—Standard and Simplified Accounts.
West's California Judicial Council Forms GC-400(G), Schedule G, Liabilities at End of Account Period—Standard and Simplified Accounts.
West's California Judicial Council Forms GC-400(NI), Net Income from Trade or Business—Standard Account.
West's California Judicial Council Forms GC-400(NL), Net Loss from Trade or Business—Standard Account.
West's California Judicial Council Forms GC-400(OCH), Other Charges—Standard and Simplified Accounts.
West's California Judicial Council Forms GC-400(OCR), Other Credits—Standard and Simplified Accounts.
West's California Judicial Council Forms GC-400(PH)(1), Cash Assets on Hand at Beginning of Account Period—Standard and Simplified Accounts.
West's California Judicial Council Forms GC-400(PH)(2), Non-Cash Assets on Hand at Beginning of Account Period—Standard and Simplified Accounts.
West's California Judicial Council Forms GC-400(SUM), Summary of Account—Standard and Simplified Accounts.
West's California Judicial Council Forms GC-405(A), Schedule A, Receipts—Simplified Account.
West's California Judicial Council Forms GC-405(AP), Additional Property Received During Period of Account— Standard and Simplified Accounts.
West's California Judicial Council Forms GC-405(B), Schedule B, Gains on Sales—Standard and Simplified Accounts.
West's California Judicial Council Forms GC-405(C), Schedule C, Disbursements—Simplified Account.
West's California Judicial Council Forms GC-405(D), Schedule D, Losses on Sales—Standard and Simplified Accounts.
West's California Judicial Council Forms GC-405(DIST), Distributions to Conservatee or Ward—Standard and Simplified Accounts.

§ 2620

West's California Judicial Council Forms GC–405(E)(1), Cash Assets on Hand at End of Account Period—Standard and Simplified Accounts.
West's California Judicial Council Forms GC–405(E)(2), Non-Cash Assets on Hand at End of Account Period—Standard and Simplified Accounts.
West's California Judicial Council Forms GC–405(F), Schedule F, Changes in Form of Assets—Standard and Simplified Accounts.
West's California Judicial Council Forms GC–405(G), Schedule G, Liabilities at End of Account Period—Standard and Simplified Accounts.
West's California Judicial Council Forms GC–405(OCH), Other Charges—Standard and Simplified Accounts.
West's California Judicial Council Forms GC–405(OCR), Other Credits—Standard and Simplified Accounts.
West's California Judicial Council Forms GC–405(PH)(1), Cash Assets on Hand at Beginning of Account Period—Standard and Simplified Accounts.
West's California Judicial Council Forms GC–405(PH)(2), Non-Cash Assets on Hand at Beginning of Account Period— Standard and Simplified Accounts.
West's California Judicial Council Forms GC–405(SUM), Summary of Account—Standard and Simplified Accounts.

§ 2620.1. Guidelines to be developed

The Judicial Council shall, by January 1, 2009, develop guidelines to assist investigators and examiners in reviewing accountings and detecting fraud. *(Added by Stats.2007, c. 553 (A.B.1727), § 21.)*

§ 2620.2. Failure to file account; notice; citation; contempt; removal

(a) Whenever the conservator or guardian has failed to file an accounting as required by Section 2620, the court shall require that written notice be given to the conservator or guardian and the attorney of record for the conservatorship or guardianship directing the conservator or guardian to file an accounting and to set the accounting for hearing before the court within 30 days of the date of the notice or, if the conservator or guardian is a public agency, within 45 days of the date of the notice. The court may, upon cause shown, grant an additional 30 days to file the accounting.

(b) Failure to file the accounting within the time specified under subdivision (a), or within 45 days of actual receipt of the notice, whichever is later, shall constitute a contempt of the authority of the court as described in Section 1209 of the Code of Civil Procedure.

(c) If the conservator or guardian does not file an accounting with all appropriate supporting documentation and set the accounting for hearing as required by Section 2620, the court shall do one or more of the following and shall report that action to the bureau established pursuant to Section 6510 of the Business and Professions Code:

(1) Remove the conservator or guardian as provided under Article 1 (commencing with Section 2650) of Chapter 9 of Part 4 of Division 4.

(2) Issue and serve a citation requiring a guardian or conservator who does not file a required accounting to appear and show cause why the guardian or conservator should not be punished for contempt. If the guardian or conservator purposely evades personal service of the citation, the guardian or conservator shall be immediately removed from office.

(3) Suspend the powers of the conservator or guardian and appoint a temporary conservator or guardian, who shall take possession of the assets of the conservatorship or guardianship, investigate the actions of the conservator or guardian, and petition for surcharge if this is in the best interests of the ward or conservatee. Compensation for the temporary conservator or guardian, and counsel for the temporary conservator or guardian, shall be treated as a surcharge against the conservator or guardian, and if unpaid shall be considered a breach of condition of the bond.

(4)(A) Appoint legal counsel to represent the ward or conservatee if the court has not suspended the powers of the conservator or guardian and appoint a temporary conservator or guardian pursuant to paragraph (3). Compensation for the counsel appointed for the ward or conservatee shall be treated as a surcharge against the conservator or guardian, and if unpaid shall be considered a breach of a condition on the bond, unless for good cause shown the court finds that counsel for the ward or conservatee shall be compensated according to Section 1470. The court shall order the legal counsel to do one or more of the following:

(i) Investigate the actions of the conservator or guardian, and petition for surcharge if this is in the best interests of the ward or conservatee.

(ii) Recommend to the court whether the conservator or guardian should be removed.

(iii) Recommend to the court whether money or other property in the estate should be deposited pursuant to Section 2453, 2453.5, 2454, or 2455, to be subject to withdrawal only upon authorization of the court.

(B) After resolution of the matters for which legal counsel was appointed in subparagraph (A), the court shall terminate the appointment of legal counsel, unless the court determines that continued representation of the ward or conservatee and the estate is necessary and reasonable.

(5) If the conservator or guardian is exempt from the licensure requirements of Chapter 6 (commencing with Section 6500) of Division 3 of the Business and Professions Code, upon ex parte application or any notice as the court may require, extend the time to file the accounting, not to exceed an additional 30 days after the expiration of the deadline described in subdivision (a), where the court finds there is good cause and that the estate is adequately bonded. After expiration of any extensions, if the accounting has not been filed, the court shall take action as described in paragraphs (1) to (3), inclusive.

(d) Subdivision (c) does not preclude the court from additionally taking any other appropriate action in response to a failure to file a proper accounting in a timely manner. *(Stats.1990, c. 79 (A.B.759), § 14, operative July 1, 1991. Amended by Stats.1991, c. 1019 (S.B.1022), § 6; Stats.1992, c. 572 (S.B.1455), § 7; Stats.2001, c. 359 (S.B.140), § 4; Stats.2002, c. 664 (A.B.3034), § 178.5; Stats.2006, c. 493 (A.B.1363), § 25; Stats.2007, c. 553 (A.B.1727), § 22.)*

Cross References

Guardians and conservators, removal or resignation, see Probate Code § 2650 et seq.
Notice,
  Mailing, see Probate Code § 1215 et seq.
  Posting, see Probate Code § 1230.
  Proof of giving notice, see Probate Code § 1260 et seq.
  Special notice, see Probate Code § 1250 et seq.
  This code, generally, see Probate Code § 1200 et seq.
Service of process,
  Generally, see Code of Civil Procedure § 413.10 et seq.
  Mail, see Code of Civil Procedure §§ 415.30, 1012 et seq.
  Personal delivery, see Code of Civil Procedure § 415.10.
  Proof of service, see Code of Civil Procedure § 417.10 et seq.
  Publication, see Code of Civil Procedure § 415.50.
Temporary guardians and conservators, generally, see Probate Code § 2250 et seq.

Research References

Forms
West's California Code Forms, Probate § 2620 Form 1, [First/Second, Etc] Account for Guardianship or Conservatorship Estate and Petition for Settlement of Account [And for Compensation].

§ 2621. Notice of hearing

Notice of the hearing on the account of the guardian or conservator shall be given for the period and in the manner provided in Chapter 3 (commencing with Section 1460) of Part 1. If notice is required to be given to the Director of State Hospitals or the Director of Developmental Services under Section 1461, the account shall not be settled or allowed unless notice has been given as

GUARDIANSHIP—CONSERVATORSHIP LAW § 2626

provided in Section 1461. *(Stats.1990, c. 79 (A.B.759), § 14, operative July 1, 1991. Amended by Stats.2012, c. 440 (A.B.1488), § 47, eff. Sept. 22, 2012.)*

Cross References

Director of Developmental Services, see Welfare and Institutions Code § 4401 et seq.
Director of State Hospitals, see Welfare and Institutions Code §§ 4001, 4004.
Request for special notice, see Probate Code § 2700 et seq.

Research References

Forms

West's California Code Forms, Probate § 2630 Form 2, Order Settling Final Account of Guardian or Conservator.

§ 2622. Objections to account

The ward or conservatee, the spouse of the ward or the spouse or domestic partner of the conservatee, any relative or friend of the ward or conservatee, or any creditor or other interested person may file written objections to the account of the guardian or conservator, stating the items of the account to which objection is made and the basis for the objection. *(Stats.1990, c. 79 (A.B.759), § 14, operative July 1, 1991. Amended by Stats.2001, c. 893 (A.B.25), § 40.)*

Cross References

Domestic partner, defined, see Probate Code § 37.
Interested person, defined, see Probate Code § 1424.

Research References

Forms

West's California Code Forms, Probate § 2620 Form 1, [First/Second, Etc] Account for Guardianship or Conservatorship Estate and Petition for Settlement of Account [And for Compensation].

§ 2622.5. Objections or opposition to objections without reasonable cause or in bad faith; payment of costs and expenses; personal liability

(a) If the court determines that the objections were without reasonable cause and in bad faith, the court may order the objector to pay the compensation and costs of the conservator or guardian and other expenses and costs of litigation, including attorney's fees, incurred to defend the account. The objector shall be personally liable to the guardianship or conservatorship estate for the amount ordered.

(b) If the court determines that the opposition to the objections was without reasonable cause and in bad faith, the court may award the objector the costs of the objector and other expenses and costs of litigation, including attorney's fees, incurred to contest the account. The amount awarded is a charge against the compensation of the guardian or conservator, and the guardian or conservator is liable personally and on the bond, if any, for any amount that remains unsatisfied. *(Added by Stats.1996, c. 563 (S.B.392), § 12.)*

Cross References

Attorney's fees and costs, generally, see Code of Civil Procedure § 1021.
Costs, see Probate Code § 1002.

§ 2623. Compensation and expenses of guardian or conservator

(a) Except as provided in subdivision (b), the guardian or conservator shall be allowed all of the following:

(1) The amount of the reasonable expenses incurred in the exercise of the powers and the performance of the duties of the guardian or conservator (including, but not limited to, the cost of any surety bond furnished, reasonable attorney's fees, and such compensation for services rendered by the guardian or conservator of the person as the court determines is just, reasonable, and in the best interest of the ward or conservatee).

(2) Such compensation for services rendered by the guardian or conservator as the court determines is just, reasonable, and in the best interest of the ward or conservatee.

(3) All reasonable disbursements made before appointment as guardian or conservator.

(4) In the case of termination other than by the death of the ward or conservatee, all reasonable disbursements made after the termination of the guardianship or conservatorship, but before the discharge of the guardian or conservator by the court.

(5) In the case of termination by the death of the ward or conservatee, all reasonable expenses incurred before the discharge of the guardian or conservator by the court for the custody and conservation of the estate and its delivery to the personal representative of the estate of the deceased ward or conservatee or in making other disposition of the estate as provided for by law.

(b)(1) The guardian or conservator shall not be compensated from the estate for any costs or fees that the guardian or conservator incurred in unsuccessfully defending their fee request petition, opposing a petition, or any other unsuccessful request or action made by, or [1] behalf of, the ward or conservatee.

(2) If the court determines, by clear and convincing evidence, that the defense, opposition, or other action described in paragraph (1) was made in good faith, was based upon the best interest of the ward or conservatee, and did not harm the ward or conservatee, the court may reduce the compensation awarded for the costs or fees incurred instead of denying it completely. The court shall state the reasons for its determination in writing or on the record. *(Stats.1990, c. 79 (A.B.759), § 14, operative July 1, 1991. Amended by Stats.2006, c. 493 (A.B.1363), § 26; Stats.2021, c. 417 (A.B.1194), § 23, eff. Jan. 1, 2022.)*

[1] So in enrolled bill.

Cross References

Attorney's fees and costs, generally, see Code of Civil Procedure § 1021.
Compensation of guardian, conservator, and attorney, see Probate Code § 2640 et seq.
Independent exercise of powers, see Probate Code § 2590 et seq.
Personal representative and general personal representative, defined, see Probate Code § 58.
Termination,
 Conservatorship, see Probate Code § 1860 et seq.
 Guardianship, see Probate Code §§ 1600, 1601.

Research References

Forms

1 California Transactions Forms--Estate Planning § 6:16, Guardian of Person.
West's California Code Forms, Probate § 2620 Form 1, [First/Second, Etc] Account for Guardianship or Conservatorship Estate and Petition for Settlement of Account [And for Compensation].

§ 2625. Review of sales, purchases and other transactions

Any sale or purchase of property or other transaction not previously authorized, approved, or confirmed by the court is subject to review by the court upon the next succeeding account of the guardian or conservator occurring after the transaction. Upon such account and review, the court may hold the guardian or conservator liable for any violation of duties in connection with the sale, purchase, or other transaction. Nothing in this section shall be construed to affect the validity of any sale or purchase or other transaction. *(Stats.1990, c. 79 (A.B.759), § 14, operative July 1, 1991.)*

Cross References

Review of periodic payments of compensation to guardian, conservator or attorney, see Probate Code § 2643.

§ 2626. Termination of proceeding upon exhaustion of estate

If it appears upon the settlement of any account that the estate has been entirely exhausted through expenditures or disbursements

§ 2626

which are approved by the court, the court, upon settlement of the account, shall order the proceeding terminated and the guardian or conservator forthwith discharged unless the court determines that there is reason to continue the proceeding. *(Stats.1990, c. 79 (A.B.759), § 14, operative July 1, 1991.)*

Cross References

Termination of guardianship by emancipation, majority, death or adoption, see Probate Code §§ 1600, 1601.
Termination of proceeding upon transfer of all assets out of state, see Probate Code § 2808.

Research References

Forms

1 California Transactions Forms--Estate Planning § 6:16, Guardian of Person.
1 California Transactions Forms--Estate Planning § 6:17, Guardian of Estate or of Property.
West's California Code Forms, Probate § 1601 Form 1, Petition for Termination of Guardianship—Judicial Council Form GC-255.
West's California Code Forms, Probate § 2626 Form 1, Ex Parte Petition for Final Discharge and Order—Judicial Council Form DE-295/GC-395.
West's California Judicial Council Forms GC-255, Petition for Termination of Guardianship.
West's California Judicial Council Forms GC-260, Order Terminating Guardianship.

§ 2627. Settlement of accounts and release by ward; discharge of guardian

(a) After a ward has reached majority, the ward may settle accounts with the guardian and give the guardian a release which is valid if obtained fairly and without undue influence.

(b) Except as otherwise provided by this code, a guardian is not entitled to a discharge until one year after the ward has attained majority. *(Stats.1990, c. 79 (A.B.759), § 14, operative July 1, 1991.)*

Cross References

Age of majority, see Family Code § 6500 et seq.
Removal of property of nonresident from state, discharge of personal representative, see Probate Code § 3803.

Research References

Forms

West's California Code Forms, Probate § 1601 Form 1, Petition for Termination of Guardianship—Judicial Council Form GC-255.
West's California Code Forms, Probate § 2626 Form 1, Ex Parte Petition for Final Discharge and Order—Judicial Council Form DE-295/GC-395.
West's California Judicial Council Forms DE-295, Ex Parte Petition for Final Discharge and Order.
West's California Judicial Council Forms GC-255, Petition for Termination of Guardianship.
West's California Judicial Council Forms GC-395, Ex Parte Petition for Final Discharge and Order.

§ 2628. Public benefit payments; procedure; conditions

(a) The court may make an order that the guardian or conservator need not present the accounts otherwise required by this chapter so long as all of the following conditions are satisfied:

(1) The estate at the beginning and end of the accounting period for which an account is otherwise required consisted of property, exclusive of the residence of the ward or conservatee, of a total net value of less than fifteen thousand dollars ($15,000).

(2) The income of the estate for each month of the accounting period, exclusive of public benefit payments, was less than two thousand dollars ($2,000).

(3) All income of the estate during the accounting period, if not retained, was spent for the benefit of the ward or conservatee.

(b) Notwithstanding that the court has made an order under subdivision (a), the ward or conservatee or any interested person may petition the court for an order requiring the guardian or conservator to present an account as otherwise required by this chapter or the court on its own motion may make that an order. An order under this subdivision may be made ex parte or on such notice of hearing as the court in its discretion requires.

(c) For any accounting period during which all of the conditions of subdivision (a) are not satisfied, the guardian or conservator shall present the account as otherwise required by this chapter. *(Stats. 1990, c. 79 (A.B.759), § 14, operative July 1, 1991. Amended by Stats.1991, c. 1019 (S.B.1022), § 7; Stats.1998, c. 103 (S.B.1487), § 1; Stats.2007, c. 553 (A.B.1727), § 23.)*

Cross References

Designation of guardian or conservator as payee for public assistance payments, see Probate Code § 2452.
Guardianship and conservatorship, interested person, defined, see Probate Code § 1424.

Research References

Forms

West's California Code Forms, Probate § 1510 Form 1, Petition for Appointment of Guardian of Estate of Minor—Judicial Council Form GC-210.
West's California Judicial Council Forms GC-255, Petition for Termination of Guardianship.
West's California Judicial Council Forms GC-260, Order Terminating Guardianship.
West's California Judicial Council Forms GC-410, Request and Order for Waiver of Accounting.

ARTICLE 4. ACCOUNTS ON TERMINATION OF RELATIONSHIP

Section
2630. Continuing jurisdiction of the court.
2631. Death of ward or conservatee; disposition of assets.
2632. Account of deceased; incapacitated or absconding guardian or conservator.
2633. Order that inventory and appraisement need not be filed; account of assets in possession and control.

Cross References

Application of old and new law, see Probate Code § 3.
Termination of conservatorship, death of conservatee or court order, see Probate Code § 1860.
Termination of guardianship upon majority, death, adoption, or emancipation of ward, see Probate Code § 1600.

§ 2630. Continuing jurisdiction of the court

The termination of the relationship of guardian and ward or conservator and conservatee by the death of either, by the ward attaining majority, by the determination of the court that the guardianship or conservatorship is no longer necessary, by the removal or resignation of the guardian or conservator, or for any other reason, does not cause the court to lose jurisdiction of the proceeding for the purpose of settling the accounts of the guardian or conservator or for any other purpose incident to the enforcement of the judgments and orders of the court upon such accounts or upon the termination of the relationship. *(Stats.1990, c. 79 (A.B.759), § 14, operative July 1, 1991.)*

Cross References

Age of majority, see Family Code § 6500 et seq.
Removal or resignation of guardian or conservator, see Probate Code § 2650 et seq.
Termination,
  Conservatorship, see Probate Code § 1860 et seq.
  Guardianship, see Probate Code §§ 1600, 1601.
Trusts, judicial proceedings,
  Generally, see Probate Code § 17000 et seq.
  Continuing jurisdiction, see Probate Code § 17300 et seq.

Research References

Forms

West's California Code Forms, Probate § 1601 Form 1, Petition for Termination of Guardianship—Judicial Council Form GC-255.

West's California Code Forms, Probate § 2620 Form 1, [First/Second, Etc] Account for Guardianship or Conservatorship Estate and Petition for Settlement of Account [And for Compensation].

West's California Code Forms, Probate § 2630 Form 2, Order Settling Final Account of Guardian or Conservator.

§ 2631. Death of ward or conservatee; disposition of assets

(a) Upon the death of the ward or conservatee, the guardian or conservator may contract for and pay a reasonable sum for the expenses of the last illness and the disposition of the remains of the deceased ward or conservatee, and for unpaid court-approved attorney's fees, and may pay the unpaid expenses of the guardianship or conservatorship accruing before or after the death of the ward or conservatee, in full or in part, to the extent reasonable, from any personal property of the deceased ward or conservatee which is under the control of the guardian or conservator.

(b) If after payment of expenses under subdivision (a), the total market value of the remaining estate of the decedent does not exceed the amount determined under Section 13100, the guardian or conservator may petition the court for an order permitting the guardian or conservator to liquidate the decedent's estate. The guardian or conservator may petition even though there is a will of the decedent in existence if the will does not appoint an executor or if the named executor refuses to act. No notice of the petition need be given. If the order is granted, the guardian or conservator may sell personal property of the decedent, withdraw money of the decedent in an account in a financial institution, and collect a debt, claim, or insurance proceeds owed to the decedent or the decedent's estate, and a person having possession or control shall pay or deliver the money or property to the guardian or conservator.

(c) After payment of expenses, the guardian or conservator may transfer any remaining property as provided in Division 8 (commencing with Section 13000). For this purpose, the value of the property of the deceased ward or conservatee shall be determined after the deduction of the expenses so paid. *(Stats.1990, c. 79 (A.B.759), § 14, operative July 1, 1991. Amended by Stats.1996, c. 563 (S.B.392), § 13.)*

Cross References

Account defined, see Probate Code § 21
Attorney's fees and costs, generally, see Code of Civil Procedure § 1021.
Care of estate after death of ward or conservatee, see Probate Code § 2467.
Estate administration,
  Generally, see Probate Code § 7000 et seq.
  Payment of debts, see Probate Code § 11400 et seq.
Estate attorney, compensation, amount, see Probate Code § 10810 et seq.
Financial institution, defined, see Probate Code § 40.
Inventory and appraisal, generally, see Probate Code § 8800 et seq.
Termination of estate upon death of conservatee, see Probate Code § 1860.
Termination of guardianship upon majority, death, adoption or emancipation of ward, see Probate Code § 1600.

Research References

Forms

West's California Code Forms, Probate § 1064 Form 1, Petition for Approval of Account and for Compensation.

West's California Code Forms, Probate § 2630 Form 1, Termination of Guardianship or Conservatorship; Petition for Order Permitting Liquidation of Decedent's Estate Valued at Under $166,250.

West's California Code Forms, Probate § 2630 Form 2, Order Settling Final Account of Guardian or Conservator.

West's California Judicial Council Forms DE-295, Ex Parte Petition for Final Discharge and Order.

West's California Judicial Council Forms GC-395, Ex Parte Petition for Final Discharge and Order.

§ 2632. Account of deceased; incapacitated or absconding guardian or conservator

(a) As used in this section:

(1) "Incapacitated" means lack of capacity to serve as guardian or conservator.

(2) "Legal representative" means the personal representative of a deceased guardian or conservator or the conservator of the estate of an incapacitated guardian or conservator.

(b) If a guardian or conservator dies or becomes incapacitated and a legal representative is appointed for the deceased or incapacitated guardian or conservator, the legal representative shall, not later than 60 days after appointment unless the court extends the time, file an account of the administration of the deceased or incapacitated guardian or conservator.

(c) If a guardian or conservator dies or becomes incapacitated and no legal representative is appointed for the deceased or incapacitated guardian or conservator, or if the guardian or conservator absconds, the court may compel the attorney for the deceased, incapacitated, or absconding guardian or conservator or the attorney of record in the guardianship or conservatorship proceeding to file an account of the administration of the deceased, incapacitated, or absconding guardian or conservator.

(d) The legal representative or attorney shall exercise reasonable diligence in preparing an account under this section. Verification of the account may be made on information and belief. The court shall settle the account as in other cases. The court shall allow reasonable compensation to the legal representative or the attorney for preparing the account. The amount allowed shall be a charge against the estate that was being administered by the deceased, incapacitated, or absconding guardian or conservator. Legal services for which compensation shall be allowed to the attorney under this subdivision include those services rendered by any paralegal performing the services under the direction and supervision of an attorney. The petition or application for compensation shall set forth the hours spent and services performed by the paralegal. *(Stats.1990, c. 79 (A.B.759), § 14, operative July 1, 1991.)*

Cross References

Appointment of personal representative, generally, see Probate Code § 8400 et seq.
Attorney's fees and costs, generally, see Code of Civil Procedure § 1021.
Capacity determinations, generally, see Probate Code § 3200 et seq.
Personal representative and attorney, compensation, generally, see Probate Code § 10800 et seq.
Personal representative and general personal representative, defined, see Probate Code § 58.
Petition by attorney for compensation, see Probate Code § 2642.
Removal of guardian or conservator in case of incapacity, see Probate Code § 2650.

§ 2633. Order that inventory and appraisement need not be filed; account of assets in possession and control

Subject to Section 2630, where the guardianship or conservatorship terminates before the inventory of the estate has been filed, the court, in its discretion and upon such notice as the court may require, may make an order that the guardian or conservator need not file the inventory and appraisal and that the guardian or conservator shall file an account covering only those assets of the estate of which the guardian or conservator has possession or control. *(Stats.1990, c. 79 (A.B.759), § 14, operative July 1, 1991.)*

CHAPTER 8. COMPENSATION OF GUARDIAN, CONSERVATOR, AND ATTORNEY

Section
2640. Petition by guardian or conservator of estate.
2640.1. Person who has petitioned for appointment of conservator but was not appointed; petition for compensation and reimbursement; notice of hearing; order for compensation and costs; retroactive effect.
2641. Petition by guardian or conservator of person.
2642. Petition by attorney.
2643. Periodic payments of compensation to guardian, conservator or attorney; order.
2643.1. Professional fiduciary as guardian or conservator; court authorization of periodic payments; contents of petition; notice; objections; payments; termination of authorization.
2644. Contingent fee contract with attorney.
2645. Estate funds to compensate guardian or conservator for legal services; court approval; disclosure of relationships.
2646. Proceedings; determinations allowed.
2647. Attorney fees.

Cross References

Application of old and new law, see Probate Code § 3.

§ 2640. Petition by guardian or conservator of estate

(a) At any time after the filing of the inventory and appraisal, but not before the expiration of 90 days from the issuance of letters or any other period of time as the court for good cause orders, the guardian or conservator of the estate may petition the court for an order fixing and allowing compensation to any one or more of the following:

(1) The guardian or conservator of the estate for services in the best interest of the ward or conservatee rendered to that time.

(2) The guardian or conservator of the person for services in the best interest of the ward or conservatee rendered to that time.

(3) The attorney for services in the best interest of the ward or conservatee rendered to that time by the attorney to the guardian or conservator of the person or estate or both.

(b) Notice of the hearing shall be given for the period and in the manner provided for in Chapter 3 (commencing with Section 1460) of Part 1.

(c) Upon the hearing, the court shall make an order allowing (1) any compensation requested in the petition the court determines is just and reasonable to the guardian or conservator of the estate for services rendered or to the guardian or conservator of the person for services rendered, or to both, and (2) any compensation requested in the petition the court determines is reasonable to the attorney for services rendered to the guardian or conservator of the person or estate or both. The compensation allowed to the guardian or conservator of the person, the guardian or conservator of the estate, and to the attorney may, in the discretion of the court, include compensation for services rendered before the date of the order appointing the guardian or conservator. The compensation allowed shall be charged to the estate. Legal services for which the attorney may be compensated include those services rendered by any paralegal performing legal services under the direction and supervision of an attorney. The petition or application for compensation shall set forth the hours spent and services performed by the paralegal.

(d)(1) Notwithstanding subdivision (c), the guardian or conservator shall not be compensated from the estate for any costs or fees that the guardian or conservator incurred in unsuccessfully defending their fee request petition, opposing a petition, or any other unsuccessful request or action made by, or [1] behalf of, the ward or conservatee.

(2) If the court determines, by clear and convincing evidence, that the defense, opposition, or other action described in paragraph (1) was made in good faith, was based upon the best interest of the ward or conservatee, and did not harm the ward or conservatee, the court may reduce the compensation awarded for the costs or fees incurred instead of denying it completely. The court shall state the reasons for its determination in writing or on the record.

(e) Notwithstanding subdivision (c), the guardian, conservator, or attorney shall not be compensated with any government benefits program moneys unless deemed by the court as necessary to sustain the support and maintenance of the ward or conservatee, but in no event may this exceed the amount permitted by federal laws and regulations. *(Stats.1990, c. 79 (A.B.759), § 14, operative July 1, 1991. Amended by Stats.1992, c. 572 (S.B.1455), § 8; Stats.1998, c. 581 (A.B.2801), § 23; Stats.2006, c. 493 (A.B.1363), § 27; Stats.2019, c. 847 (S.B.303), § 6, eff. Jan. 1, 2020; Stats.2021, c. 417 (A.B.1194), § 24, eff. Jan. 1, 2022.)*

[1] So in enrolled bill.

Cross References

Appointment of legal counsel, see Probate Code § 1470 et seq.
Attorney's fees and costs, generally, see Code of Civil Procedure § 1021.
Compensation for attorney rendering account for dead, incapacitated or absconding guardian or conservator, see Probate Code § 2632.
Filing inventory and appraisement, see Probate Code § 2610.
Independent exercise of powers, see Probate Code § 2590 et seq.
Issuance of letters, see Probate Code § 2310.
Letters, defined, see Probate Code § 52.
Personal representative and attorney, compensation, generally, see Probate Code § 10800 et seq.
Presentation of account for settlement and allowance, see Probate Code § 2620.

Research References

Forms

1 California Transactions Forms--Estate Planning § 1:2, Probate System.
West's California Code Forms, Probate § 1064 Form 1, Petition for Approval of Account and for Compensation.
West's California Code Forms, Probate § 2640 Form 1, Petition for Fees.

§ 2640.1. Person who has petitioned for appointment of conservator but was not appointed; petition for compensation and reimbursement; notice of hearing; order for compensation and costs; retroactive effect

(a) If a person has petitioned for the appointment of a particular conservator and another conservator was appointed while the petition was pending, but not before the expiration of 90 days from the issuance of letters, the person who petitioned for the appointment of a conservator but was not appointed and that person's attorney may petition the court for an order fixing and allowing compensation and reimbursement of costs, provided that the court determines that the petition was filed in the best interests of the conservatee.

(b) Notice of the hearing shall be given for the period and in the manner provided in Chapter 3 (commencing with Section 1460) of Part 1.

(c) Upon the hearing, the court shall make an order to allow both of the following:

(1) Any compensation or costs requested in the petition the court determines is just and reasonable to the person who petitioned for the appointment of a conservator but was not appointed, for his or her services rendered in connection with and to facilitate the appointment of a conservator, and costs incurred in connection therewith.

(2) Any compensation or costs requested in the petition the court determines is just and reasonable to the attorney for that person, for

his or her services rendered in connection with and to facilitate the appointment of a conservator, and costs incurred in connection therewith.

Any compensation and costs allowed shall be charged to the estate of the conservatee. If a conservator of the estate is not appointed, but a conservator of the person is appointed, the compensation and costs allowed shall be ordered by the court to be paid from property belonging to the conservatee, whether held outright, in trust, or otherwise.

(d) It is the intent of the Legislature for this section to have retroactive effect. *(Added by Stats.1995, c. 730 (A.B.1466), § 5. Amended by Stats.2006, c. 493 (A.B.1363), § 28.)*

Cross References

Attorney's fees and costs, generally, see Code of Civil Procedure § 1021.
Legislative intent, construction of statutes, see Code of Civil Procedure § 1859.
Letters, defined, see Probate Code § 52.

§ 2641. Petition by guardian or conservator of person

(a) At any time permitted by Section 2640 and upon the notice therein prescribed, the guardian or conservator of the person may petition the court for an order fixing and allowing compensation for services in the best interest of the ward or conservatee rendered to that time.

(b) Upon the hearing, the court shall make an order allowing any compensation the court determines is just and reasonable to the guardian or conservator of the person for services rendered in the best interest of the ward or conservatee. The compensation allowed to the guardian or conservator of the person may, in the discretion of the court, include compensation for services rendered before the date of the order appointing the guardian or conservator. The compensation allowed shall thereupon be charged against the estate.

(c)(1) Notwithstanding subdivision (b), the guardian or conservator shall not be compensated from the estate for any costs or fees that the guardian or conservator incurred in unsuccessfully defending their fee request petition, opposing a petition, or any other unsuccessful request or action made by, or [1] behalf of, the ward or conservatee.

(2) If the court determines, by clear and convincing evidence, that the defense, opposition, or other action described in paragraph (1) was made in good faith, was based upon the best interest of the ward or conservatee, and did not harm the ward or conservatee, the court may reduce the compensation awarded for the costs or fees incurred instead of denying it completely. The court shall state the reasons for its determination in writing or on the record.

(d) Notwithstanding subdivision (b), the guardian or conservator of the person shall not be compensated with any government benefits program moneys unless deemed by the court as necessary to sustain the support and maintenance of the ward or conservatee, but in no event may this exceed the amount permitted by federal laws and regulations. *(Stats.1990, c. 79 (A.B.759), § 14, operative July 1, 1991. Amended by Stats.1992, c. 572 (S.B.1455), § 9; Stats.2006, c. 493 (A.B.1363), § 29; Stats.2019, c. 847 (S.B.303), § 7, eff. Jan. 1, 2020; Stats.2021, c. 417 (A.B.1194), § 25, eff. Jan. 1, 2022.)*

[1] So in enrolled bill.

Cross References

Accounting, compensation for guardian of person, see Probate Code § 2623.

Research References

Forms

West's California Code Forms, Probate § 2640 Form 1, Petition for Fees.

§ 2642. Petition by attorney

(a) At any time permitted by Section 2640 and upon the notice therein prescribed, an attorney who has rendered legal services to the guardian or conservator of the person or estate or both, including services rendered under Section 2632, may petition the court for an order fixing and allowing compensation for such services rendered to that time. Legal services for which the attorney may petition the court for an order fixing and allowing compensation under this subdivision include those services rendered by any paralegal performing the legal services under the direction and supervision of an attorney. The petition or application for compensation shall set forth the hours spent and services performed by the paralegal.

(b) Upon the hearing, the court shall make an order allowing such compensation as the court determines reasonable to the attorney for services rendered to the guardian or conservator. The compensation so allowed shall thereupon be charged against the estate. *(Stats. 1990, c. 79 (A.B.759), § 14, operative July 1, 1991.)*

Cross References

Accounting, allowance for attorney's fees, see Probate Code § 2623.
Appointment of legal counsel, see Probate Code § 1470 et seq.
Attorney's fees and costs, generally, see Code of Civil Procedure § 1021.
Estate attorney, compensation, amount, see Probate Code § 10810 et seq.

Research References

Forms

West's California Code Forms, Probate § 2640 Form 1, Petition for Fees.

§ 2643. Periodic payments of compensation to guardian, conservator or attorney; order

(a) Except as provided in Section 2643.1, on petition by the guardian or conservator of the person or estate, or both, the court may by order authorize periodic payments on account to any one or more of the following persons for the services rendered by that person during the period covered by each payment:

(1) The guardian of the person.

(2) The guardian of the estate.

(3) The conservator of the person.

(4) The conservator of the estate.

(5) The attorney for the guardian or conservator of the person or estate, or both.

(b) Notice of the hearing on the petition shall be given for the period and in the manner provided in Chapter 3 (commencing with Section 1460) of Part 1.

(c) The petition shall describe the services to be rendered on a periodic basis and the reason why authority to make periodic payments is requested. In fixing the amount of the periodic payment, the court shall take into account the services to be rendered on a periodic basis and the reasonable value of those services. The guardian or conservator of the estate may make the periodic payments authorized by the order only if the services described in the petition are actually rendered. The payments made pursuant to the order are subject to review by the court upon the next succeeding account of the guardian or conservator of the estate to determine that the services were actually rendered and that the amount paid on account was not unreasonable, and the court shall make an appropriate order if the court determines that the amount paid on account was either excessive or inadequate in view of the services actually rendered. *(Stats.1990, c. 79 (A.B.759), § 14, operative July 1, 1991. Amended by Stats.2013, c. 248 (A.B.1339), § 6.)*

Cross References

Attorney's fees and costs, generally, see Code of Civil Procedure § 1021.
Compensation and expenses of guardian or conservator or attorney, see Probate Code § 2623.

§ 2643

Trust administration, periodic payments of compensation to trustee, see Probate Code § 15682.

Research References

Forms

West's California Code Forms, Probate § 2640 Form 1, Petition for Fees.

§ 2643.1. Professional fiduciary as guardian or conservator; court authorization of periodic payments; contents of petition; notice; objections; payments; termination of authorization

(a) On petition by a guardian or conservator of the person or estate, or both, who is a professional fiduciary, as described in Section 2340 and who is required to be licensed under the Professional Fiduciaries Act (Chapter 6 (commencing with Section 6500) of Division 3 of the Business and Professions Code), the court may by order authorize periodic payments on account to a person described in subdivision (a) of Section 2643 for the services rendered by that person during the period covered by each payment only if that person has filed a proposed hourly fee schedule or another statement of his or her proposed compensation from the estate of the ward or conservatee for services performed as a guardian or conservator, as required by Section 2614.7, and only after the court has addressed any objections filed pursuant to subdivision (d).

(b) The petition shall describe the services to be rendered on a periodic basis, the reason why authority to make periodic payments is requested, and a good faith estimate of the fees to be charged by the professional fiduciary from the date the petition is filed up to, and including, the date of the next succeeding account required by Section 2620 or, if the next succeeding account required by Section 2620 is due in less than one year, a good faith estimate of the fees to be charged by the professional fiduciary from the date the petition is filed through the next succeeding 12 months, inclusive. Prior to ordering periodic payments or fixing the amount of the periodic payment, the court shall determine whether making periodic payments is in the best interest of the ward or conservatee, taking into consideration the needs of the ward or conservatee and the need to preserve and protect the estate. If the court determines that making periodic payments is not in the best interest of the ward or conservatee, the court shall deny the petition to authorize periodic payments. If the court determines that making periodic payments is in the best interest of the ward or conservatee, the court shall fix the amount of the periodic payment. In fixing the amount of the periodic payment, the court shall take into account the services to be rendered on a periodic basis and the reasonable value of those services.

(c)(1) Notice of the hearing on the petition and notice of how to file an objection to the petition shall be given for the period and in the manner provided in Chapter 3 (commencing with Section 1460) of Part 1.

(2) The notices required by paragraph (1) shall be made to the court investigator for the period and in the manner provided in Chapter 3 (commencing with Section 1460) of Part 1.

(d)(1) Any person entitled to notice under paragraph (1) of subdivision (c) may file with the court a written objection to the authorization of periodic payments on account. The court clerk shall set any objections for a hearing no fewer than 15 days after the date the objections are filed.

(2) If an objection is filed pursuant to paragraph (1), the guardian or conservator shall have the burden of establishing the necessity for and amount, if any, of periodic payments.

(e) The guardian or conservator of the estate may make the periodic payments authorized by the order only if the services described in the petition are actually rendered. The payments made pursuant to the order shall be reviewed by the court upon the next succeeding account of the guardian or conservator of the estate to determine that the services were actually rendered and that the amount paid on account was reasonable and in the best interest of the ward or conservatee, taking into consideration the needs of the ward or conservatee and the need to preserve and protect the estate. The court shall make an appropriate order reducing the guardian or conservator's compensation if the court determines that the amount paid on account was either unreasonable or not in the best interest of the ward or conservatee in view of the services actually rendered.

(f) The authorization for periodic payments granted pursuant to this section shall terminate on a date determined by the court, but not later than the due date of the next succeeding account required by Section 2620. Nothing in this section shall preclude a guardian or conservator from filing a subsequent petition to receive periodic payments pursuant to this section. *(Added by Stats.2013, c. 248 (A.B.1339), § 7.)*

Research References

Forms

West's California Code Forms, Probate § 2640 Form 1, Petition for Fees.

§ 2644. Contingent fee contract with attorney

(a) Where it is to the advantage, benefit, and best interest of the ward or conservatee or the estate, the guardian or conservator of the estate may contract with an attorney for a contingent fee for the attorney's services in representing the ward or conservatee or the estate in connection with a matter that is of a type that is customarily the subject of a contingent fee contract, but such a contract is valid only if (1) the contract is made pursuant to an order of the court authorizing the guardian or conservator to execute the contract or (2) the contract is approved by order of the court.

(b) To obtain an order under this section, the guardian or conservator shall file a petition with the court showing the advantage, benefit, and best interest to the ward or conservatee or the estate of the contingent fee contract. A copy of the contingent fee contract shall be attached to the petition.

(c) Notice of the hearing on the petition shall be given for the period and in the manner provided in Chapter 3 (commencing with Section 1460) of Part 1.

(d) As used in this section, "court" includes either of the following:

(1) The court in which the guardianship or conservatorship proceeding is pending.

(2) Where the contract is in connection with a matter in litigation, the court in which the litigation is pending. *(Stats.1990, c. 79 (A.B.759), § 14, operative July 1, 1991.)*

Cross References

Attorneys' fees and costs,
  Generally, see Code of Civil Procedure § 1021.
  Action on contract, see Civil Code § 1717.

Research References

Forms

West's California Code Forms, Probate § 2640 Form 1, Petition for Fees.

§ 2645. Estate funds to compensate guardian or conservator for legal services; court approval; disclosure of relationships

(a) No attorney who is a guardian or conservator shall receive any compensation from the guardianship or conservatorship estate for legal services performed for the guardian or conservator unless the court specifically approves the right to the compensation and finds that it is to the advantage, benefit, and best interests of the ward or conservatee.

(b) No parent, child, sibling, or spouse of a person who is a guardian or conservator, and no law partnership or corporation whose partner, shareholder, or employee is serving as a guardian or conservator, shall receive any compensation for legal services performed for the guardian or conservator unless the court specifically approves the right to the compensation and finds that it is to the advantage, benefit, and best interests of the ward or conservatee.

(c) This section shall not apply if the guardian or conservator is related by blood or marriage to, or is a cohabitant with, the ward or conservatee.

(d) After full disclosure of the relationships of all persons to receive compensation for legal services under this section, the court may, in its discretion and at any time, approve the right to that compensation, including any time during the pendency of any of the following orders:

(1) An order appointing the guardian or conservator.

(2) An order approving the general plan under Section 1831.

(3) An order settling any account of the guardian or conservator.

(4) An order approving a separate petition, with notice given under Section 2581. *(Added by Stats.1993, c. 293 (A.B.21), § 4.)*

§ 2646. Proceedings; determinations allowed

In proceedings under this chapter, the court shall only determine fees that are payable from the estate of the ward or conservatee and not limit fees payable from other sources. *(Added by Stats.1995, c. 730 (A.B.1466), § 6.)*

§ 2647. Attorney fees

No attorney fees may be paid from the estate of the ward or conservatee without prior court order. The estate of the ward or conservatee is not obligated to pay attorney fees established by any engagement agreement or other contract until it has been approved by the court. This does not preclude an award of fees by the court pursuant to this chapter even if the contractual obligations are unenforceable pursuant to this section. *(Added by Stats.2007, c. 553 (A.B.1727), § 24.)*

Research References

Forms

West's California Code Forms, Probate § 1064 Form 1, Petition for Approval of Account and for Compensation.

CHAPTER 9. REMOVAL OR RESIGNATION

ARTICLE 1. REMOVAL OF GUARDIAN OR CONSERVATOR

Section
2650. Causes for removal.
2651. Petition for removal.
2652. Notice of hearing.
2653. Hearing and judgment.
2654. Suspension of powers and surrender of estate pending hearing.
2655. Contempt; disobeying order of court.

Cross References

Application of old and new law, see Probate Code § 3.

§ 2650. Causes for removal

A guardian or conservator may be removed for any of the following causes:

(a) Failure to use ordinary care and diligence in the management of the estate.

(b) Failure to file an inventory or an account within the time allowed by law or by court order.

(c) Continued failure to perform duties or incapacity to perform duties suitably.

(d) Conviction of a felony, whether before or after appointment as guardian or conservator.

(e) Gross immorality.

(f) Having such an interest adverse to the faithful performance of duties that there is an unreasonable risk that the guardian or conservator will fail faithfully to perform duties.

(g) In the case of a guardian of the person or a conservator of the person, acting in violation of any provision of Section 2356.

(h) In the case of a guardian of the estate or a conservator of the estate, insolvency or bankruptcy of the guardian or conservator.

(i) In the case of a conservator appointed by a court in another jurisdiction, removal because that person would not have been appointed in this state despite being eligible to serve under the law of this state.

(j) In any other case in which the court in its discretion determines that removal is in the best interests of the ward or conservatee; but, in considering the best interests of the ward, if the guardian was nominated under Section 1500 or 1501, the court shall take that fact into consideration. *(Stats.1990, c. 79 (A.B.759), § 14, operative July 1, 1991. Amended by Stats.2014, c. 553 (S.B.940), § 26, eff. Jan. 1, 2015, operative Jan. 1, 2016.)*

Cross References

Duty to use ordinary care and diligence in management and control of estate, see Probate Code § 2401.
Inventory and accounts, see Probate Code § 2600 et seq.
Removal for failure to,
 Furnish sufficient or additional surety, see Code of Civil Procedure § 996.010.
 Produce conservatee for court investigator, see Probate Code § 1853.

Research References

Forms

West's California Code Forms, Probate § 2651 Form 1, Petition for Removal of Guardian or Conservator.

§ 2651. Petition for removal

The ward or conservatee, the spouse of the ward or the spouse or domestic partner of the conservatee, any relative or friend of the ward or conservatee, or any interested person may apply by petition to the court to have the guardian or conservator removed. The petition shall state facts showing cause for removal. *(Stats.1990, c. 79 (A.B.759), § 14, operative July 1, 1991. Amended by Stats.2001, c. 893 (A.B.25), § 41.)*

Cross References

Domestic partner, defined, see Probate Code § 37.
Interested person, defined, see Probate Code § 1424.

Research References

Forms

West's California Code Forms, Probate § 2651 Form 1, Petition for Removal of Guardian or Conservator.

§ 2652. Notice of hearing

Notice of hearing on the petition shall be given for the period and in the manner provided in Chapter 3 (commencing with Section 1460) of Part 1. *(Stats.1990, c. 79 (A.B.759), § 14, operative July 1, 1991.)*

§ 2653. Hearing and judgment

(a) The guardian or conservator, the ward or conservatee, the spouse of the ward or the spouse or registered domestic partner of the conservatee, a relative or friend of the ward or conservatee, and any interested person may appear at the hearing and support or oppose the petition.

§ 2653

(b) If the court determines that cause for removal of the guardian or conservator exists, the court may remove the guardian or conservator, revoke the letters of guardianship or conservatorship, and enter judgment accordingly and, in the case of a guardianship or conservatorship of the estate, order the guardian or conservator to file an accounting and to surrender the estate to the person legally entitled thereto. If the guardian or conservator fails to file the accounting as ordered, the court may compel the accounting pursuant to Section 2620.2.

(c) If the court removes the guardian or conservator for cause, as described in subdivisions (a) to (g), inclusive, of Section 2650 or Section 2655, all of the following shall apply:

(1) The court shall award the petitioner the costs of the petition and other expenses and costs of litigation, including attorney's fees, incurred under this article.

(2) The guardian or conservator may not deduct from, or charge to, the estate the guardian's or conservator's costs of opposing the petition for removal, and is personally liable for those costs and expenses.

(3) If the court removes a professional fiduciary as guardian or conservator for cause, the court shall report that determination and the basis for removal to the Professional Fiduciaries Bureau. If the court reports an action taken under this section, the court shall provide the bureau, at no charge, with access to the information, including confidential information, regarding its investigation of the professional fiduciary contained in court records. The bureau shall maintain the confidentiality of the information, as required by paragraph (4) of subdivision (a) of Section 6580 of the Business and Professions Code or any other applicable state or federal law.

(d) A superior court shall not be required to perform any duties imposed pursuant to the amendments to this section enacted by the measure that added this subdivision until the Legislature makes an appropriation identified for this purpose. *(Stats.1990, c. 79 (A.B. 759), § 14, operative July 1, 1991. Amended by Stats.2001, c. 893. (A.B.25), § 42; Stats.2006, c. 493 (A.B.1363), § 30; Stats.2021, c. 417 (A.B.1194), § 26, eff. Jan. 1, 2022.)*

Cross References

Domestic partner, defined, see Probate Code § 37.
Interested person, defined, see Probate Code § 1424.
Revoking letters for failure to furnish additional or sufficient surety, see Code of Civil Procedure § 996.010.

Research References

Forms

West's California Code Forms, Probate § 2620 Form 1, [First/Second, Etc] Account for Guardianship or Conservatorship Estate and Petition for Settlement of Account [And for Compensation].
West's California Code Forms, Probate § 2651 Form 1, Petition for Removal of Guardian or Conservator.

§ 2654. Suspension of powers and surrender of estate pending hearing

Whenever it appears that the ward or conservatee or the estate may suffer loss or injury during the time required for notice and hearing under this article, the court, on its own motion or on petition, may do either or both of the following:

(a) Suspend the powers of the guardian or conservator pending notice and hearing to such extent as the court deems necessary.

(b) Compel the guardian or conservator to surrender the estate to a custodian designated by the court. *(Stats.1990, c. 79 (A.B.759), § 14, operative July 1, 1991.)*

Cross References

Suspension of powers of guardians, see Code of Civil Procedure § 166.
Suspension of powers when petition for further surety or bond filed, see Probate Code § 2334.

§ 2655. Contempt; disobeying order of court

(a) A guardian or conservator may be removed from office if the guardian or conservator is found in contempt for disobeying an order of the court.

(b) Notwithstanding any other provision of this article, a guardian or conservator may be removed from office under subdivision (a) by a court order reciting the facts and without further showing or notice. *(Stats.1990, c. 79 (A.B.759), § 14, operative July 1, 1991.)*

Research References

Forms

West's California Code Forms, Probate § 2651 Form 1, Petition for Removal of Guardian or Conservator.

ARTICLE 2. RESIGNATION OF GUARDIAN OR CONSERVATOR

Section
2660. Resignation of guardian or conservator.
2662. Removal or limitation on power of guardian or conservator; appointment of responsible adult to make educational decisions for minor; conflicts of interest.

Cross References

Application of old and new law, see Probate Code § 3.

§ 2660. Resignation of guardian or conservator

A guardian or conservator may at any time file with the court a petition tendering the resignation of the guardian or conservator. Notice of the hearing on the petition shall be given for the period and in the manner provided in Chapter 3 (commencing with Section 1460) of Part 1. The court shall allow such resignation when it appears proper, to take effect at such time as the court shall fix, and may make any order as may be necessary to deal with the guardianship or conservatorship during the period prior to the appointment of a new guardian or conservator and the settlement of the accounts of the resigning guardian or conservator. *(Stats.1990, c. 79 (A.B.759), § 14, operative July 1, 1991.)*

Cross References

Appointment of successor, see Probate Code § 2670.
Continuing jurisdiction of court, settling of accounts, see Probate Code § 2630.
Resignation of temporary guardian or conservator, see Probate Code § 2258.
Resignation of trustee, see Probate Code § 15640.
Temporary guardian or conservator, appointment by court, see Probate Code § 2250.

§ 2662. Removal or limitation on power of guardian or conservator; appointment of responsible adult to make educational decisions for minor; conflicts of interest

Whenever the court grants a petition removing the guardian or conservator of a minor ward or conservatee or tendering the resignation of the guardian or conservator of a minor ward or conservatee, if the court does not immediately appoint a successor guardian or conservator, the court shall at the same time appoint a responsible adult to make educational decisions for the minor until a successor guardian or conservator is appointed. Whenever the court suspends or limits the powers of the guardian or conservator to make educational decisions for a minor ward or conservatee, the court shall at the same time appoint a responsible adult to make educational decisions for the minor ward or conservatee until the guardian or conservator is again authorized to make educational decisions for the minor ward or conservatee. An individual who would have a conflict of interest in representing the child may not be appointed to make educational decisions. For purposes of this section, "an individual who would have a conflict of interest," means a person having any interests that might restrict or bias his or her ability to make educational decisions, including, but not limited to, those conflicts of interest prohibited by Section 1126 of the Government Code, and the receipt of compensation or attorneys' fees for the provision of services pursuant to this section. A foster parent may not be deemed to have a conflict of interest solely because he or she receives compensation for the provision of services pursuant to this section. (Added by Stats.2002, c. 180 (A.B.886), § 1.)

Cross References

Dependent children, persons appointed to make educational decisions for, see Welfare and Institutions Code § 361.
Wards of court, persons appointed to make educational decisions for, see Welfare and Institutions Code § 726.

Research References

Forms

West's California Code Forms, Probate § 2651 Form 1, Petition for Removal of Guardian or Conservator.
West's California Code Forms, Probate § 2682 Form 1, Petition for Appointment of Successor Conservator.

CHAPTER 9.5. APPOINTMENT OF SUCCESSOR GUARDIAN OR CONSERVATOR

ARTICLE 1. APPOINTMENT OF SUCCESSOR GUARDIAN

Section
2670. Vacancy; appointment of successor.

Cross References

Application of old and new law, see Probate Code § 3.

§ 2670. Vacancy; appointment of successor

When for any reason a vacancy occurs in the office of guardian, the court may appoint a successor guardian, after notice and hearing as in the case of an original appointment of a guardian. *(Stats.1990, c. 79 (A.B.759), § 14, operative July 1, 1991.)*

Cross References

Conservator of person, estate or person and estate, original appointment, see Probate Code § 1801.
Original appointment of guardian, see Probate Code § 1514.

ARTICLE 2. APPOINTMENT OF SUCCESSOR CONSERVATOR

Section
2680. Vacancy; appointment of successor.
2681. Petition; filing; persons or entities authorized.
2682. Petition; contents.
2683. Notice of hearing.
2684. Court investigator; duties.
2685. Presence of conservatee at hearing; duty of court.
2686. Absence of conservatee from hearing; continuance; duties of court investigator.
2687. Persons authorized to support or oppose petition.
2688. Appointment; determination; law governing.
2689. Absentee conservatee; applicable provisions.

§ 2680. Vacancy; appointment of successor

When for any reason a vacancy occurs in the office of conservator, the court may appoint a successor conservator in the manner provided in this article. *(Stats.1990, c. 79 (A.B.759), § 14, operative July 1, 1991.)*

Research References

Forms

West's California Judicial Council Forms GC–310, Petition for Appointment of Probate Conservator.

§ 2681. Petition; filing; persons or entities authorized

A petition for appointment of a successor conservator may be filed by any of the following:

(a) The conservatee.

(b) The spouse or domestic partner of the conservatee.

(c) A relative of the conservatee.

(d) Any interested state or local entity or agency of this state or any interested public officer or employee of this state or of a local public entity of this state.

(e) Any other interested person or friend of the conservatee. *(Stats.1990, c. 79 (A.B.759), § 14, operative July 1, 1991. Amended by Stats.2001, c. 893 (A.B.25), § 43.)*

Cross References

Domestic partner, defined, see Probate Code § 37.
Guardianship and conservatorship, interested person, defined, see Probate Code § 1424.
Petitions and other papers, see Probate Code § 1020 et seq.

Research References

Forms

West's California Code Forms, Probate § 2682 Form 1, Petition for Appointment of Successor Conservator.

§ 2682. Petition; contents

(a) The petition shall request that a successor conservator be appointed for the person or estate, or both, and shall specify the name and address of the proposed successor conservator and the name and address of the conservatee.

(b) The petition shall set forth, so far as they are known to the petitioner, the names and addresses of the spouse or domestic partner and of the relatives of the conservatee within the second degree.

(c) If the petition is filed by one other than the conservatee, the petition shall state whether or not the petitioner is a creditor or debtor of the conservatee.

(d) If the conservatee is a patient in or on leave of absence from a state institution under the jurisdiction of the State Department of State Hospitals or the State Department of Developmental Services and that fact is known to the petitioner, the petition shall state that fact and name the institution.

(e) The petition shall state, so far as is known to the petitioner, whether or not the conservatee is receiving or is entitled to receive benefits from the Veterans Administration and the estimated amount of the monthly benefit payable by the Veterans Administration for the conservatee.

(f) The petition shall state whether or not the conservatee will be present at the hearing. *(Stats.1990, c. 79 (A.B.759), § 14, operative July 1, 1991. Amended by Stats.2001, c. 893 (A.B.25), § 44; Stats. 2012, c. 440 (A.B.1488), § 48, eff. Sept. 22, 2012.)*

Cross References

Domestic partner, defined, see Probate Code § 37.

§ 2682

Petitions and other papers, see Probate Code § 1020 et seq.

Research References

Forms

West's California Judicial Council Forms GC–310, Petition for Appointment of Probate Conservator.

§ 2683. Notice of hearing

(a) At least 15 days before the hearing on the petition for appointment of a successor conservator, notice of the time and place of the hearing shall be given as provided in this section. The notice shall be accompanied by a copy of the petition.

(b) Notice shall be delivered pursuant to Section 1215 to the persons designated in Section 1460 and to the relatives named in the petition.

(c) If notice is required by Section 1461 to be given to the Director of State Hospitals or the Director of Developmental Services, notice shall be delivered pursuant to Section 1215 as required.

(d) If notice is required by Section 1461.5 to be given to the Veterans Administration, notice shall be delivered pursuant to Section 1215 as required. *(Stats.1990, c. 79 (A.B.759), § 14, operative July 1, 1991. Amended by Stats.1994, c. 806 (A.B.3686), § 19; Stats.2012, c. 440 (A.B.1488), § 49, eff. Sept. 22, 2012; Stats.2017, c. 319 (A.B.976), § 50, eff. Jan. 1, 2018.)*

Cross References

Absentee conservatees,
  Defined, see Probate Code § 1403
  Notice, see Probate Code §§ 1842, 2689.
Computation of time, see Code of Civil Procedure §§ 12 and 12a; Government Code § 6800 et seq.
Notice of hearing,
  Generally, see Probate Code §§ 1200 et seq., 1460 et seq.
  Delivery of notice instead of mailing, see Probate Code § 1215.
  Mailing, see Probate Code § 1215 et seq.
  Posting, see Probate Code § 1230.
  Proof of giving notice, see Probate Code § 1260 et seq.
  Special notice provisions, see Probate Code §§ 1250 et seq., 2700 et seq.
Service of process,
  Generally, see Code of Civil Procedure § 413.10 et seq.
  Mail, see Code of Civil Procedure §§ 415.30, 1012 et seq.
  Personal delivery, see Code of Civil Procedure § 415.10.
  Proof of service, see Code of Civil Procedure § 417.10 et seq.
  Publication, see Code of Civil Procedure § 415.50.

Research References

Forms

West's California Code Forms, Probate § 2651 Form 1, Petition for Removal of Guardian or Conservator.

West's California Code Forms, Probate § 2682 Form 1, Petition for Appointment of Successor Conservator.

§ 2684. Court investigator; duties

Unless the petition states that the conservatee will be present at the hearing, the court investigator shall do all of the following:

(a) Interview the conservatee personally.

(b) Inform the conservatee of the nature of the proceeding to appoint a successor conservator, the name of the person proposed as successor conservator, and the conservatee's right to appear personally at the hearing, to object to the person proposed as successor conservator, to nominate a person to be appointed as successor conservator, to be represented by legal counsel if the conservatee so chooses, and to have legal counsel appointed by the court if unable to retain legal counsel.

(c) Determine whether the conservatee objects to the person proposed as successor conservator or prefers another person to be appointed.

(d) If the conservatee is not represented by legal counsel, determine whether the conservatee wishes to be represented by legal counsel and, if so, determine the name of an attorney the conservatee wishes to retain or whether the conservatee desires the court to appoint legal counsel.

(e) Determine whether the appointment of legal counsel would be helpful to the resolution of the matter or is necessary to protect the interests of the conservatee in any case where the conservatee does not plan to retain legal counsel and has not requested the appointment of legal counsel by the court.

(f) Report to the court in writing, at least five days before the hearing, concerning all of the foregoing, including the conservatee's express communications concerning representation by legal counsel and whether the conservatee objects to the person proposed as successor conservator or prefers that some other person be appointed.

(g) Deliver pursuant to Section 1215, at least five days before the hearing, a copy of the report referred to in subdivision (f) to all of the following:

(1) The attorney, if any, for the petitioner.

(2) The attorney, if any, for the conservatee.

(3) Any other persons as the court orders. *(Stats.1990, c. 79 (A.B.759), § 14, operative July 1, 1991. Amended by Stats.2017, c. 319 (A.B.976), § 51, eff. Jan. 1, 2018.)*

Cross References

Absentee conservatee,
  Applicable provisions, see Probate Code § 2689.
  Defined, see Probate Code § 1403.
Appointment of legal counsel, see Probate Code § 1471.

Research References

Forms

West's California Code Forms, Probate § 1454 Form 2, Order Appointing Court Investigator—Judicial Council Form GC-331.

West's California Code Forms, Probate § 2682 Form 1, Petition for Appointment of Successor Conservator.

West's California Code Forms, Probate § 2688 Form 1, Order Appointing Successor Conservator.

West's California Judicial Council Forms GC–331, Order Appointing Court Investigator (Review and Successor Conservator Investigations).

§ 2685. Presence of conservatee at hearing; duty of court

If the conservatee is present at the hearing, prior to making an order appointing a successor conservator the court shall do all of the following:

(a) Inform the conservatee of the nature and purpose of the proceeding.

(b) Inform the conservatee that the conservatee has the right to object to the person proposed as successor conservator, to nominate a person to be appointed as successor conservator, and, if not represented by legal counsel, to be represented by legal counsel if the conservatee so chooses and to have legal counsel appointed by the court if unable to retain legal counsel.

(c) After the court so informs the conservatee, the court shall consult the conservatee to determine the conservatee's opinion concerning the question of who should be appointed as successor conservator. *(Stats.1990, c. 79 (A.B.759), § 14, operative July 1, 1991.)*

Cross References

Appointment of legal counsel, see Probate Code § 1471.

Research References

Forms

West's California Code Forms, Probate § 2688 Form 1, Order Appointing Successor Conservator.

§ 2686. Absence of conservatee from hearing; continuance; duties of court investigator

If the petition states that the conservatee will be present at the hearing and the conservatee fails to appear at the hearing, the court shall continue the hearing and direct the court investigator to perform the duties set forth in Section 2684. *(Stats.1990, c. 79 (A.B.759), § 14, operative July 1, 1991.)*

Research References

Forms

West's California Code Forms, Probate § 1454 Form 2, Order Appointing Court Investigator—Judicial Council Form GC-331.

West's California Judicial Council Forms GC-331, Order Appointing Court Investigator (Review and Successor Conservator Investigations).

§ 2687. Persons authorized to support or oppose petition

The conservatee, the spouse, the domestic partner, or any relative or friend of the conservatee, or any other interested person may appear at the hearing to support or oppose the petition. *(Stats.1990, c. 79 (A.B.759), § 14, operative July 1, 1991. Amended by Stats.2001, c. 893 (A.B.25), § 45.)*

Cross References

Domestic partner, defined, see Probate Code § 37.
Interested persons, see Probate Code § 1424.
Objections to petition, see Probate Code § 1043.

§ 2688. Appointment; determination; law governing

(a) The court shall determine the question of who should be appointed as successor conservator according to the provisions of Article 2 (commencing with Section 1810) of Chapter 1 of Part 3.

(b) The order appointing the successor conservator shall contain, among other things, the names, addresses and telephone numbers of the successor conservator, the conservatee's attorney, if any, and the court investigator, if any. *(Stats.1990, c. 79 (A.B.759), § 14, operative July 1, 1991.)*

Cross References

Final order, effect, see Probate Code § 2103.
Hearings and orders, generally, see Probate Code § 1040 et seq.
Jury trial, right to, see Probate Code § 1452.
Petitions and other papers, generally, see Probate Code § 1020 et seq.
Rules of practice, see Probate Code § 1000 et seq.

Research References

Forms

West's California Code Forms, Probate § 2682 Form 1, Petition for Appointment of Successor Conservator.

West's California Code Forms, Probate § 2688 Form 1, Order Appointing Successor Conservator.

West's California Judicial Council Forms GC-340, Order Appointing Probate Conservator.

§ 2689. Absentee conservatee; applicable provisions

If the conservatee is an "absentee" as defined in Section 1403:

(a) The petition for appointment of a successor conservator shall contain the matters required by Section 1841 in addition to the matters required by Section 2682.

(b) Notice of the hearing shall be given as provided by Section 1842 in addition to the requirements of Section 2683, except that notice need not be given to the conservatee.

(c) An interview and report by the court investigator is not required. *(Stats.1990, c. 79 (A.B.759), § 14, operative July 1, 1991.)*

Cross References

Notice provisions,
 Generally, see Probate Code §§ 1200 et seq., 1460 et seq.
 Proof of giving notice, see Probate Code § 1260 et seq.
 Special notice provisions, see Probate Code § 2700 et seq.

CHAPTER 10. REQUESTS FOR SPECIAL NOTICE

Section
2700. Written request; persons authorized.
2701. Modification or withdrawal of request; new request.
2702. Petitioner required to give special notice.

§ 2700. Written request; persons authorized

(a) At any time after the issuance of letters of guardianship or conservatorship, the ward, if over 14 years of age or the conservatee, the spouse of the ward or the spouse or domestic partner of the conservatee, any relative or creditor of the ward or conservatee, or any other interested person, in person or by attorney, may file with the court clerk a written request for special notice.

(b) The request for special notice shall be so entitled and shall set forth the name of the person and the address to which notices shall be delivered pursuant to Section 1215.

(c) Special notice may be requested of any one or more of the following matters:

(1) Petitions filed in the guardianship or conservatorship proceeding.

(2) Inventories and appraisals of property in the estate, including any supplemental inventories and appraisals.

(3) Accounts of the guardian or conservator.

(4) Proceedings for the final termination of the guardianship or conservatorship proceeding.

(d) Special notice may be requested of:

(1) Any one or more of the matters in subdivision (c) by describing the matter or matters.

(2) All the matters in subdivision (c) by referring generally to "the matters described in subdivision (c) of Section 2700 of the Probate Code" or by using words of similar meaning.

(e) A copy of the request shall be delivered pursuant to Section 1215 to the guardian or conservator or to the attorney for the guardian or conservator. If personally delivered, the request is effective when it is delivered. If mailed or electronically delivered, the request is effective when it is received.

(f) If the original of the request is filed with the court clerk, it shall be accompanied by a written admission or proof of service. *(Stats. 1990, c. 79 (A.B.759), § 14, operative July 1, 1991. Amended by Stats.2001, c. 893 (A.B.25), § 46; Stats.2017, c. 319 (A.B.976), § 52, eff. Jan. 1, 2018.)*

Cross References

Accounts, see Probate Code § 2620 et seq.
Conveyance or transfer of property, see Probate Code § 850.
Domestic partner, defined, see Probate Code § 37.
Guardianship and conservatorship, interested person, defined, see Probate Code § 1424.
Inventory and appraisement of estate, see Probate Code § 2610 et seq.
Notice requirements,
 Generally, see Probate Code § 1460.
 Mailing, see Probate Code § 1215 et seq.
 Posting, see Probate Code § 1230.
 Proof of notice, see Probate Code § 1260.
 Special notice, administration of estates of decedents, see Probate Code § 1250.
This code, generally, see Probate Code § 1200 et seq.
Removal or resignation of guardian or conservator, see Probate Code § 2650 et seq.
Request for special notice pursuant to this section, superior court filing fees, see Government Code § 70662.
Service of process,
 Generally, see Code of Civil Procedure § 413.10 et seq.
 Mail, see Code of Civil Procedure §§ 415.30, 1012 et seq.
 Personal delivery, see Code of Civil Procedure § 415.10.

§ 2700
PROBATE CODE

Proof of service, see Code of Civil Procedure § 417.10 et seq.
Publication, see Code of Civil Procedure § 415.50.

Research References

Forms

West's California Code Forms, Probate § 2700 Form 1, Request for Special Notice (Probate)—Judicial Council Form GC-035.

§ 2701. Modification or withdrawal of request; new request

(a) A request for special notice may be modified or withdrawn in the same manner as provided for the making of the initial request.

(b) A new request for special notice may be served and filed at any time as provided in the case of an initial request. *(Stats.1990, c. 79 (A.B.759), § 14, operative July 1, 1991. Amended by Stats.2006, c. 493 (A.B.1363), § 31.)*

Cross References

Notice,
  Mailing, see Probate Code § 1215 et seq.
  Posting, see Probate Code § 1230.
  Proof of giving notice, see Probate Code § 1260 et seq.
  Special notice, see Probate Code § 1250 et seq.
  This code, generally, see Probate Code § 1200 et seq.
  This division, generally, see Probate Code § 1460 et seq.
Service of process,
  Generally, see Code of Civil Procedure § 413.10 et seq.
  Mail, see Code of Civil Procedure §§ 415.30, 1012 et seq.
  Personal delivery, see Code of Civil Procedure § 415.10.
  Proof of service, see Code of Civil Procedure § 417.10 et seq.
  Publication, see Code of Civil Procedure § 415.50.

Research References

Forms

West's California Code Forms, Probate § 2700 Form 1, Request for Special Notice (Probate)—Judicial Council Form GC-035.

§ 2702. Petitioner required to give special notice

(a) Unless the court makes an order dispensing with the notice, if a request has been made pursuant to this chapter for special notice of a hearing, the person filing the petition, account, or other paper shall give written notice pursuant to Section 1215 of the filing, together with a copy of the petition, account, or other paper, and the time and place set for the hearing, to the person named in the request at the address set forth in the request, at least 15 days before the time set for the hearing.

(b) If a request has been made pursuant to this chapter for special notice of the filing of an inventory and appraisal of the estate or of the filing of any other paper that does not require a hearing, the inventory and appraisal or other paper shall be delivered pursuant to Section 1215 not later than 15 days after the inventory and appraisal or other paper is filed with the court. *(Stats.1990, c. 79 (A.B.759), § 14, operative July 1, 1991. Amended by Stats.2017, c. 319 (A.B.976), § 53, eff. Jan. 1, 2018.)*

Cross References

Computation of time, see Code of Civil Procedure §§ 12 and 12a; Government Code § 6800 et seq.
Inventory and appraisement of the estate, see Probate Code § 2610 et seq.
Mailing, completion, see Probate Code § 1467.

Research References

Forms

West's California Code Forms, Probate § 2700 Form 1, Request for Special Notice (Probate)—Judicial Council Form GC-035.

CHAPTER 12. TRANSFER OF PERSONAL PROPERTY OUT OF STATE

Section
2800. Foreign guardian or conservator.
2801. Order for transfer of assets out of state.
2802. Petition; persons authorized to file.
2803. Petition; contents.
2804. Notice of hearing.
2805. Objections to petition.
2806. Order for transfer.
2807. Manner of transfer; terms and conditions.
2808. Termination of guardianship or conservatorship.

§ 2800. Foreign guardian or conservator

As used in this chapter, "foreign guardian or conservator" means a guardian, conservator, committee, or comparable fiduciary in another jurisdiction. *(Stats.1990, c. 79 (A.B.759), § 14, operative July 1, 1991.)*

Cross References

Fiduciary, defined, see Probate Code § 39.
Trusts, judicial proceedings,
  Generally, see Probate Code § 17000 et seq.
  Transfer from another jurisdiction, see Probate Code § 17450 et seq.

§ 2801. Order for transfer of assets out of state

Subject to the limitations and requirements of this chapter, the court in which the guardianship of the estate or conservatorship of the estate is pending may order the transfer of some or all of the personal property of the estate to a foreign guardian or conservator in another jurisdiction outside this state where the ward or conservatee resides at the time the petition for the order authorizing the transfer is filed. *(Stats.1990, c. 79 (A.B.759), § 14, operative July 1, 1991.)*

Cross References

Administration of trusts, transfer of assets to another jurisdiction, see Probate Code § 17400 et seq.

§ 2802. Petition; persons authorized to file

A petition for an order authorizing a transfer may be filed by any of the following:

(a) The guardian of the estate or the conservator of the estate.

(b) The ward or conservatee.

(c) A foreign guardian or conservator. *(Stats.1990, c. 79 (A.B. 759), § 14, operative July 1, 1991.)*

§ 2803. Petition; contents

The petition shall set forth all of the following:

(a) The name and address of:

(1) The foreign guardian or conservator, who may but need not be the guardian or conservator appointed in this state.

(2) The ward or conservatee.

(3) The guardian or conservator, so far as is known to the petitioner.

(b) The names, ages, and addresses, so far as they are known to the petitioner, of the spouse of the ward or the spouse or domestic partner of the conservatee and of relatives of the ward or conservatee within the second degree.

(c) A brief description of the character, condition, value, and location of the personal property sought to be transferred.

(d) A statement whether the foreign guardian or conservator has agreed to accept the transfer of the property. If the foreign guardian or conservator has so agreed, the acceptance shall be attached as an exhibit to the petition or otherwise filed with the court.

(e) A statement of the manner in which and by whom the foreign guardian or conservator was appointed.

(f) A general statement of the qualifications of the foreign guardian or conservator.

(g) The amount of bond, if any, of the foreign guardian or conservator.

(h) A general statement of the nature and value of the property of the ward or conservatee already under the management or control of the foreign guardian or conservator.

(i) The name of the court having jurisdiction of the foreign guardian or conservator or of the accounts of the foreign guardian or conservator or, if none, the court in which a proceeding may be had with respect to the guardianship or conservatorship if the property is transferred.

(j) Whether there is any pending civil action in this state against the guardian or conservator, the ward or conservatee, or the estate.

(k) A statement of the reasons for the transfer. *(Stats.1990, c. 79 (A.B.759), § 14, operative July 1, 1991. Amended by Stats.2001, c. 893 (A.B.25), § 47.)*

Cross References

Domestic partner, defined, see Probate Code § 37.
Trusts, judicial proceedings,
    Generally, see Probate Code § 1700 et seq.
    Transfer from another jurisdiction, see Probate Code § 17450 et seq.

§ 2804. Notice of hearing

At least 30 days before the hearing, the petitioner shall deliver pursuant to Section 1215 a notice of the time and place of the hearing and a copy of the petition to each person required to be listed in the petition at the address stated in the petition. *(Stats.1990, c. 79 (A.B.759), § 14, operative July 1, 1991. Amended by Stats.2017, c. 319 (A.B.976), § 54, eff. Jan. 1, 2018.)*

Cross References

Computation of time, see Code of Civil Procedure §§ 12 and 12a; Government Code § 6800 et seq.
Mailing, completion, see Probate Code § 1467.
Notice,
    Mailing, see Probate Code § 1215 et seq.
    Posting, see Probate Code § 1230.
    Proof of giving notice, see Probate Code § 1260 et seq.
    Special notice, see Probate Code § 1250 et seq.
    This code, generally, see Probate Code § 1200 et seq.
    This division, generally, see Probate Code § 1460 et seq.
Service of process,
    Generally, see Code of Civil Procedure § 413.10 et seq.
    Mail, see Code of Civil Procedure §§ 415.30, 1012 et seq.
    Personal delivery, see Code of Civil Procedure § 415.10.
    Proof of service, see Code of Civil Procedure § 417.10 et seq.
    Publication, see Code of Civil Procedure § 415.50.

§ 2805. Objections to petition

Any of the following may appear and file written objections to the petition:

(a) Any person required to be listed in the petition.

(b) Any creditor of the ward or conservatee or of the estate.

(c) The spouse of the ward or the spouse or domestic partner of the conservatee or any relative or friend of the ward or conservatee.

(d) Any other interested person. *(Stats.1990, c. 79 (A.B.759), § 14, operative July 1, 1991. Amended by Stats.2001, c. 893 (A.B.25), § 48.)*

Cross References

Domestic partner, defined, see Probate Code § 37.

Interested person, defined, see Probate Code § 1424.

Research References

Forms

West's California Code Forms, Probate § 278 Form 1, Disclaimer.

§ 2806. Order for transfer

The court may grant the petition and order the guardian or conservator to transfer some or all of the personal property of the estate to the foreign guardian or conservator if the court determines all of the following:

(a) The transfer will promote the best interests of the ward or conservatee and the estate.

(b) The substantial rights of creditors or claimants in this state will not be materially impaired by the transfer.

(c) The foreign guardian or conservator is qualified, willing, and able to administer the property to be transferred. *(Stats.1990, c. 79 (A.B.759), § 14, operative July 1, 1991.)*

Cross References

Appealable orders, see Probate Code § 1300 et seq.

§ 2807. Manner of transfer; terms and conditions

If a transfer is ordered, the court may direct the manner of transfer and impose such terms and conditions as may be just. *(Stats.1990, c. 79 (A.B.759), § 14, operative July 1, 1991.)*

§ 2808. Termination of guardianship or conservatorship

(a) If the court's order provides for the transfer of all of the property of the estate to the foreign guardian or conservator, the court, upon settlement of the final account, shall order the guardianship of the estate or the conservatorship of the estate terminated upon the filing with the clerk of the court of a receipt for the property executed by the foreign guardian or conservator.

(b) Unless notice is waived, a copy of the final account of the guardian or conservator and of the petition for discharge, together with a notice of the hearing, shall be delivered pursuant to Section 1215 at least 30 days before the date of the hearing to all persons required to be listed in the petition for transfer, including the foreign guardian or conservator. *(Stats.1990, c. 79 (A.B.759), § 14, operative July 1, 1991. Amended by Stats.2017, c. 319 (A.B.976), § 55, eff. Jan. 1, 2018.)*

Cross References

Appealable orders, see Probate Code § 1300 et seq.
Computation of time, see Code of Civil Procedure §§ 12 and 12a; Government Code § 6800 et seq.
Mailing, completion, see Probate Code § 1467.
Notice,
    Mailing, see Probate Code § 1215 et seq.
    Posting, see Probate Code § 1230.
    Proof of giving notice, see Probate Code § 1260 et seq.
    Special notice, see Probate Code § 1250 et seq.
    This code, generally, see Probate Code § 1200 et seq.
    This division, generally, see Probate Code § 1460 et seq.
    To directors, see Probate Code § 1461.
Service of process,
    Generally, see Code of Civil Procedure § 413.10 et seq.
    Mail, see Code of Civil Procedure §§ 415.30, 1012 et seq.
    Personal delivery, see Code of Civil Procedure § 415.10.
    Proof of service, see Code of Civil Procedure § 417.10 et seq.
    Publication, see Code of Civil Procedure § 415.50.

§ 2808

Termination of proceeding upon exhaustion of estate, see Probate Code § 2626.

Research References

Forms

2 California Transactions Forms--Family Law § 6:2, Governing Law.

CHAPTER 14. NOTIFICATION TO COURT BY INSTITUTIONS

Section
2890. Guardian or conservator taking possession or control of asset; filing of statement by institution; contents of statement.
2891. Affidavit; application of chapter; fee.
2892. Guardian or conservator changing name of account of safe-deposit box; filing of statement by financial institution; contents of statement.
2893. Affidavit; disclosure.

§ 2890. Guardian or conservator taking possession or control of asset; filing of statement by institution; contents of statement

(a) When a guardian or conservator, pursuant to letters of guardianship or conservatorship of the estate, takes possession or control of any asset of the ward or conservatee held by an institution, as defined in subdivision (c), the institution shall file with the court having jurisdiction of the guardianship or conservatorship a statement containing the following information:

(1) The name of the ward or conservatee.

(2) The name of the guardian or joint guardians or conservator or joint conservators.

(3) The court case number.

(4) The name of the institution.

(5) The address of the institution.

(6) The account number of the account, if any, in which the asset was held by the ward or conservatee.

(7) A description of the asset or assets held by the institution. If an asset is a life insurance policy or annuity, the description shall include the policy number, if available. If the asset is a security listed on a public exchange, the description shall include the name and reference number, if available.

(8) The value, if known, or the estimated value otherwise, of the asset on the date the letters were issued by the court to the guardian or conservator, to the extent this value is routinely provided in the statements from the institution to the owner.

(b) Taking possession or control of an asset includes, for purposes of this chapter, changing title to the asset, withdrawing all or any portion of the asset, or transferring all or any portion of an asset from the institution.

(c) For purposes of this chapter, "institution" means an insurance company, insurance broker, insurance agent, investment company, investment bank, securities broker-dealer, investment adviser, financial planner, financial adviser, or any other person who takes, holds, or controls an asset subject to a conservatorship or guardianship that is not a "financial institution" as defined in Section 2892. *(Added by Stats.2001, c. 563 (A.B.1286), § 7.)*

Cross References

Security, defined, see Probate Code § 70.

Research References

Forms

West's California Code Forms, Probate § 2890–2893 Comment.

West's California Judicial Council Forms GC–050, Notice of Taking Possession or Control of an Asset of Minor or Conservatee.
West's California Judicial Council Forms GC–150, Letters of Temporary Guardianship or Conservatorship.
West's California Judicial Council Forms GC–250, Letters of Guardianship.

§ 2891. Affidavit; application of chapter; fee

(a) The statement filed pursuant to Section 2890 shall be an affidavit by a person having authority to make the statement on behalf of the institution, as defined in Section 2890, and shall include that fact in the statement.

(b) If the affidavit and any accompanying information to be filed pursuant to this section also contains the ward or conservatee's social security number or any other personal information, including financial information regarding the ward or conservatee which would not be disclosed in an accounting, an inventory and appraisal, or any other nonconfidential pleading filed in the action, the information shall be kept confidential and subject to disclosure to any person only upon order of the court.

(c) This chapter does not apply to any trust arrangement described in subdivision (b) of Section 82 except paragraph (4) of that subdivision relating to assets held in Totten trust.

(d) No fee shall be charged by the court for the filing of the affidavit or related information as required by this section.

(e) The affidavit required by Section 2890 is not required to be filed in a proceeding more than once for each asset. However, all assets held by institutions may be listed in a single affidavit filed with the court.

(f) When a guardian or conservator takes possession or control of an asset in an institution, as defined in Section 2890, the institution may then file with the court the statement required by Section 2890 as to any or all other assets of the ward or conservatee held in the institution. *(Added by Stats.2001, c. 563 (A.B.1286), § 7.)*

Cross References

Affidavits, see Code of Civil Procedure § 2009 et seq.
Totten trust account, defined, see Probate Code § 80.

§ 2892. Guardian or conservator changing name of account of safe-deposit box; filing of statement by financial institution; contents of statement

(a) When a guardian or conservator, pursuant to letters of guardianship or conservatorship of the estate, opens or changes the name to an account or safe-deposit box in a financial institution, as defined in subdivision (b), the financial institution shall send to the court identified in the letters of guardianship or conservatorship a statement containing the following information:

(1) The name of the person with whom the account or safe-deposit box is opened or changed.

(2) The account number or reference number.

(3) The date the account or safe-deposit box was opened or changed ownership pursuant to letters of guardianship or conservatorship.

(4) If the asset is held in an account in a financial institution, the balance as of the date the account was opened or changed.

(5) If the asset is held in a safe-deposit box, and the financial institution has been given access to the safe-deposit box, a list of the contents, including, for example, currency, coins, jewelry, tableware, insurance policies or certificates, stock certificates, bonds, deeds, and wills.

(6) The name and address of the financial institution in which the asset is maintained.

(b) For purposes of this chapter, "financial institution" means a bank, trust, savings and loan association, savings bank, industrial bank, or credit union. *(Added by Stats.2001, c. 563 (A.B.1286), § 7. Amended by Stats.2003, c. 888 (A.B.394), § 7.)*

Cross References

Account defined, see Probate Code § 21
Governmental access to financial records, authorized acts, see Government Code § 7480.

Research References

Forms

West's California Judicial Council Forms GC–051, Notice of Opening or Changing a Guardianship or Conservatorship Account or Safe-Deposit Box.

§ 2893. Affidavit; disclosure

(a) The written statement provided pursuant to Section 2892 by the financial institution shall be in the form of an affidavit signed by an officer of the financial institution and the officer shall provide his or her name and title in the affidavit.

(b) The affidavit required by this section is subject to disclosure under the circumstances described in subdivision (*l*) of Section 7480 of the Government Code under the California Right to Financial Privacy Act (Chapter 20 (commencing with Section 7460) of Division 7 of Title 1 of the Government Code).

(c) This chapter does not apply to any trust arrangement described in subdivision (b) of Section 82 except paragraph (4) of that subdivision relating to assets held in a Totten trust.

(d) The affidavit described in Section 2892 is not required to be filed in a proceeding more than once for each asset. However, all assets held by the financial institution may be listed in a single affidavit filed with the court.

(e) If the affidavit and any accompanying information to be filed pursuant to this section also contains the ward or conservatee's social security number or any other personal information, including financial information regarding the ward or conservatee which would not be disclosed in an accounting, an inventory and appraisal, or other nonconfidential pleading filed in the action, the information shall be kept confidential and subject to disclosure to any person only upon order of the court. *(Added by Stats.2001, c. 563 (A.B.1286), § 7.)*

Cross References

Affidavits, see Code of Civil Procedure § 2009 et seq.
Governmental access to financial records, authorized acts, see Government Code § 7480.
Totten trust account, defined, see Probate Code § 80.

Research References

Forms

West's California Code Forms, Probate § 2890–2893 Comment.
West's California Judicial Council Forms GC–150, Letters of Temporary Guardianship or Conservatorship.
West's California Judicial Council Forms GC–250, Letters of Guardianship.

Part 5

PUBLIC GUARDIAN

CHAPTER 1. TAKING TEMPORARY POSSESSION OR CONTROL OF PROPERTY

Section
2900. Loss, injury, waste or misappropriation of property; control or possession of property; restraint of persons from disposal of property held in trust; removal of occupants; hearing.
2901. Certificate of authority; standardized form; effect; surrender of property; discharge of liability.

Section
2901.5. Restraint of disposal of real or personal property held in trust; written certificate of authority.
2902. Costs and fees.
2903. Application of chapter; continuing application of repealed provisions.

Application

Application to possession or control of property by a public guardian on or after July 1, 1989, see Probate Code § 2903.

§ 2900. Loss, injury, waste or misappropriation of property; control or possession of property; restraint of persons from disposal of property held in trust; removal of occupants; hearing

(a)(1) If the public guardian or public conservator determines that the requirements for appointment of a guardian or conservator of the estate are satisfied and the public guardian or public conservator intends to apply for appointment, the public guardian or public conservator may take possession or control of real or personal property of a person domiciled in the county that is subject to loss, injury, waste, or misappropriation, and, subject to subdivision (b), may deny use of, access to, or prohibit residency in, the real or personal property, by anyone who does not have a written rental agreement or other legal right to the use of, or access to, the property.

(2)(A) Except as provided in subparagraph (C), if the public guardian or public conservator determines that the requirements for appointment of a guardian or conservator of the estate are satisfied and the public guardian or public conservator intends to apply for appointment as the guardian or conservator of a person domiciled in the county, the public guardian or public conservator may restrain any person from transferring, encumbering, or in any way disposing of any real or personal property held in a trust, provided all of the following requirements are met:

(i) The real or personal property held in the trust is subject to loss, injury, waste, or misappropriation.

(ii) The proposed ward or conservatee is a settlor of the trust.

(iii) The proposed ward or conservatee has a beneficial interest in the trust to currently receive income or principal from the trust.

(iv) The proposed ward or conservatee holds a power to revoke the trust.

(B) During the period of any restraint under this paragraph, the property subject to the restraint shall continue to be retained as property of the trust pending termination of the restraint or further court order. The public guardian or public conservator shall provide notice of any action taken under this paragraph to all of the persons required to be noticed pursuant to Section 17203, to the extent the public guardian or public conservator has access to the trust documents or is otherwise able to determine the persons entitled to receive notice. Any settlor, trustee, or beneficiary may petition the court for relief from any action taken by the public guardian or public conservator under this paragraph.

(C) This paragraph shall not apply if a current trustee or cotrustee is a spouse of the proposed ward or conservatee and that spouse is also a settlor of the trust, unless the public guardian or public conservator determines that the real or personal property held in the trust is subject to substantial loss, injury, waste, or misappropriation.

(b) The authority provided to the public guardian and public conservator in subdivision (a) includes the authority to terminate immediately the occupancy of anyone living in the home of an intended ward or conservatee, other than the intended ward or conservatee, and the authority to remove any such occupant residing therein, subject to the following requirements:

§ 2900
PROBATE CODE

(1) The public guardian or public conservator shall first determine that the person whose occupancy is to be terminated has no written rental agreement or other legal right to occupancy, and has caused, contributed to, enabled, or threatened loss, injury, waste, or misappropriation of the home or its contents. In making this determination, the public guardian or public conservator shall contact the intended ward or conservatee and the occupant, advise them of the proposed removal and the grounds therefor, and consider whatever information they provide.

(2) At the time of the removal, the public guardian or public conservator shall advise the intended ward or conservatee and the occupant that a hearing will be held as provided in paragraph (3).

(3) The public guardian or public conservator shall file a petition regarding removal, showing the grounds therefor, to be set for hearing within 10 days of the filing of the petition and within 15 days of the removal. The person removed and the intended ward or conservatee shall be personally served with a notice of hearing and a copy of the petition at least five days prior to the hearing, subject to Part 2 (commencing with Section 1200) of Division 3. The right of the public guardian or public conservator to deny occupancy by the removed person to the premises shall terminate 15 days after removal, unless extended by the court at the hearing on the petition. The court shall not grant an extension unless the public guardian or public conservator has filed a petition for appointment as guardian or conservator of the estate.

(c) If the public guardian or public conservator takes possession of the residence of an intended ward or conservatee under this section, then for purposes of Section 602.3 of the Penal Code, the public guardian or public conservator shall be the owner's representative. *(Added by Stats.1992, c. 572 (S.B.1455), § 11. Amended by Stats. 2011, c. 370 (A.B.1288), § 1.)*

§ 2901. Certificate of authority; standardized form; effect; surrender of property; discharge of liability

(a) A public guardian who is authorized to take possession or control of property under this chapter may issue a written certification of that fact. The written certification is effective for 30 days after the date of issuance.

(b) The written recordable certification shall substantially comply with the following form:

"CERTIFICATE OF AUTHORITY

THIS IS AN OFFICIAL CERTIFICATE ENTITLING THE PUBLIC GUARDIAN TO TAKE POSSESSION OF ANY AND ALL PROPERTY BELONGING TO THE FOLLOWING INDIVIDUAL:

(Name of Individual) _____

This Certificate of Authority has been issued by the Public Guardian pursuant to and in compliance with Chapter 1 (commencing with Section 2900) of Part 5 of Division 4 of the California Probate Code. Under California law, this Certificate of Authority authorizes the Public Guardian to take possession or control of property belonging to the above-named individual.

SPECIAL NOTE TO FINANCIAL INSTITUTIONS:
State law requires that upon receiving a copy of this Certificate of Authority, financial institutions shall provide the public guardian with information concerning property held by the above-named individual and surrender the property to the Public Guardian if requested.

This Certificate of Authority shall only be valid when signed and dated by the Public Guardian or a deputy Public Guardian of the County of _____ and affixed with the official seal of the Public Guardian below.

This Certificate of Authority expires 30 days after the date of issuance.

Signature of Public Guardian:
Date:
Official Seal"

(c) The public guardian may record a copy of the written certification in any county in which is located real property of which the public guardian is authorized to take possession or control under this chapter.

(d) A financial institution or other person shall, without the necessity of inquiring into the truth of the written certification and without court order or letters being issued:

(1) Provide the public guardian information concerning property held in the sole name of the proposed ward or conservatee.

(2) Surrender to the public guardian property of the proposed ward or conservatee that is subject to loss, injury, waste, or misappropriation.

(e) Receipt of the written certification:

(1) Constitutes sufficient acquittance for providing information and for surrendering property of the proposed ward or conservatee.

(2) Fully discharges the financial institution or other person from any liability for any act or omission of the public guardian with respect to the property. *(Stats.1990, c. 79 (A.B.759), § 14, operative July 1, 1991. Amended by Stats.2001, c. 232 (A.B.1517), § 2; Stats.2011, c. 370 (A.B.1288), § 2.)*

§ 2901.5. Restraint of disposal of real or personal property held in trust; written certificate of authority

(a) A public guardian or public conservator, who is authorized to restrain any person from transferring, encumbering, or in any way disposing of any real or personal property held in a trust in accordance with paragraph (2) of subdivision (a) of Section 2900, may issue a written certification of that fact. The written certification is effective for 30 days after the date of issuance.

(b) The written recordable certification shall substantially comply with the following form:

"CERTIFICATE OF AUTHORITY

THIS IS AN OFFICIAL CERTIFICATE ENTITLING THE PUBLIC GUARDIAN/PUBLIC CONSERVATOR TO RESTRAIN ANY PERSON FROM TRANSFERRING, ENCUMBERING, OR IN ANY WAY DISPOSING OF ANY REAL OR PERSONAL PROPERTY HELD IN THE FOLLOWING TRUST:

(Name of Trust) _____

THE PUBLIC GUARDIAN/PUBLIC CONSERVATOR HAS DETERMINED THAT IT HAS AUTHORITY TO ISSUE THIS CERTIFICATE WITH RESPECT TO THE ABOVE-NAMED TRUST AND IN CONNECTION WITH PROCEEDINGS THAT

ARE OR WILL BE PENDING RELATED TO THE FOLLOWING INDIVIDUAL:

_____(Name of Individual)_____

This Certificate of Authority has been issued by the Public Guardian/Public Conservator pursuant to and in compliance with Chapter 1 (commencing with Section 2900) of Part 5 of Division 4 of the California Probate Code. Under California law, this Certificate of Authority authorizes the Public Guardian/Public Conservator to restrain any person from transferring, encumbering, or in any way disposing of any real or personal property held in the above-named trust.

SPECIAL NOTE TO FINANCIAL INSTITUTIONS:
State law requires that, upon receiving a copy of this Certificate of Authority, financial institutions shall provide the public guardian/public conservator with information concerning property held in the above-named trust and shall restrain any person from transferring, encumbering, or in any way disposing of any real or personal property held in the above-named trust.

This Certificate of Authority shall only be valid when signed and dated by the Public Guardian/Public Conservator or a deputy Public Guardian/Public Conservator of the County of ____ and affixed with the official seal of the Public Guardian/Public Conservator below.

This Certificate of Authority expires 30 days after the date of issuance.

Signature of Public Guardian/Public Conservator:
Date:
Official Seal"

(c) The public guardian or public conservator may record a copy of the written certification in any county in which is located real property held in a trust as to which the public guardian or public conservator has determined it has authority to issue the written certification.

(d) A financial institution or other person who is provided with the written certification by the public guardian or public conservator shall, without the necessity of inquiring into the truth of the written certification and without court order or letters being issued:

(1) Provide the public guardian or public conservator information concerning any real or personal property held in the trust identified in the written certification.

(2) Restrain any person from transferring, encumbering, or in any way disposing of any real or personal property, held in the trust identified in the written certification.

(e) Receipt of the written certification:

(1) Constitutes sufficient acquittance for providing information and for restraining any person from transferring, encumbering, or in any way disposing of any real or personal property held in the trust identified in the written certification.

(2) Fully discharges the financial institution or other person from any liability for any act or omission of the public guardian or public conservator with respect to the property. *(Added by Stats.2011, c. 370 (A.B.1288), § 3.)*

§ 2902. Costs and fees

A public guardian who takes possession or control of property pursuant to this chapter is entitled to reasonable costs incurred for the preservation of the property, together with reasonable compensation for services, in case of the subsequent appointment of another person as guardian or conservator of the estate. The costs and compensation are a proper and legal charge against the estate of the ward or conservatee. *(Stats.1990, c. 79 (A.B.759), § 14, operative July 1, 1991.)*

§ 2903. Application of chapter; continuing application of repealed provisions

This chapter applies only to possession or control of property by a public guardian on or after July 1, 1989. Possession or control of property by a public guardian before July 1, 1989, is governed by the applicable law in effect before July 1, 1989, notwithstanding its repeal by Chapter 1199 of the Statutes of 1988. *(Stats.1990, c. 79 (A.B.759), § 14, operative July 1, 1991.)*

CHAPTER 2. PREFILING INVESTIGATION BY PUBLIC GUARDIAN

Section
2910. Petition for appointment of public guardian as conservator; investigation; notice and service of process.
2911. Contents of order issued in response to petition.

§ 2910. Petition for appointment of public guardian as conservator; investigation; notice and service of process

(a) Upon a showing of probable cause to believe that a person is in substantial danger of abuse or neglect and needs a conservator of the person, the estate, or the person and estate for his or her own protection, the public guardian or the county's adult protective services agency may petition for either or both of the orders of the court provided in subdivision (b) in connection with his or her investigation to determine whether a petition for the appointment of the public guardian as conservator of the person, estate, or the person and estate of the person would be necessary or appropriate.

(b) The petition may request either or both of the following orders for the limited purposes of the investigation concerning a person:

(1) An order authorizing identified health care providers or organizations to provide private medical information about the person to the public guardian's authorized representatives.

(2) An order authorizing identified financial institutions or advisers, accountants, and others with financial information about the person to provide the information to the public guardian's authorized representatives.

(c) Notice of the hearing and a copy of the petition shall be served on the person who is the subject of the investigation in the manner and for the period required by Section 1460 or, on application of the public guardian contained in or accompanying the petition, on an expedited basis in the manner and for the period ordered by the court. The court may dispense with notice of the hearing only on a showing of facts demonstrating an immediate threat of substantial harm to the person if notice is given. *(Added by Stats.2007, c. 553 (A.B.1727), § 25.)*

§ 2911. Contents of order issued in response to petition

A court order issued in response to a public guardian's petition pursuant to Section 2910 shall do all of the following:

(a) Authorize health care providers to disclose a person's confidential medical information as permitted under California law, and also authorize disclosure of the information under federal medical privacy regulations enacted pursuant to the Health Insurance Portability and Accountability Act of 1996.

§ 2911 PROBATE CODE

(b) Direct the public guardian or the adult protective services agency to keep the information acquired under the order confidential, except as disclosed in a judicial proceeding or as required by law enforcement or an authorized regulatory agency.

(c) Direct the public guardian or the adult protective services agency to destroy all copies of written information obtained under the order or give them to the person who was the subject of the investigation if a conservatorship proceeding is not commenced within 60 days after the date of the order. The court may extend this time period as the court finds to be in the subject's best interest. *(Added by Stats.2007, c. 553 (A.B.1727), § 25.)*

CHAPTER 3. APPOINTMENT OF PUBLIC GUARDIAN

Section
2920. Application for appointment; court order; notice and hearing.
2921. Persons under jurisdiction of Department of State Hospitals or Department of Developmental Services; consent to application.
2922. Letters; bond and oath.
2923. Continuing education requirements.

§ 2920. Application for appointment; court order; notice and hearing

(a) If any person domiciled in the county requires a guardian or conservator and there is no one else who is qualified and willing to act and whose appointment as guardian or conservator would be in the best interests of the person, then either of the following shall apply:

(1) The public guardian shall apply for appointment as guardian or conservator of the person, the estate, or the person and estate, if there is an imminent threat to the person's health or safety or the person's estate.

(2) The public guardian may apply for appointment as guardian or conservator of the person, the estate, or the person and estate in all other cases.

(b) The public guardian shall apply for appointment as guardian or conservator of the person, the estate, or the person and estate, if the court so orders. The court may make an order under this subdivision on motion of an interested person or on the court's own motion in a pending proceeding or in a proceeding commenced for that purpose. The court shall order the public guardian to apply for appointment as guardian or conservator of the person, the estate, or the person and estate, on behalf of any person domiciled in the county who appears to require a guardian or conservator, if it appears that there is no one else who is qualified and willing to act, and if that appointment as guardian or conservator appears to be in the best interests of the person. However, if prior to the filing of the petition for appointment it is discovered that there is someone else who is qualified and willing to act as guardian or conservator, the public guardian shall be relieved of the duty under the order. The court shall not make an order under this subdivision except after notice to the public guardian for the period and in the manner provided for in Chapter 3 (commencing with Section 1460) of Part 1, consideration of the alternatives, and a determination by the court that the appointment is necessary. The notice and hearing under this subdivision may be combined with the notice and hearing required for appointment of a guardian or conservator.

(c) The public guardian shall begin an investigation within two business days of receiving a referral for conservatorship or guardianship. *(Stats.1990, c. 79 (A.B.759), § 14, operative July 1, 1991. Amended by Stats.2006, c. 493 (A.B.1363), § 32.)*

§ 2921. Persons under jurisdiction of Department of State Hospitals or Department of Developmental Services; consent to application

An application of the public guardian for guardianship or conservatorship of the person, the estate, or the person and estate, of a person who is under the jurisdiction of the State Department of State Hospitals or the State Department of Developmental Services shall not be granted without the written consent of the department having jurisdiction of the person. *(Stats.1990, c. 79 (A.B.759), § 14, operative July 1, 1991. Amended by Stats.2012, c. 440 (A.B.1488), § 50, eff. Sept. 22, 2012.)*

Cross References

Department of Developmental Services, see Welfare and Institutions Code § 4400 et seq.

§ 2922. Letters; bond and oath

If the public guardian is appointed as guardian or conservator:

(a) Letters shall be issued in the same manner and by the same proceedings as letters are issued to other persons. Letters may be issued to "the public guardian" of the county without naming the public guardian.

(b) The official bond and oath of the public guardian are in lieu of the guardian or conservator's bond and oath on the grant of letters. *(Stats.1990, c. 79 (A.B.759), § 14, operative July 1, 1991.)*

§ 2923. Continuing education requirements

On or before January 1, 2008, the public guardian shall comply with the continuing education requirements that are established by the California State Association of Public Administrators, Public Guardians, and Public Conservators. *(Added by Stats.2006, c. 493 (A.B.1363), § 33.)*

CHAPTER 4. ADMINISTRATION BY PUBLIC GUARDIAN

Section
2940. Funds; deposit or investment.
2941. Private attorneys; cost of employment.
2942. Payments from estate.
2943. Appraisal of inventory property; sale of residence.
2944. Liability for failure to take possession.

§ 2940. Funds; deposit or investment

All funds coming into the custody of the public guardian shall be deposited or invested in the same manner and subject to the same terms and conditions as deposit or investment by the public administrator of money in an estate pursuant to Article 3 (commencing with Section 7640) of Chapter 4 of Part 1 of Division 7. *(Stats.1990, c. 79 (A.B.759), § 14, operative July 1, 1991.)*

§ 2941. Private attorneys; cost of employment

The public guardian may, if necessary and in the public guardian's discretion, employ private attorneys where the cost of employment can be defrayed out of estate funds or where satisfactory pro bono or contingency fee arrangements can be made. *(Stats.1990, c. 79 (A.B.759), § 14, operative July 1, 1991.)*

§ 2942. Payments from estate

The public guardian shall be paid from the estate of the ward or conservatee for all of the following:

(a) Reasonable expenses incurred in the execution of the guardianship or conservatorship.

(b) Compensation for services of the public guardian and the attorney of the public guardian, and for the filing and processing services of the county clerk or the clerk of the superior court, in the amount the court determines is just and reasonable. In determining what constitutes just and reasonable compensation, the court shall, among other factors, take into consideration the actual costs of the services provided, the amount of the estate involved, the special value of services provided in relation to the estate, and whether the compensation requested might impose an economic hardship on the estate. Nothing in this section shall require a public guardian to base a request for compensation upon an hourly rate of service.

(c) An annual bond fee in the amount of twenty-five dollars ($25) plus one-fourth of 1 percent of the amount of an estate greater than ten thousand dollars ($10,000). The amount charged shall be deposited in the county treasury. This subdivision does not apply if the ward or conservatee is eligible for Social Security Supplemental Income benefits. *(Stats.1990, c. 79 (A.B.759), § 14, operative July 1, 1991. Amended by Stats.1994, c. 472 (A.B.2725), § 2; Stats.1998, c. 103 (S.B.1487), § 2; Stats.1999, c. 866 (A.B.1152), § 1.)*

§ 2943. Appraisal of inventory property; sale of residence

(a) Notwithstanding subdivision (c) of Section 2610, the property described in the inventory may be appraised by the public guardian and need not be appraised by a probate referee if the public guardian files with the inventory an appraisal showing that the estimated value of the property in the estate does not exceed the amount prescribed in Section 13100.

(b) If the conservator seeks authority pursuant to subdivision (b) of Section 2540 to sell the conservatee's personal residence, whether or not it is real property, or if the conservator seeks authority pursuant to Section 2590 to sell the conservatee's real property, valued in excess of ten thousand dollars ($10,000), or an item of personal property valued in excess of ten thousand dollars ($10,000) that is not a security sold pursuant to subdivision (a) of Section 2544, that property shall be appraised by a probate referee. *(Stats.1990, c. 79 (A.B.759), § 14, operative July 1, 1991. Amended by Stats.1996, c. 86 (A.B.2146), § 3.)*

§ 2944. Liability for failure to take possession

The public guardian is not liable for failing to take possession or control of property that is beyond the ability of the public guardian to possess or control. *(Stats.1990, c. 79 (A.B.759), § 14, operative July 1, 1991.)*

CHAPTER 5. FINANCIAL ABUSE OF MENTALLY IMPAIRED ELDERS

ARTICLE 1. GENERAL

Section
2950. Legislative intent; coordination with existing programs.
2951. Definitions.

§ 2950. Legislative intent; coordination with existing programs

(a) It is the intent of the Legislature to do all of the following:

(1) Reduce the incidence of financial abuse perpetrated against mentally impaired elder adults.

(2) Minimize monetary losses to mentally impaired elder adults as a result of financial abuse.

(3) Facilitate timely intervention by law enforcement, in collaboration with the public guardian, to effectively protect mentally impaired elder adult victims of financial abuse, and to recover their assets.

(b) Any peace officer or public guardian of a county that has both of the following, as determined by the public guardian of that county, may take the actions authorized by this chapter:

(1) The existence of sufficient law enforcement personnel with expertise in the assessment of competence.

(2) The existence of a law enforcement unit devoted to investigating elder financial abuse and the enforcement of laws applicable to elder abuse.

(c) This chapter shall be coordinated with existing mandated programs affecting financial abuse of mentally impaired elders that are administered by the adult protective services agency of the county. *(Added by Stats.2000, c. 813 (S.B.1742), § 1.)*

Cross References

Financial abuse defined for purposes of this Chapter, see Probate Code § 2951.

§ 2951. Definitions

The definitions contained in this section shall govern the construction of this chapter, unless the context requires otherwise.

(a) "Declaration" means a document that substantially complies with the requirements of Section 2954, and is signed by both a peace officer and a supervisor from the county's adult protective services agency and provided to the public guardian in accordance with subdivision (b) of Section 2952.

(b) "Elder person" means any person residing in this state, 65 years of age or older.

(c) "Financial abuse" means a situation described in Section 15610.30 of the Welfare and Institutions Code.

(d) "Financial abuse POST training" means an elder financial abuse training course certified by the Commission on Peace Officer Standards and Training.

(e) "Financial institution" means any bank, savings and loan, thrift, industrial loan company, credit union, or any branch of any of these institutions doing business in the state, as defined by provisions of the Financial Code.

(f) "Peace officer" means a sheriff, deputy sheriff, municipal police officer, or a peace officer authorized under subdivision (b) of Section 830.1 of the Penal Code, duly sworn under the requirements of state law, who satisfies any of the following requirements:

(1) The sheriff, deputy sheriff, municipal police officer, or peace officer authorized under subdivision (b) of Section 830.1 of the Penal Code has completed or participated as a lecturer in a financial abuse POST training program within the last 36 months. The completion of the course may be satisfied by telecourse, video training tape, or other instruction. The training shall, at a minimum, address relevant elder abuse laws, recognition of financial abuse and fraud, assessment of mental competence in accordance with the standards set forth in Part 17 (commencing with Section 810) of the Probate Code, reporting requirements and procedures for the investigation of financial abuse and related crimes, including neglect, and civil and criminal procedures for the protection of victims. The course may be presented as part of a training program that includes other subjects or courses.

(2) The sheriff, deputy sheriff, municipal police officer, or peace officer authorized under subdivision (b) of Section 830.1 of the Penal Code, has consulted with a sheriff, deputy sheriff, municipal police officer, or peace officer authorized under subdivision (b) of Section 830.1 of the Penal Code, who satisfies the requirements of paragraph (1) concerning the declaration defined in subdivision (a) and obtained the signature of that sheriff, deputy sheriff, municipal police officer, or peace officer authorized under subdivision (b) of Section 830.1 of the Penal Code on a declaration that substantially complies with the form described in Section 2954.

(g) "Property" means all personal property and real property of every kind belonging to, or alleged to belong to, the elder. *(Added by Stats.2000, c. 813 (S.B.1742), § 1.)*

ARTICLE 2. ESTATE PROTECTION

Section
2952. Issuance of declaration by peace officer; certificate of authority; standardized form; authority and responsibility; liabilities for actions under certificate; expiration; investigation by county adult protective services agency.
2953. Petition for costs and fees; duties of public guardian; petition for order to quash certification.
2954. Form of declaration.
2955. Powers of public guardian to undertake other proceedings.

§ 2952. Issuance of declaration by peace officer; certificate of authority; standardized form; authority and responsibility; liabilities for actions under certificate; expiration; investigation by county adult protective services agency

(a) A peace officer may issue a declaration, as provided in Section 2954, concerning an elder person if all of the following conditions are satisfied:

(1) There is probable cause to believe that the elder person is substantially unable to manage his or her financial resources or to resist fraud or undue influence.

(2) There exists a significant danger that the elder person will lose all or a portion of his or her property as a result of fraud or misrepresentations or the mental incapacity of the elder person.

(3) There is probable cause to believe that a crime is being committed against the elder person.

(4) The crime is connected to the inability of the elder person to manage his or her financial resources or to resist fraud or undue influence, and that inability is the result of deficits in the elder person's mental functions.

(5) The peace officer has consulted with an individual qualified to perform a mental status examination.

(b) If the requirements of subdivision (a) are satisfied, the peace officer may provide a signed declaration to the public guardian of the county. The declaration provided by the peace officer under this subdivision shall be signed by both the peace officer and a supervisor from the county's adult protective services agency. The declaration shall be transmitted to the public guardian within 24 hours of its being signed, and may be transmitted by facsimile.

(c)(1) Upon receiving a signed declaration from a peace officer, the public guardian is authorized to rely on the information contained in the declaration to take immediate possession or control of any real or personal property belonging to the elder person referred to in the declaration, including any property that is held jointly between the elder person and a third party that is subject to loss, injury, waste, or misappropriation, and may issue a written recordable certification of that fact pursuant to this section. The written recordable certification shall substantially comply with the following form:

"CERTIFICATE OF AUTHORITY

THIS IS AN OFFICIAL CERTIFICATE ENTITLING THE PUBLIC GUARDIAN TO TAKE POSSESSION OF ANY AND ALL PROPERTY BELONGING TO THE FOLLOWING INDIVIDUAL:

(Name of Victim) _____

This Certificate of Authority has been issued by the Public Guardian pursuant to and in compliance with the Financial Abuse of Mentally Impaired Elders statute, Chapter 4 (commencing with Section 2950) of Part 5 of Division 4 of the California Probate Code. Under California law, this Certificate of Authority authorizes the Public Guardian to take possession or control of property belonging to the above-named individual.

SPECIAL NOTE TO FINANCIAL INSTITUTIONS:
State law requires that upon receiving a copy of this Certificate of Authority, financial institutions shall provide the public guardian with information concerning property held by the above-named individual and surrender the property to the Public Guardian if requested.

This Certificate of Authority shall only be valid when signed and dated by the Public Guardian or a deputy Public Guardian of the County of _____ and affixed with the official seal of the Public Guardian below.

Signature of Public Guardian:
Date:
Official Seal"

(2) The mere issuance of the declaration provided by this section shall not require the public guardian to take possession or control of property and shall not require the public guardian to make a determination that the requirements for the appointment of a conservator are satisfied.

(3) The authority provided to the public guardian in paragraph (1) includes the authority to deny use of, access to, or prohibit residency in the home of the elder, by anyone who does not have a written rental agreement or other legal right to the use of, or access to, the residence, and, subject to the requirements of subdivision (b) of Section 2900, the authority to terminate the occupancy of anyone living in the home of the elder person, and the authority to remove that occupant residing therein.

(4) The public guardian shall serve, or cause to be served, a copy of the certification issued pursuant to this section on the elder person by mail within 24 hours of the execution of the certification, or as soon thereafter as is practical, in the manner provided in Chapter 4 (commencing with Section 413.10) of Title 5 of Part 2 of the Code of Civil Procedure.

(5) Receipt of a certification issued under this section constitutes sufficient acquittance to financial institutions and others in possession of an elder person's property to provide information and surrender property of the elder person to the public guardian. Any financial institution or other person who provides information or surrenders property pursuant to this section shall be discharged from any liability for any act or omission of the public guardian with respect to the property.

(6) A public guardian acting in good faith is not liable when taking possession or control of property pursuant to this section.

(7) A certification issued pursuant to this section is valid for 15 days after the date of issuance. Upon ex parte petition to the superior court, the public guardian may seek additional 15-day certifications. The court shall grant that petition only if it determines that the additional certification is necessary to protect the elder from financial abuse and the elder's property from loss, injury, waste, or misappropriation.

(d)(1) If the public guardian takes possession of an elder person's property pursuant to this section, the public guardian shall attempt to find agents pursuant to the use of durable powers of attorney or successor trustees nominated in trust instruments, or other persons having legal authority under existing legal instruments, to manage the elder person's estate.

(2) If the public guardian is unable to find any appropriate person to manage the elder person's estate pursuant to paragraph (1), the public guardian shall attempt to find appropriate family members willing to manage the elder person's estate. If no documents exist appointing appropriate fiduciaries, the public guardian shall follow the priorities set forth in Article 2 (commencing with Section 1810) of Chapter 1 of Part 3.

(3) The public guardian shall take the steps described in paragraphs (1) and (2) within 15 days of taking possession of an elder person's property pursuant to this section.

(e) Nothing in this section prevents the county's adult protective services agency from conducting an investigation regarding the elder person named in the declaration and providing appropriate services, in coordination with any actions taken with the public guardian under this section or an investigation conducted by law enforcement regarding the elder person. *(Added by Stats.2000, c. 813 (S.B.1742), § 1. Amended by Stats.2001, c. 232 (A.B.1517), § 3.)*

Cross References

Declaration defined for purposes of this Chapter, see Probate Code § 2951.
Elder person defined for purposes of this Chapter, see Probate Code § 2951.
Financial abuse defined for purposes of this Chapter, see Probate Code § 2951.
Peace officer defined for purposes of this Chapter, see Probate Code § 2951.
Property defined for purposes of this Chapter, see Probate Code § 2951.

§ 2953. Petition for costs and fees; duties of public guardian; petition for order to quash certification

(a)(1) A public guardian who has taken possession or control of the property of an elder person pursuant to this chapter is entitled to petition a court of competent jurisdiction for the reasonable costs incurred by the public guardian for the protection of the person or the property, together with reasonable fees for services, including, but not limited to, reasonable attorneys' fees. These fees shall be payable from the estate of the elder person if the person is not deemed competent by the court and if any of the following apply:

(A) The public guardian or someone else is appointed as the temporary or general conservator of the estate.

(B) An attorney-in-fact, under a durable power of attorney, or a trustee, takes steps, or is notified of the need to take steps, to protect the estate of the elder person.

(C) An action is brought against the alleged financial abuser by the elder person, his or her conservator, a trustee, a fiduciary, or a successor in interest of the elder person, arising from a harm that the public guardian taking charge was intended to prevent or minimize.

(2) Any costs incurred by the public guardian pursuant to paragraph (1) shall be compensable as provided in Section 2902. Fees collected by the public guardian pursuant to this chapter shall be used for the activities described in this chapter.

(b) When a public guardian has taken possession or control of the property of an elder person pursuant to this chapter, the public guardian shall exercise reasonable care to ensure that the reasonable living expenses and legitimate debts of the elder person are addressed as well as is practical under the circumstances.

(c) Any person identified as a victim in a declaration described in Section 2954 may bring an ex parte petition in the superior court for an order quashing the certification issued by the public guardian as provided in subdivision (c) of Section 2952.

(1) Upon request by the petitioner, the court may defer filing fees related to the petition, and order the public guardian to authorize the release of funds from a financial institution to reimburse the petitioner the filing fees from assets belonging to the petitioner, but shall waive filing fees if the petitioner meets the standards of eligibility established by subparagraph (A) or (B) of paragraph (6) of subdivision (a) of Section 68511.3 of the Government Code for the waiver of a filing fee.

(2) The court shall quash the certification if the court determines that there is insufficient evidence to justify the imposition on the alleged victim's civil liberties caused by the certification.

(3) If the court determines that there is sufficient evidence to justify the imposition on the alleged victim's civil liberties caused by the certification, the court may, in its discretion, do one or more of the following:

(A) Order disbursements from the alleged victim's assets, as are reasonably needed to address the alleged victim's needs.

(B) Appoint a temporary conservator of the alleged victim's estate, where the facts before the court would be sufficient for the appointment of a temporary conservator under Section 2250.

(C) Deny the petition.

(D) Award reasonable attorney's fees to the respondent's attorney from the victim's estate. *(Added by Stats.2000, c. 813 (S.B.1742), § 1. Amended by Stats.2001, c. 232 (A.B.1517), § 4.)*

Cross References

Declaration defined for purposes of this Chapter, see Probate Code § 2951.
Elder person defined for purposes of this Chapter, see Probate Code § 2951.
Peace officer defined for purposes of this Chapter, see Probate Code § 2951.
Property defined for purposes of this Chapter, see Probate Code § 2951.

§ 2954. Form of declaration

A declaration issued by a peace officer under this chapter shall not be valid unless it substantially complies with the following form:

DECLARATION

PRINT OR TYPE

1. My name is: _____
   My badge number is: _____
   My office address and telephone number are:
   _____
   _____

2. I am a duly sworn peace officer presently employed by _____, in the County of _____, in the State of California.

3. On _____ (date) I personally interviewed _____ (victim) at _____ a.m./p.m. at _____ (address). The victim resides at _____ (address, telephone number, and name of facility, if applicable).

4. There is probable cause to believe that:
   (a) _____ (Victim) is substantially unable to manage his or her financial resources or to resist fraud or undue influence, and
   (b) There exists a significant danger the victim will lose all or a portion of his or her property as a result of fraud or misrepresentations or the mental incapacity of the victim, and
   (c) There is probable cause to believe that a crime is being committed against the victim, and
   (d) The crime is connected to the victim's inability to manage his or her financial resources or to resist fraud or undue influence, and
   (e) The victim suffers from that inability as a result of deficits in one or more of the following mental functions:

INSTRUCTIONS TO PEACE OFFICER: CHECK ALL BOXES THAT APPLY:

[A] ALERTNESS AND ATTENTION
   ☐ 1. Levels of arousal. (Lethargic, responds only to vigorous and persistent stimulation, stupor.)
   ☐ 2. Orientation. Person _____ Time _____ (day, date, month, season, year), Place _____ (address, town, state), Situation _____ (why am I here?).
   ☐ 3. Ability to attend and concentrate. (Give detailed answers from memory, mental ability required to thread a needle.)

§ 2954   PROBATE CODE

[B] **INFORMATION PROCESSING**
Ability to:
☐ 1. Remember, i.e., short- and long-term memory, immediate recall. (Deficits reflected by: forgets question before answering, cannot recall names, relatives, past presidents, events of past 24 hours.)
☐ 2. Understand and communicate either verbally or otherwise. (Deficits reflected by: inability to comprehend questions, follow instructions, use words correctly or name objects; nonsense words.)
☐ 3. Recognize familiar objects and persons. (Deficits reflected by: inability to recognize familiar faces, objects, etc.)
☐ 4. Understand and appreciate quantities. (Perform simple calculations.)
☐ 5. Reason using abstract concepts. (Grasp abstract aspects of his or her situation; interpret idiomatic expressions or proverbs.)
☐ 6. Plan, organize, and carry out actions (assuming physical ability) in one's own rational self-interest. (Break complex tasks down into simple steps and carry them out.)
☐ 7. Reason logically.

[C] **THOUGHT DISORDERS**
☐ 1. Severely disorganized thinking. (Rambling, nonsensical, incoherent, or nonlinear thinking.)
☐ 2. Hallucinations. (Auditory, visual, olfactory.)
☐ 3. Delusions. (Demonstrably false belief maintained without or against reason or evidence.)
☐ 4. Uncontrollable or intrusive thoughts. (Unwanted compulsive thoughts, compulsive behavior.)

[D] **ABILITY TO MODULATE MOOD AND AFFECT**
Pervasive and persistent or recurrent emotional state which appears severely inappropriate in degree to the patient's circumstances. Encircle the inappropriate mood(s):

Anger	Euphoria	Helplessness
Anxiety	Depression	Apathy
Fear	Hopelessness	Indifference
Panic	Despair	

5. The property at risk is identified as, but not limited to, the following:
Bank account located at: _____
(name, telephone number, and address of the bank branch)
Account number(s): _____
Securities/other funds located at: _____
(name, telephone number, and address of financial institution)
Account number(s): _____
Real property located at: _____
(address)
Automobile described as: _____
(make, model/color)
_____
(license plate number and state)
Other property described as: _____
Other property located at: _____
6. A criminal investigation will ☐ will not ☐ be commenced against: _____
(name, address, and telephone number)
for alleged financial abuse.

BLOCKS 1, 2, AND 3 MUST BE CHECKED IN ORDER FOR THIS DECLARATION TO BE VALID:
☐ 1. I am a peace officer in the county identified above.
☐ 2. I have consulted concerning this case with a supervisor in the county's adult protective services agency who has signed below, indicating that he or she concurs that, based on the information I provided to him or her, or based on information he or she obtained independently, this declaration is warranted under the circumstances.
☐ 3. I have consulted concerning this case with an individual qualified to perform a mental status examination.

_____
Signature of Declarant Peace Officer

_____
Date

_____
Signature of Concurring Adult Protective Services Supervisor

(Added by Stats.2000, c. 813 (S.B.1742), § 1.)

Cross References

Declaration defined for purposes of this Chapter, see Probate Code § 2951.
Financial abuse defined for purposes of this Chapter, see Probate Code § 2951.
Peace officer defined for purposes of this Chapter, see Probate Code § 2951.
Property defined for purposes of this Chapter, see Probate Code § 2951.

§ 2955. Powers of public guardian to undertake other proceedings

Nothing in this chapter shall prohibit or restrict a public guardian from undertaking any other proceeding authorized by law. (Added by Stats.2000, c. 813 (S.B.1742), § 1.)

Part 6

MANAGEMENT OR DISPOSITION OF COMMUNITY PROPERTY WHERE SPOUSE LACKS LEGAL CAPACITY

Cross References

Management and control of community property, one or both spouses having conservatory of estate or lacking legal capacity, see Family Code § 1103.

CHAPTER 1. DEFINITIONS AND GENERAL PROVISIONS

ARTICLE 1. DEFINITIONS

Section
3000. Application of definitions.
3002. Community property.
3004. Conservator.
3006. Conservatorship estate.
3008. Conservatorship proceeding.
3012. Legal capacity with respect to community property.

1052

§ 3000. Application of definitions

Unless the provision or context otherwise requires, the definitions contained in this article govern the construction of this part. (Stats.1990, c. 79 (A.B.759), § 14, operative July 1, 1991.)

Cross References

Application of chapter regarding powers and duties of guardians or conservators of the estate, see Probate Code § 2407.

Research References

Forms

7PT1 Am. Jur. Pl. & Pr. Forms Community Property § 77, Statutory References.
7PT1 Am. Jur. Pl. & Pr. Forms Community Property § 84, Petition or Application—By Spouse of Incompetent—To Sell Community Property to Pay for Care—No Guardian Appointed.
West's California Code Forms, Probate § 1820 Form 1, Attachment Requesting Special Orders Regarding a Major Neurocognitive Disorder.

§ 3002. Community property

"Community property" means community real property and community personal property, including, but not limited to, a community property business that is or was under the primary management and control of one of the spouses. (Stats.1990, c. 79 (A.B.759), § 14, operative July 1, 1991. Amended by Stats.1992, c. 163 (A.B.2641), § 125, operative Jan. 1, 1994; Stats.1996, c. 877 (A.B.1467), § 1.)

Cross References

Community property business under the sole management and control of one of the spouses, see Family Code § 1100.

§ 3004. Conservator

"Conservator" means conservator of the estate, or limited conservator of the estate to the extent that the powers and duties of the limited conservator are specifically and expressly provided by the order appointing the limited conservator, and includes the guardian of the estate of a married minor. (Stats.1990, c. 79 (A.B.759), § 14, operative July 1, 1991.)

Cross References

Limited conservator, appointment, see Probate Code §§ 1801, 1828.5.
Order appointing limited conservator, contents, see Probate Code § 1830.

§ 3006. Conservatorship estate

"Conservatorship estate" includes the guardianship estate of a married minor. (Stats.1990, c. 79 (A.B.759), § 14, operative July 1, 1991.)

§ 3008. Conservatorship proceeding

"Conservatorship proceeding" means conservatorship of the estate proceeding and includes a guardianship of the estate proceeding of a married minor. (Stats.1990, c. 79 (A.B.759), § 14, operative July 1, 1991.)

§ 3012. Legal capacity with respect to community property

(a) Unless the spouse lacks legal capacity under the applicable standard prescribed in subdivision (b), a spouse has legal capacity to:

(1) Manage and control community property, including legal capacity to dispose of community property.

(2) Join in or consent to a transaction involving community property.

(b) A spouse lacks legal capacity to:

(1) Manage and control, including legal capacity to dispose of, community property if the spouse is substantially unable to manage or control the community property.

(2) Join in or consent to a transaction involving community property if the spouse does not have legal capacity for the particular transaction measured by principles of law otherwise applicable to the particular transaction.

(3) Do any act, or engage in any activity, described in paragraph (1) or (2) if the spouse has a conservator.

(c) Nothing in this section shall be construed to deny a spouse, whether or not lacking legal capacity, any of the following:

(1) The right to control an allowance provided under Section 2421.

(2) The right to control wages or salary to the extent provided in Section 2601.

(3) The right to make a will.

(4) The right to enter into transactions to the extent reasonable to provide the necessities of life to the spouse, the other spouse, and the minor children of the spouses. (Stats.1990, c. 79 (A.B.759), § 14, operative July 1, 1991.)

Cross References

Community property defined for purposes of this Part, see Probate Code § 3002.
Conservator defined for purposes of this Part, see Probate Code § 3004.
Legal capacity of conservatee for other purposes, see Probate Code § 1870 et seq.

Research References

Forms

West's California Code Forms, Probate § 3051(c) Form 1, Consent to Inclusion of Community Property in Conservatorship Estate.
West's California Code Forms, Probate § 3121 Form 1, Petition for Order Authorizing Proposed Transaction and Joinder of Conservator.

ARTICLE 2. GENERAL PROVISIONS

Section
3020. Preservation of community property interests.
3023. Determination of character of property.

§ 3020. Preservation of community property interests

(a) The proceeds, rents, issues, and profits of community property dealt with or disposed of under this division, and any property taken in exchange for the community property or acquired with the proceeds, are community property.

(b) Except as provided in this part for the management, control, and disposition of community property, nothing in this division alters the rights of the spouses in community property or in the proceeds, rents, issues, or profits of community property. (Stats.1990, c. 79 (A.B.759), § 14, operative July 1, 1991.)

Cross References

Community property defined for purposes of this Part, see Probate Code § 3002.
Management, control, and disposition of community property, see Probate Code § 3051.

§ 3023. Determination of character of property

(a) Except as provided in subdivisions (b) and (c), where one or both of the spouses has a conservator, the court in which any of the conservatorship proceedings is pending may hear and determine whether property is community property or the separate property of either spouse when the issue is raised in any proceeding under this division.

(b) Any person having or claiming title to or an interest in the property, at or prior to the hearing on the issue, may object to the hearing if the court is not the proper court under any other provision of law for the trial of an action to determine the issue. If the objection is established, the court shall not hear and determine the issue.

(c) Except as provided in subdivision (d), if a civil action is pending with respect to the issue and jurisdiction has been obtained in the court in which the civil action is pending, upon request of any party to the civil action, the court shall abate the hearing until the conclusion of the civil action.

(d) The court need not abate the hearing if the court determines that the civil action was filed for the purpose of delay. *(Stats.1990, c. 79 (A.B.759), § 14, operative July 1, 1991.)*

Cross References

Community property defined for purposes of this Part, see Probate Code § 3002.
Conservator defined for purposes of this Part, see Probate Code § 3004.
Conservatorship proceeding defined for purposes of this Part, see Probate Code § 3008.
Nature of property in proceeding for particular transaction, determination, see Probate Code § 3101.
Title to property of decedent, see Probate Code § 850.

CHAPTER 2. MANAGEMENT, CONTROL, AND DISPOSITION

ARTICLE 1. MANAGEMENT, CONTROL, AND DISPOSITION GENERALLY

Section
3051. Community property.
3054. Authority of court.
3055. Effect on consent of death or subsequent lack of legal capacity.
3056. Manner of management, control and disposition of property or a part of conservatorship estate.
3057. Protection of rights of spouse lacking legal capacity.

§ 3051. Community property

(a) Subject to Section 3071, the right of a spouse to manage and control community property, including the right to dispose of community property, is not affected by the lack or alleged lack of legal capacity of the other spouse.

(b) Except as provided in subdivision (c), if one spouse has legal capacity and the other has a conservator:

(1) The spouse who has legal capacity has the exclusive management and control of the community property including, subject to Section 3071, the exclusive power to dispose of the community property.

(2) The community property is not part of the conservatorship estate.

(c) If one spouse has legal capacity and the other has a conservator, the spouse having legal capacity may consent, by a writing filed in the proceeding, that all or part of the community property be included in and, subject to Section 3071, be managed, controlled, and disposed of as a part of the conservatorship estate.

(d) Except as provided in subdivision (e), if both spouses have conservators, an undivided one-half interest in the community property shall be included in and, subject to Section 3071, be managed, controlled, and disposed of as a part of the conservatorship estate of each spouse.

(e) If both spouses have conservators, when authorized by order of the court in which any of the conservatorship proceedings is pending, the conservators may agree in writing that all or specific parts of the community property shall be included in the conservatorship estate of one or the other of the spouses and, subject to Section 3071, be managed, controlled, and disposed of as a part of the conservatorship estate of that spouse. *(Stats.1990, c. 79 (A.B.759), § 14, operative July 1, 1991.)*

Cross References

Community property, succession, see Probate Code § 100 et seq.
Community property defined for purposes of this Part, see Probate Code § 3002.
Community property interests, extent to which affected, see Probate Code § 3020.
Conservator defined for purposes of this Part, see Probate Code § 3004.
Conservatorship estate defined for purposes of this Part, see Probate Code § 3006.
Conservatorship proceeding defined for purposes of this Part, see Probate Code § 3008.
Determination whether property community or separate, see Probate Code § 3023.
Duty of good faith in managing and controlling property, see Family Code § 1100.
Legal capacity of spouse, see Probate Code § 3012.
Protection of rights of spouse lacking legal capacity, see Probate Code § 3057.

Research References

Forms

2 California Transactions Forms--Estate Planning § 8:9, Purpose; Alternatives to Durable Powers of Attorney for Asset Management.
West's California Code Forms, Probate § 3051(c) Form 1, Consent to Inclusion of Community Property in Conservatorship Estate.
West's California Code Forms, Probate § 3080 Form 1, Petition for Support; for Injunctive Orders; for Determination of the Character of Property; for an Accounting; for Employment of Counsel; and for Attorney Fees and Costs.

§ 3054. Authority of court

When community property is included or proposed to be included in the conservatorship estate of a spouse, the court in which the conservatorship proceeding is pending, upon its own motion or upon petition of a spouse having legal capacity or the conservator of either spouse and upon such notice to such persons as the court prescribes, may do any of the following:

(a) Determine that the inclusion of some or all of the community property that is proposed to be included in the conservatorship estate would not be in the best interest of the spouses or their estates and order that such property not be included.

(b) Permit revocation of a written consent for inclusion of property in the conservatorship estate, with or without terms or conditions.

(c) Determine that the continued inclusion of some or all of the community property in the conservatorship estate is not in the best interest of the spouses or their estates and order that the inclusion of such property in the conservatorship estate be terminated, with or without terms or conditions.

(d) Make such other orders as may be appropriate for the orderly administration of the conservatorship estate or to protect the interests of the spouses. *(Stats.1990, c. 79 (A.B.759), § 14, operative July 1, 1991.)*

Cross References

Community property defined for purposes of this Part, see Probate Code § 3002.
Community property interests, extent to which affected, see Probate Code § 3020.
Conservator defined for purposes of this Part, see Probate Code § 3004.
Conservatorship estate defined for purposes of this Part, see Probate Code § 3006.
Conservatorship proceeding defined for purposes of this Part, see Probate Code § 3008.
Determination whether property is community or separate, see Probate Code § 3023.

Legal capacity defined, see Probate Code § 3012.

§ 3055. Effect on consent of death or subsequent lack of legal capacity

(a) If consent is given under this article that community property be included in the conservatorship estate of a spouse, the death of either spouse terminates the consent.

(b) If a spouse consents under this article that community property be included in the conservatorship estate of the other spouse:

(1) Subject to paragraph (2), the subsequent lack of legal capacity of the spouse giving the consent has no effect on the inclusion of the property in the conservatorship estate of the other spouse.

(2) The appointment of a conservator for the spouse giving the consent terminates the consent. *(Stats.1990, c. 79 (A.B.759), § 14, operative July 1, 1991.)*

Cross References

Community property defined for purposes of this Part, see Probate Code § 3002.
Conservator defined for purposes of this Part, see Probate Code § 3004.
Conservatorship estate defined for purposes of this Part, see Probate Code § 3006.
Legal capacity defined, see Probate Code § 3012.

§ 3056. Manner of management, control and disposition of property or a part of conservatorship estate

Except as otherwise provided in this part and subject to Section 3071, when community property is included in a conservatorship estate under this article for the purpose of management, control, and disposition, the conservator has the same powers and duties with respect to such property as the conservator has with respect to other property of the conservatorship estate. *(Stats.1990, c. 79 (A.B.759), § 14, operative July 1, 1991.)*

Cross References

Community property defined for purposes of this Part, see Probate Code § 3002.
Conservator defined for purposes of this Part, see Probate Code § 3004.
Conservatorship estate defined for purposes of this Part, see Probate Code § 3006.

§ 3057. Protection of rights of spouse lacking legal capacity

(a) Where a spouse lacks legal capacity and does not have a conservator, any interested person who has knowledge or reason to believe that the rights of such spouse in the community property are being prejudiced may bring an action on behalf of such spouse to enforce the duty imposed by Sections 721 and 1100 of the Family Code with respect to the management and control of the community property and to obtain such relief as may be appropriate.

(b) If one spouse has a conservator and the other spouse is managing or controlling community property, the conservator has the duty to keep reasonably informed concerning the management and control, including the disposition, of the community property. If the conservator has knowledge or reason to believe that the rights of the conservatee in the community property are being prejudiced, the conservator may bring an action on behalf of the conservatee to enforce the duty imposed by Sections 721 and 1100 of the Family Code with respect to the management and control of the community property and to obtain such relief as may be appropriate. *(Stats. 1990, c. 79 (A.B.759), § 14, operative July 1, 1991. Amended by Stats.1992, c. 163 (A.B.2641), § 126, operative Jan. 1, 1994.)*

Cross References

Community property defined for purposes of this Part, see Probate Code § 3002.
Conservator defined for purposes of this Part, see Probate Code § 3004.

Definitions,
   Interested person, see Probate Code § 1424.
   Legal capacity, see Probate Code § 3012.
Duty of good faith in managing and controlling community property, see Family Code § 1100.

ARTICLE 2. SUBSTITUTE FOR JOINDER OR CONSENT REQUIREMENTS

Section
3070. Satisfaction or requirements of this article; effect on other statutes.
3071. Satisfaction of joinder or consent requirements.
3072. Joinder or consent by conservator; authority; court order.
3073. Manner of joinder or consent.
3074. Good faith purchaser or encumbrancer for value.

§ 3070. Satisfaction or requirements of this article; effect on other statutes

If the requirements of this article are satisfied with respect to a transaction described in Section 3071, the transaction is deemed to satisfy the joinder or consent requirements of the statute referred to in that section. *(Stats.1990, c. 79 (A.B.759), § 14, operative July 1, 1991.)*

§ 3071. Satisfaction of joinder or consent requirements

(a) In case of a transaction for which the joinder or consent of both spouses is required by Section 1100 or 1102 of the Family Code or by any other statute, if one or both spouses lacks legal capacity for the transaction, the requirement of joinder or consent shall be satisfied as provided in this section.

(b) Where one spouse has legal capacity for the transaction and the other spouse has a conservator, the requirement of joinder or consent is satisfied if both of the following are obtained:

(1) The joinder or consent of the spouse having legal capacity.

(2) The joinder or consent of the conservator of the other spouse given in compliance with Section 3072.

(c) Where both spouses have conservators, the joinder or consent requirement is satisfied by the joinder or consent of each such conservator given in compliance with Section 3072.

(d) In any case, the requirement of joinder or consent is satisfied if the transaction is authorized by an order of court obtained in a proceeding pursuant to Chapter 3 (commencing with Section 3100). *(Stats.1990, c. 79 (A.B.759), § 14, operative July 1, 1991. Amended by Stats.1992, c. 163 (A.B.2641), § 127, operative Jan. 1, 1994.)*

Cross References

Community property, succession, see Probate Code § 100 et seq.
Conservator defined for purposes of this Part, see Probate Code § 3004.
Legal capacity, see Probate Code § 3012.
Management, control, and disposition of community property, see Probate Code § 3051.
Manner of management, control and disposition of property or a part of conservatorship estate, see Probate Code § 3056.

Research References

Forms

West's California Code Forms, Probate § 3051(c) Form 1, Consent to Inclusion of Community Property in Conservatorship Estate.

§ 3072. Joinder or consent by conservator; authority; court order

(a) Except as provided in subdivision (b), a conservator may join in or consent to a transaction under Section 3071 only after authorization by either of the following:

(1) An order of the court obtained in the conservatorship proceeding upon a petition filed pursuant to Section 2403 or under Article 7

§ 3072 PROBATE CODE

(commencing with Section 2540) or 10 (commencing with Section 2580) of Chapter 6 of Part 4.

(2) An order of the court made in a proceeding pursuant to Chapter 3 (commencing with Section 3100).

(b) A conservator may consent without court authorization to a sale, conveyance, or encumbrance of community personal property requiring consent under subdivision (c) of Section 1100 of the Family Code if the conservator could sell or transfer the property under Section 2545 without court authorization if the property were a part of the conservatorship estate. *(Stats.1990, c. 79 (A.B.759), § 14, operative July 1, 1991. Amended by Stats.1992, c. 163 (A.B.2641), § 128, operative Jan. 1, 1994; Stats.1993, c. 219 (A.B.1500), § 223.)*

Cross References

Conservator defined for purposes of this Part, see Probate Code § 3004.
Conservatorship estate defined for purposes of this Part, see Probate Code § 3006.
Conservatorship proceeding defined for purposes of this Part, see Probate Code § 3008.
Protection of rights of spouse who lacks legal capacity, see Probate Code § 3057.

§ 3073. Manner of joinder or consent

(a) The joinder or consent under Section 3071 of a spouse having legal capacity shall be in a manner that complies with Section 1100 or 1102 of the Family Code or other statute that applies to the transaction.

(b) The joinder or consent under Section 3071 of a conservator shall be in the same manner as a spouse would join in or consent to the transaction under the statute that applies to the transaction except that the joinder or consent shall be executed by the conservator and shall refer to the court order, if one is required, authorizing the conservator to join in or consent to the transaction. *(Stats.1990, c. 79 (A.B.759), § 14, operative July 1, 1991. Amended by Stats.1992, c. 163 (A.B.2641), § 129, operative Jan. 1, 1994; Stats. 1993, c. 219 (A.B.1500), § 224.)*

Cross References

Conservator defined for purposes of this Part, see Probate Code § 3004.
Legal capacity, see Probate Code § 3012.

§ 3074. Good faith purchaser or encumbrancer for value

Notwithstanding any other provision of this article, a transaction that affects real property, entered into by a person acting in good faith and for a valuable consideration, is not affected by the fact that one or both spouses have conservators unless a notice of the establishment of the conservatorship or conservatorships, as the case may be, has been recorded prior to the transaction in the county in which the property is located. *(Stats.1990, c. 79 (A.B.759), § 14, operative July 1, 1991.)*

Cross References

Conservator defined for purposes of this Part, see Probate Code § 3004.
Mode of recording, see Civil Code § 1169 et seq.

ARTICLE 3. ENFORCEMENT OF SUPPORT OF SPOUSE WHO HAS CONSERVATOR

Section
3080. Petition for order.
3081. Notice of hearing.
3082. Citation to and examination of spouse managing or controlling community property.
3083. Support pendente lite, effect of order; modification or revocation.
3084. Current income, expense and property declarations; service and filing; forms.
3085. Ex parte protective orders.

Section
3086. Continuance; preparation for hearing.
3087. Character of property; determination.
3088. Application of income and principal for support and maintenance; circumstances; periodic payments; jurisdiction to modify or vacate; orders.
3089. Division of community property; transfer of property to conservator of estate; after-acquired property.
3090. Enforcement of orders.
3091. Rules for practice and procedure.
3092. Use of other procedures for enforcement of support obligation; authority.

§ 3080. Petition for order

If one spouse has a conservator and the other spouse has the management or control of community property, the conservator or conservatee, a relative or friend of the conservatee, or any interested person may file a petition under this article in the court in which the conservatorship proceeding is pending for an order requiring the spouse who has the management or control of community property to apply the income or principal, or both, of the community property to the support and maintenance of the conservatee as ordered by the court. *(Stats.1990, c. 79 (A.B.759), § 14, operative July 1, 1991.)*

Cross References

Community property defined for purposes of this Part, see Probate Code § 3002.
Conservator defined for purposes of this Part, see Probate Code § 3004.
Conservatorship proceeding defined for purposes of this Part, see Probate Code § 3008.

Research References

Forms

West's California Code Forms, Probate § 3080 Form 1, Petition for Support; for Injunctive Orders; for Determination of the Character of Property; for an Accounting; for Employment of Counsel; and for Attorney Fees and Costs.
West's California Code Forms, Probate § 3084 Form 1, Notice of Taking Possession or Control of an Asset of Minor or Conservatee—Judicial Council Form FL-150.

§ 3081. Notice of hearing

(a) Notice of the hearing on the petition shall be given for the period and in the manner provided in Chapter 3 (commencing with Section 1460) of Part 1.

(b) If the spouse who has the management or control of community property is not the conservator, the petitioner shall also cause notice of the hearing and a copy of the petition to be served on that spouse in accordance with Title 5 (commencing with Section 410.10) of Part 2 of the Code of Civil Procedure. *(Stats.1990, c. 79 (A.B.759), § 14, operative July 1, 1991.)*

Cross References

Community property defined for purposes of this Part, see Probate Code § 3002.
Conservator defined for purposes of this Part, see Probate Code § 3004.

Research References

Forms

West's California Code Forms, Probate § 3080 Form 1, Petition for Support; for Injunctive Orders; for Determination of the Character of Property; for an Accounting; for Employment of Counsel; and for Attorney Fees and Costs.

§ 3082. Citation to and examination of spouse managing or controlling community property

Upon the filing of a petition under this article, the court may cite the spouse who has the management or control of community property to appear before the court, and the court and the petitioner may examine the spouse under oath concerning the community property and other matters relevant to the petition filed under this article. If the person so cited refuses to appear and submit to an examination, the court may proceed against the person as provided in Article 2 (commencing with Section 8870) of Chapter 2 of Part 3 of Division 7. Upon such examination, the court may make an order requiring the person cited to disclose his or her knowledge of the community property and other matters relevant to the petition filed under this article, and if the order is not complied with the court may proceed against the person as provided in Article 2 (commencing with Section 8870) of Chapter 2 of Part 3 of Division 7. *(Stats.1990, c. 79 (A.B.759), § 14, operative July 1, 1991.)*

Cross References

Community property defined for purposes of this Part, see Probate Code § 3002.

Research References

Forms

West's California Code Forms, Probate § 3080 Form 1, Petition for Support; for Injunctive Orders; for Determination of the Character of Property; for an Accounting; for Employment of Counsel; and for Attorney Fees and Costs.

§ 3083. Support pendente lite, effect of order; modification or revocation

In any proceeding under this article, the court may, after notice and hearing, order the spouse who has the management or control of community property to pay from the community property such amount as the court determines is necessary to the support and maintenance of the conservatee spouse pending the determination of the petition under this article. An order made pursuant to this section does not prejudice the rights of the spouses or other interested parties with respect to any subsequent order which may be made under this article. Any order made under this section may be modified or revoked at any time except as to any amount that may have accrued prior to the date of filing of the petition to modify or revoke the order. *(Stats.1990, c. 79 (A.B.759), § 14, operative July 1, 1991.)*

Cross References

Community property defined for purposes of this Part, see Probate Code § 3002.

Research References

Forms

West's California Code Forms, Probate § 3080 Form 1, Petition for Support; for Injunctive Orders; for Determination of the Character of Property; for an Accounting; for Employment of Counsel; and for Attorney Fees and Costs.

§ 3084. Current income, expense and property declarations; service and filing; forms

When a petition is filed under this article, the spouse having the management or control of community property shall serve and file a current income and expense declaration and a current property declaration on the forms prescribed by the Judicial Council for use in family law proceedings. *(Stats.1990, c. 79 (A.B.759), § 14, operative July 1, 1991.)*

Cross References

Community property defined for purposes of this Part, see Probate Code § 3002.

Research References

Forms

West's California Code Forms, Probate § 3084 Form 1, Notice of Taking Possession or Control of an Asset of Minor or Conservatee—Judicial Council Form FL-150.

§ 3085. Ex parte protective orders

During the pendency of any proceeding under this article, the court, upon the application of the petitioner, may issue ex parte orders:

(a) Restraining the spouse having the management or control of community property from transferring, encumbering, hypothecating, concealing, or in any way disposing of any property, real or personal, whether community, quasi-community, or separate, except in the usual course of business or for the necessities of life.

(b) Requiring the spouse having the management or control of the community property to notify the petitioner of any proposed extraordinary expenditures and to account to the court for all such extraordinary expenditures. *(Stats.1990, c. 79 (A.B.759), § 14, operative July 1, 1991.)*

Cross References

Community property defined for purposes of this Part, see Probate Code § 3002.

Research References

Forms

West's California Code Forms, Probate § 3080 Form 1, Petition for Support; for Injunctive Orders; for Determination of the Character of Property; for an Accounting; for Employment of Counsel; and for Attorney Fees and Costs.

§ 3086. Continuance; preparation for hearing

Any person interested in the proceeding under this article may request time for filing a response to the petition, for discovery proceedings, or for other preparation for the hearing, and the court shall grant a continuance for a reasonable time for any of such purposes. *(Stats.1990, c. 79 (A.B.759), § 14, operative July 1, 1991.)*

§ 3087. Character of property; determination

In a proceeding under this article, the court may hear and determine whether property is community property or the separate property of either spouse if that issue is raised in the proceeding. *(Stats.1990, c. 79 (A.B.759), § 14, operative July 1, 1991.)*

Cross References

Community property defined for purposes of this Part, see Probate Code § 3002.

Research References

Forms

West's California Code Forms, Probate § 3080 Form 1, Petition for Support; for Injunctive Orders; for Determination of the Character of Property; for an Accounting; for Employment of Counsel; and for Attorney Fees and Costs.

§ 3088. Application of income and principal for support and maintenance; circumstances; periodic payments; jurisdiction to modify or vacate; orders

(a) The court may order the spouse who has the management or control of community property to apply the income or principal, or both, of the community property to the support and maintenance of the conservatee, including care, treatment, and support of a conservatee who is a patient in a state hospital under the jurisdiction of the State Department of State Hospitals or the State Department of Developmental Services, as ordered by the court.

(b) In determining the amount ordered for support and maintenance, the court shall consider the following circumstances of the spouses:

(1) The earning capacity and needs of each spouse.

(2) The obligations and assets, including the separate property, of each spouse.

(3) The duration of the marriage.

(4) The age and health of the spouses.

(5) The standard of living of the spouses.

(6) Any other relevant factors which it considers just and equitable.

(c) At the request of any interested person, the court shall make appropriate findings with respect to the circumstances.

(d) The court may order the spouse who has the management or control of community property to make a specified monthly or other periodic payment to the conservator of the person of the conservatee or to any other person designated in the order. The court may order the spouse required to make the periodic payments to give reasonable security therefor.

(e)(1) The court may order the spouse required to make the periodic payments to assign, to the person designated in the order to receive the payments, that portion of the earnings of the spouse due or to be due in the future as will be sufficient to pay the amount ordered by the court for the support and maintenance of the conservatee. The order operates as an assignment and is binding upon any existing or future employer upon whom a copy of the order is served. The order shall be in the form of an earnings assignment order for support prescribed by the Judicial Council for use in family law proceedings. The employer may deduct the sum of one dollar and fifty cents ($1.50) for each payment made pursuant to the order. Any such assignment made pursuant to court order shall have priority as against any execution or other assignment unless otherwise ordered by the court or unless the other assignment is made pursuant to Chapter 8 (commencing with Section 5200) of Part 5 of Division 9 of the Family Code. An employer shall not use any assignment authorized by this subdivision as grounds for the dismissal of that employee.

(2) As used in this subdivision, "employer" includes the United States government and any public entity as defined in Section 811.2 of the Government Code. This subdivision applies to the money and benefits described in Sections 704.110 and 704.113 of the Code of Civil Procedure to the extent that those moneys and benefits are subject to a wage assignment for support under Chapter 4 (commencing with Section 703.010) of Division 2 of Title 9 of Part 2 of the Code of Civil Procedure.

(f) The court retains jurisdiction to modify or to vacate an order made under this section where justice requires, except as to any amount that may have accrued before the date of the filing of the petition to modify or revoke the order. At the request of any interested person, the order of modification or revocation shall include findings of fact and may be made retroactive to the date of the filing of the petition to revoke or modify, or to any date subsequent thereto. At least 15 days before the hearing on the petition to modify or vacate the order, the petitioner shall deliver pursuant to Section 1215 a notice of the time and place of the hearing on the petition, accompanied by a copy of the petition, to the spouse who has the management or control of the community property. Notice shall be given for the period and in the manner provided in Chapter 3 (commencing with Section 1460) of Part 1 to any other persons entitled to notice of the hearing under that chapter.

(g) In a proceeding for dissolution of the marriage or for legal separation, the court has jurisdiction to modify or vacate an order made under this section to the same extent as it may modify or vacate an order made in the proceeding for dissolution of the marriage or for legal separation. *(Stats.1990, c. 79 (A.B.759), § 14, operative July 1, 1991. Amended by Stats.1992, c. 163 (A.B.2641), § 130, operative Jan. 1, 1994; Stats.2004, c. 520 (A.B.2530), § 7; Stats.2012, c. 440 (A.B.1488), § 51, eff. Sept. 22, 2012; Stats.2017, c. 319 (A.B.976), § 56, eff. Jan. 1, 2018.)*

Cross References

Assignment of wages, validity and exceptions, see Labor Code § 300.
Community property defined for purposes of this Part, see Probate Code § 3002.
Conservator defined for purposes of this Part, see Probate Code § 3004.
Department of Developmental Services, see Welfare and Institutions Code § 4400 et seq.
Wage garnishment, definitions, see Code of Civil Procedure § 706.011.

Research References

Forms

3 California Transactions Forms--Business Transactions § 16:83, Exclusions.
West's California Code Forms, Probate § 3080 Form 1, Petition for Support; for Injunctive Orders; for Determination of the Character of Property; for an Accounting; for Employment of Counsel; and for Attorney Fees and Costs.

§ 3089. Division of community property; transfer of property to conservator of estate; after-acquired property

If the spouse who has the management or control of the community property refuses to comply with any order made under this article or an order made in a separate action to provide support for the conservatee spouse, upon request of the petitioner or other interested person, the court may, in its discretion, divide the community property and the quasi-community property of the spouses, as it exists at the time of division, equally in the same manner as where a marriage is dissolved. If the property is so divided, the property awarded to each spouse is the separate property of that spouse and the court shall order that the property awarded to the conservatee spouse be transferred or paid over to the conservator of the estate of that spouse to be included in the conservatorship estate and be managed, controlled, and disposed of as a part of the conservatorship estate. The fact that property has been divided pursuant to this section has no effect on the nature of property thereafter acquired by the spouses, and the determination whether the thereafter-acquired property is community or separate property shall be made without regard to the fact that property has been divided pursuant to this section. *(Stats.1990, c. 79 (A.B.759), § 14, operative July 1, 1991.)*

Cross References

Community property defined for purposes of this Part, see Probate Code § 3002.
Conservator defined for purposes of this Part, see Probate Code § 3004.
Conservatorship estate defined for purposes of this Part, see Probate Code § 3006.

Research References

Forms

West's California Code Forms, Probate § 3080 Form 1, Petition for Support; for Injunctive Orders; for Determination of the Character of Property; for an Accounting; for Employment of Counsel; and for Attorney Fees and Costs.

§ 3090. Enforcement of orders

Any order of the court made under this article may be enforced by the court by execution, the appointment of a receiver, contempt, or by such other order or orders as the court in its discretion may from time to time deem necessary. *(Stats.1990, c. 79 (A.B.759), § 14, operative July 1, 1991.)*

§ 3091. Rules for practice and procedure

Notwithstanding any other provision of law, the Judicial Council may provide by rule for the practice and procedure in proceedings under this article. *(Stats.1990, c. 79 (A.B.759), § 14, operative July 1, 1991.)*

§ 3092. Use of other procedures for enforcement of support obligation; authority

Nothing in this article affects or limits the right of the conservator or any interested person to institute an action against any person to enforce the duty otherwise imposed by law to support the spouse having a conservator. This article is permissive and in addition to any other procedure otherwise available to enforce the obligation of support. (Stats.1990, c. 79 (A.B.759), § 14, operative July 1, 1991.)

Cross References

Conservator defined for purposes of this Part, see Probate Code § 3004.

Research References

Forms

West's California Code Forms, Probate § 3080 Form 1, Petition for Support; for Injunctive Orders; for Determination of the Character of Property; for an Accounting; for Employment of Counsel; and for Attorney Fees and Costs.

CHAPTER 3. PROCEEDING FOR PARTICULAR TRANSACTION

ARTICLE 1. GENERAL PROVISIONS

Section
3100. Transaction.
3101. Nature of proceeding.
3102. Transaction as subject of proceeding.

Cross References

Fee for filing petition and opposition papers concerning internal affairs of certain trusts or first accounts of trustees of certain testamentary trusts, see Government Code § 70652.

§ 3100. Transaction

(a) As used in this chapter, "transaction" means a transaction that involves community real or personal property, tangible or intangible, or an interest therein or a lien or encumbrance thereon, including, but not limited to, those transactions with respect thereto as are listed in Section 3102.

(b) However, if a proposed transaction involves property in which a spouse also has a separate property interest, for good cause the court may include that separate property in the transaction. (Stats. 1990, c. 79 (A.B.759), § 14, operative July 1, 1991. Amended by Stats.1996, c. 877 (A.B.1467), § 2.)

Cross References

Community property,
  Defined, see Probate Code § 3002.
  Succession, see Probate Code § 100 et seq.
Fee for filing petition commencing or opposition papers concerning certain probate proceedings, see Government Code § 70655.
Joinder or consent by conservator, see Probate Code § 3072.
Satisfaction of joinder or consent requirements, see Probate Code § 3071.

Research References

Forms

1 California Transactions Forms--Estate Planning § 2:21, Execution of Documents Under Durable Power of Attorney; Substituted Judgment.
3 California Transactions Forms--Estate Planning § 17:12, Spouse in Long-Term Care.
West's California Code Forms, Probate § 3121 Form 1, Petition for Order Authorizing Proposed Transaction and Joinder of Conservator.

§ 3101. Nature of proceeding

(a) A proceeding may be brought under this chapter for a court order authorizing a proposed transaction, whether or not the proposed transaction is one that otherwise would require the joinder or consent of both spouses, if both of the following conditions are satisfied:

(1) One of the spouses is alleged to lack legal capacity for the proposed transaction, whether or not that spouse has a conservator.

(2) The other spouse either has legal capacity for the proposed transaction or has a conservator.

(b) A proceeding may be brought under this chapter for a court order declaring that one or both spouses has legal capacity for a proposed transaction.

(c) One proceeding may be brought under this chapter under both subdivision (a) and subdivision (b).

(d) In a proceeding under this chapter, the court may determine whether the property that is the subject of the proposed transaction is community property or the separate property of either spouse, but such determination shall not be made in the proceeding under this chapter if the court determines that the interest of justice requires that the determination be made in a civil action.

(e) This chapter is permissive and cumulative for the transactions to which it applies. (Stats.1990, c. 79 (A.B.759), § 14, operative July 1, 1991.)

Cross References

Appointment of conservator for other spouse not required, see Probate Code § 3113.
Community property, succession, see Probate Code § 100 et seq.
Community property defined for purposes of this Part, see Probate Code § 3002.
Conservator defined for purposes of this Part, see Probate Code § 3004.
Determination of validity of character of property, see Probate Code § 3023.
Inconsistent allegations and alternative relief, see Probate Code § 3120.
Legal capacity defined, see Probate Code § 3012.
Order authorizing transaction, see Probate Code § 3144.
Persons who may file or join in petition, see Probate Code § 3111.
Protection of rights of spouse who lacks legal capacity, see Probate Code § 3057.
Satisfaction of joinder or consent requirements, see Probate Code § 3071.
Several proposed transactions may be included in one proceeding, see Probate Code § 3120.
Transaction defined for purposes of this Chapter, see Probate Code § 3100.

Research References

Forms

West's California Code Forms, Probate § 3154 Form 1, Order Vacating Order of Sale.

§ 3102. Transaction as subject of proceeding

The transactions that may be the subject of a proceeding under this chapter include, but are not limited to:

(a) Sale, conveyance, assignment, transfer, exchange, conveyance pursuant to a preexisting contract, encumbrance by security interest, deed of trust, mortgage, or otherwise, lease, including but not limited to a lease for the exploration for and production of oil, gas, minerals, or other substances, or unitization or pooling with other property for or in connection with such exploration and production.

(b) Assignment, transfer, or conveyance, in whole or in part, in compromise or settlement of an indebtedness, demand, or proceeding to which the property may be subject.

(c) Dedication or conveyance, with or without consideration, of any of the following:

(1) The property to this state or any public entity in this state, or to the United States or any agency or instrumentality of the United States, for any purpose.

(2) An easement over the property to any person for any purpose.

(d) Conveyance, release, or relinquishment to this state or any public entity in this state, with or without consideration, of any access rights to a street, highway, or freeway from the property.

§ 3102

(e) Consent as a lienholder to a dedication, conveyance, release, or relinquishment under subdivision (c) or (d) by the owner of property subject to the lien.

(f) Conveyance or transfer, without consideration, to provide gifts for such purposes, and to such charities, relatives (including one of the spouses), friends, or other objects of bounty, as would be likely beneficiaries of gifts from the spouses. *(Stats.1990, c. 79 (A.B.759), § 14, operative July 1, 1991.)*

Cross References

Community property, succession, see Probate Code § 100 et seq.
Dedication of real property for public purposes, see Government Code § 7050.
Easements, generally, see Civil Code § 801 et seq.
Lease of property in administration of estates, see Probate Code § 9945.
Liens, generally, see Civil Code § 2872 et seq.
Oil, gas and mineral leases,
 Generally, see Public Resources Code § 6801 et seq.
 Duration, see Civil Code § 718.
Order authorizing transaction, see Probate Code § 3144.
Power of legislative body to acquire easements for public interest, see Streets and Highways Code § 10102.
Transaction defined for purposes of this Chapter, see Probate Code § 3100.

Research References

Forms

West's California Code Forms, Probate § 3121 Form 1, Petition for Order Authorizing Proposed Transaction and Joinder of Conservator.

ARTICLE 2. COMMENCEMENT OF PROCEEDING

Section
3110. Jurisdiction and venue.
3111. Persons authorized to file or join in petition.
3112. Legal capacity of petitioning spouse; determination; authority of court.
3113. Appointment of conservator for other spouse not required.

§ 3110. Jurisdiction and venue

(a) A proceeding under this chapter shall be brought by a petition filed in the superior court.

(b) The proper county for commencement of the proceeding is the county in which a conservatorship proceeding of one of the spouses is pending. If a conservatorship proceeding is not pending, then in either of the following:

(1) The county in which one or both of the spouses resides.

(2) Any other county as may be in the best interests of the spouses. *(Stats.1990, c. 79 (A.B.759), § 14, operative July 1, 1991. Amended by Stats.1994, c. 806 (A.B.3686), § 20.)*

Cross References

Conservatorship proceeding defined for purposes of this Part, see Probate Code § 3008.
Venue for conservatorship proceeding, see Probate Code §§ 2201, 2202.

Research References

Forms

West's California Code Forms, Probate § 3121 Form 1, Petition for Order Authorizing Proposed Transaction and Joinder of Conservator.

§ 3111. Persons authorized to file or join in petition

(a) Except as provided in subdivision (b), any of the following persons may file, or join in, a petition under this chapter:

(1) Either spouse, whether or not the spouse has legal capacity.

(2) The conservator of either spouse.

(b) If the petition requests approval of a proposed transaction, at least one of the petitioners shall be either a conservator or a spouse having legal capacity for the transaction. *(Stats.1990, c. 79 (A.B.759), § 14, operative July 1, 1991.)*

Cross References

Conservator defined for purposes of this Part, see Probate Code § 3004.
Legal capacity defined, see Probate Code § 3012.
Nature of proceeding, see Probate Code § 3101.
Transaction defined for purposes of this Chapter, see Probate Code § 3100.

Research References

Forms

West's California Code Forms, Probate § 3121 Form 1, Petition for Order Authorizing Proposed Transaction and Joinder of Conservator.

§ 3112. Legal capacity of petitioning spouse; determination; authority of court

(a) If a petitioning spouse is one whose legal capacity for the proposed transaction is to be determined in the proceeding, the court may do any of the following:

(1) Permit the spouse to appear without a representative.

(2) Appoint a guardian ad litem for the spouse.

(3) Take such other action as the circumstances warrant.

(b) If a petitioning spouse lacks legal capacity for the proposed transaction, the court may do either of the following:

(1) Require the spouse to be represented by the conservator of the spouse.

(2) Appoint a guardian ad litem for the spouse. *(Stats.1990, c. 79 (A.B.759), § 14, operative July 1, 1991.)*

Cross References

Conservator as representative in actions and proceedings, see Probate Code § 2462.
Conservator defined for purposes of this Part, see Probate Code § 3004.
Parties to civil actions,
 Guardian ad litem, appointment procedure, see Code of Civil Procedure § 373.
 Minors, incompetent persons or persons for whom conservator appointed, see Code of Civil Procedure § 372.
Protection of rights of spouse who lacks legal capacity, see Probate Code § 3057.
Representation of spouse alleged to lack legal capacity, see Probate Code § 3140.
Transaction defined for purposes of this Chapter, see Probate Code § 3100.

§ 3113. Appointment of conservator for other spouse not required

A proceeding may be brought under this chapter by the conservator of a spouse, or by a spouse having legal capacity for the proposed transaction, without the necessity of appointing a conservator for the other spouse. *(Stats.1990, c. 79 (A.B.759), § 14, operative July 1, 1991.)*

Cross References

Conservator defined for purposes of this Part, see Probate Code § 3004.
Legal capacity, see Probate Code § 3012.
Transaction defined for purposes of this Chapter, see Probate Code § 3100.

ARTICLE 3. PETITION

Section
3120. Permissible allegations.
3121. Required contents.
3122. Petition for court order authorizing transaction.
3123. Petition for court order declaring legal capacity for transaction.

§ 3120. Permissible allegations

(a) Several proposed transactions may be included in one petition and proceeding under this chapter.

(b) The petition may contain inconsistent allegations and may request relief in the alternative. *(Stats.1990, c. 79 (A.B.759), § 14, operative July 1, 1991.)*

Cross References

Petitions and other papers, generally, see Probate Code § 1020 et seq.
Transaction defined for purposes of this Chapter, see Probate Code § 3100.

§ 3121. Required contents

The petition shall set forth all of the following information:

(a) The name, age, and residence of each spouse.

(b) If one or both spouses is alleged to lack legal capacity for the proposed transaction, a statement that the spouse has a conservator or a statement of the facts upon which the allegation is based.

(c) If there is a conservator of a spouse, the name and address of the conservator, the county in which the conservatorship proceeding is pending, and the court number of the proceeding.

(d) If a spouse alleged to lack legal capacity for the proposed transaction is a patient in or on leave of absence from a state institution under the jurisdiction of the State Department of State Hospitals or the State Department of Developmental Services, the name and address of the institution.

(e) The names and addresses of all of the following persons:

(1) Relatives within the second degree of each spouse alleged to lack legal capacity for the proposed transaction.

(2) If the petition is to provide gifts or otherwise affect estate planning of the spouse who is alleged to lack capacity, as would be properly the subject of a petition under Article 10 (commencing with Section 2580) of Chapter 6 of Part 4 (substituted judgment) in the case of a conservatorship, the names and addresses of the persons identified in Section 2581.

(f) A sufficient description of the property that is the subject of the proposed transaction.

(g) An allegation that the property is community property, and, if the proposed transaction involves property in which a spouse also has a separate property interest, an allegation of good cause to include that separate property in the transaction.

(h) The estimated value of the property.

(i) The terms and conditions of the proposed transaction, including the names of all parties thereto.

(j) The relief requested. *(Stats.1990, c. 79 (A.B.759), § 14, operative July 1, 1991. Amended by Stats.1996, c. 877 (A.B.1467), § 3; Stats.2003, c. 32 (A.B.167), § 3; Stats.2012, c. 440 (A.B.1488), § 52, eff. Sept. 22, 2012.)*

Cross References

Community property defined for purposes of this Part, see Probate Code § 3002.
Conservator defined for purposes of this Part, see Probate Code § 3004.
Conservatorship proceeding defined for purposes of this Part, see Probate Code § 3008.
Department of Developmental Services, see Welfare and Institutions Code § 4400 et seq.
Legal capacity defined, see Probate Code § 3012.
Petitions and other papers, see Probate Code § 1020 et seq.
Transaction defined for purposes of this Chapter, see Probate Code § 3100.

Research References

Forms

West's California Code Forms, Probate § 3121 Form 1, Petition for Order Authorizing Proposed Transaction and Joinder of Conservator.

§ 3122. Petition for court order authorizing transaction

If the proceeding is brought for a court order authorizing a proposed transaction, the petition shall set forth, in addition to the information required by Section 3121, all of the following:

(a) An allegation that one of the spouses has a conservator or facts establishing lack of legal capacity of the spouse for the proposed transaction.

(b) An allegation that the other spouse has legal capacity for the proposed transaction or has a conservator.

(c) An allegation that each spouse either: (1) joins in or consents to the proposed transaction, (2) has a conservator, or (3) is substantially unable to manage his or her financial resources or resist fraud or undue influence.

(d) Facts that may be relied upon to show that the authorization sought is for one or more of the following purposes:

(1) The advantage, benefit, or best interests of the spouses or their estates.

(2) The care and support of either spouse or of such persons as either spouse may be legally obligated to support.

(3) The payment of taxes, interest, or other encumbrances or charges for the protection and preservation of the community property.

(4) The providing of gifts for such purposes, and to such charities, relatives (including one of the spouses), friends, or other objects of bounty, as would be likely beneficiaries of gifts from the spouses. *(Stats.1990, c. 79 (A.B.759), § 14, operative July 1, 1991.)*

Cross References

Community property defined for purposes of this Part, see Probate Code § 3002.
Conservator defined for purposes of this Part, see Probate Code § 3004.
Satisfaction of joinder or consent requirements, see Probate Code § 3071.
Transaction defined for purposes of this Chapter, see Probate Code § 3100.

Research References

Forms

West's California Code Forms, Probate § 3121 Form 1, Petition for Order Authorizing Proposed Transaction and Joinder of Conservator.
West's California Code Forms, Probate § 3144 Form 1, Order Authorizing Transaction.

§ 3123. Petition for court order declaring legal capacity for transaction

If the proceeding is brought for a court order declaring that one or both spouses has legal capacity for a proposed transaction, the petition shall set forth, in addition to the information required by Section 3121, an allegation of the legal capacity of such spouse or spouses for the proposed transaction. *(Stats.1990, c. 79 (A.B.759), § 14, operative July 1, 1991.)*

Cross References

Authorization of proceeding, lack of legal capacity, see Probate Code § 3101.
Legal capacity, see Probate Code § 3012.
Transaction defined for purposes of this Chapter, see Probate Code § 3100.

ARTICLE 4. CITATION AND NOTICE OF HEARING

Section
3130. Citation for nonpetitioning spouse alleged to lack legal capacity; notice to conservator in lieu of citation.
3131. Notice to nonpetitioning spouse and other persons.

§ 3130. Citation for nonpetitioning spouse alleged to lack legal capacity; notice to conservator in lieu of citation

(a) Except as provided in subdivision (b), upon the filing of the petition, the clerk shall issue a citation to each nonpetitioning spouse alleged to lack legal capacity for the proposed transaction, setting forth the time and place of hearing. The citation and a copy of the petition shall be served upon the spouse at least 15 days before the hearing.

(b) Unless the court otherwise orders, if a spouse alleged to lack legal capacity for the proposed transaction has a conservator, no citation to the spouse need be issued, and the petitioner shall cause a notice of the time and place of the hearing on the petition, accompanied by a copy of the petition, to be served on the conservator at least 15 days before the hearing.

(c) Service under this section shall be made in the manner provided in Section 415.10 or 415.30 of the Code of Civil Procedure or in such other manner as may be authorized by the court. If the person to be served is outside this state, service may also be made in the manner provided in Section 415.40 of the Code of Civil Procedure. *(Stats.1990, c. 79 (A.B.759), § 14, operative July 1, 1991.)*

Cross References

Citations, see Probate Code § 1240 et seq.
Conservator defined for purposes of this Part, see Probate Code § 3004.
Duty of conservator to appear and represent spouse, see Probate Code § 3140.
Mailing, completion, see Probate Code § 1467.
Notice of hearing,
  Generally, see Probate Code § 1200 et seq.
  Proof of giving notice, see Probate Code § 1260 et seq.
Notice to,
  Directors, see Probate Code § 1461.
  Veterans Administration, see Probate Code § 1461.5.
Transaction defined for purposes of this Chapter, see Probate Code § 3100.

Research References

Forms

7PT1 Am. Jur. Pl. & Pr. Forms Community Property § 87, Citation—To Incompetent Spouse—Notice of Hearing on Petition by Incompetent's Spouse for Sale of Community Real Property.

§ 3131. Notice to nonpetitioning spouse and other persons

(a) At least 15 days before the hearing on the petition, the petitioner shall cause a notice of the time and place of the hearing and a copy of the petition to be served upon any nonpetitioning spouse not alleged to lack legal capacity for the proposed transaction.

(b) Service under subdivision (a) shall be made in the manner provided in Section 415.10 or 415.30 of the Code of Civil Procedure or in such other manner as may be authorized by the court. If the person to be served is outside this state, service may also be made in the manner provided in Section 415.40 of the Code of Civil Procedure.

(c) At least 15 days before the hearing on the petition, the petitioner shall deliver pursuant to Section 1215 a notice of the time and place of the hearing on the petition to those persons required to be named in the petition at the addresses set forth in the petition. *(Stats.1990, c. 79 (A.B.759), § 14, operative July 1, 1991. Amended by Stats.1996, c. 877 (A.B.1467), § 4; Stats.2017, c. 319 (A.B.976), § 57, eff. Jan. 1, 2018.)*

Cross References

Mailing, completion, see Probate Code § 1467.
Notice of hearing,
  Generally, see Probate Code § 1200 et seq.
  Appointment of conservator, see Probate Code § 1822.
  Proof of giving notice, see Probate Code § 1260 et seq.
Notice to,
  Directors, see Probate Code § 1461.
  Veterans Administration, see Probate Code § 1461.5.
Transaction defined for purposes of this Chapter, see Probate Code § 3100.

Research References

Forms

7PT1 Am. Jur. Pl. & Pr. Forms Community Property § 88, Notice of Hearing—Petition of Spouse of Incompetent Spouse—For Sale of Community Real Property.

West's California Code Forms, Probate § 3121 Form 1, Petition for Order Authorizing Proposed Transaction and Joinder of Conservator.

ARTICLE 5. HEARING AND ORDER

Section
3140. Representation of spouse alleged to lack legal capacity; appointment of investigator, guardian, or legal counsel; fees and costs.
3141. Presence of spouse at hearing.
3142. Information to be given spouse by court.
3143. Order declaring legal capacity.
3144. Order authorizing transaction.
3145. Effect of determination of lack of legal capacity.

§ 3140. Representation of spouse alleged to lack legal capacity; appointment of investigator, guardian, or legal counsel; fees and costs

(a) A conservator served pursuant to this article shall, and the Director of State Hospitals or the Director of Developmental Services given notice pursuant to Section 1461 may, appear at the hearing and represent a spouse alleged to lack legal capacity for the proposed transaction.

(b) The court may, in its discretion and if necessary, appoint an investigator to review the proposed transaction and report to the court regarding its advisability.

(c) If the court determines that a spouse alleged to lack legal capacity has not competently retained independent counsel, the court may in its discretion appoint the public guardian, public administrator, or a guardian ad litem to represent the interests of the spouse.

(d)(1) If a spouse alleged to lack legal capacity is unable to retain legal counsel, upon request of the spouse, the court shall appoint the public defender or private counsel under Section 1471 to represent the spouse and, if that appointment is made, Section 1472 applies.

(2) If the petition proposes a transfer of substantial assets to the petitioner from the other spouse and the court determines that the spouse has not competently retained independent counsel for the proceeding, the court may, in its discretion, appoint counsel for the other spouse if the court determines that appointment would be helpful to resolve the matter or necessary to protect the interests of the other spouse.

(e) Except as provided in paragraph (1) of subdivision (d), the court may fix a reasonable fee, to be paid out of the proceeds of the transaction or otherwise as the court may direct, for all services rendered by privately engaged counsel, the public guardian, public administrator, or guardian ad litem, and by counsel for such persons.

(f) The court may order the cost of the review and report by a court investigator pursuant to subdivision (b) to be paid out of the proceeds of the transaction or otherwise as the court may direct, if the court determines that its order would not cause a hardship. *(Stats.1990, c. 79 (A.B.759), § 14, operative July 1, 1991. Amended by Stats.2008, c. 293 (A.B.1340), § 10; Stats.2009, c. 140 (A.B.1164), § 153; Stats.2009, c. 596 (S.B.556), § 2; Stats.2012, c. 440 (A.B.1488), § 53, eff. Sept. 22, 2012.)*

Cross References

Conservator defined for purposes of this Part, see Probate Code § 3004.
Public administrators, see Probate Code § 7601 et seq.
Representation of petitioning spouse, see Probate Code § 3112.
Transaction defined for purposes of this Chapter, see Probate Code § 3100.

§ 3141. Presence of spouse at hearing

(a) If a spouse is alleged to lack legal capacity for the proposed transaction and has no conservator, the spouse shall be produced at the hearing unless unable to attend the hearing.

(b) If the spouse is not able to attend the hearing because of medical inability, such inability shall be established (1) by the affidavit or certificate of a licensed medical practitioner or (2) if the spouse is an adherent of a religion whose tenets and practices call for reliance upon prayer alone for healing and is under treatment by an accredited practitioner of the religion, by the affidavit of the practitioner.

(c) Emotional or psychological instability is not good cause for absence of the spouse from the hearing unless, by reason of such instability, attendance at the hearing is likely to cause serious and immediate physiological damage. *(Stats.1990, c. 79 (A.B.759), § 14, operative July 1, 1991.)*

Cross References

Conservator defined for purposes of this Part, see Probate Code § 3004.
Representation of petitioning spouse, see Probate Code § 3112.
Transaction defined for purposes of this Chapter, see Probate Code § 3100.

§ 3142. Information to be given spouse by court

(a) If a spouse is alleged to lack legal capacity for the proposed transaction and has no conservator, the court, before commencement of the hearing on the merits, shall inform the spouse of all of the following:

(1) A determination of lack of legal capacity for the proposed transaction may result in approval of the proposed transaction.

(2) The spouse has the right to legal counsel of the spouse's own choosing, including the right to have legal counsel appointed by the court if unable to retain legal counsel.

(b) This section does not apply if the spouse is absent from the hearing and is not required to attend the hearing under the provisions of subdivision (a) of Section 3141 and any showing required by Section 3141 has been made. *(Stats.1990, c. 79 (A.B.759), § 14, operative July 1, 1991.)*

Cross References

Appointment legal of counsel, see Probate Code §§ 1470 et seq., 3140.
Conservator defined for purposes of this Part, see Probate Code § 3004.
Establishment of conservatorship,
 Information to proposed conservatee by court, see Probate Code § 1828.
 Petition, supplemental information, see Probate Code § 1821.
Transaction defined for purposes of this Chapter, see Probate Code § 3100.

§ 3143. Order declaring legal capacity

(a) If the petition requests that the court make an order declaring a spouse to have legal capacity for the proposed transaction and the court determines that the spouse has legal capacity for the proposed transaction, the court shall so order.

(b) If the petition alleges that a spouse having no conservator lacks legal capacity for the proposed transaction and the court determines that the spouse has legal capacity for the transaction, the court shall make an order so declaring. *(Stats.1990, c. 79 (A.B.759), § 14, operative July 1, 1991.)*

Cross References

Authorization of proceedings, see Probate Code § 3101.
Conservator defined for purposes of this Part, see Probate Code § 3004.
Hearings and orders, see Probate Code § 1040 et seq.
Legal capacity, see Probate Code § 3012.
Transaction defined for purposes of this Chapter, see Probate Code § 3100.

§ 3144. Order authorizing transaction

(a) The court may authorize the proposed transaction if the court determines all of the following:

(1) The property that is the subject of the proposed transaction is community property of the spouses, and, if the proposed transaction involves property in which a spouse also has a separate property interest, that there is good cause to include that separate property in the transaction.

(2) One of the spouses then has a conservator or otherwise lacks legal capacity for the proposed transaction.

(3) The other spouse either has legal capacity for the proposed transaction or has a conservator.

(4) Each of the spouses either (i) joins in or consents to the proposed transaction, (ii) has a conservator, or (iii) is substantially unable to manage his or her own financial resources or resist fraud or undue influence. Substantial inability may not be proved by isolated incidents of negligence or improvidence.

(5) The proposed transaction is one that should be authorized under this chapter.

(b) If the proposed transaction is to provide gifts or otherwise affect estate planning of the spouse who is alleged to lack capacity, as would be properly the subject of a petition under Article 10 (commencing with Section 2580) of Chapter 6 of Part 4 (substituted judgment) in the case of a conservatorship, the court may authorize the transaction under this chapter only if the transaction is one that the court would authorize under that article.

(c) If the court determines under subdivision (a) that the transaction should be authorized, the court shall so order and may authorize the petitioner to do and perform all acts and to execute and deliver all papers, documents, and instruments necessary to effectuate the order.

(d) In an order authorizing a transaction, the court may prescribe any terms and conditions as the court in its discretion determines appropriate, including, but not limited to, requiring joinder or consent of another person. *(Stats.1990, c. 79 (A.B.759), § 14, operative July 1, 1991. Amended by Stats.1996, c. 877 (A.B.1467), § 5; Stats.2003, c. 32 (A.B.167), § 4.)*

Cross References

Community property defined for purposes of this Part, see Probate Code § 3002.
Conclusiveness of judgment, see Code of Civil Procedure § 1908.
Conservator defined for purposes of this Part, see Probate Code § 3004.
Determination of character of property, see Probate Code § 3101.
Fraud, see Civil Code § 1571 et seq.
Hearings and orders, generally, see Probate Code § 1040 et seq.
Negligence, see Civil Code § 1714.
Protection of rights of spouse who lacks legal capacity, see Probate Code § 3057.
Rights of spouses in proceeds of transaction, see Probate Code § 3020.
Satisfaction of joinder or consent requirements, see Probate Code § 3071.
Transaction defined for purposes of this Chapter, see Probate Code § 3100.
Undue influence, see Civil Code § 1575.

Research References

Forms

7PT1 Am. Jur. Pl. & Pr. Forms Community Property § 89, Order—Permitting Spouse of Incompetent Person to Sell Community Property.
West's California Code Forms, Probate § 3144 Form 1, Order Authorizing Transaction.

§ 3145. Effect of determination of lack of legal capacity

A court determination pursuant to this chapter that a spouse lacks legal capacity for the proposed transaction affects the legal capacity of the spouse for that transaction alone and has no effect on the legal capacity of the spouse for any other purpose. *(Stats.1990, c. 79 (A.B.759), § 14, operative July 1, 1991.)*

Cross References

Conclusiveness of judgment, see Code of Civil Procedure § 1908.
Legal capacity, see Probate Code § 3012.

§ 3145

Transaction defined for purposes of this Chapter, see Probate Code § 3100.

ARTICLE 6. CONSUMMATION OF TRANSACTION

Section
- 3150. Bond.
- 3151. Execution, delivery and recordation of documents.
- 3152. Validity of conveyance or other disposition.
- 3153. Liability of conservator.
- 3154. Further proceedings if transaction not consummated.

§ 3150. Bond

(a) Unless the court for good cause dispenses with the bond, the court shall require the petitioner to give a bond, in the amount fixed by the court, conditioned on the duty of the petitioner to account for and apply the proceeds of the transaction to be received by the petitioner only as the court may by order direct.

(b) Unless the court for good cause fixes the amount of the bond in a lesser amount, if given by an admitted surety insurer, the bond shall be in an amount not less than the value of the personal property (including cash and any notes) to be received by the petitioner, as determined by the court.

(c) If the sureties on the bond are personal sureties, the bond shall be approved by the court and shall be for twice the amount required for a bond given by an admitted surety insurer.

(d) Section 2328 is applicable to the bond of the petitioner under this chapter. *(Stats.1990, c. 79 (A.B.759), § 14, operative July 1, 1991.)*

Cross References

Bond and Undertaking Law, see Code of Civil Procedure § 995.010 et seq.
Transaction defined for purposes of this Chapter, see Probate Code § 3100.

§ 3151. Execution, delivery and recordation of documents

(a) The petitioner shall, upon receipt of the consideration therefor, execute, acknowledge, and deliver any necessary instruments or documents as directed by the court, setting forth therein that they are made by authority of the order.

(b) The petitioner shall cause a certified copy of the order to be recorded in the office of the recorder of each county in which is located any real property affected by the order or any real property upon which there is a lien or encumbrance affected by the order.

(c) If a sale is made upon a credit pursuant to the order, the petitioner shall take the note of the person to whom the sale is made for the amount of the unpaid balance of the purchase money, with such security for the payment thereof as the court shall by order approve. The note shall be made payable to the petitioner or, if the petition was made by a conservator, to the petitioner as conservator. *(Stats.1990, c. 79 (A.B.759), § 14, operative July 1, 1991.)*

Cross References

Acknowledgment of instruments, see Civil Code § 1180 et seq.
Conservator defined for purposes of this Part, see Probate Code § 3004.
Documents to be recorded, see Government Code § 27280 et seq.
Recording transfers, see Civil Code § 1169 et seq.

§ 3152. Validity of conveyance or other disposition

A sale, conveyance, assignment, transfer, exchange, encumbrance, security interest, mortgage, deed of trust, lease, dedication, release, or relinquishment, and any instrument or document, made pursuant to the court's order, is as valid and effectual as if the property affected thereby were the sole and absolute property of the person making it. *(Stats.1990, c. 79 (A.B.759), § 14, operative July 1, 1991.)*

§ 3153. Liability of conservator

Notes, encumbrances, security interests, mortgages, leases, or deeds of trust, executed as provided in this chapter by a petitioning conservator create no personal liability against the conservator so executing, unless the conservator is one of the spouses and then only to the extent that personal liability would have resulted had both spouses had legal capacity for the transaction and joined in the execution. *(Stats.1990, c. 79 (A.B.759), § 14, operative July 1, 1991.)*

Cross References

Conservator defined for purposes of this Part, see Probate Code § 3004.
Legal capacity defined, see Probate Code § 3012.
Transaction defined for purposes of this Chapter, see Probate Code § 3100.

§ 3154. Further proceedings if transaction not consummated

(a) If any party to the transaction, other than the petitioner, does not consummate a transaction authorized by the court, the court, on application of the petitioner, after such notice to the parties to the transaction as the court directs, may vacate the order authorizing the transaction.

(b) If the order authorized the sale or encumbrance of property, the petitioner may by supplemental petition apply to the court for an order authorizing any other sale or encumbrance of the property to the advantage, benefit, or best interests of the spouses or their estates. The supplemental petition and a notice of the time and place of the hearing shall be served and mailed as provided in Article 4 (commencing with Section 3130) except that (1) no further citation shall be issued and (2) a copy of the supplemental petition and a notice of the time and place of the hearing shall be served upon any person who has appeared as representative of a nonpetitioning spouse or upon counsel of record for a nonpetitioning spouse or as the court may otherwise direct.

(c) If it appears to the court that the other sale or encumbrance is to the advantage, benefit, or best interests of the spouses or their estates and that the request in the supplemental petition that the transaction be authorized should be granted, the court may so order and may authorize the petitioner to do and perform acts and to execute and deliver all papers, documents, and instruments necessary to effectuate the order. *(Stats.1990, c. 79 (A.B.759), § 14, operative July 1, 1991.)*

Cross References

Notice of hearing, generally, see Probate Code § 1200 et seq.
Proof of giving notice, see Probate Code § 1260 et seq.
Transaction defined for purposes of this Chapter, see Probate Code § 3100.

Research References

Forms

7PT1 Am. Jur. Pl. & Pr. Forms Community Property § 77, Statutory References.
West's California Code Forms, Probate § 1820 Form 1, Attachment Requesting Special Orders Regarding a Major Neurocognitive Disorder.
West's California Code Forms, Probate § 3154 Form 1, Order Vacating Order of Sale.

Part 7

CAPACITY DETERMINATIONS AND HEALTH CARE DECISIONS FOR ADULT WITHOUT CONSERVATOR

Section
- 3200. Definitions.
- 3201. Petition.
- 3202. Jurisdiction and venue.
- 3203. Persons authorized to file petition.
- 3204. Contents of petition.
- 3205. Appointment of legal counsel.
- 3206. Notice of hearing and copy of petition; service; exceptions; considerations by court.

GUARDIANSHIP—CONSERVATORSHIP LAW § 3203

Section	
3207.	Submission for determination on medical declarations.
3208.	Order authorizing health care.
3208.5.	Patient with capacity to consent; court findings and orders.
3209.	Continuing jurisdiction of court.
3210.	Procedure supplemental and alternative.
3211.	Prohibition against placement in mental health treatment facility; restrictions on treatment.
3212.	Treatment by spiritual means.

§ 3200. Definitions

As used in this part:

(a) "Health care" means any care, treatment, service, or procedure to maintain, diagnose, or otherwise affect a patient's physical or mental condition.

(b) "Health care decision" means a decision regarding the patient's health care, including the following:

(1) Selection and discharge of health care providers and institutions.

(2) Approval or disapproval of diagnostic tests, surgical procedures, programs of medication.

(3) Directions to provide, withhold, or withdraw artificial nutrition and hydration and all other forms of health care, including cardiopulmonary resuscitation.

(c) "Health care institution" means an institution, facility, or agency licensed, certified, or otherwise authorized or permitted by law to provide health care in the ordinary course of business.

(d) "Patient" means an adult who does not have a conservator of the person and for whom a health care decision needs to be made. *(Stats.1990, c. 79 (A.B.759), § 14, operative July 1, 1991. Amended by Stats.1999, c. 658 (A.B.891), § 15, operative July 1, 2000.)*

Cross References

Fee for filing petition commencing or opposition papers concerning certain probate proceedings, see Government Code § 70655.
Medical treatment of ward or conservatee, consent, see Probate Code § 2353 et seq.
Powers and duties of guardian or conservator of the person, see Probate Code § 2350 et seq.

Research References

Forms

West's California Code Forms, Probate § 1820 Form 1, Attachment Requesting Special Orders Regarding a Major Neurocognitive Disorder.
West's California Code Forms, Probate § 3204 Form 2, Medical Declaration of Patient's Physician.

§ 3201. Petition

(a) A petition may be filed to determine that a patient has the capacity to make a health care decision concerning an existing or continuing condition.

(b) A petition may be filed to determine that a patient lacks the capacity to make a health care decision concerning specified treatment for an existing or continuing condition, and further for an order authorizing a designated person to make a health care decision on behalf of the patient.

(c) One proceeding may be brought under this part under both subdivisions (a) and (b). *(Stats.1990, c. 79 (A.B.759), § 14, operative July 1, 1991. Amended by Stats.1995, c. 842 (S.B.730), § 9; Stats. 1996, c. 178 (S.B.1650), § 9; Stats.1999, c. 658 (A.B.891), § 16, operative July 1, 2000.)*

Cross References

Health care decision defined for purposes of this Part, see Probate Code § 3200.
Health care defined for purposes of this Part, see Probate Code § 3200.
Medical treatment of ward, see Probate Code § 2353 et seq.
Order authorizing treatment, see Probate Code § 3208.
Patient defined for purposes of this Part, see Probate Code § 3200.
Petitions and other papers, generally, see Probate Code § 1020 et seq.

Research References

Forms

2 California Transactions Forms--Business Transactions § 15:3.50, Ethical Considerations.
2 California Transactions Forms--Estate Planning § 8:8, Ethical Considerations.
West's California Code Forms, Probate § 3204 Form 2, Medical Declaration of Patient's Physician.

§ 3202. Jurisdiction and venue

The petition may be filed in the superior court of any of the following counties:

(a) The county in which the patient resides.

(b) The county in which the patient is temporarily living.

(c) Such other county as may be in the best interests of the patient. *(Stats.1990, c. 79 (A.B.759), § 14, operative July 1, 1991.)*

Cross References

Guardianship and conservatorship proceedings, jurisdiction and venue, see Probate Code § 2200 et seq.
Patient defined for purposes of this Part, see Probate Code § 3200.

Research References

Forms

West's California Code Forms, Probate § 3204 Form 2, Medical Declaration of Patient's Physician.

§ 3203. Persons authorized to file petition

A petition may be filed by any of the following:

(a) The patient.

(b) The patient's spouse.

(c) A relative or friend of the patient, or other interested person, including the patient's agent under a power of attorney for health care.

(d) The patient's physician.

(e) A person acting on behalf of the health care institution in which the patient is located if the patient is in a health care institution.

(f) The public guardian or other county officer designated by the board of supervisors of the county in which the patient is located or resides or is temporarily living. *(Stats.1990, c. 79 (A.B.759), § 14, operative July 1, 1991. Amended by Stats.1999, c. 658 (A.B.891), § 17, operative July 1, 2000.)*

Cross References

Health care defined for purposes of this Part, see Probate Code § 3200.
Health care institution defined for purposes of this Part, see Probate Code § 3200.
Interested person defined, see Probate Code § 1424.
Patient defined for purposes of this Part, see Probate Code § 3200.

§ 3203

Public guardian, generally, see Probate Code § 2900 et seq.

Research References

Forms

West's California Code Forms, Probate § 3204 Form 2, Medical Declaration of Patient's Physician.

§ 3204. Contents of petition

The petition shall state, or set forth by a medical declaration attached to the petition, all of the following known to the petitioner at the time the petition is filed:

(a) The condition of the patient's health that requires treatment.

(b) The recommended health care that is considered to be medically appropriate.

(c) The threat to the patient's condition if authorization for the recommended health care is delayed or denied by the court.

(d) The predictable or probable outcome of the recommended health care.

(e) The medically available alternatives, if any, to the recommended health care.

(f) The efforts made to obtain consent from the patient.

(g) If the petition is filed by a person on behalf of a health care institution, the name of the person to be designated to give consent to the recommended health care on behalf of the patient.

(h) The deficit or deficits in the patient's mental functions listed in subdivision (a) of Section 811 that are impaired, and an identification of a link between the deficit or deficits and the patient's inability to respond knowingly and intelligently to queries about the recommended health care or inability to participate in a decision about the recommended health care by means of a rational thought process.

(i) The names and addresses, so far as they are known to the petitioner, of the persons specified in subdivision (b) of Section 1821. *(Stats.1990, c. 79 (A.B.759), § 14, operative July 1, 1991. Amended by Stats.1995, c. 842 (S.B.730), § 10; Stats.1996, c. 178 (S.B.1650), § 10; Stats.1996, c. 563 (S.B.392), § 15; Stats.1999, c. 658 (A.B.891), § 18, operative July 1, 2000.)*

Cross References

Affidavits, see Code of Civil Procedure §§ 2003, 2009 et seq.
Court ordered medical treatment of ward or conservatee, see Probate Code § 2353 et seq.
Health care defined for purposes of this Part, see Probate Code § 3200.
Health care institution defined for purposes of this Part, see Probate Code § 3200.
Patient defined for purposes of this Part, see Probate Code § 3200.
Petitions and other papers, generally, see Probate Code § 1020 et seq.

Research References

Forms

2 California Transactions Forms--Business Transactions § 15:3.50, Ethical Considerations.
2 California Transactions Forms--Estate Planning § 8:8, Ethical Considerations.
West's California Code Forms, Probate § 3204 Form 2, Medical Declaration of Patient's Physician.

§ 3205. Appointment of legal counsel

Upon the filing of the petition, the court shall determine the name of the attorney the patient has retained to represent the patient in the proceeding under this part or the name of the attorney the patient plans to retain for that purpose. If the patient has not retained an attorney and does not plan to retain one, the court shall appoint the public defender or private counsel under Section 1471 to consult with and represent the patient at the hearing on the petition and, if such appointment is made, Section 1472 applies. *(Stats.1990, c. 79 (A.B.759), § 14, operative July 1, 1991.)*

Cross References

Appointment legal of counsel, see Probate Code § 1470 et seq.
Patient defined for purposes of this Part, see Probate Code § 3200.
Public defender, duty to represent persons not financially able to employ counsel, see Government Code § 27706.

Research References

Forms

West's California Code Forms, Probate § 3204 Form 2, Medical Declaration of Patient's Physician.

§ 3206. Notice of hearing and copy of petition; service; exceptions; considerations by court

(a) Not less than 15 days before the hearing, notice of the time and place of the hearing and a copy of the petition shall be personally served on the patient, the patient's attorney, and the agent under the patient's power of attorney for health care, if any.

(b) Not less than 15 days before the hearing, notice of the time and place of the hearing and a copy of the petition shall be delivered pursuant to Section 1215 to the following persons:

(1) The patient's spouse, if any, at the address stated in the petition.

(2) The patient's relatives named in the petition at their addresses stated in the petition.

(c) For good cause, the court may shorten or waive notice of the hearing as provided by this section. In determining the period of notice to be required, the court shall take into account both of the following:

(1) The existing medical facts and circumstances set forth in the petition or in a medical declaration attached to the petition or in a medical declaration presented to the court.

(2) The desirability, where the condition of the patient permits, of giving adequate notice to all interested persons. *(Added by Stats.1996, c. 563 (S.B.392), § 17. Amended by Stats.1999, c. 658 (A.B.891), § 19, operative July 1, 2000; Stats.2017, c. 319 (A.B.976), § 58, eff. Jan. 1, 2018.)*

Cross References

Affidavits, see Code of Civil Procedure §§ 2003, 2009 et seq.
Health care defined for purposes of this Part, see Probate Code § 3200.
Notices,
  Generally, see Probate Code § 1460 et seq.
  Proof of giving notice, see Probate Code § 1260 et seq.
Patient defined for purposes of this Part, see Probate Code § 3200.

Research References

Forms

West's California Code Forms, Probate § 3204 Form 2, Medical Declaration of Patient's Physician.

§ 3207. Submission for determination on medical declarations

Notwithstanding Section 3206, the matter presented by the petition may be submitted for the determination of the court upon proper and sufficient medical declarations if the attorney for the petitioner and the attorney for the patient so stipulate and further stipulate that there remains no issue of fact to be determined. *(Stats.1990, c. 79 (A.B.759), § 14, operative July 1, 1991. Amended by Stats.1999, c. 658 (A.B.891), § 20, operative July 1, 2000.)*

Cross References

Notice of hearing generally, see Probate Code § 1200 et seq.

Patient defined for purposes of this Part, see Probate Code § 3200.

Research References

Forms

West's California Code Forms, Probate § 3204 Form 2, Medical Declaration of Patient's Physician.

§ 3208. Order authorizing health care

(a) Except as provided in subdivision (b), the court may make an order authorizing the recommended health care for the patient and designating a person to give consent to the recommended health care on behalf of the patient if the court determines from the evidence all of the following:

(1) The existing or continuing condition of the patient's health requires the recommended health care.

(2) If untreated, there is a probability that the condition will become life-endangering or result in a serious threat to the physical or mental health of the patient.

(3) The patient is unable to consent to the recommended health care.

(b) In determining whether the patient's mental functioning is so severely impaired that the patient lacks the capacity to make any health care decision, the court may take into consideration the frequency, severity, and duration of periods of impairment.

(c) The court may make an order authorizing withholding or withdrawing artificial nutrition and hydration and all other forms of health care and designating a person to give or withhold consent to the recommended health care on behalf of the patient if the court determines from the evidence all of the following:

(1) The recommended health care is in accordance with the patient's best interest, taking into consideration the patient's personal values to the extent known to the petitioner.

(2) The patient is unable to consent to the recommended health care. *(Stats.1990, c. 79 (A.B.759), § 14, operative July 1, 1991. Amended by Stats.1990, c. 710 (S.B.1775), § 12, operative July 1, 1991; Stats.1995, c. 842 (S.B.730), § 11; Stats.1999, c. 658 (A.B.891), § 21, operative July 1, 2000.)*

Cross References

Health care decision defined for purposes of this Part, see Probate Code § 3200.
Health care defined for purposes of this Part, see Probate Code § 3200.
Patient defined for purposes of this Part, see Probate Code § 3200.

Research References

Forms

2 California Transactions Forms--Business Transactions § 15:3.50, Ethical Considerations.

2 California Transactions Forms--Estate Planning § 8:8, Ethical Considerations.

West's California Code Forms, Probate § 3204 Form 2, Medical Declaration of Patient's Physician.

West's California Code Forms, Probate § 3208 Form 1, Order Determining that Patient Lacks Capacity to Make Health Care Decision and Authorizing Designated Person to Make Health Care Decision on Behalf of Patient.

§ 3208.5. Patient with capacity to consent; court findings and orders

In a proceeding under this part:

(a) Where the patient has the capacity to consent to the recommended health care, the court shall so find in its order.

(b) Where the court has determined that the patient has the capacity to consent to the recommended health care, the court shall, if requested, determine whether the patient has accepted or refused the recommended health care, and whether the patient's consent to the recommended health care is an informed consent.

(c) Where the court finds that the patient has the capacity to consent to the recommended health care, but that the patient refuses consent, the court shall not make an order authorizing the recommended health care or designating a person to give consent to the recommended health care. If an order has been made authorizing the recommended health care and designating a person to give consent to the recommended health care, the order shall be revoked if the court determines that the patient has recovered the capacity to consent to the recommended health care. Until revoked or modified, the order is effective authorization for the recommended health care. *(Added by Stats.1999, c. 658 (A.B.891), § 22, operative July 1, 2000.)*

Cross References

Health care defined for purposes of this Part, see Probate Code § 3200.
Patient defined for purposes of this Part, see Probate Code § 3200.

Research References

Forms

West's California Code Forms, Probate § 3208 Form 1, Order Determining that Patient Lacks Capacity to Make Health Care Decision and Authorizing Designated Person to Make Health Care Decision on Behalf of Patient.

§ 3209. Continuing jurisdiction of court

The court in which the petition is filed has continuing jurisdiction to revoke or modify an order made under this part upon a petition filed, noticed, and heard in the same manner as an original petition filed under this part. *(Stats.1990, c. 79 (A.B.759), § 14, operative July 1, 1991.)*

§ 3210. Procedure supplemental and alternative

(a) This part is supplemental and alternative to other procedures or methods for obtaining consent to health care or making health care decisions, and is permissive and cumulative for the relief to which it applies.

(b) Nothing in this part limits the providing of health care in an emergency case in which the health care is required because (1) the health care is required for the alleviation of severe pain or (2) the patient has a medical condition that, if not immediately diagnosed and treated, will lead to serious disability or death.

(c) Nothing in this part supersedes the right that any person may have under existing law to make health care decisions on behalf of a patient, or affects the decisionmaking process of a health care institution. *(Stats.1990, c. 79 (A.B.759), § 14, operative July 1, 1991. Amended by Stats.1999, c. 658 (A.B.891), § 23, operative July 1, 2000.)*

Cross References

Health care decision defined for purposes of this Part, see Probate Code § 3200.
Health care defined for purposes of this Part, see Probate Code § 3200.
Health care institution defined for purposes of this Part, see Probate Code § 3200.
Patient defined for purposes of this Part, see Probate Code § 3200.

Research References

Forms

West's California Code Forms, Probate § 3204 Form 2, Medical Declaration of Patient's Physician.

§ 3211. Prohibition against placement in mental health treatment facility; restrictions on treatment

(a) No person may be placed in a mental health treatment facility under the provisions of this part.

§ 3211

(b) No experimental drug as defined in Section 111515 of the Health and Safety Code may be prescribed for or administered to any person under this part.

(c) No convulsive treatment as defined in Section 5325 of the Welfare and Institutions Code may be performed on any person under this part.

(d) No person may be sterilized under this part.

(e) The provisions of this part are subject to a valid advance health care directive under the Health Care Decisions Law, Division 4.7 (commencing with Section 4600). *(Stats.1990, c. 79 (A.B.759), § 14, operative July 1, 1991. Amended by Stats.1996, c. 1023 (S.B.1497), § 399, eff. Sept. 29, 1996; Stats.1999, c. 658 (A.B.891), § 24, operative July 1, 2000.)*

Cross References

Health care decision defined for purposes of this Part, see Probate Code § 3200.
Health care defined for purposes of this Part, see Probate Code § 3200.
Wards or conservatees, involuntary placement in mental health treatment facility, see Probate Code § 2356.

Research References
Forms

West's California Code Forms, Probate § 3204 Form 2, Medical Declaration of Patient's Physician.

§ 3212. Treatment by spiritual means

Nothing in this part shall be construed to supersede or impair the right of any individual to choose treatment by spiritual means in lieu of medical treatment, nor shall any individual choosing treatment by spiritual means, in accordance with the tenets and practices of that individual's established religious tradition, be required to submit to medical testing of any kind pursuant to a determination of capacity. *(Added by Stats.1999, c. 658 (A.B.891), § 25, operative July 1, 2000.)*

Research References
Forms

West's California Code Forms, Probate § 1820 Form 1, Attachment Requesting Special Orders Regarding a Major Neurocognitive Disorder.

Part 8

OTHER PROTECTIVE PROCEEDINGS

Cross References

Recovery by minor under uninsured motorists' coverage, see Insurance Code § 11580.3.

CHAPTER 1. GENERAL PROVISIONS

Section
3300. Accounting by parent to minor for money received.
3303. Effect on Uniform Transfers to Minors Act.

§ 3300. Accounting by parent to minor for money received

A parent who receives any money or property belonging to a minor under any provision of this part shall account to the minor for the money or other property when the minor reaches the age of majority. *(Stats.1990, c. 79 (A.B.759), § 14, operative July 1, 1991.)*

Cross References

Age of majority, see Family Code § 6500 et seq.
Money or property belonging to minor, see Probate Code § 3400 et seq.
Transfers to minors, accounts and accounting, see Probate Code §§ 3912, 3919.

Uniform Transfers to Minors Act, see Probate Code § 3900 et seq.

Research References
Forms

1 California Transactions Forms--Estate Planning § 1:29, Options Involving Gifts to Minors.

§ 3303. Effect on Uniform Transfers to Minors Act

Nothing in this part limits the provisions of the California Uniform Transfers to Minors Act, Part 9 (commencing with Section 3900). *(Stats.1990, c. 79 (A.B.759), § 14, operative July 1, 1991.)*

CHAPTER 2. MONEY OR PROPERTY BELONGING TO MINOR

ARTICLE 1. TOTAL ESTATE NOT IN EXCESS OF $5,000

Section
3400. Total estate of minor; deductions.
3401. Delivery of money or property to parent.
3402. Written receipt of parent; effect.

§ 3400. Total estate of minor; deductions

(a) As used in this article, "total estate of the minor" includes both the money and other property belonging to the minor and the money and other property belonging to the guardianship estate, if any, of the minor.

(b) In computing the "total estate of the minor" for the purposes of this article, all of the following shall be deducted:

(1) "Custodial property" held pursuant to the California Uniform Transfers to Minors Act, Part 9 (commencing with Section 3900).

(2) Any money or property subject to court order pursuant to subdivision (c) of Section 3602 or Article 2 (commencing with Section 3610) of Chapter 4. *(Stats.1990, c. 79 (A.B.759), § 14, operative July 1, 1991.)*

Cross References

Custody, services and earnings of minors, see Family Code §§ 7500, 7503.

Research References
Forms

1 California Transactions Forms--Estate Planning § 6:15, Minors' Capacity to Take Devised Property.
1 California Transactions Forms--Estate Planning § 6:53, Matters to Consider in Drafting Gifts to Minors.
1 California Transactions Forms--Estate Planning § 6:79, Distribution of Minor's Bequest to Parents.
2 California Transactions Forms--Estate Planning § 10:34, Multiple Party Accounts.
West's California Code Forms, Probate § 3410 Comment, Court Ordered Transfer of Money Belonging to a Minor.

§ 3401. Delivery of money or property to parent

(a) Where a minor does not have a guardian of the estate, money or other property belonging to the minor may be paid or delivered to a parent of the minor entitled to the custody of the minor to be held in trust for the minor until the minor reaches majority if the requirements of subdivision (c) are satisfied.

(b) Where the minor has a guardian of the estate, all the money and other property belonging to the guardianship estate may be paid or delivered to a parent entitled to the custody of the minor to be held in trust for the minor until the minor reaches majority if the requirements of subdivision (c) are satisfied.

(c) This section applies only if both of the following requirements are satisfied:

(1) The total estate of the minor, including the money and other property to be paid or delivered to the parent, does not exceed five thousand dollars ($5,000) in value.

(2) The parent to whom the money or other property is to be paid or delivered gives the person making the payment or delivery written assurance, verified by the oath of such parent, that the total estate of the minor, including the money or other property to be paid or delivered to the parent, does not exceed five thousand dollars ($5,000) in value. *(Stats.1990, c. 79 (A.B.759), § 14, operative July 1, 1991.)*

Cross References

Cities and counties, unclaimed money, see Government Code § 50052.5.
Duty of parent to account to minor, see Probate Code § 3300.
Payment of money belonging to minor, see Probate Code §§ 3412, 3413.
Payment of wages of minors, see Family Code § 7503.
Payment or delivery of proceeds of judgment, see Probate Code § 3611.
Right of parent to child's earnings, see Family Code § 7500.
Termination of guardianship by court, see Probate Code § 2626.

Research References

Forms

1 California Transactions Forms--Estate Planning § 6:15, Minors' Capacity to Take Devised Property.
1 California Transactions Forms--Estate Planning § 6:53, Matters to Consider in Drafting Gifts to Minors.
1 California Transactions Forms--Estate Planning § 6:79, Distribution of Minor's Bequest to Parents.
4 California Transactions Forms--Estate Planning § 20:10, Devises to Minors.
West's California Code Forms, Probate § 3401 Form 1, Declaration by Parent Under Probate Code §3401.
West's California Code Forms, Probate § 6240 Form 1, California Statutory Will.

§ 3402. Written receipt of parent; effect

The written receipt of the parent giving the written assurance under Section 3401 shall be an acquittance of the person making the payment of money or delivery of other property pursuant to this article. *(Stats.1990, c. 79 (A.B.759), § 14, operative July 1, 1991.)*

Cross References

Custody, services and earnings of minors, see Family Code §§ 7500, 7503.

Research References

Forms

West's California Code Forms, Probate § 3401 Form 1, Declaration by Parent Under Probate Code §3401.

ARTICLE 2. PROPERTY IN THE FORM OF MONEY

Section
3410. Application of article; computation of money belonging to minor.
3411. Filing of petition; venue.
3412. Court-ordered termination of guardianship where sole asset of guardianship estate is money; additional orders within court's discretion.
3413. Order of court if no guardianship exists.

§ 3410. Application of article; computation of money belonging to minor

(a) This article applies to both of the following cases:

(1) Where the minor has a guardian of the estate and the sole asset of the guardianship estate is money.

(2) Where the minor has no guardian of the estate and there is money belonging to the minor.

(b) This article does not apply to, and there shall be excluded in computing "money belonging to the minor" for the purpose of this article, all of the following:

(1) Money or property which is or will be held as "custodial property" pursuant to the California Uniform Transfers to Minors Act, Part 9 (commencing with Section 3900).

(2) Any money or property subject to court order pursuant to subdivision (c) of Section 3602 or Article 2 (commencing with Section 3610) of Chapter 4. *(Stats.1990, c. 79 (A.B.759), § 14, operative July 1, 1991.)*

Research References

Forms

West's California Code Forms, Probate § 3401 Form 1, Declaration by Parent Under Probate Code §3401.
West's California Code Forms, Probate § 3410 Comment, Court Ordered Transfer of Money Belonging to a Minor.

§ 3411. Filing of petition; venue

(a) A parent of a minor entitled to custody of the minor, the guardian of the estate of the minor, or the person holding the money belonging to the minor may file a petition requesting that the court make an order under this article.

(b) The petition shall be filed in the superior court of:

(1) The county where the minor resides if the minor has no guardian of the estate.

(2) The county having jurisdiction of the guardianship estate if the minor has a guardian of the estate. *(Stats.1990, c. 79 (A.B.759), § 14, operative July 1, 1991.)*

§ 3412. Court-ordered termination of guardianship where sole asset of guardianship estate is money; additional orders within court's discretion

If the minor has a guardian of the estate and the sole asset of the guardianship estate is money, the court may order that the guardianship of the estate be terminated and, if the court so orders, the court in its discretion shall also order any one or more of the following:

(a) That the money be deposited in an insured account in a financial institution in this state, or in a single-premium deferred annuity, subject to withdrawal only upon authorization of the court.

(b) That all or any part of the money be transferred to a custodian for the benefit of the minor under the California Uniform Transfers to Minors Act, Part 9 (commencing with Section 3900).

(c) If the money of the guardianship estate does not exceed twenty thousand dollars ($20,000), that the money be held on any other condition that the court in its discretion determines to be in the best interests of the minor.

(d) If the money of the guardianship estate does not exceed five thousand dollars ($5,000), that all or any part of the money be paid to a parent of the minor, without bond, upon the terms and under the conditions specified in Article 1 (commencing with Section 3400).

(e) That the remaining balance of any money paid or to be paid be deposited with the county treasurer, if all of the following conditions are met:

(1) The county treasurer has been authorized by the county board of supervisors to handle the deposits.

(2) The county treasurer shall receive and safely keep all money deposited with the county treasurer pursuant to this subdivision, shall pay the money out only upon the order of the court, and shall credit each estate with the interest earned by the funds deposited less the county treasurer's actual cost authorized to be recovered under Section 27013 of the Government Code.

(3) The county treasurer and sureties on the official bond of the county treasurer are responsible for the safekeeping and payment of the money.

(4) The county treasurer shall ensure that the money deposited is to earn interest or dividends, or both, at the highest rate which the county can reasonably obtain as a prudent investor.

(5) Funds so deposited with the county treasurer shall only be invested or deposited in compliance with the provisions governing the investment or deposit of state funds set forth in Chapter 5 (commencing with Section 16640) of Part 2 of Division 4 of Title 2 of the Government Code, the investment or deposit of county funds set forth in Chapter 4 (commencing with Section 53600) of Part 1 of Division 2 of Title 5 of the Government Code, or as authorized under Chapter 6 (commencing with Section 2400) of Part 4. *(Stats.1990, c. 79 (A.B.759), § 14, operative July 1, 1991. Amended by Stats.1991, c. 413 (A.B.934), § 1; Stats.2004, c. 67 (A.B.1851), § 1.)*

Cross References

Cities, and other agencies, deposit of funds, local agency fund audit reports, see Government Code § 53686.
Definitions, single-premium deferred annuity, see Probate Code § 1446.

Research References

Forms

West's California Code Forms, Probate § 3410 Comment, Court Ordered Transfer of Money Belonging to a Minor.

§ 3413. Order of court if no guardianship exists

If the minor has no guardian of the estate and there is money belonging to the minor, the court may order that a guardian of the estate be appointed and that the money be paid to the guardian or the court may order any one or more of the following:

(a) That the money be deposited in an insured account in a financial institution in this state, or in a single-premium deferred annuity, subject to withdrawal only upon authorization of the court.

(b) That all or any part of the money be transferred to a custodian for the benefit of the minor under the California Uniform Transfers to Minors Act, Part 9 (commencing with Section 3900).

(c) If the money belonging to the minor does not exceed twenty thousand dollars ($20,000), that the money be held on any other condition that the court in its discretion determines to be in the best interests of the minor.

(d) If the money belonging to the minor does not exceed five thousand dollars ($5,000), that all or any part of the money be paid to a parent of the minor, without bond, upon the terms and under the conditions specified in Article 1 (commencing with Section 3400).

(e) That the remaining balance of any money paid or to be paid be deposited with the county treasurer, if all of the following conditions are met:

(1) The county treasurer has been authorized by the county board of supervisors to handle the deposits.

(2) The county treasurer shall receive and safely keep all money deposited with the county treasurer pursuant to this subdivision, shall pay the money out only upon the order of the court, and shall credit each estate with the interest earned by the funds deposited less the county treasurer's actual cost authorized to be recovered under Section 27013 of the Government Code.

(3) The county treasurer and sureties on the official bond of the county treasurer are responsible for the safekeeping and payment of the money.

(4) The county treasurer shall ensure that the money deposited is to earn interest or dividends, or both, at the highest rate which the county can reasonably obtain as a prudent investor.

(5) Funds so deposited with the county treasurer shall only be invested or deposited in compliance with the provisions governing the investment or deposit of state funds set forth in Chapter 5 (commencing with Section 16640) of Part 2 of Division 4 of Title 2 of the Government Code, the investment or deposit of county funds set forth in Chapter 4 (commencing with Section 53600) of Part 1 of Division 2 of Title 5 of the Government Code, or as authorized under Chapter 6 (commencing with Section 2400) of Part 4. *(Stats.1990, c. 79 (A.B.759), § 14, operative July 1, 1991. Amended by Stats.1991, c. 413 (A.B.934), § 2; Stats.2004, c. 67 (A.B.1851), § 2.)*

Cross References

Cities, and other agencies, deposit of funds, local agency fund audit reports, see Government Code § 53686.
Definitions,
    Money belonging to the minor, see Probate Code § 3410.
    Single-premium deferred annuity, see Probate Code § 1446.

Research References

Forms

1 California Transactions Forms--Estate Planning § 6:15, Minors' Capacity to Take Devised Property.
West's California Code Forms, Probate § 3401 Form 1, Declaration by Parent Under Probate Code §3401.
West's California Code Forms, Probate § 3410 Comment, Court Ordered Transfer of Money Belonging to a Minor.

CHAPTER 3. COMPROMISE BY PARENT OF MINOR'S DISPUTED CLAIM

Section
3500. Parental right to compromise minor's claim.
3505. Hearing on petition for compromise of minor's disputed claim.

§ 3500. Parental right to compromise minor's claim

(a) When a minor has a disputed claim for damages, money, or other property and does not have a guardian of the estate, the following persons have the right to compromise, or to execute a covenant not to sue on or a covenant not to enforce judgment on, the claim, unless the claim is against such person or persons:

(1) Either parent if the parents of the minor are not living separate and apart.

(2) The parent having the care, custody, or control of the minor if the parents of the minor are living separate and apart.

(b) The compromise or covenant is valid only after it has been approved, upon the filing of a petition, by the superior court of either of the following counties:

(1) The county where the minor resides when the petition is filed.

(2) Any county where suit on the claim or matter properly could be brought.

(c) Any money or other property to be paid or delivered for the benefit of the minor pursuant to the compromise or covenant shall be paid and delivered in the manner and upon the terms and conditions specified in Chapter 4 (commencing with Section 3600).

(d) A parent having the right to compromise the disputed claim of the minor under this section may execute a full release and satisfaction, or execute a covenant not to sue on or a covenant not to enforce judgment on the disputed claim, after the money or other property to be paid or delivered has been paid or delivered as provided in subdivision (c). If the court orders that all or any part of the money to be paid under the compromise or covenant be deposited in an insured account in a financial institution in this state, or in a single-premium deferred annuity, the release and satisfaction or covenant is not effective for any purpose until the money has been deposited as directed in the order of the court. *(Stats.1990, c. 79 (A.B.759), § 14, operative July 1, 1991.)*

Cross References

Bank accounts by or in name of minors, see Financial Code § 1400.
Definitions, single-premium preferred annuity, see Probate Code § 1446.
Deposit of funds and assets in trust company, see Financial Code § 1586.
Insured savings associations, legal investment, see Financial Code § 7000 et seq.
Life and disability insurance, insurance of minors, see Insurance Code § 10112.
Money or property as delivered pursuant to compromise or judgment, see Code of Civil Procedure § 372.

Research References

Forms

3 California Transactions Forms--Business Transactions § 18:6, Capacity.
3 California Transactions Forms--Business Transactions § 18:16, Settlements that Require Court Approval.
West's California Code Forms, Probate § 2500–2507 Form 1, Petition by Guardian or Conservator to Approve Compromise of Disputed Personal Injury Claim of Minor or Incompetent Person—Judicial Council Form MC-350.
West's California Code Forms, Probate § 3500 Form 1, Petition by Parent to Compromise Disputed Personal Injury Claim of Minor Without a Guardian of the Estate—Judicial Council Form MC-350.
West's California Code Forms, Probate § 3600 Comment, Disposition of Compromise or Judgment Amount on Behalf of an Incompetent Person Without a Conservator of the Estate.
West's California Judicial Council Forms MC–350, Petition for Approval of Compromise of Claim or Action or Disposition of Proceeds of Judgment for Minor or Person With a Disability.
West's California Judicial Council Forms MC–350(A–12b(5)), Additional Medical Service Providers Attachment to Petition for Approval of Compromise of Claim or Action or Disposition of Proceeds of Judgment.
West's California Judicial Council Forms MC–350EX, Petition for Expedited Approval of Compromise of Claim or Action or Disposition of Proceeds of Judgment for Minor or Person With a Disability.
West's California Judicial Council Forms MC–351, Order Approving Compromise of Disputed Claim or Pending Action or Disposition of Proceeds of Judgment for Minor or Person With a Disability.
West's California Judicial Council Forms MC–355, Order to Deposit Money Into Blocked Account.
West's California Judicial Council Forms MC–356, Acknowledgment of Receipt of Order and Funds for Deposit in Blocked Account.

§ 3505. Hearing on petition for compromise of minor's disputed claim

The court shall schedule a hearing on a petition for compromise of a minor's disputed claim pursuant to Section 3500 within 30 days from the date of filing. If the petition is unopposed, the court shall issue a decision on the petition at the conclusion of the hearing. (Added by Stats.2021, c. 214 (S.B.241), § 8, eff. Jan. 1, 2022.)

CHAPTER 4. MONEY OR PROPERTY PAID OR DELIVERED PURSUANT TO COMPROMISE OR JUDGMENT FOR MINOR OR DISABLED PERSON

Application

For application of this chapter, see Probate Code § 3600.

Cross References

Destruction of court records, notice, retention periods, see Government Code § 68152.
Life and disability insurance, insurance of minors, see Insurance Code § 10112.

ARTICLE 1. GENERAL PROVISIONS

Section
3600. Application of chapter.
3601. Order directing payment of expenses, costs and fees.
3602. Disposition of remaining balance.
3603. Reference to "person with a disability".
3604. Payment to special needs trust; petition for order; trust requirements; jurisdiction of court; court orders.
3605. Statutes of limitation; death of beneficiary; notice of death; payment of claims; application of section.

Application

For application of this chapter, see Probate Code § 3600.

Cross References

Fee for filing petition and opposition papers concerning internal affairs of certain trusts or first accounts of trustees of certain testamentary trusts, see Government Code § 70652.

§ 3600. Application of chapter

This chapter applies whenever both of the following conditions exist:

(a) A court (1) approves a compromise of, or the execution of a covenant not to sue on or a covenant not to enforce judgment on, a minor's disputed claim, (2) approves a compromise of a pending action or proceeding to which a minor or person with a disability is a party, or (3) gives judgment for a minor or person with a disability.

(b) The compromise, covenant, or judgment provides for the payment or delivery of money or other property for the benefit of the minor or person with a disability. (Stats.1990, c. 79 (A.B.759), § 14, operative July 1, 1991. Amended by Stats.2004, c. 67 (A.B.1851), § 3.)

Cross References

Fee for filing petition commencing or opposition papers concerning certain probate proceedings, see Government Code § 70655.
Money or property as delivered pursuant to compromise or judgment, see Code of Civil Procedure § 372.
Payment of wages to minors until notice by guardian to employer, see Family Code § 7503.
References to "person with a disability" within this Chapter, see Probate Code § 3603.

Research References

Forms

Asset Protection: Legal Planning, Strategies and Forms ¶ 14.05, Planning Strategies for the Elderly and the Disabled.
3 California Transactions Forms--Business Transactions § 18:31, Delivery and Disposition of Settlement Proceeds.
3 California Transactions Forms--Estate Planning § 17:2, Types of Special Needs Trusts.
3 California Transactions Forms--Estate Planning § 17:13, Overview [Prob. Code §§3600 to 3613].
3 California Transactions Forms--Estate Planning § 17:14, Person With a Disability.
3 California Transactions Forms--Estate Planning § 17:15, Required Findings [Prob C § 3604(B)].
3 California Transactions Forms--Estate Planning § 17:32, Medi-Cal Reimbursement Claims.
3 California Transactions Forms--Estate Planning § 17:34, Notice.
3 California Transactions Forms--Estate Planning § 17:41, Types of Special Needs Trusts Requiring Payback Provisions (Self-Settled Trusts Established on or After October 1, 1993).
West's California Code Forms, Probate § 3401 Form 1, Declaration by Parent Under Probate Code §3401.
West's California Code Forms, Probate § 3410 Comment, Court Ordered Transfer of Money Belonging to a Minor.
West's California Code Forms, Probate § 3500 Form 1, Petition by Parent to Compromise Disputed Personal Injury Claim of Minor Without a Guardian of the Estate—Judicial Council Form MC-350.
West's California Code Forms, Probate § 3500 Form 2, Order Authorizing Parent to Compromise Claim of Minor Without Guardian—Judicial Council Form MC-351.
West's California Code Forms, Probate § 3600 Comment, Disposition of Compromise or Judgment Amount on Behalf of an Incompetent Person Without a Conservator of the Estate.

§ 3600

West's California Judicial Council Forms MC–350, Petition for Approval of Compromise of Claim or Action or Disposition of Proceeds of Judgment for Minor or Person With a Disability.

West's California Judicial Council Forms MC–350(A–12b(5)), Additional Medical Service Providers Attachment to Petition for Approval of Compromise of Claim or Action or Disposition of Proceeds of Judgment.

West's California Judicial Council Forms MC–350EX, Petition for Expedited Approval of Compromise of Claim or Action or Disposition of Proceeds of Judgment for Minor or Person With a Disability.

West's California Judicial Council Forms MC–351, Order Approving Compromise of Disputed Claim or Pending Action or Disposition of Proceeds of Judgment for Minor or Person With a Disability.

West's California Judicial Council Forms MC–355, Order to Deposit Money Into Blocked Account.

West's California Judicial Council Forms MC–356, Acknowledgment of Receipt of Order and Funds for Deposit in Blocked Account.

§ 3601. Order directing payment of expenses, costs and fees

(a) The court making the order or giving the judgment referred to in Section 3600, as a part thereof, shall make a further order authorizing and directing that reasonable expenses, medical or otherwise and including reimbursement to a parent, guardian, or conservator, costs, and attorney's fees, as the court shall approve and allow therein, shall be paid from the money or other property to be paid or delivered for the benefit of the minor or person with a disability.

(b) The order required by subdivision (a) may be directed to the following:

(1) A parent of the minor, the guardian ad litem, or the guardian of the estate of the minor or the conservator of the estate of the person with a disability.

(2) The payer of any money to be paid pursuant to the compromise, covenant, or judgment for the benefit of the minor or person with a disability. *(Stats.1990, c. 79 (A.B.759), § 14, operative July 1, 1991. Amended by Stats.2004, c. 67 (A.B.1851), § 4.)*

Application

For application of this chapter, see Probate Code § 3600.

Cross References

Contingent fee contract with attorney, see Probate Code § 2644.
Disposition of remaining balance where no guardianship or conservatorship, see Probate Code § 3610.
References to "person with a disability" within this Chapter, see Probate Code § 3603.

Research References

Forms

3 California Transactions Forms--Business Transactions § 18:18, Approval and Limitation of Attorney's Fees.
3 California Transactions Forms--Business Transactions § 18:31, Delivery and Disposition of Settlement Proceeds.
West's California Code Forms, Probate § 3500 Form 1, Petition by Parent to Compromise Disputed Personal Injury Claim of Minor Without a Guardian of the Estate—Judicial Council Form MC–350.

§ 3602. Disposition of remaining balance

(a) If there is no guardianship of the estate of the minor or conservatorship of the estate of the person with a disability, the remaining balance of the money and other property, after payment of all expenses, costs, and fees as approved and allowed by the court under Section 3601, shall be paid, delivered, deposited, or invested as provided in Article 2 (commencing with Section 3610).

(b) Except as provided in subdivisions (c) and (d), if there is a guardianship of the estate of the minor or conservatorship of the estate of the person with a disability, the remaining balance of the money and other property, after payment of all expenses, costs, and fees as approved and allowed by the court under Section 3601, shall be paid or delivered to the guardian or conservator of the estate.

Upon application of the guardian or conservator, the court making the order or giving the judgment referred to in Section 3600 or the court in which the guardianship or conservatorship proceeding is pending may, with or without notice, make an order that all or part of the money paid or to be paid to the guardian or conservator under this subdivision be deposited or invested as provided in Section 2456.

(c) Upon ex parte petition of the guardian or conservator or upon petition of any person interested in the guardianship or conservatorship estate, the court making the order or giving the judgment referred to in Section 3600 may for good cause shown order one or more of the following:

(1) That all or part of the remaining balance of money not become a part of the guardianship or conservatorship estate and instead be deposited in an insured account in a financial institution in this state, or in a single-premium deferred annuity, subject to withdrawal only upon authorization of the court.

(2) If there is a guardianship of the estate of the minor, that all or part of the remaining balance of money and other property not become a part of the guardianship estate and instead be transferred to a custodian for the benefit of the minor under the California Uniform Transfers to Minors Act, Part 9 (commencing with Section 3900).

(3) That all or part of the remaining balance of money and other property not become a part of the guardianship estate and, instead, be transferred to the trustee of a trust which is either created by, or approved of, in the order or judgment described in Section 3600. This trust shall be revocable by the minor upon attaining 18 years of age, and shall contain other terms and conditions, including, but not limited to, terms and conditions concerning trustee's accounts and trustee's bond, as the court determines to be necessary to protect the minor's interests.

(d) Upon petition of the guardian, conservator, or any person interested in the guardianship or conservatorship estate, the court making the order or giving the judgment referred to in Section 3600 may order that all or part of the remaining balance of money not become a part of the guardianship or conservatorship estate and instead be paid to a special needs trust established under Section 3604 for the benefit of the minor or person with a disability.

(e) If the petition is by a person other than the guardian or conservator, notice of hearing on a petition under subdivision (c) shall be given for the period and in the manner provided in Chapter 3 (commencing with Section 1460) of Part 1.

(f) Notice of the time and place of hearing on a petition under subdivision (d), and a copy of the petition, shall be delivered pursuant to Section 1215 to the State Director of Health Care Services, the Director of State Hospitals, and the Director of Developmental Services at the office of each director in Sacramento at least 15 days before the hearing. *(Stats.1990, c. 79 (A.B.759), § 14, operative July 1, 1991. Amended by Stats.1992, c. 355 (A.B. 3328), § 2; Stats.1996, c. 563 (S.B.392), § 18; Stats.2004, c. 67 (A.B.1851), § 5; Stats.2012, c. 440 (A.B.1488), § 54, eff. Sept. 22, 2012; Stats.2017, c. 319 (A.B.976), § 59, eff. Jan. 1, 2018.)*

Application

For application of this chapter, see Probate Code § 3600.

Cross References

Computation of money belonging to the minor, see Probate Code § 3410.
References to "person with a disability" within this Chapter, see Probate Code § 3603.
Single-premium deferred annuity, see Probate Code § 1446.

Total estate of minor, deductions, see Probate Code § 3400.

Research References

Forms

3 California Transactions Forms—Business Transactions § 18:31, Delivery and Disposition of Settlement Proceeds.

3 California Transactions Forms—Estate Planning § 17:16, Court's Continuing Jurisdiction.

West's California Code Forms, Probate § 3600 Comment, Disposition of Compromise or Judgment Amount on Behalf of an Incompetent Person Without a Conservator of the Estate.

§ 3603. Reference to "person with a disability"

Where reference is made in this chapter to a "person with a disability," the reference shall be deemed to include the following:

(a) A person for whom a conservator may be appointed.

(b) Any of the following persons, subject to the provisions of Section 3613:

(1) A person who meets the definition of disability as defined in Section 1382c(a)(3) of Title 42 of the United States Code, or as defined in Section 416(i)(1) of Title II of the federal Social Security Act (42 U.S.C. Sec. 401 et seq.) and regulations implementing that act, as set forth in Part 416.905 of Title 20 of the Federal Code of Regulations.

(2) A person who meets the definition of disability as defined in paragraphs (1), (2), and (3) of subsection (d) of Section 423 of Title II of the federal Social Security Act (42 U.S.C. Sec. 401 et seq.) and regulations implementing that act, as set forth in Part 404.1505 of Title 20 of the Federal Code of Regulations.

(3) A minor who meets the definition of disability, as set forth in Part 416.906 of Title 20 of the Federal Code of Regulations.

(4) A person with a developmental disability, as defined in Section 4512 of the Welfare and Institutions Code. *(Stats.1990, c. 79 (A.B.759), § 14, operative July 1, 1991. Amended by Stats.2004, c. 67 (A.B.1851), § 6.)*

Application

For application of this chapter, see Probate Code § 3600.

Cross References

Continuing jurisdiction of court over trusts of persons with a disability who have reached the age of majority, see Probate Code § 3613.

Research References

Forms

3 California Transactions Forms—Estate Planning § 17:14, Person With a Disability.

§ 3604. Payment to special needs trust; petition for order; trust requirements; jurisdiction of court; court orders

(a)(1) If a court makes an order under Section 3602 or 3611 that money of a minor or person with a disability be paid to a special needs trust, the terms of the trust shall be reviewed and approved by the court and shall satisfy the requirements of this section. The trust is subject to continuing jurisdiction of the court, and is subject to court supervision to the extent determined by the court. The court may transfer jurisdiction to the court in the proper county for commencement of a proceeding as determined under Section 17005.

(2) If the court referred to in subdivision (a) could have made an order under Section 3602 or 3611 to place that money into a special needs trust, but that order was not requested, a parent, guardian, conservator, or other interested person may petition a court that exercises jurisdiction pursuant to Section 800 for that order. In doing so, notice shall be provided pursuant to subdivisions (e) and (f) of Section 3602, or subdivision (c) of Section 3611, and that notice shall be given at least 15 days before the hearing.

(b) A special needs trust may be established and continued under this section only if the court determines all of the following:

(1) That the minor or person with a disability has a disability that substantially impairs the individual's ability to provide for the individual's own care or custody and constitutes a substantial handicap.

(2) That the minor or person with a disability is likely to have special needs that will not be met without the trust.

(3) That money to be paid to the trust does not exceed the amount that appears reasonably necessary to meet the special needs of the minor or person with a disability.

(c) If at any time it appears (1) that any of the requirements of subdivision (b) are not satisfied or the trustee refuses without good cause to make payments from the trust for the special needs of the beneficiary, and (2) that the State Department of Health Care Services, the State Department of State Hospitals, the State Department of Developmental Services, or a county or city and county in this state has a claim against trust property, that department, county, or city and county may petition the court for an order terminating the trust.

(d) A court order under Section 3602 or 3611 for payment of money to a special needs trust shall include a provision that all statutory liens in favor of the State Department of Health Care Services, the State Department of State Hospitals, the State Department of Developmental Services, and any county or city and county in this state shall first be satisfied. *(Added by Stats.1992, c. 355 (A.B.3328), § 3. Amended by Stats.2004, c. 67 (A.B.1851), § 7; Stats.2012, c. 440 (A.B.1488), § 55, eff. Sept. 22, 2012.)*

Application

For application of this chapter, see Probate Code § 3600.

Cross References

Department of Developmental Services, see Welfare and Institutions Code § 4400 et seq.

Department of Health Care Services, generally, see Health and Safety Code § 100100 et seq.

References to "person with a disability" within this Chapter, see Probate Code § 3603.

Research References

Forms

3 California Transactions Forms—Estate Planning § 17:15, Required Findings [Prob C § 3604(B)].

3 California Transactions Forms—Estate Planning § 17:16, Court's Continuing Jurisdiction.

3 California Transactions Forms—Estate Planning § 17:17, Provisions Required for Medi-Cal Qualification.

3 California Transactions Forms—Estate Planning § 17:43, Litigation Settlement Trust Introductory Paragraph.

West's California Code Forms, Probate § 3500 Form 1, Petition by Parent to Compromise Disputed Personal Injury Claim of Minor Without a Guardian of the Estate—Judicial Council Form MC-350.

West's California Code Forms, Probate § 3500 Form 2, Order Authorizing Parent to Compromise Claim of Minor Without Guardian—Judicial Council Form MC-351.

West's California Code Forms, Probate § 3600 Comment, Disposition of Compromise or Judgment Amount on Behalf of an Incompetent Person Without a Conservator of the Estate.

§ 3605. Statutes of limitation; death of beneficiary; notice of death; payment of claims; application of section

(a) This section applies only to a special needs trust established under Section 3604 on or after January 1, 1993.

(b) While the special needs trust is in existence, the statute of limitations otherwise applicable to claims of the State Department of Health Care Services, the State Department of State Hospitals, the State Department of Developmental Services, and any county or city

§ 3605

and county in this state is tolled. Notwithstanding any provision in the trust instrument, at the death of the special needs trust beneficiary or on termination of the trust, the trust property is subject to claims of the State Department of Health Care Services, the State Department of State Hospitals, the State Department of Developmental Services, and any county or city and county in this state to the extent authorized by law as if the trust property is owned by the beneficiary or is part of the beneficiary's estate.

(c) At the death of the special needs trust beneficiary or on termination of the trust, the trustee shall give notice of the beneficiary's death or the trust termination, in the manner provided in Section 1215, to all of the following:

(1) The State Department of Health Care Services, the State Department of State Hospitals, and the State Department of Developmental Services, addressed to the director of that department at the Sacramento office of the director.

(2) Any county or city and county in this state that has made a written request to the trustee for notice, addressed to that county or city and county at the address specified in the request.

(d) Failure to give the notice required by subdivision (c) prevents the running of the statute of limitations against the claim of the department, county, or city and county not given the notice.

(e) The department, county, or city and county has four months after notice is given in which to make a claim with the trustee. If the trustee rejects the claim, the department, county, or city and county making the claim may petition the court for an order under Chapter 3 (commencing with Section 17200) of Part 5 of Division 9, directing the trustee to pay the claim. A claim made under this subdivision shall be paid as a preferred claim prior to any other distribution. If trust property is insufficient to pay all claims under this subdivision, the trustee shall petition the court for instructions and the claims shall be paid from trust property as the court deems just.

(f) If trust property is distributed before expiration of four months after notice is given without payment of the claim, the department, county, or city and county has a claim against the distributees to the full extent of the claim, or each distributee's share of trust property, whichever is less. The claim against distributees includes interest at a rate equal to that earned in the Pooled Money Investment Account, Article 4.5 (commencing with Section 16480) of Chapter 3 of Part 2 of Division 4 of Title 2 of the Government Code, from the date of distribution or the date of filing the claim, whichever is later, plus other accruing costs as in the case of enforcement of a money judgment. *(Added by Stats.1992, c. 355 (A.B.3328), § 4. Amended by Stats.2012, c. 440 (A.B.1488), § 56, eff. Sept. 22, 2012.)*

Application

For application of this chapter, see Probate Code § 3600.

Cross References

Department of Developmental Services, see Welfare and Institutions Code § 4400 et seq.
Department of Health Care Services, generally, see Health and Safety Code § 100100 et seq.

Research References

Forms

Asset Protection: Legal Planning, Strategies and Forms ¶ 14.05, Planning Strategies for the Elderly and the Disabled.
3 California Transactions Forms--Estate Planning § 17:17, Provisions Required for Medi-Cal Qualification.
3 California Transactions Forms--Estate Planning § 17:34, Notice.
3 California Transactions Forms--Estate Planning § 17:44, Payback Provisions Required in Self-Funded Special Needs Trusts.
West's California Code Forms, Probate § 3500 Form 2, Order Authorizing Parent to Compromise Claim of Minor Without Guardian—Judicial Council Form MC-351.

ARTICLE 2. DISPOSITION OF MONEY OR OTHER PROPERTY WHERE NO GUARDIANSHIP OR CONSERVATORSHIP

Section
3610. Disposition of remaining balance.
3611. Order of court.
3612. Continuing jurisdiction until minor reaches majority; continuing jurisdiction over trust of person with a disability who reaches majority.
3613. Orders or judgments with respect to adults who have capacity to consent.

Application

For application of this chapter, see Probate Code § 3600.

§ 3610. Disposition of remaining balance

When money or other property is to be paid or delivered for the benefit of a minor or person with a disability under a compromise, covenant, order or judgment, and there is no guardianship of the estate of the minor or conservatorship of the estate of the person with a disability, the remaining balance of the money and other property (after payment of all expenses, costs, and fees as approved and allowed by the court under Section 3601) shall be paid, delivered, deposited, or invested as provided in this article. *(Stats.1990, c. 79 (A.B.759), § 14, operative July 1, 1991. Amended by Stats.2004, c. 67 (A.B.1851), § 8.)*

Application

For application of this chapter, see Probate Code § 3600.

Cross References

Authority of parent, guardian, conservator to compromise claims and actions, see Code of Civil Procedure § 372; Probate Code §§ 2500 et seq., 3500.
Computation of money belonging to the minor, see Probate Code § 3410.
Payment of wages to minors until notice by guardian to employer, see Family Code § 7503.
References to "person with a disability" within this Chapter, see Probate Code § 3603.
Total estate of minor, deductions, see Probate Code § 3400.
Trustee's standard of care, see Probate Code § 16040 et seq.

Research References

Forms

Asset Protection: Legal Planning, Strategies and Forms ¶ 14.05, Planning Strategies for the Elderly and the Disabled.
3 California Transactions Forms--Business Transactions § 18:31, Delivery and Disposition of Settlement Proceeds.
West's California Code Forms, Probate § 3600 Comment, Disposition of Compromise or Judgment Amount on Behalf of an Incompetent Person Without a Conservator of the Estate.

§ 3611. Order of court

In any case described in Section 3610, the court making the order or giving the judgment referred to in Section 3600 shall, upon application of counsel for the minor or person with a disability, order any one or more of the following:

(a) That a guardian of the estate or conservator of the estate be appointed and that the remaining balance of the money and other property be paid or delivered to the person so appointed.

(b) That the remaining balance of any money paid or to be paid be deposited in an insured account in a financial institution in this state, or in a single-premium deferred annuity, subject to withdrawal only upon the authorization of the court, and that the remaining balance of any other property delivered or to be delivered be held on conditions the court determines to be in the best interest of the minor or person with a disability.

(c) After a hearing by the court, that the remaining balance of any money and other property be paid to a special needs trust established under Section 3604 for the benefit of the minor or person with a disability. Notice of the time and place of the hearing and a copy of the petition shall be mailed to the State Director of Health Care Services, the Director of State Hospitals, and the Director of Developmental Services at the office of each director in Sacramento at least 15 days before the hearing.

(d) If the remaining balance of the money to be paid or delivered does not exceed twenty thousand dollars ($20,000), that all or any part of the money be held on any other conditions the court in its discretion determines to be in the best interest of the minor or person with a disability.

(e) If the remaining balance of the money and other property to be paid or delivered does not exceed five thousand dollars ($5,000) in value and is to be paid or delivered for the benefit of a minor, that all or any part of the money and the other property be paid or delivered to a parent of the minor, without bond, upon the terms and under the conditions specified in Article 1 (commencing with Section 3400) of Chapter 2.

(f) If the remaining balance of the money and other property to be paid or delivered is to be paid or delivered for the benefit of the minor, that all or any part of the money and other property be transferred to a custodian for the benefit of the minor under the California Uniform Transfers to Minors Act, Part 9 (commencing with Section 3900).

(g) That the remaining balance of the money and other property be paid or delivered to the trustee of a trust which is created by, or approved of, in the order or judgment referred to in Section 3600. This trust shall be revocable by the minor upon attaining the age of 18 years, and shall contain other terms and conditions, including, but not limited to, terms and conditions concerning trustee's accounts and trustee's bond, as the court determines to be necessary to protect the minor's interests.

(h) That the remaining balance of any money paid or to be paid be deposited with the county treasurer, if all of the following conditions are met:

(1) The county treasurer has been authorized by the county board of supervisors to handle the deposits.

(2) The county treasurer shall receive and safely keep all money deposited with the county treasurer pursuant to this subdivision, shall pay the money out only upon the order of the court, and shall credit each estate with the interest earned by the funds deposited less the county treasurer's actual cost authorized to be recovered under Section 27013 of the Government Code.

(3) The county treasurer and sureties on the official bond of the county treasurer are responsible for the safekeeping and payment of the money.

(4) The county treasurer shall ensure that the money deposited is to earn interest or dividends, or both, at the highest rate which the county can reasonably obtain as a prudent investor.

(5) Funds so deposited with the county treasurer shall only be invested or deposited in compliance with the provisions governing the investment or deposit of state funds set forth in Chapter 5 (commencing with Section 16640) of Part 2 of Division 4 of Title 2 of the Government Code, the investment or deposit of county funds set forth in Chapter 4 (commencing with Section 53600) of Part 1 of Division 2 of Title 5 of the Government Code, or as authorized under Chapter 6 (commencing with Section 2400) of Part 4.

(i) That the remaining balance of the money and other property be paid or delivered to the person with a disability. *(Stats.1990, c. 79 (A.B.759), § 14, operative July 1, 1991. Amended by Stats.1991, c. 413 (A.B.934), § 3; Stats.1992, c. 355 (A.B.3328), § 5; Stats.1993, c. 978 (S.B.305), § 4; Stats.1996, c. 563 (S.B.392), § 19; Stats.2004, c. 67 (A.B.1851), § 9; Stats.2012, c. 440 (A.B.1488), § 57, eff. Sept. 22, 2012.)*

Application

For application of this chapter, see Probate Code § 3600.

Cross References

Accounting by parent to minor for money received, see Probate Code § 3300.
Cities, and other agencies, deposit of funds, local agency fund audit reports, see Government Code § 53686.
Delivery of money or property to parent, see Probate Code § 3401.
Payment of wages to minors until notice by guardian to employer, see Family Code § 7503.
References to "person with a disability" within this Chapter, see Probate Code § 3603.
Special needs trusts, requirements, see Probate Code § 3604.

Research References

Forms

West's California Code Forms, Probate § 3500 Form 1, Petition by Parent to Compromise Disputed Personal Injury Claim of Minor Without a Guardian of the Estate—Judicial Council Form MC-350.
West's California Code Forms, Probate § 3500 Form 2, Order Authorizing Parent to Compromise Claim of Minor Without Guardian—Judicial Council Form MC-351.
West's California Code Forms, Probate § 3600 Comment, Disposition of Compromise or Judgment Amount on Behalf of an Incompetent Person Without a Conservator of the Estate.

§ 3612. Continuing jurisdiction until minor reaches majority; continuing jurisdiction over trust of person with a disability who reaches majority

(a) Notwithstanding any other provision of law and except to the extent the court orders otherwise, the court making the order under Section 3611 shall have continuing jurisdiction of the money and other property paid, delivered, deposited, or invested under this article until the minor reaches 18 years of age.

(b) Notwithstanding subdivision (a), the trust of an individual who meets the definition of a person with a disability under paragraph (3) of subdivision (b) of Section 3603 and who reaches 18 years of age, shall continue and be under continuing court jurisdiction until terminated by the court. *(Stats.1990, c. 79 (A.B.759), § 14, operative July 1, 1991. Amended by Stats.2004, c. 67 (A.B.1851), § 10.)*

Application

For application of this chapter, see Probate Code § 3600.

Cross References

References to "person with a disability" within this Chapter, see Probate Code § 3603.

Research References

Forms

Asset Protection: Legal Planning, Strategies and Forms ¶ 14.05, Planning Strategies for the Elderly and the Disabled.
West's California Code Forms, Probate § 3500 Form 2, Order Authorizing Parent to Compromise Claim of Minor Without Guardian—Judicial Council Form MC-351.

§ 3613. Orders or judgments with respect to adults who have capacity to consent

Notwithstanding any other provision of this chapter, a court may not make an order or give a judgment pursuant to Section 3600, 3601, 3602, 3610, or 3611 with respect to an adult who has the capacity within the meaning of Section 812 to consent to the order and who has no conservator of the estate with authority to make that decision, without the express consent of that person. *(Added by Stats.2004, c. 67 (A.B.1851), § 11.)*

§ 3613

Application

For application of this chapter, see Probate Code § 3600.

Research References

Forms

3 California Transactions Forms--Estate Planning § 17:13, Overview [Prob. Code §§3600 to 3613].

3 California Transactions Forms--Estate Planning § 17:14, Person With a Disability.

3 California Transactions Forms--Estate Planning § 17:15, Required Findings [Prob C § 3604(B)].

West's California Judicial Council Forms MC–350, Petition for Approval of Compromise of Claim or Action or Disposition of Proceeds of Judgment for Minor or Person With a Disability.

West's California Judicial Council Forms MC–350(A–12b(5)), Additional Medical Service Providers Attachment to Petition for Approval of Compromise of Claim or Action or Disposition of Proceeds of Judgment.

West's California Judicial Council Forms MC–350EX, Petition for Expedited Approval of Compromise of Claim or Action or Disposition of Proceeds of Judgment for Minor or Person With a Disability.

West's California Judicial Council Forms MC–351, Order Approving Compromise of Disputed Claim or Pending Action or Disposition of Proceeds of Judgment for Minor or Person With a Disability.

West's California Judicial Council Forms MC–355, Order to Deposit Money Into Blocked Account.

West's California Judicial Council Forms MC–356, Acknowledgment of Receipt of Order and Funds for Deposit in Blocked Account.

CHAPTER 5. PROPERTY OF ABSENT FEDERAL PERSONNEL

ARTICLE 1. DEFINITIONS

Section
3700. Meaning of terms used in chapter.

Cross References

Conservator of estate of missing persons, see Probate Code § 1804.

Death of persons not heard from in five years, presumption, see Evidence Code § 667.

Special conservatorship provisions where proposed conservatee is a missing person, see Probate Code § 1845 et seq.

§ 3700. Meaning of terms used in chapter

As used in this chapter:

(a) "Absentee" is defined in Section 1403.

(b) "Certificate of missing status" means the official written report complying with Section 1283 of the Evidence Code and showing the determination of the secretary of the military department or the head of the department or agency concerned or the delegate of the secretary or head that the absentee is in missing status.

(c) "Eligible spouse" means the spouse of an absentee who has not commenced an action or proceeding for judicial or legal separation, annulment, adjudication of nullity, or dissolution of the marriage of the spouse and the absentee.

(d) "Family of an absentee" means an eligible spouse, if any, or if no eligible spouse, the child or children of an absentee, equally, or if no child or children, the parent or parents of an absentee, equally, provided these persons are dependents of the absentee as defined in Section 401 of Title 37 of the United States Code, and the guardian of the estate or conservator of the estate of any person bearing such relationship to the absentee.

(e) "Secretary concerned" is defined in Section 1440. *(Stats.1990, c. 79 (A.B.759), § 14, operative July 1, 1991.)*

Cross References

Dissolution of marriage, see Family Code §§ 310, 2300 et seq.

Judicial determination of void or voidable marriage, see Family Code § 2200 et seq.

Research References

Forms

1¶ 1 Am. Jur. Pl. & Pr. Forms Absentees § 1, Introductory Comments.

ARTICLE 2. COURT PROCEEDING TO SET ASIDE PERSONAL PROPERTY OF ABSENTEE

Section
3701. Setting aside personal property of absentee.
3702. Persons authorized to petition.
3703. Contents of petition.
3704. Notice of hearing.
3705. Hearing and order.
3706. Jurisdiction of court; amount.
3707. Joint tenancy property.
3708. Accounting.

§ 3701. Setting aside personal property of absentee

Upon petition as provided in this chapter, the court may set aside to the family of an absentee personal property of the absentee situated in this state for the purpose of managing, controlling, encumbering, selling, or conveying, or otherwise engaging in any transaction with respect to the property, if the court determines that to do so will be in the best interest of the absentee, including the interest of the absentee in providing for shelter, food, health care, education, transportation, or the maintenance of a reasonable and adequate standard of living for the family of the absentee. The absentee's interest in the property set aside shall not exceed twenty thousand dollars ($20,000). *(Stats.1990, c. 79 (A.B.759), § 14, operative July 1, 1991.)*

Cross References

Absentee defined, see Probate Code §§ 1403, 3700.
Contents of petition, see Probate Code § 3703.
Family of an absentee defined for purposes of this Chapter, see Probate Code § 3700.

§ 3702. Persons authorized to petition

A petition that personal property of an absentee be set aside as provided in this chapter may be filed by any of the following persons:

(a) A person in whose favor the personal property of the absentee may be set aside.

(b) A person to whom the absentee has issued a general power of attorney while serving in the armed forces of the United States or while an employee of any agency or department of the United States, provided the power of attorney was valid and effective at the time issued, regardless whether it has expired or terminated. *(Stats.1990, c. 79 (A.B.759), § 14, operative July 1, 1991.)*

Cross References

Absentee defined, see Probate Code §§ 1403, 3700.

§ 3703. Contents of petition

(a) The petition shall contain all of the following:

(1) A statement that the petition is filed under this chapter.

(2) In its caption, the last known military rank or grade and the social security account number of the absentee.

(3) A specific description and estimate of the value of all of the absentee's property, wherever situated (including all sums due the absentee from the United States).

(4) A designation of the property to be set aside, and the facts establishing that setting aside the property is necessary and in the best interest of the absentee.

(5) If the property is to be set aside for the benefit of the spouse of the absentee, an allegation that the spouse is an eligible spouse.

(6) So far as known to the petitioner, the names and addresses of all persons comprising the family of the absentee, and an allegation whether a guardian of the estate or a conservator of the estate of any member of the family of the absentee has been appointed.

(b) There shall be attached to the petition a certificate of missing status. The certificate of missing status shall be received as evidence of that fact and the court shall not determine the status of the absentee inconsistent with the status shown in the certificate. *(Stats.1990, c. 79 (A.B.759), § 14, operative July 1, 1991.)*

Cross References

Absentee defined, see Probate Code §§ 1403, 3700.
Eligible spouse defined, see Probate Code § 3700.
Family of an absentee defined for purposes of this Chapter, see Probate Code § 3700.

§ 3704. Notice of hearing

(a) Notice of the nature of the proceedings and the time and place of the hearing shall be given by the petitioner at least 15 days before the hearing date by all of the following means:

(1) By delivery pursuant to Section 1215, together with a copy of the petition, to all persons comprising the family of the absentee.

(2) By delivery by a method that would be sufficient for service of summons in a civil action, together with a copy of the petition, to the secretary concerned or to the head of the United States department or agency concerned.

(3) By publication pursuant to Section 6061 of the Government Code in a newspaper of general circulation in the county in which the proceedings will be held.

(b) If notice to an officer or agency of this state or of the United States is required under Section 1461 or 1822 upon petition for appointment of a conservator, notice shall be given of the petition under this chapter. *(Stats.1990, c. 79 (A.B.759), § 14, operative July 1, 1991. Amended by Stats.2017, c. 319 (A.B.976), § 60, eff. Jan. 1, 2018.)*

Cross References

Absentee defined, see Probate Code §§ 1403, 3700.
Family of an absentee defined for purposes of this Chapter, see Probate Code § 3700.
Secretary concerned defined, see Probate Code § 1440.
Service of summons, civil actions, see Code of Civil Procedure § 413.10 et seq.

§ 3705. Hearing and order

(a) Upon the hearing of the petition, any officer or agency of this state or the United States or the authorized delegate of the officer or agency, or any relative or friend of the absentee, may appear and support or oppose the petition.

(b) If the court determines that the allegations of the petition are true and correct, the court may order set aside to the family of the absentee personal property of the absentee situated in this state (excluding any sums due the absentee from the United States) in which the absentee's interest does not exceed twenty thousand dollars ($20,000). The property set aside shall be specified in the order.

(c) No bond shall be required of any person to whom property of the absentee has been set aside by order of the court pursuant to this chapter. *(Stats.1990, c. 79 (A.B.759), § 14, operative July 1, 1991.)*

Cross References

Absentee defined, see Probate Code §§ 1403, 3700.
Family of an absentee defined for purposes of this Chapter, see Probate Code § 3700.

§ 3706. Jurisdiction of court; amount

A determination by the court that the value of all of the absentee's property, wherever situated, exceeds twenty thousand dollars ($20,000) or that the absentee owns or has an interest in real property, wherever situated, does not deprive the court of jurisdiction to set aside to the family of the absentee personal property of the absentee situated in this state in which the absentee's interest does not exceed twenty thousand dollars ($20,000), and the court shall order set aside such personal property to the family of the absentee if the court finds that all of the other provisions of this chapter have been complied with. The property set aside shall be specified in the order. *(Stats.1990, c. 79 (A.B.759), § 14, operative July 1, 1991.)*

Cross References

Absentee defined, see Probate Code §§ 1403, 3700.
Family of an absentee defined for purposes of this Chapter, see Probate Code § 3700.

§ 3707. Joint tenancy property

For the purposes of this chapter, any property or interest therein or lien thereon that the absentee holds as joint tenant shall be included in determining the property of the absentee and its value. The joint tenancy interest may be set aside to the family of the absentee as provided in this chapter but may only be set aside to a member of the absentee's family who was a joint tenant with the absentee in the property. *(Stats.1990, c. 79 (A.B.759), § 14, operative July 1, 1991.)*

Cross References

Absentee defined, see Probate Code §§ 1403, 3700.
Family of an absentee defined for purposes of this Chapter, see Probate Code § 3700.
Joint tenancy, definition, method of creation, see Civil Code § 683.

§ 3708. Accounting

(a) Within six months after the absentee has returned to the controllable jurisdiction of the military department or civilian agency or department concerned, or within six months after the determination of death of the absentee by the secretary concerned or the head of the department or agency concerned or the delegate of the secretary or head, the former absentee or the personal representative of the deceased absentee may, by motion in the same proceeding, require the person or persons to whom the property of the absentee was set aside to account for the property and the proceeds, if any. The time of return to the controllable jurisdiction of the military department or civilian department or agency concerned or the determination of the time of death of the absentee shall be determined by the court under 37 United States Code, Section 556, or 5 United States Code, Section 5566. An official written report or record of the military department or civilian department or agency that the absentee has returned to its controllable jurisdiction or is deceased shall be received as evidence of that fact.

(b) This section does not in any manner derogate the finality and conclusiveness of any order, judgment, or decree previously entered in the proceeding. *(Stats.1990, c. 79 (A.B.759), § 14, operative July 1, 1991.)*

Cross References

Absentee defined, see Probate Code §§ 1403, 3700.
Secretary concerned defined, see Probate Code § 1440.

ARTICLE 3. MANAGEMENT AND DISPOSITION OF PERSONAL PROPERTY OF ABSENTEE WITHOUT COURT PROCEEDING

Section
3710. Transactions relating to absentee's personal property.

PROBATE CODE

Section
3711. Transfer of property; certificate; affidavit.
3712. Limitation of actions.

§ 3710. Transactions relating to absentee's personal property

The family of an absentee may collect, receive, dispose of, or engage in any transaction relating to the absentee's personal property situated in this state without any judicial proceeding if all the following conditions are satisfied:

(a) The absentee owns no real property situated in this state.

(b) The aggregate value of all of the absentee's personal property situated in this state is five thousand dollars ($5,000) or less, excluding any money owed the absentee by the United States.

(c) The family of the absentee needs to dispose of such personal property to provide for shelter, food, health care, education, transportation, or the maintenance of a reasonable and adequate standard of living for the family of the absentee. *(Stats.1990, c. 79 (A.B.759), § 14, operative July 1, 1991.)*

Cross References

Absentee defined, see Probate Code §§ 1403, 3700.
Family of an absentee defined for purposes of this Chapter, see Probate Code § 3700.

§ 3711. Transfer of property; certificate; affidavit

(a) If the conditions set forth in Section 3710 are satisfied, the family of the absentee may have any evidence of interest, indebtedness, or right attributable to the absentee's personal property transferred to the family of the absentee, or transferred to the person to whom the property is to be sold or transferred by the family of the absentee, upon furnishing the person (including any governmental body) having custody of the property both of the following:

(1) A certificate of missing status.

(2) An affidavit stating under oath that the provisions of this article are applicable and that the aggregate value of all property received pursuant to this affidavit, together with all other property previously received under this article, does not exceed five thousand dollars ($5,000).

(b) The receipt of a certificate of missing status and affidavit under subdivision (a) constitutes sufficient acquittance for any payment of money or delivery of property made pursuant to this article and fully discharges the recipient from any further liability concerning the money or property without the necessity of inquiring into the truth of any of the facts stated in the affidavit. *(Stats.1990, c. 79 (A.B.759), § 14, operative July 1, 1991.)*

Cross References

Absentee defined, see Probate Code §§ 1403, 3700.
Family of an absentee defined for purposes of this Chapter, see Probate Code § 3700.

§ 3712. Limitation of actions

The time within which an absentee may commence an action against any person who executes an affidavit and receives property pursuant to this article commences to run on the earlier of the following dates:

(a) Ninety days after the absentee returns to the United States after the termination of the condition that caused the classification of an absentee.

(b) Two years after the termination of the condition that caused the classification of an absentee. *(Stats.1990, c. 79 (A.B.759), § 14, operative July 1, 1991.)*

ARTICLE 4. ABSENTEE'S POWER OF ATTORNEY

Section
3720. Termination of power; liability for relying or acting on power.
3721. Actual knowledge of principal's death or incapacity while absent; revocation by absent principal.
3722. Dissolution of marriage, annulment or legal separation; absentee's spouse acting as attorney-in-fact.

§ 3720. Termination of power; liability for relying or acting on power

If an absentee executed a power of attorney that expires during the period that occasions absentee status, the power of attorney continues in full force and effect until 30 days after the absentee status is terminated. Any person who acts in reliance upon the power of attorney when accompanied by a copy of a certificate of missing status is not liable for relying and acting upon the power of attorney. *(Stats.1990, c. 79 (A.B.759), § 14, operative July 1, 1991.)*

Cross References

Absentee defined, see Probate Code §§ 1403, 3700.

§ 3721. Actual knowledge of principal's death or incapacity while absent; revocation by absent principal

For the purposes of Chapter 5 (commencing with Section 4300) of Part 2 of Division 4.5, in the case of a principal who is an absentee, an attorney-in-fact or third person shall be deemed to be without actual knowledge of the following:

(a) The principal's death or incapacity while the absentee continues in missing status and until the attorney-in-fact or third person receives notice of the determination of the absentee's death by the secretary concerned or the head of the department or agency concerned or the delegate of the secretary or head.

(b) Revocation by the principal during the period described in subdivision (a). *(Added by Stats.1994, c. 307 (S.B.1907), § 14.)*

Cross References

Absentee defined, see Probate Code §§ 1403, 3700.

§ 3722. Dissolution of marriage, annulment or legal separation; absentee's spouse acting as attorney-in-fact

If after the absentee executes a power of attorney, the principal's spouse who is the attorney-in-fact commences a proceeding for dissolution, annulment, or legal separation, or a legal separation is ordered, the attorney-in-fact's authority is revoked. This section is in addition to the provisions of Sections 4154 and 4697. *(Added by Stats.1994, c. 307 (S.B.1907), § 15. Amended by Stats.1999, c. 658 (A.B.891), § 26, operative July 1, 2000.)*

Cross References

Absentee defined, see Probate Code §§ 1403, 3700.

CHAPTER 6. REMOVAL OF PROPERTY OF NONRESIDENT

Section
3800. Petition; filing; conservatorship transferred to another state.
3801. Notice.
3802. Certificate of nonresident fiduciary.
3803. Order for removal.

GUARDIANSHIP—CONSERVATORSHIP LAW

§ 3800. Petition; filing; conservatorship transferred to another state

(a) If a nonresident has a duly appointed, qualified, and acting guardian, conservator, committee, or comparable fiduciary in the place of residence and if no proceeding for guardianship or conservatorship of the nonresident is pending or contemplated in this state, the nonresident fiduciary may petition to have property owned by the nonresident removed to the place of residence.

(b) The petition for removal of property of the nonresident shall be filed in the superior court of the county in which the nonresident is or has been temporarily present or in which the property of the nonresident, or the principal part thereof, is located.

(c) If a conservatorship was transferred from this state to another state pursuant to Article 3 (commencing with Section 2001) of Chapter 8 of Part 3, the foreign conservator may remove the conservatee's personal property from this state without seeking a petition under this chapter. (Stats.1990, c. 79 (A.B.759), § 14, operative July 1, 1991. Amended by Stats.2014, c. 553 (S.B.940), § 27, eff. Jan. 1, 2015, operative Jan. 1, 2016.)

Cross References

Transfer of assets of pending guardianship to another jurisdiction, see Probate Code § 2800 et seq.

§ 3801. Notice

(a) The petition shall be made upon 15 days' notice, by delivery pursuant to Section 1215, to all of the following persons:

(1) The personal representative or other person in whose possession the property may be.

(2) Persons in this state, known to the petitioner, who are obligated to pay a debt, perform an obligation, or issue a security to the nonresident or the estate of the nonresident.

(b) The petition shall be made upon additional notice, if any, as the court may order. (Stats.1990, c. 79 (A.B.759), § 14, operative July 1, 1991. Amended by Stats.2017, c. 319 (A.B.976), § 61, eff. Jan. 1, 2018.)

Cross References

Request for special notice, see Probate Code § 2700 et seq.

§ 3802. Certificate of nonresident fiduciary

(a) The nonresident fiduciary shall produce and file one of the following certificates:

(1) A certificate that the fiduciary is entitled, by the laws of the place of appointment of the fiduciary, to the possession of the estate of the nonresident. The certificate shall be under the hand of the clerk and seal of the court from which the appointment of the fiduciary was derived and shall show a transcript of the record of appointment and that the fiduciary has entered upon the discharge of the duties of the fiduciary.

(2) A certificate that the fiduciary is entitled, by the laws of the place of residence, to custody of the estate of the nonresident, without the appointment of any court. The certificate shall be under the hand of the clerk and seal of either (i) the court in the place of residence having jurisdiction of estates of persons that have a guardian, conservator, committee, or comparable fiduciary or (ii) the highest court in the place of residence.

(b) In the case of a foreign country, the certificate shall be accompanied by a final statement certifying the genuineness of the signature and official position of (1) the court clerk making the original certificate or (2) any foreign official who has certified either the genuineness of the signature and official position of the court clerk making the original certificate or the genuineness of the signature and official position of another foreign official who has executed a similar certificate in a chain of such certificates beginning with a certificate of the genuineness of the signature and official position of the clerk making the original certificate. The final statement may be made only by a secretary of an embassy or legation, consul general, consul, vice consul, or consular agent of the United States, or a diplomatic or consular official of the foreign country assigned or accredited to the United States. (Stats.1990, c. 79 (A.B.759), § 14, operative July 1, 1991.)

Cross References

Statements certifying genuineness of attestation to accuracy of copy of a writing, see Evidence Code § 1530.

§ 3803. Order for removal

(a) Upon the petition, if the court determines that removal of the property will not conflict with any restriction or limitation on the property or impair the right of the nonresident to the property or the rights of creditors or claimants in this state, the court shall make an order granting to the nonresident fiduciary leave to remove the property of the nonresident to the place of residence unless good cause to the contrary is shown.

(b) The order is authority to the fiduciary to sue for and receive the property in his or her own name for the use and benefit of the nonresident.

(c) The order is a discharge of the personal representative or other person in whose possession the property may be at the time the order is made and of the person obligated to pay a debt, perform an obligation, or issue a security to the nonresident or the estate of the nonresident, upon filing with the clerk of the court the receipt of the nonresident fiduciary for the property and transmitting a duplicate receipt, or a certified copy of the receipt, to the court, if any, from which the nonresident fiduciary received his or her appointment. (Stats.1990, c. 79 (A.B.759), § 14, operative July 1, 1991.)

Part 9

CALIFORNIA UNIFORM TRANSFERS TO MINORS ACT

Section	
3900.	Short title.
3901.	Definitions.
3902.	Application of part.
3903.	Nomination of custodian; creation of custodial property.
3904.	Transfer by gift or exercise of power of appointment.
3905.	Transfer authorized by will or trust.
3906.	Other transfer by fiduciary.
3907.	Transfer by obligor.
3908.	Acknowledgment of delivery.
3909.	Creation of custodial property; designation of initial custodian; control.
3910.	Single custodianship.
3911.	Validity and effect of transfer.
3912.	Duties of custodians; standard of care; records.
3913.	Rights, powers, and authority of custodians over custodial property; liability.
3914.	Use of custodial property.
3915.	Custodian's expenses, compensation and bond.
3916.	Exemption of third person from liability.
3917.	Liability to third persons.
3918.	Substitute and successor custodians.
3919.	Petition for accounting; determination of liability of custodian; removal of custodian.
3920.	Termination of custodianship.
3920.5.	Delay in transfer of custodial property until after minor attains age eighteen; transfers not specifying age.

PROBATE CODE

Section	
3921.	Proceedings on petition; place.
3922.	Transfers made under Uniform Gifts to Minors Act or Uniform Transfers to Minors Act of other state.
3923.	Effect on existing custodianships.
3925.	Part not exclusive.

Cross References

Devises subject to this act, see Probate Code § 6341 et seq.
Golden State Scholarshare Trust,
 Definitions, see Education Code § 69980.
 Ownership rights under participation agreements, see Education Code § 69986.

§ 3900. Short title

This part may be cited as the "California Uniform Transfers to Minors Act." *(Stats.1990, c. 79 (A.B.759), § 14, operative July 1, 1991.)*

Cross References

Minor defined for purposes of this Part, see Probate Code § 3901.
Transfer defined for purposes of this Part, see Probate Code § 3901.

Research References

Forms

12C Am. Jur. Pl. & Pr. Forms Gifts § 34, Introductory Comments.
4 California Transactions Forms--Business Transactions § 26:30, Drafting Signature Cards.
1 California Transactions Forms--Estate Planning § 1:29, Options Involving Gifts to Minors.
1 California Transactions Forms--Estate Planning § 6:18, Custodian Under Uniform Transfers to Minors Act.
1 California Transactions Forms--Estate Planning § 6:78, Devise to Custodian for Child Who is Minor at Testator's Death Under California Uniform Transfers to Minors Act.
1 California Transactions Forms--Estate Planning § 7:39, California Uniform Transfers to Minors Act.
2 California Transactions Forms--Estate Planning § 10:21, Life Insurance Generally.
2 California Transactions Forms--Estate Planning § 10:23, Third Party or Irrevocable Trust as Owner of Life Insurance Policy.
2 California Transactions Forms--Estate Planning § 10:34, Multiple Party Accounts.
3 California Transactions Forms--Estate Planning § 13:64, Methods of Distribution.
3 California Transactions Forms--Estate Planning § 14:24, Incorporation of CUTMA.
3 California Transactions Forms--Estate Planning § 14:52, Limited Power to Designate Remainder Beneficiaries.
3 California Transactions Forms--Estate Planning § 14:58, Provisions Typically Requested by Corporate Trustees.
3 California Transactions Forms--Estate Planning § 18:53, Irrevocable Asset Protection Discretionary Trust for Children With Spendthrift Provisions.
3 California Transactions Forms--Estate Planning § 18:54, Revocable Trust Agreement.
4 California Transactions Forms--Estate Planning § 19:134, Determining Manner of Distribution to Minors and Others.
4 California Transactions Forms--Estate Planning § 20:10, Devises to Minors.
4 California Transactions Forms--Estate Planning § 21:19, Accumulation Trust for Children.
4 California Transactions Forms--Estate Planning § 21:22, Trust Provision for Spouse With Remainder to Issue Partly Outright and Partly in Trust.
4 California Transactions Forms--Estate Planning § 21:23, Trust Provision for Spouse With Secondary Trust for Children and General Power of Appointment.
4 California Transactions Forms--Estate Planning § 21:24, Trust Provision for Children With Limited Powers of Appointment.
West's California Code Forms, Probate § 3500 Form 1, Petition by Parent to Compromise Disputed Personal Injury Claim of Minor Without a Guardian of the Estate—Judicial Council Form MC-350.
West's California Code Forms, Probate § 6240 Form 1, California Statutory Will.

§ 3901. Definitions

In this part:

(a) "Adult" means an individual who has attained the age of 18 years.

(b) "Benefit plan" means an employer's plan for the benefit of an employee or partner.

(c) "Broker" means a person lawfully engaged in the business of effecting transactions in securities or commodities for the person's own account or for the account of others.

(d) "Conservator" means a person appointed or qualified by a court to act as general, limited, or temporary guardian of a minor's property or a person legally authorized to perform substantially the same functions.

(e) "Court" means the superior court.

(f) "Custodial property" means (1) any interest in property transferred to a custodian under this part and (2) the income from and proceeds of that interest in property.

(g) "Custodian" means a person so designated under Section 3909 or a successor or substitute custodian designated under Section 3918.

(h) "Financial institution" means a bank, trust company, savings institution, or credit union, chartered and supervised under state or federal law or an industrial loan company licensed and supervised under the laws of this state.

(i) "Legal representative" means an individual's personal representative or conservator.

(j) "Member of the minor's family" means the minor's parent, stepparent, spouse, grandparent, brother, sister, uncle, or aunt, whether of the whole or half blood or by adoption.

(k) "Minor" means:

(1) Except as provided in paragraph (2), an individual who has not attained the age of 18 years.

(2) When used with reference to the beneficiary for whose benefit custodial property is held or is to be held, an individual who has not attained the age at which the custodian is required under Sections 3920 and 3920.5 to transfer the custodial property to the beneficiary.

(*l*) "Person" means an individual, corporation, organization, or other legal entity.

(m) "Personal representative" means an executor, administrator, successor personal representative, or special administrator of a decedent's estate or a person legally authorized to perform substantially the same functions.

(n) "State" includes any state of the United States, the District of Columbia, the Commonwealth of Puerto Rico, and any territory or possession subject to the legislative authority of the United States.

(*o*) "Transfer" means a transaction that creates custodial property under Section 3909.

(p) "Transferor" means a person who makes a transfer under this part.

(q) "Trust company" means a financial institution, corporation, or other legal entity, authorized to exercise general trust powers.
(Stats.1990, c. 79 (A.B.759), § 14, operative July 1, 1991.)

Research References

Forms

1 California Transactions Forms--Estate Planning § 6:18, Custodian Under Uniform Transfers to Minors Act.
1 California Transactions Forms--Estate Planning § 6:78, Devise to Custodian for Child Who is Minor at Testator's Death Under California Uniform Transfers to Minors Act.

1 California Transactions Forms--Estate Planning § 7:39, California Uniform Transfers to Minors Act.
4 California Transactions Forms--Estate Planning § 19:47, Appointment of Custodian.
West's California Code Forms, Probate § 3918 Form 1, Petition for Order Designating Successor Custodian.
West's California Code Forms, Probate § 3918 Form 2, Petition for Removal of Custodian and Designation of Successor Custodian.

§ 3902. Application of part

(a) This part applies to a transfer that refers to this part in the designation under subdivision (a) of Section 3909 by which the transfer is made if at the time of the transfer, the transferor, the minor, or the custodian is a resident of this state or the custodial property is located in this state. The custodianship so created remains subject to this part despite a subsequent change in residence of a transferor, the minor, or the custodian, or the removal of custodial property from this state.

(b) A person designated as custodian under this part is subject to personal jurisdiction in this state with respect to any matter relating to the custodianship.

(c) A transfer that purports to be made and which is valid under the Uniform Transfers to Minors Act, the Uniform Gifts to Minors Act, or a substantially similar act, of another state is governed by the law of the designated state and may be executed and is enforceable in this state if at the time of the transfer, the transferor, the minor, or the custodian is a resident of the designated state or the custodial property is located in the designated state. *(Stats.1990, c. 79 (A.B.759), § 14, operative July 1, 1991.)*

Cross References

Custodial property defined for purposes of this Part, see Probate Code § 3901.
Custodian defined for purposes of this Part, see Probate Code § 3901.
Minor defined for purposes of this Part, see Probate Code § 3901.
Person defined for purposes of this Part, see Probate Code § 3901.
State defined for purposes of this Part, see Probate Code § 3901.
Transfer defined for purposes of this Part, see Probate Code § 3901.
Transferor defined for purposes of this Part, see Probate Code § 3901.

Research References

Forms

1 California Transactions Forms--Estate Planning § 7:39, California Uniform Transfers to Minors Act.

§ 3903. Nomination of custodian; creation of custodial property

(a) A person having the right to designate the recipient of property transferable upon the occurrence of a future event may revocably nominate a custodian to receive the property for a minor beneficiary upon the occurrence of the event by naming the custodian followed in substance by the words:

"as custodian for _____
(Name of Minor)
under the California Uniform Transfers to Minors Act."

The nomination may name one or more persons as substitute custodians to whom the property must be transferred, in the order named, if the first nominated custodian dies before the transfer or is unable, declines, or is ineligible to serve. The nomination may be made in a will, a trust, a deed, an instrument exercising a power of appointment, or in a writing designating a beneficiary of contractual rights which is registered with or delivered to the payor, issuer, or other obligor of the contractual rights.

(b) A custodian nominated under this section must be a person to whom a transfer of property of that kind may be made under subdivision (a) of Section 3909.

(c) The nomination of a custodian under this section does not create custodial property until the nominating instrument becomes irrevocable or a transfer to the nominated custodian is completed under Section 3909. Unless the nomination of a custodian has been revoked, upon the occurrence of the future event, the custodianship becomes effective, and the custodian shall enforce a transfer of the custodial property pursuant to Section 3909. *(Stats.1990, c. 79 (A.B.759), § 14, operative July 1, 1991.)*

Cross References

Custodial property defined for purposes of this Part, see Probate Code § 3901.
Custodian defined for purposes of this Part, see Probate Code § 3901.
Minor defined for purposes of this Part, see Probate Code § 3901.
Person defined for purposes of this Part, see Probate Code § 3901.
Powers of appointment, generally, see Probate Code § 600 et seq.
Transfer defined for purposes of this Part, see Probate Code § 3901.

Research References

Forms

1 California Transactions Forms--Estate Planning § 1:29, Options Involving Gifts to Minors.
1 California Transactions Forms--Estate Planning § 6:15, Minors' Capacity to Take Devised Property.
1 California Transactions Forms--Estate Planning § 6:18, Custodian Under Uniform Transfers to Minors Act.
1 California Transactions Forms--Estate Planning § 6:53, Matters to Consider in Drafting Gifts to Minors.
1 California Transactions Forms--Estate Planning § 6:78, Devise to Custodian for Child Who is Minor at Testator's Death Under California Uniform Transfers to Minors Act.
1 California Transactions Forms--Estate Planning § 7:40, Form Drafting Principles.
1 California Transactions Forms--Estate Planning § 7:42, Matters to Consider When Making Transfer Under California Uniform Transfers to Minors Act.
1 California Transactions Forms--Estate Planning § 7:43, Nomination of Custodian.
West's California Code Forms, Probate § 3909 Form 1, Creation of Custodial Property.

§ 3904. Transfer by gift or exercise of power of appointment

A person may make a transfer by irrevocable gift to, or the irrevocable exercise of a power of appointment in favor of, a custodian for the benefit of a minor pursuant to Section 3909. *(Stats.1990, c. 79 (A.B.759), § 14, operative July 1, 1991.)*

Cross References

Custodian defined for purposes of this Part, see Probate Code § 3901.
Minor defined for purposes of this Part, see Probate Code § 3901.
Person defined for purposes of this Part, see Probate Code § 3901.
Powers of appointment,
    Generally, see Probate Code § 600 et seq.
    Revocability, see Probate Code § 695.
Transfer defined for purposes of this Part, see Probate Code § 3901.

Research References

Forms

1 California Transactions Forms--Estate Planning § 6:18, Custodian Under Uniform Transfers to Minors Act.

§ 3905. Transfer authorized by will or trust

(a) A personal representative or trustee may make an irrevocable transfer pursuant to Section 3909 to a custodian for the benefit of a minor as authorized in the governing will or trust.

(b) If the testator or settlor has nominated a custodian under Section 3903 to receive the custodial property, the transfer shall be made to that person.

(c) If the testator or settlor has not nominated a custodian under Section 3903, or all persons so nominated as custodian die before the transfer or are unable, decline, or are ineligible to serve, the personal representative or the trustee, as the case may be, shall designate the custodian from among those eligible to serve as custodian for property of that kind under subdivision (a) of Section 3909. *(Stats.1990, c. 79 (A.B.759), § 14, operative July 1, 1991.)*

§ 3905

Cross References

Custodial property defined for purposes of this Part, see Probate Code § 3901.
Custodian defined for purposes of this Part, see Probate Code § 3901.
Minor defined for purposes of this Part, see Probate Code § 3901.
Person defined for purposes of this Part, see Probate Code § 3901.
Personal representative defined for purposes of this Part, see Probate Code § 3901.
Transfer defined for purposes of this Part, see Probate Code § 3901.

Research References

Forms

1 California Transactions Forms--Estate Planning § 6:18, Custodian Under Uniform Transfers to Minors Act.
4 California Transactions Forms--Estate Planning § 19:47, Appointment of Custodian.

§ 3906. Other transfer by fiduciary

(a) Subject to subdivision (c), a personal representative or trustee may make an irrevocable transfer to another adult or trust company as custodian for the benefit of a minor pursuant to Section 3909, in the absence of a will or under a will or trust that does not contain an authorization to do so.

(b) Subject to subdivision (c), a conservator may make an irrevocable transfer to another adult or trust company as custodian for the benefit of the minor pursuant to Section 3909.

(c) A transfer under subdivision (a) or (b) may be made only if all of the following requirements are satisfied:

(1) The personal representative, trustee, or conservator considers the transfer to be in the best interest of the minor.

(2) The transfer is not prohibited by or inconsistent with provisions of the applicable will, trust agreement, or other governing instrument. For the purposes of this subdivision, a spendthrift provision (such as that described in Section 15300) shall not prohibit or be inconsistent with the transfer.

(3) The transfer is authorized by the court if it exceeds ten thousand dollars ($10,000) in value; provided, however, that such court authorization shall not be required when the transfer is to a custodian who is either (A) a trust company or (B) an individual designated as a trustee by the terms of a trust instrument which does not require a bond. *(Stats.1990, c. 79 (A.B.759), § 14, operative July 1, 1991. Amended by Stats.1996, c. 862 (A.B.2751), § 13.)*

Cross References

Adult defined for purposes of this Part, see Probate Code § 3901.
Conservator defined for purposes of this Part, see Probate Code § 3901.
Court defined for purposes of this Part, see Probate Code § 3901.
Custodian defined for purposes of this Part, see Probate Code § 3901.
Minor defined for purposes of this Part, see Probate Code § 3901.
Personal representative defined for purposes of this Part, see Probate Code § 3901.
Transfer defined for purposes of this Part, see Probate Code § 3901.
Trust company defined for purposes of this Part, see Probate Code § 3901.

Research References

Forms

1 California Transactions Forms--Estate Planning § 6:18, Custodian Under Uniform Transfers to Minors Act.
3 California Transactions Forms--Estate Planning § 13:64, Methods of Distribution.
4 California Transactions Forms--Estate Planning § 21:19, Accumulation Trust for Children.
4 California Transactions Forms--Estate Planning § 21:22, Trust Provision for Spouse With Remainder to Issue Partly Outright and Partly in Trust.
4 California Transactions Forms--Estate Planning § 21:23, Trust Provision for Spouse With Secondary Trust for Children and General Power of Appointment.
4 California Transactions Forms--Estate Planning § 21:24, Trust Provision for Children With Limited Powers of Appointment.

§ 3907. Transfer by obligor

(a) Subject to subdivisions (b) and (c), a person not subject to Section 3905 or 3906 who holds property of, or owes a liquidated debt to, a minor not having a conservator may make an irrevocable transfer to a custodian for the benefit of the minor pursuant to Section 3909.

(b) If a person having the right to do so under Section 3903 has nominated a custodian under that section to receive the custodial property, the transfer shall be made to that person.

(c) If no custodian has been nominated under Section 3903, or all persons so nominated as custodian die before the transfer or are unable, decline, or are ineligible to serve, a transfer under this section may be made to an adult member of the minor's family or to a trust company unless the property exceeds ten thousand dollars ($10,000) in value. *(Stats.1990, c. 79 (A.B.759), § 14, operative July 1, 1991.)*

Cross References

Adult defined for purposes of this Part, see Probate Code § 3901.
Conservator defined for purposes of this Part, see Probate Code § 3901.
Custodial property defined for purposes of this Part, see Probate Code § 3901.
Custodian defined for purposes of this Part, see Probate Code § 3901.
Member of the minor's family defined for purposes of this Part, see Probate Code § 3901.
Minor defined for purposes of this Part, see Probate Code § 3901.
Person defined for purposes of this Part, see Probate Code § 3901.
Transfer defined for purposes of this Part, see Probate Code § 3901.
Trust company defined for purposes of this Part, see Probate Code § 3901.

§ 3908. Acknowledgment of delivery

A written acknowledgment of delivery by a custodian constitutes a sufficient receipt and discharge for custodial property transferred to the custodian pursuant to this part. *(Stats.1990, c. 79 (A.B.759), § 14, operative July 1, 1991.)*

Cross References

Custodial property defined for purposes of this Part, see Probate Code § 3901.
Custodian defined for purposes of this Part, see Probate Code § 3901.

§ 3909. Creation of custodial property; designation of initial custodian; control

(a) Custodial property is created and a transfer is made whenever any of the following occurs:

(1) An uncertificated security or a certificated security in registered form is either:

(A) Registered in the name of the transferor, an adult other than the transferor, or a trust company, followed in substance by the words:

"as custodian for _____
(Name of Minor)
under the California Uniform Transfers to Minors Act."

(B) Delivered if in certificated form, or any document necessary for the transfer of an uncertificated security is delivered, together with any necessary endorsement to an adult other than the transferor or to a trust company as custodian, accompanied by an instrument in substantially the form set forth in subdivision (b).

(2) Money is paid or delivered, or a security held in the name of a broker, financial institution, or its nominee is transferred, to a broker or financial institution for credit to an account in the name of the transferor, an adult other than the transferor, or a trust company, followed in substance by the words:

"as custodian for _____
(Name of Minor)
under the California Uniform Transfers to Minors Act."

(3) The ownership of a life or endowment insurance policy or annuity contract is either:

(A) Registered with the issuer in the name of the transferor, an adult other than the transferor, or a trust company, followed in substance by the words:

"as custodian for _____
(Name of Minor)
under the California Uniform Transfers to Minors Act."

(B) Assigned in a writing delivered to an adult other than the transferor or to a trust company whose name in the assignment is followed in substance by the words:

"as custodian for _____
(Name of Minor)
under the California Uniform Transfers to Minors Act."

(4) An irrevocable exercise of a power of appointment or an irrevocable present right to future payment under a contract is the subject of a written notification delivered to the payor, issuer, or other obligor that the right is transferred to the transferor, an adult other than the transferor, or a trust company, whose name in the notification is followed in substance by the words:

"as custodian for _____
(Name of Minor)
under the California Uniform Transfers to Minors Act."

(5) An interest in real property is recorded in the name of the transferor, an adult other than the transferor, or a trust company, followed in substance by the words:

"as custodian for _____
(Name of Minor)
under the California Uniform Transfers to Minors Act."

(6) A certificate of title issued by a department or agency of a state or of the United States which evidences title to tangible personal property is either:

(A) Issued in the name of the transferor, an adult other than the transferor, or a trust company, followed in substance by the words:

"as custodian for _____
(Name of Minor)
under the California Uniform Transfers to Minors Act."

(B) Delivered to an adult other than the transferor or to a trust company, endorsed to that person followed in substance by the words:

"as custodian for _____
(Name of Minor)
under the California Uniform Transfers to Minors Act."

(7) An interest in any property not described in paragraphs (1) through (6) is transferred to an adult other than the transferor or to a trust company by a written instrument in substantially the form set forth in subdivision (b).

(b) An instrument in the following form satisfies the requirements of subparagraph (B) of paragraph (1) and paragraph (7) of subdivision (a):

"TRANSFER UNDER THE CALIFORNIA UNIFORM
TRANSFERS TO MINORS ACT

I, _____
(Name of Transferor or Name and Representative
Capacity if a Fiduciary)

hereby transfer to _____,
(Name of Custodian)

as custodian for _____
(Name of Minor)

under the California Uniform Transfers to Minors Act, the following: (insert a description of the custodial property sufficient to identify it).

Dated: _____
_____
(Signature)

_____ acknowledges receipt of the
(Name of Custodian)
property described above as custodian for the minor named above under the California Uniform Transfers to Minors Act.

Dated: _____
_____"
(Signature of Custodian)

(c) A transferor shall place the custodian in control of the custodial property as soon as practicable. *(Stats.1990, c. 79 (A.B. 759), § 14, operative July 1, 1991. Amended by Stats.1991, c. 1055 (S.B.271), § 17.)*

Cross References

Adult defined for purposes of this Part, see Probate Code § 3901.
Broker defined for purposes of this Part, see Probate Code § 3901.
Custodial property defined for purposes of this Part, see Probate Code § 3901.
Custodian defined for purposes of this Part, see Probate Code § 3901.
Financial institution defined for purposes of this Part, see Probate Code § 3901.
Minor defined for purposes of this Part, see Probate Code § 3901.
Person defined for purposes of this Part, see Probate Code § 3901.
State defined for purposes of this Part, see Probate Code § 3901.
Transfer defined for purposes of this Part, see Probate Code § 3901.
Transferor defined for purposes of this Part, see Probate Code § 3901.
Trust company defined for purposes of this Part, see Probate Code § 3901.

Research References

Forms

1 California Transactions Forms--Estate Planning § 6:18, Custodian Under Uniform Transfers to Minors Act.
1 California Transactions Forms--Estate Planning § 6:78, Devise to Custodian for Child Who is Minor at Testator's Death Under California Uniform Transfers to Minors Act.
1 California Transactions Forms--Estate Planning § 7:39, California Uniform Transfers to Minors Act.
1 California Transactions Forms--Estate Planning § 7:40, Form Drafting Principles.
1 California Transactions Forms--Estate Planning § 7:42, Matters to Consider When Making Transfer Under California Uniform Transfers to Minors Act.
1 California Transactions Forms--Estate Planning § 7:44, Transfer of Certificated or Uncertificated Securities or Tangible Personal Property Not Subject to Title Certification to Custodian for Minor.
West's California Code Forms, Probate § 3909 Form 1, Creation of Custodial Property.

§ 3910. Single custodianship

A transfer may be made only for one minor, and only one person may be the custodian. All custodial property held under this part by the same custodian for the benefit of the same minor constitutes a single custodianship. *(Stats.1990, c. 79 (A.B.759), § 14, operative July 1, 1991.)*

Cross References

Custodial property defined for purposes of this Part, see Probate Code § 3901.
Custodian defined for purposes of this Part, see Probate Code § 3901.
Minor defined for purposes of this Part, see Probate Code § 3901.
Person defined for purposes of this Part, see Probate Code § 3901.
Transfer defined for purposes of this Part, see Probate Code § 3901.

Research References

Forms

1 California Transactions Forms--Estate Planning § 6:18, Custodian Under Uniform Transfers to Minors Act.

§ 3910

West's California Code Forms, Probate § 3909 Form 1, Creation of Custodial Property.

§ 3911. Validity and effect of transfer

(a) The validity of a transfer made in a manner prescribed in this part is not affected by any of the following:

(1) Failure of the transferor to comply with subdivision (c) of Section 3909.

(2) Designation of an ineligible custodian, except designation of the transferor in the case of property for which the transferor is ineligible to serve as custodian under subdivision (a) of Section 3909.

(3) Death or incapacity of a person nominated under Section 3903 or designated under Section 3909 as custodian, or the disclaimer of the office by that person.

(b) A transfer made pursuant to Section 3909 is irrevocable, and the custodial property is indefeasibly vested in the minor, but the custodian has all the rights, powers, duties, and authority provided in this part, and neither the minor nor the minor's legal representative has any right, power, duty, or authority with respect to the custodial property except as provided in this part.

(c) By making a transfer, the transferor incorporates in the disposition all the provisions of this part and grants to the custodian, and to any third person dealing with a person designated as custodian, the respective powers, rights, and immunities provided in this part.

(d) A person is not precluded from being a custodian for a minor under this part with respect to some property because the person is a conservator of the minor with respect to other property.

(e) A person who is the conservator of the minor is not precluded from being a custodian for a minor under this part because the custodial property has or will be transferred to the custodian from the guardianship estate of the minor. In such case, for the purposes of Section 3909, the custodian shall be deemed to be "an adult other than the transferor."

(f) In the cases described in subdivisions (d) and (e), with respect to the property transferred to the custodian, this part applies to the extent it would apply if the person to whom the custodial property is transferred were not and had not been a conservator of the minor. *(Stats.1990, c. 79 (A.B.759), § 14, operative July 1, 1991.)*

Cross References

Adult defined for purposes of this Part, see Probate Code § 3901.
Conservator defined for purposes of this Part, see Probate Code § 3901.
Custodial property defined for purposes of this Part, see Probate Code § 3901.
Custodian defined for purposes of this Part, see Probate Code § 3901.
Legal representative defined for purposes of this Part, see probate Code § 3901.
Minor defined for purposes of this Part, see Probate Code § 3901.
Person defined for purposes of this Part, see Probate Code § 3901.
Transfer defined for purposes of this Part, see Probate Code § 3901.
Transferor defined for purposes of this Part, see Probate Code § 3901.

Research References

Forms

1 California Transactions Forms--Estate Planning § 7:39, California Uniform Transfers to Minors Act.
1 California Transactions Forms--Estate Planning § 7:42, Matters to Consider When Making Transfer Under California Uniform Transfers to Minors Act.

§ 3912. Duties of custodians; standard of care; records

(a) A custodian shall do all of the following:

(1) Take control of custodial property.

(2) Register or record title to custodial property if appropriate.

(3) Collect, hold, manage, invest, and reinvest custodial property.

(b) In dealing with custodial property, a custodian shall observe the standard of care that would be observed by a prudent person dealing with property of another and is not limited by any other statute restricting investments by fiduciaries except that:

(1) If a custodian is not compensated for his or her services, the custodian is not liable for losses to custodial property unless they result from the custodian's bad faith, intentional wrongdoing, or gross negligence, or from the custodian's failure to maintain the standard of prudence in investing the custodial property provided in this section.

(2) A custodian, in the custodian's discretion and without liability to the minor or the minor's estate, may retain any custodial property received from a transferor.

(c) A custodian may invest in or pay premiums on life insurance or endowment policies on (1) the life of the minor only if the minor or the minor's estate is the sole beneficiary or (2) the life of another person in whom the minor has an insurable interest only to the extent that the minor, the minor's estate, or the custodian in the capacity of custodian, is the irrevocable beneficiary.

(d) A custodian at all times shall keep custodial property separate and distinct from all other property in a manner sufficient to identify it clearly as custodial property of the minor. Custodial property consisting of an undivided interest is so identified if the minor's interest is held as a tenant in common and is fixed. Custodial property subject to recordation is so identified if it is recorded, and custodial property subject to registration is so identified if it is either registered, or held in an account designated, in the name of the custodian, followed in substance by the words:

"as a custodian for _____
(Name of Minor)
under the California Uniform Transfers to Minors Act."

(e) A custodian shall keep records of all transactions with respect to custodial property, including information necessary for the preparation of the minor's tax returns, and shall make them available for inspection at reasonable intervals by a parent or legal representative of the minor or by the minor if the minor has attained the age of 14 years. *(Stats.1990, c. 79 (A.B.759), § 14, operative July 1, 1991.)*

Cross References

Custodial property defined for purposes of this Part, see Probate Code § 3901.
Custodian defined for purposes of this Part, see Probate Code § 3901.
Legal representative defined for purposes of this Part, see Probate Code § 3901.
Minor defined for purposes of this Part, see Probate Code § 3901.
Person defined for purposes of this Part, see Probate Code § 3901.
Transfer defined for purposes of this Part, see Probate Code § 3901.
Transferor defined for purposes of this Part, see Probate Code § 3901.

Research References

Forms

1 California Transactions Forms--Estate Planning § 1:29, Options Involving Gifts to Minors.
1 California Transactions Forms--Estate Planning § 6:18, Custodian Under Uniform Transfers to Minors Act.
1 California Transactions Forms--Estate Planning § 6:78, Devise to Custodian for Child Who is Minor at Testator's Death Under California Uniform Transfers to Minors Act.
1 California Transactions Forms--Estate Planning § 7:39, California Uniform Transfers to Minors Act.

§ 3913. Rights, powers, and authority of custodians over custodial property; liability

(a) A custodian, acting in a custodial capacity, has all the rights, powers, and authority over custodial property that unmarried adult owners have over their own property, but a custodian may exercise those rights, powers, and authority in that capacity only.

(b) This section does not relieve a custodian from liability for breach of Section 3912. *(Stats.1990, c. 79 (A.B.759), § 14, operative July 1, 1991.)*

Cross References

Adult defined for purposes of this Part, see Probate Code § 3901.
Custodial property defined for purposes of this Part, see Probate Code § 3901.
Custodian defined for purposes of this Part, see Probate Code § 3901.

Research References

Forms

1 California Transactions Forms--Estate Planning § 1:29, Options Involving Gifts to Minors.
1 California Transactions Forms--Estate Planning § 6:18, Custodian Under Uniform Transfers to Minors Act.
1 California Transactions Forms--Estate Planning § 7:39, California Uniform Transfers to Minors Act.

§ 3914. Use of custodial property

(a) A custodian may deliver or pay to the minor or expend for the minor's benefit as much of the custodial property as the custodian considers advisable for the use and benefit of the minor, without court order and without regard to (1) the duty or ability of the custodian personally, or of any other person, to support the minor or (2) any other income or property of the minor which may be applicable or available for that purpose.

(b) On petition of an interested person or the minor if the minor has attained the age of 14 years, the court may order the custodian to deliver or pay to the minor or expend for the minor's benefit so much of the custodial property as the court considers advisable for the use and benefit of the minor.

(c) A delivery, payment, or expenditure under this section is in addition to, not in substitution for, and does not affect, any obligation of a person to support the minor.

(d) In lieu of the powers and duties described in subdivision (a), a transferor who is also the custodian may elect to govern his or her custodial powers and duties under this subdivision. If such election is made, the custodian shall not pay over to the minor for expenditure by the minor, and shall not expend for the minor's use or benefit, any part of the custodial property for any purpose prior to the time specified in Section 3920, except by order of the court upon a showing that the expenditure is necessary for the support, maintenance, or education of the minor. When the powers and duties of the custodian are governed by this subdivision, the transferor-custodian shall file with the clerk of the court a declaration in substantially the following form:

Declaration Under the California Uniform Transfers to Minors Act

I, _____
      (Name of Transferor-Custodian)
as custodian for _____
      (Name of Minor)
under the California Uniform Transfers to Minors Act, hereby irrevocably elect to be governed under subdivision (d) of Section 3914 of the Probate Code in my custodial capacity over the following described property

_____
(Description of Custodial Property)

I declare under penalty of perjury that the foregoing is true and correct.

Dated: _____, 19____

_____
(Signature of Transferor-Custodian)

(Stats.1990, c. 79 (A.B.759), § 14, operative July 1, 1991.)

Cross References

Court defined for purposes of this Part, see Probate Code § 3901.
Custodial property defined for purposes of this Part, see Probate Code § 3901.
Custodian defined for purposes of this Part, see Probate Code § 3901.
Minor defined for purposes of this Part, see Probate Code § 3901.
Person defined for purposes of this Part, see Probate Code § 3901.
Transfer defined for purposes of this Part, see Probate Code § 3901.
Transferor defined for purposes of this Part, see Probate Code § 3901.

Research References

Forms

1 California Transactions Forms--Estate Planning § 1:29, Options Involving Gifts to Minors.
1 California Transactions Forms--Estate Planning § 6:18, Custodian Under Uniform Transfers to Minors Act.
1 California Transactions Forms--Estate Planning § 6:78, Devise to Custodian for Child Who is Minor at Testator's Death Under California Uniform Transfers to Minors Act.
1 California Transactions Forms--Estate Planning § 7:47, Transferor-Custodian's Declaration of Election that Court Order be Required for Payment to or Expenditure for Minor.
West's California Code Forms, Probate § 3914 Form 1, Petition for Order Directing Custodian to Deliver Custodial Property to Minor.
West's California Code Forms, Probate § 3914 Form 2, Declaration Under the California Uniform Transfers to Minors Act.

§ 3915. Custodian's expenses, compensation and bond

(a) A custodian is entitled to reimbursement from custodial property for reasonable expenses incurred in the performance of the custodian's duties.

(b) Except for one who is a transferor under Section 3904, a custodian has a noncumulative election during each calendar year to charge reasonable compensation for services performed during that year.

(c) Except as provided in subdivision (f) of Section 3918, a custodian need not give a bond. *(Stats.1990, c. 79 (A.B.759), § 14, operative July 1, 1991.)*

Cross References

Custodial property defined for purposes of this Part, see Probate Code § 3901.
Custodian defined for purposes of this Part, see Probate Code § 3901.
Transferor defined for purposes of this Part, see Probate Code § 3901.

Research References

Forms

1 California Transactions Forms--Estate Planning § 1:29, Options Involving Gifts to Minors.
1 California Transactions Forms--Estate Planning § 6:18, Custodian Under Uniform Transfers to Minors Act.
1 California Transactions Forms--Estate Planning § 7:40, Form Drafting Principles.
1 California Transactions Forms--Estate Planning § 7:42, Matters to Consider When Making Transfer Under California Uniform Transfers to Minors Act.

§ 3916. Exemption of third person from liability

A third person in good faith and without court order may act on the instructions of, or otherwise deal with, any person purporting to make a transfer or purporting to act in the capacity of a custodian and, in the absence of knowledge, is not responsible for determining any of the following:

(a) The validity of the purported custodian's designation.

(b) The propriety of, or the authority under this part for, any act of the purported custodian.

(c) The validity or propriety under this part of any instrument or instructions executed or given either by the person purporting to make a transfer or by the purported custodian.

§ 3916

(d) The propriety of the application of any property of the minor delivered to the purported custodian. *(Stats.1990, c. 79 (A.B.759), § 14, operative July 1, 1991.)*

Cross References

Court defined for purposes of this Part, see Probate Code § 3901.
Custodian defined for purposes of this Part, see Probate Code § 3901.
Minor defined for purposes of this Part, see Probate Code § 3901.
Person defined for purposes of this Part, see Probate Code § 3901.
Transfer defined for purposes of this Part, see Probate Code § 3901.

§ 3917. Liability to third persons

(a) A claim based on (1) a contract entered into by a custodian acting in a custodial capacity, (2) an obligation arising from the ownership or control of custodial property, or (3) a tort committed during the custodianship, may be asserted against the custodial property by proceeding against the custodian in the custodial capacity, whether or not the custodian or the minor is personally liable therefor.

(b) A custodian is not personally liable for either of the following:

(1) On a contract properly entered into in the custodial capacity unless the custodian fails to reveal that capacity and to identify the custodianship in the contract.

(2) For an obligation arising from control of custodial property or for a tort committed during the custodianship unless the custodian is personally at fault.

(c) A minor is not personally liable for an obligation arising from ownership of custodial property or for a tort committed during the custodianship unless the minor is personally at fault. *(Stats.1990, c. 79 (A.B.759), § 14, operative July 1, 1991.)*

Cross References

Custodial property defined for purposes of this Part, see Probate Code § 3901.
Custodian defined for purposes of this Part, see Probate Code § 3901.
Minor defined for purposes of this Part, see Probate Code § 3901.

Research References

Forms
West's California Code Forms, Probate § 3919 Form 1, Petition for Accounting.

§ 3918. Substitute and successor custodians

(a) A person nominated under Section 3903 or designated under Section 3909 as custodian may decline to serve by delivering a valid disclaimer under Part 8 (commencing with Section 260) of Division 2 to the person who made the nomination or to the transferor or the transferor's legal representative. If the event giving rise to a transfer has not occurred and no substitute custodian able, willing, and eligible to serve was nominated under Section 3903, the person who made the nomination may nominate a substitute custodian under Section 3903; otherwise the transferor or the transferor's legal representative shall designate a substitute custodian at the time of the transfer, in either case from among the persons eligible to serve as custodian for that kind of property under subdivision (a) of Section 3909. The custodian so designated has the rights of a successor custodian.

(b) A custodian at any time may designate a trust company or an adult other than a transferor under Section 3904 as successor custodian by executing and dating an instrument of designation before a subscribing witness other than the successor. If the instrument of designation does not contain or is not accompanied by the resignation of the custodian, the designation of the successor does not take effect until the custodian resigns, dies, becomes incapacitated, or is removed. The transferor may designate one or more persons as successor custodians to serve, in the designated order of priority, in case the custodian originally designated or a prior successor custodian is unable, declines, or is ineligible to serve or resigns, dies, becomes incapacitated, or is removed. The designation either (1) shall be made in the same transaction and by the same document by which the transfer is made or (2) shall be made by executing and dating a separate instrument of designation before a subscribing witness other than a successor as a part of the same transaction and contemporaneously with the execution of the document by which the transfer is made. The designation is made by setting forth the successor custodian's name, followed in substance by the words: "is designated [first, second, etc., where applicable] successor custodian." A successor custodian designated by the transferor may be a trust company or an adult other than a transferor under Section 3904. A successor custodian effectively designated by the transferor has priority over a successor custodian designated by a custodian.

(c) A custodian may resign at any time by delivering written notice to the minor if the minor has attained the age of 14 years and to the successor custodian and by delivering the custodial property to the successor custodian.

(d) If the transferor has not effectively designated a successor custodian, and a custodian is ineligible, dies, or becomes incapacitated without having effectively designated a successor and the minor has attained the age of 14 years, the minor may designate as successor custodian, in the manner prescribed in subdivision (b), an adult member of the minor's family, a conservator of the minor, or a trust company. If the minor has not attained the age of 14 years or fails to act within 60 days after the ineligibility, death, or incapacity, the conservator of the minor becomes successor custodian. If the minor has no conservator or the conservator declines to act, the transferor, the legal representative of the transferor or of the custodian, an adult member of the minor's family, or any other interested person may petition the court to designate a successor custodian.

(e) A custodian who declines to serve under subdivision (a) or resigns under subdivision (c), or the legal representative of a deceased or incapacitated custodian, as soon as practicable, shall put the custodial property and records in the possession and control of the successor custodian. The successor custodian by action may enforce the obligation to deliver custodial property and records and becomes responsible for each item as received.

(f) A transferor, the legal representative of a transferor, an adult member of the minor's family, a guardian of the person of the minor, the conservator of the minor, or the minor if the minor has attained the age of 14 years, may petition the court to remove the custodian for cause and to designate a successor custodian other than a transferor under Section 3904 or to require the custodian to give appropriate bond.

(g) At least 15 days before the hearing on a petition under subdivision (d) or (f), the petitioner shall deliver notice pursuant to Section 1215 to each of the following persons:

(1) The minor.

(2) The parent or parents of the minor.

(3) The transferor.

(h) Upon consideration of the petition under subdivision (d) or (f), the court may grant the relief that the court finds to be in the best interests of the minor. *(Stats.1990, c. 79 (A.B.759), § 14, operative July 1, 1991. Amended by Stats.1992, c. 871 (A.B.2975), § 7; Stats.2017, c. 319 (A.B.976), § 62, eff. Jan. 1, 2018.)*

Cross References

Adult defined for purposes of this Part, see Probate Code § 3901.
Conservator defined for purposes of this Part, see Probate Code § 3901.
Court defined for purposes of this Part, see Probate Code § 3901.
Custodial property defined for purposes of this Part, see Probate Code § 3901.
Custodian defined for purposes of this Part, see Probate Code § 3901.
Legal representative defined for purposes of this Part, see Probate Code § 3901.

Member of the minor's family defined for purposes of this Part, see Probate Code § 3901.
Minor defined for purposes of this Part, see Probate Code § 3901.
Person defined for purposes of this Part, see Probate Code § 3901.
Transfer defined for purposes of this Part, see Probate Code § 3901.
Transferor defined for purposes of this Part, see Probate Code § 3901.
Trust company defined for purposes of this Part, see Probate Code § 3901.

Research References

Forms

1 California Transactions Forms--Estate Planning § 1:95, Nomination of Successor Custodian.
1 California Transactions Forms--Estate Planning § 6:18, Custodian Under Uniform Transfers to Minors Act.
1 California Transactions Forms--Estate Planning § 7:39, California Uniform Transfers to Minors Act.
1 California Transactions Forms--Estate Planning § 7:40, Form Drafting Principles.
1 California Transactions Forms--Estate Planning § 7:42, Matters to Consider When Making Transfer Under California Uniform Transfers to Minors Act.
1 California Transactions Forms--Estate Planning § 7:45, Custodian's Resignation and Designation of Successor.
West's California Code Forms, Probate § 3909 Form 1, Creation of Custodial Property.
West's California Code Forms, Probate § 3918 Form 1, Petition for Order Designating Successor Custodian.
West's California Code Forms, Probate § 3918 Form 2, Petition for Removal of Custodian and Designation of Successor Custodian.

§ 3919. Petition for accounting; determination of liability of custodian; removal of custodian

(a) A minor who has attained the age of 14 years, the minor's guardian of the person or legal representative, an adult member of the minor's family, a transferor, or a transferor's legal representative may petition the court for any of the following:

(1) An accounting by the custodian or the custodian's legal representative.

(2) A determination of responsibility, as between the custodial property and the custodian personally, for claims against the custodial property unless the responsibility has been adjudicated in an action under Section 3917 to which the minor or the minor's legal representative was a party.

(b) A successor custodian may petition the court for an accounting by the predecessor custodian.

(c) The court, in a proceeding under this part or in any other proceeding, may require or permit the custodian or the custodian's legal representative to account.

(d) If a custodian is removed under subdivision (f) of Section 3918, the court shall require an accounting and order delivery of the custodial property and records to the successor custodian and the execution of all instruments required for transfer of the custodial property.

(e) The right to petition for an accounting shall continue for one year after the filing of a final accounting by the custodian or the custodian's legal representative and delivery of the custodial property to the minor or the minor's estate. *(Stats.1990, c. 79 (A.B.759), § 14, operative July 1, 1991.)*

Cross References

Adult defined for purposes of this Part, see Probate Code § 3901.
Court defined for purposes of this Part, see Probate Code § 3901.
Custodial property defined for purposes of this Part, see Probate Code § 3901.
Custodian defined for purposes of this Part, see Probate Code § 3901.
Legal representative defined for purposes of this Part, see Probate Code § 3901.
Member of the minor's family defined for purposes of this Part, see Probate Code § 3901.
Minor defined for purposes of this Part, see Probate Code § 3901.
Person defined for purposes of this Part, see Probate Code § 3901.
Transfer defined for purposes of this Part, see Probate Code § 3901.
Transferor defined for purposes of this Part, see Probate Code § 3901.

Research References

Forms

4 California Transactions Forms--Business Transactions § 26:30, Drafting Signature Cards.
1 California Transactions Forms--Estate Planning § 1:29, Options Involving Gifts to Minors.
West's California Code Forms, Probate § 3918 Form 2, Petition for Removal of Custodian and Designation of Successor Custodian.
West's California Code Forms, Probate § 3919 Form 1, Petition for Accounting.

§ 3920. Termination of custodianship

The custodian shall transfer in an appropriate manner the custodial property to the minor or to the minor's estate upon the earlier of the following:

(a) The minor's attainment of 18 years of age unless the time of transfer of the custodial property to the minor is delayed under Section 3920.5 to a time after the time the minor attains the age of 18 years.

(b) The time specified in the transfer pursuant to Section 3909 if the time of transfer of the custodial property to the minor is delayed under Section 3920.5 to a time after the time the minor attains the age of 18 years.

(c) The minor's death. *(Stats.1990, c. 79 (A.B.759), § 14, operative July 1, 1991.)*

Cross References

Custodial property defined for purposes of this Part, see Probate Code § 3901.
Custodian defined for purposes of this Part, see Probate Code § 3901.
Minor defined for purposes of this Part, see Probate Code § 3901.
Transfer defined for purposes of this Part, see Probate Code § 3901.

Research References

Forms

4 California Transactions Forms--Business Transactions § 26:30, Drafting Signature Cards.
1 California Transactions Forms--Estate Planning § 1:29, Options Involving Gifts to Minors.
1 California Transactions Forms--Estate Planning § 6:18, Custodian Under Uniform Transfers to Minors Act.
1 California Transactions Forms--Estate Planning § 7:39, California Uniform Transfers to Minors Act.
3 California Transactions Forms--Estate Planning § 14:24, Incorporation of CUTMA.
4 California Transactions Forms--Estate Planning § 19:47, Appointment of Custodian.

§ 3920.5. Delay in transfer of custodial property until after minor attains age eighteen; transfers not specifying age

(a) Subject to the requirements and limitations of this section, the time for transfer to the minor of custodial property transferred under or pursuant to Section 3903, 3904, 3905, or 3906, may be delayed until a specified time after the time the minor attains the age of 18 years, which time shall be specified in the transfer pursuant to Section 3909.

(b) To specify a delayed time for transfer to the minor of the custodial property, the words

"as custodian for _____
(Name of Minor)
until age _____
(Age for Delivery of Property to Minor)
under the California Uniform Transfers to Minors Act" shall be substituted in substance for the words
"as custodian for _____
(Name of Minor)

under the California Uniform Transfers to Minors Act" in making the transfer pursuant to Section 3909.

(c) The time for transfer to the minor of custodial property transferred under or pursuant to Section 3903 or 3905 may be delayed under this section only if the governing will or trust or nomination provides in substance that the custodianship is to continue until the time the minor attains a specified age, which time may not be later than the time the minor attains 25 years of age, and in that case the governing will or trust or nomination shall determine the time to be specified in the transfer pursuant to Section 3909.

(d) The time for transfer to the minor of custodial property transferred by the irrevocable exercise of a power of appointment under Section 3904 may be delayed under this section only if the transfer pursuant to Section 3909 provides in substance that the custodianship is to continue until the time the minor attains a specified age, which time may not be later than the time the minor attains 25 years of age.

(e) The time for transfer to the minor of custodial property transferred by irrevocable gift under Section 3904 may be delayed under this section only if the transfer pursuant to Section 3909 provides in substance that the custodianship is to continue until the time the minor attains a specified age, which time may not be later than the time the minor attains 21 years of age.

(f) The time for transfer to the minor of custodial property transferred by a trustee under Section 3906 may be delayed under this section only if the transfer pursuant to Section 3909 provides that the custodianship is to continue until a specified time not later than the time the minor attains 25 years of age or the time of termination of all present beneficial interests of the minor in the trust from which the custodial property was transferred, whichever is to occur first.

(g) If the transfer pursuant to Section 3909 does not specify any age, the time for the transfer of the custodial property to the minor under Section 3920 is the time when the minor attains 18 years of age.

(h) If the transfer pursuant to Section 3909 provides in substance that the duration of the custodianship is for a time longer than the maximum time permitted by this section for the duration of a custodianship created by that type of transfer, the custodianship shall be deemed to continue only until the time the minor attains the maximum age permitted by this section for the duration of a custodianship created by that type of transfer. *(Stats.1990, c. 79 (A.B.759), § 14, operative July 1, 1991. Amended by Stats.1996, c. 862 (A.B.2751), § 14.)*

Cross References

Custodial property defined for purposes of this Part, see Probate Code § 3901.
Custodian defined for purposes of this Part, see Probate Code § 3901.
Minor defined for purposes of this Part, see Probate Code § 3901.
Transfer defined for purposes of this Part, see Probate Code § 3901.

Research References

Forms

4 California Transactions Forms--Business Transactions § 26:30, Drafting Signature Cards.
1 California Transactions Forms--Estate Planning § 1:29, Options Involving Gifts to Minors.
1 California Transactions Forms--Estate Planning § 6:18, Custodian Under Uniform Transfers to Minors Act.
1 California Transactions Forms--Estate Planning § 7:39, California Uniform Transfers to Minors Act.
3 California Transactions Forms--Estate Planning § 14:24, Incorporation of CUTMA.
4 California Transactions Forms--Estate Planning § 19:47, Appointment of Custodian.
4 California Transactions Forms--Estate Planning § 20:10, Devises to Minors.

4 California Transactions Forms--Estate Planning § 20:43, General Pecuniary Devise to Custodian for Minor.

§ 3921. Proceedings on petition; place

Subject to the power of the court to transfer actions and proceedings as provided in the Code of Civil Procedure, a petition filed under this part shall be heard and proceedings thereon held in the superior court in the proper county, which shall be determined as follows:

(a) If the minor resides in this state, in either of the following counties:

(1) Where the minor resides.

(2) Where the custodian resides.

(b) If the minor does not reside within this state, in any of the following counties:

(1) Where the transferor resides.

(2) Where the custodian resides.

(3) Where the estate of a deceased or legally incapacitated custodian is being administered.

(4) Where a parent of the minor resides.

(c) If neither the minor, nor the transferor, nor any parent resides within this state, and no estate of a deceased or legally incapacitated custodian is being administered within this state, in any county. *(Stats.1990, c. 79 (A.B.759), § 14, operative July 1, 1991.)*

Cross References

Court defined for purposes of this Part, see Probate Code § 3901.
Custodian defined for purposes of this Part, see Probate Code § 3901.
Minor defined for purposes of this Part, see Probate Code § 3901.
State defined for purposes of this Part, see Probate Code § 3901.
Transfer defined for purposes of this Part, see Probate Code § 3901.
Transferor defined for purposes of this Part, see Probate Code § 3901.

§ 3922. Transfers made under Uniform Gifts to Minors Act or Uniform Transfers to Minors Act of other state

This part applies to a transfer within the scope of Section 3902 made on or after January 1, 1985, if either of the following requirements is satisfied:

(a) The transfer purports to have been made under the California Uniform Gifts to Minors Act.

(b) The instrument by which the transfer purports to have been made uses in substance the designation "as custodian under the Uniform Gifts to Minors Act" or "as custodian under the Uniform Transfers to Minors Act" of any other state, and the application of this part is necessary to validate the transfer. *(Stats.1990, c. 79 (A.B.759), § 14, operative July 1, 1991.)*

Cross References

Custodian defined for purposes of this Part, see Probate Code § 3901.
Minor defined for purposes of this Part, see Probate Code § 3901.
State defined for purposes of this Part, see Probate Code § 3901.
Transfer defined for purposes of this Part, see Probate Code § 3901.

§ 3923. Effect on existing custodianships

(a) As used in this section, "California Uniform Gifts to Minors Act" means former Article 4 (commencing with Section 1154) of Chapter 3 of Title 4 of Part 4 of Division 2 of the Civil Code.

(b) Any transfer of custodial property, as now defined in this part, made before January 1, 1985, is validated, notwithstanding that there was no specific authority in the California Uniform Gifts to Minors Act for the coverage of custodial property of that kind or for a transfer from that source at the time the transfer was made.

(c) This part applies to all transfers made before January 1, 1985, in a manner and form prescribed in the California Uniform Gifts to Minors Act, except insofar as the application impairs constitutionally vested rights.

(d) To the extent that this part, by virtue of subdivision (c), does not apply to transfers made in a manner prescribed in the California Uniform Gifts to Minors Act or to the powers, duties, and immunities conferred by transfers in that manner upon custodians and persons dealing with custodians, the repeal of the California Uniform Gifts to Minors Act does not affect those transfers or those powers, duties, and immunities. *(Stats.1990, c. 79 (A.B.759), § 14, operative July 1, 1991.)*

Cross References

Custodial property defined for purposes of this Part, see Probate Code § 3901.
Custodian defined for purposes of this Part, see Probate Code § 3901.
Minor defined for purposes of this Part, see Probate Code § 3901.
Person defined for purposes of this Part, see Probate Code § 3901.
Transfer defined for purposes of this Part, see Probate Code § 3901.

§ 3925. Part not exclusive

This part shall not be construed as providing an exclusive method for making gifts or other transfers to minors. *(Stats.1990, c. 79 (A.B.759), § 14, operative July 1, 1991.)*

Cross References

Minor defined for purposes of this Part, see Probate Code § 3901.
Transfer defined for purposes of this Part, see Probate Code § 3901.

Research References

Forms

1 California Transactions Forms--Estate Planning § 6:18, Custodian Under Uniform Transfers to Minors Act.
1 California Transactions Forms--Estate Planning § 6:78, Devise to Custodian for Child Who is Minor at Testator's Death Under California Uniform Transfers to Minors Act.
1 California Transactions Forms--Estate Planning § 7:39, California Uniform Transfers to Minors Act.
3 California Transactions Forms--Estate Planning § 13:64, Methods of Distribution.
4 California Transactions Forms--Estate Planning § 19:134, Determining Manner of Distribution to Minors and Others.

Division 6

WILLS AND INTESTATE SUCCESSION

Cross References

Transitional provisions, see Probate Code § 3.

Part 1

WILLS

CHAPTER 3. REVOCATION AND REVIVAL

Section
6122. Dissolution or annulment of marriage; provisions revoked; other change in circumstances.
6122.1. Domestic partnership of testator; revocation by termination.

§ 6122. Dissolution or annulment of marriage; provisions revoked; other change in circumstances

(a) Unless the will expressly provides otherwise, if after executing a will the testator's marriage is dissolved or annulled, the dissolution or annulment revokes all of the following:

(1) Any disposition or appointment of property made by the will to the former spouse.

(2) Any provision of the will conferring a general or special power of appointment on the former spouse.

(3) Any provision of the will nominating the former spouse as executor, trustee, conservator, or guardian.

(b) If any disposition or other provision of a will is revoked solely by this section, it is revived by the testator's remarriage to the former spouse.

(c) In case of revocation by dissolution or annulment:

(1) Property prevented from passing to a former spouse because of the revocation passes as if the former spouse failed to survive the testator.

(2) Other provisions of the will conferring some power or office on the former spouse shall be interpreted as if the former spouse failed to survive the testator.

(d) For purposes of this section, dissolution or annulment means any dissolution or annulment which would exclude the spouse as a surviving spouse within the meaning of Section 78. A decree of legal separation which does not terminate the status of spouses is not a dissolution for purposes of this section.

(e) Except as provided in Section 6122.1, no change of circumstances other than as described in this section revokes a will.

(f) Subdivisions (a) to (d), inclusive, do not apply to any case where the final judgment of dissolution or annulment of marriage occurs before January 1, 1985. That case is governed by the law in effect prior to January 1, 1985. *(Stats.1990, c. 79 (A.B.759), § 14, operative July 1, 1991. Amended by Stats.2001, c. 893 (A.B.25), § 50; Stats.2002, c. 664 (A.B.3034), § 179; Stats.2016, c. 50 (S.B.1005), § 86, eff. Jan. 1, 2017.)*

Cross References

Powers of appointment, generally, see Probate Code § 600 et seq.

Research References

Forms

1 California Transactions Forms--Estate Planning § 2:14, Failure to Properly Designate Disposition of Assets, Provide for Pretermitted Heirs, and Plan for Dissolution of Marriage.
1 California Transactions Forms--Estate Planning § 6:30, Effect of Dissolution or Annulment of Marriage.
1 California Transactions Forms--Estate Planning § 6:51, Matters to Consider in Drafting Dispositions to Beneficiaries.
1 California Transactions Forms--Estate Planning § 6:100, Spouse Omitted If Marriage is Terminated by Dissolution or Annulment.
4 California Transactions Forms--Estate Planning § 19:42, Nature and Purpose; Governing Law.
4 California Transactions Forms--Estate Planning § 22:9, Overview.
4 California Transactions Forms--Estate Planning § 22:15, Revocation as a Result of Dissolution or Annulment.
West's California Code Forms, Probate § 8250 Form 1, Contest of Will and Objection to Probate.
West's California Code Forms, Probate § 8270 Form 1, Petition for Revocation of Probate of Will.

§ 6122.1. Domestic partnership of testator; revocation by termination

(a) Unless the will expressly provides otherwise, if after executing a will the testator's domestic partnership is terminated, the termination revokes all of the following:

(1) Any disposition or appointment of property made by the will to the former domestic partner.

§ 6122.1

(2) Any provision of the will conferring a general or special power of appointment on the former domestic partner.

(3) Any provision of the will nominating the former domestic partner as executor, trustee, conservator, or guardian.

(b) If any disposition or other provision of a will is revoked solely by this section, it is revived by the testator establishing another domestic partnership with the former domestic partner.

(c) In case of revocation by termination of a domestic partnership:

(1) Property prevented from passing to a former domestic partner because of the revocation passes as if the former domestic partner failed to survive the testator.

(2) Other provisions of the will conferring some power or office on the former domestic partner shall be interpreted as if the former domestic partner failed to survive the testator.

(d) This section shall apply only to wills executed on or after January 1, 2002. *(Added by Stats.2001, c. 893 (A.B.25), § 51.)*

Application

For application of this section, see its terms.

Research References

Forms

1 California Transactions Forms--Estate Planning § 2:14, Failure to Properly Designate Disposition of Assets, Provide for Pretermitted Heirs, and Plan for Dissolution of Marriage.
1 California Transactions Forms--Estate Planning § 6:30.50, Effect of Termination of Domestic Partnership.
1 California Transactions Forms--Estate Planning § 6:51, Matters to Consider in Drafting Dispositions to Beneficiaries.
4 California Transactions Forms--Estate Planning § 22:9, Overview.
4 California Transactions Forms--Estate Planning § 22:15.50, Revocation as a Result of Termination of a Domestic Partnership.

Part 2

INTESTATE SUCCESSION

Cross References

Biomedical and Behavioral Research, actions for physical or mental injuries or wrongful death, see Penal Code § 3524.
Claims and actions against public entities and employees, collateral source payments, see Government Code § 985.

CHAPTER 2. PARENT AND CHILD RELATIONSHIP

Section
6450. Relationship existence.
6451. Adoption.
6452. Conditions preventing a parent from inheriting from or through a child.
6453. Natural parents.
6454. Foster parent or stepparent.
6455. Equitable adoption; application.

§ 6450. Relationship existence

Subject to the provisions of this chapter, a relationship of parent and child exists for the purpose of determining intestate succession by, through, or from a person in the following circumstances:

(a) The relationship of parent and child exists between a person and the person's natural parents, regardless of the marital status of the natural parents.

(b) The relationship of parent and child exists between an adopted person and the person's adopting parent or parents. *(Added by Stats.1993, c. 529 (A.B.1137), § 5.)*

Research References

Forms

1 California Transactions Forms--Estate Planning § 6:11, Existence of Relationship.
1 California Transactions Forms--Estate Planning § 6:52, Matters to Consider in Drafting Class Gifts.
4 California Transactions Forms--Estate Planning § 19:116, Will for Single Person.
4 California Transactions Forms--Estate Planning § 19:144, Adopted Persons Included.
4 California Transactions Forms--Estate Planning § 19:145, Adopted Persons Excluded.
2 California Transactions Forms--Family Law § 6:18, Intestate Succession Rights.

§ 6451. Adoption

(a) An adoption severs the relationship of parent and child between an adopted person and a natural parent of the adopted person unless both of the following requirements are satisfied:

(1) The natural parent and the adopted person lived together at any time as parent and child, or the natural parent was married to or cohabiting with the other natural parent at the time the person was conceived and died before the person's birth.

(2) The adoption was by the spouse of either of the natural parents or after the death of either of the natural parents.

(b) Neither a natural parent nor a relative of a natural parent, except for a wholeblood brother or sister of the adopted person or the issue of that brother or sister, inherits from or through the adopted person on the basis of a parent and child relationship between the adopted person and the natural parent that satisfies the requirements of paragraphs (1) and (2) of subdivision (a), unless the adoption is by the spouse or surviving spouse of that parent.

(c) For the purpose of this section, a prior adoptive parent and child relationship is treated as a natural parent and child relationship. *(Added by Stats.1993, c. 529 (A.B.1137), § 5.)*

Research References

Forms

1 California Transactions Forms--Estate Planning § 6:12, Natural Parents of Adopted Child.
1 California Transactions Forms--Estate Planning § 6:52, Matters to Consider in Drafting Class Gifts.
4 California Transactions Forms--Estate Planning § 19:101, Adopted Children and Stepchildren.
2 California Transactions Forms--Family Law § 6:18, Intestate Succession Rights.
2 California Transactions Forms--Family Law § 6:114, Consent of Noncustodial Parent.

§ 6452. Conditions preventing a parent from inheriting from or through a child

(a) A parent does not inherit from or through a child on the basis of the parent and child relationship if any of the following apply:

(1) The parent's parental rights were terminated and the parent-child relationship was not judicially reestablished.

(2) The parent did not acknowledge the child.

(3) The parent left the child during the child's minority without an effort to provide for the child's support or without communication from the parent, for at least seven consecutive years that continued until the end of the child's minority, with the intent on the part of the parent to abandon the child. The failure to provide support or to communicate for the prescribed period is presumptive evidence of an intent to abandon.

(b) A parent who does not inherit from or through the child as provided in subdivision (a) shall be deemed to have predeceased the child, and the intestate estate shall pass as otherwise required under Section 6402. *(Added by Stats.2013, c. 39 (A.B.490), § 2.)*

Research References

Forms

1 California Transactions Forms--Estate Planning § 6:13, Conditions Preventing Parent from Inheriting from a Child.
1 California Transactions Forms--Estate Planning § 6:52, Matters to Consider in Drafting Class Gifts.

§ 6453. Natural parents

For the purpose of determining whether a person is a "natural parent" as that term is used in this chapter:

(a) A natural parent and child relationship is established where that relationship is presumed and not rebutted pursuant to the Uniform Parentage Act (Part 3 (commencing with Section 7600) of Division 12 of the Family Code).

(b) A natural parent and child relationship may be established pursuant to any other provisions of the Uniform Parentage Act, except that the relationship may not be established by an action under subdivision (c) of Section 7630 of the Family Code unless any of the following conditions exist:

(1) A court order was entered during the parent's lifetime declaring parentage.

(2) Parentage is established by clear and convincing evidence that the parent has openly held out the child as that parent's own.

(3) It was impossible for the parent to hold out the child as that parent's own and parentage is established by clear and convincing evidence, which may include genetic DNA evidence acquired during the parent's lifetime.

(c) A natural parent and child relationship may be established pursuant to Section 249.5. *(Added by Stats.1993, c. 529 (A.B.1137), § 5. Amended by Stats.2004, c. 775 (A.B.1910), § 9; Stats.2018, c. 116 (S.B.1436), § 1, eff. Jan. 1, 2019.)*

Research References

Forms

1 California Transactions Forms--Estate Planning § 6:11, Existence of Relationship.
1 California Transactions Forms--Estate Planning § 6:52, Matters to Consider in Drafting Class Gifts.

§ 6454. Foster parent or stepparent

For the purpose of determining intestate succession by a person or the person's issue from or through a foster parent or stepparent, the relationship of parent and child exists between that person and the person's foster parent or stepparent if both of the following requirements are satisfied:

(a) The relationship began during the person's minority and continued throughout the joint lifetimes of the person and the person's foster parent or stepparent.

(b) It is established by clear and convincing evidence that the foster parent or stepparent would have adopted the person but for a legal barrier. *(Added by Stats.1993, c. 529 (A.B.1137), § 5.)*

Research References

Forms

1 California Transactions Forms--Estate Planning § 2:14, Failure to Properly Designate Disposition of Assets, Provide for Pretermitted Heirs, and Plan for Dissolution of Marriage.
1 California Transactions Forms--Estate Planning § 6:14, Foster or Stepparent.
1 California Transactions Forms--Estate Planning § 6:52, Matters to Consider in Drafting Class Gifts.

4 California Transactions Forms--Estate Planning § 19:101, Adopted Children and Stepchildren.

§ 6455. Equitable adoption; application

Nothing in this chapter affects or limits application of the judicial doctrine of equitable adoption for the benefit of the child or the child's issue. *(Added by Stats.1993, c. 529 (A.B.1137), § 5.)*

Research References

Forms

1 California Transactions Forms--Estate Planning § 6:11, Existence of Relationship.
3 California Transactions Forms--Estate Planning § 14:31, Issue Defined, Including "Technotots".

Part 3

FAMILY PROTECTION

CHAPTER 1. TEMPORARY POSSESSION OF FAMILY DWELLING AND EXEMPT PROPERTY

Section
6500. Possession of family dwelling; exempt property; duration.
6501. Petition for order.

§ 6500. Possession of family dwelling; exempt property; duration

Until the inventory is filed and for a period of 60 days thereafter, or for such other period as may be ordered by the court for good cause on petition therefor, the decedent's surviving spouse and minor children are entitled to remain in possession of the family dwelling, the wearing apparel of the family, the household furniture, and the other property of the decedent exempt from enforcement of a money judgment. *(Stats.1990, c. 79 (A.B.759), § 14, operative July 1, 1991.)*

Cross References

Conservatorships and other protective proceedings, educational requirements for court-appointed, nonprofessional conservators and guardians, see Probate Code § 1457.
Enforcement of money judgments, exemptions, see Code of Civil Procedure § 703.010 et seq.

Research References

Forms

3 California Transactions Forms--Estate Planning § 18:31, Homestead Exemption.
4 California Transactions Forms--Estate Planning § 19:6, Law Governing Meaning and Effect of Will.
4 California Transactions Forms--Estate Planning § 19:7, Overview.
4 California Transactions Forms--Estate Planning § 19:8, Exempt Property.

§ 6501. Petition for order

A petition for an order under Section 6500 may be filed by any interested person. Notice of the hearing on the petition shall be given as provided in Section 1220. *(Stats.1990, c. 79 (A.B.759), § 14, operative July 1, 1991.)*

Research References

Forms

West's California Code Forms, Probate § 6501 Form 1, Petition for Order Authorizing Extended Temporary Possession of Family Dwelling and Other Exempt Property by Decedent's Family.

CHAPTER 2. SETTING ASIDE EXEMPT PROPERTY OTHER THAN FAMILY DWELLING

Section
6510. Exempt property; setting apart by court.
6511. Petition; notice.

§ 6510. Exempt property; setting apart by court

Upon the filing of the inventory or at any subsequent time during the administration of the estate, the court in its discretion may on petition therefor set apart all or any part of the property of the decedent exempt from enforcement of a money judgment, other than the family dwelling, to any one or more of the following:

(a) The surviving spouse.

(b) The minor children of the decedent. *(Stats.1990, c. 79 (A.B.759), § 14, operative July 1, 1991.)*

Cross References

Enforcement of money judgments, exemptions, see Code of Civil Procedure § 703.010 et seq.
Family allowance, generally, see Probate Code § 6540 et seq.

Research References

Forms

1 California Transactions Forms--Estate Planning § 6:32, Exceptions to Omitted Child Statute.
4 California Transactions Forms--Estate Planning § 19:8, Exempt Property.
West's California Code Forms, Probate § 6510 Form 1, Petition for Order Setting Apart Exempt Property Other Than Family Dwelling.

§ 6511. Petition; notice

A petition for an order under Section 6510 may be filed by any interested person. Notice of the hearing on the petition shall be given as provided in Section 1220. *(Stats.1990, c. 79 (A.B.759), § 14, operative July 1, 1991.)*

Research References

Forms

West's California Code Forms, Probate § 6510 Form 1, Petition for Order Setting Apart Exempt Property Other Than Family Dwelling.

CHAPTER 3. SETTING ASIDE PROBATE HOMESTEAD

Section
6520. Authority; setting aside probate homestead.
6521. Persons for whose use homestead shall be set apart.
6522. Property out of which selected; preference.
6523. Facts considered; conditions.
6524. Period; rights of parties.
6525. Petition; notice.
6526. Liability for claims against estate; homestead exemption.
6527. Modification, terms and conditions; termination; petition for order; notice of hearing.
6528. Relationship to existing law.

§ 6520. Authority; setting aside probate homestead

Upon the filing of the inventory or at any subsequent time during the administration of the estate, the court in its discretion may on petition therefor select and set apart one probate homestead in the manner provided in this chapter. *(Stats.1990, c. 79 (A.B.759), § 14, operative July 1, 1991.)*

Cross References

Exemptions generally, see Code of Civil Procedure § 703.010 et seq.
Protection of homesteads, see Cal. Const. Art. 20, § 1.5.
Recordation of order setting apart homestead, see Probate Code § 7263.

Research References

Forms

4 California Transactions Forms--Estate Planning § 19:3, Legislative Control Over Testation.
4 California Transactions Forms--Estate Planning § 19:9, Probate Homestead.
West's California Code Forms, Probate § 6520 Form 1, Petition for Order Setting Apart Probate Homestead to Surviving Spouse.
West's California Code Forms, Probate § 6602 Form 1, Petition to Set Aside Small Estate.

§ 6521. Persons for whose use homestead shall be set apart

The probate homestead shall be set apart for the use of one or more of the following persons:

(a) The surviving spouse.

(b) The minor children of the decedent. *(Stats.1990, c. 79 (A.B.759), § 14, operative July 1, 1991.)*

Cross References

Declared homesteads, see Code of Civil Procedure § 704.910 et seq.
Recordation of order setting apart homestead, see Probate Code § 7263.
Small estate set-aside, see Probate Code § 6600 et seq.

Research References

Forms

1 California Transactions Forms--Estate Planning § 6:32, Exceptions to Omitted Child Statute.
4 California Transactions Forms--Estate Planning § 19:9, Probate Homestead.
West's California Code Forms, Probate § 6520 Form 1, Petition for Order Setting Apart Probate Homestead to Surviving Spouse.

§ 6522. Property out of which selected; preference

(a) The probate homestead shall be selected out of the following property, giving first preference to the community and quasi-community property of, or property owned in common by, the decedent and the person entitled to have the homestead set apart:

(1) If the homestead is set apart for the use of the surviving spouse or for the use of the surviving spouse and minor children, out of community property or quasi-community property.

(2) If the homestead is set apart for the use of the surviving spouse or for the use of the minor children or for the use of the surviving spouse and minor children, out of property owned in common by the decedent and the persons entitled to have the homestead set apart, or out of the separate property of the decedent or, if the decedent was not married at the time of death, out of property owned by the decedent.

(b) The probate homestead shall not be selected out of property the right to possession of which is vested in a third person unless the third person consents thereto. As used in this subdivision, "third person" means a person whose right to possession of the property (1) existed at the time of the death of the decedent or came into existence upon the death of the decedent and (2) was not created by testate or intestate succession from the decedent. *(Stats.1990, c. 79 (A.B.759), § 14, operative July 1, 1991. Amended by Stats.1990, c. 710 (S.B.1775), § 17, operative July 1, 1991.)*

Research References

Forms

West's California Code Forms, Probate § 6520 Form 1, Petition for Order Setting Apart Probate Homestead to Surviving Spouse.

§ 6523. Facts considered; conditions

(a) In selecting and setting apart the probate homestead, the court shall consider the needs of the surviving spouse and minor children, the liens and encumbrances on the property, the claims of creditors, the needs of the heirs or devisees of the decedent, and the intent of the decedent with respect to the property in the estate and the estate plan of the decedent as expressed in inter vivos and testamentary transfers or by other means.

(b) The court, in light of subdivision (a) and other relevant considerations as determined by the court in its discretion, shall:

(1) Select as a probate homestead the most appropriate property available that is suitable for that use, including in addition to the dwelling itself such adjoining property as appears reasonable.

(2) Set the probate homestead so selected apart for such a term and upon such conditions (including, but not limited to, assignment by the homestead recipient of other property to the heirs or devisees of the property set apart as a homestead) as appear proper. *(Stats.1990, c. 79 (A.B.759), § 14, operative July 1, 1991.)*

§ 6524. Period; rights of parties

The property set apart as a probate homestead shall be set apart only for a limited period, to be designated in the order, and in no case beyond the lifetime of the surviving spouse, or, as to a child, beyond its minority. Subject to the probate homestead right, the property of the decedent remains subject to administration including testate and intestate succession. The rights of the parties during the period for which the probate homestead is set apart are governed, to the extent applicable, by the Legal Estates Principal and Income Law, Chapter 2.6 (commencing with Section 731) of Title 2 of Part 1 of Division 2 of the Civil Code. *(Stats.1990, c. 79 (A.B.759), § 14, operative July 1, 1991.)*

Cross References

Apportionment of receipts and expenditures, tenants and remainder-men, see Civil Code § 731.04.

Research References

Forms

4 California Transactions Forms--Estate Planning § 19:9, Probate Homestead.
4 California Transactions Forms--Estate Planning § 19:10, Family Allowance.
West's California Code Forms, Probate § 6520 Form 1, Petition for Order Setting Apart Probate Homestead to Surviving Spouse.

§ 6525. Petition; notice

(a) A petition to select and set apart a probate homestead may be filed by any interested person.

(b) Notice of the hearing on the petition shall be given as provided in Section 1220 to all of the following persons:

(1) Each person listed in Section 1220.

(2) Each known heir whose interest in the estate would be affected by the petition.

(3) Each known devisee whose interest in the estate would be affected by the petition. *(Stats.1990, c. 79 (A.B.759), § 14, operative July 1, 1991.)*

Research References

Forms

West's California Code Forms, Probate § 6520 Form 1, Petition for Order Setting Apart Probate Homestead to Surviving Spouse.

§ 6526. Liability for claims against estate; homestead exemption

(a) Property of the decedent set apart as a probate homestead is liable for claims against the estate of the decedent, subject to the probate homestead right. The probate homestead right in property of the decedent is liable for claims that are secured by liens and encumbrances on the property at the time of the decedent's death but is exempt to the extent of the homestead exemption as to any claim that would have been subject to a homestead exemption at the time of the decedent's death under Article 4 (commencing with Section 704.710) of Chapter 4 of Division 2 of Title 9 of Part 2 of the Code of Civil Procedure.

(b) The probate homestead right in the property of the decedent is not liable for claims against the person for whose use the probate homestead is set apart.

(c) Property of the decedent set apart as a probate homestead is liable for claims against the testate or intestate successors of the decedent or other successors to the property after administration, subject to the probate homestead right. *(Stats.1990, c. 79 (A.B.759), § 14, operative July 1, 1991.)*

Cross References

Protection of homesteads, see Cal. Const. Art. 20, § 1.5.

Research References

Forms

4 California Transactions Forms--Estate Planning § 19:9, Probate Homestead.
West's California Code Forms, Probate § 6520 Form 1, Petition for Order Setting Apart Probate Homestead to Surviving Spouse.
West's California Code Forms, Probate § 6520 Form 2, Order Setting Apart Probate Homestead to Surviving Spouse.

§ 6527. Modification, terms and conditions; termination; petition for order; notice of hearing

(a) The court may by order modify the term or conditions of the probate homestead right or terminate the probate homestead right at any time prior to entry of an order for final distribution of the decedent's estate if in the court's discretion to do so appears appropriate under the circumstances of the case.

(b) A petition for an order under this section may be filed by any of the following:

(1) The person for whose use the probate homestead is set apart.

(2) The testate or intestate successors of the decedent or other successors to the property set apart as a probate homestead.

(3) Persons having claims secured by liens or encumbrances on the property set apart as a probate homestead.

(c) Notice of the hearing on the petition shall be given to all the persons listed in subdivision (b) as provided in Section 1220. *(Stats.1990, c. 79 (A.B.759), § 14, operative July 1, 1991.)*

Research References

Forms

4 California Transactions Forms--Estate Planning § 19:9, Probate Homestead.

§ 6528. Relationship to existing law

Nothing in this chapter terminates or otherwise affects a declaration of homestead by, or for the benefit of, a surviving spouse or minor child of the decedent with respect to the community, quasi-community, or common interest of the surviving spouse or minor child in property in the decedent's estate. This section is declaratory of, and does not constitute a change in, existing law. *(Stats.1990, c. 79 (A.B.759), § 14, operative July 1, 1991.)*

CHAPTER 4. FAMILY ALLOWANCE

Section
6540. Persons entitled to allowance.
6541. Grant or modification; petition; hearing; notice.
6542. Commencement; retroactive allowances.
6543. Termination; limitation; continuation.
6544. Costs.
6545. Perfection of appeal; stay of proceedings.

PROBATE CODE

Cross References

Application of old and new law, see Probate Code § 3.

§ 6540. Persons entitled to allowance

(a) The following are entitled to such reasonable family allowance out of the estate as is necessary for their maintenance according to their circumstances during administration of the estate:

(1) The surviving spouse of the decedent.

(2) Minor children of the decedent.

(3) Adult children of the decedent who are physically or mentally incapacitated from earning a living and were actually dependent in whole or in part upon the decedent for support.

(b) The following may be given such reasonable family allowance out of the estate as the court in its discretion determines is necessary for their maintenance according to their circumstances during administration of the estate:

(1) Other adult children of the decedent who were actually dependent in whole or in part upon the decedent for support.

(2) A parent of the decedent who was actually dependent in whole or in part upon the decedent for support.

(c) If a person otherwise eligible for family allowance has a reasonable maintenance from other sources and there are one or more other persons entitled to a family allowance, the family allowance shall be granted only to those who do not have a reasonable maintenance from other sources. (Stats.1990, c. 79 (A.B.759), § 14, operative July 1, 1991.)

Cross References

Order of payment of expenses, charges and debts, see Probate Code § 11420.
Sale of property to pay family allowance, see Probate Code §§ 10252, 10259.

Research References

Forms

1 California Transactions Forms--Estate Planning § 1:2, Probate System.
1 California Transactions Forms--Estate Planning § 6:32, Exceptions to Omitted Child Statute.
2 California Transactions Forms--Estate Planning § 9:151, Ird is Principal for Trust Accounting Purposes.
4 California Transactions Forms--Estate Planning § 19:3, Legislative Control Over Testation.
4 California Transactions Forms--Estate Planning § 19:10, Family Allowance.
4 California Transactions Forms--Estate Planning § 19:80, Overview.
4 California Transactions Forms--Estate Planning § 21:20, Surviving Spouse's Trust Income Withheld to Extent of Family Allowance.
West's California Code Forms, Probate § 6541 Form 1, Petition for Family Allowance.

§ 6541. Grant or modification; petition; hearing; notice

(a) The court may grant or modify a family allowance on petition of any interested person.

(b) With respect to an order for the family allowance provided for in subdivision (a) of Section 6540:

(1) Before the inventory is filed, the order may be made or modified either (A) ex parte or (B) after notice of the hearing on the petition has been given as provided in Section 1220.

(2) After the inventory is filed, the order may be made or modified only after notice of the hearing on the petition has been given as provided in Section 1220.

(c) An order for the family allowance provided in subdivision (b) of Section 6540 may be made only after notice of the hearing on the petition has been given as provided in Section 1220 to all of the following persons:

(1) Each person listed in Section 1220.

(2) Each known heir whose interest in the estate would be affected by the petition.

(3) Each known devisee whose interest in the estate would be affected by the petition. (Stats.1990, c. 79 (A.B.759), § 14, operative July 1, 1991.)

Cross References

Time for and place of filing inventory, see Probate Code § 8800.

Research References

Forms

West's California Code Forms, Probate § 6541 Form 1, Petition for Family Allowance.
West's California Code Forms, Probate § 6541 Form 3, Petition to Modify Order for Family Allowance by Reducing or Terminating Allowance.

§ 6542. Commencement; retroactive allowances

A family allowance commences on the date of the court's order or such other time as may be provided in the court's order, whether before or after the date of the order, as the court in its discretion determines, but the allowance may not be made retroactive to a date earlier than the date of the decedent's death. (Stats.1990, c. 79 (A.B.759), § 14, operative July 1, 1991.)

Research References

Forms

West's California Code Forms, Probate § 6541 Form 2, Order for Family Allowance.

§ 6543. Termination; limitation; continuation

(a) A family allowance shall terminate no later than the entry of the order for final distribution of the estate or, if the estate is insolvent, no later than one year after the granting of letters.

(b) Subject to subdivision (a), a family allowance shall continue until modified or terminated by the court or until such time as the court may provide in its order. (Stats.1990, c. 79 (A.B.759), § 14, operative July 1, 1991.)

Research References

Forms

4 California Transactions Forms--Estate Planning § 19:10, Family Allowance.
West's California Code Forms, Probate § 6541 Form 2, Order for Family Allowance.

§ 6544. Costs

The costs of proceedings under this chapter shall be paid by the estate as expenses of administration. (Stats.1990, c. 79 (A.B.759), § 14, operative July 1, 1991.)

Cross References

Costs, discretion to order payment by parties or from estate, see Probate Code § 1002.

§ 6545. Perfection of appeal; stay of proceedings

Notwithstanding Chapter 2 (commencing with Section 916) of Title 13 of Part 2 of the Code of Civil Procedure, the perfecting of an appeal from an order made under this chapter does not stay proceedings under this chapter or the enforcement of the order appealed from if the person in whose favor the order is made gives an undertaking in double the amount of the payment or payments to be made to that person. The undertaking shall be conditioned that if the order appealed from is modified or reversed so that the payment or any part thereof to the person proves to have been unwarranted, the payment or part thereof shall, unless deducted from any preliminary or final distribution ordered in favor of the person, be repaid and refunded into the estate within 30 days after the court so orders following the modification or reversal, together with interest and costs. (Stats.1990, c. 79 (A.B.759), § 14, operative July 1, 1991.)

WILLS AND INTESTATE SUCCESSION § 6604

Research References

Forms

1 California Transactions Forms--Estate Planning § 1:2, Probate System.
4 California Transactions Forms--Estate Planning § 19:3, Legislative Control Over Testation.
4 California Transactions Forms--Estate Planning § 19:7, Overview.

CHAPTER 6. SMALL ESTATE SET–ASIDE

Section
6600. Decedent's estate defined.
6601. Minor child.
6602. Petition requesting order to set aside estate; maximum value.
6603. Venue.
6604. Contents of petition.
6605. Procedure for filing petition; time for filing.
6606. Who may file.
6607. Notice of hearing; concurrent with hearing of petition for probate or administration.
6608. Inventory and appraisal; filing.
6609. Determination of whether to make order; assignment of estate; unpaid liabilities; title to property.
6610. Effect of order.
6611. Unsecured debts; liability; actions and proceedings.
6612. Determinations not to make order under § 6609; action on petition for probate or administration.
6613. Attorney's fees.
6614. Application of law.
6615. References to former sections deemed references to comparable provisions of this chapter.

Application

Provisions applicable to decedents who died on or after July 1, 1987, see Probate Code § 6614.

Cross References

Application of old and new law, see Probate Code § 3.
Timing of dollar amount adjustments, adjustment based on Consumer Price Index for All Urban Consumers, publication of dollar amounts, see Probate Code § 890.

§ 6600. Decedent's estate defined

(a) Subject to subdivision (b), for the purposes of this chapter, "decedent's estate" means all the decedent's personal property, wherever located, and all the decedent's real property located in this state.

(b) For the purposes of this chapter:

(1) Any property or interest or lien thereon which, at the time of the decedent's death, was held by the decedent as a joint tenant, or in which the decedent had a life or other interest terminable upon the decedent's death, shall be excluded in determining the estate of the decedent or its value.

(2) A multiple-party account to which the decedent was a party at the time of the decedent's death shall be excluded in determining the estate of the decedent or its value, whether or not all or a portion of the sums on deposit are community property, to the extent that the sums on deposit belong after the death of the decedent to a surviving party, P.O.D. payee, or beneficiary. As used in this paragraph, the terms "multiple-party account," "party," "P.O.D. payee," and "beneficiary" have the meanings given those terms in Article 2 (commencing with Section 5120) of Chapter 1 of Part 2 of Division 5. (Stats.1990, c. 79 (A.B.759), § 14, operative July 1, 1991.)

Research References

Forms

2 California Transactions Forms--Estate Planning § 11:50, Rights of Surviving Spouse that May be Waived [Prob C § 141].
4 California Transactions Forms--Estate Planning § 19:7, Overview.
4 California Transactions Forms--Estate Planning § 19:12, Small Estate Set-Aside.
4 California Transactions Forms--Estate Planning § 19:15, Waiver of Family Protection.
West's California Code Forms, Probate § 6602 Form 1, Petition to Set Aside Small Estate.

§ 6601. Minor child

As used in this chapter, "minor child" means a child of the decedent who was under the age of 18 at the time of the decedent's death and who survived the decedent. (Stats.1990, c. 79 (A.B.759), § 14, operative July 1, 1991.)

Research References

Forms

4 California Transactions Forms--Estate Planning § 19:12, Small Estate Set-Aside.
West's California Code Forms, Probate § 6602 Form 1, Petition to Set Aside Small Estate.

§ 6602. Petition requesting order to set aside estate; maximum value

A petition may be filed under this chapter requesting an order setting aside the decedent's estate to the decedent's surviving spouse and minor children, or one or more of them, as provided in this chapter, if the net value of the decedent's estate, over and above all liens and encumbrances at the date of death and over and above the value of any probate homestead interest set apart out of the decedent's estate under Section 6520, does not exceed eighty-five thousand nine hundred dollars ($85,900), as adjusted periodically in accordance with Section 890. (Stats.1990, c. 79 (A.B.759), § 14, operative July 1, 1991. Amended by Stats.2019, c. 122 (A.B.473), § 2, eff. Jan. 1, 2020.)

Cross References

Decedent's estate defined for purposes of this Chapter, see Probate Code § 6600.
Fee for filing petition commencing or opposition papers concerning setting aside decedent's estate of small value, see Government Code § 70656.
Minor child defined for purposes of this Chapter, see Probate Code § 6601.

Research References

Forms

4 California Transactions Forms--Estate Planning § 19:12, Small Estate Set-Aside.
West's California Code Forms, Probate § 890, Comment: Timing of Dollar Amount Adjustments and Periodic Adjustments.
West's California Code Forms, Probate § 6602 Form 1, Petition to Set Aside Small Estate.

§ 6603. Venue

The petition shall be filed in the superior court of a county in which the estate of the decedent may be administered. (Stats.1990, c. 79 (A.B.759), § 14, operative July 1, 1991.)

Research References

Forms

West's California Code Forms, Probate § 6602 Form 1, Petition to Set Aside Small Estate.

§ 6604. Contents of petition

(a) The petition shall allege that this chapter applies and request that an order be made setting aside the estate of the decedent as provided in this chapter.

§ 6604

(b) The petition shall include the following:

(1) If proceedings for administration of the estate are not pending, the facts necessary to determine the county in which the estate of the decedent may be administered.

(2) The name, age, address, and relation to the decedent of each heir and devisee of the decedent, so far as known to the petitioner.

(3) A specific description and estimate of the value of the decedent's estate and a list of all liens and encumbrances at the date of death.

(4) A specific description and estimate of the value of any of the decedent's real property located outside this state that passed to the surviving spouse and minor children of the decedent, or any one or more of them, under the will of the decedent or by intestate succession.

(5) A specific description and estimate of the value of any of the decedent's property described in subdivision (b) of Section 6600 that passed to the surviving spouse and minor children of the decedent, or any one or more of them, upon the death of the decedent.

(6) A designation of any property as to which a probate homestead is set apart out of the decedent's estate under Section 6520.

(7) A statement of any unpaid liabilities for expenses of the last illness, funeral charges, and expenses of administration.

(8) The requested disposition of the estate of the decedent under this chapter and the considerations that justify the requested disposition. *(Stats.1990, c. 79 (A.B.759), § 14, operative July 1, 1991.)*

Cross References

Decedent's estate defined for purposes of this Chapter, see Probate Code § 6600.
Minor child defined for purposes of this Chapter, see Probate Code § 6601.
Probate of will, petition, see Probate Code § 8006.
Verification of pleadings, see Code of Civil Procedure § 446.

Research References

Forms

West's California Code Forms, Probate § 6602 Form 1, Petition to Set Aside Small Estate.

§ 6605. Procedure for filing petition; time for filing

(a) If proceedings for the administration of the estate of the decedent are pending, a petition under this chapter shall be filed in those proceedings without the payment of an additional fee.

(b) If proceedings for the administration of the estate of the decedent have not yet been commenced, a petition under this chapter may be filed concurrently with a petition for the probate of the decedent's will or for administration of the estate of the decedent, or, if no petition for probate or for administration is being filed, a petition under this chapter may be filed independently.

(c) A petition may be filed under this chapter at any time prior to the entry of the order for final distribution of the estate. *(Stats.1990, c. 79 (A.B.759), § 14, operative July 1, 1991.)*

§ 6606. Who may file

(a) A petition may be filed under this chapter by any of the following:

(1) The person named in the will of the decedent as executor.

(2) The surviving spouse of the decedent.

(3) The guardian of a minor child of the decedent.

(4) A child of the decedent who was a minor at the time the decedent died.

(5) The personal representative if a personal representative has been appointed for the decedent's estate.

(b) The guardian of a minor child of the decedent may file the petition without authorization or approval of the court in which the guardianship proceeding is pending. *(Stats.1990, c. 79 (A.B.759), § 14, operative July 1, 1991.)*

Cross References

Decedent's estate defined for purposes of this Chapter, see Probate Code § 6600.
Minor child defined for purposes of this Chapter, see Probate Code § 6601.

Research References

Forms

4 California Transactions Forms--Estate Planning § 19:12, Small Estate Set-Aside.
West's California Code Forms, Probate § 6602 Form 1, Petition to Set Aside Small Estate.

§ 6607. Notice of hearing; concurrent with hearing of petition for probate or administration

(a) Where proceedings for the administration of the estate of the decedent are not pending when the petition is filed under this chapter and the petition under this chapter is not joined with a petition for the probate of the decedent's will or for administration of the estate of the decedent, the petitioner shall give notice of the hearing on the petition as provided in Section 1220 to (1) each person named as executor in the decedent's will and to (2) each heir or devisee of the decedent, if known to the petitioner. A copy of the petition shall be sent with the notice of hearing to the surviving spouse, each child, and each devisee who is not petitioning.

(b) If the petition under this chapter is filed with a petition for the probate of the decedent's will or with a petition for administration of the estate of the deceased spouse, notice of the hearing on the petition shall be given to the persons and in the manner prescribed by Section 8003 and shall be included in the notice required by that section.

(c) If proceedings for the administration of the estate of the decedent are pending when the petition is filed under this chapter and the hearing of the petition for probate of the will or administration of the estate of the decedent is set for a day more than 15 days after the filing of the petition filed under this chapter, the petition under this chapter shall be set for hearing at the same time as the petition for probate of the will or for administration of the estate, and notice of hearing on the petition filed under this chapter shall be given by the petitioner as provided in Section 1220. If the hearing of the petition for probate of the will or for administration of the estate is not set for hearing for a day more than 15 days after the filing of the petition under this chapter, (1) the petition filed under this chapter shall be set for hearing at least 15 days after the date on which it is filed, (2) notice of the hearing on the petition filed under this chapter shall be given by the petitioner as provided in Section 1220, and (3) if the petition for probate of the will or for administration of the estate has not already been heard, that petition shall be continued until that date and heard at the same time unless the court otherwise orders. *(Stats.1990, c. 79 (A.B.759), § 14, operative July 1, 1991.)*

Research References

Forms

West's California Code Forms, Probate § 6602 Form 1, Petition to Set Aside Small Estate.

§ 6608. Inventory and appraisal; filing

If a petition is filed under this chapter, the personal representative, or the petitioner if no personal representative has been appointed, shall file with the clerk of the court, prior to the hearing of the petition, an inventory and appraisal made as provided in Part 3 (commencing with Section 8800) of Division 7. The personal representative or the petitioner, as the case may be, may appraise the assets which a personal representative could appraise under Section 8901. (Stats.1990, c. 79 (A.B.759), § 14, operative July 1, 1991.)

Research References

Forms

West's California Code Forms, Probate § 6602 Form 1, Petition to Set Aside Small Estate.

§ 6609. Determination of whether to make order; assignment of estate; unpaid liabilities; title to property

(a) If the court determines that the net value of the decedent's estate, over and above all liens and encumbrances at the date of death of the decedent and over and above the value of any probate homestead interest set apart out of the decedent's estate under Section 6520, does not exceed eighty-five thousand nine hundred dollars ($85,900), as adjusted periodically in accordance with Section 890, as of the date of the decedent's death, the court shall make an order under this section unless the court determines that making an order under this section would be inequitable under the circumstances of the particular case.

(b) In determining whether to make an order under this section, the court shall consider the needs of the surviving spouse and minor children, the liens and encumbrances on the property of the decedent's estate, the claims of creditors, the needs of the heirs or devisees of the decedent, the intent of the decedent with respect to the property in the estate and the estate plan of the decedent as expressed in inter vivos and testamentary transfers or by other means, and any other relevant considerations. If the surviving spouse has remarried at the time the petition is heard, it shall be presumed that the needs of the surviving spouse do not justify the setting aside of the small estate, or any portion thereof, to the surviving spouse. This presumption is a presumption affecting the burden of proof.

(c) Subject to subdivision (d), if the court makes an order under this section, the court shall assign the whole of the decedent's estate, subject to all liens and encumbrances on property in the estate at the date of the decedent's death, to the surviving spouse and the minor children of the decedent, or any one or more of them.

(d) If there are any liabilities for expenses of the last illness, funeral charges, or expenses of administration that are unpaid at the time the court makes an order under this section, the court shall make the necessary orders for payment of those unpaid liabilities.

(e) Title to property in the decedent's estate vests absolutely in the surviving spouse, minor children, or any or all of them, as provided in the order, subject to all liens and encumbrances on property in the estate at the date of the decedent's death, and there shall be no further proceedings in the administration of the decedent's estate unless additional property in the decedent's estate is discovered. (Stats.1990, c. 79 (A.B.759), § 14, operative July 1, 1991. Amended by Stats.2019, c. 122 (A.B.473), § 3, eff. Jan. 1, 2020.)

Cross References

Administration of estates of decedents, see Probate Code §§ 7000, 7001.
Burden of proof, generally, see Evidence Code § 500 et seq.
Decedent's estate defined for purposes of this Chapter, see Probate Code § 6600.
Family allowance, see Probate Code § 6540 et seq.
Minor child defined for purposes of this Chapter, see Probate Code § 6601.

Research References

Forms

4 California Transactions Forms--Estate Planning § 19:12, Small Estate Set-Aside.
West's California Code Forms, Probate § 890, Comment: Timing of Dollar Amount Adjustments and Periodic Adjustments.
West's California Code Forms, Probate § 6602 Form 1, Petition to Set Aside Small Estate.

West's California Code Forms, Probate § 6602 Form 2, Order Setting Aside Small Estate.

§ 6610. Effect of order

Upon becoming final, an order under Section 6609 shall be conclusive on all persons, whether or not they are then in being. (Stats.1990, c. 79 (A.B.759), § 14, operative July 1, 1991.)

§ 6611. Unsecured debts; liability; actions and proceedings

(a) Subject to the limitations and conditions specified in this section, the person or persons in whom title vested pursuant to Section 6609 are personally liable for the unsecured debts of the decedent.

(b) The personal liability of a person under this section does not exceed the fair market value at the date of the decedent's death of the property title to which vested in that person pursuant to Section 6609, less the total of all of the following:

(1) The amount of any liens and encumbrances on that property.

(2) The value of any probate homestead interest set apart under Section 6520 out of that property.

(3) The value of any other property set aside under Section 6510 out of that property.

(c) In any action or proceeding based upon an unsecured debt of the decedent, the surviving spouse of the decedent, the child or children of the decedent, or the guardian of the minor child or children of the decedent, may assert any defense, cross-complaint, or setoff which would have been available to the decedent if the decedent had not died.

(d) If proceedings are commenced in this state for the administration of the estate of the decedent and the time for filing claims has commenced, any action upon the personal liability of a person under this section is barred to the same extent as provided for claims under Part 4 (commencing with Section 9000) of Division 7, except as to the following:

(1) Creditors who commence judicial proceedings for the enforcement of the debt and serve the person liable under this section with the complaint therein prior to the expiration of the time for filing claims.

(2) Creditors who have or who secure an acknowledgment in writing of the person liable under this section that that person is liable for the debts.

(3) Creditors who file a timely claim in the proceedings for the administration of the estate of the decedent.

(e) Section 366.2 of the Code of Civil Procedure applies in an action under this section. (Stats.1990, c. 79 (A.B.759), § 14, operative July 1, 1991. Amended by Stats.1990, c. 140 (S.B.1855), § 4.1, operative July 1, 1991; Stats.1992, c. 178 (S.B.1496), § 32.)

Cross References

Minor child defined for purposes of this Chapter, see Probate Code § 6601.

Research References

Forms

4 California Transactions Forms--Estate Planning § 19:12, Small Estate Set-Aside.

§ 6612. Determinations not to make order under § 6609; action on petition for probate or administration

If a petition filed under this chapter is filed with a petition for the probate of the decedent's will or for administration of the estate of the decedent and the court determines not to make an order under Section 6609, the court shall act on the petition for probate of the decedent's will or for administration of the estate of the decedent in the same manner as if no petition had been filed under this chapter, and the estate shall then be administered in the same manner as if no

§ 6612

petition had been filed under this chapter. *(Stats.1990, c. 79 (A.B.759), § 14, operative July 1, 1991.)*

Cross References

Administration of estates of decedents, see Probate Code § 7000 et seq.

Research References

Forms

West's California Code Forms, Probate § 6602 Form 1, Petition to Set Aside Small Estate.

§ 6613. Attorney's fees

The attorney's fees for services performed in connection with the filing of a petition and the obtaining of a court order under this chapter shall be determined by private agreement between the attorney and the client and are not subject to approval by the court. If there is no agreement between the attorney and the client concerning the attorney's fees for services performed in connection with the filing of a petition and obtaining of a court order under this chapter and there is a dispute concerning the reasonableness of the attorney's fees for those services, a petition may be filed with the court in the same proceeding requesting that the court determine the reasonableness of the attorney's fees for those services. If there is an agreement between the attorney and the client concerning the attorney's fees for services performed in connection with the filing of a petition and obtaining a court order under this chapter and there is a dispute concerning the meaning of the agreement, a petition may be filed with the court in the same proceeding requesting that the court determine the dispute. *(Stats.1990, c. 79 (A.B.759), § 14, operative July 1, 1991.)*

§ 6614. Application of law

Sections 6600 to 6613, inclusive, do not apply if the decedent died before July 1, 1987. If the decedent died before July 1, 1987, the case continues to be governed by the law applicable to the case prior to July 1, 1987. *(Stats.1990, c. 79 (A.B.759), § 14, operative July 1, 1991.)*

Application

For law applicable if decedent died before July 1, 1987, see Probate Code § 6615 and Law Revision Commission Comments under heading and sections of this chapter.

§ 6615. References to former sections deemed references to comparable provisions of this chapter

A reference in any statute of this state or in a written instrument, including a will or trust, to a provision of former Sections 640 to 647.5, inclusive, repealed by Chapter 783 of the Statutes of 1986, shall be deemed to be a reference to the comparable provisions of this chapter. *(Stats.1990, c. 79 (A.B.759), § 14, operative July 1, 1991.)*

Division 11

CONSTRUCTION OF WILLS, TRUSTS, AND OTHER INSTRUMENTS

Part 6

FAMILY PROTECTION: OMITTED SPOUSES AND CHILDREN

Application

Part 6 is not applicable where decedent died before Jan. 1, 1998, see Probate Code § 21630. For provisions applicable to estates of decedents who died before Jan. 1, 1998, see Chapter 5, Probate Code § 6560 et seq.

CHAPTER 1. GENERAL PROVISIONS

Section
21600. Application of part.
21601. Definitions.

Application

Part 6 is not applicable where decedent died before Jan. 1, 1998, see Probate Code § 21630. For provisions applicable to estates of decedents who died before Jan. 1, 1998, see Chapter 5, Probate Code § 6560 et seq.

§ 21600. Application of part

This part shall apply to property passing by will through a decedent's estate or by a trust, as defined in Section 82, that becomes irrevocable only on the death of the settlor. *(Added by Stats.1997, c. 724 (A.B.1172), § 34.)*

Application

Part 6 is not applicable where decedent died before Jan. 1, 1998, see Probate Code § 21630. For provisions applicable to estates of decedents who died before Jan. 1, 1998, see Chapter 5, Probate Code § 6560 et seq.

Cross References

Estate defined for purposes of this Part, see Probate Code § 21601.

Research References

Forms

1 California Transactions Forms--Estate Planning § 2:14, Failure to Properly Designate Disposition of Assets, Provide for Pretermitted Heirs, and Plan for Dissolution of Marriage.
1 California Transactions Forms--Estate Planning § 6:25, In General.
1 California Transactions Forms--Estate Planning § 6:27, Omitted Spouse Statute.
1 California Transactions Forms--Estate Planning § 6:56, Matters to Consider in Drafting Disinheritance Clause.
1 California Transactions Forms--Estate Planning § 6:94, Omission of Specific Heir.
4 California Transactions Forms--Estate Planning § 19:7, Overview.
4 California Transactions Forms--Estate Planning § 19:13, Protection from Unintentional Disinheritance.
4 California Transactions Forms--Estate Planning § 22:9, Overview.
4 California Transactions Forms--Estate Planning § 22:13, Revocation as Result of Application of Statute Governing Omitted Spouse.
4 California Transactions Forms--Estate Planning § 22:14, Revocation as Result of Application of Statute Governing Omitted Child.
4 California Transactions Forms--Estate Planning § 22:16, Partial Revocation.

§ 21601. Definitions

(a) For purposes of this part, "decedent's testamentary instruments" means the decedent's will or revocable trust.

(b) "Estate" as used in this part shall include a decedent's probate estate and all property held in any revocable trust that becomes irrevocable on the death of the decedent. *(Added by Stats.1997, c. 724 (A.B.1172), § 34.)*

CONSTRUCTION OF WILLS, TRUSTS, AND OTHER INSTRUMENTS § 21611

Application

Part 6 is not applicable where decedent died before Jan. 1, 1998, see Probate Code § 21630. For provisions applicable to estates of decedents who died before Jan. 1, 1998, see Chapter 5, Probate Code § 6560 et seq.

Research References

Forms

1 California Transactions Forms--Estate Planning § 6:27, Omitted Spouse Statute.

1 California Transactions Forms--Estate Planning § 6:28, Exceptions to Omitted Spouse Statute.

1 California Transactions Forms--Estate Planning § 6:29, Manner of Satisfying Omitted Spouse's Share.

1 California Transactions Forms--Estate Planning § 6:31, Omitted Child Statutes.

1 California Transactions Forms--Estate Planning § 6:32, Exceptions to Omitted Child Statute.

1 California Transactions Forms--Estate Planning § 6:33, Manner of Satisfying Omitted Child's Share.

4 California Transactions Forms--Estate Planning § 19:13, Protection from Unintentional Disinheritance.

4 California Transactions Forms--Estate Planning § 22:13, Revocation as Result of Application of Statute Governing Omitted Spouse.

CHAPTER 2. OMITTED SPOUSES

Section
21610. Share of omitted spouse.
21611. Spouse not to receive share; circumstances.
21612. Manner of satisfying share of omitted spouse; intention of decedent.

Application

Part 6 is not applicable where decedent died before Jan. 1, 1998, see Probate Code § 21630. For provisions applicable to estates of decedents who died before Jan. 1, 1998, see Chapter 5, Probate Code § 6560 et seq.

§ 21610. Share of omitted spouse

Except as provided in Section 21611, if a decedent fails to provide in a testamentary instrument for the decedent's surviving spouse who married the decedent after the execution of all of the decedent's testamentary instruments, the omitted spouse shall receive a share in the decedent's estate, consisting of the following property in said estate:

(a) The one-half of the community property that belongs to the decedent under Section 100.

(b) The one-half of the quasi-community property that belongs to the decedent under Section 101.

(c) A share of the separate property of the decedent equal in value to that which the spouse would have received if the decedent had died without having executed a testamentary instrument, but in no event is the share to be more than one-half the value of the separate property in the estate. (Added by Stats.1997, c. 724 (A.B.1172), § 34.)

Application

Part 6 is not applicable where decedent died before Jan. 1, 1998, see Probate Code § 21630. For provisions applicable to estates of decedents who died before Jan. 1, 1998, see Chapter 5, Probate Code § 6560 et seq.

Cross References

Decedent's testamentary instruments defined for purposes of this Part, see Probate Code § 21601.

Estate defined for purposes of this Part, see Probate Code § 21601.

Research References

Forms

1 California Transactions Forms--Estate Planning § 2:14, Failure to Properly Designate Disposition of Assets, Provide for Pretermitted Heirs, and Plan for Dissolution of Marriage.

1 California Transactions Forms--Estate Planning § 6:27, Omitted Spouse Statute.

1 California Transactions Forms--Estate Planning § 6:28, Exceptions to Omitted Spouse Statute.

1 California Transactions Forms--Estate Planning § 6:29, Manner of Satisfying Omitted Spouse's Share.

1 California Transactions Forms--Estate Planning § 6:96, Omission of Existing Spouse.

1 California Transactions Forms--Estate Planning § 6:97, Omission of Future Spouse.

1 California Transactions Forms--Estate Planning § 6:99, Omitted Spouse Made Valid Agreement Waiving Right to Share in Decedent's Estate.

4 California Transactions Forms--Estate Planning § 19:3, Legislative Control Over Testation.

4 California Transactions Forms--Estate Planning § 19:13, Protection from Unintentional Disinheritance.

4 California Transactions Forms--Estate Planning § 19:30, Republication by Codicil.

4 California Transactions Forms--Estate Planning § 22:13, Revocation as Result of Application of Statute Governing Omitted Spouse.

§ 21611. Spouse not to receive share; circumstances

The spouse shall not receive a share of the estate under Section 21610 if any of the following is established:

(a) The decedent's failure to provide for the spouse in the decedent's testamentary instruments was intentional and that intention appears from the testamentary instruments.

(b) The decedent provided for the spouse by transfer outside of the estate passing by the decedent's testamentary instruments and the intention that the transfer be in lieu of a provision in said instruments is shown by statements of the decedent or from the amount of the transfer or by other evidence.

(c) The spouse made a valid agreement waiving the right to share in the decedent's estate.

(d)(1) If both of the following apply:

(A) The spouse was a care custodian, as that term is defined in Section 21362, of the decedent who was a dependent adult, as that term is defined in Section 21366, and the marriage commenced while the care custodian provided services to the decedent, or within 90 days after those services were last provided to the decedent.

(B) The decedent died less than six months after the marriage commenced.

(2) Notwithstanding paragraph (1), a spouse described by this subdivision shall be entitled to receive a share of the estate pursuant to Section 21610 if the spouse proves by clear and convincing evidence that the marriage between the spouse and the decedent was not the product of fraud or undue influence. (Added by Stats.1997, c. 724 (A.B.1172), § 34. Amended by Stats.2019, c. 10 (A.B.328), § 3, eff. Jan. 1, 2020.)

Application

Part 6 is not applicable where decedent died before Jan. 1, 1998, see Probate Code § 21630. For provisions applicable to estates of decedents who died before Jan. 1, 1998, see Chapter 5, Probate Code § 6560 et seq.

Cross References

Decedent's testamentary instruments defined for purposes of this Part, see Probate Code § 21601.

§ 21611

Estate defined for purposes of this Part, see Probate Code § 21601.

Research References

Forms

1 California Transactions Forms--Estate Planning § 2:14, Failure to Properly Designate Disposition of Assets, Provide for Pretermitted Heirs, and Plan for Dissolution of Marriage.

1 California Transactions Forms--Estate Planning § 6:27, Omitted Spouse Statute.

1 California Transactions Forms--Estate Planning § 6:28, Exceptions to Omitted Spouse Statute.

1 California Transactions Forms--Estate Planning § 6:94, Omission of Specific Heir.

1 California Transactions Forms--Estate Planning § 6:95, Omission of Heir Provided for by Transfer Outside of Testamentary Instrument.

1 California Transactions Forms--Estate Planning § 6:96, Omission of Existing Spouse.

1 California Transactions Forms--Estate Planning § 6:98, Omitted Spouse Provided for by Transfer Outside of Testamentary Instrument.

1 California Transactions Forms--Estate Planning § 6:99, Omitted Spouse Made Valid Agreement Waiving Right to Share in Decedent's Estate.

1 California Transactions Forms--Estate Planning § 6:102, Omission of Child Born or Adopted After Execution of Instrument.

2 California Transactions Forms--Estate Planning § 11:50, Rights of Surviving Spouse that May be Waived [Prob C § 141].

4 California Transactions Forms--Estate Planning § 19:14, Exceptions to Pretermission.

4 California Transactions Forms--Estate Planning § 19:99, Disinheritance Provision.

4 California Transactions Forms--Estate Planning § 19:121, Contemplated Marriage Not to Revoke Will.

4 California Transactions Forms--Estate Planning § 22:13, Revocation as Result of Application of Statute Governing Omitted Spouse.

§ 21612. Manner of satisfying share of omitted spouse; intention of decedent

(a) Except as provided in subdivision (b), in satisfying a share provided by this chapter:

(1) The share will first be taken from the decedent's estate not disposed of by will or trust, if any.

(2) If that is not sufficient, so much as may be necessary to satisfy the share shall be taken from all beneficiaries of decedent's testamentary instruments in proportion to the value they may respectively receive. The proportion of each beneficiary's share that may be taken pursuant to this subdivision shall be determined based on values as of the date of the decedent's death.

(b) If the obvious intention of the decedent in relation to some specific gift or devise or other provision of a testamentary instrument would be defeated by the application of subdivision (a), the specific devise or gift or provision may be exempted from the apportionment under subdivision (a), and a different apportionment, consistent with the intention of the decedent, may be adopted. *(Formerly § 26112, added by Stats.1997, c. 724 (A.B.1172), § 34. Renumbered § 21612 and amended by Stats.2003, c. 32 (A.B.167), § 17.)*

Application

Part 6 is not applicable where decedent died before Jan. 1, 1998, see Probate Code § 21630. For provisions applicable to estates of decedents who died before Jan. 1, 1998, see Chapter 5, Probate Code § 6560 et seq.

Cross References

Abatement of shares of beneficiaries, exception to abatement requirements for omitted spouse or omitted children, see Probate Code § 21401.

Decedent's testamentary instruments defined for purposes of this Part, see Probate Code § 21601.

Estate defined for purposes of this Part, see Probate Code § 21601.

Research References

Forms

1 California Transactions Forms--Estate Planning § 2:14, Failure to Properly Designate Disposition of Assets, Provide for Pretermitted Heirs, and Plan for Dissolution of Marriage.

1 California Transactions Forms--Estate Planning § 6:29, Manner of Satisfying Omitted Spouse's Share.

CHAPTER 3. OMITTED CHILDREN

Section

21620. Child born or adopted after execution of will; share in estate.
21621. Child not to receive share; circumstances.
21622. Decedent's erroneous belief or lack of knowledge; child's share of estate.
21623. Manner of satisfying share of omitted child; intention of decedent.

Application

Part 6 is not applicable where decedent died before Jan. 1, 1998, see Probate Code § 21630. For provisions applicable to estates of decedents who died before Jan. 1, 1998, see Chapter 5, Probate Code § 6560 et seq.

§ 21620. Child born or adopted after execution of will; share in estate

Except as provided in Section 21621, if a decedent fails to provide in a testamentary instrument for a child of decedent born or adopted after the execution of all of the decedent's testamentary instruments, the omitted child shall receive a share in the decedent's estate equal in value to that which the child would have received if the decedent had died without having executed any testamentary instrument. *(Added by Stats.1997, c. 724 (A.B.1172), § 34.)*

Application

Part 6 is not applicable where decedent died before Jan. 1, 1998, see Probate Code § 21630. For provisions applicable to estates of decedents who died before Jan. 1, 1998, see Chapter 5, Probate Code § 6560 et seq.

Cross References

Decedent's testamentary instruments defined for purposes of this Part, see Probate Code § 21601.

Estate defined for purposes of this Part, see Probate Code § 21601.

Research References

Forms

1 California Transactions Forms--Estate Planning § 2:14, Failure to Properly Designate Disposition of Assets, Provide for Pretermitted Heirs, and Plan for Dissolution of Marriage.

1 California Transactions Forms--Estate Planning § 6:31, Omitted Child Statutes.

1 California Transactions Forms--Estate Planning § 6:32, Exceptions to Omitted Child Statute.

1 California Transactions Forms--Estate Planning § 6:33, Manner of Satisfying Omitted Child's Share.

1 California Transactions Forms--Estate Planning § 6:68, Afterborn Children to Participate in Devise.

1 California Transactions Forms--Estate Planning § 6:101, Omission of Living Child.

1 California Transactions Forms--Estate Planning § 6:102, Omission of Child Born or Adopted After Execution of Instrument.

4 California Transactions Forms--Estate Planning § 19:3, Legislative Control Over Testation.

4 California Transactions Forms--Estate Planning § 19:13, Protection from Unintentional Disinheritance.

4 California Transactions Forms--Estate Planning § 22:14, Revocation as Result of Application of Statute Governing Omitted Child.

§ 21621. Child not to receive share; circumstances

A child shall not receive a share of the estate under Section 21620 if any of the following is established:

(a) The decedent's failure to provide for the child in the decedent's testamentary instruments was intentional and that intention appears from the testamentary instruments.

(b) The decedent had one or more children and devised or otherwise directed the disposition of substantially all the estate to the other parent of the omitted child.

(c) The decedent provided for the child by transfer outside of the estate passing by the decedent's testamentary instruments and the intention that the transfer be in lieu of a provision in said instruments is show by statements of the decedent or from the amount of the transfer or by other evidence. *(Added by Stats.1997, c. 724 (A.B. 1172), § 34.)*

Application

Part 6 is not applicable where decedent died before Jan. 1, 1998, see Probate Code § 21630. For provisions applicable to estates of decedents who died before Jan. 1, 1998, see Chapter 5, Probate Code § 6560 et seq.

Cross References

Decedent's testamentary instruments defined for purposes of this Part, see Probate Code § 21601.

Estate defined for purposes of this Part, see Probate Code § 21601.

Research References

Forms

1 California Transactions Forms--Estate Planning § 2:14, Failure to Properly Designate Disposition of Assets, Provide for Pretermitted Heirs, and Plan for Dissolution of Marriage.

1 California Transactions Forms--Estate Planning § 6:31, Omitted Child Statutes.

1 California Transactions Forms--Estate Planning § 6:32, Exceptions to Omitted Child Statute.

1 California Transactions Forms--Estate Planning § 6:33, Manner of Satisfying Omitted Child's Share.

1 California Transactions Forms--Estate Planning § 6:94, Omission of Specific Heir.

1 California Transactions Forms--Estate Planning § 6:95, Omission of Heir Provided for by Transfer Outside of Testamentary Instrument.

1 California Transactions Forms--Estate Planning § 6:101, Omission of Living Child.

1 California Transactions Forms--Estate Planning § 6:103, Omission of Child Provided for by Transfer Outside of Testamentary Instrument.

1 California Transactions Forms--Estate Planning § 6:104, Disposition of Estate to Parent of Omitted Child.

4 California Transactions Forms--Estate Planning § 19:14, Exceptions to Pretermission.

4 California Transactions Forms--Estate Planning § 19:99, Disinheritance Provision.

4 California Transactions Forms--Estate Planning § 22:14, Revocation as Result of Application of Statute Governing Omitted Child.

§ 21622. Decedent's erroneous belief or lack of knowledge; child's share of estate

If, at the time of the execution of all of decedent's testamentary instruments effective at the time of decedent's death, the decedent failed to provide for a living child solely because the decedent believed the child to be dead or was unaware of the birth of the child, the child shall receive a share in the estate equal in value to that which the child would have received if the decedent had died without having executed any testamentary instruments. *(Added by Stats.1997, c. 724 (A.B.1172), § 34.)*

Application

Part 6 is not applicable where decedent died before Jan. 1, 1998, see Probate Code § 21630. For provisions applicable to estates of decedents who died before Jan. 1, 1998, see Chapter 5, Probate Code § 6560 et seq.

Cross References

Decedent's testamentary instruments defined for purposes of this Part, see Probate Code § 21601.

Estate defined for purposes of this Part, see Probate Code § 21601.

Research References

Forms

1 California Transactions Forms--Estate Planning § 6:31, Omitted Child Statutes.

1 California Transactions Forms--Estate Planning § 6:102, Omission of Child Born or Adopted After Execution of Instrument.

4 California Transactions Forms--Estate Planning § 19:13, Protection from Unintentional Disinheritance.

§ 21623. Manner of satisfying share of omitted child; intention of decedent

(a) Except as provided in subdivision (b), in satisfying a share provided by this chapter:

(1) The share will first be taken from the decedent's estate not disposed of by will or trust, if any.

(2) If that is not sufficient, so much as may be necessary to satisfy the share shall be taken from all beneficiaries of decedent's testamentary instruments in proportion to the value they may respectively receive. The proportion of each beneficiary's share that may be taken pursuant to this subdivision shall be determined based on values as of the date of the decedent's death.

(b) If the obvious intention of the decedent in relation to some specific gift or devise or other provision of a testamentary instrument would be defeated by the application of subdivision (a), the specific devise or gift or provision of a testamentary instrument may be exempted from the apportionment under subdivision (a), and a different apportionment, consistent with the intention of the decedent, may be adopted. *(Added by Stats.1997, c. 724 (A.B.1172), § 34. Amended by Stats.2003, c. 32 (A.B.167), § 16.)*

Application

Part 6 is not applicable where decedent died before Jan. 1, 1998, see Probate Code § 21630. For provisions applicable to estates of decedents who died before Jan. 1, 1998, see Chapter 5, Probate Code § 6560 et seq.

Cross References

Abatement of shares of beneficiaries, exception to abatement requirements for omitted spouse or omitted children, see Probate Code § 21401.

Decedent's testamentary instruments defined for purposes of this Part, see Probate Code § 21601.

Estate defined for purposes of this Part, see Probate Code § 21601.

Research References

Forms

1 California Transactions Forms--Estate Planning § 2:14, Failure to Properly Designate Disposition of Assets, Provide for Pretermitted Heirs, and Plan for Dissolution of Marriage.

1 California Transactions Forms--Estate Planning § 6:33, Manner of Satisfying Omitted Child's Share.

1 California Transactions Forms--Estate Planning § 6:68, Afterborn Children to Participate in Devise.

4 California Transactions Forms--Estate Planning § 22:13, Revocation as Result of Application of Statute Governing Omitted Spouse.

§ 21623 PROBATE CODE

4 California Transactions Forms--Estate Planning § 22:14, Revocation as Result of Application of Statute Governing Omitted Child.

CHAPTER 4. APPLICABILITY

Section
21630. Decedent's death before January 1, 1998; application of part.

Application

For provisions applicable to estates of decedents who died before Jan. 1, 1998, see Chapter 5, Probate Code § 6560 et seq.

§ 21630. Decedent's death before January 1, 1998; application of part

This part does not apply if the decedent died before January 1, 1998. The law applicable prior to January 1, 1998, applies if the decedent died before January 1, 1998. (Added by Stats.1997, c. 724 (A.B.1172), § 34.)

Application

For provisions applicable to estates of decedents who died before Jan. 1, 1998, see Chapter 5, Probate Code § 6560 et seq.

Cross References

Estate defined for purposes of this Part, see Probate Code § 21601.

Research References

Forms

1 California Transactions Forms--Estate Planning § 2:14, Failure to Properly Designate Disposition of Assets, Provide for Pretermitted Heirs, and Plan for Dissolution of Marriage.

1 California Transactions Forms--Estate Planning § 6:25, In General.

1 California Transactions Forms--Estate Planning § 6:27, Omitted Spouse Statute.

1 California Transactions Forms--Estate Planning § 6:28, Exceptions to Omitted Spouse Statute.

1 California Transactions Forms--Estate Planning § 6:29, Manner of Satisfying Omitted Spouse's Share.

1 California Transactions Forms--Estate Planning § 6:31, Omitted Child Statutes.

1 California Transactions Forms--Estate Planning § 6:32, Exceptions to Omitted Child Statute.

1 California Transactions Forms--Estate Planning § 6:33, Manner of Satisfying Omitted Child's Share.

1 California Transactions Forms--Estate Planning § 6:56, Matters to Consider in Drafting Disinheritance Clause.

1 California Transactions Forms--Estate Planning § 6:94, Omission of Specific Heir.

1 California Transactions Forms--Estate Planning § 6:96, Omission of Existing Spouse.

4 California Transactions Forms--Estate Planning § 19:13, Protection from Unintentional Disinheritance.

4 California Transactions Forms--Estate Planning § 22:13, Revocation as Result of Application of Statute Governing Omitted Spouse.

4 California Transactions Forms--Estate Planning § 22:14, Revocation as Result of Application of Statute Governing Omitted Child.